COMMON LAW MARRIAGE

COMMON LAW MARRIAGE

A LEGAL INSTITUTION FOR COHABITATION

GÖRAN LIND

OXFORD
UNIVERSITY PRESS
2008

OXFORD
UNIVERSITY PRESS

Oxford University Press, Inc., publishes works that further Oxford University's objective of excellence in research, scholarship, and education.

Oxford New York
Auckland Cape Town Dar es Salaam Hong Kong Karachi Kuala Lumpur
Madrid Melbourne Mexico City Nairobi New Delhi Shanghai Taipei Toronto

With offices in
Argentina Austria Brazil Chile Czech Republic France Greece
Guatemala Hungary Italy Japan Poland Portugal Singapore
South Korea Switzerland Thailand Turkey Ukraine Vietnam

Published by Oxford University Press, Inc. 198 Madison Avenue, New York, New York 10016
www.oup.com

Library of Congress Cataloging-in-Publication Data

Lind, Göran.
Common law marriage : a legal institution for cohabitation / Göran Lind.
p. cm.
Originally presented as the author's thesis (doctoral)—Uppsala University, Uppsala. 2006.
Includes bibliographical references and index.
ISBN 978-0-19-536681-5 ((clothbound): alk. paper) 1. Common law marriage—United States. 2. Unmarried couples—Legal status, laws, etc.—United States. 3. Common law marriage. 4. Conflict of laws—Common law marriage. 5. Concubinage. I. Title.
KF516.L5'6 2008
346.73016—dc22
2007043688

1 2 3 4 5 6 7 8 9

Printed in the United States of America
on acid-free paper

Note to Readers

This publication is designed to provide accurate and authoritative information in regard to the subject matter covered. It is based upon sources believed to be accurate and reliable and is intended to be current as of the time it was written. It is sold with the understanding that the publisher is not engaged in rendering legal, accounting, or other professional services. If legal advice or other expert assistance is required, the services of a competent professional person should be sought. Also, to confirm that the information has not been affected or changed by recent developments, traditional legal research techniques should be used, including checking primary sources where appropriate.

(Based on the Declaration of Principles jointly adopted by a Committee of the American Bar Association and a Committee of Publishers and Associations.)

To Kerstin,
Magnus, and Johan

Preface

The research that is the basis of this work has taken me on a uniquely inspiring journey from Ancient Rome to today's international debate concerning the legal regulation of cohabitation.

For their generous companionship, good advice, and readings of the manuscript on this journey, and for the spontaneous response and support I have received in the international legal academic family, I thank Professors Anders Agell and Stig Strömholm, Uppsala University; Professor J. Thomas Oldham, University of Houston; Professor David Westfall, Harvard Law School; Professor Martha Baily, Queen's University, Kingston; Professor Marsha Garrison, Brooklyn Law School; Professor Thomas R. Andrews, University of Washington; Professor Eric M. Clive, University of Edinburgh; Professor Bill Atkin, Victoria University of Wellington; Professor Kathleen Kiernan, London School of Economics and Political Science; and Dr. Jens M. Scherpe, Max-Planck Institute for Foreign and International Private Law.

For their excellent and courteous library assistance, I give thanks to Professor James B. Leonard, Director of the Law Library, University of Alabama, previously Ohio Northern University; Librarian Birgitta Köhler, Uppsala University; as well as the entire staff at the Law Library of Congress, Washington, D.C., where I have had the pleasure of conducting some of my research. Particular thanks must also be given to my translator, Laura Carlson, an American and Swedish Doctor of Law.

Financial support for this project has been gratefully received from the Faculty of Law, Uppsala University; Emilj Heijnes Stiftelse för Rättsve tenskaplig Forskning; G. Huselius Stiftelse and Jura Law Institute.

GÖRAN LIND
Washington D.C.
April 2007

Contents

COMMON LAW MARRIAGE

CHAPTER 1

INTRODUCTION

Marriage is a great institution – but who wants to live in an institution?

Old Vaudeville Joke

1.1 BACKGROUND

Several of the most characteristic developments affecting family law in the Western world during the last thirty years have been the decreasing rates of marriage, the increasing numbers of unmarried cohabiting couples, and the increasing numbers of children born in such relationships. The legal problems that these developments entail have catalyzed significant activity at both the judicial and legislative levels in several countries. In the United States, Northern and Western Europe, Canada, Australia, and New Zealand, the courts have attempted to resolve the family law problems of cohabiting parties through the application of property law principles. On the legislative level, several jurisdictions have enacted cohabitation legislation that, with respect to its legal effects, has increasingly come to resemble formal marriage. Some laws are based on the cohabitation, others on a registration. Couples of the same sex have also been included more and more. The need for legislation is discussed in even more countries. For example, in the United States, the American Law Institute (ALI) recommended legislation in 2002 concerning the division of property and maintenance upon the dissolution of "the relationship of domestic partners" inter vivos.[1] According to the proposed ALI Principles, cohabiting unmarried couples, of both different and the same sexes, in principle are equated with married couples. Today, states in the United States are considering and discussing whether this legislation ought to be adopted. In the Western world in general, the courts and other governmental authorities are confronted with issues concerning the application of laws, including to whom the regulatory systems are to be

1 *See* AMERICAN LAW INSTITUTE (ALI), PRINCIPLES OF THE LAW OF FAMILY DISSOLUTION: ANALYSIS AND RECOMMENDATIONS (2002). For a critique, *see* Reconceiving the Family. Critique on the American Law Institute's Principles of the Law of Family Dissolution (Robin Fretwell Wilson ed., 2006).

applied and, with respect to the future course of the law, the appropriateness of legislation as a method.[2]

1.2 THE OBJECT OF THIS EXAMINATION

Common law marriage is a long-standing American legal institution that highlights several of the questions that the modern development has raised. This informal marriage is the ultimate legal solution for cohabiting couples who have not formally entered into marriage in that it entails all the legal effects of marriage. This legal construction, the primary object of this investigation, has its origins in the two legal systems in the Western world that historically have had the broadest international application, namely, Roman law and medieval canon law. At the Council of Trent in 1563, the Roman Catholic Church established an unconditional form requirement for the commencement of a marriage, a resolution that was subsequently enacted in most other European legal systems. Although the majority of these systems have diverged from their historical beginnings, common law marriage has remained tied to its roots. The renaissance of legal solutions for informal cohabitation that in the Western world has gained ground during the last thirty years has been little influenced by common law marriage or its historical predecessors. There is scant awareness that "all roads lead to Rome."

The term common law marriage has no etymological connection with the English common law, as this legal institution stems nearest from English ecclesiastic and therewith medieval canon law.[3] The designation, however, is adequate to the extent that the legal institution in American law has developed, not through legislation, but in the main through case law that in this area has created an American common law.[4] Even in states in which the doctrine has been codified to a limited extent, the designation common law marriage is ordinarily used. Other terms used are

2 The international development is presented more closely below in Part III.

3 The expression *common law marriage* already appears in JAMES KENT, COMMENTARIES ON AMERICAN LAW 2 (New York, William Kent 1826) and in the case law in *Grisham & Ligan v. The State,* 10 Tenn. 589 (1831); *Cheney v. Arnold,* 15 N.Y. 345, 69 Am. Dec. 609 (1857); and *Carmichael v. State,* 12 Ohio St. 553 (1861).

4 Even if the recognition of a common law marriage must take into consideration whether the form requirements existing in the legislation with respect to the ceremonial marriages create impediments, the doctrine rests on the common law. The court in the case of *In re Marriage of Phelps and Robinson,* 74 P.3d 506 (Colo.App. 2003), consequently is correct when it maintains that "(a) determination of the existence of a common law marriage is governed by the common law, not by the UMA," in other words, the UNIFORM MARRIAGE AND DIVORCE ACT. West's C.R.S.A. § 14-2-101 *et seq.* (West. 2003). Already in *Meister v. Moore,* 96 U.S. 76, 78 (1877), the United States Supreme Court speaks of "a marriage at common law."

informal marriage,[5] irregular marriage, consensual marriage,[6] unsolemnized marriage, and nonceremonial marriage.[7] Given this historical perspective, the expression common law marriage is preferable, and is most commonly used in both the academic literature and the case law. It has been said that it is unusual for cohabiting couples to use this expression in describing their relationship.[8]

A closer definition of common law marriage will unfold in the material analyzed herein. As a starting point, however, in the broadest sense, let us characterize common law marriage as a legal institution that gives the legal effects of formal marriage to qualified couples who, without formally

5 OTTO E. KOEGEL, COMMON LAW MARRIAGE AND ITS DEVELOPMENT IN THE UNITED STATES 7 (1922), uses as synonyms to common law marriage *informal or irregular marriages.* The latter terms are most common in Scottish law, *see* Chapter 11 *infra.* CHESTER G. VERNIER, AMERICAN FAMILY LAWS I, 103 (1931), speaks of the validity of *common-law or informal marriages.* Thirty years later, the expression recurs in Walter O. Weyrauch's essays, *see,* e.g., *Informal Marriage and Common Law Marriage,* in SEXUAL BEHAVIOUR AND THE LAW 297 (R. Slovenko ed. 1965). *See also* Nancy Rebecca Shaw, Note, *Common Law Marriage and Unmarried Cohabitation: An Old Solution to a New Problem,* 39 U. PITT. L. REV. 579 (1977), who speaks of "common law or informal marriage." In Texas, where common law marriage has been codified, the applicable chapter is entitled: "Subchapter E. Marriage without formalities" and section 2.401 "Proof of Informal Marriage," *see* TEX. FAM. CODE ANN. (Vernon 2005). Both expressions are used in the case law, even if *common law marriage* there is more common. In *Russell v. Russell,* 838 S.W.2d 909, 913 (Tex.App.-Beaumont 1992), the court states: "In this opinion we use the terms 'informal marriage' and 'common- law marriage' interchangeably." The expressions *informal or common-law marriage* also appear in case law from Iowa, *see* e.g., *In re Stopps' Estate,* 244 Iowa 931, 57 N.W.2d 221, 224 (Iowa 1953).

6 The expression *consensual marriage* appears particularly in older decisions, which can be explained by that the elements of the contract played a greater role before than today. *See,* e.g., *State v. McFarland,* 38 Kan. 664, 17 P. 654, 655 (1888); and *Matney v. Linn,* 59 Kan. 613, 54 P. 668 (1898). Ordinarily, the expression *consensual marriage* is used alternately with *common law marriage, see Schuchart v. Schuchart,* 61 Kan. 597, 60 P. 311 (1900); and *Shorten v. Judd,* 60 Kan. 73, 55 P. 286, 287 (1898). The expression can also be found even in more modern cases such as *Driscoll v. Driscoll,* 220 Kan. 225, 552 P.2d 629, 630 (1976), which discusses *common law or consensual marriage.* In *Morrison v. Sunshine Mining Co.,* 64 Idaho 6, 127 P.2d 766 (1942), the court speaks in a similar manner of a "consent marriage." A somewhat longer and more descriptive expression with the historical background is *pre-Tridentine canonical consensual marriage, see Mueggenborg v. Walling,* 836 P.2d 112, 115 (Okla. 1992).

7 In Utah, where common law marriage was reinstated in 1987 through legislation, the heading to UTAH CODE ANN. § 30-1-4.5 (Supp. 1987) uses the term "Validity of marriage not solemnized." Its Supreme Court speaks in *Whyte v. Blair,* 885 P.2d 791, 792 (Utah 1994), of "unsolemnized or common law marriage." These expressions can also be found in case law from other states and at different points of time, *see,* e.g., *People v. Spencer,* 199 Mich. 395, 165 N.W. 921, 923 (1917), *Bolz v. Bolz,* 325 Mass. 726, 92 N.E.2d 365 (1950), *Matter of Estate of Wagner,* 126 Idaho 848, 893 P.2d 211, 212 (1995) and *Baynes v. Baynes,* 219 Ga.App. 848, 467 S.E.2d 195 (1996) (*common law marriage* and *nonceremonial marriage*). In *Williams v. Williams,* 46 Wis. 464, 1 N.W. 98, 101, 102, 32 Am.Rep. 722 (1879) and in *Travers v. Reinhardt,* 205 U.S. 423, 436, 27 S. Ct. 563, 51 L.Ed. 865, 871 (1906), the term *marriage in fact* appears.

8 It happens that unmarried cohabiting persons call themselves *common law wife* or *common law husband* respectively, despite the fact that they live in a state not recognizing such marriages, *see* Ellen Kandoian, *Cohabitation, Common Law Marriage, and the Possibility of a Shared Moral Life,* 75 GEO. L.J. 1829, 1862 (1987).

having entered into marriage, are in agreement and live together under marriage-like conditions.[9]

Common law marriage is not, as sometimes assumed, a legal construction with the limited objective of reaching solutions in particularly exceptional cases. A common law marriage entails in principle all the legal effects of formal marriage.[10] The parties in such a marriage consequently have the same obligations to each other during the marriage as do spouses. The dissolution of the relationship inter vivos occurs through marital divorce. Consequently, the establishment of a common law marriage is informal but its dissolution is formal. A common law marriage is not terminated merely by separation.[11] A common case is the petition by a party for a marital divorce, child custody, maintenance, or the division of an estate, based on a common law marriage, while the other party denies the existence of such a marriage.[12] Maintenance obligations against a previous

---

9 The lack of form concerns both the absence of requirements for a wedding ceremony as well as requirements for a marriage license, *see* e.g. *Grigsby v. Reib*, 105 Tex. 597, 153 S.W. 1124, 1130 (Tex. 1913).

10 General statements appear already in *Askew v. Dupree*, 30 Ga. 173 (1860), in which it was ascertained that a formless marriage "is to all intents and purposes a valid marriage." In *Beggs v. State*, 55 Ala. 108, 112 (1876), the court stated that the parties in a common law marriage "stand to each other in the relation of husband and wife, having all the rights, and subject to all the duties, flowing from a marriage..." In *Holmes v. Pere Marquette R. Co.*, 28 Ohio App. 297, 162 N.E. 675 (1928), the court explained that the parties in a common law marriage are "husband and wife as fully and to the same extent as if there had been a statutory and ceremonial marriage." The court stated in a similar manner in *Stump v. Stump*, 111 Pa.Super. 541, 546 (1934): "It has the same force, effect and sanctity as one performed by a minister or magistrate." In *McClish v. Rankin*, 14 S.2d 714, 718 (Fla. 1943), the court stated that: "It is patent that no distinction exists between the obligations and responsibilities of a marriage by ceremony and one consensus." In *Turner v. Turner*, 251 Ala. 295, 37 So.2d 186, 188-189 (1948), the court stated that one cannot be "a little bit married." In *Nat'l Union Fire Ins. Co. v. Britton*, 187 F.Supp. 359 (D.D.C. 1960), it was maintained that a common law marriage is equally "lawful, solemn, and binding" as a ceremonial marriage. In *Piel v. Brown*, 361 So.2d 90, 93 (Ala. 1978), the court stated that "such a marital device exists in this state, not as an exception, but as a coequal, alternate method of validating the connubial union of two people." *See also Barron v. Apfel*, 209 F.3d 984, 986 (7th Cir. 2000).

11 In *Dickey v. Office of Personnel Management*, 419 F.3d 1336 (C.A.Fed. 2005), the court held that it was clear legal error to hold that a common law marriage can be terminated merely by separation. *See also Bell v. Ferraro*, 849 A.2d 1233 (Pa.Super. 2004); *Buford v. Buford*, 874 So.2d 562 (Ala.Civ.App. 2003); *Eris v. Phares*, 39 S.W.3d 708 (Tex.App.-Houston, 1 Dist. 2001); *Stringer v. Stringer*, 689 So.2d 194 (Ala.Civ.App. 1997); *Cann v. Cann*, 632 A.2d 322 (Pa.Super. 1993); *Winfield v. Renfro*, 821 S.W.2d 640 (Tex.App.-Houston 1991); *Villegas v. Griffin Industries*, 975 S.W.2d 745 (Tex.App.-Corpus Christi 1998); *Matter of Estate of Stodola*, 519 N.W.2d 97, 100 (Iowa App. 1994); and *Prevatte v. Prevatte*, 297 S.C. 345, 377 S.E.2d 114 (App. 1989) (divorce based on infidelity). In *Skipworth v. Skipworth*, 360 So.2d 975, 977 (Ala. 1978), the court stated that: "A party cannot legally terminate the marriage by simply changing his or her mind and moving out or by telling selected individuals, 'We're not really married.'"

12 *Young-Jones v. Bell*, 905 A.2d 275 (D.C.App. 2006); *Cardwell v. Cardwell*, 195 S.W.3d 856 (Tex.App.-Dallas 2006); *Bevan v. Bevan*, 2006 WL 1519654 (Ohio App. 11 Dist. 2006); *Callen v. Callen*, 365 S.C. 618, 620 S.E.2d 59 (2005); *Toom v. Toom*, 710 N.W.2d 258 (Iowa App. 2005); *Perotti v. Meredith*, 868 A.2d 1240 (Pa.Super. 2005); *Lewis v. Anderson*,

spouse can cease when the latter commences a new common law marriage.[13] The same regulations for spouses concerning inheritance, wills, and the administration of estates are applicable.[14] Children in a common law marriage are legitimate, and their parents have the same rights and responsibilities as formally married parents.[15] A common law marriage constitutes an impediment against a later marriage, both ceremonial and common law. In some states, a person is guilty of bigamy when, knowing he or she

---

173 S.W.3d 556 (Tex.App.-Dallas 2005); *Sulfridge v. Kindle*, 2005 WL 1806482 (Ohio App. 4 Dist. 2005); *Reyes v. Vasquez*, 2005 WL 1389076 (Ohio App. 6 Dist. 2005); *Faison v. Faison*, 2005 WL 1303344 (Ohio App. 8 Dist. 2005); *Harris v. Harris*, 2004 WL 2896422 (Ohio App. 9 Dist. 2004); *DeMelo v. Zompa*, 844 A.2d 174 (R.I. 2004); *In re Marriage of Lenz*, 715 N.W.2d 770 (Iowa App. 2006); *In re Marriage of Martin*, 681 N.W.2d 612 (Iowa 2004); *Ward v. Ward*, 268 Ga.App. 394, 601 S.E.2d 851 (2004); *In re Marriage of Phelps and Robinson*, 74 P.3d 506 (Colo.App. 2003); *Clark v. Clark*, 423 Utah Adv. Rep. 3, 2001 UT 44, 27 P.3d 538 (Utah 2001); *Fritz v. Mork*, 2001 Iowa App. LEXIS 594 (2001); *Standefer v. Standefer*, 26 P.3d 104 (Okla. 2001); *In re Estate of Antonopoulos*, 268 Kan. 178, 993 P.2d 637 (1999); *Earnheart v. Earnheart*, 979 P.2d 761 (Okla.Civ.App. Div. 3 1999); *Hansen v. Hansen*, 958 P.2d 931 (Utah App. 1998) (divorce, custody, maintenance, a division of the estate); *In re Custody of Nugent*, 955 P.2d 584 (Colo.App. 1997) (divorce, custody, maintenance, a division of the estate); *Kowalik v. Kowalik*, 118 Ohio App.3d 141, 691 N.E.2d 1152 (1997); *Krier v. Krier*, 676 So.2d 1335 (Ala.Civ.App. 1996); *Matter of Estate of Alcorn*, 868 P.2d 629 (Mont. 1994); *Lyon v. Lyon*, 86 Ohio App.3d 580, 621 N.E.2d 718 (1993); *Cann v. Cann*, 632 A.2d 322 (Pa.Super. 1993); *Mueggenborg v. Walling*, 836 P.2d 112 (1992); *Waller v. Waller*, 567 So.2d 869 (Ala.Civ.App. 1990); *In re Marriage of Mahaffey*, 801 P.2d 1335 (Mont. 1990); *Bochette v. Bochette*, 386 S.E.2d 475 (S.C.App. 1989); *Prevatte v. Prevatte*, 377 S.E.2d 114 (App. 1989); *In re Marriage of Stogdill*, 428 N.W.2d 667 (Iowa 1988); *East v. East*, 536 A.2d 1103 (D.C. App. 1988) (maintenance to children); *In re Marriage of Gebhardt*, 426 N.W.2d 651 (Iowa App. 1988); *In re Marriage of Geertz*, 755 P.2d 34 (Mont. 1988); *In re Marriage of Winegard*, 278 N.W.2d 505 (Iowa 1979); and *Com. ex rel. McDermott v. McDermott*, 236 Pa.Super. 541, 345 A.2d 914 (1975) (support).

13 *Jackson v. Culp*, 583 A.2d 1236 (Pa.Super. 1990); *Whitley v. Whitley*, 778 S.W.2d 233 (Mo.App. 1989); *In re Marriage of Cargill & Rollins*, 843 P.2d 1335 (Colo. 1993); *Cathcart v. Cathcart*, 414 S.E.2d 811 (S.C.App. 1992); *In re Marriage of Dwyer*, 825 P.2d 1018 (Colo.App. 1991); *Doyle v. Doyle*, 497 S.W.2d 846 (Mo.App. 1973); *Rogers v. Rogers*, 197 S.E.2d 921 (S.C. 1973); and *Jeanes v. Jeanes*, 255 S.C. 161,177 S.E.2d 537 (S.C. 1970).

14 *Matter of Estate of Marson*, 328 Mont. 348, 120 P.3d 382 (Mont. 2005), remanded for further proceedings; *Pike v. Estate of Pike*, 2005 WL 2248347 (Tex.App.-Ft. Worth 2005); *In re Estate of Love*, 274 Ga.App. 316, 319, 618 S.E.2d 97, 100 (2005); *Matter of Estate of Crenshaw*, 100 P.3d 568 (Colo.App. 2004); *In re Ober*, 2003 MT 7, 314 Mont. 20, 62 P.3d 1114 (2003); *Wilkins v. Wilkins*, 48 P.3d 644 (Idaho 2002); *In re Estate of LeGrand*, 259 Ga.App. 67, 576 S.E.2d 54 (2002); *Gray v. Bush*, 835 So.2d 192 (Ala.Civ. App. 2001); *Creel v. Creel*, 763 So.2d 943 (Ala. 2000); *In re Estate of Sky Dancer*, 13 P.3d 1231 (Colo.App. 2000); *Matter of Estate of Hunsaker*, 968 P.2d 281 (Mont. 1998); *Butler v. Coonrod*, 671 So.2d 750 (Ala.Civ.App. 1995); *Matter of Estate of Alcorn*, 868 P.2d 629 (Mont. 1994); *Adams v. Boan*, 559 So.2d 1084 (Ala. 1990); *Coleman v. Aubert*, 531 So.2d 881 (Ala. 1988); *Matter of Estate of Giessel*, 734 S.W.2d 27 (Tex.App.-Houston (1st Dist.) 1987); and *Nestor v. Nestor*, 15 Ohio St.3d 143, 15 O.B.R. 291, 472 N.E.2d 1091 (1984).

15 *S.J.S. v. J.O.S.*, 2006 WL 2089193 (Ala.Civ.App. 2006) (right to contest adoption); *Hart v. Webster*, 2006 WL 1707975 (Tex.App.-Austin 2006) (the presumption of paternity); *In the Interest of D.C.*, 279 Ga.App. 889, 632 S.E.2d 744 (2006) (parental rights); *Reed v. Madry*, 585 So.2d 909 (Ala. 1991); and *Edwards v. Edwards*, 136 Ga.App. 668, 222 S.E.2d 169 (1975).

is common law married, the person purports to marry or cohabits with another person.[16] The regulations for spouses concerning joint liability for certain debts are applicable as to parties in a common law marriage.[17] A party in such a marriage has the same rights as those of a formal spouse for damages or loss of consortium if the other spouse was injured or died because of an assault or other cause by a third party.[18] The parties, in addition, have the same right to social and insurance benefits as formally married spouses.[19] From a tax perspective, they are viewed as formally married; in criminal cases, a party in a common law marriage has the same privilege as a spouse to refrain from witnessing against the other party.[20] These are only a few examples of the implications of common law marriage.

1.2.1 Jurisdictions Recognizing Common Law Marriage

There is somewhat varying information concerning the number of states recognizing common law marriage. Certain differences are attributable to the different definitions that have been used and somewhat different

---

16 *Pike v. Estate of Pike*, 2005 WL 2248347 (Tex.App.-Ft. Worth 2005); *Phillips v. Dow Chemical Co.*, 186 S.W.3d 121 (Tex.App.-Houston (1 Dist.) 2005); *Lee v. Lee*, 201 A.2d 873, 875 (D.C.App. 1964); *In re Zemmick's Estate*, 17 Ohio Supp. 15, 76 N.E.2d 902, 905 (Ohio App. 1946); *State v. Green*, 99 P.3d 820 (Utah 2004) (bigamy); and *State v. Thompson*, 76 N.J.L. 197, 68 A. 1068 (1908) (bigamy).

17 *Warren Gen. Hosp. v. Brink*, 80 Ohio App.3d 793, 610 N.E.2d 1128 (1992); *Richland Memorial Hosp. v. English*, 369 S.E.2d 395 (S.C.App. 1988).

18 *Drake v. Hinds*, 2006 WL 1562511 (N.D.Iowa 2006); *Phillips v. Dow Chemical Co.*, 186 S.W.3d 121 (Tex.App.-Houston (1 Dist.) 2005); *Dickey v. Office of Personnel Management*, 419 F.3d 1336 (C.A.Fed. 2005); *Nava v. Reddy Partnership/Quail Chase*, 988 S.W.2d 346 (Tex.App.-Houston (1st Dist.) 1999); *Dalworth Trucking Co. v. Bulen*, 924 S.W.2d 728 (Tex.App.-Texarkana (1996); and *Mattison v. Kirk*, 497 So.2d 120 (Ala. 1986).

19 *Coleman v. Nicholson*, 2006 WL 1523178 (Vet.App. 2006) (death benefits); *Snyder-Murphy v. City of Cedar Rapids*, 695 N.W.2d 44 (Iowa App. 2005) (workmen's compensation); *Int'l Painters and Allied Traders Ind. Pensions Fund v. Calabro*, 312 F.Supp.2d 697 (E.D.Pa. 2004) (death benefits); *Thompson v. Barnhart*, 2005 WL 23347 (D.Kan. 2005) (widow's benefits); *Reusser v. Mulvane Cooperative Union*, 119 P.3d 705 (Kan. App. 2005) (workmen's compensation); *Brandywine Paper Bd. v. W.C.A.B. (Zittle)*, 751 A.2d 1205 (Pa.Cmwlth. 2000) (workmen's compensation); *Matter of Death of Boyd*, 959 P.2d 612 (Okla.Civ.App. Div. 1 1998) (workmen's compensation); *Blessing v. Deere & Co.*, 985 F.Supp. 899 (S.D.Iowa 1997) (pension rights); *White v. State Farm Mut. Auto. Ins. Co*, 907 F.Supp. 1012 (E.D.Tex. 1995) (insurance benefits); and *Matter of Estate of Stodola*, 519 N.W.2d 97 (Iowa App. 1994) (health insurance). In *Scott v. Bd. of Trustees Mobile S.S. Ass'n*, 859 F.2d 872, 875 (11th Cir. 1988), it was found that insurance terms that refused common law marriages the same status as ceremonial marriages were invalid as they violated public policy. *See also Whyte v. Blair*, 885 P.2d 791, 792 (Utah 1994) (automobile insurance); *Gordon v. Railroad Retirement Bd.*, 225 U.S.App.D.C. 49, 696 F.2d 131 (1983) (social security); *Freiburghaus v. Freiburghaus*, 103 Idaho 679, 651 P.2d 944 (App. 1982) (life insurance); and *Carter v. Firemen's Pension Fund*, 634 P.2d 410 (Colo. 1981) (the right to pension).

20 *Hartfield v. Commissioner of Internal Revenue*, 2006 WL 1280961 (U.S.Tax.Ct. 2006); *Mesa v. United States*, 875 A.2d 79 (D.C.App. 2005); *Brown v. State*, 108 P.3d 1018 (Kan.App. 2005); *Davis v. State*, 103 P.3d 70 (Okla.Cr.App. 2004); *State v. Mireles*, 904 S.W.2d 885 (Tex.App.-Corpus Christi 1995); *Weaver v. State*, 855 S.W.2d 116, 120 (Tex.App.-Houston (14 Dist.) 1993); and *People v. Lucero*, 747 P.2d 660 (Colo. 1987).

interpretations of the case law. Others are based on misunderstandings.[21] If one begins with the jurisdictions that generally recognize common law marriage and give it all the legal effects of marriage, common law marriage today, based on a selection of the most recent decisions, can legally be established in Alabama,[22] Colorado,[23] the District of Columbia,[24]

---

21 In *Kelley v. Kelley*, 9 P.3d 171, 183 (Utah App. 2000), which describes the situation in 1987, Idaho, Georgia, South Carolina, Ohio, and District of Columbia were omitted incorrectly. *See further* Mary D. Feighny, *Common Law Marriage: Civil Contract or "Carnal Commerce,"* 70 KAN. B.J. 20 (2001), who only mentions eight states. She fails to include Oklahoma and does not mention the District of Columbia. Texas and Utah are referred to only as "variations of the doctrine" together with New Hampshire. Even Cynthia Grant Bowman, *A Feminist Proposal to Bring Back Common Law Marriage*, 75 OR. L. REV. L. REV. 709, 715 (1996), fails to include Oklahoma and mentions 11 states as well as the District of Columbia, wherewith is included Idaho, in which common law marriage was repealed from 1996, *see* note 34 *infra*. The author fails to include Oklahoma also in *Legal Treatment of Cohabitation in the United States*, 26 LAW & POLICY 119, 122 (2004). Oklahoma was omitted also in David F. Crabtree, *Family Law Recognition of Common-Law Marriages*, 149 UTAH L. REV. 273, 275-276 (1988), and in GRAHAM DOUTHWAITE, UNMARRIED COUPLES AND THE LAW 11 (1979). Nevertheless, Oklahoma recognizes common law marriage, *see* note 28 *infra*. *See further* Lawrence W. Waggoner, *Marital Property Rights in Transition*, 59 MO. L. REV. 21, 75 note 133 (1994), who mentions Ohio, despite the fact that common law marriage was repealed there in 1991, *see* note 33 *infra*. Also in JUDITH AREEN, CASES AND MATERIALS ON FAMILY LAW 76 (3d ed. 1992), Ohio is taken up and Utah absent. Other sources that do not appear to have noted that common law marriage has been enacted in Utah are: Kathryn S. Vaughn, Comment, *The Recent Changes to the Texas Informal Marriage Statute: Limitation or Abolition of Common Law Marriage?*, 28 HOUS. L. REV. 1131, 1132, 1135 (1991) and Jack B. Helitzer, *State Developments in Employee Benefits: Common-Law Marriage*, 4 BENEFITS L.J. 95, 98, 104 note 48 (1991); and Joseph W. McKnight, *Husband and Wife*, 21 TEX. TECH. L. REV. 911, 937 (1990). Nevertheless, common law marriage was enacted in Utah through legislation in 1987, *see* note 32 *infra*. Finally in Sonya C. Garza, *Common Law Marriage: A Proposal for the Revival of a Dying Doctrine*, 40 NEW ENG. L. REV. 541, 545 (2005), incorrectly includes Idaho and Pennsylvania, *compare infra* notes 34 and 36 *infra*, and fails to include Oklahoma, *compare supra* note 28 *infra* and *In re Marriage of J.M.H. and Rouse*, 143 P.3d 1116, 1117 (Colo.App. 2006), incorrectly includes Idaho.

22 *S.J.S. v. J.O.S.*, 2006 WL 2089193 (Ala.Civ.App. 2006); (*Buford v. Buford*, 874 So.2d 562 (Ala.Civ.App. 2003); *Gray v. Bush*, 835 So.2d 192 (Ala.Civ.App. 2001); and *Creel v. Creel*, 763 So.2d 943 (Ala. 2000).

23 *In re Marriage of J.M.H. and Rouse*, 143 P.3d 1116 (Colo.App. 2006); *Matter of Estate of Crenshaw*, 100 P.3d 568 (Colo.App. 2004); *In re Marriage of Phelps and Robinson*, 74 P.3d 506 (Colo.App. 2003); *In re Estate of Sky Dancer*, 13 P.3d 1231 (Colo.App. 2000); *In re Custody of Nugent*, 955 P.2d 584 (Colo.App. 1997); *Whitenhill v. Kaiser Permanente*, 940 P.2d 1129 (Colo.App. 1997); *In re Marriage of Cargill & Rollins*, 843 P.2d 1335 (Colo. 1993); *In re Marriage of Dwyer*, 825 P.2d 1018 (Colo.App. 1991); *Crandell v. Resley*, 804 P.2d 272 (Colo.App. 1990); and *People v. Lucero*, 747 P.2d 660 (Colo. 1987).

24 *Young-Jones v. Bell*, 905 A.2d 275 (D.C.App. 2006); *Crane v. Puller*, 169 Md.App. 1, 899 A.2d 879 (Md.App. 2006) (applying District of Columbia law); *Mesa v. United States*, 875 A.2d 79 (D.C.App. 2005); *Dickey v. Office of Personnel Management*, 419 F.3d 1336 (C.A.Fed. 2005); *Coates v. Watts*, 622 A.2d 25 (D.C. App. 1993); *Robinson v. Evans*, 554 A.2d 332 (D.C.App. 1989); and *East v. East*, 536 A.2d 1103 (D.C. App. 1988).

Iowa,[25] Kansas,[26] Montana,[27] Oklahoma,[28] Rhode Island,[29] South Carolina,[30] Texas,[31] and Utah.[32] Four additional states considered in this investigation repealed common law marriage during the 1990s and the beginning of

---

25 *In re Marriage of Lenz*, 715 N.W.2d 770 (Iowa App. 2006); *Drake v. Hinds*, 2006 WL 1562511 (N.D.Iowa 2006); *Toom v. Toom*, 710 N.W.2d 258 (Iowa App. 2005); *Snyder-Murphy v. City of Cedar Rapids*, 695 N.W.2d 44 (Iowa App. 2005); and *In re Marriage of Martin*, 681 N.W.2d 612 (Iowa 2004).

26 *Thompson v. Barnhart*, 2005 WL 23347 (D.Kan. 2005); *Reusser v. Mulvane Cooperative Union*, 119 P.3d 705 (Kan.App. 2005); *Brown v. State*, 108 P.3d 1018 (Kan.App. 2005); *In re Marriage of Kuzanek*, 82 P.3d 528 (Kan.App. 2004); *In re Marriage of Kopac*, 30 Kan.App.2d 735, 47 P.3d 425 (2002); and *In re Estate of Antonopoulos*, 268 Kan. 178, 993 P.2d 637 (1999).

27 *Matter of Estate of Marson*, 328 Mont. 348, 120 P.3d 382 (2005); *In re Ober*, 2003 MT 7, 314 Mont. 20, 62 P.3d 1114 (2003); *Matter of Estate of Hunsaker*, 968 P.2d 281 (Mont. 1998); and *Matter of Estate of Alcorn*, 868 P.2d 629 (Mont. 1994).

28 *Davis v. State*, 103 P.3d 70 (Okla.Cr.App. 2004); *Standefer v. Standefer*, 26 P.3d 104 (Okla. 2001); *Mueggenborg v. Walling*, 836 P.2d 112 (Okla. 1992); *Matter of Estate of Stinchcomb*, 674 P.2d 26 (Okla. 1983); *Tatum v. Tatum*, 736 P.2d 506 (Okla. 1982); *In re Estate of Hornback's Estate*, 475 P.2d 184 (Okla. 1970); *Hill v. Shreve*, 448 P.2d 848 (Okla. 1968); and *Parkhill Truck Co. v. Row*, 383 P.2d 203 (Okla. 1963).

29 *DeMelo v. Zompa*, 844 A.2d 174 (R.I. 2004); and *Sardonis v. Sardonis*, 106 R.I. 469, 261 A.2d 22 (1970).

30 *Callen v. Callen*, 365 S.C. 618, 620 S.E.2d 59 (2005); *Pirri v. Pirri*, 369 S.C. 258, 631 S.E.2d 279 (App. 2006); *Barker v. Baker*, 330 S.C. 361, 499 S.E.2d 503 (App. 1998); *Owens v. Owens*, 466 S.E.2d 373 (S.C.App. 1996); and *Kirby v. Kirby*, 270 S.C. 137, 241 S.E.2d 415 (1978).

31 *Hart v. Webster*, 2006 WL 1707975 (Tex.App.-Austin 2006); *Cardwell v. Cardwell*, 195 S.W.3d 856 (Tex.App.-Dallas 2006); *Pike v. Estate of Pike*, 2005 WL 2248347 (Tex.App.-Ft. Worth 2005); *Lewis v. Anderson*, 173 S.W.3d 556 (Tex.App.-Dallas 2005); *Phillips v. Dow Chemical Co.*, 186 S.W.3d 121 (Tex.App.-Houston (1 Dist.) 2005); *Nichols v. Lightle*, 153 S.W.3d 563 (Tex.App.-Amarillo 2004); *Canady v. Russell*, 138 S.W.3d 412 (Tex.App.-Tyler 2004); *Mills v. Mest*, 94 S.W.3d 72 (Tex.App.-Houston (14th Dist.) 2002); *Ganesan v. Vallabhaneni*, 96 S.W.3d 345 (Tex.App.-Austin 2002); *In re Estate of Loveless*, 64 S.W.3d 564 (Tex.App.-Texarkana 2001); *Jenkins v. Jenkins*, 16 S.W.3d 473 (Tex.App.-El Paso 2000); *Ballesteros v. Jones*, 985 S.W.2d 485 (Tex.App.-San Antonio 1998); *Shepherd v. Ledford*, 962 S.W.2d 28 (Tex. 1998); *Crowson v. Wakeham*, 897 S.W.2d 779 (Tex. 1995); *Flores v. Flores*, 847 S.W.2d 648 (Tex.App.-Waco 1993); *Russell v. Russell*, 838 S.W.2d 909 (Tex.App.-Beaumont 1992), *rev'd*, 865 S.W.2d 929 (Tex. 1993); and *Lorensen v. Weaber*, 840 S.W.2d 644 (Tex.App.-Dallas 1992) rev'd 865 S.W.2d 929 (Tex. 1993). *See also* TEX. FAM. CODE ANN. § 2.401 (Vernon 2005).

32 *State v. Green*, 99 P.3d 820 (Utah 2004); *Clark v. Clark*, 423 Utah Adv. Rep. 3, 2001 UT 44, 27 P.3d 538 (2001); *Kelley v. Kelley*, 9 P.3d 171 (Utah App. 2000); and *In re Marriage of Gonzalez*, 387 Utah Adv. Rep. 89, 2000 UT 28, 1 P.3d 1074 (2000). Common law marriage was reinstated in Utah 1987 after having been repealed 1888, *see* UTAH CODE ANN. § 30-1-4.5 (Supp. 1987), effective April 27, 1987.

the 2000s, namely Ohio,[33] Idaho,[34] Georgia,[35] and Pennsylvania.[36] The latter are included in our investigation because the repeals were not retroactive

33 OHIO REV. CODE ANN. § 3105.12 (B) (1, 2) (West. 1991). *See Bevan v. Bevan*, 2006 WL 1519654 (Ohio App. 11 Dist. 2006); *Sulfridge v. Kindle*, 2005 WL 1806482 (Ohio App. 4 Dist. 2005); *Reyes v. Vasquez*, 2005 WL 1389076 (Ohio App. 6 Dist. 2005); *Faison v. Faison*, 2005 WL 1303344 (Ohio App. 8 Dist. 2005); *Harris v. Harris*, 2004 WL 2896422 (Ohio App. 9 Dist. 2004); *Cunningham v. Apfel*, 12 Fed.App. 361 (C.A.6 (Ohio) 2001); *Kowalik v. Kowalik*, 118 Ohio App.3d 141, 691 N.E.2d 1152 (1997): *State v. Phelps*, 100 Ohio App.3d 187, 652 N.E.2d 1032 (1995); *In re Estate of Shepherd*, 646 N.E.2d 561 (Ohio App. 3 Dist. 1994); *Lyon v. Lyon*, 86 Ohio App.3d 580, 621 N.E.2d 718 (1993); *Warren Gen. Hosp. v. Brink*, 80 Ohio App.3d 793, 610 N.E.2d 1128, 1129 (1992) ("Ohio will no longer recognize common-law marriages initiated in Ohio after October 10, 1991"); and *Nestor v. Nestor*, 15 Ohio St.3d 143, 15 O.B.R. 291, 472 N.E.2d 1091 (1984).

34 In Idaho, common law marriage has been repealed effective 1996, *see* H.B. 176; Chap. 104, 1995 Idaho Session Laws; IDAHO CODE ANN. § 32-201 (2) (Michie 2003): "The provisions of subsection (1) of this section requiring the issuance of a license and a solemnization shall not invalidate any marriage contract in effect prior to January 1, 1996." *See also Wilkins v. Wilkins*, 48 P.3d 644 (Idaho 2002); *Matter of Estate of Wagner*, 126 Idaho 848, 893 P.2d 211 (1995); and *McCoy v. McCoy*, 868 P.2d 527 (Idaho App. 1994).

35 GA. CODE ANN. §§ 19-3-1, 19-3-1.1 (West 2003): "No common-law marriage shall be entered into in this state on or after January 1, 1997. Otherwise valid common-law marriages entered into prior to January 1, 1997, shall not be affected by this Code section and shall continue to be recognized in this state." *Compare In the Interest of D.C.*, 279 Ga.App. 889, 632 S.E.2d 744 (2006); *In re Estate of Love*, 274 Ga.App. 316, 618 S.E.2d 97 (2005); *Ward v. Ward*, 268 Ga.App. 394, 601 S.E.2d 851 (2004); *In re Estate of LeGrand*, 259 Ga.App. 67, 576 S.E.2d 54 (2002); *Finch v. Dasgupta*, 251 Ga.App. 637, 555 S.E.2d 22 (2001); *In re Estate of Wilson*, 236 Ga.App. 496, 512 S.E.2d 383 (1999); *Wright v. Goss*, 229 Ga.App. 393, 494 S.E.2d 23, 25 (1997); and *Ridley v. Grandison*, 260 Ga. 6, 389 S.E.2d 746 (1990).

36 *Perotti v. Meredith*, 868 A.2d 1240 (Pa.Super. 2005); *Bell v. Ferraro*, 849 A.2d 1233 (Pa.Super. 2004); *Stackhouse v. Stackhouse*, 862 A.2d 102, 2004 Pa.Super. 427 (2004); *Int'l Painters and Allied Traders Ind. Pensions Fund v. Calabro*, 312 F.Supp.2d 697 (E.D.Pa. 2004); and *Staudenmayer v. Staudenmayer*, 714 A.2d 1016 (Pa. 1998). *Compare PNC Bank Corp. v. Workers' Comp. Appeal Bd. (Stamos)*, 831 A.2d 1269 (Pa.Cmwlth. 2003), in which the court attempted to repeal common law marriage. The attempt was not accepted in *Bell* and *Stackhouse* with reference to that it is a matter for the legislature. The Pennsylvania Supreme Court has not taken a stance after *Staudenmayer*. The most common understanding in the case law is that legislation is required in order to repeal common law marriage, *see*, e.g., from Pennsylvania, *Interest of Miller*, 301 Pa.Super. 511, 448 A.2d 25 (1982); *Buradus v. Gen. Cement Products Co.*, 159 Pa. Super. 501, 506, 48 A.2d 883 (1946), *aff'd*, 356 Pa. 349, 52 A.2d 205 (1947); *Fisher v. Sweet & McClain*, 154 Pa.Super. 216, 35 A.2d 756, 760 (1944), and from other states, *In re Marriage of J.M.H. and Rouse*, 143 P.3d 1116, 1118 (Colo.App. 2006); *Goode v. Goode*, 396 S.E.2d 430 (W.Va. 1990); *In re Stopps' Estate*, 244 Iowa 931, 57 N.W.2d 221, 223 (1953); *Hoage v. Murch Bros Const. Co.*, 60 App. D.C. 218, 50 F.2d 983, 986 (D. C.Cir. 1931); *Offield v. Davis*, 100 Va. 250, 40 S.E. 910 (1902); *Hulett v. Carey*, 66 Minn. 327, 69 N.W. 31, 34 (1896); and *United States v. Simpson*, 4 Utah 227, 7 P. 257, 258 (1885). Common law marriage was finally abolished in Pennsylvania by legislation, effective January 1, 2005. Common law marriages entered into after this date are not valid, but relationships entered into on or before January 1, 2005, would be recognized. *See* 23 PA. CONS. STAT. ANN. § 1103 (West 2005); Amendment A3597, House Bill 2719, Senate Bill 985 (Pa. Leg. 2004). In *Costello v. Workers' Comp. Appeal Bd.* (*Kinsley Constr., Inc.*), 2006 WL 4043525 (Pa.Cmwlth. 2006), the court accepted that the case of *PNC Corp.* was overruled by the legislation. Therefore a common law marriage established after *PNC Corp.*, but before the legislation was effective, was valid.

and the law in these states will, therefore, be of interest for a long time into the future. The investigation of current law primarily focuses on these fifteen jurisdictions, which have approximately 75 million inhabitants. In addition, common law marriage enjoys partial recognition in New Hampshire, where, in the event of a death, the surviving party in a common law marriage is granted the same rights as a surviving spouse, assuming that the parties lived together during the three last years prior to the death.[37]

Because of applicable choice of law rules between states, common law marriage has significance in all American states. The majority of these rules recognize common law marriages that have been established in a state in which such marriages can legally be established, which is of great practical significance, given how much people move from state to state. For example, as discussed subsequently, a short visit to a common law marriage state can give rise to a marriage without the parties' awareness. The chapter on conflict rules addresses all the states.

A large number of states are also considered in tracing the reception of common law marriage in order to fully show how common law marriage evolved in the United States. Moreover, many cases from other states contributed to the developments of the 1800s. Thus, this investigation encompasses all states and territories that have had their own legal systems.

In "Part III, The Future," United States common law marriage is compared with cohabitation law in the Western world in general, including the legal systems in Northern and Western Europe, Canada, Australia, and New Zealand.

1.2.2 The Need for a More In-Depth Legal Discourse

Common law marriage has not been the object of any extensive academic legal investigation since Otto Koegel's meritorious dissertation of 172 pages, Common Law Marriage, dating from 1922.[38] Articles with a mainly legal policy focus have treated the subject sporadically. However, those interested in current law have primarily been referred to treatises. The most often-cited during the last fifty years has been a twenty-five-page section in Homer Clark's The Law of Domestic Relations, published in 1968 and updated in 1987.[39] At the same time, the case law has been overwhelming since 1922. Approximately one hundred new judgments on common law marriage have been issued each decade in each state and

37 It is notable that the legislation speaks of *cohabitation* and the courts *common law marriage*, *see*, e.g., *Gray v. Gray*, 379 A.2d 442, 445 (N.H. 1977); *In re Estate of Buttrick*, 597 A.2d 74 (N.H. 1991); and N.H. Rev. Stat. Ann. 457:39 (West 2003). The legislation has a long heritage, *see* already RS 149:11 (1842).

38 *See* Koegel, *supra* note 5. *Compare* Robert. E. Dillon, Common Law Marriage (1942), who treats the Catholic Church's attitude.

39 Homer H. Clark, Jr., The Law of Domestic Relations in the United States 45-58 (1968), I, 100-124 (2d ed. 1987).

at the federal level; in other words, approximately one thousand cases. This flood of decisions has, to a great extent, lain unanalyzed. The state of the law has been and is complex, uncertain, and difficult to assess.

Occasionally, in the courts' decisions, there are more or less desperate cries concerning the legal uncertainty in the applicable principles as well as the numerous and often drawn-out lawsuits to which the legal regulations give rise. For example, in Ridley v. Grandison (1990), Justice Weltner at the Georgia Supreme Court exclaimed: "Plainly, the law of common law marriage is chaos that cries out for order."[40] Another example can be found in *Russell v. Russell* (1992), in which Chief Justice Walker at the Court of Appeals in Beaumont, Texas, begins the judgment with the statement that "this case is a trial judge's nightmare."[41] The problems the courts point to are also expressed in the legal academic scholarship. When Stuart Stein, in his 1969 article concerning informal marriage, states that "the law is highly uncertain and seemingly in a continued state of flux," his assessment sums up the prevailing understanding during the 1900s.[42]

It is fair to ask whether contemporary rules regarding cohabitation will face similar problems. The hasty international development within private law has endeavored to reach solutions as to cohabiting parties' legal problems in country after country and has caused the courts to apply far-reaching analogies and, at times, pure fictions to attempt to resolve these problems. This indicates a need for academic legal reflection. The sudden international development of cohabitation legislation with legal effects that increasingly come to resemble common law marriage also occasionally gives the impression that urgent political desires have precluded allowing the time for contemplation that is necessary for academic legal analysis. There appears to be a need for a legislative and judicial "time out." A historical, comparative, and sociological perspective as to the developments is needed in order to assess the appropriate legal strategy for the future.

---

40 *Ridley v. Grandison*, 260 Ga. 6, 389 S.E.2d 746, 749 (1990).

41 *Russell v. Russell*, 838 S.W.2d 909, 911 (Tex.App.-Beaumont 1992).

42 Stuart J. Stein, *Common-Law Marriage: Its History and Certain Contemporary Problems*, 9 J. FAM. L. 271, 290 (1969). VERNIER, *supra* note 5, p. 103, described in 1931 the state of the law as chaos: "There is too much confusion, conflict and uncertainty." Thirty years later, Walter O. Weyrauch, *Informal and formal marriage - an appraisal of trends in family organization*, 28 U. CHI. L. REV. 88, 91 (1960) noted: "Whatever hazy notions we have vary not only from jurisdiction to jurisdiction but from case to case within a recognizing jurisdiction." *See further* Olen E. Adams, Note, *Common Law Marriage in Oklahoma*, 14 OKLA. L. REV. 291, 292 (1961): "[T]here is no point of civil law concerning domestic relations, which is more confusing and upon which one will find more contradictory decisions than common-law marriage." The same assessment recurs 18 years later in William W. Hood, Jr., *Common-law marriage in Oklahoma: A Survey*, 49 OKLA. B.J. 1505, 1506 (1978) and in the beginning of the 1980's it was said as to the term "common law marriage" that "its conceptual equivalents are hazy," *see* WALTER O. WEYRAUCH & SANFORD N. KATZ, AMERICAN FAMILY LAW IN TRANSITION 118 (1983).

1.3 Objective, Method, Materials, and Outline

Die reichte Quelle aller Entdeckungen in jeder Erfahrungswissenschaft ist Vergleichung und Konstruktion.

Anselm Feuerbach

As is evident from the title, the objective of this work on a more general level is to investigate common law marriage, its historical origins, current status, and future. The general methodological starting point is in a legal investigation that without preconceptions seeks relevant knowledge through historical, comparative, and sociological perspectives. Within the framework imposed by domestic legal systems and other societal contexts, the aim is to use this knowledge to investigate the current status of the law, but primarily to discuss the future course of the law.

This open attitude to the search for knowledge is not free of objections. One certainly is reminded of Montesquieu's influential statement concerning the difficulties of comparing and transferring rules from one legal system to another: "Les Loix Politiques & Civiles de chaque Nation doivent être tellement propres au Peuple pour lequel elles sont faites, que c'est un très grand hasard si celles d'une Nation peuvent convenir à une autre."[43] The author's skepticism naturally rests on the environmental factors, such as "le climat, la Religion, les Loix, les maximes du Gouvernement, les exemples des choses passées, les moeurs, les manieres," taken up in his celebrated catalog.[44] Montesquieu's admonition of the "très grand hasard," the very great risk, is usually viewed as particularly pertinent to family law – and in particular marital law – with its close connections to ethical, religious, social, and cultural fundamental conditions. Distinguished comparativists, even in modern times, have certainly warned of the difficulties in this area of family law.[45]

The general viability of Montesquieu's skepticism today can be questioned with reason, at least as long as the comparison is limited to the Western world. A voluminous flow of news, ideas, values, and cultural manifestations via modern media washes over with the speed of light throughout the world and is assimilated in people's thoughts and actions irrespective of national boundaries. The family and family law have not remained unaffected. In a manner that probably would amaze Montesquieu, radical winds, for better or worse, have swept through family law systems

---

43 Charles de Montesquieu, L'Esprit des Lois, Liv. I, Chap. III (Genève, Barillot & Fils 1748).

44 Montesquieu, *id.*, Liv. XIX, Chap. IV.

45 H.C. Gutteridge, Comparative Law 32 (2d ed. 1949); *Stig Strömholm, Användningen av utländskt material i juridiska monografier.* Några anteckningar och förslag, 56 SvJT 260 (1971); *Otto Kahn-Freund,* On Uses and Misuses of Comparative Law, 37 Mod. L. Rev. 1 (1974); and Mary Ann Glendon, State, Law and Family. Family Law in Transition in the United States and Western Europe 17 (1977).

since the late 1970s. No-fault divorce has been adopted throughout the Western world, even in Catholic countries where divorce previously was not permitted. Attitudes toward cohabitation outside of marriage and same-sex relationships have undergone considerable changes. Who, today, could have predicted that a Catholic country such as Spain would permit marriages between persons of the same sex?

In the Western world today, religious, cultural, ideological, social, and economic conditions appear sufficiently similar to actually be considered variations of one and the same culture. At the same time, legal systems vary sufficiently, so that a comparative perspective is fruitful. On the legislative level, purely political deadlocks can certainly impose impediments.[46] Montesquieu's understanding, therefore, has a certain continued relevance with respect to politics, which encompass not only "[la] principe du Gouvernement qui est établi" but also "qu'on veut établir."[47] The task of legal scholarship, however, is broader and more long term than fulfilling the desires of temporary officeholders. In legal scholarship, a comparative perspective ought not be only a right, but also, perhaps more appropriately, an obligation. The simple but fundamental epistemological understanding is that legal scholarship should further the knowledge that a comparative investigation can provide and that sometimes can be utilized within one's own or another legal system.

On the judicial level, there is reason to encourage greater caution. For example, if the Roman jurist Ulpian has anything material to say to a court in Washington, D.C., Stockholm, or Sydney, it is the task of legal scholarship to convey the message.[48] There are human values and conceptions that are relatively independent of time and space and the limits of environment. The consequences of these general methodological perspectives are illustrated more closely in the three parts of this work.

The objective and materials for each part are given below. In addition, each chapter has an introduction that explains its objective. Each chapter, in addition, has a summary of conclusions in which the chapter's significance is explained in terms of its interconnectedness with the treatise's other parts. A reader only interested in certain features of this investigation may choose to read the introductions and conclusions of the chapters he or she finds most pertinent. Each part is also set up so that a reader only interested in a certain part can limit his or her reading to that section.

46 Despite the homogeneity concerning fundamental societal conditions and values characterizing, for example, the Nordic countries in Europe, at times it has been difficult to reach mutual solutions for political reasons, *see* SOU 1981:85, ÄKTENSKAPSBALK, p. 118.

47 MONTESQUIEU, *id.*, Liv. I, Chap. III.

48 *See, e.g.*, Ulpian's maxim: *Consensus facit nuptias*, with respect to the Roman law *see* Section 2.4.2, with respect to the Medieval Canon law, Chapter 3.3.3, with respect to common law marriage, Section 6.1 and with respect to the discussion concerning the constituent elements facing the future, Section 13.2, *supra*.

The idea, however, is that the three parts enrich one another and are best read entirely.

Part I. The Origins

The Objective and the Outline

The objective of the two first chapters in Part I, Chapter 2, "Informal Marriages in Roman Law," and Chapter 3, "Informal Marriages in Canon Law," is to seek the origins of common law marriage in the ancient Roman and medieval canon law. Of interest in these chapters is how these worldwide legal systems, over approximately fifteen hundred years, attempted to solve the problems of a declining number of marriages and increasing informal cohabitation. These chapters study how legal effects were tied to different types of informal relationships, some recognized as marriage and others as concubinage. Of particular interest is investigating the legal requirements that had to have been fulfilled in order for legal effects to attach to informal relationships, and how the line of demarcation was drawn for relationships that fell outside of the systems. In a world of thought in which fundamental distinctions were made between body and soul, idea and action, subject and object, will and manifestation, it became natural within the legal scholarship to distinguish between the elements animus and corpus; and in marital laws, to distinguish between the parties' marital intent, *affectio maritalis*, and their actual objective cohabitation. Several of the fundamental ideas underlying the Western understanding of marriage were laid down in these systems. The legal significance attributed to these two elements was established by different relationships recurring in both legal systems, as with the related evidentiary issues. The criminal law used to enforce the rules fall outside the framework of this presentation.

The Roman and canon law concepts and distinctions are later utilized in Part II, which investigates the marriage contract's structure and content in current law (Chapters 6 and 7). The use in the future of a subjective contractual element with the establishment of a cohabitation relationship is specifically discussed in Chapter 13, Section 13.2. This concerns quite simply the question of whether the parties' own intentions in their relationship are to be given any significance in the establishment of a legal relationship. The role of contract law, therefore, becomes a central issue in the legal policy discussion as to the appropriateness of future common law marriage and cohabitation legislation as investigated in Chapter 14.

The second element, in other words, the corpus element or the cohabitation, and its significance as a legal element and as evidence in both the Roman and canon law free marriage and concubinage, is revisited in Part II. Cohabitation as an evidentiary fact is discussed in Chapter 7; its character as an element in a marital presumption is analyzed in Chapter 9; and its character as a necessary requisite is examined in Chapter 8. All are treated within the framework of common law marriage. The possible future use of cohabitation as a basis for rights and obligations is discussed in Part III in Chapters 13 and 14. The discussion with respect to the future in Part III draws on past experiences in the application of the historical legal systems.

Chapter 4, "The Reception of Common Law Marriage in United States, maps the states and courts reception of this legal construction from the early 1800s and investigates the broader underlying reasons and causes for this development. The reasons why certain courts did not recognize common law marriage and the initial criticism that the institution met are also of interest. The investigation addresses the laws of all the states and certain territories, not only the states that today recognize common law marriage. A complete historical perspective requires an examination of the influence of many cases from many jurisdictions that influenced the development of common law marriage during the 1800s. The colonial period, to which very few references are made in later American case law, falls outside of this investigation.

The question of whether the historical reasons, causes, and critical views are tenable in today's society, as well as other modern arguments for and against common law marriage and cohabitation legislation, are critically reviewed and discussed in Part III.

The Material

The first two chapters on Roman and canon law are based on the Roman and canon sources of law and the research of scholars in these fields. The task of this work has not been to question the results of this research, but rather to seek, in these comprehensive legal historic materials, the origins of common law marriage. The material in Chapter 4, with the exception of individual legislation, consists almost entirely of extensive case law from all states and territories. Relevant academic literature and articles have naturally been taken into consideration.

PART II. THE CURRENT LAW

The Objective and the Outline

The boundaries between legal history, current law, and the future course of the law are somewhat tenuous in a legal system based on approximately two hundred years of case law, in which the uncertainty concerning that which may be viewed as the current law is significant. The objective of Part II is to identify the applicable common law based on case law and limited legislation. Of particular interest is investigating the conditions necessary and sufficient for the establishment of a common law marriage. These requisites mark the line between, on one side, informal cohabitation recognized as a complete marriage and, on the other side, cohabitation entirely lacking legal effect, which until modern times, has even been criminally punishable.[49] Many cases have attempted to determine whether a woman was a man's common law wife or simply a man's intimate friend;[50] whether parties were husband and wife or simply friends and sweethearts;[51] whether they, after a thirty-year cohabitation, were man and spouse or simply lover and paramour;[52] whether a relationship was marriage or simply a love affair;[53] or whether the relationship had undergone a formless "metamorphosis from concubinage to marriage."[54] Similar questions are raised in Part III, which addresses the attempts in modern cohabitation legislation to determine whether a couple's cohabitation is marriage-like enough to give rise to legal effects.

Chapter 5, "Legal Capacity and Common Law Marriage," introduces Part II. Each legal system imposes a requirement of legal capacity to marry in order to prevent unsuitable relationships, given that the creation of families constitutes one of the cornerstones of the Western concept of marriage. Such requirements are also applicable to common law marriage. Ceremonial marriages are preceded by an assessment of whether impediments against marriage exist, but for common law marriages, these questions are often raised afterwards, for example, if one party presents a claim based on the common law marriage, upon separation or death of the other.

The objective of this chapter is to investigate how the system of first afterwards assessing the requirements of legal capacity has been applied in the case law and assess the outcomes, taking into consideration the objectives of the requirements. Specific attention is given to the age

---

49 *See, e.g., Smith v. Smith*, 161 K.I, 165 P.2d 593 (1946).

50 In *Dowell v. Welch*, 574 P.2d 1089 (Okla.App. 1978), Presiding Judge Brightmire in the Court of Appeals in Oklahoma stated: "Was appellee Orpha Welch, the paramour or common-law wife of the late Chester A. Dowell when he died April 8, 1976? Decedent's son, Chester Ralph Dowell, says she was no more than an intimate friend. The court that heard the evidence found, however, that she was the senior Dowell's surviving spouse. We affirm." *Compare Brinckle v. Brinckle*, 12 Phila. 232, 236 (1877), in which the court stated: "That the plaintiff was either the mistress or the wife of the defendant admits of no doubt."

51 *In the Matter of Estate of Koshman*, 288 P.2d 652, 656 (Idaho 1955). In *Texas Employers' Ins. Ass. v. Elder*, 274 S.W.2d 144, 146 (Texas 1954), the man stated that the parties had lived together for nine years, while the woman maintained that she never did more than "sweetheart around" with the man and that she spent "an occasional night" with him.

52 *McSweeney c. Celebrezze*, 253 F.Supp. 100, 101 (U.S.Dist.N.Y. 1966).

53 *Guardians of the Poor v. Nathans*, 2 Brewster 149, 177 (1845). The court found a common law marriage proven. In *Duncan v. Duncan*, 10 Ohio St. 181, 188, 1859 WL 67 (1859), the court expressed concern over that "God-ordained matrimony" and simply "meretricious cohabitation" were being placed on an all too equal footing.

54 *McClish v. Rankin*, 14 S.2d 714, 717 (Fla. 1943). *Compare Wilkins v. Wilkins*, 48 P.3d 644, 650 (Idaho 2002), in which the court found that the parties considered each other as "something less than a spouse and more like a 'good friend'."

requirements and the requirement that a party not be married to another person, whether through a previous ceremonial marriage or a common law marriage. For instance, a party may not be aware that he or she is in a common law marriage, and may separate without formally dissolving the marriage. If that party then enters into a new common law marriage or a ceremonial marriage, a number of intricate questions arise as to the validity of the new relationship.

The legal effects of modern cohabitation legislation include addressing the difficulty of achieving the objectives of the regulations concerning legal capacity without a licensing procedure, as well as resolving the evidentiary and legal certainty problems presented by assessments made afterwards. These questions are therefore revisited and discussed in terms of the future in Chapter 14, "Arguments For and Against Common Law Marriage and Cohabitation Law" of Part III.

Chapter 6, "The Common Law Marriage Contract," focuses on a central inheritance from the Roman and canon law, namely the maxim, *consensus facit nuptias*. This concept that the parties' mutual intent is the basis for the marriage has always been one of the cornerstones of common law marriage. In all the jurisdictions recognizing such marriages today, the parties' marital *consensus*, in principle, constitutes one of the necessary requisites for establishing such a marriage. Wedding ceremonies or other forms are not necessary.

The objective of this chapter, therefore, is to investigate certain fundamental questions regarding the agreement that is the basis for a common law marriage. These are the nature of the marriage contract; the content of the intent; the distinction between an agreement de praesenti, in other words, an immediately valid agreement, and an agreement de futuro, in other words, an agreement concerning a future marriage; express agreements and the application of general contract law principles regarding offer and acceptance as to these; and certain issues with respect to the lack of agreement between intent and declaration of intent. Other sections in Part III, Section 13.2, "The Parties' *Consensus* as a Necessary Element," and Section 14.3.1, "Limitation of the Freedom of the Parties," consider the need for a marriage contract as a constitutive element and the functions of different contract constructions within the framework of common law marriage and cohabitation legislation, with respect to the future course of the law.

As it is very unusual for the parties in a common law marriage to enter into an express marriage contract, either oral or written, Chapter 7, "Implied Marriage Agreements," is included. Typically, the parties quite simply move in and live together under marriage-like circumstances. It has even been asserted that the majority of such couples are not aware that their relationships are common law marriages.[55] This chapter begins

55 See Graham Kirkpatrick, *Common-Law Marriages: Their Common Law Basis and Present Need,* 6 St. Louis U. L.J. 30, 47 (1960).

by focusing on the reasons behind the acceptance of implied or inferred agreements with the establishment of a common law marriage, the development of the law during 1800s and the 1900s, and the state of the law today. A presentation follows of the evidentiary facts most commonly cited in the case law in support of inferred agreements. In addition, the courts' reasoning in a number of cases is more closely analyzed to ascertain how, from the facts cited, the courts establish the existence of an inferred marriage agreement and how they reason in those cases in which no agreement is proven. The question arises whether, in accepting inferred agreements, the courts must abandon the idea of a sharply defined contract, in which the parties at a certain point of time and a certain place entered into the agreement, and instead accept the Roman idea of a continual consent, *consensus continuus*.

Chapter 13, "The Constitutive Requisites in the Future," addresses the issue of whether an application of the principles as to inferred agreements in the future is necessary in order for common law marriage to be able to give the protection intended by the legal institution, and whether this objective, in the future, can be met in another manner, as well as other more general issues. The reasons stated by the courts, as well as the reasons for and against an application of the principles as to inferred agreements, are critically reviewed.

Chapter 8, "Cohabitation, Holding Out, and Reputation as Spouses," concerns the marriage concept's corpus element, objective circumstances that are historically diverse and highly debated. One issue is whether these circumstances constitute necessary requisites, in addition to the marriage *contract*, for the establishment of a common law marriage or whether they simply have the character of evidentiary facts for the parties' marital *consensus*. The latter is the pure contract principle. To fully grasp current law, it is necessary to examine the historically controversial aspects of this question, including the underlying reasons why and to what extent cohabitation has been accepted as a necessary requisite. The structure and elements of the concept of cohabitation are analyzed. The application problems associated with the objective element are also evaluated in this chapter.

The future function of cohabitation and the other objective elements within the framework of common law marriage or cohabitation legislation is discussed from an international perspective in Chapters 12, "Common Law Marriage and Cohabitation Law," and 13, "The Constitutive Requisites in the Future."

Chapter 9, "Burdens of Proof and Presumptions," illustrates how the application of the substantive regulations is affected by burdens of proof and legal presumptions. At the same time, the underlying evidentiary rules and reasons reflect the attitudes of the courts and legislators toward the entire legal institution of common law marriage. The objective of this chapter, therefore, is to investigate which rules the courts actually apply and for which reasons. Of particular interest is the marriage presumption, its origins and underlying values, the requirements for its application, its legal effects, and its relationship to the substantive law and to the fundamental regulations concerning the burden of proof and the standard of evidence. Chapter 13 discusses the use of the burdens of proof and legal presumptions from a future perspective. For instance, is it reasonable, today, to presume the existence of a marriage if a couple lives together under marriage-like circumstances?

Chapter 10, "Conflicts of Laws and Choice of Law," assumes that common law marriage is of interest beyond the boundaries of those jurisdictions in the United States into which such marriages can be legally entered. This premise takes into consideration the significant mobility of people between states and the circumstance that all states under certain conditions recognize common law marriages that have been established in a state where such marriages can be entered into legally and according to their applicable regulations. Add to this that the courts in many states do not require that the parties have either a domicile or residence in a common law marriage state. Thus, even a short visit to such a state may establish a common law marriage with all the legal effects of marriage without the couple being aware thereof. This chapter, naturally, is of significant practical interest, but also raises technical, theoretical questions regarding the application of the principle lex loci contractus to inferred agreements. Questions are: In which state does the marital *consensus* exist? Can the parties be seen to have a continual *consensus* if they move from state to state? In addition, is evidence in the form of cohabitation in a state other than the common law marriage state relevant? Can the marriage presumption be based on such evidence? This chapter also shows how the substantive law of the common law marriage state is applied by courts in other states. The issues raised are based on a review of approximately two hundred fifty cases from all American states, which have scarcely received any previous academic legal attention.

Chapter 11, "Scottish Irregular Marriages," is of interest because of the historical influence of Scottish law on American common law marriage,[56] but also because of the remnant of formless marriages that persisted in Scotland, namely, "marriage by cohabitation with habit and repute." This legal concept, its underlying reasons, as well as its legal nature, content and legal effects, are considered. Paradoxically, in December 2005, the Scottish parliament simultaneously repealed this surviving law in Scotland, and adopted cohabitation legislation. The discussion of the future in Chapter 14 considers why the institution of irregular marriage was supported in Scotland, the criticism directed against it, as well as the rationale for the new cohabitation legislation.

---

56 *See* Chapter 4, The Reception of Common Law Marriage in the United States and Chapter 7, Implied Marriage Agreements, *infra*.

The Material

The examination in Part II primarily concerns the American common law spanning over two centuries from the first leading case of *Fenton v. Reed* (1809), a period during which the higher courts have decided more than one thousand cases concerning common law marriage. Though not all these cases are cited, a large number are, which bears explanation. First, civil law lawyers primarily work within codified legal systems focusing on legislation and its preparatory works; case law only constitutes examples of how a legal rule has been applied. Part II, on the other hand, primarily is based on the common law as the primary source of law and therefore the cases are the basis for the applicable legal principles. As seen from Chapter 4, "The Reception of Common Law Marriage in the United States," understanding legislation's secondary role entails understanding that common law marriage during the 1800s was recognized by many courts, despite the fact that all states had form requirements for the commencement of marriage. These regulations were not considered mandatory but simply "directory" as long as legislation did not expressly invalidate common law marriage. As individual cases at times simply illustrate one aspect of a problem, several cases often are required in order to formulate a principle. Second, Part II primarily concerns the fifteen jurisdictions that, in modern times, recognize common law marriage, though cases taking up different questions are also described for each state. Third, the treatise spans a period of time of two hundred years, and different cases from different times are presented to illuminate the development of the law. Fourth, the state of the law, as mentioned above, is often uncertain and in a state of flux. At times, the decisions differ not only from state to state, but also within the same state from court to court, and at times within the same court.

It ought to be mentioned that the courts, when addressing the same issue, as a rule appear to have attempted to adhere to stare decisis, according to which a court is bound by its own decisions and the decisions of higher courts in the same jurisdiction. The application of this principle in the United States courts, however, is less rigid than the tradition of English courts.[57] Moreover, the facts often differ from case to case. It is often difficult to determine whether the court's reasoning has the character of a ratio decidendi or obiter dicta[58] and how the circumstances in the cases cited have qualified as legal facts, evidentiary facts, or the elements in a presumption. The statement of the content that "each case rests on its

57 *Helvering v. Hallock*, 309 U.S. 106, 119, 121, 60 S.Ct. 444, 84 L.Ed. 604 (1940). *Compare* Melvin Aron Eisenberg, The Nature of the Common Law 47 (1988); and Edward H. Levi, An Introduction to Legal Reasoning, passim. (1948).

58 *Compare* the critical stance of Arthur Goodhart, *Determining the Ratio Decidendi of a Case*, 40 Yale L.J. 161, 182 f (1930).

own bottom"[59] is symptomatic in those cases in which higher controlling decisions have not existed. The courts, in their assessment of common law marriage, ordinarily have searched rather freely for guidance among judgments handed down throughout the United States, which often are given persuasive authority. Fifth, the discussions in Chapters 4 and 10 include all American states. The latter considers two hundred fifty cases.

With such voluminous case law, there has been restraint in giving lengthy descriptions of individual cases, and effort to cite only the core of the courts' reasoning. An exception is the Chapter 10 discussion of inferred marriage agreements. In order to be able to analyze how the courts allowed certain facts to be used to prove an inferred marriage agreement, a somewhat more detailed presentation of certain cases is necessary. To illustrate the issues about legal capacity in Chapter 5, in which several aspects of the relationships have been discussed, shorter summaries of the facts in a number of cases are given. Similarly, in Chapter 10, the conflicts of law between different jurisdictions are illustrated with cases in which the parties have had ties to different states.

The gathering of the case law for this investigation has occurred through a review primarily of the seven regional reporters that cover all American states and are included in West's Regional Reporters,[60] as well as The New York Supplement and The California Reporter. Federal cases have been obtained from The Federal Reporter and with respect to those cases that have been decided by the United States Supreme Court, The United States Reports, The Supreme Court Reporter and United States Supreme Court Reports, Lawyers edition (L.Ed.) have been used. Particularly with respect to older cases, investigations have been made of all the states' own official reports as well as certain private collections. With respect to the most recent case law, Internet searches have been made with the help of West Law and Lexis Nexis. See the section, "Abbreviations," at the back of this book for an explanation of how the reporters are cited.

To a limited extent, legislation is an object for this investigation. This concerns Texas, which codified common law marriage in 1969, and Utah, where the doctrine was reinstated through legislation in 1987.[61]

---

59 *Carmichael v. State*, 12 Ohio St. 553 (1861); and *Jackson v. United States*, 14 F.Supp. 132 (1936), *aff'd*, 89 F.2d 572 (1937), *aff'd*, 302 U.S. 628, 82 L.Ed 488, 58 S.Ct. 390 (1938).

60 The North Western Reporter, The North Eastern Reporter, The Atlantic Reporter, The South Western Reporter, The South Eastern Reporter, The Southern Reporter and The Pacific Reporter.

61 The legislation both in Texas and in Utah limits itself to several individual regulations, *see* "Subchapter E. Marriage without formalities," section 2.401-2.404, TEX. FAM. CODE ANN. (Vernon 2005) and § 30-1-4.5, "Validity of marriage not solemnized," UTAH CODE ANN. (Supp. 1987). Before the repeal, effective January 1, 2005, Pennsylvania's marital legislation prescribes only: "This part shall not be construed to change the existing law with regard to common-law marriage," *see* § 1103, "Common-law marriage," PA. CONS. STAT. ANN. (West 2003). A similar regulation

Historically, common law marriage in the 1800s gained recognition in legislation in California, Idaho, the Dakota Territory, and Montana. Legislation, in general, has played a secondary role.

Part III. The Future

The Objective and the Outline

The objective of Part III is to conduct from historical, comparative, and sociological perspectives a legal policy discussion concerning the future of common law marriage and modern cohabitation law. This expansion of the perspective is motivated by the developments of the last thirty years and the perception that cohabitation law constitutes an alternative that fulfills comparable purposes, as does common law marriage. The historical perspective highlights several of the issues and experiences stemming from Roman and canon law and from two hundred years of common law marriage in the United States. Reason exists to learn from history!

This perspective compares developments in the United States, Northern and Western Europe, Canada, Australia, and New Zealand; in other words, countries in the Western world with sufficient similarity for a fruitful comparison. All jurisdictions in Part III are placed on an equal footing, meaning that material of interest is taken from them all. The exposition is directed at legislators and others around the world contemplating a strategy to face declining marriage rates; increasing numbers of unmarried, cohabiting couples; and the increasing number of children born outside of marriage.

The Western world faces a family law challenge during the twenty-first century that raises the following questions: Ought cohabiting unmarried couples, through the application of common law marriage or cohabitation legislation, be entirely equated with couples who formally marry? Or, in addition to marriage, should specific legal systems be constructed for unmarried cohabiting persons with legal effects other than those of marriage, and ought these be based upon cohabitation alone or on a registration? Or, ought cohabiting persons be encouraged to marry, and how? Or, ought unmarried cohabiting parties' legal problems be solved by the application of general civil law principles and agreements entered into by them and tailored to suit them best? Or, ought formal marriage be reformed to better fulfill the needs of families that are different because

---

exists in Montana, *see* Mont. Code Ann. § 40-1-403 (Mont. Leg. Serv. Div. 2003). Individual regulations are applied in other states as to common law marriage. With respect to Idaho, *see* Idaho Code Ann. § 32-201 (1985); H.B. 176; Chap. 104, Idaho Session Laws (1995). With respect to Iowa, *see* Iowa Code Ann. 595.1 (West 2003). With respect to Georgia, *see* Ga. Code Ann. §§ 19-3-1, 19-3-1.1 (West 2003). With respect to Kansas, *see* Kan. Stat. Ann. 23-101 (2003).

of the specific situations and desires of the parties? The questions can continue.

Chapter 12, "Common Law Marriage and Cohabitation Law," gives a background and a basis for the three chapters that follow it, and begins with the sociological perspective. Section 12.2, "Statistical and Demographic Data," focuses on statistical data concerning the demographic development during the last thirty years in those above-mentioned countries. The objective is to assess the gravity of the Western trends in rates of marriage, numbers of children born to unmarried mothers, and the number of unmarried cohabiting couples. The goal is also to utilize the sociological research regarding cohabitation as a social phenomenon. Can this population be viewed as a homogeneous group in which all or the majority have the same needs and desire for legal regulations, or is it a heterogeneous group that requires a range of solutions? How does the sociological concept of cohabiting persons relate to common law marriage and legally regulated cohabitations?

Section 12.3, "Property Law Solutions in the Case Law," addresses the property law solutions for unmarried cohabiting persons that, in the countries named, have grown in the private law case law outside of family law during the last thirty years. Here, solutions based on traditional, express agreements that the parties in a cohabitation relationship enter into are not presented. Instead, cases are discussed in which the courts considered cohabitation through the lenses of property law, looking at how cohabitation was interpreted in agreements and other legal actions, or is otherwise finding remedies that offer legal protection. In certain cases, the courts' reasoning rested on fictions that concealed the true basis of decisions, namely, cohabitation. The boundary between property law and family law has tended to become unclear, to the point that it has been said that common law marriage was let in through a back door.[62] This section concludes with an attempt to clarify this boundary, and evaluate developments in these countries from a legal and political perspective.

Section 12.4, "Family Law Regimes for Unmarried Cohabiting Persons," focuses on the intense development of cohabitation legislation that has occurred in the Western world during the last thirty years and its relationship to common law marriage. Is the development of cohabitation legislation simply on the way towards a common law marriage? Considered are the legal systems in which the cohabitation constitutes a basis for the rights and obligations, as well as those that require registration. A specific analysis of the concepts that have come to use are made in Chapter 13 and the reasons behind the new cohabitation legislation is discussed in Chapter 14.

Chapter 13, "The Constitutive Requisites in the Future," is directed *inter alia* at legislators who intend to preserve or introduce common law

62 *Hewitt v. Hewitt*, 77 Ill.2d 49, 31 Ill.Dec. 827, 394 N.E.2d 1204, 1207-1211 (1979). *See also* Homer H. Clark, Jr., *The New Marriage*, 12 WILLAMETTE L.J. 441, 449 (1976).

marriage or cohabitation legislation. The chapter focuses, therefore, on an analysis of the different elements that today constitute and in the future can be thought to constitute necessary requisites in the legislation. The function and effects of different elements are discussed. The requisites are significant as they determine which relationships fall within and outside of the regulatory systems' scope of application. The historical perspective, everything from the Roman and canon law to the lengthy American experience with common law marriage, evokes the question of whether, in the future, the parties' *consensus* ought to constitute a necessary requisite with the establishment of a legal relationship between persons cohabiting. This question has not received the attention it deserves in the modern cohabitation legislation, as seen in Section 13.2. The modern cohabitation legislation's requirements for cohabitation as well as the comparable experiences hereof within the framework for common law marriage are presented in Section 13.3, "Cohabitation as a Necessary Requisite." The historical experiences also motivate contemplation of the use of burdens of proof and legal presumptions as discussed in Section 13.4. The issue of the consideration that ought to be given to the intentions of the parties with the establishment of a legal relationship affects other ideological questions concerning the state's power and the parties' autonomy, as discussed in Chapter 14.

Chapter 14, "Arguments For and Against Common Law Marriage and Cohabitation Law," is primarily directed at legislatures in the Western world contemplating enacting or repealing common law marriage or cohabitation legislation, presenting and discussing arguments for and against these legal figures. The historical perspective invokes an assessment of whether the reasons underlying the medieval canon law marriage and the recognition of common law marriage during the 1800s in the United States are tenable in the future, as based on Chapter 4. In addition, the reasons that can be assumed to have lain behind the repeal of common law marriage in many of the American states during the 1900s are considered. The comparative perspective entails that the reasons that have been the basis for the enactment of or proposals concerning cohabitation legislation in Northern and Western Europe, Australia, New Zealand, Canada, and the United States, as well as the criticism that these meet, are reviewed. From the sociological perspective, the data presented in Chapter 12 add to the discussion.

All of the concerned legal systems are treated equally, however, though not necessarily in individual sections. Reasons and arguments stemming from the different legal systems are addressed by issue; the exposition is thematic. This chapter thus gives a legal comparative presentation, and a basis for a legal policy discussion of the reasons for and against common law marriage and cohabitation legislation.

Chapter 15, "A New of Model Marriage," raises the final question of whether a reformed formal marriage can constitute an alternative to the legalization of informal relationships through common law marriage and existing cohabitation legislation. This alternative is seen as a plausible way to avoid the significant problems that a legal regulation of informal relationships entails, as discussed in Chapter 14. Another objective is to expand spouses' freedom of choice among different formal regulations. As this subject falls somewhat outside of the framework of this treatise, which primarily focuses on the informal relationships, this chapter is an excursion into the future of formal marriage. However sketchy, these preliminary ideas are the basis of a discussion about alternatives, a primary concern in the Western world.

The Material

With respect to common law marriage, the materials presented in Parts I and II are utilized in Part III, as well as certain legislation that has repealed the institution. With respect to the sociological perspective, the material consists of sociological reports, academic literature, and articles. With respect to the comparative perspective, the material concerning the property law development outside of family law primarily consists of cases from the concerned countries. With respect to cohabitation legislation, the material consists primarily of legislation and the legislative preparatory works from the examined jurisdictions, as well as academic literature and the spirited legal policy debate in the legal periodicals.

PART I

The Origins

CHAPTER 2

INFORMAL MARRIAGES IN ROMAN LAW

The Censor: Ut tu ex animi tui sententia uxorem habes?
(Have you, to the best of your knowledge and belief, a wife?)
Aulus Gellius, *Attic Nights*, IV, 20, 4-5

2.1 INTRODUCTION

Few areas of Roman law have evinced as wide a range of opinions as classical matrimonial law. On one end, it is considered "perhaps the most imposing achievement of the Roman legal genius."[1] On the other, the classical marriage has been thought to provide "the true explanation of how the formerly so powerful Roman Empire could easily be overthrown once the foundation of society - the family - had been broken."[2] Regardless of the accuracy of these views, it may be confidently said that Roman matrimonial law was fundamentally different from its modern European equivalents, which in recent centuries have been subjected to alien influences, primarily from canon law. Historically, therefore, there has been little interest in comparing Roman matrimonial law with the legal treatment of marriage in modern times. As late as 1950, Fritz Schulz stated that classical matrimonial law "bides its time."[3] Today, over fifty years later, the Roman models of marriage, although partly veiled in prehistoric obscurity,[4] effectively shed light on questions raised by common law marriage and the development of concepts of cohabitation in recent years in the Western world.

The course of development within family law in ancient Rome has certain characteristics in common with the progression in the Western world during the latter part of the 1900s and the beginning of the twenty-first century, albeit that these similarities ought not be exaggerated. At the end of the Roman Republic and in the beginning of the Principate, the Roman

---

1 FRITZ S. SCHULZ, CLASSICAL ROMAN LAW 103 (1951).
2 S.R.D.K. OLIVECRONA, OM MAKARS GIFTORÄTT I BO 32 (5th ed. 1882).
3 SCHULZ, CLASSICAL, *supra* note 1, at 10.
4 The Classical jurists did not present any collective theory of marriage. Their view as to marriage instead is found in the sporadic answers given to practical questions. The fragmentary nature of the sources and the peculiarities of Roman matrimonial law have given rise to considerable differences of opinion concerning its true content.

traditions with respect to the formation of families underwent considerable change. Ceremonial forms for the commencement of marriage fell into disuse and the number of marital divorces increased. Ceremonies were only a supplement to marriages for spouses who wished such an order. Formless relationships were recognized as marriages and cohabitation was given legal effects. The Western world today faces a similar development with decreasing rates of marriage and increasing numbers of unmarried cohabiting persons, to which the legislators respond with increasing legislation regulating these relationships.

This chapter focuses on the degree to which common law marriage can find its origins in Roman family law, whether the Roman concepts can contribute to explaining the legal structure of common law marriage, and whether, in our time, there is anything to learn from the Roman experiences in the enactment of cohabitation legislation. Of particular interest with respect to the formless relationships in Roman family law is the *usus* marriage, the free Roman marriage, and concubinage.

2.2 The Roman Understanding of Marriage

2.2.1 The Definition of Marriage

The characteristic feature of the Roman view of marriage, *matrimonium* or *nuptiae*,[5] is Modestinus' definition: "Nuptiae sunt coniunctio maris et feminae et consortium omnis vitae divini et humani iuris communicatio."[6] Thus, marriage is conceived of as a monogamous union of a man and a woman,

5 *Nuptiae* originally seems to have denoted only the actual wedding ceremony, from *nubo* = cover, veil oneself for the bridegroom, but also denoted the marriage relationship, *see* Lewis and Short, Latin Dictionary 1222 and 1229 (1998). Modestinus used *nuptiae* for the ceremonial marriage between Roman citizens that had many legal effects, while he used *matrimonium* to denote a marriage where neither or just one of the parties was a citizen. The latter marriage was informal and had restricted legal effects. Justinian later used the two words synonymously; *compare* Justinian's definition in the following note. With respect to the legal etymology of both words, *see* Christian Friedrich Glück, Ausfürlichen Erläuterungen der Pandecten nach Hellfeldt, ein Kommentar, Bd. 23, at 119-121 (1822). *Compare* Max Kaser, Das Römische Privatrecht I, 73 n.5 (1966).

6 *See* D. 23, 2, 1. *Compare* Justinian's similar definition in Inst. 1, 9, 1: "Nuptiae autem sive matrimonium est viri et mulieris coniunctio individuam consuetudinem vitae continens." *Compare* C. 9, 32, 4, Corpus Iuris Civilis I, Institutiones, Digesta (P. Krueger-T. Mommsen eds. 1905), and II Codex Iustinianus (P. Krueger ed. 1900). Modestinus' definition has been assumed to have been influenced by Greek philosophy, *see* W.G. Becker, Platons Gesetze und das Griechiche Familienrecht 31 (1932); and Fritz Schulz Prinzipien der Römischen Rechts 32 n.32 (1934). *Compare*, Arnold Ehrhardt, *Consortium omnis vitae*, SZ 357 (1937). The Roman definition in its turn, despite its pre-Christian origins, has been thought to have influenced canon law. Gutzwiller describes it as "die schönste Definition der Ehe, eine Definition, welche noch immer als unübertroffen zu gelten hat" in Festgabe der Universität Freiburg für die Schweizer Katholiken 208 (1954), cit. according to Wolfram Müller-Freienfels, Ehe und Recht 6 (1962).

a total community of life, a partnership according to both human and divine laws. The nub of the material content of this definition consists of the idea of marriage as a lifelong companionship, a participation in the whole of life, a *consortium omnis vitae*,[7] not simply a liaison for the purpose of meeting a limited need, such as the satisfaction of sexual urges or the production of legitimate offspring, although the latter was emphasized during certain epochs.[8] Indeed, this definition is not an empirical, universally valid description of matrimonial relationships in Rome, but rather a normative picture of ideal marriage. Moreover, the Roman concept of marriage was derived not only from positive law but also from ethics and natural law. This partly non-legal concept of marriage also finds expression in the reality that classical marriage had few legal consequences. Strictly speaking, wedding and divorce did not require the cooperation of any governmental authority or the observance of any formalities. For this reason, Roman marriage has been characterized with some justification as *verwirklichte Lebensgemeinschaft*.[9] From a legal viewpoint, this community of life according to prevaling opinion appears as a relevant legal ground for certain legal consequences.

2.2.2 The Legal Effects

The extent of the legal consequences depended, however, on the type of marriage involved. Early Roman law distinguished between two kinds of civil marriage, *matrimonium iustum*,[10] the *manus* marriage; and the free

7 The idea of an undivided community also recurs in Justinian's definition quoted above in note 5, *supra*, "individuam consuetudinem vitae." The wholeness is usually understood not only as a sharing of everything in life but also as a union for the whole of life. Yet the fact that this intended permanence did not exclude the possibility of divorce emerges already from the circumstance that marriage could be freely dissolved from Modestus' time onwards, *see* GLÜCK, *supra* note 5, at 126 and 131, who assumes "die Absicht einer lebenslänglichen Vereinigung." *See also* Max Kaser, 1 IURA 64, 71 (1960) ("Ehe und "conventio in manum"); and KASER I, *supra* note 5, at 73. *Compare* C.W. WESTRUP, INTRODUCTION TO EARLY ROMAN LAW I, 10 (1944).

8 At the height of the Republic, and particularly in the time of the Augustine marriage reform when nativity was low and a wife was often described as *uxor liberorum quaerendorum (procreandorum) causa*, the objective of producing legitimate offspring was accentuated, *see, e.g.*, Ulp. 3, 3; Gell. 4, 32 and 17, 21, 44; and C. 5, 4, 9. *See also* Wolfgang Kunkel, *Matrimonium*, 14 PAULUS REAL-ENZYKLOPÄDIE DER CLASSISCHEN ALTERTUMS WISSENSCHAFT sp. 2259, 2260 (1930), with references. *Compare* the Greek Aristotelian philosophy, according to which marriage appears as something more than a liaison for the sole purpose of continuing the family, *see* ARISTOTLE, THE NICOMACHEAN ETHICS, VIII, 12, 7 (H. Rackham ed. 1947).

9 LUDWIG MITTEIS, RÖMISCHES PRIVATRECHT 131 note 19 (1908).

10 Gai. 1, 76 in GAI INSTITUTIONES (P. Krueger-G. Studemund eds. 5th ed. 1905); GAIUS, THE INSTITUTES OF GAIUS I (crit. notes & trans. by Francis de Zulueta 1946); and Ulp. 5, 2: ("Iustum matrimonium est, si inter eos qui nuptias contrahunt conubium sit") in ULPIANI LIBER SINGULARIS REGULARUM. PAULI LIBRI QUINQUE SENTENTIARUM. FRAGMENTA MINORA (P. Krueger ed. 1878).

marriage without *manus*.[11] The former entailed the woman's legal entry into the man's family under his conjugal authority, *manus*, while the wife in the free marriage remained legally in the family to which she previously had belonged, emancipated *vis-à-vis* her husband. Legal consequences not governed by the *manus* relationship ensued with both forms of wedding, including the status of children as born in wedlock.[12]

The forms of solemnization possible for the *manus* relationship were either *confarreatio*, *coemptio*, which were formal acts, or *usus*, which conferred *manus* on the basis of the parties' actual cohabitation.[13] In contrast, the free marriage was entirely informal. It could be freely entered into and freely dissolved without interference by any authority or mandatory formalities. Thus, for the purposes of this discussion, there is reason to closely scrutinize both *usus* and the constituent elements of the free marriage.

A deeper understanding of these two concepts of marriage and their mutual relationship requires examining the historical context of these institutions. The answers to pertinent questions, however, are largely obscure and consequently highly controversial.[14] For our purposes, it suffices to consider only the more probable assumptions. It seems reasonable that the *manus* marriage is the older of the two forms, and consequently, according to the earliest Roman law, typically involved the woman's submission to the man's authority. If this assumption is correct, marriage and *manus* originally composed one and the same concept. *Usus*, mentioned already in the Twelve Tables (app. 450 BC),[15] is discussed at the end of the republic by Cicero[16] and referred to by Quintus Scaevola[17] as still-valid law. According to Gaius,[18] however, it fell into disuse in classical times. During this period, it still was formally possible via *confarreatio* and *coemptio* to effect *conventio in manum*.[19] The Justinian legislation, however, no longer contained any provisions for the *manus* marriage. Part of the explanation for this development seems to be the emergence of free marriage, the

11 Cic. Top. 3, 14; Ulp. 26, 7; and Gell. 18, 6, 9 in Gellius, Noctes Atticae (Hosius ed. 1903).

12 Gai. I, 55; and D. 1, 6, 4, Inst. 1, 9, 3.

13 Gai. I, 110-4; Ulp. 9, 1; Gell. 3, 2, 12-3; Serv. in Georg. 1, 31; Serv. in Aen. 4, 103; Boeth. in Cic. Top. 3, 14; and Isid. Or. 5, 24 and 26. *See also* Fontes Iuris Romani Antiqui II, Scriptores (C.G. Bruns ed. 1909).

14 August Rossbach, Untersuchungen über die Römische Ehe 155 (1853); Otto Karlowa, Römische Rechtsgeschichte ii, 164 (1901); Otto Karlowa, Die Formen der Römischen Ehe und Manus (1868); Joachim Marquardt, Das Privatleben der Römer i, 32 (2d ed. 1886); Pietro Bonfante, Corso di Diritto Romano 42 (1963); C.W. Westrup, Recherches sur les Formes Antiques de Mariage dans L'Encienne Droit Romaine (1943); Percy Ellewood Corbett, The Roman law of Marriage 68 (1930); and Kaser, Iura, *supra* note 7, at 64.

15 Leges XII Tabularum, Tabula VI, Fontes Iuris Romani Antiqui I, Leges et Negotia 25 (C.G. Bruns ed. 1909).

16 Cic. Pro Flacco 34 and 84.

17 According to Gell. 3, 2 and 12.

18 Gai. 1 and 111.

19 Gai. 1, and 112-3; and Ulp. 9 and 1.

obscure origins of which may be in the preclassical period, but which is clearly documented in classical and postclassical times.[20] Thus, at least throughout the classical era, citizens were free to choose marriage with or without *manus*. A conceptually significant consequence of the development of the free marriage is that the concepts of matrimony and *manus* were separated, so that *confarreatio* and *coemptio* supplemented marriage according to the desire of couples.[21] Notwithstanding, this choice was used less and less frequently during the classical period.[22]

2.2.3 The Legal Capacity to Enter into a Marriage

The *manus* marriage and the free marriage shared a common ground in that the validity of both required the fulfillment of certain external conditions independent of the parties' intentions. These requirements were closely connected with the structure of the Roman society and its division according to ethnic affiliation, class, and rank, and so several are alien to modern law. Some of them, however, are of interest because they contributed not only to the definition of marriage, but also to the generation of new extramarital forms of cohabitation and, paradoxically enough, to demarcating the boundaries between these different forms. Thus, the fundamental prerequisite for a *matrimonium iustum* was that the parties were competent to enter into marriage with each other, *conubium*,[23] a right in principle confined to Roman citizens [24] and originally not even existing between patricians and plebeians.[25] At the end of the republic, the free born,

---

20 *See* Section 2.4, *infra*.

21 Tacitus reports on Tiberius' difficulties in recruiting qualified candidates for the office of *Flamen Dialis*. The holder thereof had to be born in a *confarreatio* marriage, *see* Tac. Ann. 4 and 16.

22 *See* Section 2.4, *infra*.

23 Gai. 1, 56; Gai. 1, 76; and Ulp. 5, 2. *Conubium* appears in the Roman legal sources in a wider sense and then also comprises the impediments to marriage, *see* Gai. 1, 59; KUNKEL, *supra* note 8 col. 2262; and PAUL FREDERIC GIRARD, MANUEL ELEMENTAIRE DE DROIT ROMAIN 157 (1929).

24 Thus the civil law concept of marriage did not cover a union between a Roman citizen and a foreigner, or a marriage between two aliens, *peregrini*, provided that these had not been granted *ius conubii* by special decree, *see* Ulp. 5, 4; Gai. 1, 57. Non-Roman marriages were described as *matrimonium iniustum*; and later as *matrimonium iuris gentium*, *see* D. 38, 11,1, pr.; and D. 50, 1, 37, 2. One such marriage that was well known was the one between Antony and Cleopatra, *see* PAUL JÖRS AND WOLFGANG KUNKEL, RÖMISCHES PRIVATRECHT 272 note 3 (3rd ed. 1949) with references. Nor did the Roman marriage concept cover cohabitation between slaves and free born, and liaisons between slaves, *contubernium*, *see* Ulp. 5, 5; C. 5, 5, 3; D. 22, 2, 14, 3; and D. 40, 4, 59 pr. *See also* Joseph N. Perry, *Canonical Concept of Marital Consent: Roman Law Influence*, 25 CATHOLIC LAW 228 (1980), who has stated: "*Iustae nuptiae* described marriages of Roman citizens only, not those of foreigners (*peregrini*) or slaves (*servi*)." *see* also BARRY NICHOLAS, AN INTRODUCTION TO ROMAN LAW 83 (1962). *Conubium* lost much of its erstwhile significance by the extension of the right to citizenship, particularly by *Constitutio Antoniniana* in 212 A.D.

25 *Lex Canuleia* in 445 B.C. allowed marriage between patricians and plebeians, *see* Cic. De Rep. 2, 37 and 63.

the *ingenui*, were still not permitted to wed freedmen, the *liberti*.[26] It was chiefly the Augustine matrimonial legislation that introduced several further prohibitions on marriage for special categories, such as senators and soldiers, but also for citizens in general.[27] These limitations of *ius conubii*, together with the fact that cohabitations of long duration often occurred, despite the prohibitions, promoted the emergence of extramarital relationships, among which concubinage, *concubinatus*[28] is further examined below. Apart from *conubium*, a varying number of impediments to marriage were imposed from time to time. The following were the most important: The parties desiring to marry must have reached the age of puberty, fourteen years for the man and twelve for the woman.[29] If either was subject to *patria potestas*, the consent of his or her *pater familias* was required.[30] In accordance with the definition of matrimony presented above, the Roman marriage was monogamous. An existing marriage, therefore, was an impediment to a later marriage,[31] as were close kinship,[32] affinity,[33] and guardianship.[34] Apart from these impediments, marriage was not permitted for couples found guilty of adultery, *adulterium*,[35] with each other. It is of special interest that requirements, partly analogous to the aforesaid impediments to marriage, came to be external delimiting criteria to the extramarital *concubinatus*. There is reason to return later to this double function of the external delimiting criteria.[36]

Roman marriages, given their highly non-legal nature, were entered into without any official control as to whether the parties possessed *ius conubii*, and whether other matrimonial impediments existed. A legal test of the external matrimonial prerequisites ensued, but, apart from penal cases, was used only when the validity of a marriage was subject to prejudicial scrutiny. Declaratory judgments concerning the existence of a marriage were evidently not available.[37] As a rule, if there was a lack of positive conditions for the marriage or the existence of matrimonial impediments, the marriage was regarded as null and void, invalid as

---

26 Theodor Mommsen, Römisches Staatsrecht III 429 (1893).

27 D. 23, 2, 23; and Ulp. 13, 1.

28 Ulp. 13, 2; D. 23, 2, 43; and Paul Meyer, Der Römische Konkubinat 25 (1895).

29 Ulp. 5, 2 and 11, 28; Gai. 1, 196; Inst. 1, 10 pr. amd 1, 22 pr.; and C. 5, 4, 24 and 5, 60, 3. If the cohabitation was begun when either party was still too young, marriage ensued *ipso facto* when the minor had reached the required age, *see* D. 12, 4, 8; and 23, 2, 4.

30 Ulp. 5, 2; D. 23, 2, 2; D. 23, 2, 35; Inst. 1, 10 pr.; and C. 5, 4, 25. Regarding the guardian's consent, *compare* Ulp. 11 and 27.

31 Gai. 1, 63; D. 3, 2, 1; C. 5, 5, 2 and 9, 9, 18; and Inst. 1, 10, 6 ("duas uxores eodem tempore habere non licet").

32 Gai. 1, 59; Ulp. 5, 6; and Inst. 1, 10, 1.

33 Gai. 1, 63; and D. 23, 2, 40.

34 D. 23, 2, 59.

35 D. 48, 5, 41 (40) pr.; and Nov. 134, 12.

36 *See* Section 2.5 *infra*.

37 *See* Kaser I, *supra* note 5, at 71; and II, at 311.

regards both the relationship between the parties and any child's legal status.[38]

2.3 The *Manus* Marriage

2.3.1 Introduction

According to the earliest Roman law, a *matrimonium iustum* usually involved *manus*, a legal relationship analogous to *patria potestas*. The woman entering into her husband's *manus*, *conveniebat in manum mariti*, legally left the family to which she had belonged and the *patria potestas* to which, so long as she had not been *sui iuris*, she was subject to as a maiden. She instead became a member of her husband's family and subject to his patriarchal authority.[39] The wife was, however, described as *mater familias* and honored with *mater familias honestatem*.[40] She entered among the man's agnatic kin according to the laws of inheritance, and was thereby regarded as her husband's daughter and her children's sister.[41] Thus, the woman acquired the right to inherit[42] from her husband and his relatives but lost her hereditary rights and her other agnatic rights with respect to the members of the family to which she had belonged. All that the wife owned when she entered into the *manus* marriage, and all that she later acquired, became the sole property of her husband.[43]

Of the three ways whereby these legal consequences could ensue, *confarreatio* and *coemptio* are in general disregarded here, while *usus* as a

38 D. 24, 1, 3, 1; Inst. 1, 10, 12; and C. 5, 8. If a widow, despite the ban during the year of mourning after her husband's death, entered into a new marriage, it was not regarded as a *nullum matrimonium*, *see* Nov. 22, 22; and C. 5, 17, 8-9. In exceptional cases, consideration was given to a party's good faith concerning the absence of an impediment, insofar as the marriage was not adjudged null and void so far as regarded the spouse in question. On these putative marriages, *matrimonium putativum*, *see* C. 5, 5, 4; D. 23, 2, 57a; and D. 24, 3, 22, 13. With respect to putative marriages in Canon and American law, *see* Section 14.2.5 *infra*. It is a moot point whether violations of the Augustine marital prohibitions originally resulted in the invalidity of the marriage. It seems clear that nullity later ensued, *see e.g.*, D. 23, 1, 16; D. 23, 2, 16 pr.; MOMSEN, RÖM. STAATSRECHT, *supra* note 26, at 472; and Kunkel, *Matrimonium*, *supra* note 8, col. 2262. In the event that a matrimonial impediment that actually had existed no longer did so, the marriage could *ipso facto* become valid, *see* regarding age note 29 *supra*.

39 Gai. 1, 136; and Tac. Ann. 4, 16. The father's *patria potestas* over the children was matched by his *manus*, literally = hand, over his wife. The *manus* marriage is sometimes called the "strict" marriage, *see* GLÜCK, *supra* note 5, at 134; EDWARD HAMBRO, DEN ROMERSKE FAMILIE- OG ARVERET 6 (1923); and OLIVECRONA, *supra* note 2, at 22.

40 The wife in a *manus* marriage originally seems to have been described as *mater familias* to distinguish her from a wife in a free marriage, who was called *uxor*, *see*, *e.g.*, Ci. Top. 3, 14; D. 50, 16, 46, 1; D. 48, 5, 14 (13) pr.; D. 23, 2, 41, 1; D. 47, 10, 15, 5; GLÜCK, *supra* note 5, at 133; and MEYER, *supra* note 28, at 13.

41 Gai. 1, 111 ("filiae locum optinet"); 1, 114; 2, 159; and 3, 3. Regarding assumed deviations from the main rule, *compare* KARLOWA, RÖM. RG. II, *supra* note 14, at 152.

42 Gai. 3, 3; and Ulp. 22, 14.

43 Gai. 2, 90; 2, 96; 2, 98. For exceptions *see* Gai. 3, 83 and *compare* Cic. Top. 4, 23.

constituent legal fact is more closely examined. The controversial issue of whether *usus* was only a way whereby *manus* could be acquired, or also a way of wedding, is part of the wider complex pertaining to the general relationship between the concepts of marriage and *manus*, and is illustrated below. For our purposes, this preclassical construction is of considerable interest, regardless of whether *usus* was a legal fact for all the consequences of marriage, or only for the woman's legal entry into the man's family and conjugal authority, which alone would have been a significant legal effect.

2.3.2 The Commencement of Marriage

1. *Confarreatio* [44]

The characteristic feature of the rite of *confarreatio*, evidently long a prerogative of the patricians, was its sacred, very solemn nature. The ceremony was attended, apart from the man and the woman, by two officiating high priests, the Pontifex Maximus and the Flamen Dialis, and ten witnesses. The rite included the offering of a spelt-cake, *panis farreus*, to Jupiter, the patron of marriage, as well as certain verbal responses, *certa verba*.[45] In classical times, *confarreatio* had fallen into almost total disuse but still was practiced to some extent among the high priesthood.[46] The *confarreatio* marriage, or its *manus* relationship, could be dissolved according to the principle of a rite *contrarius actus* to *confarreatio*, through *diffarreatio*.[47]

2. *Coemptio* [48]

The second form of marriage, *coemptio*, whereby the woman could enter *in manum mariti*, took the form of a fictitious purchase.[49] It evolved from *mancipatio*,[50] a formal act devised for the transfer of ownership of an object used in diverse judicial proceedings. The ceremony was held in the presence of at least five witnesses and a paymaster, *libripens*. A copper coin was

44 Gai. 1, 112; and Ulp. 9, 1.

45 Neither Gaius nor Ulpian state what these *certa verba* were, and what other rites accompanied the *confarreatio*. Nevertheless, certain assumptions have been made with the help of Serv. in Georg. 1, 31, Serv. in Aen. 4, 105 and 4, 374 and other literary sources. *See* Rossbach, *supra* note 14, at 156; Danz, I, p. 153; Marquardt, *supra* note 14, at 33; Karlowa, Die Formen, *supra* note 14, at 25; Röm. Rg. II, *supra* note 14, at 154; Corbett, *supra* note 14, at 68; and Westrup, Recherces, *supra* note 14, at 9.

46 Tac. Ann. 4, 16.

47 Festus P. 74, Bruns Fontes II, *supra* note 13, at 25; Plut. Quaest. Rom. p. 50; and Westrup, Recherces, *supra* note 14, at 16.

48 Gai. 1, 113; Boeth. Cic. Top. 3, 14; Serv. in Georg. 1, 31; Serv. in Aen. 4, 103; and Isid. Or. 5, 24, 26.

49 It has been asserted that *coemptio* originates in a prehistoric bride-purchase, *see* Rossbach, *supra* note 14, at 77 and 156; and Westrup, Recherces, *supra* note 14, at 49. *Compare* Karlowa, Die Formen, *supra* note 14, at 45.

50 Gai. 1, 119.

laid upon a scale[51] as a symbolic payment for the bride. The woman and the man asked each other: *an sibi mulier mater familias esse vellet?* To which they then must reply *Volo!*[52] During the preclassical period, *coemptio* seems to have been the most common form of *manus* transfer [53] among plebeians, who were debarred from *confarreatio*. It was still in use in the classical era, albeit that then, free marriage was totally predominant. *Coemptio* is not mentioned in *Corpus Iuris Civilis*. The legal relationship constituted by *coemptio* was most likely dissolved by *remancipatio*.[54]

3. *Usus as a Constituent Legal Fact*

Usus, based on a prescription concerning moveable property, *usucapio*,[55] signified that after one year of uninterrupted prescription, the woman legally entered into the man's family and conjugal *manus*.[56] What then is characteristic of this *usus*, regarded as a constituent legal fact? What objective or subjective circumstances must prevail for the year of *usus* to elapse and for the woman, after the expiry of the period of prescription, to enter *in manum mariti?*

In view of the fragmentary, indeterminate nature of the sources available, it is not surprising that *usus* as a legal fact came to be described in the literature on Roman law in somewhat general, somewhat abstract, and extremely vague terms. Be that as it may, certain definitions by Nordic scholars appear to be unduly insubstantial. Lassen speaks laconically of the woman's "ophold i mandens hus i et helt aar," a sojourn in the man's

51 Controversy exists as to which of the parties should be considered the buyer or seller, *see, e.g.*, ROSSBACH, *supra* note 14, at 77; KARLOWA, RÖM. RG. II, *supra* note 14, at 159; CORBETT, *supra* note 14, at 80; and WESTRUP, RECHERCES, *supra* note 14, at 61.

52 *Compare* Cicero who associates *coemptio* with the man's question, "Quaenam vocaris?" and the woman's response, "Ubi to Gaius, ego Gaia!," *see* Cic. Pro Murena 12, 27 in CICERO, IN CATILINAM I-IV, PRO MURENA, PRO FLACCO, PRO SULLA (eng. trans. ed. Louis E. Lord 1953). *Compare* Quintilian who refers the formula to the marriage by *confarreatio, see* 1, 7, 28. However, the formula does not seem to have been a legal requisite for the act, *see* KARLOWA, RÖM. RG. II, *supra* note 14, at 161; and CORBETT, *supra* note 14, at 74.

53 Once marriage between patricians and plebeians was permitted by Lex Canuleia in 445 B.C., *coemptio* seems to have been used for such mixed marriages, *see* Cic. de Rep. 2, 37, 63.

54 Gai. 1, 137; Festus P. 277; and BRUNS FONTES II, *supra* note 13, at 31. *Compare* Gai. 1, 132; 1, 115; 1, 115a; 1, 166; 1, 195; 1, 118; and 1, 118a. Once marriage and *manus* had become separate concepts, the wife was entitled to dissolution of the *manus* relationship in the event of divorce, *see* Gai. 1, 137a.

55 Gai. 1, 111; and ROSSBACH, *supra* note 14, at 147.

56 Gai. 1, 111: ("in familiam viri transibat filiaeque locum optinebat ... eo modo in manum mariti convenire"). According to prevailing opinion, the *manus* relationship constituted by *usus* was probably dissolved in the same way as *coemptio*, through *remancipatio, see supra* note 16 with source references; CORBETT, *supra* note 14, at 188; and Kunkel, *Matrimonium, supra* note 8, col. 2278. *Compare* Constantin Tomulescu, *Gaius 1, 111 und die Ehe usu*, in SEIN UND WERDEN IM RECHT, FESTGABE FÜR ULRICH VON LÜBTOW ZUM 70 GEBURTSTAG 401, 409 (1970), who assumes that the *manus* relationship was dissolved by *trinoctium*.

house for an entire year,[57] without focusing on whether there were any requirements as to her relationship with him beyond her actual stay under his roof. There is a failure to take into account the practical reality in Olivecrona's negative concept that signified that *usus* existed "when the woman had not been away from the man,"[58] although a conclusion *e contrario* implies that she must in any case have been present or at home. Apart from the requirement of the woman's sojourn in the man's house, Levy seems to postulate a union existing where, "Manus durch usus ist Ehe durch die blosse Tatsache der Hausgemeinschaft."[59] It is far more usual and somewhat more substantiated to present, as a legal fact, one year of uninterrupted dwelling together or cohabitation between the man and the woman. Mitteis speaks of "ein schlechthin formlos begründetes Zusammenleben."[60] Accarias declares that the man "par une cohabitation continue" after one year acquired *manus* over his wife,[61] and Westrup refers to the objective requisites in terms of, e.g., *cohabitation* and *un an de vie commun.*[62] Similarly, Nicholas asserts that the legal consequences ensued "by one year's cohabitation."[63] Regarding the legal fact via the term used by French and English scholars, which in both languages can denote dwelling together, and living together as husband and wife,[64] no deliberate distinction can be found between the concepts of dwelling together and living together. Another definition of *usus* as a legal fact that is prevalent in the literature refers to marriage in its social sense. Thus, Volterra asserts that *usus* arose *ipso iure* "après une année de marriage." It is clear that he means matrimony in a social sense.[65] Jörs-Kunkel speaks in general terms of the ending of the informal marriage through "Herstellung der

57 Jul Lassen, Laerebog i Romersk privatret 73 (1911).

58 Olivecrona, *supra* note 2, at 23.

59 Ernst Levy, Der Hergang der Römischen Ehescheidung 68 (1925).

60 Mitteis, *supra* note 9, at 252. see *also* Karlowa, Röm. Rg. II, *supra* note 14, at 162; Rudolf Köstler, *Raub- und Kaufehe bei den Römern*, 65 Zeitschrift der Savigny-Stiftung für Rechtsgeschichte (SZ) 43, 50 (1947); Tomulescu, *supra* note 56, at 409; and Hans Friedrich C. Thomas, Formlose Ehen 18 (1973) (establishes as a legal fact one year of uninterrupted "Zusammenleben").

61 C. Accarias, Precis de Droit Romain II 280 (1882). Henri Levy & Bruhl, *Les origines du mariage sine manu*, 14 Tijdschrift voor Rechtsgeschiedenis 453 (1936), also states with regard to the objective circumstances that a man and a woman could not "cohabiter ... sans que la femme, au bout d'un an, tombat sous la manus du mari."

62 C.W. Westrup, Quelques observations sur les origines du mariage par "usus" et du mariage sans "manus," dans lÁncien droit romain 5 and 12 (1926).

63 Nicholas, *supra* note 24, at 82. *Compare* Corbett, *supra* note 14, at 86.

64 Both the Frech and the English word "cohabitation" comes from the latin *cohabitare. See* Grand Larousse de la Langue Francais 2, at 782 (1972); Emile Littré, Dictionnaire de la Langue Francais 2, at 440 (1956); The Oxford-Hachette French Dictionary 163 (3d ed. 2001); Black's Law Dictionary 254 (7th ed. 1999); and Webster's New Encyclopedic Dictionary 191 (1993).

65 E. Volterra, La Conception du Mariage d'apres les Juristes Romains 31 (1940). *Compare* Kaser, who understands *manus* as a supplement to marriage and consequently declares that the woman entered by *usus* into the man's *manus* when she "in gültiger Ehe gelebt hat" with him for one year, *see* Kaser I, *supra* note 5, at 78.

ehelichen Gemeinschaft" at the same time as he, unfortunately without adducing supporting evidence, defines the legal fact of the woman's affiliation to the household: the man acquired *manus* by one year of uninterrupted "Zugehörigkeit der Frau zu seinem Haushalt."[66] It also happens that the definition of *usus* incorporates the concepts of both living together and marriage. Thus, Sohm states, indeed with a hint at a definition of the relationship between the man and woman, that *manus* was acquired by one year of unbroken "Gebrauch der Ehe" and adds "[d]as ununterbrochene Zusammenleben ist das Kennzeichnen ehelicher Gemeinschaft."[67]

The majority of these definitions of *usus* as a legal fact, however, seem not to be derived from a reported analysis in which an attempt was made to establish a clear distinction between the concepts of dwelling together, living together, and marriage, and their components and legal nature. The accounts tend to indicate that, with regard to these connotations, the different expressions are used more or less synonymously, and that they refer to essentially the same objective circumstances. Notwithstanding the fact that none of these expressions can be said to be a synonym for any of the others—all actual marriages do not involve living together and all cases of living together do not involve marriage—it must be said that the cohabitation of a man and a woman who had *conubium* in a sense is synonymous with marriage as a social institution. One reason to describe a legal fact in such general and vague terms is that the sparse source material hardly allows any far-reaching definitions.

It is not feasible to seek more detail from the sources. With regard to the objective circumstances, it appears that during the *usus* year, the woman must indeed have been with the man, *cum viro ... fuisset.*[68] From this, it follows that an agreement by the parties, or any other *consensus* between them, did not suffice as a legal fact. Furthermore, the woman must not only have stayed with, but must also have been with the man. The sources do not directly say what form this being together must take for the period of prescription to pass. Nevertheless, a possessive element, which indicates intimacy, can be discerned in the requisite living together of the parties. The woman must, so to speak, have been in the man's power.[69] The location of the common life is not explicitly mentioned in the sources. It seems natural to assume, as above, that in practice it usually occurred in

66 Jörs & Kunkel, supra note 24, p. 280. *Compare also* Karlowa, Die Formen, *supra* note 14, at 66; and Röm. Rg. II, *supra* note 14, at 162.

67 Rudolph Sohm, Institutionen 505 (1949).

68 Servius, In Georg. 1, 3: ("*cum viro... fuisset*"). *Compare* Gell. 3, 2, 12: ("*apud virum ... esse coepisset*").

69 Gai. 1, 111: "quia enim veluti annua possessione usucapiebatur." As emerges from Karlowa, the analogy with possession of an object should not be driven too far: "Auch beim usus ist aber nicht an eine sächliche Ersitzung der Frau, an ein uti muliere im Sinn des Gebrauchens derselben, wie einer Sache, zu denken. Die Frau giebt sich dem Manne factisch zur ehelichen Gemeinschaft hin," *see* Karlowa, Die Formen, *supra* note 14, at 66. *Compare* Rossbach, *supra* note 14, at 156.

the man's house or home. It would therefore appear justifiable in objective terms, albeit not wholly convincing, to describe the couple's life together during the *usus* year as *dwelling* or *living* together.

Under these circumstances, should we follow Mitteis and regard *usus* as "ein schlechthin formlos begründetes Zusammenleben;" consequently, "ein gewöhnliches Konkubinat"?[70] Moreover, is Levy's characteristic of *usus* as "[e]he durch die blosse Tatsache der Hausgemeinschaft"[71] at all apt? It would hardly seem so. The importance these authors attach to the purely factual circumstances is not worthy of unreserved acceptance. Judging by the legal sources, it seems feasible to distinguish a subjective element allowing certain specification. According to a comment by Scaevola, restated by Gellius and frequently neglected in the literature, the *usus* year began to run on the day when the woman "apud virum matrimonii causa esse coepisset."[72] It is thereby clear that concubinage *anno continuo* could not without further ado give rise to *usus*. The union must have been established *matrimonii causa*, with a view to marriage. This source gives no further explanation of the content of this matrimonial intent. The few Romanists who have seen fit to linger on the subjective element must resort to hypotheses. Yet, it may be said with some degree of certainty that *matrimonii causa* can hardly have involved an intention to achieve any particular legal consequence. As emerges later in the discussion of *usurpatio trinoctii*, it was even possible to continue to live together year after year, *matrimonii causa* and at the same time ensure that the legal effect of *usus*, *conventio in manum*, would not supervene.[73] It also seems strange to postulate an intention to achieve a completely different legal consequence as a subjective requirement for *usus* and thereby for the transformation into *manus*. *Matrimonii causa* better refers to marriage in a social rather than legal sense. It is probably this social concept of marriage that impels Karlowa to presume that the man and woman embarked on their life together as husband and wife "in der Absicht eine Ehe miteinander *zu führen*" (italics added).[74] What form, then, would a social marriage take according to this intention? Karlowa goes no further in his explanation. However, Westrup does to some extent, inasmuch as he assumes that "selon les termes de Q. Mucius, cette cohabitation s'ètablissait matrimonii causa, c'est-à-dire liberorum (= lib.legitimorum) quaerendorum causa."[75] The idea that the parties' intention must have been to produce legitimate

70 Mitteis, *supra* note 9, at 252. Regarding the concept of concubinage, *compare* Chapter 2.5, *infra*.

71 Levy, *supra* note 59, at 68.

72 Gell. 3, 2, 12. *See* Weiss' translation "zum Zweck der Ehe" in Die Attischen Nächte des Aulus Gellius I-II 177 (Fritz Weiss ed. 1875/76). *Compare* Gai. 1, 111: ("*nupta perseverabat*").

73 *See* Section 2.3.2 *infra*.

74 Karlowa, Röm. Rg. II, *supra* note 14, at 162; and Die Formen, *supra* note 14, at 68.

75 Westrup, Mariage, *supra* note 62, at 12. *Compare* Tomulescu, *supra* note 56, at 403: "Wir können uns höchstens auf den Ausdruck matrimonii causa des Aulus Gellius

offspring accords well with the purposes of marriage particularly emphasized during the heyday of the republic and the period of Augustus' matrimonial reform, when the wife was often described as *uxor liberorum quaerendorum (procreandorum) causa.*[76] Furthermore, it is compatible with the importance that could be attached in an evidentiary aspect to the parties' concentration on procreation.[77] Nevertheless, there is some doubt about the general validity of Westrup's assumption. Procreation, as found above, was not the only purpose attributed to the Roman marriage.[78]

4. *Breach of Usus via Trinoctium*

In the event the woman did not wish to enter into the man's family and marital *manus* after the expiry of the *usus* year, she was entitled to interrupt the period of prescription, *usurpation,* and thereby prevent the legal consequences of *usus.* According to the law of the Twelve Tables, the woman, to effect such an interruption, has to have been absent from the man, *abesse a viro,*[79] for three successive nights, *trinoctium.* If their life together then continued *matrimonii causa,* a new period of prescription began to run. This legal construction, incorporated in the Twelve Tables, albeit at variance with family law, is based on the *usurpatio* of the institution of prescription in property law and presumably rested on an earlier, customary law.

The absence of the woman as a legal fact for *usurpatio* has come to be somewhat differently described in the literature on Roman law. Several authors cite the woman's absence from the man's house or home as an objective requirement for a break in the period of prescription. Kaser states that the one-year term was adjudged broken when the woman "vom Haus des Mannes ferngebleiben ist"[80] during the *trinoctium.* Westrup states that if she "s'éloignait trois nuits de suite de la maison du mari," she broke the *usus* and prevented the establishment of *manus.*[81] The place from which the woman should be absent is occasionally described as *conjugal.* Thus, Jörs-Kunkel comments that the woman spent three successive nights

3.2. berufen: zum Zwecke der Eheschliessung, also mit dem Ziele, legitime Kinder zu erzeugen, denn der Zweck der Ehe war liberorum quaerendorum causal."

76 Kunkel, *Matrimonium, supra* note 8, col. 2260.

77 Gai. 1, 29; Ulp. 3, 3; Gell. 4, 32 and 17, 21, 44; and C. 5, 4, 9.

78 *See* Section 2.2.1 *supra.*

79 Gai. 1, 111; and Gell. 3, 2, 13.

80 KASER I, *supra* note 5, at 78. *Compare* SOHM, *supra* note 67, at 505 ("[N]icht im Hause des Mannes war"); Tomulescu, *supra* note 56, at 405 ("[V]om Hause des Mannes fernblieb"); Kunkel, *Matrimonium, supra* note 8, col. 2261 ("[A]usser dem Hause des Mannes verweilte"); FRITZ SCHWIND, RÖMISCHES RECHT I, at 168 (1950) ("[D]as Hause des Gatten verlassen"); and THOMAS, *supra* note 60, at 18 ("Abwesenheit vom Hause des Mannes"). *Compare* Jörstad's translation of Gaii Inst. 1, 111: "[V]aere borte fra hjemmet" (was away from home), GAIUS INSTITUSJONER 23 (Norwegian trans. Jacob Jorstad 1927).

81 WESTRUP, *supra* note 62, at 6.

"ausserhalb der ehelichen Wohnung."[82] Levy & Bruhl declare that the woman could effect *usurpatio trinoctii* "en quittant trios nuits de suite le domicile conjugal."[83] According to Hambro, the prescription was broken if she was "borte fra egteskapshuset" (away from the conjugal home) for three successive nights.[84] The most frequent case in reality would seem to have been that the woman left the house or home described above as conjugal for *trinoctium*. The assumption that during her absence she usually stayed with her parents and participated in their *gentilsacra* has the ring of probability.[85] Nevertheless, it may be mentioned that, strictly speaking, the sources quoted say only that during the *trinoctium*, the woman is to be away from the man, *abesse a viro*,[86] and that the absence from house and home, be it conjugal or not, is not explicitly stated as a necessary and sufficient requisite for *usurpatio*. Assume, for example, that the woman left the man's home and spent three successive nights at her parents' house, but that her husband accompanied her. In such a case, the woman can be said to have been absent from home but hardly from the man. This circumstance may have had some practical significance when the man and the woman were traveling long distances.

Did the woman's mere absence from the man for the *trinoctium* invariably then involve a breach of *usus*? This presumably was not the case. As found with regard to *usus*, as well as the objective circumstances, a subjective element here often neglected would seem to have been required for the accomplishment of *usurpatio*. According to Scaevola, during the *trinoctium*, the woman must be absent from the man *usurpandi causa*, *i.e.*, in order to break *usus*.[87] From this follows the natural conclusion, now supported by the subjective requirement, that the woman's objective absence merely for the purpose of, e.g., visiting her parents did not break the

82 Jörs & Kunkel, *supra* note 24, at 280. *Compare* Köstler, *supra* note 60, at 51 ("Fernbleiben von der ehelichen Wohnung"); and Schulz, Prinzipien, *supra* note 6, at 130 ("Abwesenheit von der Ehewohnung").

83 Levy & Bruhl, *supra* note 61, at 463.

84 Hambro, *supra* note 39, at 8.

85 Jörs & Kunkel, *supra* note 24, at 280; and Sohm, *supra* note 67, at 506 n. 4 with references.

86 Gell. 3, 2, 13. *Compare* Gai. 1,111 and de Zulueta's translation thereof, whereby a woman not wishing to come under her husband's *manus* should stay away from him for three nights, *see* The Institutes of Gaius I 35 (crit. notes & trans. by Francis de Zulueta 1946). Karlowa, closely following the sources, correctly assumes that the woman would "vom Mannen abwesend sind," *see* Röm. Rg. II, *supra* note 14, at 163. Nicholas is less specific than the sources allow, saying that a woman could prevent the establishment of *manus* "by absenting herself for three nights," without stating from what or whom she should be absent, *see* Nicholas, *supra* note 24, at 82. Accarias is similarly justifiably laconic although more concrete when he remarks that the woman "en d'ecouchant" for three successive nights could achieve *usurpatio*, *see* Accarias, *supra* note 61, at 280.

87 Gell. 3, 2, 13. *Compare* Rolfe's translation: "[F]or the purpose of gaining her independence" in The Attic Nights of Aulus Gellius I-III, 243 (John C. Rolfe trans. 1927) and Weiss': "[U]m.. ihre Freiheit zu bewahren" in Die Attischen Nächte des Aulus Gellius I-II, 178 (Fritz Weiss ed. 1875/76).

period of prescription notwithstanding that the visit lasted longer than a *trinoctium.* Through the requirement that the purpose of the woman's absence was to break the period of prescription and thereby prevent a legal consequence, her entry into the man's conjugal *manus,* the woman's action to some extent resembles a legal act in the modern sense. Regardless, it was not a matter of a mutual agreement since the act was wholly dependent on the woman and her intentions.[88] The legal possibility for the woman to break *usus* each year by *usurpatio* and at the same time still continue *usus* raises the question of how her aforesaid purpose, *usurpandi causa,* is related to her matrimonial intent, *matrimonii causa,* to continue the cohabitation. Can these two subjective elements be reconciled? Could the woman intend both to break and to continue *usus*? This question must be answered in the affirmative. Westrup correctly states that the annual exercise of *ius trinoctii* was a repetition "par laquelle la femme manifestait sa volonté non point de rompre effectivement la vie commune—puisqu'au contraire celle-ci devait se poursuivre—mais simplement de ne pas se soumettre à la *manus de* son mari ..."[89] This presumes, however, a separation of the concepts of matrimony and *usus.* Either the woman by exercising *ius trinoctii* could avoid submission to *manus* at the same time as the marriage was constituted after the expiry of the one-year term, whereby the other legal consequences of marriage ensued, or as seems more likely, the possibility already existed of constituting a free marriage which, however, for avoidance of *manus* still required resort to *ius trinoctii.*[90]

5. *Usus and the Free Marriage*

It should be clear from the above that the institution of *usus* is veiled to a great extent in the obscurity of prehistory. The fragmentary source material, however, allows certain conclusions. Once a man and a woman, having *conubium,* lived together *matrimonii causa, i.e.,* for the purpose of marriage, for one entire year, the woman legally entered the man's family and submitted to his conjugal *manus.* Yet, the woman could avoid this legal consequence by deliberately spending three successive nights, *trinoctium,* away from the man and thereby breaking the period of prescription, *usurpatio.* There was, however, no obstacle to the cohabitation continuing, thereafter, *matrimonii causa.* A new period of prescription could then begin to run. Consequently, by annually exercising the *ius trinoctii,* the woman could already in preclassical times permanently cohabit with a man without

88 Gai, 1, 111: ("ut si qua nollet").

89 WESTRUP, *supra* note 62, at 7.

90 Added to the distinction between the two subjective elements may be that the element *usurpandi causa* is also intended to shed light on the concept *matrimonii causa per se.* It follows from the said content of the former element, and the possibility of simultaneously uniting of the two objectives, that the purpose of marriage, *matrimonii causa,* cannot have denoted an intent on the legal consequences comprising the woman's entry into the man's manus. Accordingly *usus* did not presume *a priori* the legal consequence of *usus,* entry into *manus. Compare* Chapter 2.3.2.3, *supra.*

legally entering his family and without submitting to his authority. This arrangement prefigured the free marriage that later became prevalent in the classical period, during which the wife, without having to practice *trinoctium* each year, remained emancipated, freed from her husband's *manus* authority.

2.3.3 The Legal Nature of the Relationship during the *Usus* Year

The question of how the relationship between the parties could be legally described before the period of prescription had elapsed, during the actual *usus* year and in the event of the annual exercise of *ius trinoctii,* has been extensively debated. The differences of opinion fall into two main camps.

In one, it is argued that the liaison during this period was a purely factual relationship without legal relevance, and not only the woman's entry into the man's family and conjugal *manus* but all the legal consequences of marriage should be referred to at the time of expiry of the *usus* year. Thus, Meyer states: "es besteht noch kein *matrimonium.*"[91] Karlowa, who also considers that the relationship was only transformed into a genuine *iustum matrimonium* after the expiry of the set year, describes the liaison during the *usus* year as a *matrimonium iuris gentium.*[92] This main view is also advocated by Tomulescu, who during the *annus cohabitationis* describes the woman as "konkubine *matrimonii causa,*" legally defining the relationship as marriage only when the *usus* year is at an end.[93] There is some support in the legal sources for the belief that *usus* together with *confarreatio* and *coemptio* was a means of entering into marriage. Servius states: "Tribus enim modis apud veteres nuptiae fiebant: use ... farre ... coemptione."[94] Boethius agrees, stating: "*Tribus modis uxor habebatur, use farreo* coremptione."[95]

The other camp argues that *usus* was only a legal ground for the woman's entry into the man's family and conjugal *manus,* and should be distinguished from the wedding and its legal consequences. In accordance with this stance, which seems to presume the existence of a free marriage *solo consensu* already at the time of the Twelve Tables, the women's *conventio in manum* followed after one year of valid marriage, while the other legal consequences of matrimony ensued already when the parties informally wed one year earlier. Schwind distinguishes thus between marriage and *manus*: "Das einjährige Bestehen der Ehe führt zur Begründung der manus."[96] The presence of a legally valid marriage during the *usus* year is

---

91 Meyer, *supra* note 28, at 15.
92 Karlowa, Röm. Rg. II, *supra* note 14, at 162; and Die Formen, *supra* note 14, at 65.
93 Tomulescu, *supra* note 56, at 401.
94 Georg. 1, 31 in Bruns Fontes II, *supra* note 13, at 78.
95 Ciceronis Topica, 3, 14, *id.* at 73.
96 Schwind, *supra* note 80, at 168.

clearly maintained by Kaser who states that by *usus*, the woman entered into the man's *manus* when she had "in gültiger Ehe gelebt"[97] for one year. Nor does this second main view lack support in the sources. Thus, Gaius describes *usus* as a way whereby the woman entered into the man's *manus*: "Olim itaque tribus modis in manum conveniebant, use farreo coemptione" (Gai. 1, 110). He goes on to say: "eo modo in manum mariti convenire" (Gai.1, 111). Gaius' use of the word *nupta* in the clause: "Use in manum conveniebat quae anno continuo nupta perseverabat" (Gai. 1, 111) is of particular interest. It is clear that the woman entered into the man's *manus* when she *nupta perseverabat* for one full year. The fact that *nupta* denotes a matron and that when she thus entered into the man's *manus*, she had already been legally married to him for one year has been adduced as evidence that the relationship between the parties already during the *usus* year constitutes a legal marriage.[98] This interpretation is linguistically supported in several standard Latin dictionaries. Thus, *nupta*, the perfect passive participle of *nubo*, as adjective or as a noun, is translated from Latin to French as *mariée, épouse*;[99] from Latin to English as *married, wedded, married woman, bride, wife*;[100] from Latin to German as *verheiratet, vermählt, Ehefrau, Gattin, Braut;* [101] and from Latin to Swedish as *gift, hustru,* and *brud.*[102] The lexical significance gains some support, albeit not without reservations, from translations of *Gai Institutiones.* Thus, in his translation of Gai 1, 111, Jorstad declares that the woman *vaert gift* (had been married)[103] for one year, while de Zulueta states that she *cohabited*[104] with her *husband* for a similar period. It may be recalled, however, that Gaius' own usage, so far as it is now relevant, does not appear to be legally convincing or consistent. Thus, in other texts, he uses *nuptia* and *nupta* of and in relationships which did not constitute a *iustum matrimonium*, e.g., a liaison invalid and incestuous (Gai. 1, 64) and in a relationship between an alien and a Roman citizen (Gai. 1, 68). According to Westrup, the word *nupta*, as Gaius uses it, has no specific technical significance but may denote either a married or a single woman as "la fiancée acquise *matrimonii causa*,

97 KASER I, *supra* note 5, at 78. *See further* ROSSBACH, *supra* note 14, at 147; SOHM, *supra* note 67, at 506; WESTRUP, *supra* note 62, at 7; KUNKEL, *supra* note 8 col. 2261; and NICHOLAS, *supra* note 24, at 83. For deviations from the main tenets, *compare* Köstler who characterizes the relationship during the *usus* year as an incomplete marriage, "eine unvollkommene Ehe," *see* Köstler, *supra* note 60, at 51, and Mitteis, who alleges that the function of *usus* was originally to remedy formal errors at the wedding, *see* Mitteis, *supra* note 9, at 252.

98 Köstler, *supra* note 60, at 51.

99 FELIX GAFFIOT, DICTIONNAIRE ILLUSTRÉ LATIN FRANCAIS 1048 (1934).

100 LEWIS AND SHORT, *supra* note 5, at 1222.

101 LANGENSCHEIDTS GROSSWÖRTERBUCH LATEINISCH TEIL I, LATEINISCH-DEUTSCH, 508 (Hermann Menge ed., 20th ed. 1978).

102 CHRISTIAN CAVALLIN, LATINSKT LEXIKON II col. 67 (1888).

103 Jorstad, *supra* note 80, at 23.

104 de Zulueta, *supra* note 86, at 35.

mais non encore definitivement épousée."[105] Jurists other than Gaius used the word *nupta* in extramarital relationships. Ulpian and Pomponius thus describe an unmarried girl who was too young legally to enter into marriage, but who cohabited with a man, as *nupta.*[106] Consequently, there is no unequivocal legal interpretation of the word *nupta* extant.

It is clear from the above that the fragmentary sources lend a certain support to the two main opinions. The contradiction between them disappears, however, if viewed from a temporal perspective. It is equally correct to assume that marriage and *manus* were originally inseparable concepts, that marriage then always involved the man's *manus* authority over his wife, and that the formalities for the wedding, the foundation of *manus,* and the dissolution of the marriage and the *manus* relationship, always coincided.[107] The couple then, as married, always belonged to the same *familia.* With the later recognition of the free marriage, *solo consensu* and *sine manu* as an *iustum matrimonium,* it may also be assumed that the concepts of marriage and *manus* diverged and had, in principle, become separate concepts, by Gaius' time, when free marriage predominated, and *usus* according to the testimony of Gaius had fallen into disuse. *Confarreatio* and *coemptio* then became a supplement to the free marriage for couples desiring a *manus* relationship. A certain link persisted between the concepts in that the woman's possibility of dissolving the *manus* relationship seems to have presumed a divorce (Gai. 1,137). This, too, is no more than an assumption, however, since the date of the appearance of the free marriage[108] cannot be fixed with certainty. Yet, it may confidently be said that after one year of unbroken *usus,* the man acquired *manus* authority over the woman.

---

105 WESTRUP, *supra* note 62, at 6.

106 Ulpian (D. 23, 1, 9; D. 48, 5, 14 (13) 8) and Pomponius (D. 23, 2, 4), respectively. *Compare* Durrey, who describes *"nupta"* as "verehelichte," *see* RIDA 2, 1955 at 263 and RIDA 3, 1956 at 227. Garcia & Garrido, who consider that *"nupta"* denotes an unmarried woman who lives with a man without any sexual intercourse, *see* Labeo 3, 1957 at 76.

107 *See* BONFANTE, *supra* note 14, at 42. *Compare* KARLOWA, RÖM. RG. II, *supra* note 14, at 164 and 151; and CORBETT, *supra* note 14, at 86.

108 The expression "free marriage" has its equivalents in other languages, *compare* FIRMIN LAFERRIÉRE, HISTOIRE DU DROIT CIVIL DE ROME ET DU DROIT FRANCAIS III 67 (Paris 1847) ("le mariage libre"); CORBETT, *supra* note 14, at 90 ("free marriage"); LEVY, *supra* note 59, at 67 ("die freie Ehe"); M. GROSSE, FREIE RÖMISCHE EHE UND NICHTEHELICHE LEBENSGEMEINSCHAFT (1991) ("die freie Ehe"); and LASSEN, *supra* note 57, at 350 ("det 'frie' Aegteskab"). The expression "det laxa äktenskapet" also occurs in Nordic scholarship. Other authors start from the absence of the man's *manus* authority over his wife in the free marriage and describe this as "le mariage sine manu," *see* Levy & Bruhl, *supra* note 61, at 453. *See also* WESTRUP, *supra* note 62, at 5 ("mariage sans 'manus'"); and KUNKEL, *supra* note 8 col. 2271 ("die Gewaltfreie Ehe").

2.4 The Free Roman Marriage

2.4.1 Introduction

Roman customs with respect to forming families underwent many changes at the end of the Roman Republic and in the beginning of the Roman Empire.[109] The frequency of marriage declined and the number of divorces increased. If we believe Seneca, there were women who no longer counted the years by the number of consuls but by how many husbands they had had.[110] More Romans than ever chose to live alone or in more or less temporary extramarital liaisons rather than form a family. The birth rate fell and threatened the Roman population base of the realm. Attempts to stem this development through legislation proved fruitless.[111] Concubinage became

---

109 Gell. I, 6, 1; Ludwig Friedländer, Darstellungen aus der Sittengeschichte Roms 248 and 285 (1922); Wilhelm Kroll, *Die Kultur der Ciceronischen Zeit*, in Das Erbe der Alten II 51 (1933); Westrup, Introduction, *supra* note 7, at 89 and 154; and H. Vandenberghe, De Juridische Betekenis vanhet Concubinaat 3 (1970). *Compare* Schulz, Classical, *supra* note 1, at 105, who did not assume the existence of any widespread aversion to marriage. *Compare* the same author, *id.* at 133.

110 De Beneficiis, III, 16. *Compare* Juvenal, who reports that many wives resorted to divorce even before the green boughs that decked the house as the newlyweds entered had withered, *see id.* at 6, 227. Notwithstanding the fact that these poets' satirical descriptions of the manners (*see also* Martial's epigrams and Ovid's Ars Amandi) and morals of Roman women—note that it is the women—seem exaggerated and, as Jörs & Kunkel have maintained, do not allow for any far-reaching generalizations, there was indisputably an unusual mutual frivolity, see Jörs & Kunkel, *supra* note 24, at 274 n. 2. The inscription *Laudatio Turiae*, in memory of a woman who died after 41 years of matrimony, shows that marriages dissolved by death and not by divorce were rare, *see* Bruns Fontes I, *supra* note 15, at 126; and Friedländer, *supra* note 109, at 286. *Compare*, Kaser I, *supra* note 5, at 72: "Die Macht der *mores* hielt die römischen Ehen nicht weniger stark zusammen als andernorts das Gebot des Rechts."

111 The most comprehensive was Augustus' matrimonial legislation that sought to strengthen citizenship, family, and marriage, and increase the frequency of wedlock and nativity. The chief laws were *Lex Iulia de maritandis ordinibus* and *Lex Iulia de adulteriis* from 18 B.C. and *Lex Papia Poppaea* from 9 A.D. (sometimes cited as one single law). According to these provisions, men between the ages of 25–60 years and women between the ages of 20–50 years in principle were obliged to live as married, *see* Ulp. 16, 1. In addition, freeborn parents were to produce three children in the marriage and freed parents four. Violations of the regulations were punished *inter alia* by limitations in the right to inherit and bequests. At the same time, married citizens with the requisite number of children born in wedlock were favored in special respects, from precedence in appointment to office to priority in the booking of theatre seats, *see* Gell. 2, 15, 4; Tac. Ann. 2, 51 and 15, 19; D. 4, 4, 2; Ulp. 17, 1; Gai.2, 111; 2, 144; 2, 286; and Jörs, H 13-8. The provisions concerning moral issues included penalties for adultery, *adulterium*, *see* D. 48, 5; and D. 23, 2, 43, and various forms of lewdness, *stuprum*, such as sexual intercourse with a free, unmarried, respectable woman, *see* D. 48, 5, 35, 5; D. 25, 7, 1, 1; and D. 25, 7, 3,11. At the same time as marriage was promoted, a number of prohibitions on matrimony, particularly for citizens of senatorial rank, were introduced to strengthen citizenship and protect it from unworthy elements, *see* Ulp. 13, 2; and D. 23, 2, 43. Marriages in violation of these prohibitions were originally considered invalid only when these laws were enforced, which meant that the parties were affected by the negative consequences for unmarried individuals there prescribed, *see* Ulp. 16, 2; Jörs at 20; and Kaser I, *supra* note 5, at 319. These marriages later became generally null and

increasingly common and more and more of those who desired to live as married chose free marriage rather than with *manus*, which thereby fell into disuse, but not as a result of legislation.[112] Throughout the classical and postclassical epochs, the free marriage held pride of place.

There is no reason to scrutinize this ontological development, its underlying principles, and its effects on the Roman society for the purposes here.[113] It may suffice with respect to the free marriage to state that it probably emerged under the influence of both Greek individualistic philosophy and native Roman *humanitas*, which held that women should have a freer,

---

void, *see* D. 23, 2, 16 pr.; D. 23, 1, 16; D. 24, 1, 3, 1; and D. 23, 2. 41, 1. The Augustine matrimonial legislation does not seem to have achieved its purpose of increasing the frequency of marriage and the birth rate, *see* Tac. Ann. 3, 25; Friedländer, *supra* note 109, at 248; Marquardt, *supra* note 14, at 75; Kaser I, *supra* note 5, at 318; and Jörs & Kunkel, *supra* note 24, at 274. Paradoxically enough, it instead gave rise to new extramarital relationships, more on this below concerning concubinage. It may be observed that Augustus' reform did not include any change with regard to the form of entry into the free marriage, and only set minor limitations on the possibility of dissolving this by divorce, *see* Kaser I, *supra* note 5, at 321. Even in Augustus' time, the free marriage could be entered into and dissolved freely without the observation of any formalities. The registration of births that Augustus introduced had no equivalent registration pertaining to marriages.

112 Kaser, Iura, *supra* note 7 at 87; and Schulz, Classical, *supra* note 1, at 104. Throughout the classical era, the old Roman *manus* marriage existed as a legal phenomenon but, like an empty suit of armor, remained well nigh unused. The Justinian legislation lacked provisions on *manus*.

113 The source material is meager and the historical causal connections difficult to analyze. Under these circumstances, and with reference to the highly moral potency of the issues, it is not surprising that the free marriage, like the development of the Roman customs of forming families in general, have aroused so widely divergent views in the scholarship. Olivecrona states: "The lax marriages destroyed all order in family relationships and resulted in further immorality which pervaded all levels of society. This immorality again nurtured a general slackness in both physical and moral respects; and this situation gives the true explanation of why the formerly so powerful Roman Empire, once the foundation of the society, the family, had been destroyed, easily collapsed, and how the weakened, morally depraved Romans were subdued without obvious difficulty by barbarian invaders," *see* Olivecrona, *supra note* 2, at 32. It may be remarked that the author's far-reaching conclusions with regard to the effects of the free marriage on the Roman society hardly do full justice to the complexity of the historical causal connections, and that the evidence he adduces has its shortcomings. Yet Olivecrona's account deserves its place as a representative of early to mid-twentieth century scholarship, and as an echo of the ideas widespread on the Continent in the mid-nineteenth century. *Compare* Laferrière, *supra* note 108, at 197; Paul Gide, *De la Condition de l'enfant naturel et de la concubine dans la législation romaine*, R.H.D. 337 (1880); Rudolph Ihering, Geist des Römischen Rechts II 183 (Leibzig, Breitkopf und Härtel, 2d ed. 1866); and Georg Friedrich Puchta, Cursus der Institutionen I-II 394 (Leipzig, 10th ed. 1893). If free marriage was regarded in patriarchal circles as a manifestation of decadence and demoralization, it aroused greater enthusiasm in the liberal camp. A typical representative thereof is Schulz who, somewhat uncritically, views classical matrimonial law as an expression of Roman humanist ideas: "The Classical law of marriage is an imposing, perhaps the most imposing, achievement of the Roman legal genius. For the first time in the history of civilization there appeared a purely humanistic idea of marriage as being a free and freely dissoluble union of two equal partners for life," *see* Schulz, Classical, *supra* note 1, at 103. *Compare* his Prinzipien at 128.

less dependent status *vis-à-vis* men than the patriarchal structure of the *manus* marriage allowed, and that the official legal system should not intrude into a family's autonomy but, in principle, end at the threshold of the home.[114]

In accordance with these ideas, the free marriage was characterized by a considerable freedom from legal consequences. Thus, the woman did not enter into her husband's *manus* and did not have to avoid such entry by the exercise the *ius trinoctii.* She was not legally a member of her husband's family and did not acquire right of inheritance under civil law, *ius sui heredis,* after him and his relatives.[115] The marriage did not involve an economic union between the parties.[116] Anything owned by a spouse at the time of the wedding, or acquired later, was retained by the spouse outright.[117] Similarly, each spouse was responsible for his or her debts.[118] As a result, an order prevailed resembling the modern system of separation of goods, applied in England since 1882, the German "Gütertrennung" and the Swedish arrangement of private property. It was customary upon marriage for the wife, or others on her behalf, to bring with her a dowry, *dos,*[119] that was returned when the marriage was dissolved.[120] Other gifts between the spouses were in principle illegal, which frequently provoked disputes as to whether a marriage existed when the gift was bestowed.[121]

114 Levy & Bruhl, *supra* note 61, at 454 and 464: "Mais les choses changèrent au moment où les influences grecques développèrent à Rome l'individualisme et le féminisme, où l'antique famille patriarcale tendit à se dissocier." *Compare* WESTRUP, RECHERCES, *supra* note 14, at 32; and Kroll, *supra* note 109, at 121. Regarding the interest of wealthy Roman women in Greek education and their aversion to the *manus* marriage, *see* Tomulescu, *supra* note 56, at 407; and MARQUARDT, *supra* note 14, at 61. Regarding the influence of native Roman *humanitas, see* SCHULZ, CLASSICAL, *supra* note 1, at 103; and PRINZIPIEN at 128.

115 In the event of a lack of other heirs, however, the couple had a limited praetorian right of inheritance from each other, *bonorum possession, see* D. 38, 11; and Inst. 3, 9, 3-7. Postclassical law bestowed on a widow or widower without means a certain right of inheritance, even in competition with other heirs, but this comprised at most one-fourth of the estate, *see* Nov. 53, 6, and later even less, *see* Nov. 117, 5.

116 Consequently by "coniunctio maris et feminae et consortium omnis vitae divini et humani iuris communicatio," Modestinus meant something different from the property relationship of positive law between the parties to a free marriage.

117 According to *praesumptio Muciana,* property *in dubio* was considered to belong to the man, *see* D. 24, 1, 51.

118 KASER I, *supra* note 5, at 329.

119 D. 23, 3, 3. The dowry was originally intended as a contribution to defray the living costs, *onera matrimonii,* and in the event of the dissolution of the marriage as a contribution to the woman's maintenance. The wife's property apart from the *dos* was hers alone and described as *parapherna* or *paraphernalia, see* C. 5, 14, 8. Under classical law, there evidently was no legal obligation to bring a *dos, see* C. 5, 3, 20, C. 5, 17, 11 pr.; KASER I, *supra* note 5, at 80; CORBETT, *supra* note 14, at 153; and H.F. JOLOWICZ, ROMAN FOUNDATIONS OF MODERN LAW 151 note 1 (1957). *Compare* on the other hand, OLIVECRONA, *supra* note 2, at 29.

120 D. 23, 3, 42.

121 D. 24, 1, 1; C. 5, 16. The purpose of the ban on gifts seems to have been to prevent unduly extravagant self-sacrifice by reason of matrimonial affection. On this point, and on the exceptions from the ban on gifts, *see* CORBETT, *supra* note 14, at 144.

Nor was there a legal obligation of maintenance between the spouses, although they were considered morally bound to contribute to each other's support.[122]

The personal legal consequences of marriage were also limited. The lack of entry into *manus* meant that the wife was not subject to her husband's authority in a personal respect. If she had been under *patria potestas* before the marriage, she formally continued even afterwards.[123] If she had been *sui iuris*, she remained independent or emancipated; nor did she bear the man's family name.[124] Nevertheless, as a result of the marriage, the woman acquired the dignity of matron, *honor matrimonii*,[125] and shared her husband's class, rank, and domicile.[126] In principle, the couple owed each other fidelity.[127] Finally, it may be mentioned that they were freed from the obligation to testify against each other.[128]

The most significant legal effect of the free marriage presumably pertained not to the relationship between the spouses but to the status of their children. Children born in wedlock were legitimate and became Roman citizens. Legally they belonged to their father's family and shared his class and rank. They had the right of inheritance from their father and other members of his family, and were subject to his *patria potestas*.[129]

The free Roman marriage was nevertheless free chiefly insofar as it could be freely entered into and dissolved without interference by any authority and without the observance of any formalities. This *libertas matrimonii*, a counterpart of the freedom of testamentary disposition and contractual freedom *inter vivos*, represented a cornerstone of the liberal classical concept of marriage. As stated above, no official check was made *ipso iure* of whether matrimonial impediments existed at the wedding.[130] Moreover, the marriage did not have to be celebrated before a religious or secular authority, nor did any other formalities have to be unconditionally observed.

---

122 Kaser I, *supra* note 5, at 80 and 329, and II at 118. However, if the *dos* had been handed over, the wife was adjudged to be entitled to maintenance from it, *see* D. 24, 3, 22, 8; D. 23, 3, 73, 1; and C. 5, 12, 29.

123 In practice, *patria potestas* usually seems to have been exerted over married women, *see* D. 43, 30, 1, 5; D. 48, 5, 12, 1; and Paul. Sent. 5, 6, 15.

124 *See* Schulz, Classical, *supra* note 1, at 115, who remarks that Cicero's wife was called Terentia. *See* further Marquardt, *supra* note 14, at 17.

125 D. 24, 1, 32, 13; D. 32, 49, 4 ("dignitas"). Regarding the significance of *honor matrimonii* as an evidentiary fact of the intent to marry, *see* Section 2.4.2.2, *infra*.

126 D. 1, 9, 1, 1 and 8; and C. 5, 4, 10; C. 12, 1, 13. Schulz, Classical, *supra* note 1, at 115, assumes that sharing a rank only applied to the wives of senators.

127 The woman's infidelity already in classical law could be punished as *adulterium*, *see* D. 48, 5; and C. 9, 9. The man's infidelity could be of significance for the return of the dowry but only resulted in punishment in postclassical law under influence from the Church, *see* Nov. 134, 10. *Compare* Nov. 117, 9, 5; C. 5, 17, 8, 2; and Gell. 10, 23, 3-5.

128 D. 22, 5, 4.

129 D. 1, 6, 4; Inst. 1, 9, 3; and Gai. 1, 55.

130 *See* Section 2.2.3, *supra*.

By the same token, if the marriage was ended by divorce, *divortium*,[131] no legal process or cooperation of any authority was required where the parties had to present legally acceptable grounds for dissolving the marriage. Even agreements excluding or curtailing the possibility of divorce, or stipulating damages in the event thereof, were invalid.[132] Divorce was a purely private act.

The absence of every formality for either entry into a marriage or its dissolution accentuates the question of what positive requisites needed to be present for a marriage to be adjudged legally established, existing, or dissolved.

2.4.2 Entry into Marriage

1. Consensus or Affectio Maritalis as the Constituent Elements

The parties' mutual matrimonial intent, expressed in the maxim *consensus facit nuptias*, was the fundamental legal element for the constitution of a free marriage.[133] This congruent matrimonial intent had to be temporally focused on a present, not merely a future marriage, to be given constituent effect.[134] The crux of this marital consensualism consisted in the parties' *affectio maritalis*,[135] a concept that, due to its uniqueness, is not be

131 D. 24, 1, 32, 13. Dissolution of a marriage could ensue either from mutual agreement, *communi consensu, bona gratia* or *divortium sensu stricto, see* D. 24, 2, 2; C. 5, 17, 9; C. 5, 13, 16; and Nov. 22, 4, or from a unilateral declaration of divorce, *repudium, see* D. 24, 2, 9. Special grounds on which dissolution of a marriage by *repudium* was allowed were first introduced in the postclassical period under the influence of the Church. Divorce in violation of these grounds could result in punishment and other sanctions but the marriages nevertheless were dissolved under civil law. These grounds therefore were more in the nature of rules for exemption from punishment than grounds for divorce in the modern sense. Regarding the number of such grounds for divorce varying with time, *see* D. 45, 15, 8; D. 45, 1, 19; C. Th. 3, 10, 1; C. Th. 3, 16, 1; C. 5, 17, 8-11; Nov. 22, 3; and Nov. 117 and 127, 4. Dissolution of a marriage by mutual agreement was permitted during a long period. It was Justinian who first attempted to drastically limit the possibility thereof, *see* Nov. 117, 10. The limitation was repealed shortly afterwards by his successor, *see* Nov. 140.

132 C. 8, 38, 2.

133 D. 50, 17, 30 ("Nuptias non concubitus, sed consensus facit") (not copulation, but consent creates marriage); and D. 35, 1, 15.

134 Thus it would be a question of a *consensus in praesenti* and not *consensus in futuro*. In the latter case, when the parties had agreed to marry in the future, it was a betrothal, *sponsalia, see* D. 23, 1; C. 5, 1 that was not compulsory from a legal viewpoint, nor accompanied by any formalities: *sufficit nudus consensus ad constituenda sponsalia, see* D. 23, 1, 4. *Compare* the Mediaeval Canon law whereby a matrimonial *consensus in futuro* could acquire constituent significance, *see* Section 3.3.3 *infra*.

135 D. 24, 1, 32, 13 ("non enim coitus matrimonium facit, sed maritalis affection"). *Compare* D. 24, 1, 32, 13; D. 24, 1, 66 pr.; D. 25, 7, 4; D. 39, 5, 31 pr.; D. 48, 20, 5, 1; C. 2, 7, 23, 4; C. 5, 4, 13; C. 5, 4, 22; C. 5, 17, 1; C. 5, 17, 8 pr.; 5, 17, 11 pr.; C. 5, 27, 11 pr.; C. Th. 3, 6, 1; C. Th. 3, 7, 3; C. Th. 7, 13, 6; Nov. 22, 3; Nov. 74, 4; Nov. 117, 4-6; Inst. Orat. 5, 11, 32; and Paul. Sent. 2, 20, 1. Regarding interpellations of the

encompassed within the modern concept of contract.[136] In both its character and content, the concept of *affectio maritalis* appears to have been extremely indefinite, in the view of a various scholars.

Notwithstanding the lexical meaning,[137] few authors have understood *affectio* as a marital emotion, sentiment, attitude, conduct, state of mind, or temperament, with which the parties more or less unconsciously are expected to be filled, afflicted, or seized. *Affectio* has in different languages indeed been described on occasions as *état de l'homme*,[138] *Gesinnung*,[139] *state of mind*,[140] and *geestelijke ingesteldheid, een mentaliteit.*[141] As a rule, however, *affectio* has been understood as a *consciousness*, an *intention* or a *will* with a certain matrimonial content, albeit that the distinctions between the said subjective entities are rarely maintained.[142] Müller-Freienfels postulates for the constitution of the free marriage that a "freien Bewusstsein der beiden Ehepartner, dass ihre Gemeinschaft eine Ehe sei."[143] We also find this idea, of the parties' awareness of the nature of their union, or the way they think of and regard each other, in the content of the *affectio maritalis* in Corbett, who declares "[t]hey must regard each other as man and wife."[144] Thus, if we follow Corbett, persons are not legally married until they have begun to see each other in this light. Others place a heavier emphasis on the parties' intention with regard to the union than their

---

sources, *see* Kuebler in SZ, 11 (1890) at 49; LEVY, *supra* note 59, at 70; and CORBETT, *supra* note 14, at 93.

136 Regarding the conception in modern civil law of how the wedding is related to the general concept of contract, *see* Heinz Hübner, *Eheschliessung und allgemeine Wirkungen der Ehe als dogmatische Problem*, FamRZ 1 (1962), who regards entry into marriage as "Rechtsgeschäft, ja als Vertrag im Sinne eines contractus sui generis."

137 *See, e.g.*, LEWIS AND SHORT, LATIN DICTIONARY 65 (1998): affectio (adf-), onis, f. [adficio]. I. The relation to or disposition toward a thing produced in a person by some influence. II. A. A change in the state or condition of body or mind, a state of frame of mind, feeling. B. A permanent state of mind, a frame of mind, a state of feeling. Also of body, as anal. to the mind, a fixed, permanent constitution. C. Esp., a favorable disposition toward any one, love, affection, good-will. D. In the Lat. of Pandects, ability of willing, will, volition, inclination.

138 VOLTERRA, *supra* note 65, at 38.

139 KASER I, *supra* note 5, at 73; Kaser, IURA, *supra* note 7 at 80 and 18 in STUDIA ET DOCUMENTA HISTORIAE ET IURIS 304 (1952).

140 JOLOWICZ, *supra* note 119, at 143.

141 VANDENBERGHE, *supra* note 109, at 10. *Compare* RICCARDO ORESTANO, LA STRUTURA GIURIDICA DEL MATRIMONIO ROMANO DAL DIRITTO CLASSICO AL DIRITTO GIUSTINIANEO 300 (1951), using the expression: "elemento spirituale."

142 *See e.g.* Kaser, who describes *affectio maritalis* sometimes as both parties "Bewusstsein," *see* Kaser, I at 321, sometimes as their "dauernder Willen," *see* KASER I, *supra* note 5, at 73, and sometimes, which could imply the establishment of an interesting relationship between the elements, as "die eheliche Gesinnung," in which "der auf Begründung and Erhaltung der Ehe gerichtete Wille" becomes concrete, *see* Kaser, IURA, *supra* note 7 at 80 n. 49. In STUDIA ET DOCUMENTA, *supra* note 139, at 304, the author interprets this "Dauerwille" as an "eheliche Gesinnung," as an "Entschollenheit" and as a "Haltung," without apparently differentiating between them.

143 MÜLLER-FREIENFELS, *supra* note 6, at 8.

144 CORBETT, *supra* note 14, at 92.

comprehension thereof.[145] Thus, Jolowicz, who characterized *affectio* as a state of mind, asserts that the marriage comes into being through the parties' intentions, indeed their firm intentions to be man and wife.[146] Others also understand *affectio* as an intent, albeit an intent that seems singular in its legal nature. Thus, it differs from the *consensus* of most modern voluntative schools chiefly in that it was not based on a single verbal declaration, but rather was manifested by the parties' temperament throughout their life together. Thus, it was not a question of a once-congruent intent, an initial intent, but a continuous *consensus*, sometimes aptly described by German-speaking scholars as *Dauerkonsens*,[147] which was more in the nature of an enduring, subjective prerequisite, like *animus* with regard to possession, rather than an element in a contract.[148] A modern marriage, once sealed, legally endures, irrespective of whether the spouses' matrimonial intent and actual cohabitation have ceased, until it is dissolved by divorce. The Roman marriage was dependent for both its constitution and its continuance on the mutual will of the parties. Pacchioni fully articulated this difference as follows: "Die moderne Ehe wird geschlossen, die romische gelebt."[149] The aphorism however, is more convincing if *erlebt* replaces *gelebt* to reflect the subjective nature of the *consensus* requisite.

The sources state that the *affectio* should be matrimonial, *maritalis*. Many Roman scholars stop short by laconically remarking that it must be a question of matrimonial intent or the like. Thus, e.g., Kunkel speaks of the parties' "Ehewillen" and "Willen zur Ehe."[150] The question arises, however, whether the intention to marry is to be focused on marriage as a social phenomenon or marriage as a legal institution.[151] Does the object of the intent to marry consist of the legal consequences of marriage, or of the marital cohabitation? Few authors have been disposed to regard the

145 *Compare* Vandenberghe, who by *affectio maritalis* understands both the intention and the decision to live as man and wife: "[D]e bedoeling en de overtuiging, als man en vrouw to leven," *see* VANDENBERGHE, *supra* note 109, at 10.

146 Jolowicz, *supra* note 119, at 143, 145 and 151. *Compare* Nicholas, who speaks of a "common intention to be married," *see* NICHOLAS, *supra* note 24, at 81; and Glück, who *a contrario* seems to presume an "[a]bsicht vollständiger Lebensgemeinschaft," *see* GLÜCK, *supra* note 5, Bd. 28 at 360.

147 KASER II, *supra* note 5, at 108. *Compare* VOLTERRA, *supra* note 65, at 38, who speaks of "une volonté durable, continue."

148 Schulz asserts that the marriage is sealed by an "informal agreement" but finds that it did not constitute a consensual contract, maintaining that the constituent element is the man's and the woman's free will but does not expatiate the nature and the character thereof, *see* SCHULZ, CLASSICAL, *supra* note 1, at 111. *Compare* Lassen, who in a subjective respect laconically states that marriages were made "ved formlös Overenskomst," *see* LASSEN, *supra* note 57, at 350. Similarly, Sundberg remarks that marriage is entered into "avtalsvis," *see* JACOB W.F. SUNDBERG, FAMILJERÄTT I OMVANDLING 20 (1969).

149 Quoted from SCHWIND, *supra* note 80, at 177.

150 KUNKEL, *supra* note 8 col. 2271; and JÖRS & KUNKEL, *supra* note 24, at 278. *See also e.g.* KARLOWA, RÖM. RG. II, *supra* note 14, at 180; and PUCHTA II, *supra* note 113, at 400.

151 Regarding marriage in the two different senses, *see* Section 2.2 *supra*

matrimonial intent as an intention to achieve all or some of the legal consequences of marriage. Yet Meyer starts from "die zum Ausdruck gebrachte Willenseinigung der Ehegatten ('maritalis affectio') rechtliche Wirkungen zu erzeugen," at least with respect to the status of the children.[152] Nicholas, who finds a common purpose "to be married" necessary for the constitution of a marriage and contrasts such an intention with a desire "merely to live together," also seems, although he does not dwell on the distinction, to have understood the former as a wish to be legally wed.[153]

It has more commonly been held that matrimonial intent should focus on marriage in the sense of the social institution through the actual marital cohabitation. Thus, Schwind formulates the mutual matrimonial intent as "dem Willen, mit einander als Eheleute *zu leben*" (italics added) but sometimes varies the definition to "den Willen der Familienbildung,"[154] Likewise, with the social institution in mind, Sohm postulates that the parties' *consensus* must be focused on an "eheliche Gemeinschaft."[155] Scholars seldom discuss the details of how the spouses live or should live, or what form the creation of a family or the connubial fellowship takes or should take. Nevertheless, Kaser somewhat extends his exposition of the object of the intent and asserts that *affectio* must be focused on "eine lebenslange, monogamische, mit Hausgemeinschaft verbundene Lebensgemeinschafte zum Zweck der Kindererzeugnung,"[156] and adds that only a union so qualified won legal recognition. Kaser's specification of the object of the matrimonial intent inevitably brings to mind the Roman definitions of marriage presented above in the introduction to this chapter, to which, surprisingly enough, he makes no explicit mention. Volterra, however, does and considers that the expression *consortium omnis vitae* in Modestinus'

152 Meyer, *supra* note 28, at 87.

153 Nicholas, *supra* note 24, at 81. *Compare* Pringsheim, who regarding the *animus* concept in Roman law in general asserts that the concept is probably Byzantine and that it comprised an intention to attain a legal result. Unfortunately, Pringsheim does not express himself clearly on the content of the intention with regard to the *affectio maritalis* of matrimonial law, *see* Fritz Pringsheim, *Animus in Roman law*, 49 L.Q.R. 43, 379 and 399 (1933).

154 Schwind, *supra* note 80, at 176 and 181. *Compare* equivalent expressions in Vandenberghe, *supra* note 109, at 10: "als man en vrouw to leven." Instead of an intention "to live as," others use the expression of an intention or purpose "to be" man and wife. Thus Jolowicz presumes the parties' intention "to be man and wife," *see* Jolowicz, *supra* note 19, and Hambro, refers to their unanimity in wishing "vaere aegtefolk," *see* Hambro, *supra* note 39, at 8. Although naturally, it is entirely logically possible to be, or to intend to be, man and wife without living, or intending to live, as man and wife and vice versa—thus if "to be" denotes "legally to be"—the authors, who have not made any explicit distinction in the relation in question between "to be" and "to live," seem by the former expression to have meant rather "actually or socially to be," so that the difference from "to live" as man and wife is considerably reduced.

155 Sohm, *supra* note 67, at 508.

156 Kaser I, *supra* note 5, at 73. *Compare* similar descriptions, *id.* at 321. In the author's view, the social circumstances for a visiting marriage without a common home are lacking, *see id.* at 73 n. 10.

definition very well reproduces the concept *affectio maritalis*,[157] the material content of which he characterizes as "la volonte d'etablir un union monogamique, durable, pour toute la duree de l'existence, ayant comme but la formation d'une famille, c'est à dire d'une société domestique pour la procréation et l'éducation des enfants issus de cette union, fondée sur des rapports mutuels de protection et d'assistance."[158] Volterra's reference to the general definition of marriage as the object of the matrimonial intent is convincing. However, he does not linger on the questions of whether all or only some; and of those which (or perhaps none) of the elements are necessary and sufficient to constitute the legally required matrimonial intent. Thus, there is doubt as to the absolute necessity of all the elements in every case. Notwithstanding that the production of legitimate offspring was emphasized in Rome from time to time[159] as a purpose of marriage, there must also have been those who were childless by choice. Nonetheless, Modestinus' definition does not explicitly mention this purpose either. The crux must have been that the partners' aim was not to establish a liaison with a limited purpose but rather to constitute a full community of life,[160] a sharing of everything in life, a *consortium omnis vitae*, in which procreation must have been important although not always necessary and sufficient.

Although, as emerges from the above, different opinions are expressed by scholars concerning the true character and content of the concept *consensus v. affectio maritalis*, it is generally agreed that this subjective requisite was absolutely necessary for the legal constitution of a marriage.

---

157 VOLTERRA, *supra* note 65, at 37. Regarding the definition of marriage in Roman law, *see* Chapter 2.2 *supra*.

158 VOLTERRA, *supra* note 65, at 35. *Compare* the author's succinct definitions of the object of matrimonial intent as "d'etablir une union durable, pour toute la duree de l'existence," *see id.* at 37, further as "de constituer un rapport conjugal perpetuel," *see id.* at 38, and as "d'établir une union conjugal stable, juridiquement valable," *see id.* at 42. It may be observed that Volterra's stated requirements for an intention "pour toute la duree de l'existence" mean neither that this purpose must be permanent nor exclude divorce. This would be confusing the object of the intention with its duration. The requirement of an intention to establish a union for life simply means that as long as the intention persists, it must pertain to a permanent union. Thus it follows that the union, according to the couples' intentions, may not be conditional or temporary, *see id.* at 35. *Compare* Kaser, who in agreement herewith as regards the focus of the intention on a life-long community of life, asserts that "Lebenslänglichkeit, die Scheidbarkeit nicht ausschliesst, gehört zum Wesen der Ehe," and that a trial marriage which is dissolved in the event of childlessness is unknown, *see* KASER I, *supra* note 5, at 73 n. 9; and Kaser, IURA, *supra* note 7 at 71.

159 As we found above, it happened that the wife was described as *uxor liberorum quaerendorum* (*procreandorum*) *causa*, *see supra* note 8.

160 *Compare* Glück, who *e contrario* seems to articulate the necessary matrimonial intent as a *consensus* "zur ungetheilten Gemeinsamkeit des ganzen Lebens and der Schicksale," *see* GLÜCK, *supra* note 5, Bd. 28 at 373.

2. *Objective Prerequisites or Evidentiary Facts*

On the other hand, there is the highly controversial issue of whether the subjective prerequisite was sufficient as a legal fact, or whether an objective prerequisite was also needed. Such a prerequisite could be a marriage that had de facto come into existence socially, a cohabitation in a *consortium omnis vitae* that had actually begun. The former opinion, which is particularly relevant in earlier scholarship,[161] has a chief modern adherent in Volterra, who maintains that in both classical and Justinian law, only *consensus* was necessary.[162]

Levy took up arms against this marked subjectivism and made a major contribution to laying the foundation of the accepted but far from predominant theory whereby, just as legal possession[163] in classical times involved both the elements *animus* and *corpus*, the constitution of a marriage also required an indispensable objective circumstance. Already Modestinus' general definition of marriage can be considered to support this belief because of his requirement of *coniunctio maris et feminae* and *consortium omnis vitae*.[164] A community of life is indeed feasible as an ethical kinship perceived only inwardly[165] but undoubtedly appears more realistic in the idea of the essence of marriage as "verwirklichte Lebensgemeinschaft,"[166] presented at the beginning of this chapter, which

---

161 *See, e.g.*, ALOIS BRINZ, LEHRBUCH DER PANDEKTEN III, 672 (Erlangen, 2d ed. 1874); ACCARIAS, *supra* note 61, at 174; and JÖRS & KUNKEL, *supra* note 24, at 278 n. 9. *Compare* Glück, who apart from *affectio maritalis* presumed an "ungeteilten Lebensgemeinschaft," *see* GLÜCK, *supra* note 5, Bd. 28 at 372.

162 VOLTERRA, *supra* note 65, at 25 and succinctly at 39, and after him, ORESTANO, *supra* note 141.

163 D. 41, 2, 3, 1: ("Et apiscimur possessionen corpore et animo, neque per se animo aut per se corpore").

164 D. 23, 2, 1. *See* further D. 39, 5, 31 pr.: ("vitae coniunctione considerata perpendendum esse respondi").

165 *Compare* Bonfante, who is inclined to interpret the community of life of *corpus* element, not literally or materialistically, but in an ethical and social sense: "[N]on pas dans une signification littérale et matérialiste, mais dans une signification éthique et sociale," *see* quoted from VOLTERRA, *supra* note 65, at 25. *Compare* Kaser, who considers that the concept of community of life comprises not only external elements such as the parties' personal presence and their cohabitation but also "die Anerkennung, dass diese äussere Gemeinschaft eine von solcher Art ist, wie sie dem Wesen der Ehe entspricht," *see* STUDIA ET DOCUMENTA, *supra* note 139, at 303.

166 *See* MITTEIS, *supra* note 9, at 131 n. 19, whose definition of the nature of marriage was given before Levy's investigation. *Compare* GLÜCK, *supra* note 5, Bd. 28 at 372; and PUCHTA II, *supra* note 113, at 400. The emphasis on the constituent significance and actual nature of the community of life recurs in several authors. Kunkel speaks of "die Herstellung der tatsächlichen Lebensgemeinschaft," *see* Kunkel, *Matrimonium, supra* note 8, col. 2271; Sohm of "tatsächlichen Beginn der ehelichen Gemeinschaft," *see* SOHM, *supra* note 67, at 508; and Plassard of "La communauté d'existence de deux personnes," *see* J. PLASSARD, LE CONCUBINAT ROMAIN SOUS LE HAUT EMPIRE 35 (1921). Jolowicz considers that the objective element can be described as "the beginning of life together," *see* JOLOWICZ, *supra* note 119, at 144. Vandenberghe declares that marriage is the "in praktijk gebrachte levensgemeenschap," *see* VANDENBERGHE, *supra* note 109, at 10, and Lassen asserts that marriage is made by

seems to presume a life actually spent together. How, then, would such a community of life between a man and a woman actually be launched and developed in order, together with the presence of the subjective prerequisite, to constitute a marriage? Levy declares: "Keine Eheschliessung ohne räumliche Verbindung," and also uses paraphrases such as "raumliche Vereinigung," "Vergemeinschaftung des Hauses," and "Vergemeinschaftung der Wohräume."[167]

It is beyond all doubt that this spatial union of the spouses in Roman law did not consist of *copula carnalis.*[168] Its constituent importance for marriage is first stipulated in canon law. The crucial significance was usually attached rather to the fact that the woman entered her husband's house, *deductio in domum mariti,*[169] particularly when deciding on the time at which the marriage should be adjudged sealed. In an analogy with real contracts in property law, we may say that the *deductio* of the woman *in domum* corresponded to a tradition of some kind. It would seem clear that this possessive *corpus* element, together with the presence of the subjective prerequisite, could suffice for the constitution of a marriage. Whether the moving together of the parties by *deductio in domum* should also be considered always necessary is moot.[170] In principle, the legal creation of the free

---

informal agreement in association with "Livfaelleskabets faktiske Begyndelse," *see* LASSEN, *supra* note 57, at 350.

167 LEVY, *supra* note 59, at 67 and 71; and VOLTERRA, *supra* note 65, at 39 and 49.

168 D. 24, 1, 32, 13: ("non enim coitus matrimonium facit"). *Compare* D. 50, 17, 30: ("Nuptias non concubitus ... facit"). Nor does Levy, who considers these fragments to be interpolated, allege that in classical law, the couple's physical union founds the marriage, *see* LEVY, *supra* note 59, at 67 and 71. *Compare* the importance thereof in Medieval Canon law, Chapter 3.3.3 *infra.*

169 *See particularly* C. 5, 3, 6; D. 24, 1, 66; Paul. Sent. 2, 19, 8; and D. 23, 2, 5-6. *Compare* D. 35, 1, 15; and D. 24, 132, 13. Wedding is sometimes described in the sources as "*uxorem ducere,*" *see* VIR II 404, 52.

170 According to C. 5, 3, 6, gifts made after *domum deductio* were invalid as made between man and wife, *inter virum et uxorem.* Yet according to D. 24, 1, 66, there are indications that the marriage would, notwithstanding that the woman had entered the man's house, be constituted at another time, if the parties were so agreed. In such a situation, gifts could be valid even if they were made after *domum deductio.* The seemingly incompatible fragments have given rise to different opinions on the necessity of *deductio.* However, as the requisites for the constitution of a marriage must in the latter case be considered lacking in a subjective respect, the content of D. 24, 1, 66 need not deprive *domum deductio* of its objective character of crucial fact. Thus the two sources can be considered compatible. *See* Levy, *supra* note 59, at 72; and CORBETT, *supra* note 14, at 92, quoting chiefly D. 23, 2, 5 and Paul. Sent. 2, 19, 8: ("vir absens uxorem ducere potest; femina absens non potest"), which deal with the possibility of a wedding in the man's absence, compare *traditio brevi manu,* considered that *domum deductio* was indispensable at least in classical times. *Compare* Volterra, who asserts that the sources in question actually deal with the possibility of executing not the wedding but the *deductio* in the man's absence, and further cites *inter alia* D. 35, 1, 15; D. 23, 2, 6; and D. 24, 1, 32, 13 as well as D. 24, 1, 66 pr., postulating that *deductio in domum mariti* was not essential but only significant "en tant qu'elle peut démontrer l'existence de la volonté des conjoints," as an evidentiary fact of the couple's intent, see VOLTERRA, *supra* note 65, at 45. *Compare* Volterra, who elsewhere, somewhat inconsistently, did not even stipulate that the intention must be explicit, *see id.* at 39.

marriage did not require a duration of the cohabitation corresponding to the one-year term laid down for the *usus* marriage. It was sufficient that the community of life had actually begun. It was another matter that, in accordance with the content of the subjective prerequisite, an enduring community of life as a rule must have been intended by the couple. From the requirement of actual cohabitation follows the conclusion, maybe trivial but perhaps therefore occasionally overlooked, that simply the parties' rarely well-documented verbal or written agreement on marriage did not suffice for the legal constitution thereof in the classical period. Through the victory of the animus theory within legal scholarship and legislation during the postclassical and Justinian times, the concept *affectio maritalis,* abstracted as from a community of life in general, appears to have been given greater significance as a legal fact, while the objective views assumed a lesser role in the background. It appears that, upon the commencement of a marriage, it no longer was required that a marriage, in order to be viewed as legally established, actually had to be effectuated in an objective action. It ought to have been satisfactory that the parties' marital intent had been expressed verbally, either orally or in writing.[171]

Another means of legally qualifying cohabitation and the constituent elements thereof is to regard them not as necessary objective prerequisites but as evidentiary facts for something else which is sought, the parties' *consensus vel affectio maritalis,* which would then represent the only legal requirement for the constitution of a marriage.[172] The nature of these elements as evidentiary facts of the matrimonial intent naturally does not exclude the possibility that according to the above, they are also

171 C. 2, 7, 23, 4: ("Quotiens de nuptiis quis sine dotalibus instrumentis mutuo contrahendi matrimonium animo celebratis super ad fectu suo"); C. 5, 17, 11 pr.; ("ad fectu matrimonia contrahuntur"); and Nov. 22, 3: ("nudus animus nuptialis").

172 VOLTERRA, *supra* note 65, at 45. Thus according to Orestano, community of life ("la convinenza"), like the other external manifestations of marriage, are only evidence of its existence *per se, see* ORESTANO, *supra* note 141, at 85 and 388. Schwind asserts that religious formalities and *deductio in domum mariti* can be regarded as "äussere Kennzeichnen" of the matrimonial intent, *see* SCHWIND, *supra* note 80, at 182. *Compare* WESTRUP, *supra* note 62, at 18; Joyce, at 53; and Karlowa, in principle, *see* RÖM. RG. II, *supra* note 14, at 180. *Compare* Kaser, who does not seem to accept the idea of proof, although his somewhat hesitant mode of expression has been so understood, *see* THOMAS, *supra* note 60, at 19 n. 4. Kaser describes *deductio* as "das typische Anzeichen" of the presence of a matrimonial union, *see* KASER I, *supra* note 5, at 322, and as "ein besonders wirksames Indiz" of the end of a marriage, *see* STUDIA ET DOCUMENTA, *supra* note 139, at 307. Kaser suggests that matrimonial intent can also appear from other "Indizien," *see* KASER I, *supra* note 5, at 322. *Compare* Kaser, IURA, *supra* note 7 at 80, where the author alleges that the judicial system uses certain indications for the establishment of "die Herstellung der ehelichen Gemeinschaft, die eheliche Gesinnung and die Herstellung des häuslichen Lebens." That which Kaser here calls "Anzeichen" and "Indizien" he nevertheless does not seem to regard merely as evidentiary facts but rather as valid elements inherent in the concept of marriage, whereby the community of life must be unconditionally realized but among which *deductio* is one of several sufficient albeit not essential formalities, *see* STUDIA ET DOCUMENTA, *supra* note 139, at 304, 307 and KASER I, *supra* note 5, at 74.

objective prerequisites.[173] Yet, if in the following, we begin only with the former attribute, the different elements of the *corpus,* such as the woman's *deductio in domum mariti,* have no independent significance. In a number of cases, they possess evidentiary value insofar as they may be considered to express the matrimonial intent. So free an evidentiary evaluation is also consistent with the Roman principle of free examination of evidence.[174] Typical not individual viewpoints seem, however, chiefly to have been taken into account. Apart from the parties moving in together, it is clear that most evidentiary value is attached to the duration of the cohabitation. The social position the woman actually occupied in the home was also important. If a woman acted as a wedded wife, with *honor matrimonii,*[175] it would be a typical evidentiary fact of the parties' matrimonial intent.

It follows from the above that a matrimonial intent could be deduced from facts other than those inherent in the actual cohabitation. This was also the case in Roman law, in which the principle of a free examination of evidence included both free evaluation and free adduction of evidence.[176] Among these other *indicia,* some also seem to have been regarded as typical. Although not enjoined by Roman law, Roman customs that had developed in connection with weddings contained several rites and ceremonies, *celebritas nuptiarum, pompa nuptialis, nuptiarum festivitas, ritus nuptiarum,*[177] composed of sacred and profane elements, in which the parties'

---

173 Thus to all appearances Puchta considers it necessary for the marriage to come into being but nevertheless finds that *deductio in domum* is only of importance as "Beweis der affectio maritalis," *see* PUCHTA II, *supra* note 113, at 400. Similarly Kunkel, characterizes *deductio in domum* as "äusseres Symptom" of intent to marry, which he nevertheless does not find sufficient without creation of the matrimonial union, *see* Kunkel, *Matrimonium, supra* note 8, col. 2271. *Compare* Glück, who maintains that *deductio in domum,* together with other circumstances, could serve "zum Beweis des animus maritalis," *see* GLÜCK, *supra* note 5, Bd. 28 at 374, Bd. 22 at 400, and that everything depended on merely "das äusserlich erkennbare Dasein jenes consensus matrimonialis," *see id.* at Bd. 28, at 373.

174 D. 22, 5, 3, 2.

175 D. 35, 1, 15; D. 25, 2, 15 pr.; D. 24, 1, 32, 13; VOLTERRA, *supra* note 65, at 39 and 49; and LEVY, *supra* note 59, at 75. Regarding the significance of respectability as a constituent element in the concept of concubinage, *see* Section 2.5, *infra.*

176 D. 22, 5, 3, 2, 176.

177 The ceremonies occasionally held in association with the entry into the free marriage must be distinguished from the formalities of *confarreatio* and *coemptio,* unconditionally prescribed for matrimony with *conventio in manum,* which varied in both content and extent with the status and rank of the parties. However, it was not unusual for the ceremonies to begin in the brides' parental home. Her costume included a scarlet bridal veil with which her head was covered, *compare nubo* = to cover oneself, to wed. Sacrifices were offered and the outcome of *auspicia,* signs from the gods, proclaimed. Sometimes a marriage contract, *tabula nuptialis,* was drawn up. At nightfall, when the evening star had risen, the groom must symbolically snatch the bride from her mother's arms. The bride could then be led in a torchlight procession, accompanied by flute playing and songs, to the groom's home, where she was carried with mock resistance over the threshold. Beside the marriage bed, the bride then prayed to the groom's family gods that she would be granted the privilege of bearing many children to continue the family. Since these ceremonies and similar rites in the Roman tradition did not represent legal

congruent matrimonial intent could be manifested. If the parties had drawn up marriage papers, *tabulae nuptiales*, such as documents referring to the dowry, *dotis instrumenta*,[178] these could serve as evidence that their liaison was conjugal. The couple's oath[179] before the censor and the attestation of friends, *amicorum fide firmari*,[180] also may be mentioned as evidence, which was wont to be adduced to confirm the existence of a marriage. Nevertheless, so much importance seems to have been attached to the cohabitation compared with other *prima facie* facts that the existence of a marriage was presumed from cohabitation between a free man and a free woman who were competent to marry.[181] This presumption, which could be refuted, acquired great practical significance in distinguishing marriage from concubinage and other extramarital relationships, as discussed further below.

requirements for the wedding, they appear chiefly in non-legal sources, *see, e.g.*,: Catullus, 62, 1; and Festus, P. 289, P. 94, P. 2 (*"aqua et igni"*). *Compare coemptio*; BRUNS FONTES II, *supra* note 13, at 3, 10, 30; Plutarch, Quest. Rom. 29; Servius In Aen. 6, 603; Tac. Ann. 11, 27, 30; D. 24, 1 66, 1; C. Th. 3, 7, 3. Litt.: ROSSBACH, *supra* note 14, at 254; KARLOWA, DIE FORMEN, *supra* note 14; MADELEINE RAGE-BROCARD, RITES DE MARIAGE: LA DEDUCTIO IN DOMUM MARITI *passim* (1934); ERNST SAMTER, FAMILIENFESTE DER GRIECHEN UND RÖMER (1901); MARQUARDT, *supra* note 14, at 36; and JÖRS & KUNKEL, *supra* note 24, at 278. The symbolical ceremonies are not now thought to have originated in a marriage by rape, *see id. Compare* ROSSBACH, *supra* note 14, at 360. Regarding the use of formulae, *see, e.g.*, Plutarch, Quest. Rom. 30; Cicero, Pro Murena, 12, 27 (*compare* coemptio *supra*); and THEODOR MOMMSEN, RÖMISCHE FORSCHUNGEN I, at 11 (1864). LEVY, *supra* note 59, at 74, asserts that the couple's *consensus* was usually not explicit.

178 Ulp. 3, 3; C. 5, 4, 9 and 13; C. 5, 4, 22; C. 5, 27, 10 ("dotalia instrumenta"); C. 5, 27, 11 ("nuptialia instrumenta"); C. Th. 3, 7, 3; C. 5, 3, 20; D. 24, 1, 66 pr.; Tac. Ann. 11, 27, 30; and HANS JULIUS WOLFF, WRITTEN AND UNWRITTEN MARRIAGES IN HELLENISTIC AND POSTCLASSICAL ROMAN LAW 87 (1939). As found above, *dos* in the classical period seems to have been a voluntary dowry. The wife could regain her *dos* by *restitutio dotis* if the marriage was dissolved. With this in mind, an *instrumentum dotale*, listing the properties included in the *dos*, was sometimes drawn up when the dowry was handed over.

179 Gell. 4, 20, 3 and 4, 3, 2.

180 C. Th. 3, 7, 3.

181 D. 23, 2, 24: (*"In liberae mulieries consuetudine non concubinatus sed* nuptiae intelligendae sunt, si non corpore quaestum fecerit"). According to accepted opinion, *liberae* should be read as *ingenuae, see* LEVY, *supra* note 59, at 75. The presumption, as Orestano explains, was not a *praesumptio iuris et de iure* but a *praesumptio iuris*, which could thus be refuted. The presumptive elements in the cohabitation that must be present for the presumption to be valid are rarely specified. Karlowa seems in general to assume that the parties must have "ehelich zusammenlebt," *see* RÖM. RG. II, *supra* note 14, at 180. CORBETT, *supra* note 14, at 95, postulates "cohabitation," Levy a "Verbindung," *see supra* note 59, at 75, and Volterra a "union" between the man and the woman, *see* VOLTERRA, *supra* note 65, at 35.

2.4.3 Divorce

1. Affectio Maritalis in Absentia *or the Existence of an Intention to Divorce*

Since, in the classical period, there was as little need for cooperation by any authority or other observance of certain formalities in the case of the dissolution of marriage by divorce, *divortium*,[182] as on the occasion of the wedding, it may appear consistent to regard the nonexistence of the aforesaid prerequisites for the constitution of a marriage as a legal fact of its dissolution. The concept of divorce is then the reverse of the concept of marriage. Such a correspondence also emerges with regard to *divortium*, although specific viewpoints on divorce also come into play. Thus, in the subjective respect, it was required that the couple's matrimonial *consensus vel affectio maritalis* no longer was present. Schwind says that, in accordance with its essence, the marriage was dissolved when "der Wille zur ehelichen Gemeinschaft weggefallen war."[183] Similarly, Kaser presumes "die Beendigung ihres Ehekonsenses"[184] with regard to the couples' subjective conditions. However, the subjective element is also occasionally described not as a suspension of the parties' matrimonial *consensus* but as the appearance of a new element, a special intention to separate notwithstanding that the distinction de facto has not reportedly been observed. Thus, Kaser speaks of "den Willensbestimmung dass die Ehe beendet sein soll" and the couple's "Scheidungswillen."[185] In contrast to the situation at the wedding, when the congruent *consensus* of both parties was required to constitute the marriage, the intention of only one or the cessation of matrimonial intent sufficed at its dissolution.

Different degrees of significance have been attached by Roman scholars to the subjective element in connection with divorce. Some, like Schwind,[186] have considered that it is the only necessary prerequisite for the dissolution of the marriage, provided it is explicit and can be proved. The most far-reaching in his subjectivism is Volterra, who maintains that the spouses need not even manifest their intention to dissolve the marriage. It sufficed that they no longer intended to be joined in matrimony.

---

182 *See* Section 2.4.1 *supra*.

183 SCHWIND, *supra* note 80, at 185.

184 KASER I, *supra* note 5, at 326.

185 *Id.* at 81 and 327. Karlowa and Sohm also use the expression "Scheidungswille." It may appear that the distinction is purely linguistic and lacks any true reference in fact since an intention to dissolve the marriage is irreconcilable with a simultaneous intention to continue it and vice versa. Yet, it can be argued that there may be cases where one spouse's matrimonial *consensus* has lapsed but has not been replaced by a definite intention to divorce (actually!). The spouse in question perhaps has no intention whatsoever at present, or stands in doubt, or has an intention but has not decided, or indeed has not pondered the matter.

186 SCHWIND, *supra* note 80, at 185; SOHM, *supra* note 67, at 524; KARLOWA, RÖM. RG. II, *supra* note 14, at 189; and PUCHTA II, *supra* note 113, at 404.

Thus, in his view, it was not necessary "que les conjoints manifestent leur volonté de dissoudre le mariage. Il suffit que l'un des deux Wait plus la volonté d'être uni en mariage pour que le rapport conjugal soit considere dissous. Le droit classique ne prévoit aucune forme pour accomplir le divorce."[187] This exclusivity of intention is now, however, accepted by the prevalent opinion according to which the subjective element was indeed adjudged necessary but not sufficient.

2. *Objective Requisites and Evidentiary Facts*

Apart from the subjective elements, a *divortium*, like a wedding, also presupposed an objective requisite. As against the requirement of an actual community of life for the establishment of the marriage, its dissolution called for a cessation of the cohabitation. Thus, for Kaser, divorce, in terms of the essence of Roman marriage, consisted, so far as is now at issue, in that "die eheliche Lebensgemeinschaft von einem oder beiden Ehegatten aufgehoben wird."[188] In agreement with his idea of the conditions for the wedding, Levy declares for his part: "Keine Ehescheidung ohne räumliche Trennung."[189] According to Levy, in an analogy with the terms for loss of possession, the parties' spatial separation is the requisite *corpus* element. So long as they shared a home, the marriage could not be dissolved, any more than could an explicit but not executed *possidere nolle* at the loss of possession.[190] *Animus* theory, however, appears to have also influenced the conditions for the dissolution of the marriage. According to the Justinian code, the spouses' actual separation no longer constitutes a condition for divorce. It was sufficient that the intent to separate was expressed in another manner.[191]

Although the objective elements were frequently self-evident, so to speak, certain usages, which were not obligatory from a legal standpoint

187 Volterra, *supra* note 65, at 34.

188 *Id.* at 81 and 326. *Compare* likewise Shulz, who assumes the necessity of the "dissolution of the common life" *see* Schulz, Classical, *supra* note 1, at 134.

189 Levy, *supra* note 59, at 67. Kunkel follows Levy, *see* Kunkel, *Matrimonium*, *supra* note 8, col. 2278.

190 Levy, *supra* note 59, at 77. The author examines various elements inherent in the spatial separation and finds, not surprisingly, that not every separation of the spouses can be approved, such as *e.g.* each journey to another place during a shorter or longer period, or each separate sojourn at different places or even at the same place, *compare* D. 7, 8, 4, 1. His explanation thereof is of greater interest, however, in that the act of separation must be "ehewidrig," which is not always the case in the examples given. He thereby discusses *inter alia* cases where the separation must be adjudged to have a "böslichen Charakter," *see id.* at 81. This emphasis on the act of separation *per se* and its nature is characteristic of Levy's objectivism. It should be noted, however, that it is entirely possible to justify the conclusions reached by Levy instead by the subjective breach of the requirements. One then accepts the act of separation *per se* but does not find sufficient ground for divorce since its purpose was not to dissolve the marriage and no such intent was thus present. Regarding dissolution of the *usus* marriage, *see* Levy, *supra* note 59. Regarding the comparison with *nolle possidere*, *see* D. 41, 2, 17, 1.

191 D. 24, 2, 3; D. 50, 17, 48; and Levy, *supra* note 59, at 98.

but could serve as evidence, were long-standing in the Roman custom concerning a spouse's announcement of an intention to separate, *repudium.*[192] Typical declarations of intent are extant, such as the one spouse's injunction to the other to leave home, *baete foras;*[193] or pack his or her bags, *tuas res tibi habeto* or *agito;*[194] or his or her confiscation of the keys to the house, *claves adimere.*[195] The classic declaration of divorce was informal and could be made orally or in writing, personally or by proxy.[196] In a legal system with free examination of evidence, it is clear that the facts were assigned much or little evidentiary value depending on the case, and other facts could also come into question. The points of special interest in this respect are the parties' actual separation and its inherent elements, and whether these could, notwithstanding that they were or were not necessary objective requisites, be regarded as acts from which the presence of an intention to divorce could be deduced, or whether this intention must be explicitly declared. Opinions seem to have differed on this matter in Cicero's time, at least when the acts consisted of one party entering into a new marital relationship unbeknown to the other.[197] The classical differences of opinion have their equivalents in modern times. Thus, Levy asserts that *repudium* could be inherent in the act of separation itself, e.g., if the man physically drove his wife out of the house,[198] while Sohm

---

192 D. 50, 16, 191; D. 24, 2, 2 pr.

193 Varro, Ap. Non. (77); Plaut Cas. 210; Mart. Ep. 11, 104, 1; Juv. Sat. 6, 146; and BRUNS FONTES I, *supra* note 15, at 22.

194 D. 24, 2, 2, 1; Plaut. Amph. 928, Trin. 266; Cic. Phil. 2, 28, 69; Mart. Ep. 10, 41, 2: and BRUNS FONTES, I, *supra* note 15, at 22.

195 Cic. Phil. 2, 28, 69; and BRUNS FONTES I, *supra* note 15, at 22.

196 D. 23, 2, 45, 4; D. 24, 1, 32, 19; and Cic. Top. 4 Ad Att. The written declaration which in classical times constituted documentary evidence and would then rarely gave rise in postclassical law to a bill of divorce, *libellus repudii*, which, together with divorce witnesses, later came to be a formal requirement, *see* D. 24, 2, 7; C. 5, 17, 6 and 8 pr.; and LEVY, *supra* note 59, at 55 and 104. *Compare* CORBETT, *supra* note 14, at 228, who with reference to *inter alia* D. 24, 2, 9, alleges that the witness requirement was mandatory already in classical law.

197 Cicero tells of a *pater familias* who left his pregnant wife in Spain and went to Rome where, without explicitly notifying his wife of the dissolution of their marriage, he entered into a new matrimonial liaison with a woman who bore him a son, *see* De Orat. 1, 40, 183, CICERO, DE ORATORE I-II (eng. trans. E.W. Sutton, introd. H. Rackman 1942). The man died intestate, so that the question arose whether the first marriage could only be dissolved with the use of *certis quibusdam verbis*, or whether this could also ensue concludently from *novis nuptiis.* Cicero states that there were differences of opinion on this legal issue in the most erudite circles, "fuit inter peritissimos homines summa de iure dissension," *see* De Orat. 1, 56, 238. Following Meyer in drawing certain conclusions in favor of one opinion only citing this source therefore seems to lack justification.

198 LEVY, *supra* note 59, at 15 and 84. *Compare* D. 25, 2, 11 pr. and Vat. Frag. 106. There may be doubt regarding the general validity of Levy's argument. The example he gives can be contradicted insofar as the man who drove his wife out of the house need not thereby have expressed an intention to divorce. He may have intended, as was perhaps customary in the family's practice of marital intercourse, to drive her in again. The objection can, however, be refuted if the only point to be made was that the evidentiary value of action together with other facts must be assessed

seems to assume that *repudium* took place only by an explicit declaration of divorce.[199] It may be added here that the difference between an explicit and implied declaration of intent may be limited. Thus, the *claves adimere* mentioned above may be described as a kind of act that, insofar as it was accepted, acquired the nature of an intended verbal act.[200]

In view of the subjective and objective requirements discussed herein, it is not surprising that difficulties could arise in assessing whether, and if so, when a marriage was actually dissolved. This must have been the case particularly in the event of a long drawn-out, gradual dissolution of a community of life, possibly with repeated reconciliations, separations, and reunions. Already the imposition of the double requirement for both a subjective and an objective requisite meant, however, that in cases in which the conditions could indeed be questioned in the one respect but obviously broke down in the other, the divorce was not legally valid. If, e.g., the sharing of bed and board did not cease, the intention to divorce was not sufficient, however explicit in injunctions to leave home, *baete foras*. These were regarded, so long as the act of separation had not occurred, as harmless quarrels, *iurgium*,[201] which were not sufficient legally to dissolve the marriage. The same situation prevailed if the conditions were indeed objectively present per se, such as if the couple lived apart, but not as a result of a proven intention to separate but because one party worked elsewhere.[202]

Even in cases in which both the subjective and the objective requisites for dissolution of the marriage existed per se, it could nevertheless happen that *divortium* did not ensue, e.g., even if, perchance, an intent to divorce had been unequivocally expressed and followed by the spouses' actual separation. During the immediately subsequent period, a kind of "suspended legal situation" prevailed[203] that could be resolved in different ways. If the parties were reconciled during this time, the marriage was adjudged not dissolved but newly constituted. No *verum divortium*[204] then came into being. The marriage had rather persisted throughout. The same applied

---

from case to case. *Compare* Corbett, *supra* note 14, at 233, who regards the actual separation as one piece of evidence among other *indicia* of the intent to divorce.

199 Sohm, *supra* note 67, at 524.

200 *Compare* Mitteis, who asserts that to be effective, a declaration of *inteni* must have been addressed to the other party, *see* Mitteis, *supra* note 9, at 152.

201 D. 23, 3, 31; D. 24, 2, 3; and D. 23, 4, 27.

202 *Compare* D. 7, 8, 4, 1.

203 *Compare* Levy regarding classical divorce as a "gestreckten" actual situation, and as a "Schwebezustand," *see* Levy, *supra* note 59, at 91.

204 D. 24, 1, 64; D. 23, 4, 26, 5; D.24, 2, 3; D. 23, 2, 33; and Frag, Vat. 106. All the sources cited here pertain to cases where separated spouses were reconciled and the principle of *verum divortium* was applied to examination of the question of whether the marriage should be adjudged dissolved or still in existence. In the first case, which concerned the much, discussed divorce of Maecenas and his temperamental wife-Terentia, the situation, which is not unusual even today, was such that *repudium* injunctions, which were not confined to innocuous *iurgium*, were daily pronounced and one spouse left the home but returned. No *verum divortium* had then come into being, *compare* Seneca, Dial. 1, 3, 10; Ep. 114, 6; and Levy, *supra* note 59, at 86.

in the event of repeated reconciliations of the spouses. On the other hand, if a separation became permanent, the marriage was dissolved. The judge decided on the issue of when the critical moment of the suspended situation occurred after considering the circumstances of the individual case.[205] If, during the period in question, one party entered into a new marriage with a third person, the suspended legal situation came to a premature end, so to speak, and the separation became a *verum divortium.*[206] Since the former marriage, in such cases, was dissolved at the same moment as the new one was constituted, bigamy did not ensue.[207]

2.4.4 The Effect of the *Animus* Theory on the Concept of Marriage

When analyzing the concept of the free marriage above, we employ distinctions such as those between subjective and objective requisites, intent and object, intent and expression, legal fact and evidentiary fact—pairs of concepts that, so to speak, compose some of the modern lenses through which we study the structure of the Roman concept of marriage. The purpose is to elicit findings that may be of interest in the discussion of modern law.

This method is not wholly innocuous. One danger naturally is that modern lenses are not suited to the historical phenomena under scrutiny. There is a risk that the picture will be blurred. This risk may be diminished, however, by taking the temporal perspective into account. If we consider the Roman concept of marriage with this in mind, we find that, despite efforts to prove the contrary,[208] it was not static but rather underwent significant changes that explain some of the differences of opinion reported above as to its true nature.

Thus, it is worth noting that in the classical world of ideas, these distinctions were not as manifest as they later became. For the classical jurists, the concept of declaration of intent in contract theory was not yet fully developed.[209] As regards the concept of matrimony, it has even been alleged that "Wille and Vollzug" formed "eine untrennbare Einheit" [210] for both the making and the breaking of the marriage. Notwithstanding that this statement seems too far-reaching—even its articulation comprises two

205 The sources quoted in note 2 *supra* imply that the period in question may not be *longum* or *multum tempus* but was short as a rule.
206 D. 23, 2, 33.
207 *Compare* D. 3, 2, 1.
208 Thus *e.g.* VOLTERRA, *supra* note 65, at 25, and ORESTANO, *supra* note 141, at 211, who seek to give a consistent reply in favor of the exclusivity of the subjective requisite as a legal fact, and JOLOWICZ, *supra* note 119, 141, who emphasizes both the subjective and objective elements of classical and Justinian law.
209 *Compare* JÖRS & KUNKEL, *supra* note 24, at 80.
210 KASER I, *supra* note 5, at 326. *Compare* likewise Jörs & Kunkel regarding the unity of the *animus* and *corpus* of possession, *see* JÖRS & KUNKEL, *supra* note 24, at 113.

subjects—it would have been alien to the classical jurists; their perception of the practice of law did not include attaching crucial importance to an inner intent not shown by any objective facts. On the whole, the definition of marriage as "verwirklichte Lebensgemeinschaft" appears more apt. The aforesaid objectively colored opinions,[211] whereby the marriage indeed required *consensus* but was nevertheless adjudged to be legally constituted only if and when it was de facto sealed by an objectively realized community of life, and whereby its dissolution by divorce presumed the couple's actual separation, appear well founded, provided that we confine ourselves to classical law. As regards this period, there is nothing to prevent us from legally qualifying the said *corpus* elements as necessary objective requisites.

The postclassical world of ideas, however, had its greater interest in abstract theory, especially after the introduction of Christianity. Long before the Cartesian dualism of body and soul, the distinctions between heaven and earth, body and soul, form and content, thought and action, subject and object, intent and declaration, appear to quite clearly constitute tenets of Justinian thought. At the same time, the subjective elements in the pairs of concepts increasingly came to the fore. This tradition of thought in jurisprudence and legislation evolved into an *animus* theory, which was adopted in widely divergent legal fields. In, e.g., contract law, the consensual agreement became increasingly widespread already from the classical period onwards. Contractual intent was abstracted from its outward expression and assigned increasing importance in different types of contract, a development that paved the way for the theory of tacit contracts, and gave rise to much thinking about the presumptions and fictions pertaining to the existence of parties' implicit intentions.[212] Moreover, increasing significance was attached to the *animus* elements within the theory of possession. Possession could be acquired *nudo animo* without any change in the *corpus* element.[213] The development in both private and penal law of the concepts of *dolus* and *culpa* provides further evidence of the spread of the *animus* theory. Concerning the individual responsibility in private law in the postclassical period, it has even been said that "states of mind were judged instead of conduct."[214]

Under these circumstances, it is not surprising that the *animus* theory impinged on matrimonial law as well. The concept *affectio maritalis*, abstracted from the community of life in general, occurs more frequently

---

211 *See* Section 2.4.2 *supra*.

212 Regarding consensual contracts such as *mandatum* and *societas*, verbal and quasi contracts *see* Pringsheim, *supra* note 153, at 381.

213 JÖRS & KUNKEL, *supra* note 24, at 114. *Compare* classical law, where possession was acquired *corpore et animo*, *see* D. 41, 2, 3, 1, and where possession once founded persisted so long as both the subjective and the objective elements were present.

214 Pringsheim, *supra* note 153, at 50. *Compare* MITTEIS, *supra* note 9, at 322, and regarding the responsibility under penal law, *see* THEODOR MOMMSEN, RÖMISCHES STRAAFRECHT 86 (1899).

in the postclassical and Justinian legal sources than in the classical.[215] The former seems to have assumed far greater significance as a crucial legal fact, while the importance of objective viewpoints declined further and further. Thus, it was evidently no longer required at the wedding that the marriage, to be regarded as legally constituted, must have been reified by an objective action. It seems to have sufficed that the parties' marital intent was articulated, either orally or in writing.[216] Similarly, the *animus* theory appears to have influenced the conditions needed for the dissolution of a marriage. In classical law, the marriage was dissolved by the departure of one of the parties, when we may assume that the couple's actual cohabitation came to an end; in Justinian law it continued to exist provided that their *animus* did not cease.[217] If the marriage was dissolved by *divortium*, the parties' actual separation no longer seems to have been a condition for the divorce. It evidently sufficed that the intention to part was otherwise expressed.[218]

As a result, the opinions reported above,[219] whereby the subjective features of the concept of marriage were emphasized, are supported by the development of the *animus* theory as regards postclassical and Justinian law. Nevertheless, the subjectivistic efforts in Roman matrimonial law had not yet reached the point of dispensing with every expression of *animus*.[220] Consequently, the temporal perspective does not offer any sudden, radical change in the structure of the concept of marriage. Indeed, there is a gradual development from an accentuation of the objective to an emphasis on the subjective viewpoints.

2.4.5 Application Problems and Conflicts

The free Roman marriage resulted in extensive application problems, finally causing Emperor Justinian to react through legislation.[221] The ability

---

215 *Compare* regarding classical law: D. 39, 5, 31 pr.; Paul. Sent. 2, 20, 1; D. 25, 7, 4; D. 23, 2, 65, 1; D. 25, 7, 1, 1; D. 48, 5, 14 (13), 6; D. 24, 1, 58 pr.; D. 24, 1, 3, 1; D. 48, 20, 5, 1; D.25, 7, 3 pr.; D. 23, 2, 24; D. 50, 17, 30; and regarding postclassical law: C. 5, 4, 6; C. 5, 17, 8 pr.; C. 5, 4, 26, 1; and Pringsheim, *supra* note 153, at 400. *Compare* KASER I, *supra* note 5, at 321 n. 2; and VOLTERRA, *supra* note 65, at 43; and WOLFF, *supra* note 178, at 94. Regarding interpolations of the expression, *see* LEVY, *supra* note 59, at 70; and CORBETT, *supra* note 14, at 93.

216 C. 2, 7, 23, 4;C. 5, 17, 11 pr.; and Nov. 22, 3.

217 Under classical law, deportation involved loss of citizenship, *capitis deminutio media*, which dissolved the marriage by civil law, *see* D. 48, 20, 5, 1; D. 24, 3, 56; and D. 24, 1, 43. *Compare* C. 5, 17, 1. Already in classical law, certain legal consequences of marriage seem to have remained in force despite deportation, *see* D. 24, 1, 13, 1. When Justinian declares that *deportatio ... non solvit matrimonia*, *see* Nov. 22, 13, he presumably confirms a rule introduced already by Constantine, *see Compare* C. 5, 16, 24, 2. Similarly regarding captivity, *see* D. 49, 15, 9; C. 8, 50, 1; and imprisonment by reason of crime, *see* Nov. 22, 7.

218 D. 24, 2, 3; D. 50, 17, 48; and LEVY, *supra* note 59, at 98.

219 *See* Section 2.4.2 *supra.*

220 *Compare*, VOLTERRA, *supra* note 65, at 34.

221 Nov. 74, 4 in CORPUS IURIS CIVILIS III, NOVELLAE (R. Schoell-G. Kroll eds. 1904): "Illud quoque melius arbitramur constituere competenter, quod ex plurimo causarum

to cite as a basis for a marriage an informal relationship, founded on the parties' *affectio maritalis* and their cohabitation, gave rise to extensive evidentiary problems. The country was filled with fraudulent marriages, *falsatis contractibus,* that had never been commenced. Witnesses were cited, who without risk testified that the parties called each other husband and wife and on the basis of such statements a marriage that actually never existed could be found. This gave rise to extensive and long drawn-out litigation, *multae quidem et continuae lites,* which Justinian attempted to resolve by enacting requirements such as formal marriage contracts and the conveyance of a dowry.

Much later, comparable application problems were one of the main reasons why informal marriages were repealed under canon law (see chapter 3) and why common law marriage has been abolished in many American states. These issues are discussed in "Part III, The Future," along with the reasons for and against common law marriage and cohabitation law in the future.

2.5 The Roman Concubinage

2.5.1 Introduction

Roman concubinage does not present a consistent picture from either a sociological or legal perspective. The legislator's attitude to this extramarital phenomenon has varied from a censorious, indifferent tolerance, to benevolent neutrality, to legal recognition of a second-class marriage, all

experimento cognovimus; *multae quidem et continuae lites* nuntiatae nostrae maiestati ad opus nos deduxerunt legis. Quia enim et antiquis promulgatum est legibus et a nobis ipsis sunt haec eadem constituta, ut nuptiae et *extra dotalia documenta ex solo affectu* valeant et ratae sint, sed *falsatis contractibus nostra ex hoc est completa respublica* (nam introeunt testes sine periculo mentientes, *quia vir vocabat dominam cohaerentem et istum illa similiter nominabat, et sic eis finguntur matrimonia non pro veritate confecta*), hoc aestimavimus oportere secundum naturales definire leges ... Haec ergo casta lege sancire bene se habere credidimus ... 1 In maioribus itaque dignitatibus et quaecumque usque ad nostros est senatores et magnificentissimos illustres neque fieri haec omnino patimur, sed sit omnino et dos et antenuptialis donatio et alia omnia quae honestiora decet nomina" (italics added). In S.P. Scott's translation "the numerous and incessant lawsuits" and marriages entered into "by affection alone" are mentioned, and that the country was full of "fraudulent contracts ... for witnesses are constantly introduced who, incurring no risk, testify that a man has called a woman with whom he is living his wife, and that she has also alluded to him as her husband," *see* Corpus Iuris Civilis Vol. 16, 282-284 (S.P. Scott trans. 1973). In the German version, "viele und anhaltende Prozesse" is mentioned, and that the witnesses said that "der Mann die bei ihm lebende Frauensperson Herrin, und sie ihn Herr genannt habe," that marriage was established "durch die blosse Neigung" and that the country was full of "untergeschobenen Verträgen," *see* Das Corpus Iuris Civilis, Bd. 7 at 372-374 (C.E. Otto, B. Schilling, C.F.F. Sintenis eds. 1833). With respect to the significance in the case law concerning common law marriage of that the parties referred to each other as husband and wife, *see* Chapters 7 and 8, *infra.*

depending on the nature of the concubinage and its placement in the republican, classical, or postclassical period.

Early Roman law made no clear distinction between different liaisons that, according to Roman lawmakers, were not recognized as *matrimonium.* During the republic, at the end of which the number of extramarital liaisons steeply increased,[222] the expression *pelicatus*[223] was used to denote both temporary and permanent relationships between men and women, regardless of whether the parties were single, or the liaison existed alongside a marriage. The relative want of precision in the formation of the concept, however, can hardly have involved any inconvenience in the enforcement of the law since concubinage, in any case, essentially lacked legal significance.[224]

In classical times when, as we found, the Augustinian matrimonial legislation *inter alia* was passed for the purpose of increasing the frequency of wedlock, the classical concubinage, *concubinatus*[225] arose, paradoxically enough, as an undesirable consequence of all the prohibitions on marriage laid down in these laws.

---

222 Kroll, *supra* note 109, at 38; JOSEPH DUVAL, LE CONCUBINAT 13 (1895); and PLASSARD, *supra* note 166, at 190 and 195.

223 *Paelex* originally seems to have denoted a woman who lived for a long time with a bachelor without being his *uxor.* Towards the end of the republic, however, *paelex* also was used referring to a spinster who had a liaison with a married man, *see* D. 50, 16, 144. *Regarding* the etymological development of prostitution, *see* MEYER, *supra* note 28, at 7.

224 L. D'Haucour, *L'Évolution Historique du Concubinat Romain,* 16 NOUVELLE REVUE HISTORIQUE DE DROIT FRANCAIS ET ÉTRANGER 730 (1894).

225 Regarding the lexical significance, *see* LEWIS AND SHORT, LATIN DICTIONARY 404 (1998): *Concubinatus, us,* m. [id.]. I. Union of a man with an unmarried woman (usu. Of a lower social grade than himself), concubinage (opp. *Matrimonium* on the one hand, and *adulterium* or *stuprum* on the other. II. Adulterous intercourse: *nuptarum,* i.e. with the betrothed. *Compare concubinus,* i, m., and *concubina,* ae, f. [concubo], one who lives in concubinage (cf. concubinatus), a concubine (male or female), a less reproachful designation than *paelex. Compare* French usage which distinguishes between "*le concubinat*" and "*le concubinage,*" whereby the former denotes the Roman *concubinatus* and the latter the modern French equivalent, *see* PLASSARD, *supra* note 166, at 15. *Compare* German usage, which has both "*der Konkubinat*" and "*das Konkubinat,*" the former usually denoting the Roman mode of cohabitation, *see* A. BAUMANN, DIE ZIVILRECHTLICHE BEDEUTUNG DES KONKUBINATES 3 (1932). *Compare* Swedish usage, SV. AKAD. ORDB. (1936) K 2126: *konkubin* kon [1]kubi [4]n, also kon [1] -, 1. -ku- (kånnkubi'n Dalin), f.: best. -en, vard. (except in Southern Sweden) also =; p,- -er; formerly also *konkubina,* f; def. -an; pl. -or 1. -er (formerly also written *concubin* 1610 (:Concubiner, pl.), 1621 etc. -bina 1614-1771. -bine 1658-1807) ... (especially with regard to ancient conditions) lover, mistress, concubine; secondary wife. "Absalom went in unto his father's concubines in the sight of all Israel" (2 Sam. 16:22). Rauman Ryning 16 (1610). At the Skänninge Assembly, the clergy were forbidden to keep public concubines, *see* Botin, Hem. 2, 201 (1915). Derivation: *Konkubinage,* n. (from Fr. concubinage) (Ger.) konkubinat. Wedberg HD 449 (in documents from 1832). Gynther ConvHlex. (1845) -*konkubinat,* n. (esp. regarding ancient conditions) cohabitation with a mistress 1, concubine. ConvLex. (1821)... Olivecrona, Lagb Gift. 15 (1851). NoK 85:71 (1928). *See* further Drafts Legislation Committee, LB I (1913) at 89, which uses the expression 'concumbenterna,' from *concumbo,* not *concubo.*

Concubinage represented a substitute institution for all those who, by reason of this or later legislation, were not legally competent to enter into matrimony, *conubium*, [226] but who nevertheless wished to live in a relationship like marriage. These parties included soldiers in general; officials in the provinces involved with native women; senators involved with freed women and actresses; and all free-born citizens involved with certain other, not respectable, women. However, concubinage came to represent an alternative also for those who per se were legally competent to wed but who refrained from doing so for economic or other reasons, despite the benefits under Augustinian laws that accrued to those who married.[227] Consequently, concubinage covered couples who wished to marry but could not, and couples who could but did not want to. The two categories had in common that the parties were nevertheless living together, in some sense, in a relationship like marriage. This cohabitation seems eventually to have gained greater social recognition and became more common. In classical times, concubinage had spread through all social classes and already in the first century A.D., could count on what has been described as a "welwillende neutraliteit"[228] on the part of the Roman society.

The social recognition was balanced in the classical period by a certain legal recognition. Concubinage was now introduced as a legal concept in the legislation[229] and a legal distinction was thereby made between it and

226 *Compare* Chapter 2.2.3, *supra*; and Schulz: "Thus the soldiers were inevitably doomed to concubinage," *see* SCHULZ, CLASSICAL, *supra* note 1, at 113.

227 Concubinage could obviously appear as financially more advantageous than matrimony for a man who in a previous marriage had enjoyed the benefits thereof conferred by the Augustine legislation, and who after his wife's death intended to enter into a new relationship without adding any rivals over the estate to the children born of the marriage, *see* Kübler, SZ 17 (1896) at 360. *Compare* Emperor Marcus Aurelius, who after his wife's death chose to not remarry since he did not wish to give his children a stepmother. Instead he lived with a concubine who in the emperor's opinion was a better mother than a new wedded wife would have been, *see* Marcus Aurelius 29: "Enisa est Fabia, ut Faustina mortua in eius matrimonium coiret, sed ille concubinam sibi adscivit procuratoris uxoris suae filiam, ne tot liberis superduceret novercam."

228 VANDENBERGHE, *supra* note 109, at 16. Opinions have differed on the question of the extent to which concubinage was considered socially acceptable, *see* SCHULZ, CLASSICAL, *supra* note 1, at 137. A. ESMEIN, LE MARIAGE EN DROIT CANONIQUE II, 106 (2d ed. 1935), maintains that concubinage did not violate Roman morality. DUVAL, *supra* note 223, at 6, asserts that the attitude to the concubine fell between distaste for a prostitute and the respect which accrued to the wedded wife. *Compare* Gide, *supra* note 113, at 398 who states that concubinage would not have been morally tolerated. Here it may merely be added that the attitude must have been dependent on the nature of the concubinage, particularly its duration and whether it was adulterous. It is a fact that concubines were included in several epitaphs, as reproduced by Meyer, *see* MEYER, *supra* note 28, at 67. Concubinage also seems to have occurred in all classes of society, *see* PLASSARD, *supra* note 166, at 190 and 195; and MEYER, *supra* note 28, at 89. Thus even respected emperors, such as Antoninus Pius and Marcus Aurelius had concubines, *see* FRIEDLÄNDER, *supra* note 109, at 65; and MEYER, *supra* note 28, at 89.

229 D. 25, 7 - *de concubinis*; D. 25, 7, 3, 1: ("concubinatus per leges nomen assumpsit"). Already Cicero uses the epithet *concubina* as a description of a spinster who lived

other extramarital liaisons. The legal consequences were limited, however. The most important was the exemption from the punishment for *stuprum*, [230] that was otherwise prescribed for sexual intercourse outside marriage. Furthermore it may be mentioned that, in conformity with what was generally the case for wives, a soldier's gifts to his concubine were invalid.[231] Otherwise, concubinage in general lacked significance in civil law in classical times.[232]

In the postclassical era, under the influence of Christianity, the legislature again sought to limit the spread of concubinage by legal penalties, and rewards to those who married, but these efforts proved futile, and the lawmakers changed their tactics *vis-à-vis* concubinage. The objective then seems to have been to assimilate each respectable de facto family under a legal regulation. [233] Roman concubinage thereby, if not before, evolved into a second-class marriage, an *inaequale conubium*.[234] This was favored

---

with a man who had abandoned his wife, *see* De Orat. 1, 183, CICERO, DE ORATORE I-II (Eng. trans. E.W. Sutton, intro. H. Rackman 1942).

230 D. 25, 7, 1, 1; D. 25, 7, 3,1; D. 48, 5, 35: ("Stuprum committit, qui liberam mulierem consuetudinis causa non matrimonii continet, excepta videlicet concubina"); and MOMMSEN, *supra* note 214, at 691. An abundance of literary and epigraphical sources testify that even concubinage with free-born, respectable women was not punishable under Lex Iuliae de Adulteriis, *see* thereon PLASSARD, *supra* note 166, at 160; and Ludwig Mitteis, *Romanistische Papyrusstudien*, 23 ZEITSCHRIFT DER SAVIGNY-STIFTUNG FÜR RECHTSGESCHICHTE (SZ), 274, 310 (1902). Opinions differ concerning the time to which the exceptions refer. MEYER, *supra* note 28, at 27 asserts that they go back to Augustus' regulations. Kübler, *supra* note 227, at 361, maintains that they can date from the second century at the earliest but is inclined to believe that they were added in Justinian's time. It may be observed that already Papinian and Paul mention concubinage with women who are *ingenua et honesta, see* D. 34, 9, 16, 1; and D. 34, 2, 36 pr. *Compare* Ulpian, D. 25, 7, 1, 1.

231 C. 5, 16, 2.

232 Concubinage between a freed woman and her patron had special status. She was placed on a par with a wife in certain respects. Like a wife she could be charged with adultery, *adulterium*. She had certain advantages under the law of inheritance and acquired *nomen matronae* and *materfamilias honestatem, see* D. 48, 5, 14 (13) pr.; D. 23, 2, 41, 1; and D. 25, 7, 1, 1, pr. It has been assumed, however, that the legal consequences were founded rather on the patronage relationship than the concubinage *per se, see* GLÜCK, *supra* note 5, Bd. 28 at 361; MEYER, *supra* note 28, at 86; and PLASSARD, *supra* note 166, at 188. *Regarding* the social picture of this concubinage, *see* Kroll, *supra* note 109, at 41.

233 The Emperor Constantine's sanctions on concubinage in penal law pertained particularly to those who by reason of the ban on marriage lived in such a relationship, and to those who sought by adoption to improve the position of their bastards, *see e.g.*, C. 5, 27, 12, 3; C. Th. 4, 6, 2-3; C. 5, 27, 1; GLÜCK, *supra* note 5, Bd. 28 at 384; MEYER, *supra* note 28, at 25; KASER II, *supra* note 5, at 125; and VANDENBERGHE, *supra* note 109, at 12. According to BAUMANN, *supra* note 225, at 13 and 15, the legislator's efforts were impeded by the appreciation of concubinage among the ranks of the people.

234 C. 5, 27, 3, 2. According to an earlier view, represented by Accarias, who refers to "un mariage inférieur," *see* ACCARIAS, *supra* note 61, at 224; D'Haucour, *supra* note 224, at 730; and MOMMSEN, *supra* note 214, at 693, concubinage is described already in Augustus' time as a second class marriage. According to a later opinion that gained support from the results of interpolation research, *see* VANDENBERGHE, *supra* note 109, at 5 with references, concubinage first merits this definition through

particularly under Justinian legislation, which also conferred recognition on concubinage in civil law. This was partly expressed in the legal consequences attached to concubinage. These included *inter alia* the limited right of inheritance from the man—one-sixth of his estate—which under certain circumstances was bestowed on his concubine and the children she had borne to him.[235] The offspring of concubinage, *liberi naturals*,[236] thereby came to assume an especially favorable position compared with other bastards, *vulgo quaesiti, vulgo concepti, spurii.* Moreover, the former could claim maintenance[237] from their father and were entitled by *legitimatio*[238] to acquire the same legal status as children born in wedlock, and thereby could be placed under the father's *patria potestas.*

The legal nature of concubinage as *inaequale coniugium*, however, appears most distinctly in the inward and outward conditions that constituted legal facts necessary for the legal consequences and the delimiting criteria *vis-à-vis* for both marriage and other extramarital liaisons.

Despite the fact that the Roman concubinage partly was an *inaequale coniugium*, conditions somewhat analogous to the obstacles to marriage came to apply as external delimiting criteria for Roman concubinage.[239] Thus, the parties must have reached a certain age.[240] Kinship[241] in the direct line of descent and actual affinity [242] prevented the liaison from being legally regarded as concubinage. Yet the most characteristic feature of concubinage as a relationship like marriage was that it was presumed to be a monogamous union. In contrast to what seems to have been the case

---

Justinian's legislation. *See* GIRARD, *supra* note 23, at 200, who with reference thereto speaks of "une inaequale conjugium, une legitima conjunction." SOHM, *supra* note 67, at 509 and BAUMANN, *supra* note 225, at 14, describe concubinage as an "Ehe minderen Rechts" and an "Ehe minderen Grades" respectively. *Compare* MEYER, *supra* note 28, at 20 and 143.

235 Assuming the lack of a wife and children of the marriage, *see* Nov. 18, 5; Nov. 89, 12, 4; and GLÜCK, *supra* note 5, Bd. 28 at 391. Apart from the legal right of inheritance, the laws extended the possibilities for a man to provide for his concubine and her children by gifts and testamentary dispositions, *see* C. Th. 4, 6, 4; C. 5, 27, 2 (together with 8 and 12); and Nov. 89, 12, 2-3.

236 Nov. 89 ("de naturalibus liberis"); C. 27, 5; C. Th. 4, 6, 7; and MEYER, *supra* note 28, at 126. *Compare* Sundberg, who does not seem to have observed any move in Rome to equate children born in wedlock and bastards, *see* SUNDBERG, *supra* note 148, at 20.

237 Nov. 89, 12, 4; and Nov. 89, 13 and 15.

238 *Legitimatio* could ensue *per subsequens matrimonium, see* C. 7, 15, 3; and Nov. 18, 11, *per rescriptum principis, see* C. 5, 27, 11; and Nov. 74, and *per oblationem curiae, see* C. 5, 27, 8 pr.

239 C. 5, 27, 10; and Nov. 12, 4. *Compare* Chapter 2.2.3, *supra* regarding impediments to marriage. Several of the impediments arising by reason of imperfect *conubium*, like the Augustine bans on marriage, had been abolished before Justinian's time, *see* KASER II, *supra* note 5, at 111 and 126.

240 D. 25, 7, 1,4: ("Cuiusque aetatis concubinam habere posse palam est, nisi minor annis duodecim sit").

241 D. 23, 2, 56.

242 D. 25, 7, 1, 3. *Compare* C. 5, 4, 4.

from the outset in classical law, the Justinian legislation did not permit a married man to have a concubine.[243] Nor was the possession of several concubines acceptable.[244]

2.5.2 The Constituent Elements of Concubinage

What, then, was objectively and subjectively necessary for a man and a woman, who were competent to do so, to be legally regarded as living in concubinage? A study of the definitions of Roman concubinage, insofar as these pertain to legal facts (a good many also address legal consequences and other circumstances), indicate that, objectively, in contrast to definitions of the concept of marriage,[245] considerable significance was attached to the parties' sexual cohabitation. Only a few authors, however, characterize concubinage as a relationship that is exclusively sexual in nature, and these regularly emphasize that it could not be a purely temporary liaison. Thus, Glück speaks of "fortdauernder Geshlechtsverbindung."[246] It is more usual, however, for the concept of concubinage to be widened to include a more complete union between the man and the woman. Thus, Kaser presumes a "dauernde Lebens- und Geschlechtsgemeinschaft."[247] The characteristic feature of this community of life is usually considered to be its similarity to marriage. Thus, Mommsen defines the relationship as an "ehegleiche Zusammenleben,"[248] and Accarias describes the woman as "une maitresse vivant maritalement

243 Paul. Sent. 2, 20, 1: ("eo tempore, quo quis uxorem habet, concubinam habere non potest") (Probably interpolated). *Compare* SCHULZ, CLASSICAL, *supra* note 1, at 138, asserting when referring to the classical era that a married man could indeed only have one wife but that he could at the same time have a concubine, and that a bachelor then and still under Constantine could have two concubines, *see id.* at 140. *Compare*, Baumann, who maintains the monogamous nature of concubinage already in classical law, *see* BAUMANN, *supra* note 225, at 10. *Regarding* the postclassical period *see* C. 5, 26, 1: ("Nemini licentia concedatur, constante matrimonio, concubinam penes se habere"). *Compare* C. 7, 15, 2. Regarding the mild punishment for the man's adultery, *see* PLASSARD, *supra* note 166, at 46.

244 Nov. 18, 5: ("Atque haec dicimus, si unam concubinam habuerit"); and Nov. 89, 12, 4-5. *Compare* C. 7, 15, 3.

245 D. 50, 17, 30: ("consensus non concubitus facit nuptias") (consent not copulation creates marriage); and D. 35, 1, 15.

246 GLÜCK, *supra* note 5, Bd. 28 at 372 and 360; PUCHTA II, *supra* note 113, at 396; and MEYER, *supra* note 28, at 88 who also mention a "Geschlechtliches Zusammenleben" and Jörs & Kunkel, who characterize concubinage as a "dauernder Geschlechtsgemeinschaft," *see* JÖRS & KUNKEL, *supra* note 24, at 282. *Compare* Meyer, who elsewhere, does not limit concubinage to a purely sexual relationship but attributes to the female concubine a position in the home like that of a wife, *see* MEYER, *supra* note 28, at 91.

247 KASER I, *supra* note 5, at 328; VANDENBERGHE, *supra* note 109, at 3: ("een stabiele geslachts—en levensgemeenchap van een man en een vrouw"); and SOHM, *supra* note 67, at 509.

248 MOMMSEN, *supra* note 214, at 693 n. 2. Sohm similarly describes the community of life in a concubinage as a "der Ehe gleiches Zusammenleben," *see* SOHM, *supra* note 67, at 509 n. 9.

avec un amant."[249] That the similarity to marriage did not only presume sexual cohabitation of long duration is emphasized by Mitteis, who maintains that the male concubine "seine Geliebte gleich einer Hausfrau hielt."[250] Against the background of the exhaustive discussion concerning the necessity of the wife's *deductio in domum mariti*[251] at her wedding, it is not surprising that when the concept of concubinage was defined, the question of whether a community of bed and board should be required for concubines hardly roused any attention from scholars. Since, as has already been explained, different definitions seemed to allow for different opinions, it is worth emphasizing that Roman legal sources support the notion that a common home was a requirement of concubinage.[252] The element of legal concubinage constantly emphasized, regardless of whether concubinage is conceived as a sexual liaison, a community of life, or a relationship like marriage, is, as stated, its permanence[253] or intended permanence.[254] This element has been regarded as an essential criterion delimiting concubinage from more temporary extramarital liaisons, *fornicantium* (Nov. 18, 5). It is fitting that we sometimes find, as an element abstracted from permanence, a requirement of stability; a relationship may, of course, be long term but always labile; or, conversely, brief, perhaps by reason of the death of one party, but stable as long as it lasted. Thus, Plassard sets first and foremost "la permanence et la durée des relations"[255] as a constituent element of concubinage. Furthermore, there has occasionally been a demand for the presence of a pronounced ethical element,

249 Accarias, *supra* note 61, at 224. *See also* Schulz, who, referring to the female concubine, speaks of a spinster who lived with a man "as his wife," *see* Schulz, Classical, *supra* note 1, at 137.

250 Mitteis, *supra* note 231, at 310. *See also* Meyer, who states: "Die Konkubine vertritt im Hause die Stelle der fehlenden Gattin," *see* Meyer, *supra* note 28, at 91. Meyer states as regards Emperor Marcus Aurelius' concubine, that she "in Bezug auf ihre persönliche Stellung dem Kaiser gegenüber and in der Hauslichkeit einer Ehefrau nicht nachstand. Ja sie wird nach seiner Meinung seinen Kindern eine bessere Mutter sein als eine zweite Gattin," *see id.*

251 *See* Section 2.2.4, *supra.*

252 D. 50, 16, 144:("quosdam eam quae uxoris loco sine nuptiis in domo sit").

253 C. 5, 27, 10 pr.; and Nov. 12, 4 (*consuetudo*). *Compare* Nov. 18, 5; Nov. 89, 12 4; C. 7, 15, 3; Glück, *supra* note 5, Bd. at 360 and 372; Puchta II, *supra* note 113, at 396; Meyer, *supra* note 28, at 89; Sohm, *supra* note 67, at 509 n. 9; Mitteis, *supra* note 231, at 308; Plassard, *supra* note 166, at 191; Kaser I, *supra* note 5, at 328 and II, at 126; Jörs & Kunkel, *supra* note 24, at 282; and Schwind, *supra* note 80, at 177. Regarding the increasing significance attached to permanence in postclassical law, *see* Meyer, *supra* note 28, at 88 and 154.

254 The distinction between permanence and intended permanence has not been further discussed by scholars. It may, however, be remarked that Sohm, *supra* note 67, at 509 n. 9, speaks briefly of a cohabitation which is "auf Dauer gewolltes," and that Hambro, *supra* note 39, at 10, equally laconically presumes a "paa varighed anlagt" relationship.

255 Plassard, *supra* note 166, at 191. *Compare* Schulz, Classical, *supra* note 1, at 137; and Vandenberghe's statement concerning "een stabiele" union, *see* Vandenberghe, *supra* note 109, at 3.

which Plassard describes as "un élément d'honorabilité,"[256] and according to Mitteis presumed that the relationship be such as to appear "Gesellschaftsfähig." It is difficult to discern the individual factors that carried weight in the assessment of this element of respectability, which must be distinguished from the *honor matrimonii*,[257] which only accrued to the wedded wife. It is only reasonable that stability and permanence must have been taken into account. The honor of the matron was of more independent significance in that *inter alia* the parties thereby made their relationship public. Relations demonstrated outwardly were adjudged respectable while covert liaisons were condemned.[258] Concealment, which in modern times has been praised by the puritanical spirit as discretion, was censured as shameful in antiquity.

It should be clear from the above that the various elements inherent in the concept of concubinage are extremely vague. Nor do the sources give any unequivocal answer to the question of which elements were adjudged necessary and sufficient, or their order of importance. It is obvious, however, that in an overall assessment they could be considered significant, and the presence of at least some *corpus* element was necessary for the constitution of concubinage. Even if concubinage on the whole appears diffuse in its outlines, the aforesaid elements were intended to distinguish this concept from other, brief, labile, temporary, extramarital liaisons. Roman concubinage could be dissolved either by the disappearance of the constituent elements or the onset of circumstances which transformed it into marriage.[259]

---

256 PLASSARD, *supra* note 166, at 191 and 73. *See* particularly Mitteis' shrewd analysis of Papiniani's pregnant response concerning a testamentary issue, D. 34, 9, 16 pr., which indicates that the testator, a senator, loved his concubine "*honore pleno,*" *see* Mitteis, *supra* note 231, at 304. Regarding interpretations of the source by earlier scholars, *see* Glück's summary, GLÜCK, *supra* note 5, Bd. 382. n. 65. *Compare* SOHM, *supra* note 67, at 509 n. 9; and HAMBRO, *supra* note 39, at 10, laconic definitions of concubinage as an "offenes" and an "aapenlyst" relationship respectively. *Compare* the struggle of the Mediaeval Church against secret weddings, *matrimonium clandestinum,* Chapter 3.4, *infra* and the importance of "reputation" in the modern concept of common law marriage, Chapters 8 and 9, *infra.*

257 *See* Section 3.3, *supra. Compare* Accarias, who states that concubinage differed from marriage both by the parties' intentions and "par une affection moins digne dans sa vivacité et moins respectueuse pour la femme," *see* ACCARIAS, *supra* note 28, at 224. For a modern observer, it seems risky in practice to correctly value this "affection" and measure the degree of respectability.

258 *Compare* the strict judgements passed on a young slave girl's nocturnal visits to the aged Cato, *see* Plutarch, Caton l'Ancien, 37 in THE ROMAN QUESTIONS OF PLUTARCH (H.J. Rose trans. and comm. 1924).

259 The dissolution of concubinage rarely involves special procedures. Moreover, the sources are surprisingly silent on this point. Even if the dissolution is regarded merely as the negative side of all the actual constituent elements, it was obviously not without legal problems. Such concern *e.g.* the establishment of the occasion of the dissolution in the event of intermittent separations. *Compare* divorce, Chapter 2.4.3, *supra.*

2.5.3 The Difference between Concubinage and Marriage

If the dividing line between concubinage and other extramarital liaisons seems somewhat diffuse, the substantive delimitation of concubinage from the free marriage, the constitution of which, as we have found, did not require any formalities,[260] could be even trickier. This was particularly true in cases in which the parties were per se competent to marry each other, so that no external criteria excluded matrimony as was the case in many concubinages. In objective terms, these two modes of cohabitation could appear wholly similar.[261] What is the legal difference? Indeed, the fundamental distinction pertained to the parties' purely subjective *animus*. There is no dispute that concubinage lacked the *consensus vel affectio maritalis*[262] necessary for the constitution of a marriage. Only in this subjective respect did the necessary constituent elements of concubinage essentially differ from those of marriage. A more detailed specification of the difference between concubinage and marriage, so far as it is now at issue, therefore depends on the significance to be attached to the concept *affectio maritalis*. If, without repeating the above analysis,[263] we refer to some of these divergent results, we find that the consequences of the scope of the concept of concubinage, which are seldom realized, are different. Thus, if a marriage existed as soon as the parties themselves consciously saw each other as spouses, or their relationship as matrimonial,[264] the difference between concubinage and matrimony is subjectively dependent on the idea of marriage that the couple themselves hold in each individual case, and what conditions they think must be fulfilled before they are justified in regarding their union as a marriage. In cases in which the parties actually live together as husband and wife, concubinage would be present if they nevertheless did not regard each other as man and wife, or they still lacked a free awareness that their union was a marriage. If we ignore cases

---

260 *See* Section 2.4.2, *supra*.

261 In fact, a matrimonial *corpus* was required for the constitution of concubinage, while the necessity thereof at a wedding has been questioned, *see* Section 2.4.2, *supra*.

262 D. 25, 7, 4: ("Concubinam ex sola animi destinatione aestimari oportet"); Paul. Sent. 2, 20, 1: ("concubina igitur ab uxore solo dilectu separator"); D. 24, 1, 3, 1-2: ("quia non erat affectione uxoris habita, sed magis concubinae"); and D. 23, 2, 65, 1: ("si in eadem voluntate perseverat"). There is a somewhat contradictory statement by Puchta in which he first correctly maintains that concubinage was "nur ein rein faktisches Verhältnis" for its existence but continues "er besteht nur durch den fortgesetzten Willen," *see* PUCHTA II, *supra* note 113, at 397. *See* the same contradiction in Meyer, *see* MEYER, *supra* note 28, at 88, who follows Puchta. Perry, supra note 24, at 233 states: "*Affectio maritalis* distinguished *iustae nuptiae* from concubinage in Roman common law of the classical period."

263 *See* Section 2.4.3.1, *supra*.

264 Thus e.g. CORBETT, *supra* note 14, at 92, and MÜLLER-FREIENFELS, *supra* note 6, at 8. Unfortunately, these authors do not specify the possible importance attached by the parties of the content of *affectio maritalis*, and the consequences thereof for the concept of concubinage. In order to avoid trans-intentional misunderstandings, we shall here refrain from analyzing possible specifications.

in which the parties are mistaken about facts, the possibility of establishing the distinction between concubinage and marriage requires, that the parties consider matrimony to be something, more or less, different from the matrimonial cohabitation. The consequences of this idea of *affectio maritalis* is that the concept of concubinage cannot be unequivocally developed with respect to its individual character. Subjectively, concubinage could take peculiar forms, at least if the parties' conception of marriage were accepted, whatever it was; the parties might even think they were living as husband and wife only when all possible matrimonial cohabitation has ceased.

Again, if *affectio maritalis* is regarded as an intent, in terms of its legal consequences, the distinction is easy; couples could be thought to live in concubinage if they actually lived together as man and wife but lacked a common intent, or, indeed if they had a common intent not to incur the legal consequences of marriage.[265] If, on the other hand, the object of the parties' intent should be the matrimonial cohabitation, which is the prevailing opinion,[266] the distinction is more difficult to maintain. Yet, it is possible to make a distinction if it is assumed that in concubinage, in contrast to marriage, no complete community of life, no *consortium omnis vitae*, was intended, but that the liaison instead was designed to satisfy some more limited purpose.[267] So long as the cohabitation takes a plausible form, the difference appears also subjectively conceivable despite uncertainty about the limited purpose of the relationship. Assume, however, that the concubines, in accordance with the aforesaid criteria, actually lived together in a stable, honorable, permanent union closely akin to marriage, a *consortium omnis vitae*. Can the existence of a marriage be refuted under such circumstances by reference to the lack of matrimonial intent which has cohabitation as its object?

Surely it is theoretically possible in this case to also assert that if the parties' intent was nevertheless to fulfill a more limited purpose, a marriage could not be adjudged constituted. This would presume that their subjective intent did not cover the whole of the objective matrimonial cohabitation, or, in other words, that the parties did not wish to live as they did in fact. The thought of such an objective excess seems to have little to do with the realities of Roman family life. Another plausible explanation of the difference between concubinage and marriage in such cases is that the object of the matrimonial intent must include a future as well as an actual,

---

265 Meyer, who regards the matrimonial intent as an intent as to legal consequences, logically states of concubinage: "der Wille and die Absicht der Parteien ist auf ein anderes Ziel gerichtet. Der Konkubinat ... geht nicht auf ein rechtliches Ziel," *see* MEYER, *supra* note 28, at 88.

266 *Compare* Chapter 2.4.3, *supra.*

267 Thus clearly Glück, who states that concubinage could be differentiated from the free marriage only by "mangelnde Absicht vollständiger Lebensgemeinschaft," *see* GLÜCK, *supra* note 5, Bd. at 360. *Compare id.* at 372.

current, cohabitation. A temporary or long-term cohabitation, very like marriage, would not constitute matrimony but only concubinage, provided it was not the parties' common intention to continue the said liaison in the future. This line of thought in explaining the difference between the two forms of cohabitation, in cases such as those at issue, with the help of a future subjective expectation, has not been explicitly stated in the Roman legal sources. Nor does the explanation seem to have attracted the direct attention of scholars. Nevertheless, it is compatible with Modestinus' definition of marriage as a *consortium omnis vitae*, inasmuch as this may thereby be understood not only as a sharing of everything in life but, if there is some evidence, a union "for the whole of life."[268]

Notwithstanding that Roman law had an impressive intellectual readiness for assessing the *animus* phenomenon now at issue, there is reason to assume that a material distinction between the concepts of marriage and concubinage, based on a fine subjective requisite, should have led to difficulties in the application of the law, particularly given that an *affectio concubinam habendi* could gradually be transformed into an *affectio maritalis*. Such difficulties were diminished, however, by typical, not individual, *indicia*, which carry particular evidentiary value for the examination of whether or not *affectio maritalis* was present. These included, as we saw above,[269] *inter alia* the woman's more or less ceremonial *deductio in domum mariti*, other solemn *festivitas nuptiarum*,[270] and the drafting of marriage documents such as *dotis instrumenta*, etc. In the event that such *indicia* did not exist, or despite their existence there was doubt as to whether or not *affectio maritalis* was present, if a free man and a free woman who were competent to marry had lived together for a long time in a relationship like marriage, a presumption ensued that the union was matrimonial.[271] It is clear that this presumption must have reduced the difficulties of the law's application, notwithstanding that it would not have involved their total removal. The application thereof indeed required the presence of a presumptive circumstance, *consuetudo*, which appears weak and has not been narrowly specified. Glück mentions the man who had taken to himself a woman with whom he "fortwährend wie mit einer Ehefrau zusammenlebte."[272] Karlowa seems to assume that the parties must have

268 *See* Section 2.2.1, *supra*.
269 *See* Section 2.4.2.2, *supra*.
270 Regarding the significance that could be attached to the lack of ceremony particularly among the nobles, where the expectations of such were greater, *see* Mitteis' excellent analysis of Papiniani's pregnant response in D. 34, 9, 16 pr., which concerns a senator, *vir clarissimi*, who, according to Mitteis, had "in Ehren 'geliebt' aber nicht in Ehren gefreit," which, Mitteis thought constituted crucial evidence that the relationship was a concubinage, not a marriage, *see* Mitteis, *supra* note 231, at 312.
271 D. 23, 2, 24: ("In liberae mulieris consuetudine non concubinatus sed nuptiae intelligendae sunt, si non corpore quaestum fecerit"). According to accepted opinion, 'liberae' should be read as 'ingenuae', *see* Levy, *supra* note 59, at 75.
272 Glück, *supra* note 5, Bd. 28 at 375.

ehelicht zusammenlebt.[273] Corbett postulates *cohabitation*,[274] Levy a *Verbindung*,[275] and Volterra a *union*[276] between the man and the woman for the presumption to be applicable. Since it comprised not a *praesumptio iuris et de iure* but a *praesumptio iuris*, it could be refuted.[277] It follows from the above that the Roman concepts of marriage and concubinage well nigh merge.

2.6 Summary and Conclusions

The family law development in ancient Rome, albeit the similarities ought not be over-exaggerated, had certain common features with the development in the Western world during the latter part of the 1900s and the beginning of the twenty-first century. At the end of the Roman Republic and in the beginning of the Principate, the Roman traditions with respect to family building underwent significant changes. The rate of marriage decreased, and the number of marital divorces increased. The ceremonial forms for the commencement of marriage fell into disuse and were replaced by the free Roman marriage and concubinage. Ceremonies were only a supplement to marriages for spouses who so wished. During the entire classical and postclassical epochs, free marriage came to constitute the dominant model of marriage. Today, the Western world encounters a similar development with decreasing rates of marriage and an increasing number of unmarried cohabiting persons, circumstances that lawmakers are meeting with increasing legislation regulating formless cohabitations. The question of whether this strategy is effective is discussed in Part III.

Certain Roman principles as to marriage, as seen in the following chapters, came to influence much later legal thinking concerning marriage in general and common law marriage in particular.

1. *Marriage as a Contract*

A significant inheritance from Roman family law is the concept that the commencement of marriage is basically a contract. The principle *consensus facit nuptias*[278] in modern times would become fundamental for the establishment of both ceremonial and common law marriages, but in reality the principle received its greatest significance with respect to the latter form of marriage. In the leading American cases in which common law

273 Karlowa, Röm. Rg. II, *supra* note 14, at 180.
274 Corbett, *supra* note 14, at 95.
275 Levy, *supra* note 59, at 75.
276 Volterra, *supra* note 65, at 35.
277 Regarding the legal nature of the presumption, *see* Orestano, *supra* note 141, at 376. Regarding the possibility for the man to declare before witnesses that he had taken the woman as his concubine, not his wife, *see* D. 25, 7, 3 pr.
278 D. 50, 17, 30: ("Nuptias non concubitus, sed consensus facit") (not copulation, but consent creates marriage); and D. 35, 1, 15.

marriage was established in the United States during the 1800s, the court cited these Roman law principles.[279] In accordance with Roman law, the parties' shared marital intent, in order to be granted constitutive effect, had to be temporally focused on a present, not simply a future, marriage, as described above.[280] In addition, a characteristic of the Roman marriage contract was that the parties' shared intent consisted of their *affectio maritalis*,[281] in other words, a shared intent, in some sense, to be married. The issue arises whether the object of this intent is the marriage's legal effects or the marital cohabitation. Despite the plausibility of different interpretations, it appears logical to tie this intent to the Roman definition of marriage and allow the object of the parties' shared intent to consist of a *consortium omnis vitae*, in other words, a community in everything in life for the entire life.

Therewith, the Roman contract approach has raised questions that are material for the following presentation. The issue of the role that different objects for the marital intent play today within the framework of the common law marriage case law is examined in Chapters 6, "The Common Law Marriage Contract," and 7, "Implied Marriage Agreements."[282] The issue of what effects the different types of shared intentions in the future can have within this doctrine and within cohabitation law are discussed in Chapters 13, "The Constitutive Requisites in the Future," and 14, "Arguments For and Against Common Law Marriage and Cohabitation Law."[283]

Also characteristic in the Roman marriage contract was that the parties' *affectio maritalis* did not need to come to expression with a sharply delineated verbal act. Instead, this *affectio* encompassed the parties' state of mind continuously exhibited in all circumstances during the entire cohabitation. Consequently, it was not a question of a one-time shared intent, an initial intent, but rather of a continuous *consensus*, which had more the

---

279 *See, eg.*, *Askew v. Dupree*, 30 Ga. 173, 178 (1860), in which the court states: "Consensus, non concubitus, faciat matrimonium, the maxim of the Roman civil law is, in truth, the maxim of all law upon the subject." *See also James Kent*, who in a commentary as to his own judgment in *Fenton v. Reed*, 4 Johns. 52 (N.Y. 1809), states that: "The Roman lawyers strongly inculcated the doctrine, that the very foundation and essence of the contract consisted freely given, by parties competent to contract. *Nihil proderit signasse tabulas, simentem matrimonii non fuisse constabit. Nuptias non concubitus, sed consensus*," *see* James Kent, Commentaries on American Law 2, 75 (1826). Regarding the Reception of Common Law Marriage in the United States, *see* Chapter 4 *infra*. With respect to The Common Law Marriage Contract, *see* Chapter 6 and Implied Marriage Agreements, Chapter 7, *infra*.

280 This would consequently be a question of a *consensus in praesenti* and not *consensus in futuro*. Compare the Medieval Canon law, according to which even a marital *consensus in futuro* could be attributed constitutive effect, *see* Chapter 3, *infra*.

281 D. 24, 1, 32, 13: ("non enim coitus matrimonium facit, sed maritalis affectio").

282 *See* Chapter 6, The Common Law Marriage Contract and Chapter 7, Implied Mariage Agreements, *infra*.

283 *See* Chapter 13, The Constitutive Requisites in the Future and Chapter 14, Arguments For and Against Common Law Marriage and Cohabitation Law, *infra*.

character of a permanent subjective requisite, similar to *animus* in questions of possession. The modern formal marriage is entered into; the Roman marriage was lived.

This idea of a continuous *consensus* ought to fit well in a reality in which the parties do not enter into any express agreement, but the relationship, as is the case with common law marriage, commonly is based on an inferred agreement that rests upon the parties' actual cohabitation. Whether and to what extent American courts, which during two hundred years formed the case law concerning common law marriage, partook of the idea of a continuous *consensus* will be more closely examined in Chapters 6 and 7.[284]

For the commencement of both Roman marriage and concubinage, the parties had to be legally competent. In accordance with the largely non-legal character of the Roman marriage, however, the state exercised no control over the commencement of relationships concerning whether *ius conubii* arose as to the parties or whether impediments against the marriage in general existed. Any legal assessment of the parties' legal capacity arose afterwards, when the validity of a marriage or a concubinage became the object of a legal assessment. Today, the situation is the same with respect to both common law marriage and modern cohabitation legislation. Chapter 5, "Legal Capacity and Common Law Marriage," addresses the problems that arise when new informal relationships are established consecutively and an early relationship is not formally dissolved, which then constitutes an impediment against a later marriage.[285] Whether regulations concerning legal capacity can prevent unsuitable relationships without an advance hearing is discussed in Chapter 14, with respect to both common law marriage and today's cohabitation legislation.[286]

2. *Cohabitation as an Objective Requisite and as an Evidentiary Fact*

The institution of *usus*, mentioned already in the law of the Twelve Tables, which fell in disuse during the classical period, is the oldest Roman form of cohabitation that entailed marital legal effects. The woman entered in the man's family and under his marital authority, *manus*, and their children attained legitimacy. It, however, ought to be noted that the *usus* construction could not avoid a subjective element. Consequently, it was required that the parties during a one-year period lived together *matrimnii causa*, in other words, with a marital purpose. The woman, furthermore, could avoid these legal effects by being absent during three consecutive nights, *trinoctium*, from the man, although her intentions also were considered.

284 *See* Chapter 6, The Common Law Marriage Contract and Chapter 7, Implied Marriage Agreements, *infra*.
285 *See* Chapter 5, Legal Capacity and Common Law Marriage, *infra*.
286 *See* Chapter 14, Arguments For and Against Common Law Marriage and Cohabitation Law, specifically § 14.3.5, *infra*.

The function of a subjective element within the modern concept of marriage and cohabitation law is treated in Chapter 13.[287]

A debated issue has been whether cohabitation, the outward appearance of being spouses, or another objective element in addition to the marriage contract was also required for the establishment of the free Roman marriage, or whether these facts only constituted evidentiary facts for the existence of the marriage contract. In accordance with the dominant view, it appears that in the classical period, analogous to the requirement of tradition within private property law, the woman was required to enter into the man's house, *deductio in domum mariti*, particularly for determining the point at which the marriage would be viewed as commenced. No period of cohabitation or *copula carnalis* was required. It was sufficient that a community of life actually was commenced. With the victory of the *animus* theory within legal scholarship and legislation during the postclassical and Justinian periods, it appears sufficient that the parties' marital intent came to expression in words, either orally or in writing.

The question of whether cohabitation, outward appearance, or reputation as spouses would be required for the creation of a common law marriage in addition to the marriage contract would, as seen below, become the object of divided opinions over the following centuries.[288]

It has further been seen in this chapter that the cohabitation as well as other facts are given significance as evidentiary facts for the existence of the parties' *consensus vel affectio maritalis*. Such a free evidentiary evaluation is consistent with the Roman principle concerning free evidentiary assessments. Even the woman's actual social status was material, *i.e.*, whether she acted as a true wife, in other words with *honor matrimonii*, this one typical evidentiary fact was proof of the parties' marital intent. The significance to American case law, substantively[289] and evidentiarily, [290] of the parties' reputations as spouses will be more closely investigated below.

In those cases in which the parties availed themselves of voluntary celebrations and solemnities, *celebritas nuptiarum, pompa nuptialis, nuptiarum festivitas, ritus nuptiarum*, or drafted marriage documents, *tabulae nuptiaes*, it is clear that these could constitute evidence of their marital *consensus*. Even the parties' oath in front of the Censor and the attestation of friends, *amicorum fide firmari*, may be mentioned as examples of evidence, customarily cited as proof that a marriage was at hand.

Cohabitation, however, appears to have been taken as such strong evidence that it became the basis of a presumption about the existence of

287 *See* Chapter 13, The Constitutive Requisites in the Future, *infra*.

288 *See* the discussion in Chapter 8, Cohabitation, appearance outwardly and reputation as spouses, *infra*.

289 *See* Chapter 8, *infra*.

290 *See* Chapter 7, Implied Marriage Agreements and Chapter 9, Burdens of Proof and Presumptions, *infra*.

a marriage. This presumption, which could be rebutted, assumed considerable practical importance in delimiting between marriage, concubinage, and other out-of-wedlock relationships.

The use of presumptions based on the parties' cohabitation and outward appearance as spouses would later assume considerable practical importance with the establishment of an informal marriage in canon law. In modern times, it has had an important function to fulfill both with respect to formal marriage and common law marriage. The application of presumptions in the American case law is examined below in Chapters 7, and 9, "Burdens of Proof and Presumptions."

3. The Legal Effects of the Free Marriage

A characteristic feature in the development of the Roman understanding of marriage was the idea that the state legal system ought not encroach upon the family's autonomy but rather in principle should end at the threshold of the home. According to this, a more individual perspective is the basis from which the legal effects of marriage ought to be limited. The woman, thereby, took a freer and more independent status in relation to the man than that granted by the *manus* marriage's patriarchical structure. She did not legally become a member of the man's family and did not acquire any civil law right to inherit, *ius sui heredis*, after the man and his family. The marriage did not entail any economic community between the spouses. There consequently was an order; some modern law is reminiscent: the English "system of separation of goods," applied in 1882; the German "Gütertrennung"; and the Swedish system of individual property.

Personally, the woman was not subjected to the man's authority and she did not take his name. Through the marriage, however the woman was honored as a true spouse, *honor matrimonii*. The children born in such a marriage were legitimate and became Roman citizens. They had the right to inherit after their father and other members of his family, as well as to be placed under the father's *potestas patria*.

4. Martial Divorce

In addition, characteristic for the free Roman marriage was that even divorce, *divortium*, occurred without the participation of any authority or the observance of certain forms. Here, the free Roman marriage differs from present-day common law marriage, which is dissolved by divorce in the same formal way as ceremonial marriage. In this respect, the Roman system, on the other hand, resembles modern cohabitation legislation, according to which the relationships usually are dissolved formlessly. It is possible that the constructors of cohabitation legislation today have something to learn from the Roman scheme. Although cohabitation legislation today usually assesses whether a couple has separated based only on objective criteria, the Roman law also employed a subjective element. It consequently required that one of the parties had given expression of an intent to be divorced. The requirement of a subjective element made it possible to make exceptions for cases in which the parties did not maintain the cohabitation, for other reasons; for example due to employment or military service in another place. The exceptions concerning temporary quarrels, *iurgium*, and the requirement of a true intent to divorce, *verum divortium*, were also instruments that could facilitate the assessment of intent to divorce.

For spouses, the notification of the intent to divorce, *repudium*, in Rome had developed certain customs, which from a legal perspective were not mandatory, but which could serve as evidence; for example, of one spouse's request to the other to leave the home, *baete foras*, or to clear out his or her belongings, *tuas res tibi habeto* or *agito*, as well as one spouse's repossession of the keys to the home, *claves adimere*. Even the parties' termination of the cohabitation or one party's commencement of a new relationship could serve as evidence for the existence of an intent to divorce.

With the application of modern cohabitation legislation today, it is often risky to try to assess whether and at which point a cohabitation actually was dissolved. The Roman law's employment of subjective and objective requisites is of interest in resolving these problems.

5. *The Roman Concubinage*

As a consequence of the Augustinian marital legislation's several marriage prohibitions, the classical concubinage, *concubinatus*, arose. For those who, based on these laws, lacked the legal capacity to enter into a marriage, *conubium*, concubinage was a substitute. Concubinage, however, came to be an alternative even for those who had the legal capacity to marry, but refrained for economic or other reasons. In both categories, it was common that the parties, in some sense, lived together in marriage-like circumstances. Such cohabitation appears afterwards to have won a wide social acceptance and became an expanding phenomenon. From the first century on, it appears that concubinage was regarded with benign neutrality within Roman society.

During the classical period, concubinage was introduced as a legal concept in the legislation and a legal distinction was made between concubinage and other out-of-wedlock relationships. The legal effects, however, were limited. The greatest significance was the exemption from criminal punishment for *stuprum*, which otherwise was imposed for sexual intercourse outside of marriage. In addition to this, as was the case for spouses, a soldier's gifts to his concubine were invalid.

Legislation in the postclassical period, under Christian influence, once again attempted to impose criminal law sanctions against concubinage and to reward those who married, to limit the expansion of concubinage, but these endeavors were not successful. The legislators' tactics *vis-à-vis* concubinage then changed. The objective later appears to have been to assimilate every de facto family within a legal regulation. With this, the

Roman concubinage developed into a marriage of second rank, an *inaequale coniugium.* The woman in concubinage was granted the right to inherit after the man; their children received the right to inherit and the right to maintenance after the father; as well as a right through *legitimatio* to become entirely legally, the equal of children born within wedlock and within the father's *patria potestas.*

The vacillating Roman strategy in relation to concubinage is easy to trace when one studies it in relation to common law marriage and cohabitation as they developed in the Western world during 1800s and 1900s, as examined further below.[291]

6. *The Constituent Elements of Concubinage*

A man and a woman who were legally competent, in other words, who fulfilled the terms and conditions similar to those applicable to spouses, could establish a legal concubinage if they lived in a marriage-like relationship, and it was intended that they were cohabiting and that they had an ongoing sexual relationship. In order to distinguish concubinage from other loose or temporary relations, a cohabitation that was permanent and stable appears to have been required. The marriage-like character of concubinage made it, objectively, very similar to free marriage. The difference was subjective. For the establishment of a concubinage, the existence of *affectio maritalis*—in other words, an intent in any sense to be married—was not required. Somewhat simplified, one can state that the free Roman marriage most resembled common law marriage, while concubinage resembled cohabitation in accordance with modern legislation. However, in ancient Rome, in reality, it was hazardous to distinguish between free marriage and concubinage, just as today it is hazardous in a common law marriage state to distinguish between common law marriage and cohabitation. These latter differences are investigated more closely in Chapters 7 and 13.[292]

7. *Application Problems and Disputes*

Finally, it has been seen in this chapter that the free Roman marriage and concubinage gave rise to extensive application problems, which caused Emperor Justinian to act through legislation. The possibility of citing an informal relationship as the basis for a marriage caused significant evidentiary problems and tempted parties to use fraudulent agreements to prove marriages that were never entered into. All this gave rise to

---

291 With respect to the reasons for and the criticism of common law marriage in the United States during the 1800s, *see* Chapter 4, The Reception of Common Law Marriage in the United States, *infra.* With respect to the arguments for and against common law marriage in the future, *see* Chapter 14, The Arguments For and Against Common Law Marriage and Cohabitation Law, *infra.*

292 *See* Chapter 7, Implied Marriage Agreements and Chapter 13, The Constitutive Requisites in the Future, *infra.*

numerous, drawn-out litigations, which Justinian sought to resolve by laying down requirements for formal marriage contracts and the conveyance of dowries.

These historical experiences would also, in the future, be repeated by later civilizations. The Roman Catholic Church, during the second millennium in the year 1563, repealed the canon law's informal marriages, in part to resolve problems of application.[293] The same reasons also played a large role when the English formless marriage was repealed through Lord Hardwicke's Act, in 1753. One of the main disclosures of this investigation into American case law from the 1800s and 1900s, encompassing more than one thousand cases concerning common law marriage, is the extensive application problems, both legal and evidentiary. These problems have caused many disputes and led to the doctrine's repeal in certain states. Every legislator who, today, during the third millennium is contemplating enacting common law marriage or cohabitation legislation in general has good reason to consider these disputes, the costs, and the legal uncertainty of legislation concerning formless relationships.

293 *See* Chapter 3, The Reception of Common Law Marriage in the United States, *infra.*

CHAPTER 3
Informal Marriages in Canon Law

Of all people in the world lovers are the least likely to distinguish precisely between the present and the future tenses.

Pollock and Maitland

3.1 Introduction

Marriage was one of the main objects of legal regulation in the medieval canon law governing the entire Christian world. The church considered the legal regulation of the marital community in accordance with Christian conceptions to be its rightful task. Marriage was held to be part of the order of creation given by God, based on Genesis 1:28 and 2:18, in which marriage took a place as one of the seven sacraments. The young Christian church endeavored to more extensively legalize marriage, in contrast to the classical Roman understanding that state legal systems ought not encroach upon the family's autonomy but rather, in principle, stopping at the threshold to the home.

The regulation of marriage exemplified the power of the church's growing strength. During the High Middle Ages, the heyday of canon law, marriage constituted one of the main objects of papal legislative activity as well as academic studies at the law schools in Bologna and Paris. The result was an extensively developed and refined legal marital system, which for centuries would come to dominate in the medieval world. Canon legal scholarship contributed to a high degree to the construction of this system. Pioneer contributions were made by Master Gratian himself, the father of the canonists, who in approximately 1140 completed his great work, *Concordantia discordantium canonum*, which later came to be designated as *Decretum Gratiani*.[1] Among the founders of this marriage law system, Peter Lombard also deserves to be mentioned, who in 1150–1152 released his *Sententiae*. Pope Alexander III (1159–1181) further developed and through

1 With respect to the title and date of this work, *see* Peter-Josef Kessler, Die Entwicklung der Formvorschriften Für die kanonische Eheschliessung, 21 note 48 and 22 note 50 (1934).

legislation gave papal sanction to the system, which later was taken up in Pope Gregorius IX's decretal collection *Liber Extra* published in 1234.[2]

The canon law marital system and the experiences associated with it influenced modern law. Both Gratian and Peter Lombard drew distinctions that still serve as instruments of explanation and analysis of the structure of the concept of marriage. The reason for this ought partly be found in the scholastic method's highly abstract character. Its strict adherence to authoritative sources and its objective of achieving a system free of contradictions were its strength as well as its weakness. Canon law, as a consequence, was, on one hand, to a high degree free from historical considerations, and barely considered the realities of the medieval society in which it arose. On the other hand, the abstract distinctions made in canon law can be of interest to other societies. Despite the insularity of the canon law system, it was not altogether removed from the world. The church's own interests and a compelling necessity required *inter alia* consideration of the diversity within local marital traditions and customs, which since ancient times had been dominant within different parts of the church's extensive jurisdiction. In order to achieve the church's far-reaching marriage law goals, these considerations had to be assessed in different legal policy strategies, which also ought to be of interest for modern legislators. The canon law doctrinal system, though primarily the church's own product, was influenced by Germanic, Jewish, and Roman law.

The highest priority in the legalization of the canon law marriage was the indissolubility of marriage and marital impediments, not the form requirements for the commencement of a marriage. Canon law and papal authority held a dominant position in the Christian world during the Middle Ages. Strikingly, however, not until the Council of Trent in 1563, did the by-then Roman Catholic branch decree—by what modern authors ordinarily called *Tametsi*—that entering into a marriage through a church wedding ceremony was an unconditional prerequisite for the validity of the marriage.[3]

The absence, in over more than one thousand years of pre-Tridentine canon law, of any form requirement raises the question of why the Christian medieval church had, during this millennium, accepted relationships as marriages which were entered into without the use of any religious forms. In addition, the question arose as to what requirements had to be fulfilled in order to establish a valid marriage between legally competent persons. What significance was attributed to the parties' *consensus* and cohabitation with the establishment of an informal marriage, and how were these

---

2 Liber decretalium vagantium extra Decretum Gratiani or Gregoriana, decretales Gregorii IX. *See* CORPUS JURIS CANONICI, EMENDATUM ET NOTIS ILLUSTRATUM. GREGORII XIII. PONTIF. MAX. JUSSU EDITUM COLONIAE MUNATIANAE, M.DC.XCVI. (C.J.C)

3 c. 1, Trid. Sess. XXIV, *De reformatione matrimonii*, CANONES ET DECRETA SACROSANTI OECUMENICI CONCILII TRIDENTI SUB PAULO III, IULIO III, ET PIO IV (1903); CANONS AND DECREES OF THE SACRED AND OECUMENICAL COUNCIL OF TRENT 196-97 (J. Waterworth trans., Dolman, London 1848).

elements more precisely formulated? Was the cohabitation a necessary requisite or did it simply constitute an evidentiary fact for the parties' *consensus* or for a presumption that they were married? In which manner do the origins of common law marriage appear in this canon law system? What were the experiences of the application of the laws that occurred and for which reasons was the system eventually repealed? This chapter focuses on these questions.

3.2 The Canon Law Understanding of Marriage

3.2.1 The Definition of Marriage

The Roman legal influence, which at times was more visible than actual, is clearly expressed in the canon law definition of marriage. Very often, the church fathers began their descriptions of the essence of marriage by primarily restating the Justinian Roman definition, which, as stated above, reads: *Nuptiae sive matrimonium est viri et mulieris coniunctio individuam vitae consuetudinem continens.*[4] This understanding of marriage, as an *individua consuetudem vitae,* an undivided cohabitation for a lifetime, echoes Augustine and Gratian, among others who came later.[5]

The definitions in the Roman law had the character more of normative pictures of marriage as an ideal type, whose realization to a high degree was delegated to the spouses themselves, whereas, in the canon law marriage was given a more material content with legal effects supervised by the Papal See. In contrast to Roman law, the church fathers by interpreting the concept of cohabitation, *consuetudo,* emphasized the sexual element *copula carnalis* and its dual purpose to satisfy sexual desire, and produce legitimate heirs of the body.[6] The most radical difference appears,

4 Inst. 1, 9, 1. *Compare* Modestinus' definition: *Nuptiae sunt coniunctio maris et feminae et consortium omnis vitae* divini *et humani iuris communicatio* (D. 23, 2, 1). *Compare supra* Chapter 2.2.1.

5 Augustine said according to c. 3, C. 27, qu. 2: *Beata Maria ... Consensus ergo cohabitandi & individuam vitae consuetudinem retinendi interveniens, eos conjuges fecit. Individua vero vitae consuetudo est, talem se in omnibus exhibero viro, qualis ipsa sibi est, et e converso.* Gratian stated in the exposition to C. 27, qu. 2: *Sunt enim Nuptiae, sive matrimonium, viri mulierisque conjunctio, individum vitae consuetudinem retinens. See* C.I.C., *supra* note 2, *Decretum Gratiani,* col. 927. *See also* Liber Extra: *cum matrimonium fit maris & feminae conjunctio, individuam vitae consuetudinem retinens,* c. 11 X, II, 23, C.I.C., *supra* note 2, *Decretales Gregorii,* col. 284. *Compare* Eduard Wichmann, Lehrbuch des Kirchenrechts auf Grund des Codex Iuris Canonici II at 66 (3 Aufl. 1930): "Die Ehe ist also die rechtsmässige Verbindung eines Mannes und einer Frau zu völligen, ungeteilten Lebensgemeinschaft."

6 Marriage's dual purpose has been expressed by Gratian, (c. 1-16, C. 32, qu. 2), since he, in the scholastic manner citing authorities for and against, maintains that marriage was not only established for the acquisition of a *proles,* but that also women, *quae sola causa incontinentiae ducitur,* are to be viewed as wives. *See* C.I.C, *supra* note 2, Decretum *Gratiani,* col. 978. *Compare* Plöchl, who maintains that marriage "bildete eine vollkommene und grundsätzlich unauflösliche Lebens- und Leibesgemeinschaft,

however, to be in the *passus*, in which marriage is designated as a cohabitation *individua vitae*. From the representation of marriage as a legal, undivided, and indissoluble union between a man and a woman for a lifetime, followed the canon law understanding that marriage was not only monogamous, but indissoluble. The latter characteristic is in stark contrast to the Roman legal principle of *libertas matrimonii*, which by definition protected the possibility of marital divorce.[7] The church certainly did not lack theological support for its understanding of marriage's indissolubility. Ordinarily cited in the holy scriptures were the recurring explanations that spouses after the commencement of marriage were no longer two, but rather one flesh (*una caro*), and that which God consequently has joined, let no man sunder (*quod ergo Deus conjunxit, homo non separet*).[8] Support for the understanding of marriage's indissolubility was also obtained in the representation of marriage as a sacrament and as a symbol for Christ's eternal and indissoluble union with his congregation (*sacramentum, quia nullum divortium*).[9]

3.2.2 Legal Capacity to Enter into Marriage

With the delineation of that which ought to be recognized as a *matrimonium legitimum*, the church gave high priority to imposing external requisites that would apply with respect to the parties' legal capacity to enter into marriage. The church's interest hereof can be explained by the close connection between marriage's moral essence and its indissolubility. Afterwards, canon law was based consequently on a very extensive and increasingly refined system of marriage impediments (*impedimenta*), a system in which the distinction *inter alia* was introduced between dissoluble impediments (*impedimenta dirimenta*) and indissoluble impediments (*impedimenta impedientia*).[10] Marriages entered into in conflict with a dissoluble

---

die ausser dem ursprünglichen Zweck der Fortpflanzung des Menschengeschlechts auch die legitime Befriedigung des Geschlechtstriebs umfasste," *see* Willibald M. Plöchl, Geschichte des Kirchenrechts II, Das Kirchenrecht der abendländischen Christenheit 1055 bis 1517, 268 (1955).

7 *See* Section 2.4.3.

8 Matt 19:6 and Mark 10:9. *Cf.* Matt 19:5, Mark 10:8, Eph, 5:31 and Genesis 2:23.

9 *Sacramentum, quia nullum divortium,* Augustine states according to c. 10, C. 27, qu. 2. *See* C.I.C., *Decretum Gratiani,* col. 929.

10 In addition to the difference between dissoluble and indissoluble impediments, a distinction that has remained to modern times also arose between true and false impediments. Included in the latter are *inter alia* relationships which according to the modern system do not even belong in the category of marital impediments, e.g., the absence of marital intent (*dissensus*) and certain deficiencies in the same such as conditional intent (*impedimentum conditions appositae*), involuntary consent (*impedimentum vis ac metudd*), and misrepresentation (*impedimentum erroris*). We return to these below when discussing marital intent. As to specifics with respect to marital impediments, *see* Joseph Freisen, Geschichte des Canonischen

impediment were considered a nullity (*matrimonium nullum*), while relationships that were entered into in ignorance of an indissoluble impediment constituted a valid, albeit impermissible, marriage (*matrimonium illicitum*). At the Fourth Council of the Lateran in 1215, the requirement of banns was adopted in order to assure that impediments against an intended marriage did not exist. The failure to call banns could entail criminal punishment for the priest as well as for the parties themselves, but did not affect the validity of a an informal marriage entered into without publishing the banns.[11] The validity of the informal marriage, however, depended on there being no fatal impediment.

As certain of the canon law marital impediments appear alien to the modern legal understanding, e.g., spiritual affinity, impediment due to impotence, or differences in faith, there is no reason to more closely review the entire system. Several of the most important *impedimentia dirimentia* deserve, however, to be mentioned. As the requisite marital age (*impedimentum aetatis*), the canon law, as did the Roman, used the threshold of puberty, which as long as nothing to the contrary was proven, was presumed to be achieved for the woman at twelve years of age and for the man at fourteen. These age requirements, as late as the 1900s, were applied as to common law marriage in certain cases.[12] Affinity (*cognatio*) within the seventh degree (the canon basis of calculation) and within the fourth degree after the Fourth Council of the Lateran in 1215, constituted an impediment, which can be compared with the Roman law's limit at the fourth degree (civil basis of calculation). Affinity through marriage (*impedimentum affinitas*) was treated in the comparable manner, based upon the representation in the holy scriptures that the man and woman through marriage became one flesh (*una caro*) and affinity through marriage therefore became identical with family relationships.

Of greater interest for our purposes is that an existing marriage constituted a marriage impediment (*impedimentum ligaminis*).[13] From the outset,

---

EHERECHTS DIS ZUM VERFALL DER GLOSSENLITTERATUS 227 (Paderborn, Druck und Verlag von Ferdinand Schöningh, 2 Aufl.1893) and A. ESMEIN, LE MARIAGE EN DROIT CANONIQUE I, 227 (R. Génestal ed., 2nd ed. 1929).

11 c. 3 X, IV, 3, C.J.C., *supra* note 2, Decretales Gregorii, col. 552. The requirement as to banns was also included in a papal letter immediately after the Council. *See*, e.g., Pope Innocentius III's letter dated 5 April 1216 to the Archbishop in Uppsala, *see* Diplomatarium Suecanum I at 182 DS-nr 156 (Joh. Gusth. Liljegren ed., Stockholm 1829).

12 *See* Chapter 5.

13 The principle concerning marriage's monogamous character can be seen from a large number of sources, including Hieronumus: *unius uxoris virum, id est, monogamum* (c. 1, D. 26), *see* C.J.C., *supra* note 2, Decretum Gratiani, col. 85; Innoceentius III: *Nec ulli unuquam licuit insimul plures uxores habere nisi cui fuit divina relevatione concessum, see* c. 8 X, IV, 19, C.J.C, *supra* note 2, Decretales Gregorii, col. 591. It is common that existing marriages as a marriage impediment are directly tied to marriage's indissolubility. The canon law therefore had a broader concept of monogamy than modern law. One, consequently, spoke of *polygamia simultanae,* in other words, polygamy. [*See, e.g.*, Gratian in c. 1, D. 26]. The principle of monogamy also

under canon law, marriage was monogamous, in contrast to the Jewish and Germanic traditions, but similar to Greek and Roman law. Already the story of Adam and Eve in paradise served as a dogmatic basis for the church to maintain monogamy as a principle.[14] This assumed significant practical importance as an impediment because the church praised the principle of marriage's indissolubility, which presented a danger of bigamy.[15] Certainly the spouses on certain grounds could receive a separation as to bed and home (*separatio quod mensam et thorum*), but the bonds of marriage still remained (*vinculum matrimonii*) and this constituted an impediment against a new marriage. First, a marriage could be dissolved through a spouse's death. If the other spouse entered into a new marriage before this, it was considered adultery (*adulterium*). There was a possibility of being able to enter into a new marriage by alleging a fatal marriage impediment to get the previous marriage declared null. If the danger for bigamy was considerable because of marriage's indissolubility, entirely formless marriages also constituted an impediment against a new marriage. A common law marriage in the United States today still constitutes an impediment against both a new informal marriage and a ceremonial marriage.[16]

3.3 The Informal Marriages

3.3.1 Introduction

Although the difference between Roman and canon law was most apparent regarding marriage's dissolution, the continuity with Rome was strongest with respect to canon law's constitutive requisites for the commencement of marriage. For our purposes, it is of particular interest to ascertain that

---

can be seen indirectly from many statements that directly concern the possibility of receiving a separation as to bed and home and the impossibility of getting the bonds of marriage (*vinculum*) dissolved. *See* c. 2, C. 32, qu. 7, C.J.C, *supra* note 2, Decretum Gratiani, col. 995. *See, e.g.*, Alexander III's letter dated 6 July 1161 to King Carl Sverkersson and Sweden's bishops, Dipl. Suec, *supra* note 11, nr 41 p. 60. The idea of monogamy can be seen clearly from Innocentius III's letter dated 3 October 1213 to the bishop in Lund in reply to the latter's question of whether priests who have had two concubines (*successive duas concubinas habentes*) could be viewed as having committed bigamy. The pope answered in the negative (Dipl. Suec, *supra* note 11, DS-nr 150 p. 175).

14 Genesis 2:24, Genesis 1:27ff; Matt 19:4 ff; Cor 6:16, Eph 5:31 ff and 5:32.

15 Before the distinction between *sponsalia de praesenti* and *sponsalia de futuro* was introduced, *copula carnalis* was required to enter into a marriage that would be an *impedimentum dirimens*. Since the distinction was included, a *sponsalia de praesenti* alone, as a *sponsalia de futuro* with thereafter *copula carnalis*, was an *impedimentum ligaminis*. *Sponsalia de futuro* alone constituted an impediment against a later *sponsalia de futuro*, while on the other hand, not a later *sponsalia de praesenti*. That said now was applicable also in cases in which the marriage was entered into entirely formlessly. *See* c. 2 X, IV, 3, and c. 10 X, IV, 17, C.J.C., *supra* note 2, Decretales Gregorii, col. 552 and 582; c. 1 pr., C. 30, qu. 5, C.J.C., *supra* note 2, Decretum Gratiani, col. 963.

16 *See* Chapter 5.

the Christian church, consistent with the Roman law, originally did not apply any unconditional form requirements for the establishment of a valid marriage between legally competent persons. This meant, in part, an acceptance of the different locally prevailing marriage traditions within the church's jurisdiction;[17] in part, a tolerance of entirely formless and even clandestine marriages (*matrimonia clandestina*).[18] The church certainly looked with increasing disapproval upon these clandestine relationships and recommended that marriages ought to be entered into before the church (*in facie Eccleiae*),[19] but the failure to enter into a *matrimonium manifestum* did not invalidate the marriage.[20] Entirely formless, already commenced marriages were indissoluble. They constituted impediments against new marriages and lent legitimacy to any children born therein. Given that the canon law only recognized one cohabitation form, marriage, and that no unconditional form requirement for its commencement existed, it followed that informal cohabitation under marriage-like conditions came, after the principles examined below more closely, to be legally qualified either as a marriage or as an impermissible out-of-wedlock relation (*concubitus illicitus*), which could be criminally punishable as *fornicatio*.[21]

3.3.2 The Reasons behind the Lack of Form

The church's reasons for the lack of form cannot be determined with certainty. It is, however, clear that the holy scriptures, which primarily treat marriage as a *morae essence*, did not expressly prescribe anything regarding

---

17 Plöchl II, *supra* note 6 at 269.

18 The term *matrimonium clandestinum* appears in several meanings. It consequently can denote (1) a marriage for which no evidence is available outside of the parties' own information. It is also used as a designation for (2) a marriage entered into in the presence of witnesses but not *in facie Ecclesiae*. In the German-speaking areas "heimliche Ehen" has also meant (3) marriages that have been entered into without parental consent. After the Fourth Council of the Lateran in 1215, wherewith was prescribed that marriage would be proceeded by banns, the term often was used as a designation for (4) marriages that had been entered into without preceding banns. Common for the different meanings appears to have been partly marriages that nevertheless were valid. With this the term came to reflect at different times specified form requirements that were not followed. With respect to the terminology, *see* EMIL FRIEDBERG, DAS RECHT DER EHESCHLIESSUNG IN SEINER GESCHICHTLICHEN ENTWICKLUNG 72 (Leipzig 1865); GEORGE HAYWARD JOYCE, CHRISTIAN MARRIAGE: AN HISTORICAL AND DOCTRINAL STUDY 108 note 2 (2nd ed. 1948); KESSLER, *supra* note 1 at 3, 18 note 31, 11 note 38, 8 note 17, and 45; J. FR. SCHULTE, HANDBUCH DES KATOLISCHEN EHERECHTS 41 (Giessen 1855).

19 *See* Pope Alexander III (1159-1181) in c. 4, Comp. I, IV, 4, QUINQUE COMPILATIONES ANTIQUAE I at 46 (Aemilius Friedberg, ed., Lipsiae 1882). *Cf.* c. 7 X, II, 27, C.J.C, *supra* note 2, Decretales Gregorii, col. 317.

20 c. 1, 4, 5, 6, 9, 38, C. 27, qu. 2, princ. C. 30, qu. 5, C.J.C, *supra* note 2, Decretum Gratiani, col. 927-928, 937, 963.

21 c. 4, C. 32, qu. 4 and c. 16, C. 33, qu. 2, C.J.C, *supra* note 2, Decretum Gratiani, col. 978 and 985.

the form for the commencement of marriage. With this starting point, it appears that the church at its initial legalization of marriage, primarily focused on the regulations concerning marriage impediments and marital divorce rather than form questions, because the former were thought to be more immediately connected to marriage's moral essence. In addition, it deserves to be stressed that the church did not enter into a newly created world, but rather a world that already existed and was full of varying and ancient rooted family traditions. Before the church had gained the requisite strength, there ought to have been a compelling necessity to adapt to the established customs.[22] At the same time, the sources available state that parties often, because of poverty, started families without observing any solemnities whatsoever. This circumstance is an often-overlooked reason why the church refrained from any unconditional form requirements.[23] It is reasonable to assume that if the church had ambitiously introduced a form requirement earlier, the canon marital system in the beginning would have been applicable to a faithful, but very limited flock.

By refraining from form requirements, the church could, under the conditions examined below more closely, within the canon doctrinal system and its indissoluble sacrament, capture both cohabiting couples who had chosen profane rather than religious wedding rites, as well as cohabiting couples who for financial or other reasons entirely refrained from any formality. Thus, the church legalized informal cohabitation. The doors to marriage stood open for admittance, while the exits in principle were closed. The given order also entailed tangible benefits from the families' perspective. Through informal concubinage, that under certain conditions could be considered marriage, the children of such relationships were spared the stigma of illegitimacy, and the parents avoided the ignominy of living in sin.[24] Protecting the children and capturing the "lost sheep" would later also be used to justify the reception of common law marriage in the United States[25] and are of interest in current discussions concerning the legal regulation of informal relationships in general.[26]

---

22 *Cf.* RUDOLPH SOHM, DAS RECHT DER EHESCHLIESSUNG 107 (Weimar 1875); AUGUST KNECHT, HANDBUCH DES KATHOLISCHEN EHERECHTS 603 and 606 (1928); FERDINAND SCHÖNSTEINER, GRUNDRISS DES KIRCHLICHEN EHERECHTS 658 (2d ed. 1937); KESSLER, *supra* note 1 at 5.

23 In a letter to the Bulgars in the year 866 AD, Pope Nicolaus I describes the Roman Catholic Church's customary formalities with the commencement of marriage, whereafter he explains that none are necessary for the marriage's validity, particularly because the parties often, due to poverty, were prevented from observing any special occasions. *See* Nicolaus I, Responsa ad Consulta Bulgarorum, JEAN HARDOUIN, ACTA CONCILIORUM ET EPISTOLAE DECRETALES AC CONSTITUTIONES SUMMORUM PONTIFICIUM IX at 354 (A. Cotillon et Cie, Paris 1715).

24 J. A. Andrews, *Common law marriage*, 22 MOD. L. REV. 396 (1959).

25 *See* Chapter 4.

26 *See* Chapter 14.

3.3.3 Marriage's Constitutive Elements

In accordance with the canon and natural law understandings, the substantive requirements for the establishment of a marriage were considered to be so closely tied to the marriage's essence – to the point of being understood as "ll'essence même du mariage"[27] – and being axiomatically given *ex iure naturale.* Nevertheless, it is an undeniable fact that the church's own understanding, or to use a natural law expression, insight into these conditions, has been neither uniform nor invariable. Consequently, the constitutive significance at the commencement of marriage of the *animus* and *corpus* elements is a theme running through the entire pre-Tridentine canon legal scholarship. As in the comparable Roman discussion, the question has primarily concerned whether, for the establishment of a marriage, in addition to the uncontested *animus* element, a *corpus* element should also unconditionally be required.[28] Both elements, however, in the canon law receive a partially different character, different content and different legal effect than in the Roman law, even if direct points of connection are not wanting. The discussion anticipates the lengthy comparisons in the American case law concerning the question of whether cohabitation is a necessary requisite in addition to the parties' *consensus* or simply an evidentiary fact for the latter with the establishment of a common law marriage.[29]

1. *The Parties' Consensus as a Constitutive Element*

In close agreement with the Roman maxim *consensus facit nuptias*[30] and at times citing this, both the old fathers of the church as well as the Papal See cited early the principle: *Voluntas facit matrimonium.*[31] This agreeing marital intent of the parties later in the canon law constituted an indispensable legal element for the establishment of a marriage. No sacred or profane rituals or other formalities were necessary. The marriage was entered into *solo consensu.* Similar to the Roman law, according to which an actual cohabitation with *affectio maritalis* in the preclassical period could constitute a *usus*-marriage, and in the classical and Justinian law, a free marriage,

27 ESMEIN I, *supra* note 10 at 97.
28 With respect to Roman law, *see* Chapter 2.
29 *See* Chapter 8.
30 With respect to Roman law, *see* Chapter 2.
31 Chrysostomus said in c. 1, C. 27, qu. 2: *Matrimonium quidem non facit coitus, sed voluntas.* Even Isidor states: *Consensus facit matrimonium. See* princ. C. 27, qu. 2. Pope Nicolaus I also refers to this maxim in a reply given by him the year 866 to the Bulgar Christians, who asked whether the holy blessing was required for the validity of marriage. The pope answered with reference to the Roman law (leges): *Sufficiat secundum leges solus eorum consensus, de quorum conjunctionibus agitur. Qui consensus, si in nuptiis solus forte defuerit, caetera omnia etiam cum ipso coitu celebrata frustrantur. (Item Nicolaus Papa ad consulta Bulgarorum). See* c. 2, C. 27, qu. 2, C.J.C., *supra* note 2, Decretum Gratiani, col. 927; FREISEN, *supra* note 10 at 152. *See* also ROBERT. E. DILLON, COMMON LAW MARRIAGE 25 (1942).

both legally recognized as *matrimonium justum*,[32] according to the canon law an actual cohabitation could constitute a recognized marriage (*matrimonium legitimum*) assuming that the parties' marital intent existed.[33] The canon law recognized, however, only one form of cohabitation – marriage. No other legal institution equipped with legal effects in addition thereto, no *coniugium inaequale*, comparable to the Roman *concubinatus*[34] was recognized in principle by the canon law. Actual cohabitation relationships not categorized as marriage constituted impermissible concubinage (*concubinatus illicitus*)[35] and were, in certain cases, criminally punishable.

The *consensus* requisite according to the canon law understanding assumed the parties' free, serious, and well-considered intent to marry.[36] The marriage was invalid if the marital intent was absent with both or one party. Herein lies a marked difference *vis-à-vis* certain Germanic marriages, in which agreements could be entered into between the families, but not between the parties to be wedded. In addition, the *consensus* requisite of the canon legal scholarship does not, as in the classical Roman law, originally appear to have been understood as an *affectio maritalis* in the sense that one of the parties, during the entire cohabitation, under all circumstances, continuously manifested a marital state of mind. Consequently, it was not a question of a continual *consensus* (*consensus continuus*), or that which in the German doctrine customarily is designated as a *Dauerkonsens*, and in the French theory as "une volonte durable, continue," all of which have more the character of a subjective requisite, similar to *animus* in questions as to the possession of property. The canon law marital intent is modeled on the Justinian law and appears instead originally, in principle, to have constituted an initial intent that later was developed as an element in a sharply defined contractual conclusion. This understanding was possible to maintain as long as a verbal agreement was required. It is common that marriage is designated as a contract in the canon law.[37]

Even though certain attempts have been made in the modern case law of common law marriage to require a defined contractual conclusion, the

---

32 Chapter 2.2.

33 With respect to the development of the term *matrimonium legitimum*, *see* FREISEN, *supra* note 10 at 72.

34 *Compare* Chapter 2.5.

35 c. 4, C. 32, qu. 4 and c. 16, C. 33, qu. 2. *See* C.J.C., *supra* note 2, Decretum Gratiani, col. 985 and col. 1010.

36 The church often maintains that it is to be a question of a *consensus liber*, *see* c. 5 X, IV, 5, C.J.C., *supra* note 2, Decretales Gregorii, col. 556.

37 *See*, e.g., Gregorius IX's decrees, IV, 5: *De conditionibus appositiis in desponsatione, vel in aliis contractibus*, in which (c. 1) *contractu matrimonii* is mentioned. *See* C.J.C, *supra* note 2, Decretales Gregorii, col. 555. *Compare* the older church fathers, who speak of marriage as a *pactio conjugalis*, Ambrosius according to c. 5, C. 27, qu. 2. *See* C.J.C, *supra* note 2, Decretum Gratiani col. 928. Even the modern Catholic ecclesiastical law designates marriage as a contract, EDUARD EICHMANN & KLAUS MÖRSDORF, LEHRBUCH DES KIRCHENRECHTS II at 131 (11th ed. 1969).

acceptance of inferred agreements based on the parties' cohabitation has made this impossible. Instead, the American case law during 1800s and 1900s has leaned towards the Roman law reasoning of employing a continual *consensus*.[38]

What, then, was the assumed intent's object? A given starting point was obviously that the intent should be marital (*consensus matrimonialis*), in other words, focused on marriage in some sense. But, to what, more precisely, were the parties assumed to give their consent? Gratian poses the question: *An consensus cohabitationis, an carnalis copulae, an uterque?* If an agreeing intent to cohabit were sufficient, then, Gratian maintains, a brother would be able to enter into a marriage with his sister. If, again, a *consensus carnalis copulae* were necessary for the establishment of a marriage, then, Gratian continues, the relationship between Joseph and the Holy Virgin Mary would not have been a marriage.[39] Gratian answers the question by tying the necessary marital intent's content to the marriage's essence as expressed in the above definition of marriage. It follows that the object for the parties' agreeing intent was not allowed to be limited to only a joint residence, a sexual relationship, a friendship, or an association for some other determined spiritual, artistic, financial, or societal purpose. The agreeing intent would rather be focused as to a complete and undivided community in all aspects for a lifetime.[40] If this content of the intent existed, it was a question of a *consensus matrimonialis*. If deficiencies in the marital intent (*dissensus*) existed, no marriage existed.

In actuality, Gratian initiated a debate concerning the marital intent and its object that today is as important to the delineation of common law marriage (see Chapter 6, "The Common Law Marriage Contract") and that in a discussion concerning the future is also relevant concerning the legal significance of the parties' intentions with cohabitations in a broader context (see Chapter 13, "The Constitutive Requisites in the Future").

The partial contractual character that the canonists lent marriage and the related possibility of applying general contract legal principles, in practice the Roman law, to the marriage contract, meant the canon law, in principle, had to allow conditional marriages (*matrimonium sub conditione*).[41]

38 With respect to the development in the American case law, *see* Chapters 6 and 7.

39 Gratian states in dictum ad c. 2, C. 27, qu. 2: *Si cohabitationis consensus matrimonium facit, tunc frater cum sorore matrimonium potest contrahere: Si carnalis copulae, inter Mariam et Joseph non fuit conjugium. See* C.J.C., *supra* note 2, Decretum Gratiani, col. 927.

40 Gratian states in c. 3, C. 27, qu. 2: *Consensus ergo cohabitandi & individuam vitae consuetudinem retinendi interveniens, eos conjuges fecit. Individua vero vitae consuetudo est, talem se in omnibus exhibere viro, qualis ipsa sibi est, & e converso. See* C.J.C., *supra* note 2, Decretum Gratiani, col. 927; KNECHT, *supra* note 22 at 115 ff; EICHMANN II, *supra* note 37 at 112-113.

41 Pope Gregorius IX's decree contains a specific titulus in the subject: *De conditionibus adpositis in desponsatione, vel in aliis contractibus* (IV, 5). *See* C.J.C., *supra* note 2, Decretales Gregorii, col. 555. A man could enter into an agreement as to marriage with woman under the condition that the woman's parents provided an acceptable dowry (c. 3). If the marriage was consummated through *copula carnalis*, the condition

Because of the close ties of the object of the intent to the essence of marriage, however, contractual freedom was limited. Marriages that were entered into with terms and conditions that were *contra substantiam matrimonii* were consequently invalid.[42] For example, if the parties entered into a marriage under the condition that they would refrain from consummation (*copula carnalis*) or under the condition that the relationship would be dissoluble, the marriage was a nullity. Nothing ought, however, have prevented spouses, after the commencement of a marriage, to agree to actually practice sexual abstinence. From that, it follows that all terms of dissolution were in conflict with marriage's essence because they assumed the dissolution of the marriage.

Even if the parties internally possessed an agreeing intent that, in accordance with that stated was to be viewed as a *consensus matrimonialis*, it was not sufficient to constitute a marriage. The marriage contract, in the canon law more than in the Roman, had developed into a legal act in the modern sense and, therefore, assumed in principle two declarations of intent. It followed that each party's marital intent had to be outwardly manifested to receive constitutive effect. If one party only internally, in his or her *forum internum*, consented to the marriage, it did not come into existence. The intent must, through a declaration of intent, come to expression in the parties' *forum externum* and be answered by the other party.

It was originally maintained that the agreeing intent was not allowed to come to expression in any manner whatsoever but that, in principle, it should be expressed in words (*per verba expressus*).[43] With respect to deaf and mute persons, however, signs (*signis*) were sufficient.[44] During the 1200s, it appears that opinion was divided as to whether words could be dispensed with as an expression of marital intent for other groups. The understanding that later appears to have prevailed is that it was sufficient that the parties' *consensus matrimonialis* came to expression through words, signs, or in whatever manner was sufficiently demonstrative.[45] With this,

---

was considered therewith revoked (c. 6 X, IV, 5). *Cf.* Gratian in c. 7-8, C. 27, qu. 2. *See* C.J.C, *supra* note 2, Decretum Gratian, col. 928.

42 C. 7 X, IV, 5. *See* C.J.C, *supra* note 2, Decretum Gratiani, col. 557.

43 Peter Lombard: *Efficiens autem causa matrimonii est consensus, non quilibet sed per verba expressus* (Sent. IV, D. 27 § c). *See* PETRI LOMBARDI LIBRI IV SENTENTIARUM I-II (2 ed. 1916). The same emphasis that the marital intent should come to expression in words we find again in the papal decrees of Innocentius III, who speaks of: *verba consensum exprimentia de praesenti* (c. 25 X, IV, 1). *See* C.J.C., *supra* note 2, Decretales Gregorii, col. 544 and Alexander III, who speaks of: *consensu verbis consuetis expresse recipiat* (c. 3 X, IV, 4), C.J.C., *supra* note 2, Decretales Gregorii, col. 554.

44 C. 23 X, IV, 1, in fine: *Cum quod verbis non potest signis valeat declarare. See* C.J.C., *supra* note 2, Decretales Gregorii, col. 543.

45 c. 25 X, IV, 1: *matrimonium per consensum mutuum sine verbis*), C.J.C., *supra* note 2, Decretales Gregorii, col. 544; TANCREDI SUMMA DE MATRIMONIO 8 (Agaton Wunderlich ed., Göttingen 1841). A. VON SCHEURL, DIE ENTWICKLUNG DES KIRCHLICHEN EHESCHLIESSUNGSRECHT 93 (Erlangen 1877), maintains that the marital intent "ohne gelobende verba de praesenti ... durch eine der Einsegnung vorhergehende blosse 'verjahung', jedenfalls durch tatsächliche Empfangnahme des Weibes bei der Traung,

the marriage contract's character as a consensual contract was strengthened. The parties' cohabitation, thereby, became relevant as an expression for their marital intentions.

In the American case law concerning common law marriage over the last two hundred years, the phrase that has continuously been repeated is that it is to be an agreement *per verba de praesenti.* Nevertheless, few courts have actually required a verbal agreement. Instead, they have accepted implied agreements and an application of the marriage presumption based on the parties' cohabitation and reputation as spouses.[46]

That the declarations of intent need not occur in the presence of both parties shows the contractual character of the agreement. In contrast to Roman law, according to which marriage could be entered into in the man's but not in the woman's absence,[47] both parties' marital declarations of intent could be given by proxy.[48]

Deficiencies in the parties' *consensus matrimonialis,* which could prevent a marriage from being established, need not have been manifested in express terms. Such was the case, e.g., with *simulation* and *mental reservation.* Lack of agreement then existed between the content of the intent and the given declaration of intent. If the parties, after the agreement, through a declaration of intent, expressed a marital intent that did not exist, it was considered a simulation. If either of the parties, without agreement between themselves, through a declaration of intent, gave expression to a marital intent that he or she deep down did not possess, this was categorized as a mental reservation.[49] The comparable was true if the marital intent certainly was not entirely absent but partially characterized with material deficiencies. Such was the case if the object of the man's marital intent was a marital relationship with a woman, but only a temporary one. It must be stressed, however, that, in order to invalidate a marriage because of either simulation or mental reservation, the preexistence of these deficiencies had to be proven, which could be tricky, particularly if a long time had passed since the declaration of intent. The marriage's contractual character also allowed it to be declared invalid based on a

---

und etwa auch durch (beiderseits freiwilliges) concubitus erklärt werden können." SOHM, *supra* note 22 at 149, states that from the beginning of the 1200s was accepted "der irgendwie erklärte consensus de praesenti." *See also* FRIEDBERG, *supra* note 18 at 11 and 102.

46 It is primarily the courts in Pennsylvania that appear to have maintained the requirement as to a contract "per verba," *see* Section 6.2.2, but as an alternative they have been able to apply the marriage presumption based on the parties' cohabitation and reputation as spouses, *see* Chapter 9. Most common, however, is that the courts accepted "implied agreements," *see* Chapter 7.

47 *See supra* Section 2.2.3.

48 c. 14 X, III, 32. Se C.J.C., *supra* note 2, Decretales Gregorii, col. 468.

49 Peter Lombard: *Si autem verbis explicant, quod tarnen vorde nonvolunt* (Sent. IV, D. 27 §, *see supra* note 43.) *See also* c. 26 X, IV, 1, C.J.C., *supra* note 2, Decretales Gregorii, col. 544.

misunderstanding (*error*) as well as a series of other grounds when a *consensus liber* did not exist.[50]

Chapter 6 takes up questions concerning the existence of a common law marriage when there is lack of agreement between the intent and the declaration of intent (sham marriages).[51]

2. *Copula Carnalis as a Constitutive Element*

If the parties' *consensus matrimonialis* in the canon law was accepted as a necessary requisite to legally establish an informal marriage, a more highly debated question was whether, in addition to this *animus* element, a *corpus* element should also be required, as in the Roman law. The questioned *corpus* element, however, was not identical in the two legal systems. The Roman law discussion concerned the question of whether a marriage more generally, de facto, would have been established; in other words, whether there was an actual cohabitation in a *consortium omnis vitae* in any manner. With the woman's entrance in the man's home (*deductio in domum mariti*), it appears to have been necessary in any case with the commencement of marriage in the man's absence.[52] Nevertheless, the object for the canon law discussion was of a more specific nature, namely, the constitutive significance of consummation (*copula carnalis*). The question was whether, in addition to the *conjunctio spitiitualis* that was created through the parties' mutual marital intent, a *conjunctio corporalis* would be required.

In the pre-Gratian ecclesiastical law, it was argued, on one hand, that the *copula* constituted a necessary requisite for the establishment of a marriage. Support was absent in both the holy scriptures and the writings of the church fathers. Already, with the drafting of the general definition of marriage as applied by the church, as we have found, the sexual element was emphasized, motivated by marriage's dual purpose, to satisfy sexual desire and to produce legitimate descendents. As long as the parties did not fulfill this dual purpose, it could be argued that no marriage existed.[53] The most-often-cited reasoning as support for the necessity of *copula carnalis*, however, was that the parties through consummation became one flesh (*una caro*), and that this union symbolized Christ's eternal and indissoluble union with his congregation. First, through the *copula*, the relationship received status as a sacrament and thereby became a completed

---

50 C. 29, qu. 1, *see* C.J.C., *supra* note 2, Decretum Gratiani, col. 952.

51 *See* Section 6.3.2.

52 With respect to Roman law, *see* Section 2.2. *Compare* Lombard law, according to which simply *consensus* was not sufficient for the establishment of a marriage and according to which *consensus* must be combined with formal *traditio* or the actual assumption of the marital cohabitation (*ambulavit ad maritum*), as to this *see* ESMEIN I, *supra* note 10 at 171.

53 c. 12, C. 32, qu. 1 and c. 27, C. 32, qu. 7 (*sterilem uxorem*). *See* C.J.C., *supra* note 2, Decretum Gratiani, col. 976 and 1001.

and indissoluble marriage.[54] It was even argued, throughout the first Christian centuries, that *copula carnalis* should be the only always-necessary requisite for the establishment of a marriage between legally competent parties, though this view does not appear to have been dominant.[55]

On the other hand, the diametric understanding that *copula carnalis* was not at all necessary for the establishment of a marriage was also argued in the pre-Gratian ecclesiastical law. Several authorities offered theological support thereto. The commonly cited theological basis was that the relationship between Joseph and the Holy Virgin Mary, whose virtue was beyond all doubt, constituted a true marriage. The only necessary requisite for the establishment of a marriage between common citizens ought also therefore be the parties' marital *consensus*.[56]

During the swift development of the canon law in the middle of the 1100s, the question of whether marriage required consummation for validity was a focus. Gratian treated the question extensively in his decree (approximately 1140). In the scholastic manner, he first clarified the questions, gave thereafter authoritative support both for as well as against the requirement of consummation, and finally attempted to bring the different views into harmony through a distinction, namely that between *matrimonium*

54 As stated above, the idea recurs at different places in the holy scriptures that spouses after the commencement of marriage are no longer two but rather one flesh (above p 4). This idea is clearly combined in the scriptures with the representation of Christ's eternal and indissoluble union with his congregation (Eph 5: 31-32). *Compare* Freisen, who believes that the requirement as to *copula* stems from the Jewish tradition (FREISEN, *supra* note 10 at 154 f.). Gratian states: *Non est inter eos matrimonium, quos non copulat commistio sexus*, c. 16, C 27, qu. 2 *compare* ESMEIN, *id.* p. 99 f.

55 Pelagius rebutted that marriage was formed, not through the wedding ceremony (*velata*), but rather through *copula carnalis*. First through the consummation *sponsa* became a true *nupta* (dictum ad c. 29, C. 27, qu. 2 § 1. *See* C.J.C., *supra* note 2, Decretum Gratiani, col. 935. *compare* FREISEN, *id.* p. 158).

56 With reference thereto Ambrosius (333-397) consequently explicitly states: *non defloratio virginitatis facit conjugium, sed pactio conjugalis* (c. 5, C. 27, qu. 2); Chrysostomus (354-407), in agreement herewith makes the following statement: *Matrimonium non facit coitus sed voluntas* (c. 1, C. 27, qu. 2). With reference *inter alia* to Chrysostomus, Pope Nicolaus I, who was a contemporary of the Archbishop Hincmar of Reims and in counterpoint to him the year 866 repeats: *Matrimonium non facit coitus sed voluntas* (c. 2, C. 27, qu. 2). *See* C.J.C., *supra* note 2, Decretum Gratiani, col. 927-928. Freisen, who is of the understanding that *copula carnalis* in pre-Gratian law was necessary for the establishment of a marriage, argues that Ambrosius simply meant that *defloratio* alone did not constitute marriage, that Chrysostomus denies that the relationship between Joseph and Mary was of a marital nature, and that Nicolaus maintains that *consensus* under the obvious presumption that *coitus* soon would follow. In his in generally penetrating analysis, however, Freisen does not give any true arguments as support for Nicolaus, despite his explicit statement that *coitus non facit*, nevertheless considered *coitus* to be an obvious, not only consequence, but also prerequisite (*id.* p. 151 ff, particularly 162 f). *Compare* Sohm, who also maintains that *consensus* was not sufficient, however, but rather ascribes to Nicolaus several implicit conditions with respect to *coitus* (SOHM, *supra* note 22 at 147), as well as Joyce, who on the other hand has the understanding that *consensus* alone constituted marriage (JOYCE, *supra* note 18 at 43.)

initiatum and *matrimonium ratum*.[57] The former marriage was formed through the parties' simple *consensus*. As the distinction between *sponsalia de praesenti praesenti* and *de futuro* was unknown to Gratian, it appears that *consenus initiatum* had included both agreements as to the present, in other words, immediately effective, as well as future marriages.[58] A *matrimonium ratum* on the other hand in addition to the *consensus* also required consummation through *copula carnalis carnalis*. The most apparent difference with respect to the legal effects between the two marriages was that the unconsummated one could be dissolved while the consummated was indissoluble. Through this distinction, Gratian referred all legal maxims that permitted dissolution of marriage to *matrimonium initiatum* and all legal maxims that concerned marriage's indissolubility to *matrimonium ratum*.[59] The relationship between Joseph and the Holy Virgin Mary could then be said to have been a marriage, namely, a *matrimonium initiatum*, at the same time that a marriage became an indissoluble *matrimonium ratum* through consummation. From this distinction, it followed that if a man and a woman entered into a marriage agreement and the woman, before they commenced any cohabitation, promised herself to another man and consummated the bond with the latter, then the first agreement was set aside and the consummated agreement was declared to be a true marriage.

The canonists of the Bologna School sided with the Gratian understanding. His distinction also gained expansion in the application of the law, particularly with the ecclesiastical courts in Italy in which the influence of Bologna was strongest. No final solution on the issue of the constitutive significance of *copula carnalis* upon the commencement of marriage was achieved, however, with the Gratian distinction.

---

57 *Dictum* ad c. 34, C. 27, qu. 2: *Unde inter sponsum et sponsam conjugium est, sed initiatum; inter copulatos est conjugium ratum. See* C.J.C., *supra* note 2, Decretum Gratiani, col. 936).

58 With respect to the importance Gratian ascribes *consensus, see* expositio ad C. 27, qu. 2, and dictum ad C. 29, qu. 1, C.J.C., *supra* note 2, Decretum Gratiani, col. 927, 952-953. That Gratian did not distinguish between *betrothal consensus* and *marital consensus* can be explained by that Peter Lombard first later introduced the distinction between *consensus de praesenti* and *consensus de futuro* which was taken up in his Sentences approximately 1150-1152, *supra* note 43 at 164).

59 With respect to the indissolubility of a *matrimonium ratum*, which also was designated as *conjugium ratum*, or *matrimonium perfectum* or *matrimonium consummatum, see* particularly dictum ad c. 39, C. 27, qu. 2., C.J.C, *supra* note 2, Decretum Gratiani, col. 937: *Matrimonium perfectum ... tale videlicet quod habeat in se Christi et Ecclesiae sacramentum. See also* c. 17, C. 28, qu. 1, *id. Compare* Plöchl, who with reference to that the relationship between Joseph and the Holy Virgin Mary according to Gratian had marriage's three benefits, fides, proles, and sacramentum, maintains that *consensus* was sufficient for the creation of the sacrament, *see* WILLIBALD M. PLÖCHL, DAS EHERECHT DES MAGISTERS GRATIANUS 37(1935). *Compare* on the other hand a convincing JOYCE, *supra* note 18 at 58 note 3.

The idea that *consensus* alone constituted marriage had never lost its anchoring within the church, particularly within the French church.[60] However, it was Peter Lombard who, in his *Sententiae* (1150–1152) and in direct contrast to Gratian, maintained anew that consummation was not necessary for the establishment of a sacramental and indissoluble marriage. The parties' simple *consensus* should be sufficient. He did not accept, however, any marital *consensus* whatsoever, but rather introduced a distinction between *sponsalia de praesenti* and *sponsalia de futuro.*[61] A promise of the first named type; in other words, the promise of a present or immediately effective marriage was required to create an indissoluble marriage. Such an agreement (*consensus de praesenti*) was considered to have created the true marriage.[62] If the vows, on the other hand, were of the latter type and the agreement consequently concerned a future marriage (*consensus de futuro*), it simply constituted a betrothal and was dissoluble. In both cases, the parties consented to marriage, but the one consent was given in the presens tempus, while the other was given in the future. From this distinction, it followed that if a woman gave a vow of marriage *de praesenti* to a man, and, thereafter, prior to the marriage being consummated, gave an identical vow to another man and consummated the agreement with the latter, the first named agreement need not give way. According to Peter Lombard, however, a prerequisite that this *consensus* would constitute marriage was that it came to expression either through words or signs.[63] Nothing, however, prevented this from occurring entirely formlessly or even in secret, assuming that such an expression could in some manner be proven.[64]

Through his distinction, Peter Lombard, as had Gratian, attempted to bring the conflicting sources into harmony. Wherever marriage's indissolubility is discussed, the concern is *consensus de praesenti*; on the other hand, wherever the possibility of dissolving a relationship is discussed, it is a question of *consensus de futuro.*[65] With respect to theological symbolism, it was now possible to apply the distinction to maintain that the unconsummated relationship between Joseph and the Holy Virgin Mary

60 In close agreement with Pope Nicolaus I and the tradition he represented, Petrus Damianus (death 1072), Ivo of Chartres (death 1116), and Hugo of St. Victor (death 1141) maintained consequently that *copula carnalis* was not necessary for the establishment of an indissoluble marriage. *Consensus* was sufficient thereto. *See* as to this more closely JOYCE, *supra* note 18 at 61 f.

61 Sent. IV, 27 § c., *supra* note 43: *Efficiens autem causa matrimonii est consensus, non quilibet, sed per verba expressus: nec de futuro, sed de praesenti.*; JOYCE, *supra* note 18 at 62 f.; ESMEIN I, *supra* note 10 at 122; FREISEN, *supra* note 10 at 181.

62 *Cf.* FREISEN *id.* at 197, and SOHM, *supra* note 22 at 122, who designate both *consensus de praesenti* and *consensus de futuro* as "Verlobung."

63 Sent. IV, D. § c: *Si consentiunt mente et non expremant verbis vel aliis certis signis, nec talis consensus afficit matrimonium, supra* note 43.

64 Sent. IV, D. 28 § B., *id.*

65 Sent. IV, D.27 § j and k., *id.*

constituted a true marriage.[66] With respect to the sacramental symbolism of Christ's union with his congregation, Peter Lombard tried to further distinguish between a *sacramentum spirituale* and a *sacramentum corporale* by arguing that only the former, which did not require consummation, was necessary for the establishment of a sacramental and indissoluble marriage.[67]

For a man and a woman who had declared that they take each other as husband and wife, without more closely defining when this was intended to occur, the crucial significance that this distinction ascribes to the tense in which the consent has been given can naturally appear somewhat academic. The distinction certainly has been criticized, for example, by Martin Luther with respect to its application in the German language. In his writing "von Ehesachen," he states: "Gleichwie sie auch ein lauter Narrenspiel getrieben haben cum verbis de praesenti vel futuro ... Denn diese Wort: 'Accipio te in uxorem, ich nehme Dich zu meinem Ehemann.' Und haben nicht gesehen noch gemerkt, dass dies nicht im Brauch ist, deutsch zu reden, wenn man de praesenti redet; sondern das heisst de praesenti geredt: 'Ich will Dich haben.'"[68] Pollock and Maitland comment on the distinction that it is "certainly no masterpiece of human wisdom. Of all people in the world, lovers are the least likely to distinguish precisely between the present and the future tenses."[69]

As to the general viability of these statements, doubt can prevail. The question is whether, in actuality, exactly the opposite is true. Anyone ought hardly be more aware as to the difference between the present and the future than two engaged persons who look forward in the future to being able to fulfill their vows. There are linguistic complications and the evidentiary difficulties in the distinction, particularly in cases in which consent has been given entirely formlessly, as when given in the presence of only the parties themselves. Nevertheless, it ought to be stressed that the distinction was thought to serve the interest of clarity and, for centuries, would be incorporated into the structure of the concept of marriage. From its inception, Peter Lombard's theory became dominant in the school of law in Paris, where he was a teacher, and in the French courts, over which he, as a bishop, had influence.[70]

---

66 Sent. IV, D. 30 § b-c, and D 26 § g, *supra* note 43.

67 Sent. IV, D. 26 § f-g, *id.*

68 Martin Luther, Werke 23 at 102 (Erlangen 1838). *Compare* Sohm, *supra* note 22 at 139, who declares that he does not really know how a farmhand and housemaid with the use of German language ought or could become engaged *per verba de futuro* (*id*). *Compare* that which Sohm explained as a practical impossibility of Scheurl "für damalige praktische Wirklichkeit" (Scheurl, *supra* note 45 at 85).

69 Frederick Pollock and Frederic W. Maitland, History of English Law II, 368 f. (London, 2d ed. 1898). *Compare* Sohm, *supra* note 22 at 127, who with the distinction maintains that it "im wirklichen Leben keinerlei Anhalt fand." With respect to the distinction's application in American law today, *see* Section 6.4.

70 The varying application of the law can be seen from *Summa Rufini* (1157-1159), *Summa Coloniensis* (1169-1170) and *Summa Parisiensis* (c:a 1170), republished by Freisen, *supra* note 10 at 182.

The divergence in understanding between the schools in Bologna and Paris, and the varying case law that developed over the long run, became untenable for the church and required an authoritative decision from the Papal See. Pope Alexander III (1151–1181), who previously had sided with the Gratian understanding, nevertheless, in his capacity as pope, declared that *consensus* alone constituted marriage.[71] The pope gave an opinion to the bishop in Norwich concerning a case in which a woman first entirely formlessly commenced a relationship with a man and before sexual intercourse had been established between them married another man, wherewith the customary solemnities were observed and the relationship was consummated with *carnalem commixtionem.* The pope stated that if the woman and the first man had taken each other through a mutual *consensus de praesenti* stating, respectively: I take you as my (*meum*) and I take you as my (*meam*), the woman must then be reunited to this man, even if no solemnities were observed and even if the relationship was not consummated. After such a consent, she was not authorized to marry another.[72]

According to this final papal decision, the principle, *contractus perfectum est per solum consensum,* was confirmed.[73] Marriage consequently, in principle, qualified as a consensual contract, entered into through the parties' simple *consensus.* Neither the solemnities imposed by the church nor marriage's consummation through *copula carnalis* was necessary for the establishment of a marriage. At the same time, the Gallic distinction between *sponsalia de praesenti* and *de futuro,* wherewith the former in principle was necessary for the creation of a marriage, was taken up in the papal legislation.[74] Even though *copula carnalis* in principle did not come to constitute a necessary requisite for the establishment of a marriage, the *copula* theory was retained. Through the parties' given *sponsalia de praesenti,* in principle, an indissoluble marriage was certainly created. As long as the marriage was not consummated through *copula carnalis,* however, there was a limited possibility of dissolving the marriage after the giving of monastic vows and through a papal dispense. After *copula carnalis* had taken place, the possibility of dissolving the marriage was absent entirely.[75] More

71 Sententiae at 271.

72 c. 6 (8), Comp. I, IV, 4, *supra* note 19 at 47; FREISEN, *supra* note 10 at 193. *Compare* c. 3 X, IV, 4 and c. 2 X, IV, 16; C.J.C., *supra* note 2, col. 554 and 578-579. *Compare* Alexander's earlier view in c. 2, Comp. I, IV, 1, *supra* note 19 at 44 and c. 7 X, III, 32, C.J.C., *supra* note 2, col. 466, which is presented well by JEAN DAUVILLIER, LE MARIAGE DANS LE DROIT CLASSIQUE DE L'ÉGLISE 17 (1933) and FREISEN, *id.* at 190. It may be noted that the words used in the declaration of intent "*ego te recipio in meam (meum)*" (c. 6 (8)), did not constitute any necessary wording for the establishment of a marriage (SCHEURL, *supra* note 45 at 93).

73 Dictum ad c. 39, C. 27, qu. 2, C.J.C., *supra* note 2, Decretum Gratiani, col. 937.

74 c. 3 X, IV, 4, C.J.C. *supra* note 2, Decretum Gregorii, col. 554; c. 6 (8), Comp. I, IV, 4, *supra* note 19 at 47.

75 c. 5 (7), Comp. I, IV, 4, *supra* note 19 at 47; c. 2, 7 X, III, 32; c. 16 X, IV, 1; c. 4 X, IV, 4, C.J.C, *supra* note 2, col. 464-466. Due to this possibility in a very special case and

significant, however, was the constitutive effect that came to be added to the *copula carnalis* following a betrothal (*sponsalia de futuro*). More discussion on this follows. With this, the medieval canon law came to constitute a compromise between the pure *consensus* principle and the *copula* theory.[76]

The great interest in the medieval canon law in *copula carnalis,* despite its theological and historical causes, appears somewhat obsolete against the background of today's sexual mores. It ought, however, be noted that in the modern case law on common law marriage, the *copula* recurs as a relevant element in the assessment of whether the requirement of cohabitation has been fulfilled.[77] As will be seen in Chapter 13 and in Chapter 14, "Arguments For and Against Common Law Marriage and Cohabitation Law," the modern cohabitation legislation has not been able to avoid *copula's* relevance in the assessment of whether a relationship is a cohabitation or simply a friendship or other relationship.[78]

3. Marriage through Consensus de Futuro and Copula Carnalis

The canon law reception of the Gallic distinction between *consensus de praesenti* and *consensus de futuro* meant that the canon law betrothal (*consensus de futuro*), in contrast with the Germanic,[79] became consistent with the Roman *sponsalia* theory,[80] and constituted not the marriage contract itself, but rather a *pactum de contrahendo*; in other words, a specific agreement as to a future commencement of the actual marriage creating agreement.[81]

---

in general by way of exception after a papal dispense to dissolve a marriage, that after the parties' "*sponsalia de praesenti*" was not still consummated, far-reaching conclusions have been drawn as to the content that such a relationship did not constitute a true marriage but simply a betrothal. *See* Sohm, *supra* note 22 at 126. *Cf.* Esmein I, *supra* note 10 at 143 ff; Freisen, *supra* note 10 at 195, 212. *Compare* Pope Innocentius III's letter the 12 January 1206 to the Archbishop Andreas in Lund regarding a woman, who after *sponsalia per verba de praesenti* gave monastic vows in order to avoid the marriage's consummation with the man, who suffered from leprosy. The pope declared that she could choose between consummating the marriage or for always entering the cloister, *see* Dipl. Suec, *supra* note 11, DS-nr 123 p. 151. With respect to the *copula* theory's influence in Sweden, *see* the papal letters dated 24 July 1254 (*id.* DS-nr 419), 21 May 1288 (*id.* DS-nr 962), 18 March 1299 (*id.* DS-nr 1270) and 7 November 1303 (*id.* DS-nr 1412).

76 *Compare* Freisen, *supra.*Note 10, at 208 n. 8, who prefers to not characterize the Medieval Canon law's final stance as a compromise, as *copula's* constitutive significance remained.

77 *See* Chapter 8.

78 *See* Chapter 13. With respect to those problems concerning personal integrity that investigations of the parties' sexual relationships entail, *see* Section 14.3.7.

79 With respect to the Germanic betrothal's legal character, *see* Emil Friedberg, Verlobung und Trauung (Leipzig 1876), passim.

80 With respect to the Roman *consensus sponsalitius, see* Dauvillier, *supra* note 72 at 8 and Esmein I, *supra* note 10 at 137.

81 c. 3 X, IV, 4., *cf.* c. 16 X, IV, 1, C.J.C., *supra* note 2, Decretum Gregorii, col. 554 and 541. *Compare* Freisen, who based on his understanding that marriage in the canon law was established through *copula carnalis* with the parties' *consensus matrimonialis* as

Already, however, an agreement *de futuro* to enter into marriage entailed certain legal effects. *Sponsalia de futuro* could be dissolved through the parties' mutual consent. In those cases in which the parties disagreed, the party who wished such dissolution was required to cite specific grounds.[82] Simply an agreement per *verba de futuro* to enter into marriage with each other did not, however, constitute an impediment to entering into marriage with another, even if the broken marriage vows could entail sanctions.[83] On the other hand, *consensus de futuro* for the parties would constitute an impediment against marriage with the other's relatives.[84]

Even if *copula carnalis*, according to the view that became dominant in the medieval canon law, did not come to constitute a necessary requisite for the establishment of a marriage, the *copula* received indirectly constitutive significance. If *sponsalia de futuro* was followed by *copula carnalis*, it was presumed that the *copula ipso facto* included a *sponsalia de praesenti* and that the relationship, consequently, was a marriage.[85] When this marital presumption by Pope Gregorius IX (1227–1234) was raised to a *praesumtio iuris et de iure*, in other words, a presumption against which no counterevidence was permitted,[86] *copula carnalis* received a constitutive effect that was highly material. The c*opula* was certainly not always a

---

conditio sine qua non maintains that the object for *sponsala de futuro* consisted of both the marriage contract *de praesenti* as *copula carnalis*, in other words, both of these according to him were marriage creating moments (FREISEN, *supra* note 10 at 207). *Compare* SOHM, *supra* note 22 at 146, who argues that the canon law received the Germanic betrothal and not the distinguish between *sponsalia de futuro* and *sponsalia de praesenti* ("Wir können uns deutlicher dahin ausdrücken, dass die s.g. *Sponsalia de futuro Sponsalia de praesenti sind*"), whose content of the intent (*essentialia negotii*) he finds consists of a present marital relationship, while a future marital community (p. 134 f., 129); *compare* Scheurl, who states that *sponsalia de futuro* means "eheversprechende Verlobung" and *sponsalia de praesenti* "eheschliessende Verlobung," both species of the term "Verlobung" (SCHEURL, *supra* note 45 at 83, 89, 93).

82 Several grounds corresponded to those applied for the dissolution of a *matrimonium initatum*. Similar to other agreements, *consensus de futuro* could be dissolved through the parties entering into an agreement as to this. In addition the relationship could be dissolved against the one party's will by citing a series of specific grounds, of which can be mentioned infidelity, unjust postponement of marriage, long lasting sickness, physical handicap, bad breath and odor, etc. (*see* as to this, JOYCE, *supra* note 18 at 93).

83 c. 6, Comp. I, IV, 4, e contrario, *supra* note 19 at 47.

84 c.c. 4-6 X, IV, 2, C.J.C., *supra* note 2, Decretales Gregorii, col. 547-548; *Cf.* already Gratian in c. 11, C. 27, qu. 2, C.J.C., *supra* note 2, Decretum Gratiani, col. 929

85 Both Innocentius III (1198-1216) and Gregorius IX (1227-1234) gave expression for this presumption in their decrees. The former states that when after *sponsalia de futuro* followed *copula*, so was *pro matrimonio vehementer quidem praesemendum* (c. 6 X, IV, 5, C.J.C., *supra* note 2, Decretales Gregorii, col. 556). *Compare* DAUVILLIER, *supra* note 92 at 56, who argues that Innocentius' decree can be traced back to Hugoccio (death 1210). Joyce's statement that "betrothal, if followed by copula, was declared by Alexander III to constitute marriage" (JOYCE, *supra* note 18 at 89) appears too far-reaching; it ought to be noted that the presumption assumes that *copulan* follows after *sponsalia de futuro. Copula carnalis* with subsequent *sponsalia de futuro* was not accepted (c. 2, Comp. III, IV, 1, *supra* note 19 at 126).

86 c. 30 X, IV, 1: A betrothed person after *sponsalia de futuro* and *copula carnalis* had entered into marriage with another *in facie ecclesiae* and consummated marriage.

necessary requisite, but it was, with *sponsalia de futuro*, sufficient for the establishment of a marriage. With a such marriage, a *matrimonium praesumtum*, all of marriage's legal effects also followed.[87] From this construction, the presumed intent for an immediate marriage (*consensus de praesenti*) assumed the character of a fiction. Despite Scheurl's assumption, which undeniably appears optimistic, "(d)ass die Verlobten zur copula carnalis nur schritten indem sie zugleich stillschweigend zu dem consensus de praesenti sich vereinigten,"[88] the possibility existed that two engaged persons found themselves in a marriage with each other, despite the fact that neither actually possessed any present intent to be married to the other. It is clear that this possibility of marriage, without the parties' marital *consensus de praesenti* as the basis, from a principle view entails a remarkable departure from the *consensus* that since ancient times characterized the ecclesiastical marital laws. As this construction assumed a vow of marriage, albeit a vow with respect to the future, consideration of the parties' intent was not entirely lacking.

The presumption's construction and its possibility of establishing a marriage through only *sponsalia de futuro* followed from the fact that *copula carnalis* also entails consequences for *sponsalia futuro* itself and its legal character. This vow of marriage can no longer be said to have constituted a *pactum de contrahende* in the sense that a subsequent primary agreement *de praesenti* actually must come into existence. It was known to be sufficient that the prior presence could be presumed.[89]

Gregorius stated: *contra praesumptionem tarnen hujusmodi non est probatio admittenda*, C.J.C., *supra* note 2, Decretales Gregorii, col. 546.

87 c. 30, 32 X, IV, 1; c. 6 X, IV, 5, C.J.C., *supra* note 2, Decretales Gregorii, col. 545-546.

88 Scheurl, *supra* note 45 at 91. *Compare* Joyce, who argues that Gregorius IX through the presumption attempted to make it impossible for a man to win a woman through marriage vows and thereafter abandon her, as "very often, no doubt, copula had taken place without any intention of contracting a marriage. In this case the man found that he was committed beyond recall to the woman." (Joyce, *supra* note 18 at 90). The idea that *copulan* can be seen to give expression for the marital intent can also be found even in Swedish law. With the enactment of the betrothal regulations in 1 Chapter 1 § GB 1920, which concern *sponsalia de futuro*, LB stated that the regulation also included cases in which the woman allowed herself to rely upon the man's marriage vows. LB found certainly that doubt could arise *inter alia* for the reason that the man's offer as to marriage often appeared as a means to remove the woman's misgivings with respect to sexual relations and on this basis did not to the same degree as an ordinary proposal of marriage testify as to his intent to take her as a spouse. LB however found that from a contractual law perspective it ought not face any principle impediment that within the concept of betrothal was included also such cases, in which the woman under the circumstances and in the manner that recently had been stated accepted the man's offer of marriage (Lagberedningens förslag till revision av Giftermålsbalken och vissa delar av Ärvdabalken I at 117 (1913).

89 *Compare* Sohm, *supra* note 22 at 142-143, who argues that *copula carnalis* worked, not "weil aus ihr der consensus matrimonialis, d.h. die Eingehung von Sponsalia de praesenti gesetzlich gefolgert würde." Instead the author who finds the canon law strongly influenced by Germanic law, allocates *copulan* and *sponsalia de futuro* a more independent significance: "Damit ist ausgesprochen, dass auch die Sponsalia de

The two variations of entering into an informal marriage that the canon law consequently established, either *per verba de praesenti* or *per verba de futuro cum copula carnalis*, would come to endure long after the canon law through the Council of Trent in 1563 repealed the informal marriage within the Roman Catholic jurisdiction. As seen in the next chapter, it was still alive when common law marriage appeared in the United States during the 1800s. The American case law, however, in principle accepted only the first named variation.[90] The courts today still have to distinguish between the two types of *consensus*, which can be tricky when cohabiting couples, not uncommonly, have had plans to enter into a ceremonial marriage, but have not actually done so.[91]

3.3.4 Proving the Informal Marriage

Difficulties arose concerning proving the existence of an informal and, in particular, a clandestine marriage (*matrimonium clandestinum*). Often, with the evidentiary proving, the parties' own information (*confessio*) was simply cited. If these were consistent, they were accepted by Gratian, in principle, as complete evidence.[92] Exceptions had to be made, however, to account for the danger of abuse arising in a system where the parties' own information was admitted without further investigation. If a man stated that he first, in secrecy, entered into a clandestine marriage with a woman but thereafter entered into marriage with another woman, the latter relationship had precedence, even if all three parties were in agreement that the clandestine marriage was entered into first. If both parties in the first marriage denied that they, in secrecy, had entered into a marriage, they could not be forced into a marital cohabitation with each other. If they submitted conflicting information concerning the presence of a clandestine marriage, the evidentiary burden of proof was on the party alleging that a marriage was established. If he or she could not present complete evidence, no marriage was considered to have been established.[93] No presumption that cohabitation under marriage-like circumstances constituted

futuro der Consummirung fähig sind, und dass es nach Abschluss der selben zur Entstehung der Ehe nicht mer der Eingehung von Sponsalia de praesenti, sondern nur noch ihrer Consummirung bedarf." If one sees only to the practical result of the presumption, Sohm's view is reasonable. It leads however to that the contract of betrothal constituted the primary agreement and *copulan* its consummation, and ignores therewith the intention of the parties with *sponsalia de futuro* and from the circumstance that the presumption, albeit that it was not rebuttable, actually was construed as a presumption. The rule as known in the decrees could directly be formulated so that *consensus de futoro* and *copula carnalis* constituted marriage. This however did not occur. Sohm's view therefore is not tenable.

90 *See* Chapter 4.

91 *See* Chapter 6.

92 Dictum ad c. 11, C. 30, qu. 5, C.J.C., *supra* note 2, Decretum Gratiani col. 966.

93 c. 1 X, IV, 3, C.J.C., *supra* note 2, Decretales Gregorii, col. 552: *Pro clandestino matrimonio non praesumitur.*

marriage, comparable to the one that was applied in the Roman law, appears to have been taken up in the medieval canon law. The reason ought *inter alia* to have been that the risk that temporary sexual relations (*fornicatio*) could then be presumed to be marriage.

On the other hand, it is clear that the actual circumstances surrounding the cohabitation and different elements were given, according to the canon law understanding, great value as evidentiary facts. If it was a question of a continuous cohabitation (*cohabitatio diutina*), this could even constitute complete evidence that a marriage existed. Such cohabitation was considered, however, as a rule to exist first after more than ten years of cohabitation. With the assessment of the cohabitation's evidentiary value, it appears that particular weight has been given to the three elements of *nominatio, tractatus,* and *fama.*[94] *Nominatio* meant that consideration was given to whether the man and woman characterized each other as spouses, while *tractatus* meant the consideration of whether they treated each other as spouses. With respect to the parties' relationship to each other, particular weight was placed on whether the cohabitation included a community of both bed and board (*in lecto et mensa*). This dual requirement recurs even in older Nordic law, and up to the present day in Scottish law, and has been given great significance with the assessment of whether an irregular marriage existed.[95] In addition, the importance of the parties' relationship public reputation (*publica fama*) as married was often emphasized. This element had particular weight as evidence in combination with a continuous cohabitation. In addition to these circumstances, a series of others of a more secondary significance were also considered, such as whether the woman wore a ring and provided a dowry (*donatio propter nuptias*).[96]

---

94 c. 11, X, II, 23, C.J.C., *supra* note 2, Decretales Gregorii, col. 284: *Per cohabitationem diutinam et famam de matrimonio et contractibus matrimonialibus ac alia adminicula probatur matrimonium.* The requirement as to durability that ought to be applied however was the object of divided opinions. (Panormitanus, id: *decem annorum*). *Compare* c. 28 X, IV, 1,5 (*id.*) in which Hostiensis maintains that marriage cannot be proven through cohabitation, as long as it has not lasted for a long period of time, for example 40 years (*per 40 annos*). That *nominatio* only was given limited evidentiary value can be seen from the warnings that were given for that even concubines could call each other spouses (Panormitanus ad c. 11 X, II, 23).

95 With respect to the significance of the community of bed and board, *see* c. 11 X, II, 23, C.J.C., *supra* note 2, Decretales Gregorii, col. 284: ... *vir ipsam in lecto et in mensa. See also* Hostiensis, who, in order for that a durable cohabitation would be able to constitute evidence as to marriage, assumes that the man *tenuisset earn in lecto et mensa ut uxorem* (Panormitanus, ad c. 28 X, IV, 1, 5). *Compare* Esmein, who from the sources does not highlight the community *in lecto et mensa,* ESMEIN I, *supra* note 10 at 222. With respect to the significance that a community "at bed and board" to the present date has been given in Scottish law with the assessment of whether an irregular marriage existed, *see* Chapter 11.

96 c. 11 X, II, 23, C.J.C., *supra* note 2, Decretales Gregorii, col. 284. *Cf.* c. 7, C 30, qu. 5, C.J.C., *supra* note 2, Decretum Gratiani, col. 965; ESMEIN I, *supra* note 10 at 224 note 5.

Even if the evidentiary value of the stated elements and combinations of elements were discussed in the canon law, as well as whether, e.g., *confessio* and *cohabitatio*, particularly if they existed in combination with *publica fama*, could constitute complete evidence of a marriage, it does not appear to have been a question of any legal evidentiary assessment with formally stipulated evidentiary values determined in advance. It appears rather to have been a question of an assessment *in casu* of all of the circumstances, in which no fact could always be said to be necessary or, if the circumstances indicated otherwise, sufficient for the establishment of a marriage. This, in actuality, is consistent with the notion that these named circumstances simply had the character of evidentiary facts and that they therefore were cited as support for something other than that sought, namely, the parties' *consensus matrimonialis*; in other words, the marital intent that constituted an unconditionally necessary requisite for the establishment of a marriage. In actuality, it appears that any manner whatsoever that was sufficiently demonstrative was accepted as an expression of the marital intent.[97] This evidentiary approach considered a series of different circumstances, and isolated those that were not sufficient as evidence, but which taken together were accepted as complete evidence for the existence of a marriage, and appears generally to have been accepted among both the canonists as well as legists.[98]

With the assessment of whether a marriage has arisen through *consensus de futuro* with subsequent *copula carnalis*, the courts had to try not only the existence of the subjective requisite in accordance with the above named principles,[99] but also the existence of *copula carnalis*. If disputes existed, the presentation of evidence often became intrusive. Even physical inspections could be required as proof of a woman's virginity.

As can be seen from the following chapters, many of these stated evidentiary circumstances have had striking longevity in the determination of a common law marriage, even up to modern times. A durable cohabitation (*cohabitatio diutina*), a community of bed and board (*mensa et lecto*), the parties' treatment of each other (*tractatus*), their designations of each other (*nominatio*), and their reputation as spouses (*fama*), recur within the

---

97 A. Scheurl argues that *consensus de praesenti* could create a marriage "eben auch ohne verba de praesenti, jedenfalls ohne gelobende verba de praesenti, er sollte auch durch eine der Einsegnung vorhergehende blosse 'Verjahung,' jedenfalls durch tatsächliche Empfangnahme des Weibes bei der Trauung, und etwa auch durch (beiderseits freiwilligen) concubitus erklärt werden können" (SCHEURL, *supra* note 47 at 93 with reference to Summa Coloniensis § 23).

98 Esmein states that the theory that was developed in c. 11, X, 23 (*De praesumptionibus*) was tentative and complicated, but that it "était là un trait general de la théorie des preuves, telle que ll'avaient construite les légistes et les canonistes, cela venait surtout de ce qu'ils admettaient qu'on pouvait composer une preuve complète par la réunion de divers éléments, qui, pris isolément, n'araient point force probante; ces combinaisons possibles étaient assez nombreuses et assez mal déterminees" (ESMEIN I, *supra* note 10 at 225).

99 ESMEIN I, *id.*

framework for common law marriage as evidentiary facts supporting the existence of a marriage contract (Chapter 7), as elements in the requirement as to cohabitation and appearance outwardly as the spouses (Chapter 8, "Cohabitation, Holding Out, and Reputation as Spouses"), and as elements in the marriage presumption (Chapter 9, "Burdens of Proof and Presumptions").

3.4 The Canon Law's Concubinage

The canon law concept of concubinage during the Middle Ages, like the Roman concept, always had something in common with the concept of marriage, and simultaneously something that distinguished it. This varied somewhat depending because the concept of concubinage in the canon law was not applied uniformly.

3.4.1 Occasional and Long-Term Concubinage

The early church assumed a tolerant attitude concerning concubinage. Against this, however, vis-à-vis marriage, the church maintained the principle of monogamy. Already, with the Council of Toledo in 400 AD, concubinage was allowed, but it was not permissible for a man to have several concubines or to have a concubine in addition to a wife.[100] Still, in the ninth century, concubinage was often treated as a marriage as far as the principle of monogamy was concerned.[101]

The church's tolerance had its equivalent in the secular law that, in certain aspects, accepted the system of concubines. Long-term relationships, in which the man was not married and had only one concubine,

---

100 The Council arranged so that a man who had a concubine would not be excluded from communion; *ceterum is qui non habet uxorem et pro uxore concibinam habet, a communione non repellatur* (c. 4, D. 34). *Compare* Augustine's tolerant attitude to concubinage in c. 19 *id.* as well as c. 6, C. 32, qu. 2, C.J.C., *supra* note 2, Decretum Gratiani, col. 112 and 928. *Compare* the critical stance to concubinage that Pope Leo I assumed in a letter dated the year 458-459 to Bishop Rusticus of Narbonne, however without forbidding the same, c. 12, C. 32, qu. 2, C.J.C., *supra* note 2, Decretum Gratiani, col. 980. *Compare* H. Vandenberghe, Den juridische betekenis van het concubinat 19 (1970): "De door het concilie van Toledo bedoelde concubinerenden iurecivile, zijn, iure canonico, werkelijke echtgenoten." With respect to the principle of monogamy's application as to concubinage, *see also* c. 5, D. 34, C.J.C., *supra* note 2, Decretum Gratiani, col. 112: *Christiano non dicam plurimas, sed nec duas simul habere licitum est, nisi unam tantum, aut uxorem out certe, loco uxoris (si conjux deest) concubinam.* The impediment against successive bigamy with respect to marriage was applicable also to concubinage in accordance with c. 1-2, D. 33, C.J.C., *supra* note 2, Decretum Gratiani, col. 109-110. *Compare* Pope Innocentius III's reply dated 3 Oct 1213 to the Archbishop Andreas in Lund as to his question whether priests that have had two concubines successively (*successive duas concubinas habentes*) could be viewed as having committed bigamy. The pope answered in the negative, *see* Dipl. Suec., *supra* note 11, DS-nr 150 p. 175.

101 *See* Joyce, *supra* note 18 at 606.

appear during the early Middle Ages to have been tolerated, at least in the Nordic countries. Such arrangements also appear to have commonly existed, even in the highest classes of society.[102] In Danish law, the legal effects of marriage could be effected if a man publicly had a woman in his home for three years, living there as his wife, with whom he had a community of board and bed, and who carried the keys to the home. Similar regulations existed in Norwegian law but with a required period of twenty and thirty years, respectively. These time periods had equivalents in the property law of possession and prescription concepts, as had the Roman *usus* marriage.[103] The children of concubines certainly were not legitimate, but were given a limited right to inherit from the father during the later Middle Ages.[104]

Even if the canon law originally tolerated concubinage, it was not a question of equipping it with the legal effects of marriage and raising it to any *inaequale coniugium* similar to the Roman concubinage.

All relationships that did not constitute marriage, however, were viewed as concubinage. As was the case in the Roman law, canon law included an interest in distinguishing concubinage as against more temporary sexual relationships. Therefore, a distinction was made, albeit that it was not generally extensive, between long-term concubinage (*concubinatus perpetuus*) and temporary concubinage (*concubinatus temporarius*). The latter, which did not constitute true concubinage, was criminally punishable as fornication (*fornicatio*).[105]

3.4.2 Concubinage without *Affectus Maritalis*

No uniform view existed with respect to the inner constitutive elements of the canon law concept of concubinage. Consequently, concubinage was understood to be relationships that had been established through the parties'

102 *See* LIZZIE CARLSSON, JAG GIVER DIG MIN DOTTER 231 (1965).

103 The danish Jyske lov, I, 27 prescribes: Hvis en mand har en slegfred (= frilla) i huset hos sig i 3 år, og han åbenbart deler seng med hende; og hun råder over lås og lukke og åbenlyst spiser og drikker samrnen med ham, så skal hun vaere (at betragte som) hans aegtehustru og retmaessige husfrue. *See* DANMARKS GAMLE LANDSKAPSLOVE II at 68 (J. Brøndum-Nielsen & P.J. Jørgensen eds. 1933-41). For the comparable regulation in Skåne law, *see* Tillägg VIII: 2, SVENSKA LANDSKAPSLAGAR IV, SKÅNELAGEN AND GUTALAGEN at 153 (Åke Holmbäck & Elias Wessen eds.1979). The norwegian Gulatingslov 125 prescribes: Um ein mann bur saman med frilla si i 20 vetrar eller lengher enn 20 vetrar, lever saman med henne openbart, og vert det ingen skilnad millom dei i den tidi og kjem det ingi lysing um noko anna i dei fyrste 20 åri, då er borni deira rettkomne till arv, og lovi legg felaget deira. *See* GULATINGSLOVI (Knut Robberstad ed. 1952). *Cf.* Æeldre Borgarthings Christenret, II:10 and the therein prescribed 30 years' period, *see* NORGES GAMLE LOVE I at 356 (R. Keyser & P.A. Munch et al. 1846-1895). *Compare* the Roman *usus*-marriage, Chapter 2.3.2.3.

104 *See* the Skåne law, *id.*, Tillägg IV: 6 at 150.

105 c. 5, C. 32, qu. 2: *Concubinae ad tempus adhibitae, nec etiamsi causa filiorum concumbant, justum faciunt concubinatum suum,* C.J.C., *supra* note 2, Decretum Gratiani, col. 979. *Cf.* c. 6, *id.*

mutual marital intent, but which had been entered into without the observance of the forms imposed for the commencement of marriage. This actually meant that which we above designated as informal or clandestine marriages, which received the legal effects of marriage.[106]

The relatively open attitude that the church early assumed in relation to concubinage was more closely defined and became more fixed under Gratian. The canon law recognized now only one form of cohabitation – marriage – and the criteria of demarcation in relation to concubinage became the parties' *affectus maritalis*. Informal relationships entered into with marital *affectus* were considered marriages and received the legal effects of marriage, while others were considered *concubitus illicitus*, which was criminally punishable.[107] No institution in addition to marriage was equipped with legal effects, an *inaequale coniugium*, comparable to the Roman *concubinatus*. It is therefore somewhat misleading when Freisen claims that, "Was nach römischem Recht Concubinat war, das konnte nach kirchlichem Recht Ehe sein, vorausgesetzt den *affectus maritalis,*" as the stated conditions that Freisen calls the Roman concubinage was not any *concubinatus*, but rather a Roman marriage.[108] That which was concubinage in accordance with Roman law was also concubinage in accordance with the canon law, but with the difference that the canon law concubinage did not entail any positive legal effects for the parties.[109]

Pope Leo X criminalized concubinage in 1516. The Council of Trent imposed limitations on the concept of marriage. The concept of concubinage was broadened to a comparable degree and came to include all relationships entered into without the observance of the form requirements; in other words, everything from durable relationships, which had been entered into formlessly with *affectus maritalis*, to more temporary sexual relationships. And thus, the concept of concubinage has remained until the present day, in jurisdictions in which an unconditional form requirement has been enacted.[110]

---

106 FRIEDBERG, *supra* note 18 at 21 note 1.

107 Dicta ad c. 6 and c. 8, D. 34; c. 5, C. 32, qu. 2; c. 4, C. 32, qu. 4, C.J.C., *supra* note 2, Decretum Gratiani, col. 112, 114, 979, 985; FREISEN, *supra* note 10 at 65. *Compare* Esmein, who finds that the differentiation of concubinage in actuality is a later distinction, arising in order to cloak the church's contradictory attitude in the issue of concubinage. *See* A. ESMEIN, LE MARIAGE EN DROIT CANONIQUE II, 136 (R. Génestal & J. Dauvillier eds., 2nd ed. 1935).

108 FREISEN, *supra* note 10 at 68.

109 The children resulting from a concubinage, however, in contrast with other out-of-wedlock children had the right to maintenance from the father's side, *see* c. 5, X, IV, 7, C.J.C., *supra* note 2, Decretales Gregorii, col. 561.

110 HARDOUIN, *supra* note 23 at 1878; c. 8, Trid. Sess. XXIV. De reformatione matrimonii, *supra* note 3; FREISEN, *supra* note 10 at 70.

3.5 THE IMPLEMENTATION OF THE COUNCIL OF TRENT

3.5.1 Evidentiary Problems and Disputes

It is not surprising that the medieval canon law's informal marriages led to problems in the application of the law. The decisive constitutive significance that was attributed to the applied concept of marriage's subjective elements created particular evidentiary difficulties. It must, e.g., have been tempting for a man, after a vow given in secrecy, which was consummated through *copula carnalis,* to abandon the woman and deny that any vow had been given. If the woman in such a case alleged that a marriage had been established, the evidentiary burden of proof rested on her, and she would have had difficulty proving her assertion. If this, as we have found, was combined with the academic and linguistic difficulties of distinguishing between *consensus de praesenti* and *consensus de futuro,* the obstacles were so much the greater to presenting evidence concerning which type of *consensus* existed in the concrete case. The evidentiary problems were not eliminated through the marriage presumption applied in cases of a betrothal, even if it did not permit counterevidence, because the party who then prosecuted the lawsuit had to prove the previous existence of both *consensus de futuro* and *copula carnalis,* which often must have been difficult. Certainly the evidence was facilitated in cases of permanent cohabitation (*cohabitatio diutina*) that enjoyed general reputation (*publica fama*). It may, however, be repeated that in such a case, the cohabitation in principle was not attributed independent significance. It was cited as support for something else that was sought, namely, the parties' *consensus matrimonialis.* Even if the cohabitation could constitute complete evidence, the possibility of presenting counterevidence existed.

The recently mentioned evidentiary difficulties led to extensive litigation and, from a legal certainty perspective, an unsatisfactory situation.[111] The lack of form also appears to have given rise to impermissible relationships between relatives[112] and to a growing incidence of bigamy, as Luther so clearly depicted:

111 This can already be seen in a decree from Pope Alexander III, 1159-1181, concerning clandestine marriages, which begins with the words: *Solet frequenter, ut audiuimus, euenire, ut super clandestinis coniugiis, que in archiepiscopatu tuo sepissime contrahuntur, multa litigantium questionepulseris...* (c. 4, Comp. I, IV, 4, *supra* note 19 at 46). From a considerably later date can be mentioned, that of 320 cases that for the year 1349 were taken up in the book of judgments in Augsburg, 111, in other words, approximately one-third, concerned the question of whether a marriage had been entered into based on *consensus de praesenti.* Over 80 of these cases were dismissed primarily due to evidentiary difficulties. (*See* as to this, KNECHT, *supra* note 22 at 611 n. 1). *Cf.* with respect to evidentiary difficulties, DAUVILLIER, *supra* note 72 at 103.

112 FRIEDBERG, *supra* note 18 at 101.

Also ging mir's im Kloster auch; oder wo man fur den Official kam, so schwur sich Eines vom Andern freieten wieder. Darnach kamen sie zu mir oder einem Andern in der Beichte und sprachen: Lieber Herr, ich habe itzt eine Frau, der habe ichs heimlich gelobt; wie thue ich ihm immermehr? Helft mir lieber Herr Doctor, dass ich nicht verzweifle, denn Greta mit der ich mich am ersten verlobt hab, ist mein recht Eheweib. Aber diese Barbara die mir darnach vertrauet, ist nicht mein Weib, und muss doch bei ihr schlafen? Jene darf ich nicht nehmen, die ich doch gerne möcht haben, då es sein könnte; aber ich kann nu nicht; denn ich habe eine Andere, so hat sie auch einen Andern; doch weiss es Niemand, dass sie mein Weib ist, denn allein Gott im Himmel, dem ist's bewusst. O, ich werde verdampt, ich weiss keinen Rath!"[113]

The canonists' learned presentations in evidentiary issues during the Middle Ages became increasingly extensive. The clandestine marriage, without doubt, constituted one of the main problems of medieval church family law, and evidentiary difficulties were a strong contributing factor to the church's often-repeated prohibitions and recommendations against it.[114]

3.5.2 The Proposal Concerning an Obligatory Form Requirement

Pope Alexander III (1159–1181) forbade clandestine marriage at the risk of excommunication and required that marriages be entered into publicly

113 *See* Luther's "Tischreden," MARTIN LUTHER, WERKE 62 at 229 (Erlangen 1838). Likewise Luther states in "von Ehesachen": "Es ist oft geschehn, dass für mich kommen ein ehelich Paar Volks, da eins oder alle beide sich vorhin heimlich mit Andern verlobet hatten, da war Jammer und noth. Da haben wir Beichtväter und Theologen sollen rathen solschen gefangenen Gewissen; wie konnten wir aber? Da stund der Official Recht und Brauch, und urtheilet, das erste heimliche Verlöbniss sollt eine rechte Ehe sein fur Gott, und die andere ein offentlicher Ehebruch." (WERKE 23 at 98). With respect to bigamy's expansion in Germany, *see* FRIEDBERG, *id.* at 101 n. 2 with references.

114 DIE SUMMA MAGISTRI ROLANDI 153 f. (Friedrich Thaner ed., Innsbruck 1874). Kessler, who researched the development of the form requirement during the Middle Ages, maintains that as a basis for the prohibition against clandestine marriage "erscheint jedoch nur noch die der Eheschliessung unter vier Augen immanente Gefahr, dass bei Bestreiten des einen Ehepartners die tatsächlich vorgenommene Eheschliessung nicht bewiesen werden kann... Was den Kanonisten eben als das Motiv aller dieser capitula erscheint, ist die Frage der Beweissicherung." From this the author draws the far-reaching conclusion: "Deswegen, und nur deswegen sind nach ihrer Ansicht die klandestinen Ehen durch die Kirche verpönt." (KESSLER, *supra* note 1 at 21.) These prohibitions at times simply had the character of advice and did not affect the validity of the clandestine marriages. *See also* JOYCE, *supra* note 18 at 113 note 1.

and preferably *in facie ecclesia*.[115] In the numerous provincial councils and synods held throughout the Middle Ages, the problems of clandestine marriage were treated, and the prohibitions against it were continuously sharpened.[116] After the Fourth Lateran Council in 1215, the requirement of a public wedding ceremony also included the requirement that the marriage be preceded by banns.[117] The regulations, from the beginning, often simply had the character of advice, but later were tied to sanctions. Priests who presided over clandestine marriages were threatened with suspension, and the parties risked everything from fines to excommunication, refusal of sacraments, as well as exclusion from communion and church burial. The church, however, did not take the step of repealing the validity of clandestine marriages. Ecclesiastical legislation had little effect, despite continuously repeated prohibitions and recommendations during the Middle Ages and the reasons given for them, penal options, and growing

---

115 c. 4, Comp. 1, IV, 4, *supra* note 19 at 46; c. 2, Comp. II, IV, 3, *supra* note 19 at 92; c. 7 X, II, 27, C.J.C., *supra* note 2, Decretales Gregorii, col. 315.

116 Schulte states correctly: "Es sind der Concilien zu viele, als dass sie alle genannt werden können" (SCHULTE, *supra* note 18 at 40 n. 10). Of these as examples may be mentioned, with respect to England: Winton 1076, Londin 1102, Westmonast 1175, Londin 1200, Oxon 1212, Dunelm 1220, Conventr 1237, Cicestr 1246, Bridport 1256, Exon 1287, Sodor 1291, Ossor 1321, Cantuar 1328, Londin 1342, Eborac 1367, Lamehith 1455, Cantuar 1460, Eborac 1518, Edinburg 1551. *See* DAVID WILKINS, CONCILIA MV (London 1737). With respect to France: Rotomagense 1072, Gopnteri 1231, Salmur 1235, Arelatense 1260, Andegavenss 1270, Langesiense 1278, Bituricense 1286, Sylvanectense 1326, Vauriennse 1368, Narben 1374, Andegavense 1448, Toulouse 1515, Senonense 1528, Narbon 1551. *See* PHILIPPE LABBÉ, SACROSANTA CONCILIA IX-XV (Lutetise, Parisiorum 1671-72). With respect to Germany: Trevir 1227, Magdeburg 1266, Leod 1287, Herebip 1298, Trevir 1310, Olomuc 1318, Salisb 1420, Herbip 1446, Constant 1463, Magdeburg 1463, Varmiens 1495, Basileens 1503, Misn 1504, Tornac 1520, Hildesheim 1539. *See* JOSEPH HARTZHEIM, CONCILIA GERMANIAE II-IV (Köln 1759-1763). With respect to Spain: Valentinae 1255, Toledo 1335, Arandense 1473 and 1512. *See* JOSEPH SAENZ DE AGUIRRE, COLLECTIO MAXIMA CONCILIORUM OMNIUM HISPANIAE ET NOVI ORBIS V (Salamanca 1686). A similar picture appears in Portugal, Italy, the Netherlands, and the Slavic countries. With respect to Sweden can be mentioned Pope Alexander III's letter dated 11 September 1165-81 to the Archbishop in Uppsala with restrictions *inter alia* that marriages were not allowed to be entered into without a priest officiating wedding ceremony: "*Caeterum clandestina & absque sacerdotali benedictione non debere contrahi coniugia*" (Sv. Dipl.). After 1215, several restrictions concerned the importance of that the commencement of marriage was preceded by the calling of banns. *See* for example Pope Innocentius III's letter dated 5 April 1216 to the Archbishop in Uppsala (Sv. Dipl.). Not before the end of the Middle Ages was the requirement as to a church participation upon the commencement of marriage combined with criminal punishment in the form of fines. *See* for example the Arboga parish meeting decision dated 14 September 1412 that prescribes fines of three marks for priests who have blessed a person who has not proven the absence of marriage impediments. (Sv. Dipl). *See* further Arboga parish meeting decision 14 September 1417.

117 The failure to observe the thrice calling of banns required in the year 1215 however did not entail the marriage's invalidity, *see* c. 3 X, IV, 3, C.J.C., *supra* note 2, Decretales Gregorii, col. 552-553.

support from secular legislation.[118] The marital behavioral patterns simply did not conform to legislated rules.

Despite the increasingly obstinate application problems that the informal marriages entailed during the Middle Ages, it would not be until the Council of Trent, 1542–1563, before the church – now the Roman Catholic branch – would, as a requisite for the validity of marriage, introduce an obligatory form requirement upon commencement of the marriage.[119] The *consensus* about the importance of not impeding access to marriage was not deterred by the inconveniences of the applicable system, as reported above, which were also widely acknowledged among the delegates at the council.[120] On the other hand, a dogmatic issue of the highest

---

118 It can be seen from Alexander III's (1159-1181) above cited statement that clandestine marriages during his time commonly existed (*solet frequenter, see supra* note 111). Already the large number of councils and synods that thereafter followed and with which the church anew was forced to sharpen the prohibition against *matrimonii clandestina* give support for that they were very frequent during the entire Middle Ages. Despite the continuously repeated prohibitions and the all-the-more-strict sanctions that came to be tied to these, complaints were made at the councils and synods continuously over the often-existing violations. Such was the case, for example, with the synod in Toulouse:... *quod matrimonium contrahentes in loco privato, clandestine per laicos. See* Jean de Launoy, Concilia Antiqua Galliae 417 (Paris 1639), another example can be found in Spain, where despite the prohibitions against clandestine marriages that were issued *inter alia* at the councils in Toledo 1335 and Arandense 1473 and despite a strong, secular legislation there in 1505, which for the parties in clandestine marriages was prescribed *inter alia* the loss of their collective assets, expulsion from Spain and the death penalty in the event they returned, a provincial council in 1512 was forced again to sharpen the prohibition:... *quia dictaprohibitio iuris, nec poenae quae rigore...non sufficiunt ad obviandum magnis periculis et scandalis... See* Aguirre V, *id.* 373. Even the modern academic literature is in fair agreement that the medieval church's legislation against clandestine marriages to a considerable extent was without effect. Schulte states that the requirements of public finalization of marriage, despite the fact that they so often were repeated, became "sehr oft ausser Acht gesetzt, wie schon die mehrfachen Publicationen in denselben Diöcesen beweisen würden, wenn nicht manche Concilien selbst laut darüber Klage erhoben hätten" (Schulte, *supra* note 18 at 44). Kessler states as to the regulations governing the calling of banns that "der verhältnissmässig scharfe Zugriff durch die Bestimmung des 4. Laterankonzils hat zur Erreichung des Zieles öffentlicher Eheschliessung so wenig gefruchtet wie die Vorschriften der früheren Zeit" (Kessler, *supra* note 1 at 49 f). Joyce maintains in agreement herewith with respect to the 1500s that "the problem was acute and had been long felt to be such: and the remedies hitherto employed had had but a very limited success" (Joyce, *supra* note 18 at 116); Knecht, *supra* note 22 at 611; and Friedberg, *supra* note 18 at 32, 39, 65, 70 f, 75, 77 f.

119 In general with respect to the discussions at the Council, *see* Esmein II, *supra* note 107 at 157, G. Schreiber, Weltkonzil von Trient I-II (1951) passim. Even the Protestant reformers were critical with respect to clandestine marriages, but emphasized for their part after the Germanic role model the requirement of parental consent upon the commencement of marriage, *see* as to this Joyce, *supra* note 18 at 113.

120 The situation that clandestine marriages created is reflected in the introduction of decree adopted by the Council, which after the ingress came to be called *Tametsi*, but which actually was designated "*Decretum de reformatione matrimonii*"; "*Tametsi dubitandum non est, clandestina matrimonial, libera contrahentium consensu facta, rata et vera esse matrimonia...* " (c. 1, Trid. Sess. XXIV, De reformations matrimonii,

theological degree became very controversial, namely, the question of whether the church had the authority to decide the marital sacrament's form, given that Christ himself in the holy scriptures had not laid down any form requirement.[121] The dogmatic misgivings, however, had to give way in the interest of eliminating the application problems. On November 11, 1563, with 133 votes against 59, the decree *Tametsi* was finally adopted, after months of discussion, different compromise proposals, and eventually, pressure from the French king. According to the decree, marriage was to be entered into before a priest and in the presence of two or three witnesses (*coram parocho et duobus vel tribus testibus*), and marriages entered into without the observance of these forms were invalid (*et hujusmodi contractus irritos et nullos esse decernit*).[122] It followed that a formless *consensus de praesenti* or a *consensus de futuro* with subsequent *copula carnalis* no longer could constitute marriage. The formal act would rest on contractual grounds to such an extent that the parties during the formal act were required to give expression to their marital *consensus de praesenti*. The declaration of intent, however, was not tied to any defined word formulations.[123] Openings were left for local traditions. Through the decree, the requirement of the calling of banns was made a prerequisite for the validity of marriage, as well the registration of the marriage, required in a marriage book particularly intended for that purpose.[124] Both latter requirements were also intended to facilitate the proving of a marriage, as well as to allow control of marital impediments and thus to prevent bigamous relationships.

Esmein calls the Council of Trent a *revolution veritable*, hardly an exaggeration.[125] For the first time in the church's history, a mandatory form requirement at the commencement of marriage was enacted as a prerequisite for the validity of marriage. This broke over one thousand years of

---

supra note 3). With respect to the individual delegates' statements, *see* ESMEIN II, *id.* at 179 f., 187 f.; FRIEDBERG, *supra* note 18 at 113.

121 Several delegates considered that decisions in sacramental issues fell within the church's jurisdiction, others maintained the opposite view and still others argued that a form requirement upon the commencement of marriage did not affect marriage as a sacrament. The church's hesitation as to the idea of subjecting the sacrament of marriage to a form not prescribed by Christ himself – the master of the sacrament – already could be found with authorities such as THOMAS AQUINAS, P. THOMAE AQUINATIS DOCTORIS ANGELICI SUMMA THEOLOGICA III., qu. 64 art. 2 ad 1 (Augustae Taurinorum, ed. 1903). With respect to the delegates' statements in sacramental issues, *see* FRIEDBERG, *supra* note 18 at 108. *Cf.* JOYCE, *supra* note 18 at 118.

122 c. 1, Trid. sess. XXIV, *De reformatione matrimonii, supra* note 3.

123 *Tametsi, id.*

124 *Id.* Already with the Fourth Council of the Lateran in the year 1215, it was required that the commencement of marriage be proceeded by banns having been called three times in the church. The failure to observe the requirement however did not entail the marriage's invalidity (c. 3 X, IV, 3, C.J.C., *supra* note 2, Decretales Gregorii, col. 552-553).

125 ESMEIN II, *supra* note 107 at 176.

canon law tradition and would, in the future, decisively influence the structure of the concept of marriage.

The form requirement, in different variations, successively became a part of the majority of national legal systems in Europe and in the Christian world in general.[126] In our culture, to the present day, the requirement of a wedding ceremony is a notable characteristic of the Christian marriage.

The requirement of a wedding ceremony did not, however, come to be a necessary prerequisite for the establishment of marriage in all of the countries within our culture. The informal marriage persisted in a few legal systems in different variations, and includes the institution of common law marriage, which was considerably influenced by the pre-Tridentine canon models of marriage. This institution, which retained its traditional gestalt in England up to 1754 and in Scotland up to 1940, has been identifiable in a renewed form in Scotland up to 2006, and is still applicable in ten American states as well as the District of Columbia.

3.6 Summary and Conclusions

If one views medieval canon law from a comparative perspective, it is clear that the church's legal policy objective, after rising from the catacombs, spread across the world, legalizing the marital community more extensively than Roman law ever had, and bringing it in accordance with Christian values. The object of the church's interest was the marital community, whether formalized or not, which is predictable, given that the holy scriptures did not impose any form requirements for the commencement of marriage. In the church's endeavors to legally regulate the marital relationship, it appears to have applied a two-fold strategy.

126 That the *forma tridentina* did not receive any immediate effect also depended partially on the somewhat specific regulations applicable to its enactment and that prescribed that the decree would be applied only in parishes in which it had been published (c. 1). In parishes and countries in which the Protestant teachings were dominant, the Catholic decree was not published, consequently the old Catholic teachings according to which formless marriages were valid there until further notice would have been applicable. This was the case, for example, in Great Britain, Prussia, Saxen, and the Scandinavian countries. Different countries on the continent with both Catholic and Protestant populations in varying majorities would create an uneven map of parishes which applied or did not apply, respectively, the *Council of Trent*. As a result, application difficulties, not in the least in cases of mixed marriages, and a significant legal uncertainty ensued. Schönsteiner speaks of "ein wahres Chaos" (Schönsteiner, *supra* note 22 at 666). The picture is also complicated in that hand in hand with this development, the jurisdiction in litigation concerning marriage was successively transferred from the ecclesiastical to secular courts. Eventually, however, *forma tridentina* also came to be a part of the Protestant and secular marital laws. Through the decree *Ne Temere* from the year 1907, a uniform system was created for all Catholics based on *Tametsi* and which, in 1917, was taken up in Codex Juris Canonici.

1. *The Goal of Increasing the Rate of Marriage*

On one side, the church constructed a legal marriage, a *matrimonium legitimum*, through which it attempted to encourage the parties to subject themselves formally to the church's authority before entering into a *matrimonium manifestum*. With gradually increasing intensity during the Middle Ages, the church reiterated the prohibition against clandestine marriages (*matrimonia clandestina*), as well as the requirement to formally enter the marriage through the church. Similarly to the Roman legislator, the church during the Middle Ages, despite the use of penal sanctions, had little success in its endeavors. Over one thousand years of Roman and canon law experiences provide a warning against optimism to every modern legislator who is facing decreasing rates of marriage and observing, with concern, a growing number of cohabitations outside of marriage. History teaches that legislation can be fraught with significant difficulties as it attempts to influence marital attitudes and behavioral patterns.

2. *The Goal of Capturing the "Lost Sheep"*

On the other side, the church also considered marriages that had been entered into without the observance of the forms imposed by the church as completely valid (*matrimonia legitima*). Through this strategy, the church, within the canon law teachings and its indissoluble sacrament, could capture both those who chose profane wedding rites as well as those who for financial or other reasons entered into marriage entirely formlessly. Given that prevailing marriage traditions persisted so relentlessly, the church ought to have been compelled to adapt. With a dual strategy, on one side to forbid and on the other side to recognize clandestine marriages, the church could have imposed its marriage law system on those who violated the prohibition and therefore on a much larger number of families. Of the legal effects of marriage to which the parties were subjected, marriage's indissolubility was the most important for the church. The doors to marriage stood open for admittance, while the exits, in principle, were closed.

If the canon law system had given parties freedom of choice with respect to the form of the commencement of marriage, they would have been able to regulate what they considered most desirable. But the issue was never one of legislative neutrality; the same regulations would apply regardless of the form of the commencement of marriage.

The reasons of protecting children and capturing the parents, "lost sheep," within the legal marital fold in order to exercise control and imposing obligations upon them recur later as justifications for common law marriage in the United States[127] and are pertinent to a discussion of current legal regulations for informal relationships in general.[128]

---

127 *See* Chapter 4.
128 *See* Chapter 14.

3. *The Acceptance of the Roman Definition of Marriage*

We have in this chapter, in addition, made the remarkable observation that the old fathers of the church, rising from the ruins of the disintegrated Roman culture, utilized the Roman definition of marriage, which was understood to be a complete shared life for a lifetime (*individua consuetudo vitae* eller *consortium omnis vitae*) between a man and a woman. Instead of considering the definition as simply a normative view of marriage as an ideal, the church gave the definition more substantive content. Canon law understood the husband and wife to be one flesh (*una coro*) and therefore could not accept the Roman principle of *libertas matrimonii.* Instead, the definition of marriage emphasized indissolubility (*quod ergo Deus conjunxit, homo non separet*). Still, the definition's core survived for more than one thousand years, both among the Roman heathen and medieval Christian cultures. The universal constancy of this definition lends itself to natural law, whose viability in modern times will be explored below.

4. *Marital Impediments and Informal Relationships*

The reality was that even though marriage, according to the medieval canon law, was indissoluble, parties separated and entered into new relationships, making the risk for bigamy considerable. This risk was particularly great when even entirely formless marital relationships constituted impediments against new marriages. A common law marriage in the United States still today constitutes an impediment against both a new common law marriage and against a ceremonial marriage.[129] Clearly, problems arise if the parties begin new relationships successively without knowing that they have previously established a common law marriage. The problems addressed in American case law are treated in Chapter 5, "Legal Capacity and Common Law Marriage." The question of society's future possibilities of exercising control over the legal capacity to commence a formless cohabitation relationship and the dissolution of marriages is discussed in Chapter 14.

5. *The Elements of the Contract*

In this chapter, it has further been seen that the medieval canon law inherited from the Roman law not only its definition of marriage, but also the principle that marriage is based on the parties' agreement (*voluntas facit matrimonium*). This definition underwent development, despite its striking external constancy and undeniable ability to cast this concept of marriage as a natural law. In contrast to classic Roman law, it appears that the canon law legal scholarship, at least originally, did not understand the marital intent as an *affectio maritalis* in the meaning of a continuously

129 *See* Chapter 5.

manifested state of mind by one of the parties during the entire cohabitation in all circumstances (*consensus continuus*). The canon law marital intent appears instead, with Justinian law as a role model, to have originally constituted an initial intent, which was developed as an element in a sharply defined contractual conclusion. This understanding became difficult to maintain when the requirement of a verbal agreement no longer was applied and the cohabitation was recognized as evidence of the parties' marital intentions.

Even if certain attempts were made in modern case law with respect to common law marriage about requiring a defined contractual conclusion, the acceptance of inferred agreements based on the parties' cohabitation has made this impossible. Instead, as can be seen below, American case law during 1800s and the 1900s has leaned towards the reasoning of Roman law by employing a continual *consensus*.[130]

In this chapter, we have also highlighted that Gratian raised a central issue concerning the marital intent's object when he questioned what the parties actually agreed to in order for a marriage to be established. The canon law tied herewith the object of the intention of the parties to the essence of marriage as came to expression in the definition of marriage. Consequently, the parties must have a mutual intent to establish a complete and undivided community in all aspects of life for a lifetime (*individua consuetudo vitae, consortium omnis vitae*). Gratian initiated a discussion about the object of the marital intent that today is equally important with the delineation of common law marriage (see Chapter 6, below) and that in an assessment concerning the future is also relevant in a discussion concerning the legal significance of the parties' intentions with cohabitations in a broader context (see Chapter 13).

Peter Lombard's distinction between *consensus de praesenti* and *consensus de futuro* was also fundamental to the modern development, which meant that only the former, an agreement to a present or immediately effective marriage, would be able to constitute marriage, while the latter constituted an agreement to enter into a marriage contract in the future (*pactum de contrahendo*).

The canon legal scholarship further developed the marriage contract into a legal act in the modern sense which, in contrast with the Roman concept, applied general contract law, in practice Roman legal principles, *inter alia* simulation, mental reservation, misunderstanding, etc. The contractual freedom, however, was limited to the extent that terms in conflict with the essence of marriage were invalid inasmuch as the spouses could not terminate the agreement through a request for marital divorce. The marriage was, in principle, indissoluble.

130 With respect to the development in the American case law, *see* Chapters 6 and 7.

6. *The Significance of Copula Carnalis*

In addition, it has been seen from this chapter that the significance of *copula carnalis* with the establishment of an informal marriage was one of the most debated questions in the medieval canon law. At the same time as the *copula* was considered to be a notable characteristic feature of marriage, it was considered, absent the other elements, to be a sign of something entirely despicable, namely fornication (*fornicatio*). The discussions appear to have resulted in a compromise, according to which, on one side, *copula carnalis* was not required for the establishment of a marriage. It could consequently be established only through the parties' mutual intentions (*consensus de praesenti*). On the other side, a marriage could also be established through the intentions of the parties in the future to enter into a marriage (*consensus de futuro*) being supplemented with *copula carnalis.* The intentions of the parties were presumed to have been transformed into an intent to be immediately married. Because the presumption could not be rebutted, in other words, it was a *praesumtion juris et de jure, copulan* retained a constitutive effect to such an extent that it, with *consensus de futuro,* was sufficient albeit not always necessary for the establishment of a marriage.

The two variations of entering into an informal marriage that the canon law consequently established, either *per verba de praesenti* or *per verba de futuro cum copula carnalis,* would come to remain long after the canon law through the Council of Trent in 1563 repealed informal marriages within the Roman Catholic jurisdiction. As seen in the next chapter, the distinction was still alive when common law marriage was received in the United States during the 1800s. However, in principle, only the first named variation became acceptable in American case law.[131] The courts today still have to distinguish between the two types of *consensus,* which can be difficult when cohabiting couples have had certain plans to enter into a ceremonial marriage, but these have not yet been realized.[132]

The great interest in the medieval canon law as to *copula carnalis,* which has theological and historical causes, can appear somewhat obsolete nowadays, against the background of today's sexual mores. It ought, however, be noted that the *copula* in modern case law with respect to common law marriage continuously recurs as a relevant element in the assessment of whether the requirement of cohabitation has been fulfilled.[133] As seen in Chapters 13 and 14, modern cohabitation legislation has not been able to avoid the *copula's* relevance with the assessment of whether a cohabitation relationship, and not simply a friendship or other relationship, exists.[134] In light hereof, one is tempted to agree with Horatius when he declares

131 *See* Chapter 4.
132 *See* Chapter 6.
133 *See* Chapter 8.
134 *See* Chapter 13. With respect to those problems concerning the personal integrity as investigations of the parties' sexual relationships entail, *see* Chapter 14.

that one can exorcise natural law with a pitchfork, but it nevertheless continuously returns: *naturam expellas furca tamen usque recurret.*

7. *The Cohabitation as an Evidentiary Fact*

Even if the actual cohabitation in the canon system did not have the character of a legal element, in other words, a necessary prerequisite for the establishment of a marriage between legally competent persons, it was not without significance in the legal assessment of whether or not a marriage existed. Despite the fact that the canon principles spoke of a marriage contract *per verba* and originally appear to have required a verbal agreement, inferred agreements were later accepted, whose existences were proven with the support of the parties' cohabitation and other circumstances.

The cohabitation could consequently even in the canon law be attributed significance as an evidentiary fact supporting the parties' marital intentions. Unlike Roman law, the canon law does not appear to have laid down any actual presumption that cohabitation under marriage-like circumstances constituted marriage. The evidentiary burden of proof thereto rested on the party alleging that a marriage was established. However, if it was a question of a permanent cohabitation (*concubitus diutina*), this could, particularly if it enjoyed general reputation (*publica fama*), even constitute complete evidence that a marriage existed. And what can actually be better proof that the parties agree to live together in a *consortium omnis vitae* or a *individua consuetudo vitae* than that they actually lived in such a relationship? In principle, the cohabitation, however, was not necessary or when other circumstances indicated otherwise, sufficient for the establishment of a valid marriage.

As seen from the following chapters, the modern case law with respect to common law marriage does not ordinarily require verbal agreements despite the fact that the parties' mutual intention is still formulated as a *consensus per verba de praesenti.* Nowadays, it is almost exclusively a question of inferred agreements. The longevity that many of the medieval evidentiary circumstances have had in the determination of a common law marriage still in modern times is striking. A durable cohabitation (*cohabitatio diutina*), a community of bed and board (*mensa et lecto*), the parties' treatment of each other (*tractatus*), their designations of each other (*nominatio*), and their reputation as spouses (*fama*), recur within the framework of common law marriage as evidentiary facts supporting the existence of a marriage contract (Chapter 7), as elements in the requirement as to cohabitation and appearance outwardly as spouses (Chapter 8), and as relevant elements with the application of the marriage presumption (Chapter 9).

8. *The Canon Law Concubinage*

The application of the principle *consensus facit nuptias* as criteria with the delineation of the concept of marriage meant, as in the Roman *usus* marriage and the Roman free marriage, that a subjective requisite was a necessary condition for the establishment of a valid marriage between legally competent persons. In contrast with the *usus* marriage, which also required one years' cohabitation, in accordance with the medieval canon law, the parties' *consensus matrimonialis* was not only necessary, but in principle also sufficient for the establishment of a valid marriage. If no marital intent existed, the cohabitation was categorized in accordance with the canon law, as was the case with the Roman law of concubinage. However, although Roman concubinage came to constitute an institution equipped with legal effects in addition to the informal marriage, an *inaequale coniugium*, the canon law concubinage, after initially having been tolerated, afterwards became the object of even stricter criminalization.

9. The Application Problems

That the medieval canon law's informal marriage gave rise to extensive application problems was also seen in this chapter. The disadvantages that permeate contract principles are predictable. They arise partly from the danger of abuse that lies in the possibility that the parties may state that a marriage contract had been entered into without needing to prove their intentions through an effected agreement, and partly from the evidentiary difficulties that arise if one party denies the existence of an informal marriage agreement entered into secretly.

The recently mentioned application problems, as we have found, also gave rise to extensive litigation and expanded legal uncertainty. With respect to the problem of bigamy, which Luther so clearly depicted as a result of clandestine marriages, it ought be noted that widespread bigamy was not only a consequence of the lack of form, but also, to a material extent, a consequence of the fact that the canon marriage was indissoluble. As we have learned from Cicero with respect to the Roman law, and as we will find with respect to several of the modern concepts of cohabiting persons, the problems of bigamy do not arise in legal systems in which a marital relationship is dissolved as soon as one of the parties begins a new relationship with another. As seen in Chapter 5, however, the issue of bigamy is a current problem in the American states recognizing common law marriage, which is dissolved first through formal marital divorce.

The difficulties that arise in investigating and proving that *copula carnalis* occurred, as well as the invasion in the individual's personal integrity that can be anticipated, urge restraint with the use of the *copula* as a constitutive element. Certainly the evidentiary forms used in the canon law, e.g., physical inspections as proof of the woman's virginity, appear drastic and unacceptable to a modern legal understanding. Moreover, given today's sexual mores, such investigations would have limited evidentiary value in the majority of cases. The medieval evidentiary forms demonstrate, however, the consequences to which such a system can ultimately lead. The need to present evidence with respect to the *copula* is a logical consequence of the *copula's* being given constitutive effect. No evidence concerning an element such as *copula carnalis* can avoid coming into conflict with the protection of personal integrity.

Every modern legislator contemplating enacting legislation on informal marriages or cohabitation has reason to study the previously mentioned evidentiary difficulties arising from the church's repeated prohibitions and recommendations against informal marriage and the problems of enforcing those prohibitions that arose during the Middle Ages. All these difficulties contributed to the church's decision, finally and despite serious dogmatic misgivings, to break over one thousand years of canon law tradition by introducing an obligatory form requirement as a requisite for the validity of marriage. To disregard the church's third strategy would be turning a blind eye to historical reality.

The legal application problems that follow from common law marriage and cohabitation legislation are highlighted in the discussion concerning the future in Chapter 14.[135]

10. Forma Tridentina

The implementation of the Council of Trent certainly meant that the application problems tied to the informal marriage concept could be avoided. It ought, however, be stressed that the form requirement on the other hand did not constitute any guarantee that the parties also availed themselves of the prescribed form. The danger would always exist that the parties commenced a cohabitation without observing the specified form requirements and that they consequently fell outside of the system imposed by the legislator. This problem, the Tridentine dilemma, constitutes a latent danger in all countries in which the form requirements of a religious or civil wedding ceremony have been part of the national legal system. In modern times, in several countries it has an immediacy as a result of decreasing rates of marriage. Legal policy assessments, in addition to form requirements, are the two other canon law strategies treated in the introduction of this concluding section, in order to either increase the rate of marriage or regulate informal relationships. The possibility of solving the Tridentine dilemma, without using form requirements but still maintaining the rate of marriage, is discussed in Chapter 15.[136]

From this chapter, it ought to have been seen that the canon law concept and historical experiences with the canon law of marriage cast light on several of the issues raised by the development of common law marriage and the modern concepts of cohabiting persons. This concerns issues of a more general legal policy nature with respect to the concept of marriage. Modern common law marriage must be assessed in the framework of the modern sources of law and society. Still, there is reason to consider how canon law thought and experiences can benefit modern legal thinking about common law marriage and cohabitation. We will return to these questions.

---

135 Chapter 14.
136 *See* Chapter 15.

CHAPTER 4

The Reception of Common Law Marriage in the United States

4.1 Introduction

Common law marriage has its origins in old English ecclesiastical law and medieval canon law, which in turn was influenced by Roman law, as discussed in the previous chapter.[1] This resulted from the fact that the ecclesiastical courts in England administered the canon marital laws. Consequently, the term *common law marriage* did not have its origins in the English common law courts, and a strict interpretation of the term is not entirely accurate. However, in a broader sense, the canon law has also been viewed as part of the English common law.[2] In American law, the term *common law marriage* appears to have originated with the American jurist James Kent,[3] and common law marriage has been primarily developed in the case law, creating an American common law in this area.[4]

---

1 Roman Law, *see* Chapter 2, and Canon Law, *see* Chapter 3 *supra.*

2 William Holdsworth, A History of English Law 595 (7th ed. 1966) states that common law in the wider context could include "such canons and constitutions ecclesiastical as have been allowed by general consent and custom within the realm, and form … the king's ecclesiastical law." *See also* William Blackstone, Commentaries on the Law of England 79-80 (R.M. Kerr, London 1884).

3 The term "common law marriage" appears in the literature already with James Kent, Commentaries on American Law 2 (New York, William Kent 1826) and in the case law in *Grisham & Ligan v. The State,* 10 Tenn. 589 (1831); *Cheney v. Arnold,* 15 N.Y. 345, 69 Am.Dec. 609 (1857); and *Carmichael v. State,* 12 Ohio St. 553 (1861). A somewhat peculiar situation arose in Texas, in which the Mexican Congress, to which Texas then belonged, decided in 1840 that the common law of England would be applied as long as no domestic legislation prescribed otherwise. Despite the fact that English common law in 1840 did not recognize common law marriage, the Texas Supreme Court held that by English common law would be understood the common law that in several American states recognized such marriages. *See Grigsby v. Reib,* 105 Tex. 597, 153 S.W. 1124, 1125 (Tex. 1913).

4 The United States Supreme Court also stated in *Meister v. Moore,* 96 U.S. 76, 78 (1877), with reference to a formless marriage contract, that "such a contract constitutes a marriage *at common law*" (italics added).

This chapter gives a background on current American law and a discussion of the future of common law marriage by focusing on the reception of the doctrine in the United States during the 1800s and the beginning of the 1900s. The survey of cases here is only intended to show that the courts in the different states originally more or less adopted the doctrine, with no attempt to be exhaustive state by state. More detailed analyses of several of these older cases are given in the chapters specifically treating different aspects of the current law, for example, in Chapter 6, "The Common Law Marriage Contract;" Chapter 7, "Implied Marriage Agreements;" cohabitation as a necessary requisite in Chapter 8, "Cohabitation, Holding Out, and Reputation," as well as the different burdens of proof and legal presumptions presented in Chapter 12, "Common Law Marriage and Cohabitation Law." A greater number of cases, as later adjudicated, particularly in states that up to the present day recognize common law marriage, are also presented in these chapters.

The objective of this chapter is the presentation of the causes that can be assumed to underlie the American reception of common law marriage. These historical causes and their continuing relevance today in society, as well as other more modern issues, are critically reviewed and discussed in "Part III, The Future," of this exposition, addressing the future of common law marriage. Even if this chapter concerns the reception of the doctrine in the United States, attention is also briefly given to the initial criticism against the same surfacing already in the 1800s. A closer discussion and review of the viability of this criticism in today's society as well as other modern reasons against common law marriage are postponed to Part III in the discussion as to the future of the doctrine.

4.2 The Historical Background

4.2.1 The Origins in English Ecclesiastical Law

The origins of common law marriage can already be traced to William the Conqueror, who separated the jurisdiction of the English Church from that of the secular courts in 1085, giving the English Church jurisdiction to adjudicate issues concerning marriage.[5] During the Reformation, England freed itself of the Roman Catholic Church; in 1534, the Anglican Church assumed jurisdiction in cases concerning marriage, and retained the

5 Franklin C. Setaro, *A History of English Ecclesiastical Law (Part I)*, 18 B.U. L. Rev. 102, 104-107 (1938). The property law issues concerning *inter alia* dowries were tried on the other hand by the secular courts, which paradoxically required that the church forms for the commencement of a marriage were observed. The common law courts consequently did not apply common law marriage. As to this *see* Frederick Pollock and Frederic W. Maitland, History of English Law II, 367 (Cambridge, University Press, 2d ed. 1898); Emil Friedberg, Das Recht der Eheschliessung in seiner geschichtlichen Entwicklung 49 (Leipzig 1865); and Robert Black, *Common Law Marriage*, 2 U. Cin. L. Rev. 113, 126 (1928).

medieval canon law's principles as to the commencement of marriage.[6] Later, in 1563, the Roman Catholic Church reintroduced the *Forma Tridentina,* but was powerless in Protestant England. Paradoxically, the canon law that predated the Council of Trent still applied.[7] England certainly allowed marriages to be entered *in facie Ecclesiae.* The validity of a marriage, however, was not dependent upon any form requirement. The English Church consequently recognized both (1) marriage commenced through the parties' contract as to a present, in other words, an immediately effective marriage, *consensus de praesenti,* and (2) marriage commenced through the parties' contract as to a future marriage as well as a subsequent consummation, *consensus de futuro cum copula carnale.*[8] The first method did not originally require cohabitation. In principle, the agreement was sufficient.[9] In American law, cohabitation as a necessary requisite in addition to the agreement was developed later.[10] There are different views as to what extent spouses in England actually refrained from the forms imposed by the church. Actual cohabitation without formal marriage appears, however, to have been most common in the lower economic classes of society.[11]

---

6 SUPREMACY ACT, St. 26 Hen. VIII ch. 1, as well as St. 25 Hen. VIII ch. 19.

7 Thus at the Anglican Church's synod in London in 1597, it was demanded that marriages commenced without the church's participation be valid. *See* DAVID WILKINS, CONCILIA IV, 398 (London 1737).

8 POLLOCK AND MAITLAND, *supra* note 5, at 368.

9 In *dictum* in *Lindo v. Belisario,* (1795) 1 Hagg.Cons.Rep. 216, in which Scottish law was applied, Lord Stowell (later Sir William Scott) stated with reference to the canon, older English and Scottish law: "The vinculum follows on the contract, without consummation." From the same time, *see also Reed v. Passer,* (1790) Peake 303, N.D.Cas. 231, 170 Eng.Rep. 164 (1794), stating that the marriage contract is *ipsum matrimonium.* In *Dalrymple v. Dalrymple,* (1811) 2 Hagg.Cons. 54, 103, 161, Eng.Rep. 665, 682, Sir William Scott stated: "The contract *de praesenti* does not require consummation in order to become 'very matrimony'" and that the contract "*ipso facto, et ipso jure,* constitutes the relation of man and wife!" *See also M'Adam v. Walker,* (1813) 1 Dow. 148, 184-185, 3 Eng.Rep. 654, 666. The man in the case had orally before his servants declared that his mistress actually was his wife and that their children were legitimate, after which the woman gave him her hand, however without saying anything. Several hours later the man committed suicide. From the same time *see also Lautour v. Teesdale,* (1816) 8 Taunt. 830, 2 Marsh. 243, 17 Rev.Rep. 518, 12 Eng.Rul.Cas. 729, in which the court held that a contract *per verba de praesenti* constituted a marriage without subsequent cohabitation. *See also* HOLDSWORTH, *supra* note 2, at 622.

10 Regarding the development of cohabitation as a necessary requisite, *see* Chapter 8 *infra.* Regarding cohabitation as an evidentiary fact, *see* Chapter 7 *infra.* Regarding cohabitation as an element in the marriage presumption, *see* Chapter 9 *infra.*

11 According to POLLOCK AND MAITLAND, *supra* note 5, at 375, at Bracton's time (death 1268) it was "usual to go to church when one is to be married; all decent persons do this..." *Compare* on the other hand OTTO E. KOEGEL, COMMON LAW MARRIAGE AND ITS DEVELOPMENT IN THE UNITED STATES 12 (1922); G.H. JOYCE, DIE CHRISTLICHE EHE 131 (1934); and FRIEDBERG, *supra* note 5, at 317. P.M. BROMLEY, FAMILY LAW 86 (4th ed. 1997) maintains that in the middle of the 1700s, there was a danger that in certain parts of society such marriages "would become the rule rather than the exception."

An informal marriage was indissoluble and constituted an impediment against a later ceremonial marriage.[12]

The enactment in England of Lord Hardwicke's Act in 1753 introduced a mandatory form requirement as a requisite for the validity of a marriage.[13] The law prescribed that only marriages entered into after banns had been called three times, in the presence of a clergyman and two witnesses, were valid. In addition, violations could be punished by fourteen years' service on the royal estates. Consequently, 190 years after the Council of Trent, the *Forma Tridentina* was also enacted in England. The *ratio legis* behind Lord Hardwicke's Act, as well as the reasons behind the *Forma Tridentina*, are largely a result of application difficulties and the chaos caused by the lack of form. It was hazardous to assess whether an informal marriage had been established. A later formal marriage could be invalid due to a previous informal relationship that the parties did not know constituted an impediment against the former.[14] Although objections against the enactment of the *Forma Tridentina* in 1563 had been mostly theological, the

---

12 BROMLEY, *id.* ("Whilst such a marriage would no longer produce all the legal effects of coverture at common law, it was nevertheless valid for many purposes").

13 LORD HARDWICKE'S ACT of June 6, 1753, which came into force March 25, 1754, 26 Geo. II c. 33 stated that "in no case whatsoever shall any suit or proceeding be had in any ecclesiastical court in order to compel a celebration *in facie ecclesiae* by reason of any contract of matrimony whatsoever, whether *per verba de praesenti* or *per verba de futuro.*"

14 The law was the result of a long-term reform, ongoing since the last of the Stuarts. Previous proposals as to reform had failed because of the opposition in the House of Commons. *See* FRIEDBERG, *supra* note 5, at 346. When Lord Chancellor Hardwicke presented his "Bill for the better preventing of clandestine marriage," whose purpose primarily was to prevent secret marriages which during the 1700s had become more common and quickly spread in the area of Fleet in London and the prison there. According to PHILLIPE YORKE, THE LIFE OF LORD CHANCELLOR HARDWICKE 58 (1913), a prison priest of the name Gainham performed 36,000 secret weddings between the years 1709 and 1740 while another named Keith performed 1,190 during one year. *See also* GEORGE ELLIOTT HOWARD, A HISTORY OF MATRIMONIAL INSTITUTIONS I, 435 (1904). It has even been argued that the purpose of the law was only to limit the "Fleet marriages" and that open common law marriages unintentionally were affected due to the chosen form of construction. Consequently it has been maintained, however without convincing support, that common law marriage in England was repealed "almost by accident," *see* Stuart J. Stein, *Common-Law Marriage: Its History and Certain Contemporary Problems,* 9 J. FAM. L. 271, 274 (1969). In addition to dissatisfaction with secretly commenced marriages, there was also dissatisfaction as to the difficulties in application and the chaos created by informal marriages, *see, e.g.*, parliament member Ryder's speech in the debate in the House of Commons in 1753 in William Ferguson, *Introduction to the Scots and Parliament,* 15 PARLIAMENTARY HISTORY 1 (1996); and FRIEDBERG, *supra* note 5, at 350. Even the unjust consequences to which a revocation of a wedded marriage could lead, when it was found invalid due to a previous formless marriage entered into by one of the spouses with someone else, ought to have played a role. *See* the case tried in 1753 in the House of Lords, *Cochrane v. Campbell*; and Ferguson *id.* LAWRENCE STONE, THE FAMILY, SEX AND MARRIAGE IN ENGLAND 1500-1800 (1990) states that: "It is not too much to say that the marriage law as it operated in practise in England from the fourteenth to the nineteenth century was a mess. The root cause of the trouble was that there was no consensus within the society at large about how a legally binding marriage should be carried out."

criticism against Lord Hardwicke's legislative proposal was primarily related to economics and class. Only the upper class, the critics argued, had the means and the possibility of entering into ceremonial marriages. They feared that marriage, in reality, would be accessible only to a small portion of the population.[15] The majority in parliament, however, was not persuaded by these objections.

Even though informal marriage was still recognized in England during a relatively short time, *i.e.*, until Lord Hardwicke's Act, the development of the law in England has importance that persists to the present day. The period in question, namely, constituted an important phase in the colonization of North America, during which English legal ideas were exported to the colonies. Lord Hardwicke's Act did not become applicable in the colonies,[16] although domestic form requirements for the commencement of marriage were enacted.[17] However, to the extent that these form requirements were not considered unconditional, the door stayed open for common law marriage.[18] Despite examples of cases in which the courts during the colonial period applied the doctrine,[19] it is

15 *See, e.g.*, the speeches in the House of Commons by Parliamentary Members Fox, Nugent, Holdane, and Townsend, in Ferguson, *id.* at 1; and FRIEDBERG, *supra* note 5, at 350.

16 *Cf. Sneed v. Ewing*, 5 Ky. (1 J.J.Marsh.) 460 (1831). *Dyer v. Brannock*, 66 Mo. 391, 27 Am.Rep. 359 (1877), refers to BLACKSTONE, *supra* note 2, at 86. For specific instances regarding the reception in the colonies, *see* GEORGE ELLIOTT HOWARD, A HISTORY OF MATRIMONIAL INSTITUTIONS II 125-327, III 170-185 (1904); KOEGEL, *supra* note 11, at 58; Cook, *supra* note 16, at 352; Chilton Powell, *Marriage in Early New England*, 1 N.E.Q. 331 (1928); and John E. Semonche, *Common Law Marriage in North Carolina: A Study in Legal History*, 9 AM. J. LEGAL HIST. 320 (1965). With respect to the application of Lord Hardwicke's Act in American law, *see Cheney v. Arnold*, 15 N.Y. 345, 69 Am.Dec. 609 (1857). In *Vaigneur v. Kirk*, 2 S.C.Eq. (2 Des.) 640, 644 (1817), the court held that Lord Hardwicke's Act was not applicable in South Carolina, stating: "We must therefore resort to the law as it stood in England prior to the statute..."

17 Regarding the development of the form requirements, *see* WILLYSTINE GOODSELL, HISTORY OF THE FAMILY AS A SOCIAL AND EDUCATIONAL INSTITUTION 376 (1924); and HOWARD III, *id.* at 170. The question whether those form requirements enacted in the colonies were to be seen mandatory or simply directory has been contested, as to this specifically, *see* Fred S. Hall, *Common Law Marriage in New York State*, 30 COLUM. L. REV. 1, 2 (1930) and is unclear, *see* W.J. BROCKELBANK, LA FORMATION DU MARIAGE DANS LE DROIT DES ETATS-UNIS 250 (1935).

18 In *Rose v. Clark*, 8 Paige 574 (1841), it is stated that common law marriage constituted a part of the common law which the first English colonists brought with them to New York.

19 *See Cheseldine v. Brewer*, 1 H. & McH. 152 (1739), in which the parties lived together for 5 years and had a mutual son. Decisive for whether the son should be viewed as born within wedlock and therewith be entitled to inherit, according to the court's opinion, was whether the parties prior to the birth of the child had "consented and agreed to be man and wife, and had cohabited and copulated as such." The agreement and the cohabitation as the basis for the marriage indicate recognition of common law marriage. Nothing is said whether these circumstances would only be evidence for the existence of a ceremonial marriage. *See also* HOWARD III, *supra* note 16, at 180 fn. 1. *Compare* KOEGEL, *supra* note 11, at 76-77, who argues that *Cheseldine* only concerned the evidence of a marriage. *Cheseldine* much later was overruled in *Denison v. Denison*, 35 Md. 361 (1872), in which the court stated: "We think we are safe in

unclear to what extent it occurred in American case law during this period.[20]

Lord Hardwicke's Act became applicable in England and Wales. In Ireland and Scotland, on the other hand, the old system remained. As no new English cases arose after 1753, it was the Irish and Scottish cases heard by the House of Lords in London that primarily influenced American case law.[21] During the 1800s, when common law marriage appeared in the United States, the English cases ought to have had a greater influence than domestic decisions of the colonial period. It was the courts, however, and not legislators, that took the initiative.[22]

A consequence of the enactment of Lord Hardwicke's Act in England was that Gretna Green and other Scottish villages near the English border became refuges for English couples wishing to enter into marriage without observing the form requirements presented by Lord Hardwicke.[23] One of the historically leading cases, cited even today in American cases

---

saying that there never has been a time in the history of the State, whether before its independence of Great Britain, or since, when some ceremony or celebration was not deemed necessary to a valid marriage." The marriage however could be proven in another manner, *see Jackson v. Jackson*, 80 Md. 176 (1894). *See also Richardson v. Smith*, 80 Md. 89, 30 A. 568 (1894), for the marriage presumption as to a ceremonial marriage. The court held that "marriage can be proved by general reputation, cohabitation and acknowledgment, and when these exist it will be inferred that a religious ceremony has taken place..."

20 According to Frank Gaylard Cook, *supra* note 16, at 354, common law marriage was entirely rendered ineffective by the marital legislation's requirement of the participation of an authorized person to perform the wedding ceremony. GOODSELL, *supra* note 17, at 376, has with respect to informal relationships stated: "In such cases, except where the law expressly declared the marriage void, the offenders were liable to punishment for contracting an *illegal* marriage, but their union was not declared *invalid*." HOWARD, *id.* at 170, with respect to common law marriage has stated that "nor is it historically correct to say that in the English colonies it had been entirely supplanted by legislation..."

21 Belonging to the category of most cited cases are *Dalrymple v. Dalrymple*, (1811) 2 Hagg.Cons. 54, 161 Eng.Rep. 665; *Cunningham v. Cunningham*, (1814) 2 Dow. 483, 501; and *Campbell v. Campbell*, (The Breadalbane case) (1866) 4 M. 867, (1866), (1867) 5 M. (H.L.) 115. The Scottish influence is clear in *e.g. Fryer v. Fryer*, 9 S.C.Eq. (Rich.Cas.) 85 (1832); *Yardley's Estate*, 75 Pa. 207 (1874); *Hynes v. McDermott*, 91 N.Y. 451, 459, 43 Am.Rep. 677 (1883); and *Cargile v. Wood*, 63 Mo. 501 (1876).

22 Even if there are exceptions, it has been maintained that the courts not only follow previous case law but rather that there was even support for common law marriage. *See* MICHAEL GROSSBERG, GOVERNING THE HEART: LAW AND THE FAMILY IN NINETEENTH-CENTURY AMERICA 89 (1985): "Most of the bench and bar, though, endorsed common-law marriage not because of slavish adherence to precedent but rather because they agreed with the doctrine itself."

23 Thousands of trips to Gretna Green were taken annually, where, in the event the parties so wished, the local village blacksmith was rumored to have functioned as a "person authorized to perform a wedding ceremony." The number of trips was rumored to have been reduced when the requirement was passed in Lord Brougham's Act in 1856 that the couple must have stayed in Scotland at least three weeks in order to be able to enter into a marriage there, *see* 19, 20 Vict. c. 96. Gretna Green marriages have been recognized in other countries, *see* ERNST RABEL, THE CONFLICT OF LAWS, A COMPARATIVE STUDY I 224 (1945). Regarding Gretna Green marriages, *see* more closely JOYCE, *supra* note 11, at 135; and FRIEDBERG, *supra* note 5, at 425.

regarding common law marriage, *Dalrymple v. Dalrymple* (1811),[24] concerns a young English nobleman, John William Henry Dalrymple, who in 1804 during service in the army stayed in Scotland. There he began a relationship with a Miss Gordon that he wished to keep secret from his parents. The young couple entered into a secret written marriage contract with respect to a present, in other words, immediately effective marriage, *sponsalia de praesenti.* The marriage was consummated thereafter through *copula carnalis.* In 1805, Dalrymple left Scotland and, in 1808, he married Miss Laura Manners, entirely in accordance with the English wedding rites. Miss Gordon filed suit, claiming that the marriage between her and Mr. Dalrymple should be declared valid; Miss Manners filed a countersuit. The question was tried in accordance with Scottish law, and Sir William Scott (Lord Stowell) wrote the 249-page judgment, which has rightly been generally recognized as "a masterpiece of legal literature."[25] The court held that the informal marriage was valid, in accordance with the canon law regulations on marriage, which prior to the Council of Trent were applicable in the Christian countries on the continent, in England prior to 1753, and in Scotland at the time of the actual marriage's commencement. Therefore, the court found that the marriage with Miss Gordon was valid and that the wedded marriage with Miss Manners, on the other hand, was invalid.

The case of *Dalrymple* was followed during the 1800s by a pair of English cases in which the result was the opposite.[26] These cases, in which it was actually posited that English law never recognized informal marriages, however, have been refuted by legal historical research[27] as well as by later case law.[28] Even if these cases received certain recognition in the American case law,[29] the majority of American courts during the 1800s followed the fundamental principles conveyed in *Dalrymple* as supplemented by independent American case law.[30]

---

24 *Dalrymple v. Dalrymple,* (1811) 2 Hagg.Con. 54, 161 Eng.Rep. 665.

25 KOEGEL, *supra* note 11, at 38 (with references).

26 In *Regina v. Millis,* (1843) 10 Cl. & F. 534, 8 Eng.Rep. 844, concerning a marriage commenced in Ireland, it was even argued that English common law never recognized marriages commenced without the participation of a clergyman. *See also Beamish v. Beamish,* (1861) 11 Eng.Rep. 735, which also had Irish origins.

27 FREDERICK POLLOCK, FIRST BOOK OF JURISPRUDENCE 328 (2d ed. 1904) argues consequently that this understanding "is now believed by most competent scholars to be without any real historical foundation." In POLLOCK AND MAITLAND, *supra* note 5, at 372, it is stated: "[If] the victorious cause pleased the lords, it is the vanquished cause that will please the historian of the middle ages." *See also* JOEL PRENTISS BISHOP, NEW COMMENTARIES ON MARRIAGE, DIVORCE AND SEPARATION I §§ 400-417 (Chicago, T.H. Flood & Co. 1891); OTTO E. KOEGEL, *supra* note 11, at 49-50: "There is now no doubt that the decisions in these two cases were incorrect."

28 *Thomas v. Holtzman,* 18 D.C. 62, 7 Mackey 62 (1888).

29 In *Denison v. Denison,* 35 Md. 361 (1872), common law marriage was not recognized with reference to *Regina v. Millis.*

30 In *Hallett v. Collins,* 51 U.S. 174, 182, 10 How. 174, 13 L.Ed. 376 (1850), the United States Supreme Court stated: "Whether such marriage was sufficient by the common

Scotland recognized informal marriages until 1940, both those entered into *sponsalia de praesenti* and those constituted *sponsalia de futuro* followed by *copula carnalis*.[31] A third form of irregular marriage has existed until 2006 in Scotland, namely "marriage by cohabitation with habit and repute"[32] and is further discussed in Chapter 11, "Scottish Irregular Marriages."

It has been argued that canon law from before the Council of Trent found its way into American case law, not only via English and Scottish law, but also via the Spanish colonies. Despite the fact that Spain adopted the *Forma Tridentina*, it should not have been applicable in the Spanish territories.[33] American jurisdictions in the Spanish territories that did not apply mandatory form requirements, therefore, could have applied common law marriage. The United States Supreme Court consequently found in *Hallett v. Collins* (1850), with respect to a cohabitation occurring between 1805 and 1810 in what is now Alabama, that the applicable form requirements ought to be interpreted in accordance with the medieval canon law and that consent alone, joined with the will to marry, constitutes marriage.[34] The question of whether the

---

law in England, previous to the marriage act, has been disputed of later years in that country, though never doubted here." In *Davis v. Stouffer*, 132 Mo.App. 555, 112 S.W. 282 (1908), it was held that *Regina v. Millis* did not give expression for English common law as understood by American courts and legislators and that these are not obligated to follow newly launched understandings in England concerning that which there had been common law. In *Carmichael v. State*, 12 Ohio St. 553 (1861), the court held that, even if *Regina v. Millis* would have correctly understood the content in English common law, it recognized on its own behalf marriage *per verba de praesenti*.

31 Marriage Act 1939, 2,3 Geo. VI, c. 34, which entered in force July 1, 1940. Marriages that before this had been entered into formlessly however remained valid, *see* sections 5 and 8. With respect to Scottish law, *see* PATRIC FRASER, HUSBAND AND WIFE ACCORDING TO THE LAW OF SCOTLAND I 294 (2 ed. 1876); W.M. GLOAG AND R. CANDLISH HENDERSON, INTRODUCTION TO THE LAW OF SCOTLAND 663 (7 ed. 1968); FREDERICK PARKER WALTON, A HANDBOOK OF HUSBAND AND WIFE ACCORDING TO THE LAW OF SCOTLAND 25 (3 ed. 1951); ERIC M. CLIVE AND JOHN G. WILSON, THE LAW OF HUSBAND AND WIFE IN SCOTLAND 107 (1974); and ERIC M. CLIVE, THE LAW OF HUSBAND AND WIFE IN SCOTLAND 40 (4th ed. 1997).

32 *See* Family Law (Scotland) Bill, SP Bill 36B, Session 2 (2005), 2A. The new law, "FAMILY LAW (SCOTLAND) ACT (2006), is not retroactively applicable as to relationships entered into prior to the law's validity. This presumed marriage, based on a rebuttable *praesumtio iuris*, has support in a parliamentary decision from 1503, c. 77. *See* FRIEDBERG, *supra* note 5, at 450.

33 *Hallett v. Collins*, 51 U.S. 174, 182, 10 How. 174, 13 L.Ed. 376 (1850). *Cf. Patton v. Philadelphia*, 1 La.Ann. 98 (1846).

34 *Hallett v. Collins*, 51 U.S. 174, 182 (1850). Other Spanish colonies applied form requirements that constituted impediments against common law marriage. *See, e.g.*, with respect to New Mexico, *In re Gabaldon's Estate*, 38 N.M. 392, 34 P.2d 672 (1934). Other states under Mexican influence recognized common law marriage, e.g. Texas, Arizona and California. Texas still recognizes common law marriage. With respect to the Spanish and Mexican influence on American law, *see* Woodrow Borah & Sherburne F. Cook, *Marriage and Legitimacy in Mexican Culture: Mexico and California*, 54 CAL. L. REV. 946 (1966); and Cynthia Grant, Bowmant, *A Feminist Proposal to Bring Back Common Law Marriage*, 75 OR. L. REV. 709 (1996).

Forma Tridentina became applicable in the Spanish colonies, however, is debated.[35]

4.2.2 The American Reception in the 1800s and at the Beginning of the 1900s

Guiding for the American development was *Fenton v. Reed* (1809), in which the New York Supreme Court, without reference to previous American case law, however citing three English cases, stated: "No formal solemnization of marriage was requisite. A contract of marriage made *per verba de praesenti* amounts to an actual marriage, and is as valid as if made in facie ecclesiae ..."[36] The decision, which was not signed individually, has been ascribed to Chancellor James Kent,[37] then the chief justice of that court, who in 1826 published his Commentaries on American Law.[38] Although the case has generated criticism due to its weak legal basis,[39] it was an *obiter dictum* that, as well as Kent's book, achieved remarkable success and regularly was cited during the entire 1800s in support of recognizing common law marriage.[40]

---

35 *See In re Gabaldon's Estate,* 38 N.M. 392, 34 P.2d 672, 679 (1934).

36 *Fenton v. Reed,* 4 Johns. 52 (N.Y. 1809). (Per Curiam). As support, bare references are given *inter alia* to three English cases without any presentation of their content. In one, *Collins v. Jessot,* (1704) 6 Mod. 155, Eng.Rep. 913, the court stated that "if the contract be *per verba de praesenti* it amounts to an actual marriage which the parties themselves cannot dissolve..." In *Reed v. Passer,* (1794) Peake's Cases 231, 170 Eng. Rep. 164, the court deemed, without committing itself, that "even an agreement *per verba de praesenti was ipsum matrimonium*"; and *Alleyn v. Gray,* (1689) 2 Salk. 437, 91 Eng.Rep. 380. In *Fenton,* cited as support for the marriage presumption is also *Morris v. Miller,* (1767) 4 Burr. 2057.

37 Koegel, *supra* note 11, at 80 fn. 1; Hall, *supra* note 17, at 4; and Grossberg, *supra* note 22, at 71.

38 Kent, *supra* note 3.

39 *Compare* Cook, *supra* note 16, at 352, who argues that the doctrine "seems hardly to have been bourne out by the English cases cited. In fact, this doctrine was novel to American courts." *See further* Hall, *supra* note 17, at 3, who has maintained that the result in *Fenton v. Reed* was based on a mistake that consisted of the court not paying attention to the fact that English colonial marital laws, containing unconditional form requirements, were still applicable, as the state of New York had not yet enacted its own legislation. Powell, *supra* note 16, at 334, argues that the judgment "was obviously without precedent in America." Other critics have based their arguments upon English cases that did not accept formless marriages such as *Regina v. Millis,* (1843) 10 Cl. & F. 534, 8 Eng.Rep. 844; and *Beamish v. Beamish,* (1861) 11 Eng.Rep. 735. *See also Milford v. Worchester,* 7 Mass. 48 (1810); and *Denison v. Denison,* 34 Md. 361 (1871).

40 References to *Fenton v. Reed* can be found in many American cases from all states during the entire 1800s, *see, e.g., Pearson v. Howey,* 6 Halstead 12 (N.J. 1829); *Newbury v. Brunswick,* 2 Vt. 151, 19 Am.D. 703 (1829); *Tarpley v. Poage's Adm'r,* 2 Tex. 139, 149 (1847); *Graham v. Bennett,* 2 Cal. 503 (1852); *Duncan v. Duncan,* 10 Ohio St. 181, 184, 1859 WL 67 (1859); *Askew v. Dupree,* 30 Ga. 173 (1860); *Carmichael v. State,* 12 Ohio St. 553 (1861); *Hutchins v. Kimmell,* 31 Mich. 126, 18 Am.Rep. 164 (1875); *Blanchard v. Lambert,* 43 Iowa 228, 22 Am.Rep. 245 (1876); *United States v. Simpson,* 4 Utah 227, 7 P. 257 (1885); *Thomas v. Holtzman,* 18 D.C. 62, 7 Mackey 62, 66 (1888); and *Odd Fellows Beneficial Ass'n v. Carpenter,* 17 R.I. 720, 24 A. 578 (1892). During the 1900s,

Even though several other American cases also cited Scottish and older English decisions,[41] it is no exaggeration to say that Kent implanted the doctrine of common law marriage in the United States, though he certainly did not create it. Kent's contribution, however, appears not to have been rooted in political conviction, but rather in the authority he ascribed to the English, canon, and Roman sources of law, as discussed further below. During the first part of the 1800s, the doctrine was also supported by other leading scholars such as Tapping Reeve[42] and Simon Greenleaf[43] and during the later part of the century, primarily by Joel Bishop.[44]

Fenton v. Reed was followed in the 1800s by several other cases in the state of New York.[45] Several years after *Fenton,* the Pennsylvania Supreme Court in *Hantz v. Sealy* (1814) gave expression to its support of common law marriage through the following statement: "Marriage is in law a civil contract, and does not require any particular form of solemnization before officers of church or state." Despite the fact that this only constituted *dictum,* it came to have repercussions in Pennsylvania, which eventually would have extensive case law in the area and which until recent years has

---

see also Travers v. Reinhardt, 205 U.S. 423, 436, 27 S.Ct. 563, 51 L.Ed 865 (1906); *Applegate v. Applegate,* 118 Misc.Rep. 359, 193 N.Y.S. 494 (Sup.Ct. 1922); *Fisher v. Fisher,* 250 N.Y. 313, 165 N.E. 460 (1929); and *Allen v. State,* 60 Ga.App. 248, 3 S.E.2d 780, 782 (1939).

41 *See, e.g., Askew v. Dupree,* 30 Ga. 173 (1860); *Carmichael v. State,* 12 Ohio St. 553 (1861); *Port v. Port,* 70 Ills. 484 (1873); *Travers v. Reinhardt,* 205 U.S. 423, 27 S.Ct. 563, 51 L.Ed 865 (1906); *Quinn v. Phipps,* 93 Fla. 805, 113 So. 419, 425, 54 A.L.R. 1173 (1927); and *Orr v. State,* 129 Fla. 398, 176 So. 510 (1937).

42 Tapping Reeve, The Law of Husband and Wife (New York 1816) (3 ed. 1867).

43 Simon Greenleaf, A Treatise on the Law of Evidence (1842); (Boston 2 ed. 1846); (3 ed. 1852); and (16 ed. 1899).

44 Joel Prentiss Bishop, Commentaries on the Law of Marriage and Divorce and Evidence in Matrimonial Suits (Boston 1852) (2d ed. 1856); and New Comm., *supra* note 27.

45 *Jackson v. Claw,* 18 Johns. 346 (1820); *Jackson v. Winne,* 7 Wend. (N.Y.) 47, 22 Am.Dec. 563 (1831); *Jenkins v. Bisbee,* 1 Edw.Ch. 377 (N.Y.1832); *Rose v. Clark,* 8 Paige 574 (N.Y. 1841); *Starr v. Peck,* 1 Hill. 270 (N.Y. 1841); *In re Taylor,* 9 Paige 611 (1842); *Hicks v. Cochran,* 4 Edw.Ch. 107 (N.Y. 1843); *Clayton v. Wardell,* 5 Barb. 2144, 4 N.Y. 230 (1850); *Tummalty v. Tummalty,* 3 Bradf. 369 (N.Y. 1855); *Grotgen v. Grotgen,* 3 Bradf. 373 (N.Y. 1855); *Cunningham v. Burdell,* 4 Bradf. 343 (N.Y. 1858); *Hayes v. People,* 25 N.Y. 390, 82 Am.Dec. 364 (1862); *Richwell v. Tunnicliff,* 6 Barb. 408 (N.Y. 1862); *O'Gara v. Eisenlohr,* 38 N.Y. 296 (1868); *Van Tuyl v. Van Tuyl,* 57 Barb. 235 (1869); *Bissell v. Bissell,* 55 Barb. 325 (N.Y. 1869); *Wright v. Wright,* 48 How.Pr. 1 (N.Y. 1874); *Davis v. Davis,* 7 Daily 308 (N.Y.1877); *People ex. rel. Comm. of Public Charities and Corrections v. Bartholf,* 24 Hun. 272 (N.Y. 1881); *Badger v. Badger,* 88 N.Y. 546, 42 Am.Rep. 263 (1882); *Betsinger v. Chapman,* 88 N.Y. 487 (1882); *Hynes v. McDermott,* 91 N.Y. 451, 453, 43 Am.Rep. 677 (1883); *Newton v. Southworth* 46 Hun 32, 7 N.Y.S.R. 130 (1887); and *Wilcox v. Wilcox,* 46 Hun 32, 10 N.Y.S.R. 746 (1887). In *Gall v. Gall,* 114 N.Y. 109, 21 N.E. 106 (1889), the court stated: "A present agreement between competent parties to take each other for husband and wife constitutes a valid marriage, even if not in the presence of witnesses ... Such marriage may be proved by showing actual cohabitation as husband and wife, acknowledgment, declarations, conduct, repute, reception among neighbors and the like." *See also Bates v. Bates,* 27 N.Y.Supp. 872 (1894); *In re Brush,* 49 N.Y.S. 803 (1 st Dep't 1898); and *Atlantic City R. Co. v. Goodin,* 72 Am.St.Rep. 652, 42 A. 333 (1898).

accepted the doctrine.[46] During the early 1800s, common law marriage received support in the case law from states spread from the north to the south. From the 1820s, it was mentioned in New Hampshire,[47] whose support after a period was reduced to a partial recognition; Kentucky;[48] and New Jersey;[49] as well as Vermont,[50] whose support was soon overruled by later decisions. During the 1830s, the stance was adopted by the courts in South Carolina, which today still recognizes common law marriage. In *Fryer v. Fryer*, the District of Columbia Court of Appeals held that the law "requires nothing but the agreement of the parties, with an intention that the agreement shall, per se, constitute the marriage."[51]

46 *Hantz v. Sealy*, 6 Binn. 405, 412 (Pa. 1814); *Chambers v. Dickson*, 2 S. & R. 475, 476 (1816); *Rodebaugh v. Sanks*, 2 Watts 9 (Pa. 1833); *Guardians of the Poor v. Nathans*, 2 Brewst. 149 (Pa. 1845); and *Physick's Estate*, 2 Brewster 179 (1862). The citation is later given *inter alia* in *Com. v. Stump*, 53 Pa. 132, 136 (1866); *Richard v. Brehm*, 73 Pa. 140 (1873); *Yardley's Estate*, 75 Pa. 207 (1874); *Greenawalt v. McEnelley*, 85 Pa. 352 (1877); *Hunt's Appeal*, 86 Pa. 294 (1878); *Markley v. Baldwin*, 112 U.S. 490 (1884); *Grimm's Est.*, 131 Pa. 199, 18 A. 1061 (1890); *Strauss's Estate*, 168 Pa. 561, 32 A. 98 (1895); *Grieve's Estate*, 165 Pa. 126 (1895); *Durning v. Hastings*, 183 Pa. 210 (1897); and *In re Hines's Estate*, 7 Pa.Dist.R. 89, 20 Pa.Co.Ct. 445 (1897), *aff'd*, 10 Pa.Super.Ct. 124 (1899).

47 *Londonderry v. Chester*, 2 N.H. 268, 278, 9 Am.Dec. 61 (1820). Compare on the other hand, *Dunbarton v. Franklin*, 19 N.H. 257 (1848). According to the legislation from 1842, New Hampshire only partially recognizes common law marriage. Upon cases of death, the surviving party receives the same rights as a spouse, assuming that the cohabitation had been at least three years, *see* RS 149:11 (1842). The law is still in force today, *see* N.H. REV. STAT. ANN. 457:39 (West 2003).

48 *Dumaresly v. Fishly*, 10 Ky. 368 (1821); and *Donnelly v. Donnelly*, 8 Ky. (1 B. Mon.) 113, 116 (App. 1847). Common law marriage was repealed by legislation in Kentucky in 1852. *See Estill v. Rogers*, 1 Bush 62 (1866); and *Harris v. Harris*, 85 Ky. 49, 2 S.W. 549 (1887). In *Robinson v. Redd*, 19 Ky. L.Rep. 1422; 43 S.W. 435 (1897), the court held that "since the adoption of the Revised Statutes, there can be no such thing as legal marriage by cohabitation and recognition alone. All marriages not solemnized or contracted in the presence of an authorized person or society are absolutely void."

49 *Wyckoff v. Boggs*, 2 Halst. 138 (1824); *Pearson v. Howey*, 6 Halst. 12 (N.J. 1829); *Applegate v. Applegate*, 45 N.J.Eq. 116, 17 A. 293 (1889); *Voorhees v. Voorhees*, 46 N.J.Eq. 411, 19 Am.St.Rep. 404 (1890); *Atlantic City R. Co. v. Goodin*, 72 Am.St.Rep. 652, 42 A. 333 (1898); *Stevens v. Stevens*, 56 N.J.Eq. 488, 38 A. 460 (1898); *Chamberlain v. Chamberlain*, 68 N.J.Eq. 736, 62 A. 813 (Ch. 1905), *aff'd*, 68 N.J.Eq. 736, 62 A. 680, 681 (E.&A. 1905); and *Travers v. Reinhardt*, 25 App.D.C. 567, 205 U.S. 423, 51 L.ed. 865, 27 Sup. Ct.Rep. 563 (1907).

50 *Newbury v. Brunswick*, 2 Vt. 151, 19 Am.D. 703 (1829). In *Mountholly v. Andower*, 11 Vt. 226 (1839), a ceremonial marriage was found invalid as the parties did not consent to the marriage. In *dictum*, the court states: "A marriage *per verba de praesenti*, followed by cohabitation, is valid, although no marriage ceremony is celebrated." *Compare Northfield v. Plymoth*, 20 Vt. 582 (1848). *See later Morrill v. Palmer*, 68 Vt. 1, 23, 33 A. 829 (1895), maintaining that common law marriage was never recognized in Vermont.

51 *Fryer v. Fryer*, 9 S.C.Eq. (Rich.Cas.) 85, 92 (1832). Regarding the significance of *Fryer* for the spread of the marriage presumption and implied agreements, *see* Chapter 7 *infra*. *See also Jewell v. Magwood*, 9 S.C.Eq. (Rich.Cas.) 113, 114 (1833) ("Certainly, by our law, marriage is regarded only as a civil contract..."); *Lucken v. Wichman*, 5 S.C. 411, 414 (1874); and *Davenport v. Caldwell*, 10 S.C. 317 (1877). Compare *Vaigneur v. Kirk*, 2 S.C.Eq. (2 Des.) 640, 644 (1817).

Support for common law marriage also came, at the same time, from Louisiana.[52]

It was, however, during the latter part of the 1800s in which recognition of common law marriage truly accelerated. In Mississippi, the doctrine was adopted in the middle of the 1850s.[53] During the 1860s, it won judicial acceptance in three states that to the present day have been true to this viewpoint. In Georgia, *Askew v. Dupree* (1860) was decided, including a thorough discussion of the issue with references to Roman, canon, English, and Scottish law, as well as American cases such as *Fenton v. Reed,* and the domestic literature mentioned above, which by now supported common law marriage.[54] Thereafter, Ohio[55] and Alabama followed. In the latter state, which has an extensive case law on this subject, its supreme court stated in *Campbell v. Gullatt* (1869): "The great weight of authority, as well as of reason, is in favor of the proposition that, marriage by mere consent of the parties, especially if followed by cohabitation, is good."[56]

52 In *Holmes v. Holmes,* 6 La. 463, 26 Am.Dec. 482 (1834), the court stated: "Marriage is regarded by our law in no other light than as a civil contract, highly favored, and depending essentially on the free consent of the parties capable by law of contracting. Our Code does not declare null a marriage not preceded by a license and not evidenced by an act signed by a certain number of witnesses and the parties." *See also Patton v. Philadelphia,* 1 La.Ann. 98 (1846). *Compare Johnson v. Raphael,* 117 La. 967, 42 So. 470 (1906), in which the court held that the legislation "surely contemplated some kind of public celebration of the contract of marriage."

53 *Hargroves v. Thompson,* 31 Miss. 211 (1856); *Dickerson v. Brown,* 49 Miss. 357 (1873); *Wilkie v. Collins,* 48 Miss. 496 (1873); *Rundle v. Pegram,* 49 Miss. 751 (1874); *Taylor v. State,* 52 Miss. 84, 2 Am.Crim.Rep. 13 (1876); and *Floyd v. Calvert,* 53 Miss. 37 (1876). Mississippi repealed common law marriage in 1956, MISS. CODE ANN. § 465.5 (1956).

54 *Askew v. Dupree,* 30 Ga. 173, 178 (1860). *Compare already Park v. Barron,* 20 Ga. 702, 65 Am.Dec. 641 (1856). *See further Clark v. Cassidy,* 64 Ga. 662 (1880); *Jenkins v. Jenkins,* 83 Ga. 286, 9 S.E. 541 (1889); *Smith v. Smith,* 84 Ga. 440, 11 S.E. 496 (1890); and *Dale v. State,* 88 Ga. 552, 15 S.E. 287, 288-289 (1891), in which the court states that "a mutual agreement to be husband and wife, by parties able to contract, followed by cohabitation, is recognized as a valid marriage." Common law marriage was repealed in Georgia in 1996, GA. CODE ANN. §§ 19-3-1, 19-3-1.1 (1996). Relationships entered into prior to January 1, 1997 are still valid. The state has an extensive case law analyzed in the following chapters.

55 *Carmichael v. State,* 12 Ohio St. 553, 560-561 (1861). After references *inter alia* to English and Scottish cases as well as domestic literature (Bishop), the court stated: "It was a contract of present marriage – openly made, and followed by cohabitation as husband and wife – and we think was a valid marriage under the laws of this state." *See also Holtz v. Dick,* 42 Ohio St. 23, 51 Am.Rep. 791 (1884); *Pearce v. Pearce,* 13 Ky. L.Rep. 67, 16 S.W. 271 (1891); *Johnson v. Dudley,* 3 Ohio N.P. 196 (1896); *Swartz v. State,* 7 Ohio C.D. 43, 13 Ohio C.C. 62 (1896); and *Wilson v. Allen,* 108 Ga. 275 (1899).

56 *Campbell v. Gullatt,* 43 Ala. 57, 63 (1869). *See* already the *dictum* in *State v. Murphy,* 6 Ala. 765, 771 (1844). *Compare Robertson v. State,* 42 Ala. 509 (1868). *See further Williams v. State,* 54 Ala. 131, 25 Am.Rep. 665 (1875); *Beggs v. State,* 55 Ala. 108, 112 (1876); *Parker v. State,* 77 Ala. 47, 54 Am.Rep. 43 (1884); *Farley v. Farley,* 10 So. 646 (Ala. 1892); *Ashley v. State,* 109 Ala. 48, 19 So. 917 (1895); *Mickle v. State,* 21 So. 66 (Ala. 1896); *Moore v. Heineke,* 119 Ala. 627, 24 So. 374 (1898); *Bynon v. State,* 117 Ala. 80, 23 So. 640 (1898); and *Tartt v. Negus,* 127 Ala. 301, 28 So. 713 (1899). Alabama has an extensive case law from the 1900s analyzed in the following chapters.

In the 1870s, common law marriage was recognized by the courts in Illinois,[57] Arkansas,[58] and Iowa, a state that still today recognizes common law marriage. In *Blanchard v. Lambert* (1876), the Iowa Supreme Court consequently held: "It is a settled rule of the common law that any mutual agreement between the parties to be husband and wife, *in presenti*, followed by cohabitation, constitutes a valid and binding marriage, if there is no legal disability on the part of either to contract matrimony." The court further held that "in this state no express form is necessary, more than at common law, to constitute a valid marriage."[59]

During the 1870s, common law marriage also gained a foothold in the legislation of several states. In California, case law had supported the common law marriage doctrine since the beginning of the 1850s,[60] but in a definitive breakthrough in 1872, the state regulated the doctrine through legislation, which was very unusual in the United States. The California Civil Code held: "Marriage is a personal relation arising out of a civil contract, to which the consent of parties capable of making it is necessary. Consent alone will not constitute marriage; it must be followed by a solemnization, or by a mutual assumption of marital rights, duties, or obligations."[61] Similar legislation was enacted in 1877 in the Territory of

---

57 *Port v. Port*, 70 Ill. 484 (1873); *Hebletwaite v. Hepworth*, 98 Ill. 126 (1880); *Bowman v. Bowman*, 24 Ill.App. 165 (1887); *Cartwright v. McGown*, 121 Ill. 388, 12 N.E. 737 (1887); and *Crymble v. Crymble*, 50 Ill.App. 544 (1893). In *Hiler v. People*, 156 Ill. 511, 47 Am.St.Rep. 221 (1895), the court held that "a marriage legal at common law is recognized as valid and binding in this State. What constitutes such common-law marriages legal and valid has been recognized by repeated adjudications." The court, however, did not find a marriage proven. *See also Laurence v. Laurence*, 164 Ill. 374, 45 N.E. 1071 (1896); *Elzas v. Elzas*, 171 Ill. 632, 49 N.E. 717 (1898); *Hooper v. McCaffery*, 83 Ill.App. 341 (1898); and *McKenna v. McKenna*, 180 Ill. 577, 54 N.E. 641 (1899). Common law marriage was repealed in Illinois through an amendment to § 4, Marriage Act, which entered in force July 1, 1905. *See Wilson v. Cook*, 256 Ill. 460, 100 N.E. 222 (1912).

58 *Jones v. Jones*, 28 Ark. 19 (1872); *Darling v. Dent*, 82 Ark. 76, 100 S.W. 747 (1907). Compare *Furth v. Furth*, 97 Ark. 272, 133 S.W.2d 1037 (1911), which did not recognize common law marriage.

59 *Blanchard v. Lambert*, 43 Iowa 228, 231, 22 Am.Rep. 245 (1876). *See also McFarland v. McFarland*, 51 Iowa 565, 2 N.W. 269 (1879); *Leach v. Hall*, 95 Iowa 611, 64 N.W. 790 (1895).

60 In *Graham v. Bennett*, 2 Cal. 503 (1852), in which the parties drafted a written marriage contract, the court stated: "Marriage is regarded as a civil contract, and no form is necessary for its solemnization. If it takes place between parties able to contract, an open avowal of the intention, and an assumption of the relative duties which it imposes on each other, is sufficient to render it valid and binding."

61 CALIFORNIA CIVIL CODE § 55 (1872), Code of March 21, 1872. *See further Estate of Beverson*, 47 Cal. 621 (1874); *In re McCausland's Estate*, 52 Cal. 568, 577 (1878); *Case v. Case*, 52 Cal. 568 (1878); *In re Jessup's Estate*, 81 Cal. 408, 21 P. 976, 22 P. 742 (1889); *Sharon v. Sharon*, 75 Cal. 1, 16 p. 345, 79 Cal. 633, 22 P. 26, (1889); *White v. White*, 82 Cal. 427, 23 P. 276 (1890); *Kilburn v. Kilburn*, 89 Cal. 46, 26 P. 636, 637 (1891); *People v. Beevers*, 99 Cal. 286, 33 P. 844 (1893); *People v. Lehman*, 104 Cal. 631, 38 P. 422 (1894); *Toon v. Huberty*, 104 Cal. 260, 37 P. 944 (1894); *Hinckley v. Ayres*, 105 Cal. 357, 38 P. 735 (1895); *Hunter v. Milam*, 41 P. 332 (Cal. 1895); *In re Ruffino*, 116 Cal. 304, 48 P. 127 (1897); *Harron v. Harron*, 128 Cal. 308, 60 P. 932 (1900); *In re Richards*, 133 Cal. 524, 65 P. 1034 (1901); and *In re Baldwin's Estate*, 162 Cal. 471, 123 P. 267, 275 (1912).

Dakota[62] and in Idaho, which recognized the doctrine until 1995 and still applies it to relationships entered into before 1995.[63] In Montana, common law marriage was also codified somewhat later through a comparable regulation that later received a different formation.[64] Montana still recognizes common law marriage today.

The United States Supreme Court, for the first time, took a stance on the validity of a common law marriage in Michigan in *Meister v. Moore* (1877). The court cited with approval a statement from *Hutchins v. Kimmel* (1875), in which the Michigan Supreme Court stated: "[I]f the parties agreed to take each other for husband and wife, and from that time lived together professedly in that relation, proof of these facts would be sufficient to constitute proof of a marriage ... This has become the settled doctrine of the American courts."[65] Even if the statement actually was *dictum*,

---

In 1895, California became the first state to repeal common law marriage through legislation, *see* Act of March 26 (1895); Assembly Bill No. 567 (1895); Senate Bill No. 91 (1895). *See also Norman v. Norman*, 121 Cal. 620, 54 P. 143 (1898).

62 *See* § 34 of THE REVISED CODES OF THE TERRITORY OF DAKOTA (Geo. H. Hand ed. 1877). Section 45 expressly prescribed that non-compliance with the form requirements did not invalidate any lawful marriage. Before the 1877 amendment, the consent of the parties was "alone necessary," *see* § 34 of the Civil Code of the Territory of Dakota (1866). According to § 37 a consent *de praesenti* was required, *i.e.* to a marriage commencing instantly, and not to an agreement to marry afterwards. When South Dakota became a state in 1889, common law marriage possessed continued recognition, *see e.g. Henry v. Taylor*, 16 S.D. 424, 93 N.W. 641 (1903); *Swendsen v. Swendsen*, 37 S.D. 353,158 N.W. 410 (1916); *Bracken v. Bracken*, 45 S.D. 430, 188 N.W. 46 (1922); *Agnew v. Agnew*, 58 S.D. 164, 235 N.W. 644 (1931); *Beuck v. Howe*, 71 S.D. 288, 23 N.W.2d 744 (1946); and *In re Erickson's Estate*, 75 S.D. 345, 64 N.W.2d 316, 318 (1954). Common law marriage was repealed in South Dakota in 1959, *see* S.D. CODE ANN. § 14.0101 (Sup. 1960).

63 1877, p. 24, § 1; R.S., § 2420; reen. R.C. & C.L., § 2611; C.S., § 4591; I.C.A., § 31-201; I.C. 32-201. *Huff v. Huff*, 20 Idaho 450, 118 P. 1080, 1083 (1911) cites R.S. § 2611, which has had the same wording to the present day: "Marriage is a personal relation arising out of a civil contract, to which the consent of parties capable of making it is necessary. Consent alone will not constitute marriage; it must be followed by a solemnization, or by a mutual assumption of marital rights, duties or obligations." Cited also in *Huff* is § 2620: "Marriage must be solemnized, authenticated and recorded as provided in this chapter, but noncompliance with its provisions does not invalidate any lawful marriage," *see* 1877, p. 24 § 8; R.S., § 2425; reen. R.C. & C.L., § 2620; C.S., § 4600; I.C.A., § 31-301; I.C. 32-301. In Idaho, common law marriage was repealed beginning 1996, *see* H.B. 176; Chap. 104, 1995 Idaho Session Laws. Common law marriage, however, is still applicable as to relationships entered into prior to 1996.

64 Montana Constitution, Code & Statutes, Civil Code, Division I, section 50 (1895): "Consent alone will not constitute marriage; it must be followed by a solemnization, or by mutual and public assumption of the marital relation." A similar regulation can be found in section 3607 R.C. (1907), section 5695 R.C. (1921) and section 48-101 R.C.M. (1947). The regulation was repealed through Session law, chapter 536 (1975). The present M.C.A. 40-1-403 (2003) has a different formation. *Cf. Hadley v. Rash*, 21 Mont. 170, 53 P. 312 (1898) regarding legal presumptions.

65 *Hutchins v. Kimmel*, 31 Mich. 126, 130, 18 Am.Rep. 164 (1875); *Peet v. Peet*, 52 Mich. 464, 18 N.W. 220 (1884) ("An actual ceremony of marriage is not essential to the establishment of the relation of husband and wife"); *Brooke v. Brooke*, 60 Mich. 464 (1884); *Clancy v. Clancy*, 66 Mich. 202, 33 N.W. 889 (1887); *People v. McQuaid*, 85 Mich. 127, 48 N.W. 161 (1891); *Williams v. Kilburn*, 88 Mich. 279, 50 N.W. 293 (1891); *Van*

the United States Supreme Court understood it to be an authoritative declaration concerning the recognition of common law marriage. The court further held that with respect to an informal marriage through a contract *per verba de praesenti*: "That such a contract constitutes a marriage at common law there can be no doubt, in view of the adjudications made in this country, from its earliest settlement to the present day."[66] In addition to *Fenton v. Reed, Meister v. Moore* is the case most cited as support for common law marriage. That same year, the courts in Missouri[67] and Minnesota[68] gave recognition to common law marriage and a couple years later, Wisconsin followed.[69]

During the 1880s, common law marriage was recognized in Florida,[70] Indiana,[71] Arizona,[72] Utah,[73] and Kansas, which still recognizes the doctrine.

Dusan v. Van Dusan, 97 Mich. 70 (1893); *People v. Mendenhall*, 119 Mich. 404, 78 N.W. 325 (1899); *Flanagan v. Flanagan*, 122 Mich. 386, 81 N.W. 258 (1899) and *Lorimer v. Lorimer*, 124 Mich. 631, 83 N.W. 609 (1900). Michigan repealed common law marriage in 1957, *see* MICH. STAT. ANN. § 25.2 (1957).

66 *Meister v. Moore*, 96 U.S. 76, 78 (1877). In *Meister*, a man had married a Native American woman at a ceremony deviating from the wedding rites valid in the state, which, in the absence of any express regulation prescribing that common law marriage was invalid, were considered to be simply directory. Compare, *Jewell v. Jewell*, 42 U.S. (1 Howard) 219 (1843), in which the Court was split and did not reach a final decision. For later cases, *see Markley v. Baldwin*, 112 U.S. 490 (1884); and *Travers v. Reinhardt*, 25 App.D.C. 567, 205 U.S. 423, 51 L.ed. 865, 27 Sup.Ct.Rep. 563 (1907).

67 *Dyer v. Brannock*, 66 Mo. 391, 27 Am.Rep. 359 (1877); *Waddingham v. Waddingham*, 21 Mo.App. 609 (1886); *State v. Bittick*, 103 Mo. 183, 15 S.W. 325 (1891); and *State v. Cooper*, 103 Mo. 266, 15 S.W. 325 (1890). *Compare Cargile v. Wood*, 63 Mo. 501 (1876).

68 *State v. Wortingham*, 23 Minn. 528 (1877); *In re Terry*, 58 Minn. 268, 59 N.W. 1015 (1894); *Hulett v. Carey*, 66 Minn. 327, 69 N.W. 31, 34 L.R.A. 384, 61 Am.St.Rep. 419 (1896); and *State v. Lowell*, 80 N.W. 877 (Minn. 1899).

69 *Williams v. Williams*, 46 Wis. 464, 32 Am.Rep. 722, 1 N.W. 98 (1879); *Spencer v. Pollock*, 83 Wis. 215 (1892); and *Becker v. Becker*, 153 Wis. 226, 140 N.W. 1082 (1913). Common law marriage was repealed in Wisconsin through "the Uniform Marriage and Marriage License Act (1917)."

70 *Daniels v. Sams*, 17 Fla. 487 (1880). *Compare Burns v. Burns*, 13 Fla. 369 (1869). *See further Caras v. Hendrix*, 62 Fla. 446, 57 So. 345 (1912); *Warren v. Warren*, 66 Fla. 138, 63 So. 726 (1913); *Green v. State*, 21 Fla. 403 (1885); *Banks v. Banks*, 42 Fla. 362, 29 So. 318 (1900); *Arendall v. Arendall*, 61 Fla. 496, 54 So. 957 (1911); *Caras v. Hendrix, 62 Fla. 446*, 57 So. 345 (1912); *Bagdads Land & Lumber Co. v. Poston*, 69 Fla. 340, 68 So. 180 (1915); *Green v. Green*, 77 Fla. 101, 80 So. 739 (1919); *Chaves v. Chaves*, 79 Fla. 602, 84 So. 672 (1920); and *Marsicano v. Marsicano*, 79 Fla. 278, 84 So. 156 (1920). Common law marriage was repealed in Florida on January 1, 1968, *see* FLA. STAT. ANN. § 741.211.

71 *Teter v. Teter*, 101 Ind. 129, 51 Am.Rep. 742 (1884); and *Meehan v. Edward Valve and Mfg. Co.*, 65 Ind.App. 342, 117 N.E. 265, 266 (1917). In *Bowers v. Van Winkle*, 41 Ind. 432 (1872), the court held: "It is a general rule that in civil suits, except for criminal conversation, cohabitation and reputation are sufficient evidence." Compare already *Dumaresly v. Fishly*, 10 Ky. 368 (1821), in which the court makes the statement with respect to Indiana law. Indiana repealed common law marriage in 1957, *see* IND. ANN. STAT. 44.111 (Supp. 1959).

72 *United States v. Tenney*, 2 Ariz. 127, 11 P. 472 (1885).

73 *United States v. Simpson*, 4 Utah 227, 7 P. 257-258 (1885): "No form or ceremony is required, and no record of marriage is kept. Marriage is left as it was at common law, and a consensual marriage is, in all respects, valid." *See also Hilton v. Roylance*, 25 Utah 129, 69 P. 660 (1902), which concerned a marriage commenced in 1872. The Utah Supreme Court held that "in case of marriage, no particular form of words is necessary.

In *State v. Walker* (1887), the Kansas Supreme Court found an informal relationship to be a valid common law marriage, despite the fact that it was criminally punishable. The court stated that "When persons who are permitted to marry 'live together as man and wife,' it may be taken as an expression of consent; and consent, under these circumstances, is sufficient as we have seen, to constitute a marriage at common law."[74] This statement raises issues concerning the function of cohabitation as an evidentiary fact and as a necessary requisite as more closely analyzed in Chapters 7, "Implied Marriage Agreements," and 8, "Cohabitation, Holding Out, and Reputation as Spouses," respectively. Even Rhode Island, the smallest state, and still recognizing common law marriage, had its first cases at the end of the 1800s, in which the courts stated a support for common law marriage.[75]

During the last decade of the 1800s, common law marriage also won recognition in Colorado, another state still recognizing the doctrine. In *Israel v. Arthur* (1897), the Colorado Supreme Court stated: "Though there was no express proof of a formal ceremony of marriage, *in facie ecclesiae*, or by a civil magistrate, yet, from all the evidence and circumstances of the case, the court was warranted in finding that plaintiff in error, had actually contracted and consummated a marriage with Israel before the death of her first husband."[76] This recognition gave rise early to different views in Colorado case law concerning the legal character of cohabitation with the

---

If, in language mutually understood, or by acts declaratory of intention, the parties accept each other as husband and wife, the marriage is consummated." *See also Riddle v. Riddle*, 26 Utah 268, 72 P. 1081 (1903). Common law marriage was repealed in Utah already in 1888 through the Act of March 8, 1888, ch. 45, § 2 (3), Utah Laws 88, 89 (1888), but was reinstated almost 100 years later through legislation in 1987, *see* Act of Feb. 25, 1987, ch. 246, effective April 27, 1987; Utah Code Ann. § 30-1-4.5. (1987). The new law is not retroactively applicable.

74 In *State v. Walker*, 36 Kan. 297, 59 Am.Rep. 556, 13 P. 279, 285 (1887), the court held that the "punishment may be inflicted upon those who enter the marriage relation in disregard of the prescribed statutory requirements, without rendering the marriage itself void." *See also State v. Hughes*, 35 Kan. 626, 12 P. 28, 57 Am.Rep. 195, 12 P. 28 (1886); *State v. McFarland*, 38 Kan. 664, 17 P. 654 (1888); *Matney v. Linn*, 59 Kan. 613, 54 P. 668 (1898); *Shorten v. Judd*, 60 Kan. 73, 55 P. 286 (Kan. 1898); *Renfrow v. Renfrow*, 60 Kan. 277, 72 Am.St.Rep. 350, 56 P. 534 (1899); and *Schuchart v. Schuchart*, 61 Kan. 597, 60 P. 311, 78 Am.St.Rep. 342 (1900).

75 *See Mathewson v. Phoenix Iron Foundry*, 20 F. 281, 282 (Cir.D.R.I. 1884), in which the court found that the form requirements according to Rhode Island law were not fulfilled, but citing English law as well as domestic case law and literature, stated: "But, while this marriage was not according to the form of the statute, it was a good contract of marriage, *per verba de praesenti*, or at common law, so called." In several cases, this statement is cited as support for common law marriage by the courts in Rhode Island, *see Peck v. Peck*, 12 R.I. 485 (1880); *State v. Boyle*, 13 R.I. 537 (1882); *Odd Fellows' Beneficial Ass'n v. Carpenter*, 17 R.I. 720, 24 A. 578 (1892); and *Williams v. Herrick*, 21 R.I. 401, 79 Am.St.Rep. 809, 43 A. 1036 (1899). The Rhode Island Supreme Court finally decided the issue in *Holgate v. United Electric Ry. Co.*, 47 R.I. 337, 133 A. 243 (1926), in which a common law marriage was found to be proven.

76 *Israel v. Arthur*, 18 Colo. 158, 164, 32 P. 68 (1893); and *Poole v. People*, 24 Colo. 510, 65 Am.St.Rep. 245, 52 P. 1025 (1898). Compare already *Kansas Pac. Ry. Co. v. Miller*, 2 Colo. 442 (1874), where a marriage was presumed.

establishment of a common law marriage, a split that would exist for a long time as further discussed in Chapter 8.[77] During the 1890s, the common law marriage doctrine was also accepted in Nebraska[78] and Nevada.[79] Even in Wyoming during the end of the 1890s, there was a tendency to support common law marriage, although it was never entirely accepted.[80]

The courts in Texas, from the time of the state's incorporation, had a relatively positive attitude towards, for example, marital relationships in which the form requirements were not fulfilled, or cases in which assessing the validity of a marriage entailed the possibility of taking into consideration circumstantial evidence.[81] This attitude prevailed even though common law marriage was not completely recognized until the end of the 1800s. Although the Texas courts rejected the doctrine in several instances,[82] it was accepted and became established during the years before and after the turn of the twentieth century.[83] Common law marriage,

---

77 *Taylor v. Taylor*, 10 Colo.App. 303, 50 P. 1049 (1897); and *Klipfel v. Klipfel*, 41 Colo. 40, 92 P. 26, 28 (1907).

78 *Gibson v. Gibson*, 24 Neb. 394, 39 N.W. 450 (1888); *Goodrich v. Cushman*, 34 Neb. 460, 51 N.W. 1041 (1892); *Haggin v. Haggin*, 35 Neb. 375. 53 N.W. 209 (1892); *Bailey v. State*, 36 Neb. 808, 55 N.W. 241 (1893); *University of Michigan v. McGuckin*, 62 Neb. 489, 87 N.W. 180, *aff'd on reh'g*, 64 Neb. 300, 89 N.W. 778 (1901); *Eaton v. Eaton*, 66 Neb. 676, 92 N.W. 995 (1902); and *Sorensen v. Sorensen*, 68 Neb. 500, 100 N.W. 930 (1904), *aff'd*, 68 Neb. 483, 103 N.W. 455 (1905). In *Collins v. Hoag & Rollins Inc.*, 241 N.W. 766 (Neb. 1932), the Nebraska Supreme Court found that common law marriage was invalid based on a regulation issued in 1923 stating that "no marriage hereafter contracted shall be recognized *as valid* unless such license has been previously obtained, and unless such marriage is solemnized by a person authorized by law to solemnize marriages" (italics added), *see* chapter 40, Laws (1923).

79 *State v. Zichfeld*, 23 Nev. 304, 46 P. 802 (1896).

80 In *Connors v. Connors*, 5 Wyo. 439, 40 P. 966 (1895), a marriage commenced without a license was found to be valid. *Compare In re Robert's Estate*, 58 Wyo. 438, 133 P.2d 492 (1943), in which the court states that common law marriage was never recognized in Wyoming.

81 *See already Tarpley v. Poage's Adm'r*, 2 Tex. 139, 149 (1847), in which the court considered the following circumstances to be relevant, "evidence of cohabitation, reputation acknowledgment of the parties, reception in the family, and other circumstances from which an inference of marriage could be drawn." The court cited *inter alia Fenton v. Reed. See also Yates v. Houston*, 3 Tex. 433 (1848); *Robertson v. Cole*, 12 Tex. 356 (1854); *Lockhart v. White*, 18 Tex. 102 (1856); *Carroll v. Carroll*, 20 Tex. 731 (1858); *Sapp v. Newson*, 27 Tex. 537 (1864); *Rice v. Rice*, 31 Tex. 174 (1868); and *Lewis v. Ames*, 44 Tex. 338 (1875). In *Cumby v. Garland*, 6 Tex.Civ.App. 519, 25 S.W. 673, 676 (1894), the court stated as to the older cases that "it can hardly be contended that there is found in those decisions, or in the laws and habits of society out of which they grew, any policy or spirit hostile to what are generally called common law marriages." Also in the case of *Ingersol v. McWillie*, 9 Tex.Civ.App. 543, 30 S.W. 56, 61 (1895), the court stated: "Our decisions have usually been broad and liberal upon the subject."

82 *Dumas v. State*, 14 Tex.Crim.App. 464, 46 Am.Rep. 241 (1883); and *Western U. Teleg. Co. v. Proctor*, 6 Tex.Civ.App. 300, 25 S.W. 811 (1894).

83 *Cumby v. Garland*, 6 Tex.Civ.App. 519, 25 S.W. 673 (1894); and *Holder v. State*, 35 Tex. Crim.Rep. 19, 29 S.W. 793 (1894). In *Ingersol v. McWillie*, 9 Tex.Civ.App. 543, 30 S.W. 56, 61 (1895), the court held that "marriage may be valid and binding upon the parties, although entered into not in accordance with the terms of the statute requiring license and solemnization by a minister or officer." *See also Coleman v. Vollmer*, 31 S.W.

still applicable in Texas, was codified there in the 1960s and supplemented with an extensive case law, which is discussed further in the following chapters.

In the beginning of the 1900s, the question of the validity of common law marriage arose in several of the newer states. One state in the Southwest, usually not receiving the attention it deserves, is Oklahoma, whose courts in the beginning of the 1900s recognized common law marriage. When Oklahoma was simply a territory, its courts had already decided cases in favor of the doctrine. In *Reaves v. Reaves* (1905), the court cited English law as well as the then-current American case law and literature in favor of common law marriage.[84] After Oklahoma became a state in 1907, new family law legislation followed, as well as an extensive case law that, today, still recognizes the doctrine.[85] In Alaska, the applicable form requirements for the commencement of marriage were considered, for a period, to be simply suggested, which allowed common law marriage; later requirements became mandatory.[86] In Hawaii, cases decided in support of common law marriage were overruled by later decisions.[87]

The jurisdiction with case law recognizing common law marriage later than all others is the District of Columbia. After new constitutional conditions in 1929 freed it of ties to Maryland, the case of *Hoage v. Murch Bros. Const. Co.* (1931) was heard. Its highest court, the Court of Appeals, somewhat reluctantly concluded that the lower court decision that invalidated

---

413 (Tex.Civ.App. 1895); *Chapman v. Chapman*, 88 Tex. 641, 32 S.W. 871 (1895); *Simmons v. Simmons*, 39 S.W. 639, 640 (Tex.Civ.App. 1897); *Galveston, Harrisburg, and San Antonio R.R. Co. v. Cody*, 20 Tex.Civ.App. 520, 50 S.W. 135 (1899); *Cuneo v. de Cuneo*, 24 Tex.Civ.App. 436, 59 S.W. 284, 285 (1900); *Lon Lee v. State*, 44 Tex.Crim. Rep. 354, 72 S.W. 1005, 61 A.L.R. 904 (1902); *Edelstein v. Brown*, 35 Tex.Civ.App. 625, 80 S.W. 1027 (1904); *Burnett v. Burnett*, 83 S.W. 238 (Tex.Civ.App. 1904); *Burks v. State*, 50 Tex.Crim.Rep. 47, 94 S.W. 1040 (1906); *Jackson v. Banister*, 47 Tex.Civ.App. 317, 105 S.W. 66 (1907); *Knight v. State*, 55 Tex.Crim.Rep. 243, 116 S.W. 56 (1909); *Harlan v. Harlan*, 125 S.W. 950 (Tex.Civ.App. 1910); *Bargna v. Bargna*, 127 S.W. 1156 (Tex.Civ.App. 1910); *Wolford v. State*, 60 Tex.Crim.Rep. 624, 132 S.W. 929 (1910); *Melton v. State*, 71 Tex.Crim.Rep. 130, 158 S.W. 550 (1913); *Berger v. Kirby*, 105 Tex. 611, 153 S.W. 1130, 1131 (1913); and *Grigsby v. Reib*, 153 S.W. 1124, 1125 (1913), which for a long time would be the leading case.

84 *Reaves v. Reaves*, 15 Okla. 240, 82 P. 490 (1905). Before Oklahoma became a state, Nebraska law formally was applied.

85 *See In re Love's Estate*, 42 Okla. 478, 142 P. 305, 307 (1914). This case was followed extensively in the case law described in the following chapters.

86 In Alaska, the form requirements applicable prior to 1917 were considered to be simply directory, *see McDaniels v. McDaniels*, 5 Alaska 107 (D.C.D. Alaska 1914); *Reed v. Harkrader*, 4 Alaska Fed. 893, 264 F. 834 (9th Cir. 1920); and *Parks v. Parks*, 6 Alaska 426 (D.C.D. 1921), while those which thereafter were applicable were viewed as "mandatory," *see Edwards v. Franke*, 364 P.2d 60 (Alaska 1961).

87 In *Godfrey v. Rowland*, 16 Haw. 377 (1905), the Hawaii Supreme Court viewed the requirement for a marriage license to be simply directory. In *Parke v. Parke*, 25 Haw. 397 (1920), the court changed its view and found the regulations to be "mandatory", despite the fact that they did not contain express words as to invalidity. Section 2905 R.L. 1915 (Sec. 1870 Civ.L. 1897) states that "it shall in no case be lawful for any person to marry in this Territory without a license..."

common-law marriages in the District of Columbia was not supported by law and was wrong.[88] This jurisdiction still recognizes the doctrine.

4.2.3 Peculiarities of American Common Law Marriage

The development of American common law marriage deviated from the classical role models. Although one of the two canon law and English variations of informal marriages appeared in the United States, the other, *sponsalia per verba de futuro cum copula,* in other words, the agreement to a future marriage with thereafter following consummation, consequently became obsolete, although the state of the law during the 1800s was somewhat unclear. Already in 1922, Otto Koegel stated: "The common law rule of marriage *per verba de futuro cum copula* is not law in any American state today." The later development of the law has not allowed this informal marriage.[89] The legal institution, however, is alive in that it still is necessary in American case law to maintain a distinction between *sponsalia per verba*

---

88 *Hoage v. Murch Bros Const. Co.*, 60 App. D.C. 218, 50 F.2d 983 (D.C.Cir. 1931). Much earlier, the marriage presumption for ceremonial marriages was applied based on cohabitation and reputation, *see Blackburn v. Crawfords,* 3 Wall. (U.S.) 175 (1865), 18 L.ed. 186 (1866); *Diggs v. Wormley,* 21 D.C. 477 (1893); and *Jennings v. Webb,* 8 App. D.C. 43 (1896). *Compare* the Maryland case of *Denison v. Denison,* 35 Md. 361 (1872), *supra* note 19.

89 With respect to the canon law, *see* Section 3.3.3 *supra.* With respect to Scottish law, *see Dalrymple v. Dalrymple,* (1911) 2 Hagg.Cons. 54, 65, 161 Eng.Rep. 665, 669. Regarding the American law's negative stance as to granting *consensus de futuro cum copula* constitutive effect, *see* already Kent, Lectures, XXVI (6) (1826), as well as the cases: *Jewell v. Magwood,* 9 S.C.Eq. (Rich.Cas.) 113 (1833); *Cheney v. Arnold,* 15 N.Y. 345, 69 Am. D. 609 (1857); *Duncan v. Duncan,* 10 Ohio St. 181 (1859). According to § 37 of the Civil Code of the Territory of Dakota (1866), a consent *de praesenti,* was required *i.e.* to a marriage "commencing instantly, and not to an agreement to marry afterwards." *In re McCausland's Estate,* 52 Cal. 568, 577 (1878); *In re Grimm's Estate,* 131 Pa. 199 (1890). *Compare Fryer v. Fryer,* 9 S.C.Eq. (Rich.Cas.) 85 (1832); *Guardians of the Poor v. Nathans,* 2 Brewster 149 (1845); *Richard v. Brehm,* 73 Pa. 140 (1873); *Peck v. Peck,* 12 R.I. 485 (1880); *In re Comly's Estate,* 185 Pa. 208 (1898); *Davis v. Stouffer,* 132 Mo.App. 555, 112 S.W. 282, 283 (1908); and *Marsicano v. Marsicano,* 79 Fla. 278, 84 So. 156 (1920). In the literature, Bishop, *supra* note 27, at §§ 353-377, has expressed approval for the principle *consensus de futuro cum copula,* however, only as a rebuttable presumption. *See also* Greenleaf, *supra* note 43, § 460 (3d. ed. 1846). Something of the reasons against a recognition of *sponsalia de futuro cum copula* one can detect with Peck at 16: "If an agreement for future marriage followed by cohabitation constituted a valid marriage, then every case of seduction under promise of marriage would be a legal marriage in fact." American case law thereafter has also expressed disapproval, *see, e.g., In re Danikas' Estate,* 76 Colo. 191, 230 P. 608 (1924); *In re Murdock's Estate,* 92 Pa.Super. 275 (1928); *Cavanaugh v. Cavanaugh,* 135 Okla. 204, 275 P. 315 (1929); and *Baker v. Mitchell,* 143 Pa.Super. 50, 17 A.2d 738, 740 (1941): "They did not import an immediate, present marriage but a promise to marry in the future; and it makes no difference, so far as a legal *marriage* is concerned, that relying on this promise and with it in expectation they had intercourse together. That did not constitute them husband and wife." The same viewpoint recurs in American case law from more recent years, *see, e.g., In re Estate of Fisher,* 176 N.W.2d 801, 802 (Iowa 1970); *McDermott v. McDermott,* 236 Pa.Super.Ct. 541, 345 A.2d 914 (1975); and *Lackey v. State,* 638 S.W.2d 439 (Tex.Crim.App. 1982).

de praesenti, giving the marriage's legal effects, and *sponsalia per verba de futuro*, which does not give it legal effects. The distinction, therefore, is discussed specifically in Chapter 6 regarding the marriage contract.

As can be seen above from *Fenton v. Reed* (1809), American common law marriage is based, in principle, on a marriage contract per *verba de praesenti*. As can be seen from the discussion below on the development in the American case law, the courts accepted inferred agreements, in which the parties' cohabitation and outward appearance as spouses in practice became decisive, while the elements of the contract in many cases more often appeared in the background as seen in Chapter 7. The marriage presumption is also based upon the cohabitation of the parties as well as their outward appearance, as examined in Chapter 9, "Burdens of Proof and Presumptions." In addition, these circumstances, over time, developed into the independent requisites required for the establishment of a common law marriage in addition to the all-the-more fictional marriage contract as discussed in Chapter 8.

4.3 The Reasons for the American Reception

The question of why common law marriage was introduced and accepted in the United States cannot be answered simply. The doctrine is not primarily a product of a legislative work, during which the underlying reasons are often stated and discussed. In all material aspects, common law marriage has grown in the case law, in which stated reasons are sparingly presented. What is clear, however, is that the theological reasons, which for more than one thousand years restrained the church from introducing terms and conditions for the marriage's validity in form requirements, as well as, e.g., the absence in the holy scriptures of an expressed form, did not constitute the *ratio legis* behind American common law marriage.[90] The stated reasons for informal marriage in American law are complex and diffuse. Nevertheless, certain primary reasons can be distinguished with some degree of certainty.

4.3.1 The Authority of Other Legal Systems

An often overlooked, but not insignificant explanation of the recognition of common law marriage, in any event, in older American case law, is the authority the English, canon, and ancient Roman law enjoyed in American law. After independence, the American courts did not have any formal obligation to apply laws that the former mother country had repealed through Lord Hardwicke's Act in 1753, but these older principles were

90 Regarding the reasons behind the informal marriage of medieval canon law, *see* Section 3.3.2 *supra*.

still cited. This can be seen *inter alia* in that American courts recognizing common law marriage usually did not provide any independent legal policy considerations and/or reasons for their recognition. Instead, they directly cited canon law principles that had come to expression in English and Scottish law and were rooted in Roman law. For example, in *Askew v. Dupree* (1860), the Georgia Supreme Court stated, after references to Roman, canon, English, and Scottish law: "*Consensus, non concubitus, faciat matrimonium,* the maxim of the Roman civil law is, in truth, the maxim of all law upon the subject."[91] This restraint, along with the domestic policy considerations that influenced many leading cases, expresses an acceptance of authority more than the judges' own personal views.[92]

91 *Askew v. Dupree,* 30 Ga. 173, 178 (1860); and *Carmichael v. State,* 12 Ohio St. 553 (1861). *See also* older leading cases, such as *Fenton v. Reed,* 4 Johns. 52 (N.Y. 1809), in which the court without providing any independent legal policy discussion states: "A contract of marriage made *per verba de praesenti* amounts to an actual marriage and is as valid as if made *in facie ecclesiae.*" As support thereof, the court directly cites the English cases of *Collins v. Jessot,* (1705) 6 Mod. 155, 87 Eng.Rep. 913; *Alleyne v. Gray,* (1689) 2 Salk. 437, 91 Eng. Rep. 380; and *Reed v. Passer,* (1794) Peake's Cases 231, 170 Eng.Rep. 164. In contrast to the leading English and Scottish cases from the same period, as well as *Dalrymple v. Dalrymple,* (1811) 161 Eng.Rep. 665, a total of 249 pages with extensive historical embellishments, the American cases are consistently short. Despite the fact that *Fenton v. Reed* scarcely constitutes more than a page of print and does not contain any extensive historical embellishments, the canon and old English principles are unmistakable from the language used as well as the content. *See also Dumaresley v. Fishly,* 10 Ky. 368 (1821); *Duncan v. Duncan,* 10 Ohio St. 181 (1859); and *Van Tuyl v. Van Tuyl,* 57 Barb. 235 (1869). In *Carmichael v. State,* 12 Ohio St. 553 (1861), the court's decision is preceded by a long discourse concerning English cases applying canon law principles. *See also Port v. Port,* 70 Ill. 484 (1873). Comparable in the literature, *see* Kent, *supra* note 3, at XXVI (6). The lack of legal policy considerations naturally is less surprising as a domestic authoritative case law was well established. However, not entirely absent under the authoritative pressure are legal policy stances. They occasionally arise as a supplement to a reluctant recognition of the institution. In *State v. Bittick,* 103 Mo. 183, 15 S.W. 325, 327 (1891), in which a common law marriage was found to be established, the court stated: "We will add that ... all marriages should be entered into publicly before those authorised by law to solemnize them, and put upon the public records." The court found it however fit to add: "But we are not here to make the law conform to what we think it ought to be, but to declare it as it is." Similar grousing under the authoritative pressure is found in *United States v. Simpson,* 4 Utah 227, 7 P: 257 (1885), in which the Utah Supreme Court states that a couple can whenever during a day meet on a country road and enter into a valid marriage, however in which the court adds: "Whether it tends to good morals to leave the matter thus loose, and completely at the will of the parties it is not for us to discuss. That is a matter for the legislature. We have to take the law as we find it." In *Mathewson v. Phoenix Iron Foundry,* 20 F. 281 (Cir.D.R.I. 1884), English law as well as domestic case law and literature is cited. In *Fisher v. Fisher,* 250 N.Y. 313, 165 N.E. 460 (1929), containing extensive historical embellishments, the court states *inter alia:* "According to the common law of all Christendom, consensual marriages – *i.e.,* marriages resting simply on consent *per verba de praesenti*—between competent parties, are valid marriages. Wharton's Conflict of Laws, §§ 171-173. 'This view prevailed and may be said to have been the common law of Christendom, as it had been of the old Roman Empire, down to the Council of Trent.' Maitland Select Essays in Anglo-American Legal History, vol. 3, p. 810."

92 *Compare* Grossberg, *supra* note 22, at 89, stating: "Most of the bench and bar, though, endorsed common-law marriage not because of slavish adherence to precedent but

The citing by the courts of canon law and Roman principles was also supported by the legal literature.

James Kent stated in his commentaries to *Fenton v. Reed* (N.Y. 1809):

> *No particular ceremonies are requisite by the common law to the valid celebration of the marriage. The consent of the parties is all that is required; and as marriage is said to be a contract* jure gentium, *that consent is all that is required by natural and public law. The Roman lawyers strongly inculcated the doctrine, that the very foundation and essence of the contract consisted in consent freely given, by parties competent to contract.* Nihil proderit signasse tabulas, simentem matrimonii non fuisse constabit. Nuptias non concubitus, sed consensus facit. *This is the language equally of the common and canon law, and of common reason.*[93]

The authority of the canon legal principles means that common law marriage is not an American innovation, though the informal marriage fit well into the American reality and the values characterizing it.[94]

4.3.2 The Freedom to Enter into Marriage without State Interference

The United States in the beginning of the 1800s was a society without a state church, where many had emigrated under state confessional oppression. The country lacked the European acceptance of the requirements given by the state and the church regarding the commencement of marriage. Joel Bishop, with respect to the English Episcopalian church, correctly noted that the Puritan dissidents fled to the western wilds for the single purpose of escaping what they regarded as the oppression and moral contagion flowing from churches.[95] Michael Grossberg, for his part, makes another point about the American liberal perspective, stating that American marital law reflected and fostered a republican ethos stemming

rather because they agreed with the doctrine itself." Compare Hall, *supra* note 17, at, who, based on the same personal perspective, maintains that Kent personally was positive to legislation excluding common law marriage.

93 KENT, *supra* note 3, at 75. Regarding the Roman law, *see* Chapter 2 and the canon law, Chapter 3 *supra.*

94 *Compare* LAWRENCE M. FRIEDMAN, A HISTORY OF AMERICAN LAW 202 (2d ed. 1985), who argues that common law marriage "was probably an American innovation."

95 BISHOP, *supra* note 44, § 166. *See also* AUGUSTE CARLIER, MARRIAGE IN THE UNITED STATES 36 (1867), referring to "the predominant view in America that the individual is superior to the community." *See further Londonderry v. Chester,* 2 N.H. 268, 278, 9 Am.Dec. 61 (1820); and *Dumaresly v. Fishly,* 10 Ky. 368, 370 (1821).

from a faith in competitive individualism and voluntary choice.[96] It then was logical that the commencement of marriage was considered a private contract between independent individuals. From this perspective, form requirements for the commencement of marriage appeared to be bureaucratic regulations that could not be allowed to jeopardize the validity of a marriage. In a similar manner, Bishop designated the form requirements for the commencement of marriage as cumbersome, artificial barriers to matrimony.[97] The institution of marriage, of such fundamental significance to humanity, could not be impeded by any form requirements.[98]

This attitude toward form requirements has also been expressed in the case law. For example, in *Carmichael v. State* (1861), the Ohio Supreme Court posited that the form requirements did not concern anything so important as the right to marry but rather simply "the exercise of that right,"[99] and in *Crawford v. State* (1895), the Mississippi Supreme Court held that no marriage that had been entered into openly and honestly ought to be declared invalid based on "some wretched formality which has been overlooked or disregarded."[100]

Evidently, people also expressed opposition to observing the new form requirements as enacted. Edmund Brown, in addressing the requirements for a marriage license enacted at the end of the 1800s, held that many persons considered the procedure indelicate, and so hesitated to go before a clerk of the court to secure a marriage license.[101] Naturally,

96 GROSSBERG, *supra* note 22, at 70. *See also* Walter O. Weyrauch, *Informal and formal marriage - an appraisal of trends in family organization,* 28 U. CHI. L. REV. 88, 109 (1960), speaking of "[t]he rugged individualism of American frontier days, which favored the growth of common law marriage..."

97 BISHOP, *supra* note 27, at 165-167.

98 *See* JAMES SCHOULER, MARRIAGE, DIVORCE, SEPARATION & DOMESTIC RELATIONS I, 42 (6th ed. 1921); and BISHOP, *id.* § 457.

99 *Carmichael v. State,* 12 Ohio St. 553, 556 (1861). The same attitude already appears in *Pearson v. Howey,* 6 Halstead 12, 18 (N.J. 1829), in which the form requirements are considered not as binding but as "laws of fashion." *See also Londonderry v. Chester,* 2 N.H. 268, 281 (1820), in which the court held that the marriage contract "will never be annulled for any accidental or designed irregularity not extending to the essential grounds of the contract." Compare *Meister v. Moore,* 96 U.S. 76, 81 (1877).

100 *Crawford v. State,* 73 Miss. 172, 178 (1895); and *Coachman v. Sims,* 36 Okla. 536, 129 P. 845 (1913). In the case of *In re Sanders' Estate,* 67 Okla. 3, 168 P. 197 (1917), the court speaks of the importance to "preserve the sanctity of the marriage relation"; and *Tiuna v. Willmott,* 162 Okla. 42, 19 P.2d 145 (1933). In *Allen v. State,* 60 Ga.App. 248, 3 S.E.2d 780 (1939), one can see how the reasons affect the principles of interpretation: "Marriage is favored in law, and statutory provisions establishing forms are to be strictly interpreted, and legislation commanding formalities and even punishing the parties themselves will not render a marriage had in disregard of it void, unless statute expressly or by necessary implication declares such consequence." In *Williams v. White,* 263 S.W.2d 666, 668 (Tex.Civ.App.-Austin 1953), the Texas Court of Appeals, Austin, stated: "It is the policy of the law to look with special favor upon marriage and to seek in all lawful ways to uphold this most important of social institutions." *Compare Gress v. Gress,* 209 S.W.2d 1003 (Tex.Civ.App. 1948); and *Nixon v. Wichita Land & Cattle Co.,* 84 Tex. 408, 19 S.W. 560 (1892).

101 EDMUND Q. BROWN, MARRIAGE IN PENNSYLVANIA UNDER THE NEW LICENSE ACT 3, 6 (1886).

it could be argued that the form requirements for the commencement of marriage, one of the most important contracts a person could enter into, are not more burdensome than those one subjects oneself to in the acquisition of an acre of land.[102] Compared with the mother country's strict requirements, the form requirements developed in the United States reflected a liberal acceptance of varying wedding forms and persons authorized to perform weddings from different religious congregations and governmental authorities.[103]

The freedom from form requirements that common law marriage offered was criticized at the turn of the century as an expression of an unveiled individualism that ignored the interests of society. George Howard exclaimed: "Verily this is individualism absolutely unrestrained!"[104] It ought, however, be noted that the freedom at issue concerns only the form for the commencement of marriage. An often-overlooked reality, however, is that with respect to the legal effects, the concern is exactly the opposite. Through common law marriage, which in reality could be based on the parties' actual cohabitation, parties were subjected to marriage's legal effects, which included not only the rights but also all of the obligations that the contract placed upon the spouses through the power of the state, acting as a third party. Among these rights is the limited possibility of marital divorce. From the perspective of the state, common law marriage, therefore, became a method of capturing "lost sheep," similar to the approach taken in medieval canon law. The freedom to enter into a marriage without state interference was, consequently, a temporary freedom; immediately after the marriage was established, the state intervened and exercised control, as it would for a ceremonial marriage. This, however, as the following chapters show, occurred with the difference that the parties in a common law marriage, in many cases, were not even conscious

102 In *Dunbarton v. Franklin*, 19 N.H. 257, 264-265 (1848), the court stated: "It is singular that the most important of all human contracts, on which the rights and duties of the whole community depend, requires less formality for its validity than a conveyance of an acre of land, a policy of insurance, or the agreement which the statute of frauds requires should be in writing."

103 Grossberg, *supra* note 22, at 75-79. Regarding the early development of the form requirements, *see* Howard I, *supra* note 14, at 300-308. It ought to be noted that the state of New York enacted new legislation as to the commencement of marriage between 1826-1830 and appears to have lacked such legislation when *Fenton v. Reed*, 4 Johns. 52 (N.Y. 1809) was decided. According to the new legislation, the form requirements were no impediment against the common law marriage: "Nor shall the provisions of this Article be construed to require the parties to any marriage, or any minister or magistrate to solemnize the same in the manner herein prescribed," *see* 3 Rev. Stat. (1 st ed. 1827-1828), at 152 App. For more on this, *see* Hall, *supra* note 17, at 6-8.

104 Howard III, *supra* note 14, at 184. *Compare* Weyrauch, *supra* note 96, at 109, who speaks of "[t]he rugged individualism of American frontier days, which favored the growth of common law marriage." *See* also, Ariele R. Duble, Note: *Governing Through Contract: Common Law Marriage in the Nineteenth Century*, 107 Yale L.J. 1885, 1907-1908 (1998).

of the legal effects, which in reality could already have arisen based on their actual cohabitation. Consequently, the freedom to enter into a marriage was partly an illusion, as is discussed in more detail in Chapters 13 and 14 regarding the future of common law marriage.

4.3.3 The Form Requirements for Ceremonial Marriages Are Not Mandatory

The wish to preserve autonomy that fueled the attitude toward form requirements also affected their interpretation. Even though form requirements existed for ceremonial marriages, they were not always perceived as creating an impediment to common law marriage. The courts distinguished between form requirements that were "mandatory" and those that were simply "directory", in other words, recommendations or advice. In those cases in which the regulations were interpreted to be the latter, there was to apply the common law marriage doctrine. James Kent gave expression to this stance early on when he maintained that the marriage contract amounts to a valid marriage in the absence of all civil regulations to the contrary.[105] The principle later was sanctioned by the United States Supreme Court in *Meister v. Moore* (1877): "No doubt, a statute may take away a common-law right; but there is always a presumption that the legislature has no such intention, unless it be plainly expressed...courts have usually held a marriage good at common law to be good notwithstanding the statutes, unless they contain express words of nullity."[106] The requirement

105 KENT, *supra* note 3, at 87 (2d ed. 1832).

106 *Meister v. Moore,* 96 U.S. 76, 79 (1877). *See* already *Dumaresly v. Fishly,* 10 Ky. 368 (1821); *Holmes v. Holmes,* 6 La. 463, 26 Am.Dec. 482 (1834); *Robertson v. Cole,* 12 Tex. 356 (1854); and *Hargroves v. Thompson,* 31 Miss. 211 (1856). The requirement that invalidity be evident from express words recurs in several decisions from the end of the 1800's, *see e.g. State v. Bittick,* 183 Mo. 183, 15 S.W. 325, 326 (1891), in which the court with respect to interpretation of similar form requirements held that common law marriage may be viewed as valid "unless the statutes contain express words of nullity" and in which the court, concerning the extent of the acceptance of this principle of interpretation, stated that it "has been adopted in nearly all the American states." Similar statements recur in other cases from the end of the 1800's, *see e.g. Daniel Sams v. Sams,* 17 Fla. 487 (1880); *Mathewson v. Phoenix Iron Foundry,* 20 F. 281 (Cir.D.R.I. 1884) (Rhode Island law); *State v. Walker,* 36 Kan. 297, 59 Am.Rep. 556, 13 P. 279 (1887); *Simon v. State,* 31 Tex.Crim.Rep. 186, 37 Am. St.Rep. 802, 20 S.W. 399, 401 (1892); *Cumby v. Garland,* 6 Tex.Civ.App. 519, 25 S.W. 673 (1894); *Ingersol v. McWillie,* 9 Tex.Civ.App. 543, 30 S.W. 56, 61 (1895); *State v. Zichfeld,* 23 Nev. 304, 46 P. 802 (1896); *Taylor v. Taylor,* 10 Colo.App. 303, 50 P. 1049 (1897); *Reaves v. Reaves,* 15 Okla. 240, 82 P. 490, (1905); and *Caras v. Hendrix,* 62 Fla. 446, 57 So. 345 (1912): "No statute of this state, expressly or by fair implication, renders invalid or void marriage contracts between competent parties that are consummated under the rules of the common law." *See also In re Love's Estate,* 42 Okla. 478, 142 P. 305, 307 (1914). Compare the Hawaii Supreme Court, which in *Godfrey v. Rowland,* 16 Haw. 377 (1905), considered the requirement for a marriage license to be simply directory but later changed view in *Parke v. Parke,* 25 Haw. 397 (1920). The principle still lives in later case law. *See e.g. Holgate v. United Electric Ry. Co.,* 47 R.I. 337, 133 A. 243 (1926); and *Hoage v. Murch Bros. Constr. Co,* 60 App. D.C. 218,

that invalidity be evident from express words also recurs in several decisions from the end of the 1800s. The form requirements were considered only recommendations and advice. The argument is classic common law in that the legislation is only considered a supplementary legal source, accepted as a supplement to or exception from common law only if the regulations can be viewed to be mandatory. This conforms to the maxim of interpretation that statutes in derogation of the common law are to be strictly construed. The form requirements do not create a new right, they simply regulate a previously existing right. Even if the form requirements of a wedding ceremony with a person authorized to officiate, witnesses, etc., are expressed with what appears to be an unconditional imperative such as *shall* and *must*, this usually has not prevented the requirements from being considered simply directory. The informal marriage, despite this, has been considered valid.[107] Even if the failure to observe form

---

50 F.2d 983 (1931), in which the court stated that "the rule now generally recognized is that statutes requiring a marriage to be preceded by a license, or to be solemnized by a religious ceremony, without express words of nullity as to marriages contracted otherwise, are directory merely, and a failure to procure the license or to go through a religious ceremony does not invalidate the marriage." Similar arguments are given in *Sturm v. Sturm*, 111 N.J.Eq. 579, 163 A. 5 (1932); *In re Redman's Estate*, 135 Ohio St. 554, 21 N.E.2d 659 (1939); and in *Lefkoff v. Sicro*, 189 Ga. 554, 6 S.E.2d 687 (1939), in which the court held that "although the legislature in Georgia has prescribed various formalities for the execution of their marriage contract, the courts of the state have uniformly held, for almost a century, that a compliance with these provisions is not essential to the validity of a marriage contract, and that an informal contract of marriage executed without such formalities is valid and binding." From that stated, it follows that it depends on the legislator that if he/she intends that the commencement of marriage without the observance of the form requirements is to result in the marriage's invalidity, to also clearly state that. Even the regulations that are criminally sanctioned have been considered to be simply directory, *see State v. Ward*, 204 S.C. 210, 28 S.E.2d 785, 786 (1944). In *Buradus v. Gen. Cement Products Co.*, 159 Pa.Super. 501, 506 (1946), in which the form requirements were found to be simply directory and therefore did not entail invalidity of a common law marriage, the court stated: "Even though the expression of an act is in general terms, only such modification will be recognized as the statute clearly and definitely prescribes. In the absence of express declaration, the law presumes that the act did not intend to make any change in the common law, for if the legislature had that design they would have expressed it." *See Marris v. Sockey*, 170 F.2d 599, 601-602 (10th Cir. 1948); and *Williams v. White*, 263 S.W.2d 666, 668 (Tex.Civ.App.-Austin 1953). From more recent years ought finally be mentioned *Souza v. O'Hara*, 121 R.I. 88, 395 A.2d 1060 (1978), in which a regulation prescribing that "[p]ersons intending to be joined together in marriage in this state must first obtain a license..." was not deemed to constitute an impediment against the validity of a common law marriage, wherein the regulations were not followed. The regulation in question can be found in GENERAL LAWS 1956 (1969 Reenactment) § 15-2-1 Rhode Island. No issue of interpretation arises certainly as to this, as earlier in Idaho, in the form requirements established that "noncompliance with its provisions does not invalidate any lawful marriage," *see* IDAHO CODE ANN. § 32-301. Common law marriage was repealed in Idaho beginning 1996, *see* H.B. 176; Chap. 104, 1995 Idaho Session Laws.

107 *See, e.g., Meister v. Moore*, 96 U.S. 76, 81 (1877), in which the legislation stated: "In every case there shall be at least two witnesses, besides the minister or magistrate, present at the same time." The regulations were considered however to be

requirements has been criminally sanctioned, the validity of the marriage is not affected, a result that is made possible by maintaining the distinction between *legality* and *validity*.[108]

The leading principle consequently has been that a common law marriage is considered invalid first if the legislation contains an express regulation of invalidity.[109] The distinction between regulations that are mandatory and those that simply are directory also rests upon legal policy considerations and adopted interpretations. The courts that favor common law marriage have found it easier to consider the form requirements to be merely directory. In addition to the above-named common law argument, one can detect, behind the stance that the form requirements for the commencement of marriage are simply recommended, several of the reasons constituting the *ratio legis* behind common law marriage, e.g., the interest of protecting marriage and children as discussed further below.[110]

---

simply directory. *See also Rodebaugh v. Sanks,* 2 Watts 9 (Pa. 1833); and *In re Love's Estate,* 42 Okla. 478, 142 P. 305 (1914). *Compare In re Robert's Estate,* 58 Wyo. 438, 133 P.2d 492 (1943), in which the Wyoming Supreme Court found that the applicable form requirements, containing the words "shall" and "must", were to be viewed as "mandatory" and therewith constituted an impediment against common law marriage. The objective of preventing "fraudulent claims" against estates of the deceased also appears to have played a role with the repeal of common law marriage in Nebraska in 1923. In *Collins v. Hoag & Rollins Inc.,* 241 N.W. 766 (Neb. 1932), the Nebraska Supreme Court found a common law marriage invalid due to a 1923 issued new regulation prescribing that "no marriage hereafter contracted shall be recognized *as valid* unless such license has been previously obtained, and unless such marriage is solemnized by a person authorized by law to solemnize marriages" (italics added), *see* Neb. Comp. Stat. § 42-104 (1929). The courts in Oregon have also said no to common law marriages through interpretation, *Huard v. McTeigh,* 113 Or. 279, 232 P. 658, 39 A.L.R. 528 (1925). Most typically, however, the repeal of common law marriage has been considered to require legislation, *see Interest of Miller,* 301 Pa.Super. 511, 448 A.2d 25, 32 (1982). It is unusual but does happen that the legislation expressly prescribes that a regulation is "mandatory" and not simply "directory", *see, e.g.,* the regulation through which common law marriage was repealed in New Jersey in 1939, L. 1939, c. 227, N.J. Stat. Ann. 37:1-10 (West 2003).

108 The distinction is still alive today. In Iowa, the failure to observe the form requirements for the commencement of marriage can result in $50 in fines for each party, *see* I.C.A. § 595.11. *See e.g. Coleman v. Graves,* 122 N.W.2d 853 (Iowa 1963). In Kansas, which also recognizes the validity of common law marriage, the comparable offense can result in fines between $500-1000, or prison of at least one and at the highest three months, *see* KAN. STAT. ANN. 23-118. *See, e.g., Smith v. Smith,* 161 K.I., 165 P.2d 593 (1946).

109 In *Askew v. Dupree,* 30 Ga. 173, 180 (1860), the court states that common law marriages are valid "except where local statutes expressly provide that marriages not made in the manner prescribed by them are void."

110 *See Meister v. Moore,* 96 U.S. 76, 81 (1877); and *Ingersol v. McWillie,* 9 Tex.Civ.App. 543, 30 S.W. 56, 60-61 (1895). Against a proposal to invalidate common law marriage, *Warren D. Harris* at the turn of the twentieth century stated: "A legislative enactment to annul a marriage *de facto* is a penal enactment – penal to the parties, in that it declares their union meretricious, envelops them in shame and disgrace, resulting in social ostracism from polite society, and rendering them liable to an indictment for fornication; penal to the innocent offspring, in that it

Cases in which the form requirements through interpretation have been found to be mandatory preclude the possibility of applying the common law marriage doctrine. This has been the case if the legislation expressly states that marriages commenced without the observance of the form requirements are invalid. However, there are also courts, if the minority, which have found the form requirements to be mandatory even in the absence of express regulations as to invalidity. This interpretation was also influenced by the legal policy considerations as discussed further below in this chapter regarding criticism of common law marriage.

4.3.4 Limited Access to Wedding Ceremonies during the Pioneer Period

The acceptance of common law marriage in American case law was also influenced by the historical realities of the pioneer period of the United States, which limited access to wedding ceremonies. In sparsely populated settlements, there was inadequate public transportation and a lack of persons legally authorized to perform wedding ceremonies. At the same time, forming families and entering into marriage facilitated the possibility of surviving the difficult living conditions of the pioneer period.[111] Under these circumstances, common law marriage was an easily accessible way to get all the legal effects of a ceremonial marriage. In *Chambers v. Dickson* (1816), the Pennsylvania Supreme Court paints the following picture of the situation: "We have no established church; a certificate from the bishop, therefore, is out of the question. We have no law compelling the keeping of a register by all persons who perform the marriage ceremony; our marriages are celebrated, sometimes by clergymen, sometimes by justices of the peace, and sometimes before witnesses, without the intervention of clergymen or justices. Many of our citizens are emigrants from foreign countries where they were married; many marriages take place in parts of our country but thinly settled. To hold a woman, therefore, to proof of her actual marriage, might be productive of very great inconvenience, without any advantage ... We must pay regard to the situation of our own country ... I am of opinion, that in the action of dower, circumstances

---

sends them out into the world as outcasts in society, branded with the stigma of illegitimacy – a stigma which the most virtuous life can never remove; and, finally, penal to society itself, in that it shocks public morality and decency with the spectacle of an unmarried man and woman living together in the relation of husband and wife, and jeopardizes the legal status of many a happy pair who are conscious of no violation of the law. Such enactments, therefore, being penal, are to be construed strictly." *See also* Warren D. Harris, *The Essentials of a Valid Marriage in Virginia*, 6 VA. L. REG. 437, 444-445 (1900).

111 LAWRENCE M. FRIEDMAN, PRIVATE LIVES: FAMILIES, INDIVIDUALS, AND THE LAW 19-20 (2004); MARY BECKER ET AL., CASES AND MATERIALS ON FEMINIST JURISPRUDENCE: TAKING WOMAN SERIOUSLY 727 (1994); TERESA AMOTT & JULIE MATTHAEI, RACE, GENDER, AND WORK: A MULTICULTURAL ECONOMIC HISTORY OF WOMAN IN THE UNITED STATES 98-100 (1991); and Bowman, *supra* note 34, at 723.

short of positive proof, are proper to be given in evidence; *cohabitation* and *reputation,* especially of an ancient date, are very strong circumstances, and ought, in this case to have gone to the jury."[112]

In *Forney v. Hallacher* (1822), another early case from Pennsylvania, the court recites *inter alia* the difficulties at that time in maintaining a requirement as to witnesses at the commencement of marriage: "[T]he boundless field for enterprise in the new States that are continually forming, renders the habits of the people of America, essentially those of migration; and beside, no inconsiderable portion of the population is made up of emigrants from abroad; many of whom are married when they come here. The witnesses to marriages celebrated here, are, in the usual course, soon dispersed over this extensive country; and neither their testimony, nor that of the witnesses to marriages abroad, can ordinarily be had, except at an expense that puts it beyond the reach of all whose circumstances are not above mediocrity. We have no parish registers in Pennsylvania; and even if we had, the same difficulty would still be found in procuring proof of the identity of the persons named in the register ..."[113]

The absence of a state church and the diversity of faiths that grew in the new world constrained the possibility of achieving a uniform and unconditional form requirement.[114] Lack of knowledge of the English language and the resulting ignorance about the content of the form requirements have been given as reasons.[115] The significance of the conditions during the pioneer period, e.g., sparsely populated settlements, poor public transportation, and lack of accessible persons authorized to perform wedding ceremonies, however, should not be exaggerated. Common law

---

112 *Chambers v. Dickson,* 2 S. & R. 475, 476 f (1816). Similar views have been expressed in *Dumaresly v. Fishly,* 10 Ky. 368 (1821), in which the court held that "there was in this country no church established by law, and consequently none that had authority to solemnise the rites of matrimony." *See also Sapp v. Newson,* 27 Tex. 537 (1864). In *McChesney v. Johnson,* 79 S.W.2d 658, 659 (Tex.Civ.App.-Fort Worth 1934), the court stated: "The sparse settlements, the long distance to places of record, bad roads, difficulties of travel, made access to officers or ministers difficult for some of our residents, lack of general education in the English language produced unfamiliarity with the laws, and in the small it was more difficult to dignify an illicit association with the name of marriage than in one of our large cities where all of us are strangers to the private life of most of its residents." Similar are the cases of *In re Estate of Soeder,* 7 Ohio App. 271, 220 N.E.2d 547, 562 (1966); and *Middlebrook v. Wideman,* 203 S.W.2d 686, 687 (Tex.Civ.App. 1947). *Compare Turner v. Turner,* 251 Ala. 295, 37 So.2d 186, 189 (1948); *Goodman v. McMillan,* 258 Ala. 125, 61 So.2d 55, 60 (1952); and *De Santo v. Barnsley,* 476 A.2d 952, 955 (Pa.Super. 1984). *See also* John B. Crawley, *Is the Honeymoon Over for Common Law Marriage: A Consideration of the Continued Viability of the Common Law Marriage Doctrine,* 29 Cumb. L. Rev. 399, 403 (1998/1999); and Alan H., Rothstein, Special Comment, *A New Look at Common Law Marriages in Florida,* 10 Miami L.Q. 87, 95 (1955).

113 *Forney v. Hallacher,* S. & R. 159, 162 (1822). *See also Commonwealth v. Murtagh,* 1 Ashm. 272, 274-275 (1831), in which the court referred to "the habits, manners, and peculiar conditions of the country."

114 Rothstein, 10 Miami L.Q. at 102; and Note, *Decline and Fall of Common Law Marriage in Pennsylvania,* 18 Temp.U.L.Q. 264, 265 (1944).

115 *McChesney v. Johnson,* 79 S.W.2d 658, 659 (Tex.Civ.App.-Fort Worth 1934).

marriage developed in the case law of several leading states, such as New York and Pennsylvania, when they had already left the conditions of the pioneer period behind them; meanwhile the sparsely populated state of Wyoming never recognized common law marriage.[116]

4.3.5 A State Instrument of Control

The above-mentioned function of common law marriage, to capture "lost sheep," is based on the doctrine's capacity to create a status as well as a contract. Common law marriage, thereby, became an instrument of control by which the state placed all the obligations of formally married spouses on couples that moved in together and created families. Recognition of this function, however, has not been particularly forthcoming. Ariela Dubler, alluding to common law marriage, has maintained that the courts during the 1800s generally used marriage as a vector of public policy.[117] The reason is intimated in American case law by way of exception.

During the 1800s, it was a family law interest that couples living together were subjected to the restrictive marital divorce regulations. This has been expressed, for example, in *Londonderry v. Chester* (1820), in which the New Hampshire Supreme Court pointed to the ease of entering into a common law marriage and the difficulty of dissolving the same.[118] If the marital relationship has well been entered into, the law steps in and holds the parties to various obligations.[119] In *Askew v. Dupree* (1860), the Georgia Supreme Court recognized the validity of common law marriage with reference *inter alia* to the welfare of society and the peace of families.[120] Even in the literature during the 1800s, there were supporters for common law marriage who maintained the importance of getting cohabiting couples within the legal marital system of regulation.[121] Through common law marriage, the considerable portion of the African-American population

---

116 *Roberts v. Roberts,* 133 P.2d 492 (Wyo. 1943). *See also* Bowman, *supra* note 34, at 723.

117 Dubler, *supra* note 104, at 1886. *Compare* Nancy F. Cott, *Giving Character to Our Whole Civil Policy: Marriage and the Public Order in the Late Nineteenth Century,* in U.S. History as Women's History: New Feminist Essays 107 (Linda K. Kerber et al. eds., 1995).

118 *Londonderry v. Chester,* 2 N.H. 268, 281, 9 Am.Dec. 61 (1820). *See also Vaigneur v. Kirk,* 2 S.C.Eq. (2 Des.) 640, 646 (1817), in which the court stated: "[T]he remarkable facility of contracting matrimony in this State, is strongly contrasted with the impracticability of dissolving the contract." The difficulty in dissolving a common law marriage has also been considered a disadvantage, *see* Elizabeth Cady Stanton, a leading feminist during the 1800s, an opponent to the courts' recognition of common law marriage as marital divorce regulations therewith became applicable as to the parties, limiting their freedom. *See* Dubler, *supra* note 104, at 1908.

119 *Maynard v. Hill,* 125 U.S. 190, 211 (1888).

120 *Askew v. Dupree,* 30 Ga. 173, 188 (1860). Compare *People v. Spencer,* 199 Mich. 395, 165 N.W. 921, 923 (1917), in which the court held that common law marriage is recognized *inter alia* "in the interest of the family..."

121 Noah Davis, *Marriage and Divorce,* 139 N. Am. Rev. 31 (1884).

that refrained from ceremonial marriage could be held to the obligations incumbent upon marriage.[122]

A similar reason also recurs in the beginning of the 1900s. Warren Harris maintained at the turn of the twentieth century that, when a man and a woman live together in a relationship as husband and wife, public interests and the general welfare of society are better advanced by holding that they are in law, as well as in fact, husband and wife.[123] Somewhat later, the Pennsylvania Superior Court in *Stump v. Stump* (1934) stated: "It is to the interest of the State that persons living together in the family relation should be married and that the relationship of husband and wife and that of the family be preserved and not be lightly destroyed."[124]

This purpose of the state, to hold cohabiting couples to the legal obligations of marriage, will play a role in a future of decreasing rates of marriage, as discussed in Chapter 14. Also discussed is the other side of the coin, namely, whether in actuality common law marriage and other cohabitation legislation are a threat to the freedom of parties.

4.3.6 Ethnic and Cultural Reasons, as well as Social Reasons

Since the 1800s, ethnic and cultural diversity in the United States have had to be accommodated in order to provide the option of legal marriage to various groups who were either prevented from formally entering into marriage or whose traditions did not include ceremonial marriage. When slavery stripped the African-American population of legal capacity, African-American women and men were prevented from entering into ceremonial marriages as well as common law marriages. This did not, however, impede the creation of families.[125] If a cohabitation continued after the parties were freed or the other impediments were removed, a common law marriage could be established, which offered a legal protection to the parties.[126] This prompted racists to work for the repeal of common law marriage.[127]

---

122 Laura F. Edwards, *The Marriage Covenant Is at the Foundation of All Our Rights: The Politics of Slave Marriages in North Carolina After Emancipation,* 14 LAW & HIST. REV. 81, 93 (1996).

123 Harris, *supra* note 110, at 443.

124 *Stump v. Stump,* 111 Pa. Super. 541, 546 (1934). The same reason can also be traced in *Bishop v. Brittain Invest. Co.*, 229 Mo. 699, 129 S.W. 668 (1910). *See also Ingersol v. McWillie*, 9 Tex.Civ.App. 543, 30 S.W. 56, 60 (1895).

125 *See* FRIEDMAN, *supra* note 94, at 496; and MAXWELL BLOOMFIELD, AMERICAN LAWYERS IN A CHANGING SOCIETY 108-109 (1976).

126 A law in Alabama from 1868 stated that "freed men and women ... living together as man and wife, shall be regarded in law as man and wife," *see* Laws Ala. Ord. No. 23 (1868); and FRIEDMAN, *supra* note 94, at 495-496. In *Cumby v. Garland,* 25 S.W. 673 (Tex.Civ.App. 1894), the court held with respect to freed slaves: "They were free to marry, and, if we are correct in the views before expressed, it required only their mutual consent to convert their previous moral union into a legal and valid marriage. That they did so assent is found by the judge below when he says they continued to live together 'as man and wife' for several months after they were freed."

127 *See* Bowman, *supra* note 34, at 737-740, who argues that the opposition in Louisiana against common law marriage was for the purpose of preventing marriages between

Even if the possibility of formal marriage was available to African-Americans, they, like other social groups, had traditions that accepted cohabitation without ceremonial marriage. It is notable that the first case concerning common law marriage tried by the United States Supreme Court, *Meister v. Moore* (1877), concerned a European man who married a Native-American woman at a ceremony that deviated from the legally applicable wedding rites.[128] Given the American melting pot of different cultures, in certain common law marriage states, imposing form requirements has taken a backseat to maintaining a more tolerant attitude to different marriage traditions.

This reasoning is also compelling in modern times, in states in which the African- American population is not significantly large. In discussions carried out in Pennsylvania concerning the possible repeal of common law marriage, an important argument for retaining the doctrine has been consideration of the African-American population and their traditions.[129]

---

white men and their slaves. *See also* Catherine Augusta Mills, Comment, *Implications of the Repeal of Louisiana Civil Code Article 1481*, 48 La. L. Rev. 1201, 1215 (1988); Bloomfield, *supra* note 125, at 496; and Kermit L. Hall, The Magic Mirror: Law in American History 155 (1989).

128 *Meister v. Moore*, 96 U.S. 76, 78 (1877). In the beginning of the 1900s, the courts often still decided cases concerning marriage according to Native American traditions, *see, e.g.*, cases from Oklahoma, *Hunt v. Hunt*, 23 Okla. 490, 100 P. 541, 22 L.R.A., N.S., 1202 (1909); *Warren v. Canard*, 30 Okla. 514, 120 P. 599 (1911); *Clarkson v. Washington*, 38 Okla. 4, 131 P. 935 (1913); *Coachman v. Sims*, 36 Okla. 536, 129 P. 845 (1913); *Bothwell v. Way*, 44 Okla. 555, 145 P. 350 (1914); *In re Love's Estate*, 42 Okla. 478, 142 P. 305, L.R.A. 1915E, 109 (1914); *Chancey v. Whinnery*, 47 Okla. 272, 147 P. 1036 (1915); *James v. Adams*, 56 Okla. 450, 155 P. 1121 (1915); *Palmer v. Cully*, 52 Okla. 454, 153 P. 154, Ann.Cas. 1918E 375 (1915); *Crickett v. Hardin*, 60 Okla. 57, 159 P. 275 (1916); *Zimmerman v. Holmes*, 59 Okla. 253, 159 P. 303 (1916); *Carney v. Chapman*, 60 Okla. 49, 158 P. 1125 (1916); *In re Sander's Estate*, 67 Okla. 3, 168 P. 197, 199 (1917); *Coleman v. James*, 67 Okla. 112, 169 P. 1064 (1917); *Linsey v. Jefferson*, 68 Okla. 156, 172 P. 641 (1918); *Hughes v. Kano*, 68 Okla. 203, 173 P. 447 (1918); *Horrigan v. Gibson*, 87 Okla. 1, 206 P. 219 (1922); *Madison v. Steckleberg*, 101 Okla. 237, 224 P. 961 (1924); *Thompson v. Smith*, 102 Okla. 150, 227 P. 77 (1924); *Sandlin v. Tiger*, 104 Okla. 107, 230 P. 905 (1925); *Baker v. Jack*, 112 Okla. 142, 241 P. 478 (1925); *Webster v. Webster*, 114 Okla. 57, 242 P. 555 (1925); and *Cordilla v. Taylor*, 181 Okla. 20, 72 P.2d 375 (1937). From Oregon, *see Kalyton v. Kalyton*, 74 P. 491 (Or. 1903). From Missouri, *see Johnson v. Johnson's Adm'r*, 30 Mo. 72 (1860); and *McBean v. McBean*, 61 P. 418 (Or. 1900). Regarding the traditions of Native Americans, *see* Henry H. Foster, *Indian and Common Law Marriages*, 3 Am. Indian L. Rev. 83 (1975) and Olen E. Adams, Note, *Common-Law Marriage In Oklahoma*, 14 Okla. L. Rev. 291 (1961).

129 Steven G. Brown, Comment, *Pennsylvania Common Law Marriage and Annulment: Present Law and Proposals for Reform*, 15 Vill. L. Rev. 134, 140 (1969): "[C]ommentators agree that the common law marriages are most prevalent among lower class Negroes and whites and the poorer segment of society where it is generally accepted. These groups, which compose a significant portion of society, must be taken into consideration before any steps are taken to deny their marriages of their viability." Nancy Rebecca Shaw, *Common Law Marriage and Unmarried Cohabitation: An Old Solution to a New Problem*, 39 U. Pitt. L. Rev. 579, 586 (1977), states: "[I]t may be noted that Pennsylvania is a state in which a wide variety of ethnic groups, cultural backgrounds and lifestyles find representation. Marital customs vary among these diverse groups and Pennsylvania's protection of the marital status extends to all of them by means of the common law tradition." As to the extent at the turn of

As will be seen from the discussion in Chapter 14 concerning the future of common law marriage, the number of families created outside ceremonial marriages during the last thirty years has increased in the United States, including among the European-American segment of the population.

A more general, but related reason that can be separately identified, is the goal of giving social protection to more vulnerable groups.[130] Common law marriage consequently offers, regardless of ethnic association, a material protection for economically, educationally, and/or socially members of vulnerable groups who did not formalize their family relationships through wedding ceremonies. The parties most in need thereby also enjoy the social benefits accruing only to families in which the men and women are or have been married to each other. In the case of *In re Redman's Estate* (1939), the court held that common law marriages are held valid by courts only to protect the rights of innocent persons.[131] In close connection hereto, Walter Weyrauch, in 1960, maintained informal marriages may aid

---

the twentieth century of common law marriage among African-American men and women, and the legislator's endeavor to encourage them to formally marry, is *Renfrow v. Renfrow*, 60 Kan. 277, 72 Am.St.Rep. 350, 56 P. 534 (1899), in which the court applied an in Missouri applicable law prescribing: "In all cases where persons of color heretofore held as slaves in the state of Missouri have cohabited together as husband and wife, it shall be the duty of persons thus cohabiting to appear before a justice of the peace of the township where they reside, or before any other officer authorized to perform the ceremony of marriage..." The court found, however, that the law did not affect the validity of common law marriage: "The statute in question does not pretend to operate upon the marriage status. It does not pretend to annul or forbid the marriage relation because not entered into in accordance with prescribed forms. It only provides penalties for noncompliance with certain ceremonies of solemnization." *See also McAdoo v. Metro. L.Ins.Co*, 233 Mo.App. 900, 110 S.W.2d 845 (1937), in which the court held concerning two African Americans who had lived together between 1902-1909 that they "were living together as husband and wife, as many of their race were wont to do, under a common-law form of marriage." *See also* Jacobus TenBroek, *California's Dual System of Family Law: Its Origin, Development, and Present Status*, 17 STAN. L. REV. 614, 617 (1965): "[C]eremonial marriage is often expensive and may not be a part of the cultural mores of various minority groups." *Cf.* José E. Arraros, *Concubinage in Latin America*, 3 J. FAM. L. 330, 333 (1963) who states that concubinage is accepted among the poor, who develop their own norms, values, and attitudes. Even MEYER F. NIMKOFF, MARRIAGE AND THE FAMILY, 219 (1947) and JOHN SIRJAMAKI, THE AMERICAN FAMILY IN THE TWENTIETH CENTURY 69 (1953), points to the extent of common law marriage among the lower classes of society's with respect to both African Americans and European Americans. *Compare* Walter O. Weyrauch, *Informal Marriage and Common Law Marriage*, in SEXUAL BEHAVIOUR AND THE LAW 297 (R. Slovenko ed. 1965) and HOMER H. CLARK, JR., THE LAW OF DOMESTIC RELATIONS IN THE UNITED STATES 57 fn. 86 (1968).

130 Even if there is a correlation between social class, race, and ethnicity, with European Americans usually the most economically privileged, *see* Wendy D. Manning & Pamela J. Smock, *Living Together Unmarried in the United States: Demographic Perspectives and Implications for Family Policy*, 26 LAW & POLICY 87, 98 (2004), it ought to be noted that a large group of European American couples are not privileged.

131 *In re Redman's Estate*, 135 Ohio St. 554, 558, 21 N.E.2d 659, 661 (1939); *Jolley v. Jolley*, 46 Ohio Misc. 40, 347 N.E.2d 557, 560 (1975); and John R. Williams, *Solemnization of Marriage: The common law marriage—never solemn and no longer common—will it remain law?*, 13 U. MIAMI L. REV. 447, 452 (1959).

and protect the poor and the ignorant in families.[132] Traditionally, cohabitation without formal marriage has been more common in the lower economic classes of society than in the middle class, but a change is under way here today.[133]

4.3.7 Protection for the More Vulnerable Party

Another social objective, also serving the purposes of social justice, regardless of the parties' ethnic association or economic conditions, is protecting the more vulnerable party in the relationship, often the woman, during the cohabitation as well as at its dissolution. This corresponds in actuality to the *ratio legis* behind the ceremonial marriage of providing, with its civil and public law legal effects, benefits including protection and fairness during a marriage as well as upon its dissolution through marital divorce or death. As the woman, most, often is the more vulnerable party, common law marriage has constituted a protection for her and became an instrument for feminist aspirations.[134] One of the primary reasons the legislature in Texas during recent years rejected the proposal to repeal the institution of common law marriage was to preserve the protection to stable family relationships of long duration, and assure the surviving party in an informal relationship the same social benefits granted to the surviving spouse in a formal marriage.[135] Similar to formal marriage, common law marriage in

---

132 Weyrauch, *supra* note 96, at 101. *See also* Williams, *id.* 453 (1959); Martha L. Fineman, *Law and Changing Patterns of Behaviour: Sanctions on Non-Marital Cohabitation,* Wis. L. Rev. 275, 322 fn. 189 (1981); and Thomas Clifford Billig and James Phillip Lynch, *Common-Law Marriage in Minnesota, A Problem in Social Security,* 22 Minn. L. Rev. 177, 178 (1938). *See also* TenBroek, *supra* note 129, at 617: "[C]eremonial marriage is often expensive and may not be a part of the cultural mores of various minority groups." *Compare* Arraros, *supra* note 129, at 333, stating that concubinage is accepted among the poor, who develop their own norms, values and attitudes. *See also* Nimkoff, *supra* note 129, at 219 and Sirjamaki, *supra* note 129, at 69 (common law marriage is common among groups with lower socio-economic status).

133 *See* Chapter 12 *infra.*

134 Dubler, *supra* note 104, at 1887 and 1916, maintains that the majority of cases concerning recognition of common law marriage during the 1800s "were claims for the material support of women left, by death or desertion, without male partners to provide for them... Women plaintiffs who came before nineteenth-century courts seeking financial support through judicial recognition of common law marriages were in dire need. In applying the doctrine to their situations, courts afforded these women monumental concrete benefits." *See also* Bowman, *supra* note 34, at 711. A leading feminist during the 1800s, Elizabeth Cady Stanton, however, was an opponent to the judicial recognition of common law marriage, as marital divorce regulations therewith became applicable as to the parties, limiting their freedom. *See* Dubler, *id.* at 1908.

135 Note, 5 Tex. Tech. L. Rev. 301 (1974). The most recent proposal as to repealing common law marriage in Texas was presented in 1989 by State Representative Patricia Hill from Dallas, House Bill No. 588, 71st Leg.Sess. (1989). The proposal was adopted by the House of Representatives, but defeated as it was not taken up by the Senate. As reason given for the proposal was primarily the uncertainty with respect to the parties' status upon the dissolution of a formless marriage, the criticism

American law has provided not only protection, but also assured the entitlement of a spouse resulting from his or her contributions to the relationship. It is argued that a woman in an informal marriage has, by working in the home and caring for children, facilitated the acquisition of property by the gainfully employed man during the cohabitation and that she, therefore, is entitled to a portion.[136]

4.3.8 A Protection for Children

The *ratio legis* behind informal marriages in American law has not only had the objective of ensuring men and women in such relationships better protection. As with the free Roman marriage and concubinage and informal marriages in medieval canon law, the institution of common law marriage in the United States also has the goal of protecting children from the stigma of illegitimacy, granting them the same rights as those given to children born in wedlock. This purpose is expressed clearly in the older case law. In *Rodebaugh v. Sanks* (Pa.1833), the Pennsylvania Supreme Court held that "a rigid execution of [the statutory requirement of a wedding ceremony] would bastardize a vast majority of the children which have been born within the state for half a century."[137] In *Fryer v. Fryer* (S.C. 1833), in which the parties had lived together for more than thirty years and had

---

against the proposal referred *inter alia* to the importance of giving children and women protection upon the dissolution of such relationships, *see* House Recording Numbers 62 and 78.

136 Shaw, *supra* note 129, at 589, states that: "The assumption is the same one that is implicit in the policy considerations underlying the spouse's statutory intestate share and an equitable division of marital property upon divorce - that the homemaking or childrearing efforts of the dependent partner aided the working partner in the accumulation of the assets during the period of cohabitation, thereby entitling the former to an equitable interest in the property jointly accumulated." *See also Seagriff v. Seagriff*, 195 N.Y.S.2d 718, 721 (Dom.Rel.Ct. 1960), in which a common law marriage was not found proven, but in which the court held that one can sympathize with the woman who after having performed "normal wifely duties" for 35 years deemed herself abandoned by the man. The court found, however, that this ought not to have been entirely unexpected for the woman and that she had not taken advantage of all the occasions that later had been available "to legalize her status." A comparable argument can be also found in Swedish case law. *See* the Swedish cases, SvJT 1974 rf. p. 71 and SvJT 1977 rf. p. 2, whose argument however was not accepted by the Swedish Supreme Court, see further Chapter 12.3.1.1 *infra*.

137 *Rodebaugh v. Sanks*, 2 Watts 9, 11 (Pa. 1833); *Bashaw v. State*, 9 Tenn. (1 Yer.) 177, 197 (1829); *Holmes v. Holmes*, 6 La. 463, 470 (1834); and *Graham v. Bennet*, 2 Cal. 503 (1852). *See further Barnett v. Kimmell*, 35 Pa. 13, 21 (1859), in which the Pennsylvania Supreme Court maintained the importance of protecting "the offspring, whether born before or after the marriage, from the stain and disabilities of illegitimacy." *See also Commonwealth v. Stump*, 53 Pa. 132, 136, 91 Am.Dec. 198 (1866). In *Armaell's Estate*, 2 Brewster 239, 246 (Penn. 1869), a university professor had a child with his servant. Upon his death, the woman and child made claims upon the estate and cited as grounds thereof a common law marriage between the woman and the deceased. Despite the fact that the man wished to hide the relationship, the court granted the claims, stating that "the policy of the state demands that this relation should not be lightly discredited and the issue bastardized." In *Lucken*

children, the South Carolina Court of Appeals questioned: "Who, then, would bastardize this whole family, unless forced, by indubitable testimony, to do so? No one."[138] In *Meister v. Moore* (1877), the United States Supreme Court gave authoritative support for this reasoning by pronouncing that any other construction of marital legislation than the one that is simply directory and, thus allows common law marriage, would compel holding illegitimate the offspring of many parents conscious of no violation of law.[139] The same reasoning supports the legal presumptions applicable to common law marriage. In *Hynes v. McDermott* (1883), the New York Court of Appeals consequently stated with respect to the marriage presumption: "The law presumes everything in favor of the legitimacy of children and it is a very powerful and overwhelming presumption."[140] This same reason is the basis for the presumption in the favor of the latter of two marriages.[141] Joel Bishop summarized the argument at the end of the 1800s by maintaining that a repeal of common law marriage would leave a family with children under the disability and disgrace of bastardy.[142]

Concern about children and their legitimacy can also be found as *ratio* in the case law throughout the 1900s.[143] Occasionally, the courts are more

---

v. Wichman, 5 S.C. 411, 414 (1874), the court notes the significance of saving "the reputation of the woman and free the children from the brand of bastardy."

138 *Fryer v. Fryer*, 9 S.C.Eq. (Rich.Cas.) 85, 108 (1832).

139 *Meister v. Moore*, 96 U.S. 76, 81 (1877). *See also Markley v. Baldwin*, 112 U.S. 490, 495, 28 L.Ed 822, 824, 5 Sup.Ct.Rep. 278 (1884), in which the Court stated: "The protection of the parties and their children and considerations of public policy require this public recognition." For state court, *see Nixon v. Wichita Land & Cattle Co.*, 84 Tex. 408, 19 S.W. 560, 563 (1892); *Holder v. State*, 35 Tex.Crim.Rep. 19, 29 S.W. 793 (1894); *Cumby v. Garland*, 6 Tex.Civ.App. 519, 25 S.W. 673 (1894); *Ingersol v. McWillie*, 9 Tex.Civ.App. 543, 30 S.W. 56, 60-61 (1895); and *State v. Zichfeld*, 23 Nev. 304, 46 P. 802 (1896). The endeavor during the 1800s to protect the legitimacy of children is also argued by Dubler, *supra* note 104, at 1894; GROSSBERG, *supra* note 22, at 196; and Black, *supra* note 5, at 114 and 132.

140 *Hynes v. McDermott*, 91 N.Y. 451, 453, 43 Am.Rep. 677 (1883). Compare *Dillon v. Dillon*, 60 Ga. 204 (1878). *See also Megginson's Estate*, 21 Ore. 387, 28 P. 388, 389 (Or. 1891).

141 *See* Section 5.3.3 *infra.*

142 BISHOP, *supra* note 27, at §§ 403 and 423. *See also* Harris, *supra* note 110, at 444-445.

143 *Reaves v. Reaves*, 15 Okla. 240, 82 P. 490, 496 (1905); *In re McCausland's Estate*, 213 Pa. 189, 62 A. 780 (1906); *Coachman v. Sims*, 36 Okla. 536, 129 P. 845, 847 (1913); and Umbenhower v. Labus, 85 Ohio St. 238, 249, 97 N.E. 832, 834 (1911), in which the Ohio Supreme Court stated: "It is the innocent offspring of such citizens that the law would mercifully protect, and rather call them heirs than bastards." *See also In re Love's Estate*, 42 Okla. 478, 142 P. 305, 308 (1914); *People v. Spencer*, 199 Mich. 395, 165 N.W. 921, 923 (1917) (common law marriage recognized "in the interest of the family and of legitimacy of offspring"); and *In re Sanders' Estate*, 67 Okla. 3, 168 P. 197 (1917). In the case of *In re Stevenson's Estate*, 272 Pa. 291, 116 A. 162, 165 (1922), the court, in a generally critical attitude, stated: "The security of homes as well as the paternity of children is at stake." *See also Dirion v. Brewer*, 20 Ohio App. 298, 301, 151 N.E. 818 (1925); *Welch v. All Persons*, 78 Mont. 370, 254 P. 179, *rev'd*, 85 Mont. 114, 278 P. 110, 115 (1929); *Tiuna v. Willmott*, 162 Okla. 42, 19 P.2d 145 (1933); *Stevens v. Woodmen of the World*, 105 Mont. 121, 71 P.2d 898, 912 (1937); and *Jones v. Kemp*, 144 F.2d 478 (1944). In *Reger v. Reger*, 242 Ind. 302, 315, 177 N.E.2d 901 (1961) (court speaking of "the policy of the common law to protect the innocent party"); *In re Gabaldon's Estate*, 38 N.M. 392, 412, 34 P.2d 672 (1934) (dissenting opinion);

emotional, as in the tone of *In re Love's Estate* (1914), in which the Oklahoma Supreme Court stated: "At the trial of this suit a little daughter, the result of this union, sat innocently by, unconscious that her very name and future status were being determined there. We infer from the record that the property involved is insignificant, and was probably little in mind, while the woman fought for the relation of wife and for a name for her little girl. She is entitled both. We do not propose to sit here, considering the most sacred relation of life, and construe away the status of this woman, who appears to have acted in good faith; neither will we turn the innocent result of this common law union out into the world a nameless thing. She was begotten by a man who had voluntarily assumed the relation of husband and she shall have the right to be called his child and bear his name."[144]

In step with the waning stigma attached to being illegitimate, the tone in the courts' decisions has changed somewhat. Initially, and even in the middle of 1900s, it appeared that the courts, in assessing whether a common law marriage existed between the parents, actively and willingly tried to avoid bastardizing their children.[145] In more modern cases, the courts speak more objectively about avoiding the disadvantages of a child's illegitimacy. In *Ridley v. Grandison* (1990), the Georgia Supreme Court, was generally critical to the doctrine, and consequently stated that common law marriage is a means for avoiding the disadvantages of "illegitimacy" that burden the child whose parents have forgone a ceremonial marriage.[146] The courts, however, have sometimes indicated that even this consideration has its limits. In *Anderson v. Anderson* (1956), the Indiana Supreme Court did not find any common law marriage to exist, and consequently stated: "It is regrettable that the parties had a child born out of wedlock, but this court does not sit as the General Assembly to legitimize all children born under such circumstances."[147] The interest of protecting children is not only anchored in the case law. One of the primary reasons

---

Gatterdam v. Gatterdam, 86 Ohio App. 29, 85 N.E.2d 526, 530 (1949); and *In re Rosenberger's Estate*, 362 Pa.153, 65 A.2d 377 (1949); *In re Wagner's Estate*, 398 Pa. 531, 533 f, 159 A.2d 495, 497 (1960) ("If children had been born of this relationship, the wisdom of regularizing it if possible would be all the more apparent"); and *Tarter v. Medley*, 356 S.W.2d 255 (Ky. 1962). *See also* Black, *supra* note 5, at 114; Weyrauch, *supra* note 96, at 101; and HOMER H. CLARK, JR., THE LAW OF DOMESTIC RELATIONS IN THE UNITED STATES 1, 50 (2d ed. 1987).

144 In the case of *In re Love's Estate*, 42 Okla. 478, 142 P. 305, 308 (1914). *See also Coachman v. Sims*, 36 Okla. 536, 129 P. 845 (1913).

145 *See, e.g.*, *In re Rosenberger's Estate*, 362 Pa. 153, 65 A.2d 377, 380 (1949); and *In re McAnany's Estate*, 91 Pa.Super. 317 (1927).

146 *Ridley v. Grandison*, 260 Ga. 6, 389 S.E.2d 746, 748 (1990). Consideration for the children also appears in *Sapp v. Solomon*, 252 Ga. 532, 314 S.E.2d 878 (1984), in which the court states: "[T]here is nothing illegitimate about any child who is brought, involuntarily, into this world. The attaint of that term should be reserved, in proper cases, for parents." *See also Johnson v. Green*, 251 Ga. 645, 309 S.E.2d 362, 363 (1983).

147 *Anderson v. Anderson*, 235 Ind. 113, 131 N.E.2d 301, 307 (1956).

for the legislator in Texas in recent years to reject the proposal concerning the repeal of the institution of common law marriage was that children born in such relationships today are legitimate.[148] In Chapter 14, "Arguments For and Against Common Law Marriage and Cohabitation Law," other methods of protecting the interests of children are also explored.

4.3.9 A Fulfillment of the Good Faith Expectations of the Parties

Common law marriage has also had the function of fulfilling the good faith expectations of the parties united in marriage and avoiding unjust results.[149] For example, suppose two parties enter into a ceremonial marriage that is later invalidated as a result of an impediment, even though one or both parties entered the marriage in good faith. If the impediment is later removed, and the cohabitation continues, a common law marriage can be established. Similarly, if the parties have acted in good faith, but their ceremonial marriage is invalid due to a mistake in form, the establishment of a common law marriage can prevent unjust results.

Even if a wedding ceremony never occurred, it appears that the courts, in certain cases, have wished to protect a woman who had lived together and perhaps had a child with a man in the belief that she was his wife. Only after the man's death, however, when his will and testament was read, might it become clear that he wanted to avoid acknowledging her rights. In *Brinckle v. Brinckle* (1877), the Pennsylvania Court of Common Pleas in Philadelphia stated: "In those cases, courts and juries, with natural indignation, have been glad to take advantage of every admission in favor of youth and innocence. They have presumed from these facts that the

148 Clarice M. Davis, Comment, *Common-Law Marriage in Texas*, 21 Sw. L.J. 647, 660 (1967): "[S]ince Texas has no paternity act, the availability of common-law marriage serves a useful function in reducing the number of children made illegitimate by the failure of their parents to marry." The same reasons as well as others against a legislative proposal in 1989 as to repealing common law marriage in Texas were given. The legislative proposal was passed by a narrow majority by the House of Representatives, but defeated when it was not taken up by the Senate. *See* House Bill No. 588, 71st Leg. Sess. (1989); House Recording Nos. 62 and 78.

149 Weyrauch, *supra* note 96, at 109, states: "Common law marriage, jointly with other kinds of informal marriages, may assume the function of a safety valve for releasing accumulated pressure and avoiding hardship in individual cases." *See also* Kathryn S. Vaughn, Comment, *The Recent Changes to the Texas Informal Marriage Statute: Limitation or Abolition of Common-law Marriage?*, 28 Hous. L. Rev. 1131, 1140 (1991), who finds that common law marriage's probably most important function is to protect the parties' "good faith expectations." *See also* Clark, *supra* note 143, at 111, who views common law marriage as a means "to make good the bona fide expectations of the parties." *See also* Graham Douthwaite, Unmarried Couples and the Law 19 (1979); Ralph B. Kelley, *Creation and Proof of Common Law Marriage Following Removal of Impediments*, 18 N.Y. Intra. L. Rev. 213, 221 (1963); and Denzil Y. Causey, Jr., Comment, *Domestic Relations - Common Law Marriage in Georgia*, 25 Ga. B.J. 225, 229-230 (1962).

woman has been misled from her confidence in the man; that she has herself thought that the marriage relation existed, and she has consequently been put in the place of an innocent third party ..."[150]

It ought to be noted that the application of the legal institution of common law marriage is not limited to relationships in which one of the parties acted in good faith or is affected in an unjust manner. The purpose of fulfilling the parties' good faith expectations can also be met with the application of legal means other than common law marriage, e.g., the putative marriage doctrine. This alternative to common law marriages is discussed more closely in Chapter 14, addressing the reasons for and against common law marriage in the future.

4.3.10 Moral Reasons

Reasons with a stronger moral tinge appear in the American case law particularly from the middle to the end of the 1800s. Then, the courts strived to salvage the honor of the parties, particularly the woman's, through the use of the common law marriage doctrine, transforming out-of-wedlock relations to legally valid and morally accepted marriages. In *Askew v. Dupree* (1860), the Georgia Supreme Court stated concerning the woman: "Her honor is saved, and this is worth more than everything, even life itself."[151] At the same time that the community, driven by moral indignation and relying on penal sanctions, attempted to stem concubinage and other "loose" relations and to induce couples to formally get married, the morality offered that formless cases of living together, which had marital appearance, could be saved to the true condition. The high respect for marriage encouraged the presumption of marriage even if no marriage

150 *Brinckle v. Brinckle*, 12 Phila. 232, 235 (1877). *See also Orr v. State*, 129 Fla. 398, 409, 176 So. 510, 514 (1937), which concerned cohabiting African Americans: "The institution of marriage is the foundation of our republic ... it is commonly acknowledged to be the best plan created by the ingenuity of man. These colored people failed to obtain a license to marry or to have a ceremony performed in conformity with our law and customs but the facts indicate a common law marriage. The admission 'We was clear to marry but got no court house papers' should not militate against them here." *Cf. Walker v. Matthews*, 191 Miss. 489, 3 So.2d 820 (1941); and *Travers v. Reinhardt*, 205 U.S. 423 (1906).

151 *Askew v. Dupree*, 30 Ga. 173, 190 (1860). From the same period, *see Kansas Pac. Ry. Co. v. Miller*, 2 Colo. 442, 463 (1874), in which the Colorado Supreme Court with respect to the parties stated: "Their conduct being susceptible of two opposite explanations, we are bound to assume it to be moral rather than immoral." In *Armaell's Estate*, 2 Brewster 239, 246 (Penn. 1869), in which the Pennsylvania Supreme Court found that a common law marriage existed, the court held that "marriage, followed by the birth of issue, lies at the very base of the social fabric and of all good morals, and looking at the consequences to society we feel unwilling to suffer an acknowledged marriage and parentage of children..." Against the criticism that common law marriage would damage marriage, the New Hampshire Supreme Court already in 1920 objected that "the purity and sacredness of the marriage contract will remain not less but rather more inviolate," *see Londonderry v. Chester*, 2 N.H. 268, 281 (1820).

contract, either formally or formlessly, could be proven. This presumption also protected marriage as an institution. In *Hynes v. McDermott* (1883), which concerned common law marriage, the New York Court of Appeals consequently stated: "The law presumes morality and not immorality; marriage, and not concubinage; legitimacy and not bastardy."[152] A comparable *ratio* appears in jurisdictions that did not recognizing common law marriage but which, on the basis of cohabitation, presumed a ceremonial marriage.[153]

Morally tinged reasoning can also be found in cases from the beginning of the 1900s. In *Reaves v. Reaves* (1905), the Oklahoma Supreme Court, in support of common law marriage stated: "This doctrine, we think, is more in accord with equity, justice, and good morals than to adopt a rule which might work irreparable injury and hold illegitimate the offspring of parties who were conscious of no violation of the law."[154] In *United States Fidelity & Guaranty Co. v. Dowdle* (1924), a dissenting judge listed the following legal policy reasons for his conclusion that a common law marriage existed: "[I]f any presumptions are to be indulged from the evidence in this case, they should lean to innocence rather than to guilt, and should support a status of matrimony rather than a status of concubinage." The majority shared this view, but came to another conclusion.[155]

In other cases, the moral acceptability of a relationship is based, not on the legal marital system, but rather in the fact that many couples live in a morally acceptable relationship deserving recognition. In *Schurler v. Industrial Comm'n* (1935), the Utah Supreme Court made the following legal policy statement: "Our society is made up largely of social units called families. Where two persons live together such as these did and perhaps have children, there is much to be said in favor of treating them in law as a family ... Illegality is not necessarily immorality ... Certainly, many cases

152 *Hynes v. McDermott,* 91 N.Y. 451, 459, 43 Am.Rep. 677 (1883). The same statement recurs in *Teter v. Teter,* 101 Ind. 129, 51 Am.R. 742 (1884). *See also Hadley v. Rash,* 21 Mont. 170, 53 P. 312 (1898). In *Cargile v. Wood,* 63 Mo. 501, 512 (1877), the court held that though the parties had lived together and outwardly presented themselves as husband and wife and there were circumstances from which one could deduce a contract, a marriage is presumed "in favour of innocence and good morals." The court added: "The law in general presumes against vice and immorality." *Compare Richard v. Brehm,* 73 Pa. 140 (1873); and *Hilton v. Roylance,* 25 Utah 129, 69 P. 660 (1902). A presumption in favor of "marriage" and against "concubinage" also recurs in *Linsey v. Jefferson,* 68 Okla. 156, 172 P. 641 (1918). *See also Jones v. Jones,* 63 Okla. 208, 164 P. 463, 31 L.R.A. 1917 E (1917); and *Nixon v. Wichita Land & Cattle Co.,* 84 Tex. 408, 19 S.W. 560, 563 (1892). *See also* Harris, *supra* note 110, at 444-445.

153 *Redgrave v. Redgrave,* 38 Md. 97 (1873), in which the presumption was made "in favour of morality and decency." *See also Vanderpool v. Ryan,* 137 Va. 445, 119 S.E. 65 (1923), in which the court "in the interest of morality and decency" presumed a ceremonial marriage between a man and a woman on the basis that they had lived together as husband and wife, acted and won acceptance as such. *Compare Reynolds v. Adams,* 125 Va. 295, 99 S.E. 695 (1919).

154 *Reaves v. Reaves,* 15 Okla. 240, 82 P. 490, 496 (1905).

155 *U.S. Fid. & Guar. Co. v. Dowdle,* 269 S.W. 119, 124, 130 (Tex.Civ.App.-Dallas 1924).

may be shown where a man and woman have lived together as *de facto* man and wife during their lives and have been more moral than those who have lived together as *de jure* man and wife."[156] Utah, however, did not recognize common law marriage at that time.

Similar arguments can also be found later. In *Gammelgaard v. Gammelgaard* (1956), concerning a common law marriage, the court declares: "In doubtful cases, courts prefer that construction of evidence which finds a legitimate marriage rather than a long period of lewd and criminal cohabitation."[157] Among the states that today recognize common law marriage, this *ratio* appears most clearly in Montana. The courts there have, since the end of the 1800s, given expression for the same view which its supreme court held in the case of *In re Estate of Swanson* (1972): "Every intendment of the law is in favor of matrimony which presumes morality and not immorality, marriage and not concubinage, legitimacy and not bastardy."[158]

Moral arguments are to a high degree also cited against common law marriage, as is seen from the section below regarding the initial criticism against these marriages. The delicate question of how the line is drawn between presumed morality and immorality in American case law is treated in subsequent chapters (see Chapters 5-9). The increasingly limited role of the moral dimension within the framework for common law marriage and modern cohabitation legislation early in the twenty-first century is discussed in Chapter 14.

---

156 *Schurler v. Industrial Comm'n,* 86 Utah 284, 43 P.2d 696, 698-699 (1935).

157 *Gammelgaard v. Gammelgaard*, 247 Iowa 978, 77 N.W.2d 479, 481 (1956). *Compare Trammell v. Trammell,* 196 S.W.2d 209, 210 (Tex.Civ.App. 1946), in which the court found a common law marriage proven instead of "condemning them to a life of unlicensed sin." *Compare also In re Wagner's Estate,* 398 Pa. 531, 533, 159 A.2d 495, 497 (1960), in which the parties after marital divorce formlessly moved in together and in which the court stated: "We regard it better to encourage remarriage than to leave such parties under judicial edict that they were living sinfully together for ten years." *Compare* Joseph W. McKnight, *Recodification and Reform of the Law of Husband and Wife,* 33 TEX. B.J. 34, 36 (1970), who points to common law marriage's function to confer upon stable personal relationships a legal status and validity.

158 *In re Estate of Swanson*, 160 Mont. 271, 502 P.2d 33, 37 (1972). *See already Hadley v. Rash,* 21 Mont. 170, 53 P. 312, 314 (1898), in which the court came to the conclusion that a marriage existed "in the interest of morality, innocence, and the sanctity of the marriage relation"; and *State v. Newman,* 66 Mont. 180, 213 P. 805 (1923). In *Welch v. All Persons,* 78 Mont. 370, 254 P. 179, 182 (1926), the Montana Supreme Court stated: "The presumption in favor of matrimony is one of the strongest known to the law ... Every presumption will be indulged in favor of the legality of a common-law marriage in the same way and to the same extent as the law indulges them in favor of a ceremonial marriage." *See also Matter of Estate of Murnion,* 212 Mont. 107, 686 P.2d 893, 897 (1984).

4.4 The Initial Criticism against Common Law Marriage

Even though this chapter primarily purports to present how and why common law marriage gained recognition in the United States, as background to the subsequent presentation, it ought to be noted that criticism of the doctrine began to arise in the case law as early as the 1800s. The criticism during the first half of the 1800s would lead to the repeal of the doctrine in many states but also to a change in attitude in those states that continued to recognize common law marriage for a long time forward. The initial criticism during the 1800s may constitute a background for the discussion in Chapter 14 with respect to the reasons for and against common law marriage in the future.

The year after *Fenton v. Reed,* the Massachusetts Supreme Judicial Court in *Milford v. Worchester* (1810), chaired by Chief Justice Theophilus Parsons, refused to recognize common law marriage by asserting that the most important form requirements were mandatory, not simply directory, even in the absence of express regulations about invalidity.[159] In *Commonwealth v. Munson* (1879), the same court – after a historical review of the state's form requirements for the commencement of marriage – held that the canon law was never adopted and never accepted here as common law; that parties could, by their own contract, without the presence of an officiating clergyman or magistrate, take each other as husband and wife; and so marry themselves.[160] Massachusetts did not later recognize common law marriage.

Parsons' criticism of common law marriage applied a principle of interpretation other than that used by James Kent. The criticism largely rested on legal policy considerations with respect to the danger to morality, risk of abuse, and legal uncertainty of the doctrine.[161] The criticism against

159 In *Milford v. Worcester,* 7 Mass. 48, 52-53 (1810). *Compare already Mangue v. Mangue,* 1 Mass. 240 (1804), in which the woman's lawsuit concerning marital divorce was dismissed with reference to that the common law did not contain any principle according to which one of the parties, without the presence of a clergyman, giving marriage vows could constitute a valid marriage: "Here is no evidence of a marriage - no such evidence as is known in law." That the court's decision was not only based on insufficient proof can be seen from the following: "The parties agreed to come together, and they may now agree to separate," *id. at* 242.

160 *Commonwealth v. Munson,* 127 Mass. 459, 460-461 (1879).

161 In *Milford v. Worcester,* 7 Mass. 48, 52-53 (1810), the court pointed to the danger for the "prostration of morals and a dissolution of manners" and the importance to "guard against fraud, surprise, and seduction." In *Bashaw v. State,* 9 Tenn. (1 Yer.) 177 (1829), the court also maintained that the interests of society must be considered. *See also State v. Samuel,* 19 N.C. 177 (1836); *State v. Hodskins,* 19 Me. 155, 36 Am.D. 743 (1841); *Ligonia v. Buxton,* 2 Greenleaf 102, 11 Am.Dec. 46 (1822); and *State v. Patterson,* 2 N.C. (1 Ired.) 346 (1836) (1836). In *Dunbarton v. Franklin,* 19 N.H. 257, 264-265 (1848), the court stated: "It is singular that the most important of all human contracts, on which the rights and duties of the whole community depend, requires less formality for its validity than a conveyance of an acre of land,

common law marriage also received support in a couple of English decisions, in which a divided House of Lords held that the presence of a clergyman always has been necessary for the creation of a marriage in England.[162] Even if the statements were historically incorrect, they came to play a role in the American criticism against common law marriage.[163] In general, criticism against the doctrine was not common during the first part of the 1800s. As can be seen from the above, the doctrine was not accepted by the courts in Tennessee,[164] North Carolina,[165] and Maine;[166] eventually,

---

a policy of insurance, or the agreement which the statute of frauds requires should be in writing." *Compare Hurley's Case*, 14 Gray 411 (Mass. 1860), in which the court as to the evidence held that "cohabitation and the conduct of the parties are in all cases competent evidence in proof of marriage."

162 In *Regina v. Millis*, (1843) 10 Cl. & F. 534, 8 Eng.Rep. 844, which concerned a marriage commenced in Ireland, it was argued that English common law never recognized marriages commenced without the participation of a clergyman. *See also Beamish v. Beamish*, (1861) 11 Eng.Rep. 735, also with Irish origins. The cases are cited *inter alia* in *Milford v. Worchester*, 7 Mass. 48 (1810) and in *Denison v. Denison*, 34 Md. 361 (1871).

163 POLLOCK, *supra* note 27, at 328, argues consequently that this view "is now believed by most competent scholars to be without any real historical foundation." In POLLOCK AND MAITLAND, *supra* note 5, at 372, it is stated: "If the victorious cause pleased the lords, it is the vanquished cause that will please the historian of the middle ages." *See also* BISHOP, *supra* note 27, at §§ 400-417; and KOEGEL, *supra* note 11, at 49-50: "There is now no doubt that the decisions in these two cases were incorrect."

164 *Bashaw v. State*, 9 Tenn. (1 Yer.) 177, 197 (1829). In *Grisham v. State*, 10 Tenn. (2 Yer.) 588, 592 (1831), the court stated: "Since the year 1741, at least, the common law mode of constituting a legal marriage is of no validity here." *Compare McCorry v. King's Heirs*, 22 Tenn. 267 (1842); *Rice v. State*, 26 Tenn. 14 (1846); *Andrews v. Page*, 50 Tenn. 653 (1871); and *Holabird v. Atlantic Mutual Life Ins. Co.*, 12 Fed.Cas. 315 No. 6, 587 (C.C.E.D. Mo 1873). The cases of *Bashaw and Grisham* finally received support in the later leading case, *Smith v. North Memphis Savings Bank*, 115 Tenn. 12, 89 S.W. 392 (1905), in which a common law marriage was considered invalid through an interpretation of form requirements lacking express regulations as to invalidity. The marriage presumption, however, received support already in *inter alia Ewell v. State*, 14 Tenn. 364, 372 (1834), in which the court stated: "Cohabitation as man and wife and general reputation, are evidence of marriage as well as relationship." *See also Johnson v. Johnson*, 41 Tenn. 626 (1860). In Tennessee, the courts later applied other solutions, *see* Robert E. Kendrick, *Informal Marriages in Tennessee – Marriage by Estoppel, by Prescription and by Ratification*, 3 VAND. L. REV. 610 (1950).

165 *State v. Samuel*, 19 N.C. 177 (1836); *State v. Patterson*, 2 N.C. (1 Ired.) 346 (1836); *Overmans v. Clemmons*, 19 N.C. 178 (1836); and *State v. Wilson*, 121 N.C. 650, 28 S.E. 416 (1897). Marriages without a license were valid in *State v. Robbins*, 28 N.C. 23, 45 Am.Dec. 507 (1845). In addition, it appears that "reputation, cohabitation and the declaration and conduct of the parties" have been competent proof of a marriage, *see Archer v. Haithcock*, 51 N.C. 421 (1859); *Jackson v. Rhem*, 59 N.C. 141 (1869), *Jones v. Reddick*, 79 N.C. 290 (1878); and *Ferrall v. Rhem*, 59 N.C. 141 (1869). *See also* Semonche, *supra* note 16, at 320.

166 *State v. Hodskins*, 19 Me. 155, 36 Am.D. 743 (1841); *Ligonia v. Buxton*, 2 Greenleaf 102, 11 Am.Dec. 46 (1822). The requirement of parental consent to a marriage of minors, however, has been considered directory, *see Hiram v. Pierce*, 45 Me. 367 (Me. 1858). *See also Gardiner v. Manchester*, 88 Me. 249, 33 A. 990 (1896). As to the evidence, *compare Taylor v. Robinson*, 29 Me. 323 (1849), in which the court held that "in all civil personal actions, except for criminal conversation, general reputation and cohabitation are sufficient evidence of marriage."

New Hampshire curtailed its acceptance with a partial recognition.[167] This development occurred despite more and more courts accepting informal marriages.

In the middle of the nineteenth century, a critical voice was raised in the academic literature. It was Chief Justice Parsons' son, Theophilus Parsons, Jr., who in his book on contracts published in 1853 carried his father's views further.[168] However, it was first during the 1870s that the criticism against common law marriage became part of an organized campaign purporting to protect society from marital instability.[169] Michael Grossberg has stated that panic over family life led to persistent efforts to compel deviant couples to adhere to orthodox republican matrimonial practices.[170] One of those eager for reform, Frank Cook, posited a requirement for a stronger state intervention through legislation within the marital laws.[171] The criticism was directed to a high degree against the divorce legislation that was considered too liberal, but a material contribution in this campaign also was the criticism against informal relationships. James Schouler spoke of "the painful uncertainty which hangs about these informal marriages" but admitted that these rested on the idea that "an institution of such fundamental importance to our race ought to be good independently of, and prior to, the formal requirements which human government imposes at an advanced stage of society."[172] Afterwards, the criticism grew and, at the turn of the century, a crusade against common law marriage had been formed, led by George Howard, who encouraged a legislative revolution.[173] Several jurists joined the campaign, active during the first part of the 1900s, such as Robert Brickell,[174] Otto Koegel,[175]

---

167 *Dunbarton v. Franklin*, 19 N.H. 257 (1848).

168 Theophilus Parsons, Jr., The Law of Contract (Boston 1853).

169 Regarding the movement for reform, *see* Grossberg, *supra* note 22, at 85; and Dubler, *supra* note 104, at 1885.

170 Grossberg, *supra* note 22, at 84.

171 Cook, *supra* note 16, at 352. *See also* M.H. Buckham, *The Relation of the Family to the State,* 13 International Review 63 (1882); Gordon A. Stewart, *Our Marriage and Divorce Laws*, 23 P.S.M. 228 (1883); Charles Noble, *A Compendium of the Laws on Marriage and Divorce* (New York 1882); Report of the National League for the Protection of the Family (Boston 1891); and William E. Bullock, The Law of Domestic Relations of the State of New York 33 (Albany, N.Y. 1898), who recommended the repeal *inter alia* because he considered common law marriage to be immoral and lead to divorces. For more concerning the movement for reform, *see* Grossberg, *supra* note 22, at 83.

172 James Schouler, A Treatise on Husband and Wife 47-50 (Boston, Little, Brown & Co. 1882). *See also* the same author in Marriage, Divorce, Separation & Domestic Relations I, 42 (6th ed. 1921).

173 Howard III, *supra* note 16, at 184. *See also* the same author in *Social Control of Domestic Relations,* 167 A.J.S. 815 (1910).

174 Robert C. Brickell, *Common-Law Marriage,* 44 Am. L. Rev. 256 (1910).

175 Koegel, *supra* note 11.

Willystine Goodsell,[176] Frank Keezer,[177] Chester Vernier,[178] and later Abraham and Maurice Freedman.[179]

During the latter part of the 1800s, the criticism against common law marriage became clearer even in the case law. Consequently, recognition was refused by the courts in Oregon,[180] Maryland,[181] Connecticut,[182] Virginia,[183] West Virginia[184] and Washington.[185] In the beginning of the 1900s,

---

176 GOODSELL, *supra* note 17, at 358, arguing that "no legislative reform is more needed than clear and positive statutes declaring such loosely contracted unions null and void."

177 In FRANK H. KEEZER, A TREATISE ON THE LAW OF MARRIAGE AND DIVORCE 81-82 (2d ed. 1923) the author stated: "There should always be either a religious ceremony or a civil celebration and all marriages by simple consent should be declared void on the ground of public policy. Such marriages are contrary to the principles of sound morality..." *See also* JOHN W. MORLAND, KEEZER ON THE LAW OF MARRIAGE AND DIVORCE, 59 (3 ed 1946) ("It cheapens marriage and gives instability to the home").

178 CHESTER G. VERNIER, AMERICAN FAMILY LAWS I, 108 (1931), proposed the repeal of common law marriage with respect to the fact that there is "too much confusion, conflict, and uncertainty."

179 ABRAHAM L. FREEDMAN AND MAURICE FREEDMAN, LAW OF MARRIAGE AND DIVORCE IN PENNSYLVANIA I, 103 (2d ed. 1957).

180 In *Holmes v. Holmes*, 1 Abb. 525 (U.S.C.C. Ore. 1870), the form requirements were considered "mandatory." In *Huard v. McTeigh*, 113 Or. 279, 232 P. 658, 39 A.L.R. 528 (1925), the Oregon Supreme Court held that "the doctrine of common-law marriage is contrary to public policy and public morals. It places a premium upon illicit cohabitation and offers encouragement to the harlot and to adventuress. We do not sanction loose marriages or easy divorces." *Compare Reed v. Harkrader*, 4 Alaska Fed. 893, 264 F. 834 (9th Cir. 1920), in which Oregon law was applied, as well as *In re Glisan*, 18 Pen.Dec. 323 (1911). *Compare also Megginson's Estate*, 21 Ore. 387, 28 P. 388 (Or. 1891), in which the marriage presumption was applied. *See also* Erroll Clarence Gilkey, *Validity of Common Law Marriage in Oregon*, 3 OREG. L. REV. 28 (1923).

181 *Denison v. Denison*, 35 Md. 361 (1872); and *Richardson v. Smith*, 80 Md. 89, 30 A. 568 (1894) ("there cannot be a valid marriage without a religious ceremony"). *Compare Cheseldine v. Brewer*, 1 H.& McH. 152 (1739). The marriage presumption however has been applied, *see Richardson*, as well as *Jackson v. Jackson*, 80 Md. 176 (1894); and *Redgrave v. Redgrave*, 38 Md. 93 (1873).

182 *In re Bartlett*, 15 Pen.Dec. 290 (1880); and *Felson v. Allen*, 129 Conn. 427, 29 A.2d 306 (1943). *Compare Erwin v. English*, 61 Conn. 502 (1892).

183 In *Beverlin v. Beverlin*, 29 W.Va. 732, 3 S.E. 36 (1887), the judge expressed in *dictum* as to the state of the law in Virginia: "I have been unable to find any case in which the courts of this state or of Virginia have ever held that *common law marriage was valid.*" On the other hand, it appears that the marriage presumption had support in older case law, *see Eldred v. Eldred*, 97 Va. 606, 34 S.E. 477 (1899). Regarding Virginia, for a historical analysis of older legislation *see* Harris, *supra* note 110. In *Offield v. Davis*, 100 Va. 250, 40 S.E. 910 (1902), the form requirements through interpretation were also considered to be "mandatory." The court stated: "The question before us involves the best interests of society, the preservation of home and family, the foundation of all society."

184 In *Beverlin v. Beverlin*, 29 W.Va. 732, 3 S.E. 36 (1887), the court stated in *dictum*: "We think our statute has wholly superseded the common law, and in effect if not in express terms renders invalid all attempted marriages contracted in this State which have not been solemnized in compliance with its provisions." *See also Kisla v. Kisla*, 124 W.Va. 220, 19 S.E.2d 609 (1942); and *Goode v. Goode*, 396 S.E.2d 430 (W.Va. 1990).

185 In the case of *In re McLaughlin's Estate*, 4 Wash. 570, 30 P. 651 (1892), the court refers to "the best interest of society and the preservation of the home and family, - the foundation of all society." *Compare In re Smith's Estate*, 4 Wash. 702, 30 P. 1059 (1892);

common law marriage was rejected by the courts in North Dakota,[186] Delaware,[187] and New Mexico, in which the form requirements were considered mandatory, despite the fact that marriages commenced in violation of them were not expressly declared invalid.[188] The majority of courts, however, still accepted the doctrine, by which the form requirements did not expressly prescribe that informal marriages were invalid.

Around the turn of the twentieth century, legislative bodies also began to intervene with legislation directly purporting to repeal common law marriage. Consequently, the doctrine was repealed in California in 1895[189] and in New York in 1901,[190] where the doctrine, however, was reinstated in 1907 in order to be repealed anew through legislation in 1933. With the final repeal, one of the reasons stated was the risk of fraudulent behavior for the purpose of claiming the estates of deceased persons.[191] Common law marriage was also repealed through legislation in Utah in 1888, which, however, ninety-nine years later reinstated the doctrine through legislation in 1987.[192] This was simply the beginning of a development. At the turn of the twentieth century, common law marriage was still recognized in two-thirds of all states.[193] Developments during the first half of the 1900s would, however, mean that more than half of all states repealed common law marriage, as will be discussed more fully in "Part III, The Future."

The criticism rested to a high degree consequently on legal policy considerations with respect to common law marriage; the moral dangers of the doctrine; the family and the community in general; as well as the application difficulties, disputes, and the legal uncertainty it entailed.[194]

---

and *In re Wilbur's Estate*, 8 Wash. 35 (1894). The same argument recurs in *Offield v. Davis*, 100 Va. 250, 40 S.E. 910 (1902).

186 *Schumacker v. Gt. Northern Ry. Co.*, 23 N.D. 231, 136 N.W. 85 (1912); and *Powers v. Buckey*, 190 N.W. 312 (1922).

187 *Wilmington Trust Co. V. Hendrixon*, 31 Del. 303, 114 A. 215 (1921); and *Owens v. Bentley*, 40 Del. 512, 14 A.2d 391 (1940).

188 *In re Gabaldon's Estate*, 38 N.M. 392, 412, 34 P.2d 672 (1934).

189 Act of March 26 (1895). *See* Charlotte K Goldberg, *The Schemes of Adventuresses: The Abolition and Revival of Common-Law Marriage*, 483 Wm. & Mary J. Women & L. 483, 505-509 (2006-2007).

190 Laws of 1901, c. 339, § 6; Domestic Relations Law § 19. Common law marriage was reinstated in New York in 1907 through Laws of 1907, c. 742, § 6. Common law marriage was repealed anew in New York in 1933 through Laws of 1933, c. 606. Domestic Relations Law § 11.

191 For more on this, *see* Section 14.3.2 *infra*.

192 Common law marriage was repealed in Utah by Act of March 8, 1888, ch. 45, § 2 (3). *See also United States v. Simpson*, 4 Utah 227, 7 P. 257 (1885); and Utah Code Ann. § 30-1-4.5. (1987), enacted through Act of Feb. 25, 1987, ch. 246, effective April 27, 1987.

193 *See also* Howard III, *supra* note 16, at 184.

194 Already in *Duncan v. Duncan*, 10 Ohio St. 181, 188, 1859 WL 67 (1859), the court held that common law marriage "would tend to weaken the public estimate of the sanctity of the marriage relation" and would further "place honest, God-ordained matrimony, and mere meretricious cohabitation too nearly on a level with each other." Observe that common law marriage was recognized two years later in Ohio, *see Carmichael v. State*, 12 Ohio St. 553 (1861). *See also Denison v. Denison*, 35 Md. 361 (1872),

That which the proponents considered to be a protection for the woman in a common law marriage was considered by the opponents to be a source of abuse. The reform endeavors were also optimistic about the possibility of family law legislation affecting patterns of behavior.[195] Many of the earlier arguments presented against common law marriage resurfaced as well as others in the efforts to repeal the doctrine in many states during the 1900s. As these arguments are of interest in the discussion today concerning the future for common law marriage and other cohabitation law, they are more closely analyzed and critically reviewed in Part III.

It is clear that the strong criticism against common law marriage primarily during the first part of the 1900s also affected attitudes towards the doctrine in jurisdictions in which it remained alive. During the 1800s, the courts could cite public policy, common justice, and humanity in support of common law marriage.[196] During the first part of the 1900s, social pressures in favor of ceremonial marriage as well as the application problems of common law marriage led the courts that recognized the doctrine to do so with a certain animosity. Typical of the attitude of many courts is *Baker v. Mitchell* (1941), in which Superior Court of Pennsylvania stated: "The law of Pennsylvania *recognizes* common law marriage. But they are a fruitful source of perjury and fraud, and, in consequence, they are to be *tolerated, not encouraged*" (italics added).[197] This same attitude is clearly

in which the court stated: "These loose and irregular contracts as a general thing, derive no support from morals or religion, but are most generally founded in a wanton and licentious cohabitation. Hence the law of the state has given them no sanction." In *Sorensen v. Sorensen*, 68 Neb. 500, 504, *aff'd*, 100 N.W. 930, 934 (1904), the court held that if it would establish a marriage on the basis of the evidence presented in the court, it would be to "open the door to fraud and perjury." In *Furth v. Furth,* 133 S.W. 1037, 1039 (Ark. 1911), the court stated that formal marriage "will best foster and protect the home, and promote the sacredness of the marriage relation, which is the foundation of the family and the origin of all forms of government."

195 *See* George Elliot Howard, *Social Control of Domestic Relations,* 167 A.J.S. 815 (1910), who argued that a good marriage act "tends to check hasty, clandestine, frivolous, and immature wedlock."

196 *See, e.g., Ingersol v. McWillie,* 9 Tex.Civ.App. 543, 30 S.W. 56, 61 (1895). In the case concerning the surviving woman's right to the man's estate, the Texas Court of Civil Appeals held that its decisions usually have been "broad and liberal upon the subject" and continued: "Since his death, we think that public policy, as well as common justice and humanity, demand that the marriage should be sustained, and her rights as survivor protected." Concerning the courts' positive attitude to common law marriage at the end of the 1800s, *see* in general those cases cited above particularly under the main headings *Moral Reasons* and *The State's Interest.*

197 *Baker v. Mitchell,* 143 Pa.Super. 50, 54, 17 A.2d 738, 741 (1941). The same statement later has recurred in a series of cases, from Pennsylvania as from other states. *See e.g., In re Erickson's Estate,* 75 S.D. 345, 64 N.W.2d 316, 318 (1954) ("Such marriages are a source of fraud and perjury. They are to be tolerated only and not encouraged"); *Anderson v. Anderson,* 235 Ind. 113, 131 N.E.2d 301, 305 (1956); *In re Blecher's Estate,* 381 Pa. 138, 112 A.2d 129 (1955); *In re Estate of Wagner,* 398 Pa. 531, 159 A.2d 495 (1960); *In re Estate of Collings,* 405 Pa. 280, 175 A.2d 62, 63 (1961); *McDermott v. McDermott,* 236 Pa.Super.Ct. 541, 345 A.2d 914, 918 (1975) ("It is true that the courts have in the past looked upon common law marriage with a somewhat jaundiced eye");

expressed by the courts in the South. In *Texas Employers' Insurance Association v. Elder* (1954), the court stated: "[T]he law does not favour, but merely tolerates, common law marriages."[198] This restrained attitude, which lies in the idea that common law marriage ought to be tolerated, not protected and even less favored, in many states has affected the formation of the evidentiary rules that place the burden of proof upon the party claiming a common law marriage, and requires that such a marriage be proven through evidence that is clear and convincing. Within this restrictive view in the evidentiary context, there naturally lies a tension in relation to the use of the legal presumptions to the benefit of the acceptance of informal marriages and the above reported reasons behind these (see Chapter 9, "Burdens of Proof and Presumptions").[199]

An exception to the requirement of clear and convincing evidence to prove the existence of a common law marriage, in certain cases, has been made when the legal consequences concerned a child's legitimacy, giving credence to the significance of this concern. [200] Furthermore, in a number of cases, it appears that the requirement of clear and convincing evidence has taken a back seat in order to favor remarriage between divorced couples through informal marriage.[201] In contrast to other states, however, note Idaho, which has never taken a negative attitude to the institution of common law marriage,[202] and Alabama, where the courts in general also appear to have never disdained this cohabitation form.[203]

In re Estate of Stauffer, 505 Pa. 626, 476 A.2d 354, 356 (1984); *Estate of Gavula*, 490 Pa. 535, 417 A.2d 168, 171 (1980); and *In re Estate of Kovalchick*, 345 Pa.Super. 229, 498 A.2d 374, 376 (1985).

198 *Texas Employers' Ins. Ass'n v. Elder*, 274 S.W.2d 144, 147 (Tex.Civ.App. 1954).

199 For more concerning the different burdens of proof, levels of proof and legal presumptions, *see* Chapter 9 *infra*.

200 *See, e.g., Richard v. Richard*, 172 Okla. 397, 45 P.2d 101, 108 (1935).

201 In the case of *In re Wagner's Estate*, 398 Pa. 531, 159 A.2d 495, 82 A.L.R.2d 681, (1960) the court stated concerning a formless reunion of divorced spouses: "In such case we think that the law's role of mere toleration of the common law relationship should be reversed and the status of remarriage favored, even if acquired with common law informality." The same view recurs in *McDermott v. McDermott*, 236 Pa.Super.Ct. 541, 345 A.2d 914, 919 (1975). By way of exception, however, cases arise in which the courts have taken the opposite view and maintained that the parties' marital divorce speaks against that they later had been rejoined in a common law marriage, *see e.g., Goodman v. McMillan*, 258 Ala. 125, 61 So.2d 55 (1952); *Turner v. Turner*, 251 Ala. 295, 37 So.2d 186 (1948); and *In re Pratt's Estate*, 233 App.Div. 200, 251 N.Y.S. 424 (1931).

202 I.C. § 32-201, Analysis: "Idaho has never viewed the doctrine of common-law marriage with disfavor." The Idaho Supreme Court also gives expression to the same stance in *Metro. Life Ins. Co. v. Johnson*, 103 Idaho 122, 645 P.2d 356, 360 (1982).

203 Crawley, *supra* note 112, at 403, stating that "the Alabama appellate courts have generally not disparaged the doctrine or given it only grudging approval."

4.5 Summary and Conclusions

1. *The Historical Background*

Common law marriage has its origins in old English ecclesiastical law and medieval canon law, which in turn was influenced by Roman law, as traced in this chapter. When England, through the Reformation, freed itself from the Roman Catholic Church, and the Anglican Church in 1534 assumed jurisdiction in cases concerning marriage, it retained the medieval canon law principles for the commencement of marriage. When the Roman Catholic Church, in 1563, introduced the *Forma Tridentina,* it was not adopted in Protestant England, but the canon law that preceded the Council of Trent was still applied. First, through Lord Hardwicke's Act of 1753, in England, a requisite was enacted for the validity of a marriage and a mandatory form was required, excluding common law marriage. Lord Hardwicke's Act did not become applicable in the colonies or in Ireland and Scotland. As no new English cases on the subject were adjudicated after 1753, it was the Irish and primarily Scottish cases that exercised influence on the American case law.[204]

2. *The American Reception*

The American courts, after independence in 1776, did not have any formal obligation to apply the legal regulations of its former mother country. England itself had abandoned the old regulations with the passage of Lord Hardwicke's Act. Nevertheless, the fundamental principles for common law marriage were received into the American case law. Guiding the American development was *Fenton v. Reed* (1809), in which the New York Supreme Court, without reference to earlier American case law, but citing three English cases, stated: "No formal solemnization of marriage was requisite. A contract of marriage made *per verba de praesenti* amounts to an actual marriage, and is as valid as if made *in facie ecclesiae...*"[205] The decision, supported by the leading scholarship, had remarkable impact on the case law during the entire 1800s.

Common law marriage spread during the first part of the 1800s to a number of states, but it was during the latter part of that century that recognition of the doctrine truly accelerated. In *Meister v. Moore* (1877), common law marriage was recognized for the first time by the United States Supreme Court, stating: "That such a contract constitutes a marriage at common law there can be no doubt, in view of the adjudications made in this country, from its earliest settlement to the present day."[206] At the end of the 1800s, common law marriage also received a foothold in

204 *See, e.g., Dalrymple v. Dalrymple,* (1811) 2 Hagg.Cons. 54, 161 Eng.Rep. 665.
205 *Fenton v. Reed,* 4 Johns. 52 (N.Y. 1809).
206 *Meister v. Moore,* 96 U.S. 76, 78 (1877).

the legislation of several states. At the turn of the twentieth century, two-thirds of the American states recognized common law marriage and, thereafter, the doctrine gained recognition in a few additional states, but by then, opposition to the doctrine had begun to have an effect.

3. Several Peculiarities in American Common Law Marriage

The development of American common law marriage would come to deviate from its classical role models. One of the two canon and English variations of formless marriage, *sponsalia per verba de futuro cum copula,* in other words, an agreement of a future marriage with thereafter following consummation, became obsolete. Even if the other variation, which gained recognition, in principle was based on a marriage contract *per verba de praesenti,* the development in the American case law would mean that the courts accepted inferred agreements, in which the parties' cohabitation and outward appearance as spouses in practice would become decisive, while the contractual elements, in many cases, would be moved further and further into the background.[207] The marriage presumption was also based on the parties' cohabitation and outward appearance as spouses.[208] In addition, these circumstances in time would develop into the independent requisites necessary for establishing a common law marriage in addition to the fictional marriage contract.[209]

4. The Reasons for the American Reception

One often-overlooked reason behind the recognition of common law marriage in the United States, as seen from this chapter, is (1) the authority enjoyed by the English and therewith canon and classical Roman law. For example, in *Askew v. Dupree* (1860), the court stated, after references to Roman, canon, English, and Scottish law: "*Consensus, non concubitus, faciat matrimonium,* the maxim of the Roman civil law is, in truth, the maxim of all law upon the subject."[210] The same partiality for Roman principles was expressed in the literature. This authority must have been facilitated by the lack of any pre-existing system in the United States that could compete with the system based on classical thought that was imported from the mother country. Common law marriage was not an American innovation, but the informal marriage fit well in the American reality and the values characterizing it.

The United States, at the beginning of the 1800s, was a community without a state church, to which many had emigrated to escape state oppression, and (2) there was sympathy for allowing the freedom to enter

207 *See* Chapter 7 *infra.*
208 *See* Chapter 9 *infra.*
209 *See* Chapter 8 *infra.*
210 *Askew v. Dupree,* 30 Ga. 173, 178 (1860).

into marriage without state interference. American marital law expressed an individualism according to which the commencement of marriage was considered a private contract between independent individuals; marriage was viewed as an institution of such fundamental significance that it could not be impeded by any form requirements.

The inclination to protect autonomy also affected the interpretation of form requirements. Even if there were form requirements for the commencement of a ceremonial marriage, (3) they were not considered mandatory, as long as they did not expressly regulate the validity of informal marriages. This is a classic common law argument that legislation is treated as a secondary source of law, to the extent that is accepted, only if the regulations are mandatory. Usually, however, they were considered to be only a directory. Even if the failure to comply with the form requirements was criminally sanctioned, the marriage's validity was not affected, which was possible by maintaining a distinction between legality and validity.

A historical reason for the growth of common law marriage in the American case law, which was significant during the pioneer period, in the United States, was (4) the limited access to formal weddings, which was caused by sparsely populated settlements, insufficient public transportation, and the lack of persons authorized to perform wedding ceremonies. Common law marriage, under these circumstances, was an easily accessible possibility to enter into a valid marriage.

It has further been seen in this chapter that common law marriage also (5) functioned as a control mechanism for the state to capture, within state regulations, as many as possible of those who actually create families without formally marrying. In contrast with the commencement of a common law marriage, the legal effects thereof were not a private contract primarily expressing the parties' individual agreements. It was in this respect a status, and entailed all the legal effects of a marriage given by the state, including the accompanying obligations, such as the divorce regulations, that applied to ceremonial marriages.

Since the 1800s in the United States, there have been (6) ethnic, cultural, and social reasons to try to make legal marriage available to groups, who have been prevented from formally entering into marriage or whose traditions do not include ceremonial marriage. During the 1800s, newly freed African-American couples, who during slavery had been prevented from entering into marriage, could establish a common law marriage if they continued to cohabitate. Common law marriage thus allowed for the traditional tolerance for cohabitation without ceremonial marriage that existed among various groups within the population.

An additional purpose, meant to serve social justice, is (7) to give the more vulnerable party in the relationship protection during the cohabitation as well as at its dissolution. Common law marriage offers a significant protection to parties in economically, educationally, and socially more vulnerable groups who did not formalize their family relationships with a wedding ceremony. The parties most in need could, thus, also enjoy the social benefits accruing to families in which the man and woman are or have been married to each other. As the woman, most often, has been the more vulnerable party, common law marriage has come to constitute a protection for her and an instrument for feminist aspirations.

Similar to the informal marriage in medieval canon law, the institution of common law marriage in the United States, from the beginning, had the objective of (8) protecting children born out of wedlock by removing the stigma of illegitimacy and granting the rights given to children born to married couples. Protecting children has continued to be one of the primary arguments supporting informal marriages.

Common law marriage has also had the function of (9) fulfilling the parties' good faith expectations about being united in marriage and, in the individual cases, has prevented unjust results. Common law marriage has here fulfilled a function similar to the putative marriage doctrine.

(10) Moral arguments appear in the American case law, particularly from the middle and the end of the 1800s, as the courts tried to salvage the honor of the parties, and especially that of the woman, by using common law marriage to transform out-of-wedlock relations into legally valid and morally accepted marriages. Morality simultaneously fueled the community's moral indignation and the use of penal measures to stem concubinage and other "loose" relations and to induce couples to formally get married, and at the same time offered salvation in cases of informal living, which nevertheless had a marital appearance.

Whether any of the above-stated causes for the reception of common law marriage still have force now, at the beginning of the twenty-first century, as well as other modern arguments against the doctrine, are questions that are more closely analyzed and discussed in Part III.

5. *The Initial Criticism against Common Law Marriage*

The criticism against common law marriage, as seen in this chapter, began to arise in the case law during the early 1800s. However, it was during the 1870s that the criticism first became a campaign that, at the turn of the twentieth century, had turned into a veritable crusade against common law marriage. The criticism rested mostly on the legal policy considerations posed by the dangers of common law marriage to morality, the family, and the community in general; as well as its application difficulties, abuse, disputes, and legal uncertainty. That which the proponents considered to be a protection for the woman in a common law marriage was considered by the opponents to be a source of fraud and abuse. This criticism, during the first half of the 1900s, led to the repeal of common law marriage by a majority of the states, and dampened conviction in those states that continued to apply the doctrine. The principle now became that common law marriages were to be tolerated, not encouraged.[211]

These critical reasons, as well as other modern arguments against common law marriage and today's cohabitation legislation, will be more closely analyzed and discussed in Part III in the discussion the future of common law marriage.

211 *Baker v. Mitchell*, 143 Pa.Super. 50, 54, 17 A.2d 738, 741 (1941).

PART II

The Current Law

CHAPTER 5
Legal Capacity and Common Law Marriage

5.1 Introduction

A cornerstone in the Western concept of marriage is the requirement that the parties possess the legal capacity to marry. Each jurisdiction imposes this requirement for the purpose of preventing unsuitable relationships and family building, based on ethical, religious, medical, and social motives.[1] Deeply rooted components of the legal capacity to enter into a ceremonial marriage stem from the Christian tradition, for example, concerning age, sex, consanguinity, monogamy, physical and psychological conditions, requirements that vary somewhat from state to state and generally are expressed in the legislation.[2]

The legislative method that lawmakers have chosen to achieve these goals with respect to ceremonial marriages is primarily preventive. Through a licensing procedure, the determination is made whether any impediments to a marriage exist, and the parties are given a marriage license as evidence of their capacity. A violation of the regulations with respect to marriage licenses is usually criminally punishable. The licensing process gives the state a strong hand in determining who is allowed to enter into a ceremonial marriage. At the same time, this procedure allows for the registration of marriages that have already commenced.[3] On the other side, lawmakers have implemented legislation making marriages between incompetent parties void, either by finding that such marriages

1 *Compare* William Hood, Jr., *Common-law Marriage in Oklahoma: A Survey*, 49 Okla. B.J. 1505, 1507 (1978), using the term "legal capability of the parties to enter into a marriage."

2 The Unif. Marriage and Divorce Act § 207, 9A Unif. L. Ann. 108 (1979) has only been adopted in a few states.

3 Common also with respect to the legislation concerning marriage licenses, even though the details differ somewhat from state to state, is the fact that the commencement of a marriage requires the permission of the state, *see* Chester G. Vernier, American Family Laws i, 59 (1931). As to the state's interest in preventing marriages involving minors as well as incestuous marriages, in promoting health and administering the registration, *see Developments in the Law – The Constitution and the Family*, 93 Harv. L. Rev. 1156, 1242 (1980).

have been so from the beginning (*void ab initio*),[4] or by creating the possibility, after petitioning a court, of having the marriage declared void (voidable).

Even the formation of a common law marriage is based on the assumption that the parties are competent to enter into marriage with each other.[5] This is based on the same conditions underlying the requirements applicable to ceremonial marriages. The requirement of capacity, consequently, is to prevent the formation of unsuitable relationships and family building. As a rule, however, there is no specific legislation regarding this issue with respect to common law marriages. The regulations, instead, often are found in either the legislation applicable to ceremonial marriages or in the case law.

The same substantive regulations are applicable to common law marriages as to ceremonial marriages.[6] Consequently, the parties historically must be of different sexes.[7] However, as attitudes towards homosexuality

---

4 The expressions *absolutely void* and *null and void* appear, *inter alia,* in *Jewett v. Jewett,* 196 Pa.Superior Ct. 305, 175 A.2d 141 (1961), citing the Divorce Code of Pennsylvania, Act of July 15, 1935, Pa.Laws § 1013. *Compare* on the other hand 23 PA. CONS. STAT. ANN. §§ 3304-3305 (West 2003), distinguishing between void and voidable marriages. The expression *absolutely void* is also used in, e.g., KAN. STAT. ANN. 23-102 (2002) and N.J. STAT. ANN. 37:1-10 (West 2003).

5 *Villegas v. Griffin Industries,* 975 S.W.2d 745 (Tex.App.-Corpus Christi 1998); *Toye v. Toye,* 170 A.2d 778 (D.C.App. 1961); *Sullivan v. Sullivan,* 196 Kan. 705, 413 P.2d 988 (1966); *Stevens v. Woodmen of the World,* 105 Mont. 121, 71 P.2d 898, 905 (1937); *Markley v. Hudson,* 143 Ohio St. 163, 28 Ohio Ops. 81, 54 N.E.2d 304 (1944); *Daniels v. Mohon,* 350 P.2d 932 (Okla. 1960); and *McKee v. State,* 452 P.2d 169 (Okla.Crim.App. 1969).

6 *See,* e.g., *McKee v. State,* 452 P.2d 169 (Okla.Crim.App. 1969); *Ex parte Tucker,* 91 Okla. Crim.App. 391, 219 P.2d 245 (1950); *Bell v. State,* 137 Tex.Cr. 401, 129 S.W.2d 664 (App. 1939); *Calhoun v. Dotson,* 32 S.W.2d 656 (Tex.Civ.App. 1930); and *Prudential Ins. Co. of America v. Lewis,* 306 F.Supp. 1177, 11 83 (D.C. Ala. 1969). In *Gillaspie v. Blair Constr. Co.,* 192 Kan. 455, 388 P.2d 647 (1964), the court stated: "The fact that Pearl's marriage to Gillaspie was a common law-marriage places it in no different posture than the marriage ceremony." *See also Jennings v. Jennings,* 20 Md.App. 369, 315 A.2d 816 (1974); and *Doyle v. Doyle,* 497 S.W.2d 846 (Mo.App. 1973). In *Howard v. Howard,* 459 S.W.2d 901, 904 (Tex.Civ.App.-Houston 1970), the court stated: "If an impediment to the creation of a lawful marriage between the parties exists, as when one is married to another, or where one is under any other lawful disability, there can be no common law marriage." *See also In re Zemmick's Estate,* 17 Ohio Supp. 15, 76 N.E.2d 902, 905 (1946).

7 Common law marriages between homosexuals, in the same manner as with ceremonial marriages, have been found invalid. In *De Santo v. Barnsley,* 328 Pa.Super. 181, 476 A.2d 952 (1984), a man petitioned for divorce from another man under the claim that the couple had lived together in a common law marriage. The Pennsylvania Superior Court found that two persons of the same sex could not enter into a common law marriage, citing 23 PA. CONS. STAT. ANN. § 206 (West 2003) and 48 §§ 1-1 et seq., 1-3. In contrast to this requirement simply speaking of a "male and female applicant," other states have express prohibitions against marriage between persons of the same sex. *See,* e.g., Georgia (GA. CODE ANN. § 19-3-3.1 (a) (West 2003)), Iowa (IOWA CODE ANN. § 595.2 (West 2003)), Kansas (KAN. STAT. ANN. §§ 23-101)(2002)), Oklahoma (OKLA. STAT. ANN. tit. 43, § 3 (West 2003)), South Carolina (S.C. CODE ANN. § 20-1-15(Law. Coop. 2003)), and Utah (UTAH CODE ANN. § 30-1-2 (5) (Michie 2003)). *See e.g. Baker v. Nelson,* 291 Minn. 310, 191 N.W.2d 185 (1971); *Jones v. Hallahan,* 501 S.W.2d 588 (Ky. App. 1973); *Singer v. Hara,* 11 Wash.App. 247, 522 P.2d 1187, 84 Wash.2d 1008 (1974); *Adams v. Howerton,* 673 F.2d 1036 (9th Cir. 1982), *cert. denied,* 458 U.S. 1111, 102

have changed,[8] some courts have rejected such provisions as unconstitutional.[9] In addition, the parties must have reached a certain age and not be married (discussed further below). They cannot be closely related (including by marriage) to each other, and must fulfill the law's requirement as to mental and, at times, physical, capacity.[10] Certain states also require that the parties have no venereal diseases or AIDS.[11] This consistency with ceremonial marriages appears logical if common law marriages are intended to be lifelong relationships with all of the legal consequences of formal marriages.

However, common law marriage is characteristically formless, with respect not only to commencement but also the requirement of capacity.

S.Ct. 3494, 73 L.Ed.2d 1373 (1982); *Bowers v. Hardwick*, 478 U.S. 186, 106 S.Ct. 2841, 92 L.Ed.2d 140 (1986); *Dean v. District of Columbia*, 653 A.2d 307 (D.C.App. 1995).

8 IRA MARK ELLMAN ET AL., FAMILY LAW: CASES, TEXT, PROBLEMS 101 (3d ed. 1998), with references.

9 *See Goodridge v. Department of Public Health*, 440 Mass. 309, 798 N.E.2d 941 (2003), wherein the Supreme Judicial Court in Massachusetts stated that "barring an individual from the protections, benefits, and obligations of civil marriage solely because that person would marry a person of the same sex violates the Massachusetts Constitution." *See also Baker v. State*, 744 A.2d 864 (Vt. 1999) and *Baehr v. Lewin*, 74 Haw. 530, 852 P.2d 44 (1993), cases that have opened the doors for legislation for same-sex couples. *See* on "domestic partnership" in Vermont 15 V.S.A. § 1201-1206 (1999). Vt Laws 91. Compare Haw. Laws, Act 383, H.B. 118; HAW. REV. STAT. ANN. § 572C-1 et seq. (1999). *Compare Romer v. Evans*, 517 U.S. 620, 116 S.Ct. 1620, 134 L. Ed.2d 855 (1996). The literature on same sex marriages is extensive, *see* HOMER H. CLARK, JR., ANN LAQUER ESTIN, CASES AND PROBLEMS ON DOMESTIC RELATIONS 165 (6th ed. 2000); ELLMAN *id.* at 103.

10 **Alabama:** ALA. CODE ANN. 30-1-19 (d) (Law. Coop. 2002); *Osoinach v. Watkins*, 235 Ala. 564, 180 So. 577 (1838); *Cross v. Rudder*, 380 So.2d 766 (Ala. 1980); *Beck v. Beck*, 286 Ala. 692, 246 So.2d 420 (1971). **Colorado:** COLO. REV. STAT. ANN. §§ 14-2-110, 14-10-111 (West 2003); *Young v. Colorado Nat'l Bank of Denver*, 365 P.2d 701 (Colo. 1961). **District of Columbia:** D.C. CODE ANN. §§ 46-401, 46-403 (West 2001). **Georgia:** GA. CODE ANN. §§ 19-3-2 (1), 19-3-3 (West 2003). **Idaho:** IDAHO CODE ANN. §§ 32-205, 32-206, 32-501 (Michie 2003). **Iowa:** IOWA CODE ANN. §§ 595.19, 598.29 (West 2003). **Kansas:** KAN. STAT. ANN. §§ 23-102 (2002); *In re Estate of Hendrickson*, 248 Kan. 72, 805 P.2d 20 (1991). **Montana:** MONT. CODE ANN. §§ 40-1-401, 40-1-402 (Mont. Leg. Serv. Div. 2003). **Ohio:** OHIO REV. CODE ANN. §§ 3101.01, 3105.31 (West 2003). **Oklahoma:** OKLA. STAT. ANN. tit. 43, § 2 (West 2003); *In re Estate of Hendrickson*, 248 Kan. 72, 805 P.2d 20 (1991) (applying Kansas law). **Pennsylvania:** PA. CONS. STAT. ANN. 23- 1304 (c)(e) (West 2003). **Rhode Island:** R.I. GEN. LAWS §§ 15-1-1, 15-1-2, 15-1-5 (Michie 2003). **South Carolina:** S.C. CODE ANN. § 20-1-10 (A)(B)(C) (Law. Coop. 2003). **Texas:** TEX. FAM. CODE ANN. §§ 6.106, 6.108, 6.201 (West 2002). **Utah:** UTAH CODE ANN. §§ 30-1-1, 30-1-2, 30-1-17.1 (Michie 2003).

11 *See*, e.g., IDAHO CODE ANN. § 32-412A (Michie 2003); MONT. CODE ANN. § 40-1-203 (Mont. Leg. Serv. Div. 2003); TEX. FAM. CODE ANN. § 2.010 (1997) and UTAH CODE ANN. § 3-1-2.3 (Michie 2003). To receive a marriage license, the parties normally must produce a physician's certificate stating that they have no venereal diseases, *see, e.g.*, D.C. CODE ANN. § 46-417 (West 2001), GA. CODE ANN. § 19-3-40 (1999), MONT. CODE ANN. §§ 40-1-203, 40-1-208 (Mont. Leg. Serv. Div. 2003). No physician's certificate is required in Colorado, Kansas, and Texas. *Compare* Pennsylvania, where the application for the license is to contain a statement that neither of the applicants "is afflicted with transmissible disease," PA. CONS. STAT. ANN. § 1302 (b) (4) (West 2003). *See* Robert Goodman, *In Sickness or in Health: The Right to Marry and the Case of HIV Antibody Testing*, 38 DEPAUL L. REV. 87 (1988).

No formal review prior to the commencement of such a marriage exists, and no marriage license is required.[12] In states recognizing common law marriage, the formal marriage regulations are viewed simply as "*directory*.[13] The fact that the regulations governing marriage licenses are criminally punishable does not render the marriage void based on the violation.[14] A ceremonial marriage that has been commenced without the required license consequently can be valid as a common law marriage.[15]

Instead, the issue of capacity with respect to a common law marriage is first addressed afterwards, for example, if one party, upon separation or death, makes a claim based on the existence of a common law marriage. The opposing party can then contest the claim of marriage on the basis that one of the parties was not competent to enter into the marriage, for example, because he or she had not yet reached the age of legal majority or because he or she was a party in an already existing ceremonial or common law marriage. The legal consequences of incapacity then can

---

12 *See*, e.g., *Africa v. Vaughan*, 998 F.Supp. 552, 556 (E.D.Pa. 1998). In *Buradus v. Gen. Cement Prod. Co.*, 356 Pa. 349, 52 A.2d 205, 208 (1947), the regulation requiring that "no person within this Commonwealth shall be joined in marriage, until a license shall have been obtained for that purpose," was found applicable only to ceremonial marriages, not common law marriages. *Compare* today 23 PA. CONS. STAT. ANN. § 1103 (West 2003). *See also White v. White*, 41 Ga.App. 394, 153 S.E. 203 (1930); *Gay v. Pantell*, 164 Ga. 738, 139 S.E. 543 (1927); *In re Estate of Antwood*, 577 N.W.2d 60, 62 (Iowa App. 1998); and *In re Stopps' Estate*, 244 Iowa 931, 57 N.W.2d 221, 224 (1953) ("[W]e do not find that the legislative intent to make void all marriages informally contracted without blood test or license sufficiently appears"). It also has been found that the legislation expressly requiring a marriage license does not constitute an impediment to a common law marriage, *see, e.g.*, MONT. CODE ANN. § 40-1-403 (Mont. Leg. Serv. Div. 2003); and S.C. CODE ANN. § 20-1-360 (Law. Coop. 2003).

13 *Meister v. Moore*, 96 U.S. 76, 79 (1877); *Mathewson v. Phoenix Iron Foundry*, 20 F. 281, 283 (Cir.D.R.I. 1884); *In re Love's Estate*, 42 Okla. 478, 142 P. 305, 306 (1914); *Smith v. Smith*, 205 Ala. 502, 88 So. 577, 578 (1921); *Holgate v. United Electric Ry. Co.*, 47 R.I. 337, 133 A. 243 (1926); *Hoage v. March Bros. Const. Co.*, 60 App.D.C. 218, 50 F.2d. 983, 985 (1931); *McClendon v. Brown*, 63 S.W.2d 746 (Tex.Civ.App.-Galveston 1933); *Portwood v. Portwood*, 109 S.W.2d 515, 522 (Tex.Civ.App.-Eastland 1937); *Cross v. Cross*, 110 Mont. 300, 102 P.2d 829 (1940); *State v. Ward*, 204 S.C. 210, 28 S.E.2d 785 (1944); *Teague v. Allred*, 119 Mont. 193, 173 P.2d 117 (1946); *Marris v. Sockey*, 170 F.2d 599, 601-602 (10th Cir. 1948); *In re Stopps' Estate*, 244 Iowa 931, 57 N.W.2d 221, 224 (1953); *Williams v. White*, 263 S.W.2d 666, 668 (Tex.Civ.App.-Austin 1953); *Robertson v. Robertson*, 262 Ala. 114, 77 So.2d 373 (1955); *Souza v. O'Hara*, 121 R.I. 88, 395 A.2d 1060, 1061 (1978); *Husband v. Pierce*, 800 S.W.2d 661, 665 (Tex.App.-Tyler 1990); *Adams v. Boan*, 559 So.2d 1084, 1086-1087 (Ala. 1990); and *In re Estate of Antwood*, 577 N.W.2d 60, 62 (Iowa App. 1998).

14 For example, in South Carolina, the legislation mandates that "a probate judge or clerk of court issuing a license contrary to the provisions, upon conviction, must be fined not more than one hundred dollars or not less than twenty-five dollars, or imprisoned for not more than thirty days or not less than ten days," *see* S.C.CODE ANN. § 20-1-220 (2002). At the same time, the legislation states: "Nothing contained in this article shall render illegal any marriage contracted without the issuance of a license," *see* S.C. CODE ANN. § 20-1-360 (Law. Coop. 2003). *See also State v. Ward*, 204 S.C. 210, 28 S.E.2d 785, 786 (1944); *Cochran v. State*, 91 Ga. 763, 18 S.E. 16 (1893); *Needam v. Needam*, 183 Va. 681, 33 S.E.2d 288 (1945); and *Hunt v. Hunt*, 23 Okla. 490, 100 P. 541 (1909).

15 *White v. White*, 41 Ga.App. 394, 153 S.E. 203 (1930).

result in the court declaring that the common law marriage is either void or voidable.

Against this background, it is appropriate to attempt to cast light on the capacity requirements applicable to common law marriage. These requirements appear fairly often in the shadows of the well-illuminated statutory regulations applicable to ceremonial marriages. The question that results is whether the typical case law method of applying requirements for capacity with respect to a common law marriage only afterwards, and perhaps after a long cohabitation, is the best and most appropriate way to serve the requirements' protective purposes.[16]

Particular attention is given to two of the requirements: first, the parties must have reached a certain age to establish a common law marriage; and, second, the parties may not already be married to another person, whether through a previous ceremonial or formless common law marriage. These requirements are of particular interest as the regulations applied to common law marriages differ somewhat from those applicable to ceremonial marriages, particularly because it often is unclear whether and when a common law marriage has been established.

5.2 The Required Marital Age

1. *The Applicability of Common Law Principles*

Prior to legislating requirements concerning the capacity to enter into marriage in the American states, females were competent to marry at the age of twelve and males at the age of fourteen according to the common law, these being the ages at which the parties were considered sexually mature. Marriages entered into by persons under these ages were not considered automatically void, however, but rather voidable, in that they could be annulled by the courts upon the petition of a party. Marriages entered into by children under the age of seven, however, were always a nullity and void.[17] This rule, with its origins in Roman law, was justified by reasoning

16 Requirements of a marriage license as applied to a common law marriage have been overruled, *see Fisher v. Sweet & McClain*, 154 Pa.Super. 216, 35 A.2d 756 (1944), *overruled by Buradus v. Gen. Cement Prod. Co.*, 356 Pa. 349, 52 A.2d 205 (1947).

17 *In re Pace*, 26 Kan.App.2d 538, 989 P.2d 297, 298 (1999); *State v. Coffman*, 260 Kan. 811, 925 P.2d 419 (1996); *State v. Sedlack*, 246 Kan. 305, 787 P.2d 709 (1990); *State v. Wade*, 244 Kan. 136, 766 P.2d 811, 815 (1989); *State v. Johnson*, 216 Kan. 445, 532 P.2d 1325, 1328 (1975); *Jewett v. Jewett*, 196 Pa.Super. 305, 175 A.2d 141, 142 (1961); *In re Zemmick's Estate*, 17 Ohio Supp. 15, 76 N.E.2d 902 (1946); *State v. Ward*, 204 S.C. 210, 28 S.E.2d 785, 786 (1944); *Needam v. Needam*, 183 Va. 681, 33 S.E.2d 288, 290 (1945); *Hitchens v. Hitchens*, 47 F.Supp. 73, 74 (D.C. 1942); *Ex parte Blizzard*, 185 S.C. 131, 193 S.E. 633 (1937); *Greene v. Brandt*, 13 Pa. D. & C. 712, 25 Luzerne Leg. Reg.R. 463, 44 York Leg.Rec. 83, 78 Pittsb.Leg.J. 732 (1930); *State v. Sellers*, 140 S.C. 66, 134 S.E. 873 (1926); *Hughes v. Kano*, 68 Okla. 203, 173 P. 447, 448 (1918); *Browning v. Browning*, 89 Kan. 98, 130 P. 852, 853 (1913); *Hunt v. Hunt*, 23 Okla. 490, 100 P. 541 (1909); *State v. Bittick*, 103 Mo. 183, 15 S.W. 325 (1891); and *Smith v. Smith*, 84 Ga. 440, 11 S.E.

that it was better to legalize a sexual relationship already begun by two minors than to stigmatize it and delegitimatize any offspring.[18] This principle in the common law has been found by several courts to be applicable if not expressly rejected by legislation.

Based on this, the common law has been applied, for example in Kansas, where legislation, KAN. STAT. ANN. § 23-106 (2002), mandates that a marriage license may not be issued to a person under the age of eighteen unless consent to the marriage is given by the parents, guardian, or a court. A marriage commenced there without such consent is not void if the parties have reached the applicable age according to the common law, *i.e.*, twelve years for girls and fourteen years for boys.[19] Men indicted for having sexual relationships with minor girls have invoked this rule fairly often, claiming that their actions are not criminally punishable because the parties were joined in a common law marriage.

In *State v. Sedlack* (1990), a man lived periodically with a fifteen-year-old girl, beginning in February 1988 and continuing during the year. They had a sexual relationship, and the girl became pregnant. The man contributed to the girl's maintenance, and they considered themselves married. The girl's parents opposed the relationship and forbade the relationship. Based on the fact that the girl was under the age of sixteen and not married, the man was indicted for having sexual relations with her under KAN. STAT. ANN. §§ 21-3503(a) and 21-4501(c). The Kansas Supreme Court, however, found that the girl, who was more than twelve years old, was competent to marry according to the common law. The court dismissed the case with reference to the fact that the man and girl were united in a common law marriage under KAN. STAT. ANN. § 21-3503(b).[20] In order to prevent the use of common law marriage as a

---

496, 498 (1890). *See also* older law, WILLIAM BLACKSTONE, COMMENTARIES ON THE LAW OF ENGLAND 436 (R.M. Kerr, ed., London 1884); FREDRICK POLLOCK AND FREDERICK W. MAITLAND, HISTORY OF ENGLISH LAW II, 389 (Cambridge University Press, 2d ed. 1889); and JOEL PRENTISS BISHOP, MARRIAGE, DIVORCE, AND SEPARATION II, § 571 (Chicago, T.H. Flood and Co. 1891).

18 GEORGE ELLIOTT HOWARD, A HISTORY OF MATRIMONIAL INSTITUTIONS I, 357-359, 399-402 (1904); *Shaffer v. Harris*, 71 Pa. D & C 587, 10 Lawrence L.J. 57 (1949); ABRAHAM L. FREEDMAN AND MAURICE FREEDMAN, LAW OF MARRIAGE AND DIVORCE IN PENNSYLVANIA I, 30 (2d ed. 1957).

19 *In re Pace*, 989 P.2d 297, 298 (Kan.App. 1999). The purpose of the legislation appears to be to prevent marriages from being entered into without consent as far as possible without rendering them invalid, *see* the early case of *Browning v. Browning*, 89 Kan. 98, 130 P. 852, 853 (1913). The fact that a violation of the regulations with respect to marriage licenses is punishable by law does not render the marriage invalid, *see State v. Ward*, 204 S.C. 210, 28 S.E.2d 785, 786 (1944).

20 *State v. Sedlack*, 246 Kan. 305, 787 P.2d 709 (1990); and *In re Pace*, 989 P.2d 297, 298 (Kan.App. 1999). *Compare State v. Coffman*, 260 Kan. 811, 925 P.2d 419 (1996), in which a man was indicted for having encouraged a 6-year old girl to have oral sex with him. The man raised the defense that the prosecutor had not proven that he was not married to the child, arguing that the action was thus not punishable. The court, however, found that the man was not married to the girl, with reference to the minimum age for girls to enter into marriage according to the common law

defense to sexual crimes against children, proposals were presented relating to the abolition of common law marriage in Kansas.[21] The legislature, however, did not go further than enacting the following amendment to the rules on the age of consent: "The State of Kansas shall not recognize a common law marriage contract if either party to the marriage contract is under 18 years of age" as expressed in KAN STAT. ANN. 23-101 (b) (2003).[22]

In a comparable manner, the courts in South Carolina earlier fell back on the principles of common law if the legislation did not expressly state that a marriage commenced in violation of the regulations was void. In *State v. Ward* (1944), a man was indicted for the rape of a thirteen-year-old girl. The man argued in his defense that he could not be convicted of rape, because the girl was his wife, according to the common law. The South Carolina Supreme Court, in assessing whether there was a common law marriage, stated that, according to the common law, the applicable age for girls is twelve, not the age given in the legislation of fourteen years, and that a violation of the legislation did not expressly result in invalidity.[23] The legislation in South Carolina, however, was amended in 1997 to state that a marriage, both ceremonial and common law, entered into by a man under the age of sixteen or a woman under the age of fourteen is *void ab initio*.[24] Therewith, the common law principles were overturned. The age limit was later changed to sixteen years for both men and women.

---

being twelve years. The man could therefore be found guilty of aggravated criminal sodomy. *See also State v. Wade*, 244 Kan. 136, 766 P.2d 811 (1989), concerning a five-year-old girl. *Compare State v. Johnson*, 216 Kan. 445, 532 P.2d 1325 (1975) and *McKinney v. McKinney*, No. 83, 410 (Kan. Ct. App. May 12, 2000) (unpublished), where the court found that a common law marriage between a thirty-four-year-old man and a fourteen-year-old girl was induced by fraud.

21 Senate Bill No. 486 (Sess. 2002). In Suppl. Note on House Sub. for SB 486 (Sess. 2002) the following background is given: "The original bill was supported by an assistant county attorney from Butler County and a rape victim who became pregnant at the age of eleven and later at the age of fourteen by a twenty-four-year-old man. The jury in a rape trial convicted the man after several hours of deliberation regarding whether the defense of common law marriage applied." For an earlier proposal for abolition, *see* House Bill No. 2689 (Sess. 1982).

22 L. 2002, ch. 143 § 1; House Sub. for SB 486 (Sess. 2002); House Bill No. 2366 (Sess. 2001); and House Bill No. 2876 (Sess. 2000).

23 *State v. Ward*, 204 S.C. 210, 28 S.E.2d 785 (1944). The court did not retry the case, but remanded the case for a new trial. *See also State v. Sellers*, 140 S.C. 66, 134 S.E. 873 (1926); and *Ex parte Blizzard*, 185 S.C. 131, 193 S.E. 633 (1937). In *Meetze v. Associated Press*, 230 S.C. 330, 95 S.E.2d 606, 610 (1956), a 20-year-old man had married an 11-year-old girl and a year after their marriage, they had a son. The event received a great amount of attention in the press and the parties filed a lawsuit claiming damages from the Associated Press on the basis that their right of privacy had been violated. The South Carolina Supreme Court stated in *dictum* that the marriage was not void despite the fact that the girl was only eleven years old when she married.

24 S.C. CODE ANN. § 20-1-100; 1997 S.C. Acts 95; Bill 3861. A legislative proposal was introduced in 2000 according to which the minimum age for both men and woman was suggested as sixteen years, *see* House Bill 3465. Today the section reads: "A common-law marriage hereinafter entered into by a person under the age of sixteen is *void ab initio*," *see* S.C. CODE. ANN. § 20-1-100 (Law. Coop. 2003).

The principles in the common law have also been applied in cases from Pennsylvania. The Pennsylvania legislation concerning age limit requirements for the commencement of a marriage has been viewed by the courts to be directory not expressly rejecting the common law.[25] In the case of *In re Miller* (1982), a thirty-six-year-old teacher entered into a common law marriage with a fifteen-year-old student, in part to avoid a criminal indictment for his relationship with the girl. The marital age given in the legislation of sixteen years for girls was not viewed as applicable to common law marriage.[26] The legislation in Pennsylvania has also since been amended to expressly state that a common law marriage is invalid if one of the parties is under the age of eighteen.[27]

The common law principles seem to have survived in Colorado. There, the statutory age of consent for marriage is eighteen. Nevertheless, persons between sixteen and eighteen years of age may marry if they obtain parental consent, or, if that is not possible, judicial approval. A person under the age of sixteen may receive judicial approval to marry if that person is capable of giving consent; or has the consent of both parents; or has the consent of his or her guardian; or, if the parents are not living together, the consent of the parent who has legal custody or decision-making responsibility concerning such matters or with whom the child is living, according to COLO. REV. STAT. ANN. §§ 14-2-106 and 108 (West 2003). However, these statutory provisions are perceived as merely directory

25 In *Buradus v. Gen. Cement Prod. Co.*, 356 Pa. 349, 52 A.2d 205, 208 (1947), a regulation stating that "no person within this Commonwealth shall be joined in marriage, until a license shall have been obtained for that purpose" was found applicable only to ceremonial marriages, not common law marriages.

26 *In re Interest of Miller*, 301 Pa.Super. 511, 448 A.2d 25, 32 fn. 6 (1982). With respect to the issue of whether the relationship was a sham marriage, *see* Chapter 6. In *Jewett v. Jewett*, 196 Pa.Superior Ct. 305, 175 A.2d 141, 142 (1961), it was found in accordance with the common law that marriages entered into by persons over the age of seven were "voidable, not void." *See also In re Zemmick's Estate*, 17 Ohio Supp. 15, 76 N.E.2d 902, 905 (1946), where the court, applying Pennsylvania law with respect to the legal capacity to enter into common law marriage, stated that according to the common law, a marriage by a person under the age of seven years was "absolutely void, and a nullity," and a marriage entered into by a person over the age of seven years, but under the age of consent, which was twelve years for women and fourteen years for men, was voidable, *citing* Am.Jur. § 103. *See also Greene v. Brandt*, 13 Pa. D. & C. 712, 25, Luzerne Leg. Reg.R. 463, 44 York Leg.Rec. 83, 78 Pittsb.Leg.J. 732 (1930); and *Shaffer v. Harris*, 71 Pa. D & C 587, 10 Lawrence L.J. 57 (1949). In the case of *In re Ward's Estate*, 30 Pitts.L.J. (O.S.) 394 (1883), a girl that had not reached the age of twelve had entered into a marriage with a man with whom she lived after she became twelve. She later married another man. When the second man died, the issue arose as to whether she was his legal widow. The court found that the marriage with the deceased was invalid as she had been previously married, *see* THE MARRIAGE LAW, Act of Aug. 22, 1953 Pa. Laws § 1344, 48 Pa. Cons. Stat. § 1-1 et seq. *Compare* today, 23 PA. CONS. STAT. ANN. § 1304 (West 2003).

27 23 PA. CONS. STAT. ANN. § 3304 (a) (4) (West 2003). Observe that common law marriage, as was mentioned in chapter 1, was repealed in Pennsylvania by legislation, effective January 1, 2005, however not retroactively, *see* 23 PA. CONS. STAT. ANN. 1103 (WEST 2005).

according to the Colorado case law. It thus appears that Colorado has adopted the common law age of consent for marriage as fourteen years of age for a male and twelve for a female. Consequently, the Colorado Court of Appeals held in the case of *In re Marriage of J.M.H. and Rouse* (2006) that a fifteen-year-old female may enter into a valid common law marriage without judicial approval.[28]

Naturally, it is repugnant to see common law marriage exploited to avoid criminal indictment for sexual relationships with minors. One explanation for this misuse is that the common law age limits, based upon sexual maturity, are too low and lack public support. Today, girls and boys, normally, upon reaching the ages of twelve and fourteen, respectively, have not reached the maturity required to enter into marriage, live as a couple, raise children, and understand the legal content of marriage. A more likely explanation is that common law marriage is established formlessly, often based upon an inferred agreement and a limited actual cohabitation. Against this background, one tempting defense to an indictment is to make the claim that the parties were united in a common law marriage.

It is unsatisfactory that the legislation is so unclear that the principles in the common law are applicable though not intended by lawmakers. There is no reason to apply different age limits to common law marriages and ceremonial marriages if the former is viewed as a long-term relationship with the same extensive consequences as the latter. This consideration should outweigh the goal to capture, at any price, minor parties within the marital regulatory system.

Thus, it is urgent that lawmakers in states such as Colorado expressly reject the common law principles in the legislation, and legislate the same age limits for parties entering into common law marriages as for those entering into ceremonial marriages.

2. *The Upper Age Limits in the Legislation*

In the majority of states, the principles in the common law have been replaced by legislation expressly specifying age limits as to the commencement of a marriage.[29] These have been found in many cases to be applicable to common law marriages even if the formal licensing procedure is not applicable to this type of marriage.[30] The proving of the age requirement then occurs afterwards. The age limits have varied from time to time and

28 *In re Marriage of J.M.H. and Rouse*, 143 P.3d 1116 (Colo.App. 2006).

29 One author two decades ago identified four age restrictions in American marriage law, *see* Lynn Wardle, *Rethinking Marital Age Restrictions,* 22 J. FAM. L. 1 (1983-84).

30 *See Evans v. Ross*, 309 Mich. 149, 14 N.W.2d 815 (1944); and *Smith v. Smith*, 84 Ga. 440, 11 S.E. 496, 8 LRA 362 (1890) (raising the age limit to fourteen years for girls and seventeen for boys). *See also Walter v. Walter*, 433 S.W.2d 183 (Tex.Civ.App. 1968) (raising the age limit to fourteen and sixteen years respectively in Texas in 1866).

from state to state.[31] There have also been reasons to distinguish between different types of age limits and legal consequences within one and the same jurisdiction, often for rather unclear reasons.

First, there is an upper age limit that did not exist in the common law, in that parties not yet reaching that age must have the consent either of parents, guardians, or the courts to enter into marriage. This age was successively raised during the first part of the 1900s, in many states to the age of twenty-one for men and eighteen for women.[32] During the latter part of the 1900s, however, there has been a tendency, in accordance with the Uniform Marriage and Divorce Act, to place the age limit at eighteen years for both men and women,[33] the age at which the majority of states have also placed the age of majority and voting rights.[34] However, there still is considerable variation with respect to the marital age.[35] If the parties have

31 *Hitchens v. Hitchens*, 47 F.Supp. 73 (D.C. 1942); *Needam v. Needam*, 183 Va. 681, 33 S.E.2d 288 (1945); and *In re Interest of Miller*, 301 Pa.Super. 511, 448 A.2d 25, 32 (1982).

32 With respect to the beginning of the 1900s, *see* VERNIER, *supra* note 3, at §§ 29-30.

33 UNIF. MARRIAGE AND DIVORCE ACT §§ 203 and 208; and 9A UNIF. L. ANN. §§ 102 and 110 (1979).

34 U.S. CONST. Amend. XXVI. There has been a division of opinion as to whether the difference in ages between men and women with respect to the legal capacity to enter into marriage violates the federal Constitution's "Equal Protection Clause," *see* U.S. CONST. Amend. XIV § 1. *See Berger v. Adornato*, 76 Misc.2d 122, 350 N.Y.S.2d 520 (1973), in which the difference was found to violate the constitution. *See also Stanton v. Stanton*, 421 U.S. 7, 95 S.Ct. 1373, 43 L.Ed.2d 688 (1975); and *Phelps v. Bing*, 58 Ill.2d 32, 316 N.E.2d 775 (1974). *Compare Friedrich v. Katz*, 76 Misc.2d 663, 341 N.Y.S.2d 932 (1973), 34 N.Y.2d 987, 360 N.Y.S.2d 415, 318 N.E.2d 606 (1974).

35 **Alabama:** If the parties are under the age of eighteen, consent from either the parents or guardian is required to receive a marriage license where they have not previously been married (ALA. CODE ANN. § 30-1-5 (Law. Coop. 2002)). **Colorado:** Persons over the age of eighteen years may marry without parental consent. Persons under the age of eighteen but over the age of sixteen may marry with the consent of the parents, guardians or the court. Persons under the age of sixteen may marry if they have the consent of both parents or the guardian, and permission from the court (COLO. REV. STAT. ANN. § 14-2-106 (West 2003)). **District of Columbia:** Under the age of eighteen, the consent of the parents or guardian is required (D.C. CODE ANN. § 46-411 (West 2001)). **Georgia:** Where one of the parties is a minor (under the age of majority), parental consent is required (GA. CODE ANN. §§ 19-3-2(2), 19-3-37 (West 2003)). **Idaho:** Men and women having reached the age of eighteen are competent to enter into marriage. Persons between the age of sixteen and eighteen may be issued a marriage license where the written consent of the parents or guardian is produced. Persons under the age of sixteen are required in addition to receive the permission of the court (IDAHO CODE ANN. § 32-202 (Michie 2003)). **Iowa:** The age of consent is eighteen years for both men and women. For parties under the age of eighteen, the consent of the parents, guardian or the court is also required (IOWA CODE ANN. § 595.2 (West 2003)). **Kansas:** The consent of the parents, guardian, or court is also required for persons under the age of eighteen (KAN. STAT. ANN. §§ 23-106 (2002)). **Montana:** Persons over the age of eighteen may enter into marriage. Persons under the age of eighteen and over the age of sixteen may marry with the consent of their parents, guardian or permission of the court (MONT. CODE ANN. §§ 40-1-202, 40-1-213, 40-1-402 (Mont. Leg. Serv. Div. 2003)). **Ohio:** Men may marry at the age of eighteen years, and women, at the age of sixteen years. Persons under the age of eighteen must, however, have the consent of their parents, guardian or the authorities (OHIO REV. CODE ANN. §§ 3101.01, 3109.01 (West 2003)). **Oklahoma:** Persons over the age of eighteen years have the right to marry.

had children together or the woman is pregnant, the legislation may allow a lower age limit. The goal of the new age limits has been to prevent marriage between younger persons not possessing the maturity or experience required to live in a marital relationship and start a family. The parties' ability to understand the content of the marital regulatory system also appears to play a role here. A further reason behind the higher age limit appears to be to create more stable relationships and therewith avoid divorce, which is common in the marriages of younger persons.[36] An exception to the higher age limit is accepted in those instances in which the parents consent to the marriage. As young couples often are not even aware of the legalities of common law marriage, it is unusual for them to request such permission from their parents.

Characteristic of the technical legal construction of this age limit is the fact that the requirement, as well as the consent, is normally directed at the public authorities (for example, the county clerk, clergy, or magistrate) issuing the marriage license. The public authority may not, according to the regulations, issue a license without the required consent of the parents, guardians, or authorities. Violations of these regulations are often

---

Persons under the age of eighteen cannot marry without the consent of their parents, guardian or a judge. Persons under the age of sixteen years are prohibited from marrying without the permission of the court (OKLA. STAT. ANN. tit. 43 § 3 (West 2003)). **Pennsylvania:** A marriage with a person under the age of sixteen years is voidable and can be declared invalid if permission was not obtained from the court (PA. CONS. STAT. ANN. 23-1304 (b) (West 2003)). For persons under the age of eighteen, a marriage license may not be issued without the consent of their parents or guardian. **Rhode Island:** To issue a marriage license, the rule in principle is the age of eighteen for men and sixteen for women. Younger persons may receive a license under special circumstances (R.I. GEN. LAWS §§ 15-2-11, 15-12-1 (Michie 2003)). **South Carolina:** A marriage license must not be issued when either applicant is under the age of sixteen. When either applicant is between the ages of sixteen to eighteen, consent is required from parents, guardian or other relatives (S.C. CODE ANN. § 20-1-250 (Law. Coop. 2003)). **Texas:** Persons under the age of eighteen may not marry without parental consent or the permission of the court. Persons under the age of fourteen years may not marry without the consent of the court (TEX. FAM. CODE ANN. §§ 2.101-2.102, 2.401 (c) (1997)). The marriage of minors between fourteen and eighteen years of age is not void but voidable (TEX. FAM. CODE ANN. § 6.102 (West 2002)). **Utah:** If the parties are under the age of eighteen and they have not previously been married, consent is required from the parents or guardian to receive a license. If the parties are fifteen, the permission of a judge or court commissioner is required (UTAH CODE ANN. § 30-1-9 (Michie 2003)). A marriage is "prohibited and declared void" if the parties are under the age of fourteen years or if they are under the age of sixteen when the parties attempt to enter into a marriage. An exception can be made for persons that are fifteen years of age and have the required consent (UTAH CODE ANN. § 30-1-2 (Michie 2003)).

36 Steven G. Brown, Comment, *Pennsylvania Common Law Marriage and Annulment: Present Law and Proposals for Reform,* 15 VILL. L. REV. 134, 147 (1969); Note, *The Uniform Marriage and Divorce Act - Marital Age Provisions,* 57 MINN. L. REV. 179, 181-186 (1972); HOMER H. CLARK, JR., THE LAW OF DOMESTIC RELATIONS IN THE UNITED STATES 162 (2d ed. 1987); and Robert Furlong, *Youthful Marriages and Parenthood: A Threat to Family Stability,* 19 HASTINGS L.J. 105, 109 (1967).

punishable by law.[37] With respect to the relationship between the parties, the courts, in contrast, have often seen these regulations as merely directory, meaning that a violation of the rule does not affect the validity of the marriage as long as the law does not expressly prohibit it.[38] This technical legal construction can be explained by the reasoning that the parental consent is to be "preventive, rather than prohibitive."[39] Even if a formal licensing procedure is not applicable to common law marriage, the significance of the requirement of parental consent is relevant even to the validity of this type of marriage.

One consequence of the lack of parental consent in a common law marriage in many cases has been no legal consequence at all. For example, in Alabama, where parental consent is required for those under the age of eighteen (Ala. Code § 30-1-5 (1975)), marriages between persons not having reached that age have been viewed as valid despite lack of consent. In *Adams v. Boan* (1990), a man had commenced a relationship with a sixteen-year old girl. They lived together for approximately two years prior to the man's death. The girl then claimed that they had lived in a common law marriage, to which the man's family raised the defense that the girl was not competent to enter into a marriage because the legislation required parental consent for those under the age of eighteen. The Alabama Supreme Court found, however, that the regulation in question was merely directory and that a violation of the regulation could not make the marriage invalid. As the age of capacity for marriage was fourteen years in Alabama (Ala. Code § 30-1-4(1975)), the sixteen-year-old girl was

37 *See,* e.g., the legislation in Texas: "A county clerk or deputy county clerk who violates or fails to comply with this subchapter commits an offense. An offense under this section is a misdemeanor punishable by a fine of not less than $200 and not more than $500," *see* Tex. Fam. Code Ann. § 2.012 (West 2002). In South Carolina, the legislation prescribes that "a probate judge or clerk of court issuing a license contrary to the provisions, upon conviction, must be fined not more than one hundred dollars or not less than twenty-five dollars, or imprisoned for not more than thirty days or not less than ten days," *see* S.C. Code Ann. § 20-1-220 (Law. Coop. 2003). *See also* Kansas (Kan. Stat. Ann. § 23-114 (2002)); Georgia (Ga. Code Ann. § 19-3-32 (West 2003)); Alabama (Ala. Code Ann. § 30-1-10 (Law. Coop. 2002)); Montana (Mont. Code Ann. § 40-1-208 (Mont. Leg. Serv. Div. 2003)); and Oklahoma (Okla. Stat. Ann. tit. 43 § 15 (West 2003)).

38 In *Needam v. Needam,* 183 Va. 681, 33 S.E.2d 288, 290 (1945), the court stated: "The general rule is that the effect of statutes prohibiting clergymen or magistrates from marrying minors without the consent of their parents or guardians, or forbidding the issuance of marriage licenses without such consent, and prescribing a penalty for the violation thereof, is not to render such marriages void or voidable, when solemnized without the required consent, the statutes being regarded as directory only, in the absence of any provision declaring such marriages void or voidable." *See also* Hood, *supra* at 1507 note 1, who, with respect to Oklahoma, viewed the criminal regulations as directed "towards the Clerk who issues the marriage license and not against the parties attempting to contract the marriage."

39 *Needam v. Needam,* 183 Va. 681, 33 S.E.2d 288, 291 (1945).

considered competent to enter into a common law marriage. The marriage was found established.[40]

The absence of any legal consequence of the lack of parental consent has great significance for the validity of common law marriage; such marriages are often entered into formlessly through inferred agreements based on the parties' actual cohabitation. Many parties, when they move in together, know nothing about either common law marriage or the fact that they are establishing such a marriage, and are unaware of any need to obtain parental consent in the same manner as for a ceremonial marriage.

In other cases, the absence of parental consent to a marriage between minors has affected the marriage's validity. Normally, the marriage has not been considered void, in other words, a nullity, but rather voidable in that it can be declared void.[41] As a rule, only the parties themselves have

---

40 **Alabama:** *Adams v. Boan*, 559 So.2d 1084, 1086-1087 (Ala. 1990). The same stance can be found in *Robertson v. Robertson*, 262 Ala. 114, 77 So.2d 373 (1955), in which the absence of parental consent was not considered to constitute grounds for declaring the marriage invalid. *See also Smith v. Smith*, 205 Ala. 502, 88 So. 577, 578 (1921), finding no invalidity despite the license being issued without the required consent: "It is recognized as a general rule that, unless a statute expressly declares a marriage contracted without the necessary consent of the parents, or other statutory requirements, to be a nullity, the statute is to be construed as directory only in this respect, so that the marriage will be held valid notwithstanding the disobedience of the statute may entail penalties on the officiating authorities." *Compare White v. Hill*, 176 Ala. 480, 58 So. 444 (1912). **Georgia:** *Cochran v. State*, 91 Ga. 763, 18 S.E. 16 (1893), a 14-year-old girl was considered competent to enter into a marriage despite the fact that the issuance of a license to a person under the age of eighteen without the required consent of the parents or guardian was criminally punishable. The court stated that "the law does not declare that a marriage is void, or in any manner impeach its validity, when the young woman, notwithstanding the unwillingness of her parents or guardian, and because of a neglect by the ordinary to perform his duty in the premises, succeeds, nevertheless, in getting married." *See also Handley v. State*, 115 Ga. 584, 41 S.E. 992 (1902); *Irby v. State*, 57 Ga.App. 717, 196 S.E. 101 (1938); and *Allen v. State*, 60 Ga.App. 248, 3 S.E.2d 780 (1939). **District of Columbia:** *Hitchens v. Hitchens*, 47 F.Supp. 73, 74 (D.C. 1942). **Montana:** In *Teague v. Allred*, 119 Mont. 193, 173 P.2d 117 (1946), a marriage entered into without parental consent by a 17-year-old girl was not declared invalid, despite the fact that such a consent was required for women under the age of eighteen, as she had reached "the legal age of consent." **Kansas:** *Browning v. Browning*, 89 Kan. 98, 130 P. 852, 853 (1913); **Oklahoma:** *Hunt v. Hunt*, 23 Okla. 490, 100 P. 541 (1909).

41 **Colorado**: A violation of the requirements concerning age and consent renders the marriage voidable, *see* COLO. REV. STAT. ANN. §§ 14-2-106 (b), 14-10-111 (c) (West 2003). **Montana:** MONT. CODE ANN. § 40-1-402 (c) (Mont. Leg. Serv. Div. 2003). **Oklahoma:** A petition for an annulment of the marriage based on age can be filed by the parties, and in addition, by the parents or guardians. A cohabitation after the required age has been reached, however, is an impediment to invalidity, *see* OKLA. STAT. ANN., tit. 43 § 128 (West 2003). **Idaho:** The absence of parental consent can constitute a ground for declaring the marriage invalid, but not if they after attaining the age of consent cohabit as husband and wife, *see* IDAHO CODE ANN. § 32-501 (Michie 2003). *See also Mays v. Folsom*, 143 F.Supp. 784 (D. Idaho 1956), in which the 16-year-old daughter entered into a marriage without the consent of her mother, the marriage was found "not void but voidable." In *Cross v. Cross*, 110 Mont. 300, 102 P.2d 829 (1940) (applying Idaho law), however, the requirement of parental consent to

standing to make a claim on this basis; others may have standing under certain conditions. Such a marriage is invalid from the date the court's judgment becomes final. In Texas, persons under the age of eighteen may not enter into marriage without parental consent or the permission of the courts.[42] A marriage entered into in violation of this rule by a person at least fourteen years of age, but not yet eighteen, is voidable. It is possible to have the marriage declared invalid by the court, but it is valid until that time.[43] A marriage entered into by a person fourteen years of age without the permission of the court is also voidable.[44] The ability to petition for an annulment, however, is limited if the minor has reached the age of eighteen, or if either of the parties is deceased.[45] In *Husband v. Pierce* (1990), neither of the parties to the marriage had petitioned for an annulment, the girl's age of fifteen years was no impediment to the establishment of a common law marriage, and the court was prevented from ordering her return to her parents.[46]

3. *The Lower Age Limit in the Legislation*

Within American jurisdictions, albeit not consistently, a lower age limit appears in the law, at which the parties are not competent to enter into a marriage even if they have parental consent. This age limit, sometimes referred to as *the minimum age for contracting marriage*[47] or *the age of consent,*[48] has varied over time and from state to state. For example, in Alabama, the current age limit is fourteen years for both men and women, *i.e.*, higher than the age applicable according to the common law.[49] The lower age

---

be in writing to receive a marriage license was found simply to be "directory." The absence of a writing therefore could not be a ground for invalidity. **Texas:** The court may grant an annulment of a marriage of a person 14 years of age but under 18 that occurred without parental consent or court order, *see* TEX. FAM. CODE ANN. § 6.102 (a) (West 2002).

42 TEX. FAM. CODE ANN. §§ 2.101, 2.102 and 2.401 (c) (West 1997).

43 *Id.* at § 6.102 (a).

44 *Id.* at § 6.101.

45 *Id.* at §§ 6.103 and 6.111. In *Williams v. White*, 263 S.W.2d 666, 668 (Tex.Civ.App.-Austin 1953), the parents were found to have no standing to file a petition for annulment, as they were not found to have any justiciable interest in the matter.

46 *Husband v. Pierce*, 800 S.W.2d 661, 665 (Tex.App.-Tyler 1990); *Williams v. White*, 263 S.W.2d 666, 668 (Tex.Civ.App.-Austin 1953); *Portwood v. Portwood*, 109 S.W.2d 515, 522 (Tex.Civ.App.-Eastland 1937); *Ex parte Nolte*, 269 S.W. 906 (Tex.Civ.App.-San Antonio 1925); and *Robertson v. Cole*, 12 Tex. 356 (1854).

47 ALA. CODE ANN. § 30-1-4 (Law. Coop. 2002).

48 D.C. CODE ANN. § 46-403 (West 2001).

49 ALA. CODE ANN. § 30-1-4 (Law. Coop. 2002). The minimum age previously was seventeen years for men and fourteen years for women, *see* ALA. CODE ANN. § 34 par. 4 (1940). *See Taylor v. Taylor*, 249 Ala. 419, 31 So.2d 579 (1947). In Georgia, a person must be sixteen years of age in order to enter into a marriage where the parties do not have mutual children born outside of the marriage, or the woman is pregnant, *see* GA. CODE ANN. § 19-3-2 (2) (West 2003). In South Carolina, where the previously applied common law principles were overturned in legislation in 1997, a minimum age of sixteen years for men and fourteen years for women was applied, *see* S.C. CODE ANN. § 20-1-100 (Law. Coop. 1997). According to a new legislative proposal,

limit has commonly had a greater significance to the marriage's validity than the upper limit, below which parental consent is required.[50] The resulting legal consequences, however, have varied within the case law.

The majority of courts appear, at times with the support of the legislation, to view a marriage between minors not reaching the minimum age, not as void, but rather simply voidable, rendering the marriage valid until it is declared by a court to be invalid.[51] If the parties continue the cohabitation until the required age, and refrain from petitioning the court for an annulment, they do not need to remarry if they wish to continue the marriage. The continued cohabitation is viewed as a ratification of the marriage contract.[52] This distinction has great practical significance, because the issue of the marriage's validity is often raised later as a prejudicial issue in a different lawsuit, sometimes upon the death of one of the parties when no one has standing to make a claim. Consequently, invalidity, as a principle cannot be declared in a different lawsuit, for example, concerning an inheritance, divorce, or a criminal case.[53] Moreover, if the invalidity has not been previously litigated, and the parties are married to each other, a marriage that is only voidable can prevent the conviction of one party for having sexual intercourse with a minor. Because the marriage is valid until declared invalid by the court, children born to the couple are considered born in wedlock and thereby legitimate.

In *Taylor v. Taylor* (1947), a sixteen-year old boy had entered into a ceremonial marriage with a minor girl. Immediately thereafter, he abandoned the girl, who was pregnant. A few months later, she gave birth to their child. No cohabitation occurred between the parties. At trial, the boy petitioned for an annulment, as he was under the age of seventeen at the time, thus not competent to enter into a marriage under ALA. CODE TITLE

---

the minimum age for both ceremonial and common law marriage has been changed to sixteen years of age for both men and women, *see* House Bill 3465 (2000). Today the section reads: "A common-law marriage hereinafter entered into by a person under the age of sixteen is void ab initio," *see* S.C. CODE. ANN. § 20-1-100 (Law. Coop 2003). *Compare* Montana, where the minimum age for both sexes is sixteen years of age, *see* MONT. CODE ANN. § 40-1-402 (c) (Mont. Leg. Serv. Div. 2003). In Rhode Island, the expression "the legal age of consent" found in R.I. GEN. LAWS § 195 (Michie 2003) has been interpreted in accordance with the common law and found to be fourteen years for men and twelve years for women, *see Capwell v. Capwell*, 21 R.I. 101, 41 A. 1005 (1898).

50 That the parties are minors and thereby not competent to enter into a contract generally does not hinder their right to enter into a marriage, *see Allen v. State*, 60 Ga.App. 248, 3 S.E.2d 780 (1939); *Needam v. Needam*, 183 Va. 681, 33 S.E.2d 288 (1945); and *Portwood v. Portwood*, 109 S.W.2d 515, 522 (Tex.Civ.App.-Eastland 1937).

51 *See, e.g.*, 23 PA. CONS. STAT. ANN. § 3305 (b) (West 2003); and *Peefer v. State*, 42 Ohio App. 276, 182 N.E. 117 (1931).

52 MONT. CODE ANN. § 40-1-402 (2)(c) (Mont. Leg. Serv. Div. 2003); IDAHO CODE ANN. § 32-501 (1) (Michie 2003); OKLA. STAT. ANN. tit. 43 § 128 (West 2003); UNIF. MARRIAGE AND DIVORCE ACT § 208 (b)(3); and 9A UNIFORM L. ANN. 110 (1979).

53 *See, e.g., Abbott v. Indus. Com.*, 80 Ohio App. 7, 35 Ohio Ops. 406, 74 N.W.2d 625 (1946); *Peefer v. State*, 42 Ohio App. 276, 182 N.E. 117 (1931); *State v. Sellers*, 140 S.C. 66, 134 S.E. 873 (1926); and *Beggs v. State*, 55 Ala. 108, 110-111 (1876).

34 § 4 (1940) (currently ALABAMA CODE § 30-1-4 (Law. Coop. 2002)). The Alabama Supreme Court found that the marriage was not void but rather voidable, declaring it invalid. As the invalidity commenced with the judgment, and the child was born prior to the judgment, the child was found to be legitimate, that is, born within the marriage. It ought to be noted that the court, in its judgment, appeared to be endeavoring to save the child's legitimacy.[54]

Other courts have had a stricter attitude, maintaining that a marriage commenced by persons that have not yet reached the age of consent is void, in other words, null and void or *void ab initio*. Such a marriage is invalid even if no petition has been filed because the marriage never existed. The invalidity then, in principle, can be invoked at any time and in any situation. In *Scott v. State* (1947), a man indicted for having sexual relations with a fourteen-year-old girl, argued that he could not be convicted as he was married to her. The Oklahoma Criminal Court of Appeals stated that a fourteen-year-old could not lawfully marry with or without parental consent, and that any marriage with her, therefore, would be "null and void."[55] No marriage constituting an impediment to a criminal conviction existed.

---

54 *Taylor v. Taylor*, 249 Ala. 419, 31 So.2d 579, 580 (1947). The same principles with respect to the parties' capacity are generally applied to common law marriage as well as ceremonial marriages, *see Prudential Ins. Co. of America v. Lewis*, 306 F.Supp. 1177, 1183 (D.C. Ala. 1969). In *Hunt v. Hunt*, 23 Okla. 490, 100 P. 541, 22 L.R.A., N.S., 1202 (1909), in which according to the then-applicable legislation, boys and girls under the age of eighteen and fifteen respectively were "forbidden and prohibited" to enter into marriage, the Oklahoma Supreme Court found that a marriage between a 16-year-old boy and a 14-year-old girl was only voidable, not void under WILSON'S REV. & ANN. ST. OKLA. § 3484 (1903). *See also Hughes v. Kano*, 68 Okla. 203, 173 P. 447, 448 (1918), regarding common law marriage and R.L. 1910 § 3885 (now OKLA. STAT. ANN. tit. 43 § 3 (West 2003)); *Andrews v. Hooper*, 138 Okla. 103, 280 P. 424 (1929); *Mantz v. Gill*, 147 Okla. 199, 296 P. 441, 444 (1931); *Puntka v. Puntka*, 174 Okla. 517, 50 P.2d 1092, 1093 (1935); and *Burdine v. Burdine*, 206 Okla. 170, 242 P. 2d 148 (1952). *See also McKee v. State*, 452 P.2d 169, 172 (Okla.Crim.App. 1969), stating that a common law marriage with a 15-year-old girl was not void but voidable. The issue however was not at trial. In Oklahoma today, a petition for an annulment based on incapacity can be filed by the parties as well as by the parents or guardian. Cohabitation after the required age has been reached is an impediment to invalidity. Children born prior to the marriage being declared void are "legitimate." *See* OKLA. STAT. ANN. tit. 43 § 128 (West 2003). *Compare* other criminal cases from Oklahoma, where the marriage was considered void. In the District of Columbia, a marriage is voidable if it is entered into by parties under "the age of consent," which is sixteen years of age. Invalidity begins from the point of time that the marriage is declared void, *see* D.C. CODE ANN. § 30-103 (West 2001). With respect to Montana, *see* MONT. CODE ANN. § 40-1-402 (c) (Mont. Leg. Serv. Div. 2003).

55 *Scott v. State*, 85 Okla.Crim.App. 213, 186 P.2d 336, 338 (1947). *See also Yeats v. State*, 30 Okla.Crim.App. 320, 236 P. 62 (1925), in which the court maintained that a common law marriage with a girl under the age of fifteen was void and that such a marriage could not prevent prosecution for "the abduction of the female child." *See also Ex parte Tucker*, 91 Okla.Crim.App. 391, 219 P.2d 245, 248 (1950), where a common law marriage with a twelve-and-a-half-year-old girl was not considered valid even with parental consent, as she had not reached the age of fifteen, *see* OKLA. STAT. ANN. tit. 43 § 3. The dominant stance in the case law from Oklahoma appears to be,

This stricter stance has also come to expression in modern legislation. In South Carolina, as seen above, where the common law principles resulting in sensational consequences were rejected in legislation in 1997, according to which both ceremonial and common law marriages are void if the relationship was entered into when the man is under the age of sixteen or the woman is under fourteen. The required age was later changed to sixteen years for both males and females in S.C.CODE ANN. § 20-1-100.[56]

It has also been the case that the legal consequence of the age of the minors is between void and voidable. A marriage between minors may begin as void (*void ab initio*) so that no petition for an annulment is necessary, but the marriage can then be ratified by the parties continuing the cohabitation until they have reached the required age.[57] The latter possibility deviates from the general legal principle that a contract, which is void, cannot be ratified and bring to life something that never existed.

This stance clearly appears in the case law from Georgia. For example, in *Hayes v. Hay* (1955), a man had entered into a marriage with a twelve-year-old girl. No cohabitation took place. The man later married another woman. When he died, the issue was which marriage was valid. The Georgia Court of Appeals found that the girl had not reached "the legal age," which according to then current legislation was fourteen years for girls; in other words, two years older than according to the common law. It found that a

---

however, that the marriage is simply voidable. *See also Evans v. Ross*, 309 Mich. 149, 14 N.W.2d 815 (1944), in which a man had entered into marriage with a 15-year-old girl. No cohabitation occurred after the girl had reached the marital age. The applicable legislation stated: "No marriage, common law or ceremonial, in this state shall be contracted where the female is under the full age of sixteen (16) years, and any such marriage, if entered into, shall be void." The Michigan Supreme Court stated that "[t]he language used strongly indicates that it was the intention of the legislature to make such marriages void," and found that the marriage at issue was a nullity. *Compare Walter v. Walter*, 433 S.W.2d 183, 193 fn. 1 (Tex.Civ.App. 1968), in which the court, in dictum, maintained that marriage by girls under the age of fourteen and by boys under the age of sixteen, which the court found to be comparable to the seven-year age limit in the common law, "should be held void."

56 S.C. CODE ANN. § 20-1-100; 1997 S.C. Acts 95; Bill 3861. A legislative proposal was introduced in 2000 according to which the minimum age for both men and women was suggested as sixteen years, *see* House Bill 3465. Today the section reads: "A common-law marriage hereinafter entered into by a person under the age of sixteen is *void ab initio*," *see* S.C. CODE. ANN. § 20-1-100 (Law. Coop. 2003). In Utah, a marriage is "prohibited and declared void" when the parties are under fourteen years or where they are sixteen when they try to commence the marriage. An exception can be made for a person under the age of fifteen, *see* UTAH CODE ANN. § 30-1-2 (Michie 2003).

57 *Compare* JAMES SCHOULER, MARRIAGE, DIVORCE, SEPARATION & DOMESTIC RELATIONS, 30 (6th ed. 1921): "Marriage within the age of consent seems therefore to be neither strictly void nor strictly voidable, but rather inchoate and imperfect"; JAMES KENT, COMMENTARIES ON AMERICAN LAW 2, 234 (14th ed. 1896); and JOEL PRENTISS BISHOP, COMMENTARIES ON THE LAW OF MARRIAGE AND DIVORCE §§ 46, 55 and 194 (1852) ("an inchoate or imperfect marriage"). *Compare* CLARK, *supra* note 36, at 167, who is critical of the distinction of void and voidable. *See also* Robert Kingsley, *The law of infants' marriages*, 9 VAND. L. REV. 593, 596 (1956), which finds this confusing and maintains that the legal consequence of an invalid marriage should depend upon "the nature of the proceeding in which the status is questioned."

marriage with a person under the legal age was invalid. That the court therewith viewed such a marriage as a nullity can be seen from its statement that "there is not and has never been a marriage between them."[58] The possibility, through a continued cohabitation between them until the parties had reached the required marital age, of ratifying an invalid marriage, can be seen in *Smith v. Smith* (1890). There, the Georgia Supreme Court stated: "The marriage of a boy in his sixteenth year, although declared by the Code to be void in the sense of being absolutely void, may nevertheless be ratified and confirmed by continuing after arriving at the age of 17 years, to cohabit with his wife as such."[59]

58 *Hayes v. Hay*, 92 Ga.App. 88, 88 S.E.2d 306, 309 (1955) addressing GA. CODE ANN. § 53-102 (1957); *Andrews v. Andrews*, 91 Ga.App. 659, 86 S.E.2d 669 (1955); *Mims v. Hardware Mut. Cas. Co.*, 82 Ga.App. 210, 60 S.E.2d 501, 503 (1950); *Jones v. Jones*, 200 Ga. 571, 37 S.E.2d 711 (1946); *Eskev v. Eskev*, 198 Ga. 513, 34 S.E.2d 697 (1945); *Morgan v. Morgan*, 148 Ga. 625, 97 S.E. 675 (1918); *Americus Gas & Electric Co. v. Coleman*, 16 Ga.App. 17, 84 S.E. 493 (1915); and *Powers v. Powers*, 138 Ga. 65, 74 S.E. 759 (1912). In *Luke v. Hill*, 137 Ga. 159, 73 S.E. 345, 346 (1911), concerning a girl under the age of fourteen, the court stated: "Such marriages partake more of the nature of voidable than void marriages. They are imperfect marriages which the party may affirm or disaffirm after reaching the age of consent." *See also Crapps v. Smith*, 9 Ga.App. 400, 71 S.E. 501 (1911). With respect to the raising of the age limit in Georgia from the common law limit for women of twelve, to fourteen years of age, *see Smith v. Smith*, 84 Ga. 440, 11 S.E. 496, 8 LRA 362 (1890). With respect to ratification today, *see* GA. CODE ANN. § 19-3-5 (b) (West 2003). Observe that common law marriage, as was mentioned in chapter 1, was repealed in Georgia January 1, 1997, however not retroactively, *see* GA. CODE ANN. §§ 19-3-1.1 (West 2003).

Even in the *Ohio* case law, it appears that the legal consequence has been *void ab initio* but with the possibility of ratification. In *Carlton v. Carlton*, 76 Ohio App. 338, 64 N.E.2d 428 (1945), a seventeen-year-old boy had entered into a marriage with a nineteen-year-old woman. After five days of cohabitation, he left the woman, who gave birth to their child four months later. The boy petitioned that the marriage be declared void as he, at the point of time of the commencement of the marriage, had not reached the age of eighteen. Section 11181 of the Ohio General Code stated: "Male persons of the age of eighteen years, and female persons of the age of sixteen years ... may be joined in marriage." As the boy was not legally competent to enter into marriage due to his age, and he did not later ratify the marriage after he reached the age of eighteen, the court found that "the marriage was void and a decree annulling it will be entered." As it was the spouses themselves that were parties to the case, it is not clear whether the court viewed the marriage as void or voidable. Even a marriage that is void can be declared so by a court. The court's reference to *Shafher v. State*, 20 Ohio St. 1 (1851), however, indicates that they viewed the marriage as *void ab initio*. In the case of *Shafher*, concerning prosecution for bigamy, the defense argued that the man, at the point of time for the commencement of the marriage, had not reached the age of eighteen, and consequently the marriage was void. The court agreed, stating: "We think these authorities very conclusively show that the contract of marriage when entered into by a person under the age fixed by law, is void." No particular petition for annulment was necessary. In the case of *In re Zemmick's Estate*, 17 Ohio Supp. 15, 76 N.E.2d 902, 905 (1946), the court stated that a marriage which is "absolutely void" can be ratified through cohabitation when the parties have reached the required age. Observe that common law marriage, as was mentioned in chapter 1, was repealed in Ohio October 10 1991, however not retroactively, *see* OHIO REV. CODE ANN. § 3105.12 (B) (1, 2) (WEST 1991).

59 *Smith v. Smith*, 84 Ga. 440, 11 S.E. 496, 8 LRA 362 (1890). The burden of proof for the existence of a ratification through cohabitation after the impediment's removal has been viewed to rest upon the party claiming such. *See Mims v. Hardware Mut. Cas. Co.*,

The uncertainty of the terminology in the case law has led certain courts to designate such marriages simply as voidable,[60] which does not appear to be accurate. It would be more correct to view these marriages as void, because they remain so unless ratification occurs. The marriage is then viewed as having never existed, *void ab initio*. No petition for an annulment needs to be filed. It must also be noted that, with this legal consequence, if a void marriage is ratified through cohabitation, the ratification is considered retroactive, so that the marriage is considered to have existed the entire time.[61]

The possibility of ratifying a void marriage has also come to expression in modern legislation. According to the Pennsylvania code, a common law marriage today is void if either of the parties is under the age of eighteen, and no "confirmation by cohabitation" has occurred after the removal of the impediment under 23 PA. CONS. STAT. ANN. § 3304 (West 2003).[62]

In the case law, the principles in the common law have been viewed as a ceiling under which the last mentioned legal consequences are invoked. For example, in *Boehm v. Rohlfs* (1937), applying Minnesota law, a nineteen-year-old man entered into marriage with a fourteen-year-old girl. As the girl was under "the age of consent," which was sixteen years, but over the age that the common law stipulated, which was twelve, the marriage was not considered void but rather voidable. The reasoning was stated as thus: "Because young people sometimes indiscreetly get married before they reach the legal age, it is not the policy of the law to impose upon them and especially their innocent offspring, the distressing penalties that would result if the marriage was held to be absolutely void, and it would be especially harsh and unwarranted to so hold if neither of the young people

---

82 Ga.App. 210, 60 S.E.2d 501, 503 (1950), in which it was claimed that the man had entered into a marriage with a girl who was twelve or thirteen years of age. The Georgia Court of Appeals found that it was not proven that a ratification of the marriage had occurred as the girl turned fourteen and therewith was competent to enter into marriage. The court stated that "the claimant failed to carry the burden of proving that this marriage was in fact ratified, since the only result to be reached from Hughes' testimony was that she was either a few months under or a few months over 14 at the time they finally separated."

60 *See, e.g., Eskev v. Eskev*, 198 Ga. 513, 34 S.E.2d 697, 698 (1945).

61 *Crapps v. Smith*, 9 Ga.App. 400, 71 S.E. 501 (1911); *Powers v. Powers*, 138 Ga. 65, 74 S.E. 759 (1912); *Eskev v. Eskev*, 198 Ga. 513, 34 S.E.2d 697 (1945); and *Jones v. Jones*, 200 Ga. 571, 37 S.E.2d 711 (1946).

62 A petition for annulment can be filed by the parties themselves, but prior to their reaching the age of eighteen, also by the parents and guardian under 23 PA. CONS. STAT. ANN. § 3303 (West 2003). A ceremonial marriage, in contrast, is not void but simply voidable. Grounds for declaring a ceremonial marriage invalid can be that one of the parties was under the age of sixteen, that the court has not approved of the marriage, or that the parties are sixteen or seventeen and have not obtained consent from the parents or guardian or court, and the parties have not "ratified the marriage" after reaching the age of eighteen, *see* 23 PA. CONS. STAT. ANN. § 3305 (West 2003).

asked to have the marriage annulled after arriving at the age where either could have it set aside."[63]

The uncertain legal consequences resulting from lack of marital age, and the descriptions in the legislation, as well as in the case law, are naturally unsatisfactory. It is necessary for lawmakers to more clearly identify the legal consequences resulting if the different age requirements are not fulfilled. Homer Clark correctly notes that the legislation generally often gives rise to confusion when it treats the "void-voidable" distinction.[64] This is even truer with respect to common law marriage. Clark suggests that marriages involving minors should be simply voidable. This, however, can be questioned with respect to common law marriage. There is a danger that minors, unaware that they are living in such a marriage, will miss the window of opportunity to file a petition for annulment. Another problem that can arise is that a marriage that has not been declared void can be used as a defense, by claiming that the parties are married to each other, to criminal charges of sexual conduct with a minor. In other situations, being able to cite the validity of a voidable marriage is less significant if it is uncertain whether the parties themselves agree about the validity of the marriage.

It appears reasonable that a common law marriage between minors not having reached the marital age is *void ab initio.* But it can be debated whether the ability to ratify a void marriage should extend to common law marriages, because the parties in such marriages have not gone through a wedding ceremony giving them reason to believe that they are married. Such a possibility is not without problems from a contractual perspective, as the original contract in a common law marriage is often an inferred agreement. A continued cohabitation should be deemed a ratification only if it is proven that an earlier marriage contract also existed.[65] In addition, under-age parties fulfilling the other requirements of a common law marriage can often, through their actions, enter into a "new" common law marriage when they reach the required age. However, in such a case, the new marriage is normally not considered retroactive, which means that any children born before the new marriage are illegitimate. The legal protection of children, however, ought to be provided for through specific

---

63 *Boehm v. Rohlfs*, 224 Iowa 226, 276 N.W. 105, 108 (1937). In *Peefer v. State*, 42 Ohio App. 276, 182 N.E. 117 (1931), a forty-one-year-old man entered into a marriage with a fourteen-year-old girl, who was competent in accordance to the common law to marry, but not according to the existing legislation which required the age of sixteen. The consent required, as she was under the age of twenty-one, was also absent. The marriage was considered voidable, but not void. The man could not be convicted of delinquency with a minor. In *Duley v. Duley*, 151 A.2d 255 (M.App.D.C. 1959), in which it was found that the marriage was voidable, the court viewed itself as having the "judicial discretion" to refuse to declare a marriage void. *Compare In re Zemmick's Estate*, 17 Ohio Supp. 15, 76 N.E.2d 902, 905 (1946); *Browning v. Browning*, 89 Kan. 98, 130 P. 852 (1913); and *State v. Bittick*, 103 Mo. 183, 15 S.W. 325 (1891).

64 CLARK, *supra* note 36, at 167.

65 With respect to the ratification of an inferred agreement, *see supra* Chapter 6.2.3.

regulations granting them legitimacy even if their parents' marriage is found to be void, or through legislation that gives them certain rights, for example, the right to inherit despite illegitimacy.

5.3 PREEXISTING MARRIAGES

5.3.1 The Principle of Monogamy

The view of marriage as a monogamous relationship between a man and woman is still, now at the beginning of the twenty-first century, fundamental in Western countries. The statement by the United States Supreme Court in *Mormon Church v. United States* (1890) is principally still valid: "The organization of a community for the spread and practice of polygamy is ... contrary to the spirit of Christianity and of the civilization which Christianity has produced in the Western world."[66] The importance of the policy against plural marriages can be seen, not in the least, from the placement it sometimes receives in the constitutions of different states. The Oklahoma Constitution currently states, with a view to governing the future: "Polygamous or plural marriages are forever prohibited."[67] The principle comes to a concrete expression in all of the American jurisdictions studied here, in that an existing marriage is an impediment to the formation of a new marriage.[68] Those persons already married, consequently,

66 *Mormon Church v. United States,* 136 U.S. 1, 49 (1890). *See also Cleveland v. United States,* 329 U.S. 14 (1946); and *Mortensen v. United States,* 322 U.S. 365, 377 (1944). In *Reynolds v. United States,* 98 U.S. 145 (1878), it was held that the constitutional protection for freedom of religion could not protect against a conviction of bigamy. *See also Potter v. Murray City,* 585 F.Supp. 1126 (D.Utah 1984); *Barlow v. Blackburn,* 798 P.2d 1360 (Ariz.App. 1990); and *Employment Div. v. Smith,* 485 U.S. 660 (1988). In *Hyde v. Hyde,* L.R. 1 P. & D. 130, 133 (1866), a monogamous marriage was defined as "the voluntary union for life of a man and a woman to the exclusion of all others." Monogamy has also been viewed as "the only natural form of marriage," *see* J.A.C. Lightner, *Common Law Marriages in Wisconsin,* 6 MARQ. L. REV. 82 (1922). *Compare* the characteristic of monogamy as found in the marital contract's required intent, Chapter 6.3.

67 OKLA. CONST. art. 1 § 2 (1998). *See also* IDAHO CONST. art. 1 § 4 (Michie 2003).

68 **Alabama:** ALA. CODE ANN. §§ 13A-13-1 (Law. Coop. 2002). **Colorado**: COLO. REV. STAT. ANN. § 14-2-110 (1) (West 2003). **District of Columbia:** D.C. CODE ANN. § 46-401 (West 2001). **Georgia:** GA. CODE ANN. § 19-3-2 (3) (West 2003). **Idaho:** IDAHO CODE ANN. §§ 32-207 and 32-501 (2) (Michie 2003). **Iowa**: IOWA CODE ANN. § 595.19 (West 2003). **Kansas:** KAN. STAT. ANN. 21-3601 (2002). **Montana:** MONT. CODE ANN. § 40-1-401 (1) (a) (Mont. Leg. Serv. Div. 2003). **Ohio:** OHIO REV. CODE ANN. §§ 3101.01, 31.05.31 (2000). **Oklahoma:** OKLA. STAT. ANN. tit. 43, § 3 (West 2003). **Pennsylvania**: PA. STAT. ANN. 23-1304 (West 2003); *In re Watt's Estate,* 409 Pa. 44, 185 A.2d 781, 785-786 (1962); *Fiedler v. Nat'l Tube Co.,* 161 Pa.Super. 155, 53 A.2d 821 (1947); *Sharpe v. Federal Window & Office Cleaning Co.,* 144 Pa.Super. 231, 19 A.2d 509, 514 (1941); *In re Cline's Estate,* 128 Pa.Super. 309, 194 A. 222 (1937); *Fitzpatrick v. Miller,* 129 Pa.Super. 324, 196 A. 83 (1937); *Thomas v. Thomas,* 124 Pa. 646, 17 A. 182 (1889); and *Heffner v. Heffner,* 23 Pa.St. 104, 106 (1854). **Rhode Island**: R.I. GEN. LAWS § 15-1-5 (Michie 2003). **South Carolina:** S.C. CODE ANN. 20-1-80 (Law. Coop. 2003). **Texas:** TEX. FAM. CODE ANN. § 6.202 (West 2002). **Utah**: UTAH CODE. ANN. §§ 30-1-2, 30-1-17.1

may not marry again until the already existing marriage is dissolved by divorce, annulment, or death. If such an impediment exists, the new marriage is void. This view of monogamy has also influenced the criminal regulations, according to which, persons who are already married but who enter into a new marriage can be found guilty of the crime of bigamy.[69] The principle of monogamy also has a central place in the regulations pertaining to the premarital controls over marriage and marriage licenses, whose purposes are to prevent bigamy and encourage parties to live monogamously.

During the later half of the 1900s, indictments for bigamy have become increasingly rare.[70] In addition, the legal system has considerably facilitated the ability to divorce and establish new marriages. This development has contributed to such a high rate of divorce and remarriage that lawmakers are viewed as accepting and approving of what is sometimes referred to as "successive polygamy."[71] Nevertheless, even though people may simultaneously have relationships with several partners, it is rare for anyone to actually live with several persons in a polygamous family.[72]

The principle of monogamy is applicable not only to ceremonial marriages but also to common law marriages. Similarly, the civil regulations concerning marital impediments and the penal regulations on bigamy apply to such marriages. An existing marriage, therefore, is an impediment against the formation of a common law marriage. The impediment

---

(Michie 2003). *See also* UNIF. MARRIAGE AND DIVORCE ACT § 207; and 9A UNIFORM L. ANN. 108 (1979).

69 The criminal regulations, which fall outside of the parameters of this study, are somewhat differently formulated in the different jurisdictions. Certain jurisdictions criminalize not only the married person entering into the latter marriage, but also their cohabitation with someone other than their lawful spouse. The boundaries are difficult to define with respect to common law marriages entered into through an "inferred agreement" based upon the parties' cohabitation. Certain regulations take into account the party's good faith with respect to the dissolution of a previous marriage. **Alabama:** ALA. CODE ANN. § 13A-13-1 (Law. Coop. 2002); *Beggs v. State*, 55 Ala. 108, 110-111 (1876). **Colorado:** COLO. REV. STAT. ANN. §§ 18-6-201, 18-6-202 (West 2003). **District of Columbia:** D.C. CODE ANN. § 22-501 (West 2001). **Georgia:** GA. CODE ANN. § 16-6-20 (West 2003). **Idaho:** IDAHO CODE ANN. §§ 18-1101, 18-1102, 18-1103 and 18-1104 (Michie 2003). **Iowa:** IOWA CODE ANN. § 726.1 (West 2003). **Kansas**: KAN. STAT. ANN. § 21-3601 (2002); *In re Marriage of Thomas*, 16 Kan.App.2d 511, 825 P.2d 1163 (1992). **Montana**: MONT. CODE ANN. §§ 45-5-611, 45-5-612 (Mont. Leg. Serv. Div. 2003). **Ohio:** OHIO REV. CODE ANN. § 2919.01 (West 2003). **Oklahoma**: OKLA. STAT. ANN. tit. 43, § 124 (West 2003). **Pennsylvania**: PA. STAT. ANN. 18-4301 (West 2003). **Rhode Island:** R.I. GEN. LAWS § 11-6-1 (Michie 2003); **South Carolina:** S.C. CODE. ANN. § 16-15-10 (Law. Coop. 2003). **Texas:** TEX. PEN. CODE ANN. § 25.01 (West 2002). **Utah:** UTAH CODE ANN. § 76-7-101 (Michie 2003).

70 Ralph Slovenko, *The De Facto Decriminalization of Bigamy*, 17 J. FAM. L. 297 (1978); CLARK, *supra* note 9, at 124, referring to one famous older case, *Williams v. North Carolina* I, 317 U.S. 287, 63 S.Ct. 207, 87 L.Ed. 279 (1942); II, 325 U.S. 226, 65 S.Ct. 1092, 89 L.Ed. 1577 (1945). *Compare State v. Green*, 99 P.3d 820 (Utah 2004).

71 Mary-Ann Glendon, *Marriage and the State: The Withering Away of Marriage*, 62 VA. L. REV. 663, 673 (1976).

72 This problem existed to a limited extent among the Mormons, *see* Orma Linford, *The Mormons and the Law: The Polygamy Cases*, 9 UTAH L. REV. 308, 543 (1964).

can consist of a previously formed ceremonial marriage,[73] but also can be a previously established common law marriage. In *McClurkin v. McClurkin* (1921), two women made separate claims on the deceased's estate, asserting that they were his widows in common law marriage. The first established the existence of a common law marriage, which was not dissolved prior to the man's death and was an impediment to the second marriage.[74]

---

73 *Phillips v. Dow Chemical Co.*, 186 S.W.3d 121 (Tex.App. 2005); *Int'l Painters and Allied Traders Ind. Pensions Fund v. Calabro*, 312 F.Supp.2d 697, 702 (E.D.Pa. 2004); *Potter v. Davie*, 275 A.D.2d 961, 713 N.Y.S.2d 627, 629 (A.D. 4 Dep't 2000); *Hall v. Duster*, 727 So.2d 834, 836 (Ala.Civ.App. 1999); *Villegas v. Griffin Industries*, 975 S.W.2d 745 (Tex.App.-Corpus Christi 1998); *Netecke v. State, through DOTD*, 715 So.2d 449 (La.App. 3 Cir. 1998); *In re Estate of Hunsaker*, 968 P.2d 281 (Mont. 1998); *State Farm Fire & Cas. Co. v. Platt*, 4 F.Supp.2d 399 (E.D.Pa. 1998); *Rowbottom v. State*, 327 Ark. 79, 938 S.W.2d 224 (1997); *Roy v. Bethlehem Steel Corp.*, 838 F.Supp. 312 (E.D.Tex. 1993); and *Johns v. Johns*, 420 S.E.2d 856 (S.C.App. 1992). At the point of time at which the parties moved in together, and during their cohabitation, the man was married to a different woman. No common law marriage could therefore be established. The court cited the South Carolina legislation applicable to common law marriages: "All marriages contracted while either of the parties has a former wife or husband living shall be void," *see* S.C. CODE. ANN. § 20-1-80 (Law. Coop. 2003). *See also In re Marriage of Thomas*, 16 Kan.App.2d 511, 825 P.2d 1163 (1992); *Crandell v. Resley*, 804 P.2d 272 (Colo.App. 1990); *Petrarca v. Castrovillari*, 448 A.2d 1286 (R.I. 1982); *Tatum v. Tatum*, 736 P.2d 506 (Okla. 1982); *Franklin v. Smallridge*, 616 S.W.2d 655 (Tex.Civ.App-Corpus Christi 1981); *Blackwood v. Kilpatrick*, 52 Ala.App. 505, 294 So.2d 753 (1974); *In re Reichert*, 95 Idaho 647, 516 P.2d 704 (1973); *Home Indemnity Co. v. Edwards*, 488 S.W.2d 561 (Tex.Civ.App.-Fort Worth 1972); *Hill v. Shreve*, 448 P.2d 848 (Okla. 1968)(impediment, however, not proven); *Lester v. Celebrezze*, 221 F.Supp. 607 (E.D.Ark. 1963); *Santill v. Rosseti*, 178 N.E.2d 633 (C.P.Ohio 1961); *Simpson v. Simpson*, 404 Pa. 247, 172 A.2d 168 (1961); *Kicklighter v. Kicklighter*, 217 Ga. 54, 121 S.E.2d 122 (1961); *Barker v. Lee*, 337 S.W.2d 637 (Tex.Civ.App. 1960); *Liberty Mut. Ins. Co. v. Ellis*, 99 Ga. App. 486, 109 S.E.2d 70 (1959); and *Di Giovanni v. Di Giovannantonio*, 98 U.S.App.D.C. 147, 233 F.2d 26 (1956). In *Warrenberger v. Folsom*, 239 F.2d 846 (3d Cir. 1956) (applying Pennsylvania law), the Pennsylvania principle, that a person guilty of adultery was prevented from marrying the person with whom they had committed adultery while the previous spouse was still alive, was also found to be applicable to entering into a common law marriage; *Grooms v. Globe Indem. Co.*, 92 Ga.App. 387, 88 S.E.2d 504 (1955); *Toole v. Gallion*, 221 Ga. 494, 144 S.E.2d 360 (1965); *Mayers v. Ewing*, 102 F.Supp. 201 (D.C.Pa. 1952); *In re Gallagher's Estate*, 35 Wash.2d 512, 213 P.2d 621 (1950); *Branch v. United States*, 83 F.Supp. 641 (D.C.Okla. 1949); *Ryan v. Ryan*, 84 Ohio App. 139, 86 N.E.2d 44 (1948); and *Clark v. Glenn*, 249 Ala. 342, 31 So.2d 507 (1947). *See also Wydra v. Philadelphia & Reading Coal & Iron Co.*, 153 Pa.Super. 529, 34 A. 2d 326 (1943); *Whitney v. Whitney*, 192 Okla. 174, 134 P.2d 357, 359 (1943); *Morrison v. Sunshine Mining Co.*, 64 Idaho 6, 127 P.2d 766 (1942); *Wilbert v. Com. Sec. Reserve Acc.*, 143 Pa.Super. 37, 17 A.2d 732 (1941); *Sharpe v. Federal Window & Office Cleaning Co.*, 144 Pa.Super. 231, 19 A.2d 509 (1941); *Wolford v. Whiterock Quarries*, 144 Pa.Super. 577, 20 A.2d 887 (1941); and *Stewart v. Shenandoah Life Ins. Co.*,144 Pa.Super. 549, 20 A.2d 246 (1941). In the case of *In re Cline's Estate*, 128 Pa.Super. 309, 194 A. 222 (1937), the court stated that it was legally impossible for the woman, who had a living spouse, to enter into a new marriage "either by a formal ceremony or by common law agreement." *See also In re Morrow's Estate*, 100 Colo. 424, 68 P.2d 36, 39 (1937); *Valdez v. Shaw*, 100 Colo. 101, 66 P.2d 325 (1937); and *Hess v. Pettigrew*, 261 Mich. 618, 247 N.W. 90 (1933).

74 *McClurkin v. McClurkin*, 206 Ala. 513, 90 So. 917 (1921); *Texas Employer's Ins. Assn. v. Elder*, 155 Tex. 27, 274 S.W.2d 144 (Civ.App. 1954), 282 S.W.2d 371 (Tex. 1955); *Harrison v. Burton*, 303 P.2d 962 (Okla. 1954); *In re Rosenberger's Estate*, 362 Pa. 153, 65 A.2d 377 (1949); *Walker v. Matthews*, 191 Miss. 498, 3 So.2d 820 (1941);

A man who has established a common law marriage with a woman and later cohabits with another woman can be charged with and convicted of bigamy if he knew he was married and had not dissolved the first marriage prior to initiating the second, which need not be a new ceremonial marriage. Simple cohabitation can already lead to the crime of bigamy. This situation was the background to *State v. Green* (2004).[75]

The principle of monogamy further entails that a common law marriage in its turn can be an impediment to entering into a ceremonial marriage. A common law marriage can then only be dissolved by a formal divorce, and until then is an impediment to any new marriage even where the parties have actually separated. The District of Columbia Court of Appeals consequently came to the following conclusion in *Lee v. Lee* (1964): "[S]ince the common-law marriage was not terminated by death or a decree of divorce, the attempted ceremonial marriage in Maryland was void in the District of Columbia."[76]

---

and *Aldana v. Aldana*, 42 S.W.2d 661 (Tex.Civ.App.-El Paso 1931). *See also Cunningham v. Cunningham*, 210 S.W. 242 (Tex.Civ.App.-Galveston 1918); *Pike v. Estate of Pike*, 2005 WL 2248347 (Tex.App.-Forth Worth 2005); and *Matter of Estate of Marson*, 328 Mont. 348, 120 P.3d 382 (Mont. 2005) (remanded for further proceedings).

75 In *State v. Green*, 99 P.3d 820 (Utah 2004), a man had established a common law marriage with a woman and later during five years cohabited with four other women. He was charged and convicted of bigamy. The Supreme Court of Utah only considered the constitutional issues. Utah's bigamy statute provides: "A person is guilty of bigamy when, knowing he has a husband or wife, the person purports to marry another person or cohabits with another person." UTAH CODE ANN. § 76-7-101(1), § 30-1-4.5 (Michie 1999). Other common law marriage states include *cohabitation* as an element of the crime of bigamy. *See, for example*, COLO. REV. STAT. ANN. § 18-6-201 (West 2003); R.I. GEN. LAWS § 11-6-1 (Michie 2003); and TEX. PEN. CODE ANN. § 25.01 (West 2002). *See also State v. Thompson*, 76 N.J.L. 197, 68 A. 1068, 1069 (1908), in which the court stated: "We are of the opinion that under the law of this state the contract, followed by cohabitation, as shown in this case, is just as lawful a marriage as if it had been ceremoniously celebrated, and that this defendant was a married man, with a wife living, when he married Nellie Reynolds, and that when he married her he committed the crime of bigamy." *Compare Umbenhour v. Umbenhour*, 12 Ohio C.C.R. (n.s.) 289 (Cir.Ct. 1909), *aff'd*, 85 Ohio St. 238, 97 N.E. 832 (1912); *Fuguay v. State*, 217 Ala. 4, 114 So. 898 (1927); and *Davis v. People*, 83 Colo. 295, 264 P. 658 (1928). In *Bynon v. State*, 117 Ala. 80, 23 So. 640 (1898), a man was convicted of bigamy, as he had entered into a ceremonial marriage despite the fact that he already was united in a common law marriage with a different women. The reverse is also true, that a person entering into a common law marriage despite the fact that he or she is already married with a different person can be found guilty of bigamy, *see Campbell v. Allen*, 208 Ga. 274, 66 S.E.2d 226, 231 (1951); *Allen v. State, 17 Ga.App. 431, 87 S.E. 681 (1916); Green v. State, 21 Fla. 403 (1885); Carmichael v. State*, 12 Ohio St. 553 (1861); and *Baker v. Mays*, 199 S.W.2d 279 (Tex.Civ.App. 1946). *See also* Hugh A. Ross, *The Ohio Law of Marriage*, 14 WESTERN RESERV. L. REV. 724, 730 (1963); and Walter O. Weyrauch, *Informal and formal marriage - an appraisal of trends in family organization*, 28 U. CHI. L. REV. 88, 91 (1960). According to Henrik Hartog, *Marital Exits and Marital Expectations in Nineteenth-Century America*, 80 GEO. L.J. 95, 107 (1991), the courts during the 19th century were reluctant to characterize common law marriage cases as bigamy. *See also* Timothy J. Gilfoyle, *The Hearts of Nineteenth-Century Men: Bigamy and Working Class Marriage in New York City, 1800-1890*, 19 PROSPECTS 135, 151 (1994).

76 *Lee v. Lee*, 201 A.2d 873, 875 (D.C.App. 1964); *Barron v. Apfel*, 209 F.3d 984 (7th Cir. 2000) (applying Social Security Act, 42 U.S.C. § 402 (e)) (if a common law marriage

Specific problems arise with the application of the principle of monogamy to common law marriages. The issuance of a marriage license typically must be preceded by an assessment of whether impediments to the marriage exist, but these regulations are not applicable to common law marriages. Consequently, as regards such a marriage, the issue of impediments first commonly arises in lawsuits filed after, perhaps many years after, the relationship was commenced. Moreover, since common law marriages are not registered, evidentiary issues are difficult to assess. For example, in order to prove whether a person was born within a marriage, or has a right to inherit, a court may need to determine whether the parents, who perhaps

---

was established, it was an impediment to the three formal marriages the woman later entered into); *In re Estate of Lymon*, 542 N.Y.S.2d 168 (A.D. 1989) (common law marriage, however, not proven); *Baker v. Musa*, 170 Ga.App. 77, 316 S.E.2d 178 (1984); *Yarbrough v. Yarbrough*, 280 S.C. 546, 314 S.E.2d 16, 18 (App. 1984) (dictum); *Tatum v. Tatum*, 736 P.2d 506 (Okla. 1982) (dictum); and *In re Estate of Claveria v. Claveria*, 615 S.W.2d 164, 165 (Tex. 1981); *Rodriguez v. Avalos*, 567 S.W.2d 85, 87 (Tex.Civ.App.-El Paso 1978); and *Byers v. Mount Vernon Mills, Inc.*, 268 S.C. 68, 231 S.E.2d 699 (1977) (common law marriage not proven). *Compare In re Estate of Benjamin*, 34 N.Y.2d 27, 355 N.Y.S.2d 356, 311 N.E.2d 495 (1974) (in which the marital presumption, according to which a common law marriage was presumed based on the parties' cohabitation and representation outwardly as spouses, was found subordinate to the presumption in favor of a later ceremonial marriage); *Gallegos v. Wilkerson*, 79 N.M. 549, 445 P.2d 970 (1968); and *Foix v. Jordan*, 421 S.W.2d 481 (Tex.Civ.App.-El Paso 1967). *See also Parkhill Truck Co. v. Row*, 383 P.2d 203 (Okla. 1963) (in which a common law marriage was found to be an impediment to the forming of a later ceremonial marriage, despite the fact that the applicable presumption was in favor of the later marriage); *Campbell v. Christian*, 235 S.C. 102, 110 S.E.2d 1, 5 (1959); and *Hackmeyer v. Hackmeyer*, 268 Ala. 329, 106 So.2d 245 (1958). In *Skinner v. Skinner*, 4 Misc.2d 1013, 150 N.Y.S.2d 739 (1956), a common law marriage was found established through short visits in Pennsylvania and Washington, D.C. An impediment therefore existed as to a later ceremonial marriage. In *Harrison v. Burton*, 303 P.2d 962 (Okla. 1954), a common law marriage was an impediment to a ceremonial marriage. In *Earley v. State Indus. Comm'n*, 269 P.2d 977, 979 (Okla. 1954), a common law marriage was also found to be an impediment to a ceremonial marriage: "Thus, when Audrey and Walter Early attempted to be married, Audrey was not capable to so contract because she was the undivorced common-law wife of Gillum." *See also Nyhuis v. Pierce*, 65 O.L.Abs. 73, 114 N.E.2d 75 (Ohio App. 1952). In *Dibble v. Dibble*, 88 Ohio App. 490, 100 N.E.2d 451 (1950), a common law marriage was found to be an impediment against a later ceremonial marriage, which was considered void. A common law marriage could only be dissolved by death or divorce, not "by estoppel." *See also In re Tersip's Estate*, 86 Cal.App.2d 43, 194 P.2d 66 (1948). In *Abbott v. Indus. Com.*, 80 Ohio App. 7, 35 Ohio Ops. 406, 74 N.W.2d 625 (1946), a woman had entered into a ceremonial marriage, after that a common law marriage and finally a ceremonial marriage with different men. The court found the first marriage void because there was no consent from the parents. As this marriage was void only from the date of the declaration of annulment, it was an impediment to the two later marriages. The court further stated that if the first marriage was *void ab initio*, then the second marriage (the common law marriage) was an impediment to the last marriage. *See also In re Zemmick's Estate*, 17 Ohio Supp. 15, 76 N.E.2d 902, 905 (1946); and *Sloss-Sheffield Steel & Iron Co. v. Watford*, 245 Ala. 425, 17 So.2d 166 (1944). In *Craddock's Case*, 37 N.E.2d 508 (Mass. 1941) (applying Pennsylvania law), a common law marriage was an impediment to a ceremonial marriage. *See also Walker v. Matthews*, 191 Miss. 498, 3 So.2d 820 (1941); *Sam v. Sam*, 172 Okla. 342, 45 P.2d 462 (1935); *Boyd v. Boyd*, 252 N.Y. 422 (N.Y. 1930); and *Chapman v. Chapman*, 16 Tex.Civ. App. 382, 41 S.W. 533 (1897).

are deceased, had entered into a formless common law marriage decades previously. The court may need to determine whether that marriage was invalid because one parent entered into an even earlier common law marriage that was not dissolved.

The evidentiary difficulties are not minimized by the fact that the majority of common law marriages are entered into by inferred agreements in the form of the parties' cohabitation.[77] The time of the commencement of the marriage, therefore, often is not clear. Such a marriage may have been established after a period of cohabitation without the knowledge of the parties.[78] This is understandable, particularly if many couples are generally unaware of the legal doctrine of common law marriage.[79] This situation has created considerable legal uncertainty. The parties' lack of knowledge means that they also are unaware that they must

---

77 For more on this, *see* Chapter 7. Certain courts have maintained, however, that for a common law marriage to be an impediment to a ceremonial marriage, it cannot be based on the presumption with the support of "cohabitation and reputation" but must be "properly proven." *See* from Georgia, *Cooper v. Cooper*, 88 Ga.App. 335, 76 S.E.2d 726, 728 (1953); *Carter v. Graves*, 206 Ga. 234, 56 S.E.2d 917, 920 (1949), 207 Ga. 308, 61 S.E.2d 282 (1950); and *Addison v. Addison*, 186 Ga. 155, 197 S.E. 232, 234 (1938). In such cases, the party claiming the impediment must prove "every element necessary to the validity of such a prior marriage, by proving not only that the prior marriage was consummated in accordance with the foregoing rules of law, but that such alleged former spouse was single and possessed every other qualification for a valid marriage." *See also Barney v. Barney*, 43 Ga.App. 545, 548, 159 S.E. 595 (1931); *Norman v. Goode*, 113 Ga. 121, 38 S.E. 317, 318-319 (1901); and *Jenkins v. Jenkins*, 83 Ga. 286, 9 S.E. 541, 20 Am.St.Rep. 316 (1889) ("The true doctrine of the authorities is that where two alleged marriages compete, and one of them is proved as a fact, whether by direct or circumstantial evidence, the other cannot be left to stand upon the mere legal presumption founded on cohabitation and repute.") *Compare Dixon v. State*, 217 Ga.App. 267, 456 S.E.2d 758, 760 (1995). It ought to be noted that a later ceremonial marriage can constitute evidence that no common law marriage had existed, *see, e.g., McClurkin v. McClurkin*, 206 Ala. 513, 90 So. 917 (1921); and *Moore v. Heineke*, 119 Ala. 627, 24 So. 374 (1898). *Compare Crosson v. Crosson*, 668 So.2d 868 (Ala.Civ.App. 1995), in which a common law marriage was found established despite the fact that the man thereafter entered into a ceremonial marriage with a different woman. At trial, the woman claimed that the man was guilty of bigamy and adultery, which however, were not issues at trial.

78 American and Swedish sociologists are in agreement that cohabitation without formal marriage is seldom the result of a conscious decision, *see, for example,* JAN TROST, UNMARRIED COHABITATION, 63-64 (1979). *See also* Eleanor D. Macklin, *Nonmarital Heterosexual Cohabitation,* MAR. FAM. REV. March/April, at 1, 6 (1978) ("Living together is seldom the result of a considered decision... Most cohabitation evolves from a drift of sleeping more and more frequently together and the gradual accumulation of possessions in one residence"); and David S. Caudill, *Legal Recognition of Unmarried Cohabitation: A Proposal to Update and Reconsider Common-Law Marriage,* 49 TENN. L. REV. 537, 565 (1982).

79 The situation is rather common as found in *Lorensen v. Weaber*, 840 S.W.2d 644, 646 (Tex.App.-Dallas 1992), where the woman was questioned: "And at that point in time, what was the agreement between the two of you as to living together?" She answered: "I don't understand." In *Hawkins v. Weinberger*, 368 F.Supp. 896, 899 (D.Kan. 1973), the woman was asked: "Q. Did you believe that your living together made you legally married? A. Yes. Later on I learned about common law marriage."

dissolve the marriage through a formal divorce.[80] Therefore, it is common for them to separate, without filing for divorce, and then commence a new relationship, oblivious to the reality that their common law marriage is an impediment to establishing either a new common law marriage or a ceremonial marriage.[81] Therefore, there is reason to assume that bigamy, in the civil meaning, is not unusual, though the parties may be unaware of it, in cases in which a common law marriage precedes a later marriage. (For comparison, see on the other hand the presumption in favor of a later marriage, *infra*). When a party in a ceremonial marriage petitions for divorce, claiming a division of the property and maintenance, they consequently can be met by the objection that the marriage was invalid because the other spouse had lived in a earlier common law marriage which had not been dissolved by a formal divorce.[82] This problem challenges the legal system.

5.3.2 The Legal Consequences of the Impediment

A common law marriage entered into despite the fact that one or both of the parties were already married is not only voidable in the majority of jurisdictions, that is, it can be declared void by the court,[83] but also *void ab initio*, a nullity.[84] The legal consequence is the same regardless of whether

80 OTTO E. KOEGEL, COMMON LAW MARRIAGE AND ITS DEVELOPMENT IN THE UNITED STATES, 102 (1922), stated in the 1920s that "very few, if any, of these persons really believe that they are married. Scarcely any of these persons believe that a divorce is necessary to dissolve the marriage." *Compare Barron v. Apfel*, 209 F.3d 984 (7th Cir. 2000), in which the court stated that a common law marriage could not be dissolved through separation but only through formal divorce, and that if such a such marriage was established, it was an impediment to the three formal marriages the woman later entered into.

81 *See also* Clarice M. Davis, *Common Law Marriage in Texas*, 21 S.W.L.J. 647, 655 (1967), stating: "Frequently several informal relationships are involved, any of which may or may not be a marriage."

82 *See, e.g., Yarbrough v. Yarbrough*, 280 S.C. 546, 314 S.E.2d 16, 18 (App. 1984); and *Hackmeyer v. Hackmeyer*, 268 Ala. 329, 106 So.2d 245 (1958). Even where two ceremonial marriages compete with each other and a spouse in the later marriage petitions for divorce and claims maintenance, the other spouse can object that the marriage is void due to the previous undissolved marriage, *see, e.g., Kirk v. Kirk*, 238 P.2d 808 (Okla. 1951).

83 **Idaho:** In *Nicholas v. Idaho Power Co.*, 63 Idaho 675, 125 P.2d 321 (1942), the Idaho Supreme Court found, in its interpretation of the applicable regulations, that a marriage entered into despite the fact that one of the parties was already married, could only be voidable despite the fact that IDAHO CODE ANN. § 31-207 (currently § 32-207 (Michie 2003)) stated that a marriage entered into by a person already married is "illegal and void from the beginning." *Compare Morrison v. Sunshine Mining Co.*, 64 Idaho 6, 127 P.2d 766, 769 (1942), where a common law marriage, as long as the impediment existed, was found "absolutely void at the time."

84 **Alabama:** *Blackwood v. Kilpatrick*, 52 Ala.App. 505, 294 So.2d 753 (1974); *Metro. Life Ins. Co. v. Spearman*, 344 F.Supp. 665, 668 (M.D.Ala. 1972); *Barker v. U.S.*, 3 F.Supp. 545 (D.C.Ala. 1933); *Dorsey v. Dorsey*, 259 Ala. 220, 66 So.2d 135, 140 (1953); *Sloss-Sheffield Steel & Iron Co. v. Watford*, 245 Ala. 425, 17 So.2d 166 (1944); *Bell v. Tennessee Coal, Iron & R. Co.*, 240 Ala. 422, 199 So. 813, 814 (1941); *Rogers v. McLeskey*, 225 Ala.

the impediment consists of a prior ceremonial marriage or a common law marriage. In *Villegas v. Griffin Industries* (1998), in which a ceremonial marriage was an impediment to a common law marriage, the latter was consequently found to be *void ab initio.*[85] From *Nyhuis v. Pierce* (1952), it can be seen that a ceremonial marriage is also a nullity if one or both of the parties are united in a previous common law marriage with a different person.[86]

As this case demonstrates, no specific petition for annulment needs to be filed, even if it is possible to do so.[87] As the new marriage is a nullity, it never legally existed and therefore does not need to be declared void.

148, 142 So. 526 (1932); and *Walker v. Walker*, 218 Ala. 16, 117 So. 472 (1928). **Colorado:** *In re Morrow's Estate*, 100 Colo. 424, 68 P.2d 36, 39 (1937); *Valdez v. Shaw*, 100 Colo. 101, 66 P.2d 325 (1937); and *Poole v. People*, 24 Colo. 510, 52 P. 1025 (1898). **District of Columbia:** *Lee v. Lee*, 201 A.2d 873, 875 (D.C.App. 1964); and *Koonin v. Hornsby*, 140 A.2d 309 (Md.App. 1958). **Georgia:** *Zurich Ins. Co. v. Craft*, 103 Ga.App. 889, 120 S.E.2d 922 (1961); *Campbell v. Allen*, 208 Ga. 274, 66 S.E.2d 226 (1951); *Graves v. Carter*, 207 Ga. 308, 61 S.E.2d 282 (1950) ("an absolute nullity"); and *Gearllach v. Odom*, 200 Ga. 350, 37 S.E.2d 184 (1946). **Iowa:** *DeWall v. Rhoderick*, 258 Iowa 433, 138 N.W.2d 124 (1965). **Kansas:** *Johnson County Nat. Bank & Trust Co. v. Bach*, 189 Kan. 291, 369 P.2d 231 (1962). **Montana:** *Elliott v. Indus. Accident Bd.*, 101 Mont. 246, 53 P.2d 451 (1936). **Ohio**: *Detroit Diesel Corp. v. Lane-Smith*, 39 F.Supp.2d 852, 858 (E.D.Mich. 1999) (applying Ohio law); *Darling v. Darling*, 44 Ohio App.2d 5, 335 N.E.2d 708, 710 (1975); *Nyhuis v. Pierce*, 65 O.L.Abs. 73, 114 N.E.2d 75 (Ohio App. 1952); *In re Zemmick's Estate*, 17 Ohio Supp. 15, 76 N.E.2d 902, 905 (1946); and *Cartwright v. McGown*, 121 Ill. 388, 12 N.E. 737 (1887) (applying Ohio law). **Oklahoma:** *Whitney v. Whitney*, 192 Okla. 174, 134 P.2d 357, 360 (1943). *Compare In re Rogers' Estate*, 569 P.2d 536, 538 (Okla.App. 1977), in which the Oklahoma Court of Appeals found that a marriage entered into within the six month waiting period after a divorce was "voidable rather than void." **Pennsylvania:** *In re Watt's Estate*, 409 Pa. 44, 185 A.2d 781, 785-786 (1962); *Simpson v. Simpson*, 404 Pa. 247, 172 A.2d 168, 171 (1961); *Visconti v. Sec'y of Health, Ed., and Welfare*, 374 F.Supp. 1272 (D.C.Pa. 1974); *Fiedler v. Nat'l Tube Co.*, 161 Pa.Super. 155, 53 A.2d 821 (1947); *Sharpe v. Federal Window & Office Cleaning Co.*, 144 Pa.Super. 231, 19 A.2d 509, 514 (1941); *Fitzpatrick v. Miller*, 129 Pa.Super. 324, 196 A. 83 (1937); *Thomas v. Thomas*, 124 Pa. 646, 17 A. 182 (1889); and *Heffner v. Heffner*, 23 Pa.St. 104, 106 (1854). **Rhode Island:** *Keidel v. Keidel*, 119 R.I. 726, 383 A.2d 264, 265 (1978); *Holgate v. United Electric Ry. Co.*, 47 R.I. 337, 133 A. 243 (1926); and R.I. GEN. LAWS. § 15-1-5. **South Carolina:** *Johns v. Johns*, 420 S. E.2d 856 (S.C.App. 1992); *Day v. Day*, 216 S.C. 334, 58 S.E.2d 83 (1950); *Ex parte Blizzard*, 185 S.C. 131, 193 S.E. 633 (1937); *Lemon v. Lemon*, 158 S.C. 71, 155 S.E. 285 (1930); and *Bannister v. Bannister*, 150 S.C. 411, 148 S.E. 228 (1929). **Texas:** *Villegas v. Griffin Industries*, 975 S.W.2d 745 (Tex.App.-Corpus Christi 1998); *Price v. Travelers Inc. Co.* 111 F.2d 776 (5th Cir. 1949); and *Papoutsis v. Trevino*, 167 S.W.2d 777 (Tex.Civ. App.-San Antonio 1942). **Utah:** *In re Dalton's Estate*, 167 P.2d 690, 692 (Utah 1946).

85 In *Patterson v. Gaines*, 47 U.S. (6 How.) 550, 12 L.Ed. 553 (1848), the U.S. Supreme Court stated: "(A) marriage between a woman and a man who had then another wife living was void, and the woman could marry again without waiting for a judicial sentence to be pronounced declaring the marriage to be void." *See also Villegas v. Griffin Industries*, 975 S.W.2d 745 (Tex.App.-Corpus Christi 1998).

86 *Nyhuis v. Pierce*, 65 O.L.Abs. 73, 114 N.E.2d 75 (Ohio App. 1952). In the case of *In re Zemmick's Estate*, 17 Ohio Supp. 15, 76 N.E.2d 902, 905 (1946), a common law marriage was also found to be an impediment to a ceremonial marriage, which was found to be a nullity.

87 *Whitney v. Whitney*, 192 Okla. 174, 134 P.2d 357, 360 (1943). In the District of Columbia, it appears from the text of the legislation that a marriage which is *void ab initio* can be declared void by the court, *see* D.C. CODE ANN. § 46-402 (West 2001).

The objection that a new marriage is void based on a previous marriage can be made whenever and wherever a party wishes to claim a right based upon the existence of the latter marriage. For example, if one spouse petitions for divorce and claims maintenance and a division of the property because the parties had lived in a common law marriage, the other spouse can object that no common law marriage existed due to a previous undissolved marriage.[88] The parties' understanding in good faith that they were competent to enter into a new marriage has been considered irrelevant if the legislation has not specifically prescribed a different result.[89] If the impediment concerns one spouse, the other spouse is free to enter into a new marriage without needing to take any further action to have the interim marriage dissolved or declared void. The same opportunity is available to the other spouse after the removal of the impediment. The principle that the marriage is viewed as *void ab initio* has great practical significance in cases in which the invalidity is invoked many years after the commencement of the marriage. For example, it can concern a lawsuit regarding inheritance or a child's marital status, when one or both of the parents are dead. In such cases, it can be difficult to prove a petition for annulment. Consequently, there are considerable differences with regard to the legal effects of whether a marriage is *void ab initio* or merely *voidable*.

A consequence of the fact that the latter of two marriages is invalid has traditionally been that children born in the second marriage are considered illegitimate. In the case of *In re Cline's Estate* (1937), in which six children born in the second marriage were found illegitimate as one of the parents had a previously, undissolved marriage, the court stated: "The sins of the parents are still visited on the children."[90] However, there is a trend, supported by legislation, to grant legitimacy to children born in a marriage later proven to be void, under certain circumstances, so that those children need not bear their taint of their parents' "sins."[91] This has

88 *Johns v. Johns*, 420 S.E.2d 856 (S.C.App. 1992); and *Rutledge v. Rutledge*, 41 Tenn.App. 158, 293 S.W.2d 21 (1954).

89 *Anonymous v. Anonymous*, 67 Misc.2d 982, 325 N.Y.S.2d 499 (1971). The new marriage was found to be void even though the one spouse gave false information as to the fact that they were competent to marry, *Wehner v. Wehner*, 66 N.Y.S.2d 703 (1946); *Johnson v. J.H. Terry & Co.*, 182 Pa.Super. 258, *aff'd*, 389 Pa. 586, 133 A.2d 234 (1957); and *Dorsey v. Dorsey*, 259 Ala. 220, 66 So.2d 135, 140 (1953). As the parties were in good faith with respect to the existence of an impediment, they could not be convicted for bigamy, *see Chamberlain v. Chamberlain*, 68 N.J.Eq. 736, 62 A. 680 (1905).

90 *In re Cline's Estate*, 128 Pa.Super. 309, 194 A. 222 (1937); and *Warrenberger v. Folsom*, 239 F.2d 846, 849 (3d Cir. 1956). *Compare Graham v. Bennet*, 2 Cal. 503 (1852), where children were found to be legitimate in spite of the fact that the parents' common law marriage was void because of an impediment.

91 The regulations, however, are formulated somewhat differently with respect to both the circumstances and the effects. Support exists in the legislation, for example, in **Alabama:** ALA. CODE ANN. § 26-11-2 (Law. Coop. 2002), the father to out-of-wedlock children can petition for legitimacy and therewith give the child the right to inherit from him. **Colorado:** COLO. REV. STAT. ANN. §§ 14-2-110 (2), 14-10-111 (4) (West 2003), children born within a marriage later declared void are legitimate;

been particularly true in cases in which one party acted in good faith regarding the non-existence of marital impediments. The principle has also been applied with respect to children born in a common law marriage that was later found to be void because one parent was already married. The children in such a common law marriage have been given the right to inherit from their father.[92]

A prerequisite for an earlier marriage being an impediment to a later marriage is that the former, in its turn, must be valid. If the first marriage is a nullity, *void ab initio*, for example, because one party had not dissolved a prior marriage, the other party can, without dissolving the marriage, enter into a new valid marriage. A judgment of invalidity is not required.[93]

Mund v. Rehaume, 51 Colo. 129, 117 P. 159 (1911). With respect to inheritance rights under certain conditions, *see Valdez v. Shaw*, 100 Colo. 101, 66 P.2d 325 (1937) (citing Colo.L. §§ 5151, 5158). **District of Columbia:** D.C. CODE ANN. §§ 16-97, 16-98 (West 2001). **Georgia**: GA. CODE ANN. §§ 19-3-2 (3), 19-3-5, 19-4-1 (West 2003); *Campbell v. Allen*, 208 Ga. 274, 66 S.E.2d 226 (1951) (children born in a void marriage considered legitimate.) **Idaho**: IDAHO CODE ANN. § 32-503 (Michie 2003). **Iowa:** IOWA CODE ANN. § 598.31 (West 2003) (children born in a void marriage legitimate.) **Montana:** MONT. CODE ANN. § 40-1-401 (3) (Mont. Leg. Serv. Div. 2003). **Ohio:** *Wolf v. Gardner*, 386 F.2d 295 (6th Cir. 1967) (applying Ohio law) (children born in a common law marriage, void due to an impediment, considered legitimate despite the fact that the parties were not in good faith concerning the impediment.) *Compare Santill v. Rosseti*, 178 N.E.2d 633 (C.P.Ohio 1961); *Folsom v. Furber*, 6 Ohio Ops.2d 509, 256 F.2d 120 (6th Cir. 1958). **Oklahoma:** OKLA. STAT. ANN. tit. 84, § 215 (West 2003) (children born in void marriage legitimate); *Green v. Green*, 309 P.2d 276, 278 (Okla. 1957). **Pennsylvania:** PA. STAT. ANN. 48-169.1 (West 2003). **South Carolina:** S.C. CODE. ANN. § 20-1-90 (v) (children legitimate if one of the parents entered into the marriage not knowing the other was married). **Rhode Island:** R.I. GEN. LAWS. § 15-8-1 (Michie 2003). **Texas:** *Whaley v. Peat*, 377 S.W.2d 855 (Tex.Civ.App.-Houston 1964) (children born in invalid common law marriage considered legitimate). *Compare Lester v. Celebrezze*, 221 F.Supp. 607 (E.D.Ark. 1963) (applying Texas law); *Esparza v. Esparza*, 382 S.W.2d 162 (Tex.Civ.App.-Corpus Christi 1964) (assuming that the child was born after the commencement of the void marriage); and *Home of the Holy Infancy v. Kaska*, 397 S.W.2d 208 (Tex. 1965) (assuming the parents were in good faith). There is also a trend that goes further, making all children the legitimate children of their parents, thereby receiving the same rights as children born in wedlock, *see* ARIZ. REV. STAT. § 8-601 (Supp. 1986); and ALASKA STAT. ANN. § 25.20.050 (Supp. 1984). In *Kasey v. Richardson*, 462 F.2d 757 (4th Cir. 1972) (applying Virginia law), a child born in a common law marriage, which due to an impediment was invalid, was found to be legitimate, despite the fact that the parents were aware of the impediment and that common law marriage was not recognized in Virginia (VA. CODE ANN. §§ 64.1-7 (1957)). *See also* UNIF. PARENTAGE ACT, 9A Unif.L.Ann. 588 (1979). *Compare* UNIF. MARRIAGE AND DIVORCE ACT § 208 (D); and 9A Unif. L. Ann. 11 (1979).

92 *Santill v. Rosseti*, 178 N.E.2d 633 (C.P.Ohio 1961).

93 In the case of *In re Dalton's Estate*, 167 P.2d 690 (Utah 1946), the man, Orion, first married Mildred Jolley. They divorced in 1940. Prior to the finalization of the judgment of divorce, and before Orion was competent to enter into a new marriage, he married Valhalla in 1941. Thereafter, he married a third woman, Minnie, in 1943, who died that same year, and the issue arose as to whether Orion was her surviving spouse. As the marriage between Orion and Valhalla was a nullity, as Orion had not, at that point of time, yet been divorced from Mildred Jolley, the marriage to Valhalla was no impediment to the marriage with Minnie. Orion's marriage to Mildred Jolley was also no impediment to his marriage to Minnie, as it was dissolved prior to his

The party is then not guilty of bigamy.[94] If the first marriage, on the other hand, is voidable and can be declared void by a judgment of the court, it generally is an impediment against entering into a new marriage. The parties can thus be guilty of bigamy. The impediment stands until the first marriage is dissolved.[95] If the first marriage is valid, but is dissolved after the new marriage has been commenced, the latter can be valid as a common law marriage if the requisites have been fulfilled.[96]

5.3.3 The Presumption in Favor of the Later Marriage

1. Background and Motivations

Not uncommonly, a lack of clarity can exist as to whether a previous marriage has been dissolved. This can be explained by the fact that the formally married spouses have simply separated and moved, perhaps to another state, without filing a petition for divorce.[97] Naturally, this is more

---

marrying Minnie. The Utah Supreme Court therefore found that Orion was Minnie's surviving spouse.

94 In *Williams v. Williams*, 90 Ohio App. 369, 106 N.E.2d 655 (1951), the court stated that as the woman had previously entered into a "bigamous marriage, such marriage was void and she could legally marry defendant without waiting for dissolution of bigamous union either by death or divorce." *See also Mims v. Hardware Mut. Cas. Co.*, 82 Ga.App. 210, 60 S.E.2d 501, 503 (1950); *In re Rosenberger's Estate*, 362 Pa. 153, 65 A.2d 377 (1949); *Taegen v. Taegen*, 61 N.Y.S.2d 869 (1946); *In re Dalton's Estate*, 167 P.2d 690 (Utah 1946); *State v. Sellers*, 140 S.C. 66, 134 S.E. 873 (1926); and *Peet v. Peet*, 52 Mich. 464, 18 N.W. 220 (1884).

95 The basis for the crime of bigamy is always first a valid marriage. For example, if a man enters into a marriage with a first wife, and thereafter with a second wife, and the first marriage is later proven invalid, he has not committed bigamy. If the first marriage is valid, and he enters into a second marriage, thereafter the first marriage becomes dissolved either by death or divorce and he then enters into a third marriage, he can have committed bigamy with respect to the second marriage, but not with respect to the third, as the second is a nullity. If, after the first marriage's dissolution, the cohabitation continues in the second relationship and a common law marriage is established, it can be an impediment to the establishment of the third marriage. The commencement of the third marriage can then be bigamous. *See State v. Sellers*, 140 S.C. 66, 134 S.E. 873, 874 (1926). A common law marriage is not only an impediment against the establishment of a later ceremonial marriage, a person entering into the latter can be guilty of bigamy and even prostitution, *see State v. Grimes*, 215 Iowa 1287, 247 N.W. 664 (1933), in which an indictment was filed for adultery but in which no common law marriage, however, was found proven.

96 For more on the establishment of a common law marriage after the impediment's removal, *see* Chapter 7, Implied Marriage Agreements and Chapter 9, Burdens of Proof and Presumptions. In states not recognizing common law marriage, the removal of the impediment is required to enter into a new ceremonial marriage.

97 Previously, when it was almost impossible to get a formal decree of divorce, many couples seem to have found their own solution to their "marital unhappiness" by *de facto* dissolving their relationship and after that entering into formless unions. *See* Gilfoyle, *supra* note 73, at 136-137; Norma Basch, *Relief in the Premises: Divorce as a Woman's Remedy in New York and Indiana, 1815-1870*, 8 L. HIST. REV. 1, 17 (1990). It is estimated that approximately 100,000 men abandoned their families in 1957, *see supra* note 73, at 103 fn. 79.

common among couples that have lived in a common law marriage, perhaps not even aware that they were married at all. The parties later enter into new relationships and, after a time, one of the parties dies. Competition can then arise between the earlier and later marriages, and certain presumptions are applied in order to resolve such conflicts.

One presumption strongly anchored by both American legislation and case law, and extensively applied by the courts, is *in favor of the latter of two marriages*. All of the jurisdictions examined here appear to principally recognize this presumption, however, with a restrictive application in Alabama, Georgia, Iowa, and Pennsylvania, and only in the exceptional case in Ohio.[98] This presumption is also applicable in favor of the most

98 **Alabama:** *Lott v. Toomey*, 477 So.2d 316, 320 (Ala. 1985); *James v. James*, 260 Ala. 511, 71 So.2d 62 (1954); and *Freed v. Sallade*, 245 Ala. 505, 17 So.2d 868 (1944). **Colorado:** *Deter v. Deter*, 484 P.2d 805 (Colo.App. 1971). **District of Columbia:** *Gordon v. Railroad Retirement Bd.*, 225 U.S.App.D.C. 49, 696 F.2d 131 (1983); *Johnson v. Young*, 372 A.2d 992, 994 (D.C.App. 1977); *Mayo v. Ford*, 184 A.2d 38, 41 (D.C.App. 1962); *Brantley v. Skeens*, 105 App.D.C. 246, 266 F.2d 447, 454 (1959); *Di Giovanni v. Di Giovannantonio*, 98 U.S.App.D.C. 147, 233 F.2d 26 (1956); *Harsley v. United States*, 88 U.S.App.D.C. 150, 187 F.2d 213, 214 (1951); and *United States v. Warner*, 84 F.Supp. 607 (D.D.C. 1949). **Georgia:** *Baker v. Musa*, 170 Ga.App. 77, 316 S.E.2d 178 (1984). **Idaho:** *Nicholas v. Idaho Power Co.*, 63 Idaho 675, 125 P.2d 321 (1942). **Iowa:** *In re Estate of Weems*, 258 Iowa 711, 139 N.W.2d 922, 924 (1966). **Kansas:** *Chandler v. Central Oil Corp., Inc.*, 253 Kan. 50, 853 P.2d 649 (1993); *In re Estate of Frazier*, 145 P.3d 75 (Kan.App. 2006); *Hawkins v. Weinberger*, 368 F.Supp. 896 (D.Kan. 1973); and *Haywood v. Nichols*, 99 Kan. 138, 160 P. 982 (1916). **Montana:** According to the applicable Montana legislation concerning the marital presumption, "a lawful contract of marriage" is presumed where the parties "deported themselves as husband and wife," *see* MONT. REV. CODE ANN. § 93-1301-7 (1947), currently MONT. CODE ANN. § 26-1-602 (30) (Mont. Leg. Serv. Div. 2003). In *Spradlin v. United States*, 262 F.Supp. 502, 505 (D.C.Mont. 1967), the court maintained that the presumption of "a lawful contract of marriage" also encompassed the fact that the parties had the "capacity to marry." A later common law marriage was therefore presumed to be valid and the previous ceremonial marriage dissolved. *See also Welch v. All Persons*, 78 Mont. 370, 254 P. 179, *rev'd*, 85 Mont. 114, 278 P. 110 (1929); and *Hadley v. Rash*, 21 Mont. 170, 53 P. 312 (1898). *See also In re Marriage of Mahaffey*, 8245 Mont. 424, 801 P.2d 1335, 47 St.Rep. 1172 (1990), in which the man objected that "there was no showing that he was competent to enter into a marriage." The court however shifted the burden of proof and stated: "In the absence of any evidence that Boyd was incompetent, we conclude that no finding was necessary on that point." *Compare In re Estate of Hunsaker*, 968 P.2d 281, 285 (Mont. 1998), in which the party claiming the existence of a common law marriage was given the burden of proof with respect to whether the parties "were competent to enter into a marriage." **Ohio:** *Detroit Diesel Corp. v. Lane-Smith*, 39 F.Supp.2d 852 (E.D.Mich. 1999) (applying Ohio law); *In re Zemmick's Estate*, 17 Ohio Supp. 15, 76 N.E.2d 902, 906 (1946). **Oklahoma:** *Hill v. Shreve*, 448 P.2d 848 (Okla. 1968); *Marcum v. Zaring*, 406 P.2d 970 (Okla. 1965); *Norton v. Coffield*, 357 P.2d 434, 435 (Okla. 1960); *In re Blackhawk's Estate*, 195 Okla. 390, 158 P.2d 168, 173 (1944); *Sam v. Sam*, 172 Okla. 342, 45 P.2d 462 (1935); *Templeton v. Jones*, 127 Okla. 1, 259 P. 543 (1927). **Pennsylvania:** *Com. ex rel. Alexander v. Alexander*, 445 Pa. 406, 289 A.2d 83 (1971); *In re Estate of Holben*, 93 Pa.Super.Ct. 472 (1928). **South Carolina:** *Yarbrough v. Yarbrough*, 280 S.C. 546, 314 S.E.2d 16 (App. 1984). **Texas:** *Villegas v. Griffin Industries*, 975 S.W.2d 745 (Tex.App.-Corpus Christi 1998). **Utah:** *Martin v. Martin*, 29 Utah 2d 413, 510 P.2d 1102 (1973); *In re Estate of Pilcher*, 114 Utah 72, 197 P.2d 143 (1948). **Rhode Island:** *Rhode Island Hosp. Trust Co. v. Thorndike*, 24 R.I. 105, 52 A. 873 (1902). *See also* the cases cited in Peter

recently commenced marriage in which a party has entered into more than one marriage.[99] The effect is that the earlier common law marriage is presumed to have been dissolved, which is why separation in such a marriage sometimes has been referred to as the "poor man's divorce."[100]

In Texas, where this presumption has been codified in TEX. FAM. CODE ANN. § 1.102) (West 2002), the legislation states: "When two or more marriages of a person to different spouses are alleged, the most recent marriage is presumed to be valid as against each marriage that precedes it until one who asserts the validity of a prior marriage proves the validity of the prior marriage."[101] This presumption must be distinguished from the *putative marriage doctrine*, which gives some rights to a spouse in a latter marriage, despite the fact it is void and the latter is valid.

Behind the presumption in favor of the most recent marriage lies a motive that is also a basis for the general presumption in favor of marriage: *Semper praesumitur pro matrimonio.*[102] Both presumptions are based on the endeavor, wherever possible, to rescue any commenced marriage to protect the parties themselves and the legitimacy of

---

Nash Swisher & Melanie Diana Jones, *The Last-in-Time Marriage Presumption, 29* FAM. L.Q. 409 (1995). With respect to older cases, *see* Robert A. Allen, *Presumption of the Validity of a Second Marriage*, 20 BAYLOR L. REV. 206 (1968); J. E. Keefe, Jr., Annotation, *Presumption as to Validity of Second Marriage*, 14 A.L.R.2d 7 (1950); and 52 Am.Jur.2d Marriage §§ 140-167 (1979).

99 *Matthews v. Matthews*, 259 Ala. 332, 67 So.2d 22 (1953).

100 *See* Weyrauch, *supra* note 73, at 103.

101 The law is the equivalent of the earlier TEX. FAM. CODE ANN. § 2.01, recodified as § 1.102. Acts 1997, 75th Leg., ch. 7 § 1, 1997 Tex. Gen. Laws 8, eff. April 17, 1997; *Phillips v. Dow Chemical Co.*, 186 S.W.3d 121 (Tex.App. 2005); *In re Estate of Loveless*, 64 S.W.3d 564 (Tex.App.-Texarkana 2001); *Chandler v. Chandler*, 991 S.W.2d 367, 393 (Tex.App.-El Paso 1999); *Villegas v. Griffin Industries*, 975 S.W.2d 745 (Tex.App.-Corpus Christi 1998); *In re Estate of Claveria v. Claveria*, 615 S.W.2d 164 (Tex. 1981); *Franklin v. Smallridge*, 616 S.W.2d 655 (Tex.Civ.App-Corpus Christi 1981); *Rosetta v. Rosetta*, 525 S.W.2d 255 (Tex.Civ.App.-Tyler 1975); *Davis v. Davis*, 521 S.W.2d 603 (Tex. 1975); *In re Interest of R.L.*, 622 S.W.2d 660 (Tex.App.-Forth Worth 1981); *Caruso v. Lucius*, 448 S.W.2d 711 (Tex.Civ.App. 1969); *Texas Employers' Ins. Ass'n v. Elder*, 155 Tex. 27, 282 S.W.2d 371 (1955); *Hudspeth v. Hudspeth*, 198 S.W.2d 768 (Tex.Civ.App.-Amarillo 1946); *Nixon v. Wichita Land 6 Cattle Co.*, 84 Tex. 408, 19 S.W. 560 (1892); *Texas Employers' Ins. Assoc. v. Gomez*, 313 S.W.2d 956 (Tex.Civ.App.-Eastland 1958); *Carroll v. Carroll*, 20 Tex. 731 (1858); *Lockhart v. White*, 18 Tex. 102 (1856); and *Yates v. Houston*, 3 Tex. 433 (1848). *Compare Netecke v. State, through DOTD*, 715 So.2d 449 (La.App. 3 Cir. 1998), in which the Louisiana Court of Appeals, applying Texas law, did not raise the presumption but instead placed the burden of proof on the surviving man claiming to have lived in a common law marriage with the deceased. The court stated that the man "failed to prove that his prior marriage was legally dissolved. Therefore, an impediment to his common law marriage existed." *see id.* at 451.

102 With respect to the marital presumption and its contradiction to the general rules concerning the burden of proof, *see* Chapter 9.

their children.[103] Spouses, after a short marriage that was not formally dissolved,

103 *Chandler v. Central Oil Corp., Inc.*, 253 Kan. 50, 853 P.2d 649 (1993); *Com. ex rel. Alexander v. Alexander*, 445 Pa. 406, 289 A.2d 83, 86 (1971); *Caruso v. Lucius*, 448 S. W.2d 711, 714 (Tex.Civ.App. 1969) ("This presumption is based on sound public policy that favors morality, innocence, marriage and legitimacy"); *Schacht v. Schacht*, 435 S.W.2d 197, 201 (Tex.Civ.App.-Dallas 1968); *Dolan v. Celebrezze*, 381 F.2d 231, 237 (2d Cir. 1967); *Cupler v. Sec'y of Health*, 252 F.Supp. 178, 182 (W.D.Pa. 1966); and *Yarbrough v. United States*, 341 F.2d 621, 625 (Ct.Cl. 1965) ("It arises because the law will assume morality and legitimacy and that parties who have lived together as man and wife for a number of years do so legally.") In *Mayo v. Ford*, 184 A.2d 38, 41 (D.C.App. 1962), the court maintained that the presumption in its turn was based on "the presumption of innocence of the crime of bigamy, on the presumption of the regularity of the acts of licensing and officiating officers, and in the strong public policy of fostering respectability and protecting offspring from the taint of illegitimacy." In the case of *In re Watt's Estate*, 409 Pa. 44, 185 A.2d 781, 785 (1962), "the presumption of innocence" and "the presumption of legitimacy" were referred to, strengthening the presumption in favor of the later marriage. *See also Marcum v. Zaring*, 406 P.2d 970, 973 (Okla. 1965); *In re Adams' Estate*, 362 Mich. 624, 107 N.W.2d 764 (1961); *Norton v. Coffield*, 357 P.2d 434, 435 (Okla. 1960) ("morality, marriage and legitimacy"); *Harper v. Dupree*, 185 Kan. 483, 345 P.2d 644 (1959); *Tatum v. Tatum*, 241 F.2d 401, 406 (9th Cir. 1957) (applying Texas law) ("The purpose is not only to preserve the relationship of the parties and prevent the stigmatization of offspring as illegitimate, but also to protect and strengthen the social and moral standards of the community"); *Woodum v. American Mut. Liab. Ins. Co.*, 212 Ga. 386, 93 S.E.2d 12 (1956); *Warner v. Warner*, 76 Idaho 399, 283 P.2d 931, 934-935 (1955); *Texas Employers' Ins. Ass'n v. Elder*, 274 S.W.2d 144 (Tex. App. 1954), *aff'd*, 155 Tex. 27, 282 S.W.2d 371, 373 (1955) ("morality, innocence, marriage, and legitimacy"); *Matthews v. Matthews*, 259 Ala. 332, 67 So.2d 22, 23 (1953); *Ashley v. Ashley*, 255 Ala. 313, 51 So.2d 239 (1951). In *Headen v. Pope & Talbot, Inc.*, 252 F.2d 739, 742 (3d Cir. 1958) (applying Pennsylvania law), the court stated that the presumption represents "a strong social policy in favor of reaching a particular result in the close and doubtful cases." *See also In re Estate of Pilcher*, 114 Utah 72, 197 P.2d 143, 148 (1948) ("When a second marriage is shown, it is clothed with every presumption of validity. The law presumes innocence, not guilt; morality, not immorality; marriage, not concubinage"); *Marris v. Sockey*, 170 F.2d 599, 603 (10th Cir. 1948) ("It enhances the morals and standards of the community and serves the ends of society if marriages are regarded as valid and the issue thereof as legitimate"); *Faggard v. Filipowich*, 248 Ala. 182, 27 So.2d 10, 12 (1946); *Hudspeth v. Hudspeth*, 198 S.W.2d 768 (Tex.Civ.App.-Amarillo 1946); *Sloss-Sheffield Steel & Iron Co. v. Alexander*, 241 Ala. 476, 3 So.2d 46, 48 (1941) ("innocence, morality, legitimacy"); *Mauldin v. Sunshine Mining Co.*, 61 Idaho 9, 97 P.2d 608, 611 (1939); *Carter v. Green*, 64 S.W.2d 1068, 1070 (Tex.Civ.App.-Texarkana 1933); *Holman v. Holman*, 288 S.W. 413 (Tex.Comm'n App. 1926); *Fowler v. Texas Exploration Co.*, 290 S.W. 818 (Tex.Civ.App. 1926); *Kinney v. Woodmen of the World*,110 Kan. 323, 325, 203 P. 723 (1922); *Smith v. Smith*, 32 Idaho 478, 185 P. 67, 68-69 (1919); *Chancey v. Whinnery*, 47 Okla. 272, 147 P. 1036, 1038 (1915) ("Every intendment of law is in favor of matrimony."); *Adams v. Wm. Cameron & Co.*, 161 S.W. 417, 420 (Tex.Civ.App.-Texarkana 1913); *Coachman v. Sims*, 36 Okla. 536, 129 P. 845, 847 (1913) ("The law is astute to preserve the sanctity of the marriage relation, the legitimacy of children, and stability of descent and distribution, and therefore presumes innocence and virtue, in the absence of proof"); *Shepard v. Carter*, 86 Kan. 125, 130, 119 P. 533 (1911); *In re Thewlis' Estate*, 217 Pa. 307, 66 A. 519 (1907) ("Thus, if the decedent continued to be her husband, they were both guilty of bigamy, and the children by her second marriage were all illegitimate. But the presumption against crime, and still more the presumption in favor of legitimacy, forbid such a result"); *In re McCausland's Estate*, 213 Pa. 189, 194, 110 Am.St.Rep. 540, 62 A. 780 (1906) ("*Semper praesumitur pro matrimonio*"); *In re Colton's Estate*, 129 Iowa 542, 105 N.W. 1008, 1010 (1906); *State v. Rocker*, 130 Iowa 239, 106 N.W. 645 (1906); *Pittinger v. Pittinger*, 28 Colo. 308,

may later enter into one or more new marriages, or live in a new family for a long period of time. It has been argued that the consequences would be egregious if, in such situations, the new marriages were invalidated and any children born to those marriages were considered illegitimate.[104]

A reasonable objection to this argument is that the presumption addresses the competition between two marriages, and that favoring the later marriage invalidates the first marriage and imposes illegitimacy on the children born to the first marriage. This objection, however, is not completely tenable, as the presumption does not raise the issue of whether the first marriage has been entered into. Instead, it presumes that it has been dissolved prior to the commencement of the later marriage. With the support of the presumption, both marriages thereby can be rescued, as legitimacy is established with respect to the children in both marriages.[105] However, this presumes that the earlier marriage was dissolved after the birth of any children. This elegant solution in favor of the children, however, does not resolve the competition between spouses in different marriages in the event of a divorce or death, where the presumption favors the later marriage at the cost of the former.

Further specific reasons are given for the presumption in favor of the later marriage. It is argued that no one should be assumed guilty of a crime (*i.e.*, bigamy),[106] an argument which has limited legal force, despite its moral value since a conviction for bigamy is not based on civil legal presumptions, but on the premise that the accused is innocent until proven guilty.[107] In contrast, a more significant factor in forming the

---

64 P. 195, 197 (1901); *Hadley v. Rash*, 21 Mont. 170, 53 P. 312 (1898); *In re Wile's Estate*, 6 Pa.Super. 435 (1898) ("[H]e would otherwise be guilty of bigamy"); *Lampkin v. Travelers' Ins. Co.*, 11 Colo.App. 249, 52 P. 1040 (1898); *Banks v. State*, 96 Ala. 78, 11 So. 404 (1892); *Leach v. Hall*, 95 Iowa 611, 64 N.W. 790 (1895); *Nixon v. Wichita Land & Cattle Co.*, 84 Tex. 408, 19 S.W. 560 (1892); *Hynes v. McDermott*, 91 N.Y. 451, 459, 43 Am.Rep. 677 (1883); *Patterson v. Gaines*, 47 U.S. (6 How.) 550, 597, 12 L.Ed. 553 (1848) (applying Pennsylvania law); and *Breiden v. Paff*, 12 S. & R. 430, 431 (1825) ("[F]or the law will not gratuitously impute crime to anyone, the presumption being in favor of innocence.") For older cases, *see* Keefe, *supra* note 98, at 14; BISHOP, *supra* at 457 note 17, 946-948, 956, 958. *Compare* modern legislation in TEX. FAM. CODE ANN. § 1.101. (West 2002): "In order to provide stability for those entering into the marriage relationship in good faith and to provide legitimacy and security for the children of the relationship, it is the policy of this state to preserve and uphold each marriage against claims of invalidity unless strong reasons exist for holding it void or voidable." *See also* Stuart J. Stein, *Common-law marriage: its history and certain contemporary problems*, 9 J. FAM. L. 271, 287 (1969).

104 *Ashley v. Ashley*, 255 Ala. 313, 51 So.2d 239 (1951). In *Ray v. Soc. Sec. Bd.*, 73 F.Supp. 58 (D.C.Ala. 1947), the court maintained that the presumption was beneficial to society and that it was sound policy to protect an existing new family whose members had lived together for many years. The interest of finding children legitimate was so strong that it motivated an independent presumption as to the legitimacy of children.

105 *Sam v. Sam*, 172 Okla. 342, 45 P.2d 462 (1935).

106 *See* note 69 *supra*.

107 Keefe, *supra* note 98, at 19; Stein, *supra* note 103, at 287, referring to "the belief that a person will not commit bigamy and the general desire of the courts, where possible, to uphold marriages."

presumption concerns which party can most easily produce evidence. It is argued, with good reason, that it would be an unreasonable burden on a spouse to require that they prove that their spouse's previous marriage was dissolved by divorce.[108] Normally, it would be easier for the spouse from the previous marriage to prove the continued existence of that marriage at the point of the commencement of the later marriage. Without a doubt, however, it is a difficult task to prove the negative of a proposition, *i.e.*, that the first marriage *was not* dissolved. The weight attributed to whether the parties were in good faith also appears to have influenced the arguments behind the presumption in favor of the later of two marriages.[109]

Whether these arguments are sufficient to apply the presumption in favor of the later *common law marriage* is debatable. Certain courts have found that the presumption is not applicable in favor of such a marriage. This is particularly true in the older case law in Texas.[110] In these cases, the party claiming the existence of an impediment against a common law marriage needed only prove that a previous marriage existed. The party claiming the existence of the later common law marriage had the burden of proving that the prior marriage was dissolved. This stance seems to spring from the general ambivalence toward the entire legal institution of common law marriage, and the reasoning that such marriages ought to be tolerated, but not protected or favored.[111] Further, it has been argued that it would be wrong for society to prefer a formless cohabitation to an existing marriage and thus favor a loose moral perspective that violates the obligations of marriage.

The understanding that a common law marriage is a complete marriage that therefore ought to be given the same legal consequences as its formal equivalent, however, has displaced this argument. The Texas Supreme Court, in later decisions, consequently found the presumption applicable even in favor of a common law marriage. In *Employers' Insurance Association v. Elder* (1954), in which the objection was made that the presumption should not be applicable to such marriages, the court stated: "We can perceive of no valid reason for a distinction between a subsequent

---

108 *Pittinger v. Pittinger*, 28 Colo. 308, 64 P. 195, 197 (1901).

109 CLARK, *supra* note 36, at 137.

110 Keefe, *supra* note 98, at 19, § 5; *Lopez v. Missouri, K. & T. Ry. Co.*, 222 S.W. 695, 697 (Tex.Civ.App. 1920); *Dowdle v. U.S. Fid. & Guar. Co.*, 242 S.W. 771 (Tex.Civ.App. 1922), 255 S.W. 388 (Tex. Comm'n App. 1923); *Holman v. Holman*, 288 S.W. 413 (Tex.Comm'n App. 1926); *Shaw v. Shaw*, 28 S.W.2d 173 (Tex.Civ.App. 1929); and *Calhoun v. Dotson*, 32 S.W.2d 656 (Tex.Civ.App. 1930). *See also Rosetta v. Rosetta*, 525 S.W.2d 255, 256 (Tex.Civ.App 1975), in which the court in its summary stated that the presumption would only be applicable in favor of formal marriages. *Compare Bolash v. Heid*, 733 S.W.2d 698, 699 (Tex.Civ.App.-San Antonio 1987).

111 With respect to the motivations behind common law marriage, *see* Section 4.3.

common-law marriage and a subsequent ceremonial marriage in so far as the efficacy of the presumption is concerned."[112]

One can also trace a hesitant attitude towards applying the presumption to common law marriages in the case law from the District of Columbia, and in the cases in which it has been applied, it has been relatively easily rebutted.[113] This negative stance can also be found in certain statements by the courts in Utah[114] and Georgia.[115] The dominant stance in Georgia, as well as the other states examined here, however, appears to be that the presumption is applicable even in favor of a later common law marriage. If one of the parties in such a marriage has earlier entered into a ceremonial marriage, it consequently is presumed to be dissolved.[116]

---

112 *Employers' Ins. Ass'n v. Elder*, 274 S.W.2d 144 (1954), *aff'd*, 155 Tex. 27, 282 S.W.2d 371 (1955), discussed *infra*; *Pike v. Estate of Pike*, 2005 WL 2248347 (Tex.App.-Forth Worth 2005) (two common law marriages); *Phillips v. Dow Chemical Co.*, 186 S.W.3d 121 (Tex.App. 2005) (presumption defeated by evidence that the first marriage was not dissolved); *In re Interest of R.L.*, Tex.App. 622, S.W.2d 660 (Tex.App.-Forth Worth 1981); *In re Estate of Claveria v. Claveria*, 615 S.W.2d 164 (Tex. 1981); and *Villegas v. Griffin Industries*, 975 SW.2d 745, 750 (Tex.App.-Corpus Christi 1998). *Compare, Netecke v. State, through DOTD*, 715 So.2d 449 (La.App. 3 Cir. 1998) (applying Texas law), in which the court did not raise the issue of the presumption but instead placed the burden of proof on the surviving man claiming to have lived in a common law marriage with the deceased. The court stated that the man "failed to prove that his prior marriage was legally dissolved. Therefore, an impediment to his common law marriage existed." *Id.* at 451.

113 *See Brantley v. Skeens*, 105 App.D.C. 246, 266 F.2d 447, 454 (1959), in which the presumption was applied, but with reference to the evidence cited in the case, was considered rebutted. Hesitation as to the applicability of the presumption to common law marriages has also come to expression in *Di Giovanni v. Di Giovannantonio*, 98 U.S.App.D.C. 147, 233 F.2d 26 (1956).

114 *Re Wo-Gin-Up*, 57 Utah 29, 192 P. 267 (1920) (applying Utah Territory law to Native American marriages).

115 In *Lumbermens Mut. Cas. Co. v. Reed*, 84 Ga.App. 541, 66 S.E.2d 360, 364 (1951), the Georgia Court of Appeals stated, concerning a woman who had formlessly lived together with a man: "[S]ince she did not enter into any regularly solemnized ceremonial marriage she is not entitled to the benefit of the presumption that the former marriage terminated in divorce." The woman therefore must prove that no impediment existed as to her common law marriage with the man, with which she was not successful. *See also Belle Isle v. Belle Isle*, 47 Ga.App. 168, 170 S.E. 211 (1933), in which the court maintained that a later marriage based on the presumption of "cohabitation and repute" could not take precedence to a previous formal marriage. *Compare Carr v. Walker*, 205 Ga. 1, 52 S.E.2d 426 (1949) and *Brown v. State*, 208 Ga. 304, 66 S.E.2d 745 (1951), in which the Georgia Supreme Court applied the presumption in favor of a common law marriage. After the new formulation of the presumption in 1957, it appears as a rule to also be applied to formless marriages, *see, e.g., Zurich Ins. Co. v. Craft*, 103 Ga.App. 889, 120 S.E.2d 922, 924 (1961). In *Gates v. State*, 120 Ga.App. 518, 171 S.E.2d 375 (1969), it appears that the presumption in favor of a later common law marriage was not applied as the woman at the same time stated that the previous marriage had not been dissolved by divorce and that her husband was still alive. However, the presumption appears to have been applied, but in the reverse, *compare* GA. CODE ANN. § 53-102(1)(1957).

116 *Villegas v. Griffin Industries*, 975 S.W.2d 745 (Tex.App.-Corpus Christi 1998) (presumption rebutted); *Lott v. Toomey*, 477 So.2d 316 (Ala. 1985); *In re Estate of Claveria v. Claveria*, 615 S.W.2d 164, 167 (Tex. 1981); *Franklin v. Smallridge*, 616 S.

There is reason to note, however, that certain of the above-mentioned motivations do not have the same force concerning the application of the presumption with respect to favoring a later common law marriage. This is the case with respect to the parties' expectations in good faith that their marriage is valid. Many couples simply drift into such marriages based on the parties' actual cohabitation, unaware that they live in a common law marriage. They can scarcely claim in good faith that they have relied upon receiving these rights and obligations. The parties' lack of awareness that they live in a common law marriage ought to mean that they separate more often and formlessly than formally married couples. The presumption, that the first marriage was dissolved through divorce, therefore is less appropriate in those cases in which the first marriage is a common law marriage. This is true regardless of whether the later marriage is a new common law or ceremonial marriage.

2. The Legal Effects of the Presumption

If a party has entered into two marriages, whether ceremonial or common law marriages, and the issue arises whether the former marriage is an impediment to the latter, the presumption favors the latter marriage over the former, assuming that the earlier marriage has been dissolved. The party claiming that the latter marriage is void due to an impediment has, according to the dominant view, the burden of proof not only to establish

---

W.2d 655, 657 (Tex.Civ.App-Corpus Christi 1981); *Hawkins v. Weinberger*, 368 F. Supp. 896, 900 (D.Kan. 1973) (a common law marriage was not established as no contract was proven); *Deter v. Deter*, 484 P.2d 805 (Colo.App. 1971); *Caruso v. Lucius*, 448 S.W.2d 711 (Tex.Civ.App. 1969); *Hill v. Shreve*, 448 P.2d 848 (Okla. 1968); *Spradlin v. United States*, 262 F.Supp. 502 (D.C.Mont. 1967); *Yarbrough v. United States*, 341 F.2d 621, 624 (Ct.Cl. 1965) (applying Alabama law); *Zurich Ins. Co. v. Craft*, 103 Ga.App. 889, 120 S.E.2d 922, 924 (1961); *Baker v. Lee*, 337 S.W.2d 637, 639 (Tex.Civ.App. 1960) (presumption rebutted); *Brantley v. Skeens*, 105 App.D.C. 246, 266 F.2d 447, 454 (1959) (presumption rebutted); *Troxel v. Jones*, 45 Tenn.App. 264, 322 S.W.2d 251 (1958); *Texas Employers' Ins. Assoc. v. Elder*, 274 S.W.2d 144 (1954), *aff'd*, 155 Tex. 27, 282 S.W.2d 371, 375 (1955); *Warner v. Warner*, 76 Idaho 399, 283 P.2d 931 (1955); *Anderson-Tully Co. v. Wilson*, 221 Miss. 656, 74 So.2d 735 (1954); *Matthews v. Matthews*, 259 Ala. 332, 67 So.2d 22 (1953); *Brown v. State*, 208 Ga. 304, 66 S.E.2d 745 (1951); *Carr v. Walker*, 205 Ga. 1, 52 S.E.2d 426 (1949); *Nicholas v. Idaho Power Co.*, 63 Idaho 675, 125 P.2d 321 (1942); *Sillart v. Standard Screen Co.*, 119 N.J.L. 143, 194 A. 787 (1937); *Puntka v. Puntka*, 174 Okla. 517, 50 P.2d 1092 (1935) (presumption rebutted); *Shepherd & Pierson Co. v. Baker*, 81 Mont. 185, 262 P. 887 (1927); *Templeton v. Jones*, 127 Okla. 1, 259 P. 543 (1927); *Madison v. Steckleberg*, 101 Okla. 237, 224 P. 961 (1924) (presumption rebutted); *Welch v. All Persons*, 78 Mont. 370, 254 P. 179, *rev'd*, 85 Mont. 114, 278 P. 110 (1929) (assuming that the parties' "matrimonial consent" was clearly demonstrated); Keefe, *supra* note 98, at 19 § 5; *In re De Bois*, 7 N.J.Misc. 1029, 148 A. 10 (1929); *Shepherd & Pierson Co. v. Baker*, 81 Mont. 185, 262 P. 887 (1927); *Holman v. Holman*, 288 S.W. 413 (Tex. Comm'n App. 1926); *Phillips v. Wilson*, 298 Mo. 186, 250 S.W. 408 (1923); *Hamlin v. Grogan*, 257 F. 59 (8th Cir. 1919) (applying Missouri law); *Thomas v. James*, 69 Okla. 285, 171 P. 855 (1918) (the later common law marriage presumed before the earlier); *Greenwood v. Frick*, 233 F. 629 (6th Cir 1916); *Zimmerman v. Holmes*, 59 Okla. 253, 159 P. 303 (1916); and *Blanchard v. Lambert*, 43 Iowa 228, 229, 22 Am.Rep. 245 (1876).

the existence of the previous marriage but also that the marriage has not been dissolved by divorce, annulment, or death.[117] The party contesting the latter marriage consequently has the heavy burden of proving a negative. If the party is successful in proving both that the earlier marriage was established and not dissolved, the former marriage is an impediment against the latter, which is then viewed as void.[118]

In *Warner v. Warner* (1955), the woman married and divorced her first husband twice. Thereafter, she married and divorced another man. During the latter marriage, she began a relationship again with the first husband and lived with him for a period after the marriage with the second husband was dissolved. Thereafter, she separated again from her first husband and married a third man. She again lived together with her first husband. She requested a divorce from him again, claiming that a common law marriage had been established between the parties. The man objected, arguing that an impediment existed against the formation of a common law marriage because the woman, during their final cohabitation, was married to the third husband. This argument was accepted by the trial court. The Idaho Supreme Court, however, held that as the parties lived together as husband and wife, the validity of their common law marriage

---

117 *Prater v. Aftra Health Fund*, 23 F.Supp.2d 505, 508 (D.N.J. 1998) ("by death, divorce, or annulment"); *Lott v. Toomey*, 477 So.2d 316 (Ala. 1985); *Yarbrough v. Yarbrough*, 280 S.C. 546, 314 S.E.2d 16 (App. 1984) ("by death or divorce"); *Baker v. Musa*, 170 Ga.App. 77, 316 S.E.2d 178 (1984); and *Gordon v. Railroad Retirement Bd.*, 225 U.S.App. D.C. 49, 696 F.2d 131 (1983). According to *In re Estate of Claveria v. Claveria*, 615 S.W.2d 164, 165 (Tex. 1981), the legal consequences of the presumption continued until evidence of "the impediment of a prior marriage and its continuing validity." *See also Jones v. Transamerica Ins. Co.*, 154 Ga.App. 408, 409, 268 S.E.2d 444 (1980); *Davis v. Davis*, 521 S.W.2d 603 (Tex. 1975); *Hawkins v. Weinberger*, 368 F. Supp. 896 (D.Kan. 1973); *Deter v. Deter*, 484 P.2d 805 (Colo.App. 1971); *Hill v. Shreve*, 448 P.2d 848 (Okla. 1968); *In re Estate of Weems*, 258 Iowa 711, 139 N.W.2d 922, 924 (1966); *Yarbrough v. United States*, 341 F.2d 621, 624 (Ct.Cl. 1965) (applying Alabama law); *In re Watt's Estate*, 409 Pa. 44, 185 A.2d 781 (1962); *Norton v. Coffield*, 357 P.2d 434 (Okla. 1960); *Brantley v. Skeens*, 105 App.D.C. 246, 266 F.2d 447 (1959); *Tatum v. Tatum*, 241 F.2d 401, 406 (9th Cir. 1957) (applying Texas law) ("death, divorce or annulment"); *Texas Employers' Ins. Ass'n v. Elder*, 274 S.W.2d 144 (1954), *aff'd*, 155 Tex. 27, 282 S.W.2d 371 (1955) ("annulment or divorce"); *Warner v. Warner*, 76 Idaho 399, 283 P.2d 931 (1955); *Dorsey v. Dorsey*, 259 Ala. 220, 66 So.2d 135 (1953) ("divorce or death"); *Walker v. Matthews*, 191 Miss. 498, 3 So.2d 820 (1949); *Longstreet v. Longstreet*, 205 Ga. 255, 53 S.E.2d 480 (1949); *In re Estate of Pilcher*, 114 Utah 72, 197 P.2d 143 (1948); *Shreyer v. Shreyer*, 113 Colo. 219, 155 P.2d 990 (1945); *In re Blackhawk's Estate*, 195 Okla. 390, 158 P.2d 168, 173 (1944); *Lea v. Galbraith*, 64 Idaho 724, 137 P.2d 320 (1943); *Nicholas v. Idaho Power Co.*, 63 Idaho 675, 125 P.2d 321 (1942); *Titus v. Titus*, 151 Kan. 824, 101 P.2d 872 (1940); *Welch v. All Persons*, 78 Mont. 370, 254 P. 179, *rev'd*, 85 Mont. 114, 278 P. 110 (1929); *Hallums v. Hallums*, 74 S.C. 407, 54 S.E. 613 (1905); and *Rhode Island Hosp. Trust Co. v. Thorndike*, 24 R.I. 105, 52 A. 873 (1902).

118 *Mauldin v. Sunshine Mining Co.*, 61 Idaho 9, 97 P.2d 608, 612 (1939). *Compare* the earlier cases from the same court, *Smith v. Smith*, 32 Idaho 478, 185 P. 67, 69 (1919) (a common law marriage found established despite the man's uncontested statement that the entire time he was married to another woman); *Nicholas v. Idaho Power Co.*, 63 Idaho 675, 125 P.2d 321 (1942); *In re estate of Tormey*, 44 Idaho 299, 256 P. 535 (1927) and the later case of *Warner v. Warner*, 76 Idaho 399, 283 P.2d 931 (1955).

must be presumed "in the absence of sufficient evidence to establish that her husband by ceremonial marriage had not died and had not secured a divorce from her."[119] The woman consequently was entitled to receive a divorce with respect to their common law marriage due to "extreme cruelty" and therewith could claim spousal maintenance and property division.

There are courts that apply the presumption in favor of a later marriage only with respect to the establishment of the first marriage, but not to its dissolution. If the previous marriage can be proven to have been established, it is presumed to have continued. It then rests upon the party claiming that the later marriage is valid to prove that the first marriage was dissolved. If the party is not successful, the first marriage is an impediment to the latter. The negative of a fact need not be proven. Among the jurisdictions examined here, it appears today that only the courts in *Ohio* apply this limited version of the presumption.

If the existence of the first marriage has been proven, the courts in Ohio have presumed that the marriage has continued if the opposite has not been proven, even in the instance of a common law marriage. In the absence of such proof, a common law marriage has been found to be an impediment against a later ceremonial marriage. For example, in the case of *In re Zemmick's Estate* (1946), a sixteen-year-old boy, William, began a common law marriage in 1928 with a fourteen-year-old girl, Sarah. They lived together until 1940, when William married Mary Katherine in a ceremonial wedding. William and Mary lived together approximately one year. William, however, continued to live with Sarah on weekends until his death in 1944. The issue then arose as to who was his legal widow, Sarah or Mary Katherine.

The Ohio Court of Appeals found a common law marriage had been established between William and Sarah. Mary Katherine argued that the presumption in favor of a later ceremonial marriage ought to be applied and that the common law marriage established between William and Sarah ought to be presumed to have been dissolved prior to William marrying Mary Katherine. The court instead applied the presumption that the valid common law marriage between the appellee and the decedent continued until the latter's death. The burden of proof consequently was placed upon Mary Katherine, who claimed that the ceremonial marriage was valid. She was not successful in proving that the first marriage had been dissolved prior to the later marriage.[120] The court found that it was not proven that

119 *Warner v. Warner*, 76 Idaho 399, 283 P.2d 931 (1955). Observe that common law marriage, as was mentioned in chapter 1, was repealed in Idaho January 1, 1996, *see* IDAHO CODE ANN. § 32-201 (2) (Michie 2003).

120 *In re Zemmick's Estate*, 17 Ohio Supp. 15, 76 N.E.2d 902, 906 (1946). In *Detroit Diesel Corp. v. Lane-Smith*, 39 F.Supp.2d 852, 859 (E.D.Mich. 1999) (applying Ohio law), concerning the competition between spouses from two ceremonial marriages, the court stated that there was a presumption in favor of the validity of the latter marriage, but that the burden of proof then rested on the spouse in the latter marriage where evidence was produced as to the existence of the first marriage. The spouse in the latter marriage must then demonstrate that the first marriage

the established common law marriage had been dissolved at the commencement of the ceremonial marriage or at the time of the man's death.

3. *A Strong Presumption Traditionally*

Even if the presumption favoring the validity of the latter marriage is not absolute nor conclusive,[121] but instead refutable, it traditionally has been viewed as strong,[122] very strong,[123] and even one of the strongest

had been dissolved. Applying this principle, the court found the existence of the first marriage, and that "the burden is now shifted to defendant Spivey to show that Smith's prior marriage to Lane-Smith had been in some way dissolved." This could not, however, be proven. *Compare In re Estate of Soeder*, 7 Ohio.App. 271, 220 N.E.2d 547, 554 (1966), in which the presumption in favor of the first marriage was applied, and the burden of proof rested with the party claiming the validity of the latter marriage to demonstrate that the first had been dissolved. In *Dibble v. Dibble*, 88 Ohio App. 490, 100 N.E.2d 451, 461 (1950), in which the Court of Appeals found that a common law marriage had been established, stating: "The burden of proof is then on the one who claims its dissolution to prove it." As no such evidence could be produced, the marriage was an impediment to the later ceremonial marriage. *See also Machransky v. Machransky*, 31 Ohio App. 482, 166 N.E. 423 (1927); and *Olijan v. Lubin*, 50 N.E.2d 264, 38 Ohio.L.Abs. 393, 143 Ohio.St. 417, 55 N.E.2d 658 (1943). Older cases from Ohio have rejected the presumption, *see Heath v. Heath*, 25 Ohio.N.P.N.S. 123 (1924); *Indus. Comm'n of Ohio v. Dell*, 104 Ohio St. 389, 135 N.E. 669, 674 (1922); *McHenry v. McHenry*, 19 Ohio.App. 187 (1923); *Evans v. Reynolds*, 32 Ohio.St. 163 (1877); *Smith v. Smith*, 5 Ohio.St. 32 (1855); and 26 Ohio Jurisprudence, 81, Section 72, ("But in Ohio it cannot be presumed that parties once married have been divorced, in the absence of proof, and there is no presumption of divorce in support of the legality of a later marriage"). *Compare Metro. Life Ins. Co. v. Spearman*, 344 F.Supp. 665, 667-668 (M.D.Ala. 1972), in which court on one side held that the presumption in favor of the latter marriage meant that the party attacking it must prove that the first marriage existed and that it was not dissolved by "death, divorce or annulment," but on the other side, when trying the case, found that the first marriage had existed and that it was presumed to continue "in the absence of evidence of its dissolution by death or divorce." The court consequently appears to have shifted the burden of proof after the existence of the first marriage had been proven.

121 *Fuguay v. State*, 217 Ala. 4, 114 So. 898 (1927); *Brokeshoulder v. Brokeshoulder*, 84 Okla. 249, 204 P. 284 (1921); *Adams v. Wm. Cameron & Co.*, 161 S.W. 417 (Tex.Civ.App. 1913).

122 *Jones v. Jones*, 63 Okla. 208, 164 P. 463, 464 (1917) ("A strong presumption exists ... which is not overcome by mere proof of a prior marriage and that the wife had not obtained a divorce before her second marriage. The parties attacking such a second marriage have the burden of proof to show that neither party to the first marriage had obtained a divorce"). With respect to the fact that a six-month period existed in which the former spouse could have obtained a divorce in the county where the spouses resided, the presumption was not found rebutted. *See also Chancey v. Winnery*, 47 Okla. 272, 147 P. 1036, 1037 (1915). In *Haile v. Hale*, 40 Okla. 101, 135 P. 1143 (1913), it was not found sufficient to produce evidence from the courts in four counties in two different states where the previous spouse had resided to demonstrate that he had not obtained a divorce. The court found it not proven that these counties were the only ones in which he had resided and found that other courts could have granted a divorce. The presumption therefore was not found rebutted. *See also Prater v. Aftra Health Fund*, 23 F.Supp.2d 505 (D.N.J. 1998) ("a strong presumption").

123 *Yarbrough v. United States*, 169 341 F.2d 621 (Ct.Cl. 1965) (applying Alabama law); and *In re Adams' Estate*, 362 Mich. 624, 107 N.W.2d 764 (1961).

presumptions in the law.[124] Several attempts have been made to more narrowly define the required degree of proof. The case of *Sy Joc Lieng v. Sy Quia* (1913) concerned whether a marriage entered into in China was an impediment to a later marriage established in the Philippines. The Court required "proof so clear, strong and unequivocal as to produce a moral conviction of the existence of that impediment."[125] A similar description of the requirement can be found in the case law of the different states. For example, in *Chandler v. Central Oil Corp., Inc.* (1993), the Kansas Supreme Court maintained that the party seeking to attack the later marriage had assumed a burden of producing evidence "so cogent as to compel conviction" that the earlier marriage had not been dissolved. According to the court's opinion, the evidence must be "clear, strong, and satisfactory and so persuasive as to leave no room for reasonable doubt." In the case of *In re Estate of Frazier* (2006), in which the same standard was applied, no common law marriage was proven.[126] In a similar manner, the Georgia Court of Appeals described the requirement in *Baker v. Musa* (1984), stating that the presumption could only be defeated by the existence of evidence that is "clear, distinct, positive, and satisfactory."[127] That it is the evidence

124 *Pike v. Estate of Pike*, 2005 WL 2248347 (Tex.App.-Ft. Worth 2005); *Fisher v. Toombs County Nursing Home*, 223 Ga.App. 842, 479 S.E.2d 180 (1996) (applying Florida law); *Chandler v. Central Oil Corp., Inc.*, 253 Kan. 50, 853 P.2d 649, 654 (1993); *Wood v. Paulus*, 524 S.W.2d 749 (Tex.Civ.App.-Corpus Christi 1975); *Panzer v. Panzer*, 87 N.M. 29, 528 P.2d 888 (1974); *Jackson v. Jackson*, 49 Ala.App. 702, 275 So.2d 683 (1973); *Marcum v. Zaring*, 406 P.2d 970, 973 (Okla. 1965); *Norton v. Coffield*, 357 P.2d 434, 435 (Okla. 1960); *Harper v. Dupree*, 185 Kan. 483, 345 P.2d 644, 648 (1959); *Texas Employers' Ins. Ass'n v. Elder*, 155 Tex. 27, 282 S.W.2d 371, 373 (1955) ("one of the strongest, if indeed, not the strongest"); *Troxel v. Jones*, 45 Tenn.App. 264, 322 S.W.2d 251, 257 (1958) ("one of the strongest"); *Matthews v. Matthews*, 259 Ala. 332, 67 So.2d 22 (1953) ("one of the strongest"); *In re Blackhawk's Estate*, 195 Okla. 390, 158 P.2d 168, 173 (1944); *Sloss-Sheffield Steel & Iron Co. v. Alexander*, 241 Ala. 476, 3 So.2d 46, 48 (1941) ("one of the strongest"); *Ashley v. Ashley*, 255 Ala. 313, 51 So.2d 239 (1951) ("very satisfactory evidence" was required to rebut the presumption); *Sloss-Sheffield Steel & Iron Co. v. Watford*, 245 Ala. 425, 17 So.2d 166 (1944); *Chancey v. Whinnery*, 47 Okla. 272, 147 P. 1036 (1915) ("one of the strongest presumptions known to the law"); and *Shepard v. Carter*, 86 Kan. 125, 130, 119 P. 533 (1911).

125 *Sy Joc Lieng v. Sy Quia*, 228 U.S. 335, 57 L.Ed. 862, 33 S.Ct. 514 (1913).

126 *Chandler v. Central Oil Corp., Inc.*, 253 Kan. 50, 853 P.2d 649, 654-655 (1993). The court did not, however, try the case but remanded it for a new trial. *See also In re Estate of Frazier*, 145 P.3d 75 (Kan.App. 2006) (established). A similar description of the requirement with respect to the evidence can be found in *Marcum v. Zaring*, 406 P.2d 970, 974 (Okla. 1965) ("clear, cogent and convincing evidence"); *Harper v. Dupree*, 185 Kan. 483, 345 P.2d 644, 648 (1959) ("proof so cogent as to compel conviction"); *Williamson v. Williamson*, 48 Del. 379, 104 A.2d 463, 464 (1954) ("evidence so clear, cogent and conclusive as to fairly preclude any other result"); *Lea v. Galbraith*, 64 Idaho 724, 137 P.2d 320 (1943) ("clear, cogent and satisfactory"); *Mauldin v. Sunshine Mining Co.*, 61 Idaho 9, 97 P.2d 608 (1939); *Sam v. Sam*, 172 Okla. 342, 45 P.2d 462 (1935); *Kinney v. Woodmen of the World*, 110 Kan. 323, 203 P. 723 (1922); *In re estate of Tormey*, 44 Idaho 299, 256 P. 535 (1927); *Marris v. Sockey*, 170 F.2d 599, 603 (10th Cir. 1948) (applying Tribal common law); and *Carr v. Carr*, 724 So.2d 937, 941 (Miss.App. 1998).

127 *Baker v. Musa*, 170 Ga.App. 77, 316 S.E.2d 178, 179 (1984); *see also Jones v. Transamerica Ins. Co.*, 154 Ga.App. 408, 409, 268 S.E.2d 444 (1980); *McCormick v. Denny*, 213 Ga.

required with respect to the dissolution of the previous marriage, which is the most important and most difficult to produce, can be seen in *Schacht v. Schacht* (1968). There, the Texas Court of Appeals required evidence negating the effective operation of every possible means by which the dissolution of a previous marriage could have occurred.[128] In certain cases, the presumption has been considered stronger if a long period of time has passed since the parties in the first marriage separated and a child was born within the second marriage.[129]

28, 96 S.E.2d 600, 601 (1957); *Johnson v. Johnson*, 96 Ga.App. 84, 99 S.E.2d 352, 353 (1957); *Woodum v. American Mut. Liab. Ins. Co.*, 212 Ga. 386, 93 S.E.2d 12 (1956); *Robertson v. Robertson*, 210 Ga. 346, 83 S.E.2d 619, 625 (1954); *Cooper v. Cooper*, 88 Ga.App. 335, 76 S.E.2d 726, 728 (1953); *Lumbermens Mut. Cas. Co. v. Reed,* 84 Ga. App. 541, 66 S.E.2d 360 (1951); *Longstreet v. Longstreet*, 205 Ga. 255, 53 S.E.2d 480, 482 (1949); *Reed v. Reed*, 202 Ga. 508, 43 S.E.2d 539, 543 (1947); *Brown v. Hogan*, 72 Ga.App. 691, 34 S.E.2d 619 (1945); *Bituminous Casualty Corp. v. Harris*, 68 Ga.App. 889, 24 S.E.2d 803, 804 (1943); *State Highway Bd. v. Lewis*, 46 Ga.App. 162, 167 S.E. 219 (1932); *Brown v. Parks*, 173 Ga. 228, 160 S.E. 238 (1931); and *Murchinson v. Green*, 128 Ga. 339, 57 S.E. 709, 710 (1907). In other cases from Georgia, Utah, and above all else, the District of Columbia, a narrower description can be found, according to which the courts require "strong, distinct, satisfactory, and conclusive evidence." *See Gordon v. Railroad Retirement Bd.*, 225 U.S.App.D.C. 49, 696 F.2d 131, 132 (1983); *Johnson v. Young*, 372 A.2d 992, 994 (D.C.App. 1977); *Mayo v. Ford*, 184 A.2d 38, 41 (D.C.App. 1962); *Wheeler v. Terell*, 238 F.2d 29, 30 (1956), 99 U.S.App. D.C. 168, *cert. denied*, 352 U.S. 1018, 77 S.Ct. 581, 1 L.Ed.2d 557 (1957); *Harsley v. United States*, 88 U.S.App.D.C. 150, 187 F.2d 213, 214 (1951); and *In re Estate of Pilcher*, 114 Utah 72, 197 P.2d 143, 148 (1948). *Compare In re Adams' Estate*, 362 Mich. 624, 107 N.W.2d 764, 766 (1961) ("clear and positive proof"); and *In re Thewlis' Estate,* 217 Pa. 307, 66 A. 519 (1907) ("positive, affirmative proof"). In the cases of *Prater v. Aftra Health Fund*, 23 F.Supp.2d 505, 508 (D.N.J. 1998) and *Panzer v. Panzer*, 87 N.M. 29, 528 P.2d 888 (1974), the courts required "clear and convincing evidence," a degree of evidence common with respect to proving the existence of a common law marriage, *see* Chapter 9 *infra.*

128 *Schacht v. Schacht*, 435 S.W.2d 197, 201 (Tex.Civ.App.-Dallas 1968) (the presumption, however, was rebutted); *Pike v. Estate of Pike*, 2005 WL 2248347 (Tex.App.-Forth Worth 2005); *see also Texas Employers' Ins. Assn. v. Gomez*, 313 S.W.2d 956 (Tex.Civ.App-Eastland 1958); *Hudspeth v. Hudspeth*, 198 S.W.2d 768 (Tex.Civ.App.-Amarillo 1946); *Brown v. Phillips Petroleum Co.*, Tex.Civ.App., 144 S.W.2d 358 (1940); and *Holman v. Holman*, 288 S.W. 413, 414 (Tex.Comm'n App. 1926). *See also Robertson v. Robertson*, 210 Ga. 346, 83 S.E.2d 619, 620 (1954) ("by disproving every reasonable possibility" against the marriage's validity); *Lumbermens Mut. Cas. Co. v. Reed,* 84 Ga.App. 541, 66 S.E.2d 360, 363 (1951); *Azar v. Thomas,* 206 Ga. 588, 57 S.E.2d 821, 822 (1950); *Longstreet v. Longstreet*, 205 Ga. 255, 53 S.E.2d 480, 482 (1949); *Reed v. Reed,* 202 Ga. 508, 43 S.E.2d 539, 543 (1947); *Travelers Ins. Co. v. Lester*, 73 Ga.App. 465, 36 S.E.2d 880 (1946); *Callaway v. Cox*, 74 Ga.App. 555, 40 S.E.2d 578 (1946); and *Brown v. Parks*, 173 Ga. 228, 160 S.E. 238 (1931).

129 In *Appeal of O'Rourke*, 310 Minn. 373, 246 N.W.2d 461 (1976), the presumption was not applied as the latter marriage was very short. *See also Wood v. Paulus*, 524 S.W.2d 749 (Tex.Civ.App. 1975); *Marcum v. Zaring*, 406 P.2d 970, 973 (Okla. 1965); *Norton v. Coffield*, 357 P.2d 434, 435 (Okla. 1960); *In re Watt's Estate*, 409 Pa. 44, 185 A.2d 781 (1962); *In re Adams' Estate*, 362 Mich. 624, 107 N.W.2d 764 (1961); and *Woodum v. American Mut. Liab. Ins. Co.*, 212 Ga. 386, 93 S.E.2d 12, 15 (1956). In *Texas Employers' Ins. Ass'n v. Elder*, 274 S.W.2d 144 (1954), *aff'd*, 155 Tex. 27, 282 S.W.2d 371 (1955), it was noted that the latter marriage had lasted eighteen years. *See also Azar v. Thomas,* 206 Ga. 588, 57 S.E.2d 821, 822 (1950); *Brown v. Parks*, 173 Ga. 228,

The strength of the presumption can also be seen from the fact that it is commonly considered stronger than other, competing presumptions.[130] Consequently, it has been considered stronger than the presumption in favor of an already-existing marriage, meaning that the party attacking such a marriage has the burden of proving that it is invalid.[131] The presumption in favor of the later marriage has even been considered stronger than the presumption of continued life (for a certain period, usually seven years) applicable to missing persons. If the missing person was married, and his or her spouse later remarries, the earlier marriage to the missing person is presumed to be dissolved by death even if seven years have not yet passed when the second marriage was commenced.[132] The presumption

---

160 S.E. 238 (1931); and *Nixon v. Wichita Land & Cattle Co.*, 84 Tex. 408, 19 S.W. 560 (1892).

130 *Fuguay v. State*, 217 Ala. 4, 114 So. 898 (1927); and *Murchinson v. Green*, 128 Ga. 339, 57 S.E. 709 (1907). In *Boze v. Boze*, 96 Colo. 309, 42 P.2d 470 (1935), the Colorado Supreme Court remarked upon the competition between the presumption in favor of the earlier relationship not being criminal, and children of that relationship being legitimate. That issue, however, was not tried. *Compare Sharpe v. Federal Window & Office Cleaning Co.*, 144 Pa.Super. 231, 19 A.2d 509 (1941), in which the presumption in favor of the latter marriage was not considered stronger as the marriage began "meretriciously."

131 *Chandler v. Central Oil Corp., Inc.*, 253 Kan. 50, 853 P.2d 649, 654 (1993); *Gordon v. Railroad Retirement Bd.*, 225 U.S.App.D.C. 49, 696 F.2d 131, 132 (1983); *Ellis v. Ellis*, 50 Ala.App. 67, 277 So.2d 102, 103 (1973); *Schacht v. Schacht*, 435 S.W.2d 197, 201 (Tex.Civ.App.-Dallas 1968); *Ventura v. Ventura*, 53 Misc.2d 881, 280 N.Y.S.2d 5 (Sup. Ct. 1967); *Mayo v. Ford*, 184 A.2d 38, 41 (D.C.App. 1962); *In re Adams' Estate*, 362 Mich. 624, 107 N.W.2d 764 (1961); *Norton v. Coffield*, 357 P.2d 434 (Okla. 1960); *Watson v. Todd*, 322 S.W.2d 422 (Tex.Civ.App.-Ft. Worth 1959); *Harper v. Dupree*, 185 Kan. 483, 345 P.2d 644, 647 (1959); *Headen v. Pope & Talbot, Inc.*, 252 F.2d 739, 743 (3d Cir. 1958) (applying Pennsylvania law); *Tatum v. Tatum*, 241 F.2d 401, 406 (9th Cir. 1957) (applying Texas law); *Woodum v. American Mut. Liab. Ins. Co.*, 212 Ga. 386, 93 S.E.2d 12, 15 (1956); *Di Giovanni v. Di Giovannantonio*, 98 U.S.App.D.C. 147, 233 F.2d 26 (1956); *Texas Employers' Ins. Ass'n v. Elder*, 274 S.W.2d 144 (1954), *aff'd*, 155 Tex. 27, 282 S.W.2d 371 (1955); *Harrison v. Burton*, 303 P.2d 962 (Okla. 1954); *Matthews v. Matthews*, 259 Ala. 332, 67 So.2d 22 (1953); *Ashley v. Ashley*, 255 Ala. 313, 51 So.2d 239 (1951); *Caroll v. Hill*, 80 Ga.App. 576, 56 S.E.2d 821 (1949); *Longstreet v. Longstreet*, 205 Ga. 255, 53 S.E.2d 480, 481 (1949); *Faggard v. Filipowich*, 248 Ala. 182, 27 So.2d 10 (1946); *Shreyer v. Shreyer*, 113 Colo. 219, 155 P.2d 990 (1945); *Nash v. Nash*, 198 Ga. 527, 32 S.E.2d 379, 381 (1944); *Modern Woodmen of America v. Barnes*, 61 F.Supp. 660 (D.C.Minn. 1945); *Sloss-Sheffield Steel & Iron Co. v. Alexander*, 241 Ala. 476, 3 So.2d 46, 48 (1941); *Boze v. Boze*, 96 Colo. 309, 42 P.2d 470 (1935); *Jones v. Milliken*, 96 Colo. 279, 42 P.2d 467 (1935); *Note*, 82 U. PA. L. REV. 508, 512 (1934); *Brown v. Parks*, 173 Ga. 228, 160 S.E. 238, 240 (1931); *Welch v. All Persons*, 78 Mont. 370, 254 P. 179, *rev'd*, 85 Mont. 114, 278 P. 110 (1929); *Ex parte Young*, 211 Ala. 508, 101 So. 51 (1924); *Shepard v. Carter*, 86 Kan. 125, 130, 119 P. 533 (1911); *In re Colton's Estate*, 129 Iowa 542, 105 N.W. 1008 (1906); *Goodwin v. Goodwin*, 113 Iowa 319, 85 N.W. 31 (1901); *Pittinger v. Pittinger*, 28 Colo. 308, 64 P. 195 (1901); and *In re Pickens' Estate*, 163 Pa. 14, 29 A. 875, 876 (1894). *See also* the dictum in older cases, *Senser v. Bower*, 1 Pa. 450 (1830); *Breiden v. Paff*, 12 S. & R., 430 (1825); and Keefe, *supra* note 98, at 7.

132 *See Longstreet v. Longstreet*, 205 Ga. 255, 53 S.E.2d 480, 482 (1949), in which the evidence demonstrated that the "former spouse of the defendant was last seen by her in 1927, about six months after their separation, which was slightly less than seven years prior to the second marriage; and that neither party to the present litigation

in favor of the latter of two marriages in certain cases has been considered stronger than the marital presumption based on "cohabitation and reputation" in favor of the first marriage.[133] There certainly are courts, however, that have found that the presumption in favor of the latter marriage requires the opposing party to prove that the first marriage was commenced and not dissolved by divorce or death, but not that it is invalid, particularly if invalidity would conflict with the presumption that the children from the first marriage were legitimate.[134]

4. *Required Counter-Evidence*

Against the background of superlatives used to describe the strength of the presumption, the issue arises whether the evidence necessary to defeat it, as required in the case law, particularly as the opposing party, must prove the negative of a supposition. With respect to the assumption of the presumption that the first marriage is dissolved *inter vivos,* the question arises as to the type of evidence that has been viewed as necessary to demonstrate that a divorce or court judgment has not occurred at the time of the commencement of the latter marriage.[135] The answer concerning both the quality and quantity of evidence, as well as other related evidentiary issues, is that it "has no certain measures."[136] Certain aspects, however, can

---

knew whether the former spouse was living or dead. Such evidence was clearly insufficient to overcome the presumption that the former marriage had been dissolved by death." *See Nash v. Nash,* 198 Ga. 527, 32 S.E.2d 379 (1944); *Bituminous Casualty Corp. v. Harris,* 68 Ga.App. 889, 24 S.E.2d 803, 804 (1943); *Murchinson v. Green,* 128 Ga. 339, 57 S.E. 709 (1907), 11 L.R.A., N.S., 702 ("Where the presumption of the validity of a marriage, arising from the performance of a ceremony, conflicts with the presumption of the continued life of a former spouse of one of the parties, if neither is aided by proof of facts or circumstances corroborating it, the presumption of the validity of the second marriage will prevail over the presumption of the continuance of life of the former spouse"); *Smith v. Fuller,* 138 Iowa 91, 108 N.W. 765 (1906) (a remarriage three years after the disappearance); *Stymiest v. Stymiest,* 4 Pa.Dist. 305, 16 Pa.Co. 236 (1895); *Nixon v. Wichita Land & Cattle Co.,* 84 Tex. 408, 19 S.W. 560 (1892); *Carroll v. Carroll,* 20 Tex. 731 (1858); *Lockhart v. White,* 18 Tex. 102 (1856); and *Yates v. Houston,* 3 Tex. 433 (1848) (a remarriage approximately four years after the disappearance).

133 *Williamson v. Williamson,* 48 Del. 379, 104 A.2d 463, 464 (1954); *In re Blackhawk's Estate,* 195 Okla. 390, 158 P.2d 168, 173 (1944); *In re Sloan's Estate,* 50 Wash. 88, 96 P. 684 (1908); and *Clayton v. Wardell,* 4 N.Y.230 (1858). The presumption in favor of the latter marriage, however, has not been given precedence to the presumption based on "cohabitation and repute" arising after an invalid wedding, *see Clark v. Clark,* 189 P. 676, *aff'd,* 194 P. 96 (Nev. 1920). With respect to the presumption based on cohabitation and reputation, *see* Chapter 9 *infra.*

134 *Faggard v. Filipowich,* 248 Ala. 182, 27 So.2d 10 (1946), concerning two ceremonial marriages, in which the court did not find that the presumption "should be extended to the point of overcoming not only the presumption of the continuance of respondent's first marriage but also the legitimacy of her son by Filipowich. We are of the opinion that the burden of proving the invalidity of her marriage to Filipowich must rest upon respondent."

135 With respect to annulments, *see Texas Employers' Ins. Assoc. v. Gomez,* Tex. Civ. App., 313 S.W.2d 956 (1958).

136 *Jones v. Case,* 266 Ala. 498, 97 So.2d 816, 818 (1957).

be gleaned from the case law. The clearest have been instances in which the placement of the burden of proof resulted in the production of no or little evidence with respect to the existence of the previous marriage.[137] Evidence that one party's former spouse was alive at the time of the commencement of the latter marriage, as a rule, has been not considered sufficient.[138] Neither has it been considered sufficient to demonstrate with the evidence that one spouse has not obtained a divorce. Evidence that the other spouse has not done so has also been required. Because of this, the testimony of only one spouse generally has not been considered sufficient.[139]

---

137 In *Mauldin v. Sunshine Mining Co.*, 61 Idaho 9, 97 P.2d 608 (1939), the parties had lived together for approximately nine months and outwardly represented themselves as spouses. Certain information arose in the case with respect to the fact that the woman had twice been previously married. No investigation as to whether these marriages had been dissolved was conducted. The Idaho Supreme Court stated: "The presumption that impediments have been removed casts the burden upon the party attacking the validity of a marriage to show by clear, cogent and satisfactory evidence, not only the fact of the former marriage but the further fact that no divorce has been obtained from the former spouse ... and that death has not removed the former spouse." With respect thereto, the court found that the evidence produced was too insufficient to prove that an impediment existed to the marriage. A common law marriage consequently was found established. In *Smith v. Smith*, 32 Idaho 478, 185 P. 67, 69 (1919), a common law marriage was found established, despite the man's unproven statement that he was married to a different woman the entire time.

138 *James v. James*, 260 Ala. 511, 71 So.2d 62 (1954); *Dorsey v. Dorsey*, 259 Ala. 220, 66 So.2d 135,137 (1953); *Freed v. Sallade*, 245 Ala. 505, 17 So.2d 868 (1944); *Nash v. Nash*, 198 Ga. 527, 32 S.E.2d 379 (1944); *Sloss-Sheffield Steel & Iron Co. v. Alexander*, 241 Ala. 476, 3 So.2d 46 (1941); and *Franklin v. Franklin*, 247 S.W.329 (Tex.Civ.App. 1922). The circumstance that the previous spouse was still alive, however, was decisive in the application of the presumption as revised in Georgia in 1957.

139 *Prater v. Aftra Health Fund*, 23 F.Supp.2d 505 (D.N.J. 1998) (applying New York law); *Jackson v. Jackson*, 49 Ala.App. 702, 275 So.2d 683 (1973); *Yarbrough v. United States*, 341 F.2d 621, 624 (Ct.Cl. 1965) (applying Alabama law); *Jordan v. Copeland*, 272 Ala. 336, 131 So.2d 696 (1961); *Troxel v. Jones*, 45 Tenn.App. 264, 322 S.W.2d 251 (1958); *Texas Employers' Ins. Ass'n v. Elder*, 274 S.W.2d 144 (1954), *aff'd*, 155 Tex. 27, 282 S.W.2d 371 (1955); and *Warner v. Warner*, 76 Idaho 399, 283 P.2d 931 (1955). The only counter-evidence produced in *Dorsey v. Dorsey*, 259 Ala. 220, 66 So.2d 135,137 (1953) comprised of "the testimony of the respondent herself and admissions made by her," which was not found sufficient. *See also Brown v. State*, 208 Ga. 304, 66 S.E.2d 745, 749 (1951); *Longstreet v. Longstreet*, 205 Ga. 255, 53 S.E.2d 480, 482 (1949); and *In re Estate of Pilcher*, 114 Utah 72, 197 P.2d 143, 148 (1948). In *Marris v. Sockey*, 170 F.2d 599, 603 (10th Cir. 1948), the man's only counter-evidence comprised of his own testimony "that he had not obtained a divorce and had not been served with process in a divorce proceeding," which was not found sufficient to rebut the presumption. *See also Reed v. Reed*, 202 Ga. 508, 43 S.E.2d 539, 543 (1947); *Hudsperth v. Hudspeth*, 198 S.W.2d 768 (Tex.Civ.App. 1946); *Shreyer v. Shreyer*, 113 Colo. 219, 155 P.2d 990 (1945); *Brown v. Hogan*, 68 Ga.App. 889, 24 S.E.2d 803 (1945); *Freed v. Sallade*, 245 Ala. 505, 17 So.2d 868 (1944); *Nicholas v. Idaho Power Co.*, 63 Idaho 675, 125 P.2d 321, 325 (1942) ("Mere proof of a prior marriage and that one party had not obtained a divorce is not sufficient, for the other might have obtained such divorce and left him or her free to contract the second marriage"); *Brown v. Parks*, 173 Ga. 228, 236, 160 S.E. 238 (1931); *Holman v. Holman*, 288 S.W. 413 (Tex.Comm'n App. 1926); *Madison v. Steckleberg*, 101 Okla. 237, 224 P. 961 (1924); *Jones v. Jones*, 63 Okla. 208, 164 P. 463, 464 (1917); *Chancey v. Whinnery*,

Texas Employers' Insurance Association v. Elder (1955) concerned two common law marriages. The woman, Ethel Mae Elder, lived for approximately nine years with Allen Dade, and they represented themselves outwardly as husband and wife. After they separated, Ethel lived with Grover Cleveland Elder from 1934 until his death in 1952, approximately eighteen years. Ethel then claimed worker's compensation death benefits in her capacity as Grover's widow and cited as grounds that she had lived in a common law marriage with the deceased.

At trial, the insurance company contested her claim, arguing that the presumption in favor of the later marriage was not applicable to common law marriages and that if it was applicable, it was rebuttable. As evidence, the company cited the fact that the woman herself had stated that "she never got a divorce" from her first husband, and that he, as a witness at the trial, said nothing about a divorce. The former common law marriage, consequently, was an impediment against the latter.

The Texas Court of Civil Appeals, finding that the requirements for the establishment of a common law marriage were fulfilled in both relationships, stated that the presumption was applicable, even in favor of a later common law marriage, as the regulations concerned both types of marriage. The party contesting the latter common law marriage must therefore endeavor "throughout and in every particular plainly to make the fact appear, against the constant pressure of the presumption, that it is illegal and void." According to the court's stance, the strength of the presumption increases the longer the parties have cohabited. To rebut it, evidence "which negatives the effective operation of every possible means by which a dissolution of the prior marriage could have taken place" is required. The opposing party, therefore, had to prove that the woman's previous common law marriage had been established and that it was not dissolved. Despite the woman's statement, the court found that the presumption was not rebutted, as it was not demonstrated that the first marriage was not dissolved by divorce—the man, who had himself remarried, could have obtained a divorce.[140] The Texas Supreme Court agreed with the lower court's view that, in the absence of evidence, it will be presumed that the subsequent marriage was legal, and that the prior marriage had been dissolved, stating: "The presumption in favor of the validity of a marriage which, as in this case, has been duly shown to have been

---

47 Okla. 272, 147 P. 1036 (1915); and *Haile v. Hale*, 40 Okla. 101, 135 P. 1143 (1913). *See also Pittinger v. Pittinger*, 28 Colo. 308, 64 P. 195, 197 (1901), in which the man had entered into two formal marriages prior to his death. The presumption in favor of the latter marriage was not considered broken, despite the fact that the first wife was alive and testified that no divorce had occurred between them. The court could not rule out that the deceased had received a divorce. *See also* Keefe, *supra* note 98, at 50 § 21.

140 *Texas Employers' Ins. Ass'n v. Elder*, 274 S.W.2d 144 (Tex.Civ.App. 1954), *aff'd*, 282 S.W.2d 371 (Tex. 1955); *compare Gress v. Gress*, 209 S.W.2d 1003 (Tex.Civ. App.-Galveston 1948).

contracted is one of the strongest, if, indeed, not the strongest, known to the law."[141]

If, in *Elder*, the counter-evidence was not found sufficient, the question becomes what is required to rebut the presumption in favor of the latter marriage. The evidence given the greatest weight in the case law appears to be court records demonstrating that neither of the parties in the first marriage has received a divorce or an annulment of the marriage.[142] The quantity needed, however, has varied. On one side, it is unusual to require court records from all of the jurisdictions in the entire United States in which either party has had the right to petition for a divorce or annulment.[143] On the other side, as a rule, it has been found not sufficient to simply accept records from some jurisdictions in which the parties have resided[144] or from the first spouse's home state.[145]

---

141 *Texas Employers' Ins. Ass'n v. Elder*, 282 S.W.2d 371, 373 (Tex. 1955). The case is referred to without comment in Clair Getty, Jr., *Marriage - Presumption in favor of a subsequent common law marriage - Evidence* -, 2 ST. L.J. 191 (1956). With respect to later cases decided by the Texas Supreme Court, *see also In re Estate of Claveria v. Claveria*, 615 S.W.2d 164 (Tex. 1981). *Compare* a somewhat different stance taken by the Court of Appeals in *Villegas v. Griffin Industries*, 975 S.W.2d 745, 750 (Tex.App.-Corpus Christi 1998) and *Franklin v. Smallridge*, 616 S.W.2d 655, 657 (Tex.Civ.App-Corpus Christi 1981).

142 In *Brantley v. Skeens*, 105 App.D.C. 246, 266 F.2d 447, 454 (1959), in which the presumption in favor of a later common law marriage was found rebutted, it was found proven that the first marriage, which was ceremonial, was not dissolved. The following evidence was cited: (1) A copy of the marriage license and certificate with respect to the first marriage; (2) An affidavit by the man in the first marriage stating that he never received a divorce from the deceased woman; and (3) a certificate under seal from a deputy clerk for the United States District Court for the District of Columbia, stating that a search of the District of Columbia court records from 1938 to 1956 failed to disclose a divorce or annulment of the marriage and (4) comparable evidence from a county in South Carolina. In addition, there was an admission by the man in the claimed common law marriage that the relationship was "illegal" and that the children were "illegitimate." *See also Mayo v. Owen*, 208 Ga. 483, 67 S.E.2d 709 (1951); *In re Cox*, 95 Okla. 14, 217 P. 493 (1923); and Keefe, *supra* note 98, at 54 § 22.

143 *Compare* Hood, *supra* note 1, at 1509, arguing that a skilled attorney can place the opposing party in a difficult situation with the need to obtain "a certified statement from every divorce court in the nation" proving that no divorce has occurred.

144 *In re Estate of Loveless*, 64 S.W.3d 564 (Tex.App.-Texarkana 2001). In *Metro. Life Ins. Co. v. Manning*, 568 F.2d 922 (2d Cir. 1977) (applying Connecticut law), an investigation in two counties was not sufficient as there was information that the spouses in the first marriage had also lived elsewhere. Even in *Dixon v. Gardner*, 302 F.Supp. 395 (E.D.Pa. 1969) (applying North Carolina law), it was unclear in which counties the spouses resided. *See also Norton v. Coffield*, 357 P.2d 434 (Okla. 1960). In *Haywood v. Nichols*, 99 Kan. 138, 160 P. 982 (1916), evidence with respect to the county where the parties had once lived and where the former spouse died nineteen years later was insufficient. *Compare Smith v. Fuller*, 138 Iowa 91, 108 N.W. 765 (1906), in which it was considered sufficient with a listing from only one court, as it was the only court with jurisdiction.

145 *Miller v. A.M.F. Harley-Davidson Motor Co.*, 328 N.W.2d 348 (Iowa App. 1982). When counsel for the party stated that there was no court record demonstrating that the woman in the first marriage had received a divorce in the state, the court found that she could have received a divorce in another state or country.

In *Nicholas v. Idaho Power Co.* (1942), the man and woman formally entered into a marriage less than six months after the man's divorce from his previous wife. Since remarrying was not allowed at this time in Idaho, the new marriage was void. Because the parties, after the removal of the impediment until the man's death, a period of approximately six years, continued the cohabitation, the woman claimed that a common law marriage was established between them. The issue arose as to whether a further impediment existed as to the marriage between the parties because the woman had also earlier entered into a marriage with another man. Two years before she married the deceased, she had filed for divorce from her previous husband, who personally attended the hearings. No divorce was granted. This evidence, however, was found insufficient to rebut the presumption in favor of the latter marriage. The former marriage consequently was presumed dissolved either through divorce or death. The court stated: "The courts of the forty-four counties of the state were open to them to prosecute a divorce action during all this time."[146] A common law marriage consequently was found to have been established.

Commonly, records have been required from courts having jurisdiction during the first marriage, as well as from all jurisdictions in which the parties have resided during the period beginning with the separation and up to the commencement of the later marriage.[147] Such a requirement

---

146 *Nicholas v. Idaho Power Co.*, 63 Idaho 675, 125 P.2d 321, 325 (1942). With respect to the application of the marital presumption to the parties' cohabitation, *see* Chapter 9 *infra*. Neither in *Shreyer v. Shreyer*, 113 Colo. 219, 155 P.2d 990 (1945), was the presumption in favor of the latter marriage, which was a formal marriage, considered defeated with the support of the fact that a petition for divorce was filed but never heard with respect to the previous marriage.

147 According to *Lott v. Toomey*, 477 So.2d 316, 320 (Ala. 1985), the courts in Alabama prefer "court records from all of the places where the first marriage partners are shown to have resided." One method to defeat the presumption, according to *Ellis v. Ellis*, 50 Ala.App. 67, 277 So.2d 102, 104 (1973), is to produce "appropriate court records from the places where the parties to the first marriage have lived" which show that a divorce was not granted for either of the spouses in the first marriage. No such evidence was presented in *Yarbrough v. United States*, 341 F.2d 621, 625 (Ct.Cl. 1965) (applying Alabama law) where the court stated: "In most cases an examination of the records of the divorce courts of all the counties where the parties had lived and where domicile for divorce could have been obtained has been held sufficient proof to rebut the presumption of dissolution of the prior marriage." *See also Dorsey v. Dorsey*, 259 Ala. 220, 66 So.2d 135 (1953); *Ashley v. Ashley*, 255 Ala. 313, 51 So.2d 239 (1951); *Whitman v. Whitman*, 253 Ala. 643, 46 So.2d 422 (1950); *Lindsey v. Lindsey*, 48 Ala.App. 495, 266 So.2d 298 (1972); *compare Ray v. Soc. Sec. Bd.*, 73 F.Supp. 58 (D.C.Ala. 1947) (applying Alabama law). In *Azar v. Thomas*, 206 Ga. 588, 57 S.E.2d 821, 822 (1950), the court required evidence that neither of the parties had received a divorce "in any counties of jurisdiction where it should have been granted," but found it sufficient with "a general search of the court records of the State in which the spouse effecting the second marriage has established residence, that no divorce has been granted." In *Troxel v. Jones*, 45 Tenn.App. 264, 322 S.W.2d 251, 257 (1958), the court required records from "any of the divorce courts in any of the counties where either of the spouses might have obtained such divorce." Where such evidence was not produced, the presumption in favor of the latter common law marriage was applied. In *Lumbermens Mut. Cas. Co. v. Reed*, 84

naturally entails problems in which one of the spouses has lived in many states and/or counties. There are cases in which it has not been possible with any certainty to establish where one of the spouses has resided, and the presumption has still been applied. It has not then been sufficient in the jurisdictions in which the spouse could have been expected to obtain a divorce.[148] The same concrete requirement in practice has been applied if the courts have simply required records from jurisdictions in which it is reasonable to believe that the parties could have filed a petition for divorce or annulment.[149]

In *Lott v. Thomey* (1985), Barbara and Clarence had entered into a ceremonial marriage in 1954 in Mobile County, Alabama. Thereafter, they moved to Chicago, Cook County, Illinois, where they lived until 1959 when they separated. Barbara then moved to California and lived in Los Angeles County. In 1962, she moved back to Alabama where she, until her death,

---

Ga.App. 541, 66 S.E.2d 360, 363 (1951), the court required divorce records from "the counties of the jurisdiction where it should have been granted." *See also Travelers Ins. Co. v. Lester,* 73 Ga.App. 465, 36 S.E.2d 880 (1946); *Sloss-Sheffield Steel & Iron Co. v. Watford,* 245 Ala. 425, 17 So.2d 166 (1944); and *Bell v. Tennessee Coal, Iron & R. Co.,* 240 Ala. 422, 199 So. 813 (1941). In the case, *In re McLaughlin's Estate,* 314 Pa. 574, 172 A. 107, 108 (1934), the presumption was found rebutted by evidence that "no divorce had been granted either to John W. McLaughlin or Cordelia Reed in any of the jurisdictions in which they had been respectively domiciled and where they were entitled to sue for divorce." In *Woods v. Hardware Mut. Cas. Co.,* Tex.Civ. App., 141 S.W.2d 972 (1940), no investigation was required in the locations where the parties had only lived for a short period of time. *See also Fowler v. Texas Exploration Co.,* 290 S.W. 818 (Tex.Civ.App. 1926); *In re Cox,* 95 Okla. 14, 217 P. 493 (1923); *Brokeshoulder v. Brokeshoulder,* 84 Okla. 249, 204 P. 284, (1921); *Smith v. Fuller,* 138 Iowa 91, 108 N.W. 765 (1906); *In re Colton's Estate,* 129 Iowa 542, 105 N.W. 1008, 1010 (1906); and *Barnes v. Barnes,* 90 Iowa 282, 57 N.W. 851 (1894). It is uncommon that the court records from those places where the spouses in the first marriage have resided are found to be insufficient. In *Rutledge v. Rutledge,* 41 Tenn.App. 158, 293 S.W.2d 21 (1954), the presumption, however, was found to not be rebutted by evidence which was "cogent and convincing" despite the production by the man of "certificates that no proceedings dissolving the first marriage were of record," as there was no evidence, besides the man's statements, as to in which counties he had resided. *See also Spears v. Spears,* 178 Ark. 720, 12 S.W.2d 875 (1928).

148 *Norton v. Coffield,* 357 P.2d 434, 435, 439 (Okla. 1960). In *Marcum v. Zaring,* 406 P.2d 970, 973 (Okla. 1965), the production of county records from several counties in three states was found insufficient.

149 In *Davis v. Davis,* 521 S.W.2d 603, 605 (Tex. 1975), the wife in the first marriage was not obliged to prove that a divorce had not occurred in each jurisdiction in which such an event "could have been possible," but simply in those jurisdictions in which the man "might reasonably have been expected to have pursued them." The presumption was considered rebutted as court records from those places in which the spouses in the first marriage had lived demonstrated that they had not received a divorce. In *Caruso v. Lucius,* 448 S.W.2d 711 (Tex.Civ.App. 1969), the presumption in favor of the later common law marriage was found rebutted by the statement from the deceased "that he could not send his first wife money because it would incriminate him and by certificates that proved there was no record of any divorce or annulment in any jurisdiction in which the decedent had resided." *See also Parkhill Truck Co. v. Row,* 383 P.2d 203 (Okla. 1963); and *Dockery v. Brown,* Tex.Civ. App. 209 S.W.2d 801 (1947).

resided in Mobile and Elmore Counties. From the time of the marriage until Barbara's death, Clarence had only lived in Mobile and Cook Counties. After the separation from Clarence, Barbara commenced a common law marriage with Lott. When Barbara died in 1979, the issue was whether Lott or Clarence was Barbara's surviving spouse. According to the presumption in favor of the later marriage, Barbara's common law marriage to Lott, the party claiming the invalidity had to demonstrate, not only that Barbara married Clarence in 1954, but also that the marriage was not dissolved. Evidence was produced, "affidavits from each of the four counties where the evidence shows Clarence and Barbara to have lived, indicating the lack of any record of divorce." The Alabama Supreme Court found that the ceremonial marriage between Barbara and Clarence was an impediment to her common law marriage with Lott.[150]

The presumption has been found rebutted even in cases in which the latter marriage was a ceremonial marriage and the former was a common law marriage. If the dissolution of the former marriage requires personal service, and none has occurred, this has been sufficient evidence to rebut the presumption. For example, in *Parkhill Truck Company v. Row* (1963), Marie and James formlessly lived together as husband and wife beginning in January 1954 until December 1958, barely four years, when they separated. Four months later, James entered into a ceremonial marriage with Opal, with whom he lived for five months until September of the same year, when he died in a work-related accident. Both Marie and Opal requested death benefits under the claim that they were the deceased's surviving spouses.

The Oklahoma Supreme Court found that a common law marriage had been formed between James and Marie and that the evidence was sufficient to rebut the presumption that the marriage had been dissolved by a judgment of divorce prior to the commencement of the ceremonial marriage between James and Opal. The court referred to the fact that Marie and James, at the time of his death, had been separated for less than ten months, a period during which both resided in Oklahoma. The court further referred to the fact that a divorce required personal service as to the petition and that Marie testified that she had not been served. Given that fact, the court concluded that the evidence clearly overcame the presumption that the common-law marriage in controversy was terminated by divorce.[151]

---

150 *Lott v. Toomey*, 477 So.2d 316 (Ala. 1985). The court did not wish, however, to exclude any other method for rebutting the presumption.

151 *Parkhill Truck Co. v. Row*, 383 P.2d 203, 208 (Okla. 1963). The court, however, did not address the issue of the strength of the presumption here, but has done so in several other cases, *see, e.g., Norton v. Coffield*, 357 P.2d 434, 440 (Okla. 1960), where it speaks of "the strong presumption." *Compare In re Estate of Claveria v. Claveria*, 615 S.W.2d 164, 167 (Tex. 1981), in which the Texas Supreme Court, remanding the case, stated: "Certificates from the district clerks of Bexar and Dallas Counties show

5. *The Presumption in the Case Law – A Moderate Application*

Despite the traditional strength of the presumption, the courts have sought to limit its effects. This has occurred in different ways, including by modifying the specific requirements for application of the presumption, and by limiting the legal consequences of its application. The presumption has been eroded to the point that there is reason to question whether it actually is applicable and ought to be applied.

The courts in Alabama are among those urging caution in the application of the presumption by not wishing to place too heavy a burden of proof on the party claiming that a former marriage *was not* dissolved and is an impediment against the latter. In the above-mentioned case of *Lott v. Thomey* (1985), the Alabama Supreme Court consequently stated: "A rule of law which allows an artificial or technical force to be given evidence which warrants such presumptions, beyond its natural tendencies to convince the mind, and requires court and juries to presume as true that which is false, cannot but be fraught with dangerous consequences."[152] In the endeavor to maintain the principally high evidentiary requirements applied above, the court instead found that the presumption ought to be rebutted "when the facts and circumstances, in light of all *reasonable inferences,* show that the first marriage was not dissolved." (Italics added). Court records had been produced from those jurisdictions in which the spouses from the first marriage had resided, demonstrating that the marriage had not been dissolved by divorce and rebutting the presumption. However, this occurred, according to the court, without "foreclosing any other method of rebutting the presumption."[153]

---

that there has been no divorce or annulment decree from either of those counties," in other words, where the parties had resided.

152 *Lott v. Toomey,* 477 So.2d 316, 320 (Ala. 1985). The same caution is found in *Hammond v. Shipp,* 292 Ala. 113, 289 So.2d 802 (1974), in which the presumption that the first marriage was dissolved was found rebutted with support of "evidence, including power of attorney of such woman stating that she was lawful wife of homesteader and deed where homesteader recognized such woman as his wife." In *Yarbrough v. United States,* 341 F.2d 621, 624-625 (Ct.Cl. 1965) (applying Alabama law), the United States Court of Claims found that the presumption was "strong" or "very strong," but applied a requirement of "a reasonable inference" as well as evidence which was "reliable and convincing." *See also Jordan v. Copeland,* 272 Ala. 336, 131 So.2d 696, 701 (1961) (simply one spouse's own testimony that the first marriage according to the court records had not been dissolved was found to be hearsay and could not defeat the presumption); *James v. James,* 260 Ala. 511, 71 So.2d 62 (1954); *Dorsey v. Dorsey,* 259 Ala. 220, 66 So.2d 135, 137 (1953); *Matthews v. Matthews,* 259 Ala. 332, 67 So.2d 22 (1953); *Clark v. Glenn,* 249 Ala. 342, 31 So.2d 507, 511 (1947) ("The court will not give artificial or technical force to evidence which is supposed to warrant the presumption that a divorce was granted beyond the natural tendencies to convince the mind"); *Freed v. Sallade,* 245 Ala. 505, 17 So.2d 868, 869 (1944); *Sloss-Sheffield Steel & Iron Co. v. Watford,* 245 Ala. 425, 17 So.2d 166, 168 (1944); *Bell v. Tennessee Coal, Iron & R. Co.,* 240 Ala. 422, 199 So. 813 (1941); and *Ex parte Young,* 211 Ala. 508, 101 So. 51 (1924).

153 *Lott v. Toomey,* 477 So.2d 316, 320 (Ala. 1985).

There is no lack of cases in Alabama in which other methods were applied, and the *dictum* consequently took on authority as a holding, *ratio decidendi.* The evidence then has rested on the statements and actions of the parties in the first marriage in which they have testified that they had not obtained a divorce. Of particular significance has been the continued cohabitation. In *Sloss-Sheffield Steel & Iron Co. v. Watford* (1944),[154] the presumption in favor of the later ceremonial marriage was found rebutted both in favor of a previous common law marriage by the wife, and in favor of a former ceremonial marriage by the husband. The woman, Maggie Lee Watford, claimed worker's compensation benefits in her capacity as the widow of Will, who died in 1942 from injuries received at work. The insurance company contested the claim, arguing that impediments existed against the marriage for both spouses. The issue was whether Maggie and Will truly were married at the time of his death. The following can be seen from the marital history of the spouses.

Maggie and Will had lived together since 1929 and formally married in 1932. Thereafter, they lived together as husband and wife until Will's death, and had seven mutual children. However, Maggie had previously married Allan in 1922 for the purpose of preventing his indictment for seduction. They never cohabited before or after the wedding, and, in 1923, received a divorce without the right for Maggie to remarry.[155] Allan, prior to meeting Maggie, had formlessly lived together with Louise. They appeared outwardly as spouses, and their cohabitation continued after Allan's marriage with Maggie. Allan and Louise's relationship fulfilled the requirements for the formation of a common law marriage. After the divorce from Allan, Maggie had for several months in 1924 lived together with John, who soon thereafter disappeared from her life; he was never heard from again.

---

154 *Sloss-Sheffield Steel & Iron Co. v. Watford,* 245 Ala. 425, 17 So.2d 166 (1944). *See also Jones v. Case,* 266 Ala. 498, 97 So.2d 816, 818 (1957), in which, in addition to the spouses' own testimony, it was noted that the spouses in the first marriage approximately twelve years after the separation jointly owned property. In *James v. James,* 260 Ala. 511, 71 So.2d 62, 64 (1954), the presumption in favor of the later marriage was found rebutted based on the fact that the one spouse in the first marriage stated that no divorce had occurred and that the other spouse after the commencement of the second marriage according to the court records filed a petition for divorce in the first marriage. In *Williams v. Wilson,* 210 Ala. 289, 97 So. 911 (1923), the husband in the first marriage had not returned after a commandeering during war. The wife remarried. The first husband, however, was alive and had also entered into a new marriage with different woman. When the first husband returned after twenty years, the spouses again cohabited for a period. The presumption in favor of the later marriage was not applied as it could not be presumed that the parties in the first marriage received a divorce. The court was not persuaded by the circumstance that the woman later left the first husband and returned to the second.

155 With respect to the issue of the interest of avoiding criminal prosecution and not hindering the formation of a marriage due to a lack of marital intent, *see* Chapter 6 *infra.*

After the death of his first wife, Will had been formally married to Mary since 1920. They had four mutual children. Will and Mary separated in 1923, but according to Mary's testimony at the trial, they never obtained a divorce.

The Alabama Supreme Court found, in trying the issue of whether there was an impediment to Maggie's marriage with Will, that a common law marriage had been formed between Allan and Louise.[156] With the assessment of the issue of whether this marriage was an impediment against Allan's marriage to Maggie, the court found that the presumption in favor of the latter of two marriages was rebutted, given that the formless marriage between Allan and Louise was presumed dissolved. In its decision the court particularly noted that Allan and Louise had not separated but had continued their cohabitation after Maggie's marriage to Allan. The common law marriage established between Louise and Allan was an impediment to the marriage between Allan and Maggie. Because that marriage was void, and because John was presumed to be dead, due to his unexplainable absence of seven years, Maggie was competent to enter into marriage with Will.

With respect to Will's capacity to enter into marriage with Maggie, the court noted that the presumption in favor of the latter marriage definitely resulted in Will's marriage with Mary being dissolved by divorce. The Alabama Supreme Court, however, found that the presumption was also rebutted with respect to this relationship. The court supported its finding by referring to the fact that Will, during his life, had only lived in four counties, and the court records demonstrated that no divorce had occurred between Will and Mary. Consequently, their marriage was an impediment to Will's marriage with Maggie. The latter, therefore, was not married to Will at the time of his death and could not receive workers' compensation.

In the case law from Pennsylvania, which correctly has been perceived as giving a "confused impression,"[157] a moderate and flexible presumption is also indicated by the low standard of evidence applied. According to the Pennsylvania Supreme Court in the case of *In re Watt's Estate* (1962), the presumption can be rebutted by the production of "proof of some nature" that the first marriage, at the commencement of the second, had not been dissolved by divorce or death. The court found the presumption to have been rebutted, and noted that a judgment of divorce with respect to the first marriage was declared null, indicating that it was not dissolved by divorce.[158]

---

156 With respect to the issue of whether the conditions for the formation of a common law marriage are fulfilled, *see* Chapter 7 *infra*.

157 Homer H. Clark, Jr. & Carol Glowinsky, Cases and Problems on Domestic Relations 138 (4th ed. 1990).

158 *In re Watt's Estate*, 409 Pa. 44, 185 A.2d 781, 786 (1962). *See also Cupler v. Sec'y of Health*, 252 F.Supp. 178, 184 (W.D.Pa. 1966), in which the presumption, however,

The weakness of the presumption can also be seen in the court finding that simply the existence of a later marriage is not always sufficient to apply the presumption against an earlier marriage. Circumstances in support of the later marriage have also been required. The following are considered relevant: the passage of a long period of time between the separation of the parties in the first marriage and the commencement of the second; the remarriage of the other party in the first marriage; the good faith of the parties in the second marriage; a formal marriage; a long cohabitation between the spouses of the second marriage; and the effect on the legitimacy of the children in the marriage.[159]

The relative weakness of the presumption in Pennsylvania law can further be seen from its inability to compete with other presumptions. In relation to the presumption that the establishment of a marriage is assumed until one of the parties has died or the marriage is dissolved by divorce, the courts appear to prefer an equitable assessment from case to case in which the presumption "which from the evidence and inferences

---

was not found rebutted. *Compare In re Estate of Lymon*, 542 N.Y.S.2d 168 (A.D. 1989)(applying Pennsylvania law), in which the court spoke of the "very strong presumption." *Compare* older case law, *In re Thewlis' Estate*, 217 Pa. 307, 66 A. 519 (1907), in which the Pennsylvania Supreme Court required "positive, affirmative proof" and in which the presumption was not rebutted, as well as *In re McLaughlin's Estate*, 314 Pa. 574, 172 A. 107, 108 (1934), in which the presumption according to the same court was found rebutted by evidence that "no divorce had been granted either to John W. McLaughlin or Cordelia Reed McLaughlin in any of the jurisdictions in which they had been respectively domiciled and where they were entitled to sue for divorce."

159 *In re Watt's Estate*, 409 Pa. 44, 185 A.2d 781, 786 (1962). The Pennsylvania Supreme Court, however, found that the presumption was not rebutted in *Com. ex rel. Alexander v. Alexander*, 445 Pa. 406, 289 A.2d 83 (1971). Neither was it rebutted in *Headen v. Pope & Talbot, Inc.*, 252 F.2d 739, 743-745 (3d Cir. 1958)(applying Pennsylvania law), in which it was noted that the later marriage was ceremonial, entered into in good faith, a long period had occurred between the separation from the first spouse and the marriage with the second, the parties in the second marriage lived together for fifteen years, the second marriage was accepted among friends and acquaintances, the former spouse was found competent to enter into a new marriage, and that the second marriage's invalidity would affect the legitimacy of nine children. *See also Madison v. Lewis*, 151 Pa.Super. 138, 30 A.2d 357, 360 (1943), in which the court with respect to the presumption in favor of the latter marriage maintained that it "does not of itself destroy the first but requires some proof of facts and circumstances to be given the effect of overcoming the first; as for instance, the long lapse of time during which the other party may be presumed to have died, the question of legitimacy of a child of the second marriage, the fact that the other spouse had likewise remarried, proof that the decedent, whose heirs are attacking the second marriage, had himself recognized the validity of it." *See* a similar reasoning in *Hudek v. United Engineering & Foundry Co.*, 152 Pa.Super. 493, 33 A.2d 41 (1943). *Compare Sharpe v. Federal Window & Office Cleaning Co.*, 144 Pa.Super. 231, 19 A.2d 509 (1941), in which the presumption in favor of a later common law marriage was not applied, as only approximately one year had passed between the separation in the first marriage and the commencement of the second, the spouse in the previous marriage was still alive, neither of the parties had any grounds for divorce, and the issue concerned the legitimacy of children. *See also In re Estate of Holben*, 93 Pa.Super.Ct. 472 (1928); *In re Divers's Estate*, 22 Pa.Super. 436 (1903); and *In re Wile's Estate*, 6 Pa.Super. 435 (1898).

there from render it the least probable to sustain"[160] ought to win. At the same time that the application of the presumption in Pennsylvania expands to reach a materially reasonable result in each case, the presumption is robbed of its fixedness and durability.

The presumption has also been modified in the case law from Iowa. First, in a manner similar to that in Pennsylvania, specific conditions have been required for the presumption to be applicable. The courts, consequently, have required that both of the spouses in the first marriage in some manner must have acted as if their marriage had been dissolved. In the case of *In re Estate of Weems* (1966), in which both of the spouses in the first of two ceremonial marriages later remarried, the Iowa Supreme Court consequently required "something based on the acts and conduct of both parties inconsistent with the continuance of the marriage relation."[161] The parties' actions in the later marriages were also considered.[162] If the presumption is applicable, strong and persuasive evidence is required to rebut it, but court records, demonstrating that the parties in the first marriage had not been granted a divorce, have not always been required. In *Weems,* it was sufficient upon the man's death that the wife in the first marriage testified that no divorce had been granted in their marriage and that the deceased's second wife testified that she knew that the deceased had never received a divorce from his first wife. With this direct evidence, the presumption was found rebutted, and the first marriage was deemed an impediment to the second.[163] The case law gives the impression that, if the

---

160 *See Cupler v. Sec'y of Health,* 252 F.Supp. 178, 184 (W.D.Pa. 1966); and *In re Watt Estate,* 409 Pa. 44, 185 A.2d 781, 786 (1962). In *Fritsche v. O'Neill,* 147 Pa.Super. 153, 24 A.2d 157 (1942), it was suggested that any decision between the two presumptions should take into consideration, from case to case, the legitimacy of children and the criminalization of the actions of the parties.

161 *In re Estate of Weems,* 258 Iowa 711, 139 N.W.2d 922, 924 (1966). The presumption was applied and found not defeated in *Miller v. A.M.F. Harley-Davidson Motor Co.,* 328 N.W.2d 348, 352 (Iowa App. 1982); and *Eygabrood v. Gruis,* 247 Iowa 1346, 79 N.W.2d 215 (1956). The principle has support in older case law: *see for example Casley v. Mitchell,* 121 Iowa 96, 96 N.W. 725 (1903); *Tuttle v. Raish,* 116 Iowa 331, 90 N.W. 66 (1902); and *Goodwin v. Goodwin,* 113 Iowa 319, 85 N.W. 31 (1901). In *Leach v. Hall,* 95 Iowa 611, 64 N.W. 790 (1895), the court required "something based upon the acts and conduct of both parties inconsistent with the continuance of the marriage relation." *See also Gilman v. Sheets,*78 Iowa 499, 43 N.W. 299 (1889). In *Ellis v. Ellis,* 58 Iowa 720, 13 N.W. 65 (1882), in which the wife in the first marriage claimed to be the deceased's widow, the presumption was found rebutted as she, according to her testimony, did not know of the man's second marriage, had not taken out a divorce and did not know that the man should have done so. In *Blanchard v. Lambert,* 43 Iowa 228, 229, 22 Am.Rep. 245 (1876), in which both of the spouses in the first marriage entered into a new marriage, the presumption in favor the later marriage was applied. *Compare Barnes v. Barnes,* 90 Iowa 282, 57 N.W. 851 (1894).

162 In *Miller v. A.M.F. Harley-Davidson Motor Co.,* 328 N.W.2d 348, 352 (Iowa App. 1982), the parties' long-term cohabitation was considered.

163 *In re Estate of Weems,* 258 Iowa 711, 139 N.W.2d 922, 924 (1966). *See also Eygabrood v. Gruis,* 247 Iowa 1346, 1350, 79 N.W.2d 215 (1956). *Compare, Miller v. A.M.F. Harley-Davidson Motor Co.,* 328 N.W.2d 348, 352 (Iowa App. 1982), where the party's counsel could not find any court records demonstrating that a valid divorce had

legitimacy of children is not involved, the courts allow the two persons competing as legal spouses to do so on more equal terms.[164]

Another method to limit the scope of the presumption has been used in Georgia, where the presumption earlier was applied with few exceptions without any limitations.[165] The Georgia courts, since the end of the 1950s, have not presumed that the previous marriage was dissolved by divorce if it could be shown that the spouse in the previous marriage was still alive. In this case, the burden of proof is on the party claiming that the later marriage is valid. That party must then prove that the previous marriage was dissolved by divorce.[166] On the other hand, if it cannot be

---

occurred in California between the parties in the first of two ceremonial marriages. The court maintained that it was entirely possible that the wife in the first marriage could have received a divorce in another state or in Mexico or another country. The application of the presumption was also motivated by the fact that the parties in the later marriage lived many years together as husband and wife in Iowa.

164 *In re Colton's Estate,* 129 Iowa 542, 105 N.W. 1008 (1906). In *Parsons v. Grand Lodge,* 108 Iowa 6, 78 N.W. 676 (1899), concerning a widow's rights under an insurance policy, the presumption was applied. *See also Farr v. Farr,* 190 Iowa 1005, 181 N.W. 268 (1921).

165 *See* prior to the 1957 amendment to the GA. CODE ANN. § 53-102 (1) (1957), where a previous marriage was presumed to be dissolved either through death or divorce. *See also Murchinson v. Green,* 128 Ga. 339, 57 S.E. 709 (1907); *Ward v. Ward,* 24 Ga.App. 695, 102 S.E. 35 (1920); and *Brown v. Parks,* 173 Ga. 228, 160 S.E. 238, 240 (1931) ("If it is shown that a party to a marriage has contracted a previous marriage and that his or her former spouse is still living, this has been held not to destroy the prima facie validity of the second marriage. In such a case it has been presumed that the first marriage has been dissolved by divorce"); *Bituminous Casualty Corp. v. Harris,* 68 Ga.App. 889, 24 S.E.2d 803, 804 (1943); *Nash v. Nash,* 198 Ga. 527, 32 S.E.2d 379 (1944); *Brown v. Hogan,* 72 Ga.App. 691, 34 S.E.2d 619 (1945); and *Longstreet v. Longstreet,* 205 Ga. 255, 53 S.E.2d 480, 482 (1949). In *Carr v. Walker,* 205 Ga. 1, 9, 52 S.E.2d 426 (1949), the presumption in favor of the later common law marriage was applied, with which the party contesting had to prove that the first marriage had not been dissolved. They were not successful. *See Azar v. Thomas,* 206 Ga. 588, 57 S.E.2d 821, 822 (1950) ("To overcome the presumption of validity of the subsequent marriage, there must be plenary proof that neither party to the previous marriage had obtained a divorce"); *Brown v. State,* 208 Ga. 304, 66 S.E.2d 745, 749 (1951); *Mayo v. Owen,* 208 Ga. 483, 67 S.E.2d 709 (1951); *Cooper v. Cooper,* 88 Ga.App. 335, 76 S.E.2d 726, 729 (1953); *Woodum v. American Mut. Liab. Ins. Co.,* 212 Ga. 386, 93 S.E.2d 12 (1956); *Wheeler v. Terell,* 238 F.2d 29 (1956), 99 U.S.App. D.C. 168, *cert. denied,* 352 U.S. 1018, 77 S.Ct. 581, 1 L.Ed.2d 557 (1957); *Johnson v. Johnson,* 96 Ga.App. 84, 99 S.E.2d 352, 353 (1957); and *McCormick v. Denny,* 213 Ga. 28, 96 S.E.2d 600, 601 (1957). *See also Edwards v. Edwards,* 136 Ga.App. 668, 222 S.E.2d 169, 170 (1975), in which Court of Appeals gave the presumption in favor of the later marriage the content that the previous marriage was presumed to be dissolved either by death or divorce. However, the presumption was found rebutted due to the evidence brought in the case. In older cases, the presumption is not always applied, *see, e.g., Neely v. Tennessee, G. & A.R. Co.,* 145 Ga. 363, 89 S.E. 325 (1916) (burden of proof on the party filing the complaint and claiming that the first marriage was dissolved); and *Wilson v. Allen,* 108 Ga. 275, 33 S.E. 975 (1899). However, *Neely* must be viewed as overruled, *see Woodum v. American Mut. Liab. Ins. Co.,* 212 Ga. 386, 93 S.E.2d 12, 15 (1956).

166 The presumption's new formulation has its basis on the statutory text, GA. CODE ANN. § 53-102 (1) (1957): "The dissolution of a previous marriage in divorce proceedings must be affirmatively established and will not be presumed." This section has been interpreted in the case law as that the burden of proof rests upon the

proven that the previous spouse is still alive, the presumption in favor of the later marriage is applied.

For example, in *Baker v. Musa* (1984), Berry married Ruth in 1935. Berry married again to Willie Mae in 1946. He received a divorce from Ruth a year later. Berry and Willie Mae continued to live together as husband and wife and had a daughter in 1948. Berry and Willie Mae later separated. Thereafter, Berry formally married another woman named Margie Vera in 1953, living together until her death in 1973. Berry formally married Margie in 1974. They divorced in 1975 but remarried that same year and lived together thereafter until Berry's death in 1981.

Upon Berry's death, Margie claimed maintenance from his estate (a year's support) based on the claim that she was the deceased's widow. The issue arose whether the marriage between Berry and Margie was valid or whether the marriage between Berry and Willie Mae was an impediment, and whether the relationship between the latter two in turn was a valid marriage or whether an impediment to it existed, based on the relationship between Berry and Ruth.

First, the Georgia Court of Civil Appeals found that Berry's first marriage was an impediment to Berry's second marriage with Willie Mae at the time of its commencement in 1945. However, as Berry and Willie Mae continued their cohabitation after the removal of the impediment, a common law marriage was formed between the parties. The issue then arose whether this marriage was an impediment to Berry's marriage with Margie in 1974. The court then applied the presumption in favor of the

---

party claiming that the later marriage is valid first if the spouse from the first marriage is still alive. In *Liberty Mut. Ins. Co. v. Ellis*, 99 Ga. App. 486, 109 S.E.2d 70, 71 (1959), the court stated: "The language of the quoted Code section is explicit that where there is proof that one of the parties to a ceremonial marriage has a living spouse, there is no presumption that a divorce has been previously granted dissolving the former marriage." *See also Zurich Ins. Co. v. Craft*, 103 Ga.App. 889, 120 S.E.2d 922 (1961) (however, it could not be proven that the former spouse was still alive); and *American Mutual Liab. Ins. Co. v. Copeland*, 113 Ga.App. 707, 149 S.E.2d 402 (1966). In *Smith v. Smith*, 230 Ga. 616, 198 S.E.2d 307 (1973), the court did not shift the burden of proof, as it was not proven that the earlier spouses were alive. The court stated: "The introduction in evidence by Leon Smith of evidence of two ceremonial marriages by Tommy Smith, prior to his marriage with her, without any evidence that these former spouses are living, did not place the burden of evidence on Ethel Miller Smith to prove that these marriages had been dissolved by divorce." *See also Patrick v. Simon*, 237 Ga. 742, 229 S.E.2d 746 (1976), in which the presumption in favor of a later commenced marriage was applied, but in which, when it was proven that the first spouse was alive, the later spouse must prove that the earlier marriage was dissolved by divorce. The last mentioned spouse, prior to the marriage with the deceased, had entered into three ceremonial marriages of which none could be proven to have been dissolved by divorce. In *Johnson v. Johnson*, 239 Ga. 714, 238 S.E.2d 437 (1977), the spouse from the first of two ceremonial marriages was alive. The burden of proof shifted as the spouse in the second marriage had to prove that the first marriage was dissolved by divorce, which they succeeded in doing. *See also Baker v. Musa*, 170 Ga.App. 77, 316 S.E.2d 178 (1984); *Scott v. Jefferson*, 174 Ga.App. 651, 331 S.E.2d 1, 3 (1985); *Dismuke v. C & S Trust Co.*, 261 Ga. 525, 407 S.E.2d 739, 740 (1991); and GA. CODE ANN. § 19-3-2(3) (West 2003).

later marriage, but as Willie Mae was alive at the time of Berry's marriage with Margie, the burden of proof was on Margie to prove that the common law marriage formed between Berry and Willie Mae was dissolved through divorce. Because she could not produce any evidence with respect to this issue, the common law marriage was an impediment to the marriage between her and Berry. Margie, consequently, was not married at the time of Berry's death and was not entitled to maintenance from the estate.[167]

This formulation of the presumption naturally limits the protection granted to the latter of two marriages. At the same time, it has the advantage that neither of the parties needs to prove the negative of any premise; no one needs to prove that a divorce has not occurred at any time or place. Instead, the party claiming that the marriage was dissolved by divorce must prove it. On the other hand, in Georgia, if the spouse from the earlier marriage is not alive and the other spouse bases a claim on that marriage, the presumption in favor of the later marriage is applied. The spouse making the claim must prove that the earlier marriage had been commenced, and that it had not been dissolved with evidence that is "clear, distinct, positive and satisfactory proof."[168]

Further, cases arise in which the courts have departed from the traditional understanding by applying in principle a lower evidentiary standard with respect to the evidence required to rebut the presumption. For example, in *Yarbrough v. Yarbrough* (1984), the South Carolina Court of Appeals appears to have applied the presumption in favor of a latter marriage, which was ceremonial, but only required a preponderance of evidence to prove that one of two claimed former marriages were established and not dissolved by divorce or death. The man making the claim, however, was not successful in rebutting the presumption in favor of the latter commenced marriage, despite this evidentiary standard.[169] It has also been argued that the presumption has full effect only if counter-evidence is absent, and as soon as such evidence is produced, a different principle comes into play, such that either the first or the second marriage can win with support of a preponderance of evidence.[170]

The traces of a more moderate application of the presumption than that previously expounded by the Texas Supreme Court can also be seen

167 *Baker v. Musa*, 170 Ga.App. 77, 316 S.E.2d 178 (1984).

168 In *Jones v. Transamerica Ins. Co.*, 154 Ga.App. 408, 409, 268 S.E.2d 444 (1980), concerning two ceremonial marriages, the presumption in favor of the later marriage was applied, as the spouse from the first marriage was not alive. The other spouse from the first marriage did not succeed in rebutting the presumption.

169 *Yarbrough v. Yarbrough*, 280 S.C. 546, 314 S.E.2d 16 (App. 1984). Of the two marriages claimed to be an impediment to the existence of a third, the first was ceremonial and the second a common law marriage. The latter, however, was found not proven, and with respect to the former, it could not be proven against the presumption that it was not dissolved.

170 CLARK, *supra* note 36, at 141.

in the decisions of the Texas Court of Appeals.[171] For example, in *Villegas v. Griffin Industries* (1998), the woman claimed that she was the deceased's wife in a common law marriage. At the same time, she testified that the man was already married when they began their relationship, and that he, thereafter, continued to have contact with and supported his first family. However, she "did not know" whether the man's first marriage had been dissolved. In this situation, an application of the presumption in favor of the later marriage would entail the opposing party proving that the first marriage had not been dissolved. The Texas Court of Appeals, however, reversed the burden of proof and gave the woman the burden of proving that the previous marriage had been dissolved. As she could not produce such evidence, the court found that her common law marriage was invalid.[172] The presumption, consequently, was rebutted simply on the basis of the woman's testimony solely based on the fact that a previous marriage had been commenced, not on the fact that it was not dissolved.

This decision, along with *Franklin v. Smallridge* (1981), is scarcely in line with the principles set out by the Texas Supreme Court. In *Franklin*, the Court of Appeals similarly considered the presumption in favor of a later marriage rebutted based on the testimony from the one spouse that she had previously been married and, in addition, that the marriage had not been dissolved.[173] In, *Elder*, as noted above, the court emphasized the strength of the presumption, and found it had not been rebutted based on one spouse's testimony about a previous marriage.[174] One distinction

171 *Compare* the Texas Supreme Court's decisions in *Texas Employers' Ins. Ass'n v. Elder*, 274 S.W.2d 144 (Tex. 1954); *Davis v. Davis*, 521 S.W.2d 603 (Tex. 1975); and *In re Estate of Claveria v. Claveria*, 615 S.W.2d 164, 165 (Tex. 1981).

172 *Villegas v. Griffin Industries*, 975 S.W.2d 745, 750 (Tex.App.-Corpus Christi 1998).

173 *See Franklin v. Smallridge*, 616 S.W.2d 655, 657 (Tex.Civ.App.-Corpus Christi 1981), in which the parties entered into a common law marriage, but in which the woman stated that she had earlier entered into a ceremonial marriage and that it had not been dissolved by divorce. With respect to this, the Court of Civil Appeals shifted the burden of proof, making the woman prove that she was competent to enter into a common law marriage, which she did not succeed in doing. In *Baker v. Lee*, 337 S.W.2d 637, 639 (Tex.Civ.App. 1960), the Texas Court of Civil Appeals also found that the presumption in favor of a later common law marriage was rebutted. The court stated that the evidence showed that the ceremonial marriage preceding the formless marriage "was never dissolved by divorce or annulment." The woman, who had earlier been married, had lived in the same place as the previous man and knew his address. She and her daughter testified that she had not received a divorce and no service by publication could have occurred. *See also Phillips v. Dow Chemical Co.*, 186 S.W.3d 121 (Tex.App. 2005), where a man first entered into a ceremonial marriage with a woman and later cohabited with another. When the latter woman died, the man claimed that they had lived in a common law marriage. After the death of the latter, the man's spouse from the first marriage sued for divorce. In his sworn answer to that petition, the man admitted the fact of the marriage and referred to the petitioner as "my wife." This defeated the presumption.

174 *Texas Employers' Ins. Ass'n v. Elder*, 274 S.W.2d 144 (Tex.Civ.App. 1954). *See also Davis v. Davis*, 521 S.W.2d 603, 605 (Tex. 1975), concerning the competition between two ceremonial marriages and in which the Texas Supreme Court found the presumption rebutted as it was shown that according to the court records the parties

that can be drawn between this case and the two cases from the Court of Appeals is certainly that the former concerned the competition simply between two common law marriages, while the two latter cases concerned later common law marriages competing with earlier ceremonial marriages. This fact, however, is not stated as a reason in the later decisions and ought not to be attributed relevance according to the Texas Supreme Court, which, with the application of the presumption, has principally chosen to not draw a distinction between ceremonial and common law marriages.[175] It remains to be seen whether the Texas Supreme Court is prepared to accept this weakening of the presumption to which the decisions of the Court of Appeals give expression.

6. *The Required Counter-Evidence in Cases of Death*

As stated above, the presumption in favor of a later marriage has the legal consequence that an earlier marriage is presumed to be dissolved, not only through divorce or annulment, but also upon the death of one of the spouses.[176] The party attacking the later marriage, consequently, has the burden of proving that the other spouse in the earlier marriage was not deceased at the time of the formation of the later marriage.[177] If it can be proven that the spouses from the first marriage were alive, the second marriage is invalid.[178] In other cases, no impediment to the later marriage exists. Certain courts have found that the presumption of the death of a spouse can only be applied in favor of a new marriage by the abandoned

---

in the first marriage could not have received a divorce in the places where they had lived, as well as *In re Estate of Claveria v. Claveria*, 615 S.W.2d 164, 165 (Tex. 1981), in which the court stated that the presumption would continue until evidence of "the impediment of a prior marriage and its continuing validity" was produced.

175 *See* note 112 *supra*. In *Pike v. Estate of Pike*, 2005 WL 2248347 (Tex.App.-Ft. Worth 2005), the presumption was not rebutted as no evidence was offered to show that the first of two common law marriages was not dissolved or annulled. Consequently the later common law marriage was valid.

176 *Davis v. Davis*, 255 Ala. 488, 51 So.2d 876 (1975); *Goset v. Goset*, 112 Ark. 47, 164 S.W. 759 (1914); *Mayo v. Owen*, 208 Ga. 483, 67 S.E.2d 709 (1951); *Smith v. Fuller*, 138 Iowa 91, 108 N.W. 765 (1906); *Welch v. All Persons*, 78 Mont. 370, 254 P. 179, *rev'd* 85 Mont. 114, 278 P. 110 (1929); and Keefe, *supra* note 98, at 20 § 7.

177 According to certain courts, it is sufficient that it is proven that the absent spouse was alive at the time the validity is tried by the court, even if it is more than seven years after a disappearance. *See In re Estate of Holben*, 93 Pa.Super.Ct. 472 (1928); *Day v. Day*, 216 S.C. 334, 58 S.E.2d 83 (1950) (11 years); and *White v. Indus. Comm'n*, 102 Ohio App. 236, 142 N.E.2d 549 (1956). In certain jurisdictions, a five-year time frame is applied, and in others, the marriage is only voidable, *see, e.g.*, *In re Harrington*, 140 Cal. 244, 73 P. 1000 (1903); *Gof v. Gof*, 52 Cal.App.2d 23, 125 P.2d 848 (1942); *Ventura v. Ventura*, 53 Misc.2d 881, 280 N.Y.S.2d 5 (Sup.Ct. 1967); and *Davis v. Whitlock*, 90 S.C. 233, 73 S.E. 171 (1911). According to *Campbell v. Allen*, 208 Ga. 274, 66 S.E.2d 226 (1951), the presumption gives protection against an indictment for bigamy.

178 *Smith v. Fuller*, 138 Iowa 91, 108 N.W. 765 (1906); and *Hill v. Shreve*, 448 P.2d 848 (Okla. 1968).

spouse, not by the absent spouse.[179] Other courts have required that the presumption not be applied to an unexplainable absence, but to the abandonment of the spouse in the previous marriage.[180]

It ought to be noted that in addition to the presumption in favor of the later of two marriages, another presumption, at the same time, has the same legal consequence. According to the common law, and according to the legislation of many states, a person who has disappeared and not been heard from for seven years is presumed to be dead.[181] If the person who has disappeared was married, the marriage is, consequently, presumed to be dissolved and cannot be an impediment to a later marriage.[182] This presumption, which does not require that the presumed death of the spouse be declared by a court, is also applicable to later common law marriages.

The presumption of the death of a spouse is then applied if one spouse has petitioned for a marital dissolution and the other spouse has objected that the marriage is invalid because he or she was previously married. In *Cann v. Cann* (1993), Charles had entered into a ceremonial marriage with Ilonka in 1968. They had a mutual child. Ilonka disappeared in 1970 without being heard from again. Charles began to live with Grace in 1971, who in 1987 petitioned for a divorce, maintenance, and a division of property, claiming that they had lived in a common law marriage. Charles objected, arguing that no common law marriage had been established because Ilonka had not been declared dead, and his marriage with her was an impediment to the marriage with Grace. The Pennsylvania Superior Court stated that, in accordance with the presumption that a person was presumed dead after an absence of seven years, Charles' marriage with Ilonka was dissolved. Any impediment to the common law marriage between Charles and Grace was removed in 1977; a common law marriage,

---

179 *In re Duncan's Estate*, 190 S.C. 211, 2 S.E.2d 388, 390 (1939); and *Williams v. Williams*, 63 Wis. 58, 23 N.W. 110 (1885).

180 *Day v. Day*, 216 S.C. 334, 58 S.E.2d 83 (1950).

181 *See* 22 Am.Jur.2d (1970), Death § 304; 23 PA. CONS. STAT. ANN. § 1701 (West 2003); *In re Estate of Claveria v. Claveria*, 615 S.W.2d 164, 165 (Tex. 1981). *Compare* today TEX. FAM. CODE ANN. § 1.102 (West 2002); *Walker v. Walker*, 218 Ala. 16, 117 So. 472 (1928) (if the parties have entered into a ceremonial marriage prior to the passing of seven years after the disappearance of a previous spouse, and the cohabitation continues after the seven-year time period, a common law marriage can be established); *Scott v. Jefferson*, 174 Ga.App. 651, 331 S.E.2d 1, 3-4 (1985); *Brown v. State*, 208 Ga. 304, 66 S.E.2d 745 (1951); *see also* GA. CODE ANN. § 24-4-21 (West 2003). It has been stated that the person in question must be absent from the place of residency and not heard from for seven years, and that the actual residence be unknown. The person cannot have contact with those persons with whom they usually communicate, *see Francis v. Francis*, 180 Pa. 644, 646-47 (1897). Certain states apply a five-year period, *see, e.g.*, UTAH CODE ANN. § 75-1-107 (Michie 2003).

182 *Davis v. Whitlock*, 90 S.C. 233, 73 S.E. 171 (1911); *Smith v. Fuller*, 138 Iowa 91, 108 N.W. 765 (1906); *In re Duncan's Estate*, 190 S.C. 211, 2 S.E.2d 388 (1939); *Day v. Day*, 216 S.C. 334, 58 S.E.2d 83 (1050); *Hill v. Shreve*, 448 P.2d 848 (Okla. 1968); and *Barnett v. Barnett*, 262 Ala. 655, 80 So.2d 626 (1955).

thereafter, was established; and Grace was entitled to a divorce in the marriage.[183]

The presumption that the spouse in the previous marriage is deceased has also been applied in cases in which the other spouse has died and the spouse of the second marriage has claimed to be the administrator of the estate in the capacity of the deceased's widow. In *Hill v. Shreve* (1968), Nell first formally married Roy and they had a mutual son. Nell began a relationship with Curtis directly after Roy left their home in 1928, without obtaining a divorce. Roy's last contact with his son was sometime between 1930 and 1935. Nell and Curtis lived together, thereafter, until Nell's death in 1967. The Oklahoma Supreme Court found that no evidence had been produced concerning whether Roy was alive at the time of Nell's death. The son, who naturally ought to have had some communication with his father, had not seen him after a visit seven years after Roy had left the family. The court found that Nell and Curtis, who had lived together for approximately forty years, were united in a common law marriage at the time of her death.[184]

The presumption of the spouse's death can be rebutted with evidence that the spouse was alive at the time of the commencement of the later marriage,[185] or in certain cases, that there was a reason for the absence. However, not every kind of counter-evidence is accepted. In *Brown v. State* (1951), the parties had lived in a claimed common law marriage for eleven years. Both of the parties, however, had previously entered into ceremonial marriages with other spouses, and then separated. As the previous spouses had not been heard from for more than seven years, and the cohabitation continued after the expiration of the period, the parties were presumed to be competent to form a common law marriage.[186] One spouse testified that she had heard that her previous spouse "was in Kirkland, Georgia,"

183 *Cann v. Cann,* 632 A.2d 322 (Pa.Super. 1993). Among older cases, *see In re McCausland's Estate,* 213 Pa. 189, 110 Am.St.Rep. 540, 62 A. 780, 781 (1906), in which only two years proceeded the later marriage and in which the court found that, when the seven-year period expired, there was no presumption stating when during the seven-year period the former spouse is presumed to have died, and that it was possible to presume that the death had occurred prior to the marriage, at least in cases concerning the legitimacy of children. In other cases, the death has been presumed to have occurred at the end of the seven-year period. *Compare Sharpe v. Federal Window & Office Cleaning Co.,* 144 Pa.Super. 231, 19 A.2d 509 (1941), in which the presumption was not applied, as only approximately one year had passed since the disappearance and the commencement of a common law marriage.

184 *Hill v. Shreve,* 448 P.2d 848 (Okla. 1968). With respect to the presumption in favor of the later marriage, *see also Norton v. Coffield,* 357 P.2d 434 (Okla. 1960).

185 *Thomas v. Thomas,* 124 Pa. 646, 17 A. 182 (1889).

186 *Brown v. State,* 208 Ga. 304, 66 S.E.2d 745 (1951). *See also* GA. CODE ANN. § 24-4-21 (West 2003). A similar principle is applied in certain jurisdictions to persons imprisoned sentenced to the death penalty or for life. Their spouses can remarry without dissolving the marriage, *see Zizzo v. Zizzo,* 41 Misc.2d 928, 247 N.Y.S.2d 38 (1964); and *Brookman v. Brookman,* 161 Misc. 741, 292 N.Y.S. 918 (1937).

but she had not investigated the rumor. This was not considered sufficient to rebut the presumption. Certain courts have drawn a distinction between cases in which one has "heard from" and "heard of" the former spouse. With the former, but not the latter, the presumption has been found rebutted.[187]

If a person has been absent for a period shorter than seven years, the opposite presumption has been applied, that the person is still alive. With respect to married persons, this presumption collides with the presumption in favor of the later marriage, based on the assumption that the first marriage was dissolved by death. In this competing situation, the courts, as a rule, have found the latter presumption to be stronger. A spouse from a previous marriage who has been absent fewer than seven years is consequently presumed dead.[188] Certain courts have attempted to harmonize the presumptions by holding that the period of seven years does not specify precisely when in the period the spouse is considered to have become deceased.[189]

5.4 Summary and Conclusions

1. *Generally on the Requirement of Capacity*

This chapter began with a discussion as to how the state, for the purpose of preventing unsuitable relationships and family building, has always had a strong interest in defining the capacity to marry. The legislation, therefore, has always contained requirements concerning age, sex, consanguinity, monogamy, physical and mental conditions, etc., requirements based on ethical, religious, medical, and social mores. The legislative method chosen by lawmakers to guard this interest has primarily been preventive. Through licensing procedures, the state seeks to prevent ceremonial marriages between parties who lack capacity, as defined by law.

Even the formation of a common law marriage is based on the capacity of the parties to be able to enter into a marriage with each other. The capacity requirements applied to such marriages are principally the same as those applicable to ceremonial marriages. The requirements are based on the same fundamental values and serve the same purpose as for

187 *Moore v. Miller*, 147 Pa. 378 (1892). Neither has the statement that someone "supposed him to be living" been seen as sufficient, *see Whiteside's App.*, 23 Pa. 114, 116 (1854).

188 *Shepard v. Carter*, 86 Kan. 125, 119 P. 533 (1911); *Murchinson v. Green*, 128 Ga. 339, 57 S.E. 709 (1907); *Smith v. Fuller*, 138 Iowa 91, 108 N.W. 765 (1906); *In re McCausland's Estate*, 213 Pa. 189, 110 Am.St.Rep. 540, 62 A. 780, 781 (1906); and *Chapman v. Cooper*, S.C.L. (5 Rich.) 452 (S.C. 1852). The presumption naturally is rebutted if it is shown that the former spouse is alive, *see Thomas v. Thomas*, 124 Pa. 646, 17 A. 182 (1889).

189 *Smith v. Fuller*, 138 Iowa 91, 108 N.W. 765 (1906).

ceremonial marriages, namely, to prevent unsuitable relationships and family building. This is natural to the extent that common law marriages are viewed as lifelong relationships with all of the legal consequences of formal marriages.

Characteristic for common law marriages, however, is the fact that such marriages are formless, not only with respect to their commencement, but also with respect to the requirement of capacity. No licensing procedure exists for a beforehand assessment of whether any impediments to the marriage exist, and no marriage license is required. Instead, in a common law marriage, the issue of capacity arises afterwards, for example, in connection with a claim by one party upon separation or the death of the other. Another party then can contest the claim on the basis that one or both of the parties were not competent to enter into a marriage, for example, based on age or an already existing ceremonial or common law marriage. This type of chain of events raises the question of whether the capacity requirements, by proving only afterwards that capacity existed, effectively protect the interests for which the capacity requirements were created.

2. *The Age Limit According to the Common Law*

The traditional principle at common law, that a twelve-year-old girl and a fourteen-year-old boy can enter into marriage, continues to be applied, as seen in this chapter, by the courts in the beginning of the 2000s. Determining age limits on the basis of sexual maturity has a historical basis, but appears today to be inappropriate. Individuals, at these ages normally do not have the maturity and experience required to live in a marriage and build a family. As a rule, they most likely know nothing about the regulations pertaining to marriage. The common law principle also has had offensive consequences in case law in which men, indicted for sexual relationships with minor children, are found not guilty based on the defense that they have lived in a common law marriage with the minor child. The explanation, as we have seen, is not only low age limits but also that a common law marriage can be established based on an inferred agreement and a limited actual cohabitation. It is then tempting, as a defense to prosecution, to claim that the parties are united in a common law marriage.

As long as common law marriage is viewed as a lifelong relationship with the same legal consequences as formal marriage, it is natural to adopt the same age requirements for parties entering into such marriages as for those persons entering into ceremonial marriages. This must outweigh the interest of capturing minor children within the marital regulatory system at any price.

3. *The Legislation's Upper Age Limit*

The principles in the common law in the majority of the jurisdictions examined here have been replaced by legislation expressly specifying the age limits for the commencement of a marriage. These age limits, in many cases, have also been found applicable to common law marriages, albeit the formal license requirement has not been applied to these marriages. However, the issue of marital age with respect to common law marriages is addressed after the marriage has been commenced.

To begin with, the upper age limit, which did not exist according to the common law, requires that parties not reaching that age must have the consent of parents, guardians, or the courts to enter into marriage. Even if the legislation of the different states differs as to this limit, the trend during the second half of the 1900s, in accordance with the Uniform Marriage and Divorce Act, has been to adopt the age limit of eighteen years for both men and women, an age limit at which a majority of states have also placed the age of majority and voting rights. As young couples often are not aware of the legal institution of common law marriage, it is unusual for them to seek the consent of their parents.

The legal consequences of a violation of this age limit have varied. Normally, the regulations are directed not at the parties themselves, but at the governmental authorities issuing marriage licenses. A person issuing a marriage license in violation of the specified age limit can consequently be fined. With respect to the parties themselves, the courts have often viewed these regulations as merely directory, with the result that, unless proscribed by law, violations do not affect the validity of the marriage. This legal construction can be explained by the purpose of the regulations as being "preventive, rather than prohibitive." As a consequence, a common law marriage, for example, as can be seen in the cases from Alabama, can be formed without a license and without parental consent without affecting the validity of the marriage at all.

However, as also seen in this chapter, there are jurisdictions in which the lack of parental consent to a marriage between minors affects the validity of the marriage. This is the case, for example, with respect to the new legislation in Texas. Commonly, such a marriage has not been viewed as void, *i.e.*, a nullity, but rather as voidable, *i.e.*, one that can be declared void. A party's standing to file a petition with respect to such a declaration, as a rule, has been limited to the parties themselves, and under certain circumstances, others. The invalidity as a principle begins first when the court's judgment becomes final.

4. *The Lower Age Limits of the Legislation*

As also seen in this chapter, a lower age limit has appeared in American state law below which the parties are not competent to enter into marriage even with the consent of guardians. This age limit, sometimes referred to as the "minimum age for contracting marriage," has varied from case to case and state to state. For example, the age is fourteen years for both men and women in Alabama, today.

A violation of this age limit generally has more impact on the validity of the marriage than a violation of the upper limit at which parental consent is required. The legal consequences applied, however, have varied in the case law.

Certain courts have viewed marriages between persons under this age as simply voidable, not void, meaning that the marriage is valid until it is declared invalid by a court. This stance appears in the case law from Alabama and Oklahoma, but can also be found in legislation elsewhere. The distinction has great practical significance because the issue of the validity of a common law marriage is often raised in a separate lawsuit, sometimes upon the death of one party, at which time no one has standing to petition on validity. The marriage is then viewed as valid until it is declared not so. If the parties have continued their cohabitation until the required age and refrained from petitioning as to validity, they do not need to remarry if they desire to remain married. They are considered to have ratified the marriage contract through the continued cohabitation. The fact that they themselves have not previously petitioned for invalidity can depend on their general lack of awareness that they have lived in a common law marriage. As the marriage is valid until it is declared not so by the court, any children born within the marriage prior to this declaration are legitimate.

Other courts have adopted a stricter stance, finding that a marriage commenced by persons not reaching "the age of consent" is a nullity, *i.e.*, null and void or *void ab initio*. This stance in recent years appears to be gaining a wider acceptance in the legislation. For example, according to South Carolina legislation, a ceremonial as well as common law marriage is a nullity if the man or the woman is under the age of sixteen. No petition for annulment needs to be filed. In any litigation, whenever and wherever it may occur, the fact that the common law marriage is a nullity must be considered. This can be with respect to a petition for divorce, inheritance rights, or a criminal case concerning bigamy or sexual relations with a minor. This is of great significance in those cases in which the issue of the existence of a common law marriage arises many years after the commencement of the marriage.

Further, situations have arisen in which the legal consequence of the minor age of the parties is between void and voidable. A marriage between minors is void from its commencement (*void ab initio*) and no petition as to validity needs to be filed, but the marriage can be brought to life through the continued cohabitation of the parties after they have reached the required age. This is a deviation from the general civil principle that a contract that is a nullity cannot be ratified because something that has never existed is brought to life.

An unsatisfactory uncertainty characterizes the legal consequences of lack of age, and its results, within the legislation as well as the case law.

Lawmakers need to adopt legislating clarifying the legal consequences arising from age requirements that are not fulfilled. Homer Clark has correctly noted that the legislation generally gives rise to confusion when treating the void-voidable distinction.[190] With respect to common law marriages entered into by persons not having reached the minimum age for the commencement of a marriage, we have found, in contrast to Clark, that it is reasonable that such a marriage be void and not voidable. There is a risk that the parties, unaware that they are living in such a marriage, will miss the statute of limitations for petitioning as to invalidity. Further, we have questioned whether the ratification of such a marriage is possible, finding that the need of children for legal protection can be provided through specific legislation granting them legitimacy or in another manner.

5. *The Principle of Monogamy*

As seen in this chapter, the principle of monogamy is also applied to those parties entering into a common law marriage. This appears natural if common law marriages are viewed as lifelong relationships equipped with all of the legal consequences of formal marriage. The civil legal regulations with respect to marital impediments, as well as the criminal regulations as to bigamy, are applicable to such marriages. A previous ceremonial or common law marriage, consequently, is an impediment to the establishment of a new common law marriage, which in its turn can be an impediment to a later ceremonial marriage. As a common law marriage can only be dissolved by formal divorce, such an impediment to a new marriage can exist even if the parties have actually been separated for a long period. As many couples are not aware of the fact that they actually lived in a common law marriage, and therefore separated without formally dissolving the marriage prior to entering into a new common law or ceremonial marriage, bigamy, in the civil law meaning, may not be unusual.

Because the legal consequence is that the later marriage is *void ab initio*, *i.e.*, a nullity, the objection that a new marriage is invalid due to such an impediment can be made in any situation whatsoever, and whenever any party wishes to claim a right based on the existence of the new marriage. Even if it is possible to file for divorce or annulment, there is no requirement to do so. For example, if a party files for divorce from a ceremonial marriage and requests maintenance and a division of property, the opposing party can object, arguing that the marriage is invalid due to a previous formless common law marriage that was never formally dissolved. This legal consequence, in many cases, ought to be viewed as controversial.

---

190 Clark, *supra* note 36, at 167.

If the impediment concerns only one spouse, the other spouse is free to enter into a different marriage without taking any measures to have the interim marriage dissolved or annulled. The principle that the marriage is considered *void ab initio* has great practical significance in cases in which the invalidity is claimed many years after the commencement of the marriage. In such cases, it ought to be difficult to prove a petition for invalidity. This, however, is compensated for by the presumption in favor of the latter of two marriages, which means that an earlier marriage is presumed to be dissolved. Because of this presumption, a de facto separation of a common law marriage sometimes has been called a "poor man's divorce."

It has further been seen in this chapter that a significant evidentiary problem arises in proving whether an impediment existed, perhaps many years after the commencement of the formless marriage. This is a problem specific to common law marriages, which can be formed formlessly through the parties' inferred agreement and which are not registered. The lack of clarity regarding if and when such a marriage was formed entails considerable legal uncertainty. The problems with respect to the evidence and legal certainty, and the conflicts they give rise to, as well as the risk for bigamy, are strong arguments in any discussion concerning the dismantling in the future of the legal institution of common law marriage as discussed further in Chapter 14, "Arguments For and Against Common Law Marriage and Cohabitation Law."

6. *The Presumption in Favor of the Later Marriage*

The presumption in favor of a later marriage, according to the dominant position presented in this chapter, has also been applied in favor of a common law marriage. If one of the parties previously had entered into a ceremonial marriage, it is presumed dissolved. The party maintaining that the later common law marriage is invalid, consequently, must prove not only that the previous marriage was formed, but also that it was not dissolved by divorce, annulment, or death. This results in a heavy burden of proof that traditionally rests on the party attacking the later marriage. The burden is heavy partly as a result of the difficulty of proving the negative of a fact, and also because the evidentiary standard required for rebuting the presumption has been high. The courts traditionally have characterized the presumption as very strong, even as "one of the strongest presumptions in law."

However, as seen here, a significant modification of the traditionally strong presumption has occurred in the case law in two ways. Assessing the evidence "in light of all reasonable inferences," the courts – particularly in Alabama, Iowa, and Pennsylvania – have first invoked specific requirements for the application of the presumption. Second, the strength of the presumption has been weakened by the reduction of the requirements of counter-evidence to rebut the presumption. The most persuasive counter-evidence still consists of records from competent courts as well as from the courts in all the places in which the parties have lived or been listed under from the time of the separation until the commencement of the later marriage, demonstrating that no divorce or annulment had been granted. Other counter-evidence, however, has been found relevant and occasionally sufficient. From this presentation, it can also be seen that the courts have chosen to modify the traditionally strong presumption by requiring the evidentiary standard of a preponderance of evidence for the rebuttal.

The moderate and flexible application of the presumption developed in the case law without a doubt testifies that each individual case can create opportunities to reach a materially reasonable result. At the same time, such an application robs the presumption of its fixedness and function. The more additional requirements exacted to apply the presumption, the easier it becomes to rebut it and the less its value.

The erosion that the presumption has undergone raises the question of whether there are sufficient reasons to retain it and, moreover, whether the interests behind the presumption of favoring a later common law marriage can also be questioned. It can be noted here that the good faith belief of parties that their marriage was valid does not have the same weight with respect to a common law marriage as to a ceremonial marriage. Many couples are not even aware that they have established and live in a common law marriage. This lack of awareness further entails that they, more often than formally married couples, separate without obtaining a formal divorce. Thus, the presumption's premise that an earlier common law marriage had been dissolved, in many cases, lacks a basis in reality. The civil law presumption that a proven, previous marriage continues does not necessarily result in a criminal presumption of bigamy. The revocation of the presumption would entail the uncontestable advantage that no party would be required to prove a negative. The party attacking the validity of a later marriage would then be forced to prove that the earlier marriage was formed. The party claiming that it was dissolved would then need to produce evidence of such a dissolution. In the majority of cases, such a division as to the production of evidence is reasonable from the perspective of the party having the easiest access to the evidence. A disadvantage with the revocation of the presumption would be the effect on the legitimacy of children born in the later marriage; they would receive a less protection. This legal protection, however, ought not to rest upon an assumption which in many cases is not true. The protection instead should be given through specific legislation that legitimizes children despite the invalidity of their parents' marriage or, alternatively, that they be granted certain rights, for example, with respect to inheritance, despite their illegitimate status, in certain states.

A revocation of the presumption would also resolve the contradiction with respect to the seven-year prescription period presumption, that a person is presumed dead after an absence of seven years, but before that is presumed to be alive. This last presumption appears reasonable, and adds weight to the argument in favor of revoking the presumption in favor of the latter of two marriages. The presumption in favor of an already commenced marriage, which gives the party attacking the marriage the burden of proving that it is invalid, ought to be the law.

7. *The Absence of a Licensing Procedure for Common Law Marriages*

The absence of a licensing procedure with respect to common law marriages, as seen in this chapter, appears to seriously jeopardize the state's ability to protect the interests that capacity requirements are meant to protect. Without a prior assessment of whether an impediment to the marriage exists, it is difficult to attempt to prevent unsuitable common law marriages from forming. It is illusory to believe that the parties themselves, at the commencement of the formless relationship, consider the requirements of capacity.

As seen from the cases discussed above, the issue of capacity in alleged common law marriages normally arises first long after the relationship began, for example in connection with one party's claim upon separation or death, based on a common law marriage. The issue of whether the parties, perhaps a long time earlier, were competent to enter into marriage may be difficult to investigate. Such litigation has been characterized by evidentiary difficulties and considerable legal uncertainty.

The problem lies not only with the lack of a licensing procedure, but also with the fact that the relationships are in most cases begun formlessly. A common law marriage can be based on inferred agreements and a short-term cohabitation, having the consequence that the parties themselves in many cases are not even aware of the fact that they have entered into a common law marriage. Few minors presumably request parental consent to enter a common law marriage, and bigamy in a civil meaning is not too unusual among parties who enter into subsequent new common law or ceremonial marriages. Negative consequences pertain not only to the two capacity requirements (age and monogamy) discussed fully in this chapter. The concerns discussed above are also applicable to the other capacity requirements. The licensing procedures that require blood tests, in the interest of preventing the spread of venereal disease and AIDS, are inapplicable and, therefore, ineffective for common law marriages.[191] Impediments based on consanguinity, in general, however, are so anchored

191 In the exceptional case, it has been argued that the requirement of a physician's certificate to receive a marriage license ought to make a common law marriage void. *See* John W. Roxborough, *Antenuptial Physical Examination on Common Law Marriages in Michigan*, 16 U. DET. L.J. 174 (1953). *Compare Woodward Iron Co. v. Dean*, 217 Ala. 530, 117 So. 52 (1928), in which the court considered the regulation to be merely "directory."

in the public legal consciousness that there is no reason to believe that the pertinent regulations are violated to any great extent.[192]

This presentation raises the issue of whether a licensing procedure is of interest even with respect to common law marriage. For many, it appears illogical and unjust that persons entering into a ceremonial marriage are required to fulfill capacity requirements beforehand, while the parties to a common law marriage can avoid the controls imposed by public authority.

Even if there are good reasons to support a licensing procedure for common law marriage, it is important that lawmakers have no illusions about its effects. It is one thing to prevent the formation of a common law marriage, and another to prevent parties from actually cohabiting and building families. Unsuitable relationships and family building will most likely occur without the parties formally satisfying any specified licensing requirements. This civil law method has its limitations. With respect to the penal system, its capabilities are outside of the framework of this work.

However, in the absence of any licensing requirements for common law marriage, it is difficult to protect the interests for which the capacity requirements were created. This, as well as the problems concerning evidence and legal certainty, resulting from an assessment conducted afterwards, are weighty arguments in any discussion concerning the revocation in the future of the legal institute of common law marriage, as discussed further below in Chapter 14, which also addresses capacity issues as to cohabitation legislation.

192 *Compare In re Estate of Stiles*, 59 Ohio St.2d 73, 13 O.Ops.3d 62, 391 N.E.2d 1026 (1979), in which a common law marriage between an uncle and his niece was found *void ab initio.*

CHAPTER 6
The Common Law Marriage Contract

6.1 Introduction

The canon law, as we have seen, applied in a close parallel to Roman law the maxim: *consensus facit nuptias.*[1] That same requirement, of a mutual marital *consensus,* is also used as the determinative factor within the formation of common law marriages. The early leading Scottish case, *Dalrymple v. Dalrymple* (1811) stated: "Marriage being a contract is of course consensual ... for it is of the essence of all contracts to be constituted by the consent of parties ... the consent of two parties expressed in words of present mutual acceptance constituted an actual and legal marriage technically known by the name of *sponsalia per verba de praesenti.*"[2]

The lack of any requirement that the parties express their intent to marry in a ceremony or other formal action, as a determinative factor in a common law marriage, is also made clear in the early American case law. In *Fenton v. Reed* (1809), the New York Supreme Court stated: "No formal solemnization of marriage was required. A contract of marriage made *per verba de praesenti* amounts to an actual marriage, and is as valid as if made *in facie ecclesiae.*"[3] The view expressed in *Fenton,* that within a common law marriage, as with canon law, marriage is considered a contract, also can be found in the leading case of *Meister v. Moore* (1877), where the Supreme Court stated: "That such a contract (*per verba de praesenti*) constitutes a

---

1 *See supra* at 3.3.3.

2 *Dalrymple v. Dalrymple,* 2 Hagg.Cons. 54, 62-64, 161 Eng.Rep. 665, 668-669 (1811). *See also Fryer v. Fryer,* 9 S.C.Eq. (Rich.Cas.) 85, 92 (1832).

3 *Fenton v. Reed,* 4 Johns. 52, 4 Am.D. 244 (N.Y. 1809). *See also Hantz v. Sealy,* 6 Binn. 405 (1814); and *Londonderry v. Chester,* 2 N.H. 268, 278, 9 Am.Dec. 61 (1820). In *Newbury v. Brunswick,* 2 Vt. 151, 160, 19 Am.D. 703 (1829), the court stated that marriage "is viewed both in this State and in England in no other light than a civil contract." *See also Holmes v. Holmes,* 6 La. 463, 470 (1834). In *Mountholly v. Andower,* 11 Vt. 226, 227 (1839), the court stated: "Marriage is a civil contract, and requires the *consensus animorum* as much as any other contract." *See also Ponder v. Graham,* 4 Fla. 23 (1851); *Graham v. Bennett,* 2 Cal. 503, 506 (1852); *Askew v. Dupree,* 30 Ga. 173, 189 (1860) (marriage "is founded in the law of nature" and in society "is a civil contract"); *Physick's Estate,* 2 Brewster 179 (1862); and *Com. v. Stump,* 53 Pa. 132, 136 (1866).

marriage at common law there can be no doubt, in view of the adjudications made in this country, from its earliest settlement to the present day ... Marriage is everywhere regarded as a civil contract."[4]

The principle that informal marriages, as well as formal marriages, are to be based on a marital *consensus*, was accepted in American law during the entire twentieth century. The marriage contract therefore has been a requisite, *i.e.*, a necessary requirement in the establishment of a common law marriage. In each jurisdiction studied in this work, the marital *consensus* of the parties is the most fundamental requirement for the formation of common law marriages.[5]

---

4 *Meister v. Moore,* 96 U.S. 76, 78, 24 L.Ed. 826 (1877). Already in *Hallett v. Collins,* 51 U.S. 174, 181-182 (1850), the Supreme Court stated, in accordance with the medieval canon law principles applied in the Spanish colonies, that "consent alone, joined with the will to marry, constitutes marriage." *See later Maryland v. Baldwin,* 112 U.S. 490, 494, 28 L.Ed. 822, 5 SCt.. 278 (1884); *Travers v. Reinhardt,* 205 U.S. 423, 440, 27 S.Ct. 563, 51 L.Ed 865, 873 (1906). *Compare* The Uniform Marriage and Divorce Act (1970), which defined marriage as "a personal relationship between a man and a woman arising out of a civil contract."

5 **Alabama**: *Buford v. Buford,* 874 So.2d 562 (Ala.Civ.App. 2003); *Creel v. Creel,* 763 So.2d 943, 946 (Ala. 2000); *Hall v. Duster,* 727 So.2d 834, 836 (Ala.Civ.App. 1999); *Krier v. Krier,* 676 So.2d 1335 (Ala.Civ.App. 1996); and *Adams v. Boan,* 559 So.2d 1084, 1085 (Ala. 1990). **Colorado**: *Salzman v. Bachrach,* 996 P.2d 1263 (Colo. 2000); *In re Marriage of Cargill & Rollins,* 843 P.2d 1335, 1339 (Colo. 1993); *People v. Lucero,* 747 P.2d 660, 663 (Colo. 1987); *Crandell v. Resley,* 804 P.2d 272, 276 (Colo.App. 1990); and *In re Custody of Nugent,* 955 P.2d 584, 588 (Colo.App. 1997). **District of Columbia**: *Mesa v. United States,* 875 A.2d 79 (D.C.App. 2005); *Coates v. Watts,* 622 A.2d 25 (D.C.App. 1993); and *East v. East,* 536 A.2d 1103 (D.C.App. 1988). **Georgia**: *In re Estate of Love,* 274 Ga.App. 316, 618 S.E.2d 97 (2005); *Finch v. Dasgupta,* 251 Ga.App. 637, 555 S.E.2d 22 (2001); *Ridley v. Grandison,* 260 Ga. 6, 389 S.E.2d 746 (1990); *In re Estate of Wilson,* 512 S.E.2d 383 (Ga.App. 1999); and Ga. Code Ann. § 19-3-1. Observe that common law marriage, as was mentioned in chapter 1, was repealed in Georgia January 1, 1997, however not retroactively, *see* Ga. Code Ann. §§ 19-3-1.1 (West 2003). **Idaho**: *In re Estate of Wagner,* 126 Idaho 848, 893 P.2d 211, 214 (1995); *Metro. Life Ins. Co. v. Johnson,* 103 Idaho 122, 645 P.2d 356, 360 (1982); and Idaho Code Ann. § 32-201 (Michie 2003). Observe that common law marriage, as was mentioned in chapter 1, was repealed in Idaho January 1, 1996, however not retroactively, *see* Idaho Code Ann. § 32-201 (2) (Michie 2003). **Iowa**: *Toom v. Toom,* 710 N.W.2d 258 (Iowa App. 2005); *Snyder-Murphy v. City of Cedar Rapids,* 695 N.W.2d 44 (Iowa App. 2005); *In re Marriage of Martin,* 681 N.W.2d 612, 617 (Iowa 2004); *In re Marriage of Winegard,* 278 N.W.2d 505, 510 (Iowa 1979); *In re Estate of Stodola,* 519 N.W.2d 97, 98 (Iowa App. 1994); *Conklin v. MacMillan Oil Co.,* 557 N.W.2d 102, 105 (Iowa App. 1996); *Fritz v. Mork,* 2001 Iowa App. Lexis 594 (2001); and Iowa Code Ann. § 595.1 (West 2003). **Kansas**: *In re Estate of Antonopoulos,* 268 Kan. 178, 993 P.2d 637 (1999); *Chandler v. Central Oil Corp., Inc.,* 253 Kan. 50, 853 P.2d 649, 650 (1993); *Dixon v. Certainteed Corp.,* 915 F.Supp. 1158, 1160 (D.Kan. 1996); *In re Pace,* 26 Kan.App.2d 538, 989 P.2d 297 (1999); *Thompson v. Barnhart,* 2005 WL 23347 (D.Kan. 2005); and Kan. Stat. Ann. § 23-101 (2002). **Montana**: *In re Ober,* 314 Mont. 20, 62 P.3d 1114 (2003); *In re Estate of Hunsaker,* 968 P.2d 281, 285 (Mont. 1998); and Mont. Code Ann. 40-1-103 (Mont. Leg. Serv. Div. 2003). **Ohio**: *Nestor v. Nestor,* 150 Ohio St.3d 143, 15 O.B.R. 291, 472 N.E.2d 1091, 1094 (1984); *Bevan v. Bevan,* 2006 WL 1519654 (Ohio App. 11 Dist. 2006); *Sulfridge v. Kindle,* 2005 WL 1806482 (Ohio App. 4 Dist. 2005); *Reyes v. Vasquez,* 2005 WL 1389076 (Ohio App. 6 Dist. 2005); *Faison v. Faison,* 2005 WL 1303344 (Ohio App. 8 Dist. 2005); *Harris v. Harris,* 2004 WL 2896422 (Ohio App. 9 Dist. 2004); and *Kowalik v. Kowalik,* 118 Ohio App.3d 141, 691 N.E.2d 1152 (1997). Observe that common law marriage, as was mentioned in chapter 1, was repealed in Ohio

The marriage contract originally was the only required element for the formation of a common law marriage between two persons possessing the legal capacity to marry. This pure contract principle, however, has been somewhat displaced by the evolution of the parties' cohabitation and reputation as husband and wife as a necessary element in addition to the contract, a development discussed in Chapter 8, "Cohabitation, Holding Out, and Reputation as Spouses." These same elements, together with other circumstances, have been accepted as circumstantial evidence from which the courts have inferred a marriage contract. This is of the greatest practical significance, as most couples living in common law marriages have never entered into an explicit contract. These inferred contracts, therefore, are the subject of a specific chapter below, Chapter 7, "Implied Marriage Agreements." That a common law marriage can also be established with the application of presumptions, according to which a marital *consensus* is presumed based on the parties' cohabitation and reputation as husband and wife, is the subject of Chapter 9, "Burdens of Proof and Presumptions." The possibility of establishing inferred agreements in common law marriages has also influenced the actual structure of the contract, an issue discussed in this chapter.

This chapter focuses on certain basic issues with respect to the contract forming a common law marriage, namely the nature of the marriage contract, the content of the marital intent, the distinction between contracts *de praesenti* and *de futuro*, the express contract, and specific issues arising with respect to disparities between the actual intent and the expression of intent (sham marriages). The future need for the marriage contract as the determinative element of a common law marriage, as well as the different

October 10, 1991, however not retroactively, *see* OHIO REV. CODE ANN. § 3105.12 (B) (1, 2) (WEST 1991). **Oklahoma**: *Standefer v. Standefer,* 26 P.3d 104 (Okla. 2001); *Davis v. State,* 103 P.3d 70, 82 (Okla.Cr.App. 2004); *In re Estate of Stinchcomb,* 674 P.2d 26 (Okla. 1983); *Earnheart v. Earnheart,* 979 P.2d 761, 763 (Okla.Civ.App.Div. 3 1999); and 43 OKLA. STAT. § 1 (1999). **Pennsylvania**: *Staudenmayer v. Staudenmayer,* 714 A.2d 1016 (Pa. 1998); 23 PA. STAT ANN. § 1102 (West 2003); *Int'l Painters and Allied Traders Ind. Pensions Fund v. Calabro,* 312 F.Supp.2d 697 (E.D.Pa. 2004); and *Perotti v. Perotti,* 868 A.2d 1240 (Pa.Super. 2005). Observe that common law marriage, as was mentioned in chapter 1, was repealed in Pennsylvania in 2005, however not retroactively, *see* 23 PA. CONS. STAT. ANN. 1103 (WEST 2005). **Rhode Island**: *DeMelo v. Zompa,* 844 A.2d 174, 177 (R.I. 2004); and *Sardonis v. Sardonis,* 106 R.I. 469, 261 A.2d 22, 24 (1970). **South Carolina**: *Callen v. Callen,* 365 S.C. 618, 620 S.E.2d 59, 62 (2005); *Kirby v. Kirby,* 270 S.C. 137, 241 S.E.2d 415, 416 (1978); *Cathcart v. Cathcart,* 414 S.E.2d 811 (S.C.App. 1992); and *Barker v. Barker,* 330 S.C. 361, 499 S.E.2d 503, 506 (App. 1998). **Texas**: *Claveria v. Claveria,* 615 S.W.2d 164, 166 (Tex. 1981); *Brooks v. State,* 686 S.W.2d 952, 954 (Tex.Crim.App. 1985); *Durand v. State,* 881 S.W.2d 569, 576 (Tex.App. 1994); *Dalworth Trucking Co. v. Bulen,* 924 S.W.2d 728, 737 (Tex.App. Texarkana 1996); *Ballesteros v. Jones,* 985 S.W.2d 485, 490 (Tex.App.-San Antonio 1998); *Nava v. Reddy Partnership/Quail Chase,* 988 S.W.2d 346 (Tex.App.-Houston 1st District 1999); *Eris v. Phares,* 39 S.W.3d 708 (Tex.App.-Houston, 1 Dist. 2001); *Ganesan v. Vallabhaneni,* 96 S.W.3d 345 (Tex.App.-Austin 2002); *Nichols v. Lightle,* 153 S.W.3d 563, 570 (Tex.App.-Amarillo 2004); and TEX. FAM. CODE ANN. § 2.401(a)(2) (Vernon 2005). **Utah**: UTAH CODE ANN. § 30-1-4.5 (Supp. 1987); and *Whyte v. Blair,* 885 P.2d 791 (Utah 1994).

functions different contractual constructions can assume, are discussed in Chapter 13, "The Constitutive Requisites in the Future."

6.2 The Nature of the Marriage Contract

6.2.1 A Contract *sui generis*

Despite the fact that formal and informal marriages in American law are principally considered contracts, they are not typical civil contracts. Instead, they are contracts *sui generis*, contracts of a peculiar or unique nature. The uniqueness of the marriage contract is characterized by both the contracting parties' intimacy with each other and how the legal ramifications of the contract affect personal relationships. Moreover, in American law, marriage confers a special status, based on the idea that marriage is entered into not only for the benefit of the parties, but also for the benefit of any children, the family as a unit, and society. Thus, marriage is not considered to simply pertain to the parties, but is also one of the fundamental institutions in a civilized, Christian society. The state, therefore, has a strong interest in both formal and informal marriages, and, in some cases, is even considered a third party to the contract.[6]

6 *West v. West,* 294 Ill.App.3d 356, 689 N.E.2d 1215, 1218 (1998) ("Marriage is a three party contract between the man, the woman, and the state"); *Rogers v. Webb,* 558 N. W.2d 155, 157 (Iowa 1997) ("preservation of marital relationship is fundamental public policy"); and *Randolph v. Randolph,* 937 S.W.2d 815, 821 (Tenn. 1996) ("the State has an interest and is party to every marriage"). In *Elden v. Sheldon,* 46 Cal.3d 267, 250 Cal.Rptr. 254, 758 P.2d 582 (1988), the court held that "marriage is a civil contract of so solemn and binding a nature ... that the consent of the parties alone will not constitute marriage ... the consent of the state is also required." *See also In re Estate of Bivians,* 98 N.M. 722, 652 P.2d 755, 748 (1982) ("in New Mexico, marriage is a civil contract ... It is also a contract in which the public is interested and to which the state is a party"). In the case of *In re Estate of Stiles,* 59 Ohio St. 2d 73, 391 N.E.2d 1026, 1027 (1979), concerning a common law marriage, the court stated: "The state has an interest in all marriages and is virtually a party to them." *See also Loving v. Virginia,* 338 U.S. 1, 7 (1967) ("marriage is a social relation subject to the State's police power"); *In re Binger's Estate,* 158 Neb. 444, 63 N.W.2d 784 (1954); *Catlett v. Chestnut,* 146 So. 241 (Fla. 1933); *Collins v. Hoag & Rollins Inc.*, 241 N.W. 766, 767 (Neb. 1932); and *Potter v. Potter,* 133 So. 94 (Fla. 1931). *See also Parke v. Parke,* 25 Haw. 397, 404 (1920); *Lauer v. Banning,* 131 N.W. 783, 784 (Iowa 1911) ("Marriage under our law is a contract – a civil contract. But it is *sui generis*...The state has a peculiar interest in such a contract..."). In the case of *In re McLaughlin's Estate,* 4 Wash. 570, 30 P. 651, 657 (1892), the court opined that marriage represents "the best interests of society and the preservation of the home and family – the foundation of all society." In *Maynard v. Hill,* 125 U.S. 190, 211, 8 S.Ct. 723, 31 L.Ed. 654 (1888) the Court stated: "It is an institution, in the maintenance of which in its purity the public is deeply interested, for it is the foundation of the family and of society, without which there would be neither civilization nor progress." *See also Noel v. Ewing,* 9 Ind. 37 (1857) ("an object of the deepest public concern"). In *Stevenson v. Gray,* 17 Mon. 193 (1856), the court held that marriage is not only a contract, but is also grounded in nature and forms a fundamental basis for society. *See also Dunbarton v. Franklin,* 19 N.H. 257, 264-265 (1848) (the marriage contract "on which the rights and duties of the whole community depend").

The resulting contractual rights and obligations are seldom based on negotiations.[7] Consequently, the legal ramifications of the agreement to the parties themselves are secondary, while those resulting from the legislation and case law take precedence.[8] Many of these latter legal ramifications cannot be amended by agreement or contract between the parties,[9] albeit the freedom to contract has been expanded in modern times.[10]

7 RESTATEMENT (SECOND) OF CONTRACTS 190 (1981) states that "the marital relationship has not been regarded by the common law as contractual in the usual sense. Many terms of the relationship are seen as largely fixed by the state and beyond the power of the parties to modify." *See also* Ira Mark Ellman, *Contract Thinking Was Marvin's Fatal Flaw,* 76 NOTRE DAME L. REV. 1365 (2001).

8 *See Milford v. Worchester,* 7 Mass. 48 (1810); *Grisham v. State,* 10 Tenn. 589 (1831); *Ditson v. Ditson,* 4 R.I. 87, 101 (1856); *Noel v. Ewing,* 9 Ind. 37 (1857) ([A] status or institution. As such, it is not so much the result of private agreement, as of public ordination); *Adams v. Palmer,* 51 Me. 481, 483 (1863); and *Wade v. Kalbfleisch,* 58 N.Y. 282, 284 (1874). *Compare Hendrick v. Hendrick,* 976 P.2d 1071, 1072 (Okla.App. 1999), where the Court of Civil Appeals states, with respect to ceremonial marriages: "Marriage and divorce are creatures of statute with the State having exclusive control over the establishment, maintenance and termination of the marital relationship." *See further* Note, *Marriage, Contracts and Public Policy,* 54 HARV. L. REV. 473 (1941); Leonore J. Weitzman, *Regulation of Marriage: Tradition and Change,* 62 CAL. L. REV. 1169 (1974); and Howard O. Hunter, *An essay on contract and status: Race, marriage, and the meretricious spouse,* 64 VA. L. REV. 1039, 1045 (1978).

9 An early statement reflecting this can be found in Joseph Story, COMMENTARIES ON THE CONFLICT OF LAWS 101 (Boston, Billiard & Gray Co. 1834): "The contract of marriage is the most important of all human transactions. It is the very basis of the whole fabric of civilized society ... But it differs from other contracts in this: That the rights, obligations, or duties arising from it are not entirely to be regulated by the agreements of parties, but are, to a certain extent, matters of municipal regulation, over which the parties have no control by any declaration of their will." *See also Sheffield v. Sheffield,* 3 Tex. 86 (1848), where the first Chief Justice of the Texas Supreme Court stated: "The parties have pledged themselves, not only for their own happiness, but for purposes important to society, to live together during the term of their natural lives ... It is regarded by all Christian nations as the basis of civilized society, of sound morals and of the domestic affections: and the relationships, duties, obligations, and consequences flowing from the contract are so important to the peace and welfare of society as to have placed it under the control of special municipal regulations, independent of the will of the parties." *See also Ditson v. Ditson,* 4 R.I. 87, 101 (1856); *Adams v. Palmer,* 51 Me. 481, 483 (1863); *Wade v. Kalbfleisch,* 58 N.Y. 282, 284 (1874); *Maynard v. Hill,* 125 U.S. 190, 210, 8 S.Ct. 723, 31 L.Ed. 654, 659 (1888)("Other contracts may be modified, restricted, or enlarged, or entirely released, upon consent of the parties. Not so with marriage"). *Compare also Baehr v. Lewin,* 852 P.2d 44, 58 (Haw. 1993), in which the court states: "By its very nature, the power to regulate the marriage relation includes the power to determine the requisites of a valid marriage contract and to control the qualifications of the contracting parties, the forms and procedures necessary to solemnize the marriage, the duties and obligations it creates, its effect upon property and other rights, and the grounds for marital dissolution."

10 *See Hudson v. Hudson,* 350 P.2d 596 (Okla. 1960); and *Posner v. Posner,* 233 So.2d 381 (Fla. 1970). *See also* THE UNIFORM PREMARITAL AGREEMENT ACT (1983); Elisabeth S. Scott and Robert E. Scott, *Marriage as Relational Contract,* 84 VA. L. REV. 1225 (1998); Sanford N. Katz, *Marriage as Partnership,* 73 NOTRE DAME L. REV. 1251, 1256 (1998); Ariela R. Dubler, Note, *Governing through Contract: Common Law Marriage in the Nineteenth Century,*107 YALE L.J. 1885, 1907-08 (1998)(status contract); MARGARET F. BRINIG, FROM CONTRACT TO COVENANT: BEYOND THE LAW AND ECONOMICS OF THE FAMILY 6 (2000). *Compare* Marsha Garrison, *Is Consent Necessary? An Evaluation of*

The marriage contract as a contract *sui generis* has been the basis for the conservative application of general contract principles. For our purposes, however, it is important to note that the contractual nature of the agreement is pivotal to the determination of a common law marriage; the marriage contract, in principle, is a necessary requirement for the formation of the legal relationship, while the status of the agreement becomes most important after the marriage has been formed.[11] The parties' rights to freely contract to enter or specifically not enter into a marital relationship, or to participate or not in the applicable marital regulations, belongs to the contractual aspect of their agreement. The choice, however, is limited to the prepackaged rights and obligations made available by the third contractual. As with respect to the "status" package, the principle is mainly, "Take it or leave it!"[12] The general contractual principles that can and ought to be applied to the parties' formless contract to establish a common law marriage are discussed below.[13]

---

the Emerging Law of Cohabitant Obligation, 52 UCLA L. Rev. 815, 826 (2005), who holds that "marital obligation derives from marital commitment."

11 *Randall v. Kreiger,* 23 Wall. 137, 23 L.Ed. 124, 126 (1874) ("Marriage is an institution founded upon mutual consent"); and *Hilton v. Roylance,* 25 Utah 129, 69 P. 660, 663 (1902) ("Marriage, strictly speaking, is not a mere civil contract, but a status created by contract"); and *Hulett v. Carey,* 66 Minn. 327, 69 N.W. 31 (1896) ("The law views marriage as being merely a civil contract, not different from any other contract, except that it is not revocable or dissoluble at the will of the parties. The essence of the contract of marriage is the consent of the parties, as in the case of any other contract"). *See also Riddle v. Riddle,* 26 Utah 268, 72 P. 1081, 1084 (1903). In *Chirelstein v. Chirelstein,* 12 N.J.Super. 468, 79 A.2d 884, 893 (1951), the court stated: "Our cases continue to reiterate that marriage is a civil contract, but the expression means little except that entrance into the marriage state comes only with the simultaneous, voluntary consent of both parties." An excellent summary of the discussion concerning status and contract can be found in Hunter, *supra* note 8, at 1044, in which the author states: "One may be free to choose a status, but one does not necessarily have the right or the power to affect the impact of that status on legal capacity ... Contracting parties have the opportunity, on the other hand, to determine for themselves the parameters of their transaction. They create their own status; they do not simply choose it." With respect to the development of the status principle, *see* D. Engdahl, *Proposal for a Benign Revolution in Marriage Law and Marriage Conflicts Law,* 55 Iowa L. Rev. 56 (1969). *Compare* Leonore J. Weitzman, The Marriage Contract (1981), positing with respect to formal marriage that "there is an implicit contract that governs every marriage - an unwritten contract that is imposed by law," *id. at* XV, and that marriage has been changed from "from a status to a status-contract," *id. at* XIX. Reservations against the idea that marriage is to be viewed as a contract historically have also been made based on the fact that marriages existed before civil laws, *see* Michael F. Walsh, *Marriage and Civil Law,* 23 St. John's L. Rev. 209, 215 (1949).

12 John Austin discusses how "status" is the basis for a "bundle of duties and privileges," *see* John Austin, 2 Lectures on Jurisprudence 697 (5th ed. 1885). *See also* in modern time *In re Estate of Wilson,* 512 S.E.2d 383, 385 (Ga.App. 1999), *In re Estate of Dunn,* 236 Ga.App. 211, 511 S.E.2d 575 (1999), *Wright v. Goss,* 229 Ga.App. 393, 494 S.E.2d 23, 25 (1997) and *Baynes v. Baynes,* 219 Ga.App. 848, 467 S.E.2d 195 (1996) ("legal relationship constituting common law marriage cannot be partial or periodic").

13 *See* § 6.5 regarding express contracts.

With respect to the spouses' legal capacity to enter into a marriage and their ability to terminate the contract, legislation mandates the terms that the parties cannot change.[14] With respect to dissolution, the same regulations are applicable to both common law marriages and formal marriages. Based on the principle that the parties' intent is to be free, voluntary, and understanding,[15] it is possible for a contract to be declared void based on mistake, force, or other grounds. Once a common law marriage has been established, it is protected in the same manner as a formal marriage by the presumption rules until invalidity is established.[16]

The goal of not giving the parties too much contractual freedom has led to the development in the legislation and case law of other requirements for establishing a common law marriage. Thus, the requirement of cohabitation is motivated by the legal ramifications of marriage that result not only from the parties' contract, but also the regulations found in the legislation and case law in which society has a strong interest.[17]

6.2.2 An Express or Implied Contract

In American case law, it has been legio to discuss, in the same manner taught by Peter Lombard in medieval canon law,[18] the marriage contract in terms of *per verba de praesenti,* or *per verba, by verba, by words in,* and *in words of* an immediate consent. This appears in the older case law, for example, in the above mentioned *Fenton v. Reed* (1809) and *Meister v. Moore* (1877), as well as in more modern cases, for example, *Smereczynski v. Secretary* (1991) and *Cann v. Cann* (1993).[19] Despite these terms, it is rare

14 *Maynard v. Hill,* 125 U.S. 190, 210, 8 S.Ct. 723, 31 L.Ed. 654, 659 (1888) ("Other contracts may be ... entirely released, upon consent of the parties. Not so with marriage"). That marriage is considered to be more than just a contract is made clear in *Bishop v. Brittain Invest Co.,* 229 Mo. 699, 129 S.W. 668 (1910) ("only a court can dissolve it; it may not be rescinded at will, like other contracts; only one such can exist between near blood kin; it legitimizes children; it touches the laws of inheritance; it affects title to real estate; it provides for the perpetuity of the race; it makes a hearthstone, a home, a family; it marks the line between the morals of the barnyard and the morals of civilized men, between reasoning affection and animal lust"). *See also Jackson v. United States,* 14 F.Supp. 132 (1936), *aff'd,* 89 F.2d 572 (1937), *aff'd,* 302 US 628, 82 L.Ed 488, 58 S.Ct 30 (1938) ("Marriage in South Carolina is not a civil contract, but a status"); and *Silva v. Merritt Chapman & Scott Corporation,* 52 R.I. 30, 156 A. 512, 513 (1931), where the court emphasizes the state's interest in the marriage contract, "[a] lthough marriage is of the nature of a civil contract, it is a contract which is subject to the regulation of the state, in which in its inception or its dissolution the state has a vital interest."

15 *See Johnson v. Johnson,* 104 N.W.2d 8 (N.D. 1960).

16 With respect to invalidity due to lack of legal capacity, *see* Chapter 5.

17 *Grigsby v. Reib,* 105 Tex. 597, 153 S.W. 1124 (1913). *See* Section 8.3.1.

18 Peter Lombard: *non quilibet sed per verba expressus* (Sent IV, D 27 § c). With respect to the canon law's attitude towards the requirement of a verbal expression, *see* Section 3.3.

19 *Fenton v. Reed,* 4 Johns. 52, 4 Am.D. 244 (N.Y. 1809); *Dalrymple v. Dalrymple,* (1811) 2 Hagg.Cons. 54, 62-64, 161 Eng.Rep. 665, 668-669; *Com. v. Stump,* 53 Pa. 132, 136 (1866) ("by words in"); *Meister v. Moore,* 96 U.S. 76, 78 (1877); *Baker v. Mitchell,* 143 Pa.

for the courts to require a verbal contract. The courts in Pennsylvania, however, require that the parties' marital *consensus* be expressed in a verbal contract,[20] and even in that jurisdiction, the courts appear willing to make exceptions to the rule.[21] For example, in *Staudenmayer v. Staudenmayer* (1998), the Pennsylvania Supreme Court required an exchange of words in the present tense, and, in that case, a common law marriage could not be established because no such exchange was proven.[22] Whether a

---

Super. 50, 17 A.2d 740 (1941) ("by words in"); *In re Erickson's Estate,* 75 S.D. 342, 64 N.W.2d 316, 319 (1954) ("consent by words of the present tense"); *Rager v. Johnstown Traction Co.*, 184 Pa.Super. 474, 134 A.2d 918, 920 (1957); *Smereczynski v. Sec'y, DHHS,* 944 F.2d 296, 298 (6th Cir. 1991) ("words of present intent"); and *Cann v. Cann,* 632 A.2d 322, 325 (Pa.Super.Ct. 1993); *See also* Caleb Foot et al., Cases and Materials on Family Law 17 (3d ed. 1985) ("words of the present tense").

20 In *Bell v. Ferraro,* 849 A.2d 1233 (Pa.Super. 2004), the court required "an exchange of words in the present tense" and did not find a common law marriage proven. In *Brandywine PaperBd. v. W.C.A.B. (Zittle),* 751 A.2d 1205 (Pa.Cmwlth. 2000), the court found an oral contract proven. In *Staudenmayer v. Staudenmayer,* 714 A.2d 1016, 1020 (Pa. 1998), because of the absence of "an exchange of words in the present tense," the court found that a common law marriage did not exist. *See also Africa v. Vaughan,* 998 F.Supp. 552, 556 (E.D.Pa. 1998); *State Farm Fire & Cas. Co. v. Platt,* 4 F.Supp.2d 399, 404 (E.D.Pa. 1998); *Com. v. Wilson,* 672 A.2d 293, 301 (Pa. 1996); *Cann v. Cann,* 632 A.2d 322, 325 (Pa.Super. 1993); *Eagle v. W.C.A.B. (Bahorich),* 602 A.2d 387, 388 (Pa.Commw.Ct. 1992); *Com. v. Gorby,* 588 A.2d 902, 907 (Pa. 1991); *Com. v. McLean,* 387 Pa.Super. 354, 564 A.2d 216, 220 (1989); and *Canute v. Canute,* 384 Pa.Super. 60, 557 A.2d 772, 774 (1989). In *Com. v. Smith,* 511 Pa. 343, 513 A.2d 1371, 1375-1376 (1986), the Pennsylvania Supreme Court stated that common law marriage "must be created by an exchange of words in the present tense" and that "no such exchange of words occurred." *See also Steadman v. Turner,* 357 Pa.Super. 361, 516 A.2d 21, 23 (1986), *appeal denied,* 531 A.2d 431 (Pa. 1987); *In re Estate of Kovalchick,* 345 Pa. Super. 229, 498 A.2d 374, 377 (1985); and *In re Estate of Rees,* 331 Pa.Super. 225, 480 A.2d 327, 328 (1984). In *Com. v. Sullivan,* 484 Pa. 130, 398 A.2d 978, 980 (1979), the Pennsylvania Supreme Court stated: "The trial court justifiably found that the required words in the present tense were not uttered." *See also In re Gower's Estate,* 445 Pa. 554, 284 A.2d 742, 743 (1971); *Brown v. Atlantic & Gulf Stevedores, Inc.,* 2 Pa. Commw. 481, 279 A.2d 372, 373 (1971); *Donaldson v. P.J. Oesterling & Sons, Inc.,* 199 Pa.Super. 637, 186 A.2d 653, 655-656 (1962); *In Manfredi Estate,* 399 Pa. 285, 159 A.2d 697, 700 (1960); *Wagner's Estate,* 398 Pa. 531, 159 A.2d 495, 498 (1960); *Rager v. Johnstown Traction Co.,* 184 Pa.Super. 474, 134 A.2d 918 (1957); *In re Blecher's Estate,* 381 Pa. 138, 112 A.2d 129 (1955); *In re Stauffer's Estate,* 372 Pa. 537, 94 A.2d 726, 728 (1953); *In re Rosenberger's Estate,* 362 Pa. 153, 65 A.2d 377, 379 (1949); *Fiedler v. Nat'l Tube Co.,* 161 Pa.Super. 155, 53 A.2d 821, 822-823 (1947); *Wagner v. Wagner,* 152 Pa.Super 4, 30 A.2d 659, 661 (1943); *Wolford v. Whiterock Quarries,* 144 Pa.Super. 577, 20 A.2d 887, 888 (1941); *Baker v. Mitchell,* 143 Pa.Super. 50, 17 A.2d 738, 740 (1941); *Balanti v. Stineman Coal & Coke Co.,* 131 Pa.Super. 344, 200 A. 236 (1938); *Caddy v. Johnstown Firemen's Relief Ass'n,* 129 Pa.Super. 493, 196 A. 590 (1938); *In re Osterling's Estate,* 323 Pa. 23, 185 A. 790 (1936); *In re McGrath's Estate,* 319 Pa. 309, 179 A. 599, 602 (1935); *In re Krystkiewicz's Estate,* 310 Pa. 298, 165 A. 230, 231 (1933); *In re Ward's Estate,* 296 Pa. 20, 145 A. 676, 677 (1929); *Murdock's Estate,* 92 Pa.Super. 275 (1927); *In re Craig's Estate,* 273 Pa. 530, 117 A. 221, 222 (1922); *Com. v. Haylow,* 17 Pa.Super. 541, 547 (1901); and *Com. v. Stump,* 53 Pa. 132, 136 (1866).

21 *See* Section 7.4.

22 *Staudenmayer v. Staudenmayer,* 714 A.2d 1016, 1022 (Pa. 1998). *See also Perotti v. Meredith,* 868 A.2d 1240 (Pa.Super. 2005); *Int'l Painters and Allied Traders Ind. Pensions Fund v. Calabro,* 312 F.Supp.2d 697, 702 (E.D.Pa. 2004); and *In re Veneziale,* 267 B.R. 695, 700 (Bkrtcy.E.D.Pa. 2001).

common law marriage in Pennsylvania can be established if no evidence can be offered with respect to an actual contract, and by applying a presumption based on cohabitation and reputation, is a separate issue discussed further in Chapter 9, "Burdens of Proof and Presumptions." The courts in the District of Columbia also require that the parties' marital *consensus* be expressed in a verbal contract. In *Coates v. Watts* (1993), the Court of Appeals for the District of Columbia found that no evidence had been presented demonstrating that the parties "agreed, in words of the present tense, to be married," thus no common law marriage could be found to exist.[23] If the parties have entered into such a contract despite the existence of an impediment, no new contract is required after the removal of the impediment.[24] In case law from the District of Columbia, an exception to the requirement of an express marriage contract has been made if both of the parties are unavailable to testify, for example, because of death. The contract, under certain circumstances, can then be proven simply with the support of the cohabitation and general reputation as a married couple.[25] The requirements used by the courts in cases

---

23 The requirement of an express contract dates back in the District of Columbia to the case of *Hoage v. Murch Bros. Const. Co.*, 60 App.D.C. 218, 50 F.2d 983, 985 (1931), where the Court of Appeals stated that "an agreement between a man and a woman *per verba de praesenti* to be husband and wife, consummated by cohabitation as husband and wife," created a valid marriage, without more specifically stating whether an expressed contract was a necessary requirement. That issue has not come before the court in its entirety. The United States Court of Appeals went somewhat further in *U.S. Fid. & Guar. v. Britton*, 106 U.S.App.D.C. 58, 269 F.2d 249 (1959), holding that "an express mutual agreement to be husband and wife" must exist, and that a contract had not be proven. The requirement of an express agreement was revisited in *Nat'l Union Fire Ins. Co. v. Britton*, 187 F.Supp. 359 (D.D.C. 1960), where the contract was found proven, and in *Toye v. Toye*, 170 A.2d 778 (D.C.App. 1961), where the contract was not proven. The District of Columbia Court of Appeals went a step further in *McCoy v. District of Columbia*, 256 A.2d 908 (D.D.C. 1969), interpreting *Hoage* to require the existence of a contract *per verba praesenti* and finding that such a contract could not "be inferred from proof of cohabitation and reputation." The court found no evidence of such a contract. The requirement of a verbal contract is seen again in *Marcus v. Director, Office of Wkrs' Comp. Prog.*, 548 F.2d 1044 (D.C.Cir. 1976), in which the United States Court of Appeals stated that a common law marriage can only be established if the parties "mutually agree, in words of the present tense" and no such contract had been proven. The requirement of a verbal contract was reiterated by the District of Columbia Court of Appeals in *East v. East*, 536 A.2d 1103 (D.C.App. 1988), where the contract was proven and in *Coates v. Watts*, 622 A.2d 25 (D.C..App. 1993), where the evidence was considered insufficient. *See also Dickey v. Office of Personnel Management*, 419 F.3d 1336, 1340 (C.A.Fed. 2005). No precise formulations of the contract have been required, however, *see Nat'l Union Fire Ins. Co. v. Britton*, 187 F.Supp. 359 (D.D.C. 1960).

24 *Matthews v. Britton*, 112 U.S.App.D.C. 397, 303 F.2d 408 (1962). *See* Section 7.6.3 *infra*. *See also Lee v. Lee*, 201 A.2d 873 (D.C. App. 1964)(no information as to the original contract), and *Jennings v. Jennings*, 20 Md.App. 369, 315 A.2d 816, 823 (1974)(ceremonial wedding when an impediment existed).

25 The parties' cohabitation and reputation does not, however, demonstrate the existence of a contract if the party alleging the formation of a common law marriage omits a claim as to the existence of a contract or denies the existence of one, *see In re Veneziale*, 267 B.R. 695, 700 (Bkrtcy.E.D.Pa. 2001); *Jackson v. Bowen*, 690 F.Supp. 58, 59

of verbal contracts are discussed in Section 8.5, "The Requirement of Cohabitation," *infra.*

It is worth noting that the parties usually do not enter into any express contract, whether orally or in writing, and courts in jurisdictions other than Pennsylvania and the District of Columbia do not require a verbal contract for establishing a common law marriage.[26] The courts appear, instead, to accept that the parties' marital *consensus* is expressed through inferred or implied agreements evidenced circumstantially. A typical example of this can be found in *Russell v. Russell* (1993), where the Texas Supreme Court, after considerable legislative and judicial debate, declared that a marriage contract for establishing a common law marriage could be proven by "direct or circumstantial evidence."[27] This aspect of the nature of informal marriages is of such import that a later chapter has been devoted to its discussion, Chapter 7, "Implied Marriage Agreements," regarding inferences established by the actions of the parties.

6.2.3 *Consensus Continuus*

It would appear logical for the informal marriage contract upon which a common law marriage is formed to be based upon an agreement existing at a specific point of time – an initial intent – which would be an element in a clearly defined contractual conclusion, as with the majority of other kinds of civil contracts.[28] This would also appear logical according to either the canon law's informal marriage contract, or formal marriage, in which the final contract is considered to be entered into during the

(D.D.C. 1988); *U.S. Fid. & Guar. v. Britton,* 106 U.S.App.D.C. 58, 269 F.2d 249, 252 (1959); *Nat'l Union Fire Ins. Co. v. Britton,* 187 F.Supp. 359 (D.D.C. 1960) (*dictum*); *McCoy v. District of Columbia,* 256 A.2d 908, 910 (D.C. App. 1969) (*dictum*); and *Marcus v. Director, Office of Wkrs.' Comp.. Prog.*, 548 F.2d 1044, 1048 (D.C.Cir. 1976) (*dictum*). In the case of *In re Estate of Foster,* 376 S.E.2d 144, 148 (W.Va. 1988), where both parties were deceased, the West Virginia Supreme Court of Appeals, applying the law of the District of Columbia, found a contract evidenced with the aid of the parties' cohabitation and reputation. In a dictum in *Mesa v. United States,* 875 A.2d 79, 83 (D.C.App. 2005), the court more generally seems to accept circumstantial evidence; and *Dickey v. Office of Personnel Management,* 419 F.3d 1336, 1340 (C.A.Fed. 2005) (direct or circumstantial evidence).

26 A typical viewpoint can be found in *Dibble v. Dibble,* 88 Ohio App. 490, 100 N.E.2d 451, 458-459 (1950) ("there must be a contract in words of present tense" and that such a contract "can be implied from conduct of the parties" and "may be established by circumstantial evidence"). A common law marriage can be established where no verbal contract has been entered into. *See also Gatterdam v. Gatterdam,* 86 Ohio App. 29, 85 N.E.2d 526, 527 (1949); *Markley v. Hudson,* 143 Ohio St. 163, 54 N.E.2d 304 (1944); as well as the Sixth Circuit's application of Ohio law in *Smith-Wilkins v. Sec'y of DHHS,* 880 F.2d 864, 866 (6th Cir. 1989).

27 *Russell v. Russell,* 865 S.W.2d 929, 933 (Tex. 1993), *see also* Section 7.4 *infra.*

28 This has been the basic premise in such classic cases as *Dalrymple v. Dalrymple,* (1811) 2 Hagg.Cons. 54, 62-64, 161 Eng.Rep. 665, 668-669; *Compare Fenton v. Reed,* 4 Johns. 52, 4 Am.D. 244 (N.Y. 1809) (no requirement for a new contract after the removal of the hinder).

wedding ceremony. This reasoning can also be seen in the case law, in which the courts, in examining the question of whether a common law marriage exists, interpret the marriage contract as a formless conclusion of the contract. This is especially true of courts, as in Pennsylvania, that require an express contract. Important issues in such cases are usually when, where, and how the parties entered into the contract.

For example, in *Commonwealth v. Stump* (1866), a woman, after twenty years of cohabitation, alleged that she and the man had entered into a marriage contract, the Pennsylvania Supreme Court raised the following issues: "When was this promise and agreement made?... [I]f that relation were subsequently established, in what words was the contract formed—when was it made, and who witnessed it?"[29] In the absence of evidence, the court did not find that the existence of a contract had been proven and that a common law marriage had been formed. The same view is also expressed in modern case law. In *Africa v. Vaughan* (1998), the United States District Court for the Eastern Division of Pennsylvania required an express agreement and exchange of words. The court found that the man alleging the existence of a common law marriage had not given any evidence as to "when, where or how such a marriage was entered" and that the words stated did "not 'plainly' show the making of a 'civil contract' or 'actual agreement' to form the legal relationship of husband and wife."[30]

---

29 *Com. v. Stump*, 53 Pa. 132, 136 (1866). *See also Young v. Gen. Baking* Co., 104 Ind.App. 658, 662, 12 N.E.2d 1016, 1018 (1938), in which the court states that the woman had not testified that she "at any certain time or place, orally or by written instrument, agreed to take each other as consorts. There is, however, some evidence in the record which tends to prove such fact indirectly; and such facts may be proven by circumstantial evidence." The lack of knowledge as to common law marriage often creates confusion during interrogations. For example, in *French v. State Indus. Accident Comm'n*, 156 Ore. 443, 68 P.2d 466 (1937), the surviving woman was asked: "Q. I am trying to find out as to when, where and how you married Mr. French, if you can tell; did you have a second marriage in 1929? A. If you call that marriage we must have because we were over there a second time. Q. Didn't you marry him the second time and not the first time? A. I don't know. Q. Is that correct? A. I guess so." From later cases, *see also Seagriff v. Seagriff*, 195 N.Y.S.2d 718 (1960); *Peart v. T.D. Bross Line Constr.s Co.*, 45 A.D.2d 801, 357 N.Y.S.2d 53 (1974); and *Com. v. Sullivan*, 484 Pa. 130, 398 A.2d 978 (1979).

30 *Africa v. Vaughan*, 998 F.Supp. 552, 555-556 (E.D.Pa. 1998). *See also Staudenmayer v. Staudenmayer*, 714 A.2d 1016, 1022 (Pa. 1998) (Pennsylvania Supreme Court found that the woman "was unable to recall the specific instance of when she and Theodore said to each other, 'we are husband and wife'." The court could not find for the existence of a contract). In *Brown v. Atlantic & Gulf Stevedores, Inc.*, 279 A.2d 372, 373 (Pa.Commw. Ct. 1971), the court found that there was no evidence supporting the conclusion that "on any specific date there occurred the necessary words in present tense evidencing a marriage contract." *Compare Matter of Estate of McClelland*, 541 P.2d 780, 783 (Mont. 1975) ("The marriage must take place immediately and it cannot be created piecemeal. It comes instantly into being, or it does not come at all"). *See also Matter of Estate of White*, 212 Mont. 228, 686 P.2d 915, 916 (1984). *Compare Matter of Estate of Alcorn*, 868 P.2d 629 (Mont. 1994); and *Matter of Estate of Hunsaker*, 968 P.2d 281 (Mont. 1998); and *Skipworth v. Skipworth*, 360 So.2d 975, 977 (Ala. 1978) ("the operative time is when the agreement is initially entered into"). *See also Adams v. Boan*,

As courts in other jurisdictions generally do not require an express marriage contract to establish a common law marriage, it has not been tenable to require a clearly defined time for the conclusion of the contract. The prevalent acceptance of inferred agreements in the case law has instead contributed to the development of what could be termed a *consensus continuus* or a continued consent, a continuous intent displayed during the cohabitation, similar to the classic Roman law concept of *affectio maritalis.*[31] With this model for consent, establishing when, where, and how the marriage contract has been formed becomes more difficult. The courts have not enforced any strict requirements in this area. Reasoning based on the model of offer and acceptance as part of the marriage contract is not given in these cases.[32] This *consensus* appears to mainly have the function, in different situations, establishing a marriage if no express marriage contract is at hand, or if a contract has been entered into, but is considered invalid.

The Roman *animus* theory can be traced in older and more modern American case law, a fact that has not been given the attention it deserves. This influence in American law appears to be derived from certain Scottish cases that lean toward accepting a *consensus continuus.* In the Scottish case of *Elder v. M'Lean* (1829), the court found that the man's consent was established by the fact that the woman took the place of and was referred to as his wife.[33]

---

559 So.2d 1084, 1087 (Ala. 1990) and *Crossom v. Crossom*, 668 So.2d 868, 872 (Ala.Civ. App. 1995).

31 With respect to Roman law, *see* Section 2.4.2.

32 Examples of exceptional cases where the contractual models of offer and acceptance are mentioned can be found in *Rager v. Johnstown Traction Co.*, 134 A.2d 918, 922 (Pa. Super. 1957); *Anderson v. Anderson,* 131 N.E.2d 301 (Ind. 1956); and *In re Rosenberger's Estate,* 65 A.2d 377, 380 (Pa. 1949). *Compare* The Uniform Commercial Code, § 2-206 (a) (1962): "[A]n offer to make a contract shall be construed as inviting acceptance in any manner and by any medium reasonable in the circumstances."

33 *Elder v. M'Lean,* (1829) 8 S. 62 *See also De Thoren v. Wall,* (1876) 3 R. (H.L.) 28, 33, in which an invalid wedding ceremony was performed. The court found that the parties had come to an unquestionable agreement to live together as man and wife. Their cohabitation was proof of a "continued consent." In the case, the marital consent was considered to exist as soon as the impediment was removed: "It must be inferred that the matrimonial consent was interchanged as soon as the parties were enabled, by the removal of the impediment, to enter into the contract." This same view is expressed in *Campbell v. Campbell,* (The Breadalbane case), (1866) 4 M. 867; (1867) 5 M. (H.L.) 115, where Lord Westbury stated: "You must infer the consent to have been given at the first moment when you find the parties able to enter into the contract." *See also Chamberlain v. Chamberlain,* 68 N.J.Eq. 736, 62 A. 680 (E & A 1905) referring to *Campbell. See also Smith v. Smith,* 84 Ga. 490, 11 S.E. 496 (1890) (parties entered into a ceremonial marriage which was invalid due to the fact that the man was of a minor age and parental consent had not been given. The parties continued their cohabitation. When the minor reached the age of majority, the issue of whether an "informal marriage" was established was raised. The court stated that it could occur through ratification when the parties reached their legal majority and that continuous cohabitation could be sufficient proof of such a ratification). *See also*

Older American case law, as with the Scottish case law, began to apply the principle in cases of the ceremonial marriage deemed invalid because of a legal impediment, despite parties' expression of a marital *consensus.* If the parties, after the removal of the impediment, continued their cohabitation, it considered by the courts to be evidence of a continued marital *consensus.* For example, *in Addison v. Addison* (1938), the Georgia Supreme Court stated that the continued cohabitation of the parties as husband and wife resulted in the "original declaration of intent to be treated as continuing."[34] The use of *consensus continuus,* in these cases, naturally is explained in part by the strong expression the parties' marital *consensus* given by the formal wedding ceremony. However, if the marriage is invalid, and no new express contract has been entered into after the removal of the impediment, the use of the principle *consensus continuus* can be explained by the acceptance of the cohabitation as an expression of *consensus.* The absence of a final contractual conclusion on a certain day, in the majority of the cases, raises the question of at what time the marriage came into existence.[35] A common law marriage generally has been

---

Smith v. Reed, 145 Ga. 724, 89 S.E. 815 (1916), with a somewhat deviating reasoning as recounted in the next note, in which reference is made to *Campbell.*

34 *Addison v. Addison,* 186 Ga. 155, 197 S.E. 232, 233 (1938) (an impediment to the ceremonial marriage existed due to a previous marriage that later was dissolved). In *Applegate v. Applegate,* 118 Misc. 359, 193 N.Y.S. 494, 496 (Sup.Ct. 1922), the court noted that the parties "always intended to be husband and wife in ignorance of the impediment thereto and regardless of its removal." For a situation similar to that of the early Georgian case, *see Smith v. Reed,* 145 Ga. 724, 89 S.E. 815, 816 (1916), where the court stated: "The declaration of intent to be husband and wife should be treated as continuing." *See Gorman v. Gorman,* 166 S.W. 123 (Tex.Civ.App. 1914) and *Chamberlain v. Chamberlain,* 68 N.J.Eq. 736, 62 A. 680 (E & A 1905) (the ceremonial marriage was invalid due to an impediment. As soon as it was removed, the court found "the lawful intent still continuing"). Among later cases, *see Robertson v. Robertson,* 90 Ga.App. 576, 83 S.E.2d 619 (1954) ("but where the matrimonial cohabitation continues after the impediment is removed, it is to be presumed that the intent continues...") *Compare* a somewhat different reasoning in *Smith v. Smith* in the previous note. In *Bolz v. Bolz,* 92 N.E.2d 365 (1950), the court found that the intent the parties gave expression to during the wedding ceremony which was invalid due to an impediment "could be found to continue." *See also Albina Engine and Machine Works v. O'Leary,* 328 F.2d 877, 881 (9th Cir. 1964) (applying Idaho law) in which a ceremonial marriage was invalid due to an impediment. The court stated that "consent is a continuing thing," and consequently found that a common law marriage existed when the impediment had been removed.

35 In *Adger v. Ackerman,* 114 Fed. 124, 129 (8th Cir. 1902), the court stated that "slight circumstances may be sufficient to establish a change from an illicit to a legal relationship, and proof of its time or place is not indispensable." *See also Badger v. Badger,* 88 N.Y. 554, 42 Am.Rep. 263 (1882) ("a change may occur and be satisfactorily established, although the precise time or occasion cannot be clearly ascertained"); and *Russell v. Russell,* 838 S.W.2d 909 (Tex.App. 1992) (a common law marriage was found to exist, but the Court of Appeals found that the trial court had insufficient evidence "to uphold a finding that March 22, 1972 was the beginning date of the common law-marriage"). In *Hurley v. Hurley,* 222 Mont. 287, 721 P.2d 1279 (1986), the woman stated that "[a]t some point, there was a decision to become man and wife" occurring "when I agreed to move to Corning." The Montana Supreme Court found that the trial court had not erred in finding that the parties had entered into a common

considered to exist at the point of the removal of the impediment, assuming that the other requirements for the establishment of the marriage are also fulfilled. The impediment can be removed, for example, by the death of a previous spouse, without any clear conclusion of the contract between the parties. The parties perhaps did not even have knowledge about the removal of the impediment.[36]

In certain cases of an invalid ceremonial marriage, the courts' reasoning has referred back to the original contract, which is then "ratified and adopted" through cohabitation. In several cases, however, the continued cohabitation has been viewed as an expression of the marital intent in a manner similar to an expressed intent, without referring to ratification.[37]

The use by the courts of *consensus continuus* also appears in cases in which the original contract was not made during a ceremonial wedding, but was an informal marriage deemed invalid due to the existence of an impediment. No new conclusion of a contract has been considered necessary after the removal of the impediment. In *Matthews v. Britton* (1962), the majority for the court stated: "It is not to be expected that parties once having agreed to be married will deem it necessary to agree to do so again when an earlier marriage is terminated or some other bar to the union is eliminated."[38] A concurring judge, requiring the renewal of the contract

law marriage in April of 1973. In *Rodgers v. Herron*, 226 S.C. 317, S.E.2d 104, 113 (1954), the court noted the difficulty in establishing "precisely the time at which the common law marriage may be said to have come into being." In *Webster v. Webster*, 114 Okla. 57, 242 P. 555, 557 (1925), the court stated: "In fact, there is no foundation in right reason for the contention that the matrimonial consent necessary to create the status of marriage must be referred to the commencement of the cohabitation solely, or to any other particular point of time." With respect to the requirement that other conditions must be met simultaneously, *see* cohabitation as a requirement, Chapter 8.5.2.9.

36 *See* note 3 *supra*.

37 *Fenton v. Reed*, 4 Johns. 52 (N.Y. 1809); *Campbell v. Campbell* ("The Breadalbane case"), (1866) 4 M. 867 (1866), (1867) 5 M. (H.L.) 115; *Smith v. Smith*, 84 Ga. 490, 11 S.E. 496 (1890) (ratification); *Travers v. Reinhardt*, 205 U.S. 423, 27 S.Ct. 563, 51 L.Ed. 865 (1906); *Prince v. Edwards*, 175 Ala. 532, 57 So. 714 (1912); *Johnson v. Wolford*, 117 Ohio St. 136, 157 N.E. 385 (1927); *White v. White*, 41 Ga.App. 394, 153 S.E. 203 (1930); *Chance v. Chance*, 60 Ga.App. 889, 5 S.E.2d 399 (1939); *Nicholas v. Idaho Power Co.*, 63 Idaho 675, 125 P.2d 321, 323 (1942) (ratified and adopted); *Ryan v. Ryan*, 84 Ohio App. 139, 86 N.E.2d 44, 47 (1948); *Williams v. Williams*, 90 Ohio App. 369, 106 N.E.2d 655, 657 (1951); *In re Schneider's Will*, 206 Misc. 18, 131 N.Y.S.2d 215 (Surr.Ct. 1954); *Johnson v. Johnson*, 96 Ga.App. 84, 99 S.E.2d 353 (1957); *Ventura v. Ventura*, 53 Misc.2d 881, 280 N.Y.S.2d 5 (Sup.Ct. 1967); *Metro. Life Ins. Co. v. Holding*, 293 F.Supp. 854 (E.D.Va. 1968); and *In re Frost's Estate*, 316 N.Y.S.2d 372, 35 A.D.2d 1069 (1970). In *Prevatte v. Prevatte*, 377 S.E.2d 114, 177 (App. 1989), the court stated that with respect to the actions of the parties after the removal of the impediment, "it is clear from their conduct that they thereafter gave every indication of their agreement to be married." In the cases of *In re Haffner's Estate*, 254 N.Y. 238, 172 N.E. 483, 484 (1930) and in *Farber v. U.S. Trucking Corp.*, 26 N.Y.2d 44, 308 N.Y.S.2d 358, 256 N.E.2d 521 (1970), the courts referred, with respect to the evidence concerning the parties' marital intent, directly to the invalid wedding ceremonies.

38 *Matthews v. Britton*, 303 F.2d 408 (D. C. Cir. 1962). *Compare Bochette v. Bochette*, 386 S.E.2d 475 (S.C.App. 1989). For a case with the requirement of an expressed

after the removal of the impediment, but accepting that the actions of the parties gave rise to an implied contract, clearly expressed the principle of *consensus continuus*: "Furthermore a continuing intention and agreement to be man and wife is implicit in the parties' very manner of living day by day for six years after the removal of the impediment."[39]

Nevertheless, *consensus continuus* has filled a special function if the parties have entered into an informal marriage that is invalid because it was formed in a state not recognizing common law marriages. If the parties subsequently continued to cohabit in another state recognizing such marriages, without entering into a new express contract, the question is whether a common law marriage can be established in the second state. The requirement of *consensus* has been found to exist in a number of cases with reference to the argument that consent is a continuing thing.[40] In the case of *In re Estate of Murnion* (1984), the parties entered into an oral marriage contract in the state of Washington, which does not recognize common law marriage; they then moved to Montana, which recognizes such marriages. The Montana Supreme Court found that each of the requirements for establishing a common law marriage was fulfilled during the parties' six-month cohabitation in Montana, and with respect to the requirement of a contract, the court referred to their "continuing agreement."[41] The particular ramifications of short visits to states recognizing common law marriages are discussed in Chapter 10, "Conflict of Laws and Choice of Law," as well as the courts' use of *consensus continuus* in such cases.[42]

The cases that stretch the development of the use of an independent *consensus continuus* are those in which there originally was no express contract, ceremonial or informal. The parties simply began a cohabitation that the courts, under the circumstances, have inferred to be a marriage contract. In such cases, the courts do not identify the conclusion of a contract on a specific day. Among the older cases, in *Consolidated Underwriters v. Kelly* (1929), the Texas appellate court posited that the parties' cohabitation

---

contract, *see Donaldson v. P.J. Oesterling & Sons, Inc.*, 199 Pa.Super. 637, 186 A.2d 653, 656 (1962) where the court found that clear and convincing evidence existed in the case to support the claim that after the impediment to marriage had been removed, the parties "by words *in praesenti*" expressed the intent to presently enter into a new contract in contrast to "a continuance of the agreement" which had existed from the period before the impediment had been removed. The new contract was deemed to come into existence during a conversation in the bedchamber of the couple.

39 *Matthews* at 410.

40 *In re Foster*, 77 Idaho 26, 32, 287 P.2d 282, 285 (1955).

41 *Matter of Estate of Murnion*, 212 Mont. 107, 686 P.2d 893, 906 (1984).

42 *See* Chapter 10 with respect to short visits in common law marriage states *infra*. *See also Ram v. Ramharack*, 571 N.Y.S.2d 190, 192 (N.Y. Sup. Ct. 1991) and *Hickman v. T.J. Hughes Constr. Co.*, 11 A.D.2d 828, 202 N.Y.S.2d 77 (1960), in which the court meant that the parties' invalid "marital agreement" in New York ought to be given "some evidentiary effect" as to their "continued consent" in Florida. A common law marriage therefore was found established.

as husband and wife after the removal of the impediment was evidence of "a continued intention and agreement day by day to be husband and wife." A common law marriage was found proven.[43] In *Le Blanc v. Yawn* (1930), no express marriage contract existed in the beginning of the relationship. The Florida Supreme Court appears to have found that a contract arose from moving in together, expressed as "[i]t is in effect that an agreement was made in the beginning to live together as man and wife, and that such an agreement was actually carried out by more than ten years of cohabitation as such."[44] When, in *Dibble v. Dibble* (1950), objection was made that no evidence was presented as to when, where, and how the marriage contract was formed, the Ohio Court of Appeals stated that an inferred agreement was proven based on the circumstantial evidence.[45]

Development within the case law during the most recent years has followed the same direction. In *Boswell v. Boswell* (1986), the parties had lived together for thirty-seven or thirty-eight years, of which only one year was without an impediment. The Alabama Supreme Court found that the parties continued to live together, holding themselves out as husband and wife, thereby mutually agreeing to a common law marriage.[46] In the case of *In re Estate of Hunsaker* (1998), the objection was made that the parties' consent and agreement must occur "at a set time." The Montana Supreme Court, however, stated that the party alleging the existence of a common law marriage did not need to prove the exact day that this occurred and found that a marriage contract had been formed.[47] Another recent case in which the court abandoned the requirement of a specific time and place for the formation of the contract is *Ballesteros v. Jones* (1998), in which the parties entered into an informal cohabitation lacking an express contract, at a point of time that an impediment to the marriage existed. The cohabitation continued after the removal of the impediment for a period of seventeen years. The Texas Court of Appeals, San Antonio, stated that "an ongoing agreement to be married" could be proven by the circumstantial evidence demonstrated in the parties' continual cohabitation as husband and wife and their representation to the world as spouses.[48] A common law marriage was proven. In other cases in which no original agreement existed, and the parties simply entered into a long marital cohabitation, the courts have referred neither to a specific contractual conclusion occurring on a specific date, nor to a *consensus continuus*. Instead, the courts have simply, with reference to the actual cohabitation, found that a contract must have been entered into within a

---

43 *Consolidated Underwriters v. Kelly*, 15 S.W.2d 229, 230 (Tex. Comm'n App. 1929).

44 *Le Blanc v. Yawn*, 99 Fla. 328, 126 So. 789, 790 (1930).

45 *Dibble v. Dibble*, 88 Ohio App. 490, 100 N.E.2d 451 (1950).

46 *Boswell v. Boswell*, 497 So.2d 479, 480 (Ala. 1986).

47 *Matter of Estate of Hunsaker*, 968 P.2d 281, 286 (Mont. 1998). A similar case before the same court is *Matter of Estate of Alcorn*, 868 P.2d 629 (Mont. 1994).

48 *Ballesteros v. Jones*, 985 S.W.2d 485, 490 (Tex.App.-San Antonio 1998) (applying Tex. Fam. Code Ann. § 2.22, presently renumbered as § 6.202 (Vernon 2005)).

certain year, or without any reference to any time frame, that the parties had a mutual intent and desire to be husband and wife.[49]

A deeper analysis of how the courts have reasoned from the circumstantial evidence to a *consensus continuus*, based on a more detailed presentation of the circumstances in the actual cases, is given in Chapter 7. At this point, it is sufficient to state that the courts work with the concept of *consensus continuus* and that, apart from the law of Pennsylvania and of the District of Columbia, it is a distinguishing feature of the informal marriage contract. It is debatable whether this contractual model has grown from the case law. It is unclear whether the contract has led to the use of this category of evidence, or whether the category of evidence has influenced the contract; it is a chicken-and-egg question, although the latter theory appears most likely. This contractual model, used as a requirement, makes it possible to establish marriages in cases in which the ceremonial wedding or the informal but express marriage contract was invalid, as well as cases in which an express contract was never made, and the evidence consists solely of the actions of the parties and their cohabitation. Of interest here is the court's reasoning in the case, *In re Estate of Alcorn* (1994), in which the opposing party maintained that a contract could not be formed "in a piecemeal fashion," but instead must be formed at a certain time or not at all. The Montana Supreme Court found that the contract had been established, stating that cohabitation and public repute are "continuing factors" resulting from the marital existence.[50]

The use of the principle *consensus continuus* also serves a function in that the different requirements for establishing a common law marriage

49 In *Lewis v. Anderson*, 173 S.W.3d 556 (Tex.App.-Dallas 2005), the appellant contended that there was no evidence of the date of the marriage found by the jury and the appellee testified that they had an agreement that they were married every year. The court found that a common law marriage was established after five years of cohabitation on the date an adoption petition was filed. In *White v. State Farm Mut. Auto. Ins. Co.*,907 F.Supp. 1012, 1014 (E.D.Tex. 1995), in which the issue as to the existence of a common law marriage was not dispositive to the case, the plaintiff could not identify the point of time for the contract more closely than "we were common-law married sometime during 1986 or 1987." In *Russell v. Russell*, 838 S.W.2d 909. 913 (Tex.App.-Beaumont 1992), the woman alleged that a common law marriage was entered into on April 17, 1964. The trial court found instead that it had been established on March 22, 1972. The Texas Court of Appeals found that it had been entered into, but that the date could not be more closely established. *See also Georgia Osteopathic Hosp. v. O'Neal*, 198 Ga.App. 770, 403 S.E.2d 235 (1991); and *Coleman v. Aubert*, 531 So.2d 881 (Ala. 1988). The court required in the case of *In re Estate of Fischer*, 176 N.W.2d 801 (Iowa 1970), "intent and agreement" without further determining when the contract had been formed, but stated that it must have existed before as well as after the woman's divorce from another man. In *United States v. Michaelson*, 58 F.Supp. 796, 798 (D.Minn. 1945), the court found that the parties had "entered into a common law marriage some time in the year 1927." In *Clayton Coal Co. v. Indus. Comm'n*, 93 Colo. 145, 25 P.2d 170, 171 (1933), a common law marriage was proven despite the fact that the woman could not state if it was spring, summer, or fall during which she became the man's wife.

50 *Matter of Estate of Alcorn*, 868 P.2d 629, 630 (Mont. 1994).

must exist simultaneously.[51] In addition to the requirement of a marriage contract, most states require cohabitation and reputation, the latter of which is discussed more fully in Chapter 8, *infra.* For the requirements to be considered fulfilled, the cohabitation must have been for a certain longer or shorter period of time, which also affects the requirement of a marriage contract. In those cases in which the relationship began with a verbal contract with respect to a marriage *de praesenti* in connection with the parties moving in together, the requirement for cohabitation and reputation are not fulfilled until the parties have cohabited for a certain period of time, represented themselves to the world as spouses, and been accepted as such. At this point, the verbal contract is usually not repeated. A possible way of finding that the requirement for a marriage contract has been fulfilled, then, is the use of a *consensus continuus, i.e.,* that the contract is deemed to have continued with respect to the circumstances. The use of *consensus continuus* has facilitated the ability to synchronize the requirements and find that they have been simultaneously fulfilled.

The development in the case law, entailing that the courts have set aside the requirement of an express marriage contract with a sharply defined contractual conclusion, has created problems for both the parties and any third party wishing to determine when and where a contract has actually been formed. Such a system naturally creates serious issues of legal certainty, which are discussed in Chapters 13, "The Constitutive Requisites in the Future," and 14, "Arguments For and Against Common Law Marriage and Cohabitation Law," *infra,* where the function of the informal marriage contract in the future is discussed.

6.2.4 The Significance of the Parties' Affection

Even though the parties' affection for each other often is the most fundamental motive for their intent to enter into a marriage – whether a formal ceremonial marriage or an informal, common law marriage – the courts have been opposed to using affection as a determinative factor in the legal establishment of a marriage. In *Price v. Price* (1978), for example, divorced spouses resumed cohabitating. The woman stated that she felt she had "entered into again a marital relationship" after several months in the "housekeeping relationship." The Oklahoma Court of Appeals, however, found that neither the emotion, the reunion, nor the woman's hidden intent was sufficient to establish a marriage. A mutual intent was required.[52]

---

51 As to the requirement that "cohabitation and reputation" exist simultaneously with the marriage contract, *see* Section 8.5.2.9 *infra.*

52 *Price v. Price,* 579 P.2d 843, 844 (Okla.App. 1978). *See also Reppert v. Reppert,* 214 Iowa 17, 241 N.W. 487 (1932), where the parties after their divorce continued their cohabitation and the woman stated: "I feel that you are my husband and I am your wife as though nothing had happened." A common law marriage was not proven.

In *Sears v. Sears* (1999), the parties' "'pre-sex' ritual wherein they expressed their love for each other" did not constitute a marriage contract as the purpose therewith was not to create the legal relationship of husband and wife.[53]

Even though the parties' marital affections are not a substantive requirement in the constitution of a common law marriage, they have been given evidentiary weight in establishing the parties' marital *consensus.* In the case of *In re Estate of Alcorn* (1994), for example, the woman was asked, "Did you feel that you were married to Fritz Alcorn?" She answered, "Yes, I did." The Montana Supreme Court found, that with respect to the woman's information, as well as other circumstances, a marriage contract had been formed.[54] A remarkably high evidentiary weight was accorded by the same court to the feelings of the parties in the case of *In re Estate of Hunsaker* (1998), in which the court found that a marriage contract had been formed as the woman wore an engagement ring given to her by the man, the parties had a grandfather clock engraved with their initials, and the woman had stated she "felt married to him" and that she believed he "felt married to her."[55]

The evidentiary weight given to such facts naturally varies from case to case. In *Brown v. Brown* (1975), for example, the woman stated that she had, during the cohabitation, "felt married" and that she "considered herself married." She further stated that she had wished to have a ceremonial wedding but that had not occurred.[56] The Georgia Supreme Court found, without directly referring to her feelings, that a common law marriage had been formed. It is not clear from the court's reasoning which aspect was given the greatest weight, that which the woman "felt" or that which she "considered." The later appears to win support in *Lorensen v. Weaber* (1992), in which the woman during trial testified that when they met, she "did not consider them to be married," but she later did not see the need for a ceremonial wedding as "she felt as if she were married." The Texas Court of Appeals in Dallas naturally did not discuss the distinction between "to consider" and "to feel," and did not find that a marriage contract had been proven.[57] Significant evidentiary weight was accorded to the woman's own understanding of the relationship in *Howard v. Howard* (1970),

---

53 *Sears v. Sears,* 267 A.D.2d 988, 700 N.Y.S.2d 626, 628 (A.D. 4 Dep't 1999). *See also Payne v. Payne,* 1999 Tenn.App.Lexis 844 (1999), in which the woman testified that she used the man's last name "because I felt in my heart that I was married to him." The court did not discuss this statement, and did not find any marriage contract proven.

54 *Matter of Estate of Alcorn,* 868 P.2d 629, 631 (Mont. 1994).

55 *Matter of Estate of Hunsaker,* 968 P.2d 281, 286 (Mont. 1998). *Compare In re Estate of Wilson,* 512 S.E.2d 383, 386 (Ga.App. 1999), where the circumstance that the woman wore an engagement ring was cited as evidence of the fact that the parties intended to marry in the future.

56 *Brown v. Brown,* 234 Ga. 300, 215 S.E.2d 671, 674 (1975).

57 *Lorensen v. Weaber,* 840 S.W.2d 644, 646-647 (Tex.App.-Dallas 1992).

in which the Texas Court of Civil Appeals in Houston stated: "The strongest evidence of a common law marriage is Tressie's direct and explicit testimony that she considered herself to be the wife of A.D. Howard."[58]

The objection can be raised against this that the parties' understanding about the character of the relationship can be incorrect. A correct assessment as to the nature of the relationship assumes legal postulations of which the parties can scarcely be expected to have knowledge. In *State v. Mireles* (1995), a common law marriage was proven despite the fact that the woman "did not consider herself married."[59] However, skepticism is warranted in assessing both the feelings of the parties and their own judgments with respect to their situation, and the evidentiary weight of these circumstances must be assessed from case to case. It is their marital intent that is legally relevant. The issue of whether the parties had a *consensus* that can be adjudged marital requires a closer analysis of marital *consensus*, which is discussed below.

6.2.5 A Mutual Consent

Characteristic for the informal marriage, as for other contracts, is that the marital intent must be mutual. The meaning here is the same with respect to common law marriage as with contracts in general.[60] A promise to marry by one of the parties naturally is insufficient to form a marriage. In the case, *In re Pratt's Estate* (1931), the court correctly stated: "Like any other contract which requires for its validity the full and free consent of both parties, there can be no marriage, ceremonial or nonceremonial, without the mutual acquiescence of both the man and the woman. A promise by one, which is not joined in by the other cannot be made the basis of a legal union for life."[61] Instead, as with the fundamental requirement in general contract law, a "meeting of the minds" is often required by the courts. In *Callen v. Callen* (2005), the South Carolina Supreme Court stated: "The fact finder is to look for mutual assent: the intent of each party to be married to the other and a mutual understanding of each party's intent."[62]

58 *Howard v. Howard*, 459 S.W.2d 901, 904 (Tex.Civ.App.-Houston 1970). *See also Atkins v. Heckler*, 574 F.Supp. 634 (E.D.Pa. 1983), where both parties declared that they "considered" each other husband and wife, and that a common law marriage was proven.

59 *State v. Mireles*, 904 S.W.2d 885, 888 (Tex.App.-Corpus Christi 1995). *Compare State v. Moore*, 882 S.W.2d 253, 263 (Mo.App. E.D. 1994), where the woman stated that she "never believed she was appellant's wife," evidencing that there was no contract between the parties. *See also State v. Burkitt*, 624 N.E.2d 210, 219 (Ohio App. 1993).

60 *In re Estate of Fisher*, 176 N.W.2d 801, 806 (Iowa 1970).

61 *In re Pratt's Estate*, 233 App.Div. 200, 251 N.Y.Supp. 424, 427 (1931). *See also Mayes v. Mayes*, 84 Ind.App. 90, 147 N.E. 630, 631 (1925), in which the court maintained that "there must be mutuality to such contract and that the minds of both parties must meet in mutual consent to said marital status."

62 *Callen v. Callen*, 365 S.C. 618, 620 S.E.2d 59, 62 (S.C. 2005). In *Matter of Estate of Atwood*, 577 N.W.2d 60 (Iowa App. 1998), the Iowa Court of Appeals stated that

The special evidentiary problems of this rather self-evident requirement deserve mention. In the claim of a common law marriage, the contract usually is not expressed and the parties have not exchanged their marital intent in any clearly defined contractual conclusion. The courts must determine whether and when a meeting of the minds occurred and an implied contract was formed.[63] That this leads to considerable evidentiary problems can be seen in the following chapters. A *consensus continuus* certainly does not need to exist during the entire cohabitation or during a specific period of time. The required period of time is determined, case by case. However, that required is that the parties, at some point of time, by their actions, their cohabitation, and other circumstances, give expression to a mutual and coinciding intent to marry, *i.e.*, that a meeting of the minds has occurred. If that has occurred, a marriage has been formed if the other requirements are fulfilled. If it can be proven that the parties lacked marital intent immediately after this point, the marriage cannot be

---

"all that is required is that the minds of the parties meet in mutual consent," referring to the Iowa Supreme Court's decision of *In re Estate of Fisher*, 176 N.W.2d 801, 807 (Iowa 1970). *See* already *In re Boyington's Estate*, 157 Iowa 467, 137 N.W. 949, 950 (1912). In *Nestor v. Nestor*, 150 Ohio St.3d 143, 15 O.B.R. 291, 472 N.E.2d 1091, 1094 (1984), the Ohio Supreme Court stated that the fundamental requirement in establishing the existence of a common law marriage is "a meeting of the minds between the parties who enter into a mutual contract to presently take each other as man and wife." *Nestor* is cited in *Bevan v. Bevan*, 2006 WL 1519654 (Ohio App. 11 Dist. 2006). In *Gary v. Gary*, 490 S.W.2d 929, 934 (Texas App. 1973), the Texas Court of Civil Appeals in Tyler stated: "There must be a meeting of the minds or there is no contract." The requirement of mutuality follows from general contract principles, *see Reppert v. Reppert*, 214 Iowa 17, 241 N.W. 487 (1932). *See also In re Keig's Estate*, 59 Cal. App.2d 812, 140 P.2d 163 (1943) (intent to marry not deemed mutual "unless each party agrees in the same sense on the terms of the agreement"); *In re Estate of Fisher*, 176 N.W.2d 801, 807 (Iowa 1970) (mutuality was considered to be "that the minds of the parties had met"); *In re Dittman's Estate*, 124 Ind.App. 198, 209, 115 N.E.2d 125, 130 (1953) ("the minds of both parties must meet in mutual consent to said marital status"); and *Henry v. Taylor*, 16 S.D. 424, 433, 93 N.W. 641, 643 (1903) ("Such a marriage must be evidenced by words disclosing a meeting of the minds"). However, there are cases in which it scarcely can be argued that a "meeting of the minds" had occurred, but that a common law marriage was established anyway. In those cases, only one party alleged a marital intent, but the other party, by their actions, had given the first party the impression that they had the same intent. This good faith situation can be seen in *McFarland v. McFarland*, 51 Iowa 565, 2 N.W. 269, 273-274 (1879), where the court found that the woman could receive the benefits of the marriage "if she intends present marriage, and the man does not, provided they cohabit, and provided his conduct is such as to justify her in believing that he intends present marriage." This attitude recurs even in the *dictum* of more modern case law in Iowa, *see In re Marriage of Winegard*, 257 N.W.2d 609, 616 (Iowa 1977); and *Conklin v. MacMillan Oil Co.*, 557 N.W.2d 102, 105 (Iowa App. 1996). *Compare In re Estate of Trigg*, 102 Ariz. 140, 426 P.2d 637 (1967), in which one party's secret intention not to constitute a common law marriage did not effect the validity of the marriage when the other requirements were met. *See also Stafford v. Stafford*, 41 Tex. 111 (1874); and *Bonds v. Foster*, 36 Tex. 68 (1871).

63 In *Adger v. Ackerman* 115 F. 124, 126 (8th Cir. 1902), the court stated that an implied agreement is entered into "whenever the minds of the parties meet in a common understanding of and consent to the present and future existence of the relation of husband and wife between them."

found invalid.[64] The parties must then, if they so desire, dissolve the marriage by divorce.

6.3 The Marital Intent's *Essensialia*

In assessing whether a marriage contract has been entered into, it is, of course, important to more closely determine to what the parties have agreed. The importance of the parties demonstrating the correct marital intent to establish a common law marriage can be seen in *Green's Estate* (1885), in which the court stated: "The intention with which the parties came together is the test."[65] A more in-depth determination of the contents of the required marital intent is significant not only to establishing the substantive requirements for a common law marriage, but also as to the direction the evidence should take in a contested case. The more drawn-out cases, with many and long witness examinations, demonstrate a lack of precision in determining the legal content of the marital intent.

The question then arises as to the objectification the assumed intent should take according to American case law. The frame of reference, of course, is that the marital intent should be focused on marriage in some form. In the case of *In re Marriage of Jones* (1989), it was not considered sufficient by the court that the parties, who had cohabited during a period of four years, had simply intended to have a monogamous "marital-type relationship."[66] If this is not sufficient, the question arises about what the parties must agree to, or *i.e.*, what is the required content of the marital intent, the *essensialia negotii*. In answering this question, it certainly can be seen as reasonable, but not especially informative, to state that the contract must give expression to the intent "to be married ... as it is ordinarily understood."[67] The problem arises with the expression "be married," which can scarcely has a clear or accepted definition.

Case law gives further indications, if somewhat limited and contradictory, of the requirements for the objectification. In cases in which the existence of a marriage contract has been the subject of litigation, certain descriptions of the content of the marital intent can be discerned from the judgments, however much they differ. Nevertheless, descriptions in terms of the marital intent's *essensialia* are seldom present, and the analysis as to this issue is often found in *dictum*. Two main inquiries appear to dominate. The courts appear to either require that the parties' mutual intent be focused on something *actual*, namely, the marital relationship between the parties, or something *legal*, namely, the legal relationship

64 *State v. Johnson*, 216 Kan. 445, 532 P.2d 1325, 1329 (1975).
65 *Green's Estate*, 5 Pa.Co.Ct. 605 (1888).
66 *In re Marriage of Jones*, 451 N.W.2d 25, 27 (Iowa App. 1989).
67 *United States v. Rubenstein*, 151 F.2d 915, 919 (2d Cir. 1945).

between the parties. Glimpses into the case law occasionally show a requirement of both legal and actual intent, with several variations occurring within each framework. Moreover, the case law includes additional approaches that do not easily fit into either category, as further discussed below.

6.3.1 Cohabitation as the Object of the Marital Intent

The object of the required intent to marry is commonly the actual relationship between the parties, the marital cohabitation. Outside of the concept of marriage, relationships created simply for sexual purposes or to establish a common household, have, as a rule, been captured in the wide definition given to the intent to cohabit. Gratian, as previously mentioned, as early as the Middle Ages, was anxious to maintain that a *consensus matrimonialis* meant more than a *consensus cohabitationis* or a *consensus carnalis copulae,* namely, the mutual intent to establish a *consortium omnis vitae* and an *individua vitae consuetudo,* a common existence with respect to all facets of life and an inseparable shared existence for a lifetime.[68]

This same concept can be seen again in the early leading Scottish case of *Dalrymple v. Dalrymple* (1811), in which the court stated that marriage must contain an agreement between the parties "looking to the *consortium vitae*."[69] During this period in history, procreation was an important aspect of this intended mutual existence. Lord Stowell stated in *Lindo v. Belisario* (1845) that: "A marriage is not every carnal commerce; nor would it be so even in the law of nature; A mere carnal commerce, without the intention of cohabitation and bringing up of children, would not constitute marriage under any supposition. But when two persons agree to have that commerce for the procreation of and bringing up of children, and for such lasting cohabitation—that, in a state of nature, would be a marriage; and, in the absence of all civil and religious institutions, might safely be presumed to be, as it is properly called, a marriage in the sight of God."[70]

68 *See* Section 3.3.2.

69 *Dalrymple v. Dalrymple,* (1811) 2 Hagg.Con. 54, 161 Eng.Rep. 665. The required intent in cases where the parties have participated in a ceremony is presumed. In *McAdam v. Walker,* (1813) 1 Dow. 190, 3 Eng.Rep. 654, Lord Redesdale stated that: "There was no proof that Mr. McAdam did not intend a *consortium vitae.*"

70 *Lindo v. Belisario,* (1795) 1 Hagg.Con. 216; Eng. Ec. 367, 374. *See also* the English case, *D. v. A.*, (1845) 1 Rob.Ecc. 279, 298, stating that the purpose of marriage is "a lawful indulgence of passions" and "the procreation of children." *Compare Baxter v. Baxter* A.C. 274, 286, 298 (1948), where, according to the House of Lords, the procreation of children is not the main function: "It is indisputable that the institution of marriage generally is not necessary for the procreation of children." *Compare Weatherley v. Weatherley,* (1946) 2 All E.R. 1, 4. The purpose of procreation is the main theme of Raphael Powell, *The Concept of Marriage in Ancient and Modern Law,* 3 CURRENT LEGAL PROBLEMS 46, 63 (1950). He maintains that historically, procreation has been marriage's most important goal, and suggests three purposes presently for marriage, namely (1) the procreation of children, (2) sexual intercours, and (3) life companionship. An exception to the first can be made,

The purpose of a shared life as husband and wife also recurs in the American case law, although procreation, as a rule, is not specifically emphasized.[71] An early example from the mid 1800s can be seen in *Sheffield v. Sheffield* (1848), in which the Texas Supreme Court stated: "The parties have pledged themselves, not only for their own happiness, but for purposes important to society, to live together during the term of their natural lives."[72] In the same fashion as in medieval canon and Scottish law, the contract, according to American law, if one follows *Askew v. Dupree* (1860), must be a contract "looking to the *consortium vitae.*"[73] If the parties in any way have given expression to the intent "to cohabit as husband and wife," no other evidence was deemed to be required.[74]

Living together as husband and wife as the object of the marital intent can be also seen in cases from the beginning of the twentieth century. In *Chamberlain v. Chamberlain* (1905), the court found in the evidence the expression of the intent "to live together as husband and wife."[75]

---

according to the author, in cases of sterility or other problems. An exception to the second purpose can be made due to the age of the parties.

71 *Compare White v. White,* 4 How.Pr. 102, 107 (1849) ("Marriage is defined to be a contract between a man and a woman for the procreation and education of children"). On the other side, *see Griswold v. Connecticut,* 381 U.S. 479 (1956) and *Eisenstadt v. Baird,* 405 U.S. 438 (1972), in which the Court stated that prohibiting the use and sale of contraceptives was in violation of the Constitution's right of privacy.

72 *Sheffield v. Sheffield,* 3 Tex. 79, 85 (1848). *See also Com. v. Litzenberger,* 15 Phila. 414 (1882), where the man's admission that he and the woman "lived together as man and wife" was considered not only evidence of their coexistence, but even as with respect to a legally valid marriage. In *State v. Bittick,* 103 Mo. 183, 15 S.W. 325, 11 L.R.A. 587 (1891), the parties had drafted a written contract in which they had agreed "to live together so long as we may both live, to live together as man and wife." The court, insisting on "consent for life, for the discharge, to each other and to the community, of the duties legally incumbent on those whose association is founded on the distinction of sex," found, despite the fact that the contract did not contain any express intent with respect to the duties and obligations of the law, that the contract fulfilled these requirements, and that a common law marriage had been formed. *Compare Letters v. Cady,* 10 Cal. 533 (1858).

73 *Askew v. Dupree,* 30 Ga. 173, 178 (1860), which also speaks of two persons united "by mutual contract to live together."

74 *Green's Estate,* 5 Pa.C. 605, 606 (1888). The parties' oral agreement was not considered a marriage contract as it did not express the intent "to cohabit as husband and wife," which was evidenced by the fact that the parties, during their sixteen-year-long relationship, never had a common home. With respect to Pennsylvania, *compare* more modern cases using an intent to establish "a legal relationship," § XX *infra,* note 110.

75 *Chamberlain v. Chamberlain,* 68 N.J.Eq. 736, 62 A. 813 (E & A 1905), *aff'd,* 68 N.J.Eq. 736, 62 A. 680, 681, 3 L.R.A., N.S., 244 (E.&A. 1905). In the case, *In re Strauss's Estate,* 168 Pa. 561, 32 A. 98 (1895), the court found that no evidence had been presented as to a contract between the parties that they should "live and cohabit together as husband and wife." In *Porter v. United States,* 7 Ind. 616, 104 So. 855 (1907), the court stated that a marriage is valid when the parties are of an age of majority and without any impediment "agree to live together as man and wife" and then later perform the contract. In *Grigsby v. Reib,* 105 Tex. 597, 153 S.W. 1124 (1913), the court described the parties' intent as both the intent "to become husband and wife" and the intent "to live and cohabit together as such." Also, in *Dirion v. Brewer,* 20 Ohio App. 298, 151 N.E. 818 (1925), the marital intent was described as the intent "to live together as

The requirement naturally gives protection against contracts, which under the guise of a marriage contract are formed for entirely different reasons, for example, to give one party the opportunity to receive benefits to which they may not otherwise be entitled, or to avoid criminal sanctions. In *Pegg v. Pegg* (1908), in which the parties appeared to have entered into a written marriage contract to prevent being prosecuted for "illicit cohabitation," the court stated that the fact that: "A mere written or oral agreement to be husband and wife, without present intention to assume that relation in fact, does not constitute a marriage between the parties, especially if the agreement is entered into for some other purpose, is well settled."[76]

The marital cohabitation recurs as an object of the marital intent even in modern case law. In the case of *In re Estate of Love* (2005), the court held that, in order for a common law marriage to come into existence, the parties must agree to "live together as man and wife." In *Ram v. Ramharack* (1991), the required intent to marry was found in evidence that the parties had entered into an agreement "to live like husband and wife." In the case of *In re Estate of Abbott* (1993), no evidence was found that the parties intended "to cohabit as husband and wife," therefore, no common law marriage was formed.[77] The requirement of an intent to live as husband

---

husband and wife." *See also Wristen v. Wristen*, 119 S.W.2d 1104 (Tex.Civ.App.-Eastland 1938), referring to *Grigsby*. In *Matthews v. Britton*, 112 U.S.App.D.C. 397, 303 F.2d 408 (D.C.Cir. 1962) the woman declared that she had taken the man "as (her) husband" and that he had asked her to come and live with him "as man and wife," to which she consented. The contract did not immediately establish a marriage between them as an impediment existed. However, when the impediment was removed, the majority of the court found that an additional contract was not needed to establish a common law marriage. It was sufficient that they continued their shared living arrangements and that they lived together as man and wife. *Id.* at 409. Even one of the dissenting justices spoke of the parties' intent "to live as husband and wife." *Id.* at 410. In *Rodgers v. Herron*, 226 S.C. 317, 85 S.E.2d 104, 113 (1954), the court spoke of a contract "to live together as husband and wife." *Compare Johnson v. Johnson*, 235 S.C. 542, 112 S.E.2d 647, 651 (1960), in which the same court required a contract "to assume toward each other the relation of husband and wife." *See also In re Estate of Dallman*, 228 N.W.2d 187, 190 (Iowa 1975), where the court speaks of a contract "to live as husband and wife."

76 *Pegg v. Pegg*,138 Iowa 572, 115 N.W. 1027, 1028 (1908). In the case, *Edwards v. Enterprise Mfg. Co.*, 283 Pa. 420, 129 A. 449 (1925), the woman was asked if the parties had talked "about going together and living as man and wife," to which she answered "Nothing that I know of." In addition, she informed the court that she "just went to live with him because [she] cared for him and thought he cared for [her]." The court found that no marriage contract had been formed.

77 *In re Estate of Love*, 274 Ga.App. 316, 319, 618 S.E.2d 97, 100 (2005), *citing In re Estate of LeGrand*, 259 Ga.App. 67, 576 S.E.2d 54 (2002); *Ram v. Ramharack*, 571 N.Y.S.2d 190, 192 (Sup. 1991); and *Matter of Estate of Abbott*, 592 N.Y.S.2d 729, 730 (A.D. 1 Dep't 1993). In *Matter of Estate of Stodola*, 519 N.W.2d 97 (Iowa App. 1994), the parties had declared in a document that they "agreed to live as husband and wife." The court found that the "present intent and agreement to be married" was evidenced. *See also Brown v. Carr*, 198 Ga.App. 549, 417 S.E.2d 296, 298 (1991), where the court declared that the trial court had jurisdiction to determine if the parties "had intended to live together as husband and wife." In *Georgia Osteopathic Hosp. v. O'Neal*, 198 Ga.App. 770, 403 S.E.2d 235, 243 (1991), the court stated that in order to form a common law marriage, the parties must "agree to live together as man and wife."

and wife has often been motivated, as in Scottish law, by the desire to not accept, through the institution of common law marriage, relationships limited only to sexual purposes. The courts have, at times, interpreted their task to be the unmasking of relationships that have the façade of the parties living together as husband and wife.[78] The courts' clear distancing from relationships created solely for sexual purposes has made them cautious about expressly requiring such purposes as a requirement of intent. Naturally, however, the intent to live together as husband and wife includes sexual as well as procreational purposes.[79]

See also Holmes v. Holmes, 232 Ga.App. 434, 502 S.E.2d 294, 295 (1998) (the parties "must agree to live together as man and wife"); *In re Estate of Benjamin*, 34 N.Y.2d 27, 355 N.Y.S.2d 356, 311 N.E.2d 495, 497 (1974) ("The agreement to live as man and wife is what needs be shown"); and *Renshaw v. Heckler*, 787 F.2d 50, 53 (2d Cir. 1986) ("intent to live as husband and wife"). *Compare Goldin v. Goldin*, 48 Md.App. 154, 426 A.2d 410, 415 (1981), where the parties' intent "to enter into that status" is discussed. In the last two mentioned cases, Pennsylvania law was applied with respect to couples that had made short visits to the state. Caution is warranted with respect to the fact that the courts' formulations do not always appear to be meticulously chosen. For example, in *Whitworth v. Whitworth*, 256 Ala. 296, 54 So.2d 575 (1951), the court spoke of a contract between the parties "to live with each other as husband and wife," citing for that proposition *Turner v. Turner*, 251 Ala. 295, 37 So.2d 186, 188 (1948), where a contract "to take each other as man and wife" is discussed. In *Gordon v. Gordon*, 211 N.Y.S.2d 265, 266 (1960), the court applied the law of Texas law both as to a contract "to enter into marriage" and a contract "to live as man and wife." In *Stratos v. Stratos*, 317 Mich. 113, 26 N.W.2d 729 (1947), the man was asked during the cross-examination: "This agreement you had, was that you were going to live together? A. Yes, sir. Q. And that she was going to be known as your wife and that you were going to be known as her husband, is that right? A. Yes, sir." Referring to this testimony, the court found that the contract was evidenced and that a common law marriage was established between the parties, who had cohabited for approximately ten years. In *Trammel v. Trammel*, 196 S.W.2d 209 (Tex.Civ.App.-San Antonio 1946), the court found that a common law marriage was formed based on the contract "to live together as husband and wife," despite the fact that the parties intended in the future to have a wedding ceremony.

78 *See Thimgan v. Mathews*, 74 Colo. 93, 219 P. 211 (1923). *Compare Foley v. Gavin*, 76 Colo. 286, 230 P. 618 (1924), where the man stated in front of his friends, "We have agreed to live together as man and wife." The man, however, made a fatal additional statement which gave the court pause as to the whether it actually was a marriage contract the parties had formed, namely "[a]nd we don't care what the family thinks." According to the court, if it had been a question of a true marriage contract, it would have been natural for the man to say "Don't complain anymore; we are married." Evidence of a marriage contract, with respect to this evidence and even other circumstances, was found insufficient. *Compare Fisher v. Sweet & McClain*, 154 Pa.Super. 216, 35 A.2d 756, 761 (1944), in which the court stated that the requirement for a marriage license even for common law marriages would "establish a present intention on the part of the applicants to be *married*, and not merely an intent to have sexual relationships."

79 *See Duggan v. W.C.A.B. (Litchfield TP.)*, 569 A.2d 1022, 1023 (Pa.Cmwlth. 1990), in which the court found that the parties had a very friendly relationship, did many things together, and had mutual respect for each other. However, the evidence did not establish that the deceased "wished to marry and share either his bed or his property with the Claimant." If one spouse has expressly stated to the other a willingness to contribute to a pregnancy, and then, after the marriage has been entered into, refused to cooperate thereto, the other spouse, assuming that they are not living together when the circumstances become known, can not only have the

The courts have also imposed requirements pertaining to the intended length of the relationship. The Christian view of marriage as principally a lifetime relationship has influenced the courts in that they have not accepted marriage contracts in which the intent is an "on again, off again situation,"[80] an agreement between the parties to live together "so long as mutual affection shall exist,"[81] or "so long as they desired."[82] As a rule, the courts have instead emphasized that the intended marital relationship should be lifelong,[83] or, in any case, permanent and

---

marriage dissolved, but even annulled. *See McCann v. McCann*, 593 N.Y.S.2d 917 (Sup. 1993); and *Rich v. Rich*, 40 A.D.2d 846, 337 N.Y.S.2d 530 (2d Dep't 1972). In a Comment, *Fundamental Interests and the Question of Same-Sex Marriage*, 15 TULSA L.J. 141, 150 (1979), marriage is described as "the public and voluntary commitment of one individual to spend a lifetime with another ... If no children are born, the bond nevertheless remains."

80 *Earnheart v. Earnheart*, 979 P.2d 761, 763 (Okla.Civ.App. Div. 3 1999). *See also McChesney v. Johnson*, 79 S.W.2d 658, 660 (Tex.Civ.App-Ft. Worth 1934), in which the court did not accept a relationship expressed as: "We are husband and wife today and we will be again next week, but since it suits our convenience we will deny that relation in the interim." Proposals have arisen concerning the implementation of a "term marriage" in which the parties must renew the marriage if it is to continue, *see* WALTER WADLINGTON AND RAYMOND F. O'BRIAN, CASES AND MATERIALS ON DOMESTIC RELATIONS 24 (4th ed. 1998).

81 *Peck v. Peck*, 155 Mass. 479, 30 N.E. 74 (1892); *see also Perkins v. Silverman*, 284 Mo. 238, 223 S.W. 895 (1920); *Arnold v. Arnold*, 219 Mo.App. 8, 267 S.W. 950 (1924); and *Perales v. Flores*, 147 S.W.2d 974 (Tex.Civ.App.-San Antonio 1941).

82 *See Swingle v. Keifer*, 105 Tex. 609, 153 S.W. 1132, 1133 (1913), where the court stated that a contract according to which the parties should live together as husband and wife "so long as they desired" and according to which one or both of the parties "could dissolve the contract at will," could not legally be considered a marriage contract.

83 *See* the early case of *Sheffield v. Sheffield*, 3 Tex. 79, 85 (1848), in which the parties agreed "to live together during the term of their natural lives." In *Letters v. Cady*, 10 Cal. 533, 534, 537 (1858), the parties agreed to temporarily live together "as man and wife." The court found that the relationship between them "was intended to be temporary, and the connection one to which it would be a perversion of language to apply the name of marriage." *Compare Hyde v. Hyde*, (1866) L.R. 1 P. & D. 130. *See also Topper v. Perry*, 197 Mo. 531, 114 Am.St.Rep. 777, 95 S.W. 203, 207 (1906), which speaks of "a civil contract ... for husband and wife during their joint lives." Even in *Adger v. Ackerman*, 115 F. 124 (8th Cir. 1902), the court required a contract to be husband and wife "during their joint lives" for a valid marriage. In *Swingle v. Keifer*, 105 Tex. 609, 153 S.W. 1132, 1133 (1913), the court spoke of "an absolute agreement to be husband and wife during their lives." In *Salvini v. Salvini*, 2 S.W.2d 963, 965 (Tex. Civ.App.-El Paso 1928), the court required a contract between the parties, either express or implied "to take each other for husband and wife during their natural lives" for a common law marriage to be formed. In the case of *In re Pratt*, 233 App. Div. 200, 251 N.Y.Supp. 424, 427 (1931), the court stated that a common law marriage cannot be formed if there is no mutual intent "to enter into the bonds of matrimony until one or the other dies." Similar language can be found in *Wristen v. Wristen*, 119 S.W.2d 1104, 1105 (Tex.Civ.App.-Eastland 1938): "[T]o take each other as husband and wife during the remainder of their lives." In *De Shazo v. Christian*, 191 S.W.2d 495, 496 (Tex.Civ.App.-Amarillo 1946), the court also spoke of a contract "during their natural lives." *See also Lutwak v. United States*, 195 F.2d 748 (7th Cir. 1952), *aff'd*, 344 U.S. 684, 73 S.Ct. 481, 97 L.Ed. 593, 600 (1953) ("to establish a life together"); *Rager v. Johnstown Traction Co.*, 184 Pa.Super. 474, 134 A.2d 918, 922 (1957) ("that the parties intended to live with each other as man and wife until death

continuous.[84] The requirement of a lifelong relationship as an object of the marital intent appears to have survived the rising rate of divorces in recent decades.[85] The strength of this aspect of intent is reflected in

---

did them part"); *Svendsen v. Svendsen,* 158 N.W. 410 (S.D. 1916) (requirement that the parties had the intent to continue the marital relationship "during the remainder of their lives"); and *In re Erickson's Estate,* 75 S.D. 345, 64 N.W.2d 316, 321 (1954) (the marital intent was not proven, despite the cohabitation of the couple for twenty-five years later dissolved by a separation, as no evidence existed that they took each other "as husband and wife *forever*") (*italics added*). In *Tatum v. Tatum,* 241 F.2d 401, 407 (9th Cir. 1957), the court stated that the essential elements in a common law marriage included a contract or mutual "to be husband and wife as a lifelong relationship." In Comment, *Fundamental Interests and the Question of Same-Sex Marriage,* 15 TULSA L.J. 141, 150 (1979), marriage is described as "the public and voluntary commitment of one individual to spend a lifetime with another."

84 In *Dickey v. Office of Personnel Management,* 419 F.3d 1336, 1340 (C.A.Fed. 2005), the court stated in dictum that both spouses must intend and expressly covenant to enter into "a permanent relationship of husband and wife." In *Buford v. Buford,* 874 So.2d 562, 566 (Ala.Civ.App. 2003) and *Stringer v. Stringer,* 689 So.2d 194, 195 (Ala. Civ.App. 1997), the courts speak of a contract "to permanently enter the marriage relationship." *See also People v. Schmidt,* 579 N.W.2d 431, 434 (Mich.App. 1998); and *Crosson v. Crosson,* 668 So.2d 868, 870 (Ala.Civ.App. 1995). *Compare Hall v. Duster,* 727 So.2d 834, 836 (Ala.Civ.App. 1999), in which the court excludes the word "permanently." In *Cornell v. Mabe,* 206 F.2d 514, 517 (5th Cir. 1953), the court stated that the parties must have an agreement and intend "that their relationship as husband and wife be permanent." As evidence that neither party, despite their cohabitation of several years, intended a permanent relationship, the court referred to the fact that the man, shortly after the separation of the couple, underwent a ceremonial marriage with a different woman and took out a "license" to marry a third woman, without petitioning for a divorce from the first woman with whom he had cohabited. The court also referred to the fact that the woman, shortly after the man had left her, stated that she was "single" and that she later moved in with another man whom she later married. *See also Monroe v. Prophet,* 49 F.2d 1021 (5th Cir. 1931); *Schwingle v. Keifer,* 105 Tex. 609, 153 S.W. 1132 (1913); *Bell. v. Southern Casualty Co.,* 267 S.W. 531 (Tex.Civ.App. 1924); *Arnold v. Arnold,* 219 Mo.App. 8, 267 S.W. 950 (1924); *Cavanaugh v. Cavanaugh,* 135 Okla. 204, 275 P. 315 (1929); *In re Pratts Estate,* 251 N.Y.S. 424, 427 (1931) (the contract must be to enter into "a permanent marital relationship"); *McChesney v. Johnson,* 79 S.W.2d 658 (Tex.Civ.App.- Ft. Worth 1934); and *Orr v. State,* 129 Fla. 398, 176 So. 510, 514 (1937) ("a matrimonial relationship, permanent and exclusive of all others"). The same formulation recurs in *Chapman v. State,* 84 Okla. Crim.App. 41, 178 P.2d 638, 640 (1947); *Ridgeway v. Logan,* 205 Okla. 603, 239 P.2d 778 (1952); *In re Blackhawk's Estate,* 195 Okla. 390, 158 P.2d 168 (1944); *Vann v. Vann,* 186 Okla. 42, 96 P.2d 76, 79 (1939); *Owens v. Bentley,* 40 Del. 512, 14 A.2d 391 (1941); *Perales v. Flores,* 147 S.W.2d 974 (Tex.Civ.App.-San Antonio 1941); *Sloss-Sheffield Steel & Iron Co. v. Watford,* 245 Ala. 425, 17 So.2d 166 (1944); *De Shazo v. Christian,* 191 S.W.2d 495 (Tex.Civ.App.-Amarillo 1946); and *Ridley v. Compton,* 215 Miss. 532, 61 So.2d 341 (1952).

85 For cases from the past twenty-five years, *see,* e.g., *In re Estate of Hammonds,* 39 Ohio Misc. 96, 315 N.E.2d 843, 847 (1973) (a contract for "not merely a temporary arrangement, but an agreement for life"). An ambivalence towards the requirement of duration for a lifetime can be seen in *Jolley v. Jolley,* 46 Ohio Misc. 40, 347 N.E.2d 557 (1975), where the court had no statement from the plaintiff and her witnesses concerning a contract in which "they agreed to be husband and wife from that certain day forward and that they would live together for the rest of their lives as such," but the court in another place spoke as to "assume the relationship of marriage." *Compare Knaus v. Relyea,* 746 S.W.2d 289 (Ark.App. 1988), in which the woman stated that she and the deceased man expressed their intent during an informal ceremony "to remain together forever," but the court found that there was

studies that show that, although couples correctly presumed that half of all marriages will end in divorce, they believe that the risk in their own marriages is zero.[86]

The requirement, that the contract concerns a continuing relationship, an agreement between a man and woman to enter into a marital relationship on a trial basis as an expression of marital intent. In *Leal v. Moreno* (1987), the woman alleged that she had entered into a common law marriage with a man who was now deceased. At trial, she testified that we "were planning to get married" and that they had moved in together to "try out" their relationship. The court found that no marriage contract *de praesenti* had been formed because the parties agreed to move in together for a trial period and, then, if everything worked out, marry.[87] Sociologists have noted a trend in two-step marriages, which begin with a trial period of cohabitation, followed by a legal marriage.[88] One party's promise to try need not be considered insufficient marital intent that applies only to a trial marriage. It can simply be an expression of the intent to seriously try.[89]

At times, it is unclear what the intent is in an agreement that includes a trial marriage. It can either be a definite decision concerning a permanent

---

insufficient "objective evidence" to prove that a contract existed between the parties forming a common law marriage in accordance with Colorado law.

86 *See* AMERICAN LAW INSTITUTE, PRINCIPLES OF THE LAW OF FAMILY DISSOLUTION: ANALYSIS AND RECOMMENDATIONS § 7.07 (2001).

87 *Leal v. Moreno,* 733 S.W.2d 322 (Tex.Civ.App.-Corpus Christi 1987). The same outcome can be found in *Turner v. Turner,* 251 Ala. 295, 37 So.2d 186 (1948), where divorced spouses moved in together and were reunited, conditioned on the man being able to demonstrate that he could "straighten up and show her that he could be a good husband." The court stated that Alabama did not recognize "trial marriages" and that no common law marriage had been formed. Even in *Robertson v. State,* 42 Ala. 509 (1868), the court found the marriage contract to be conditioned as the man promised to marry the woman "as soon as the new licenses came in." *Compare Huffmaster v. Huffmaster,* 279 Ala. 594, 188 So.2d 552 (1966), in which the court did not view the reunion as conditional.

88 *See* Dudley, *Rainbows and Realities: Current Trends in Marriage and Its Alternatives,* THE FUTURIST, Feb. 23 (1979).

89 *See Benson v. Tom Williams Buick, Inc.,* 551 So.2d 355 (Ala. 1989), in which divorced spouses moved back in together and cohabited for approximately five years. The question arose as to whether a common law marriage had been formed between them. In connection with their reunion, the man said: "Come and be my wife," to which the woman promised that she would "try harder" in dealing with the man's daughter. It was argued at trial that the woman's promise made the relationship conditional and demonstrated an insufficient marital intent. The court found, however, that her promise could as easily be interpreted as an expression of "a good faith intention to make the marriage work." A common law marriage was proven. *See also Taylor v. Taylor,* 298 N.Y.S. 912, 164 Misc. 401 (1937); and *Com. v. Haylow,* 17 Pa. Super. 541, 546 (1901)(the parties' cohabitation "was under an agreement that if they got along harmoniously they would be married, if not they would separate, it is scarcely necessary to say that this was not marriage"). *Compare Lannamann v. Lannamann,* 171 Pa.Super. 147, 89 A.2d 897 (1952), in which the parties had entered into a ceremonial marriage that they agreed would be a "trial marriage" in that each of them had the right to within six months dissolve the marriage. The marriage was found to be valid.

or lifelong relationship or a definite decision concerning a legal relationship. In *Rosetta v. Rosetta* (1975), divorced spouses lived together for three years, after which the woman married another man. The question arose whether the divorced spouses could be considered to have entered into an informal marriage and whether a common law marriage was formed. The court stated: "From the entire record the most that can be said is that there may have been an agreement that after some trial period, if things worked out, or if appellee got medical help or counseling, then the appellant and the appellee might remarry. Present agreement to be married is a necessary element of common law marriage, and it is not sufficient to agree on present cohabitation."[90] The marriage contract is not considered to fulfill the requirements if the *essensialia negotii* is characterized by a present cohabitation but marriage only in the future. The court did not further elaborate the distinction between the intent concerning cohabitation and marriage. A possible interpretation is that the intent to cohabit is short-term and only encompasses the present cohabitation on a trial basis, whereas an intent encompassing marriage would be more long term and include a long marital life together. The facts that the parties, on a trial basis, continued to cohabit for a shorter period of time, and the woman then married another man, supports the premise that they did not have the intent to continue a marital existence together for the long term. Another possible and more reasonable interpretation is that the court distinguishes, on the one hand, between the intent of a person to cohabit, whether the intent is short term or long term, and on the other, the intent encompassing marriage in the sense of a legal relationship.

The requirement that the intended relationship be exclusive can also be seen in the case law. A preexisting marriage, as noted above, is an impediment to the formation of a common law marriage. If the parties enter into the relationship while one of them is married to a third party, the marital intent is considered inadequate because the object of the intent is not a monogamous relationship. The intent is usually then termed as "illicit" or "meretricious."[91] In such cases, the object of the intent is sometimes termed "concubinage" as opposed to "a matrimonial union."[92]

---

90 *Rosetta v. Rosetta,* 525 S.W.2d 255, 261 (Tex.Civ.App.-Tyler 1975). *Compare Schrader v. Schrader,* 207 Kan. 349, 484 P.2d 1007 (1971), where divorced spouses again lived together for about two years. The woman testified that she wanted to be able to get out of the relationship if things did not work out and the man testified that they would remarry only if they could repair their relationship. The court found that they had no agreement or understanding that they were married.

91 The term "meretricious" was considered in 1927 to mean "lustful and pertaining to the character of prostitution, and involving knowledge that the relation was not intended to be matrimonial but wanton," *see* Note, *Common-law marriage after removal of impediment to valid ceremonial marriage,* 12 CORNELL L.Q. 513, 518 (1927).

92 The frame of reference is given in *Clark v. Barney,* 24 Okla. 455, 103 P. 598, 600 (1909): "Common-law marriage grows out of good faith, honest intentions, and proper purposes." *See also Jones v. Kemp,* 144 F.2d 478 (10th Cir. 1944); *Hoese v. Hoese,* 205 Iowa 313, 217 N.W. 860 (Iowa 1928)("Common law marriage does exist.

The circumstance that one of the parties believes that the other is still married to a third party has been considered sufficient to hinder a true marital intent. In *Durand v. State* (1994), the court stated that the man "could not have agreed to enter into a common law marriage with appellant if she believed that appellant was still married to Jeannine."[93] Should the impediment be removed, some courts, especially if the parties had knowledge of the impediment, have presumed a continuing inadequate intent. After the removal of the impediment, the parties must demonstrate that they have changed their intent to one of true marital intent to establish a common law marriage. They are obligated to show the "metamorphosis from concubinage to marriage."[94] Simply the continuation of their cohabitation has been found insufficient.[95] Other courts have applied

---

Concubinage also exists"); *Prince v. Edwards*, 175 Ala. 532, 57 So. 714, 715 (1912) (the parties' relationship was "with matrimonial, and not with meretricious, intent"); and *Adger v. Ackerman*, 115 Fed. 124, 129 (8th Cir. 1902) (the parties had the desire and intent "to live in a matrimonial union rather than in a state of concubinage"). *Compare Reading Fire Ins. & Trust Co.'s Appeal*, 113 Pa. 204, 6 A. 60, 63 (1886), in which the woman's previous relationship with another man was considered in the finding that a common law marriage had not been formed. *Compare also Hawkins v. Weinberger*, 368 F.Supp. 896 (D.Kan. 1973).

93 *Durand v. State*, 881 S.W.2d 569, 576 (Tex.App. Houston 1994). In *McKee v. State*, 452 P.2d 169 (Okla.Crim.App. 1972), the contract was found to not be proven with respect to the fact that one of the parties was uncertain as to whether he was divorced. In *Winn v. Wiggins*, 47 N.J.Super. 215, 135 A.2d 673, 677 (1957), the court required a *consensus* "of matrimonial character," which could not be fulfilled if the parties were aware of the impediment.

94 *McClish v. Rankin*, 153 Fla. 324, 14 So.2d 714, 717 (Fla. 1943).

95 In *Abramson v. Abramsom*, 161 Neb. 782, 74 N.W.2d 919 (1956), the court spoke of an intent "to change that relationship into the legitimate relation of husband and wife." In *Canute v. Canute*, 384 Pa.Super. 60, 557 A.2d 772, 774 (1989), the court named a "clear evidence of a change in status." *See also State v. Grimes*, 215 Iowa 1287, 247 N.W. 664 (1933) and *In re Boyington's Estate*, 157 Iowa 467, 137 S.W. 949 (1912). The presumption is old, and can be found, for example, in *Williams v. Williams*, 46 Wis. 464, 1 N.W. 98, 105 (1879), where the court stated: "The presumption against marriage, where the connection between the parties is shown to have been illicit in origin, may however, be overcome by proofs, showing that the original connection has changed in its character, and a subsequent marriage may be established by circumstances, without actual proof of a marriage in fact." *See also Edelstein v. Brown*, 35 Tex.Civ.App. 625, 80 S.W. 1027 (1904); and *Barnes v. Barnes*, 90 Iowa 282, 57 N.W. 851 (1894). As to the origin of the presumption, *see Jackson v. Claw*, 18 Johns. Rep. 346 (1820); *Physicks Estate*, 4 Am.L.Reg. (N.S.) 418 (1862); *Starr v. Peck*, 1 Hill. 270 (1841); *Clayton v. Wardell*, 4 N.Y. 230 (1858); *Canjolle v. Ferrie*, 23 N.Y. 90 (1861); *O'Gara v. Eisenlohr*, 38 N.Y. 296 (1868); and *Foster v. Hawley*, 8 Hun. 68 (N.Y.1876). A number of cases have been characterized by a tangible moral indignation that the new relationship was begun "meretriciously." A somewhat more substantial reasoning regarding the question of an inadequate intent can be found in *Brinson v. Brinson*, 233 La. 417, 96 So.2d 653 (1957). The requirement of a renewed marriage contract after the removal of the impediment has been most stringent where both of the parties had knowledge as to the existence of the impediment, *see, e.g., Pierce v. Pierce*, 355 Pa. 175, 49 A.2d 246 (1946) and *Canute v. Canute*, 384 Pa.Super. 60, 557 A.2d 772 (1989). *See generally Metro. Life Ins. Co. v. Chase*, 294 F.2d 500 (3d Cir. 1961); and *Dandy v. Dandy*, 234 So.2d 728 (Fla.App. 1970). In *U.S Fid. & Guar. Co. v. Britton*, 269 F.2d 249 (D.C.Cir. 1959), in which the parties had lived together for a period of eleven years as husband and wife, the woman was found to not have any true marital intent as she,

the opposite presumption, that a continued cohabitation is the basis for a presumption of true marital intent. A new contract, therefore, has not been found necessary, especially in cases in which the parties were not aware of the impediment. However, even if the parties have had knowledge thereof, certain courts have maintained that the distinction must be made between the intent and the ability to marry, and that the parties can have had a correct marital intent but lack the ability to marry.[96]

Even in cases in which no such impediment has existed, but the parties have agreed to establish a bigamous or polygamous relationship, the contract has been found insufficient and, therefore, unable to form a new marriage, because the object of the intent of the parties is not an exclusive marital relationship. As a result, common law marriages are not established in cases concerning Mormons who have the intent to establish polygamous relationships.[97] Even if the intent to enter into a polygamous relationship is not obvious, there may be elements of such an intent that contradict the required monogamous intent. In *Gray v. Bush* (2001), in which the deceased man, during his life, had maintained relationships with other women, the court found that the surviving partner failed to produce substantial evidence indicating "a present mutual agreement to permanently enter a marriage relationship to the exclusion of all others."[98] The principle of monogamy is

---

even though it was mistaken, believed herself to be married with another man and therefore "never intended to marry" the man with whom she lived. *See also Foster v. Hawley*, 8 Hun. 68 (N.Y. 1876)(24 years of cohabitation); *Lemon v. Lemon*, 158 S.C. 71, 155 S.E. 285 (1930)(25 years); *compare Kersey v. Gardner*, 264 F.Supp. 887 (M.D.Ga. 1967).

96 *See already Fenton v. Reed*, 4 Johns. 52 (N.Y. 1809), where the parties married each other in the belief that the woman's first husband was dead. He was alive, however, and died several years later. The parties found out after the wedding that he was alive, but simply continued to live together until after the first husband's death. A common law marriage was found established. *See also Bull v. Bull*, 29 Tex.Civ.App. 364, 68 S.W. 727 (1902); *Johnson v. Wolford*, 117 Ohio St. 136, 157 N.E. 385 (1927); *Jenkins v. Jenkins*, 30 Ohio App. 336, 164 N.E. 790 (1928); *In re Haffner's Estate*, 254 N.Y. 238, 172 N.E. 483 (1930); *Thomas v. Murphy*, 71 U.S.App.D.C. 69, 107 F.2d 268 (1939); *Parella v. Parella*, 74 App.D.C. 161, 120 F.2d 728 (1941); *Thomey v. Thomey*, 67 Idaho 393, 181 P.2d 777, 779 (1947); *In re Walls' Estate*, 358 Mich. 148, 99 N.W.2d 599 (1959); *Reger v. Reger*, 242 Ind. 302, 177 N.E.2d 901 (1961); *Matthews v. Britton*, 112 U.S.App.D.C. 397, 303 F.2d 408, 409 (1962); and Note, *Common Law Marriage and Annulment*, 15 Vill. L. Rev. 134 (1969).

97 In *Riddle v. Riddle*, 72 P. 1081, 1085 (Utah 1903), a man simultaneously lived with three women. The Utah Supreme Court found that a common law marriage could not be established as the parties did not have a mutual intent to live together as husband and wife "to the exclusion of all others." The court found that the existence of "a monogamous marriage, uniting the contracting parties in wedlock for life, to the exclusion of all others, or that the parties mentally agreed that the appellant should observe or be bound by the legal obligations of a monogamic marriage," was not probable. *See also Hyde v. Hyde*, (1866) L.R. 1 P. & D. 130: "It is inconsistent with marriage as understood in Christendom that the husband should have more than one wife"; and *In re Bethell*, (1888) 38 Ch.D. 220, naming "the voluntary union for life of one man and one woman, to the exclusion of all others."

98 *Gray v. Bush*, 835 So.2d 192, 197 (Ala.Civ.App. 2001); *Buford v. Buford*, 874 So.2d 562, 566 (Ala.Civ.App. 2003); *Stringer v. Stringer*, 689 So.2d 194, 195 (Ala.Civ.App. 1997);

one of the essential elements for the object of the marital intent. In the case of *In re Estate of Shepherd* (1994), in which the existence of a marriage contract was not proven, the court considered that the man dated other women.[99] Most couples living together without formally marrying appear to want to live in monogamous relationships with a requirement of marital fidelity.[100] Intent contrary to this requirement can also be deemed an insufficient marital intent, because it is contradictory to the obligations of marriage, a subject further discussed in the next section.

However, if a common law marriage has already been formed, the marital status of the parties is not changed by any liaison of one spouse outside the marriage, even if the outside relationship can be the grounds for a divorce. In *Adams v. Boan* (1990), the allegation was that a mutual marital intent did not exist between the parties because the man had a sexual

---

Turner v. State, 708 So.2d 232, 234 (Ala.Crim.App. 1997) (evidence indicating that the relationship was not "exclusive of all others"); *People v. Schmidt,* 579 N.W.2d 431, 434 (Mich.App. 1998) (applying Alabama law); and *Crosson v. Crosson,* 668 So.2d 868, 870 (Ala.Civ.App. 1995). This element appears quite clearly in the case law in Alabama, Florida and Oklahoma. *See, for example, Adams v. Boan,* 559 So.2d 1084, 1087 (Ala. 1990) ("permanent and exclusive of all others"); *Richardson v. State,* 744 S.W.2d 65, 74 (Tex.Cr.App. 1987) (applying Oklahoma law); *Ridgeway v. Logan,* 205 Okla. 603, 239 P.2d 778 (1952); *Sloss-Sheffield Steel & Iron Co. v. Watford,* 245 Ala. 425, 17 So.2d 166 (1944); *King v. King,* 269 Ala. 468, 114 So.2d 145 (1959); *Owens v. Bentley,* 40 De. 512, 14 A.2d 391 (1941); and *Vann v. Vann,* 186 Okla. 42, 96 P.2d 76, 79 (1939). In *Orr v. State,* 129 Fla. 398, 176 So. 510, 514 (1937) the court refers to "a matrimonial relationship, permanent and exclusive of all others." The same formulation is used in *McKee v. State,* 452 P.2d 169 (Okla.Crim.App. 1969); *Downs v. Newman,* 500 So.2d 1062 (Ala. 1986); and *Boswell v. Boswell,* 497 So.2d 479 (Ala. 1986). *See* the Texas case, *Middlebrook v. Wideman,* 203 S.W.2d 686, 688 (Tex. Civ.App.-Texarkana 1947): "Then she consorted with various and sundry other members of the opposite sex, with manifest fruition, according to her testimony." The court did not find that a common law marriage had been proven, and further stated: "Courts do not view with an approving eye the conduct of one who treats lightly the most serious and sacred of all human relationships." *Compare* the Ohio case, *Minnix v. Brantner,* 48 Ohio Ops. 450, 64 Ohio L.Abs. 327, 107 N.E.2d 562 (1952), in which the parties divorced after a marriage of 24 years, but continued to live together an additional six years until the woman died. No contract forming a common law marriage after the divorced was found evidenced. It appears that the court also took into consideration the woman's interest in other men. *See also* the Pennsylvania case, *In re Stevenson's Estate,* 272 Pa. 291, 116 A. 162, 163 (1922), where the man had a relationship with another woman. During visits to her, the woman alleging the common law marriage had to wait outside the other woman's house. A marriage contract within the framework for common law marriages was not found to be evidenced. *Compare* Nancy Rebecca Shaw, *Common law marriage and unmarried cohabitation: an old solution to a new problem,* 39 U. Pitt. L. Rev. 579, 580 (1977), which with respect to Pennsylvania law assumes a couple living together "intending permanence and exclusiveness."

99 *In re Estate of Shepherd,* 646 N.E.2d 561, 564 (Ohio App. 1994).

100 A survey conducted showed that more than 90% of the couples "did not date" outside of their relationships, *see* Nancy Catlin et al., *Commitment and Relationship Factors in Consensual Cohabitation,* 8 Int.L.J. Soc. Fam. 185, 188-189 (1978). A different survey showed that a majority of those persons living together wished to live in a "sexually monogamous marriage," *see* Newcomb, *Cohabitation in America: An Assessment of Consequences,* 41 J. Marriage & Fam. 597, 600 (1979).

relationship with another woman and, therefore, lacked the intent to form a relationship "permanent and exclusive of all others." The court found, however, that the man, at the point at which the parties entered into their marriage contract, was not involved in a relationship with another woman, and, therefore, there was a mutual intent to enter into a marriage permanent and exclusive of all others.[101] The reasoning is logical if the frame of reference is the initial intent, *i.e.*, the agreed intent existing at a specific point, and not a *consensus continuus*. If the latter intent, stretching over a certain period of time, is assumed, it is more difficult to establish the point at which the contract was formed, and more likely that the above-mentioned outside sexual relationships can influence the parties' intent and, thereby, the formation of a marriage. Outside sexual relationships can also affect the possibility of fulfilling the other requirements necessary for the formation of a common law marriage. The outcome in *Adams*, therefore, is even more remarkable in that the parties were considered to have fulfilled the requirements of "public recognition of existence of marriage" and "cohabitation or mutual assumption openly of marital duties and obligations," as discussed further *infra*.

6.3.2 A Legal Relationship as the Object of the Marital Intent

An early expression of the principle that the cohabitation between the parties ought not be the object of the marital intent can be found in *Letters v. Cady* (1858), in which the court stated: "Living together 'as man and wife', is not marriage, nor is an agreement so to live a contract of marriage." The court, however, did not further elaborate as to the requirements of the content of the intent, but came to the conclusion that a marriage had not been formed.[102]

It is not unusual for the courts to describe the marriage contract, in a manner parallel to that of the ceremonial wedding's formulations,[103] as a

101 *Adams v. Boan*, 559 So.2d 1084, 1087 (Ala. 1990). *See also Krug v. Krug*, 296 So.2d 715, 718 (Ala. 1974), *Goodman v. McMillan*, 258 Ala. 125, 61 So.2d 55, 59 (1952), *Turner v. Turner*, 251 Ala. 295, 37 So.2d 186, 188-89 (1948) and *Abramson v. Abramson*, 161 Neb. 782, 74 N.W.2d 919, 924 (1956). *Compare Winfield v. Renfro*, 821 S.W.2d 640 (Tex.App. Houston 1991), in which the man admitted he had sexual relationships with other women. The court, referring to the "circumstantial evidence," found that the parties had fulfilled the requirement of an agreement to be married and the requirement of living together as man and wife, but that a common law marriage was not proven as the requirement of holding out to the public as man and wife was not fulfilled. *See also Russell v. Russell*, 838 S.W.2d 909 (Tex.App. Beaumont 1992), in which a common law marriage was proven despite the fact that the man had relationships and children with other women. *Compare Beals v. Beals*, 203 Ga.App. 81, 416 S.E.2d 301 (1992).

102 *Letters v. Cady*, 10 Cal. 533, 537 (1858). In the case, cohabitation was recognized as evidence of marriage.

103 A common wedding vow reads: "I, N.N. take thee N.N. to be my lawfully wedded wife/husband." The continuation, however, focuses more on the actual than the

contract between the parties to "take each other" as husband and wife, to "become" or to "be," husband and wife, or a contract to marry. In the case of *In re Meredith's Estate* (1937), the court required "a present agreement ... to take each other as husband and wife."[104] In *Krier v. Krier* (1996), the court characterized the content of the intent as "to be husband and wife."[105] In *Abramson v. Abramson* (1956), the court names the intent "to become husband and wife"[106] while in the case of *Interest of Miller* (1982), it is the intent "to marry."[107] These formulations leave the field open as to whether an actual or legal relationship is to be understood. To take each other, or to become or to be husband and wife can encompass an actual relationship as easily as a legal relationship. The expression, "to be husband and wife," can naturally include both "to live as" husband and wife and an actual relationship. In those cases in which the courts have expressed views as to this issue, it appears, however, that a legal or status relationship was envisioned and, consequently, something more than actually living together was intended.

In *Gary v. Gary* (1973), divorced spouses continued to live together. The court, with respect to their agreement to continue to live together, found that it "did not include the further agreement to become again husband and wife." The court found that the evidence in the record with respect to the marriage contract demonstrated only that the parties had

---

legal relationship: "[T]o have and to hold from this day forward, for better, for worse, for richer, for poorer, in sickness and in health, to love and to cherish till death us do part." The form of the ceremony varies from state to state and can in most states be individualized for each wedding. That which is most important is that the parties are present before an authorized official who declares that they take each other as husband and wife. *See* HOMER H. CLARK, JR., THE LAW OF DOMESTIC RELATIONS IN THE UNITED STATES 91 (2d ed. 1987).

104 *In re Meredith's Estate,* 279 Mich. 298 (1937). In *Turner v. Turner,* 251 Ala. 295, 37 So.2d 186, 188 (1948), the court describes common law marriage as a contract "to take each other as man and wife."

105 *Krier v. Krier,* 676 So.2d 1335, 1339 (Ala.Civ.App. 1996); *Aaberg v. Aaberg,* 512 So.2d 1375, 1376 (Ala. 1987); *Coleman v. Aubert,* 531 So.2d 881, 882 (Ala. 1988); *Kirk v. Mattison,* 497 So.2d 120, 123 (Ala. 1986); *Piel v. Brown,* 361 So.2d 90, 93 (Ala. 1978); *Smith v. Smith,* 247 Ala. 213, 23 So.2d 605, 609 (1945); *Sloss-Sheffield Steel & Iron Co. V. Watford,* 245 Ala. 425, 17 So.2d 166, 168 (1944); *Gilbreath v. Lewis,* 242 Ala. 510, 513, 7 So.2d 485, 488 (1942); *Tartt v. Negus,* 127 Ala. 301, 28 So. 713, 715 (1899); *Davis v. State,* 103 P.3d 70 (Okla.Cr.App. 2004); *Matter of Estate of Stinchcomb,* 674 P.2d 26, 29 (Okla. 1983); *In re Estate of Phifer,* 629 P.2d 808, 809 (Okla.App. 1981); and *Chirelstein v. Chirelstein,* 12 N.J.Super. 468, 79 A.2d 884, 893 (1951). In *Anderson v. Anderson,* 235 Ind. 113, 131 N.E.2d 301, 306 (1956), the court speaks of a contract "to be married or to be husband and wife" but also of a "consent to said marital status," *id.* at 305. Even in *Fritz v. Mork,* 2001 Iowa App. LEXIS 594 (2001), in which an 18-year cohabitation did not give rise to a common law marriage, the court speaks of an intent "to be married."

106 *Abramson v. Abramson,* 161 Neb. 782, 74 N.W.2d 919, 924 (1956); *Gary v. Gary,* 490 S.W.2d 929, 934 (Tex.Civ.App.-Tyler 1973); and *In re Redman's Estate,* 135 Ohio St. 554, 21 N.E.2d 659 (1939).

107 *Interest of Miller,* 301 Pa.Super. 511, 448 A.2d 25 (1982). The court did not further elaborate as to whether the intent "to marry" was in reference to an intent to live together, to establish a marital status or simply to perform a ceremony.

decided to resume living together in the same manner as they had before.[108] As the spouses previously had been married, the court clearly required an intent that encompassed something more, namely, to become husband and wife. Even if the court did not expressly state that it should encompass a legal relationship, *i.e.*, legally becoming husband and wife, this appears probable.

It is also common that courts characterize the marriage contract as a contract through which the parties intend to create a *marital relationship, matrimonial relationship, marriage relationship,* or a *matrimonial relation.* Even these expressions leave open the issue of whether an actual or legal relationship is intended. Both interpretations have support in the case law. In *Stringer v. Stringer* (1997), the parties had lived together for fifteen years

---

108 *Gary v. Gary,* 490 S.W.2d 929, 934 (Tex.Civ.App. Tyler 1973). *Compare Eagle v. W.C.A.B. (Bahorich),* 602 A.2d 387, 389 (Pa.Commw. 1992), in which divorced spouses moved in together and continued to live together for five years until the death of the man. The court found that a common law marriage had not been formed as the parties had only the intent "to reconciliate." *See also In re Redman's Estate,* 135 Ohio St. 554, 21 N.E.2d 659 (1939), in which the surviving party testified as to a meeting between the parties: "We agreed to live as man and wife ... We said we would live together as man and wife." When questioned whether they had at any time discussed "any marriage" between them, the man answered: "We talked about marriage but not for her and I." The court stated that it was necessary to prove the existence of a contract "to become husband and wife, to establish a marriage at common law" and that there was insufficient evidence as to both the contract and the intent. Indeed, the court found the opposite situation, that the parties were in agreement that "marriage" was nothing for them and that they "did not desire that status." Even if what the parties meant with the term "marriage" is not clear from the record, whether they simply meant a ceremonial wedding, the question was not raised and the court appears to accept that the content of the intent concerned the parties' "status" and not that the content could be with respect to their lives together. *Compare Young v. Gen. Baking Co.,* 104 Ind. App. 658, 12 N.E.2d 1016, 1018 (1938), in which the court found that the parties' relationship was not of such a nature as to form a common law marriage. As reason, the court stated "that appellant and decedent never considered themselves actually married; that they intended to be 'formally married' (by ceremony) at some future date, but were content to live together as husband and wife until they would be formally married; that they had not entered into an agreement of marriage." The parties' mutual intent "to live together as husband and wife" was clearly insufficient to establish an immediate marriage contract. This raises the question as to what the parties' future marital intent should have encompassed more than a ceremony. The court does not elaborate as to whether it should be the intent with legal ramifications, an intent to be bound or an intent to achieve a certain status that lay *de futuro* but is missing *de praesenti.* In the case of *In re Keimig's Estate,* 215 Kan. 869, 528 P.2d 1228, 1230 (1974), the Kansas Supreme Court found that it was not sufficient with a "consent to cohabit." The court reiterated the view expressed in *Fleming v. Fleming,* 221 Kan. 290, 559 P.2d 629, 331 (1977), in which an "agreement to marry" was not evidenced, despite the fact evidence as to the "consent to cohabit" existed in the record. The requirement of a "marriage agreement" was also posited. In *Commerce Bank of Kansas City v. Odell,* 16 Kan.App.2d 704, 827 P.2d 1205 (1992), it was a lack of "intent or agreement to be married." *See also Lackey v. Texas,* 638 S.W.2d 439, 443 (Tex.Crim.App. 1982) ("to agree on present cohabitation and future marriage" is insufficient as evidence for a valid informal marriage); *Hightower v. State,* 629 S.W.2d 920, 924 (Tex.Crim.App. 1982); and *Rosetta v. Rosetta,* 525 S.W.2d 255, 261 (Tex.Civ.App.-Tyler 1975).

and had mutual children. Their intent to live together was clear. However, the man had stated that he was not "ready to commit to a marriage." The court stated that for the creation of a common law marriage, a "mutual agreement to permanently enter the marriage relationship to the exclusion of all others" was required, and found that the evidence was sufficient to support the trial court's conclusion that the parties had no mutual assent to be married. The court appears to be referring to a legal intent or an intent to have a marital-like status.[109]

There are cases, however, in which the courts have expressly required an intent to enter into a legal relationship of marriage. This sort of expression is often used by the courts in Pennsylvania. In *Staudenmayer v. Staudenmayer* (1998), the Pennsylvania Supreme Court required an agreement with the purpose "that the legal relationship of husband and wife is created." The court did not more closely discuss the concept of *legal relationship*, but found that no such contract was proven in the case.[110]

---

109 *Stringer v. Stringer*, 689 So.2d 194, 195 (Ala.Civ.App. 1997). The courts in Alabama often use these terms without any closer explanation. In many cases, the content is unclear, *see, for example, Hall v. Duster*, 727 So.2d 834, 836 (Ala.Civ.App. 1999); *Crosson v. Crosson*, 668 So.2d 868, 870 (Ala.Civ.App. 1995); *Rickard v. Trousdale*, 508 So.2d 260, 261 (Ala. 1987); *Coleman v. Aubert*, 531 So.2d 881, 882 (Ala. 1988); *Baker v. Townsend*, 484 So.2d 1097 (Ala.Civ.App. 1986); *Boswell v. Boswell*, 497 So.2d 479, 480 (Ala. 1986); *Luther v. M & M Chemical Co.*, 475 So.2d 191, 193 (Ala.Civ.App. 1985); *Cluxton v. Cluxton*, 431 So.2d 1296 (Ala.Civ.App. 1983); *Eaton v. State*, 423 So.2d 352 (Ala.Cr.App. 1982); *Walton v. Walton*, 409 So.2d 858 (Ala.Civ.App. 1982); *Golden v. Golden*, 360 So.2d 994 (Ala.Civ.App. 1978); *Skipworth v. Skipworth*, 360 So.2d 975, 976 (Ala. 1978); *Piel v. Brown*, 361 So.2d 90, 94 (Ala. 1978); *Humphrey v. Humphrey*, 293 Ala. 118, 120, 300 So.2d 376, 377 (1974); *Beck v. Beck*, 286 Ala. 692, 697, 246 So.2d 420, 425 (1971); *Brown v. Brown*, 276 Ala. 153, 155, 159 So.2d 855, 856 (1964); *Reynolds v. Scott*, 257 Ala. 670, 60 So.2d 690 (1952); *Goodman v. McMillan*, 258 Ala. 125, 61 So.2d 55, 59 (1952); *Turner v. Turner*, 251 Ala. 295, 37 So.2d 186 (1948); *Smith v. Smith*, 247 Ala. 213, 23 So.2d 605, 609 (1945); *Sloss-Sheffield Steel & Iron Co. V. Watford*, 245 Ala. 425, 17 So.2d 166, 168 (1944); *Gilbreath v. Lewis*, 242 Ala. 510, 513, 7 So.2d 485, 487 (1942); *Rogers v. McLeskey*, 225 Ala. 148, 142 So. 526 (1932); *White v. Hill*, 176 Ala. 480, 58 So. 444, 447 (1912); and *Tartt v. Negus*, 127 Ala. 301, 28 So. 713, 715 (1899). In other cases, the term "marital relationship" has been used to denote the actual relationship. *See, e.g., Renshaw v. Heckler*, 787 F.2d 50, 52 (2d Cir. 1986), in which the court spoke of the "marital relationship" and referred to the parties' "intent to live as husband and wife." *See also Com. v. Sullivan*, 484 Pa. 130, 398 A.2d 978, 980 (1978). *Compare Steadman v. Turner*, 357 Pa.Super. 361, 516 A.2d 21 (1986).

110 *Staudenmayer v. Staudenmayer*, 714 A.2d 1016, 1020 (Pa. 1998). *See also Perotti*, 868 A.2d 1240 (Pa.Super 2005); *Bell v. Ferraro*, 849 A.2d 1233, 1235 (Pa.Super. 2004); *Africa v. Vaughan*, 998 F.Supp. 552, 556 (E.D.Pa. 1998); *In re Veneziale*, 267 B.R. 695, 700 (Bkrtcy.E.D.Pa. 2001); and *In re Marriage of Mosher*, 243 Ill.App.3d 97, 612 N.E.2d 838 (1993). In *Marino v. Anheuser-Bush*, Inc., 583 N.Y.S.2d 68, 70 (A.D. 4 Dep't 1992), a common law marriage was not established as it was not proven that the parties, during their visits to Pennsylvania, "sought to establish the legal relationship of husband and wife". *See also Canute v. Canute*, 384 Pa.Super. 60, 557 A.2d 772, 775 (1989); *Com. v. Smith*, 511 Pa. 343, 513 A.2d 1371 (1986); *In re Estate of Stauffer*, 504 Pa. 626, 476 A.2d 354, 357 (1984); *Estate of Gavula*, 490 Pa. 535, 417 A.2d 168, 171 (1980); and *In re Estate of Garges*, 474 Pa. 237, 378 A.2d 307, 309 (1977). With respect to the law of Pennsylvania, *compare Green's Estate*, 5 Pa.C. 605, 606 (1888), in which the court simply required the intent

Without deviating in meaning, the object of the marital intent has also been characterized as the intent "to create a marital status." That the status formulation also focuses on the legal relationship between the parties can be clearly seen in the older case of *State v. Walker* (1887), in which the parties had agreed to live together without subjecting themselves to the state's or society's regulations. They had conversely declared, in a ceremony, that they "repudiated all powers legally conferred upon husbands and wives," they were "opposed to the making of promises," and that they desired to remain free in the same manner as before their union. The man stated, "I abdicate in advance all the so-called marital rights," and the woman agreed. Justice Valentin, sitting in the Supreme Court of Kansas, wrote that the parties had lived together as husband and wife, but "without any intention of being such in legal contemplation. That is, they lived together, but had no intention of creating that relation or status known and defined by law and by the customs and usages of all civilized society as marriage." A cohabitation under such circumstance could not, according to Justice Valentin, constitute a valid marriage.[111] However, in cases in which a mutual intent to reach the legal status of marriage exists, a common law marriage can be found to be immediately formed despite the fact that the cohabitation is short and the parties shortly thereafter undergo a ceremonial wedding.[112]

"to cohabit as husband and wife." *See also State v. Grimes*, 215 Iowa 1287, 247 N.W. 664-666 (1933), in which the parties, in a written agreement, had agreed "to live as Husband and Wife until such time that we are Lawfully married," but the court found that no common law marriage had been formed as the contract contained no expression of the intent to assume "the legal relationship." In *Sears v. Sears*, 267 A.D.2d 988, 700 N.Y.S.2d 626, 628 (A.D. 4 Dep't 1999), the parties "pre-sex ritual wherein they expressed their love for each other" was not found to constitute a contract for the purpose of creating "the legal relationship of husband and wife." In *Abramson v. Abramson*, 161 Neb. 782, 74 N.W.2d 919, 925 (1956), the court speaks of "the legitimate relation of husband and wife." *Baker v. Mitchell*, 143 Pa.Super. 50, 17 A.2d 738 (1941) concerns a contract to create "the legal relation of husband and wife." *See also In re Pratt's Estate*, 233 App.Div. 200, 251 N.Y.Supp. 424, 427 (1931), in which the court speaks of "a legal union for life." In *Mpiliris v. Hellenic Lines, Ltd.*, 323 F.Supp. 865, 881- 882 (S.D.Tex. 1979), the court appears to require that the intent encompass the fact that the marriage would be given "legal significance." In *Skinner v. Skinner*, 150 N.Y.S.2d 739, 741 (1956), the parties were found to have the intent "to live in lawful wedlock."

111 *State v. Walker*, 36 Kan. 297, 13 P. 279, 288-289 (1887). *Compare* Joel Prentiss Bishop, New Commentaries on Marriage, Divorce, and Separation II § 14 (Chicago, T.H. Flood and Co. 1891), maintaining that the parties' contract to marry is to "assume the marital status" and that the contract is terminated as soon as this is achieved. The spouses are thereafter bound by marital regulations. *See* Joel Prentiss Bishop, Commentaries on the Law of Marriage and Divorce §§ 29 and 42 (Boston 1852). As with respect to Bishop's views, *see* Henry T. Blake, *The Gospel of Marriage according to Bishop*, 13 Ill. L. Rev. 33 (1918/19). According to *In re Boyington's Estate*, 157 Iowa 467, 137 S.W. 949, 950 (1912), the fundamental question is whether their minds have met in mutual consent to "the status of marriage."

112 *See United States v. Dorto*, 5 F.2d 596, 597 (1st Cir. 1925), where the parties' primary intention with the marriage was to impede the deportation of the woman, *see infra*

The status formulation also recurs in modern case law, which accepts that a man and a woman can fall in love and live together without having the intent to establish a legal marital status. In *Owens v. Owens* (1996), a common law marriage was found constituted despite the fact that the parties had stated that they lived in an "open concubinage" and in a "nonmarriage." The court stated that the parties' statements could have been in response to the concept of a ceremonial marriage, and not for the purpose of denying "the marital status."[113] Another similar, but significantly more unusual, general description of the required marital intent that appears in the case law is that the parties are to have the intent to clothe themselves in "the bonds of matrimony."[114] These marital bonds comprise the central portions of the parties' marital status.

The common element for these formulations is that the content of the marital intent focuses on something legal. In accordance with this understanding, the distinction between the intent "to cohabit" and the intent "to create a legal relationship or a legal status" must be made. Questions then arise about the focus of the parties' legal intent, the extent of the intent as required by the courts, and whether it is the legal ramifications of marriage itself that are required. Moreover, do the parties have to agree to all the legal ramifications of marriage or is it sufficient to intend to achieve a few, for example, those that follow from the mandatory legislation? Does it make any difference whether their intent is focused on the

---

for a discussion on sham marriages. *See also Great Northern Ry. v. Johnson*, 166 C.C.A. 181, 254 F. 683, 684 (8th Cir. 1918), in which the court stated: "Mutual assent to the present institution of the status is all sufficient."

113 *Owens v. Owens,* 466 S.E.2d 373, 375 (S.C.App. 1996). The marriage presumption based on cohabitation and reputation was applied in the case, which meant that the burden of proof was placed on the party alleging that the marriage contract did not exist. As with respect to presumptions, *see* Chapter 9 *infra*. *See also Matter of Estate of Carroll,* 749 P.2d 571, 574 (Okla. App. 1987) ("a man and a woman can fall in love and live together without agreeing to create a marital status"); *Goldin v. Goldin,* 48 Md.App. 154, 426 A.2d 410, 415 (1981) (an intent to "enter into that status"); and *In re Estate of Gower,* 445 Pa. 554, 284 A.2d 742, 743-744 (1971) (the parties had the intent of "establishing marriage status"). *Compare Collier v. City of Milford,* 537 A.2d 474, 479 (Conn. 1988) concerning an agreement "to change the status of the relationship of the parties." In *Schibi v. Schibi,* 136 Conn. 196, 69 A.2d 831 (1949), the court speaks of an intent to create "the status of marriage" as differing from an intent only concerning a "future cohabitation." The status formulation occurs in *In re Dittman's Estate,* 124 Ind.App. 198, 209, 115 N.E.2d 125, 130 (1953), where it is stated that the parties' intent must meet "in mutual consent to said marital status." The last named phrase reoccurs in *Anderson v. Anderson,* 235 Ind. App. 113, 131 N.E. 2d 301, 305 (1956). In *Fiedler v. Nat'l Tube Co.,* 161 Pa. Super. 155, 53 A.2d 821, 823 (1947), the court found that the parties, after the hinder to their marriage had been removed, "resumed cohabitation under a new arrangement and with the intent to create a new status." *See also In re Redman's Estate,* 135 Ohio St. 554, 21 N.E.2d 659 (1939); and *Mayes v. Mayes,* 84 Ind.App. 90, 147 N.E. 630, 631 (1925).

114 *In re Pratt's Estate,* 233 App.Div. 200, 251 N.Y.Supp. 424, 427 (1931). *See also In re Marriage of Mosher,* 243 Ill.App.3d 97, 612 N.E.2d 838 (1993), in which the man did not want something that was "legal and binding" and *Stringer v. Stringer,* 689 So.2d 194, 195 (Ala.Civ.App. 1997), in which the man, despite a 15-year cohabitation, was not "ready to commit to a marriage."

rights of marriage or on its obligations? Is the intent of the parties sufficient if they seek only to obtain a single legal consequence, for example, the right to immigrate or avoid military service? What happens if the parties clearly have a negative intent, *i.e.*, not to receive certain legal consequences, for example, the right to fidelity or divorce? Perhaps the parties have refrained from participating in a formal ceremony in order to be freer. These questions, which will be revisited in the discussion as to the future of the institute of common law marriage in Chapter 13, "The Constitutive Requirements in the Future," have not received close attention in case law. A few points of view, however, do appear.

Certain courts have gone so far as to require that the object of the parties' mutual intent encompass the legal ramifications of marriage. One such case is *Williams v. Williams* (1879), in which the court stated that the contract must encompass the relationship between the husband and wife "with all the responsibilities and duties which the law attaches to such relationship."[115] However, other courts have rejected the requirement of a

---

115 *Williams v. Williams*, 46 Wisc. 464, 1 N.W. 98, 101(1879) *cited in Welch v. All Persons*, 78 Mont. 370, 254 P. 179, *rev'd*, 85 Mont. 114, 278 P. 110, 115 (1929). The requirement of legal ramifications also appears in other cases from this period, *see Clark v. Cassidy*, 64 Ga. 662 (1880), in which the Georgia Supreme Court, without proving the content of the contract, assumed a "mutual intent to observe towards society and each other those duties which result from the relation of husband and wife." *See* the above-mentioned case, *Sapp v. Newsom*, 27 Tex. 537, 540 (1864), in which the court spoke of an "intention to enter into the state of matrimony and to assume its duties and obligations." In *State v. Bittick*, 103 Mo. 183, 15 S.W. 325 (1891), the parties had drafted a written agreement in which they agreed "to live together so long as we may both live, to live together as man and wife." The court, requiring "consent for life, for the discharge, to each other and to the community, of the duties legally incumbent on those whose association is founded on the distinction of sex," found that despite the fact that the contract did not contain any express intent with respect to the obligations of the law, that the contract fulfilled these requirements and that a common law marriage was proven. In *Riddle v. Riddle*, 26 Utah 268, 72 P. 1081, 1084 (1903), the Utah Supreme Court spoke of a contract in which the parties agreed "to be bound by the 'various obligations and liabilities' which by operation of law arise from the relation of the contracting parties." In *Topper v. Perry*, 197 Mo. 531, 95 S.W. 203, 207 (1906), the court characterized marriage as "a civil contract by which a man and a woman agree to take each other for husband and wife during their joint lives ... and to discharge towards each other the duties and imposed by law upon such relationship." This case is cited in *In re Stevenson's Estate*, 272 Pa. 291, 116 A.2d 162, 165 (1922). In *Scalzi v. Folsom*, 156 F.Supp. 838, 840 (D.R.I. 1957), the woman testified: "I wanted to marry Mr. Scalzi and he wanted to marry me but we did not do so as I did not want the property in the name of Campagnone to be changed to Scalzi. His children caused a great deal of trouble in money matters and I did not want them to have any interest in my property." The court found that no marriage contract had been proven, however, without directly referring to that statement. In *Abramson v. Abramson*, 161 Neb. 782, 74 N.W.2d 919 (1956), the man, according to the woman's testimony, was of the understanding that they were married as they "slept together," and she considered herself married "because of having lived with him and had three children." The court found, however, that the marriage contract had not been sufficiently evidenced. In *Jambrone v. David*, 16 Ill.2d 32, 156 N.E.2d 569, 571 (1959), the court required a contract "to be husband and wife and assume all the rights and duties of the marital relationship," which was found to not be proven. *Compare Jolley v. Jolley*, 46 Ohio Misc. 40,

focus on legal ramifications as the object of the marital intent. One example can be found in *Tartt v. Negus* (1899), in which the Alabama Supreme Court stated that "the law established the relation of marriage without regard to what the parties considered the legal effect to be."

A similar understanding came to expression over a century later in *Callen v. Callen* (2005), in which the family court found the parties' intent to be as a married couple clear, even though they may not have understood the legal consequences of their intentions and actions. The South Carolina Supreme Court, however, held that the family court misapprehended the meaning of intent to marry, and maintained that a party need not understand every nuance of marriage or divorce law, but must at least know that his actions will render him married as that word is commonly understood. If a party does not comprehend that his intentions and actions will "bind him in a legally binding marital relationship," then, according to the court, he lacks the intent to be married. The court maintained that South Carolina does not impose marriage upon a couple merely because they intend "to be together forever."[116]

The requirement of fidelity is among the obligations that are connected to marriage. A marriage contract accepting polygamy is viewed to be

---

347 N.E.2d 557 (C.P.Ohio 1975), in which the plaintiff did not believe that any marriage contract was required for establishing a common law marriage and in which she did not even claim that such a contract had been executed. No common law marriage was found proven. *Compare Ex parte Ver Pault*, 86 F.2d 113, C.C.A.N.Y. (2d Cir. 1936).

116 *Callen v. Callen*, 365 S.C. 618, 620 S.E.2d 59, 63 (2005); and *Tartt v. Negus*, 127 Ala. 301, 28 So. 713, 715 (1899). The case is discussed positively in James Schouler, A Treatise on the Law of Marriage, Divorce, Separation and Domestic Relations II § 1177 (6th ed. 1921). The same formulation appears in *McClurkin v. McClurkin*, 206 Ala. 513, 90 So. 917, 918 (1921); *White v. White*, 225 Ala. 155, 142 So. 524, 525 (1932); and *Smith v. Smith*, 247 Ala. 213, 23 So.2d 605, 609 (1945). *See also Fryer v. Fryer*, 9 S.C.Eq. (Rich.Cas.) 85, 97 (1832), in which Justice Johnson of the South Carolina Court of Appeals states that the parties must be conscious of the fact that they have entered into a contract, but adds: "I do not say, that they must have a full understanding of the legal consequences of the contract." The level of consciousness required is not elaborated upon in the case. *See also Gammelgaard v. Gammelgaard*, 247 Iowa 979, 77 N.W.2d 479 (1956), in which the man and woman lived together for twelve years, and the woman stated that she did not have any knowledge that the marriage created any legal ramifications or that such a thing as a common law marriage existed, but where the court found the existence of a marriage contract based upon their cohabitation, and thereby the formation of a common law marriage. A lack of knowledge as to the legal ramifications of the marriage ought to be distinguished from a lack of knowledge as to regulations with respect to the entering into of such a marriage. In *Elliott v. Indus. Accident Bd.*, 101 Mont. 246, 53 P.2d 451, 454 (1936), the court found that "the evidence is sufficient to establish a common-law marriage, even though the parties had no knowledge of what constitutes such a marriage." In *Shelton v. Belknap*, 155 Tex. 37, 282 S.W.2d 682, 685 (1955), the court found that a silent marriage contract had been formed, despite the fact that the man mistakenly believed that such a contract was not necessary and that living together for six months was all that was required to form a common law marriage: "The fact that he was mistaken as to how the law would be applied to the facts in interpreting the relationship should not be held to destroy the agreement for a present and continuing relationship of husband and wife."

invalid, not only because it embraces an unacceptable cohabitation, but also because it is in violation of a fundamental legal obligation within marriage.[117] In *Hansen v. Hansen* (1998), the woman, during her cohabitation with the man, had a sexual relationship with a friend of the couple. The Utah Court of Appeals stated that this circumstance indicated that she "did not want or consent to the rights and responsibilities that accompany a legally recognized marital relationship." Given this and other circumstances, the court found that the required elements of the marriage contract had not been proven.[118]

The legal ramifications resulting of a marriage include the obligation, upon termination of the relationship, to observe the legal formalities of marital divorce. Consequently, marriage contracts have not been recognized that allow for the relationship to be terminated as soon as either party so desires. One party's stated unwillingness to be subject to the regulations governing divorce, has been considered by the court in its finding that a marriage contract was not proven. For example, in *People v. Badgett* (1995), the woman testified that she did not enter into a marriage because she "did not want to have to get a divorce if the relationship did not work out." The California Supreme Court, applying Texas law, found, without any significant discussion concerning the required content of marital intent, that the trial court's judgment that no marriage contract had been entered into by the parties was correct, especially as supported by this statement, and that a common law marriage had not been proven.[119]

---

117 In *Riddle v. Riddle*, 26 Utah 268, 72 P. 1081, 1084 (1903), a Mormon man lived with three women. The Utah Supreme Court stated: "One of the essential obligations of a valid marriage contract is that which binds the parties to keep themselves separate and apart from all others, and cleave to each other during their joint lives. Therefore any contract in which the parties fail to consent and agree to so live together is void."

118 *Hansen v. Hansen*, 958 P.2d 931, 936 (Utah App. 1998). It should be noted that the requirement of cohabitation was fulfilled with respect to the same circumstances not discussed in the case.

119 *People v. Badgett*, 41 Cal.Rptr.2d 635, 895 P.2d 877, 898 (1995). *See also Perales v. Flores*, 147 S.W.2d 974 (Tex.Civ.App.-San Antonio 1941), in which the court found that the man intended an agreement that created the status of "terminable at will." The court could not accept as a marriage contract an arrangement "which could be terminated by him without the intervention or approval of the governmental agencies of society." *See also Ridley v. Compton*, 215 Miss. 532, 61 So.2d 341, 342 (1952), in which the court stated that the contract must be free of every reservation so that nothing, aside from "a decree of divorce pronounced by a court of competent jurisdiction can dissolve the relationship." *See also Ferrell v. Celebrezze*, 232 F.Supp. 281 (S.D.Tex. 1964), in which the woman, according to the findings of the court, "rejected the risk inherent in binding wedlock" and that a marriage contract was not proven based on her "reluctance and refusal to accept the legal status of a wife." *Compare Cornell v. Mabe*, 206 F.2d 514, 517 (5th Cir. 1953). *See also Swingle v. Keifer*, 105 Tex. 609, 153 S.W. 1132, 1133 (1913), in which the court refers to a contract according to which the parties would live together as husband and wife "so long as they desired" and according to which one or both of the parties "could dissolve the contract at will," and found that the contract could not legally be found to form a marriage contract.

A consequence of the fact that such a contract is not accepted is that the relationship can be terminated at will as the parties originally wished, because a marriage has not been entered into and the regulations concerning divorce are not applicable. A simple statement by one party, that they do not wish a certain legal ramification, for example, losing pension rights, has been interpreted by the courts as evidence against a true marital intent.[120]

If the parties have entered into the marriage only for the purposes of obtaining a legal benefit, for example, the right to immigrate, and generally do not have the intention to live together as spouses, but instead intend to dissolve the union as soon as the intended benefit is received, it is a sham marriage.[121] The finding of a lack of a marital intent in such cases can be dependent upon the required content of the intent, whether it is insufficient because the parties did not have the intent to accept all the legal ramifications of marriage, or because they did not have the intent to cohabit. In contrast, if the parties have the intent to form a complete legal marriage, move in together, and live as spouses, but one of the motives behind their intention is to achieve a specific legal benefit, the underlying motive is not always considered to be an impediment to the formation of a marriage. In the case of *In re Estate of Gower* (1971), the parties had drafted a written marriage contract, in which they stated that they had the intent of "establishing marriage status." It later become known that one of the motives behind their intent was to prevent the man from being called to military duty. They lived together for thirty years. The court, finding that the underlying motive did not prevent the formation of a common law marriage, stated: "We do not believe that the appellants establishing marriage ... in order to avoid conscription for military service renders invalid his otherwise valid common law marriage. The reason or motive underlying the decision to marry is not relevant to a finding of the *intention* to marry."[122]

An intent that is found to be insufficient at the commencement of the relationship can later be transformed, however, into an acceptable marital intent. In the case of *In re Erickson's Estate* (1954), the court makes the distinction between, on one side, the "consent to marriage," and on the other side, the "intention simply to live together in fornication or concubinage."[123] The court, which more closely defined consent to marriage as

120 In *Matter of Estate of Atwood*, 577 N.W.2d 60 (Iowa App. 1998), no discussion as to the intent with respect to legal ramifications was made by the court. The Iowa Court of Civil Appeals stated: "The notion that she was married for some purposes and not for others is in flagrant contradiction of the public policy behind the high standard of proof required to establish a valid marriage. We conclude, on this record, that no marriage contract was intended."

121 Sham marriages are discussed in 6.6.5 *infra.*

122 *See In re Estate of Gower,* 445 Pa. 554, 284 A.2d 742, 743-744 (1971); and *Interest of Miller,* 301 Pa.Super. 511, 448 A.2d 25 (1982).

123 *In re Erickson's Estate,* 75 S.D. 345, 64 N.W.2d 316, 317 (1954).

the parties' intent to take each other "as husband and wife forever," found, despite the fact that the parties had lived together as husband and wife approximately twenty-five years, and outwardly enjoyed the reputation of being man and wife, such *consensus* had not been proven by the evidence in the case. Instead, the evidence demonstrated, according to the court's unusually conservative assessment, "an impulsive venture into, or a continuation of, an illicit relationship."[124] In accordance with the discussion in Chapter 2, "Informal Marriages in Roman Law," *supra*, under Roman law, an *affectio concubinam habendi* could easily be transformed into an *affectio maritalis*,[125] so that the parties' ability to form a common law marriage, in the present case, with a change in their *animus* during twenty-five years, was not so distant. The court stated: "With a little change in fortune and attitude of mind it might have ripened into marriage."[126]

6.3.3 Both Cohabitation and a Legal Relationship as the Objects of the Marital Intent

Support exists in the American case law for the proposition that the parties, in order to form a common law marriage, must have both the intent to live as husband and wife and the intent to establish a legal relationship, even though it is unusual for the courts to discuss this issue and clearly refer to this double requirement. That the required marital intent must contain both of these objects appears, for example, in *Lutwak v. United States* (1953). The United States Supreme Court stated that the normal definition of marriage, which Congress must have relied upon when legislation concerning alien spouses in the War Brides Act was passed, was that "the two parties have undertaken to establish a life together and assume certain duties and obligations."[127]

This double requirement can be extracted with an extensive interpretation of some of the above-mentioned formulations. This is true, for example,

124 *Id.* at 321.

125 *See* Section 2.4.2 *supra.*

126 *Erickson's Estate* at 321.

127 *See also Lutwak v. United States,* 195 F.2d 748 (7th Cir. 1952), *aff'd,* 344 U.S. 604, 611, 73 S.Ct. 481, 97 L.Ed. 593 (1953), *discussed in* 2 U. Chi. L. Rev. 710 (1953); War Brides Act, February 5 (1917); 59 Stat. 659, 8 U.S.C., §232). For a further discussion of this case, see 6.5.3 *infra. See also Grigsby v. Reib,* 105 Tex. 597, 153 S.W. 1124, 1125 (1913), in which the lower court, vacillating in its instructions to the jury, required that the parties "mutually consented and agreed together with each other to become husband and wife, with the intention at that time of living and cohabiting with each other as husband and wife." The Texas Supreme Court found the court's instructions to be correct, although it ought to be noted that it was not the content of the parties' intentions which was the object of the trial, but rather whether the cohabitation should be a necessary requirement in addition to the contract. In *Wristen v. Wristen,* 119 S.W.2d 1104 (Tex.Civ.App.-Eastland 1938), the Court of Appeals appears to have accepted the statement made in *Grigsby* concerning the parties' intentions. Compare *State v. Bittrick,* 103 Mo. 183, 15 S.W. 325, 11 L.R.A. 587 (1891).

if a court speaks of the intent to live together as husband and wife,[128] which can be interpreted to mean a requirement that the parties have not intended any type of cohabitation but a shared life in accordance with the regulation governing married spouses. Simultaneously, this formulation focuses only on the aspect of life together. The parties' intent, for example, with respect to the application of legislation concerning divorce and the division of property upon dissolution, can hardly be considered included in such a formulation. A mutual intent to be bound by these central legal effects is significant, particularly now, when it is becoming more common and socially acceptable for couples to live together outside the marital regulatory system. It is then important to require that the parties' mutual intent be formulated so that those wishing to live within or outside of the system can be distinguished.

If one unites the intent to the actual life together, with the intent to establish a legal relationship, the requirement for the formation of a common law marriage would then be a mutual intent to live together as husband and wife in a monogamous, lifelong, or at least long-term relationship in which the spouses are bound by the applicable marital regulatory system. The requirement here of a legal intent is aimed at insuring that neither party in the relationship is forced to accept a regulatory system to which he or she did not wish or agree to be bound. The requirement of an intent to live together is to distinguish between those relationships that are marital, and those created solely for sexual purposes or for a temporary cohabitation, and to insure that the legal effects of marriage are given only to those intending a lifelong relationship. At the same time, this requirement hinders the recognition of sham marriages. It should be noted that a requirement of the intent to form a legal relationship probably has the effect, however, of encouraging many couples to simply move in and continue their lives together, outside the concept of marriage.

This discussion of the intent as an element of a marriage contract, and the consequences of the different alternatives, is revisited in Chapter 13, *infra.*[129]

6.4 *Consensus de Praesenti* and *Consensus de Futuro*

As seen from the cases discussed above, for the parties' marital *consensus* to be allowed to form the basis of a marriage, the *consensus* – in accordance with the distinction posited by Peter Lombard – must concern the present, *i.e.*, an immediately valid marriage (*consensus de praesenti*).[130] The other

---

128 *See* 6.3.1 *supra.*
129 *See generally* Chapter 13.2 *infra.*
130 With respect to Peter Lombard's distinction, *see* Section 3.3 *supra.*

type of canon marriage contract concerned a future marriage (*consensus de futuro*), which according to the canon law before the Council of Trent, through an irrebuttable presumption, formed a marriage after *copula carnalis.* This second type of marriage was early recognized as a common law marriage in England and Scotland, but did not gain acceptance in the American case law.[131] The question of whether a marriage contract contains a *consensus de praesenti* or simply a *consensus de futuro,* however, has been given significant practical meaning in American law. Only contracts of the first nature have resulted in recognized marriages.

The decisive significance of the tense in which the consent is given, under the canon law distinction, led Martin Luther to characterize it as a pure farce, "ein lauter Narrenspiel;" and Pollock and Maitland to exclaim: "Of all people in the world lovers are the least likely to distinguish precisely between the present and the future tenses."[132] Similar criticism has been made of this distinction as it exists in American law. Luther noted the difficulty of maintaining the canon law distinction between *accipio* and *accipiam,* and, consequently, distinguishing between "Ich nehme Dich" and "Ich will Dich haben" in German. Similarly, the American case law points to the fact that it can simply be a matter of luck whether the parties actually say "I do take you" or "I will take you" as husband and wife, respectively. In *Caddy v. Johnstown Firemen's Relief Ass'n* (1938), the court states, not without reason, that "[u]nlettered persons frequently become confused in the use of tenses."[133] Freedman maintains that the distinction is theoretical and utterly unrealistic.[134] This situation has been the focus of criticism directed at the courts for rejecting the possibility in American law of allowing *consensus de futuro cum copula carnalis* to form a common law marriage. Dickinson argues for this: "The object of the rule ... is to prevent the injustice of making the validity of the marriage depend upon the tense of a verb, in other words to prevent the purely verbal formalism which would be enthroned by the rule of *Murdock's Estate,* the effect of which is to invalidate what would otherwise be a perfectly valid common

131 With respect to Canon law, *see id.* With respect to Scottish law, *see, e.g., Dalrymple v. Dalrymple,* (1811) 2 Hagg.Con. 54, 65, 161 Eng.Rep. 665, 669 and Chapter 11 *infra.* With respect to the rejection in American law of the recognition of *consensus de futuro cum copula, see* Section 4.2.3 *infra.* As to modern case law, *see, for example, Holmes v. Holmes,* 232 Ga.App. 434, 502 S.E.2d 294 (1998), in which the man, according to the woman's testimony, had asked her "to move in with him and maybe, you know, the marriage would come later." A marriage contract *de praesenti* was not proven. Before *Peacock v. Peacock,* 196 Ga. 441, 26 S.E.2d 608 (1943), there were *dicta* supporting marriage *per verba de futuro com copula, see, for example, Lefkoff v. Sicro,* 189 Ga. 554, 6 S.E.2d 687 (1939); and *Askew v. Dupree,* 30 Ga. 173 (1859).

132 With respect to the criticism by Luther, Pollock and Maitland of the canon law distinction, *see* Section 3.3.2 *supra.*

133 *Caddy v. Johnstown Firemen's Relief Ass'n,* 129 Pa.Super. 493, 499, 196 A. 590, 592 (1938).

134 Abraham L. Freedman and Maurice Freedman, Law of Marriage and Divorce in Pennsylvania I, 120 (2d ed. 1957).

law marriage merely because of the form of verbal expression in which it had its inception."[135]

This criticism leads to the question of to what the extent the courts' reasoning has truly been influenced by the inevitable verbal formalism that the critics believe is intertwined in this distinction. In response, there is support in the American case law for the argument that the courts' reasoning has been based on a literal application of the law. For example, in *Pierce v. Pierce* (1946), the man said to the woman, "I will take you for my wife," to which the woman answered, "If that is the case, I will take you for my husband." They thereafter lived together as husband and wife and enjoyed a reputation as such. The court, however, found that a common law marriage had not been formed, based on the fact that the words used were *in futuro,* not *in praesenti.*[136] Limiting an assessment to simply the words expressed by the parties is not, however, representative of the American case law as a whole.

In the majority of cases, the assessment addresses the meaning of the words, and the intent of the parties, whether *de praesenti* or *de futuro,* is viewed in a much broader context. In the case of *In re Comly's Estate* (1898), the man said to the woman: "Would you be willing to marry me in this way, that you and I are to live together until death separate us; I take you to be my wife, and you take me to be your husband?" The woman answered: "Yes, sir; unless death separate us." The man thereafter asked: "Are you willing for that?" The woman answered: "I guess I would be; but don't you think we had better be married by a minister?" The man responded by saying: "It is just as lawful in this state as if we were married by a minister; do what is right; but if we live together and do what is right, we are just as lawfully married as if a dozen ministers married us." Despite the fact that this conversation could be a conditional consent, based on the future tense expressed in the words ("Would you be willing to," and "I guess I would"), and despite the hesitation reflected in the woman's words and the hint that she is interested in a church ceremony, the court found that a *consensus de praesenti* had been proven and, as a consequence, a common law marriage had been formed.[137] In the case of *In re Ward's Estate* (1929), the man and woman had known each other for a period of less than eighteen months, during which the man on several occasions had suggested marriage without receiving a positive answer. The parties, on one occasion, were with some friends at a restaurant, when the man said to the woman: "Helen, will you be my wife," to which the woman answered,

---

135 *In re Murdock's Estate,* 92 Pa.Super. 275 (1927).

136 *Pierce v. Pierce,* 355 Pa. 175, 49 A.2d 346, 347, 349 (1946). *See also Hantz v. Sealy,* 6 Binn. 405 (1814), in which the man said "I take you for my wife" and the woman answered: "To be sure he is my husband good enough." The court found that the words referred to a previous contract, not to a contract *de praesenti.*

137 *In re Comly's Estate,* 185 Pa. 208, 39 A. 890 (1898); and *Com. ex rel. McDermott v. McDermott,* 236 Pa.Super.Ct. 541, 345 A.2d 914, 917 (1975).

"Yes, Jack, I will." The man then stated: "All right, from this time on, consider yourself my wife." The parties lived together until the death of the man. The court found, specifically with reference to the man's last statement to which, according to the record, the woman did not respond, that "the intention was to make a present contract." A valid marriage contract thus existed, and the woman at the time of the man's death, was his legal wife.[138]

The tendency to consider circumstances other than just the formulations of the parties can also be seen in the case of *In re Seifert's Estate* (1931), in which the man, before the woman and her mother stated: "Flora and me are going to get married... Now, Flora, I am going to take you for my lawful wife forever," to which the woman answered: "Well now, William, I am going to marry you and take you for my lawful husband as long as we both live." Both parties used the expression, "I am going to," without further defining a point of time at which that would occur, and the woman's express intent was "to marry" – an expression commonly used during ceremonial weddings. Nevertheless, the court found that the words used by the parties, followed by their living together and appearance as husband and wife, "with all the attending circumstances indicated a present intention, " meant that a common law marriage was proven.[139]

An example of a case in which the court distanced itself from a verbal formulation is *Moffat Coal Co. v. Industrial Commission* (1941).[140] The parties in question had lived together approximately three years and had two children together. Upon the death of the man, the question arose whether a common law marriage had been formed. The woman testified as to the marital intent of the parties: "Well, I thought if he would come and live with me, he would marry me, and he kept putting it off, and he never did." Q: "Then, you intended at some later date to be married?" A: "Yes." Q: "You didn't consider you were married then?" A: "I couldn't because I wasn't." The court found, however, that the woman's use of the word *marriage* was simply referring to the *ceremony of marriage*. Her own legal conclusion, that she could not be considered married, according to the court, was based on her erroneous understanding that a wedding ceremony was a condition for the existence of a marriage. A common law marriage was proven, an outcome that appears to be based on the assumption that the woman had a marital intent to which she herself lacked insight and to which her verbal formulation did not give evidence.

The endeavor to assess the words in a wider context in the application of the distinction can also be seen in more recent cases. In *McDermott v. McDermott* (1975), a divorced man, who had gone back to his former wife, announced his arrival with the words: "Here I am. You want to be

138 *In re Ward's Estate,* 296 Pa. 20, 145 A. 676, 677 (1929).
139 *In re Seifert's Estate,* 302 Pa. 447, 153 A. 722 (1931).
140 *Moffat Coal Co. v. Ind. Comm'n,* 108 Colo. 388, 118 P.2d 769 (1941).

my wife again?" The woman answered, "Yes," after which they lived together five years and enjoyed the appearance of husband and wife until they separated again. The woman petitioned for alimony from the man based on their common law marriage, formed after the man's return. The trial court rejected her claim because the man's statement, as given above, was not made in the present tense. On appeal, a minority in the Superior Court agreed and found that the couple had referred to a marriage "at some future time," words that were insufficient to form a common law marriage. The court's majority, however, after finding that the trial court's judgment was an "overly technical adherence to a 'black letter' rule," found that the man's words, "when considered in the context of the situation," gave expression of "a clear present intent," supported by the facts of the cohabitation thereafter and the appearance they enjoyed as husband and wife. A common law marriage had, therefore, been formed.[141]

The reasoning given above, which can be found in many additional cases,[142] ought to demonstrate that the courts have not been reduced to the verbal formalism, as claimed by critics of the distinction claim. The explanation appears to be that the courts, to a degree greater than that assumed by the critics, have assessed situations not simply on the tense of the words used by the parties, but also on the intent of the parties.[143] This is also consistent with the general principle expressed in the American case law, that the parties' intent ought to be interpreted in a wider context than the words exchanged between them, which is generally applicable, and not only to the interpretation of the distinction between contracts *de praesenti* and *de futuro*. In *Commonwealth v. Haylow* (1901), the court stated, "it is not the duty of the courts to seek for an interpretation of the words used by the parties which would be inconsistent with an honorable intention as well as with their subsequent conduct and declarations, when an interpretation consistent with the formation of an honorable relation is possible,

141 *Com. ex rel. McDermott v. McDermott*, 236 Pa.Super.Ct. 541, 345 A.2d 914, 915, 919 (1975).

142 *In re Hines's Estate*, 10 Pa.Super. 124 (1899); and *In re Murdock's Estate*, 92 Pa.Super. 275 (1927). In *Brown v. Nolen*, 298 Pa. 384, 148 A. 498 (1930), the court stated that the expression in question could not be strictly construed as *de praesenti* but found that the parties' intent was that a marriage would immediately be formed: "The intention of the parties may not be disregarded. The words used to formulate the marriage contract express a present intent to create an immediate relation of husband and wife." *See also Rhoads v. Stoltzfus*, 18 Lehigh 297 (Pa. D. 1939); and *In re Neafie's Estate*, 12 Pa.Dist. 749 (1903). In *Wydra v. Philadelphia & Reading Coal & Iron Co.*, 153 Pa.Super. 529, 34 A. 2d 326, 328 (1943), the court stated that after a review of the statements made and the circumstances in general: "It was not a betrothal dinner. It was a wedding dinner."

143 *See, e.g., Rhoads v. Stoltzfus*, 18 Lehigh 297, 300 (Pa. D. 1939), in which the court correctly stated that "it is not the tense of the verb that counts, but the intention of the parties."

and in the light of all the circumstances, more probably expresses their intention."[144]

The sharp criticism of the distinction by Luther, Pollock and Maitland, Freedman, and Dickinson appears unwarranted against the background stated above, at least as applied in the American case law. This is partially explained because the critics themselves appear to be victims of the formalism that they are warning against. Even though it can generally be accepted that unlettered persons can become confused with respect to the verbal use of tenses, the distinction is completely realistic and suitable for the purpose of clarification. It is natural, for unlettered persons, as for others, to distinguish between the present and the future, between an immediate marriage and a marriage that will occur sometime in the future, and between the intent to enter into a marriage and the intent to do so sometime in the future. Despite that which Luther, Pollock and Maitland maintain, no one should be more conscious of the difference between the present and the future than two engaged lovers looking forward to exchanging their vows in the future.

The problem appears to be not so much the time aspect of the distinction as the true content of the intent of the marriage contract, the *essensialia negotii.* The relative lack of definition, which as seen above is inherent in the canon law as well as in the American law, is reflected particularly clearly in the attempt to define the boundary between contracts *de praesenti* and contracts *de futuro.* The question arises: What in the contract refers to a present intent to form a contract, *de praesenti* and what refers to the future intent to form a contract, *de futuro*? Is it the marital cohabitation or is it the legal relationship?

The lack of clarity with respect to the content of the intent is reflected in the cases, in which, strikingly often, the parties are asked if they agreed "to marry" or "to be married," immediately or in the future, respectively, without the examiner more closely defining the meanings assigned these words. The parties commonly become confused, and the danger is great that the person asking the questions and the person answering them are talking about different things.[145] If the problem simply were linguistic,

---

144 *Com. v. Haylow,* 17 Pa.Super, 541, 547 (1901); and *Chambers v. Dickson,* 2 S & R. 475 (Pa. 1816).

145 For example, in *Rosetta v. Rosetta,* 525 S.W.2d 255, 258 (Tex.Civ.App.-Tyler 1975), divorced spouses moved back together, and the man alleged that the parties had entered into a marriage contract *de praesenti* and therefore a common law marriage had been formed. During the cross-examination, the man testified: "Q: Okay. But, you did talk about sometime in the future remarrying, isn't that right? A: Yes... Q: Didn't you all have an agreement, one time, when you got ready to move back in the house that you asked her for a trial living together so that you might marry sometime if it worked out? A: Back when we first, just before, we moved in together, we discussed the possibility of a trial situation between the two of us. Q: So to see if some day you might marry in the future, isn't that right? A: Yes, go through a ceremony... Q: Did you not tell me on – during cross-examination two days ago that you entered this household under an agreement to marry in the future? Isn't that

it could be easily resolved by more closely defining the inquiry. A further definition requires taking a position, however, about which alternative is correct with respect to the object of the marital intent.

Despite the fact that there are few in-depth discussions as to the assessments made by the courts with respect to the marital intent's *essensialia*, cases exist in which the courts have taken a stance as to the object the intent is to have with reference to the parties' *consensus de praesenti* and *de futuro*, respectively. Cases can be found, for example, in which the parties have planned or simply agreed, in the future, to enter into a ceremonial marriage through a wedding ceremony. The question arises whether

---

what you told me, right there? A: I said that we might have an agreement to marry in the future. Q: That's right. An agreement to marry in the future and I asked you specifically that and you said, yes, that is right. Then, just a few minutes ago, you told me that you agreed to be married when you entered into the house. A: As far as I was concerned we were still married.... Q: If you didn't consider yourself divorced, why would you enter into an agreement to marry? A: Just for the ceremony... Q: But, you had no intent to presently be husband and wife? You were going to marry in the future, isn't that right? A: We had intent to be husband and wife. Q: Then, why would you make an agreement to marry in the future? A: She said we might. Q: Might marry in the future, right? A: Yes... Q: Okay, you also agreed to be married in the future, ceremonial, is that correct? A: I didn't agree to it. Q: But, that was Janice's condition, wasn't it? A: Not a condition, no. Q: What was it then? A: It was a maybe. Q: A maybe you would marry in the future?... A: Yes... Q: With reference to this business about marrying in the future, explain what that term meant? I mean, what were you talking about? A: Marrying in the future? Q: This—let's get our time frame right. Before you commenced living together again, on or about July 1st, 1970, and you said you had this conversation when she said, maybe we'll marry in the future? A: Yes. Q: Did she say the statement that she would be your wife? A: No. It was a little while later. Q: What was she talking about? I mean was she talking about going before a preacher or – A: Yes, a preacher, going before a preacher. Q: Is that what you understood it to mean? A: That is what I understood it to be." – The noticeable difficulties arising in the verbal communication here of course can certainly have been deliberately created. It is difficult to distance oneself from the thought that the lawyer is exploiting the power of speech over thought, and the double meaning the verb "marry" can have. By not clearly defining that which the lawyer intends with the term "marry", whether it simply is in reference to the parties' participation in a ceremony, or, that which is most likely, that the parties become husband and wife, he encourages the party to answer affirmatively, even when the party himself is referring simply to the ceremony.

Another illustrative example can be found in *Campbell v. Christian*, 235 S.C. 102, 110 S.E.2d 1, 3-4 (1959), in which the woman successfully alleged that a common law marriage had been formed. During the cross-examination, she was asked: "Q: And he never did tell you that you were his wife, did he? A: I had sense enough to know that I didn't marry him. Q: Both of you were not married then were you? A: No, we weren't married... Q: You don't think you had any right to take out a warrant against him for marrying Betty? A: No, I didn't. Q: That was because you didn't consider you and he were married? A: That is right." It is probable that the woman, with the term "married," referred to a ceremonial wedding. That explains how the court, despite the testimony, found that a common law marriage had been formed. In the case of *In re Estate of Hornback* 475 P.2d 184, 187 (Okla. 1970), the court refers to the parties' intent "to marry at some future date," without further elaborating as to whether the term "marry" meant a wedding ceremony, establishing the legal relationship, or both. The court's reasoning in *Baker v. Mitchell*, 143 Pa.Super. 50, 17 A.2d 738, 740 (1941), displays similar difficulties in the use of the expression "a promise to marry in the future."

they can be considered to have already formed a common law marriage prior to the wedding. This situation is not uncommon, as many persons living in common law marriages at some point have considered a ceremonial marriage. The theoretical question arises whether it is possible to have the intent to enter into marriage through a ceremony in the future, and, simultaneously, the intent to immediately form a common law marriage.

6.4.1 A Planned Ceremonial Marriage Prevents a Common Law Marriage

On one hand, a number of cases within the American case law stand for the proposition that a planned future wedding bars the formation of a common law marriage between the parties. A rationale is that, according to the courts, the intent to form a marriage contract includes the requirement to establish a legal relationship and, in individual cases, that intent has been with reference to a future wedding. No immediate common law marriage can consequently be formed. However, the courts' reasoning is seldom so lucid.

The required content of marital intent is often not clearly defined. If deficiencies are found in the cohabitation, it can be difficult, in assessing the reasoning of the courts, to determine whether the parties' intent is insufficient as a result of the cohabitation or the legal relationship. In the case of *In re Grimm's Estate* (1889), the woman testified that she and the deceased had lived together for a week before he died, and that they had intended to enter into a ceremonial marriage the week after he died. The court found that the intent to be married in the future was proven, and that no common law marriage had been formed at the time of the man's death.[146] Nothing was specifically stated as to the required content of the

146 *In re Grimm's Estate,* 131 Pa. 199, 18 A. 1061 (1889). *See also In re Estate of Hornback* 475 P.2d 184, 187 (Okla. 1970), concerning divorced spouses, who after the divorce lived in different geographical areas. They resumed their relationship, in that the woman lived with the man on weekends. About six months after the divorce judgment, the man died. On the same day that the man died, the woman had stated to a witness: "We were going to be married in two or three days." The man had also spoke to a witness about plans to remarry. The woman argued that she was the deceased's common law wife. The court stated: "A common law marriage is based on a present assumption of an existing relationship, not upon what the parties intended or have agreed to do at a future time" and found, based on the evidence in the record, that the parties "intended and planned to marry at some future date," the consequence of which was that no common law marriage had been formed. The court did not refer to the requirements that ought to be fulfilled as to the marital intent's *essensialia,* but instead referred only to the contract "to become husband and wife." As the parties lived together only on weekends, one cannot, according to the court's reasoning, with certainty state that the lack of intent *de praesenti* was with reference to the living together or to the legal relationship. *See also In re Danikas' Estate,* 76 Colo.191, 230 P. 608 (1924). *Compare Fryer v. Fryer,* 9 S.C.Eq. (Rich.Cas.) 85 (1832).

marital intent. Because the parties had lived together for only one week, the lack of *de praesenti* cannot with certainty be ascribed to the intent to live together or establish a legal relationship. An impediment to a marriage contract *de praesenti* has also been found if vague plans have been made to have a future wedding, undefined as to time or place. In the case of *In re Estate of Shepard* (1994), the parties divorced after being formally married for five years. However, they continued to live together for a few months, with a few interruptions, and made plans to formally marry again. When the man died, the woman alleged that she was the deceased's common law wife. The trial court found that the woman's testimony gave support only for an intent to marry in the future, which the appellate court affirmed. However, the court did not more closely define what was meant by intent to marry.[147]

In other cases in jurisdictions with required content of the marriage contract, the courts have not accepted an intent to live together as sufficient without further elaboration about what, instead, was required. In *Young v. General Baking Co.* (1938), the parties lived together as husband and wife for approximately three years before the man died. The court found that their relationship was not the basis of a common law marriage. As reasons, the court stated that appellant and decedent never considered themselves actually married; that they intended to be "formally married" (by ceremony) at some future date, but were content to live together as husband and wife until then; and that they had not entered into an agreement of marriage.[148] It can be deduced that a mutual intent to live together as husband and wife, according to the court, was clearly not acceptable as *essensialia* for the marital intent.[149] Unfortunately, the court does not state what was required instead, with respect to the parties' marital intent. It is not possible to rule out that the insufficiency was the intent to live together for life. Nevertheless, the court probably required the intent to establish a legal relationship, which, according to the court, the parties intended to give effect to at the planned wedding.

Without directly rejecting the idea that living together can be deemed the marriage contract's *essensialia*, the courts, in other cases, have described the necessary content as the intent to establish a legal relationship.

147 *In re Estate of Shepard*, 646 N.E.2d 561, 564 (Ohio App. 1994). *See also Potter v. Davie*, 275 A.D.2d 961, 713 N.Y.S.2d 627, 629 (A.D. 4 Dep't 2000). *Compare In re Estate of Wilson*, 512 S.E.2d 383, 386 (Ga.App. 1999), in which the circumstance that the woman wore an engagement ring was cited as support for the fact that the parties intended to marry in the future.

148 *Young v. Gen. Baking Co.*, 104 Ind.App. 658, 12 N.E.2d 1016, 1018 (1938). *See also Sullivan v. Sullivan*, 196 Kan. 705, 413 P.2d 988 (1966). In *Pittney v. Pittney*, 151 Kan. 848, 101 P.2d 933 (1940), where the parties lived together for 18 years without the required holding out as spouses, the court found that the they cohabited together "upon the promise of the defendant to marry plaintiff in the future – that summer." *Compare Rosetta v. Rosetta*, 525 S.W.2d 255, 261 (Tex.Civ.App.-Tyler 1975).

149 With respect to the marriage contract's *essensialia*, *see generally* 6.3 *supra*.

For example, in *Baker v. Mitchell* (1941), the woman testified to a conversation occurring between the parties during a car ride: "Well, he asked me if I would become his wife, and I said I would. Then we agreed to be man and wife ... that he would become my husband and I would become his wife." During the cross-examination, it became evident that the parties had planned, on a certain day six months after the car ride, to enter into a ceremonial marriage. Several days prior to that date, the man died. The woman, who, during this time, had lived together with him at her parents' house and become pregnant, argued that a common law marriage had been formed. The court, without elaborating as to the required content of the marital intent, however, found that the parties' contract was not an agreement concerning a marriage *de praesenti,* but a promise to marry in the future.[150] The court seems to have defined the marriage contract as a contract concerning their legal relationship,[151] and appears to have found that the intent of the parties with respect to such a relationship was postponed until their ceremonial wedding.

The reasoning of the courts is clearest in those cases in which the parties rejected cohabitation and accepted the legal relationship as the object of the marital intent. An example is *State v. Grimes* (1933), in which the parties executed a written contract according to which they agreed "to live as husband and wife until such time that we are lawfully married." No common law marriage was found proven because the contract did not include a *consensus de praesenti* to take up the legal relationship.[152]

The choice of words should not be given too much significance. Cases can be found in which the parties' wording indicates an agreement *de praesenti,* but with respect to their plans for a future wedding ceremony, has been interpreted as a *consensus de futuro.* In *Wolford v. Whiterock Quarries, Inc.* (1941), when he had opened a letter stating that he had received his divorce from his wife, the man said to the woman he was living with: "My divorce went through. Now you are my wife," to which the woman answered "That will be fine."[153] The man also stated that now they could go through with their plans to get married on Christmas day. The court found that a common law marriage had not been formed.

---

150 *Baker v. Mitchell* 143 Pa.Super. 50, 17 A.2d 738, 740 (1941). *Compare Wheaton v. State,* 85 Okla.Crim.App. 132, 185 P.2d 931 (1947), in which the parties lived together as husband and wife, but categorically declared that they were not married, but intended to marry in the future. The court, requiring for the formation of a common law marriage a contract to enter into "a matrimonial relationship," found that no common law marriage had been formed.

151 *Baker* at 741.

152 *State v. Grimes,* 215 Iowa 1287, 247 N.W. 664, 666 (1933).

153 *Wolford v. Whiterock Quarries,* 144 Pa.Super. 577, 20 A.2d 887. 889 (1941).

6.4.2 A Planned Ceremonial Marriage Does Not Prevent a Common Law Marriage

Cases also exist in the American case law standing for the proposition that a planned future wedding is not a bar to the formation of a common law marriage prior to the ceremony. The fact these cases have in common is that the parties, despite plans for a future wedding, have been found to have a mutual intent prior to the wedding to form a common law marriage.[154] It is difficult to extrapolate what is considered the required marriage contract's *essensialia* from the courts' reasoning.[155] One rationale

154 *Coney v. R.S.R. Corp.*, 563 N.Y.S.2d 211 (A.D. 3 Dep't 1990): "[D]esire for a future ceremonial marriage does not in and of itself preclude a finding that a valid common-law marriage exists." In *Metro. Life Ins. Co. v. Johnson*, 103 Idaho 122, 645 P.2d 356 (1982), the intent to have a ceremonial wedding in the future and other circumstances were not found sufficient to rebut the presumption of a common law marriage. *See also Howard v. Howard,* 459 S.W.2d 901 (Tex.Civ.App.-Houston 1970): "There is nothing necessarily inconsistent between an implied agreement to enter into a common law marriage immediately and an intention to have a ceremonial marriage at a definite future date." *Compare Gillaspie v. Blair Constr. Co.*, 192 Kan. 455, 388 P.2d 647, 649 (1964), in which the man, during the entire relationship between the parties, promised that a ceremonial wedding would take place in the future and in which a common law marriage was found to have been immediately formed. In *McIlveen v. McIlveen*, 332 S.W.2d 113, 117 (Tex.Civ. App.-Houston 1960), the court stated: "In the instant case there is nothing inconsistent with appellant's agreement in September to enter into a common-law marriage with the deceased and her intention later to enter into a ceremonial marriage in the Catholic church." *See also Butler v. Butler*, 296 S.W.2d 635 (Tex.Civ.App. 1956); *Shelton v. Belknap*, 155 Tex. 37, 282 S.W.2d 682, 684 (1955); and *Goldman's Estate*, 109 Pa.Super. 288 (1933). The circumstance that the parties from time to time discussed a future ceremonial wedding did not bar the formation of an immediate common law marriage in *Le Blanc v. Yawn*, 99 Fla. 328, 126 So. 789 (1930). *See also Radovich v. Radovich*, 84 Colo. 250, 269 P. 22, 23 (1928). *Compare* the Scottish case, *Shaw v. Henderson*, 1982, S.L.T. 63, in which the parties lived together slightly more than ten months when the man died on January 31 and the couple clearly "had made arrangements to be married on the 24th of February." The court (Outher House) found, without making a distinction between *consensus de praesenti* and *consensus de futuro*, "sufficient material from which the inference of consent to marriage can properly be drawn." A common law marriage was formed before the death with the support of the marriage presumption "by cohabitation, habit and repute."

155 For example, in *Brown v. Brown*, 215 S.E.2d 671, 234 Ga. 300 (1975), the man and woman had lived together from 1962 until 1973. In 1972, however, the man married another woman and they were divorced in March of 1972. The man continued living with the first woman until April of 1973. In July, she petitioned for divorce and alimony. As grounds, she alleged that a common law marriage had been formed between them during the years they lived together after the man's divorce from his first wife. The woman testified that she, during the time together, told the man of her desire to have a ceremonial wedding, to which the man had replied it was not necessary and that they did not need a "piece of paper" because they already were married. The woman also testified that she "felt married" to the man and that she "considered herself married." The court found that "her desire for a ceremonial marriage did not preclude the existence of a common law marriage." Even if the parties in the case did not have a mutual agreement to in the future have a wedding, it is worth noting that with respect to the woman's testimony, her one-sided desire was no impediment to her being able to in their mutual contract

for the outcomes in these cases is that the courts have required as to the content of the marital intent an intent, not to establish a legal relationship, but to live together as husband and wife. If the later intent is found

---

have an intent *de praesenti* to immediately form a common law marriage. The court did not further elaborate as to what the parties' mutual intent *de praesenti* must contain in order for it to constitute a marriage contract, but simply spoke of the requirement of a "marriage contract" and a mutual intent "to marry." *Compare* other Georgia cases where the content of the contract is more clearly defined, *e.g. Georgia Osteopathic Hosp. v. O'Neal,* 198 Ga.App. 770, 403 S.E.2d 235, 243-244 (1991). *See also Aaberg v. Aaberg,* 512 So.2d 1375, 1376 (Ala. 1987), in which the parties lived together for eleven years, of which eight were without any impediment. During the time, the man had wished to "formalize" his marriage with a civil ceremony. The court, requiring a contract "to be husband and wife," found a common law marriage proven. Using the same contract definition, the court in *Kirk v. Mattison,* 497 So.2d 120, 123 (Ala. 1986), in which the parties had lived together for ten years, found that a common law marriage had been formed, despite the fact that they had plans for a ceremonial wedding. *See also Crosson v. Crosson,* 668 So.2d 873 (Ala.Civ.App. 1995), in which the marriage contract was termed an agreement "to permanently enter the marriage relationship" and a common law marriage, with the support of a marriage presumption, had been formed despite the fact that the parties discussed getting formally married. *See also King v. King,* 269 Ala. 468, 114 So.2d 145, 147 (1959), in which the court stated: "The mere fact that the parties could not get together on the time when and the place where they were to have another ceremonial marriage is not sufficient to overcome the presumption of a common-law marriage." *Compare Skipworth v. Skipworth,* 360 So.2d 975, 977 (Ala. 1978), in which the contract was described as a contract to enter into "a marriage relationship"; and *Huffmaster v. Huffmaster,* 279 Ala. 594,188 So.2d 552 (1966), in which the court found that plans for a future wedding ceremony did not create a bar to the immediate formation of a common law marriage. In *Coleman v. Aubert,* 176 N.W.2d 801, 806, 807(Ala. 1988), the man stated: "Well she asked me if I wanted to get married and I said yes, I do." The man further stated that the woman, before her death, had said that "she wanted a ceremony." The court, stating that a contract "to be husband and wife" was required to form a common law marriage, found it evidenced as the parties had agreed to enter into "a marriage relationship" and that a marriage contract *de praesenti* existed. *Compare Stringer v. Stringer,* 689 So.2d 194 (Ala.Civ.App. 1997), in which the parties' plans to formally marry were not completed. The man said that he was not "ready to commit to a marriage." Despite the fact that they lived together for 15 years, it was found that the parties "had no mutual assent to be married." *See also Moffat Coal Co. v. Ind. Comm'n,* 108 Colo. 38, 118 P.2d 769 (1941)(the woman stated: "I thought if he would come and live with me he would marry me, and he kept putting it off and he never did." The court found, that the woman with the term "marriage" meant a future wedding ceremony, which was not a hinder to the formation of a common law marriage *de praesenti*). *Compare Gonzalez v. Satrustegui,* 870 P.2d 1188, 1197 (Ariz.App.Div. 1 1993), in which the woman answered to the question as to why they never married: "I don't know. Just one of those things. To us, it wasn't that important. It's one of those things you put off. We talked about it a lot. Wherever we went, we thought, well, we should. In Phoenix when we stayed down there in the condo, we thought we ought to get married. In fact, just the night before Frank passed away we were talking about it." Based on this, no marriage contract was found proven. *See also Winder v. Winder,* 98 Cal.App.2d 78, 219 P.2d 18 (1950), in which the court did not find that a common law marriage proven, referring to the fact that "there was no intention either on his part or her part to contract a common-law marriage." The court noted the circumstance that the woman left the man when he did not fulfill his promise to get a marriage license for a ceremonial wedding and the man directly thereafter ceremonially married another woman. *See also Employer's Mut. Ins. Co. v. Morgulski,* 69 Colo. 223, 193 P. 725 (1920).

to be evidenced *de praesenti*, a common law marriage can be immediately formed, despite the parties' *de futuro* plans for a future wedding.

A case indicating this is *Trammel v. Trammel* (1946), in which the parties together planned a future wedding. The court found that they simultaneously had a mutual marital intent *de praesenti*. The parties, during a conversation in the man's car, had agreed to be husband and wife in accordance with common law and sometime in the future confirm their relationship with a legal ceremony. They lived together thereafter for approximately thirteen years as husband and wife, enjoyed a reputation as such, where after the man abandoned the woman and married another. The court stated: "The fact that the parties were to live together as husband and wife in accordance with their agreement to do so, and at some time in the future, when their affairs made it feasible or practical, they would solemnize their relation by engaging in a lawful ceremony, cannot be construed into a modification of the marriage agreement, rendering it void and condemning them to a life of unlicensed sin."[156] Even if the court did not more closely elaborate as to the legal requirements of the marriage contract's *essensialia*, the characteristic of the contract as a contract to live together as husband and wife points to the fact that the object of the parties' marital intent was the marital cohabitation. A contract *de praesenti* concerning the cohabitation constituted the marriage, the consequence thereof is that the planned wedding ceremony was a mere technicality. The court in *Wright v. Goss* (1997) is clearer in its assessment with respect to the required intent, in that the parties, for the formation of a common law marriage, must agree to live together as man and wife.[157] The circumstance that they had talked about getting married was not considered a hindrance to the formation of a common law marriage.

Another possible explanation for the outcome in these cases is that the courts have separated the wedding into a contract concerning the legal formation of a marriage and simply the ceremony.[158] The courts then must

156 *Trammel v. Trammel*, 196 S.W.2d 209 (Tex.Civ.App. San Antonio 1946); *Tompkins v. State*, 774 S.W.2d 195, 209 (Tex.Cr.App. 1987); and *Aquilar v. State*, 715 S.W.2d 645, 648 (Tex.Cr.App. 1986). *Compare In re Foster*, 77 Idaho 26, 287 P.2d 282, 285 (1955), in which the court's majority found that the parties' consent to the marriage was evidenced by the mutual assumption of marital obligations and benefits and added: "Their intention of later solemnizing the marriage by a civil ceremony could not operate to defeat the marriage already accomplished." A dissenting justice maintained, however, that a contract to immediately cohabit and later marry is not marital when the parties' "marital status" is intended to be established in the future.

157 *Wright v. Goss*, 229 Ga.App. 393, 494 S.E.2d 23, 24 (1997); and *Georgia Osteopathic Hosp. v. O'Neal*, 198 Ga.App. 770, 403 S.E.2d 235, 243-244 (1991). *See also Brown v. Carr*, 198 Ga.App. 567, 402 S.E.2d 296, 298 (1991), in which the court found that the parties "intended to live together as husband and wife," and stated: "The fact that they planned at some point in the future to secure a license and formalize their union with a ceremonial marriage did not negate the existence of a common-law marriage under these circumstances."

158 This dichotomy is suggested in *Sorensen v. Sorensen*, 68 Neb. 483, 103 N.W. 455 (1903), in which a contract *de praesenti* was not proven. In *Guardians of the Poor v.*

find that the parties have had an intent *de praesenti* to immediately form a legal relationship, while their intent *de futuro* has simply been to undergo a ceremony. The cohabitation then does not constitute an element of the marital intent in the common law marriage.

In most of the cases in which this dichotomy can be seen, the reasoning is not especially explicit. For example, in the case of *In re Estate of Murnion* (1984), a common law marriage was proven. The parties had lived together for approximately ten months. To satisfy the wishes of his parents and their circle of acquaintances, they planned to formally marry. The court stated that this intention to formalize did not conflict with the agreement they had made to become husband and wife.[159] The court's reference to the fact that the parties had the intent to change their relationship to "a lawful relationship" and the description of the contract as "a lawful contract" suggests that the understood intent to become husband and wife was an intent to create a legal relationship.

A similar reasoning can be found in the case of *In re Estate of Fisher* (1970), in which the parties cohabited approximately five months, two of which were without any impediment. Despite the fact that the court found evidence that the parties were planning a ceremonial marriage *in futuro*, it simultaneously found a proven present agreement to form a common law marriage.[160] The intent of the parties was of the greatest importance according to the court, which nevertheless does not more closely discuss the required content of the marital intent. The reference to the intent of the parties to transform their relationship to a "legitimate relationship," however, gives the impression that the required content of the marriage contract's *essensialia* can be satisfied by the intent to establish

---

Nathans, 2 Brewster 149 (1845), in which the parties had the intent to go through a ceremonial wedding first after the man's father died, a common law marriage was found established before that. The court unfortunately does not discuss the issue more closely in that which in general is a very well thought out and well formulated judgment.

159 *Matter of Estate of Murnion*, 212 Mont. 107, 686 P.2d 893, 897 (1984). In *Brandywine PaperBd. v. W.C.A.B. (Zittle)*, 751 A.2d 1205 (Pa.Cmwlth. 2000), the parties had entered into an oral marriage contract during a private ceremony and thereafter lived together for approximately five years. A planned church wedding could not be performed due to the man's death. The purpose of that was, according to the woman was "basically, just to be married in the eyes of God, and for the children's sake." A common law marriage was found established.

160 *In re Estate of Fischer*, 176 N.W.2d 801, 806, 807 (Iowa 1970). *See also Ganesan v. Vallabhaneni*, 96 S.W.3d 345 (Tex.App.-Austin 2002), in which a common law marriage was established, despite the fact that the parties were "contemplating a formal marriage"; *Skipworth v. Skipworth*, 360 So.2d 975, 977 (Ala. 1978); *Cain v. Cain*, 160 Kan. 672, 165 P.2d 221 (1946); *Radovich v. Radovich*, 84 Colo. 250, 269 P. 22, 23 (1928); and *Huffmaster v. Huffmaster*, 279 Ala. 594, 188 So.2d 552 (1966), in which the courts did not consider plans for a future ceremonial wedding to hinder an immediate common law marriage. *Compare Gillaspie v. Blair Constr. Co.*, 192 Kan. 455, 388 P.2d 647, 649 (1964), in which the man, during the entire relationship of the parties, promised that a ceremonial wedding would be performed and in which a common law marriage was found to be immediately constituted.

a *legal* relationship. The manner by which the courts determine the existence of a legal intent, as evidenced by the actual cohabitation, is discussed in Chapter 7, "Implied Marriage Agreements."

A clearer formulation by a court can be found in *United States v. Dorto* (1925), in which the parties had not only agreed upon a future wedding, but also participated in one. Despite this, they were found to have entered into an agreement with respect to an immediately valid marriage. As a consequence, a common law marriage was formed prior to the ceremonial wedding of the parties. The parties were, thus, at the time of the wedding, already married to one another. Legally, the wedding was simply a formality. The explanation appears to be that the parties had the intent to immediate assume the legal status of marriage.[161] The conclusion, that the planned wedding was a mere formality, was evidenced by the parties' understanding that they had to get "a piece of paper." The ceremonial marriage has also been held to be legally irrelevant in cases in which its only purpose is to reach social status. In *Crane v. Puller* (2006), in which the parties had gone through a formal wedding ceremony, the court, discussing different motives, held that such a ceremony "might simply represent a desirable 'upgrade' in social status and official acceptability." Prior to the wedding, a common law marriage had been established under District of Columbia law.[162]

Regardless of whether the object of the parties' marital intent must be a marital cohabitation or a legal relationship, a marriage contract *de futuro* exists if an event must occur or a condition must be fulfilled before the marriage can be formed. A planned future wedding is only one example of such an event.[163] If the parties have agreed that the marriage shall be

161 *United States v. Dorto,* 5 F.2d 596, 597 (1st Cir. 1925). *Compare State v. Burkitt,* 624 N.E.2d 210, 219 (Ohio App. 1993).

162 *Crane v. Puller,* 169 Md.App. 1, 899 A.2d 879, 919 (2006). *Compare Mission Ins. Co. v. Indus. Comm'n,* 114 Ariz. 170, 559 P.2d 1085 (1976) (applying Kansas law), where the wedding was said to be "a piece of paper." *See also In re Estate of Antonopoulos,* 268 Kan. 178, 993 P.2d 637 (1999), where the parties had entered into a ceremonial marriage in 1992, but where the court found that they were married already in 1987 by a common law marriage.

163 *See, e.g., Regina v. Millis,* (1843) 8 Eng.Rep. 844, 10 Clark and Finally Reports 534, 708, 730 (Lord Brougham), 748, 783, 797 (Lord Campbell); *Stewart v. Menzies,* (1841) 2 Rob.App. 547, 590 (Lord Cottenham); *Clark v. Field,* 13 Vt. 460 (1841); and *Grotgen v. Grotgen,* 3 Bradf. 373 (N.Y. 1854). *Compare Odd Fellows' Beneficial Ass'n v. Carpenter,* 17 R.I. 720, 24 A. 578 (1892): "In order to constitute a marriage *per verba de praesenti* ... The consent ... must not be attended by an agreement that some intervening thing shall be done before the marriage takes effect, or that it be publicly solemnized. That is to say, it must contemplate a present assumption of the marriage status, in distinction from a mere future union." The passage "or that it be publicly solemnized" can appear to mean that the contract would unconditionally create an impediment to the immediate formation of a marriage. The conclusion that follows, however, appears to give support for the proposition that the clause "before the marriage takes effect" ought to be added. A more appropriate word choice would have been to exchange "or" with "as," or even more clear, "as for example." *See* in the older literature, OTTO E. KOEGEL, COMMON LAW

formed first with the wedding ceremony, no marriage can immediately be formed by the contract. However, simply the intent to have a wedding in the future in itself can be a barrier to the immediate formation of a marriage.

If the decisive element for the parties' *consensus* is the intent to establish a legal relationship, and the parties have agreed in the future to have a wedding ceremony, and have even set the date, this naturally is strong evidence that it is the intent of the parties that the marriage shall also be formed at the time of the wedding ceremony.[164] Such a mutual intent can somewhat safely be assumed to be the norm in the majority of the cases in which men and women go through a ceremonial wedding, whether

---

Marriage and Its Development in the United States, 108 (1922). *Compare* modern case law, *e.g. Miller v. Townsend Lumber* Co., 448 P.2d 148, 152 (Mont. 1968). A conditional marriage contract, creating a promise *de futuro*, for example, exists where a man promises to marry a woman if she bears him a child. *See, e.g., Stewart v. Menzies*, 2 Rob.App. 547 (1841). *Compare Turner v. Turner*, 251 Ala. 295, 37 So.2d 186 (1948), in which divorced spouses planned to remarry, however, under the condition that the man behaved himself and stopped drinking. A common law marriage *de praesenti* was not found to be formed. *See also Rosetta v. Rosetta*, 525 S.W.2d 255, 261 (Tex.Civ.App.-Tyler 1975), in which, with respect to the issue of the contract, the court stated that all that was evidenced was that "there may have been an agreement that after some trial period, if things worked out, or if appellee got medical help or counseling, then the appellant and the appellee might remarry." *Compare Com. v. Fick*, 27 Berks Co. L.J. 69 (1934), in which divorced spouses moved back in together. In connection with the reunion, the man said to the woman: "We don't need to get married again, we were married, and that is enough," – with which he clearly meant by "get married" a ceremonial wedding, to which the woman answered: "All right, we will try it over again," referring to their married life. A contract *de praesenti* was found to exist and therewith a common law marriage formed. A similar situation existed in the case of *In re Lambert's Estate*, 116 Ind. App. 293, 62 N.E.2d 871 (1945), in which divorced spouses began to live together again and agreed to "try it over again." During three years, until the man's death, the parties lived together as husband and wife and enjoyed the reputation as husband and wife. A common law marriage was found to be formed, with the result that the woman in her capacity as widow could receive a portion of the deceased's estate.

164 The planned wedding ceremony's character as simply an evidentiary fact appears clearly in *Knaus v. Relyea*, 746 S.W.2d 289 (Ark.App. 1988) (applying Colorado law). Even if future plans for a formal ceremony are no hinder to a present contract to be husband and wife, the court stated that there was nothing "which prevents considering such future plans as evidence of what the intent of the parties was." *See also Hamby v. Simplot* Co., 94 Idaho 794, 498 P.2d 1267 (1972), even though the distinction between contracts *de praesenti* and contracts *de futuro* does not arise. The parties, who had planned a ceremonial wedding, had lived together for a total of 13 days before the man died. During the first ten of those days, an impediment to the marriage existed due to the woman's pre-existing marriage with another man. The court, finding that no common law marriage had been formed during the three remaining days, stated that the parties' planned wedding was one of the several pieces of evidence that supported the fact that they "held themselves out as single persons intending to become married." *Compare Com. v. Stump*, 53 Pa. 132, 137 (1866), in which the court found that "the marriage ceremony, openly performed after the birth of the sons, was a further admission" as support for the fact that the parties, prior to that time, were not married to each other.

religious or civil.[165] Many would be surprised to find that before they had been declared husband and wife, they had already actually formed a common law marriage. However, the formation of a common law marriage is not hindered if it can be proven that the parties had already agreed to form such a legal relationship prior to the wedding, and, as a result, understood their wedding ceremony to be a formality. It naturally can be debated whether such a solution actually responds to any practical need. The American case law, however, includes cases in which the parties agreed to immediately establish a common law marriage, and anticipated a future solemnization of their relationship, at a time suitable in terms of financial and other practical considerations.[166]

If the decisive element in the parties' *consensus,* instead, is to establish marital cohabitation, their plans for a future wedding are naturally less significant. If it can be proven that the parties agreed to begin their lives together with the wedding ceremony, no marriage is formed prior to the wedding. The most common situation, however, is that the parties agree to immediately begin their lives together, which they do, and eventually, some time in the future, have a wedding. A common law marriage can then be immediately formed, and the wedding ceremony is considered simply a formality.

6.5 Express Contracts

Even if the parties internally possess a mutual and united intent, a marital *consensus,* their intent alone is not sufficient for the formation of a common law marriage. As in canon law, American law has required that each party's marital intent, to be given effect, must also be outwardly manifested in the relationship with the other party. In the case of *In re Erickson's Estate* (1954), the court consequently stated: "The law ... requires not only consent but an expression of consent."[167] As seen in the above section concerning the nature of the marriage contract, it is unusual for the parties to enter into

165 *See State v. Burkitt,* 624 N.E.2d 210, 219 (Ohio App. 1993), in which the parties later underwent a ceremonial wedding and the court stated: "It is plain that the April 1991 wedding was not a mere solemnization of an existing marriage, but created a marriage where none had existed before."

166 *Trammel v. Trammel,* 196 S.W.2d 209 (Tex. App. 1946).

167 *In re Erickson's Estate,* 75 S.D. 345, 64 N.W.2d 319 (1954). *Compare* Patrick S. Atiyah, An Introduction to the Law of Contracts, 9 (5th ed. 1995): "The question is not whether the parties have really agreed, or what they really intended, but whether their conduct and language are such as would lead reasonable people to assume that they have agreed." *Compare* Lord Denning in *Storer v. Manchester City Council,* (1974) 3 All E.R. 824, 828: "In contracts you do not look into the actual intent in a man's mind. You look at what he said and did."

verbal contracts and for the courts to require them. In most cases, the courts accept inferred agreements or implied agreements.[168]

Cases appear, however, in which the parties have entered into express marriage contracts, the majority of which are oral, but some are written.[169] At the same time, the courts in Pennsylvania and the District of Columbia continue to require, as a main rule, as seen above, that the contract must be *per verba, i.e.*, through "an exchange of words" between the parties.[170] This raises the question of how these contracts actually are constituted and what requirements are imposed by the courts with respect to the verbal expressions used within these contracts. The general proposition as cited in the beginning of this chapter, that common law marriage is founded upon a civil legal contract, raises the question of to what degree the courts, in the same manner as within general contract law, require an expression of intent in the form of offer and acceptance for a verbal marriage contract to be considered to exist.[171] The requirement of a verbal contract also raises the issue about to what extent the courts assess the words used by the parties in a broader context and thereby take into account, for example, the actions of the parties generally, their lives together, their reputation as spouses, and other circumstances.

Even though in a common law marriage, the character as a contract is particularly evident at the formation of the relationship, it should be noted that it is still a question of a contract *sui generis*. General contractual principles must therefore be applied cautiously. The contractual requirement to more closely define the terms to be regulated (price, quantity,

---

168 *See* Chapter 7 *infra*. With respect to the marriage presumption, *see generally* Chapter 9 *infra*.

169 With respect to written contracts, *see In re Estate of Gower*, 445 Pa. 554, 284 A.2d 742 (1971).

170 With respect to Pennsylvania case law, *see* note 20 *supra*. With respect to the marriage presumption, *see generally* Chapter 9 *infra*. The requirement of a verbal contract has also been maintained in cases where the parties have undergone a ceremonial wedding that was invalid due to an impediment. When the impediment has been removed, the parties must enter into a new oral marriage contract. In *Fiedler v. Nat'l Tube Co.*, 161 Pa.Super. 155, 53 A.2d 821, 822-823 (1947), John and Mary had married each other in a ceremony performed in 1940. The marriage, however, was invalid because John was still married to another woman. When John received his divorce, he called Mary on the telephone. As to the conversation, she testified: "He wanted me for his wife and I said I wanted him for my husband ... he said that he didn't think it was necessary to go through another ceremony and would I, at that time, take an apartment and go and live with him as man and wife ... and I said, all right, I would." Thereafter, they lived as husband and wife and enjoyed the reputation of being such until the man died in 1944. The Pennsylvania Superior Court found that the words that the parties had used to create their new status gave expression of an intent to create an immediate relationship between the man and the woman and that they had entered into a valid common law marriage.

171 *Compare* Uniform Commercial Code § 2-206(a): "An offer to make a contract shall be construed as inviting acceptance in any manner and by any medium reasonable in the circumstances." That the courts, in accepting inferred agreements, have lower or no requirements has been discussed above, *see also* Chapter 7 *infra*.

conditions for delivery, etc.) in the offer and acceptance in a civil contract, naturally is not as stringently applied when it comes to common law marriage.[172] The state provides the contract with a preexisting package of legal regulations that become the legal terms of the contract. The basic requirement of offer and acceptance, however, has an important function to perform because marriage and its accompanying legal system should not be forced upon the parties who have not agreed to it. The basic contractual mechanism, that a contract first exists when one party accepts the offer of the other party, therefore, is of interest even with respect to the contracts under discussion herein.

6.5.1 Oral Contracts

That the marital intent can be expressed verbally has the consequence that oral marriage contracts are valid. If no exchange of words is cited or evidenced, for example, because the parties' testimony has not been found credible, a contract cannot be found to exist.[173] However, there are no fixed statutory formulations, and the courts have not required any

---

172 *Compare* G. H. TREITEL, THE LAW OF CONTRACT 8 (19th Ed. 1995), which defines an acceptance as "an expression of willingness to contract on specified terms, made with the intention that it shall become binding as soon as it is accepted by the person to whom it is addressed" and offer as "a final and unqualified expression of assent to the terms of an offer." *Id.* at 16. *Compare* WILLIAM REYNELL ANSON, THE LAW OF CONTRACT 8 (1995), in which offer is defined as "an intimation, by words or conduct, of a willingness to enter into a legally binding contract, and which in its terms expressly or impliedly indicates that it is to become binding on the offeror as soon as it has been accepted by an act, forbearance or return promise on the part of the person to whom it is addressed." The notion of the intent to be bound can also be found in RESTATEMENT (SECOND) OF CONTRACTS § 26 (1981). *Compare* with respect to common law marriage, *In re Pratt's Estate,* 233 App.Div. 200, 251 N.Y.Supp. 424, 427 (1931), in which the court speaks of the intent to assume "the bonds of matrimony." *See already Regina v. Millis,* (1843) 8 Eng.Rep. 844, 10 Clark and Finally Reports 534, 708, in which Lord Brougham states that marriage is only valid "where the force and effect of the *verba de praesenti* are to bind the parties by this contract."

173 *Duggan v. W.C.A.B. (Litchfield TP.),* 569 A.2d 1022, 1023 (Pa.Cmwlth. 1990); *Canute v. Canute,* 384 Pa.Super. 60, 557 A.2d 772, 775 (1989); and *Com. v. Smith,* 511 Pa. 343, 513 A.2d 1371, 1376 (1986). In the case of *In re Estate of Kovalchick,* 345 Pa.Super. 229, 498 A.2d 374 (1985), the surviving woman claimed that the parties entered into a marriage contract in 1981 in the forest behind the man's house. The parties' cohabitation and appearance outwardly as spouses were not consistent. The court found that the woman did not prove with clear and convincing evidence the existence of a marriage contract. *See also Bowden v. Workmen's Comp. Appeal Bd,* 376 A.2d 1033 (Pa.Cmwlth. 1977). In *Marcus v. Director,* 548 F.2d 1044, 1049 (D.C.Cir. 1976), the credibility was questioned. In *Com. v. Drebot,* 199 Pa.Super. 439, 185 A.2d 617 (1962), the woman alleged that a marriage contract had been entered into in a ceremony before a "squire." The Pennsylvania Superior Court, however, stated that the evidence must be clear and convincing, and it must be evaluated with "caution and scrutiny," and found the evidence in the record "inconsistent, confused, contradicted, and unsubstantiated," and insufficient to establish a common law marriage. *See also Pierce v. Pierce,* 355 Pa. 175, 49 A.2d 346 (1946).

specific wording.[174] In cases in which the parties have arranged a private ceremony for the purpose of marrying, it is not uncommon that the expressions used are similar to those used in a wedding ceremony. In the majority of cases, however, the oral contract arises in situations of great privacy. It can be in a restaurant, in the car, at home in the kitchen, through the telephone, or in the bedroom. The formulations vary greatly. As the parties in such situations take no notes and there usually are no witnesses, difficulties often arise with respect to the evidence concerning what has been said. The courts must rely on information given in the testimony of the parties, perhaps several years after the contract has been formed. The danger is great that the persons present will have rather vague memories of what was said, and that a party, having an interest in proving the fact that a contract was or was not formed, perhaps testifies with questionable reconstructions.[175] The courts must therefore assess the testimony and its credibility "with scrutiny." It should be noted that the person alleging the existence of a common law marriage has the burden of proof, and the existence of such a marriage in several states must be proven with clear and convincing evidence.[176]

It is unusual for the parties' oral expression of intent to take the form of offer and acceptance, as would generally occur in contract law.[177] However, there are several cases in which the parties' oral exchange is questions and answers with respect to their relationship, and can, without much difficulty, be viewed as falling into the rudimentary categories of offer and acceptance. In certain cases, the parties have borrowed phrases

174 As early as in the case of *Chambers v. Dickson*, 2 Serr. & Rawles 475 (Pa. 1816), the court stated: "It is unquestioned that our courts will give effect to the intention of the parties and find a valid marriage where no direct testimony is offered as to the precise words of the marriage contract." In *Patterson v. Gaines*, 47 U.S. (6 How.) 550, 587, 12 L.Ed. 553 (1848), the Court gave its support hereto: "Marriage is a civil contract in Pennsylvania, to be completed by any words in the present tense, without regard to form." A similar attitude can be found in *Com. v. Haylow*, 17 Pa.Super. 541, 547 (1901), in which the court stated that the marriage contract can be formed "by any words in the present time without regard to form." In *Hilton v. Roylance*, 25 Utah 129, 69 P. 660 (1902), the court stated: "The consent constituting the basis of a marriage contract does not depend upon any particular form of words." *See also Consolidated Underwriters v. Kelly*, 15 S.W.2d 229 (Tex. Comm'n App. 1929); *In re McKanna's Estate*, 106 Cal.App.2d 126, 234 P.2d 673, 675 (1951); *Nat'l Union fire Ins. Co. v. Britton*, 187 F.Supp. 359, 364 (C.D.C. 1960); *Com. ex rel. McDermott v. McDermott*, 236 Pa.Super.Ct. 541, 345 A.2d 914, 917 (1975); *Estate of Gavula*, 490 Pa. 535, 417 A.2d 168, 171 (1980); *In re Estate of Stauffer*, 504 Pa. 626, 476 A.2d 354, 355 (1984) ("civil contract of common law marriage does not require any specific form of words"); *Cann v. Cann*, 632 A.2d 322, 325 (Pa.Super. 1993); *Coates v. Watts*, 622 A.2d 25 (D.C.App. 1993) ("no set formula required"); and *Staudenmayer v. Staudenmayer*, 714 A.2d 1016, 1022 (Pa. 1998).

175 *East v. East*, 536 A.2d 1103 (D.C.App. 1988).

176 *See generally* Chapter 9 *infra* with respect to burdens of proof and evidentiary requirements.

177 *Compare* UNIFORM COMMERCIAL CODE § 2-206(a) (1962): "An offer to make a contract shall be construed as inviting acceptance in any manner and by any medium reasonable in the circumstances."

used in the wedding ceremony, the meanings of which are unmistakable. That which is significant to the courts' analysis about whether a marriage contract has been formed is the courts' assessment of the broader context of the exchange of words between the parties. The case law gives the impression that the courts have applied a principle of interpretation according to which the parties' intent plays a larger role than the verbal expression of that intent.[178]

An example in which the parties, using short questions and answers, can be considered to have made an offer and an acceptance in a marriage can be seen in *Cann v. Cann* (1993). There, the woman testified that the parties, on June 19, 1982, had exchanged vows as the man, in the presence of the woman's parents, asked her "to marry him," and the woman had "responded affirmatively."[179] The parties lived together for approximately sixteen years, of which ten were without any impediment. They had named each other as beneficiaries in their insurance policies and filed joint marital tax returns between the years 1982 and 1985. The man had stated on an insurance policy that the woman was his wife. The Pennsylvania Superior Court stated that the couple had "expressed a present intention to marry" and found that the evidence supported the trial court's determination that the parties had entered into contract *per verba de praesenti* with the purpose of establishing marriage.[180]

Cases also appear in which the parties' questions and answers are more extensive and encompass the considered marital existence, as well as the rights and obligations of marriage. In such cases, the offer and acceptance concern the two central elements of the required marital intent as discussed, *supra* in Section 8.3, even though the words reflect this somewhat laconically. For example, in *McKanna's Estate* (1951), the man met the woman in connection with a business vacation in Texas. After the man's death, the woman testified that the parties had decided to not have a ceremonial wedding and the following verbal exchange had occurred during the man's visit in Texas: "Mr. McKanna asked me if I would live with him

178 *See, e.g., Com. v. Haylow,* 17 Pa.Super. 541, 547 (1901): "It is not the duty of the courts to seek for an interpretation of the words used by the parties which would be inconsistent with an honorable intention as well as with their subsequent conduct and declarations, when an interpretation consistent with the formation of an honorable relation is possible, and, in the light of all the circumstance[s], more probably expresses their intention." *See also In re Estate of Seifert,* 302 Pa. 477, 153 A. 722 (1931).

179 *Cann v. Cann,* 632 A.2d 322, 325 (Pa.Super. 1993). The marriage presumption is not applicable where the parties commenced living together during the existence of a marital impediment. With respect to presumptions, *see generally* Chapter 9 *infra.* The issue of marital impediments is discussed in Chapter 5 *supra.* In *Brandywine PaperBd. v. W.C.A.B. (Zittle),* 751 A.2d 1205 (Pa.Cmwlth. 2000), the woman testified at trial: "And he handed me a ring and said he wanted me to be his wife. And that was it. Q. Did you accept - A. Yes." The parties had lived together approximately five years. A common law marriage was found established.

180 *Cann* at 325.

as his wife and assume the duties as wife to him, and I said I would; and he said he would live with me as my husband." With this statement, the fact of the cohabitation, and the holding out as husband and wife, the California Court of Appeals found that a common law marriage had been formed.[181] It is notable that the parties' agreement encompassed a mutual intent to live together as well as the intent to have a legal effect, namely the woman's "duties as wife." It is not evident from the exchange of words whether the parties agreed with respect to the man's duties as husband, but that should be assumed based on the record in general. Of course, the marriage contract's legal effects are determined by the rights and obligations set forth in the legislation. There is no case in which a court has required a recitation of these rights and duties in the conclusion of the oral contract, which, with respect to the parties' often-incomplete knowledge, appears to be a wise approach. It has generally been considered by the courts to suffice with a few words that can be connected to the legal relationship.

The parties' rather terse statements often are vague and ambiguous, even though they take the form of questions and answers. For example, in *Caddy v. Johnstown Firemen's Relief Association of Pennsylvania* (1938), the woman testified that a verbal exchange occured during a visit to the movie theater: "He asked me if I was willing to live that way," to which the woman, according to the court, meant "to live together in the relation of man and wife without any ceremony by preacher or priest." To this, she replied, "Yes." Thereafter, the man said, "We can live together as common law people," to which the woman said, "I am satisfied," and the man placed a wedding ring on her finger. On the basis of the exchange of words between the man and woman, and the fact that they lived together until the man's death and had the appearance of husband and wife, the Pennsylvania Superior Court found that a common law marriage had been formed.[182] Naturally, it is debatable whether a vague offer "to live

---

181 *In re McKanna's Estate,* 106 Cal.App.2d 126, 234 P.2d 673, 674 (1951)(applying Texas law). In the case of *In re Neafie's Estate,* 12 Pa.Dist. 749 (1903), divorced spouses reunited, during which the man said: "I am willing to take you back as my wife if you are willing to take me back as your husband," to which the woman said: "Yes." They lived together thereafter until the man's death. The expressed words together with their marital cohabitation and reputation were sufficient to form a common law marriage.

182 *Caddy v. Johnstown Firemen's Relief Ass'n of Pennsylvania,* 129 Pa.Super. 493196 A. 590, 591-592 (1938). The words used in *Nyhuis v. Pierce,* 65 O.L.Abs. 73, 114 N.E.2d 75, 76 (1952) were also rather general. The parties had obtained a "marriage license," where after the man said: "Now we are tied up for good." The woman assumed she was married to him. Thereafter, the man had stated to his friends from work that the couple met that same day: "I want you folks to meet my wife. We were just married this morning." The court found that the parties had entered into a marriage contract *in praesenti.* In *Com. ex rel. McDermott v. McDermott,* 236 Pa.Super.Ct. 541, 345 A.2d 914, 915 (1975), a divorced man, who had returned to his previous wife, stated upon his arrival: "Here I am. You want to be my wife again?" The woman answered "Yes," after which they lived together for five years and enjoyed a

that way," which the woman accepted, contains any legal intent, or whether the parties had agreed to live together without any intent to establish a legal relationship. The court did not elaborate on the required content of the marital intent to form a common law marriage. If the court considered an intent to live together to be sufficient, the court's conclusion that the parties' statements were supported by their subsequent cohabitation is not surprising. More doubtful is the conclusion that the court required a legal intent. The exchange of rings between the parties and the intent to live "in the relationship of" husband and wife can certainly support the latter intent. It is doubtful, however, that the parties expressly agreed with clear and convincing evidence that the marital regulatory scheme, with all its legal responsibilities, as well as the regulations with respect to divorce and the division of marital property, would apply to them.

The requirement of a verbal contract appears, in certain cases, to be simply the requirement of a verbal offer, while the acceptance can be inferred. The issue of whether an inferred acceptance ought to be accepted, however, is dependent upon the content required of the parties' marital *consensus* in finding that a marriage contract has been formed (see Section 8.3, *supra*). In *Rager v. Johnstown Traction Company* (1957), the man, before the parties had moved in together, said to the woman: "Come and live with me and make a home." During their living together, he often stated: "Between the eyes of God, we are husband and wife." There is no evidence in the record of whether the woman gave any oral response to the man's request or statements. During the witness examination at trial, the woman was asked whether she and the man had entered into any contract in connection with the commencement of their cohabitation. She answered, "Sure. To be husband and wife, that's the way we made it out, as long as he lived and as long as I lived." The parties lived together for eleven years and represented themselves outwardly to be husband and wife until the man died in an accident at work. The Pennsylvania Superior Court required, as a condition for the formation of a common law marriage, the existence of "a contract *per verba de praesenti*, uttered with a view to establish the relation of husband and wife." The court found that with respect to what the parties had said to each other, and what the woman testified to during trial, they "intended to live with each other as man and wife until death did them part." A common law marriage was proven. The woman was, therefore, entitled to workmen's compensation in connection with the man's death.[183]

---

reputation as husband and wife, before they separated again. A common law marriage was proven.

183 *Rager v. Johnstown Traction* Co., 184 Pa.Super. 474, 134 A.2d 918, 921-922 (1957). Three judges concurred, stating that the offer "[c]ome and live with me and make a home" was not a proposal of marriage "but a request merely that she become his housekeeper in exchange for her keep ... What was offered and accepted was a place

The question of whether the court made a correct assessment appears to be intertwined with the content of the marital intent required to find that a marriage contract has been formed. To begin with, if one assumes that the requirement is simply a mutual intent to live together, the man's request of the woman to, "come and live with me and make a home," legally fulfills the requirement of a verbal offer. The record does not indicate whether the woman gave any oral acceptance, but the fact that she moved in with the man and that they cohabitated a period of eleven years, must speak for the fact that she, through her actions, can be inferred to have accepted the offer. The court's conclusion that the parties "intended to live with each other as man and wife until death did them part" appears correct. A marriage contract is then formed, assuming that the requirement for a verbal contract requires simply an oral offer and that the acceptance can be inferred.

On the other hand, if the required marital intent must contain a legal intent including the intent that the entire marital regulatory scheme be applicable to their relationship, *i.e.*, to establish the legal relationship of husband and wife, it is more dubious whether any contract had been formed. If we first examine the man's offer, "come and live with me and make a home," it scarcely can be viewed as giving expression to the intent to establish a legal marriage. Neither does the record contain any indication that the woman gave any answer that could be interpreted as accepting the offer to form a legal relationship, and her moving in and living together with the man has little or no evidentiary weight with respect to the issue of legal intent.[184] The man's statements made during their cohabitation, that "in the eyes of God, we are husband and wife," appear rather ambiguous, because they can be understood to mean either that the parties are married only "in the eyes of God," but not "in the eyes of law," or that they, despite the fact they have not undergone any ceremonial wedding, are legally married and have entered into a marriage "in the eyes of God." Aside from the ambiguity of the intent, the question also arises whether the man's statements can be considered an offer. His statements were made neither in any particular situation nor with the purpose of forming a marriage, but rather, occasionally during the cohabitation, clearly without the man expecting any response. The record also shows that the woman did not offer any response to the statements. The fact that the parties cohabited offers little or no evidentiary support of their legal intent. The woman's testimony that she was certain that they had entered into a marriage contract, a statement that is a legal conclusion, appears to be have been based on their life together. Consequently, it is doubtful,

of abode, a place of residence, a place in which to live and perhaps of refuge, with no intention of entering into a family relationship by marriage." *Id.* at 925.

184 *See generally* Chapter 7 *infra* with respect to the evidentiary weight ascribed the cohabitation on the issue of the marriage contract.

assuming that a legal intent is required, that a marriage contract had been formed, as result of both the insufficient marital intent and the unfulfilled requirement of a verbal contract.[185] The record, in any event, does not support the proposition that a common law marriage was formed with support of clear and convincing evidence.

The exchange of words between the parties, in other cases, has not been questions and answers, but rather of assertions of facts. That which must be assessed from case to case is whether the parties have actually made an offer and acceptance with respect to the formation of a marital relationship. It is not uncommon for the situation in which the statements were made, as well as the parties' own actions, to be considered in the findings of whether the parties have made an offer and acceptance. The occasion in question may be the parties' planning to enter into a marriage, including the arrangements for a ceremony with the exchange of rings or a similar act. Such a situation illustrates that, clearly, choice of words is not solely determinative; that which literally is an assertion of fact can, in actuality, be a legally acceptable offer and acceptance.

For example, in the case of *In re Rosenberger's Estate* (1949), the woman was at the hospital giving birth to the parties' child. When the man visited her, he suggested that they marry before the child was born. He left the hospital and shortly thereafter returned with four or five wedding rings and asked her to choose one. After the woman chose a ring, the man put it on her finger and said, "Pretty soon we will have the baby. Now you have the ring, and you are my wife." She answered, "That is fine. I love it." The parties' statements can scarcely be considered a contractual offer and acceptance. They, instead, are assertions, first, by the man stating the facts that she had the ring, and that she actually was married; and, second, by the woman expressing her satisfaction with these facts. Nevertheless, the court found that, within a broader context, a marriage contract had been formed, with the consequence of the formation of a common law marriage. The woman, after the death of the man, was thus entitled to a portion of the man's probate estate, and was favored over the interest of another woman. The man, after the birth of the child, had entered into a similar and actually clearer marriage contract with a second woman. That contract was found to be invalid because the man was already united in a common law marriage.[186]

---

185 The requirement for a legal intent and an intent for a marital cohabitation is discussed *supra* in 6.3, the marital intent's *essensialia*.

186 *In re Rosenberger's Estate*, 362 Pa. 153, 65 A.2d 377, 378 (1949). It can be added that after she discovered that the man had had an "intimate affair" with another woman, she left him. He entered into a new verbal contract with another woman. At the conclusion of that contract, he stated: "Marie, do you take me for your husband?" and she answered, "Yes, George, I do." She said, thereafter, "Do you take me for your wife?" and he replied, "Yes I do, Marie. I love you very much." Thereafter they lived together until she left him. When the man died several months later, both women claimed to be his common law wife. The court, finding that a common law

Cases also exist in which the parties' assertions with respect to their relationships are sufficient to form a marriage contract without the statements being planned for the formation of a marriage. The statements can have been made on occasions that for other reasons have been of legal interest with respect to the relationship. For example, in the case of *In re Estate of Garges* (1977), after eighteen years of cohabitation with the woman, the man received a divorce from his former wife. When he showed the woman the divorce judgment, he said, "Now we're legally married," to which she answered, "It's about time. That's just what we were waiting for." The woman thereafter began to wear a ring given to her earlier by the man. They lived together for an additional six years, and enjoyed a reputation as spouses until the death of the man. They had named each other as spouses on their life insurance policy. The man's statement literally was an assertion of fact, but was not an offer; and the woman's statement was not an acceptance, but a statement of the parties' expectations. Nevertheless, the Pennsylvania Supreme Court found that, with respect to the exchange of words and other circumstances, a marriage contract was proven to have existed. The woman, therefore, in the capacity of a wife, could claim her portion of the man's probate estate.[187] At the same time, it appears

---

marriage had been formed based on the contract with the first woman, found that their marriage had never been dissolved, and that the later contract was void and that the man had committed bigamy. The case concerned the right to the probate estate, to which the first woman and her son were found entitled. In *Atkins v. Heckler*, 574 F.Supp. 634 (E.D.Pa. 1983), the man gave the woman a wedding ring and said: "I consider you to be my wife," to which the woman answered, that she considered him her husband. The court found a common law marriage was proven. *See also In re Zemmick's Estate*, 17 Ohio Supp. 15, 76 N.E.2d 902, 904 (1946). That the evidentiary weight accorded the exchange of rings can vary can be seen in the court's reasoning in *Green's Estate*, 5 Pa.C. 605, 607 (1888). *See also Guardians of the Poor v. Nathan*, 2 Brexster 149, 158 (1845), in which the man gave the woman a ring in secret. In *Mainor v. Midvale* Co., 192 Pa.Super. 367, 162 A.2d 27 (1960), the immediate giving of a ring was not considered sufficient to form a marriage contract. *Compare In re Estate of Antonopoulos*, 268 Kan. 178, 993 P.2d 637 (1999), where a common law marriage was established at a private ceremony with witnesses and the exchange of rings. *Compare DeMelo v. Zompa*, 844 A.2d 1, 174, 177 (R.I. 2004), in which a picture was presented as evidence showing that the woman wore her ring on her right hand, not her left.

187 *In re Estate of Garges*, 474 Pa. 237, 378 A.2d 307 (1977). The marriage presumption was found not applicable as the relationship began while the man was still married to another woman. In *Nat'l Union Fire Ins. Co. v. Britton*, 187 F.Supp. 359, 363 (D.D.C. 1960), the woman testified during trial: "I thought we was married ... because he said he was my husband and I said I was his wife; so I just figured we was married." The United States District Court for the District of Columbia found that a "mutual agreement in words of present tense to be husband and wife" had been proven. The required proof with respect to the exchange of words appears to have been rather minimal in the case of *In re Stauffer's Estate*, 372 Pa. 537, 94 A.2d 726 (1953), in which the parties, according to the woman's testimony, had entered into an oral marriage contract on the stairs to the courthouse when they left the building after having received a marriage license. The record unfortunately does not note the actual words used. The Pennsylvania Supreme Court found, after expressing several doubts, that the evidence gave support for the fact that a marriage contract had been entered into and that a common law marriage had been formed.

probable that the parties actually had the intent to be united in marriage, and that the intent was given a verbal expression in the exchange of words.

Contracts have been created in certain cases in which one party has made a statement concerning marriage and the other party, through an action, has given a silent consent. For example, in *Howard v. Central Nat. Bank of Marietta* (1926), the man said to the woman, "Now we are man and wife." Despite the fact that the woman did not expressly give an answer, she was considered through her actions to silently have accepted the marriage. The woman testified concerning the events after the man's statement, "[A]nd he kissed me, and after that we went in to my mother—of course, he had talked about marriage so much—and he told my mother we had gotten married, and she said she wasn't surprised, and he put his hand on my shoulder, and my mother shook hands with us and kissed us both."[188]

The courts have considered not only the situation in which the parties' statements have been made, but also the character of the subsequent cohabitation. If the parties, after the formation of the contract, lived together for a long period as husband and wife and enjoyed a general and consistent reputation as spouses, the actual words exchanged at the occasion giving rise to the contract appear to be given less consideration.[189] In *Donaldson v. P.J. Oesterling & Sons, Inc.* (1962), the woman, according to her testimony after the death of the man, stated that she, when they were alone in the bedroom, said to the man, "Whether we're married by a preacher or not, I'm your wife," to which the man responded, "Yes, you are my wife and I am your husband." The parties lived together afterwards for twelve years until the death of the man, and they had a mutual child. The court found clear and convincing evidence that the parties "by words *in praesenti*" expressed an intent to enter into a marriage contract.[190]

In *Dozack v. Dozack*, 137 A.D.2d 317, 528 N.Y.S.2d 712, 713-714 (1988), the woman testified: "Well, we just decided that we would from that day on, as far as we were concerned in our hearts, we were man and wife, and we would consider ourselves a family and continue thus." The New York Supreme Court, Appellate Division, applying Pennsylvania law, found that a common law marriage had been formed.

188 *Howard v. Cntr. Nat'l Bank of Marietta*, 21 Ohio App. 74, 152 N.E. 784 (1926). *Compare In re Comly's Estate*, 185 Pa. 208, 39 A. 890 (1898).

189 *Compare In re Erickson's Estate*, 75 S.D. 345, 64 N.W.2d 316 (1954).

190 *Donaldson v. P.J. Oesterling & Sons, Inc.*, 199 Pa.Super. 637, 186 A.2d 653, 655 (1962). *Compare In re Blecher's Estate*, 381 Pa. 138, 112 A.2d 129 (1955), in which the man, during a car ride with his ex-wife, said: "You are my wife; I am your husband and we are going to live together the same as we did before," to which the woman said: "You are my husband and I am your wife." They lived together thereafter for thirteen years until the death of the man. A common law marriage was found to have been formed. *Compare Boykin v. State Indus. Acc. Comm'n*, 224 Or. 76, 355 P.2d 724, 726 (1960), in which the woman testified as to the following conversation between her and the man during their three to five month visit to Idaho: "'Well,' he said, 'We are married now.' He says, 'We have lived here and' he said, 'I guess we are really married." Well, later that night, then, why, as we were getting ready for bed

A literal interpretation of the parties' statements, that they already were married to each other, naturally raises questions of when, where, and how they had previously entered into a marriage contract. The court appears, however, not to base its conclusion on a literal interpretation of the words exchanged, but considered instead that the contract came into existence at that moment in which the parties mutually gave expression to their understanding, or, as the court meant, their intent with respect to their relationship. It is clear that the parties' twelve-year cohabitation and reputation as spouses is convincing evidence for the supposition that they had agreed to live together as spouses. The evidentiary weight attributable to that intent, however, is not as strong. Their cohabitation and their reputation as spouses certainly suggest that they also lived in accordance with the regulations governing spouses. Despite this, the question arises whether the woman's statement, "I'm your wife," constitutes an offer in which she expressed her intent to be legally bound and with which she wished to create a legal relationship as husband and wife under the regulations governing, for example, divorce and the division of property. It is vitally important to distinguish between those persons choosing to live without marital legal regulation and those who have entered into an agreement to be bound by such, particularly given the current tendency for couples to live together in long-term relationships without formally entering into a marriage.

On the other hand, the exchange of words as the basis of an oral marriage contract may be undermined if, for example, the parties' cohabitation was not continuous, or their reputation as spouses was inconsistent. The effect of such evidence is significant, especially in those jurisdictions where cohabitation and the reputation as spouses are not necessary requirements for the formation of a common law marriage.[191] Historically, the situation has arisen, in certain cases, of a man entering into a long-term, emotionally intense relationship with a "mistress." The couple may have often traveled together and spent time at hotels; and, technically, could be viewed as having lived together, but often the man has maintained another private, permanent home. In certain social circles, for example, among the woman's or work acquaintances, the couple could have enjoyed the reputation as husband and wife, while other circles, for example, the man's relations and friends, may not have even known about the relationship. The man, however, has chosen not to take the final step of moving in with

---

he says, 'Well,' he says, 'it's all legal now.' And I said, 'Well, not only by law,' I said, 'it's always been in the eyes of God, too.'" The court, whose reasoning as to the contract issues is virtually nonexistent, states that the parties "lived together in sickness and in health" during a period of ten years. A common law marriage was found to have been formed.

191 For example, in Pennsylvania, cohabitation and reputation as spouses are not necessary requirements for the formation of a common law marriage, *see generally* Chapter 8.4 *infra*.

the woman, and, formally marrying her. Despite this, an exchange of words between them can raise the issue of whether a common law marriage has been formed.

For example, in the case of *In re Craig's Estate* (1922),[192] according to the woman's testimony, the man had said to her one night: "I don't want you to ever use your name again; this is your name; you are my wife; and I want you to thoroughly understand that." The woman testified that she "agreed with him thoroughly," and that, on the night they "married," she received a ring from him. The parties lived together for a long period of time, but also lived apart for a long period of time. They had a mutual child, but their reputation as spouses was split. The man did not wish to introduce the woman into his social circle. Nevertheless, even when they lived separately, a total of twenty-four years, in Washington and Philadelphia, respectively, they visited each other often and exchanged no fewer than 4,046 letters. The Pennsylvania Supreme Court stated that a marriage contract must be proven by words in the present tense uttered with a view to establishing the relationship of husband and wife. The court found that the words exchanged did not clearly show a contract of marriage and that the tone in the letters did not indicate a relationship between husband and wife but rather between a "man and mistress." A marriage was not found proven, and the child, therefore, was illegitimate.

The courts have sometimes accepted, as a marriage contract, statements that cannot be viewed as expressions of intent directed by the parties to each other, but instead to a third party, and, therefore, can be seen as an offer and acceptance with difficulty. In *East v. East* (1988), the parties commenced their cohabitation in 1977.[193] They had two mutual children,

---

192 *In re Craig's Estate*, 273 Pa. 530, 117 A. 221, 222 (1922). *See also In re Stevenson's Estate*, 272 Pa. 291, 116 A. 162, 163, 165 (1922), in which according to the woman's testimony after his death, the man had stated: "Nancie, as long as you live I would not give you up ... from tonight on I am going to give you my name and protect you ... you are my wife ... from tonight on we are married." The woman consented to this. The parties' cohabitation and reputation as spouses, however, were inadequate. The trial court found that the woman had been the man's "mistress" and no marriage contract had been proven. The Supreme Court agreed. In the case of *Green's Estate*, 5 Pa.C. 605 (1888), the man gave the woman a box with a ring inside. When she asked him what was inside, he said: "That is to bind you and I together as long as we live"; to which she responded, "That is all right." During the sixteen years of their relationship, the man lived with his parents. He was known as a single man in the area. He visited her often, however, and for many years. They had two mutual children. The woman occasionally used either the man's or her previous husband's last name. She did not visit the man during his illness before he died and did not attend the funeral. The court stated that the parties' intent is decisive: "If they in any manner expressed a purpose to cohabit as husband and wife, no other evidence is needed." The court, after consideration of the parties' lives together, their admissions and reputations, found that the evidence was insufficient to prove a marriage. *See also Bicking's Appeal*, 2 Brewster 202 (1868).

193 *East v. East*, 536 A.2d 1103 (D.C.App. 1988). *See also Hoffman v. Hoffman*, 285 Ky. 55, 146 S.W.2d 347, 348 (1940), in which three witnesses to a party at the woman's apartment in Ohio in 1927 testified that "finally Dorothy and Emil went into the

born in 1978 and 1981. After six years of cohabitation, they separated, in 1983. In connection with the separation, the woman petitioned for custody and support. The question arose whether the parties lived in a common law marriage. At trial, the woman testified that the man, during a dinner party on October 31, 1977 said, "From here on in, Margaret and I are married." The man denied making the statement, and testified that the woman said to a guest that they "had been married at noon that day by a justice of the peace." He further testified that he did not protest the statement to avoid the embarrassment that would have resulted from exposing the woman's lies. The trial court found that a common law marriage had been formed, and awarded custody and support to the woman. The Court of Appeals stated that the requirement to prove a common law marriage was an express mutual agreement to be husband and wife, in words of the present tense, provable by a preponderance of the evidence, and followed by a cohabitation. The Court of Appeals found that the trial court's findings were not plainly wrong or without evidence to support them, and that the judgment therefore could not be disturbed.[194]

No discussion as to any terms of an offer or acceptance can be found in *East.* The trial court clearly found the man's statement to the guests proven by the woman's testimony. Even if the statement was an assertion that they were married, it gives the impression that he meant that they became married at the time it was spoken, "[f]rom here on in." There is no reason to question whether the statement was an expression of his intent to be married. In contrast, his statement can scarcely be characterized as an offer of marriage. It was not addressed to the woman and nothing in the situation indicates that he expected an answer from her. No response, express or implied, which could be characterized as an acceptance, is mentioned in the record. The parties simply continued their cohabitation. To accept, as binding, a silent acceptance to an offer, construed from a statement not even addressed to the woman, appears to be going too far. Even if one accepts the trial court's evaluation of the evidence, the legal conclusion that the parties had entered into a marriage contract *per verba de praesenti* can scarcely be considered contractually correct and ought to have been deemed by the Court of Appeals as plainly wrong. A contract's basic requirement of an offer and acceptance guarantees that the contract is mutual and that neither party, against his or her will, is forced into a legal relationship. Such protective mechanisms have a function even in a legal marriage contract.

---

kitchen of the apartment and stayed a while; that they then came back in and Emil told her to show her ring and the guests would know they were married and that Dorothy thereupon said that she and Emil were married and exhibited a ring." With reference to the fact that a contract was found entered into and that the parties lived together approximately three months in Ohio, the Kentucky Court of Appeals found a common law marriage established.

194 D.C. CODE ANN. § 17-305(a) (1981).

The requirement of an oral marriage contract is not fulfilled if the parties' oral statements concerning their relationship are too loose or vague. As early as *Hantz v. Sealy* (1814), the Pennsylvania Supreme Court refused to accept a marriage contract as the evidence was too slight and too equivocal to constitute a marriage.[195] If the parties' statements about their relationship cannot be identified as contractual, and instead are conversational, they normally do not fulfill the requirements of a verbal contract.[196] This can be with respect to statements which are repeated occasionally, but not for the purpose of binding the parties or creating a contract, and which do not fall within the categories of offer and acceptance. A tentative, preliminary proposal that does not definitely display the intent to be bound cannot be considered an offer.[197] It is another matter if such statements can be considered admissions and declarations offered in support of the parties' marital *consensus*. In *DeMelo v. Zompa* (2004), the Rhode Island Supreme Court found that the plaintiff did not present any evidence of a serious intent between her and the defendant to enter into the relationship of husband and wife. She merely testified that they "had discussions about spending their lives together, not necessarily as a married couple."[198]

In *Eagle v. W.C.A.B. (Bahorich)* (1992), for example, the parties had participated in a ceremonial wedding in 1952. They lived together thereafter for twenty-five years and had six children. The marriage was dissolved by

---

195 *Hantz v. Sealy*, 6 Binn. 405 (1814).

196 *Compare Ram v. Ramharack*, 571 N.Y.S.2d 190, 191-192 (Sup. 1991), in which the woman asked the man if he would accompany her to a Marriage License Bureau to obtain a marriage license before the ceremonial wedding. The man replied: "We are living happily together like husband and wife. It's no big deal not having a piece of paper." Despite the fact that her statement was a proposal to go to a Marriage License Bureau and his statement was a literal statement of his view concerning marriage licenses and the value of such, as well as a statement as to satisfaction in their present lives, the New York Supreme Court found, in applying D.C. law, that the parties had entered into a marriage contract. It should be noted at the same time that if the court appears to have gone too far, there is no requirement in Washington, D.C., law for a verbal contract. The contract could not be the basis for a common law marriage in New York, as New York did not recognize common law marriage. The court found that it "continued to be their agreement" when they continued to live together and outwardly appear as spouses in Washington, D.C., a jurisdiction recognizing common law marriage. *Compare Com. v. Haylow*, 17 Pa. Super. 541 (1901), in which the man gave the woman a "marriage license" and said that it was all that was needed, a ceremony was not necessary. The parties lived together for four years. A common law marriage was found established.

197 *Compare* the requirement within general civil law that a contract must be "certain and final" and that an offer must be definite and given with the intent from the offeror to be bound. *See, e.g.*, TREITEL, *supra* note 172, at 8; ANSON, *supra* note 172, at 25. *See also* RUDOLF B. SCHLESINGER, FORMATION OF CONTRACTS I 329 (1968), which states that an offer has not been made if "the words of commitment are weak." *Compare Stringer v. Stringer*, 689 So.2d 194 (Ala.Civ.App. 1997), in which the man stated that he was not "ready to commit to a marriage" and in which Alabama Court of Civil Appeals found that the required intent to enter into a common law marriage was lacking.

198 *DeMelo v. Zompa*, 844 A.2d 174, 177 (R.I. 2004).

divorce in 1977. In 1979, the parties met at a restaurant. The man testified as to the meeting, "Oh yeah, I said this is where we're going to start from where we left off. We made a bond of some type and, you know, we're husband and wife again as of right now and we toasted coffee to it and we enjoyed the rest of the evening."[199] The parties' cohabitation thereafter was until 1984, when the woman died as a result of an accident at work. The man claimed workmen's compensation benefits and cited as grounds that he had been united in a common law marriage with the deceased. The Commonwealth Court of Pennsylvania found that the man did not prove the exchange of words *in praesenti* sufficient to support the conclusion of a common law marriage.[200] The court's conclusion naturally is entirely correct. The man's statements, however, could also be seen as being altogether too vague and preliminary to constitute an offer with respect to marriage, whether the intent is to a marital cohabitation or to the legal consequences following marriage. There is no evidence in the record, either, that the woman in any fashion accepted the offer.

If the verbal expression is vague and the parties during the cohabitation have, in addition, behaved as unmarried persons, for example, in order to enjoy a social benefit, difficulties arise with respect to the issue of proving the existence of a marriage contract. In the case of *In re Cummings Estate* (1984), the parties met in 1972 and moved in together in December of 1974. During a visit to a restaurant in August of 1975, the man gave the woman a diamond ring. When the man bought a new house in his name in 1977, he called the woman and said: "I bought you a home ... You are my wife. You are going to move."[201] She and her two sons moved in with him

---

199 *Eagle v. W.C.A.B. (Bahorich)*, 602 A.2d 387, 388 (Pa.Cmwlth. 1992). The marriage presumption was not applicable if testimony with respect to the formation of the contract is available. With respect to presumptions, *see generally* Chapter 9 *infra.*

200 *Eagle* at 390.

201 *In re Cummings Estate*, 330 Pa.Super. 255, 479 A.2d 537, 540 (1984). The marriage presumption was found not applicable as the couple from the commencement of their relationship lived together as unmarried persons, *see generally* Chapter 9 *infra.* In *Toye v. Toye*, 170 A.2d 778 (D.C. App. 1961), the woman testified that the parties "agreed to live under the same household," that "it was just one of those things where we just didn't bother to go through any ceremony," and that they had agreed to get an apartment "and get married later on." The Municipal Court of Appeals for the District of Columbia found that "evidence that the parties never expressly agreed to be husband and wife and that the defendant made a promise to marry the plaintiff which he never kept" was insufficient to form a common law marriage. In *Murdock's Estate*, 92 Pa.Super. 275, 277 (1927), the woman testified that the man said, "Will you be good to me?" To that the woman answered, "Yes, I will do everything that a wife is supposed to do." The court found, however, that the parties had not entered into a marriage contract, but instead simply a contract "to create the pretense of a marriage, not to be married." The woman had consented only to entering into "a meretricious relationship." *Compare Tholey's Appeal*, 93 Pa. 36 (1880), in which the court found that the words "he will claim me as his wife, take care of me and the children" were insufficient to establish a marriage contract, but rather were an expression of "an intent to enter into a meretricious relationship and to masquerade as a married couple." *Compare Fireman's Fund Ins. Co. v. Smith*, 151 Ga.App. 270, 259 S.E.2d 675 (1979), in which the parties agreement that they

and lived there until his death in 1979. During the two years they lived together, the man had presented the woman to different persons as his wife and the children as "my boys." When a friend from work suggested that they formally marry, the man said, "I don't need a piece of paper to prove I'm married. I am married." The man had said to his father and brothers on several occasions, however, that he was not married. The woman received welfare benefits as an unmarried person, based on the information that the man was her "paramour." They had no joint checking or savings accounts. She did not use the man's last name, and he declared that he was unmarried on his tax returns.

The Pennsylvania Superior Court stated that no specific word formulations were required to create a contract. All that is necessary is proof of an agreement to enter into the legal relationship of marriage. The court found, however, that the man's statements alone could not form a present marriage agreement. The evidence with respect to the parties' reputation also failed to support such a finding. The woman had not demonstrated by clear and convincing evidence that the parties had entered into a marriage contract. She therefore was not entitled to a portion of the man's probate estate.[202]

The court's judgment appears to be correct. With respect to the man's statements, those concerning the purchase of the house and the suggestion that she move in, at best, can be deemed an offer for a cohabitation. There is no evidence in the record of any oral acceptance by the woman. Her moving in with him, at best, can be considered an implied acceptance to his offer of cohabitation, and though the cohabitation continued, it appears to be rather weak evidence of an implied acceptance. An offer to form a legal relationship of husband and wife cannot be considered evidence, and an oral acceptance is not named. On the contrary, the fact that the woman with respect to other entitlements acted as an unmarried person ought to have had considerable evidentiary weight.

Even though statements can be deemed assertions of fact and viewed as sufficient according to the cases above, they may be conversationally uttered statements not connected to any specific contractual occasion. They can be occasionally repeated without having the purpose of entering into a contract. For example, in *Staudenmayer v. Staudenmayer* (1998), the parties lived together from 1976 to 1984, after which they underwent a ceremonial wedding. The question arose whether the parties had already entered into a common law marriage, during their cohabitation, prior to their wedding, through the exchange of words *de praesenti*. The woman testified at trial that they had a mutual child and that they had said to each

"would take care of each other" and that they did not wish any formal marriage but "to be common law." A contract with respect to a common law marriage was found created.

202 *Id.* at 543.

other, "we are husband and wife." She could not, however, specify when these statements were made, other than most likely "off and on" during their relationship. She had not informed her parents that they were "married." On the contrary, she had stated at the birth of her daughter that she was "not married." However, the woman began to use the man's last name in different situations. They had also submitted joint tax returns. The Pennsylvania Supreme Court stated that a common law marriage can only be created by an exchange of words in the present tense made for the specific purpose of creating "the legal relationship of husband and wife."[203] The court found that the woman could not testify when they had stated to each other, "we are husband and wife." The court found that the record as a whole supported the trial court's conclusion that the woman's testimony on this issue lacked credibility, and that she failed to prove the existence of a common law marriage through the exchange of words *de praesenti* between her and her man by clear and convincing evidence.

Cases also exist in which the long cohabitation between the parties has been given a limited evidentiary weight and the words exchanged between the parties have been reviewed with considerable scrutiny. For example, in the case of *In re Erickson's Estate* (1954), a man claimed Selma Erickson's entire probate estate, on the theory that he had been her husband in a common law marriage. The parties, both immigrants from Sweden, had met in Chicago. The man then moved to South Dakota where he farmed. After one year, Selma arrived unannounced at the farm. According to the man's testimony at trial, the following conversation occurred between the parties upon Selma's arrival in which she stated, "I've come out here to help you out." The man then said, "Why didn't you write to me and let me know you were going to come so I could get things ready?" He said, "People here would begin to talk." Selma answered, "Well, they'll forget that after a while," and added, "That part is all right. We can tell the people here we got married in Chicago." The man answered, "Well, if you want it that way ... if you're going to do that, you've got to drop your name and take the name of Erickson." He also stated, "I'll introduce you to my friends and everybody as Mrs. Erickson," and, "After this you're Mrs. Erickson," to which she gave her silent assent.

The parties thereafter lived together for twenty-five years as husband and wife, represented themselves as man and wife and received reputation as such. The relationship was terminated when the man began a relationship with Selma's sister, who also had emigrated from Sweden. The man and the sister moved to Minnesota and lived there together until Selma died. During that period of more than twenty years, the man had no contact with Selma.

---

203 *Staudenmayer v. Staudenmayer*, 714 A.2d 1016, 1020 (Pa. 1998). The marriage presumption was inapplicable as the woman was available to testify as to the contract. With respect to presumptions, *see generally* Chapter 9.3 *infra*.

The man's claim in the probate estate was rejected by the Supreme Court of South Dakota, because nothing in the words presumed to have been spoken indicates any intention by the parties to take each other as husband and wife forever. Neither was such intention demonstrated by the actions of the parties. No common law marriage was established. The unanswered question is how the court could consider the fact that the parties had lived approximately twenty-five years together as husband and wife without finding that they had the intent to do so. The explanation is not that the parties, because the relationship was terminated by separation, lacked the intent to live together "forever." Instead the explanation appears to be that the court, allowing the cohabitation only a limited evidentiary weight, required a consent by words in the present tense for the formation of a common law marriage. The court's assessment of the parties' *consensus* was almost exclusively based on what they *per verba* uttered during the conversation, recited above, at the commencement of their cohabitation. The court determined that the words exchanged between the parties were not a satisfactory expression of a marital *consensus*. The evidence, according to the court's reasoning, instead supports the proposition that the conversation concerned an impulsive venture, or the continuation of an illicit relationship that the parties hid, using marriage as camouflage.[204] Despite the fact that the parties lived together thereafter as husband and wife for approximately twenty-five years, they had not during this time, according to the record, given any verbal expression to a marital *consensus* outside the above-recited conversation. The explanation for the court's conclusion appears to be based on the fact that with a marital *consensus*, the purpose ought to have been a mutual intent to establish a legal relationship and that the man's words, "[a]fter this you're Mrs. Erickson," to which the woman silently assented, were insufficient to constitute a legal relationship.

Another case in which no marriage contract was found proven despite a long-term cohabitation is *Anderson v. Anderson* (1956), in which the parties met for the first time in 1940 in Marion, Indiana, a state that at that time recognized common law marriage.[205] They commenced a relationship, had sexual relations, but did not live together. Later that same year, they moved in together in the city of Anderson. During the trial, the woman stated, "He told me if I come over and live with him I wouldn't have nothing to worry about. That he would take care of me." She further testified, "[H]e told me he was going to marry me, but he didn't ever do it. He kept putting it off."[206] They lived together thereafter for sixteen years and appeared outwardly as husband and wife. He presented her

204 *In re Erickson's Estate,* 75 S.D. 345, 64 N.W.2d 316, 321 (1954).

205 *Anderson v. Anderson,* 235 Ind. 113, 131 N.E.2d 301 (1956). According to INDIANA CODE ANN. 31-11-8-5 (Burns Code Ed.Repl. 1997), common law marriages entered into in Indiana after January 1, 1958, are invalid.

206 *Id. at* 304.

as Mrs. Anderson. She was listed as his wife an their federal income tax returns and insurance policy. The woman petitioned for divorce in 1950, but withdrew the application. The next year they had a daughter. The woman again petitioned for divorce in 1956, claiming maintenance from the man under the claim that they had lived together in a common law marriage, to which the man objected.

The Indiana Supreme Court stated that two requirements must be fulfilled for that a common law marriage could be created, namely (1) that the parties entered into a marriage contract and (2) that they, if there were no witnesses to the contract, outwardly appeared as spouses (holding out). The court stated that the marriage contract must be expressed, even though it did not need to be in writing or contain certain words. The court further stated, "Cohabitation, reputation, or other conduct may corroborate evidence that there was a contract," but "cannot constitute words which were never spoken or used." The court found that the complaint in this case did not allege that there was any contract of marriage *per verba de praesenti,* and that the evidence when viewed in favor of the appellee (the woman), with all reasonable inferences that could be drawn therefrom, failed to show such a contract. Since there was no common law marriage, there could be no divorce.

An interpretation of the judgment must begin with the man's promise that the woman "wouldn't have nothing to worry about" if she came over and "lived with him," as well as the circumstance that the woman actually moved in with him and that they thereafter, for sixteen years, lived together as husband and wife and received reputation as spouses. If the court meant by a mutual intent "to be married or to be husband and wife," an intent to live together as spouses, the man's oral offer and the woman's actual acceptance by moving in with him and continuing to live together for so long a period ought to have been sufficient to create a marriage contract. However, the court's judgment was reasonable if the court required a legal intent to achieve a marital status, which appears probable, and the man's offer as well as the woman's actual acceptance with respect to the cohabitation were insufficient.

6.5.2 Written Contracts

The parties naturally can give a verbal expression of their marital *consensus* in a written contract.[207] Such a contract has legal effect, assuming that it

207 In *Mathewson v. Phoenix Iron Foundry,* 20 F. 281, 282 (Cir.D.R.I. 1884), the parties had drafted a written document containing the following: "This is to certify that we, H.C. Mathewson and Sarah D. Mathewson, both of Providence, R.I., do hereby acknowledge ourselves before the following witnesses to be man and wife." The document was found to be the basis for a common law marriage. *See also State v. Bittick,* 103 Mo. 183, 15 S.W. 325, 326, 11 L.R.A. 587 (1891) (the parties had agreed in writing "to live together so long as we may both live, to live together as man and

does not solely contain a promise concerning a future marriage, but an agreement *de praesenti, i.e.*, a present and immediately valid marriage. Written contracts are generally accorded great evidentiary weight.[208] The parties often more closely define their marital intent if the contract is in writing. The use of written contracts is limited, however, because these voluntary forms can scarcely be considered attractive to those persons who have opted to refrain from a wedding.[209] During World War I, soldiers frequently entered into common law marriages through letters.[210] There was no requirement that both parties be present during the signing.[211] As with medieval canon law, according to American case law, common law marriages can be entered into by representatives of the parties.[212]

If there is a written contract, it is not unusual for the parties to avail themselves of the formulations found in the formal wedding ceremony. For example, in the case of *Great Northern Ry. v. Johnson* (1918), a man from Minnesota sent a signed written contract to a woman in Missouri stating, "It is hereby agreed, by and between E.R. Spiers and Mayme Woodall from this date henceforth to be husband and wife, and from this date henceforth to conduct ourselves towards each other as husband and wife, the said E.R. Spiers to contribute to the support and maintenance of the said Mayme Woodall as her husband and the said Mayme Woodall to conduct herself towards the said E.R. Spiers as a dutiful wife."[213] The woman

---

wife," which grounded a common law marriage); *Hilton v. Roylance*, 25 Utah 129, 69 P. 660, 663 (1902) (the court stated generally that the parties' *consensus* "may be given in writing"); *Great Northern Ry. v. Johnson*, 166 C.C.A. 181, 254 F. 683 (8th Cir. 1918) (a written contract was the subject of the litigation); *Com. v. Amann*, 58 Pa. D & C 669 (1947); and *In re Estate of Gower*, 445 Pa. 554, 284 A.2d 742 (1971) (a common law marriage formed on the basis of the written contract). *See also Hulett v. Carey*, 66 Minn. 327, 69 N.W. 31 (1896); and *Sharon v. Sharon*, 75 Cal. 633, 22 P. 26, 131 (1889).

208 *State v. Blair*, 885 P.2d 791, 794 (Utah 1994); and *Metro. Life Ins. Co. v. Johnson*, 103 Idaho 122, 645 P.2d 356, 361 (1982).

209 This investigation has only found a few written contracts. *See also* Note, *Common Law Marriage - A Legal Anachronism*, 32 Ind. L.J. 99, 106 note 31 (1956), in which a thorough investigation of the cases from Indiana did not reveal any marriages "based on a written or witnessed contract."

210 *In re Estate of Gower*, 445 Pa. 554, 284 A.2d 742, 743 (1971).

211 *Com. v. Amann*, 58 Pa. D & C. 669 (Q.S.Camb. 1947).

212 *United States v. Layton*, 68 F.Supp. 247 (S.D.Fla. 1946). *Compare* with respect to "proxy marriages" Clark, *supra* note 103, at 124.

213 *Great Northern Ry. v. Johnson*, 166 C.C.A. 181, 254 F. 683, 684 (8th Cir. 1918). With respect to the issue of whether cohabitation between the parties is a necessary requirement in addition to the existence of the marriage contract, *see* Section 8.4 *infra*. Compare *Clancy v. Clancy*, 66 Mich. 202, 33 N.W. 889 (1887), where the parties had in a written document contracted: "We mutually and jointly from now henceforth and forever, agree to live as man and wife, but each party retains the right to buy, sell, and transfer their respective properties without question of the other party." The majority of the Michigan Supreme Court found that this was not a marriage agreement and stated that the contract "will be found to provide only for a concubinage intercourse between the parties. It does not in terms purport to be a marriage agreement, nor an agreement to live together as husband and wife."

signed the contract. In connection with the death of the man, the woman alleged that she had lived in a common law marriage with the man and cited as grounds the written contract.

The Eighth Circuit Court of Appeals, applying Missouri law, stated: "Mutual assent to the present institution of the status is all sufficient. No other act, such as cohabitation ... is necessary to complete the institution of the status where the mutual assent contemplates a marriage *in praesenti.*"[214] The offer and contract, respectively, do not mention all the legal effects of marriage, but only the man's obligation to contribute to the woman's maintenance, and that the parties generally bind themselves to act as spouses to each other. Nevertheless, as the court found, this should be considered sufficient to constitute a marriage contract. The legal ramifications of marriage are principally not separable, but must instead be accepted in their entirety or not at all. Take it or leave it! Their agreement to be husband and wife appears to cover the entirety.

In a more recent case, *In re Estate of Gower* (1971), the man wished to obtain "marriage status" and thereby avoid military duty. In a written document drafted in 1942, he declared the following: "I, William Charles Gulick, hereby say and declare that I consider and regard Ada Gower Gulick, nee Ada Gower, as my wife ... do now, and will forever hereafter, assume all of her living expenses and provide her with the necessities of life, as well as endow her with full rights and all privileges of a wife, together with a wife's legal right to, and interest in, whatsoever property I am now possessed of or should hereafter acquire ... pursuant to an understanding by and between us that we are in all respects to be husband and wife." The woman gave her written consent as follows: "I ... have read the declaration and statements of my husband ... made for purpose of establishing marriage status ... and I hereby subscribe to his statements in every particular and respect." Prior to the execution of the contract, the parties had lived together without any marital hindrance for approximately ten years, and afterward, until the woman's death twenty years later. The man claimed he was the deceased's spouse based on this contract.

The Pennsylvania Supreme Court stated that a common law marriage is established by words in the present tense, uttered with a view and for the purpose of establishing a relationship of husband and wife. The contract, in which the parties openly accepted each other as husband and wife, was sufficient to constitute a common law marriage.[215] The court does not more closely analyze the conditions set forth in the offer, which, with respect to the woman, set forth certain of her rights but not her obligations, and with respect to the man, certain of his obligations but not his rights. It is clear, however, that their general purpose was to be husband

214 *Great Northern Ry.* at 685.
215 *In re Estate of Gower*, 445 Pa. 554, 284 A.2d 742 (1971).

and wife in all respects and establish a marriage status. This appears to be sufficient to form a common law marriage.

Another more recent case is *In re death of Boyd* (1998), in which the parties drafted and signed a written declaration that: "We, the undersigned, on or about 3rd October 92 ('Marriage Date') agreed to be married, and since that date, we have lived together continuously as husband and wife and represented ourselves to others and developed a reputation as husband and wife." The document even contained a declaration that no marital impediments existed. The Oklahoma Court of Civil Appeals found that the document was competent evidence sufficient to establish an actual mutual agreement between the parties to be husband and wife. As competent evidence had been presented as to the other requirements for a finding of a common law marriage in the case, the court found that the lower court's determination that a common law marriage had been formed was correct.[216]

6.5.3 A Lack of Agreement between the Marital Intent and Its Expressions

As can be gleaned from the above discussion, it is necessary that a marital *consensus* exists and that it be expressed for the formation of a common law marriage. A marriage cannot be formed, consequently, if the marital intent exists but is not expressed. The same is true if the expression exists, but the marital intent is missing. Already in Roman law sham marriages were invalid (*simulatae nuptiae nullius momenti sunt*).[217] This principle can also be found in medieval canon law, which proscribed that "that which the words express where the heart is not willing is not valid" (*si autem verbis explicant, quod tamen corde non volunt*).[218] These principles have their correspondence in the modern case law, and are interesting because they set out requirements with respect to the parties' marital *consensus*.

With respect to the lack of agreement between the intent and the expression of the intent, there are no material differences between cases concerning formal and informal marriages,[219] even though the question

216 *Matter of Death of Boyd*, 959 P.2d 612, 614 (Okla.Civ.App. 1998). In *Matter of Estate of Marson*, 328 Mont. 348, 120 P.3d 382 (2005), the man had executed a handwritten declaration of a common law marriage with one of the purported common law wives. *See also Costello v. Workers' Comp. Appeal Bd (Kinsley Constr., Inc.)*, 2006 WL 4043525 (Pa.Cmwlth.), where the parties had notarized a document entitled "Confirmation of Common Law Marriage," which stated in part: "We, the undersigned, do affirm that our relationship is intended to comply with Pennsylvania Law Creating a Common Law Marriage. It is our intent to have a marital relationship. We have co-habited or will co-habitate as husband and wife and hold ourselves out to the community as married..."

217 *See* Section 2.4.

218 *Id.*

219 In the Scottish case, *Orlandi v. Castelli*, 1961 S.C. 113, Lord Ordinary (Cameron) correctly stated that: "On principle I do not see that there should be any difference

has the most practical significance for the former. The majority of persons entering into sham marriages undergo formal wedding ceremonies, as the ceremony strengthens the façade. In addition, a ceremonial marriage can be formed without the wedding ceremony being followed by any actual cohabitation.[220] Certainly one of the problems with formal marriages today is that the system can be exploited by parties entering into a marriage *pro forma* simply with the intent of enjoying one of the legal benefits of marriage without having the intent to actually live together. This issue is less significant with respect to informal marriages in those jurisdictions requiring cohabitation in addition to a marriage contract, because the absence of cohabitation prevents the formation of a common law marriage. In those jurisdictions in which an informal marriage can be formed simply based on the parties' formless marriage contract *per verba de praesenti*, as under Pennsylvania or Scottish law prior to 1940, sham marriages are an interesting legal problem even though they are entered informally. If neither a form nor a cohabitation is required as a necessary condition for the formation of a common law marriage, the danger of a sham transaction is greater in informal marriages than in formal marriages, in which the form itself can act as a restraint.

The question arises about how a lack of agreement between the intent and the expression of that intent is manifested. The most obvious cases are those in which the expression exists, but the marital intent, regardless of how its content is defined, is completely absent. For example, if a man and a woman jokingly participate in a wedding, everyone knows that a marriage is not formed, because an actual marital *consensus* does not exist.[221] For the same reason, a legal marriage cannot be entered into by actors in a theatrical play, regardless of an explicit and emotional expression of marital intent. The parties have no intent to either enter

---

in the grounds on which a regular as opposed to an irregular marriage can be set aside. In both cases it is consent, and not the form in which consent is given or evidenced, that makes marriage."

220 *Schibi v. Schibi*, 136 Conn. 196, 69 A.2d 831 (1948); and *Hilton v. Roylance*, 25 Utah 129, 69 P. 660 (1902).

221 In *Davis v. Davis*, 119 Conn. 194, 175 A. 574 (1934), the parties, both nineteen years old and of the age of marital consent, found themselves at a party. To everyone's surprise, the woman jokingly proposed to the man, and the group got into an automobile, drove to another state, and the couple participated in a wedding ceremony. When the night was over, the parties separated. They never lived together. When the question later was raised whether the parties were married as they obviously, during a valid wedding ceremony, had taken each other as husband and wife, the court – reminding the parties that an issue as serious as marriage was nothing to joke about – found that as no marital *consensus* existed with the parties, the marriage was invalid. *Compare Crouch v. Wartenburg*, 91 W.Va. 91, 112 S.E. 234 (1922); *Goldman v. Dithrich*, 131 Fla. 408, 179 So. 715 (1938); *McClurg v. Terry*, 21 N.J.Eq. 225 (1870) ("[m]ere words without any intention corresponding to them, will not make a marriage or any other civil contract"); and *Meredith v. Shakespear*, 96 W.Va. 229, 122 S.E. 520 (1921). A different outcome but also different circumstances can be found in *Hand v. Berry*, 170 Ga. 743, 154 S.E. 239 (1930). *Compare* Scottish law, *Dunn v. Dunn's Trs.*, 1930 S.C. 131.

into a marital cohabitation or form a legal marriage and, consequently, no marital *consensus* exists. The same is naturally true if the parties, jokingly, or without any serious intent, enter into an informal marriage contract. Serious declarations of love have not been accepted as serious marriage contracts.[222] A serious intent has also been found lacking if the parties, under the influence of alcohol, have entered into a marriage contract.[223]

Situations have arisen, however, that fall somewhere between theatre and reality. This can be occur, for example, if the parties, living together and having the intent to enter into a marriage, during a festival, participate in an old-fashioned wedding not recognized today as a ceremonial wedding. Can the parties be construed to have entered into an informal marriage contract? In *Allison Park Contractors v. W.C.A.B.* (1999), the parties, Louise and Stephen, moved in together in 1993. They planned to have a ceremonial wedding in September of 1995. In September of 1994, during the Providence Plantation Colonial Festival, they participated in an eighteenth-century colonial wedding ceremony. Present at the ceremony were Louise's parents and sister, as well as Stephen's mother and grandmother. At trial, Louise testified to the following with respect to the ceremony, "We had a minister, an actual minister in charge of the ceremony. We exchanged rings and vows." The minister testified that he had informed the parties that the ceremony was not legally valid. According

222 No serious marital *consensus* was expressed in the Scottish case *Maloy v. Macadam*, (1885) 12 R. 431, in which the man, after living with the woman for years, stated to a stranger that he was united in marriage with her. The woman thanked the man for the admission and explained that she intended to call the stranger as a witness as to the existence of the marriage. The man stamped his foot and said: "Damn it." The court found that a marriage had not been formed. In a similar Scottish case, *Taylor v. Taylor*, (1786) 3 Paton 56, the woman had in writing declared to the man: "I hereby solemnly declare you, Patric Taylor, in Birkenshaw, my just and lawful husband, and remain your affectionate wife, Agnes Kello." It was demonstrated that the man, on the other side, did not understand woman's statement as more than a sign of her love for him and as a promise with respect to a future marriage. The Court of Session found that a marriage had been formed, while the House of Lords, with reference to the lack of *copula* and to the parties' actions generally, did not find that the parties had understood the document as a final agreement as to a marriage *de praesenti*.

223 In the Scottish case, *Steuart v. Robertson*, (1875) 2 R. (H.L.) 80, the man stated: "Maggie, you are my wife before Heaven, so help me, O God." The statement, which certainly can be said to be very expressive and was not refuted on the grounds that it did not intend a marriage *de praesenti* and in this lifetime, was instead found to not be an expression of a serious marital *consensus*, as the man at the time he uttered the statement was heavily influenced by alcohol. The circumstances in general, before as well as after the statement, supported the conclusion that the parties did not consider each other as husband and wife. In a similar case, *Gall v. Gall*, 1870 9 M. 177, the man made the following statements in writing: "Dear Sir,— I bind and oblige myself to keep and support that woman through life, I consider her my lawful wife. William Gall." Evidence was presented as to the fact that Gall, as well as the person helping him with the document, were at that point of time heavily influenced by alcohol. The statement therefore was found to not be an expression of a serious marital *consensus*.

to Louise, Stephen had presented her to his friends as his wife, while she usually said that they were engaged and that they acted like husband and wife. According to her, they had a joint credit card and bank account, and had also jointly purchased an automobile. During 1994, they filed individual federal income tax returns. Stephen died as a result of a work accident in May 1995. Louise claimed workers' compensation benefits based on the assertion that she was the deceased's widow based on a common law marriage. The Pennsylvania Commonwealth Court stated that the person alleging a common law marriage must prove "an actual intention of the parties to form a marriage contract" and found that Louise had not met the burden of proof showing that she was the deceased's common law wife.

The court does not elaborate on the missing element. Was it the content of the marital intent, the point of time for the creation of the marriage (*de praesenti* or *de futuro*), or the expression of the intent? Even though the record does not clearly state exactly what was said by the parties during the wedding ceremony, the court's reasoning indicates that they exchanged marital vows that fulfilled the requirements of a contract *per verba*. The minister's testimony was that the ceremony was not a valid ceremonial wedding, not whether it established a common law marriage. Neither is there any reason to assume that the parties did not possess marital intent. The court's conclusion should probably be interpreted to have found that the woman had not proven, by their participation in the ceremony, that they had changed their plans for a future wedding a year after the festival. She had not proven that the parties had changed their marital intent *de futuro* to a marital *consensus de praesenti*.

Of more practical significance are cases involving sham marriages, in which the parties wish to give the façade that they actually have entered into a true marriage, despite a lack of agreement on their marital *consensus*. Cases belonging here are those in which the parties neither have the intent to cohabit nor to legally form a marriage. This can be if the parties, for example, to obtain housing or employment, enter into a ceremonial wedding or an informal marriage contract.[224] In this type of case, no marital *consensus* exists.

---

224 In a number of cases in Scottish case law, a lack of a marital *consensus* was grounds for invalidity. In *More v. McInnes,* (1782) 2 Paton 598, a man wrote to a woman expecting his child: "Mrs. Fairbairn, I hereby acknowledge that you are my lawful wife, and you may from this date use my name ... Alex More." The Court of Session found that the document was sufficient evidence of a marriage, but the House of Lords came to the conclusion that the document was not prepared for the purpose of forming a marriage. It instead was written to make it possible for the woman, during her pregnancy, to live with her brother, who would not have accepted her had she been unmarried and pregnant. A marriage was not formed. A purpose other than the formation of a marriage also existed in *Lockyer v. Sinclair,* (1846) 8 D. 582, 595, despite the fact that the woman declared in writing: "I declare Edmund Beatty Lockyer to be my husband." At trial, she testified that she signed the document at the request of the man simply for the purpose of convincing his father

More difficult to assess are cases of sham marriage, in which the parties have entered into the marriage simply to obtain a certain legal consequence, for example, the right of one of the parties to immigrate, avoid military service, or to give a child legitimacy. Significantly, in a sham marriage, the parties have agreed to participate in a formal wedding, possibly for payment. At the same time, the parties have agreed to not live as husband and wife, and to dissolve the marriage as soon as possible. Sham marriage even occurs among informal marriages. Two main approaches as to the validity of these marriages appear in the case law.

According to the first approach, the marriages are invalid because the parties' marital *consensus* is insufficient. They do not possess a true marital intent. The inadequacies of the parties' *consensus*, in these cases, of course are dependent upon the requirements made of the courts as to the content of the intent. Against the background given above concerning the marital intent's *essensialia,* the question immediately arises whether the parties lack an intent to live together, or the intent to establish a complete legal relationship. The courts' reasoning with respect to this question often leaves much unanswered.

Among the cases in which sham marriages have been deemed invalid, two prototypes of sham marriage typically involve ceremonial weddings. In *United States v. Rubenstein* (1945), the parties had a wedding only to prevent the woman from being deported. The parties had agreed to never live together and dissolve the marriage within six months. The woman paid the man $200 for the inconvenience. The Second Circuit Court of Appeals found that the parties had never consented to enter into a marital relationship "as it is ordinarily understood," and that the limited intent

---

that they were engaged and that he should contribute to the son's living expenses. In the extensive correspondence between the parties, references to their future marriage were made. With respect to this and the fact that *copula* had not occurred between the parties, the court found that the statement was made for a purpose other than to form a marriage, thus no marriage had been formed. In *Stewart v. Menzies,* (1841) 2 Rob. 547, a farmer had stated in a written document to his housekeeper: "Christi, you and I having lived together as man and wife for some time, I hereby declare you to be my lawful wife, in the event of a child being borne in consequence of the present connection betwixt us." Despite the fact that the expression of intent was conditional, the House of Lords found that the document had been prepared for a purpose other than to form a marriage, namely to allow him to break an engagement with another woman, which he did. No marriage was found proven between the farmer and his housekeeper. The case of *Bradly v. Murray,* (1933) 1933 S.L.T. 534 can also be mentioned. The man had been previously married. The parties, Catholics, in order to encourage the Catholic Church to marry them, went through a private ceremony and before witnesses declared that they took each other as husband and wife. The parties immediately separated after the ceremony and never cohabited. Lord Moncreiff granted the claim as to the marriage's invalidity, partially on the ground that the parties had "by joint arrangement withheld actual consent to marry, and only interchanged, for a purpose remote from the marriage, a formal and ostensible consent." *See also Dorgeloh v. Murtha,* 156 N.Y.S. 2d 181 (1945), in which the parties met before the wedding ceremony but never again thereafter.

did not give expression to an agreement "to be married" and, therefore, no marriage had been formed.[225] If the spouses consent to a marriage only to create the appearance that they are spouses, and have an intent to dissolve the marriage as quickly as possible after the purpose for the marriage has been served, they have never, according to the court, agreed to actually be married. The wedding was, therefore, invalid.

The question of whether the *consensus* is inadequate because there is no intent to form either a marital cohabitation or a complete legal relationship is not further elaborated upon by the court, a silence that supports either argument. If the insufficiency was with respect to the intent to live together, it would have been simple for the Court of Appeals to say so. It would have been more complicated to refer to the insufficiency with respect to the lack of intent to form a complete legal relationship. On one side, it can be argued that the parties intended to achieve just one of the legal consequences of marriage, namely, the right to immigrate, and that they intended to form not a legally binding marriage, but a relationship that could be dissolved at any point in time. On the other side, their understanding of the need to dissolve their relationship through divorce indicates that they intended to form a complete legal marriage that would later be dissolved. More precise reasoning than simply a reference to the marital relationship "as it is ordinarily understood" would have clarified this issue.

The Seventh Circuit Court of Appeals took the same stance in *United States v. Lutwak* (1953),[226] in which several war veterans were prosecuted

---

225 *United States v. Rubenstein*, 151 F.2d 915, 918, 919 (2d Cir. 1945); *United States v. Lutwak*, 195 F.2d 748 (7th Cir. 1952), *aff'd*, 344 U.S. 604, 73 S.Ct. 481, 97 L.Ed. 593 (1953); *Johl v. United States*, 370 F.2d 174 (9th Cir. 1966); *Faustin v. Lewis*, 85 N.J. 507, 427 A.2d 1105 (1981); and *Conley v. Conley*, 14 Ohio Supp. 22 (1943). In *Lederkremer v. Lederkremer*, 173 Misc. 587, 18 N.Y.S.2d 725 (Sup.Ct. 1940), the marriage was viewed as invalid as it arose for the purpose of making it possible for the woman to emigrate from Poland to the United States and the parties did not intend to live together as husband and wife. In *Stone v. Stone*, 159 Fla. 624, 32 So.2d 278 (1947), the parties went through a wedding ceremony to "give the child a name" and they agreed to never consummate the marriage. A marriage was not formed. *See also Amsden v. Amsden*, 110 N.Y.S.2d 307 (1952).

226 *United States v. Lutwak*, 195 F.2d 748 (7th Cir. 1952), *aff'd*, 344 U.S. 604, 73 S.Ct. 481, 97 L.Ed. 593 (1953), *cited in* 2 U. Chi. L. Rev. 710 (1953). *See also Faustin v. Lewis*, 85 N.J. 507, 427 A.2d 1105 (1981); and *Rubman v. Rubman*, 140 Misc. 658, 251 N.Y.S. 474 (1931), where the man's intention was to avoid deportation. *Compare Osborne v. Osborne*, 134 A.2d 438 (D.C. 1957), where the man had no intention to live with his wife. *Compare* the Scottish case, *Orlandi v. Castelli*, 1961 S.C. 113, in which a British woman and her Italian fiancé had stayed in Scotland. When his visa expired, the parties went through a regular civil wedding ceremony simply to get his visa renewed. As the parties were Catholic, a civil ceremony was found to not form a marriage between them. Neither *copula carnalis* nor a marital cohabitation had occurred between the parties. The woman filed a lawsuit to have the marriage declared invalid, which was granted by the House of Lords. Lord Ordinary (Cameron) stated that simply the observation of the formalities in a civil ceremony is not sufficient for the formation of a marriage: "On principle I do not see that there should be any difference in the grounds on which a regular as opposed to an

after World War II for entering into marriages in Paris in exchange for payment to facilitate their spouses' immigration to the United States. The parties generally agreed to not live together and dissolve the relationships as soon as their purpose was served. The Seventh Circuit Court of Appeals found, with reference to the Second Circuit Court of Appeals' decision in *Rubenstein*, that no valid marriages had been formed.

Lutwak was appealed to the United States Supreme Court. The Court found no reason to retry the issue of the validity of the marriages. The Court, however, stated that Congress must have had in mind the common understanding of marriage when it enacted the War Brides Act. The regulations in this law concerning alien spouses state, "the two parties have undertaken to establish a life together and assume certain duties and obligations." The Court found that the parties, in the case, had not done so. The Court's analysis consequently leaves open the possibility referring back to the lack of intent with respect to either "a life together" or establishing "certain duties and obligations," or both.

Cases exist, however few, in which an informal marriage contract has been found invalid on the grounds that it was entered into for a limited purpose. A common law marriage, in such cases, has not been formed. In *Pegg v. Pegg* (1908), the parties executed a written marriage contract for the purpose of preventing prosecution for an "illicit cohabitation." The court stated, "That a mere written or oral agreement to be husband and wife, without present intention to assume that relation in fact, does not constitute a marriage between the parties, especially if the agreement is entered into for some other purpose, is well settled."[227] It appears from this reasoning that the court found that the lack of intent was with respect to the parties' relationship in fact, or, more precisely, the actual marital cohabitation.

---

irregular marriage can be set aside. In both cases it is consent, and not the form in which consent is given or evidenced, that makes marriage." However, in cases concerning regular marriages, as opposed to cases concerning irregular marriages, the burden of proof for invalidity of the marriage on the basis of an inadequate marital *consensus* as a rule lies with the party contesting the validity of the marriage. The performance of a wedding ceremony consequently creates a presumption for the fact that the parties possessed a mutual marital *consensus*.

227 *Pegg v. Pegg*, 138 Iowa 572, 115 N.W. 1027, 1028 (1908). The court, as a necessary requisite for the formation of a common law marriage also required cohabitation and could have also found the evidence insufficient on the basis of the lack of a cohabitation. *Compare* the Scottish case, *Bradly v. Murray*, 1933 S.L.T. 534, in which the man had previously been married. The parties, Catholics, in order to encourage the Catholic Church to marry them, went through a private ceremony and before witnesses declared that they took each other as husband and wife. The parties immediately separated after the ceremony and never cohabited. Lord Moncreiff granted the claim as to the marriage's invalidity, partially on the ground that the parties had "by joint arrangement withheld actual consent to marry, and only interchanged, for a purpose remote from the marriage, a formal and ostensible consent."

A recent case is *Bell v. Ferraro* (2004), in which the parties had signed an "Affidavit of Common Law Marriage." Given that the affidavit was intended solely to allow the woman to be added to the man's health insurance, and by also referring to other circumstances, the court found that no common law marriage was proven.[228]

According to the second approach in the case law, sham marriages entered into for limited purposes are valid, but the side agreements of the spouses to never live together and to dissolve the relationship as soon as possible are invalid.[229] Of those cases in which the parties, without the intent to live together, have gone through a wedding to form a sham marriage that were found valid, *United States v. Diogo* (1963)[230] can be mentioned. Diogo was prosecuted for false representations regarding his

---

228 *Bell v. Ferraro*, 849 A.2d 1233 (Pa.Super. 2004). Compare *In re Estate of Gowers*, 445 Pa. 554, 284 A.2d 742 (1971).

229 This stance appears to have its origins in English law, *see Bell v. Graham*, (1859) 13 Moore P.C. 242, 15 Eng.Rep. 91; and Joseph Jackson, The Formation and Annulment of Marriage 196 (2d ed. 1969). In *Gregg v. Gregg*, 133 Misc. 109, 231 N.Y.S. 221 (1928), the parties agreed that they would not live together, that the man would not contribute to the woman's living expenses, and that he would be free to live with other women. The court stated: "The parties to a marriage may not vary or diminish the obligations which the law attaches to the relationship by private agreements between themselves ... The parties here concededly went through a marriage ceremony. Any private reservations they may have made in regard to their respective obligations under the marital status which resulted are void and of no effect." As to immigration cases, *United States v. Diogo*, 320 F.2d 898 (2d Cir. 1963), can be mentioned. The Second Circuit Court of Appeals stated that a marriage entered into in exchange for payment and for the purpose of facilitating an immigration to the United States, is valid in accordance with applicable New York state law, as long as the marriage is not proven invalid. In *Campbell v. Moore*, 189 S.C. 497, 1 S.E.2d 784 (1939), a written agreement between the parties to not live together and not contest any legal action to void the marriage made by the other party, was considered to negate the existence of a marital intent. As to the cases with respect to establishing the legitimacy of a child, *Franklin v. Franklin*, 154 Mass. 515, 28 N.E. 681 (1891) can be mentioned. A man and woman entered into a temporary relationship resulting in a pregnancy. In order to give legitimacy to the child, ("giving the child a name"), the parties agreed to participate in a wedding but not to assume any marital cohabitation or any of the obligations accompanying marriage, and dissolve the marriage as quickly as possible. The court, finding that the parties did not possess the right, through contract, to avoid marital obligations, found that a valid marriage had been formed. *See also Schibi v. Schibi*, 136 Conn. 196, 69 A.2d 831 (1949), in which the parties entered into a marriage for "giving the child a name" and without any intention to live together as husband and wife. The parties were to dissolve the marriage six weeks after the ceremony. A marriage was found formed. The parties were considered to have the intent to create "the status of marriage" in any case for the limited period of time. *See also Erickson v. Erickson*, 48 N.Y.S.2d 588 (1944), in which the parties entered into a marriage for the sole purpose of legitimizing the child. The parties agreed to never live together. The marriage was found to be valid. *See also DeVries v. DeVries*, 195 Ill.App. 4 (1915); 14 A.L.R.2d 624 (1952); *Barker v. Baker*, 88 Misc. 300, 151 N.Y.S. 811 (Sup.Ct. 1914); *Hanson v. Hanson*, 287 Mass. 154, 191 N.E. 673 (1934); *Campbell v. Moore*, 189 S.C. 497, 1 S.E.2d 784 (1939); *Delfino v. Delfino*, 35 N.Y.S.2d 693 (Sup.Ct. 1942); *Bishop v. Bishop*, 308 N.Y.S.2d 998 (1970); and *Mpiliris v. Hellenic Lines, Ltd.*, 323 F.Supp. 865, 881-882 (S.D.Tex. 1979).

230 *United States v. Diogo*, 320 F.2d 898 (2d Cir. 1963).

marital status. The prosecutor argued that Diogo had entered into a sham marriage. Diogo, a Portuguese citizen, came to the United States in 1951 and received a temporary visa. When his visa was about to expire, he married Clara Heredia, an American citizen, in April 1957, in order to be able to stay in the United States. The parties agreed that Clara would receive a sum of money for the inconvenience and that there was to be no sexual relationship. No cohabitation was commenced. The marriage was dissolved by divorce in Mexico in January 1958. The Second Circuit Court of Appeals found that a marriage entered into for money and the purpose of hindering a deportation was valid in accordance with the law of New York, as long as the marriage was not proven invalid. The court found, in accordance with the evidence presented in the case, that at the trial below, the government had failed, as a matter of law, to sustain its burden of proof that the marriage was invalid at the time Diogo made his statements concerning his marital status.

The proposition that there is a presumption that a valid marriage has been formed through a wedding ceremony, until the contrary is proven, can be seen from *Diogo*, meaning that the burden of proof rests with the party alleging that the marriage is invalid. However, *Diogo* is interesting not only from an evidentiary viewpoint. Without explicit discussion the court appears to have indirectly taken a stance with respect to the required content of the parties' marital *consensus*. As it was clear that the parties had no intent to live together[231] and a marriage was formed, the court does not appear to have required that kind of marital intent. The outcome in *Diogo* can be seen as contradictory to the reasoning of the court, albeit in dictum, in *United States v. Lutwak* (1953), in which, as discussed above, the Court stated that the common understanding of marriage is that the two parties have undertaken to establish a life together.[232]

The court in *Diogo* appears instead, albeit not expressly stated, to have assumed that the required element of intent is a legal relationship. As the parties' only purpose was to prevent the man's deportation, it certainly can be questioned whether they had an extensive legal intent.[233] Still, the parties clearly believed that a divorce would be required, which is evidence in support of their understanding that a legal marriage had been formed.

231 A co-defendant in the case, Gonzales, for the purpose of staying in the United States, entered into a similar marriage to Yvette Garces. The woman accepted the arrangement on the conditions that she received payment and that the parties "would not live together as man and wife." The court made the same assessment in the case as with respect to Diogo.

232 *United States v. Lutwak*, 195 F.2d 748 (7th Cir. 1952), *aff'd*, 344 U.S. 604, 611, 73 S.Ct. 481, 97 L.Ed. 593 (1953), *cited in* 2 U. CHI. L. REV. 710 (1953).

233 A true marital *consensus* does not appear to have existed if the parties have expressed such only for the purpose of allowing one party to obtain some economic benefit. In *Hamilton v. Hamilton,* 1 Bell.App. 736 (1842), the parties' intent was found to be to receive a pension from the War Office, which was insufficient to form a marriage.

If the marital *consensus* is interpreted in this fashion, and the burden of proof is placed as in the case, the court's conclusion that the marriage was not proven to be invalid is not surprising. The court's reasoning does not, however, elaborate its requirements with respect to marital intent.[234]

However, in many cases, the parties ought to be willing to accept all legal consequences of a marriage, if only temporarily, even though only a single legal consequence is important to them. Those that marry, for example, to legitimize a child, ought to be willing to accept the other aspects of marital status.[235] Often, the parties have agreed to dissolve the marriage as quickly as possible, which assumes that they have had the intent to form a marriage. The parties' intent to achieve a marital status for a limited time has, in certain cases, not hindered the formation of a marriage.[236] If they have the intent to assume a marital status, a marriage is formed, regardless of whether the primary motive behind the intent is to obtain a certain legal consequence. Courts, with reference to the fact that the achievement of the parties' underlying purpose assumes marriage, have found, in several cases, that the parties must have intended to create a marital status.[237]

Cases also exist in which the informal marriage has been found to be valid despite the fact that it was entered into for a limited purpose. All too often, however, the courts' reasoning with respect to the consensual requirements is dissatisfactory. In the case of *Interest of Miller* (1982),[238] a thirty-six-year-old male teacher began a relationship with a fourteen-year old girl who was a pupil at the school. In order to avoid criminal prosecution for sexual conduct with a minor, but also, according to his testimony, as accepted by the court, because of his love for her, the teacher entered into a common law marriage with the student. The student was at the age of consent despite being only fourteen years old.[239] The informal marriage

---

234 It has been argued that the courts' judgment have been influenced by politics and a desire to protect the legitimacy of children, a glimpse of which can be found if one looks at the requirements of marital intent the courts actually ought to have applied. *See* Clark, *supra* note 103, at 217.

235 *See, e.g., Wagner v. Wagner*, 59 Pa.D.C. 90 (1947). As the intent of the parties was to legitimize the child, the court found that their intent must also have been to enter into a valid marriage. *See also Schibi v. Schibi*, 136 Conn. 196, 69 A.2d 831 (1949), in which the parties participated in a wedding ceremony for the purpose of giving the child a name and in which the court found that the parties had the intent to create "the status of marriage." *See also Mpiliris v. Hellenic Lines, Ltd.*, 323 F.Supp. 865, 881-882 (S.D.Tex. 1979) (a marriage entered into for a limited purpose was valid if it is the parties' intent that the marriage be given "legal significance"); *compare Anonymous v. Anonymous*, 49 N.Y.S.2d 314 (Sup. Ct. 1944).

236 *Schibi v. Schibi*, 136 Conn. 196, 69 A.2d 831 (1949) ("In principle, it would make no difference whether the status so created by the terms of the agreement was to continue for six weeks or six years").

237 *Wagner v. Wagner*, 136 Conn. 196, 69 A.2d 831 (1949); and *Anonymous v. Anonymous*, 49 N.Y.S.2d 314 (Sup.Ct. 1944).

238 *Interest of Miller*, 301 Pa.Super. 511, 448 A.2d 25, 26 (1982).

239 The 14-year-old student had not reached the age of legal consent in accordance with Pennsylvania law to enter into a formal marriage, that age being sixteen, but had

was entered into in a little ceremony at three o'clock in the morning, witnessed by the man's sister and brother-in-law, as well as a thirteen-year-old friend of the girl. In accordance with the instructions the man had received from a lawyer, he said: "I marry you." With that, the man, according to his testimony, intended that the girl would "be my wife" and it was his intent "to take her home to live with me as my wife." According to his testimony, he also intended to assume his obligations "to take her, provide a home and all the necessities that you would normally provide for your wife."

The trial court found that the marriage was invalid, but on appeal, the Pennsylvania Superior Court stated that the purpose of avoiding criminal prosecution does not invalidate a common law marriage if the parties also have the intention to marry. A dissenting judge found that it was not evidenced in the record by clear and convincing evidence that the parties had entered into a mutual contract or that they had the intent to establish a relationship of husband and wife. The dissent referred to the fact that the parties immediately after the ceremony went their separate ways and never lived together, indicating that they, with the "intention to marry" did not intend an actual marital cohabitation.

Unfortunately, the Superior Court does not elaborate on the meaning of intention to marry. The question arises whether the court considered that the intention to marry simply meant going through a ceremony, or whether the court meant that the parties intended to live together or assume marital status with the accompanying legal obligations and rights. If the court required an intent to establish marital status, it must have found that the parties had a legal intent that was more extensive than simply avoiding prosecution. The man's testimony as to the duties he believed he had assumed, consequently, must have been given some weight by the court. If the court, on the other hand, required that the intent include marital cohabitation, the court must have accepted the man's testimony that he had the intent "to take her home to live with me." (Compare the dissenting justice's evaluation of the evidence.) Clearer reasoning by the court would have been beneficial. Regardless of which stance the court has taken with respect to the marital intent's essence, it appears that the court's conclusion that a valid marriage had been formed rests fragilely on the evidence in the record.

In cases in which the parties have had a clear intent to live together, and, in addition, obtain a marital status, the common law marriage has been found valid, despite the fact that their intentions originally were limited to a specific purpose. In such cases, it is dubious to view the marriage

---

reached the age required to enter into a common law marriage, which is seven. *Miller* at 26. *See also Jewett v. Jewett*, 196 Pa.Super. Ct. 305, 175 A.2d 141 (1951). *Compare Sloss-Sheffield Steel & Iron Co. v. Watford*, 245 Ala. 425, 17 So.2d 166 (1944), in which one of several ceremonial marriages was found valid "even though he married her to escape prosecution for seduction" and no marital cohabitation had occurred.

as a sham. Logically, what part of the marriage is to be considered a sham? For example, in the case of *In re Estate of Gower* (1971), the man, having the intent to avoid military duty, in a written document in 1942 declared, "I, William Charles Gulick, hereby say and declare that I consider and regard Ada Gower Gulick, nee Ada Gower, as my wife ... do now ... endow her with full rights and all privileges of a wife." The woman consented to this in writing. When she died in 1962, the man claimed that he was her surviving spouse. The trial court found that the marriage was invalid, because the man's purpose in the marriage had been to avoid military duty. The Pennsylvania Supreme Court, after stating that the required marital intent was "establishing the relation of husband and wife," found that the parties' contract was sufficient to form a common law marriage.[240] If the court, with the term *relationship of husband and wife*, referred to the actual relationship with respect to the marital cohabitation between the parties, the outcome of the case is not at all surprising. The parties, at the point of the formation of the contract, had lived together for ten years after the woman's divorce from a previous marriage, and, after the formation of the contract, the parties continued to live together for another twenty years. Neither is the outcome surprising if the court instead focused on the legal relationship, as the intent of the parties was not simply to avoid military duty but also to assume a marriage status.[241] Further elaboration by the court in this case would also have been interesting.

The court in *United States v. Dorto* (1925)[242] more clearly delineates what satisfies the intent to establish marital status. In *Dorto*, the parties' primary goal with the informal marriage contract was to hinder the woman's deportation, and their cohabitation was only for a short period of time. Emilie Carlevale Dorto arrived in New York in June of 1922. Her attorneys informed her that if she wished to avoid deportation, she should marry an American citizen and thereby obtain American citizenship. The Cable Act was about to take effect, as of September 22, 1922, and would limit the ability to obtain American citizenship based upon marriage. Around August 1, 1922, the woman met Dorto in Providence, Rhode Island. She told him about her situation, and he consented to marry her. Two or three

240 *In re Estate of Gowers*, 445 Pa. 554, 284 A.2d 742 (1971). *Compare* the Scottish case, *Imrie v. Imrie* (1891), 19 R. 185, in which the parties had exchanged declarations in writing that they took each other as husband and wife. *Copula carnalis* had occurred before and after the declarations. At trial, it was argued that the man's expression of intent made when he was seriously ill, was for purpose of making the woman a beneficiary of the man's insurance. The court found, however, with respect to the parties' actions before as well as after the signing of the document, that they had given an expression for a marital *consensus* and that a marriage had been formed. *See also Hoggan v. Craigie*, (1839) Macl. & Rob. 942, where it was argued that the man's admission of the marriage was motivated by the desire that the woman, after his death, would receive a widow's pension. The parties were found to have had the intent to form a marriage.

241 *Gowers* at 743. *Compare Bell v. Ferraro*, 849 A.2d 1233 (Pa.Super. 2004).

242 *United States v. Dorto*, 5 F.2d 596 (1st Cir. 1925).

days later, they began to live as husband and wife in the man's home. He introduced her to his acquaintances as his wife. On September 23, 1922, the day after the new law took effect, the parties participated in a ceremonial wedding. Thereafter, they lived together as husband and wife. The record reveals that there was mutual love between the parties, and that the woman, as of June 1924, was expecting their mutual child.

The ceremony performed on September 23, 1922, was not seen as an impediment to a deportation in accordance with the legislation enacted the prior day. The question then arose whether the parties had instead entered into a common law marriage prior to September 22, which would be an impediment to a deportation. The court required, for the formation of a common law marriage, that the parties must "agree to become husband and wife presently." The court held that an immediate marriage had been the goal of the parties from the beginning, despite also finding that the woman's primary and initial desire was to receive the legal status of marriage as a bar to deportation.[243] In addition, the parties had actually lived as husband and wife, and represented themselves as such. A common law marriage had been formed prior to September 22, 1922. Consequently, the parties were married to each other prior to the wedding ceremony and the enactment of the legislation.

It appears from *Dorto* that a marriage contract existed at the commencement of their relationship. No reference was made to their verbal statements upon the formation of the contract, or their intent for the future, aside from the goal of avoiding the woman's deportation. The court simply states that she told the man about her situation and he "agreed to marry." It naturally can be argued that even though the parties' primary purpose originally was to prevent deportation, their intent could, at a later date, have developed into a marital *consensus*. The court, however, found that the parties' intent, to immediately form a marriage, existed from the beginning. Despite the fact that the parties participated in a ceremonial wedding on September 23, and prior to that date had the intent to do so, the contract was not interpreted by the court as an agreement as to a future marriage *per verba de futuro*. The fact that the parties' primary intent, from the beginning, was to hinder her deportation was not sufficient to confer the status of a sham marriage. The relatively low requirements with respect to the marital intent and its expression were not counterbalanced by the requirements of a long-term marital cohabitation and a lengthy reputation as husband and wife. The parties' cohabitation had only been for a period of six weeks. Nevertheless, the parties had formally married, albeit a few days too late; lived as a married couple; and were expecting a child. Given this background, it is difficult to think that the court, equitably, could find it appropriate to allow the woman's deportation. There is no support for this hypothesis, however, in the reasoning

243 *Id.* at 597.

given by the court. The opposite is true, as the court states that the ceremonial wedding has little or no influence on its conclusions and that "love, mutual attraction, and a child" are to be seen as "fortunate results."[244] The decisive fact in *Dorto* is that the parties, to prevent the woman's deportation, were willing to assume the legal status of marriage.

The assessment of whether a sham marriage exists, and the lack of agreement between the intent and the expression of the intent, is different in the instance of an informal marriage, in which a cohabitation between the parties is deemed a necessary requirement for the formation of the marriage. If the parties have actually lived together, the longer the cohabitation, the more difficult it ought to be to maintain that the marriage was entered into as a joke or a sham. A marital cohabitation as husband and wife reasonably ought to remove any doubts about whether the parties have entered into an agreement as to such a cohabitation. One of the advantages of an informal marriage, in which marital cohabitation is a necessary requirement for the formation of the marriage, is that the requirement hinders sham marriages.[245] This assumes, however, that the required marital intent concerns the parties' cohabitation. If, on the other hand, the content of the contract must include the intent to establish a legal relationship or complete a marital status, the cohabitation naturally is accorded lesser weight.

There are American cases involving long-term cohabitations in which the reasoning by the courts is similar to that found in typical cases of sham marriages. For example, in the above-mentioned case, *In re Erickson's Estate* (1954), the court made a distinction between, on one side, a marital *consensus,* and on the other, an "intention simply to live together in fornication or concubinage and to cover up this socially unacceptable status by falsely representing a marriage relationship to the public."[246] The court in *Erickson's Estate* found that no common law marriage had been formed, because the intent to take "each other as husband and wife forever" was not proven.[247] The evidence demonstrated instead, according to the court's reasoning, that it was a question of "an impulsive venture into, or a continuation of, an illicit relationship" and that the parties "covered it with the cloak of marriage."[248] The facts that the parties actually lived together for twenty-five years and represented themselves as spouses, and enjoyed a reputation as husband and wife, were deemed by the court to be "falsely representing a marriage relationship to the public." The basis of

244 *Id.*

245 A separate issue is whether the requirement of cohabitation causes other problems, for example with respect to the length of time required, etc. The case law appears to be uncertain in this area, *see generally* Chapter 8 *infra* with respect to cohabitation as a necessary requirement for the formation of a common law marriage.

246 *In re Erickson's Estate,* 75 S.D. 345, 64 N.W.2d 316, 317 (1954).

247 *Id.* at 321.

248 *Id.*

the court's finding, that the case concerned an illegitimate relationship which the parties hid with the cloak of marriage, is not further elaborated, especially as to whether that which was hidden was an illicit relationship in that the cohabitation was not marital. This appears inconsistent with the fact that the parties, according to the court, actually lived together as husband and wife for about twenty-five years and enjoyed a reputation as such. The court instead seems to have viewed the marriage contract as a sharply defined conclusion, and that the parties' marital *consensus* must be an initial intent to which they give expression *per verba de praesenti* at the time of the formation of the contract. As such intent was not given, the parties' relationship was found to be an illicit relationship, and what the parties hid was the absence of an expressed marriage contract *per verba de praesenti*. The absence was hidden by the marriage as a camouflage, which the court concludes by relying on statements such as, "We can tell the people here we got married in Chicago."[249] Moreover, the parties generally did represent themselves as married. The court appears to have found these actions to have been a false representation made to the public.

Even if the court's reasoning here is similar to that found in cases concerning the more traditional forms of sham marriages, significant differences arise. In the usual sham marriage, the façade is an express marriage contract entered into *pro forma* – privately or by wedding ceremony—the insufficiency of which is the absence of a true marital *consensus*, including the intent to live together. In the present case, the façade appears to be the parties' marital cohabitation, the statements they made, and the reputation they enjoyed as husband and wife, even though they lacked either the intent to establish a legal relationship or an express marriage contract in which they *per verba de praesenti* gave expression to a marital *consensus*. In this instance, the appearance and reality of expressions of marital intent have reversed roles.[250]

A lack of agreement between the intent and the expression of intent can be only on the side of one party. The typical case falling into this category concerns a significant disparity in age between the parties, commonly referred to as winter and spring, in which one party marries to gain access to the other's wealth. In the typical case, both spouses have a legal intent to assume the legal consequences of a marriage, but one party does not have the intent to enter into a long-term marital relationship. The ability to invalidate such a marriage, aside from the argument that the marriage is based on mistaken assumptions, is to argue that no marital

249 *Id.* at 317.

250 *Compare Tholey's Appeal*, 93 Pa. 36 (1880), in which the court found that the words, "he will claim me as his wife, take care of me and the children" were insufficient to establish a marriage contract but rather gave expression to "an intent to enter into a meretricious relationship and to masquerade as a married couple."

consensus existed, because there was no mutual intent to live together.[251] The longer such a relationship lasts, however, the harder it becomes to make the argument that the intent was missing.

Another situation in which the parties' intent can diverge is if one party enters into the marriage simply for a limited purpose, for example to be allowed to immigrate, while the other marries for love and intends to live together in a complete legal relationship. In this instance, in contrast to the above, the party possessing the intent to have a complete marriage has an interest in proving that a marriage has been formed. The problem lies in the fact that the parties have not had a mutual intent to live together. However, if the party with the limited intent, through his or her actions, gives the other party reason to believe that they have a mutual intent to live together and establish a complete legal relationship, the wronged party ought to have the possibility, under a good faith argument, to have the marriage declared valid.[252]

The courts' vacillating analyses with respect to the issue of sham marriages is driven by the lack of definition of the required content of the marital intent's *essensialia.* Greater precision in the requirements would facilitate the assessments made by the courts and create clarity within the field. The requirement that a marriage contract, to be valid, must contain a mutual intent to live together, would protect against sham marriages. The requirement that a marriage contract, to be valid, must instead include a mutual intent to establish a complete legal relationship or a marital status in a wider context, would also hinder sham marriages in cases in which the parties' intent is limited to a specific legal consequence. However, the parties in such situations ought to be prepared to accept, albeit temporarily, a marital status in a broader context and the accompanying legal consequences. Those that marry, for example, to legitimize a child, are generally willing to assume the other aspects of marital status.[253]

---

251 In the Scottish case, *McLeod v. Adams,* 1920 1 S.L.T. 229, the man, a deserter from the army, had given a widow false information as to his name, work, and position, as well as declaring that he took her as his wife. The court found, however, that the man's intent was to take refuge in the woman's home, get access to her savings, and then abandon her. The man's statement, that he had taken the woman as his wife, the court found was not an expression of a marital *consensus,* but rather a part of a plan to swindle the woman of her savings through false information.

252 *Compare McFarland v. McFarland,* 51 Iowa 565, 2 N.W. 269, 273-274 (1879); *In re Marriage of Winegard,* 257 N.W.2d 609, 616 (Iowa1977); and *Conklin v. MacMillan Oil Co.*, 557 N.W.2d 102, 105 (Iowa App. 1996). *Compare In re Estate of Trigg,* 102 Ariz. 140, 426 P.2d 637 (1967) (one party's secret intention to not constitute a common law marriage did not effect the validity of the marriage when the other requirements of such a marriage were met); *Stafford v. Stafford,* 41 Tex. 111 (1874) and *Bonds v. Foster,* 36 Tex. 68 (1871).

253 *See, e.g., Wagner v. Wagner,* 59 Pa. D. C. 90 (1947). As the parties' intent was to legitimize the child through the wedding ceremony, the court found that their intent was to enter into a valid marriage. *See also Schibi v. Schibi,* 136 Conn. 196, 69 A.2d 831 (1949), in which the parties underwent a wedding ceremony for the purpose of giving the child "a name" and in which the court found that the parties

Parties often agree, based on an intent to constitute a legal marriage, to dissolve the marriage by divorce. A marriage contract containing such an intent consequently does not hinder sham marriages, if the lack of agreement arises from the absence of the intent to live together, compare *Diogo* and *Dorto.*

6.6 Summary and Conclusions

1. *The Nature of the Marriage Contract*

American law, as shown in this chapter, consistent with Roman and canon law, has, from the beginning, applied the principle of *consensus facit nuptias.* As a result, the marriage contract has always been viewed as a necessary requirement for the formation of a common law marriage. This is true in all American jurisdictions recognizing such marriages, despite the fact that other requirements may have arisen in addition to the contract.

The marriage contract does not constitute a typical civil contract. Many of the legal consequences, for example, the requirement of legal capacity and the conditions for dissolution, result not from the contract, but from mandatory legislation governing these issues. Nevertheless, the contractual nature of the marriage contract is particularly prevalent with respect to the function of the contract as a determinative element in the formation of a common law marriage. Even with respect to the conclusion of the marriage contract, it is apparently a contract *sui generis.*

As discussed above, only the Pennsylvania courts require that the parties' marital *consensus* be expressed in a verbal contract. One of the unique characteristics of the nature of the informal marriage contract is the fact that the parties typically do not actually enter into a contract, whether orally or in writing. The courts in the other jurisdictions examined do not even require a verbal contract. Instead, they usually accept inferred agreements or implied agreements, in which the parties' cohabitation and the circumstances generally are considered.

This stance appears to have influenced the nature of the marriage contract. The idea of an initial intent that comes to expression at a sharply defined time and place for a contractual conclusion, appears, as we have seen, to be upheld by courts in jurisdictions that require a verbal contract. The courts that have accepted inferred agreements based on circumstantial evidence to a large degree have abandoned this stance.

---

had the intent to create "the status of marriage"; and *Mpiliris v. Hellenic Lines, Ltd.*, 323 F.Supp. 865, 881-882 (S.D.Tex. 1979), in which the court found that a marriage entered into for a limited purpose was valid if it was the parties' intent that the marriage should be granted "legal significance." *Compare Anonymous v. Anonymous*, 49 N.Y.S.2d 314 (Sup.Ct. 1944).

Instead, they have found a *consensus continuus*, or a continued consent, *i.e.*, a continual marital intent during the cohabitation similar to Roman law's *affectio maritalis*. With this *consensus* model, it is more difficult to precisely determine when, where, and how the contract has been formed. The courts have not upheld any strict requirements. In reality, with the majority of the contracts viewed as inferred agreements, it is more logical and easier to find a continued, day-to-day, intention and agreement, to be husband and wife, or an ongoing agreement to be married, than to find the specific time and place of a definite contractual execution. The choice of contractual construction is significant to the possible establishment of a common law marriage. The use of *consensus continuus* has the function mainly of finding the formation of a common law marriage in cases in which the ceremonial wedding, or the informal but express marriage contract, was invalid. It is used more commonly in cases in which there is the absence of an express contract, and the evidence comprises the actions of the parties and their cohabitation. The use of *consensus continuus* also fills the function of allowing the different requisites for a common law marriage to be fulfilled simultaneously. In addition to a marriage contract, the majority of states recognizing common law marriages require cohabitation and reputation as discussed below in Chapter 8, "Cohabitation, Holding Out, and Reputation as Spouses." As these elements must coexist, for a certain period of time, the use of a *consensus continuus* facilitates the possibility of synchronizing the requirements and finding that they were fulfilled simultaneously.

Though the parties' affections for each other are often the most fundamental motivation for their intent to enter into a marriage – whether formal or informal – the courts have been reluctant to recognize these feelings as a constituting element in the legal formation of a marriage. Marital affections, in certain cases, however, have been given a surprisingly high evidentiary weight in the proving of the parties' marital *consensus*.

This development in the case law has without doubt created difficulties both for the parties themselves and for any third party attempting to establish when and where a contract has been formed. Such a method also has serious repercussions with respect to the question of legal certainty, further discussed in Chapters 13 and 14 with respect to the function of the informal marriage contract in the future.

As further discussed in Chapter 7, the acceptance of inferred agreements has also resulted in the fact that the cohabitation and circumstances in general become more significant, while the contract appears more in the background. The development in the case law gives witness to a considerable erosion of the marriage contract as a necessary requirement for the formation of a common law marriage. A more in-depth analysis of the courts' reasoning, with respect to findings based on circumstantial evidence of a *consensus continuus*, requires a more detailed presentation of the facts in the specific cases and is given in Chapter 7.

2. *The Marital Intent's Essensialia*

The courts have seldom closely examined what the parties have agreed upon, *i.e.*, the marital intent's *essensialia,* despite its importance in an assessment of whether a marriage contract has been formed. In contrast to the wedding ceremony, in which the consent can be viewed to a large extent as fossilized in form, the informal marriage contract ought, one would think, be more open to discussion as to the required content of marital intent in the formation of a common law marriage. The lack of precision as to the legal requirements of marital intent, without doubt, has led to unnecessary and expensive trials with lengthy witness examinations in which the parties, lawyers, and judges appear to be discussing different concepts. Despite this lack of precision, one can find two main approaches to the marital intent's *essensialia* in the case law as discussed in this chapter. First, the parties' mutual intent can be focused on an actual relationship, namely, the marital cohabitation, which is lifelong, or in any event, permanent and long term. The requirement of an intent for a marital cohabitation is often motivated by the desire to exclude relationships created for sexual purposes or simply for cohabitation. American courts have, therefore, followed the examples of medieval canon law and Scottish law by requiring that the intent of a marital cohabitation meant an intent to establish a *consortium omnis vitae* and an *individua vitae consuetudo, i.e.*, a mutual life in all respects, and an inseparable coexistence for a lifetime. Despite the courts' modern cautiousness in allowing the required marital intent to also include a sexual relationship and procreation, these elements must be viewed as naturally forming a part of such an intent. As discussed above, the requirement of an intended long-term relationship means that agreements between men and women to enter into a marriage on a trial basis have not been found to be an acceptable marital intent. In addition, the case law principle of monogamy has resulted in a requirement that the required marital intent must include the intent to form an exclusive relationship.

The second approach requires that the mutual intent be focused on something legal, namely, the creation of a legal relationship between the parties. The intent to simply live together is insufficient, even if the parties intend a lifelong coexistence. They must have the intent to enter into a legal relationship or, as several courts have expressed it, to create a marital status. The depth of the required intention, however, is not clear. Whether the intent must be to a legal consequence or to the bundle of legal consequences resulting from marriage has been the object of different interpretations in the case law. The legal consequences that ought to be included in the intent have not been closely discussed.

There is certain support in the American case law for the principle that the parties must possess both the intent for a marital cohabitation and the intent to establish a legal relationship in order to form a common law marriage. If these two intents are combined, the parties must have a mutual intent for a marital cohabitation as husband and wife in a monogamous and lifelong or at least long-term continual relationship, to which the marital regulatory system would be applicable. The existence of this intent would then be the basis of the formation of a common law marriage. The requirement of such a legal intent is to guarantee that neither party in the relationship is forced to accept a regulatory system to which they did not wish to submit and to which they did not agree. This is important, especially at a time in which living outside of marriage has become more common and socially acceptable, and many couples face the choice of living together informally or accepting the marital system. The requirement of an intent to live together thus assures that relationships based on sexual purposes or a temporary cohabitation are not given the legal consequences resulting from marriage. At the same time, a requirement of the intent for a marital cohabitation inhibits the formation of sham marriages. It should, however, be noted that a requirement for an intent encompassing the creation of a legal relationship most likely would have the effect that many couples, who have simply moved in together and continue their cohabitation, fall outside the marital regulations. Further discussion about the required content that the marital intent ought to have as a basis for the marriage contract, as well as the different consequences the different alternatives have, can be found in Chapter 13.

3. Consensus de Praesenti and Consensus de Futuro

As discussed above, American law has upheld the distinction first postulated by Peter Lombard between *consensus de praesenti* and *consensus de futuro*. For the formation of a common law marriage, only a marriage contract *de praesenti*, one concerning an immediately valid marriage, is acceptable. The second type of canon law marriage contract, with respect to a future marriage, *consensus de futuro*, in accordance with the canon law prior to the Council of Trent, could constitute a marriage in conjunction with a subsequent *copula carnalis*. This type of contract was recognized early as a common law marriage in England and Scotland, but has never won acceptance in American law.

The sharp criticism levied by Luther, Pollock and Maitland, Freedman, and Dickinson against the distinction made of the tense of the words used, has been to a large extent unwarranted as shown above. The reasoning of the courts demonstrates that, contrary to the belief of critics, formalism has not limited the distinction. An explanation may be that the courts, to a higher degree than predicted by the critics, have taken the view that it is not the actual words or their tense that is most meaningful, but rather the intention of the parties adjudged in a wider context. The critics, instead, appear to have fallen victim to the formalism they predicted. For unlettered persons as well as others, it must be natural to distinguish between the present and the future, between an immediate and a future marriage.

As seen, the problem lies not in the distinction based on tense, but with the actual content of the marital intent (*essensialia negotii*). The lack of precision of this question is reflected most clearly in attempts to distinguish between contracts *de praesenti* and contracts *de futuro*. What in the contract should be viewed as referring to the present and future, respectively, allowing for the creation of either a contract *de praesenti* or *de futuro?* Is it the marital cohabitation or the creation of the legal relationship? Clear answers to these questions would facilitate the application of the distinction. The courts' readiness, in cases in which the parties have planned a future wedding, to accept the formation of a prior common law marriage, can be explained either by the fact that the parties, in accordance with the courts' requirements, have had a *consensus de praesenti* to begin a marital cohabitation, or by the fact that the courts have divided the wedding ceremony into an intent to establish a legal relationship and an intent to undergo a ceremony, and that the parties have been found to have a mutual *consensus de praesenti* to establish the legal relationship.

4. *Express Contracts*

Despite the fact that the courts in the American case law traditionally referred to a contract *per verba* with respect to informal marriage contracts, only the courts in Pennsylvania principally uphold the requirement of a verbal contract in cases in which the marriage presumption is not applicable. Occasions arise, however, in which the parties have entered into a verbal contract, orally or in writing, raising the question of how these contracts actually are created and the requirements by the courts with respect to such contracts.

As seen above, no special formulations are actually used or required by the courts if the parties have entered into *oral contracts*. If the parties have arranged a private ceremony, it is not unusual for the words expressed to mirror those used in wedding ceremonies. In the majority of cases, however, the contract has arisen in a situation of the greatest privacy, leading to a large variation in the terms. It often is a question of statements made conversationally, resulting in very subjective boundaries between oral contracts and conversations. The lack of a writing or witnesses in most of these cases creates evidentiary difficulties. The standard of review of great scrutiny and the standard of proof by clear and convincing evidence appear to be well justified. As seen above, the courts regularly evaluate the exchange of words between the parties in a broader context, and thereby also consider the situation in which the statements were made, the actions of the parties, their cohabitation and reputation as spouses as well as the circumstances generally. The courts appear as a rule, in their interpretation of what was said, to attach more weight to that which the parties intended rather than their verbal expression of that intent.

Despite the general proposition that common law marriages are based on a legal civil contract, the application by the courts of general contractual principles is rudimentary. A closer, if cautious, consideration of these principles with respect to the contract as the basis of a common law marriage would be beneficial. Such an application would be designed to guarantee that neither party in the relationship was forced to submit to regulations to which they had not agreed. The fundamental requirements of offer and acceptance would prevent this, and could be used to delineate the fluctuating boundary between an expressed intent to be bound, and that which is simply conversationally uttered with respect to the parties' relationship. This is of significance at a time when it is more common and socially acceptable to live together, and many face the choice whether to live outside ceremonial marriage.

The question of whether the requirement of a verbal contract has a function to fulfill depends upon the required marital intent. If the marital intent includes a continual marital cohabitation, it is clear that the parties' cohabitation, their reputation as spouses, and their actions generally are of great significance in finding whether a contract has been formed. A woman, moving in with a man and living together with him her entire life, has, through her actions, given the best indication of her wishes. The parties' actions can be more expressive than words! If the marital intent, on the other hand, is focused on being legally bound and the intent to form a legal marriage, the actions of the parties are of less significance. One can certainly state that a man and a woman are living together as husband and wife in accordance with the norms applicable to spouses, but one cannot state with certainty that they intended that important regulations, for example, with respect to divorce and the division of marital property, would be applicable. They can have decided to live together without any legal ties. The words, then, are meaningful in showing the parties' legal intent. There is no reason, however, to go as far as in the case of civil contracts, by requiring clearer definitions with respect to the conditions regulated by offer and acceptance.[254] The state provides the contract with a pre-packaged set of rights and obligations, which become the legal consequences of the marriage contract. A requirement to list all of these at the verbal conclusion of the contract would be entirely unrealistic given the parties' insufficient legal knowledge. The requirement of a minimum of words associated with the legal relationship, however, appears to be justified.

As noted above, the use of written contracts has been limited, which can be explained by the fact that this voluntary form is probably not an attractive alternative to parties consciously refraining from ceremonial weddings. At the same time, the function of the written contract must be noted, especially in situations in which the parties are geographically separated from each other and do not both have the possibility to be present at a wedding or the formation of an informal contract. A written contract,

254 *Compare* Treitel, *supra* note 172, at 8.

adequately drafted and signed by both parties, serves the interest of legal certainty. The parties have reason to seriously consider that which they have consented to in writing, and the existence of a written document can help avoid potential legal conflicts.

5. *The Lack of Agreement between the Intent and the Expression of the Intent*

Even if a clearly written or oral expression of intent exists, a marriage is not formed if a true marital intent does not exist. Roman law recognized early that if the expression of intent is not in agreement with the intent, the simulated marriages were invalid (*simulatae nuptiae nullius momenti sunt*). This principle was also used in canon law, which stated that which the words express but the heart does not wish, is not valid (*si autem verbis explicant, quod tamen corde non volunt*).

One of the problems arising with respect to formal marriages today, as seen, is that the system can be exploited by the parties entering into a marriage *pro forma* with the intent to simply enjoy one of the consequences of marriage, for example, the right to immigrate, without intending to actually enter into a marital cohabitation. Their intent instead is to dissolve the relationship as soon as the benefit has been received. This problem of sham marriages also exists in those jurisdictions in which an informal marriage can be formed simply on the basis of the parties' contract *per verba de praesenti.*

The courts' treatment of the problem of sham marriages, as seen above, is characterized by a lack of definition with respect to the content of the marriage contract. It would be preferable if the courts, in this area, more closely elaborated on what a lack of *consensus* is, instead of simply referring, for example, to the marriage relationship "as it is ordinarily understood."[255] A higher degree of precision here would impart greater clarity to this area of the law.

A marriage contract requiring that the parties have the mutual intent to live together is a protection against this type of marriage. This function, however, can also be fulfilled by a direct requirement of cohabitation as a necessary requirement for the formation of a marriage, as discussed further below. A marriage contract, requiring instead a mutual intent to establish a complete legal relationship or marital status in a wider context, can also hinder sham marriages if the intent of the parties is limited to a single legal consequence. However, the parties are often prepared to accept, albeit temporarily, other legal consequences of marriage, *i.e.*, the marital status. It appears that parties often agree to dissolve the relationship as quickly as possible through divorce, an agreement that presupposes they have the intent to enter into a marriage. A marriage contract with such required content does not, in such cases, bar the formation of a

255 *United States v. Rubenstein,* 151 F.2d 915, 918, 919 (2d Cir. 1945).

sham marriage, if the insufficiency consists of the lack of the intent to cohabit. The diverging functions of the different elements with respect to marital intent, and the consequences of these different solutions, even in the future, for example, with respect to sham marriages, are further discussed in Chapter 13.

CHAPTER 7
Implied Marriage Agreements

7.1 Introduction

Despite the requirement of a marriage contract being a necessary requisite for the establishment of a common law marriage in all of the jurisdictions recognizing such marriages, it is very unusual for the parties in such a relationship to actually enter into an express contract, whether in writing or orally. This absence is consistent with the view that many couples drift into a common law marriage.[1] They simply begin to live together. Later at trial, when questioned by attorneys about the existence of a marriage contract, they are at a complete loss.[2] It has even been claimed that

1 Similar assumptions recur at different periods of time. In 1955, Alan H. Rothstein, Special Comment, *A New Look at Common Law Marriages in Florida*, 10 Miami L.Q. 87, 100 (1955), stated that in "most instances there is no clear evidence as to the alleged agreement," and in 1967, that "[i]t is indisputable that in most cases the agreement is more judicially inferred than actually made." *See* Claris M. Davis *Common-Law-Marriage in Texas*, 21 S.W.L.J. 647, 662 (1967). *Compare* Homer H. Clark. Jr., The Law of Domestic Relations in the United States, 49 (1968), stating that the parties "in many cases" have not entered into any express marital contract, which commonly leads the courts "to infer an agreement from the fact that they have lived together for all intents and purposes as husband and wife." In 1974, it was asserted that "no genuine agreement to be married exists in the vast majority of situations when an informal marriage is asserted," an argument for the repeal of common law marriage in Texas, *see* 5 Tex. Tech. L. Rev. 301 (1974). About fifteen years later, it was noted that "normally an agreement is inferred by courts when a couple engages in cohabitation and acquires a reputation as husband and wife." *See* Ellen Kandoian, *Cohabitation, Common Law Marriage, and the Possibility of a Shared Moral Life*, 75 Geo. L.J. 1829, 1842-1843 (1987). The fact that the parties in many cases lack an express contract can also be seen from the case law, *see People v. Lucero*, 747 P.2d 660, 664 (Colo. 1987); and *Russell v. Russell*, 838 S.W.2d 909, 913 (Tex.App.-Beaumont 1992). American and Swedish sociologists agree that a cohabitation outside of a formal marriage is rarely the result of a considered decision, *see* Jan Trost, Unmarried Cohabitation, 63-64 (1979). *See also* Eleanor D. Macklin, *Nonmarital Heterosexual Cohabitation*, Mar. & Fam. Rev. March/April, at 1, 6 (1978) ("Living together is seldom the result of a considered decision ... Most cohabitation evolves from a drift of sleeping more and more frequently together and the gradual accumulation of possessions in one residence"); and David S. Caudill, *Legal Recognition of Unmarried Cohabitation: A Proposal to Update and Reconsider Common-Law Marriage*, 49 Tenn. L. Rev. 537, 565 (1982).

2 The situation in *Lorensen v. Weaber*, 840 S.W.2d 644, 646 (Tex.App.-Dallas 1992) is rather typical, where the woman was asked: "And at that point in time, what was the agreement between the two of you as to living together?" The woman answered: "I don't understand."

the majority of couples living together in a common law marriage are not even aware of the fact that they are doing so.[3]

In those cases in which the contract requirement is found to have been fulfilled and a common law marriage established, the courts have based their reasoning on the existence of an inferred or implied agreement. A common law marriage consequently can be established by the actions of the parties, from which the existence of a marital contract can be inferred.

Although the legal terms *implied* and *inferred* are used as synonyms,[4] there are hints of a certain difference in emphasis. An implied contract refers to the commencement of a contract that has not been entered into expressly, but rather is implied, for example, by the actions of the parties, the cohabitation, and the outward representation. An inferred contract is based on the evidence introduced afterwards to prove the contract, and which the contract is said to be "inferred from."[5] In *Berger v. Kirby* (1913), the court defined an *implied agreement* as an agreement in which the parties "with reference to the subject matter is such as to induce the belief, in the minds of the contracting parties, that they intend to do that which their acts indicate they have done."[6] In the event that the contract has not generally been verbally expressed, but rather depends on the actions of the parties, one can also speak of a silent contract, *i.e.*, silent or tacit agreements.[7]

In *Hawkins v. Weinberger*, 368 F.Supp. 896, 899 (D.Kan. 1973), the woman was asked: "Did you believe that your living together made you legally married?" Answer: "Yes. Later on I learned about common law marriage."

3 *See* Graham Kirkpatrick, *Common-Law Marriages: Their Common Law Basis and Present Need*, 6 St. Louis U. L.J. 30, 47 (1960).

4 For example, in *Howard v. Howard*, 459 S.W.2d 901, *903* (Tex.Civ.App.-Houston 1970) and in *Humphreys v. Humphreys*, 364 S.W.2d 177 (Tex. 1963), the courts stated that a contract to marry "may be implied or inferred from evidence." In *Jolley v. Jolley*, 46 Ohio Misc. 40, 347 N.E.2d 557, 560-561 (C.P. Ohio 1975), the court stated that an agreement to marry "can be implied from the testimony of witnesses as to acts, declarations, admissions, and cohabitation of parties," and that a common law marriage "can be proved by the acts, declarations, and conduct of the parties."

5 According to Black's Law Dictionary 757 (7th ed. 1999), the expression "implied" means "not directly expressed; recognized by law as existing inferentially <implied agreement>". The term "inferred," on the other hand, is derived from evidentiary law and entails a conclusion drawn from one fact to another: "[I]nference" is "1. A conclusion reached by considering other facts ans deducting a logical consequence from them 2. The process by which such a conclusion is reached; the process of thought by which one moves from evidence to proof." *Id.* at 781. In *U.S. Fid. & Guar. Co. v. Dowdle*, 269 S.W. 119 (Tex.Civ.App. 1924), the court stated that marriage can be proved "by circumstantial as well as by direct evidence. It may in a proper case be *inferred from* continuous cohabitation and repute" (*italics added*).

6 *Berger v. Kirby*, 105 Tex. 611, 153 S.W. 1130, 1131 (1913). A similar definition can be found in *Cuneo v. de Cuneo*, 24 Tex.-Civ.App. 436, 59 S.W. 284, 285 (1900).

7 *Dalworth Trucking Co. v. Bulen*, 924 S.W.2d 728, 737 (Tex.App.-Texarkana 1996) ("tacit agreement"); and *Flores v. Flores*, 847 S.W.2d 648, 652 (Tex.App.-Waco 1993). Also, in the few cases where an express contract exists, as stated in the examples in Chapter 6, they often are entered into in a situation of the greatest privacy, which is why the courts afterwards have referred to indirect and "circumstantial evidence" concerning

This chapter focuses on several aspects concerning inferred agreements. Section 7.2, "The Reasons for Implied Agreements," addresses the reasons for accepting inferred agreements, with the establishment of a common law marriage; Section 7.3, "The Development of the Law," considers the development of the law with respect to inferred agreements during the 1800s and 1900s. Section 7.4, "The Current State of the Law in Different States," addresses the status of inferred agreements today. Thereafter, a presentation concerning the most common evidentiary facts cited as support for inferred agreements is provided in Section 7.5, "Evidentiary Facts as Support for Implied Agreements." The courts' reasonings in a number of cases are further discussed in order to explore how the facts cited are used in the finding of the existence of an inferred marriage contract in Section 7.6, "Cases in Which Implied Agreements Have Been Proven," as well as the reasonings given in the cases in which no contract was found proven, as discussed in Section 7.7, "Cases in Which an Implied Agreement Have Not Been Found Proven." This chapter ends with a summary and conclusions as to the present status of the law with respect to inferred agreements in Section 7.8, "Summary and Conclusions."

The issue of whether the principles with respect to inferred agreements are necessary to give common law marriage the legal protection it is intended to give, and whether this purpose can be satisfied in another manner, as well as more general issues, is discussed in Chapter 13, "The Constitutive Requisites in the Future," concerning the future direction of the law. In that chapter, we will critically review the motivations cited and discuss the reasons for and against the principles of inferred agreements.

7.2 THE REASONS FOR IMPLIED AGREEMENTS

The most significant reason behind inferred marital agreements is that they give legal protection to couples who have not formalized their relationship through marriage. This reason, one of the main motivations for the entire institution of common law marriage, has great practical significance today. The parties, as stated above, often drift into formless relationships without entering into any express contract therein. Common law marriage, in its present form, but without the acceptance of inferred agreements, would then exclude the majority of these couples from the legal protections that the legal institution is intended to provide. As the examples in the previous chapter show, the few cases of express

the existence of a contract. *See also* Grace Ganz Blumberg, *Cohabitation without Marriage: A Different Perspective*, 28 UCLA L. REV. 1125, 1128 note 21 (1981), maintaining that the evidence is often "indirect and circumstantial." *See further* Kirkpatrick, *supra* note 3, at 46, stating that in the majority of cases, it is only the parties themselves who have knowledge as to the existence of an express contract.

contracts were entered into in extreme privacy, which is why the courts afterwards refer to the indirect and circumstantial evidence concerning their existence.[8]

In several cases, for example, concerning a child's legitimacy and claim to an estate, sometimes several years after the parents entered into the marriage, there is no evidence other than circumstantial evidence. Even in cases in which one party survives, in certain jurisdictions, his or her testimony may be inadmissible under a dead man's statute, because the survivor can be perceived as having an interest in the outcome of the case and "the dead man's lips are sealed." Circumstantial evidence can then be decisive at trial.[9]

A special group of cases are those in which the parties have entered into a ceremonial marriage, which is invalid as the result of an impediment, and they continue to live together after the removal of the impediment without formally renewing their relationship. Many courts, albeit not all, have the intent to give legal protection in such situations by accepting the continued cohabitation as circumstantial evidence supporting a common law marriage.[10]

The intent to provide legal protection can clearly be seen in the case law. To ignore circumstantial evidence as to whether a common law marriage existed according to *Laurence v. Laurence* (1896) would "threaten the legitimacy of children and the rights of heirs, and endanger the social fabric which rests on the institution of marriage."[11] This same motivation is given by several authors. Nancy Shaw stated: "That the parties be precluded from all protection merely because they have never verbalized their commitment to one another, although their conduct towards one another clearly indicated that such a commitment in fact existed, is

---

8 With respect to examples of expressed contracts, *see supra* at 6.5.1. *See also* Blumberg, *id.* at 1128 fn. 21, maintaining that the evidence is often "indirect and circumstantial." *See further* Kirkpatrick, *supra* note 3, at 46, stating that in the majority of cases, it is only the parties themselves which have knowledge as to whether a contract has been entered into.

9 In Pennsylvania, a reason given for the marital presumption has been the effects of the "Dead Man's Act," 42 Pa.C.S. § 5930, *see Staudenmayer v. Staudenmayer*, 714 A.2d 1016, 1020 (Pa. 1998); and *In re Estate of Stauffer*, 476 A.2d 354, 357 (Pa. 1984). *See Wagner's Estate*, 398 Pa. 531, 159 A.2d 495, 498 (1960), in which the survivor's lips were sealed under the Dead Man's Act, May 23, 1887, P.L. 158, 35 (e), 28 PS § 322. *See also Dibble v. Dibble*, 88 Ohio App. 490, 100 N.E.2d 451 (1950); and *Edelstein v. Brown*, 35 Tex.Civ.App. 625, 80 S.W. 1027 (1904). *Compare* on the other hand, for example, Idaho, where a common law marriage can be proven by the testimony of the surviving spouse, *see Metro. Life Ins. Co. v. Johnson*, 103 Idaho 122, 645 P.2d 356 (1982).

10 Ralph B. Kelley, *Creation and Proof of Common Law Marriage Following Removal of Impediments*, 18 N.Y.U. Intra. L. Rev. 213 (1963).

11 *Laurence v. Laurence*, 164 Ill. 367, 45 N.E. 1071, 1072 (1896). *See also* in more Gen. terms, *In re Estate of Kovalchick*, 345 Pa.Super. 229, 498 A.2d 374, 376 (1985), in which the court stated: "Because it is often difficult to prove a civil contract of marriage, the law has permitted that it be established by circumstantial evidence." *See* with respect to older law, Clark, *supra* note 1, at 49-50 (1968) and 106-107 (2d ed. 1987).

unduly rigid."[12] Kathryn Vaughn, criticizing the repeal in Texas in 1989 of the legislation accepting the cohabitation of the parties and the outward representation as evidence of the existence of a marriage contract, maintained that the burden of proving an express agreement is simply too high for most persons attempting to establish a common law marriage and that changes in the legislation would lead to a number of unjust results.[13]

This motivation is sometimes given a moral overtone. To find, based on the cohabitation and the representation of the parties, the existence of a marriage contract according to the court in *Leibrock v. Leibrock* (1952) is consistent with and to the benefit of "morality and decency."[14] A closely related motivation is the community's interest in presumptions in favor of marriage and against concubinage.[15] That there is, in the view of the community, a value in accepting the parties' cohabitation and reputation can already be seen in *Tummalty v. Tummalty* (1855), in which the court gave the ten-year cohabitation a higher evidentiary weight than the man's "stale conversations and private statements" by referring to the fact that the community "would not be safe for a moment."[16]

The motivation behind the possibility to be able to find the existence of a marriage contract from the parties' actions also rests on the belief that "certain acts may speak as loudly as words."[17] Sometimes added to the notion of a higher evidentiary weight for such actions is a nearly related reason, namely, that it would be an expression of an exaggerated

---

12 Nancy Rebecca Shaw, *Common law marriage and unmarried cohabitation: an old solution to a new problem*, 39 U. PITT. L. REV. 579, 592 (1977).

13 Kathryn S. Vaughn, Comment, *The Recent Changes to the Texas Informal Marriage Statute: Limitation or Abolition of Common Law Marriage?* 28 HOUS. L. REV. 1132, 1155 and 1159 (1991).

14 *Leibrock v. Leibrock*, 63 Ohio Law Abs. 565, 107 N.E.2d 418, 423 (Ohio Com.Pl. 1952).

15 *Linsey v. Jefferson*, 68 Okla. 156, 172 P. 641, 642 (1918).

16 *Tummalty v. Tummalty*, 3 Bradf. 369, 371 (N.Y. 1855).

17 *In re Wagner's Estate*, 398 Pa. 531, 159 A.2d 495, 498 (1960). *See also Navarro Inc. v. Baker*, 54 So.2d 59, 60 (Fla. 1951), in which the court, as support for the finding that the parties had entered into a marriage contract, stated that "the circumstances surrounding their meeting were more eloquent and forceful than formal language." In *Brown's Adm'r v. Brown*, 308 Ky. 796, 215 S.W.2d 971, 975 (1948), the parties had lived together and appeared outwardly as spouses. With respect to certain statements which the man had made and which contradicted the existence of a common law marriage, the court stated: "His conduct speaks louder, and more convincingly, than his words." That the parties' actions can be viewed as meaningful in an evidentiary assessment as their words can already be seen in JOHN HUBBACK, A TREATISE ON THE EVIDENCE OF SUCCESSION TO REAL AND PERSONAL PROPERTY AND PEERAGES 247 (London, W. Benning 1844): "The parties' assertions of marriage and the Gen. reputation of the fact may be evidenced with as much strength and distinctness by actions as by words." The same attribution to the ability of actions to speak recurs in the case of *In re Thewlis Estate*, 217 Pa. 307, 309, 66 A. 519 (1907): "[B]ut each day during these many years that they thus lived together there was an assertion by acts and conduct which in law is as efficacious as words for establishing a contract by implication." In *Henderson v. Henderson*, 199 Md. 449, 87 A.2d 403, 408 (App. 1952), the court stated that: "Cohabitation as husband and wife is a manifestation that the couple had consented to contract that relation."

formalism to require something in addition. Michael Grossberg, investigating the development during the 1800s, speaks of "a clear policy decision favoring practice over form."[18] Homer Clark includes both aspects, stating: "It would place a wholly unjustifiable emphasis on form to require the parties to say 'we hereby agree to be husband and wife,' when they are already giving ample evidence by their conduct that this is their understanding."[19]

Finally, to ignore circumstantial evidence in the assessment of the existence of a common law marriage has been viewed as a way by which to open the door to fraud and imposition, and invite perjury.[20] As discussed in Chapter 14 below, this is in general one of the main reasons against admitting the existence of common law marriage.

7.3 The Development of the Law

7.3.1 The Development during the Early 1800s

The ability to find, from the actions of the parties, the existence of a marriage contract is not an American innovation. Already during the Middle Ages, as discussed above, Peter Lombard's view that the marital intent must be expressed verbally was replaced by Hostiensi's view, according to which the parties' *consensus*, as with other consensual contracts, could be expressed in any manner and therewith, also through the cohabitation of the parties.[21] This view was also later adopted in Scottish law.[22]

One also finds early support in the American case law for the view that cohabitation can be used as evidence of the marital intent or for the marriage. With this acceptance during the 1800s, however, the courts occasionally reluctantly spoke of the fact that, as evidence of the marital relationship,

---

18 Michael Grossberg, Governing the Hearth: Law and the Family in Nineteenth Century America, 79-80 (1985).

19 Clark, *supra* note 1, at 52 (1968) and 112 (2d ed. 1987).

20 *Laurence v. Laurence*, 164 Ill. 367, 45 N.E. 1071, 1073 (1896).

21 With respect to the canon law's required form of expression for marital intent, *see supra* Chapter 3.3.4.

22 *See, e.g., Hoggan v. Craigie*, (1889) Macl. & Rob. 942, 965, in which Lord Chancellor Cranworth, concerning the marriage contract *per verba de praesenti* stated: "It is not necessary to prove the contract itself; it is sufficient if the facts of the case are such as to lead to satisfactory evidence of such a contract having taken place; upon this principle the acknowledgement of the parties, their conduct towards each other, and the repute consequent upon it may be sufficient to prove a marriage ... Everything, therefore, is pertinent and relevant in an inquiry like the present, which indicates the present or previous consent of the parties." *See further* Lord Westbury in *Campbell v. Campbell* (The Breadalbane Case)(1867) L.R. 1 H.L.Scot.App. 182, 192, 196, 211: "[C]ohabitation as husband and wife is a manifestation of the parties having consented to contract that relation *inter se*. It is a holding forth to the world, by the manner of daily life, by conduct, demeanor, and habit, that the man and the woman who live together have agreed to take each other in marriage and to stand in the mutual relation of husband and wife."

they had accepted the same sort of evidence with which men seek to enforce "the most trifling pecuniary obligations."[23]

Already in *Fenton v. Reed* (1809), in which no verbal contract of marriage had been entered into after the woman's marriage with another man was dissolved, but in which the parties cohabited together as husband and wife, and under the reputation and understanding that they were such, from 1800 to 1806, the New York Supreme Court stated that a marriage "may be proved ... from cohabitation, reputation, acknowledgment of the parties, reception in the family and other circumstances from which a marriage may be inferred."[24] The court made an exception, however, with respect to an indictment for bigamy and civil cases concerning criminal conversation. Because the case before the court did not concern these two matters, the court found that the trial court had sufficient basis to conclude that, with reference to the circumstances in the case, a marriage existed.[25] It should be noted that the court accepted as evidence both the "acknowledgment of the parties," *i.e.*, that commonly was termed as "admissions and declarations," as well as the "cohabitation and reputation." It should further be noted that a continued cohabitation after the removal of an impediment was sufficient, despite the fact that the parties had knowledge of the impediment, not at the wedding but later. The presumption that the relationship continued to be "meretricious," a presumption that would need to be rebutted by evidence of a change in their intent, was not raised in the court's reasoning. Another early case is *Chambers v. Dickson* (1816), in which the Pennsylvania Supreme Court accepted evidence cited in the form of circumstances and stated "that cohabitation and reputation, especially of an ancient day," constituted very strong evidence for the proof of a marriage. Based on this, the trial court's decision was rejected, as this type of evidence had not been considered.[26]

23 *Green's Estate,* 5 Pa.C. 605, 606 (1888). *Compare Askew v. Dupree,* 30 Ga. 173, 178 (1860), in which the court expressed its concern with reference to the fact that "the *concubitas* may take place for the mere gratification of present appetite, without a view to any thing further."

24 *Fenton v. Reed,* 4 Johns. 52, 54 (N.Y. 1809).

25 *Id.* The court cites in dictum the case of *Morris v. Miller,* (1767) 4 Burr. 2057, concerning criminal conversation (adultery), as support that a marriage can be proven with evidence of a cohabitation and other circumstances. In dictum, however, Lord Mansfield stated that "reputation" is sufficient except in cases of bigamy and criminal conversation. Another early case is *Hammack v. Bronson,* 5 Day 290, 293 (Conn. 1812), in which the judge, with respect to the acceptance of cohabitation and reputation as evidence, stated: "I take it to be fully settled both in this state, and in Great Britain, that the fact of marriage may be proved by evidence of this kind."

26 *Chambers v. Dickson,* 2 S. & R. 475, 476 (1816). The recital of cohabitation and reputation as particularly strong evidence can be the embryo of the acceptance of a presumption. However, nothing is stated as to whether these circumstances constitute necessary and sufficient elements for the application of the presumption, and that they entail a rebuttal of the burden of proof. The court cites *Fenton v. Reed* as well as *Morris v. Miller. Compare also Hantz v. Sealy,* 6 Binn. 405 (Pa. 1814).

The court made no exception, in contrast with *Fenton v. Reed*, for bigamy and criminal conversation.[27]

The *per curiam* judgment issued in *Fenton v. Reed* has been attributed to Chief Judge James Kent, later Chancellor of New York, who expressed the same view in his COMMENTARIES ON AMERICAN LAW. This book was first published in 1826 and was highly respected. Kent stated there that the parties' consent can afterwards be "confessed or acknowledged" and that "the marriage may even be inferred from continual cohabitation, and reputation as husband and wife." However, he made exceptions for civil cases concerning adultery and indictments of bigamy or adultery, adding that "illicit intercourse or concubinage" will not raise any such presumption of marriage.[28]

Even though legal support for the judgment in *Fenton v. Reed* and for Kent's conclusions has been justifiably criticized,[29] there is no doubt that the judgment, as well as Kent's commentaries, were significant, influential legal sources throughout the 1800s.[30]

The development, as an exception rather than a rule, had direct support in the legislation. In *Houpt v. Houpt* (1832), the Ohio Supreme Court stated with respect to the state's legislation: "Section 4 of the divorce act, 29 Ohio L. 432, authorizes the court, in its discretion, to admit proof of cohabitation and reputation as evidence of the marriage of the parties."[31] However, the development occurred primarily within the case law.

---

27 The exceptions with respect to bigamy and criminal conversation, which go back to *Morris v. Miller*, (1767) 4 Burr 20, 57 and which would come to have an anchoring in American case law up until the 1900s, was received reluctantly by the courts in Pennsylvania. *See, e.g., Forney v. Hallacher*, 8 S. & R. 159, 162 (1822); *Com. v. Murtagh*, 1 Ashm. 272 (1831); *Com. v. Wyman*, 3 Brews. 338 (1869); *Com. v. Henning*, 10 Phila. 209 (1874); and *Durning v. Hastings*, 183 Pa. 210 (1897). The same stance recurs in the cases from Pennsylvania during the 1900s, *see, e.g., Com. v. Bockes*, 103 Pa.Super. 378 (1931).

28 JAMES KENT, COMMENTARIES ON AMERICAN LAW, 2, (New York, William Kent 1826), Lec. XXVI (6). As support for his views, Kent cites *Morris v. Miller* and *Fenton v. Reed*. It ought to be noted that common law marriage received its support in the literature already with TAPPING REEVE, THE LAW OF HUSBAND AND WIFE (1816).

29 As to the criticism, *see* Section 4.2.2 *supra*.

30 *Id.*

31 *Houpt v. Houpt*, 5 Ohio 539 (1832). The regulation at issue was later taken up in Sec.5698, R.S., and thereafter in Sec. 11989, G.C., which unchanged was incorporated in Sec. 8003-13 G.C., in its turn incorporated unchanged in Sec. 3105.12, enacted as of October 10, 1991, stating: "[P]roof of cohabitation and reputation of the marriage of a man and woman is competent evidence to prove their marriage, and, in the discretion of the court, that proof may be sufficient to establish their marriage for a particular purpose." From the same time period, *see also Fryer v. Fryer*, 9 S.C.Eq. (Rich.Cas.) 85, 92-93 (1832), in which the court stated that the contract of marriage is "susceptible to an infinite variety of proof. It may be proved by those who witnessed it when it took place. It may be proved by the subsequent declarations or acknowledgement of the parties. It may be evidenced by their conduct, and the attitude they maintain towards each other and the world." A couple consequently can "express their agreement by parol, they may signify it by whatever ceremony their whim, or their taste, or their religious belief, may select." If, however, the parties' relation from the beginning is "illicit," the presumption is that "the intercourse

In *Tarpley v. Poage's Adm'r* (1847), the Texas Supreme Court gave the jury extensive authority to consider circumstantial evidence in determining whether a marriage existed. The court referred to evidence of cohabitation, reputation, acknowledgment of parties, reception in the family, and other circumstances from which an inference of marriage could be drawn.[32]

When Bishop published his first edition of the COMMENTARIES ON THE LAW OF MARRIAGE AND DIVORCE in 1852, he echoed Kent's understanding. Bishop maintained that "proof of cohabitation and repute is sufficient evidence of marriage ... the marriage may be sufficiently inferred from the cohabitation of the parties as husband and wife." Bishop also made an exception for certain criminal indictments (polygamy and adultery) and certain civil complaints (criminal conversation).[33] During the later part of the 1800s, a number of court decisions gave support to this understanding.

7.3.2 The Development during the Latter Half of the 1800s

One can begin to see the case law following two distinct paths during the latter half of the 1800s in the treatment of circumstantial evidence of the parties' cohabitation in proving a common law marriage. First, circumstantial evidence was considered in the proving of the marriage contract. Less far-reaching on this path was accepting such evidence as complementary evidence in support of an expressed contract. For example, in *Carmichael v. State* (1861), the Ohio Supreme Court stated that: "The circumstances of

is carried on in the same character, unless the contrary is made appear," *id.* at 98. *See also Jewell v. Magwood*, 9 S.C.Eq. (Rich.Cas.) 113, 114 (1833); *Senser v. Bower*, 1 Pa. 450 (1830) ("For civil purposes reputation and cohabitation are sufficient evidence of marriage"); *Holmes v. Holmes*, 6 La.Rep. 463 (1833); and *Rose v. Clark*, 8 Paige 574, 579 (N.Y. 1841) ("That an actual marriage may be inferred in ordinary cases, from cohabitation, acknowledgments of the parties ... there can be no room to doubt"). In *Guardians of the Poor v. Nathis*, 2 Brewster 149, 168, 171 (1845), the court stated that it is clearly accepted that "cohabitation and reputation prove a marriage" and found that marriage proved between the parties "by their own acknowledgment, coupled with the fact of cohabitation for at least a period of about two months." In *Purchell v. Purchell*, 4 Va. (1 Hen. & M.) 507, 512 (1810), the court stated that a marriage can be proven "by cohabitation, name, reputation, and other circumstances."

32 *Tarpley v. Poage's Adm'r*, 2 Tex. 139, 149 (1847). The court cites, among other cases, *Fenton v. Reed*. *See also Trimble v. Trimble*, 2 Ind. 76, 78 (1850), in which the Indiana Supreme Court stated that "the marriage may even be inferred from continual co-habitation and reputation as husband and wife, except in cases of civil actions for adultery or public prosecutions for bigamy." *See also Donnelly v. Donnelly*, 8 Ky. (1 B. Mon.) 113 (App. 1847), where the court held that cohabitation and the recognition of the parties as man and wife, is competent evidence to establish marriage in a civil suit.

33 JOEL PRENTISS BISHOP, COMMENTARIES ON THE LAW OF MARRIAGE AND DIVORCE AND EVIDENCE IN MATRIMONIAL SUITS § 324 (Boston 1852). As support, Bishop cites, *inter alia*, *Clayton v. Wardell*, 5 Barb. 2144 (1858) and *Holmes v. Holmes*, 6 La.Rep. 463 (1833). From the same period, *see* SIMON GREENLEAF, A TREATISE ON THE LAW OF EVIDENCE, II, § 462 (Boston, 3 ed. 1846), which adopted the same view as KENT, *supra* note 28, (17th ed. 1899). Kent was cited in a number of cases during the entire 1800s.

publicity in entering into the contract, and of cohabitation thereafter as husband and wife, are most important to show the intent with which any words were used."[34]

A more far-reaching aspect of this approach placed greater faith in the evidentiary weight of the cohabitation, meaning that a contract of marriage can be proven only by circumstantial evidence. For example, in *Tummalty v. Tummalty* (1855), the New York Court of Appeals held that the cohabitation between the parties outweighed the other evidence, and maintained that giving conversations and statements by the parties more weight than their cohabitation as husband and wife would create substantial uncertainty in the community: "Society would not be safe for a moment, in this, the most sacred of its relations, if an open and public cohabitation as man and wife for ten years, continued with all the conventional usages of married life, and followed by the procreation of children, could be overturned by relating stale conversations and private statements of the husband as to the particular mode and the inception of the relation."[35] Common to both possibilities is that the existence of a marriage contract must be evidenced, albeit that a contract based only upon circumstantial evidence can, to a certain extent, be fictional.

34 *Carmichael v. State*, 12 Ohio St. 553, 560 (1861). With respect to the issue as to whether the parties' cohabitation according to this case was also a necessary requisite, *see infra* Chapter 6. *See also Lehigh Valley R.R. Co. v. Hall*, 61 Pa. 361, 366 (1869), in which the court stated that "[m]arriage is provable in all civil actions by cohabitation, reputation, acknowledgment of the parties, reception of the family, and any other circumstances from which it may be inferred." The cohabitation's function as an evidentiary fact appears at this time also more clearly expressed in *Askew v. Dupree*, 30 Ga. 173, 180 (1869), in which the court stated that the marriage "may even be inferred from continual cohabitation and reputation as husband and wife." The court, however, makes an exception for civil cases concerning adultery and criminal cases concerning adultery and bigamy. *See also Physick's Estate*, 2 Brewster 179 (1862) ("Reputation and cohabitation are sufficient evidence of marriage in Pennsylvania for all civil purposes"). According to *Vincent's Appeal*, 10 P.F. Smith 228, 60 Pa. 228 (1869), clear and repeated admissions of the marriage, as well as a long-term cohabitation and the reputation as spouses normally are satisfactory evidence concerning marriage. In *Richard v. Brehm*, 73 Pa. 140, 144 (1873), the Pennsylvania Supreme Court stated that the marriage "may be proved in civil cases, by reputation, declarations, and conduct of the parties, and other circumstances usually accompanying that relation." If both cohabitation and reputation exist, according to the court a marital presumption is created. For more on this, see Chapter 9 *infra*. In *Lucken v. Wichman*, 5 S.C. 411, 415 (1874), the court states that the marriage can be based on an "express contract, or inferred from circumstances."

35 *Tummalty v. Tummalty*, 3 Bradf. 369, 371 (N.Y. 1855). In *Thorndell v. Morrison*, 25 Pa. 326, 328, 1 Casey 326 (1855), the court stated that marriage "may be shown by evidence of long-continued cohabitation as man and wife." *See also infra Richard v. Brehm*, 73 Pa. 140, 144, 13 Am.Rep. 733 (1873); *Reading Fire Ins. & Trust Co.'s Appeal*, 113 Pa. 204, 6 A. 60, 63 (1886); and *Green's Estate*, 5 Pa.C. 605, 606 (1888). In *Letters v. Cady*, 10 Cal. 533, 537 (1858), the court stated that the cohabitation as husband and wife was "*prima facie* evidence of a marriage." However, a marriage was not found proven.

The second primary path, as influenced by Scottish law,[36] entails that the courts apply a legal presumption according to which the party claiming the existence of a common law marriage, in principle, does not need to prove the existence of a marriage contract. It is sufficient that the existence of cohabitation and reputation is demonstrated. The law then presumes that a marriage exists, and shifts the burden of proof to the party contesting the existence of the common law marriage. That party must then prove that no marriage contract existed. (See Chapter 9, "Burdens of Proof and Presumptions," for more on the legal marital presumption.)[37] This distinction is not always clear. Certain authors consider both applications presumptions.[38]

When the United States Supreme Court had to take a stance on the validity of a common law marriage for the first time, it clearly found that such a marriage could be based solely upon evidence of the parties' cohabitation and their reputation as spouses. In *Hutchins v. Kimmell* (1875), the Michigan Supreme Court stated in a civil case that: " [I]f the parties agreed presently to take each other for husband and wife, and from that time lived together professedly in that relation, proof of these facts would be sufficient to constitute proof of a marriage ... This has become the settled doctrine of the American courts."[39] Even though the principle was not

36 The Scottish influence is most clear in two of America's most historically significant cases, namely *Yardley's Estate*, 75 Pa. 207 (1874), adjudged by the Pennsylvania Supreme Court and *Hynes v. McDermott*, 91 N.Y. 451, 459, 43 Am.Rep. 677 (1883), adjudged by the New York Court of Appeals. *See also Cargile v. Wood*, 63 Mo. 501 (1876) and *Fryer v. Fryer*, 9 S.C.Eq. (Rich.Cas.) 85 (1832).

37 *Richard v. Brehm*, 73 Pa. 140, 141, 13 Am.Rep. 733 (1873). The case, in which a common law marriage was found established, is a good example of how a court reasons with the application of a legal presumption with a reversed evidentiary burden based on the parties' "cohabitation and reputation." The opposing party was not successful in proving that a contract of marriage was not entered into: "His declaration made upon one occasion, when angry at his wife, to her sister, that they were not married, after more than thirty-five years of apparent wedded life was certainly very weak evidence to rebut the presumption of marriage." *Id.* at 145. *Compare* from the same time period *Yardley's Estate*, 75 Pa. 207, 211 (1874) ("Neither cohabitation nor reputation of marriage, nor both, is marriage. When conjoined they are evidence from which a presumption of marriage arises.") *See* the same court in *Com. v. Stump*, 53 Pa. 132, 91 Am.Dec. 198 (1866). Early in the 1800s, the courts in Pennsylvania accepted the parties' "cohabitation and reputation" as a very strong and even sufficient evidence for the marriage contract, without expressly creating a legal presumption to shift the evidentiary burden. *See supra Chambers v. Dickson*, 2 S. & R. 475 (1816); *Senser v. Bower*, 1 Pa. 450 (1830); *Guardian of the Poor v. Nathis*, 2 Brewster 149 (1845); *Covert v. Herzog*, 4 Pa. 145 (1846); *Thorndell v. Morrison*, 25 Pa. 326 (1855); and *Physick's Estate*, 2 Brewster 179 (1862). *Compare* ABRAHAM L. FREEDMAN AND MAURICE FREEDMAN, LAW OF MARRIAGE AND DIVORCE IN PENNSYLVANIA I, 130 (2d ed. 1957), who consider these cases presumption cases.

38 *See, e.g.*, JOEL PRENTISS BISHOP, NEW COMMENTARIES ON MARRIAGE, DIVORCE, AND SEPARATION, I § 927 (Chicago, T.H. Flood & Co. 1891), which discusses presumptions of different degrees.

39 *Hutchins v. Kimmel*, 31 Mich. 126, 130, 18 Am.Rep. 164 (1875). The court cited almost thirty cases as support for its stance in addition to *Fenton v. Reed*. *Compare* from the same time *McFarland v. McFarland*, 51 Iowa 565, 2 N.W. 269 (1879),

applied in the actual case, which concerned adultery, this statement would be given great significance. When the United States Supreme Court, a few years later in *Meister v. Moore* (1877), needed to take a stance on the validity of a common law marriage, the Court certainly did not retry the evidence. Neither did it further expound on its position on the evidentiary issues. However, it cited the above statement from *Hutchins v. Kimmell*, not as *obiter dictum*, but rather as authority with respect to the current law.[40]

The acceptance of the cohabitation as an evidentiary fact for the marital contract received support at the end of the 1800s in Bishop's New Commentaries, a treatise that would, for a long period of time, exert considerable influence upon the case law. The author stated: "Not even words are in all circumstances necessary. Or it is sufficient that the parties, in language mutually understood, or in any way declaratory of intention, accept each other as husband and wife."[41] According to the author, even if the parties knew that an impediment to the marriage existed, there is no requirement to enter into a renewed contract upon the removal of the impediment: "If the parties desire marriage and do what they can to render their union matrimonial, yet one of them is under a disability—as when there is a prior marriage undissolved—their cohabitation, thus matrimonially meant, will, in matter of law, make them husband and wife from the moment when the disability is removed; and it is immaterial whether they knew of its existence, or its removal, or not."[42]

---

in which the court stated that the woman was entitled to the rights of marriage "if she intends present marriage, and the man does not, provided they cohabit, and provided his conduct is such as to justify her in believing that he intends present marriage" and found that the parties after the divorce reunited in a common law marriage. *See also Stafford v. Stafford*, 41 Tex. 111 (1874) and *Bonds v. Foster*, 36 Tex. 68 (1871).

40 *Meister v. Moore*, 96 U.S. 76, 82-83 (1877); and *Burner v. Briggs*, 39 Ohio St. 478 (1883). *Compare Brinckle v. Brinckle*, 12 Phila. 232 (1877), where the court stated that the marriage contract can be proven as all other contracts, by direct evidence, evidence concerning the parties' execution of the contract "or it can be inferred from circumstances, such as reputation, conduct and cohabitation." In *Reading Fire Ins. & Trust Co.'s Appeal*, 113 Pa. 204, 6 A. 60, 63 (1886), the court stated: "Many times marriage may be proved by acts of recognition, continued matrimonial cohabitation, and Gen. reputation." The evidence, however, was insufficient to prove the existence of an "actual agreement to form the relation of husband and wife." *See also Green's Estate*, 5 Pa.C. 605, 606 (1888) ("In a vast number of cases, respecting which the present may serve as an example, the fact of marriage must be gathered wholly from the acts of the contracting parties themselves. Their cohabitation and their admissions, and the reputation which these incidents have gained for them in the community, are all proofs that they are living in a state of wedlock"); and *Jenkins v. Jenkins*, 83 Ga. 286, 9 S.E. 541 (1889). In *Gall v. Gall*, 114 N.Y. 109, 21 N.E. 106, 118 (1889), the court found that the parties, which began to live together as "man and mistress," finally "agreed to live together as husband and wife." *See also White v. White*, 82 Cal. 427, 23 P. 276 (1890); and *Odd Fellows' Beneficial Ass'n v. Carpenter*, 17 R.I. 720, 24 A. 578 (1892).

41 Bishop, *supra* note 48, § 970. *Compare* on the other hand *Hunt's Appeal*, 86 Pa. 294 (1878).

42 Bishop *id.* In *Strauss's Estate*, 168 Pa. 561, 570 (1895), the court stated that marriage is a civil contract and that "at least, reputation and cohabitation are sufficient evidence of it."

Those courts that did not find it to be a necessary requisite also recognized cohabitation as evidence. In *Hulett v. Carey* (1896), the Minnesota Supreme Court, consequently, stated that cohabitation may be evidence of marriage.[43] To accept the cohabitation as supplementary evidence in addition to other evidence, for example, oral contracts, seems somewhat remarkable. However, in this time period, there are cases in which the courts declared that an express contract was not required and that the contract could entirely be based upon the actions of the parties. In *Renfrow v. Renfrow* (1899), the Kansas Supreme Court consequently stated that "an express agreement between the parties to take and live with each other as husband and wife is not necessary. The agreement to do so is implied from their acts and conduct in mutually recognizing and holding each other out as bound together in the matrimonial state, and proof of such acts and conduct is proof of the marriage agreement."[44]

There are also cases from this period in which the courts accept that the contract of marriage is simply proven with circumstantial evidence, even in criminal cases. In *Bynon v. State* (1898), concerning bigamy, the Alabama Supreme Court could consequently find the existence of a marriage contract "from facts and circumstances—from the cohabitation and conduct of the parties." If one party in the common law marriage later entered into a ceremonial marriage with a different partner, a prosecution for bigamy resulted.[45]

7.3.3 The Development during the Early 1900s

There are cases in the beginning of the 1900s in which the courts make nuanced statements concerning the weight of the interpretation of the parties' oral contract in light of their actions and other circumstances.[46]

43 *Hulett v. Carey*, 66 Minn. 327, 69 N.W. 31, 34 (1896). With respect to the stance in the cases as to the issue of whether cohabitation is a necessary requirement for the formation of a common law marriage, *see infra* Chapter 8.2. *See also Johnson v. Dudley*, 3 Ohio N.P. 196 (1896); *Durning v. Hastings*, 183 Pa. 210 (1897); *Taylor v. Taylor*, 10 Colo.App. 303, 50 P. 10 49 (1897); *Cox v. State*, 117 Ala. 103, 23 So. 806 (1898); and *Moore v. Heineke*, 119 Ala. 627, 24 So. 374 (1898). *Compare Collins v. Voorhees*, 47 N.J.Eq. 315, 20 A. 676 (1890).

44 *Renfrow v. Renfrow*, 60 Kan. 277, 56 P. 534, 72 Am.St.Rep. 350 (1899) (applying Missouri law).

45 *Bynon v. State*, 117 Ala. 80, 23 So. 640 (1898). *See also Parker v. State*, 77 Ala. 47, 54 Am.Rep. 43 (1884); *State v. Hughes*, 35 Kan. 626, 12 P. 28, 30 (1886); and *Simmons v. Simons*, 39 S.W. 639 (Tex.Civ.App. 1897). *Compare Jenkins v. Jenkins*, 83 Ga. 286, 9 S.E. 541 (1889); *Dumas v. State*, 14 Tex.Crim.App. 464, 46 Am.Rep. 241 (1883); *Williams v. State*, 54 Ala. 131, 25 Am.Rep. 665 (1875); *Arthur v. Broadnax*, 3 Ala. 557, 37 Am.Dec. 707 (1842); and *Patterson v. Gaines*, 47 U.S. (6 How.) 550, 12 L.Ed. 553 (1848).

46 *See, e.g., Com. v. Haylow*, 17 Pa.Super. 541, 548 (1901), in which the Pennsylvania Superior Court stated that "it is not the duty of the courts to seek for an interpretation of the words used by the parties which would be inconsistent with an honorable intention as well as with their subsequent conduct and declarations, when an interpretation consistent with the formation of an honorable relation is possible, and, in the light of all the circumstances, more probably expresses their intention."

Clearly even more extensive possibilities of finding for the existence of a common law marriage from the cohabitation and parties' outward representation can be found in the Court's decision in *Travers v. Reinhardt* (1906). Albeit that the circumstances were special in that the parties had originally performed a wedding which was found to be invalid, the court stated that their actions toward each other and outward to the public were comparable to "a declaration by each that they did, and during their joint lives were to, occupy the relation of husband and wife."[47]

During the 1910s, however, the courts in a number of states retained a cautious attitude. For example, in *Umbenhower v. Labus* (1912), the Ohio Supreme Court stated that the proving of the marriage could partially consist of "the immediate and continued course of conduct of the parties in reference to each other in their domestic and social life."[48] The majority of courts, however, were prepared to go further. One example is the short but clear case of *Hamlin v. Grogan* (1919), in which a party argued that the contract of marriage must be proven "as a *tertium quid anterior* to and independent of cohabitation, declaration of the parties, and manner of life." The Eighth Circuit Court of Appeals rejected this as the law, stating that the contract may be shown as an inference of fact from "cohabitation, declarations, and reputation among friends and kindred"

The court concluded that the testimony of the woman taken in connection with "the proved acts and declarations of defendant, and the evidence of cohabitation and reputation" was sufficient to sustain a finding that the woman took the man to be her husband and that he took her to be his wife.

47 *Travers v. Reinhardt*, 205 U.S. 423, 440, 27 S.Ct. 563, 51 L.Ed 865, 873 (1906), summarized *infra*. *Compare Thewli's Estate*, 217 Pa. 307, 66 A. 519 (1907), in which the court stated that the parties' actions and behavior is "as efficacious as words for establishing a contract by implication." Another case from the same time period, which would have influence on the development in Georgia, is *Drawdy v. Hesters*, 130 Ga. 161, 168, 60 S.E. 451, 454 (1908), in which the Georgia Supreme Court stated: "Marriage may be inferred from proof of cohabitation, and that the parties held themselves out to the world as husband and wife, and such proof may be made by Gen. repute among neighbors and others in a position to know the facts." *See also Pegg v. Pegg*, 138 Iowa 572, 115 N.W. 1027 (1908). In *Tyner v. Schoonover*, 79 Kan. 573, 100 P. 478, 479 (1909), in addition to the testimony by acknowledgment, there was cohabitation, conduct, and Gen. reputation, "all tending to show" the marriage by the parties. *See also Brisbin v. Huntington*, 128 Iowa 166, 103 N.W. 144 (1905).

48 *Umbenhower v. Labus*, 85 Ohio St. 238, 97 N.E. 832, 833 (1912). *See* earlier *Carmichael v. State*, 12 Ohio St. 553 (1861). *See also* from the 1910's, *Bishop v. Brittain Invest. Co.*, 229 Mo. 699, 129 S.W. 668 (1910); and *Miller v. State*, 9 Ga.App. 827, 72 S.E. 279 (1911). In *Alexander v. Gibson*, 57 So. 760 (Ala. 1912), the court stated that "cohabitation as man and wife, the rearing of children, the recognition of the relation by the parties themselves, and by their friends and relatives, and their declarations and conduct, holding themselves out to the world as husband and wife, are manifestations of the parties having consented to contract that relation *inter se*, and therefore circumstances from which the trier of the fact may infer that a marriage had in fact been entered into." *See also Berger v. Kirby*, 105 Tex. 611, 153 S.W.1130, 1131 (1913); *Fender v. Segro*, 41 Okla. 318, 137 P. 103, 105 (1913) ("Marriage, it is true, may be proved by circumstantial evidence"); *In re Estate of Wittick*, 164 Iowa 485, 493, 145 N.W. 913, 916 (1914); *Peery v. Peery*, 27 Colo.App. 533, 150 P. 329 (1915); and *Smith v. Reed*, 145 Ga. 724, 89 S.E. 815, 816 (1916).

and found that the actual marriage contract was proven as a fact by circumstances.[49]

Legal scholars in the beginning of the 1920s refer to implied agreements with respect to marriage, but the subject was not further investigated. James Schouler states laconically that the contract of marriage "may be implied."[50] Otto Koegel, in his doctoral thesis from 1922, addressed whether cohabitation should be considered a necessary requisite for the formation of a common law marriage, and answered the question in the negative, but did not more closely analyze the function of cohabitation as an evidentiary fact. As a passing comment, he states, however, that: "The only function of evidence of cohabitation is to show consent."[51] Consistent with this, the Colorado Supreme Court stated, in *Peters v. Peters* (1923): "The habit and repute of marriage are not an essential of the legality of the relationship, but merely evidence of an essential—i.e., consent." By then, cohabitation was widely accepted as evidence for the marriage contract in the case law.[52]

---

49 *Hamlin v. Grogan*, 257 F. 59, 60-61 (8th Cir. 1919)(applying Missouri law). *See also Meehan v. Edward Valve and Mfg. Co.*, 65 Ind.App. 342, 117 N.E. 265, 266 (1917), in which the Indiana Appellate Court stated that the contract, when it cannot be proven by written evidence or witnesses, "may be proven by cohabitation, reputation, conduct and all other circumstances having to do with the acts and conduct of the parties with respect to the marriage relation." *Compare* the restrictive stance by the Indiana Supreme Court in *Anderson v. Anderson*, 235 Ind. 113, 131 N.E.2d 301, 306 (1956). *See also Tedder v. Tedder*, 108 S.C. 271, 94 S.E. 19, 20, 2 A.L.R. 438 (1917), in which the parties' moral reputation was given weight, as well as *Smith v. People*, 64 Colo. 290, 170 P. 959, 960 (1918), where there was not an express marriage contract but the Colorado Supreme Court stated that "mutual consent may be inferred from cohabitation and repute, of which there is ample evidence in this case." *See also Linsey v. Jefferson*, 68 Okla. 156, 172 P. 641, 642 (1918)("It is also well settled that marriage may be proven by circumstantial evidence"); and *Love v. Love*, 185 Iowa 930, 171 N.W. 257 (1919). In *Brewer v. Brewer's Estate*, 68 Colo. 84, 188 P. 725 (1919), a common law marriage was found established based on a cohabitation of two and one-half years. *See also Marsicano v. Marsicano*, 79 Fla. 278, 84 So. 156 (1920).

50 JAMES SCHOULER, MARRIAGE, DIVORCE, SEPARATION & DOMESTIC RELATIONS 1427 (6th ed. 1921). The author cited the above-mentioned cases of *Adger v. Ackerman*, 115 F. 124 (8th Cir. 1902); *Tedder v. Tedder*, 108 S.C. 271, 94 S.E. 19 (1917) and *McKenna v. McKenna*, 180 Ill. 577, 54 N.E. 641 (1899).

51 OTTO E. KOEGEL, COMMON LAW MARRIAGE AND ITS DEVELOPMENT IN THE UNITED STATES, 127 (1922). *See also* FRANK H. KEEZER, A TREATISE ON THE LAW OF MARRIAGE AND DIVORCE § 135 (2d ed. 1923).

52 *Peters v. Peters*, 73 Colo. 271, 215 P. 128, 129 (1923). It can be seen from *Cordas v. Ryan*, 72 Colo. 521, 212 P. 490, 491 (1923), that the same court had contemplated that a marriage contract could be proven simply by evidence concerning the actions of the parties. For such cases, the court applied as a requirement that the proof demonstrate something that is "not merely consistent with marriage, but inconsistent with any other relation." *See further Applegate v. Applegate*, 118 Misc. 359, 193 N.Y.S. 494, 495 (Sup.Ct. 1922), in which the New York Supreme Court, concerning the parties, stated that "their actions were an expression of their intentions." *Compare In re Craig's Estate*, 273 Pa. 530, 117 A. 221, 222 (1922), in which the Pennsylvania Supreme Court stated in the event the evidence was not sufficient with respect to a written marriage contract, which could be proven by the signature of the parties, and if witnesses could neither prove an oral contract, the marriage could be established "by proof of reputation and cohabitation, declarations and conduct of the

Nevertheless, a number of courts at this time took a more restricted attitude toward the acceptance of circumstantial evidence. In *State v. Newman* (1923), the Montana Supreme Court accepted that the marriage agreement could be "implied from the conduct of the parties," but required that the parties be conscious that the marriage is a result thereof: "[M]arriage cannot be said to steal upon them unaware. One cannot become married unwittingly or accidentally."[53]

The issue of cohabitation as an evidentiary fact was raised in the 1930s by the Florida Supreme Court in *Le Blanc v. Yawn* (1930). The court found that the parties had entered into a contract when they commenced their cohabitation as husband and wife and that the contract was actually carried out by more than ten years of cohabitation.[54] In a similar fashion, the Texas Appellate Court in *Wingfield v. Pool* (1931) stated that a marriage may be "circumstantially established" by the fact that a man and woman have, for a considerable period of time, openly cohabited as husband and

---

parties, and such other circumstances as usually accompany the marriage relation." Evidence concerning an oral contract was presented in the case, which was however found insufficient. In *U.S. Fid. & Guar. Co. v. Dowdle*, 269 S.W. 119, 126 (Tex.Civ. App. 1924), the court stated that the marriage "may be shown by circumstantial as well as by direct evidence. It may in a proper case be inferred from continuous cohabitation and repute." However, no marriage was found proven. *Cf. Brooks v. Hancock*, 256 S.W.2d 296 (Tex.Civ.App.-Texarkana 1923); *In re Estate of Medford*, 197 Iowa 76, 196 N.W. 728 (1924); and *Edwards v. Enterprise Mfg. Co.*, 283 Pa. 420, 129 A. 449, 450 (1925). In *Dirion v. Brewer*, 20 Ohio App. 298, 151 N.E. 818 (1925), the court referred to the legislation as support for the possibility to cite o the parties' cohabitation and the reputation as spouses as evidence, albeit their own conclusions also rested upon the direct evidence which was presented in the case. The court cited Ga.Code § 11989: "Proof of cohabitation, and reputation of the marriage of the parties, shall be competent testimony to prove such marriage, and may be, within the discretion of the court, sufficient evidence thereof." The regulation, which in the first place was applicable to cases concerning marital divorce, but not to criminal cases, was applied in *Dirion*, an inheritance case. The evidentiary weight of the cohabitation naturally was reduced if direct evidence to the contrary was produced. This can be the case, for example, where the parties themselves state that no contract had been entered into, *see State v. Martinez*, 43 Idaho 180, 250 P. 239 (1926). In the case of *In re Murdock's Estate*, 92 Pa.Super. 275, 277 (1927), the Pennsylvania Superior Court consequently stated hypothetically that if the actual conversation in the case between the parties really constituted a contract, the parties' cohabitation and reputation could be accepted as supplementary evidence as support for the fact that a marriage contract had actually been entered into. However, if the woman herself testified that no valid marriage contract had been entered into between them, the evidence concerning cohabitation and reputation lacked weight. *Compare In re Estate of Holben*, 93 Pa.Super.Ct. 472 (1928), where cohabitation and reputation could be given decisive consideration, criticized by the Pennsylvania Supreme Court in *Pierce v. Pierce*, 355 Pa. 175, 49 A.2d 346, 349 (1946). *Compare Holgate v. United Electric Ry. Co.*, 47 R.I. 337, 133 A. 243, 244 (1926), in which the Rhode Island Supreme Court more freely accepted, based on "cohabitation, declarations, reputation among friends and kindred," the existence of a common law marriage. *See also Walker v. Walker*, 218 Ala. 16, 117 So. 472 (1928); and *Consolidated Underwriters v. Kelly*, 15 S.W.2d (Tex.Com.App. 1929).

53 *State v. Newman*, 66 Mont. 180, 213 P. 805, 807 (1923). It should be observed that this was a criminal case. As to Montana civil law, *see* § 7.4 *infra*.

54 *Le Blanc v. Yawn*, 99 Fla. 328, 126 So. 789 (1930).

wife and recognized and treated each other as such so that they are generally reputed to be married among those who have come in contact with them.[55]

The previously applied exceptions in civil cases concerning criminal conversation, and criminal bigamy and adultery were not applied as much as before. An example is *Comm. v. Bockes* (1931), in which the Pennsylvania Supreme Court stated: "There is no reason ... why evidence which is competent to prove a marriage in a civil case should not be competent in a criminal case. The fact to be proved is the same.... proof of marriage by cohabitation and reputation ... may be sufficient to sustain a conviction of adultery or bigamy." The court meant that the difference between civil and criminal cases, instead, lies in the evidentiary standard applied.[56] The same court stated in the civil case, *In re McGrath's Estate* (1935), that evidence concerning cohabitation and reputation, even in cases in which the evidence is not sufficient for an application of the marital presumption, can be considered "as corroborating claimant's testimony as to marriage, if provable as ordinary contract."[57] The Georgia Court of Appeals went considerably further in *Chance v. Chance* (1939) by stating that: "Marriage may be inferred from proof that parties cohabited and held themselves out to the world as husband and wife."[58]

---

55 *Wingfield v. Pool*, 38 S.W.2d 422, 423 (Tex.Civ.App.-Galveston 1931). *Compare supra Consolidated Underwriters v. Kelly*, 15 S.W.2d 229 (Tex.Com.App. 1929); and *In re Krystkiewicz's Estate*, 310 Pa. 298, 165 A. 230 (1933).

56 *Com. v. Bockes*, 103 Pa.Super. 378, 380-383 (1931). In the case of *In re Graham's Estate*, 169 Okla. 568, 37 P.2d 964, (1934), the Oklahoma Supreme Court adds, as evident, that the contract "might be implied from this action and conduct."

57 *In re McGrath's Estate*, 319 Pa. 309, 179 A. 599, 600 (1935). *See also In re Murdock's Estate*, 92 Pa.Super. 275 (1927). With respect to the marital presumption, *see* Chapter 9 *infra. See also Sam v. Sam*, 172 Okla. 342, 45 P.2d 462 (1935); *James v. James*, 97 Colo. 413, 50 P.2d 63, 64 (1935); and *Richard v. Richard*, 172 Okla. 397, 45 P.2d 101 (1935).

58 *Chance v. Chance*, 60 Ga.App. 889, 5 S.E.2d 399 (1939). The court there cited *Drawdy v. Hesters*, 130 Ga. 161, 168, 60 S.E. 451, 454 (1908). *See also Norell v. Norell*, 220 Ind. 398, 404, 44 N.E.2d 97, 99 (1942); *Associated Indemnity Corporation v. Billberg*, 172 S.W.2d 157 (Tex.Civ.App.-Amarillo 1943); and *Jamison v. Williams*, 164 Pa.Super. 344, 348, 64 A.2d 857 (1949). In *Young v. Gen. Banking Co.*, 104 Ind.App. 658, 12 N.E.2d 1016, 1018 (1938), the Indiana Appellate Court stated that the woman in the case could not testify as to whether the parties at some specific occasion or place orally or in writing "agreed to take each other as consorts." However, the court stated at the same time that such facts could be proven through circumstantial evidence. The evidence, however, was not sufficient to prove such a contract. The stance of accepting cohabitation as circumstantial evidence appears at this time to even be accepted by a court in Pennsylvania, on the condition that the circumstances are sufficiently strong and convincing. In *dictum* in *Caddy v. Johnstown Firemen's Relief Ass'n*, 129 Pa.Super. 493, 196 A. 590 (1938), the Pennsylvania Superior Court stated: "Cohabitation and reputation that the parties are married do not constitute a legal marriage—not even a common law marriage—but they are evidence from which a marriage may be found, if the circumstances are sufficiently strong and convincing to satisfy the triers of fact." An oral contract was found proven partially with the support of circumstantial evidence. *See also Manire v. Burt*, 121 S.W.2d 630 (Tex.Civ.App.-Austin 1938) and *Drummond v. Benson*, 133 S.W.2d 154 (Tex.Civ.App.-San Antonio 1939).

The courts had reason to take a stance on cohabitation's significance as an evidentiary fact even during the 1940s. In *Moffat Coal Co. v. Industrial Commission* (1941), the Colorado Supreme Court maintained that evidence with respect to "habit and repute" always is usable, and that such evidence in itself may properly be the basis for inferring consent to a contract of marriage.[59] A marriage contract was found proven and a common law marriage established. In *Markley v. Hudson* (1944), the Ohio Supreme Court emphasized the necessity of proving an agreement between the parties to become husband and wife. The court maintained, however, that this does not mean that such proof must establish an express agreement resulting in a contract, or that such result may not be established by circumstances from which an agreement *in praesenti* may be inferred.[60] It is clearly expressed in *Sloss-Sheffield Steel & Iron Co. v. Watford* (1944) that those circumstances that most often come into play are the parties' cohabitation and outward representation as spouses. There, the Alabama Supreme Court stated that the mutual contract to be husband and wife "may be inferred from cohabitation and reputation."[61]

However, there is no shortage of cases in which the courts have been reluctant, based on the parties' cohabitation, to find the existence of the marriage contract. This has been true, for example, in cases in which direct evidence was contrary to such a conclusion, most commonly because the parties themselves testified that no such marriage existed despite the fact that they lived together. A somewhat more delicate situation occurred in *Clack v. Williams* (1945), in which the spouses, after a divorce, had continued the cohabitation as before. After the death of the woman, the man claimed that they were united in a common law marriage. The Texas Court of Appeals, San Antonio, stated that an agreement to marry, which is an essential basis for a common law marriage, certainly could be inferred from the surrounding facts and circumstances. Nevertheless, the court found that the inference of the existence of a marriage agreement cannot be drawn from circumstances contrary to "the direct testimony of a litigant" (asserting the existence of a marriage) as to facts which, if true,

---

59 *Moffat Coal Co. v. Indus. Comm'n*, 108 Colo. 388, 118 P.2d 769 (1941). With respect to the significance of the parties' plans to later formally marry, *see* Section 6.4 *supra. See also Craddock's Estate*, 310 Mass. 116, 37 N.E.2d 508, 512 (1941) ("assent may be implied from the conduct of the parties"); and *Baker v. Mitchell*, 143 Pa.Super. 50, 17 A.2d 738, 740 (1941). *See further Gilbreath v. Lewis*, 242 Ala. 510, 7 So.2d 485 (1942), in which the parties' negative moral reputation was considered. *See previously also Berger v. Kirby*, 105 Tex. 611, 153 S.W. 1130 (1913). In the case of *In re Keig's Estate*, 140 P.2d 163 (D.C.App. 1943), the court stated: "Evidence of cohabitation is admissible as proof tending to show mutual consent."

60 *Markley v. Hudson*, 143 Ohio St. 163, 28 O.O. 81, 54 N.E.2d 304, 306 (1944).

61 *Sloss-Sheffield Steel & Iron Co. v. Watford*, 245 Ala. 425, 17 So.2d 166 (1944). *See also Smith v. Smith*, 247 Ala. 213, 217, 23 So.2d 605, 609 (1945); *In re Blackhawk's Estate*, 195 Okla. 390, 158 P.2d 168 (1944); *De Shazo v. Christian*, 191 S.W.2d 495, 496 (Tex. Civ.App–Amarillo 1945); and *Baker v. Mays & Mays*, 199 S.W.2d 279, 284 (Tex.Civ. App.-Ft. Worth 1946).

demonstrate that no marriage agreement was entered into.[62] The man had himself stated that he did not know, prior to the death of the woman, that she had received a divorce from him. In this situation, it was difficult for him to assert that he, after the divorce, through the continued cohabitation, had entered into a contract of marriage with his wife.

Certain courts have been restrictive in accepting circumstantial evidence in cases in which the relationship from the beginning was meretricious because of an impediment to the marriage. In *Pierce v. Pierce* (1946), the Pennsylvania Supreme Court considered a relationship commenced when an impediment existed against the marriage such that the relationship was meretricious from the beginning. The court stated that changing the relationship into a valid marriage "may be established by circumstantial evidence" only if the evidence is strong enough to overturn the presumption that the original relationship continued, and satisfactorily proves that the relationship "was changed to matrimonial union by parties' mutual consent." Cohabitation and reputation, alone, were found to be insufficient. No contract was proven, despite a cohabitation of seventeen years after the removal of the impediment.[63] In the majority of cases, however, the circumstance that the relationship from the beginning was meretricious has not been an impediment to an inferred agreement based on cohabitation and reputation.[64]

7.3.4 The Development in the Mid 1900s

It appears that, in the mid 1900s, the different developments led to more concrete positions. On one hand, a number of courts took a restrictive view and were not willing to go beyond accepting the cohabitation between the parties as more than corroborating evidence supporting an oral

62 *Clack v. Williams*, 189 S.W.2d 503, 505 (Tex.Civ.App.-San Antonio 1945). A similar reasoning can be found in *Mares v. Heckler*, 1985 U.S.Dist. LEXIS 23303 (N.D.Ind. 1985). *Compare United States v. Michaelson*, 58 F.Supp. 796 (D.Minn. 1945), in which the marital contract was found proven to a high degree based on circumstantial evidence when applying Minnesota law, which recognizes common law marriages commenced before 1941 and applies the pure contract principle. *See Hulett v. Carey*, 66 Minn. 327, 69 N.W. 31 (1896), *see* Section 8.2 *infra*. In *Middlebrook v. Wideman*, 203 S.W.2d 686 (Tex.Civ.App.-Texarkana 1947), the court certainly accepted that a common law marriage could be proven circumstantially, but found the proof insufficient.

63 *Pierce v. Pierce*, 355 Pa. 175, 49 A.2d 346 (1946). The court criticizes the case of *In re Estate of Holben*, 93 Pa.Super.Ct. 472 (1928), where cohabitation and reputation were attributed decisive significance. No common law marriage was found proven. *Compare Edwards v. Enterprise Mfg. Co.*, 283 Pa. 420, 129 A. 449, 450 (1925); and *Faggard v. Filipowich*, 248 Ala. 182, 27 So.2d 10 (1946). *Compare also In re Rosenberger's Estate*, 362 Pa. 153, 65 A.2d 377, 379 (1949), in which the court, in cases where the relationship from the beginning was "illicit," appears to require an oral contract or evidence of "a marriage by mutual consent, effected by words *in praesenti*." Such a contract was found proven, for more on this, *see* Section 6.5.1 *supra*.

64 *See* § 7.6 *infra*.

contract between the parties. The cohabitation, according to this understanding, was not allowed to replace words that were not stated. These courts commonly kept the requirement of a verbal contract, in any event, at least with respect to the offer, while the cohabitation was accepted as supplementary evidence. An example appears in *Anderson v. Anderson* (1956), in which the Indiana Supreme Court stated: "Cohabitation, reputation, or other conduct may corroborate evidence that there was a contract, or in the absence of testimony by one of the parties as to what the agreement was, if any, it might, in a strong case, be sufficient to draw the inference that there was a contract to marry in the present tense, but the contract must be formed by what was said and done by the parties, and when the testimony of the party asserting and relying upon the contract discloses there was no language in the present tense constituting a contract to marry, then cohabitation, reputation and other conduct cannot constitute words which were never spoken or used."[65]

On the other hand, it appears that the majority of the courts strengthened the cohabitation as an evidentiary fact for the marriage contract. This development had support in the legal literature,[66] and was manifested also in the statutory codification of the principles. In *Leibrock v. Leibrock* (1952), the Ohio Court of Common Pleas stated that "cohabitation and

65 *Anderson v. Anderson*, 235 Ind. 113, 131 N.E.2d 301, 306 (1956). Common law marriage was later repealed in Indiana and could not be entered into after January 1958, *see* IND. CODE ANN. 31-11-8-5 (Michie 1997). *See also Carretta v. Carretta,* 58 So.2d 439, 441 (Fla. 1952), in which the Florida Supreme Court stated: "The best evidence to establish common-law marriage would be the testimony of the contracting parties, or others who may have been present when the agreement was entered into. In *Le Blanc v. Yawn* (1930, 99 Fla. 328, 126 So. 789) we held that proof of Gen. repute and cohabitation as man and wife will support a presumption of marriage when the agreement is denied and cannot be proven by the best evidence." Common law marriage was repealed in Florida through Fla.Stat. § 741.211 (1987): "No common law marriages entered into after January 1, 1968, shall be valid." Another example of this restrictive stance can be found in *Rager v. Johnstown Traction Co.,* 184 Pa.Super. 474, 134 A.2d 918, 922 (1957), in which the parties had entered into an oral contract and in which the Pennsylvania Superior Court stated that "the cohabitation and reputation evidence corroborates an agreement to live together as man and wife." In *U.S. Fid. & Guar. Co. v. Britton,* 269 F.2d 249, 252 (D.C.Cir. 1959), the District of Columbia Court of Appeals stated that the best proof with respect to an expressed contract to be husband and wife is the parties' testimony, but if neither of them are available to testify, under certain circumstances "proof of cohabitation and Gen. reputation as a married couple ... [can] be sufficient to warrant an inference of marriage by consent." However, if one of the parties is claiming that it is a marriage, but either denies or omits to states that there was a mutual *consensus* or a contract, such a conclusion is not permitted. The case is over-interpreted somewhat in *East v. East,* 536 A.2d 1103, 1105 (D.C.App. 1988), in which the court understood the requirement for an expressed contract as a requirement for a verbal contract. In *Matter of Estate of Foster,* 376 S.E.2d 144 (W.Va. 1988), in which both of the parties were deceased, evidence regarding "cohabitation and Gen. reputation as a married couple" was viewed as sufficient for proving the existence of a marital contract.

66 JOHN W. MORLAND, KEEZER ON THE LAW OF MARRIAGE AND DIVORCE §§ 739-741 (3d ed. 1946); FREEDMAN AND FREEDMAN, *supra* note 37, Chapter 35.

reputation are evidential facts."[67] As support thereto, the court cited, *inter alia,* the new Ohio legislation, which repeated the older principle: "Proof of cohabitation, and reputation of the marriage of the parties, is competent evidence to prove such marriage, and within the discretion of the court, may be sufficient therefore."[68]

Moreover, cohabitation was codified as an evidentiary fact for the marriage contract in Texas. The Texas Supreme Court had paved the way by applying established case law, *inter alia,* in *Shelton v. Belknap* (1955). The court maintained that the parties' contract did not need to be express and that their cohabitation could constitute evidence of the contract: "The agreement necessary to the validity of a common law marriage need not be an express agreement; it may be implied ... an implied agreement ordinarily may be inferred from ... the living and cohabiting together and the holding out to the public."[69] An implied agreement between the parties

67 *Leibrock v. Leibrock,* 63 Ohio Law Abs. 565, 107 N.E.2d 418, 422 (Com.Pl. 1952). For earlier case law from Ohio, *see, e.g., Dibble v. Dibble,* 88 Ohio App. 490, 100 N.E.2d 451, 458-459 (1950)(an agreement to marry "can be implied from conduct of the parties" and that it "may be established by circumstantial evidence"); *Gatterdam v. Gatterdam,* 86 Ohio App. 29, 85 N.E.2d 526 (1949); *Markley v. Hudson,* 143 Ohio St. 163, 54 N.E.2d 304, 306 (1944); *Dirion v. Brewer,* 20 Ohio App. 298, 151 N.E. 818 (1925); *Umbenhower v. Labus,* 85 Ohio St. 238, 97 N.E. 832 (1912); *Carmichael v. State,* 12 Ohio St. 553 (1861); and *Houpt v. Houpt,* 5 Ohio 539 (1832). *Compare Brown v. State,* 208 Ga. 304, 66 S.E.2d 745, 748 (1951).

68 Sec. 8003-13, G.C. The regulation corresponds to the previous Sec. 11989, G.C., which corresponded to the older § 5698, R.S. The thought of accepting cohabitation as a form of implied action and not requiring an express verbal statement of intentions with the formation of a common law marriage was expressed early in the case of *In re Schneider's Will,* 206 Misc. 18, 131 N.Y.S.2d 215, 220 (Surr.Ct. 1954), in which the court stated: "[T]heir conduct.... established the agreement." *Compare Applegate v. Applegate,* 118 Misc. 359, 361, 193 N.Y.S. 494, 495 (Sup.Ct. 1922), in which the court, with respect to the parties, stated that "their actions...were an expression of their intention." *Compare further Skinner v. Skinner,* 4 Misc.2d 1013, 150 N.Y.S.2d 739, 741 (1956), in which the court had not stated that the parties' actions "established," but rather that they "evidenced" their intent: "Their conduct evidenced their intent...to live in lawful wedlock." *See also Graham v. Graham,* 130 Colo. 225, 274 P.2d 605, 606 (1954) and *Rodgers v. Heron,* 226 S.C. 317, 85 S.E.2d 104 (1954). In *Gammelgaard v. Gammelgaard,* 247 Iowa 979, 77 N.W.2d 479, 480 (1956), the Iowa Supreme Court stated: "Proof of cohabitation ... as well as evidence of conduct and of Gen. repute in the community where the parties reside is admissible as tending to strengthen a showing of a present agreement to be husband and wife, and as bearing upon the question of intent." *See also Rodgers v. Herron,* 226 S.C. 317, 85 S.E.2d 104 (1954). The requirement for a verbal contract however arose in *Whitworth v. Whitworth,* 256 Ala. 296, 54 So.2d 575 (1951), which is not representative of the courts in Alabama. *See infra Piel v. Brown,* 361 So.2d 90 (Ala. 1978).

69 *Shelton v. Belknap,* 155 Tex. 37, 282 S.W.2d 682, 684 (1955). *See also Humphreys v. Humphreys,* 364 S.W.2d 177, 178 (Tex. 1963), in which the court stated: "A contract to marry may be implied or inferred from evidence which establishes the second and third element of the marriage." The fact that the court in the actual case did not find any contract proven is a separate issue. The ability to "infer" the marriage contract can also be found in other cases from the same time period. *See, e.g., McIlveen v. McIlveen,* 332 S.W.2d 113 (Tex.Civ.App.-Houston 1960); *Gordon v. Gordon,* 27 Misc.2d 948, 211 N.Y.S.2d 265 (1960)(applying Texas law); *Potter v. Potter,* 342 S.W. 2d 800 (Tex.Civ.App. 1961); *Hinojos v. Railroad Retirement Bd.,* 323 F.2d 227,

was found proven. When common law marriage was codified in 1969, the legislation established not only the constituting elements of a common law marriage, namely, that the parties must have (1) agreed to be married, (2) lived together in this state as husband and wife, and (3) there represented to others that they were married.[70] The legislation in addition also adopted the principle established in the case law with respect to the evidence of the contract: "The agreement to be married may be inferred from the evidence used to establish the other two elements."[71] However, after the codification of the principle, the marriage contract could not be inferred from the parties' cohabitation and outward representation if direct evidence, e.g., in the form of the parties' own information, clearly demonstrated that there was no contract. In *Gary v. Gary* (1973), the Texas Court of Civil Appeals, Tyler, stated that the agreement to become husband and wife certainly may be implied or inferred, but found that this could not occur when direct testimony of the appellee negates such an agreement.[72] On the other hand, if there is direct evidence for the

---

230 (5th Cir. 1963); *Rosales v. Rosales*, 377 S.W.2d 661 (Tex.Civ.App.-Corpus Christi 1964); and *Ferrell v. Celebrezze*, 232 F.Supp. 281 (S.D.Tex. 1964). *Compare also Johnson v. Johnson*, 235 S.C. 542, 112 S.E.2d 647, 651 (1960).

70 Act of June 2, 1969, 61 st Leg., R.S., ch. 888, § 1, 1969, effective Jan 1, 1970. Tex.Gen. Laws 2707, 2717; Tex. Fam. Code Ann. § 1.91 (a)(2). The three elements are to exist simultaneously, *see Winfield v. Renfro*, 821 S.W.2d 640, 646 (Tex.App.-Houston 1991); *Bolash v. Heid*, 733 S.W.2d 698, 699 (Tex.Civ.App.-San Antonio 1987); and *Gary v. Gary*, 490 S.W.2d 929, 934 (Tex.App.-Tyler 1973). Comparable principles were codified in Utah in 1987, *see* Act of Feb. 25, 1987, ch. 246; Utah Code Ann. § 30-1-4.5 (Supp. 1987).

71 Tex. Fam. Code Ann. § 1.91 (b) (Vernon's 1975), consistent with the case law from Texas, *see Humphreys* in note 69 as well as the cases cited there. *See also* the earlier cases such as *Ex parte Threet*, 160 Tex. 482, 333 S.W.2d 361 (1960); *Shelton v. Belknap*, 155 Tex. 37, 282 S.W.2d 682 (1955); *Baker v. Mays & Mays*, 199 S.W.2d 279 (Tex.Civ. App.-Ft. Worth 1946); *Consolidated Underwriters v. Kelly*, 15 S.W.2d 229 (Tex.Com. App. 1929); and *U.S. Fid. & Guar. v. Dowdle*, 269 S.W. 119, 126 (Tex.Civ.App. 1924), in which the court stated that the marriage "may be shown by circumstantial as well as by direct evidence. It may in a proper case be inferred from continuous cohabitation and repute," despite the fact that no marriage was found proven in the case. *See* already *Tarpley v. Poage's Adm'r*, 2 Tex. 139 (1847). As examples of the case law following the enactment of the legislation, *see Howard v. Howard*, 459 S.W.2d 901 (Tex.Civ. App. 1970); *Morris v. Morris*, 463 S.W.2d 295 (Tex.Civ.App.-Houston 1971); *Collora v. Navarro*, 574 S.W.2d 65 (Tex. 1978); and *Rodriguez v. Avalos*, 567 S.W.2d 85, 86 (Tex. Civ.App.-El Paso 1978). In the case of Estate of *Claveria v. Claveria*, 615 S.W.2d 164, 166 (Tex. 1981), the Texas Supreme Court stated that the marriage could be proven with the same type of evidence as other facts, and as a consequence thereof, "proof of common-law marriage may be shown by the conduct of the parties."

72 *Gary v. Gary*, 490 S.W.2d 929 (Tex.Civ.App-Tyler 1973). *See* earlier *Rush v. Travelers Ins. Co.*, 347 S.W.2d 758, 760 (Tex.Civ.App-Texarkana 1961), in which the court admitted that a marriage contract could certainly be implied or inferred, but in which the court at the same time stated that this could not occur "contrary to direct evidence which definitely shows that there was no such agreement." *See also Ferrell v. Celebrezze*, 232 F.Supp. 281, 283 (S.D.Tex. 1964), where the formation of a common law marriage was prevented based on direct evidence of the content that the woman had not desired a "binding wedlock." *See supra also Clack v. Williams*, 189 S.W.2d 503, 504 (Tex.Civ.App.-San Antonio 1945).

existence of a marriage contract, it is clear that cohabitation and holding out to the public as husband and wife can constitute excellent corroborative evidence as proof of the same.[73] The above-mentioned Texas legislation with respect to the proof was later amended, which will be further discussed below.

7.4 The Current State of the Law in the Different States

The cohabitation between the parties is accepted today as an evidentiary fact for the marriage contract in all of the jurisdictions recognizing common law marriage, albeit to a greater or lesser extent. Today, the development in the case law and the legislation has strong support in the legal literature. Not least, Homer Clark has, in several editions of his books, maintained that it is necessary to consider the parties' actions in proving the marriage agreement because the parties seldom enter into any formal contract and consequently, their actions have significant evidentiary weight.[74] An overview of the current status of the law, which is primarily based on the development during the latter portion of the 1900s and the beginning of the 2000s, reveals the following.

If we first look west, beginning with **Montana** as the most far north and west, the Montana Supreme Court, on repeated occasions, has made the principle statement that the parties' marital *consensus* does not need to be expressed in any predetermined form, but can be seen in the actions of the parties. Consequently, in the case of *In re Matter of Estate of Hunsaker* (1998), the court stated that mutual consent could be implied from the conduct of the parties. The court also applied this principle in the case at hand.[75]

In the neighboring state of **Idaho**, common law marriage was codified and the requisites for the formation of such a marriage were regulated by the legislation.[76] Moreover, a provision in Idaho Code § 32-203 (1985), addressed the proof more generally by stating: "Consent to and subsequent consummation of marriage may be manifested in any form, and

73 *Collora v. Navarro*, 574 S.W.2d 65 (Tex. 1978).

74 Clark, *supra* note 1, at 49-52 (1968), 107-112 (2d ed. 1987). *See also* Davis, *supra* note 1, at 662; Kandoian, *supra* note 1, at 1842-1843; and Vaughn, *supra* note 13, at 1155 and 1159.

75 *Matter of Estate of Hunsaker*, 968 P.2d 281, 286 (Mont. 1998). Similar statements can be found, *e.g.*, in *Miller v. Townsend Lumber Co.*, 448 P.2d 148, 151 (Mont. 1968). Without giving any principle statement, the court applied the same principle in the cases of *Matter of Estate of Alcorn*, 868 P.2d 629 (Mont. 1994) and *In re Ober*, 2003 MT 7, 314 Mont. 20, 62 P.3d 1114 (2003). *Compare* the restrictive view in *State v. Newman*, 66 Mont. 180, 213 P. 805, 807 (1923), a criminal case, *supra* note 53.

76 Idaho Code Ann. § 32-201 (1985). In Idaho, common law marriage has been repealed effective 1996, however not retroactivily, *see* H.B. 176; Chap. 104, 1995 Idaho Session Laws; Idaho Code Ann. § 32-201 (2) (Michie 2003).

may be proved under the same general rules of evidence as facts in other cases."[77] From this, it follows that circumstantial evidence is also permitted. That this includes the cohabitation of the parties and their actions in general has clearly been established by the Idaho Supreme Court, which, in the case of *In re Matter of Estate of Wagner* (1995), *inter alia*, stated that consent may be express or implied from the parties' conduct and, further, that proof of the cohabitation of the parties and holding oneself out as being married are two of the best methods for proving that there was consent to the contract.[78] Even though the common law marriage statute was repealed in Idaho in 1996, this legislation still applies to relationships entered into before this date.[79]

In **Utah**, where common law marriage had been repealed for ninety-nine years,[80] the legal institution was reintroduced by legislation in 1987. The new legislation, which is largely similar to that of Idaho, states with respect to the proving: "Evidence of a marriage ... may be manifested in any form, and may be proved under the same general rules of evidence as facts in other cases."[81] In *Whyte v. Blair* (1994), the Utah Supreme Court stated that general reputation, cohabitation, and the assumption of marital rights and duties can constitute evidence with respect to the parties' consent, even if such circumstances alone are not sufficient.[82]

In the neighboring state of **Colorado**, the Colorado Supreme Court stated in *People v. Lucero* (1987) that, in many cases, common law marriages'

---

77 Idaho Code Ann. § 32-203 (1985); 1877, p. 24, § 1; R.S. § 2420; reen. R.C. & C.L., § 2611; C.S., § 4591; I.C.A., § 31-201; am. 1995, ch. 104, § 3, p. 334.

78 *Matter of Estate of Wagner*, 126 Idaho 848, 893 P.2d 211, 214 (1995). *See also Metro. Life Ins. Co. v. Johnson,* 103 Idaho 122, 645 P.2d 356, 362 (1982), in which the court stated that "consent to enter into a common law relationship may be implied and established from the circumstances and facts of the parties' relationship in cohabiting, assuming the rights, duties and obligations of marriage, and holding out of themselves as husband and wife." *Wagner* and *Metropolitan Life* are cited in *Wilkins v. Wilkins,* 48 P.3d 644, 649 (Idaho 2002). *See also McCoy v. McCoy,* 868 P.2d 527, 530 (Idaho App 1994); *Freiburghaus v. Freiburghaus,* 103 Idaho 679, 651 P.2d 944, 946-947 (App. 1982); *In re Estate of Brock,* 94 Idaho 111, 482 P.2d 86 (1971); *In re Foster,* 77 Idaho 26, 287 P.2d 282 (1955); *Nicholas v. Idaho Power Co.,* 63 Idaho 675, 125 P.2d 321 (1942); *Mauldin v. Sunshine Mining Co.,* 61 Idaho 9, 97 P.2d 608 (1939); and *State v. Martinez,* 43 Idaho 180, 250 P. 239 (1926).

79 In Idaho, common law marriage was repealed in 1996, *see* H.B. 176; Chap. 104, 1995 Idaho Session Laws (1995).

80 Common law marriage was repealed in Utah by the Act of March 8, 1888, ch. 45 § 2(3).

81 Utah Code Ann. § 30-1-4.5 (1987); Act of Feb. 25, 1987, ch. 246, effective April 27, 1987.

82 *Whyte v. Blair,* 885 P.2d 791 (Utah 1994). As to the application, *see Clark v. Clark,* 423 Utah Adv. Rep. 3, 2001 UT 44, 27 P.3d 538, 542 (Utah 2001); *Kelley v. Kelley,* 9 P.3d 171, 178 fn. 6 (Utah App. 2000); and *Hansen v. Hansen,* 958 P.2d 931, 936 (Utah App. 1998). *Compare* from the period prior to the repeal of common law marriage, *Hilton v. Roylance,* 25 Utah 129, 69 P. 660 (1902), in which the Utah Supreme Court stated that the parties' *consensus* "may be inferred from the acts of the parties ... With reference to consent, in case of marriage, no particular form of words is necessary. If, in language mutually understood, or by acts declaratory of intention, the parties accept each other as husband and wife, the marriage is consummated."

lack of express contracts causes substantial evidentiary difficulties. The court stated that if the contract was contested or could not be proven, its existence could be inferred from evidence of cohabitation and general repute and, in such a case, the conduct of the parties provides truly reliable evidence of the nature of their understanding or agreement.[83]

With respect to **Kansas**, the issue of cohabitation as an evidentiary fact has not specifically been addressed in the most recent cases decided by the state courts. In *Fleming v. Fleming* (1977), however, the Kansas Supreme Court stated that a present marriage agreement between the parties may be shown by circumstantial evidence.[84] This same position was adopted by the United States District Court; in applying Kansas law, in *Dixon v. Certainteed Corp.* (1996), the court stated that the agreement may be evidenced by the acts and conduct of the parties.[85]

---

83 *People v. Lucero*, 747 P.2d 660, 664 (Colo. 1987). *See also Deter v. Deter*, 484 P.2d 805, 806 (Colo.Ct.App. 1971), in which the court stated: "It is clear that cohabitation and repute are evidentiary of a marriage contract." *Compare earlier Taylor v. Taylor*, 10 Colo.App. 303, 50 P. 1049 (1897): "It is also agreed that in cases where the contract or agreement is denied, and cannot be shown, its existence may be proven by, and presumed from, evidence of cohabitation as husband and wife, and Gen. repute." The same understanding in principle can be found in *Klipfel v. Klipfel*, 41 Colo. 40, 92 P. 26 (1907); *Smith v. People*, 64 Colo. 290, 170 P. 959, 960 (1918); *Peters v. Peters*, 73 Colo. 271, 215 P. 128, 129 (1923); *Cordas v. Ryan*, 72 Colo. 521, 212 P. 490, 491 (1923); *James v. James*, 97 Colo. 413, 50 P.2d 63, 64 (1935); *Moffat Coal Co. v. Indus. Comm'n*, 108 Colo. 388, 118 P.2d 769 (1941); *Zuzich v. Leyden Lignite Co.*, 120 Colo. 21, 30, 206 P.2d 833, 839 (1949) and *Graham v. Graham*, 130 Colo. 225, 274 P.2d 605, 606 (1954). The same stance recurs in later cases, such as *Knaus v. Relyea*, 746 S.W.2d 389, (Ark.App. 1988), in which Colorado law was applied. No marriage contract was proven, but the court stated that the parties' actions constitute "important evidence of the existence of mutual agreement." *See also Crandell v. Resley*, 804 P.2d 272, 276 (Colo.App. 1990), in which the court stated that a common law marriage is established through the parties' mutual consent or agreement to be husband and wife "as manifested by conduct that gives evidence of the mutual understanding and intent of the parties."

84 *Fleming v. Fleming*, 221 Kan. 290, 559 P.2d 329 (1977); and *In re Estate of Keimig*, 215 Kan. 869, 528 P.2d 1228, 1230 (1974). *See also Driscoll v. Driscoll*, 220 Kan. 225, 552 P.2d 629 (1976), in which the court made a more Gen. reference that the existence of a common law marriage is an evidentiary fact as any other evidentiary fact. *See also Whetstone v. Whetstone*, 178 Kan. 595, 290 P.2d 1022, 1023 (1955), in which the Kansas Supreme Court stated that the legislation (G.S. 1949, 60-1508) partially gave support for the premise that evidence concerning "cohabitation and reputation of the marriage" may be cited as evidence of the marriage. *See also Cain v. Cain*, 160 Kan. 672, 165 P.2d 221, 223 (1946); and already *Renfrow v. Renfrow*, 60 Kan. 277, 56 P. 534, 72 Am.St.Rep. 350 (1899). *Compare In re Estate of Freeman*, 171 Kan. 211, 231 P.2d 261, 263 (1951), where the court stated that the Gen. reputation of the parties with respect to being married or single does not prove or disprove the marriage agreement itself.

85 *Dixon v. Certainteed Corp.*, 915 F.Supp. 1158, 1160 (D.Kan. 1996). *See also Gonzalez v. Satrustegui*, 870 P.2d 1188, 1197 (Ariz.App.Div. 1 1993) (applying Kansas law). In the case of *Freeman*, 171 Kan. 211, 231 P.2d 261, 263 (1951), the court does not seem willing to accept the reputation of the parties as evidence for the marriage contract.

The courts in **Oklahoma**, where the principles concerning common law marriage to a large extent are consistent with those applied in Kansas,[86] despite extensive case law, have also long been reticent to make statements of principles concerning the cohabitation's function as an evidentiary fact. However, in *Standefer v. Standefer* (2001), the Oklahoma Supreme Court stated: "Some evidence of consent to enter into a common-law marriage are cohabitation, actions consistent with the relationship of spouses, recognition by the community of the marital relationship, and declarations by the parties."[87]

The state of the law in **Texas** is more complicated and deserves deeper analysis. As stated above, the legislature at the end of the 1960s codified the principle that the marriage contract could be proven by the fact that the parties lived together as husband and wife and represented to others that they were married, in TEX. FAM. CODE ANN. § 1.91 (b) (West 1993).[88] This paragraph was applied in *Garduno v. Garduno* (1988), in which the Texas Court of Appeals, Corpus Christi, with the support of the above-named principle, found sufficient evidence to show a common law marriage agreement. Because the other requisites were also fulfilled, it was found that a common law marriage had been established.[89] At the same

86 The consistency between Kansas and Oklahoma law was noted by the Oklahoma Supreme Court in *Matter of Estate of Hendrickson*, 248 Kan. 72, 805 P.2d 20, 23 (1991), in which the court applied Oklahoma law.

87 *Standefer v. Standefer*, 26 P.3d 104 (Okla. 2001). See earlier the case of *In re Estate of Hornback*, 475 P.2d 184 (Okla. 1970), where the court stated: "Both cohabitation and reputation are admissible as circumstantial evidence of a common-law contract of marriage." In *Quinton v. Webb*, 207 Okla. 133, 248 P.2d 586, 589 (1952), the Oklahoma Supreme Court stated that "open and notorious cohabitation of the parties is evidentiary of a marriage agreement, other elements being present, while lack of such open cohabitation of the parties may be evidence tending to discredit the alleged agreement." *See also In re Blackhawk's Estate*, 195 Okla. 390, 158 P.2d 168 (1944). In *Richard v. Richard*, 172 Okla. 397, 45 P.2d 101 (1935), the Oklahoma Supreme Court stated that evidence of cohabitation and reputation is admissible as circumstantial evidence with respect to a common law contract of marriage. The court had as a requirement that "such cohabitation must be matrimonial and not meretricious, and must not be irregular, limited, or partial cohabitation." In the case of *In re Graham's Estate*, 169 Okla. 568, 37 P.2d 964, 967 (1934), the Oklahoma Supreme Court interjected as almost obvious that an intention, consent, or agreement "might be implied from this action and conduct." *See Howell v. Adams*, 158 Okla. 239, 13 P.2d 577 (1932) ("Common law marriage may be established by circumstantial evidence"); and *Fender v. Segro*, 41 Okla. 318, 137 P. 103, 105 (1913) ("Marriage, it is true, may be proved by circumstantial evidence"). An earlier case is *Reaves v. Reaves*, 15 Okla. 240, 82 P. 490, 2 L.R.A., N.S., 353 (1905). The requirement for direct evidence existed as an exception, *see, e.g.*, the criminal case, *United States v. Eaton*, 485 F.2d 102 (10th Cir. 1973), in which the United States Court of Appeals stated that the case law in Oklahoma indicated that there must be "direct evidence of a contract." The court referred to *Rainey v. Thomas*, 203 Okla. 401, 222 P.2d 510 (1950). This case in its turn referred to *Richard v. Richard*, 172 Okla. 397, 45 P.2d 101 (1935), which, however, can scarcely be seen as requiring direct evidence as an immutable requirement.

88 Act of June 2, 1969, 61 st Leg., R.S. ch. 888, § 1.91, 1969 Tex.Gen.Laws 2707, 2717.

89 *Garduno v. Garduno*, 760 S.W.2d 735, 739 (Tex.App.-Corpus Christi 1988). The regulation was also applied in *Leal v. Moreno*, 733 S.W.2d 322 (Tex.App.-Corpus

time, the court stated that such a conclusion could not occur contrary to direct evidence which definitely shows that there was no such agreement.[90]

In *Winfield v. Renfro* (1991), the same principles were also applied to a marital contract that was claimed to have been executed in 1982. The Texas Court of Appeals, Houston, stated as its principal stance that evidence concerning an agreement to be married may be inferred from cohabitation and representations, and found, in concurring with the trial court, that the proof in the case at hand was sufficient to prove such a contract.[91] However, no common law marriage was found established, as it was not demonstrated that the parties, in addition, represented to others in Texas that they were married.[92]

Winfield set off a legislative and judicial storm in Texas that requires deeper explanation. Already, during the trial in 1989, in the District Court of Harris County, the case attracted considerable attention from the mass media as well as the Texas legislature.[93] The case generated interest because one party to the case was David Winfield, a famous baseball player. Nevertheless, the case also gave rise to a debate about the principles concerning the formation and very existence of common law marriages. The attention did not diminish after the trial court found that a common law marriage was established based on the relationship that existed between Winfield and his former girlfriend, Sandra Renfro.[94]

Christi 1987), albeit no marriage contract was there found proven. *Cf. Farley v. M.M. Cattle Co.*, 529 S.W.2d 751, 755 (Tex. 1975).

90 *Garduno*, 760 S.W.2d at 739. Other cases from Texas, in which the direct proof was emphasized, are *e.g. Gary v. Gary*, 490 S.W.2d 929, 934 (Tex.Civ.App.-Tyler 1973); *Rush v. Travelers Ins. Co.*, 347 S.W.2d 758, 760 (Tex.Civ.App.-Texarkana 1961); *Clack v. Williams*, 189 S.W.2d 503, 505 (Tex.Civ.App.-San Antonio 1945); and *Perales v. Flores*, 147 S.W.2d 974, 975-976 (Tex.Civ.App.-San Antonio 1941).

91 *Winfield v. Renfro*, 821 S.W.2d 640, 641, 646 (Tex.App.-Houston 1991). Remarkably enough, the court made no reference to § 1.91 (b), a fact that can be explained in two different ways. One alternative is that the court applied the law current as after the legislative amendment enacted on September 1, 1989. In such a case, it is somewhat surprising that the court did not consider the new law or even take notice of the legislative amendments. Another alternative is that the court applied the law applicable prior to the legislative amendment without expressly citing the legislative text. The content of the text as cited above by the court appears to be closer to the second alternative, which is also supported by the court's reference to two cases from the period prior to the legislative amendments, namely *Collora v. Navarro*, 574 S.W.2d 65 (Tex. 1978) and *Matter of Estate of Giessel*, 734 S.W.2d 27 (Tex.Civ. App.-Houston 1987). This is also consistent with the transition regulations, according to which the older law would be applied to those cases brought but not decided as of September 1, 1989 (Act of June 14, 1989 ch. 369, Section 10(b) 1989, Tex. Gen.Laws 1458, 1461). *Winfield* was filed prior to September 1, and the jury gave its verdict in the trial court finding that a common law marriage existed in July of 1989

92 *Winfield*, 821 S.W.2d at 651.

93 *See e.g.* Houston Post Mar. 23, 1990, B-6, col. 1.

94 *Winfield*, 821 S.W.2d at 641.

A proposal to repeal common law marriage was presented to the legislature,[95] but the outcome was a compromise.[96] The institution survived, but was amended on two issues. First, the legislature repealed the regulation that expressly stated that the courts could find the existence of a marriage contract based on the facts that the parties lived together as husband and wife and that they represented to others that they were married, TEX. FAM. CODE ANN. § 1.91(b)(Vernon supp. 1991).[97] Further, a new

---

95 State Representative Patricia Hill from Dallas presented a proposal in 1989 concerning the repeal of common law marriage in Texas, House Bill (H.B.) No. 588, 71st Leg. Sess. (1989). The primary motivation for the proposal was the legal uncertainty concerning the parties' status with the dissolution of a common law marriage (Patricia Hill, floor debate remarks, 71st Leg.Sess., House Recording No. (H.R.) 62 and 78). H.B. 588 was adopted by barely a majority (73 votes to 61) in the House of Representatives, but was never taken up by the Senate. The objections to the repeal of common law marriage were based, *inter alia,* on references to the needs of any children and of women for protection in the formless relationship. Among the critics was State Representative Ron Wilson, who characterized the proposal as "the yuppie shackin' up insurance bill."

96 Senate Bill, (S.B.) No. 307 (Senate Author: Bob Glasgow, House Sponsor: Patricia Hill). Senate Recording No. 127.

97 Act of June 14, 1989, 71 st Leg., R.S., ch. 369 § 9, 1989, effective Sept. 1, 1989, Tex. Gen.Laws 1458, 1461. TEX. FAM. CODE ANN. § 1.91(b) (Vernon Supp. 1991). The enactment of a one-year statute of limitations was designed to prevent the parties from having the risk of a trial hanging over their heads their entire future. A one year period, according to which "a proceeding in which a marriage is to be proved under this section must be commenced not later than one year after the date on which the relationship ended" was commenced from the date that the parties' "cohabitation" ceased, *see Georgiades v. Di Ferrante,* 871 S.W.2d 878, 881 (Tex.App.-Houston, 14th Dist. 1994); *Riley v. State,* 849 S.W.2d 901, 902 (Tex.App.-Austin 1993); *Villages of Greenbriar v. Torres,* 874 S.W.2d 259 (Tex.App.-Houston, 1 Dist. 1994); and *White v. State Farm Mut. Auto. Ins. Co.,* 907 F.Supp 1012, 1017 (E.D.Tex. 1995). In *Mossler v. Shields,* 818 S.W.2d 752 (Tex. 1991), according to Texas Supreme Court, this period was not found to be in conflict with State or public policy. Neither according to the Texas Court of Appeals in *Dannelly v. Almond,* 827 S.W.2d 582, 585 (Tex.App.-Houston 1992), was the period found to be in conflict with any constitutional rights. *Compare* however *White v. State Farm Mut. Auto. Ins. Co.,* 907 F.Supp 1012, 1017-119 (E.D.Tex. 1995), in which the United States District Court found that the period was in conflict with the Equal Protection clause of the United States Constitution. The Court has taken the same stance with respect to statutes of limitations governing the legitimacy of children, *see Mills v. Habluetzel,* 456 U.S. 91, 102 S. Ct. 1549, 71 L.Ed.2d 770 (1982). The one year period in § 1.91(b) was repealed by the Act of May 24, 1995, 74th Leg., R.S., ch. 891, § 1, 1995. The amendment, however, did not have any retroactive effect, *see White v. State Farm Mut. Auto. Ins. Co.,* 907 F.Supp. 1012, 1016 (E.D.Tex. 1995). The one year period has not been viewed as being in conflict with the two-year period according to the Medical Liability and Insurance Improvement Act, *see Shepherd v. Ledford,* 962 S.W.2d 28 (Tex. 1998). In *Nava v. Reddy Partnership/Quail Chase,* 988 S.W.2d 346, 350 (Tex.App.-Houston 1999), a widow did not need to file a wrongful death action within one year from the death of the man, as she had within this period applied for widow benefits. The period was later extended to two years, after which it is presumed that the parties have not entered into a marriage contract and the regulation was placed in § 2.401 (b), *see* Act of April 17, 1997, 75th Leg., R.S., ch. 7, § 1, 1997 Tex.Sess.Law.Serv. 15 (Vernon 1997). Today the regulations are found in TEX. FAM. CODE ANN. § 2.401(b) (Vernon Pamph. 1998) (Vernon 2005). In *Amaye v. Oravetz,* 57 S.W.3d 581 (Tex.App.-Houston, 14 Dist., 2001), the presumption was not rebutted. In *Lopez-Rodriguez v. City of Levelland,* 2004 WL 1746045 (N.D.Tex. 2004), the court held that the plaintiff must

enactment required that a complaint with respect to a common law marriage must be filed during a prescribed period of one year from the date that the relationship was terminated. Later, the period was extended to two years. In addition, the two-year period is no longer an absolute bar to the filing of a complaint; after two years, it is rebuttably presumed that the partiers did not enter into an agreement to be married according to TEX. FAM. CODE ANN. § 2.401(b) (Vernon 1998 and Supp. 2004).

The repeal of the legislation with respect to the ability of the courts to find, from the parties' cohabitation and reputations, the existence of a marriage contract raises the issue of whether inferred agreements are still permitted. Different interpretations have been expressed in the legal literature. On the one hand, according to Kathryn Vaughn, who appears to have understood the reform as a requirement for an express marital contract, the amendment should effectively abrogate common law marriage in Texas because the burden of proving an express agreement is simply too high for most persons attempting to establish a common law marriage.[98] Joseph McKnight, on the other hand, has maintained that the courts, in many cases, still could find a tacit agreement to be married based solely on circumstantial evidence, but that the evidence with respect to a holding out in the future must be "more convincing" than before the 1989 amendment.[99]

The development in the case law appears to have followed McKnight's view, albeit the courts have displayed considerable uncertainty about the content of the 1989 legislation. In *Russell v. Russell* (1992), the Texas Court of Appeals, Beaumont, stated that an agreement to be married "may be inferred from direct or circumstantial evidence which preponderates that parties lived together in state of Texas and did, in Texas, represent to others that they were married." The court, however, understood the 1989 legislative amendment as a challenge to the courts to give a more detailed review of evidence on issues of common law marriage.[100] The court found a marriage contract proven, albeit the date of its commencement could not be established. During the same time, the Court of Appeals, Dallas,

---

have initiated either a proceeding to declare the existence of the common law marriage or filed a wrongful death/survival action within two years of the decedent's death.

98 Vaughn, *supra* note 13, at 1161. According to *Sampson,* the purpose of the amendment was "to restore to the fact finding process the issue of whether there was agreement to be married," *see* John J. Sampson, *Legislation Affecting Family Law Practice,* The 71 st Legislature Regular Session 89-1, STATE BAR SEC. FAM. L. REPT. 1,8 (1989). With respect to the legislative proposal and the debate in the Senate, *see* Senate Bill No. 307 and Senate Recording No. 127, 71st Leg.Sess. (1989); and DON KOON, HANDBOOK OF TEXAS FAMILY LAW § 2.2 (1996). *See also* the dissenting opinion in *Russell v. Russell,* 865 S.W.2d 929, 933 (Tex. 1993).

99 Joseph McKnight, *Family Law: Husband and Wife,* 44 SW. L.J. 1, 2 (1990). *See* the same author in Texas Family Code Symposium-Title 1. *Husband and wife,* 21 TEX. TECH L. REV. 911, 939 (1990).

100 *Russell v. Russell,* 838 S.W.2d 909, 913 (Tex.App.-Beaumont 1992).

in deciding *Lorensen v. Weaber* (1992), expressed uncertainty about the evidentiary requirement that was to be applied after the 1989 amendment, but viewed it as clear that such evidence did not exist in the present case.[101] In *Flores v. Flores* (1993), the Court of Appeals, Waco, stated with reference to general principles, that the marital legislation allowed an agreement to be married to be proven through wholly circumstantial evidence.[102] Unsurprisingly, however, the court did not find that a marriage contract was proven with reference to the circumstances of the case.

The cases of *Russell v. Russell* and *Lorensen v. Weaber* were appealed and heard together by the Texas Supreme Court (1993). The court found that the law did not require direct evidence with respect to an agreement to be married in order to establish a common law marriage. According to the view of the court, it could be proven by circumstantial evidence. The court further stated that proof of cohabitation and representations to others that the couple is married may constitute circumstantial evidence of an agreement to be married, but maintained that sufficient evidence with respect to the elements of "cohabitation and public representations" were not necessarily sufficient evidence with respect to a marriage contract. Both cases were remanded for a new trial.[103]

The case naturally raises questions about the changes introduced by the 1989 amendment. Two dissenting judges on the Texas Supreme Court did not share the majority's view that an agreement to be married could still be proved by circumstantial evidence, but rather interpreted the amendments so that the legislation now requires direct evidence, either written or oral, of a contract. Such an interpretation, according to the dissent, should prevent "accidental marriages" in which cohabitation and holding out are used to bind a party that has never intended to enter into a marriage. They further maintained that the majority opinion was congruent with the system that the legislature had repealed, and thus ignored the intent of the legislature to make it more difficult to prove an informal marriage. According to the dissent, the majority's view conflicted with the separation of powers doctrine of the United State Constitution, according to which the legislature has the power to amend the law, which the courts then do not have the right to amend. According to the dissent, the majority's interpretation was also in conflict with the presumption that the legislature does nothing without a purpose.[104]

---

101 *Lorensen v. Weaber*, 840 S.W.2d 644 (Tex.App.-Dallas 1992). The actual circumstances in the case, however, were such that it was altogether clear that a marriage contract could not be viewed as proven, either under the new or the old law.

102 *Flores v. Flores*, 847 S.W.2d 648, 652 (Tex.App.-Waco 1993). Also in *Quinonez-Saa v. State*, 860 S.W.2d 704, 710 (Tex.App.-Houston (1 Dist.) 1993), the court accepted an implied contract by maintaining that the parties must have entered into an express or implied agreement.

103 *Russell v. Russell*, 865 S.W.2d 929, 933 (Tex. 1993).

104 *Id.* at 935-936, with reference to *Hunter v. Fort Worth Capital Corp.*, 620 S.W.2d 547, 551 (Tex. 1981); and *Cameron v. Terrell 6 Garrett*, Inc., 618 S.W.2d 535, 540 (Tex. 1981).

It is possible to object to the reasoning of the dissent. First, the constitutional concerns appear unwarranted. If the 1989 reform is interpreted from an historical perspective, it is noteworthy that the repealed regulation, originally enacted in 1969, expressly allowing a formless marriage contract to be inferred from parties' cohabitation and representation, was simply a codification of the previously applicable case law.[105] Consequently, the actual regulation was nothing more than a clarification. When the regulation in question was taken out of the system in 1989, one was back to the situation applicable prior to 1969, *i.e.*, without any express clarification in the legislation. Consequently, the current law addresses only the substantive elements to be fulfilled, of which one is the marriage contract, but is silent as to the proving. Therefore, it does not follow that there is any prohibition against citing circumstantial evidence, nor does the absence of an express regulation mean that there is a prohibition for citing direct evidence. From the general principles, just the opposite can be derived, namely, both types of evidence can be cited as long as the legislature does not prohibit it. The legislature, naturally, has the power to enact limitations concerning the ability to present evidence, but only by express regulation.[106] The intent of the legislature is, of course, interesting to the interpretation of a statute, but the purpose alone does not constitute the regulation. The legislature's intent to limit the ability to establish a common law marriage was enacted through the creation of the one-year statute of limitations. In contrast, no regulation was enacted with respect to the proving. As no such rule was enacted, the Texas Supreme Court's stance in *Russell* cannot be seen to be in conflict with the legislation. The constitutional objections, thus, appear to have no weight.

Has the status of the law changed in Texas after the 1989 amendment in general with respect to the proving of a formless marriage contract? This does not appear to be the case. It certainly is of pedagogical value that McKnight notes that circumstantial evidence in the form of the parties' cohabitation and holding out must be "convincing" to prove the existence of an agreement to be married and that, the court notes that such evidence does not necessarily constitute sufficient evidence of a contract. However, this requirement does not appear to be new. During the

105 Act of June 2, 1969, 61 st Leg., R.S., ch. 888, § 1, 1969, effective Jan 1, 1970. Tex. Gen.Laws 2707, 2717; TEX. FAM. CODE ANN. § 1.91(b) (Vernon 1975).

106 *Compare* the historically well based principle in the case law according to which form requirements with respect to the commencement of a marriage were considered simply a "directory," and not mandatory, holding the door to common law marriage open as long as the legislature, through express regulations, does not declare the commencement of a relationship in conflict with the form requirements to be invalid. *See, e.g., Meister v. Moore*, 96 U.S. 76, 78 (1877). With respect to Texas case law, *see, e.g., Ingersol v. McWillie*, 9 Tex.Civ.App. 543, 30 S.W. 56, 61 (1895); *Cumby v. Garland*, 6 Tex.Civ.App. 519, 25 S.W. 676 (1894); *Simon v. State*, 31 Tex. Crim.Rep. 186, 37 Am.St.Rep. 802, 20 S.W. 399, 401 (1892); and *Robertson v. Cole*, 12 Tex. 356 (1854). For more as to this, *see* Section 4.3 *supra*.

twenty years that the statute was in effect, 1969 to 1989,[107] as well as prior to its enactment,[108] finding the existence of a marital contract from the parties' cohabitation and representation did not include the possibility that the existence of certain circumstances could automatically allow a legal presumption that there was a contract. Instead, the courts have had to determine, case by case, whether a marriage contract, as well as the elements of cohabitation and holding out, have been proven. Therewith, they have been able to consider direct evidence as well as circumstantial evidence. The latter could be the facts of the parties' cohabitation and representations, but also other circumstances. The concepts *cohabitation* and *representations* have not limited the ability to present circumstantial evidence, but rather have been examples of two related groups of relevant circumstances. The removal of the statutory paragraph, therefore,

---

107 *See, e.g., Howard v. Howard,* 459 S.W.2d 901 (Tex.Civ.App. 1970); *Morris v. Morris,* 463 S.W.2d 295 (Tex.Civ.App.-Houston 1971); *Collora v. Navarro,* 574 S.W.2d 65 (Tex. 1978); *Rodriguez v. Avalos,* 567 S.W.2d 85, 86 (Tex.Civ.App.-El Paso 1978); and *In re Glasco,* 619 S.W.2d 567, 570-571 (Tex.Civ.App.-San Antonio 1981) ("We hold that there was sufficient evidence to uphold the trial court's implied findings that the parties agreed to be husband and wife"). In the case of *Estate of Claveria v. Claveria,* 615 S.W.2d 164, 166 (Tex. 1981), the Texas Supreme Court stated that the marriage can be proven with the same type of evidence as other facts, and as a consequence thereof, "proof of common-law marriage may be shown by the conduct of the parties." *See also Leal v. Moreno,* 733 S.W.2d 322 (Tex.Civ.App. 1987) (contract not proven); *Garduno v. Garduno,* 760 S.W.2d 735, 740 (Tex.App.-Corpus Christi 1988) (contract proven after evidence presented); and *Winfield v. Renfro,* 821 S.W.2d 640, 644 (Tex.App.-Houston 1991) (contract and cohabitation proven, however not holding out).

108 *See,* e.g., *Humphreys v. Humphreys,* 364 S.W.2d 177, 178 (Tex. 1963), in which the court first found that the evidence "shows without dispute that Oscar and Hazel cohabited and held themselves out to the public as husband and wife." Thereafter the court heard the evidence concerning the marital contract and drew the following conclusion: "In view of this evidence, the trial court could reasonably conclude that Oscar and Hazel did not agree to become husband and wife." In *Shelton v. Belknap,* 155 Tex. 37, 282 S.W.2d 682, 684 (1955), the court stated that the contract necessary for the formation of a common law marriage "need not be an express agreement; it may be implied" and that such a contract "ordinarily may be inferred from the evidence which establishes ... the living and cohabiting together and the holding out to the public." After the court found the requisites of cohabitation and holding out proven, there was no automatic conclusion with respect to the existence of a marital contract. The court instead tried this question separately and found that the "evidence was sufficient to support jury finding that deceased and alleged wife mutually and unequivocally agreed to become husband and wife." In *Baker v. Mays & Mays,*199 S.W.2d 279, 284 (Tex.Civ.App.-Ft. Worth 1946), the court stated: "That, proof of living together under the same name, introducing each other as husband and wife respectively, recognizing their children and in many other respects tending to show their marital status, is sufficient to prove a marriage." In other cases where cohabitation and holding out have principally been accepted as evidence for the contract, after the separate evidentiary hearing, no contract has been found proven, *see, e.g., Clack v. Williams,* 189 S.W.2d 503 (Tex.Civ.App.-San Antonio 1945). In the older cases, *see, e.g., U.S. Fid. & Guar. v. Dowdle,* 269 S.W. 119, 126 (Tex.Civ.App. 1924), in which the court stated that the marriage "may be shown by circumstantial as well as by direct evidence. It may in a proper case be inferred from continuous cohabitation and repute," albeit no marriage was found proven.

has linguistically but not substantively expanded the evidentiary possibilities. Given the long and rich case law in Texas concerning the proving of marriage contracts, it is therefore appropriate to revisit *Tarpley v. Poage's Adm'r* (1847), in which the court recommended a consideration of evidence of cohabitation, reputation, acknowledgment of parties, reception in the family, and other circumstances from which an inference of marriage could be drawn.[109]

Now that the legislative and judicial storm fueled by the 1989 amendment in Texas has cooled, it can be argued that nothing has actually happened with respect to the status of the law.[110] Nevertheless, there is reason to reconsider the issue of the evidentiary importance of cohabitation and holding out, respectively. A valuation thereof assumes a picture of that to be proven, *i.e.*, of that which the marriage contract actually ought to contain.[111]

If we now turn to the three states in the Southeast, the issue of whether a verbal marital contract is required for the formation of a common law marriage has been the object of decisions in **Alabama**. In *Piel v. Brown* (1978), a party argued that a verbal contract was required. The Alabama Supreme Court, however, stated that the court had never required actual words and that the parties' intent to establish a common law marriage can be inferred from the circumstances.[112] There are even cases in which the

109 *Tarpley v. Poage's Adm'r*, 2 Tex. 139, 149 (1847).

110 Later case law appears to have followed *Russell*, *see Welch v. State*, 908 S.W.2d 258, 265 (Tex.App.-El Paso 1995); *Dalworth Trucking Co. v. Bulen*, 924 S.W.2d 728, 737 (Tex.App.-Texarkana 1996); *Villegas v. Griffin Industries*, 975 S.W.2d 745, 749 (Tex. App.-Corpus Christi 1998); and *Lee v. Lee*, 981 S.W.2d 903 (Tex.App.-Houston 1998). In *Eris v. Phares*, 39 S.W.3d 708, 714 (Tex.App.-Houston (1 Dist.) 2001), the court stated that evidence of an agreement to be married "may be inferred from cohabitation and representations." In *Mills v. Mest*, 94 S.W.3d 72 (Tex.App.-Houston (14th Dist.) 2002), the court maintained that an agreement to be married may be established by circumstantial evidence, but did not find a common law marriage proven. In *Lewis v. Anderson*, 173 S.W.3d 556, 559 (Tex.App.-Dallas 2005), the court held that the proponent of a common law marriage may prove an agreement to be married by circumstantial evidence as well as direct evidence and that evidence of cohabitation, and representations that the couple is married, may constitute circumstantial evidence. A common law marriage was established. In *Hart v. Webster*, 2006 WL 1707975 (Tex.App.-Austin 2006), the court remanded a paternity case and held that no reasonable fact-finder could have ignored the uncontested evidence that the parties lived together and represented themselves as married. Moreover, the court held that no reasonable fact-finder could have determined that the parties did not implicitly agree to be married after the two had divorced their prior spouses and exchanged wedding rings. The court held that legally there was insufficient evidence to support the district court's finding that there was no marriage. Under §§ 160.204(a)(3) and (a)(4)(C), TEX. FAM. CODE ANN. (West Supp. 2005), a person is presumed the father if he was married to the child's mother at the birth of the child, or if he (1) marries the child's mother after the child is born, (2) voluntarily asserts paternity, and (3) promises in a record to support the child as his own.

111 For more on the content of the marital contract, *see* Section 6.3.

112 *Piel v. Brown*, 361 So.2d 90, 94 (Ala. 1978). As support for the requirement of a verbal contract, *Whitworth v. Whitworth*, 256 Ala. 296, 54 So.2d 575 (1951) was cited,

cohabitation was given a very high evidentiary weight, and the marriage contract was found to be in the actual cohabitation. In *Boswell v. Boswell* (1986), the court consequently found that the parties, after an impediment to the marriage had been removed, continued to live together, holding themselves out as husband and wife, thereby mutually agreeing to a common law marriage.[113] The courts today follow these decisions. Not only is the parties' cohabitation and holding out as spouses relevant, but so are all the surrounding circumstances.[114]

Of the large number of cases concerning common law marriage decided in **Georgia**, there are relatively few cases in which the courts have more directly addressed the issue of the value of the cohabitation as an evidentiary fact. In *Brown v. Brown* (1975), the Georgia Supreme Court, however, stated that the existence of a marriage contract "may be shown by such circumstances as the act of living together as man and wife, holding themselves out to the world as such, and repute in the vicinity and among neighbors and visitors that they are such, together with all such facts as usually accompany the marriage relation and indicate the factum of marriage."[115] A common law marriage was found proven based on a

---

in which the court cited the following from a case in Florida: "There must be words of present assent *per verba de praesenti.*" *See In re Price's Estate,* 127 Fla. 467, 176 So. 492, 493 (1937). The court in *Piel v. Brown,* however, referred *inter alia* to *Sloss-Sheffield Steel & Iron Co. v. Watford,* 245 Ala. 425, 17 So.2d 166 (1944) and *Beck v. Beck,* 286 Ala. 692, 697, 246 So.2d 420, 425 (1971) ("no particular words are necessary to constitute a valid common-law marriage"). *See also Smith v. Smith,* 247 Ala. 213, 23 So.2d 605, 609 (1945) and later *Skipworth v. Skipworth,* 360 So.2d 975 (Ala. 1978). Among the older cases, *see Bynon v. State,* 117 Ala. 80, 23 So. 640 (1898) and *Prince v. Edwards,* 175 Ala. 532, 57 So. 714 (1912).

113 *Boswell v. Boswell,* 497 So.2d 479, 480 (Ala. 1986).

114 *Hall v. Duster,* 727 So.2d 834, 836 (Ala.Civ.App. 1999) ("an agreement may be inferred from all the surrounding circumstances"); and *Waller v. Waller,* 567 So.2d 869 (Ala.Civ.App. 1990) ("present intention is inferred from cohabitation and public recognition"). *Compare Crosson v. Crosson,* 668 So.2d 868, 869 (Ala.Civ.App. 1995) (the marital presumption was applied); and *Butler v. Coonrod,* 671 So.2d 750, 751 (Ala.Civ.App. 1996). For older cases *see, e.g., Etheridge v. Yeager,* 465 So.2d 378 (Ala. 1985); *Walton v. Walton,* 409 So.2d 858 (Ala.Civ.App. 1982); *Barnett v. Barnett,* 262 Ala. 655, 80 So.2d 626 (1955); *Vinson v. Vinson,* 260 Ala. 254, 69 So.2d 431, 433 (1953); *Sloss-Sheffield Steel & Iron Co. v. Watford,* 245 Ala. 425, 17 So.2d 166 (1944); and *Walker v. Walker,* 218 Ala. 16, 117 So. 472 (1928).

115 *Brown v. Brown,* 234 Ga. 300, 215 S.E.2d 671, 672 (1975). The court cited *Drawdy v. Hesters,* 130 Ga. 163, 60 S.E. 451, 452 (1908). *See also Chance v. Chance,* 60 Ga. App. 889, 5 S.E.2d 399 (1939); *Carr v. Walker,* 205 Ga. 1, 9, 52 S.E.2d 426 (1949); *Mortensen v. Mortensen,* 225 N.Y.S.2d 323 (Sup.Ct. 1962) (applying Georgia law); *Murray v. Clayton,* 151 Ga.App. 720, 261 S.E.2d 455 (1979); and *Scott v. Jefferson,* 174 Ga.App. 651, 653 (2), 331 S.E.2d 1 (1985). The statement in *Brown* is cited in later cases such as *Baynes v. Baynes,* 219 Ga.App. 848, 467 S.E.2d 195, 196 (1996); *Wright v. Goss,* 229 Ga.App. 393, 494 S.E.2d 23, 25 (1997); and *In re Estate of Wilson,* 512 S.E.2d 383, 385 (Ga.App. 1999) and *In re Estate of Love,* 274 Ga.App. 316, 319, 618 S.E.2d 97, 100 (2005). *Compare Foster v. Foster,* 178 Ga. 791, 174 S.E. 532 (1934). Without any more principle statements concerning the value of circumstantial evidence, a common law marriage was found proven based on such evidence as in *Beals v. Beals,* 203 Ga.App. 81, 416 S.E.2d 301 (1992) and in *Brown v. Carr,* 198 Ga.App. 567, 402 S.E.2d 296 (1991), despite the fact that in the latter case,

ten-year cohabitation, of which, only one year was without an impediment to the marriage.

In the third state in the Southeast, namely **South Carolina,** the court in *Kirkby v. Kirkby* (1978) tried the issue of whether a marriage contract existed, despite the fact that no express agreement had been entered into. In the case, the parties had commenced their relationship while the woman was still married to another man. Their relationship was therefore illicit and still presumed to be illicit when the impediment was removed four years later through a marital divorce. This presumption had to, therefore, be broken by a new marriage agreement. After the impediment was removed, the parties continued to cohabit for sixteen years. They had four mutual children and represented themselves outwardly as husband and wife. The South Carolina Supreme Court stated that such a contract "may just rest in circumstances" and found that the proving "demonstrates the parties' new mutual agreement to enter into a common law marriage."[116] The South Carolina Court of Appeals, in *Yarbrough v. Yarbrough* (1984), later adopted the same stance, in principle, albeit no contract was found proven. The court stated that a cohabiting couple must, to establish a common law marriage after the removal of an impediment to the marriage, be in agreement to enter into such a marriage and added that an agreement thereof may be gathered from the conduct of the parties.[117]

---

an impediment to the marriage existed when the cohabitation was commenced. A clear example of the older law can be found in *Jenkins v. Jenkins*, 83 Ga. 286, 9 S. E. 541 (1889). Even if common law marriage was repealed in Georgia in 1997, relationships contracted before January 1, 1997 are recognized, see GA. CODE ANN. §§ 19-3-1, 19-3-1.1 (1997).

116 *Kirkby v. Kirkby*, 270 S.C. 137, 241 S.E.2d 415, 416, 417 (1978). With respect to the older case law, *see Fryer v. Fryer*, 9 S.C.Eq. (Rich.Cas.) 85, 98 (1832); *Stringfellow v. Scott*, 9 S.C.Eq. (Rich.Cas.) 109 (1832); *Lucken v. Wichman*, 5 S.C. 411 (1874); *Blackburn v. Crawfords*, 3 Wall. 195, 18 L.Ed. 186 (1886); *Tedder v. Tedder* 108 S.C. 271, 94 S.E. 19, 20, 2 A.L.R. 438 (1917); *Jackson v. United States*, 14 F.Supp. 132 (D.C.S.C. 1936), *aff'd*, 89 F.2d 572 (1937), *aff'd*, 302 U.S. 628, 82 L.ed 488, 58 S.Ct. 390 (1938) (applying South Carolina law); *Rodgers v. Heron*, 226 S.C. 317, 85 S.E.2d 104 (1954); and *Johnson v. Johnson*, 235 S.C. 542, 112 S.E.2d 647, 651 (1960).

117 *Yarbrough v. Yarbrough*, 280 S.C. 546, 551, 314 S.E.2d 16, 19 (App. 1984). Even if the court in *Yarbrough* had not found any contract proven, the statement was later cited in *Prevatte v. Prevatte*, 297 S.C. 345, 377 S.E.2d 114, 117 (App. 1989) and *Johns v. Johns*, 420 S.E.2d 856, 858 (S.C.App. 1992). *See also Bochette v. Bochette*, 386 S.E.2d 475, 477 (S.C.App. 1989), in which the court, with reference to *Prevatte v. Prevatte*, stated that "the agreement may be shown by conduct of the parties." *Compare Jennings v. Hurt*, 554 N.Y.S.2d 220 (A.D. 1 Dep't 1990), in which the parties lived together for two months and ten days in South Carolina and in which the plaintiff claimed that she and the defendant had entered into a common law marriage "by virtue of having held themselves out as husband and wife." The New York Supreme Court, Appellate Division, stated with reference to *Collier v. City of Milford*, 537 A.2d 474, 478-479 (Conn. 1988), that the mutual agreement "must be conveyed with such a demonstration of intent and with such a clarity on the part of the parties that marriage does not creep up on either of them and catch them unawares. One cannot be married unwittingly or accidentally" and found that there was neither a mutual intent nor an agreement to enter into a marriage contract,

The South Carolina Supreme Court in *Callen v. Callen* (2005) stated that today no express contract is necessary and the agreement may be inferred from the circumstances, and it seems to be common that a common law marriage is proven with the support of circumstantial evidence.[118]

With respect to Iowa, the **Iowa** Supreme Court stated in the case of *In re Marriage of Martin* (2004) that: "An implied agreement may support a common law marriage where one party intends present marriage and the conduct of the other party reflects the same intent."[119] There are also cases in which the courts have maintained that the parties' marital *consensus* cannot be proven simply through their cohabitation. In addition, evidence of their actions in relation to each other and their understanding of their relationship are also required.[120] Iowa case law contains cases in which a

---

and as a consequence thereof, no common law marriage was established. With respect to a cohabitation of six weeks in South Carolina after the removal of an impediment to the marriage, *see Parker v. Parker*, 46 N.C.App. 254, 265 S.E.2d 237 (1980). *Compare Richland Memorial Hosp. v. English*, 295 S.C. 511, 369 S.E.2d 395, 396 (1988), in which the court appears rather to have applied the marital presumption. *See also Jeanes v. Jeanes*, 255 S.C. 161, 177 S.E.2d 537 (1970); and *In re Greenfield's Estate*, 245 S.C. 595, 141 S.E.2d 916 (1965).

118 *Callen v. Callen*, 365 S.C. 618, 620 S.E.2d 59 (2005); and *Barker v. Baker*, 330 S.C. 361, 499 S.E.2d 503, 507 (App. 1998) ("Thus, the existence of a common law marriage frequently is proved by circumstantial evidence").

119 *In re Marriage of Martin*, 681 N.W.2d 612 (Iowa 2004). In *Conklin v. MacMillan Oil Co.*, 557 N.W.2d 102, 105 (Iowa App. 1996), the court stated: "Proof of cohabitation, as well as evidence of conduct and Gen. repute in the community where the parties reside, tends to strengthen the showing of present agreement to be husband and wife, as well as bearing upon the question of intent." *See also In re Marriage of Gebhardt*, 426 N.W.2d 651, 652 (Iowa App. 1988). The court cited *Gammelgaard v. Gammelgaard*, 247 Iowa 979, 980, 77 N.W.2d 479, 480 (1956), where the Iowa Supreme Court made a similar statement. *See further In re Marriage of Winegard*, 257 N.W.2d 609, 617 (Iowa 1977), in which the Iowa Supreme Court stated that "it is well established circumstantial evidence may be relied upon to demonstrate a common law marriage." *See further In re Marriage of Winegard*, 278 N.W.2d 505, 511 (Iowa 1979); *In re Estate of Fisher*, 176 N.W.2d 801, 806 (Iowa 1970); *State v. Lawson*, 165 N.W.2d 838, 839 (Iowa 1969); *In re Estate of Malli*, 260 Iowa 252, 256, 149 N.W.2d 155, 158 (1967); *Coleman v. Graves*, 255 Iowa 396, 402, 122 N.W.2d 853 (1963); and *In re Estate of Allen*, 251 Iowa 177, 182, 100 N.W.2d 10, 12 (1959). *Compare Jambrone v. David*, 16 Ill.2d 32, 156 N.E.2d 569 (1959), in which the Illinois Supreme Court, applying Iowa law, considered the parties' conduct and reputation as "evidential factors," but in which no common law marriage was found proven. *See also State v. Grimes*, 215 Iowa 1287, 247 N.W. 664 (1933); *In re Estate of Medford*, 197 Iowa 76, 196 N.W. 728 (1924); *In re Estate of Wittick*, 164 Iowa 485, 493, 145 N.W. 913, 916 (1914); *Pegg v. Pegg*, 138 Iowa 572, 115 N.W. 1027 (1908); *Brisbin v. Huntington*, 128 Iowa 166, 103 N.W. 144 (1905); and *McFarland v. McFarland*, 51 Iowa 565, 2 N.W. 269, 273-274 (1879).

120 *See In re Estate of Fisher*, 176 N.W.2d 801, 806 (Iowa 1970), in which the Iowa Supreme Court stated: "[N]either such intention nor consent can be inferred from cohabitation alone." *See also State v. Lawson*, 165 N.W.2d 838 (Iowa 1969). *Compare* already *Brisbin v. Huntington*, 128 Iowa 166, 103 N.W. 144, 145 (1905), applying Nebraska law and in which the court, in addition to the parties' cohabitation, noted "the acts of the parties," their treatment of each other and their reputation among others. The court cited a case from Pennsylvania, namely *In re Grimm's Estate*, 131 Pa. 199, 18 A. 1061 (1889), which is a presumption case, as well as one from Illinois, *McKenna v. McKenna*, 180 Ill. 577, 584, 54 N.E. 641 (1899).

couple of months of cohabitation has been sufficient to infer a present intent and agreement to be married and cases in which eighteen years of cohabitation was not enough.[121]

In **Ohio**, the Ohio Supreme Court (per curiam) stated, as to the issue in *Nestor v. Nestor* (1984), that the contract of marriage may be proven by way of "proof of cohabitation, acts, declarations, and the conduct of the parties and their recognized status in the community in which they reside." In a fairly nuanced commentary, the court further stated that if there was no direct evidence concerning the commencement of the contract, "testimony regarding cohabitation and community reputation tends to raise an inference of the marriage. This inference is given more or less strength according to the circumstances of the particular case. The inference is generally strengthened with the lapse of time during which the parties are living together and cohabiting as man and wife." However, it ought to be noted that there was an oral contract between the spouses in the case, with respect to which the court added that "the evidence of long-time cohabitation and reputation of living together as man and wife should be given even greater weight to further strengthen the inference of marriage."[122] If direct evidence exists in the case, for example, in the form of the parties' own statements of the content that no marriage contract existed, or by the party claiming the existence of a common law marriage that a marriage had been entered into, the parties' cohabitation and reputation as husband and wife, however, are not sufficient to establish a common law marriage.[123] Even the Ohio 1991 legislation recognizes the value of

121 *Compare In re Estate of Fisher*, 176 N.W.2d 801, 806 (Iowa 1970) and *Fritz v. Mork*, 2001 Iowa App. LEXIS 594 (2001).

122 *Nestor v. Nestor*, 15 Ohio St.3d 143, 15 O.B.R. 291, 472 N.E.2d 1091, 1094-1095 (1984) (per curiam). The main issue, however, was whether the parties fulfilled the requirement of outwardly appearing as spouses. The case is therefore discussed *infra* concerning holding out, *see* Section 8.6. The statement concerning the cohabitation's function as an evidentiary fact is cited later by the Ohio Court of Appeals in *Fields v. Fields*, 530 N.E.2d 933, 936 (Ohio App. 1987), *Fitzgerald v. Mayfield*, 584 N.E.2d 13, 17 (Ohio App. 4 Dist. 1990), *In re Estate of Hall*, 588 N.E.2d 203, 206 (Ohio App. 4 Dist. 1990), *Warren Gen. Hosp. v. Brink*, 80 Ohio App.3d 793, 610 N.E.2d 1128, 1130 (1992); *Reyes v. Vasquez*, 2005 WL 1389076 (Ohio App. 6 Dist. 2005); *Faison v. Faison*, 2005 WL 1303344 (Ohio App. 8 Dist. 2005); and *Bevan v. Bevan*, 2006 WL 1519654 (Ohio App. 11 Dist. 2006). In *Warren Gen. Hosp.*, the court found that there was "evidence that they cohabited and that they held themselves out to the community as husband and wife and were considered as such." The court's conclusion from these facts as to the existence of a contract was clear: "From this, the present agreement could be inferred." *See* already *Houpt v. Houpt*, 5 Ohio 539 (1832); *Carmichael v. State*, 12 Ohio St. 553 (1861); *Johnson v. Dudley*, 3 Ohio N.P. 196 (1896); *Umbenhower v. Labus*, 85 Ohio St. 238, 97 N.E. 832 (1912); *Dirion v. Brewer*, 20 Ohio.App. 298, 151 N.E. 818 (1925); *Markley v. Hudson*, 143 Ohio St. 163, 28 O.O. 81, 54 N.E.2d 304, 306 (1944); *Dibble v. Dibble*, 88 Ohio App. 490, 100 N.E.2d 451 (1950); *Leibrock v. Leibrock*, 63 Ohio Law Abs. 565, 107 N.E.2d 418 (Ohio Com.Pl. 1952); *In re McLaughlin's Estate*, 197 N.E.2d 578 (Ohio P.Ct. 1963); and *Merritt v. Chevrolet Tonawanda Div.*, G.M.C., 50 A.D.2d 1018, 377 N.Y.S.2d 663 (1975) (applying Ohio law).

123 *Jolley v. Jolley*, 46 Ohio Misc. 40, 347 N.E.2d 557 (C.P.Ohio 1975).

cohabitation and reputation as competent evidence to prove a marriage, albeit common law marriages established after the enactment of the legislation are forbidden.[124]

In the case law from **Pennsylvania**, the traditional requirement for a verbal contract was in principle maintained, as discussed in Chapter 6, "The Common Law Marriage Contract," albeit the courts at times were prepared to make exceptions.[125] In certain cases, a common law marriage can also be established with the support of the marital presumption,[126] which is based upon "constant cohabitation and general reputation." The cohabitation's function as an element in this rebuttable presumption is discussed in Chapter 9. Even in cases in which the claim for the common law marriage is based upon evidence concerning a verbal contract, the cohabitation between the parties and other circumstances, however, can be cited as supplementary evidence for proving that a marriage contract has been created. In the case of *In re Estate of Kovalchick* (1985), the Pennsylvania Superior Court stated that evidence with respect to the parties' cohabitation and reputation could be considered "in corroboration of testimony that a contract of marriage was in fact entered into." The Pennsylvania Supreme Court expressed the same stance in *Staudenmayer v. Staudenmayer* (1998).[127] The issue of the significance of circumstantial

124 The legislation, enacted on October 10, 1991, states: "[P]roof of cohabitation and reputation of the marriage of a man and woman is competent evidence to prove their marriage, and, in the discretion of the court, that proof may be sufficient to establish their marriage for a particular purpose." (Sec. 3105.12. G.C.). 1991 H 32. Previous laws: Sec. 8003-13, G.C., replacing Sec. 11989 G.C., replacing Sec. 5698 R.S., replacing Sec. 4, 29 Ohio L. 432, *see Houpt v. Houpt*, 5 Ohio 539 (1832).

125 In *Globe Sec. Systems Co. v. W.C.A.B.*, 520 A.2d 545, 547 (Pa.Cmwlth. 1987), the trial court maintained that the parties' intent to enter into a common law marriage "may be expressed in other, nonverbal ways" when it was a case of favoring remarriage between parties which previously had been married to each other. The Pennsylvania Supreme Court agreed, but did not further develop its views as to this issue, *see* 544 A.2d 953, 954, note 1 (Pa. 1988). *See also Fragapane v. Fragapane*, 131 P.L.J. 421 (1983); and *Com. ex rel. Rubin v. Rubin*, 201 Pa.Super. 517, 193 A.2d 639 (1963). In *Wagner's Estate*, 398 Pa. 531, 159 A.2d 495 (1960), where the court viewed it as important "to encourage remarriage," it found that the proof in the form of circumstantial evidence was sufficient "to establish intention of the parties to remarry and to establish common-law remarriage." In other cases concerning a remarriage, oral contracts have existed between the parties, *see, e.g., Com. ex rel. McDermott v. McDermott*, 236 Pa.Super.Ct. 541, 345 A.2d 914, 919 (1975); *In re Blecher's Estate*, 381 Pa. 138, 112 A.2d 129 (1955); and *In re Neafie's Estate*, 12 Pa. Dist. 749 (1903).

126 *See* Chapter 9 *infra*.

127 *Staudenmayer v. Staudenmayer*, 714 A.2d 1016, 1021 (Pa. 1998); and *In re Estate of Kovalchick*, 345 Pa.Super. 229, 498 A.2d 374, 377 (1985). In close connection thereto, the New York Supreme Court, Appellate Division, applying Pennsylvania law in *Dozack v. Dozack*, 137 A.D.2d 317, 528 N.Y.S.2d 712, 714 (A.D. 3 Dep't 1988), stated the following: "Where the direct proof purports to establish an oral marriage contract, however, the Pennsylvania courts examine all of the proof, including the circumstantial evidence, to determine whether to credit the proof of an oral contract." This same stance was adopted by the courts in the cases of *Globe Sec. Systems Co. v. W.C.A.B.*, 520 A.2d 545, 547 (Pa.Cmwlth. 1987), *aff'd*, 544 A.2d 953

evidence with the proving of an oral contract as a basis for a common law marriage is treated more closely in Section 6.5, "Express Contracts," of Chapter 6. The recognition of common law marriage has recently been questioned in Pennsylvania case law.[128]

With respect to the courts in the **District of Columbia**, it appears that the principles that were expressed in *United States Fidelity & Guaranty v. Britton* (1959) are still highly valid in the current case law. The requirement of an expressed contract is maintained. The best proof concerning such is, consequently, the parties' testimony, but if neither of them is available as witnesses, proof of cohabitation and general reputation as a married couple can be sufficient. In the case of *In re Matter of Estate of Foster* (1988), just this specific exception was at issue because both of the parties were deceased. The West Virginia Supreme Court of Appeals, applying the law of the District of Columbia, found that proof of cohabitation and general reputation as a married couple may be sufficient to warrant a finding of marriage by consent. A common law marriage was also found established based on such proof.[129] In *Mesa v. United States* (2005), the District of Columbia Court of Appeals held, without mentioning special requirements, that the existence of an agreement may be inferred from the character and duration of cohabitation, or from other circumstantial evidence such as testimony by relatives and acquaintances as to the general reputation regarding the parties' relationship.[130]

(Pa. 1988); *In re Estate of Garges,* 474 Pa. 237, 378 A.2d 307, 309 (1977); *Com. ex rel. McDermott v. McDermott,* 236 Pa.Super. 541, 345 A.2d 914, 919 (1975); *Rager v. Johnstown Traction Co.,* 184 Pa.Super. 474, 134 A.2d 918, 922 (1957); *In re Stauffer's Estate,* 372 Pa. 537, 94 A.2d 726 (1953); *Fiedler v. Nat'l Tube Co.,* 161 Pa.Super. 155, 53 A.2d 821, 823 (1947); *Com. ex rel. Kolish v. Kolish,* 154 Pa.Super. 59 1, 593, 36 A.2d 857 (1944); and *Baker v. Mitchell,* 143 Pa.Super. 50, 17 A.2d 738, 740 (1941). *See also Rhoads v. Stoltzfus,* 18 Lehigh 297, 301 (1939), in which a common law marriage was found proven and in which the proof concerning the parties' cohabitation was viewed as "cumulative and corroborative." In the case of *In re McGrath's Estate,* 319 Pa.Super. 309, 179 A. 599, 602 (1935), the court stated that evidence concerning cohabitation and reputation can, even in cases where the evidence is not sufficient for an application of the marital presumption, be considered "as corroborating claimant's testimony as to marriage, if provable as ordinary contract." *See also In re Murdock's Estate,* 92 Pa.Super. 275, 277 (1927): "If the alleged conversation constitutes a contract of marriage, evidence of cohabitation and reputation is received in corroboration of her testimony that a marriage contract was in fact entered into."

128 *See PNC Bank Corp. v. Workers' Comp. Appeal Bd (Stamos),* 831 A.2d 1269 (Pa.Cmwlth 2003), where the court refused to recognize a common law marriage.

129 *U.S. Fid. & Guar. v. Britton,* 106 U.S.App.D.C. 58, 269 F.2d 249 (1959); and *Matter of Estate of Foster,* 376 S.E.2d 144, 148 (W.Va. 1988).

130 *Mesa v. United States,* 875 A.2d 79, 83 (D.C.App. 2005), citing *Marcus v. Director, Office of Wkrs' Comp. Prog.,* 548 F.2d 1044, 1048 n. 9 (D.C.Cir. 1976). *See further Dickey v. Office of Personnel Management,* 419 F.3d 1336, 1340 (C.A.Fed. 2005), where the United States Court of Appeals, Federal Circuit, stated that the existence of the agreement to become husband and wife may, like any other fact, be established either by direct or circumstantial evidence. *See also Jennings v. Jennings,* 20 Md. App. 369, 315 A.2d 816, 823 (1974), in which the Maryland Court of Special Appeals applied District of Columbia law. With respect to cohabitation after the

Finally, in **Rhode Island**, the court in *Sardonis v. Sardonis* (1970) gave a rather correct description of acceptable evidentiary facts, stating consequently that the parties' intent to enter into a husband-wife relationship can be shown by inference from cohabitation, declarations, reputation among kindred and friends, and other competent circumstantial evidence.[131]

7.5 Evidentiary Facts as Support for Implied Agreements

From an evidentiary perspective, inferred agreements can be proven by two basic types of evidence, namely, circumstantial evidence and direct evidence in the form of admissions and declarations.

7.5.1 Circumstantial Evidence

Circumstantial evidence[132] is understood to be those facts proving the existence of other facts.[133] Included with respect to the contract of marriage

---

removal of a marriage impediment, *see Utterback v. Utterback*, 71 F.Supp. 231 (D.D.C. 1947).

131 *Sardonis v. Sardonis*, 106 R.I. 469, 261 A.2d 22, 24 (1970). *See also* H*olgate v. United Electric Ry. Co.*, 47 R.I. 337, 133 A. 243, 244 (1926); and *Silva v. Merritt*, 52 R.I. 30, 156 A. 512, 513 (1931).

132 *See, e.g., In re Marriage of Winegard*, 257 N.W.2d 609, 617 (Iowa 1977), in which the Iowa Supreme Court stated that "it is well established circumstantial evidence may be relied upon to demonstrate a common law marriage." *See also Young v. Gen. Baking Co.*, 104 Ind.App. 658, 662, 12 N.E.2d 1016, 1018 (1938), in which the Indiana Appellate Court stated: "Appellant testified concerning the relation which existed but she did not testify that she and decedent at any certain time or place, orally or by written instrument, agreed to take each other as consorts. There is, however, some evidence in the record which tends to prove such fact indirectly; and such fact may be proven by circumstantial evidence."

133 In *Russell v. Russell*, 865 S.W.2d 929, 933 (Tex. 1993), the Texas Supreme Court stated: "A fact is established by circumstantial evidence when the fact may be fairly and reasonably inferred from other facts proved in the case." *See further Flores v. Flores*, 847 S.W.2d 648, 652 (Tex.App.-Waco 1993), in which the Texas Court of Appeals, Waco, stated: "Gen.ly, any ultimate fact may be established by circumstantial evidence as well as by direct evidence ... An ultimate fact may be conclusively shown by wholly circumstantial evidence." The court viewed these principles as also applicable within the law of marriage. In *Winfield v. Renfro*, 821 S.W.2d 640, 644 (Tex.App.-Houston 1991), the Texas Court of Appeals, Houston, correctly stated concerning the difference between direct evidence and circumstantial evidence: "A fact may be established by direct evidence or by circumstantial evidence or both. A fact is established by direct evidence when proved by witnesses who saw the act done or heard the words spoken or by documentary evidence. A fact is established by circumstantial evidence when it may be fairly and reasonably inferred from other facts proved." *See from* older case law, *Hilton v. Roylance*, 25 Utah 129, 69 P. 660, 663 (1902), where the Utah Supreme Court stated: "Such consent, which, as we have seen, constitutes the contract to marry, may be given in writing or verbally, or may be inferred from the acts of the parties or the ceremony performed." In *Jenkins v. Jenkins*, 83 Ga. 286, 9 S.E. 541 (1889), in which the Georgia Supreme

are the parties' actions or conduct, which, within American evidentiary theory, is sometimes termed a *habit.* The parties' cohabitation is very significant evidence that is understood not only as their common residence and their shared living but also in a broader sense.[134] The cohabitation, as well as the therein-constituting elements can be cited as evidence. As important is their reputation as spouses. The umbrella terms for these evidentiary facts, when used with respect to the marriage contract, therefore, are *cohabitation and reputation* or *habit and repute.*[135]

It ought, however, to be noted that any relevant circumstances can be cited as evidence for the existence of a marital contract.[136] An illustrative example of this among the older cases is *Meehan v. Edward Valve and Manufacturing Co.* (1917), in which the court stated that a common law marriage "may be proven by cohabitation, reputation, conduct, and all other circumstances having to do with the acts and conducts of the parties with respect to the marriage relation."[137] This same evidentiary freedom

---

Court accepted the use of both direct evidence and circumstantial evidence, the same was stated: "Circumstantial evidence is that which tends to prove the fact in question by the proof of other facts from which it may be inferred. If the fact to be proved were a marriage, an instance of direct testimony would consist in the sworn statement of a witness who was present at the marriage, and observed the performance of the ceremony. An example of circumstantial evidence in a case of that kind would consist in such a set of facts surrounding the parties supposed to be man and wife in their relation to each other, and attendant upon their lives, as that, from these facts, it could be reasonably inferred that a marriage had occurred."

134 The dictionary definition of the word "cohabitation" in American and English usage, as with the French correspondence to *cohabitation*, are not solely limited to the actual living together, but rather are synonymous with "cohabitation" in a broader sense, and more closely, cohabitation as husband and wife. Both the Frech and the English word "cohabitation" comes from the latin *cohabitare. See* GRAND LAROUSSE DE LA LANGUE FRANCAIS 2, at 782 (1972); EMILE LITTRÉ, DICTIONNAIRE DE LA LANGUE FRANCAIS 2, at 440 (1956); THE OXFORD-HACHETTE FRENCH DICTIONARY 163 (3d ed. 2001); BLACK'S LAW DICTIONARY 254 (7th ed. 1999); and WEBSTER'S NEW ENCYCLOPEDIC DICTIONARY 191 (1993). *Compare* with respect to the terminology in the case law, *Ridley v. Compton*, 215 Miss. 532, 61 So.2d 341 (1952), in which the court stated: "The word 'cohabitation' as used in the marriage laws means the public assumption by a man and woman of the marital relation and dwelling together thereby holding themselves out to the public as being man and wife." *Compare* a similar statement in *O'Malley v. O'Malley*, 46 Mont. 549, 129 P. 501, Ann.Cas. 1914B, 662 (1913), in which the court, as to the meaning of "mutual and public assumption of the marital relation" stated: "To us it means a course of conduct on the part of both man and wife towards each other and toward the world as that people Gen.ly would take them to be married. Indispensable to this is cohabitation."

135 JOHN WIGMORE, TREATISE ON EVIDENCE 2, § 268 (J. Chadbourn rev. 1979).

136 *Fiedler v. Nat'l Tube Co.*, 161 Pa.Super. 155, 53 A.2d 821, 823 (1947); and *In re McGrath's Estate*, 319 Pa. 309, 179 A. 599 (1935).

137 *Meehan v. Edward Valve & Mfg. Co.*, 165 Ind.App. 342, 344, 177 N.E. 265, 266 (1917). In Alfred Appel, Note, *Common law marriage after removal of impediment to valid ceremonial marriage*, 12 CORNELL L.Q. 513, 515-516 (1927), it is argued that the parties' mutual consent can be implied in fact from cohabitation, reputation, treatment of each other as husband and wife, or any other conduct naturally tending to show the existence of the marriage relation. The idea that the marital intent may be expressed in any manner can also be found in the case of *In re Green's Estate*,

can also be seen in modern cases such as *Hall v. Duster* (1999), in which the court maintained that a marriage agreement may be inferred from all the surrounding circumstances.[138] The ability to consider all other circumstances in individual cases therefore supports Brockelbanc's somewhat drastic statement that "le mariage peut ... se contracter ... tout comme on achèterait une voiture ou un sac de farine."[139] In other words, to contract a marriage can be similar to buying a car or bag of flour. Somewhat better anchored in American custom, at least as an older southern state tradition, is to marry by hopping over a pistol placed on the ground before witnesses. Nevertheless, the practical significance of being able to enter into a common law marriage through certain actions appears to lie in the ability to find the existence of a marriage contract in the cohabitation.

The function the parties' cohabitation and reputation as an evidentiary fact must be distinguished from its function as a requisite in addition to the marriage contract, a function discussed in Chapter 8, "Cohabitation, Holding Out, and Reputation as Spouses." Even in jurisdictions in which these circumstances constitute necessary requirements for the formation of a common law marriage, they can at the same time serve as evidentiary facts for the marriage contract. This double function appears clearly in

---

5 Pa.C. 605, 606 (1888), in which the court as to the parties stated: "If they, *in any manner*, expressed a purpose to cohabit as husband and wife, no other evidence is needed" (*italics added*). *See* already *Tarpley v. Poage's Adm'r*, 2 Tex. 139 (1847).

138 *Hall v. Duster*, 727 So.2d 834, 836 (Ala.Civ.App. 1999). In *Standefer v. Standefer*, 26 P.3d 104 (Okla. 2001), the Oklahoma Supreme Court stated: "Some evidence of consent to enter into a common-law marriage are cohabitation, actions consistent with the relationship of spouses, recognition by the community of the marital relationship, and declarations by the parties." In *Kelley v. Kelley*, 9 P.3d 171, 178 note 6 (Utah App. 2000), concerning divorced spouses that were reunited, the court found that the man had demonstrated his consent to a common law marriage "by filing a joint 1994 tax return, making statements to Dr. Hood at the parenting class, continuing financial support far above the level ordered in the original decree, maintaining joint accounts with Sonia, continuing cohabitation and sexual relations with Sonia, giving Sonia an anniversary card expressing his love and desire for another fifteen years together and failing to tell anyone in the community about the divorce." *See also Bishop v. Bishop*, 57 Ala.App. 619, 330 So.2d 443, 445 (1976), in which the court stated: "The marriage relationship may be shown in any way that can be known by others, such as living together as man and wife, referring to each other in the presence of others as being in that relation, declaring the relation in various types of documents and transactions, sharing household duties and expenses, and Gen.ly engaging in 'all of the numerous aspects of day-to-day mutual existence of married persons'."

139 W. J. Brockelbanc, La formation du mariage dans le droit des Etats-Unis 260 (1935). As to the old southern state tradition, *see In re Estate of Soeder*, 7 Ohio App. 271, 220 N.W.2d 547, 562 (1966). The breadth of possible evidence was clearly demarcated already in *Fryer v. Fryer*, 9 S.C.Eq. (Rich.Cas.) 85, 92-93 (1832), in which the court stated that the marital contract is "susceptible to an infinite variety of proof." A couple can consequently "express their agreement by parol, they may signify it by whatever ceremony their whim, or their taste, or their religious belief, may select."

the case law from Texas prior to 1989.[140] In cases in which cohabitation is not a necessary requirement, but is recognized as an evidentiary fact for the contract of marriage, the latter can be proven other than through cohabitation.[141]

A further distinction is warranted with respect to those functions attributed to the parties' cohabitation and reputation. The function of these circumstances as evidentiary facts ought to distinguish them from their function as elements in a legal presumption, as discussed in Chapter 9. This difference consists of the fact that, if the parties' cohabitation and reputation are used as evidentiary facts for the marriage contract, these circumstances as well as other evidence must lead to proving a marital *consensus* in the individual case to find that a common law marriage was established. If these circumstances are used as evidentiary facts, they are then not necessary for the formation of a common law marriage, because the marriage contract can be proven in other ways. If the parties' cohabitation and reputation are instead used as an element in a *presumption*, a *praesumptio juris*, these circumstances are then necessary for the consequences of the presumption to be invoked, namely, that a marital *consensus* is presumed to have existed. This *consensus*, however, does not need to be proven in the individual case. The party claiming the existence of a common law marriage need only prove that cohabitation and reputation exist, after which the evidentiary burden is shifted to the other party. A common law marriage is established, then, if this party is not successful in rebutting the presumption by proving that no marital *consensus* existed. The court does not need to conclude that a marriage contract is proven based on the circumstances. The law already does this. The parties' cohabitation and reputation constitute the elements that typically are grounds for the presumption that a marital *consensus* existed. Even in jurisdictions in which the presumption is applied, the contract of marriage can, alternatively, be proven by direct evidence. The distinction between the parties' cohabitation and reputation as an evidentiary fact and as an element in a *praesumptio juris* is theoretically motivated, but also has considerable practical importance, because it affects the evidence that both parties need to present. It is a separate issue that the courts, in their reasoning, do not always appear to maintain this distinction with the precision that is desirable.[142] It is not uncommon for the courts to use language that is unclear

140 *See, e.g.*, *Shelton v. Belknap*, 155 Tex. 37, 282 S.W.2d 682, 684 (1955); *Consolidated Underwriters v. Kelly*, 15 S.W.2d 229 (Tex.Com.App. 1929) and *Humphreys v. Humphreys*, 364 S.W.2d 177 (Tex. 1963).

141 *See, e.g.*, *Love v. Love*, 185 Iowa 930, 171 N.W. 257 (1919).

142 It is rare for the courts to expressly discuss the difference between the function of cohabitation as a required element in a presumption and its function as an evidentiary fact. In *Hamlin v. Grogan*, 257 F. 59 (8th Cir. 1919), however, the Eighth Circuit Court of Appeals stated entirely correctly that "the contract may be shown as an inference of fact from cohabitation, declarations, and reputation among friends and kindred. In such a case the fact of contract is not a 'presumption',

about whether they have applied the presumption or not. There are examples in which the court has stated that a marriage contract has been found "presumed from" the cohabitation as husband and wife, without applying a correct *praesumptio juris* with the shifted burden of proof. By using "presumed from," the court could have meant that it found or did not find the contract "proven by" or "inferred from" the cohabitation, which consequently is used as an evidentiary fact.[143]

In the next section, we will explore the evidentiary importance of the parties' cohabitation and reputation, as well as the separate elements and the attributions given to them by the case law in assessing the existence of an inferred marriage agreement.

7.5.2 Admissions and Declarations

In addition to circumstantial evidence, the second category of evidentiary facts that is also invoked in support of an inferred or implied agreement, is, namely, admissions and declarations, *i.e.*, admissions and statements that the parties have made during the cohabitation.[144] Not included are

---

but is a fact proven by circumstantial evidence. Such circumstantial evidence, if clear and persuasive, establishes the existence of the contract of marriage between the parties as satisfactorily as if the contract had been reduced to writing, or had been expressed in the presence of living witnesses in the plainest form of contractual words." The court found consequently that in the case the actual marital contract "is proven as a fact by circumstances, and does not rest upon a presumption." Another case where the court appears to have correctly understood the difference without more closely addressing the issue is *Holgate v. United Electric Ry. Co.*, 47 R.I. 337, 133 A. 243, 244 (1926), in which the Rhode Island Supreme Court stated: "A common law marriage may be shown as an inference of fact from cohabitation, declarations, and reputation among friends and kindred. In such a case the fact of contract is not a presumption, but is a fact proven by circumstantial evidence. Such circumstantial evidence, if clear and persuasive, establishes the existence of the contract of marriage between the parties as satisfactorily as if the contract had been reduced to writing or had been expressed in the presence of living witnesses in the plainest form of contractual words." *See also Jenkins v. Jenkins*, 83 Ga. 286, 9 S.E. 541 (1889).

143 *See e.g. Taylor v. Taylor*, 10 Colo.App. 303, 50 P.2d 1049 (1897); and *People v. Lucero*, 747 P.2d 660, 664 (Colo. 1987). In *Faggard v. Filipowich*, 248 Ala. 182, 27 So.2d 10, 15 (1946), the court appears to hold both methods open: "Cohabitation, reputation, the acknowledgment of the parties themselves, and reception as man and wife by their relations may be sufficient proof of the fact or at least raise a presumption that a marriage took place until the contrary is shown." *See also Richard v. Brehm*, 73 Pa. 140, 144 (1873). *Compare* BISHOP, *supra* note 38, § 927, which uses the expressions "presumptive evidence" and "proof by presumption" without therewith referring to a legal presumption that facilitates a conclusion of law.

144 In the case of *In re Estate of Wilson*, 512 S.E.2d 383, 386 (Ga.App. 1999), the fact that the man claiming a common law marriage existed between him and the deceased had stated after the woman's death that he had never been "common law married" with the woman was attributed great significance. In addition to cohabitation and reputation, admissions and declarations have long been the most common type of evidence for proving a common law marriage, *see* already *Vincent's Appeal*, 10 P.F. Smith 228, 60 Pa. 228 (1869) and *Richard v. Brehm*, 73 Pa. 140, 144 (1873). As long as the statements were made during the cohabitation, they could not be rejected as not belonging to the *res gestae*, *see Drawdy v. Hesters*, 130 Ga. 161, 60 S.E. 451,

those statements that can constitute an offer or an acceptance, respectively, in an oral contract, but rather more indirect statements concerning the parties' marital status.[145] Admissions and declarations are normally characterized as direct evidence.[146] The boundary with circumstantial evidence, however, is fluid as actions sometimes are considered admissions and declarations. The circumstance that one party applied for a divorce, but then recalled the petition, consequently has been understood as an admission that the parties were united in a common law marriage.[147]

Examples of statements commonly cited in support of the existence of a marriage agreement are as follows: That the parties between themselves, in front of other persons or a governmental authority, orally or in writing, called each other "Mrs. and Mr."[148] or "husband

---

15 L.R.A., N.S. 190 (1908); *Smith v. Fuller*, 138 Iowa 91, 108 N.W. 765 (1906); and *Reppert v. Reppert*, 214 Iowa 17, 241 N.W. 487 (1932). Statements concerning the parties' status could not be rejected as hearsay in those cases in which the statements were made "against interest," *see Greenawalt v. McEnelley*, 85 Pa. 352 (1877) or where they were evidence concerning "family relations or pedigree," *see Topper v. Perry*, 197 Mo. 531, 95 S.W. 203 (1906). Gen. statements made by a third party that a marriage existed have as a rule, however, been given little evidentiary value, *see, e.g., Faggard v. Filipowich*, 248 Ala. 182, 27 So.2d 10 (1946).

145 The boundary between oral offers and acceptances on one side, and conversationally uttered statements on the other is, however, fluid. With respect to oral contracts, *see* Section 6.5.1.

146 *Com. v. Haylow*, 17. Pa.Super. 541, 547 (1901) ("The admissions by the parties of their marriage is in the nature of direct proof, and is certainly competent evidence of the fact"). *See also Greenawalt v. McEnelly*, 85 Pa. 352, 356-357 (1877); *Vann v. Vann*, 186 Okla. 42, 96 P.2d 76 (1939); *Coleman v. James*, 67 Okla. 112, 169 P. 1064, 1066 (1917) ("It is well settled that repeated acknowledgments by the man of his marriage with a certain woman, are direct evidence of a marriage"); *Linsey v. Jefferson*, 68 Okla. 156, 172 P. 641, 642 (1918); and *In re Comly's Estate*, 185 Pa. 208, 39 A. 890 (1898). *Compare Applegate v. Applegate*, 118 Misc. 359, 193 N.Y.S. 494, 496 (Sup.Ct. 1922), in which the court distinguishes between "direct proof, as distinguished from proof of matrimonial cohabitation and acknowledgment of the status."

147 *See Beals v. Beals*, 203 Ga.App. 81, 416 S.E.2d 301 (1992). In the case of *In re Torrence's Estate*, 47 Pa.Super. 509, 515 (1911), the court stated: "It was a distinct admission by one of the parties of the marriage, the libel in divorce being in itself an implied admission of the formation of a tie which the application sought to sever." *See also Strauss's Estate*, 168 Pa. 561 (1895). *Compare Anderson v. Anderson*, 235 Ind. 113, 131 N.E.2d 301 (1956), in which the woman previously had petitioned for a marital divorce and a number of other admissions and explanations were made, but in which no common law marriage was found proven. In *Com. v. Stump*, 53 Pa. 132, 137, 91 Am.Dec. 198 (1866), the parents' attempts to legitimize their "illegitimate sons" constituted an admission that the relationship of the parents was not a marriage. Also in the case of *In re Physick's Estate*, 2 Brews. 179 (1863), the statements as to the illegitimacy of the children constituted an admission that the parents' relationship was not a marriage.

148 *Ballesteros v. Jones*, 985 S.W.2d 485, 490 (Tex.App.-San Antonio 1998); *In re Marriage of Mahaffey*, 801 P.2d 1335, 1337 (Mont. 1990); *In re Marriage of Gebhardt*, 426 N.W.2d 651 (Iowa App. 1988); and *Sardonis v. Sardonis*, 106 R.I. 469, 261 A.2d 22, 24 (1970). The court's list of admissions and declarations in the case of *In re Stauffer's Estate*, 372 Pa. 537, 94 A.2d 726, 727 (1953) is typical: "Decedent mailed postal cards addressed to claimant as his wife; six other postal cards were mailed to them as Mr. and Mrs. Russell F. Stauffer and another card was mailed to claimant, addressed as 'Mrs. Russell F. Stauffer'." *See also In re Clark's Estate*, 228 Iowa 75,

and wife;"[149] that the woman used the man's last name;[150] that they stated that they were "married," that they lived in marriage,[151] or that their intent was to "marry."[152]

---

290 N.W. 13 (1940); *Blair v. Howell*, 68 Iowa 619, 28 N.W. 199 (1886); and *Guardians of the Poor v. Nathis*, 2 Brewster. 149,178 (1845).

149 *Hall v. Duster*, 727 So.2d 834, 837 (Ala.Civ.App. 1999); *Stringer v. Stringer*, 689 So.2d 194, 197 (Ala.Civ.App. 1997); *Cann v. Cann*, 632 A.2d 322, 325 note 4 (Pa.Super. 1993); *In re Estate of Fisher*, 176 N.W.2d 801 (Iowa 1970); and *In re Marriage of Mahaffey*, 801 P.2d 1335, 1337 (Mont. 1990). In *Clayton Coal Co. v. Indus. Comm'n*, 93 Colo. 145, 25 P.2d 170, 172 (1933), the court referred to the fact that the man called the woman "his wife." In *Walton v. Walton*, 203 S.W. 133, 134 (Tex.Civ.App.-Galveston 1918), the court referred to the fact that the man in several letters had addressed them to the woman as his wife. *See* already *Com. v. Litzenberger*, 15 Phila. 414 (1882), in which an admission from the man that he and the woman in question "lived together as man and wife" was found not only to be an admission concerning cohabitation, but also concerning a legal marriage. In the case of *In re Pyle's Estate* 15 Lanc.Bar 17, 18 (1883), the man in his will used the expression "my beloved wife," which was found to constitute permissible evidence. *Compare In re Marriage of Mosher*, 243 Ill.App.3d 97, 612 N.E.2d 838 (1993), in which the woman stated that the man presented her as his "wife," while the man claimed that he had presented her as the "mother of my children" and "my woman." The court's majority found, in contrast with the minority, that no "intent and agreement" to be married had been proven. *See also United States v. Dorto*, 5 F.2d 596 (1st Cir. 1925). *Compare* on the other hand, *Matter of Estate of Carroll*, 749 P.2d 571 (Okla.App. 1987), in which the court as support for its conclusion that no marriage agreement had been proven, stated that the man, neither privately or publicly, referred to the woman as his wife and that she never referred to the man as her husband.

150 *In re Marriage of Gebhardt*, 426 N.W.2d 651 (Iowa App. 1988); and *Grigsby v. Grigsby*, 757 S.W.2d 163 (Tex.App.-San Antonio 1988). In the case of *In re Stauffer's Estate*, 372 Pa. 537, 94 A.2d 726, 729 (1953), it was noted that the woman, in different registers, used the man's last name: "[S]he registered claimant as a voter in the name of Marie B. Stauffer; claimant was registered for social security in that name." In *Com. v. Allen*, 63 Dauph. 40, 44-45 (1952), the woman's use of the man's last name in different documents was given significant evidentiary weight. In the case of *In re Redman's Estate*, 135 Ohio St. 554, 21 N.E.2d 659 (1939), in which no common law marriage was found proven, the woman had used the man's last name. *See also Abramson v. Abramson*, 161 Neb. 782, 74 N.W.2d 919 (1956); *Anderson v. Anderson*, 235 Ind. 113, 131 N.E.2d 301 (1956); as well as *Bowden v. Workmen's Comp. Appeal Bd*, 376 A.2d 1033 (Pa.Cmwlth. 1977).

151 In *Eris v. Phares*, 39 S.W.3d 708, 714 (Tex.App.-Houston (1Dist.) 2001), the woman's statement that the parties "didn't have to be married to be married" was evidence for the existence of a marriage contract; *Stringer v. Stringer*, 689 So.2d 194, 197 (Ala. Civ.App. 1997); *Campbell v. Christian*, 235 S.C. 102, 110 S.E.2d 1 (1959); *In re Redman's Estate*, 135 Ohio St. 554, 21 N.E.2d 659 (1939); *Richard v. Brehm*, 73 Pa. 140, 13 Am.Rep. 733 (1873); and *Teter v. Teter*, 101 Ind. 129, 51 Am.R. 742 (1884). In the case of *In re Drinkhouse's Estate*, 151 Pa. 294, 300 (1892), the notation "married May 2, 1874" was found to constitute a permissible "direct proof of marriage." In the case of *In re Estate of Fisher*, 176 N.W.2d 801 (Iowa 1970), great weight was given to the fact that the wife presented herself as the man's wife. Another case in which Iowa law was applied is *Jambrone v. David*, 16 Ill.2d 32, 156 N.E.2d 569 (1959), in which the man wrote checks to the woman under the name "Mrs. Gorra," but in which no common law marriage was found proven. In *Bochette v. Bochette*, 386 S.E.2d 475 (S.C.App. 1989), the parties' contract was found manifested through their actions "holding themselves out as husband and wife, including filing tax returns indicating they were married persons filing jointly." With respect to the evidentiary weight of joint tax returns, *see also Day v. Day*, 421 S.W.2d 703 (Tex.Civ. App.-Austin 1967) and *Deo v. State*, 272 P.2d 473 (Okla. 1954).

152 *In re Estate of Kovalchick*, 345 Pa.Super. 229, 498 A.2d 374 (Pa.Super. 1985); and *U.S. Fid. & Guar. Co. v. Britton*, 106 U.S.App.D.C. 58, 269 F.2d 249 (1959).

As evidence invoked, on the other hand, against the existence of a marriage agreement, the following is typically cited: That the woman called herself "Ms.," that she used her maiden name,[153] or her name from a previous marriage; that the parties had stated that they were "single"[154] or that

---

153 *Barker v. Baker*, 330 S.C. 361, 499 S.E.2d 503, 505 (App. 1998) (marital presumption found not applicable); and *Butler v. Coonrod*, 671 So.2d 750, 752 (Ala.Civ.App. 1995). In *Frazier v. State*, 219 Ga.App. 768, 467 S.E.2d 338 (1995), the court referred to the fact that the parties did not have the same last name. *See also McCoy v. McCoy*, 868 P.2d 527, 530 (Idaho App. 1994) (maiden name); *Lee v. Cotten*, 793 P.2d 1369 (Okla.App. 1990); and *Etheridge v. Yeager*, 465 So.2d 378, 379 (Ala. 1985). In the case of *In re Estate of Kovalchick*, 345 Pa.Super. 229, 498 A.2d 374 (1985), the witness testified that the woman called herself the man's "fiancée." *See also In re Estate of Malli*, 260 Iowa 252, 149 N.W.2d 155, 157-158 (1967); *In re Greenfield's Estate*, 245 S.C. 595, 141 S.E.2d 916 (1965); *Coleman v. Graves*, 255 Iowa 396, 122 N.W.2d 853 (1963); *In re Long's Estate*, 251 Iowa 1042, 102 N.W.2d 76, 80 (1960); *Chaachou v. Chaachou*, 73 So.2d 830 (Fla. 1954); and *In re Trope's Estate* 190 Okla. 453, 124 P.2d 733, 736 (1942). In *Foley v. Gavin*, 76 Colo. 286, 230 P. 618, 620 (1924), no marriage contract was found proven, based *inter alia* on reference to the fact that the woman used her name from a previous marriage. *See also Thimgan v. Mathews*, 74 Colo. 93, 219 P. 211, 212 (1923). In the cases of *In re Smith's Estate*, 3 Lack.Leg. News 122 (1895) and *Laurence v. Laurence*, 164 Ill. 367, 45 N.E. 1071 (1896), the use of the woman's maiden name was given great significance. *See also Brinckle v. Brinckle*, 12 Phila. 232, 235 (1877); and *Physick's Estate*, 2 Brewster 179, 194 (1863) (man's use in his will of woman's maiden name given only limited evidentiary weight). *See further Letters v. Cady*, 10 Cal. 533, 534, 537 (1858), in which the parties agreed to temporarily live together "as man and wife" and in which the court stated: "From the character of the allegations, and the pregnant fact that the plaintiff does not even sue in her marital name, except under alias, we are led to the inference that the arrangement between her and the deceased was intended to be temporary, and the connection one to which it would be a perversion of language to apply the name of marriage."

154 In *DeMelo v. Zompa*, 844 A.2d 174, 178 (R.I. 2004), the court held that there was a lack of clear and convincing evidence that plaintiff considered herself married, stating: "There were many documents introduced in evidence, such as tax returns, a mortgage application, and insurance applications in which she listed herself as single." *See also Fritz v. Mork*, 2001 Iowa App. LEXIS 594 (2001); *Kelley v. Kelley*, 9 P.3d 171, 178 note 6 (Utah App. 2000) (joint 1994 tax return); *In re Estate of Wilson*, 512 S.E.2d 383, 386 (Ga.App. 1999); *In re Estate of Dunn*, 236 Ga.App. 211, 511 S.E.2d 575, 577 (1999) (separate tax returns as single); *Hansen v. Hansen*, 958 P.2d 931, 936 (Utah App. 1998) (separate tax returns as single); *Barker v. Baker*, 330 S.C. 361, 499 S.E.2d 503, 505 (S.C.App. 1998); *Butler v. Coonrod*, 671 So.2d 750, 752 (Ala.Civ.App. 1995) (different documents); *McCoy v. McCoy*, 868 P.2d 527, 531 (Idaho App. 1994) (separate tax returns); and *Coates v. Watts*, 622 A.2d 25, 27 (D.C.App. 1993); and *Grossman v. Gangel*, 192 A.D.2d 396, 596 N.Y.S.2d 53, 55, 625 N.E.2d 590 (1993). *Compare Krier v. Krier*, 676 So.2d 1335 (Ala.Civ.App. 1996), in which the parties, after a marital divorce, for a period of ten months lived together, wore rings and submitted a joint tax return. A common law marriage was found proven. *See further Cann v. Cann*, 632 A.2d 322, 325 note 4 (Pa.Super. 1993), in which the circumstance that the parties had filed joint tax returns was corroborative evidence in support that the parties' oral contract was a marriage agreement. *See also Beals v. Beals*, 203 Ga.App. 81, 416 S.E.2d 301 (1992). In the cases, *Lee v. Cotten*, 793 P.2d 1369 (Okla.App. 1990) and *Mueggenborg v. Walling*, 836 P.2d 112, 114 (Colo. 1992),the courts attributed the circumstance that the parties had filed separate tax returns considerable significance as support for the conclusion that no common law marriage was found proven. *See further, Jennings v. Hurt*, 554 N.Y.S.2d 220, 221 (1990); *Smith-Wilkins v. Sec'y of HHS*, 880 F.2d 864, 866 (6th Cir. 1989); *In re Marriage of Gebhardt*, 426 N.W.2d 651 (Iowa App. 1988); *In re Marriage of Geertz*, 232 Mont. 141, 755 P.2d 34, 37 (1988); and *In re Estate of Dodge*, 361 Pa.Super. 188, 522 A.2d 77 (1987). In the case of *In re Matter of Estate of White*, 212 Mont. 228,

they were "not married;"[155] or that they called each other "fiancé(e)," "girlfriend" or "boyfriend," respectively;[156] that the woman was simply the

686 P.2d 915 (1984), the woman had received Social Security benefits as unmarried. *See also In re Estate of Stinchcomb*, 674 P.2d 26, 29 (Okla. 1983); *In re Estate of Malli*, 260 Iowa 252, 149 N.W.2d 155, 157 (1967); and *Coleman v. Graves*, 255 Iowa 396, 122 N.W.2d 853 (1963). In the case of *In re Gholson's Estate*, 83 Idaho 270, 361 P.2d 791 (1961), the woman had filed tax returns as single and had also received public assistance as single. She then could not upon the man's death claim that she was his surviving spouse. *See also In re Long's Estate*, 251 Iowa 1042, 102 N.W.2d 76, 80 (1960); *Cornell v. Mabe*, 206 F.2d 514, 517 note 2 (5th Cir. 1953); *Com. ex rel. De Marco v. De Marco*, 166 Pa.Super. 69, 70 A.2d 384 (1950); *In re Trope's Estate*, 190 Okla. 453, 124 P.2d 733, 736-737 (1942); *Ghelin v. Johnson*, 186 Minn. 405, 243 N.W. 443 (1932); and *Foley v. Gavin*, 76 Colo. 286, 230 P. 618, 619 (1924).

155 *Fritz v. Mork*, 2001 Iowa App. Lexis 594 (2001); and *In re Estate of Wilson*, 512 S.E.2d 383, 386 (Ga.App. 1999). In the case of *In re Estate of Dunn*, 236 Ga.App. 211, 511 S.E.2d 575, 577 (1999), the court noted *inter alia* that the woman had stated that the man was not "her husband." In *Payne v. Payne*, 1999 Tenn.App. Lexis 844 (1999), decisive weight was given to the fact that the woman, with the purchase of real estate, was not named in "the deed to the property." In *Hansen v. Hansen*, 958 P.2d 931, 936 (Utah App. 1998), the court observed that the parties had not referred to each other as husband and wife. In *Butler v. Coonrod*, 671 So.2d 750, 752 (Ala.Civ.App. 1995), the court referred to the fact that the parties had not stated to the man's family that they were "married" and found that the man never "indicated intention to marry," however, without clarifying what was meant by the expressions "marry" and "married" respectively. *See also In re Estate of Glover*, 882 S.W.2d 789 (Tenn.App. 1994)(applying Alabama law); *In re Estate of Dodge*, 361 Pa.Super. 188, 522 A.2d 77, 79 (1987); and *Etheridge v. Yeager*, 465 So.2d 378 (Ala. 1985). *In Eaton v. Johnston*, 9 Kan.App. 63, 672 P.2d 10 (1983); *aff'd*, 235 Kan. 323, 681 P.2d 606 (1984), both of the parties had filed separate tax returns as unmarried head of household. No common law marriage was found proven. See also *In re Long's Estate*, 251 Iowa 1042, 102 N.W.2d 76, 80 (1960)(man in a purchase agreement stated he was unmarried); *Scalzi v. Folsom*, 156 F.Supp. 838, 840 (D.R.I. 1957); *In re Foster*, 77 Idaho 26, 287 P.2d 282 (1955); and *In re Kapuchinski's Estate*, 318 Pa. 314, 178 A. 465 (1935). In the case of *In re Swartley's Estate*, 19 D. & C., 388, 389 (1933), the woman, claiming that she had lived in a common law marriage with the deceased man, upon several occasions had made statements indicating that they were not husband and wife even if they lived together. The court stated: "The claimant cannot be an unmarried woman for one purpose ... and the common law wife of the decedent for the purpose of claiming his estate." *See also In re Levy's Estate*, 307 Pa. 522, 161 A. 740 (1932); *Welch v. All Persons*, 78 Mont. 370, 254 P. 179, *rev'd*, 85 Mont. 114, 278 P. 110 (1929); *Foley v. Gavin*, 76 Colo. 286, 230 P. 618, 619 (1924); *Coleman v. James*, 67 Okla. 112, 169 P. 1064 (1917); and *In re Inner's Estate*, 19 York 166 (1906). In *Reading Fire Ins. & Trust Co.'s Appeal*, 113 Pa. 204, 6 A. 60, 61-62 (1886), several statements were cited in the judgment where the man stated they were "not married," however, without any further precision as to whether he thereby meant "formally" married. *See also Tholey's Appeal*, 93 Pa. 36 (1880).

156 In *Bevan v. Bevan*, 2006 WL 1519654 (Ohio App. 11 Dist. 2006), the women's assertion that a trip to Niagara Falls was a honeymoon and that she considered herself the man's wife thereafter, was accepted as direct proof of a contract to marry. *See also Brown v. State*, 108 P.3d 1018 (Kan.App. 2005)(girlfriend or fiancée). In the case of *In re Estate of Wilson*, 512 S.E.2d 383, 385 (Ga.App. 1999), the parties had consistently referred to each other as "fiancé(e)" in their conversations. In the case of *In re Matter of Estate of Micheel*, 577 N.W.2d 407, 409 (Iowa 1998), "long-time friend" was not found to indicate a common law marriage. In *Barker v. Baker*, 330 S.C. 361, 499 S.E.2d 503, 505 (App. 1998), in which the marital presumption was found to be inapplicable, the woman had referred to the man as "her boyfriend,

man's "housekeeper;"[157] that "marriage" was nothing to them or that they had no intent "to marry."[158]

It is common that admissions and declarations give expression to the parties' own understanding of their marital status[159] and are accepted as evidence of the existence of a marriage contract. Even though such evidence is permissible, its value must be assessed from case to case.[160] In the

---

not her husband." In *Matter of Estate of Yao You-Xin*, 246 A.D.2d 721, 667 N.Y.S.2d 462 (1998), it was objected without success that the woman was only "one of decedent's many girlfriends." In *Fuentes v. Transamerican Nat'l Gas Corp.*, 933 S.W.2d 624 (Tex.App.-San Antonio 1996), the woman stated that she and the man were "boyfriend and girlfriend" and that they had no plans to marry. In *Frazier v. State*, 219 Ga.App. 768, 467 S.E.2d 338 (1995), the circumstance that the woman called the man her "boyfriend" was taken into consideration. In *Welch v. State*, 908 S.W.2d 258, 265 (Tex.App.-El Paso 1995), the court noted that the woman called the man, not her "husband," but her "old man." In the case of *In re Estate of Glover*, 882 S.W.2d 789, 791 (Tenn.App. 1994) (applying Alabama law), great significance was attributed to the fact that the woman identified herself as the man's "fiancée," with the conclusion that no marriage contract existed. In *Grossman v. Gangel*, 192 A.D.2d 396, 596 N.Y.S.2d 53, 55, 625 N.E.2d 590 (1993), the court, as support that a common law marriage had not been entered into, referred to that the man referred to the woman in his will as his "friend." In *Jennings v. Hurt*, 554 N.Y.S.2d 220, 221 (1990), the fact that the man called the woman his "friend" instead of his "spouse" was given significance. *See also Coates v. Watts*, 622 A.2d 25, 26 (D.C.App. 1993) ("friend"). In the case of *In re Estate of Kovalchick*, 345 Pa.Super. 229, 498 A.2d 374 (1985), the witnesses stated that the woman called herself the man's "fiancée." In the case of *In re Cumming's Estate*, 330 Pa.Super. 255, 479 A.2d 537, 543 (1984), the fact that the woman in a document to the Pennsylvania Department of Public Welfare stated that the man was her "paramour" was found significant. *See also Petrarca v. Castrovillari*, 448 A.2d 1286, 1292 (R.I. 1982) (man called the woman his "girlfriend").

157 *See* the discussed cases, *In re Estate of Kovalchick*, 345 Pa.Super. 229, 498 A.2d 374 (1985) and *Jolley v. Jolley*, 46 Ohio Misc. 40, 347 N.E.2d 557 (C.P.Ohio 1975). *See also Price v. Price*, 579 P.2d 843 (Okla.App. 1978); *Coleman v. Graves*, 255 Iowa 396, 122 N.W.2d 853, 854 (1963); *Johnson v. Johnson*, 235 S.C. 542, 112 S.E.2d 647, 650 (1960); *Odd Fellows' Beneficial Ass'n v. Carpenter*, 17 R.I. 720, 24 A. 578 (1892); *In re Horton's Estate*, 357 Pa. 30, 52 A.2d 895 (1947); *In re Trope's Estate* 190 Okla. 453, 124 P.2d 733, 735, 737 (1942); and *Reading Fire Ins. & Trust Co.'s Appeal*, 113 Pa. 204, 6 A. 60, 61-62 (1886).

158 In the case of *In re Estate of Wilson*, 512 S.E.2d 383, 386 (Ga.App. 1999), the woman had stated to her friends that she "had no intention of marrying" the man. In *Butler v. Coonrod*, 671 So.2d 750, 752 (Ala.Civ.App. 1995), the court found that the man never "indicated intention to marry," however, without stating that which was meant by the expression "marry." *See also U.S. Fid. & Guar. Co. v. Britton*, 106 U.S.App.D.C. 58, 269 F.2d 249 (1959) (the woman's statement that she "never intended to marry" the man was fatal); and *In re Estate of Dodge*, 361 Pa.Super. 188, 522 A.2d 77 (1987).

159 The parties have also been viewed as able to testify at trial as to whether they considered themselves married or not. The objection that they are then drawing a legal conclusion has not been sustained, *see In re Estate of Allen*, 251 Iowa 177, 100 N.W.2d 10 (1959); and *In re Malli's Estate*, 260 Iowa 252, 149 N.W.2d 155 (1967).

160 *Beck v. Beck*, 286 Ala. 692, 246 So.2d 420 (1971); *White v. White*, 41 Ga.App. 394, 153 S.E. 203 (1930); *Cooper v. Butler*, 223 Ga. 797, 158 S.E.2d 244 (1967); *In re Swartley's Estate*, 19 Pa. Dist. & Co. 388 (1933); *McIlveen v. McIlveen*, 332 S.W.2d 113 (Tex.Civ.App. 1960); *Dibble v. Dibble*, 88 Ohio App. 490, 100 N.E.2d 451 (1950); *Pierce v. Pierce*, 355 Pa. 175, 49 A.2d 346 (1946); In re *McGrath's Estate*, 319 Pa. 309, 179 A. 599 (1935); *Ryan v. Ryan*, 84 Ohio App. 139, 86 N.E.2d 44 (1948);

next section, the evidentiary weight attributed to different types of admissions and declarations in the case law in determining whether an inferred marriage agreement exists is examined more closely. Of what significance is it that a party's statement is made against his or her own interests? Does it make any difference whether it is a question of statements made for or against the existence of a marriage agreement and therewith a common law marriage?

7.6 Cases in Which Implied Agreements Have Been Proven

This and the following section are devoted to a further analysis of the courts' reasons about how the facts cited become a basis for finding the existence or nonexistence of an implied agreement in the formation of a common law marriage. What is the evidentiary value of the parties' cohabitation and reputation, and their admissions and declarations in cases concerning common law marriage? Is the concept that "certain acts speak as loudly as words" actually viable?

As an implied agreement is normally based on a number of facts, such an examination requires a relatively detailed description of the cases. In this and the next section, a number of cases in which the courts, on one hand, have found a contract proven, and cases, on the other, in which no marital contract was found proven, will be described.

7.6.1 Cohabitation after a Wedding Ceremony That Was Invalid due to an Error in the Formalities

To begin, *Travers v. Reinhardt* (1906) is a case in which the parties had entered into a ceremonial marriage that was invalid. The issue then arose

---

Smith v. Fuller, 138 Iowa 91, 115 N.W. 912 (1906); *State v. Hughes*, 35 Kan. 626, 12 P. 28 (1886); *Aldana v. Aldana*, 42 S.W.2d 661 (Tex.Civ.App.-El Paso 1931); *In re Miller's Estate*, 182 Okla. 534, 78 P.2d 819 (1938); *In re Trope's Estate*, 190 Okla. 453, 124 P.2d 733 (1942); and *Welch v. All Persons*, 78 Mont. 370, 254 P. 179, *rev'd*, 85 Mont. 114, 278 P. 110 (1926). For a restrictive stance, *see In re Pratt's Estate*, 233 App.Div. 200, 251 N.Y.S. 424, 425 (1931), in which the court stated: "Evidence of admissions made by deceased tending to show marital relation with person seeking to inherit as surviving husband should be scrutinized with care and acted upon with caution." *See also Faggard v. Filipowich*, 248 Ala. 182, 27 So.2d 10, 16 (1946) (the court assumed that the party making the statement was a party to the case: "[D]eclarations by a party to a suit that he had been married is competent evidence against him"); *Forney v. Hallacher*, 8 S. & R. 159 (1822); *Com. v. Murtagh*, 1 Ash. 272 (1831); *Vincent's Appeal*, 10 P.F. Smith 228, 60 Pa. 228 (1869); *Greenawalt v. McEnelly*, 85 Pa. 352 (1877); and *Drinkhouse's Estate*, 151 Pa. 294 (1892). In *Strauss's Estate*, 168 Pa. 561, 570 (1895), the court stated that the marriage is a civil contract and that "at least, reputation and cohabitation are sufficient evidence of it." *In Lehigh Valley R.R. Co. v. Hall*, 61 Pa. 361, 366 (1869), the court stated that the marriage can be proven through "cohabitation, reputation, acknowledgment of the parties, reception of the family, and any other circumstances from which it may be inferred."

whether a common law marriage was established during the cohabitation that thereafter followed. *Travers,* decided by the United States Supreme Court, would come to exercise considerable influence on the development of the case law.

In *Travers,* the parties had gone through a wedding ceremony in Virginia that was invalid as a result of an error in observing the formalities. Thereafter, they lived together for eighteen years, mainly in Maryland, but for almost one year in New Jersey, before the man died. Neither Virginia nor Maryland recognized common law marriage. The issue arose whether a common law marriage had been established during the parties' cohabitation in New Jersey, where such marriages were recognized at that time.

The Court found that it was not proven that the parties during their time in New Jersey had entered into any express marriage contract. Despite this, it found that a common law marriage had been established there. In the judgment, the court stated the following: "Their conduct towards each other in the eye of the public, while in New Jersey, taken in connection with their previous association, was equivalent, in law to a declaration by each that they did, and during their joint lives were to, occupy the relation of husband and wife. Such a declaration was as effective to establish the status of marriage in New Jersey as if it had been made in words of the present tense after they became domiciled in that state."[161]

The judgment undeniably reveals a considerable reliance on the cohabitation as an expression of the parties' marital *consensus* that is particularly striking since nothing in the cohabitation and its constituting actions is specifically, directly cited as indicators of such a *consensus.* Moreover, it is not argued that the marriage agreement occurred at a particular time or place. Rather, the facts in the case are consistent with the conclusion that the parties simply lived for one year together in New Jersey. It appears rather farfetched to equate the parties' actions to "a declaration," even if the court took into consideration not only their actions in New Jersey but also their previous association.

One cannot, however, overlook the fact that the invalid wedding ceremony could have played a role in the court's assessment. The judgment in such a case could then be explained by the Court taking into consideration

161 *Travers v. Reinhardt,* 205 U.S. 423, 440, 27 S.Ct. 563, 51 L.Ed 865, 873 (1906). *Compare* the dissent, Justice Holmes, who did not find it proven that a marriage contract had been entered into in New Jersey: "Habit and repute might be evidence of a marriage when unexplained. But they must be evidence of a contract, however informal, to have any effect." As to his views on contracts, see OLIVER WENDELL HOLMES, THE COMMON LAW 247 (Boston, Little, Brown & Co. 1881). *Compare* a similar stance in *Nat'l Union Fire Ins. Co. v. Britton,* 187 F.Supp. 359 (D. D.C. 1960); *Walker v. Matthews,* 191 Miss. 489, 3 So.2d 820 (1941); and *Cook v. Carolina Freight Carriers Corp.,* 299 F.Supp. 192 (D.Del. 1969). Support for the majority's opinion in *Travers* can be found again in CALEB FOOTE ET AL., CASES AND MATERIALS ON FAMILY LAW 20 (3d ed. 1985). The parties' visits in several states in *Travers* raises the issue of the conflict of laws, discussed in Chapter 10 *infra.*

the marital intent expressed by the parties in the invalid ceremony and further viewing the intent as constituting a *consensus continuus*, which came to expression in the parties' continued cohabitation until the man's death. Such an explanation is somewhat supported in the court's reasoning, given the reference to the fact that their agreement "was faithfully kept up" until the man's death.[162]

7.6.2 Cohabitation after a Wedding Ceremony That Was Invalid due to an Impediment

If the parties have gone through a wedding ceremony, but the marriage was invalid as a result of an impediment, typically a previous, undissolved marriage, and the parties, after the impediment's removal, continue the cohabitation, the question arises as to which evidentiary requirements should hinge on the existence of a marital *consensus*. If the parties continued the cohabitation after the impediment's removal, particularly if they were in good faith as to the impediment, a common law marriage generally is considered to have been established.[163] The reason that the requirement

162 *Travers*, 205 U.S. at 873.

163 *Jennings v. Jennings*, 20 Md.App. 369, 315 A.2d 816, 823 (1974); *Yarbrough v. United States*, 169 Ct.Cl. 589, 341 F.2d 621, 624 (Ct.Cl. 1965); *Burnett v. Burnett*, 192 Kan. 247, 387 P.2d 195 (1963); *King v. King*, 269 Ala. 468, 114 So.2d 145 (1959). The more liberal stance in the case law from Oklahoma finally led to the Oklahoma Supreme Court expressly stating that a continued cohabitation after the impediment's removal is sufficient even in cases where the parties knew of the impediment. *See Olinghouse v. Olinghouse*, 265 P.2d 711 (Okla. 1954), therewith *Clark v. Barney*, 24 Okla. 455, 103 P. 598 (1909) was finally overruled. *Compare* In *Mantz v. Gill*, 147 Okla. 199, 296 P. 441, 444 (1931), the Oklahoma Supreme Court stated: "Where a second marriage is entered into in good faith, and the parties continue to cohabit without change during and beyond the statutory six-month period of impediment, this relationship ripens into a common law marriage." *See also Andrews v. Hooper*, 138 Okla. 104, 280 P. 424 (1929); and *Burdine v. Burdine*, 206 Okla. 170, 242 P. 2d 148 (1952)(one of the parties knew of the impediment). *See further Utterback v. Utterback*, 71 F.Supp. 231 (D.D.C. 1947); *Smith v. Smith*, 247 Ala. 213, 23 So.2d 605 (1945); *McVicker v. McVicker*, 76 U.S.App.D.C. 208, 130 F.2d 837 (1942); *Morrison v. Sunshine Mining Co.*, 64 Idaho 6, 127 P.2d 766 (1942); *Nicholas v. Idaho Power Co.*, 63 Idaho 675, 125 P.2d 321 (1942); *Parella v. Parella*, 74 App.D.C. 161, 120 F.2d 728 (1941); *Thomas v. Murphy*, 71 U.S.App.D.C. 69, 107 F.2d 268 (1939); and *Defferari v. Terry*, 68 S.W.2d 253 (Tex.Civ.App.-Galveston 1933), 128 Tex. 521, 99 S.W.2d 290 (1934). *See also Hill v. Lindsey*, 223 Ala. 550, 137 So. 395 (1931). In the case of *In re Haffner's Estate*, 254 N.Y. 238, 172 N.E. 483, 484 (1930), the court stated: "The ceremonial marriage evidenced the intent of the deceased and respondent to enter into a legal and honorable state of matrimony." *See also Holgate v. United Electric Ry. Co.*, 47 R.I. 337, 133 A. 243, 244 (1926); *Mudd v. Perry*, 108 Okla. 168, 235 P. 479 (1925); *Webster v. Webster*, 114 Okla. 57, 242 P. 555 (1925); and *In re Matter of Crandall's Estate*, 214 App.Div. 363, 212 N.Y.S. 210 (4th Dep't 1925). In *Applegate v. Applegate*, 118 Misc. 359, 193 N.Y.S. 494, 495 (Sup.Ct. 1922), the parties in good faith had entered into a ceremonial marriage, which was invalid due to an impediment. When the impediment was removed, a common law marriage was established. The court stated: "[T]heir actions from the time the impediments were removed were an expression of their intention to be that which they theretofore were not but which they believed they were." *See also Wilson v. Burnett*, 105 Misc.

of a renewed contract is so low has been that the parties, through the wedding ceremony expressed their marital intent, even though it was invalid. The continued cohabitation was then sufficient to prove a marital *consensus.*

On the other hand, opinions have been split about the requirement of a renewed contract if the parties acted in bad faith as regards the existence of an impediment. If they had knowledge that one of the parties at the time of the commencement of the marriage was still married to another, there are courts, on one hand, that have strictly required the existence of a new contract after the impediment's removal. Cases which represent this restrictive attitude and its underlying reasoning are discussed in Section 7.7 "Cases in Which an Implied Agreement Has Not Been Found Proven." On the other hand, the majority of courts appear nowadays to understand that in cases in which the parties have been in bad faith with respect to the existence of an impediment, the continued cohabitation ought to be sufficient to prove a marital *consensus.*

For example, in *Prevatte v. Prevatte* (1989), the man and woman had entered into a formal marriage in 1959, despite the fact that they both knew that the woman was still married to another man. The parties lived together and appeared outwardly as husband and wife for twenty-five years and had mutual children. They filed joint tax returns and the woman was listed on the man's insurance policy as his wife. In 1985 the parties discovered that her first husband had received a divorce from her in 1977. The parties lived, with the exception of short periods in 1982 and 1983,

---

279, 172 N.Y.S. 673 (Sup.Ct. 1918); and *Smith v. Reed,* 145 Ga. 724, 89 S.E. 815, 816 (1916). In *Prince v. Edwards,* 175 Ala. 532, 57 So. 714, 715.716 (1912), the parties had entered into a ceremonial marriage in 1903, which was invalid, however, due to the fact that the woman was still married to another man. When the other man died in 1908, the impediment was removed. The parties continued their cohabitation until the death of the second man in 1911. The Alabama Supreme Court stated that "a mere cohabitation" after the impediment's removal was sufficient and found that the parties therewith had "renewed their pledges." A common law marriage was found proven. *See also In re Wells,* 123 App.Div. 79, 108 N.Y.S. 164 (1908), *aff'd,* 194 N.Y. 548, 87 N.E. 1129 (1909); *Klipfel v. Klipfel,* 41 Colo. 40, 92 P.26, 124 Am.St.Rep. 96, 113 (1907); and *Chamberlain v. Chamberlain,* 68 N.J.Eq. 736, 62 A. 680 (1905). *Compare Adger v. Ackerman,* 115 Fed. 124, 129-130 (8th Cir. 1902), in which the court stated that "slight circumstances may be sufficient to establish a change from an illicit to a legal relation, and proof of its time or place is not indispensable ... where parties who are incompetent to marry enter an illicit relation, with a manifest desire and intention to live in a matrimonial union, rather than a state of concubinage, and the obstacle to their marriage is subsequently removed, their continued cohabitation raises a presumption of an actual marriage immediately after the removal of the obstacle, and warrants a finding to that effect." *See also Eaton v. Eaton,* 66 Neb. 676, 92 N.W. 995 (1902); *Schuchart v. Schuchart,* 61 Kan. 597, 60 P. 311, 312 (1900); and *Poole v. People,* 24 Colo. 510, 52 P. 1025 (1898). *See already Fenton v. Reed,* 4 Johns. 52 (N.Y. 1809), in which the parties married in the belief that the woman's first man was dead. However, he was alive but died several years later. The parties who after the wedding ceremony found out that the first husband was still alive, simply continued to live together after his death. A common law marriage was found established, *compare* § 7.3.1 *supra.*

as husband and wife until October 1984 when they definitely separated. In April of 1985 the woman petitioned for a marital divorce based on infidelity and claimed alimony and a share of the marital property.

The South Carolina Court of Appeals stated that a relationship, which is illicit due to an impediment, is presumed to continue to be illicit after the impediment's removal. The court stated, however, that this presumption could be rebutted through the circumstance that the parties "agree[d] to enter into a common law marriage" and that such a contract "may be gathered from the conduct of the parties." In the assessment given in the case, the court referred to the fact that the man, in a previous case from 1984, admitted to the marriage and further found that it was clear from their conduct that they thereafter gave every indication of their agreement to be married.[164] A common law marriage was therefore found proven.

When the parties, as in *Prevatte*, go through a ceremonial marriage which is invalid due to an impediment and continue the cohabitation after the impediment's removal, instead of considering the invalid wedding ceremony as an expression of an incorrect intent which must be changed after the impediment's removal, certain courts in their reasoning in support of a common law marriage have instead taken the opposite stance to the invalid wedding ceremony by maintaining that the continued cohabitation led to "the original declaration of intent to be treated as continuing."[165] The use of a *consensus continuus* in these cases is explained

---

164 *Prevatte v. Prevatte*, 297 S.C. 345, 377 S.E.2d 114 (App. 1989). It can be questioned whether the case is in accordance with *Byers v. Mount Vernon Mills, Inc.*, 268 S.C. 68, 231 S.E.2d 699 (1977), in which the parties entered into a ceremonial marriage which was invalid due to an impediment and in which they lived together for eleven years after the impediment's removal. The South Carolina Supreme Court found that no new contract had been proven. *Compare Kirby v. Kirby*, 270 S.C. 137, 241 S.E.2d 515, 417 (1978), in which the parties lived together for sixteen years after the impediment's removal. The court stated that the parties' contract "may yet rest in circumstances" and found proved the parties' "new mutual agreement to enter into a common law marriage." A difference when compared with *Byers* is that the man in *Kirby*, despite the fact that he contested the existence of the common law marriage, during trial had testified concerning the woman that he "had considered her to be his wife."

165 *Addison v. Addison*, 186 Ga. 155, 197 S.E. 232, 233 (1938). In *Hess v. Pettigrew*, 261 Mich. 618, 247 N.W. 90, 91 (1933), the court stated that "consent to present marriage evidenced by the ceremony continues from day to day and becomes effective as a present taking in marriage on removal of the impediment." Similar reasoning can be found in *In re Gallagher's Estate*, 35 Wash.2d 512, 213 P.2d 621 (1950). In *Applegate v. Applegate*, 118 Misc. 359, 193 N.Y.S. 494, 496 (Sup.Ct. 1922), the court noted that the parties "always intended to be husband and wife in ignorance of the impediment thereto and regardless of its removal." A similar situation can be found in *Smith v. Reed*, 145 Ga. 724, 89 S.E. 815, 816 (1916), in which the court stated: "The declaration of intent to be husband and wife should be treated as continuing." Prior to this, *see* Gorman *v. Gorman*, 166 S.W. 123 (Tex.Civ.App. 1914) and *Chamberlain v. Chamberlain*, 68 N.J.Eq. 736, 62 A. 680 (1905), in which ceremonial marriages were invalid due to impediments and in which, after the impediments' removal, the courts found "the lawful intent still continuing." For later

by the strong expression that the parties' marital *consensus* receives in the formalized wedding ceremony, and also by the acceptance of the subsequent cohabitation as an expression of this *consensus*.

7.6.3 Cohabitation after an Express Formless Agreement That Was Invalid due to an Impediment

The requirement of a new contract has been minimal even in cases in which the parties have not entered into a ceremonial marriage but simply a formless but express marriage contract where, however, an impediment to a common law marriage existed due to an earlier, undissolved marriage. When the impediment later was removed and the parties continued the cohabitation, it has been viewed, particularly if the parties were in good faith as to the non-existence of the impediment, as requiring too much of the parties that they should then again enter into an express contract of marriage.[166] With respect to the evidentiary aspects, the formless contract has been found significant in the assessment of the parties' marital *consensus* after the impediment's removal in the same manner as the wedding ceremony and the continued cohabitation.

If the parties have been in bad faith with respect to the existence of an impediment, the opinions have been divided concerning the requirement of a renewed contract. If they had knowledge upon entering into the formless contract that one of them was already married, there are courts on one hand that have exacted a high requirement as to the existence of a new contract after the impediment's removal. The cases which represent this restrictive stance and the reasoning behind it are discussed in the next

---

cases, *see Robertson v. Robertson*, 90 Ga.App. 576, 582, 83 S.E.2d 619 (1954), where the court stated: "[B]ut where the matrimonial cohabitation continues after the impediment is removed, it is to be presumed that the intent continues." In *Bolz v. Bolz*, 92 N.E.2d 365 (1950) (applying New York law), the court maintained that the intent which the parties had given expression for in the wedding ceremony, which was invalid due to an impediment, "could be found to continue." *See also Albina Engine and Machine Works v. O'Leary*, 328 F.2d 877, 881 (9th Cir. 1964) (applying Idaho law), where the ceremonial marriage was invalid due to an impediment and where the court stated that "consent is a continuing thing," as consequence of which is that a common law marriage was found established when the impediment was removed.

166 In *Morrison v. Sunshine Mining Co.*, 64 Idaho 6, 127 P.2d 766, 769 (1942), the parties, while one was still married, had entered into a formless marriage contract, which was absolutely void. When the impediment later was removed, a common law marriage was established due to the "continuance of the marital relation and assumption of its duties." *See also In re Walls' Estate*, 358 Mich. 148, 99 N.W.2d 599 (1959); *Reger v. Reger*, 242 Ind. 302, 177 N.E.2d 901 (1961); and Steven G. Brown, Comment, *Common Law Marriage and Annulment*, 15 VILL. L. REV. 134 (1969). *Compare Smith v. Reed*, 145 Ga. 724, 89 S.E. 815, 816 (1916), in which the court, after the impediment's removal, presumed a continued marital *consensus* only after an invalid ceremonial marriage, not after a "meretricious cohabitation."

section, Section 7.7.[167] On the other hand, the majority of courts appear nowadays to have the understanding that even in cases where the parties have been in bad faith with respect to the existence of an impediment, the continued cohabitation ought to be sufficient proof of a marital *consensus*, an understanding which also has a historical anchoring.[168] To begin with, this stance has been expressed in cases where one of the parties has been in bad faith.

For example, in *Hall v. Duster* (1999), the parties, Fred and Carolyn, had met in 1973. Fred had then been recently married to another woman. In 1974, the parties moved in together. In connection therewith, Fred told Carolyn that he was divorced from his wife and suggested that they should "just live together, common law married for a while" and perhaps later have a formal wedding ceremony, which Carolyn accepted. The parties lived together thereafter and had a child in 1976. Fred's marriage with his previous wife was dissolved by divorce first in 1993. They continued to live together until 1996 when they separated. In connection therewith Carolyn petitioned for a divorce, stating that the parties lived together in a common law marriage, which Fred contested.

The circumstances were highly contested. The witnesses testified that the parties presented each other as "wife" and "husband" and that they had a joint checking account. Fred stated that he only saw himself as Carolyn's "boyfriend," that he traveled a lot in his job and that he had "a girlfriend in every state where he worked." He further stated that Carolyn "kicked him out of the bedroom" in 1988 and they had not had any sexual relationship since then, which Carolyn partially contested. He argued further that he filed single tax returns.

The trial court found that Carolyn presented clear and convincing evidence as support that a common law marriage existed between her and Fred after the impediment was removed. The case was appealed to the Alabama Court of Appeals, which stated that in order to establish a common law marriage, the parties must agree to enter into the marriage relationship. The court, however, meant that a contract may be inferred from all the surrounding circumstances. The court further stated that if the parties had tried to marry while an impediment to the marriage existed,

---

167 Cases, in which the courts required a renewed contract and in which none was found proven, as discussed *infra* in the next section, are *Weathers v. Bolt*, 293 S.C. 486, 361 S.E.2d 773 (App. 1987) and *Canute v. Canute*, 384 Pa.Super. 60, 557 A.2d 772 (1989).

168 Bishop, *supra* note 38, § 970. In *Campbell v. Campbell* (The Breadalbane case) (1867) 5 M. (H.L.) 115, the parties commenced their relationship in the highest degree of bad faith, running away when the young woman was still married to another man. The parties lived thereafter as husband and wife. After the first husband's death, the parties had a mutual child. Upon the death of the father, the question arose whether the child was born in or out of wedlock, and therewith whether a common law marriage was established between the parents. The court found that such a marriage was established when the impediment was removed. The evidence in the case as to the renewed marital contract appears very sparse.

and they continued to live together as husband and wife after the impediment was removed, the law presumed the existence of a common law marriage.[169] The court did not discuss the existence of the original marriage contract or its significance in the evidentiary perspective of a marital *consensus* after the impediment's removal, nor did it discuss the significance of the parties' good or bad faith. The court did not more closely address the issue of whether the evidence presented in the case was sufficient to find the existence of a new inferred agreement, but rather simply stated that the trial court was authorized to conclude that Duster presented clear and convincing evidence that she and Hall had a common law marriage after Hall was divorced in 1993. Neither did the court reveal whether it considered the circumstances prior to and after the impediment's removal. It is probable that the parties' long-term cohabitation, despite its insufficiencies, played a decisive and rather independent role in the court's assessment.[170] The court did not raise the issue concerning the relationship, as in *Prevatte* above, of whether after the impediment's removal the continued cohabitation must be presumed to continue to be illicit until the parties' *consensus* has undergone the required change. One sees here a distinction in the reasonings of the courts in Alabama and in South Carolina.

The case law contains cases where the requirement of a renewed contract after the impediment's removal has been avoided even where both of the parties had knowledge of the impediment. For example, in *Matthews v. Britton* (1962),[171] the parties, Ernestine and Henry Matthews, had commenced their cohabitation in Washington, D.C., in 1935 while Ernestine was still married to another man. The District of Columbia recognizes common law marriages. The first marriage was formally dissolved in 1952. Ernestine and Henry never formally married, but Ernestine testified at trial that she had taken Henry "as [her] husband," that when they began their cohabitation he asked her to live together as "as man and wife" and that she consented. The parties lived together as husband and wife and had outwardly appeared as such until the man's death in 1957.

In connection therewith, Ernestine claimed death benefits based on the fact that she was Henry's common law wife.[172] The United States

169 *Hall v. Duster*, 727 So.2d 834, 836 (Ala.Civ.App. 1999). The court referred to *Smith v. Smith*, 247 Ala. 2123, 23 So.2d 605 (1945) and *Hill v. Lindsey*, 223 Ala. 550, 552, 137 So. 395, 396 (1931). It ought, however, be noted that the parties in these cases, as distinguished from *Hall*, had entered into ceremonial weddings that were invalid due to impediments.

170 *Compare Boswell v. Boswell*, 497 So.2d 479, 480 (Ala. 1986), in which the Alabama Supreme Court based an implied contract only upon the parties' cohabitation after the impediment's removal (discussed *infra*).

171 *Matthews v. Britton*, 112 U.S.App.D.C. 397, 303 F.2d 408 (1962). *Compare Lee v. Lee*, 201 A.2d 873 (D.C. App. 1964), in which it is not clear from the facts given whether the original contract was expressed.

172 According to Longshoremen's and Harbor Workers' Compensation Act. 44 Stat. 1424, 33 U.S.C.A. § 901 et seq., applicable in the District of Columbia through 45 Stat. 600§ 36 - 501, D.C. Code 1951, 33 U.S.C.A. § 903 note.

District Court of Appeals stated that no common law marriage naturally was established as long as Ernestine was married to another man. The court found, however, regardless of whether the parties had knowledge as to the impediment, that a common law marriage was established upon the removal of the impediment through the marital dissolution. The court granted the woman's claims. A concurring judge, Judge Prettyman, wished to maintain the requirement of a new marriage contract after the impediment's removal, but was prepared to accept the actions of Ernestine and Henry after the divorce as declarations of an intent to live as husband and wife. The concurring opinion based its reasoning on the existence of *consensus continuus* and found that that it was implicit in the parties' very manner of living day by day for six years after the removal of the impediment.[173] However, the court's majority entirely refrained from the requirement of a new marriage agreement with the following reasoning as formulated by Justice Burton: "It is not to be expected that parties once having agreed to be married will deem it necessary to agree to do so again when an earlier marriage is terminated or some other bar to union is eliminated."[174] If Ernestine and Henry agreed to be married while an impediment still existed and thereafter continued to cohabit and live together as husband and wife, according to the majority a common law marriage was established when the impediment was removed.[175]

---

173 *Matthews v. Britton* 112 U.S.App.D.C. 397, 303 F.2d 408, 411 (1962). Few cases contain so clear a description of the parties' actions and their connection to the contract as given by Judge Prettyman: "Although Ernestine and Henry did not, after the divorce was granted, make a formal reaffirmation in *haec verba* of their intention to live as husband and wife, they performed acts which constituted in substance such a declaration. For example, after the divorce, Ernestine, as 'Mrs. Ernestine Matthews,' took out two insurance policies naming Henry as beneficiary. Also after the divorce she incurred bills as Mrs. Ernestine Matthews. Each of these acts was in effect a declaration that she considered herself to be Mrs. Matthews. Furthermore a continuing intention and agreement to be man and wife is implicit in the parties' very manner of living day by day for six years after the removal of the impediment." *Id.* at 410.

174 *Id.* at 409. *Cf. Thomas v. Murphy*, 71 U.S.App.D.C. 69, 107 F.2d 268 (1939). *See also Scott v. Jefferson*, 174 Ga.App. 651, 653(2), 331 S.E.2d 1 (1985), in which the court stated: "If [a] prior marriage or other impediment is shown to have been dissolved after a second common law 'marriage' by cohabitation was initiated, the party asserting the validity of the second marriage must overcome the presumption that 'cohabitation illicit in its inception is presumed to continue throughout the period of cohabitation.' This presumption can be overcome by introducing direct or *circumstantial evidence* showing the existence of all essentials to a valid marriage, including cohabitation after removal of the impediment" (*italics added*). *See also Carr v. Walker*, 205 Ga. 1, 9, 52 S.E.2d 426 (1949), in which the court stated: "[I]f after the disability has been removed the cohabitation is continued and the parties hold themselves out as man and wife, a new and valid agreement of marriage will be presumed to have been entered upon, in the absence of anything appearing to the contrary." *See also Brown v. Carr*, 198 Ga.App. 567, 402 S.E.2d 296 (1991); and *Ram v. Ramharack*, 571 N.Y.S.2d 190 (Sup. 1991).

175 *Matthews*, 112 U.S.App.D.C. at 410.

While the concurring opinion as to the contractual issue appears to have based its reasoning on the parties' cohabitation after the impediment's removal and in this found an implicit contract, the majority appears to have taken its stance from the original contract and recognized its legal effects despite the fact that an impediment to the marriage existed at the commencement of the contract. Its legal effects, however, were considered postponed until the removal of the impediment. The continued cohabitation between the spouses appears to have been a condition for these legal effects. In this manner, the cohabitation was also for the majority an implied portion of the contract.

7.6.4 Cohabitation after an Implied Agreement That Was Invalid due to an Impediment

Of course, it is easy to understand that the parties do not find it necessary to enter into a new marriage contract when they already believe that they have entered into one through a wedding ceremony or a formless but expressed agreement. However, even in cases where the original contract was based on certain actions consisting of a marital cohabitation between the parties, which ought to be a common occurrence, the requirement of a new contract after the impediment's removal many times has been minimal. The courts in these cases commonly do not frame the issue in terms of the parties' good or bad faith with respect to the existence of the impediment. In many cases, the parties' marital *consensus* has been found proven solely through their cohabitation and appearance outward as spouses after the impediment's removal, even if this is simply a short period. In certain cases, the presumption that a relation commenced while an impediment existed continues to be illicit, and after the impediment's removal, a change in the relationship is required, has been loosely applied with the requirement of a change progressively fading.

In the same manner as in *Prevatte* above, the courts in South Carolina, even in cases where the parties have not entered into any ceremonial marriage but simply began to live together while an impediment to the marriage existed, have assumed that the relationship continued to be illicit and have required a change proving a new contract when the impediment was removed. In *Campbell v. Christian* (1959), "a fundamental change" was found to have taken place in the parties' relationship as they, after the impediment's removal, moved in together.[176] In practice though, in the same manner as in *Prevatte*, considerably more modest, sometimes even unnoticeable, changes have been accepted. In certain cases, the courts have noted that the parties under the continued cohabitation had

176 *Campbell v. Christian*, 235 S.C. 102, 110 S.E.2d 1 (1959).

made certain oral statements[177] or that they considered each other husband and wife.

For example, in *Kirby v. Kirby* (1978), the parties had lived together for twenty years, of which sixteen years were after the impediment's removal. The South Carolina Supreme Court certainly assumed that the relationship continued to be illicit, but stated that the parties' contract may yet rest in the circumstances and found that the evidence proved the parties' "new mutual agreement to enter into a common law marriage." The court referred, in addition to the parties' continued cohabitation, also to the fact that the man, despite the fact that he contested the existence of a common law marriage, at trial concerning the woman testified that he "had considered her to be his wife."[178] The court later in *Callen v. Callen* (2005)

---

177 In *Bochette v. Bochette*, 386 S.E.2d 475 (S.C.App. 1989), the parties had lived together for seven years despite the fact that the man was married to another woman. The day after he received a marital divorce from his previous wife, the woman asked him when they "would be married." The man answered: "[W]e [a]re already married, ... we [a]re already man and wife ... We w[ill] get the papers later." The couple continued to live together as husband and wife and outwardly appeared as such for ten years, until 1987 when they separated. In connection therewith, the woman petitioned for a division of the marital property. The South Carolina Court of Appeals found a common law marriage proven, stating that "an illicit relationship can ripen into a common-law marriage after the impediment of a prior marriage is removed if the parties agree to enter into a common-law marriage and the agreement may be shown by conduct of the parties." The court found that the parties' relationship lost "its illicit nature" when the man answered the woman's question and the parties for ten years had "engaged in conduct manifesting to the world they were husband and wife." The court cited *Prevatte v. Prevatte*, 297 S.C. 345, 377 S.E.2d 114 (App. 1989), in which a common law marriage was found proven after the impediment's removal. One difference between the cases, however, is that the parties in the latter case had commenced their relationship with a wedding ceremony, which was invalid due to the impediment. It can be questioned whether *Prevatte* is consistent with *Byers v. Mount Vernon Mills, Inc.*, 268 S.C. 68, 231 S.E.2d 699 (1977), in which the parties entered into a ceremonial marriage which was invalid due to an impediment and in which they lived together for eleven years after the impediment's removal. The South Carolina Supreme Court found that no new contract had been proven. The principle that a relationship which from the beginning was "illicit" due to an impediment is presumed to continue to be "illicit" after the impediment's removal and that a new contract is required, one which, however, "may be gathered from the conduct of the parties," can even been seen in *Yarbrough v. Yarbrough*, 289 S.C. 546, 314 S.E.2d 16 (App. 1984), in which no new contract, however, was found proven. *See further Kirby v. Kirby*, 270 S.C. 137, 241 S.E.2d 515, 416-417 (1978), in which the parties lived together for sixteen years after the impediment's removal. The court stated that the parties' contract "may yet rest in circumstances" and found that the evidence proved the parties' "new mutual agreement to enter into a common law marriage." A difference compared with *Byers* is that the man in *Kirby*, despite the fact that he contested the existence of a common law marriage, at trial concerning the woman testified that he "had considered her to be his wife."

178 *Kirby v. Kirby*, 270 S.C. 137, 241 S.E.2d 515, 517 (1978). The principle that a relationship which from the beginning is "illicit" due to an impediment is presumed to continue to be "illicit" after the impediment's removal and that a new contract is required, which contract, however, "may be gathered from the conduct of the parties," can even been seen in *Yarbrough v. Yarbrough*, 289 S.C. 546, 314 S.E.2d 16 (App. 1984), in which, however, no new contract was found proven. There are,

found the same principle applicable also when the impediment has been the fact that the parties lived in states not recognizing common law marriage. When the parties later moved to South Carolina and the impediment disappeared, it was presumed that the relationship remained "non-marital." Consequently, the party alleging that a common law marriage was established had the burden of proving that they had entered into a marital agreement after moving to South Carolina.[179]

While the cohabitation in the last case was longer, Iowa offers cases in which the presumption that the relationship after the impediment's removal continues to be illicit is maintained almost *pro forma* and where an inferred contract was found proven with the support of a very short cohabitation as well as the parties' outward appearance as husband and wife. Despite the fact that the cohabitation had not undergone any noticeable changes, it was seen to constitute affirmative proof of an intent to change the relationship to a legitimate marriage. An example of this can be found in the case of *In re Estate of Fisher* (1970). Wilson Paul Fisher received a judgment in August 1967 for marital divorce from Cheryl Joy Fisher. In October of the same year, he became acquainted with Carroll Sue Perdue, who then was married to Platt Perdue. In January 1968 Carroll filed for divorce in a Dallas court. In June of the same year, when Wilson had certain discussions with his former wife Cheryl Joy about a possible reunion, he and Carroll moved in together in Des Moines, Iowa, a state that, like Texas, recognizes common law marriage. On August 27, Carroll and Wilson had a baby. On September 9, Carroll received a final judgment for marital divorce from Platt. At the end of October, they moved to a house near Granger, Iowa, and on November 21, 1968, Wilson died in a traffic accident.

Under the five months in which Wilson and Carroll lived together, they lived as husband and wife. After Carroll received the divorce judgment and until Wilson's death, *i.e.*, for two months, he presented her as "my wife, Carroll" and she as her husband. He gave her two rings. They had certain plans in the future to marry formally. When Wilson died, both Carroll and Cheryl Joy petitioned to be administrator of his estate. The issue then arose whether a common law marriage was established during the two months in which Wilson and Carroll lived together from the divorce judgment until his death.

The Iowa Supreme Court, stating that common law marriage must always be closely scrutinized and which, in addition to the requirement of continued cohabitation, discussed more thoroughly in Chapter 8 below, applied, as a necessary element and condition for the formation of a

---

on the other hand, cases in which the South Carolina courts have not found a new contract proven simply based on a continued cohabitation, *see Weathers v. Bolt*, 293 S.C. 486, 361 S.E.2d 773 (App. 1987).

179 *See Callen v. Callen*, 365 S.C. 618, 620 S.E.2d 59, 63 (2005).

common law marriage, the parties' marital intent and agreement *in praesenti.* The court stated that the parties' mutual consent can be achieved through their cohabitation, but neither such an intent nor such a consent can be inferred from cohabitation alone. The court found in both the parties an intent that they be considered husband and wife both before and after the divorce judgment. The court found the woman's presentation of herself to an insurance representative as the man's wife, after her divorce and in the presence of the man and uncontested by him, to constitute a strong circumstance evidencing that the minds of the parties had met and that there was mutuality of consent to establish a marriage relationship. Even if the court maintained that the parties' presentation of each other was not in itself sufficient as proof of a present agreement and intent, it found with respect thereto and with the circumstances in general that the marital relationship was proven through clear, consistent, and convincing evidence.[180]

It can be seen from *Fisher* that the parties, neither before nor after the woman received her divorce, had not entered into any express marriage contract. The court found the existence of a marital intent and agreement based on the cohabitation—a total of five months, of which only two months were without an impediment—and the parties' outward appearance as spouses—which meant, *inter alia,* that they presented each other as spouses. It should also be observed that the contract was found to be "present" despite the fact that the parties had certain plans in the future to go through a wedding ceremony.[181] It is notable that the court, in addition to the requirement of cohabitation, however short it is, required also something else to be able to find the existence of a contract, namely, admissions and declarations of the marital relationship.[182] The high

180 *In re Estate of Fisher,* 176 N.W.2d 801, 807 (Iowa 1970). *Compare In re Marriage of Mosher,* 243 Ill.App.3d 97, 612 N.E.2d 838 (1993), in which the parties lived together for five months in Iowa and in which the facts concerning their presentations were contested. The wife maintained that the man presented her as his wife, while the man maintained that he presented her as the "mother of my children" and "my woman." The court's majority found the requisites continuous cohabitation and public declaration proven, but not the requirement of intent and agreement to be married. *Compare further Newton v. Lehman,* 105 Ill.App.2d 442, 244 N.E.2d 830 (1969) and *In re Marriage of Grother,* 242 N.W.2d 1 (Iowa 1976), in which no common law marriage either was found proven.

181 Similar to the case of *In re Foster,* 77 Idaho 26, 287 P.2d 282, 285 (1955), in which the court as to the parties' intentions stated: "Their intention of later solemnizing the marriage by a civil ceremony could not operate to defeat the marriage already accomplished." *See also United States v. Dorto,* 5 F.2d 596 (1st Cir. 1925) (applying Rhode Island law law), in which the parties, after a cohabitation of six weeks, entered into a ceremonial marriage with each other, but in which a common law marriage was found established between them prior to the wedding ceremony. With respect to the distinction between a marital contract *per verba de praesenti* and *per verba de futuro, see* Section 6.4.

182 There is no shortage of cases in which the courts have contrarily stated that the parties' actions alone can be sufficient for proving the parties' marital *consensus. See, e.g., In re Zemmick's Estate,* 17 Ohio Supp. 15, 76 N.E.2d 902, 904 (1946), in

evidentiary weight the court attributed to the circumstance that the woman, upon one occasion, presented herself as the man's wife to the insurance agent, appears, however, remarkable. The court did not frame the issue of the parties' good or bad faith with respect to the existence of the impediment. It stated that if the cohabitation from the beginning was illicit, affirmative proof as to a later intent to change that relationship to a legitimate relationship between husband and wife was required to establish a common law marriage. The evidence presented does not appear, however, to prove any tangible change in their intent in and with the impediment's removal. Their cohabitation and outward appearance appear to have been as "marital" before and after the woman's divorce. The court itself maintained that the parties both before and after had the intent to be viewed as husband and wife and had not taken into consideration the requirement of change.

There are also courts within this group of cases that do not generally raise the issue of the illicit presumption or impose any requirement that the relationship or the parties' intentions after the removal of the impediment must undergo any changes. This is true, e.g., of the courts in Alabama. In *Boswell v. Boswell* (1986), the court consequently decided, in the same manner as in *Hall v. Duster* above, the issue of whether the parties entered into an inferred marriage agreement by taking into consideration the parties' cohabitation and outward appearance after the impediment's removal, without specifically examining whether any changes of their relationship had occurred. The parties, S.C. Boswell and Marjorie Boswell, began their cohabitation in 1946. Marjorie had already been formally married since 1944 to Arthur Fair, who died in 1983.[183] S.C. Boswell and Marjorie lived together until Boswell's death in 1984, i.e., for approximately

---

which the Ohio Court of Appeals, applying Pennsylvania law, stated that the parties' consent to a common law marriage "may be evidenced in any form or manner, and verbally or by conduct alone" (dictum).

183 *Boswell v. Boswell*, 497 So.2d 479 (Ala. 1986). *See also Brown v. Carr*, 198 Ga.App. 567, 402 S.E.2d 296 (1991), where the parties lived together and appeared outwardly as spouses for eleven years. During the first four years, however, the man was married to another woman. The court stated that the parties' relationship from the beginning was "illicit" and that it certainly was presumed to be illicit even after the impediment's removal, but added that the presumption can be rebutted through circumstantial evidence: "[If] after the disability has been removed the cohabitation is continued and the parties hold themselves out as man and wife, a new and valid agreement of marriage will be presumed to have been entered upon, in the absence of anything appearing to the contrary." The court cites *Scott v. Jefferson*, 174 Ga.App. 651, 653(2), 331 S.E.2d 1 (1985) and *Carr v. Walker*, 205 Ga. 1, 9, 52 S.E.2d 426 (1949). A common law marriage was found proven and the surviving widow inherited from the deceased. In *Hill v. Shreve*, 448 P.2d 848, 851 (Okla. 1968), the Oklahoma Supreme Court stated concerning the woman's knowledge of her previous husband's fate: "Whether she knew of his demise or assumed such demise after seven years is immaterial." *See also, e.g., Rocky Mountain Fuel Co. v. Reed*, 110 Colo. 88, 130 P.2d 1049 (1942); *Clark v. Clark*, 123 Colo. 285, 229 P.2d 142 (1951); and *Gillaspie v. Blair Constr. Co.*, 192 Kan. 455, 388 P.2d 647 (1964).

thirty-eight years. Consequently, for only one year during this long cohabitation was there no impediment to their marriage.

Upon S.C. Boswell's death, Marjorie claimed the statutory widow allotment in Alabama, citing as a basis that she had been the deceased's common-law wife. The Alabama Supreme Court stated that three requirements must exist in order to establish a common law marriage: (1) capacity; (2) present, mutual agreement to permanently enter the marriage relationship to the exclusion of all other relationships; and (3) public recognition of the relationship as a marriage and public assumption of the marital duties and cohabitation.[184] The court further stated that these elements can either be explicitly expressed or implicitly inferred from the circumstances. The court found that the parties, after the removal of the impediment in 1983, and until S.C. Boswell's death in 1984, continued to live together, holding themselves out as husband and wife "thereby mutually agreeing to a common-law marriage."[185]

Even if the facts cited in the case are sparse as to the actual circumstances, it can be seen that the parties had not entered into any express marriage contract from the beginning. They simply moved in together. It cannot be determined from the facts whether the parties were in good or bad faith with respect to the impediment, and the court did not raise the issue. The cohabitation certainly was long, approximately thirty-eight years, but only one year of this period was without an impediment. It appears as if this short cohabitation after the impediment's removal and their outward appearance as spouses during this same period was sufficient to establish an inferred marriage agreement. No further manifestation of the parties' *consensus* was required. The court did not point to any particular circumstances and did not more closely state that upon which it based its findings, but rather simply referred to the fact that the parties after the impediment's removal continued the cohabitation, outwardly appeared as husband and wife, and that they thereby mutually entered into an agreement, which clearly was based on the fact that they "permanently enter[ed] the marriage relationship to the exclusion of all other relationships." The entire contract consequently was an implied agreement or a silent agreement.

---

184 *Boswell*, 497 So.2d at 480. With respect to the requisites, the court cited its own prior decisions in *Etheridge v. Yeager*, 465 S.2d 378 (Ala. 1985) and *Mattison v. Kirk*, 497 So.2d 120 (Ala. 1986).

185 *Boswell*, 497 So.2d at 480. It can be noted that the appellate court applied the *ore tenus* evidentiary principle, that when the trial court has the opportunity to look witnesses in the eye and hear the inflections in their voices, the trial court's determination of the facts in a case will be presumed correct by the appellate court unless that determination is shown to be plainly and palpably erroneous or manifestly unjust. The Alabama Supreme Court stated that the trial court's judgment was presumed correct as it "is fairly supported by credible evidence under (a) reasonable aspect (of this case), and is not palpably wrong or manifestly unjust." *Id.* at 481. The trial court in its judgment had found that the parties "by habit, repute, and cohabitation ... lived in matrimonial cohabitation." *Id.* at 480.

Boswell also gives insight as to how the court reasons when it, instead of a sharp delineation of the execution of a contract, states that the parties continued to live together thereby mutually agreeing to a common law marriage, employing a *consensus continuus* as discussed above in Chapter 6 with the formation of an inferred agreement.[186] However, there are other cases in this group that clearly demonstrate how the courts reason when they find the existence of a *consensus continuus* based on circumstantial evidence.

For example, in *Consolidated Underwriters v. Kelly* (1929), the parties, Louisa and Joe Kelly, had moved in together in Beaumont in Texas in October of 1925.[187] Louisa, who came from Amelia, Louisiana, was then still married to another man, who died approximately one month later. Louisa and Joe lived together thereafter as husband and wife for approximately six weeks until January 1926 when Joe died.

As Joe's death was due to injuries received at work, Louisa applied for workmen's compensation benefits stating that she was Joe's widow. The issue then arose whether a common law marriage had been established between Louisa and Joe during the approximately six weeks that they had lived together after her previous husband's death. The Texas Court of Civil Appeals found in their first review of the case that a common law marriage was established between Louisa and Joe. The court stated, in the renewed examination: "Their continued living together as husband and wife after the removal of the impediment bespeaks a continued intention and agreement day by day to be husband and wife."[188] As to the fact that no evidence, beyond the cohabitation, was required, the court explicitly stated: "It is not necessary in addition to offer evidence of ... the actual agreement of the parties to be husband and wife." The Texas Commission of Appeals approved of the court's conclusion that the parties upon Joe's death were husband and wife, recommending the adoption of the court's judgment. In its retrial, the Texas Court of Civil Appeals adopted the recommendation.

The use of the cohabitation as an evidentiary fact for the contract is naturally more suitable as evidence for a *consensus continuus* than as evidence of the sharply defined execution of a contract. Nevertheless, the issue remains about what evidentiary weight should be attributed to a

186 Chapter 6.2.3 *infra.*

187 *Consolidated Underwriters v. Kelly,* 15 S.W.2d 229 (Tex.Com.App. 1929). It ought to be noted that the principles for proving common law marriages in Texas were codified at the end of the 1960s and that these rules were again amended in 1989.

188 *Id. Cf.* a similarly expressed statement by the dissent in *Matthews v. Britton,* 112 U.S.App.D.C. 397, 303 F.2d 408, 410 (D.C.Cir. 1962). *Cf. Wilson v. Burnett,* 105 Misc. 279, 172 N.Y.S. 673 (1918), in which the court found that after the impediment against a legal marriage was removed, they each consented and agreed to continue their relations as husband and wife, and acted accordingly. *Cf. Travers v. Reinhardt,* 205 U.S. 423, 440, 27 S.Ct. 563, 51 L.Ed 865, 873 (1906).

cohabitation lasting a few months in proving the existence of an intent to be husband and wife. Decisive for the answer to this issue is not only the length of the cohabitation, but above all else, the contents of the marital intent, its *essensialia.* If on one hand, the object of the marital intent is to "to live together as husband and wife" and the parties actually do this, it is clear that the cohabitation ought to be attributed a considerable evidentiary importance. However, it cannot be taken for granted that a cohabitation as short as the one in the case referenced above can be deemed to be an expression an intent to live an entire life together. If, on the other hand, the object of the marital intent is to be an intent invoking legal consequences, or an intent to change the parties' marital status, it is clear that the cohabitation, even if it were long, ought to be attributed a more limited evidentiary weight. The issue as to which content the marital intent's *essensialia* ought to be given is not raised in *Kelley* at all, but is more closely discussed below in the last section here. Neither did the court in its reasoning raise any discussion in terms of offer and acceptance as parties in a mutual contract of marriage.

Even if a short relationship can result in a common law marriage, the length of the cohabitation as discussed in the case law has had significance in the valuation of the evidence. Where the cohabitation has been very long, it appears that certain courts have overlooked periodic insufficiencies as to the cohabitation and the marriage-like conditions in the cohabitation. Despite such deficiencies, they have referred to "an ongoing agreement."

One example is from Texas, *Ballesteros v. Jones* (1998), in which the parties began their relationship in 1970, when both of them were married to other persons. The man lived 3-4 times a week with a woman in Laredo, but also spent a portion of his time in his house in Nuevo Laredo together with the children from a previous marriage (with respect to the requirement of cohabitation, see Chapter 8).[189] The man gave the woman a diamond ring and a wedding band. The woman received her divorce shortly thereafter. They had a mutual son. After the man's previous wife died in 1980, and no impediment to the marriage existed any longer, they continued their cohabitation for approximately seventeen years. The man lived on a regular basis with the woman, but periodically also in his own house. He presented her as his wife. On trips, they traveled as Mr. and Mrs. Monetou. The man contributed to the family's maintenance but also saw other women. He hired prostitutes who were flown in from Mexico to participate in lesbian sex with his common law wife while he watched. The parties never submitted a joint tax statement as husband and wife. The woman claimed that she believed that they had entered into an agreement to be married.

189 *See* Section 8.5 *infra.*

The Texas Court of Appeals in San Antonio stated that "an ongoing agreement to be married" may be shown by the circumstantial evidence of the parties continuing to live together as husband and wife and holding themselves out to others as being married after removal of the impediment.[190] The court found that the evidence was sufficient to support the jury's conclusion concerning the existence of a marriage agreement and a common law marriage. As the court refers to circumstantial evidence after the removal of the impediment, it appears that the court did not place much weight on the parties' exchange of rings when commencing the relationship. The parties' sexual adventures did not prevent the existence of an ongoing agreement to be married.

In other cases where the courts have used a *consensus continuus* model, they have noted circumstances that also occasionally are cited as support for oral contracts, for example, that the parties exchanged rings, that they engraved their names or had a mutual symbol in them, etc. However, here there is no issue of an oral contract as no contractual exchange of words has occurred (as to oral contracts, see Chapter 6). Neither have the courts, in their reasoning, spoken in terms of offer and acceptance, which are parts of a mutual contract. In such cases, it is an issue of an implied agreement that can also be based upon other circumstantial evidence and admissions and declarations that continually arise often over a long period. Objections that a contract must be entered into at a specific point of time and at a specific place are rejected.

An example of this can be seen in the case of *In re Matter of Estate of Hunsaker* (1998), in which the parties, Anne and Maurice, met in 1985 when Anne was still married to another man. In December of 1986, Ann moved into Maurice's mobile home. In that same month on Christmas Day, Ann received both engagement and wedding rings from Maurice. She wore the former but not the latter, as she believed she did not have the right until they were formally married. In February of 1987, she received her divorce from her previous husband. In October of 1987, the couple moved to a house near Toston, Montana, where they lived together and appeared as husband and wife for nine years until Maurice's death in 1996. They commonly presented each other as husband and wife, albeit Maurice had stated occasionally that they were not married but that she was only his "long-term girlfriend," "sweetheart," or "significant other."

190 *Ballesteros v. Jones*, 985 S.W.2d 485, 490 (Tex.App.-San Antonio 1998). According to Tex. Fam. Code Ann. § 2.22, now § 6.202 (Vernon 2005), no new contract after the removal of the impediment needs to be proven. The law presumes such a contract if the parties "have lived together as husband and wife and represented themselves to others as being married." This cohabitation, which can be of a short duration, does not need to have taken place in Texas. *See also Rogers v. Sullivan*, 795 F.Supp. 761 (E.D.N.C. 1992); *Garduno v. Garduno*, 760 S.W.2d 735 (Tex.App.-Corpus Christi 1988); *Orr v. Bowen*, 648 F.Supp. 1510 (D.Nev. 1986); and *Braddock v. Taylor*, 592 S.W.2d 40 (Tex.Civ. App.-Beaumont 1979). In *Durr v. Newman*, 537 S.W.2d 323 (Tex.Civ.App.-El Paso 1976), the court accepted a cohabitation of three days after the impediment's removal.

They had separate bank accounts and filed separate tax returns as single persons, as Maurice did not want to involve Ann in his financial problems. Together they purchased a large grandfather clock and engraved the initials "M.," "A.," and "H." on the pendulum. Ann further stated that she "felt married" and that she believed that Maurice did the same. Immediately before his death, Maurice planned to leave his property to Ann in his will because she was his common-law wife. After his death, Ann argued that she was his surviving wife in a common law marriage.

The deceased's siblings argued before the Montana Supreme Court that the parties' consent and agreement must occur "at a set time." The court stated that the parties' mutual consent and contract "can be implied from the conduct of the parties" and that the party claiming that a common law marriage existed did not need to prove the exact day that this occurred. As to whether the woman, who had the burden of proof, was successful in proving the existence of a marriage contract, the court particularly noted that she had worn the engagement ring she received from the man, that the parties on their grandfather clock had engraved their initials, that the woman stated that she "felt married to him" and that she believed he "felt married to her."[191] The court found that the woman carried her burden of proving that she and the man mutually consented and agreed to a marital relationship. The case can be compared to *Campbell v. Christian* (1959), where the parties moved in together after the removal of the impediment and where the South Carolina Supreme Court did not go further than to state that the contract was entered into "within a year or so" after the man's marital divorce from his previous wife. It does not appear that the

191 *Matter of Estate of Hunsaker*, 968 P.2d 281, 286 (Mont. 1998). A similar objection was made to the same court in the case of *Matter of Estate of Alcorn*, 868 P.2d 629, 630 (Mont. 1994), where one party maintained that "marriage cannot occur in a piecemeal fashion," but must come into existence upon a certain occasion or not at all. The court responded to this argument by stating that "cohabitation and public repute" are factors that do not arise upon a certain occasion but rather are "continuing factors." The court found a contract proven with reference, *inter alia,* to the fact that the man had given the woman a ring with two horseshoes on it, that the same symbols were cemented to the entrance of the parties' residence, and that the woman stated that the parties agreed to be husband and wife. *See also In re Matter of Estate of Murnion*, 212 Mont. 107, 686 P.2d 893, 906 (1984), in which the parties had entered into an oral marital contract in the state of Washington, a state which does not recognize common law marriage, where after they moved to Montana, which recognizes such marriage. The Montana Supreme Court found that all of the requisites for the formation of a common law marriage were fulfilled under the parties' approximately six-month cohabitation in Montana, wherewith the court referred to *inter alia* their "continuing agreement." A marriage contract was also proven in *In re Ober*, 2003 MT 7, 314 Mont. 20, 62 P.3d 1114 (2003), in which the parties had exchanged rings. The man had carried a photograph of the woman in his wallet. On the back of it he had written "my wife." Despite the facts that the parties had separate bank accounts and surnames and were "single" taxpayers, a common law marriage was established.

twenty-four years of cohabitation and outward appearance were required.[192]

7.6.5 Cohabitation without a Prior Impediment

The American case law naturally also includes cases in which no impediment to the marriage existed in the beginning, and in which the parties without entering into any express contract thereon simply moved in together, and in which the courts from the parties' cohabitation and holding out as a couple have found the existence of a marriage agreement. Among these cases, one can detect a tendency in some that the courts certainly in principle have imposed the contract requirement, but where their reasoning and conclusions in the contract portion begin to fade into the background, and where they more directly find the existence of a common law marriage from the parties' cohabitation and outward appearance as spouses. One then with justification can speak of implied agreements and even silent agreements.

An example of this is the case of *In re Marriage of Gebhardt* (1988), in which the plaintiff, Patricia Probert Gebhardt, moved into the home of the defendant Freddie L. Gebhardt in 1970, and lived there continually for approximately sixteen years. In 1986, Patt filed for marital divorce based on the claim that she and Freddie had lived together in a common law marriage. Freddie contested the existence of any common law marriage, citing as grounds thereof that the parties had not demonstrated any present intent to be husband and wife and that they did not hold themselves out to the public to be married. As support thereof, he stated that Patt in her tax returns had stated that she was single, that she applied for employment under her maiden name of Patt Probert, a single person,

---

192 *Campbell v. Christian*, 235 S.C. 102, 110 S.E.2d 1 (1959). The idea, that upon the commencement of a cohabitation as husband and wife there actually is an implied agreement which is executed through the thereafter following cohabitation, is anchored even in cases where at the beginning of the cohabitation, there was an impediment to the marriage. This has been expressly stated, for example, in *Le Blanc v. Yawn*, 99 Fla. 328, 126 So. 789, 790 (1930), in which the parties for approximately ten years lived together as husband and wife and outwardly appeared as such, but in which the man for the first six to seven years was married to another woman. The court stated: "It is in effect that an agreement was made in the beginning to live together as man and wife, and that such an agreement was actually carried out by more than ten years of cohabitation as such." In *Hurley v. Hurley*, 222 Mont. 287, 721 P.2d 1279, 1284 (1986), in which the parties lived together for eleven years, the woman was asked at trial whether she could state an exact time at which the marital contract arose, to which she answered: "At some point, there was a decision to become man and wife ... At the moment when I agreed to move to Coming." The Montana Supreme Court found that the trial court's finding that the parties had entered into a common law marriage "in April, 1973" was correct. *Compare Anderson v. Anderson*, 235 Ind. 113, 131 N.E.2d 301 (1956), in which the parties' moving in together, and the following sixteen years of cohabitation as husband and wife, were not sufficient to establish a marital contract and therewith a common law marriage.

that Patt was registered as owner of a newly acquired automobile, that she purchased shares in the name of Patt Probert, that the same name was on her driver's license, and that she as defendant in a federal case stated that her name was Patt Probert.

The Iowa Court of Appeals stated that three elements were necessary to establish a common law marriage in Iowa, namely (1) present intent and agreement to be married, (2) continuous cohabitation, and (3) public declarations that the parties are husband and wife. The court further stated that the burden of proof lies on the party asserting the existence of a common law marriage, who must prove all three of these elements by a preponderance of the evidence.[193] Concerning the cohabitation's function as an evidentiary fact for the marriage contract, the court stated: "Proof of cohabitation, as well as evidence of conduct and general repute in the community where the parties reside, tends to strengthen the showing of present agreement to be husband and wife, as well as bearing upon the question of intent."

The court found that the evidence clearly and convincingly demonstrated that the parties were holding out to the public that they were husband and wife and noted the following fifteen circumstances as support for the existence of a common law marriage: (1) Patt's intent and belief with respect to her relationship with Freddie; (2) opinions of various witnesses that the community generally regarded the parties as married; (3) continuous cohabitation by the parties for sixteen years; (4) Freddie's acquiescence in Patt's use of his name and her representations to the community that they were married; (5) Patt's receipt of a diamond engagement ring and wedding ring from Freddie; (6) payment by Freddie of charge accounts incurred by Patt as Mrs. Freddie Gebhardt; (7) mail received and sent by the parties as Mr. and Mrs. Freddie Gebhardt; (8) payment of family and business debts from a single checking account on which both parties were authorized to draw checks, including Patt's authorization to sign Freddie's name to the checks; (9) joint vacations, with the parties' purchase of airline tickets under the names of Freddie and Patt Gebhardt; (10) Freddie's introduction of Patt as his wife to friends and business associates; (11) the parties' operation of a business together; (12) a joint AAA membership listing Patt Gebhardt as a member; (13) a newspaper publication circulated throughout the area which contained an auction sale bill listing the owners as Freddie and Pat Gebhardt;

193 *In re Marriage of Gebhardt,* 426 N.W.2d 651, 652 (Iowa App. 1988). A preponderance of the evidence is the ordinary and lower of the two evidentiary standards that are commonly applied in the proving of cases concerning common law marriage. The same evidentiary standard was applied in the case of *In re Marriage of Grother,* 242 N.W.2d 1 (Iowa 1976). The higher evidentiary standard, which the majority of courts apply, is clear and convincing evidence. *Compare State v. Ware,* 338 N.W.2d 707, 711 (Iowa 1983), which required "a preponderance of clear, consistent, and convincing evidence." For a further discussion as to the burden of proof and evidentiary standards, *see* Chapter 9 *infra.*

(14) Freddie's preparation of a will which provided for Patt in much the same way as one would provide for a spouse; and (15) reference to Pat as an "in-law" by Freddie's mother and sister."

At the same time, Patt declared herself single in her tax returns. The court stated that this fact would weigh against the existence of a common law marriage, but found that the circumstances in general spoke for an opposite conclusion. The court found that the tax returns were filed by the parties as single persons in an effort to facilitate Freddie's early retirement program. Nor did the court place emphasis on the fact Patt had signed her maiden name on various documents. The court formed the impression that the parties believed that the information in certain documents could only be changed after the parties had had a ceremonial wedding. The court doubted that the parties had much particular actual knowledge about common law marriage. The court found that Patt had successfully carried her burden to prove a common law marriage existed.

If one considers the court's reasoning in light of the requirements it imposed upon the formation of a common law marriage, perhaps it is not an overstatement that the court, despite the facts that Patt in certain documents gave her maiden name and in others stated that she was single, found the requirement of "continuous cohabitation" and "public declaration that the parties are husband and wife" proven with the support of all of the facts that were presented and considered. In addition to the court's reasoning that the information in the different documents was based on a formal marriage, parties in general, as a rule, act on that assumption whenever they provide information about their marital status.

It is striking that the parties' present intent and agreement to be married is almost entirely absent in the court's reasoning. Perhaps the fact that there is no discussion regarding a contractual execution on a certain day is not so strange, but the court also does not give any conclusion about all the circumstantial evidence on an intent and agreement. Instead, the court directly found that a common law marriage existed. Under this deficient reasoning, the contractual elements take a back seat, and the contract becomes a silent agreement, even for the court. As a result of this erosion of the contractual elements, the case seems to rest on a presumption of marriage, in which cohabitation and the outward appearances are sufficient for presuming a marriage, but in which objections with regard to the parties' marital *consensus* can rebut the presumption.

In conclusion, the case of *Beals v. Beals* (1992), a case similar to *Gebhardt*, also concerns a cohabitation. The parties moved in together without entering into any express marriage contract and, for a long period, lived together and appeared outwardly as spouses, albeit, unlike *Gebhardt*, the cohabitation lasted not sixteen but seven years, and was not dissolved through divorce but by the death of the man. A marked difference between *Beals* and *Gebhardt*, though, is that a second woman claimed that she had lived with the man in a common law marriage.

The parties in *Beals*, Melvin Beals, Jr., and Patricia Johnson, decided in 1971 to live together as husband and wife. In 1972, they purchased a house together and lived there until 1978. During those seven years they cohabited, referred to each other as husband and wife, and had a joint bank account. They purchased automobiles and signed contracts jointly. They had two mutual children. However, on their tax returns, they stated that they were single persons. Patricia used her maiden name when she applied for Aid for Families with Dependent Children (AFDC) benefits. On two occasions, she petitioned for marital divorce from Melvin, but recalled the petitions. Melvin, on his side, made statements that he had no intent to divorce Patricia. However, they separated and, in 1984, signed a contract concerning child maintenance, visitation rights, and division of the marital property. Even though they did not move back in together, they continued to have sexual relations until 1990, *i.e.*, the last year of his life.

Melvin died in a train accident in 1990. In connection therewith, Patricia petitioned the Probate Court to be appointed administrator of the deceased's estate, claiming that she was his common-law wife. However, another woman filed a comparable petition, claiming that she was the deceased's surviving spouse, that she and the deceased had lived together as husband and wife in a common law marriage since 1978 and that two children had been born as a result of the marriage. The second woman argued that Patricia was appointed administrator by fraudulent representations made for the purpose of demonstrating that she was the deceased's surviving spouse. The court granted Patricia's petition, and the other woman appealed the decision. The Georgia Court of Appeals found ample evidence that a common law marriage existed between Melvin and Patricia and that the marriage was not dissolved until Melvin's death.[194]

The fact that two women were claiming to be the deceased's common law wife clearly illustrates the risk of fraudulent behavior in the application of the regulations concerning common law marriages. Such circumstances can also lead to problems in proving whether the cohabitation and the parties' repute fulfill the legal requirements, as discussed further in Chapter 8, "Cohabitation, Holding Out, and Reputation as Spouses." If, however, a common law marriage had been established between Melvin and Patricia before he met the other woman—as long as the marriage had not been dissolved through a judgment for marital divorce—an impediment existed to a new common law marriage with another person. With respect to the marriage contract, the case could have led to a discussion about whether the man had an actual intent to enter into a marital relation "to the exclusion of all others." On one hand, this could have been contested by citing the fact that he started a new relationship. On the other, it could be argued that the man, at the commencement of the first relationship, had a true intent, and that his intent to begin another

194 *Beals v. Beals*, 203 Ga.App. 81, 416 S.E.2d 301, 303 (1992).

relationship did not arise until after a common law marriage had been established and the parties had *de facto* separated. However, the court does not in general discuss the contract issue, but instead simply states that ample evidence existed proving that a common law marriage existed when the man died.

7.6.6 Cohabitation Resumed after a Marital Divorce

There are also examples in the case law in which the parties cohabit after receiving a marital divorce. In *Clark v. Clark* (2001), the spouses, Linda and Cecil, dissolved their ceremonial marriage through divorce in 1985, after eighteen years of marriage. After a separation of six months, they moved in together again and lived together for approximately ten years until 1995 when they separated again. Linda brought action to establish a common law marriage, obtain divorce, and divide marital assets. Cecil contested the existence of such a marriage and, in addition, argued that the applicable statute of limitations in Utah barred the petition.

The Utah Supreme Court found that the complaint had been filed within the prescribed time[195] and that a common law marriage had been established during the parties' cohabitation. Given the legislative requirement of "a contract between two consenting parties," it is interesting to note that the court, in its reasoning, did not make any reference to either the parties' previous ceremonial marriage and the marital intent there expressed, or the intent to divorce that later led to their divorce. Moreover, the court did not state its requirements for a marriage contract as regards the object of the marital intent or how more closely it found that the contract had been established. The court simply stated that the parties "filed joint income tax returns; established joint checking and credit accounts; jointly purchased real estate holdings, including a shared residence; jointly purchased vehicles and other personal belongings together; shared household expenses; and slept in the same bed" and that these circumstances demonstrated that the parties consented to a marital relationship.[196]

---

195 With respect to the statute of limitation, the legislation states that "(t)he determination or establishment of a marriage under this section must occur during the relationship described in subsection (1), or within one year following the termination of that relationship." *See* UTAH CODE ANN. § 30-1-4.5(2) (1998). Despite the literal requirement of "determination or establishment," the court found it sufficient that "the filing of a petition" occurred within one year. The decision, which in this part is consistent with *In re Marriage of Gonzalez*, 387 Utah Adv. Rep. 89, 2000 UT 28, 1 P.3d 1074 (2000), is judicious with respect to the risk for delaying trials that would have existed if the court had followed the legislation literally. *Compare Bunch v. Englehorn*, 906 P.2d 918 (Utah App. 1995), which was overruled by *Clark*.

196 *Clark v. Clark*, 423 Utah Adv. Rep. 3, 2001 UT 44, 27 P.3d 538, 542 (Utah 2001). The court also found the requirements of cohabitation and holding out as spouses fulfilled.

7.7 Cases in Which an Implied Agreement Has Not Been Found Proven

The American case law also includes cases in which the parties' cohabitation and reputation, as well as their admissions and declarations, have not been found to be a sufficient basis for the existence of a marital *consensus* between the parties and, therefore, no contract was found proven. In certain cases, the facts have been so weak that it is not surprising that no marital contract was established. In other cases, the courts have imposed more stringent conditions for the establishment of a marriage agreement, with reasoning that reflects a more restrictive view of the formation of a common law marriage. The courts' reasonings disclose that one and the same case often can contain a blend of reasons as to why a common law marriage has not been established.

7.7.1 Faulty Cohabitation and Reputation

To begin, there are cases in which the courts in principle have been prepared to evaluate the parties' cohabitation and reputation value as circumstantial evidence, but the actual circumstances cited as support for the existence of a marriage agreement have been insufficient. A cohabitation may have been short or not sufficiently consistent, and/or the parties' reputation as spouses may have been limited or contested. It is then not surprising that the value of these circumstances as evidence in support of the existence of a marriage contract has been low. The boundary between cohabitation and reputation, proving or not proving a contract, of course, is fluid. The nature of the circumstances naturally makes it difficult to determine whether the insufficiencies in the parties' cohabitation and reputation have been so significant that the courts have not found an inferred agreement to have been proven.

For example, the parties in the case of *In re Estate of Phifer* (1981), Kay and Henry, had a relationship for four to five years. They lived under the same roof "on a part-time basis" in Oklahoma. From time to time they separated. Upon one occasion, in 1978, Kay went to Texas with her two children where she stayed several months. Henry presented her as his wife upon certain occasions, for example, when she accompanied him to conferences. In a number of documents, however, he stated that he was not married; for example, in tax returns, registrations, loan applications, and contracts. They also had separate bank accounts.

When Henry died, Kay maintained that she was the deceased's surviving wife in a common law marriage and had the right to inherit. The Oklahoma Court of Appeals found that she had not proven by clear and convincing evidence that the claimed marriage had in fact been agreed to, consummated, and adhered to by the parties.[197]

Despite the fact that the relationship between the parties lasted four to five years, it is not surprising that the court did not find any implied marriage agreement proven, in the light of the insufficiencies in the cohabitation as well as in the parties' outward appearance. In other cases, the party objecting to the common law marriage has reasonably claimed that the other party was simply living in the house with the other, or that the woman was a housekeeper. The boundary between a live-in relationship, housekeeping relationship, unmarried cohabitation, and common law marriage, of course, is fluid. Such actual circumstances can speak against the existence of a marital *consensus* but also against the requirements of cohabitation and reputation in those states in which the latter are independent requisites.[198]

---

197 *In re Estate of Phifer*, 629 P.2d 808, 810 (Okla.App. 1981). Belonging to those cases concerning rather short cohabitations which also have not been stable and where the parties did not have the reputation as spouses is also *Jambrone v. David*, 16 Ill.2d 32, 156 N.E.2d 569 (1959), in which the Illinois Supreme Court, applying Iowa law, did not find a present intent and agreement to be husband and wife proven. The court appears herewith to have required a legal intent between the parties. For more on this *see infra*. *Compare In re Estate of Fischer*, 176 N.W.2d 801 (Iowa 1970), where a common law marriage was found proven after scarcely five months cohabitation, of which only barely two months were without an impediment to the marriage. *See also Cathcart v. Cathcart*, 414 S.E.2d 811 (S.C.App. 1992), in which the parties did not call each other husband and wife. They did not file joint tax returns. They had no joint bank accounts. They did not have the same postal address. In addition, the man dated other women. Both of the parties testified that they "had no intent to be married." The South Carolina Court of Appeals did not find any common law marriage proven.

198 *In re Estate of Kovalchick*, 345 Pa.Super. 229, 498 A.2d 374 (1985). *Compare Estate of Gavula*, 490 Pa. 535, 417 A.2d 168 (1980), in which the parties' relationship certainly lasted nine years, but in which their cohabitation and the reputation as spouses was insufficient and in which no common law marriage was found proven. *See also Price v. Price*, 579 P.2d 843 (Okla.App. 1978), in which divorced spouses moved in together in a relationship which according to the woman's understanding was from the beginning a "housekeeping relationship," but in which the woman later felt that she "had entered into again a marital relationship." The court did not find proven that the parties had again entered into a marriage contract. *See also Jolley v. Jolley*, 46 Ohio Misc. 40, 347 N.E.2d 557 (C.P. Ohio 1975), where the witness testified that the woman called herself the man's "fiancée" and that she had the position as his "housekeeper" (discussed *infra*). No common law marriage was found proven. *See further In re Estate of Dallman*, 228 N.W.2d 187 (Iowa 1975), in which the woman first had employment as a "housekeeper" and in which a marriage contract later was found proven. No common law marriage, however, was found proven due to the insufficient "holding out." In the case of *In re Estate of Swanson*, 160 Mont. 271, 502 P.2d 33 (1972), a common law marriage was established between a man and his previous "housekeeper." In *Deter v. Deter*, 484 P.2d 805 (Colo.Ct.App. 1971), the court found that the housekeeper relationship had glided into a common law marriage. *See further Coleman v. Graves*, 255 Iowa 396, 122 N. W.2d 76 (1960), in which the evidence was not sufficient to prove a common law marriage between the deceased and his previous "housekeeper." *Compare Etter v. von Aschen*, 82 O.L.A. 421, 163 N.E.2d 197 (1959), in which the parties certainly lived together for twelve years, but in which four neighbors testified that they

For example, in the case of *In re Estate of Kovalchick* (1985), the parties, Mike Kovalchick and Adele Baldwin, had begun their relationship in 1977. Adele moved to Mike's residence and lived there until 1980. According to Adele's testimony at trial, the parties, in June 1981, exchanged marital promises in the forest behind his house. Thereafter, they lived more consistently together. Their outward appearance was contested. Certain witnesses testified that Mike referred to Adele as his wife. Others testified that he had said that "marriage was not for him" and that "he would never marry." Certain witnesses testified that she called herself his "fiancée," while others stated that periodically she did not live with him, and that when she was there, she was his housekeeper, living in a separate bedroom. Mike, who died in 1982, had disposed of his estate by will. Adele contested the will, claiming she was Mike's widow in a common law marriage.

The Superior Court of Pennsylvania stated that a contract of marriage may be established by circumstantial evidence and that evidence of cohabitation and reputation may be considered in corroboration with testimony that a marriage contract actually was entered into.[199] The burden of

---

understood that the man was "a boarder and roomer" of the woman. With respect hereto and the circumstances in Gen., the court found that the evidence was insufficient to prove that the parties "were treated and reputed" as husband and wife and that the parties entered into a marriage contract. Such a marriage however was found proven despite the objection that the woman was simply the "housekeeper" in *Gammelgaard v. Gammelgaard,* 247 Iowa 979, 77 N.W.2d 479 (1956). In *Pitney v. Pitney,* 151 Kan. 848, 101 P.2d 933 (1940), a marriage agreement was not found proven between a man and his previous housekeeper, as there was not sufficient evidence of "holding out." *See also Pegg v. Pegg,* 138 Iowa 572, 115 N.W. 1027, 1030 (1908), in which the court found that the woman's relationship to the man "was that of housekeeper for him," not wife. *See further Laurence v. Laurence,* 164 Ill. 367, 45 N.E. 1071, 1074 (1896), in which the court found that the man "always treated her as a housekeeper, never as a wife" and in which no common law marriage was found established. *Compare Hulett v. Carey,* 66 Minn. 327, 69 N.W. 31 (1896), where a previous "housekeeper" was found to have become a "common law wife." *See also Com. v. Stump,* 53 Pa. 132, 91 Am.Dec. 198 (1866).

199 *In re Estate of Kovalchick,* 345 Pa.Super. 229, 498 A.2d 374, 376-377 (1985). Another case where the surviving party claimed that a marital contract was entered into during a civil ceremony and where no contract was found proven, despite the fact that the parties' actions were also cited as evidence thereof, is *Knaus v. Relyea,* 746 S.W.2d 389 (Ark.App. 1988). There the parties had a relationship for about two and one-half years, of which one and one-half were in Colorado, a state recognizing common law marriage. When the man died, the woman claimed that when they lived in Colorado, they had "informal ceremonies" in which they gave expression for "their love for one another and their intent to remain together forever" and with which "their souls were one." According to the woman, they also gave each other rings. Letters were offered in which they called each other husband and wife. They had plans, however, to through a wedding ceremony enter into a ceremonial marriage, which the woman spoke of to relatives and friends as well as in a newspaper article. The investigation also showed that the woman, in connection with a real estate purchase, was listed as single, that the parties in their visits to relatives had separate bedrooms and that they stated that they did not have any sexual relationship. Many of their friends and relatives had not heard them call each other husband and wife. The Arkansas Court of Appeals, applying Colorado

proving the existence of a common law marriage, according to the court's view, however, rested with Adele. As the relationship from the beginning was meretricious, she further had to prove the existence of a marriage contract with evidence that was clear and convincing.[200] The absence of a general reputation as husband and wife was considered significant in the assessment of the woman's credibility with respect to whether a marriage contract had been executed, even though this circumstance did not constitute a necessary requisite according to Pennsylvania law. The court's conclusion was that Adele had not succeeded in proving that she was the deceased's common law wife and, therefore, she did not have the right to take against decedent's will.

The investigation in the case has certain insufficiencies with respect to the woman's testimony that she and Mike, in June 1981, had gone to a family altar in the woods behind decedent's home and there exchanged marriage vows. Strangely enough, no inquiry was made about what was stated on this occasion between the parties. This ought to have been of interest, even if the court's majority did not expressly apply any requirement to the use of words with the commencement of the contract.[201] Mike's statement that he "would never marry" was also never clarified. Did he mean an actual ceremonial wedding? It is clear that the parties' cohabitation and reputation in cases in which the evidence concerning an oral contract is insufficient can be important as corroborative evidence. This, however, assumes that the cohabitation is more consistent and the parties' reputation as spouses is not contested. The court's conclusion, therefore, is not surprising, albeit its judgment with respect to the contractual issue is a bit terse. In a case like *Kovalchick*, in which the direct evidence and all of the circumstantial evidence is weak, the rule regarding the burden of proof as well as the requirement of clear and convincing evidence without a doubt has an important function, particularly if one party is deceased and the court is provided with information from only one party.

7.7.2 Neither Party Claims the Existence of a Marriage Agreement

At times, neither of the parties at trial even claim that they have entered into or agreed to a marriage contract. Perhaps they did not even know

---

law, stated that the parties' actions are "important evidence of the existence of mutual agreement," but found that there was not sufficient objective evidence to prove that a mutual marital contract existed.

200 *In re Estate of Kovalchick*, 498 A.2d at 377.

201 However, a dissenting judge, with reference to the case of *In re Manfredi's Estate*, 399 Pa. 285, 159 A.2d 697, 700 (1960), in which the Pennsylvania Supreme Court spoke of an express marriage agreement "*by words*—not *in futuro* or *potestae*, but—*in praesenti*," wished to remand the case for a renewed evaluation of the evidence by the trial court concerning the issue of whether words which constitute a marriage contract were stated by the parties, *id.* at 378,

about the requirement of a contract for the formation of a common law marriage or that a contract can be silent, if they believe that a contract means a verbal contract. Even courts attributing evidentiary value to the parties' actions have not found the existence of a marriage agreement in the absence of any statements by the parties, particularly if the parties' cohabitation and reputation as spouses has been short and not entirely uncontested.

For example, in *Jolley v. Jolley* (1975), the spouses, June and George Jolley, after almost five years of marriage, received a judgment for marital divorce in 1970 from the Common Pleas Court in Crawford County, Ohio.[202] The next year, they moved in together again and continued to live as husband and wife. Together, they purchased a house trailer and also appeared as spouses in different situations.

After about two years of cohabitation, June filed a petition against George and maintained that they had lived in a common law marriage after the marital divorce. George, however, denied that they outwardly appeared as spouses and maintained that she was simply his housekeeper and nothing more. The court stated that for the formation of a common law marriage, it was required that (1) an agreement to marry *in praesenti* exist; (2) followed by cohabitation as husband and wife; as well as (3) the consequence that they were treated and reputed as husband and wife in the area in which they lived. The court also stated that the plaintiff had the evidentiary burden and that she had to prove these elements with evidence that was clear and convincing.[203]

The court, in trying the evidence, found that the parties lived together as husband and wife and that they also had been treated outwardly as spouses by persons in the area. With respect to the contractual requirement, the court stated that neither the plaintiff nor any of her witnesses had stated that there was a contract in which the parties agreed to become husband and wife at a certain time and that they intended to assume the relation of marriage. The court further stated that a marriage contract certainly can be proven by the acts, declarations, and conduct of the parties,[204] but did not find that the plaintiff had produced any evidence that either any such type of agreement, even in an informal manner, or any understanding between the plaintiff and the defendant, was ever made. The court, therefore, concluded that plaintiff had not demonstrated that any marital contract had been entered into between the parties. No common law marriage had been established.

---

202 *Jolley v. Jolley*, 46 Ohio Misc. 40, 347 N.E.2d 557 (C.P. Ohio 1975). *See also U.S. Fid. & Guar. Co. v. Britton*, 106 U.S.App.D.C. 58, 269 F.2d 249 (D.C.Cir. 1959), in which the court noted that the woman had not testified as to a mutual consent or agreement.

203 *Jolley*, 347 N.E.2d at 560.

204 *Id.* at 561. In another part of the judgment, the court expresses the same thing, but takes as the basis not the evidence but the contract, stating that it "can be implied from the testimony of witnesses as to acts, declarations, admissions, and cohabitation of parties" but that it commonly is the case that neither party is heard. *Id.* at 560.

That the plaintiff had not offered any evidence concerning a contract of marriage can be explained by the fact that she did not believe that a contract was required for the formation of a common law marriage. Clearly, she was of the understanding that it was sufficient to live together and to hold oneself out as man and wife in the community, and to love the defendant and take care of him.[205] Her mistake with respect to the content of the current law regarding the constituting elements certainly ought not exclude the fact that the parties actually entered into a contract of marriage. Nevertheless, if she and her witnesses could not even state that any contract had been entered into or that they silently agreed to be husband and wife, it is not surprising that the court denied her claim, particularly because they were divorced spouses who, in connection with their marital divorce, precisely before they moved in together, expressed an intent to not be united in marriage.[206]

7.7.3 The Requirement of a New Agreement after the Removal of an Impediment to the Marriage

In those cases in which an impediment to the marriage existed when the cohabitation was commenced, the majority of courts nowadays do not appear to impose any higher evidentiary requirements on the existence of

---

205 *Id.* at 559. *Compare Abramson v. Abramson*, 161 Neb. 782, 74 N.W.2d 919 (1956), in which the man appears to have had the understanding that a common law marriage could be established as they "slept together," while the woman thought that it was sufficient that she "(had) lived with him and had three children." No marital contract was proven.

206 Another case in which divorced spouses moved in again together but where no common law marriage was established, as no marriage contract was found proven, is *In re Estate of Dunn*, 236 Ga.App. 211, 511 S.E.2d 575 (1999), where the court referred *inter alia* to the circumstances that the parties had filed single tax returns, that they did not have joint checking, savings, or credit card accounts, that the woman had a residence and car in her own name, and that they kept their bills separately, as well as that she stated that the man was not her husband. *See further Fields v. Fields*, 530 N.E.2d 933 (Ohio.App. 1987), in which after twenty-five years of marriage, the spouses received a judgment for marital divorce on May 19, 1983. Already in June, they began living together again for about six months. They shared a bed and had a joint checking account. However, they had separate safety deposit boxes and individual health insurances. In April of 1984 they filed separate tax returns for the income year 1983. The court found that no common law marriage had been proven. Other cases in which divorced spouses moved in together, but where no marriage contract was found proven, are *Price v. Price*, 579 P.2d 843 (Okla.App. 1978) and *Eaton v. Johnston*, 9 Kan.-App. 63, 672 P.2d 10 (1983); *aff'd*, 235 Kan. 323, 681 P.2d 606 (1984). There are also cases in which divorced spouses have moved in together again and a common law marriage has been found proven, *see, e.g., Compagnoni v. Compagnoni*, 591 So.2d 1080 (Fla.App. 3 Dist. 1991); *Waller v. Waller*, 567 So.2d 869 (Ala.Civ.App. 1990); *Com. ex rel. McDermott v. McDermott*, 236 Pa.Super.Ct. 541, 345 A.2d 914 (1975); *In re Wagner's Estate*, 398 Pa. 531, 159 A.2d 495 (1960); *Rowland v. State*, 75 Okla.Crim.App. 164, 129 P.2d 609 (1942); and *In re Graham's Estate*, 169 Okla. 568, 37 P.2d 964 (1934). In *Lorren v. Agan*, 2006 WL 3691568 (Ala.Civ.App. 2006), the issue arose whether the parties' cohabitation after their divorce "killed the divorce." The case was remanded to the trial court for a jury trial.

a marriage contract after the impediment has been removed, even though the parties acted in bad faith, as discussed in Section 7.6. The majority of the courts have accepted inferred agreements, and continued cohabitation has generally been sufficient as evidence.

Nevertheless, there are courts that respond to such situations by imposing higher requirements for proving the marriage contract if the impediment was later removed. If the parties, at the commencement of the cohabitation, were conscious that an impediment existed against the marriage, perhaps because one of the parties was married, the courts have found that the parties did not have a true marital intent for a monogamous relationship. On the contrary, their intent has been considered illicit or meretricious, and has been presumed to continue after the impediment was removed. The parties, therefore, must present evidence that a change in their *consensus* has arisen through a new marriage agreement.[207] These courts have refused to accept a mere lapse of time to prove such a change, even if the cohabitation has been long term and the parties in their surroundings have uncontestedly had the reputation as spouses. The courts with the highest standard have required an express contract.

This restrictive stance has been adopted by the courts in Pennsylvania, which principally have not found that the existence of a marriage contract in such cases could be proven simply by the parties' cohabitation. The presumption of marriage based on constant cohabitation and general reputation as applicable in Pennsylvania does not apply when the relationship was meretricious from the beginning, as discussed further in Chapter 9 below.

For example, in *Canute v. Canute* (1989), the parties, Doris and Jacob, had met for the first time on March 29, 1983, at the Holiday Inn in Grantville, Pennsylvania. Jacob was then married to another woman, a fact known by both parties. On April 14 they moved in together and on May 6 that same year they gave marital vows to each other in a civil ceremony in Virginia. Thereafter they lived together, had sexual relations, and had the reputation as husband and wife. They shared their income and bills and had a joint bank account. Jacob's prior marriage was dissolved through divorce on January 18, 1985. The parties separated on February 6, 1988, after almost five years of cohabitation, of which about three were without an impediment to the marriage. Doris claimed spousal support from Jacob based on the fact that they had been united in a common law marriage.

The Pennsylvania Superior Court stated that cohabitation and reputation are simply circumstances from which a marriage may be inferred and

---

207 For example, in *Drummond v. Benson*, 133 S.W.2d 154, 160 (Tex.Civ.App.-San Antonio 1939), the court stated that no evidence existed proving "an intent on the part of either C.O. Drummond or Mary Benson to change the relation that had theretofore existed."

rebutted by other facts and circumstances.[208] An impediment to the marriage existed when relationship commenced, and both parties knew that the relationship from the beginning was meretricious. The court presumed that the parties even after the impediment's removal continued to live together unmarried, as long as they did not "reaffirm" their marriage agreement. The court required clear evidence of "a change in status" and of an intent to enter into a marriage agreement to find that a common law marriage existed. With respect to the significance of the marital cohabitation, the court stated that it did not constitute the essential proof of "an agreement to enter into a legal relationship of marriage."[209] The evidence presented with respect to cohabitation and reputation did not, according to the court, contain any evidence of an agreement of marriage between the parties following the removal of the impediment in 1985 and was therefore insufficient to rebut the presumption that a state of non-marriage continued.

There is no doubt that the court takes a restrictive stance even if it in principle can attribute the parties' marital cohabitation and reputation weight as evidence. The parties' cohabitation certainly was not particularly long, but it was almost five years, of which approximately three were without an impediment, and without doubt was marital as was their reputation. The case therefore is a clear expression for the understanding that such circumstances cannot constitute sufficient evidence for the parties' marital *consensus*, in any case where the relationship due to an impediment was from the beginning meretricious. It then is required that their intent to enter marriage agreement later be clearly expressed, and that the evidence therefore was stronger. It is clear that an oral contract would have been sufficient, but it is doubtful whether the court would go so far as to actually require it.[210] The court's stance is easy to understand if, with respect to the parties' intent to enter into "a legal relationship," this actually refers to an intent concerning legal effect. This terminology, however, is not consistent, and neither does the court raise the issue of the *essensialia* of the marital intent.[211]

Other courts have in principle presumed that the relationship after the impediment's removal continues to be illicit and have required that the

---

208 *Canute v. Canute*, 384 Pa.Super. 60, 557 A.2d 772, 774 (1989). *See* already *Hunt's Appeal*, 86 Pa. 294 (1878).

209 *Canute*, 557 A.2d at 775.

210 The court goes no further than in Gen. dictum stating that the evidence concerning the parties' intentions "*may* consist of words"(*italics added*), *id.*at 774, but of course, could wish to go further in cases where an impediment to the marriage existed.

211 With respect to the marriage contract's *essensialia,* the court speaks not only of the contract "to enter into a legal relationship," *id.* at 775, it also uses the expressions "to establish a marital relationship," *id.* at 774 and "to enter into a marriage agreement," *id.* at 775, as well as "the purpose of establishing the relation of husband and wife," *id.* at. 774.

parties demonstrate that a change of their *consensus* has occurred, but have accepted that such a change can be proven through circumstantial evidence. As such evidence in reality commonly consists of the parties' cohabitation and the reputation as spouses, and the circumstances before as well as after the impediment's removal which to a large extent can be seen as marriage-like, the courts face the difficulty of pinpointing that which constitutes the change. The case law from South Carolina is illustrative of this problem.

For example, in *Weathers v. Bolt* (1987), which concerns the marital adventures of Melvin Weathers, Melvin married Dorothy Terry in 1940. Later, while he was still married with Dorothy, he began to live with, marry, and divorce Leona Head. Thereafter he married Mildred Arrowood. That marriage, however, was declared invalid in 1970 due to the fact that the marriage with Dorothy was not dissolved. That same year, Melvin began to live with a fourth woman, namely Virginia Morris. Dorothy died in 1977, which was why an impediment to the marriage no longer existed. Melvin and Virginia lived together until Virginia's death in 1985, fifteen years of which eight were without an impediment to the marriage. During the cohabitation, Virginia sometimes used the last name of Weathers. A niece to Victoria testified that Victoria after Dorothy's death did not consider herself married to Melvin.

In connection with Virginia's death, Melvin claimed that they lived in a common law marriage. The South Carolina Court of Appeals held that no new marriage contract was required after the impediment's removal for a common law marriage to be established. However, the parties, when they commenced their relationship, were conscious that an impediment to the marriage existed and the court found the evidence insufficient to establish common law marriage.[212]

The court's rather laconic conclusion that the evidence was insufficient to establish a common law marriage appears to have been based on its view that the parties' knowledge that an impediment existed from the beginning necessitated a new marriage contract after the impediment's removal. It did not find that the parties' cohabitation, despite its long term, constituted sufficient evidence for the existence of such a contract. The court in *Yarbrough v. Yarbrough* (1984) is, in principle, even clearer, stating that a relationship which, from the beginning was illicit due to an impediment, is presumed to be illicit after the impediment's removal

212 *Weathers v. Bolt*, 293 S.C. 486, 361 S.E.2d 773 (App. 1987). *See also Byers v. Mount Vernon Mills, Inc.*, 268 S.C. 68, 231 S.E.2d 699 (1977)(no new contract was found proven after the impediment's removal); and *Howell v. Littlefield*, 211 S.C. 462, 46 S.E.2d 47 (1947). *Compare Cathcart v. Cathcart*, 414 S.E.2d 811 (S.C.App. 1992), in which South Carolina Court of Appeals did not find a common law marriage established. The finding in the case, however, is not surprising as both the parties testified that they "had no intent to be married." They did not call each other husband and wife. They filed no joint tax return. They had no joint checking account and did not have the same postal address. In addition, the man dated other women.

and that, in order for a common law marriage to arise, the parties must agree to enter into a common law marriage after the impediment is removed, though such agreement may be gathered from the conduct of the parties.[213]

Just how much evidence is required can be seen from other South Carolina cases. In *Campbell v. Christian* (1959),[214] in which the parties previously had five children together, moved in together first after the impediment's removal and lived together for twenty-four years, during which time they were known and recognized as spouses. The South Carolina Supreme Court found that the relationship underwent "a fundamental change" and the parties had entered into a new mutual agreement. The most significant difference with respect to *Weathers*, consequently, is that the parties in *Campbell* moved in together after the impediment's removal. Considerably less significant was the change in *Kirby v. Kirby* (1978), in which the parties had lived together for twenty years, of which sixteen were after the impediment's removal. The court stated that the parties' contract may yet rest in circumstances and found that the evidence proved the parties' "new mutual agreement to enter into a common law marriage." A notable difference in comparison with *Weathers* is that the man in *Kirby*, despite the fact that he contested the existence of a common law marriage, at trial testified concerning the woman that he had "considered her to be his wife."[215] In other cases, it was sufficient that the parties after the impediment's removal during a continuous cohabitation made oral statements that their relation changed to a marriage.[216] The court in *Prevatte v. Prevatte* (1989) appears to scarcely require a change. The parties' continued cohabitation after the impediment's removal as well as some admissions of the marriage was accepted as a basis for an inferred agreement, even though both parties were in bad faith at the commencement of the relationship and the court had assumed that the relationship

213 *Yarbrough v. Yarbrough*, 280 S.C. 546, 551, 314 S.E.2d 16, 19 (App. 1984).

214 *Campbell v. Christian*, 235 S.C. 102, 110 S.E.2d 1 (1959). *See also further* from South Carolina *Bochette v. Bochette*, 386 S.E.2d 475 (S.C.App. 1989) and *Kirby v. Kirby*, 270 S.C. 137, 241 S.E.2d 515 (1978), in which the courts found common law marriages proven after the impediment's removal. *Compare Byers v. Mount Vernon Mills, Inc.*, 268 S.C. 68, 231 S.E.2d 699 (1977)(no new contract was found proven despite eleven years cohabitation after the impediment's removal); and *Lemon v. Lemon*, 158 S.C. 71, 155 S.E. 285 (1930)(contract not proven after twenty-five years, cohabitation). *Compare Bannister v. Bannister*, 150 S.C. 411, 148 S.E. 228 (1929). Examples of other similar cases, in which no express marriage contract was executed and in which a long term cohabitation proved the existence of a common law marriage, can be found in *Radovich v. Radovich*, 84 Colo. 250, 269 P. 22 (1928); *Moffat Coal Co. v. Indus. Comm.*, 108 Colo. 388, 118 P.2d 769 (1941); *In re Foster*, 77 Idaho 26, 287 P.2d 282 (1955); and *Chivers v. Couch Motor Lines*, 159 So.2d 544 (La.App. 1964).

215 *Kirby v. Kirby*, 270 S.C. 137, 241 S.E.2d 515, 517 (1978).

216 *Bochette v. Bochette*, 386 S.E.2d 475 (S.C.App. 1989).

continued to be illicit.[217] Common for the cases from South Carolina is the fact that the courts, in principle, wished to uphold the presumption that a relationship which was entered into while an impediment existed was presumed to continue to be illicit even after the impediment was removed. In reality, however, the requirement for a fundamental change in the relationship was low or nonexistent.

7.7.4 Direct Evidence against the Existence of an Agreement

Admissions and declarations, *i.e.*, statements which the parties themselves have made concerning their marital *consensus*, are of significant value in trying the issue of whether an inferred marriage agreement exists. If, at trial, direct evidence is produced in the form of the parties' own statements in support of a marriage contract or a marital *consensus* not existing, such evidence has generally been given a higher evidentiary weight than the circumstantial evidence concerning the parties' cohabitation and the reputation as spouses.[218] In certain cases, the latter evidence has been considered entirely insignificant in relationship to the parties' testimony.[219]

217 *Prevatte v. Prevatte*, 297 S.C. 345, 377 S.E.2d 114 (App. 1989), discussed *supra*. It is doubtful whether the case is consistent with *Weathers v. Bolt*, 293 S.C. 486, 361 S.E.2d 773 (App. 1987) or with *Byers v. Mount Vernon Mills, Inc.*, 268 S.C. 68, 231 S.E.2d 699 (1977), in which no new contract was found proven after the impediment's removal.

218 *See Caretta v. Caretta*, 58 So.2d 439, 441 (Fla. 1952), in which the court stated: "The best evidence to establish common-law marriage would be the testimony of the contracting parties, or others who may have been present when the agreement was entered into. In *Le Blanc v. Yawn*, 99 Fla. 328, 126 So. 789 (1930), we held that proof of Gen. repute and cohabitation as man and wife will support a presumption of marriage when the agreement is denied and cannot be proven by the best evidence. In this case the appellee was present before the Examiner and testified. If there was an agreement to presently become husband and wife, she could have testified as to that agreement. Her testimony would have been the best evidence. She gave no such testimony." *See further In re Blackhawk's Estate*, 195 Okla. 390, 158 P.2d 168, 173 (1944), in which the court stated: "There is ample evidence to make a prima facie case of marriage based upon circumstantial evidence. But this prima facie case is greatly weakened, if not entirely overcome, by the positive and direct denial of marriage by the mother."

219 *See U.S. Fid. & Guar. Co. v. Britton*, 106 U.S.App.D.C. 58, 269 F.2d 249, 253 (D.C.Cir. 1959) (applying South Carolina law), in which the woman stated that she "never intended to marry Grayson." In relation to this statement, all the evidence concerning the cohabitation and reputation as spouses according to the court was "not only unconvincing but also immaterial." The case appears to have had considerable influence on the modern case law and is cited *inter alia* by *McCoy v. District of Columbia*, 256 A.2d 908 (D.C.App. 1969), in which no common law marriage was either found proven. It is even cited in cases in which a common law marriage is found proven: *see Jennings v. Jennings*, 20 Md.App. 369, 315 A.2d 816, 820, 823 (1974); *Marcus v. Director*, 548 F.2d 1044 (D.C.Cir. 1976); *East v. East*, 536 A.2d 1103 (D.C.App. 1988); and *Matter of Estate of Foster*, 376 S.E.2d 144 (W.Va. 1988). *Compare Matthews v. Britton*, 112 U.S.App.D.C. 397, 303 F.2d 408 (D.C.Cir. 1962), in which the dissent, citing *U.S. Fid. & Guar. Co. v. Britton*, would impose a higher requirement of an express marriage contract after the impediment's removal than did

As the party claiming the existence of a marriage contract has the burden of proof thereof, and in addition, in many cases, must produce clear and convincing evidence, it is not surprising that the parties' own statements, as well as the contract in question could prevent the formation of a common law marriage. The intent of the parties, not their own legal conclusions, is relevant to the assessment of their statements.

For example, in the case of *In re Estate of Wilson* (1999), the parties, Teresa and Brent, had lived together from 1992 until 1995 when they moved apart. A year later, Teresa died in an airplane crash, at which time Brent applied for letters of administration with respect to the administration of the estate, under a statement that he had lived in a common law marriage with Teresa. Brent introduced certain statements as support for the existence of a common law marriage, but the trial court did not find them credible. It was shown that the parties presented each other as "fiancé(e)," that they filed single tax returns, and that the woman had kept her name from her previous marriage. In addition, Teresa had told her friends that she "had no intention of marrying" Brent and that he had stated in writing that he "was never common law married" to Teresa.[220]

---

the majority. In the former case, however, there was from the beginning an express, albeit formless contract, which was invalid due to an impediment. Should both of the parties deny the existence of a marriage contract or a shared marital intent, it is clear that no common law marriage can be based on simply the cohabitation, *see Rittger v. United States*, 154 F.2d 768, 772 (8th Cir. 1946)(applying Iowa law). *See also Schrader v. Schrader*, 207 Kan. 349, 484 P.2d 1007 (1971), where divorced spouses again lived together for around two years and held themselves out as man and wife. The court found that, standing alone, these circumstances might well have sufficed to warrant an inference that a consensual marriage had been contracted. However, the woman testified that she wanted to be able to get out of the relationship if things did not work out and the man testified that they would remarry only if they could repair their relationship. The court found that they had no agreement or understanding that they were married. Neither in *In re Estate of Keimig*, 215 Kan. 869, 528 P.2d 1228, 1230 (1974), did the court find that any marriage agreement ever existed between the parties subsequent to their divorce, even though they did later reconcile and for a considerable period of time lived together as man and wife. A common law marriage may exist even if one party denies it, *see Reilly v. Jacobs*, 536 S.W.2d 406 (Tex.Civ.App.-Dallas 1976). *See also Gonzalez v. Satrustegui*, 870 P.2d 1188, 1197 (Ariz.App.Div. 1 1993), where the court was very quick to conclude that no marriage contract was entered into with reference to the woman's answer to the question why she and the man "never married." Also in the case of *In re Estate of Dodge*, 361 Pa.Super. 188, 522 A.2d 77, 79 (1987), one party had stated that they "did not intend to marry," but it was questioned whether the party meant a formal wedding ceremony. *See also Etheridge v. Yeager*, 465 So.2d 378 (Ala. 1985). *Compare Welch v. All Persons*, 78 Mont. 370, 254 P. 179, *rev'd*, 85 Mont. 114, 278 P. 110 (1929), in which the woman in an affidavit submitted to receive a widow pension stated that her husband was deceased and that she "has not remarried since his death." With reference thereto, her relationship to another man was found to not constitute a common law marriage. The issue of whether she with "remarried" meant a ceremonial marriage or a common law marriage was not further investigated.

220 *In re Estate of Wilson*, 512 S.E.2d 383, 386 (Ga.App. 1999). *Compare Cathcart v. Cathcart*, 414 S.E.2d 811 (S.C.App. 1992), in which both of the parties testified that they "had no intent to be married." The South Carolina Court of Appeals did not

The trial court found that no common law marriage had been proven and the Georgia Court of Appeals found that the evidence supported the trial court's findings, despite maintaining that a marriage agreement may be inferred from proof of cohabitation and that the parties held themselves out to the world as husband and wife. Even if the marriage-likeness of the three years of cohabitation in *Wilson* was not convincing, it appears to have been the parties' direct statements concerning their marital intentions and the existence of a common law marriage that were decisive to the outcome in the case. The weight of the parties' statements attributed by the courts, against the weight of the existence of a contract, appear clearest in those cases in which the cohabitation has been long and the parties have enjoyed a reputation as spouses.

For example, in *Stringer v. Stringer* (1997), the parties, Lawrence and Carolyn, met in 1980. They lived together, thereafter, for fifteen years and had five mutual children. They filed joint tax returns, called each other husband and wife, and generally appeared outwardly as spouses. During one month of this long cohabitation, they lived separately. Carolyn lived with her sister, but was forcefully taken back by Lawrence. During two short periods, Carolyn and the children lived at family violence shelters because Lawrence had been physically abusive to her. She accepted the services provided under Protection from Abuse Act, which supports spouses and persons living in common law marriage relationships, but not persons only living together. At trial, Lawrence testified that he, when he and Carolyn had begun to live together, was not "ready to commit to a marriage" after his marital divorce from his first wife. When they had lived together for six or seven years, they had planned to enter into a ceremonial marriage, but when they got to the court, Carolyn did not want to get married. She gave the excuse that she had forgotten her driver's license. When Carolyn brought up the issue of marriage, he gave her "excuses and excuses" or stated that no one could force him to marry.

The majority opinion for the Alabama Court of Civil Appeals stated that for the formation of a common law marriage in Alabama, it was required *inter alia* that "mutual agreement to permanently enter the marriage relationship to the exclusion of all others" exist. The majority also found that the evidence supported the trial court's finding that the parties had no mutual assent to be married and, therefore, that no common law

---

find a common law marriage proven. Therewith it was noted that they did not call each other husband and wife. They did not file joint tax returns, did not have joint bank accounts and did not have the same address. In addition, the man dated other women. *Compare In re Estate of Kovalchick*, 345 Pa.Super. 229, 498 A.2d 374, 376 (1985), in which the witnesses testified that the man had stated that "marriage was not for him" and that "he would never marry." Even if the significance the court gave this information is unclear, no common law marriage was found proven. *See also Price v. Price*, 579 P.2d 843, 84 (Okla.App. 1978), where the man concerning a conversation the parties had before they moved in together stated: "I told her I had no intentions of being married to her." No marriage agreement was proven.

marriage existed.[221] Two dissenting judges, however, found that ample evidence supported a finding that an intent to be married and a common law marriage existed between the parties.

The Court of Civil Appeals in this case did not completely review the evidence, because it only had to decide whether the trial court's judgment was plainly and palpably wrong. Its conclusion nevertheless raises the question of what was missing for a marital *consensus*. Neither the majority nor the minority discussed this issue closely. The intent to actually live a life together could scarcely to be said to be missing here. Even though the man's behavior toward the woman upon several occasions was not exemplary, their fifteen-year cohabitation showed that they had such an intent. The court's majority appeared to instead require a legal intent. The parties' hesitation to marry and the man's reluctance to commit to marriage does not appear to have been simply hesitation about going through with a wedding ceremony but also, without a doubt, a general reluctance to be legally bound.[222] It is not clear from *Stringer* whether the hesitation to be bound pertained to a continued cohabitation or to the obligations of marriage in general. Even though they had continued to live together for a long period of time, the man may have wished to have been free to go wherever he wished.

In several cases, it also appears that the courts in Illinois, applying Iowa law, have interpreted a requirement of an intent to pertain to an intent to be legally bound, which makes it difficult, with the support of only the cohabitation, to find the existence of an inferred marriage agreement. For example, in the case of *In re Marriage of Mosher* (1993), the parties had lived together and held themselves out as husband and wife for five months in Iowa. At trial, the woman testified that the man "did not want anything that was legal and binding." The trial court found that the requirements of continuous cohabitation and public declaration were fulfilled, but that there was no evidence demonstrating that the man ever intended to be "legally married." The Illinois Appellate Court stated that

---

221 *Stringer v. Stringer*, 689 So.2d 194, 195 (Ala.Civ.App. 1997). Another case of a long term cohabitation can be found in *Fritz v. Mork*, 2001 Iowa App. LEXIS 594 (2001), in which the parties had lived together for eighteen years and had three mutual children. With respect to the fact that they stated that they were single and unmarried, the requirement of a present intent and agreement to be married was found not proven.

222 The courts in Alabama appear to not have given the issue of the *essensialia* of the marriage contract the attention it deserves. *See Boswell v. Boswell*, 497 So.2d 479 (Ala. 1986), discussed *supra*. That a deficient marital *consensus* can prevent the establishment of a common law marriage in cases where the parties live together can already be seen in *Farley v. Farley*, 10 So. 646 (Ala. 1892), in which the court stated: "As a Gen. proposition, when the nuptials are delayed with an understanding of the parties that they are not to become husband and wife until a formal ceremony takes place, marriage is not constituted by copulation without solemnization." For more on the marriage contract's *essensialia*, *see* Section 6.3 *infra*.

the conduct of the parties did not establish a mutual present intention and agreement to enter into a marital relationship.[223]

Even though the cohabitation has been short, it may have been sufficiently stable and public to fulfill the requirements of continuous cohabitation and public declaration, but not sufficient to prove a marriage contract. This can be compared with *Fisher*, discussed above, in which the parties lived together for five months, of which only approximately two months were without an impediment and in which the Iowa Supreme Court found a common law marriage. A relevant difference, however, is that the man in *Mosher* did not wish anything which was "legal and binding," which demonstrates the effects of the requirement for a legal intent on the possibility of demonstrating an inferred agreement.[224]

The same difficulties arise in cases in which, with the support of the parties' cohabitation and the reputation as spouses to prove an inferred agreement, the courts' requirement of a legal intent is formulated as an intent to reach a marriage-like status.[225] In these cases, the parties' cohabitation and reputation as spouses have been given little weight as evidence of the existence of a *consensus*, even though the cohabitation has been stable and relatively long term. Direct evidence, in the form of the parties' own statements, in which they have made utterances against such a mutual intent, has received decisive significance in such cases.

---

223 *In re Marriage of Mosher*, 243 Ill.App.3d 97, 612 N.E.2d 838 (1993). Even the Illinois Supreme Court appears to have interpreted Iowa law in a similar manner in *Jambrone v. David*, 16 Ill.2d 32, 156 N.E.2d 569, 572 (1959) (applying Iowa law), where the parties lived together for approximately one year in Iowa. The court stated that the parties' conduct and reputation certainly constituted "evidential facts which tend to prove or disprove the agreement and intend of the parties," but found that the evidence did not support the fact that the cohabitation in this case stemmed from any agreement "to assume the marital duties and obligations of husband and wife." A difference that arises in *Mosher*, however, is that the cohabitation was insufficient and no reputation as spouses had been acquired by the parties. The Illinois Supreme Court, also applying Illinois law, has given expression of the requirement of an intent as to legal effect. *See, e.g.*, *Seuss v. Schukat*, 358 Ill. 27, 192 N.E. 668, 671 (1934), in which the court spoke of an intent "to discharge towards each other the duties imposed by law upon the relation assumed." With respect to the application of Iowa law, *see also* the Nebraska Supreme Court in *Abramson v. Abramson*, 161 Neb. 782, 74 N.W.2d 919 (1956).

224 *Compare In re Estate of Fisher*, 176 N.W.2d 801, 807 (Iowa 1970); and *In re Marriage of Gebhardt*, 426 N.W.2d 651 (Iowa App. 1988). *Compare Fritz v. Mork*, 2001 Iowa App. Lexis 594 (Iowa App. 2001), in which a common law marriage was not found proven despite an eighteen-year cohabitation. In older Iowa case law, the marriage contract's *essensialia* is commonly referred to as an intent "to be husband and wife," and not an intent to receive "all the rights and duties" which are tied to marriage. *See, e.g.*, *Gammelgaard v. Gammelgaard*, 247 Iowa 979, 77 N.W.2d 479, 480 (1956); and *Pegg v. Pegg*, 138 Iowa 572, 115 N.W. 1027, 1028 (1908). *See also In re Estate of Dallman*, 228 N.W.2d 187, 190 (Iowa 1975), in which the court spoke of a contract "to live as husband and wife." *Compare State v. Grimes*, 215 Iowa 1287, 247 N.W. 664 (1933), in which the court did not accept a contract "to live as Husband and Wife until such time that we are Lawfully married," as there was no intent to constitute "the legal relation." *Compare Beach v. Beach*, 160 Iowa 346, 141 N.W. 921 (1913).

225 For more on the marital contract's *essensialia*, *see* Section 6.3 *infra*.

For example, in the case of *In re Redman's Estate* (1939), the parties, Anna Redman and Harry Hiland, had lived together for five and one-half years as spouses. They had also appeared outwardly in the community where they lived and generally had the reputation as husband and wife. Harry paid a larger portion of their living costs; Anna used his last name and, among their friends, was called by the name *Hiland.* At trial, Harry stated that they met for the first time in June of 1926 at his rooming house, where she visited him. Anna spent the night. As to this meeting, Harry further testified that, "We agreed to live as man and wife." As to the question whether they had ever discussed any marriage between them, Harry answered, "We talked of marriage but not for her and I."[226]

Anna died on December 9, 1931, without any known heirs. Seven years later, in February 1938, Harry filed a petition in which he asked the court to declare him Anna's common law husband. The Ohio Supreme Court found that the evidence proved that that the parties had lived together and were recognized as husband and wife where they lived. However, the court continued that it was necessary also to show an agreement *in praesenti* to become husband and wife to establish a marriage at common law. No such agreement or intention of these parties was shown to exist. On the contrary, the court continued, "they agreed that marriage was not for them and that they did not desire *that status* ... Their action was no more than the most casual beginning of a state of fornication (italics added)." The court found that there was complete failure of proof of an agreement *in praesenti* to enter into the relationship of husband and wife.[227] No common law marriage was found proven.

Even though entering a marriage contract upon a first meeting between the parties can appear somewhat hasty, it ought to be noted that the man's testimony in *Redman* was not disputed. The court, which consequently had to address the parties' words that they "would live together as man and wife," appears, however, with respect to the marriage contract's required content, to distinguish between on one hand an intent "(to) live together" and on the other an intent to reach "that status." Only a mutual intent to reach the latter appears to have been accepted by the court as *essensialia* in a marriage contract. It is easy to understand that the parties' cohabitation of about five years and their reputation as spouses was given low evidentiary weight in relation to the direct evidence concerning their agreement and its content. Nevertheless, it can be said that the man's statement, "We talked about marriage but not for her and I" was fatal; in particular, it appears remarkable that it was not investigated at trial whether, by "marriage," he meant marriage in general or a ceremonial wedding ceremony. If he was referring to the latter, the statement did not

226 *In re Redman's Estate*, 135 Ohio St. 554, 21 N.E.2d 659, 660 (1939).
227 *Id.* at 661-662.

constitute any impediment to the parties having the intent to establish a common law marriage.

There are also cases in which the courts, particularly in the case law from the mid 1900s, have adopted a very restrictive posture toward accepting inferred agreements as a basis for a common law marriage, even though the parties have made direct statements neither for nor against the existence of a contract. This restrictedness has been motivated by the parties' cohabitation, while reputation has captured limited evidentiary weight with respect to an intent to assume the legal bonds and obligations of marriage. This restrictive stance has been expressed even in those cases in which the parties lived together for a very long time and enjoyed a reputation as spouses.

One example is *In Erickson's Estate* (1954), decided by the South Dakota Supreme Court, a state that recognized common law marriage at that time, though not now.[228] *Erickson's Estate* concerned the estate of the deceased Selma C. Erickson, who had lived together for twenty-five years with a man.[229] The parties, both Swedish immigrants, met in Chicago. The man later moved to South Dakota where he farmed. Selma arrived a year later unannounced at the farm. According to the man's testimony at trial concerning Selma's arrival and the conversation between the parties, she stated, "I've come out here to help you out." The man then said, "Why didn't you write to me and let me know you were going to come so I could get things ready?" and further, "[P]eople here would begin to talk." Selma answered, "Well, they'll forget that after a while," and added, "That part is all right. We can tell the people here we got married in Chicago." The man answered, "Well, if you want it that way ... if you're going to do that, you've got to drop your name and take the name of Erickson." He then

228 Common law marriage was repealed in South Dakota on July 1, 1959.

229 *In re Erickson's Estate,* 75 S.D. 345, 64 N.W.2d 316 (1954). Another case with a long term cohabitation is *Abramson v. Abramson,* 161 Neb. 782, 74 N.W.2d 919 (1956) (applying Iowa law), in which the parties lived together for approximately twenty years in Nebraska, a state which does not recognize common law marriage, and approximately one year in Iowa, which recognizes such marriages. They had also acquired a reputation as husband and wife. The man appears to have had the understanding that a common law marriage could be established as they "slept together," while the woman thought it was sufficient that she "(had) lived with him and had three children." Despite the fact that the Nebraska Supreme Court, applying Iowa law, considered their cohabitation in Iowa as well as in Nebraska, it found that they had not proven "any agreement or understanding" to become husband and wife when they commenced their relationship and neither any intent to later change their relationship to a "legitimate relationship." *See also Anderson v. Anderson,* 235 Ind. 113, 131 N.E.2d 301 (1956), in which the Indiana Supreme Court appears to have required a mutual intent to reach a "marital status" and in which no contract was found proven despite sixteen years, cohabitation. *See also Stringer v. Stringer,* 689 So.2d 194, 195 (Ala.Civ.App. 1997), *supra,* where the parties lived together for fifteen years and *Fritz v. Mork,* 2001 Iowa App. LEXIS 594 (2001), in which the cohabitation was eighteen years. An older case with 30 years of cohabitation not establishing a common law marriage is *McKenna v. McKenna,* 180 Ill. 577, 54 N.E. 641 (1899).

said, "I'll introduce you to my friends and everybody as Mrs. Erickson," and "After this you're Mrs. Erickson," to which she gave her silent consent.[230]

The parties lived together thereafter about twenty-five years as husband and wife and outwardly had the reputation of being such. The relationship was dissolved when the man began a relationship with Selma's sister, who also emigrated from Sweden. The man and the sister then lived in Minnesota, where they still lived at the time of Selma's death. During that period of almost twenty years, the man had no contact with Selma.

When Selma died, however, the man claimed her estate because he had lived together with her in a common law marriage. The South Dakota Supreme Court stated that a common law marriage can be established if there is "an actual agreement to form a legal relationship of husband and wife" as well as "a marriage in fact." The court, however, emphasized that a common law marriage can only be established through exceptional facts. With respect to the evidence, the court admitted that the proof of habit and repute, *i.e.*, the parties' actions towards each other and their reputation as spouses in the community, were permitted as evidence. However, if direct evidence is produced concerning the parties' intentions, e.g., if one of them describes that which has been said, such evidence must, according to the court's view, constitute the basis of the judgment.[231] The evidentiary burden rests upon the party claiming such a marriage, and that party must prove the marriage with evidence that is clear and convincing.[232]

In assessing the evidence produced in the case, the court stated that not only consent but an expression of consent was required to establish a marriage contract. The court continued by finding that the man's testimony as to the oral contract when Selma arrived at the farm was a denial or a part of an attempt to mislead the community rather than evidence of a marriage. With respect to the cohabitation's importance as evidence, the court pointed to "the untrustworthiness of mere cohabitation and reputation as proof of marriage" and stated further: "The cohabitation of the parties in this case, clearly and beyond any question, is no better proof that they were married than it is that they were enacting a deception designed to serve a purpose of enjoying sexual union and all other pleasures of intimate association common to the marriage state but free of its bonds and ultimate responsibilities."[233]

230 *Erickson's Estate*, 64 N.W.2d at 317.

231 *Id.* at 319. A similar statement can be found in *Pierce v. Pierce*, 355 Pa. 175, 49 A.2d 346 (1946): "In civil cases, reputation and cohabitation are admitted as evidence of an actual marriage ... When, however, we have the testimony of one of the parties as to the terms of the contract, and that shows that there was no contract by words *in praesenti*, all other evidence on the subject is of no importance." *Compare Schilling v. Parsons*, Admir, 110 Ind.App. 52, 36 N.E.2d 958 (1951), in which thirty years of cohabitation did not establish a common law marriage.

232 *Erickson's Estate*, 64 N.W.2d at 318.

233 *Id.* at 320.

The court found that the evidence, taken together, did not demonstrate that consent or intention to marry existed. No intent to take "each other as husband and wife forever" was proven. The evidence in its entirety instead tended, according to the court's view, "to show an impulsive venture into, or a continuation of, an illicit relationship of the kind least offensive to society because the parties covered it with the cloak of marriage. The ultimate result and involvement were scarcely in the contemplation of the parties because of the consuming anticipation of immediate pleasure." As the man consequently could not be considered Selma's surviving spouse, he could not inherit from her.

It is difficult to resist the belief that the court's moral indignation was motivated less by the fact that the man abandoned Selma for her sister—a relationship which lasted more than twenty years – and more by his audacity, upon Selma's death, in claiming her estate as her surviving spouse after over twenty years of cohabitation with her sister. Nevertheless, apart from this indignation, the court's reasoning is also legally interesting. Even though the court had attributed evidentiary weight to the cohabitation, it is clear that it did not accept that the marriage contract was proven simply through cohabitation or habit and repute, despite a relationship lasting twenty-five years.[234] To this extent, the court can be said to have been faithful to the original content of the canon law marriage of *per verba de praesenti*, as even a verbal expression of intent was required as an expression for the parties' marital *consensus*. When the court noted the unreliability of the cohabitation as evidence, it referred to the fact that the cohabitation could as easily be seen as constituting evidence that the parties attempted to mislead the community in order to enjoy the pleasures of marriage, without needing to assume its bonds and obligations.[235] However, this is an argument that can even to a higher degree affect direct evidence. The parties' statements, even more easily than the

234 *Id.* at 321: "To find consent from mere cohabitation, or habit and repute, with the full facts of the real arrangement disclosed in words from which no marriage agreement is shown, violates the law of evidence in this jurisdiction." To not accept the man's statement, "[a]fter this you're Mrs. Erickson" and the woman's silent consent as an oral contract appears in light of the case law in Gen. a bit strict. With respect to oral contracts, *see* Section 6.5.1 *infra.*

235 *Id.* at 320. However, there is no shortage of cases in which the parties' sexual relationship was attributed significance as an evidentiary fact for their marital intent in the judgment. *See, e.g., Smith v. Smith,* 247 Ala. 213, 23 So.2d 605, 609 (1945), in which the Alabama Supreme Court stated: "It is shown without dispute that in July, 1943, appellant and appellee slept together in the same bed for one or two nights ... and this is evidence of the fact that they considered themselves to be husband and wife." *Compare O'Dell v. O'Dell,* 57 Ala.App. 185, 326 So.2d 747 (1976) ("The admitted fact of sexual intercourse does not *per se* prove the existence of a common-law marriage"); and *Gilbreath v. Lewis,* 242 Ala. 510, 7 So.2d 485 (1942). *See further In re Miller's Estate,* 182 Okla. 534, 78 P.2d 819, 827 (1938), in which the Oklahoma Supreme Court stated: "The testimony that the parties occupied the same room or bed overnight when visiting the farms near Shawnee is of little or no value as circumstantial evidence of a marriage contract."

cohabitation itself, could, of course, be used to mislead others. Naturally, an objection to the court's reasoning is that if the cohabitation is given a higher evidentiary weight, and a common law marriage therein is found established, the parties have taken upon themselves the bonds, responsibilities, and obligations of marriage.

The length and content of the cohabitation, alone, is not of decisive or evidentiary importance. The determination of what is to be evidenced is more important, *i.e.*, the requirements invoked by the courts with respect to the marital intent's *essensialia.* Suppose the court, on one hand, determines that consent or intention to marry means an intent to live a life together as husband and wife. Logically, twenty-five years of such a life can be given more evidentiary weight than that given by the court in *Erickson's Estate.* But if the court, on the other hand, determines that the marriage contract's *essensialia* requires an intent for legal effects, the court's evaluation of the evidence in *Erickson's Estate* is less surprising. The court could have meant a legal effect of some type, albeit the terminology is not consistent, in its description of marriage as "a *legal* relationship of husband and wife" (italics added). The same possibility is reflected in the court's concern that the parties lived in a relationship free from marriages "bonds and ultimate responsibilities." If the parties fulfill marital obligations as part of the cohabitation, it may indicate that they promised each other to do so, but need not prove any legal obligation. The parties could very well have had the intent to live a life together without marital rights and obligations.

7.7.5 Cohabitation and Reputation as Only Corroborating Evidence

The American case law also contains cases in which the courts in general have not accepted any inferred marriage agreement. Today, it is mostly the courts in Pennsylvania that take such a restrictive view if the marriage presumption is not applicable.[236] This can even be formulated as a requirement for a verbal contract or a contract *per verba de praesenti,* albeit no specifically determined wording has been considered necessary. Even though the cohabitation between the parties, their actions, and their reputation as spouses alone have not been viewed as sufficient evidence of a marriage contract, such circumstances have been accepted as supplementary or corroborating evidence in support of the verbal contract.[237]

---

236 *See* the summary § 7.4 *supra.* As to the marriage presumption, *see* Chapter 9, "Burdens of Proof and Presumptions."

237 *See, e.g., Staudenmayer v. Staudenmayer,* 714 A.2d 1016, 1021 (Pa. 1998); and *In re Estate of Kovalchick,* 345 Pa.Super. 229, 498 A.2d 374, 377 (1985). *See also Anderson v. Anderson,* 235 Ind. 113, 131 N.E.2d 301 (1956) in which the Indiana Supreme Court did not accept implied agreements but on the other hand was prepared to accept the parties' cohabitation and reputation as husband and wife as corroborating

These circumstances, however, have not been permitted to replace words that have not been stated. In several cases, no common law marriage has been established despite a long-term cohabitation.

For example, in *Bowden v. Workmen's Comp. Appeal Bd.* (1977), the parties had lived together for twelve years and had a mutual daughter. The woman used the man's last name and they appeared outwardly as spouses. When the man died in a work accident, the woman filed for workmen's compensation in her capacity as the deceased's surviving spouse in a common law marriage. The Workmen's Compensation Appeal Board found that she was not the deceased's widow and rejected her request for compensation.

The woman appealed this decision to the Commonwealth Court of Pennsylvania, arguing that the board had incorrectly required that she prove that the parties had exchanged words evidencing a present intent to enter into a marriage contract. The court stated that even if the exact words are not alone decisive, evidence concerning "the actual intention of the parties to form a marriage contract" is a condition for the existence of a common law marriage. The court found no reason to change the board's findings that it was not convinced that the parties had the intention to be married when they lived together. No common law marriage, therefore, was found to be established, and the woman did not receive any compensation.[238]

Shaw, who finds the outcome of the case unjust, has interpreted *Bowden* as the court requiring a verbal contract.[239] Even if the court's reasoning does not serve the interests of clarity, Shaw's interpretation is consistent with Pennsylvania case law in that, in those cases in which the marital presumption is not applicable, a contract *per verba* is required in principle, albeit no particular formulation is required.[240] As the woman had the evidentiary burden of proving the contract and her testimony was not considered credible, her claim was not granted. If the marital presumption had been applicable, a marital contract most probably would have been presumed as a result of the parties' long-term cohabitation and reputation. The evidentiary burden would then have shifted therewith to the opposing party to demonstrate that the parties had no marital *consensus*. As the evidence here was not found credible, the presumption could not be

---

evidence as support for a verbal contract. The court, however, did not find a contract proven despite the fact that the parties lived together for sixteen years. For more on oral contracts, *see* Section 6.5.1 *infra*.

238 *Bowden v. Workmen's Comp. Appeal Bd*, 376 A.2d 1033 (Pa.Cmwlth. 1977).

239 Shaw, *supra* note 12, at 592: "That the parties be precluded from all protection merely because they have never verbalized their commitment to one another, although their conduct towards one another clearly indicated that such a commitment in fact existed, is unduly rigid." *See also* Vaughn, *supra* note 13, at 1156.

240 *See, e.g.*, *Staudenmayer v. Staudenmayer*, 714 A.2d 1016, 1020 (Pa. 1998), in which the Pennsylvania Supreme Court required "an exchange of words in the present tense," and other cases as found in Chapter 6.5 *supra*.

considered rebutted and a common law marriage therewith established. The court does not state why it did not apply the presumption. One reason could have been that direct evidence concerning the existence of a contract was available.[241]

7.8 Summary and Conclusions

1. *Generally on the Development of the Law*

It can be seen from this historical overview that American case law during the entire 1800s and 1900s, in principle, accepted the parties' cohabitation and reputation as evidence of the marriage contract. According to the majority's understanding, inferred or implied agreements were accepted as long as there was no direct evidence contrary to the existence of a contract. The marked restrictedness in criminal cases during the 1800s appears to now have little anchoring in the courts. Certain courts require evidence of the marriage agreement, in addition to the cohabitation and reputation, such as the parties' admissions and declarations, while the majority is content that no circumstances speak against the existence of a contract. Several courts, however, have found a marriage contract proven based on the parties' cohabitation and reputation, despite certain admissions and declarations against a contract. Other courts, for example in Pennsylvania, have in certain situations required an express contract, but have accepted the parties' cohabitation and declaration as corroborative evidence on the side thereof.

This understanding recurs to varying degrees in the courts in those states which today recognize common law marriage; Alabama is the most liberal and Pennsylvania the strictest. The development in Texas is still unclear after the 1989 reform, which removed the legislation's express support for finding the existence of a marriage agreement in the cohabitation and the parties' outward appearance. From our historical analysis of the legislation and case law as given above, it is clear that in Texas, despite the legislative amendment, there is still good reason to accept inferred agreements.

2. *The Evidentiary Weight of Cohabitation and Reputation*

A general conclusion which can be drawn from the cases discussed above is that, in the American case law, the parties' cohabitation and reputation is given remarkably great weight as evidence for demonstrating the marriage agreement in cases concerning the existence of common law marriage. This conclusion is not undermined by those cases in which the

241 With respect to the marital presumption, *see Staudenmayer v. Staudenmayer*, 714 A.2d 1016 (Pa. 1998) and other cases as found in Chapter 9 *infra*.

courts have not found a contract proven because the parties' cohabitation has not been constant or has been insufficient and their reputation as spouses has been inconsistent. It, therefore, is not surprising that no marriage contract was found proven, for example, in cases in which the parties only lived together on a part-time basis or cases in which one party claimed, with good reason, that the other party was simply a boarder or a housekeeper. Instead, it appears more remarkable that a marital contract has been found in cases in which the parties lived together only a few months. Neither is it surprising that the courts have rejected claims of a common law marriage in cases in which the parties have not even stated that a marital contract was executed or that they silently agreed to be husband and wife.

Even though cohabitation and reputation are generally considered to have high evidentiary importance, it can be seen from the cases discussed above that inferred agreements can be arranged on a sliding scale. At the high end, the parties' cohabitation and reputation may be given great significance and a more independent role vis-à-vis the marital contract. At the same time, the contract has been moved into the background to the point of finally assuming a fictional character.

To begin, we have seen cases in which the parties from the outset entered into a formal wedding ceremony that was invalid as a result of a mistake in the formalities. For example, the Court in *Travers v. Reinhardt* (1906) found a marriage contract proven between parties, who certainly lived together for eighteen years, but scarcely only one year in a state recognizing common law marriage. The decision, clearly, gives witness to considerable faith in the cohabitation as an expression of the marital intent, and highly dilutes the requirement of a new marriage agreement. The Court decided that the parties' conduct toward each other in the eye of the public was equivalent, in law, to a declaration by each that they did, and during their joint lives were to, occupy the relation of husband and wife. Such a declaration was as effective to establish the status of marriage as if it had been made in words of the present tense..[242] One cannot, however, entirely ignore the fact that the invalid wedding ceremony had a role in the Court's assessment.

If a marriage was invalid as a result of an impediment, the courts traditionally have been reluctant to accept inferred agreements between the parties after the impediment was removed. This restraint has been motivated by the fact that the parties, particularly if they acted in bad faith, did not from the beginning have a true marital intent to establish a monogamous relationship. On the contrary, their intentions have been considered meretricious or illicit. The parties have, therefore, been obligated to present evidence that a change in their *consensus* has occurred through a new marriage agreement after the impediment's removal. Even if this

242 *Travers v. Reinhardt*, 205 U.S. 423, 440, 27 S.Ct. 563, 51 L.Ed 865, 873 (1906).

understanding is unusual today, the courts in Pennsylvania, as seen in this chapter, require that this change be demonstrated through an expressed contract, while the courts in South Carolina have accepted that the change can be demonstrated through circumstantial evidence, even though a continued cohabitation in certain cases has not been seen as sufficient. The requirement of a change, however, has become more and more diluted, which means that the continued cohabitation and holding out as spouses in practice has been sufficient in proving an inferred marriage agreement.

The majority of courts today appear to not generally raise the issue of the significance of the original impediment but rather accept the continued cohabitation after the impediment's removal as a basis for an inferred marriage agreement. This is true, for example, of the courts in Alabama. An argument for this approach is that one must distinguish between the intent and the ability to marry, and the parties from the beginning did not lack a marital *consensus*. Instead of considering an invalid wedding ceremony or an invalid formless contract as an expression of an incorrect intent that the parties must change, this reasoning calls for the exact opposite, namely, that the original intent was a marital intent, although there was an impediment to the marriage, and that the continued cohabitation led to the original declaration of intent to be treated as continuing.

The consideration of the original expression of intent has arisen in cases in which it consists of either a ceremonial wedding ceremony or a formless but expressed marital contract. In the latter, the following reasoning is typical: It is not to be expected that parties, having once agreed to be married, will deem it necessary to agree to do so again when an earlier marriage is terminated or some other bar to union is eliminated.

Entirely without the support of any original contract, either formal or formless, are those cases in which the parties simply move into together and later, after the impediment was removed, continued the cohabitation and outward representation as husband and wife. It is singular that the courts' reasoning in these cases does not raise the issue of the parties' good or bad faith with respect to the impediment. The courts can cite the moving in together of the parties and their statements about the relationship's marital character, but do not generally use particular actions carried out as part of the cohabitation as the basis of marital intent. Instead, they stop with the more sweeping reference to the fact that the parties, through living together and appearing outwardly as spouses, entered into a contract, thereby mutually agreeing to a common law marriage. One then can truly speak of a contract that is implied in the parties' actions. The inferred agreement with the support of such reasoning has been found proven even in cases in which the parties lived together only a few months.

Also unique to the courts' reasoning is that the contractual element fades more and more in the background. To begin, the courts have abandoned the idea of a sharply defined contract execution in which the parties, at a certain time and place, entered into the contract. Instead, it is natural to characterize the contract as a *consensus continuus*, which fits like a hand in a glove with evidence of the parties' cohabitation and outward appearance "day by day." Which is the chicken and which is the egg can be debated, but there is reason to assume that the acceptance of the cohabitation as evidence for the marriage contract has influenced the nature of the contract. The courts appear to have understood cohabitation and public repute as continuing factors, and adjust the marriage contract by characterizing it as an ongoing agreement. The party claiming the existence of a common law marriage, as a rule, need not prove the exact day the agreement was reached. It is unusual for the courts to attempt to define the time for the contract's execution, and typical for them to be satisfied that the contract, as was said in one case, must have come into being within a year or so. *Consensus continuus* appears to be a contractual model which—in a world in which, clearly, the majority of couples unconsciously drift into a common law marriage—is more consistent with reality than a sharply defined contract execution.

In several cases, the contractual element has been pushed a step even further back because the courts have not even generally discussed the contract in the reasoning. In their conclusion, the courts have hopped over the contractual requirement and reached a finding directly from the facts presented in the case related to the existence of a common law marriage. This development testifies to an extensive erosion of the marriage contract as a necessary requirement for the formation of a common law marriage. There are many cases, in practice, which the courts are only a step away from only proving the parties' cohabitation and reputation as a requisite for the establishment of a common law marriage. Nevertheless, it is noteworthy that, as long as the contractual element remains, it is possible to object that the parties have not entered in any marriage contract, despite the existence of cohabitation and reputation. Such an objection may be supported by other evidence, such as, e.g., admissions and declarations. The function of this contractual element in the future is further discussed in Chapter 13, "The Constitutive Requisites in the Future."

The evidentiary importance of the parties' cohabitation and reputation is also dependent on the present-day realities to which this concept is applied. Clearly, family patterns and relationships between men and women during recent decades have undergone considerable changes. Consequently, living together without formally entering into marriage is no longer the stigma it once was. Such relationships have become much more common but are varied. Certain couples live together for a test period, break up, and move on to try a new relationship with someone else. Others live together without any long-term intentions. For others, a formal marriage or a formless cohabitation that is lifelong follows. Another aspect of this picture is that the number of divorces has increased greatly.

The widely different intentions of couples in relationships has resulted in a radical reduction in the evidentiary weight of their actions, which outwardly can appear to be rather similar. How should one assess the value of the fact that a man and a woman have lived together several months or a year? Does this demonstrate that the parties, based on the cohabitation, have had an intent extending over an entire lifetime, or no longer than the actual days in which they lived together? A cohabitation today can certainly be either scenario; the first months of cohabitation can be the beginning of a long life together or living together day by day without any further intentions. The new day simply proves that the previous one has ended!

Warnings in the case law concerning the untrustworthiness of cohabitation and reputation as proof of marriage, today, have increased relevance with respect to shorter relationships. The increased mobility today among cohabiting couples generally calls for considerably greater caution in drawing conclusions about marriage-like intentions from the parties' cohabitation and reputation!

As Kathryn Vaughn anticipated with respect to the legislative development in Texas, greater caution by the courts in finding the existence of inferred marriage agreement has the consequence of putting many couples outside the legal protections offered by common law marriage.[243] However, this appears to be an unavoidable price; the alternative violates honesty by pretending that the cohabitation proves something that it does not. There are other methods of providing legal protection if it is desired. One possibility is to tie the legal consequences directly to the cohabitation, by eliminating the contractual element of common law marriage. Such a system, however, is not without problems as seen in the discussion in Chapter 13.

3. *The Evidentiary Value of Admissions and Declarations*

As the cases discussed above reveal, it is very common in trials concerning common law marriage for the parties to refer to admissions and declarations they have made concerning their marriage-like status, in addition to citing cohabitation and reputation as evidence of the existence of a marriage contract. Such statements are also cited as evidence against the existence of a contract. In several of the cases discussed above, the statements made by the parties during the cohabitation were decisive to the courts' conclusions with respect to the existence of an inferred marriage agreement and therewith a common law marriage.

In support of the existence of a marriage contract, it is common for the courts to cite that the parties, between themselves or before other persons or an authority, orally or in writing, called each other "Mrs. and Mr." or "husband and wife," that the woman used the man's last name, that they

243 Vaughn, *supra* note 13, at 1161.

stated that they were "married" or that they lived in "marriage," or that their intent was "to marry," etc. With respect to the evaluation of this kind of evidence, the courts' assessments have to a large extent varied. On one hand, we have seen cases in which the man's presentation of the woman as his "wife," on one occasion during a cohabitation which lasted only a few months, was considered by the court to constitute strong evidence that the minds of the parties had met and that there was mutuality of consent to establish a marriage relationship. Less remarkable have been the cases in which statements by the man that he "had considered her to be his wife" assumed decisive significance when the cohabitation lasted many years. On the other hand, we have seen cases in which a common law marriage was not found proven despite the fact that the woman used the man's name throughout a cohabitation of many years, and the parties outwardly appeared as spouses. In a society in which nonmarital cohabitation is far more common than it once was, a fact-finder must weigh the evidence of a tacit agreement more carefully than in the past.

It can be further seen from the cases that it is also very common in trials concerning common law marriages for statements that the parties made to be cited against the existence of a marriage contract. For example, the woman in different situations called herself "Ms.," used her maiden name or name from a previous marriage; or the parties stated that they were "single," that they were "not married," or that they called each other "fiancé(e)," "girlfriend," or "boyfriend," respectively; or that the woman only was the man's "housekeeper;" that "marriage" was nothing for them or that they had no intent "to marry."

Most significant is the direct evidence in the form of the parties' own statements which were directed at the marriage agreement and the parties' marital *consensus*. For example, the parties stated that they "was never common law married," that they "had no intention of marrying," that they "did not want anything that was legal and binding," that they were not ready "to commit to marriage," or that marriage was nothing to them. Such statements, as addressed in this chapter, often have decisive significance and generally are attributed a higher evidentiary weight than the circumstantial evidence concerning a long-term cohabitation in which the parties enjoyed the reputation as spouses.

Since it is very common at trial to cite such statements against the existence of a common law marriage, there is ample reason for caution. To begin, it appears that the statements all too often are invoked as grounds for the courts' judgment uncritically, without being investigated or even questioned. Remarkably, the parties may not even be asked what they mean when they use expressions such as "marriage" and "marry." The great danger is that the parties may refer to a ceremonial marriage or to formally marrying, respectively. This will occur since common law marriage is often unfamiliar to the parties and expressions such as ""marriage," "marry," "married," etc., are so strongly associated with the ceremonial wedding ceremony, to which their statements can frequently be assumed to refer. If so, the evidentiary importance of the statements can be very limited. Such statements certainly can express that the parties did not want to constitute a marriage either actually or legally, but they can also express that the parties merely did not or did not wish to go through a wedding ceremony. Not uncommonly, the parties' statements concerning their marriage-like status are their responses to leading questions from lawyers, questions that unfortunately, all too often, proceed without objection or any requirement for precision. Given the power of language, the great danger is that a lawyer asks one question, and the party answers another. If such answers become the basis for the courts' conclusions, legal certainty is clearly endangered. Questions regarding, for example, whether the parties had the intent "to marry," whether they thought they were "married," or whether "marriage" was anything to them, ought not to be asked without precisely defining the terms in the questions.

The evidentiary importance of such statements must naturally, to a large extent, vary with respect to the circumstances in general, such as the nature of the statement, its purpose, and the context in which the statement was made. One ought to be able, however, to generally say that statements made by a party are given a higher evidentiary weight if they conflict with the party's own interests. This can be the case, for example, if a man contesting the existence of a common law marriage at the same time states that he always considered the woman as his wife, or the reverse; or if the man is claiming the common law marriage, but at the same time admits that he was never common law married with the woman. It naturally can be questioned whether it is in conflict with one's own interest to be considered married. This, however, has been seen to be the case by the courts with respect to the obligations which marriage entails. Which of the parties is claiming and objecting to the existence of a common law marriage, respectively, ought to serve as a guide. A higher evidentiary weight also appears to be given to statements made by a party makes in the presence of the other party, without objections. The statements made by a deceased person in support of a marriage between the deceased, if cited by the party claiming the deceased's estate, are viewed with suspicion. It generally further appears that a higher evidentiary weight is given to statements with respect to the parties' status if cited in support of rather than against the existence of a common law marriage. The evidentiary value of the circumstance that a woman, today, during the cohabitation with a man, used her maiden name, stated that she is "single" or that she is not "married," can be limited. This is connected to the fact that these expressions, as noted above, are so strongly tied to the ceremonial wedding ceremony. Added to this is the fact that life's realities change through the years. Today, it is more common than before for a woman to use her maiden name and file a single tax return, regardless of whether she and a man live together for a short time on a trial basis, or decide spend a life together without a ceremony. Although the resulting development is not entirely clear, in several cases, a common law marriage has been found proven despite the fact that the parties stated that they were single and the woman used her maiden name. The general conclusion about more limited evidentiary weight, given against the existence of a common law marriage, does not apply to statements that are more directly focused on the marriage contract and the parties' marital *consensus*.

There is a different situation for statements given in support of the existence of a common law marriage. Statements by parties, which have not gone through a marriage ceremony, that they are "married" or that they are "Mr. and Mrs.," or that the woman used the man's last name, have generally been given higher evidentiary weight. Despite this, the value of such admissions and declarations must be assessed with full consideration of the circumstances in each individual case. The increased variation in cohabitation cases, which calls for greater caution in the valuation of the parties' cohabitation and reputation as evidence for the marriage agreement, also calls for greater caution in the assessment of the evidentiary importance of the parties' admissions and declarations. The notion that the parties' admissions and declarations generally ought to be given a higher evidentiary weight than their cohabitation and reputation appears, today, to be scarcely justifiable. The courts have good reason to prove the value of each piece of evidence on a case-by-case basis.

Occasionally, there are particular reasons to view the parties' statements with skepticism. The use of such epithets as "Mr. and Mrs." can be more motivated by convenience than by an intent to declare the character of a relationship. This is true, for example, when parties sign travel documents or register at a hotel. Close cases are those in which the evidentiary importance of the parties' statements are greatly reduced if the parties, choose whatever is advantageous, stating that they are married in one situation, but presenting themselves as single in another situation. In these cases, highly placed requirements in the rules concerning the burden of proof and the evidentiary standard without doubt have an important function to fulfill. As to the future, such actions point to the weakness of common law marriage, namely, that it invites fraud, as more closely discussed in Chapter 14, "Arguments For and Against Common Law Marriage and Cohabitation Law."

4. The Significance of the Agreement's Essensialia

A general defect that can be found in the courts' determinations of whether an inferred marriage agreement or a marital *consensus* exists is that, as a rule, they do not more closely state what kind of marital intent is to be proven by the parties' cohabitation, reputation, and admissions and declarations, *i.e.*, the requirements of the marital intent's *essensialia*. This is a decisive issue in the significance of evidence and evidentiary valuation, which is discussed in Chapter 6 as a contract issue with respect to the state of the law today, and with respect to the future in Chapter 13. On one hand, if the object of the marital intent is to live together as husband and wife and the parties actually do this, perhaps for many years, it is clear that the cohabitation ought to be given considerable evidentiary weight. Given such an intent, the result in several of the above cases, in which the parties lived together for a very long time and a marriage contract was found proven, is not surprising. With that same intent, it cannot be taken for granted that a short cohabitation, as in several of the cases discussed above, in which the parties lived together only a few months, expresses an intent to live an entire life together.

If, on the other hand, the object of the marital intent must be a legal intent of some type, for example, an intent to change the parties' legal status or to assume the marital duties and obligations of husband and wife, or an intent generally to be legally bound, it is clear that even long-term cohabitation is less important as evidence. With an intent so defined, it is not surprising that the courts in several of the above discussed cases, despite a long-term cohabitation, did not find a marriage agreement. The cohabitation can certainly indicate that the parties promised and did fulfill marriage-like obligations. The cohabitation, however, need not prove any legal obligation. The parties can very well have an intent to live an entire life together, but without marital rights and obligations. For instance, a court may state that a fundamental change has occurred in the parties' relationship because they moved in together. The court's conclusion is probably true with respect to the actual relationship, but may not mean that the parties intended a change in legal status.

None of the cases discussed above raised the issue of the marriage contract's *essensialia,* although the courts, in several of the cases, appear to have applied an intent with respect to legal effect. This lack of definition in the object of the marital intent often leads to drawn-out trials in which the witnesses are questioned at length about unclear evidentiary issues, and the witnesses and the lawyers are not in agreement about what is being discussed. A closer definition of the content of the intent within the marriage contract would be useful both to shorten trials and increase legal certainty. The validity of one of the premises behind the acceptance of inferred agreements, namely, that the parties' "conduct can speak as loudly as words," must today be strongly questioned with respect to the marriage contract and is highly dependent on what the parties' conduct is saying

Even if the courts would benefit from an increased degree of precision in determining the required marital intent within an inferred agreement, and even if they began to observe a greater degree of caution in the valuation of the evidence for this intent, there is still reason to anticipate considerable application difficulties and legal uncertainty. Such effects within a legal system always lead, as shown by the 1989 reform in Texas, to reactions and justified criticism of, first, the acceptance of inferred agreements, and second, common law marriage generally. As seen by the above, the American case law includes cases in which the courts, as a rule, have required an express, albeit formless, contract in which the parties' cohabitation and reputation was only accepted as corroborative evidence. However, one cannot ignore that inferred agreements, as this chapter has shown, contribute by giving legal protection to parties that live in common law marriage as well as their children. The question of whether the criticism against inferred agreements and common law marriage generally is justified and whether the inconveniences suffered are a price worth paying for the legal protections the institution gives, is discussed in Chapter 13, concerning the future function of the marriage contract, and also in Chapter 14, where the future existence of the legal institution of common law marriage is explored.

CHAPTER 8

Cohabitation, Holding Out, and Reputation as Spouses

"Boire, manger, coucher ensemble est marriage, ce me semble."

Old French Proverb[1]

8.1 Introduction

As seen in Chapter 7, "Implied Marriage Agreements," cohabitation between the parties clearly has been accepted in the American case law as an implied expression of the parties' marital *consensus* and as evidence for the existence of a marriage contract, albeit its value in this respect naturally varies somewhat. In this function, the cohabitation principally is neither sufficient nor necessary for the establishment of a common law marriage. The cohabitation instead is an expression and evidence of something else, namely, the marriage contract, which can also be expressed and evidenced in other ways. In this chapter, we will examine in contrast how cohabitation in American law is assigned a different function as a requisite, *i.e.*, as a necessary requirement for the establishment of a common law marriage in addition to the marriage contract. Logically, nothing prevents a cohabitation from simultaneously fulfilling both of these functions.[2]

The question of whether cohabitation ought to be recognized as a necessary requirement is one of the most diffuse issues in the history of common law marriage. Legal authorities have long disagreed. If the parties actually cohabited, as in the majority of cases that have been the

1 Georges Ripert & Jean Boulanger, Traité de Droit Civil, I, Para. 1254 (1956).

2 This double function appears clearly in the case law as well as in the legislation in Texas, *see, e.g.*, *Consolidated Underwriters v. Kelly*, 15 S.W.2d 299 (Tex. Comm'n App. 1929); *Shelton v. Belknap*, 155 Tex. 37, 282 S.W. 682, 684 (1955); and *Humpreys v. Humpreys*, 364 S.W.2d 177 (Tex. 1963). During the period from 1969-1989, the double function also came to expression in the legislation, *see* 1969 Tex.Gen.Laws 2707.2717, repealed by 1989 Tex.Gen.Laws 1459, 1461.

objects of litigation in the American case law, the courts' statements – regardless of the stance taken – often have the character of *obiter dicta* making any assessment of the state of the law difficult. Against this background, statements similar to those we find in *Herd v. Herd* (1915), are not surprising: "There is not only lack of unanimity, but great conflict, and, in the language of the Supreme Court of the United States, the conflict amounts almost to a state of anarchy."[3] Given that this issue has been highly debated and is difficult to assess, a review of its legal development during the 1800s and 1900s and an attempt to capture the current status of the law in the different states are warranted.

To the degree that cohabitation is accepted as a requisite, we shall further examine the underlying motives for the requirement and structure of the principle of cohabitation, as well as identify its different elements. The boundaries of the principle are significant because they determine the scope of common law marriage, which couples fall outside or inside the regulatory system, determining who receives the rights, as well as the obligations, of marriage.

Since it is common in both the legislation and case law to have a separate requirement that the parties outwardly appear as spouses in addition to the requirement of cohabitation, this requirement is specifically addressed in a section below. This requirement focuses on either the parties actions in themselves, in other words, their holding out as spouses, or on the effects thereof, *i.e.*, their reputation as husband and wife.

8.2 THE PURE CONTRACT PRINCIPLE

1. The Motivation behind the Pure Contract Principle

The traditional understanding in American law has been that a common law marriage is based solely on the parties' marital *consensus*, and therefore, that cohabitation is not necessary for the establishment of such a marriage. This understanding is the pure contract principle, based on general contract law, in which the legal relationship is principally based solely upon contracts and other legal actions. Because marriage is basically understood to be a contract,[4] nothing other than the contract is

3 *Herd v. Herd*, 194 Ala. 613, 69 So. 887 (1915).

4 The leading early English case of *Dalrymple v. Dalrymple*, (1811) 2 Hagg.Cons 54, 62-64, 161 Eng.Rep. 665, 668-669, already stated: "Marriage being a contract is of course consensual ... for it is of the essence of all contracts to be constituted by the consent of parties." *See also* WILLIAM BLACKSTONE, COMMENTARIES ON THE LAWS OF ENGLAND, 433, 439 (R.M. Kerr ed., London 1884): "Our law considers marriage in no other light than as a civil contract." This stance, that marriage is based upon a contract, can be found in each of the leading American cases from the 1800s, although whether any additional requirements existed is less certain. *See Fenton v. Reed*, 4 Johns. 52, 4 Am.D. 244 (N.Y. 1809): "A contract of marriage made *per verba de praesenti* amounts to an actual marriage, and is as valid as if made *in facie acclesiae*." The expressed understanding in that

viewed as necessary.[5] This is true of ceremonial marriages as well as common law marriages. The formal requirements constitute the only difference between these two types of marriages according to the pure contract principle. This traditional understanding is close to that of the Roman and canon principles: *consensus, non concubitus, facit nuptias,* as presented in Chapters 2, "Informal Marriages in Roman Law," and 3, "Informal Marriages in Canon Law."[6]

As the pure contract principle in American case law has gained acceptance to a large extent through its reception by legal scholars, the independent legal political motivations behind the principle, other than those as stated above, appear seldom in the judgments. An argument made in the older case law is that the distinction between marriage *per verba de praesenti* and marriage *per verba de futuro cum copula carnalis* would be rendered meaningless if a requirement of cohabitation were applied to the first category of marriage. However, that argument has since lost its significance because the distinction is no longer applied.[7] Another argument, which holds greater weight today, is that contradictions would be created in the legal system if cohabitation, on one side, is required as a requisite for the establishment of a marriage, and, on the other side, is viewed as outside of marriage, and perhaps is even criminalized, before the marriage is established. This idea was expressed by Koegel, who rather sharply maintains: "A doctrine that requires two persons to fornicate a number of times before they create a legal status is absurd. Must they live together as husband and wife before they are husband and wife and this too in the face of a provision of the criminal law that persons who do this without first being married are guilty of a crime?"[8] As to this last viewpoint, it can be

---

case, that a common law marriage, as with a canon law marriage, legally qualifies as a contract can also be seen in the later leading case of *Meister v. Moore,* 96 U.S. 76, 78, 24 L. Ed. 826 (1877) in which the United States Supreme Court stated: "Marriage is everywhere regarded as a civil contract." In *Askew v. Dupree,* 30 Ga. 173, 176, 177, 178, 179, 189 (1869), the contract principle is also adopted with the support of both Scottish and older English law.

5 Reference to general contract law as support for the proposition that cohabitation is not necessary can be found in *Great Northern Ry. Co. v. Johnson,* 166 C.C.A. 181, 254 F. 683, 684-685 (8th Cir. 1918): "[T]he rule seems to be that marriage is a civil contract ... The marriage contract possesses the elements of an ordinary contract and none other." The court in *Love v. Love,* 185 Iowa 930, 171 N.W. 257 (1919) also referred to the fact that the marriage contract "like other contracts, is complete when made." In *Fryer v. Fryer,* 9 S.C.Eq. (Rich.Cas.) 85, 92 (1832), Judge Johnson stated: "Marriage, with us, so far as the law is concerned, has ever been regarded as a mere civil contract. Our law prescribes no ceremony. It requires nothing but the agreement of the parties, with an intention that that agreement shall, per se, constitute the marriage." In *Physick's Estate,* 2 Brewster 179 (1862), the Pennsylvania Supreme Court stated that marriage "is a civil contract, and nothing more." Ceremonial marriages do not as a principle require consummation, *see United States v. Rubinstein,* 151 F.2d 915, 918, 919 (2d Cir. 1945).

6 With respect to Roman law, *see* Section 2.4.4 *supra;* Canon law, *see* Section 3.3.3 *supra.*

7 *Davis v. Stouffer,* 132 Mo.App. 555, 112 S.W. 282, 284 (1908).

8 OTTO E. KOEGEL, COMMON LAW MARRIAGE AND ITS DEVELOPMENT IN THE UNITED STATES 128 (1922). *See also Davis v. Stouffer,* 132 Mo.App. 555, 112 S.W. 282, 284 (1908).

mentioned that medieval canon law separated civil and criminal law to the extent that the civil law recognized a relationship that was criminally punishable. A somewhat more significant problem, logically, however, is the fact that cohabitation originally outside of a marriage can become a marriage. The question then can be raised at which point of time the legal ramifications of marriage arise.

As an argument for the application of the pure contract principle, Hugh Ross has also maintained that there should be no requirement of cohabitation because no such requirement exists for ceremonial marriages.[9] A compelling reason, seldom expressed in the judgments, but that appears to have influenced the outcome of the trials, is the existence of very strong evidence with respect to the marriage contracts, e.g., the contract was in writing, and no requirement of cohabitation was considered necessary.[10] Another practical reason is that cohabitation was not possible, for example, as a result of a party's military duty in another country.[11] Warnings have been issued further about the difficulties with respect to deciding when a common law marriage is to be considered established after a certain cohabitation. Koegel states: "Again, just where will the line be drawn? When do the parties cease to be fornicators and just when does the sublime institution of matrimony begin?"[12] These and other potential motivations in favor of the pure contract principle in modern society are discussed further in Chapter 13, "The Constitutive Requisites in the Future."

2. *Influence from Older Scottish Law*

Older American case law with respect to the application of the pure contract principle appears to have been influenced by older Scottish and English case law.[13] In *Lindo v. Belisario* (1795), Lord Stowell, applying Scottish law with reference to canon law as well as older English and Scottish law, stated in *dictum*: "The vinculum follows on the contract,

9 Hugh A. Ross, *The Ohio Law of Marriage*, 14 W. RESERV. L. REV. 724, 732 (1963).

10 *See, e.g.*, *Mathewson v. Phoenix Iron Foundry*, 20 F. 281, 282 (Cir. D.R.I. 1884); *State v. Bittick*, 103 Mo. 183, 15 S.W. 325, 326, 11 L.R.A. 587 (1891); *Hulett v. Carey*, 66 Minn. 327, 69 N.W. 31 (1896); *Great Northern Ry. Co. v. Johnson*, 166 C.C.A. 181, 254 F. 683, 685 (8th Cir. 1918); *Com. v. Amann*, 58 Pa.D. & C. 669 (1947); and *In re Estate of Gower*, 445 Pa. 554, 284 A.2d 742, 744 (1971).

11 In *Com. v. Amann*, 58 Pa.D. & C. 669 (1947), the man served military duty in the Philippines while the woman lived in Pennsylvania. They separately signed a written marriage contract, which constituted a common law marriage. With respect to the issue of how the courts in different states solve the problem of a required cohabitation, *see* Section 8.5.3 *infra*.

12 KOEGEL, *supra* note 8, at 128. *See also* ROSS, *supra* note 9, at 732.

13 *See, e.g.*, *Fryer v. Fryer*, 9 S.C.Eq. (Rich.Cas.) 85, 96 (1832); *Guardians of the Poor v. Nathans*, 2 Brewster 149, 152 (1845); JOEL PRENTISS BISHOP, COMMENTARIES ON THE LAW OF MARRIAGE AND DIVORCE AND EVIDENCE IN MATRIMONIAL SUITS § 67 (Boston 1852), *citing Lindo v. Belisario*, (1795) 1 Hagg.Con.Rep. 216.

without consummation."[14] This concept, that the legal binding is a result of the contract, not of the consummation, can also be found in the celebrated case of *Dalrymple v. Dalrymple* (1811), in which Lord Stowell, now Sir William Scott, applying Scottish law, also found that the "contract *de praesenti* does not require consummation in order to become 'very matrimony'" and that the contract "*ipso facto, et ipso jure*, constitutes the relation of man and wife."[15] It has been noted that this statement is *dictum* with respect to the issue of whether cohabitation between the parties existed.[16] This objection, however, appears only partially valid, as the English officer and Scottish woman in the case did have *copula carnalis* during the man's secret visits to the woman. It was not a question of an actual cohabitation. The court's reasoning, for our purposes, must, therefore, be seen as constituting a *ratio decidendi* to the extent that no official or more complete cohabitation in its true meaning was found necessary.

If the cohabitation is completely denied the effect of establishing a common law marriage, the difference with respect to a formal marriage, which generally does not require cohabitation, becomes only the absence of formal requirements. A direct comparison with a church wedding ceremony is made in *M'Adam v. Walker* (1813). In that case, the cohabitation following the oral marriage contract, and as a result of the man's suicide, was limited to only a few hours and the lack of a cohabitation after formation of the contract constituted a *ratio decidendi* to an even higher degree. The English court, represented by Lord Eldon, applying Scottish law, stated with respect to the man: "When he declared that the lady was actually his very wife, and that these were his legitimate children, *per verba de praesenti*, this formed a present contract, and they became *eo instanti*, as much husband and wife, as if the ceremony had been celebrated in the kirk; and the marriage was as valid as if a man, in returning from the kirk, immediately after his marriage there, had died of an apoplectic fit before he reached the house."[17]

---

14 *See Lindo v. Belisario, id.*. *See also Reed v. Passer*, (1794) Peake's Cases 303, 170 Eng. Rep. 164, from the same time period, stating that the marriage contract is *ipsum matrimonium*.

15 *Dalrymple v. Dalrymple*, (1811) 2 Hagg.Con. 54, 103, 161 Eng.Rep. 665, 682.

16 *See Grigsby v. Reib*, 105 Tex. 597, 153 S.W. 1124, 1128 (1913), one of the leading cases in support of the proposition that cohabitation is necessary. In *Dalrymple*, citing *Swinburne*, the court maintained: "that is a present and perfect consent, that which alone maketh the matrimony, without either public solemnization or carnal copulation, for neither is the one, nor the other, the essence of matrimony, but consent only." *See Dalrymple*, 161 Eng.Rep. at 682.

17 *M'Adam v. Walker*, (1813) 1 Dow. 148, 184-185, 3 Eng.Rep. 654, 666. The man, orally before his servants, declared that his lover was actually his wife and that their children were legitimate, at which the woman gave him her hand, however, without saying anything. Several hours later, the man committed suicide. *See also Lautour v. Teesdale*, (1816) 8 Taunt. 830, 2 Marsh. 243, 17 Rev.Rep. 518, 12 Eng.Rul.Cas. 729, from the same time period, in which the court stated that a contract *per verba de praesenti*, without a following cohabitation, constituted a marriage.

Even in the middle of the 1800s, when the canon law principles in Scottish law exercised significant influence on the American case law, the dominant understanding in Scottish law appears to be that a marriage contract *de praesenti* was sufficient to establish an informal marriage, and that no cohabitation was then necessary. In *Yelverton v. Longworth* (1864), the Lord President stated with respect to a similar contract: "It is not necessary towards the constitution of marriage in that way that it shall have been followed by cohabitation. Such I hold to be the established law of this country."[18]

3. The Application of the Pure Contract Principle in the United States in the 1800s

The Roman and canon law principle, *consensus, non concubitus, facit nuptias,*[19] won early acceptance by American courts in cases concerning common law marriage. This occurred first in *dictum,*[20] and later clearly in the holdings, *ratio decidendi.* For example, in *Dumaresly v. Fishly* (1821), the man and woman had a wedding ceremony before a priest in Indiana that was invalid because the priest did not have the authority to perform such ceremonies. No cohabitation occurred between the bride and groom because the bride refused. The issue arose whether a common law marriage had been established between the parties. With reference to the lack of cohabitation, the minority of the Kentucky Supreme Court, applying Indiana law, found that a marriage had not been established. Chief Justice Boyle, writing for the majority, in contrast found, based *inter alia* upon canon law principles, that a common law marriage had been established, stating: "Marriage is nothing but a contract; and, to render it valid, it is only necessary ... that the parties should be able to contract, willing to contract, and should actually contract... Marriage and cohabitation are

---

18 *Yelverton v. Longworth,* (1864) 4 Macq. 746, 803. *See also Bell v. Graham,* (1859) 13 Moore, P.C.C. 242, from the same time period, in which the cohabitation following the marriage was considered unnecessary if the parties understood they had agreed to an *ipsum matrimonium. Compare Campbell v. Campbell,* (1867) 5 M. (H.L.) 115, Sc.App.Cas. 182, in which Lord Cranworth in *dictum* stated: "Marriage can only exist as the result of mutual agreement. The conduct of the parties, and of their friends and neighbours, – *i.e.,* habit and repute, – may afford strong, and in Scotland, attending to the laws of marriage there existing, unanswerable, evidence that at some unascertained time a mutual agreement to marry was entered into by the parties passing as man and wife. I cannot, however, think it correct to say that habit and repute in any case make the marriage." The statement naturally supports the proposition that cohabitation is not a necessary requirement for the establishment of an informal marriage. The fact that the statement, however, does not relegate the cohabitation to simply an evidentiary fact, but rather gives it the character of a required element in a rebuttable presumption, gives reason to return to the question.

19 With respect to Roman law, *see* Section 2.4.2, with respect to Canon law, *see* Section 3.3.3.

20 In *Fenton v. Reed,* 4 Johns. 52 (N.Y. 1809), in which cohabitation existed, the court stated: "A contract of marriage made *per verba de praesenti* amounts to an actual marriage, and is as valid as if made *in facie acclesiae.*"

two things. The latter is the object to be obtained by the former, and, to make it lawful, must be preceded by the former." The majority further stated that "a marriage *per verba praesenti* is, forthwith, a marriage, and complete without cohabitation."[21] The absence of cohabitation between the parties in the case makes the statement one of the clearest examples of a *ratio decidendi* in American case law espousing the pure contract principle.

The pure contract principle was immediately accepted by American scholars. In his first edition of COMMENTARIES ON AMERICAN LAW (1826), James Kent, in agreement with the canon law basis, stated: "If the contract be made *per verba de praesenti* and remain without cohabitation it amounts to a valid marriage."[22] This stance is repeated in the later editions of his book during the entire 1800s.[23] The pure contract principle, however, did not create an impediment, as seen in the previous chapter, to cohabitation being accepted as an evidentiary fact as to the existence of a marriage contract.[24] The authors' viewpoints heavily influenced the case law during the early 1800s.[25]

---

21 *Dumaresly v. Fishly*, 10 Ky. 368, 372 (1821). In another case from that same time period, the *ratio decidendi* supported the stance that cohabitation is not necessary for the establishment of a marriage. In *Jackson v. Winne*, 7 Wend. (N.Y.) 47, 22 Am.Dec. 563 (1831), the man and woman had a police escort to a justice of the peace, who in the presence of the woman's parents asked the parties if they consented to the marriage and requested that they hold hands. The man took down his hand and turned away from the woman, who, however, took the man's hand and held it in hers until the justice of the peace declared that they were husband and wife. After the ceremony, the woman returned to the home of her parents. The man did not follow. No cohabitation ever existed between the parties. A few days later, the man married another woman. Three to six months later, both women gave birth to his child. The court found that a marriage had been established during the first ceremony. Beside the fact that the court, for the finding of a valid marriage, obviously did not require cohabitation, it must be noted that the court must have had an extremely low requirement as to the existence of a marriage contract. With respect to the man's silence, it was not a question of any expressed contract. Neither can the man be said to have, through his actions, entered into an implied contract. His gestures rather give witness to a certain repugnance. Neither can it be maintained that simply his presence at the ceremony was an implied contract, as the police escorted him there. The court appears rather to have accepted the man's passivity, the fact that he did not leave the ceremony, as an acceptance of a silent contract between the parties. However, it is difficult to rid oneself of the notion that the contractual consent in the case was allowed to calcify in the required form.

22 *See* JAMES KENT, COMMENTARIES ON AMERICAN LAW 2, Lec. XXVI (6) (New York, William Kent 1826). Kent is reputed to have made the decision in *Fenton v. Reed*, 4 Johns. 52 (N.Y. 1809). *Compare Hantz v. Sealy*, 6 Binn. 405 (Pa. 1814); *Chambers v. Dickson*, 2 S. & R. 475 (1816); and TAPPING REEVE, THE LAW OF BARON AND FEMME (New York 1816).

23 *See, e.g.*, JAMES KENT, COMMENTARIES ON AMERICAN LAW 2, 52 (7th ed. 1851), and at 119-124 (16th ed. 1901).

24 KENT, *supra* note 22, at 87: " [T]he marriage may even be inferred from continual cohabitation, and reputation as husband and wife."

25 Kent is cited in a number of cases, *see, e.g.*, *Guardians of the Poor v. Nathans*, 2 Brewster 149, 152 (1845). In *Hulett v. Carey*, 66 Minn. 327, 69 N.W. 31 (1896), a case which itself came to be a leading case in support for the proposition of a pure contract principle, the Minnesota Supreme Court cites the second edition of Kent at 87,

The pure contract principle came to an early expression in South Carolina in the case law. In *Fryer v. Fryer* (1832), Judge Johnson, sitting on the South Carolina Court of Appeals, stated that marriage is to be viewed simply as a civil contract and that it requires nothing but the agreement of the parties.[26] Apparently, this stance has never been questioned by the courts in South Carolina, where the pure contract principle appears to still be the current law. The courts in Pennsylvania also took the same stance, the second of the two states where the pure contract principle is currently the law. In *Guardians of the Poor v. Nathans* (1845), the court stated that marriage is only a civil contract and that it is valid even if it remains without cohabitation. This statement was *dictum*, but the sentiment can be found in the *ratio decidendi* of the case law of Pennsylvania.[27]

Simon Greenleaf published his book, A TREATISE ON THE LAW OF EVIDENCE, in the 1940s, stating that marriage is a civil contract that for validity simply requires the consent of the parties. Greenleaf continued almost verbatim from Kent: "If the contract is made *per verba de praesenti*, though it is not consummated by cohabitation ... it amounts to a valid marriage."[28]

---

as well as "2 *Greenl. Ev.* § 460" and "1 *Bishop*, Mar & Div. §§ 218, 227-229." The case of *Hilton v. Roylance*, 25 Utah 129, 69 P. 660, 664 (1902) cites "2 *Kent* Comm. 87-89" and "*Bish.* Mar. & Div. § 383."

26 *Fryer v. Fryer*, 9 9 S.C.Eq. (Rich.Cas.) 85, 92 (1832) (*dictum*). *See also Jewell v. Magwood*, 9 S.C.Eq. (Rich.Cas.) 113, 114 (1833).

27 *Guardians of the Poor v. Nathans*, 2 Brewster 149, 152 (1845). The parties first lived together secretly, then later openly, a consequence of which the statement constitutes *dictum*. The pure contract principle also has support in *Trimble v. Trimble*, 2 Ind. 76 (1850). *Compare Barnett v. Kimmel*, 35 Pa. 13 (1859) (the man, after the contract, refused to live together with the woman, but in which a marriage was found to be established); and *Physick's Estate*, 2 Brewster 179 (1862). In *Richard v. Brehm*, 73 Pa. 140, 144, 13 Am.Rep. 733 (1873), in which the parties lived together approximately forty years, the court stated, also in *dictum*, that if a contract is entered into *per verba de praesenti*, it is treated as a valid marriage, even if it is not consummated through cohabitation. Cohabitation and reputation as husband and wife can constitute elements in a marriage presumption (more on this in Chapter 9 *infra*) without always being necessary requisites in the informal marriage concept. This can seen from the *dictum* in *Yardley's Estate*, 75 Pa. 207, 211 (1874): "Neither cohabitation, nor reputation of marriage, nor both, is marriage. When conjoined they are evidence from which a presumption of marriage arises." No marriage contract was found proven by the direct evidence and neither could it be presumed as sufficient cohabitation and reputation did not exist for the application of the presumption. In *Green's Estate*, 5 Pa.C. 605, 606 (1885), in which the parties lived together for sixteen years, the court stated that the parties' intent, when they met, was decisive: "If they, in any manner, expressed a purpose to cohabit as husband and wife, no other evidence is needed." *Compare In re Comly's Estate*, 185 Pa. 208, 211, 39 A. 890 (1898). *See also Biesecker's Estate*, 7 Pa.D. 70 (1898). In *Gerson v. Oil City Trust Co.*, 28 Pa.Dist.R. 853 (1918), in which the evidence concerning cohabitation and reputation was not considered satisfactory, the court stated: "Cohabitation and reputation of marriage are but the natural sequence of marriage. They are not in any sense requisites of a marriage."

28 *See, e.g.*, SIMON GREENLEAF, A TREATISE ON THE LAW OF EVIDENCE, II § 460 (3d ed. 1846), citing JAMES KENT, COMMENTARIES ON AMERICAN LAW, 2, Lec. XXVI (6) (1826), *Fenton v. Reed*, 4 Johns. 52 (1809) and *Jackson v. Winne*, 7 Wend. (N.Y.) 47, 22 Am.Dec. 563 (1831). *See also Guardians of the Poor v. Nathans*, 2 Brewster 149, 152 (1845). In *Letters*

This same stance was repeated in the later editions of Greenleaf's book throughout the entire 1800s.[29]

Joel Prentiss Bishop also endorsed the pure contract principle when in 1852 he published his first edition of COMMENTARIES ON THE LAW OF MARRIAGES AND DIVORCE. According to Bishop, when two parties who have the legal capacity to marry agree to immediately be married, the marriage is complete. He added: "[T]he consummation, as it is sometimes termed, adds nothing to its validity."[30] Bishop repeated this stance in his commentaries throughout the entire 1800s.[31] The understanding that a common law marriage, as with a canon law marriage, legally qualifies as a contract was also endorsed by the United States Supreme Court in the later leading case of *Meister v. Moore* (1877), in which Justice Strong stated: "That such a contract (*per verba de praesenti*) constitutes a marriage at common law there can be no doubt, in view of the adjudications made in this country, from its earliest settlement to the present day. Marriage is everywhere regarded as a civil contract."[32] The statement that marriage is based upon a contract, naturally needs not support the pure contract principle. That cohabitation is a requisite does not call the requirement of a contract into question. The issue, however, is whether the court goes further in viewing the contract as the only necessary requirement for the establishment of a marriage between two parties with legal capacity. The formulation that the contract constitutes a marriage can be interpreted as that the contract is not only necessary, but also alone sufficient, especially if nothing else is stated. On the other hand, the court cites with approval *Hutchins v. Kimmel* (1875), in which the Michigan Supreme Court speaks of an "agreement followed by cohabitation," which can be interpreted as a cautious recognition of the significance of cohabitation.[33] Since cohabitation was present

---

v. Cady, 10 Cal. 533, 537 (1858), the court stated that "[l]iving together 'as man and wife,' is not marriage, nor is an agreement so to live a contract of marriage."

29 *See* GREENLEAF, *supra* note 28, at § 460 (16th ed. 1899).

30 BISHOP, *supra* note 13, § 67. Bishop cites the Scottish case, *Lindo v. Belisario*, (1795) 1 Hagg.Con.Rep. 216. *Compare Patrick v. Patrick*, 3 Phill. 496, *Jackson v. Winne*, 7 Wend. (N.Y.) 47, 22 Am.Dec. 563 (1831), *Dumaresly v. Fishly*, 10 Ky. 368, 377 (1821) and *Walton v. Rider*, 1 Lee. 16 (5 E.E.R. 289) (1852).

31 Bishop repeats this viewpoint in the four editions of the original COMMENTARIES, the fourth edition being printed in 1888. The same view is seen also in the author's NEW COMMENTARIES ON MARRIAGE, DIVORCE AND SEPARATION (1891), in which he states: "To render competent parties husband and wife, they must and need only mutually agree in the present tense to be such." *Id.* at § 299. He further states that with respect to a marriage contract, that "consummation adds nothing to its legal effect." *Id.* at § 317.

32 *Meister v. Moore*, 97 U.S. 76, 78 (1877). *See also Hallett v. Collins*, 51 U.S. 174, 181-182 (1850), where the United States Supreme Court, interpreting Alabama law, applied the medieval Canon law as in force in the Spanish colonies. The court stated that "consent alone, joined with the will to marry, constitutes marriage."

33 *Meister*, 97 U.S. at 82. With respect to *Hutchins v. Kimmel*, 31 Mich. 126, 18 Am.Rep. 164 (1875) *see* the next section *infra*. *Compare Lucken v. Wichman*, 5 S.C. 411, 415 (1874), in which the court maintained that marriage can be based upon an "express contract, or inferred from circumstances."

in *Meister v. Moore*, and the issue of its constitutive significance was not at trial, the statements are simply *dicta* of a limited value.

Legal scholars do not treat the pure contract principle as consistently during the late 1800s as earlier. James Schouler took the same stance as the above-mentioned authors in A Treatise on the Law of Husband and Wife (1882), stating that the current law required "a simple expression of mutual consent, and no more."[34] Bishop did not amend his stance in the new expanded commentaries published in 1891, stating: "To render competent parties husband and wife, they must and need only mutually agree in the present tense to be such." He further stated, with respect to the marriage contract, that consummation adds nothing to its legal effect.[35] The older viewpoint is also repeated in the treatises of Reeve, Kent and Greenleaf, which continued to be published in newer editions.[36]

4. *The Application of the Pure Contract Principle in the United States in the 1900s*

At the turn of the nineteenth century, the pure contract principle continued to appear to be well anchored in the American case law. For example, in *Hulett v. Carey* (1896), a man and his housekeeper had entered into a written marriage contract, in which they declared that they "hereby agree to be husband and wife, and to hereafter live together as such." Thereafter, they secretly shared a bedroom and lived together as husband and wife for six months until the man's death. However, even after the execution of the contract, the woman outwardly appeared as the man's housekeeper. It clearly was the intention of the parties to eventually move to another town, and end the secrecy of their relationship. After the man's death, the woman claimed the man's real estate, certain personal property, and maintenance from the estate, arguing that, based on their common law marriage, she was the deceased's widow. The Minnesota Supreme Court found that a common law marriage had been established between the parties, stating *inter alia:* "The law views marriage as being merely a civil contract, not differing from any other contract, except that it is not revocable or dissoluble at the will of the parties ... to render competent parties husband and wife, they must and need only agree in the present tense to be such, no time being contemplated to elapse before the assumption of the status. If cohabitation follows, it adds nothing in law,

---

34 James Schouler, A Treatise on the Law of Husband and Wife § 31 (Boston, Little, Brown & Co. 1882). From this time period, *see also Murphy v. Ramsey*, 114 U.S. 15, 42 (1885), in which the Court, in a case concerning whether bigamy was committed, stated: "Cohabitation is but one of the many incidents to the marriage relation. It is not essential to it."

35 Joel Prentiss Bishop, New Commentaries on Marriage, Divorce and Separation, II, § 299 and § 317 (1891).

36 Greenleaf, *supra* note 28, § 460 (Lewis ed. 1896): "If the contract is made *per verba de praesenti*, though it is not consummated by cohabitation ... it amounts to a valid marriage."

although it may be evidence of marriage."[37] The objection has been raised that this clear statement supporting the proposition that cohabitation is legally meaningless, is simply *dictum*, because the parties actually lived together.[38] The objection, however, is not entirely tenable, as the cohabitation between the parties, as well as the time period, was very limited. The case, therefore, stands as clear support for the proposition that cohabitation entailing a holding out before one's surroundings that the parties are husband and wife is not necessary. In addition, the court's statements, though *dicta*, actually exerted a significant influence on the later development in American case law.[39]

The unusual situation that no cohabitation at all existed between the parties was the case in *Great Northern Ry. Co. v. Johnson* (1918), as in *Dumaresly* above. The *Johnson* court, consequently, was forced to address the issue of the necessity of cohabitation for the establishment of a common law marriage. In *Johnson*, the man had drafted and signed in Minnesota two copies of a written contract, in which he and the woman

---

37 *Hulett v. Carey*, 66 Minn. 327, 69 N.W. 31, 33-34 (1896). *Compare* Ariela R. Dubler, Note, *Governing Through Contract: Common Law Marriage in the Nineteenth Century*, 107 YALE L.J. 1885, 1893 (1998), who finds that "more than contract principles guided the decision." *See also United States v. Simpson*, 4 Utah 227, 7 P. 257 (1885) from the same time period: "The marriage is complete when there is a full, free and mutual consent by the parties capable of contracting, though not followed by cohabitation." A similar statement can be found in *Hilton v. Roylance*, 25 Utah 129, 69 P. 660 (1902): "Cohabitation is not essential to the creation of the marriage status." *See also McGrecry v. Davis*, 44 S.C. 195, 22 S.E. 178 (1893). *Compare Reaves v. Reaves*, 15 Okla. 240, 82 P. 490 (1905). *See also Davis v. Stouffer*, 132 Mo.App. 555, 556, 112 S.W. 282, 284-285 (1908), in which cohabitation certainly existed, but in which the Missouri Supreme Court, after an extensive investigation, and with reference to several of the above-mentioned older cases, in a carefully considered *dictum*, stated: "No one could say that reputation of marriage was any party of the marriage for the simple reason that there could not be rightful reputation of marriage until after the marriage; and so cohabitation is not a party of the marriage, for it can only lawfully exist after the marriage, as a sequence of the marriage ... A common law marriage ... is complete with the mutual present consent. It needs nothing more ... it need not to be followed by cohabitation, either in the sense of living together or of sexual intercourse. Mutual consent, expressed, is the requisite." *Compare* the less clear case from the same state, decided a few years earlier, *Topper v. Perry*, 197 Mo. 531, 114 Am.St.Rep. 777, 95 S.W. 203, 207 (1906), in which the court on one side stated that "if the contract be made *per verba de praesenti* it is sufficient evidence of a marriage" and on the other side, somewhat contradictorily, stated: "When the consent to marry is manifested by words *de praesenti*, a present assumption of the marriage status is necessary." The court did not elaborate what it meant by "assumption of the marriage status." *Compare Davis v. Stouffer* (p. 283), in which the court by the recently named expression did not intend "cohabitation and intercourse" but simply "a recognition that by the contract the parties, in good faith, have become and are married, for the purpose of assuming and carrying out the marriage relation."

38 *See Grigsby v. Reib*, 105 Tex. 597, 153 S.W. 1124 (1913).

39 The case is cited *inter alia* in the following cases: *Hilton v. Roylance*, 25 Utah 129, 69 P. 660, 664 (1902); *Davis v. Stouffer*, 132 Mo.App. 555, 112 S.W. 282, 284 (1908); *Love v. Love*, 185 Iowa 930, 171 N.W. 257 (1919); *Peters v. Peters*, 73 Colo. 271, 215 P. 128 (1923); *Mudd v. Perry*, 108 Okla. 168, 235 P. 479 (1925); *Tiuna v. Wilmott*, 162 Okla. 42, 19 P.2d 145 (1933); and *Lefkoff v. Sicro*, 189 Ga. 554, 6 S.E.2d 687, 697 (1939).

agreed "from this day henceforth to be husband and wife, and from this day henceforth to conduct ourselves toward each other as husband and wife." Thereafter, the man sent the two copies of the contract to the woman, who resided and worked in Missouri. After she signed the contract, she sent one copy to the man and kept the other. In a rather cursory summary of the facts, the court came to the conclusion that no cohabitation occurred between the parties after the execution of the contract. When the man died, the woman claimed that she was his wife in a common law marriage, citing the contract. The federal Circuit Court of Appeals, applying Missouri law, found that a common law marriage had been established between the parties. Circuit Judge Stone stated as reason *inter alia* the following: "Mutual assent to the present institution of the status is all sufficient. No other act, such as cohabitation ... is necessary."[40]

The pure contract principle lost some of its former influence upon the case law in the beginning of the 1920s, however, the state of the law in the majority of the states at this point of time was uncertain.[41] Even in the states in which the courts appeared to have abandoned the pure contract principle, as in Colorado, Oklahoma, and Iowa, cases giving expression for this principle appeared during the 1920s and 1930s.[42] In Colorado,

40 *Great Northern Ry. Co. v. Johnson*, 166 C.C.A. 181, 254 F. 683, 685 (8th Cir. 1918). *Compare* from the same time period, *Davidson v. Ream*, 97 Misc. 89, 161 N.Y.Supp. 73 (1916), in which it was maintained that consummation after the entering into of the marriage contract was not required. *See also Chaves v. Chaves*, 79 Fla. 602, 84 So. 672 (1920) ("It is the agreement itself, and not the form in which it is couched, which constitutes the contract, and the words used or the ceremony performed are, like *cohabitation and repute*, merely evidence of marriage") (*italics added.*); *Gerson v. Oil City Trust Co.*, 28 Dist.R. 853 (1918); *Green v. Green*, 77 Fla. 101, 80 So. 739 (1919); *compare Love v. Love*, 185 Iowa 930, 171 N.W. 257 (1919) (if the parties are agreed as to the existence of a marriage contract, no evidence as to the fact that the parties lived together or had a general reputation as husband and wife is necessary).

41 KOEGEL, *supra* note 8, at 164-165, stating that the pure contract principle was accepted in four states, and that the state of law in fifteen of the nineteen states recognizing common law marriage was unclear.

42 The pure contract principle is expressed occasionally in cases from Oklahoma. In *Mudd v. Perry*, 108 Okla. 168, 235 P. 479 (1925), the Oklahoma Supreme Court stated: "Whenever the minds of the parties meet in a common consent thereto, the marriage immediately arises." The court spoke of cohabitation only as an evidentiary fact for the existence of the contract and refers, *inter alia*, to *Hulett v. Carey*, 66 Minn. 327, 69 N.W. 31 (1896), one of the leading cases representing the pure contract principle. It ought, however, be noted that the case concerned parties that had entered into a ceremonial marriage, which was invalid due to a marital impediment. The issue that arose was whether the continued cohabitation after the removal of the marital impediment established a common law marriage. With respect thereto, and to the fact that cohabitation existed in the case, extensive conclusions should not be drawn as to the court's *dictum* with respect to the significance of the contract. A similar case can be found in *Fisher v. Fisher*, 116 Okla. 129, 243 P. 730 (1926). The court in *Tiuna v. Wilmott*, 162 Okla. 42, 19 P.2d 145 (1933) appears to have gone even further in favor of the pure contract principle: "All that is necessary to make competent parties husband and wife is that they agree in present tense to be such." The court added that "it is not necessary" that such a contract follows from "holding themselves out to the public as husband and wife or that it be acted on by them professedly living together in that relation." This statement was directly taken from

isolated cases would appear far into the twentieth century.[43] It is notable, however, that the pure contract principle, despite changes in the case law, continued to be consistently discussed in the legal literature. Otto Koegel stated, in 1922, in his doctoral thesis: "It is a mistake of principle to require, in addition to consent, evidence of cohabitation as essential to the validity of an informal marriage."[44]

One of the last serious questionings of cohabitation as a necessary requirement occurred during the 1960s. By then, however, reality had already raced past theory. Professor Hugh Ross maintained that according to the understanding of majority in the country, of which he viewed himself to be representative, nothing beyond the marriage contract was required, and in Ohio, it was unclear whether or not the case law required cohabitation.[45] Already, at the time of the publication of Ross' article, the

---

Hulett v. Carey. In deciding *Tiuna*, the court determined only whether a contract could be found evidenced, which was the case. *Compare Allen v. Smith*, 177 Okla. 605, 61 P.2d 564 (1936). Even in Iowa, where the Iowa Supreme Court consistently has given expression for the requirement of cohabitation during this time period, exceptional cases can be found giving expression for the pure contract principle, *see for example Love v. Love*, 185 Iowa 930, 171 N.W. 257 (1919). *See also* Note, *Presumptions in Common Law Marriage*, 14 IOWA L. REV. 215, 216 (1929). This stance was finally overruled by *In re Estate of Dallman*, 228 N.W.2d 187 (Iowa 1975). The pure contract principle dominated the case law in Georgia even to the end of the 1930s, *see Lefkoff v. Sicro*, 189 Ga. 554, 6 S.E.2d 687 (1939).

43 In *Peters v. Peters*, 73 Colo. 271, 215 P. 128, 129 (1923), the Colorado Supreme Court stated: "The habit and repute of marriage are not an essential of the legality of the relationship but merely evidence of an essential, *i.e.*, consent." If the contract can be proven in another manner, no evidence of habit and repute is required. This was in contrast to the findings of the lower court. The pure contract principle can be found in the decisions by the same court in *Thimgan v. Mathews*, 74 Colo. 93, 219 P. 211 (1923) and *Moffat Coal Co. v. Indus. Comm'n*, 108 Colo. 388, 118 P.2d 769 (1941). The same stance was taken by the Colorado Court of Appeals in *Deter v. Deter*, 484 P.2d 805, 806 (Colo.App. 1971). The court affirmed that cohabitation and repute are evidentiary facts as to the existence of a marriage contract, "even though such showing would not be essential to a common law marriage." *See also Vandever v. Indus. Comm'n*, 148 Ariz. 373, 714 P.2d 866 (1985) (applying Colorado law).

44 KOEGEL, *supra* note 8, at 127. *See also* from the same time period L.R.A. 1915E, 16 and 24: "It is the consent and not the cohabitation, that constitutes marriage... If a mutual agreement in fact is clearly established by direct evidence, neither holding out nor cohabitation is necessary to constitute the parties husband and wife." Treatises such as GEORGE ELLIOTT HOWARD, A HISTORY OF MATRIMONIAL INSTITUTIONS, III, 175 (1904), mention somewhat more laconically a contract "by mere present consent." *See also* FRANK KEEZER, THE LAW OF MARRIAGE AND DIVORCE 26 (1906), which with respect to common law marriage states: "It may be entered into by simple consent." *Compare* the second edition, which with respect to the contract states: "This may or may not be followed by consummation through cohabitation," at 90 (2d ed. 1923). *Compare* WILLIAM MACK, CYCLOPEDIA OF LAW AND PROCEDURE, VOL. XXVI, 836 (1907), which in its account of the case law is more varying.

45 Ross, *supra* at 732 note 9. As support for his view, Ross cites in his article only the two above-referenced cases, namely *Hulett v. Carey*, 66 Minn. 327, 69 N.W. 31 (1896) and *Great Northern Ry. v. Johnson*, 166 C.C.A. 181, 254 F. 683 (8th Cir. 1918). His stance has in Ohio support in the *dictum* of only a few cases, *see Gatterdam v. Gatterdam*, 86 Ohio App. 29, 85 N.E.2d 526 (1949) and *Leibrock v. Leibrock*, 63 Ohio Law Abs. 565, 107 N.E.2d 418 (Ohio Com.Pl. 1952). Ross' view received support in the case of *In re Estate of Madia*, 6 Ohio Misc. 109, 215 N.E.2d 72 (P.Ct. 1966). The issue was proven in the case

courts in the majority of the published cases from Ohio had clearly stated in *dictum* that the necessary requirements for the establishment of a common law marriage were cohabitation as husband and wife and holding out in some form.[46] This is now the current law, albeit the formulation of the requirement of holding out varies somewhat.[47]

5. *The Application of the Pure Contract Principle Today*

With respect to the pure contract principle's existence today, the states where the principle is still applied, namely, Pennsylvania and South

---

of *In re Estate of Soeder*, 7 Ohio.App. 271, 220 N.E.2d 547 (Ohio App. 1966), in which the lower court, with reference to Ross, simply required a marriage contract and found a common law marriage established. The lower court's judgment was overturned, however, by the Ohio Court of Appeals, which also required cohabitation, holding out, and reputation, and as a result, did not find that any common law marriage had been established. Ross' view was also mentioned in *Borton v. Burns*, 11 Ohio Misc. 200, 230 N.E.2d 156 (Ohio Prob. 1967). *See also*, from the same time period, HANS-HERMANN SPIESS, DIE UNGÜLTIGE EHE IM RECHT DER VEREINIGTEN STAATEN 56 (1964), which maintains that the pure contract principle is "*heute herrschende Ansicht*" and Holland Smith, Note, *Common law marriage: What it is and how to prove it*, 12 S.C. L.Q. 355 (1960). Even ABRAHAM L. FREEDMAN AND MAURICE FREEDMAN, LAW OF MARRIAGE AND DIVORCE IN PENNSYLVANIA I, 24, 57 (2d ed. 1957), appear to support the pure contract principle. In Lowell B. Howard, *Common law marriage*, 10 OHIO S.L.J. 405, 407 (1949), cohabitation and holding out are not required when the contract is "conclusively proved by other evidence." *See also Norell v. Norell*, 220 Ind. 398, 404, 44 N.E.2d 97, 99 (1942). *Compare* HOMER H. CLARK, JR., THE LAW OF DOMESTIC RELATIONS IN THE UNITED STATES 48 (1968), 105 (2d ed. 1987), who considers the requirement of cohabitation "clear and sound."

46 *See* already in *Umbenhower v. Labus*, 85 Ohio St. 238, 97 N.E. 832 (1912), *infra* note 116 and therein cited cases.

47 *Warren Gen. Hosp. v. Brink*, 80 Ohio App.3d 793, 610 N.E.2d 1128, 1129 (1992). In *Smereczynski v. Sec'y, DHHS*, 944 F.2d 296, 298 (6th Cir. 1991), the Sixth Circuit Court of Appeals articulated the objective element as a requirement of cohabitation as husband and wife and holding out to the public as man and wife. In the cases of *Fitzgerald v. Mayfield*, 584 N.E.2d 13, 17 (Ohio App. 4 Dist. 1990), *In re Estate of Hall*, 588 N.E.2d 203, 205 (Ohio App. 4 Dist. 1990), and in *Fields v. Fields*, 530 N.E.2d 933, 935-936 (Ohio App. 1987), the Ohio Court of Appeals cites with approval *Umbenhower* and *Nestor v. Nestor*, 15 Ohio St.3d 143, 15 O.B.R. 291, 472 N.E.2d 1091, 1094-1095 (1984) In the case of *In re McLaughlin's Estate*, 197 N.E.2d 578, 581 (Ohio P.Ct. 1963), the Probate Court of Columbiana County applied three requirements in addition to the marriage contract, namely cohabitation as husband and wife, holding out of themselves as husband and wife and being regarded as husband and wife. These same three requirements were used by the Court of Common Pleas in the case of *In re Estate of Hammonds*, 39 Ohio Misc. 96, 315 N.E.2d 843, 847 (C.P.Ohio 1973) and by the Ohio Court of Appeals in the case of *In re Estate of Soeder*, 4 Misc. 96, 209 N.E.2d 175, 7 Ohio App. 271, 220 N.E.2d 547, 557 (Ohio App. 1966). It also occurs that holding out is not specifically mentioned, but that the requirement is defined as "cohabitation as husband and wife" with the result that they "were treated and reputed as husband and wife," *see Jolley v. Jolley*, 46 Ohio Misc. 40, 347 N.E.2d 557, 560 (C.P.Ohio 1975). In *Bevan v. Bevan*, 2006 WL 1519654 (Ohio App. 11 Dist. 2006) the court held that the contract is the fundamental element of common law marriage in Ohio, but recognized incidentally that cohabitation and reputation are necessary elements, and in *Sulfridge v. Kindle*, 2005 WL 1806482 (Ohio App. 4 Dist. 2005), the court required, besides the agreement, cohabitation as husband and wife and holding out by the parties to those with whom they normally come into contact, resulting in a reputation as a married couple in community. *See also Reyes v. Vasquez*, 2005 WL 1389076 (Ohio App. 6 Dist. 2005) (cohabitation and reputation).

Carolina, are of particular interest. In Pennsylvania, where the principle has been well anchored since the 1800s as seen above,[48] the continued application in the case law during the 1900s[49] was confirmed by the state's Supreme Court in *McGrath's Estate* (1935). There, the parties had entered into a marriage contract, which they read to each other at the ceremonial marriage's wedding ritual. After approximately ten years of cohabitation, the man died. The issue arose as to whether a common law marriage had been established between the parties. The lower court found, despite the fact that a marriage contract *de praesenti* was found evidenced, that no common law marriage had been established because no general reputation as husband and wife had been proven. The court found that it was not necessary, however, to evidence the reputation, stating: "If the fact of marriage has already been shown by other evidence sufficient for the purpose ... resort to proof by habit and reputation is not necessary; it is mere cumulation." *McGrath's Estate* was the leading case for an extensive period of time.[50] As in a number of other cases in which the courts have found a common law marriage evidenced, the material grounds in *McGrath's Estate* consisted simply of a marriage contract, albeit the parties' cohabitation, reputation as spouses, and other circumstances acted as further support for the agreement.[51]

The Pennsylvania Supreme Court has recently reaffirmed the pure contract principle. In the case of *In re Estate of Gower* (1971), in which a common law marriage was established based upon a written contract, the court stated: "Having decided that the writing is sufficient to establish proof of a common law marriage, we need not consider whether the proof of cohabitation and reputation either corroborates or establishes

---

48 *See Guardians of the Poor v. Nathans*, 2 Brewster 149, 152 (1845), discussed *supra* as well as the cited cases.

49 *Long v. Long*, 15 Northamp. 157 (1915). In *Gerson v. Oil City Trust Co.*, 28 Pa.Dist.R. 853 (1918), in which the evidence regarding cohabitation and reputation was found insufficient, the court stated: "Cohabitation and reputation of marriage are but the natural sequence of marriage. They are not in any sense requisites of marriage." *See also Abbott's Petition*, 27 Pa.D. & C. 205 (1935).

50 *McGrath's Estate*, 319 Pa. 309, 313, 315, 318 (1935); and *Cordora v. Cordora*, 58 Pa.D. & C. 87 (1946). The same view can also be found in *Com. v. Amann*, 58 Pa.D. & C. 669, 673 (1947): "Cohabitation is not a requisite of marriage ... cohabitation is frequently used to prove marriage, but its absence does not disprove a marriage otherwise shown to have been effected." *See also Com. v. Allen*, 63 Dauph. 40, 41 (1952): "[T]he burden of proving a common law marriage ... may be sustained either by proof of the terms of the agreement, or by proof of cohabitation and reputation of marriage from which such may be inferred." If the informal marriage is proven by "the terms of the agreement," no cohabitation is consequently necessary. *See also In re Rosenberger's Estate*, 326 Pa. 153, 65 A.2d 377 (1949) and *In re Stauffer's Estate*, 372 Pa. 537, 94 A.2d 726 (1953), in which the Pennsylvania Supreme Court based a common law marriage mainly upon the parties' oral agreements. FREEDMAN AND FREEDMAN, *supra* note 45, at 24 and 57, appear to support the pure contract principle.

51 *See McGrath's Estate*, 319 Pa. 309, 313, 315, 318 (1935).

independently the validity of the common law marriage."[52] The court has repeated this stance whenever the material ground for the common law marriage has been based on an oral contract. In the case of *In re Estate of Garges* (1977), the court stated: "All that is essential is proof of an agreement to enter into the legal relationship of marriage at the present time."[53]

These principles have been applied in Pennsylvania to date. Only the contract is a necessary requirement, while cohabitation and other circumstances are evidentiary facts from which the courts can find the existence of a contract.[54] In *Cann v. Cann* (1993), the Pennsylvania Superior Court found that the parties had orally, before the woman's parents, entered into a contract for the purpose of establishing a marriage. The parties' marriage vows were supported by their joint tax declaration; the fact that they had named each other as beneficiaries under different insurance policies; and that the man, on his life insurance policy, had stated that the woman was his wife and the mother of his son. The court found, based on this, that a common law marriage had been established.[55]

The pure contract principle in Pennsylvania has been applied not only in the civil law arena, but also within administrative law. In *Atkins v. Heckler* (1983), a widower with children began to live with a woman in 1960. Out of respect for the man's children, who feared that the woman, through marriage, would take their mother's place, the parties never entered a ceremonial marriage. Nevertheless, they planned to formalize their relationship with a wedding after the man's children moved away from the home. Up until the man's death in 1980, the woman spent the majority of her time in the man's house. At the same time, however, she had her own apartment. In about 1975, the man gave the woman a wedding ring and

52 *In re Estate of Gower*, 445 Pa. 554, 284 A.2d 742, 744 (1971).

53 *In re Estate of Garges*, 474 Pa. 237, 378 A.2d 307, 309 (1977).

54 The Pennsylvania Supreme Court repeated the same stance in *Estate of Gavula*, 490 Pa. 535, 417 A.2d 168, 171 (1980), in which no common law marriage was found established with reference to the fact that no marriage contract was proven. The court stated: "Under the law of this Commonwealth, marriage is a civil contract. The contract does not require any specific form of words, and all that is essential is proof of an agreement to enter into the legal relationship of marriage at the present time." *See also In re Estate of Stauffer*, 504 Pa. 626, 476 A.2d 354 (1984). *See further In re Estate of Kovalchick*, 345 Pa.Super. 229, 498 A.2d 374 (1985), in which the lower court clearly stated that cohabitation and reputation were necessary elements in addition to the marriage contract. The Pennsylvania Superior Court, however, stated that a common law marriage existed "whenever an agreement of marriage is entered by an exchange of words *in praesenti*. Cohabitation and reputation are merely circumstances from which the existence of a contract of marriage can be inferred." *See also Renshaw v. Heckler*, 787 F.2d 50 (2d Cir. 1986). In *Com. v. McLean*, 387 Pa.Super. 354, 564 A.2d 216 (1989), the court states that cohabitation and reputation are not "requisites *per se* to prove a common law marriage." Observe that common law marriage, as was mentioned in chapter 1, was repealed in Pennsylvania by legislation, effective January 1, 2005, however not retroactively, *see* 23 PA. CONS. STAT. ANN. 1103 (WEST 2005).

55 *Cann v. Cann*, 632 A.2d 322 (Pa.Super. 1993).

said, "I consider you to be my wife," to which the woman responded that she viewed him as her husband. In connection with the man's death, the woman claimed widow's benefits based upon the fact that a common law marriage existed between her and the deceased. The administrative law judge, hearing the woman's claim, noted that the following three requirements for finding that a common law marriage existed: an agreement to become husband and wife, cohabitation as husband and wife, and a holding out by the parties publicly that they are husband and wife. The judge her application, referring to the fact that the evidence did not prove a reputation as husband and wife. The woman appealed, and the court found, that the administrative law judge had misconstrued Pennsylvania law by requiring that the plaintiff prove a combination of requirements, namely, an agreement expressed in the present tense to become man and wife, *plus* cohabitation and reputation. Moreover, the court found that if the judge, based on the evidence with respect to the ring, etc., had found a proven the intent of the parties to be married at the present time, that alone would be sufficient evidence that a common law marriage existed.[56]

Despite the broad and consistent support that the courts in Pennsylvania have given to the pure contract principle, the courts in New York, when applying Pennsylvania law, have occasionally mistakenly assumed a requirement of cohabitation.[57] It should also be noted that the application of the

56 *Atkins v. Heckler*, 574 F.Supp. 634 (E.D. Pa. 1983), in which he court cited *McGrath's Estate*, 319 Pa. 309 (1935) and *Estate of Gavula*, 490 Pa. 535, 417 A.2d 168, 171 (1980).

57 It appears that the courts in New York have mistakenly understood Pennsylvania law to contain a requirement of cohabitation. *See, e.g., Peart v. T.D. Bross Line Constr. Co.*, 357 N.Y.S.2d 53 (App.Div. 1974) (applying Pennsylvania law), in which the New York Supreme Court, Appellate Division, stated that a common law marriage must be proven through the parties' verbally expressed intent to be married "followed by cohabitation and acknowledgement." *Compare Pecorino v. Pecorino*, 64 A.D.2d 711, 407 N.Y.S.2d 550 (1978), in which the court spoke of a contract "followed by cohabitation" but in which the cohabitation does not appear to have been viewed as necessary. *See also Cross v. Cross*, 541 N.Y.S.2d 202, 205 (App.Div. 1989) (applying Pennsylvania law), in which Supreme Court, Appellate Division, found that the woman had neither shown any "intention to be married" nor "cohabitation or reputation of the type required to evidence a common law marriage in Pennsylvania." The court certainly could have meant, but gives no indication of doing so, that "cohabitation and reputation" is required for an application of the marriage presumption. This formulation rather gives the indication that it meant that these elements are necessary in addition to the contract in Pennsylvania. This case is more closely discussed in Chapter 10, *infra*. The same view basically appears in the case of *In re Estate of Abbott*, 592 N.Y.S.2d 729, 730 (App.Div. 1993). There the parties were not successful in fulfilling "the requirements of the laws of that state" as there was a lack of evidence that they intended to live together as husband and wife and that they "held themselves out as husband and wife or established a general reputation as husband and wife in the community." *See also Dozack v. Dozack*, 137 A.D.2d 317, 528 N.Y.S.2d 712 (App.Div. 1988) and *Matter of Danza*, 188 A.D.2d 530, 591 N.Y.S.2d 197, 198 (1992), in which, according to the courts, it appears that a common law marriage can be based solely upon a contract. Also, in *Craddock's Case*, 37 N.E.2d 508, 511 (Mass. 1941), the Massachusetts Supreme Judicial Court, in applying

pure contract principle in Pennsylvania naturally does not exclude cohabitation as evidence for the marriage contract. In addition, cohabitation and reputation can be required elements of a marriage presumption, in addition to the contract principle, according to which a marriage is presumed to exist if the absence of a marriage contract cannot be proven, as discussed further in Chapter 9, "Burdens of Proof and Presumptions."

The pure contract principle does not appear as clearly in South Carolina. Still, no objections have been raised in the case law about the statement by the South Carolina Court of Appeals in *Fryer v. Fryer* (1832), that marriage is a civil contract that requires nothing but the agreement of the parties.[58] Neither does more recent case law support the proposition that the courts today would require any objective requirements for the establishment of a common law marriage. In *Owens v. Owens* (1996), in which the question certainly was not contested because the marriage presumption was applied, the South Carolina Court of Appeals stated that the establishment of a valid common law marriage requires that the facts and circumstances show an intention by both parties to enter into a marriage contract. Nothing in addition is mentioned other than as factual circumstances or as an element in the marriage presumption.[59] Somewhat clearer is the same court's *dictum* in *Barker v. Baker* (1998), stating, without naming any further conditions, that a common law marriage exists if the parties "intend to enter into a marriage contract." The Supreme Court of South

---

Pennsylvania law, mistakenly assumes a requirement of "open cohabitation" as well as reputation and assent by the parties. The same mistaken interpretation of the law of Pennsylvania occurs in cases from Ohio, *see In re Zemmick's Estate*, 17 Ohio Supp. 15, 76 N.E.2d 902, 905-906 (1946). Also in Cynthia Grant Bowman, *A Feminist Proposal to Bring Back Common Law Marriage*, 75 OR. L. REV. L. REV. 709, 713 (1996), there are statements as to requirements of both cohabitation and holding out and reputation, without support in Pennsylvania law. Also HARRY D. KRAUSE ET AL., FAMILY LAW, CASES, COMMENTS, AND QUESTIONS (5th ed. 2003), seem to accept a general requirement of "holding out' (cohabitation)."

58 *Fryer v. Fryer*, 9 S.C.Eq. (Rich.Cas.) 85, 92 (1832). *See also Jewell v. Magwood*, 9 S.C.Eq. (Rich.Cas.) 113, 114 (1833); *McGrecry v. Davis*, 44 S.C. 195, 22 S.E. 178 (1893); and *Rutledge v. Tunns*, 69 S.C. 400, 48 S.E. 297 (1903).

59 *Owens v. Owens*, 466 S.E.2d 373, 375 (S.C.App. 1996). This question remarkably enough has not explicitly been at issue in a case. It can be seen, however, from the early case law, that only the marriage contract, expressed or implied, has been the object of the trial. *See, e.g., Catchcart v. Catchcart*, 414 S.E.2d 811 (S.C.App. 1992); *Jennings v. Hurt*, 554 N.Y.S.2d 220, 221 (App.Div. 1990); *Bochette v. Bochette*, 386 S.E.2d 475 (S.C.App. 1989); *Prevatte v. Prevatte*, 297 S.C. 345, 377 S.E.2d 114 (App. 1989); *Richland Memorial Hosp. v. English*, 295 S.C. 511, 369 S.E.2d 395 (1988); *Weathers v. Bolt*, 293 S.C. 486, 361 S.E.2d 773 (App. 1987); *Yarbrough v. Yarbrough*, 280 S.C. 546, 314 S.E.2d 16 (App. 1984); *Kirby v. Kirby*, 270 S.C. 137, 241 S.E.2d 415 (1978); *Johnson v. Johnson*, 235 S.C. 542, 112 S.E.2d 647, 651 (1960); and *Ex parte Blizzard*, 185 S.C. 131, 193 S.E. 633 (1937). The case of *Jennings v. Hurt*, 554 N.Y.S.2d 220, 221 (A.D. 1 Dep't 1990), applying South Carolina law, has been seen to constitute an example that the South Carolina law requires both cohabitation and reputation, and that the court, in the absence thereof, did not find a common law marriage proven, *see* Bowman, *supra* note 57, at 717. There therefore is reason to note that the court instead based its decision on that "there was neither a mutual intent nor an agreement to enter into a marriage contract."

Carolina has finally confirmed the pure contract principle by the following *dictum* in *Callen v. Callen* (2005): "A common law marriage is formed when two parties contract to be married."[60] On the other hand, as seen from Chapter 7, "Implied Marriage Agreements," the parties' cohabitation and their outward representation can be viewed in part as evidence for the existence of such a contract, and also as an element in the marriage presumption; for more on this, see Chapter 9.[61] South Carolina appears to be, next to Pennsylvania, the only common law marriage state in which the pure contract principle has survived and, accordingly, an informal marriage can be based only upon a contract.

However, the pure contract principle, today, does not lack new supporters. In Oklahoma, where the case law historically has taken a fluctuating position, there are new signals. In *Mueggenborg v. Walling* (1992), Chief Justice Opala of the Oklahoma Supreme Court addressed whether cohabitation should be a necessary element in common law marriage: "I would today overrule the distortions scattered throughout our case law and excise from its corpus references to cohabitation as a requirement for a common law marriage."[62] However, this rule has not been adopted in any case within Oklahoma.[63]

8.3 The Development of Cohabitation as a Requisite

1. *The Motivation behind the Requirement of Cohabitation as a Requisite*

The premise that cohabitation between the parties should be a necessary requirement in addition to the marriage contract does not, in contrast to common law marriage in general, have its origins in medieval canon or English ecclesiastical law.[64] Neither has it, to the same degree as the pure contract principle, been embraced by the American legal literature.

60 *See Callen v. Callen*, 365 S.C. 618, 620 S.E.2d 59, 62 (2005), remanded for a new hearing. *See also Barker v. Baker*, 330 S.C. 361, 499 S.E.2d 503, 506 (App. 1998), concerning the marriage presumption, which was found not applicable. For more on this, *see* Chapter 9 *infra*.

61 The marriage presumption based upon the parties' cohabitation and outward representation has been applied in, *e.g.*, *Owens v. Owens*, 466 S.E.2d 373 (S.C.App. 1996); *Jeanes v. Jeanes*, 255 S.C. 161, 177 S.E.2d 537, 539 (1970); and *In re Greenfield's Estate* 245 S.C. 595, 141 S.E.2d 916 (1965).

62 *Mueggenborg v. Walling*, 836 P.2d 112, 116 (Okla. 1992).

63 *Compare Sanders v. Sanders*, 948 P.2d 719 (Okla.Civ.App. Div 3 1997); and *Matter of Death of Boyd*, 959 P.2d 612 (Okla.Civ.App. Div. 1 1998).

64 *Compare* KOEGEL, *supra* note 8, at 130: "There is absolutely no authority in any of the English cases to support the theory that cohabitation is essential to an informal marriage."

Instead, it has developed in the American case law and, to a certain degree, in the legislation.

This requirement is based on the assumption that marriage is not only a contract between two parties but also a matter concerning even the children, the entire family, and the community in general. In *Sheffield v. Sheffield* (1848), the first Chief Justice of the Texas Supreme Court stated: "The parties have pledged themselves, not only for their own happiness, but for purposes important to society."[65] In accordance therewith, marriage has been viewed as a foundation for the entire Christian civilized society. The marriage contract is entered into not just for the sake of the parties. The rights and obligations that follow from the marriage are not only a result of the agreement between the spouses. Marriage becomes a status relationship with extensive legal consequences that are not regulated in the marriage contract. Instead, they are primarily the result of legislation, but also of case law. Several of the legal ramifications cannot be influenced by the parties' declarations of intent. A natural consequence of this is that the establishment of a marriage ought to not rest solely upon the agreement of the parties. The community has an interest in ensuring that the parties' vows to live their entire lives together are followed by a cohabitation so that a marriage can be established.[66]

Furthermore, a fundamental motivation behind the requirement of cohabitation is that the majority of the legal consequences of marriage are intended for marriages that are consummated through cohabitation. An application of the pure contract principle, according to which the parties can enter into a marriage contract and receive the legal consequences of marriage without ever engaging into an actual cohabitation, can be said to be in conflict with this purpose. This is especially true if the contract is entered into secretly with or without the parties personally meeting.[67]

From the parties' perspective, the requirement of cohabitation can also be motivated by the fact that the cohabitation must often be considered to constitute a presumption for the contract, *i.e.*, the contract was entered into under the condition that cohabitation would occur.

The requirement of cohabitation can also be motivated as a protection for the parties themselves against a hasty marriage contract. Even if they already have entered into the contract, the commencement of the cohabitation can be considered to be definite proof that the agreement truly was seriously intended.[68] It is one thing to orally enter into a marriage contract

65 *Sheffield v. Sheffield*, 3 Tex. 79, 85-86 (1848).

66 *Grigsby v. Reib*, 105 Tex. 597, 153 S.W. 1124 (1913); *Catlett v. Chestnut*, 107 Fla. 498, 146 So. 241 (1933); *McChesney v. Johnson*, 79 S.W.2d 658, 659 (Tex.Civ.App.-Fort Worth 1934); and *In re McKanna's Estate*, 106 Cal.App.2d 126, 234 P.2d 673, 675 (1951).

67 *Lefkoff v. Sicro*, 189 Ga. 554, 6 S.E.2d 687, 703 (1939).

68 Clark, *supra* note 45, at 48 (1968) and 105 (2d ed. 1987): "Adding the requirement of open marital cohabitation gives assurance that some objective evidence of the relationship will have to be introduced in every case to establish that the parties did consider themselves husband and wife."

and another to execute it. This reasoning is especially compelling if the contract itself is informal and perhaps comprises more or less conversationally uttered statements.[69] The cohabitation then functions as a substitute for the form requirement. The requirement of cohabitation, and especially the requirement of the parties' holding out as spouses, has always been intended to protect against secret marriages.[70] If the parties do not announce their marriage through a wedding, they must then, through their outward actions, announce their relationship. The weight given to this requirement in the case law can be seen in the fact that the parties' outward actions are sometimes referred to as the "acid test."[71] If they have undergone this test, they are considered to have mutually decided to live together because the public nature of the relationship gives the possibility of assessing whether the cohabitation is sufficiently marriage-like. Third parties that enter into agreements with the parties also have, through the requirement of cohabitation and primarily through the requirement of the parties' outward representation as spouses, a protection against secret marriages.[72]

Moreover, the requirement of cohabitation can be seen as a protection against more or less fraudulent claims, based solely on secret contracts about which no outside parties are aware. This is particularly true if a claim is made against the estate of a deceased party. In the requirement of a holding out, a protection then exists against someone, under the assertion that he or she entered into a marriage contract with the deceased, and thereby established a common law marriage, making fraudulent claims as to the property of the deceased.[73] It has even been said that a

69 With respect to the case law concerning oral contracts, *see* Section 6.5.1 *supra.*

70 *Lefkoff v. Sicro,* 189 Ga. 554, 6 S.E.2d 687, 703 (1939) (" Even creditors might be injuriously affected, and the State hampered in the enforcement of its penal laws"); and *Matter of Estate of Vandenhook,* 855 P.2d 518, 520 (Mont. 1993). In *Golden v. Golden,* 360 So.2d 994, 996 (Ala.Civ.App. 1978), the court found that the parties, who had "occasional clandestine sexual liaisons," did not receive "public recognition as husband and wife."

71 *McChesney v. Johnson,* 79 S.W.2d 658, 659 (Tex.Civ.App.-Fort Worth 1934). Actually, the case assumes, in addition to the contract, simply "holding out to the public as man and wife." However, though this generally may be considered to assume cohabitation, it appears more important to view the requirement as a complement rather than an alternative to cohabitation. It is expressly understood to be thus in the case of *In re Estate of Soeder,* 7 Ohio.App.2d 271, 220 N.E.2d 547 (Ohio App. 1966). The understanding that the parties' outward representation is the "acid test" recurs often. *See, e.g., Miller v. Sutherland,* 131 Mont. 175, 309 P.2d 322 (1957); *McClish v. Rankin,* 14 So.2d 714 (Fla. 1943); and *In re Schneider's Will,* 206 Misc. 18, 131 N.Y.S.2d 215 (Surr.Ct. 1954).

72 *Lefkoff v. Sicro,* 189 Ga. 554, 6 S.E.2d 687, 703 (1939) ("Even creditors might be injuriously affected, and the State hampered in the enforcement of its penal laws"); and *Matter of Estate of Vandenhook,* 855 P.2d 518, 520 (Mont. 1993).

73 *People v. Lucero,* 747 P.2d 660, 664 (Colo. 1987) ("The reason for this requirement is to guard against fraudulent claims of common law marriage"); and *Schilling v. Parsons,* 110 Ind.App. 52, 36 N.E.2d 958, 961 (1941) ("To hold that a common law marriage is established without public acknowledgment of the marriage status of the contracting parties where there is an unwitnessed oral agreement would open the

contract without the requirement of cohabitation would make "the estates of wealthy men the prey of the adventuress."[74]

A significant motivation for requiring cohabitation or outward representation as spouses, in addition to the marriage contract for establishing common law marriages, has been finally to avoid evidentiary difficulties and conflicts. It has been viewed as desirable to avoid those evidentiary difficulties that can be associated with a marriage entered into, perhaps only at night between the couple without their acquaintances having any knowledge.[75] The requirement of cohabitation thereby has also been considered to be a means of avoiding disputes. The fact that a requirement of cohabitation in itself can lead to difficulties with its application is a separate issue.[76] The motivation behind the requirement of cohabitation in a future context is discussed further in Chapter 13, "The Constitutive Requisites in the Future."

2. *Cohabitation as a Requisite during the 1800s*

Despite the fact that the pure contract principle dominated the legal literature during the entire 1800s, its development in the case law and, to a certain degree, in the legislation went in another direction. The understanding that cohabitation ought to be a necessary requirement in addition to the marriage contract, grew stronger during the 1800s,

---

door to perjury and fraud, deny the parties themselves the protection to which they are each entitled, and jeopardize the sanctity of the basic institution of all civilized society, the home"). The dissent in *Lefkoff v. Sicro*, 189 Ga. 554, 6 S.E.2d 687, 703 (1939) noted: "It would enable a man and woman under spurious claim of marriage to evade the statutes of frauds, and in virtue of supposed marital relations." In *Grigsby v. Reib*, 105 Tex. 597, 153 S.W. 1124 (1913) the court maintained that the absence of holding out would "open a wide door, with strong invitation to perjury and fraud." *See also Lee v. State*, 44 Tex.Crim.Rep. 354, 72 S.W. 1005 (1902). *Compare In re Callery's Estate*, 226 Pa. 469, 75 A. 672 (1910), in which the court, with respect to the surviving woman, stated: "[W]hen Callery was dying ... she not only made no effort to assert the rights of a wife to be with him and care for him, but entered into negotiations for pecuniary settlement"; and *Sharon v. Sharon*, 79 Cal. 633, 22 P. 26, 36 (1889). There is no absence of cases in which several persons made claims on an estate based upon the fact that they were the deceased's common law spouses, *see, e.g., Matter of Estate of Akers*, 541 P.2d 284 (Okla.App. 1975), in which not less than three women maintained that they were the deceased's widow. *Compare* the following cases, in which two women claimed that they were the deceased's common law wife: *Chapman v. Chapman*, 88 Tex. 641, 32 S.W. 871 (1895); *Klipfel v. Klipfel*, 41 Colo. 40, 92 P. 26, 124 Am.St.Rep. 96 (1907); *In re Rosenberger's Estate*, 362 Pa. 153, 65 A.2d 377 (1949); *Mitchell v. Smyser*, 236 S.C. 332, 114 S.E.2d 226 (1960); *Rush v. Traveler's Ins. Co.*, 347 S.W.2d 758 (Tex.App.-Texarkana 1961); *Gary v. Gary*, 490 S.W.2d 929 (Tex.Civ.App.-Tyler 1973); *Beals v. Beals*, 203 Ga.App. 81, 416 S.E.2d 301 (1992); and *Chandler v. Central Oil Corp., Inc.*, 253 Kan. 50, 853 P.2d 649 (1993).

74 James Schouler, A Treatise on the Law of Marriage, Divorce, Separation and Domestic Relations, II § 1177 (6th ed. 1921). In *Grigsby v. Reib*, 105 Tex. 597, 153 S.W. 1130 (1913), the court maintained in a similar manner that with respect to a deceased party, the absence of a requirement of cohabitation would "make their estates the prey of the bawd and the adventuress, with no possible safeguard."

75 *See United States v. Simpson*, 4 Utah 227, 7 P. 257, 258 (1885).

76 *See* the summary of this chapter *infra*.

becoming totally dominant by the turn of the century. An early example, already discussed, is *Dumaresly*, in which the majority of the Kentucky Supreme Court, applying Indiana law, held the existence of a common law marriage, under the pure contract principle, while the dissenting Judge Mills maintained that the establishment of a common law marriage required "consummation evidenced by cohabitation."[77]

As seen in this chapter, an implied contract prevents neither the application of the pure contract principle, nor cohabitation from being given, at all times, evidentiary weight in proving the parties' marital *consensus*. This was also true in the first half of the 1800s. One eventually can find formulations that go a step further, however, without cohabitation taking the place of a constant necessary requirement. In this in-between stage, one finds reasoning such as that given in *Rose v. Clark* (1841), in which the court, endorsing the main principle that each mutual contract between the parties to be husband and wife *in praesenti* constitutes a valid and binding marriage, adds "especially where it is followed by cohabitation."[78] Despite the fact that a contract already existed, it could clearly be important in certain cases that it was followed by something, namely, cohabitation. The Georgia Supreme Court formulated its stance somewhat unclearly in *Askew v. Dupree* (1860), which can be seen as the first step in Georgia towards accepting cohabitation as a necessary condition for the establishment of a common law marriage.[79]

This doctrine found support in the American case law during the second half of the 1800s. An early example of this is *Carmichael v. State* (1861), in which the Ohio Supreme Court stated that it was to be inferred

77 *Dumaresly v. Fishly*, 10 Ky. 368, 377 (1821), applying Indiana law, but stating that Kentucky law was the same. Judge Mills considered there to be support for his view of the principles to which the English parliament had given expression. *See also Jenkins v. Jenkins*, 2 Dana 102, 26 Am.Dec. 437 (Ky. 1833).

78 *Rose v. Clark*, 8 Paige 574, 580 (1841). The court refers to 2 Kent's Com. 87, which, however, does not contain the formulation "especially where it is followed by cohabitation." This appears to be added in by the court in *Rose v. Clark*.

79 *Askew v. Dupree*, 30 Ga. 173, 178 (1860). *See also Clark v. Cassidy*, 64 Ga. 662 (1880), in which the court, without trying the question as to the requirements, states as a basis for an "informal marriage," in addition to the contract, "the consummation of that contract." The court also speaks of a mutual intent to observe the duties, which follow from the relationship between husband, and wife "coupled with cohabitation and the performance of those duties." *See also Smith v. Smith*, 84 Ga. 440, 11 S.E. 496 (1890), which with the support of the law, required consummation, *see* GA. CODE SEC. 1653 (1863), as well as *Dale v. State*, 88 Ga. 552, 15 S.E. 287, 288-289 (1891), in which the court stated that "a mutual agreement to be husband and wife, by parties able to contract, followed by cohabitation, is recognized as a valid marriage." As cohabitation existed in the case, the statement is simply *dictum*. However, it ought to not be understood only as a statement as to the proven facts, but as a statement as to the existing law. The court stated: "By the common law and the law of this state," by which the cohabitation is a fact which together with the contract is recognized as a marriage. *Compare Lefkoff v. Sicro*, 189 Ga. 554, 6 S.E. 2d 687 (1939), in which the court maintained that the statement in *Dale* only refers to the existing evidence in the case.

from the statement that the parties openly and mutually consented to a contract of present marriage, to become husband and wife, and thereafter cohabit as such, and that "this" constituted a legal marriage. It can be questioned whether the court meant something other than that cohabitation was evidence of a marriage contract, rather whether the "this" also included the cohabitation, for which a certain support in the context generally can be found, in the meaning that it also was a requisite.[80]

In *Hutchins v. Kimmell* (1875), a case important to the recognition of common law marriages in the United States, a statement appears which is pertinent to the significance of cohabitation as a necessary requirement. The Michigan Supreme Court stated there that if the parties agreed presently to take each other as husband and wife, and from that time lived together professedly in that relation, evidence with respect to these facts was sufficient to establish a marriage. The statement is not simply a description of the facts in the case, but a statement about the state of the law.[81] As cohabitation existed in the case, the statement is simply *dictum*, but still significant. The courts in Michigan have, namely, since cited *Hutchins* as support for the proposition that cohabitation, along with the contract, is not only sufficient but also necessary for the establishment of a common law marriage. This view has been expressed in actual *ratio decidendi*.[82]

80 *Carmichael v. State*, 12 Ohio St. 553 (1861). This citation is taken from the case summary. Later in the judgment, the court does not mention the circumstances but rather that "an intent to form the honorable relation of marriage could not be properly found. In this case those circumstances are clearly shown. It was a contract of present marriage—openly made, and followed by cohabitation as husband and wife—and we think was a valid marriage under the laws of this state." *Id.* at 560-561. The legal significance of the cohabitation certainly relates to the marital intent, but the court nevertheless seems to consider it necessary. It ought to be noted that the court found reason to state, not only that a contract existed, but also that it was followed by cohabitation. As a contract already existed, the last statement would not have been necessary if cohabitation was simply evidence of the contract. It is unusual for the courts in Ohio to cite this case. The case of *Umbenhower v. Labus*, 85 Ohio St. 238, 97 N.E. 832 (1912) has had greater influence.

81 *Hutchins v. Kimmell*, 31 Mich. 126, 130, 18 Am.Rep. 164 (1875). That this is a statement as to the state of the law can be seen from the court's addition: "This has become the settled doctrine of the American courts" and later " [s]uch being the law of this state..." That the statement concerns cohabitation as a necessary requirement in the same manner as the contract and not simply as evidence of the contract can be seen from the way the court treats the contract and the cohabitation side by side. *See* the heading in the summary "Present agreement followed by cohabitation," after which is stated that a contract and cohabitation "constitute a valid marriage." *Id.* at 127. However, others have understood the statement to simply be a statement of the facts in the case or an acceptance of cohabitation as an evidentiary fact. *See Hulett v. Carey*, 66 Minn. 327, 69 N.W. 31 (1896).

82 The case of *Hutchins v. Kimmel* was cited with approval three years later by the United States Supreme Court in the significant case of *Meister v. Moore*, 97 U.S. 76, 82 (1878). Even the statement as to the significance of the cohabitation was cited, albeit that issue was not at trial in either case. As to the development in Michigan, the Michigan Supreme Court interpreted its statement in *Hutchins* as support for the proposition that cohabitation is a necessary requirement in addition to the contract. *See Peet v. Peet*, 52 Mich. 464, 18 N.W. 220, 221 (1884), in which the court maintained that it is

At this point of time, the first somewhat clear *dictum* from the Iowa Supreme Court emerged. In *Blanchard v. Lambert* (1876), the court stated that each mutual contract according to which the parties should be husband and wife "followed by cohabitation" constitutes a valid and binding marriage, if no impediment exists preventing the parties from entering into a marriage. Even if the support the court referred to for its proposition was rather weak, its decision would soon be repeated and come to strengthen the proposition that cohabitation is a necessary requirement.[83] At that same time period, similar statements from the Alabama Supreme Court can be found, as in *Beggs v. State* (1876), in which the court stated that a marriage entered into simply with the parties' *consensus* "followed by cohabitation" is valid.[84]

---

sufficient that the parties "consent to take each other as husband and wife, and actually cohabit as such." *See also People v. McQuaid*, 85 Mich. 127, 85 Mich. 127, 48 N.W. 161 (1891) and *Lorimer v. Lorimer*, 124 Mich. 631, 83 N.W. 609, 610 (1900). *See also Judson v. Judson*, 147 Mich. 518, 111 N.W. 78 (1907). *Hutchins* has also had influence on the case law of other states, *see, e.g.*, with respect to Texas, *Grigsby v. Reib*, 105 Tex. 597, 153 S.W. 1124 (1913).

83 *Blanchard v. Lambert*, 43 Iowa 228, 231, 22 Am.Rep. 245 (1876). The statement is not simply a statement of the facts in the case but is also a more general statement as to the applicable law. The general features can be seen from the court's reference to "any mutual agreement ... followed by cohabitation" and the view that this "constitute[s] a valid and binding marriage." That the statement is with respect to the state of the law can be seen from court's reference that it is "a settled rule of the common law." A common law marriage was found proven in *Blanchard*. The statement, however, is only *dictum* as the parties had lived together totally approximately five years, of which approximately fourteen months were without impediment. As support for its stance, the court referred to *Rose v. Clark*, 8 Paige 514, 573-579 (1841), which, however, does not give clear support for the proposition that cohabitation ought to be viewed as a necessary requirement. In *Rose*, the court only stated that each mutual contract between a man and a woman to be husband and wife constitutes a marriage "especially if followed by cohabitation." In other words, especially if the contract is followed by cohabitation, but not only then, to establish a marriage. Cohabitation can scarcely be argued to be a necessary requirement there. The court in *Rose* cited as support for its stance 2 *Kent's*, Com. 87, which, however, lacks the above-cited wording and which defends the pure contract principle (*see* 8.2.3. *supra*). Even if the Iowa Supreme Court in *Blanchard* had little support for the proposition that cohabitation is a necessary requirement, they repeat and strengthen this stance in later decisions. The statement with the content that cohabitation is a requirement is made in *McFarland v. McFarland*, 51 Iowa 565, 2 N.W. 269 (1879) ("provided they cohabit") and in *Brisbin v. Huntington*, 128 Iowa 166, 103 N.W. 144 (1905) ("if they lived together"). The courts stated in the following cases that the contract must be "followed by cohabitation": *Pegg v. Pegg*, 138 Iowa 572, 115 N.W. 1027 (1908); *In re Estate of Medford*, 197 Iowa 76, 196 N.W. 728 (1924); *State v. Grimes*, 215 Iowa 1287, 247 N.W. 664 (1933); *Rittgers v. United States*, 154 F.2d 768 (8th Cir. 1946) (applying Iowa law); *Abramson v. Abramson*, 161 Neb. 782, 74 N.W.2d 919 (1956) (applying Iowa law); *Gammelgaard v. Gammelgaard*, 247 Iowa 979, 77 N.W.2d 919 (1956); and *Jambrone v. David*, 16 Ill.2d 32, 156 N.E.2d 569 (1959) (applying Iowa law).

84 *Beggs v. State*, 55 Ala. 108, 112 (1876). *Compare* Robert C. Brickell, *Common Law Marriage*, 44 AM. L. REV. 256, 267 (1910), who holds that the expression "followed by cohabitation" is only a presentation of facts and that the case is contrary to *Ashley v. State*, 109 Ala. 48, 19 So. 917 (1895) and *Hawkins v. Hawkins*, 142 Ala. 571, 38 So. 640, 110 Am.St.Rep. 53 (1905).

During the latter half of the 1800s, cohabitation also received an anchoring as a necessary requirement in the legislation of several northwestern states with the legislation in California appearing to lead. The California Marriage Legislation of 1875 mandated that a common law marriage was established where the parties' consent to the marriage was followed by "a mutual assumption of marital rights, duties, or obligations."[85] This statute, repealed with the entire institution of common law marriage in California, in 1895, however, came to influence the development of the law in neighboring states. Already in 1877, the legislation of the Territory of Dakota, which before only required the consent of the parties, took up a similar regulation.[86] Idaho also amended the same requirement, which even today has a correspondence.[87] The legislation in Montana also took up a similar regulation for the establishment of a common law marriage, according to which a "mutual and public

85 Cal. Civ. Code § 55 (1875). Case law developed in California in connection with this statute, according to which the requirement of "assumption of marital rights, duties and obligations" entailed a requirement of cohabitation and reputation. In *Hinckley v. Ayres*, 105 Cal. 357, 38 P. 735, 736-737 (1895), the court stated: "There is no assumption [of marital rights, duties or obligations] unless the parties live together as husband and wife, treat each other 'in the usual way with married people,' and so conduct themselves as to have full repute among their intimate friends and associates to be husband and wife." *See also In re Jessup's Estate*, 81 Cal. 408, 21 P. 976, 22 P. 742 (1889). *See* especially *Sharon v. Sharon*, 79 Cal. 633, 22 P. 26, 131 (1889), in which the statute was not viewed by the lower court as requiring "cohabitation and recognition," but in which the opposite stance was successful upon the appeal, *see* 79 Cal. 633, 22 P. 26, 36-37 (1889). In *Sharon*, the California Supreme Court stated: "Cohabitation, which is evidence of the assumption of marital rights, duties or obligations, must be a 'living together as husband and wife'... If the parties agree to marriage, and commence to dwell together, in pursuance of the contract, as husband and wife, they have assumed marital rights, duties and obligations and are legally married." In *Kilburn v. Kilburn*, 89 Cal. 46, 26 P. 636, 637 (1891), the California Supreme Court stated that "by cohabitation is not meant simply the gratification of the sexual passions, but to live or dwell together, to have the same habitation, so that where one lives and dwells there does the other live and dwell also." *See also People v. Beevers*, 99 Cal. 286, 33 P. 844 (1893); *People v. Lehman*, 104 Cal. 631, 38 P. 422 (1894); *Harron v. Harron*, 128 Cal. 308, 60 P. 932 (1900); *In re Richards*, 133 Cal. 524, 65 P. 1034 (1901); and *In re Baldwin's Estate*, 162 Cal. 471, 123 P. 267, 275 (1912). The Idaho Supreme Court often cites California decisions in their interpretation of the actual statute, *see, e.g.*, *Hamby v. Simplot Co.*, 94 Idaho 794, 498 P.2d 1267, 1269 (1972); *In re Gholson's Estate*, 83 Idaho 270, 361 P.2d 791 (1961); and *Freiburghaus v. Freiburghaus* 103 Idaho 679, 651 P.2d 944, 947 (App. 1982). Also in Montana, *see Miller v. Sutherland*, 131 Mont. 175, 309 P.2d 322, 328 (1957); and *O'Mally v. O'Mally*, 46 Mont. 549, 129 P. 501, 503 (1913), in which the court added: "To us it means a course of conduct on the part of both man and wife towards each other and towards the world as that people generally would take them to be married. Indispensable to this is cohabitation." In South Dakota, an early statute can be found comparable to those in California and Idaho and interpreted in a similar manner, *see In re Svendsens's Estate*, 37 S.D. 353, 158 N.W. 410 (1916).

86 *See* § 34 of The Revised Codes of the Territory of Dakota (Geo. H. Hand ed. 1877). Before the 1877 amendment, the consent of the parties was "alone necessary", *see* § 34 of the Civil Code of the Territory of Dakota (1866).

87 Idaho Code Ann. § 32-201 (1983), referring to: 1877, p. 24 § 1; R.S. § 2420; reen. R.C. & C.L. § 2611; C.S. § 4591; I.C.A. § 31-201 (1983).

assumption of the marital relation," must be proven in addition to the parties' consent to marriage.[88] As a rule, this requisite has been interpreted in the case law as a requirement of cohabitation and reputation.[89] The case law from California has had and still has today a significant influence primarily on the courts in neighboring states,[90] but even on the case law of other states generally.[91]

3. *The Development at the Turn of the Century*

At the end of the nineteenth century, the idea of cohabitation as a necessary requirement began to find a stronger footing even in those states in which common law marriage was not regulated by legislation and the pure contract principle had been dominant in the case law.

Two cases from *Colorado*, which became the groundwork for the development there, ought to be mentioned here. In the first, *Taylor v. Taylor* (1897), the Colorado Court of Appeals stated that only a marriage made through the agreement of the parties, followed by cohabitation as husband and wife, and such other attendant circumstances as are necessary to constitute what is termed a common law marriage, can be binding. The court further stated that "the contract alone is not sufficient, unless it is followed by its consummation; that is, by cohabitation as husband and wife."[92] *Taylor* was followed by *Klipfel v. Klipfel* (1907), in which the Colorado Supreme Court cited with approval the first of the above cited statements made in *Taylor*.[93] Even though the decisions in Colorado continued to

---

88 MONT. REV. CODE ANN. § 3607 (1907): "Consent alone will not constitute marriage; it must be followed by a solemnization, or by mutual and public assumption of the marital relation," later MONT.REV.CODE ANN. § 5695(1921) and § 48-101 (1947). The regulation was repealed in 1975 through Session Law, Chapter 536 (1975).

89 *O'Mally v. O'Mally*, 46 Mont. 549, 129 P. 501, 503, Ann.Cas. 1914B 662 (1913): "To us it means a course of conduct on the party of both man and wife towards each other and toward the world as that people generally would take them to be married. Indispensable to this is cohabitation."

90 *See* note 146 *infra*.

91 The requirement of "assumption of marital rights, duties, or obligations" is taken from the Californian case of *People v. Lehman*, 104 Cal. 631, 38 P. 422 (1894), cited in 26 *Cyclopedia of Law and Procedure*, 836, 837 (1907), which appears to have influenced the case law of Oklahoma as well as Alabama. *See for example White v. Hill*, 176 Ala. 480, 58 So. 444, 447 (1912); *Bothwell v. Way*, 44 Okla. 555, 145 P. 350 (1914); and *Herd v. Herd*, 194 Ala. 613, 69 So. 885, 887 (1915). This formulation of the requirement has since remained unchanged in these states to modern times.

92 *Taylor v. Taylor*, Colo.App. 303, 50 P. 1049 (1897). *Cf. Israel v. Arthur*, 18 Colo. 158, 164, 32 P. 68 (1893), in which the Colorado Supreme Court, without the issue of whether it was a necessary requirement being raised at trial, however stated that the parties "contracted and consummated a marriage."

93 *Klipfel v. Klipfel*, 41 Colo. 40, 92 P. 26, 28 (1907). The statement in *Taylor* that the contract is not sufficient can be seen more clearly there than in *Klipfel*. The court in *Klipfel*, however, did not give any reason as to why it was left out in the long citation from *Taylor*, but rather stated that the cases were comparable and that they agreed with the *Taylor* court. It cannot be reasonably objected that the Colorado Supreme Court in *Klipfel* only cites to the cohabitation as a proven fact or its character as an evidentiary fact for the marriage contract, *compare* A.L.R. 24, 29 (1929). From the

vacillate for a long period of time with respect to this issue, and the pure contract principle remained anchored in the courts,[94] these cases continue to exert influence over the development of the case law over one hundred years later.[95] The understanding that the parties' actions are necessary for the establishment of a common law marriage would eventually prevail in Colorado.[96]

---

reasoning in *Klipfel*, it can be seen that the court more generally and in an indeterminate form speaks of "a marriage simply by agreement of the parties, followed by cohabitation" and that it belonged to the circumstances which "are necessary to constitute" a common law marriage in Colorado. This speaks for the fact that it was the court's *understanding* that cohabitation was a necessary requirement. The fact that the statement is *dictum* and that its significance and continued application can be questioned is a separate issue. The court's statement in the case of *In re Matteote's Estate*, 59 Colo. 566, 151 P. 448, 449 (1915) is significantly weaker: "In this case there was mutual consent, followed by cohabitation as husband and wife." This is a statement only as to that which was proven in the case. Simultaneously, it raises the question as to why the court spoke of whether cohabitation existed, when it had already found proven the existence of a consent? The case, however, cannot be considered more than weak support for the proposition that cohabitation is necessary. A certain support for the acceptance of cohabitation as a necessary requisite can be found in *Employer's Mut. Ins. Co. v. Morgulski*, 69 Colo. 223, 193 P. 725, 726 (1920), in which one party argued that a contract could not constitute marriage without cohabitation and that cohabitation could not be found proven. The Colorado Supreme Court did not elaborate more closely as to which requirement was necessary to establish a common law marriage, but found, despite the lack of cohabitation, no reason to change the lower court's decision, "though the company's claim as to the kind of cohabitation, requisite in such a case to constitute marriage, be correct."

94 In *Peters v. Peters*, 73 Colo. 271, 215 P. 128, 129 (1923), the Colorado Supreme Court stated: "The habit and repute of marriage are not an essential of the legality of the relationship but merely evidence of an essential, *i.e.*, consent." If the contract can be proven in another way, according to the court's reasoning, proof of habit and repute are not required, as the lower court found. The court does not appear to be bound by *Taylor v. Taylor*, 10 Colo. App. 303, 50 P. 1049 (1897), as no marriage was ever intended, and neither by *Employer's Mut. Ins. Co. v. Morgulski*, 69 Colo. 223, 193 P. 725 (1920), as habit and repute were proven. The court does not mention *Klipfel v. Klipfel*, 41 Colo. 40, 92 P. 26, 124 Am.St.Rep. 96 (1907). The pure contract principle can be found in the decisions by the same court in *Thimgan v. Matthews*, 74 Colo. 93, 219 P. 211 (1923) and in *Moffat Coal Co. v. Indus. Comm'n*, 108 Colo. 388, 118 P.2d 769 (1941). The Colorado Court of Appeals gives expression to the same stance in *Deter v. Deter*, 484 P.2d 805, 806 (Colo.App. 1971), stating that cohabitation and repute are evidentiary facts of a marriage contract, "even though such showing would not be essential to a common law marriage." *See also Vandever v. Indus. Comm'n*, 148 Ariz. 373, 714 P.2d 866 (1985) (applying Colorado law).

95 The cases of *Taylor* and *Klipfel* are cited in, *e.g.*, *Knaus v. Relyea*, 746 S.W.2d 389, 391 (Ark.App. 1988); *People v. Lucero*, 747 P.2d 660, 663 (Colo. 1987); *In re Estate of Bivians*, 652 P.2d 744, 752 (N.M. App. 1982); *Carter v. Firemen's Pension Fund*, 634 P.2d 410, 412 (Colo. 1981); *Valencia v. Northland Ins. Co.*, 514 P.2d 789 (Colo.App. 1973); *In re Binger's Estate*, 158 Neb. 444, 63 N.W.2d 784 (1954); *Graham v. Graham*, 130 Colo. 225, 274 P.2d 605, 606 (1954); *Peery v. Peery*, 27 Colo.App. 533, 150 P. 329 (1915); and *In re Matteote's Estate*, 59 Colo. 566, 151 P. 448 (1915).

96 *In re Matteote's Estate*, 59 Colo. 566, 151 P. 448 (1915); *Employer's Mut. Ins. Co. v. Morgulski*, 69 Colo. 223, 193 P. 725 (1920) (minimum requirement of cohabitation due to evidence in the form of a document); *Foley v. Gavin*, 76 Colo. 286, 230 P. 618 (1924); *Radovich v. Radovich*, 84 Colo. 250, 269 P. 22 (1928); *Davis v. People*, 83 Colo. 295, 264 P. 658 (1928); *Clayton Coal Co. v. Indus. Comm'n*, 93 Colo. 145, 25 P.2d 170 (1933); *Moffat Coal Co. v. Indus. Comm'n*, 108 Colo. 388, 118 P.2d 769 (1941); *Clark v.*

During this same time period, similar statements were expressed in judgments from the neighboring state of Kansas, where the Kansas Supreme Court, in *Shorten v. Judd* (1898), stated that a contract followed by cohabitation is sufficient to establish a common law marriage.[97] The statement is of interest since it is not simply a summary of the facts found proven in the case but a more general statement on the applicable law, followed by an evidentiary finding as to the contract as well as the cohabitation.[98] It is, therefore, the clearest statement to date by the courts in Kansas in support of the proposition that cohabitation is a necessary requirement in addition to the contract.[99] The stance would have been even clearer if the court had stated that the cohabitation, as well as the contract, was not just sufficient but also necessary for the establishment of a marriage contract. The case then would have been even more significant if a cohabitation had not existed, and as a consequence, no common law marriage was established. However, it would not be until the 1950s that the Kansas Supreme Court would make a more clear statement on this issue.[100]

The case law from **Oklahoma** in the beginning of the 1900s is also characterized by a tendency to require a complement to the marriage contract. In *Warren v. Canard* (1911), the Oklahoma Supreme Court stated that a common law marriage existed if the parties agreed to be husband and wife and in agreement therewith "have entered into the marriage relation." The court further viewed cohabitation as significant evidence for the proof of such a marriage.[101] Three years later, the court returned to the same requirement in two cases that became significant to the development

Clark, 123 Colo. 285, 229 P.2d 142 (1951); *Graham v. Graham*, 130 Colo. 225, 274 P.2d 605, 606 (1954); *In re Estate of Bivians*, 98 N.M. 722, 652 P.2d 744, 752 (App. 1982) (applying Colorado law); *People v. Lucero*, 747 P.2d 660, 663-664 (Colo. 1987); *Knaus v. Relyea*, 746 S.W.2d 389, 391 (Ark.App. 1988) (applying Colorado law); *Crandell v. Resley*, 804 P.2d 272 (Colo.App. 1990); *In re Marriage of Cargill & Rollins*, 843 P.2d 1335, 1339 (Colo. 1993); and *In re Custody of Nugent*, 955 P.2d 584, 588 (Colo.App. 1997).

97 *Shorten v. Judd*, 60 Kan. 73, 55 P. 286, 287 (1898). A similar statement appears in *Matney v. Linn*, 59 Kan. 613, 54 P. 668, 669 (1898). *Compare* 33 ALR 1924, where these cases are considered to only accept cohabitation as evidence or to state that cohabitation was proven in the cases in question. Nor in *Schuchart v. Schuchart*, 61 Kan. 597, 60 P. 311 (1900), does the cohabitation clearly appear as a necessary prerequisite.

98 With respect to the evidence, the court referred to testimony that consent existed but also that the parties "lived together as man and wife." *Judd*, 55 P. at 287.

99 The court refers to the older decisions of *State v. Hughes*, 35 Kan. 626, 12 P. 28, 57 Am.Rep. 195, 12 P. 28 (1896), *State v. Walker*, 36 Kan. 297, 13 P. 279, 59 Am.Rep. 556 (1887) and *State v. McFarland*, 38 Kan. 664, 17 P. 654 (1888). These cases, however, do not appear to give support for more than that the cohabitation was accepted as evidence.

100 *See In re Estate of Freeman*, 171 Kan. 211, 231 P.2d 261 (1951).

101 *Warren v. Canard*, 30 Okla. 514, 120 P. 599, 600 (1911). However, the court did not retry the facts but remanded it to the lower court for a new trial in accordance with their decision.

of the law in Oklahoma. In the first, *In re Love's Estate* (1914), the requirement was formulated in a comparable manner as in *Canard*, with a requirement that the parties "enter into and maintain thereafter the marriage relation."[102] In the other, *Bothwell v. Way* (1914), the court formulated the requirement somewhat differently, maintaining that the contract should be "consummated by their cohabitation as man and wife or their mutual assumption openly of marital duties and obligations."[103] With these cases, albeit the pure contract principle would continue to be expressed in isolated cases throughout the 1920s and 1930s,[104] the groundwork was laid for the view that today is dominant in Oklahoma.

---

102 *In re Love's Estate*, 42 Okla. 478, 142 P. 305, L.R.A. 1915E, 109 (1914). The same formulation recurs in, *e.g.*, *In re Sanders' Estate*, 67 Okla. 3, 168 P. 197 (1917); *Hughes v. Kano*, 68 Okla. 203, 173 P. 447 (1918); *Baker v. Jack*, 112 Okla. 142, 241 P. 478, 479 (1925); *Cavanaugh v. Cavanaugh*, 135 Okla. 204, 275 P. 315 (1929); *Cordilla v. Taylor*, 181 Okla. 20, 72 P.2d 375, 378 (1937); and *In re Miller's Estate*, 182 Okla. 534, 78 P.2d 819, 826 (1938). The Oklahoma Criminal Court of Appeals uses the same expression in *Rowland v. State*, 75 Okla.Crim.App. 164, 129 P.2d 609, 612 (1942); *Quinton v. Webb*, 207 Okla. 133, 248 P.2d 586, 588 (1952); *Daniels v. Mohon*, 350 P.2d 932 (Okla. 1960); *McKee v. State*, 452 P.2d 169 (Okla.Crim.App. 1969); and *Matter of Estate of Bouse*, 583 P.2d 514 (Okla.App. 1978).

103 *Bothwell v. Way*, 44 Okla. 555, 145 P. 350 (1914). The Oklahoma Supreme Court does not state why it uses a different formulation in *Bothwell* than in *In re Love's Estate*, decided only four months earlier. The locution in *Bothwell* is used later by the courts, as in *Thompson v. Smith*, 102 Okla. 150, 227 P. 77 (1924). In the case of *In re Graham's Estate*, 169 Okla. 568, 37 P.2d 964, 966 (1934), the court cites the locution in *Bothwell*, speaking of a contract "followed by cohabitation as such." *See also Vann v. Vann*, 186 Okla. 42, 96 P.2d 76, 79 (1939); and *Daniels v. Mohon*, 350 P.2d 932, 935 (Okla. 1960). The Oklahoma Court of Criminal Appeals expresses the requirement in the same manner in *McKee v. State*, 452 P.2d 169 (Okla.Crim. App. 1969). *Compare Chapman v. State*, 84 Okla.Crim.App. 41, 178 P.2d 638, 640 (1947) and *Marshall v. State*, 537 P.2d 423, 429 (Okla.Crim.App. 1975), in which the court made the significant distinction that each and every one of the requirements are not expressed as either, but as both (*Chapman:* "as well as"). None of the requirements were found proven in *Marshall*. The Oklahoma Supreme Court used a somewhat different formulation again in the case of *In re Trope's Estate*, 190 Okla. 453, 124 P.2d 733, 736 (1942), requiring "holding out by the parties of themselves as husband and wife" as well as the "public assumption of the relation." The statement is later cited in *Quinton v. Webb*, 207 Okla. 133, 248 P.2d 586, 587 (1952) and in *Richardson v. State*, 744 S.W.2d 65 (Tex.Cr.App. 1987). In a similar manner, the court in *Rath v. Maness*, 470 P.2d 1011, 1013 (Okla. 1970) speaks of "consummating arrangement by cohabitation and open assumption of marital duties," a formulation later cited by the Oklahoma Supreme Court in *Mueggenborg v. Walling*, 836 P.2d 112, 113 (Okla. 1992) and by the Oklahoma Court of Civil Appeals in *Sanders v. Sanders*, 948 P.2d 719 (Okla.Civ.App. Div. 3 1997).

104 The pure contract principle was particularly suitable to several cases during the 1920s and 1930s. In *Mudd v. Perry*, 108 Okla. 168, 235 P. 479 (1925), the Oklahoma Supreme Court stated: "Whenever the minds of the parties meet in a common consent thereto, the marriage immediately arises." The court speaks of cohabitation only as an evidentiary fact for the contract and refers, *inter alia*, to *Hulett v. Carey*, 66 Minn. 327, 69 N.W. 31 (1896), one of the leading cases representing the pure contract principle (*see* note 37 *supra*). It ought, however, be noted that the case concerned parties who had entered into a ceremonial marriage that was invalid due to a marital impediment. The issue later arose as to whether the continued cohabitation after the removal of the marital impediment could constitute a common law marriage. With reference thereto, and to the fact that cohabitation

The locution used in *Bothwell* appears to be borrowed from the CYCLOPEDIA OF LAW AND PROCEDURE (1907),[105] which in turn took the expression from California law, where the legislation, as stated above, at the end of the 1800s, required "a mutual assumption of marital rights, duties, or obligations."[106] The locution used in the encyclopedia appears to have also influenced the courts in other states. For example, in Alabama, where cohabitation as a necessary requirement has had a long and solid tradition, but the requisite in the case law earlier was formulated as a requirement of cohabitation,[107] the courts at this time used this same locution.[108] This occurs even in those states that today no longer recognize common law marriage.[109]

---

existed in the case, a not altogether far-reaching conclusion was drawn by the court in the *dictum* with respect to the significance of the contract. A similar case can be found in *Fisher v. Fisher*, 116 Okla. 129, 243 P. 730 (1926). The court appears to go farther in *Tiuna v. Wilmott*, 162 Okla. 42, 19 P.2d 145 (1933), stating even more clearly in favor of the pure contract principle: "All that is necessary," to make competent husband and wife is that "they agree in present tense to be such." The court further adds that "[i]t is not necessary" that such a contract is followed by the "holding themselves out to the public as husband and wife or that it be acted on by them professedly living together in that relation." These statements are directly borrowed from *Hulett v. Carey*. When hearing the case, the court only decided the issue of whether the contract was proven, which it found to be the case.

105 In 26 CYCLOPEDIA OF LAW AND PROCEDURE, 836, 837 (1907), a contract "consummated by their cohabitation as man and wife or their mutual assumption openly of marital duties and obligations" is discussed. The author to that section, United States Supreme Court Justice John Harlan, does not discuss closer the formulation of the requirements but simply makes reference to the following cases: *Hawkins v. Hawkins*, 142 Ala. 571, 38 So. 640, 110 Am. St. Rep. 53 (1905); *People v. Lehman*, 104 Cal. 631, 38 P. 422 (1894); *Sorensen v. Sorensen*, 68 Neb. 483, 100 N.W. 930 (1904); and *Taylor v. Taylor*, 10 Colo.App. 303, 50 P. 1049 (1897). However, of the cited cases, only *People v. Lehman*, in accordance with California law, formulated the requisite as a requirement of "assumption of marital duties and obligations." In general, reference usually was made to "cohabitation" or some similar wording.

106 CAL. CIV. CODE § 55 (1875). In connection with this legislation, the case law in California developed so that the requirement of "assumption of marital rights, duties and obligations" encompassed a requirement of "cohabitation" and "reputation."

107 *Hawkins v. Hawkins*, 142 Ala. 571, 110 Am.St.Rep. 53, 38 So. 640 (1905); *Tartt v. Negus*, 127 Ala. 301, 28 So. 713 (1900); *Moore v. Heineke*, 119 Ala. 627, 24 So. 374, 380 (1898); and *Ashley v. State*, 109 Ala. 48, 19 So. 917 (1895). *See also* older cases such as *Mickle v. State*, 21 So. 66 (Ala. 1896); *Farley v. Farley* 94 Ala. 501, 33 Am.St. Rep. 141, 10 So. 646 (1891); *Beggs v. State*, 55 Ala. 108 (1876); and *Campbell v. Gullatt*, 43 Ala. 57 (1869).

108 *See White v. Hill*, 176 Ala. 480, 58 So. 444, 447 (1912) and the leading case of *Herd v. Herd*, 194 Ala. 613, 69 So. 885, 887 (1915). This formulation of the requisite has since remained unchanged to the present day.

109 *See, e.g.*, *Lorimer v. Lorimer*, 124 Mich. 631, 83 N.W. 609, 610 (1900), in which the Michigan Supreme Court stated that an informal marriage contract is not sufficient to establish a valid marriage "unless acted upon by living together and cohabiting as husband and wife." With respect to Michigan, *see* the early case of *Hutchins v. Kimmell*, 31 Mich. 126, 18 Am.Rep. 164 (1875). *See also Topper v. Perry*, 197 Mo. 531, 114 Am.St.Rep. 777, 95 S.W. 203, 207 (1906), in which the Missouri Supreme Court stated: "When the consent to marry is manifested by words *de praesenti*, a present assumption of the marriage status is necessary." *See* the early cases from

The development around the turn of the century against an acceptance of cohabitation as a necessary requirement in addition to the marriage contract can be seen clearly in the case law of Texas. In *Simmons v. Simmons* (1897), the Texas Court of Civil Appeals, in clear *dictum*, stated that the only requirement for the establishment of a common law marriage was the agreement of the man and woman to become then and thenceforth husband and wife. When this takes place, the marriage is complete.[110] The court further stated that the parties' cohabitation and other facts could be evidence for the existence of a marriage contract, but that it would be a mistake to believe that such circumstances could constitute a marriage. The court found proven that the parties agreed to marry each other, that they, thereafter, lived together, as well as recognized and treated each other as husband and wife, and a marriage was found to have been established.

A definite change in stance occurred in Texas with the case of *Grigsby v. Reib* (1913), which became the leading case in the development of this issue. The plaintiff, a woman named Jessie Stallcup Grigsby, had a rooming house in Dallas where young women lived and received male visitors. Jessie also served alcohol on the premises. The house was visited by a widower, G.M.D. Grigsby, who began a sexual relationship with Jessie. In April of 1905, Grigsby and Jessie entered into an agreement with the content that they should become husband and wife. Thereafter, and until his death, Grigsby often regularly visited Jessie, where they always shared the same room. Grigsby called Jessie his wife and also presented her as such to a number of persons. However, Jessie never took the name Grigsby until after his death. When he died in 1906, his sister, Eliza J. Reib, took possession of his property. Jessie claimed half of the property based on the fact that she had been the deceased's common law wife.

The Texas Supreme Court found that the case of *Simmons* could be distinguished, as cohabitation existed there between the parties and the

---

Missouri, *State v. Bittick*, 103 Mo. 183, 15 S.W. 325, Am.S.R. 869, 11 L.R.A. 587 (1891); *State v. Cooper*, 103 Mo. 271, 15 S.W. 327 (1891); and *Dyer v. Brannock*, 66 Mo. 391, 27 Am.Rep. 359 (1877). *Compare Davis v. Stoufer*, 132 Mo.App. 555, 112 S.W. 282 (1908), in which the Missouri Court of Appeals maintained that a common law marriage could be established even if the contract was not followed by cohabitation, as "assumption" does not mean cohabitation but simply "recognition that by the contract the parties, in good faith, have become and are married, for the purpose of assuming and carrying out the marriage relation." The pure contract principle is also applied in *Great Northern Ry. Co. v. Johnson*, 166 C.C.A. 181, 254 F. 683 (8th Cir. 1918).

110 *Simmons v. Simmons*, 39 S.W. 639, 640 (Tex.App. 1897). With respect to older cases, *see, e.g., Sapp v. Newson*, 27 Tex. 537 (1864), *dictum*, in which a marriage was based upon a written marriage contract, but in which a certain cohabitation, however, existed. The pure contract principle has support even in *Lon Lee v. State*, 44 Tex. Crim.Rep. 354, 72 S.W. 1005, 61 A.L.R. 904 (1902); *Melton v. State*, 71 Tex.Crim. Rep. 130, 158 S.W. 550 (1913); and *Reed v. State*, 95 Tex.Crim.Rep. 492, 255 S.W. 619 (1923).

above-cited statements were only *dictum*.[111] Instead, the court took the stance that an assumption of the marriage status is essential to a common law marriage and that an agreement presently to be husband and wife is not sufficient to constitute marriage until it is acted upon by the parties. A common law marriage thus is entered into through "mutual agreement with cohabitation" and cohabitation, according to the court's view, and must be "professedly as husband and wife, and public," so that, by their conduct towards each other, they may be known as husband and wife. The court found that the lower court, which had denied Jessie's claim with reference to the lack of evidence concerning the marriage-like cohabitation, had decided correctly.[112]

With the holding in *Grigsby*, two aspects of the requirement were established, namely, the requirement of cohabitation between the parties and the requirement of holding out in relation to others. Despite some variations in the subsequent case law, *Grigsby* became[113] the leading case for the

111 Even if the court in *Grigsby* was correct in its assessment that the statement in *Simmons* had the character of *dictum* and consequently its legal significance was limited, it is clear that the courts had different views as to the relevant question. While the court in *Simmons* found that "only the agreement" was required, the *Grigsby* court stated that the contract was "not sufficient," two irreconcilable views.

112 *Grigsby v. Reib*, 105 Tex. 597, 153 S.W. 1124 (1913). The Texas Supreme Court also maintained, with respect to *Simmons*, that the cohabitation that existed in *Simmons* was also a basis for the judgment. This was seen from the fact that the *Simmons* court found that the marriage commenced not with the contract but when the parties "assumed that relation." Consequently, the marriage was based, not solely upon the contract, but rather the "consent and cohabitation." This conclusion appears, however, to be faulty, and relies upon not distinguishing the character of the cohabitation as evidence or as a requisite. In *Simmons*, the cohabitation was considered an evidentiary fact for the contract and its origins. It was not considered to always be a necessary requirement. *Compare Lorimer v. Lorimer*, 124 Mich. 631, 83 N.W. 609 (1900), in which the Michigan Supreme Court found the requirement of cohabitation fulfilled between a man and a prostitute. A dissent, however, found that no common law marriage existed: "Their intercourse was purely one of sexual commerce."

113 In *Salvini v. Salvini*, 2 S.W.2d 963, 965 (Tex.Civ.App.-El Paso 1928), the court spoke of a requirement of "cohabitation and living together professedly as man and wife." *Compare McChesny v. Johnson*, 79 S.W.2d 658, 659 (Tex.App.-Fort Worth 1934), in which the court formulates the requisite as a requirement of "cohabitation" and "holding out to the public as being man and wife." A similar case can be found in *Shazo v. Christian*, 191 S.W.2d 495 (Tex.Civ.App-Amarillo 1946). In *Wristen v. Wristen*, 119 S.W.2d 1104, 1105 (Tex.Civ.App.-Eastland 1938), the same court formulated it somewhat differently, however, without deviating from the substantive meaning, stating that the contract must be followed by "cohabitation and living together professedly as man and wife." This appears, however, not to be a deviation from the substantive meaning, while the requirement that the cohabitation shall be "professedly" as husband and wife entails a requirement of "holding out." Before common law marriage was codified in Texas in 1969, the Texas Supreme Court formulated the requirement as a requirement of cohabitation and holding out, *see Smith v. Smith*, 257 S.W.2d 335 (Tex.App.-Waco 1953); *Shelton v. Belknap*, 155 Tex. 37, 282 S.W.2d 682 (1955); *Cain v. Caine*, 314 S.W.2d 137 (Tex.App.-Waco 1958); *Ex parte Threet*, 160 Tex. 482, 333 S.W.2d 361, 364 (1960); *Humphreys v. Humphreys*, 364 S.W.2d 177, 178 (Tex. 1963); and *Hinojos v. Railroad Retirement Bd.*, 323 F.2d 227, 230 (5th Cir. 1963) (applying Texas law). Without materially changing the meaning,

development of this issue in Texas until these principles were codified in the 1960s.[114] *Grigsby* even came to influence the courts of other states.[115]

Around this same time, the Ohio Supreme Court, in *Umbenhower v. Labus* (1912), spoke of a marriage contract "followed by cohabitation." This case would become the leading case for the development in Ohio.[116]

In states such as **Alabama**, where cohabitation's position as a necessary requirement had long ago been clearly expressed in *dictum*, the requirement of cohabitation would also be established in three decisions around the turn of the century in which the Alabama Supreme Court, in the *ratio decidendi*, gave expression to the requirement. In *Herd v. Herd* (1915), which became the leading case, the Alabama Supreme Court consequently stated not only that a marriage contract must be followed by cohabitation but also found, with reference to the fact that no cohabitation had existed, that no common law marriage had been established.[117]

---

the legislation was formulated as a requirement that the parties "lived together in this State as husband and wife," and that they there "represented to others that they were married." *See* Tex. Fam. Code Ann. § 1.91 (a) (West 1969), presently Tex. Fam. Code Ann. § 2.401 (a) (Vernon 2005).

114 References to *Grigsby* are legio in later case law, albeit often in *dictum*, *see, e.g., Defferari v. Terry*, 68 S.W.2d 253, 256 (Tex.App.-Galveston 1934); *Perales v. Flores*, 147 S.W.2d 974 (Tex.App.-San Antonio 1941); *Drummond v. Benson*, 133 S.W.2d 154 (Tex.Civ.App.-San Antonio 1939); *Clack v. Williams*, 189 S.W.2d 503 (Tex.App.-San Antonio 1945); *Smith v. Smith*, 257 S.W.2d 335 (Tex.App.-Waco 1953); *Shelton v. Belknap*, 155 Tex. 37, 282 S.W.2d 682 (1955); *Cain v. Caine*, 314 S.W.2d 137 (Tex. App.-Waco 1958); *Ex parte Threet*, 160 Tex. 482, 333 S.W.2d 361, 364 (1960); *Hinojos v. Railroad Retirement Bd.*, 323 F.2d 227, 230 (5th Cir. 1963); *Ferrell v. Celebrezze*, 232 F.Supp. 281, 283 (S.D.Tex. 1964); and *Walter v. Walter*, 433 S.W.2d 183, 194 (Tex. Civ.App.-Houston (1st Dist.) 1968).

115 *In re McKanna's Estate*, 106 Cal.App.2d 126, 234 P.2d 673 (1951).

116 *Umbenhower v. Labus*, 85 Ohio St. 238, 97 N.E. 832 (1912): "An agreement of marriage *in praesenti*, when made by parties competent to contract, accompanied and followed by cohabitation as husband and wife, they being so treated and reputed in the community and circle in which they move, establishes a valid marriage at common law." This *dictum* is repeated in the cases of *In re Estate of Redman*, 135 Ohio St. 554, 21 N.E.2d 659 (1939); *Markley v. Hudson*, 143 Ohio St. 163, 54 N.E.2d 304 (1944); and *Nestor v. Nestor*, 15 Ohio St.3d 143, 15 O.B.R. 291, 472 N.E.2d 1091, 1094 (1984) (the objection was made that only a marriage contract was required. The Ohio Supreme Court found that both cohabitation and reputation were necessary elements in addition to the contract). The statement in *Umbenhower* has been often cited by other courts, *see, e.g., Holmes v. Pere Marquette R. Co.*, 28 Ohio App. 297, 162 N.E. 675 (1928). In *Respole v. Respole*, 70 N.E.2d 465, 468 (C.P.Ohio 1946), the statement in *Umbenhower* was formulated as a direct requirement when the Court of Common Pleas maintained that the marriage contract "must be accompanied and followed by cohabitation as husband and wife, and they must be treated and reputed as being married in the community and circle in which they move." *See also Nyhuis v. Pierce*, 65 O.L.Abs. 73, 114 N.E.2d 75, 77 (Ohio App. 1952); *Fitzgerald v. Mayfield*, 584 N.E.2d 13, 17 (Ohio App. 1990); *In re Estate of Hall*, 588 N.E.2d 203, 205 (Ohio App. 1990); and *Warren Gen. Hosp. v. Brink*, 80 Ohio App.3d 793, 610 N.E.2d 1128, 1129 (1992).

117 *Herd v. Herd*, 194 Ala. 613, 60 So. 885, 887 (1915). Two other decisions where the reasoning has the character of *ratio decidendi* are *Hawkins v. Hawkins*, 142 Ala. 571, 110 Am.St.Rep. 53, 38 So. 640 (1904) and *Ashley v. State*, 109 Ala. 48, 19 So. 917, 918 (1896). In the latter, the marriage was considered to be invalid, as the contract was

At the same time, the stance of the Michigan Supreme Court in *Hutchins v. Kimmell* was clarified by maintaining that the agreement and the cohabitation were not only sufficient but also necessary, stating in *People v. Spencer* (1917) that: "In this state a marriage is not proven by evidence only that the parties, *inter se*, agreed to take each other for husband and wife. To establish a nonceremonial marriage, then there must be proof, not only of the agreement, but of the setting up of the relation of husband and wife by cohabitation. The parties must act in conformity with such an agreement and live together and cohabit as husband and wife—live together in that relation." As no common law marriage was found established with reference to the insufficient cohabitation, the court's reasoning constitutes the *ratio decidendi*.[118]

The understanding that cohabitation was a necessary requirement in addition to the marriage contract appears to have grown so strong in the beginning of 1920s that it was the dominant stance of the courts, while the pure contract principle continued to dominate the legal literature, as seen above, for example, with Otto Koegel, who defended it in his doctoral thesis.[119]

4. *The Development in the Mid-Twentieth Century*

The development of cohabitation as a necessary requirement is even further established in the mid-twentieth century, much as at the beginning of the century.[120] This can be seen, *inter alia*, from cases in **Georgia** in the beginning of 1950s. The majority of the Georgia Supreme Court had earlier in *Lefkoff v. Sicro* (1939) continued to champion the pure contract principle. The dissent, however, maintained that cohabitation is necessary for the establishment of a common law marriage.[121] The dissent's stance was victorious in *Drewry v. State* (1951), in which the majority maintained that the legislation's requirement of "consummation" as stated in

not followed by cohabitation. *See also* the clear *dicta* in *White v. Hill*, 176 Ala. 480, 58 So. 444, 447 (1912); *Moore v. Heineke*, 119 Ala. 627, 24 So. 374, 380 (1898); *Mickle v. State*, 21 So. 66, 67 (Ala. 1896); *Farley v. Farley*, 94 Ala. 501, 33 Am.St.Rep. 141, 10 So. 646 (1892); *Beggs v. State*, 55 Ala. 108 (1876); and *Campbell v. Gullatt*, 43 Ala. 57 (1869).

118 *People v. Spencer*, 199 Mich. 395, 165 N.W. 921, 923 (1917).

119 KOEGEL, *supra* note 8, at 127. *Compare* SCHOULER, *supra* note 74, § 1177, who holds that cohabitation is a necessary requisite citing only *Herd v. Herd*, 1194 Ala. 613, 69 So. 885 (1915).

120 *See* JOHN W. MORLAND, KEEZER ON THE LAW OF MARRIAGE AND DIVORCE 34 (3d ed. 1946), in which the requirement of cohabitation is clearly seen. *Compare* KEEZER, *supra* note 44, at 26, which, with respect to common law marriage, states: "It may be entered into by simple consent." *Compare* KEEZER at 90 (2d ed. 1923), stating, with respect to the contract: "This may or may not be followed by consummation through cohabitation."

121 *Lefkoff v. Sicro*, 189 Ga. 554, 6 S.E.2d 687, 703 (1939). *Compare Nelms v. State*, 84 Ga. 466, 10 S.E. 1087 (1890), in which bigamy was found to exist despite the fact that the other marriage was not consummated through cohabitation. It ought, however, to be noted that this marriage was ceremonial.

GA. CODE ANN. § 53-101 (1933) for the establishment of marriage was also applicable to common law marriages and that consummation meant "cohabitation."[122] This view would dominate to the present date.[123]

The state of the law in **Colorado** had been rather unclear and the pure contract principle appears to have dominated since the beginning of 1920s.[124] In the beginning of the 1950s, the Colorado Supreme Court again returned to the decisions from the turn of the century, in which the requirement of cohabitation as a requisite in addition to the marriage contract had become anchored in the case law, as discussed above. In *Graham v. Graham* (1954), the Colorado Supreme Court cited with approval long portions from *Taylor v. Taylor* (1897), stating that "the contract alone is not sufficient, unless it is followed by its consummation; that is, by cohabitation as husband and wife." Even if the issue of the requirement is not more clearly discussed in *Graham*, and sufficient, albeit limited, cohabitation existed there, the court in clear *dictum* gave expressed its views.[125] This stance, as seen in the next section, appears to dominate in Colorado even today, although there may be a fly in the ointment.[126]

After early isolated *dicta* in favor of requiring that the cohabitation between the parties be a requirement in addition to the marriage contract,[127] the Kansas Supreme Court in the beginning of the 1950s gave a clear and decisive holding. In the case of *In re Estate of Freeman* (1951), the court maintained that, for the establishment of a common law marriage, there must be, in addition to the contract, "a holding out of each other to the public as husband and wife." Because such a holding out could not be

---

122 *Drewry v. State*, 208 Ga. 239, 65 S.E.2d 916 (1951). A dissent was given to the majority's opinion.

123 *Tabor v. Fowler*, 119 Ga.App. 259, 167 S.E.2d 220 (1969); *Brown v. Brown*, 234 Ga. 300, 215 S.E.2d 671, 673 (1975); *Fireman's Fund Ins. Co. v. Smith*, 151 Ga.App. 270, 271, 259 S.E.2d 675 (1979); *Ridley v. Grandison*, 260 Ga. 6, 389 S.E.2d 746 (1990); *Georgia Osteopathic Hosp. v O'Neal*, 198 Ga.App. 770, 403 S.E.2d 235, 243 (1991); and *Brown v. Carr*, 198 Ga.App. 567, 402 S.E.2d 296, 297 (1991). *See also* Denzil Y. Causey, Jr., Comment, *Domestic Relations - Common Law Marriage in Georgia*, 25 GA. B.J. 225, 229 (1962).

124 *Peters v. Peters*, 73 Colo. 271, 215 P. 128, 129 (1923); *Thimgan v. Mathews*, 74 Colo. 93, 219 P. 211 (1923); and *Moffat Coal Co. v. Indus. Comm'n*, 108 Colo. 388, 118 P.2d 769 (1941).

125 *Graham v. Graham*, 130 Colo. 225, 274 P.2d 605 (1954).

126 After *Graham*, the same stance has since been most clearly expressed in the cases of *In re Enoch's Estate*, 52 Ill.App.2d 39, 201 N.E.2d 682 (1964), in which *Taylor* is cited; and *Valencia v. Northland Ins. Co.*, 514 P.2d 789 (Colo.App. 1973), citing both *Taylor* and *Klipfel*. The Colorado Supreme Court expressed the same stance in *Carter v. Firemen's Pension Fund*, 634 P.2d 410, 412 (Colo. 1981), citing both *Taylor* and *Klipfel*. The same view recurs in the case of *In re Estate of Bivians*, 652 P.2d 744, 752 (N.M. App. 1982), in which the New Mexico Court of Appeals, applying Colorado law, cited the cases of *Graham*, as well as *Taylor* and *Klipfel*. Both of these cases are cited with approval by the Colorado Supreme Court in *People v. Lucero*, 747 P.2d 660, 663 (Colo. 1987). The same view is later expressed in *Knaus v. Relyea*, 746 S.W.2d 289 (Ark.App. 1988) and in *Crandell v. Resley*, 804 P.2d 272 (Colo.App. 1990).

127 *See Shorten v. Judd*, 60 Kan. 73, 55 P. 286 (1898). *Matney v. Linn*, 59 Kan. 613, 54 P. 668, 669 (1898).

proven in *Freeman*, the court found that no common law marriage had been established.[128] With this, the court, in a clear *ratio decidendi*, took a stance, formulating the requirement that exists even to today.[129]

In **Oklahoma**, where the groundwork, as seen above, already had been laid in the beginning of the century, the view also became clearer during the 1940s and even more so in the 1950s. The need to clarify had existed since the Oklahoma Supreme Court during the 1920s and 1930s had made statements that could be interpreted as support more in favor of the pure contract principle[130] than of the requirement of cohabitation. In *Quinton v. Webb* (1952), the court more clearly demarcated these two main stances and adopted a position supporting the proposition that cohabitation was a necessary requirement in addition to the marriage contract. As the required cohabitation was not found proven in *Quinton*, the court's stance was formalized in a *ratio decidendi*.[131]

As regards the general description of the requisite, the court in *Quinton* appears to have borrowed the expression from one of the earliest cases in Oklahoma, holding that a common law marriage exists if the parties are in agreement to be husband and wife and thereafter enter into and maintain the marital relation.[132] When more closely defining the element,

---

128 *In re Estate of Freeman*, 171 Kan. 211, 231 P.2d 261, 263 (1951). As support for the proposition that the parties' holding out is a necessary requirement in addition to the marriage contract, the court cited *Cooper v. Cooper*, 147 Kan. 256, 76 P.2d 867 (1938) and *Pitney v. Pitney*, 151 Kan. 848, 101 P.2d 933 (1940). These cases appear, however, to not be clear expressions for this proposition.

129 The same view recurs clearly in *Whetstone v. Whetstone*, 178 Kan. 595, 290 P.2d 1022, 1023 (1955), where the required holding out was found not proven. *See also Gillaspie v. Blair Constr. Co.*, 192 Kan. 455, 388 P.2d 647, 649 (1964); *Sullivan v. Sullivan*, 196 Kan. 705, 413 P.2d 988, 992 (1966) (neither the contract nor holding out was found proven); *Schrader v. Schrader*, 207 Kan. 349, 484 P.2d 1007, 1008 (1971) (contract not found proven); *In re Estate of Keimig*, 215 Kan. 869, 872, 528 P.2d 1228, 1230 (1974); *State v. Johnson*, 216 Kan. 445, 532 P.2d 1325, 1328 (1975) (the required holding out found not proven); *Driscoll v. Driscoll*, 220 Kan. 225, 552 P.2d 629, 632 (1976) ("sporadic cohabitation" found not a sufficient holding out); *Eaton v. Johnston*, 235 Kan. 323, 672 P.2d 10, 12 (1983), 681 P.2d 606 (1984); *State v. Sedlack*, 246 Kan. 305, 787 P.2d 709, 710 (1990); *Matter of Estate of Hendrickson*, 248 Kan. 72, 805 P.2d 20 (1991) (only approximately two weeks of cohabitation, of which one week was in the hospital prior to the man's death); *Chandler v. Central Oil Corp., Inc.*, 253 Kan. 50, 853 P.2d 649 (1993); *In re Pace*, 26 Kan.App.2d 538, 989 P.2d 297 (1999); and *In re Estate of Antonopoulos*, 268 Kan. 178, 993 P.2d 637, 647 (1999).

130 *Mudd v. Perry*, 108 Okla. 168, 235 P. 479 (1925); *Fisher v. Fisher*, 116 Okla. 129, 243 P. 730 (1926); and *Tiuna v. Wilmott*, 162 Okla. 42, 19 P.2d 145 (1933).

131 *Quinton v. Webb*, 207 Okla. 133, 248 P.2d 586 (1952). Also in the case of *In re Trope's Estate*, 190 Okla. 453, 124 P.2d 733 (1942), a clear expression for the proposition that the cohabitation ought to constitute a necessary requirement in addition to the contract is made. However, cohabitation existed in that case. *See also In re Miller's Estate*, 182 Okla. 534, 78 P.2d 819 (1938), where no common law marriage was found proven due to an insufficient cohabitation. *See also In re Blackhawk's Estate*, 195 Okla. 390, 158 P.2d 168 (1944).

132 The court refers to *Cordilla v. Taylor*, 181 Okla. 20, 72 P.2d 375 (1937), but the locution actually appears to have its origins in the case of *In re Love's Estate*, 42 Okla. 478, 142 P. 305 (1914).

the formulation from later case law is used by the court, setting out the "holding out by the parties of themselves as husband and wife" and "public assumption of the relation."[133] As a synonym for the latter prong, the court also used the expression "cohabitation." This double requirement of cohabitation between the parties and "holding out" with respect to third parties is the applicable law even today, albeit the courts' formulations have varied somewhat.[134]

This double requisite also became fixed in the case law from **Iowa**, where the requirement of an objective element for the establishment of a common law marriage has had a long tradition.[135] However, the courts in Iowa have long held a requirement of cohabitation.[136] In the case of *In re Long's Estate* (1960), however, the Iowa Supreme Court chose to formulate the objective element as a requirement of both "continuous cohabitation" and "public declaration" that the parties are husband and wife. The last named requirement is comparable to that which in several other states is termed "holding out."[137] The courts in Iowa have maintained this double requirement to date.[138]

---

133 *See In re Trope's Estate*, 190 Okla. 453, 124 P.2d 733 (1942). *Compare Bothwell v. Way*, 44 Okla. 555, 145 P. 350 (1914), where the court formulated the requisite somewhat differently by requiring that the contract should be "consummated by their cohabitation as man and wife or their mutual assumption openly of marital duties and obligations."

134 *See* Section 8.6 *infra*.

135 *See Pegg v. Pegg*, 138 Iowa 572, 115 N.W. 1027 (1908), in which the Iowa Supreme Court stated that for the establishment of a common law marriage, a contract to be husband and wife "followed by cohabitation as such" must be proven. *See* the prior case of *McFarland v. McFarland*, 51 Iowa 565, 2 N.W. 269, 274 (1879), in which the court maintained that the woman could receive marriage-like rights "provided they cohabit." *See also Blanchard v. Lambert*, 43 Iowa 228, 22 Am.Rep. 245 (1876). *Compare Love v. Love*, 185 Iowa 930, 171 N.W. 257 (1919), in which it was maintained that there was no requirement that the parties lived and cohabited together or that they outwardly before the public represented themselves as husband and wife. This case, in this latter aspect, was finally overruled by the clear *ratio decidendi* in the case of *In re Estate of Dallman*, 228 N.W.2d 187 (Iowa 1975), in which the woman was not successful in proving the requirement holding out and therefore, no common law marriage was found proven.

136 *See Gammelgaard v. Gammelgaard*, 247 Iowa 979, 77 N.W.2d 479, 480 (1956), in which the Iowa Supreme Court required consent to be husband and wife "followed by cohabitation." This locution recurs in *Jambrone v. David*, 16 Ill.2d 32, 156 N.E.2d 569 (1959), in which the Illinois Supreme Court applied Iowa law. The expression had earlier been used in *Abramson v. Abramson*, 161 Neb. 782, 74 N.W.2d 919 (1956), in which the Nebraska Supreme Court, applying Iowa law, required that a contract to be husband and wife must exist, as well as "cohabitation as such." *See also Rittgers v. United States*, 154 F.2d 768 (8th Cir. 1946) (applying Iowa law). The latter expression had previously been used by the courts in Iowa in *State v. Grimes*, 215 Iowa 1287, 247 N.W. 664 (1941); *In re Estate of Medford*, 197 Iowa 76, 196 N.W. 728 (1924); and *Pegg v. Pegg*, 138 Iowa 572, 115 N.W. 1027 (1908). *Compare McFarland v. McFarland*, 51 Iowa 565, 2 N.W. 269, 274 (1879), in which the court maintained that the woman could receive marriage-like rights "provided they cohabit."

137 *In re Estate of Malli*, 260 Iowa 252, 149 N.W.2d 155 (1967).

138 *In re Long's Estate*, 251 Iowa 1042, 102 N.W.2d 76, 79 (1960); *Coleman v. Graves*, 255 Iowa 396, 122 N.W.2d 853, 856 (1963); *In re Estate of Malli*, 260 Iowa 252, 149

Despite the fact that the requirement of cohabitation in the beginning of 1960s entirely dominated the law, the legal literature continued to expound the pure contract principle.[139] In an article in 1963, Ross maintained that, according to the majority's understanding in the country, which he represented, nothing in addition to the marriage contract was required.

5. *The Development during the Latter Part of the 1900s*

Cohabitation's ever-growing importance manifested itself during the 1960s with the codification of common law marriage in Texas, with the legislation mandating cohabitation as a necessary requisite in addition to the contract. The construction was based on the double requirement that the parties "lived together in this State as husband and wife," and that they there "represented to others that they were married" as stated in TEX. FAM. CODE ANN. § 1.91 (a)(1969).[140] The legislation entailed a codification of the earlier principles as found in the case law.[141]

Cohabitation's position as a requisite was further anchored at the end of the twentieth century. When common law marriage was reintroduced in Utah legislation in 1987, after an absence of ninety-nine years, the pure

N.W.2d 155, 158 (1967); *State v. Lawson*, 165 N.W.2d 838 (Iowa 1969); *In re Estate of Fisher*, 176 N.W.2d 801, 805 (Iowa 1970); and *In re Estate of Dallman*, 228 N.W.2d 189 (Iowa 1975). The most recent case by the Iowa Supreme Court giving expression to this double requirement is *In re Marriage of Winegard*, 278 N.W.2d 505, 510 (Iowa 1979). The requirement of both "continuous cohabitation" and "public declaration" has since, however, recurred in cases from the Iowa Court of Appeals, *see, e.g., In re Marriage of Gebhardt* 426 N.W.2d 651, 652 (Iowa App. 1988); *In re Marriage of Jones*, 451 N.W.2d 25, 27 (Iowa App. 1989); and *Fritz v. Mork*, 2001 Iowa App. LEXIS 594 (2001). *See also Hurley v. Hurley*, 222 Mont. 287, 721 P.2d 1279, 1284 (1986) (applying Iowa law) and *In re Marriage of Mosher*, 183 Ill.Dec. 911, 243 Ill.App.3d 97, 612 N.E.2d 838, 841 (1993) (applying Iowa law). In the case of *Matter of Estate of Stodola*, 519 N.W.2d 97, 98 (Iowa App. 1994), the court spoke of "continuous cohabitation" and "general and substantial public declarations that the parties are husband and wife."

139 *See* Ross, *supra* note 9, at at 732, maintaining that the majority understanding is in favor of the pure contract principle.

140 Act of June 2, 1969, 61 st Leg., R.S. chap. 888 § 1.91, 1969 Tex.Gen.Laws 2707.2717 (Vernon's 1975), currently TEX. FAM. CODE ANN. § 2.401(a) (Vernon 2005). Three requirements are to be fulfilled for establishing a common law marriage: (1) An agreement to be married, (2) Living together in Texas as husband and wife, and (3) Representing to others in Texas that they are married. These three elements must exist simultaneously. *See Bolash v. Heid*, 733 S.W.2d 698, 699 (Tex.Civ.App.-San Antonio 1987); *Winfield v. Renfro*, 821 S.W.2d 640, 646 (Tex.App.-Houston 1991); and *Gary v. Gary*, 490 S.W.2d 929, 934 (Tex.Civ.App.-Tyler 1973).

141 *Humphreys v. Humphreys*, 364 S.W.2d 177 (Tex. 1963); *Hinojos v. Railroad Retirement Bd.*, 323 F.2d 227, 230 (5th Cir. 1963) (applying Texas law); *Ex parte Threet*, 160 Tex. 482, 333 S.W.2d 361 (1960); *Shelton v. Belknap*, 155 Tex. 37, 282 S.W.2d 682 (1955); *Estate of Claveria v. Claveria*, 615 S.W.2d 164, 166 (Tex. 1981); *Collora v. Navarro*, 574 S.W.2d 65 (Tex. 1978); *Morris v. Morris*, 403 S.W.2d 295, 296 (Tex.Civ.App. 1971); and *Conlon v. Schweiker*, 537 F.Supp. 158, 159 (N.D.Tex. 1982) (applying Texas law). The requirement is valid even today, *see Lorensen v. Weaber*, 840 S.W.2d 644, (Tex. App.-Dallas 1992), *rev'd*, 865 S.W.2d 929 (Tex. 1993); and *Quinonez-Saa v. State*, 860 S.W.2d 704, 710 (Tex.App.-Houston (1 Dist.) 1993).

contract principle applied earlier was abandoned. The new law introduced instead, in addition to the requirement of a contract between two parties competent to enter into a marriage, three separate requirements as to the actions of the parties. First, the parties must "have cohabited." Second, the legislation requires that the parties "assume marital rights, duties, and obligations." Third, the two parties must "hold themselves out as and have acquired a uniform and general reputation as husband and wife."[142]

8.4 THE CURRENT STATE OF THE LAW IN DIFFERENT STATES

Given that the issue of whether cohabitation ought to be recognized as a necessary requirement has been one of the most diffuse in the history of common law marriage, there is reason to attempt to define the current state of the law in the American legal systems that are the objects of this investigation. The parties' cohabitation and reputation, in some form, is currently a requisite for the establishment of a common law marriage in all of the jurisdictions recognizing such marriages except in Pennsylvania, and South Carolina; the state of the law in Oklahoma is somewhat unclear. A survey reveals the following.

If we begin with the western states and **Montana**, the most northern, its legislation for decades has contained the requirement that for the establishment of a common law marriage, a "mutual and public assumption of the marital relation" must be proven in addition to the parties' consent to marriage.[143] This requisite has been interpreted in the case law mainly as a requirement of cohabitation and reputation.[144] Despite the repeal of this

142 UTAH CODE ANN. § 30-1-4.5 (1987); Act of Feb. 25, 1987, ch. 246, effective April 27, 1987. The new law is applicable only to cases where the cohabitation commenced after the enactment of the legislation. *See Clark v. Clark*, 423 Utah Adv. Rep. 3, 2001 UT 44, 27 P.3d 538 (Utah 2001); and *Hansen v. Hansen*, 958 P.2d 931 (Utah App. 1998). Before common law marriage was repealed by the Act of March 8, 1888, ch. 45, 2 (3) (1888), this legal figure rested solely upon the case law, according to which cohabitation was not a necessary requisite for the establishment of such a marriage. Instead, the pure contract principle was applied. *See, e.g., United States v. Simpson*, 4 Utah 227, 7 P. 257-258 (1885): "The marriage is complete when there is a full, free, and mutual consent by the parties capable of contracting, though not followed by cohabitation ... Cohabitation is but one of the many incidents to the marriage relation. It is not essential to it."

143 MONT. REV. CODE ANN. § 48-101 (1947): "Consent alone will not constitute marriage; it must be followed by a solemnization, or by mutual and public assumption of the marital relation." Previously section 5695 R.C. (1921); before that section 3607 R.C. The regulation was repealed in 1975, Session Law, Chapter 536 (1975).

144 *See Miller v. Townsend Lumber Co.*, 448 P.2d 148 (Mont. 1968); *Miller v. Sutherland*, 131 Mont. 175, 309 P.2d 322 (1957); *Elliot v. Indus. Accident Bd.*, 101 Mont. 246, 53 P.2d 451 (1936); *O'Malley v. O'Malley*, 46 Mont. 549, 129 P. 501, 503 (1913): "To us it means a course of conduct on the part of both man and wife towards each other and toward the world as that people generally would take them to be married. Indispensable to this is cohabitation."

legislation in 1975, the Montana Supreme Court has since, for example, in the case of *In re Estate of Alcorn* (1994), upheld the requirement that for the establishment of a common law marriage, in addition to the parties' consent to the marriage, the fact that they "established the marriage by cohabitation and repute" must also be proven.[145]

Common law marriage is codified in the neighboring state of **Idaho**. The requirements for the establishment of such a marriage can be found in IDAHO CODE § 32-201 (1983): "Consent alone will not constitute marriage; it must be followed by a solemnization, or by a mutual assumption of marital rights, duties or obligations."[146] According to the case law that has developed in Idaho, partly influenced by older California law, this assumption can occur through the parties' cohabitation and through their holding out as husband and wife.[147] As can be seen from *In re Estate*

---

145 *Matter of Estate of Alcorn*, 868 P.2d 629, 630 (Mont. 1994). The same stance can be found in the cases of *In re Estate of Vandenhook*, 855 P.2d 518 (Mont. 1993); *In re Marriage of Mahaffey*, 801 P.2d 1335, 1336 (Mont. 1990); and *In re Marriage of Geertz*, 232 Mont. 141, 755 P.2d 34, 37 (1988). The Montana Supreme Court clearly marked its stance in the case of *Matter of Estate of Murnion*, 212 Mont. 107, 686 P.2d 893, 899 (1984): "In addition to the consent required for a valid common law marriage, there must be cohabitation and public repute of the marriage."

146 IDAHO CODE ANN. § 32-201 (1877) p. 24 § 1; R.S. § 2420; reen. R.C. & C.L. § 2611; C.S. § 4591; I.C.A. § 31-201(1983); *Metro. Life Ins. Co. v. Johnson*, 103 Idaho 122, 645 P.2d 356, 360 (1982); and *Wilkins v. Wilkins*, 48 P.3d 644 (Idaho 2002). Observe that common law marriage, as was mentioned in chapter 1, was repealed in Idaho January 1, 1996, however not retroactively, *see* DAHO CODE ANN. § 32-201 (2) (Michie 2003).

147 *Freiburghaus v. Freiburghaus*, 103 Idaho 679, 651 P.2d 944, 947 (App. 1982). In California, where common law marriage was repealed in 1895, prior to that a regulation existed in California Civil Code § 55, enacted already in 1875 and identical to the Idaho law from 1877 (R.S. §§ 2420 (1887)) and the present Idaho Code § 32-201 (1983). In connection with this regulation, case law in California developed according to which the requirement of "assumption of marital rights, duties and obligations" contained a requirement of "cohabitation" and "reputation." In *Hinckley v. Ayres*, 105 Cal. 357, 38 P. 735, 736-737 (1895), the court stated: "There is no assumption (of marital rights, duties or obligations) unless the parties live together as husband and wife, treat each other 'in the usual way with married people,' and so conduct themselves as to have full repute among their intimate friends and associates to be husband and wife." *See also In re Jessup's Estate*, 81 Cal. 408, 21 P. 976, 22 P. 742 (1889) and particularly *Sharon v. Sharon*, 75 Cal. 633, 22 P. 26, 131 (1889), in which the regulation was not considered by the lower court to require "cohabitation and recognition," but in which the opposite stance was taken upon appeal, *see* 79 Cal. 633, 22 P. 26, 36-37 (1889). In *Sharon*, the California Supreme Court stated: "Cohabitation, which is evidence of the assumption of marital rights, duties or obligations, must be a 'living together as husband and wife'... If the parties agree to marriage, and commence to dwell together, in pursuance of the contract, as husband and wife, they have assumed marital rights, duties and obligations and are legally married." In *Kilburn v. Kilburn*, 89 Cal. 46, 26 P. 636, 637 (1891), the California Supreme Court stated that "by cohabitation is not meant simply the gratification of the sexual passions, but to live or dwell together, to have the same habitation, so that where one lives and dwells there does the other live and dwell also." *See People v. Beevers*, 99 Cal. 286, 33 P. 844 (1893); *People v. Lehman*, 104 Cal. 631, 38 P. 422 (1894); *Harron v. Harron*, 128 Cal. 308, 60 P. 932 (1900); *In re Richards*, 133 Cal. 524, 65 P. 1034 (1901); and *In re Baldwin's Estate*, 162 Cal. 471, 123 P. 267, 275 (1912). These California decisions are often cited by the Idaho

of Wagner (1995), this is the applicable rule today.[148] Even though common law marriage was repealed in Idaho in 1996, this legislation is still applicable to relationships entered into before that date.[149]

Common law marriage, after being repealed for ninety-nine years, was reintroduced in **Utah** by statute in 1987. The new legislation, in addition to the requirement of a contract between two parties competent to enter into a marriage, has no less than three separate requirements for their actions. First, the parties must have cohabited. Second, the legislation requires, as in Idaho, that the parties "assume marital rights, duties, and obligations." Third, the two parties must "hold themselves out as and have acquired a uniform and general reputation as husband and wife."[150] The difference between the legislation in Utah and in Idaho appears, however, to be more a difference in technique than in materiality. The requirements of cohabitation and reputation in Utah are stated specifically; in Idaho, they are considered contained within the requirement of mutual assumption of marital rights, duties, or obligations.

In the neighboring state of **Colorado**, where common law marriage is not regulated by legislation, the law, as seen in the previous section, has long varied as to whether the parties' actions shall simply be evidence of the existence of the marriage contract or a necessary additional requirement. The pure contract principle was long anchored in the case law of Colorado.[151] However, nowadays, it appears that the Colorado Supreme Court has the understanding that the parties' actions are necessary for the establishment of a common law marriage. In *People v. Lucero* (1987) the court stated: "We affirm today that such conduct in a form of mutual public acknowledgment of the marital relationship ... is essential to the establishment of a common law marriage."[152] This principle has since been reaffirmed.[153] It is unclear how the requirement of the parties'

Supreme Court along with the interpretation of the actual regulation. *See, e.g., Hamby v. Simplot Co.*, 94 Idaho 794, 498 P.2d 1267, 1269 (1972); *In re Gholson's Estate*, 83 Idaho 270, 361 P.2d 791 (1961); and *Freiburghaus v. Freiburghaus*, 103 Idaho 679, 651 P.2d 944 (App. 1982). Also in Montana, *see Miller v. Sutherland*, 131 Mont. 175, 309 P.2d 322, 328 (1957); and *O'Malley v. O'Malley*, 46 Mont. 549, 129 P. 501, 503 (1913), in which the court adds: "To us it means a course of conduct on the part of both man and wife towards each other and toward the world as that people generally would take them to be married. Indispensable to this is cohabitation." In South Dakota, an earlier regulation existed similar to that in California and Idaho and interpreted in a similar manner, *see In re Svendsens's Estate*, 37 S.D. 353, 158 N.W. 410 (1916).

148 *Matter of Estate of Wagner*, 126 Idaho 848, 893 P.2d 211 (1995), in which the requirement, however, was not found fulfilled.

149 In Idaho, common law marriage was repealed in 1996, *see* H.B. 176; Chap. 104, 1995 Idaho Session Laws (1995); *Wilkins v. Wilkins*, 48 P.3d 644 (Idaho 2002).

150 UTAH CODE ANN. § 30-1-4.5 (1987). The new law is applicable only to cases of cohabitation commenced after the enactment of the legislation.

151 *See* notes 43 and 94 *supra*.

152 *People v. Lucero*, 747 P.2d 660, 663-664 (Colo. 1987).

153 In *Knaus v. Relyea*, 746 S.W.2d 389, 391 (Ark.App. 1988) (applying Colorado law), the Arkansas Court of Appeals stated that the marriage contract must be followed

actions should be formulated. Commonly, the courts speak of a requirement of either consummation, cohabitation, or "assumption of a marital relationship." The case law does not support the premise that the courts, with these different formulations, ntially have intended different requirements.[154] In contrast, in a number of cases, reputation as husband and wife is not required.[155]

As to **Kansas**, the Kansas Supreme Court stated in *Chandler v. Central Oil Corp., Inc.* (1993) that, in addition to a marriage contract between the parties, "a holding out of each other as husband and wife to public" is required.[156] The parties' cohabitation, in contrast, is not stated as a specific requirement in the case law from the past few years.[157] Neither is

---

by a "mutual and open assumption of a marital relationship ... The contract alone is not sufficient unless it is followed by its consummation, that is, by cohabitation as husband and wife." Also in *Crandell v. Resley*, 804 P.2d 272 (Colo.App. 1990) as well as *In re Custody of Nugent*, 955 P.2d 584, 588 (Colo.App. 1997), the Colorado Court of Appeals required the parties' "mutual and open assumption of a marital relationship." *See also In re Marriage of Cargill & Rollins*, 843 P.2d 1335, 1339 (Colo. 1993). As pointed out in Denise K. Mills, *Common Law Marriage in Colorado*, 16 COLO. LAW. 252 (1987), this offers no clarification to maintain on one side that both the marriage contract and the parties' "mutual and open assumption of a marital relationship" create the "foundation for a common law marriage" and on the other side, maintain that "cohabitation and reputation as a married couple are not essential elements of a common law marriage."

154 Already in *Taylor v. Taylor*, 10 Colo.App. 303, 50 P. 1049 (1897), the court spoke of "consummation; that is, by cohabitation as husband and wife." In *Knaus v. Relyea*, 746 S.W.2d 389, 391 (Ark.App. 1988), the court used all three expressions: "mutual and open assumption of a marital relationship ... The contract alone is not sufficient unless it is followed by its consummation, that is, by cohabitation as husband and wife." *Taylor* is cited with approval in *Graham v. Graham*, 130 Colo. 225, 274 P.2d 605, 606 (1954).

155 *Klipfel v. Klipfel*, 41 Colo. 40, 92 P. 26 (1907). Even in the cases of *Peters v. Peters*, 73 Colo. 271, 215 P. 128, 129 (1923), and *Moffat Coal Co. v. Indus. Comm'n*, 108 Colo. 388, 118 P.2d 769 (1941), the court stated that "habit and repute" are not necessary, but these cases are of lesser interest with respect to the formation of the requisite as they do not consider any actions by the parties are generally necessary for the establishment of a common law marriage, consequently, supporting the pure contract principle.

156 *Chandler v. Central Oil Corp., Inc.*, 253 Kan. 50, 853 P.2d 649, 650 (1993).

157 *See Thompson v. Barnhart*, 2005 WL 23347 (D.Kan. 2005); *In re Pace*, 26 Kan.App.2d 538, 989 P.2d 297, 298 (1999); *Dixon v. Certainteed Corp.*, 915 F.2d 1158, 1160 (D. Kan. 1996) (applying Kansas law); and *Commerce Bank of Kansas City v. Odell*, 16 Kan. App.2d 704, 827 P.2d 1205, 1207 (1992). The Kansas Supreme Court in the case of *Matter of Estate of Hendrickson*, 248 Kan. 72, 805 P.2d 20, 21 (1991) also described the requisite in addition to the contract as "holding out of each other as husband and wife." *See also State v. Sedlack*, 246 Kan. 305, 787 P.2d 709, 710 (1990); *Eaton v. Johnston*, 235 Kan. 323, 672 P.2d 10, 12 (1983), 681 P.2d 606 (1984); *Fleming v. Fleming*, 221 Kan. 290, 559 P.2d 329, 331 (1977); *Driscoll v. Driscoll*, 220 Kan. 225, 552 P.2d 629, 632 (1976) ("sporadic cohabitation" was not found to be a sufficient holding out); *State v. Johnson*, 216 Kan. 445, 532 P.2d 1325, 1328 (1975) (the required holding out was not found proven); *In re Estate of Keimig*, 215 Kan. 869, 872, 528 P.2d 1228, 1230 (1974); *Schrader v. Schrader*, 207 Kan. 349, 484 P.2d 1007, 1008 (1971) (neither the contract nor the holding out was found proven); *Sullivan v. Sullivan*, 196 Kan. 705, 413 P.2d 988, 992 (1966) (neither the contract nor the holding out was found proven); *Gillaspie v. Blair Constr. Co.*, 192 Kan. 455, 388 P.2d

reputation as husband and wife taken up as a specific requisite. The parties' marriage-like reputation, in contrast, is accepted as an evidentiary fact for the existence of holding out.[158]

Even though the principles for the establishment of a common law marriage in **Oklahoma** are considered consistent with those in Kansas,[159] the requirement of the parties' actions in the case law from Oklahoma is regularly formulated as a requirement of cohabitation as well as holding out, albeit the courts' formulations are not consistent. The Oklahoma Supreme Court has taken a very inconsistent stance as to the formulation of the requisite during the entire 1900s, creating uncertainty, to say the least.[160] In the case of *In re Estate of Stinchcomb* (1983), the Oklahoma

---

647, 649 (1964); *Whetstone v. Whetstone*, 178 Kan. 595, 290 P.2d 1022, 1023 (1955) (the required holding out not found proven); and *In re Estate of Freeman*, 171 Kan. 211, 231 P.2d 261, 263 (1951). The court appears, on the other hand, to not be prepared to accept the parties' marriage-like reputation as an evidentiary fact for the marriage contract. As support for the parties' holding out as a necessary requirement in addition to the marriage contract, the court in *Freeman* cited the cases of *Cooper v. Cooper*, 147 Kan. 256, 76 P.2d 867 (1938) and *Pitney v. Pitney*, 151 Kan. 848, 101 P.2d 933 (1940). These cases, however, are not clear expressions of this. In *Tyner v. Schoonover*, 79 Kan. 573, 100 P. 478, 479 (1909), in addition to testimony by acknowledgment, there was cohabitation, conduct, and general reputation, "all tending to show" the marriage by the parties. The reasoning by the court indicates that all these were only circumstantial evidence tending to show the "consensual or common law marriage." In *Shorten v. Judd*, 60 Kan. 73, 55 P. 286 (1898), the Kansas Supreme Court stated that a contract "followed by cohabitation" is sufficient to establish a common law marriage, however, without expressly stating whether they are necessary. A similar case can be found in *Matney v. Linn*, 59 Kan. 613, 54 P. 668, 669 (1898).

158 *In re Estate of Freeman*, 171 Kan. 211, 231 P.2d 261, 263 (1951); and *Whetstone v. Whetstone*, 178 Kan. 595, 290 P.2d 1022, 1023 (1955).

159 *Matter of Estate of Hendrickson*, 248 Kan. 72, 805 P.2d 20, 23 (1991).

160 The descriptions used by the Oklahoma Supreme Court vary somewhat. If we go back to *Warren v. Canard*, 30 Okla. 514, 120 P. 599, 600 (1911), the court requires, in addition to the contract, that the parties "have entered into the marriage relation." The court uses a similar formulation in the case of *In re Love's Estate*, 42 Okla. 478, 142 P. 305 (1914), where as a requirement for the establishment of a common law marriage, in addition to the marriage contract, it required that the parties "enter into and maintain thereafter the marriage relation." This formulation has since been repeated by the court in the cases of *In re Sanders' Estate*, 67 Okla. 3, 168 P. 197 (1917); *Hughes v. Kano*, 68 Okla. 203, 173 P. 447 (1918); *Baker v. Jack*, 112 Okla. 142, 241 P. 478, 479 (1925); *Cavanaugh v. Cavanaugh*, 135 Okla. 204, 275 P. 315 (1929); *Cordilla v. Taylor*, 181 Okla. 20, 72 P.2d 375, 378 (1937); *In re Miller's Estate*, 182 Okla. 534, 78 P.2d 819, 826 (1938); and *Quinton v. Webb*, 207 Okla. 133, 248 P.2d 586, 587 (1952). The Criminal Court of Appeals uses the same expression in *Rowland v. State*, 75 Okla.Crim.App. 164, 129 P.2d 609, 612 (1942). That same year, the Oklahoma Supreme Court decided in the case of *In re Love's Estate*, referring to *Bothwell v. Way*, 44 Okla. 555, 145 P. 350 (1914), that the marriage contract must be "consummated" in one of two ways, either through the parties' "cohabitation as man and wife" or through their "mutual assumption openly of marital duties and obligations." This formulation has been used by the court since in *Vann v. Vann*, 186 Okla. 42, 96 P.2d 76, 79 (1939), *In re Blackhawk's Estate*, 195 Okla. 390, 158 P.2d 168 (1944) and *Daniels v. Mohon*, 350 P.2d 932, 935 (Okla. 1960) (no common law marriage was found established with respect to the fact that the evidence concerning "cohabitation or assumption of marital duties and obligations" was not considered

Supreme Court, stated as a requirement that the relationship must be evidenced by a cohabitation as man and wife and the parties must hold themselves out publicly as man and wife.[161] This case is cited in later case law.[162] In *Mueggenborg v. Walling* (1992) the court cited *Rath v. Maness* (1970) in *dictum*, speaking of a consummating arrangement by cohabitation and open assumption of marital duties.[163] Chief Justice Opala in *Rath*, however, carried on the tradition in Oklahoma by questioning whether cohabitation in general was a necessary element of a common law marriage.[164] In *Standefer v. Standefer* (2001), the court stated that a common law

---

to be sufficient). The Court of Criminal Appeals expressed the requirements in a similar manner in *McKee v. State*, 452 P.2d 169 (Okla.Crim.App. 1969). The ways to consummate a marriage have been understood as alternatives in William Hood Jr., *Common Law Marriage in Oklahoma: A Survey*, 49 OKLA. B. J. 1505,1506 (1978). *Compare Chapman v. State*, 84 Okla.Crim.App. 41, 178 P.2d 638 (1947), where the court speaks of a mutual agreement consummated by their cohabitation as man and wife "as well as" their open assumption of other marital duties. *See also Marshall v. State*, 537 P.2d 423, 429 (Okla.Crim.App. 1975), in which the court made the significant distinction that each of the requirements were necessary and found that none of them were found proven. In a similar manner, the Oklahoma Supreme Court in *Mueggenborg v. Walling*, 836 P.2d 112, 113 (Okla. 1992) spoke of a "consummating arrangement by cohabitation and open assumption of marital duties," citing *Rath v. Maness*, 470 P.2d 1011, 1013 (Okla. 1970), and in turn was cited in *Sanders v. Sanders*, 948 P.2d 719 (Okla.Civ.App. Div. 3 1997). The Oklahoma Supreme Court formulated the requirement somewhat differently in the case of *In re Trope's Estate*, 190 Okla. 453, 124 P.2d 733, 736 (1942), requiring "holding out by the parties of themselves as husband and wife" as well as "public assumption of the relation." This statement is cited in *Quinton v. Webb*, 207 Okla. 133, 248 P.2d 586, 587 (1952), in which the court, as a synonym to "a public assumption of the marital relation," uses the expression "cohabitation," and also in *Richardson v. State*, 744 S.W.2d 65 (Tex.Cr.App. 1987). In the case of *In re Graham's Estate*, 169 Okla. 568, 37 P.2d 964, 966-967 (1934), the locution in *Bothwell* is cited, with the court adding a contract "followed by cohabitation as such."

161 *Matter of Estate of Stinchcomb*, 674 P.2d 26, 29 (Okla. 1983). The Oklahoma Supreme Court referred to the decision by the Court of Appeals in the case of *In re Estate of Phifer*, 629 P.2d 808, 809 (Okla.App. 1981), where a similar formulation is used. The issue of the necessity of cohabitation was decided in *United States v. Staggs*, 881 F.2d 1546, 1550 (10th Cir. 1989)(applying Oklahoma law), in which the woman testified that the parties, after the divorce, did not live together. The man did not deny this, but objected that no cohabitation was legally required for the establishment of a common law marriage in Oklahoma. The Tenth Circuit Court of Appeals, in a *ratio decidendi*, affirmed the requirement of cohabitation and that no common law marriage therefore had been established.

162 *See Richardson v. State*, 744 S.W.2d 65, 73 (Tex.Cr.App. 1987); *United States v. Staggs*, 881 F.2d 1546, 1550 (10th Cir. 1989)(applying Oklahoma law); *Earnheart v. Earnheart*, 979 P.2d 761, 763 (Okla.Civ.App. Div. 3 1999); and *Davis v. State*, 103 P.3d 70, 82 (Okla.Cr.App. 2004) (hold themselves out publicly as man and wife).

163 *Mueggenborg v. Walling*, 836 P.2d 112, 113 (Okla. 1992). The last statement has since been cited in *Sanders v. Sanders*, 948 P.2d 719, 720 (Okla.Civ.App. Div. 3 1997).

164 *Mueggenborg v. Walling*, 836 P.2d 112, 116 (Okla. 1992). Chief Justice Opala stated: "I would today *overrule* the distortions scattered throughout our case law and excise from its corpus references to cohabitation as a prerequisite for a common law marriage." *Id.* Despite this, these new signals have not won any footing in a *ratio decidendi*. *Compare Sanders v. Sanders*, 948 P.2d 719 (Okla.Civ.App. div. 3 1997); and *Matter of Death of Boyd*, 959 P.2d 612, 614 (Okla.Civ.App. Div. 1 1998).

marriage is formed when the minds of the parties meet in consent at the same time.[165]

In **Texas**, common law marriage has been codified since the end of the 1960s. The legislation contains the requirement that the parties "lived together in this State as husband and wife," and that they "represented to others that they were married" in Tex. Fam. Code Ann. § 2.401 (a)(2) (West 1998).[166] The legislation contains a codification of the early principles found in the case law.[167] Without introducing any material changes, the legislature chose, however, the expression "represented to others" instead of the usual phrase found in the case law, "holding out" as husband and wife. The expressions have been viewed as synonyms in the later case law.[168] As can be seen from the statutory wording, the parties' cohabitation and outward representation must occur within Texas.[169]

165 *Standefer v. Standefer*, 26 P.3d 104 (Okla. 2001), which cites *Reaves v. Reaves*, 82 P. 490 (Okla. 1905). *Compare Davis v. State*, 103 P.3d 70, 82 (Okla.Cr.App. 2004), requiring "a permanent relationship, an exclusive relationship – proved by cohabitation as man and wife."

166 Act of June 2, 1969, 61 st Leg., R.S. ch. 888 § 1.91, 1969 Tex.Gen.Laws 2707, 2717 (Vernon's 1975) (amended 1997). The regulations were renumbered in 1997, from § 1.91 to § 2.401, without any material changes. Three requirements are to be fulfilled in order for a common law marriage be established, namely: (1) an agreement to be married, (2) living together in Texas as husband and wife and (3) representing to others in Texas that they are married. *See* Tex. Fam. Code Ann. (Vernon 2005). These three elements must exist simultaneously. *See Ganesan v. Vallabhaneni*, 96 S. W.3d 345 (Tex.App.-Austin 2002); *Nava v. Reddy Partnership/Quail Chase*, 988 S.W.2d 346, 350 (Tex.App.-Houston (1 st Dist.) 1999); *Ballesteros v. Jones*, 985 S.W.2d 485, 489 (Tex.App.-San Antonio 1998); *Winfield v. Renfro*, 821 S.W.2d 640, 646 (Tex.App.-Houston 1991); *Bolash v. Heid*, 733 S.W.2d 698, 699 (Tex.App.-San Antonio 1987); and *Gary v. Gary*, 490 S.W.2d 929, 934 (Tex.Civ.App.-Tyler 1973). In *Canady v. Russell*, 138 S.W.3d 412 (Tex.App.-Tyler 2004), in which the parties had plans to cohabit but had not yet moved in together, a common law marriage was not established.

167 *Humphreys v. Humphreys*, 364 S.W.2d 177 (Tex. 1963); *Hinojos v. Railroad Retirement Bd.*, 323 F.2d 227, 230 (5th Cir. 1963) (applying Texas law); *Ex parte Threet*, 160 Tex. 482, 333 S.W.2d 361 (1960); *Shelton v. Belknap*, 155 Tex. 37, 282 S.W.2d 682 (1955); *Estate of Claveria v. Claveria*, 615 S.W.2d 164, 166 (Tex. 1981); *Collora v. Navarro*, 574 S.W.2d 65 (Tex. 1978); *Morris v. Morris*, 403 S.W.2d 295, 296 (Tex.Civ.App. 1971); and *Conlon v. Schweiker*, 537 F.Supp. 158, 159 (N.D.Tex. 1982) (applying Texas law). The requirement even holds today, *see Lorensen v. Weaber*, 840 S.W.2d 644 (Tex. App.-Dallas 1992), *rev'd*, 865 S.W.2d 929 (Tex. 1993); and *Quinonez-Saa v. State*, 860 S.W.2d 704, 710 (Tex.App.-Houston (1 Dist.) 1993).

168 *Nichols v. Lightle*, 153 S.W.3d 563, 570 (Tex.App.-Amarillo 2004); *Eris v. Phares*, 39 S.W.3d 708 (Tex.App.-Houston (1 Dist.) 2001); *Lee v. Lee*, 981 S.W.2d 903 (Tex. App.-Houston (1st Dist.) 1998); *Flores v. Flores*, 847 S.W.2d 648, 653 (Tex.App.-Waco 1993); *Russell v. Russell*, 838 S.W.2d 909, 914 (Tex.App.-Beaumont 1992); *Winfield v. Renfro*, 821 S.W.2d 640, 648 (Tex.App.-Houston 1991); *Matter of Estate of Giessel*, 734 S.W.2d 27, 30 (Tex.App.-Houston (1st Dist.) 1987); *Estate of Claveria v. Claveria*, 615 S.W.2d 164, 166 (Tex. 1981); and *Warren v. Kyle*, 565 S.W.2d 313, 316 (Tex.Civ.App.-Austin 1978). In Joseph W. McKnight, *Title 1. Husband and Wife*, 21 Tex. Tech. L. Rev. 911, 939 (1990), the requisite was formulated as a requirement that the parties must "hold themselves out as married in Texas." *See also Quinonez-Saa v. State*, 860 S.W.2d 704, 710 (Tex.App.-Houston (1 Dist.) 1993); *Garduno v. Garduno*, 760 S. W.2d 735 (Tex.App.-Corpus Christi 1988); and *Leal v. Moreno*, 733 S.W.2d 322, 323 (Tex.App.-Corpus Christi 1987).

169 In *Ganesan v. Vallabhaneni*, 96 S.W.3d 345 (Tex.App.-Austin 2002), the woman moved from California to Texas to live with the man. *In re Estate of Burroughs*, 486

The requirement of an objective element has a long and established tradition in the case law from **Alabama.**[170] The formulations, however, varied during the entire 1900s, without the courts displaying any intent to give the requirement different meanings. These variations have not served the interest of clarity! During the past ten years, the inconsistencies have continued. Two main formulations are most common. According to the first, the requirement is formulated, as in *Krier v. Krier* (1996), as a requirement, in part, of "cohabitation or mutual assumption openly of marital duties and obligations," and of "public recognition" of the existence of the marriage.[171] According to the other formulation, the objective element is

---

N.W.2d 113, 116 (Mich.App. 1992)(applying Texas law)("Living together in Michigan does not satisfy the Texas cohabitation element."); *Williams v. Home Indem. Co.*, 722 S.W.2d 786 (Tex.App.-Houston 1987); and *Walter v. Walter*, 433 S.W.2d 183 (Tex.Civ.App.-Houston (1st Dist.) 1968).

170 An early and clear expression of the requirement of cohabitation can be found in *Herd v. Herd*, 194 Ala. 613, 60 So. 885, 887 (1915), in which the Alabama Supreme Court, after consideration of the issue, stated that for a marriage contract to be valid as a common law marriage, it "must be followed by cohabitation." As no cohabitation existed in the case, no common law marriage was established. The requirement of cohabitation as a necessary requisite appears, however, to not be seriously questioned by the courts in Alabama. *See* previously *White v. Hill*, 176 Ala. 480, 58 So. 444, 447 (1912); *Hawkins v. Hawkins*, 142 Ala. 571, 110 Am.St.Rep. 53, 38 So. 640 (1904) (*ratio decidendi*); *Moore v. Heineke*, 119 Ala. 627, 24 So. 374, 380 (1898); and *Mickle v. State*, 21 So. 66, 67 (Ala. 1896). In *Ashley v. State*, 109 Ala. 48, 19 So. 917, 918 (1896), the marriage was considered to be invalid because the contract was not followed by cohabitation (*ratio decidendi*). *See also Farley v. Farley*, 94 Ala. 501, 33 Am.St.Rep. 141, 10 So. 646 (1892); *Beggs v. State*, 55 Ala. 108 (1876); and *Campbell v. Gullatt*, 43 Ala. 57 (1869).

171 *Turner v. State*, 708 So.2d 232, 234 (Ala.Crim.App. 1997); and *Krier v. Krier*, 676 So.2d 1335, 1339 (Ala.Civ.App. 1996). A similar formulation can be found in the following cases: *People v. Schmidt*, 579 N.W.2d 431, 434 (Mich.App. 1998)(applying Alabama law); *Stringer v. Stringer*, 689 So.2d 194, 195 (Ala.Civ.App. 1997); *Butler v. Coonrod*, 671 So.2d 750 (Ala.Civ.App. 1995)(however, without "obligations" expressly mentioned); *Crosson v. Crosson*, 668 So.2d 868, 870 (Ala.Civ.App. 1995)(however, without "obligations" expressly mentioned); *Adams v. Boan*, 559 So.2d 1084, 1086 (Ala. 1990); *Copeland v. Richardson*, 551 So.2d 353, 354 (Ala. 1989); *Coleman v. Aubert*, 531 So.2d 881, 882 (Ala. 1988); *Aaberg v. Aaberg*, 512 So.2d 1375, 1376 (Ala. 1987); *Kirk v. Mattison*, 497 So.2d 120, 122 (Ala. 1986); *Boswell v. Boswell*, 497 So.2d 479, 480 (Ala. 1986)(however, without "obligations" expressly mentioned); *Skipworth v. Skipworth*, 360 So.2d 975, 977 (Ala. 1978); *Blackwood v. Kilpatrick*, 52 Ala.App. 505, 294 So.2d 753 (1974)(the Court of Civil Appeals uses the expressions "holding out" and "reputation" instead of "public recognition"); *Brown v. Brown*, 276 Ala. 153, 159 So.2d 855 (1964); *Goodman v. McMillan*, 258 Ala. 125, 61 So.2d 55, 59 (1952); *Whitworth v. Whitworth*, 256 Ala. 296, 54 So.2d 575 (1951); *Turner v. Turner*, 251 Ala. 295, 37 So.2d 186 (1948); *Murphy v. Jacobs*, 249 Ala. 594, 32 So.2d 306 (1947); *Sloss-Sheffield Steel & Iron Co. v. Watford*, 245 Ala. 425, 17 So.2d 166 (1944); and *Gilbreath v. Lewis*, 242 Ala. 510, 7 So.2d 485, 488 (1942). The expression "or assumption of marital duties and obligations" existed as early as in *White v. Hill*, 176 Ala. 480, 58 So. 444, 447 (1912). The court appears to have been influenced by 26 Cyc. 836, 837, which in its turn appears to have been influenced by California law. Without any material changes, and probably to due a mistake in writing, the Alabama Supreme Court stated the requisite in *Downs v. Newman*, 500 So.2d 1062, 1063 (Ala. 1986) as a requirement of "public recognition of the existence of the marriage or mutual assumption openly of the marital duties and obligations," *i.e.*, without the word "cohabitation" before the "or" and if one literally follows the meanings of the words, a choice exists as to the interpretation.

stated as a requirement of consummation, which is considered to contain a requirement of public recognition that the parties live together as husband and wife.[172]

Historically, it has long been unclear whether the courts in **Georgia**, have any objective requirement for the establishment of a common law marriage.[173] Nowadays, such an element has support in the marriage legislation, which, in addition to the marriage contract, requires "consummation according to law" as stated in GA. CODE ANN. § 19-3-1 (1999).[174] The issue of whether this requisite was applicable to a common law marriage was historically open for a long period of time. Nowadays, this requirement

---

In several cases, "cohabitation as man and wife" is followed not by "or" but rather by "and" as to their "mutual assumption openly of marital duties and obligations." *See King v. King*, 269 Ala. 468, 114 So.2d 145 (1959); *Campbell v. Rice*, 245 Ala. 395, 17 So.2d 162 (1944); and *Rogers v. McLeskey*, 225 Ala. 148, 142 So. 526, 527 (1932). Despite the fact that the use of the word "or," as opposed to "and" literally excludes the one phrase and therewith the requirement, the cases do not give the appearance that this difference was intended. In *Napier v. Napier*, 555 So.2d 1112, 1113 (Ala.Civ.App. 1989), the court, without any material changes, stated that it was not "public recognition," but whether the parties "hold themselves out to the community as husband and wife." In *Rickard v. Trousdale*, 508 So.2d 260, 261 (Ala. 1987), the Alabama Supreme Court stated that the contract must be followed by "cohabitation as man and wife and a public recognition of that relationship," and therewith cited *Luther v. M & M Chemical Co.*, 475 So.2d 191, 193 (Ala.Civ.App. 1985). In the older case law, the courts sometimes only made a requirement of "cohabitation" and/or "living together as husband and wife," as in *Smith v. Smith*, 247 Ala. 213, 23 So.2d 605, 609 (1945); *White v. White*, 225 Ala. 155, 142 So. 524 (1932); *McClurkin v. McClurkin*, 206 Ala. 513, 90 So. 917, 918 (1921); *Herd v. Herd*, 194 Ala. 613, 69 So. 885 (1915); *Hawkins v. Hawkins*, 142 Ala. 571, 110 Am.St.Rep. 53, 38 So. 640 (1905); *Tartt v. Negus*, 127 Ala. 301, 28 So. 713 (1900); *Moore v. Heineke*, 119 Ala. 627, 24 So. 374, 380 (1898); *Ashley v. State*, 109 Ala. 48, 19 So. 917 (1895); *Mickle v. State*, 21 So. 66 (Ala. 1896); *Farley v. Farley* 94 Ala. 501, 33 Am.St.Rep. 141, 10 So. 646 (1891); and *Beggs v. State*, 55 Ala. 108 (1876).

172 *Hall v. Duster*, 727 So.2d 834, 836 (Ala.Civ.App. 1999). In *Waller v. Waller*, 567 So.2d 869 (Ala.Civ.App. 1990), the Alabama Court of Civil Appeals, in addition to the expression "public recognition," used the even more general expression "consummation." In *Piel v. Brown*, 361 So.2d 90, 94, 95 (Ala. 1978), the court in more general terms also spoke of consummation, therewith the court meant that the parties must "so live as to achieve public recognition of their status as husband and wife." A similar statement was made in *Beck v. Beck*, 286 Ala. 692, 246 So.2d 420 (1971): "[S]o live as to gain the recognition of the public that they are living as man and wife rather than in a state of concubinage." *See also Krug v. Krug*, 296 So.2d 715, 718 (Ala. 1974); *Humphrey v. Humphrey*, 293 Ala. 118, 300 So.2d 376 (1974); and *Huffmaster v. Huffmaster*, 279 Ala. 594, 188 So.2d 552 (1966). John B. Crawley, *Is the Honeymoon Over for Common Law Marriage: A Consideration of the Continued Viability of the Common Law Marriage Doctrine*, 29 CUMB. L. REV. 399, 405 (1998/1999) states that the parties "must live in such a way as to gain public recognition that they are living as husband and wife."

173 *See supra* notes 79, 123-124.

174 With respect to the history of the section, *see* GA. CODE § 1653 (1863); § 1697 (1868); § 1698 (1873); § 1698 (1882); § 2411 (1895); § 2930 (1910); and § 53-101 (1933). Observe that common law marriage, as was mentioned in chapter 1, was repealed in Georgia January 1, 1997, however not retroactively, *see* GA. CODE ANN. §§ 19-3-1.1 (West 2003).

is considered applicable to both ceremonial and common law marriages.[175] The requirement of consummation has commonly been viewed in the case law as containing the element of cohabitation as man and wife.[176] In contrast, it has not been thought to contain any element of holding out or reputation, such that the parties outwardly represent and enjoy a reputation as husband and wife. Consequently, the requirement includes the possibility for clandestine marriages.[177] Even though holding out and reputation are not necessary requisites, they can be circumstances that are evidence of consummation.[178] Although common law marriage was repealed in Georgia in 1997, these recently named regulations are applied to relationships commenced before that date.[179]

As can be seen from the above, the courts in **South Carolina** appear to apply the pure contract principle, which means that no cohabitation is necessary for the establishment of a common law marriage. Such a marriage ought to be based solely on a marriage contract. Separate issues

175 *In re Estate of Love*, 274 Ga.App. 316, 319, 618 S.E.2d 97, 100 (2005); *Holmes v. Holmes*, 232 Ga.App. 434, 502 S.E.2d 294 (1998); *Wright v. Goss*, 229 Ga.App. 393, 494 S.E.2d 23, 25 (1997); *Georgia Osteopathic Hosp. v O'Neal*, 198 Ga.App. 770, 403 S.E.2d 235, 243 (1991); *Brown v. Carr*, 198 Ga.App. 567, 402 S.E.2d 296, 297 (1991); *Ridley v. Grandison*, 260 Ga. 6, 389 S.E.2d 746 (1990); *Fireman's Fund Ins. Co. v. Smith*, 151 Ga.App. 270, 271, 259 S.E.2d 675 (1979); *Brown v. Brown*, 234 Ga. 300, 215 S. E.2d 671, 673 (1975); *Tabor v. Fowler*, 119 Ga.App. 259, 167 S.E.2d 220 (1969); and *Drewry v. State*, 208 Ga. 239, 65 S.E.2d 916 (1951). *See also* Causey, *supra* note 123, at 229.

176 In *Scott v. Jefferson*, 174 Ga.App. 651, 331 S.E.2d 1, 3 (1985), the Georgia Court of Appeals speaks of a contract followed by cohabitation, citing *Stewart v. Price*, 89 Ga.App. 662, 665, 81 S.E.2d 28 (1954). In *Brown v. Brown*, 234 Ga. 300, 215 S.E.2d 671, 673 (1975), the Georgia Supreme Court spoke of "consummation of the marriage; *i.e.*, cohabitation as man and wife." In *Edwards v. Edwards*, 136 Ga.App. 668, 222 S.E.2d 169, 171 (1975) and in *Kersey v. Gardner*, 264 F.Supp. 887, 889 (M.D.Ga. 1967) (applying Georgia law), the courts used the expression "consummation by cohabitation." In *Fireman's Fund Ins. Co. v. Smith*, 151 Ga.App. 270, 271, 259 S.E.2d 675 (1979), the court stated that the "fact of cohabitation is treated as essential." *See also Hayes v. Hay*, 92 Ga.App. 88, 88 S.E.2d 306 (1955); *Drewry v. State*, 208 Ga. 239, 65 S.E.2d 916 (1951); and Causey, *supra* note123, at 229.

177 *Hayes v. Hay*, 92 Ga.App. 88, 88 S.E.2d 306 (1955). The absence of a requirement of holding out has been seen as opening the door to secret marriages. *Compare Reed v. Madry*, 585 So.2d 909, 910 (Ala. 1991) (applying Georgia law), in which the Alabama Supreme Court required parties "who held themselves out to the public as husband and wife and who lived together as such." The court referred to *Campbell v. Allen*, 208 Ga. 274, 66 S.E.2d 226 (1951) which, however, applied Pennsylvania law. In addition, the court in *Campbell* appears to have misunderstood somewhat the content of Pennsylvania law, which for the establishment of a common law marriage requires either only an expressed contract or a "constant cohabitation plus general reputation" in a rebuttable presumption, but not both, *see Com. v. McLean*, 387 Pa.Super. 354, 564 A.2d 216, 221 (1989). In *Beals v. Beals*, 203 Ga.App. 81, 416 S.E.2d 301 (1992), a common law marriage was found evidenced despite the fact that the woman used her maiden name and that the parties declared themselves as single in their tax returns.

178 *See, e.g.*, *Baynes v. Baynes*, 219 Ga.App. 848, 467 S.E.2d 195 (1996); and *Fireman's Fund Ins. Co. v. Smith*, 151 Ga.App. 270, 259 S.E.2d 675 (1979).

179 GA. CODE ANN. § 19-3-1 (1999); and *Finch v. Dasgupta*, 251 Ga.App. 637, 555 S.E.2d 22 (2001).

arise. The first is whether the parties' cohabitation as spouses, and their outward representation as such, can be evidence for the existence of such a contract, as further discussed in Chapter 7. The second issue is whether the cohabitation can be viewed as a necessary element in a presumption, according to which a common law marriage is presumed, as long as evidence is not brought against the existence of a marriage contract, as further discussed in Chapter 9.

In **Iowa**, on the other hand, the requirement of an objective element for the establishment of a common law marriage has had a long tradition.[180] From a historical perspective, the formation of the requisite has shifted somewhat. The courts, for a long period, spoke of a requirement of cohabitation.[181] However, in the case of *In re Long's Estate* (1960), the Iowa Supreme Court chose to require both continuous cohabitation and public declaration that the parties are husband and wife. The courts in Iowa have maintained this double requisite to the present day.[182]

180 *See* notes 83 and 135 *supra.*

181 *See Gammelgaard v. Gammelgaard,* 247 Iowa 979, 77 N.W.2d 479, 480 (1956), in which the Iowa Supreme Court required a consent to be husband and wife "followed by cohabitation." This locution recurs in *Jambrone v. David,* 16 Ill.2d 32, 156 N.E.2d 569 (1959) (applying Iowa law). The expression had been previously used in *Abramson v. Abramson,* 161 Neb. 782, 74 N.W.2d 919 (1956), in which the Nebraska Supreme Court, applying Iowa law, required that there must exist a contract to be husband and wife as well as "cohabitation as such." *See also Rittgers v. United States,* 154 F.2d 768 (8th Cir. 1946) (applying Iowa law). The last expression had previously been used by the courts in Iowa in *State v. Grimes,* 215 Iowa 1287, 247 N.W. 664 (1941); *In re Estate of Medford,* 197 Iowa 76, 196 N.W. 728 (1924); and *Pegg v. Pegg,* 138 Iowa 572, 115 N.W. 1027 (1908). *Compare McFarland v. McFarland,* 51 Iowa 565, 2 N.W. 269, 274 (1879), in which the court maintained that the woman could receive marriage-like rights "provided they cohabit" and *Blanchard v. Lambert,* 43 Iowa 228, 231, 22 Am.Rep. 245 (1876), in which the Iowa Supreme Court stated that every mutual contract between a man and a woman to immediately be husband and wife "followed by cohabitation," constitutes a valid and binding marriage.

182 *In re Long's Estate,* 251 Iowa 1042, 102 N.W.2d 76, 79 (1960); *Coleman v. Graves,* 255 Iowa 396, 122 N.W.2d 853, 856 (1963); *In re Estate of Malli,* 260 Iowa 252, 149 N.W.2d 155, 158 (1967); *State v. Lawson,* 165 N.W.2d 838 (Iowa 1969); *In re Estate of Fisher,* 176 N.W.2d 801, 805 (Iowa 1970); *In re Estate of Dallman,* 228 N.W.2d 189 (Iowa 1975); and *In re Marriage of Grother,* 242 N.W.2d 1 (Iowa 1976). The most recent case where the Iowa Supreme Court expressed the double requirement was *In re Marriage of Winegard,* 278 N.W.2d 505, 510 (Iowa 1979). The requirement of both continuous cohabitation and public declaration has, however, since recurred in cases from the Court of Appeals, *see, e.g., In re Marriage of Gebhardt* 426 N.W.2d 651, 652 (Iowa App. 1988) and *In re Marriage of Jones,* 451 N.W.2d 25, 27 (Iowa App. 1989) and *Fritz v. Mork,* 2001 Iowa App. Lexis 594 (2001). *See also Hurley v. Hurley,* 222 Mont. 287, 721 P.2d 1279, 1284 (1986), in which the Montana Supreme Court applied Iowa law and *In re Marriage of Mosher,* 183 Ill.Dec. 911, 243 Ill.App.3d 97, 612 N.E.2d 838, 841 (1993) (applying Iowa law). In the case of *Matter of Estate of Stodola,* 519 N.W.2d 97, 98 (Iowa App. 1994), the Iowa Court of Appeals formulated the objective element as a continuous cohabitation and a "general and substantial public declarations that the parties are husband and wife." *See also Conklin v. MacMillan Oil Co.,* 557 N.W.2d 102, 105 (Iowa App. 1996) (continuous cohabitation and public declaration); *Blessing v. Deere & Co.,* 985 F.Supp. 899, 904 (S.D.Iowa

The requirement of public declaration is comparable to that which in several states is termed as holding out.[183]

Even though **Ohio** has also repealed common law marriage by statute, marriages established prior to October 10, 1991, are still valid.[184] The courts in Ohio, therefore, in the same manner as in Idaho and Georgia, will have reason in the near future to decide the validity of common law marriages alleged to have been established before the repeal. It has long been debated whether, for the establishment of a common law marriage, something in addition to the marriage contract should be required. Already at the time of the above-mentioned Ross article, the courts in the majority of referenced cases from Ohio had, in clear *dictum*, stated that a necessary requirement for the establishment of a common law marriage was "cohabitation as husband and wife" and "holding out" in some form.[185] This is currently the applicable law, albeit the formulations of the requirement of holding out vary somewhat.[186]

1997) (applying Iowa law); *In re Marriage of Martin*, 681 N.W.2d 612, 617-618 (Iowa 2004); and *Toom v. Toom*, 710 N.W.2d 258 (Iowa App. 2005).

183 *In re Malli's Estate*, 260 Iowa 252, 149 N.W.2d 155 (1967).

184 OHIO REV. CODE ANN. § 3105.13 (B) (1, 2) (1991).

185 *See* note 116 *supra*.

186 In *Kowalik v. Kowalik*, 118 Ohio App.3d 141, 691 N.E.2d 1152, 1154 (1997); *State v. Burkitt*, 624 N.E.2d 210, 219 (Ohio App. 2 Dist. 1993); and *Warren Gen. Hosp. v. Brink*, 80 Ohio App.3d 793, 610 N.E.2d 1128, 1129 (1992). In *Smereczynski v. Sec'y, DHHS*, 944 F.2d 296, 298 (6th Cir. 1991) (applying Ohio law), the Sixth Circuit Court of Appeals formulated the requisite as a requirement of "cohabitation as husband and wife" and "holding out to the public as man and wife." In the cases of *Fitzgerald v. Mayfield*, 584 N.E.2d 13, 17 (Ohio App. 4 Dist. 1990), *In re Estate of Hall*, 588 N.E.2d 203, 205 (Ohio App. 4 Dist. 1990), and *Fields v. Fields*, 530 N.E.2d 933, 935-936 (Ohio App. 1987), the Ohio Court of Appeals cited with approval the cases of *Umbenhower* and *Nestor v. Nestor*, 15 Ohio St.3d 143, 15 O.B.R. 291, 472 N.E.2d 1091, 1094-1095 (1984), the latter a leading case in which the Ohio Supreme Court spoke of "cohabitation and reputation" as a necessary element in addition to the marriage contract. The requirement of outward representation is sometimes split into a requirement of holding out as well as reputation, *see Sulfridge v. Kindle*, 2005 WL 1806482 (Ohio App. 4 Dist. 2005); *Harris v. Harris*, 2004 WL 2896422 (Ohio App. 9 Dist. 2004); *Kowalik v. Kowalik*, 118 Ohio App.3d 141, 691 N.E.2d 1152, 1154 (1997), *State v. Phelps*, 100 Ohio App.3d 187, 652 N.E.2d 1032, 1035 (1995) and *State v. DePew*, 38 Ohio St.3d 275, 528 N.E.2d 542, 549 (1988). In the case of *In re McLaughlin's Estate*, 197 N.E.2d 578, 581 (Ohio P.Ct. 1963), the Probate Court of Columbiana County stated three requirements in addition to the marriage contract, namely "cohabitation as husband and wife," "holding out of themselves as husband and wife," and "being regarded as husband and wife." This tripartite treatment is also made by the Court of Common Pleas in the case of *In re Estate of Hammonds*, 39 Ohio Misc. 96, 315 N.E.2d 843, 847 (1973) and Court of Appeals in the case of *In re Estate of Soeder*, 4 Misc. 96, 209 N.E.2d 175, 7 Ohio App. 271, 220 N.E.2d 547, 557 (Ohio App. 1966). "Holding out" sometimes is not specifically mentioned, but then the requirement is defined as "cohabitation as husband and wife" with the result that they "were treated and reputed as husband and wife," *see Jolley v. Jolley*, 46 Ohio Misc. 40, 347 N.E.2d 557, 560 (C.P.Ohio 1975). Observe that common law marriage, as was mentioned in chapter 1, was repealed in Ohio October 10 1991, however not retroactively, *see* OHIO REV. CODE ANN. § 3105.12 (B) (1, 2) (WEST 1991).

The courts in **Pennsylvania** apply the pure contract principle, as seen above, which means that cohabitation is not necessary for the establishment of a common law marriage. Such a marriage consequently can be based solely on the marriage contract. However, the parties' cohabitation as spouses, and their outward representation as such, can be considered evidence for the existence of such a contract as discussed in Chapter 7, and can also be seen as elements in the presumption, according to which a common law marriage is presumed, as long as evidence is not produced against the existence of the marriage contract as further discussed in Chapter 9.

As early as in *Hoage v. Murch Bros. Const. Co.* (1931), the United States Court of Appeals for the District of Columbia Circuit, the highest court for the **District of Columbia**, stated that a marriage contract "consummated by cohabitation" constitutes a common law marriage.[187] This statement has been cited in *United States Fidelity & Guaranty Co. v. Britton* (1959), which in turn is the currently most cited case on the law of the District of Columbia law on this question.[188] No requirement of holding out as husband and wife in addition to the requirement of cohabitation is generally required in the case law.[189] In contrast, the parties' holding out is accepted as an evidentiary fact as to the existence of the marriage contract as well as the cohabitation. The evidentiary requirement appears, however, to be lower in the District of Columbia than in many states. A common law marriage in the District of Columbia need not be proven with clear and convincing evidence, only with a preponderance of evidence, a common standard of proof for civil cases. The District of Columbia Court of Appeals expresses the current state of the law in *Mesa v. United States* (2005).[190]

---

187 *Hoage v. Murch Bros. Const. Co.*, 60 App.D.C. 218, 50 F.2d 983, 985 (1931).

188 *U.S. Fid. & Guar. Co. v. Britton*, 106 U.S.App.D.C. 58, 269 F.2d 249, 251 (D.C.Cir. 1959), in which the court maintained that the contract "must be consummated by cohabitation." This case is cited in *Toye v. Toye*, 170 A.2d 778 (D.C.App. 1961); *McCoy v. District of Columbia*, 256 A.2d 908, 910 (D.C.App. 1969); *Jennings v. Jennings*, 20 Md.App. 369, 315 A.2d 816, 820 (1974) (applying the law of the District of Columbia); *Marcus v. Director*, 548 F.2d 1044, 1048 (D.C.Cir. 1976); *Johnson v. Young*, 372 A.2d 992, 994 (D.C.App. 1977); *East v. East*, 536 A.2d 1103, 1105 (D.C.App. 1988); *Matter of Estate of Foster*, 376 S.E.2d 144, 147 (W.Va. 1988) (applying the District of Columbia law); *Cross v. Cross*, 541 N.Y.S.2d 202, 206 (App.Div. 1989) (applying the District of Columbia law); and *Coates v. Watts*, 622 A.2d 25 (D.C.App. 1993).

189 *Compare Ram v. Ramharack*, 571 N.Y.S.2d 190, 191 (Sup. 1991), in which the New York Supreme Court, applying the District of Columbia law, appears to require, in addition to a marriage contract and cohabitation, a requirement of a holding out as husband and wife. *See also* the Municipal Court of Appeals, in *Caldwell v. Caldwell*, 140 A.2d 926, 927 (D.C.App. 1958), which appears to have applied a presumption based upon cohabitation and reputation with the result that no common law marriage was found proven. *Compare Troshinsky v. Rosin*, 428 A.2d 847 (D.C.App. 1981), in which Court of Appeals did not find a common law marriage established with reference to the fact that the parties did not have "a general reputation in the community as being married." The court, however, did not state whether this reputation was a necessary requirement or simply an evidentiary fact.

190 *Mesa v. United States*, 875 A.2d 79 (D.C.App. 2005). *See also Dickey v. Office of Personnel Management*, 419 F.3d 1336, 1340 (C.A.Fed. 2005), where the court speaks of an

Finally, in **Rhode Island**, the state of the law appears to be somewhat unclear. In *Souza v. O'Hara* (1978), the Rhode Island Supreme Court stated, however, that to prove a common law marriage, evidence that the parties "considered themselves to be married" and that their actions gave rise to "a general reputation" among friends and relatives that they were married was required.[191] The parties' intentions, as well as their reputation, can be proven by circumstantial evidence.[192] In *DeMelo v. Zompa* (2004), the court stated that the parties' conduct must be of such a character as to lead to a belief in the community that they were married, but found that plaintiff had failed to satisfy the trial court that the parties held themselves out to the community as husband and wife. Longtime friends testified that the parties never planned to get married, nor did they refer to each other as husband and wife.[193]

8.5 The Requirement of Cohabitation

8.5.1 The Formulation of the Requisite of Cohabitation

The objective elements required in addition to the marriage contract for the establishment of a common law marriage are formulated somewhat differently in the legislation and case law from across the states, as seen above. From a legal perspective, the principle of cohabitation,

---

agreement "followed by cohabitation as husband and wife." As to the standards of proof, *see* Chapter 9 *infra.*

191 *Souza v. O'Hara,* 121 R.I. 88, 395 A.2d 1060, 1061 (1978). The Rhode Island Supreme Court appears to have taken the same material stance in *Sardonis v. Sardonis,* 106 R.I. 469, 261 A.2d 22 (1970), albeit the court there formulated it somewhat differently with respect to both requisites, requiring that the parties "seriously intended to enter into the husband-wife relationship" and that their conduct was of such character "as to lead to a belief in the community that they were married." That the court appears to have understood the last element also as a requirement is supported by the fact that the court names that both the contract and this belief can be proven by circumstantial evidence. The court also spoke of the prerequisite intent and belief. As support for the last named element, the court cites *Williams v. Herrick,* 21 R.I. 401, 43 A. 1036 (1899), which, however, is rather dubious support, as the case speaks of a presumption due to "cohabitation and reputation," not "reputation," as a necessary requirement in addition to the marriage contract. Other older decisions appear to be based on the marriage contract as the only necessary requirement and do not mention cohabitation in this function. *See, e.g., Scalzi v. Folsom,* 156 F.Supp. 838 (D.R.I. 1957) (applying Rhode Island law); *Silva v. Merritt,* 52 R.I. 30, 156 A. 512 (1931); *Ibello v. Sweet,* 47 R.I. 480, 133 A. 801 (1926); *Holgate v. United Electric Railways Co.,* 47 R.I. 337, 133 A. 243 (1926); *United States v. Dorto,* 5 F.2d 596 (1st Cir. 1925) (applying Rhode Island law); *Odd Fellows' Beneficial Ass'n v. Carpenter,* 17 R.I. 729, 24 A. 578 (1892); and *Matthewson v. Phoenix Iron Foundry,* 20 F. 281 (Cir. D.R.I. 1884) (applying Rhode Island law), where a written and witnessed document, in which the parties recognized that they were husband and wife constituted a common law marriage.

192 *Sardonis v. Sardonis,* 106 R.I. 469, 261 A.2d 22, 24 (1970); *Holgate v. United Electric Ry. Co.,* 47 R.I. 337, 133 A. 243, 244 (1926) and *Silva v. Merritt,* 52 R.I. 30, 156 A. 512, 513 (1931).

193 *DeMelo v. Zompa,* 844 A.2d 174 (R.I. 2004).

consequently, is divided into two main prongs. First, cohabitation in the more narrow meaning entails the relationship between the parties, as discussed here. Second is their holding out and reputation as spouses, *i.e.*, their outward representations as to others and the reputation they therewith acquire, discussed below in Section 8.6, "The Requirements of Holding Out and Reputation."

As a necessary requirement, cohabitation between the parties is described in American law rather generally, partially abstract and in extremely vague terms. Three rather similar descriptions, however, can be found. The first common formulation of the requirement of cohabitation in the more narrow meaning is cohabitation as husband and wife,[194] or living together as husband and wife.[195] The second is the "assumption of

---

194 The expression "cohabitation" is used in judgments from Montana, *see In re Ober*, 2003 MT 7, 314 Mont. 20, 62 P.3d 1114 (2003); *Matter of Estate of Alcorn*, 868 P.2d 629, 630 (Mont. 1994); *In re Marriage of Mahaffey*, 801 P.2d 1335, 1336 (Mont. 1990); and *In re Marriage of Geertz*, 232 Mont. 141, 755 P.2d 34, 37 (1988). The Montana Supreme Court clearly marked its stance in the case of *Matter of Estate of Murnion*, 212 Mont. 107, 686 P.2d 893, 899 (1984): "In addition to the consent required for a valid common law marriage, there must be cohabitation and public repute of the marriage." In the legislation from Utah, the requirement of cohabitation exists in addition to the requirement that the parties "assume marital rights, duties, and obligations," *see* UTAH CODE ANN. § 30-1-4.5 (1987). For judgments applying Colorado law, *see Knaus v. Relyea*, 746 S.W.2d 389, 391 (Ark.App. 1988), from Oklahoma, *see Earnheart v. Earnheart*, 979 P.2d 761, 763 (Okla.Civ.App. Div. 3 1999); *Matter Estate of Stinchcomb*, 674 P.2d 26, 29 (Okla. 1983); *In re Estate of Phifer*, 629 P.2d 808, 809 (Okla.App. 1981); *Matter of Estate of Bouse*, 583 P.2d 514 (Okla.App. 1978); *Chapman v. State*, 84 Okla.Crim.App. 41, 178 P.2d 638, 640 (1947); *In re Blackhawk's Estate*, 195 Okla. 390, 158 P.2d 168 (1944), *Vann v. Vann*, 186 Okla. 42, 96 P.2d 76 (1939); *Bothwell v. Way*, 44 Okla. 555, 145 P. 350 (1914), from Alabama, *see Adams v. Boan*, 559 So.2d 1084, 1086 (Ala. 1990). In Iowa today the expression "continuous cohabitation" is used, *see In re Marriage of Winegard*, 278 N.W.2d 505, 510 (Iowa 1979). In the case law from Ohio, the courts speak of "cohabitation" or "cohabitation as husband and wife," *see Nestor v. Nestor*, 15 Ohio St.3d 143, 472 N.E.2d 1091, 1094-1095 (1984) and *Warren Gen. Hosp. v. Brink*, 80 Ohio App.3d 793, 610 N.E.2d 1128, 1129 (1992).

195 The formulation "lived together as husband and wife" is used in the Texas legislation, *see* TEX. FAM. CODE. ANN. § 1.91 (a) (Vernon's 1975). The regulation was renumbered in 1997 from § 1.91 to § 2.401 without any material changes. It is a codification of older case law, *see Ex parte Threet*, 160 Tex. 482, 333 S.W.2d 361 (1960). In Joseph W. McKnight, *supra* note 168, at 939, the requisite is formulated as a requirement that the parties must cohabit. McKnight further states: "Living together as husband and wife merely connotes cohabitation." Clarice M. Davis, *Common Law Marriage in Texas*, 21 S.W. L.J. 647, 648 (1967), speaks of "cohabitation as husband and wife." In *Welch v. State*, 908 S.W.2d 258, 265 (Tex.App.-El Paso 1995), the court required that the parties "cohabited pursuant to that agreement." In *Drummond v. Benson*, 133 S.W.2d 154, 159 (Tex.Civ.App.-San Antonio 1939), the Court of Civil Appeals maintained that to "live and cohabit together as husband and wife" means "a living together, claiming to be married, in the relationship of husband and wife." *See also Humble Oil & Ref. Co. v. Jeffrey*, 38 S.W.2d 374 (Tex.Civ.App.-Austin 1931), *aff'd*, 55 S.W.2d 521 (Tex.Comm.-App. 1932). In *Sharon v. Sharon*, 79 Cal. 633, 22 P. 26, 37 (1889), the California Supreme Court stated: "Cohabitation, which is evidence of the assumption of marital rights, duties or obligations, must be a 'living together as husband and wife'." In *Brinckle v. Brinckle*, 12 Phila. 232, 234 (1877), the court stated: "Cohabitation does not mean merely living together; it means living together

the marital relation"[196] or "assumption of marital rights, duties and obligations."[197] A third construction sets up the requirement of "consummation"

---

as husband and wife." In *Grammas v. Kettle*, 306 Mich. 308, 10 N.W.2d 895 (1943), "living together as husband and wife" and "cohabitation" are used. *Compare U.S. Fid. & Guar. Co. v. Britton*, 106 App.D.C. 58, 269 F.2d 249 (D.C.Cir. 1959). Sometimes, the expression that the parties' cohabitation shall be "matrimonial in its nature" is used, *see In re Moll's Estate*, 299 S.W. 127 (Mo.App. 1927).

196 The expression "assumption of the marital relation" has long existed in Montana's legislation, *see* MONT. CODE ANN. § 48-101 (1947) (repealed in 1975). *See also* the case law, *Miller v. Townsend Lumber Co.*, 448 P.2d 148 (Mont. 1968); *Miller v. Sutherland*, 131 Mont. 175, 309 P.2d 322 (1957); *Elliot v. Indus. Accident Bd.*, 101 Mont. 246, 53 P.2d 451 (1936); and *O'Malley v. O'Malley*, 46 Mont. 549, 129 P. 501, 503, Ann.Cas. 1914B 662 (1913). A similar formulation occurs in older cases from Oklahoma, *see, e.g., Warren v. Canard*, 30 Okla. 514, 120 P. 599, 600 (1911), in which the Oklahoma Supreme Court required that the parties "have entered into the marriage relation." The court used a similar formulation in the case of *In re Love's Estate*, 42 Okla. 478, 142 P. 305 (1914), where as a requirement for the establishment of a common law marriage, the parties must "enter into and maintain thereafter the marriage relation." This formulation has since been repeated by the court in the case of *In re Miller's Estate*, 182 Okla. 534, 78 P.2d 819 (1938); and *Quinton v. Webb*, 207 Okla. 133, 248 P.2d 586, 589 (1952) ("assumption of the marital relation is an essential element"). The Oklahoma Criminal Court of Appeals used the same expression in *Rowland v. State*, 75 Okla.Crim.App. 164, 129 P.2d 609, 612 (1942). *Compare Grigsby v. Reib*, 105 Tex. 597, 153 S.W. 1124 (1913), in which the Texas Supreme Court used the expression "assumption of the marriage status."

197 The expression "assumption of marital rights, duties or/and obligations" has, due to influence from California law, long been anchored in the law of the northwestern states, as in the legislation of Idaho, *see* IDAHO CODE § 32-201(1983), and of Utah, where the requirement appears in addition to the requirement of cohabitation, *see* UTAH CODE ANN. § 30-1-4.5 (1987). In certain particularly older cases from Oklahoma, *see e.g. Bothwell v. Way*, 44 Okla. 555, 145 P. 350 (1914), the Oklahoma Supreme Court referred to the fact that the marriage contract must be consummated in one of two different ways, either through the parties' "cohabitation as man and wife" or through their "mutual assumption openly of marital duties and obligations." This formulation is later used by the court in the cases of *In re Graham's Estate*, 169 Okla. 568, 37 P.2d 964, 966 (1934), *Vann v. Vann*, 186 Okla. 42, 96 P.2d 76, 79 (1939), and *Ridgeway v. Logan*, 205 Okla. 603, 239 P.2d 778, 782 (1952). In the same manner, the Oklahoma Court of Criminal Appeals expressed the requirements in *Chapman v. State*, 84 Okla.Crim.App. 41, 178 P.2d 638, 640 (1947) and in *Marshall v. State*, 537 P.2d 423, 429 (Okla.Crim.App. 1975), however, with the significant difference that each and every one of the requirements were not expressed as either/or, but rather as both/and (*Chapman:* "as well as"). None of the requirements were found proven in *Marshall*. In a similar manner, the Oklahoma Supreme Court in *Mueggenborg v. Walling*, 836 P.2d 112, 113 (Okla. 1992) spoke of a "consummating arrangement by cohabitation and open assumption of marital duties," therewith the court cited *Rath v. Maness*, 470 P.2d 1011, 1013 (Okla. 1970). That court was cited in *Sanders v. Sanders*, 948 P.2d 719 (Okla.Civ.App. Div. 3 1997). The expression also recurs in cases from Alabama, where the general formulation nowadays is "cohabitation or mutual assumption openly of marital duties and obligations," *see Creel v. Creel*, 763 So.2d 943, 946 (Ala. 2000); *Turner v. State*, 708 So.2d 232, 234 (Ala.Crim.App. 1997); *Krier v. Krier*, 676 So.2d 1335, 1339 (Ala.Civ.App. 1996); and *Adams v. Boan*, 559 S.2d 1084, 1086 (Ala. 1990). *Compare Crosson v. Crosson*, 668 So.2d 868, 870 (Ala.Civ.App. 1995) ("public assumption of marital duties and cohabitation," where consequently "or" has been replaced by "and" and where "obligations" has been taken away, without reference to any material changes), *see also Butler v. Coonrod*, 671 So.2d 750, 751 (Ala.Civ.App. 1995).

or that the contract shall be "consummated by cohabitation."[198] In addition to these formulations, cohabitation in the more limited meaning can also be constructed not as a separate requirement but within the terms of "holding out" and reputation as spouses.[199]

It would appear natural that these different expressions give the requirements different meanings. A distinction on one hand, between rights and obligations, and on the other, the actual existence of cohabitation and consummation, would be particularly well motivated. However, no conscious distinction has been maintained in the American case law between these terms. In contrast, it appears that they have been assigned the same legal meaning.

This can be seen initially if the courts explain the meanings of the expressions they use. *Cohabitation* is used in a more narrow sense than that of the vernacular and is legally synonymous with "living together as husband and wife."[200] In *Freiburghaus v. Freiburghaus* (1982), the Idaho Court

---

198 The expression "consummation" can be found within the marriage legislation of Georgia, *see* GA. CODE ANN. § 19-3-1 (1999), which is also applicable to common law marriages, *see Drevry v. State*, 208 Ga. 239, 65 S.E.2d 916 (1951); *In re Estate of Love*, 274 Ga.App. 316,, 319, 618 S.E.2d 97, 100 (Ga.App. 2005). "Consummation" according to the Georgia case law has commonly been considered to mean "cohabitation as man and wife," *see Brown v. Brown*, 234 Ga. 300, 215 S.E.2d 671, 673 (1975). In the District of Columbia case law, a marriage contract "consummated by cohabitation" is mentioned, *see East v. East*, 536 A.2d 1103, 1105 (D.C.App. 1988); and *U.S. Fid. & Guar. Co. v. Britton*, 106 U.S.App.D.C. 58, 269 F.2d 249, 251 (D.C.Cir. 1959). *See also Knaus v. Relyea*, 746 S.W.2d 389, 391 (Ark.App. 1988), in which the Arkansas Court of Appeals, applying Colorado law, spoke of a marriage contract followed by its "consummation, that is, by cohabitation as husband and wife." The Colorado Court of Appeals used a similar expression in *Taylor v. Taylor*, 10 Colo.App. 303, 50 P. 1049 (1897). The Oklahoma Supreme Court used the expression "consummated by their cohabitation" in *Bothwell v. Way*, 44 Okla. 555, 145 P. 350 (1914). The same formulation recurs in the case of *In re Graham's Estate*, 169 Okla. 568, 37 P.2d 964, 966 (1934), *Vann v. Vann*, 186 Okla. 42, 96 P.2d 76, 77 (1939), *McArthur v. Hall*, 169 S.W.2d 724, 726 (Tex.Civ.App.-Fort Worth 1943) (applying Oklahoma law), *Chapman v. State*, 84 Okla.Crim.App. 41, 178 P.2d 638, 640 (1947), *Ridgeway v. Logan*, 205 Okla. 603, 239 P.2d 778, 782 (1952), *Daniels v. Mohon*, 350 P.2d 938 (Okla. 1960), *McKee v. State*, 452 P.2d 169 (Okla.Crim.App. 1969), *Dowell v. Welch*, 574 P.2d 1089, 1091 (Okla.App. 1978) and *In re Bouse's Estate*, 583 P.2d 514, 515 (Okla.App. 1978). In a similar manner, in *Mueggenborg v. Walling*, 836 P.2d 112, 113 (Okla. 1992), the court spoke of a "consummating arrangement by cohabitation and open assumption of marital duties," therewith citing *Rath v. Maness*, 470 P.2d 1011, 1013 (Okla. 1970), and being cited in *Sanders v. Sanders*, 948 P.2d 719 (Okla.Civ.App. Div. 3 1997). Even in certain cases from Alabama, the courts spoke more generally of "consummation," *see, e.g.*, *Waller v. Waller*, 567 So.2d 869 (Ala.Civ.App. 1990); and *Piel v. Brown*, 361 So.2d 90, 94, 95 (Ala. 1978).

199 In Kansas, the requirement of cohabitation ought to be considered contained within the requirement of "holding out of each other as husband and wife," *see Chandler v. Central Oil Corp., Inc.*, 253 Kan. 50, 853 P.2d 649, 650 (1993); and *Dixon v. Certainteed Corp.*, 915 F.Supp. 1158, 1160 (D.Kan. 1996) (applying Kansas law). In *Rhode Island*, conduct which gives rise to a general reputation that the parties are husband and wife is mentioned, *see Souza v. O'Hara*, 121 R.I. 88, 395 A.2d 1060, 1061 (1978).

200 In *Levy v. Goldsoll*, 131 S.W. 420 (Tex. Civ. App. 1910), the court stated: "Cohabitation means literally a living together, but as applied to the marriage relation it is more restricted and implies a living together as husband and wife."

of Appeals found that the parties established a "mutual assumption of the rights, duties and responsibilities of marriage" through cohabitation and through "holding themselves out to the community as husband and wife."[201] On the other side, the definition of cohabitation is explained as "assumption of the marital relation,"[202] expressions that may also said to be alternatives.[203] The Georgia Supreme Court, in *Brown v. Brown* (1975), when explaining the meaning of consummation, spoke of the "consummation of the marriage; *i.e.*, cohabitation as man and wife."[204] In *Chapman v. State* (1947), the Oklahoma Criminal Court of Appeals understood cohabitation as one of the "marital duties."[205] The fact that the courts in the same state, without any apparent motivation, use one or the other of these expressions also supports the conclusion that different meanings

---

201 *Freiburghaus v. Freiburghaus*, 103 Idaho 679, 651 P.2d 944, 947 (App. 1982). As to the influence from California law on Idaho and Montana law, *see* note 85 *supra.*

202 In *Ridley v. Compton*, 215 Miss. 532, 61 So.2d 341, 342 (1952), the Mississippi Supreme Court stated: "The word 'cohabitation' as used in the marriage laws means the public assumption by a man and woman of the marital relation, and dwelling together as such thereby holding themselves out to the public as being man and wife." In Montana, where the objective element was earlier formulated as a requirement of "mutual and public assumption of the marital relation," this was interpreted as a requirement of "cohabitation and reputation," *see Miller v. Townsend Lumber Co.*, 448 P.2d 148 (Mont. 1968); *Miller v. Sutherland*, 131 Mont. 175, 309 P.2d 322 (1957); *Elliot v. Indus. Accident Bd.*, 101 Mont. 246, 53 P.2d 451 (1936); and *O'Malley v. O'Malley*, 46 Mont. 549, 129 P. 501, 503, Ann.Cas. 1914B 662 (1913) ("To us it means a course of conduct on the part of both man and wife towards each other and toward the world as that people generally would take them to be married. Indispensable to this is cohabitation"). In *State v. Newman*, 66 Mont. 180, 213 P. 805, 807 (1923), the Montana Supreme Court expressed the matter thus, that the contract "must contemplate a present assumption of the marriage status." Despite the fact that the objective requisites in Iowa are formulated as a requirement, in part of "continuous cohabitation" and of "public declaration that the parties are husband and wife," the Montana Supreme Court stated in *Hurley v. Hurley* 222 Mont. 287, 721 P.2d 1279, 1284 (1986), that "the elements required to establish a common law marriage in Iowa and Montana are substantively identical."

203 In Alabama case law, the expression "cohabitation or mutual assumption openly of marital duties and obligations" is used, *see for example Creel v. Creel*, 763 So.2d 943, 946 (Ala. 2000); *Turner v. State*, 708 So.2d 232, 234 (Ala.Crim.App. 1997); *Krier v. Krier*, 676 So.2d 1335, 1339 (Ala.Civ.App. 1996); and *Adams v. Boan*, 559 S.2d 1084, 1086 (Ala. 1990). *Compare Crossom v. Crossom*, 668, So.2d 868, 870 (Ala.Civ.App. 1995), in which, without any substantive changes, the court speaks of the "public assumption of marital duties and cohabitation."

204 *Brown v. Brown*, 234 Ga. 300, 215 S.E.2d 671, 673 (1975). *See also Edwards v. Edwards*, 136 Ga.App. 668, 222 S.E.2d 169, 171 (1975), and *Kersey v. Gardner*, 264 F.Supp. 887, 889 (M.D.Ga. 1967) (applying Georgia law), in which the courts used the expression "consummation by cohabitation." When the Arkansas Court of Appeals, in *Knaus v. Relyea*, 746 S.W.2d 389, 391 (Ark.App. 1988) (applying Colorado law), would explain the term "consummation," they spoke of a marriage contract followed by "consummation, that is, by cohabitation as husband and wife." The Colorado Court of Appeals expressed itself in the same manner in *Taylor v. Taylor*, 10 Colo.App. 303, 50 P. 1049 (1897). The courts in the District of Columbia formulate the requisite as a requirement that the marriage contract must be "consummated by cohabitation," *see, e.g., East v. East*, 536 A.2d 1103, 1105 (D.C.App. 1988).

205 *Chapman v. State*, 84 Okla.Crim.App. 41, 178 P.2d 638, 640 (1947).

are not attributed to phrases.[206] The judgments rather give the impression that the different expressions with respect to their denotations are used relatively synonymously and that they generally refer to the same actual relationships.

8.5.2 Relevant Factors

A requirement of cohabitation naturally raises the question of how the cohabitation must occur for a common law marriage to be considered to exist. Cohabitation can manifest itself in many different ways. The marriage-like companionship can be greater or lesser. The factors usually considered by sociologists to be aspects of a marriage-like cohabitation include the following: a monogamous sexual relationship, an emotional relationship, mutual children, joint residence, common household, joint economy, leisure time spent together, as well as common friends.[207]

---

206 *See, e.g.*, *Knaus v. Relyea*, 746 S.W.2d 389, 391 (Ark.App. 1988) (applying Colorado law), in which the Arkansas Court of Appeals, in the same case used all three of the expressions: "[M]utual and open assumption of a marital relationship ... The contract alone is not sufficient unless it is followed by its consummation, that is, by cohabitation as husband and wife." Also in *Sharon v. Sharon*, 79 Cal. 633, 22 P. 26, 37 (1889), the California Supreme Court stated: "Cohabitation, which is evidence of the assumption of marital rights, duties or obligations, must be a 'living together as husband and wife'." In *Grammas v. Kettle* 306 Mich. 308, 10 N.W.2d 895 (1943), "living together as husband and wife" was used as well as "cohabitation." *Compare U.S. Fid. & Guar. Co. v. Britton*, 106 App.D.C. 58, 269 F.2d 249 (D.C.Cir. 1959). *See* generally the differences in the manner of expression from case to case in Colorado, notes 153-155 *supra*. In the case law from Oklahoma, significant differences arise as to the courts' manners of expression, *see In re Love's Estate*, 42 Okla. 478, 142 P. 305 (1914), where the Oklahoma Supreme Court, as a requirement for the establishment of a common law marriage, in addition to the marriage contract, required that the parties "enter into and maintain thereafter the marriage relation." That same year in which the court decided *In re Love's Estate*, in *Bothwell v. Way*, 44 Okla. 555, 145 P. 350 (1914) the court referred to the fact that the marriage contract must be "consummated" in one of two ways, either through the parties' "cohabitation as man and wife" or through their "mutual assumption openly of marital duties and obligations." *Compare*, *Chapman v. State*, 84 Okla.Crim.App. 41, 178 P.2d 638, 640 (1947) and *Marshall v. State*, 537 P.2d 423, 429 (Okla.Crim.App. 1975), in which the Court of Criminal Appeals drew the significant distinction that each and every one of the requirements were not expressions of either/or, but rather of both/and (*Chapman:* "as well as"). The Oklahoma Supreme Court articulated it somewhat differently in the case of *In re Trope's Estate*, 190 Okla. 453, 124 P.2d 733, 736 (1942), requiring "holding out by the parties of themselves as husband and wife" as well as "public assumption of the relation." The statement has been cited *inter alia* in *Quinton v. Webb*, 207 Okla. 133, 248 P.2d 586, 587 (1952), in which the court, as a synonym to "a public assumption of the marital relation," used the expression "cohabitation," and in *Richardson v. State*, 744 S.W.2d 65 (Tex.Cr.App. 1987). In the case of *In re Graham's Estate*, 169 Okla. 568, 37 P.2d 964, 966-967 (1934), the locution in *Bothwell* is cited, but the court adds a contract "followed by cohabitation as such."

207 With respect to different elements, *see* Jan Trost, Unmarried Cohabitation, 63-64 (1979): "[J]oint housing, joint economy, joint ownership of real and personal property, children together, meals together, vacations together, recreation together, same friends, same 'language', feeling of community and belonging together,

These factors, however, are based on how the marriage-like reality actually manifests itself, while the pertinent question here is how it ought to manifest itself in order for the marriage to be considered legally established and the legal consequences thereby invoked. A question arises as to the factors that have been considered necessary in the case law and the elements found sufficient to fulfill the requirement of cohabitation.[208]

The case law from the different states gives the impression that if the courts have sought to more clearly define the different requirements for cohabitation, there are certain factors that would generally be considered relevant. The different elements that have more or less been found significant in the assessment of whether the applicable requirements have been fulfilled are examined below. However, it would be impossible to give an exhaustive list of the relative factors that have been considered by the courts.

1. *A Sexual Relationship*

In medieval canon law, the sexual relationship between the parties was one of the two fundamental elements characterizing a cohabitation between a man and a woman. One spoke of a companionship *in lecto et in mensa*,[209] in other words, a companionship at table and bed. In a similar manner, the principle of cohabitation in Scottish law has traditionally entailed a companionship "at bed and board."[210] The courts in the American case law have also attributed significant importance to the

---

sexual relation, looking upon themselves and being looked upon by friends and family as having responsibility for each other in case of accident or illness. Most of these elements may be subsumed in the term 'economic and social integration'." Trost is also cited in Grace Ganz Blumberg, *Cohabitation without Marriage: A Different Perspective*, 28 UCLA L. REV. 1125, 1131 (1981).

208 A comparable problem arises in the treatment of cohabitation as an object of the marital intent, *see* the discussion concerning this in Chapter 6 and the future perspective given in Chapter 13.

209 *See* c. 11 X, II, 23: "*Vir eam in lecto et in mensa sicut suam uxorem aut concubinam habuerit.*" A comparison of the principle of "*cohabitatio*" to companionship "*in lecto et in mensa*" can be found in Panormitanus, ad c. 28 X, IV, 1, 5: "*praesumitur matrimonium etiam probata cohabitatione ... longo tempore, puta per 40 annos, tenuisset eam in lecto et mensa ut uxorem.*"

210 ERIC M. CLIVE AND JOHN G. WILSON, THE LAW OF HUSBAND AND WIFE IN SCOTLAND 118 (2d ed. 1982); JOHN ERSKINE, PRINCIPLES OF THE LAW OF SCOTLAND I, 6, 6 (21st ed. 1911), speak of "cohabitation, or the parties living together at bed and board." *See also* PATRIC FRASER, HUSBAND AND WIFE ACCORDING TO THE LAW OF SCOTLAND, I, 401 (Edinburgh, 2d ed. 1876), with respect to the issue of if and when "cohabitation at bed" is to be considered to exist. *See also Nicol v. Bell*, 1954 S.L.T. 314, in which the court found that the parties had lived together "at bed and board." The Marriage Law of Scotland Committee Report also mentions "cohabitation, or living together at bed and board" at 42. Bed and board companionship as a legal term can also be found in German law, where it is termed as a companionship to "*Tisch und Bett*" and older Scandinavian law, which requires that the parties "*deler seng*" as well as "*spiser og drikker sammen.*" *See* the Danish Jydske Lov I, 27 in DANMARKS GAMLE LANDSKAPSLOVE (J. Brøndum-Nilsen & P.J. Jørgensen eds. (1933-41)).

existence of a sexual relationship between the parties in assessing whether the requisite cohabitation for a common law marriage has been fulfilled.

At the same time that sexual relations outside of marriage were strongly condemned, the sexual relationship within a marriage was viewed as a fundamental characteristic and one of the central functions of marriage. A factor that can be an expression of one of marriage's most holy principles, as well as one of the most forbidden acts outside of marriage, clearly becomes problematic when used to define marriage.[211]

The courts in the American case law have gone so far as to state that the sexual relationship is a necessary element in the principle of cohabitation. In *Nestor v. Nestor* (1984), the Ohio Supreme Court, with respect to the element of cohabitation, stated that there must be proof that the parties had sexual activity in the open manner of husband and wife in a marital state.[212] This statement includes an indication that the significance of a sexual relationship is openness; clandestine relationships are not recognized as common law marriages.

The sexual relationship, however, is commonly considered neither necessary nor solely sufficient in the case law.[213] As a rule, the absence of a sexual relationship as a result of age, handicap, or disease has not been seen as an impediment against the establishment of a common law marriage.[214] Even though the sexual relationship is not considered necessary,

---

211 *Compare* Koegel, *supra* note 8, at 128: "A doctrine that requires two persons to fornicate a number of times before they create a legal status is absurd." *Compare* cases where the issue has arisen as to whether a prostitute lived in a common law marriage, *e.g. Parker v. De Bernardi*, 40 Nev. 361, 164 P. 645 (1917).

212 *Nestor v. Nestor*, 472 N.E.2d 1091, 1095 (Ohio 1984); *see also Scott v. Jefferson*, 174 Ga.App. 651, 331 S.E.2d 1, 4 (1985), in which the Georgia Court of Appeals stated that the woman "was an invalid and according to appellants' testimony 'couldn't sleep with nobody else.' Therefore, there was no proof of consummation of the marriage agreement by cohabitation as man and wife, an essential element in establishing a common law marriage."

213 In *Sharon v. Sharon*, 79 Cal. 633, 22 P. 26, 37 (1889), the California Supreme Court stated: "In our judgment sexual intercourse is not necessary to the validity of a marriage of the kind we are considering ... The commencement of true and open matrimonial cohabitation ... is a mutual assumption of marital rights, duties and obligations, while mere copulation without such cohabitation is insufficient. The courts have used the word 'consummation' generally as the completion of the marriage relation, and not necessarily as the act of sexual intercourse." In *Kilburn v. Kilburn*, 89 Cal. 46, 26 P. 636, 637 (1891), the court also stated that "by cohabitation is not meant simply the gratification of the sexual passions." *Compare Jacoby v. Jacoby*, 132 Kan. 77, 294 P. 857 (1931), in which a common law marriage was found proven despite the fact that the man objected that the woman only did household chores and that "an illicit intimacy existed between them that was merely of a lustful nature." In *Hunt v. Hunt*, 172 Miss. 732, 161 So. 119, 121 (1935), the court stated that "cohabitation may be without coition." In the case of *In re Marriage of Kuzanek*, 82 P.3d 528, 529 (Kan.App. 2004), the court held that in order for two adults to cohabitate, the must live together and assume the marital rights, duties, and obligations which are usually manifested by married people, "including but not necessarily dependent on sexual relations."

214 In *Buford v. Buford*, 874 So.2d 562, 566 (Ala.Civ.App. 2003), the court held that the parties' sexual relation is "indicative of achieving marital status" but not

it is assumed to be a natural component in a cohabitation alleged to be marriage-like and a meaningful element in the legal principle of cohabitation. Significantly, however, though the sexual relationship is an element of cohabitation, it has never been seen as solely sufficient for fulfilling the requirement of cohabitation.[215] Something more must always exist! In reality, it is those relationships that are only of a sexual nature that the courts have wished to discourage when requiring a sexual relationship for the establishment of a common law marriage.[216]

An important function of the sexual relationship is that it distinguishes common law marriages from simple friendships. It is certainly not the intention of the law to find that all friendships are common law marriages.

"absolutely necessary" to fulfill the requirement of cohabitation. In *Hall v. Duster*, 727 So.2d 834, 837 (Ala.Civ.App. 1999), the Alabama Court of Appeals stated that sexual relations between the parties are not "an indispensable element of cohabitation." However, the extent to which the parties had a sexual relationship was unclear. In the case of *Matter of Estate of Foster*, 376 S.E.2d 144, 149 (W.Va. 1988), the West Virginia Supreme Court of Appeals, in applying the law of the District of Columbia, found a common law marriage established. The court noted, among many other facts, "almost thirty years of continually living in the same home and sharing the same bedroom." In *Beck v. Beck*, 286 Ala. 692, 246 So.2d 420, 426, 429 (1971), one party in the relationship was incapable of having sexual intercourse due to a medical condition. No common law marriage had been found established as "sexual intercourse is an indispensable element of a common law marriage." However, the Alabama Supreme Court found that "under circumstances where advanced age or physical infirmity are shown to have prevented the parties from engaging in sexual intercourse, the absence of that act alone should not operate to prevent a common law marriage."

215 *See Ex parte Threet*, 160 Tex. 482, 333 S.W.2d 361 (1960), in which the man, a 20-year old youth, and the woman, a 15-year-old schoolgirl, had entered into an agreement to be husband and wife. Thereafter the parties during two months on different occasions had sex with each other in their respective parents' houses. The young pair never spent an entire night together. The girl used her maiden name. The question arose as to whether a common law marriage existed. The court required the following: "(1) an agreement to be husband and wife (2) a living together as husband and wife, and (3) a holding out to the public that the couple are husband and wife." It was found not evidenced that the young pair lived together as husband and wife. The court further found the secrecy surrounding the relationship was not compatible with the third requirement. In *State v. Wagoner*, 182 N.E.2d 328, 329 (Ohio App. 1961), the court stated: "One must not confuse the wide distinction between a harlot and one entering upon and living under a common law marriage." In the case of *In re Miller's Estate*, 182 Okla. 534, 78 P.2d 819, 827 (1938), the court stated with respect to the parties' sexual actions: "Such acts do not constitute cohabitation as that term is employed in connection with the question of informal marriage." In *Sharon v. Sharon*, 79 Cal. 633, 22 P. 26, 37 (1889), the California Supreme Court stated: "[M]ere copulation without such cohabitation is insufficient. The courts have used the word 'consummation' generally as the completion of the marriage relation, and not necessarily as the act of sexual intercourse." Also in *Kilburn v. Kilburn*, 89 Cal. 46, 26 P. 636, 637 (1891), the court stated that "by cohabitation is not meant simply the gratification of the sexual passions." *See also Grigsby v. Reib*, 105 Tex. 597, 153 S.W. 1124 (1913).

216 The courts have sometimes viewed it as their duty to expose relationships hiding behind the façade of parties living together as husband and wife. *See Thimgan v. Mathews*, 74 Colo. 93, 219 P. 211 (1923). *Compare Foley v. Gavin*, 76 Colo. 286, 230 P. 618 (1924).

A common objection against the existence of a common law marriage is that the parties simply were "close friends." This creates problems in those cases that ought to be recognized as marriages despite the fact that no sexual activity existed as a result of age, handicap, or disease. The actual circumstances in these relationships can appear to be those of friendship.[217] However, it ought to be noted that these application problems sometimes can be resolved with the help of two other requirements for a common law marriage, namely the marriage contract—expressed or implied - as well as the parties' holding out as spouses. Friends do not enter into agreements to be husband and wife living together in a legal relationship. Neither do they represent themselves to the public as husband and wife.[218] These problems are more significant in the legal systems that bind the legal consequences to simply the actual cohabitation, such as modern cohabitation law, discussed in Chapter 13, "The Constitutive Requisites in the Future," and Chapter 14, "Arguments For and Against Common Law Marriage and Cohabitation Law."

Sexual relationships as a factor in the proving of a common law marriage create serious difficulties for investigators. The facts concerning these relationships are often difficult to uncover. The courts often hear conflicting information from the parties or, upon the death of one of the spouses, information from only the surviving party. When testimony is given by outside third parties, it seldom contains the immediately relevant or intimate facts being sought. Instead, inevitably, such testimony is merely the observations of outsiders and can be ridiculous. In the case of *In re Estate of Soeder* (1966), for example, a witness testified under pressure with respect to the man that: "Well, there was times when I saw him in pajamas and a robe and house slippers."[219] The estate, which called forty-six witnesses,

217 In *Goodman v. McMillan*, 258 Ala. 125, 61 So.2d 55, 60 (1952), the parties had a relationship after their divorce. The woman stated in a letter that they ought to go separate ways and that they ought to be "merely friends." With reference to this, and to other circumstances, no common law marriage was found established.

218 *Compare In re Koshman's Estate*, 77 Idaho 96, 288 P.2d 652, 656 (1955), in which the court found the lack of a sexual relationship, an outward public representation, and a general acceptance as husband and wife. The court found that the relationship between them was one between "friends or sweethearts."

219 *In re Estate of Soeder*, 7 Ohio App. 271, 220 N.E.2d 547, 577 (Ohio App. 1966). In *Doyle v. Doyle*, 497 S.W.2d 846, 847 (Mo.App. 1973), a private detective had been hired: "He saw the house lights go off with both parties still inside indicating they had retired for night, but he could not confirm this latter fact." In *Nestor v. Nestor*, 472 N.E.2d 1091, 1095 (Ohio 1984), testimony as to the fact that the parties "slept together in the downstairs double bed" was introduced. In *de Shazo v. Christian*, 191 S.W.2d 495, 496-497 (Tex.Civ.App-Amarillo 1946), a witness testified that the woman had spent her nights at a sister's and not at the house where the man lived, while another witness testified that there were two beds in the man's house and that it was obvious that both were used. In *Foix v. Jordan*, 421 S.W.2d 481, 484 (Tex. Civ.App.-El Paso 1967), the court gave significance to the testimony that the parties' house had "one bedroom with one bed." In *Smith v. Smith*, 247 Ala.213, 23 So.2d 605 (1945), the man, a soldier, admitted that he had slept with the woman one or two nights, but denied that he had sexual relations with her. In the case of

succeeded, however, in convincing the majority in the Ohio Court of Appeals, which did not find a common law marriage proven. A more serious difficulty with such investigations is that they certainly can violate personal privacy. Objections that evidence concerning the parties' sexual relationship should not be admitted have been overruled, on the argument that such circumstances are materially relevant.[220] Nevertheless, legal investigations that invade personal privacy are troubling and require correction. The need, however, to present evidence with respect to the sexual element is a logical consequence of giving the same constitutive effect.

2. *An Exclusive Relationship*

A majority of couples living together without formally marrying nevertheless want to live in a monogamous relationship with marriage-like faithfulness.[221] We saw in Chapter 6 that in the case law with respect to marriage contracts, many courts require that the necessary marital intent include the intent to live in an exclusive relationship.[222] In a number of cases, the

---

In re Long's Estate, 251 Iowa 1042, 102 N.W.2d 76, 80 (1960), the witnessed testified that the parties often spent the night when they visited, but never "occupied the same bedroom," which was denied by one of the parties.

220 *Walter v. Walter*, 433 S.W.2d 183, 190 (Tex.Civ.App.-Houston (1st Dist.) 1968).

221 A survey showed than more than 90% of the couples "did not date" outside of their relationships, *see* Catlin et al., *Commitment and Relationship Factors in Consensual Cohabitation*, 8 INT.L.J. SOC. FAM. 185, 188-189 (1978). Another study showed that a majority of cohabiting couples wished to live in a "sexually monogamous marriage," *see* Paul R. Newcomb, *Cohabitation in America: An Assessment of Consequences*, 41 J. MAR. & FAM. 597, 600 (1979).

222 The element clearly appears in the case law from Alabama, Florida and Oklahoma, *see Davis v. State*, 103 P.3d 70 (Okla.Cr.App. 2004); *Crosson v. Crosson*, 668 So.2d 868, 870 (Ala.Civ.App. 1995); *Adams v. Boan*, 559 So.2d 1084, 1087 (Ala. 1990) ("permanent and exclusive of all others"); *Matter of Death of Boyd*, 959 P.2d 612, 614 (Okla. Civ.App. Div. 1 1998); *Richardson v. State*, 744 S.W.2d 65, 74 (Tex.Cr.App. 1987) (applying Oklahoma law); *Sloss-Sheffield Steel & Iron Co. v. Watford*, 245 Ala. 425, 17 So.2d 166 (1944); *King v. King*, 269 Ala. 468, 114 So.2d 145 (1959); and *Owens v. Bentley*, 40 Del. 512, 14 A.2d 391 (1941) (applying Delaware law). In *Orr v. State*, 129 Fla. 398, 176 So. 510, 514 (1937), the court spoke of "a matrimonial relation, permanent and exclusive of all others." The same expression recurs in *McKee v. State*, 452 P.2d 169 (Okla.Cr.App. 1969); *Downs v. Newman*, 500 So.2d 1062 (Ala. 1986); and *Boswell v. Boswell*, 497 So.2d 479 (Ala. 1986). *See* from Texas *Middlebrook v. Wideman*, 203 S.W.2d 686, 688 (Tex.Civ.App.-Texarkana 1947) ("Then she consorted with various and sundry other members of the opposite sex, with manifest fruition, according to her testimony." The court found no common law marriage proven and further stated: "Courts do not view with an approving eye the conduct of one who treats lightly the most serious and sacred of all human relationships"). *Compare*, from Ohio, *Minnix v. Brantner*, 48 Ohio Ops. 450, 64 Ohio L.Abs. 327, 107 N.E.2d 562 (1952), in which the parties, after twenty-four years of marriage, divorced but continued to cohabit for six more years until the death of the woman. No contract constituting a common law marriage after the divorce was found proven. Therewith the circumstance that the woman showed interest in other man was considered. *See also* from Pennsylvania *In re Stevenson's Estate*, 272 Pa. 291, 116 A. 162, 163 (1922), in which the man had a relationship with another woman. The woman, claiming the existence of the common law marriage, had to wait outside the other woman's

existence of relationships with others has been cited to support that the parties have not entered into a true marriage contract. The pertinent issue in this chapter is whether the requirement of cohabitation can be considered fulfilled despite the fact that a party actually has a relationship with another, third party.[223] The first-mentioned parties, when they commenced their relationship, agreed to live in an exclusive relationship, but later did not adhere to the agreement. Was a common law marriage constituted if the cohabitation from the beginning was exclusive? Such situations become particularly pertinent in states in which the requirement of cohabitation, according to the preceding, is formulated as a requirement of a "cohabitation as husband and wife,"[224] "living together as husband and wife,"[225] or particularly an "assumption of marital rights, duties and obligations."[226] Can a party having a relationship with someone other than their spouse be said to fulfill marriage-like obligations, and can they then be viewed as living together as husband and wife?

American case law does not take any clear position this issue. Courts have, with reference to marriage as the holiest of all human relationships, ruled out the establishment of a common law marriage in cases in which one of the parties has had relationships with others. In *Middlebrook v. Wideman* (1947), in which the woman had relationships with other men, the Texas Court of Appeals stated: "Courts do not view with an approving eye the conduct of one who treats lightly the most serious and sacred of all human relationships."[227] The court found no common law marriage

house during his visits. No marriage contract within the frame for a common law marriage was found proven. Compare Nancy Rebecca Shaw, *Common Law Marriage and Unmarried Cohabitation: An Old Solution to a New Problem*, 39 U. PITT. L. REV. 579, 580 (1977), which with respect to Pennsylvania assumes a common law pair, living together "intending permanence and exclusiveness."

223 A separate issue arises as to whether an actual relationship with another is evidence for the fact that their contract was insufficient. In the case of *In re Estate of Shepherd*, 646 N.E.2d 561, 564 (Ohio App. 3 Dist. 1994), in which no marriage contract was found proven, the circumstance that the man "dated other women" appears to have been considered. *See also Hansen v. Hansen*, 958 P.2d 931, 936 (Utah App. 1998). *Compare Barker v. Baker*, 330 S.C. 361, 499 S.E.2d 503, 506 (S.C.App. 1998), in which the woman had a relationship with another man and in which the marriage presumption was not found applicable. It is, however, unclear as to the significance given this circumstance, *see* Chapter 9.

224 *See* note 194 *supra*.

225 *See* note 195 *supra*.

226 *See* note 196 *supra*.

227 *Middlebrook v. Wideman*, 203 S.W.2d 686, 688 (Tex.Civ.App.-Texarkana 1947). With respect to the facts in the case, the court stated: "After she left Lem, she lived in the house with Monroe, and then on the same place in a separate dwelling, without being certain that Lem was dead. Then she consorted with various and sundry other members of the opposite sex, with manifest fruition, according to her testimony. Then, she moved into the protective fold of Joe, before the death of Monroe, and for thirty years has claimed to be Joe's spouse." In *Downs v. Newman*, 500 So.2d 1062, 1063 (Ala. 1986), in which a common law marriage was found proven, the court stated: "Neither of them dated or had sexual relations with other parties." However, it is somewhat unclear the significance the court gave to this fact in the

proven. Evidence was also introduced in *Sanders v. Sanders* (1997), showing that the woman, who alleged that she was a man's common law wife during the last months of his life, had sex with another man three to four times a week. The Oklahoma Court of Civil Appeals found that no common law marriage had been proven.[228]

There are courts, on the other hand, that in the assessment of whether a common law marriage has been established, have downplayed the significance of the parties' sexual relationships with others. For example, in Alabama, although the courts do not consider a sexual relationship between the parties necessary for establishing a common law marriage,

---

terse judgment rendered in the case. In *Marcus v. Director*, 548 F.2d 1044, 1049 (D.C.Cir. 1976), in which a common law marriage was not found proven during the eighteen months the parties lived together, it was noted that the woman during this time "continued to date other men." The circumstance that the woman was a prostitute was cited as a reason against the existence of a common law marriage in *Gilbreath v. Lewis*, 242 Ala. 510, 7 So.2d 485, 486 and 488 (1942). In *Warren v. Canard*, 30 Okla. 514, 120 P. 599 (1911), the Oklahoma Supreme Court stated, concerning a statement that the woman was a prostitute: "Proof, therefore, that the woman during the time of the cohabitation with the man, was a common prostitute would necessarily greatly weaken the probative force of the cohabitation." With respect thereto, the court allowed the introduction of evidence with respect to this fact, but did not allow evidence concerning the woman's "reputation" based on this. *See also Parker v. de Bernardi*, 40 Nev. 361, 164 P. 645 (1917); and *Matter of Estate of Stinchcomb*, 674 P.2d 26, 29 (Okla. 1983). *See also Olinghouse v. Olinghouse*, 265 P.2d 711 (Okla. 1954), where it was claimed that the man lived together with two women simultaneously. This was found not proven by the majority of the court, but the minority found it proven and maintained that cohabitation with two persons did not fulfill the requirement of cohabitation. With respect to application of the marriage presumption, *see Horrigan v. Gibson*, 87 Okla. 1, 206 P. 219 (1922), where a man had relations with two women. In the case of *In re Callery's Estate*, 226 Pa. 469, 75 A 672, 673 (1910), in which the surviving woman did not succeed in proving cohabitation and reputation, the court stated: "There is evidence that in the meantime she had relation with other men." In the case of *In re Stevenson's Estate*, 272 Pa. 291, 116 A. 162, 163 (1922), the man conducted a relationship with another woman. The woman claiming the common law marriage waited outside the other woman's house while the man visited her. No marriage contract within the frame of a common law marriage was found evidenced. The issue of whether cohabitation existed was not an issue at trial as it is not a necessary requirement in Pennsylvania and the marriage presumption was not applicable. In *Brinckle v. Brinckle*, 12 Phila. 232, 235 (1877), the court maintained that if a woman claimed to assume the role of wife, her actions must be compatible with that position. If she "admits other men to her embrace or plays the party of a wanton in the public streets," she cannot expect to be viewed as a wife.

228 *Sanders v. Sanders*, 948 P.2d 719, 721 (Okla.Civ.App. Div. 3 1997). *See also In re Estate of Glover*, 882 S.W.2d 789 (Tenn.App. 1994), in which the man, made repeated trips to Alabama clearly with several different women, where he engaged in card playing and "eating, shopping and sharing a motel room" with the women. No common law marriage was found proven. In *Eaton v. Johnston*, 9 Kan.App. 63, 672 P.2d 10 (1983); *aff'd*, 235 Kan. 323, 681 P.2d 606 (1984), in which the man "was involved with another woman," no common law marriage was found proven. *Compare Johnson v. Young*, 372 A.2d 992. 993 (D.C.App. 1977), in which Levy, who lived with Alma, dated Vonnie and "began spending nights with her on a fairly regular basis even to the point of moving some of his clothes into her apartment" and in which Levy "continued to also visit Alma, at least during the day." No common law marriage with Alma was found proven.

as seen above, the parties' relationships with others have not prevented the establishment of an informal marriage. For example, in the case of *Hall v. Duster* (1999), the man testified that he traveled a lot with his job and that he had "a girlfriend in every state" where he worked. Despite the fact that the woman testified that the man had not been faithful to her, the Alabama Court of Appeals found that a common law marriage had been established.[229]

However, if the parties have already fulfilled the requirement of cohabitation as well as any other requirements, and a common law marriage has been established, the marriage is not terminated by the sexual relationship of one party with a third party. In the above-cited case of *Nestor v. Nestor* (1984), the court considered a sexual relationship between the parties necessary for the establishment of a common law marriage and found no impediment against the establishment of a common law marriage, when the man, during the parties' twelve year cohabitation and without the woman's knowledge, had a relationship with another woman on three occasions.[230] Such a relationship, on the other hand, when it arises in a formal marriage, can be grounds for divorce and punishable for adultery. In *Walton v. Walton* (1918), the parties had lived together and had a common residence for four to five years when the man died. They had three mutual children and had outwardly appeared as spouses. The man, employed by the railroad, however, traveled for long periods. Despite the fact that the woman at trial admitted that he had a "sweetheart" in every city, and that he received many letters from other women, the Texas Court of Appeals found that the parties had been united in a common law marriage and that the woman consequently was the man's lawful wife.[231]

---

229 *Hall v. Duster*, 727 So.2d 834 (Ala.Civ.App. 1999). The point of time during which the man had relationships with other women cannot be deduced from the court's summary, which does not raise the issue of whether the man had already had relationships before fulfilling the requirement of cohabitation ("consummation"). Despite the circumstances, the court found the existence of an implied marriage contract, *see* Section 7.6.3 *supra*.

230 *Nestor v. Nestor*, 472 N.E.2d 1091, 1096 (Ohio 1984). In *Adams v. Boan*, 559 So.2d 1084, 1087 (Ala. 1990), the man had had a sexual relationship with another woman. The requirements of "public recognition of existence of marriage" and "cohabitation or mutual assumption openly of marital duties and obligations" for the establishment of a common law marriage, however, were considered to be fulfilled. *Compare Winfield v. Renfro*, 821 S.W.2d 640 (Tex.App.-Houston 1991), in which the man admitted that he had had sexual relationships with other women, but in which the court, with reference to the circumstantial evidence, found that the parties fulfilled the requirements of an agreement to be married and of living together as man and wife. However, no common law marriage was found established as the requirement of holding out to the public as man and wife was not fulfilled. *See also Beals v. Beals*, 203 Ga.App. 81, 416 S.E.2d 301 (1992), as well as *Bolash v. Heid*, 733 S.W.2d 698, 699 (Tex.Civ.App.-San Antonio 1987).

231 *Walton v. Walton*, 203 S.W. 133 (Tex.Civ.App.-Galveston 1918); *compare Jacoby v. Jacoby*, 132 Kan. 77, 294 P. 857 (1931), in which a common law marriage was found proven despite the fact that the man objected that the woman kept company with

The same liberal acceptance of relationships with others can be found in the modern case law from Texas. In *Russell v. Russell* (1992), the Texas Court of Appeals found the requirements of cohabitation and holding out fulfilled, despite the fact that the man had relationships and six children with other women, in addition to the five children he had with the woman claiming to be the man's common law wife.[232] In a recent case from Texas, *Ballesteros v. Jones* (1998), the man hired prostitutes who were flown in from Mexico to participate in lesbian sex with his common law wife while he watched. Despite this, the requirement of cohabitation as husband and wife with the woman was found to be fulfilled and a common law marriage established. The courts have sometimes been surprisingly liberal in their acceptance of other relationships, even for short cohabitations.[233] In *Crosson v. Crosson* (1995), the Alabama Court of Appeals found the requirement of public assumption of marital duties and cohabitation fulfilled, despite the fact that the man, during the parties' approximately one-year long cohabitation, dated other women.[234] The explanation for this acceptance seems to be that a common law marriage, despite the short cohabitation, was already established before the relationships with the other women were formed. In *Gray v. Bush* (2001), on the other side, the man had relationships with other women, and the same court found that his partner failed to produce substantial evidence indicating a present, mutual agreement "to permanently enter a marriage relationship to the exclusion of all others."[235]

3. *Mutual Children*

As little as the marriage contract according to American law must necessarily contain an intent to acquire children,[236] as discussed above in Chapter 6, there is no requirement whatsoever that the parties must have mutual children for the requirement of cohabitation to be considered fulfilled.[237] There are several cases, consequently, in which the parties have had mutual children, but the requirement of cohabitation was not found

other men "by day and by night." The Texas Supreme Court did not, however, indicate whether they found that assertion proven.

232 *Russell v. Russell*, 838 S.W.2d 909 (Tex.App.-Beaumont 1992).

233 *Ballesteros v. Jones*, 985 S.W.2d 485, 490 (Tex.App.-San Antonio 1998).

234 *Crosson v. Crosson*, 668 So.2d 868, 872 (Ala.Civ.App 1995). The court appears to have accepted the man's relationships. With respect to one of these relationships, it occurred at the end of the one year of cohabitation, and a common law marriage had already been established. It can be noted that the man formally married two months later with the woman he had "dated." *See also* Section 9.3. *infra*.

235 *Gray v. Bush*, 835 So.2d 192, 197 (Ala.Civ.App. 2001).

236 *See* Section 6.3.1. *supra*.

237 In the case of *Matter of Estate of Eliasen*, 105 Idaho 234, 668 P.2d 110, 114 (1983), the court stated that the parties "lived together, assumed marital rights and duties, including the conception and birth of a son." *See also Wadsworth v. Brigham*, 125 Or. 428, 259 P. 299, 91 A.L.R. 212 (1927); and *DeMedio v. DeMedio*, 215 Pa.Super. 255, 257 A.2d 290, 302 (1969).

proven, and, conversely, the parties lacked mutual children but a common law marriage was found still established.[238] The existence of mutual children, however, especially when united with other circumstances, can be a significant factor in the assessment of whether the requirement of cohabitation is fulfilled. A couple having mutual children and a mutual home and household ought to have a good basis for fulfilling the requirement of cohabitation. The suggestion has been made, however, that the circumstance that the parties have mutual children ought to be given more significance in the assessment of whether a common law marriage has been established.[239]

4. *Mutual House and Household*

In American case law, defining the second prong of companionship "at bed and board," namely, the mutual household, is more important than elucidating the sexual aspect of cohabitation.[240] To begin, it is assumed, fundamentally, that the parties have a mutual residence. An older case, *Yardley's Estate* (1874), which actually concerned the application of the marriage presumption, somewhat adequately defines the principle of cohabitation and has had great influence on later case law even in those jurisdictions where cohabitation is a necessary requirement. The court stated: "[C]onstancy of dwelling together is the chief element of cohabitation. Cohabitation is not a sojourn, a habit of visiting nor a remaining with for a time ... Cohabitation is to have the same habitation so that where one dwells there the other dwells with him."[241] Therewith, the parties are not found to share a residence where each lives in their own room or one is a boarder, even if a lease agreement does not always exclude a common law marriage.[242] Their residence must be mutual in the sense that they have a mutual home and household. The mutual residence should be in a house

238 *See, e.g., Herd v. Herd*, 194 Ala. 613, 69 So. 885 (1915). *Compare In re Craig's Estate*, 273 Pa. 530, 117 A. 221, 222 (1922) ("Proof that a man was the father of a child is of but little weight on the question of whether there was a common law marriage between the man and the child's mother"). In the case of *Green's Estate*, 5 Pa.C. 605, 607 (1888), the circumstance that the parties had a mutual child was not given any significant evidentiary weight.

239 *See Ridley v. Grandison*, 260 Ga. 6, 389 S.E.2d 746, 749 (1990).

240 In the case of *In re McLaughlin's Estate*, 197 N.E.2d 578, 579, 580, 582 (Ohio P.Ct. 1963), the expressions "the same bed and table" and "bed and board" were used.

241 *Yardley's Estate*, 75 Pa. 207 (1874). This case is cited in a number of decisions in which cohabitation was considered a necessary requirement. *See, e.g., Walter v. Walter*, 433 S.W.2d 183, 190, 195 (Tex.Civ.App.-Houston (1st Dist.) 1968). With respect to the marriage presumption, *see* Chapter 9 *infra*.

242 *Etter v. Aschen*, 82 Ohio Law Abst. 421, 163 N.E.2d 197, 199 (1959). *Compare In re Marriage of Kuzanek*, 82 P.3d 528, 530 (Kan.App. 2004), in which the parties had a significant long-term romantic relationship that included occasional sexual relations and in which the court held that a cohabitation relationship "should not be masked by use of a legal device, such as a lease agreement if, when stripped away, cohabitation clearly exists." *Cf. also Graham v. Graham*, 130 Colo. 225, 274 P.2d 605 (1954), in which the man began by renting a room from the woman, after which they lived together for four months. The Colorado Supreme Court, which for the

that the parties view as their mutual home and where they have their personal belongings.[243] A mutual household does not entail simply common meals and their planning. The parties ought be engaged in numerous aspects of the day-to-day mutual existence of married persons.[244] All the contributions that the parties make for the mutual household are to be without remuneration.[245] This constitutes the difference between a housekeeper and a common law wife. Herein lies a significant portion of the creation of the life companionship that the marriage contract is assumed to cover.

The requirement of a mutual home and household is created to distinguish common law marriages from relationships based upon sexual needs.

---

establishment of a common law marriage required, in addition to a marriage contract, "cohabitation as husband and wife," found that such a marriage was proven.

243 *Drummond v. Benson,* 133 S.W.2d 154 (Tex.Civ.App.-San Antonio 1939); *Ex parte Threet,* 160 Tex. 482, 333 S.W.2d 361 (1960); and *Winfield v. Renfro,* 821 S.W.2d 640, 648 (Tex.App.-Houston 1991). In *Botwell v. Way,* 44 Okla. 555, 145 P. 350, 354 (1914), the Oklahoma Supreme Court stated as support for the finding that no common law marriage had been established, that the parties did not have a "common home." In the case of *In re Estate of Slavens,* 162 Mont. 123, 509 P.2d 293, 294-295 (1973), significant disagreement existed as to whether the man truly lived with the woman. Even if the parties in *Matter of Estate of Brack,* 121 Mich.App. 585, 329 N.W.2d 432, 434 (1982) often lived with each other, they had separate residences, which was considered to be strong evidence against the existence of a cohabitation. In the case of *In re Marriage of Ales,* 592 N.W.2d 698, 701, note 1 (Iowa App. 1999), the court held that cohabitation is evidenced: " (1) an unrelated person of the opposite sex living or residing in the dwelling house...(2) living together in the manner of husband and wife, and (3) unrestricted access to the home."

244 *Piel v. Brown,* 361 So.2d 90, 95 (Ala. 1978). In *Beck v. Beck,* 286 Ala. 692, 246 So.2d 420 (1971), the Alabama Supreme Court stated: "We think it may or may not, under the circumstances of the particular case, include sexual activity, but it does include such things as eating together, sharing household duties, payment of household expenses, holding themselves out to the public as man and wife, and all the numerous aspects of day-to-day mutual existence of married persons." In the case of *Matter of Estate of Alcorn,* 868 P.2d 629, 631 (Mont. 1994), the court stated that the couple "invested a great deal of time and money in decorating and refurbishing their home." *See also Winfield v. Renfro,* 821 S.W.2d 640 (Tex.App.-Houston 1991), in which the court stated that the man acted "husbandly" by doing errands, working around the house, and generally acting as though he were married. This was true during several weeks in the month of August. In *Walter v. Walter,* 433 S.W.2d 183, 190 (Tex.Civ.App.-Houston (1st Dist.) 1968), the court accepted the following definition: "The term lived and cohabited together as husband and wife means living together, claiming to be married and doing those things ordinarily done by husband and wife." *See also Humble Oil & Ref. Co. v. Jeffrey,* 38 S.W.2d 374 (Tex.Civ.App.-Austin 1931), *aff'd,* 55 S.W.2d 521 (Tex.Comm.App. 1932); *compare Drummond v. Benson,* 133 S.W.2d 154 (Tex.Civ.App.-San Antonio 1939); and *Robinson v. Casey,* 272 S.W. 536 (Tex.Civ.App.-Amarillo 1925). In *James v. James,* 253 S.W. 1112 (Tex.Civ.App.-San Antonio 1923), the court used the expression "the normal relation of husband and wife."

245 In the case of *In re Miller's Estate,* 182 Okla. 534, 78 P.2d 819, 827 (1938), it was found not proven that the parties had fulfilled "any of the ordinary matrimonial duties and obligations." The woman requested and was granted compensation from the man's estate for food, shelter, and laundry. The court found this to be a direct admission that such services performed were not as a wife but in a businesslike manner.

The American case law contains innumerable cases in which the courts denied claims of a common law marriage because the relationship was mainly based on "the gratification of the sexual passions."[246] By this requirement, cases fall outside the principle of cohabitation, such as a companionship in which the parties consistently visited each other over a long period of time.[247] Separate residences have not been accepted even

---

246 In *State v. Lawson,* 165 N.W.2d 838 (Iowa 1969), the parties had a sexual relationship for over one year, but never moved in together. No common law marriage was considered to be established. In *Grigsby v. Reib,* 105 Tex. 597, 153 S.W. 1124 (1913), in which the man during a one year period constantly visited the woman at her "rooming house" and presented her to a number of persons as his wife, the court found that a marriage-like cohabitation was not proven. In *O'Malley v. O'Malley,* 46 Mont. 549, 129 P. 501, 503 (1913), cohabitation was not considered to mean "simply the gratification of the sexual passions, but to live or dwell together, to have the same habitation, so that where one lives and dwells there does the other live and dwell also." Constant visits with overnight stays did not fulfill the requirement of cohabitation.

247 In *Aleen v. Allen,* 966 S.W.2d 658, 661 (Tex.App.-San Antonio 1998), the court found that cohabitation did not encompass situations involving "a frequent overnight guest." Therefore a man's obligation to support his former wife was not terminated. In *Marshall v. State,* 537 P.2d 423, 429 (Okla.Crim.App. 1975), the court maintained that the cohabitation could not be "irregular, limited or partial" and found that the woman never stayed more than one night on each occasion she visited the man, thereafter she returned to her mother's home. The requirement of cohabitation was not found fulfilled. In the case of *In re Estate of Soeder,* 7 Ohio App. 271, 220 N.E.2d 547 (Ohio App. 1966), the parties' relationship had been approximately twenty years. They had, however, separate residences and in most situations had stated that they were single. The elements of cohabitation and holding out were found not proven. The idea that it ought to be a question of a mutual cohabitation that is permanent recurs also in *Ex parte Threet,* 160 Tex. 482, 333 S.W.2d 361, 364 (1960), in which the court, as reason for why the parties were not considered to live together as husband and wife stated: "They never moved into or occupied, publicly, a common residence or room." In *Murphy v. Jacobs,* 249 Ala. 594, 32 So.2d 306, 308 (1947), the parties lived in separate homes close to each other and no common law marriage was found proven. *See also McArthur v. Hall,* 169 S.W.2d 724 (Tex.Civ.App.-Fort Worth 1943), in which the parties' "matrimonial cohabitation" was considered to assume that they had the same habitation. The court stated: "He maintained no home within which he and Jennie lived as man and wife." *See also Drummond v. Benson,* 133 S.W.2d 154 (Tex.Civ.App.-San Antonio 1939). In the case of *In re Miller's Estate,* 182 Okla. 534, 78 P.2d 819, 827 (1938), the word "cohabitation" was considered to mean "a living or residing together of a man and woman ostensibly as husband and wife, and ordinarily carries with it the idea of a fixed residence ... and does not contemplate a casual sojourning together." *Compare Richard v. Richard,* 172 Okla. 397, 45 P.2d 101 (1935); and *Le Blanc v. Yawn,* 99 Fla. 328, 126 So. 789, 790 (1930) ("To cohabit as man and wife means to live together, to have the same habitation, so that, where one lives, there will the other live also. It does not contemplate a mere sojourn, visit, or living together for a time"). In *King v. King's Unknown Heirs* 16 S.W.2d 160, 161 (Tex.Civ.App.-San Antonio 1929), the Texas Court of Civil Appeals stated that "a common homestead" was "the most important element of the true marital state" and found that a relationship which had lasted approximately thirty years without the parties having a mutual residence did not constitute a common law marriage, as the requirement of cohabitation was not found to be fulfilled. In *Crossett v. State,* 260 S.W. 186, 188 (Tex.Cr.App. 1924) the court stated: "Cohabitation consists of a living or dwelling together in the same habitation as husband and wife, and not merely sojourning, visiting, or remaining together for a time." In *People v. Spencer,* 85 Mich. 127, 165 N.W. 921 (1917), the

though the parties had separate homes close to each other and often stayed overnight. In *Finch v. Dasgupta* (2001), the woman stayed at the man's home for several nights each week but maintained her own residence throughout the course of their ten-year relationship. In view of this and other circumstances, the court found that the woman failed to establish that a common law marriage existed.[248] On the other hand, a cohabitation has been found to exist even though one of the parties, as a result of employment, had a separate residence.[249] In contrast, a partial cohabitation, in which the parties shared a household, but one of them had another, separate household, has been accepted because the residency with the party in the informal marriage occurred on a regular basis.[250]

5. *Economic Support*

One of the most important obligations of the spouses in a marriage is their contributions to the maintenance of each other and the family. Especially in jurisdictions requiring an "assumption of marital rights, duties and obligations," the fulfillment of the obligation of maintenance ought to be a significant factor. However, it is uncommon for the courts, when reviewing this obligation, to inventory the rights and obligations of the spouses.[251]

---

court stated that cohabitation means "dwelling together; living in the usual manner of married people." *Compare Green's Estate,* 5 Pa.C. 605, 607 (1888), in which the parties lived separately for a long period of time.

248 *Finch v. Dasgupta,* 251 Ga.App. 637, 555 S.E.2d 22 (2001); *Cf. Freiburghaus v. Freiburghaus,* 103 Idaho 679, 651 P.2d 944 (App. 1982). In *Edelstein v. Brown,* 35 Tex. App. 625, 80 S.W. 1027 (1904), a housing shortage was not accepted as a compelling reason for living separately in different cities.

249 *Kelley v. Kelley,* 9 P.3d 171, 178 fn. 6 (Utah App. 2000).

250 In *Ballesteros v. Jones,* 985 S.W.2d 485, 490 (Tex.App.-San Antonio 1998), the man lived "three or four times a week" with the woman in question, and "some time" in a different place with his children from a previous marriage. He also had his clothes and personal belongings at the woman's residence. The requirement of cohabitation was considered to be fulfilled as the couple lived together "on a regular basis." A common law marriage was found established. *See also In re Glasco,* 619 S.W.2d 567 (Tex.Civ.App.-San Antonio 1981), in which the man was pastor of two churches for nearly two decades, one in San Antonio and the other in Seguin. While in Seguin the pastor always stayed at the woman's house and they represented to others that they were man and wife. A common law marriage was established. *Compare Gilbreath v. Lewis,* 242 Ala. 510, 7 So.2d 485 (1942), in which the man lived and took his meals sometimes at the woman's residence and sometimes with his brothers. No common law marriage was found proven. *See also Gray v. Bush,* 835 So.2d 192 (Ala. Civ.App. 2001), in which the parties lived together during different periods but maintained separate residences. Another important circumstance was that the man maintained relationships with other women. A common law marriage was not established.

251 In *Harris v. Harris,* 2004 WL 2896422 (Ohio App. 9 Dist. 2004), the court relied, *inter alia,* on the fact that the man financially supported the woman and their children and found that a common law marriage was established. In *Marshall v. State,* 537 P.2d 423, 429 (Okla.Crim.App. 1975), the requirement of "assumption of marital duties and obligations" was found to be not proven with reference to the fact that the man had not given "support" to the woman and she did not perform any

That the parties mutually take care of the family's economic needs and contribute to each other's and the family's maintenance is a relevant element in the concept of cohabitation. Consequently, the fact that the parties share household duties and living expenses has been given significance.[252] A circumstance indicating that the parties have a mutual economy can be a joint bank account.[253]

"duties or obligations as a wife." *See also McArthur v. Hall*, 169 S.W.2d 724 (Tex.Civ. App.-Fort Worth 1943), in which the parties' "matrimonial cohabitation" was considered to assume that they had "the same habitation." The court stated: "He maintained no home with in which he and Jennie lived as man and wife. After the baby was born, the evidence goes no further than to show that he purchased a tent for a home for Jennie and provided for her and Lena and a little son, who was born later, and that he visited them at times." *Compare In re Sander's Estate*, 67 Okla. 3, 168 P. 197, 199 (1917), in which the parties did not have a mutual residence, but in which the Sanders, a European American, made constant and according to certain witnesses, daily visits to a Native American woman named Peggy, who lived with her parents. They had a mutual child. The court stated the following with respect to the maintenance: "After the birth of the child, he furnished Peggy money with which to pay for the services of the attending physician, and at various times furnished her different sums to purchase clothes for the child ... and he told Peggy's father to take care of her, and he would pay the expense, and gave her father money at various times for that purpose." The court, which in addition to a marriage contract, for the establishment of a common law marriage required that the parties "enter into and thereafter maintain the marriage relation," found a common law marriage proven. In *O'Malley v. O'Malley*, 46 Mont. 549, 129 P. 501, 503 (1913), no common law marriage was found proven, despite constant visits and overnight stays and the fact that the man "bought supplies for her and gave her money." In *Nat'l Union Fire Ins. Co. V. Britton*, 187 F.Supp. 359, 364 (D.D.C. 1960), the court noted that the man left "support" to the woman; *see also Ballesteros v. Jones*, 985 S.W.2d 485, 490 (Tex.App.-San Antonio 1998). *Compare Barker v. Baker*, 330 S.C. 361, 499 S.E.2d 503, 506 (S.C.App. 1998), in which the man did not pay any medical bills or personal expenses of the woman and in which the marriage presumption in favor of a common law marriage was found not applicable, *see* Section 9.3 *infra*.

252 *Down v. Newman*, 500 So.2d 1062, 1063 (Ala. 1986), similarly *see Piel v. Brown*, 361 So.2d 90, 95 (Ala. 1978). *See also Nestor v. Nestor*, 15 Ohio St.3d 143, 472 N.E.2d 1091, 1096 (1984), in which the court emphasized that the parties, during a period of twelve and a half years, "lived together sharing their lives, their families, their friends, the household duties and expenses and their worldly goods." *See further Gordon v. Gordon*, 27 Misc.2d 948, 211 N.Y.S.2d 265, 270 (1960), in which the court took into consideration the man's "drawing of pay based upon the plaintiff's being his dependant and reimbursement by the government for her traveling expenses as his wife." In the case of *Beck v. Beck*, 286 Ala. 692, 246 So.2d 420 (1971), the Supreme Court of Alabama held that cohabitation includes, *inter alia*, sharing household duties and payment of household expenses.

253 In the case of *Matter of Estate of Foster*, 376 S.E.2d 144, 149 (W.Va. 1988), the West Virginia Supreme Court of Appeals, applying the law of the District of Columbia, found a common law marriage proven, noting among many factors that the parties "maintained several joint bank accounts. In the bank book to at least one of these accounts was 'to be theirs as joint owners, subject to order of either, and balance at death of either to the survivor'." *See also Rosales v. Rosales*, 377 S.W.2d 661 (Tex.Civ. App. 1964). *Compare Grigsby v. Reib*, 105 Tex. 597, 153 S.W. 1124 (1913), in which the circumstance that the parties had separate bank accounts spoke against the fact that the parties lived together as husband and wife.

This factor is given particular importance in certain cases in which many of the other factors are not present, for example, if one of the spouses, due to employment or military duty, resides outside of the country, such that economic support perhaps may be the only factor indicating shared living.[254] If a significant relationship carrying the colorable attributes of a marriage-like relationship currently exists between two individuals, one of whom is already receiving spousal support from a former spouse, the issue arises whether it is appropriate for the former spouse to be forced to continue to pay spousal support. In one such case, the court based its finding on a lease agreement between the parties in a common law marriage, according to which one party received material financial gain or benefit. The court terminated the spousal support being received by that party from a former spouse, on the grounds that the party had entered into a cohabitation, in the context of a new common law marriage.[255]

6. *Emotional Support*

The courts, during the proving of the requirement of cohabitation, sometimes consider, albeit not so often, that the parties gave each other emotional as well as financial support. That a man and a woman actually support each other is, therefore, a component of the principle of cohabitation, though spouses, as a rule, do not have any legally sanctioned obligation. The question of whether one party was helpful, for example, by visiting the other during a hospitalization, has been raised in several cases. The presence of the surviving party at the deceased's funeral has been given significance as a circumstance relevant to proving whether the necessary holding out existed.[256]

7. *Shared Recreation*

Recreation, during recent years, has become an all-important family function. If both parties in a cohabitation are employed, they will spend only

---

254 In *Krug v. Krug*, 296 So.2d 715, 717-718 (Ala. 1974), the man did military duty in Vietnam, and the relationship with the woman, who lived in Alabama, consisted of contact by letters and certain economic support which the man sent to the woman. *See also In re Sander's Estate*, 67 Okla. 3, 168 P. 197 (1917), in which the parties did not live together, but in which the man made constant visits to the woman and contributed to her support.

255 In the case of *In re Marriage of Kuzanek*, 82 P.3d 528 (Kan.App. 2004), the court terminated maintenance payments to ex-wife after divorce when she entered a cohabitation relationship with third party although she and her cohabitant had a lease agreement.

256 In *Drummond v. Benson*, 133 S.W.2d 154, 161 (Tex.Civ.App.-San Antonio 1939), in which the requirement of cohabitation was not considered to be fulfilled, the court noted that the woman had not "attended the elderly man in such illness, or at least attended his funeral." *Compare Nestor v. Nestor*, 15 Ohio St.3d 143, 472 N.E.2d 1091 (1984), discussed *infra* with respect to holding out. In *Goodman v. McMillan*, 258 Ala. 125, 61 So.2d 55, 59 (1952), the court stated with respect to the woman: "[S]he never saw or attempted to see him again. She never visited him during his fatal illness and did not attend his funeral."

their free time together. Therefore, recreation is significant to an assessment of whether a cohabitation exists. However, it is rather unusual for this to be emphasized in the court's reasoning.[257] Another aspect is that mutual leisure activities, conducted in the presence of others, can be significant in an assessment of whether the requirements of holding out and reputation are fulfilled.

8. A Summation of the Factors

It is characteristic of the factors presented above that none of them is always considered necessary or sufficient to fulfill the requirement of cohabitation, regardless of the requirement's formulation. Neither is this listing exhaustive. The legal application must constantly be open to the consideration of new factors. If cohabitation is viewed as the execution of a marriage having the purpose of *consortium omnis vitae, i.e.,* companionship in all aspects of life, there is leeway for several relevant factors.[258] The above factors, however, are relevant in that one or several of them must always exist. Their internal weighting within the courts' assessments has varied, but the sexual relationship as well as the mutual home and household have always been given the greatest weight. In the same manner as in medieval canon law, a companionship *in lecto et in mensa* in American case law, today, is consequently given the meaning of a companionship "at bed and board." The durability of this concept is surprising in a time when gender roles and family patterns have constantly been changing.

9. The Length of the Cohabitation and the Point of Time for the Establishment of a Common Law Marriage

It can be argued that, given the nature of cohabitation, there must be a time requirement for the fulfillment of the different elements. The requirement of cohabitation cannot be considered fulfilled, one can conclude, if the parties simply lived together for several hours or days. There are examples in history in which a certain period of time was required for the cohabitation. The classical Roman *usus* marriage was established after one year of unbroken cohabitation.[259] It is surprising that no minimum

257 In *Brown v. Brown*, 234 Ga. 300, 215 S.E.2d 671, 673 (1975), the Georgia Supreme Court stated that the parties, during ten years, of which, however, only approximately one year was without a marriage impediment, "lived together, slept together, ate together, took vacations together and went on business trips together." The court found that the evidence was sufficient to prove the requirement of consummation. In the case of *In re Marriage of Gebhardt*, 426 N.W.2d 651, 653 (Iowa App. 1988), the fact that the parties had joint vacations was cited among a number of facts.

258 With respect to the purpose of the marriage contract in creating a *consortium omnis vitae, see* Section 6.3.1 *supra.*

259 After a cohabitation of one year, the woman legally entered into the man's family and under its marriage-like *manus.* If the woman, after the expiration of the year of *usus* wished to avoid this legal consequence, she could, by an absence of three nights (*trinoctium*) terminate the year of *usus.* If she thereafter continued the cohabitation, a new period began to run. *See* more on this in Chapter 2.3.2 *supra.*

time limits have been set for the establishment of a common law marriage in American legislation or in the case law.[260] To the contrary, the courts have often emphasized that no minimum time period is required.[261] Instead, it appears that the content of the cohabitation has been decisive. American case law also demonstrates that the courts, in many cases, have accepted surprisingly short periods of cohabitation.

The following three typical cases can serve as examples. In the case of *In re Estate of Fisher* (1970), the parties had known each other approximately one year, had a mutual residence for only five months, and were competent to live together as husband and wife during only two months of that, after the woman's earlier marriage was dissolved through a divorce decree. The Iowa Supreme Court, in addition to the requirement of a marriage contract for the establishment of a common law marriage, required not only cohabitation, but a "continuous cohabitation," finding that such a cohabitation existed.[262] In *Dowell v. Welch* (1978), the parties had lived together for six months, during which an impediment to the marriage existed for five months. Consequently, the marriage could only be established during a period of three weeks before the man died. For the establishment of a common law marriage, the Oklahoma Court of Appeals required, in addition to a marriage contract, the consummation of that agreement by cohabitation as husband and wife. The court found that the parties' illegitimate relationship after the removal of the marital

---

260 *Compare*, however, the legislation in New Hampshire, which does not recognize common law marriage, but which recognizes the survival of some of the legal consequences, assuming that the parties have lived together at least three years, *see, e.g.*, *Bisig v. Bisig*, 124 N.H. 372, 469 A.2d 1348 (1983).

261 *In re Estate of Burroughs*, 486 N.W.2d 113, 115 (Mich.App. 1992) (" There is no specified length of time the parties must live together, but there must be a constancy of dwelling together").

262 *In re Estate of Fisher*, 176 N.W.2d 801 (Iowa 1970). The requirement of "intent and agreement" was found proven with the support of circumstantial evidence during the short cohabitation. The case is summarized in Chapter 7.6.4 *supra*. Also in the case of *In re Marriage of Mosher*, 183 Ill.Dec. 911, 243 Ill.App.3d 97, 612 N.E.2d 838, 842 (1993) (applying Iowa law), the court found that a five-month period of cohabitation in Iowa was sufficient to fulfill the requirements of "continuous cohabitation" and "public declaration." To distinguish from *Fisher*, however, the *Mosher* court could not from these facts find the existence of an implied marriage contract (in contrast, see the dissent). Also in *Garduno v. Garduno*, 760 S.W.2d 735 (Tex. App.-Corpus Christi 1988), the parties lived together for six years, but the relevant cohabitation, after the woman received her divorce from another man, was no longer than a period of three to four months. The Texas Court of Appeals found that the requirement of "living together as husband and wife" was fulfilled and that a common law marriage was established. *Compare Ganesan v. Vallabhaneni*, 96 S.W.3d 345 (Tex.App.-Austin 2002), where the parties "at times" throughout the relationship of one and one-half years, held themselves out to be married and where a common law marriage was constituted. *See also Graham v. Graham*, 130 Colo. 225, 274 P.2d 605 (1954), in which the man began by renting a room from the woman, after which they lived together for four months. The Colorado Supreme Court, which for the establishment of a common law marriage required, in addition to a marriage contract, "cohabitation as husband and wife," found that such a marriage was proven.

impediment was transformed into a common law marriage.[263] A third example is the case of *Matter of Estate of Murnion* (1984), in which the parties lived together for the first four months in Washington, which does not recognize common law marriage, and thereafter for six months in Montana, which does recognize such marriages. The Montana Supreme Court, which required, in addition to a marriage contract, "cohabitation and public repute of marriage," found that a common law marriage had been established.[264]

There are also cases in which considerably shorter periods of cohabitation have been accepted, which raises the question whether the courts have simply made an exception to the requirement of cohabitation.[265]

Even though surprisingly short periods of cohabitation have been accepted as cohabitation, the courts have often emphasized that the relationship must be continual or permanent. Repeated short periods of cohabitation, interrupted by periods during which the parties have not lived together, have therefore not been accepted.[266] In *Richard v. Richard* (1935), the Oklahoma Supreme Court used a formulation that recurs in several cases, namely, that the cohabitation may not be "irregular, limited or partial."[267] The parties should not be able to say that they are husband and wife one day, and then again a week later, but in between deny the relationship if it is convenient for them to do so.[268]

The fact that the courts in several cases have set such a low requirement for the length of the cohabitation supports the view that the requisite of cohabitation is seen as an execution of the marriage contract. From this perspective, it is appropriate, in Georgia, to speak of the cohabitation as a consummation of the contract.[269] The contract in itself is not sufficient to

---

263 *Dowell v. Welch*, 574 P.2d 1089 (Okla.App. 1978).

264 *Matter of Murnion*, 212 Mont. 107, 686 P.2d 893 (1984).

265 The courts in New York in certain cases, when applying Georgia law, have found that a cohabitation of two to five days was sufficient for fulfilling the requirement of consummation, *see for example Kellard v. Kellard*, 13 Family Law Reporter 1490 (N.Y.Sup.Ct. 1987); *Coney v. R.S.R. Corp.*, 167 A.D.2d 582, 563 N.Y.S.2d 211(A.D. 3 Dep't 1990) and *Ventura v. Ventura*, 53 Misc.2d 881, 280 N.Y.S.2d 5 (Sup.Ct. 1967). *Compare Orr v. Bowen*, 648 F.Supp. 1510 (D.Nev. 1986) (applying Texas law), in which two to three visits to Texas for a maximum of two weeks were found sufficient. For further discussion as to these cases, which are unique as they concern short visits to common law states, *see* Chapter 10 *infra.*

266 In the case of *In re Estate of Phifer*, 629 P.2d 808 (Okla.App. 1981), the parties had been "separated from time to time." The court found no common law marriage proven during the four to five years they lived together under the same roof "on a part-time basis." The requirement of a "permanent relationship" was also made in the following cases: *Marshall v. State*, 537 P.2d 423 (Okla.Crim.App. 1975); *Earnheart v. Earnheart*, 979 P.2d 761, 763 (Okla.Civ.App. Div. 3 1999); *Matter of Estate of Stinchcomb*, 674 P.2d 26, 29 (Okla. 1983); and *Matter of Death of Boyd*, 959 P.2d 612 (Okla.Civ.App. Div. 1 1998).

267 *Richard v. Richard*, 172 Okla. 397, 45 P.2d 101 (1935). The case is actually a presumption case, *see* Chapter 9 *infra.*

268 *McChesney v. Johnson*, 79 S.W.2d 658, 659-660 (Tex.Civ.App.-Fort Worth 1934).

269 *Georgia Osteopathic Hosp. v. O'Neal*, 198 Ga.App. 770, 403 S.E.2d 235, 243 (1991).

establish a common law marriage. It must be executed. It must also be proven that the relationship did not stop simply with a contract, but that a marriage had also commenced. Still, it can be debated whether the purpose of the requirement of cohabitation, namely, to prevent the exploitation of the legal system, is achieved by allowing the shorter periods of time sometimes accepted by the courts.[270] If only the necessary cohabitation is considered, there are cases that actually fall within these parameters but ought not to be recognized as common law marriages.

The requirement of cohabitation, however, should not be viewed in isolation. It is applied together with the requirements of a contract and a holding out, which can appear restrictive in cases in which the relationships are insufficient. In a legal system strictly adhering to the requirement of a contract, the need for a longer period of cohabitation is reduced as compared to a legal system in which the legal consequences are solely tied to cohabitation. The need also appears less urgent than in the application of a marriage presumption based only on cohabitation and reputation as discussed further in Chapter 9. To the extent that the marriage contract is not expressed, it can be precarious to rely on an inferred agreement based upon a cohabitation that is short or insufficient. The fact that the courts all too often rely upon an implied marriage contract based upon a too short or insufficient cohabitation is a separate issue as discussed in Chapter 7 above.[271]

The fact that the cohabitation must be of a certain longer or shorter period of time also influences the contract requirement. Each of the requisites, namely, must be fulfilled at the same time. For example, in Texas, the requirements of (1) an agreement; (2) cohabitation; and (3) holding out, must be fulfilled simultaneously.[272] In cases in which the relationship commences with an oral contract, a marriage *de praesenti*, the requirements of cohabitation and holding out are not fulfilled by the parties moving in together until after the cohabitation has commenced, and the parties have outwardly represented themselves as spouses and gained acceptance as such. At this point of time, the oral marriage contract is not usually repeated. To then fulfill the requirement of a marriage contract,

---

270 With respect to the purpose of the requirement of cohabitation, *see People v. Lucero*, 747 P.2d 660, 664 (Colo. 1987) and the other cases listed in Section 8.3.1 *supra*.

271 *See* Section 7.8.2. *supra*.

272 *Ballesteros v. Jones*, 985 S.W.2d 485, 489 (Tex.App.-San Antonio 1998); and *Winfield v. Renfro*, 821 S.W.2d 640 (Tex.App.-Houston 1991). In *Bolash v. Heid*, 733 S.W.2d 698, 699 (Tex.Civ.App.-San Antonio 1987), the requirement of holding out was not considered fulfilled at the relevant point of time, but possibly later. *See also* cases from Georgia: *In re Estate of Love*, 274 Ga.App. 316,, 319, 618 S.E.2d 97, 101 (Ga. App. 2005); *Wright v. Goss*, 229 Ga.App. 393, 494 S.E.2d 23, 25 (1997); *Baynes v. Baynes*, 467 S.E.2d 195, 196 (1996); and *Brown v. Brown*, 234 Ga. 300, 215 S.E.2d 671, 673 (1975)("all at one period in time"). *See also* cases from Kansas: *Dixon v. Certainteed Corp.*, 915 F.Supp. 1158, 1160 (D.Kan. 1996); and *Thompson v. Barnhart*, 2005 WL 23347 (D.Kan. 2005).

a *consensus continuus*[273] is employed, *i.e.*, a contract that is viewed as continual with the support of the circumstances, as discussed in more depth in Chapters 6 and 7 above.

The requirement of cohabitation, which is a continuing factor,[274] raises the question as to whether a common law marriage can be considered established from the date when the cohabitation was commenced or later. In the few cases in which the question has been given any attention, a general rule has been applied, that the marriage is considered established when the cohabitation commences.[275] It ought to be understood that it is the date on which an acceptable cohabitation has been commenced, not a more sporadic or generally insufficient cohabitation. Further, an establishment assumes that the other requirements are fulfilled at the same point of time, for example, the parties' marriage-like *consensus* and holding out. To the degree that a certain period of time is required of the cohabitation, it follows that each such common law marriage begins as a nonmarital relationship, but when it is transformed into a marriage, the transformation includes even the past, the time during which the cohabitation was nonmarital from the beginning. This raises the question of how earlier decisions, based on the parties' nonmarital status, can be retried in the light that the parties, due to the continued cohabitation, actually had a marital status from the beginning. This question, though not discussed in any of the cases, but ought to be answered positively. The practical problem is minimized if consummation is considered to exist as soon as an acceptable cohabitation exists. If the cohabitation originally is insufficient, later becomes sufficient, the marriage may not be considered established before the cohabitation is sufficient, assuming that all the other requirements are also fulfilled. If the requirement of "marriage-like *consensus*" is not fulfilled from the beginning, but in contrast the requirement of cohabitation appears to be fulfilled, a marriage is not established until the contract requirement is met.

---

273 *See, e.g., Matter of Estate of Murnion*, 212 Mont. 107, 686 P.2d 893, 899 (1984).

274 *See, e.g., Matter of Estate of Alcorn*, 868 P.2d 629, 632 (Mont. 1994); and *In re Estate of Murnion*, 212 Mont. 107, 686 P.2d 893, 899 (1984).

275 In *State v. Newman*, 66 Mont. 180, 213 P. 805, 807 (1923), the court stated: "As a general rule, when a marriage is sought to be proved by conduct, cohabitation and repute, the date of the marriage in fact, which such conduct and repute tends to establish, is the date of the commencement of such conduct and repute, and not afterwards." *See also Welch v. All Persons*, 78 Mont. 370, 254 P. 179, 183, *rev'd*, 85 Mont. 114, 278 P. 110 (1929); *Wingfield v. Pool*, 38 S.W.2d 422, 423 (Tex.Civ.App.-Galveston 1931); and *Miller v. Townsend Lumber Co.*, 448 P.2d 148, 152 (Mont. 1968). *Compare Bolash v. Heid*, 733 S.W.2d 698, 699 (Tex.Civ.App.-San Antonio 1987), in which the requirement of holding out was not considered to be fulfilled at the relevant point of time, but possibly later. In *Ganesan v. Vallabhaneni*, 96 S.W.3d 345 (Tex.App.-Austin 2002), the court found that the parties were married as of February 23, 1995, the day when the woman moved to the man from California to Texas.

If the cohabitation has been commenced and the other requirements are fulfilled, a common law marriage is established. Insufficiencies in the different elements of the cohabitation that may arise later are not relevant with respect to the establishment of the marriage. These may concern sexual relationships with others, or breaking up the mutual home, household, etc., and are circumstances that can lead to the dissolution of an established marriage through divorce. In *National Union Fire Insurance Co. v. Britton* (1960), the parties first lived together for four years in Virginia and, thereafter, for ten years in the District of Columbia before the man was shot to death outside the bar where he worked. The court correctly considered it irrelevant that the parties, during the last two years of the man's life, had lived separately.[276]

8.5.3 Cohabitation Only to the Extent Possible

American courts have applied particularly diluted requirements of cohabitation, including cases in which the requirement of cohabitation in the traditional meaning has been set aside. These have been cases in which a complete cohabitation has not been possible because one of the parties, for example, as a result of employment, military duty, studies, or health, has had a separate residence in another area or country. In these cases, the courts have been cautious about formulating a new standard. Instead, given that each case rests on its own facts or something similar, they have emphasized that no far-reaching conclusions should be drawn from these cases. Despite this, one can conclude that cohabitation has only been required to the extent possible under the circumstances.[277] The three following cases are demonstrative.

In *Winfield v. Renfro* (1991), a case that created a legislative storm in Texas, the man, a baseball star, traveled often throughout the United States. In April of 1982, he spent three days with a woman in a hotel in Dallas where the parties entered into an agreement of marriage. In August of the same year, he returned to Texas. He bought a residence in Houston and he and the woman moved in together. He brought his bed and personal belongings to the house. Their mailbox had the man's name, "Winfield," on it. The man acted "husbandly," by running errands, working around the house, and generally behaving as if he were married. During the time, the woman became pregnant with his child, who was born later. The man stayed at the residence for a few weeks in August.

---

276 *Nat'l Union Fire Ins. Co. v. Britton*, 187 F.Supp. 359, 364 (D.D.C. 1960).

277 *Compare Erickson v. Stogner*, 90 U.S.App.D.C. 278, 195 F.2d 777 (1952), in which a woman made a claim against the man's life Ins. policy. Upon his return from the war, he was in the hospital for a year before he died. No cohabitation or contact generally occurred after the impediment to the marriage was removed. The woman argued that cohabitation was not necessary "when it is impossible." The D.C. Court of Appeals, however, found that no common law marriage had been proven.

The Texas Court of Appeals found that the parties, during the period from April to August, fulfilled the requirement of cohabitation in Texas. The decisive fact, with respect to the requirement of continuity in the cohabitation, appears to have been that the parties, despite the man's travels, adventures with other women, and limited time in Texas, were together "as often as the man could be in Texas."[278]

Even though the court applied a rather limited requirement of cohabitation, it can scarcely be maintained that the court completely set aside the requirement of cohabitation or made exceptions to it. The parties actually had a mutual home and household for a few weeks, when the woman was expecting his child. More interesting than the limited requirement of cohabitation is that the court took into consideration what was possible given the demands of the man's employment.

The requirement of cohabitation appears to have been watered down even more in a different case from Texas, where the cohabitation was extremely limited or even nonexistent because of the man's foreign employment. In *Bolash v. Heid* (1987), the man and woman had previously been married to each other. The woman lived in San Antonio, Texas, while the man worked in Nigeria. While in San Antonio, the woman visited him at his hotel room. Thereafter, they went to her apartment, spent the night, had sex, and "agreed to be husband and wife." The man returned to Nigeria the next day. During the next four years, he traveled several times to Texas. On each occasion, the parties were together. The Texas Court of Appeals found that the requirement of cohabitation, requiring that the cohabitation occur in Texas, was fulfilled, as the parties had lived together as husband and wife "to the extent possible under the circumstances."[279]

---

278 *Winfield v. Renfro*, 821 S.W.2d 640 (Tex.App.-Houston 1991). It ought to be noted that the court's judgment was limited to the question presented to the jury, namely whether the parties had entered into a common law marriage "on or about April 11, 1982." The court considered a period of four months after this date. *Id.* at 646-647. With respect to the issue of whether the requirement of holding out had been fulfilled in the case, *see* Section 8.6.2. *infra.* With respect to the issue of whether a marriage contract existed, *see* Section 7.4. *supra. Compare Walton v. Walton*, 203 S.W. 133 (Tex.Civ.App.-Galveston 1918), in which the parties lived together for four to five years and had three mutual children. Continuity, however, was found insufficient as the man, employed by the railroad, was constantly traveling. In addition, the woman admitted that the man had a "sweetheart" in every city, *see supra* the section regarding exclusive relationships. The requirement of cohabitation, however, was considered to be fulfilled. As the parties also represented themselves outwardly as spouses, a common law marriage was found proven.

279 *Bolash v. Heid*, 733 S.W.2d 698, 699 (Tex.Civ.App.-San Antonio 1987). An older case, in which a very low requirement of cohabitation was applied, is *Employer's Mut. Ins. Co. v. Morgulski*, 69 Colo. 223, 193 P. 725, 726 (1920), in which the woman had lived with her parents. The man visited her upon several occasions, and the visits were sometimes weekly, and perhaps a month upon one occasion. They stayed in the same room. They had sexual relations. The man did not contribute to the woman's maintenance with the exception of a few dollars. The relationship was known to the woman's mother, but kept secret from her father. The man, when he began his employment with the Oakdale Company, filled out an employment

A different issue arises because the courts, in neither *Winfield* nor *Bolash*, found that a common law marriage was proven, because the requirement that the parties represented to others that they were married was not fulfilled, a circumstance discussed further below.

It can scarcely be argued that the parties in *Bolash* had a mutual home and household. The cohabitation was mainly limited to the man's visits to the woman. The court, therefore, made an exception to the requirement of cohabitation in its traditional meaning. However, there are cases in which the requirement is even further limited and in which the parties generally did not meet at all during the period of time they were competent to enter into a marriage, but during which a common law marriage was found to have been established. This has been the case if the parties were prevented from meeting each other because of military duty.

For example, in *Krug v. Krug* (1974), the parties had married on December 31, 1969. At that time, an impediment to the marriage existed because the woman's previous marriage to another man was not yet dissolved, and thus the new marriage was invalid. The parties lived together, however, and represented themselves outwardly as husband and wife until January 19, 1970, when the man was called to military duty in Vietnam. On February 21, the impediment against the marriage was removed, and on May 14 of the same year, the man was killed in combat. The main issue at trial was whether a common law marriage had been established between the parties during the three months of their relationship, after the removal of the marital impediment. They had not met during that time. Their relationship consisted of almost daily letters to each other. The man addressed his letters to "Mrs. Raymond H. Krug." They also sent cassette tapes to each other. He sent money for her support, and wrote asking about her desires to create a family. They planned a future together. No sexual, residential, or household relationship was possible.

The Alabama Supreme Court found that there was a sufficient living together to gain the recognition of the public that they were living as husband and wife rather than "in a state of concubinage" and that the parties therefore were entitled to the protections following from a common law

application that he signed, and from which it appeared that he was married and that his wife's name was Lillian Morgulski and that in the event of an accident, information should be left with her at her mother's address. When the woman, upon the death of the man, claimed death benefits as she was the man's widow in a common law marriage, the opposing party objected that a marriage contract did not constitute a marriage if cohabitation did not exist, and that the cohabitation must be "not merely sexual intercourse on visits of more or less length, yet temporary, but actual dwelling together in the usual manner of married people, dwelling, as one court has expressed it, 'with the habit and repute of marriage'." The Colorado Supreme Court, certainly finding that the opposing party's requirement of cohabitation was correct, however, found that the "documentary evidence" showed that the deceased considered the woman "as his wife," which gave their cohabitation the required character.

marriage.[280] It is apparent that the court required only a minimum of cohabitation, whose objective facts consisted mainly of letter contact and a certain economic support. Thus, the court, as in *Bolash*, must be said to have made an exception to the requirement of cohabitation in the traditional meaning.

From these three cases, *Winfield*, *Bolash*, and *Krug*, it can be seen that the courts, in varying degrees, have limited the requirement of cohabitation by accepting a very short cohabitation, a relationship consisting only of visits, and a cohabitation created through letter contact and a certain amount of economic support. It is common in these cases for the courts to examine the circumstances and take into consideration that no further cohabitation was possible. Of course, it is most clear that the parties did not voluntarily choose their situation in the case of the man being called to military duty. That situation can be compared to a hospital stay.[281] In all three of the cases, it can be argued that the parties lived together as a formally married couple would live in the same situation.

There is a danger of taking the requirement of cohabitation too lightly. An unintended effect of setting aside the requirement of cohabitation is

---

280 *Krug v. Krug*, 296 So.2d 715, 717-718 (Ala. 1974). With respect to the requirement of cohabitation's varying formation in the case law from Alabama, *see* Section 8.4 *supra*. A similar case where cohabitation was not possible due to military duty is *Burdine v. Burdine*, 206 Okla. 170, 242 P.2d 148 (1952), in which the man, after his return from World War II, abandoned the woman, who requested a divorce and claimed alimony with respect to the fact that a common law marriage had been established. The man contested that such a marriage existed. The Oklahoma Supreme Court, however, found that a common law marriage had been proven, despite the fact that the parties "did not dwell under the same roof." *Compare Sturm v. Sturm*, 111 N.J.Eq. 579, 163 A. 5 (1932). Naturally, this problem does not arise in a state such as Pennsylvania that does not have any requirement of cohabitation. For example, in *Com v. Amann*, 58 Pa.D. & C. 669 (1947), the man, having done military service in the Philippines, and the woman, residing in Pennsylvania, each separately signed a written marriage contract, which constituted a common law marriage. Another case, where the parties did not have a mutual home nor household, but where a common law marriage was similarly found proven, is *In re Sander's Estate*, 67 Okla. 3, 168 P. 197 (1917), concerning a European-American man named Sanders and a Native-American woman named Peggy. The man frequently visited the woman who lived with her parents during a period of seven to eight years. He contributed continually to her and their mutual children's maintenance. The Oklahoma Supreme Court, which in addition to a marriage contract required that the parties "enter into and thereafter maintain the marriage relation," found a common law marriage proven. The court stated: "Sanders would visit Peggy at the home of her parents very frequently—some of the evidence showing every Saturday and often during the week—and some of the evidence tends to show that he was there almost every day. He would frequently stay all day and all night, and he and Peggy would occupy the same bed." It cannot be seen from the summary of the fact why the parties did not live together.

281 *See In re Estate of Hendrickson*, 248 Kan. 72, 805 P.2d 20 (1991), in which the parties, in the presence of the media and TV, entered into a marriage contract at the hospital the man was staying at, and in which the parties' relationship lasted approximately two weeks before the man died. The Kansas Supreme Court, however, not more closely examining the requirement of holding out, found that a common law marriage had been established.

the very abuses that this requirement was meant to prevent. One can argue that the requirement of a contract certainly is an added restraint. However, a contract is not very meaningful if the parties do not follow it with a complete cohabitation, but instead continue with only short visits or letter contact, which could indicate that one of the parties has doubts about fulfilling the contract. To not uphold the requirement of cohabitation can, therefore, create problems as to legal certainty. A lawsuit claiming an unexecuted contract could surprise the other party. An important function here, naturally, is fulfilled by the requirement of holding out. In neither *Winfield* nor *Bolash* was a common law marriage found proven, because the requirement of holding out was not fulfilled. Even in a relationship based on short visits, the parties can, on these occasions, outwardly represent themselves so as to give a "false reputation" as spouses. Consequently, the requirement of cohabitation has a function.

8.6 THE REQUIREMENTS OF HOLDING OUT AND REPUTATION

The jurisdictions invoking cohabitation as a necessary requirement for the establishment of a common law marriage, with the exception of Georgia[282] and most probably the District of Columbia,[283] each appears to

282 *See, e.g., Hayes v. Hay*, 92 Ga.App. 88, 88 S.E.2d 306 (1955): "It is not necessary to the validity of a common law marriage that it be publicized, and the mere fact that it is kept secret does not authorize the jury to find that it did not exist." *Compare Lefkoff v. Sicro*, 189 Ga. 554, 6 S.E.2d 687 (1939), in which the court maintained that the cohabitation need not be public. Even if holding out and reputation are not necessary requirements in Georgia and in the District of Columbia, these circumstances, however, are considered as evidentiary facts for the existence of a marriage contract and for the "consummation" and "consummation by cohabitation," respectively, of the marriage contract necessary in these states. For example, in *Baynes v. Baynes*, 219 Ga.App. 848, 467 S.E.2d 195, 197 (1996), the court found that the parties' insufficient holding out as spouses was evidence that they "had not intended to enter into a binding marriage."

283 *Mesa v. United States*, 875 A.2d 79 (D.C.App. 2005). Already in *Hoage v. Murch Bros. Const. Co.*, 60 App.D.C. 218, 50 F.2d 983, 985 (1931), the court stated that a marriage contract "consummated by cohabitation" constitutes a common law marriage. This statement is cited later cited in *U.S. Fid. & Guar. Co. v. Britton* 106 U.S.App.D.C. 58, 269 F.2d 249, 251 (D.C.Cir. 1959), in which the court maintained that the contract "must be consummated by cohabitation." No requirement of holding out as husband and wife in addition to the requirement of cohabitation was generally made in the case law. In contrast, the parties' holding out is accepted as an evidentiary fact for the existence of the marriage contract as well as cohabitation. *See Caldwell v. Caldwell*, 140 A.2d 926, 927 (D.C.App. 1958), in which the Municipal Court of Appeals appears to have applied a presumption based upon "cohabitation and reputation" with the result that no common law marriage was found proven. *Compare Troshinsky v. Rosin*, 428 A.2d 847 (D.C.App. 1981), in which the Court of Appeals did not find a common law marriage established with reference to the fact that the parties did not have "a general reputation in the community as being married." The court, however, did not more closely elaborate as to whether this reputation was a necessary requirement or simply an evidentiary fact.

have the additional requirement that the parties must outwardly represent themselves as spouses with respect to third parties. This requisite focuses either upon the parties' actions in themselves, *i.e.*, their "holding out" as spouses, or upon the effects thereof, *i.e.*, their reputation as husband and wife.[284] A requirement including both of these elements also exists.[285] In exceptional cases, the courts can state the objective requirement as "holding out" or reputation instead of "cohabitation."[286]

The requirement of outward representation appears to a large degree to serve the purpose of preventing clandestine marriages.[287] If the parties

---

Compare Ram v. Ramharack, 571 N.Y.S.2d 190, 191 (Sup. 1991), in which Supreme Court in New York, applying the law of the District of Columbia, in addition to the marriage contract and the cohabitation appears to have applied a requirement of "a holding out as husband and wife."

284 *Brinckle v. Brinckle*, 12 Phila. 232, 234 (1877) ("It is the reputation arising from their holding themselves out to the world as occupying that relation to which the law refers").

285 The legislation in Utah requires in addition to the fact that the parties hold themselves out, that they also have "acquired a uniform and general reputation as husband and wife," *see* UTAH CODE ANN. § 30-1-4.5 (1987). Even in several cases in Ohio, however rather inconsistently, both holding out and reputation are mentioned. *See Kowalik v. Kowalik*, 118 Ohio App.3d 141, 691 N.E.2d 1152 (1997) ("holding of themselves out as husband and wife" and "being regarded as husband and wife"); *State v. Phelps*, 100 Ohio App.3d 187, 652 N.E.2d 1032, 1035 (1995); *State v. DePew*, 38 Ohio St.3d 275, 528 N.E.2d 542, 549 (1988); *In re McLaughlin's Estate*, 197 N.E.2d 578, 581 (Ohio P.Ct. 1963); *In re Estate of Hammonds*, 39 Ohio Misc. 96, 315 N.E.2d 843, 847 (1973); and *In re Estate of Soeder*, 4 Misc. 96, 209 N.E.2d 175, 7 Ohio App. 271, 220 N.E.2d 547, 557 (Ohio App. 1966).

286 In Kansas, the requirement of cohabitation ought to be considered included in the requirement of "holding out of each other as husband and wife," *see Chandler v. Central Oil Corp., Inc.*, 253 Kan. 50, 853 P.2d 649, 650 (1993). *Compare Brinckle v. Brinckle*, 12 Phila. 232, 234 (1877), where the court spoke of "matrimonial cohabitation, where the parties not only live together as husband and wife, but hold themselves out to the world as sustaining that honorable relation to each other." *See also McChesney v. Johnson*, 79 S.W.2d 658, 659 (Tex.Civ.App.-Fort Worth 1934), which in addition to the contract expressly required only a "holding out to the public as man and wife." However, this generally is considered to assume cohabitation. It appears more important to consider the requirement as a complement rather than an alternative to cohabitation. It is expressly understood as such in the case of *In re Estate of Soeder*, 7 Ohio.App.2d 271, 220 N.E.2d 547 (1966). In a case from Rhode Island, conduct that gives rise to a "general reputation" that the parties are husband and wife is discussed, *see Souza v. O'Hara*, 121 R.I. 88, 395 A.2d 1060, 1061 (1978).

287 In *Matter of Estate of Vandenhook*, 855 P.2d 518, 520 (Mont. 1993), the court stated: "As to repute, a common law marriage cannot be kept secret by the parties." In *Sulfridge v. Kindle*, 2005 WL 1806482 (Ohio App. 4 Dist. 2005), appellant admitted that he did not inform his own brother the parties were married because it was their "secret." This statement was a strong reason against the existence of a common law marriage. In *Wristen v. Wristen*, 119 S.W.2d 1104, 1108 (Tex.Civ.App.-Eastland 1938), the woman was asked the following at trial as to the parties' relationship: "Q: It was kept a secret? A. Yes. Q. And never was proclaimed publicly? A. No, because he didn't believe in being public." The court, which found that the requirement of cohabitation was fulfilled, however, stated that the parties had not lived together "professedly." In *Ex parte Threet*, 160 Tex. 482, 333 S.W.2d 261, 364 (1960), the court, as a condition for the establishment of a common law marriage, required "holding out to the public that the couple are husband and wife," stating with respect to the secrecy surrounding the relationship: "Under the Texas decisions,

do not wish to announce their marriage through a wedding ceremony, they must, through their actions, announce their relationship. The weight given to this requirement the case is clear in the references to the parties' outward actions as "the acid test."[288] Secrecy with respect to the marriage has rarely been accepted. This has been the case when a relationship has been kept secret for fear of the harm that would result if one of the parties' families knew.[289] The case law also demonstrates that the purpose of the requisite, to prevent abuse of the system, is endangered if the courts take the requirement of holding out too lightly.

8.6.1 The Formulation of the Requisite Holding Out

The requirement of holding out focuses on the parties' outward actions. Its formulation varies somewhat. Commonly, it is stated as a requirement of "holding out as husband and wife," *i.e.*, that the parties outwardly,

---

there can be no secret common law marriage as such. The secrecy is inconsistent and irreconcilable with the requirement of a public holding out that the couple are living together as husband and wife." With reference thereto, the court found that no common law marriage had been established. However, it may be noted, that the relationship in question was not kept secret, as the woman's nearest friends were aware of it. *Compare Quinton v. Webb*, 207 Okla. 133, 248 P.2d 586 (1952), in which the Oklahoma Supreme Court maintained that secret meetings did not fulfill the requirement of a marriage-like cohabitation: "Secret meetings or nights clandestinely spent together do not constitute cohabitation in the marital sense. Such occasional associations are meretricious and, though often repeated, do not constitute cohabitation as man and wife as the term is used in considering common law marriages." *See also James v. James*, 253 S.W. 1112 (Tex.Civ.App.-San Antonio 1923). With respect to secret relationships, *see also Tompkins v. State*, 774 S.W.2d 195 (Tex.Cr.App. 1987). In *Walter v. Walter*, 433 S.W.2d 183, 186, 191, 194 (Tex.Civ. App.-Houston (1st Dist.) 1968), the woman admitted, with respect to the parties' marriage contract, that it "has been a secret." The court stated: "There can be no secret common law marriage." *See also In re Estate of Dallman*, 228 N.W.2d 187, 190 (Iowa 1975); *In re Estate of Soeder*, 7 Ohio App.2d 271, 220 N.E.2d 547, 561-563 (1966); *In re Estate of De Witte*, 140 Ind.App. 114, 222 S.E.2d 285, 288 (1966); *Anderson v. Anderson*, 235 Ind. 113, 131 N.E.2d 301, 305-306 (1956); *In re Dittman's Estate*, 124 Ind. App. 198, 115 N.E.2d 125, 127 (1953); *In re Trope's Estate*, 199 Okla. 453, 124 P.2d 733, 736-737 (1942); and *Scilling v. Parsons*, 110 Ind.App. 52, 36 N.E.2d 958, 960-961 (1941).

288 It was understood thus in the case of *In re Estate of Soeder*, 7 Ohio.App.2d 271, 220 N.E.2d 547 (1966). The view that the parties' outward representations constitute "the acid test" recurs often. *See, e.g., Miller v. Sutherland*, 131 Mont. 175, 309 P.2d 322 (1957); *McClish v. Rankin*, 14 So.2d 714 (Fla. 1943); and *In re Schneider's Will*, 206 Misc. 18, 131 N.Y.S.2d 215 (Surr.Ct. 1954).

289 *See Shattuck v. Shattuck's Estate*, 118 Minn. 60, 136 N.W. 409 (1912), in which the parties lived together approximately three years. Very few, albeit some, persons had knowledge of the relationship. The relationship was kept secret due to the woman's well-founded fear that her family would hurt her if they were aware of the relationship. The court, which generally considered secrecy an impediment to the establishment of a common law marriage, found reason to make an exception with respect to the named reason. Secrecy for the purpose of not losing employment, in contrast, has not been accepted, *see Miller v. Sutherland*, 131 Mont. 175, 309 P.2d 322 (1957).

before others, represented themselves as husband and wife.[290] In Texas, in which the expression *holding out* was previously dominant in the case law, but where common law marriage has been regulated by statute since 1969, the law states, without any material deviation from the case law, that the parties must have "represented to others that they were married."[291] Certain courts formulate the requirement of holding out as a requirement of "public declaration" that the parties are husband and wife, thereby

290 The legislation in Utah contains the requirement that the parties "hold themselves out" as husband and wife, *see* UTAH CODE ANN. § 30-1-4.5 (1987). *See also* from Kansas, *Chandler v. Central Oil Corp., Inc.*, 253 Kan. 50, 853 P.2d 649, 650 (1993), in which the court applies the requirement of "holding out of each other as husband and wife to public"; and *Dixon v. Certainteed Corp.*, 915 F.Supp. 1158, 1160 (D.Kan. 1996). *See* from Oklahoma, where the formulations vary, but the court, in the case of *Matter Estate of Stinchcomb*, 674 P.2d 26, 29 (Okla. 1983), required that the parties "hold themselves out publicly as man and wife"; *Earnheart v. Earnheart*, 979 P.2d 761, 763 (Okla.Civ.App. Div. 3 1999); *Richardson v. State*, 744 S.W.2d 65, 73 (Tex. Crim.App. 1987)(applying Oklahoma law); and *United States v. Staggs*, 881 F.2d 1546, 1550 (10th Cir. 1989)(applying Oklahoma law). *See* from Ohio, the Sixth Circuit Court's description in *Smereczynski v. Sec'y, DHHS*, 944 F.2d 296, 298 (6th Cir. 1991) of the requirement as "holding out to the public as man and wife." It is more common, however, that the courts in Ohio formulate the requisite as a requirement of reputation, *see, e.g., Nestor v. Nestor*, 15 Ohio St.3d 143, 472 N.E.2d 1091, 1094 (1984). Only exceptionally have the courts, when applying the law of the District of Columbia, in addition to the requirement of cohabitation, formulated a requirement of holding out, *compare Ram v. Ramharack*, 571 N.Y.S.2d 190, 191 (1991). In *Napier v. Napier*, 555 So.2d 1112, 1113 (Ala.Civ.App. 1989), the court spoke of the fact that the parties "hold themselves out to the community as husband and wife." Considerably more common among the courts in Alabama, however, is to formulate the requisite as a requirement of "public recognition," *see* § 8.6.3 *infra*.

291 *See Ex parte Threet*, 160 Tex. 482, 333 S.W.2d 361 (1960), in which as a condition for the establishment of a common law marriage, in addition to an "agreement to be husband and wife" and "a living together as husband and wife," the court even required "a holding out to the public that the couple are husband and wife." The last prong was incorporated into the Texas legislation regulating common law marriage in 1969. The text states, without any material changes, the requirement that the parties must have "represented to others that they were married." *See* TEX. FAM. CODE. ANN. § 1.91(a)(2) (Vernon's 1975), currently TEX. FAM. CODE ANN. § 2.401(a)(2) (Vernon 2005). *See also Morris v. Morris*, 403 S.W.2d 295, 296 (Tex.Civ. App. 1971); and *Conlon v. Schweiker*, 537 F.Supp. 158, 159 (N.D.Tex. 1982). The requirement is applied today, *see Lorensen v. Weaber*, 840 S.W.2d 644 (Tex.App.-Dallas 1992), *rev'd*, 865 S.W.2d 929 (Tex. 1993); and *Dalworth Trucking Co. v. Bulen*, 924 S.W.2d 728, 737 (Tex.App.-Texarkana 1996). In *Welch v. State*, 908 S.W.2d 258, 265 (Tex.App.-El Paso 1995), the formulation "represented to the general public that they were married" is used. Despite statutory changes, the requirement today is sometimes described as "holding out," *see State v. Mireles*, 904 S.W.2d 885, 888 (Tex.App.-Corpus Christi 1995); *Ballesteros v. Jones*, 985 S.W.2d 485, 491 (Tex.App.-San Antonio 1998); *Lee v. Lee*, 981 S.W.2d 903, 906 (Tex.App.-Houston (1st Dist.) 1998); *Nava v. Reddy Partnership/Quail Chase*, 988 S.W.2d 346 (Tex.App.-Houston (1st Dist.) 1999); and *Ganesan v. Vallabhaneni*, 96 S.W.3d 345 (Tex.App.-Austin 2002). In *Mills v. Mest*, 94 S.W.3d 72, 75 (Tex.App.-Houston (14th Dist.) 2002), the court held that after 1989 legislation, the law requires "more convincing" evidence than before as to the holding out.

referring to their words as well as their actions.[292] The courts can also formulate the requirement in more general terms, by requiring that the cohabitation be "open"[293] or "public,"[294] or that the parties should have lived together "professedly" as husband and wife, by which it is understood that they, before the authorities, have represented themselves as such.[295] In certain cases, the courts have not made any specific requirement of holding out, but rather have intended that it be encompassed in the requirement of "assumption of the marital relation,"[296] or in the requirement of "assumption of marital rights, duties or obligations,"[297] as discussed in the previous section. Even though the literal meanings of these different expressions are distinguishable, the case law shows that the courts have generally assigned the same legal content to the different formulations.

8.6.2 Relevant Factors

The parties' holding out as spouses can consist of words as well as of actions. Naturally, it is their outward actions and behavior that is

---

292 The locution was common during the 1960s in the cases from Iowa, *see In re Long's Estate*, 251 Iowa 1042, 102 N.W.2d 76, 79 (1960); even to today, *see In re Marriage of Gebhardt*, 426 N.W.2d 651, 652 (Iowa App. 1988) and *Conklin v. MacMillan Oil Co.*, 557 N.W.2d 102, 105 (Iowa App. 1996). In the case of *Matter of Estate of Stodola*, 519 N.W.2d 97 (Iowa App. 1994), the court elaborated by stating "general and substantial public declarations that the parties are husband and wife." With the expression "public declaration" is included holding out, *see for example In re Estate of Dallman*, 228 N.W.2d 187, 190 (Iowa 1975); *Conklin v. MacMillan Oil Co.*, 557 N.W.2d 102, 105 (Iowa App. 1996); *Blessing v. Deere & Co.*, 985 F.Supp. 899, 904 (S.D.Iowa 1997) (applying Iowa law); *Fritz v. Mork*, 2001 Iowa App. LEXIS 594 (2001); *In re Marriage of Martin*, 681 N.W.2d 612, 618 (Iowa 2004); *Toom v. Toom*, 710 N.W.2d 258 (Iowa App. 2005); and *Snyder-Murphy v. City of Cedar Rapids*, 695 N.W.2d 44 (Iowa App. 2005).

293 *See Quinton v. Webb*, 207 Okla. 133, 248 P.2d 586 (1952), in which "open cohabitation" is mentioned.

294 *See O'Malley v. O'Malley*, 46 Mont. 549, 129 P. 501, Ann.Cas. 1914B, 662 (1913), in which the court stated that the commencement of a marriage-like relationship is to be "public," meaning that parties, not only to each other, but also "toward the world," behave so that "people generally would take them to be married."

295 *Salvini v. Salvini*, 2 S.W.2d 963, 965 (Tex.Civ.App.-El Paso 1928); and *De Shazo v. Christian*, 191 S.W.2d 495, 496 (Tex.App.-Amarillo 1946). As a synonym to "professedly," sometimes "avowedly" is used. The word "profess" has also been considered to mean "to make open declaration of, to make public declaration or avowal," while "professed" has been seen to mean "openly declared, avowed, acknowledged or claimed," *see Wristen v. Wristen*, 119 S.W.2d 1104, 1106 (Tex.Civ.App.-Eastland 1938). *Compare Grigsby v. Reib*, 105 Tex. 597, 153 S.W. 1124, 1130 (1913) ("The cohabitation must be professedly as husband and wife, and public, so that, by their conduct toward each other, they may be known as husband and wife"). The expression has older roots, *see Hutchins v. Kimmel*, 31 Mich. 126, 18 Am.Rep. 164 (1875).

296 *See Ridley v. Compton*, 215 Miss. 532, 61 So.2d 341 (1952), in which the court spoke of "public assumption" of the marriage-like relationship, with which is required parties "holding themselves out to the public as being man and wife."

297 *See* IDAHO CODE ANN. § 32-201 (1983), and the courts' interpretation of the statute, as found in *Freiburghaus v. Freiburghaus*, 103 Idaho 679, 651 P.2d 944, 947 (App. 1982); and *Case of Graham*, 103 Idaho 824, 654 P.2d 1377 (1982) (the requirement of holding out was not considered to be fulfilled).

relevant.[298] In almost every case, however, the parties' oral statements concerning their marital status are also cited, albeit unnecessarily.[299] Several statements, viewed as admissions and declarations constituting evidence of the existence of a marriage contract, as discussed in Chapter 7, are better categorized as holding out.[300] Holding out can include the parties presenting each other as husband and wife,[301] stating in different documents that they are married;[302] the woman using the

---

298 *Ballesteros v. Jones*, 985 S.W.2d 485, 490 (Tex.App.-San Antonio 1998); *Winfield v. Renfro*, 821 S.W.2d 640, 648 (Tex.App.-Houston 1991); *Matter of Estate of Giessel*, 734 S.W.2d 27, 31 (Tex.App.-Houston (1st Dist.) 1987); and *Rosales v. Rosales*, 377 S.W.2d 661, 664 (Tex.Civ.App.-Corpus Christi 1964).

299 *Lee v. Lee*, 981 S.W.2d 903, 906 (Tex.App.-Houston (1st Dist.) 1998); *Winfield v. Renfro*, 821 S.W.2d 640, 648 (Tex.App.-Houston 1991); and *Associated Indem. Corp. v. Billberg*, 172 S.W.2d 157, 164 (Tex.App.-Amarillo 1943).

300 The double function appears clearly, for example, in *Russell v. Russell*, 838 S.W.2d 909, 917 (Tex.App.-Beaumont 1992), in which the court stated: "We believe that this objective evidence of holding out to be husband and wife, brought about at the insistence of appellant, was evidence of sufficient weight for the trial court to 'infer' an agreement to be married."

301 *Hall v. Duster*, 727 So.2d 834, 837 (Ala.Civ.App. 1999). In *Ballesteros v. Jones*, 985 S.W.2d 485, 490 (Tex.App.-San Antonio 1998), the fact that the parties, in connection with taking flights and staying at hotels, registered as Mr. and Mrs., was cited. *See also Dalworth Trucking Co. v. Bulen*, 924 S.W.2d 728, 737 (Tex.App.-Texarkana 1996); and *Matter of Estate of Alcorn*, 868 P.2d 629, 632 (Mont. 1994). In *Conlon v. Schweiker*, 537 F.Supp. 158, 159 (N.D.Tex. 1982), it was found that the parties cohabited, but the woman's presentation of the man before her friends as "mine" was considered insufficient support for the proposition that they outwardly represented themselves as husband and wife. With respect to presentations, *see also Downs v. Newman*, 500 So.2d 1062 (Ala. 1986) (the fact that the parties often presented each other as spouses was given weight); and *Carson v. Kee*, 677 S.W.2d 283 (Tex.Civ. App.-Fort Worth 1984). In *Case of Graham*, 103 Idaho 824, 654 P.2d 1377, 1380 (1982), the requirement of holding out was found not fulfilled with reference to the fact that the woman never used the name "Mrs. Graham or represented herself as the decedent's wife." *Compare Ex parte Threet*, 160 Tex. 482, 333 S.W.2d 361, 364 (1960), in which the parties in certain situations presented each other as spouses, but in which no common law marriage was found established as the cohabitation occurred secretly in the parental home and only a few friends were informed as to the marriage. Occasional references to the parties as "husband and wife" were considered insufficient according to the *dictum* in *Gary v. Gary*, 490 S.W.2d 929, 934 (Tex.Civ.App.-Tyler 1973). *Compare Matter of Estate of Giessel*, 734 S.W.2d 27 (Tex. App.-Houston (1st Dist.) 1987) (where the parties only occasionally presented each other as spouses, but where they, during a cohabitation of twenty years, in the community received the reputation as spouses and where a common law marriage was found proven); and *Gillaspie v. Blair Constr. Co.*, 192 Kan. 455, 388 P.2d 647, 648 (1964) (presentations as married relevant).

302 This can occur, for example, in documents connecting to a loan for the purchase of a house, *Bolash v. Heid*, 733 S.W.2d 698 (Tex.Civ.App.-San Antonio 1987), a will and a power of attorney, *Flavin v. Flavin*, 523 S.W.2d 94 (Tex.Civ.App.-Houston 1975), a credit application, *Persons v. Persons*, 666 S.W.2d 560 (Tex.App.-Houston 1984), a patient's medical journal, *Ortiz v. Santa Rosa Med. Center*, 702 S.W.2d 701 (Tex.App.-San Antonio 1987), a life insurance policy, *Grigsby v. Grigsby*, 757 S.W.2d 163 (Tex.App.-San Antonio 1988), or with an instrument of adoption, *De Beque v. Ligon*, 292 S.W. 157 (Tex.Comm'n App. 1927). The fact that the parties, in their tax declarations, have stated that they were married, is often cited, *see, e.g., Russell v. Russell*, 838 S.W.2d 909, 915 (Tex.App.-Beaumont 1992); *Gillaspie v. Blair Constr. Co.*, 192 Kan. 455, 388 P.2d 647, 648 (1964); and *Aldana v. Aldana*, 42 S.E.2d 661, 664

man's family name;[303] the parties being referred to as a son-in-law or daughter-in-law by their respective parents;[304] the parties wearing rings,[305] having joint bank accounts,[306] naming each other as beneficiaries on insurance policies;[307] etc.

In a similar fashion, to support that no holding out as husband and wife existed, the following circumstances can be cited: the parties have stated that they are single or unmarried;[308] the woman is the man's fiancée,

---

(Tex.Civ.App.-El Paso 1931). An isolated statement that the woman is the man's wife has, however, limited evidentiary weight, *see, e.g., Whitworth v. Whitworth*, 256 Ala. 296, 54 So.2d 575, 577 (1951).

303 *In re Glasco*, 619 S.W.2d 567, 570 (Tex.Civ.App.-San Antonio 1981); *Kirk v. Mattison*, 497 So.2d 120 (Ala. 1986); and *Wingfield v. Pool*, 38 S.W.2d 422 (Tex.Civ.App. 1931). In *Graham v. Graham*, 130 Colo. 225, 274 P.2d 605, 607 (1954), the fact that the woman, during the four months in which she lived with the man, stated to neighbors: "I am Mrs. Dobbin," was given weight. *See also Carpenter v. Carpenter*, 617 N.Y.S.2d 903, 904 (A.D. 2 Dep't 1994) (a presumption case).

304 In *Hall v. Duster*, 727 So.2d 834, 837 (Ala.Civ.App. 1999), the fact that the funeral program, in which the man was referred to as the deceased's son-in-law, was considered relevant in the assessment as to whether the parties had been recognized as husband and wife.

305 *Matter of Estate of Alcorn*, 868 P.2d 629, 632 (Mont. 1994); *Harris v. Harris*, 2004 WL 2896422 (Ohio App. 9 Dist.).

306 *Hall v. Duster*, 727 So.2d 834, 837 (Ala.Civ.App. 1999); *Matter of Estate of Alcorn*, 868 P.2d 629, 632 (Mont. 1994); *Carpenter v. Carpenter*, 617 N.Y.S.2d 903, 905 (A.D. 2 Dep't 1994) (a presumption case); *Flores v. Flores*, 847 S.W.2d 648, 653 (Tex.App.-Waco 1993) (*dictum*); *Adams v. Boan*, 559 So.2d 1084, 1085 (Ala. 1990); *Kirk v. Mattison*, 497 So.2d 120 (Ala. 1986); and *Gillaspie v. Blair Constr. Co.*, 192 Kan. 455, 388 P.2d 647, 648 (1964). *Compare Aaberg v. Aaberg*, 512 So.2d 1375 (Ala. 1987), in which the requirement of public recognition was considered to be fulfilled despite the fact that the parties did not have joint checking accounts or cash cards. However, they had a joint business account. In the case of *Matter of Estate of White*, 212 Mont. 228, 686 P.2d 915 (1984), the district court gave the fact that the parties had separate accounts significant weight.

307 *Carpenter v. Carpenter*, 617 N.Y.S.2d 903, 905 (A.D. 2 Dep't 1994) (a presumption case).

308 *Toom v. Toom*, 710 N.W.2d 258 (Iowa App. 2005); *Snyder-Murphy v. City of Cedar Rapids*, 695 N.W.2d 44 (Iowa App. 2005); *Sulfridge v. Kindle*, 2005 WL 1806482 (Ohio App. 4 Dist. 2005); *Reyes v. Vasquez*, 2005 WL 1389076 (Ohio App. 6 Dist. 2005); and *Faison v. Faison*, 2005 WL 1303344 (Ohio App. 8 Dist. 2005). In *Eris v. Phares*, 39 S.W.3d 708, 716 (Tex.App.-Houston (1 Dist.) 2001), the conduct of the parties in connection with the transfer of a house at dispute was particularly significant, especially the fact that the warranty deed conveyed the house to the woman "a single person." A common law marriage was not established. *See further Fritz v. Mork*, 2001 Iowa App. LEXIS 594 (2001); and *Blessing v. Deere & Co.*, 985 F.Supp. 899, 905 (S.D.Iowa 1997). In *Conklin v. MacMillan Oil Co.*, 557 N.W.2d 102, 104 (Iowa App. 1996), in which the requirement of public declaration was not found fulfilled, the woman in her tax declaration had stated that she was single and divorced. In *Butler v. Coonrod*, 671 So.2d 750. 752 (Ala.Civ.App. 1995), the man had stated on several different documents that he was single and the parties had not filed a joint tax declaration. In *Flores v. Flores*, 847 S.W.2d 648 (Tex.App.-Waco 1993), the woman stated at the hospital that she was single, which was cited against the existence of a necessary holding out. In *Winfield v. Renfro*, 821 S.W.2d 640, 650 (Tex.App.-Houston 1991), the woman had stated on her tax return, and on her bank and insurance documents, that she was single. With respect thereto, and to a large degree upon other circumstances, the requirement of holding out was found not fulfilled. In the case of *In re Estate of Hall*, 588 N.E.2d 203, 207

girlfriend,[309] or housekeeper;[310] the man is the woman's boarder and roomer;[311]

(Ohio App. 1990), in which no common law marriage was found proven, the man had declared his income as single. In *Napier v. Napier*, 555 So.2d 1112, 1113 (Ala. Civ.App. 1989), the court drew far-reaching conclusions solely based on the fact that the deceased, on a purchase contract and registration documents, stated that he was a single man. The court stated: "These described him as a 'single man,' thus, failing to satisfy the requirement that a man and woman hold themselves out to the community as husband and wife in order for a common law marriage to exist." *See also Fields v. Fields*, 530 N.E.2d 933, 936 (Ohio App. 1987). In *Bolash v. Heid*, 733 S.W.2d 698, 699 (Tex.Civ.App.-San Antonio 1987), the real estate document in connection with the purchase of a house stated that the man was single. *See also State v. Ware*, 338 N.W.2d 707, 711 (Iowa 1983) (single-status tax returns); and *Freiburghaus v. Freiburghaus*, 103 Idaho 679, 651 P.2d 944, 946 (App. 1982). In *Harrison v. Racca*, 360 So.2d 974 (Ala. 1978), the man was listed as single on his tax return, rental agreement, and life insurance policy. In the case of *In re Estate of Dallman*, 228 N.W.2d 189 (Iowa 1975), the parties had lived together for twenty-four years. The woman had retained her maiden name. In their tax declarations and purchase papers they had stated that they were single. No holding out or public declaration that they were married was proven, thus no common law marriage was found to exist. The woman's claim upon the man's probate estate was denied. In the case of *In re Estate of Malli*, 260 Iowa 252, 149 N.W.2d 155, 157 (1967), the woman had stated on her tax declarations, and in an admittance to the hospital, that she was single while the man stated he was single in connection with registration of a real estate purchase. With respect to the meaning of "single," *see also In re Estate of Soeder*, 7 Ohio App. 271, 220 N.E.2d 547, 551-552 (Ohio App. 1966) (both parties, in almost all documents, stated that they were single. The majority for the court found that the requirement of holding out was not fulfilled); and *Coleman v. Graves*, 255 Iowa 396, 122 N.W.2d 853, 854 (1963). In the case of *In re Gholson's Estate*, 83 Idaho 270, 361 P.2d 791 (1961), the woman had filed tax returns stating that she was single and also received public assistance as a single person. *See also In re Long's Estate*, 251 Iowa 1042, 102 N.W.2d 76, 80 (1960) (real estate documents); *Etter v. von Aschen*, 82 Ohio Law Abs. 421, 163 N.E.2d 197, 200 (1959) (tax returns); *Murphy v. Jacobs*, 249 Ala. 594, 32 So.2d 306, 308 (1947); *In re Trope's Estate*, 190 Okla. 453, 124 P.2d 733, 736-737 (1942); and *Butler v. Butler*, 130 Kan. 186, 285 P. 627 (1930).

309 *Snyder-Murphy v. City of Cedar Rapids*, 695 N.W.2d 44 (Iowa App. 2005) (girlfriend or fiancé); *Brown v. State*, 108 P.3d 1018 (Kan.App. 2005) (girlfriend or fiancé). In *Gray v. Bush*, 835 So.2d 192 (Ala.Civ.App. 2001), the man had introduced the wife as his "better half" and "boss lady," but never as his wife. The requirement of public recognition was not fulfilled. In *Quinonez-Saa v. State*, 860 S.W.2d 704, 710 (Tex.App.-Houston (1 Dist.) 1993), the testimony that the woman was the man's "girlfriend, common law wife" as not considered to be sufficient. In *Matter of Estate of Brack*, 121 Mich.App. 585, 329 N.W.2d 432 (1982), the women stated that she was the deceased's girlfriend, which according to the court spoke against the existence of a common law marriage. In *State v. Johnson*, 216 Kan. 445, 532 P.2d 1325, 1329 (1975), the court stated as support for its conclusion that the necessary holding out did not exist, the fact, *inter alia,* that the man had called the woman his girlfriend. In *Murphy v. Jacobs* 249 Ala. 594, 32 So.2d 306, 308 (1947), the woman was known as the man's woman or mistress. In *Gilbreath v. Lewis*, 242 Ala. 510, 7 So.2d 485 (1942), in which the parties were not considered to be known as spouses "by the public," the court referred to the fact, *inter alia,* that the woman presented the man, not as her husband, but as "her man."

310 *In re Trope's Estate*, 190 Okla. 453, 124 P.2d 733, 735, 737 (1942); and *Com. v. Stump*, 53 Pa. 132, 91 Am.Dec. 198 (1866).

311 In *Etter v. Aschen*, 82 Ohio Law Abst. 421, 163 N.E.2d 197, 199 (1959), four neighbors testified that they considered the man simply as a boarder and roomer of the woman, which in addition to other circumstances, led to the finding that the requirement of holding out was not fulfilled.

the woman uses her maiden name;[312] they have separate credit cards and bank accounts;[313] or they have themselves testified that they did not hold themselves out to the world as being married.[314] In light of such circumstances, the courts have often not found that the necessary holding out has been proven.[315]

It is notable that these circumstances are not always necessary or sufficient to fulfill or negate the requirement of the holding out. There are several cases in which the requirement of holding out has been found fulfilled despite the fact that the parties stated that they were single. In *Matter of Estate of Alcorn* (1994), the requirement of holding out was met and a common law marriage established, notwithstanding that the woman kept her own name, failed to name the man as a beneficiary on insurance forms, and filed tax returns as single person, while the man referred to himself as a single man in his will. At the same time, several witnesses testified that couple held themselves out as married and had a joint bank account, and the wife wore a ring designed for her by the man.[316]

---

312 *Butler v. Coonrod*, 671 So.2d 750. 752 (Ala.Civ.App. 1995); and *Winfield v. Renfro*, 821 S.W.2d 640, 650 (Tex.App.-Houston 1991) (mother used maiden name on the daughter's birth certificate). In *Bolash v. Heid*, 733 S.W.2d 698 (Tex.Civ.App.-San Antonio 1987), the fact that the woman never used the man's last name was given weight. *See also Matter of Estate of Brack*, 121 Mich.App. 585, 329 N.W.2d 432, 434 (1982); *Freiburghaus v. Freiburghaus*, 103 Idaho 679, 651 P.2d 944, 946 (App. 1982); *In re Marriage of Grother*, 242 N.W.2d 1, 2 (Iowa 1976); *State v. Johnson*, 216 Kan. 445, 532 P.2d 1325, 1329 (1975); *In re Estate of Dallman*, 228 N.W.2d 187, 188 (Iowa 1975); *In re Estate of Malli*, 260 Iowa 252, 149 N.W.2d 155, 157 (1967); *Coleman v. Graves*, 255 Iowa 396, 122 N.W.2d 853, 855 (1963); *In re Long's Estate*, 251 Iowa 1042, 102 N.W.2d 76, 80 (1960); *Ex parte Threet*, 160 Tex. 482, 333 S.W.2d 361, 364 (1960); *Murphy v. Jacobs*, 249 Ala. 594, 32 So.2d 306, 308 (1947); *Faggard v. Filipowich*, 248 Ala. 182, 27 So.2d 10 (1946); *In re Trope's Estate*, 190 Okla. 453, 124 P.2d 733 (1942); *Pitney v. Pitney*, 151 Kan. 848, 101 P.2d 933, 935 (1940); *Wristen v. Wristen*, 119 S.W.2d 1104 (Tex.Civ.App.-Eastland 1938); *Butler v. Butler*, 130 Kan. 186, 285 P. 627, 628 (1930); *Bothwell v. Way*, 44 Okla. 555, 145 P. 350, 354 (1914); and *Brinckle v. Brinckle*, 12 Phila. 232, 235 (1877).

313 *Snyder-Murphy v. City of Cedar Rapids*, 695 N.W.2d 44 (Iowa App. 2005); *Reyes v. Vasquez*, 2005 WL 1389076 (Ohio App. 6 Dist. 2005); *Faison v. Faison*, 2005 WL 1303344 (Ohio App. 8 Dist. 2005); *Butler v. Coonrod*, 671 So.2d 750. 752 (Ala.Civ. App. 1995); *Freiburghaus v. Freiburghaus*, 103 Idaho 679, 651 P.2d 944, 946 (App. 982); and *State v. Ware*, 338 N.W.2d 707, 711 (Iowa 1983).

314 *See, e.g., Butler v. Butler*, 130 Kan. 186, 285 P. 627, 628 (1930), where the woman testified: "We held ourselves out to each other as being married but not to the world." A common law marriage was not established.

315 *See Hamby v. Simplot Co.*, 94 Idaho 794, 498 P.2d 1267 (1972).

316 *Matter of Estate of Alcorn*, 868 P.2d 629 (Mont. 1994); *Ganesan v. Vallabhaneni*, 96 S.W.3d 345 (Tex.App.-Austin 2002) (in her immigration documentation the woman held herself out as single. Despite this fact a common law marriage was established); *Hall v. Duster*, 727 So.2d 834, 837 (Ala.Civ.App. 1999) (the man filed single tax returns); and *Lancaster v. 46 NYL Partners*, 651 N.Y.S.2d 440, 446 (A.D. 1 Dep't 1996) (applying Ohio law). In the case of *Matter of Estate of Stodola*, 519 N.W.2d 97 (Iowa App. 1994), the parties were found to have fulfilled the requirement of "general and substantial public declarations that the parties are married," despite the fact that during their twenty-year cohabitation, they had upon several occasions stated that they were single or not married. In *Warren Gen. Hosp. v. Brink*, 80 Ohio App.3d 793, 610 N.E.2d 1128, 1129 (1992), the court found evidence that the

These cases can partially be explained by the fact that the couples assumed that their marital status could only be affected by a formal marriage, or that they were not aware of common law marriage.[317] There are also several cases in which the requirement of holding out has been found fulfilled despite the fact that the woman used her maiden name. During recent years, of course, this practice has also become more common among formally married women.[318] On the other hand, there are several

---

parties "held themselves out to the community as husband and wife and were considered as such," despite the fact that the man, in his social security documents, had stated that he was not married to the woman. Neither did they file joint tax declarations. *See also Waller v. Waller*, 567 So.2d 869 (Ala.Civ.App. 1990), in which the parties had separate economies and in which they, in real estate registrations and purchase documents, and in their tax returns, stated that they were single. In *Adams v. Boan*, 559 So.2d 1084, 1085 (Ala. 1990), public recognition was also found proven, despite the fact that the parties, in employment applications and tax documents stated that they were single. In the case of *In re Marriage of Gebhardt*, 426 N.W.2d 651, 653 (Iowa App. 1988), the court found that the requirement of holding out was fulfilled despite the fact that the woman had filed single tax declarations and used her maiden name. *See also Coleman v. Aubert*, 531 So.2d 881 (Ala. 1988) (public recognition found proven, despite the fact that the woman used her maiden name and had filed single tax declarations); *Aaberg v. Aaberg*, 512 So.2d 1375, 1376 (Ala. 1987) (the parties, in all document in which they had to given their marital status, had stated that they were single, but in which the requirement of public recognition considered to be fulfilled); and *Downs v. Newman*, 500 So.2d 1062, 1063 (Ala. 1986) (the requirement of public recognition was found fulfilled despite the fact that the parties in their tax declarations, loan and real estate registration documents, had stated that they were single). In *Nestor v. Nestor*, 15 Ohio St.3d 143, 472 N.E.2d 1091 (1984), the parties had lived together approximately twelve years. In all of the documents cited in the case, they were referred to as unmarried. Despite this, the majority for the Ohio Supreme Court found that the requirement of holding out was fulfilled. Two dissenting judges agreed with the findings of the lower court. In the case of *Matter of Estate of Giessel*, 734 S.W.2d 27, 31 (Tex.App.-Houston (1st Dist.) 1987), the requirement of holding out was found to be fulfilled despite the fact that the parties had, before several of their relatives, talked as if they were not married, and the woman had stated in her tax declaration that she was single. However, the parties had lived together for twenty years and were rumored to be married in their community. In *Oliver v. Estate of Landry*, 326 S.W.2d 923, 924 (Tex.App. 1959), the requirement of holding out was found to be fulfilled, despite the fact that the woman, to retain a pension, stated that she was an "un-remarried widow." In *Rosales v. Rosales*, 377 S.W.2d 661, 664 (Tex.Civ.App. 1964), where the parties had not presented each other as husband and wife, the court stated: "Proof of holding out to the general public can be shown by other evidence, including the conduct and the actions of the parties, which sometimes speak louder than words of introduction." In *Owens v. Owens*, 466 S.E.2d 373 (S.C.App. 1996), where the requirement of holding out is not a necessary requisite, but in contrast, is a necessary element in the marriage presumption, it was found fulfilled despite the fact that the parties had filed single tax declarations.

317 *Compare DeMelo v. Zompa*, 844 A.2d 174 (R.I. 2004), wherein friends of the parties witnessed that the man and the woman "never planned to get married, nor did they refer to each other as husband and wife." The requirement of reputation was not met.

318 *Lancaster v. 46 NYL Partners*, 651 N.Y.S.2d 440, 446 (A.D. 1 Dep't 1996); *Welch v. State*, 908 S.W.2d 258, 265 (Tex.App.-El Paso 1995); *Matte of Estate of Alcorn*, 868 P.2d 629 (Mont. 1994); *Coleman v. Aubert*, 531 So.2d 881 (Ala. 1988); *In re Marriage of Gebhardt*, 426 N.W.2d 651, 653 (Iowa App. 1988); and *Cain v. Cain*, 160 Kan. 672, 165 P.2d 221 (1946). *Compare Baker v. Mays*, 199 S.W.2d 279 (Tex.Civ.App.-Fort

cases in which the parties have stated that they were husband and wife but the requirement of holding out was found unfulfilled. A certain degree of continuity is required. It is a question of weighing all the circumstances from case to case.[319]

The parties must have outwardly represented themselves as spouses to a circle that is mainly relatives and friends.[320] If the parties have not even

---

Worth 1946) (the woman used her maiden name in church). In *Nestor v. Nestor*, 15 Ohio St.3d 143, 15 Ohio.B. 291, 472 N.E.2d 1091 (1984), the parties had kept their relationship secret from his mother by the woman retaining her name from a previous marriage. In all documents cited to the court, the parties were stated to be unmarried. Despite this, the Ohio Supreme Court found that the requirement of holding out was fulfilled and that the parties, who had lived together approximately twelve years, were united in a common law marriage. In the case of *In re Estate of Swanson*, 160 Mont. 271, 502 P.2d 33 (1972), the woman used her name from a previous marriage in a business setting.

319 In *Nichols v. Lightle*, 153 S.W.3d 563, 570-571 (Tex.App.-Amarillo 2004), the man had said "I am the husband of Claudia M. Lightle by common law marriage." The court, however, found: "At most, the statement reflects only isolated references, which is not evidence of 'holding out' to others that a marriage exists." *See further Flores v. Flores*, 847 S.W.2d 648, 653 (Tex.App.-Waco 1993); *Bolash v. Heid*, 733 S.W.2d 698 (Tex.Civ.App.-San Antonio 1987); *Roach v. Roach*, 672 S.W.2d 524 (Tex.App.-Amarillo 1984); *Gary v. Gary*, 490 S.W.2d 929, 934 (Tex.Civ.App.-Tyler 1973); and *Ex parte Threet*, 160 Tex. 482, 333 S.W.2d 361, 364 (1960). It has not been considered sufficient when the parties held themselves out to be man and wife "only when it was advantageous to assume a marriage posture," *see State v. Johnson*, 216 Kan. 445, 532 P.2d 1325 (1975). In *Claveria v. Estate of Claveria*, 597 S.W.2d 434 (Tex.Civ. App. 1980), a warranty deed and a deed of trust stating that the man and the woman were husband and wife were not considered sufficient to fulfill the requirement of holding out. According to Texas law, the parties' holding out must have occurred in Texas. *Compare Franzen v. Equitable Life Assur. Soc.*, 130 N.J.L. 457, 33 A.2d 599 (1943), where the parties' reputation did not need to occur in a state recognizing common law marriage, if the parties, while they were in such a state, entered into a marriage contract.

320 *McKnight, supra* note 168, at 939, which states that the circle is normally friends and relatives. In the case of *Matter of Estate of Alcorn*, 868 P.2d 629, 632 (Mont. 1994), the fact that the parties arranged barbecues and pool parties during summers for family and friends was cited. Occasionally, family photographs of the parties and their children are introduced as evidence, *see, e.g., Russell v. Russell*, 838 S.W.2d 909, 915 (Tex.App.-Beaumont 1992). In *Walter v. Walter*, 433 S.W.2d 183, 195 (Tex.Civ. App.-Houston (1st. Dist.) 1968), in which the requirement of holding out was not found fulfilled, the court stated: "The repute must be general, extending to the friends and relatives of both parties, with whom their daily lives are spent, and such repute must not be divided." In *Vinson v. Vinson*, 260 Ala. 254, 69 So.2d 431, 432 (1953), the court found no evidence that the parties' "neighbors or friends knew of them as husband and wife." The significance attributed to appearing together among friends can clearly be seen in the court's reasoning in *Consolidated Underwriters v. Kelly*, 15 S.W.2d 229 (Tex. Comm'n App. 1929): "Joe Kelly introduced her to his Beaumont friends as his wife, and she acknowledged him openly as her husband. They lived and cohabited as husband and wife, and received their friends in their home as such, and their friends recognized them as husband and wife." The requirement of holding out was found to have been fulfilled during the parties' three-month cohabitation, in which during two of the months a marital impediment existed. *See also Flavin v. Flavin*, 523 S.W.2d 94 (Tex.Civ.App.-Houston 1975), where a relatively small number of persons were aware of the parties' relation. In *Brinckle v. Brinckle*, 12 Phila. 232, 234 (1877), the court names "relatives, neighbors, friends and acquaintances."

informed their parents of their "marriage," the requirement of holding out is not fulfilled.[321] It has not been seen as sufficient that the parties have appeared as husband and wife simply before a few relatives or friends.[322] On the other hand, it is not required that the holding out be with respect to every person.[323] The requirement ought to be limited to those relatives the parties normally associate with and to friends "in the circle in which they live."[324]

---

321 In *People v. Badgett*, 41 Cal.Rptr.2d 635, 895 P.2d 877 (1995), the court stated that "the couple did not inform their parents of the 'marriage' even though they lived with Chris' mother, nor did they hold themselves out as married to any other relative or close friend while they were in Texas."

322 In *Lee v. Lee*, 981 S.W.2d 903, 906-907 (Tex.App.-Houston (1st Dist.) 1998), the woman, but not the man, stated before two friends and several customers that she was married. They did not have the reputation in the community as spouses. The requirement of holding out was not found to be fulfilled. A similar case is *Winfield v. Renfro*, 821 S.W.2d 640 (Tex.App.-Houston 1991), in which it was mainly the woman who under the period in question outwardly represented that they were married. This was with respect to her relatives. The court found that the parties had not represented to others that they were married. In *Ex parte Threet*, 160 Tex. 482, 333 S.W.2d 261, 364 (1960), the relationship was known only to the woman's nearest friends, thus the requirement of "a public holding out that the couple are living together as husband and wife" was not found fulfilled. The circumstance that the parties have entirely different circles of acquaintances can speak against the existence of a common law marriage, *see, e.g.*, *Laurence v. Laurence*, 164 Ill. 367, 45 N.E. 1071 (1896), concerning a European-American man and an African-American woman. In the case of *Green's Estate*, 5 Pa.C. 605 (1888), the court warned that the parties' repute can be limited "to a class and neighborhood so narrow as to give no real clue to the actual status of the parties affected." In *Brinckle v. Brinckle*, 12 Phila. 232, 234 (1877), the court spoke of "almost every one." *See also Bicking's Appeal*, 2 Brewster 202, 232 (1868), in which the court did not find it sufficient that the parties, among a few persons, enjoyed a reputation as spouses.

323 In the case of *In re Ober*, 2003 MT 7, 314 Mont. 20, 62 P.3d 1114 (2003), more than 30 witnesses were examined with different opinions about the marital status of the parties. The requirement of public reputation was fulfilled. *Adams v. Boan*, 559 So.2d 1084, 1088 (Ala. 1990). In *Nestor v. Nestor*, 15 Ohio St.3d 143, 15 Ohio B. 291, 472 N.E.2d 1091 (1984), the parties had kept their relationship secret from the man's mother by, *inter alia*, the woman keeping her name from a previous marriage. The requirement of holding out was found to be fulfilled. In *Employer's Mut. Ins. Co. v. Morgulski*, 60 Colo. 223, 193 P. 725 (1920), a common law marriage was found established despite the fact that the parties' cohabitation occurred at the woman's parental home, and despite the fact that the relationship was kept secret from the woman's father, but not her mother. In the case of *Matter of Estate of Giessel*, 734 S.W.2d 27, 31 (Tex.App.-Houston (1st Dist.) 1987), the requirement of holding out was found to be fulfilled despite the fact that the parties had not mentioned that they were married to several of their relatives and the woman in her tax declaration stated that she was single. However, the parties had lived together for twenty years and had the reputation in the community where they lived as being married.

324 *See Butler v. Coonrod*, 671 So.2d 750 (Ala.Civ.App. 1995), in which the woman only called witnesses that seldom came into contact with the parties, limiting the value of their testimony. The parties had not mentioned to the man's family that they were married. Neither had they, according to the man's family and friends, represented themselves outwardly as spouses. In *State v. Burkitt*, 624 N.E.2d 210, 219 (Ohio App. 2 Dist. 1993), it was noted that "the community and circle in which they moved considered them married." *See also In re McLaughlin's Estate*, 197 N.E.2d 578 (Ohio P.Ct. 1963) (the parties, in a very limited manner, appeared as spouses before the man's family, which was explained by the fact that they had very little

Normally, it is required that the parties, with respect to the community in general, also outwardly mutually represent themselves as husband and wife.[325] This can, for example, be with respect to trips, [326] albeit hotel visits are occasionally viewed skeptically[327] because they can as easily indicate a nonmarital or clearly secret relationship. There is significance in the parties being together at public gatherings, for example, by attending church, shopping, pursuing leisure or children's' activities, or appearing before the media.[328] If one party is deceased, the courts attach great weight to

---

contact with them); *Nestor v. Nestor*, 15 Ohio St.3d 143, 472 N.E.2d 1091, 1095 (1984) (the court maintained that it must be a holding out in relationship to those person with whom the parties "normally come in contact"); *State v. Phelps*, 100 Ohio App.3d 187, 652 N.E.2d 1032, 1035 (1995); and *State v. DePew*, 38 Ohio St.3d 275, 528 N.E.2d 542, 549 (1988); *Bevan v. Bevan*, 2006 WL 1519654 (Ohio App. 11 Dist. 2006) (in the couple's circle of acquaintances). In *Com. v. Stump*, 53 Pa. 132, 91 Am.Dec. 198 (1866), the court spoke of "people who have an opportunity to know the parties" (a presumption case). As to views from a neighbor, *see Graham v. Graham*, 130 Colo. 225, 274 P.2d 605, 607 (1954) and *Etter v. Aschen*, 82 Ohio Law Abst. 421, 163 N.E.2d 197, 199 (1959), and from "residents of the community," *see Jenkins v. Avery*, 257 Ala. 387, 59 So.2d 671, 672 (1952).

325 In *King v. King's Unknown heirs*, 16 S.W.2d 160 (Tex.Civ.App.-San Antonio 1929), a 30-year relationship was considered to not fulfill the requirement of holding out, as it was proven that the parties never appeared together and never attended any religious, business, or social gatherings together. In *Etter v. von Aschen*, 82 Ohio Law Abs. 421, 163 N.E.2d 197, 199 (1959), in which the requirement of holding out was not found to be fulfilled, the fact that the parties did not attend church together was cited among other circumstances. This particular circumstance was also cited by the Oklahoma Supreme Court in *Bothwell v. Way*, 44 Okla. 555, 145 P. 350, 354 (1914) as support for the finding that no common law marriage had been established. In *State v. Johnson* 216 Kan. 445, 532 P.2d 1325, 1329 (1975), where the court applied as a requirement that the parties outwardly appear as spouses "to public," it was considered insufficient that they so appeared only in relationship to the man's employer and their landlord. In exceptional cases, the requirement of holding out in relationship to the community has not been applied. In the case of *In re McLaughlin's Estate* 197 N.E.2d 578, 582 (Ohio P.Ct. 1963), the court viewed evidence that the parties appeared as husband and wife "in the community" unnecessary where evidence existed that they appeared as spouses before "persons who came in contact with them" and were understood to be so "by the circle of friends in which they lived."

326 In *Gatterdam v. Gatterdam*, 86 Ohio App. 29, 85 N.E.2d 526 (1949), the requirement of holding out was found to be fulfilled by the parties' 12-day stay at a camping sight where they, before the owner and other guests, appeared as spouses.

327 *Miller v. Sutherland*, 131 Mont. 175, 309 P.2d 322, 328 (1957); and *Ballesteros v. Jones*, 985 S.W.2d 485, 490 (Tex.App.-San Antonio 1998). In the case of *In re McKanna's Estate*, 106 Cal.App.2d 126, 234 P.2d 673, 675 (1951), the parties met mainly at a rooming house and at different hotels in Texas, where they checked in as spouses. They were also presented as spouses to certain persons. The requirement of holding out was found to be fulfilled.

328 In the case of *In re Estate of Glover*, 882 S.W.2d 789, 791 (Tenn.App. 1994) (applying Alabama law), the requirement of public recognition was found not fulfilled as the couple's only activities in Alabama were "eating, shopping and sharing a motel room." In the case of *In re Marriage of Gebhardt*, 426 N.W.2d 651, 653 (Iowa App. 1988), the fact that the parties appeared as spouses in the newspaper was cited among several circumstance. *See also Gammelgaard v. Gammelgaard*, 247 Iowa 979, 77 N.W.2d 479, 484 (1956). In the case of *Matter of Estate of Alcorn*, 868 P.2d 629, 632 (Mont. 1994), the facts that the woman, during the man's sickness lasting a period

whether the surviving party has been mentioned in the obituary and participated in the funeral.[329]

The application problems arising in connection with the principle of holding out as spouses is easily demonstrated by the above referenced case of *Winfield v. Renfro* (1991), in which the requirement of cohabitation was found to be fulfilled, but the question also arose as to whether the parties, during the period from April to August of 1982, represented themselves outwardly as spouses in Texas. The relationship between the man and woman was kept secret to the greatest extent by the man. The parties rarely appeared together before his relatives and friends. However, during a three-day visit to a hotel in Dallas, they had checked in as "M/M David Winfield." After the man bought a residence in Houston, which the woman moved into, his last name was on the mailbox. The woman had stated to her mother that they were married. In other situations, for example, on her daughter's birth certificate, the woman gave her maiden name. In her tax declaration and on her bank account and insurance policies, she stated that she was single. She did not, in a single document in which she had to give her marital status, state that she was married. The Texas Court of Appeals found that the parties had entered into a marriage contract and that they lived together as spouses.[330] Nevertheless, the court found that the evidence was insufficient to prove that the parties represented to others in Texas that they were married during the period in question.[331]

---

of eight years, was constantly by his side, and that they appeared as spouses at the race track, were cited. *Compare Green's Estate*, 5 Pa.C. 605, 608 (1888), in which the court stated that the woman claiming to be the deceased's common law wife, "never visited him in his illness, and did not even attend at the church." *See also In re Estate of Hendrickson*, 248 Kan. 72, 805 P.2d 20 (1991), in which the parties, in the presence of the press and TV, entered into a marriage contract at the hospital in which the man was staying. The parties' relationship lasted only approximately two weeks before he died. The Kansas Supreme Court, however, without further examining the requirement of holding out, found that a common law marriage had been established.

329 *Dalworth Trucking Co. v. Bulen*, 924 S.W.2d 728, 737 (Tex.App.-Texarkana 1996). A fact which was given weight in *Nestor v. Nestor*, 15 Ohio St.3d 143, 472 N.E.2d 1091, 1096 (1984), was the circumstance that the woman was mentioned as the surviving spouse in the man's obituary. In the presumption case of *Yardley's Estate*, 75 Pa. 207 (1874), the fact that the woman did not participate in the man's funeral was given weight when the court found that the necessary reputation did not exist. In *Gallo v. Steinman Coal & Coke Co.*, 93 Pittsb.Leg.J. 357 (1944), the circumstance that the woman did not participate in the man's funeral was given weight. Neither had the woman in *Walter v. Walter*, 433 S.W.2d 183, 187 (Tex.Civ.App.-Houston (1st Dist.) 1968) participated in the man's funeral. It is, however, unclear what weight was attributed to this circumstance. However, the requirement of holding out was found not fulfilled.

330 *See* Section 7.4 as well as § 8.5.3 *supra*.

331 *Winfield v. Renfro*, 821 S.W.2d 640, 651 (Tex.App.-Houston 1991). It ought to be noted that the court's judgment was limited to the question presented to the jury, namely whether the parties entered into a common law marriage "on or about April 11, 1982." The court took into consideration a period of four months after that date. *Id.* at 646-647. Several pieces of evidence were introduced, but not taken into consideration by the court, with respect to the period after August of 1982.

Winfield clearly demonstrates that the requirement of holding out has a function to fulfill in ensuring that the legal consequences of marriage, mainly intended for spouses who have lived or live together, actually are reserved for these relationships and not more sporadic associations.

In the above-named case, *Bolash v. Heid* (1987), in which the man worked in Nigeria and the woman resided in San Antonio, Texas, and in which the Texas Court of Appeals also found that the requirement of cohabitation was fulfilled, the issue of whether the requirement of holding out was fulfilled was discussed. During the four years in which he worked outside of the country, he traveled several times to Texas. Upon each such occasion, the parties were together. In connection with the purchase of a house, the man stated that he was single. The evidence further demonstrated that the woman never used the man's last name, and that she presented him only as "Andy." The woman's mother stated that the man always referred to her daughter as his wife, but that this occurred first after the purchase of the house. The Texas Court of Appeals found that the evidence was insufficient to prove the necessary holding out and that no common law marriage had been established at the time of the house purchase. Therefore, the house was not considered to be community property of which the woman, as a wife, was entitled to claim a portion.[332]

In cases in which the cohabitation has not been sporadic and the parties have for several years lived together in Texas, the requirement of a continuous holding out has also been applied by the courts. In *Lee v. Lee* (1998), the woman, but not the man, before two friends and several customers, stated that she was married. In the community, they did not have a reputation as spouses. The requirement of holding out was found to not be fulfilled.[333]

8.6.3 The Formulation of the Requisite Reputation

The other main emphasis of the parties' outward actions focuses not on their holding out in itself, but on the effects it creates, namely, their reputation as husband and wife.[334] It is, therefore, not sufficient that the parties

Compare the dissenting judge, who found the necessary holding out proven, but appears to have taken into consideration circumstances occurring after this time period. *Id.* at 653-658. *Compare Ganesan v. Vallabhaneni*, 96 S.W.3d 345 (Tex.App.-Austin 2002), where the parties "at times" throughout the relationship of one and one-half years held themselves out to be married and where a common law marriage was constituted.

332 *Bolash v. Heid*, 733 S.W.2d 698, 699 (Tex.Civ.App.-San Antonio 1987).

333 *Lee v. Lee*, 981 S.W.2d 903, 906-907 (Tex.App.-Houston (1st Dist.) 1998).

334 In *Miller v. Townsend Lumber Co.*, 448 P.2d 148, 152 (Mont. 1968), the court explained: "By repute we mean reputation, being the character and status commonly ascribed to one's actions by the public." No such repute was found proven in the cases of *Murphy v. Jacob*, 249 Ala. 594, 32 So.2d 306 (1947); *Arnold v. Arnold*, 219 Mo.App. 8, 267 S.W. 950 (1924); and *Respole v. Respole*, 70 N.E.2d 465 (C.P.Ohio 1946). With respect to the element of repute, *see* Note, *Common Law Marriage - A Legal Anachronism*,

outwardly are known as husband and wife. It is required that they are also recognized as such.[335] The requirement has, with good reason, been viewed as "the speech of the people."[336] In contrast to medieval canon law, which gave the parties' *publica fama* significant evidentiary weight when trying the issue of whether an informal marriage existed,[337] in American law, reputation as spouses is often a necessary requirement.

As a requisite, it is commonly formulated as the requirement of *repute* or *reputation as husband and wife*, an expression sometimes strengthened by the use of adjectives such as "public," "uniform," or "general."[338] The necessary effect is also described as a requirement of "public recognition," "public acknowledgment,"[339] "a belief in the community" that they are husband

---

32 IND.L.J. 99 (1956). *Compare* the use of the element in the presumption under Scottish law, Chapter 11.3 *infra*, and in American law, Chapter 9.4 *infra*.

335 Both can be seen clearly in *Edelstein v. Brown*, 95 S.W. 1126, 1129, 100 Tex. 403, 100 S.W. 129, 123 Am.St.Rep. 816 (1907), in which the court stated that the parties lived together for many years as husband and wife "during which time they declared themselves as husband and wife, and were so known and recognized by their neighbors and friends."

336 *Com. v. Stump*, 53 Pa. 132, 91 Am.Dec. 198 (1866) (a presumption case).

337 With respect to medieval Canon law, *see* Section 3.3.4 *supra*.

338 The legislation in Utah requires that the parties acquire "a uniform and general reputation as husband and wife," *see* UTAH CODE ANN. § 30-1-4.5 (1987). *See also Hansen v. Hansen*, 958 P.2d 931, 936 (Utah App. 1998). A comparable expression can be found in the cases of *In re Trope's Estate*, 190 Okla. 453, 124 P.2d 733 (1942); and *In re Gholson's Estate*, 83 Idaho 270, 361 P.2d 791, 792 (1961). In cases from Montana, the requirement of "assumption of the marital relation" as formulated earlier in the statute has been considered in the case law to contain a requirement of cohabitation and reputation, *see* Section 48-101 R.C.M. (1947); *Miller v. Townsend Lumber Co.*, 448 P.2d 148 (Mont. 1968); and *Elliot v. Indus. Accident Bd.*, 101 Mont. 246, 53 P.2d 451 (1936). After the repeal of the law in 1975, the requisite has continued to be formulated as a requirement of "cohabitation and repute," or "cohabitation and public repute," *see In re Ober*, 2003 MT 7, 314 Mont. 20, 62 P.3d 1114 (2003); *Matter of Estate of Alcorn*, 868 P.2d 629, 630 (Mont. 1994); *In re Estate of Vandenhook*, 855 P.2d 518 (Mont. 1993); *In re Marriage of Mahaffey*, 801 P.2d 1335, 1336 (Mont. 1990); *In re Marriage of Geertz*, 232 Mont. 141, 755 P.2d 34, 37 (1988); and *In re Marriage of Murnion*, 212 Mont. 107, 686 P.2d 893, 899 (1984). In *Blackwood v. Kilpatrick*, 52 Ala.App. 505, 294 So.2d 753 (1974), the Alabama Court of Civil Appeals speaks of holding out and reputation.

339 With respect to public recognition, for Alabama law, *see Buford v. Buford*, 874 So.2d 562 (Ala.Civ.App. 2003); *Gray v. Bush*, 835 So.2d 192 (Ala.Civ.App. 2001); *Creel v. Creel*, 763 So.2d 943, 946 (Ala. 2000); *People v. Schmidt*, 579 N.W.2d 431, 434 (Mich. App. 1998) (applying Alabama law); *Stringer v. Stringer*, 689 So.2d 194, 195 (Ala.Civ. App. 1997); *Krier v. Krier*, 676 So.2d 1335, 1339 (Ala.Civ.App. 1996); *Butler v. Coonrod*, 671 So.2d 750, 751 (Ala.Civ.App. 1995); *In re Estate of Glover*, 882 S.W.2d 789, 791 (Tenn.App. 1994) (applying Alabama law); *Crosson v. Crosson*, 686 So.2d 868, 870 (Ala.Civ.App. 1995); *Adams v. Boan*, 559 So.2d 1084, 1086 (Ala. 1990); *Copeland v. Richardson*, 551 So.2d 353, 354 (Ala. 1989); *Coleman v. Aubert*, 531 So.2d 881, 882 (Ala. 1988); *Aaberg v. Aaberg*, 512 So.2d 1375, 1376 (Ala. 1987); *Downs v. Newman*, 500 So.2d 1062, 1063 (Ala. 1986); *Kirk v. Mattison*, 497 So.2d 120, 122 (Ala. 1986); *Boswell v. Boswell*, 497 So.2d 479, 480 (Ala. 1986); *Skipworth v. Skipworth*, 360 So.2d 975, 977 (Ala. 1978); *Krug v. Krug*, 296 So.2d 715, 718 (Ala. 1974); *Brown v. Brown*, 276 Ala. 153, 159 So.2d 855 (1964); *Goodman v. McMillan*, 258 Ala. 125, 61 So.2d 55, 59 (1952); *Whitworth v. Whitworth*, 256 Ala. 296, 54 So.2d 575 (1951); *Turner v. Turner*, 251 Ala. 295, 37 So.2d 186 (1948); *Murphy v. Jacobs*, 249 Ala. 594,

and wife,[340] or that they are "regarded as husband and wife."[341] Certain courts hold that consummation contains a requirement that the parties enjoy "public recognition" as husband and wife.[342]

In a majority of the judgments, no sharp distinctions are made between the parties' holding out and their reputation as husband and wife, even if it is possible for the parties to outwardly appear as spouses without others noticing and without their appearance giving rise to any reputation. The reverse can also be true, that the parties have received a mistaken or undeserved reputation as spouses without any outward representation. In the case law from Texas, however, the distinction is maintained. The courts apply the requirement of holding out, meaning that the parties represented to others that they were married, as set out in the legislation, but not a requirement of reputation as spouses. The existence of such a reputation, in Texas, however, can be evidence that the parties "represented to others" that they were married.[343]

---

32 So.2d 306 (1947); *Sloss-Sheffield Steel & Iron Co. v. Watford*, 245 Ala. 425, 17 So.2d 166 (1944); and *Gilbreath v. Lewis*, 242 Ala. 510, 7 So.2d 485, 488 (1942). In *Hall v. Duster*, 727 So.2d 834, 836 (Ala.Civ.App. 1999), the court maintained that the parties must "consummate the marriage; that is, they must live in such a way as to gain public recognition that they are living as husband and wife." A similar formulation can be found in *Waller v. Waller*, 567 So.2d 869 (Ala.Civ.App. 1990). *See also Piel v. Brown*, 361 So.2d 90, 94, 95 (Ala. 1978), where the Alabama Supreme Court, in more general terms, speaks of consummation therewith the parties must "so live as to achieve public recognition of their status as husband and wife." *See also Beck v. Beck*, 286 Ala. 692, 246 So.2d 420 (1971); *Krug v. Krug*, 296 So.2d 715, 718 (Ala. 1974); *Humphrey v. Humphrey*, 293 Ala. 118, 300 So.2d 376 (1974); and *Huffmaster v. Huffmaster*, 279 Ala. 594, 188 So.2d 552 (1966). *Compare* the older case of *Maryland v. Baldwin*, 112 U.S. 490, 495 (1884). The Court, somewhat hesitantly, as characteristic of public recognition as evidence, gives the impression that it is simply understood as an evidentiary fact. However, the Court speaks of the element as "necessary" as evidence, which means that this recognition understands the elements of the principle. *Compare Norell v. Norell*, 220 Ind. 398, 404, 44 N.E.2d 97, 99 (1942), in which reputation was only considered to be a type of evidence.

340 For Rhode Island, *see Petrarca v. Castrovillari*, 448 A.2d 1286 (R.I. 1982) and *Sardonis v. Sardonis*, 106 R.I. 469, 261 A.2d 22 (1970). *Compare Souza v. O'Hara*, 121 R.I. 88, 395 A.2d 1060, 1061 (1978), in which the court uses the expression "general reputation."

341 *Kowalik v. Kowalik*, 118 Ohio App.3d 141, 691 N.E.2d 1152, 1154 (1997).

342 *See* the cases from Alabama listed in note 172 *supra*.

343 *See* TEX. FAM. CODE ANN. § 2.401 (a)(2) (Vernon 2005). In *Lee v. Lee*, 981 S.W.2d 903, 904 (Tex.App.-Houston (1st Dist.) 1998), the requirement that the parties "represented to others that they were married" was not found fulfilled. The court referred *inter alia* to the fact that they "did not have reputation in community for being married." *See also Matter of Estate of Giessel*, 734 S.W.2d 27 (Tex.App.-Houston (1st Dist.) 1987); *Rosales v. Rosales*, 377 S.W.2d 661 (Tex.Civ.App. 1964); *Oliver v. Landry*, 326 S.W.2d 923 (Tex.Civ.App. 1959); *Drummond v. Benson*, 133 S.W.2d 154 (Tex.Civ.App.-San Antonio 1939); *Wingfield v. Pool*, 38 S.W.2d 422 (Tex.Civ.App.Galveston 1931); and *Brooks v. Hancock*, 256 S.W. 296, 297 (Tex.App. 1923). In other cases, the requirement of reputation has been be dispensed with under certain circumstances. In *Vann v. Vann* 186 Okla. 42, 96 P.2d 76, 77 (1939), the Oklahoma Supreme Court stated that it was not necessary to prove reputation in cases where there was direct evidence in the form of declarations and admissions from the party against whose interest they were made, evidence of cohabitation as husband and wife, or

8.6.4 Relevant Factors

As the parties' holding out normally creates their reputation, the same circumstances as discussed above in Section 8.6.2, "Relevant Factors," are often cited as support for the existence of a holding out and of a reputation. The following statement made by the Court in *Maryland v. Baldwin* (1884) gives a summary: "[I]t may be made in any way which can be seen and known by men, such as living together as man and wife, treating each other and speaking of each other in the presence of third parties as being in that relation, and declaring the relation in documents executed by them whilst living together, such as deeds, wills, and other formal instruments. From such recognition the reputation of being married will obtain."[344]

With respect to the extent of the circle within which the parties' reputation must be exist, similar views are applicable as well as with the term *holding out*, discussed above. Already the term *reputation* requires a certain amount of publicity, strengthened by the use of adjectives such as public and general. It, therefore, is not surprising that the Utah Court of Appeals, in *Hansen v. Hansen* (1998), found that the requirement of a "uniform and general reputation as husband and wife" was not fulfilled. The parties had not been consistent in their appearance as spouses and not even their closest friends considered them such.[345] In *DeMelo v. Zompa* (2004), the plaintiff's only evidence that the parties had held themselves out as spouses was her brother's testimony that the defendant had called him "brother-in-law." The court held: "However, long-time friends of both plaintiff and defendant testified that they never planned to get married, nor did they refer to each other as husband and wife."[346] Isolated occasions of holding out before a few persons do not form a reputation as husband and wife.[347] Creating a reputation as spouses takes a reasonable amount of time.

---

evidence of "mutual assumption openly of marital duties." *See also Ridgeway v. Logan*, 205 Okla. 603, 239 P.2d 778, 782 (1952).

344 *Maryland v. Baldwin*, 112 U.S. 490, 5 S.Ct. 278, 28 L.Ed. 822 (1884). The criteria of public recognition in this case was directly applied in *Adams v. Boan*, 559 So.2d 1084, 1088 (Ala. 1990) and cited with approval, for example, in *Downs v. Newman*, 500 So.2d 1062, 1063 (Ala. 1986); *Piel v. Brown*, 361 So.2d 90, 95 (Ala. 1978); *Murphy v. Jacobs*, 249 Ala. 594, 32 So.2d 306, 307-308 (1947); and *Gilbreath v. Lewis*, 242 Ala. 510, 7 So.2d 485, 489 (1942).

345 *Hansen v. Hansen*, 958 P.2d 931, 936 (Utah App. 1998).

346 *DeMelo v. Zompa*, 844 A.2d 174, 177 (R.I. 2004).

347 In the case of *In re Estate of Phifer* 629 P.2d 808 (Okla.App. 1981), the Oklahoma Court of Appeals found that the isolated occasions in which the man referred to the woman as his wife were insufficient to achieve "a community wide reputation" that they were a married couple. *See also Miller v. Townsend Lumber Co.*, 448 P.2d 148 (Mont. 1968). It was not sufficient that the parties had a reputation as spouses at the hotel where they usually met. In the case of *In re Callery's Estate*, 226 Pa. 469, 75 A. 672, 673 (1910), the court stated: "There was a 'repute' prevailing in the Colonial hotel of their marital relations as 'Mr. and Mrs. Phillips,' but there was no pretense that this 'repute' extended to Callery's family and acquaintances until a short time before his death." *Compare In re McKanna's Estate*, 106 Cal.App.2d 126, 234 P.2d

Therewith, the requirement creates a protection against short-term relationships and short visits to states recognizing common law marriages.[348] The Court in *Maryland v. Baldwin* (1884) spoke of a reputation among "friends, associates, and acquaintances,"[349] and in *Kowalik v. Kowalik* (1997), the Ohio Court of Appeals required that the parties be viewed as husband and wife in the community in which they live.[350] The term *community* has no certain boundaries. It can even be questioned whether the socializing habits of cohabiting couples today have the same radius as before. In *Petrarca v. Castrovillari* (1982), the objection was raised that the term "belief in the community" was too broad because it implies a more widespread knowledge of the parties' circumstances than is compatible with the reality of today's suburban society. The Rhode Island Supreme Court, however, stated that the term does not include persons with whom the parties were not acquainted.[351]

Traditionally, some courts have required that the parties' reputation as spouses be not only general but also undivided.[352] In *Richard v. Richard* (1935),

---

673, 674 (1951), in which the parties' registration as spouses at a rooming house and a number of hotels in Texas was attributed great significance.

348 *See, e.g., Matter of Estate of Vandenhook*, 855 P.2d 518 (Mont. 1993), in which the requirement of cohabitation and repute was not found to be fulfilled during a short visit to Montana, for more on this, *see* Chapter 10 *infra*. *See also Conlon v. Schweiker*, 537 F.Supp. 158 (N.D.Tex. 1982), in which the parties lived together for two weeks and there the woman maintained that "Mike was introduced to friends as mine," but in which the court found that the requirement of holding out was not fulfilled. *Compare* the words of Lord Chancellor Chelmsford in *Campbell v. Campbell* (1867), L.R. 1 H.L. Sc.App. 182, 196: "Habit and repute ... arises from parties cohabiting together openly and constantly as if they were husband and wife, and so conducting themselves towards each other for such a length of time in the society or neigbourhood of which they are members as to produce a general belief that they really are married persons."

349 *Maryland v. Baldwin*, 112 U.S. 490, 5 S.Ct. 278, 28 L.Ed. 822 (1884). The criteria of public recognition in this case was directly applied in *Adams v. Boan*, 559 So.2d 1084, 1088 (Ala. 1990) and cited with approval, for example, in *Downs v. Newman*, 500 So.2d 1062, 1063 (Ala. 1986); *Piel v. Brown*, 361 So.2d 90, 95 (Ala. 1978); *Murphy v. Jacobs*, 249 Ala. 594, 32 So.2d 306, 307-308 (1947); and *Gilbreath v. Lewis*, 242 Ala. 510, 7 So.2d 485, 489 (1942).

350 *Kowalik v. Kowalik*, 118 Ohio App.3d 141, 691 N.E.2d 1152, 1154 (1997). In *Lancaster v. 46 NYL Partners*, 651 N.Y.S.2d 440, 446 (A.D. 1 Dep't 1996) (applying Ohio law), the court speaks of "in the community and circle in which they move."

351 *Petrarca v. Castrovillari*, 448 A.2d 1286, 1290 (R.I. 1982).

352 *Richard v. Richard*, 172 Okla. 397, 45 P.2d 101 (1935), which is actually a presumption case, *see* Chapter 9 *infra*. Neither in *McArthur v. Hall*, 169 S.W.2d 724, 728 (Tex. Civ.App-Fort Worth 1943), was the requirement of reputation considered fulfilled, as it was a question concerning a "divided repute." In the case of *In re Trope's Estate*, 190 Okla. 453, 124 P.2d 733 (1942), the Oklahoma Supreme Court stated that reputation must be "uniform and general and not substantially contradicted and divided" and found with respect to the relationship which had lasted twenty-eight years, that the evidence, comprising of 1124 pages, demonstrated that the parties' reputation was divided. No common law marriage was found proven. In the case of *In re Gholson's Estate*, 83 Idaho 270, 361 P.2d 791, 792 (1961), the Idaho Supreme Court stated: "Reputation must be uniform and general and not limited to particular persons or divided, in the community in which [the] parties cohabit, in order to suffice as proof of marriage." *See also Brisbin v. Huntington*, 128 Iowa 166, 103

the Oklahoma Supreme Court stated: "Proof of general reputation of such marital status must be general and not special or divided." If the parties, in order to benefit from a situation, state that they are married, and in another situation, state that they are single, obviously, their reputation is conflicted, in other words, divided.[353] No common law marriage can then be established.

Nevertheless, as in the assessment of holding out, there is support in the case law for subjectivity, according to which the requirement of general reputation is limited to those with whom the parties normally come into contact, or the community and circle in which they move.[354] This subjectivity raises the question of whether a couple, lacking relatives, friends, and acquaintances, generally need to have any reputation. Some minimum of holding out and reputation ought, however, be required. The requirement of an undivided reputation as spouses has not been consistently upheld.[355]

A case illustrating the application problems entailed with the term *reputation* is *Nestor v. Nestor* (1984).[356] The parties, Eleanor Clark Nestor, a widow, and Hobart Nestor, a divorcee, met in 1963. Eleanor lived in a rental apartment, and Hobart lived with his mother. They discussed marriage but never acted on their discussions. In 1969, Hobart purchased an

---

N.W. 144 (1905). In *Walter v. Walter*, 433 S.W.2d 183, 194 (Tex.Civ.App.-Houston (1st Dist.) 1968), the parties' general reputation was considered to be divided. *See also Miller v. Sutherland*, 131 Mont. 175, 309 P.2d 322 (1957); *White v. White*, 82 Cal. 427, 23 P. 276 (1890); *Jackson v. Jackson*, 82 Md. 17, 33 A. 317 (App. 1895); and *Bishop v. Brittain Invest. Co.*, 229 Mo. 699, 129 S.W. 668 (1910). *Compare* the presumption cases in Scottish law. In *Cunningham v. Cunningham*, (1814) 2 Dow 482, 483, the court stated that repute must "be founded on general, not singular opinion" and that "a divided repute is, on such a subject, no evidence at all." *See also Lapsley v. Grierson*, (1845) 8 D. 34, 61 ("the repute must have been undivided during the whole period"); and *Nicol v. Bell*, (1954) S.L.T. 314, 315 ("there must be a general and not a divided repute").

353 In the case of *In re Trope's Estate*, 190 Okla. 453, 124 P.2d 733, 735-736 (1942), the trial court suspected that the parties outwardly appeared as spouses to have others believe that a common law marriage existed.

354 In *Nestor v. Nestor*, 15 Ohio St.3d 143, 472 N.E.2d 1091, 1095 (1984), the court spoke of reputation in relation to those with whom the parties "normally come in contact." *In Respole v. Respole*, 70 N.E.2d 465 (C.P.Ohio 1946), the court limited the public to which the parties should appear as married to "the community and circle in which they move." In *Richard v. Richard*, 172 Okla. 397, 45 P.2d 101 (1935), reputation was required "among such relatives and acquaintances of both parties as have come in contact with them." In *Klipfel v. Klipfel*, 41 Colo. 40, 92 P. 26, 124 Am.St.Rep. 96 (1907), the Colorado Supreme Court maintained that with reputation is intended an understanding among "the neighbors and acquaintances with which the parties associate in their daily life." *Compare*, with respect to holding out, *In re McLaughlin's Estate*, 97 N.E.2d 578, 582 (Ohio P.Ct. 1963), where the court speaks of "the circle of friends in which they lived."

355 In *Peet v. Peet*, 52 Mich. 464,18 N.W. 220 (1884), the Michigan Supreme Court could have made an allowance for the fact that the parties' reputation was divided, as they had lived together approximately twenty years and had thirteen children. *Compare In re Trope's Estate*, 190 Okla. 453, 124 P.2d 733 (1942), note 297 *supra*.

356 *Nestor v. Nestor*, 15 Ohio St.3d 143, 472 N.E.2d 1091 (1984).

older house in Akron, Ohio, and began restoring it. He and Eleanor, together, chose a new refrigerator and stove for the house. Hobart bought dining room furniture and bathroom fixtures. They also decided that Eleanor would move from her apartment to his residence. Eleanor moved all of her belongings on July 1, 1970, to the house, including furniture, kitchen utensils, porcelain, clothes, and other personal belongings. Later that evening, Hobart asked Eleanor to marry him, and she accepted. Immediately thereafter, they called Eleanor's daughter and son-in-law and informed them that they were married. Later that same week, Hobart and Eleanor visited a number of married couples that were friends of Hobart's. Upon these occasions, Hobart stated that he and Eleanor were married. From the findings of fact, however, it can be seen that Hobart asked Eleanor not to disclose their marriage to Hobart's mother. Further, he suggested that Eleanor retain the name "Clark" from her previous marriage, on their tax returns, bank accounts, customer accounts, and retirement accounts, which she did.

Eleanor testified that after she moved into the new home, they cooked most meals and cleaned the house together. They often ate dinner out, and enjoyed visiting together families and friends. When vacationing in Ohio and on other occasions, they registered at hotels as husband and wife. Hobart was retired, and his only income came from leasing a gas station, which he previously had managed and occasionally still helped out at with repair work. Eleanor was employed the first years they lived together, but later became unemployed when her employer closed the factory. The findings further showed that Hobart paid their grocery bills and other living expenses, and that he paid for the trips they made together.

In 1979, it became clear that Hobart had amyotrophic lateral sclerosis. His condition quickly declined. Before he died, he was partially incapable of moving himself. Eleanor cared for him and took care of his daily needs, including administering his medicines and oxygen until his death on January 21, 1983. Eleanor participated in the funeral together with members of Hobart's family, who thought she should be named as Hobart's spouse in the obituary published in the *Akron Beacon Journal.* The funeral director, however, listed her as a "close friend."

Several facts about the parties' cohabitation were contested at trial. Eleanor stated that she slept together with the deceased as his wife, and that she had a sexual relationship with him until several weeks before he died. Several of Hobart's children, however, testified that Eleanor simply rented a room from the deceased. Eleanor rejected the claim that she lived in Hobart's home as a renter and stated that she never paid any rent. No evidence was introduced proving any rental payments. In contrast, evidence was produced demonstrating that Hobart, on all of his documents, stated he was single.

After Hobart died, Eleanor claimed the estate as the surviving spouse in a common law marriage, which the man's heirs contested. The case was first heard by the Court of Common Pleas, which, in assessing the parties' marriage-like status, referred to documents stating that they were unmarried. Not a single document listed the couple as married. The court noted that the evidence demonstrated that Eleanor and Hobart represented themselves as friends to his family and others. Eleanor did not use the name "Nestor," and explained that Hobart did not wish his family to know that they were married. The court found that the parties had entered into a marriage contract on July 1, 1970, and that they agreed to outwardly appear as unmarried and that a common law marriage did not exist because the parties did not hold themselves out as being married. The judgment was appealed to the Court of Appeals, which affirmed the lower court's judgment.

The Ohio Supreme Court stated that to establish a common law marriage, cohabitation and reputation were required in addition to the marriage contract. In evaluating the facts in the case, the court stated that the existence of a marriage contract *in praesenti* could not be questioned. With respect to the element of cohabitation, according to the court's view, more than ample evidence demonstrated that the parties lived openly as a married couple. The court referred to Eleanor's testimony that, after she moved into Hobart's home, she always slept with him in the bedroom on the lower level, and to their registration and sleeping arrangements in hotels in connection with their trips. Further, evidence was introduced that when a relative stayed at Hobart and Eleanor's home, she slept in the bedroom on the lower level, while the host and hostess slept together in a double bed on the same level.

With respect to the third and undoubtedly most difficult element to judge, namely the parties' holding out, the court began with reference to the fact that the parties had notified Eleanor's daughter of their contract, that the parties during the same week had visited several of Hobart's married friends whom they informed as to the marriage, while Eleanor was presented to other friends by Hobart as his wife.

According to the court, evidence certainly existed that Eleanor was in agreement with Hobart that his mother should not be notified, and therefore, Eleanor kept the name of Clark on several documents. However, the court found that these facts alone could not prevent the establishment of a common law marriage, noting that many married women today keep their maiden or previous marital name, and there is no obligation for a married woman to take her husband's family name.

The court further stated that the parties, during their entire life together, had before their friends appeared as husband and wife. Family members and friends had sent cards to Eleanor addressed to "Mrs. Eleanor Nestor" or "Eleanor Nestor." With the assessment as to the parties' marriage-like status, the court gave significant weight to the relationship, the fact that the parties during a long period of time, twelve and a half years, lived together and shared their lives, families, friends, household chores and expenses, and their worldly goods. Even if evidence existed that Hobart, upon three occasions during the parties' cohabitation had a relationship with another woman, this was unknown to Eleanor. She had continued in her faithful relationship to Hobart. She supported him during his difficult illness and until his death, even when his physical and psychological needs become all the more taxing. According to the court's view, there was no evidence that Eleanor performed these duties in the capacity of a housemaid, as there was no evidence that she received payment for these services. Neither could it be reasonably assumed, according to the court, that she did this only as a close friend to Hobart. These were duties performed by a wife for her husband. The court found it even more convincing that Hobart's family, after his death, agreed that his obituary should name Eleanor as his surviving spouse. The abrupt change in the family's position as to Eleanor's status first came after a period of reflection that followed his death. The court, in light of the evidence presented, and in contrast to the lower courts' conclusions, found that a common law marriage had been established between Eleanor and Hobart Nestor.[357] Two judges dissented on the issue of whether the requirement of holding out was fulfilled, referring to the evidence presented at the trial court and maintaining that insufficient reason existed to overrule it.

There are cases in which the requirement of reputation was also not found fulfilled despite rather long cohabitations. In *Butler v. Coonrod* (1995), the parties had lived together for nine years until the death of the man, after which the woman made a claim on the estate in the capacity of surviving spouse in a common law marriage. However, the evidence showed that the woman, on several occasions, had left the man; the parties never informed the man's family that they were married; the woman used her maiden name except upon one occasion; they did not file joint tax returns and did not have joint credit cards; and the deceased's marital status was given as single on several documents. The parties did not present each other as spouses, and the deceased's friends and family members were not of the understanding that the parties outwardly appeared as spouses. The Alabama Court of Civil Appeals found that they cohabited but did not hold themselves out or refer to each other as husband and wife, thus no common law marriage had been established.[358] The requirement of reputation or "public recognition," as it is called in Alabama, was not found fulfilled.

A double requirement of both holding out and reputation exists in Utah, where the legislation requires that the parties "hold themselves out as and have acquired a uniform and general reputation as husband and wife." In the case of *Clark v. Clark* (2001), the spouses Linda and Cecil divorced in 1985 after eighteen years of marriage. After a half-year separation,

357 *Id.* at 1096.
358 *Butler v. Coonrod*, 671 So.2d 750 (Ala.Civ.App. 1995).

they resumed living together for a period of more than ten years until 1996, when they separated. Linda then brought an action to establish a common law marriage, obtain a divorce, and divide the marital assets. The Supreme Court of Utah held that Linda's filing of a petition to establish marriage less than one year after termination of the marriage tolled the statute of limitation. Further, the court held that the evidence was sufficient to establish that parties held themselves out and had acquired reputation as husband and wife, and supported trial court's finding of cohabitation in action to establish an unsolemnized marriage. The court referred to the facts that Linda retained her married name of "Clark," and both Linda and Cecil routinely introduced each other as husband and wife. Furthermore, the court referred to the fact that at least two witnesses believed that the Clarks were married. The witnesses made that assumption because the Clarks were the "[Clark children's] mom and dad," and because the Clarks acted as a husband and wife would act.[359]

8.7 Summary and Conclusions

1. *The Pure Contract Principle*

The issue of whether cohabitation between the parties ought to be recognized as a necessary requirement, or whether the establishment of a common law marriage ought to be solely based on the marriage contract, has been one of the most diffuse in the history of common law marriage. The latter understanding, the pure contract principle, has its basis in general contract law, where legal relationships are principally based on the contract and other legal actions. As marriages, both formal as well as informal, are principally understood to be contracts, nothing in addition to the contract has been considered necessary. This traditional understanding is close to the Roman and canon laws' principle: *consensus, non concubitus, facit nuptias* as discussed in Chapters 2, "Informal Marriages in Roman Law," and 3, "Informal Marriages in Canon Law."

As the pure contract principle gained acceptance to a large extent in the American legal literature, legal political motivations behind the principle, beyond those given above, rarely appear in the judgments. One argument against cohabitation as a requisite has been, however, that it would create contradictions within the legal system if cohabitation, on one side, was required as a condition for the establishment of a marriage, and, on the other side, was viewed as outside of marriage and even criminalized before the marriage had time to be established. In addition, warnings have been given about potential application difficulties.

---

359 *Clark v. Clark*, 423 Utah Adv.Rep. 3, 2001 UT 44, 27 P.3d 538, 542 (Utah 2001).

The pure contract principle, as seen in this chapter, has been consistently discussed in the legal literature. In recurring editions of their treatises, Kent, Greenleaf, and Bishop, during the entire 1800s, supported the idea that only the contract, and not the cohabitation, was required to establish a common law marriage. Towards the end of the nineteenth century, and in the beginning of 1900s, this idea was carried forward by Schouler in his treatise, and by Koegel in his doctoral thesis published in 1922. Even in the 1960s, Ross maintained that no cohabitation was necessary, according to the dominant thinking.

Despite this support from legal scholars, the pure contract principle has been displaced in the case law by the understanding that cohabitation ought to be a necessary requirement in addition to the contract. This latter understanding has prevailed in both the case law and the legislation. The pure contract principle is applied today only by the courts of two of the fifteen jurisdictions examined here, namely, *Pennsylvania* and *South Carolina.*

The application of the pure contract principle, it can be noted, does not preclude cohabitation being given weight as an evidentiary fact for the existence of a marriage contract as seen in Chapter 7. Moreover, cohabitation, in addition to reputation, can be a necessary element in the marriage presumption, according to which a marriage is presumed to exist as long as the absence of a marriage contract cannot be proven, as discussed below in Chapter 9. The future function that the pure contract principle can have in modern society is be discussed in Chapter 13.

2. *Cohabitation's Development as a Necessary Requirement*

The uncertainty which has prevailed over the question of whether cohabitation should be considered a necessary requirement justified the above review of the legal developments of the 1800s and 1900s, and an attempt to ascertain the state of the law today in those jurisdictions which have been examined herein. The result shows that the reasoning about the necessity of cohabitation in addition to the marriage contract during the 1800s grew progressively stronger in the case law as well as the legislation, and, around the turn of the century, became dominant despite the support the pure contract principle received in the legal literature. In the beginning of 1920s, the notion that cohabitation was necessary dominated in the courts, while the pure contract principle continued to dominate in the literature, for example, in Koegel's thesis. In several states, the development of this doctrine fluctuated and then stabilized by the middle of the century. Today, cohabitation is a necessary requirement in thirteen of the fifteen jurisdictions examined: Montana, Idaho, Utah, Colorado, Kansas, Oklahoma, Texas, Alabama, Georgia, Iowa, Ohio, District of Columbia, and Rhode Island. In Texas, the requirement of cohabitation for the establishment of a common law marriage has been codified in the legislation since the end of the 1960s and in Utah, since the late 1980s.

3. *The Motivations behind the Requirement of Cohabitation*

Unlike common law marriage, cohabitation as a necessary requirement does not have its roots in medieval canon law or in English ecclesiastical law. And unlike the pure contract principle, it has not been taken up by the legal literature. Thus, the motivation behind the requirement must be found in American case law and the legislation in which it has been adopted.

This motivation, as seen above, rests on the premise that marriage is not simply a contract between two parties but rather a matter concerning the entire community. Therefore, this conforms to the understanding of marriage as a status relationship, whose legal ramifications follow primarily not from the marriage contract but from legislation and case law. These legal consequences concern not only the parties themselves, but also their entire families and third parties. A natural consequence of this is that the establishment of a marriage ought not to rest solely upon the parties' agreement. The community has a stake in ensuring a marriage is established not only by the taking of vows to live together but also by a subsequent cohabitation. Moreover, the majority of the legal consequences of marriage are intended for marriages that are enacted through cohabitation.

From the parties' perspective, the majority of persons assume that they are to live together and therefore, cohabitation must be considered a condition of the contract. From this perspective, the requirement of cohabitation has also been viewed as a protection for the parties themselves against a hasty marriage contract. The commencement of cohabitation, consequently, can be considered definite evidence that the agreement was the result of serious intent. The cohabitation then acts as a substitute for the form requirement. The requirements of cohabitation and holding out as spouses have always been intended to prevent secret marriages. The significance of these requirements in the case law can be seen from the description of the parties' outward actions as "the acid test."

A cohabitation, which is outwardly apparent, can also constitute a protection for third parties entering into contracts with the parties. The requirement of cohabitation further has been seen as a protection against fraudulent claims directed against one party, an estate. or the state. Finally, a requirement of cohabitation has been viewed as a means of avoiding evidentiary difficulties and conflicts, albeit that such a requirement can also give rise to these same problems. This motivation behind the requirement of cohabitation and its relevance in the future is discussed in Chapter 13.

4. *The Requirement of Cohabitation*

The boundaries of the requirement of cohabitation are significant because they affect the areas of application for common law marriages and determine which relationships confer the rights as well as the obligations of marriage, and which relationships fall outside the regulatory system. Cohabitation as a legal requisite is formulated in different ways in the legislation and case law of different states, as seen in this chapter. The principle of cohabitation, from a legal perspective, has two main elements. On one side is cohabitation in the more narrow sense, covering the relationship between the parties; on the other side, is the holding out and reputation of the parties as spouses, *i.e.*, their outward representation to others and the reputation thus acquired.

As regards the relationship between the parties, different formulations of the requirement of cohabitation appear in American law. One construction speaks of "cohabitation," "cohabitation as husband and wife," or "living together as husband and wife." A second formulation of the requisite is "assumption of the marital relation" or "assumption of marital rights, duties and obligations." The third construction requires "consummation" or that the contract shall be "consummated by cohabitation." In addition, cohabitation, in this more narrow sense, instead of being a separate requirement, is encompassed in the terms *holding out* and *reputation as spouses.* Even though it is predictable that these different formulations might give the requirement different meanings, there are no such distinctions among the expressions in the case law. In contrast, it appears that they have all come to generally have the same legal definition.

Against this background, it is interesting to review a number of the factors that have been considered relevant in the case law in assessing whether the requirement of cohabitation has been fulfilled. Regardless of the formulation of the requirement of cohabitation as cited above, the courts have generally considered the same factors. These have been (1) sexual relations, (2) an exclusive relationship, (3) mutual children, (4) mutual home and household, (5) economic maintenance, (6) personal support, (7) mutual recreation. Of course, this list is not exhaustive. The requirement of cohabitation is best understood as an open requisite with room for new factors that arise from developments in the concept of family, gender roles, etc. The reality that a couple has lived together as man and wife should not be undermined by the fact that, in many marriages today, the parties may not play traditional roles or carry out the tasks once closely identified with marital status.[360]

None of the factors listed herein can be considered always necessary or sufficient as elements of the requirement of cohabitation, despite the support they lend in individual cases. Nevertheless, in principle, one or several of them must always exist. How they are weighted by the courts also varies. Sexual relations, as well as mutual home and household, are two significant factors that, together, are normally considered to fulfill the requirement of cohabitation. Just as medieval canon law spoke of a companionship *in lecto et in mensa,* in American case law today, there is a

360 Barbara A. Kazen, FAMILY LAW: TEXAS PRACTICE AND PROCEDURE 3-11 (1990).

companionship "at bed and board." This pair of factors is intended to separate common law marriages from relationships that are either friendships or relationships that are purely sexual. The historical durability of these two factors is striking in a world in which gender roles and family concepts are constantly changing. Even today, the old French proverb has a significant degree of relevance: "Boire, manger, coucher, ensemble, est marriage ce me semble."

It is striking that neither the American legislation nor the case law stipulate a required minimum time for the cohabitation, as is often the case in modern cohabitation law. Compare Chapter 12, "Common Law Marriage and Cohabitation Law", and Chapter 13, "The Constitutive Requisites in the Future." Instead the quality of the cohabitation has been decisive. American case law also demonstrates that the courts, in many cases, have accepted surprisingly short periods of cohabitation, often only a period of a few months or sometimes even shorter.

The fact that the courts in several cases have set a low requirement for the length of cohabitation gives the impression that the cohabitation is the execution of the marriage contract. It appears, against this background, appropriate, as in Georgia, to speak of cohabitation as the consummation of the marriage contract. It must also be demonstrated that the relationship did not stop with simply the contract but that a marriage had also been commenced, but no more! If only the necessary cohabitation is considered, some relationships that should not be recognized as common law marriages will fall within the parameters.

The requirement of cohabitation should not, however, be viewed in isolation. It is applied together with the requirements of a contract and holding out, which can be restraints in cases in which the relationships are insufficient. In a legal system that strictly enforces the contract requirement, the need for a cohabitation over a long period of time is less compelling than in a system in which the legalities are simply tied to the requirement of cohabitation. The need also appears to be less compelling than if the application of the marriage presumption based only upon "cohabitation and reputation," as discussed further in Chapter 9.

That the cohabitation must still have been for a certain, albeit undefined, period of time in order to fulfill the requirement of cohabitation also influences the requirement of a contract to the extent that it creates the need to work with a *consensus continuus, i.e.*, a continuous contract that comes to expression through the cohabitation.

The requirement of cohabitation, as a continuing factor, also becomes an issue in the question of whether a common law marriage is considered to have been established from the time the cohabitation commences or at a later date. In the few cases in which the question has received any attention, a general rule has been that the marriage ought to be considered established when the cohabitation commenced. This, of course, is understood to mean the point at which an acceptable, rather than a sporadic or otherwise insufficient, cohabitation commences. Further, the establishment of a marriage assumes that the other requirements also are fulfilled at the same time, *i.e.*, the parties' marriage-like *consensus* and holding out. To the extent a cohabitation is required for a certain period, it follows that each such common law marriage begins as a nonmarital relationship, but when this relationship is transformed to a marriage, the transformation dates from the time that the nonmarital relationship began.

This raises a question about how an earlier decision based upon the parties' nonmarital status can be retried in the light that the parties, as a result of their continued cohabitation, actually had a marital status from the beginning. This question has not been raised in the cases, but should be answered affirmatively. The practical problem is minimized if consummation is equated with an acceptable cohabitation. If the cohabitation is insufficient at its commencement, but later becomes sufficient, a marriage is not established before the cohabitation is sufficient, assuming that the other requirements are fulfilled. If the requirement of marital *consensus* is not fulfilled from the beginning, but the requirement of cohabitation is, no marriage is established until the contract requirement is fulfilled.

If the cohabitation has begun, and the other requirements are fulfilled, a common law marriage is established. Deficiencies that arise thereafter in any of the elements of the cohabitation are not relevant to the establishment of a common law marriage. These elements may pertain to sexual relationships with others, the dissolution of the mutual home or household, etc. The fact that such deficiencies can be the basis of a divorce is a separate issue.

As can be seen in this chapter, the requirement of cohabitation also creates problems for relationships that, for different reasons, ought to be considered eligible to receive the legal consequences of marriage, but will instead fall outside the protection of marriage. This has caused the courts, in certain cases, to apply very diluted requirements of cohabitation, as in, for example, *Winfield, Bolash,* and *Krug.* This has been true in cases in which a more complete cohabitation has not been possible because one of the parties, for example, as a result of work, military duty, studies, or health conditions, has had a residence or household that is geographically distant from the other party. Certain courts, thus, have applied the principle that cohabitation is only required to the extent it is possible under the circumstances. As this principle appears to have been applied in cases in which no cohabitation has generally been possible, the courts actually appear to have abandoned the requirement of cohabitation.

5. *The Requirement of Holding Out and Reputation*

Each of the jurisdictions that apply an element of cohabitation as a necessary requirement for the establishment of a common law marriage, except for Georgia and most probably, the District of Columbia, appear to require, in addition, that the parties appear outwardly as spouses.

This requirement focuses either on the parties' actions in themselves, their holding out as spouses, or the effects thereof, *i.e.*, their reputation as husband and wife. One or both of these additional requirements can be applied.

The requirement of holding out, as seen here, commonly is formulated as a requirement of holding out as husband and wife, *i.e.*, that the parties appear as husband and wife before others, or that the parties must have represented to others that they were married. Several courts formulate the requirement of holding out as a requirement of public declaration that the parties are husband and wife, by their words as well as by their actions. Courts have also formulated the requirement in more general terms, by a requirement that the cohabitation be open or public, or that the parties have lived together professedly as husband and wife, by which is understood that they have appeared outwardly as such before authorities. In several cases, courts have not applied any explicit requirement of holding out, but instead have found it within the requirement to assume marital rights, duties, or obligations.

Even though the different manners of expression differ linguistically and, therefore, could assume different nuances of meaning, the case law demonstrates that the courts have generally assigned them the same legal content.

Further, we have seen in this chapter, the parties' holding out as spouses can comprise words as well as actions. Several of the admissions and declarations, evidence for the existence of a marriage contract, belong to the category of circumstances considered as holding out. Also included are instances in which the parties present each other as husband and wife or state in different documents that they are married; the woman uses the man's family name; the parties wear rings, have joint bank accounts, name each other as beneficiaries on insurance policies; etc.

Similarly, the finding that no holding out as husband and wife existed can be supported by citing circumstances such as the following: The parties have stated that that they are single or unmarried; that the woman was the man's fiancée, girlfriend, or housekeeper; or that the man was the woman's boarder and roomer. Other relevant facts are that the woman used her maiden name, or the parties had separate bank accounts or credit cards. In the presence of such circumstances, the courts have often found that the necessary holding out did not exist.

Nevertheless, it is noteworthy that the kinds of circumstances mentioned above are, alone, neither always necessary nor sufficient to fulfill or negate the requirement of holding out. Caution is called for because the parties' statements about their marital status may reflect that they have not entered into a formal marriage, and perhaps do not understand that they have a common law marriage. Therefore, there are cases in which the requirement of holding out was found to be fulfilled despite the fact that the parties, for example, stated that they were single or the woman used her maiden name. All the circumstances must be weighed from case to case.

As noted above, the circle in which the parties live, and to which the parties must outwardly appear as spouses, is primarily made up of relatives and friends. It is commonly required that the parties also outwardly, with respect to the community in general, appear as husband and wife. This can pertain, for example, to religious gatherings, shopping, recreational or children's activities, as well as appearances before the media. If one party is deceased, the courts have considered how the surviving party was identified in obituaries and his or her participation in the funeral.

The other main aspect with respect to the parties' outward actions focuses, as stated above, not on the holding out itself, but its effect, namely, their reputation as husband and wife. Thus, it is not sufficient that the parties outwardly are known as husband and wife. It is also required that they be recognized as such. This requirement therefore has been termed "the speech of the people."

The requisite is commonly formulated as a requirement of repute or reputation as husband and wife, expressions that can be strengthened by the adjectives public, uniform or general. The necessary effect can even be described as a requirement of public recognition, public acknowledgment, or a belief in the community that they are husband and wife. Normally, the parties' holding out is considered to create their reputation, so that the same circumstances are often cited to support the existence of both the holding out and the reputation, however, in addition, it is required that the parties' outward representation in their environment gives rise to a reputation as spouses.

With respect to the extent of the circle throughout which the parties' reputation must be spread, the applicable viewpoints are similar to those that apply to holding out. The Court, in *Maryland v. Baldwin* (1884), spoke of reputation among friends, associates, and acquaintances.[361] However, reputation also includes an element of publicity, meaning that the reputation is public or general. The requirement has also, in the case law, been based on the fact that the parties' reputation is to be undivided, a requirement that has proven difficult to maintain.

The requirements of holding out and reputation, which reasonably take a certain period of time to fulfill, certainly have a significant function to fulfill as they ensure that the legal consequences of marriage are reserved for spouses who are living or having lived together, and not to more sporadic relationships. The significance of the requirement becomes particularly clear if the courts fail to take it seriously. Common law marriages were not found in either *Winfield* or *Bolash*, in which the requirement of cohabitation was considered to be fulfilled even though the cohabitation was sporadic, because the requirement of holding out was

361 *Maryland v. Baldwin*, 112 U.S. 490, 5 S.Ct. 278, 28 L.Ed. 822 (1884).

not fulfilled. In a state such as Georgia, which has no requirement of holding out, secret marriages and abuses of the system are a risk, albeit the absence of holding out as spouses in a concrete case can be seen as evidence of the fact that no consummation existed.[362] At the same time, a requirement of holding out and reputation can be difficult to fulfill with respect to a couple that continuously moves from one place to another.[363]

6. *Application Problems*

One of the purposes of the requirement of cohabitation is to diminish the application problems that the pure contract principle is assumed to create. We have seen in this chapter that an unconditional requirement of cohabitation can contribute to reducing these problems, especially if the marriage contract is secret or consists of inferred agreements. Based upon approximately one thousand cases, however, a significant conclusion is that a requirement of cohabitation also creates extensive application problems. These concern the application of the requirement of cohabitation as well as the requirement of holding out, regardless of the concrete formulations in the legislation and in the case law. The question of when the relationship between a man and a woman legally crosses the threshold from nonmarital to marital has not been given any satisfactory answer in the case law.

The requirement, as well as the different factors in it, are so loosely defined that there is considerable room for different interpretations. This has often entailed long and drawn-out trials with extensive witness testimony. Application problems have also been aggravated by reality, *i.e.*, relationships between men and women are not easily categorized into cohabiting and not cohabiting. The relationships of couples living together without formally having entered into a marriage vary. Certain couples live together for a period of time to test a relationship. Certain couples live together before they separate and establish new relationships with different parties. Others have more or less limited their cohabitation as a result of work or studies in different areas (*Bolash*, *Winfield*, and *Krug*). Others allow themselves to have relationships with others. Not surprisingly, it is difficult, with the application of the requirement of cohabitation, to separate those that ought to have the rights and assume the obligations of marriage from those who ought to fall outside of the system.

In light of the difficulties accompanying the application of the requisite, a significant problem arises as regards legal certainty. It is often difficult for the parties themselves to know whether they are married, and to predict when legal regulations are applicable. Many parties first become

---

362 With respect to short visits to Georgia which gave rise to common law marriages, *see* Chapter 10 *infra*.

363 Steven G. Brown, Comment, *Pennsylvania Common Law Marriage and Annulment: Present Law and Proposals for Reform*, 15 Vill. L. Rev. 134, 135 (1969).

aware of common law marriage only after they separate or one party has died. An attorney then advises them that perhaps they lived in a common law marriage with the complete legal effects of a marriage. Certainly, a stringently applied contract requirement can contribute to diminishing legal uncertainty. Still, as long as the courts, to the significant extent as seen in Chapter 7, accept rather dubious grounds as an implied contract, the potential effectiveness of this element is undermined.

One of the obstacles in applying the requirement of cohabitation is the difficulty of proving several of the factors that the courts consider materially relevant at trial. This problem arises foremost with respect to proving the sexual relationships of the parties with each other as well as with outsiders. In many cases, the courts have to assess conflicting information from the parties themselves, or in the case of a deceased, from only one party. A further difficulty is the danger that "pajamas investigations" (see, e.g., *Nestor, Scott, Soeder, Russell,* and *Doyle*) can violate personal privacy. A legal system based on investigations so invasive of personal integrity must be viewed as flawed and in need of attention. A question that arises is whether the rules concerning evidentiary burdens and presumptions have a role in solving the above-mentioned application problems, which is discussed further in Chapter 9.

As all modern cohabitation legislation enacted today throughout the Western world is based on the element of cohabitation, the experiences analyzed in this chapter ought to be useful for any legal policy discussion. These problems with respect to the future are revisited later in Chapter 12, "Common Law Marriage and Cohabitation Law, Chapter 14, "The Constitutive Requisites in the Future," and Chapter 14, "Arguments For and Against Common Law Marriage and Cohabitation Law."

CHAPTER 9
Burdens of Proof and Presumptions

9.1 Introduction

The substantive requisites necessary for the formation of a common law marriage were examined in the previous chapters, Chapters 6, "The Common Law Marriage Contract," and 7, "Implied Marriage Agreements," were devoted to the elements of the marriage contract, while Chapter 8, "Cohabitation, Holding Out, and Reputation as Spouses," discussed the objective elements of cohabitation and reputation as necessary substantive requirements.

However, as every practitioner knows, the possibility of success in a lawsuit is often highly dependent upon the procedural requirements resulting from the applicable evidentiary rules pertaining to burdens of proof and presumptions. This is just as true for claims regarding the existence of common law marriages.[1] At the same time, these rules and their underlying intentions reflect the attitudes of both the courts and legislatures toward the legal concept of common law marriage. This is of interest both in the application of the law as well as in any discussion as to the future direction of the law such as the one found in the conclusion of this work.

This chapter, therefore, examines the evidentiary rules pertaining to burdens of proof and presumptions, their purposes, and their application by the courts. Of particular interest is the marriage presumption; its origin and underlying values; the elements that must be proved to invoke its application, and its legal effects and relationship to the substantive law and fundamental evidentiary rules with respect to the burden of proof and the standard of persuasion. Based on the discussion, we shall draw certain conclusions. Chapters 13, "The Constitutive Requisites in the Future," and 14, "Arguments For and Against Common Law Marriage and Cohabitation Law," address the future use of burdens of proof and presumptions.

---

1 *See, e.g.*, William Hood Jr., *Common Law Marriage in Oklahoma: A Survey*, 49 Okla. B. J. 1505, 1506 (1978), referring to "the awesome burden of proof."

9.2 Burdens and Standards of Proof

Consistent with general American evidentiary theory, the starting point of the issue of whether a common law marriage has been formed is that the burden of proof rests with the party alleging the existence of the marriage.[2] This is true for each of the necessary requisites, namely, the parties' legal capacity, the marriage contract, and the required cohabitation and reputation as spouses.

Many courts have traditionally applied a stricter standard to the measure of persuasion of the proof in cases in which one party bases the complaint on the existence of a common law marriage. This is particularly true in cases in which one spouse is deceased, and the surviving spouse is claiming a portion of the deceased's estate. The stricter standard is often justified by the fact that common law marriage is a fruitful source of fraud and perjury, and claims of the existence of such marriages must, therefore, be closely scrutinized. If one party is deceased, his or her lips are sealed, which is a second reason for applying a strict standard. Therefore, the courts and public authorities, often, must rely primarily on the surviving party's testimony.[3]

If the parties refrained from a ceremonial wedding despite being "in the shadow of the county clerk's office and within the sound of church bells", wariness and a careful investigation of the facts in these cases is called for.[4] This suspicious attitude toward common law marriages is based on the principle that these marriages "are to be tolerated not encouraged."[5] This attitude is not common in the case law from the 1800s, but can be found in cases covering the entirety of the 1900s, especially the courts in Pennsylvania, the District of Columbia, Ohio, Iowa, Alabama, and Texas,[6]

---

2 *Compare Clark v. Cassidy,* 64 Ga. 662, 667 (1880): "The burden generally lies on the party who asserts or affirms a fact, and sometimes a negative affirmation is essential, and when it is so, the proof of such negative rests on the party affirming it."

3 *See, e.g., In re Stevenson's Estate,* 272 Pa. 291, 116 A. 162, 165 (1922), where the court stated that "when the lips of a man are sealed by death, and he leaves no satisfactory evidence as to the existence of such contract, courts will be very slow to establish it in derogation of the undoubted rights of those who follow him." *See also* the case of *Com. ex rel. McDermott v. McDermott,* 236 Pa.Super.Ct. 541, 345 A.2d 914, 918 (1975) ("Courts are properly skeptical of the claims of a surviving common law spouse which may rest on testimony designed to elevate the casual or illicit affair to the level of the legally recognized estate of marriage"); and *Estate of Gavula,* 490 Pa. 535, 417 A.2d 168, 171 (1980).

4 *McChesney v. Johnson,* 79 S.W.2d 658, 659 (Tex.Civ.App-Ft. Worth 1934).

5 *Baker v. Mitchell,* 143 Pa.Super. 50, 17 A.2d 738, 741 (1941).

6 In the case of *In re Redman's Estate,* 135 Ohio St. 554, 21 N.E.2d 659, 661 (1939), the Supreme Court of Ohio stated: "So-called common law marriage contravenes public policy and should not be accorded any favor; indeed, it is quite generally condemned." *See also In re Osterling's Estate,* 323 Pa. 23, 185 A. 790, 792 (1936); *In re McGrath's Estate,* 319 Pa. 309, 179 A. 599, 603 (1935); *McChesney v. Johnson,* 79 S.W.2d 658, 659 (Tex.Civ. App-Ft. Worth 1934); *In re Krystkiewicz's Estate,* 310 Pa. 298, 300, 165 A. 230 (1933); *In re Craig's Estate,* 273 Pa. 530, 117 A. 221, 224 (1922); *Boyd v. Boyd,* 252 N.Y. 422, 169 N.E. 632, 634 (N.Y. 1930); *In re Stevenson's Estate,* 272 Pa. 291, 116 A. 162, 164-165 (1922); *In re Davis's Estate,* 204 Pa. 602, 54 A. 475 (1903). Already in *Brinckle v. Brinckle,*

albeit such declarations appear to have once again become less common during the 1980s and 1990s.[7] A separate issue arises from the fact that these principles are not strictly upheld in their practical application.

A case that significantly influenced the development of the case law is *Baker v. Mitchell* (1941), in which the Pennsylvania Superior Court stated: "The law of Pennsylvania recognizes common law marriages. But they are a fruitful source of perjury and fraud, and, in consequence, they are to be tolerated, not encouraged ... the professed contract should be examined with great scrutiny." This statement is cited in a number of cases from Pennsylvania as well as by courts in other states, even today, and is also referenced by legal scholars.[8]

This negative attitude lives on in the case law from the 1970s. For example, in the case *In re Marriage of Winegard* (1979), which is often cited by other courts, the Iowa Supreme Court stated: "The burden of proof lies on the party asserting its existence, and such a claim of marriage will be regarded with suspicion, there being no public policy in Iowa favoring common law marriage."[9] In the beginning of the 1990s, the courts still expressed the same position. In *Coates v. Watts* (1993), the District of Columbia Court of Appeals stated: "Since ceremonial marriage is readily available and provides unequivocal proof that the parties are husband and

---

12 Phila. 232 (1877) and *Guardians of the Poor v. Nathans*, 2 Brewster 149, 153 (1845), in which the courts underlined the need of "great scrutiny."

7 With regard to the initial criticism against common law marriage, *see* Section 4.4 *supra*.

8 *Baker v. Mitchell*, 143 Pa.Super. 50, 17 A.2d 738, 741 (1941). *Baker* is cited, for example, in Caleb Foote et al., Cases and Materials on Family Law 17-18 (3d ed. 1985).

9 *In re Marriage of Winegard*, 278 N.W.2d 505, 510 (Iowa 1979). In *Bodde v. State*, 568 S.W.2d 344 (Tex.Cr.App. 1978), the Texas Court of Criminal Appeals stated: "A claim of common law marriage is closely scrutinized by the courts." In *Piel v. Brown*, 361 So.2d 90, 95 (Ala. 1978), the Supreme Court of Alabama held: "It has been said that due to the serious nature of the marriage relationship, the courts will closely scrutinize a claim of common law marriage and require clear and convincing proof thereof..." In the case of *In re Marriage of Grother*, 242 N.W.2d 1, (Iowa 1976), the Iowa Supreme Court stated: "A claim of common law marriage is regarded with suspicion and is closely scrutinized." *See also In re Marriage of Reed*, 226 N.W.2d 795, 796 (Iowa 1975); *Chatman v. State*, 513 S.W.2d 854 (Tex.Cr.App. 1974); *In re Estate of Hammonds*, 39 Ohio misc. 96, 315 N.E.2d 843, 847 (1973); *Gary v. Gary*, 490 S.W.2d 929, 935 (Tex. Civ.App.-Tyler 1973); *In re Estate of Fisher*, 176 N.W.2d 801, 805 (Iowa 1970); *State v. Lawson*, 165 N.W.2d 838 (Iowa 1969); *In re Estate of Malli*, 260 Iowa 252, 149 N.W.2d 155 (1967); *In re Estate of Collings*, 405 Pa. 280, 175 A.2d 62, 63 (1961); *In re Long's Estate*, 251 Iowa 1042, 102 N.W.2d 76, 79 (1960); *Mainor v. Midvale Co.*, 192 Pa.Super. Ct. 367, 162 A.2d 27, 30 (1960); *In re Wagner's Estate*, 398 Pa. 531, 159 A.2d 495, 497 (1960); *In re Manfredi's Estate*, 399 Pa. 285, 159 A.2d 697, 701 (1960); *Krzesinski v. State*, 169 Tex. Cr.R. 178, 333 S.W.2d 149 (App. 1960); and *Etter von Aschen*, 82 Ohio Law Abst. 421, 163 N.E.2d 197, 198 (1959). In *Texas Employers' Ins. Ass'n v. Elder*, 274 S.W.2d 144, 147 (Tex.Civ.App. 1954), the Texas Court of Civil Appeals held: "[T]he law does not favor, but merely tolerates, common law marriage." *See also In re Blecher's Estate*, 381 Pa. 138, 112 A.2d 129, 131 (1955); *In re Stauffer's Estate*, 372 Pa. 537, 94 A.2d 726, 728 (1953); *Goodman v. McMillan*, 258 Ala. 125, 61 So.2d 55, 59 (1952); *Welch v. State*, 151 Tex.Cr.R. 356, 207 S.W.2d 627 (1948); and *In re Nikitka's Estate*, 346 Pa. 63, 29 A.2d 521, 523 (1943).

wife, claims of common law marriage should be closely scrutinized, especially where one of the purported spouses is deceased and the survivor is asserting such a claim to promote his financial interest."[10]

Even during recent years, the courts with reference to previous case law repeat similar statements. For example, in *Staudenmayer v. Staudenmayer* (1998), the Pennsylvania Supreme Court confirms that claims for this type of marriage are disfavored,[11] and in the case of *In re Marriage of Martin* (2004), the court, referring to *Winegard,* holds that "claims of common law marriage are carefully scrutinized and the burden of proof rests with the party asserting the claim."[12]

It appears, however, that this type of negative proclamation has become less common during recent years because the attitude to cohabitation without formal marriage has become more positive. In those cases that include statements about the evidentiary proof, they appear to be more motivated by the difficult evidentiary situation than by a morally tinged hostility to common law marriage.[13]

---

10 *Coates v. Watts,* 622 A.2d 25, 27 (D.C.App. 1993). However, the court just required a preponderance of evidence. *Coates* is cited in *Mesa v. United States,* 875 A.2d 79, 83 (D.C.App. 2005) and in *Dickey v. Office of Personnel Management,* 419 F.3d 1336 (C.A.Fed. 2005). In *Lofton v. Estate of Weaver,* 611 So.2d 335, 336 (Ala. 1992), the Alabama Supreme Court stated: "Courts of this state closely scrutinize claims of common law marriage." *See also Matter of Danza,* 188 A.D.2d 530, 591 N.Y.S.2d 197, 198 (1992), applying Pennsylvania law. In the case of *In re Estate of Corace,* 527 A.2d 1058, 1060 (Pa.Super. 1987), the Superior Court of Pennsylvania held that "while this Commonwealth tolerates common law marriage, the same is not encouraged ... because common law marriage is a fruitful source of perjury and fraud, the law imposes a heavy burden on one who grounds his or her claim on an allegation of common law marriage." *See also In re Estate of Dodge,* 361 Pa.Super. 188, 522 A.2d 77, 78 (1987); *Baker v. Townsend,* 484 So.2d 1097, 1098 (Ala.Civ.App. 1986); *In re Estate of Kovalchick,* 345 Pa.Super. 229, 498 A.2d 374, 376 (1985); *Etheridge v. Yeager,* 465 So.2d 378, 380 (Ala. 1985); *De Santo v. Barnsley,* 328 Pa.Super. 181, 476 A.2d 952, 955 (1984); *In re Estate of Stauffer,* 504 Pa. 626, 476 A.2d 354, 356 (1984); *In re Cummings Estate,* 330 Pa.Super. 255, 479 A.2d 537, 542-543 not 3 (1984); *Estate of Gavula,* 490 Pa. 535, 417 A.2d 168, 171 (1980); *Hightower v. State,* 629 S.W.2d 920 (Tex.Cr.App. 1981); *Lackey v. State,* 638 S.W.2d 439, 443 (Tex.Cr.App. 1982); and *Walton v. Walton,* 409 So.2d 858 (Ala.Civ.App. 1982).

11 *Staudenmayer v. Staudenmayer,* 714 A.2d 1016, 1020 (Pa. 1998); and *Africa v. Vaughan,* 998 F.Supp. 552, 556 (E.D.Pa. 1998). For the grudging attitude of Texas courts, *see Shepherd v. Ledford,* 962 S.W.2d 28, 31 (Tex. 1998); *Stringer v. Stringer,* 689 So.2d 194, 197 (Ala.Civ.App. 1997); *Conklin v. MacMillan Oil Co.,* 557 N.W.2d 102, 105 (Iowa App. 1996); and *State v. Burkitt,* 624 N.E.2d 210, 219 (Ohio App. 2 Dist. 1993) ("have never been favored in Ohio").

12 *In re Marriage of Martin,* 681 N.W.2d 612, 617 (Iowa 2004); *Bell v. Ferraro,* 849 A.2d 1233 (Pa.Super. 2004); and *In re Veneziale,* 267 B.R. 695, 700 (Bkrtcy.E.D.Pa. 2001).

13 Aside from statements in the criminal cases, *Lackey v. State,* 638 S.W.2d 439, 443 (Tex. Cr.App. 1982) and *Bodde v. State,* 568 S.W.2d 344 (Tex.Cr.App. 1978), in Texas one has to go back to *Texas Employers' Ins. Ass'n v. Elder,* 274 S.W.2d 144, 147 (Tex.Civ. App. 1954) and *McChesney v. Johnson,* 79 S.W.2d 658, 659 (Tex.Civ.App-Ft. Worth 1934), in order to find a clear expression of a negative attitude. The rather extensive civil case law that has developed after the 1969 legislation, Act of June 2, 1969, 61st Leg., R.S. ch. 888 § 1.91, 1969, Tex.Gen.Laws 2707.2717 (Vernon 1975), assumes a more neutral stance. *Compare People v. Badgett,* 41 Cal.Rptr.2d 635, 895 P.2d 877, 897 (1995) (applying Texas law). With respect to Alabama, it appears that the principle

Despite the strength in the above-stated principles for the evidentiary proof, it ought to be noted that these are not always strictly applied in practice. There are, however, boundaries to the courts' ability to counteract common law marriages. Naturally, they cannot, as stated in Freedman, "legislate against them by a harsh refusal to recognize their existence."[14]

9.2.1 Clear and Convincing Evidence

Without doubt, there is a clear relationship between the courts' attitude toward common law marriage and the measure of persuasion required of the parties with respect to the burden of proof. The courts, in applying a stricter standard, usually require that the evidence shall be clear and convincing, a standard higher than a preponderance of the evidence, which is typically applied in civil cases,[15] but lower than beyond a reasonable doubt, which is applied in criminal cases.[16] In the case of *In re Estate of Stodola* (1994), the Iowa Court of Appeals found that the elements of a common law marriage between James and Joyce were established by clear and convincing evidence,[17] while the Pennsylvania Supreme Court in the case of *Staudenmayer v. Staudenmayer* (1998) found that the woman failed to prove the establishment of a common law marriage by clear and convincing evidence.[18] In approximately half of the states recognizing common law marriages, the courts have required clear and convincing evidence or a similar standard.[19]

---

stance has not received a complete effect in the practical application of the law. John B. Crawley, *Is the Honeymoon Over for Common Law Marriage: A Consideration of the Continued Viability of the Common Law Marriage Doctrine*, 29 CUMB. L. REV. 399, 404 (1998/1999) states that "the Alabama appellate courts have generally not disparaged the doctrine or given it only grudging approval."

14 ABRAHAM L. FREEDMAN AND MAURICE FREEDMAN, LAW OF MARRIAGE AND DIVORCE IN PENNSYLVANIA I, 108 (2d ed. 1957). *See also In re Blecher's Estate*, 381 Pa. 138, 112 A.2d 129 (1955).

15 *See Hansen v. Hansen*, 958 P.2d 931, 934-935 (Utah App. 1998); *East v. East*, 536 A.2d 1103, 1105 (D.C.App. 1988); and *Renfroe v. Hamilton*, 193 Ga. 194, 17 S.E.2d 709, 713 (1941).

16 *Jolley v. Jolley*, 46 Ohio Misc. 40, 347 N.E.2d 557, 560 (1975); *In re McLaughlin's Estate*, 197 N.E.2d 578, 581 (Ohio P.Ct. 1963); *Cross v. Ledford*, 161 Ohio App. 469, 120 N.E.2d 118 (1954); and *Dirion v. Brewer*, 20 Ohio App. 298, 151 N.E. 818, 819 (1925).

17 *Matter of Estate of Stodola*, 519 N.W.2d 97, 99 (Iowa App. 1994).

18 *Staudenmayer v. Staudenmayer*, 714 A.2d 1016, 1022 (Pa. 1998). In *Faber v. TGI-Friday's Inc.*, 148 F.Supp.2d 556, 559 (E.D.Pa. 2001), the proof consisted only of the woman's statement that the parties had lived together as husband and wife for more than ten years. The court stated: "Without more, these averments are insufficient to sustain the heavy burden placed on them to establish a common law marriage..."

19 **Kansas:** *Chandler v. Central Oil Corp. Inc.*, 253 Kan. 50, 853 P.2d 649, 655 (1993); *Cerretti v. Flint Hills Roral Electric Co-op Ass'n*, 251 Kan. 347, 367, 837 P.2d 330 (1992); *Barbara Oil Co. v. Kansas Gas Supply Corp.*, 250 Kan. 438, 448, 827 P.2d 24 (1992). **Oklahoma law**: In *Standefer v. Standefer*, 26 P.3d 104 (Okla. 2001), the Oklahoma Supreme Court stated: "The person seeking to establish a common law marriage espousal relationship has the burden to show by clear and convincing evidence the existence of the marriage." *See also Davis v. State*, 103 P.3d 70 (Okla.Cr.App. 2004);

Attempts have been made to more closely define the meaning of the standard. As a rule, however, the results have consisted mainly of rewriting the phrase and have not contributed greatly to any explanation of

Matter of Death of Boyd, 959 P.2d 612 (Okla.Civ.App. Div. 1 1998) (clear and convincing evidence existed). *Compare Sanders v. Sanders*, 948 P.2d 719, 720 (Okla.Civ.App. Div. 3 1997); *Mueggenborg v. Walling*, 836 P.2d 112, 114 (Okla. 1992); *Lee v. Cotten*, 793 P.2d 1369 (Okla.App. 1990) ("A claim of common law marriage must be supported by clear and convincing proof of the elements thereof"); and *Richardson v. State*, 744 S.W.2d 65, 73 (Tex.Cr.App. 1987) (applying Oklahoma law). In *Matter of Estate of Stinchcomb*, 674 P.2d 26, 29 (Okla. 1983), the court found that the party had "failed to prove a pre-existing common law marriage by clear and convincing evidence." *Compare Hill v. Shreve*, 448 P.2d 848, 851 (Okla. 1968), in which the court stated: "By a preponderance of the evidence, Nell Shreve was the common law wife of Stephen Curtis Shreve." **Texas:** In certain older cases, the Texas courts have required evidence that is clear and satisfactory. This standard was used by the Court of Civil Appeals in *King v. King's Unknown Heirs*, 16 S.W.2d 160, 162 (Tex.Civ.App. 1929), with respect to "decency and good morals." The same standard recurs in *Perales v. Flores*, 147 S.W.2d 974, 976 (Tex.Civ.App.-San Antonio 1941) and *Middlebrook v. Wideman*, 203 S.W.2d 686 (Tex.Civ.App. 1947). *Compare* note 33 *infra.* **Alabama:** *Buford v. Buford*, 874 So.2d 562, 566 (Ala.Civ.App. 2003); *Gray v. Bush*, 835 So.2d 192, 197 (Ala.Civ.App. 2001); *Hall v. Duster*, 727 So.2d 834, 837 (Ala.Civ.App. 1999); *Stringer v. Stringer*, 689 So.2d 194, 197 (Ala.Civ.App. 1997); *Butler v. Coonrod*, 671 So.2d 750 (Ala.Civ.App. 1995); *Lofton v. Estate of Weaver*, 611 So.2d 335, 336 (Ala. 1992) (clear and convincing proof); *Baker v. Townsend*, 484 So.2d 1097, 1098 (Ala.Civ. App. 1986); *Etheridge v. Yeager*, 465 So.2d 378, 380 (Ala. 1985); and *Piel v. Brown*, 361 So.2d 90, 95 (Ala. 1978). *Compare* cases in which the court appears to have accepted a preponderance of the evidence, *infra* note 33. **Ohio:** *Bevan v. Bevan*, 2006 WL 1519654 (Ohio App. 11 Dist.); *Faison v. Faison*, 2005 WL 1303344 (Ohio App. 8 Dist. 2005); *Harris v. Harris*, 2004 WL 2896422 (Ohio App. 9 Dist. 2004); *Kowalik v. Kowalik*, 118 Ohio App.3rd 141, 691 N.E.2d 1152, 1155 (1997); *State v. Phelps*, 100 Ohio App.3rd 187, 652 N.E.2d 1032, 1036 (1995); *In re Estate of Shepherd*, 646 N.E.2d 561, 564 (Ohio App. 3 Dist. 1994); *State v. Burkitt*, 624 N.E.2d 210, 219 (Ohio App. 2 Dist. 1993); and *Warren Gen. Hosp. v. Brink*, 80 Ohio App.3d 793, 610 N.E.2d 1128, 1129 (1992). In the case of *In re Estate of Hall*, 588 N.E.2d 203 (Ohio App. 4 Dist. 1990), the measure of persuasion of clear and convincing evidence was unsuccessfully contested. *See also Fitzgerald v. Mayfield*, 584 N.E.2d 13, 17 (Ohio App. 4 Dist. 1990); *Smith-Wilkins v. Sec'y of HHS*, 880 F.2d 864, 866 (6th Cir. 1989); *Fields v. Fields*, 530 N.E.2d 933, 936 (Ohio App. 1987); and *Nestor v. Nestor*, 15 Ohio St.3rd 143, 15 O.B.R. 291, 472 N.E.2d 1091, 1094 (1984). In *Umbenhower v. Labus*, 85 Ohio St. 238, 97 N.E. 832, 833 (1912), the court spoke of the evidence as clear and satisfactory. **Pennsylvania:** *Staudenmayer v. Staudenmayer*, 714 A.2d 1016, 1022 (Pa. 1998); *Perotti v. Meredith*, 868 A.2d 1240 (Pa.Super. 2005); *State Farm Fire & Cas. Co. v. Platt*, 4 F. Supp.2d 399 (E.D.Pa. 1998); *In re Veneziale*, 267 B.R. 695, 700 (Bkrtcy.E.D.Pa. 2001); *Stuck Leasing Co. v. W.C.A.B. (Ziegler)*, 125 Pa. 237, 557 A.2d 808, 811 (Pa.Cmwlth. 1989); *In re Estate of Kovalchick*, 345 Pa.Super. 229, 498 A.2d 374, 377 (1985); *In re Cummings Estate*, 330 Pa.Super. 255, 479 A.2d 537, 542 (1984); *In re Estate of Garges*, 474 Pa. 237, 378 A.2d 307, 309 (1977); and *In re Gower's Estate*, 445 Pa. 554, 284 A.2d 742, 744 (1972). In the case of *In re Krystkiewicz's Estate*, 310 Pa. 298, 165 A. 230 (1933), a party argued that a preponderance of the evidence was insufficient, instead the standard of clear, consistent, and convincing evidence should be required. The court stated: "We agree that claims of this sort will only be upheld upon evidence sufficient to satisfy the mind of the chancellor that there was an actual agreement to form the lawful relation of husband and wife ... but it was never suggested or intended that the evidence presented in support of the claim must be uncontroverted." **Rhode Island:** *DeMelo v. Zompa*, 844 A.2d 174, 177 (R.I. 2004) (clear and convincing evidence); *Souza v. O'Hara*, 121 R.I. 88, 395 A.2d 1060, 1061 (1978); and *Sardonis v. Sardonis*, 106 R.I. 469, 472, 261 A.2d 22, 24 (1970).

the term. Consequently, one court has stated that this standard of proof, which actually does not refer to the quantity, but rather the quality of the evidence, entails "a firm belief or conviction."[20] Another court has maintained that clear and convincing evidence is "certain, unambiguous and plain to the understanding and so reasonable and persuasive as to cause the trier of fact to believe it."[21] Unconfirmed information from the plaintiff concerning a conversation between the parties has not been viewed as constituting clear and convincing evidence of the existence of an oral marriage contract.[22] It probably is most satisfactory to simply state, as did Homer Clark, that this standard requires "evidence of a more reliable and persuasive quality than that of the ordinary civil lawsuit."[23]

On occasion, the courts include a third element by requiring that the evidence be "clear, consistent and convincing" without, however, intending to materially heighten the requirement with respect to the evidence.[24] This is particularly true in cases from Colorado and Iowa.[25] In Pennsylvania, during the past few years, the courts, on occasion, have used the expression,

---

20 *Cerretti v. Flint Hills Rural Electric Co-op Ass'n*, 251 Kan. 347, 367, 837 P.2d 330 (1992); and *Cross v. Ledford*, 161 Ohio App. 469, 120 N.E.2d 118, 123 (1954). In the later case, the Ohio Supreme Court stated: "The degree of proof required is determined by the impression which the testimony of the witnesses makes upon the trier of facts, and the character of the testimony itself. Credibility, intelligence, freedom from bias or prejudice, opportunity to be informed, the disposition to tell the truth or otherwise, and the probability or improbability of the statements made, are all tests of testimonial value. Where the evidence is in conflict, the trier of facts may determine what should be accepted as the truth and what should false." In *Brastein v. Sedivy*, 11 Ohio Misc. 200, 230 N.E.2d 156 (1957), the court speaks of a degree of evidence "though not necessarily conclusive, which will produce in the mind of the Court a firm belief or conviction."

21 *Chandler v. Central Oil Corp., Inc.*, 253 Kan. 50, 853 P.2d 649, 655 (1993).

22 *Milburn v. Milburn*, 694 N.E.2d 738, 740 (Ind.App. 1998).

23 HOMER H. CLARK, JR. THE LAW OF DOMESTIC RELATIONS IN THE UNITED STATES, 106 (2d ed. 1987).

24 **Colorado**: *see People v. Lucero*, 747 P.2d 660, 664 (Colo. 1987), in which the expression "clear, consistent and convincing evidence" was not considered to entail a higher standard of proof, instead it simply referred to the fact that the parties must present "more than vague claims unsupported by competent evidence." *See also*, *Employer's Mutual Liab. Ins. Co. of Wisconsin v. Indus. Comm'n*, 124 Colo. 68, 234 P.2d 901, 903 (1951); and *Peery v. Peery*, 27 Colo. 271, 150 P.329, 330 (1915). *Compare Klipfel v. Klipfel*, 41 Colo. 40, 92 P.26, 29 (1907), which spoke of the need for "convincing and positive evidence." **Iowa:** *Blessing v. Deere & Co.*, 985 F.Supp. 899, 904 (S.D.Iowa 1997). In the case *Conklin v. MacMillan Oil Co.*, 557 N.W.2d 102 (Iowa App. 1996), the court required "a preponderance of clear, consistent and convincing evidence." *See also Matter of Estate of Stodola*, 519 N.W.2d 97, 98 (Iowa App. 1994); *In re Marriage of Gebhardt*, 426 N.W.2d 651, 652 (Iowa App. 1988); *State v. Ware*, 338 N.W.2d 707, 711 (Iowa 1983); *In re Estate of Dallman*, 228 N.W.2d 187 (Iowa 1975); *In re Estate of Fisher*, 176 N.W.2d 801, 805 (Iowa 1970); *In re Estate of Malli*, 260 Iowa 252, 149 N.W.2d 155, 158 (1967); *Coleman v. Graves*, 255 Iowa 396, 122 N.W.2d 853, 856 (1963) ("We conclude plaintiff's burden to establish a common law marriage by clear consistent and convincing evidence is not met"); and *In re Long's Estate*, 251 Iowa 1042, 102 N.W.2d 76, 79 (1960) ("When one party is dead, the essential elements must be shown by clear, consistent and convincing evidence").

25 *People v. Lucero*, 747 P.2d 660, 664 (Colo. 1987).

"clear evidence of a change in status" instead of the term "clear and convincing evidence."[26] It is common, however, that the courts, in determining the issue of whether a common law marriage has been formed, have chosen a higher than usual standard from among the above-mentioned possibilities.

A separate issue is that the principally high standard of proof, in many cases, is not accompanied by an equally strict application. Consequently, as shown in Chapter 7, the standard of proof is not an impediment to the court, with the support of circumstantial evidence, for finding the existence of a marriage contract. In *Piel v. Brown* (1978), the parties had lived together for nine years and enjoyed a reputation as spouses. The woman filed her tax returns as single and had her own bank account. The parties had not entered into any express marriage contract. The Alabama Supreme Court began by stating that, given the serious nature of the marriage relationship, the courts closely scrutinize a claim of common law marriage and require clear and convincing proof. Nevertheless, the court found that the parties' intent to form a common law marriage could be inferred from the circumstances and, therefore, that such a marriage had been proven.[27] The cohabitation in the case of *In re Estate of Fisher* (1970) was considerably shorter. The parties had cohabited five months, two without any marital impediment, and had presented themselves as spouses. The Iowa Supreme Court, following the principle that a common law marriage always must be closely scrutinized, found that the marital relationship was proven by clear, consistent, and convincing evidence.[28]

It has been occasionally argued that the courts, in trying cases concerning common law marriages, should set the standard of proof lower in certain types of cases, for example, if the issue concerns the legitimacy of

26 **Pennsylvania:** *Cann v. Cann*, 632 A.2d 322, 325 (Pa.Super. 1993); *Canute v. Canute*, 384 Pa.Super. 60, 557 A.2d 772 (1989); and *Steadman v. Turner*, 357 Pa.Super. 361, 516 A.2d 21, 23 (1986).

27 *Piel v. Brown*, 361 So.2d 90, 95 (Ala. 1978). *See, e.g., Krier v. Krier*, 676 So.2d 1335 (Ala. Civ.App. 1996), in which the parties, after being divorced for a period of ten months, cohabited together again, then separated again. Despite the man's objection that the parties "had no intent to resume a marital relationship" the court directly relied upon the cohabitation and the parties' holding out to reach the conclusion that a common law marriage existed. No closer assessments were made by the court with respect to the contractual issue. *See also, e.g., Dibble v. Dibble*, 88 Ohio App. 490, 100 N.E.2d 451 (1950), in which a common law marriage was proven with clear and convincing evidence despite the fact that the contract was inferred and based on circumstantial evidence.

28 *In re Estate of Fisher*, 176 N.W.2d 801, 807 (Iowa 1970). *Compare In re Marriage of Mosher*, 243 Ill.App.3d 97, 612 N.E.2d 838 (1993), in which the parties had cohabited five months in Iowa and the facts with respect to their presentations were contested. The woman alleged that the man presented her as his "wife," while the man alleged that he presented her as the "mother of my children" and as "my woman." The majority for the court found that the requisites of continuous cohabitation and public declaration were proven, but not the requisite of intent and agreement that they were married. *Compare Newton v. Lehman*, 105 Ill.App.2d 442, 244 N.E.2d 830 (1969), in which a common law marriage also was not proven.

a child[29] or workers' compensation,[30] as opposed to whether the claim is entitlement to a probate estate or for alimony in connection with a divorce. Even though the actual evaluation of the evidence varies from case to case, there is scarcely any support in the case law for the argument that the courts, with rare exceptions, as a matter of principle should apply a different standard of proof in such cases.[31] The fact that the protection of the legitimacy of any children is a justification behind the marriage presumption is a separate issue discussed further below.

9.2.2 A Preponderance of Evidence

The fact that many courts have not applied a standard of proof to common law marriage that is higher than that applied to other civil cases is often overlooked. The courts instead have only required a preponderance of evidence or similar wording. In several cases, the application of this standard of proof has been supported by the court stating expressly that it does not have a negative attitude towards common law marriage. Consequently, in *Metropolitan Life Ins. Co. v. Johnson* (1982), the Idaho Supreme Court stated: "In contrast with other jurisdictions, Idaho has never viewed the doctrine of common law marriage with disfavor. Together with a small number of other states, Idaho permits a non-ceremonial marriage to be proven by a preponderance of the evidence."[32] The number of states applying this standard of proof is not as limited as the court assumes, because approximately half the states recognizing common law marriages apply this standard.[33] In Utah, common law marriage is regulated by

29 CLARK, *supra* note 23, at 109, which refers to the Ohio Court of Appeals' decision in *Gatterdam v. Gatterdam*, 86 Ohio App. 29, 85 N.E.2d 526 (1949) and to *Tarter v. Medley*, 356 S.W.2d 255 (Ky. 1962). It ought, however, be noted that the Ohio Supreme Court in the case of *In re Redman's Estate*, 135 Ohio St. 554, 21 N.E.2d 659, 661 (1939), stated that the requirement of clear and convincing evidence was also applicable to cases concerning the legitimacy of children.

30 ALBERT C. JACOBS AND JULIUS GOEBEL, JR., CASES AND OTHER MATERIALS ON DOMESTIC RELATIONS 96-97 (4th ed. 1961).

31 In the case, *Richard v. Richard*, 172 Okla. 397, 45 P.2d 101, 108 (1935), the Oklahoma Supreme Court required evidence that was clear and convincing, but was prepared to make an exception in cases concerning the legitimacy of children. *Compare Chapman v. State*, 84 Okla.Crim.App. 41, 178 P.2d 638, 641 (1947), where the Criminal Court of Appeals required evidence that was clear and convincing as the parties had no mutual children.

32 *Metro. Life Ins. Co. v. Johnson*, 103 Idaho 122, 645 P.2d 356, 360 (1982); and *Wilkins v. Wilkins*, 48 P.3d 644 (Idaho 2002). Observe, however, that Idaho repealed the recognition of common law marriage beginning 1996, *see* H.B. 176; Chap. 104, Idaho Session Laws (1995).

33 **Montana:** *Miller v. Townsend Lumber Co.*, 448 P.2d 148 (Mont. 1968); *Miller v. Sutherland*, 131 Mont. 175, 309 P.2d 322, 327 (1957). **Idaho:** *Matter of Estate of Wagner*, 126 Idaho 848, 893 P.2d 211, 214 (1995); *Freiburghaus v. Freiburghaus*, 103 Idaho 679, 651 P.2d 944, 946 (App. 1982); *Metro. Life Ins. Co. v. Johnson*, 103 Idaho 122, 645 P.2d 356, 360 (1982); *Mauldin v. Sunshine Mining Co.*, 61 Idaho 9, 97 P.2d 608 (1939)(this is the same burden of proof as with respect to other cases, IDAHO CODE ANN. § 32-203 (1985). **Utah:** UTAH CODE ANN. § 30-1-4.5(2)(1987); *Hansen v. Hansen*, 958 P.2d 931

a statute that states that such a marriage may be proved under the same general rules of evidence as facts in other cases.[34] In *Hansen v. Hansen* (1998), the question was how this standard should be interpreted. The lower court had tried the case according to a standard of clear and

---

(Utah App. 1998); *State v. Johnson,* 856 P.2d 1064, 1069 (Utah 1993). **Colorado:** In *Knaus v. Relyea,* 746 S.W.2d 389, 391 (Ark.App. 1988), the Arkansas Court of Appeals stated, when applying Colorado law: "In the case at bar, there simply is not enough 'objective evidence' to hold that by a preponderance of evidence a present agreement existed between the appellant and Mark Relyea to be husband and wife." In *Taylor v. Taylor,* 10 Colo.App. 303, 50 P. 1049, 1050 (1897): "[T]he proof failed to sustain the allegations of plaintiff and any other finding and judgment would have been against the great weight and preponderance of the evidence." With respect to Colorado, *compare* note 23 *supra.* **Kansas:** *Chandler v. Central Oil Corp., Inc.,* 253 Kan. 50, 853 P.2d 649, 654 (1993). To break the presumption for the advantage of the later of two marriages, the court in Kansas required clear and convincing evidence. **Texas:** In *Jenkins v. Jenkins,* 16 S.W.3rd 473, 480 (Tex.App.-El Paso 2000), the court stated that the woman "had the burden to establish her alleged common law marriage by a preponderance of the evidence." *See also Welch v. State,* 908 S.W.2d 258, 265 (Tex.App.-El Paso 1995); *In re Marriage of Britton,* 970 S.W.2d 389,390 (Mo.App.S.D. 1998) (applying Texas law); *Weaver v. State,* 855 S.W.2d 116, 120 (Tex.App.-Houston (14th Dist.) 1993); *Richardson v. State,* 744 S.W.2d 65, 73 (Tex.Cr.App. 1987); and *Carson v. Kee,* 677 S.W.2d 283, 284 (Tex.App.-Fort Worth 1984). In *Daniel v. Daniel,* 676 S.W.2d 666, 669 (Tex.App.-Beaumont (9 Dist.) 1984), it was found correct to question the jury as to each of the necessary requisites for a common law marriage: "Do you find from a preponderance of the evidence that..." **Alabama:** *Coleman v. Nicholson,* 2006 WL 1523178 (Vet.App. 2006) (death benefits) and *Rogers v. McLeskey,* 225 Ala. 148, 142 So. 526, 529 (1932), *compare* the general rule, note 19 *supra.* **Georgia law:** In the case of *In re Estate of Wilson,* 512 S.E.2d 383, 385 (Ga.App. 1999), the burden of proof was allocated to the party alleging the common law marriage. *See also Wright v. Goss,* 229 Ga.App. 393, 394 (1), 494 S.E.2d 23 (1997). In *Frazier v. State,* 219 Ga.App. 768, 467 S.E.2d 338, 341 (1995), the court stated that the party alleging the existence of a common law marriage must prove it with a preponderance of the evidence. *See also Dismuke v. C & Strust Co.,* 407 S.E.2d 739, 740 (Ga. 1991). This is also true when the defendant in a criminal case argues that the crime of kidnapping cannot be committed within a common law marriage, despite the fact that the burden of proof according to the general rule rests with the prosecutor, *see Dixon v. State,* 217 Ga.App. 267, 456 S.E.2d 758, 760 (1995). In *Jenkins v. Jenkins,* 83 Ga. 286, 9 S.E. 541, 542 (1889), the Georgia Supreme Court stated "the greater weight of evidence." **South Carolina:** *Callen v. Callen,* 365 S.C. 618, 620 S.E.2d 59, 62 (2005); *Barker v. Baker,* 330 S.C. 361, 499 S.E.2d 503, 508 (App. 1998); *Owens v. Owens,* 466 S.E.2d 373 (S.C.App. 1996); *Jeanes v. Jeanes,* 255 S.C. 161, 177 S.E.2d 537 (1970); *Yarbrough v. Yarbrough,* 280 S.C. 546, 314 S.E.2d 16 (App. 1984); *Kirby v. Kirby,* 270 S.C. 137, 241 S.E.2d 415 (1978); and *Ex Parte Blizzard,* 185 S.C. 131, 193 S.E. 633 (1937). **Iowa:** *In re Marriage of Gebhardt,* 426 N.W.2d 651 (Iowa App. 1988); *In re Marriage of Grother,* 242 N.W.2d 1 (Iowa 1976). *Compare* note 24 *supra.* **District of Columbia:** *Mesa v. United States,* 875 A.2d 79 (D.C.App. 2005); *Dickey v. Office of Personnel Management,* 419 F.3d 1336, 1340 (C.A.Fed. 2005); *Coates v. Watts,* 622 A.2d 25, 27 (D.C.App. 1993); and *Robinson v. Evans,* 554 A.2d 332, 337 (D.C.App. 1989). The question can be raised whether the standard of proof was the object for the differing opinions in *East v. East,* 536 A.2d 1103, 1105 (D.C.App. 1988), in which the Court of Appeals simply required a preponderance of the evidence to overcome the presumption to the advantage of the later of two marriages. Generally, in the District of Columbia, the standard of clear and convincing evidence is required. *See Gordon v. Railroad Retirement Bd.,* 225 U.S.App.D.C. 49, 50, 696 F.2d 131, 132 (1983); and *Johnson v. Young,* 372 A.2d 992, 994 (D.C. 1977).

34 UTAH CODE ANN. § 30-1-4.5(2) (Michie 1987).

convincing evidence. The Court of Appeals, however, found that a correct interpretation of the regulation was by the preponderance of the evidence. The court's application of the lower standard resulted, however, in no change to the trial court's conclusion that no common law marriage had been established by the evidence.[35]

In an attempt to more closely define this standard of proof, the Kansas Supreme Court in *Chandler v. Central Oil Corp., Inc.* (1993), stated that the trier of fact had to be convinced by "a preponderance of the credible evidence that the party's position on an issue is more probably true than not true based upon the whole record."[36] The application of this lower standard of proof does not entail the courts' failure to uphold the requirement of an especially thorough examination in cases concerning common law marriages.[37]

These burdens of proof result in the party alleging the existence of a common law marriage having to either prove each of the requisites necessary for the formation of a common law marriage with clear and convincing evidence or a preponderance of the evidence. The party basing the claim on the existence of such a marriage, according to Pennsylvania law, consequently must prove the existence of a marital *consensus* with evidence that is clear and convincing, while the party alleging the existence of a common law marriage according to Texas law has to prove with a preponderance of the evidence that the parties 1) agreed to be married, 2) lived together, and 3) represented to others that they were married.[38]

The discussion above concerns the burden of proof with respect to the establishment of informal marriages. Alternatively, whether an already existing common law marriage is invalid, an issue that is outside this

---

35 *Hansen v. Hansen*, 958 P.2d 931 (Utah App. 1998). Neither the requirement of a marriage contract or of a reputation as spouses was found to be proven.

36 *Chandler v. Central Oil Corp., Inc.*, 253 Kan. 50, 853 P.2d 649, 654 (1993). *Compare Jeanes v. Jeanes*, 255 S.C. 161, 177 S.E.2d 537 (1970), in which the South Carolina Supreme Court named a "preponderance or greater weight of evidence." In *Brastein v. Sedivy*, 11 Ohio Misc. 200, 230 N.E.2d 156 (1957), the court stated that preponderance was not "determined by the number of witnesses but by the weight of the evidence which weight is determined by the witnesses' opportunity for knowledge, the information actually possessed and related, and the manner in which the testimony is given." *Compare Jenkins v. Jenkins*, 83 Ga. 286, 9 S.E. 541, 542 (1889), in which the Georgia Supreme Court used the phrase "the greater weight of evidence."

37 *See, e.g.*, with respect to Texas law, *People v. Badgett*, 41 Cal.Rptr.2d 635, 895 P.2d 877, 897 (1995) (applying Texas law); *Hightower v. State*, 629 S.W.2d 920 (Tex.Cr.App. 1981); and *Gary v. Gary*, 490 S.W.2d 929, 935 (Tex.Civ.App.-Tyler 1973). For Iowa law, *see In re Marriage of Grother*, 242 N.W.2d 1 (Iowa 1976).

38 *Flores v. Flores*, 847 S.W.2d 648, 651 (Tex.App.-Waco 1993) ("Peggy bore the burden of proof on all of the elements of her alleged common law marriage"); *Chandler v. Central Oil Corp., Inc.*, 253 Kan. 50, 853 P.2d 649, 654 (1993); and *Warren Gen. Hosp. v. Brink*, 80 Ohio App.3d 793, 610 N.E.2d 1128, 1129 (1992) ("all three of the essential elements must be established by clear and convincing evidence"). In the case *Matter of Estate of Stodola*, 519 N.W.2d 97, 98 (Iowa App. 1994), the court required that the party alleging the existence of a common law marriage "must prove three elements by a preponderance of clear, consistent and convincing evidence."

discussion, generally relies on the principle that the burden of proof falls on the party alleging the invalidity of the marriage. The party maintaining that a common law marriage is invalid because one party is already united with a third party in either marriage by a ceremonial wedding or a common law marriage, consequently has the burden of proof with respect to both the existence of the previous marriage and the fact that it had not been dissolved by divorce.[39]

9.3 The Marriage Presumption

9.3.1 The Background

Beginning early in the American case law, the courts have applied the legal marriage presumption that two parties are presumed to be married to each other: *maxim semper praesumitur pro matrimonio* if they have lived together and had a reputation as spouses.[40] In *Richard v. Brehm* (1873), the Pennsylvania Supreme Court stated that the parties' cohabitation and reputation as spouses was necessary to establish a presumption of marriage.[41] The Pennsylvania Superior Court refers to the same presumption

39 *Lott v. Toomey*, 477 So.2d 316 (Ala. 1985); and *Cross v. Rudder*, 380 So.2d 766 (Ala. 1979). In *Roy v. Ind. Comm'n*, 397 P.2d 211, 214 (Ariz. 1964), the Arizona Supreme Court found, applying Texas law, that the parties had established a common law marriage and: "Once established there is a strong presumption that the marriage continued, and this record does not contain sufficient evidence to rebut it." *See also Clark v. Glenn*, 249 Ala. 342, 31 So.2d 507 (1947); *Sloss-Sheffield Steel & Iron Co. v. Alexander*, 241 Ala. 476, 3 So.2d 46 (1941); *Bell v. Tennessee Coal, Iron & R. Co.*, 240 Ala. 422, 199 So. 813 (1941); *Lea v. Galbraith*, 64 Idaho 724, 137 P.2d 320 (1943); *Hadley v. Rash*, 21 Mont. 170, 53 P. 312 (1898); *Brokeshoulder v. Brokeshoulder*, 84 Okla. 249, 204 P. 284, 34 ALR 441 (1921); *Tedder v. Tedder*, 108 S.C. 271, 94 S.E. 19, (1917) (*cited in* 2 A.L.R. 438); *King v. King*, 269 Ala. 468, 114 So.2d 145 (1959); *Thomey v. Thomey*, 67 Idaho 393, 181 P.2d 777 (1947) ("When a marriage has been shown in evidence, whether regular or irregular, and whatever form of proof, law raises a strong presumption of its legality casting the burden of proof upon the party objecting"); *Mauldine v. Sunshine Mining Co.*, 61 Idaho 9, 97 P.2d 608, 611 (1939); *Texas Employers' Ins. Ass'n. v. Elder*, 155 Tex. 27, 282 S.W.2d 371 (1955); and *Nixon v. Wichita Land & Cattle Co.*, 84 Tex. 408, 19 S.W. 560 (1892). The burden of proof is considered to lie with the party objecting to the validity of an already existing common law marriage also in cases where the marriage is based on a presumption or circumstantial evidence, *see for example Thomson v. Thomson*, 236 Mo.App. 1223, 163 S.W.2d 792 (1942).

40 We meet this principle as early as in the legal scholarship of Joel Prentiss Bishop, New Commentaries on Marriage, Divorce, and Separation I, § 77 (Chicago, T.H. Flood & Co. 1891). *See also Hilton v. Roylance,* 25 Utah 129, 69 P. 660, 663 (1902).

41 *Richard v. Brehm*, 73 Pa. 140, 141 (1873). The case, in which a common law marriage was found formed, is a good example of how a court reasons with the application of a legal presumption with the reallocation of the burden of proof based on the parties' cohabitation and reputation. The opposing party was not successful in proving that the marriage contract had not been entered into: "His declaration made upon one occasion, when angry at his wife, to her sister, that they were not married, after more than thirty-five years of apparent wedded life was certainly very weak evidence to rebut the presumption of marriage." *Id.* at 145. *Compare* from the same time

in *Commonwealth v. McLean* (1989) when it states that there is a rebuttable presumption of marriage.[42] The presumption is unique in that it reallocates the burden of proof with respect to the elements of the marriage contract. The party contesting the existence of a common law marriage has to prove that no marriage contract was formed.

This presumption, which became a fixture in the American case law already during the 1800s, appears to have originated in Scottish law,[43] which until 2006 allowed the formation of an irregular marriage "by cohabitation, habit and repute," a reminiscence of the original marriage presumption applied in Scotland, discussed further in Chapter 11, "Scottish Irregular Marriages." The American marriage presumption is applied both in states recognizing common law marriages and in states only recognizing ceremonial marriages. However, the application in the latter states falls outside the framework of this analysis.[44]

Among the states recognizing common law marriages, the legal marriage presumption currently is most supported and consistently applied by courts

---

period *Yardley's Estate*, 75 Pa. 207, 211 (1874): "Neither cohabitation nor reputation of marriage, nor both, is marriage. When conjoined they are evidence from which a presumption of marriage arises." *See* the same court in *Com. v. Stump*, 53 Pa. 132, 91 Am.Dec. 198 (1866). Early in the 1800s, the courts in Pennsylvania accepted the parties' cohabitation and reputation as very strong and even sufficient evidence of a marriage contract, without expressly creating a presumption reallocating the burden of proof. *See Chambers v. Dickson*, 2 S. & R. 475 (Pa. 1816); *Senser v. Bower*, 1 Pa. 450 (1830); *Guardian of the Poor v. Nathans*, 2 Brewster 149 (1845); *Covert v. Herzog*, 4 Pa. 145 (1846); *Thorndell v. Morrison*, 25 Pa. 326 (1855); and *Physick's Estate*, 2 Brewster 179 (1862). *Compare* FREEDMAN, *supra* note 14, at 130, which views these as presumption cases.

42 *Com. v. McLean*, 387 Pa.Super. 354, 564 A.2d 216 (1989).

43 A Scottish influence can be clearly seen in two of the most historically significant cases with respect to presumptions in American case law, namely *Yardley's Estate*, 75 Pa. 207 (1874), heard by the Pennsylvania Supreme Court and *Hynes v. McDermott*, 91 N.Y. 451, 459 (1883) *cited in* 43 Am.Rep. 677, heard by the New York Court of Appeals. *See also Cargile v. Wood*, 63 Mo. 501 (1876) and *Fryer v. Fryer*, 9 S.C.Eq. (Rich. Cas.) 85 (1832).

44 The presumption's application in cases with ceremonial marriages in different states is rather unclear. In OTTO E. KOEGEL, COMMON LAW MARRIAGE AND ITS DEVELOPMENT IN THE UNITED STATES, 151 (1922), the author during the 1920s stated that "it is a presumption prevailing everywhere." *See also* Walter O. Weyrauch, *Informal and formal marriage - an appraisal of trends in family organization*, 28 U. CHI. L. REV. 88, 105 fn. 83 (1960), stating in 1960 that "marriage by presumption is available in all American jurisdictions, particularly all those that purportedly do not recognize common law marriage." *Compare* Walter O. Weyrauch, Sanford N. Katz, AMERICAN FAMILY LAW IN TRANSITION 137 (1983): "The presumption of marriage is available in all American jurisdictions, regardless of whether or not they still recognize common law marriage." *See, e.g., Matter of Estate of Lowney* 543 N.Y.S.2d 698 (A.D. 2 Dep't 1989); and *Douglas Northwest v. Bill O'Brian & Sons*, 828 P.2d 565 (Wash.App. 1992). *See also In re Estate of Buttrick*, 597 A.2d 74 (1991). *Compare* HARRY D. KRAUSE ET AL., FAMILY LAW, CASES, COMMENTS, AND QUESTIONS 87 (5th ed. 2003), who states: "There is no presumption that persons are married."

in Pennsylvania,[45] Montana,[46] Idaho,[47] South Carolina,[48] and Alabama,[49] while it is applied more sporadically, often in older case law, in Georgia,[50]

---

45 In Pennsylvania case law, the marriage presumption has arisen in several cases, albeit that the conditions for its application have not always been present, *see, e.g.*, *In re Veneziale*, 267 B.R. 695, 700 (Bkrtcy.E.D.Pa. 2001); *Staudenmayer v. Staudenmayer*, 714 A.2d 1016, 1020-1021 (Pa. 1998); *Africa v. Vaughan*, 998 F.Supp. 552 (E.D.Pa. 1998); *State Farm Fire & Cas. Co. v. Platt*, 4 F.Supp.2d 399 (E.D.Pa. 1998); *Com. v. Wilson*, 672 A.2d 293, 301 (Pa. 1996); *Eagle v. W.C.A.B (Bahorich)*, 602 A.2d 387, 388 (Pa.Cmwlth. 1992); *Stuck Leasing Co. v. W.C.A.B. (Ziegler)*, 557 A.2d 808 (Pa.Cmwlth. 1989); *Estate of Gavula*, 490 Pa. 535, 417 A.2d 168, 171 fn. 7 (1980); *In re Estate of Garges*, 474 Pa. 237, 378 A.2d 307, 309 (1977); *Baker v. Mitchell*, 143 Pa.Super. 50, 17 A.2d 738 (1941); *In re Craig's Estate*, 273 Pa. 530, 117 A. 221, 222 (1922); *In re Stevenson's Estate*, 272 Pa. 291, 297, 116 A. 162, 164 (1922); *Com. v. Haylow*, 17 Pa.Super. 541 (1901); *In re Grimm's Estate*, 131 Pa. 199, 18 A. 1061 (1889); *Appeal of Reading Fire Ins. & Trust Co.*, 113 Pa. 204, 6 A. 60 (1886); *Hunt's Appeal*, 86 Pa. 294 (1878); *Brinckle v. Brinckle*, 12 Phila. 232 (1877); *Yardley's Estate*, 75 Pa. 207 (1874); *Richard v. Brehm*, 73 Pa. 140, 145 (1873); *Bicking's Appeal*, 2 Brewster 202 (1868); and *Com. v. Stump*, 53 Pa. 132, 91 Am.Dec. 198 (1866). Observe that common law marriage, as was mentioned in chapter 1, was repealed in Pennsylvania in 2005, however not retroactively, *see* 23 PA. CONS. STAT. ANN. 1103 (WEST 2005).

46 In Montana, the presumption is legislated, MONT. CODE ANN. § 26-1-602(30) MCA (1999), which is comparable to older law, § 93-1301-7 RCM (1947) and §§ 10606 (30) Rev. Code (1935) and (1921): "All other presumptions are 'disputable presumptions' and may be controverted by other evidence. The following are of that kind:...(30) 'A man and a woman deporting themselves as husband and wife have entered into a lawful contract of marriage'." In the case of *In re Ober*, 2003 MT 7, 314 Mont. 20, 62 P.3d 1114 (2003), the court stated that "public policy, as well as statutory law, favors the finding of a valid marriage." *See also Matter of Estate of Alcorn*, 868 P.2d 629 (Mont. 1994)(dictum); *In re Marriage of Geertz*, 755 P.2d 34, 37 (Mont. 1988); and *Matter of Estate of Murnion*, 212 Mont. 107, 686 P.2d 893, 41 St.Rep. 1627 (1984).

47 *See, e.g.*, *Wilkins v. Wilkins*, 48 P.3d 644 (Idaho 2002); *McCoy v. McCoy*, 868 P.2d 527 (Idaho App. 1994); *Matter of Estate of Eliasen*, 105 Idaho 234, 668 P.2d 110 (1983); *Freiburghaus v. Freiburghaus*, 103 Idaho 679, 651 P.2d 944, 946 (App. 1982); and *Metro. Life Ins. Co. v. Johnson*, 103 Idaho 122, 645 P.2d 356, 361 (1982). Observe that common law marriage, as was mentioned in chapter 1, was repealed in Idaho January 1, 1996, however not retroactively, *see* IDAHO CODE ANN. § 32-201 (2) (Michie 2003).

48 *See Callen v. Callen*, 365 S.C. 618, 620 S.E.2d 59, 62 (2005)(dictum). The clearest case is *Barker v. Baker*, 330 S.C. 361, 499 S.E.2d 503 (App. 1998), in which, however, the requisites for the application of the presumption were not fulfilled. *See also Owens v. Owens*, 466 S.E.2d 373 (S.C.App. 1996) and *Jeanes v. Jeanes*, 255 S.C. 161, 177 S.E.2d 537, 539-540 (1970). *Compare In re Greenfield's Estate*, 245 S.C. 595, 141 S.E.2d 916 (1965). *See also* Judge Goolsby's separate opinion in *Richland Memorial Hosp. v. English*, 295 S.C. 511, 369 S.E.2d 395 (1988). For older case law, *see Fryer v. Fryer*, 9 S.C.Eq. (Rich.Cas.) 85 (1832)(dictum).

49 *See, e.g.*, *Crosson v. Crosson*, 668 So.2d 868, 872 (Ala.Civ.App. 1995); *Rickard v. Trousdale*, 508 So.2d 260, 261 (Ala. 1987); *Steele v. Steele*, 522 So.2d 269 (Ala. 1988); and *Krug v. Krug*, 296 So.2d 715 (Ala. 1974).

50 The presumption is referred to in *Edwards v. Edwards*, 136 Ga.App. 668, 222 S.E.2d 169, 171 (1975); *Simeonides v. Zervis*, 127 Ga.App. 506, 194 S.E.2d 324, 326 (1972); *Cooper v. Cooper*, 88 Ga.App. 335, 76 S.E.2d 726, 728 (1953); *Brown v. State*, 208 Ga. 304, 66 S.E.2d 745, 748 (1951); *Addison v. Addison*, 186 Ga. 155, 197 S.E. 232, 233 (1938); *Adger v. Ackerman*, 115 F. 124, 129 (8th Cir. 1902); *Norman v. Good*, 113 Ga. 121, 38 S.E. 317 (1901); *Jenkins v. Jenkins*, 83 Ga. 286, 9 S.E. 541 (1889); *Clark v. Cassidy*, 64 Ga. 662 (1880); and *Dillon v. Dillon*, 60 Ga. 204 (1878). Observe that common law marriage, as was mentioned in chapter 1, was repealed in Georgia

Oklahoma,[51] and Ohio.[52] In other states, for example, in Texas, where the presumption is not applied, the parties' cohabitation and reputation as spouses has been viewed as evidence in cases concerning common law marriages. However, the existence of these circumstances, without the support of the legal marriage presumption, does not reallocate the burden of proof with respect to the elements of the marriage contract as further discussed in Chapter 7.[53]

9.3.2 The Motivations for the Presumption

The marriage presumption, in contrast to the burden of proof discussed in the previous section, is based on entirely different considerations. While the strict burden of proof rests on a negative and restrained view of common law marriage, the presumption is meant to be the basis of a positive attempt to rescue the cohabiting couple, and give them the status of marriage. This endeavor, which can be seen most clearly in the case law from the latter 1800s, has a moral tinge. The community, fueled by moral indignation, enforced criminal laws pertaining to concubinage and other "loose" relationships. Simultaneously, however, the community offered a morally acceptable redemption that elevated informal cohabitations with a marital reputation, giving these relationships the status of marriage.

January 1, 1997, however not retroactively, *see* GA. CODE ANN. §§ 19-3-1.1 (West 2003).

51 *See, e.g., Tower v. Towie,* 368 P.2d 488 (Okla. 1962); *Burdine v. Burdine,* 206 Okla. 170, 242 P.2d 148 (1952); and *Olinghouse v. Olinghouse,* 265 P.2d 711 (Okla. 1954).

52 The presumption has questionable support in the cases from Ohio, *see, e.g., In re Maynard's Estate,* 117 Ohio.App. 315, 192 N.E.2d 281, *appeal denied* 174 Ohio St. 211 187 N.E.2d 883 (1962); *Ryan v. Ryan,* 84 Ohio App. 139, 86 N.E.2d 44 (1948); *Lumas v. Lumas,* 26 Ohio App. 502, 160 N.E. 480 (1927); *Dirion v. Brewer,* 20 Ohio App. 298, 151 N.E. 818 (1925); and *Johnson v. Dudley,* 3 Ohio N.P. 196 (1896). Observe that common law marriage, as was mentioned in chapter 1, was repealed in Ohio October 10, 1991, however not retroactively, *see* OHIO REV. CODE ANN. § 3105.12 (B) (1, 2) (WEST 1991).

53 With respect to Texas law, *see, e.g., Russell v. Russell,* 865 S.W.2d 929, 933 (Tex. 1993), where the Texas Supreme Court accepted circumstantial evidence as evidence of a marriage contract, but clearly emphasized the weight that each of the requisites should be accorded in the evidentiary valuation. With respect to Colorado, *see People v. Lucero,* 747 P.2d 660, 664 (Colo. 1987). With respect to Iowa, *see Note, Presumptions in Common Law Marriage,* 14 IOWA L. REV. 215, 217 (1929), which discusses presumptions, but cites cases from other states. *Compare Conklin v. MacMillan Oil Co.,* 557 N.W.2d 102, 105 (Iowa App. 1996), in which the court states: "A continuous cohabitation of the parties and the declaration or holding out to the public they were, in fact, husband and wife constitutes circumstantial evidence which tends to create a fair presumption that a common law marital relationship existed." A presumption resulting in the reallocation of the burden of proof, however, was not discussed. *See also In re Marriage of Winegard,* 257 N.W.2d 609, 617 (Iowa 1977); and *Blessing v. Deere & Co.,* 985 F.Supp. 899, 904 (S.D.Iowa 1997). In Utah, where common law marriages are regulated by legislation, it appears that there is no leeway for the application of a marriage presumption reallocating the burden of proof, as each element, including the marriage contract, the cohabitation, reputation, etc., must be demonstrated, *see for example Hansen v. Hansen,* 958 P.2d 931, 935 (Utah App. 1998).

The great dignity assigned to marriage by the legal system was a central premise of the presumption. Michael Grossberg argues that the judicial incorporation of the marriage presumption was driven by a persistent inclination to find matrimony whenever a man and woman lived together.[54] This inclination is especially pronounced in situations involving in protecting the interests of children and their legitimacy; surviving spouses and children upon the death of a spouse; and upholding the principles favoring remarriage. Thus, the presumption is viewed as constituting an offshoot of the more general presumption, namely, the presumption of innocence, which means that the parties are presumed not to be violating the order of society and breaking either criminal or civil law.[55] Consequently, the underlying basis of the presumption strongly resembles the factors underlying the entire concept of common law marriage.[56]

The marriage presumption, a court stated: "The law presumes morality and not immorality; marriage, and not concubinage; legitimacy, and not bastardy."[57] This and similar language recur even in the modern case law.[58]

---

54 Michael Grossberg, Governing The Hearth: Law and the Family in Nineteenth Century America 79 (1985), with references.

55 Bishop, *supra* note 40, §§ 931-932, and Joel Prentiss Bishop, Commentaries on the Law of Marriage and Divorce, and Evidence in Matrimonial Suits § 324 (Boston 1852).

56 As to the underlying factors behind the legal principle of common law marriage, *see* Chapter 4 *supra* and the future perspective presented in Chapter 14 *infra*.

57 *Hynes v. McDermott*, 91 N.Y. 451, 459 (1883) *cited in* 43 Am.Rep. 677. The named underlying factors are cited with approval in number of cases even today. As to jurisdictions that presently recognize common law marriage, particularly cases from Idaho and South Carolina, *see, e.g., Huff v. Huff*, 20 Idaho 450, 118 P. 1080 (1911); *Ollschlager v. Widmer*, 55 Or. 145, 105 P. 717 (1909); *Thomas v. James*, 69 Okla. 285, 171 P. 855, 858 (1918) (Oklahoma law); *Labonte v. Davidson*, 31 Idaho 644, 175 P. 588 (1918); *Smith v. Smith*, 32 Idaho 478, 482, 185 P. 67, 69 (1919); *Mauldin v. Sunshine Mining Co.*, 61 Idaho 9, 17, 97 P.2d 608, 611 (1939); *Nicholas v. Idaho Power Co.*, 63 Idaho 675, 125 P.2d 321 (1942); *Warner v. Warner*, 76 Idaho 399, 282 P.2d 931, 934 (1955); *Thomey v. Thomey*, 67 Idaho 393, 181 P.2d 777, 779 (1947); *Jeanes v. Jeanes*, 255 S.C. 161, 177 S.E.2d 537, 539-540 (1970); *In re Estate of Brock*, 94 Idaho 111, 482 P.2d 86, 90 (1971); and *Metro. Life Ins. Co. v. Johnson*, 103 Idaho 122, 645 P.2d 356, 361 (1982).

58 *See* the Montana Supreme Court in *Matter of Estate of Murnion*, 212 Mont. 107, 686 P.2d 893, 41 St.Rep. 1627 (1984); *In re Estate of Slavens*, 162 Mont. 123, 509 P.2d 293, 294-295 (1973); and *In re Estate of Swanson*, 160 Mont. 271, 502 P.2d 33, 37 (1972) ("Every intendment of the law is in favor of matrimony which presumes morality and not immorality, marriage and not concubinage, legitimacy and not bastardy"). In *Thomas v. Murphy*, 71 App. D.C. 69, 107 F.2d 268, 269 (1938), the court stated that it was socially sound to favor marriage between parties before "concubinage." The marriage presumption, however, was not expressly mentioned. *See, e.g., Welch v. All Persons*, 78 Mont. 370, 254 P. 179, 182 (1926) ("Every presumption will be indulged in favor of the legality of a common law marriage in the same way and to the same extent as law indulges them in favor of a ceremonial marriage"); and *Coachman v. Sims*, 36 Okla. 536, 129 P. 845, 847 (1913) ("The law is astute to preserve the sanctity of the marriage relation, the legitimacy of children, and stability of descent and distribution, and therefore presumes innocence and virtue, in the absence of proof"). *Compare Gammelgaard v. Gammelgaard*, 247 Iowa 978, 77 N.W.2d 479 (1956) in which the court stated that: "In doubtful cases, courts prefer that construction of evidence which finds a legitimate marriage rather than a long period of lewd and criminal cohabitation." The case, however, concerned an inferred agreement rather than a presumption. As to the legitimacy of children, *see Dirion v.*

Today, we also find examples of ponderous reasoning in which marriage is named as the fundamental basis of Christian civilization. In *Johnson v. Lincoln Square Properties* (1990), the court stated that the presumption arises out of the concern of all civilized societies over the legitimacy of children, the descent and distribution of property, and the sanctity of marriage as the keystone of Christian governments.[59]

Addressing the practical evidentiary difficulties that arise in proving the marriage contract in certain situations must also be included as justifications for the presumption. These difficulties can arise in cases in which a surviving party claims entitlement to the deceased's estate based on the existence of a common law marriage. The surviving party can be prevented from testifying by law.[60] It is possible that the only available evidence concerns the cohabitation and reputation of the parties.

The contrast to the motives behind the stricter burden of proof becomes especially clear when the difficulties in proving a common law marriage are cited as a justification for the presumption. The stricter standard of proof makes it more difficult to prove a common law marriage, while the marriage presumption facilitates its proving. This naturally reflects a consistent attitude where the courts, as in Idaho, apply a lower standard of proof and at the same time are disposed to apply the marriage presumption.[61] A number of courts, however, apply both the stricter standard of proof as well as the presumption, as is the case in Pennsylvania. This creates troublesome tension in the legal system, an issue that will be discussed further below.

Brewer, 20 Ohio App. 298, 151 N.E. 818, 819 (1925). In *Com. ex rel. Rubin v. Rubin*, 201 Pa.Super. 517, 193 A.2d 639, 640 (1963), the Pennsylvania Superior Court stated: "It is highly desirable that the birth of this child be legitimized." As to favoring remarriage, *see In re Wagner's Estate*, 398 Pa. 531, 533, 159 A.2d 495, 497 (1960), in which the parties, after a divorce, moved back in together: "We regard it better to encourage remarriage than to leave such parties under judicial edict that they were living sinfully together for ten years." *See also Com. ex rel. Rubin v. Rubin*, 201 Pa.Super. 517, 193 A.2d 639 (1963). The favoring of remarriages has been criticized, *see* CLARK, *supra* note 23, at 106.

59 *Johnson v. Lincoln Square Properties*, 571 So.2d 541, 542 (Fla.App. 2 Dist. 1990).

60 *See, e.g., Staudenmayer v. Staudenmayer*, 714 A.2d 1016, 1020 (Pa. 1998); *State Farm Fire & Cas. Co. v. Platt*, 4 F.Supp.2d 399, 404 (E.D.Pa. 1998) ("In light of the difficulties involved in proving a common law marriage, the law has created a rebuttable presumption of marriage"); *In re Estate of Garges*, 474 Pa. 237, 378 A.2d 307, 309 (1977); and *In re Wagner's Estate*, 398 Pa. 531, 159 A.2d 495, 498 (1960) (the surviving party's lips were sealed due to the Dead Man's Act, May 23, 1887, P.L. 158, 35 (e), 28 PS § 322; 42 Pa.C.S. § 5930 (1960)). *See also Eagle v. W.C.A.B. (Bahorich)*, 602 A.2d 387, 388 (Pa.Cmwlth. 1992); *Com. v. McLean*, 387 Pa.Super. 354, 564 A.2d 216, 221 (Pa.Super. 1989); *In re Estate of Kovalchick*, 345 Pa.Super. 229, 498 A.2d 374, 376 (1985); *In re Estate of Rees*, 331 Pa.Super. 225, 480 A.2d 327, 328 (1984); *In re Cummings Estate*, 330 Pa.Super. 255, 479 A.2d 537, 542 (1984); *Estate of Gavula*, 490 Pa. 535, 417 A.2d 168, 171 fn. 7. (1980) ("Because it is often difficult to prove a common law marriage, the law has created a rebuttable presumption of marriage"); *In re Manfredi's Estate* 399 Pa. 285, 159 A.2d 697, 700 (1960); and FOOTE ET AL., *supra* note 8, at 18.

61 *See* the Idaho Supreme Court in *Metro. Life Ins. Co. v. Johnson*, 103 Idaho 122, 645 P.2d 356, 360 (1982). This stance is repeated by the Court of Appeals in *Freiburghaus v. Freiburghaus*, 103 Idaho 679, 651 P.2d 944, 946 (App. 1982).

9.4 COHABITATION AND REPUTATION

From the presentation above, we have seen how the paired term, *cohabitation and reputation*, is used for different functions. Cohabitation and reputation, and other circumstances can create circumstantial evidence supporting the existence of an inferred marriage contract, as seen in Chapter 7. The paired term is discussed in Chapter 8, "Cohabitation, Holding Out, and Reputation as Spouses," as a necessary requirement in addition to the contract for the formation of a common law marriage. The term's legal function, as discussed in the previous section, is to form one of the elements necessary for the application of the marriage presumption. In the case of *In re Estate of Garges* (1977), the Pennsylvania Supreme Court stated: "Cohabitation of a man and a woman, both of whom are capable of contracting marriage, and a reputation as husband and wife in their community together raise a presumption that the parties have contracted marriage."[62]

Cohabitation and reputation as elements necessary for the application of the presumption are not in general, in contrast with circumstantial evidence, used to prove the existence of a common law marriage contract. Rather, they are specific circumstances established by the case law; they and no other elements are necessary to the application of the presumption. They are typical elements viewed as *prima facie* evidence of the existence of a marital *consensus*. In contrast to the inference of an implied marriage agreement, analyzed in Chapter 7, under the marriage presumption a

62 *In re Estate of Garges*, 474 Pa. 237, 378 A.2d 307, 309 (1977). That cohabitation and reputation are not just sufficient but also necessary elements for the application of the presumption can clearly be seen in the case of *In re Estate of Kovalchick*, 345 Pa. Super. 229, 498 A.2d 374, 376 (1985), in which the Pennsylvania Superior Court assumed that "two absolutely essential elements co-exist." A similar approach can be seen in the case of *In re Estate of Rees*, 331 Pa.Super. 225, 480 A.2d 327 (1984). In the case, *In re Horton's Estate*, 357 Pa. 30, 52 A.2d 895, 897 (1947), the Pennsylvania Supreme Court stated: "Reputation and cohabitation are facts required to be proved." No inconsistency is created when the same court stated in *Pierce v. Pierce*, 355 Pa. 175, 49 A.2d 346, 248 (1946) that: "Cohabitation and reputation are not marriage. They are merely circumstances from which a marriage may be presumed." In *Richard v. Richard*, 172 Okla. 397, 45 P.2d 101, 108 (1935), the Oklahoma Supreme Court spoke of cohabitation and reputation as two separate and necessary steps for the application of the presumption. There are, however, older cases in which the elements can be viewed as more open. For example, in the case, *In re Craig's Estate*, 273 Pa. 530, 533, 117 A. 221, 222 (1922), the court used the description "proof of reputation and cohabitation, declarations and conduct of the parties, and such other circumstances as usually accompany the marriage relation." *Compare In re Bisbing's Estate*, 266 Pa. 529, 531, 109 A. 670, 671 (1920) ("Cohabitation and reputation are not marriage; they are but circumstances from which marriage may be presumed"). *Contra Yardley's Estate*, 75 Pa. 207, 212 (1874) (the court spoke of the two elements as necessary steps); *Richard v. Brehm*, 73 Pa. 140 (1873) *cited in* 13 Am.Rep. 733 ("Both cohabitation and reputation are necessary to establish a presumption of marriage"); and *Com. v. Stump*, 53 Pa. 132, 91 Am.Dec. 198 (1866) ("Where there is no proof of actual marriage, cohabitation and reputation are necessary to ground a presumption of marriage").

marital *consensus* need not be proven in every single case; if the elements of cohabitation and reputation exist, such a *consensus* is presumed to exist. Consequently, under the presumption a common law marriage contract is determined by law, not judicially. The elements resemble the necessary requirements of a material legal rule, in contrast to circumstantial evidence, because they are necessary to the application of the presumption. Still, these elements are not always sufficient for the formation of a common law marriage. This legal consequence is conditional; if the party contesting the marriage can prove that no marital *consensus* existed, no common law marriage will be established, despite the existence of cohabitation and reputation, as further discussed below in Section 9.5, "The Legal Effects of the Marriage Presumption."

9.4.1 Constant Cohabitation

Even though the requirement of cohabitation is formed differently by the different courts, it often is simply a requirement of cohabitation between the parties.[63] However, not just any cohabitation is accepted. As early as the influential case of *In re Yardley's Estate* (1874), the Pennsylvania Supreme Court determined, influenced by Scottish law, that "constancy of dwelling together" is the chief element of cohabitation.[64] It is not sufficient that the parties have lived separately and visited each other regularly. It must be a continuous and joined living together. Based on this, later case law has used, without changing the effect, the expressions *continuous cohabitation*[65] or, more commonly, *constant cohabitation* in the description of the element of cohabitation. In *Commonwealth v. McLean* (1989), the Pennsylvania Superior Court consequently maintained that the cohabitation must be constant, not irregular or inconstant.[66]

63 *Eagle v. W.C.A.B. (Bahorich)*, 602 A.2d 387 (Pa.Cmwlth. 1992) (cohabitation); *Jackson v. Culp*, 583 A.2d 1236 (Pa.Super. 1990); *Canute v. Canute*, 557 A.2d 772 (Pa.Super. 1989); *Stuck Leasing Co. v. W.C.A.B. (Ziegler)*, 125 Pa. 237, 557 A.2d 808 (Pa.Cmwlth. 1989); *Steadman v. Turner*, 357 Pa.Super. 361, 516 A.2d 21 (1986); *Bowden v. Workmen's Compensation Appeals Bd.*, 376 A.2d 1033 (Pa.Cmwlth. 1977); *In re Estate of Garges*, 474 Pa. 237, 378 A.2d 307 (1977); *Rager v. Johnstown Traction Co.*, 184 Pa.Super. 474, 134 A.2d 917 (1957); *In re Craig's Estate*, 273 Pa. 530, 117 A. 221 (1922); *Appeal of Reading Fire Ins. & Trust Co.*, 113 Pa. 204, 6 A. 60 (1886); and *Yardley's Estate*, 75 Pa.207 (1874).

64 *Yardley's Estate*, 75 Pa. 207 (1874). *See also Proctor v. Foster*, 107 Okla. 95, 230 P. 753 (1925).

65 *Simeonides v. Zervis*, 127 Ga.App. 506, 194 S.E.2d 324, 326 (1972); *Brown v. State*, 208 Ga. 304, 66 S.E.2d 745, 748 (1951); *Chance v. Chance*, 60 Ga.App. 889, 5 S.E.2d 399, 400 (1939); *Addison v. Addison*, 186 Ga. 155, 197 S.E. 232, 233 (1938); and *Drawdy v. Hesters*, 130 Ga. 161, 60 S.E. 451 (1908).

66 In *Com. v. McLean*, 387 Pa.Super. 354, 564 A.2d 216, 221 (Pa.Super. 1989), the requirement of "constant cohabitation" was not considered fulfilled, as the parties had lived together sporadically. The requirement that the parties' cohabitation be "constant" recurs in a number of cases from Pennsylvania: *see, e.g., In re Veneziale*, 267 B.R. 695, 700 (Bkrtcy.E.D.Pa. 2001); *Staudenmayer v. Staudenmayer*, 714 A.2d 1016, 1020-1021 (Pa. 1998); *State Farm Fire & Cas. Co. v. Platt*, 4 F.Supp.2d 399,

Even though shared living is one of the main elements of the cohabitation, a marital cohabitation, from a wider perspective, is understood to include the parties recognizing and treating each other as husband and wife. A common way to denote this, as the Supreme Court of South Carolina does in *Callen v. Callen* (2005), is to use the expression "cohabitation, apparently matrimonial."[67] In Montana, where the presumption is legislated, the statutory text captures this in its description of a man and a woman "deporting themselves as husband and wife."[68]

---

404 (E.D.Pa. 1998); *Africa v. Vaughan*, 998 F.Supp. 552, 556 (E.D.Pa. 1998); *Com. v. Wilson*, 672 A.2d 293, 301 (Pa. 1996); *In re Estate of Dodge*, 361 Pa.Super. 188, 522 A.2d 77. 79 (1987); *In re Cummings Estate*, 330 Pa.Super. 255, 479 A.2d 537, 542 (1984); and *In re Estate of Kovalchick*, 345 Pa.Super. 229, 498 A.2d 374, 376 (1985). In the case, *In re Estate of Rees*, 331 Pa.Super. 225, 480 A.2d 327, 329 (1984), the woman could not prove the existence of a "constant, as distinguished from an irregular or inconstant, cohabitation" as she lived mainly in Florida and he in Pennsylvania. *See also In re Estate of Gavula*, 490 Pa. 535, 417 A.2d 168 (1980); and *Com. ex rel. McDermott v. McDermott*, 236 Pa.Super.Ct. 541, 345 A.2d 914 (1975). *Compare In re Estate of Garges*, 474 Pa. 237, 378 A.2d 307, 309 (1977) and *McKenzie v. Harris*, 679 F.2d 8, 10 (3d. Cir. 1982), in which the court used the expression "cohabitation of a man and a woman." In the latter case, the presumption was applied after nine years of cohabitation. *See also In re Estate of Slavens*, 162 Mont. 123, 509 P.2d 293, 294-295 (1973), in which there were significant differences of opinion as to whether the man actually lived with the woman. In the case of *In re Manfredi's Estate*, 399 Pa. 285, 159 A.2d 697, 700 (1960), the Pennsylvania Supreme Court spoke of "constant, as distinguished from irregular or inconstant, cohabitation." A similar requirement can be found in the case law from Oklahoma, *see McArthur v. Hall*, 169 S.W.2d 724 (Tex.Civ.App.-Fort Worth 1943) (applying Oklahoma law) ("irregular, limited or partial cohabitation is not sufficient to create presumption in favor of 'common law marriage', but it must be continuing and complete and such as is usual between persons lawfully married ... To constitute 'matrimonial cohabitation' which will give rise to a common law marriage, under Oklahoma law, parties must have the same habitation"); *Richard v. Richard*, 172 Okla. 397, 45 P.2d 101, 106 (1935) ("The evidence in this case clearly shows that the cohabitation between plaintiff and defendant was at all times irregular, limited, and partial, and, therefore, such evidence was not sufficient as to cohabitation to create a presumption of the marriage contract and marital status"); and *Proctor v. Foster*, 107 Okla. 95, 230 P. 753 (1925) ("it must be shown that the parties have openly cohabited as husband and wife for a considerable time"). *See also Fender v. Segro*, 41 Okla. 318, 137 P. 103, 105 (1913). In the case of *In re Callery's Estate*, 226 Pa. 469, 75 A. 672, 673 (1910), the court found that the parties "were not 'constantly' living together."

67 *Callen v. Callen*, 365 S.C. 618, 620 S.E.2d 59, 62 (2005); *see also Barker v. Baker*, 330 S.C. 361, 499 S.E.2d 503 (App. 1998); *Owens v. Owens*, 466 S.E.2d 373, 375 (S.C.App. 1996); *Jeanes v. Jeanes*, 255 S.C. 161, 177 S.E.2d 537, 539 (1970); and *In re Greenfield's Estate*, 245 S.C. 595, 141 S.E.2d 916, 920 (1965). The term is also used by the Oklahoma Supreme Court in *Tower v. Towie*, 368 P.2d 488, 491 (Okla. 1962) and by the Idaho Supreme Court in the following cases: *In re Foster*, 77 Idaho 26, 287 P.2d 282 (1955) and *Warner v. Warner*, 76 Idaho 399, 283 P.2d 931, 934 (1955). *See also Mauldin v. Sunshine Mining Co.*, 61 Idaho 9, 17, 97 P.2d 608, 611 (1939); *Smith v. Smith*, 32 Idaho 478, 185 P. 67, 69 (1919); and *Adger v. Ackerman*, 115 F. 124 (8th Cir. 1902) ("matrimonial cohabitation"). As to older case law, *see* the historically significant case, *Hynes v. McDermott*, 91 N.Y. 451 (1883). *Compare Hilton v. Roylance*, 25 Utah 129, 69 P. 60 (1902), which describes the necessary elements as "when a man and woman are living together as husband and wife."

68 MONT. CODE ANN. § 26-1-602(30) (1999). *See also Matter of Estate of Alcorn*, 868 P.2d 629 (Mont. 1994) (dictum); *In re Marriage of Geertz*, 755 P.2d 34, 37 (Mont. 1988);

Without exacting additional proof, the Idaho Supreme Court, in the case of *In re Estate of Wagner* (1995), set out, as an element of the presumption, that the party alleging the existence of the common law marriage *prima facie*, by a preponderance of the evidence, must demonstrate that the parties assumed marital rights, duties, and obligations, and cohabited. This description is commonly used by the Idaho courts.[69] It is also closer to the definition of the objective requisites, in addition to the parties' marital *consensus*, necessary for the formation of a common law marriage in Idaho in cases in which the presumption is not applicable,[70]

In Alabama, where the objective requirement for cohabitation with the formation of a common law marriage is typically described as "cohabitation or mutual assumption openly of marital duties and obligations,"[71] the courts also speak of a presumption based on cohabitation.[72]

As a rule, there is no requirement for the length of time of the cohabitation.[73] The presumption, therefore, can be applied in cases in which the

---

Matter of Estate of Murnion, 212 Mont. 107, 686 P.2d 893 (1984); and *Spradlin v. United States*, 262 F.Supp. 502 (D.C.Mont. 1967).

69 *Matter of Estate of Wagner*, 126 Idaho 848, 893 P.2d 211, 215 (1995); *McCoy v. McCoy*, 868 P.2d 527, 531 (Idaho App. 1994); *In re Estate of Eliasen*, 105 Idaho 234, 668 P.2d 110 (1983); *Freiburghaus v. Freiburghaus*, 103 Idaho 679, 651 P.2d 944, 946 (App. 1982); and *Metro. Life Ins. Co. v. Johnson*, 103 Idaho 122, 645 P.2d 356, 361 (1982). In older Idaho case law, a presumption "from a cohabitation, apparently matrimonial" is fairly often instead mentioned, *see e.g., In re Foster*, 77 Idaho 26, 287 P.2d 282 (1955); *Warner v. Warner*, 76 Idaho 399, 283 P.2d 931, 934 (1955); *Mauldin v. Sunshine Mining Co.*, 61 Idaho 9, 17, 97 P.2d 608, 611 (1939); and *Smith v. Smith*, 32 Idaho 478, 185 P. 67, 69 (1919). The expression appears to be derived from the historical case, *Hynes v. McDermott*, 91 N.Y. 451, 43 Am.Rep. 677, 681 (1883).

70 IDAHO CODE ANN. § 32-201 (1985); 1877, p. 24 § 1; R.S. § 2420; reen. R.C. & C.L. § 2611; C.S. § 4591; I.C.A. § 31-201; *Matter of Estate of Wagner*, 126 Idaho 848, 893 P.2d 211, 214 (1995); and *Metro. Life Ins. Co. v. Johnson*, 103 Idaho 122, 645 P.2d 356, 360 (1982). According to the case law developed in Idaho, influenced in part by older California law, this assumption occurs through the parties' cohabitation and their holding out as husband and wife. *See Freiburghaus v. Freiburghaus*, 103 Idaho 679, 651 P.2d 944, 947 (App. 1982).

71 *Krier v. Krier*, 676 So.2d 1335, 1339 (Ala.Civ.App. 1996).

72 *Crosson v. Crosson*, 668 So.2d 868, 872 (Ala.Civ.App. 1995); *Matthews v. Matthews*, 259 Ala. 332, 67 So.2d 22 (1953); *White v. White*, 225 Ala. 155, 142 So. 524 (1932) (cohabitation); *Moore v. Heineke*, 119 Ala. 627, 24 So. 374 (1898) (cohabitation and conduct); *Weatherford v. Weatherford*, 20 Ala. 548, 56 Am.Dec. 206 (1852); *Krug v. Krug*, 296 So.2d 715 (Ala. 1974); *Hackmeyer v. Hackmeyer*, 268 Ala. 329, 106 So.2d 245 (1958) (cohabit as man and wife); *Barnett v. Barnett*, 262 Ala. 655, 658, 80 So.2d 626 (1955); *Hunter v. Lynn*, 256 Ala. 501, 506, 55 So.2d 849 (1951); and *Hill v. Lindsey*, 223 Ala. 550, 137 So. 395, 397 (1931).

73 *Compare* New Hampshire, a state which does not recognize common law marriages, requires a three-year cohabitation prior to the death of one party for the marriage presumption to be applied, *see* N.H. REV. STAT. ANN. § 457:39 (1955). *Compare Clark v. Cassidy*, 64 Ga. 662, 667 (1880) ("presumptions do arise in favor of marriage where parties have lived together in such apparent relation, and after a great lapse of time the offspring thereof are likely to be bastardized"); and *Dillon v. Dillon*, 60 Ga. 204, 206 (1878) ("for a long period"). *Compare also* the medieval canon law right according to which *cohabitatio diutina* as a rule was considered to exist first after ten years of cohabitation, *see* Section 3.3.4 *supra*. Also, in older Scottish case law, the cases in which the presumption has been applied are those in which cohabitations of

cohabitation varies from several months to over forty years.[74] Nevertheless, in Oklahoma, where the presumption appears predominantly in older case law, the courts note that the cohabitation should be open and long-standing for the presumption to be applied. In the case of *Fender v. Segro* (1913), the Oklahoma Supreme Court stated that the parties had openly lived together as husband and wife for a considerable length of time, a statement that recurs in later case law. Despite this distinction, cases in Oklahoma have accepted cohabitation of less than one year.[75] Remarkably, even the courts in Alabama have accepted shorter periods of cohabitation as the basis of the presumption. In *Crosson v. Crosson* (1995), the parties had been together approximately one year, of which they had lived together only for eight months and, in addition, the man had dated other women. The Alabama Court of Appeals found that their cohabitation was sufficient to presume a common law marriage.[76] Contradictory evidence in that case is discussed, *infra*. Even shorter

---

between 10 and 30 years existed, *see* Chapter 11, *infra*. During the 1900s, however, the time requirement has been considerably shortened in the Scottish case law, and in most recent years, cases exist in which the requirement of continuation is no longer than that found in American law.

74 *Owens v. Owens*, 466 S.E.2d 373 (S.C.App. 1996) (10 years cohabitation); *Crosson v. Crosson*, 668 So.2d 868 (Ala.Civ.App. 1995) (approximately 8 months); *Rickard v. Trousdale*, 508 So.2d 260 (Ala. 1987) (8 years, 6 without marital impediment); *Matter of Estate of Eliasen*, 105 Idaho 234, 668 P.2d 110 (1983) (3 years before they formally married); and *Metro. Life Ins. v Johnson*, 103 Idaho 122, 645 P.2d 356 (1982) (1 year 2 months); *Krug v. Krug*, 296 So.2d 715 (Ala. 1974) (the presumption was applied after an approximately four-month relationship during which the man did military duty in Vietnam while the woman was in the United States); *In re Estate of Swanson*, 160 Mont. 271, 502 P.2d 33 (1972) (8 years); *Jeanes v. Jeanes*, 255 S.C. 161, 177 S.E.2d 537 (1970) (approximately 2 years); *Com. ex rel. Rubin v. Rubin*, 201 Pa.Super. 517, 193 A.2d 639 (1963) (4 years); *Tower v. Towie*, 368 P.2d 488, 491 Okla. (1962) (several years); *In re Wagner's Estate*, 398 Pa. 531, 159 A.2d 495 (1960) (10 years); *King v. King*, 269 Ala. 468, 114 So.2d 145 (1959) (6 years, of which only 4 months were without marital impediment); *Rager v. Johnstown Traction Co.*, 184 Pa.Super. 474, 134 A.2d 917 (1957) (11 years); *Spradlin v. United States*, 262 F.Supp. 502 (D.C.Mont. 1967) (3 years); *Mauldin v. Sunshine Mining Co.*, 61 Idaho 9, 17-18, 97 P.2d 608, 612 (1939) (approximately 9 months); *Howell v. Adams* 158 Okla. 239, 13 P.2d 577 (1932) (8 months); *Hill v. Lindsey*, 223 Ala. 550, 139 So. 395 (1931) (almost one year); *Ollschlager v. Widmer*, 55 Or. 145, 105 P. 717, 721 (1909) (17 years); *Hynes v. McDermott*, 91 N.Y. 451, 464, 43 Am.Rep. 677 (1885) (3 years); and *Richard v. Brehm*, 73 Pa. 140, 145, 13 Am.Rep. 733 (1873) (almost 40 years).

75 *Fender v. Segro*, 41 Okla. 318, 137 P. 103, 105 (1913). The court repeated the statement in *Coleman v. James*, 67 Okla. 112, 169 P. 1064, 1066 (1917); *Lindsey v. Jefferson*, 68 Okla. 156, 172 P. 641, 642 (1918); and *Proctor v. Foster*,107 Okla. 95, 230 P. 753, 754 (1925). In *Howell v. Adams*, 158 Okla. 239, 13 P.2d 577, 578 (1932), the presumption was applied after barely eight months of cohabitation prior to the man's death. In *Richard v. Richard*, 172 Okla. 397, 45 P.2d 101, 105-106 (1935), the court found that the evidence clearly demonstrated that the parties' cohabitation was "at all times irregular, limited, and partial" and that it was insufficient "to create a presumption of the marriage contract and marital status." *See also McArthur v. Hall*, 169 S.W.2d 724, 726 (Texas App. 1943) (applying Oklahoma law).

76 *Crosson v. Crosson*, 668 So.2d 868 (Ala.Civ.App. 1995) (app. 8 months). The court notes that the man's contacts with other women occurred at the end of the parties' marital existence.

periods of cohabitation, sometimes simply a few days or weeks, have been accepted as grounds for the application of the marriage presumption if the cohabiting couple, living in another state, has visited a common law marriage state.[77] Because particular circumstances arise in these cases, they are treated separately in Chapter 10, "Conflict of Laws and Choice of Law."

It can be questioned whether there is reason to use a different definition of cohabitation in applying the presumption than in cases in which the presumption is not applicable. In the latter cases, the cohabitation is usually a necessary requirement in addition to the marriage contract, as noted in Chapter 8, "Cohabitation, Holding Out, and Reputation as Spouses." In applying the presumption, where no marriage agreement has to be proved, there is an argument for setting the requirement of cohabitation higher. In a state such as Pennsylvania, where a common law marriage can be established either by only proving the existence of a marriage contract *per verba de praesenti*, or by applying the marriage presumption based on cohabitation and reputation, several of the older presumption cases have exerted influence upon the application of the requirement of cohabitation outside the presumption's application area. A more in-depth analysis of the principle of cohabitation is provided in Chapter 8, where the principle is discussed as a necessary requirement in addition to the marriage contract.

9.4.2 General Reputation

In addition to the internal marital cohabitation between the parties, certain courts have posited that the parties also have to outwardly represent themselves as husband and wife for the application of the marriage presumption.[78] In the case of *In re Estate of Wagner* (1995), the Idaho Supreme Court examined the question of whether the parties held themselves out to the community as husband and wife.[79] In Montana, where the presumption

---

77 *See, e.g., Carpenter v. Carpenter*, 617 N.Y.S.2d 903 (A.D. 1994), in which the parties, residing in New York, visited Pennsylvania for a week in 1969 and another four days in 1989. The New York Supreme Court, Appellate Division, applying Pennsylvania law, found with the support of the marriage presumption that a common law marriage had been formed. The fact that the parties had a 25-year cohabitation in New York also was cited in the judgment.

78 In contrast in the older law, it has happened that reputation alone has been viewed as sufficient for an application of the presumption, assuming that the reputation was "uniform and general," *see* BISHOP, *supra* note 40, I § 936.

79 *Matter of Estate of Wagner*, 126 Idaho 848, 893 P.2d 211, 215-216 (1995); *McCoy v. McCoy*, 868 P.2d 527, 531 (Idaho App. 1994); *Matter of Estate of Eliasen*, 105 Idaho 234, 668 P.2d 110 (1983); *Freiburghaus v. Freiburghaus*, 103 Idaho 679, 651 P.2d 944, 946 (App. 1982); *Metro. Life Ins. Co. v. Johnson*, 103 Idaho 122, 645 P.2d 356, 361 (1982); and *Mauldin v. Sunshine Mining Co.*, 61 Idaho 9, 17, 97 P.2d 608, 611 (1939). That material requisite, in addition to the parties' marital *consensus*, is necessary for the formation of a common law marriage in Idaho which requires "a mutual assumption of marital rights, duties or obligations" which can be fulfilled by the parties'

is codified in the statute, the act simply refers to a man and woman "deporting themselves as husband and wife," which ought to even include their holding out in relation to others.[80]

It appears more common, however, that the formulation of this requisite refers not to the parties' outward actions, but to the effect of their actions on the requirement that the parties should enjoy the reputation as man and wife. This is true, for example, with the courts in Pennsylvania.[81] The parties' reputation has been considered to be the shadow of the marital cohabitation.[82] In South Carolina, *social acceptance*, a synonym for *reputation*, also appears.[83]

The courts occasionally mention both holding out and reputation. In Oklahoma, where the presumption appears predominantly in the older case law, the Oklahoma Supreme Court required in *Fender v. Segro* (1913) that the parties "holding each other out and recognizing and treating each other as such by declarations, admissions, or conduct, and are accordingly generally reputed to be such among their relatives and acquaintances and those who come in contact with them," a phrasing repeated in later case law.[84]

It has been argued, not without basis, that reputation is "the speech of the people."[85] However, one question concerns the extensiveness of the circle within which the parties must outwardly have appeared as or enjoyed the reputation as spouses. Typically, the courts have stated that it must be

---

cohabitation and holding out as spouses, *see e.g., Freiburghaus v. Freiburghaus*, 103 Idaho 679, 651 P.2d 944, 947 (App. 1982) and Chapter 8 *supra. Compare In re Estate of Brock*, 94 Idaho 111, 482 P.2d 86, 91 (1971), in which the presumption was based on the fact that the parties "considered they were married."

80 MONT. CODE ANN. § 26-1-602(30), (1999). In the case, *In re Estate of Slavens*, 162 Mont. 123, 509 P.2d 293, 294-295 (1973), no holding out was found to exist on the woman's side.

81 *Staudenmayer v. Staudenmayer*, 714 A.2d 1016, 1020 (Pa. 1998); *State Farm Fire & Cas. Co. v. Platt*, 4 F.Supp.2d 399, 404 (E.D.Pa. 1998); *Eagle v. W.C.A.B. (Bahorich)*, 602 A.2d 387 (Pa.Cmwlth. 1992); *Canute v. Canute*, 557 A.2d 772 (Pa.Super. 1989); *Steadman v. Turner*, 357 Pa.Super. 361, 516 A.2d 21 (1986); *McKenzie v. Harris*, 679 F.2d 8, 10 (3d. Cir. 1982); *Com. ex rel. McDermott v. McDermott*, 236 Pa.Super.Ct. 541, 345 A.2d 914 (1975); *Rager v. Johnstown Traction Co.*, 184 Pa.Super. 474, 134 A.2d 917 (1957); and *In re Horton's Estate*, 357 Pa. 30, 52 A.2d 895, 897 (1947).

82 BISHOP, *supra* note 40, I § 936.

83 *Jeanes v. Jeanes*, 255 S.C. 161, 177 S.E.2d 537, 539 (1970).

84 *Fender v. Segro*, 41 Okla. 318, 137 P. 103, 105 (1913). The court repeated the statement in *Coleman v. James*, 67 Okla. 112, 169 P. 1064, 1066 (1917); *Lindsey v. Jefferson*, 68 Okla. 156, 172 P. 641, 642 (1918); and *Proctor v. Foster*, 107 Okla. 95, 230 P. 753, 754 (1925). In *Howell v. Adams*, 158 Okla. 239, 13 P.2d 577, 578 (1932), the presumption was applied based on an approximately eight-month cohabitation and despite the fact that several friends and acquaintances to the deceased had never heard that he had a wife. In *Richard v. Richard*, 172 Okla. 397, 45 P.2d 101, 106 (1935), the court in contrast found that no evidence had been presented that the parties enjoyed a "reputation, general or special, in the vicinity of defendant's home at Richardsville" as husband and wife. *See also McArthur v. Hall*,169 S.W.2d 724, 726 (Tex.Civ.App.-Fort Worth 1943) (applying Oklahoma law).

85 *Com. v. Stump*, 53 Pa. 132, 91 Am.Dec. 198 (1866); and *In re Hines' Estate*, 10 Pa.Super. 124, 130 (1899).

a question of a general reputation. In the case, *Commonwealth v. McLean* (1989), the Pennsylvania Superior Court maintained that the parties' reputation as spouses should be "broad and general, not partial or divided."[86] In contrast, it has not, as a rule, been considered sufficient that the parties

---

86 *Com. v. McLean*, 387 Pa.Super 354, 564 A.2d 216, 221 (1989), in which the requirement of "general reputation" was not found fulfilled as the parties had lived together only sporadically. In *Africa v. Vaughan*, 998 F.Supp. 552, 556 (E.D.Pa. 1998), the court stated that there was no evidence that plaintiff and the woman in question "enjoyed a general reputation of marriage." *See also Com. v. Wilson*, 672 A.2d 293, 301 (Pa. 1996) (the requirement of general reputation not met); and *Matter of Estate of Wagner*, 126 Idaho 848, 893 P.2d 211 (1995). In *Sears v. Sears*, 267 A.D.2d 988, 700 N.Y.S.2d 626, 628 (A.D. 4 Dep't 1999), the plaintiff could not demonstrate that her reputation as married in Pennsylvania was "broad and general" rather than "partial or divided." In the case *In re Estate of Corace*, 527 A.2d 1058, 1061 (Pa.Super. 1987), the fact, *inter alia,* that the woman was at the hospital immediately before the man's death did not prove that she was his spouse. *See also Jackson v. Culp*, 583 A.2d 1236 (Pa.Super. 1990) (reputation missing); *In re Estate of Dodge*, 361 Pa.Super. 188, 522 A.2d 77, 79 (1987); and *In re Estate of Kovalchick*, 345 Pa.Super. 229, 498 A.2d 374, 376 (1985). In the case of *In re Estate of Rees*, 331 Pa.Super. 225, 480 A.2d 327 (1984), the parties had a close and intimate relationship for more than two decades. They had mainly lived apart, in Florida and Pennsylvania respectively, but traveled together on many occasions. Only a few of their neighbors and friends could witness as to their relation. The court found that the requirement of general reputation was not fulfilled. *See also In re Cummings Estate*, 330 Pa.Super. 255, 479 A.2d 537, 542 (1984); *Estate of Gavula*, 490 Pa. 535, 417 A.2d 168, 171 (1980) ("Instantly, the record does not reveal any evidence of constant cohabitation and general reputation; accordingly, no such presumption of common law marriage has been established"); and *In re Manfredi's Estate*, 399 Pa. 285, 159 A.2d 697, 700 (1960). In the case *McArtur v. Hall*, 169 S.W.2d 724, 728 (Tex.Civ.App.-Fort Worth 1943), the court found that the parties' reputation as spouses only could be viewed as "divided repute." In the case of *In re Osterling's Estate*, 323 Pa. 23, 185 A. 790 (1936), the deceased had presented the woman as his wife only to a few persons. Sufficient evidence for the application of the presumption for a common law marriage was not found to exist. *See also In re Craig's Estate*, 273 Pa. 530, 117 A. 221 (1922); *Hilton's Estate*, 263 Pa. 16, 106 A. 69 (1919) ("Proof of reputation for such purpose must be general and not confined to a few persons in the immediate neighborhood, as the relationship may be established merely for the purpose of deceiving others") *cited with approval in In re Nikitka's Estate*, 346 Pa. 63, 29 A.2d 521, 523 (1943); *In re Boyington's Estate*, 157 Iowa 467, 137 S.W. 949 (1912) and *Hynes v. McDermott*, 91 N.Y. 451, 453, 43 Am.Rep. 677 (1883) (the parties' reputation may not be "divided" but rather must be "general, and consistent with matrimonial cohabitation"). The court in *Green's Estate*, 5 Pa.C. 605 (1888) cautioned that the parties' repute could be limited "to a class and neighborhood so narrow as to give no real clue to the actual status of the parties affected." In the case *Brinckle v. Brinckle*, 12 Phila. 232 (1877), the court maintained that the parties' reputation must be general and continued: "The conduct of the parties must be such as to make almost every one infer that they were married." In the case *Yardley's Estate*, 75 Pa. 207 (1874), where the parties lived separately but during a period of many years the man continuously visited the woman and where the woman felt she was known as the man's "shirtwoman," according to the court's view, neither the required cohabitation nor reputation were evidenced. *Compare Lyle v. Ellwood*, Law.Rep. 19 Eq. 98 (1871), in which a marriage was found formed despite the fact that the parties' reputation was divided. *See also Bicking's Appeal*, 2 Brewster 202, 232 (1868), in which the court did not find it sufficient that the parties, among a few person, enjoyed the reputation as spouses; and *Com. v. Stump*, 53 Pa. 132, 91 Am.Dec. 198 (1866). In the case *Fryer v. Fryer*, 9 S.C.Eq. (Rich.Cas.) 85 (1832), the parties' reputation was found to be divided, therefore the presumption could not be applied.

have only appeared as spouses in a hotel in connection with a trip or before a few acquaintances.[87] Typically, it is required that they, in their normal circles of relatives, friends, neighbors, work acquaintances and in public situations, represent themselves and act as married spouses.[88] However, it is not normally required that the parties need enjoy a reputation as spouses before all or a majority of the persons that they meet. In certain cases, it has been considered sufficient to consider persons having the opportunity to form an opinion about the parties and their relationship.[89] Whether the requirement of holding out or reputation is fulfilled has been difficult to judge in many cases.[90]

It is in the nature of the requirement that the parties need time to be accepted as husband and wife. This was expressed in the formulation of the requirement given by the South Carolina Court of Appeals in *Owens v. Owens* (1996), "social acceptance over a long period of time."[91] A predetermined time period has never been expressed. Remarkably short periods of cohabitation have sometimes been viewed as sufficient for creating a reputation. In the above-mentioned case *Crosson v. Crosson* (1995), the parties had a relationship approximately one year, during which they cohabited only eight months. During that time, the man dated other women with whom he also publicly appeared, and two months later married one of them. Nevertheless, during the relationship, the parties, who had previously been married to each other, had filed a joint tax return. They had also shared the household duties. Further, the woman had presented the man as her husband. The requirement of public recognition of

---

87 In the case *In re Callery's Estate*, 226 Pa. 469, 75 A. 672, 673 (1910), the court stated: "There was a 'repute' prevailing in the Colonial hotel of their marital relations as 'Mr. and Mrs. Phillips,' but there was no pretense that this 'repute' extended to Callery's family and acquaintances until a short time before his death."

88 *In re Craig's Estate*, 273 Pa. 530, 117 A. 221 (1922); *Appeal of Reading Fire Ins. & Trust Co.*, 113 Pa. 204, 6 A. 60 (1886); *compare Brinckle v. Brinckle*, 12 Phila. 232, 234 (1877) ("Marital cohabitation is generally evidenced by the parties being received into the society of their friends as man and wife—being entertained by them as such - being visited by respectable families in their neighborhood, and addressing each other as persons actually married, and bearing openly the same name"). In the case *Yardley's Estate*, 75 Pa. 207 (1874), where the woman did not participate in the man's funeral and she felt she was known as the deceased's "shirtwoman," the court found that the requirement of reputation was not fulfilled. Joint vacation was not enough in *Manfredi's Estate*, 399 Pa. 285, 159 A.2d 697 (1960) and *Miller v. Sutherland*, 131 Mont. 175, 309 P.2d 322 (1957).

89 *In re Greenfield's Estate*, 245 S.C. 595, 141 S.E.2d 916, 920 (1965). In the case, *Com. v. Haylow*, 17 Pa.Super. 541, 546 (1901), the required reputation was found proven despite the fact that the parties "lived in a large city" and "their immediate circle of mutual acquaintances was somewhat limited."

90 *See, e.g., Case of Graham*, 103 Idaho 824, 654 P.2d 1377 (Idaho 1982), in which the majority for the Idaho Supreme Court (Bakes, McFadden and Shepard) found that the requirement of holding out was not fulfilled, while the dissent (Bistline), after a detailed review of the facts in the case, argued that the presumption should be applied.

91 *Owens v. Owens*, 466 S.E.2d 373, 375 (S.C.App. 1996); *see also Jeanes v. Jeanes*, 255 S.C. 161, 177 S.E.2d 537, 539 (1970).

the relationship as a marriage and the public assumption of marital duties and cohabitation was considered fulfilled. The Alabama Court of Appeals, therefore, found that a common law marriage had been formed based on the presumption.[92]

On the other side, cases exist in which the parties, despite a long cohabitation, did not establish the required reputation.[93] Naturally, it is not the time period alone that is decisive but the nature of the relationship. In *Barker v. Baker* (1998), the parties had lived together for more than twenty years until the woman died. However, their reputation as spouses was inconsistent, and included the following circumstances: The woman always used her maiden name; she called the man her boyfriend, not her husband; they never had a joint checking account; he never paid for her medical or personal costs; they never filed a joint tax return; she stated in several documents that she was single; she kept in contact with another man during a long period; and the man was not named in the woman's obituary. The South Carolina Court of Appeals found that the marriage presumption was not applicable because the requirement of social acceptance over a long period of time was not fulfilled.[94] In an examination of "the speech of the people," during trial, it is possible to gather testimony from neighbors and acquaintances of the parties both for and against the existence of a reputation as husband and wife.[95]

A number of facts are relevant evidence in evaluating whether the requirement of reputation has been fulfilled including whether the parties have presented each other as husband and wife, filed joint tax returns, declared each other to be beneficiaries under insurance policies, plus all circumstances supporting that they have appeared in the same manner as married spouses usually do.[96] A closer analysis of the terms, holding out and reputation, can be found in Chapter 8, where the terms are discussed as necessary requisites in addition to the marriage contract.[97]

The marriage presumption is not applicable if cohabitation and holding out and reputation do not exist. A third requirement, comparable to the requirement of a marriage contract for the substantive formation of a

92 *Crosson v. Crosson*, 668 So.2d 868 (Ala.Civ.App. 1995). The court notes that the man's contacts with other women were mainly towards the end of the parties' marital cohabitation.

93 *See, e.g., Eagle v. W.C.A.B. (Bahorich)*, 602 A.2d 387 (Pa. Cmwlth. 1992), where reputation did not exist despite the five-year cohabitation, or *Yardley's Estate*, 75 Pa. 207 (1874), where the parties lived separately but the man during a period of many years continuously visited the woman and where she felt she was known as the man's "shirtwoman," the court found neither the required cohabitation nor reputation existed.

94 *Barker v. Baker*, 330 S.C. 361, 499 S.E.2d 503, 508 (App. 1998).

95 *In re Hines' Estate*, 10 Pa.Super. 124, 130 (1899).

96 *In re Horton's Estate*, 357 Pa. 30, 52 A.2d 895, 897 (1947).

97 *See* Chapter 6 *supra*.

common law marriage, however, is not required for the application of the presumption.[98]

9.5 THE LEGAL EFFECTS OF THE MARRIAGE PRESUMPTION

In accordance with the preceding discussion, the burden of proof with respect to proving the existence of cohabitation and reputation rests with the party alleging the existence of a common law marriage. If the party is not successful in proving these elements, the marriage presumption generally is not applicable and, consequently, no common law marriage is found to have been formed. On the other side, if the party is successful in proving that cohabitation and reputation exist, the legal consequences of the presumption are invoked: The parties are presumed to have entered into an informal marriage contract[99] and the burden of proof shifts to the other party,[100] which must then prove that such a contract was

98 *See* with respect to Pennsylvania, *Com. v. McLean*, 564 A.2d 216 (Pa.Super. 1989); and *In re McGrath's Estate*, 319 Pa. 309, 179 A. 599, 602 (1935) ("no other proof is needed"). With respect to the application of the presumption in Montana, the Montana Supreme Court's statement in *Matter of Estate of Alcorn*, 868 P.2d 629, 630 (Mont. 1994) raises some hesitation. The court maintained that a rebuttable presumption exists "when '(a) man and woman deporting themselves as husband and wife have entered into a lawful contract of marriage'." The statement, by the use of the word "when," can give the impression that an application of the presumption is based on a contract. Instead, it is the contract itself that is presumed. The presumption's legal consequences appear to be a prerequisite for its application. The legislation, under the heading "Disputable presumptions" states: "A man and a woman deporting themselves as husband and wife have entered into a lawful contract of marriage," *see* MONT. CODE ANN. § 26-1-602(30) (1999).

99 According to *In re Estate of Dodge*, 361 Pa.Super. 188, 522 A.2d 77 (1987), the court presumed that the parties "contracted common law marriage." In Montana, where the presumption is legislated, it is formulated as: "A man and a woman deporting themselves as husband and wife have entered into a lawful contract of marriage," *see* MONT. CODE ANN. § 26-1-602(30)(1999). *See also Spradlin v. United States*, 262 F.Supp. 502, 505 (D.C.Mont. 1967). In *Metro. Life Ins. Co. v. Johnson*, 103 Idaho 122, 645 P.2d 356, 362 (1982), the Idaho Supreme Court found that the evidence presented in the case was sufficient to presume a marriage "including the element of consent." In *Coleman v. James*, 67 Okla. 112, 169 P. 1064 (1917), the court spoke of a presumption "that they have previously entered into an actual marriage, although there be no direct testimony to that effect."

100 It is unusual for the courts to expressly state that the burden of proof has shifted in these cases. *Compare McCoy v. McCoy*, 868 P.2d 527, 531 (Idaho App. 1994). Note that the court in *Rickard v. Trousdale*, 508 So.2d 260, 261 (Ala. 1987), presumed a common law marriage based on the parties' cohabitation and admission as spouses, and that the opposing party was not successful in disproving the presumption by demonstrating that the parties lacked a marital *consensus*. *See also Matter of Estate of Eliasen*, 105 Idaho 234, 668 P.2d 110, 114 (1983) ("We hold that sufficient evidence meeting the evidentiary requirements raised the presumption of marriage and thereafter the burden shifted to the estate to disprove the validity of the asserted common law marriage"); *Freiburghaus v. Freiburghaus*, 103 Idaho 679, 651 P.2d 944, 946 (App. 1982); *Metro. Life Ins. Co. v. Johnson*, 103 Idaho 122, 645 P.2d 356, 361

not executed.[101] Consequently, the party alleging the existence of a common law marriage does not, in principle, need to prove a marital *consensus*.[102] The presumption does not, as with the medieval canon law's

(1982); *In re Estate of Watts*, 31 N.Y.2d 491, 294 N.E.2d 195, 198 (1973); *King v. King*, 269 Ala. 468, 114 So.2d 145 (1959); and *In re Foster*, 77 Idaho 26, 287 P.2d 282 (1955). In *Faggard v. Filipowich*, 248 Ala. 182, 27 So.2d 10, 15 (1946), the court stated that the parties' cohabitation, *inter alia*, at least raised a presumption that a marriage took place until the contrary was shown. In *Mauldin v. Sunshine Mining Co.*, 61 Idaho 9, 17-18, 97 P.2d 608, 612 (1939), the court found that the evidence "was sufficient to establish their relationship of husband and wife, raising the strong presumption of its legality, and casting the burden of proof upon respondents to repel such presumption." In the case of *In re Craig's Estate*, 273 Pa. 530, 117 A. 221 (1922), the Pennsylvania Supreme Court stated that the presumption "is always open to rebuttal by proof that no marriage had, in fact, taken place"; *see also Appeal of Reading Fire Ins. & Trust Co.*, 113 Pa. 204, 6 A. 60, 62 (1886); *Hunt's Appeal*, 86 Pa. 294, 297 (1878); and *Port v. Port*, 70 Ills. 484 (1873); *Physick's Estate*, 2 Brewster 179 (1862); and *Guardians of the Poor v. Nathans*, 2 Brewster 149 (1845).

101 *See In re Cummings Estate*, 330 Pa.Super. 255, 479 A.2d 537, 542 (1984); *Com. ex rel. McDermott v. McDermott*, 236 Pa.Super.Ct. 541, 345 A.2d 914. 915 (1975) (the presumption can be disproved and that it "will wholly disappear in the face of proof that no marriage existed"); *Rager v. Johnstown Traction Co.*, 184 Pa.Super. 474, 134 A.2d 917, 920 (1957) ("presumption of marriage arising from reputation and cohabitation will give way to positive proof that no contract was made"); *Caddy v. Johnstown Firemen's Relief Ass'n of Pennsylvania*, 129 Pa.Super. 493, 496, 196 A. 590 (1938); *White v. White*, 225 Ala. 155, 142 So. 524 (1932); *In Re Murdock's Estate*, 92 Pa. Super. 275, 277 (1927) ("if she herself proves that no valid marriage contract was actually entered into between them, evidence as to cohabitation and reputation goes for nothing"); *Rogers v. McLeskey*, 225 Ala. 148, 142 So. 526 (1932); *Hill v. Lindsey*, 223 Ala. 550, 139 So. 395 (1931); *In re McGrath's Estate*, 319 Pa. 309, 179 A. 599, 602 (1935) ("the presumption of marriage, that such evidence might raise must give way to the positive proof of the party that no contract was made"); and *In re Bisbing's Estate*, 266 Pa. 529, 109 A. 670, 671 (1920) ("Cohabitation and reputation are not marriage; they are but circumstances from which marriage may be presumed, and such presumption may always be rebutted and will wholly disappear in the face of proof that no marriage in fact has taken place"). *Compare* Scottish law, *e.g.*, *Campbell v. Campbell*, (The Breadalbane case) (1867) 5 M. (H.L.) 115, from which it appears that the presumption is "rebutted by proving that there was no consent at all"; and *Nicol v. Bell*, 1954 S.L.T. 314, 326 in which Lord Mackintosh stated: "This presumption, though often a very strong one, is ... rebuttable by proving that there was no consent at all."

102 With respect to the presumption as applied in Montana, a particular case gives rise to a hesitation as to whether the legal effect is a shift in the burden of proof, *see In re Marriage of Geertz*, 755 P.2d 34, 37 (Mont. 1988), where the Montana Supreme Court stated: "Although the public policy of this state, as demonstrated by the presumption contained within § 26-1-602(30), MCA, generally favors a finding of a valid marriage, the burden of proof remains upon the person asserting a common law marriage." As the presumption simply requires that the parties are "deporting themselves as husband and wife," that which is presumed is that they "have entered into a lawful contract of marriage." The law, however, ought to reasonably be interpreted so that the burden of proof is with respect to the actions of the parties, "deporting themselves as husband and wife," and, assuming that the presumption is applicable, not the marriage contract. The law presumes such, and that it is rebuttable presumption can be seen from the heading of the legislation, "Disputable presumptions." Another Supreme Court case has also interpreted it as a "rebuttable presumption," *see Matter of Estate of Alcorn*, 868 P.2d 629, 630 (Mont. 1994). In *Spradlin v. United States*, 262 F.Supp. 502, 505 (D.C.Mont. 1967), the court seems to have applied the Montana presumption correctly. The lower court, the Appeals

sponsalio de futuro cum copula, create a *praesumptio iuris et de iure, i.e.*, a non-rebuttable presumption, but rather a *praesumptio iuris*, which is rebuttable. If the opposing party succeeds in proving that an informal marriage contract did not exist, the presumption is disproved and no common law marriage is found. If the opposing party is unsuccessful, the marriage is found to have been established based on the presumption.[103] Such a common law marriage, with certain exceptions, has all the legal effects of a formal marriage.[104]

The presumption consequently entails that in states that, in addition to the legal capacity of the parties,[105] mandate three necessary requisites for

---

Council in Montana, had found that no common law marriage had existed between the parties as, *inter alia*, no marital intent or present consent to be husband and wife was proven. The United States District Court, however, found that the lower court ought to have applied the marriage presumption, as it only required that the parties were "deporting themselves as husband and wife."

103 *Callen v. Callen*, 365 S.C. 618, 620 S.E.2d 59 (2005) ("a lack of intent to be married overrides the presumption of marriage that arises from cohabitation and reputation"); *Meeks v. W.C.A.B. (Louis Cicconi Auto)*, 720 A.2d 162 (Pa. Cmwlth. 1998); *Barker v. Baker*, 330 S.C. 361, 499 S.E.2d 503, 507 (App. 1998); *Owens v.Owens*, 466 S.E.2d 373 (S.C.App. 1996); *Crosson v. Crosson*, 668 So.2d 868, 872 (Ala.Civ.App. 1995); *Carpenter v. Carpenter*, 617 N.Y.S.2d 903 (A.D. 2 Dep't 1994); *Rickard v. Trousdale*, 508 So.2d 260 (Ala. 1987); *Matter of Estate of Eliasen*, 105 Idaho 234, 668 P.2d 110 (1983); *Metro. Life Ins. v Johnson*, 103 Idaho 122, 645 P.2d 356 (1982); *Krug v. Krug*, 296 So.2d 715 (Ala. 1974); *In re Estate of Swanson*, 160 Mont. 271, 502 P.2d 33 (1972); *Jeanes v. Jeanes*, 255 S.C. 161, 177 S.E.2d 537 (1970); *Com. ex rel. Rubin v. Rubin*, 201 Pa.Super. 517, 193 A.2d 639 (1963); *Tower v. Towie*, 368 P.2d 488, 491 (Okla. 1962); *In re Wagner's Estate*, 398 Pa. 531, 159 A.2d 495 (1960); *King v. King*, 269 Ala. 468, 114 So.2d 145 (1959); *Rager v. Johnstown Traction Co.*, 184 Pa.Super. 474, 134 A.2d 917 (1957); *Spradlin v. United States*, 262 F.Supp. 502 (D.C. Mont. 1967); *Mauldin v. Sunshine Mining Co.*, 61 Idaho 9, 17-18, 97 P.2d 608, 612 (1939); *Howell v. Adams* 158 Okla. 239, 13 P.2d 577 (1932); *Hill v. Lindsey*, 223 Ala. 550, 139 So. 395 (1931); *Ollschlager v. Widmer*, 55 Or. 145, 105 P. 717, 721 (1909); *Hynes v. McDermott*, 91 N.Y. 451, 464, 43 Am.Rep. 677 (1885); and *Richard v. Brehm*, 73 Pa. 140, 145, 13 Am.Rep. 733 (1873).

104 However, a common law marriage based on the application of the presumption has not been viewed by some courts as an impediment to a later ceremonial wedding, *see, e.g., Edwards v. Edwards*, 136 Ga.App. 668, 222 S.E.2d 169, 171 (1975); *Cooper v. Cooper*, 88 Ga.App. 335, 76 S.E.2d 726, 728 (1953); *Carter v. Graves*, 206 Ga. 234, 56 S.E.2d 917, 920 (1949); *Addison v. Addison*, 186 Ga. 155, 197 S.E. 232, 233 (1938); *White v. White*, 41 Ga.App. 394, 153 S.E. 203, 204 (1930); *Norman v. Good*, 113 Ga. 121, 38 S.E. 317 (1901); and *Jenkins v. Jenkins*, 83 Ga. 286, 9 S.E. 541, 20 Am.St.Rep. 316 (1889). A later common law marriage based on the presumption has also, in contrast with a proven common law marriage, difficulties with respect to competing with previous ceremonial marriages, *see Lumbermen's Mut. Cas. Co. v. Reed*, 84 Ga.App. 541, 66 S.E.2d 360, 363 (1951).

105 The marriage presumption in certain cases has been applicable even to the legal capacity of the parties to enter into a marriage. Their marital cohabitation and representation outwardly as spouses has thus created a presumption that they had the legal capacity to enter into a marriage with each other. In *Spradlin v. United States*, 262 F.Supp. 502, 505 (D.C.Mont. 1967), that court maintained that the applicable marital presumption in Montana, according to which "a lawful contract of marriage" is presumed if the parties "deported themselves as husband and wife," means that even the parties' capacity to marry is presumed. In *Langdon v. Langdon*, 204 Ind. 321, 183 N.E. 400 (1932), the Indiana Supreme Court found that a ceremonial wedding was invalid due to a lack of mental competence by one

the formation of a common law marriage, namely, (1) a marriage contract, (2) cohabitation, (3) and reputation as spouses, a party alleging the existence of a common law marriage has to only prove requisites two and three. In a state such as Pennsylvania, on the other hand, a common law marriage can be established either by only proving the existence of a marriage contract *per verba de praesenti* (the first requisite), or by applying the marriage presumption based on cohabitation and reputation, after which the burden of proof shifts to the other party, who must prove that a contract was not formed. It ought to be noted that the presumption's discharge from the primary obligation of proving the formation of a marriage contract is inconsistent with the general rules about burdens of proof, as stated in the previous section. The courts, therefore, have particular cause to note and rule on the legal conflict between the rules concerning the burden of proof and the application of the marriage presumption.

In American case law, as influenced by Scottish precedents, the marriage presumption is considered to be strong, which has come to expression in the courts' different formulations of the standard of proof required for its rebuttal.[106] In *Hynes v. McDermott* (1883), the court stated: "The presumption of marriage from a cohabitation, apparently matrimonial, is one of the strongest presumptions known to the law ... it can be repelled only by the most cogent and satisfactory evidence."[107] The strength of the presumption is considered to increase with the length of the marital cohabitation and the arrival of children, especially in cases concerning legitimacy.[108]

---

of the parties, but that the presumption of a continued mental incompetence was subordinated to the marriage presumption, and in accordance, a common law marriage was found formed after 5½ years of cohabitation. In *DeMedio v. DeMedio*, 215 Pa.Super. 255, 257 A.2d 290, 302-303 (1969), the Pennsylvania Superior Court reasoned hypothetically in accordance with the principles applied in *Langdon*. In *Elliott v. Indus. Accident Bd.*, 101 Mont. 246, 53 P.2d 451, 454 (1936), the issue was whether a common law marriage had been formed and if so, whether it created an impediment for a later common law marriage. For further discussion as to this issue, *see* Chapter 5 *supra* with respect to the parties' legal capacity to enter into a marriage.

106 The presumption's strength in Scottish law can be seen, for example, in *Campbell v. Campbell,* (The Breadalbane case) (1867) 5 M. (H.L.) 115, 201: "Habit and repute afford by the Law of Scotland ... evidence of marriage always strong, and in Scotland, unless met by counter evidence, generally conclusive." In *Morris v. Davies* (5 Cl. & F. 163) Lord Lyndhurst stated: "The presumption of law is not lightly to be repelled. It is not to be broken in upon, or shaken by a mere balance of probability. The evidence for the purpose of repelling it must be strong, distinct, satisfactory and conclusive." In *Piers v. Piers* (2 H.L. Cas. 331), Lord Campbell stated that the presumption can be broken only "by disproving every reasonable possibility," and in the same case, Lord Brougham stated, with respect to the counter evidence, that it must be "clear, distinct and satisfactory." These statements can also be found cited in American case law, *see, e.g., Hynes v. McDermott,* 91 N.Y. 451, 459, 43 Am.Rep. 677 (1883); and *Teter v. Teter,* 101 Ind. 129, 51 Am.R. 742 (1884).

107 *Hynes v. McDermott,* 91 N.Y. 451, 459, 43 Am.Rep. 677 (1883).

108 *Owens v. Owens,* 466 S.E.2d 373, 375 (S.C.App. 1996); *Brown v. State,* 208 Ga. 304, 66 S.E.2d 745 (1951); *Chance v. Chance,* 60 Ga.App. 889, 5 S.E.2d 399, 400 (1939); *Salvini v. Salvini,* 2 S.W.2d 963 (Tex.Civ.App.-El Paso 1928); *Tarleton v. Thompson,*

Hynes has had a strong influence on later American case law, even in modern times,[109] such that the requirement of the most cogent and satisfactory evidence remains intact today.[110] Even though the formulation with respect to the standard of proof varies somewhat, the purpose, clearly, is to maintain the strict requirement of proof. Many courts require clear and positive evidence. For example, in *Metropolitan Life Ins. Co. v. Johnson* (1982), in which the presumption was considered applicable based on the parties' cohabitation during one year and two months, the Idaho Supreme Court found that the opposing party had not succeeded in overthrowing the presumption by introducing clear and positive evidence. As a consequence, a common law marriage was found.[111] This case can be compared

---

125 S.C. 182, 118 S.E. 421 (1922); *Drawdy v. Hesters*, 130 Ga. 161, 60 S.E. 451 (1908); *Pooler v. Smith*, 73 S.C. 102, 52 S.E. 967 (1904). In *Tower v. Towie*, 368 P.2d 488, 491 (Okla. 1962), where the issue was whether a child was legitimate and therefore entitled to inherit, the court found that the parties had lived together for several years, they outwardly appeared as spouses, and that the counter-evidence was not sufficiently "clear, convincing and cogent" to disprove the presumption. In *Dillon v. Dillon*, 60 Ga. 204, 206-207 (1878), the court stated: "When persons for a long period act, habitually, as married people generally act, there is a strong presumption that they have, at some time, and in some way, entered the state—that they have acquired the rights, and assumed the obligations, of the marriage relation." *Compare Dixon v. State*, 217 Ga.App. 267, 456 S.E.2d 758, 760 (1994), in which the court states: "There is no presumption that two persons who cohabited and produced a child were married at common law; more must be shown." The court however does not elaborate as to what else must be proven.

109 The case is cited with approval in a number of American cases, *see, e.g., Smith v. Smith*, 32 Idaho 478, 482, 185 P. 67, 69 (1919); *Mauldin v. Sunshine Mining Co.*, 61 Idaho 9, 17-18, 97 P.2d 608, 611 (1939); *Nicholas v. Idaho Power Co.*, 63 Idaho 675, 125 P.2d 321 (1942); *Thomey v. Thomey*, 67 Idaho 393, 181 P.2d 777, 779 (1947); *Warner v. Warner*, 76 Idaho 399, 282 P.2d 931, 934 (1955); *In re Foster*, 77 Idaho 26, 287 P.2d 282, 286 (1955); *Jeanes v. Jeanes*, 255 S.C. 161, 177 S.E.2d 537, 539-540 (1970); and *Metro. Life Ins. Co. v. Johnson*, 103 Idaho 122, 645 P.2d 356, 361 (1982).

110 *Smith v. Smith*, 32 Idaho 478, 482, 185 P. 67, 69 (1919); *Mauldin v. Sunshine Mining Co.*, 61 Idaho 9, 17, 97 P.2d 608, 611 (1939); *Warner v. Warner*, 76 Idaho 399, 282 P.2d 931, 934 (1955); *In re Foster*, 77 Idaho 26, 287 P.2d 282, 286 (1955); *see also* the dissent in *Case of Graham*, 103 Idaho 824, 654 P.2d 1377, 1383 (Idaho 1982). *See also Jeanes v. Jeanes*, 255 S.C. 161, 177 S.E.2d 537, 540 (1970), in which the South Carolina Supreme Court required as rebuttal evidence "strong, cogent, satisfactory or conclusive evidence." *Compare also Owens v. Owens*, 466 S.E.2d 373, 375 (S.C.App. 1996), in which the South Carolina Court of Appeals states that it is "a strong presumption" that can only be disproved by evidence that is "clear, distinct and satisfactory," an expression taken from Scottish law, *see Morris v. Davies* (5 Cl. & F. 163). *Compare In re Greenfield's Estate*, 245 S.C. 595, 141 S.E.2d 916, 919 (1965), in which the court more generally speaks of "the strong presumption of marriage"; and *Johnson v. Lincoln Square Properties*, 571 So.2d 541, 542 (Fla.App. 2 Dist. 1990) ("one of the strongest of all legal presumptions").

111 *Metro. Life Ins. Co. v. Johnson*, 103 Idaho 122, 645 P.2d 356, 362-363 (1982); *Freiburghaus v. Freiburghaus*, 103 Idaho 679, 651 P.2d 944, 947 (App. 1982); *Case of Graham*, 103 Idaho 824, 654 P.2d 1377, 1379 (Idaho 1982) (the majority's opinion); *Eliasen v. Fizgerald*, 105 Idaho 234, 668 P.2d 110, 114 (1983); *McCoy v. McCoy*, 868 P.2d 527, 531 (Idaho App. 1994); and *Matter of Estate of Wagner*, 126 Idaho 848, 893 P.2d 211, 214 (1995). *Compare* older Idaho cases, where the Supreme Court formulates the standard of proof somewhat differently and requires "the most cogent and satisfactory evidence," *see* note 109.

to *Wilkins v. Wilkins* (2002), in which the court found that the woman presented sufficient evidence to establish a *prima facie* case of common law marriage, with which the burden of proof shifted to the estate of the deceased. The court found later that the estate proved, by clear and convincing evidence, that there was no common law marriage.[112] In contrast, in the case of *Owens v. Owens* (1996), the presumption was not rebutted, despite the fact that the parties had stated that they lived in an "open concubinage" and a "nonmarriage." The court, requiring proof that was clear, distinct, and satisfactory, explained that the parties' statements could easily have been made with respect to a ceremonial marriage, and not for the purpose of denying the existence of a marital status. Consequently, a common law marriage was, therefore, found to have been formed.[113] Other courts have required clear evidence[114] or satisfactory evidence,[115] but despite these more generalized formulations, they have desired to maintain a strict standard of proof in disproving the presumption.

The courts' reasoning about the marriage presumption does not always follow the logic of the reversed burden of proof. Instead of first stating that the party alleging the existence of a common law marriage must prove cohabitation and reputation and, thereafter, that the opposing party must prove that no marriage contract existed, many courts draw the direct conclusion that a marriage contract has been proven.[116] An example of

112 *Wilkins v. Wilkins*, 48 P.3d 644, 650 (Idaho 2002).

113 *Owens v. Owens*, 466 S.E.2d 373, 375 (S.C.App. 1996).

114 *Simeonides v. Zervis*, 127 Ga.App. 506, 194 S.E.2d 324, 326 (1972); *Brown v. State*, 208 Ga. 304, 66 S.E.2d 745, 748 (1951); *Chance v. Chance*, 60 Ga.App. 889, 5 S.E.2d 399, 400 (1939); and *Drawdy v. Hesters*, 130 Ga. 161, 60 S.E. 451 (1908).

115 *See* the Montana Supreme Court's opinions in the cases of *Matter of Estate of Murnion*, 212 Mont. 107, 686 P.2d 893, 897, 41 St.Rep. 1627 (1984) and *In re Estate of Swanson*, 160 Mont. 271, 502 P.2d 33, 37 (1972), which for rebuttal evidence required "satisfactory evidence," referring to *Welch v. All Persons*, 78 Mont. 370, 384, 254 P. 179, 182 (1926): "The presumption in favor of matrimony is one of the strongest known to the law." *See also Elliot v. Indus. Accident Bd.*, 101 Mont. 246, 53 P.2d 451 (1936).

116 *See*, e.g., *Carpenter v. Carpenter*, 617 N.Y.S.2d 903 (A.D. 2 Dep't 1994), in which the New York Supreme Court, Appellate Division, in applying Pennsylvania law, found that "the plaintiff overwhelmingly demonstrated, without rebuttal from the defendant (except for various blanket denials), that the parties entered into a valid common law marriage." In the case of *In re Estate of Swanson*, 160 Mont. 271, 502 P.2d 33, 34 (1972), the Montana Supreme Court stated that a "presumption of marriage arose and decedent's brother who sought letters of administration could repel presumption only by satisfactory evidence." The court does not, thereafter, retry the issue of whether the party had managed to disprove the presumption but instead states that: "Evidence supported finding that petitioner for letters of administration who lived with decedent at time of his death was married to decedent *by verbal consent* and by mutual and public assumption of the marital relation" (*italics added*). In *Howell v. Adams*, 158 Okla. 239, 13 P.2d 577 (1932), the Oklahoma Supreme Court, in application of the presumption, concluded that "defendant in error was and is the surviving widow of the decedent." *Compare Com. v. Haylow*, 17 Pa.Super. 541, 548 (1901), in which a common law marriage was found formed. It also appears that where ambiguity exists, the presumption has not been applied. If the normal presumption had been applied, the court could have stated that cohabitation and reputation were proven and that the opposing party had not

a correct application can be seen in *Jeanes v. Jeanes* (1970). After finding that cohabitation and reputation existed, the South Carolina Supreme Court, with an application of older Scottish principles, came to the following conclusion: "We do not find in the record any strong, cogent, satisfactory or conclusive evidence tending to show that appellant and Swygert *are not,* in fact, married"(italics added).[117]

The opposing party's tasks—of rebutting with evidence according to the strict burden of proof and, in addition, proving the negative of a fact, namely, that the parties did not ever enter into a marriage contract—can appear to be difficult. Nevertheless, in reality, the parties are often rigorously cross-examined about the marriage contract and their marital *consensus.* The parties' own testimony can prove that they never entered into a contract or that the contract they entered into did not have the required content. In *McCoy v. McCoy* (1994), under cross-examination, the woman had testified that she never consented to be Clinton's wife and never considered herself married. The Idaho Court of Appeals stated that even

demonstrated that a marriage contract did not exist. The court found instead, with reference to the woman's testimony, that "the proved acts and declarations of the defendant, and the evidence of cohabitation and reputation" proved that the woman, together with the man, took him "to be her husband and he took her to be his wife." Therefore, it appears to be rather a question of an inferred agreement, *see also* Chapter 7 *supra.*

117 *Jeanes v. Jeanes,* 255 S.C. 161, 177 S.E.2d 537, 540 (1970). *Compare Crosson v. Crosson,* 668 So.2d 868, 872 (Ala.Civ.App. 1995), in which the Alabama Court of Appeals stated that the arguments presented to disprove the presumption were "insufficient to rebut the facts suggesting a common law marriage." In the case of *Matter of Estate of Eliasen,* 105 Idaho 234, 668 P.2d 110, 114 (1983), the Idaho Supreme Court stated that the cited circumstance "was insufficient to meet the clear and positive proof standard. Hence ... we hold that a common law marriage existed." In *Metro. Life Ins. Co. v. Johnson,* 103 Idaho 122, 645 P.2d 356, 362-363 (1982), the same court came to the following conclusion: "The evidence of the respondent was either not probative of the element of the consent of the parties on October 22, 1976, or insufficient to overcome the presumption of marriage." In *McKenzie v. Harris,* 679 F.2d 8, 11 (3d. Cir. 1982), the court found that the evidence presented against the existence of the common law marriage was not sufficient "to rebut the presumption of marriage raised by the evidence in this case." In *Rager v. Johnstown Traction Co.* 184 Pa.Super. 474, 134 A.2d 917, 921 (1957), where the woman's testimony was cited as counter-evidence, the Pennsylvania Superior Court stated: "If she clearly testified that there was no contract, then her claim would fall. We do not believe that she so testified." In *Mauldin v. Sunshine Mining Co.,* 61 Idaho 9, 17-18, 97 P.2d 608, 612 (1939), the court found that the evidence presented in the rebuttal was not "so cogent and satisfactory as would rebut this strong presumption"; in *Ollschlager v. Widmer,* 55 Or. 145, 105 P. 717, 721 (1909), the counter-evidence "falls far short of overcoming the presumption in favor of the marriage of decedent and petitioner." *Compare Richard v. Brehm,* 73 Pa. 140, 145, 13 Am.Rep. 733 (1873), in which the man stated to his sister-in-law, when angry at his wife, that the parties were not married. The court, in assessing the statement, stated that "after more than thirty-five years of apparent wedded life, [it] was certainly very weak evidence to rebut the presumption of marriage." In *Hynes v. McDermott,* 91 N.Y. 451, 464, 43 Am.Rep. 677 (1885), the court stated with respect to the counter evidence: "These circumstances were either contradicted or did not conclusively repel the presumption."

though the evidence was sufficient to establish a presumption of marriage and shift the burden of proof to the woman, the clear and positive evidence presented by her was sufficient to rebut the presumption.[118] In assessing the contractual evidence relevant for disproving the presumption, issues, discussed in Chapter 6, again arise about the content of the marriage contract. Even though the parties can be seen as having entered into a marriage contract, it can be viewed as a contract *de futuro*, with the consequence of disproving the presumption. The question also arises whether the parties had an intent to cohabit or an intent to form a legal relationship. With respect to these issues, reference is made to the discussions in Chapters 6 and 13.

Despite the strict standard of proof, many courts have accepted circumstantial evidence as proof that a marriage contract was not formed.[119] The circumstances cited here are often the same as those used to prove

---

118 *McCoy v. McCoy*, 868 P.2d 527, 531 (Idaho App. 1994). The record in the case shows that the woman had also filed a single tax return, used her maiden name and had her own bank account. In *Eagle v. W.C.A.B. (Bahorich)*, 602 A.2d 387 (Pa.Cmwlth. 1992), divorced spouses had moved in together again, living together for five years until the death of the man. They were, however, found only to have come to an agreement to "reconciliate," not marry. Reputation was also not proven. In the case of *In re Mann's Estate*, 24 Lehigh 261 (1951), the woman testified that the parties never considered themselves married to each other, as a consequence, no marriage contract was found to be formed. In *Com. v. Deogard*, 33 Erie 183, 185 (1949), despite a 25-year cohabitation, no marriage was found formed, due to the woman's statement that "I wanted to get married on account of the children's sakes and he would never do it." In *Elliott v. Indus. Accident Bd.*, 101 Mont. 246, 53 P.2d 451 (1936), in which the parties lived together and outwardly appeared as spouses in a manner that appears to have been satisfactory for the formation of a common law marriage, the woman was asked the following leading question: "Q. You did not consider that you were his wife? A. I did not want to be." No common law marriage was found formed, therefore, no impediment existed as to a common law marriage entered thereafter. *See also Morris v. McKeesport Coal & Coke Co.*, 99 Pa.Super. 112 (1930); and *Welch v. All Persons*, 85 Mont. 114, 278 P. 110 (1929). In the case *In re Murdock's Estate*, 92 Pa.Super. 275, 277 (1927), the court stated, with respect to the woman's testimony concerning the contract that "if she herself proves that no valid marriage contract was actually entered into between them, evidence as to cohabitation and reputation goes for nothing." In *Edwards v. Enterprise Mfg. Co.*, 283 Pa. 420, 129 A. 449 (1925), the woman was asked: "Was there anything said between you about going together and living as man and wife?," to which she answered: "Nothing that I know of." In the case of *In re Bisbing's Estate*, 266 Pa. 529, 109 A. 670, 671 (1920), the woman was asked during the trial the following leading question: "Q. He asked you to get married? A. Yes. Q. And you declined? A. Yes." With respect to this and the fact that the woman admitted that the relationship was "illicit," the presumption could not be applied. In the case of *In re Bott's Estate*, 10 Dist. 122 (1901), the presumption was rebutted as the party admitted that a marriage was intended first in the future.

119 *See McCoy v. McCoy*, 868 P.2d 527, 531 (Idaho App. 1994), previous footnote. In the case, *In re Marriage of Geertz*, 232 Mont. 141, 755 P.2d 34, 37 (1988), the court referred to the actual circumstances, for example, "single income tax returns, separate insurance and bank accounts," which were considered sufficient "to rebut any statutory or common law presumption of marriage." An alternative reasoning could have been that the court instead stated that the parties, with respect to the demonstrated circumstances, could not be viewed as having "deported themselves as husband and wife" and that the presumption therefore was not applicable.

that the parties did not, through their outward representations, fulfill the requirement of holding out as spouses. Other circumstances, which can suggest that the parties never had a true marital intent are, for example, the fact that their cohabitation was terminated through separation and that one of the parties immediately thereafter formally married another person. The evidentiary weight given such circumstances must, of course, be determined case by case.[120]

For example, in *Crosson v. Crosson* (1995), the parties, Bruce and Barbara, after eleven years of formal marriage, divorced in June of 1993. A few months later, around August, Bruce asked Barbara to return and, as previously, be his wife. They once again lived in a marital cohabitation that lasted about one year. During the four final months, Barbara, however, had her own home because her job was relocated to another area. The parties resumed their sexual relations, shared household chores, and filed a joint tax declaration. Barbara presented Bruce as her husband in several different situations. They had plans to renew their marriage vows during a ceremony. However, during this time Bruce "dated other women," with whom he also publicly appeared. After one year, August 1994, the cohabitation between Bruce and Barbara was terminated; two months later, he formally married another woman.

Barbara petitioned for divorce based on the claim that she was his common law wife and argued that the man had committed adultery and bigamy. The Alabama Court of Appeals, in determining whether a common law marriage had been formed, found that the requirements of public recognition of the relationship as a marriage and public assumption of marital duties and cohabitation had been fulfilled. The presumption, based on the parties' cohabitation could, therefore, be applied. The circumstances that the man dated other woman and formally married one of them two months after the termination of the cohabitation, were not considered sufficient to disprove the presumption. The reasoning was also based on the fact that the parties, when they resumed their marital cohabitation, agreed to permanently enter the marriage relationship to the exclusion of all other relationships. A common law marriage was, therefore, found to have been formed.[121]

Bruce dated others during the marital cohabitation and immediately thereafter formally married a different woman. Therefore, it is easy to question whether he had the intent to permanently enter the marriage

120 *White v. White,* 225 Ala. 155, 142 So. 524 (1932): "Presumption of actual marriage from cohabitation is rebutted by subsequent permanent separation without apparent cause and actual marriage by one party." For similar statements, *see Moore v. Heineke,* 119 Ala. 627, 24 So. 374, 380 (1898); and *Weatherford v. Weatherford,* 20 Ala. 548, 56 Am.Dec. 206 (1852). *Compare Crosson v. Crosson,* 668 So.2d 868, 872 (Ala.Civ. App. 1995). As to precedence between this presumption and the presumption in favor of a later marriage, the latter has generally been considered to be stronger, *see* Section 5.3.3 *supra.*

121 *Crosson v. Crosson,* 668 So.2d 868 (Ala.Civ.App. 1995).

relationship to the exclusion of all other relationships, which is the contract requirement in Alabama. Nevertheless, it ought to be noted that the burden of proof, as a result of the presumption, shifted to the party contesting the existence of the common law marriage. He did not prove that a true marriage contract had not been formed. The court found that the arguments presented to disprove the presumption were insufficient to rebut the facts suggesting a common law marriage.

9.6 The Marriage Presumption – Not Applicable

Three exceptions have been made in American case law in certain jurisdictions as to the application of the marriage presumption. These are cases in which (1) a marital impediment has previously existed and the impediment was later removed, (2) the relationship clearly was nonmarital from its commencement, and (3) direct evidence exists as to the marriage contract. In these cases, the burden of proof with respect to the marriage contract has remained with the party alleging the existence of the common law marriage.

9.6.1 Marital Impediment Previously Existed

If the parties, at the beginning of their relationship, lacked the legal capacity to enter into a marriage with each other, for example, because one party was already married to another, and the relation at issue was consequently considered "meretricious" or "illicit,"[122] several courts have found the marriage presumption inapplicable, even though the marital impediment was later removed. In these cases, a common law marriage could not be presumed based on cohabitation and reputation. Instead, the courts have assumed that, from the beginning, the relationship was impermissible

122 A "meretricious" relationship is defined as a "relation sustained by persons who contract a marriage that is void by reason of legal incapacity." *See Cann v. Cann*, 632 A.2d 325 (Pa.Super. 1993); *Steadman v. Turner*, 357 Pa.Super. 361, 516 A.2d 21, 23 (1986); *Pierce v. Pierce*, 355 Pa. 175, 49 A.2d 346, 348 (1946); *Wagner v. Wagner*, 152 Pa.Super. 4, 30 A.2d 659 (1943). *Compare* Black's Law Dictionary 1002 (7th ed. 1999), where a "meretricious relationship" means "1. Involving prostitution; of an unlawful sexual nature <a meretricious encounter>. 2. (Of a romantic relationship) involving either two people of the same sex or lack of capacity on the part of one party 'a meretricious marriage'..." In Freedman, *supra* note 14, at 138 and 140, the expression "illicit" is used as a synonym for "meretricious." The expression has also been used in the case law with respect to unmarried cohabitation, *see* § 2 *infra*. *Compare* the unusual definition in *Connell v. Francisco*, 127 Wash.2d 339, 346, 898 P.2d 831, 834 (Wash. 1995), where the community property system for spouses was applied to a "meretricious relationship," and where the relationship was defined as "a stable, marital-like relationship where both parties cohabit with knowledge that a lawful marriage between them does not exist..."

by clear and satisfactory evidence,[123] and by applying a reverse presumption, that the parties' relationship was presumed to continue as "illicit and meretricious."[124] The fundamental rules governing the burden of proof have, thus, been applied.

---

123 The required standard of proof was not met, *see, e.g., Knecht v. Knecht*, 261 Pa. 410 (1918); *In re Hine's Estate*, 10 Pa.Super. 124 (1899); *Drinkhouse's Estate*, 151 Pa. 294, 24 A. 1083 (1892); and *Vincent's Appeal*, 10 P.F. Smith 228, 60 Pa. 228 (1869). *See also* Freedman, *supra* note 14, at 140.

124 **Montana:** *Stevens v. Woodmen of the World*, 105 Mont. 121, 71 P.2d 898 (1937) (the contract, however, was proven: "Originally illicit relations between man and woman are presumed to continue so until contrary is shown, and burden rests on party asserting valid marriage between them to show that such relations changed to lawful relation by marriage"); *Welch v. All Persons*, 78 Mont. 370, 254 P. 179 (1929); and *Shepherd & Pierson Co. v. Baker*, 81 Mont. 185, 262 P. 87 (1927). *Compare Matter of Estate of Alcorn*, 868 P.2d 629 (Mont. 1994) (no mention of the presumption if the relationship continued as illicit despite the fact that an impediment existed from the beginning: "persons who cohabit after the removal of the impediment may become lawfully married as of the date of the removal of the impediment." All three elements were proven). **Georgia:** *Dismuke v. C & Trust Co.*, 407 SE.2d 739, 740 (Ga. 1991) ("Where as here, the relationship between the appellant and the decedent began illicitly, appellant had the burden of showing that the illicit relationship ended and that she and the decedent had entered into a marriage contract"); *Scott v. Jefferson*, 174 Ga.App. 651, 331 S.E.2d 1, 3 (1985); *Brown v. Brown*, 234 Ga. 300, 215 S.E.2d 671, 673 (1975). **South Carolina:** *Johns v. Johns*, 309 S.C. 199, 420 S.E.2d 856, 858 (App. 1992) (informal marital cohabitation, impediment existed however during the entire relationship: "A relationship illicit at its inception does not ripen into a common law marriage once the impediment to marriage is removed. Instead, the law presumes that the relationship retains its illicit character after removal of the impediment") *citing Prevatte v. Prevatte*, 297 S.C. 345, 377 S.E.2d 114, 117 (App. 1989) (invalid wedding, cohabitation during twenty five years, seven of which without impediment) *citing Yarbrough v. Yarbrough*, 280 S.C. 546, 314 S.E.2d 16, 19 (App. 1984) (informal cohabitation with respect to the second of the relationships, impediment, presumption of a continued illicit relationship); *Kirby v. Kirby*, 270 S.C. 137, 241 S.E.2d 415, 416 (1978) (informal cohabitation, impediment at the commencement: "the presumption of fact is that the illicit relationship continued after the impediment to marriage was removed"); and *Byers v. Mount Vernon Mills, Inc.*, 268 S.C. 68, 231 S.E.2d 699 (1977). **Ohio:** *Dirion v. Brewer*, 20 Ohio App. 298, 151 N.E. 818 (1925) ("a relationship having been established as illicit, the presumption is that it remains illicit so long as the cohabitation remains ... Agreement of parties to live together as husband and wife followed by present cohabitation constituted common law marriage"); *Lumas v. Lumas*, 26 Ohio App. 502, 160 N.E. 480 (1927); and *In re Maynard's Estate*, 117 Ohio.App. 315, 192 N.E.2d 281, *app. dism.* 174 Ohio St. 211 187 N.E.2d 883 (1962). **Pennsylvania:** *Int'l Painters and Allied Traders Ind. Pensions Fund v. Calabro*, 312 F.Supp.2d 697 (E.D.Pa. 2004); *State Farm Fire & Cas. Co. v. Platt*, 4 F.Supp.2d 399, 404 (E.D.Pa. 1998); *Canute v. Canute*, 557 A.2d 772, 774 (Pa.Super. 1989) ("Where the relationship began while at least one of the parties was married to a third person, the courts will presume that the parties continued to live together unmarried even after the impediment to their marriage had been removed unless thereafter they reaffirm their marriage agreement"); *In re Estate of Dodge*, 361 Pa.Super. 188, 522 A.2d 77, 79 (1987) ("However, an inference of marriage does not arise from cohabitation and reputation where the relationship between a man and a woman was illicit and meretricious at its inception. On the contrary, a relationship which is meretricious at its inception is presumed to continue in like manner during subsequent cohabitation"); *Steadman v. Turner*, 357 Pa.Super. 361, 365, 516 A.2d 21, 23 (1986); *In re Estate of Garges*, 474 Pa. 237, 378 A.2d 307 (1977); *Donaldson v. P.J. Oesterling & Sons, Inc.*, 199 Pa.Super. 637, 186 A.2d 653 (1962) ("Being a meretricious relationship in its inception,

The reason for this reversed presumption appears to be that the parties, when they began their cohabitation, could not be viewed as having a true marital intent, especially if they knew that one or both of them were already married to other persons.[125] To simply continue the cohabitation in the same manner as before, after the removal of the impediment, has been viewed as insufficient. The parties must prove a change in their intentions.[126] In addition, that the courts have wished to punish the parties for their immoral and sometimes criminal actions must also be considered.[127]

To disprove the presumption that the relationship continued to be "illicit and meretricious," the party alleging the existence of the common law marriage must demonstrate that the parties, after the removal of the marital impediment, expressed a marital *consensus*.[128] The majority of courts discuss this in terms similar to those discussed in Section 9.2, "Burdens and Standards of Proof," above, that the required standard of proof is

---

no presumption of marriage is raised from proof of its continuance"). **Rhode Island:** *Sardonis v. Sardonis*, 106 R.I. 469, 261 A.2d 22, 24 (1970) ("the law presumes that what was meretricious in its origins continues thus"); *Silva v. Meritt Scapman and Scott Co.* 52 R.I. 30, 156 A. 512 (1931); and *Ibello v. Sweet*, 47 R.I. 480, 133 A. 801 (1926).

125 *Canute v. Canute*, 557 A.2d 772, 774 (Pa.Super. 1989) ("The relationship was therefore meretricious because both partners were aware of the impediment"). *See also Steadman v. Turner*, 357 Pa.Super. 361, 365, 516 A.2d 21, 23 (1986); and *Brown v. Sheridan*, 83 Ga.App. 725, 64 S.E.2d 636 (1951). With respect to the parties' knowledge as the existence of an impediment, the question has been raised as to the significance this should be ascribed to whether the parties knew that the impediment had been removed. *See U.S. Fid. & Guar. Co. v. Dowdle*, 269 S.W. 119, 124 (Tex. Civ.App. 1925) ("Without knowledge of the removal of the impediment, they could not have intended a second marriage or have attempted to enter into another marriage"). *See also Lester v. Celebrezze*, 221 F.Supp. 607 (E.D.Ark. 1963). In *Lawrence v. Lawrence*, 86 Ga.App. 8, 70 S.E.2d 549 (1952), the relationship was presumed "illicit" as the woman, however mistakenly, believed that the man was married. *Compare In re Gallagher's Estate*, 35 Wash.2d 512, 213 P.2d 621 (1959). In FREEDMAN, *supra* note 14, at 142, older cases are systemized in accordance to when one, or both, or none, of the parties had knowledge of the impediment.

126 Among older cases, *see, e.g., Williams v. Williams*, 46 Wis. 464, 1 N.W. 98, 102, 105 (1879), in which the court required something more than a continued cohabitation to demonstrate a change in the parties' relation after the removal of the impediment. The court did not elaborate as to what was required, but simply stated a requirement of "some affirmative evidence." A marriage, however, appears to be able to be proven formed "by circumstances." *Compare* CLARK, *supra* note 23, at 112 fn. 53, which appears to interpret the case as making a requirement of an explicit agreement.

127 CLARK, *supra* note 23, at 112: "The parties are thus punished for their sins by withholding legal recognition of their marriage."

128 In *Dismuke v. C & Trust Co.*, 407 SE.2d 739, 740 (Ga. 1991), the court stated that the parties, after the removal of the impediment, must enter into a marriage contract. In *Kirby v. Kirby*, 270 S.C. 137, 241 S.E.2d 415, 416 (1978), the court required a new mutual agreement and in *Canute v. Canute*, 557 A.2d 772, 774 (Pa.Super. 1989), the court stated that the parties must "reaffirm their marriage agreement." The inadequacies that exist with respect to the analyses regarding the marriage contract's intent, as discussed in Chapter 6 *supra*, also appear in cases where the parties must prove the existence of a marital *consensus* after the removal of the impediment. What is it that the parties must be in agreement upon? With respect to this issue, reference is made to the discussion in Chapter 6.3, and the future perspective given in Chapter 13.

with clear evidence[129] or clear and convincing evidence,[130] while others have applied a preponderance of the evidence.[131] In *Cann v. Cann* (1993), the Pennsylvania Superior Court stated that if a relationship is meretricious at its inception, there must be clear evidence of a change in status to rebut the presumption that the nonmarriage continued after the impediment to the marriage was removed.[132]

Nowadays, few courts require that the new contract be expressed.[133] The majority of courts accept circumstantial evidence[134] or an implied

---

129 *Cann v. Cann*, 632 A.2d 322, 325 (Pa.Super 1993). *See also Canute v. Canute*, 557 A.2d 772, 774 (Pa.Super. 1989) (standard of proof "clear evidence of a change in status"). The same formulation can be found in *Steadman v. Turner*, 357 Pa.Super. 361, 365, 516 A.2d 21, 23 (1986); *Sardonis v. Sardonis*, 106 R.I. 469, 261 A.2d 22, 24 (1970) (clear proof); and *Ibello v. Sweet*, 47 R.I. 480, 133 A. 801 (1926).

130 *Int'l Painters and Allied Traders Ind. Pensions Fund v. Calabro*, 312 F.Supp.2d 697, 703 (E.D.Pa. 2004); *State Farm Fire & Cas. Co. v. Platt*, 4 F.Supp.2d 399, 404 (E.D.Pa. 1998); *Marino v. Anheuser-Bush, Inc.*, 583 N.Y.S.2d 68, 69 (1992); and *Estate of Gavula*, 490 Pa. 535, 417 A.2d 168 (1980). In the case of *In re Estate of Garges*, 474 Pa. 237, 378 A.2d 307, 309 (1977), the Pennsylvania Supreme Court required evidence that was clear and convincing to disprove the presumption that the parties continued to live together as unmarried also after the removal of the impediment. The court found the contract proven. *See also In re Estate of Gower*, 445 Pa. 554, 284 A.2d 742 (1971); *Brown v. Atlantic & Gulf Stevedores, Inc.*, 2 Pa.Commw. 481, 279 A.2d 372 (1971); *Donaldson v. P.J. Oesterling & Sons, Inc.*, 199 Pa.Super. 637, 186 A.2d 653 (1962) ("The presumption is for the continuance of the meretricious relationship, and it can be overcome only by clear and convincing evidence that both parties consented to a new agreement after the removal of the obstacle to their marriage"); *Com. v. Drebot*, 199 Pa.Super. 439, 185 A.2d 617, 618 (1962); *Mainor v. Midvale Co.*, 192 Pa.Super.Ct. 367, 162 A.2d 27, 30 (1960); *In re Stauffer's Estate*, 372 Pa. 537, 94 A.2d 726, 727-728 (1953); *Com. ex rel. DeMarco v. DeMarco*, 166 Pa.Super. 69, 70 A.2d 384, 386 (1950); *Pierce v. Pierce*, 355 Pa. 175, 49 A.2d 346, 348 (1946); and *Wagner v. Wagner*, 152 Pa.Super. 4, 30 A.2d 659, 661 (1943). *See also* Foote et al., *supra* note 8, at 18. In *Brown v. Brown*, 115 S.W.2d 786 (Tex.Civ.App.-Galveston 1938), evidence which was "positive and satisfactory" was required as the relationship from the beginning was "meretricious." No such evidence was presented. The marriage presumption was, however, not mentioned. *See also Silva v. Merritt, Chapman & Scott Corp.*, 52 R.I. 30, 156 A. 512 (1931).

131 *Kirby v. Kirby*, 270 S.C. 137, 241 S.E.2d 415, 416 (1978).

132 *Cann v. Cann*, 632 A.2d 322, 325 (Pa.Super. 1993); *State Farm Fire & Cas. Co. v. Platt*, 4 F.Supp.2d 399 (E.D.Pa. 1998); *Canute v. Canute*, 384 Pa.Super. 60, 557 A.2d 772 (1989); *Steadman v. Turner*, 357 Pa.Super. 361, 516 A.2d 21 (1986); *In re Estate of Garges*, 474 Pa. 237, 378 A.2d 307, 309 (1977); and *Donaldson v. P.J. Oesterling & Sons, Inc.*, 199 Pa.Super. 637, 186 A.2d 653 (1962).

133 In *Anderson v. Anderson*, 235 Ind. 113, 131 N.E.2d 301 (1956), the Indiana Supreme Court required in principle evidence of an express contract after the removal of the impediment, but added that "such contract may be proved by circumstances." In *Donaldson v. P.J. Oesterling & Sons, Inc.*, 199 Pa.Super. 637, 186 A.2d 653 (1962), where the Pennsylvania Superior Court required "a new marriage agreement" after the removal of the impediment, the parties had proven that they entered into an express contract, a consequence of which was that a common law marriage was proven. It is not clear from the case, however, how the court would have reacted if the new contract had not been express. *Compare* Clark, *supra* note 23, at 112 fn. 53, which cites the case as support for the proposition of the requirement for an explicit contract. With respect to Pennsylvania *see* the next footnote.

134 **Georgia:** *Scott v. Jefferson*, 174 Ga.App. 651, 331 S.E.2d 1, 3 (1985) ("This presumption can be overcome by introducing direct or circumstantial evidence showing the

agreement.[135] In *Johns v. Johns* (1992), the South Carolina Court of Appeals stated: "In order for a common law marriage to arise, the parties must agree to enter into a common law marriage after the impediment is removed though such agreement may be gathered from the conduct of the parties."[136] Certain courts have considered such evidence alone sufficient.[137] Other courts, accepting circumstantial evidence, maintain that the new contract may not solely rest on such evidence, which is, however, accepted as corroborative evidence in support of a new contract. Not uncommonly in such cases, oral statements made by the parties

---

existence of all essentials to a valid marriage"); *Evans v. Marbut*, 140 Ga.App. 329, 231 S.E.2d 94 (1976), *cert. dismissed*, 238 Ga. 583, 234 S.E.2d 506 (1977); *Brown v. Brown*, 234 Ga. 300, 215 S.E.2d 671, 673 (1975); *Brown v. State*, 208 Ga. 304, 66 S. E.2d 745, 748 (1951); *Pickren v. Pickren*, 190 Ga. 609, 10 S.E.2d 40 (1940); *Addison v. Addison*, 186 Ga. 155, 197 S.E. 232, 233 (1938); *Foster v. Foster*, 178 Ga. 791, 174 S.E. 532, 534 (1934); *Drawdy v. Hesters*, 130 Ga. 161, 60 S.E. 451 (1908) and *Clark v. Cassidy*, 64 Ga. 662, 667 (1880). **South Carolina:** *Johns v. Johns*, 309 S.C. 199, 420 S.E.2d 856, 858 (App. 1992) (dictum). Circumstantial evidence is cited in the following cases from South Carolina and discussed in Chapter 7 above, *Prevatte v. Prevatte*, 297 S.C. 345, 377 S.E.2d 114, 117 (App. 1989) (contract proven); *Weathers v. Bolt*, 293 S.C. 486, 361 S.E.2d 773 (App. 1987) (contract not proven); *Yarbrough v. Yarbrough*, 280 S.C. 546, 314 S.E.2d 16, 19 (App. 1984) (contract not proven); *see also Kirby v. Kirby*, 270 S.C. 137,241 S.E.2d 415, 416 (1978) (contract proven); *Byers v. Mount Vernon Mills, Inc.*, 268 S.C. 68, 231 S.E.2d 699 (1977) (contract not proven); *Campbell v. Christian*, 235 S.C. 542, 112 S.E.2d 647 (1960) (contract proven); and *Howell v. Litlefield*, 211 S.C. 462, 46 S.E.2d 47 (1947) (contract not proven). **Pennsylvania:** *Int'l Painters and Allied Traders Ind. Pensions Fund v. Calabro*, 312 F. Supp.2d 697, 703 (E.D.Pa. 2004); *Cann v. Cann*, 632 A.2d 322, 325 (Pa.Super. 1993); *Canute v. Canute*, 384 Pa.Super. 60, 557 A.2d 772 (1989); *Steadman v. Turner*, 357 Pa.Super. 361, 516 A.2d 21 (1986); *In re Estate of Garges*, 474 Pa. 237, 378 A.2d 307, 309 (1977); *Donaldson v. P.J. Oesterling & Sons, Inc.*, 199 Pa.Super. 637, 186 A.2d 653 (1962); *Pierce v. Pierce*, 355 Pa. 175, 49 A.2d 346 (1946) ("A change of meretricious relationship between man and woman to lawful marriage may be established by circumstantial evidence," however not simply cohabitation and reputation); *Edward v. Enterprise Mfg. Co.*, 283 Pa. 420, 129 A. 449, 450 (1925); and *In re Thewlis' Estate*, 217 Pa. 307, 66 A. 519 (1907). **District of Columbia:** *United States Fidelity & Guar. Co. v. Britton*, 106 U.S.D.C. 58, 269 F.2d 249 (1959); and *Smith v. Smith*, 61 App.D.C. 157, 58 F.2d 883 (1932). **Rhode Island:** *Sardonis v. Sardonis*, 106 R.I. 469, 261 A.2d 22, 24 (1970) (parties lived together three years, two without impediment. The presumption was considered disproved with evidence that was clear and convincing); *Silva v. Meritt Scapman and Scott Co.*, 52 R.I. 30, 156 A. 512 (1931) (continued cohabitation after removal of impediment insufficient evidence); *Ibello v. Sweet*, 47 R.I. 480, 133 A. 801 (1926) (the man, after the death of his first wife, said to the woman he was living with, "Now you are my wife" and the parties thereafter together with friends celebrated the fact they were married. The court found that the presumption was disproved).

135 In *Stevens v. Woodmen of the World*, 105 Mont. 121, 71 P.2d 898, 905-906 (1937), the lower court had found impliedly that a common law marriage existed after the removal of the impediment and the Montana Supreme Court stated that ample evidence existed to support this conclusion.

136 *Johns v. Johns*, 420 S.E.2d 856, 858 (App. 1992) (dictum).

137 *See, e.g., Adger v. Ackerman*, 115 F. 124 (8th Cir. 1902) ("A relation, illicit in its inception, is presumed to continue, in the absence of countervailing evidence. But slight circumstances may be sufficient to establish a change from concubinage to matrimony"); and *Prince v. Edwards*, 175 Ala. 532, 57 So. 714 (1912) (a marriage "may be found from mere cohabitation," without visible changes after the removal of the impediment).

are cited.[138] On the other hand, other courts, in finding a common law marriage proven formed solely based on circumstantial evidence, emphasize that this evidence must demonstrate that the parties' relation truly has changed to a matrimonial union after the removal of the marital impediment through their new, mutual intent.[139] Under this approach, it is common that the courts have not accepted simply a continued cohabitation or a lapse of time.

The ability to consider circumstantial evidence in the proof of the new contract naturally minimizes the actual difference between applying the marriage presumption based on cohabitation and reputation. A principal difference, however, is that, under the marriage presumption, the law draws the conclusion about a marriage; with circumstantial evidence, the courts, in the individual cases, after hearing the evidence, draw the conclusion about the existence of a contract. Further, it appears that various courts, in more recent cases, take into consideration only the circumstances that have occurred after the removal of the marital impediment.[140]

---

138 *Cann v. Cann*, 632 A.2d 322, 325 (Pa.Super. 1993) ("cohabitation and reputation alone will not suffice"); *Canute v. Canute*, 384 Pa.Super. 60, 557 A.2d 772 (1989); *Steadman v. Turner*, 357 Pa.Super. 361, 516 A.2d 21 (1986); *In re Estate of Garges*, 474 Pa. 237, 378 A.2d 307, 309, fn. 8 (1977) (common law marriage proven to exist after removal of the impediment: "While post-1962 cohabitation and reputation cannot by themselves establish a marriage here because of the presumption that the appellee and decedent continued their prior unmarried relationship, these facts can corroborate other evidence of an agreement to marry entered into after both parties became competent to marry"). *Compare Pierce v. Pierce*, 355 Pa. 175, 49 A.2d 346 (1946), in which the court stated that "a change of meretricious relationship between man and woman to lawful marriage may be established by circumstantial evidence, but circumstances must be such as to exclude presumption that original relation continued and prove satisfactorily that it was changed to matrimonial union by parties' mutual consent." Standing alone, the statement can be seen as giving support for the principle that the contract can be entirely based upon circumstantial evidence. In the case, where an alleged oral contract was not proven, a cohabitation lasting seventeen years was insufficient to form a common law marriage. The court distinguished its reasoning from the case of *In re Estate of Holben*, 93 Pa.Super.Ct. 472 (1928), in which the Superior Court considered cohabitation and reputation occurring after the removal of the impediment as sufficient to prove the existence of a new contract.

139 *Foster v. Foster*, 178 Ga. 791, 174 S.E. 532, 534 (1934) ("Such presumption may be overcome by direct or circumstantial evidence affirmatively showing that, pending the illicit relation, the parties entered into an agreement to become husband and wife, and thereafter continued the cohabitation in the new relation. The burden of proof is upon the party asserting the agreement"), *cited in Drawdy v. Hesters*, 130 Ga. 161, 60 S.E. 451 (1908). *See also Prevatte v. Prevatte*, 297 S.C. 345, 377 S.E.2d 114, 117 (App. 1989) (where the parties "represented to the court that that they were married, and acted in ways indicating agreement to be married"); *Kirby v. Kirby*, 270 S.C. 137, 241 S.E.2d 415, 416 (1978) (the parties "consistently represented themselves as husband and wife in their community, and the parties appeared as husband and wife on their children's birth certificate and filed joint federal income tax returns").

140 *Cann v. Cann*, 632 A.2d 322, 325 (Pa.Super. 1993); *Johns v. Johns*, 309 S.C. 199, 420 S.E.2d 856, 858 (S.C.App. 1992) (dictum); *Canute v. Canute*, 384 Pa.Super. 60, 557 A.2d 772 (1989); *Steadman v. Turner*, 357 Pa.Super. 361, 516 A.2d 21, 23 (1986) ("Appellant's evidence of cohabitation and reputation of marriage which

In addition, the legal consequence of an application of the presumption is preliminary in that the burden of proof is shifted to the opposing party, who then has the possibility to demonstrate that a marriage contract did not exist.

In certain cases, in which the presumption based on the cohabitation and reputation was inapplicable because the relationship was illicit and meretricious from the beginning, a marriage contract has nevertheless been found proven.[141] In other cases, the presumption of a continued meretricious or illicit relationship could not be disproved.[142]

The manner in which the courts, basing their reasoning on circumstantial evidence, have found the existence of a marriage contract is more closely discussed above in Chapter 7, "Implied Marriage Agreements."

In American case law, exceptions to the marriage presumption do not occur uniformly in cases in which the parties married or commenced a relationship while a marital impediment existed. Instead, several courts have applied the marriage presumption if the parties continued their marital cohabitation after the impediment was removed. The courts' view has not been that the parties lacked a marital intent or that their relationship was meretricious as a result of the impediment, but rather that either the parties did not know about the impediment and therefore acted in good faith, or the impediment was understood to be simply a superficial

---

occurred after removal of the impediment is equally unavailing to rebut the presumption that the non-marriage continued"); *Prevatte v. Prevatte,* 297 S.C. 345, 377 S.E.2d 114, 117 (App. 1989); and *Yarbrough v. Yarbrough,* 280 S.C. 546, 314 S.E.2d 16, 19 (App. 1984). In certain cases, such circumstances have been attributed significant evidentiary weight particularly where the cohabitation after the removal of the impediment has been long term, *see, e.g., Thewlis's Estate,* 217 Pa. 307, 309 (1907), in which the cohabitation was thirteen years, Judge Penrose stated that though there certainly was no formalized contract, "each day during these many years that they thus lived together there was an assertion by acts and conduct which in law are as efficacious as words for establishing a contract by implication."

141 *Cann v. Cann,* 632 A.2d 322 (Pa.Super. 1993); *Stuck Leasing Co. v. W.C.A.B. (Ziegler),* 557 A.2d 808 (Pa. Cmwlth. 1989); *Prevatte v. Prevatte,* 297 S.C. 345, 377 S.E.2d 114, 117 (App. 1989); *Dozack v. Dozack,* 137 A.D.2d 317, 528 N.Y.S.2d 712 (A.D. 3 Dep't 1988); *Kirby v. Kirby,* 270 S.C. 137, 241 S.E.2d 415, 416 (1978); *In re Estate of Garges,* 474 Pa. 237, 378 A.2d 307 (1977); *Donaldson v. P.J. Oesterling & Sons, Inc.,* 199 Pa. Super. 637, 186 A.2d 653 (1962); *In re Estate of Gower,* 445 Pa. 554, 284 A.2d 742 (1972); *Sinclair v. Sinclair,* 197 Pa.Super. 59, 176 A.2d 123 (1961); *Campbell v. Christian,* 235 S.C. 542, 112 S.E.2d 647 (1960); and *Stevens v. Woodmen of the World,* 105 Mont. 121, 71 P.2d 898, 905 (1937).

142 *Matter of Danza,* 188 A.D.2d 530, 591 N.Y.S.2d 197 (1992); *Canute v. Canute,* 557 A.2d 772 (Pa.Super. 1989); *In re Estate of Dodge,* 361 Pa.Super. 188, 522 A.2d 77 (1987); *Weathers v. Bolt,* 293 S.C. 486, 361 S.E.2d 773 (App. 1987); *Steadman v. Turner,* 357 Pa.Super. 361, 516 A.2d 21 (1986); *Yarbrough v. Yarbrough,* 280 S.C. 546, 314 S.E.2d 16, 19 (App. 1984); *Byers v. Mount Vernon Mills, Inc.,* 268 S.C. 68, 231 S.E.2d 699 (1977); *David v. Bellevue Locust Garage,* 317 A.2d 341 (Pa.Cmwlth. 1974); *Brown v. Atlantic & Gulf Stevedores, Inc.,* 2 Pa. 481, 279 A.2d 372 (1971); *Com. ex. rel. De Marco v. DeMarco,* 166 Pa.Super. 69, 71, 70 A.2d 384, 386 (1950); *Howell v. Litlefield,* 211 S.C. 462, 46 S.E.2d 47 (1947). *Pierce v. Pierce,* 355 Pa. 175, 49 A.2d 346 (1946); *Wagner v. Wagner,* 152 Pa.Super. 4, 30 A.2d 659 (1943); and *In re McLaughlin's Estate,* 314 Pa. 574, 172 A. 107 (1934).

legal requirement.[143] After the removal of the impediment, no changes in the relationship or a new marital *consensus* were necessary; the continued marital cohabitation was sufficient.

Such cases involved the parties entering into a formal marriage that was invalid as a result of a marital impediment. For example, in *Rickard v. Trousdale* (1987), the parties, Leon and Isephene, entered into a formal marriage in 1976. The marriage, however, was invalid because the man was already married to another woman, a marriage that dissolved in 1978. Thereafter, Leon and Isephene lived, together, until her death in 1984. The Alabama Supreme Court stated: "It is the well-settled rule that if parties in good faith (attempt to) marry at a time when in fact a legal impediment exists to their marriage, and they continue to live together as husband and wife after the removal of the impediment to their lawful union, the law presumes a common law marriage." The court found that the parties had cohabited in a common law marriage. No reference about whether the relationship was presumed to be "illicit and meretricious" appeared in the case. The opposing party did not succeed in disproving the marriage presumption by demonstrating that the parties lacked a marital *consensus*.[144]

---

143 *Holgate v. United Electric Ry. Co.*, 47 R.I. 337, 133 A. 243, 244 (1926) ("The fact that the marriage was void because final decree had not been entered at the time divorcing Mr. Holgate from his former wife would not prove that the parties did not then intend to and consent to become husband and wife").

144 *Rickard v. Trousdale*, 508 So.2d 260, 261 (Ala. 1987). The principle has a long tradition in Alabama. **Alabama**, *see Steele v. Steele*, 522 So.2d 269 (Ala. 1988); *Krug v. Krug*, 296 So.2d 715 (Ala. 1974); *Morgan v. Richardson*, 325 F.Supp. 128 (D.C.Ala. 1971); *Matthews v. Matthews*, 259 Ala. 332, 67 So.2d 22 (1953); *King v. King*, 269 Ala. 468, 114 So.2d 145 (1959); *Hackmeyer v. Hackmeyer*, 268 Ala. 329, 106 So.2d 245, 248 (1958) (one party in good faith); *Barnett v. Barnett*, 262 Ala. 655, 658, 80 So.2d 626 (1955); *Hunter v. Lynn*, 256 Ala. 501, 506, 55 So.2d 849 (1951); *Smith v. Smith*, 247 Ala. 213, 23 So.2d 605, 608-609 (1945); *Hill v. Lindsey*, 223 Ala. 550, 137 So. 395, 397 (1931); *White v. White*, 225 Ala. 155, 142 So. 524 (1932); *compare Prince v. Edwards*, 175 Ala. 532, 57 So. 714 (1912). **Oklahoma:** *Olinghouse v. Olinghouse*, 265 P.2d 711, 712 (Okla. 1954) ("The acts of living together and holding themselves out as husband and wife, after removal of a legal impediment to marriage, constitute a common law marriage, even though both parties knew of the impediment"); *compare* older case law, *Clark v. Barney*, 24 Okla. 455, 103 P. 598 (1909); *Webster v. Webster*, 114 Okla. 57, 242 P. 555 (1925) ("When parties in good faith comply with the forms of law which would give rise to their marriage but for one being under a disability, the law infers that the matrimonial consent was interchanged between them as soon as the disability is removed, and stamps their relation with the status of a valid marriage"). **Georgia:** *Johnson v. Johnson*, 96 Ga.App. 84, 99 S.E.2d 352, 353 (1957); *Chance v. Chance*, 60 Ga.App. 889, 5 S.E.2d 399 (1939); *White v. White*, 41 Ga.App. 394, 153 S.E. 203 (1930); *Heflinger v. Heflinger*, 161 Ga. 867, 132 S.E. 85 (1926); *Harper v. Atlantic & W.P.R. Co.*, 33 Ga.App. 259, 125 S.E. 885 (1924); and *Smith v. Reed*, 145 Ga. 724, 89 S.E. 815 (1916). **Ohio:** *Ryan v. Ryan*, 84 Ohio App. 139, 86 N.E.2d 44 (1948) ("While a ceremonial marriage is invalid if, at the time, one of the parties has an existing marriage status, but cohabitation is continued after the termination of the previous marriage, a valid marriage is then in force"). **District of Columbia:** *Parella v. Parella*, 74 App.D.C. 161, 33 F.Supp. 614, 120 F.2d 728 (1941) (invalid wedding, continued cohabitation after the removal of the impediment sufficient to form a common law marriage. The relationship was not

Cases exist in which the marriage presumption, comparable to its Scottish precedent,[145] has been applied after the removal of the marital impediment even though the parties have entered into an informal relationship. For example, in *Thomas v. Murphy* (1938), the parties had entered into an informal cohabitation while a marital impediment existed. The relationship was not termed meretricious and the presumption of a continued status as meretricious was not applied. When the impediment was later removed, a change in the parties' intents was not required, even though both knew about the impediment. Their continued cohabitation was sufficient to form a common law marriage: "The removal of an impediment while the parties continue to live together as husband and wife, gives rise to a 'common law marriage,' even though one or both of the parties knew of the impediment." One aspect of the reasoning behind this approach is that the parties, from the beginning, had a true marital *consensus*, while a marital impediment existed. Moreover, from a legal policy perspective, it is considered socially sound to favor marriage between parties over concubinage.[146]

---

termed "meretricious"); *Williams v. Williams*, 74 App.D.C. 396, 33 F.Supp. 612, *aff'd*, 121 F.2d 737 (1940); *McVicker v. McVicker*, 76 U.S.App.D.C. 208, 130 F.2d 837 (1942); *Utterback v. Utterback*, 71 F.Supp. 231 (D.D.C. 1947); *Lee v. Lee*, 201 A.2d 873 (D.C.App. 1964); and *Jennings v. Jennings*, 20 Md.App. 369, 315 A.2d 816, 823 (1974) (applying D.C. law). *Compare Friedenwald v. Friedenwald*, 57 App.D.C. 13, 16 F.2d 509 (1926) (no cohabitation evidenced after the removal of the impediment). **Rhode Island:** *Holgate v. United Electric Ry. Co.*, 47 R.I. 337, 133 A. 243, 244 (1926) ("It is a principle of law that where parties who are incompetent to marry enter an illicit relation with a manifest desire and intention to live in a matrimonial union rather than in a state of concubinage, and the obstacle to their marriage is subsequently removed, their continued cohabitation raises a presumption of an actual marriage immediately after the removal of the obstacle"). **Idaho:** *Nicholas v. Idaho Power Co.*, 63 Idaho 675, 125 P.2d 321 (1942); and *Huff v. Huff*, 20 Idaho 450, 118 P. 1080, 1084 (1911).

145 With respect to Scottish law, *see Campbell v. Campbell*, (1867) L.R.I.H.L. Sc.App. 182, in which the parties began their relationship with the highest degree of bad faith as they eloped when the young woman was still married to another. The parties thereafter lived together as husband and wife. After the husband from which the woman had fled died, the parties had a mutual child. With the death of the child's father, the question arose as to whether the child was born within wedlock and whether a common law marriage had been formed between the parties. The court found that such a marriage was formed after the removal of the impediment. The evidence in the case as to a renewed marriage contract appears to have been rather sparse.

146 **District of Columbia:** *Thomas v. Murphy*, 71 App. D.C. 69, 107 F.2d 268, 269 (1938). *See also Matthews v. Britton*, 112 U.S.App.D.C. 397, 303 F.2d 408, 409 (D.C.Cir. 1962); *Lee v. Lee*, 201 A.2d 873 (D.C.App. 1964); *compare U.S. Fid. & Guar. Co. v. Britton*, 106 U.S.App.D.C. 58, 269 F.2d 249 (D.C.Cir. 1959). **Alabama:** *Rogers v. McLeskey*, 225 Ala. 148, 142 So. 526 (1932) (the court stated that the parties certainly would have married, but no evidence was introduced). **Idaho:** *Hamby v. Simplot Co.*, 94 Idaho 794, 498 P.2d 1267 (1972) (no discussion of the presumption of "illicit" despite the fact that an impediment existed at the commencement of the relationship). In *Albina Engine and Machine Works v. Oleary*, 328 F.2d 877, 882 (9th Cir. 1964), the court takes a stance against a requirement of "a new marriage agreement in addition to mere continuance of the prior relationship." *See also Warner v. Warner*, 76

The presumption that a relationship begun while a marital impediment existed continues as "illicit and meretricious" after the removal of the impediment has been criticized. Homer Clark has questioned the psychological basis behind the presumption and maintains that the parties, in many cases, can have commenced their lives together meretriciously simply because the divorce laws prevented them from dissolving an earlier marriage and that their intent can very well have been to live together as husband and wife as allowed by the law.[147] Also, it can be argued that the presumption ought not, above all else, be based on the parties' marital intent when they began the relationship with respect to the marital impediment. To not wish to be married is one thing, to not be able to marry is another! Because the intent to live together or the intent to create a legal relationship is included in the assessment of marriage contracts, as discussed in Chapter 6 above, such intent can exist despite the existence of the impediment. The question about whether the parties knew about the impediment then becomes less interesting. In contrast, an argument can be made in support of the presumption, namely, that the parties ought to have the burden of proving that a marital intent existed when the marital impediment was removed and a marriage could be formed. It has been stated that it cannot be expected that parties, having once agreed to be married, will believe it necessary to reiterate their agreement once an earlier marriage is terminated or some other bar to the union is eliminated. Their intent, however, may have changed, especially if a long period of time has passed. Therefore, it is reasonable to request that the parties prove the existence of a marital intent after the removal of the impediment. This should be possible with evidence of an express contract or circumstantial evidence under the condition it reaches the required standard of proof. It ought, in that case, to be possible to consider circumstances both before and after the removal of the impediment, assuming that the marital intent can be attributed the period after the removal.

9.6.2 The Relationship was Meretricious from the Beginning

Another group of cases, on the side of the impediment cases, in which the parties' relationship is considered to be "illicit" or "meretricious" are cases

---

Idaho 399, 283 P.2d 931, 935 (1955); and *Thomey v. Thomey*, 67 Idaho 393, 181 P.2d 777, 779 (1947). **Oklahoma:** *Burdine v. Burdine*, 206 Okla. 170, 242 P.2d 148 (1952) ("The removal of a legal impediment to marriage, where parties continue to live together, recognizing each other as husband and wife, ripens into a common law marriage as of the time of the removal of the impediment, though one of the parties knew of the impediment"); and *Hess v. Hess*, 198 Okla. 130, 176 P.2d 804 (1947) ("The removal of a legal impediment to marriage while parties continue to live together as husband and wife gives rise to a 'common law marriage,' even though one or both of the parties knew of the impediment").

147 Clark, *supra* note 18, at 113. *See also* Freedman, *supra* note 9, at 143 fn. 11 and Bishop, *supra* note 40, § 970.

in which the parties' from the beginning had no marital *consensus* and the relationship therefore was non-marital at its commencement.[148] In these cases certain courts, especially those in Pennsylvania, have not applied the marriage presumption based on cohabitation and reputation. Perhaps the parties admitted that their relationship was non-marital from the beginning.[149] This group of cases ought to be distinguished from the cases that address marital impediments, despite the fact that the courts seldom maintain the distinction with any clarity.[150] In the non-marital cases, it has not been seen as sufficient that the parties later demonstrate a continued cohabitation and reputation. In these cases, the relationship is also presumed to continue as illicit or meretricious. The party alleging the existence of a common law marriage must prove that a change occurred in the relationship and that a marital *consensus* existed with evidence that is clear and convincing.[151]

---

148 *See, e.g., In re Cummings Estate*, 330 Pa.Super. 255, 264, 479 A.2d, 542 (1984); *Brown v. Atlantic & Gulf Stevedores, Inc.*, 2 Pa.Commw. 481, 279 A.2d 372, 373 (1971); *Mainor v. Midvale Co.*, 192 Pa.Super.Ct. 367, 162 A.2d 27 (1960), in which both expressions are used synonymously. In the case of *In re Stauffer's Estate*, 372 Pa. 537, 539, 94 A.2d 726, 727 (1953), the court refers to a relationship which is "illicit and meretricious"; and *Matter of Estate of Murnion*, 212 Mont. 107, 686 P.2d 893, 897 (1984), "illicit" and "meretricious" are used synonymously.

149 The inadequacies discussed in Chapter 6 *supra* with respect to the analysis of the content of the marriage contract's intent also exist in the cases in which the parties' relationship from the beginning is considered non-marital due to an insufficient marital *consensus* and where they must prove the later existence of such a *consensus*. What is it that the parties had not been, but later must be in agreement upon? With respect to this question, reference is made to the presentation in Chapter 6.3 *supra* and the discussion in Chapter 13 *infra*.

150 In many cases concerning impediments, non-marital cases are cited, and vice versa. *See, e.g., In re Estate of Garges*, 474 Pa. 237, 378 A.2d 307, 309 (1977), an impediment case, referring to *In re Stauffer's Estate*, 372 Pa. 537, 539, 94 A.2d 726 (1953) and *In re Rosenberger's Estate*, 362 Pa. 153, 65 A.2d 377 (1949), both of which are non-marital cases, and *Matter of Estate of Murnion*, 212 Mont. 107, 686 P.2d 893, 897 (1984), which is an non-marital case, *citing Stevens v. Woodmen of the World*, 105 Mont. 121, 71 P.2d 898 (1937), which is an impediment case. The distinction between relationships which are "illicit" due to impediment or due to an insufficient marital intent, respectively, can be clearly seen in *Thomas v. Murphy*, 71 App. D.C. 69, 107 F.2d 268, 269 (1938). *See also Smith v. Reed*, 145 Ga. 724, 89 S.E. 815 (1916).

151 *Milburn v. Milburn*, 694 N.E.2d 738 (Ind.App. 1998); and *In re Cumming's Estate*, 330 Pa.Super. 255, 479 A.2d 537, 542-543 (1984). In the case of *In re Estate of Kovalchick*, 345 Pa.Super. 29, 235, 498 A.2d 374, 377 (1985), the court stated: "A presumption of marriage based on cohabitation and reputation will not arise where the parties admit that they lived together unmarried up to the time of the alleged agreement to create a marriage relationship ... Where a relationship between a man and a woman is 'illicit and meretricious' in its inception, it is presumed to so continue during the cohabitation of the parties ... [T]he court could find that it continued to be meretricious unless appellant proved by evidence that was clear and convincing that the meretricious relationship had been superseded by a consensual agreement of marriage." *See also In re Stauffer's Estate*, 372 Pa.537, 94 A.2d 726 (1953) ("Being a meretricious relationship in its inception, no presumption of marriage is raised from proof of its continuance"); *Gilbreath v. Lewis*, 242 Ala. 510, 7 So.2d 485, 488 (1942) ("If intercourse between persons of opposite sex was illicit in its inception because of their failure to enter into a marriage by ceremony or by

In the case of *In re Cummings Estate* (1984), the parties, Patricia and Rodney, met in 1972. They dated and, in 1974, Patricia and her two sons moved in to Rodney's home in Manheim, Pennsylvania. Nevertheless, they did not outwardly present themselves as spouses. During a restaurant visit in 1975, Rodney gave Patricia a diamond ring and declared that he felt he was a married man. In 1977, Rodney bought a home in Renovo, Clinton County. Patricia was hesitant about moving, but Rodney said to her: "You are my wife. You are going to move." She moved in, along with her two sons. It was found proven that Rodney presented Patricia as his wife and that they outwardly appeared as spouses, albeit evidence existed to the contrary. When Rodney died in 1979, Patricia claimed the probate estate based on the fact that she was his common law wife.

The lower court, the Court of Common Pleas, Orphans' Court Division, Clinton County, found that no marriage contract was proven in connection with the restaurant visit in 1975, but that the marriage presumption could be applied based on the parties' cohabitation and reputation after moving to Renovo and that a common law marriage could, therefore, be presumed. The Pennsylvania Superior Court reversed, finding that the marriage presumption was not applicable because the parties' relationship originally was illicit and meretricious. The court stated: "It is clear then that Rodney and Patricia lived together *unmarried* for a number of years at the outset of their relationship; thus, their relationship began meretriciously." Instead, it was presumed that the parties continued to live together as unmarried. Patricia did not succeed in demonstrating, by clear and convincing evidence, that they had changed their relationship and had entered into an agreement to establish a marital relationship.[152]

---

agreement, it is presumed to continue so, and the burden of proving a subsequent intermarriage rests on the party asserting it"). *Compare Thomas v. Murphy*, 71 App. D.C. 69, 107 F.2d 268, 269 (1938) where the court stated that "it is reasonable to require some evidence of a change of intention." *Compare also In re Patterson's Estate*, 237 Pa. 24, 85 A. 75, 76 (1912) ("when, as in this case, the relation between the parties was illicit in its inception, a marriage will not be presumed, because of cohabitation and reputation, without proof of a change of the relation"); *Barnes v. Barnes*, 90 Iowa 282, 57 N.W. 851 (1894); and *Appeal of Reading Fire Ins. & Trust Co.*, 113 Pa. 204, 6 A. 60, 62 (1886) ("When the relation between a man and a woman living together is illicit in its commencement, it is presumed to so continue until a changed relation is proved. Without proof of subsequent actual marriage, it will not be presumed from continued cohabitation and reputation of a relation between them which is of illicit origin") *citing Hunt's Appeal*, 86 Pa. 294 (1878). *See also* the older case, *Brickle v. Brinckle*, 12 Phila. 232, 234 (1877) ("The mere fact of a man and a woman living together, and carrying on an illicit intercourse, is wholly insufficient to raise a legal presumption of marriage").

152 *In re Cummings Estate*, 330 Pa.Super. 255, 479 A.2d 537, 542-543 (1984). For other cases in which the presumption that the relationship continued as "illicit" was not disproved through evidence of a new contract, *see, e.g., In re Estate of Kovalchick*, 345 Pa.Super. 29, 235, 498 A.2d 374 (1985); *In re Stevenson's Estate*, 272 Pa. 291, 116 A. 162, 164 (1922); *In re Patterson's Estate*, 237 Pa. 24, 85 A. 75, 76 (1912); *In re Callery's Estate*, 226 Pa. 469 (1910); *Appeal of Grimm*, 131 Pa.St. 199, 18 A. 1061, 1062 (1890);

In cases in which the parties have successfully disproved the presumption that the relationship continued as illicit or meretricious by demonstrating that a marriage contract was formed, it has usually been through an oral contract supported by the circumstances. In the case of *In re Estate of Murnion* (1984), the Montana Supreme Court held, with respect to the woman's statement that her nonmarital relationship with the man became a common law marriage: "We determine that Pauline has met that burden by showing that their original meretricious relationship changed into a lawful one with their agreement to marry."[153]

Nevertheless, just as in cases involving a marital impediment, nothing prevents a new contract from being based solely on circumstantial evidence.[154] A continued cohabitation can change in a manner that demonstrates that the parties have entered into a marriage contract. This can happen, for example, by showing that the cohabitation became considerably more marital, because the parties had children, organized their existence in anticipation of a long life together, or outwardly represented themselves in a manner demonstrating a marital *consensus*. The required standard of proof, however, must be met.

The exception from the application of the marriage presumption recently discussed naturally raises the issue of whether the presumption can be applied in the cases of cohabiting partners. In the older case of *Appeal of Grimm* (1890), the court stated, with respect to the woman's claim of a common law marriage, that: "In the case in hand the relation between the parties was illicit at its commencement, and known to be such by the parties.... It would have been better for her had the cohabitation been later

---

Appeal of Reading Fire Ins. & Trust Co., 113 Pa. 204, 6 A. 60, 62 (1886); and *Hunt's Appeal*, 86 Pa. 294 (1878).

153 *Matter of Estate of Murnion*, 212 Mont. 107, 686 P.2d 893, 897 (1984); *In re Stauffer's Estate*, 372 Pa.537, 94 A.2d 726 (1953); *In re Rosenberger's Estate*, 362 Pa. 153, 65 A.2d 377 (1949); and *Rhoads v. Stoltzfus*, 18 Lehigh 297 (1939) (evidence with respect to cohabitation was simply "cumulative and corroborative"). In the case of *In re Estate of Kovalchick*, 345 Pa.Super. 29, 235, 498 A.2d 374, 377 (1985), the court stated: "Evidence of cohabitation and reputation may be received and considered in corroboration of testimony that marriage contract was in fact entered into." With respect to oral contracts, *see* Section 6.5 *supra*.

154 *In re Estate of Kovalchick*, 345 Pa.Super. 29, 235, 498 A.2d 374 (1985) (*dictum*, "Because it is often difficult to prove a civil contract of marriage, the law has permitted that it be established by circumstantial evidence"); *compare* the impediment cases, for example, *Pierce v. Pierce*, 355 Pa. 175, 49 A.2d 346 (1946) ("A change of meretricious relationship between man and woman to lawful marriage may be established by circumstantial evidence"). *See also Sandlin v. Tiger*, 104 Okla. 107, 230 P. 905 (1925) ("Illicit intercourse during courtship does not, as a matter of law, incapacitate the parties from afterwards assuming marriage relations, and where it is shown that the parties afterwards cohabited together in good faith and held themselves out as husband and wife, the presumption obtains in harmony with the general policy of the law to promote and encourage good morals that the parties had reformed, and the change from illicit to matrimonial relations may occur, although the occasion or precise time of the change has not been clearly ascertained").

or the marriage earlier."[155] The question is whether the majority of relationships actually begin meretriciously, *i.e.*, before the cohabitation deepens and the parties begin to enjoy a reputation as spouses, and before they decide more definitely on the future. In other words, at what point does the relationship on one hand continue to be illicit and meretricious and on the other hand, become eligible to apply the marriage presumption?

Perhaps the application of the presumptions can be illustrated by the following three cases. If it is clear that the parties had no marital *consensus* when they began their cohabitation, the marriage presumption based on cohabitation and reputation is not applicable to their continued relationship. A continued illicit and meretricious state is presumed and the parties must prove a later marital *consensus*. On the other hand, if it is clear that the parties had a marital *consensus* when the relationship commenced, there is no need to apply the marriage presumption because that which is presumed is already proven. If it is unclear whether the parties had a marital *consensus* when the relationship was commenced, the marriage presumption is applicable. A marriage contract can then be presumed based on cohabitation and reputation, however, the presumption can be rebutted in accordance with the above.

If the legal system is to apply a marriage presumption according to which a marital *consensus* can be presumed based on cohabitation and reputation, there is good reason not to apply the presumption if a *consensus* is shown to have not existed when the relationship was begun. The presumption that the relationship continues as illicit and meretricious is more strongly justified in these cases than in the impediment cases discussed above. This situation concerns parties who originally did not have a marital intent and, therefore, must demonstrate that they acquired one. In actuality, the fundamental rules governing the burden of proof and the measure of persuasion are applicable here with respect to each of the requirements necessary to form a common law marriage.

The presumption that the relationship has continued as illicit and meretricious has been criticized with respect to the difficulties entailed in proving a new marital *consensus*. Nancy Rebecca Shaw has maintained that it can lead to many harsh and inequitable results.[156] However, these results appear to be difficult to avoid as long as the legal system requires a marriage contract. The question of the function such a requirement can have in the future is discussed in Chapter 13, "The Constitutive Requisites in the Future."

9.6.3 Direct Evidence Is Available

There are cases in American case law, particularly within Pennsylvania, in which the courts have found that the marriage presumption was not applicable because direct evidence existed with respect to the marriage contract. If it is alleged that the parties entered into a marriage contract at

155 *Appeal of Grimm*, 131 Pa.St. 199, 18 A. 1061, 1062 (1890).
156 Nancy Rebecca Shaw, *Common Law Marriage and Unmarried Cohabitation: An Old Solution to a New Problem*, 39 U. Pitt. L. Rev. 579, 592 (1977).

a specific point of time and place, and direct evidence exists in the form of the parties' testimony on these facts, they have been deemed estopped from citing the presumption. Determinative for the result has been whether the marriage contract can be proven. Nothing prevents citing cohabitation and reputation in such cases, not as circumstances for the application of the presumption, but as corroborative evidence to support the existence of a marriage contract.[157]

For example, in *Eagle v. W.C.A.B.* (*Bahorich*) (1992), the man, with the support of the marriage presumption based on cohabitation and reputation, was granted workmen's compensation benefits as a surviving spouse in a common law marriage. The judgment, heard on appeal by the Workmen's Compensation Appeal Board, was appealed again by the employer to the Commonwealth Court of Pennsylvania, which stated: "Here, there was no basis to resort to the presumption, because claimant was available to testify to the words he allegedly exchanged with decedent. Because proof was available to find an exchange of words *in praesenti*, and the referee did not make a specific finding of an exchange of words *in praesenti* or a present intention to be married, the referee could not, as a matter of law, find a common law marriage. Therefore, the referee and board erred in evaluating evidence of cohabitation and reputation of marriage, and finding a common law marriage based on that evidence."[158]

---

157 *Staudenmayer v. Staudenmayer*, 714 A.2d 1016, 1021 (Pa. 1998). In the case of *In re Veneziale*, 267 B.R. 695, 700 (Bkrtcy.E.D.Pa. 2001), the court found that the presumption was not applicable, and gave as reason thereto: "There is no evidence that the debtor was not available to testify in this case, and her proffered testimony indicates that the debtor and Mr. Corliss never exchanged words in the present tense to create a common law marriage." *Compare Tornese v. Tornese*, 649 N.Y.S.2d 177, 179 (A.D. 2 Dep't 1996), in which the New York Supreme Court, Appellate Division, applying Pennsylvania law, in a case based on the parties' testimony with respect to an oral marriage contract, appears to have mistakenly applied the marriage presumption with a shift in the burden of proof. It would have been more correct in the reasoning to use the parties' cohabitation and reputation as corroborative evidence of an oral contract.

158 *Eagle v. W.C.A.B.* (*Bahorich*), 602 A.2d 387, 388-390 (Pa. Cmwlth. 1992). In the case of *In re Estate of Rees*, 331 Pa.Super. 225, 228, 480 A.2d 327 (1984) concerning a will, the Pennsylvania Superior Court stated: "The rule which permits a finding of marriage duly entered into based upon reputation and cohabitation alone is one of necessity to be applied only in cases where other proof is not available," *citing In re Nikitka's Estate*, 346 Pa. 63, 65, 29 A.2d 521, 522 (1943) (court rejected a claim based on cohabitation and reputation with reference to the fact that the plaintiff "was available to testify to the precise form of the alleged marriage contract between her and the decedent but this she did not do, from which it may properly be assumed that no contract was in fact entered into"). *See also Mainor v. Midvale Co.*, 192 Pa.Super.Ct. 367, 162 A.2d 27, 30 (1960) ("Since claimant here relied on the alleged contract of marriage in 1953, evidence of cohabitation and reputation is of no avail"); and *In re Estate of Stauffer*, 476 A.2d 354, 357 (Pa. 1984) (a common law marriage can be based on evidence of a marriage contract, but "where there is no such proof available, the law permits a finding of marriage based upon reputation and cohabitation"). In the case, *In re Horton's Estate*, 357 Pa. 30, 52 A.2d 895, 897 (1947), the woman, claiming a portion of a probate estate, alleged being the deceased's surviving wife based on a common law marriage. They had lived together approximately

The man could not prove a marriage contract and, even though the presumption would have been applicable, the court found that the evidence was insufficient to fulfill the requirement of general reputation, and the presumption in any case would have been rebutted by the parties contemporaneous representation to government agencies of their unmarried status.

A later case of interest is *Staudenmayer v. Staudenmayer* (1998), in which both parties were alive and able to testify as to the formation of the marriage contract. The Pennsylvania Supreme Court found that the marriage presumption was not applicable and stated that the presumption applies only if testimony regarding the exchange of *verba de praesenti* is unavailable. The woman, alleging that a common law marriage existed between the parties, therefore, had the burden of proving that they had entered into a verbal marriage contract. She was unsuccessful, despite the fact that the parties' cohabitation and reputation was considered in the assessment.[159]

The approach, that a party must choose between basing the claim on the contract or on cohabitation and reputation in accordance with the presumption, appears rather rigid. The boundary between direct evidence as to the contract and circumstantial evidence is often difficult to draw. On one side, the contract is often no more than statements uttered

---

fifteen years. The woman testified during trial, but no express marriage contract was cited. The Pennsylvania Supreme Court stated that if "there is no proof of an actual contract," evidence must be introduced with respect to cohabitation and reputation and found that no common law marriage was proven. *See also Fiedler v. Nat'l Tube Co.*, 161 Pa.Super. 155, 53 A.2d 821, 823 (1947); *In re McGrath's Estate*, 319 Pa. 309, 179 A. 599, 602 (1935) ("It is settled in this state that, if other proof is not available 'the marriage may be established ... by proof of reputation and cohabitation, declarations and conduct of the parties, and such other circumstances as usually accompany the marriage relation'"); *In re Murdock's Estate*, 92 Pa.Super. 275 (1927) ("The claimant testified to the precise form of the contract of marriage between her and the decedent, and by this she must stand or fall. If the alleged conversation constitutes a contract of marriage, evidence of cohabitation and reputation is received in corroboration of her testimony that a marriage contract was in fact entered into. But if she herself proves that no valid marriage contract was actually entered into between them, evidence as to cohabitation and reputation goes for nothing"); *In re Craig's Estate*, 273 Pa. 530, 117 A. 221, 222 (1922) ("But if such evidence is not available, the marriage may be established by proof of reputation and cohabitation, declarations and conduct of the parties"); *Tholey's Appeal*, 93 Pa. 36 (1880); and *Richard v. Brehm*, 73 Pa. 140, 144 (1873) ("Both cohabitation and reputation are necessary to establish a presumption of marriage, where there is no proof of actual marriage"). *See also Com. v. Stump*, 53 Pa. 132, 91 Am.Dec. 198 (1866) and FOOTE ET AL., *supra* note 8, at 17-18.

159 *Staudenmayer v. Staudenmayer*, 714 A.2d 1016, 1021-1022 (Pa. 1998). *See also Perrotti v. Meredith*, 868 A.2d 1240 (Pa.Super. 2005), where the Superior Court of Pennsylvania held that because both parties were available to testify as to the agreement *verba de praesenti*, the woman could not rely primarily upon cohabitation (5 years) and reputation evidence to support her contention that a common law marriage existed, *i.e.*, she was not "entitled to any rebuttable presumption in favor of a common law marriage through evidence of cohabitation and reputation of marriage," *citing Staudenmayer. See also Int'l Painters and Allied Traders Ind. Pensions Fund v. Calabro*, 312 F.Supp.2d 697, 672 (E.D.Pa. 2004), and *compare, supra* note 124.

conversationally, often best understood through circumstantial evidence. The parties' marital *consensus* perhaps is best seen in the totality of the circumstances surrounding their statements and actions upon many different occasions. On the other side, the presumption's requirement of reputation is often dependent upon the parties' statements surrounding their relation and its character. If the presumption's requirement of cohabitation and reputation is fulfilled, it is reasonable that the legal consequences in these cases also come into play, *i.e.*, that the parties are presumed to have entered into a marriage contract and the burden of proof shifts to the opposing party. It ought, however, to be noted that the opposing party has the opportunity to rebut the presumption through evidence that a marriage contract was not formed or that no marital *consensus* existed. The opposing party ought to have the opportunity to cite the direct evidence that the other party has refrained from presenting, and, thereby, to demonstrate the lack of a contract. With reference thereto there are reasons to repeal the exception to the marriage presumption discussed in this section. A separate issue, whether the reasons for the marriage presumption can also be questioned today, is discussed further below.

9.7 SUMMARY AND CONCLUSIONS

Every practitioner is conscious of the fact that the possibility of success in a lawsuit often is highly dependent on the procedural requirements resulting from the applicable evidentiary rules pertaining to burdens of proof and presumptions. At the same time, these rules and their underlying motivations reflect the attitudes of the courts and the legislatures with respect to the legal concept of common law marriage.

1. *The Burden and Standards of Proof*

It can be seen from the discussion presented in this chapter that the allocation of the burden of proof as regards the issue of the formation of a common law marriage is consistent with general American evidentiary theory, because it principally lies with the party alleging the existence of such a marriage. This is true for each of the necessary requisites; the parties' legal capacity, the marriage contract and, if required, their cohabitation and reputation as spouses.

The survey presented here shows that many courts apply the standard of great scrutiny and clear and convincing evidence in considering each of the constituting elements, a posture that, at its nadir, is suspicious and often hostile toward common law marriage. At the same time, the survey has shown that American case law is not uniform on this point. Almost as many courts have been satisfied with the requirement of a preponderance of evidence when determining the issue of a common law marriage, which the courts in Idaho have justified by never having adopted a hostile attitude to such marriages. Regardless of the attitude of the legal system toward common law marriages, the potential for abuse is a strong argument for maintaining a strict standard of proof (issues as to the burden of proof and the measure of persuasion are further discussed in Chapter 13).

2. The Marriage Presumption

This chapter has also demonstrated the tension between the rules governing the burden of proof and the application of the marriage presumption, based on the existence of cohabitation and reputation, shifting the burden of proof about the marriage contract to the party contesting the existence of the marriage. Consequently, the opposing party has to prove that no marital *consensus* existed between the parties. In many cases, this legal consequence determines the outcome of the case, given the difficulty of proving a subjective requisite and, in addition, the negative of a fact.

The survey demonstrates that this tension also exists in the underlying justifications of the presumption. Although the rules regarding the burden of proof and the high standard of proof required are based on a negative attitude toward common law marriage, the marriage presumption is based on a positive attitude, facilitating the evidence and thereby capturing the behavior of the parties in a more morally acceptable format, within marriage. This gives the parties, and their children the protection of marriage. The opposition to the reasons behind the strict burdens of proof is particularly clear where the difficulties of proving a common law marriage are cited as the basis for the marriage presumption.[160] This fundamental structural contradiction within the legal system demands the attention of the legislator. (For a further discussion of the presumption in the future, see Chapter 13.)

3. Exceptions to the Marriage Presumption

If the parties, when they began their relationship, lacked the legal capacity to enter into marriage with each other, for example, because one of the parties was already married to a third party, some courts have found, as we have seen, the marriage presumption inapplicable even if the impediment is later removed, see the exceptions under subsection 9.6.1. "Marital Impediment Previously Existed," above. The courts, in these cases, have instead applied an opposite presumption, that the parties' relationship is presumed to continue as illicit or meretricious. The fundamental rules concerning the burden of proof have then been applied.

160 *Eagle v. W.C.A.B. (Bahorich)*, 602 A.2d 387, 388 (Pa.Cmwlth. 1992); *Com. v. McLean*, 387 Pa.Super. 354, 564 A.2d 216, 221 (1989); *In re Estate of Kovalchick*, 345 Pa.Super. 229, 498 A.2d 374, 376 (1985); *In re Estate of Rees*, 331 Pa.Super. 225, 480 A.2d 327, 328 (1984); *In re Cummings Estate*, 330 Pa.Super. 255, 479 A.2d 537, 542 (1984); *Estate of Gavula*, 490 Pa. 535, 417 A.2d 168, 171 fn. 7. (1980) ("Because it is often difficult to prove a common law marriage, the law has created a rebuttable presumption of marriage"); and *In re Manfredi's Estate* 399 Pa. 285, 159 A.2d 697, 700 (1960).

The reason for this reverse presumption appears, as shown above, to stem from the fact that the parties, when they began their cohabitation, were not considered to have a true marital intent. The party alleging the existence of a common law marriage must, therefore, demonstrate that the parties, after the removal of the impediment, have expressed a marital *consensus*. American case law, however, is not uniform on this point. Several courts, as our survey has demonstrated, have chosen to apply the marriage presumption instead of the presumption that the relationship has continued as illicit and meretricious.

Good arguments also exist for finding that the existence of a marital impediment ought not automatically lead to an insufficient marital intent, whether it refers to an intent to live together or an intent to create a legal relationship. To not wish to be married is one thing, to not be able to marry is another! The existence of a marital impediment when the relationship is commenced is, therefore, not sufficient for the presumption that, after the removal of the marital impediment, the relationship continues to be illicit and meretricious. On the other hand, the preservation of the burden of proof can be justified by the need to prove that the parties still had a marital *consensus* when the impediment was removed, and that a marriage could be formed. This ought to be able to occur without any express contract and with the support of circumstantial evidence as long as the required standard of proof is met. It ought to be possible to consider evidentiary circumstances that existed before, as well as after, the removal of the impediment, assuming that the marital intent is with respect to the time thereafter.

If the legal system applies a marriage presumption according to which a marital *consensus* is based on cohabitation and reputation, good reason exists, according to the second exception above, for not applying the presumption in cases in which it is demonstrated that such a *consensus* did not exist when the relationship was commenced. The reasons behind the presumption that the relationship continues as illicit and meretricious is stronger than in the previously discussed impediment cases. Here, it is a case of parties that have not had a marital intent and, therefore, must prove that they have acquired one. In actuality, the fundamental rules with respect to the burden of proof and the measure of persuasion are applied with respect to each of the requisites necessary for the formation of a common law marriage.

The approach, especially applied in Pennsylvania, upon which the third exception, above, is based, namely, that the parties should have to choose either between basing their claim on the contract or upon cohabitation and reputation in accordance with the presumption, appears somewhat rigid. If the presumption's requirement of cohabitation and reputation is fulfilled, it appears reasonable that the legal consequences also become invoked in the case, *i.e.*, that the parties are presumed to have entered into a marriage contract and that the burden of proof shifts to the opposing party.

It ought to be noted that the opposing party has the opportunity to rebut the presumption by proving that no marriage contract had been entered into or that no marital *consensus* existed. The opposing party ought to then have the opportunity to cite any direct evidence the other party may have refrained from presenting, and, thereby, the opportunity to demonstrate the absence of a contract. With reference thereto there are reasons to repeal the exception to the marriage presumption.

4. *The Marriage Presumption Can Be Questioned*

In the preceding presentation, the legal consequences of the marriage presumption have been discussed. If the party alleging the existence of a common law marriage is successful in proving cohabitation and reputation, the parties are consequently presumed to have entered into an informal marriage contract and the burden of proof shifts to the opposing party, who must then prove that no informal marriage contract had been formed. The party alleging the existence of a common law marriage consequently does not need, in principle, to prove a marital *consensus*. With respect to the difficulties of proving a subjective requisite, and, in addition, the negative of a fact, these legal consequences often determine the outcome of the case.

However, the question can be raised whether the elements of cohabitation and reputation today are appropriate as requirements for the application of a legal marriage presumption having such significant legal consequences. Can these elements, in the typical case, be seen as *prima facie* evidence of the existence of a marital *consensus*? Today, it is not unusual for a couple to live together without any intent whatsoever to establish a legal relationship. Is there reason, in a time during which cohabitation outside of marriage has been more and more decriminalized, to maintain a presumption of innocence? Moreover, is there sufficient reason for the legal system to apply a marriage presumption that conflicts with the fundamental rules governing burdens of proof and the underlying justifications for these rules. These questions are further discussed in Chapter 13.

CHAPTER 10

CONFLICT OF LAWS AND CHOICE OF LAW

10.1 INTRODUCTION

Common law marriage is of interest not only in the ten states, together with the District of Columbia, where such marriages can be entered into legally. Because all states in United States and many foreign countries recognize marriages that have been established in a common law marriage state, assuming compliance with the law valid there, the institution has significance far outside of these states' borders. Courts and authorities in and outside of the United States, consequently, have to decide whether a common law marriage is constituted between a man and a woman who previously have been domiciled in a state where such marriages can be entered into legally.

Added to this, the courts in many states do not require that the parties have had their residence or even been living in a common law marriage state. A formless marriage, thus, can be established during a short visit by cohabiting couple in such a state.[1] Moreover, it is not always required that the parties traveled for the purpose of marrying or expressly entered into a marriage contract. Many times, it has been sufficient that the parties lived together during a short visit and held themselves out as husband and wife. Without being aware of it, they have been united in a common law marriage with all the legal effects of a marriage. This has been the case, for example, when unmarried cohabiting couples from New York, a state where common law marriage no longer can be entered into, have taken a business or vacation trip to or through Pennsylvania, Washington, D.C., or Georgia. During such a single several-day visit, a cohabitation can be transformed into a common law marriage.[2] Nevertheless, there are also several cases in which

---

1 *Compare* William A Reppy, Jr., *Property and Support Rights of Unmarried Cohabitants: A Proposal for Creating a New Legal Status*, 44 LA. L. REV. 1677, 1706 note 109 (1984), stating that "temporary visitors in a state recognizing the doctrine are unable to effectuate a common law marriage under local law."

2 *See Kellard v. Kellard*, 13 Family Law Reporter 1490 (N.Y.Sup.Ct. 1987) (One night in South Carolina and two nights in Georgia on a trip to Disney World); *Blaw-Knox Constr. Equip. Co. v. Morris*, 596 A.2d 679 (Md.Spec.App. 1991) (2-day visit in Pennsylvania);

a short visit has not given rise to any such marriage, witness to the fact that the courts apply different legal principles.[3]

Coney v. R.S.R.Corp. 63 N.Y.S.2d 211 (A.D. 3 Dept. 1990) (3 days in Georgia); *Ventura v. Ventura,* 53 Misc.2d 881, 280 N.Y.S.2d 5 (Sup.Ct. 1967) (3 days in Georgia); *Pecorino v. Pecorino,* 64 A.D.2d 711, 407 N.Y.S.2d 550, 551 (1978) (3 days in Pennsylvania); *Steinreich v. Steinreich,* 270 N.Y. 668, 244 App.Div. 780, 280 N.Y.S. 791, 1 N.E.2d 989 (1936) (3 days in New Jersey); *Bloch v. Bloch,* 473 F.2d 1067, 1069 (3d Cir. 1973) (3-4 days in Florida); *Renshaw v. Heckler,* 787 F.2d 50 (2d Cir. 1986) (8 overnight stops in Pennsylvania): *Ram v. Ramharack,* 571 N.Y.S.2d 190 (Sup. 1991) (2-3 times per year in Washington D.C.); *Carpenter v. Carpenter,* 617 N.Y.S.2d 903 (A.D. 2 Dept. 1994) (one week in Pennsylvania); *Madewell v. United States,* 84 F.Supp. 329 (E.D.Tenn. 1949) (a number of days and nights in Alabama); *Old Republic Ins. Co. v. Christian,* 389 F.Supp. 335 (E.D.Tenn. 1975) (up to 10 days in Georgia and Alabama); *Boltz v. Boltz,* 325 Mass. 726, 92 N.E.2d 365 (1950) (4-18 days in New York); *In re Frost's Estate,* 35 A.D.2d 1069, 316 N.Y.S.2d 372 (4th Dept. 1970) (2 weeks in Florida); *Tornese v. Tornese,* 649 N.Y.S.2d 177 (A.D.2 Dep't 1996) (weekends and repeated trips to Pennsylvania); *Succession of Marinoni,* 177 La. 592, 148 So. 888 (1933) (one week or more in Mississippi); *Orr v. Bowen,* 648 F.Supp. 1510, 1513 (D.Nev. 1986) (2-3 visits to Texas of at the most 2 weeks); *In re Schneider's Will,* 206 Misc. 18, 131 N.Y.S.2d 215, 220 (Surr.Ct. 1954) (visit to New Jersey and several weeks in Florida); *Skinner v. Skinner,* 4 Misc.2d 1013, 150 N.Y.S.2d 739, 741 (1956) (3 weeks in Pennsylvania and one month in Washington D.C.); *Metro. Life Ins. Co. v. Holding,* 293 F.Supp. 854, 858 (E.D.Va. 1968) (one month in Florida and Ohio respectively); *Gunter v. Dealer's Transp. Co.,* 120 Ind.App. 409, 91 N.E.2d 377 (1950) (one month in Colorado); *Albina Engine & Machine Works v. O'Leary,* 328 F.2d 877 (9th Cir. 1964), *cert. denied,* 379 U.S. 817, 85 S.Ct. 35, 13 L.Ed.2d 29 (1964) (1-2 weeks per year in Idaho); *Farber v. U.S. Trucking Corp.,* 26 N.Y.2d 44, 308 N.Y.S.2d 358, 256 N.E.2d 521 (1970) (three weeks in Florida); *McCullon v. McCullon,* 96 Misc.2d 962, 410 N.Y.S.2d 226 (Sup.Ct. 1978) (2-4 weeks per year in Pennsylvania); *Smart v. Smart,* 676 P.2d 1379 (Okla.Civ.App. 1983) (2-3 times per year during 16 years Oklahoma); *Peirce v. Peirce,* 379 Ill. 185, 39 N.E.2d 990 (1942) (one month in Nevada); *Boykin v. State Indus. Acc. Comm'n,* 224 Or. 76, 355 P.2d 724, 726 (1960) (3-5 months in Idaho); *Tarter v. Medley,* 356 S.W.2d 255 (Ky. 1962) (4-5 months in Ohio); *Bowlin v. Bowlin,* 55 N.C.App. 100, 285 S.E.2d 273 (1981) (6 months in South Carolina); and *Ray v. Ray,* 1996 Tenn.App. LEXIS 314 (1996) (8 months in Alabama).

3 *Matter of Estate of Brack,* 121 Mich.App. 585, 329 N.W.2d 432 (1982) (one night at a motel in Georgia); *Kelderhaus v. Kelderhaus,* 467 S.E.2d 303 (Va.App. 1996) (one night in Texas and one in Oklahoma); *Matter of Heitman's Estate,* 154 Misc. 838, 279 N.Y.S. 108 (1935) (one night in Pennsylvania); *Cruickshank v. Cruickshank,* 93 Misc. 366, 82 N.Y.S.2d 522 (1948) (16 hours in Texas); *Matter of Estate of Necastro,* 1990 Del.Ch. LEXIS 123 (1990) (one visit to Pennsylvania and several in Texas); *Matter of Grossman v. Gangel,* 192 A.D.2d 396, 596 N.Y.S.2d 53, 55, 625 N.E.2d 590 (A.D. 1 Dep't 1993) (two nights in South Carolina); *Cross v. Cross,* 146 A.D.2d 302, 541 N.Y.S.2d 202 (A.D. 1 Dep't 1989) (weekends in Pennsylvania and Washington, D.C.); *Payne v. Payne,* 1999 Tenn.App. LEXIS 844 (1999) (2-3 nights in Georgia); *In re Estate of Stahl,* 13 Ill.App.3rd 680, 301 N.E.2d 82 (1973) (three days in Texas); *Peart v. T.D. Bross Line Constr. Co.,* 45 A.D.2d 801, 357 N.Y.S.2d 53, 54 (3d Dep't 1974) (3-4 days in Pennsylvania); *Walker v. Hildenbrand,* 243 Or. 117, 410 P.2d 244 (1966) (four fishing trips to Idaho each for 2-7 days); *Taegen v. Taegen,* 61 N.Y.S.2d 869 (1946) (upon three occasions 3-4 days in New Jersey); *Etienne v. DKM Enterprises, Inc.,* 136 Cal.App.3rd 487, 186 Cal.Rptr. 321 (1982) (7-8 days in Texas); *In re Enoch's Estate,* 52 Ill.App.2d 39, 201 N.E.2d 682, 689 (1964) (two weeks in Colorado); *Laikola v. Engineered Concrete,* 277 N.W.2d 653, 655-656 (Minn. 1979) (three weeks in Montana); *Hesington v. Estate of Hesington,* 640 S.W.2d 824 (Mo.App. 1982) (weekends in Oklahoma); *Matter of Estate of Lamb,* 99 N.M. 157, 655 P.2d 1001, 1003 (1982) (overnight in Texas); *In re Estate of Bivians,* 98 N.M. 722, 652 P.2d 744, *cert. quashed,* 652 P.2d 1213, 98 N.M. 762 (1982) (trips to Texas and Colorado); *In re Estate of Glover,* 882 S.W.2d 789, 791 (Tenn.

Moreover, because individuals and families move frequently and take trips between states even more frequently, knowledge concerning common law marriage is of great practical significance in all states.[4] This chapter, therefore, is devoted to how the conflict of laws principles are applied to the issue of whether a common law marriage has been established between parties with connections to states other than the common law state, through domicile, residence, or in another manner. In addition, the reasons supporting the principles as applied are discussed below in Section 10.2, "The Choice of Applicable Law."

This chapter further examines how the substantive law of common law marriage states is applied. The question of when such a marriage is to be considered commenced is commonly not as easy to answer as with a ceremonial marriage, which clearly occurred. The situation can certainly be similar if the parties in a common law marriage have entered into an express marriage contract as discussed below in Section 10.3.1, "Expressed Contracts in a Common Law Marriage State." However, if such a marriage is based on an inferred agreement or a presumption that in turn is based on the parties' cohabitation and holding themselves out as spouses, such circumstances may have existed not only in the common law marriage state but also in other states. If the parties' marriage contract, as in Chapter 7, "Implied Marriage Agreements," above, consists of a marital *consensus* that has been expressed day-by-day, in which state is the contract then considered to have been commenced?[5] With such an assessment, whether only events taking place in the common law marriage state may be considered, or whether circumstances relating to the other states are also relevant is further discussed in Sections 10.3.2, "Inferred Marriage Agreements," to Section 10.3.3, "The Marriage Presumption." Common law marriage states, may require cohabitation and reputation in addition to the marriage contract as necessary requirements for the establishment of such a marriage, raising the further question of whether these requirements must be fulfilled during the parties' visit there, or whether their actions in other states, for example, in their state of domicile, are also relevant, an issue addressed in Section 10.4, "The Requirement of Cohabitation and Reputation as Spouses."

App. 1994) (repeated trips to Alabama); *In re Estate of Wilson*, 512 S.E.2d 383, 385 (Ga.App. 1999) (2-3 overnight stops in Georgia); *Seagriff v. Seagriff*, 195 N.Y.S.2d 718, 721 (Dom.Rel.Ct. 1960) (3-4 times per year in New Jersey); *Burger v. Burger*, 136 Cal. App.2d 360, 288 P.2d 926 (1955) (three weeks in Oklahoma); *Bridgman v. Stout*, 5 Ore. App. 558, 485 P.2d 1101 (1971) (approximately one month in Ohio); *Parker v. Parker*, 46 N.C.App. 254, 265 S.E.2d 237 (1980) (6 weeks in South Carolina); *In re van Schaick's Estate*, 256 Wis. 214, 40 N.W.2d 588 (1949) (5 vacations in Texas); *In re Estate of Watts*, 31 N.Y.2d 491, 341 N.Y.S.2d 609, 294 N.E.2d 195 (1973) (winter months three years in Florida); and *Darling v. Dent*, 82 Ark. 76, 100 S.W. 747 (1907) (8 months in Texas).

4 *See also* Gary Taylor, *Increased Mobility Adds to Common Law Claims*, NAT'L L.J. 24 (Aug. 14, 1989).

5 *See* Chapter 7 *supra* concerning implied marriage agreements.

Because no registration normally occurs as to the commenced common law marriage, the courts outside of common law marriage states have to not only recognize but also to decide, afterwards, whether a common law marriage has been established. These trials area not made easier by the need to address conflict of laws issues, an area of law, characterized by "uncertain purposes and manipulatable methodology."[6] The resulting difficulty is particularly challenging as regards the principles for the establishment of a common law marriage.

10.2 THE CHOICE OF APPLICABLE LAW

1. The General Rule: Lex Loci Contractus

According to the doctrine of choice of law, the majority rule is that the validity of a common law marriage is determined, as with ceremonial marriage,[7] by the law of the place in which the marriage was entered into (*lex loci contractus*). If a couple, domiciled in a common law marriage state, enters into such a marriage in accordance with the regulations valid there, the marriage is commonly recognized in all other states.[8] In *Loughran v. Loughran* (1933), the

6 Michael S. Finch & Lora J. Smeltzly, *The Restatement Second and Conflict of Laws: Extending the Bishop Approach to Problems in Contracts,* 16 STETSON L. REV. 261 (1987).

7 As a designation of the law of the place for the marriage's commencement with respect to the ceremonial marriages, the expression *lex celebrationis* is commonly used. This expression is not as adequate with respect to common law marriage, but is used also with respect to such marriages, *see, e.g.,* Charles W. Taintor, *Marriage in the Conflict of Laws,* 9 VAND. L. REV. 607 (1956).

8 In the classic case, *Dalrymple v. Dalrymple,* 2 Hagg.Cons. 54, 161 Eng.Rep. 665 (1811), wherein the parties entered into a common law marriage in Scotland, the English Court found by application of *lex loci contractus,* i.e., Scottish law, that the marriage was valid, despite the fact that such marriages could not be entered into in England after Lord Harwicke's Act (1753). The English couple's trips to Scotland for the purpose of entering into a formless marriage resulted in Lord Brougham's Act (1856), in which the requirement was made that the couple must have been in Scotland at least three weeks to be able to enter into marriage there. *See also Medway v. Needham,* 15 Mass.Rep. 157, 8 Am.Dec. 131 (1819). In *Patterson v. Gaines,* 47 U.S. (6 How.) 550, 587, 12 L.Ed. 553, 557 (1848), the Court stated that: "Marriage is to be decided by the laws of the place where celebrated." In *Redgrave v. Redgrave,* 38 Md. 93, 97-98 (1873), the court stated: "In this case, proof has been offered from which marriage can be inferred; and, in such case, the presumption is, that the marriage was duly and legally contracted according to the law of the place or country in which it occurred; and, when contracted in a foreign state or Country, the validity of such marriage is recognized here, although it may not have been attended with the same formal ceremonies as are required for the celebration of a valid marriage by the law of this state." *See also Meister v. Moore,* 96 U.S. 76, 24 L.Ed. 826 (1877); *Travers v. Reinhardt,* 205 U.S. 423, 27 S.Ct. 563, 51 L.Ed. 865, 867 (1906); *Great Northern Ry. v. Johnson,* 166 C.C.A. 181, 254 F. 683, 684 (8th Cir. 1918); and *Yarbrough v. United States,* 341 F.2d 621 (Ct.Cl. 1965). RESTATEMENT (SECOND) OF CONFLICT OF LAWS § 283 (2) (1971) states that: "A marriage which satisfies the requirements of the state where the marriage was contracted will everywhere be recognized as valid..."; JAMES KENT, COMMENTARIES ON AMERICAN LAW, 2, (1826), Lec. XXVI (7); JOSEPH STORY, COMMENTARIES ON THE CONFLICT OF LAWS §§ 79-81 (1834); JOEL PRENTISS BISHOP,

United States Supreme Court stated that a marriage "will if valid by the law of the State where entered into, be recognized as valid in every other jurisdiction."[9] Because no registration occurs in the establishment of a common law marriage, the courts in other states, to which the parties may later move, have to determine whether such a marriage is established in accordance with *lex loci contractus*. This doctrine is well established in all of the states.[10]

A more controversial point is that a marriage that is invalid in the state in which it was entered into is not recognized as valid in other states.[11] If a couple

---

COMMENTARIES ON THE LAW OF MARRIAGE AND DIVORCE AND EVIDENCE IN MATRIMONIAL SUITS § 125 (1852); RORER, AMERICAN INTER-STATE LAW, 177 (1878); MINOR, CONFLICT OF LAWS, 150 (1901); ALBERT A. EHRENZWEIG, A TREATISE ON THE CONFLICT OF LAWS § 138 (1962); EUGENE F. SCOLES, PETER HAY, CONFLICT OF LAWS 436 (2d ed. 1992); Reese, *Marriage in American Conflict of Laws*, 26 INT'L & COMP. L.Q. 952 (1977); Annotation, 71 A.L.R. 2D 687 (1960); Charles W. Taintor, *Marriage in the Conflict of Laws*, 9 VAND.L. REV. 607, 617 (1956). *Compare* U.S. CONST. art. IV § 1.; M.C.L.A. A common law marriage which has been entered into in the United States has also been recognized in European countries, *see* ERNST RABEL, THE CONFLICT OF LAWS, A COMPARATIVE STUDY, I, 224 (1945).

9 *Loughran v. Loughran*, 292 U.S. 216, 223, 54 S.Ct. 684, 78 L.Ed. 1219 (1934).

10 Case law from each of the states within the United States is presented in a register at the end of this chapter.

11 In *Gamez v. Indus. Comm'n*, 114 Ariz. 179, 559 P.2d 1094 (1976), *lex loci contractus* was applied, Mexican law, which does not recognize common law marriage. *Compare In re Estate of Dauenhauer*, 167 Mont. 83, 535 P.2d 1005 (1975), in which the court did not recognize a common law marriage entered into in California, where such marriages cannot be entered into legally. The parties however, were not domiciled in Montana, where such marriages could be entered into legally. In *Young v. Viruet de Garcia*, 172 So.2d 243 (Fla.3rd DCA 1965), the court applied Puerto Rican law according to which an alleged common law marriage was found to be invalid. *See Jewett v. Jewett*, 196 Pa.Super. 305, 175 A.2d 141, 142 (1961). In *Abramson v. Abramson*, 161 Neb. 782, 74 N.W.2d 919, 924 (1956), the court reasoned as to the marriage that "if invalid by the *lex loci contractus*, it will be invalid wherever the question may arise." In *Bolkovac v. State*, 229 Ind. 294, 98 N.E.2d 250, 254-255 (1951), a common law marriage could not be established in England. In *Ferraro v. Ferraro*, 77 N.Y.S.2d 246 (Dom. Rel.Ct. 1948), the parties had entered into a marriage by proxy in the District of Columbia. The court did not find that a common law marriage had been established as the parties never lived there as husband and wife. On the other hand, a marriage by proxy was found established according to the District of Columbia law. In *Respole v. Respole*, 70 N.E.2d 465 (C.P.Ohio 1946), in which the court applied *lex loci contractus*, i.e., West Virginia law, presumed to be the same as Ohio law, an invalid wedding ceremony by proxy was considered to not constitute a common law marriage with regards to the lack of cohabitation and reputation as husband and wife. *See also Knight v. Shields*, 19 Ohio Law Abs. 37 (1935); and *Huard v. McTeigh*, 113 Or. 279, 232 P. 658, 663 (1925). *Compare Hynes v. McDermott*, 91 N.Y. 451, 459, 43 Am.Rep. 677 (1883), in which an American citizen with domicile in New York entered into a formless marriage contract with an English woman in London in 1871. The parties lived together several months in Paris and thereafter in London until the man's death in 1874. They had two mutual children and appeared outwardly as husband and wife. English law did not recognize common law marriage. Faced with a lack of evidence concerning the content of French law, the court applied the man's *lex domicili*, i.e., New York law, according to which common law marriage could be established. *Compare Phillips v. Gregg*, 10 Watts 158, 36 Am.Dec. 158 (Pa. 1840). Certain authors have suggested that marriages which are invalid according to *lex loci contractus*, but valid according to *lex fori* or *lex domicili*, ought to be able to be maintained

domiciled in a state recognizing common law marriage enters into a formless marriage contract in a state in which no such marriages can legally be entered into, no marriage can be established.[12] Such a marriage can later be established, however, on the basis of the parties' actions in the state of domicile, and certain evidentiary weight can be attributed to the invalid contract concerning their marital intentions.[13] Suppose the parties have their domicile in a common law marriage state in which such marriages can only be entered into through a marriage contract, for example, Pennsylvania, and they enter into a contract during a visit to another common law marriage state that, in addition, requires cohabitation and reputation as spouses. According to the rule, no marriage is established unless the last-named requirements are fulfilled.

The motivations behind the principle concerning the application of *lex loci contractus* are mixed. On a more general level, respect for or civility toward other states' legal systems, *comitas gentium*, has played a role in the event that the parties were domiciled in the state in which the marriage

---

with the support of the "Rule of Validation," *see* ALBERT A. EHRENZWEIG, A TREATISE ON THE CONFLICT OF LAWS § 139 (1962) and Charles W. Taintor, *Marriage in the Conflict of Laws*, 9 VAND.L. REV. 607, 608-609 (1956).

12 *In re Marriage of Reed*, 226 N.W.2d 795 (Iowa 1975); and *Bobb v. Sec'y, Dep't of Health, Educ. & Welfare*, 312 F.Supp. 225 (S.D.N.Y. 1970).

13 In *Sullivan v. American Bridge Co.*, 115 Pa.Super. 536, 176 A. 24 (1935), the parties, who were living in New Jersey, traveled to Maryland where they entered into an expressed but formless marriage contract in 1925. A common law marriage could not be established according to *lex loci contractus*, as Maryland did not recognize common law marriage. The parties lived thereafter as husband and wife in New Jersey and Pennsylvania, two states in which such marriages could be entered into legally. Upon the man's death in 1933, the Superior Court in Pennsylvania held that the woman was the deceased's surviving widow in a common law marriage and entitled to workmen's compensation. It has been argued that the court applied Pennsylvania law "to effectuate the exchange of vows in Maryland" and that invalidity according to *lex loci contractus* consequently could not entail invalidity. *See Goldin v. Goldin*, 48 Md.App. 154, 426 A.2d 410, 413 (1981). The court in *Sullivan* appears, however, to have based its decision on the parties' "subsequent conduct" in New Jersey and in Pennsylvania. These actions were considered to be "equivalent to a declaration by each that they did, and during their joint lives were to, occupy the relation of husband and wife," *id.* at 540. *See also Cook v. Carolina Freight Carriers Corp*, 299 F.Supp. 192 (D.C.Del. 1969), in which the parties commenced their relationship and agreed upon a common law marriage in West Virginia, a state in which such marriages could not be entered into legally. The parties later moved to Florida, in which they lived together and outwardly appeared as husband and wife. A common law marriage was found to be established according to Florida law. *See also Navarro Inc. v. Baker*, 54 So.2d 59 (Fla. 1951), in which the parties commenced their common law marriage in Connecticut, a state not recognizing common law marriage. They later moved to Florida where the parties lived as husband and wife. Despite the fact that the parties did not enter into any express marriage contract, the court found that a common law marriage had been established given that "the circumstances surrounding their meeting were more eloquent and forceful than formal language." *See also Boykin v. State Indus. Acc. Comm'n*, 224 Or. 76, 355 P.2d 724, 727 (1960); and *Huard v. McTeigh*, 113 Or. 279, 287, 232 P. 658 (1925). *Compare Travers v. Reinhardt*, 205 U.S. 423, 27 S.Ct. 563, 51 L.Ed. 865 (1906) as well as several cases, there the invalid marriage contract was given evidentiary weight as discussed further *infra*.

was entered into.[14] The conception of the marriage as a contract, *consensus facit nuptias,*[15] has also rendered it natural, in accordance with that applicable to contracts in general, to apply *lex loci contractus.*[16] The intentions of the parties are also the basis for the understanding that the actual principles of conflict of law are based on the presumption that the parties have subjected themselves to that law.[17] Lord Brougham stated that it is "*ex debito justitiae* the parties agreeing to have the contract formed and its validity determined according to that law."[18] Similar understandings have been expressed in modern American case law. In *George v. George* (1980), the Mississippi Supreme Court reasoned that the parties cannot be required to have their domicile in the state in which they enter into a common law marriage and, moreover, cited the basic right of all persons to choose their place of marriage.[19] This reasoning is based on the idea that the marriage's essence is consent, which the form proves. Considering the parties' expectations also serves the purpose of ensuring reasonable requirements of predictability and legal certainty.

These reasons, however, have limited relevance in the cases in which the parties, during a visit to a common law marriage state, did not enter into any expressed marriage contract. Rather, the question is whether a marriage has been established with the application of legal presumptions and inferred agreements based on the parties' cohabitation and reputation as spouses. It then is difficult to maintain that the parties subjected themselves to *lex loci contractus.* Perhaps they did not travel to a common law marriage state for the purpose of entering into a marriage at all. They can even be unaware of the fact that a common law marriage can be

---

14 *Carpenter v. Carpenter,* 617 N.Y.S.2d 903, 904 (A.D. 2 Dep't 1994); *In re Estate of Bivians,* 98 N.M. 722, 652 P.2d 744, 748, *cert. quashed,* 98 N.M. 762, 652 P.2d 1213 (1982); *Hesington v. Estate of Hesington,* 640 S.W.2d 824, 826 (Mo.App. 1982); *Brinson v. Brinson,* 233 La. 417, 96 So.2d 653 (1957); *Henderson v. Henderson,* 199 Md. 449, 87 A.2d 403, 408, 409 (App. 1952); *Anonymous v. Anonymous,* 7 Terry 458, 85 A.2d 706, 716 (1951); *Gunter v. Dealer's Transp. Co.,* 120 Ind.App. 409, 91 N.E.2d 377 (1950); *Walker v. Matthews,* 191 Miss. 498, 3 So.2d 820, 824 (1941); *Succession of Marinoni,* 177 La. 592, 148 So. 888 (1933); and *Tryling v. Tryling,* 53 S.W.2d 725, 727 (Ky. 1932).

15 For more concerning the marriage contract, *see* Chapter 6 *supra.*

16 JOEL PRENTISS BISHOP, COMMENTARIES ON THE LAW OF MARRIAGE AND DIVORCE AND EVIDENCE IN MATRIMONIAL SUITS § 142 (1852); *Rea v. Fornan,* 46 N.E.2d 649 (Ohio App. 1942); and *Knight v. Shields,* 19 Ohio Law Abs. 37 (1935).

17 J.A. Andrews, *Common law marriage,* 22 MOD. L. REV. 396, 404 (1959). The author cites *Kochanski v. Kochanska* (1958) P. 147, which however, is unique as that case concerned Polish prisoners of war in Germany as to whose marriage *lex loci celebrationis,* i.e., German law, was not applicable. *See also Ruding v. Smith,* 2 Hagg. Cons. 371 (1821), which concerned soldiers in one of the conquered countries. *See also* RESTATEMENT (SECOND) OF CONFLICT OF LAWS § 283 cmt. b (1971): "To the extent that they think about the matter, they would usually expect that the validity of their marriage would be determined by the local law of the state where it was contracted."

18 *Warrender v. Warrender,* 2 Cl. & Fin. 488, 529, 530. *Compare* Charles W. Taintor, *Marriage in the Conflict of Laws,* 9 VAND. L. REV. 607, 618 (1956), in which he speaks of "the idea that where persons believe themselves to be married, they should be held to be married, unless their union is very offensive to the law of the intended family domicile."

19 *George v. George,* 389 So.2d 1389, 1391 (Miss. 1980).

entered into there and, therefore, did not expect that such a marriage would be established during the visit. The question of whether a common law marriage was established may be raised many years later, for example, if the parties separate, one of them dies, or a question arises about the legitimacy of a child.

An important reason behind the rules concerning recognition is also to create uniformity with respect to the parties' status.[20] Uniformity is of great significance in a country with extensive interstate mobility.[21] The parties then do not risk being considered married in one state and unmarried in another. Children are not considered legitimate in one state and illegitimate in another. The parties do not need to remarry as soon as they come to a new state. Their and their children's legal status is the same regardless of where they find themselves.

The reasons in the substantive law underlying the application of the marriage presumption, *maxim semper praesumitar pro matrimonio*,[22] discussed

---

20 In *Crane v. Puller*, 169 Md.App. 1, 899 A.2d 879, 912 (2006), the court, citing *Henderson*, held that it is desirable that there should be uniformity in the recognition of the marital status, so that persons legally married according to the laws of one State will not be held to be living in adultery in another State, and that children begotten in lawful wedlock in one State will not be held illegitimate in another. In *Johnson v. Lincoln Square Properties*, 571 So.2d 541, 543 (Fla.App. 2 Dist. 1990), the court reasoned as support for the application of *lex loci contractus* that if the legislation which repealed common law marriage in Florida in 1968 would also affect marriages entered into outside of Florida, then the legislation would "have the effect of converting lawful marriages into adulterous relationships and bastardizing children from those relationships." *See also Henderson v. Henderson*, 199 Md. 449, 87 A.2d 403, 408 (App. 1952); *Anonymous v. Anonymous*, 7 Terry 458, 85 A.2d 706, 716 (1951); *In re Lando's Estate*, 112 Minn. 257, 127 N.W. 1125 (1910); *Darling v. Dent*, 82 Ark. 76, 100 S.W. 747 (1907); and *Medway v. Needham*, 15 Mass.Rep. 157, 8 Am.Dec. 131 (1819).

21 *See, e.g., Old Republic Ins. Co. v. Christian*, 389 F.Supp. 335 (E.D.Tenn. 1975), in which the parties within the course of approximately two years had lived in Tennessee, Florida, Georgia, Alabama, Virginia, and West Virginia. A common law marriage was found established during their visits to Georgia and Alabama, which lasted up to ten days. *See also Dupre v. Rochester Ropes*, 216 So.2d 589 (La.App. 1968), in which the parties lived in Louisiana, Mississippi, Texas, and Oklahoma.

22 In *Hynes v. McDermott*, 91 N.Y. 451, 459, 43 Am.Rep. 677 (1883), the court reasoned: "The law presumes morality and not immorality; marriage, and not concubinage; legitimacy, and not bastardy." An American man with his domicile in New York met an English woman in London in 1871, where they entered into a formless marriage contract. The parties lived several months in Paris and thereafter in London until the man's death in 1874. They had two mutual children and appeared outwardly as husband and wife. English law did not recognize common law marriage. In the absence of evidence concerning the content of French law, the court applied the man's *lex domicili*, i.e., New York law, according to which common law marriage could be established. The case is cited with approval in *Shea v. Shea*, 268 App.Div. 677, 53 N.Y.S.2d 756, 762, 294 N.Y. 909, 63 N.E.2d 113 (1945). *See also Medway v. Needham*, 15 Mass.Rep. 157, 8 Am.Dec. 131 (1819), in which the court stated that *lex loci contractus* "is founded in principles of policy, to prevent the great inconvenience and cruelty of bastardizing the issue of such marriages, and to avoid the public mischief which would result from the loose state in which people so situated would live." The statement is cited in *Haviland v. Halstead*, 34 N.Y. 643, 646, 647 (1886) and in *Shea supra*. It ought to be noted that the last cited case was decided after the state of New York repealed common law marriage in 1933 (N.Y.Laws of 1933, c. 606). *See also Johnson v.*

more closely in Chapter 9, "Burdens of Proof and Presumptions," also appear to play a role within the choice of law. The choice between *lex loci contractus* and *lex domicili*, thus, has often been affected by the objective of maintaining the validity of existing marriages.[23] Against this interest, the courts often balance the suspicion against common law marriages that often motivates strict evidentiary burdens of proof.[24]

In support of the recognition of common law marriages entered into in another state, certain courts have cited the full faith and credit clause in the United States Constitution.[25] To recognize ceremonial marriages but not common law marriages entered into in other states, in some cases, has also been viewed as constituting discrimination that conflicts federal as well as state constitutional requirements of equal protection.[26]

Lincoln Square Properties, 571 So.2d 541, 542 (Fla.App. 2 Dist. 1990), in which the recognition of the marriage presumption in Florida appears to have spoken against, with reference to public policy, refusing to recognize a common law marriage which was entered into in another state.

23 In *Madewell v. United States*, 84 F.Supp. 329, 332 (E.D.Tenn. 1949), the court stated that: "The public policy of Tennessee and, this Court believes, the public policy of the civilized world, is to sustain marriages, not to upset them." A common law marriage was found established during the man's military service in Alabama, where the parties on different occasions lived "for a number of days and nights." A common law marriage was found established with the support of *lex loci contractus*, i.e., Alabama law. *See also Shea v. Shea*, 268 App.Div. 677, 53 N.Y.S.2d 756, 762, 294 N.Y. 909, 63 N.E.2d 113 (1945). In *Gradias v. Gradias*, 51 Ariz. 35, 74 P.2d (1937), it was unclear where an alleged common law marriage had been entered into. The court stated that: "Since there is nothing in the record to show where the marriage found to exist by the court was contracted, we must assume that the evidence shows it was contracted in a state where such marriages were valid." *Compare* ALBERT A. EHRENZWEIG, A TREATISE ON THE CONFLICT OF LAWS § 138 (1962), which speaks of the "Rule of Validation," which points to whatever law which works for a marriage's validity.

24 With respect to the attitudes towards common law marriages and evidentiary burdens applied in states in which such marriages can be entered into, *see* Chapter 9 *supra*. The suspicion against common law marriages recurs even in cases from other states in which the courts have had to recognize marriages that have been entered into in a common law marriage state. *See, e.g., Boyd v. Boyd*, 252 N.Y. 422, 428, 169 N.E. 632 (1930), in which the New York Court of Appeals stated: "The validity of any alleged common law marriage is always open to suspicion. Especially is doubt justified when one of the parties is dead." From more recent years, *see, e.g., Matter of Grossman v. Gangel*, 192 A.D.2d 396, 596 N.Y.S.2d 53, 55, 625 N.E.2d 590 (A.D. 1 Dep't 1993).

25 U.S.C.A. Const. Art. 4 § 1. *See* the courts in Louisiana, *Fritsche v. Vermilion Parish Hosp. Service District*, 893 So.2d 935 (La.App. 3 Cir. 2005); *Netecke v. State, through DOTD*, 715 So.2d 449, 450 (La.App. 3 Cir. 1998); *Succession of Rodgers*, 499 So.2d 492, 495 (La. App. 2 Cir. 1986); and *Parish v. Minvielle*, 217 So.2d 684, 688 (La.App. 3d Cir. 1969).

26 In *Bowers v. Wyoming State Treasurer ex. rel. Workmen's Comp. Div.*, 593 P.2d 182 (Wyo. 1979), it was considered to be discrimination, and in conflict with the federal as well as the state constitution's requirement of equal protection, to recognize ceremonial marriages but not common law marriages entered into in another state. *See* Article 1 § 2, Wyoming Constitution and Section One of the Fourteenth Amendment to the Constitution of the United States.

2. *The Strong Public Policy Exception*

Respect for *lex loci contractus* has its limits.[27] Given that each state in the United States is sovereign with respect to marital laws, certain states have refused to recognize marriages entered into by their residents in another state or recognize such marriages only under certain conditions.[28] Consequently, recognition can be refused if the marriage is viewed as conflicting with strong public policy in the state that had the most significant relationship with both the parties and the marriage at the point of time of the marriage's commencement, for example, in the forum state or the state in which the parties or one of them had their domicile and where they immediately thereafter formed their home.[29]

---

27 *Brinson v. Brinson*, 233 La. 417, 96 So.2d 653, 659 (1957); and *Henderson v. Henderson*, 199 Md. 449, 87 A.2d 403, 408, 409 (App. 1952).

28 *United States v. Costigan*, 2000 U.S.Dist. Lexis 8625 (2000). In *Trammel v. United States*, 445 U.S. 40, 50, 63 L.Ed.2d 186, 100 S.Ct. 906 (1980), the Court stated that "the laws of marriage and domestic relations are concerns traditionally reserved to the states." *See also Sosna v. Iowa*, 419 U.S. 393, 404, 42 L.Ed.2d 532, 95 S.Ct. 553 (1975); *Maynard v. Hill*, 125 U.S. 190, 210, 8 S.Ct. 723, 31 L.Ed. 654 (1888); *Wilson v. Cook*, 256 Ill. 460, 100 N.E. 222 (1912); and *Ross v. Bryant*, 90 Okla. 300, 217 P. 364, 365 (1923). In *Larsen v. Erickson*, 222 Minn. 363, 24 N.W.2d 711, 713 (1946), the court stated: "To each state belongs the exclusive right and power of determining upon the status of its resident and domiciled citizens and subjects, in respect to the question of marriage and divorce...." *See In re Duncan*, 83 Idaho 254, 360 P.2d 987 (1961); *Henderson v. Henderson*, 199 Md. 449, 87 A.2d 403, 409 (App. 1952); *First Nat'l Bank v. N. D. Workmen's Comp. Bureau*, 68 N.W.2d 661 (N.D. 1955); *Catalano v. Catalano*, 148 Conn. 288, 291, 170 A.2d 726 (1961); *Johnson v. Johnson*, 104 N.W.2d 8 (N.D. 1960); and *Fattibene v. Fattibene*, 183 Conn. 433, 441 A.2d 3 (1981). In *Hesington v. Estate of Hesington*, 640 S.W.2d 824, 826 (Mo.App. 1982), the court stated: "A state is fully sovereign with respect to the control and regulation of marriages for the purpose of promoting public morality and the moral and physical development of the parties, and every state has the power to determine not only who shall assume, but also who shall occupy, the matrimonial relationship within its borders."

29 Restatement (Second) of Conflict of Laws § 283 (2) (1971) makes an exception to *lex loci contractus* when it conflicts with "the strong public policy of another state that had the most significant relationship to the spouses and the marriage at the time of the marriage." In *Metro. Life Ins. Co. v. Manning*, 568 F.2d 922 (2d Cir. 1977), the deceased's state of domicile at the point of time of the death was considered to be "most significant." In *Henderson v. Henderson*, 199 Md. 449, 87 A.2d 403, 409 (App. 1952), the court stated that: "Marriages that are tolerated in another State but are condemned in by the State of Maryland as contrary to its public policy will not be held valid in this State." The court, however, accepted the principle that a common law marriage which is valid where it was entered into is valid all over, "unless contrary to the public policy of the forum." The court recognized a common law marriage that was established during the parties' visit approximately one year in Washington, D.C. It cannot be seen from the summary of the facts whether the parties became domiciled there. In *Beddow v. Beddow*, 257 S.W.2d 45 (Ky.App. 1952), *lex domicili* was applied, i.e., Kentucky law, with respect to the mental capacity concerning a person who had entered into a ceremonial marriage in Mississippi. *See* with respect to public policy, *Gilbert v. Gilbert*, 275 Ky. 559, 122 S.W.2d 137, 139 (App. 1938); *Damron v. Damron*, 301 Ky. 636, 192 S.W.2d 741 (App. 1946); and *Delaney v. Delaney*, 35 Conn. Sup. 230, 405 A.2d 91 (1979). In *Plunk v. Plunk*, 224 Tenn. 495, 457 S.W.2d 522 (1970), which concerned a man's marriage with his stepdaughter, the court deemed that the general principle concerning exceptions from *lex loci contractus* was applicable to cases "where our statute prohibiting the marriage is expressive of settled

One example is parties who commenced a marriage while domiciled in a common law marriage state and then moved to a state that did not recognize such marriages. Despite a hostile attitude to common law marriages in many states,[30] it has normally not been sufficient to refuse recognition on grounds of public policy simply because the parties moved and their new state of domicile repealed common law.[31] Stronger reasons in general have been required, such as incest or polygamy.[32] As seen in

---

public policy regarding public morals or good order in society." In the case of *In re Campbell's Estate*, 260 Wis. 625, 51 N.W.2d 709 (1952), the validity of a ceremonial marriage which did not fulfill the form requirements according to Wisconsin law was recognized, but which was valid according to *lex loci contractus* (Illinois law). No reason existed to make an exception with regards to "the law of nature" or "public policy." In *Lederkremer v. Lederkremer*, 173 Misc. 587, 18 N.Y.S.2d 725 (Sup.Ct. 1940), New York law was applied to a marriage entered into in Poland, which was found to be invalid because it came into existence for the purpose of making it possible for the woman to immigrate from Poland to the United States, and the parties did not intend to live together as husband and wife.

30 With respect to the attitudes towards common law marriage and the affect thereof upon the evidentiary burdens of proof, *see* Chapter 9 *supra.*

31 Common law marriage was repealed in Florida in 1968, with such marriages entered into after January 1, 1968, being invalid, *see* § 741.211, Florida Statutes (1987). In connection therewith, the Florida Attorney General stated that the regulation did not change the principle that a marriage's validity was determined in accordance with the law of the place in which the marriage was commenced. Even if this statement cannot be viewed as binding, but only persuasive, it became guiding in *Johnson v. Lincoln Square Properties*, 571 So.2d 541 (Fla.App. 2 Dist. 1990), in which the court did not find that public policy motivated an application of *lex domicili*, but found that with an application of *lex loci contractus* (Texas law) that a common law marriage had been established. It ought to be noted that the parties in the case entered into their common law marriage while residents in Texas, and that the court unfortunately did not more closely define whether it also meant marriages of couples who had their domicile in Florida. In *Bowers v. Wyoming State Treasurer ex. rel. Workmen's Comp. Div.*, 593 P.2d 182, 184 (Wyo. 1979), in which the court found it unconstitutional to not recognize a common law marriage which was entered into in another state, it was also considered to not serve any "established state purpose" to recognize only ceremonial marriages. In *Delaney v. Delaney*, 35 Conn.Sup. 230, 405 A.2d 91 (1979), the parties had entered into a common law marriage in Rhode Island where they lived for approximately seven years. As the marriage did not violate strong policy in Connecticut (only incestuous marriages), the marriage was recognized. The woman received therefore a marital divorce. In the case of *In re Kinkead's Estate*, 239 Minn. 27, 57 N.W.2d 628, 631 (1953), which concerned a ceremonial marriage, the court accepted *lex loci contractus*, "unless it violates a strong public policy of the domicile of the parties"; and *Whitehurst v. Whitehurst*, 156 Md. 610, 145 A. 204 (1929). In *Shea v. Shea*, 294 N.Y. 909, 63 N.E.2d 113 (1945), it was stated that common law marriage could not be likened to incest or polygamy; *Butterfield v. Ennis*, 193 Mo.App. 638, 186 S.W. 1173 (1916); *In re Houston*, 48 Mont. 524, 139 P. 458 (1914); *Gibson v. Gibson*, 24 Neb. 394, 39 N.W. 450 (1888); *In re Wells*, 123 App.Div. 79, 108 N.Y.S. 164 (1908), *aff'd*, 194 N.Y. 548, 87 N.E. 1129 (1909); and *Nelson v. Carlson*, 48 Wash. 651, 94 P. 477 (1908). *Compare Lynch v. Bowen*, 681 F.Supp. 506 (N.D.Ill. 1988).

32 In *Loughran v. Loughran*, 292 U.S. 216, 223, 54 S.Ct. 684, 78 L.Ed. 1219 (1934), the Court stated that: "Marriages not polygamous or incestuous, or otherwise declared void by statute, will if valid by the law of the State where entered into, be recognized as valid in every other jurisdiction." In *Hager v. Hager*, 3 Va.App. 415, 416, 349 S.E.2d 908 (1986), the parties had entered into a marriage in South Carolina, which according to South Carolina law was voidable as it was bigamous. As the parties resided in Virginia, the court however, applied Virginia law, according to which the

Chapter 5, "Legal Capacity and Common Law Marriage," persons of the same sex may not enter into a common law marriage in any state where such marriages can be established.[33] If this were to be possible in the future, other states might argue for the right to refuse the recognition of the same-sex common law marriage.[34]

---

marriage was *void ab initio.* In *Brinson v. Brinson,* 233 La. 417, 96 So.2d 653 (1957), Willie Leon Brinson in 1921 had entered into a ceremonial marriage with Annie Lillian Taylor in Mississippi. Without this marriage being dissolved, he entered into a new ceremonial marriage with Zeola Lee Koen in Mississippi in 1931, there they lived together. After Willie Leon in 1933 received a marital divorce from Annie Lillian, he continued the cohabitation with Zeola Lee. Willie Leon entered into a third ceremonial marriage with Effie Mae King in Louisiana in 1946, and they lived together until his death in 1952. Zeola Lee then made claims on the estate of the deceased on the ground that a common law marriage had been established between her and the deceased in Mississippi after his marriage with Annie Lillian was dissolved and that the common law marriage constituted an impediment against his marriage with Effie Mae which was then invalid. The latter argued that she was the deceased's legal widow. The Louisiana Supreme Court stated that common law marriages, which are valid in the state in which they have been entered into, are given as a rule recognition by the courts in Louisiana. The court, however, did not find that a common law marriage had been established according to Mississippi law, a conclusion which can be discussed, *compare Sims v. Sims,* 122 Miss. 745, 85 So. 73 (1920), but stated, that which is interesting here, that even if a common law marriage had been established according to Mississippi law, the court did not intend to recognize it as it violated public policy in Louisiana. The reason moreover was that the parties in bad faith, i.e., aware that the man was married, entered into the ceremonial marriage and that their relationship after the removal of the impediment could not be transformed into a common law marriage only through continued cohabitation but rather required a new express marriage contract. *Compare* however, *In re May's Estate,* 305 N.Y. 486, 114 N.E.2d 4 (1953), in which "an uncle and his niece," who were of the Jewish faith and domiciled in New York, were married by a Jewish rabbi in Rhode Island. The marriage was considered by the court's majority valid despite the fact that it was incestuous according to *lex domicili,* as the marriage was valid according to *lex loci contractus.* A dissenting judge however, found that the marriage violated strong public policy in New York.

33 *See* Section 5.3.1 *supra.*

34 Congress passed "The Defense of Marriage Act," DOMA, in 1996 which provides that no State shall be required to give effect to a law of any other state with respect to a same-sex marriage. The Act for purposes of federal law further defines "marriage" as the legal union of a man and a woman as husband and wife and "spouse" as a husband or wife of the opposite sex, *see* Pub. L. No. 104-199, 110 Stat. 2419; 28 USCA § 1738 C; 1 U.S.C. 7, Supp. II 1997. Many states have also passed their own "Defense of Marriage Acts" and constitutional amendments providing that same-sex marriages are not allowed. These conflicts are anticipated to increase after Massachusett's recognition of same-sex marriages, *see Goodridge v. Department of Public Health,* 440 Mass. 309, 798 N.E.2d 941 (2003), 2004 Mass. LEXIS 35, wherein the Supreme Judicial Court of Massachusetts held that "barring an individual from the protections, benefits, and obligations of civil marriage solely because that person would marry a person of the same sex violates the Masachusetts Constitution." *Compare* further the provinces of Ontario and British Columbia in Canada, where courts have authorized same sex marriages, *see Barbeau v. British Columbia (Attorney General),* 2003 BCCA 406 (BC Court of Appeals, July 8, 2003); *Halpern v. Canada (A.G.),* (2003) O.J. No. 2268 (Ontario Court of Appeals, June 10, 2003). *Compare* Belgium and *the* Netherlands, where same sex couples are allowed to get married.

Other states have passed legislation for same-sex couples that is comparable to marriage, *e.g.* the legislation for "civil unions" in Vermont and "domestic partnerships" in California. *See* on Vermont, 15 V.S.A. § 1201-1206 (1999), Vt Laws 91, and on California, THE DOMESTIC PARTNER RIGHTS AND RESPONSIBILITIES ACT (2003). To avoid

With respect to the parties' legal capacity to enter into a marriage, the case law is more inconsistent. In certain cases, *lex loci contractus* has been applied.[35] In others, the state of domicile has been viewed as having the

certain conflicts of law problems, the California legislation requires the couples to agree to jurisdiction by the California courts even if they move out of the state. The legislation also provides that partnerships entered into in other jurisdictions where they are valid will be recognized in California, *see* § 299.2 (2003). At the same time, it should be noted that California has passed a "Defense of Marriage Act," prohibiting same-sex marriages, *see* CAL. FAM. CODE § 308.5 (2002).

Other countries in Europe, *e.g.* the Nordic countries, Australia and New Zealand, have passed legislation for same-sex couples, *see* Chapter 12 *infra.* As to conflicts of laws, *see* Cynthia Grant Bowman, *Legal Treatment of Cohabitation in the United States*, 26 LAW & POLICY 119, 133-134 (2004); Comment, *Developments - The Law of Marriage and Family*, 116 HARV. L. REV. 1996 (2003); Christopher D. Sawyer, *Practise What You Preach: California's Obligation to Give Full Faith and Credit to the Vermont Civil Union*, 54 HASTINGS L.J. 727 (2003); William A. Reppy, Jr., *Choice of Law Problems Arising When Unmarried Cohabitants Change Domicile*, 55 S.M.U. L. REV. 273, 303 (2002); Ann Laquer Estin, *When Baehr Meets Romer: Family Law Issues After Amendment 2*, 68 U. COLO. L. REV. 349 (1997); Kramer, *Same-Sex Marriage, Conflict of Laws, and the Unconstitutional Public Policy Exception*, 106 YALE L.J. 1965 (1997); Andrew Koppelman, *Dumb and DOMA: Why the Defense of Marriage Act Is Unconstitutional*, 83 IOWA L. REV. (1997); Jennifer Gerarda Brown, *Competitive Federalism and the Legislative Incentives to Recognize Same-Sex Marriage*, 68 S.C. L. REV. 745 (1995); Joseph Hovermill, *A Conflict of Law and Morals: The Choice of Law Implications of Hawaii's Recognition of Same-Sex Marriages*, 53 MD. L. REV. 450 (1994); and Barbara Cox, *Same-Sex Marriage and Choice of Law: If We Marry in Hawaii, Are We Still Married When We Return Home?*, 1994 WIS. L. REV. 1033.

35 In *Guidry v. McZeal*, 487 So.2d 780 (La.App. 1986), the parties had stayed 8 months in Texas. Applying Texas law, a common law marriage could not be established, as the man during the visit was married to another woman. In *Seabold v. Seabold*, 84 Ohio App. 83, 84 N.E.2d 521 (1948), the one party's mental capacity to enter into a ceremonial marriage in Kentucky was proven according to *lex loci contractus. See also In re Gallagher's Estate*, 35 Wash.2d 512, 213 P.2d 621 (1950), where the determination of one party's mental capacity was in accordance with Michigan law. Also in *Jewett v. Jewett*, 196 Pa.Super. 305, 175 A.2d 141, 142 (1961), a ceremonial marriage's invalidity was decided based on a lack of parental consent in accordance with *lex loci contractus*, i.e., Maryland law. *See also Boehm v. Rohlfs*, 224 Iowa 226, 276 N.W. 105 (1937) (applying Minnesota law); and *In re Chase*, 26 R.I. 351, 58 A. 978 (1904). In *Hiram v. Pierce*, 45 Me. 367 (Me. 1858), the validity of a ceremonial marriage based on lack of age and a previously undissolved marriage was decided in accordance with *lex loci contractus*, Massachusetts law. On the other hand, *see Cruickshank v. Cruickshank*, 93 Misc. 366, 82 N.Y.S.2d 522 (1948), in which the court applied *lex loci contractus*, California law, with respect to the requirements of age and parental consent, which resulted in that the marriage could be declared invalid. In accordance with New York law, the parties were competent to enter into a marriage. Also in *Hitchens v. Hitchens*, 47 F.Supp. 73 (D.D.C. 1942), *lex loci contractus* (Maryland law) was applied with respect to the age requirement, which entailed that the marriage could not be declared invalid. *See also State v. Graves*, 228 Ark. 378, 307 S.W.2d 545 (1957), in which a 14-year-old girl and a 17-year-old boy, who were not competent to enter into a marriage in Arkansas, with the parents' consent formally married in Mississippi, whereafter they returned to Arkansas. The court applied *lex loci contractus* and did not find the marriage to be invalid. *See also Mangrum v. Mangrum*, 310 Ky. 226, 220 S.W.2d 406 (App. 1949); *Koonin v. Hornsby*, 140 A.2d 309 (Mun.Ct.App.D.C. 1958); and *Kitzman v. Kitzman*, 167 Wis. 308, 166 N.W. 789 (1918).

most significant relationship to the parties and the marriage when deciding the validity of the marriage, thus *lex domicili* is applied.[36]

3. Short Visits to Common Law Marriage States

If the parties, on the other hand, had their domicile in a state where a common law marriage could not be entered into, different views exist regarding whether they, during a short visit to a common law marriage state, can enter into such a marriage and have it recognized in the state of domicile.

On one side, the courts in certain states, for example, New York, Delaware, Indiana, Tennessee, Mississippi, Nevada, New Mexico, North Carolina, and Oregon, have applied *lex loci contractus* even when the parties have made short visits to a common law marriage state, *i.e.*, as though it were a question of a man and woman who had traveled to another state only to enter into a ceremonial marriage there. Certain courts have considered it to be possible even if the marriage was entered into in a common law marriage state for the purpose of avoiding invalidity in accordance with the parties' *lex domicili*. In *Shea v. Shea* (1945), the New York Court of Appeals stated that a common law marriage is valid even though both parties, domiciled in New York, leave it for the purpose of evading its laws and enter into a common law marriage in a state where such marriage is lawful and then immediately return to New York.[37] These courts have not found

36 Restatement (Second) of Conflict of Laws § 283 (1) (1971). In *First Nat'l Bank v. N. D. Workmen's Comp. Bureau*, 68 N.W.2d 661 (N.D. 1955), *lex domicili* was applied with respect to mental capacity to enter into a marriage; and *Holland v. Holland*, 212 N.Y.S.2d 805 (1961), with respect to age. In *Portwood v. Portwood*, 109 S.W.2d 515 (Tex.Civ.App.-Eastland 1937), it appears that the court, in deciding whether the parties with regards to their age were competent to enter into a common law marriage in Oklahoma, applied Texas law. *See also Wilkins v. Zelichowski*, 26 N.J. 370, 140 A.2d 65 (1958). In *Headen v. Pope & Talbot, Inc.*, 252 F.2d 739, 742 (3d Cir. 1958), the court stated that the presumption in accordance with *lex domicili* to the benefit of the latter of two marriages represents "a strong social policy in favor of reaching a particular result in the close and doubtful cases" and that Pennsylvania "as the domicile was the state primarily concerned with the legal incidents of this union." Therefore, Pennsylvania law was applied to a marriage commenced in Maryland. The federal district court had also applied Pennsylvania law, but as it found it to be a procedural evidentiary issue, found that it ought to be decided in accordance with the parties' *lex forii*. *See also In re Estate of Holben*, 93 Pa.Super. 472 (1928), which concerned the validity of an in New York commenced and another in Michigan commenced marriage. In both cases, Pennsylvania law was applied. *See also Schmeizl v. Schmeizl*, 184 Md. 584, 42 A.2d 106 (1945), which concerned a marriage commenced in California, whose validity was decided in accordance with Maryland law. For more concerning the parties' legal capacity to enter into a marriage, *see* Chapter 5 *supra*.

37 *Shea v. Shea*, 268 App.Div. 677, 53 N.Y.S.2d 756, 763, 294 N.Y. 909, 63 N.E.2d 113 (1945). In *George v. George*, 389 So.2d 1389 (Miss. 1980), the fact that the parties had their domicile in Mississippi did not prevent them from entering into a common law marriage in Georgia. Even in *Sturgis v. Sturgis*, 51 Or. 10, 93 P. 696, 698 (1908), the Oregon Supreme Court maintained that a marriage which is valid where it was entered into is valid "in the state of the domicile of the parties, even when they have left their own state to marry elsewhere for the purpose of avoiding the laws of the state of their domicile."

that such recognition conflicts with the resident state's public policy.[38] The recognition has rested, instead, on those reasons underlying *lex loci contractus*, as stated above.[39] It perhaps is less surprising that the courts in a common law marriage state recognize marriages entered into during a short stay there between parties who have had their domicile in another state.[40]

These states commonly do not apply any particular rules for an application of *lex loci contractus*. In the majority of cases, it has been sufficient with a statement that a marriage contract, expressed or inferred, has been entered into during the parties' visit to a common law marriage state for the courts to have jurisdiction to decide whether such a marriage has been established in accordance with that state's regulations. With respect to the case law from New York, this can be clearly seen in cases in which a common law marriage has been found proven,[41] as well as in those cases

38 In *Gallegos v. Wilkerson*, 79 N.M. 549, 445 P.2d 970, 974 (1968), the parties were living in New Mexico, a state where a common law marriage cannot be entered into legally. With reference thereto, a party argued that public policy ought to prevent them from avoiding the state's requirement of a ceremonial marriage by entering into a common law marriage in Texas. The New Mexico Supreme Court however, did not find that the fact that common law marriages cannot be entered into in New Mexico is an expression of "such an overriding public policy" that it requires that a marriage valid in Texas where it was entered into must be seen invalid in New Mexico. The court therefore recognized the marriage with the support of New Mexico's legislation concerning recognition of marriages, *see* §§ 57(1)-(4) N.M.S.A. 1953). In *Madewell v. United States*, 84 F.Supp. 329, 332 (E.D.Tenn. 1949), the court stated that: "The public policy of Tennessee and, this Court believes, the public policy of the civilized world, is to sustain marriages, not to upset them." A common law marriage was found established during the man's military service in Alabama, where the parties on different occasions lived "for a number of days and nights." The court stated that "domicile has no bearing on the validity of a foreign marriage." A common law marriage was found established with the support of *lex loci contractus*, *i.e.*, Alabama law. *See also Old Republic Ins. Co. v. Christian*, 389 F.Supp. 335 (E.D.Tenn. 1975), in which a common law marriage was established between between a man and woman who had their domicile in Tennessee and who took short trips of up to ten days in Georgia and Alabama. In *Gunter v. Dealer's Transp. Co.*, 120 Ind.App. 409, 91 N.E.2d 377 (1950), a common law marriage was recognized which arose during a month's military service in Colorado. In *Matter of Estate of Necastro*, 1990 Del.Ch. LEXIS 123 (1990), the issues was whether a common law marriage had been established between a man and a woman who had their domicile in Delaware and who had visited Pennsylvania and Texas. The court applied *lex loci contractus*, but did not find any marriage proven.

39 *See inter alia Shea v. Shea*, 268 App.Div. 677, 53 N.Y.S.2d 756, 763, 294 N.Y. 909, 63 N.E.2d 113 (1945); and *George v. George*, 389 So.2d 1389 (Miss. 1980) *supra*.

40 In *Smart v. Smart*, 676 P.2d 1379 (Okla.Civ.App. 1983), a common law marriage was found established between two individuals who had their domicile and their residence in California, but who during a period of 16 years annually made 2-3 visits to Oklahoma, a state in which such marriages can be entered into legally.

41 *Coney v. R.S.R.Corp.* 63 N.Y.S.2d 211 (A.D. 3 Dep't 1990)(3 days in Georgia); *Ventura v. Ventura*, 53 Misc.2d 881, 280 N.Y.S.2d 5 (Sup.Ct. 1967)(3 days in Georgia); *Pecorino v. Pecorino*, 64 A.D.2d 711, 407 N.Y.S.2d 550, 551 (1978)(3 days in Pennsylvania); *Steinreich v. Steinreich*, 270 N.Y. 668, 244 App.Div. 780, 280 N.Y.S. 791, 1 N.E.2d 989 (1936)(3 days in New Jersey); *Renshaw v. Heckler*, 787 F.2d 50 (2d Cir. 1986)(8 overnight stops in Pennsylvania); *Tornese v. Tornese*, 649 N.Y.S.2d 177 (A.D.2 Dep't

in which such marriages have not been found proven in accordance with *lex loci contractus*.[42] In *Renshaw v. Heckler* (1986), the United States Second Circuit Court of Appeals stated: "Since plaintiff claims that she contracted a common-law marriage with her husband in Pennsylvania during their travels through the state, the appropriate law to apply is the law of Pennsylvania." Compare with *In re Landolfi* below.[43]

On the other side, the courts in other states, for example, Arkansas, Illinois, Minnesota, Missouri, Nebraska, New Jersey, and Wisconsin, have found that an application of *lex loci contractus* to couples making short visits to a common law marriage state would conflict with the public policy in the state of domicile that had repealed common law marriage. Recognition then has been viewed as in conflict with the purpose of the repeal. For example, in *Lynch v. Bowen* (1988), the United States District Court for the District of Illinois stated that the recognition of marriages which come into existence through short visits to a common law marriage state "could significantly erode Illinois' prohibition on common law marriage. Validity of those marriages would turn on the happenstance of which state a couple choose to visit (however, briefly)."[44]

1996) (weekends and repeated trips to Pennsylvania); *Carpenter v. Carpenter*, 617 N.Y.S.2d 903 (A.D. 2 Dep't 1994) (one week in Pennsylvania); *Farber v. U.S. Trucking Corp.*, 26 N.Y.2d 44, 308 N.Y.S.2d 358, 256 N.E.2d 521 (1970) (3 weeks in Florida); and *Skinner v. Skinner*, 4 Misc.2d 1013, 150 N.Y.S.2d 739, 741 (1956) (3 weeks in Pennsylvania and one month in Washington D.C.).

42 *Mott v. Duncan Petroleum Trans.*, 51 N.Y.2d 289, 434 N.Y.S.2d 155, 414 N.E.2d 657 (1980) (weeks in Georgia) *cert. denied*; *Cruickshank v. Cruickshank*, 93 Misc. 366, 82 N.Y.S.2d 522 (1948) (16 hours in Texas); *Matter of Grossman v. Gangel*, 192 A.D.2d 396, 596 N.Y.S.2d 53, 55, 625 N.E.2d 590 (A.D. 1 Dep't 1993) (two nights in South Carolina); *Cross v. Cross*, 146 A.D.2d 302, 541 N.Y.S.2d 202 (A.D. 1 Dep't 1989) (weekends in Pennsylvania and Washington D.C.); *Peart v. T.D. Bross Line Constr. Co.*, 45 A.D.2d 801, 357 N.Y.S.2d 53, 54 (3rd Dep't 1974) (3-4 days in Pennsylvania); *Taegen v. Taegen*, 61 N.Y.S.2d 869 (1946) (upon three occasions 3-4 days in New Jersey); *Lieblein v. Charles Chips, Inc.*, 32 A.D.2d 1016, 301 N.Y.S.2d 743 (1969) (approximately one week in Georgia) *cert. denied*; and *In re Estate of Watts*, 31 N.Y.2d 491, 341 N.Y.S.2d 609, 294 N.E.2d 195 (1973) (winter months three years in Florida).

43 *Renshaw v. Heckler*, 787 F.2d 50, 52 (2d Cir. 1986). Observe that common law marriage, as was mentioned in chapter 1, was repealed in Pennsylvania January 1, 2005, however not retroactively, *see* 23 Pa. Cons. Stat. Ann. 1103 (West 2005)

44 *Lynch v. Bowen*, 681 F.Supp. 506, 512 (N.D.Ill. 1988). In *Winn v. Wiggins*, 47 N.J.Super. 215, 135 A.2d 673, 678 (1957), the court stated in dictum that "we are of the opinion that the strong public policy evidenced by the enactment of the 1939 statute, N.J.S.A. 37:1-10, is best effectuated by declaring that persons domiciled in New Jersey cannot leave this State, enter into a common law marriage in a state where such marriages are allowed, and then return home and ask our courts to recognize that marriage." It ought to be noted that the law by which common law marriage was repealed in New Jersey in 1939 did not contain any expressed prohibitions against recognizing a common law marriage of a party domiciled in New Jersey and entered into in another state. The statement appears to have been followed in *Metro. Life Ins. Co. v. Chase*, 294 F.2d 500, 505 (3d Cir. 1961), in which the parties' "law of the domicile at the time their alleged common law marriage took place" was applied, i.e., the law of New Jersey, which then no longer recognized common law marriages. If the parties, on the other hand, at the commencement of the marriage had their domicile in a common law marriage state, it appears that public policy in New Jersey does

At one time, inspiration for this view could be found in the Uniform Marriage Evasion Act, which sought to prevent persons who lived in and had the intent to live in a certain state from avoiding that state's requirements concerning the commencement of a marriage by entering into a marriage in another state.[45] The act was entirely or partially enacted in only a few states before it was repealed. Even though the Uniform Marriage Evasion Act served other purposes, for example, preventing couples from avoiding the domicile state's requirements for marital age and prohibition against remarriage, the principles, in certain cases, were used to prevent the entering into of a common law marriage through short visits to other states. The parties' intentions of avoiding the domicile state's requirements, however, were not relevant.

These states have laid down specific and somewhat varying requirements in order to apply *lex loci contractus* and recognize a common law marriage entered into in another state.[46] In order to recognize a common

---

not place impediments in the path for a recognition of the marriage, *see Tegenborg v. Tegenborg*, 26 N.J.Super. 467, 98 A.2d 105 (1953). In *Stein v. Stein*, 641 S.W.2d 856 (Mo.App. 1982), the parties, who had their domicile in Missouri, had participated in a bus tour to *inter alia* Pennsylvania, where they, according to the woman, one night "exchanged rings and marriage vows." The court stated that it would be in conflict with the public policy of Missouri and against the purpose of the law which there repealed common law marriage to recognize such a marriage between two Missouri residents, even if it were commenced when the parties visited Pennsylvania, which recognized such marriages. *See also Hesington v. Estate of Hesington*, 640 S.W.2d 824 (Mo.App. 1982), which concerned a temporary visit to Oklahoma. The court stated that: "To forbid a common law marriage in this state but recognize a strictly common law marriage of domiciliaries and residents of Missouri on a sojourn in a common law state, of which there are several, would defeat that purpose."

45 The Uniform Marriage Evasion Act § 1 was adopted between 1912-1943 in **Illinois, Louisiana, Massachusetts, Vermont**, and **Wisconsin**. 9A U.L.A. XXI (1957). It can be questioned whether the law was applicable to couples who had entered into a common law marriage in a state other than their state of domicile, as long as they had not been "disabled or prohibited" from entering into a marriage in their state of domicile. Today, THE UNIFORM MARRIAGE AND DIVORCE ACT § 210, 9A U.L.A. 147, 176-77 (1987) and RESTATEMENT (SECOND) OF CONFLICT OF LAWS § 283 (1971) have greater significance. This type of legislation has received decreased significance during later years, *see* EUGENE F. SCOLES, PETER HAY, CONFLICT OF LAWS 453 (2d ed. 1992).

46 *See* already Sir George Hay in *Harford v. Moris*, 2 Hagg.C.R. 423 (4 E.E.R. 575); and *Ruding v. Smith*, 2 Hagg. Cons. 371 (1821). This stance appears to be common in countries outside of the United States, *Rabel, Ernst*, The Conflict of Laws, A Comparative Study, I, 240 (1958). It has anchorage in American states. **Arkansas:** *Brissett v. Sykes*, 313 Ark. 515, 855 S.W.2d 330 (1993), which requires that the parties "actually resided" in a common law marriage state, see ARKANSAS CODE ANN. § 9-11-107 (1987). **Illinois:** *Lynch v. Bowen*, 681 F.Supp. 506 (N.D.Ill. 1988); *In re Enoch's Estate*, 52 Ill.App.2d 39, 201 N.E.2d 682, 689 (1964); and *In re Estate of Stahl*, 13 Ill. App.3rd 680, 301 N.E.2d 82 (1973). The courts in Illinois, however, recognize a common law marriage that was entered into in another state if the parties had their domicile there. *See, e.g., Peirce v. Peirce*, 379 Ill. 185, 39 N.E.2d 990 (1942), in which the parties had their domicile in Nevada. *See also In re Marriage of Mosher*, 243 Ill. App.3d 97, 612 N.E.2d 838 (1993), where the parties resided 5 months in Iowa. A common law marriage however, was not found to be proven in accordance with Iowa law. **Massachusetts:** *Boltz v. Boltz*, 325 Mass. 726, 92 N.E.2d 365 (1950). **Minnesota:** In *Laikola v. Engineered Concrete*, 277 N.W.2d 653, 655-656 (Minn. 1979),

law marriage, Illinois courts have required the parties to have their domicile in a common law marriage state at the time of the marriage's commencement. In *Lynch v. Bowen* (1988), the parties had lived as husband and wife in Illinois for thirty-eight years. During this time, they made short visits to Pennsylvania, Georgia, and the District of Columbia, jurisdictions that recognized common law marriage. As they had their domicile in Illinois the entire time, according to the court's view, a common law marriage could not be established during the short visits. The intent to avoid the domicile state's regulations, however, was not required.[47] The Arkansas

it appears that the court has made a distinction between "residence" and "domicile." The court stated that: "Minnesota residents may not enter into a common law marriage by temporarily visiting a state that allows common law marriages ... However, the court will recognize a common law marriage if the couple takes up residence (but not necessarily domicile) in another state that allows common law marriages..." The court's statement that this "is consistent with the elements of a common law marriage" does not appear to be entirely correct with respect to all common law marriage states, *see* Pennsylvania and South Carolina, Chapter 8.4. **Missouri:** *Stein v. Stein*, 641 S.W.2d 856 (Mo.App. 1982); and *Hesington v. Estate of Hesington*, 640 S.W.2d 824 (Mo.App. 1982). **Nebraska:** *In re Binger's Estate*, 158 Neb. 444, 63 N.W.2d 784, 785 (1954). **New Jersey:** *Winn v. Wiggins*, 47 N.J.Super. 215, 135 A.2d 673, 678 (1957); and *Metro. Life Ins. Co. v. Chase*, 294 F.2d 500, 505 (3d Cir. 1961). If the parties, on the other hand, had their domicile in a common law marriage state at the commencement of the marriage, it appears that public policy in New Jersey does not place impediments on the path for a recognition of the marriage, *see Tegenborg v. Tegenborg*, 26 N.J.Super. 467, 98 A.2d 105 (1953). **Utah:** *In re Vetas' Estate*, 110 Utah 187, 170 P.2d 183 (1946). It ought to be noted that Utah after 1987 recognizes common law marriage. **Virginia:** *Metro. Life Ins. Co. v. Holding*, 293 F.Supp. 854 (E.D.Va. 1968). **Wisconsin:** *In re Van Schaick's Estate*, 256 Wis. 214, 40 N.W.2d 588 (1949). In accordance with Wisconsin law, a common law marriage cannot be entered into in another state if the parties live and have the intention to continue living in Wisconsin. The court cites the UNIFORM MARRIAGE EVASION ACT § 1. This law, however, has not constituted an impediment in *Boltz v. Boltz*, 325 Mass. 726, 92 N.E.2d 365 (1950) or in *Peirce v. Peirce*, 379 Ill. 185, 39 N.E.2d 990 (1942). In many cases, questions concerning the burden of proof and the standard of evidence have been assessed in accordance with *lex loci contractus*, *see, e.g.*, *Matter of Danza*, 591 N.Y.S.2d 197 (1992), in which Pennsylvania law was applied. With respect to the application of *lex fori* with the valuation of the evidence, *see* Charles W. Taintor, *Marriage in the Conflict of Laws*, 9 VAND. L. REV. 607 (1956). According to RESTATEMENT (SECOND) OF CONFLICT OF LAWS § 283 cmt. d (1971), the courts commonly apply *lex fori* to issues which involve "process, pleadings, joinder of parties, and the administration of the trial." In *Ponzi v. Ponzi*, 157 Cal.App.2d 772, 321 P.2d 847, 850 (1958), the District Court of Appeals in California stated that "California law governs the presumptions and inferences to be drawn from the evidence" with respect to the issue concerning whether a couple entered into a common law marriage with a visit to Texas and Oklahoma.

47 *Lynch v. Bowen*, 681 F.Supp. 506 (N.D.Ill. 1988); and *In re Enoch's Estate*, 52 Ill.App.2d 39, 201 N.E.2d 682, 689 (1964). In the case of *In re Estate of Stahl*, 13 Ill.App.3rd 680, 683, 301 N.E.2d 82 (1973), the court maintained that a person can have only one domicile and must fulfill two criteria to receive it. First, the person must "physically go to the new home and live there." Second, this must occur "with the intention of making it the permanent home." A three-day visit to Texas was considered therefore insufficient, despite the fact that the parties had the intent to in the future live in Texas; RESTATEMENT (SECOND) OF CONFLICT OF LAWS § 18 (1971). The courts in Illinois have recognized, however, a common law marriage that was entered into in another state if the parties had their domicile there, *see, e.g.*, *Peirce v. Peirce*, 379 Ill. 185, 39

Supreme Court has required that the parties have actually resided in a common law marriage state.[48] In cases in which the parties have had a stable and long-term relationship, the marriage has been recognized. The requirement of actual residence has been maintained even though the state visited did not require cohabitation to establish a common law marriage.[49] The courts in other states have also taken into consideration the intentions of the parties during the visit. In Wisconsin, one of the few states that adopted the Uniform Marriage Evasion Act, a common law marriage is not established in another state as long the parties lived and have had the intention to live in Wisconsin.[50] In a similar manner, the Nebraska Supreme Court has required that the parties intend to change their domicile or residence to the common law marriage state they visited.[51]

N.E.2d 990 (1942), in which the parties had their domicile in Nevada. The court defines "domicile" in accordance with the following: "The domicile is the place where a person lives and has his true, permanent home, to which, whenever he is absent, he has an intention of returning," *id.* at 993. *See Acklin v. Employees' Ben. Ass.*, 222 Ill.App. 369 (1920); and *Young v. Young*, 213 Ill.App. 402 (1918). *See also* Utah law prior to 1987, when common law marriage could not legally be entered into there and such marriages which were entered into in other states neither were recognized if the parties had their domicile in Utah. On the other hand, Utah recognized marriages which were "solemnized" in other states, not including common law marriages, *see e.g., In re Vetas' Estate*, 110 Utah 187, 170 P.2d 183 (1946). *Compare Tetterton v. Arctic Tankers*, 116 F.Supp. 429 (E.D.Pa. 1953).

48 Short visits *inter alia* to Pennsylvania were not sufficient in *Brissett v. Sykes*, 313 Ark. 515, 855 S.W.2d 330, 332 (1993) as the parties did not "actually reside" there, *see* ARKANSAS CODE ANN. § 9-11-107 (1987).

49 *See Standridge v. Standridge*, 298 Ark. 494, 769 S.W.2d 12, 15 (1989), which concerned short visits to Oklahoma. *Compare Walker v. Yarbrough*, 257 Ark. 300, 516 S.W.2d 390 (1974), in which "mere visits or sojourns" in Colorado were considered insufficient to constitute a common law marriage. The legislation in Arkansas required that the parties "actually resided" in the foreign state, but the marriage was not found to be established based on the requirement of a marriage contract according to *lex loci contractus* (Colorado law); and *In re Enoch's Estate*, 52 Ill.App.2d 39, 201 N.E.2d 682, 689 (1964) (two weeks in Colorado considered not sufficient). *Compare Stilley v. Stilley*, 219 Ark. 813, 244 S.W.2d 958 (1952), in which the court recognized a common law marriage after nine years' cohabitation in Kansas. *Compare* also *Darling v. Dent*, 82 Ark. 76, 100 S.W. 747 (1907), in which approximately eight months' cohabitation in Texas was sufficient.

50 In the case of *In re van Schaick's Estate*, 256 Wis. 214, 40 N.W.2d 588 (1949), the parties during five winters in the 1940s had spent their vacation at a "tourist camp" in Texas, where they appeared as husband and wife. A common law marriage, however, could not be established based on Wisconsin law as the parties lived and had the intent to continue living in Wisconsin. *See* St. 1947 § 245.04 which corresponds to the UNIFORM MARRIAGE EVASION ACT § 1. The issue whether the requirements for the establishing of a common law marriage according to Texas law were fulfilled therefore needed not to be decided.

51 *See In re Binger's Estate*, 158 Neb. 444, 63 N.W.2d 784, 790 (1954), which concerned short visits to Colorado during which the parties lived and outwardly appeared as spouses. *Compare Allen v. Allen*, 121 Neb. 635, 237 N.W. 662 (1931), in which a common law marriage was considered established since the parties lived together for six years and outwardly presented themselves as spouses in Colorado. *See also Ragan v. Ragan*, 158 Neb. 51, 62 N.W.2d 122 (1958).

Even in a state such as New—York where, as noted above, the parties' statement that a marriage contract has been entered into in a common law marriage state, in general, has been sufficient for an application of *lex loci contractus*, —a new type of reasoning arises in the case law from a later period, by which a choice of law rule with a minimum requirement for ties to the common law marriage appears to have been applied. In the case of *In re Landolfi* (2001), in which the parties lived in New York, the woman claimed upon the man's death that she was his surviving widow based on a common law marriage formed in connection with several visits the couple made to family in Pennsylvania. At best, they stayed overnight on one such occasion. The New York Supreme Court, Appellate Division, however, found that the woman did not present sufficient evidence of cohabitation in Pennsylvania to motivate an application of Pennsylvania law in deciding her marital status.[52] It ought to be noted that the court herewith does not appear to have relied upon the Pennsylvania law requirement of constant cohabitation for application of the marital presumption. Instead, the court appears to have applied choice of law rules. It remains to be seen if this new reasoning is accepted by the New York Court of Appeals.

A requirement of domicile or permanent residence is also a method for preventing marriages based on inferred agreements or presumptions leading to situations where the parties are married without having knowledge thereof. Other methods with the same purpose focus instead on the local common law marriage rules, and further comments on this are made below.

4. *Conflict of Law Principles or Lex Loci Contractus?*

From the conflict of law requirements discussed above, the eventual requirement of residence that the courts have to decide according to *lex loci contractus* must be distinguished; see the sections that follow. In several cases, however, it cannot be clearly seen from the courts' reasoning whether they refused to recognize a common law marriage with the support of the choice of law rules laying down specific conditions for an application of *lex loci contractus* or whether they, with the application of this law, did not find a common law marriage. This is true, for example, of certain

52 *In re Landolfi*, 724 N.Y.S.2d 470, 472 (N.Y.A.D. 2 Dep't 2001). *See also Ram v. Ramharack*, 571 N.Y.S.2d 190 (Sup. 1991), in which the parties 2-3 times per year made visits to Washington D.C. and in which the court stated: "Minimum contacts with a common law marriage jurisdiction ... are sufficient to activate the foreign law..."

decisions from California,[53] New Mexico,[54] and Louisiana,[55] in which the courts carried out conflict of law reasoning, but in which the holding finally appears to be obtained from *lex loci contractus.* Even the courts in Oregon, in a similar manner, have sometimes adopted reasoning meant to prevent a common law marriage based on temporary visits to a common law marriage state, but in the final analysis, did not wish to make an exception to the main principle and, instead, rejected such a marriage with

53 In *Etienne v. DKM Enterprises, Inc.*, 136 Cal.App.3rd 487, 186 Cal.Rptr. 321 (1982), the parties, who were domiciled in California, took short trips of 7-8 days in Texas, a state recognizing common law marriage. The court to a certain extent carried out a reasoning of a conflict of law character by stressing that a short visit of "a non-domiciliary couple" in a state in which common law marriage can be entered into is insufficient, and that the parties did not have an intent to acquire "either a Texas domicile or residence." Decisive to the holding, however, was that the requirements according to Texas law of cohabitation and appearance outwardly "in the State of Texas" were not fulfilled. *Compare Ponzi v. Ponzi,* 157 Cal.App.2d 772, 321 P.2d 847, 850 (1958), in which the parties previously had been married to each other, and in May and June of 1951, stayed in Oklahoma and Texas, two states recognizing common law marriage. The court did not find a common law marriage proven given that no discussion had been held between them "indicating that they intended to remarry" in Texas or Oklahoma, wherewith, one must assume, the court applied "*lex loci contractus.*" It is however, somewhat unclear if the court's reference that the parties "maintained their residence" in California was an attempt to lay down a conflict of law requirement according to California law or if the court interpreted residence in the state of the visit as a requirement according to Texas and Oklahoma law. The last-named state does not appear to require that the cohabitation occurred there. Probably the circumstance constituted only an evidentiary fact as the parties did not live together in the last-named states. It is clear on the other hand that the court applied California law with respect to the valuation of the evidence and the use of presumptions. With respect to the importance according to Texas law of that the parties' cohabitation occurred in Texas, *see* Section 8.4 *supra.* A similar lack of clarity in the courts' reasoning exists in other cases that concerned visits to Texas, *see, e.g., In re McKanna's Estate,* 106 Cal.App.2d 126, 234 P.2d 673, 674 (1951); and *Tatum v. Tatum,* 241 F.2d 401, 409-410 (9th Cir. 1957). *Compare Burger v. Burger,* 136 Cal. App.2d 360, 288 P.2d 926 (1955), in which the parties entered into a ceremonial marriage in Arizona, which was invalid based on an impediment. After the impediment was removed, the parties stayed three weeks in Oklahoma. When the woman as support that their relationship was then transformed into a common law marriage cited a case from Oklahoma, the court stated that: "Such authorities declare the law of Oklahoma, not of California." At the same time as the court appears to reject an application of *lex loci contractus,* it ought to be noted that the woman according to the court "pleaded no common law marriage" but rather cited only the invalid marriage in Arizona.

54 *See* the somewhat unclear standpoint of the courts in New Mexico, which do not appear to have required domicile or even residence in Texas according to New Mexico law. Even if the New Mexico Supreme Court in *Matter of Estate of Lamb,* 99 N.M. 157, 655 P.2d 1001, 1003 (1982) required significant contacts with Texas, this does not appear to have its basis in a conflict of law principle but almost rather in the requirement according to Texas law of cohabitation in Texas. This requirement was found to not be fulfilled in *Lamb,* but, on the other hand, it was in the case of *In re Matter of Estate of Willard,* 93 N.M. 352, 600 P.2d 298 (1979) and in *Gallegos v. Wilkerson,* 79 N.M. 549, 445 P.2d 970, 972 (1968). In the case of *In re Estate of Bivians,* 98 N.M. 722, 652 P.2d 744, *cert. quashed,* 652 P.2d 1213, 98 N.M. 762 (1982), the requirement of contracts in Texas was not found to be fulfilled.

55 With respect to Louisiana, *see* particularly *Dupre v. Rochester Ropes,* 216 So.2d 589 (La.App. 1968), and *Franzen v. E.I. du Pont De Nemours & Co.,* 146 F.2d 837 (3d. Cir. 1944).

a conflict-of-law-influenced interpretation of *lex loci contractus*.[56] In other cases, the courts, in contrast, have searched for support for a denial of a claim of common law marriage in *lex loci contractus*, but ultimately based their decisions on conflict of law principles.[57] In still other cases, although

56 Already in *Sturgis v. Sturgis*, 51 Or. 10, 93 P. 696, 698 (1908), the Oregon Supreme Court argued that a marriage which is valid where it was entered into is valid "in the state of the domicile of the parties, even when they have left their own state to marry elsewhere for the purpose of avoiding the laws of the state of their domicile." No exception from this principle with regards to public policy in Oregon was found by the United States Court of Appeals to be motivated with respect to common law marriage in *Albina Engine & Machine Works v. O'Leary*, 328 F.2d 877 (9th Cir. 1964), in which the parties, who were domiciled in Oregon, annually for fourteen years had stayed one to two weeks in Idaho. The court found a common law marriage proven applying Idaho law. *Compare Boykin v. State Indus. Acc. Comm'n*, 224 Or. 76, 355 P.2d 724, 726 (1960), in which the parties had spent 3-5 months in Idaho. A common law marriage was found to be proven. The parties had at that point of time no domicile in Oregon, but commenced soon thereafter a ten-year cohabitation in that state. There is in Oregon case law also expression of a more critical public policy with respect to the recognition of common law marriages entered into in other states. This policy, however, appears to not have manifested itself in any new conflict of law principles. The courts namely in these cases have continued to follow the main rule and applied *lex loci contractus*, but with the interpretation hereof utilized a reasoning of a conflict of law character. In *Huard v. McTeigh*, 113 Or. 279, 232 P. 658, 663 (1925), the Oregon Supreme Court stated that "the doctrine of common law marriage is contrary to public policy and public morals." It ought, however, be noted that the statement was directed to the possibility of entering into common law marriage in Oregon and not against the recognition of common law marriages entered into in other states. In *Walker v. Hildenbrand*, 243 Or. 117, 410 P.2d 244, 246 (1966), in which the parties upon four occasions made fishing trips to Idaho, the court stated that something so serious and vital for the community's well-being as the decision whether a marriage exists ought not rest on something so "insubstantial" as a short visit to a common law marriage state, particularly when there is no evidence "that the parties were aware that any change in their marital status would result or that the visit was made for the purpose of consummating a marriage." Despite this conflict-of-law-influenced reasoning, the court rejected the alleged marriage given that "Idaho courts would hold that no common law marriage was consummated." Even in *In re Marriage of Wharton*, 55 Or.App. 564, 639 P.2d 652 (1982), the parties, who were domiciled in Oregon, during a ten-year period had annually taken short trips of on average 10 days in Idaho. During the visits as well as during the parties' twelve years' cohabitation in Oregon, they appeared outwardly as husband and wife. Despite the fact that the legislation in Idaho did not expressly require cohabitation in the state for the establishment of a common law marriage, the Oregon Court of Appeals found that in the state of Idaho, "the parties' contacts with Idaho were insufficient to constitute the basis of a common law marriage under Idaho law." This indicates that the court applied a conflict of law rule according to Oregon law, but the conclusion indicates instead that the court applied Idaho law, but made a conflict of law interpretation thereof. Oregon law, however, appears to not contain any such conflict of law rule and the legislation in Idaho contains no rule in which the requirement of cohabitation is limited to Idaho, *see* IDAHO CODE § 32-201. Even in *Bridgman v. Stout*, 5 Ore.App. 558, 485 P.2d 1101 (1971), in which the parties stayed in Ohio approximately one month, a common law marriage was rejected with the support of Ohio law. With respect to the requirement of cohabitation in Idaho and other states, *see* Section 8.4 *supra*.

57 *See Laikola v. Engineered Concrete*, 277 N.W.2d 653, 656 (Minn. 1979), in which the parties, who had their domicile in Minnesota, had made visits to Montana. The court considered whether the requirements according to Montana law of cohabitation and reputation for the establishing of a common law marriage were fulfilled,

the prerequisites according to applicable choice of law for an application of *lex loci contractus* have not been found fulfilled, the courts nevertheless decided whether the requirements according to the last-named rules were fulfilled.[58]

Against this background, it would serve the interest of clarity if the courts more clearly separated the determination of the issue of choice of law and the application of the foreign law. This could occur by first determining, with the support of applicable choice of law rules, which state's law is to be applied. Then, it would be appropriate to consider whether the parties have sufficient ties to the common law marriage state through domicile, residence, contracts, mutual intentions, or other manner, and if sufficient ties exist, decide the case by correctly applying the *lex loci contractus* without the influences of conflict of law. As seen in the following sections, such influences have not been avoided in the case law.

---

despite the fact that the court appears to have based its decision on a requirement according to Minnesota conflict of law of residence in Montana, which was not fulfilled. The court made a distinction between residence and domicile and stated: "Minnesota residents may not enter into a common law marriage by temporarily visiting a state that allows common law marriages... However, the court will recognize a common law marriage if the couple takes up residence (but not necessarily domicile) in another state that allows common law marriages..." *Compare Kennedy v. Damron*, 268 S.W.2d 22, 24 (Ky..App. 1954), which concerned short visits to Ohio, in which the court did not require a legal domicile in a common law marriage state in the meaning of a residence intended to be permanent, but on the other hand "an established place of abode with which the parties may be identified as members of the community." Despite the fact that the reasoning appears to be of a conflict of law character, the court cited cases from Ohio, *see Dibble v. Dibble*, 88 Ohio App. 490, 100 N.E.2d 451 (1950).

58 *See, e.g., In re Estate of Stahl*, 13 Ill.App.3rd 680, 683, 301 N.E.2d 82 (1973), in which the parties made a three-day visit to Texas, and neither the requirement according to Illinois law of domicile in Texas or the requirement according to Texas law of cohabitation in Texas were considered fulfilled. In *Walker v. Yarbrough*, 257 Ark. 300, 516 S.W.2d 390 (1974), mere visits or sojourns in Colorado were considered to be insufficient to constitute a common law marriage. Despite the fact that the court gave a reasoning of a conflict of law character and the legislation in Arkansas requires that the parties "actually resided" in the foreign state, *see* Ark.Stat.Ann. § 55-110 (Repl. 1971), the court rejected the existence of a common law marriage given that the requirement of a marriage contract according to *lex loci contractus* (Colorado law) was not fulfilled. *Compare State ex rel. Smith v. Superior Court for King County*, 23 Wash.2d 357, 161 P.2d 188 (1945), which concerned short visits to Idaho. The Washington Supreme Court made the following statement often cited by other courts concerning short visits to common law marriage states: "Parties who live for years in illicit relationship in a state in which they were domiciled will not find themselves married to each other if they happen to sojourn for a short time and hold themselves out as man and wife in a state where common law marriage is recognized." The court, however, appears to not have refused to recognize the alleged common law marriage with the support of any choice of law principles but rather applying *lex loci contractus* (Idaho law). The statement is cited by courts in states in which specific conditions are placed for an application of *lex loci contractus, see In re Binger's Estate*, 158 Neb. 444, 63 N.W.2d 784, 790 (1954); *Walker v. Yarbrough*, 257 Ark. 300, 516 S.W.2d 390, 397 (1974); and *Brissett v. Sykes*, 313 Ark. 515, 855 S.W.2d 330, 332 (1993). *See also* CALEB FOOTE ET AL., CASES AND MATERIALS ON FAMILY LAW 25 (3d ed. 1985).

10.3 The Marriage Contract

10.3.1 Expressed Contracts in a Common Law Marriage State

We found in Chapter 6, "The Common Law Marriage Contract," that the marriage contract, based on the parties' marital *consensus*, in accordance with the Roman principle *consensus facit nuptias*, constitutes the fundamental requirement for the establishment of a common law marriage in all of the jurisdictions recognizing such marriages.[59] Even though American case law traditionally spoke of a contract *per verba*, we found that, today, only the courts in Pennsylvania and the District of Columbia, in principle, maintain the requirement of a verbal agreement.[60] No predetermined word formulations are prescribed, nor do they arise when the parties enter into oral agreements. Despite general declarations that a common law marriage rests upon a civil law contract, we found, further, that the courts' application of general contract law principles as regards the commencement of agreements, must be designated as rudimentary. In our analysis of the case law, we could *inter alia* ascertain that it is unusual for the courts to reason in terms of offer and acceptance.[61] In Chapter 6, we criticized the courts for all too seldom deciding whether an agreement has been established by more thoroughly defining the agreement's required intent. Nevertheless, it appears from the case law that there are two main understandings. One is based on an intent to live together, and the other, on an intent to create a legal relationship between the parties.[62] We further found in the same chapter that the agreement must be with respect to a present, in other words an immediately effective marriage, *consensus de praesenti*, not a future marriage or *consensus de futuro*.[63]

The question in this chapter is how the courts in other jurisdictions, commonly the parties' state of domicile, have applied the preceding contractual principles to cases in which the parties have made short visits to a common law marriage state. The issue arises whether a marriage has been established in accordance with that state's law, *lex loci contractus*. Naturally, it is possible for a cohabiting couple, for example, in New York, to travel to Philadelphia to enter into a common law marriage. If they enter into an oral agreement there, perhaps before witnesses, in which they agree to

---

59 *See* Section 6.1 *supra*.

60 *See Peart v. T.D. Bross Line Constr. Co.*, 45 A.D.2d 801, 357 N.Y.S.2d 53, 54 (3rd Dep't 1974); and *Cross v. Cross*, 146 A.D.2d 302, 541 N.Y.S.2d 202 (A.D. 1 Dep't 1989). For more concerning the requirement of verbal agreements in Pennsylvania and the District of Columbia, *see* Section 6.2.2 *supra*. The requirement of a verbal agreement is applicable *e.g.* to a relationship that from the beginning is "illicit or meretricious" and the marriage presumption based on cohabitation and reputation is not applicable. With respect to the marriage presumption, *see* Chapter 9 *supra*.

61 *See* Section 6.1 *supra*.

62 *See* Section 6.3.2 *supra*.

63 *See* Section 6.4 *supra*.

enter into a legal relationship and to live a marital life together in accordance with valid legal marital regulations, there ought not be any doubt that a common law marriage has been established, because Pennsylvania, beyond the requirement of a contract, does not impose any requirements of cohabitation nor any requirement of domicile in that state.[64] For example, in *Pecorino v. Pecorino* (1978), the parties, in 1953, had traveled to Pennsylvania for the specific purpose of entering into a common law marriage. When they arrived, they exchanged verbal marriage vows. Three days later, they returned to New York, where they lived together and held themselves out as spouses for twenty years until the man's death. A common law marriage was established.[65] It is clear that the lack of a requirement of cohabitation for the establishment of a common law marriage facilitates the existence of such marriages with short visits to a state such as Pennsylvania. On the other side, the requirement for a verbal agreement appears restrictive. However, it is rare that a couple travels to a common law marriage state for the purpose of formlessly marrying in this manner.

It is unusual for the parties to enter into a written marriage contract, which, as we found in Chapter 6, ought to be given a high evidentiary weight. In those cases in which the parties have been in different states during their correspondence, the contract has been viewed as having been established in the state in which the offer is accepted.[66]

---

64 *Dozack v. Dozack*, 137 A.D.2d 317, 528 N.Y.S.2d 712, 713 (A.D. 3 Dep't 1988).

65 *Pecorino v. Pecorino*, 64 A.D.2d 711, 407 N.Y.S.2d 550 (1978). In *Matter of Catapano*, 17 A.D.3d 672, 794 N.Y.S.2d 401 (A.D. 2 Dep't 2005), witnesses testified that on June 29, 2001, the parties had expressed marriage vows at the home in Pennsylvania. A common law mariage was established. *Compare Bloch v. Bloch*, 473 F.2d 1067, 1069 (3d Cir. 1973), in which the parties had their residence and their domicile in the Virgin Islands, which does not recognize common law marriage. In 1965 they made a 3-4 days' visit to Florida, which in those days recognized such marriages. According to Florida law, no cohabitation was required but rather only a marriage contract to establish a common law marriage. Against the man's denial, the United States District Court of the Virgin Islands found that the parties "vowed and consented to be husband and wife in Florida" and the United States Third Circuit Court of Appeals found that the court's conclusion was not clearly erroneous.

66 In *Great Northern Ry. v. Johnson*, 166 C.C.A. 181, 254 F. 683 (8th Cir. 1918), a man in Minnesota had sent to the woman in Missouri a written marriage contract signed by him, which the woman then signed. Her acceptance was considered to constitute a valid marriage according to Missouri law. Upon the man's death, therefore the woman was considered his widow in Minnesota. In *Ray v. Ray*, 193 Misc. 131, 83 N.Y.S.2d 126 (S.Ct. 1948), a marriage was considered invalid despite the fact that it fulfilled the form requirements in the state in which the acceptance was received. The reason moreover was that it did not fulfill the form requirements in the state from which the acceptance was sent. *See Commonwealth v. Amann*, 58 Pa. D & C. 669 (Q.S.Camb. 1947). *Compare* Charles W. Taintor, *Marriage in the Conflict of Laws*, 9 VAND. L. REV. 607, 619 (1956), who argues that the state in which the acceptance "is put in mail" is decisive. With respect to a written marriage contract, *see* Section 6.5.2 *supra*.

1. *The Oral Agreement*

The basis for the assessment of whether an oral agreement has been entered into naturally is the parties' statements during the visit to a common law marriage state, for more concerning oral agreements, see Section 6.5, "Express Contracts," above. Even though the courts have not maintained any strict requirements of offer and acceptance for the creation of a marriage contract, the parties' marital *consensus* must have some expression.[67] If they, in general, have not discussed the issue,[68] or only considered marriage but not given expression to any final position, an agreement normally will not be established.[69] The courts have directly

---

67 *See* Section 6.5 *supra.*

68 For example, in *Marino v. Anheuser-Bush,* Inc., 182 A.D.2d 1078, 583 N.Y.S.2d 68, 70 (A.D. 4 Dep't 1992), the parties, who lived in New York, during the weekends had taken trips to Pennsylvania to visit friends and watch football games. During the visits, they were presented as husband and wife. When the man died, the woman claimed "compensation for death of a putative husband" on the basis that a common law marriage had been established during the visits to Pennsylvania. The New York Supreme Court, Appellate Division, stated that the woman did not even allege that they discussed marriage plans in Pennsylvania and found that a common law marriage was not established as evidence was lacking that the parties during their trips there "sought to establish the legal relationship of husband and wife." The court adjudged a visit that the parties made to Texas in a similar manner. No evidence whatsoever that the parties "agreed to marry" had been presented. *See also Peart v. T.D. Bross Line Constr. Co.,* 45 A.D.2d 801, 357 N.Y.S.2d 53, 54 (3rd Dep't 1974), in which the parties, who lived in New York, for 3-4 days in September of 1958 had visited an old friend in Camp Hill, Pennsylvania, a state recognizing common law marriage. From the investigation in the case, it appears that during the visit there, they "cohabitated together, conducted and held themselves out generally as husband and wife to their hosts and to others they had occasion to meet." The court, which required "a verbal expression of an intention to be married," did not find any common law marriage proven. With respect to the requirement for verbal agreements in Pennsylvania and the District of Columbia, *see* Section 6.2.2 *supra.* The requirement of a verbal agreement is applicable *e.g.* when a relationship from the beginning is "illicit or meretricious" and the marriage presumption based on cohabitation and reputation is not applicable. With respect to the marriage presumption, *see* Chapter 9 *supra. See also Cross v. Cross,* 146 A.D.2d 302, 541 N.Y.S.2d 202 (A.D. 1 Dep't 1989), in which the parties had commenced their cohabitation in New York in 1965, when they both still were married to others. After the impediments were removed, they continued the cohabitation until 1983 when they separated. The issue arose then whether they lived in a common law marriage which would have been established either during a weekend visit (1-2 nights) in 1982 in Pennsylvania or during another weekend (two nights) in Washington, D.C. The Supreme Court (Appellate Division) in New York stated that the parties' relationship to begin with was "illicit and meretricious" and reasoned with respect to the visit to Pennsylvania that the woman did not through evidence that was clear and convincing show that the parties during their visit there "agreed to enter into a valid marriage" or that there was even the smallest indication of an intention to be married. The court cited *inter alia, Peart v. Bross supra,* which required a verbal agreement. With respect to the visit to Washington, D.C., the court found that Regina did not present the "minutest of evidence" that they there had entered into any "present tense agreement to be husband and wife." The court's conclusion was that no common law marriage existed.

69 In *Gonzalez v. Satrustegui,* 178 Ariz. 92, 870 P.2d 1188, 1197 (App.Div. 1 1993), the court found, applying Kansas law, that the parties simply "contemplated marriage."

pointed out, in individual cases, that the parties have not given any marital vows. For example, in *Hutton v. Brink* (2005), the court considered parties' toast to one another as "husband" and "wife" during a dinner in Pennsylvania along with a public avowal of their mutual commitment to one another as a loving married couple. The court held, however, that the toast did not contain an exchange of words manifesting a specific, present intent to enter into marriage sufficient to create a common law marriage under Pennsylvania law.[70] A requirement for expressed vows naturally is a protection against parties, without their knowledge, becoming married and therewith governed by an entire system of regulations that they did not desire. In *State ex rel. Smith v. Superior Court for King County* (1945), the court stated that: "Parties who live for years in illicit relationship in a state in which they were domiciled will not find themselves married to each other if they happen to sojourn for a short time and hold themselves out as man and wife in a state where common law marriage is recognized."[71]

As to the issue why they never married, the woman stated: "I don't know. Just one of those things. To us, it wasn't that important. It's one of those things you put off. We talked about it a lot. Wherever we went, we thought, well, we should. In Phoenix when we stayed down there in the condo, we thought we ought to get married. In fact, just the night before Frank passed away we were talking about it." To use this statement as the reason that no marriage contract had been entered into as the court did is dubious, as the woman's testimony in actuality appears to have concerned a ceremonial marriage, not a common law marriage. With respect to the prerequirements for the establishing of a common law marriage according to Kansas law, *see* Chapter 6 *supra* with respect to the requirement of an agreement, and with respect to the requirement of holding out, *see* Section 8.4 *supra.*

70 *Hutton v. Brink*, 798 N.Y.S.2d 378 (A.D. 1 Dept 2005). In the case of *In re Matter of Danza*, 188 A.D.2d 530, 591 N.Y.S.2d 197 (1992), the parties, Susan and Rudolph T., who were from New York, had commenced their cohabitation while the man was still married to another woman. In February 1983, they made a 3-day "honey-moon" visit to the Poconos in Pennsylvania. When Rudolph later died, Susan claimed that she was the deceased's common law wife. The New York Supreme Court, Appellate Division, which in accordance with Pennsylvania law required clear and convincing evidence for the establishment of a common law marriage, found that there was no evidence that showed that the deceased ever consented to enter into a valid common law marriage with Susan. Just the opposite appeared from the evidence, that the deceased did not consider himself as married to her. *See also Taegen v. Taegen*, 61 N.Y.S.2d 869 (1946), in which the parties, who lived in New York, had made three short visits of three to four days in New Jersey. The New York Supreme Court stated: "There is not a scintilla of evidence that on any of those visits to New Jersey ... Mary and Walter ever said to each other, in words or substance, that they thereby agreed to or did take each other as husband and wife." As neither of the parties said that there was a marriage contract, the court deemed that it would be "logically absurd and ridiculous for a trier of facts nevertheless to presume or infer that such agreement was made." *See also State ex rel. Smith v. Superior Court*, 23 Wash.2d 357, 161 P.2d 188, 192 (1945). In *Norcross v. Norcross*, 155 Mass. 425, 29 N.E. 506 (1892), the parties lived together as husband and wife in Massachusetts, a state that does not recognize common law marriage. They made two visits, however, one for one week, the other three days, to New York, which in those days recognized common law marriage. The court stated that: "But there was no evidence that the parties while in New York entered into any contract of marriage between themselves."

71 *State ex rel. Smith v. Superior Court*, 23 Wash.2d 357, 161 P.2d 188, 192 (1945). *Compare Albina Engine & Machine Works v. O'Leary*, 328 F.2d 877 (9th Cir. 1964), in which a

The case shows, even though it is not representative for common law marriage in general, the function of an expressed agreement from the perspective of legal certainty.

It is unusual for the courts to discuss the agreement's required intent thoroughly. In certain cases, there is no doubt that the exchanges of words has arisen between the parties which would fulfill the requirements of a marriage contract, regardless of whether one intends an agreement to live together or a contract to establish a legal relationship. For more on this topic, see Chapter 6. For example, in *McKanna's Estate* (1951), the man, who lived in California, had met a woman in connection with a business and vacation trip to Texas. At trial, the woman testified that the parties decided not to enter into any ceremonial marriage; rather the following exchange of words occurred during the man's visit to Texas: "Mr. McKanna asked me if I would live with him as his wife and assume the duties as wife to him, and I said I would; and he said he would live with me as my wife." Taking this into consideration, along with the fact that the requirements of cohabitation and holding out as husband and wife were fulfilled, the California Court of Appeals, applying Texas law, found that a common law marriage had been established.[72]

In other short visit cases, the courts have found that a common law marriage was not established, because the parties did not show an intent to establish the legal relationship of husband and wife. In *Sears v. Sears* (1999), the parties' "pre-sex ritual," wherein they expressed their love for each other during visits to different common law marriage states, did not therefore constitute a marriage contract.[73] Even though the parties' feelings do not have a constitutive effect, they sometimes are given certain evidentiary weight.[74] In several cases, however, the requirements of the oral contract have been noticeably low. Exchanges of words that can best be characterized as conversational

---

common law marriage was found to be established based on 1-2 week visits to Idaho during a number of years.

72 *In re McKanna's Estate*, 106 Cal.App.2d 126, 234 P.2d 673, 674 (1951).

73 *Sears v. Sears*, 267 A.D.2d 988, 700 N.Y.S.2d 626, 628 (A.D. 4 Dep't 1999). The parties had visited South Carolina, Pennsylvania, and the District of Columbia. For example, in *Marino v. Anheuser-Bush*, Inc., 182 A.D.2d 1073, 583 N.Y.S.2d 68, 70 (A.D. 4 Dep't 1992), the New York Supreme Court, Appellate Division, found a common law marriage not established, as evidence was lacking that the parties, during their visits to Pennsylvania, "sought to establish the legal relationship of husband and wife." The marriage presumption was not found to be applicable in the case as the woman during the first visits was married to another man. With respect to the marriage presumption, *see* Chapter 9 *supra*. *Compare Dozack v. Dozack*, 137 A.D.2d 317, 528 N.Y.S.2d 712, 713 (A.D. 3 Dep't 1988), in which the court speaks of "a legal relationship of marriage" and in which a common law marriage was found to be proven. The court cited *Estate of Gavula*, 490 Pa. 535, 417 A.2d 168, 171 (1980). For more concerning the requirement of a legal intent in Pennsylvania case law, *see* Section 6.3.2 *supra*.

74 *See* Section 6.2.4 *supra*.

utterances sometimes have been accepted as a contract.[75] In other cases, the courts have been more restrictive.[76]

75 For example, in *Boykin v. State Indus. Acc. Comm'n*, 224 Or. 76, 355 P.2d 724, 726 (1960), the parties for ten years had lived together as husband and wife and outwardly presented themselves as such in Arizona, Arkansas, Nevada, Utah, and primarily in Oregon, states that at that time did not recognize common law marriage. In 1951, they spent 3-5 months in Idaho, which recognized such marriages. At trial, the woman testified as to the following conversation between her and her husband during their visit to Idaho: "'Well', he said, 'We are married now.' He says 'We have lived here and' he said, 'I guess we are really married.'...Well, later that night, then, why, as we were getting ready for bed he says, 'Well', he says, 'it's all legal now.' And I said, 'Well, not only by law' I said, 'it's always been in the eyes of God, too.'" The Oregon Supreme Court, whose reasoning in the issue concerning the agreement was almost non-existent, stated that the parties for ten years also "lived together in sickness and in health." A common law marriage was found established. The woman received therefore widow's benefits upon the man's death. In the case of *In re Neafie's Estate*, 12 Pa.Dist. 749 (1903), divorced spouses had met anew wherewith the man had said: "I am willing to take you back as my wife if you are willing to take me back as your husband," after which the woman answered: "Yes." They lived thereafter together until the man's death. The stated words together with their cohabitation and reputation were sufficient to constitute a common law marriage. *See also Hoffman v. Hoffman*, 285 Ky. 55, 146 S.W.2d 347, 348 (1940), in which three witnesses testified concerning a party in the woman's apartment in Ohio 1927 that "finally Dorothy and Emil went into the kitchen of the apartment and stayed a while; that they came back in and Emil told her to show her ring and the guests would know they were married and that Dorothy thereupon said that she and Emil were married and exhibited a ring." With regards to that a contract was found to be commenced and the parties lived together approximately three months in Ohio, the Kentucky Court of Appeals found that a common law marriage had been established.

76 For example, in *Milburn v. Milburn*, 694 N.E.2d 738 (Ind.App. 1998), the parties, Marlene and Gerald, had commenced their cohabitation in Indiana in 1965, a state that had repealed common law marriage. Later, Marlene adopted the last name Milburn and began to wear a gold wedding ring on her left ring finger. They had two mutual children in 1966 and 1968. In November 1970, Gerald moved to Pennsylvania since his employer ceased its operations in Indiana. He testified that he there rented a house for six months and that Marlene and the children occasionally visited him. Marlene, on the other hand, testified that she actually lived with Gerald during this period, which she estimated to be ten months. At trial, Marlene maintained that the parties on December 24, 1970, in Pennsylvania entered into a marriage contract based on the following exchange of words: "Well, it was, —we lived in like a three tiered house and the Christmas tree and everything was downstairs where we had got the kids' toys ready and we just kind of was looking at each other and said 'You are my wife.' And I said 'You are my husband.' And, after that we went to bed." The Indiana Court of Appeals found that the relationship between the parties to begin with was "meretricious." Consequently, Marlene had the evidentiary burden of proof for that the parties in Pennsylvania consented to a valid marriage and that a change occurred in their legal status. The court found that Marlene's unconfirmed testimony concerning the conversation on December 24, 1970, could not solely constitute clear and convincing evidence as required according to Pennsylvania law. With respect to the evidence connected to the state of domicile, Indiana, *see* the text *infra*. *Compare Matter of Estate of Necastro*, 1990 Del.Ch. LEXIS 123 (1990), in which the parties lived together approximately 20 years in Delaware. One day, they visited a jeweler in Philadelphia, Pennsylvania, where the man bought a diamond ring for the woman. During the visit to the shop, the man said to the jeweler and possibly also to the woman that they "would soon be getting married" or "will make" or "be making it legal soon." The court did not find proven with clear and convincing evidence "a present intention to contract marriage" but rather only an intent to be engaged.

2. *Evidence Relating to the Common Law Marriage State*

Evidence relating to the state in which the visit occurred and the contract was executed is of primary interest in proving an oral agreement. Direct evidence concerning the parties' statements on the occasion on which the contract was entered into is of greatest interest; see, e.g., *Boykin* and *Milburn*, as referenced in notes 75 and 76. Particular weight should be attributed to circumstances that have ties to the contractual situation, for example, their exchange of rings, the witnesses who were present or that during the visit, how they arranged a wedding party, or something similar.[77] However, other events taking place in the state of the visit can also constitute corroborative evidence in support of the contract. For example, there may be evidence that the parties lived together and held themselves out as spouses during the visit.

In *Dozack v. Dozack* (1988), the parties had exchanged wedding rings in the presence of witnesses in Pennsylvania. Concerning the event, the woman testified the following: "Well, we just decided that we would from that day on, as far as we were concerned in our hearts, we were man and wife, and we would consider ourselves a family and continue thus."[78] The man denied at trial that they exchanged rings and could not recall the event in question. The parties later moved to New York, where the issue arose whether a common law marriage had been established upon the occasion in question. The New York Supreme Court, Appellate Division, applying Pennsylvania law, found that the woman, by clear and convincing evidence, had proven the existence of a common law marriage.

Another case in which the court appears to have limited its determination to the events taking place in the state of the visit, but in which no oral

---

For more concerning the difference between *consensus de praesenti* and *consensus de futuro*, *see* Section 6.4 *supra*.

77 *Farber v. U.S. Trucking Corp.*, 26 N.Y.2d 44, 308 N.Y.S.2d 358, 256 N.E.2d 521 (1970). In *Matter of Estate of Yao You-Xin*, 246 A.D.2d 721, 667 N.Y.S.2d 462 (1998), two witnesses testified that they were invited to a common law marriage ceremony in the parties' residence in Philadelphia, Pennsylvania, on December 31, 1990, wherewith the man said to the woman: "From now on you are my wife." The woman answered that she was happy to be his wife, after which the man gave her a gold wedding ring. The parties referred to each other and were "by general reputation in the community" known as husband and wife.

78 *Dozack v. Dozack*, 137 A.D.2d 317, 528 N.Y.S.2d 712, 713 (A.D. 3 Dep't 1988). *See also Seagriff v. Seagriff*, 195 N.Y.S.2d 718, 721 (Dom.Rel.Ct. 1960), in which the parties lived together as husband and wife in New York from 1921 to 1957. Until 1928, the man was married to another woman and according to the judgment of marital divorce, forbidden to remarry in the state of New York. During the years 1928 to 1933, the couple 3-4 times per year had traveled to New Jersey, where they visited a couple they knew. Upon one occasion, they spent the night. New Jersey at that time recognized common law marriage. The court stated that to constitute a common law marriage in New Jersey, "an agreement ... in words of the present tense to live together as husband and wife" was required, and found that the parties never "made an agreement" in New Jersey. *Compare Steinreich v. Steinreich*, 270 N.Y. 668, 244 App. Div. 780, 280 N.Y.S. 791, 1 N.E.2d 989 (1936), in which a 3-day visit to New Jersey was sufficient to constitute a common law marriage.

contract was found proven, is *Vandever v. Industrial Comm'n of Arizona* (1985). The parties lived together for approximately seven years in Arizona and the woman's statement that the parties during a visit to Colorado "decided they were married," was not considered sufficient as proof according to the Arizona Court of Appeals that the parties entered into a marriage contract. *Vandever* is discussed in more detail below with respect to presumptions.[79]

3. *Evidence Relating to the State of Domicile*

The courts appear to have different attitudes towards evidence relating to the state of domicile, *i.e.*, the state that does not recognize common law marriage. On one side, certain courts have refused to consider such evidence. A reason for this stance, even if not expressly discussed, is that a common law marriage cannot be entered into in the domicile state. For example, in *Milburn v. Milburn* (1998), in which no common law marriage was found proven by clear and convincing evidence through an exchange of words occurring between the parties during a visit to Pennsylvania, the woman testified that the man in Indiana presented her as his wife on thousands of occasions. In addition, she presented evidence that the parties had submitted joint federal tax statements, bought real estate together, and had joint bank accounts. The Indiana Court of Appeals objected however, that the additional evidence with respect *inter alia* to the parties' reputation that the woman presented did not specifically concern the period during which the man (and possibly the woman) lived in Pennsylvania.[80]

The majority of courts, on the other side, appear to consider even evidence related to the state of domicile, despite the fact that the marriage

79 *Vandever v. Indus. Com'n of Arizona*, 714 P.2d 866 (Ariz.App. 1985). With respect to short visits to Colorado, *see also In Re Enoch's Estate*, 52 Ill.App.2d 39, 201 N.E.2d 682 (1964), in which a court in Illinois found that two weeks in Colorado, during which the woman had introduced the man as her spouse, was insufficient to constitute a valid common law marriage. *See also In re Binger's Estate*, 158 Neb. 444, 63 N.W.2d 784 (1954), in which the court found that pleasure trips of 3-4 days to Colorado were insufficient to constitute a common law marriage, as they did not change their domicile and neither entered into any agreement while they found themselves in Colorado. *Compare Bourelle v. Soo-Crete Inc.*, 165 Neb. 731, 87 N.W.2d 371 (1958), in which the parties between 1945-1946 lived In Iowa where the parties "on numerous occasions repeated their vows and stated to each other that according to the Bible and in the eyes of God they were man and wife." As a marriage contract was considered commenced and the parties lived together as husband and wife and outwardly presented themselves as such, a common law marriage was found established, which was recognized by the Nebraska Supreme Court.

80 *Milburn v. Milburn*, 694 N.E.2d 738, 740 (Ind.App. 1998). *Compare State ex rel. Smith v. Superior Court*, 23 Wash.2d 357, 161 P.2d 188 (1945), in which the court stated that a marriage contract can be proven through "an inference ... from conduct, and the holding out of each other as husband and wife." However, the court continued, if the parties during a long period lived together as husband and wife in another state and the relationship there was "illicit," then no such deduction can be made from a "mere continuance of the illicit relationship."

was not entered into there. Circumstances, which have a direct connection to the commencement of the formless marriage, of course, have significant evidentiary weight. An example would be that the parties in the home state, before their trip, planned for their formless common law marriage by acquiring wedding rings or inviting family members and friends to a wedding party in the state of the visit. Because such arrangements are unusual, it is of great practical importance that the parties' cohabitation in the state of domicile, which may have been lengthy, is considered circumstantial evidence that they entered into a formless marriage contract in the state of the visit. In the above-named case of *Pecorino v. Pecorino* (1978),[81] in which the parties entered into a marriage contract in Pennsylvania and thereafter lived in New York for twenty years, the court deemed that the agreement was ratified by their every act in Pennsylvania, New York, and elsewhere. A cohabitation, which is not recognized as marriage in New York, consequently serves as evidence for finding that the parties entered into a common law marriage in Pennsylvania. It also appears reasonable that no principal impediments can be placed against such evidence relating to the state of domicile or to other states. A separate issue, however, is that the value of such evidence to a large extent can vary from case to case.[82]

The creation of a common law marriage in the state of the visit assumes, as seen above, that the evidentiary requirements are fulfilled. The party

---

81 *Pecorino v. Pecorino*, 64 A.D.2d 711, 407 N.Y.S.2d 550, 551 (1978). In *Boykin v. State Indus. Acc. Comm'n*, 224 Or. 76, 355 P.2d 724, 726 (1960), the court stated that the parties for ten years "lived together in sickness and in health." *See also Franzen v. Equitable Life Assur. Soc. of United States*, 130 N.J.L. 457, 33 A.2d 599 (1943), in which the parties, according to the testimony, entered into an informal marriage contract in New Jersey, a state recognizing common law marriage at that time. Two days later, the parties moved to Louisiana, where for a couple of years until the man's death, they continued their marital cohabitation. Despite the fact that a common law marriage could not be established according to Louisiana law, the New Jersey Supreme Court found that the parties' cohabitation and reputation in Louisiana were relevant factors in assessing whether a common law marriage had been established in New Jersey. In *Dozack v. Dozack*, 137 A.D.2d 317, 528 N.Y.S.2d 712, 713 (A.D. 3 Dep't 1988), the court stated that the parties' cohabitation and appearance outwardly as spouses in New York were relevant, albeit not solely sufficient, as circumstantial evidence of proof that a common law marriage had been entered into before in Pennsylvania. The oral evidence with respect to the contract, however, was sufficient as proof of a common law marriage. *See supra* in the text.

82 *Compare* Charles W. Taintor, *Marriage in the Conflict of Laws*, 9 VAND. L. REV. 607, 621 (1956), who argues that if "cohabitation and repute is merely corroboratory of the exchange of consents," there is no reason why the place for the cohabitation should be decisive. In *George v. George*, 389 So.2d 1389, 1391 (Miss. 1980), the parties had their domicile in Mississippi but lived temporarily in Georgia. When trying whether they entered into a marriage contract in Georgia, the court considered their cohabitation and appearance outwardly as spouses in Mississippi, but noted at the same time that "standing alone, it would not prove that they entered into a common law marriage in Georgia." However, "in conjunction with" the parties' cohabitation and appearance outwardly even in Georgia, a marriage contract was found to be commenced.

claiming such a marriage was established, moreover, commonly has the evidentiary burden of proof. With respect to the required standard of proof, approximately half of the jurisdictions require evidence that is clear and convincing, while others apply a preponderance of the evidence standard. (For more concerning burdens of proof, see Chapter 9.)[83] As can be seen from the previous section, the state of domicile sometimes applies its own evidentiary burdens of proof.

10.3.2 Inferred Marriage Agreements

As seen in the previous section, it is unusual for a couple to travel to a state recognizing such marriages for the purpose of achieving a common law marriage and then entering into an express marriage contract. Nevertheless, there is extensive acceptance in American case law for inferred agreements or implied agreements, as discussed more in Chapter 7, "Implied Marriage Agreements." These have come to play a large and debatable role when the courts have to assess whether a common law marriage has been established during a short visit taken by a couple into a common law marriage state.

Although the courts do not require any express marriage contract, the requirement of a sharply defined contractual conclusion is not maintained. It has been neither important nor necessary to more thoroughly establish where, when, and how the marriage contract has been entered into during the short visit. In the litigation in general, neither has any reasoning in terms of offer and acceptance as aspects of the marriage contract been presented. The court's statement in the case of *In re Schneider's Will* (1954) is rather typical: The circumstances "are not weighed as evidence of the fact that at some time or other the parties said to each other, 'I take you to be my wife' or 'husband', but rather the circumstances are treated as evidence of their common desire and intention to be man and wife."[84] The acceptance of inferred agreements in the case law, which has rendered the contractual construction a *consensus continuus*, in other words, a continued consent, as discussed in Chapters 6 and 7, is also

---

83 In *Gilbert v. Gilbert*, 275 Ky. 559, 122 S.W.2d 137 (Ky.App. 1938), the woman asserted that the parties during a short visit to Cincinnati, Ohio, in March 1927 entered into a marriage contract in a hotel by placing their hands on a Bible and declaring that they as from that day were husband and wife. The man, however, denied that they entered into any agreement and that they were in Ohio at the point of time in question. The court, which required that a common law marriage must be proven with clear and convincing evidence, found that the parties had not been in Cincinnati at the occasion in question. For more concerning the burden of proof and the standard of the evidence, *see* Chapter 9 *supra*.

84 *In re Schneider's Will*, 206 Misc. 18, 131 N.Y.S.2d 215, 220 (Surr.Ct. 1954), citing *Chirelstein v. Chirelstein*, 12 N.J.Super. 468, 79 A.2d 884, 893 (1951).

applied when deciding cases in which the parties made visits to common law marriage states.[85]

In support of the existence of a marital *consensus*, the parties, in such cases, in part, cite circumstantial evidence, namely, their cohabitation and their reputation as spouses, but actually all other circumstances having to do with the acts and conduct of the parties with respect to the marriage relation. Second, in part, their admissions and declarations are cited, *i.e.*, the admissions and statements which the parties made during the cohabitation.[86] It is unusual but possible for the courts to require something more than merely living together to prove the existence of a marital *consensus*.[87] The extent of the relevant evidentiary basis is influenced strongly by whether the courts simply consider circumstances related to the visit to a common law marriage state or whether they have taken into consideration circumstances related to other states.

1. The Parties' Actions in a Common Law Marriage State

With respect to the evidence of an inferred marriage contract established during a visit to a common law marriage state, the circumstances that occurred in that state of course are clearly relevant. The understanding that the determination must be limited only to such circumstances has also been expressed. Thus, Taintor has asserted that when the cohabitation and repute is the sole foundation for a conclusion that the parties did

85 For more concerning *consensus continuus*, *see* Section 6.2.3 *supra*.

86 For more concerning circumstantial evidence and admissions and declarations, *see* Section 7.5 *supra*.

87 In the case of *In re Estate of Bivians*, 98 N.M. 722, 652 P.2d 744, *cert. quashed*, 652 P.2d 1213, 98 N.M. 762 (1982), the parties had commenced their cohabitation in New Mexico in 1969, a state not recognizing common law marriage. They were then both married to others, but these marriages were later dissolved. Robert bought a wedding ring for Diana. They continued to live together until they separated and remained separated until Robert's death in 1979. During 1972, they made several business and pleasure trips to Texas and Colorado, two states recognizing common law marriage. There they had outwardly presented themselves as husband and wife. The Court of Appeals in New Mexico stated that New Mexico for the recognition of such marriages already entered into in other states applies its own high evidentiary burdens of proof. The court stated that in addition, Texas as well as Colorado require for the establishment of a common law marriage *inter alia* a marriage contract and that the existence of a common law marriage must be proven by something more than "mere living together." The court found that the evidence was insufficient to prove that the parties "formulated a present agreement to become husband and wife in Texas" or to "establish a present intention of the parties to become married in the State of Colorado." The court did not decide whether the remaining requirements were fulfilled. The necessary requirements for the establishment of a common law marriage in Texas are (1) an agreement presently to be husband and wife; (2) living together as husband and wife in Texas; and (3) holding each other out there to the public as such (TEX. FAM. CODE ANN. § 1.91 (a)(2) (Vernon 1975). In *Colorado*, (1) "a contract or agreement of marriage *in praesenti*" constitutes a necessary requirement. In addition to this, in certain cases (2) "cohabitation as husband and wife" has also been applied as a necessary requirement, *see Bivians* and *Graham v. Graham*, 130 Colo. 225, 274 P.2d 605 (1954). *Compare Vandever v. Indus. Com'n of Arizona*, 714 P.2d 866 (Ariz.App. 1985) with references.

actually consent to marriage, the holding out must occur in a state recognizing such consent, without an exchange of express consents, as a sufficient form.[88] As the local law in general does not appear to apply any such limitations with respect to a couple domiciled in a common law marriage state, these courts make an application of *lex loci contractus* influenced by conflict of law. This application means not only that the issue of choice of law is based on the parties' actions in the state of the visit,[89] which is the obvious place for an inferred agreement determined by the parties' actions. It also means that when the choice of applicable law is made, with the application, thereof, only events taking place in the common law marriage state are considered.

Such a limitation on the evidence may appear too tenuous to establish any certain conclusions concerning the parties' marital intentions.[90] The parties often have stayed only several days or weeks in connection with a business or pleasure trip. There are, nevertheless, cases in which the parties' actions during the short visit to a common law marriage state have

---

88 Charles W. Taintor, *Marriage in the Conflict of Laws*, 9 VAND. L. REV. 607, 621 (1956). As support for his understanding, he cites *Rittger v. United States*, 154 F.2d 768, 772 (8th Cir. 1946), which is not a typical short visit case, as the parties in *Rittger* from the beginning had their domicile in a common law marriage state. The parties, after an impediment against the marriage was removed, had a relationship in Iowa, a state recognizing common law marriage, for approximately eight months. They moved thereafter to Minnesota, a state no longer recognizing such marriages. They lived together there and appeared outwardly as spouses. The lower court, the United States District Court of Minnesota, instructed the jury that the parties' actions in Minnesota could not be considered in assessing whether a common law marriage had been established. The Eighth Circuit Court of Appeals stated: "From such facts no presumption was warranted as to the relation of the parties in the State of Iowa." Taintor also cites *In re Foster*, 77 Idaho 26, 32, 287 P.2d 282, 285 (1955). It ought to be noted, however, that the parties in *Foster* entered into an oral marriage contract, which was invalid because it was commenced in the state of Washington, which does not recognize common law marriage, but which played a role in the court's reasoning.

89 By "state where the marriage was contracted" is meant, according to RESTATEMENT (SECOND) OF CONFLICT OF LAWS (1971), the state in which the marriage was celebrated or "where some other act was done that is claimed to have resulted in the creation of a marriage status." *See* RESTATEMENT (SECOND) OF CONFLICT OF LAWS § 283 cmt. e (1971). *See also* comment g, from which it can be seen that the marriage cannot be viewed as invalid if "the acts relied upon to create the marriage meet the requirements of the state where the acts took place."

90 *See Kennedy v. Damron*, 268 S.W.2d 22, 24 (Ky..App. 1954), which concerned short visits to Ohio. The court stated that a marriage contract *in praesenti* certainly "may be implied from the conduct of the parties in holding themselves out to the public as man and wife, in the community in which they reside," and that if a relationship is to be presumed from "conduct and reputation," it must "be in identification with an established home." The court, however, did not require "a legal domicile" in a common law marriage state in the meaning of a residence with an intent to be permanent, but on the other hand, "an established place of abode with which the parties may be identified as members of the community." *Compare Tarter v. Medley*, 356 S.W.2d 255 (Ky. 1962), in which a common law marriage was found established in Ohio, after a visit there of 4-5 months during which the parties had their own household and outwardly appeared as husband and wife.

been viewed as sufficient to prove the existence of a marriage contract. For example, in the case of *In re Schneider's Will* (1954), in 1938, the parties entered into a ceremonial marriage that was invalid.[91] They lived, thereafter, as husband and wife in New York until the man's death in 1952. They acted as spouses and were perceived as such by their family members and by others who knew them. They submitted joint income tax returns and otherwise represented that they were married. During this period, common law marriage was not recognized in New York, but the courts recognized such marriages that had been legally entered into in other states. During their cohabitation, the parties for several weeks had visited Florida and even made visits to New Jersey, two states that recognized common law marriage at that time. During these visits, they held themselves out as husband and wife.

When the man died, the woman made claims on the estate in the capacity of surviving spouse under the assertion that a common law marriage had been established during their visits to Florida or New Jersey. The Surrogates Court, Kings County, in New York, stated that no expressed agreement was necessary for the establishing of a common law marriage as "their conduct in those states established the agreement...."[92] The court found that the parties, sometime after the invalid wedding in New York, consented to be man and wife in New Jersey or Florida. A common law marriage was thus established. It ought to be noted that the court's reasoning did not, at least not expressly, make any connections to the invalid wedding in New York in a way that other courts have done, as discussed further in the next section. The parties' actions in the states visited appear to have been decisive.

91 *In re Schneider's Will*, 131 N.Y.S.2d 215 (1954). *See also In re Frost's Estate*, 35 A.D.2d 1069, 316 N.Y.S.2d 372 (4th Dep't 1970), in which the parties in New York entered into an invalid wedding ceremony and thereafter visited Florida for a few months. As they believed that they were married, the cohabitation in Florida was sufficient to constitute a common law marriage. *See also Bowlin v. Bowlin*, 55 N.C.App. 100, 285 S.E.2d 273 (1981), in which the parties entered into a ceremonial marriage which was invalid based on an impediment. After the impediment's removal, they lived together approximately four years in North Carolina and Alaska, two states not recognizing common law marriage, but also six months in South Carolina, a state recognizing such marriages. The court found that their cohabitation and holding out in South Carolina was sufficient to constitute a common law marriage that ought to be recognized in North Carolina. *See also Parker v. Parker*, 46 N.C.App. 254, 265 S.E.2d 237 (1980), in which the parties were residents of North Carolina, but in which they lived together as husband and wife six weeks in South Carolina.

92 *In re Schneider's Will*, 131 N.Y.S.2d 215, 220 (1954). The idea that the cohabitation does not need evidence that the parties, at a certain point of time, entered into an express marriage contract, but rather instead, of their desire and intent to be husband and wife, recurs even in *Chirelstein v. Chirelstein*, 12 N.J.Super. 468, 79 A.2d 884, 893 (1951). There the court stated that the cohabitation and other circumstances "are not weighed as evidence of the fact that at some time or other the parties said to each other, 'I take you to be my wife' or 'husband.' But rather the circumstances are treated as evidence of their common desire and intention to be man and wife."

One of the most far-reaching cases in which the parties' actions in the state of the visit were sufficient is *Coney v. R.S.R. Corp.* (1990),[93] in which a common law marriage was recognized based on a three-day visit to Georgia. The parties had lived together in New York from 1979 to 1984, until the man died. They shared family expenses, considered themselves as husband and wife, and held themselves out as such. They had certain plans in the future to formalize their relationship through a wedding ceremony that were never realized. At this time, a common law marriage could not be entered into in New York, but the state recognized that such marriages might be formed in other states.

The parties spent three days with family members in Georgia in 1981. During their visit there, they held themselves out as husband and wife. When the man in 1984 was killed while employed by R.S.R. Corporation, the woman filed for workers' compensation benefits in the capacity as the man's widow. The New York Supreme Court, Appellate Division, stated that three requirements exist for a valid marriage in Georgia: (1) the parties must be able to contract; (2) an actual contract existed; and (3) consummation occurred according to the law.[94] In deciding whether these conditions were fulfilled, the court stated that the parties' plans in the future to enter into a ceremonial marriage did not in itself rule out that a common law marriage existed, a finding supported by earlier case law.[95] The court, however, went entirely past the question of whether any actual contract had been established, simply stating that the parties lived together and held themselves out as married during the three days in Georgia. The court deemed this period, though short, to be sufficient because Georgia did not require any minimum period of time to establish a common law marriage.

Common to the decisions in *Schneider* and *Coney* is an apparent reliance on circumstances that simply were related to the common law marriage state visited by the parties. This conflict of law limitation on the trial evidence with the application of *lex loci contractus* also arises in *Ray v. Ray* (1996) and other cases from *Tennessee*.[96] In addition, it is remarkable that

93 *Coney v. R.S.R. Corp.*, 167 A.D.2d 582, 563 N.Y.S.2d 211 (A.D. 3 Dep't 1990). *Compare Mott v. Duncan Petroleum Trans.*, 51 N.Y.2d 289, 434 N.Y.S.2d 155, 414 N.E.2d 657 (1980).

94 GA. CODE ANN. § 19-3-1 (1982). Observe that common law marriage, as was mentioned in chapter 1, was repealed in Georgia January 1, 1997, however not retroactively, *see* GA. CODE ANN. §§ 19-3-1.1 (West 2003).

95 *See Brown v. Brown*, 234 Ga. 300, 215 S.E.2d 671 (1975).

96 For example, in *Ray v. Ray*, Tenn.App. LEXIS 314 (1996), the parties, William and Susan, had divorced in 1970, but reassumed the cohabitation and lived together for 18 years in Tennessee, Florida, and Alabama. They had a mutual daughter. When the parties later separated, Susan requested a portion of the estate on the basis that a common law marriage had been established during their six-month cohabitation in Alabama. Susan testified that the parties lived together as husband and wife in Tuscumbia, Alabama, from June to December 1978 and that William presented her to their landlord and work acquaintances as his wife. They had joint bank accounts

the courts did not more closely explain how the marriage contract had been established. Cohabitation and other circumstances were not presented as evidence for the existence of a marital *consensus.* Rather, they were regarded as independently significant for the establishment of a common law marriage. Nothing indicated that the parties traveled to the common law marriage states for the purpose of entering into such a marriage there or that, during the visit, they were aware that such a marriage could be established there. The absence in the facts of an inference of an agreement, which was a general conclusion in Chapter 7 concerning the creation of inferred agreements, appears even more obvious when this contractual construction is applied to short visits to common law marriage states.[97] The courts' terse reasonings in these cases gives rise to misgivings from the perspective of legal certainty. It is a serious flaw in a legal system if the parties become married to each other without having knowledge thereof!

---

and submitted joint married tax returns that year. She was acknowledged as his wife in his health insurance and in different medical documents. Their daughter testified that the parents, when they lived in Alabama, referred to each other as husband and wife and that they lived as a "normal family." The Tennessee Court of Appeals, appearing to have only reviewed the parties' documents in Alabama as the basis for its decision, found that the requirement in Alabama of present agreement was fulfilled. The court did not describe more closely how from the existence of the above presented actual circumstances it came to the conclusion of the existence of an inferred marriage contract. *See also In re Estate of Glover*, 882 S.W.2d 789, 791 (Tenn. App. 1994), which also concerned short visits to Alabama. In *Glover*, the same court stated applying Alabama law that "the requirement elements necessary to establish a valid common law marriage must have occurred in the State of Alabama." *See also Andrews v. Signal Auto Parts Inc.*, 492 S.W.2d 222 (Tenn. 1972). With respect to the question of credibility, on the other hand, the court in *Glover* found the parties' documents in Tennessee relevant. The court did not find any marriage contract proven during the visits to Alabama, wherewith considerable significance was attributed to the circumstance that the woman identified herself as the man's fiancée. With respect to the acceptance in Alabama law of inferred agreements, *see* Section 7.4 *supra.* With respect to the requirement of cohabitation and public recognition in addition to the marriage contract, *see* Section 8.4 *supra. Compare Payne v. Payne*, 1999 Tenn.App. Lexis 844 (1999), in which the parties commenced their relationship while the man was still married to another woman. After the impediment was removed, they lived together approximately 16 years. In transit they had spent the night 2-3 times at a motel in Georgia, a state recognizing common law marriage at that time. As to the issue why her name did not exist on conveyances to the property they lived on in Tennessee, the woman answered: "Because Mr. Payne told me he would see that I was always taken care of, that I would always have a home as long as I didn't marry someone else." According to the court, their discussion showed the absence of an intent with Tony Payne to enter into a marriage contract. A common law marriage was not found to be proven. The conveyance drafted in Tennessee could consequently constitute evidence that the man did not have an intent in Georgia to enter into a marriage contract. With respect to inferred agreements according to Georgia law, *see* Section 7.4 *supra.*

97 For more concerning implied marriage agreements, *see* Chapter 7 *supra.*

2. *The Parties' Actions in States Other than a Common Law Marriage State*

When deciding whether an inferred marriage contract has been established by the parties' visits to a common law marriage state, the courts commonly have also considered circumstances related to other states. Once the courts have determined the applicable law, they then have not allowed limiting conflicts principles to affect the application of *lex loci contractus.* The possibility of considering the parties' long cohabitation in their state of domicile naturally may facilitate the finding of a common law marriage based on a visit to a state where such marriages can be entered into legally.

This issue was the focus in *Mott v. Duncan Petroleum Trans.* (1980), in which the parties, who lived together nine years in New York, had made short visits to Georgia, a state where common law marriage at that time could be entered into legally.[98] The New York Court of Appeals stated that the lower court failed to even consider the behavior of the parties in New York as evidence of their intent to marry.[99] Even if such evidence was not by itself decisive and naturally secondary to the parties' actions in the visited state, the court deemed the evidence at least relevant to demonstrating whether the parties considered themselves husband and wife during their trips to Georgia. Because the lower court had erroneously applied the law, the court remanded the case.

Even though the evidence of an inferred agreement always means a collective assessment of all relevant circumstances, certain actions that the

98 With respect to Georgia law and inferred agreements, *see* Section 7.4 and with respect to the requirement of cohabitation, Section 8.4, *supra.*

99 *Mott v. Duncan Petroleum Trans.*, 51 N.Y.2d 289, 434 N.Y.S.2d 155, 158, 414 N.E.2d 657 (1980). The case had first been tried by the Workers' Compensation Board and thereafter by the Supreme Court, Appellate Division, which affirmed. *See also Gordon v. Gordon*, 27 Misc.2d 948, 211 N.Y.S.2d 265, 270 (1960), in which the parties moved together in New York in 1940 and lived there as husband and wife until 1958. During the man's 14-month military service in 1942-43, the parties lived together in Texas, a state recognizing common law marriage. The court found such a marriage established during their visit to Texas and also considered with its assessment the parties' 18-year cohabitation in New York. *See also Kellard v. Kellard*, 13 Family Law Reporter 1490 (N.Y.Sup.Ct. 1987), in which the parties on a trip to Disneyland, Florida, made a two-night stay in a Georgia motel. A common law marriage was found established and the court also considered their cohabitation in New York. *See also Matter of Grossman v. Gangel*, 192 A.D.2d 396, 596 N.Y.S.2d 53, 55, 625 N.E.2d 590 (A.D. 1 Dep't 1993), in which the parties' actions in New York were considered in deciding whether the parties entered into a common law marriage in South Carolina and Pennsylvania. *See also Brown's Adm'r v. Brown*, 308 Ky. 796, 215 S.W.2d 971, 975 (1948), in which the parties, who were living in Kentucky, a state that did not recognize common law marriage, had spent four winters in Florida, a state that at that time recognized such marriages. Despite the fact that the relationship was considered "illicit" in Kentucky, the court considered not only that the parties lived and outwardly presented themselves as spouses in Florida, but also that they "lived together, after their return from Florida in 1942, as man and wife, openly and avowedly." A common law marriage was found to be proven.

parties take outside of a common law marriage state, however, are of particular interest as evidence of the parties' marital *consensus*.

2.1 *An Invalid Wedding Ceremony in a State Other than a Common Law Marriage State*

Such a particular event in the home state occurs when the parties there entered into a ceremonial wedding ceremony, in which they expressed their marital *consensus*, but which was invalid, for example, based on an impediment.[100] If the parties, after the removal of the impediment, visit a common law marriage state, their cohabitation there has been viewed as constituting evidence for a continued marital *consensus*. The reference back to the invalid wedding ceremony in the courts' reasoning has been more or less strong. A more direct connection is found in those cases in which the courts assume that the marital *consensus* expressed in the invalid wedding ceremony continues. The use of the *consensus continuus* model, in these cases, is motivated to an extent by the strong expression of the parties' marital *consensus* in the formalized wedding. This, however, was invalid and no new expressed agreement was entered into after the removal of the impediment. The use of the model also has its explanation in the acceptance of the subsequent cohabitation as an expression of the parties' *consensus*. It ought to be noted, however, that the invalid wedding in the home state is not substantive but has only evidentiary significance in deciding whether a common law marriage has been entered into in the state of the visit. The circumstance that the parties believed that the formal wedding had been valid has been taken into consideration in individual cases by the courts, but has not constituted any premise for an evidentiary consideration of the same.[101] The idea that an invalid wedding ceremony in another state can be given evidentiary weight in deciding whether the

100 *Travers v. Reinhardt*, 205 U.S. 423, 440, 27 S.Ct. 563, 51 L.Ed. 865 (1906), invalid wedding ceremony in another state; *Boltz v. Boltz*, 325 Mass. 726, 92 N.E.2d 365 (1950), invalid wedding ceremony in a common law marriage state; *Albina Engine and Machine Works v. O'Leary*, 328 F.2d 877, 881 (9th Cir. 1964), invalid wedding ceremony in a common law marriage state; *Ventura v. Ventura*, 53 Misc.2d 881, 280 N.Y.S.2d 5 (Sup.Ct. 1967), invalid wedding ceremony in the state of domicile; and *Farber v. U.S. Trucking Corp.* 26 N.Y.2d 44, 308 N.Y.S.2d 358, 256 N.E.2d 521 (1970), invalid wedding ceremony in the state of domicile.

101 *See, e.g.*, *In re Frost's Estate*, 35 A.D.2d 1069, 316 N.Y.S.2d 372 (4th Dep't 1970). In *Skinner v. Skinner*, 4 Misc.2d 1013, 150 N.Y.S.2d 739 (1956), the parties had entered into a ceremonial marriage in New York in 1948. The marriage, however, was invalid based on the man's previous not-yet-dissolved marriage. The court found given that the parties' "conduct evidenced their intent, in good faith, to live in lawful wedlock," and that a common law marriage had been established both during the parties' one-month-long visit to the District of Columbia and during their three weeks in Pennsylvania. That common law marriage constituted therefore an impediment against a ceremonial marriage that the man later entered into. It cannot be seen whether the court by "conduct" also referred to the parties' behavior in New York. *See also Metro. Life Ins. Co. v. Holding*, 293 F.Supp. 854 (E.D.Va. 1968), in which the parties did not have knowledge of the existence of an impediment against their marriage.

parties entered into an inferred marriage contract in a common law marriage state has also been accepted by Rhode Island's courts.[102]

An often-cited case is *Travers v. Reinhardt* (1906), in which the United States Supreme Court reviewed a case in which the parties had ties to several states.[103] The man, who was domiciled in the District of Columbia, and the woman, who was domiciled in Virginia, had undergone a wedding ceremony in the latter state that proved invalid because of a mistake in form. Even though the wedding ceremony was invalid and Virginia did not recognize common law marriage, the court noted that the parties' agreement "was faithfully kept up" until the man's death. These events had occurred during more than fifteen years of cohabitation in Maryland, a state not recognizing common law marriage, and finally during barely one year in New Jersey, a state that recognized such marriages.[104] The Court found that the parties' actions in New Jersey "taken in connection with their *previous association,* was equivalent, in law, to a declaration by each that they did and during their joint lives were to occupy the relation of husband and wife" (*italics added*).

Of particular interest in the Court's reasoning is its reference to the invalid wedding ceremony and its consideration, not only of the parties' actions in New Jersey, but also of their previous association. Although the case is often cited, it ought to be noted that it is unique to the extent that there was an invalid wedding ceremony at the bottom and it was not a typical case involving short visits. The parties actually maintained their domicile in New Jersey and lived there almost one year until the man's death.

Later developments in the case law have gone considerably further. In certain cases in which the parties have celebrated an invalid wedding ceremony in the state of domicile, the courts have found that a common law marriage has been established in connection with their making a short visit of only a few days in a state recognizing such marriages. For example, in *Ventura v. Ventura* (1967), the parties lived together for fourteen years in New York, where they underwent a wedding ceremony that was invalid as

---

102 *See Holgate v. United Electric Ry. Co.*, 47 R.I. 337, 133 A. 243, 244 (1926), in which the parties during a temporary visit to Massachusetts entered into a wedding ceremony, which was invalid because of an impediment. After the impediment was removed, they lived together for 17 years until the man's death in Rhode Island, a state in which common law marriage can be entered into legally. The Rhode Island Supreme Court stated that there could be no doubt that the parties at the point of time of the invalid wedding ceremony possessed an intent to become husband and wife. The only conclusion which was consistent with the evidence concerning the parties' "intent, conduct, declarations and reputation" was that the parties entered into a common law marriage as soon as the impediment was removed.

103 *Travers v. Reinhardt*, 205 U.S. 423, 440, 27 S.Ct. 563, 51 L.Ed. 865 (1906). As the case is of general interest, it is also discussed in Chapter 7 concerning Implied Marriage Agrements, *supra.*

104 *Id.* at 873. *Compare In re Foster*, 77 Idaho 26, 287 P.2d 282 (1955), in which the court maintained that "consent is a continuing thing."

a result of an impediment. A common law marriage could not be entered into in the state of New York at that time but, for three days, the parties visited Atlanta, Georgia, a state where such marriages were legal.

The Supreme Court, Queens County, New York, found, with respect to the elements of the contract, using the same reasoning as in *Travers*, that their actions during the three days in Atlanta "taken in connection with their *previous association*, was equivalent, in law, to a declaration by each that they did and during their joint lives were to occupy the relation of husband and wife" (italics added).[105] The reference to the invalid wedding ceremony was justified through the court's reliance on case law from Georgia and New York; thus, their continued cohabitation after the impediment's removal caused the original declaration of intent to be considered continuing.

The argument that the parties' marriage contract consists of a *consensus continuus* having its origin in an invalid ceremonial marriage is also clearly expressed in the cases in which a wedding ceremony, invalid as a result of an impediment, occurred in a common law marriage state and in which the parties' cohabitation without impediment occurred primarily in a state not recognizing common law marriage. Recurring short visits to a common law marriage state have then given rise to a common law marriage. For example, in *Albina Engine and Machine Works v. O'Leary* (1964),[106]

105 *Ventura v. Ventura*, 53 Misc.2d 881, 280 N.Y.S.2d 5 (Sup.Ct. 1967). Another case in which the period of cohabitation had been limited but in which the court's reasoning is terse is *Madewell v. United States*, 84 F.Supp. 329, 335 (E.D.Tenn. 1949). The parties, Orville O. Madewell and Mary Jean Madewell, had in Georgia in March of 1942 entered into a ceremonial marriage, which was invalid as the man was still married to another woman. They later lived primarily in Tennessee. During his military service, Orville for a period was stationed in Alabama, a state recognizing common law marriages. Mary Jean and their oldest child visited him there several times. They lived together then in a home outside of the military base on different occasions "for a number of days and nights." They stated there that they were husband and wife and were received and perceived as such by the home's residents and by Orville's friends. To judge from the summary of the facts, the court does not mention the requirements in Alabama for the establishment of a common law marriage and neither the assessments which it makes, but rather simply finds "on the basis of the foregoing" that Mary Jean was Orville's legal widow and that therefore she was entitled to insurance benefits. Even in *Old Republic Ins. Co. v. Christian*, 389 F.Supp. 335, 338 (E.D.Tenn. 1975) a common law marriage was found to be established between a man and a woman who had their domicile in Tennessee and who took short trips of up to ten days in Georgia and Alabama. The court states the requirements in Georgia and Alabama for a marriage contract, but gives no conclusion from the facts in the case as to the existence of a contract.

106 *Albina Engine and Machine Works v. O'Leary*, 328 F.2d 877, 881 (9th Cir. 1964). Even in *Boltz v. Boltz*, 325 Mass. 726, 92 N.E.2d 365 (1950), the parties in a state that recognized common law marriages (New York 1918) had entered into a wedding ceremony which was invalid due to an impediment. They also had their domicile there. When the impediment was removed, they continued the cohabitation there for 4-18 days. The Supreme Judicial Court of Massachusetts found that the wedding ceremony was strong proof that the parties intended that the woman would become "a wife not merely a mistress" and that this intent "could be found to continue" during the short time they lived in New York after the impediment

the parties had entered into a ceremonial marriage in Idaho, in 1938, which was invalid based on an impediment. In 1942, the couple moved to Oregon. A year later the impediment was removed. They lived there together as husband and wife until the man's death in 1961. Together they had three children. Oregon did not recognize common law marriage. The parties with their children, however, had returned to Idaho every year between 1942 and 1956, spending one or two weeks with their parents. Idaho recognized common law marriages.

When the man died, the woman filed for death benefits in her capacity as his surviving spouse.[107] The issue arose then whether a common law marriage had been established during the family's annual visits to Idaho. With respect to the requirement of consent, the court stated that "consent is a continuing thing,"[108] which calls for a "continuation ... of conduct" sufficient to fulfill the requirements of consent and mutual assumption of marital rights, duties, or obligations. The court found that a common law marriage had been established.

An invalid wedding ceremony in a state not recognizing common law marriages has also been given considerable evidentiary weight in cases in which the parties not only made a short visit but also lived together several years in a common law marriage state. In the case of *In re Gallagher's Estate* (1950), the parties, in 1925, had entered into a ceremonial marriage in Seattle, Washington. The marriage was invalid, however, because the woman's previous marriage was not dissolved. A common law marriage could not be entered into in Washington. The parties later lived as husband and wife for approximately five years in Detroit, Michigan, a state where a common law marriage at that time could be entered into legally. After the woman's previous marriage was dissolved in 1929, there were approximately three years during which there was no impediment against the marriage in Detroit. The parties then moved to California and finally again to the state of Washington, where the man died in 1944. The Washington Supreme Court found that, with the application of *lex loci*

---

was removed. A common law marriage was found established. The woman therefore received spousal maintenance from the man when they separated in 1948. The State of New York introduced common law marriages through law 1907 (N.Y.Laws of 1907, c. 742) and repealed the institution through law 1933 (N.Y.Laws of 1933, c. 606). From January 1, 1908, until April 29, 1933, common law marriages could be established in New York. *See also Sturm v. Sturm*, 111 N.J.Eq. 579, 163 A. 5 (1932) in which the court stated: "If the marriage was void in Galicia, it became valid as a continuing contract upon the transfer of the domicile to this state, the fact of continuing consent having been proved."

107 According to Section 909 of the Longshoremen's and Harbor Workers' Compensation Act, 44 Stat. 1424 (1927), 33 U.S.C.A. §§ 901-950. This federal law, however, does not more closely define "surviving wife." The interpretation of the term becomes dependent of the states' general principles.

108 *In re Foster*, 77 Idaho 26, 32, 287 P.2d 282, 285 (1955). *See also Boykin v. State Indus. Acc. Comm'n*, 244 Or. 76, 85, 355 P.2d 724, 728 (1960). *Compare Tatum v. Tatum*, 241 F.2d 401, 409-410 (9th Cir. 1957); and *In re Binger's Estate*, 158 Neb. 444, 63 N.W.2d 784, 788-789 (1954).

contractus, i.e., Michigan law, a common law marriage had been established in Detroit and that the woman consequently was the deceased's widow. As support thereof the court stated that: "The consent and taking manifested by the former ceremony, coupled with continued cohabitation thereunder, operated as a present taking, and they thereupon entered into a common-law marriage ...."[109]

From the cases cited above, it can be seen that the courts in their reasoning as support that the parties entered into a marriage contract in the state of the visit related back to an invalid wedding ceremony. This can be seen in *Travers,* with the court maintaining that the agreement the parties entered into later "was faithfully kept up" through their actions.[110] Also, in *Ventura* and *Albina Engine,* the courts characterized their marital *consensus* as a "continued consent"[111] which has been expressed through their conduct. Perhaps most clearly, as in *Gallagher,* the courts related back to the invalid wedding ceremony, through maintaining that it together with the cohabitation, operated as a present taking of each other as husband and wife.[112] An additional reason offered by the courts, as in *Stilley,* is that a common law marriage has been established by ratification,[113] or as in *Farber,* by public recognition of the invalid contract.[114] The invalid wedding ceremony's effect in all of these cases, in principle, is not substantive but rather simply evidentiary.

109 *In re Gallagher's Estate,* 35 Wash.2d 512, 213 P.2d 621, 624 (1950). *Compare Hess v. Pettigrew,* 261 Mich. 618, 247 N.W. 90, 91 (1933).

110 *Travers v. Reinhardt,* 205 U.S. 423, 440, 27 S.Ct. 563, 51 L.Ed. 865, 873 (1906).

111 *Albina Engine and Machine Works v. O'Leary,* 328 F.2d 877, 881 (9th Cir. 1964); and *Ventura v. Ventura,* 53 Misc.2d 881, 280 N.Y.S.2d 5 (Sup.Ct. 1967).

112 *In re Gallagher's Estate,* 35 Wash.2d 512, 213 P.2d 621, 624 (1950).

113 *See Stilley v. Stilley,* 219 Ark. 813, 244 S.W.2d 958, 960 (1952), in which the parties in Arkansas entered into a ceremonial marriage, which was invalid because the woman had already been married for 15 years. The parties later lived 9 years in Kansas, a state recognizing common law marriage. The court found that the parties "had by ratification and by common law become lawfully married in the State of Kansas." *See also Darling v. Dent,* 82 Ark. 76, 100 S.W. 747 (1907).

114 In *Farber v. U.S. Trucking Corp.* 26 N.Y.2d 44, 308 N.Y.S.2d 358, 256 N.E.2d 521 (1970), the parties had undergone a wedding ceremony in New York in January of 1949, which however, was invalid due to an impediment. In August the same year, as the impediment against the marriage no longer existed, the parties visited Florida, a state that at that time recognized common law marriage. During the visit there, which lasted three weeks, they lived together and appeared outwardly as husband and wife. They arranged a "wedding party" where they received presents. When the man died 12 years later in 1961, the woman filed for death benefits on the basis that she was the deceased's widow. The Workmen's Compensation board found that the parties in Florida had entered into a valid common law marriage according to Florida law. The New York Court of Appeals found that the invalid ceremonial marriage was evidence for "an intention then to enter a marital relation" and that the parties' actions and statements in Florida clearly demonstrated, "not the initiation" of, but "a public recognition" of a marriage and found that the lower court's conclusion was supported by substantial evidence.

The court's reasoning in *In re Frost's Estate,* 35 A.D.2d 1069, 316 N.Y.S.2d 372 (4th Dep't 1970) was similar, in which a man and a woman entered into a ceremonial marriage in New York in 1963, which however, was invalid based on an impediment. The couple lived thereafter together as husband and wife until the man's

The parties' cohabitation in the state of domicile appears to have greater significance for the establishment of the inferred marriage contract than the relation back to the invalid wedding ceremony. As seen from the cases, the courts consider not only the parties' actions during the visit to a common law marriage state, which in *Ventura* lasted only three days; *Albina Engine*, one to two weeks every year for fourteen years; *Metropolitan Life Insurance Company*, one month; *Singer*, a honeymoon; *Travers*, scarcely one year; and *Gallagher*, five years. The courts also took into consideration their long-term cohabitation outside of the common law marriage state, which in *Ventura* lasted fourteen years; *Travers*, eighteen years; *Albina Engine* and *Gallagher*, nineteen years; *Metropolitan Life Insurance Company*, twenty-one years; and *Singer*, thirty years. Despite the fact that the states in which these cohabitations occurred did not recognize common law marriage, it was considered proof that the parties in a common law marriage state entered into such a marriage.

There are also cases in which a common law marriage has been established in the state of the visit without the parties' marital *consensus* being connected to the invalid wedding ceremony in the courts' reasoning. The cohabitation between the parties thereby receives a more independent significance as evidence of the parties' marital intentions.[115] In certain cases, the reasoning concerning the existence of a marital *consensus* has also more or less faded away while the cohabitation was used more directly as the basis for the existence of a common law marriage.[116]

---

death in 1967. New York did not then recognize common law marriage entered into in that state. In December 1963 or in January 1964, however, the parties for two weeks had stayed in Florida, a state that at that time recognized common law marriage. The New York Supreme Court (Appellate Division) found that the parties had lived together as husband and wife in Florida and stated that any expressed agreement was not required as the parties believed that they were validly married, continuing: "Continued cohabitation under an assumed valid but, in fact, invalid, ceremonial marriage is sufficient to validate a common law marriage under Florida law." A valid common law marriage was found consequently established in Florida.

115 In the case of *In re Singer's Estate*, 138 N.Y.S.2d 740 (Surr.Ct. 1955), the parties in New York had undergone a wedding ceremony, which was invalid because the woman was prohibited from remarrying according to a previous divorce judgment. The parties spent their "honeymoon" in New Jersey, where they also later many times lived in a hotel. The parties lived together as husband and wife and appeared outwardly as such in New York and in Florida. Both New Jersey and Florida at that time recognized common law marriage. The court stated that the divorce judgment in New York did not have any extra-territorial effect and found that a common law marriage had been established as the requirements in New Jersey of "cohabitation accompanied by matrimonial intent and repute" were fulfilled. The court also considered the parties' 30-year cohabitation in New York and Florida as corroborative evidence. In *Weisel v. Nat'l Transp. Co.*, 14 A.D.2d 621, 218 N.Y.S. 2d 725 (1961), the parties in New York had undergone a wedding ceremony, which was invalid due to an impediment. The parties stayed 10 months in Florida. A common law marriage was found established simply based on the parties' cohabitation as husband and wife after the removal of the impediment.

116 For example, in *Metro. Life Ins. Co. v. Holding*, 293 F.Supp. 854, 858 (E.D.Va. 1968), the parties in 1946 had entered into a ceremonial marriage in Paris, which was

2.2 Formless Agreements in a State Other than the Common Law Marriage State

If the parties entered into a formless marriage contract in the state in which they are domiciled, invalid because that state does not recognize common law marriage, and the parties later made a visit to a common law marriage state, the invalid contract, in the same manner as an invalid wedding ceremony, as well as their cohabitation and holding out as spouses, has been given weight as evidence of the fact that the parties, during the visit, have had a continued marital *consensus*. A common law marriage then has been able to be established without the parties there entering into any new expressed agreement.

For example, in *Ram v. Ramharack* (1991),[117] the parties had commenced their cohabitation in New York, in 1978, while both were still married to others. When their previous marriages were dissolved in 1984, the woman asked the man to accompany her to the marriage license bureau in New York to obtain a marriage license prior to a ceremonial wedding ceremony. The man then answered that a license is "only a piece of paper," and added, "We are living happily together like husband and wife. It's no big deal not having a piece of paper." They, therefore, never acquired any license nor entered any ceremonial marriage. They lived, however, as husband and wife and held themselves out as such in New York and other places. They had two mutual children, often traveled together, bought and sold property in joint names, and lived together until 1990, when the woman petitioned for marital divorce.

New York did not recognize common law marriage, so the complaint could not be based on a marriage commenced in New York. The parties, however, had visited the woman's family in the city of Washington, D.C., two to three times per year. The District of Columbia is a jurisdiction recognizing such marriages. During the visits, they lived together and held

---

invalid based on an impediment. The parties, which did not have knowledge thereof, continued the cohabitation in Virginia and in different directions in the world until the man's death in 1967. The parties, who traveled much, spent one month in 1961 in Florida and one month in Ohio, two states recognizing common law marriage. The court found that a common law marriage had been established "by virtue of their living together as man and wife in Florida and in Ohio during 1961 and by holding themselves out as such thereafter whereever they lived." *See also Steinreich v. Steinreich*, 270 N.Y. 668, 244 App.Div. 780, 280 N.Y.S. 791, 1 N.E.2d 989 (1936), in which a three-day visit to New Jersey was sufficient to constitute a common law marriage. In *Smart v. Smart*, 676 P.2d 1379 (Okla.Civ.App. 1983), the parties in Arizona had entered into a marriage which was invalid based on an impediment. After the impediment was removed, they continued the cohabitation for nearly 30 years in California, where they had their domicile. For 16 years, they had 2-3 times per year visited Oklahoma, a state in which common law marriage could be entered into legally. Once they stayed there 2-5 weeks. The court found with reference to that the parties in Oklahoma outwardly presented themselves as spouses, that a common law marriage had been established. No reasoning in the issue concerning the agreement was presented.

117 *Ram v. Ramharack*, 571 N.Y.S.2d 190 (Sup. 1991).

themselves out as husband and wife. The woman, therefore, based her complaint on the fact that a common law marriage had been established during their visits to Washington, D.C. The man objected that no such marriage had ever been established because no express mutual agreement to be husband and wife had been entered into in Washington, D.C.

The court stated that three requirements must be proven for a common law marriage to be established, namely: (1) a present intent to be married, (2) a holding out as husband and wife to others in both New York and the other state, and (3) cohabitation. With respect to the two last-named conditions, the court stated briefly that the parties to numerous people in New York and other places outwardly presented themselves as husband and wife and that they cohabited together during their visits to Washington. With respect to the requirement of an agreement, the court posed the question of whether the parties' original agreement had to be expressly repeated and answered: "The answer obviously is, NO! Their agreement to be husband and wife, as expressed in 1984, *continues to be their agreement* as long as they continue to cohabit and hold themselves out to others as husband and wife"(italics added).[118] A common law marriage was found established, which then must be dissolved through marital divorce.

In addition to the invalid contract in New York, the court, in the same manner as in the cases discussed earlier, considered the parties' cohabitation and holding out not only during the short visits a couple times per year in Washington, D.C., *i.e.*, in a state recognizing common law marriage, but also their actions in New York and other places, which combined becomes a cohabitation of approximately twelve years.

---

118 *Id.*, at 192. If one works from general civil law principles, it is doubtful whether any original agreement in general had been established in *Ram*. It can be questioned whether the woman's request to the man to go to a Marriage License Bureau and the man's answer, "We are living happily together like husband and wife. It's no big deal not having a piece of paper," fulfills the requirements of offer and acceptance. The man's statement appears in a literal light as a value judgment concerning marriage licenses as well as a statement concerning the happiness in their cohabitation. Even in other cases in which the parties entered into oral agreements, the requirements as to the expression of the mutual marital intent have scarcely been stringent. In the case of *In re Foster*, 77 Idaho 26, 32, 287 P.2d 282, 285 (1955), the parties, according to the woman's testimony after the man's death, during a car trip in the state of Washington "had decided to get married." Based on this, a formless agreement was found commenced, which however, was invalid, as the state of Washington did not recognize common law marriage. In *Matter of Estate of Murnion*, 212 Mont. 107, 686 P.2d 893, 902 (1984), the invalid contract came into existence in the same state. The contract was based on the following conversation between the parties: "Michael then asked Pauline if she would come to Montana as his wife. Pauline told him that she would. He said he wanted to bring her out here and introduce her as his wife, and she so agreed." For more concerning oral agreements, *see* Section 6.5.1 *supra*. *Compare In Re Matter of Grossman v. Gangel*, 192 A.D.2d 396, 596 N.Y.S.2d 53, 55, 625 N.E.2d 590 (A.D. 1 Dep't 1993), in which the parties entered into a formless marriage contract in New York, but in which the court does not appear to have attributed the contract any significance in deciding whether the parties entered into a common law marriage in Pennsylvania.

As the District of Columbia law, in principle, requires a verbal agreement (*per verba*) for a common law marriage to be established, and no such agreement was entered into there, it ought to be noted that the court in *Ram*, with the application of *lex loci contractus*, appears to have accepted that the agreement's verbal element was referable to New York.[119] The issue whether the requirements in the District of Columbia of cohabitation and holding out for the establishment of a common law marriage were fulfilled is treated below in Section 11.5, "Exceptions to the Marriage Presumption," and also in Chapter 8, "Cohabitation, Holding Out, and Reputation as Spouses."

American case law also demonstrates other types of cases in contrast to *Ram*, because the parties there have had their domicile in a state recognizing common law marriage but entered into a formless but invalid contract in another state not recognizing such marriages. When they returned to the state of their domicile and continued the cohabitation there without entering into any new marriage contract, a common law marriage could be established in the same manner as in *Ram*, on the theory that consent is continuing.[120] In other cases, the parties have had their domicile in and even entered into the formless marriage contract in a state not recognizing common law marriage. When they later have been domiciled in a state recognizing common law marriage, the original contract has been attributed evidentiary weight in deciding whether a marriage has been entered into in the new state.[121] In still other cases, the parties have entered into

119 With respect to the requirement of a contract *per verba* in Washington D.C. and in Pennsylvania, *see* Section 6.2.2 *supra*.

120 *See In Re Matter of Estate of Murnion*, 212 Mont. 107, 686 P.2d 893, 906 (1984), in which the parties had entered into an oral marriage contract in the state of Washington, a state not recognizing common law marriage, whereafter they moved to Montana, which recognizes such marriages. The Montana Supreme Court found that all the requirements for the establishment of a common law marriage were fulfilled during the parties' approximately 6-month long cohabitation in Montana, wherewith the court with respect to the requirement of an agreement referred to their "continuing agreement." *See also In re Foster*, 77 Idaho 26, 32, 287 P.2d 282, 285 (1955), in which the parties, who were living in Idaho, a state at that time recognizing common law marriage, had made a 3-day visit to Washington, a state not recognizing such marriages. The woman testified that the parties during the visit had "decided to get married." After the return to Idaho, they lived together approximately three and a half months before the man died. The Idaho Supreme Court stated: "Assuming the marriage was consented to and consummated in Washington, consent is a continuing thing, and it follows that the parties also consented to and consummated the marriage in Idaho upon their return." *See further Grammas v. Kettle*, 306 Mich. 308, 10 N.W.2d 895, 897 (1943), in which the parties entered into an oral marriage contract in Illinois, a state not recognizing common law marriage. The parties moved thereafter to Michigan, a state that at that time recognized such marriages. There they lived together and appeared outwardly as husband and wife. The Michigan Supreme Court stated that "the agreement can be said to have continued from day to day, or its existence inferred ... from such facts as the holding out as being married and acceptance as such by the public..."

121 *See, e.g., Nat'l Union Fire Ins. Co. v. Britton*, 187 F.Supp. 359, 364 (D.D.C. 1960), *aff'd*, 110 U.S.App.D.C. 77, 289 F.2d 454, *cert. denied*, 368 U.S. 832, 82 S.Ct. 54, 7 L.

a formless agreement in the state in which they are domiciled but the contract has been found invalid based on an impediment.[122] Wherever the parties have expressed a marital *consensus*, it has been given weight as evidence to prove that the parties in a common law marriage state entered into an inferred marriage contract.

2.3 The Parties' Cohabitation in States Other than the Common Law Marriage State

There are also cases in which neither a contractual tie to an invalid wedding ceremony nor a formless agreement has been present. The evidence instead rested primarily on a lengthy cohabitation in the state of domicile, which together with the parties' marital appearance during the

---

Ed.2d 34 (1961), in which the parties had entered into an oral marriage contract in Virginia, which was invalid because the state did not recognize common law marriage. The parties moved, however, to Washington D.C., a district recognizing such marriages and lived together there approximately 10 years until the man's death. The court stated that as the relationship continued "pursuant the agreement entered into previously," a common law marriage had been established "as soon as the couple moved to the District of Columbia and continued living there." *See further Cook v. Carolina Freight Carriers Corp*, 299 F.Supp. 192 (D.C.Del. 1969), in which the parties after a wedding ceremony in Kentucky and later divorce in 1962, reunited in West Virginia, a state not recognizing common law marriage. There they entered into a common law marriage and agreed to continue the cohabitation as husband and wife. Two months later they moved to Florida, a state in which common law marriage at that time could be entered into legally. There they lived together until 1966 when the man due to an accident died in Delaware. In connection therewith, the question arose whether the parties could be viewed as having entered into a common law marriage in Florida when they commenced their relationship in West Virginia. Further, the question also arose whether West Virginia law or Florida law would be applied. The court applied Florida law, which recognizes the validity of a common law marriage even if the marital relationship "originated" in a state that did not recognize such marriages but in which the parties continued to cohabit and consider each other as husband and wife. The court found that the parties had entered into "an agreement or contract of marriage." *Compare Travers v. Reinhardt*, 205 U.S. 423, 440, 27 S.Ct. 563, 51 L.Ed. 865 (1906). In *O'Benar v. O'Benar*, 410 S.W.2d 214 (Tex.Civ.App.-Dallas 1966), the parties had commenced their relationship in Illinois, a state not recognizing common law marriage. They continued the relationship in Texas, where the court, without reference to the circumstances in Illinois, found that the parties entered into a new agreement in Texas.

122 *See, e.g., Hickman v. T.J. Hughes Constr. Co.*, 11 A.D.2d 828, 202 N.Y.S.2d 77 (1960), in which the parties had moved together and entered into a "marital agreement" in New York in 1929, a state that at that time recognized common law marriage. As an impediment existed against the marriage, however, their marriage contract was invalid. After the impediment was removed and New York repealed common law marriage, the parties in 1937 stayed approximately one year in New Jersey, a state that at that time recognized common law marriage. The parties lived thereafter together in New York until the man's death in 1957. The court found that the parties' invalid agreement and their cohabitation in New York after the removal of the impediment proved their intent to live in a valid marriage. The court stated that the parties' invalid "marital agreement" in New York ought to be attributed "some evidentiary effect" for their continued consent. A common law marriage was found therefore to be established.

short visit of several days in a common law marriage state, was sufficient to prove the existence of an inferred marriage contract.

For example, in *Renshaw v. Heckler* (1986), the parties had commenced their cohabitation in Baltimore, Maryland, in 1958. They did not enter into any ceremonial marriage, but agreed to live as though they were married and considered each other husband and wife. Shortly after they commenced the cohabitation, the woman received a wedding ring from the man. She adopted the last name of Renshaw and they presented each other to family, friends, and acquaintances as husband and wife. The year after they moved to Buffalo, New York, where they lived for twenty years until the man's death in 1979. They submitted their joint income tax statements as husband and wife. The man named the woman as the beneficiary of his life insurance. Neither Maryland nor New York could recognize a common law marriage entered into at that time.

Nevertheless, upon approximately eight occasions between the years 1968 and 1975, the couple, together with a daughter and sometimes the man's mother, visited family members in Virginia and North Carolina. On the way there, the family always spent one night at Port Motel in Port Treverton, Pennsylvania, a state recognizing common law marriage. At least upon one occasion, the man at the motel had booked a room for himself, "his wife," and their daughter. When they arrived, they checked into their room, ate dinner at the restaurant, retired for the evening, and continued their journey the morning after. During their trips through Pennsylvania, the couple held themselves out as husband and wife. Besides the daughter and the man's mother, they never met anyone they knew, with the exception of the woman's brother, who believed that she and the man were married to each other.

After the man's death, the woman claimed that she was entitled to the insurance benefits due a widow according to New York's Social Security Act, citing as grounds that she was the deceased's common law wife. The issue arose whether a common law marriage had been established in connection with the couple's motel visits to Pennsylvania. The authority deciding such insurance benefits, the Secretary of Health and Human Services, and the Federal District Court, to which the case was appealed, found that the woman was not the man's common law wife.

The decision was appealed to the United States Second Circuit Court of Appeals, which stated that the woman presented evidence with respect to cohabitation and reputation and that the parties' "conduct while in Pennsylvania and elsewhere" gave sufficient support to find a declaration that they had assumed a relationship as husband and wife.[123] The Second

123 *Renshaw v. Heckler*, 787 F.2d 50, 54 (2d Cir. 1986). In the case of *In Re Matter of Estate of Foster*, 376 S.E.2d 144 (W.Va. 1988), the parties had lived together for approximately five years in Washington, D.C., where a common law marriage legally could be entered into, and thereafter for approximately 22 years in Virginia, a state in which this is not possible. The court found that the parties entered into an inferred

Circuit concluded that the parties during their travels through Pennsylvania had entered into a common law marriage in accordance with valid Pennsylvania law[124] and that the woman consequently was entitled to a widow's insurance benefits.

This reasoning resembles that of *Travers v. Reinhardt*. However, in contrast to *Renshaw*, it was not a question of a short visit but rather of a cohabitation of almost one year in a common law marriage state in which the parties were domiciled. Had the court in *Renshaw* considered only the parties' actions during the trips through Pennsylvania, no common law marriage ought to have been established. As the court also took into consideration their conduct "elsewhere," it could consider the parties' cohabitation and holding themselves out as spouses during twenty years in New York. The court does not appear to have strictly applied the marital presumption Pennsylvania law offers by which the court, *i.e.*, from the existence of constant cohabitation and general reputation, presumes the existence of a marriage contract as long as the opposite is not proven.[125] Instead, the court finds a declaration that the parties in Pennsylvania had assumed a relationship as husband and wife.[126]

---

agreement and cited as support moreover not only the cohabitation in Washington D.C. but also the one that occurred in Virginia. In *Brown's Adm'r v. Brown*, 308 Ky. 796, 215 S.W.2d 971, 975 (1948) the parties, who were living in Kentucky, a state not recognizing common law marriage, had spent four winters in Florida, a state that at that time recognized such marriages. Despite the fact that the relationship was considered "illicit" in Kentucky, the court not only considered that the parties lived and outwardly presented themselves as spouses in Florida, but also that they "lived together, after their return from Florida in 1942, as man and wife, openly and avowedly." A common law marriage was found to be proven. In *Tryling v. Tryling*, 53 S.W.2d 725, 728 (Ky. 1932), the court considered the parties' actions in Kentucky as support for that they in Ohio entered into a marriage contract.

124 *Compare* with respect to Pennsylvania law, *Skinner v. Skinner*, 4 Misc.2d 1013, 150 N.Y.S.2d 739 (1956) and *McCullon v. McCullon*, 96 Misc.2d 962, 410 N.Y.S.2d 226 (N.Y.Sup.Ct. 1978), in which 3 weeks and 2-4 weeks per year in Pennsylvania respectively were sufficient to constitute a common law marriage there. *Compare Cross v. Cross*, 541 N.Y.S.2d 876 (A.D. 1 Dep't 1984)(1-2 days), *Chlieb v. Heckler*, 777 F.2d 842 (2d Cir. 1985)(2 nights), *Peart v. T.D. Bross Line Constr. Co.*, 45 S.D.2d 801, 357 N.Y.S.2d 53 (3rd Dep't 1974)(3-4 days), and *Goldin v. Goldin*, 48 Md.App. 154, 426 A.2d 410 (1981)(ski trips), in which short trips to Pennsylvania were not considered sufficient to there constitute a common law marriage. With respect to the courts' reasoning, *see infra* in this chapter.

125 *Compare* with respect to the marriage presumption's application with short visits to common law marriage states, Section 11.4 *infra*.

126 A difference in the nuances in the reasonings of *Travers v. Reinhardt* and *Renshaw v. Heckler* is that the court in the former case found that the parties' actions were "equivalent to" a declaration by them both that they entered into a relationship as husband and wife, while the court in the latter found that the parties' actions in a similar manner were sufficient to "support finding such a declaration here." In both cases, however, the requirement of a contract was applied, with or without explanation. *Compare* on the other side the court's admission that "there is no evidence of some present tense intent to create the marriage while in Pennsylvania," *Renshaw*, 787 F.2d at 53.

3. *Objections with Respect to the Marriage Contract's Essensialia*

It happens, albeit too rarely, that the courts conclude that the actual circumstances relating to the parties' visit to a common law marriage state have not been sufficient for the conclusion that an inferred marriage contract has been established.[127] In certain cases in which this has occurred, it has been explained by the fact that the parties' actions have not been sufficiently marriage-like.[128] However, even though the parties, during the visit to a common law marriage state, lived together and held themselves out as husband and wife, these circumstances have not always been sufficient to prove the existence of an inferred marriage contract. One might think that a cohabiting couple's crossing of the border of a common law marriage state should not be sufficient to become married to each other. In the case of *In re Binger's Estate* (1954), the court stated that the parties, who lived in Nebraska, made short pleasure trips over the border to Colorado "without ever intending to contract or contracting a common-law marriage...."[129]

The parties in these cases commonly have made admissions and declarations that speak against the existence of a marriage contract.[130] However, even

---

127 *See, e.g., Ponzi v. Ponzi*, 157 Cal.App.2d 772, 321 P.2d 847, 850 (1958), in which the parties entered into a ceremonial marriage in Arizona, which was invalid based on an impediment. After the impediment was removed, the parties in May and June of 1951 stayed in Oklahoma and Texas. The court finding that the parties lived together as husband and wife, however, stated that they retained "their residence" in California and that there had not arisen any discussion which indicated that they "intended to remarry" in Texas or Oklahoma. No common law marriage was found to be proven. *See also Carroll v. Carol*, 251 S.W.2d 989, 991 (Ky.Ct.App. 1952), in which the parties lived together as husband and wife in Kentucky, a state that no longer recognized common law marriage. However, they spent the winters in 1946-1950 in Florida, a state in which such marriages at that time could be entered into legally. No other evidence than that the parties lived together and outwardly appeared as spouses in Florida existed. No attempt was made to prove any agreement in Florida. The court found therefore nothing in the case supported the understanding that the parties' relationship "rose to the dignity of marriage merely because they crossed the state line into Florida!"

128 For example, in *Merritt v. Chevrolet Tonawanda Div., G.M.C.*, 50 A.D.2d 1018, 377 N.Y.S.2d 663, 665 (1975), the parties, who were resident in New York, had lived together for approximately five years. However, they had not submitted joint tax returns and did not designate each other as beneficiaries on life insurances. The woman did not use the man's name and had also stated that she was single. The parties had made short visits to Ohio, where they stayed overnight with friends, who believed that they were married. The court stated that: "Claimant's actions and conduct following those trips negate clear and convincing proof of such a marital agreement."

129 *In re Binger's Estate*, 158 Neb. 444, 63 N.W.2d 784, 789 (1954); and *Doyle v. Doyle*, 497 S.W.2d 846 (Mo.App. 1973).

130 In *Mares v. Heckler*, 1985 U.S.Dist. LEXIS 23303 (N.D.Ind. 1985), the parties, domiciled in Texas, had received a marital divorce in 1955. When they did not receive any divorce paperwork, they continued the cohabitation in Texas until 1960, in accordance with which the woman testified as to the belief that they still were married. After a separation in 1960, the woman moved to Indiana. Upon the man's

though the parties have made such statements, their cohabitation and holding out as spouses during the visit to a common law marriage state, as well as in the state of domicile, have been attributed a higher evidentiary weight. In *Brown's Adm'r v. Brown* (1948), the court stated, concerning statements which the man had made against the existence of a common law marriage: "His conduct speaks louder, and more convincingly than his words." The courts must always make a collective assessment of all the present circumstances.[131]

In assessing the issue of the evidentiary weight that ought to be attributed to the parties' cohabitation and reputation, as well as their admissions and declarations, in proving an inferred marriage contract, it is decisively important to precisely define that which is to be proven. In Chapter 6, which discusses the content of the marriage contract, we found that it is unusual for the courts in common law marriage states to closely discuss and define what constitutes the marital intent. We found, in

death in 1977, she claimed that she was the deceased's widow in a common law marriage. The court found, applying Texas law, that no inferred marriage contract could be viewed as proven with regards to the woman's understanding that the parties never received a marital divorce. The court cited *Clack v. Williams*, 189 S.W.2d 503 (Tex.Civ.App.-San Antonio 1945); *Gary v. Gary*, 490 S.W.2d 929 (Tex.App.-Tyler 1973); and *Rush v. Travelers Ins. Co.*, 347 S.W.2d 758, 760 (Tex.Civ.App-Texarkana 1961), by which the court certainly admitted that a marriage contract can be implied or inferred, but in which the court at the same time stated that it cannot occur "contrary to direct evidence which definitely shows that there was no such agreement." *See also Ferrell v. Celebrezze*, 232 F.Supp. 281, 283 (S.D.Tex. 1964), in which the establishment of a common law marriage was prevented based on direct evidence of the content that the woman did not wish a "binding wedlock." For more concerning inferred agreements in Texas, *see* Section 7.4 *supra*.

131 In *Brown's Adm'r v. Brown*, 308 Ky. 796, 215 S.W.2d 971, 975 (1948), the parties, who were living in Kentucky, a state not recognizing common law marriage, had spent four winters in Florida, a state that at that time recognized such marriages. Despite the fact that the relationship was considered "illicit" in Kentucky, the court considered not only that the parties lived and outwardly presented themselves as spouses in Florida, but also that they "lived together, after their return from Florida in 1942, as man and wife, openly and avowedly." The court stated that with respect to the man's statements against the existence of a common law marriage: "His conduct speaks louder, and more convincingly than his words." A common law marriage was found to be proven. *See also Hoffman v. Hoffman*, 285 Ky. 55, 146 S.W.2d 347, 349 (1940), in which the court stated: "Of course evidence that these parties lived together as husband and wife in Kentucky could not establish a common law marriage, which is not recognized in Kentucky, but unquestionably such evidence is competent as corroboration of evidence that they lived together as husband and wife in the State of Ohio before moving to Kentucky." *See further In Re Matter of Estate of Foster*, 376 S.E.2d 144 (W.Va. 1988), in which the parties' cohabitation of approximately five years in a common law marriage jurisdiction, the District of Columbia, and 22 years in Virginia, where such marriages cannot be entered into, weighed more heavily than certain circumstances which spoke against the existence of a common law marriage, *inter alia*, that the man stated that he was single and that the woman used her maiden name. An inferred agreement with respect to common law marriage was found to exist.

Chapter 7, that this was a general deficiency in the courts' analysis of the existence of inferred marriage agreement.[132]

The question is how the intent of the marriage contract is put to the test when the issue is whether a contract has been entered into during a short visit to a common law marriage state. If, on one hand, the object of the marital intent is to live together as husband and wife, and the parties actually did this, perhaps for many years, it is clear that the cohabitation ought to be given a considerable evidentiary weight. On the other hand, with the same intent, it cannot be taken for granted that a short coexistence during a visit to a common law marriage state needs to express an intent to live an entire life together. The question of whether the courts consider only the parties' cohabitation during the short visit or whether they also take into consideration their cohabitation in the home state receives considerable significance here.

On the other side, if the object of the marital intent must be a legal intent of some type, for example, an intent to change the parties' legal status or assume the marital duties and obligations of husband and wife, or an intent in general to be legally bound, it is clear that the cohabitation, even though lengthy, ought to be attributed a more limited evidentiary weight. The cohabitation, if the parties thereby fulfill marital obligations, certainly can indicate that they also promised each other to do this. The cohabitation, however, need not prove any legal obligation. The parties can very well have had the intention to live an entire life together, but without marital rights and obligations.

Moreover, it does not appear, when deciding cases concerning short visits to common law marriage states, that the marital intent's *essensialia* has received the attention it deserves. Behind the courts' stances, however, one can discern different understandings of the issue. In several cases, it appears that the courts in Illinois, applying Iowa law, have interpreted a requirement for a legal intent to be bound, so that supporting the existence of an inferred marriage contract with the cohabitation then becomes more tenuous. For example, in the case of *In re Marriage of Mosher* (1993), for five months, the parties had lived together and held themselves out as husband and wife in Iowa. At trial, the woman however, testified that the man "did not want anything that was legal and binding." The lower court found that the requirements of continuous cohabitation and public declaration were fulfilled, but on the other hand, that there was no evidence that the man "ever intended to be legally married." The Illinois Appellate Court stated that the conduct of the parties does not establish a mutual present intention and agreement to enter into a marital relationship.[133] As the courts in Iowa do not appear to have been equally

132 *See* Section 6.3 and 7.8 *supra*.

133 *In re Marriage of Mosher*, 243 Ill.App.3d 97, 612 N.E.2d 838 (1993). The Illinois Supreme Court appears to have interpreted Iowa law in a similar manner in

unequivocal in their interpretation of Iowa law, one can characterize the Illinois court's reasoning as a conflict of laws' influenced application.[134]

The requirement of a legal marital intent also appeared when the Connecticut Supreme Court has applied *Alabama* and *South Carolina* law, albeit these jurisdictions do not give any clear support thereof.[135] The consequence has been that visits to these states do not result in a common law marriage. In *Collier v. City of Milford* (1988), the parties had begun to live together in Bridgeport, Connecticut, in 1962, a state not recognizing common law marriage. The woman was then married to another man who died in 1968. In 1966, the couple had a mutual daughter. They continued the cohabitation in Bridgeport until the man's death in 1978.

The parties annually made vacation trips of approximately two weeks to either South Carolina or Alabama, two states recognizing common law marriage. During these visits, they slept together, held themselves out as if they were married to each other, and were perceived in general as married by those with whom they came in contact. On one occasion, however, the man informed his mother that they were not married.

When the man died, the woman applied for workers' compensation in the capacity of surviving spouse, and the issue arose whether a common law marriage had been established during their visits to South Carolina and Alabama. The Connecticut Supreme Court stated that, as a minimum for the establishment of a common law marriage, evidence was required of a mutual intention to marry when the parties found themselves in South Carolina or Alabama. By intent, the court meant an intent to change the status of the relationship.[136] Because the woman's story did not contain

---

Jambrone v. David, 16 Ill.2d 32, 156 N.E.2d 569, 572 (1959), in which the parties lived approximately one year in Iowa. The court stated certainly that the parties' conduct and reputation constituted "evidential facts which tend to prove or disprove the agreement and intend of the parties," but found that the evidence did not give support for that the cohabitation in this case stemmed from any agreement "to assume the marital duties and obligations of husband and wife." In contrast to *Mosher*, however, the cohabitation was deficient and neither had they acquired any reputation as spouses.

134 *See, e.g., In re Estate of Fisher*, 176 N.W.2d 801, 807 (Iowa 1970). *See further In re Estate of Dallman*, 228 N.W.2d 187, 190 (Iowa 1975), in which the court speaks of a contract "to live as husband and wife."

135 For example, in *Rodgers v. Herron*, 226 S.C. 317, 85 S.E.2d 104, 113 (1954), the South Carolina Supreme Court speaks of a contract "to live together as husband and wife," while the same court in *Johnson v. Johnson*, 235 S.C. 542, 112 S.E.2d 647, 651 (1960), requires a contract "to assume toward each other the relation of husband and wife," *see* Section 6.3 *supra*. With respect to the courts in Alabama's vague descriptions of the marital intent's *essensialia*, *see* Section 6.3 *supra*.

136 *Collier v. City of Milford*, 537 A.2d 474, 479 (Conn. 1988). *See also Walker v. Hildenbrand*, 243 Or. 117, 410 P.2d 244, 246 (1966), in which the Oregon Supreme Court did not find any common law marriage proven, *inter alia*, given that there was no evidence "that the parties were aware that any change in their marital status would result or that the visit was made for the purpose of consummating a marriage." *See also Bridgman v. Stout*, 5 Ore.App. 558, 485 P.2d 1101 (1971). In *McGrath v. McGrath*, 387 S.W.2d 239 (Mo.App. 1965), which concerned a couple who lived together and outwardly appeared as spouses for approximately 8 years in Missouri, a state at that

any such evidence, no common law marriage was found, despite the fact that the parties lived together for sixteen years, of which ten years were without an impediment.

The courts' differing understandings concerning the marital intent's *essensialia* appear also to have received decisive significance for the results in the cases when they apply Pennsylvania law. In the cases in which the courts have required a legal intent, it has been more difficult with a short stay in a state to prove the establishment of a common law marriage than if the courts have required an intent to live as husband and wife.[137] A case in which the former intent was decisive is *Goldin v. Goldin* (1981), in which several ski trips to Pennsylvania did not give rise to a common law marriage. The parties had commenced their relationship in Buffalo, New York, in 1954 or 1955, while both were still married to others. These marriages were dissolved in 1956. For religious reasons, they never entered into any ceremonial marriage with each other. In 1958, the couple moved to Virginia and seven years later to Maryland where they lived for approximately fifteen years. They bought a house together, had two mutual children, submitted joint tax returns, had joint bank accounts, and lived in general as husband and wife. Neither New York, Virginia, nor Maryland recognize common law marriage.

During the period from 1964 to 1969, they traveled, however, almost every weekend and several holidays, together with the children, to Seven Springs, Pennsylvania, to ski. Pennsylvania recognizes common law marriage. They lived mostly in a motel where they registered as "Mr. and Mrs. Goldin." All four slept in the same room. The woman claimed that the couple had sexual relations there, which the man contested.

Later, the woman requested a divorce *a mensa et thoro* from the man. The issue arose whether a common law marriage had been established during their visits to Pennsylvania. The Court of Special Appeals in Maryland was reluctant to maintain that a man and woman who had traveled to a state recognizing common law marriages and lived there together several few days legally shall be considered to be husband and wife, unless a clear intent to enter into that status is shown. The court found that the evidence presented did not show that the parties intended their weekend or holiday ski trips to be construed as entry into a common law marriage.[138] The legal effects of marriage includes the duty in a marital

---

time not recognizing common law marriage, the parties had visited many states among which was Texas, where they outwardly presented themselves as spouses. The court stated that: "No suggestion is made and no evidence is submitted that any new or fresh agreement was made to become husband and wife in Texas or in any other state." In *Winn v. Wiggins*, 47 N.J.Super. 215, 135 A.2d 673, 677 (1957), the court required a *consensus* "of matrimonial character," which could not be fulfilled if the parties knew of a marriage impediment.

137 *See Renshaw v. Heckler*, 787 F.2d 50, 54 (2d. Cir. 1986).

138 *Goldin v. Goldin*, 48 Md.App. 154, 426 A.2d 410, 415 (1981). *See also Marino v. Anheuser-Bush*, Inc., 182 A.D.2d 1078, 583 N.Y.S.2d 68, 70 (A.D. 4 Dep't 1992), in

divorce to observe the imposed forms. Because the marriage contract was not accepted, it was a contract to establish a relationship that could be terminated as soon as any of the parties wished. Statements by a party revealing an unwillingness to be subjected to the regulations concerning

---

which the New York Supreme Court, Appellate Division, stated that the woman did not even allege that they discussed marriage plans in Pennsylvania and found that no common law marriage was established as evidence was lacking that the parties during their visits there "sought to establish the legal relationship of husband and wife." The court judged in a similar manner a visit that the parties made to Texas. Any evidence whatsoever that that the parties "agreed to marry" had not been presented. With respect to expressed agreements, *see In re McKanna's Estate,* 106 Cal. App.2d 126, 234 P.2d 673 (1951); *Sears v. Sears,* 267 A.D.2d 988, 700 N.Y.S.2d 626, 628 (A.D. 4 Dep't 1999); and *Dozack v. Dozack,* 137 A.D.2d 317, 528 N.Y.S.2d 712, 713 (A.D. 3 Dep't 1988). *See also In Re Matter of Grossman v. Gangel,* 192 A.D.2d 396, 596 N.Y.S.2d 53, 55, 625 N.E.2d 590 (A.D. 1 Dep't 1993), in which the parties made a stop of two nights in South Carolina en route to Florida. The court found that "any intent to assume marital status is contradicted by documentary evidence." *See also Cruickshank v. Cruickshank,* 93 Misc. 366, 82 N.Y.S.2d 522, 525 (1948), in which the court did not find a common law marriage established during the 16-hour stop the parties made in Texas based on poor weather conditions for flying. The court stated that the parties' appearance outwardly as spouses during their visit there "was not an act that was intended to result in a new status, a common law marriage." In *Abramson v. Abramson,* 161 Neb. 782, 74 N.W.2d 919 (1956), the parties had lived together approximately 20 years in Nebraska, a state not recognizing common law marriage, and approximately two years in Iowa, which recognizes such marriages. They had also received a reputation as husband and wife. The man appears to have been of the understanding that a common law marriage could be established based on that they "slept together," while the woman believed that it was sufficient with that she "(had) lived with him and had three children." Despite the fact that the Nebraska Supreme Court, which applied Iowa law, considered their cohabitation in Iowa as well as in Nebraska, the court did not find proven that they had "any agreement or understanding" to be husband and wife when they commenced their relationship and neither any intent to later change the relationship to a "legitimate relationship." In *Winder v. Winder,* 98 Cal.App.2d 78, 219 P.2d 18 (1950), the parties had lived together two years in Nebraska, a state that at that time recognized common law marriage. The court found however, that such a marriage had not been established and referred to that "there was no intention either on his part or her part to contract a common law marriage." The court pointed *inter alia* to the circumstance that the woman left the man when he did not keep his promise to acquire a license for a ceremonial marriage and that the man soon thereafter married ceremonially another woman. *Compare Ponzi v. Ponzi,* 157 Cal. App.2d 772, 321 P.2d 847, 850 (1958), in which the parties entered into a ceremonial marriage in Arizona, which was invalid due to an impediment. After the impediment was removed, the parties in May and June 1951 stayed in Oklahoma and Texas. The court found that the parties lived together as husband and wife, but stated that they retained "their residence" in California and that no discussion had arisen which indicated that they "intended to remarry" in Texas or Oklahoma. No common law marriage was found to be proven. *Compare Nevarez v. Bailon,* 287 S.W.2d 521 (Tex.Civ.App.-El Paso 1956), in which the parties in Mexico entered into an agreement "to live together" and did so for 13 years. The court found that they in accordance with Mexican law did not enter into a marriage but rather a "concubinage" which *inter alia* entailed certain rights to inheritance. The relationship however, could not upon the man's death be recognized as marriage in Texas.

marital divorce have been taken into consideration when the courts have rejected alleged marriage contracts.[139]

On the other hand, there are cases in which the courts did not require an intent during the short visit to Pennsylvania to change their status but only an intent to live as husband and wife. Apparently, the court in *Goldin* came to a conclusion other than those of the courts in the above cases of *McCullon* and *Renshaw*, which also concerned short visits to Pennsylvania, for reasons other than what the court itself appears to believe, namely, that it depended on the facts of each particular case. Rather, the differences reflect the courts' shifting assessments and uncertainty about the state of the law. In *Renshaw*, the court stated that there was no evidence that the parties, during eight trips through Pennsylvania, had any intent to create the marriage. However, the court did not apply such an intent as a requirement. It was sufficient that the parties, during their twenty-one-year relationship, had an intent to live as husband and wife and that their actions in Pennsylvania and "elsewhere" were the equivalent of a declaration of this intent. Consequently, the relevant difference between these cases and *Goldin* lies not so much in the facts but rather in the courts' legal understanding about the marital intent's *essensialia*.

Again, in *McCullon*, in which the parties stayed in Pennsylvania two to four weeks each year, the entire contract issue is in the background of the court's reasoning. The court instead found that the parties entered into a common law marriage by focusing on their holding out of each other as husband and wife in Pennsylvania. The court, on the other hand, did not otherwise refer to the parties' cohabitation, in the same manner as in *Renshaw*. The differences, consequently, are not so much in the facts as in the legal assessment.

The courts' vacillating attitudes are illustrated by the fact that the federal courts, as well as the courts in New York, in other cases in which a common law marriage has not been found proven, even though the issue is not more closely discussed, have leaned more toward legal intent.[140]

Generally, the increased mobility today of cohabiting couples evokes considerably greater caution in drawing conclusions from the parties'

---

139 In *People v. Badgett*, 41 Cal.Rptr.2d 635, 895 P.2d 877, 898 (1995), the woman stated at trial that she did not enter into marriage as she "did not want to have to get a divorce if the relationship did not work out." The California Supreme Court, applying Texas law, taking this and other circumstances into consideration, found that no marriage contract had been entered into and that no common law marriage had been established.

140 *Compare* the cases commented on below, *Chlieb v. Heckler*, 777 F.2d 842, 845 (2d Cir. 1985), in which the same court as in *Renshaw* stated that the marriage contract is a contract by which the parties enter into "the legal relationship of marriage." *See also In re Landolfi*, 724 N.Y.S.2d 470 (N.Y.A.D., 2 Dep't 2001), in which the man's unwillingness to formally marry "because of the dissension it would create in his family" entirely undermined the woman's statement that the parties intended to create "the legal relationship of husband and wife." With respect to the marital intent's *essensialia* in Pennsylvania law, *see* Section 6.3.2 *supra.*

cohabitation and reputation concerning their marital intentions! Certain couples can have the intention to simply live together for a trial period or perhaps only to take a trip together. Others can have the intention to live together without any legal ties. A short visit to a common law marriage state need not mean that the parties subjected themselves to its law. The warnings in the case law concerning "the untrustworthiness of mere cohabitation and reputation as proof of marriage" have increased the relevance of short visits to common law marriage states.[141]

There is another method, in addition to the choice of law applied requirement of domicile or permanent residence in a common law marriage state, for preventing the creation of marriages based on inferred agreements and on presumptions and the inconvenience of parties unknowingly becoming married. It is to require a legal intent, *i.e.*, an intent to receive the legal effects of marriage or to change their marital status. Such an intent is difficult to prove with the support of the parties' cohabitation and holding out, particularly if the evaluation is limited to the parties' actions during a short visit to a common law marriage state. However, even though the parties lived together many years in their state of domicile, they can have chosen to live together without legal ties.

10.3.3 The Marriage Presumption

The marriage presumption as introduced in Chapter 9, "Burdens of Proof and Presumptions," is also applicable to cases in which couples make short visits to common law marriage states. An application of the presumption, consequently, assumes constant cohabitation and a general reputation as spouses. No inferred marriage contract need be proven. If these conditions exist, the presumption's legal effects mean that the parties, during the short visit, are presumed to have entered into a formless marriage contract or to have possessed a marital *consensus*. Because the presumption is rebuttable, the evidentiary burden of proof shifts to the opposing party, who has to prove that such an agreement has not been executed. If that party is not successful, a common law marriage is established. Because the presumption can be viewed as strong, the opposing party has a heavy burden of proof. Commonly, the presumption has not been viewed as applicable if the relationship from the beginning has been "meretricious,"[142] or it has been alleged that the parties entered into a marriage

141 *In re Erickson's Estate*, 75 S.D. 345, 64 N.W.2d 316, 320 (1954).

142 For example, in *McGrath v. McGrath*, 387 S.W.2d 239 (Mo.App. 1965), which concerned a couple who lived together and outwardly appeared as spouses for approximately 8 years in Missouri, a state that at that time did not recognize common law marriage, the parties had visited many states among which was Texas, where they outwardly presented themselves as spouses. The court cited a case from Missouri from the period in which common law marriages could be entered into there as support for a presumption that "the status existing upon the inception of the relationship is presumed to continue absent proof to the contrary," *see Cargile v. Wood*,

contract at a certain point of time and place and there is direct evidence concerning these facts in the form of the parties' statements.[143] For more concerning the marriage presumption, see Chapter 9 *supra.*

With the application of the presumption to cases in which the parties took short trips to a state where a common law marriage could be entered into, the question arises about how the requirements of constant cohabitation and general reputation can be viewed as fulfilled because both elements reasonably can only come into existence over a certain period. A significant issue in these assessments is whether the courts have considered their cohabitation in the state in which they were domiciled as well as the parties' actions in the state of the visit, or only the latter.

1. *The Parties' Actions in the Common Law Marriage State*

Limiting the evidence to simply the parties' actions during the short visit to a common law marriage state appears to be a conflict of law influenced application of *lex loci contractus.* This means that not only is the issue of choice of law based on the parties' actions in the state of the visit,[144] but also that, with the application of the local law, only events taking place in the common law marriage state are considered.[145] Such a limitation as to the evidence can appear to make it difficult to prove the existence of constant cohabitation and general reputation. Even though the parties, during a several-day visit to such a state, act as spouses, one can ask whether

---

63 Mo. 501 (1876). No new marriage contract was found to be proven in Texas. No presumption based on cohabitation and appearance outwardly was applied. *See also In re Estate of Watts,* 31 N.Y.2d 491, 341 N.Y.S.2d 609, 294 N.E.2d 195 (1973). *Compare McCullon v. McCullon,* 410 N.Y.S.2d 226 (1978), summarized below in the text. For more concerning the exceptions, *see* Section 9.6 *supra.*

143 In the case of *In re Landolfi,* 724 N.Y.S.2d 470, 473 (N.Y.A.D., 2 Dep't 2001), the woman, according to the New York Supreme Court, Appellate Division, could not cite the presumption applicable in Pennsylvania as she testified concerning a verbal agreement. With respect to Pennsylvania law, *see In re Veneziale,* 267 B.R. 695, 700 (Bkrtcy.E.D.Pa. 2001); *Staudenmayer v. Staudenmayer,* 714 A.2d 1016, 1021 (Pa. 1998); *Eagle v. W.C.A.B. (Bahorich),* 602 A.2d 387, 388-390 (Pa. Commw. 1992); *In re Estate of Rees,* 331 Pa.Super. 225, 228, 480 A.2d 327 (1984); *In re Nikitka's Estate,* 346 Pa. 63, 65, 29 A.2d 521, 522 (1943); *Mainor v. Midvale Co.,* 192 Pa.Super.Ct. 367, 162 A.2d 27, 30 (1960); *In re Estate of Stauffer,* 476 A.2d 354, 357 (Pa. 1984); *In re Horton's Estate,* 357 Pa. 30, 52 A.2d 895, 897 (1947); *Fiedler v. Nat'l Tube Co.,* 161 Pa.Super. 155, 53 A.2d 821, 823 (1947); *In re McGrath's Estate,* 319 Pa. 309, 179 A. 599, 602 (1935); *In re Murdock's Estate,* 92 Pa.Super. 275 (1927); *In re Craig's Estate,* 273 Pa. 530, 117 A. 221, 222 (1922); *Richard v. Brehm,* 73 Pa. 140, 144 (1873); and *Comw. v. Stump,* 53 Pa. 132, 91 Am.Dec. 198 (1866). For more concerning these cases, *see* Chapter 9 *supra.*

144 By "state where the marriage was contracted" is meant according to Restatement (Second) of Conflict of Law (1971), the state in which the marriage was celebrated or "where some other act was done that is claimed to have resulted in the creation of a marriage status." *See* Restatement (Second) of Conflict of Laws § 283 cmt. e (1971). *See also* comment g, from which it can be seen that the marriage cannot be viewed as invalid if "the acts relied upon to create the marriage meet the requirements of the state where the acts took place."

145 *Compare* Charles W. Taintor, *Marriage in the Conflict of Laws,* 9 Vand. L. Rev. 607, 621 (1956); Restatement (Second) of Conflict of Laws § 283 cmt. e (1971).

their actions fulfill the requirement of a cohabitation in which the main element is "constancy of dwelling together" and whether, during this short time, they succeed in acquiring a reputation as spouses that is "broad and general, not partial and divided."[146]

Nevertheless, the case law demonstrates, on one side, cases, in which a common law marriage has been established simply based on the actions of the man and woman in the state of the visit. For example, in *McCullon v. McCullon* (1978), the parties, in 1948, had moved in together in Buffalo, New York. The woman was then still married to another man, from whom she received a marital divorce in 1953. The couple never entered into any ceremonial marriage with each other. However, they lived together as husband and wife and had three mutual children. The woman received a wedding ring from the man and took his last name. She was introduced among their friends as his wife. They had joint bank accounts and bought their residence in New York together. They submitted their tax returns as husband and wife. The woman was a housewife and the man was responsible for the family's maintenance. For twenty-eight years, they lived together as husband and wife in New York, a state not recognizing common law marriage. However, for two to four weeks every year during the period from 1948 to 1977, that parties visited family and friends in Cresco, Pennsylvania, a state recognizing common law marriage. During the visits to Cresco, they shared a bedroom. The woman was presented as the man's wife and in general they held themselves out as husband and wife.

When the couple separated in 1977, the woman petitioned for spousal maintenance from the man and cited as grounds that a common law marriage had been established during their visits to Pennsylvania. The New York Supreme Court, Erie County, found that the parties entered into a valid common law marriage resulting from their holding out each other as husband and wife in Pennsylvania after her divorce in 1953.[147]

Of the two methods that Pennsylvania law offers for establishing a common law marriage, it is clear that the court did not apply the one entailing that

---

146 In *Sears v. Sears*, 267 A.D.2d 988, 700 N.Y.S.2d 626, 628 (A.D. 4 Dep't 1999), the parties who had lived together in New York for approximately 12 years, made short visits to South Carolina, Pennsylvania, and the District of Columbia. The woman, who petitioned for divorce, could not demonstrate that her reputation as married was "broad and general" rather than "partial or divided." No common law marriage was considered established. *Compare French v. State Indus. Accident Comm'n*, 156 Ore. 443, 68 P.2d 466 (1937), in which only the fact that the parties during their visits to Idaho, a state in which common law marriage could be entered into at that time, did not do more than live together, was insufficient for an application of the marriage presumption. For more concerning the requirement of reputation with the application of the marriage presumption, *see* Chapter 9 *supra*.

147 *McCullon v. McCullon*, 410 N.Y.S.2d 226, 227 (1978). The court's reasoning in *Goldin v. Goldin*, 48 Md.App. 154, 426 A.2d 410, 413 (1981) appears to have been incorrectly understood so that the court also considered the "New York cohabitation."

such a marriage is based on the existence of a verbal marriage contract.[148] The parties' "holding out ... as husband and wife" was not cited as evidence for an expressed agreement or for a marital *consensus.* Instead, it appears that the court, despite the fact that the relationship from the beginning was meretricious, applied the marriage presumption. The reasoning, however, is terse. The court carries out no extensive scrutiny of whether the two conditions, constant cohabitation and general reputation, are fulfilled. Rather, it concludes in more sweeping terms the existence of a marriage from their holding out as husband and wife. It ought herewith to be noted that the court in its stated reasons only refers to their cohabitation during the visits to Pennsylvania. Even though the visits there lasted two to four weeks every year between 1953 and 1977, the court undeniably gives the parties' holding out during the visits a strikingly high evidentiary weight.

The case law also includes, on the other hand, cases in which the courts' consideration of only the parties' actions in the state of the visit have resulted in the presumption's requirements for cohabitation and reputation not being found fulfilled. For example, in *Vandever v. Industrial Comm'n of Arizona* (1985), the parties had their domicile in Arizona, a state not recognizing common law marriage. They lived there and held themselves out as spouses for approximately seven years. They had two mutual children.

In 1978, the parties stayed three weeks in Colorado to attend a family wedding and to look for employment. Colorado recognizes common law marriage. During the visit, they were presented as husband and wife to everyone they met. They were even in a local newspaper, which drew attention to the wedding, designated as Mr. and Mrs. Vandever. They lived in the newlyweds' apartment while the couple was on their honeymoon. During their visit to Colorado, they were listening to a radio program concerning common law marriage and drew the conclusion that they actually were married according to valid law in Colorado. In 1979, they again visited Colorado for two weeks so that the man could look for employment. Thereafter, they lived in other states and later resided again in Arizona, living there until the man's death in 1983. By then, they had lived together for approximately seven years.

Upon the man's death, the question arose whether the woman was entitled to workers' compensation on the basis of a common law marriage established during their visits to Colorado. The Arizona Court of Appeals, finding no oral marriage contract proven during the parties' visits to Colorado,[149] ruled that the woman did not present clear and positive

148 *See, e.g., Staudenmayer v. Staudenmayer,* 714 A.2d 1016, 1020 (Pa. 1998), in which the Pennsylvania Supreme Court required "an exchange of words in the present tense" in several cases in Chapter 6.2.2 *supra.*

149 *See* Section 6.5 *supra.*

evidence of both cohabitation and general repute in Colorado. The circumstance that the parties, in connection with the wedding ceremony, an isolated event, held themselves out as husband and wife, was not deemed sufficient by the court to apply the marriage presumption.[150] If the court had also taken into consideration the parties' seven-year cohabitation in Arizona, a common law marriage probably would have been established based on the presumption.

2. *The Parties' Actions in States Other than the Common Law Marriage State*

The courts, when applying the marriage presumption to short visits to common law marriage states, commonly consider not only their actions there, but also their conduct in the state in which they are domiciled and in other states, even those in which such marriages cannot be formed. This naturally facilitates the possibility of establishing such marriages. The parties may have lived together solely in the home state as husband and wife for many years without formally entering into marriage.

For example, in *Tornese v. Tornese* (1996), the parties, who were living in New York, two months after they had received a judgment of marital divorce, visited Pennsylvania during a weekend. During the visit, according to the plaintiff, the man had said to her that "their divorce about two month[s] earlier had been a mistake." The woman had agreed and, according to her, they decided that "they were married." The man objected that they agreed to be married anew. During the following fifteen years, they lived together in New York and held themselves out as husband and wife, but also made additional trips to Pennsylvania.

The New York Supreme Court, Appellate Division, did not decide whether the plaintiff succeeded in proving the existence of an expressed marriage contract, but rather applied the marriage presumption and found overwhelming evidence that the requirements of constant cohabitation and general reputation were fulfilled. The evidentiary burden of proof, consequently, was shifted to the defendant, who had to demonstrate that no marriage contract had been established. Because the man did not succeed in rebutting the presumption, a common law marriage was found established.[151]

---

150 *Vandever v. Indus. Com'n of Arizona*, 714 P.2d 866 (Ariz.App. 1985). With respect to short visits to Colorado, *see also In Re Enoch's Estate*, 52 Ill.App.2d 39, 201 N.E.2d 682 (1964), in which the Illinois court found that two weeks in Colorado, during which the woman had introduced the man as her husband, were insufficient to constitute a valid common law marriage. *See also In re Binger's Estate*, 158 Neb. 444, 63 N.W.2d 784 (1954), in which a Nebraska court found that pleasure trips of 3-4 days to Colorado were insufficient to constitute a common law marriage, as the couple did not change their domicile and neither entered into any agreement while they were in Colorado.

151 *Tornese v. Tornese*, 649 N.Y.S.2d 177 (A.D.2 Dep't 1996). The court's conclusion with a reversal of the evidentiary burden of proof is an entirely correct application of

It naturally can be questioned whether the relationship between the parties during their short trips to Pennsylvania lawfully ought to be considered a constant cohabitation and whether, during these trips, they truly could be viewed as having acquired a reputation as spouses which was broad and general, not partial or divided. A certain period reasonably is required to fulfill both requirements. The answer to the issue, however, is that the court, in assessing both elements, considered not only their conduct during the visits to Pennsylvania but also their actions at home in New York, both before as well as after the trips. The parties, after the first trip to Pennsylvania, lived together for fifteen years, so it is not so surprising that the court found the requirements for an application of the presumption fulfilled.[152]

---

the presumption. *Compare* the above commented case, *Renshaw v. Heckler*, 787 F.2d 50, 54 (2d Cir. 1986), in which the court did not equally strictly adhere to the reasoning according to the presumption. Instead, the court there finds "a declaration" that the parties in Pennsylvania had assumed a relationship as husband and wife.

152 The same court, with the application of the marriage presumption, comes to the same conclusion, however, with a less clean reasoning, in *Carpenter v. Carpenter*, 617 N.Y.S.2d 903 (A.D. 2 Dep't 1994). There the parties lived together as husband and wife in New York for 25 years. They took the same last name, had and raised two mutual children, and had joint bank accounts. They submitted joint income tax statements and the woman was listed as beneficiary of the man's insurances. The parties appeared outwardly as spouses and had the reputation as such. The man in a birthday card called the woman his "wife" and his mother called her "daughter-in-law." The couple had made two short visits to Pennsylvania, one week in 1969 and four days in 1989. When they later separated, the woman petitioned that the court should declare that a valid common law marriage had been established during their visits to Pennsylvania. The New York Supreme Court, Appellate Division, found with the application of the marriage presumption, which requires "constant cohabitation" and "general reputation" as spouses, that the plaintiff "overwhelmingly demonstrated, without rebuttal from the defendant (except for various blanket denials), that the parties entered into a valid common law marriage in June 1969 when they held themselves out as husband and wife while staying in Pennsylvania." It is obvious that the court considered the parties'conduct in New York both prior to and after the visit to Pennsylvania. A more correct reasoning ought to have first contained a statement that the plaintiff demonstrated the existence of "constant cohabitation" and "general reputation" and thereafter a statement that the defendant did not demonstrate that a marriage contract was not established. *Compare Sears v. Sears*, 267 A.D.2d 988, 700 N.Y.S.2d 626, 628 (A.D. 4 Dep't 1999), in which the parties, who lived together in New York approximately 12 years, had made short visits to South Carolina, Pennsylvania, and the District of Columbia. The court found that the woman did not demonstrate that the parties outwardly appeared as husband and wife in Pennsylvania or that her reputation as married was "broad and general" rather than "partial or divided." Even the parties' reputation in New York was considered. *See also In re Landolfi*, 724 N.Y.S.2d 470 (N.Y.A.D., 2 Dep't 2001), in which the parties lived 26 years in New York and made an overnight visit to Pennsylvania. Despite the fact that the court did not find the presumption applicable and not Pennsylvania law in general, it made a statement indicating that it was prepared to also take into consideration the parties' actions in New York, but still did not find the requirement of "broad and general reputation" fulfilled as the testimony from several few neighbors and friends was not considered sufficient. *Compare In Re Matter of Estate of Abbott*, 592 N.Y.S.2d 729, 730 (A.D. 1 Dep't 1993), in which the parties spent one night in Pennsylvania, and had

More surprising is the great weight as evidence that the parties' cohabitation and reputation during a short visit has been attributed in some cases. In, e.g., *Blaw-Knox Construction Equip. Co. v. Morris* (1991), the parties were domiciled in Maryland and had lived together and held each other out as husband and wife there for more than thirty years. They had six children, submitted joint tax returns, and the man named the woman as the beneficiary of his life insurance. In 1983, they visited Pennsylvania for a funeral, staying two nights at a motel. During the visit, they met several of the man's relatives.

When he died in 1985 in an accident at work, the woman filed for compensation in her capacity as the deceased's surviving spouse in a common law marriage constituted during the their visit in Pennsylvania. The court held: "Although the Morris' stay in Pennsylvania was certainly brief, Mrs. Morris did present evidence of reputation in Pennsylvania, *i.e.*, holding themselves out as husband and wife to all the Pennsylvania friends and relatives and cohabitation in Pennsylvania, *i.e.*, the two nights in the Pennsylvania motel." A common law marriage was found constituted.[153]

3. Counter-evidence Rebutting the Presumption

If the elements of cohabitation and reputation exist, this invokes the presumption's legal effects, as seen in Chapter 9, that the parties during the visit to a common law marriage state are presumed to have entered into an informal marriage contract or to have possessed a marital *consensus*. As the presumption is rebuttable, the evidentiary burden of proof shifts to the other party, who has to prove that no such agreement has been executed. Despite the presumption's strength and the difficulties of proving the negative of a fact, there is no lack of cases in which it has been successfully rebutted. As evidence for finding that the parties did not possess any marital *consensus* with a visit to a common law marriage state, the courts have also accepted facts stemming from other states.

For example, in *Chlieb v. Heckler* (1985), the parties lived together in New York from 1958 to 1976, when the relationship was dissolved through separation. During these eighteen years, they had two mutual children. Directly before they commenced the cohabitation, the woman declined

a relationship for 25 years in New York during which they often lived together. The court did not find proven that the parties "held themselves out as husband and wife or established a general reputation as husband and wife in the community..." The court does not state whether it also considered the cohabitation in New York. It ought to be noted that an impediment existed against the marriage. In *Matter of Heitman's Estate*, 154 Misc. 838, 279 N.Y.S. 108, 113 (1935), a woman claimed that the parties had entered into a common law marriage during a one night stay in Pennsylvania. After the visit, the parties had separate residences. The woman's reputation was questioned. The court held that the acts of the parties did not show "that they were living together as husband and wife" and found that no common law marriage existed. For more concerning the marriage presumption, *see* Chapter 9, *supra*.

153 *Blaw-Knox Construction Equip. Co. v. Morris*, 596 A.2d 679 (Md.Spec.App. 1991).

the man's marriage proposal; when she proposed marriage after the birth of her first child in 1959, the man said that, "he felt it too late to marry."[154]

The couple spent one night in Ohio and two nights in Pennsylvania in August of 1973 in connection with traveling through these states. In both Ohio and Pennsylvania, a common law marriage could be entered into legally. In deciding whether such a marriage had been established during their travels and whether the woman for reason thereof was entitled to spousal benefits, the Court of Appeals found that the evidence showed that the parties did not have any intent to marry when they spent their nights in Pennsylvania and Ohio. Because they had not entered into any common law marriage, the woman was not entitled to the benefits.

The reason that the Court of Appeals in *Chlieb*, in which the parties lived together in New York for eighteen years and took short trips to Pennsylvania and Ohio, comes to a conclusion different from the one in *Renshaw*, in which the parties lived together for twenty years in New York and took short trips to Pennsylvania, appears to be that each of the parties in *Chlieb* had refused marriage proposals from the other. It ought to be noted that this occurred in the state of New York, where they were domiciled and long before the actual trips occurred. In some cases, the counter-evidence has not been sufficient to rebut the presumption.[155]

In Chapter 9, it was questioned whether there is reason, in those jurisdictions in which common law marriages can be entered into, to maintain, in general, a legal marriage presumption that is the opposite of the basic evidentiary rules about the burden of proof, which place a heavy burden on the party alleging the existence of a common law marriage. It can be seen in this section that the presumption's application in cases in which the parties have made short visits to common law marriage states has given further fuel to questions about whether the elements of cohabitation and reputation today, typically, can be viewed as constituting *prima facie* evidence for the presence of a marital *consensus*. It is not unusual, today, for couples to live together without any intent to establish a legal relationship. The future of the marriage presumption is discussed in Chapter 13, where it is suggested that it be repealed.

4. *A Special Presumption According to Texas Law*

A special presumption is applied according to the legislation in Texas. It applies to cases in which the parties entered into a common law marriage in accordance with the requirements there; agreed to be married; "lived

154 *Chlieb v. Heckler*, 777 F.2d 842, 845-846 (2d Cir. 1985).

155 In *Blaw-Knox Construction Equip. Co. v. Morris*, 596 A.2d 679 (Md.Spec.App. 1991), the woman witnessed that the man "kept telling me he was gonna marry me." These plans to marry in the future were assumed only to connote a formal ceremony, not the marriage. The statement therefore did not prevent the parties from becoming common law married during the two-days-visit in Pennsylvania.

together in this state as husband and wife"; and there "represented to others that they were married,"[156] but the marriage is invalid because one of the parties was already married. If the previous marriage is dissolved, the new marriage becomes valid if the parties "have lived together as husband and wife and represented themselves to others as being married," see TEX. FAM. CODE ANN. § 6.202 (1988).[157] No new agreement is required after the removal of the impediment. The parties' cohabitation and holding out as spouses need not, in contrast to the original cohabitation, occur in Texas but rather can occur in another state recognizing common law marriage. In *Orr v. Bowen* (1986), the United States District Court in Nevada stated that: "Under Texas law the necessary acts need not take place in Texas, but they must occur in a state where common law marriage can be contracted."[158] It therewith has been sufficient with short visits.[159]

This presumption deviates entirely from the law in the majority of other states in which the marriage presumption may not be applied because the parties lived together while either of them are still married to another. In most states, it is presumed that, after the removal of the impediment, the relationship continues to be illicit or meretricious, which means that a new marriage contract must be proven for a common law marriage to be able to be established.[160] However, it ought to be noted that an application of § 6.202 assumes that the parties have a previous mutual history when they fulfilled the requirements of establishing a common law marriage in Texas, albeit that the marriage was invalid.[161]

156 TEX. FAM. CODE ANN. § 2.401 (a)(2) (Vernon 2005). Comparable to the previous § 1.91 (a)(2)(Vernon's 1975).

157 Comparable to the previous § 2.22 and *see also Ballesteros v. Jones*, 985 S.W.2d 485, 490 (Tex.App.-San Antonio 1998); *Garduno v. Garduno*, 760 S.W.2d 735 (Tex.App.-Corpus Christi 1988); *Braddock v. Taylor*, 592 S.W.2d 40 (Tex.Civ.App.-Beaumont 1979); and *Rodriguez v. Avalos*, 567 S.W.2d 85 (Tex.Civ.App. 1978).

158 *Orr v. Bowen*, 648 F.Supp. 1510, 1513 (D.Nev. 1986), citing *Braddock v. Taylor*, 592 S.W.2d 40, 42 (Tex.Civ.App.-Beaumont 1979), in which cohabitation in California was not accepted in accordance with § 2.22.

159 In *Rogers v. Sullivan*, 795 F.Supp. 761 (E.D.N.C. 1992), it was sufficient with nine visits of typically three days with family members in South Carolina. It ought to be noted that a common law marriage was not found to be established in accordance with South Carolina law, which requires a new agreement after the removal of the impediment. In *Orr v. Bowen*, 648 F.Supp. 1510 (D.Nev. 1986), it was sufficient that the parties after the removal of the impediment made two or three return visits to Texas to visit family members. The longest lasted two weeks. *Compare Durr v. Newman*, 537 S.W.2d 323 (Tex.Civ.App.-El Paso 1976), in which three days in Nevada was sufficient, probably due to a procedural error.

160 For more on this, *see* Chapter 9 *supra*.

161 *Compare* William W. Morris, *Common Law Marriage and Palimony* (May 1990), p. B-22, unpublished paper, Marriage Dissolution Institute, Houston, which uses the expression "springing marriages" to demonstrate that § 2.22 "causes a valid marriage to 'spring' from an invalid marriage."

10.4 The Requirement of Cohabitation and Reputation as Spouses

It has been seen that the parties' cohabitation and reputation as spouses is taken into consideration as evidence for the existence of an inferred marriage contract as discussed in Section 10.3.2, "Inferred Marriage Agreements," and also as an element in the marriage presumption in Section 10.3.3, "The Marriage Presumption," when *lex loci contractus* is applied in the case law. As we found in Chapter 8, however, the parties' cohabitation and reputation as spouses, today, also constitutes a necessary requirement in addition to the contract in all of these jurisdictions in which a common law marriage can be entered into with the exceptions of Pennsylvania[162] and South Carolina, albeit that it appears that the courts in New York do not always correctly interpret Pennsylvania law on this point.[163]

162 Pennsylvania law offers two methods of establishing a common law marriage. The party claiming the existence of such a marriage can either try to prove the existence of a verbal marriage contract, which if it succeeds is sufficient, or in accordance with the marriage presumption, try to prove the existence of cohabitation and reputation, whereafter the evidentiary burden of proof shifts to the opposing party which has to prove that no agreement has been established. The party claiming that a common law marriage has been established consequently needs not demonstrate both the existence of a contract and cohabitation and reputation. With respect to the requirement in Pennsylvania of a verbal expression of the parties'marital intent, *see* Section 6.2.2 *supra.* With respect to the lack in the same state of a requirement for "cohabitation and acknowledgment" as a necessary requisite, *see* Section 8.4 *supra.* With respect to the marriage presumption, *see* Chapter 9 *supra.*

163 *See, e.g., Peart v. T.D. Bross Line Constr. Co.*, 357 N.Y.S.2d 53, 54-55 (3rd Dep. 1974), in which the New York Supreme Court, Appellate Division, stated that a common law marriage in accordance with Pennsylvania law must be proven through "a verbal expression of an intention to be married" and further that it be followed by "cohabitation and acknowledgment." *See also Cross v. Cross*, 541 N.Y.S.2d 202, 205 (A.D. 1 Dep't 1989), in which the same court found that the woman neither had shown any "intention to be married" or "cohabitation or reputation of the type required to evidence a common law marriage in Pennsylvania." The court certainly could have intended, but gives no indication of doing so, that "cohabitation and reputation" are required for an application of the marriage presumption. Their manner of expression gives rather the impression in the situation that it intended that these elements in Pennsylvania are necessary in addition to the contract. The court in the case of *In Re Matter of Estate of Abbott*, 592 N.Y.S.2d 729, 730 (A.D. 1 Dep't 1993) appears to have taken the same principal stance. There the parties did not succeed in fulfilling "the requirements of the laws of that state" in the absence of evidence that they had the intent to live together as husband and wife and in the absence of evidence that they "held themselves out as husband and wife or established a general reputation as husband and wife in the community." *Compare Dozack v. Dozack*, 137 A.D.2d 317, 528 N.Y.S.2d 712 (A.D. 3 Dep't 1988) and *In Re Matter of Danza*, 188 A.D.2d 530, 591 N.Y.S.2d 197, 198 (1992), in which according to the courts a common law marriage appears to be able to be based on only a contract. *See also In re Landolfi*, 724 N.Y.S.2d 470 (N.Y.A.D., 2 Dep't 2001), according to which a common law marriage entirely correctly can be entered into either through a verbal agreement or with the support of the presumption. In *Craddock's Case*, 37 N.E.2d 508, 511-512 (Mass. 1941), it also appears that the Supreme Judicial Court

As seen in Chapter 8, the legal concept of cohabitation can be divided into two main components, *cohabitation*, in a narrower meaning encompassing the relationship between the parties, and their *holding out* and *reputation* as spouses, *i.e.*, their appearance to others and the reputation they thereby acquired.

The requirement of cohabitation is sometimes formulated as a requirement of cohabitation, cohabitation as husband and wife, or living together as husband and wife. Another commonly existing formulation is assumption of the marital relation or assumption of marital rights, duties and obligations. Normally, a mutual residence and a marital cohabitation are required for the requirement of cohabitation to be seen as fulfilled. A third construction has been a requirement of consummation or that the agreement shall be consummated by cohabitation. In addition to this, cohabitation in this more limited sense is not always constructed as a particular requirement but rather is contained in the concepts of holding out and reputation as spouses. With respect to the more defined classification of the concept of cohabitation and its different component elements, refer to Chapter 8.[164]

Chapter 8, in addition, shows that, of the jurisdictions applying a requirement of cohabitation as a necessary requirement for the establishment of a common law marriage, it appears that all, except Georgia and probably the District of Columbia, also apply a requirement that the parties must appear as spouses outwardly to others. This requirement either takes aim at the parties' actions themselves, in other words, their holding out as spouses, or at the effect thereof, *i.e.*, their reputation as husband and wife.

With respect to the requirement of holding out, it is commonly applied as a requirement of holding out as husband and wife; in other words, that the parties outwardly, before others, appeared as husband and wife, or without changing the content, that the parties must have represented to others that they were married. Certain courts formulate the requirement of holding out as a requirement of a public declaration that the parties are husband and wife, including words as well as actions. Courts also frame the requirement in more general terms by requiring that the cohabitation be open or public, or that the parties have lived together professedly as husband and wife, such that it is understood how they outwardly appeared before the public. Normally, reputation requires that the parties, before family members, friends, and acquaintances, and outwardly in the community in which they

in Massachusetts, incorrectly applying Pennsylvania law, required "open cohabitation" and "reputation," as well as "assent by the parties." The same incorrect interpretation of the state of the law in Pennsylvania recurs in the case law from Ohio, *see e.g., In re Zemmick's Estate*, 17 Ohio Supp. 15, 76 N.E.2d 902, 905-906 (1946). For more concerning the application of the pure contract principle and of the marriage presumption in Pennsylvania, *see* Section 8.2 and Chapter 9 *supra.*

164 *See* Section 8.5 and 8.6 *supra.*

live, appear as husband and wife. In certain cases, the courts had no particular requirement of holding out, but rather found that this was contained in the requirement of assumption of the marital relation, or in the requirement of assumption of marital rights, duties or obligations.[165] Building a reputation normally requires more time than a short visit allows.[166]

The question is raised here about how the above-named requirements in accordance with *lex loci contractus* have been applied to couples who have their domicile in, or another tie to, states other than the common law marriage state. For example, the parties, during a several-day visit to a common law marriage state, act as spouses, and there is no requirement of a minimum time of cohabitation. Nevertheless, one can question whether their actions fulfill the requirement of a cohabitation if the main element is constancy of dwelling together; and whether, during that short time, they have succeeded in acquiring a reputation as spouses that is broad and general, not partial and divided. Both elements ought reasonably to require a certain period of time in order to come into existence. The requirements of cohabitation and holding out can, therefore, serve the purpose of preventing the creation of common law marriages with temporary visits, and ensure that the legal effects of marriage are given only to couples who truly live together. A significant question in these assessments is whether the courts have taken into consideration the parties' actions only in the state of the visit or whether they also considered their cohabitation in the state in which they are domiciled.

1. The Parties' Actions in a Common Law Marriage State

Charles Taintor has maintained that if both the contract and cohabitation are necessary for the establishment of a common law marriage, both must occur in a state in which a common law marriage can be entered into legally.[167] This stance can appear natural from a conflict of laws' perspective. The place for the marriage's commencement is determined consequently by both the contract and cohabitation. The principle that both elements must have occurred in a common law marriage state is not equally obvious if the choice of law question has been decided and concerns the application of local law, as discussed further below. Still, it appears that the principle commonly has been guiding even with the last-named examinations. Moreover, the legal grounds have varied.

In *Texas*, this principle has even been expressed in the legislation, which is unusual. In addition to a requirement that the parties agreed to be married, the legislation in Texas contains an explicit requirement that they

165 *See* Section 8.6 *supra.*
166 *Id.*
167 Taintor, *supra* note 7, at 621. As support hereof, the author cites *Ferraro v. Ferraro*, 77 N.Y.S.2d 246 (Dom.Rel.Ct. 1948).

"lived together *in this state* as husband and wife and there represented to others that they were married" (italics added).[168] This requirement, which appears to be a codification of earlier case law,[169] naturally limits the possibilities of constituting a common law marriage through a short visit to Texas.[170] No minimum time of cohabitation is required according to Texas

---

168 *See* TEX. FAM. CODE ANN. § 2.401 (a)(2) (Vernon 2005), which corresponds to the previous § 1.91 (a)(2)(Vernon's 1975); Common law marriage was codified in Texas through Act of June 2, 1969, 61 st Leg., R.S. ch. 888 § 1.91, 1969 Tex.Gen. Laws 2707.2717, which came into force in 1970. *See also Matter of Estate of Burroughs*, 486 N.W.2d 113 (Mich.App. 1992). In *Jones v. Int'l Tel. & Tel. Corp.*, 462 So.2d 1348 (La.App. 3 Cir. 1985), the parties who for 20 years resided in Texas, after their divorce continued the cohabitation there approximately nine months until the man's death. The Court of Appeals in Louisiana found that a common law marriage was established.

169 For example, in *Grant v. Superior Court*, 27 Ariz.App. 427, 555 P.2d 895 (1976), the parties, who were living in Arizona, together with another couple traveled to El Paso, Texas, where they checked into a motel. During the hotel visit, which lasted three hours, the parties, according to the woman, entered into "an agreement to be husband and wife and consummated the marriage." Thereafter they left the hotel and told the other couple that they were married. The group spent the remainder of the day in Juarez, Mexico. They returned to Arizona, where they since then lived together as husband and wife. The man bought wedding rings and the couple appeared outwardly as spouses. In a lawsuit concerning spousal maintenance on the basis that a common law marriage had been established during the parties' visit to Texas, the question arose whether the requirement according to Texas law of "cohabitation as husband and wife" was fulfilled. The Arizona Court of Appeals stated that cohabitation means "dwelling together" as husband and wife and that the requirement includes "the many facets of married life in addition to sexual relations." To allow the couple in Arizona to fulfill the requirement of cohabitation would be, according to the court, "frustrating the laws of Texas." In *Marek v. Flemming*, 192 F.Supp. 528, 533 (S.D.Tex. 1961), trips to Texas did not result in a valid common law marriage as the parties did not have any intent "of acquiring residence in Texas." In *Cruickshank v. Cruickshank*, 93 Misc. 366, 82 N.Y.S.2d 522 (1948), the court stated that "no valid common law marriage between Robert and Josephine resulted by reason of their acts at the time of the sixteen hours stop-over in the State of Texas." *See also Kelly v. Consolidated Underwriters*, 300 S.W. 981 (Tex.Civ.App. 1927), *aff'd*, 15 S.W.2d 229 (Tex.Com.App. 1929). *Compare Gallegos v. Wilkerson*, 79 N.M. 549, 445 P.2d 970 (1968), in which the parties, who were living in New Mexico, in November of 1937 rented an apartment in El Paso, Texas, where they came to agreement as to marriage and lived together and outwardly appeared as husband and wife. The lower court found a common law marriage proven and the New Mexico Supreme Court found that this conclusion had the support of substantial evidence. *See also Parish v. Minvielle*, 217 So.2d 684 (La.App. 3d Cir. 1969), in which a common law marriage was found to be proven.

170 In *Kelderhaus v. Kelderhaus*, 467 S.E.2d 303 (Va.App. 1996), one night in Texas and one night in Oklahoma were not sufficient to constitute a common law marriage. In the case of *In Re Matter of Estate of Necastro*, 1990 Del.Ch. LEXIS 123 (1990), the parties, who lived together approximately 20 years in Delaware, had upon several occasions visited Texas. As they did not live together in Texas, the Court of Chancery of Delaware found no common law marriage proven. *See also Etienne v. DKM Enterprises, Inc.*, 136 Cal.App.3rd 487, 186 Cal.Rptr. 321 (1982), where 7-8 days in Texas was not sufficient. In the case of *In Re Matter of Estate of Lamb*, 99 N.M. 157, 655 P.2d 1001 (1982), the parties had stayed 1-2 days at a hotel in El Paso, Texas, where they according to the woman's testimony, repeated earlier made marital vows. The court found, however, that this was insufficient to constitute a common law marriage. In the case of *In re Estate of Stahl*, 13 Ill.App.3rd 680, 683, 301 N.E.2d

law, but there must exist a constancy of dwelling together.[171] For a closer look at the content of the requirements of cohabitation and representation to others as spouses according to Texas law, refer to Chapter 8.[172] However, it ought to be noted that it is not necessary that the parties have their domicile or legal residence in Texas. Without such a requirement, the question then arises about how much living together and holding out is required in Texas. Two cases from courts outside of Texas illuminate how hazardous it is to more closely define this requirement.

In the case of *In Re Matter of Estate of Burroughs* (1992), the parties had resided in Michigan since the middle of the 1960s. During ten months in 1982 and 1983, the woman worked in Houston, where she rented an apartment. The man remained in their residence in Michigan, but visited the woman in Texas one weekend a month. He also spent his vacation there. In October 1983, the woman moved back to Michigan. For one more year, she commuted to her employment in Houston. Neither of the parties, however, had a permanent residence in Texas. When the man died in 1989, the woman filed a lawsuit claiming that she was the deceased's common law wife.

The Michigan Court of Appeals stated that neither of the parties was a permanent resident of Texas. The fact that the man retained the family home in Michigan, according to the court, spoke against cohabitation in Texas. The court shared the lower court's understanding that the woman could not transplant her long-term relationship with the man to Texas on the basis of the facts which were presented and stated: "Living together in Michigan does not satisfy the Texas cohabitation element."[173]

This case can be compared to the case of *In Re Matter of Estate of Willard* (1979), in which the parties had commenced their cohabitation in New Mexico in 1969, where they also had their domicile and their residence. The man was then married to another woman but received a marital divorce in 1970. Because the man, for a period of seven years until his death in 1977, worked in the oilfields in Texas, the couple often stayed there. During a visit to Texas, they agreed formlessly to be married and exchanged rings as a confirmation. Several times every year, they visited family and friends in Texas. They had also a joint bank account in that state. During the visits, they held themselves out as husband and wife. After the man's death, the question arose whether the parties entered into

---

82 (1973), in which the parties made a three-day visit to Texas, the requirement according to Texas law of cohabitation in Texas was considered not fulfilled.

171 *See Walter v. Walter*, 433 S.W.2d 183 (Tex.Civ.App.-Houston 1968).

172 *See* Section 8.4 *supra*.

173 *Matter of Estate of Burroughs*, 486 N.W.2d 113, 116 (Mich.App. 1992). *See also Williams v. Home Indemnity Co.*, 722 S.W.2d 786 (Tex.Civ.App.-Houston 1987), in which the parties lived together in New York and Virginia. The man received employment in Houston, Texas, and rented an apartment for the family. Before the woman and their mutual children had time to move in, the man was murdered. The woman was found to not be the deceased's common law widow.

a common law marriage in Texas and whether the requirement of cohabitation was fulfilled there. The New Mexico Court of Appeals found that the man and the woman lived and cohabited together in Texas.[174] A common law marriage was found proven.

A comparison of the two cases demonstrates that the man's seven-year employment period in Texas in *Willard* was considerably longer than the ten months that the woman in *Burroughs* spent there. In addition, the other party's visits to Texas were more frequent and longer in *Willard*. However, it is remarkable that the parties in *Willard* did not appear to have had a mutual permanent residence in Texas.

The situation is different if one party had his or her domicile in and actually was resident in Texas and received visits of the other party, who was domiciled in another state. In these cases, it appears that the requirement of cohabitation in Texas has been more limited. In certain cases, several weeks have been sufficient.[175] In addition, however, it has always been required that the parties in Texas also outwardly represent themselves as spouses.[176] The requirements of cohabitation and holding out in Texas serve, therefore, the purpose of preventing the creation of common law marriages with temporary visits to that state.

Without legislative support, similar to that in Texas, the courts apply requirements for both cohabitation and holding out or reputation as spouses. The determination of whether these requirements have been fulfilled is limited to the parties' actions during the visit to the common law marriage state, even though support has been scarce in the common law marriage states' case law. The creation of such marriages with short visits could thereby be prevented. This has been the case when the courts in Kentucky[177] apply Ohio law, and when the courts in New York apply the District of Columbia law.

---

174 *Matter of Estate of Willard*, 93 N.M. 352, 600 P.2d 298 (1979); *Matter of Estate of Burroughs*, 486 N.W.2d 113 (Mich.App. 1992); *In re Estate of Bivians*, 98 N.M. 722, 652 P.2d 744, 750, *cert. quashed*, 652 P.2d 1213, 98 N.M. 762 (1982); and *In re Marriage of Wharton*, 55 Or.App. 564, 639 P.2d 652 (1982). In the case of *In re Estate of Stahl*, 13 Ill.App.3rd 680, 683, 301 N.E.2d 82 (1973), the court maintained that a person can only have one domicile and must fulfill two criteria in order to receive this. First, the person must "physically go to the new home and live there." Second, the person must do this "with the intention of making it the permanent home."

175 With respect to assessments made by the courts in Texas, *see Winfield v. Renfro*, 821 S.W.2d 640, 650 (Tex.App.-Houston 1991), in which the requirement of cohabitation but not the requirement of holding out in Texas was found to be fulfilled during the man's visits of several weeks there. *See also Bolash v. Heid*, 733 S.W.2d 698 (Tex.Civ.App.-San Antonio 1987).

176 In *People v. Badgett*, 41 Cal.Rptr.2d 635, 895 P.2d 877 (1995), the court states that "the couple did not inform their parents of the 'marriage'even though they lived with Chris's mother, nor did they hold themselves out as married to any other relative or close friend while they were in Texas."

177 For example, in the case of *Vaughn v. Hufnagel*, 473 S.W.2d 124 (Ky.App.), *cert. denied*, 405 U.S. 1041, 31 L.Ed.2d 582 (1971), a couple who resided in Kentucky, a state not recognizing common law marriage, for less than 24 hours had visited Ohio, a state in which such marriages can be entered into legally. There they

For example, in *Cross v. Cross* (1989), the parties had commenced their cohabitation in New York in 1965, when both were still married to others. After the impediments were removed, they continued the cohabitation until 1983, when they separated. The issue arose then, whether they lived in a common law marriage that was established during one weekend visit (two nights) in Washington, D.C. The District of Columbia requires, in addition to a marriage contract, that it also is "consummated by cohabitation."[178] The New York Supreme Court, Appellate Division, stated with respect to the parties' visit to Washington, D.C., that the plaintiff cannot establish cohabitation and reputation in Washington, D.C., on the basis of a two-day visit.[179] The court was clearly prepared to take into consideration

---

checked into a hotel as husband and wife and formlessly made marital vows. The day after they returned to Kentucky wherewith the woman was "regaled with customary diamond ring and wedding band." They lived until the man's death together as husband and wife in Kentucky. The court, whose reasoning exhibits considerable deficiencies, stated that Kentucky recognizes a common law marriage established in a state in which such relations legally can be entered into, but maintained that "it takes more than riding across the Ohio River to make one legal." In general, the court states that it leaves it for the authors of textbooks and others to more closely discuss common law marriage. That which the court did not go into is the question of whether the requirements for the establishing of a common law marriage according to Ohio law were fulfilled, namely the requirements of a marriage contract and of cohabitation. A contract probably ought to have come into existence through the parties' marital vows. On the other hand, it is clear that the requirement of cohabitation was not fulfilled through the parties' less than 24-hour visit to Ohio. Should their several year cohabitation in Kentucky also have been viewed as relevant, the requirement probably would have been fulfilled. *Compare Kennedy v. Damron*, 268 S.W.2d 22, 24 (Ky..App. 1954), which concerned week-long visits to Ohio during a period of several years. The court did not require a legal domicile in a common law marriage state in the meaning of a residence with an intent to be permanent, but on the other hand "an established place of abode with which the parties may be identified as members of the community," which the parties lacked. Despite the fact that the reasoning appears to be of a conflict of law character, the court cited cases from Ohio. *See Dibble v. Dibble*, 88 Ohio App. 490, 100 N.E.2d 451 (1950). It ought to be noted that the conclusion that no common law marriage was established was ultimately based on the lack of a marriage contract. *Compare Tarter v. Medley*, 356 S.W.2d 255 (Ky. 1962), in which a common law marriage was found established in Ohio, after a visit there of 4-5 months during which the parties had their own household and outwardly appeared as husband and wife. *See also Hoffman v. Hoffman*, 285 Ky. 55, 146 S.W.2d 347, 349 (1940), in which a common law marriage was found to be proven since the parties lived together and outwardly presented themselves as spouses during approximately three months in Ohio. The parties' ten-year cohabitation in Kentucky was attributed value only as an evidentiary fact for that they lived together in Ohio as spouses. The question of whether cohabitation is necessary for establishing a common law marriage in Ohio is debated, *see* Section 8.2 *supra.*

178 *See U.S. Fid. & Guar. Co. v. Britton*, 106 U.S.App.D.C. 58, 269 F.2d 249, 251 (D.C.Cir. 1959).

179 *Cross v. Cross*, 146 A.D.2d 302, 541 N.Y.S.2d 202, 206 (A.D. 1 Dep't 1989). *See also Ferraro v. Ferraro*, 77 N.Y.S.2d 246 (Dom.Rel.Ct. 1948), in which a wedding ceremony occurred in Washington, D.C., in 1945. The woman was personally present and the man, due to his military service, was represented by proxy. When the man, after a couple years of cohabitation with the woman in New York, abandoned her, she petitioned for maintenance. The issue arose then whether a marriage was established.

only the parties' cohabitation in Washington, D.C., not their cohabitation outside of the common law marriage state, which encompassed eighteen years with impediments and four years without impediments in New York. This stance appears to have certain support in the District of Columbia law.[180] On the other hand, this jurisdiction ought not apply any requirement of holding out.[181] Such a requirement, however, appears to have been applied by the court in New York.

The possibility of fulfilling the requirement of cohabitation during a visit to a common law marriage state naturally is dependent upon the requirement's closer formation. In Georgia, it has been easier than in other states to fulfill it during a short visit because this requirement is considered a realization of the marriage contract and therefore is formulated as a requirement of consummation.[182] What must be demonstrated is that the relationship did not stop with simply a contract, but that the marriage also commenced—however, not more! Because Georgia law applies a separate requirement for neither holding out nor reputation, and the courts, as seen above, place low requirements as to the inferred agreements, the door is open for the creation of a common law marriage in connection with remarkably short visits to Georgia.

For example, in the cases above, *Coney v. R.S.R. Corp.* (1990)[183] and *Ventura v. Ventura* (1967),[184] the parties lived together five and fourteen

---

The court found that a common law marriage could not be established in Washington, D.C., as the parties' cohabitation in its entirety occurred in New York. The court on the other hand found that a valid "ceremonial proxy marriage" had been established. It ought to be noted that the court did not cite District of Columbia law with respect to the principles for the establishment of a common law marriage, but rather the provisions in New York law which in 1933 repealed common law marriage, *see* Dom.Rel. Law § 11. There are, however, cases from New York, in which even the parties' cohabitation in the home state are taken into consideration, *see Ram v. Ramharack*, 571 N.Y.S.2d 190 (Sup. 1991). With respect to the requirement in the District of Columbia that the marriage contract in a common law marriage is consummated by cohabitation, *see* Section 8.4 *supra.*

180 *See Johnson v. Young*, 372 A.2d 992, 994 (D.C.App. 1977), in which the parties lived together approximately three years in Virginia, a state not recognizing common law marriage, and approximately four years in Washington D.C., in which such marriages can be entered into legally. The court, which did not find any marriage proven, appears to have based its decision only on the parties' insufficient cohabitation in Washington, D.C. *Compare Ram v. Ramharack*, 571 N.Y.S.2d 190 (Sup. 1991) and *In Re Matter of Estate of Foster*, 376 S.E.2d 144 (W.Va. 1988).

181 *See* Section 8.4 *supra.*

182 *Georgia Osteopathic Hosp. v. O'Neal*, 403 S.E.2d 235, 243 (Ga.App. 1991). With respect to the use of the concept "consummation" in the case law, *see* Section 8.4 *supra.*

183 *Coney v. R.S.R. Corp.*, 563 N.Y.S.2d 211 (A.D. 3 Dep't 1990); *compare Mott v. Duncan Petroleum Trans.*, 51 N.Y.2d 289, 434 N.Y.S.2d 155, 414 N.E.2d 657 (1980).

184 *Ventura v. Ventura*, 53 Misc.2d 881, 280 N.Y.S.2d 5 (Sup.Ct. 1967). Another case in which the period of cohabitation was limited but in which the court's reasoning is insufficient is *Madewell v. United States*, 84 F.Supp. 329, 335 (E.D.Tenn. 1949). The parties, Orville O. Madewell and Mary Jean Madewell, in March of 1942 in Georgia had entered into a ceremonial marriage, which was invalid due to the man being still married to another woman. They later lived primarily in Tennessee. During his military service, Orville was for a period stationed in Alabama, a state recognizing

years, respectively, in New York, a state in which common law marriage could not be entered into legally. In both cases, during three days, the parties visited Georgia where they lived together and held themselves out as spouses. In both cases, a common law marriage was found established. The courts, as seen in the previous section, also considered the parties' actions in New York when assessing whether an inferred marriage contract had been established, yet it appears that the requirement of consummation had been fulfilled during the visit to Georgia. A requirement for a more extensive cohabitation or holding out and reputation in Georgia would have limited the possibility of establishing a common law marriage during the visit.

This can be seen in the comparison between *Coney* and *Cross*, both of which were decided by the New York Supreme Court, Appellate Division. In the latter case, two days in the District of Columbia were not considered to be sufficient. Though the visit in *Cross* was one day shorter, the more compelling explanation for the decision is that the New York court's interpretation, rightly or wrongly, was that the District of Columbia law has a requirement of both cohabitation and reputation.

The courts in common law marriage states, where the evaluation is limited to the parties' actions during a short visit, have not found the requirements of cohabitation and reputation to be fulfilled. For example, in the case of *In Re Matter of Estate of Vandenhook* (1993), the man lived in Montana and the woman in Oklahoma. They met in Utah at the end of 1990. All three states recognize common law marriage. On two occasions during 1991, the woman visited the man in Montana, one visit lasting five days and the other four days. On the last day, the woman received a diamond ring from the man and afterward they ate lunch together with a girlfriend. They did not, however, mention that they considered themselves as married at the lunch. In general, they kept contact with each other by letter and telephone. The man drew up a will to benefit the woman. Upon the man's death in October of 1991, she maintained that she was the deceased's common law wife. The Montana Supreme Court did not decide the question of whether a marriage contract had been established in connection with

common law marriage. Mary Jean and their oldest child visited him there several times. They then lived together in a home outside of the military station on different occasions "for a number of days and nights." They stated there that they were husband and wife and were received and perceived as such by the home's residents and by Orville's friends. To judge from the summary of the facts, the court does not mention the requirements in Alabama for the establishment of a common law marriage and neither states the assessments it made, but rather finds simply "on the basis of the foregoing," that Mary Jean was Orville's legal widow and that she therefore was entitled to the insurance benefits. Even in *Old Republic Ins. Co. v. Christian*, 389 F.Supp. 335, 338 (E.D.Tenn. 1975), a common law marriage was found to be established between a man and woman who had their domicile in Tennessee and who took short trips of up to ten days in Georgia and Alabama. The court mentions the requirements in Georgia and Alabama of a marriage contract, but gives no conclusion from the facts in the case as to the existence of a contract.

the delivery of the ring. The court found, however, that the Montana statutory requirement of cohabitation and repute for the establishment of a common law marriage was not fulfilled through the parties' coexistence that last afternoon after the delivery.[185]

Also as to visits in common law marriage states with no requirements that the cohabitation must have occurred there, either through the legislation or the case law, such a requirement has still been applied by courts outside of the common law marriage state, for example, in the parties' state of domicile, with a conflict of law influenced interpretation of *lex loci contractus*. This means that not only is the issue of choice of law based on the parties' actions in the state of the visit,[186] but also, with the application of the local law, only events taking place in the common law marriage state are considered.[187] If the marriage is seen as having commenced in the common law marriage state, it is logical that not only the marriage contract, expressed or inferred, but the other requirements for a common law marriage, have also been fulfilled there.

Such an interpretation appears *inter alia* with the courts in Tennessee applying Alabama law. In addition to the requirement of a marriage contract, expressed or inferred, Alabama law commonly also apply requirements for both cohabitation and public recognition[188] without requiring that the cohabitation occurs in Alabama.[189] In the case of *In re Estate of*

---

185 *In Re Matter of Estate of Vandenhook*, 855 P.2d 518, 520 (Mont. 1993). *See also In Re Matter of Estate of Murnion*, 212 Mont. 107, 686 P.2d 893, 899 (1984), in which the court stated: "In addition to the consent required for a valid common law marriage, there must be cohabitation and public repute of the marriage." For more concerning the requirement of cohabitation and repute in Montana, *see* Section 8.5 *supra*.

186 By "state where the marriage was contracted" is meant, according to RESTATEMENT (SECOND) OF CONFLICT OF LAW (1971), the state in which the marriage was celebrated or "where some other act was done that is claimed to have resulted in the creation of a marriage status." *See* RESTATEMENT (SECOND) OF CONFLICT OF LAWS § 283 cmt. e (1971). *See also* comment g, from which it can be seen that the marriage cannot be viewed as invalid if "the acts relied upon to create the marriage meet the requirements of the state where the acts took place."

187 *Compare* Charles W. Taintor, *Marriage in the Conflict of Laws*, 9 VAND. L. REV. 607, 621 (1956); RESTATEMENT (SECOND) OF CONFLICT OF LAWS § 283 cmt. e (1971).

188 According to Alabama case law, different ways to formulate the requirement of cohabitation arise. A common wording, as in *Krier v. Krier*, 676 So.2d 1335, 1339 (Ala.Civ.App. 1996), is to as a requirement, in part for "cohabitation or mutual assumption openly of marital duties and obligations," in part, public recognition of the marriage's existence. Another common way is to formulate the objective requirement as a requirement of consummation, which can be viewed as including a requirement for public recognition that the parties live as husband and wife. *See, e.g., Hall v. Duster*, 727 So.2d 834, 836 (Ala.Civ.App. 1999). In *Waller v. Waller*, 567 So.2d 869 (Ala.Civ.App. 1990), the Court of Civil Appeals in addition to the expression "public recognition" also used the more general expression "consummation." For more concerning the formation of the requirement of cohabitation according to Alabama law, *see* Section 8.4 *supra*.

189 In *Krier v. Krier*, 676 So.2d 1335, 1339 (Ala.Civ.App. 1996), the parties after a divorce had reassumed the cohabitation and outwardly presented themselves as spouses first approximately three months in Kansas, a state recognizing common law

Glover (1994), however, which concerned short visits to Alabama, the Court of Appeals in Tennessee, applying Alabama law, stated that the required elements necessary to establish a valid common law marriage must have occurred in Alabama. The requirement of public recognition was not considered fulfilled in *Glover* as the couple's only activities in Alabama were eating, shopping, and sharing a motel room.[190]

However, if the visits to Alabama have been somewhat longer, a common law marriage has been able to be established. For example, in *Ray v. Ray* (1996), the parties divorced in 1970, but resumed a cohabitation that continued for eighteen years in Tennessee, Florida, and Alabama. They had a mutual daughter. When they later separated, the woman petitioned for part of the estate on the basis that a common law marriage had been established during their six-month cohabitation in Alabama. The woman testified that the parties lived together as husband and wife in Tuscumbia, Alabama, from June to December of 1978 and that the man presented her to their landlord and work acquaintances as "his wife." They had joint bank accounts and submitted joint tax statements that year as if they were married. She was acknowledged as his wife in his health insurance and in different medical documents. Their daughter testified that the parents referred to each other as husband and wife when they lived in Alabama, and that they lived as a normal family. The Tennessee Court of Appeals, which appears to have only used the parties' actions in Alabama as the basis for their decision, found that the Alabama requirements of public recognition and cohabitation were fulfilled.[191]

It appears that the courts in Oregon have used a similar approach in applying Idaho law, albeit the state of the law in the last-named jurisdiction

---

marriage, thereafter approximately five months in Arkansas, a state not recognizing such marriages, and finally approximately two months in Alabama, in which common law marriages can be entered into legally. The Alabama Court of Civil Appeals found that a common law marriage had been established. Even if the court's reasoning as support thereof is scant, it appears that it had considered the parties' cohabitation in all three states.

190 *In re Estate of Glover*, 882 S.W.2d 789, 791 (Tenn.App. 1994). *See also Andrews v. Signal Auto Parts Inc.*, 492 S.W.2d 222 (Tenn. 1972), in which a couple who lived together in Tennessee took a 3-week trip to Alabama, where they were presented as husband and wife for family and friends. Public reputation was considered not to exist. *Compare Old Republic Ins. Co. v. Christian*, 389 F.Supp. 335 (E.D.Tenn. 1975), in which the parties within the course of approximately two years had lived in Tennessee, Florida, Georgia, Alabama, Virginia, and West Virginia. A common law marriage was found established during their visits to Georgia and Alabama, which lasted up to ten days. In *Madewell v. United States*, 84 F.Supp. 329, 332 (E.D.Tenn. 1949), a common law marriage was found to be established during the man's military service in Alabama, in which the parties on different occasions lived "for a number of days and nights." With respect to the requirement in Alabama law of cohabitation and public recognition in addition to the marriage contract, *see* Section 8.4 *supra*.

191 *Ray v. Ray*, 1996 Tenn.App. Lexis 314 (1996). *Compare In re Marriage of Smyklo*, 180 Cal.App.3rd 1095 (1986), in which an approximately three-year cohabitation in Alabama was sufficient.

is somewhat unclear. For example, in the case of *In re Marriage of Wharton* (1982), the parties, who were domiciled in Oregon, during a ten-year period had annually taken short trips of an average of ten days in Idaho, a state recognizing common law marriage. During the visits as well as at home in Oregon, the parties held themselves out as husband and wife. Although Idaho law did not expressly require that the cohabitation must have occurred in Idaho for the establishment of a common law marriage,[192] the court found that the parties' contact with Idaho was insufficient to constitute the basis of a common law marriage under Idaho law.[193] It ought to be noted that Oregon law does not appear to contain any conflict of law rule with such a restriction. One can, therefore, speak of a conflict of law-influenced interpretation of *lex loci contractus*.

The case of *Wharton* can be compared with *Albina Engine & Machine Works v. O'Leary* (1964), in which the parties, during four years, lived together in Idaho. No common law marriage could then be established because an impediment against the marriage existed there. After the parties became domiciled in Oregon and the impediment was removed, they stayed annually during fourteen years for one to two weeks in Idaho. The Ninth Circuit found that the Idaho requirements of consent and assumption of marital rights, duties, and obligations were fulfilled, even if one limited the assessment to the parties' conduct during the visits to Idaho.[194]

Of the above-referred cases, it has been seen that the requirements of cohabitation and holding out or reputation as spouses, regardless of whether they are based on legislation or the case law in a common law

---

192 IDAHO CODE ANN., § 32-201 (1947). Observe that common law marriage, as was mentioned in chapter 1, was repealed in Idaho January 1, 1996, however not retroactively, *see* IDAHO CODE ANN. § 32-201 (2) (Michie 2003).

193 *In re Marriage of Wharton*, 55 Or.App. 564, 639 P.2d 652 (1982). *See also Walker v. Hildenbrand*, 243 Or. 117, 410 P.2d 244, 246 (1966), in which the parties for nine years lived together in Oregon and Washington, states not recognizing common law marriage. The parties upon four occasions, however, had made fishing trips to Idaho, a state that at that time recognized common law marriage. The Oregon Supreme Court did not find any common law marriage proven and stated *inter alia* that nothing so serious and vital for the community's welfare as the decision whether a marriage exists ought to rest on something so "insubstantial" as a short visit to a common law marriage state. The court rejected the alleged marriage with reference to that "Idaho courts would hold that no common law marriage was consummated." With respect to the requirement of cohabitation according to Idaho law, *see* Section 8.4 *supra*. In *Bridgman v. Stout*, 5 Ore.App. 558, 485 P.2d 1101 (1971), the parties, who lived together in Oregon for 15 years, had stayed in Ohio approximately one month. The court did not find that a common law marriage was established with the support of Ohio law.

194 *Albina Engine & Machine Works v. O'Leary*, 328 F.2d 877, 882 (9th Cir. 1964). *See also Boykin v. State Indus. Acc. Comm'n*, 224 Or. 76, 355 P.2d 724, 727-728 (1960), in which the parties for ten years had lived together as husband and wife and outwardly presented themselves as such in Arizona, Arkansas, Nevada, Utah, and primarily in Oregon, states which at that time did not recognize common law marriage. In 1951 they spent 3-5 months in Idaho, a state recognizing such marriages. The Oregon Supreme Court, stating that "the real issue" concerned the "events in Idaho" found that a common law marriage had been established.

marriage state or on a conflict of law-influenced interpretation, have been aimed at preventing the creation of common law marriages with short visits to states in which such marriages can be entered into legally. No such impediments exist in common law marriage states, such as Pennsylvania, in which any requirement of cohabitation, in principle, is not a necessary requirement in addition to the marriage contract. On the other hand, a stricter requirement of the marriage contract can fulfill the same function, either so that the requirement of an expressed contract is sharpened or so that the marriage contract's content is formulated as a requirement of a legal intent.

In those states recognizing common law marriage, the requirements of cohabitation and reputation, as seen from Chapter 8, also have a significant function. They strive to give the legal effects of marriage, to spouses who live or have lived together and for whom they are primarily intended and not to couples who live in more sporadic relationships.[195] However, it is not a given that such limits effectuate this purpose. The parties can have lived in a stable relationship for many years in another state and traveled to a common law marriage state for the purpose of in a private ceremony entering into an expressed but formless marriage contract there. In such cases, the requirements of cohabitation and holding out in the state of the visit hinders giving the legal effects of marriage to those who live together.

2. *The Parties' Actions in States Other than the Common Law Marriage State*

The understanding that both the marriage contract and the cohabitation must have occurred in a common law marriage state is not equally obvious if one more clearly separates the conflict of laws' assessment on one side, and the application of the local law on the other side. The issue of choice of law can be decided with the support of an expressed marriage contract uncontestedly entered into in a private ceremony in a common law marriage state. If the law of the common law marriage state is found applicable and the court applies it, it is not a given that the local law ought to limit the consideration only to circumstances that occurred in that state. These courts can decide whether a common law marriage was established between the state's own residents by taking into consideration not only that the parties lived together in the home state, but also, for example, that they held themselves out as spouses during trips to other states. The parties' cohabitation and holding out in other states can also demonstrate a stable relationship that ought to be given the legal effects of marriage. A correct application of the common law marriage state's law on visitors should then have the same result.

---

195 With respect to the purpose of the requirements of cohabitation and holding out, *see* Section 8.3.1 *supra*.

Even though the recently named principles do not appear to have been more closely developed in the case law concerning visits to common law marriage states, there are exceptional cases in which the courts have taken into consideration the cohabitation outside of the state of the visit. For example, in the case of *In Re Matter of Estate of Foster* (1988), the parties had lived together approximately five years in Washington, D.C., and, thereafter, for approximately twenty-two years in Virginia. In assessing whether the parties fulfilled the requirement of cohabitation according to the District of Columbia law, the lower court, the Circuit Court, Berkeley County, took into consideration the parties' cohabitation in Virginia. On appeal, the West Virginia Supreme Court of Appeals found that the lower court's decision was based on a correct analysis of the applicable law.[196]

In the case referred to above, *Ram v. Ramharack* (1991),[197] it also appears that the court has taken into consideration the parties' actions outside of the state of the visit. In this case, the parties had entered into a formless marriage contract in New York and lived there together, holding themselves out as spouses for approximately twelve years, of which six were without an impediment. Two to three times per year, the parties had visited the woman's family in Washington, D.C. During the visits, they lived together and appeared outwardly as husband and wife.

The New York Supreme Court, I.A. Term, Queens County, stated that for the establishment of a common law marriage, in addition to a present intent to be married, a holding out as husband and wife to others in both New York and the other state and cohabitation are required. As regards the latter two requirements, the court stated briefly that the parties held themselves out as husband and wife to numerous people in New York and other places, and that during their visits to Washington they cohabited together. A common law marriage was found established that had to be dissolved through divorce. Consequently, the court made an entirely different interpretation of the District of Columbia law than that which the New York Supreme Court, Appellate Division, made in the above named case, *Cross v. Cross* (1989).

The parties' actions in states other than in the common law marriage state have been given value by other courts simply as evidence that the parties in a common law marriage state lived together and outwardly

196 *Matter of Estate of Foster*, 376 S.E.2d 144 (W.Va. 1988). *Compare Smart v. Smart*, 676 P.2d 1379 (Okla.Civ.App. 1983), in which the parties in Arizona had entered into a marriage which was invalid due to an impediment. After the impediment was removed, they continued the cohabitation for nearly 30 years in California, where they had their domicile. During a period of sixteen years, they had 2-3 times per year visited Oklahoma, a state in which common law marriage can be entered into legally. One time they stayed two to five weeks. The court pointed to that the parties "lived together as man and wife for 20 years and during that time held themselves out as such" and that they in Oklahoma outwardly presented themselves as spouses. A common law marriage was found established.

197 *Ram v. Ramharack*, 571 N.Y.S.2d 190 (Sup. 1991).

appeared as husband and wife. For example, in *Brown's Adm'r v. Brown* (1948), in which the parties were residing in Kentucky, a state not recognizing common law marriage, they had spent four winters in Florida, a state that recognized such marriages at that time. Even though the relationship was considered illicit in Kentucky, the court considered not only that the parties lived together and held themselves out as spouses in Florida, but also that they lived together, after their return from Florida in 1942, as man and wife, openly and avowedly. A common law marriage was found proven. The parties' cohabitation in Kentucky, however, appears to have merely constituted evidence for finding that they consummated their marriage in Florida.[198]

Even in *Hoffman v. Hoffman* (1940), the cohabitation outside of the common law marriage state had evidentiary weight. The parties, who were residents in Kentucky, had lived together for approximately three months and held themselves out as spouses in Ohio. Nevertheless, their ten-year cohabitation in Kentucky was given weight as evidence for the fact that they lived together as spouses in Ohio. The court stated that: "Of course evidence that these parties lived together as husband and wife in Kentucky could not establish a common law marriage, which is not recognized in Kentucky, but unquestionably such evidence is competent as corroboration of evidence that they lived together as husband and wife in the State of Ohio before moving to Kentucky."[199]

10.5 Summary and Conclusions

As seen in this chapter, common law marriage is of interest not only in those jurisdictions in which such marriages can be lawfully entered into

---

198 *Brown's Adm'r v. Brown*, 308 Ky. 796, 215 S.W.2d 971, 975 (1948). Common law marriage was repealed in Florida in 1968. *See* section 741.211, Florida Statutes (1987): "No common law marriages entered into after January 1, 1968, shall be valid..." Before this, a marriage contract and cohabitation were required for the establishment of such a marriage. *See Lowe v. Broward County*, 766 So.2d 1199, 1211 (Fla.App. 4 Dist. 2000); *Phillips v. Phillips*, 215 So.2d 83, 84 (Fla.App. 1968); *Budd v. J.Y. Gooch Co.*, 157 Fla. 716, 27 So.2d 72, 74 (1946); and *McClish v. Rankin*, 153 Fla. 324, 14 So.2d 714, 718 (Fla. 1943). In *Le Blanc v. Yawn*, 99 Fla. 328, 126 So. 789, 790 (1930), the court stated that: "To cohabit as man and wife means to live together, to have the same habitation, so that, where one lives, there will the other live also. It does not contemplate a mere sojourn, visit, or living together for a time." *Compare* the older case law, *Green v. Green*, 77 Fla. 101, 80 So. 739 (1919) and *Chaves v. Chaves*, 79 Fla. 602, 84 So. 672 (1920).

199 *Hoffman v. Hoffman*, 285 Ky. 55, 146 S.W.2d 347, 349 (1940). Observe that common law marriage, as was mentioned in chapter 1, was repealed in Ohio on October 10, 1991, however not retroactively, *see* Ohio Rev. Code Ann. § 3105.12 (B) (1, 2) (West 1991).

but also in other jurisdictions. Courts and governmental authorities in all of the states within the United States and many foreign countries may have to determine whether such a marriage has been established between a man and a woman who previously had been domiciled in a common law marriage state. In addition, courts in many states do not require that the parties have had their domicile or even been residing in a common law marriage state. A formless marriage, thus, can be established during a short visit by a cohabiting couple to such a state. With regards to individuals and families who move frequently and take trips between states even more frequently, the knowledge of common law marriage in all the states is of great practical significance.

1. *The Choice of Applicable Law*

According to the dominant doctrine of choice of law, the main rule is that the validity of a common law marriage is determined by *lex loci contractus, i.e.*, the law of the place where the marriage was entered into is applied. If a couple, domiciled in a common law marriage state, enters into such a marriage in accordance with the valid regulations, the marriage is commonly recognized as valid in all other states.[200] The general reason for the recognition is respect for or civility to other states' legal systems, *comitas gentium.*

One of the reasons behind the principle concerning the application of *lex loci contractus* is the conception of marriage as a contract, *consensus facit nuptias.* The parties are viewed as having the right to choose their place of marriage. By entering into the marriage contract in a common law marriage state, they have subjected themselves to that law. Taking into consideration the expectations made in good faith by the parties supports reasonable requirements of predictability and legal certainty. These principles appear to be sound as regards a common law marriage based on an express marriage contract. If the parties travel to a common law marriage state for the purpose of entering such a marriage by participating in a private ceremony, it appears reasonable that the marriage is also recognized in other states.

However, as seen in this chapter, these arguments have little relevance to a formless marriage premised on legal presumptions or inferred agreements based on the parties' cohabitation and reputation as spouses. Perhaps the couple has not traveled to the common law marriage state for the purpose of entering into a marriage at all. They can even be unaware that a common law marriage can be entered into and, therefore, are not expecting that such a marriage would be established during the visit. Under such circumstances, it cannot be argued that the parties subjected themselves to the law of the common law marriage state. In such cases, the

---

200 For cases from all the states, *see* infra at the end of this chapter the register of cases.

recognition of such a marriage fails to fulfill the parties' good faith expectations. Against the background that the majority of common law marriages are based on inferred agreements and presumptions, there is reason to strongly question the application of *lex loci contractus* without specific requirements.

On the other hand, a strong reason behind the regulations concerning recognition is the value of creating uniformity in the parties' status to eliminate the parties taking the risk of being considered married in one state and unmarried in another. For example, children are not considered legitimate in one state and illegitimate in another. The family's legal status is the same regardless of where they find themselves.

It appears that even the reason underlying the general marriage presumption, *maxim semper praesumitur pro matrimonio, i.e.*, the interest of maintaining the validity of marriage, has also had an influence on the choice of law. However, there is reason in the future to question whether the marriage presumption has played its role, as discussed further below. In support of the recognition of a common law marriage entered into in another state, the courts have cited the full faith and credit clause of the United States Constitution. To recognize ceremonial marriages but not common law marriages entered into in other states, in individual cases, has also been considered discriminatory and in conflict with the constitutional requirement for equal protection. What is fundamental is the states' sovereign right to independently determine which marriages they wish to recognize.

The courts have had different views, as seen here, about the practical situation of parties who have had their domicile in a state where a common law marriage cannot be entered into and who have made a short visit to a state in which such marriages can be established. In certain states, the courts also have applied *lex loci contractus* in these cases, while other courts have laid down particular, additional requirements. The requirements have commonly been that the parties must have their domicile, or actually have resided, or have had the intention to live in a common law marriage state. If the parties had their domicile in a state that repealed common law marriage and they made a short visit to a common law marriage state without the intent to live there, these courts have refused to recognize the marriage given that an application of *lex loci contractus* would conflict with the purpose of the repeal and therewith against public policy in the state of domicile. A requirement for domicile or permanent residence is, therefore, a method of preventing marriages based on inferred agreements or presumptions and the implications that may result if the parties unknowingly become married. At the same time, it also inevitably hinders couples traveling to a common law marriage state only for the purpose of entering into an expressed common law marriage in a private ceremony there.

Certain courts wishing to prevent the creation of a common law marriage with temporary visits to a common law marriage state, as seen above, do not do this with the support of choice of law rules with particular requirements for an application of *lex loci contractus.* Rather, instead, these courts reject such a marriage through a conflict of law-influenced interpretation of the local law as discussed further below.

2. *Expressed Marriage Contracts*

It is completely possible, as seen above, for a cohabiting couple to travel to a common law marriage state for a private ceremony entered into by an oral agreement, perhaps before witnesses, according to which they agree to enter into a legal relationship and to live a marital life together in accordance with valid legal marital regulations. If no requirements are applied as to cohabitation or domicile in the state of the visit, a common law marriage is established already based on the contract. However, expressed marriage contracts, oral or written, are very unusual. A requirement for expressed vows is naturally a protection against the parties unknowingly becoming married and thus subject to an entire system of regulation that they perhaps did not desire.

With respect to the evidence of an oral agreement, of interest first is the evidence relating to the state of the visit in which the contract was executed. Of the greatest significance is direct evidence concerning the parties' statements upon the occasion of the execution of the contract. Particular importance also ought to be to circumstances having a connection to the contractual situation, for example, the circumstance that they exchanged rings, that there were witnesses or that during the visit they arranged a wedding party or something similar. However, even other events taking place in the state of the visit can constitute corroborative evidence supporting the contract. For example, it may be important that the parties lived together during the visit and held themselves out as spouses.

With respect to evidence relating to the state of domicile, certain courts have been reluctant to take this into consideration, which possibly can be motivated by the fact that common law marriages cannot be entered into their own jurisdictions legally. This restraint, however, appears unwarranted. As the contract to be proven must be connected to the common law marriage state, there must not be any principal impediment against taking into consideration circumstantial evidence from other states. Of course, significant evidentiary weight is given to circumstances having direct connections to the formless execution, for example, the circumstance that the parties before their journey planned for their formless common law marriage by purchasing wedding rings or inviting family and friends to a wedding party in the state of the visit. The circumstance that the parties actually lived together in the state of domicile has more indirect evidentiary weight. In these cases, with respect to the proof of a common law marriage, the general evidentiary burdens of proof are applicable.

3. *Inferred Marriage Contracts*

Since it is unusual for a couple to travel to a state recognizing common law marriage and there enter into an expressed marriage contract, inferred or implied agreements have received extensive acceptance as seen above in the American case law. These come to play a large and debatable role if the courts have had to assess whether a common law marriage has been established during a short visit made by a couple to a common law marriage state. The extent of the relevant evidentiary basis is strongly influenced by whether the courts consider only circumstances related to the visit to the common law marriage state or whether they also have taken into consideration circumstances relating to other states. Here, the understandings diverge.

On one side, a number of courts, in the manner Taintor advised,[201] limit the evidentiary basis only to circumstances relating to the common law marriage state through a conflict of laws' influenced application of *lex loci contractus*,. Despite this limitation on the evidence, it appears hazardous to draw any certain conclusions concerning the parties' marital intentions—the parties, often, have stayed there only several days or weeks in connection with a business or pleasure trip. There are cases in which the parties' actions during the short visit have been viewed as sufficient to prove the existence of a marriage contract.

Several of these cases have given rise to criticism. The courts have not mentioned any closer scrutiny of how the marriage contract has been established. The cohabitation and other circumstances have not been stated as evidence for the existence of a marital *consensus*, but rather, to a large extent, have been independent significance in the establishment of a common law marriage. In many cases, nothing indicates that the parties traveled to the common law marriage state for the purpose of entering into such a marriage there or that, during the visit, they were conscious that such a marriage could be established there. The absence of inference from the facts about the existence of an agreement, a general conclusion in Chapter 7 concerning the creation of inferred agreements, is even more evident when this contractual construction is used with short visits to common law marriage states. In these cases, the courts' lack of reasoning raises misgivings from the perspective of legal certainty. It is a serious deficiency in a legal system for parties to become married to each other without knowing it! It then is easy to understand the court's reluctance in the case of *In re Estate of Bivians* (1982) to find a marriage contract proven simply based on the parties' living together during a short visit. The court there referred to the mobility of modern society, the possibility of fraud

201 Taintor, *supra* note 7, at 621.

arising from claims of common law marriage, and the uncertainty injected into the affairs of individuals by such claims of marriage.[202]

On the other side, it appears that the courts, in deciding whether an inferred marriage contract has been established with the parties' visits to common law marriage states, have commonly also considered circumstances related to other states. The possibility of citing circumstances from a long cohabitation in the parties' state of domicile naturally facilitates the possibility of establishing a common law marriage. Even though the evidence of an inferred agreement always means a collective assessment of all relevant circumstances, it is certain actions that have been of particular interest as evidence of the parties' marital *consensus*.

The courts, as seen here, have taken into particular consideration two special events in the home state. The first is that the parties entered into a ceremonial wedding ceremony, which was invalid, for example, based on an impediment. The second is a formless marriage contract that is invalid because the state in question does not recognize common law marriage. These expressions of the parties' marital *consensus* have been given weight as evidence that the parties upon their visit to the common law marriage state still possessed a marital *consensus*. The continued cohabitation and holding out as spouses in the common law marriage state has then been an expression of a *consensus continuus, i.e.*, a continued marital consent. In this explanatory model, however, the invalid wedding ceremony and the invalid contract in the state of domicile are not material but rather simply evidentiary in deciding whether an inferred contract has been established in a common law marriage state.

The parties' cohabitation in the home state, which in many cases has been lengthy, appears to have had greater significance in the creation of the inferred marriage contract than the connection to the invalid agreements. There are cases in which the evidence rested primarily on a lengthy cohabitation in the state of domicile, which together with the parties' marital appearance during the short visit of several days in a common law marriage state has been sufficient to prove the existence of an inferred marriage contract. This ought to be an unknown fact because many unmarried cohabiting couples in states have repealed common law marriage.

4. *The Marriage Contract's Essensialia*

In many cases in which the inferred contract rested on the parties' cohabitation, the question of the intent required for the marriage contract, the *essensialia*, has not received the attention it deserves. As maintained above, it is with the assessment of the evidentiary weight given to the parties' cohabitation and reputation, as well as their admissions and declarations

---

202 *In re Estate of Bivians*, 98 N.M. 722, 652 P.2d 744, *cert. quashed*, 652 P.2d 1213, 98 N.M. 762 (1982).

with the proof of an inferred marriage contract, that is of more decisive importance than that which more precisely is to be proven.

The question of the intent of the marriage contract is placed at its extreme when the issue arises whether a contract has been entered into during a short visit to a common law marriage state. On one side, if the object of the marital intent is to live together as husband and wife, and the parties actually did this, perhaps for many years, it is clear that the cohabitation ought to be attributed a considerable evidentiary weight. On the other side, with the same intent, it is not a given that a short co-existence during a visit to a common law marriage state need be an expression of an intent to live an entire life together. As can be seen from the referred cases, this receives considerable significance if the courts consider only the parties' cohabitation during the short visit or whether they also take into consideration their cohabitation in the home state.

On the other hand, if the object of the marital intent must be a legal intent of some type, for example, an intent to change the parties' legal status or to assume the marital duties and obligations of husband and wife, or an intent in general to be legally bound, it is clear that the cohabitation, even if lengthy, ought to be attributed a more limited evidentiary weight. The cohabitation, if the parties thereby fulfill marital obligations, certainly can indicate that they also promised each other to do this. The cohabitation, however, need not prove any legal obligation. The parties can very well have had the intention to live an entire life together, but without marital rights and obligations.

Neither in deciding cases concerning short visits to common law marriage states does it appear that the question of the marital intent's *essensialia* has received the attention it deserves. Behind the courts' stances, however, one can discern different understandings of the issue.

Seen generally, the increased mobility today among cohabiting couples motivates a considerably greater caution when it comes to drawing conclusions from the parties' cohabitation and reputation concerning their marital intentions! Certain couples can have the intention to simply live together for a trial period or perhaps simply take a trip together. Others can have the intention to live together without any legal ties. The warnings in the case law concerning the untrustworthiness of mere cohabitation and reputation as proof of marriage have become more urgent particularly with respect to short visits to common law marriage states.

There is a method, in addition to that within the choice of law applied requirement of domicile or permanent residence in the common law state, for preventing the creation of marriages based on inferred agreements or on presumptions and the inconvenience of the parties' becoming married without having knowledge thereof. This consequently is to require a legal intent, i.e., an intent to receive the legal effects of marriage or to change their marital status. It is easy to have sympathy for the Oregon Supreme Court when in *Walker v. Hildenbrand* (1966) it did not find any common law marriage proven during the parties' four fishing trips to Idaho. The court stated that: "Common sense would indicate that something as serious and vital to the welfare of society as a determination of the marriage relation should not rest on something as insubstantial as a holiday visit to a common law marriage state with a person of the opposite sex during which the participants held themselves out as husband and wife. This is particularly so where there is no evidence that the parties were aware that any change in their marital status would result or that the visit was made for the purpose of consummating a marriage."[203] Such an intent is difficult to prove with the support of the parties' cohabitation and holding out, particularly if the assessment is limited to the parties' actions during a short visit to a common law marriage state. However, even if the parties lived together many years in their state of domicile, they can have chosen to live together without legal ties.

5. *The Marriage Presumption*

The marriage presumption as presented in Chapter 9 is also applicable to cases in which couples make short visits to common law marriage states as seen above. An application of the presumption consequently assumes that constant cohabitation and general reputation as spouses is at hand. An inferred marriage contract needs not be proven. If these conditions exist, the presumption's legal effects mean that the parties during the short visit are presumed to have entered into an informal marriage contract or to have possessed a marital *consensus*. As the presumption is rebuttable, the evidentiary burden of proof shifts to the opposing party, who has to prove that no such contract has been executed. If the party is not successful, a common law marriage has been established.

It has been argued that if both constant cohabitation and general reputation are necessary for the establishment of a common law marriage, both must have occurred in a common law marriage state. Despite the fact that the elements of constant cohabitation as well as general reputation reasonably ought to require a certain period of time to come into existence, we have seen that there are cases in which a common law marriage has been established simply based on the actions of the man and woman in the state of the visit.

However, the courts with the application of the marriage presumption to short visits to common law marriage states commonly consider not only their actions there but also their conduct in the state in which they are domiciled and in other states, even if such marriages cannot be entered into there. This naturally facilitates the possibility of establishing such marriages. The parties in the home state can have lived together as husband and wife for many years without formally having entered into marriage. As the presumption is rebuttable, the evidentiary burden of proof

203 *Walker v. Hildenbrand*, 243 Or. 117, 410 P.2d 244, 246 (1966).

shifts to the opposing party, who has to prove that no such contract has been executed. Despite the presumption's strength and the difficulties of proving anything in the negative, there is no absence of cases in which it has been rebutted. As evidence that the parties with the visit to a common law marriage state did not possess any marital *consensus*, the courts have also accepted facts stemming from other states.

It was questioned in Chapter 9 whether there is reason, in those jurisdictions where common law marriage can be entered into, to employ a legal marriage presumption in conflict with the fundamental rules concerning evidentiary burdens that place a heavy burden of proof on the party alleging the existence of a common law marriage. It has been seen from this chapter that the application of the presumption in cases in which the parties have made short visits to common law marriage states gives additional reason for questioning whether the element of cohabitation and reputation as typically seen today can be viewed as constituting *prima facie* evidence for the presence of a marital *consensus*. It is not unusual today for a couple to live together without any intention to establish a legal relationship. The future of the marriage presumption is discussed in Chapter 13, in which it is even suggested that it be repealed.

6. The Requirements of Cohabitation, Holding Out, and Reputation as Spouses

The parties' cohabitation, holding out, and reputation as spouses today constitute necessary requirements in addition to the contract in all the jurisdictions in which a common law marriage can be entered into with the exceptions of Pennsylvania and South Carolina.

These requirements, formulated somewhat differently in the different states, as can be seen from Chapter 8, however, serve *inter alia* the purpose that the legal effects of marriage are granted only to couples truly living together. This chapter has shown that the requirements also serve the purpose of preventing couples from other states, with short visits to a common law marriage state, becoming married to each other. The possibility of ensuring these purposes are to a large extent dependent upon whether the courts take into consideration the parties' actions only in the state of the visit or whether they also consider their cohabitation in the state in which they are domiciled.

The majority of the courts, in accordance with Taintor's understanding, consider only the parties' actions in the common law marriage state. [204] The idea then has been that if both the contract and the cohabitation are necessary for the establishment of a common law marriage, both must occur in a state where a common law marriage can be entered into legally. The place for the marriage's commencement is consequently determined

---

204 Taintor, *supra* note 7, at 621. As support hereof, the author cites *Ferraro v. Ferraro*, 77 N.Y.S.2d 246 (Dom.Rel.Ct. 1948).

by both the contract and the cohabitation. This stance can appear natural from a conflict of laws' perspective.

The legal grounds moreover have varied. In *Texas*, the principle has come to expression in the legislation, while in other common law marriage states, it can be seen from the case law. In still other cases, such a requirement has been maintained by the courts outside of the common law marriage state, a conflict of law influenced interpretation of *lex loci contractus*, which has meant that not only the issue of choice of law but also the application of the local law is based on the parties' actions in the state of the visit.

If one views the purpose of preventing couples from other states from becoming married to each other with short visits to a common law marriage state, it can be seen from the above referred cases that the requirements of cohabitation and holding out or reputation as spouses have had this function. It is clear that the requirement of a cohabitation in which the main element is constancy of dwelling together as well as the requirement of a reputation as spouses that is broad and general, not partial and divided is difficult to fulfill during a short visit. These requirements, in addition to the above named requirements of domicile and of a legal intent within the framework for the marriage contract, create a third method of preventing the creation of common law marriages with short visits to states in which such marriages can be entered into legally.

The possibility through a requirement of cohabitation of preventing the creation of a common law marriage in connection with short visits, however, is dependent upon the requirement's closer formation. In *Georgia*, where this requirement is formulated as a requirement of consummation and where there are no separate requirements for holding out or reputation, the doors have been opened to the creation of a common law marriage in connection with remarkably short visits of only three days.

On the other hand, one can scarcely maintain that a consideration of simply the parties' actions in a common law marriage state effectuates the purpose that the legal effects of marriage are attributed to those who live or have lived together and not to couples who live in more sporadic relations. The parties can have lived in a stable relationship for many years in another state and traveled to a common law marriage state for the purpose of in a private ceremony entering into an expressed but formless marriage contract there. In such cases, the requirements of cohabitation and holding out in the state of the visit prevent the legal effects of marriage being given to those who live together.

Exceptions in the case law include cases in which the courts have taken into consideration the parties' cohabitation and holding out as spouses not only in the common law marriage state but also in other states, e.g., the parties' state of domicile where they perhaps for many years lived together. Even if the courts did not more closely develop the motivation moreover, it is, as we found, possible to reach such a stance by more clearly holding separate the conflict of laws' assessment on one side and the application of the local law on the other side. The issue of choice of law can have been decided with the support of an express marriage contract, which uncontestedly has been entered into in a private ceremony in a common law marriage state. When the common law marriage state's law has been found applicable, it is not taken for granted that the local law ought to limit the consideration only to circumstances occurring in that state. The courts can very well in deciding whether a common law marriage was established between the state's own residents be seen as taking into consideration not only that they lived together in the home state but also that they, for example, during trips to other states, there also held themselves out as spouses. The parties' cohabitation and appearance outwardly in other states can also demonstrate that it is a question of a stable relationship that ought to be attributed the legal effects of marriage. A correct application of the common law marriage state's law to visitors there should then give the same result.

10.6 Register: *Lex Loci Contractus* in Common Law Marriage Cases from the Different American States

Lex loci contractus is well anchored in the states, albeit that certain states also require that other conditions be fulfilled, such as that the parties had their domicile in the common law marriage state or something similar. **Alabama:** *Prudential Ins. Co. of America v. Lewis*, 306 F.Supp. 1177 (D.C. Ala. 1969). **Alaska:** *Burgess Constr. Co. v. Lindley*, 504 P.2d 1023 (Alaska 1972) (dictum). **Arizona:** *Gonzalez v. Satrustegui*, 870 P.2d 1188 (Ariz.App. Div. 1 1993); *Grant v. Superior Court*, 27 Ariz.App. 427, 555 P.2d 895 (1976); *Mission Ins. Co. v. Indus. Comm'n*, 114 Ariz. 170, 559 P.2d 1085 (1976); *Gamez v. Indus. Comm'n*, 114 Ariz. 179, 559 P.2d 1094 (1976); *Atkinson v. Valley Nat'l Bank of Arizona*, 22 Ariz.App. 297, 526 P.2d 1252 (1974); *In re Estate of Trigg*, 102 Ariz. 140, 426 P.2d 637 (1967); and *Gradias v. Gradias*, 51 Ariz. 35, 74 P.2d (1937). **Arkansas:** *Brissett v. Sykes*, 313 Ark. 515, 855 S.W.2d 330, 332 (1993); *Standridge v. Standridge*, 298 Ark. 498, 769 S.W.2d 12 (1989); *Stilley v. Stilley*, 219 Ark. 813, 244 S.W.2d 958 (1952); *Woods v. Bell*, 218 Ark. 307, 236 S.W.2d 63 (1951); *Blickford v. Carden*, 215 Ark. 560, 221 S.W.2d 421 (1949); *Orsburn v. Graves*, 213 Ark. 727, 210 S.W. 496 (1948); *Evatt v. Miller*, 114 Ark. 84, 169 S.W. 817 (1914); and *Darling v. Dent*, 82 Ark. 76, 100 S.W. 747 (1907). **California:** *Knight v. Superior Court*, 128 Ca.App.4th 14, 26 Cal.Rptr.3d 687, 691 (Cal.App. 2005) (dictum); *Burks v. Apfel*, 233 F.3d 1220, 1225 (10th Cir. 2000) (dictum); *People v. Badgett*, 41 Cal.Rptr.2d 635, 895 P.2d 877, 897 (Cal. 1995); *In re Marriage of Smyklo*, 180 Cal.App.3d 1095 (Cal.App. 1Dist. 1986); *Etienne v. DKM Enter.*,

Inc., 136 Cal.App.3d 487, 490, 186 Cal.Rptr. 321 (1982); *Chatman v. Ribicoff*, 196 F.Supp. 931 (N.D.Cal. 1961); *Tatum v. Tatum*, 241 F.2d 401, 407 (9th Cir. 1957); *Ponzi v. Ponzi*, 157 Cal.App.2d 772, 321 P.2d 847 (1958); *In re McKanna's Estate*, 106 Cal.App.2d 126, 234 P.2d 673 (1951); *In re Tersip's Estate*, 86 Cal.App.2d 43, 194 P.2d 66 (1948); and *In re Keig's Estate*, 59 Cal. App.2d 812, 816, 140 P.2d 163 (1943). **Colorado:** *Spencer v. People*, 133 Colo. 196, 292 P.2d 971 (1951). **Connecticut:** *Collier v. Milford*, 537 A.2d 474, 477 (Conn. 1988); *Delaney v. Delaney*, 35 Conn.Sup. 230, 405 A.2d 91, 92 (1979); *Parker v. Parker*, 29 Conn.Sup. 41, 270 A.2d 94 (1970); *Catalano v. Catalano*, 148 Conn. 288, 291, 170 A.2d 726 (1961); and *Davis v. Davis*, 119 Conn. 194, 175 A. 574 (1934). **Delaware:** *Matter of Estate of Necastro*, 1990 Del.Ch. LEXIS 123 (1990); *Cook v. Carolina Freight Carriers Corp*, 299 F.Supp. 192 (D.C.Del. 1969); *Harleysville Mut. Cas. Ins. Co. v. Carroll*, 123 A.2d 128 (Del. 1956); *DuPont v. DuPont*, 8 Terry 231, 90 A.2d 468 (Sup. Ct.Del. 1952); *Anonymous v. Anonymous*, 7 Terry 458, 85 A.2d 706 (1951); and *Petras v. Petras*, 30 Del. 29, 105 A. 835 (1919). **District of Columbia:** *Rosenbaum v. Rosenbaum*, 210 A.2d 5 (D.C.App. 1965); *Hitchens v. Hitchens*, 47 F.Supp. 73 (D.D.C. 1942); and *Rhodes v. Rhodes*, 68 App.D.C. 313, 96 F.2d 715 (1938). **Florida:** *Gonzales-Jiminez de Ruiz v. United States*, 378 F.3d 1229 (11th Cir. 2004); *Am. Airlines, Inc. v. Mejia*, 766 So.2d 305 (Fla. 4 Dist. Ct.App. 2000); *Anderson v. Anderson*, 577 So.2d 658 (Fla.App. 1 Dist. 1991); *Johnson v. Lincoln Square Properties*, 571 So.2d 541 (Fla.App. 2 Dist. 1990); *Guelman v. De Guelman*, 453 So.2d 1159, 1160 (Fla. 3 Dist.Ct.App. 1984); and *Young v. Viruet de Garcia*, 172 So.2d 243, 244 (Fla. 3 Dist.Ct.App. 1965). **Georgia:** *Fisher v. Toombs County Nursing Home*, 223 Ga.App. 842, 479 S.E.2d 180, 183 (1996); *White v. White*, 41 Ga.App. 394, 153 S.E. 203 (1930); and *Harper v. Atlanta & W.P.R. Co.*, 33 Ga.App. 259, 125 S.E. 885 (1924). **Hawaii:** *State v. Clyde*, 47 Haw. 345, 388 P.2d 846 (1964). **Idaho:** *Huff v. Huff*, 20 Idaho 450, 118 P. 1080 (1911); and *Morrison v. Sunshine Mining Co.*, 64 Idaho 6, 127 P.2d 766 (1942). **Iowa:** *In re Marriage of Reed*, 226 N.W.2d 795 (Iowa 1975); and *Boehm v. Rohlfs*, 224 Iowa 226, 276 N.W. 105 (1937). **Illinois:** *In re Marriage of Mosher*, 612 N.E.2d 838 (Ill.App. 3 Dist. 1993); *Allen v. Storer*, 235 Ill.App.3d 5, 175 Ill.Dec. 805, 600 N.E.2d 1263 (1992); *Jambrone v. David*, 16 Ill.2d 32, 156 N.E.2d 569, 570 (1959); *Peirce v. Peirce*, 379 Ill. 185, 39 N.E.2d 990, 993 (1942); *Acklin v. Employees' Ben. Ass.*, 222 Ill.App. 369 (1920); *Young v. Young*, 213 Ill.App. 402 (1918); *Stevens v. Stevens*, 3 Ill. 297, 136 N.E. 785 (1922); and *Wilson v. Cook*, 256 Ill. 460, 100 N.E. 222 (1912). **Indiana:** *Mares v. Heckler*, 1985 U.S.Dist. LEXIS 23303 (N.D.Ind. 1985); *Milburn v. Milburn*, 694 N.E.2d 738 (Ind.App. 1998) (does not take a stance); *Bolkovac v. State*, 229 Ind. 294, 98 N.E.2d 250 (1951); *Gunter v. Dealer's Transp. Co.*, 120 Ind.App. 409, 91 N.E.2d 377 (1950); and *Roche v. Washington*, 19 Ind. 557 (1862). **Kansas:** *Westerman v. Westerman*, 121 Kan. 501, 247 P. 863 (1926). **Kentucky:** *Vaughn v. Hufnagel*, 473 S.W.2d 124 (Ky.App.) *cert. denied* 92 S.Ct. 1313, 405 U.S. 1041, 31 L.Ed.2d 582 (1971); *Tarter v. Medley*, 356 S.W.2d 255 (Ky. 1962); *Kennedy v. Damron*,

268 S.W.2d 22 (Ky.App. 1954); *Carroll v. Carroll*, 251 S.W.2d 989 (Ky.App. 1952); *Brown's Adm'r v. Brown*, 308 Ky. 796, 215 S.W.2d 971, 975 (1948); *Damron v. Damron*, 301 Ky. 636, 192 S.W.2d 741 (App. 1946); *Hoffman v. Hoffman*, 285 Ky. 55, 146 S.W.2d 347 (1940); *Gilbert v. Gilbert*, 275 Ky. 559, 122 S.W.2d 137 (App. 1938); *Tryling v. Tryling*, 53 S.W.2d 725, 727 (Ky. 1932); *Hopkins County Coal Co. v. Williams*, 219 Ky. 156, 292 S.W. 1088 (1927); *Scott v. Scott*, 200 Ky. 153, 252 S.W. 1019 (1923); and *Klenke v. Noonan*, 118 Ky. 436, 81 S.W. 241 (1904). **Louisiana:** *Fritsche v. Vermilion Parish Hospital Service District*, 893 So.2d 935 (La.App. 3 Cir. 2005); *Netecke v. State, through DOTD*, 715 So.2d 449, 450 (La.App. 3 Cir. 1998); *Howard v. Keohane*, 898 F.Supp. 459 (D.C.Ky. 1995), *dictum*; *Strawder v. Zapata Haynie Corp.*, 649 So.2d 554, 561 (La.App. 3 Cir. 1994); *Succession of Rodgers*, 499 So.2d 492, 495 (La.App. 2 Cir. 1986); *Jones v. In'l Tel. & Tel. Corp.*, 462 So.2d 1348 (La.App. 3 Cir. 1985); *Parish v. Minvielle*, 217 So.2d 684 (La. App. 3rd Cir. 1969); *Dupre v. Rochester Ropes*, 216 So.2d 589 (La.App. 1968); *Chivers v. Couch Motor Lines*, 159 So.2d 544 (La.App. 1964); *Brinson v. Brinson*, 233 La. 417, 96 So.2d 653 (1957); *Bloom V. Willis*, 221 La. 803, 60 So.2d 415, 417 (1952); *Franzen v. E.I. du Pont De Nemours & Co.*, 146 F.2d 837 (3d. Cir. 1944); *Honore v. Jones*, 180 La. 109, 156 So. 191 (1934); and *Succession of Marinoni*, 177 La. 592, 148 So. 888 (1933). **Maine:** *Hiram v. Pierce*, 45 Me. 367 (1858). **Maryland:** *Crane v. Puller*, 169 Md.App. 1, 899 A.2d 879 (Md.App. 2006); *Blaw-Knox Constr. Equip. Co. v. Morris*, 596 A.2d 679 (Md.Spec.App. 1991); *Goldin v. Goldin*, 48 Md.App. 154, 426 A.2d 410 (1981); *Jennings v. Jennings*, 20 Md.App. 369, 315 A.2d 816 (1974); *Marshall v. Stefanides*, 17 Md.App. 364, 302 A.2d 682 (1973); *Lacetti v. Lacetti*, 245 Md. 97, 225 A.2d 266 (1967); *Henderson v. Henderson*, 199 Md. 449, 87 A.2d 403 (App. 1952); *Bannister v. Bannister*, 181 Md. 177, 29 A.2d 287 (1942); *Jackson v. Jackson*, 82 Md. 17, 33 A. 317 (App. 1895); and *Redgrave v. Redgrave*, 38 Md. 93 (1873). **Massachusetts:** *Boltz v. Boltz*, 325 Mass. 726, 92 N.E.2d 365 (1950); *Craddock's Case*, 310 Mass. 116, 37 N.E.2d 508 (1941); and *Norcross v. Norcross*, 155 Mass. 425, 29 N.E. 506 (1892). **Michigan:** *Matter of Estate of Burroughs*, 194 Mich.App. 196, 486 N.W.2d 113 (1992); *People v. Schmidt*, 579 N.W.2d 431, 434 (Mich.App. 1998); and *Matter of Estate of Brack*, 121 Mich.App. 585, 329 N.W.2d 432 (1982). **Mississippi:** *Enis v. State*, 408 So.2d 486 (Miss. 1981); *George v. George*, 389 So.2d 1389 (Miss. 1980); *Potts v. Bryant*, 194 So.2d 495 (Miss. 1969); and *Walker v. Matthews*, 191 Miss. 498, 3 So.2d 820 (1941). **Missouri:** *Hesington v. Estate of Hesington*, 640 S.W.2d 824 (Mo.App. 1982); *Pope v. Pope*, 520 S.W.2d 634 (Mo.App. 1975); *Doyle v. Doyle*, 497 S.W.2d 846 (Mo.App. 1973); *Preston v. Preston*, 342 S.W.2d 956 (Mo.App. 1961); and *Butterfield v. Ennis*, 193 Mo.App. 638, 186 S.W. 1173 (1916). **Minnesota:** *Laikola v. Eng'd Concrete*, 277 N.W.2d 653, 656 (Minn. 1979); *Kinkead's Estate*, 239 Minn. 27, 57 N.W.2d 628, 631 (1953). **Montana:** *In re Estate of Dauenhauer*, 167 Mont. 83, 535 P.2d 1005 (1975); *Cross v. Cross*, 110 Mont. 300, 102 P.2d 829 (1940); and *In re Houston*, 48 Mont. 524, 139 P. 458 (1914). **Nebraska:** *Bourelle v. Soo-Crete Inc.*, 165

Neb. 731, 87 N.W.2d 371 (1958); *Abramson v. Abramson*, 161 Neb. 782, 74 N.W.2d 919, 924 (1956); *In re Binger's Estate*, 158 Neb. 444, 63 N.W.2d 784 (1954); *Ragan v. Ragan*, 158 Neb. 51, 62 N.W.2d 122 (1958); *Scott v. Scott*, 153 Neb. 906, 46 N.W.2d 627 (1951); *Riddle v. Peters Trust Co.*, 147 Neb. 578, 24 N.W.2d 434 (1946); *Forshay v. Johnson*, 144 Neb. 525, 13 N.W.2d 873 (1944); *Allen v. Allen*, 121 Neb. 635, 237 N.W. 662 (1931); and *Gibson v. Gibson*, 24 Neb. 394, 39 N.W. 450 (1888). **Nevada:** *Hilt v. State*, 91 Nev. 654, 541 P.2d 645, 649 (1975). **New Hampshire:** *Smith v. Smith*, 99 N.H. 362, 111 A.2d 531 (1955). **New Jersey:** *Metro. Life Ins. Co. v. Chase*, 294 F.2d 500 (3rd Cir. 1961); *Winn v. Wiggins*, 47 N.J.Super. 215, 135 A.2d 673 (1957); *Sturm v. Sturm*, 111 N.J.Eq. 579, 163 A. 5 (Ch.N.J. 1932); *Travers v. Reinhardt*, 205 U.S. 423, 27 S.Ct. 563, 51 L.Ed 865, 866 (1906); and *Clark v. Clark*, 52 N.J.Eq. 650, 30 A. 81 (Ch.Div. 1894). **New Mexico:** *In re Estate of Bivians*, 98 N.M. 722, 652 P.2d 744, *cert. quashed* 652 P.2d 1213, 98 N.M. 762 (1982); *Matter of Estate of Lamb*, 99 N.M. 157, 655 P.2d 1001 (1982); *Matter of Estate of Willard*, 93 N.M. 352, 600 P.2d 298 (1979); and *Gallegos v. Wilkerson*, 79 N.M. 549, 445 P.2d 970, 974 (1968). **New York:** *Mott v. Duncan Petroleum Trans.*, 51 N.Y.2d 289, 434 N.Y.S.2d 155, 414 N.E.2d 657 (1980); *Knox v. Palestine Lib. Org.*, 442 F.Supp.2d 62, 75 (S.D.N.Y. 2006); *Matter of Catapano*, 17 A.D.3d 672, 794 N.Y.S.2d 401 (A.D. 2 Dept. 2005); *Hutton v.* Brink, 798 N.Y.S.2d 378 (A.D. 1 Dept 2005) *Matter of Estate of Gernold*, 9 Misc.3d 427, 800 N.Y.S.2d 329 (Surr.Ct. 2005); *Matter of Steiner*, 12 A.D.3d 682, 786 N.Y.S.2d 83 (A.D. 2 Dept. 2004); *Langan v. St. Vincent Hosp.*, 196 Misc.2d 440, 765 N.Y.S.2d 411, 414 (N.Y.Sup.Ct. 2003), *rev'd on other grounds*, 25 A.D.3d 90, 802 N.Y.S.2d 476 (2d Dep't 2005); *In re Landolfi*, 724 N.Y.S.2d 470 (N.Y.A.D., 2 Dept. 2001); *Black v. Moody*, 276 A.D.2d 303, 304, 714 N.Y.S.2d 30, 31 (1 st Dep't 2000); *Matter of Estate of Yao You-Xin*, 246 A.D.2d 721, 667 N.Y.S.2d 462 (1998); *Tornese v. Tornese*, 649 N.Y.S.2d 177 (A.D.2 Dept. 1996); *Lancaster v. 4 NYL Partners*, 228 A.D.2d 133, 651 N. Y.S.2d 440 (A.D. 1 Dept. 1996); *Matter of Grossman v. Gangel*, 192 A.D.2d 396, 596 N.Y.S.2d 53, 55, 625 N.E.2d 590 (A.D. 1 Dept. 1993); *Dozack v. Dozack*, 137 A.D.2d 317, 528 N.Y.S.2d 712, 713 (A.D. 3 Dep't 1988); *Hulis v. M. Foschi & Sons*, 124 A.D.2d 643, 507 N.Y.S.2d 898 (1986); *Matter of Estate of Jenkins*, 133 Misc.2d 420, 506 N.Y.S.2d 1009 (Sur. 1986); *Mott v. Duncan Petroleum Transp.*, 51 N.Y.2d 289, 434 N.Y.S.2d 155, 414 N.E.2d 657 (1980); *Matter of Tabler's Will*, 426 N.Y.S.2d 132, 73 A.D.2d 101 (1980); *Pecorino v. Pecorino*, 64 A.D.2d 711, 407 N.Y.S.2d 550 (1978); *Merritt v. Chevrolet Tonawanda Div., G.M.C.*, 50 A.D.2d 1018, 377 N.Y.S.2d 663 (1975); *Peart v. T.D. Bross Line Constr. Co.*, 45 A.D.2d 801, 357 N.Y.S.2d 53, 54 (3d Dep't 1974); *In re Estate of Watts*, 31 N.Y.2d 491, 341 N.Y.S.2d 609, 294 N.E.2d 195 (1973); *Farber v. U.S. Trucking Corp.*, 26 N.Y.2d 44, 308 N.Y.S.2d 358, 256 N.E.2d 521 (1970); *Lieblein v. Charles Chips, Inc.*, 32 A.D.2d 1016, 301 N.Y.S.2d 743 (1969); *Ventura v. Ventura*, 53 Misc.2d 881, 280 N.Y.S.2d 5 (Sup.Ct. 1967); *Mortensen v. Mortensen*, 225 N.Y.S.2d 323 (Sup.Ct. 1962); *Gibson v. Hughes*, 192 F.Supp. 564 (S.D.N.Y. 1961); *Weisel v. National Transp. Co.*,

14 A.D.2d 621, 218 N.Y.S.2d 725 (1961); *In re Gibson's Will*, 212 N.Y.S.2d 335 (Surr.Ct. 1961); *Gordon v. Gordon*, 27 Misc.2d 948, 211 N.Y.S.2d 265, 270 (1960); *Welsh v. Surface Transp. Co.*, 7 Misc.2d 167, 161 N.Y.S.2d 190 (1957); *Skinner v. Skinner*, 4 Misc.2d 1013, 150 N.Y.S.2d 739 (1956); *In re Singer's Estate*, 138 N.Y.S.2d 740 (Surr.Ct. 1955); *In re May's Estate*, 305 N.Y. 486, 114 N.E.2d 4 (1953); *Cruickshank v. Cruickshank*, 93 Misc. 366, 82 N.Y.S.2d 522 (1948); *Taegen v. Taegen*, 61 N.Y.S.2d 869 (1946); *Shea v. Shea*, 52 N.Y.S.2d 756, 63 N.E.2d 113 (1945); *In re Sokoloff*, 166 Misc. 403, 2 N.Y.S.2d 602 (1938); *Matter of Heitman's Estate*, 154 Misc. 838, 279 N.Y.S. 108 (1935); and *In re Wells*, 123 App.Div. 79, 108 N.Y.Supp. 164, *aff'd.* 194 N.Y. 548, 87 N.E. 1129 (1909). **North Carolina:** *Harris v. Harris*, 257 N.C. 416, 126 S.E.2d 83, 85 (1962); *Rogers v. Sullivan*, 795 F.Supp. 761 (E.D.N.C. 1992); *Bowlin v. Bowlin*, 55 N.C.App. 100, 285 S.E.2d 273 (1981); and *Parker v. Parker*, 46 N.C.App. 254, 265 S.E.2d 237 (1980). **North Dakota:** *First Nat'l Bank v. N. D. Workmen's Comp. Bureau*, 68 N.W.2d 661 (N.D. 1955). **Ohio:** *Ryan v. Ryan*, 84 Ohio App. 139, 86 N.E.2d 44, 47 (1948); *Abbott v. Indus. Com.*, 80 Ohio App. 7, 35 Ohio Ops. 406, 74 N.W.2d 625 (1946); *Rea v. Fornan*, 46 N.E.2d 649 (Ohio App. 1942); *Knight v. Shields*, 19 Ohio Law Abs. 37 (1935); and *Howard v. Cntr. Nat'l Bank of Marietta*, 21 Ohio App. 74, 152 N.E. 784 (1926). **Oklahoma:** *Lopez v. Bonner*, 439 P.2d 687 (Okla. 1967). **Oregon:** *In re Marriage of Wharton*, 55 Ore.App. 564, 639 P.2d 652 (1982); *Matter of Booker's Estate*, 27 Ore.App. 779, 557 P.2d 248 (1976); *Bridgman v. Stout*, 5 Ore.App. 558, 485 P.2d 1101 (1971); *Garrett v. Chapman*, 252 Or. 361, 449 P.2d 856 (1969); *Walker v. Hildenbrand*, 243 Or. 117, 410 P.2d 244 (1966); *Albina Engine & Machine Works v. O'Leary*, 328 F.2d 877 (9th Cir. 1964), *cert. denied* 379 U.S. 817, 85 S.Ct. 35, 13 L.Ed.2d 29 (1964); *Boykin v. State Indus. Acc. Comm'n*, 244 Or. 76, 85, 355 P.2d 724, 728 (1960); *Huard v. McTeigh*, 113 Or. 279, 232 P. 658 (1925); *Ollschlager v. Widmer*, 55 Or. 145, 105 P. 717 (1909); and *Sturgis v. Sturgis*, 51 Or. 10, 93 P. 696, 698 (1908). **Pennsylvania:** *Bobb v. Sec'y, Dept. of Health, Educ. and Welfare*, 312 F. Supp. 225 (S.D.N.Y. 1970); *Jewett v. Jewett*, 196 Pa.Super. 305, 175 A.2d 141 (1961); *Com. v. Custer*, 145 Pa.Super. 535, 21 A.2d 524 (1941); *Sullivan v. American Bridge Co.*, 115 Pa.Super 536, 176 A. 24 (1935); and *Schofield v. Schofield*, 51 Pa.Super. 564, 568 (1912). **Rhode Island:** *In re Chase*, 26 R.I. 351, 58 A. 978 (1904). **South Carolina:** *Zwerling v. Zwerling*, 270 S.C. 685, 244 S.E.2d 311 (1978). **South Dakota:** 25-1-38 S.D.Code.Ann (2002). **Tennessee:** *Payne v. Payne*, 1999 Tenn.App. Lexis 844 (1999); Ray *v. Ray*, 1996 Tenn.App. Lexis 314 (1996); *In re Estate of Glover*, 882 S.W.2d 789 (Tenn.App. 1994); *Old Republic Ins. Co. v. Christian*, 389 F.Supp. 335 (E.D.Tenn. 1975); *Shelby County v. Williams*, 510 S.W.2d 73 (Tenn. 1974); *Andrews v. Signal Auto Parts Inc.*, 492 S.W.2d 222 (Tenn. 1972); *Lightsey v. Lightsey*, 56 Tenn.App. 394, 407 S.W.2d 684 (1966); *Troxel v. Jones*, 45 Tenn. App. 264, 322 S.W.2d 251 (1958); *Madewell v. United States*, 84 F.Supp. 329, 335 (E.D.Tenn. 1949); *Smith v. Mitchell*, 185 Tenn. 57, 202 S.W.2d 979 (1947); *Keith v. Pack*, 182 Tenn. 420, 187 S.W.2d 618 (1945); *Pennegar v.*

State, 87 Tenn. 244, 10 S.W. 305 (1889); and *Morgan v. McGhee*, 24 Tenn. 13 (1844). **Texas:** *O'Benar v. O'Benar*, 410 S.W.2d 214 (Tex.Civ.App.-Dallas 1966); and *Nevarez v. Bailon*, 287 S.W.2d 521 (Tex.Civ.App.-El Paso 1956). **Utah:** *Schurler v. Indus. Comm'n*, 86 Utah 284, 43 P.2d 696 (1935). **Washington:** *In re Marriage of Pennington*, 142 Wash.2d 592, 14 P.3d 764 (2000); *Peffley-Warner v. Bowen*, 778 P.2d 1022 (Wash. 1989); *In re Warren*, 40 Wash.2d 342, 243 P.2d 632 (1952); *In re Gallagher's Estate*, 35 Wash.2d 512, 213 P.2d 621 (1950); *State ex rel. Smith v. Superior Court for King County*, 23 Wash.2d 357, 161 P.2d 188 (1945); *Nelson v. Carlson*, 48 Wash. 651, 94 P. 477 (1908); and *Willey v. Willey*, 2 Wash. 115, 60 P. 145 (1900). **Vermont:** *Morrill v. Palmer*, 68 Vt. 1, 33 A. 829 (1895); HRS 572-3. **West Virginia:** *Griffis v. Griffis*, 503 S.E.2d 516 (W.Va. 1998); *Matter of Estate of Foster*, 376 S.E.2d 144 (W.Va. 1988); and *State v. Bragg*, 152 W.Va. 372, 163 S.E.2d 685 (1968); *Goode v. Goode*, 396 S.E.2d 430, 435 (W.Va. 1990). **Virginia:** *Metro. Life Ins. Co. v. Holding*, 293 F.Supp. 854, 857 (E.D.Va. 1968); **Virgin Islands:** *Bloch v. Bloch*, 473 F.2d 1067 (3rd Cir. 1973). *Kelderhaus v. Kelderhaus*, 467 S.E.2d 303 (Va.App. 1996). **Wisconsin:** *Xiong v. Xiong*, 2002 WI.App. 110, 648 N.W.2d 900 (2002); *In re Estate of Ferguson*, 25 Wis.2d 75, 130 N.W.2d 300 (1964); *In re Campbell's Estate*, 260 Wis. 625, 51 N.W.2d 709 (1952); and *In re van Schaick's Estate*, 256 Wis. 214, 40 N.W.2d 588 (1949). **Wyoming:** *Bowers v. Wyoming State Treasurer ex. rel. Workmen's Comp. Div.*, 593 P.2d 182 (Wyo. 1979); *Jim's Water Service v. Eayrs*, 590 P.2d 1346 (Wyo. 1979); and *Hoagland v. Hoagland*, 27 Wyo. 178, 193 P. 843 (1920).

CHAPTER 11
Scottish Irregular Marriages

11.1 Introduction

Scottish law is especially significant because of its influence on the American reception of common law marriage during the 1800s[1] and the lingering remnants of formless marriage that have persisted in Scotland up to the present.

Lord Hardwicke's Act of 1753, in which a mandatory form requirement was introduced in England, as seen in Chapter 4, "The Reception of Common Law Marriage in the United States," was not applicable to marriages entered into in Scotland. On several occasions during the 1700s and the 1800s, similar legislative proposals with respect to Scotland were rejected as a result of strong Scottish resistance resting primarily on economic and class grounds. Only the upper class, the critics argued, had the means and opportunity to enter into ceremonial marriages,[2] entailing that two medieval canon law models of marriage were valid in Scotland. The first was marriage *per verba de praesenti,* in other words, marriage through an agreement as to a present or immediately valid marriage; the second was marriage *per verba de futuro cum copula caralis,* in other words, marriage through an agreement as to a future marriage with subsequent consummation.

In Scotland, these two medieval forms were customarily called *irregular marriages* and were not repealed until 1940.[3] One of the leading reasons for the repeal was the application problems, in the broadest sense. The legislative history reveals a preoccupation with the difficulty of proving the existence of such marriages, as well as the dangers of fraud, deception,

---

1 *See* Chapter 4, The Reception of Common Law Marriage in the United States and Chapter 7, Implied Marriage Agreements, *supra.*

2 With respect to the enactment of Lord Hardwicke's Act, June 6, 1753, 26 Geo. II. c. 33, *see* Section 4.2 *supra.* With respect to the subsequent legislative propositions up to the 1860's, *see* Emil Friedberg, Das Recht der Eheschliessung in seiner geschichtlichen Entwicklung 453 (1865).

3 Marriage (Scotland) Act 1939, 2, 3 Geo. VI, c. 34, which came into force 1 July 1940 states: "No irregular marriage by declaration *de praesenti* or by promise *subsequente copula* contracted after the commencement of this Act shall be valid." Marriages entered into formlessly before this however remain valid (Sections 5 and 8).

and other misuse, reasons similar to those that in 1563 led to the implementation of *Forma Tridentina*. These same reason also prompted, in 1753, the enactment of the mandatory form requirement in England.[4] In 1939, the Secretary of State acknowledged the seriousness of changing a long-standing Scottish law that had an aura of "glamour and romance," but nevertheless proposed a repeal "for the happiness of many people in Scotland in the future."[5]

Nevertheless, there should have been few problems in Scotland, quantitatively, given its tradition of high rates of marriage and rare disputes concerning irregular marriages.[6] It is notable that, during the 1980s and 1990s, the marriage rate in Scotland, similar to that of Western Europe in general, decreased tangibly and the number of cases of unmarried cohabiting couples increased.[7] The two now-repealed irregular models of marriage in Scottish law will not be more closely examined in the current chapter. To a certain extent, the Scottish case law developed in connection with a marriage *per verba de praesenti* has already been considered above in the treatment of the American law.

The Scottish law, however, has also had room for a third form of irregular marriage that was not repealed through the 1939 legislation, namely, "marriage by cohabitation with habit and repute,"[8] valid in Scotland

---

4 The Secretary of State stated with respect to marriage through *consensus per verba de praesenti*: "Marriage by the mere interchange of consent without any previous notice or formality introduces large possibilities of uncertainty which may have deplorable results." *See* Hansard, Vol. 345, House of Commons 1938-39 Session, sp. 2249. There is no doubt that the Scottish legislator now wished to halt the embarrassing marriage trips to the smithy in Gretna Green. These trips had been "a kind of aristocratic fashion" in marrying, used *inter alia* by Lord Deerhurst and Lord Chief Justice Erskine, *id.* col. 22698. *Compare* the reasons behind *Forma Tridentina* and Lord Hardwick's Act, Chapter 4.2 *supra.*

5 Hansard, *id.* at 2252.

6 According to the Marriage Law of Scotland, Committee Report (1969) at 43, on the average only 12 irregular marriages are established per year through judgments. In 1939, the Secretary of State spoke of "the extremely rare case of a marriage established by habit and repute," *see* Hansard, *id.* In 2000, six and in 2001, four irregular marriages were registered in Scotland. *See* Annual Report of the Registrar General for Scotland, Table 7.7.

7 The number of registered weddings in Scotland in 1951 was up to 41,000 and in 2002, 29,000. The number of "cohabiting couple families" increased from 4% in 1991 to 7% in 2001. *See* Legal Studies Research Programme Findings No. 43 (2004). With respect to the demographic development in the Western world in general, *see* Chapter 12 *infra.*

8 In addition to the designation "marriage by cohabitation with habit and repute" as used here, the expressions "marriage by cohabitation and habit and repute" and "marriage by habit and repute" are also used without any substantive differences. The designation "marriage by cohabitation" is also used, see The Secretary of State, Hansard, *supra* note 4, col. 2249. *Compare Shaw. v. Henderson*, 1982 S.L.T. 211, in which the Outer House (Lord Stott) speaks of both marriages "by habit and repute," as "cohabitation ... and the habit and repute arising therefrom" as "common law marriage." *Compare* D.I.C. Ashton-Cross, *Cohabitation with Habit and Repute,* Jurid. Rev. 21, 30 (1961), who speaks of "marriage by consent inferred from cohabitation with habit and repute" and W.D.H. Sellar, *Marriage by cohabitation with habit and repute: review and*

until 2006. The legal character of this concept is addressed here, including an attempt to more closely define its content and identify its legal effects. It is appropriate to begin, however, by briefly considering its historical background and *ratio legis.*

The origins of the institution are debated. The traditional Scottish view traces it back to domestic Scottish tradition. The legal institution is thought to have origins in a Scottish law dating from 1503, according to which a woman who lived together with a man during his life was presumed, upon the man's death, to be his wife and was entitled to the rights granted a widow. This legal construction was of the same type of rebuttable presumption we have seen in American law in Chapter 9, "Burdens of Proof and Presumptions." A marriage was presumed as long as the opposite was not proven.[9] Another view, however, is that marriage by cohabitation with habit and repute originated in medieval canon law, according to which, as mentioned above, marriage could be proven through long-term cohabitation, *cohabitatio diutina,* with particular consideration to the elements *nominatio, tractatus,* and *fama,* as discussed in Chapter 3.3.4, "Proving the Informal Marriage." Added support for the latter view, as proposed by Clive-Wilson[10] and determinedly maintained by W.D.H. Sellar,[11] is that the more exact formation of the elements in the Scottish presumption closely agree with the medieval canon law equivalents, discussed further below. Irregular marriage later developed in the case law, in addition to the other two now-repealed kinds of marriage. All three have the same legal effects as a ceremonial marriage.

In connection with the 1939 reform, the committee responsible for the investigation proposed that marriage by cohabitation with habit and repute should also be abolished.[12] The secretary of state, whose proposal

---

requiem? in Comparative and Historical Essays in Scots Law 117 (D.L. Carey Miller and D.W. Meyers eds. 1992).

9 David Hume, Lectures on the Law of Scotland 1786-1822, I, 55-56 (G.C.H. Paton ed. 1939-1958). Viscount Stair, The Institutions of the Law of Scotland I, 4, 6 (5th ed. 1832) (D.M. Walker ed., reprinted 1981), refers to "our custom" and cites the law 1503, c. 77. John Erskine, An Institute of the Law of Scotland I, 6, 6 (J.B. Nicholson ed., 8th ed. 1870), maintains that the presumption has its basis, not only in the law from 1503, c. 77, but also in "the nature of things." *Compare* Patric Fraser, A Treatise on the Law of Scotland I, 393 (Edinburgh 1846); F.P. Walton, A Handbook of Husband and Wife according to the Law of Scotland 34 (W.E.R. Hendry and Alistair M. Johnston eds., 3d ed. 1951); T. B. Smith, A Short Commentary on the Law of Scotland 313 (1962); and D. M. Walker, Principles of Scottish Private Law 240 (4th ed. 1988).

10 Eric M. Clive, and John G. Wilson, The Law of Husband and Wife in Scotland 116 (1974); and Eric M. Clive, The Law of Husband and Wife in Scotland 48 (4 ed. 1997).

11 Sellar, *supra* note 8, at 117, 119 and 128, who argues that the law from 1503 "concerned fee and heritage and not status" and that the doctrine was an inheritance from the canon law.

12 O.R.(H.L.) Vol. III No. 16, 14th December 1938.

was adopted by the parliament, however, wished to preserve the institution and stated: "[W]e have come to the conclusion that this form of marriage may serve a useful purpose and that on balance it would be better not to do away with it ... there would be a risk of hardship if we abolished this form of marriage."[13] The risk to which he referred is one of the leading reasons behind the American legal institution of common law marriage as seen above, namely, the desire to protect the interests of children and the more vulnerable party traceable in both American and Scottish law.[14] As in the United States, Scotland had an interest in salvaging the validity of a marriage that might otherwise be rendered invalid as a result of minor form deficiencies or previously existing impediments at the commencement of the marriage.[15] The question of a repeal in Scotland of marriage by cohabitation with habit and repute was raised anew by the Kilbrandon Committee, which nevertheless did not find reason to propose a repeal in its 1967 legislative committee report.[16] In the beginning of the 1990s, however, the Scottish law commission recommended its abolition[17] and, in December 2005, the Scottish parliament decided to repeal this last remnant of common law marriage in Scotland, at the same time that it introduced cohabitation legislation, as discussed further below.

11.2 THE LEGAL NATURE OF THE INSTITUTION

It has been shown how the paired concepts of cohabitation and reputation serve different functions in American law. Chapter 7, "Implied Marriage Agreements," shows how cohabitation and reputation, as well as other circumstances, can serve as circumstantial evidence in the proving of an inferred marriage agreement. Chapter 8, "Cohabitation, Holding Out, and Reputation as Spouses," shows that the conceptual pair is treated as a necessary requisite in addition to the agreement for the establishment of a common law marriage. In Chapter 9, "Burdens of Proof and Presumptions," we investigated its function as an element in the American marriage presumption. The Scottish institution of "marriage by cohabitation with habit and repute" is of particular interest for our purposes as it invites different understandings concerning its legal nature. Prior to the 1939 reform, its relationship to the two other forms of irregular marriage was featured, conceptually, by a certain lack of clarity. Moreover, questions

13 HANSARD, *supra* note 4, col. 2249; Marriage Law of Scotland, Committee Report (1969) at 43.
14 STAIR, *supra* note 9, I, 4, 6; Marriage Law of Scotland, Committee Report at 43; HANSARD, *supra* note 4, col. 2253.
15 Marriage Law of Scotland, Committee Report at 43.
16 *Id.* at 43.
17 The Scottish Law Commission, Report on Family Law, No. 135, Part VII (1992).

remain about how the repeal of the two other forms has affected its own legal character.

1. *The Legal Element Theory*

On one side, the institution can be perceived as a method of substantively constituting a marriage. The theory embedded in this method, let us call it the legal element theory, is that cohabitation with habit and repute materially constitutes a legal element; in other words, they are the only necessary and sufficient conditions for the establishment of an irregular marriage between legally competent persons. From this it follows that the parties' marital *consensus* lacks significance as an independent element in the concept. According to the cohabitation legislation that has been enacted in many jurisdictions in the Western world during the latest thirty years, the parties' rights are ordinarily based only on their actual cohabitation, as discussed further in Chapters 12, "Common Law Marriage and Cohabitation Law," and 13, "The Constitutive Requisites in the Future." In a number of states recognizing common law marriage in the United States, the requirements of cohabitation and reputation have developed in addition to but not instead of the marriage contract, even though the contract, as an inferred agreement has moved to the background.[18] It has also been argued, on the other hand, that the establishment of a Scottish marriage by cohabitation with habit and repute requires both "mutual consent to marry" and "cohabitation by habit and repute."[19]

2. *The Evidentiary Theory*

On the other side, the Scottish institution has been understood as a method to prove the existence of a marriage contract. This method starts with the theory, let us call it the evidentiary theory, which maintains that the parties' marital *consensus* constitutes the only necessary and sufficient condition for the establishment of an irregular marriage between legally competent parties. Cohabitation with habit and repute is, thus, not granted any independent constitutive significance, but simply constitutes an evidentiary fact of the parties' marital consent. In pure terms, the evidentiary theory asserts that cohabitation with habit and repute is neither necessary nor always sufficient for the establishment of an irregular marriage. Understood as such, the institution has an equivalent in the original gestalt of American common law marriage.[20]

---

18 With respect to the development in the United States of the parties' cohabitation and appearance outwardly as necessary requisites in addition to the agreement, *see* Section 8.3 *supra.* With respect to inferred marriage agreements, *see* Chapter 7 *supra.*

19 CLIVE, *supra* note 10, at 51.

20 With respect to the pure contract principle in American law, *see* Section 8.2 and inferred marriage agreements, *see* Chapter 7, *supra.*

The question of the legal nature of the Scottish institution has been highlighted by D.I.C. Ashton-Cross, who makes a large number of distinctions between establishing and proving the existence of a marriage. He argues that even the committee responsible for the investigation that formed the basis for the 1939 reform, and the secretary of state, who presented the legislative proposal, as well as the Scottish parliament that passed the measure, would have understood cohabitation with habit and repute as a method to establish a marriage and, thus, entirely misunderstood the institution's legal nature.[21] The author explains the legislators' mistake was the result, *inter alia*, of the careless use in the case law of expressions such as "marriage by habit and repute," and less well-thought-out references to the institution as a form of marriage.[22] According to that author's view, the institution was never a method for establishing a marriage. He adopts the evidentiary theory, instead, by maintaining that the institution "merely proved" a previous "tacit or inferred consent," which in its turn constituted marriage. Ashton-Cross prefers to speak of "marriage by consent inferred from cohabitation with habit and repute."[23] The idea that the parties' marital *consensus* constitutes the only necessary and sufficient element for the establishment of an irregular marriage has also received support from W.D.H. Sellar.[24]

The issue raised by Ashton-Cross concerning the Scottish marriage by cohabitation with habit and repute and its legal nature is certainly also interesting, for the sake of comparison, in that there is reason to pause and review the sources he cites in support of his view and test the viability of his conclusions.

3. The Presumption Theory

Let us, however, first put forth a third explanation not highlighted by Ashton-Cross in his article about the Scottish institution's legal character. It is, namely, that cohabitation with habit and repute constitutes a method neither to substantively establish nor simply prove a marriage, but rather a method of presuming a marriage. According to this method, if the party claiming the existence of a marriage simply proves the existence of cohabitation with habit and repute, the parties' marital *consensus* is presumed to exist. The legal consequences come into play when the evidentiary burden of proof shifts to the party denying the marriage's existence. A marriage is considered to have been established as long as a party cannot prove that a

21 Ashton-Cross, *supra* note 8, at 21.

22 *Id.* at 30.

23 *Id. See also* SMITH, *supra* note 9, at 314, who states: "Habit and repute is a method of proving consent and this may not have been realised by the legislature in 1939."

24 Sellar, *supra* note 8, at 117, 129, 134-135 states that "the consent of the parties is enough by itself to constitute marriage..." and "consent is both necessary and sufficient."

marital *consensus* did not exist. Consequently, this would be a question of a rebuttable *praesumtio iuris.*

If examined somewhat more closely, the presumption theory includes the notion that cohabitation with habit and repute are not any evidence whatsoever. They are not merely circumstantial evidence, but particularly chosen circumstances to be requirements for the application of the presumption. From this, it follows that exactly these and no other elements are necessary to constitute an irregular marriage between thereto legally competent parties. The elements are particularly chosen, because they typically constitute *prima facie* proof of the existence of a marital *consensus.* To that extent, the presumption theory resembles the evidentiary theory in that cohabitation with habit and repute constitutes evidence of something else. According to the presumption theory, however, no marital *consensus* need be proven in each individual case. If the presumed typical elements exist, the law presumes such consent.

Given that the elements are necessary for the establishment of an irregular marriage, the constitutive elements of the presumption theory resemble those of the legal element theory more closely than those of the evidentiary theory. If, however, the institution is a substantive and constitutive legal regulation, the elements in question would be required to be not simply necessary but also sufficient for the establishment of an irregular marriage. To such an extent, cohabitation with habit and repute is also certainly sufficient under the presumption theory, in that an irregular marriage can be established if the party claiming the existence simply proves that the elements in question exist. The legal consequence, however, is conditioned in that it does not apply if the party contesting the marriage proves that no marital consent existed. Consequently, the parties' *consensus* has legal significance primarily as a counterfact. Thus, cohabitation with habit and repute is not always sufficient for the establishment of an irregular marriage. Therefore, the institution, in accordance with the presumption theory and in contrast to the legal element theory, cannot be characterized as a substantive constitutive legal regulation; it is a rebuttable presumption, in other words, a *praesumtio iuris.*[25]

4. *A Critical Assessment of the Evidentiary Theory*

With the background given above, we can revisit Ashton-Cross for an assessment of the support he cites for his conclusion, *inter alia* the case of *Nicol v. Bell* (1954), which he believes expresses the understanding that cohabitation with habit and repute "*makes* the marriage" (italics added); in other words, it is the legal element theory. Ashton-Cross is clearly particularly critical of the court's conclusion that the parties were found to be married "by cohabitation from 1930 until 1950 and the habit and

25 *Compare* the American legal presumptions, Chapter 9 *supra.*

repute arising therefrom."[26] The use of the preposition *by* can certainly give the impression that the court assumed that cohabitation, habit, and repute constituted marriage in the sense that these elements would be necessary and sufficient conditions for the establishment of a marriage. A consequence is that the parties' marital *consensus* entirely lacked significance as an independent element of the concept. If, however, we use the presumption theory as the explanation of the case, we find that the party alleging the existence of a marriage had proven the existence of cohabitation, habit, and repute, that the party contesting the marriage did not prove that any marital consent did not exist, and that the court, under such circumstances, found a marriage established by cohabitation, habit, and repute. The party alleging the marriage's existence did not have to prove any marital *consensus*.[27] Such a consent was presumed by the law, given the elements. Therefore, the court could find the existence of a marriage directly from cohabitation, habit, and repute without going on a detour via an actual *consensus*. The presumption theory's application is also expressed, in that the court in the case stated that "marriage is presumed or inferred from cohabitation."[28] The language used by the court in its conclusion that the parties were found to be married "by cohabitation..." etc., appears, albeit not as complete, to be acceptable, comprehensible, and correct in substance, if one simply recognizes the assumed unspoken conclusion, that the party contesting the marriage's existence was not successful in proving the absence of marital *consensus*.[29]

---

26 *Nicol v. Bell*, 1954 S.L.T. 314. *Compare* as may be the case even more clearly Lord Blades, who there states that cohabitation with habit and repute is still a recognized "mode of establishing an irregular marriage in Scotland."

27 Pursuant to Lord (Blades) Ordinary, *Nicol* at 317, the woman as plaintiff had "fulfilled the conditions precedent to a declarator of marriage based on cohabitation and repute. She has established that there was continuous cohabitation with the defender for nearly twenty-two years, when the defender and she lived openly at bed and board, as husband and wife do; and she has further established that during that cohabitation the defender and she were reputed to be married persons." When the plaintiff consequently satisfactorily had proven cohabitation and repute, the parties' marital *consensus* was presumed. *Compare* Lord Patrick, *Nicol* at 323: "The burden of proof resting on the pursuer being therefore the normal one in cases of this kind, no heavier and no lighter, it remains to consider whether there was evidence before the Lord Ordinary upon which he was entitled to hold that the pursuer and the defender cohabited as man and wife for such sufficient period of time, and that there was such sufficient repute that they were man and wife as to entitle the pursuer to a declarator of marriage." Neither does Lord Patrick apply any requirements as to proving the previous existence of marital *consensus*.

28 *Nicol* at 314, 319, in which Lord Justice-Clerk (Thomson) cites Erskine.

29 Lord Mackintosh: "This presumption ... is ... rebuttable by proving that there was no consent at all," *see Nicol* at 326. The defendant alleged certainly "that no inference of consent to marry could be drawn from the association," *see Nicol* at 314, 318. Lord Patrick turned the question, however, and stated: "[T] here is in this case no proof of an intention on the part of the defender to remain a single man throughout his cohabitation with the pursuer," *id.* at 323. It was certainly uncontested in the case that the man had not wanted to formally marry the woman, either in the church

Ashton-Cross directs a comparable criticism against the court's conclusion in *A.B. v. C.D.* (1957), in which the parties were found by Lord Ordinary (Guthrie) to be married "by cohabitation ... and the habit and repute arising therefrom."[30] Ashton-Cross declares that he cannot see how the court's conclusion can mean anything other than that such a marriage is constituted by cohabitation with habit and repute, which he considers "nonsense." The court, in this case, however, does not appear to have found that cohabitation with habit and repute constituted marriage in the sense that these elements were the only necessary and sufficient requirements for the establishment of an irregular marriage between legally competent parties, as a consequence of which the parties' marital consent entirely lacked significance. The court's conclusion, however, can mean something else if one begins with the presumption theory. Then, one realizes that a marital *consensus* was presumed to result from a cohabitation with habit and repute, the party contesting the marriage's existence did not prove the absence of a marital consent and the court, taking all this into consideration, found a marriage established.[31] No consent need be proven in the case. Such was presumed and, as the presumption was not rebutted by evidence from the party contesting the existence of the marriage, the court could then directly find the existence of a marriage based on cohabitation with habit and repute. Therefore, we cannot share Ashton-Cross' view when he claims that it is obviously through an error of wording that the court found that the parties were married "by cohabitation ... and the habit and repute arising therefrom," even though Lord Guthrie cannot be said to have particularly clearly developed the presumption theory in the case.[32]

If we review the cases which, according to Ashton-Cross, express the evidentiary theory as represented by him, according to which cohabitation with habit and repute simply is evidence of the parties' marital *consensus*, which in its turn is the constitutive element, he cites *inter alia De Thoren v. Wall* (1876), in which Lord Chelmsford states: "A marriage is established by habit and repute on the ground that the cohabitation as husband and wife is proof that the parties have consented to contract the relation."[33] The statement that the cohabitation "is proof" of the parties' consent naturally could be interpreted so that their marital *consensus* would be the only necessary and sufficient requisite for the establishment of a marriage, that the court's conclusion must lead to a finding that this

---

or civilly. This fact however Lord Patrick considered simply as "evidence of his intention not to take part in a ceremony of regular marriage," *id.*.

30 *A.B. v. C.D.*, 1957 S.C. 415 (reported sub nom. *Woodward v. Woodward*), 1958 S.L.T. 213, 214, 220; Ashton-Cross, *supra* note 8, at 29.

31 The woman in the case had claimed that she "did not consent, after her sixteenth birthday, to be married," *A.B. v. C.D.* at 215.

32 *Id.* at 214 and 220; and Ashton-Cross, *supra* note 8, at 29.

33 *De Thoren v. Wall* (1876) 3 R. (H.L.) 28, 33; and Ashton-Cross, *id.* at 26.

consensus has been found proven and that cohabitation with habit and repute simply constitute evidence thereto. Nevertheless, it appears that the presumption theory better explains the content of the case. Lord Chelmsford's statement, generally held, does not constitute a conclusion in the concrete case. It appears, as well, to be able to be interpreted as an assertion that the cohabitation typically seen "is proof" of the parties' consent and that, therefore, no marital *consensus* need exactly be proven in the concrete case. Neither does he state that the marriage was established by the parties' consent, but rather, instead, that "[a] marriage is established by habit and repute." That the court actually applied the presumption model with the reversal of the evidentiary burden of proof can certainly be furthermore seen in that the court found that the marriage presumption based on habit and repute had not been rebutted.[34]

As support for the evidentiary theory, Ashton-Cross cites, in addition, a statement by Lord Westbury in *Campbell v. Campbell* (1867): "It is not pretended by any of the learned judges [of the Court of Session] that marriage is constituted by cohabitation with habit and repute but they, one and all, I think treat the evidence upon that subject as evidence to prove that which alone constitutes marriage, namely, the consent of the parties..."[35] The statement that the parties' marital *consensus* alone constitutes marriage is undeniable support for the stance argued by Ashton-Cross. However, Lord Westbury, as well as Lord Chelmsford in *De Thoren*, could have meant that cohabitation with habit and repute *typically* is seen to constitute evidence to prove the spouses' marital *consensus*. This interpretation wins support from another statement by Lord Westbury, in which he states that it is a question of a consent "which the law will infer" when he characterizes cohabitation with habit and repute as "a mode of making manifest to the world that tacit consent which the law will infer to have been already interchanged."[36] On this basis and despite the claim that consent alone constituted marriage, it was "marriage" and not *consensus* the court found had been established by the proof of cohabitation.[37]

As support for that the parties' *consensus* is the constitutive element, Ashton-Cross, in addition, states that the point in time for the marriage's establishment is determined, not at the point of time for the acquisition of habit and repute but rather at the point of time for the parties' consent. He refers to Lord Westbury, who continues: "[T]hat inference of consent, when drawn, must be of consent at some particular period..."[38] The statement could give the impression that at a certain point of time an actually entered into marriage agreement must be proven. According to Lord

34 *Id.*
35 *Campbell v. Campbell* (1866) (The Breadalbane case) 4 M. 867, (1867) 5 M.(H.L.) 115, 140 f.
36 *Id.*
37 *Id.*
38 (1866) 4 M. 867, (1867) 5 M. (H.L) 115; and Ashton-Cross, *supra* note 8, p. 25.

Westbury, however, this does not appear to be the case in that the marriage in question "in theory of law" was presumed to have been commenced when the parties became legally competent to enter into marriage with each other: "The marriage, therefore, in theory of law, took place at the time when [the parties] became competent to enter into the contract."[39] The present case also asserts that habit and repute create a presumption that shifts the burden of proof to the party contesting the existence of the marriage. If that presumption is not rebutted, a marriage is established. Lord Cranworth stated: "Habit and repute afford by the law of Scotland, as indeed of all countries, evidence of marriage always strong, and in Scotland, unless met by counter evidence, generally conclusive."[40]

That a marriage agreement entered into at a certain point of time need not be proven is also maintained by T. B. Smith, who expresses the understanding that a judgment about marriage can be given though it cannot single out with certainty any particular date on which mutual consent to marriage was approved.[41] The difficulties of fixing the point at which the marriage's establishment by cohabitation with habit and repute clearly appear in *Nicol v. Bell* (1954), which questioned the point of time a household servant relationship would be viewed as having glided over into an informal marriage. Lord Ordinary (Blades) found that the parties lived together as husband and wife from the day of the birth of their child on June 2, 1930, and that the marital *consensus* was reached at or approximately at the point when the man sent the woman to the hospital as "Mrs. Bell" to give birth to the child. Lord Patrick found no support for defining the point during the day when the woman was sent to the hospital, but rather concluded that a marital consent could be presumed sometime during 1930. Lord Justice-Clerk (Thomson) declared himself content with the point fixed by Lord Ordinary at which the relationship could be said to have become marital. Still, he added that he was equally willingly to use the day when the man's sister moved out of the house and the entire household was reorganized *inter alia* so that the woman could move her sleeping place in the kitchen to a bedroom shared with the man, an event that occurred prior to the birth of the child. He declared, however, that it was not necessary to fix a certain day when the marriage is to be seen as having come into existence: "[I]t may not always be possible for the Court, which ultimately comes to pronounce a decree of declarator, to single out with any certainty any incident or even point of time in

39 *Compare* (1866) 4 M. 867, 902, which with respect to the presumption is stated: "It does not necessarily refer to any particular time or place at which the marriage must have been contracted." *Compare* G. J. BELL, PRINCIPLES OF THE LAW OF SCOTLAND 1516 (W. Guthrie ed, 10th ed. 1899), who in the question of *consensus de praesenti* maintains that this can establish a marriage "without proof of the precise time and place when such consent was interchanged..."

40 *Id.* at 201.

41 SMITH, *supra* note 9, at 790.

the association of the parties from which the married state should run. For practical reasons, the Court has to do its best to fix a point of time but the inability of a party to designate any particular incident or any particular day is no legal impediment to obtaining decree." The court found that the parties had lived together "by cohabitation from 1930 until 1950 and the habit and repute arising therefrom."[42]

In support of the evidentiary theory, Ashton-Cross finally cites *Wallace v. Fife Coal Co.* (1909), in which Lord Ardwall refers to the following *dictum* of Lord Moncreiff in the case of *Lapsley v. Grierson*: "Marriage is not constituted by the mere fact of cohabitation with the assumption of the characters of husband and wife, and repute to that effect. The proper doctrine is that the consent by which marriage is constituted by the law of Scotland may be proved by such habit and repute."[43] Despite this apparently clear support for the evidentiary theory, it can be noted that Lord Moncreiff continues his dictum by laying down certain requirements concerning the parties' cohabitation that must be fulfilled in order for the legal consequence to be invoked. The circumstance that cohabitation with habit and repute was considered to constitute a necessary element for the legal consequence's invocation according to this third form of irregular marriage gives the result that the elements were not seen as any evidence whatsoever; neither were they constitutive elements in the sense that they were the only necessary and sufficient requirements for the establishment of an irregular marriage. However, they were elements in a presumption, meaning that they also were sufficient for the establishment of an irregular marriage, assuming that the opposing party could not prove the absence of any marital *consensus*. Lord Moncreiff did not more clearly denote that cohabitation, habit, and repute constitute necessary elements because, by that time, in contrast to the situation after 1939, it was possible to also constitute an irregular marriage without the recently mentioned element, namely, only through consent *per verba de praesenti*. The institution in this case was understood as a method of presuming marriage, which can also be seen from the statement of Lord Justice-Clerk (Hope), although an impediment against the marriage existed and the presumption therefore could not be applied.[44] Today, Lord Moncreiff's statement does not appear completely correct and could lead to misunderstanding. After 1939 it became more correct to say that cohabitation with habit and repute were necessary elements for the establishment of an irregular marriage. If these elements existed, such a marriage was also established as long as the other party could not prove the absence of any marital *consensus*. The institution, in other words, was a *praesumtio iuris*.

---

42 *Nicol v. Bell*, 1954 S.L.T. 314, 316, 317, 319, 321, 325 f.

43 Ashton-Cross, *supra* note 8, at 26; *Wallace v. Fife Coal Co.*, 1909 S.C. 682, 1909 1 S.L.T. 509, 611; and *Lapsley v. Grierson*, (1845) 8 D. 34, 61.

44 *Id.*, at 37 and 50.

Ashton-Cross, however, can be seen as receiving support for his view from a case decided after the publication of his article and which he, therefore, did not mention. In *Shaw v. Henderson* (1982), Lord Stott in the Outer House declared that he shared the defendant's understanding that marriage is constituted not by cohabitation and repute but by the consent of parties to be inferred therefrom.[45] In the case, the parties had lived together approximately ten months and Lord Stott found that there was sufficient material from which the inference of consent to marriage could properly be drawn.[46] The reasoning, which is surprising, can undeniably be seen as an expression of the evidentiary theory. Consequently, it provides that the parties' marital consent would be the only necessary and sufficient requisite for the establishment of an informal marriage between legally competent persons. Cohabitation and repute would not be granted any independent significance, but simply constitute an evidentiary fact for the parties' marital consent. A consequence is that a marital *consensus* must always be proven. Another consequence of the evidentiary theory is that if the parties' marital consent can be proven in another manner, e.g., through an oral or a written agreement, no cohabitation and repute is necessary. Such was certainly the state of the law in Scotland prior to the 1939 reform, when marriage could formlessly be established through simply a marriage contract *per verba de praesenti*.[47]

Nevertheless, this type of marriage was repealed through the reform. The only, thereafter, recognized formless marriage in Scotland has been marriage by cohabitation with habit and repute established through a *praesumptio iuris*. After 1939, it follows that these elements must be seen as necessary for the establishment of an informal marriage. They are the required elements in a presumption. If the existence of cohabitation with habit and repute is not proven, no formless marriage comes into existence, even though a marital *consensus* is proven in another manner, e.g., through an oral or written marriage agreement. If no cohabitation with habit and repute exists, strictly speaking, the existence of a marital consent need not be considered, even though certain courts appear to do so.[48]

If, however, the plaintiff is able to prove the previous existence of cohabitation with habit and repute, the parties' marital consent is presumed to exist. No further proof is required of the plaintiff. Consequently, no marital *consensus* needs be proven in the concrete case. It is the law,

45 *Shaw v. Henderson*, 1982 S.L.T. 211, 212.

46 *Id.* at 213.

47 Observe that Lord Stott as support for his assertion that "marriage is constituted not by cohabitation and repute but by the consent of parties to be inferred therefrom" cites *Lynch v. Lynch*, 1926 S.N. 172, which however was decided prior to the 1939 reform.

48 *See, e.g., Walker v. Roberts*, 1998 S.L.T. 1133, 1136-1137; and *Ackerman v. Logan's Exr.* (2002) S.L.T. 37.

not the court, which draws the conclusion.[49] It, therefore, does not appear correct to maintain, as Eric Clive did, that the irregular marriage requires both "mutual consent" and "cohabitation by habit and repute."[50] It is sufficient that the elements for such a consent exist. The presumption's character of a *praesumptio iuris* then means that the presumption is rebuttable and the evidentiary burden of proof shifts to the defendant, who has to prove the absence of a marital *consensus*. If he or she is not successful with this, an irregular marriage has been established by cohabitation with habit and repute. If he or she succeeds, however, no marriage is established. Consequently, cohabitation with habit and repute is always necessary, but not always sufficient for the establishment of an informal marriage.

Can Lord Stott's reasoning then be reconciled with the presumption theory? He appears to have considered the presumption, yet his reasoning is not too clear, as can be seen from the following statement: "Presumption arising from habit and repute must receive effect unless there is cogent evidence to the contrary..."[51] However, if Lord Stott requires that the plaintiff must prove the existence of a marital *consensus* between the parties, the question arises about what the defendant in this situation has to prove with "cogent evidence"? In this situation, if the defendant, according to Lord Stott, has to prove the absence of a marital *consensus*, the presumption is illogical because it places the burden of proof on both sides. It is, however, not ruled out that Lord Stott when he finds that "the inference of consent to marry can properly be drawn" simply means that a marital consent can be presumed, not that such is proven. In support, when he draws the conclusion that there is a "consent to marriage," we can assume that he does not find proven a commenced marriage agreement at a certain time, place, and manner, but simply a "consent to marriage" sometime during the approximately ten months' long cohabitation period. The plaintiff's burden of proof would then be lower than the "cogent evidence" that the defendant has to present as counter-evidence, and the presumption becomes logically acceptable and meaningful. The language used by Lord Stott appears, however, in such a case to be somewhat unfortunate and carries the reasoning further than necessary by leading to a conclusion about the existence of the parties' marital *consensus*. In Lord Stott's place with the application of the presumption to the case, we would have chosen to state in the court's reasoning that the plaintiff had proven the existence of cohabitation and repute, that the defendant had not proven the absence of a marital consent, as well as that, under such circumstances, a marriage was established between the parties.

---

49 *Campbell v. Campbell*, (1966) 4 M. 867, p. 925: "The law infers mutual consent in the minds of the parties from their living so long together as man and wife, and allowing themselves to be reputed man and wife."

50 Clive 1997, *supra* note 10, at 51.

51 *Id.* at 213.

In support of his view that cohabitation with habit and repute never has been "a mode of marriage," Ashton-Cross also cites certain authors. He refers consequently to Stair, who in the fifth edition of his INSTITUTIONS from 1832, states that "marriage is proved by cohabitation."[52] That Stair, however, does not represent any pure evidentiary theory can be seen that, in his presentation, he refers to the law of 1503 c. 77, which included the above-mentioned marriage presumption. Stair furthermore continues: "Cohabitation, and behaving as man and wife for a considerable time, *presumeth* marriage"[53] (italics added). Ashton-Cross also cites Erskine, who, in his brief presentation from 1828, states: "Marriage may also be entered into where the consent is not expressed but is discovered *rebus ipsis et factis.* In this way it is *presumed*"[54] (italics added). Erskine herewith appears to have assumed the presumption theory can be seen not only from the choice of words, which is also confirmed in his reference to the law of 1503 c. 77. Primarily, he explicitly states that habit and repute raise a presumption, which is rebuttable and entails the legal consequence that the evidentiary burden of proof shifts to the party contesting the marriage: "[T]he presumption of habit and repute is not so strong an evidence of marriage as to exclude a contrary proof; it only throws the burden of it on him who denies the marriage."[55] Bell is also cited by Ashton-Cross in the tenth edition in 1899 of his work, in which Bell states that cohabitation, habit, and repute always means strong evidence for a marriage, to the point that such evidence in general must be seen as conclusive that marriages can come into existence "without proof of the precise time and place when such consent was interchanged." Bell's statement also expresses that the parties' marital *consensus* need not be proven; it is presumed, assuming that the proper circumstances exist. Bell articulates the presumption theory, not the evidentiary theory.[56] Ashton-Cross also cites works published after the 1939 reform. He refers, consequently, to a statement by F.P. Walton, in 1952, which states that "consent to be inferred from proof of cohabitation and habit and repute."[57] It can clearly be seen, however, that Walton starts with the presumption theory when he continues: "This method raises a presumption of law that the necessary consent has been exchanged." Walton actually means a presumption that can also be seen from the continuation of the statement not cited by Ashton-Cross: "[B]ut deliberate or formal interchange of consent is not an essential requisite of proof of marriage by habit and repute."[58] Walton did not mean that the parties' consent lacks significance, but simply that

52 STAIR, *supra* note 9, 3, 42.
53 *Id.*, 4, 45, 19.
54 ERSKINE, *supra* note 9, 1, 6, 6.
55 *Id.*
56 BELL, *supra* note 39, at 1516.
57 WALTON, *supra* note 9, at 24.
58 *Id.*

the evidentiary burden of proof shifts to the party contesting the existence of the marriage if the required elements are shown, as can be seen with clarity from the following statement: "[T]he onus of showing that the relation between them is concubinage, and not marriage, shall lie on the person who makes that assertion."[59] Even Clive-Wilson designates, in the work published after Ashton-Cross' article, the institution in question as "marriage by cohabitation with habit and repute," and categorizes it prior to 1940 as one of "three forms of irregular marriage."[60] There is reason to assume that Ashton-Cross would have found Clive-Wilson to represent the view that cohabitation with habit and repute constituted marriage. It ought, however, be stressed that Clive-Wilson notes exactly the opposite, in other words, that these circumstances cannot constitute marriage, but rather raise the strong presumption of an inferred consent, a presumption which can, however, be rebutted: "But the cohabitation with habit and repute does not of itself constitute marriage. It raises a strong presumption that there has been tacit consent to marriage, but, as with other forms of marriage, the presumption of consent can be rebutted or displaced by the evidence."[61] However, it ought to be added that Ashton-Cross later received support for his view from Sellar, who found that the parties' marital intention is the only necessary and sufficient requisite for the establishment of an irregular marriage according to Scottish law.[62]

Our analyses has led us to the conclusion that the cases Ashton-Cross cites as support for the view that cohabitation with habit and repute "makes marriage" actually support the presumption theory. The criticism by Ashton-Cross that the cases express understandings that are "nonsense" and that the courts "are ... to blame for the confusion of thought"[63] that has arisen concerning the institution's legal character, therefore appear unjustified. In addition, even the cases that Ashton-Cross cites as support for the view he represents, namely, that cohabitation with habit and repute simply constitutes evidence of the parties' marital *consensus*, which constitutes the only necessary and sufficient condition for the establishment of a marriage, in other words, for the evidentiary theory, in actuality also appear to express the presumption theory. Such a theory undeniably renders the cases cited both comprehensible and consistent.

The views expressed in the academic literature also support the notion that the institution in question does not constitute a material method of establishing a marriage, despite one using the expression "marriage by cohabitation with habit and repute" and spoke of this as a "form of marriage." Neither, however, does the literature support the views of Ashton-Cross and Sellar that the circumstances in question simply constitute evidence

59 Walton, *supra* note 9, at 34.
60 Clive-Wilson, *supra* note 10, at 116 and 96.
61 *Id.* at 116. *See also* Clive, *supra* note 10, at 51.
62 Sellar, *supra* note 8, at 134-135.
63 Ashton-Cross, *supra* note 8, at 28.

of the parties' marital *consensus*, which in turn constitutes marriage. Instead, the academic literature in all material aspects has strengthened the presumption theory, in other words, that the circumstances in question raise a presumption, which entails shifting the burden of proof to the party contesting the existence of the marriage and means that a marriage is established if he or she cannot rebut the presumption by proving the absence of a marital consent.

Against the preceding background, we can connect this back to the assertion made by Ashton-Cross, as restated in the introduction to the present section, that the investigative committee, as well as the secretary of state and the Scottish parliament, would have understood the institution as "a method of constituting marriage" and therefore entirely misunderstood the legal character of the institution. To begin with, it may be repeated that the legislative bodies did not more closely develop their views about the institution's legal character.[64] In addition, it ought to be noted that the committee in another place actually speaks of marriage "proved in this way."[65] Ashton-Cross is justified in that the language used has not always served the interests of clarity. However, that stated above gives us reason to find that, in the case law, terms such as "marriage by cohabitation with habit and repute" and the characterization of the institution as "a form of marriage" can well be reconciled with the understanding of the institution as a *praesumtio iuris*. If the views of the legislature about the legal character of the institution have been affected by the case law, this has not caused any misunderstandings.

The misunderstanding can rather be attributed to Ashton-Cross himself. Despite certain objective validity, the explanation for his misunderstanding of the institution's legal character appears to partly lie on his reliance upon the language of the sources rather than the true meaning of the content. Ashton-Cross apears to have let himself be hypnotized by the dichotomy between establishing and proving a marriage and therefore overlooked the solution that lies between these two, namely, to presume marriage. In light of the presumption theory, the institution does not appear as "confusing and demoralising" as Ashton-Cross believes it to be. We will not upbraid him for his misunderstanding, because his objective of attempting to bring clarity to the Scottish institution's legal character is admirable, deviating from the all-too-common somewhat resigned and incorrect assertion that, from a practical perspective, it makes

64 *Id.* at 21 consequently refers to a statement by the committee, in which it recommends that a marriage lacking valid effect could be able to be "constituted ... in accordance with the existing doctrines of Scottish law known as marriage ... (iii) by habit and repute," *see* Report December 15, 1936, at 12. In addition, Ashton-Cross refers to several statements by the Secretary of State where, when the legislative proposal was discussed in the parliament, he designates the institution as "marriage by cohabitation or habit and repute" and as "a form of marriage," *see* HANSARD, *supra* note 4, at 2246.

65 Report December 15,1936, at 12.

no difference whether one is establishing or proving a marriage.[66] Neither has it been our main objective to seek to refute the conclusions to which Ashton-Cross has arrived. In our comparative perspective, the Scottish institution and discussion concerning its legal character have cast light over the informal marriage's many faceted structure.

11.3 Cohabitation with Habit and Repute

The prerequisites for the presumption, "cohabitation with habit and repute" do not comprise any evidence whatsoever. Rather, it is a question of particular circumstances in the case law; just these, and no other elements, are necessary for the presumption to be applicable. The elements are chosen because they typically have been considered *prima facie* evidence of the existence of a marital *consensus*. To a certain extent, the elements resemble the evidentiary facts usually cited as support for the existence of an inferred marriage agreement, as discussed in Chapter 7. With the application of the presumption, however, no marital *consensus* needs be proven in each individual case. If the elements exist, such a consent is presumed. Consequently, it is the law, not the courts, that draws the conclusion.[67]

The required elements of the presumption resemble constitutive elements in a material legal regulation, in contrast to circumstantial evidence, in that they are necessary for the application of the presumption. The elements, however, are not always sufficient for the establishment of a common law marriage. The legal consequence, namely, is conditioned such that it does not occur if the party contesting the existence of the marriage proves that no marital *consensus* existed, as discussed further below in Section 11.4, "The Legal Effects of the Presumption."

The requirements specified in the Scottish law for the application of the presumption have several aspects in common with the medieval canon and American laws, the latter of which, as we noted in Chapters 7 and 9, refer to Scottish case law.

1. Cohabitation

To begin with, an application of the Scottish presumption assumes "cohabitation," in other words, an actual cohabitation between the parties. As seen in Chapter 9, "Burdens of Proof and Presumptions," American courts, influenced by older Scottish law, found, in the application of the

66 *See, e.g., Campbell v. Campbell* (1867), L.R.1 H.L. Sc. App. 182, 201, in which Lord Cranworth states: "Whether habit and repute make marriage or afford only evidence of marriage is, perhaps, one rather of words than of substance..."

67 *Campbell v. Campbell,* (1966) 4 M. 867, p. 925: "The law infers mutual consent in the minds of the parties from their living so long together as man and wife, and allowing themselves to be reputed man and wife."

marriage presumption's requirement of cohabitation, that "constancy of dwelling together is the chief element of cohabitation."[68] Based on this, the American case law has often used the expression *constant cohabitation.*[69] The Scottish law has applied a similar requirement. It, therefore, is not sufficient that the parties live at different places and visit each other, even regularly. They must continuously reside and live together. Even cohabitation that has occurred at the home of the parents of one of the parties is relevant.[70]

With attempts to more closely define the concept of cohabitation, the requirement appears in the Scottish case law that the parties are to live together "at bed and board," in other words, that they have a community both as to bed and board.[71] It is striking how closely this conceptual pair agrees with the description in the medieval canon law of cohabitation as a community *in lecto et in mensa*, a relationship that in the Scottish law does not appear to have received the attention it deserves.[72] Community of bed and board as a legal conceptual pair can also be found even in the Germanic law, in which it is designated as a community at *Tisch und Bett* and in older Nordic law which assumes that the parties both *deler seng* as well as *spiser og drikker sammen.*[73] In the American case law, the courts have

68 *Yardley's Estate*, 75 Pa. 207 (1874). For more on this, *see* Chapter 9, Burdens of Proof and Presumptions, *supra*. *Compare Lowrie v. Mercer* (1840) 2 D. 953, 983, in which Lord Medwyn speaks of "cohabitation according to what is usual with married persons."

69 *Com. v. McLean*, 387 Pa.Super. 354, 564 A.2d 216, 221 (Pa.Super. 1989).

70 *Dewar v. Dewar*, 1995 S.L.T. 467.

71 Erskine speaks of "cohabitation, or the parties living together at bed and board," *see* ERSKINE, *supra* note 9, I, 6, 6. *See also* FRASER, *supra* note 9, at 401; W. M. GLOAG AND R. CANDLICH HENDERSON, INTRODUCTION TO THE LAW OF SCOTLAND 665 (7 ed. 1968); and CLIVE-WILSON, *supra* note 10, at 118. With respect to the question of whether and when "cohabitation at bed" is to be seen as existing, *see Nicol v. Bell*, 1954 S.L.T. 314, in which the woman, when she moved into the man's residence, first had her sleeping place in the kitchen and after several months shared a bedroom with him and in which the parties both prior to the move as thereafter had sexual relations with each other. The man testified as to the sexual relations, but objected that the woman merely had been his housekeeper already from the move and during the 20 years she thereafter lived in his residence. The court found that the parties had lived together "at bed and board" without that the point of time was more closely defined than that it occurred in 1930. In The Marriage Law of Scotland Committee Report 42 (1969),"cohabitation, or living together at bed and board" is also discussed. *See also Dewar v. Dewar*, 1995 S.L.T. 467, 473, where the court found that the parties "lived together at bed and board."

72 *See* c. 11 X, II, 23: "*Verum, quia in huiusmodi dubietate fama viciniae magis debet attendi, tuae sollicitudinis erit famam loci diligenter inquirere, utrum praedictus vir eam in lecto et in mensa sicut suam uxorem aut concubinam habuerit; et si fama loci habet, quod vir ipsam in lecto et in mensa sicut uxorem tenuerit...*" The comparable definition of the term "cohabitatio" to a community "*in lecto et in mensa*" can also be found in Panormitanus, ad c. 28 X, IV, 1, 5: "*praesumitur matrimonium etiam probata cohabitatione ... longo tempore, puta per 40 annos, tenuisset eam in lecto et mensa ut uxorem...*"

73 With respect to the Germanic concept "*Tisch und Bett*," *see* Section 8.5.2 *supra*. With respect to older Nordic law, *see* the Danish Jyske lov I, 27: "*Hvis en mand har en slegfred (= frilla) i huset hos sig i 3 år, og han åbenbart deler seng med hende; og hun råder over lås og lukke og åbenlyst spiser og drikker sammen med ham, så skal hun vaere (at betragte som) hans*

also assigned considerable significance to the existence of a sexual community and a shared household between the parties in the assessment of the question of whether the cohabitation requisite in a common law marriage had been fulfilled.[74] The requirement of a shared household, which today is a particular requisite in French law and also certain Swedish legislation, is intended to exclude cases in which each of the parties has a residence or a community that includes close visits to each other but not a joint household.[75] Both tenant relationships and visits to prostitutes fall outside of the scope of the rules.[76] However, objectively, cases in which it is less well motivated, to the extent that the requirement of a community of household or board is interpreted strictly, can also fall outside the scope of the rules. Belonging here are, e.g., cases, in which one party, as a result of work, studies, military service, or disease has his or her residence in another area.

In addition to a community at bed and board, the Scottish law, along with American law, require that the relationship in its entirety constitutes a cohabitation "as man and wife,"[77] which ordinarily is understood to mean that the parties consider and treat each other as husband and wife, which has meant *inter alia* a consideration of how the parties actually enjoyed the rights and fulfilled the obligations that accrue and lie with husband and wife, respectively.[78] Household servant relationships fall outside of this concept, but problems have resulted in defining boundaries when such relationships become marriage-like.[79] The attempt was

---

aegtehustru og retmaessige husfrue," *see* Danmarks Gamle Landskapslove (J. Bröndum-Nielsen & P.J. Jörgensen ed. (1933-41).

74 *See* Section 8.5.2 *supra.*

75 With respect to modern cohabitation legislation, *see* Section 13.3 *supra.*

76 Without a different material content, two elements are occasionally applied: "[T]hat there has been cohabitation at bed and board between the defender and herself as husband and wife over a considerable period" and "that during that cohabitation they were reputed substantially, though not necessarily uniformly, to be married persons." With respect to close visits, *see* Lowrie v. Mercer (1840), 2 D. 953; with respect to the reasoning in cases involving prostitution in Scottish law, *see Farrel v. Barrie* (1828) 6 p. 472. *Compare* with respect to American law, *Grigsby v. Reib,* 105 Tex. 597, 153 S.W. 1124 (Tex. 1913).

77 For example, in *Hamilton v. Hamilton* (1839) 2 D. 89, 120, the court assumed "behaving of the parties to each other as man and wife." *Compare Lowrie v. Mercer* (1840), 2 D. 953, 983 (Lord Medwyn): "[T] here must be cohabitation according to what is usual with married persons..." *See also Campbell v. Campbell* (Breadalbane Case) (1867) L.R. 1 H.L. Sc. App. 182, 196: "[P]arties cohabiting together openly and constantly as if they were husband and wife." *See further Cunningham v. Cunningham* (1814) 2 Dow 482; *Nicol v. Bell* 1954 S.L.T. 314, 317("continued cohabitation as man and wife") (Lord Patrick).

78 *See Campbell v. Campbell,* (1867) 5 M. (H.L.) 115, 135, in which by habit is understood "the daily acts of persons living together, which imply that they consider each other as man and wife, and it may be taken as implying an agreement to be what they represent themselves as being." *Compare* the requirement in American law as to "mutual assumption of marital rights, duties and obligations," Chapter 8 *supra.*

79 *See Nicol v. Bell* 1954 S.L.T. 314, in which the man without success objected that the woman had been his housekeeper for 22 years.

made in *Walker v. Roberts* (1998) to distinguish between cohabitation and "cohabitation as man and wife," wherewith the court *inter alia* noted that the relationship at issue in the case was only cohabitation because the parties had separate bank accounts, acquired property in their own names, and the woman did not use the man's last name.[80] These same circumstances are also cited diligently and with varying success in American trials. The evidentiary value can be questioned especially since even formally married spouses act individually. The cohabitation required according to the Scottish presumption must have occurred in Scotland.[81]

2. A Durable Cohabitation

In order to exclude temporary relationships, in addition to cohabitation, it must be characterized by such continuity that it constitutes a cohabitation "with habit."[82] Although the American case law, in certain cases, laid down very low requirements for the cohabitation's durability – approximately two months in *Fischer*[83] – it appears that the Scottish law, similar to the medieval canon law, traditionally has taken a more restrictive attitude. The Roman *usus* marriage required one year's cohabitation and according to the canon law, *cohabitatio diutina* as a rule was considered to exist first after more than ten years' cohabitation.[84] Even in older Scottish case law, in those cases in which the presumption has been applied, they concerned a cohabitation of several years.[85] During the 1900s, however, the time requirement has been considerably reduced in the Scottish case law and there are cases in the most recent years in which the requirement of durability has not been placed higher than in the American law. Consequently, in *Shaw v. Henderson* (1982), an approximately ten-month cohabitation was considered to be sufficient for the establishment of a marriage by cohabitation with habit and repute, while a comparable period of cohabitation in the beginning of that century was

80 *Walker v. Roberts*, 1998 S.L.T. 1133, 1135.

81 *Dysart Peerage Case* (1881) L.R. 6 App. Cas. 489, 537. In *Walker v. Roberts*, 1998 S.L.T. 1133, a cohabitation in Swaziland could not be considered.

82 *Campbell v. Campbell, id.*

83 *See* Section 8.5.2.9 *supra.*

84 C XI, X, II, 23: "*Unde dico ponendo unum intellectum hujus capituli quod diutina cohabitatio, puta decem annorum, cum fama non solum de matrimonio, sed etiam de tractatibus matrimonialibus, una cum aliis adminiculis plene probat matrimonium.*" *Compare* c. 28 X, IV, 1, 5, in which Hostiensis maintains that marriage cannot be presumed through cohabitation, as long as the cohabitation does not last for a long period of time, for example 40 years: "*dicit Hostiensis quod non praesumitur matrimonium etiam probata cohabitatione ... nisi longo tempore, puta per 40 annos*" With respect to the Roman *usus* marriage, *see* Section 2.3.2.3, *supra.*

85 FRASER, *supra* note 9, at 400, speaks of 10-30 years. *Compare Campbell v. Campbell*, (1866) 4 M. 867, 926, in which one was prepared to accept a three-year cohabitation. *Compare Lapsley v. Grierson* (1845), 8 D. 34, 61, in which Lord Moncreiff means that the cohabitation must have been "for a considerable period."

considered insufficient.[86] According to the Marriage Law of Scotland (Committee Report), nothing prevents the time requirement from differing from case to case, e.g., instances of a wedding ceremony that occurred but later was proven invalid, and for which the Committee declared that a minimum cohabitation could be sufficient.[87] No definite point of time, however, has been recognized as a minimum in Scottish law. Fraser's statement that so long a time should have passed that it is possible "to test the conduct and intentions of parties, and to afford rational grounds for building up habit and repute"[88] still appears justified. In *Kamperman v. MacIver* (1994), the court stated that no legal requirements existed about a minimum period of cohabitation that must always be fulfilled, but that "a considerable time" is required that is dependent upon the nature and the quality of the parties' cohabitation and reputation as spouses during the period.[89] In *Mullen v. Mullen* (1991), several months after a divorce, the couple had resumed the cohabitation. The woman suggested marriage, but the man did not wish to formally marry again; he did not recognize the divorce for religious reasons. After approximately six months of cohabitation, the woman's reservations against a continued cohabitation had ceased, and a marriage was considered established by cohabitation with habit and repute.[90] From the requirement of a certain durability, it follows that all relationships in the beginning of the cohabitation *ex hypothesi* are concubinage and not marriage.

3. General Reputation as Spouses

In medieval canon law, in the proving of a marriage, particular consideration was given to whether the parties' relationship enjoyed general reputation (*publica fama*) as marriage.[91] In the American law, the parties' "reputation as husband and wife" was even viewed as constituting "the

86 *Shaw v. Henderson*, 1982, S.L.T. 211; *Wallace v. Fife Coal Co.*, 1909 1 S.L.T. 509, 1909 S.C. 682; *see further A.B. v. C.D.* 1957 S.C. 415, sub nom.; *Woodward v. Woodward*, 1958 S.L.T. 213, in which a cohabitation of approximately six years was accepted. *Compare Nicol v. Bell*, 1954 S.L.T. 314, in which the presumption was applied on the basis of a 22-year cohabitation. *Compare Wood's Trustees v. Findlay* 1909 1 S.L.T.. 156, in which the presumption was applied on the basis of a 42-year cohabitation. *Compare Low v. Gorman* 1970 S.L.T. 356, 359. A common expression in the case law is that the cohabitation is to have lasted "for a considerable time." *See, e.g., Elder v. M'Lean*, 1829, 85, p 62 and *Nicol v. Bell*, 1954 S.L.T. 314. Lord Ordinary: "a considerable period of years." *Compare id.* 322 Lord Patrick "a substantial period of time."

87 Marriage Law of Scotland, Committee Report (1969) at 43.

88 Fraser, *supra* note 9, at 400.

89 *Kamperman v. MacIver*, 1994 S.L.T. 763, 764. The court refused to accept that a period of approximately six months could never be legally acceptable. The requirement that the cohabitation must have been "a considerable time" also has support in older sources. *See Campbell v. Campbell*, (1866) 4 M. 867, 926; *Lapsley v. Grierson* (1845), 8 D. 34, 61; Erskine, *supra* note 9, I, 6, 6; and Stair, *supra* note 9, IV, 14, 19. I.

90 *Mullen v. Mullen*, 1991 S.L.T. 205.

91 *See* Section 3.3.4 *supra.*

acid test."[92] Similarly, a required element in the marriage in Scottish law is whether the parties enjoy the reputation (*repute*) as husband and wife.[93] Consequently, it is not sufficient for them to outwardly present themselves as spouses—they must also have gained the reputation of being husband and wife.

Typically, the reputation as spouses must be general and undivided. In the older case law, it often was said that it must be "substantially unvarying and consistent."[94] In a modern case such as *Gow v. Lord Advocate* (1992), in which the presumption was not applied, the court found that the parties' reputation as spouses was "in no sense general and undivided."[95]

Particular weight is given to the reputation *inter familiares*, in other words, among family relatives and close friends in the same social group as the parties.[96] Consideration is also given, however, to the reputation that they enjoy with work acquaintances, neighbors, and people in general.[97] Along with the valuation of the evidence, it is logical to assess

---

92 In the American law, the requirement was formed both as a requirement as to holding out and as a requirement which was tied to the effect thereof, in other words, a requirement as to general reputation as spouses, appear. With respect to different formulations in the American law of this requirement as a necessary requisite in addition to the marriage contract, *see* Chapter 8, Cohabitation, Holding Out, and Reputation as Spouses, *supra*. With respect to the American requirement of general reputation as a prerequisite for an application of the marriage presumption, *see* Chapter 9, Burdens of Proof and Presumptions, *supra*.

93 *Davis v. Sutherland's Exrx.*, 1990 G.W.D. 8-433 (the requirement as to repute not fulfilled).

94 The expression can also be found *e.g.* in *Petrie v. Petrie* 1911 S.C. 360, 366; *Nicol v. Bell* 1954 S.L.T. 314, 316; WALTON, *supra* note 9, at 35; CLIVE-WILSON, *supra* note 10, at 120; A similar formulation is in GLOAG & HENDERSON, *supra* note 71, at 665: "The repute must be general and consistent, so preponderating as to leave no substantial doubt." *Compare also* Marriage Law of Scotland, Committee Report (1969), p. 42 f. If exceptions are allowed, traditionally it has been maintained that the reputation as husband and wife must be general and that a divided reputation lacks evidentiary value. In *Cunningham v. Cunningham* (1814) 2 Dow 482, 483, the repute must "be founded on general, not singular opinion" and that "a divided repute is, on such a subject, no evidence at all." In *Hamilton v. Hamilton* (1839), 2 D. 89, 120: "There can be no room, in such a case for a divided evidence of habit and repute." *Compare Lapsley v. Grierson* (1845), 8 D. 34, 61("The repute must have been undivided during the whole period"); *Darsie v. Sceales* (1867) 39 Sc.Jur. 191; and *Nicol v. Bell*, 1954 S.L.T. 314, 315 ("There must be a general and not a divided repute").

95 *Gow v. Lord Advocate*, 1993 S.L.T. 275, 276. *Compare Low v. Gorman*, 1970 S.L.T., 357, 359: "Although the repute need not be universal, it must be general, substantially unvarying and consistent, and not divided."

96 In *Ackerman v. Logan's Exr.* (2002), 37, 39, in which the woman stated that the parties were believed to be married "by all except their close family," the requirement as to general reputation was not fulfilled. *See also Cossar v. Cossar* (1901), 9 S.L.T. 44, 45; *Hendry v. Lord Advocate*, 1930 S.L.T. 793, 1930 S.C. 1027, 1029 f; WALTON, *supra* note 9, at 35; and *Lang v. Lang*, (1841) 3 D. 980.

97 In *Hamilton v. Hamilton* (1839), 2 D. 89, wherein neighbors and business associates, but on the other hand, not the man's work acquaintances, had the understanding that the woman was the man's wife, sufficient repute was not found to exist.

how close the witnesses were and whether they actually possessed knowledge about the parties' relationship.[98]

The requirement that the reputation is to be general, however, does not entail that it needs to be either universal or without exception.[99] A specific problem, even in American law, is that changes in language use and behavior patterns justify a certain caution in the interpretation of older cases. For example, it may not be decisive that the parties do not have a shared last name or joint bank accounts because, nowadays, often, neither do formally married spouses.[100]

Another problem highlighted in the American case law and also appearing in the Scottish cases is that the courts, at times, base their decisions uncritically on statements in which witnesses have stated that they believed that the parties were not "married" or that they did not live in "marriage," without clarifying what the witnesses were actually saying. Not uncommonly, the statements were based on the witnesses knowing that the parties had not gone through a formal wedding ceremony. Statements by the parties themselves that they were "single" or "not married" can also reflect that they did not formally marry. This means that the witness examinations, at times, have been unclear and misleading.[101] The circumstance that relatives did not consider the parties married because they knew that they never went through any formal wedding ceremony did not mean that the necessary reputation was considered to exist in *Shaw v. Henderson* (1981). This was explained by the nonexistence of reputation among family relatives concerned about the lack of a formal ceremony rather than "the marriage state."[102] The clarification of concepts and evidentiary

98 *Lynch v. Lynch,* 1926 S.N. 172; *Hendry v. Lord Advocate,* 1930 S.L.T. 793, 1930 S.C. 1027; *Nicol v. Bell* 1954 S.L.T. 314, 316; *Thomas v. Gordon,* (1829) 7 p. 872; *Dysart Peerage Case* (1881) L.R. 6 App.Cas. 489; and *Cossar v. Cossar,* (1901), 9 S.L.T. 44.

99 *Cunningham v. Cunningham* (1814) 2 Dow 482; *Hamilton v. Hamilton* (1842) 1 Bell App. 736; *Low v. Gorman* 1970 S.L.T. 356, 358; *Donnelly v. Donnelly's Exr.,* 1992 S.L.T. 13; *Gow v. Lord Advocate,* 1993 S.L.T. 275; and *Dewar v. Dewar,* 1995 S.L.T. 467.

100 In *Donnelly v. Donnelly's Exr.,*1992 S.L.T. 13, in which the parties in general outwardly presented themselves as husband and wife, the requirement as to general reputation was considered fulfilled despite the fact that the woman used her maiden name with governmental authorities. *Compare Walker v. Roberts,* 1998 S.L.T. 1133, in which the woman both on official documents and with many relatives and acquaintances used her maiden name. The parties in addition had separate bank accounts and had acquired property in their own names. The court found that the evidence concerning the parties' reputation as husband and wife "was seriously divided and was not general." For the extensive American case law, *see* Chapters 8 and 7 *supra.*

101 *See* with respect to the American law, Chapter 7.8 *supra. Compare* the Scottish case *Ackerman v. Logan's Exr.,* (2002), 37, 42, in which a witness had the impression that the parties "were living together as husband and wife" but could not say "whether they were married" and in which another witness said that he always "thought of them as a couple, married or living together as husband and wife." *See also* the witness testimony in *Mackenzie v. Scott,* 1980 S.L.T. (Notes) 9.

102 *Shaw v. Henderson,* 1982 S.L.T. 211. *See also Dewar v. Dewar,* 1995 S.L.T. 467 in which the man's family and several acquaintances did not consider the parties as husband and wife as there had not been any formal wedding ceremony. The court found the

themes would have been beneficial for both procedural efficiency and legal certainty.

Even though it is consequently possible in the case law to distinguish the requisites of cohabitation, habit, and repute, and their elements, there is reason to stress that they are closely tied to each other and that the courts, as a rule, make the assessment based on the facts as a whole.[103] Lord Chancellor Chelmsford's words in *Campbell v. Campbell* (1867) serves as a summation: "Habit and repute ... arises from parties cohabiting together openly and constantly as if they were husband and wife, and so conducting themselves towards each other for such a length of time in the society or neighbourhood of which they are members as to produce a general belief that they really are married persons."[104]

11.4 The Legal Effects of the Presumption

If the required elements of the presumption exist, the legal effects take effect, which means that a marital *consensus* is presumed to exist. Because the presumption constitutes a *praesumtio iuris*, the evidentiary burden of proof shifts to the party contesting the existence of the marriage, who must rebut the presumption by proving that no marital consent existed.[105] If he or she is not successful, a marriage is established. It is regularly emphasized in the case law that this concerns a strong presumption that, in order to be rebutted, requires considerable counterevidence. This stance in Scottish law has also been adopted in the American case law.[106]

---

requirement as to repute was fulfilled despite this. With respect to the American case law, *see* Chapters 8 and 7 *supra.*

103 The importance of an assessment of the facts as a whole is emphasized in *e.g. Nicol v. Bell*, 1954 S.L.T. 314.

104 (Breadalbane case) (1867), L.R. 1 H.L. Sc.App. 182, 196.

105 *See, e.g., Cunningham v. Cunningham* (1814) 2 Dow 482; *Campbell v. Campbell* (Breadalbane case) (1867) 5 M. (H.L.) 115, from which it can be seen that the presumption becomes "rebutted by proving that there was no consent at all." *Compare Nicol v. Bell*, 1954 S.L.T. 314, 326, in which Lord Mackintosh states: "This presumption, though often a very strong one, is ... rebuttable by proving that there was no consent at all." ERSKINE, *supra* note 9, I,6,6, maintains that "the presumption of habit and repute is not so strong an evidence of marriage as to exclude a contrary proof; it only throws the burden of it on him who denies the marriage."

106 The presumption's strength can be seen *e.g.* from *Campbell v. Campbell* (Breadalbane case) (1867) 5 M. (H.L.) 115, 201: "Habit and repute afford by the Law of Scotland ... evidence of marriage always strong, and in Scotland, unless met by counter evidence, generally conclusive." In *Morris v. Davies* (5 Cl. & Fin. 163), Lord Lyndhurst states: "The presumption of law is not lightly to be repelled. It is not to be broken in upon, or shaken by a mere balance of probability. The evidence for the purpose of repelling it must be strong, distinct, satisfactory and conclusive." In *Piers v. Piers* (2 H.L. Cas. 331), Lord Campbell states that the presumption can be rebutted only "by disproving every reasonable possibility," and in the same case Lord Brougham states concerning the counterevidence that it must be clear, distinct and satisfactory. The cited statements in the two last-mentioned cases are

Simple information from one party that he or she did not have any marital intentions is not usually sufficient.[107] The Scottish law, however, gives reason for pause with respect to the issue of which type of marriage is addressed by the more closely defined presumption. Is it a marital *consensus* expressed through a regular religious or civil wedding ceremony? Or is it a marital consent that has been expressed *per verba de praesenti*? Or is it an inferred marital *consensus* that constitutes the presumption's object? The question is not only academic, because the answer determines which counterevidence must be presented by the party contesting the marriage in order to rebut the presumption. The question received new light to a certain extent after the 1939 reform, in which both the material irregular marriages *per verba de praesenti* and *per verba de futuro cum copula carnalis* were repealed.

11.4.1 The State of the Law Prior to 1939

If we begin with the situation prior to the 1939 reform, it is clear that cohabitation with habit and repute in Scottish law, as is the case today in American and also English law,[108] could be the basis of the presumption of a regular wedded marriage, in other words, a presumption that the parties at a valid wedding ceremony have expressed their marital consent. Fraser states as to this: "The law presumes that all legal solemnities were duly observed."[109] This presumption is applicable even though the party claiming the existence of such a marriage cannot more closely designate the time and place of the presumed ceremony.[110] If cohabitation with habit and repute exists, the burden of proof shifts from the party claiming the existence of a regular marriage to the party contesting the same. He or

---

also cited in the American case law, *see, e.g., Hynes v. McDermott*, 91 N.Y. 451, 459, 43 Am.Rep. 677 (1883), Chapter 9 *supra.*

107 *Nicol v. Bell*, 1954 S.L.T. 314; *Donnelly v. Donnelly's Exr.*, 1992 S.L.T. 13. In *Dewar v. Dewar*, 1995 S.L.T. 467, 473, the man had explained to a number of witnesses that he was "against the idea of marriage." The court found that "whatever his words may have been that was not his intention. Any such words are totally inconsistent with his actings over the years." *Compare Gow v. Lord Advocate*, 1993 S.L.T. 275, in which the court found proven that the woman did not have any marital intention. *See also Craig v. Simpson*, (1869) 6 S.L.R. 639; *Bairner v. Fels*, 1931 S.C. 674; 1931 S.L.T. 489.

108 With respect to the American law, *see* Chapter 9 *supra.* With respect to the English law, *see* P.M. Bromley, Family Law 65 (4th ed. 1971), who states: "It has long been established law that, if a man and woman cohabit and hold themselves out as husband and wife, this in itself raises a presumption that they are legally married." Bromley maintains that the English presumption actually consists of two legal presumptions, one that the parties went through "a valid form of marriage," and that they then had "the capacity to marry."

109 Fraser, *supra* note 9, at 392; *Campbell v. Campbell* (1866) 4 M. 867, 918: "In a country where marriage could take place only by celebration, the presumption arising from cohabitation and repute is, that at some time or other a celebration took place."

110 Fraser, *id.* at 391.

she then has to prove that no such marriage had ever been entered into between the parties. Against the background *inter alia* of the reliability of the Scottish registration system concerning weddings, it appears that, for the party having the burden of proof, the information is easier to find than in the United States. If both parties admit that they never went through a ceremony, it appears that the presumption, as a rule, is rebutted. However, if the party contesting the marriage fails to prove that there was no wedding ceremony in which the parties expressed their marital consent, a marriage is established based on the presumption. As long as irregular marriages can also be presumed based on "cohabitation with habit and repute," it appears that there is little practical significance to being able to presume a regular marriage. This may explain why the presumption so far has received minor attention in the Scottish academic literature.[111] The latter presumption, however, has a certain function to fulfill in those cases in which the parties, e.g., after going through a wedding ceremony, have lived together for a long period of time and the question thereafter arises whether the ceremony was invalid in some respect. This is particularly true about marriages that have been entered into abroad, where irregular marriages, according to the Scottish law, cannot be established.

The presumption based on cohabitation with habit and repute, however, primarily has had significance with respect to the irregular marriage.[112] Traditionally, the presumed statement appears as a *tacit consent*; in other words, an inferred marital *consensus*.[113] That which is presumed is stated to be an inferred consent and, prior to 1940, this is also natural. An irregular marriage could then be established either through an express agreement *per verba de praesenti* or through cohabitation with habit and repute entailing a presumed tacit consent. The boundary between the two irregular kinds of marriage, however, is not sharp. A marriage *per verba de praesenti* could be entered into, in addition through an oral and written marriage agreement,[114] also through inferred actions as for example signs,

---

111 *Compare id.*

112 *Campbell v. Campbell* 4 M. 867, 918-919 (1866): "In a country where marriage could take place only by celebration, the presumption arising from cohabitation and repute is, that at some time or other a celebration took place; and if in any way it can be shewn, which is not always very easy, that a celebration never took place, then the presumption will yield to the truth. In a country where marriage may be effected in other ways than by celebration the presumption is that there was a marriage either by celebration or in some other of those recognised ways, and the presumption will only be overcome if it can be shewn that no marriage took place in any way."

113 Stair consequently distinguishes between marital *consensus* "by words expressly; or tacitly, by marital cohabitation or acknowledgement," *see* STAIR, *supra* note 9, I, 4, 6. *Compare* Erskine, who speaks of a consent that is not expressed "but is discovered *rebus ipsis et factis*," *see* ERSKINE, *supra* note 9, I, 6, 6.

114 With respect to written agreements, *see, e.g., Richardson v. Irving*, 1785; *Mackenzie v. Stewart*, 1848, 10 D. 611; and *Imrie v. Imrie*, 1891, 19 R. 185.

nods, curtsies,[115] even through one party's tacit acceptance of the other party's explicit declaration of intent.[116] A structural difference between the concepts still appears. The difference is, in part, because the only necessary and sufficient prerequisite for the establishment of a marriage *per verba de praesenti* is that the parties' marital *consensus* be proven through a contract. Another aspect of the difference is that marriage through cohabitation with habit and repute requires that the recently named elements existed even though, on the other hand, no defined contractual conclusion was required. Consequently, there are cases in which the parties' inferred actions have not been sufficient to constitute cohabitation with habit and repute. Nevertheless, on the other hand, the same actions together with verbal acts can prove that an agreement *per verba de praesenti* had been entered into.[117] Against this background, it is not surprising that the party in the dispute alleging the existence of an irregular marriage often cites both irregular forms.[118]

11.4.2 The State of the Law after 1939

If one looks at the situation after the 1939 reform, in which marriages *per verba de praesenti* were repealed, it can be maintained with justification that the presumption based on "cohabitation and repute" ought to have included only a regular marriage. Arguably, presuming a marriage *per verba de praesenti* presumes something that is invalid, and the opposing party is forced to present evidence that nothing invalid existed. It could certainly be reasonable to maintain that, if the informal marriage agreements were repealed, they ought neither to be able to be presumed to have occurred nor would a marriage come into existence because of such a presumption. This stance, however, is based on cohabitation with habit and repute as simply an evidentiary question. For those, such as Ashton-Cross, who represent the evidentiary theory, such a premise appears logical. Ashton-Cross did not address the issue of the object of the presumption, and so we shall not ascribe any view to him. Furthermore, it certainly was not the legislator's intent to limit the content of the presumption to this extent, [119] nor has the presumption in the case law,

115 *Walker v. McAdam* (1813) 5 Pat. 675. *See also Hoggan v. Craigie*, Martin Macl. & Rob. 942, 965, in which Lord Chancellor Cranworth states: "It is not necessary to prove the contract itself; it is sufficient if the facts of the case are such as to lead to satisfactory evidence of such a contract having taken place."

116 *Aitchison v. Solicitors-at-Law* (1838) 1 D. 42.

117 *Glass v. Glass's Trs.* (1907) 15 S.L.T. 716; and *Petrie v. Petrie*, 1911 S.C. 360.

118 *Robertson v. Inglis* (1787) 3 Pat. 53. *Compare De Thoren v. Wall* (1876), 3 R. (H.L.) 28, 33: "[T]he ceremony which took place, although invalid, was undoubtedly a consent by the parties to live together as husband and wife. And their subsequent cohabitation was a proof of continued consent."

119 HANSARD, *supra* note 4, col. 2246, albeit that the question was not more closely discussed by the legislator.

since the 1939 reform, been limited to addressing regular marriage.[120] Apparently, this has not been the case because cohabitation with habit and repute does not simply constitute evidence of a marriage agreement, but is also a required element in a presumption with a more independent significance.

1. *A Marital Intent de praesenti*

The presumption's applicability after the 1939 reform to irregular marriages raises the question of how the object of the presumption ought to be more closely determined. If, as before 1940, it was presumed based on cohabitation with habit and repute, it could with reason be said to be the parties' tacit consent, which is not obvious after the reform. However, even after the reform the presumed object is stated thus. As a result, Clive-Wilson argues that cohabitation with habit and repute raises a strong presumption "that there has been *tacit* consent to marriage"[121] (italics added). Assuming, however, a case in which the parties orally or in writing entered into an expressed marriage agreement *per verba de praesenti,* the question arises of whether an irregular marriage exists. No marriage *per verba de praesenti* has then naturally been established. However, assume *mutatis mutandis* that the question arises of whether a marriage by cohabitation with habit and repute has been established between the parties. If the recently named elements exist and the parties have expressly entered into a marriage contract, it appears somewhat curious to presume a tacit consent, unless there is no question of whether an agreement exists between the intent and the declaration of intent. For us, it appears more natural that, after the 1939 reform, that which ought to be presumed is not a tacit consent but rather a marital *consensus,* pure and simple.[122] We assume, in addition, although the question in the Scottish law has not received the attention it deserves, the presumed marital intent must be a *consensus de praesenti.* What the opposing party must prove is that no such *consensus* existed, either tacit or expressed.[123]

---

120 *See A.B. v. C.D.,* 1957 S.C. 415, 1958 S.L.T. 213; *Low v. Gorman,* 1970 S.L.T. 356; and *Nicol v. Bell,* 1954 S.L.T. 314. Observe however that in *Nicol* the cohabitation between the parties occurred both before as after 1940. *See also Shaw v. Henderson,* 1982 S.L.T. 211.

121 CLIVE-WILSON, *supra* note 10, at 116 and 122; CLIVE, *supra* note 10, at 49, 51 and 55. *See also* the case *Shaw v. Henderson,* 1982 S.L.T. 211.

122 If cohabitation with habit and repute exists, it appears that the party contesting the existence of the marriage has to prove that no marital *consensus* existed, neither expressed through a regular wedding ceremony, through an express agreement or through an inferred consent. The requirement for the party contesting the marriage to present counterevidence in the recently mentioned aspects appears – albeit that the question has not received the attention it deserves – to assume that the party maintaining the existence of the marriage in any case claims that the parties' marital *consensus* has come to expression in such a manner.

123 *Compare Nicol v. Bell,* 1954 S.L.T., 314, 326, in which Lord Mackintosh with respect to the possibilities of rebutting the presumption states: "It will not, however, be rebutted by merely showing that no consent had been expressly interchanged,

If the opposing party can show that the object of the intention of the parties was a future marriage, the presumption is rebutted. A common situation is that the couple has more or less made plans for a future formal wedding ceremony. As can be seen from the American law, however, the significance cannot be taken for granted.[124] On one side, such plans can be indicative that the parties only had a marital intent *de futuro*.[125] On the other side, the parties can have abandoned their plans or considered the future wedding ceremony as only a ceremony, while they have the intent to immediately become husband and wife.[126] To decide the presumed object in this manner does not conflict with the 1939 reform. Through this, marriage constituted simply through *consensus per verba de praesenti* was repealed. For establishing an irregular marriage according to the Scottish law, cohabitation with habit and repute is always required, which raises a presumption that a marital *consensus de praesenti* existed. The burden of proof shifts to the party contesting the existence of the marriage. If he or she cannot prove that no marital consent existed, a marriage is established.[127]

---

for the law of Scotland recognises cohabitation and repute if sufficiently established to be a tacit expression of matrimonial consent." *See also Donnelly v. Donnelly's Exr.*, 1992 S.L.T. 13, in which the court presumed that the parties "had tacitly consented to be married." Also in *Walker v. Roberts,* 1998 S.L.T. 1133, 1137, the court uses the expression "tacit consent."

124 With respect to the significance in the American case law of that the parties contemplated a formal wedding ceremony in the future, *see* the discussion in Chapter 6.4 *supra.*

125 In *Ackerman v. Logan's Exr.*, (2002) S.L.T. 37, the woman had consented to marry the man. She had received a ring and they had celebrated this with a "champagne dinner." The woman maintained that the ring was a wedding ring and that the parties thereafter considered themselves married. The court found that the parties "had agreed to become married at some future date, that they had thus become engaged to be married and that what was under discussion was an event which would take place at a future date." In *Walker v. Roberts,* 1998 S.L.T. 1133, 1137, the parties were found to view the engagement as showing that they considered marriage first in the future. *Compare Cossar v. Cossar,* (1901), 9 S.L.T. 44; and *Elder v. McLean* (1829) 8 p. 56, p. 62. In *Mackenzie v. Scott,* 1980 S.L.T. (Notes) 9, the parties were found to have an intent that they would become married persons "in the future."

126 *Compare* the case *Shaw v. Henderson,* 1982 S.L.T., in which the parties, who as unmarried persons lived together approximately 10 months, clearly planned to go through a formal wedding ceremony on 24 February 1979, but in which the man died on 31 January that same year. A marriage was found to be established "by cohabitation with habit and repute." The issue of whether the planned future wedding ceremony constituted an impediment against a *consensus de praesenti* appears however to not have been the object of court's assessment. *Compare Dewar v. Dewar,* 1994 S.L.T. 467, 469 and *Hendry v. Lord Advocate,* 1930 S.C. 1027. In *Mullen v. Mullen,* 1991 S.L.T. 205, divorced spouses had reassumed cohabitation. For religious reasons, the man did not wish to remarry as he did not recognize divorce. The parties were found to be married based on cohabitation with habit and repute. *Compare Nicol v. Bell,* 1954 S.L.T. 314.

127 *Compare Low v. Gorman,* 1970 S.L.T. 356, 360, in which no marriage through cohabitation with habit and repute was found to be established. Lord Robertson stated that neither of the parties had "consented to marriage" during the period of

A specific intent-based problem arises if divorced spouses move in again together and continue the cohabitation. On one side, as we noted in the American case law, there is an endeavor to favor remarriage with the support of the marriage presumption by that the parties were considered to have established a common law marriage.[128] On the other side, it can be argued that the parties through the divorce have expressed a strong intent to legally not be married and that resuming only the cohabitation need not indicate a new intent to be remarried. In *Mullen v. Mullen* (1991), several months after their divorce, the parties had resumed their cohabitation. After a period of hesitation, the woman suggested marriage, but the man did not wish to formally marry again because he did not recognize the divorce for religious reasons. After an approximately six-month cohabitation, when the woman's reservations against a continued cohabitation ceased, a marriage was considered established by cohabitation with habit and repute.[129]

2. *An Intent to Live Together or to Establish a Legal Relationship*

A distinction in the marital intent's *essensialia* between an intent to live as husband and wife and an intent to legally be married was discussed in the American case law. Nevertheless, in modern Scottish law, it does not appear to have received the attention it deserves. This distinction has considerable practical significance because it determines which types of evidence are relevant in rebutting the presumption.

As seen in Chapter 6, two main views can be discerned in the American case law that the courts did not expressly discuss. One, similar to that in the medieval canon law, concerned an intent to live together, to establish a *consortium omnis vitae* and a *individua vitae consuetude;* in other words, a community in everything in life and an undivided cohabitation for a lifetime.[130] This requirement was intended to distinguish temporary sexual relationships and marriages on a trial basis from common law marriage. According to the second view, the parties must have an intent to enter into a legal relationship or, as several courts have expressed it, to create a marital status. To what extent such an intent must include an intent to accomplish the legal effects of marriage appears unclear. The requirement of a legal intent is intended to distinguish between cases of cohabitation in

---

10 months that the parties lived together after the man received a marital divorce from his former wife. It appears however that one could argue that the presumption never had been raised, as the cohabitation in question was not found by the court to be "such as could be sufficient for a marriage by habit and repute," *see id.* at 361. Strictly speaking, according to our view, any assessment of the issue of whether the parties consented to the marriage therefore was not necessary. *Compare Bairner v. Fels,* 1931 S.C. 674, 1931 S.L.T. 489.

128 *See* Chapter 9 *supra.*

129 Mullen v. Mullen, 1991 S.L.T. 205.

130 *See* Section 6.3 *supra.*

which the parties simply have an intent to live together and cases in which they want legal effects. In certain cases, the American courts appear to have started with the premise that both types of marital intent must exist.

In the Scottish case law, the distinction appears to not have been the object of any closer discussion. In the older case law, there is a certain support for the idea that the marital intent can be focused on the actual cohabitation. For example, in *Dalrymple v. Dalrymple* (1811), the court maintained that a marriage must include an agreement between parties "looking to the *consortium vitae,*"[131] and in *Lowrie v. Mercer* (1840), Lord Medwyn speaks of "a consent of the parties to live together in the character of husband and wife."[132] In connection with the 1939 reform, through which cohabitation with habit and repute was retained, there are statements that point to the actual significance of the cohabitation.[133] In *Dewar v. Dewar* (1994), the man had said that he "was against the idea of marriage," but the court found that "whatever his words may have been that was not his intention. Any such words are totally inconsistent with his actings over the years."[134] Unfortunately, what the man was rejecting was not more clearly investigated in the case. Was he against living as and appearing outwardly as a spouse, or did he have something against the legal system of marriage? The court's reasons can be interpreted two ways. It may be that the man, through his cohabitation, actions, and appearance outwardly during eight years demonstrated that his intent was to live a marital life and then this was decisive, such that it did not matter whether he was against marriage as a legal idea. Alternatively, the court could also interpret the man's actions of presenting himself as a spouse, etc., showed that he had a "legal" intent to be married. Even though the latter interpretation appears less likely, there are other cases that indicate requirement of a *legal* intent, expressed by the courts in cases such as *Gow v. Lord Advocate* (1992), speaking of an intent to achieve "the status of marriage," "the marriage state," or "the married state."[135] The requirement of an intent to achieve a legal status can underlie these expressions. This interpretation

131 *Dalrymple v. Dalrymple,* (1811) 2 Hagg.Con. 54, 161 Eng.Rep. 665.

132 *Lowrie v. Mercer,* (1840) 2 D. 953, 983.

133 In the parliamentary treatment, Mr. Buchanan stated: "If a man without any legal ceremony lives with a woman and carries out all his social duties without the power of the law which compels the rest of us to do so, then I say that that man is just as good a husband and father as any other member of the community," *see* HANSARD, *supra* note 4, col. 2283.

134 *Dewar v. Dewar,* 1995 S.L.T. 467, 473.

135 In *Gow v. Lord Advocate,* 1993 S.L.T. 275, 276, the court notes the woman's reluctance to formally marry and that she "was at pains to secure that her own children got such money as she had at her death." *Compare Lapsley v. Grierson* (1845), 8 D. 34, 61, in which Lord Moncreiff speaks of "consent to be married." *See also* Lord MacKintosh in *Nicol v. Bell,* 1954 S.L.T. 314, 326, who uses the expression "consent to be husband and wife." *See also* FRASER, *supra* note 9, at 435, who states: "The essential in every marriage is the consent of parties to its constitution ... it must be serious, and with the intention to enter into marriage."

can be seen most clearly in *Mackenzie v. Scott* (1980), in which Lord Ross found that the woman began the cohabitation with the man without any intent to achieve "the legal status of his wife." Instead, their relationship was seen as only "one of concubinage." [136] With the application of the presumption, the other party in such a case must demonstrate that the couple did not have an intent to legally be married. The distinction is of great significance in separating cases that are to fall within the regulatory system from those that fall without, because many unmarried couples today can be assumed to have an intent to live together in a *consortium omnis vitae*, yet it is uncertain what legal regulation they prefer.

Despite the fact that with the assessment of the question of whether a marriage contract has been established or not, it is of the greatest weight to more closely define that which it is that the parties must have entered into an agreement about, it is remarkable how seldom the courts analyzed or addressed the issue of the marital intent's *essensialia*. This lack of precision with respect to the marital intent's legal content without a doubt has caused unnecessary and expensive lawsuits with drawn-out witness examinations, in which the parties, legal counsel, and courts tended to speak past each other.

3. The Point of Time for the Establishment of the Marriage

In those cases in which the invocation of a right is based on the parties' cohabitation and reputation as spouses, a predictable question concerns the point at which the marriage is deemed established. Is it the day when the cohabitation was commenced, or is it first when the necessary cohabitation has existed and a required marital reputation has been created? The American courts, as seen in Chapter 8 above, in those few cases in which they have tried the question, have leaned toward the point of time of the cohabitation's commencement.[137] To the extent that a certain period of cohabitation is required, it follows that every such common law marriage begins as an out-of-wedlock relationship, but the marriage that results from the transformation also includes the past, starting from when the cohabitation from the beginning was outside of marriage.

This retroactive transformation also appears in the Scottish case law with the application of the marriage presumption. It has, however, received considerable criticism. Eric Clive, after an in-depth analysis of the case law, has stated: "The only logical date for such a marriage is the date by which there has been sufficient relevant cohabitation ... and reputation to satisfy the law's requirements."[138] This interpretation makes sense if the cohabitation does not constitute simply an evidentiary fact supporting the existence of a marital *consensus* but also a necessary requisite either in addition

136 *Mackenzie v. Scott*, (1980) S.L.T. (Notes) 9.
137 *See* Section 8.5.2 *supra*.
138 CLIVE, *supra* note 10, at 63.

to the agreement or in a presumption. It can possibly be prompted by verification that the cohabitation, once commenced, was sufficiently marriage-like. It is not surprising that, in the individual case, there are additional difficulties in determining such a point of time. In certain cases, the courts have stopped at pure guesses about when the marital legal relationship began.[139]

Neither a decision of a court or registration is necessary to constitute a marriage by cohabitation, with habit and repute. The parties, however, have the possibility of filing a petition about the declaration of an already-existing irregular marriage, "a court declarator." This declares that a marriage was established at a somewhat earlier occasion. An irregular marriage can be registered only after such a decision, "a decree of declarator" by the court of session.[140]

11.5 Exceptions to the Marriage Presumption

Parties may lack the legal capacity to enter into a marriage with each other when they commenced their relationship because for example, one party was married to a third party. In this instance several American courts, as seen Chapter 9, have not found the marriage presumption applicable even though the impediment was later removed.[141] The explanation appears to be that the parties, when they commenced their cohabitation, were not viewed as having had a true marital intent. The party alleging the existence of a common law marriage in such cases has had to show that the parties, after the removal of the impediment, have expressed a new marital *consensus*. Other American courts, however, have chosen to also apply the marriage presumption in these cases. There are other good

139 In *Nicol v. Bell*, 1954 S.L.T. 314, 319, Lord Justice Clerk Thomson stated that "it may not always be possible for the court, which ultimately comes to pronounce a decree of declarator, to single out with any certainty any incident or even point of time in the association of the parties from which the married state should run. For practical reasons, the Court has to do its best to fix a point of time." In *Donelly v. Donnelly's Exr.*, 1992 S.L.T. 13,15, the parties had begun to live together "in or about 1979." The court stated that a precise date "was not ascertainable," but found that the parties were married with each other "on 1 January 1980". *See also Dewar v. Dewar*, 1995 S.L.T. 467, 473, in which the parties lived together for eight years and in which Lord Abernethy stated: "It appears that they moved in at around the end of 1974 or beginning of 1975. In these circumstances I think it appropriate to fix 1 February 1975 as the date of the marriage." That some marriage agreement entered into at a certain point of time need not be proven is maintained by *T. B. Smith*, who gives expression for the stance that a judgment as to marriage can be issued "though it cannot single out with certainty any particular date on which mutual consent to marriage was approved," *see* Smith, *supra* note 9, at 790.

140 *Morris v. Morris*, 1987 G.W.D. 39-1437; *Forbes v. House of Clydesdale Ltd.*, 1987 S.C.L.R. 136. In 2000, six and in 2001 four irregular marriages were registered in Scotland. *See* Annual Report of the Registrar General for Scotland, Table 7.7.

141 *See* Section 9.6.1 *supra*.

reasons for why the existence of an impediment against the marriage ought not lead to the marital intent being seen as having deficiencies. To not want to be married is one thing, to not be able to is another!

It also appears that originally, in the Scottish law, there was an unwillingness to apply the marriage presumption in those cases in which an impediment against the marriage initially existed but later was removed.[142] Nowadays, however, the dominant view appears to be that the presumption is applied even in these cases, assuming naturally that cohabitation with habit and repute exists.[143] Eric Clive states: "There is no reason why consent, originally ineffective because of an impediment to the marriage, should not emerge and become effective after the impediment is removed."[144] The question has thus arisen about whether the cohabitation that occurred prior to the impediment's removal is irrelevant in the assessment of an irregular marriage that was thereafter established. In *Kamperman v. MacIver* (1994), the court did not wish to accept that such facts and circumstances would be wholly irrelevant.[145] Even a marital intent expressed in a formal wedding ceremony, invalid because the woman was not of age, has been considered relevant when the age impediment later was removed and the parties continued the cohabitation. In *Woodward v. Woodward* (1958), the court stated: "Their participation in the invalid ceremony was, after all, a public declaration of their wish to be married to each other, which clearly persisted after the sixteenth birthday of the woman."[146] This reasoning resembles the use in the American case law of a *consensus continuus,* according to which the parties' express a marital *concensus* in the formalized wedding ceremony, as well in the cohabitation that follows.[147]

11.6 SUMMARY AND CONCLUSIONS

The medieval canon law models of marriage, marriage *per verba de praesenti,* in other words, marriage through an agreement regarding a present marriage, and marriage *per verba de futuro cum copula carnalis,* in other words, marriage through an agreement regarding a future marriage with subsequent consummation survived in Scotland until relatively recently. Nevertheless, as a result of application problems in the broadest sense,

142 *Cunningham v. Cunningham,* (1814) 2 Dow. 482; *Lang v. Lang* (1841) 3 D. 980; and *Lapsley v. Grierson* (1845) 8 D. 34.
143 *Shaw v. Henderson,* 1982 S.L.T. 211; *Nicol v. Bell,* 1954 S.L.T. 314; *Hendry v. Lord Advocate,* 1930 S.C. 1027; *Campbell v. Campbell* (1866) 4 M. 867, 5 M. (H.L.) 115; and *De Thoren v. Wall* (1876) 3 R. (H.L.) 28.
144 CLIVE, *supra* note 10, at 57.
145 *Kamperman v. MacIver,* 1994 S.L.T. 763, 765.
146 *Woodward v. Woodward,* 1958 S.L.T. 213.
147 With respect to American law, *see* Section 7.1.2 *supra.*

these models were repealed in the 1939 reform. Today, in Scotland, a third type of irregular marriage, namely, marriage by cohabitation with habit and repute, was valid until 2006.

1. *Marriage's Legal Character*

Even though the legal sources provide support for different views of the legal character of marriage by cohabitation with habit and repute, our analysis has ruled out the evidentiary theory, according to which the institution is simply a method of proving the existence of a marriage contract, which would constitute the only necessary and sufficient condition for the establishment of an irregular marriage. Nor have we accepted the legal element theory, according to which cohabitation with habit and repute would constitute the only necessary and sufficient requirement for the establishment of such a marriage.

Instead, our discussion has led us to the conclusion that marriage by cohabitation with habit and repute, after the 1939 reform, is a method of presuming marriage. From this presumption theory, it follows that cohabitation with habit and repute always constitutes the necessary requisite for the establishment of an irregular marriage. If the existence of these elements is not proven, no formless marriage exists, even though the parties' marital *consensus* would be able to be proven in another manner, e.g., through an oral or written marriage agreement. If the party claiming the existence of an irregular marriage is able to show cohabitation with habit and repute, the law presumes the presence of a marital consent. No concrete consent needs to be proven in the individual case.

The burden of proof then shifts to the party contesting the existence of the marriage, who can rebut the presumption by proving that no marital *consensus* existed. Consequently, it is a question of a rebuttable presumption, in other words, a *praesumptio iuris,* according to which the parties' marital *consensus* does not constitute a necessary requisite for the establishment of an irregular marriage but rather functions as counter-evidence. If the opposing party succeeds in rebutting the presumption, no marriage is established. If he or she, on the other hand, is not able to do this, a marriage by cohabitation with habit and repute is established.

2. *The Object of the Marital Intent*

The question can be posed as to what is the more closely defined object of the marital *consensus* after 1939 that is presumed through cohabitation with habit and repute and must be rebutted by the opposing party? To begin with, it is clear that, after 1939, consistent with American law, marital intent is *de praesenti,* in other words, a mutual intent to immediately become spouses. Consequently, the presumption is rebutted if it is shown that the parties entered into a marriage contract *de futuro,* in other words, to be married in the future. The application problems that have arisen in American law when cohabiting couples have had more or less stated plans for a future wedding ceremony have also appeared in the Scottish case law. In addition, the presumption is not, as is the case in many jurisdictions not recognizing common law marriage, limited to presuming that the parties have entered into a formal wedding ceremony; the existence of a marital *consensus* is presumed.

The difference between an intent to live as husband and wife and an intent to be legally married is a distinction within the marital *consensus* that is of great practical significance because it determines the type of evidence that is relevant to rebutting the presumption. This distinction has already been discussed in American case law, but does not appear to have received the attention it deserves in the modern Scottish law. On one side, there are cases that, in accordance with Roman and canon law, indicate that the object of the mutual intent must be to live in a *consortium omnis vitae;* in other words, to establish a community in everything in life and for the entire life. On the other side, there are cases indicating that the object of the mutual intent is to reach the legal effects of marriage. The requirement of a legal intent makes it possible to distinguish between parties who simply have an intent to live together and those who wish to achieve a legal community. The future use of different objects of the parties' marital *consensus* and their effects is discussed in Chapter 13, "The Constitutive Requisites in the Future."

The value of a presumption based on cohabitation with habit and repute naturally is dependent on what is to be presumed. If the object of the parties' marital *consensus* is their marital cohabitation, it is clear that the applied presumption appears primarily suitable, but if the object is to obtain a legal marital status, it can be questioned whether cohabitation with habit and repute actually and typically expresses such an intent. Today, a number of couples may choose to not formally marry just in order to avoid the legal effects of marriage. The danger of failing to consider the parties' own legal intentions in this construction of the common law marriage and cohabitation legislation is discussed in Chapter 14, "Arguments for and Against Common Law Marriage and Cohabitation Law."[148]

3. *From Agreement to Cohabitation*

The development of the irregular marriage in Scottish law during the 1900s shares tangible similarities with the development of common law marriage in the United States, in which the parties' cohabitation has different functions to play and an even greater role in the legal establishment of a formless marriage, while the marriage contract has receded into the background. Specifically, however, the Scottish development differs from the American. Characteristically, in almost all of the states recognizing common law marriage, the American concept of marriage is that the

148 *See* Chapter 14 Arguments for and Against Common Law Marriage and Cohabitation Law, *infra.*

cohabitation and the parties' outward appearance as spouses are necessary, in addition to the marriage contract, as seen in Chapter 8, "Cohabitation, Holding Out, and Reputation as Spouses." Moreover, the cohabitation has gained significant value as an expression of the parties' marital *consensus* and as evidence of the existence of an inferred marriage agreement as seen in Chapter 7, "Implied Marriage Agreements." The *praesumptio iuris* applied in Scottish law, as with the comparable presumption in American law discussed in Chapter 9, in principle goes a step farther so that the party claiming the existence of a marriage only has to prove the presence of cohabitation with habit and repute, while the parties' marital *consensus*, or more correctly stated the absence thereof, has the character of a counter fact.

The American courts, as we have found, have come to attribute to the cohabitation ever-greater evidentiary value. In several cases, their conclusions been disinclined to pursue the proving of the existence of a concrete marriage agreement, demonstrating that the difference between proving and presuming a marriage contract, in reality, is no longer very great.

The ever-stronger value of cohabitation in proving the establishment of an informal marriage, in both American and Scottish law, naturally raises the question of whether the parties' marital *consensus* can entirely be avoided in this context. The only necessary requisite would then, as is commonly the case in all the cohabitation legislation in the West during the last thirty years, as seen in Chapter 12, "Common Law Marriage and Cohabitation Law," consist of the parties' cohabitation. The answer, however, is not a given, as seen in Chapter 13, which discusses the function that the marriage contract and other elements in the future could have in the establishment of informal relationships that give legal effects.

4. *The Reasons for and Problems with the Scottish Presumption*

The application problems that followed from the formless marriage in the Roman and medieval canon law and which for a couple of hundred years have been associated with common law marriage in the United States, have also visited the Scottish irregular marriage. As seen in this chapter, the risk of misuse and the lack of legal certainty constituted leading reasons for why two of the Scottish forms of irregular marriages were repealed in 1939. Despite the fact that the Scottish legislator intended to create a law that was "simple" and "certain,"[149] the application of the third form, marriage by cohabitation with habit and repute, has revealed problems similar to those of many others. Even though the number of cases in which one has attempted to get an irregular marriage established through judgment has been surprisingly few, the difficulty of determining whether the cohabitation has been sufficiently marriage-like and whether the parties

149 HANSARD, *supra* note 4, col. 2288.

have had sufficient reputation as spouses has been obvious. Often, the lawsuits have been drawn out with many, long witness examinations that question the credibility of the parties and witnesses on both sides.[150] It has even been argued that the law is like a cohabitants' lottery in which a few winners are picked up by a complicated process involving considerable public expense, and that it is restricted to those who have been guilty of lies, deceit, or concealment of the truth.[151] It does not serve the interests of legal certainty if the courts face great difficulties in determining whether and when a legal relationship as significant as marriage has been established.

The presumption's requirement that the parties must have lived together as husband and wife, or "at bed and board," and not only as friends or as man and housekeeper, in several cases has required exhaustive investigations of the parties' sexual relationship, constituting a danger to privacy.[152] These, as with common law marriage and cohabitation legislation, are discussed in the comparative perspective in Chapter 14.

During the 1900s, the inconveniences of marriage by cohabitation with habit and repute in Scotland have caused several proposals concerning its repeal[153] and, in December 2005, the parliament finally adopted one.[154]

Scotland, today, experiences problems similar to those of Western Europe in general with a decreasing rate of marriage and an increasing number of cohabitations outside of marriage.[155] Based on this, Scotland enacted cohabitation legislation that serves purposes similar to those of marriage by cohabitation with habit and repute, in other words, giving legal protection to the more vulnerable party and children upon the dissolution of the relationship through separation or death. The legal protection, however, is more limited in the new legislation.

With respect to the application problems that the Scottish legislator wished to avoid, it can be noted that the courts now and in the future have

---

150 For example, in *Walker v. Roberts,* 1998 S.L.T. 1133, 27 witnesses were heard. The parties, who provided less than correct information as best suited them, were not considered credible.

151 *See* CLIVE, *supra* note 10, at 65.

152 *See, e.g., Nicol v. Bell,* 1954 S.L.T. 314, 315-316, in which was exhaustively investigated who was in the house and/or when the parties had sexual intercourse for the purpose of assessing whether a housekeeper relationship had glided into a marriage by cohabitation, habit, and repute.

153 The Scottish Law Commission's Report on Family Law, No. 135, Part VII (1992); The Marriage Law of Scotland, Committee Report (1969); O.R.(H.L.) Vol. III No. 16, 14th December 1938.

154 *See* Family Law (Scotland) Bill, SP Bill 36B, Session 2 (2005), 2A. The new law FAMILY LAW (SCOTLAND) ACT (2006), is not retroactively applicable as to relationships entered into prior to the law's validity.

155 The number of registered weddings in Scotland was 41,000 in 1951 and in 2002, 29,000. The number of "cohabiting couple families" increased from 4% in 1991 to 7% in 2001. *See* Legal Studies Research Programme Findings No. 43 (2004). With respect to the demographic development in the Western world in general, *see* Chapter 12 *infra.*

to try, not whether the parties lived together "by cohabitation with habit and repute" but rather, instead, whether a couple is "living together as if they were husband and wife."[156] One can question whether the new definition solves any application problems.

Typically, it is also questionable whether cohabitation legislation based on the parties' cohabitation is a good alternative to cohabitation with habit and repute. The frequent absence of a marital *consensus* in Western legal concepts about cohabiting persons makes it difficult to distinguish between cohabitations that ought to fall within the regulation systems and temporary relationships, friendships, etc. The danger in a system that does not consider the parties' own objectives for the relationship is that they can be subjected to a system not of their own choosing. Certain couples may have chosen to not formally marry in order to avoid the legal effects of marriage.

The courts, applying the different requirements for marriage-like cohabitation in the cohabitation legislation, face the same problems that the Scottish courts have had with the application of the requirements as to a community "at bed and board" and of "reputation." Neither has cohabitation legislation avoided the problems of the Scottish case law when it comes to determining when a relationship is established. Questions about legal certainty are at issue even with the application of modern cohabitation legislation.

The repeal in Scotland of marriage by cohabitation with habit and repute and, at the same time, the enactment of cohabitation legislation for couples living together as if they were husband and wife reflects, in a nutshell, the development during the 1900s. These questions are treated in a broader comparative perspective in Chapters 13 and 14, in which the arguments for and against common law marriage and cohabitation legislation are more closely discussed.[157]

156 See Family Law (Scotland) Bill, SP Bill 36B, 18, Session 2 (2005), sections 18-22. According to the new law, the parties are presumed *inter alia* to have a right to an equal share of the household goods acquired during the cohabitation and to money and property that is tied to their mutual household expenditures. The residence is not included in such property. In cases of death, the surviving cohabiting partner can receive a capital sum from the deceased's estate.

157 *See* Sections 13.4 and 14.3.8 *infra*.

PART III

The Future

CHAPTER 12

Common Law Marriage and Cohabitation Law

12.1 Introduction

Two paradoxical developments have characterized the family law regulations of formless couple relationships during the twentieth century. The first is that common law marriage, particularly during the first part of the century, was repealed in many American states. At the turn of the twentieth century, two-thirds of the American states recognized common law marriage;[1] in 1930, approximately one-half;[2] in 1950, one-third;[3] and in 1970, thirteen states as well as the District of Columbia recognized the institution.[4] Common law marriage was not repealed in any state between 1970 and 1990. Instead, the institution was adopted in Utah in 1987. During the 1990s and the beginning of the 2000s, four additional states repealed common law marriage[5] and, in 2008, eleven jurisdictions recognize the same.

The other development is that many states have enacted cohabitation legislation increasingly since the 1970s, because of decreasing rates of marriage and an increasing number of unmarried cohabiting persons and children born to these relationships. A characteristic feature in this development is that homosexual couples have also been given more equality with married and cohabiting couples under the law. Jurisdictions in Northern and Western Europe, Australia, New Zealand, Canada, and

---

1 George Elliott Howard, A History of Matrimonial Institutions III, 184 (1904).

2 Fred S. Hall, *Common Law Marriage in New York State*, 30 Colum. L. Rev. 1, 11 (1930).

3 John R. Williams, *Solemnization of Marriage: The common law marriage-never solemn and no longer common-will it remain law?*, 13 U. Miami L.Rev. 447, 453 (1959). Albert C. Jacobs & Julius Goebel, Jr., Cases and Other Materials on Domestic Relations 115 (3d ed. 1952), approximately twenty states.

4 Hans Friedrich C. Thomas, Formlose Ehen 150 (1973).

5 *Ohio*, Ohio Rev. Code Ann., § 3105.12 (B) (1, 2) (1991) ("common law marriages are prohibited"); *Idaho*, Session Laws, c. 104 (1995) ("No common-law marriage after January 1, 1996"); Idaho Code Ann. § 32-201 (2) (Michie 2003); *Georgia*, Ga. Code Ann. §§ 19-3-1, 19-3-1.1 (West 1996) ("No common-law marriage shall be entered into in this state on or after January 1, 1997"). *Pennsylvania*, Pa. Cons. Stat. Ann. § 1103 (West 2005) ("No Common-law Marriage, contracted after January 1, 2005, shall be valid").

the United States have enacted or plan to enact regulations with legal effects that will increasingly come to resemble common law and formal marriage. At the same time, though the problems of cohabiting parties are family law issues, the courts have demonstrated inventiveness and responsibility in attempting to reach resolutions by the application of property law principles within general private law. An additional feature in the development of the law has been that the scope of cohabitation legislation has been to some extent extended beyond relationships concerning couples, to those of parents and children, siblings, or friends living together.[6]

The notable increase in the number of unmarried cohabiting persons occurring during the last thirty years, as well as the endeavors by legislator and courts, respectively, to provide family law and property law solutions to the problems of cohabiting parties, have tested the limits of the legal terminology and the formation of concepts. In this process, it is unfortunate that the 200 years of experience with common law marriage, in the United States, have received surprisingly little attention with respect to the legislative work that has been carried out around the world during the latter part of the 1900s. The dominant understanding is that common law marriage is an anachronism, and cohabitation legislation is something entirely new. This conceptual disarray also makes itself felt in jurisdictions in which couples of the same or different sexes are offered the choice between marriage and registered partnership with nearly identical forms and legal effects.

The chapter, intended as a background and foundation for the chapters that follow, first addresses in Section 12.2, "Statistical and Demographic Data," the demographic developments during the last thirty years. Section 12.3, "Property Law Solutions in the Case Law," concerns the legal solutions for unmarried cohabiting couples that, in a number of countries, have grown out of property case law during the past thirty years. In this process, the boundary between the private law and family law spheres has tended to lose its clarity. The section concludes with suggestions about how to keep this boundary open, and, from a legal policy perspective, evaluate the development in the property law that has occurred. Section 12.4, "Family Law Regimes for Cohabiting Persons," gives an overview of the modern legislation regarding cohabition development. The chapter, in order to serve its purpose, concentrates on the main features of cohabitation law and its relationship to common law marriage. Part of the section compares the legal systems in which the cohabitation itself constitutes grounds for rights and obligations and those that require registration. Chapter 13, "The Constitutive Requisites in the Future," includes a discussion of the different subjective and objective requisites

6 *See, e.g.,* legislation in Norway, Belgium, Canada, Australia, and Hawaii, *infra* under 12.4 and 13.3.2.

and the function these can have with defining the concept cohabitation. Chapter 14, "Arguments for and Against Common Law Marriage and Cohabitation Law," focuses on a presentation and discussion of the named arguments and other cohabitation legislation; Chapter 15, "A New Model of Marriage," addresses a reformation of formal marriage. A new marriage model is presented for the purpose of resolving the problems stemming from the decreasing rate of marriage.

12.2 STATISTICAL AND DEMOGRAPHIC DATA

A given premise for any discussion concerning the future of common law marriage and other cohabitation law must be the statistical data available concerning the rate of marriage, the number of children born to various types of relationships, and the number of unmarried persons cohabiting. Demographic data concerning, e.g., age, social group, duration, the frequency of dissolution, and other data concerning unmarried cohabiting persons as a social phenomena can, as well as the parties' own legal prioritizations, also serve as the basis of assessing the need for legal solutions.

Prior to the following presentation, it ought to be noted that the selection of facts presented is based on statistical and demographic investigations performed at different points of time and sometimes with different methods and definitions, e.g., of the concept "cohabiting." Despite these reservations, the data available is of interest as a basis for the legal policy discussion.

12.2.1 Rates of Marriage

This diagram reveals that the Western world from 1966 to 2004 has had a dramatic decline in the rate of marriage, which has been correctly designated as a part of a social revolution.[7] This remarkable development appears to have had its origins in the Nordic countries in Europe, in which Sweden (SE) has occupied a particular position since the end of the 1960s. The frequency of marriage in Sweden was 7.8 in 1966, and in 1973, it had decreased to 4.7. Thereafter, the level has steadily been the lowest among comparable countries. A deviation from this trend occurred, however, in 1989 in that the number of marriages more than tripled to 12.8, which can be explained by the circumstance that the media then had asserted that couples that did not marry would lose the

---

7 Martha Bailey states with reference as to the development in Canada: "The tendency to reject marriage as a conjugal choice is evidently part of a social revolution, one of a series of rejections of institutions founded on a social order that is falling out of fashion..." *See Marriage and Marriage-Like Relationships* (Ottawa: Law Commission of Canada, 1999) at 27.

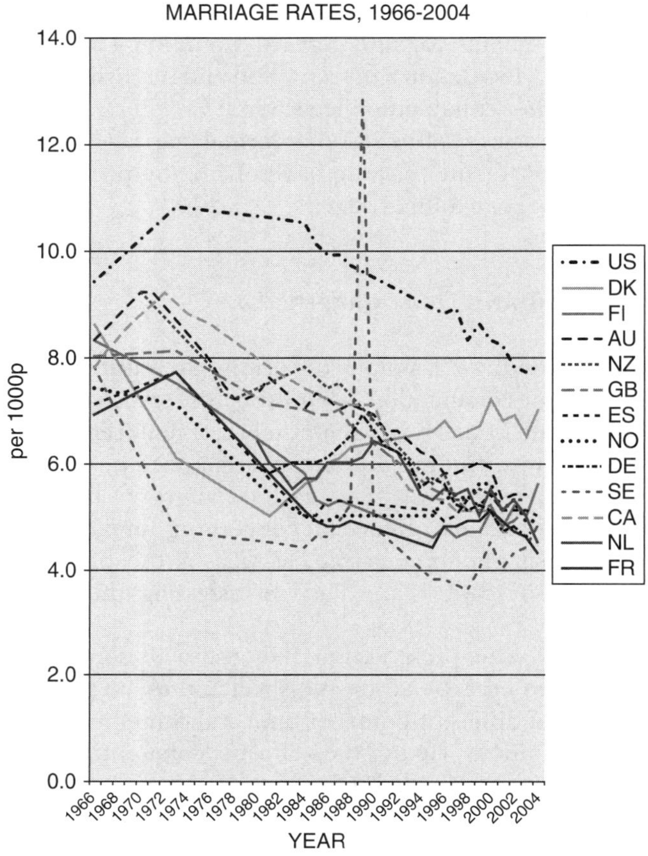

FIGURE 1: The rates of marriage during 1966–2004 as per 1,000 inhabitants.
The diagram is based on data from the UN Demographic Year Book.

widow's pension. This, however, was only partially correct, but indicates the effect information concerning a single right can have as to behavioral patterns. Thereafter, the frequency decreased again down to a bottom level in 1998 of 3.6. Denmark (DK) has followed Sweden at its heels during the 1970s, as did Norway (NO) and Finland (FI). However, it should be noted that Denmark, from the middle of the 1980s, has had an increasing rate of marriage, which in 2004 was at the highest within the EU with 7.0, a relationship that ought to be of interest for demographic science to more closely analyze.[8]

8 According to Danish sociologists, the reasons for the increased statistics as to the rate of marriage in Denmark still have not been analyzed. It therefore is too early to speak of a break in the trend. According to e-mails to Göran Lind from Professor Mai Ottesen with Socialforskningsinstitutet and from Anna Qvist at Denmark's Statistik in Copenhagen.

Western Europe, in general, met the same decline as the Nordic countries later. The majority of countries in 2004 went down to similar marriage rates, in other words, Finland 5.6, Great Britain (GB) 5.1 in 2003, Spain (ES) 5.0, Norway (NO) 4.9, Germany (DE) 4.8, and Sweden 4.8. It should be observed that Sweden was surpassed in 2004 by the Netherlands (NL) with 4.5 and France (FR) with 4.3, which took the lead.

Australia (AU) and New Zealand (NZ) have had the same development as in Europe. From very high levels of 9.2 in 1970, the rate of marriage has raced downwards to Western European levels, with Australia having 5.4 in 2003, and New Zealand 5.3 in 2003. Similarly, the marriage rate in Canada (CA) went from equally high numbers of 9.2 in 1972, and thirty years later, the rate had decreased to 4.7 in 2002.

The United States, which traditionally has had the highest rate of marriage, 10.8 in 1973, also experienced a rapid decrease in frequency. Even though the levels are still comparatively high, the curve goes steeply downwards in the past few years to 7.8 in 2004. It ought to be noted that the rate of marriage, which in the United States is based on ceremonial marriage, does not deviate from the average in the United States in the states that recognize common law marriage. A pervasive feature in the development is also that the age for the first marriage has greatly risen in the Western world since the 1970s.[9]

12.2.2 The Number of Children Born to Non-Marital Relationships

The decreasing rate of marriage in the Western world is met by an equally dramatic increase in the number of children born outside of marriage, indicating that marriage between the parents has not been viewed as a prerequisite for having children in the same manner as previously. Radical changes in attitude have occurred. Fifty years ago, having a child outside of marriage was a disgrace and imposed the stigma of illegitimacy on the child; today, being born to unwed parents is widely accepted.

The number of children born outside of marriage, commonly referred to as *children of unwed mothers*, was 55 percent (40 percent in 1980), in Sweden in 2000.[10] As a result of the parents' cohabitation, 75 percent of these children were born in a family with their father and their mother. That year, in Great Britain, the number of children born to unwed mothers was 40 percent (12 percent in 1980). In 2001, 63 percent of the parents

---

9 Kelly Raley, *Recent Trends and Differentials in Marriage and Cohabitation: The United States,* in THE TIES THAT BIND: PERSPECTIVES ON MARRIAGE AND COHABITATION 19 (Linda Waite et al. eds., 2000).

10 European Social Statistics: Demography 2002, table E-9; and Demographic Statistics 1997, table E-4.

of these children cohabited.[11] Denmark, in contrast to other Western countries, has had an increasing rate of marriage since the middle of the 1980s; during the 1990s, it had a decreasing number of children born to unwed mothers, from 47 percent in 1990 to 44 percent in 2000.[12] In Spain, where the rate of marriage decreased later than in the other Western European countries, the number of out-of-wedlock children in 2000 was up to 17 percent, a quadrupling in twenty years from 4 percent in 1980.[13]

In Australia, the number of children born outside of marriage increased from 14 percent in 1982 to 31 percent in 2002,[14] and, in New Zealand, the number of ex-nuptial births in 2001 was up to 44 percent, a quadrupling during the most recent twenty years.[15] In Canada, the number of non-marital births was one-third of all births in 1994, compared with only 6 percent in 1974.[16] Finally, in the United States, the comparable numbers in 1999 were 33 percent (17 percent in 1979), which among Anglo-Americans was 22 percent; Hispanics, 42 percent; and African-Americans, 69 percent.[17] In approximately 40 percent of the American non-martial births, the unmarried mother lived together with the father at the time of the birth.[18]

The increasing number of out-of-wedlock children can be partly explained by the increasing number of unmarried cohabiting persons, which to a high degree is now an accepted way to start a family and have children. A majority of these children are, consequently, born in a family that includes their father and mother. The attitudes toward unmarried families in different countries vary to a large extent according to the number of cohabiting persons. In the Nordic countries that have a large number of unmarried cohabiting persons, a cohabiting couple with children is considered as a "family" by approximately 90 percent of the population, while the comparable number in Western Europe in general is approximately 60 to 70 percent.[19]

---

11 *Id. See also* Kathleen Kiernan, *Unmarried Cohabitation and Parenthood in Britain and Europe*, 26 LAW & POLICY 33, 36 (2004).

12 European Social Statistics: Demography 2002, table E-9; and Demographic Statistics 1997, table E-4.

13 *Id.*

14 ABS Births Australia (2002).

15 Statistics New Zealand, Births and Deaths (March 2002).

16 *See* Law Commission of Canada (2001). *Beyond Conjugality*, at 127. Ottawa: Law Commission of Canada.

17 *Family Research Report*, 15 J. FAM. RES. INST. No. 7 (Nov. 2000). The number of births to unmarried mothers in the United States was 18% in 1980, 28% in 1990, and 34% in 2002. *See* National Vital Statistics Reports, Vol. 52, No. 10, December 17, 2003.

18 Larry Bumpass & Hsien-Hen Lu, *Trends in Cohabitation and Implications for Children's Family Contexts in the United States*, 54 POPULATION STUD. 29, 34 (2000). According to Wendy D. Manning & Pamela J. Smock, *Living Together Unmarried in the United States: Demographic Perspectives and Implications for Family Policy*, 26 LAW & POLICY 87, 102 (2004), 50% of unmarried parents cohabit.

19 Kiernan, *supra* at note 11, at 49.

12.2.3 The Number of Unmarried Cohabiting Persons

As cohabitation is not an object for registration in the same manner as marriage, available statistics concerning these numbers are uncertain. Comparisons are made more difficult in that different definitions of the concept of cohabitation have been used in the research that has been carried out in different countries and at different times. Kathleen Kiernan, who has researched the developments in Northern and Western Europe, has stated that "cohabitation is complex and diverse, and includes a range of living arrangements of varying durations that may or may not include children, that may or may not convert into marriage, that may be full-time or more part-time, and that may be but one of a portfolio of coresidential partnerships."[20] In general, it may still be possible to say that the decreasing rates of marriage and the increasing number of children born to unwed mothers cancel each other out and can be explained by the dramatic increase in unmarried cohabiting couples throughout the entire Western world. Unmarried cohabitation has become increasingly socially accepted, though the picture is not without ambiguities.[21]

Seen generally, available data indicate that unmarried cohabiting couples in modern times first received a foothold in Northern Europe, countries that still, today, have the highest share. Sweden, which at the end of the 1960s had approximately 6 to 7 percent and at the end of the 1970s approximately 15 percent, today has approximately 30 to 35 percent cohabiting persons who are not married.[22] The number of unmarried cohabiting persons is estimated in Denmark to be 18 percent, and in Norway and Finland both 15 percent.[23] The development experienced in

20 Kathleen Kiernan, *Redrawing the Boundaries of Marriage,* 66 J. MAR. & FAM. 980, 981 (2001).

21 *See* Arland Thornton and Linda Young-Demarco, *Four Decades of Trends in Attitudes Toward Family Issues in the United States: The 1960s through the 1990s,* 63 J. MAR. & FAM. 1009 (2001). *See also* Manning, *supra* note 18, at 90. DAVID BRADLEY, FAMILY LAW AND POLITICAL CULTURE: SCANDINAVIAN LAWS IN COMPARATIVE PERSPECTIVE 95 (1996), states: "A comparatively recent demographic analysis of Western Europe suggests that, in general, unmarried cohabitation has been merely or barely tolerated in the South. Acceptance has been greater further north and most marked in the Nordic countries." *Compare* Grace Ganz Blumberg, *The Regularization of Nonmarital Cohabitation: Rights and Responsibilities in the American Welfare State,* 76 NOTRE DAME L. REV. 1265, 1296 (2001), who argues that cohabitation has become socially acceptable at all levels of society. David Popenoe, *The Problem of Cohabitation,* 3 (1999-2001), cites Sociologist Andrew Cherlin: "It was unacceptable a couple of decades ago. It is acceptable now." Andrew J. Cherlin, *Toward a New Home Socioeconomics of Union Formation,* in THE TIES THAT BIND: PERSPECTIVES ON MARRIAGE AND COHABITATION 126, 127 (Linda Waite et al. eds., 2000), states that cohabitation outside of marriage has become increasingly common and acceptable among the general population.

22 Prop. 2002/03:80, at 24; SOU 1978:55, at 45.

23 *See* SVEND DANIELSEN, NORDISK BØRNERET II, 33 (2003); Linda Nielsen, *Family Law in Denmark,* in FAMILY LAW IN EUROPE 90 (Carolyn Hamilton and Alison Perry, eds., 2d ed. 2002), approximately 20%. In 2004 the number of unmarried cohabitants in Norway was estimated to be 20%, *see* Høringsnotat, January 2007. Ministry of Justice. Snr. 200405522 EP.

Western Europe, in general, was also experienced by Australia, New Zealand, and Canada primarily in the 1980s and the 1990s. The number of unmarried cohabiting couples there still lies at a somewhat lower level. In 2002, the number of unmarried cohabiting persons in Great Britain was estimated at approximately 12 percent of all cohabiting persons. Even in Australia, in 2001, the number of unmarried persons was estimated to be 12 percent, while the number ten years previously was 8 percent.[24] In Canada, the number of unmarried cohabiting persons (common-law relationships) increased from 6 percent in 1981 to 14 percent in 1996. The province of Quebec in 1996 had the highest share, with 24 percent unmarried cohabiting persons.[25] In the United States, the number of unmarried cohabiting couples for the entire population is still lower than in the above-named countries, but the increase has been dramatic from a thirty-year perspective. In 1970, the total was estimated at 523,000; in 2003 it was 5.05 million, in other words, a tenfold increase. It has been estimated that, of all couples, unmarried partners now comprise about 10 percent of all couples.[26]

The preceding statistics concern the average in the adult population. The number of unmarried cohabiting couples is considerably larger among younger than older couples. One age group of cohabiting persons that is of particular interest to study is couples thirty to forty years old. The majority in this group has entered into couple relationships and either married or continued to live together as unmarried. Many also have had children. Kathleen Kiernan, who has researched unmarried cohabiting couples in different age groups in Northern and Western Europe, reports the statistical results in Table 1.

It can be seen from the table that Sweden has been in a class by itself with the lowest rate of marriage, but also in terms of the highest number of cohabiting persons. The age group investigated to a large extent is equally as many (48 percent) unmarried cohabiting persons as married (52 percent). Consequently, approximately one-half of all couples live together outside of marriage. The following group of countries consists of Finland, Denmark, and France, with approximately one-third cohabiting. The Danish decrease in unmarried cohabiting couples can be tied to the increase in the rate of marriage. The next group of between 20 and 30 percent, in other words, approximately one-fourth cohabiting persons, includes Great Britain,

24 ABS, Marital Status and Living Arrangements, Marriages and Divorces, Australia 3310.0 (2002).

25 *See* Bailey, *supra* note 7, at 35. *See also* Céline Le Bourdais & Évelyne Lapierre-Adamcyk, *Changes in conjugal life in Canada: Is cohabitation progressively replacing marriage?,* 66 J. Mar. & Fam. 929 (2004); Law Commission of Canada (2001). *Beyond Conjugality,* at 2, notes 4 and 6. Ottawa: Law Commission of Canada.

26 Married-Couple and Unmarried-Partner Households: 2000, Census 2000, Special Reports, tbl 1, the United States Census 2000 (2003); and the United States Bureau of the Census, Unmarried-Couple Households, by Presence of Children: 1960 to Present, Table UC-1 (2004).

TABLE 1. The Percentage of Unmarried Couples Among All Cohabiting Persons 30 – 39 Years Old.

	Percent		*Percent*
Sweden	48	West Germany	15
Finland	36	Italy	14
Denmark	33	Spain	14
France	31	Luxemburg	13
Great Britain	28	Ireland	12
The Netherlands	25	Portugal	9
East Germany	24	Greece	8
Austria	22		
Belgium	20		

Source: 2002 to 2003 Kathleen Kiernan's analyses of Eurobarometer Surveys.[27]

The Netherlands, East Germany, Austria, and Belgium. Thereafter, is a group with 12 to 15 percent, approximately one-seventh cohabiting persons, in West Germany, Italy, Spain, Luxemburg, and Ireland. Finally there is Portugal and Greece, having only 8 to 9 percent unmarried couples, approximately one-tenth cohabiting persons in the actual age group. Unmarried cohabiting couples, consequently, are the most common in Northern Europe and least common in Southern Europe.

If one chooses the age group 25 to 34 years, instead, the number of unmarried cohabiting persons seen generally is much higher (in Sweden 85 percent, in Western Europe approximately 50 percent),[28] but many in this group choose to marry later.

The number of couples who lived together before marriage has steadily increased and is calculated to be 99 percent in Sweden,[29] 77 percent (6 percent at the end of the 1960s) in Great Britain,[30] 73 percent in Australia.[31] Even if a good many marry, there is a tendency toward an increasing number of long-term cohabitations.

The dramatic decrease in the rates of marriage and the increasing number of unmarried cohabiting couples invites questions about the causes of these developments. Legislators who believe that these developments are issues that need statutory solutions can look to the parties'

27 Kiernan, *Supra* note 11, at 38, and Kiernan, *supra* note 20, at 982. *Compare* Norway (another investigation) where the number of unmarried cohabitants 30-39 years old was estimated in 2004 to be 32%, *See* Høringsnotat, Ministry of Justice, January 2007. Snr. 200405522 EP.

28 Kiernan, *supra* note 11, at 38.

29 99% already in the 1970's. *See* JAN TROST, UNMARRIED COHABITATION 79-102, 191 (1979).

30 Kiernan, *supra* note 11, at 35.

31 ABS, Marital Status and Living Arrangements, Marriages and Divorces, Australia 3310.0 (2002).

own explanations about why they choose unmarried cohabitation instead of marriage for possible answers to the problem. Nevertheless, it is illusory to believe that couples that refrain from marrying always have rational legal reasons for their actions or inaction. Many "drift into" cohabitation, without conscious consideration and decisions about the choices involved in cohabitation.[32] The Swedish Sociologist Jan Trost stated in the 1970s "couples do not choose to cohabit instead of to marry. They just cohabit."[33] In order to take the step to marry, on the other hand, couples need reasons. Therefore, one can state that many cohabiting parties simply choose to cohabit because they did not have sufficient reason to marry. The same is often true today, both in Europe and in the United States,[34] a situation that does not rule out that some couples are more rational.

The causes ought rather be found in more general changes in attitude toward marriage and weddings. The social pressures that previously existed about marrying are not as strong in today's secularized world as they were forty years ago, even though there are variations among different social groups. Many that marry do so out of tradition but also in order to indicate or confirm the ties in the relationship.[35] There can be a general difference in relation to certain cohabitations that are assumed to represent a more individualized lifestyle.[36] There ought to be cohabiting persons, e.g., middle-aged couples who already have one marriage behind

---

32 *Cf.* Homer H. Clark, Jr. The Law of Domestic Relations in the United States 57 (1968) ("drift into"); Carol S. Bruch, *Property Rights of De Facto Spouses Including Thoughts on the Value of Homemakers' Services,* 10 Fam. L.Q. 101, 135 (1976), maintains that the majority probably choose to cohabit as unmarried persons "either 1. In ignorance of the legal consequences of either marriage or nonmarriage (perhaps the majority of non-lawyers believe that common law marriage exists in all jurisdictions and that protection is granted to stable nonmarital relationships), 2. under the assumption that some legal protections are available, or 3. with absolutely no thought given to the legal consequences of their relationship." *Cf.* Bill Atkin, *The Rights of Married and Unmarried Couples in New Zealand: Radical New Laws on Property and Succession,* International Society of Family Law World Conference, unpublished paper, Copenhagen/Oslo, (august 2002), at 4, who maintains that de facto couples do not give vows in the same manner as spouses, but that they "do make a choice to live together."

33 Trost, *supra* note 29, at 186. *See also* Eleanor D. Macklin, *Nonmarital Heterosexual Cohabitation,* Mar. Fam. Rev., March-April 1978 at 1, 6: "Living together is seldom the result of a considered decision ... Most cohabitation evolves from a drift of sleeping more and more frequently together and gradual accumulation of possessions in one residence..."; David S. Caudill, *Legal Recognition of Unmarried Cohabitation: A Proposal to Update and Reconsider Common-Law Marriage,* 49 Tenn. L. Rev. 537, 565 (1982); Kathleen Kiernan, *The Rise of Cohabitation and Childbearing Outside Marriage in Western Europe,* 15 Int'l J.L. Pol'y & Fam. 1, 3 (2001); and Blumberg, *supra* note 21, at 1296. In Wendy Manning & Pamela J. Smock, *Measuring and Modeling Cohabitation: New Perspectives from Qualitative Data,* 67 J. Marriage S. Fam. 989, 995 (2005), the authors held that "the process of deciding to cohabit is not necessarily planned or deliberate" and that movement into cohabitation often is described as "a gradual or unfolding process."

34 Blumberg, *supra* note 21, at 1296.

35 Trost, *supra* note 29, at 190.

36 Ulla Björnberg, *Cohabitation and Marriage in Sweden - Does Family Form Matter?,* 15 IJLPF 350, 356 (2001).

them and prefer a higher degree of independence than is allowed by the economic sharing of marriage. At the same time, there are cohabiting persons who anticipate being covered by the same regulations as those that apply to married persons. The high rate of marital divorce also appears to play a role because couples that have experienced their own parents' divorce may themselves choose to cohabitate without marrying in order to avoid the possibility of divorce. This is a somewhat paradoxical relationship given that the frequency of dissolution is much higher among cohabiting persons than among married persons.[37] With little knowledge about legal regulations, many couples do not make conscious choices about cohabitation in general. As a result, it is necessary to be cautious about drawing conclusions based on assumptions about the parties' understandings of the long-term effects of the legal regulations.

12.2.4 Cohabitation as a Social Phenomenon

Cohabitation outside of marriage in the Western world is not a homogenous social phenomenon. This group includes temporary relations or couples living together on a trial basis in order to see whether they are compatible and then later separate or marry.[38] Much cohabitation lasts only two to four years, but many tend to be all the more long term.[39] Included also are couples who begin to cohabitate, having already decided to marry later. Finally, more and more couples intend to live together for the long term, unmarried, and do so.[40] The number of couples having children during the cohabitation is increasing.[41]

In a country such as Sweden—which, during the last thirty years, until 2004 has had the lowest rate of marriage and the highest number of cohabitations outside of marriage in the Western world—unmarried cohabitation since the 1970s has been considered "normal" behavior and not in any manner a "deviant phenomenon." Cohabitations within or outside of

37 *See* Popenoe, *supra* note 21, at 2.

38 LYNNE M. CASPER & SUZANNE M. BIANCHI, CONTINUITY AND CHANGE IN THE AMERICAN FAMILY 44-59 (2002)(at the end of 1980s, 61% of cohabiting persons considered their relationship as on a trial basis).

39 Kiernan, *supra* note 11, at 35. According to M.D. BRAMSLETT & W.D. MOSHER, COHABITATION, MARRIAGE, DIVORCE, AND REMARRIAGE IN THE UNITED STATES 22 (2002), 60% of persons cohabiting marry within 5 years.

40 STEPHEN CRETNEY, FAMILY LAW IN THE TWENTIETH CENTURY, A HISTORY 518 (2003), who speaks of a substantial increase in long-term cohabitation by couples who have no intention of marrying and never do so; and that the increase in cohabitation has taken place at the expense of the numbers marrying. *See also* J. Haskey, *Demographic Aspects of Cohabitation in Great Britain*, 15 IJLPF 51, 56 (2001). Larry L. Bumpass, *The Changing Significance of Marriage in the United States*, in THE CHANGING FAMILY IN COMPARATIVE PERSPECTIVE: ASIA AND THE UNITED STATES 63, 71 (K.O. Mason et al. eds., 1998) ("the probability of marrying following cohabitation is declining, as is the probability of marrying a cohabiting partner").

41 Judith A. Seltzer, *Families Formed Outside of Marriage*, 62 J. MAR. & FAM. 1247, 1251 (2000).

marriage also have, to a large degree, been considered identical phenomena. Several decades ago, disregarding age differences, according to Swedish sociologists, it was thought that marriage and cohabitation were characterized by the same indicators, and were comparable social institutions.[42] Daily life appears, to a large extent, to be the same for married and unmarried parties and their families.[43]

A somewhat different picture appears today, indicating that unmarried couples in Sweden represent a more individualized lifestyle, meaning that, more than married couples, they prefer separate finances, and the frequency of dissolution is much higher than in marriage. In both the family and the labor market, the situation appears to be less stable for unmarried couples than for married couples.[44]

During most recent years, extensive demographic and social research has been conducted concerning unmarried cohabiting couples and their families in Western Europe and the United States.[45] The results, as far as

---

42 Trost, *supra* note 29, at 186. *See* the same author in *A Renewed Social Institution: Non Marital Cohabitation,* 21 Acta Sociologica 303 (1978); and in *Cohabitation without Marriage in Sweden,* in Marriage and Cohabitation in Contemporary Societies 16, 19 (John M. Eekelaar, Sanford N. Katz eds., 1980). *See also* SOU 1978:55, at 140 and 144.

43 *See* Björnberg, *supra* note 36, at 356. *Compare* Trost, *supra* note 29, at 192.

44 *See* Björnberg, *id.* at 356-358. Life in "reconstituted families" appears to be less satisfactory, particularly for mothers. The risk for separation is particularly high among unmarried couples where the parties previously lived in another relationship and in which the man has children from a previous relationship. According to Björnberg, cohabiting couples tend to have a more equal allocation of work in the home, but more conflicts concerning raising children and the division of work and money than married couples. Unmarried couples are commonly less educated and have a less secure status in the labor market than married women and men. According to Kristen R. Heimdal & Sharon K. Houseknecht, *Cohabiting and Married Couples' Income Organization: Approaches in Sweden and the United States,* 65 J. Mar. & Fam. 525, 534 (2003), separate economies are more common among cohabiting persons than among spouses both in Sweden and the United States.

45 A good overview of the results with respect to demographic and social research as to cohabiting unmarried heterosexual couples and their children can be found in Manning, *supra* note 18. *See* further Linda J. Waite, *Trends in Men's and Women's Well-Being in Marriage,* in The Ties that Bind: Perspectives on Marriage and Cohabitation 368, 386 (Linda Waite et al. eds., 2000), states: "Married men and women generally do better than unmarried people on the dimensions we looked at and never do worse. We see little erosion of the long-term advantage of married men and women across a range of dimensions from happiness to health to satisfaction with job and family life, and financial well-being." *See also* Manning, *supra* note 18; Mary Parke, *Are Married Parents Really Better for Children? What Research Says About the Effects of Family Structure on Child-Wellbeing,* 3 Clasp Policy Brief, Couples and Married Series 1 (2003); Wendy Sigle-Rushton and Sarah McLanahan, *For Richer or Poorer? Marriage as an Anti-Poverty Strategy in the United States,* 57 Population 509 (2002); and Martha S. Hill et al., *Childhood Family Structure and Young Adult Behaviours,* 14 J. Pop. Econ. 271 (2001). *See* regarding sociological aspects as to cohabiting, Ann Laquer Estin, *Ordinary Cohabitation,* 76 Notre Dame L. Rev. 1381-1390 (2000-2001); Pamela J. Smock, *Cohabitation in the United States: An Appraisal of Research Themes, Findings, and Implications,* 26 Ann. Rev. Soc. 1, 7 (2000); Linda Waite and Maggie Gallagher, The Case for Marriage (2000); Larry L. Bumpass et al., *The Role of Cohabitation in Declining Rates of Marriage,* 53 J. Mar. & Fam. 913, 917 (1991); Seltzer *supra* note 41, at 1251;

the United States is concerned, indicate that cohabiting couples compared with married couples are younger, have less education, lower wages, poorer health, and, in general, experience a lower degree of well-being. They are less disposed to support each other economically and place more value on independence. Joint finances are more unusual than among married couples and cohabiting pairs espouse a strong "individualistic ethic."[46] They feel less secure in their relationships and demonstrate less sexual fidelity toward each other than married couples.[47] Conflicts and physical abuse are more common than in a married family.[48] The results indicate that the children of unmarried parents are more emotionally unhealthy and suffer from a higher degree of family instability than the children of married couples.

Traditionally, unmarried cohabitation in the United States has been considerably more common among African-Americans and Hispanics than in the Anglo-American population.[49] Cohabitation has also been considerably more common in the lower classes of society than in the higher. Nevertheless, since the 1970s, cohabitation outside of marriage, expanded so that it no longer limits itself to the named ethnic and

---

Jay D. Teachman et al., *The Changing Demography of America's Families*, 62 J. MAR. & FAM. 1234 (2000); Bumpass *supra* note 18; Steven L. Nock, *A Comparison of Marriages and Cohabiting Relationships*, 16 J. FAM. ISSUES 53 (1995); CASPER, *supra* note 38, at 44-45; and BRAMSLETT, *supra* note 39, at 11.

46 *See* Kathryn Edin et al., *A Peek Inside the Black Box: What Marriage Means for Poor Unmarried Parents*, 66 J. MARIAGE & FAM. 1007, 1010 (2004); Heimdal, *supra* note 44, at 532; Anna E. Winkler, *Economic Decision-Making by Cohabitors: Findings Regarding Income Pooling*, 29 APPLIED ECON. 1079 (1997); Marin Clarkberg et al., *Attitudes, Values, and Entrance into Cohabitational Versus Marital Unions*, 74 SOC. FORCES 609 (1995); PHILIP BLUMSTEIN & PEPPER SCHWARTZ, AMERICAN COUPLES: MONEY, WORK, SEX 94-101 (1983); William G. Axinn & Arland Thornton, *The Relationship between Cohabitation and Divorce: Selectivity or Causal Influence?*, 29 DEMOGRAPHY 357, 361 (1992); Nock, *supra* note 45, at 65; Scott M. Stanley, *Maybe I Do: Interpersonal Commitment and Premarital or Nonmarital Cohabitation*, 25 J. FAM. ISSUES 496 (2004); and Elisabeth Thomson & Ugo Colella, *Cohabitation and Marital Stability: Quality or Commitment*, 54 J. MAR. & FAM. 259, 266 (1992). *See* similar results regarding Australia, Helen Glezer & Eva Mills, *Controlling the Purse Strings*, 29 FAM. MATTERS 35, 36 (1991).

47 Linda J. Waite, & Kara Joyner, *Emotional and Physical Satisfaction with Sex*, in SEX, LOVE, AND HEALTH IN AMERICA 239, 268 (Edward O. Laumann & Robert T. Michael eds., 2001); Judith Treas & Deidre Giesen, *Sexual Infidelity Among Married and Cohabiting Americans*, 62 J. MAR. & FAM. 48, 58 (2000); Renata Forste & Koray Tanfer, *Sexual Exclusivity Among Dating, Cohabiting, and Married Women*, 58 J. MAR. & FAM. 33, 38 (1996); and BLUMSTEIN, *supra* note 46, at 274.

48 Regarding relationships in conflict, *see* Larry L. Bumpass et al., *The Role of Cohabitation in Declining Rates of Marriage*, 53 J. MAR. & FAM. 913, 923 (1991); and Susan L. Brown & Alan Booth, *Cohabitation Versus Marriage: A Comparison of Relationship Quality*, 58 J. MAR. & FAM. 668, 674 (1966). Regarding violence, *see* Miner Salari & Bret M. Baldwin, *Verbal, Physical, and Injurious Aggression Among Intimate Couples Over Time*, 23 J. FAM. ISSUES 523 (2002); WAITE *supra* note 45, at 155; Todd K. Shackelford, *Cohabitation, Marriage and Murder: Woman-Killing by Male Romantic Partners*, 27 AGGRESSIVE BEHAVIOR 284 (2001); and Jan E. Stets, *Cohabiting and Marital Aggression: The Role of Social Isolation*, 53 J. MAR. & FAM. 669, 674 (1991).

49 Raley, *supra* note 9, at 23-28; and Wendy D. Manning & Pamela J. Smock, *Why Marry? Race and the Transition to Marriage Among Cohabitors*, 32 DEMOGRAPHY 509 (1995).

social groups. In line with changing attitudes, the phenomenon has spread to all classes of society, even though it still sometimes is viewed as a "poor man's marriage."[50] It is also considerably more common among African-Americans and Hispanics than among Anglo-Americans for the parties to have children during their cohabitation,[51] which indicates that long-term cohabitation is more common among these groups and is more often seen as an alternative to marriage, while the cohabitation among Anglo-Americans more often is a trial marriage or the initial phase of a marriage.[52] Economic instability has also been shown to reduce the probability of the parties marrying.[53] Despite the above-reported differences between unmarried cohabiting couples and spouses, it appears that the majority of cohabiting persons have had plans to marry at some time.[54]

---

50 Manning, *supra* note 18, at 97-98, states that Anglo-Americans, African-Americans, and Hispanics report similar levels of cohabitation experience and that cohabitation is commonplace in all these groups. According to the authors, it is however more common with children in "black and Hispanic cohabiting households" than in Anglo-American households. *See* in addition Kathryn S. Vaughn, Comment, *The Recent Changes to the Texas Informal Marriage Statute: Limitation or Abolition of Common-law Marriage?,* 28 HOUS. L. REV. 1131, 1142 (1991)(cohabitation recently has become common with middle and upper class couples). *See also* MARY ANN GLENDON, THE TRANSFORMATION OF FAMILY LAW 277 (1989), who states that cohabitation is spread in the different social groups and notes that it also concerns upper-middle class cohabitation. *Compare* Cynthia Grant Bowman, *A Feminist Proposal to Bring Back Common Law Marriage,* 75 OR. L. REV. 709, 766 (1996), who still in 1996 argued that informal unions were simply more frequent among lower income groups than among middle class. *Compare also* William A. Reppy, Jr., *Property and Support Rights of Unmarried Cohabitants: A Proposal for Creating a New Legal Status,* 44 LA. L. REV. 1677, 1681 (1984); Wand, *The Relevance of Premarital Cohabitation to Property Division Awards in Divorce Proceedings: An Evaluation of Present Trends and a Proposal for Legislative Reform,* 63 B.U. L. REV. 105, 106 (1983); LEONORE WEITZMAN, THE MARRIAGE CONTRACT 361-363 (1981); and Arlene Skolnick, *The Social Contexts of Cohabitation,* 29 AM. J. COMP. L. 339, 399 (1981).

51 Fifty-five percent of African American children, 40% of Hispanic children and 30% of Anglo-American children can be assumed to have experienced parents who are unmarried cohabiting persons. *See* Manning, *supra* note 18, at 98; and Bumpass, *supra* note 18.

52 Raley, *supra* note 9, at 23-28, states: "At the marriage rates for 1992-1995, about 60% of white women and about 30% of black women will marry by age 25. This 30 point gap narrows only slightly by age 50, at which time 92% of white women and 66% of black women will have ever married." *See also* Manning, *supra* note 49, at 509.

53 Marin Clarkberg, *The Prize of Partnering: The Role of Economic Well-Being in Young Adult's First Union Experiences,* 77 SOC. FORCES 945 (1999); Raley, *supra* note 9, at 23-28; Casper *supra* note 38, at 52-53; Valerie K. Oppenheimer, *Cohabiting and Marriage During Men's Career-Development Process,* 40 DEMOGRAPHY 127 (2003); and Yu Xie et al., *Economic Potential and Entry into Marriage and Cohabitation,* 40 DEMOGRAPHY 351, 361 (2003).

54 John D. Cunningham & John K. Antill, *Cohabitation and Marriage: Retrospective and Predictive Comparisons,* 11 J. SOC. & PERS. REL. 77 (1994)(more than 90% answered that they planned to marry sometime). *Compare* Lixia Qu, *Expectations of Marriage Among Cohabiting Couples,* 64 FAM. MATTERS 35 (2003), who found that between 50-60% of the cohabiting persons have stated that marriages between them were likely or very likely with their partner. Approximately 25% said that marriages were unlikely or very unlikely.

An alarming fact is that the frequency of dissolution of cohabitations is considerably higher than for marriage even if the parties have children. This is proven in both American and European investigations. In Sweden, in 1991, the frequency of dissolution among cohabiting persons with children was three times as high as among married couples with children. According to an investigation of the year 1997, the risk for separation was almost twice as large among cohabiting persons as among married persons.[55] A similar situation exists in Western Europe in general.[56] Over 50 percent of the cohabitation relationships in the United States are dissolved through separation within five years, compared with approximately 20 percent of marriages.[57] Even long-term cohabitations are less stable than marriages.[58] These results have given rise to an extensive social academic scholarship undertaken for the purpose of protecting marriage.[59]

Every legislator contemplating legal solutions based upon the socioeconomic differences between marriage and cohabitation ought to consider the difference between correlation and causality.[60] The correlations that the investigations have proven between unmarried cohabitation and the above-named facts need not necessarily demonstrate that there is causality between them. The circumstances under which the unmarried family lives (finances, health, etc.) need not necessarily be caused by the parties' marital status and the system of regulations under which they live. There is little certain academic evidence that the situation would have been otherwise if the same couple had married.

Despite the meritorious research already done about unmarried cohabitation, there is a need for further legal sociological research. Particularly

---

55 *See* Be 13, SM 9401, SCB 1994 and Demografiska rapporter, SCB 1999:1.

56 Kiernan, *supra* note 11, at 46-47, estimates that cohabiting unions are more fragile than marital unions and that children born within marriage were less likely to see their parents separate than those born in a cohabiting union (not shown).

57 *See* BRAMSLETT, *supra* note 39, at 22; Bumpass, *supra* note 18; Seltzer, *supra* note 41, at 1252; Julie Brines and Kara Joyner, *The Ties That Bind: Commitment and Stability in Modern Union,* 64 AM. SOC. REV. 333 (1999); Larry L. Bumpass et al., *The Role of Cohabitation in Declining Rates of Marriage,* 53 J. MAR. & FAM. 913, 917 (1991); Smock, *supra* note 45, at 13; Raley, *supra* note 9, at 23-28; and Fragile Families, *Union Formation and Dissolution in Fragile Families,* FRAGILE FAMILIES RESEARCH BRIEF, No. 14 January, Princeton, N.J. (2003). Even according to Canadian research, marriage is more stable than unmarried cohabitation, *see* Bailey, *supra* note 7, at 30 and 35.

58 Susan L. Brown, *Relationship Quality Dynamics of Cohabiting Unions,* 24 J. FAM. ISSUES 583 (2003).

59 A considerable body of social academic scholarship has been devoted to efforts to protect marriage and to encourage unmarried couples to marry, *see, e.g.,* M. Robin Dion and Barbara Devaney, *Strengthening Relationships and Supporting Healthy Marriage Among Unwed Parents,* 1 BUILDING STRONG FAMILIES IN BRIEF 1 (2003); JAMES Q. WILSON, THE MARRIAGE PROBLEM: HOW OUR CULTURE HAS WEAKENED FAMILIES (2002); MAGGIE GALLAGHER, THE MARRIAGE MOVEMENT: A STATEMENT OF PRINCIPLES (2000); WAITE *supra* note 45; BARBARA DAFOE WHITEHEAD, THE DIVORCE CULTURE: RETHINKING OUR COMMITMENTS TO MARRIAGE AND FAMILY (1996); and William A. Galstone, *Divorce American Style,* 124 THE PUBLIC INTEREST 12 (1996).

60 *See* Manning, *supra* note 18, at 103.

meaningful would be investigations about the manner and degree to which the legal marital system of regulation affects behavioral patterns. What is the significance for family stability of the parties' formal vows at the commencement of marriage, the spouses' obligations to support each other, and marital divorce regulations?[61] If such questions can be answered, the question remains whether the suitable solution is common law marriage, in which all of marriage's regulations become applicable to cohabiting couples, or whether the solution lies in encouraging the parties to formally marry, and if so, how that is to occur.

12.2.5 Cohabitation and Common Law Marriage

Many Americans are reputed to believe that the "mere passage of time transforms cohabitation into common-law marriage."[62] The preceding discussion demonstrates the heterogeneity of cohabitations clearly shows that only a portion fall within the system of regulations that common law marriage offers. Also the most of the cohabitation legislation that has been enacted in the Western world over the last thirty years is applicable only to a portion of the relationships. These legal institutions purport, as does common law marriage, to provide regulations for more long-term, stable, and marriage-like cohabitations or relationships that have had such a purpose. How, more precisely, the different doctrines have succeeded in the problematic if not impossible task of drawing a bright line between, on one side, cohabitations that fall within the regulation system and, on the other side, the relationships that fall outside, is treated in the following chapters.

The lack of uniform definitions of both common law marriage and cohabitation, as reflected in the demographic data, it is risky to more precisely estimate to what degree cohabiting couples are included in the legal concept of common law marriage. Certain authors have found that cohabiting couples, today, do not fulfill the requirement of holding out as spouses in order to constitute a common law marriage, because they no longer feel compelled to present themselves as husband and wife.[63]

A reasonable estimation ought, however, to be that the majority of couples with families and the intent to permanently live together are included in the concept of common law marriage as it has developed in the case law. This estimation is based on the courts' use of implied agreements and legal presumptions, as found in Chapters 7 and 9, based on the parties' cohabitation, which often results in findings of the existence of a common law marriage under requirements of cohabitation that are limited to a

61 *Compare* the investigations described *supra* in note 49.

62 American Law Institute, Principles of the Law of Family Dissolution: Analysis and Recommendations (2002), § 6.02.

63 *See* Cynthia Grant Bowman, *Legal Treatment of Cohabitation in the United States*, 26 Law & Policy 119, 123 (2004); and Harry D. Krause et al., Family Law, Cases, comments, and questions 221 (5th ed. 2003).

few months.[64] In the majority of jurisdictions, the parties are also required to outwardly appear as spouses and gain the reputation as such, as discussed in Chapter 8. Nevertheless, the circumstance that they do not call each other husband and wife need not, as we have found, prevent the creation of a common law marriage if the couples associated these expressions with formal marriage. Therefore, several cases in which the parties stated that they were "single" or "unmarried," nevertheless resulted in the finding that a common law marriage had been established.[65] Falling outside common law marriage, however, are cases of cohabitation in which the parties live together on a trial basis.

Because the cohabitation legislation that has been enacted in many countries during the past few years is directed primarily at the same group of cohabiting persons as common law marriage, there is reason to compare these legal solutions.

12.2.6 The Legal Challenge

The dramatic decline in the rate of marriage, the rising number of children born outside of marriage, and the increasing number of unmarried cohabiting couples in the Western world is a wake-up call and challenge to every concerned legislator. These developments mean that a large number of families, parents as well as children, at some point in their lives, risk being outside of the legal marital systems. Cohabiting couples and their children, thereby, will not enjoy the legal protection they need at different stages of their lives. Moreover, the state loses the prerogative of defining and imposing obligations and controls over which, previously, it had held a monopoly on behalf of public policy. This creates a need for legal solutions abut the problems created by cohabitation.

In light of the heterogeneity of unmarried cohabiting persons, the solutions are not predictable. It is risky to construct uniform legal regulations for a category if certain persons live on a trial basis for a period before they break up or marry, while others already have decided to marry, and still others have decided to live together for the long term without marrying. The differences are not restricted to the actual situations. Different couples can be assumed to have entirely different understandings about which legal solution best fits them, and the state's interests in its capacity as third party to the contract can be assumed to vary according to the kind of cohabitation in question. Added issues arise about the freedoms the parties ought to have in order to either legally regulate their

64 *See, e.g., Matter of Estate of Burroughs*, 486 N.W.2d 113, 115 (Mich.App. 1992): "There is no specified length of time the parties must live together, but there must be a constancy of dwelling together."

65 *See* Section 7.5 and 7.8 as well as Section 8.5.2.9 *supra*.

situation or choose a legal system as further discussed in Chapter 15, "A New Model of Marriage."

The sociological picture raises many questions of strategic importance to legislators. Should cohabiting unmarried couples through common law marriage or other cohabitation legislation be completely equated with couples through common law marriage who formally marry? Or ought, in addition to marriage, specific legal systems be constructed for cohabiting unmarried persons, systems with legal effects that differ from those of marriage? How ought the category *cohabitation* be defined with respect to the group's heterogeneous character? Are legal mechanisms needed to distinguish different kinds of cohabitation with respect to the intentions of the parties and the gestalt of their actual cohabitation?

What legal conclusion should be drawn from the fact that cohabiting persons help each other to a lesser extent than spouses, are unfaithful, and separate more often? Ought the conclusion be that the same system of regulations applicable to spouses therefore does not fit cohabiting persons or ought the opposite conclusion be that cohabiting persons need the norms of marriage in order to work and keep the relationship together? Is the canon law strategy of capturing lost sheep in marriage's norms relevant today? Should persons who are cohabiting be encouraged to marry and in such a case, how is that to proceed, or is registration a suitable alternative? Is there a need to reform marriage so that it meets the needs of families in actual situations and parties with actual desires? Or, ought the legal problems of cohabiting parties be resolved through the application of general private law?

12.3 Property Law Solutions in the Case Law

The notable increase in the Western world in the proportion of unmarried cohabiting persons during the last thirty years and the circumstance that these relationships, to a high degree, have become socially accepted, did not immediately lead to family law legislation purporting to solve the cohabiting parties' internal legal problems. Instead, the courts, in the absence of common law marriage and other family law alternatives, took a community responsibility by applying civil law principles outside of family law, offering a protection for the parties, e.g., in the event of separation or death.

The issue, therefore, has been raised whether this judicial development, in actuality, has been a way for American states to reintroduce common law marriage, after it has previously been repealed.[66] At the same

66 *Hewitt v. Hewitt*, 77 Ill.2d 49, 31 Ill.Dec. 827, 394 N.E.2d 1204, 1207-1211 (1979); *Morone v. Morone*, 50 N.Y.2d 481, 429 N.Y.S.2d 592, 596, 407 N.E.2d 438, 442 (1980); and *Merrill v. Davis*, 673 P.2d 1285, 1286-1287 (N.M. 1983). *See also* Homer H. Clark, Jr.,

time, in states recognizing common law marriage, proposals to repeal it have been justified by referring to the existence of solutions within general civil law.[67] This section, therefore, focuses on the question of how these private law remedies relate to common law marriage and the question of whether they constitute an alternative to family law solutions based upon common law marriage or other cohabitation legislation.

12.3.1 Cohabitation Through Property Law Lenses

The property law solutions discussed in this section do not refer to traditional explicit agreements entered into by both parties in a cohabitation with third parties with respect to the acquisition of property, or entered into with each other concerning the transfer or division of property. Today, there is no doubt that two cohabiting persons can together purchase real estate or a car from any third party by both signing the contract and paying the purchase price. Neither does any doubt exist that one party, through a purchase or gift, can convey half of his or her real estate to his or her cohabiting partner, by which both become owners. Neither are explicit agreements concerning compensation for work performed or for financial contributions treated here. Such traditional civil law transactions are naturally of great practical interest for unmarried cohabiting persons because they can offer legal protection, but fall outside of the framework for this exposition.

Instead, of interest here are those cases in which the assets in an estate through explicit agreements have been acquired in one person's name and the other party directly or indirectly has provided financial contributions to the acquisition or to the family's economy, or has contributed with work in the home and care of the children. In the event that their relationship dissolves, unmarried cohabiting couples do not enjoy the legal protection provided by ceremonial and common law marriages to the economically weaker party in the form *inter alia* property divisions and maintenance, the courts, over the last thirty years, have been confronted by the question of whether, in these situations, there are any property law remedies that can protect cohabiting persons.

The New Marriage, 12 WILLAMETTE L.J. 441, 449 (1976); Reiland, *Hewitt v. Hewitt: Middle America, Marvin and Common-Law Marriage*, 60 CHI. B. REC. 84, 88-90 (1978); and John B. Crawley, *Is the Honeymoon Over for Common Law Marriage: A Consideration of the Continued Viability of the Common Law Marriage Doctrine*, 29 CUMB. L. REV. 399, 400 (1998/1999).

67 After the recommendation of the Family Law Advisory Committee in Kansas, the Judicial Council in 1981 presented a proposal as to the repeal of common law marriage in Kansas. Three reasons were cited as support for the proposal: (1) the difficulty in proving the relationship, (2) the availability of causes of actions, other than divorce, to address the division of property between cohabitants, and (3) the easy availability of obtaining a marriage license, *see* House Bill No. 2689 (1982); Nancy G. Maxwell, *Can Kansas Live Happily Ever After Without Common Law Marriage?*, 20 THE CIRCUIT RIDER No. 3 (1981).

In order to be able to obtain a positive answer to this question, it has been necessary for the courts to consider family relations through new lenses. The marriage-like cohabitation, which from sociological and general human nature perspectives traditionally has been described in the nonlegal terms of love, mutual support, cooperation and care, services and reciprocal services, gifts and reciprocal gifts, has come to be defined as a conglomerate of legal actions. This development was not possible without an impressive feat of legal engineering, requiring far-reaching analogies with legal institutions originally intended for purposes other than family law. Traditional concepts were exposed to extensive interpretations that, at times, have had the character of pure fictions. Implicit agreements concerning compensation for services, hidden ownership rights, and partnership constructions have arisen from marriage-like cohabitations. Moreover, new types of constructive trusts, into which no explicit agreements had ever been entered, have appeared within the common law tradition. Through these new lenses, the parties' family behavior could be viewed *inter alia* as unjust enrichment; the parties' contributions and services to each other and on behalf of the relationship legally relevant circumstances that can be cited as the basis for new types of claims to compensation and property. Many courts have strived to reach solutions. As the Court of Appeals in London expressed the matter, "whenever justice and good conscience required it."[68]

1. The Modern Developments Outside of the United States

In Nordic countries, which since the end of the 1960s have had the lowest rate of marriage and the highest number of unmarried cohabiting couples, different property law remedies have grown in the case law within general civil law to protect the more vulnerable party in a cohabitation.

Sweden took the initiative early in family law legislation with respect to relationships between cohabiting persons. As seen below, however, it would not be until 1987 before the country received its first more extensive cohabitation legislation. Before this, it was the courts that sought to reach solutions in the event of the dissolution of a cohabitation relationship. Several cases concerned spouses with separate property who found themselves in the same unfair situation as unmarried cohabiting persons. The remedy for both categories, in the Swedish case law, was the finding of "hidden" ownership rights. If, e.g., property was purchased in the man's name, the woman was able to receive a hidden ownership right in it based on the existence of an inferred agreement between the parties. The man then has been viewed as having purchased the property as an agent on her behalf. The woman's financial contribution to the acquisition has been considered most meaningful for the occurrence of a hidden ownership right, but other contributions have also been considered. The Swedish

68 *Hussey v. Palmer* (1972) 1 W.L.R. 1286, 1290.

Supreme Court has rejected the attempts of certain lower courts to give the woman's work in the home independent significance in assessing the existence of a hidden ownership right.[69] Despite the fact that the hidden owner's financial contribution has been small, in several cases, her portion has been presumed to be one-half.[70] To find a hidden ownership right, the Swedish Supreme Court has laid down three requirements: (1) The property is to be purchased for joint use; (2) The party who did not outwardly present himself or herself as owner is to have provided a financial contribution to the purchase; and (3) The parties are to have had a mutual intent that the ownership rights be shared.[71] The circumstances at the point of time of the acquisition are decisive in this assessment, even though subsequent circumstances can have evidential value. Hidden property rights have not been recognized in relation to creditors and other third parties.[72]

The Swedish courts have not awarded financial compensation for work in the home in those cases in which agreements have not been entered into. The motivation, which is interesting for determining the boundary between property and family law, has been that the work, to a high degree, has been performed in the parties' common interests, a step in the cohabitation.[73] No cases concerning unjust enrichment in the relationship between cohabiting persons have yet been decided in Sweden. On the other hand, it appears that the Supreme Court in **Denmark** has preferred this legal basis to co-ownership, opening the possibility for compensation for the contributions of the party working at home.[74] The Swedish case law in the general private law, as well as the Swedish cohabitation legislation in this area appears to be fairly conservative from an international perspective.

A comparison between the property law co-ownership rights as tenants in common and the family law legislation for cohabiting persons in Sweden demonstrates that financial circumstances are also relevant to the assessment of whether a cohabitation exists in accordance with the Swedish Cohabitees Act. In accordance with the law's legislative preparatory works,

---

69 SvJT 1974 rf. p. 71; SvJT 1977 rf. p. 2; NJA 1980 p. 705; and NJA 1981 p. 693.

70 NJA 1980 p. 705; NJA 1981 p. 693; NJA 1982 p. 589; NJA 1983 p. 550; NJA 1983 p. 410 I-II; NJA 1986 p. 83 (tax law); RÅ 1986 ref. 179 II (tax law); NJA 1987 p. 137; NJA 1986 p. 513; NJA 1988 p. 112; NJA 1988 p. 197; NJA 1989 p. 114; NJA 1990 p. 702; NJA 1992 p. 163; NJA 1993 p. 324 (not cohabiting persons or spouses); NJA 2000 p. 3 (presumption, open co ownership); and NJA 2004 p. 397. *See also* ANDERS AGELL, ÄKTENSKAP, SAMBOENDE, PARTNERSKAP 69-78 (3 ed. 2004), with references; ANDERS AGELL, ÄGANDERÄTTEN TILL FASTIGHET FÖR MAKAR AND SAMBOENDE (1985); and EVA RYRSTEDT, BODELNING AND BOSTAD 64-87 (1998).

71 *See* NJA 2004 p. 397, 405-406, in which the court did not find proven a joint intent of the parties to own the real estate together.

72 NJA 1984 p. 772; NJA 1985 p. 615; NJA 2001 p. 511; and NJA 1985 p. 97.

73 NJA 1975 p. 298. The surviving cohabiting partner did not receive compensation for her care of the man.

74 *See* 1977 UfR 814 and 1980 UfR 480 H. *See also* Nielsen, *supra* note 23, at 57.

consideration ought to be given *inter alia* to the parties' cooperation in carrying out daily tasks in the home, and any economic cooperation that argues that there is a shared household.[75] However, it ought to be noted that these circumstances are not necessary or sufficient for the establishment of a cohabitation.

In the Nordic countries, it appears that **Norway** has gone farthest in developing remedies within the general private law. There, the courts have accepted that work on a farm and in the home can constitute not only evidence of the existence of an inferred agreement,[76] but also a direct basis for both co-ownership[77] and a demand for compensation for unjust enrichment.[78] In Norway, in contrast to Sweden, this type of co-ownership is valid against third parties such as creditors. The need for property law remedies may have been greater in Denmark and Norway than in Sweden, because the former two countries do not confer any rights that correspond to those given in the Swedish Cohabitees' Act as to the division of the residence and household goods acquired during the cohabitation, regardless of which of the parties owns the property.[79]

German *law* does not have any unified legislation concerning the relationship between couples that live in "non-marital life communities" (*nichteheliche Lebensgemeinschaften*). Paradoxically, however, the expression "marriage-like life communities" (*eheähnliche Lebensgemeinschaften*) is also used for the same phenomena.[80] The difference is that the first focuses on the legal effects of marriage and the latter on the cohabitation.

Since moral impediments no longer exist, in several cases, the German courts have used property law solutions to resolve the problems of

75 Prop. 2002/03:80, at 28. More as to the definition, *see* Section 13.3.2.

76 Rt. 1956 p. 264; TONE SVERDRUP, STIFTELSE AV SAMEIE I EKTESKAP OG UGIFT SAMLIV 469 (1997).

77 Rt. 1975 p. 220. The obligation with the assessment as to property rights of assets that the spouses used jointly, to take into consideration a spouse's work in the home has been codified in Ekteskapsloven (1991) § 31. The principle is also applied as to individual property, *see* Rt. 1980 p. 1430. Rt. 1966 p. 874. The same principles are also applicable as to unmarried cohabiting couples, *see* Rt. 1978 p. 1352; Rt. 1984 p. 497. *See also* Tone Sverdrup, Marriage and Cohabitation: Community of Life or Community of Work? Working Papers in Women's Law No. 51 (Nov. 1999), Institute of Women's' Law, Department of Public and International Law, University of Oslo (unpublished); and PETER LØDRUP, FAMILIERETTEN § 11 (4 utg. 2001), with references.

78 Rt. 2000 p. 1089; Rt. 1984 p. 497 (dicta). A surviving cohabiting partner received compensation from the estate of the deceased for taking care of him for five years. *Compare* on the other hand the Swedish case NJA 1975 p. 298. As to the validity against creditors, *see* the Norwegian cases Rt. 1978 p. 871; Rt. 1980 p. 1430, and *compare* the Swedish cases, NJA 1984 p. 772 and NJA 1985 p. 615.

79 In January 2007, the Norwegian Ministry of Justice sent out a proposal to different institutions to get feedback concerning a proposed minimum inheritance right and a right to keep the estate undivided as to residence and household goods for surviving cohabitants, *see* Høringsnotat, January 2007, Snr. 200405522 EP.

80 Extensive references, *see* Andreas Wacke, *Zivilrechtsfragen der nichtehelichen Lebensgemeinschaft*, in MÜNCHENER KOMMENTAR, BGB 7, 100 (4th ed. 2000).

cohabiting couples.[81] In contrast to the Nordic countries, the German courts have applied partnership law regulations. In the event that the parties, through mutual efforts, have acquired or built a house, a leasehold, a vehicle, or a business, in several cases, a partnership (*BGB-Gesellschaft*) has been considered entered into by the courts, despite the fact that the acquisition occurred only in one party's name (§§ 705 ff. BGB).[82] In an ordinary case in which no formal agreement has been executed, an inferred partnership agreement has been considered entered into in the relationship between the parties (*Innengesellshaft*).[83] Not uncommonly, the inferred agreements have a more or less fictional character.[84] It is not unusual that assets covered by the partnership objective have become objects for an equal division.

According to the dominant view, however, the purpose of cohabiting has not been accepted as a partnership objective.[85] One argument,

---

81 In the older case law, moral impediments were considered to exist as against private law solutions, *see* BGH, NJW 1968, 932; FamRZ 1968, 241, 243; BGH, FamRZ 1970, 19. During the 1970s, the attitude as to civil law claims began to change, *see* OLG, NJW 1978, 224, 225; LG, NJW 1976, 1690, 1691; NJW 1980, 1520, 1521; FamRZ 1980, 664, 665. For more on this, *see* Rainer Frank, *The Status of Cohabitation in the Legal Systems of West Germany and Other West European Countries,* AM. J. COMP. L. 185 (1985).

82 BGH, FamRZ 1992, 408 f.; OLG, FamRZ 1988, 58; BGH, NJW 1986, 51 f.; BGH, FamRZ 1987, 676; BB 1986, 1522; BGH, FamRZ 1985, 1232; BGHZ 84, 388; KG, FamRZ 1983, 271; BGH, FamRZ 1983, 791; BGH, FamRZ 1983, 349; BGH, FamRZ 1982, 1065; OLG, FamRZ 1982, 265; KG, NJW 1982, 1886; FamRZ 1983, 271; OLG, NJW 1982, 1885; FamRZ 1982, 265; BGH, FamRZ 1981, 530; BGH, NJW 1981, 1502; BGH, FamRZ 1980, 664; OLG, NJW 1980, 1530; OLG, NJW 1979, 1509; FamRZ 1979, 581; OLG, FamRZ 1978, 109; OLG, FamRZ 1978, 109; BGH, FamRZ 1965, 368; and BGH, WM 1962, 1086.

83 In, *e.g.*, BGH, FamRZ 1965, 368, the objective of the partnership was "*die gemeinsame Errichtung eines Hauses.*" When the man died and the real estate was sold, the woman received a portion of the purchase price, despite the fact that the house was built on the man's lot and the man during the cohabitation was married to another woman. The property law relationship was not in conflict with good practice. The case is commented also in Robert Battes, *Die rechtliche Behandlung der nichtehelichen Lebensgemeinschaften in der Bundesrepublik Deutschland,* in ENTWICKLUNG IM RECHT DER FAMILIE UND DER AUSSEREHELICHEN LEBENSGEMEINSCHAFT 21, 34 (Uwe Blaurock, Hrsg., 1989).

84 *Compare* Wolfram Müller-Freienfels, *Tendenzen zur Verechtlichung Nichtehelicher Lebensgemeinschaften* in ZEITSCHRIFT FÜR EVANGELISCHE ETHIK 55, 68 (1979).

85 OLG, FamRZ 1988, 58; LG, FamRZ 1988, 717, 718; BGH, FamRZ 1985, 1232, NJW 1986, 51; OLG, FamRZ 1984, 1013; LG, FamRZ 1983, 271; BGH, FamRZ 1983, 271; OLG, FamRZ 1982, 265; BGHZ, FamRZ 1980, 664; BGH, FamRZ 1981, 1010; OLG, FamRZ 1979, 581; and OLG, FamRZ 1979, 796. *See further* Wacke, *supra* note 80, at 114; HERBERT GRZIWOTZ, NICHEHELICHEN LEBENSGEMEINSCHAFT § 5, 12. (3 ed. 1999) (only concrete limited purposes for a BGB-Gesellschaft have been recognized); Battes, *supra* note 83, at 35; Dieter Schwab, *Eheschliessungsrecht und nichteheliche Lebensgemeinschaft,* in DIE NICHTEHELICHE LEBENSGEMEINSCHAFT 68 (Götz Landwehr, Hrsg. 1978); Manfred Lieb, *Empfiehlt es sich, die rechtlichen Fragen der nichtehel. Lebensgemeinschaften gesetzlich zu regeln?,* Gutachten, DJT 57, 69 f. (1988); Coester-Waltjen, *Die Lebensgemeinschaft: Strapazierung des Parteiwillens oder staatliche Bevormundung?,* NJW 2085, 2088 (1988); Uwe Diederichsen, *Die nichteheiche Lebensgemeinschaft im Zivilrecht,* NJW 1017, 1022 (1983); Frank, *supra* note 81, at 185; Rainer Frank, *Gesellschaften zwischen Ehegatten und Nichtehegatten,* FamRZ 541, 544

therefore, is that the BGB partnership is considered to be limited to the property law aspects of the parties' relationship. There are also misgivings about whether civil law solutions compete with marriage, though they are meant for unmarried cohabiting persons and reach outside of the economic sphere. It is ordinarily accepted as a partnership objective that there is a purpose to jointly acquire and own tangible property for the parties' common use during their relationship. Robert Battes has stated: Battes and Wackes cit. "*Gesellschaftsrecht soll nur anwendbar sein, wenn es sich um einzelne Vermögenswerte handelt und die Partner dabei die Absicht verfolgt haben, einen – wenn auch nur wirtschaftlich – gemeinsamen Wert zu schaffen, der für die Dauer der Partnerschaft nicht nur gemeinsam genutzt, sondern Ihnen nach ihrer Vorstellung auch gemeinsam gehören sollte.*"[86] An additional economic objective is also supported in the case law as an implicit agreement to create a partnership for the purpose of acquiring assets and creating financial security for the parties through work and monetary contributions, with the added purpose of sharing the profits and losses.[87]

Others have wished to go farther and argue that the cohabitation ought to be sufficient as a partnership objective in itself, because, for unmarried cohabiting persons, there is no *lex specialis* in the form of marital laws that place impediments in the way. Andreas Wacke has stated: "*Das Zusammenleben, bestehend aus dem miteinander Wohnen und gemeinsamen Wirtschaften, sollte als zulänglicher 'Zweck' … genügen,*" in other words, the living together containing the joint cohabitation and economy should be sufficient as an objective. Because even trivial and daily undertakings have been recognized as a partnership, one ought according to Wacke "*den jahre-, ja oft jahrzehntelang währenden Lebensgemeinschaften die Anerkennung als Gesellschaft Bürgerliches Rechts nich versagen,*"[88] meaning that the year-long and often decade-long life companionship should not be denied the recognition of being a partnership under the civil law. Even though the cohabitation is not recognized as a partnership objective, it naturally has certain significance as evidence of the existence of an implicit

---

(1983); Wilfried Schlüter, Die nichteheliche Lebensgemeinschaft 25 (1981); Peter Finger, *Wohngemeinschaft, Partnerschaft, Lebensgemeinschaft,* JZ 497, 502 (1981); Peter Derleder, *Vermögenskonflikte zwischen Lebensgefährten bei der Auflösung der Gemeinschaft,* NJW 545, 547 (1980); Hans-Wolfgang Strätz, *Rechtsfragen des Konkubinats im Überblick,* FamRZ 434, 436 (1980); Dietrich V. Simon, *Rechtsprobleme der nichtehelichen Lebensgemeinschaft,* JuS 253 (1980); and Martin Lipp, *Die nichteheliche Lebensgemeinschaft und das bürgerliche Recht,* 180 AcP 537, 572 (1980).

86 *Id.*

87 *See, e.g.,* BGH, NJW 1982, 2863, 2864; FamRZ 1982, 1065, 1066; BGH, NJW 1981, 1502, 1503; FamRZ 1981, 530; BGH, NJW 1980, 1520; and FamRZ 1980, 664.

88 Wacke, *supra* note 80, at 115; Uwe Diederichsen, *Rechtsprobleme der nichtehelichen Lebensgemeinschaft,* FamRZ 889, 895 (1988); Robert Battes, Nichteheliches Zusammenleben im Zivilrecht 9 (1983); Anne Gudrun Meier-Scherling, *Die eheähnliche Lebensgemeinschaft,* DRiZ 296 (1979); Appel, Die eheähnliche Gemeinschaft, insbesondere inhre Bewertung und ihre Abwicklung 180 (1981); and Robert Battes, *Gesellschaftsrechtliche Überlegungen zur nichtehelichen Lebensgemeinschaft,* ZHR 394 (1979).

partnership agreement. On the other hand, it ought to be noted that there are also cohabiting couples who have chosen to not marry precisely in order to avoid financial sharing.

In **France**, which after the Nordic countries has had the highest number of unmarried cohabiting persons during most recent years, the application of general civil law principles as to concubinage or *union libre*, a free union, has old traditions.[89] There, the courts have ordered compensation for both unjust enrichment (*l'enrichissement sans cause*)[90] and damages.[91] The French courts, in addition, have applied the regulations concerning de facto partnerships (*société de fait and société créée de fait*) to the division of property between cohabiting persons. These regulations

---

89 Historically, extramarital relationships between women and men in France have legally been divided into three categories 1) pure temporary relations (adultery), 2) "concubinage" designating long-term love relationships limited to a sexual congress (*la communauté de lit*) without cohabitation, *see* AUBRY ET RAU, PAR ESMEIN, t. VII, § 491, 370 (7 ed. 1962), and 3) relationships characterized by a proper shared life that resembles marriage (*un véritable communauté de vie revêtant lápparence du mariage*). For this third category, most interesting here, different designations arise, but nowadays it appears that "*concubinage*" and "*union libre*" ordinarily are used synonymously. NICOLE JEANMART, LES EFFETS CIVILS DE LA VIE COMMUNE EN DEHORS DU MARIAGE 18 (1974), uses both the terms "*pour désigner la situation de fait dans laquelle see trouvent deux personnes de sexe différent vivant ensemble sans être mariées et constituant ce que l'on apelle aujourd'hui un couple.*" Even Esmein states: "*L'union libre ou concubinage est le fait par un homme et par une femme de vivre ensemble en ménage comme mari et femme,*" *see* AUBRY ET RAU, PAR ESMEIN, t. XII, § 491, No 261 (7 ed. 1962): Louis Josserand, *L'avénement du concubinat*, D.H. Cronique 45 (1932); Paul Esmein, *L'union libre*, D.H. Cronique 49 (1935); and BERNARD DEMAIN, LA LIQUIDATION DE BIENS DE CONCUBINS 7 (1968). Certain authors have maintained the contractual aspect as to the relationship, *see* HENRI BRON, LES CONSÉQUENCES JURIDIQUES DE L'UNION LIBRE NOTAMMENT À L'ÉGARD DES TIERS, No 56 (1940), while others argue that one does not assume the obligation to become a concubine, one simply becomes one, *see* JEANMART, *id.* at 14.

90 The unmarried woman with the support of the principles as to "*l'enrichissement sans cause*" has been given compensation for her work in the man's business. The case law is not consistent with respect to work in the home. *See* Civ. 12 novembre 1998, Dr. Fam. 99, No 12; Civ. 4 mars 1997, Dr. Fam., No 67, note Lécuyer; Civ. 15 oct. 1996, D. 97, Somm. 177, R.T., 97, 102; Civ. 18 juin 1980, Bull., No 191; Civ. 19 mai 1969, Bull., No 187; trib. Alés, 9 novembre 1966, D. 68, 329; Civ. 25 janvier 1965, G.P., 65, 1, 198; Aix, 23 décembre 1933, D. 1935, 2, 41; Dijon, 7 févruar 1928, D. 28, 2, 169, note Voirin; and Req. 17 mai 1870, at 1871, 1, 52. *See* commentaries of Danielle Huet-Weiller, *La Cessation du concubinage*, in LES CONCUBINAGES: APPROCHE SOCIO-JURIDIQUE II 119 (Jaqueline Rubellin-Devichi ed. 1986); JEAN CARBONNIER, DROIT CIVIL 2, LA FAMILLE 710 (21 ed. 2002).

91 *See* Paris 18 March 1932, D. 1932, 2, 88, note Voirin (damages to a deceased man's two concubines). Josserand has criticized the case, *supra* note 89. In the case of J.C.P. 1970.II.16305, note Parlange, D. 1970. J.201, note Combaldieu, a suit for damages by a surviving cohabiting partner was permitted assuming that the cohabitation "*offrait des garanties de stabilité et ne présentait pas de caractère délictueux.*" *Compare* HENRI MAZEAUD ET. AL., LECON DE DROIT CIVIL I TOME, 3 VOL. 55 (1972). A surviving cohabiting person has had the right to a suit for damages even in cases where the person or deceased has been married to another during the cohabitation, *see* Cass. Crim. 20 April 1972, J.C.P. 1972.II.17278, note Vidal; Cass. Crim. 19 June 1975, D. 1975.679, note Tinc; Cass. Crim. 8 January 1976, D. 1976; Paris 10 January 1976, D. 1978.458, note Bosquet-Denis; J.C.P. 1978.II.18859, note Savatier; and J.C.P. 1979.II.19107, note Almairac.

assume the existence of a contract between two or several parties to form a partnership, contribute with capital or work, and share the profits and losses.[92] The first is a partnership containing imperfections of form while the latter is based on an inferred agreement (*contrat tacite*) that has arisen only through the parties' actions, which, through an extensive interpretation of the regulations, makes it possible to capture the cohabitees' financial dealings.[93] The application of the regulations concerning the liquidation of de facto partnerships resemble those that are applicable to property divisions between spouses, and, in certain cases, have led to an equal division of the cohabiting parties' assets, e.g., the residence and household goods.[94]

With respect to the relationship between the property law and family law reasonings, it appears that the courts in France have been more disposed to apply the principles of de facto partnerships to unmarried cohabiting persons if the relationship has been stable, monogamous, and marriage-like, or as *Cour d'Appel de Montpellier* (1982) expressed it *"la situation des concubins est empreinte d'une stabilité imitée du mariage et dépendant en partie des mœurs monogamiques qui sont celles de la majorité de la population."*[95] The importance attributed to these characteristics, which are scarcely relevant in a commercial partnership, demonstrates how close the property law reasoning has come to that of family law in considering whether a common law marriage or a legal cohabitation has been established. The same circumstances can be used as a basis for the legal ramifications within both property law and family law. Nevertheless, it should be noted that the actual cohabitation, in itself, is not viewed as sufficient to constitute a de facto partnership, while the marriage creates a marital community.

---

92 Code Civile Article 1382; Carbonnier, *supra* note 90, at 710 speaks of "*un apport, au moins en travail, des deux côtés, et l'intention de participer aux gains et aux pertes*". Alain Bénabent, Droit Civil, La Famille 30 note 22 (7th ed. 1995), emphasizes the following elements: "*apports en capital ou travail de chacun, participation aux résultats et intention de s'associer*"; Henri Mazeaud et al., Lecons de Droit Civil, 4 Tome, I Vol., 12 (3d ed. 1969), mentions the following constitutive elements: "*L'intention de de collaborer à une entreprise commune, lorsqu'ils ont eu la volonté de participer aux bénéfices et aux pertes.*" *See also* Com. 9 octobre 2001, Dr. Fam. 02, 18; Grenoble, 10 janvier 2000; Riom, 4 juille 2000, Dr. Fam., 00, No 12, note Beignier; Com. 7 avril 1998, Dr. Fam., 98, No 82; Rennes, 4 juin 1998, R.T., 99, 819; Civ. 11 févruar 1997, J.C.P., 97, 2, 22820, note Garé; Paris, 20 mars 1996, Dr. Fam., 96, No 1, note Lécuyer ("*société de fait*" applicable with separation between cohabiting persons); Civ. 18 juille 1995, R.T. 96, 133; Paris 9 nov. 1992, R.T., 93, 330; Paris, 17 avril 1991, J.C.P., 92, 2, 275; Civ. 23 juin 1987, D. 87, I.R. 169; Civ. 5 mars 1985, Bull., No 85; Crim. 13 octobre 1981, D. 82, I.R., 96 (common household "ménage commun" not sufficient); Civ. 4 novembre 1975, Bull., No 328 (intent to share the profits and the losses is required); Com. 30 juin 1970, D. 70, Somm. 196; Civ. 30 avril 1954, J.C.P. 54, 2, 8319 (common property "communs en bien" not approved of as joint venture); and Com. 3 novembre 1953, D. 53, 731.

93 Civ. 1 20 mai 1957, D. 57, som. 101; Civ. 1 decembre 1952, D. 53, 90.

94 Demain, *supra* note 89, at 10-12; Joseph Hemard, Théorie et Pratique des nullités des Sociétés et Sociétés de fait N. 154 (1926); and Huet-Weiller, *supra* note 90, at 107.

95 Cour d'Appel de Montpellier, 8 juin 1982, D. 1983 Jur. 607, note Odile Dhavernas.

Jean Carbonnier states: "*Le seul fait d'avoir vécu en concubinage ne suffit pas á créer une société de fait, tandis que le seul fait de se marier crée une communauté conjugale.*"[96] Neither is the cohabitation a necessary prerequisite for the application of partnership regulations.

Despite the increase in the number of unmarried cohabiting persons in Europe during the 1970s, in **England**, early radical attempts by the Court of Appeals were made under the leadership of Lord Denning to introduce a "constructive trust of a new model"[97] to give the more vulnerable party in the dissolution of a cohabitation a way to claim property and compensation. The new model is not tied to the intentions of the parties as the traditional predecessor was, but rather is based more on what was "reasonable and fair," opening the possibility for compensation for work in the home and the care of children, and financial contributions not made directly to the disputed property but rather to the family as a whole. The model, considered too vague and lacking support in previous case law, however, did not gain acceptance in later case law.[98]

The English courts appear instead to wish to maintain a contractual or quasi-contractual stance according to which a constructive trust is based on the parties' common intention.[99] As a rule, the parties do not enter into any expressed agreements, the courts have accepted implied agreements that could be proven *inter alia* through the parties' financial contributions to the property's acquisition, either initially or through payment

96 CARBONNIER, *supra* note 90; Civ. 23 juin 1987, Bull., No 205; Crim. 13 oct. 1981, D. 82, I.R., 96; and D. 1968, 330.

97 *See, e.g., Hall v. Hall,* (1982) 3 FLR 379, 381, in which Lord Denning concerning the woman's contributions stated: "It depends on the circumstances and how much she has contributed—not merely in money—but also in keeping up the house and, if there are children, in looking after them"; *DHN Food Distributors v. London Borough of Tower Hamlets* (1976) 1 W.L.R. 852; *Eves v. Eves,* (1975)3 All E.R. 768 (1/4 share in the house, without monetary contributions as to the acquisition, but after work as to the house); 1 W.L.R. 1338; *Re Densham* (1975) 1 W.L.R. 1519; *Binions v. Evans,* (1972) Ch 359; *Cooke v. Head,* (1972) 1 W.L.R. 518, 520 ("Whenever two parties by their joint efforts acquire property to be used for their joint benefit, the courts may impose or impute a constructive or resulting trust"); *Hussey v. Palmer* (1972) 1 W.L.R. 1286, 1289 ("constructive trust of a new model"); *Heseltine v. Heseltine,* (1971) 1 W.L.R. 342; *Appleton v. Appleton* (1965) 1 W.L.R. 25.

98 Regarding "common intentions trusts," *see Gissing v. Gissing,* (1971) A.C. 886, H.L. *Pettitt v. Pettitt,* (1970) A.C. 777; JOHN MEE, THE PROPERTY RIGHTS OF COHABITEES 175 (1999); S.M. CRETNEY AND J.M. MASSON, PRINCIPLES OF FAMILY LAW 132-148 (6th ed. 1997); ROBERT PEARCE AND JOHN STEVENSON, THE LAW OF TRUSTS AND EQUITABLE OBLIGATIONS 638 (1995).

99 A trust often more generally is described as "a relationship recognised by equity which arises where property is vested in a person (or persons) called trustee, which those trustees hold for the benefit of other persons called *cestuis que trust* or beneficiaries," *see* JILL HANBURY, AND HAROLD GREVILLE MARTIN, MODERN EQUITY 45 (15th ed. 1997). A traditional resulting trust is based with purchasing of property as to both the parties' contributions as to the purchase price. The contribution creates a presumption for ownership rights in proportion to the financial contribution, *see, e.g., Sekhon v. Alissa* (1989) 2 FLR 94.

of the mortgage.[100] In return for the contributions made by the informal owner, he or she may request a portion of the property. In certain cases, the portion has been in proportion to the contribution.[101] In other cases, the parties have been given equal shares even though the contributions have been different.[102] Financial contributions to the family's economy on the whole, or work in the home, on the other hand, have not been considered relevant.[103]

In other common law countries, the development has gone farther in order to create legal protections. The principles applied have been somewhat varying, but all are strikingly vague. In Australia, the courts, have also accepted work in the home as evidence of a constructive trust based on the parties' mutual intentions.[104] The **Australian** courts, in addition,

---

100 *See Lambert v. Lambert* (2003) EWCA Civ 1685, 1 FLR 139; *Lissimore v. Downing* (2003) 2 FLR 308; *Jennings v. Rice* (2002) EWCA 159; *Chan Pui Chun v. Leug Kam Ho* (2002) EWCA Civ 1075; *Woolwich Plc v. Le Foe & Le Foe* (2001) 2 FLR 970 ("contributions to the mortgage"); *Cowan v. Cowan* (2001) EWCA Civ 679, 2 FLR 192; *Gillett v. Holt & Another* (2000) 2 FLR 267; *Drake v. Whipp* (1996) 1 FLR 826; *Ivin v. Blake* (1995) 1 FLR 70; *Clough v. Killey,* (1996) 72 P & CR D22; *Halifax Building Society v. Brown* (1996) 1 FLR 103; *Midland Bank plc v. Cooke,* (1995) 4 All E.R. 562, 2 FLR 915; *McHardy v. Warren* (1994) 2 FLR 338; *Savill v. Goodall* (1993) 1 FLR 755; *Springette v. Defoe,* (1992) 2 FLR 388; *Lloyds Bank v. Rosset* (1991) 1 AC 107, HL; (1990) 2 W.L.R. 867; (1990) 1 All E.R. 1111; *Hammond v. Mitchell,* (1991) 1 W.L.R. 127, (1992) 2 All E.R. 109 ("common intention"; "financial contributions"); *Stokes v. Anderson* (1991) 1 FLR 391; *H. V. M.* (1992) 1 FLR 229; *Ungurian v. Lesnoff* (1990) Ch 206; *Windeler v. Whitehall* (1990) 2 FLR 505; *Thomas v. Fuller-Brown* (1988) 1 FLR 237; *Passee v. Passee* (1988) 1 FLR 263; *Higgins v. Winfiled* (1987) V.R. 689; *Austin v. Keele* (1987) 61 A.L.J.R. 605 (PC); *Grant v. Edwards* (1986) 2 All E.R. 426; 1 Ch. 638; 3 W.L.R. 114 ("common intention"; "contributions to the mortgage"); *Maharaj v. Chand* (1986) 1 AC 898; *Re Basham* (1986) 1 W.L.R. 1498; *Midland Bank plc v. Dobson,* (1986) 1 FLR 171; *Layton v. Martin,* (1986) 2 FLR 227 (agreement not proven); *Thwaites v. Ryan,* (1984) V.R. 65; *Burns v. Burns,* (1984) Ch 317; 2 W.L.R. 582; 14 Fam Law 224; 1 All E.R. 244; FLR 216; *William & Glyns Bank v. Boland* (1981) AC 487; *Haslemere Estate Ltd v. Baker* (1982)1 W.L.R. 1109; *Re Sharp* (1980) 1 W.L.R. 219; *Cowcher v. Cowcher* (1972) 1 W.L.R. 425; *Gissing v. Gissing,* (1971) A.C. 886, H.L. ("common intention trust"); *Pettitt v. Pettitt,* (1970) A.C. 777; *Nat'l Provincial Bank v. Ainsworth* (1965) A.C. 1175; *Re Rogers' Question* (1948) 1 All E.R. 328; Mee, *supra* note 98, at 117; Cretney, *supra* note 98, at 132-148; A.J. Oakley, Constructive Trusts (3d ed. 1997); and Pearce, *supra* note 98.

101 *Passee v. Passee* (1988) 1 FLR 263.

102 *Midland Bank plc v. Cooke,* (1995) 4 All E.R. 562, 2 FLR 915 (50% share despite minimal direct financial contributions); and *Grant v. Edwards* (1986) 1 Ch 638.

103 *Burns v. Burns,* (1984) Ch 317; 2 W.L.R. 582; 14 Fam Law 224; 1 All E.R. 244; FLR 216 ("housekeeping and child raising do not carry with them any implication of a common intention that the plaintiff should have an interest in the house"); *Lloyds Bank v. Rosset* (1991) 1 A.C. 107, H.L.; (1990) 2 W.L.R. 867; and (1990) 1 All E.R. 1111 ("constructive trust"; "implied agreement may be inferred from direct financial contribution, whether initially or by payment of mortgage installments, not from renovating work").

104 *Penzikis v. Brown* (2005) N.S.W.S.C. 215 ("common intention," based, *inter alia,* upon one party's contributions to the installments on the mortgage); *Carruthers v. Manning* (2001) N.S.W.S.C. 1130 ("common intention" or "unconscionable conduct" not proven); *Rasmussen v. Rasmussen* (1995) 1 V.R. 613 ("common intention"); *Bennet v. Tairua* (1992) 15 Fam. L.R. 317 ("common intention"); and *Green v. Green,* (1989) 17 N.S.W.L.R. 343, 355 ("common intention"; "such common

have gone a step farther by using constructive trusts as a remedy for "unconscionable conduct" without citing any ties to the parties' mutual intentions.[105] Circumstances relevant to the application of this construction have not only been the parties' contributions in money and work to the acquisition and improvement of property, but also in support, homemaking, and family care.[106] The issue has been whether it is "unconscionable" that one party retains the benefit of the wealth created during the cohabitation. In the Australian case law, the courts have also long since analogously applied the general private law principle of joint venture as to certain projects of the cohabiting persons, e.g., the acquisition or improvement of certain property.[107] The courts in certain later cases have considered the entire personal relationship between the parties to be a joint venture. The contributions associated with the acquisition or the

---

intention can be inferred from the making of contributions to the cost of a property, or meeting expenses in maintaining it"). *Compare Maharaj v. Chand* (1986) A.C. 898 ("common intention"; "a constructive trust may be established by an inferred common intention subsequently acted upon by the making of contributions or other action to the detriment of the claimant party").

105 The application of the principle of "unconscionable conduct" when considering whether a "constructive trust" was established has been discussed in many cases from Australia. The solutions have resembled those that have been applied with the dissolution of partnerships and joint ventures. *See Lance & Anor v. Lance* (2004) W.A.S.C. 234 (not a constructive trust); *Lloyd v. Tedesco* (2002) 25 W.A.R. 360; *Parij v. Parij* (1997) 72 S.A.S.R. 153; *Bell v. Elliot* 26 November 1996 (LEXIS, NSV Sup. Ct.); *Re Sabri* (1996) 21 Fam. L.R. 213; *Renton v. Youngman* (1995) 19 Fam. L.R. 450; *Bell v. Bell* (1995) 19 Fam. L.R. 690; *Stowe & Devereaux Holdings Pty Ltd v. Stowe* (1995) 19 Fam. L.R. 409; *Re Popescu* (1995) 55 F.C.R. 583; *Kais v. Turvey* (1994) 17 Fam. L.R. 498; *AAT case No 9763* (1994) 29 A.T.R. 1151; *Booth v. Beresford* (1993) 17 Fam. L.R. 147; *Kidner v. Sec'y, Dep't of Soc. Sec.* (1993) 31 Adm. Law Decisions 63; *Bryson v. Bryant* (1992) 29 N.S.W.L.R. 188; *Woodward v. Johnston* (1991) 14 Fam. L.R. 828; *Miller v. Sutherland* (1990) 14 Fa. L.R. 416; *Carville v. Westbury* (1990) 102 Fed. L.R. 223; *Public Trustee v. Kukula* (1990) 14 Fam. L.R. 97; *Hibberson v. George* (1989) 12 Fa. L.R. 725; *Atkinson v. Burt* (1989) 12 Fam. L.R. 800 (resulting trust); *Lipman v. Lipman* (1989) 13 Fam. L.R. 1; *Re Osborne* (1989) 25 F.C.R. 547; *Balnaves v. Balnaves* (1988) 12 Fa. L.R. 488; *Arthur v. Public Trustee* (1988) 90 Fed. L.R. 203; *Austin v. Keele* (1987) 10 N.S.W.L.R. 283; 61 A.L.J.R. 605; 72 ALR 579; *Baumgartner v. Baumgartner*, (1987) 164 C.L.R. 137; *Muschinski v. Dodds* (1985) 160 C.L.R. 583; *Calverley v. Green* (1984) 155 C.L.R. 242; *Mallet v. Mallet* (1984) 156 C.L.R. 605; *Smith v. Smith*, (1984) 9 Fam. L.R. 1014 (S.A. Sup.Ct.); *Hohol v. Hohol* (1980) 6 Fam. L.R. 1014 (S.A. Sup.Ct.); and *Brown v. Wylie* (1980) 6 Fam. L.R. 519 (N.S.W. Sup.Ct.). *See also* Michael Bryan, *Constructive Trusts and Unconscionability in Australia: On the Endless Road to Unattainable Perfection*, 8 TRUST LAW INTERNATIONAL 74 (1994); M. Neave, *The New Unconscionability Principle – Property Disputes Between de Facto Partners*, 6 AUSTRALIAN J. FAM. L. 185 (1991); J. Dodds, *The New Constructive Trust: An Analysis of Its Nature and Scope*, 16 MELBOURNE UNIV. L. REV. 482 (1988); Ashley Black, *Baumgartner v. Baumgartner, The Constructive Trust and the Expanding Scope of Unconscionability*, 11 N.S.W. L.J. 117 (1988); and Patrick Parkinson, *Intention, Reliance and Contribution in the De Facto Cases*, 5 AUSTRALIAN J. FAM. L. 268 (1991).

106 *Baumgartner v. Baumgartner*, (1987) 164 C.L.R. 137 (joint venture; unconscionable conduct; constructive trust); and *Muschinski v. Dodds* (1985) 160 C.L.R. 583 (joint venture; unconscionable conduct; constructive trust; "contributions in money and labour and indirect contributions in other forms such as support, homemaking and family care").

107 *See Muschinski v. Dodds* (1985) 160 C.L.R. 583, 610.

improvement of property have been relevant, but so have indirect contributions in the form of money and work for the benefit of the personal relationship.[108]

In **New Zealand,** a constructive trust is often based on the parties' direct or indirect contributions to the property and their reasonable expectation of an interest therein. The contributions need not be monetary. They can consist of services or work, but there must be a causal connection between the contribution and the assets' acquisition, retention, or improvement.[109] Most important, therefore, have been the contributions to assets. In certain cases, however, work in the home has been considered a relevant contribution, for example, to same-sex relationships which have been analogized to the situation of ceremonially married spouses. Thorough investigations have been necessary in order to map and evaluate the parties' contributions during a long cohabitation.[110] In New Zealand, the domestic housekeeping and child care services a cohabiting person has performed in the mutual home have also constituted a basis for compensation in the form of monetary compensation as a result of quantum meruit and unjust enrichment. Even though the parties' reasonable expectations are the most common basis for a constructive trust today, there are also cases in which it is based upon the parties' common intentions.[111]

108 *See Baumgartner v. Baumgartner*, (1987) 164 C.L.R. 137. *See* the thorough analysis of the case law in MEE, *supra* note 98, at 261-264.

109 Regarding "reasonable expectations," *see Potter v. Potter* (2003) N.Z.C.A., 12 June 2003 (agreement impediment for "constructive trust"); *King v. Church* (2002) N.Z.C.A., 25 April 2002 (same sex partners; work in the home relevant); *Horsfield v. Giltrap* (2001), C.A. 207/00, 28 May 2001; *McMahon v. McMahon* (1997) N.Z.F.L.R. 145; *Hamilton v. Jurgens* (1996) N.Z.F.L.R. 350 (same sex partners); *Dickson v. Dickson* (1996) N.Z.F.L.R. 539; *Lankow v. Rose* (1995) 1 N.Z.L.R. 277, 294-295; 1 N.Z.F.L.R. 1, 20 ("I would allow as a contribution any payment or service by the claimant which either (1) of itself assists in the acquisition, improvement or maintenance of the property or its value ... it can be seen that contributions in the home may qualify as contributions to the home"); *Burney v. Burney* (1995) N.Z.F.L.R. 787; *Nuthall v. Heslop* (1995) N.Z.F.L.R. 755; *Phillips v. Phillips* (1993) 3 N.Z.L.R. 159 (housework relevant); *Gibb v. MacDonnell* (1992) 3 N.Z.L.R. 475; *Cossey v. Bach* (1992) 3 N.Z.L.R. 612, N.Z.F.L.R. 673; *Ireland v. Hepburn* (1991), CP 221/89; *Partridge v. Moller* (1990) 6 F.R.N.Z. 147; *Gillies v. Keogh* (1989) 2 N.Z.L.R. 327; *Stratulatos v. Stratulatos* (1988) 2 N.Z.L.R. 424 ("Standing in the shoes of plaintiff as claimant would a reasonable person have understood that their efforts would result in the property? The answer must be, yes..."); *Pasi v. Kamana* (1986) 1 N.Z.L.R. 603; *Hayward v. Giordani* (1983) N.Z.L.R. 140; *Avondale Printers & Stationers Ltd v. Haggie* (1979) 2 N.Z.L.R. 124 (not family law); and *Haldane v. Haldane* (1976) 2 N.Z.L.R. 715; *Carly v. Farrelly* (1975) 1 N.Z.L.R. 356. *See also* Nicky Richardson, *Dishonesty, Constructive Trusts and De Facto Relationships,* INT. FAM. L.J. 182 (2002); Nicky Richardson, *Defeating De Facto Partner's Claims to Property in New Zealand,* INT. FAM. L.J. 107 (2003); BILL ATKIN, LIVING TOGETHER WITHOUT MARRIAGE 99-104 (1991); and Mee, *supra* note 98, at 267-293 (1999).

110 *King v. Church* (2002) N.Z.C.A., 25 April 2002 (work in the home relevant); and *Buysers v. Dean* (2001) H.C., 6 November 2001. *Compare Lankow v. Rose* (1995) 1 N.Z.L.R. 277, 294; *Gillies v. Keogh* (1989) 2 N.Z.L.R. 327, 335.

111 *Buysers v. Dean* (2001) H.C., 6 November 2001. *Compare Daly v. Gilbert* (1993) 3 N.Z.L.R. 731; *Gillies v. Keogh* (1989) 2 N.Z.L.R. 327. 332; and *Day v. Mead* (1987)

Finally, it should be noted that the new act for de facto partners (*infra* Section 12.4) has made the remedy by way of constructive trust neither necessary nor proper in certain cases.[112]

In **Canada,** the courts have used the legal institutions of constructive trusts and quantum meruit to prevent one party from being unjustly enriched at the other party's expense; not only direct and indirect economic contributions have been taken into consideration, but also whether one party has taken care of the children, home, and household.[113] The fundamental condition, however, has been that one party has become enriched at the expense of the other, which easily gives rise to the comparable assertion from the latter. The courts, in principle, have required a connection between the financial contribution or work, and the acquisition or improvement of the property. The Canadian courts have also ordered compensation in monetary terms for worked performed.

A comparison between the property law remedies and the family law legislation for cohabiting persons in *Australia* and *New Zealand* demonstrates that economic circumstances are also relevant to an assessment of whether a de facto partnership exists. As guidance for the assessment of whether the parties live together as a couple, the legislation mentions as

---

2 N.Z.L.R. 443. *Brown v. Stokes* (1980) 1 N.Z.C.P.R. 209(common intentions); and *Gough v. Frazer,* (1977) 1 N.Z.L.R. 279 (common intentions).

112 Bill Atkin, *Reflections on New Zealand's Property Reforms 'Five Years On,'* in THE INTERNATIONAL SURVEY OF FAMILY LAW 217, 234 (Bill Atkin, gen. ed., 2007).

113 In the case law in Canada, unmarried cohabiting persons have been able to cite contract, partnership and unjust enrichment law, *see, e.g., S.C. v. P.G.* (2001) J.Q. No 3817 (Qué. C.A.); *Toronto Dominion Bank v. Carotenuto* (1998) 154 D.L.R. (4th) 627; *Soulos v. Korkontzilas* (1997) 146 D.L.R. (4th) 214; *Baird v. Iaci* (1997) 18 E.T.R. (2d) 103 (B.C. S.C.) (monetary compensation); *Pickelein v. Gillmore* (1997) 27 R. F.L. (4th) 51 (BC CA); *Nowell v. Town Estate* (1997) 30 R.F.L. (4th) 107 (Ont CA); *Clarkson v. McCrossen Estate* (1995) 122 D.L.R. (4th) 239; *Crick v. Ludwig* (1994) 117 D.L.R. (4th) 228; *Harrison v. Kalinocha* (1994) 112 D.L.R. (4th) 43; *Peter v. Beblow,* (1993) 101 D.L.R. (4th) 621 (unjust enrichment; "The notion that household and child care services are not worthy of recognition by the courts fails to recognize the fact that these services are of great value, not only to the family but to the other spouse"); *Forrest v. Price* (1992) 48 E.T.R. 72 (B.S. S.C.); *Thibert v. Thibert* (1992) 39 R.F.L. (3d) 376 (BC CA); *McDonald v. Adams* (1989) 64 D.L.R. (4th) 476; *Everson v. Rich* (1988) 53 D.L.R. (4th) 470 (monetary compensation); *Rochefoucauld v. Boustead,* (1987) 1 Ch. 196; *Sorochan v. Sorochan* (1986) 29 D.L.R. (4th) 1 (unjust enrichment; work in the home taken into consideration); *Kshywieski v. Kunka Estate* (1986)21 E.T.R. 229 (C.A.) (housekeeping services gratuitous and not compensable); *Milne v. MacDonald Estate* (1986) 3 R.F.L. (3d) 206 (CA) (housekeeping services gratuitous and not compensable); *Beaudoin-Daigneault v. Richard,* (1984) 1 S.C.R. 2; *Herman v. Smith* (1984) 42 R.F.L. (2d) 154 (QB) (*quantum meruit*; housekeeping services); *Petkus v. Becker* (1980) 117 D.L.R. (3d) 257 (unjust enrichment); *Rathwell v. Rathwell,* (1978) 2 SCR 436 (unjust enrichment); *Dwyer v. Love* (1976) 9 Nfld & PEIR 325 (CA) (*quantum meruit*; housekeeping services in *de facto* union); *Murdoch v. Murdoch,* (1974) 41 D.L.R. (3d ed.) 367 (common intention trust); and *Holli v. Kost* (1972) R.F.L. 77 (*quantum meruit*; housekeeping services). *See also* BEREND HOVIUS AND TIMOTHY G. YOUDAN, THE LAW OF FAMILY PROPERTY CHAP. 7 (1991); AND Morris M. Litman, *The Emergence of Unjust Enrichment as a Cause of Action and the Remedy of Constructive Trust,* 26 ALBERTA L. REV. 407 (1988).

relevant elements the degree of financial dependence or interdependence, and any arrangement for financial support, between the parties, the ownership, use, and acquisition of property, the performance of household duties.[114] A comparable definition and elements can also be found in family law legislation from New South Wales, Australia.[115] Even in accordance with the cohabitation legislation that has been recently enacted in the province of Manitoba, Canada, the courts have, with the assessment of whether two persons are "common law partners," taken into consideration a multitude of factors, including whether the parties share household chores or perform any personal services for one another.[116] Nevertheless, it should be noted that these circumstances are not necessary or sufficient prerequisites for the establishment of a family law "de facto relationship" or a "common law relationship," respectively. For the property law solutions, on the other hand, the parties' contributions have been necessary prerequisites for the invocation of the legal consequences.

The judicial spiritedness and wealth of invention that the courts in the Western world have displayed, as discussed above, have given results worthy of consideration because they offer remedies that provide certain economic compensation and the right to property for cohabiting unmarried persons exactly in those situations in which marital legislation and common law marriage have had the objective of protecting spouses, primarily during the dissolution of a relationship. Even though a gainfully employed man formally acquired the property in the estate, a woman who has made monetary contributions toward an acquisition or mortgage payments; contributed money or work to improve the property or toward the family's expenditures; or taken care of the home, household, and children, in certain cases, has been able to receive certain compensation thereof or a certain right to division of the property.

2. *The Marvin Doctrine in the United States*

At the same time that courts in the Western world in general developed civil law remedies in order to solve unmarried cohabiting couple's legal problems, a solution called the Marvin doctrine arose in the American case law. In *Marvin v. Marvin* (1976), the California Supreme Court stated

114 *See New Zealand's* Property (Relationships) Act 1976, in its new wording effective February 1, 2002, section 2D. It ought in addition be noted that the legislation in New Zealand makes an exception to the requirement of a three-year cohabitation if the parties have children or if one of them has made "a substantial contribution to the *de facto* relationship," see *id.* Sections 14 A.

115 *See* Property (Relationships) Act (1984), N.S.W. ACTS § 4 (1)(2) that for the purpose *inter alia* of also including homosexual couples most recently has been changed by The Property (Relationships) Amendment Act (1999). N.S.W. ACTS § 3. Similar legislation has been enacted in a number of legal areas in Australia's other jurisdictions.

116 *See* Manitoba Justice, Changes to Property Laws affecting Common-Law Partners effective June 30, 2004, see: http://www.gov.mb.ca/justice/family/commonlaw/commonlawproperty.html.

that "the mores of the society have indeed changed so radically in regard to cohabitation that we cannot impose a standard based on alleged moral considerations that have apparently been so widely abandoned by so many."[117] Thereafter, the court opened the doors to a series of different possibilities for unmarried cohabiting persons to seek property law solutions for their conflicts, stating that the parties' actions during the cohabitation, in principle, could give support for "an implied contract, agreement of partnership or joint venture, or some other tacit understanding" between the parties. The court, in addition, stated that courts were unimpeded from applying the doctrine of quantum meruit or other remedies based on equity such as constructive or resulting trusts, for the purpose of protecting the parties' expectations. The court, however, was not prepared to recognize expressed agreements based to any degree on sexual services.[118]

---

117 *Marvin v. Marvin*, 18 Cal.3d 660, 134 Cal. Rptr. 815, 557 P.2d 106, 122 (1976).

118 *Id.* Sexual services need not deal with prostitution. Such considerations have made bringing a lawsuit impossible even if the services constituted only a part of a considerably broader sharing. However, it is hazardous to distinguish the parties' emotional relationship from their relationship in general. The one ought not uncommonly constitute a prerequisite for the other. *Compare* J. Simitian, *Property Rights and the Unmarried Homemaker: Marvin v. Marvin, and the California Experience*, 5 COM. PROP. J. 3, 7 (1978). In e.g. *Schwegmann v. Schwegmann*, 441 So.2d 316 (La. App. 1983), the woman maintained that during the parties' twelve-year cohabitation, she rendered services as a companion, housekeeper and cook, as well as a mother to Mr. Schwegmann's children, and as a business advisor, political assistant, and confidante to him and his corporation. The court stated: "Louisiana law clearly disallows claims in *quantum meruit* by concubines for domestic services when the services are interwoven with sexual relationship." In *Rehak v. Mathis*, 239 Ga. 541, 238 S.E.2d 81 (1977), the parties had lived together for 18 years. When they separated, the woman petitioned for monthly compensation for the period of the cohabitation as well as ownership rights in a house. As basis thereof she cited that she had paid the mortgage for the house as well as cooked, cleaned, and in general, cared for the comforts, needs, and pleasures of the man. Despite the fact that Georgia at the time of their relationship recognized common law marriage, which was not petitioned, the court found that the claims were immoral and in violation of the state's public policy as they were based upon a "meretricious relationship." Decisive for the court appears to have been the woman's admission that the parties' sexual relationship constituted a part of her performance in the contract. Therefore one cannot as *Mary Ann Glendon* says that the case is an example of "extreme disapproval" of the Marvin doctrine, *see* GLENDON, *supra* note 50, at 280. *Compare Latham v. Latham*, 274 Or. 421, 547 P.2d 144, 147 (1976), in which the court stated: "We are not validating an agreement in which the only or primary consideration is sexual intercourse. The agreement here contemplated all the burdens and amenities of married life." In *Jones v. Daly*, 122 Cal.App.3d 500, 176 Cal.Rptr. 130, 131 (1981), there was a contract between two men according to which the plaintiff would offer his services "as a lover, companion, homemaker, traveling companion, housekeeper, and cook." The court found that the parties' sexual relationship was an inseparable part of the agreement and refused to enforce it. In *Combs v. Tibbitts*, 148 P.3d 430 (Colo.App. 2006), the court, citing *Salzman v. Bachrach*, 996 P.2d 1263 (Colo. 2000), stated that cohabiting couples may legally contract with each other so long as sexual relations are "merely incidental" to the agreement. *See also Zoppa v. Zoppa*, 86 Cal.App.4th 1144, 103 Cal.Rptr.2d 901 (2001). In those cases in which the personal part of the agreement can be severed from the business, it appears

The case of *Marvin* did not actually introduce any new principles, and was not even the first to raise the issue of application as to cohabitations,[119] and the plaintiff did not finally prevail as to her claims.[120] Nevertheless, the court's principle statements and the positive attention raised[121] by the case inspired similar cases in which the Marvin doctrine was cited. As a result, the more vulnerable parties were offered a form of legal protection. In *Wilbur v. DeLapp* (1993), for example, the parties had lived together for eighteen years when they separated. The man had legal title to the house and was solely responsible for the mortgage payments. The woman contributed, financially and otherwise, to improving and maintaining the home. The court stated that the regulations concerning property divisions between spouses of matrimonial property were not applicable because

---

that the majority of courts have found the latter part to be valid, *see, e.g., Tyranski v. Piggins*, 44 Mich.App. 570, 205 N.W.2d 595, 596 (1973); *Burns v. Koellmer*, 11 Conn. App. 375, 527 A.2d 1210 (1987); *Lovinger v. Anglo California Nat. Bank*, 243 P.2d 561 (Cal.App. 1952) (contract with maid); and *Stewart v. Waterman*, 97 Vt. 408, 123 A. 524 (1924). In *Whorton v. Dillingham*, 202 Cal.App.3d 447, 248 Cal.Rptr. 405 (1988), the court deemed that a written agreement between homosexual men was valid as the sexual relationship could be severed from the remainder of the contract, which concerned services as a secretary, driver, bodyguard, and business partner. Regarding the sexual element within the requirement of cohabitation for the establishment of a common law marriage, *see* Section 8.5.2.1 *supra*.

119 The Washington Supreme Court has given unmarried cohabiting persons rights based upon *e.g.* resulting trusts, *Walberg v. Mattson*, 38 Wash.2d 808, 232 P.2d 827 (1951) (contract theory); *Dahlgren v. Blomeen*, 49 Wash.2d 47, 298 P.2d 479 (1956) (tracing source of funds); *West v. Knowles*, 50 Wash.2d 311, 311 P.2d 689 (1957) (tenancy in common); *Shull v. Shepherd*, 63 Wash.2d 503, 387 P.2d 767 (1963) (constructive trusts); *Humphries v. Riveland*, 67 Wash.2d 376, 407 P.2d 967 (1965) (implied partnership/joint venture); *In re Estate of Thornton*, 81 Wash.2d 72, 499 P.2d 864 (1972); and *Omer v. Omer*, 523 P.2d 957 (Wash.App. 1974) (constructive trust). The courts in Texas have long since recognized property rights for cohabiting unmarried persons, *see, e.g., Hayworth v. Williams*, 102 Tex. 308, 116 S.W. 43 (1909) (resulting trust not proven); *Watson v. Harris*, Tex.Civ.App. 263, 130 S.W. 237 (1910) (resulting trust, the parties are presumed to own one-half each of personal property acquired during the cohabitation); *Perales v. Flores*, 147 S.W.2d 974 (Tex. Civ.App.-San Antonio 1941) (resulting trust); and *Timmons v. Timmons*, 222 S.W.2d 339 (Tex.Civ.App.-Galveston 1949) (partnership, not based on cooking and washing). As to other states, *see* from Massachusetts, *Green v. Richmond*, 337 N.E.2d 691 (Mass. 1975) (*quantum meruit*); and from California, *Schneider v. Schneider*, 183 Cal. 335, 191 P. 533 (1920); *Coats v. Coats*, 160 Cal. 671, 118 P. 441 (1911); *Sanguinetti v. Sanguinetti*, 9 Cal.2d 95, 69 P.2d 845 (1937) (quasi-contract); and *Lazzarevich v. Lazzarevich*, 86 Cal.App.2d 708, 200 P.2d 49 (1948) (quasi-contract).

120 In *Marvin v. Marvin*, 5 Fam. L. Rep. (BNA) 3077 (Cal.Super.Ct. 1979), neither an implied agreement nor unjust enrichment were proven and in *Marvin v. Marvin*, 122 Cal.App.3d 871, 176 Cal.Rptr. 555 (App. 1981), the woman's claim as to an equitable remedy was dismissed. *See* comment in Henry H. Foster, Jr. & Doris Jonas Freed, *Marvin v. Marvin: New Wine in Old Bottles*, 5 FAM. L. REP. 4001 (1979).

121 *See, e.g.*, Herma Kay and Carol Amyx, *Marvin v. Marvin, Preserving the Options*, 65 CAL. L. REV. 937, 976 (1977). With respect to the Marvin doctrine's anchorage in different states, *see, e.g.*, Katherine Gordon, Note, *The Necessity and Enforcement of Cohabitation Agreements: When Strings Will Attach and How to Prevent Them – A State Survey*, 37 BRANDEIS L. J. 245 (1998-1999); and George L. Blum, Annotation, *Property Rights Arising from Relationship of Couple Cohabiting Without Marriage*, 69 A.L.R.5th 219 (1999).

Oregon did not recognize common law marriage, but found that it was the intent of the parties for the plaintiff to have an interest in the house and, as a matter of equity, the court held that she was entitled to a one-half interest. Another example is *Sullivan v. Rooney* (1989), in which the parties had lived together for seven years and purchased a house in the man's name. With the support of the principles of constructive trusts, the woman received ownership rights to one-half of the house, which the man had promised her. A third example is *Cook v. Cook* (1984), where the parties had lived together for twelve years. The court held that although isolated acts of joint participation such as cohabitation or the opening of a joint account may not suffice to create a contract, the fact finder may infer an exchange of promises, and the existence of the contract, from the entire course of conduct between the parties. Thus, the court found that there was ample evidence to support a finding that the parties agreed to pool their resources and share equally in certain accumulations, and that their course of conduct may be seen as consistently demonstrating the existence of such an agreement.[122] The results of the cases, however,

---

122 *Latham v. Latham*, 274 Or. 421, 547 P.2d 144 (1976); *Carlson v. Olson*, 256 N.W.2d 249 (Minn. 1977); and *Edgar v. Wagner*, 572 P.2d 405 (Utah 1977) (*quantum meruit*). In *McCullon v. McCullon*, 96 Misc.2d 962, 410 N.Y.S.2d 226 (N.Y.Sup.Ct. 1978), a common law marriage was found proven in Pennsylvania and an implied agreement in New York by the woman to forbear employment and to provide household services for the man for over 28 years in consideration of his conduct and promises to provide a home and future support. *See also Beal v. Beal*, 282 Or. 115, 577 P.2d 507 (1978) (implied contract, joint interest in property); *Faglie v. Williams*, 569 S.W.2d 557 (Tex.Civ.App.-Austin 1978) (resulting trust and partnership recognized, but not proven); *Huniston v. Bushnell*, 118 N.H. 759, 394 A.2d 844 (1978) (*quantum meruit*); *Kozlowski v. Kozlowski*, 80 N.J. 378, 403 A.2d 902 (1979) (express contract); *Rissberger v. Gorton*, 597 P.2d 366 (Or.App. 1979); *In re Estate of Steffes*, 95 Wis.2d 490, 290 N.W.2d 697 (1980) (express and implied contract); *Bramlett v. Selman*, 268 Ark. 457, 597 S.W.2d 80 (1980) (constructive trust); *Glasgo v. Glasgo*, 410 N.E.2d 1325 (Ind.App. 1980); *McHenry v. Smith*, 45 Or.App. 813, 609 P.2d 855 (1980); *Suggs v. Norris*, 88 N.C.App. 539, 364 S.E.2d 159, *cert. denied*, 322 N.C. 486, 370 S.E.2d 236 (1980); *Joan S. v. John S.*, 121 N.H. 96, 427 A.2d 498, 500 (1981); *Kinkenon v. Hue*, 207 Neb. 698, 301 N.W.2d 77 (1981); *Small v. Harper*, 638 S.W.2d 24 (Tex.App.-Houston 1982) (partnership); *Estate of Eriksen*, 337 N.W.2d 671 (Minn. 1983) (constructive trust); *Harbour v. Cogburn*, 646 S.W.2d 330 (Tex.App.-Eastland 1983); *Knauer v. Knauer*, 470 A.2d 553 (Pa.Super.Ct. 1983) (express contract); *Spafford v. Coates*, 118 Ill.App.3d 566, 455 N.E.2d 241 (1983) (implied trust); *Cook v. Cook*, 142 Ariz. 573, 691 P.2d 664 (1984) (implied contract); *Hay v. Hay*, 100 Nev. 196, 678 P.2d 672 (1984) (implied contract); *Johnston v. Mabrey*, 677 S.W.2d 235 (Tex.App.-Corpus Christi 1984) (constructive trust); *Metten v. Benge*, 366 N.W.2d 577 (Iowa 1985); *Carroll v. Lee*, 148 Ariz. 10, 712 P.2d 923 (1986); *Pickens v. Pickens*, 490 So.2d 872 (Miss. 1986) (equity); *Harman v. Rogers*, 510 A.2d 161 (Vt. 1986); *Boland v. Catalano*, 202 Conn. 333, 521 A.2d 142 (Conn. 1987) (express agreement is required); *Hudson v. DeLonjay*, 732 S.W.2d 922 (Mo.App. 1987); *Watts v. Watts*, 137 Wis.2d 506, 405 N.W.2d 303 (1987) (implied contract); *Watts v. Watts*, 448 N.W.2d 292 (Wis.App. 1989) (unjust enrichment); *Evans v. Wall*, 542 So.2d 1055 (Fla. Dist. Ct.App. 1989) (constructive trust); *Sullivan v. Rooney*, 533 N.E.2d 1372 (Mass. 1989) (constructive trust); *Goode v. Goode*, 396 S.E.2d 430 (W.Va. 1990) (allowing implied contracts); *Williams v. Mason*, 556 So.2d 1045 (Miss. 1990) (quantum meruit); *Shuraleff v. Donnelly*, 108 Ore.App. 707, 817 P.2d 764 (1991) (equity); *Bass v.*

are uncertain both because of the legal vagueness of the principles and their evidentiary complications. Cohabiting couples may have varying expectations with regard to sharing of property, income, and expenses. Still, it has been assumed that the doctrine would make unmarried cohabitation a more attractive and flexible arrangement.[123] The courts applying the Marvin doctrine tend to emphasize that these solutions do not reinstate common law marriage, while conceding that the doctrine signals that society's mores have changed.[124]

Other courts, on the other hand, for example, the Illinois Supreme Court, have refused to apply the Marvin doctrine. The court in *Hewitt v. Hewitt* (1979) stated that the doctrine damages marriage as an institution by offering an alternative, and that an application thereof would be the same as reintroducing common law marriage through the back door, which would be in conflict with the legislation repealing this legal institution. According to the Illinois Supreme Court, the Marvin doctrine is in conflict with public policy, which is the obligation of the legislature, not the courts, to change. The court further stated that it would be more honest to "to acknowledge the return of varying forms of common law marriage than to continue displaying the naiveté we believe involved in the assertion that there are involved in these relationships contracts separate and independent from the sexual activity, and the assumption that those contracts would have been entered into or would continue without that activity." The result was that a woman after a fifteen-year cohabitation, during which she had borne three children, could not be offered any legal protection.[125]

Bass, 814 S.W.2d 38 (Tenn. 1991) (implied partnership); *Western States Const. Inc. v. Michoff,* 108 Nev. 931, 840 P.2d 1220 (1992) (implied contract) *Ellis v. Berry,* 19 Kan.App.2d 63 (1983) (implied contract); *Wilbur v. DeLapp,* 119 Or.App. 348, 850 P.2d 1151 (1993) (equity); *Wallender v. Wallender,* 870 P.2d 232, 234 (Or.App. 1994) (implied agreement); *Friedman v. Friedman,* 20 Cal.App.4th 876, 24 Cal. Rptr.2d 892 (1993) (implied contract concerning maintenance not proven, a granting would then be to reintroduce common law marriage); *Bright v. Kuehl,* 650 N.E.2d 311 (Ind.App. 1995); *Byrne v. Laura,* 60 Cal.Rptr.3d 908 (App. 1997); *Schultz v. Kelly,* 581 N.W.2d 594 (Wis.App. 1998); *In re Estate of Palmen,* 588 N.W.2d 493 (Minn. 1999) (unjust enrichment); *Kaiser v. Fleming,* 735 N.E.2d 144 (Ill.App. 2000) (*quantum meruit*); *Salzmann v. Bachrach,* 996 P.2d 1263 (Colo. 2000) (*quantum meruit*); and *Keeton v. Daniel,* 2006 WL 2818238 (Tenn.App. 2006) (resulting trust). *See also* Carol S. Bruch, *Cohabitation in the Common Law Countries a Decade After Marvin: Settled In or Moving Ahead?,* 22 U.C. Davis L. Rev. 717 (1989).

123 Comment, *Property Rights Upon Termination of Unmarried Cohabitation: Marvin v. Marvin,* 90 Harv. L. Rev. 1708, 1714 (1977). *See also* Christina M. Fernández, Note, *Beyond Marvin: A Proposal for Quasi-Spousal Support,* 30 Stan. L. Rev. 359 (1978). Cases after *Marvin* are taken up in J. Thomas Oldham, Divorce, Separation and the Distribution of Property 1.02 (2002).

124 *Kozlowski v. Kozlowski,* 80 N.J. 378, 403 A.2d 902 (1979). Common law marriage was repealed in New Jersey in 1939, *see* N.J. Stat. Ann. 37:1-10 (West 2003). *See also Marvin v. Marvin,* 18 Cal.3d 660, 134 Cal. Rptr. 815, 557 P.2d 106, 122-123 (1976).

125 *Hewitt v. Hewitt,* 77 Ill.2d 49, 31 Ill. Dec. 827, 394 N.E.2d 1204, 1207-1211 (1979). Common law marriage was repealed in Illinois by statute in 1905. *Compare* the Court of Appeals, which made an entirely different assessment of public policy and which was prepared to adopt the Marvin doctrine *inter alia* with reference to that

The New York Court of Appeals stated similar reasons in *Morone v. Morone* (1980), in which a woman filed a lawsuit after an eight-year cohabitation, during which the parties had three children. New York's highest court stated that an implied contract between an unmarried couple living together is "contrary to both New York decisional law and the implication arising from our Legislature's abolition of common-law marriage," which occurred in 1933.[126] In the absence of an expressed agreement, the woman's lawsuit was dismissed.[127] The idea that this doctrine in practice would

---

the parties had lived a most conventional, respectable, and ordinary family life and that the woman's actions had not so affronted public policy that she should be denied any and all relief (*Hewitt v. Hewitt,* 62 Ill.App.3d 861, 863 and 869). It can be noted that the man told the woman that no formal marriage was necessary as they commenced their relationship in Iowa, a state recognizing common law marriage. No claim that such a marriage had been established in Iowa, however, was presented strangely enough. Even in *Carnes v. Sheldon,* 311 N.W.2d 747 (Mich.App. 1981), the court stated that recovery based on principles of contracts implied in law essentially would resurrect the old common-law marriage doctrine as specifically was abolished by the Legislature. The case of *Hewitt* was followed in *Ayala v. Fox,* 206 Ill.App.3d 538, 151 Ill.Dec. 465, 564 N.E.2d 920 (1990) and later in *Costa v. Oliven,* 365 Ill.App.3d 244, 849 N.E.2d 122, 302 Ill.Dec. 507 (2006). Several courts that have not judged in accordance with the Marvin doctrine when the claims have been based on the parties' family relationships have granted a cohabiting parties' claims with respect to a joint business transaction, *see Glidewell v. Glidewell,* 790 S.W.2d 925 (Ky.App. 1990); and *Schwegmann v. Schwegmann,* 441 So.2d 316 (La. App. 1983). *Compare Davis v. Davis,* 643 So.2d 931 (Miss. 1994); *In re Estate of Alexander,* 445 So.2d 836 (Miss. 1984); and *Grishman v. Grishman,* 407 A.2d 9 (Me. 1979).

126 *Morone v. Morone,* 50 N.Y.2d 481, 429 N.Y.S.2d 592, 596, 407 N.E.2d 438, 442 (1980). The idea that the Marvin doctrine would mean a recognition of common law marriage also recurs in *Merrill v. Davis,* 673 P.2d 1285, 1286-1287 (N.M. 1983). *Compare Slocum v. Hammond,* 346 N.W.2d 485 (Iowa 1984), in which the claims *inter alia* of unjust enrichment as well as a resulting trust and constructive trust were dismissed, and in which the circumstance that Iowa recognizes common law marriage appears to have been given significance.

127 Regarding earlier case law in New York, which did not accept implied agreements, but on the other hand expressed agreements (oral or written) with respect to household services, which were not hindered by the cohabitation, but which could not include a sexual relationship, *see Matter of Adams,* 1 A.D.2d 259, 149 N.Y.S.2d 849, *aff'd,* 2 N.Y.2d 796, 159 N.Y.S.2d 698, 140 N.E.2d 549 (1956). *Compare Dombrowski v. Somers,* 41 N.Y.2d 858, 393 N.Y.S.2d 706, 362 N.E.2d 257 (1977); *Rhodes v. Stone,* 63 Hun. 624, 17 N.Y.S. 561 (1892); *Vincent v. Moriarty,* 31 App.Div. 484, 52 N.Y.S. 519 (1898); *Matter of Gordon,* 8 N.Y.2d 71, 75, 202 N.Y.S.2d 1, 168 N.E.2d 239 (1960); and *Donnell v. Stogel,* 560 N.Y.S.2d 200 (N.Y.App.Div. 1990).

An expressed agreement has been required even in cases from other states, *see, e.g., Aehegma v. Aehegma,* 797 P. 2d 74 (Hawaii App. 1990) ("no postcohabitation rehabilitative support or equitable division of separate property in absence of express agreement"); *In re Estate of Alexander,* 445 So.2d 836 (Miss. 1984); *Merrill v. Davis,* 673 P.2d 1285 (N.M. 1983); *Tapley v. Tapley,* 122 N.H. 727, 449 A.2d 1218 (1982); *Donovan v. Scuderi,* 443 A.2d 121 (Md.Ct.Spec.App. 1982) and accepted in *Wilcox v. Trautz,* 427 Mass. 326, 693 N.E.2d 141 (1998) (written contract); *Kinnison v. Kinnison,* 627 P.2d 594 (Wyo. 1981); *Kinkenon v. Hue,* 301 N.W.2d 77 (Neb. 1981); *Levar v. Elkins,* 604 P.2d 602 (Alaska 1980) (express agreement recognized); and *Dominguez v. Cruz,* 95 N.M. 1, 617 P.2d 1322 (App. 1980). Expressed agreements may not be too general. The promise to "take care of" another person has been considered too vague, *see Estate of Lasek,* 144 Misc.2d 813, 545 N.Y.S.2d 668 (Surr.Ct. 1989); and *Friedmann v. Friedmann,* 20 Cal.App.4th 876, 24 Cal.Rptr.2d 892 (1993).

entail a reinstatement of common law marriage has also been articulated in the academic literature. Homer Clark consequently maintained that the effect of these cases is "to reinstitute common-law marriage in California after it has been abolished by the legislature."[128]

The American case law also includes cases in which the same family law circumstances cited as support for the existence of a common law marriage are also cited as support for the existence of an inferred agreement with respect to the division of property. Such circumstances include the parties' long-term cohabitation and their outward appearance as spouses. For example, in *Goode v. Goode* (1990), a woman alleged that, during twenty-eight years, she provided a wide range of homemaker services that materially contributed to the economic well-being of the defendant and their children. She argued that the man, thereby, was able to pursue full-time employment, which enabled him to amass his own assets. In reply to questions from the lower court, the Supreme Court of Appeals in West Virginia stated that the state did not recognize common law marriage, but that a court "may order a division of property acquired by a man and a woman who are unmarried cohabitants, but who have considered themselves and held themselves out to be husband and wife." The court continued a line of reasoning based on family law by pointing out that the following factors can be relevant to such a division of property: "the purpose, duration, and stability of the relationship and the expectations of the parties." At the same time, the court stated that a division of the property is to be based on "principles of contract, either express or implied, or upon a constructive trust."[129] In the academic literature, it has been argued

---

Compare on the other hand *Sopko v. Estate of Roccomonte*, 346 N.J.Super. 107, 787 A.2d 198 (App.Div. 2001), *aff'd*, 174 N.J. 381, 808 A.2d 838 (2002).

128 Clark, *supra* note 66, at 449. *See also* Charlotte K. Goldberg, *The Schemes of Adventuresses: The Abolition and Revival of Common-Law Marriage*, 483 Wm. & Mary J. Women & L. 483, 537 (2006-2007), who maintains that the revival of common law mariage "will likely take the form of determining which relationships are enough like traditional marriage to warrant extension of shared property rights." *See also* Reiland, *supra* note 66, at 88-90 and Crawley, *supra* note 66, at 400.

129 *See, e.g., Goode v. Goode*, 396 S.E.2d 430, 438 (W.Va. 1990). *See also Wallender v. Wallender*, 870 P.2d 232, 234 (Or.App. 1994), in which the court with the assessment of whether an implied agreement existed took into consideration family law circumstances such as how the parties held themselves out to their community, the nature of the cohabitation, and joint acts of financial nature, if any, how title to the property was held, and the respective financial and nonfinancial contributions of each party. *See also Schultz v. Kelly*, 581 N.W.2d 594 (Wis.App. 1998), in which the woman after an 18-year cohabitation petitioned for compensation on the basis of unjust-enrichment. The trial court did not grant the claim, in part with reference to the relevant arguments which primarily were based upon that the woman had not demonstrated that she "gave more than she got," in part with reference to family law arguments that actually are attributable to common law marriage or cohabitation law, namely that the parties had no children, she did not change her surname to Kelly, she and Kelly did not file joint tax returns; she was not carried on Kelly's insurance, and hers and Kelly's property was titled individually rather than jointly. The Court of Appeals, however, did not find that the trial court had found these factors to be necessary. *Compare Pickens v. Pickens*, 490 So.2d 872 (Miss. 1986),

that the probability of succeeding with a lawsuit in accordance with the Marvin doctrine increases if the parties have had a long-term relationship in which they outwardly appeared as husband and wife. Thus, Charlotte Goldberg has stated: "Whatever the doctrines used, whether implied-in-fact contract in California or meretricious relationship in Washington, the heart of the problem is whether the relationship in question is enough like marriage to provide rights similar to those of married people."[130]

At the same time that the family law aspects of the parties' relationship are cited in property law cases, economic circumstances, which often are decisive for a property law lawsuit, are found relevant to family law cases. Examples are the assessment of whether a common law marriage exists, as discussed in Chapters 7 and 8 above, and whether a "domestic partnership" exists in accordance with those principles proposed by the American Law Institute (ALI) 2002 for the division of property and compensatory payments upon the separation of cohabiting persons.[131] *Domestic partners* is defined as two persons of the same or different sex, not married to each other, who "for a significant period of time share a primary residence and a life together as a couple." The circumstances mentioned in the ALI principles include the extent to which the parties intermingled their finances, the extent to which their relationship fostered the parties' economic interdependence, or the economic dependence of one party upon the other, and the parties' maintenance of a common household.[132] The American reasoning is consistent here with that of the Western world in general, as seen above, in the assessment of whether a cohabitation exists.

In a number of American family law cases, the courts have considered economic circumstances in assessing the existence of a domestic partnership. The Washington Supreme Court has drawn an analogy to the community property system applicable to spouses in order to apply it to

---

in which the court did not apply a family law solution, but in which the result was similar. The parties had after a divorce lived together for 20 years. Upon their separation, the court applied analogously the principles for common law business partnership and ordered an equitable division of property that they had acquired during the cohabitation. With the division, the court took into consideration not only the parties' cash contributions with the purchases of the property, but also other contributions such as *e.g.* works and services generally regarded as domestic in nature. *See also Taylor v. Taylor*, 317 So.2d 422 (Miss. 1975); and *Chrismond v. Chrismond*, 211 Miss. 746, 52 So.2d 624 (1951).

130 Goldberg, *supra* note 128, at 537. *See also* Laquer Estin, *supra* note 45, at 1393-1394, who states: "Recovery is more likely where the parties had a long-term relationship, where they represented themselves as husband and wife, and where they combined their financial resources. Joint bank accounts, jointly owned property, joint purchases, and jointly filed income tax returns seem particularly significant." *See also* Mee, who with respect to Canadian case law states that the probability of success in a lawsuit increases greatly if the parties have had a relationship "tantamount to spousal," in MEE, *supra* note 98, at 194. *Compare* regarding the relevant factors as support for an implied common law marriage agreement, Chapter 7.5 *supra.*

131 *See* the ALI PRINCIPLES, *supra* note 62, particularly Chapter 6, The Common Law Marriage Contract.

132 *Id.* § 6.03, paragraph (7).

the dissolution of relationships between unmarried cohabiting persons,[133] which are intended to be "a stable, marital-like relationship where both parties cohabit ..." The relevant factors with the assessment of whether such a relationship exists according to the court's view are not only continuous cohabitation, duration of the relationship, purpose of the relationship, but also "pooling of resources and services for joint projects."[134] Thus, the Washington Supreme Court has made a family law assessment that is in contrast to the Marvin doctrine.[135] The parties' cohabitation is the basis, under a family law analysis, for a status with certain marital legal effects. The parties' economic dealings are relevant, in a manner similar to those of the ALI principles, but not necessary and never sufficient conditions for the creation of legal effects.

12.3.2 The Property Law Remedies and Common Law Marriage

As seen above, certain circumstances can be cited to support lawsuits concerning either common law marriage or property law remedies. Nevertheless, it appears possible and significant to maintain the distinction between the family law and property law methods. In states recognizing common law marriage, it is not unusual for the courts to apply private law principles in cases in which such a marriage has not been proven.[136] Given that the Marvin doctrine has sometimes been used to give protection comparable to that provided by formal and common law marriages, it may be understandable that critics believe that accepting the Marvin doctrine would reintroduce common law marriage. This criticism also appears unwarranted whether based on the legal grounds or legal consequences.

1. *A Comparison of Legal Grounds*

Initially, a claim to the existence of a common law marriage rests on a marriage contract, as examined in Chapter 6. According to this contract,

133 *See* § 12.3.1 *supra.*

134 *Connell v. Francisco,* 127 Wash.2d 339, 346, 898 P.2d 831 (1995).

135 *Compare Marvin v. Marvin,* 18 Cal.3d 660, 557 P.2d 106 (1976), in which the California Supreme Court considered that community property law was not analogously applicable as to cohabiting unmarried persons. *See* on the other hand previously *In re Marriage of Cary,* 109 Cal. Rptr. 862, 866-867 (App. 1973) and *Estate of Atherley,* 44 Cal.App.3d 758, 119 Cal.Rptr. 41 (1975), in which the California Court of Appeals applied the Family Law Act as to an unmarried couple.

136 In *Eaton v. Johnston,* 235 Kan. 323, 328, 681 P.2d 606 (1984), the Supreme Court of Kansas stated that a trial court has the same power to divide property accumulated during a nonmarital relationship as it would have in dissolution of a business partnership and in *Hill v. Gould,* 142 P.3d 752 (Kan.App. 2006), the court held that the trial court did not err in utilizing partnership principles in determining how to distribute the parties' property. *See also Matter of Marriage of Beitzinger,* 121 P.3d 1003 (Kan.App. 2005), where the court awarded the woman a lump sum as an equitable distribution of the couple's property.

the parties must have a mutual intent to live together as husband and wife in a monogamous and lifelong, or in any event, durable relationship encompassing everything in life (a *consortium omnis vitae* and a *individua vitae consuetudo*), which is subject to the applicable regulations for spouses. Ordinarily, the marriage contract, as seen in Chapter 7, is an implied agreement based on the parties' cohabitation and outward appearance as spouses. Such an agreement is valid if it has been entered into in a common law marriage state, but invalid if it has been entered into in another state.[137] Legislation concerning how to assess whether a cohabitation exists may include exceptions that take into consideration subjective elements, which often concern whether the intent is to include a long lasting relationship or "a shared life."[138]

On the other hand, according to the Marvin doctrine, an implied agreement does not focus on the cohabitation, but instead typically includes a mutual intent with respect to the parties' economic affairs, for example, the acquisition of or division of property, and compensation for worked performed or for contributions made.[139] Therefore, it appears not entirely correct to state, as did William Reppy, that a cohabiting person can cite "the same agreement upon which common-law marriage is founded as a Marvin-style claim."[140] Cohabiting unmarried persons have the legal right to enter into property law agreements concerning

137 In *Thomas v. La Rosa*, 400 S.E.2d 809, 814 (W.Va. 1990), the West Virginia Supreme Court stated that a contract between a man and a woman under which the two agree to hold themselves out as husband and wife, the woman agrees to cohabit, keep house and entertain friends, while the man agrees to support the woman and take care of her for life, amounts to a contract of common law marriage not valid in this State. *Compare Kozlovski v. Kozlowski*, 80 N.J. 378, 385, 388, 403 A.2d 902 (N.J. 1979), in which a married man lived together for approximately 15 years with a woman other than his wife. According to an oral agreement between the cohabiting persons, the woman would take care of defendant, his children and his home; to cook and keep house for him, and to help entertain his friends and business associates while the man promised that he would take care of her for the rest of her life. When the parties separated, the court granted her a lesser amount comparable to future maintenance.

138 *See* with respect to New Zealand, Section 2D PROPERTY (RELATIONSHIPS) ACT 1976, in its new wording that entered into force the 1st of February 2002. In paragraph (f) is discussed the degree of mutual commitment to a shared life. The same element can also be found in section 4 (2) PROPERTY (RELATIONSHIPS) ACT 1976 (N.S.W.). Even according to the Swedish cohabitation legislation, consideration ought to be given to the intentions of the parties with respect to the relationship's durability and consequence and their desire that the relationship be considered as cohabitation relationship, *see* Prop. 1986/87:1, at 253, 368, Prop. 2002/03:80, at 43. Regarding the United States, the ALI points among a number of objective circumstances also to that consideration ought to be given to the parties' statements or promises to each other. *See also Connell v. Francisco*, 127 Wash.2d 339, 346, 898 P.2d 831, 834 (1995), in which the court argues that the intent of the parties and the purpose of the relationship ought to also be given relevance.

139 English case law concerning "common intention trusts" is a rich source concerning the requirements that ought to be made as to the parties' intentions with assessments of the parties' property rights.

140 Reppy, *supra* note 50, at 1689 and 1707.

economic affairs as long as their sexual relationship is not included in the agreement.[141] For example, if a man in a cohabitation purchases a car, and the court finds that the parties shared equally in paying the cost of the car, as the parties must be seen as having entered into an implied agreement to equally share ownership of the car. Still, the agreement does not constitute a common law marriage, even though the value of the car in such a marriage would have been divided equally under family law regulations. A common law marriage is not required with respect to joint ownership of a car. Therefore, the Marvin doctrine can give a legal protection in cases to which common law marriage principles do not extend. On the other hand, common law marriage gives a right to the division of property of the car even though the parties do not specifically enter into a relevant agreement. Nevertheless, the common law marriage agreements come close to a private law partnership agreement, such as, e.g., the French *société de fait* and *société creé de fait*, entered into for mutual benefit and with an intent to contribute capital or work and share the profits and the losses.[142] Still, the difference between a marital intent, *affectio maritalis*, and the desire to form a partnership, *affectio societatis* should be noted. The object of the former is the parties' cohabitation; for the latter, it is their financial dealings. Even though the partnership agreement can, but need not, include a large part of the parties' mutual affairs, the marriage contract is broader and concerns the entirety of the cohabitation.

In addition to the marriage contract, as seen from Chapter 8, the parties' cohabitation and outward appearance as spouses constitute necessary prerequisites for the establishment of a common law marriage in the majority of jurisdictions recognizing such marriages. The same chapter explained that the parties' sexual relationship is a significant, albeit not always necessary and never solely sufficient element in the requirement as to cohabitation.[143] Even the cohabitation legislation that has been enacted in many countries requires cohabitation and similarly considers the parties' sexual relationship as an important factor in the existence of a cohabitation.[144] The sexual relationship is an important element that distinguishes the family law institutions from the property law!

In applying property law remedies, it may be not only irrelevant but forbidden to take into consideration the parties' sexual relationship;[145]

---

141 Restatement of Contracts, §§ 589, 597 (1932); 31 A.L.R.2d 1255 (1953).

142 Sanford N. Katz, *Marriage as Partnership*, 73 Notre Dame L. Rev. 1251, 1270 (1998), states: "Like some commercial partnerships, one person may contribute capital, the other may contribute human resources."

143 Regarding the sexual community's relevance in cohabitation legislation, *see* Section 13.3.2 and Section 14.3.7 *infra*.

144 Regarding the sexual community's relevance in common law marriage, *see* Section 8.5.2.1 *supra* and Chapter 14.3.7 *infra*.

145 *Compare* David L. Chambers, *The "Legalization" of the Family: Towards a Policy of Supportive Neutrality*, 18 U. Mich. J.L. Reform 805, 824-825 (1985), who is concerned that the *Marvin* doctrine invites evidentiary assessments concerning *inter alia* infidelity.

any other approach could be viewed as accepting prostitution. Moreover, in a broader context, the cohabitation is not a necessary prerequisite for a claim according to the Marvin doctrine or comparable doctrines in other countries, even though the cohabitation may have evidentiary value; compare *Goode v. Goode* and the French partnership agreement above. The parties' cohabitation alone, however, cannot be cited as an independent basis for a property law claim. In certain cases, only the unjust consequences of the cohabitation can be the basis of a claim.

Property law remedies ordinarily include requirements regarding direct or indirect financial contributions or work, performed on the property or in the home, or agreements concerning the division of the property. No such requirements need be fulfilled in the application of common law marriage or cohabitation legislation. In accordance with legislation in Sweden, Canada, New Zealand, and Australia, as well as in accordance with the principles proposed by the ALI and applied by the Washington Supreme Court, such circumstances are relevant, but neither necessary and nor sufficient for the establishment of a legal cohabitation. A point of family law legislation is just that even a party who cannot contribute either money or work to the relationship as a result of illness, handicap, destitution, or unemployment is still legally protected by marriage, whether ceremonial, common law, or de facto.

This comparison shows that, in principle, it is important to maintain the distinction between family law and general private law methods and solutions even though, to a certain extent, the same facts can be relevant in both cases. The distinction is decisive to the basis of the litigation and the presentation of evidence in disputes, but can also contribute to clarifying the discussion about legal policy alternatives.

2. *A Comparison of the Legal Effects*

The Marvin doctrine and comparable doctrines in other countries offer spouses and cohabiting unmarried couples protection that is both limited and highly uncertain compared with the legal effects of the family law systems. In the case law, the property law methods have not included analogously applying the legal effects that follow from formal or common law marriage. From case to case, the property law remedies required exhaustive investigations of the parties' contributions in the form of money or work, their sacrifices, expectations, and their implicit agreements. It is necessary to evaluate these circumstances and their benefit to the parties. The amount of that was finally awarded has varied from case to case. Sometimes, a wronged party has received a fair share of a certain piece of property or limited compensation or has had to be satisfied with a fair lump sum. In the cases, both the legal and evidentiary results have consistently been highly unpredictable. A party who, as a result of illness or handicap, cannot contribute either financially or through work in the home commonly enjoys no protection. In the cases, the uncertain results strongly contrast to the well-settled rights to property division, maintenance, etc., that ordinarily follow from ceremonial marriage, common law marriage, and cohabitation legislation, even though the latter are discretionary solutions, with justice as a guiding principle, and do not always serve the interest of clarity.

During recent years, the enactment of specific family law legislation for cohabiting unmarried couples in Sweden, Canada, Australia, and New Zealand, in part, has provided the legal protection that the property law remedies have provided, as discussed below in Section 12.4. Moreover, the property law doctrines do not concern rights to public benefits, which are, on the other hand, often protected by cohabitation legislation and still more often by common law marriage.[146] Therefore, there is no justification for maintaining that the legal effects of the Marvin doctrine constitute a principal alternative to or threat against marriage.

12.3.3 The Problems with Property Law Solutions

It has been seen above that, of the cases in which the courts attempted to reach property law solutions, many have been based on contractual or quasi-contractual reasoning. Based on the parties' actual actions, the courts have found the existence of an implied agreement concerning, for example, compensation for work performed, contributions made, or a division of property. It should be observed with this development that even an implied agreement is a contract that requires a mutual intent even if it is inferred from the parties' actions! To the extent that behavior actually discloses a mutual intent, it of course is the best basis for a solution. For example, suppose that property is purchased in one party's name but with direct financial contributions from the other in connection with the acquisition. As long as the contribution is not a loan or a gift, it is strong evidence for the existence of a mutual intent to together acquire the property, but not always conclusive. Ordinarily the parties have never discussed, considered, or even thought about their ownership rights. Therefore, there is a risk that the courts force upon the parties fictional agreements that they never entered into and which, therefore, are deceptions and against their mutual intent, or one of the parties' intent. Spouses or cohabiting persons who do not desire financial sharing of any kind are forced, for the sake of certainty, and based on the legal development in the case law, to enter into agreements that exclude both the family law and property law regimes. If the courts choose to make contractual conclusions, this risk for fictional agreements ought to encourage a stringent

146 *Cf.* Sonya C. Garza, *Common Law Marriage: A Proposal for the Revival of a Dying Doctrine,* 40 New Eng. L. Rev. 541, 552 (2005-2006); and Twila L. Perry, *The "Essentials of Marriage": Reconsidering the Duty of Support and Services,* 15 Yale J. L. & Feminism 1, 48 (2003).

application of the laws and evaluation of evidence, for the purpose of clarifying what the parties actually agreed to and their mutual intent.[147]

There is a real danger of fictional agreements even in conclusions concerning the implied agreements on which common law marriage often rests, as seen in Chapter 7.[148] The parties' cohabitation, however, appears to be given a greater evidentiary value concerning a marriage contract, in which the object of the marital intent is a long-lasting cohabitation than when concerning property law agreements, compensation for work performed, or other financial issues. The evidentiary value of cohabitation as support for a contract is limited in families in which members performing tasks and reciprocal services for each other without anticipating any compensation is taken for granted. The cohabitation's evidentiary value concerning a marriage contract requiring a legal intent, however can also be limited. The problems with marriage agreements upon which common law marriage rests are discussed more closely in Sections 13.2 and 14.3.1.

These evidentiary problems can be avoided with a requirement that the parties draft explicit or, as is necessary in Texas and Minnesota,[149] written agreements concerning property and financial relations. First, such a requirement allows a precise consideration of the intentions of the parties; and second, it avoids evidentiary problems and disputes.[150] Nevertheless, expressed agreements between cohabiting unmarried persons are unusual.[151] In addition, drafting ordinarily requires the time, knowledge, and assistance of legal expertise, to which many couples do not have access.

---

147 Critical of artificial contracts are also, inter alia, Grace Ganz Blumberg, *Cohabitation without Marriage: A Different Perspective*, 28UCLA L. REV. 1125, 1166 (1981) and Ira Mark Ellman, *"Contract Thinking" Was Marvin's Fatal Flaw*, 76 NOTRE DAME L. REV. 1365 (2001).

148 *See supra* Chapter 7.8 *supra*.

149 According to MINN. STAT. ANN. § 513.075 (West 2005), enacted in 1980, agreements between parties who have a sexual relationship concerning property and financial relations must be in writing and executable after the dissolution of the relationship. The law has been applied in *Hollom v. Carey*, 343 N.W.2d 701 (Minn.App. 1984); *Obert v. Dahl*, 574 N.W.2d 747 (Minn.App. 1998). The law, on the other hand, has not prevented claims based upon constructive trust or unjust enrichment *e.g.* in those cases in which property has been acquired in the one party's name but with financial contributions from the other party, as these requirements have been wholly independent of any service contract related to cohabitation, *see Estate of Eriksen*, 337 N.W.2d 671, 674 (Minn. 1983) (constructive trust); and *Estate of Palmen*, 588 N.W.2d 493 (Minn. 1999) (unjust enrichment). *See also* Mary L. Knoblauch, *Minnesota's Cohabitation Statute*, 2 LAW & INEQ. 335 (1984); and Kim Kantorowicz, Comment, *Contracts – Cohabitation in Minnesota: From Love to Contract-Public Policy Gone Away in In Re Estate of Palmen*, 588 N.W.2d 493 (Minn. 2000), 26 WM. MITCHELL L. REV. 213 (1999). For cases from other states, *see Kohler v. Flynn*, 493 N.W.2d 647 (N.D. 1992); and *Posik v. Layton*, 695 So.2d 759 (Fla.Dist.Ct.App. 1997). *See also* TEX. FAM. CODE ANN. 1.108 (Vernon 2005).

150 *See* Twila L. Perry, *Dissolution Planning in Family Law: A Critique of Current Analyses and a Look Toward the Future*, 24 FAM. L.Q. 77, 116 (1990).

151 Several authors have testified that expressed agreements are unusual, *see, e.g.*, Elizabeth Scott, *Domestic Partnerships, Implied Contracts, and Law Reform*, in

In those cases in which the parties do not enter into expressed agreements, it appears to be more realistic to base the private law solutions on doctrines of mistaken conctractual conditions than on quasi-contractual reasoning. The work that is to be performed on the property and in the home, as well as the financial contributions that the parties make during the cohabitation, ordinarily ought to be based upon the presumed conditions that the relationship will be lifelong or at least long-lasting. This presumption ought to be one of the explanations for why couples ordinarily do not enter into specific agreements with respect to the services they perform for each other and the family. It is unlikely that either party would perform comparable services for anyone else, for example, a neighbor; Typically, both parties understand that the cohabitation is a prerequisite for these contributions. It is predictable that if the parties later separate, each will seek compensation or shares in the wealth accumulated during the cohabitation for his or her contributions of work performed and incurred costs. The decisions in the case law vary widely. The parties' contributions do not always give rise to an asset that is preserved and allows for restitution.

A plausible assertion has been made, that the private law remedies created in the case law can achieve solutions tailored for the individual case.[152] Still, that strength is also their weakness. The case law from the entire Western world discloses how difficult it is, in each individual case, to investigate and evaluate the parties' contributions during a long cohabitation. In certain cases, a total accounting and day-by-day evaluation has been required to trace, over a long cohabitation, the parties' contributions in the form of work in the home, financial contributions, purchases of property, and consumption. At the same time, claims have been made about how to deduct the benefits that accrued to one party from the contributions of the other.

These investigative difficulties, as well as the lack of clarity that ordinarily permeates the relevant private law principles, has created extensive application difficulties, disputes, and, above all, considerable legal uncertainty. Such criticism is brought against the Marvin doctrine in both the case law[153]

Reconceiving the Family, Critique on the American Law Institute's Principles of the Law of Family Dissolution 337 (Robin Fretwell Wilson ed., 2006); and Blumberg, *supra* note 148, at 1164.

152 Tone Sverdrup has maintained that the courts here "have a law-making role that can hardly be completely supplanted by the legislator. The conflict embraces a complex collection of norms and values, which only becomes apparent in specific cases." *See* Tone Sverdrup, *Maintenance as a Separate Issue – The Relationship between Maintenance and Matrimonial Property,* in Common Core and Better Law in European Family Law 119, 124 (K. Boele-Woelki ed., European Family Law Series No. 10, Antwerp 2005).

153 *Hewitt v. Hewitt,* 77 Ill.2d 49, 31 Ill.Dec. 827, 394 N.E.2d 1204, 1211 (1979); *Morone v. Morone,* 50 N.Y.2d 481, 429 N.Y.S.2d 592, 407 N.E.2d 438, 441 (1980); *Rehak v. Mathis,* 239 Ga. 541, 238 S.E.2d 81 (1977); and *Taylor v. Polackwich,* 194 Cal.Rptr. 8 (App. 1983). In *Thomas v. La Rosa,* 400 S.E.2d 809 (W.Va. 1990), the contract

and the academic literature,[154] and is directed even against other countries' property law remedies.[155] The interests of legal certainty are not served if courts, faced with complex facts and the applicable principles, simply render decisions case-by-case.[156] Today, in the majority of cases, it is risky, not to say impossible, for cohabiting couples to predict if and to what extent they can rely on private law protections in the event that the relationship is dissolved. Altogether too often, the results of the cases rest on the courts' application of vague fictions, but what couple wants to live a life together in the expectation of a fiction?

Considerably more predictability characterizes the remedies that have been enacted through family law legislation, for example, within the framework of ceremonial marriage and registered forms of cohabitation, even though the results in property disputes, at times, can be uncertain. It seems most appropriate to use family law solutions to solve family law problems.[157] The legislative method offers better opportunities to clearly

---

between cohabitants was not considered to be enforceable as the man was married to another woman. *See also Taylor v. Fields*, 178 Cal.App.3d 653, 224 Cal.Rptr. 186 (1986), in which the parties' sexual relationship was considered inseparable from their considerations concerning the agreement. *See also Bergen v. Wood*, 14 Cal. App.4th 854, 18 Cal.Rptr.2d 75 (1993); and *Maria v. Freitas*, 73 Haw. 266, 832 P.2d 259 (1992). *Compare* on the other hand *Kozlowski v. Kozlowski*, 80 N.J. 378, 403 A.2d 902 (1979), in which the woman received compensation for breach of contract. *Compare Mullen v. Suchko*, 279 Pa.Super. 499, 421 A.2d 310 (1980); and *Collins v. Davis*, 68 N.C.App. 588, 315 S.E.2d 759, *aff'd*, 312 N.C. 324, 321 S.E.2d 892 (1984).

154 Regarding the criticism against the *Marvin* doctrine *inter alia* taking into consideration the danger for legal uncertainty and disputes, *see also* Margaret F. Brinig, *Status, Contract and Covenant*, 79 CORNELL L. REV. 1573, 1594-1599 (1994); Ira Mark Ellman, *The Theory of Alimony*, 77 CAL. L. REV. 1, 13-24 (1989); Reppy, *supra* note 50, at 1689 and 1722 ("The outcome of litigation under the implied contract theory usually will be impossible to prognosticate"); J. O'DONNELL & D. JONES, THE LAW OF MARRIAGE AND MARITAL ALTERNATIVES 190 (1982); Carol S. Bruch, *Nonmarital Cohabitation in the Common Law Countries: A Study in Judicial - Legislative Interaction*, 29 AM. J. COMP. L. 217, 243 (1981); Blumberg, *supra* note 148, at1163-1166; H. A. Finlay, *The Informal Marriage in Anglo-Australian Law*, in MARRIAGE AND COHABITATION IN CONTEMPORARY SOCIETIES 156, 166 (John M. Eekelaar, Sanford N. Katz eds., 1980); Ruth Deech, *The Case Against Legal Recognition of Cohabitation*, in MARRIAGE AND COHABITATION IN CONTEMPORARY SOCIETIES 300, 309 (John M. Eekelaar, Sanford N. Katz eds., 1980); Walter O. Weyrauch, *Metamorphoses of Marriage: Formal and Informal Marriages in the United States*, in MARRIAGE AND COHABITATION IN CONTEMPORARY SOCIETIES 265, 271 (John M. Eekelaar, Sanford N. Katz eds., 1980); and Robert C. Casad, *Unmarried Couples and Unjust Enrichment: From Status to Contract and Back Again?*, 77 MICH. L. REV. 47, 59 (1978).

155 Regarding the criticism against private law solutions in common law states, *see* Mee, *supra* note 98, at 310. Atkin, *supra* note 32, at 2, states regarding private law solutions: "The results have not however been easy to predict and some claimants have been left with little or nothing."

156 *See, e.g., Kozlowski v. Kozlowski*, 80 N.J. 378, 403 A.2d 902, 910 (1979).

157 Ellen Kandoian argues with justification that marriage law, domestic relations law, and normative morality are better equipped than contract law to address the unique features of such relationships, *see Cohabitation, Common Law Marriage, and the Possibility of a Shared Moral Life*, 75 GEO. L.J. 1829, 1869 (1987). *See also* Clare Dalton, *An Essay in the Deconstruction of Contract Doctrine*, 94 YALE L.J. 997, 1002 (1985).

define the requirements for the use of a certain solution. Even informal relationships, such as common law marriage and cohabitations regulated by law, generally offer more reliable financial remedies for the dissolution of a relationship than does private law case law. The law-regulated informal relationships lead to other application problems, disputes, and a legal uncertainty, however, that primarily are related to the question of whether and when such a relationship exists, issues that are discussed in Chapters 13 and 14 below.

12.4 Family Law Regimes for Cohabiting Persons

A characteristic feature in the development since the 1970s is that many jurisdictions in the Western world have created specific legal regimes for unmarried couples with rights and obligations, either based on the parties' cohabitation or on the registration of their relationship. Such regimes commonly have arisen through legislation but also as exceptions in the case law. Certain systems are intended for heterosexuals, others for homosexual couples, and others for both groups. It is common in all that the parties do not enter into marriage and the main purpose of the systems is to protect the more vulnerable party in the relationship. Ordinarily, these regimes have fewer legal effects than marriage and common law marriage, but the systems are in the midst of development. The two following sections in this chapter focus on an overall presentation of several representative regimes and compare them with common law marriage. A closer analysis of the concepts of cohabiting persons as used is made in Chapter 13 and the reasons behind the development of the law are discussed in Chapter 14.

12.4.1 Cohabitation as a Basis for Rights and Obligations

A comparison of common law marriage and the status-based regimes giving rights and obligations based upon the parties' cohabitation shows the following.

If one begins with the legal facts that constitute the relationships, common law marriage and cohabitation regimes have in common that they ordinarily are formless, in contrast with ceremonial marriage. A ceremonial wedding is not necessary for the invocation of legal effects. Nevertheless, determining boundaries based on form requirements is not always clear. There is some European cohabitation legislation having registration that is obligatory or optional.[158] In a few states in the United States,

158 Regarding obligatory registration in the Netherlands and the optional registration in the Spanish province of Catalonia, *see* § 12.4.2 *infra*.

even common law marriage can voluntarily be registered,[159] and thus resembles formal marriage.

A fundamental difference between the institutions is that common law marriage, in principle, is based on an agreement between the parties, *consensus, non concubitus, facit matrimonium,* while cohabitation legislation is based on the parties' cohabitation. If one ignores the lack of form, common law marriage, in this respect, resembles ceremonial marriage. The distinction from cohabitation legislation, in practice, however, has decreased, in part because of the extensive use of implied agreements and legal presumptions. As discussed in Chapters 7 and 9 above, the establishment of a common law marriage primarily is based on the parties' cohabitation. Moreover, in the majority of jurisdictions, cohabitation, in addition to the agreement, has become a necessary requisite in the majority of jurisdictions recognizing common law marriage, as seen in Chapter 8. At the same time, cohabitation legislation has not been able avoid the use of subjective elements in the establishment of the relationships, discussed further in Chapter 13. In practice, however, the parties' cohabitation constitutes, in the broadest sense, the most important actual basis for the establishment of the relationships and thus for the invocation of the legal effects of both common law marriage and cohabitation regimes. Of those cohabiting couples included within the cohabitation legislation that has been enacted in different states, approximately 80 percent fall within the regulations for common law marriage. The contractual requirement's functions when facing the future are analyzed more closely in Chapter 13.

If one begins, instead, with the legal effects, both common law marriage and cohabitation legislation purport to give solutions to the problems facing cohabiting couples. It is characteristic of common law marriage that it entails the ceremonial marriage's legal effects, rights, as well as obligations, both during the relationship and upon its dissolution through marital divorce or death. Cohabitation legislation, on the other hand, ordinarily entails more limited legal effects. Cohabitation legislation, therefore, can be said to be a partial recognition of common law marriage, *i.e.*, common law marriage is the ultimate form of cohabitation legislation. This distinction, however, seems to be more a difference of degree than substance. A feature of the development is that cohabitation legislation will increasingly approach common law marriage. It is not an unusual opinion that cohabitation ought to be given the same legal effects as marriage.[160] Neither is the extent of marriage's legal effects given one time

---

159 Regarding voluntary registration of common law marriage in *Texas* and *Montana*, *see* § 13.2.2 *infra*.

160 Michael Freeman, *Family Values and Family Justice*, in CURRENT PROBLEMS. LAW AND OPINION AT THE END OF THE TWENTIETH CENTURY (Michael Freeman ed., 1997), at 357, assumes that cohabitation and marriage will be increasingly similar in the future. Caudill, *supra* note 33, at 543, suggests that the traditional burdens and benefits of

for all. The private law institutions can also provide solutions to the problems that cohabiting unmarried couples face, but, on the other hand, as seen above, the solutions vary and are not primarily intended for family law relationships.

1. *The Modern Developments in Northern and Western Europe*

As can be seen from the statistics presented above, **Sweden** is the country in the Western world that from the end of the 1960s up to 2004 has had the lowest rate of marriage and the highest number of cohabiting unmarried couples. Early on, the Swedish legislature took the initiative by addressing the relationship between cohabiting partners. The Swedish development, therefore, has since the 1970s attracted considerable attention and appears to have inspired international debate. Mary Ann Glendon has written, "Sweden: Where all Roads Lead?"[161] Even if the historical chapters above have shown that all paths actually lead, not to Sweden, but rather to Rome, however the Swedish development is interesting in that it constitutes a new start for the development of modern cohabitation legislation concerning the relationship between the parties.[162]

In Sweden the initiative was taken in 1969 by the country's Minister of Justice, who launched an ideology of neutrality, according to which the state would be neutral in relation to the different forms of cohabitation and different moral understandings. Marriage had and ought to have a central place in family law, but the family law legislation ought not include any regulations that create unnecessary difficulties for those who have children and start families without marrying.[163] From the beginning, it was noted that this ideology could be interpreted in two diametrically

---

marriage should be imposed upon all unmarried cohabitators whose relationship have taken on the essential characteristics of marriages. Blumberg, *supra* note 148, at 1159-1170, advocates a "legal status" for long term and abiding cohabitations with both rights as obligations. Nancy Rebecca Shaw, *Common Law Marriage and Unmarried Cohabitation: An Old Solution to a New Problem,* 39 U. PITT. L. REV. 579, 586, 595 (1977), proposes complete equality with marriage under certain conditions.

161 MARY ANN GLENDON, STATE, LAW AND FAMILY. FAMILY LAW IN TRANSITION IN THE UNITED STATES AND WESTERN EUROPE 100 (1977); *see* the same author in THE TRANSFORMATION OF FAMILY LAW 273 (1989). *Compare* Anders Agell, *Family Forms and Legal Policies,* 38 SC. ST. L. 197, 206 (1999), who states: "Sweden seems to be the country in Western Europe that has chosen the clearest and most positive attitude towards cohabitation."

162 Even Sweden and other European countries have an older history of formless marriage with roots in the Middle Ages.

163 Ministry of Justice, Abstract of Protocol on Justice Department Matters 4 (1969): "New legislation ought (so far) as possible to be neutral in relation to the different forms of living together and different moral views. Marriage has and ought to have a central position in the family law, but one should try to see that the family law legislation does not create any provisions which create unnecessary hardship or inconveniences for those who have children and build families without marrying."

different ways.[164] One interpretation is that the same regulations apply to both unmarried cohabiting persons and married couples. The entire legal marital system would, in the same manner as common law marriage, become applicable to cohabiting couples, even though they did not formally marry. This interpretation of ideological neutrality in Sweden, however, came to be implemented largely in social and tax law, which, under the social welfare state, has long had the objective of reaching out to all families regardless of whether the parties had formalized their relationship through a wedding ceremony.[165]

In the relationship between the parties, on the other hand, neutrality was interpreted to mean that different regulations would be applicable to spouses and cohabiting unmarried persons with the possibility of the parties choosing systems by marrying or simply cohabiting. The first law (1973:651) concerning the mutual residence of unmarried cohabiting parties gave the cohabiting party who was most in need only a right, upon separation or death of the other party, to take over the joint residence. If the residence had an economic value, this party had to pay for the residence. This right to assume did not include an apartment house. The Act on Cohabitee's Mutual Residence (1987:232) went considerably farther by granting the parties a limited right to a division (equal division) of certain property, namely, in practice, the permanent residence and the household goods that the parties had acquired during the cohabitation relationship. A requirement of consent would be applicable to the disposition of property that is covered by the law. This system, however, is considerably more limited than the extensive matrimonial property system that, in Sweden, applies to spouses, according to which all property (not only the residence and household goods) is shared equally, including property acquired prior to the marriage and through inheritance or gift. The spouses also have, in contrast to cohabiting unmarried persons, the right to inherit and maintenance obligations.

This half-way progress toward a system resembling common law marriage has been recently confirmed by the Swedish legislature with The Swedish COHABITEES ACT (2003:376), applicable to two persons who live together long-term in a couple relationship having a common household and is therefore directly applicable even to couples of the same sex. Despite a proposal thereon, the law in principle stretches no further than the previous act.[166] The main purpose of both laws has only been to give

164 *See* Anders Agell, *Cohabitation Without Marriage in Swedish Law*, in MARRIAGE AND COHABITATION IN CONTEMPORARY SOCIETIES 245 (John M. Eekelaar and Sanford N. Katz eds. 1980); and *The Swedish law on marriage and cohabitation*, 24 S.C. S.T. L. 9, 22 (1980).

165 Anders Agell, *The Swedish Law on Marriage and Cohabitation*, 24 SC. ST. L. 9, 30 (1980); and AGELL, *supra* note 70, at 242-269.

166 In the legislative preparatory committee work that was submitted to the government (SOU 1999:104, at 199), it was suggested that the division of property should be expanded to include, not only the residence and household goods that were

minimal protection to the more vulnerable party in the event of a separation or death and provide a practical method for dividing assets that have been combined during the cohabitation. Couples who do not wish this system can contract out of the regulations concerning the division of property. Couples wishing a more extensive financial sharing are advised to formally marry.[167]

The restrictions of the Swedish ideology of neutrality have not received the attention they deserve. Persistent misunderstandings about the content of the Swedish cohabitation legislation compared to common law marriage has attracted international attention.[168] Today, several countries have enacted cohabitation legislation with more far-reaching legal effects than that of Sweden, such that it is no longer the country to which all roads lead.

Scotland, which has had a long historical experience of common law marriage, through a decision in December 2005, repealed the last remnants of "marriage by cohabitation with habit and repute," as shown in the preceding chapter. Paradoxically, at the same time, the Scottish parliament adopted a law giving rights to couples "living together as if they were

---

acquired during the cohabitation relationship, but also automobiles, boats, and other motor-driven transportation vehicles. Cautious statements, however, were made that the time ought to be ripe to go further and allow the same regulations concerning property division be applicable for unmarried cohabiting persons as well as for married persons. *See* Ryrstedt, *supra* note 70, at 429. Almost one-half of all cohabiting persons believe that the same regulations are applicable to them as for married persons, *see* Statskontoret 1993:24, at 18.

167 *See* Prop. 2002/03:80, Ny Sambolag, at 25.

168 *Compare* Bowman, *supra* note 50, at 776-777, who maintains that "Sweden has gone to the extreme of essentially eliminating any distinctions between formal and informal marriage…" The author states further that Sweden "mandating formal neutrality of treatment between couples who are married and those who are not, essentially eliminating distinctions between marriage and cohabitation of all sorts. Thus in Sweden there would be no need for the doctrine of common law marriage." *See also* Kiernan, *supra* note 11, at 50, who maintains that family law in Sweden, Finland, and Denmark, with time "has come to be applied to married and cohabiting couples in the same way." It ought to be noted that Finland and Denmark have not implemented legislation concerning the relationship between cohabiting persons in the same manner as in Sweden. *Compare* Glendon, *supra* note 50, at 276, who argues: "When one considers how few couples in the Swedish high-tax society acquire substantial assets apart from the marital home, the similarity to the property situation of married persons is strong indeed." It deserves to be noted that in the division of property between cohabiting persons, assets acquired prior to the cohabitation relationship are not included, as are neither assets acquired during the cohabitation relationship that are not the residence and household, e.g., money, shares, automobiles, boats, vacation homes, real estate. It ought further be noted that the number of automobiles, boats, and vacation homes per capita is very high in Sweden and that Swedes are the most share-investing people in the world, which means that 80% own shares in some form. A more realistic assessment is made by Matthew Fawcett, *Taking the Middle Path: Recent Swedish Legislation Grants Minimal Property Rights to Unmarried Cohabitants,* 24 Fam. L.Q. 179 (1990) and in Bradley, *supra* note 21, at 100, who states: "In comparison with property and succession rights in marriage, the rights of cohabitees are limited."

husband and wife."[169] The new legislation, The Family Law (Scotland) Act (2006), was enacted in an environment in which cohabitation has become a dominant type of family, and both the number and durability of cohabitations is expected to increase. The law's purpose is to give legal safeguards to cohabitants and protect vulnerable parties, either during the breakdown of a relationship, or if a partner dies.[170] One difference, however, is that the new regulations do not give all the legal effects of marriage in the same way as common law marriage. According to the new law, it is presumed that the parties *inter alia* have a right to an equal share of the household goods acquired during the cohabitation, as well as the money and property tied up in their mutual household expenditures. The residence is not included in such property. In the event of death, the surviving cohabiting partner can receive a capital sum from the deceased's estate. The legislator's objective has been to create greater certainty, fairness, and clarity in the law.[171] The question of whether this objective is reached by substituting the definition "cohabitation with habit and repute" for "living together as if they were husband and wife" is discussed in the next chapter.

In **Spain,** cohabitation legislation during recent years has been enacted in several provinces. In Catalonia, a law was adopted in 1998 concerning long-lasting couple relationships (*d'unions estables de parella*) in which the persons are legally competent to marry. The law equates unmarried cohabiting persons with spouses in several aspects.[172] The objective was primarily to give a protection to the more vulnerable party, but not as extensively as under the matrimonial property regime applicable to spouses. However, the parties can enter into agreements concerning the cohabitation and its dissolution. They are obligated to contribute to the household, mutual expenditures, and each other's maintenance. Upon separation, the party who has taken care of the household or worked without wages for the other party has the right to financial compensation in order to avoid

169 *See* THE FAMILY LAW (SCOTLAND) ACT (2006); and Family Law (Scotland) Bill, SP Bill 36B, 18, Session 2 (2005), sections 18-22.

170 Policy Memorandum, Family Law (Scotland) Bill (SP Bill 36) (2005), at 13.

171 *Id.*

172 LEY 10/1998, de 15 de Julio, D'UNIONS ESTABLES DE PARELLA (DOGC num. 2687, 23.07.1998). Thereafter similar legislation has been enacted in three additional provinces that have the authority to legislate within civil law. Regarding *Aragonia, see* Lay6/1999, de 26 de marzo, relativa a parejas estables no casados (BOE num. 112, 10.05.2001). Regarding *Navarra, see* Ley Foral 6/2000, de 3 de julio, para la igualdad juridica las parejas estables (BOE num. 214, 6.09.2000). Regarding *Balearic Islands, see* Ley 18/2001, de 19 de diciembre, de Parejas Estables (BOE num. 14, 16.01.2002). *See also* a number of autonomous areas. Regarding *Valencia, see* Ley 1/2001, de 6 de abril, por la que see refgulan las uniones de hecho (BOE num. 112, 10.05.2001). Regarding *Madrid, see* Ley 11/2001, de 19 de diciembre, de Uniones de Hecho de la Communidad de Madrid (BOE num. 55,.05.03.2002). Regarding *Asturien, see* Ley 4/2002, de 23 de mayo, de Parejas Estables (BOE num. 157, 02.07.2002). For more on this, *see* Miquel Martín-Casals, *Same-Sex Partnerships in the Legislation of Spanish Autonomous Communities, EU ERA Conference,* unpublished paper, Uppsala 19-20 (September 2002) at 2.

unfair enrichment. The dissolution of the relationship also raises issues concerning maintenance as well as the custody and maintenance of children. In the event of death, the surviving party has the right to continue to live in the residence for one year as well as the right to household goods that belonged to the common residence. The law is also applicable to homosexual couples, who, in addition, have the right to inherit between one-fourth and one-half of the estate, depending upon which relatives compete, as well as the entirety of the estate, if there are no relatives. Heterosexual couples receive the right to inherit only if they marry.

The legal effects of the Spanish system are less than those of common law marriage, meaning that the parties receive a fundamental legal protection even though the same regulations are not applicable as to spouses. The legislation for heterosexual couples becomes an alternative to marriage for those wishing a less extensive sharing than that offered by marriage. The system of regulation becomes applicable to heterosexual couples who lived together in a marriage-like state during an uninterrupted period of two years or who have mutual children. The law is also applicable to both heterosexual and homosexual couples through registration. The law in question does not give heterosexual cohabiting persons the right to contract out of their minimum rights and responsibilities.

An example of a very limited family law regulation for unmarried cohabiting persons can also be found in **Norway.** Despite the fact that the country, as in the other Nordic countries, has had low rates of marriage and a high number of unmarried cohabiting persons during the last thirty years, there is only a limited family law regulation of these relationships, but on the other hand, an extensive legal protection within the public law. The family law legislation is applicable not only to men and women who live together, but also as to two or several unmarried persons over eighteen years who have lived in a common household, for example homosexual couples, siblings, students, or friends. If the parties have lived together for at least two years or have mutual children, a member of the household upon the relationship's dissolution can have the right, under certain circumstances, to assume possession of the residence and household goods that have been used jointly. If the assets that are taken over have value, the assuming party must pay for them. The law gives no right to a division of estates, inheritance, or maintenance.[173]

Despite the hasty development as to cohabitation legislation in Northern and Western Europe, a number of countries have taken a hesitant attitude. An example is **England,** which certainly has a rather extensive cohabitation legislation within the public law, but which has been hesitant to regulate

173 Lag No. 45, 4 July 1991. *See* Peter Lødrup, *Family Law in Norway*, in FAMILY LAW IN EUROPE 353 (Carolyn Hamilton et al. eds., 1995). A proposal has been presented giving couples who have children or who have lived together for two years a stronger protection. Complete equality however has not been sought with spouses in consideration of freedom of choice. *See* NOU 1999:25, Samboerne og samfunnet.

property right relationships between the parties. The Law Commission for England and Wales for a long time has been studying the issue, but the legislation, with few exceptions, still has not been enacted. The lack of convincing argument as well as the common law tradition's conservative skepticism towards legislative solutions has probably been constraining.[174]

The latest proposal during the beginning of 2007 came from **Italy,** where the Italian government proposed new legislation for same-sex and unmarried heterosexual couples. The law, referred to as DICO (*Diritti di coppie conviventi*), upon separation gives the parties *inter alia* maintenance rights after three years of cohabitation, with the surviving cohabitant gaining inheritance rights after nine years of cohabitation. The surviving party inherits one-third if there is only one child, and one-fourth if there are two or more children. If the deceased is survived only by parents or siblings, one-half is taken by the cohabitant. If there are no children, parents, or siblings, the surviving party takes two-thirds, and if there are no relatives closer than the third degree (second cousins), the surviving cohabitant takes the entire estate. The law has been strongly criticized by Pope Benedict XVI.[175] The proposed law (Art. 1) requires the parties to be united by mutual emotional bonds, cohabit continuously, and give each other support and solidarity, materially as well as morally. Cohabiting partners will have to go to the registry office to declare their de facto union.

2. *The Developments in Australia and New Zealand*

The radical developments in Australia and New Zealand which first meant that unmarried cohabiting heterosexual couples were mostly equated with married persons, and later meant that homosexual couples also received the same rights, went considerably further toward becoming common law marriage. For example, legislation equating a "de facto relationship"

---

174 *See, e.g.*, a surviving cohabiting person's right to maintenance from the estate, assuming that the parties during two years immediately prior to the death had lived together as husband and wife, *see* LAW REFORM (SUCCESSION) ACT 1995 Sh. 2, amending INHERITANCE (PROVISION FOR FAMILY AND DEPENDANTS) ACT 1975 Sh. 25. *Compare* Lawrence W. Waggoner, *Marital Property Rights in Transition*, 59 MO. L. REV. 21, 78 (1994), who proposes legislation as to inheritance for unmarried couples who have lived in a "marriage like relationship." Regarding the English stance, *see* CRETNEY, *supra* note 40, at 520, who finds that the stance as to reforms is characterized by hesitancy and uncertainty. *See also* David Bradley, *Regulation of Unmarried Cohabitation in West-European Jurisdictions – Determinants of Legal Policy*, 15 IJLPF 22 (2001); John M. Eekelaar, *The Family Law Bill – The Politics of Family Law*, 26 FAM. L. 45 (1996); CRETNEY, *supra* note 98, at 243; LAW COMMISSION 44 (1995); and GLENDON, *supra* note 50, at 268, who speaks of a politics of cautious accommodation. Later during 2007 the Law Commission is expected to publish a report on cohabitation law.

175 DISEGNO DI LEGGE, SENATO DELLA REPUBLICA, XV LEGISLATURA N. 1339 (2007). As to the criticism, *see* Section 14.3.3 *infra*. Because of the requirement of registration, the law also belongs to the next section. *See* Göran Lind, *Legislation for the Surviving Cohabitant in Comparative Perspective*, in EUROPEAN CHALLENGES IN CONTEMPORARY FAMILY LAW (K. Boele-Woelki and T. Sverdrup eds., European Family Law Series No. 10, Antwerp 2008).

(both heterosexual and homosexual) with marriage after two and three years' respective cohabitation regarding such significant issues as property division (the equal division of property acquired during the relationship), inheritance, and maintenance was enacted in **New South Wales** in 1999[176] and in **New Zealand** in 2002.[177] The extensive nature of these reforms can also be seen in that the regulations were not carried out through separate legislation supplementing the marital legislation but rather by the latter becoming directly applicable to the new relationships. The reforms, therefore, have entailed extensive modifications to the concepts created in this area of law. In New Zealand, where the Matrimonial Property Act (1976) has also been applied to cohabiting unmarried couples, both homosexual and heterosexual, the term *matrimonial property* consequently has been replaced by *relationship property*. The law applicable as to all three categories has also been renamed the Property (Relationships) Act 1976. It is therefore logical that marital status is considered to entail not only marriage but also a "relationship in the nature of a marriage."

3. The Developments in the United States and Canada

American law also contains family law cohabitation legislation that becomes applicable through the parties' cohabitation, but that gives more limited legal effects than the ceremonial marriage and common law marriage. One example is **New Hampshire,** which does not recognize common

176 Regarding *New South Wales*, Australia, *see* PROPERTY (RELATIONSHIPS) ACT (1984), which for the purpose *inter alia* of also including homosexual couples, most recently has been changed through THE PROPERTY (RELATIONSHIPS) AMENDMENT ACT (1999). Within the concept "domestic relationship" falls not only "*de facto* relationships," but also a "close personal relationship" that is not marriage, or "*de facto* relationship" between two adult persons who live together, regardless of whether they are related to each other or not, in which the one or both without compensation provides the other with domestic support and personal care. Similar legislation in a number of legal areas has been enacted for Australia's other jurisdictions. For more on this, *see* DOROTHY KOVACS, DE FACTO PROPERTY PROCEEDINGS IN AUSTRALIA (1998); Linda Wilmott et al., *De facto Relationships Property Adjustment Law – A National Direction,* 17 AUST. J. FAM. L. 1 (2003); Reg Graycar & Jenni Millbank, *The Bride Wore Pink ... to the Property (Relationships) Legislation Amendment 1999: Relationship Law Reform in New South Wales,* 17 CAN. FAM. J. L. 227 (2000); and Rebecca Bailey-Harris, *A decade of reforms in Australia,* 9 IJLF 233 (1995); *Law and unmarried couple–oppression or liberation,* 8 C.F.L.Q. 137 (1996). Regarding the older developments, *compare* Bruch, *supra* note 154, at 227 and 234-235.

177 PROPERTY (RELATIONSHIPS) ACT (1976), amended by law 2001, which came into force 1 February 2002. *See* PROPERTY (RELATIONSHIPS) AMENDMENT ACT, 2001. Regarding the development in New Zealand, *see* Bill Atkin, *The Challenge of Unmarried Cohabitation–The New Zealand Response,* 37 FAM. L.Q. 303 (2003); M. HENAGHAN AND B. ATKIN, FAMILY LAW POLICY IN NEW ZEALAND (2d ed. 2002); Virginia Grainer, *What's Yours Is Mine: Reform of the Property Division Regime for Unmarried Couples in New Zealand,* 11 PAC. RIM. L. & POL'Y. J. 287 (2002); Nicky Richardson, *The New Property (Relationships) Act in Practise,* INT. FAM. L.J. 221 (2003); BILL ATKIN AND WENDY PARKER, RELATIONSHIP PROPERTY IN NEW ZEALAND (2001); Bill Atkin, *Reforming Property Division in New Zealand: From Marriage to Relationships,* 3 E.J.L.R. 349 (2001); and Wendy Parker, *New Zealand's property rights legislation: A changing landscape,* 57 FAM. MATT. 62 (2000); Bill Atkin, *Reflections, supra* note 112, at 217.

law marriage completely,[178] but which since the 1800s has had legislation concerning the surviving party's rights in the deceased's estate, a situation which calls for protection.[179] Under this rule, if the parties lived together during the three years prior to the death of one, the, surviving party is then granted all the rights that would accrue to a surviving spouse. This concerns both the right to the estate as well as the right to social benefits. On the other hand, the law does not include any protection upon the separation of the parties.[180] When considering principles, it is interesting to note that the applicable legal regulation in New Hampshire speaks of "cohabitation" while the courts use the term "common law marriage" for the same concept.[181] Usually, individual regulations concerning the relationship between cohabiting couples are not designated as common law marriage,[182] but nothing prevents speaking here of a partial recognition of common law marriage.

178 *DeLisle v. Smalley*, 63 A.2d 240 (N.H. 1949).

179 A majority of all cohabiting persons in the United States, both homosexual and heterosexual, prefer that a part of their estate be distributed to their surviving cohabiting partner, *see* Mary Louise Fellows et. al., *Committed Partners and Inheritance: An Empirical Study*, 16 LAW & INEQUALITY 1, 9 (1998). Approximately 30% of heterosexual couples and approximately 60% of homosexual couples draft wills, *see* Jennifer K. Robbenholt and Monica Kirkpatrick Johnson, *Legal Planning for Unmarried Committed Partners: Empirical Lessons for a Preventive and Therapeutic Approach*, 41 ARIZ. L. REV. 417, 441 (1999). The question of a legal right to inherit for heterosexual cohabiting persons has been an object of divided opinions with different legislators. In Scandinavia, which since the 1970s has been leading with respect to low rates of marriage and high number of cohabiting unmarried persons, the legislation in Sweden includes extensive regulations concerning the division of property between cohabiting persons, but no right to inherit. In Denmark, on the other hand, which does not have any cohabitation legislation regulating the relationship between the parties, the possibility of enacting legislation that would be limited to the right to inherit has been examined. *Compare* a surviving cohabiting person's right to maintenance from the estate in accordance with English law, assuming that the parties during two years immediately prior to the death lived together as husband and wife, *see* LAW REFORM (SUCCESSION) ACT 1995 Sh. 2, which amended INHERITANCE (PROVISION FOR FAMILY AND DEPENDANTS) ACT 1975 Sh. 25. *Compare* Waggoner, *supra* note 174, at 78, who proposes legislation as to inheritance for unmarried couples who have lived in a "marriage like relationship."

180 *Joan S. v. John S.*, 121 N.H. 96, 427 A.2d 498 (1981).

181 *See, e.g., Gray v. Gray*, 379 A.2d 442, 445 (N.H. 1977), in which the New Hampshire Supreme Court found that the plaintiff was the deceased's wife "by common-law marriage … and as such entitled to all the rights of a widow in the estate of the decedent." She received therefore a widow's intestate share of his estate. The result was the same in the case of *In re Estate of Buttrick*, 597 A.2d 74 (N.H. 1991). The applicable legal regulation speaks of persons "cohabiting and acknowledging each other as husband and wife, and generally reputed to be such, for the period of 3 years, and until the death of one of them…", *see* N.H. REV. STAT. ANN. 457:39 (West 2003). The legislation has old roots, *see* already RS 149:11 (1842). The application of the regulation requires that the parties were legally competent to enter into a marriage with each other, *see Hilliard v. Baldwin*, 76 N.H. 142, 80 A. 139 (1911); and *Emerson v. Shaw*, 56 N.H. 418 (1876).

182 *See, e.g.*, a surviving cohabiting person's right to maintenance from the estate in accordance with English law, assuming that the parties during two years immediately prior to the death lived together as husband and wife, *see* LAW REFORM

Without closer ties to or discussion of the common law marriage tradition, but inspired by the developments in Europe since the 1980s years, the legal literature in the United States has raised different proposals as to the enactment of regulations for cohabiting couples. As early as 1976, Jay Folberg and William Buren proposed "domestic partnership" with rights and obligations for unmarried cohabiting persons.[183] In 1978, Nancy Rebecca Shaw recommended a revival and expansion of the common law doctrine to more accurately conform to contemporary needs and social reality. She stated that any such change could be easily accomplished by judicial decision, without resort to the legislative process. She also maintained that a new standard is desirable if the protection of the essential element of the marriage relationship – commitment – is to be accorded the highest value.[184] In 1981, Grace Blumberg proposed that stable and long-term cohabitations ought, in the same manner as marriage, be given "a legal status" with rights and obligations both *inter se* and in relation to third parties, as long as the parties had not contracted otherwise.[185] This same author, who participated in the drafting of the ALI Principles as discussed further below, stated twenty years later: "To fulfill its welfare function, family law should cover all marriage-like relationships, the ceremonial and the nonceremonial alike."[186] In 1981, Judith Younger recommended a doctrine that she designated "engaging in marital conduct."[187] A couple of years later, William Reppy proposed a new legal status similar to common law marriages that he referred to as "lawful cohabitation" with extensive rights and obligations for cohabiting unmarried persons.[188] In 1987, Ellen Kandoian presented a proposal with

---

(Succession) Act 1995 Sh. 2, that amended Inheritance (Provision for Family and Dependants) Act 1975 Sh. 25. *Compare* Waggoner, *supra* note 174, at 78, who proposes legislation as to inheritance for unmarried couples who have lived in a "marriage like relationship."

183 H. Jay Folberg & William P. Buren, *Domestic Partnership: A Proposal for Dividing the Property of Unmarried Families,* 12 Willamette L.J. 453 (1976).

184 Nancy Rebecca Shaw, Note, *Common Law Marriage and Unmarried Cohabitation: An Old Solution to a New Problem,* 39 U. Pitt. L. Rev. 579, 595 (1977).

185 Blumberg, *supra* note 148, at 1125. *See also* H. Jay Folberg & William P. Buren, *Domestic Partnership: A Proposal for Dividing the Property of Unmarried Families,* 12 Willamette L.J. 453 (1976); and Nancy Rebecca Shaw, Note, *Common Law Marriage and Unmarried Cohabitation: An Old Solution to a New Problem,* 39 U. Pitt. L. Rev. 579, 595 (1977).

186 Blumberg, *supra* note 21, at 1306. This author was also included in the group of reporters drafting the principles that the American Law Institute adopted in the year 2000.

187 Judith T. Younger, *Marital Regimes: A Story of Compromise and Demoralization, Together with Criticism and Suggestions for Reform,* 67 Cornell L. Rev. 45, 99 (1981).

188 Reppy, *supra* note 50, at 1678. His proposed status is intended to arise either through official recordation (or even a ceremony) or through "common-law cohabitation" and give limited regulations concerning support, property and associated rights and obligations corresponding to the expectations of typical cohabitants. The author also expresses the hope that his proposed status would be accepted on the federal level with the application of taxation, bankruptcy, and some aspects of social security law. This status appears to be intended for those who

legal solutions for couples who had agreed to "carry on a shared life."[189] In 1994, Lawrence Waggoner presented a proposal for legislation concerning legal rights of inheritance for "de facto partners," who lived together with the deceased in a "marriage-like relationship."[190]

Other authors have more clearly favored a common law marriage tradition. David Caudill, who believes that the state ought to have an equally great interest in unmarried cohabiting couples as in traditional marriage, proposed in the beginning of the 1980s the enactment of a modified common law marriage that he calls "constructive marriage"[191] and in 1987, Homer Clark stated with respect to a 35-year cohabitation that the parties ought to be considered as married.[192] In the beginning of the 1990s, Kathryn Vaughn proposed the retention of common law marriage in Texas with reference to that this doctrine also today serves many important purposes[193] and at the end of the 1990s, John Crawley cautioned about the uncertainty that a repeal of common law marriage in Alabama could entail.[194] In 1996, based on a feminist perspective, Cynthia Bowman proposed the reinstatement of common law marriage in Illinois maintaining that it protects women's interests, particularly poor women and women of color. In 2005, Sonya C. Garza maintained that the increase in cohabitation among nonmarital couples has created a need for a recognition of common law marriage by more American jurisdictions,[195] and Marsha Garrison pleaded for a "revivified common law marriage," strongly emphasizing the significance that the application of the regulations be based on the parties' free will and commitment. Therefore, she is critical of legislation such as the ALI Principles based on the cohabitation of the parties, but accepts that the parties' *consensus* can be seen from the objective circumstances of the life the parties share. Also critical to the technical solutions of the ALI Principles, but accepting their motives, in 2006, Elizabeth Scott proposed the application of a presumption closely related to the common law marriage presumption.[196] The motives of the

---

have doubts about the lifelong and greater commitment of persons who elect to marry.

189 Kandoian, *supra* note 157, at 1870; *see also* Amy Lim, Comment, *In Defense of Washington's Equitable Treatment of Pseudomarital Property*, 29 IDAHO L. REV. 975, 995-998 (1992).

190 Waggoner, *supra* note 174, at 78. The proposed rights of inheritance are more limited than those applicable to spouses.

191 Caudill, *supra* note 33, at 564. *See also* Thomas Oldham & David S. Caudill, *A Reconnaissance of Public Policy Restrictions upon Enforcement of Contracts Between Cohabitants*, 18 FAM. L.Q. 93 (1984).

192 HOMER H. CLARK, JR. THE LAW OF DOMESTIC RELATIONS IN THE UNITED STATES 122 (2d 1987).

193 Vaughn, *supra* note 50, at 1169.

194 Crawley, *supra* note 66, at 425.

195 Bowman, *supra* note 50, at 779; Garza, *supra* note 146, at 552-553.

196 Marsha Garrison, *Is Consent Necessary? An Evaluation of the Emerging Law of Cohabitant Obligation*, 52 UCLA L. REV. 815, 885-890 (2005); and Elizabeth S. Scott, *Domestic Partnerships, Implied Contracts, and Law Reform*, in RECONCEIVING THE FAMILY, CRITIQUE

above-mentioned proposals and their technical solutions are analyzed below in Chapters 14 and 13, respectively.

The idea of partially tying marital legal effects to the parties' cohabitation during recent years has also received attention in proposals for American legislation as well as in the case law. Through a number of decisions, the **Washington** Supreme Court has, with certain exceptions, made the community property system applicable to spouses analogously applicable also upon the dissolution of a relationship between unmarried cohabiting persons.[197] Property that constitutes community property upon a separation or death is to be divided under fair and equitable distribution, and property acquired during the cohabitation is presumed owned by both parties.[198] Certain research indicates that many cohabiting couples want shared ownership rights as regards assets acquired during the cohabitation.[199] It ought to be noted that the court's stance is not based on private law regulations and institutions outside of family law that it previously, prior to many other courts,[200] applied to unmarried cohabiting persons. Instead, the court has taken the radical step, without support in the legislation, of basing the right to the division of property, on "a stable,

---

ON THE AMERICAN LAW INSTITUTE'S PRINCIPLES OF THE LAW OF FAMILY DISSOLUTION 331, 342-345 (Robin Fretwell Wilson ed., 2006).

197 *Marriage of Lindsey*, 101 Wash.2d 299, 678 P.2d 328 (1984); *Warden v. Warden,* 676 P.2d 1037 (Wash.App. 1984); *Foster v. Thilges*, 812 P.2d 523 (Wash.App. 1991); *Connell v. Francisco,* 127 Wash.2d 339, 898 P.2d 831 (1995); *Chesterfield v. Nash,* 96 Wash.App. 103, 978 P.2d 551 (1999); and *In re Marriage of Pennington,* 142 Wash.2d 592, 14 P.3d 764 (2000). *Compare In re Marriage of Cary,* 109 Cal. Rptr. 862, 866-867 (App. 1973) and *Estate of Atherley,* 44 Cal.App.3d 758, 119 Cal.Rptr. 41 (1975), in which the California Court of Appeals applied the Family Law Act to an unmarried couple, an analogy not accepted in *Marvin v. Marvin.* Not included in this group of cases is *Pickens v. Pickens,* 490 So.2d 872 (Miss. 1986), as the court did not apply the legal marital regulations as to unmarried cohabiting persons but rather instead equity principles concerning common law business partnerships. In this presentation, the case therefore is included in the *Marvin* doctrine, which includes not only contract principles but also the application of equity within private law. *Wilbur v. DeLapp,* 119 Or.App. 348, 850 P.2d 1151 (1993) (implied agreement) also ought to be included in the Marvin doctrine. Even Laquer Estin, *supra* note 45, at 1391, refers *Pickens* to "general equitable principles." *Compare* on the other hand, Blumberg, *supra* note 21, at 1293 note 106 and David Westfall, *Forcing Incidents of Marriage on Unmarried Cohabitants: The American Law Institute's Principles of Family Dissolution,* 76 NOTRE DAME L. REV. 1467, 1473 note 36 (2001). Exceptions from the analogy are made with respect to separate property that is not divided in the same manner as for formally married spouses, *see* Thomas Andrews, *Property Rights of Domestic Partners in the United States and Scandinavia: A Comparative Study* (2003) (unpublished paper, University of Washington).

198 *In re Marriage of Pennington,* 142 Wash.2d 592, 14 P.3d 764, 770 (2000); and *Connell v. Francisco,* 127 Wash.2d 339, 351, 898 P.2d 831 (1995).

199 *See* Weitzman, *supra* note 50, at 427; Blumberg, *supra* note 148, at 1136-1137; and Reppy, *supra* note 50, at 1720.

200 Already long before the classic case of *Marvin v. Marvin,* 18 Cal.3d 660 (1976), the Washington Supreme Court had given unmarried cohabiting persons rights, *see* note 119.

marital-like relationship where both parties cohabit …"[201] Strangely enough, the court designates the relationship as a "meretricious relationship," an expression that within the framework of the common law marriage doctrine referred to a relationship that is not marriage-like and that did not entail marital legal effects. Because of the term's negative connotation, some courts have used the expression "committed intimate relationship."[202] The court has taken an additional radical step in the United States by maintaining that equitable division of property is possible even upon dissolution of a relationship between persons of the same sex if one of them has deceased.[203] The constitutive elements that are the basis for the rights and the application problems that they entail are analyzed in Chapters 13 and 14.[204]

In contrast with the Marvin doctrine, the Washington Supreme Court has consequently made a family law assessment.[205] Both the legal facts as well as the legal effects pertain to family law. The parties' cohabitation is the basis for a family law status with certain of marriage's legal effects with respect to the relationship between them, a system that becomes applicable as long as the parties have not contracted otherwise. Given this doctrine,

---

201 *Connell v. Francisco*, 127 Wash.2d 339, 346, 898 P.2d 831 (1995). The case is commented in Gavin M. Parr, *What Is a "Meretricious Relationship"? - An Analysis of Cohabitant Property Rights Under Connell v. Francisco*, 74 Wash. L. Rev. 1243 (1999).

202 *See, e.g., Olver v. Fowler*, 131 Wash.App. 135, 126 P.3d 69 (2006). The term "meretricious" was considered in 1927 to mean "lustful and pertaining to the character of prostitution, and involving knowledge that the relation was not intended to be matrimonial but wanton," *see* Note, *Common-law marriage after removal of impediment to valid ceremonial marriage*, 12 Cornell L.Q. 513, 518 (1927). *Compare* Black's Law Dictionary 1002 (7th ed. 1999), in which a "meretricious relationship" means "1. Involving prostitution; of an unlawful sexual nature <a meretricious encounter>. 2. (Of a romantic relationship) involving either two people of the same sex or lack of capacity on the part of one party <a meretricious marriage>. 3. Superficially attractive but fake nonetheless; alluring by false show <meretricious advertising claims>."

203 *Vasquez v. Hawthorne*, 99 Wash.App. 363 (2000), *rev'd*, 145 Wash.2d 103, 107 (2001). The court did not decide the case finally but rather remanded it for decision as to whether the relationship was sufficiently "stable." Thomas Andrews has found that the case has set out two principles: "First, equitable division of property under Connell is available at the end of a same-sex relationship in Washington if it is sufficiently long-term and stable to justify such equitable treatment. Second, equitable division of property is available under Connell regardless of whether the relationship ends during the life of both partners, or at the death of one," *see* Andrews, *supra* note 196, at 37-38. The community property laws were applied by analogy at death also in *Olver v. Fowler*, 131 Wash.App. 135, 126 P.3d 69 (2006). *Compare Peffley-Warner v. Bowen*, 113 Wash.2d 243, 778 P.2d 1022 (1989), in which a cohabiting person did not receive status as surviving spouse.

204 Regarding the application problems, *see, e.g., In re Marriage of Pennington*, 142 Wash.2d 592, 14 P.3d 764, 770 (2000).

205 *Compare Marvin v. Marvin*, 18 Cal.3d 660, 557 P.2d 106 (1976), in which the California Supreme Court considered that community property law was not analogously applicable as to cohabiting unmarried persons. *See* on the other hand previously *In re Marriage of Cary*, 109 Cal. Rptr. 862, 866-867 (App. 1973) and *Estate of Atherley*, 44 Cal.App.3d 758, 119 Cal.Rptr. 41 (1975), in which the California Court of Appeals applied Family Law Act as to an unmarried couple.

the Washington case law distinguishes cases in which unmarried cohabiting persons through a contract, not cohabitation, are permitted to achieve a community property regime as though the parties were married. In actuality, the difference is not so great if the courts, as in Nevada, accept implied agreements that *inter alia* are based on the parties' cohabitation and outward appearance as spouses.[206] Compared with the common law marriage doctrine, according to which an implied agreement must include an intent to live together or attain the legal effects of marriage as seen in Chapters 6 and 7 above, the Nevada Supreme Court accepts an intent that concerns a certain legal consequence, namely, marriage's community property regime.

The development in the Washington case law appears to have influenced the American Law Institute (ALI), such that, in 2002, the ALI recommended legislation concerning the division of property when "the relationship of domestic partners" is dissolved through separation *inter vivos.*[207] The principles, considered to represent a radical departure from traditional principles of family obligations,[208] mostly equate unmarried cohabiting persons, both homosexual and heterosexual, with married couples. That which is divided is "domestic partnership property," which corresponds to marital property if the parties are formally married.[209] The principle that is recommended is a presumptively equal division of the property acquired during the relationship, which is supplemented with several exceptions.[210] In contrast with the Washington case law, no regulations are proposed to address the dissolution of the relationship upon the death of one party. On the other hand, in accordance with ALI's principles, a domestic partner is also entitled to compensatory payments on the same basis as spouses.[211] Through a contract, the parties can avoid an application of the regulations concerning property division.[212] In contrast

206 *See Western States Const. Inc. v. Michoff*, 108 Nev. 931, 840 P.2d 1220 (1992), in which the parties were considered to have entered into an implied agreement by which the applicable regulations concerning community property for the spouses became analogously applicable. The woman received thereby the right to one-half of the assets. Other authors therefore have referred to the case as the Washington doctrine, *see, e.g.*, Laquer Estin, *supra* note 45, at 1381.

207 *See* the ALI PRINCIPLES, *supra* note 62, particularly Chapter 6, Domestic Partners and Chapter 4. The influence of the state of Washington's case law can be seen directly by the regulations' formation, but is confirmed also by the ALI. Andrews, *supra* note 196: "It seems clear that the new ALI Principles have been heavily influenced by the development of the law of Washington state."

208 Garrison, *supra* note 196, at 819.

209 *Id.* § 6.04.

210 *Id.* § 4.09.

211 *Id.* § 6.06.

212 *Id.* § 6.01. In David Westfall, *Forcing Incidents of Marriage on Unmarried Cohabitants: The American Law Institute's Principles of Family Dissolution*, 76 NOTRE DAME L. REV. 1467, 1480 (2001), the author performs an exhaustive critical analysis of the possibilities and difficulties for the parties to contract out of domestic partnership status.

to common law marriage, the principles do not create any rights in relation to third parties or the public law. The constitutive elements that are the basis of a "domestic partnership" and the application problems they entail are analyzed more closely in Chapter 13. The reasons for and against this type of legislation are analyzed and discussed more closely in Chapter 14.

In areas of the law in the United States other than family law, for example within tort, social, and tax law, the picture is very split when it comes to the courts' willingness, in American states not recognizing common law marriage, to grant cohabiting couples rights based upon their cohabitation. On one side, federal legislation in general has required that the parties have been united in matrimony or common law marriage.[213] Typically, the parties have not been entitled to social benefits upon a party's death[214] or to unemployment insurance benefits as spouses.[215] They have not been able to file lawsuits concerning compensation for wrongful death, negligent infliction of emotional distress (NIED), or loss of consortium if a partner has been injured or killed.[216] They have not been entitled to the same benefits as spouses with respect to inheritance and gift tax.[217] On the other side, there are cases, in states not recognizing common law marriage in which the cohabiting unmarried person has also been considered entitled to different benefits. This has primarily concerned workers' compensation benefits,[218] but, in certain cases, even compensation from group

213 DEFENSE OF MARRIAGE ACT, 1 U.S.C.A. § 7 (2000).

214 *Califano v. Boles,* 443 U.S. 282, 99 D.Ct. 2767, 61 L.Ed.2d 541 (1979).

215 *Norman v. Unemployment Ins. Appeals Bd.*, 34 Cal.3d 1, 192 Cal.Rptr. 134, 663 P.2d 904 (1983). *Compare* on the other hand *MacGregor v. Unemployment Ins. Appeals Bd.*, 689 P.2d 453 (Cal. 1984) (unemployment insurance benefits).

216 *Garcia v. Douglas Aircraft Co.*, 133 Cal.App.3d 890, 184 Cal.Rptr. 390 (1982); and *Medley v. Strong,* 558 N.E.2d 244 (Ill.App. 1990). In *Elden v. Sheldon,* 46 Cal.3d 267, 279, 250 Cal.Rptr. 254, 758 P.2d 582 (Cal. 1988), a cohabitating person was denied compensation for negligent infliction of emotional distress after having witnessed the partner's death in a car accident. The court motivated its decision *inter alia* with that a granting would injure marriage and require investigations of the parties' intimate relationship. *Compare* on the other hand *Dunphy v. Gregor,* 136 N.J. 99, 642 A.2d 372 (1994), in which the court did not see any problems with granting a cohabiting person compensation.

217 *Cory v. Edgett,* 111 Cal.App.3d 230, 168 Cal.Rptr. 686 (1980).

218 In contrast with the case in the majority of states, unmarried cohabiting persons have been given workers' compensation benefits in the capacity as "dependants" in **Alaska**: *Burgess Construction Co. v. Lindley,* 504 P.2d 1023 (Alaska 1972). **California**: *Butcher v. Superior Court,* 139 Cal.App.3d 58, 188 Cal.Rptr. 503 (1983); *State v. Worker's Comp. Appeal Bd,* 156 Cal.Rptr. 183 (App. 1979); *Donovan v. Workers' Comp. App. Bd.*, 138 Cal.App.3d 323, 187 Cal.Rptr. 869 (1982); *Holland America Ins. Co. v. Rogers,* 313 F.Supp. 314, 320 (N.D.Cal. 1970). **Louisiana**: *Henderson v. Travelers Ins. Co.*, 354 So.2d 1031, 1032 (La. 1978), **Maryland**: *Kendall v. Housing Auth.*, 76 A.2d 767 (Md. 1950), **Michigan**: *West v. Barton-Malow Co.*, 230 N.W.2d 545 (Mich. 1975). **New Jersey:** *Parkinson v. J. & S., Tool Co.*, 313 A.2d 609 (N.J. 1974); *Dawson v. Hatfield Wire & Cable Co.*, 280 A.2d 173 (N.J. 1971); *Bulloch v. United States,* 487 F.Supp. 1978 (D.N.J. 1980). Oregon: *Bowlin v. State Accident Ins. Fund Corp.*, 726 P.2d 1186 (Or. App. 1986); *Cottrell v. EBI Cos.*, 743 P.2d 716 (Or. 1987); *Thomas v. State Accident Ins. Fund,* 8 Ore.App. 414, 495 P.2d 46 (1972); *Hewitt v. State Accident Ins. Fund Corp.*,

life insurance[219] and different benefits within health care.[220] This has been a question, however, of individual cases concerning individual benefits and not more overarching principle solutions. The state of the law is uncertain and undergoing constant change.[221] With respect to benefits based on registration, see below.

Both the legislative as well as judicial developments within family law have been intense in **Canada** during recent years. The courts have opened the constitutional doors for legislation on cohabiting unmarried couples, both heterosexual and same sex, and the legislators have adopted laws based either on cohabitation or registration.[222] This development has had the support of many jurists.[223] Canada's Supreme Court prepared the way through the statement that marital status and sexual orientation can constitute a basis for discrimination according to the constitution.[224] Federal legislation, to a great extent, has equated homosexual couples and common-law partners with spouses.[225] Legislation that previously concerned only spouses has been extended to couples of different or the same sex that have lived in a "conjugal relationship" of at least one year.[226] During recent years, Canada has enacted legislation at a brisk pace that allows registered partnerships, while opening the doors to marriages between persons of the same sex.

The different provinces have enacted more or less extensive legislation. For example, in Alberta, in 2002, legislation was adopted as to "adult interdependent partners" that to a certain extent equates cohabiting

---

653 P.2d 970 (Or. 1982). *See* more closely the analysis of Crawley, *supra* note 66, at 415-425 and therein stated sources; *see also* Bowman, *supra* note 63, at 139.

219 *Jackson v. Continental Cas. Co.*, 412 So.2d 1364 (La. 1982) ("cohabitant treated as 'spouse' under a group life insurance policy").

220 Several cities, municipalities, and private employers offer different benefits within health care also for cohabiting unmarried persons, particularly for same-sex couples. *See* Jonathan Andrew Hein, *Caring for the Evolving American Family: Cohabiting Partners and Employer Sponsored Health Care,* 30 N.M. L. Rev. 19 (2000); Robbenholt, *supra* note 179, at 426; and Bowman, *supra* note 63, at 142.

221 Regarding older law, *see* Graham Douthwaite, Unmarried Couples and the Law (1979).

222 The constitutional basis was laid down by Canada's Supreme Court in *M. v. H.*, (1999) D.L.R. 577 and was followed by *Barbeau v. British Columbia (Attorney General),* (2003) BCCA 406 (BC Court of Appeals 2003) and *Halpern v. Canada (A.G.),* (2003) O.J. No. 2268 (Ontario Court of Appeal 2003).

223 *See, e.g.,* Winifred Holland, *Intimate Relationships in the New Millennium: The Assimilation of Marriage and Cohabitation?,* 17 Can. J. Fam. L. 114 (2000); Brenda Cossman and Bruce Ryder, *What Is Marriage-Like Like? The Irrelevance of Conjugality,* 18 Can. J. Fam. L. 269 (2001); and Martha Bailey, *Regulation of Cohabitation and Marriage in Canada,* 26 Law & Policy 153, 156 (2004).

224 *See Miron v. Trudel* (1995) 2 S.C.R. 418; and *Egan v. Canada* (1995) 2 S.C.R. 513.

225 *See* Law Commission of Canada (2001). *Beyond Conjugality,* at 15. Ottawa: Law Commission of Canada. Available at http://www.lcc.gc.ca/en/themes/pr/cpra/report.asp. *See also* Brenda Cossman and Bruce Ryder, *The Legal Regulation of Adult Personal Relationships: Evaluating Policy Objectives and Legal Options in Federal Legislation* (Ottawa: Law Commission of Canada, 2000).

226 *See* Modernization of Benefits and Obligations Act, S. C. 2000, c. 12.

unmarried persons of the same or different sex with spouses. The term *adult interdependent partners* concerns persons who have lived together for at least three years, or who have had children in a relationship of a certain duration, or who have entered into a written agreement. The term also includes relationships between siblings, friends, or a parent and an adult child who are economically and emotionally dependent upon each other. This legislation gives legal effects concerning *inter alia* maintenance, damages, and workers' compensation, but does not contain regulations concerning property division.[227] The legislators have hesitated to enact this type of legislation in the light that the parties have not given their consent to a relationship in the same manner as spouses.[228] Neither have different regulations as to married and cohabiting unmarried couples with respect to matrimonial property law been considered to conflict with the constitution because cohabiting persons have chosen to avoid the legal effects of marriage.[229]

In several provinces, there is, therefore, legislation that partially equates cohabiting unmarried couples with married persons with respect to spousal-support obligations. For example, in **Ontario,** the term *spouse* includes a man or woman not married to each other who have cohabited, (1) continuously for a period of not less than three years, or (2) in a relationship of some permanence if they are the natural or adoptive parents of a child. The obligation to provide support is also applicable to parties of the same sex under the same conditions.[230] Comparable legislation in British Columbia, which also includes both parties of the different or the same sex, gives them the right to spousal support, assuming that during two years they have lived together in a "marriage-like relationship."[231] In Saskatchewan, legislation has also been enacted that gives both heterosexual as well as homosexual couples many of the rights accruing to spouses, assuming that they have lived together continuously for at least two years.[232]

The province that seems to have gone the farthest in the development of common law marriage appears to be **Manitoba.** Through legislation adopted in 2002 and effective as of June 30, 2004, the regulations became applicable to common law partners that concern family maintenance

---

227 ADULT INTERDEPENDENT RELATIONSHIPS ACT, S.A. (2002), c. A-4.5.

228 Quebec's Minister of Justice has stated: "*S'il s'est abstenu de le faire, c'est par respect pour la volonté des conjoints: quand ils ne see marient pas, c'est qu'ils ne veulent pas see soumettre au régime légal du mariage.*" *See* National Assembly *Debates of the National Assembly.* June 18, Bill 84 (1998). *See also* Bailey, *supra* note 223, at 155.

229 *Attorney Gen. of Nova Scotia v. Walsh* (2000), 4 S.C.R. 325.

230 ONTARIO FAMILY LAW REFORM ACT of 1986, R.S.O., ch. F-3, §§ 29, 30 (1990); *see also M v. H* (1999) 2 S.C.R. 3, in which Canada's Supreme Court stated that the legal definition of "spouse" must be expanded to include couples of the same sex.

231 FAMILY RELATIONS ACT OF BRITISH COLUMBIA, R.S.B.C., ch. 128, § 1 (1996), amended Oct. 1, 1998.

232 *See* Bailey, *supra* note 223, at 162.

along with a large number of laws concerning different rights and obligations outside of family law and all regulations that concern married persons' property rights.[233] Upon separation, the parties are entitled to half the value of the property that they acquired during the period they lived together, including pensions. If a party dies without having drawn up a will, the surviving party receives all or most of the deceased party's property.[234] If a will exists to the benefit of someone else, the surviving party is still entitled to a "fair share" of the couple's *family property*. The extensive nature of this reform can also be seen in that the term *marital property* has been removed and replaced by the term *family property* applicable to formally married couples.

The new legislation is applicable to a person who is a common law partner, which is commonly intended to be a person who either has registered his or her "common law relationship" with another or who cohabited with him or her "in a conjugal relationship" during a period of at least three years. In many of the laws, e.g., with respect to maintenance obligations and inheritance, a one-year cohabitation is sufficient if the parties have mutual children. According to other laws, it is sufficient with less than a one-year cohabitation. In contrast to parties in the American common law marriage, the parties in a common law relationship in Manitoba can be of the same sex. A common law relationship that has been registered is dissolved through registration and only after one year's separation. A relationship that is not registered is dissolved commonly after three years' separation. For more concerning these definitions, see Chapter 13 below.

12.4.2 Registration as a Basis for Rights and Obligations

Registration as a basis for rights and obligations within family law is closer to the formal marriage's civil form than is common law marriage, which is formless.[235] An agreement between the parties lies at the heart of

---

233 The Common-Law Partner's Property and Related Amendments Act, S.M. 2002, c. 48, has the objective of equating "common-law partners" with spouses entailed changes of The Anatomy Act; The Civil Service Superannuation Act; The Court of Queen's Bench Act; The Court of Queen's Bench Surrogate Practice Act; The Dependants Relief Act; The Family Maintenance Act; The Farm Lands Ownership Act; The Fatal Accidents Act; The Highway Traffic Act; The Homesteads Act; The Human Tissue Act; The Insurance Act; The Intestate Succession Act; The Law of Property Act; The Legislative Assembly Act; The Marital Property Act; The Mental Health Act; The Off-Road Vehicles Act; The Pension Benefits Act; The Manitoba Public Insurance Corporation Act; The Teachers' Pensions Act; The Victims' Bill of Rights; The Vital Statistics Act; The Vulnerable Persons Living with a Mental Disability Act; The Wills Act; The City of Winnipeg Charter; The Workers Compensation Act; and Conditional Amendments Re The Charter Compliance Act.

234 The Intestate Succession Act, C.C.S.M. C. 185, 13(2).

235 Common law marriage however can be registered in Texas and in Montana, *see* Section 13.2.2 *infra*.

registration, which requires consent for both parties for formal marriage and common law marriage. In this respect, registration differs from cohabitations that are regulated by legislation. The registration, however, is, as certain French commentators have expressed it, *un contrat strictement réglementé*,[236] in other words, a strictly regulated contract. Even though registration systems are not the main object of this dissertation, they warrant attention because many of these laws contain mixed requirements for either cohabitation or registration, and the latter, in addition, functions as a contrast and alternative to the formless relationships. From the beginning, the registration procedure has to a great extent been used as a method for couples of the same sex to enter into partnerships and thereby legally be equated with spouses. Later, however, registered partnerships have been able to be entered into in several countries, even between persons of different sexes, who can choose between registering partnerships and marrying. Ordinarily, requirements of legal capacity concerning *inter alia* age and family relationships, similar to those applicable to marriage and common law marriage, are applied for the registration of partnerships. In the same manner as formal marriage, the requirements of legal capacity are assessed in advance. The state, thereby, in contrast to common law marriage and legislation based on cohabitation, has control over which formal relationships are permitted. The actual procedures greatly resemble the forms for the civil wedding ceremony. Through registration, a status is created for the parties, from which follows certain legal effects given by the law, which in different legal systems are more or less extensive. The intent has been for couples of the same sex to receive the same rights and obligations as spouses, which also has been the case in certain exceptions ordinarily concerning the status of children.[237] In order to prevent "partnership tourism," registration requirements of citizenship or residence are ordinarily applied in certain states.[238] A registered partnership resembles marriage and also common law marriage in that it is dissolved either through one party's death or *inter vivos* ordinarily through a formal, albeit in certain systems less rigorous, procedure.

1. *The Developments in Northern and Western Europe*

In several of the Northern and Western European jurisdictions, legislation concerning registered partnerships has been enacted since the 1990s.

---

236 CARBONNIER, *supra* note 90, at 703.

237 Exceptions have often been made with respect to the presumption of paternity, the regulations concerning artificial insemination and fertilization outside of the body, as well as the right to joint adoption, which however during recent years has become increasingly accepted. *See* Caroline Forder, *European Models of Domestic Partnership Laws: The Field of Choice*, 17 CAN. J. FAM. L. 371, 411 (2000).

238 The requirements concerning nationality and residence vary in different jurisdictions, *see* Forder, *supra id.* at 394-402. The international private law question of whether other countries are prepared to recognize the partnerships must be distinguished from these requirements.

These reforms have not been driven by judicial decisions in the same manner as in the United States.[239] Legislation on registered partnerships was enacted first in the Nordic countries, with **Denmark** enacting the first such law in 1989,[240] **Norway** in 1993,[241] **Sweden** in 1994,[242] **Iceland** in 1996,[243] and **Finland** in 2001.[244] In contrast to common law marriage, that is only available for relationships between women and men, the Nordic partnership legislation intends to equate couples of the same sex with spouses. In accordance with the principle "separate but equal" these legislations give rights and obligations to same sex couples, without opening the possibility of marriage. Certain exceptions commonly have been made with respect to the application of the regulations concerning children, e.g., the presumption of paternity, as well as regulations concerning artificial insemination and fertilization outside of the body. The right to joint adoption has often been another exception. These rights, however, have received greater acceptance during recent years.[245] It ought to be noted that the Nordic laws do not require that couples are homosexual or even that they are cohabiting persons for their application. A legal partnership arises by two persons of the same sex registering.

---

239 The European Court of Justice has stated that Article 12 in the European Convention of Human Rights, which guarantees the right to marriage, concerns two persons of different sexes. Neither does the EU require that registered partnerships be equated with marriage with respect to employment benefits, *see D. Et Royaume de Suède c. Conseil de L'union européenne,* T-264/97 (C.F.I.E.C., 28 January 1999).

240 Law no. 372 the 7 June 1989, in force 1 October 1989. *See* Linda Nielsen, *Family Rights and the "Registered Partnership" in Denmark,* 4 IJLPF 297 (1990); Ingrid Lund-Andersen, *Moving towards the Individual Principle in Danish Law,* 4 Int. IJLPF 328 (1990); *Cohabitation and Registered Partnership in Scandinavia: The Legal Position of Homosexuals,* in The Changing Family 397 (John Eekelaar and Thandabantu Nhlapo eds. 1998); and *The Danish Registered Partnership Act,* in Legal Recoginition of Same-sex Couples in Europe 13 (Katharina Boele-Woelki and Angela Fuchs, eds., 2003).

241 Law no. 40, 30 April 1993, in force 1 August 1994. *See* Peter Lødrup, *Registered Partnership in Norway,* in The International survey of Family Law for 1994 387 (Andrew Bainham, ed. 1996).

242 Lag (1994:1117) Om Registrerat Partnerskap, in force 1 January 1995. *See* Anders Agell, *Is There One System of Family Law in the Nordic Countries?,* 3 E.J.L.R. 313, 316 (2001).

243 Law 12 June 1996, in force 27 June 1996. *See* David Thór Björgvinsson, *General Principles and Recent Development in Icelandic Family Law,* in The International Survey of Family Law for 1995, 225 (Andrew Bainham, ed. 1997).

244 Law the 13 December 2001 No. 1226; Cossman, *supra* note 225, at 130-132; Matti Savolainen, *The Finnish and the Swedish Partnership Acts-Similarities and Divergencies,* in Legal Recognition of Same-sex Couples in Europe 24 (Katharina Boele-Woelki and Angela Fuchs, eds., 2003).

245 Regarding the issue of adoption in Europe, *see* Forder, *supra* note 237, at 411. The Swedish partnership act did not from the beginning give the right for couples of the same sex to jointly adopt children. Through later legislation, however, this has become possible. *See* SFS 2002:603, Prop. 2001/02:123, LU 27. From and with 1 July 2005 in Sweden assisted fertilization with donated sperm may be performed on a woman who is a registered partner or cohabiting partner with another woman. The latter is together with the fertilized woman to be viewed as parent to the child, assuming that she consented to the treatment. *See* Prop 2004/05:137, Assisterad befruktning and föräldraskap.

Legislation based on registration has been enacted also in other Western European countries, the **Netherlands** in 1997,[246] **Belgium** in 1998,[247] **Spain** in 1998,[248] **France** in 1999,[249] **Germany** in 2001,[250] and in **England** in 2004.[251] The German legislation for life partnerships, *Eingetragene Lebenspartnerschaften*, resembles the Nordic equivalents in such a manner that it is applicable only to persons of the same sex. Amendments enacted in 2005, give homosexual couples most of the same rights and obligations as married couples. The relationship is entered into by the parties personally declaring that they wish to enter into a lifelong partnership, which is

---

246 BOOK 1 OF THE NETHERLANDS CIVIL CODE was supplemented with a Chapter 5a with the title "Registered partnership"; Act of 17 December 1997, Staatsblad 1997, 660, which came into force 1 January 1998. The law appears to rest upon liberal streams in Dutch law that also sought support in the European Convention of Human Rights. *See* Katharina Boele-Woelke, *Registered Partnerships: Legislation of the Netherlands,* in CIEC CURRENT PROBLEMS IN THE LAW OF PERSONS 44 (1999); Wendy M. Schrama, *Registered partnership in the Netherlands,* 13 IJLPF 315, 317 (1999); P. Vlaadingerbroek, *Marriage, divorce and family living in the Netherlands,* 29 FAM. L.Q. 635, 636 (1995); M. Rood de Boer, *The Netherlands,* 28 J. FAM. L. 571, 572 (1989/90); and Bradley, *supra* note 175, at 28. The basis for the neutrality in relation to different cohabitation forms appears to have been laid already in the beginning of the 1970s. A.M. van de Wiel points to the reform as to marital divorce regulations that occurred in 1971 and states that: "[F]rom 1971 attitudes have become increasingly neutral: in the eyes of the law no one form of cohabitation is, by definition, better than another," *see Cohabitation outside marriage in Dutch law,* in MARRIAGE AND COHABITATION IN CONTEMPORARY SOCIETIES 156, 215 (John M. Eekelaar, Sanford N. Katz eds., 1980).

247 The law was adopted by the Belgian parliament 29 October 1998 and entered into force 1 January 2000. *See* Gedr. St., Senaat, 1997-1998, nr. 1-916/6 d.d. 8 July 1998.

248 The law that in 1998 was enacted in Catalonia concerning long-lasting couple relationships (*d'unions estables de parella*) and which in several aspects equates unmarried cohabiting persons with spouses, is also applicable as to homosexual cohabiting persons assuming that certain form requirements are observed. For heterosexual cohabiting persons, on the other hand, it is sufficient with a two-year cohabitation. LEY 10/1998, de 15 de juliol, D'UNIONS ESTABLES DE PARELLA (DOGC num. 2687, 23.07.1998); Act 10/1998 of 15th July, Regarding Stable Pair Relationships, *see* Article 19. Thereafter, similar legislation has been enacted in an additional three provinces that have the authority to legislate within civil law as well as in a number of autonomous areas. Regarding *Valencia, see* Ley 1/2001, de 6 de abril, por la que see refgulan las uniones de hecho (BOE num. 112, 10.05.2001). Regarding *Madrid, see* Ley 11/2001, de 19 de diciembre, de Uniones de Hecho de la Communidad de Madrid (BOE num. 55,.05.03.2002). Regarding *Asturien, see* Ley 4/2002, de 23 de mayo, de Parejas Estables (BOE num. 157, 02.07.2002). For more on this, *see* Martín-Casals, *supra* note 172, at 2.

249 DU PACTE CIVIL DE SOLIDARITÉ ET DU CONCUBINAGE (PACS), Law no 99-944 of 15 November 1999, Recueil Dalloz 1999 L 515-517.

250 GESETZ ÜBER DIE EINGETRAGENE LEBENSPARTNERSCHAFT, 16 February 2001, BGBl. I 2001, at 266, that entered into force 1 August, 2001, amended 12 February 2005, BGBl. I 2005, at 203. The legislation has been found by the court (*Bundesverfassungsgericht*) to be consistent with the constitution and not in violation of the specific protections that marriage and the family enjoy. *See* judgment 17 July 2002, 1 BvF 1/01, 1 BvF 2/01.; BverfG 17.7.2002, NJW 2002, 2543, 2547.

251 CIVIL PARTNERSHIP ACT 2004, Chapter 33, which entered into force 5 December 2005. Bill 53 (HL), Bill 132 (HC) 2003-2004. The Act covers the entirety of the United Kingdom, but certain specific procedural regulations are applicable in Scotland and Northern Ireland.

registered at a governmental authority (ordinarily, *Standesamt*), if there is no impediment to the partnership. The partnership is dissolved in a formal procedure before the courts in a manner similar to that for the dissolution of marriage. The legal effects between the parties are almost the same as for spouses. The parties have, among other things, maintenance obligations, rights with respect to names, rights with respect to co-decisions, property sharing with the right to a division of the estate (*Zugewinnengemeinschaft*), and the right to inherit. The one party has the right to adopt the other's children. Outside of family law, the legal effects are more limited.[252]

The English legislation as to civil partnerships is also only applicable to persons of the same sex. In general, the same requirements exist for registration with respect to age, consanguinity, and marital status as for the legal capacity to marry. The parties become civil partners by signing a document at the registration office before a registrator and two witnesses. The legal effects of a civil partnership are the same as for marriage when it comes to the rights to property, maintenance, division of the estate, divorce, rights upon death, responsibility for the other partner's children, adoption, social benefits, pensions, life insurance, tax regulations, etc.[253]

A significant characteristic of the other Western European legislations is that they, in contrast to the English, German, and the Nordic partnership legislations, have been made available also to persons of different sexes, who have the choice between marriage and registered partnership. In a country such as the **Netherlands,** this choice, from a legal perspective, appears fairly illusory because the alternatives are largely identical.[254] Because the country applies obligatory civil marriage, reducing the religious participation to a voluntary blessing afterwards, both marriage and partnership are entered into with a registrar, before whom the parties, in both cases, declare in the presence of witnesses that they wish to enter into the relationship.[255] To a large extent, the legal effects are the same.

---

252 *See* Karsten Thorn, *The German Law on Same-Sex Partnerships*, in Legal Recognition of Same-Sex Couples in Europe 84, 85 (Katharina Boele-Woelki and Angelika Fuch eds. 2003).

253 *See* the Civil Partnership Act 2004, *supra* note 251..

254 In addition, a man and a woman, as well as two persons of the same sex, in accordance with Dutch law, can choose to sign an agreement that has been executed by a notary public. Accordingly both heterosexual and homosexual couples in the Netherlands have three formal options: marriage, registered partnership, and cohabitation agreement drawn up by a notary. On the other hand, there is no legislation regulating the relationship between cohabiting persons who have not formalized their relationship either through marriage, partnership, or agreements. *See* Masha Antokolskaia and Katharina Boele-Woelki, *Dutch Family Law in the 21st Century: Trend-Setting and Straggling Behind at the Same Time*, in Dutch Reports for the XVIIth Conference of Comparative Law, Intersentia 53-74 (2002).

255 According to Art. 1:67, Civil Code, future spouses are required in front of a registrar to take each other as spouses and declare that they will faithfully fulfill all duties attributed by law to the married state. With the registration of partnerships, the parties in front of a registrar and before witnesses declare that they wish to register the

Both marriage and partnership require a formal procedure for dissolution *inter vivos,* albeit that it is somewhat simpler to dissolve a partnership.[256] Despite the similarities, one legal relationship between men and women is designated as "marriage" and the other as "partnership." One can question whether a registered partnership of this kind fulfills any important function in addition to marriage for heterosexual couples.

For persons of the same sex, on the other hand, the partnership legislation during the first years had a function to fulfill in the Netherlands, because it gave homosexual couples a regulation they would not otherwise have had. In 2000, only a couple of years later, the Netherlands became the first country in the world that allowed homosexual couples to enter into marriage.[257] Since the partnership law was retained, the same illogical situation was created for persons of the same sex as for heterosexuals. Because the country imposes an obligatory civil marriage before a registrar, there is no legal obligation for the church to assist with marriages between homosexuals. The church itself decides whether it wishes to assist with the voluntary blessing of marriage that the parties desire. The legal capacity to enter into a partnership is, in principle, the same as for married persons with respect to age, consanguinity, etc. A partnership that has not been dissolved constitutes an impediment against a new partnership or marriage.[258] Concerning the legal effects, the partnerships become almost entirely equated with ceremonial marriages. Even homosexual couples in

---

partnership. The choice of words is free, but nothing prevents that they exchange marriage vows. *See* Schrama, *supra* note 246, at 326; and Boele-Woelke, *supra* note 246, at 46.

256 In connection with the enactment of the law concerning partnerships in the Netherlands, the Ministry of Justice described marriage and partnerships as "equivalent ... [t]he consequences are virtually identical." *See* Netherlands Ministry of Justice, *Registered Partnership,* 3 (1997). Partnership entails in principle the same personal legal effects as marriage, with the obligations to cohabit, to show each other fidelity and to support each other. The parties are obligated to contribute to each other's maintenance. Consent is required with dispositions as to the mutual residence. The community property system applicable to spouses, which also includes property acquired prior to the relationship, is also applied as to registered partners. The parties have the same right to a division of the estate and inheritance as spouses. The partnership entails nowadays also joint custody as to children. One difference is that it is easier to dissolve a partnership. Based on this, married couples contemplating divorce, choose to first transform their marriage to a partnership in order to thereafter be able to receive "lightning-divorces" without requirements for irretrievable breakdown of marriage (Art. 1:151, DUTCH CIVILE CODE). *See* Katharina Boele-Woelki, *Registered Partnership and Same-Sex Marriage in the Netherlands,* in LEGAL RECOGNITION OF SAME-SEX COUPLES IN EUROPE 41, 49 (Katharina Boele-Woelki and Angela Fuchs eds. 2003). A legal separation is possible only for spouses. *See* Antokolskaia, *supra* note 254, at 53-74.

257 Article 1:30, DUTCH CIVIL CODE. The law entered into force 1 April 2001; Staatsblad 2001, 9. *See* C. Forder, *To marry or not to marry: That is the question,* in THE INTERNATIONAL SURVEY OF FAMILY LAW 301 (A. Bainham ed. 2001); and K. Waaldijk, *Civil Developments: Patterns of Reform in the Legal Position of Same-Sex Partners in Europé,* 17 CAN. J. FAM. L. 62 (2000).

258 Boele-Woelke, *supra* note 246, at 319; Schrama, *supra* note 246, at 319.

the Netherlands have the right to joint adoption.[259] Registered partnerships for cohabiting persons are equated with marriage also within the public law, for example, social and tax law.[260]

Even though there are minor differences between marriages and partnerships, it appears that the double institutions for both heterosexuals and homosexual couples in Dutch law have not been a result of rational legal analysis. The conceptual lenses through which the marital realities are observed do not accurately distinguish between what is actually occurring and what appears to be occurring. The legislative development in the Netherlands appears to be an example of how a highly spiked eagerness to legislate can create disorder in the legal structures and the formation of concepts, which are difficult for the public to understand. Even though the Dutch situation has been seen as ideal,[261] there is reason to question whether the partnership law, viewed in the light of the hasty enactments, has already served its legal purpose.[262]

It appears, at times, that the legal development is steered more by mysticism and symbolism than by objective assessments of rights and obligations. This appears to be the case in the use of the word *marriage*, which appears to be surrounded by a blinding cultural and presumed historical valuation. Consequently, there ought to be heterosexual couples who accept the civil form for the commencement of marriage and desire its legal effects, but prefer to call their relationship a partnership, not a marriage.[263] On the other hand, there are homosexual couples who not only wish to have marriage's forms and legal effects but also want the right to call their relationship a marriage.

The legislation enacted in 1998 in **Belgium** became effective in January 2000 and is applicable to both homosexual and heterosexual couples, but to other relationships as well, for example, a parent and children or two siblings.[264] The legal relationship is entered into and dissolved through formal proceedings, which, however, are less rigorous than for marriage.[265] The legal effects are limited.[266] The parties have a certain joint liability for debts. They are obligated to share the costs of the cohabitation.

---

259 Regarding the right to joint adoption in *The Netherlands*, *see* Act on the Opening of Adoption to Same-Sex Persons of 21 December 2000, Staatsblad 2001, 10. *See* Antokolskaia, *supra* note 254, at 53-74. Regarding the issue of adoption in Europe, *see* Forder, *supra* note 237, at 411.

260 Regarding the legal effects, *see* Schrama, *supra* note 246, at 319-322; and Boele-Woelke, *supra* note 246, at 48.

261 Bowman, *supra* note 63, at 146.

262 *See also* Agell, *supra* note 161, at 207, who finds the possibility of the registration of heterosexual relationships especially surprising as it gives, as a matter of principle, the same effects as marriage.

263 *See* Antokolskaia, *supra* note 254, at 53-74; and Forder, *supra* note 237, at 394 ("a symbolic rejection of marriage").

264 Article 1475, Code Civile.

265 Article 1479, *id.*

266 Article 1477-1488, *id.*

Consent is required with the disposition of mutual residences and household goods. Each party owns the assets, but, in the event that a property right cannot be proven, the parties own the property jointly. The parties have no maintenance obligations or right to inherit after each other. Through limited legal effects, the Belgian registered partnership, in contrast to that of the Dutch, can constitute a more authentic alternative for a man and a woman who do not wish the far-reaching legal effects of marriage. In that homosexual couples nowadays also have the right to marry in Belgium,[267] the registered partnership constitutes a true and more limited alternative to marriage for them also.

Even the legislation that was enacted in **France** in 1998 concerning Pacte Civil de Solidarité (PACS) through registration became applicable not only to homosexual but also as to heterosexual couples.[268] The French form of partnership[269] is entered into through a public procedure, not with the mayor, for those who marry, but rather in front of the courts, a *tribunal d'instance*.[270] In order to be able to enter into a partnership, the parties must be legally competent in a similar manner as spouses. Even the French partnership ceases *inter vivos* through a procedure, which is, however, simpler than a marital divorce or through the parties marrying.[271]

The legal effects of PACS are considerably more limited than those that follow from marriage. They are also less extensive than those following from the Dutch partnership, but more than the Belgian system's legal effects, particularly within the public law. PACS also give a more comprehensive legal protection than that which cohabiting heterosexual couples living in concubinage received in French case law.[272] The parties are obligated to provide each other with material assistance and have joint liability for household debts.[273] Nevertheless, they have no property regulation system with principles for the division of property comparable to the *régime primaire* applicable to spouses. Instead, certain legal presumptions as to

---

267 Law the 13 February 2003 (M.B. 28.2. 2003), in force 1 June 2003.

268 DU PACTE CIVIL DE SOLIDARITÉ ET DU CONCUBINAGE (PACS), Law No 99-944 of 15 November 1999; Livre 1, Titre XII, CODE CIVILE; Recueil Dalloz 1999 L 515-517.

269 PACS have not by Caroline Forder been characterized as a partnership but rather as a "contract," as it does not create a new civil status and does not lead to all the legal effects of marriage, *see* Forder, *supra* note 237, at 386. Against this can be objected that the legal effects of PACS follow, not from the agreement between the parties, but rather from the legislation that becomes applicable through registration. Therefore it appears appropriate to speak of a status based on registration, albeit a status with more limited legal effects than marriage. Partnerships in different countries can have more or less comprehensive legal effects.

270 Article 515, CODE CIVILE.

271 The partnership is dissolved then after either a joint application to a "*tribunal d'instance*," or three months after a unilateral application from a party. *See* Article 515, *id.*

272 *See* § 12.4.2 *supra.*

273 Article 515, *id. See also* Eva Steiner, *The spirit of new French registered partnership law*, 12 C.F.L.Q. 1, 7 (2000).

co-ownership[274] and other property law solutions are applied.[275] The parties lack the right to inherit from each other. Still, the parties are equated with spouses to a high extent within social law and tax law.[276]

The French PACS, as with the Belgian variation, however, in contrast to the Dutch partnership, can constitute a truer alternative for a man and a woman not wishing the equally extensive legal effects to which marriage gives rise. It concerns a legal institution that regulates the relationship between a man and a woman intending to live together. Moreover, this legal relationship arises and is dissolved through a formal action in which the parties participate. Thus, it is plausible to argue that it is a marriage of a lower dignity, not in any pejorative sense, but rather simply to denote that it concerns an institution with fewer legal effects. Which regime in the future will be most attractive in France—marriage or *pacte civil de Solidarité*—remains to be seen. For couples of the same sex, there is only the latter.

The legislation enacted in the Spanish province of **Catalonia** in 1998 and applicable as to heterosexual couples living together two years or who have mutual children, can become applicable as to both heterosexual and homosexual couples through registration (*escriptura pública*). For heterosexual couples desiring a more limited community, this legislation is an alternative to marriage. The same is true for couples of the same sex, who, in Spain after 2005, received the right to enter into marriage. Thus, Spain became the fourth country after the Netherlands, Belgium, and Canada, permitting marriage between homosexual couples. This significant change was simple from a legal technical perspective. Added to the Spanish Civil Law's regulations as to marriage simply were the words: "Marriage will have the same requirements and effects whether the couple are members of the same sex or of different sexes."[277] Included in these legal effects is the right to adopt children.

2. *The Developments in the United States and Canada*

In certain American states recognizing common law marriage, it is possible to register the relationship. In **Texas,** the marital legislation regulations

274 Household goods that are acquired after the commencement of a partnership are owned consequently as to equal parts if nothing to the contrary has been contracted. A presumption as to ownership rights as to equal parts is applied also to other property as long as nothing to the contrary has been specified with the acquisition. The parties have to agree as to the financial resolution when the relationship ceases. *See* Xavier Tracol, *The Pacte Civil de Solidarité (PACS),* in Legal Recognition of Same-Sex Couples in Europe 68, 73 (Katharina Boele-Woelki and Angelika Fuchs eds. 2003).

275 Glendon, *supra* note 50, at 260.

276 Xavier Tracol, *supra* note 274, at 74-76; Jean-Jacques Lemouland, *Présentation de la loi No. 99-944 du 15 novembre relative au pacte civil de solidarité,* 43 Receuil Dalloz 483, 486 (1999); Claude Martin & Irène Thery, *The PACS and Marriage and Cohabitation in France,* 15 IJLPF 35 (2001); R. Nerson, *Les couples non-mariés en France,* in Marriage and Cohabitation in Contemporary Societies 198, 207 (John M. Eekelaar, Sanford N. Katz eds., 1980).

277 Article 44, Civil Code (2005).

give cohabiting couples the right to a declaration and registration of Informal Marriage.[278] The declaration, which is in writing and entered on a form in front of a county clerk, includes the following: "I solemnly swear (or affirm) that we, the undersigned, are married to each other by virtue of the following facts: On or about (date) we agreed to be married, and after that date we lived together as husband and wife and in this state we represented to others that we were married. Since that day of marriage to the other party I have not been married to any other person." The parties also certify that they have the legal capacity to enter into marriage. After the declaration is registered, it constitutes *prima facie* evidence of the parties' marriage.[279] This ought to rebut any presumption supporting a subsequent ceremonial marriage or common law marriage between one of the parties and a third party.[280] As can be seen from Chapter 5, persons of the same sex are not authorized to enter into a common law marriage in any of the states recognizing such marriages.

The American development concerning rights of persons of the same sex began somewhat later than in Europe and was initiated, in contrast to the European system, primarily by courts faced with the question of whether such rights were consistent with the Constitution. In the wake of judicial decisions, the legislation followed. The question of whether persons of the same sex are entitled to enter into a partnership (civil union) and even marriage remains quite controversial in the United States.

On one side, many states have distanced themselves from such legislation, often with explicit provisions in the state constitutions. None of the states recognizing common law marriage accept status relationships between persons of the same sex.[281] In connection with the presidential election of 2004, referendums appeared in eleven states, of which all said no to marriage between homosexual couples, while three were prepared to accept what are termed *civil unions*. On the federal level, the Defense of Marriage Act (DOMA) was enacted in 1996, according to which marriage is defined as a relationship between a man and a woman when applying

---

278 TEX. FAM. CODE ANN. § 2.402 (Vernon 2005). The Texas option to use the "declaration form" has sometimes been misunderstood as a requirement, *see* Marsha Garrison, *Marriage Matters: What's Wrong with the ALI's Domestic Partnership Proposal*, in RECONCEIVING THE FAMILY, CRITIQUE ON THE AMERICAN LAW INSTITUTE'S PRINCIPLES OF THE LAW OF FAMILY DISSOLUTION 316 fn. 70 (Robin Fretwell Wilson ed., 2006). Even in the state of *Montana*, there is a possibility for couples not wishing to enter into a ceremonial marriage, to instead give a written declaration of marriage before an official (the county clerk) at a district court, *see* MONT. CODE ANN. § 40-1-311 (Mont. Leg. Serv. Div. 2003).

279 TEX. FAM. CODE ANN. § 2.404 (d) (Vernon 2005).

280 Common law marriage constitutes an impediment against a later ceremonial marriage or common law marriage, *see* Section 5.3 *supra*.

281 Regarding the legal capacity to enter into a common law marriage, *see* Chapter 5 *supra*.

the federal law and according to which no state is obligated to recognize a marriage between homosexual couples entered into in another state.[282]

On the other side, regulations have been enacted in several states systems for couples of the same sex. A far-reaching example of this, in parity with the Nordic partnership legislation, is the legislation in **Vermont** concerning civil unions, which entered into force in 2000.[283] The Vermont Supreme Court had prepared the way by determining that such legislation was not in conflict with the state's constitution, particularly the Equal Benefits Clause, which is a controversial question in many states.[284] The commencement of a civil union, in principle, imposes the same requirements as for spouses with respect to a license, ceremony, and registration. The parties may not be married or a party in another civil union. Couples of the same sex, who enter into a civil union, are equated with spouses with respect to all state legal effects such as, e.g., the division of property, maintenance, inheritance, damages, insurance benefits, social benefits, taxation, and even adoption. The relationship is dissolved upon separation through a judicial procedure, in the same manner as a marriage or through one party's death.

In 2005, a similar civil union legislation was enacted in **Connecticut,** where parties to such a relationship have all the same benefits, protections, and responsibilities under law, whether derived from the general statutes, administrative regulations or court rules, policy, common law, or any other source of civil law, as those granted to spouses in a marriage, which is defined as the union of one man and one woman. In principle, the same requirements for spouses apply with regard to the capacity to enter a union, license, and registration. The statute creates a procedure for establishing and dissolving civil unions that parallels the state's marriage and divorce laws. Any person refusing to join persons in a civil union is not to be subject to any fine or other penalty. All civil unions celebrated in a foreign country, in which one or both parties are citizens of Connecticut, are to be valid under certain conditions.[285]

The rapid legislative development in the United States reached **New Jersey** in 2006, where, as in Vermont, a civil union law was passed in response to a state supreme court decision. In *Lewis v. Harris* (2006), the court held that the equal protection guarantee of Article 1, paragraph 1 of the New Jersey State Constitution was violated by denying to committed same-sex couples rights and benefits which were statutorily given to their

---

282 In 1996 Congress adopted The Defense of Marriage Act, DOMA, prescribing that no state is obligated to recognize marriage between persons of the same sex. As to the application of the federal legislation, marriage is defined as "the legal union of a man and a woman as husband and wife" and the expression "spouse" as "a husband or wife of the opposite sex", *see* Pub. L. No. 104-199, 110 Stat. 2419; 28 U.S.C.A. § 1738 C (West 1996); and 1 U.S.C. 7, Supp. II 1997.

283 15 Vt. Stat. Ann. §§ 1201-1206 (1999); and Vt. Laws 91.

284 *Baker v. State,* 744 A.2d 864 (Vt. 1999).

285 Conn. Gen. Stats. § 46b-38pp (2007), eff. October 1, 2005. Senate Bill 963.

heterosexual counterparts. The court stated that the "State can fulfill that constitutional requirement in one of two ways. It can either amend the marriage statutes to include same-sex couples or enact a parallel statutory structure by another name, under which same-sex couples would not only enjoy rights and benefits, but would also bear the burdens and obligations of civil marriage." The legislature has chosen the latter option and created a new equivalent status for same-sex couples. Formal procedures apply to the commencement and the dissolution of the civil union. Parties to a civil union are to receive the same benefits, protections, and responsibilities under law, whether derived from statute, administrative or court rule, public policy, common law, or any other source of civil law, as are granted to spouses in a marriage, but not the title of civil marriage.[286]

The turbulent situation in the United States is clearly reflected in **California,** where marriage between persons of the same sex was prohibited by legislation as of 2000,[287] but where a law concerning "domestic partnerships" was adopted in 2003. The latter law, which came into force in January 2005, superseding previous more limited legislation for homosexual couples, is as far-reaching as the law concerning civil unions in Vermont.[288] Consequently, the California law prescribes that registered domestic partners are to have the same rights, protection, and benefits, and be subjected to the same responsibilities, obligations, and duties under law that are granted and placed upon marital spouses.[289] The relationship is entered into through registration and is dissolved, as with a marriage, through a formal procedure. In contrast with the regulations in Vermont, the California law is also applicable to heterosexual couples having reached the age of sixty-two years. Consequently, these couples can choose to marry or to register as domestic partners and receive comparable legal effects regardless of which choice they make. Such a system appears,

---

286 N.J. STAT. ANN. § 37:1, 37:2 (2007), eff. February 19, 2007. Assembly Bill A3787 and Senate Bill S2407 2006. *See also Lewis v. Harris,* 188 N.J. 415, 463 (2006).

287 DEFENSE OF MARRIAGE ACT, CAL. FAM. CODE § 308.5 (2002) (added by initiative measure, Prop. 22, § 2, eff. Mar. 8, 2000): "Only marriage between a man and a woman is valid or recognized in California."

288 The DOMESTIC PARTNER RIGHTS AND RESPONSIBILITIES ACT (2003); (Stats. 2003, ch. 421 (Assem. Bill No. 205), § 4, eff. Jan. 1, 2005); CAL. FAM. CODE § 297 (West 2005). The law replaces DOMESTIC PARTNER REGISTRATION ACT, Former CAL. FAM. CODE § 297 (2000), (Stats. 1999, ch. 588 (Assem. Bill No. 26), § 2.), which granted couples of the same sex limited rights concerning *inter alia* social benefits, health care, the right to claim damages, the right to adopt the other party's children and the right to administer the other party's estate.

289 *Id.* § 297.5. In *Knight v. Superior Court,* 128 Cal.App.4th 14, 26 Cal.Rptr.3d 687 (2005), the court held that (1) the domestic partnership statute did not amend the voter initiative, and thus did not violate constitutional provision, and (2) the enactment of the statute was not a legislative creation of "same sex marriage" under the guise of another name. In fact, domestic partners do not receive a number of marital rights and benefits. For example, they may not file joint tax returns, their earned income is not treated as community property for state income tax purposes, and they are not entitled to numerous benefits provided to married couples by the federal government, *see id.* at § 297.5, subd. (g)(k).

in the same manner as the Dutch, to be structurally illogical, not serving the interest of clarity, even though there are smaller differences in the legal effects.

A more limited system for domestic partners can also exist on the state level, but more ordinarily on the municipal level and/or with different employers in the United States. Such systems exist, for example, in the **District of Columbia, Hawaii,** and **Maine,** and have been replaced by more far-reaching regulations in California and New Jersey.[290] These systems have opened the possibility for both heterosexual and homosexual couples, not only through cohabitation, as can be seen above, but also through registration, to become entitled to limited social benefits and other rights. The relationship between the parties is not ordinarily affected.[291]

Massachusetts has gone farther than the other American states in granting rights for persons of the same sex. In *Goodridge v. Department of Public Health* (Mass. 2003), the Supreme Judicial Court stated that there is no rational reason for excluding couples of the same sex from the benefits tied to marital status.[292] Several months later, the same court, after the legislature requested an Advisory Opinion, stated that no impediment existed against marriage between persons of the same sex, and that the

---

290 *District of Columbia* has recognized domestic partnerships since 1992. According to The DOMESTIC PARTNERSHIP EQUALITY AMENDMENT ACT of 2006, D.C. Law 16-79, eff. April 4, 2006, a domestic partner will have the same rights as a spouse regarding inheritance, probate, guardianship, and other rights traditionally accorded to spouses. Since the *Hawaii* Supreme Court pronounced that legislation for persons of the same sex did not conflict with the state constitution, and that both parties ought to have the right to a marriage license in accordance with the state's "Equal Rights Amendment," *see Baehr v. Lewin,* 852 P.2d 44, 875 P.2d 225 (Haw. 1993), an amendment to the constitution was enacted, which defines marriage as a relationship between two persons of different sexes, *see* HAWAII CONST., Art I § 23. The case, however, opened the doors for limited legislation concerning certain rights and benefits, which came into force in 1997. The registration is also open to persons who are not couples, e.g. siblings, *see* Haw. Laws, Act 383, H.B. 118; HAW. REV. STAT. ANN. § 572C-1 (1999). *See also* Dee Ann Habegger, *Living in Sin and the Law: Benefits for Unmarried Couples Dependent Upon Sexual Orientation?,* 33 IND. L. REV. 991 (2000). In *Alaska,* a court opened the possibility to marriage for couples of the same sex with reference to a constitutional right to choose a partner, see *Brause v. Bureau of Vital Statistics,* WL 88743 (Alaska Super Ct. 1998). The possibility was stopped, however, through changes to the constitution, *see* ALASKA CONST., Art §I 25. In *Maine* the legislation permits same-sex and opposite-sex couples to register as domestic partners, thereby obtaining rights with respect to probate, guardianships, conservatorships, inheritance, protection from abuse, and health insurance and related matters, *see* 2003 ME. LAWS 672, eff. July 30, 2004.

291 *See* Bowman, *supra* note 63, at 134; Blumberg, *supra* note 21, at. 1280-1281; Hein, *supra* note 220, at 19; and Craig A. Bowman and Blake M. Cornish, *Note, a More Perfect Union: A Legal and Social Analysis of Domestic Partnership Ordinances,* 92 COLUM. L. REV. 1164 (1992).

292 In *Goodridge v. Department of Public Health,* 440 Mass. 309, 798 N.E.2d 941 (2003), the court stated: "The question before us is whether, consistent with the Massachusetts Constitution, the Commonwealth may deny the protections, benefits, and obligations conferred by civil marriage to two individuals of the same sex who wish to marry. We conclude that it may not." Homosexual couples received the right to adopt children already with the case, *Adoption of Tammy,* 416 Mass. 205 (1993).

state had to begin to issue marriage licenses for such couples. The same laws and procedures that govern traditional marriage also apply to same-sex marriages. A constitutional amendment, however, to overturn *Goodridge* and the Advisory Opinion of the justices has been proposed.[293] How the American federal government will react is still an open question.

The development in **Canada** during the beginning of the twenty-first century has also been intense. A characteristic feature of the legislation concerning domestic partnerships, as enacted in several of Canada's provinces, is that, in contrast to Vermont's regulation of civil unions and the Nordic systems with registered partnerships, it is directed at both homosexual and heterosexual couples in the same manner as the Dutch partnership act. In addition, the legislators have wished to emphasize the value of registration as a basis for the partnership instead of the parties' cohabitation. The Law Commission in Canada stated in 2001: "Instead of focusing mainly on married couples and couples deemed to be 'marriage-like,' governments should establish registration schemes to facilitate the private ordering of both conjugal and nonconjugal relationships."[294] In the province of **Nova Scotia,** legislation was adopted, in 2001, granting couples of the same or opposite sex, who register their domestic partnership, many of the rights accruing spouses.[295] **Quebec** has enacted legislation that goes farther and equates couples of the same or the opposite sex with spouses with respect to the majority of rights and obligations, also with respect to fatherhood and adoption, assuming that they register their relationship.[296] The extensive legislation with respect to common law partners of the same or different sex that came into force in **Manitoba** in 2004, becomes applicable not only after a certain period's cohabitation, but also through registration.[297]

The possibility of marriage between homosexual couples has received growing support during recent years in the Canadian courts. In the provinces of **British Columbia, Ontario** and **Quebec,** the appellate courts in 2002 and 2003 stated that marriages between persons of the same sex are consistent with the constitution.[298] The principle "separate but equal," applied,

---

293 2004 Mass. LEXIS 35; 802 N.E.2d 565 (Mass. 2004). The United States Supreme Court has found that legislation criminalizing sexual actions between persons of the same sex is in conflict with the Constitution's due process clause, *see Lawrence v. Texas,* 539 U.S. 558, 123 S.Ct. 2472, 156 L.Ed.2d 508 (2003). The question concerned the TEX. PEN. CODE ANN. § 21.06(a) (West 2003). Even if the issue did not concern whether homosexual couples have the right to enter into a marriage, it has been assumed that the decision will be used as support thereof, *see* Andrews, *supra* note 196, at 23.

294 *See* Law Commission of Canada (2001). *Beyond Conjugality,* at 131. Ottawa: Law Commission of Canada.

295 *See* Bailey, *supra* note 223, at 162; and Law Reform (2000) Act, S.N.S. 2000, c. 29.

296 Bailey *id.*, at 162-63.

297 THE COMMON-LAW PARTNER'S PROPERTY AND RELATED AMENDMENTS ACT, S.M. 2002, c. 48, with amendments in the Vital Statistics Act.

298 *Halpern v. Canada,* 225 D.L.R. (4th) 529 (Ont. C.A.) (2003); and *Egale v. Canada,* 225 D.L.R. (4th) 472 (2003); 228 D.L.R. (4th) 416 (B.C. C.A.) (2003). These two

for example, in Vermont and California, giving couples of the same sex the same rights as married persons, has not been considered sufficient. The courts have also considered the symbolic value in a couple of the same sex being allowed to enter into a ceremonial marriage. At the same time, the federal government requested an opinion from Canada's Supreme Court concerning the question of whether a legislative proposal allowing marriage between persons of the same sex in the entire country conflicts with the constitution.[299] The court, in its reply dated 9 December 2004, stated that marriages between persons of the same sex are consistent with the constitution, but that representatives for religious groups have the freedom to refuse to officiate at such weddings if doing so is not consistent with their religious beliefs.[300] With this limitation in the obligation to officiate a wedding, legislation was enacted in 2005, according to which "[m]arriage, for civil purposes, is the lawful union of two persons to the exclusion of all others." The law further proscribes that a marriage is not void or voidable only because the spouses are of the same sex.[301]

3. The Developments in New Zealand

For the purpose of avoiding discrimination, legislation was enacted allowing civil unions for couples of the same sex in **New Zealand,** in 2004.[302] Such a union is entered into through a formal ceremony in front of a registrar or officiator and witnesses. The legislation to a large extent entails the same legal effects as formal marriage with the exception of the right to adoption.

A structural circumstance that deserves attention is that this legislation is also applicable to couples of different sexes. Thus, a man and a woman

---

cases were not appealed to the Supreme Court. *See* on the other hand, *Hendricks v. Quibeck*, R.J.Q. (Sup.Ct.) (2002) *aff'd*, Quibeck C.A., March (2004).

299 Justice Canada Newsroom (2003), *Minister of Justice Announces Reference to Supreme Court of Canada*, July 17, *see* http://canada.justice.gc.ca/en/news/nr/2003/doc-30944.html.

300 *See Hendricks v. Quibeck*, R.J.Q. (Sup.Ct.) (2002), *aff'd*, Quibeck C.A., March (2004). Canada's federal government presented a proposal that opened the possibility for couples of the same sex to enter into civil marriage and requested an opinion from the Canadian Supreme Court as to its compatibility with the constitution. The Supreme Court decided the case and issued its judgment on December 9, *see* 2004 S.C.C. 79. *See also* Bailey, *supra* note 223, at 155. The Canadian Supreme Court has also found that it is a violation of the constitution to discrimination with respect to homosexuals in issues of family support, *see* M. v. H. (1999), 2 S.C.R. 3. *See also* Bailey & Bala, *Canada: Reforming the Definition of Spouse and Child Related Laws*, in The International Survey of Family Law 65 (A. Bainham, ed. 2000); and Nicholas Bala, *Controversy Over Couples in Canada: The Evolution of Marriage and Other Adult Interdependent Relationships*, 29 Queen's L.J. 41, 45 (2003).

301 Marriage for Civil Purposes Act, c. 33 (2005). The Act, which opened up civil marriage to same-sex couples across the country, is commented by Martha Bailey, *Marriage and Morals*, in The International Survey of Family Law 53 (Bill Atkin gen. ed., 2007).

302 *See* Civil Union Act (2004), which entered into force 26 April 2005.

who are cohabiting in New Zealand have the following possibilities of choice: (1) They can enter into a formal marriage through a religious ceremony; (2) They can enter into a formal marriage through a civil ceremony with the same legal effects; (3) They can enter into a civil union through a civil ceremony to a large extent with the same legal effects; and (4) If they do not choose any of the three comparable alternatives and lived together for three years, similar legal effects are applicable anyway in important matters, as a result of the legislation concerning de facto relationships, discussed above in Section 12.4.1.

The legislative development in New Zealand raises the question of the outcome for freedom of choice in the face of similar legal effects. The parties certainly have the possibility of avoiding the legal consequences through a contract, but the legislation, as in the above-mentioned Dutch legislation, appears to have been enacted with such haste; that sufficient time was not set aside for academic legal analysis and reflection. One can ask why a man and a woman ought to be able to choose between civil ceremonies, to either enter into marriage or a civil union, each with largely the same legal results. The answer appears to be the fear that civil unions that can only be entered into by persons of the same sex could be understood as discriminating against couples of different sexes, something which would be inappropriate at a point when all legislative efforts purport to prevent discrimination. The consequence has been that the state, in its capacity as the good provider, by piling the same benefits again and again on couples of different sexes, has ironically caused the loss of part of the parties' freedom of choice.

12.5 Summary and Conclusions

1. *The Demographic Development – A Challenge for Each Legislator*

The dramatic decrease in the rate of marriage, the increasing number of children born outside of marriage, and the increasing number of unmarried cohabiting couples in the Western world is a wake-up call and challenge for every concerned legislator, because the developments mean that a substantial percentage of families, both parents and children, risk being excluded from the family law systems for some part of their life. Cohabiting couples and their children risk not having the benefit of the legal protection they need at different stages of their lives. The state loses its previous power to impose obligations and control as the third party to the marriage contract and the only entity capable of setting public policy. Moreover, there is a need for legal solutions to the problems that arise around cohabitation.

Taking into consideration that the group of unmarried cohabiting persons is so heterogeneous, how these solutions ought to appear is not a given. It is risky to construct a uniform legal regulation given that certain persons live on a trial basis for a period before they break up or marry, while others have already decided to marry, and still others have decided to live together for the long term without marrying. In addition, different couples can be assumed to have entirely different understandings about which legal solution fits them best while the state's interests can be assumed to vary, considering the type of cohabitation in question.

Different jurisdictions in the Western world have achieved a spectrum of legal solutions in order to face these problems, as seen in the chapter. In certain cases, the eagerness to legislate has been so great that different systems have been piled upon each other, and informal and formal regimes have been confused. In order to receive a right, registration can be required, while for another cohabitation is sufficient. The definitions of the concept of cohabitation vary at times within the same jurisdiction. This diverse picture is partially the result of the tendency of legislators and courts to immediately arrive at solutions, without academic legal analysis and structural assessments. The ensuing consequences are difficult to summarize, making it difficult for many cohabiting unmarried couples to understand whether they are on a par with married persons and whether they have a right or not and how to adapt themselves to the situation.

2. *The Property Law Solutions*

The notable increase in the number of unmarried cohabiting persons in the Western world over the past thirty years did not immediately give rise to family law legislation purporting to give solutions as to the cohabiting parties' internal legal problems, as evidenced here. Instead, the courts took responsibility by applying civil law principles outside of family law, offering a protection for the parties, e.g., in the event of separation or death.

Such application became possible because the courts considered the family relationships through new lenses. The marriage-like cohabitation came to be defined as a conglomerate of legal actions, which required far-reaching analogies with legal institutions that originally were intended for purposes other than family law. Traditional concepts were exposed to extensive interpretations that, at times, have had the character of pure fiction. From the marriage-like cohabitation, implicit agreements arose concerning compensation for services, hidden ownership rights, and partnership constructions. New types of constructive trusts, in which no express agreement was required, arose in the common law tradition. Without any contractual considerations in general, the courts have cited legal grounds that gave monetary compensation for the parties' contributions in the form of work and money. Many courts strived to reach solutions "whenever justice and good conscience required it."[303]

This judicial development has raised the issue of whether property law solutions within the general civil law can be an alternative to common law marriage and cohabitation legislation. Our comparative analysis has answered these questions in the negative. The Marvin doctrine does not mean, as has been alleged, a reinstatement of common law marriage.

Even though certain circumstances can be cited both in support of a claim concerning common law marriage and a claim concerning the property law remedies, we have found that it is, first of all, a difference in the legal bases. Common law marriage rests on a marriage contract that can be inferred, according to which the parties have a mutual intent to live together as husband and wife in a monogamous and lifelong or at least long-lasting relationship that encompasses everything in life, a *consortium omnis vitae* and a *individua vitae consuetudo,* in which the system of regulation for spouses is applicable. An implied agreement according to the Marvin doctrine, on the other hand, does not focus on the cohabitation but rather ordinarily contains a mutual intent concerning the parties' financial affairs, for example, the acquisition or division of property, compensation for work performed, or for contributions made.[304]

In addition, the parties' cohabitation and outward appearance as spouses are necessary prerequisites for the establishment of a common law marriage in the majority of jurisdictions recognizing such marriages. Even a legally recognized cohabitation relationship requires cohabitation. The parties' sexual relationship is a significant, albeit not always necessary and never solely sufficient, element in the requirement as to cohabitation. The sexual relationship is an important element that distinguishes the family law institutions from the property law! Neither the sexual relationship nor the cohabitation in a broader context is a necessary prerequisite for a claim based on property law remedies. Only unjust consequences of the cohabitation can be the bases for claims. On the other hand, contributions in the form of work or money, or agreements as to such contributions, or agreements concerning division of property can be necessary prerequisites for a claim in accordance with the property law remedies, while these circumstances are not necessary as the basis of a common law marriage or a legally recognized cohabitation relationship.

---

303 *Hussey v. Palmer* (1972) 1 W.L.R. 1286, 1290 (new constructive trust model). These far-reaching ambitions, however, have not received complete recognition in the English case law. Instead, it appears that "common intentions trusts" have become dominant. *See Gissing v. Gissing,* (1971) AC 886, HL; and *Pettitt v. Pettitt,* (1970) A.C. 777. *See also* Mee, *supra* note 98, at 175; CRETNEY, *supra* note 98, at 132-148; and PEARCE, *supra* note 98, at 638.

304 The English case law concerning "common intention trusts" is a rich source concerning the requirements that ought to be placed as to the parties' intentions with considerations as to the parties' property rights.

A point of family law legislation is that a party, due to sickness, handicap, destitution, or unemployment, who has not been able to provide any contribution to the community, either in monetary terms or work, is still given legal protection through marriage, whether ceremonial, common law marriage, or de facto marriage.

With respect to the legal effects, the protection the Marvin doctrine and comparable doctrines in other countries offer the parties is both limited and highly uncertain compared with the family law systems' legal effects, even though the discretionary solutions of the latter lack clarity. Therefore, there is no reason to maintain that the Marvin doctrine's legal effects constitute a principle alternative to or threat against marriage.

Property law solutions entail problems seen in this chapter. To the extent that the parties' behavior actually discloses a mutual intent, it is clearly the best basis for a solution. Ordinarily, however, the parties have never discussed, considered, or even thought about ownership rights. There is a risk that the courts may force upon parties fictional agreements that they never entered into and which can be viewed as a deceptive and against their intent, or at least against one party's intent. The danger of fictional agreements, however, is a reality even in conclusions concerning the implied agreements upon which common law marriage often rests.

The investigative difficulties ordinarily associated with general civil law cases as well as the lack of clarity that ordinarily permeates the private law principles have created extensive application difficulties, disputes, and, most of all, a considerable legal uncertainty. Today, it is risky, if not impossible, for cohabiting couples to predict whether and to what extent they can count upon private law protection if a relationship is dissolved. All too often, case decisions rest on the courts' application of vague fictions, that ignore that few couples wish to live a life together in the expectation of a fiction.

The Marvin doctrine and comparable remedies within other legal systems are therefore not satisfactory general solutions to unmarried cohabiting persons' legal problems, even though they can provide just results in individual cases. The need for property law solutions, however, lessens if family legislation is adopted. A considerably higher degree of predictability characterizes the remedies that have been enacted through such legislation. It ought not be surprising that it is most often most appropriate to use family law solutions for family law problems.

3. *Cohabitation as a Basis for Rights and Obligations*

Since the 1970s, one of the most significant developments in family law throughout the Western world has been the growth of legislation for cohabiting unmarried couples, legislation that has meant an altogether far-reaching equality to common law marriage. Many jurisdictions have created specific legal regimes with rights and obligations for unmarried couples that are based on the parties' cohabitation as seen in this chapter. These regimes have often come into existence through legislation but as exceptions, as in the state of Washington for the United States, and also through the case law.

A comparison between this modern cohabitation legislation and common law marriage with regard to the necessary *requisites for the establishment* of the relationships as a starting point shows a common denominator in the lack of form in their establishment. On the other hand, a fundamental difference between the institutions is that common law marriage, in principle, is based on an agreement between the parties, *consensus, non concubitus, facit matrimonium,* while cohabitation legislation is based on the parties' cohabitation. The difference with cohabitation legislation, however, in practice has decreased, in part through the extensive use of implied agreements and legal presumptions, which rest upon the parties' cohabitation as discussed in Chapters 7 and 9 above, and also, in part, because the majority of jurisdictions recognizing common law marriage require cohabitation as a necessary requisite in addition to the agreement as seen in Chapter 8 above. At the same time, the cohabitation legislation has not been able to avoid the use of subjective elements with the establishment of the relationships as further discussed in Chapter 13 below. The most important factor in both cases in practice is the parties' cohabitation. Of the cohabiting couples that are included within the cohabitation legislation that has been enacted in different states, at least 80 percent of the cases ought to fall within the regulations of common law marriage. The use of the different elements in common law marriage and the legal concepts of cohabiting persons and their effects in different aspects are discussed in Chapter 13 below more closely from a future perspective. Additionally, a feature in the development of the law has been that cohabitation legislation is being stretched to be applicable, not only to couple relationships, but also to parents and children, or siblings, living together.

If one begins, instead, with *the legal effects* of the institutions, we have found that both common law marriage and cohabitation legislation have the purpose of providing solutions to the problems cohabiting couples face. It is characteristic of common law marriage that it entails all the legal effects of ceremonial marriage, in terms of both rights as well as obligations. Cohabitation legislation, on the other hand, as can be seen above, ordinarily entails more limited legal effects. This is illustrated clearly by the Scottish legal development in which common law marriage now has been replaced by cohabitation legislation with a broader area of application but with more limited legal effects. For example, the Swedish legislators contemplated complete neutrality in marriage, as is the case in common law marriage. Nevertheless, the Swedish system stopped halfway by a giving a minimal protection to the more vulnerable party, which *inter alia* contains a right to a division of the estate of certain property, the residence and household goods. Other partial systems that give basic protection are the system proposed by the American Law Institution, according to which that the same regulations for spouses are offered, i.e., in the dissolution *inter vivos* of relationships between domestic partners, but not in cases of death. The system adopted by the Washington Supreme Court offers a division of the estate in the same manner as for spouses in instances of separation and death.

We have determined above that there is no justification for the stance that the application of the property law institutions within the framework of the Marvin doctrine to unmarried cohabiting persons would allow common law marriage to enter through a back door. On the other hand, it appears that the development by the Washington Supreme Court and the ALI principles are a way of admitting common law marriage through the main entrance, albeit partially. Characteristic of the decisions and, in part the basis thereof, are the parties' family law cohabitation, and the legal effects of family law through an analogous application of the regulations applicable to community property systems for spouses. Also belonging here is the application in New Hampshire of common law marriage, but only upon the death of one party. An even more limited system occurs in the Spanish province of Catalonia concerning long-lasting couple relationships (*d'unions estables de parella*); the minimal right to the residence for cohabiting persons is observable in Norwegian law. Through these partial systems, cohabiting unmarried persons are offered a basic protection in certain situations, however, reference is made to marrying if they desire a more extensive legal system.

The developments in Australia and New Zealand have gone considerably farther toward common law marriage, with de facto relationships, both heterosexual and homosexual, that are equated with marriage after two and three years of cohabitation, respectively, in terms of matters such as the division of the estate in the form of an equal division of property acquired during the relationship, inheritance, and maintenance. The farthest in the development toward common law marriage appears to have occurred in certain provinces in Canada. For example, Manitoba not only has regulations concerning family maintenance and a large number of laws concerning different rights and obligations outside of family law, but also all the regulations that concern married persons property rights have become applicable as to common-law partners. The extensive nature of the reforms can also be seen in that the expression *marital property* in New Zealand and Canada has been replaced by the expressions *relationship property*, and *family property*, even for spouses.

A significant difference between the *legal effects* of common law marriage and the legislation that has been enacted for cohabiting unmarried persons is that common law marriage entails the same regulations for divorce as for ceremonial marriage, while the cohabitation legislation ordinarily entirely lacks such regulations. There is an inherent contradiction in a legal system that considers children and family stability on one side, imposes restrictive divorce regulations for spouses, but, on the other side, through legislation, recognizes long-term cohabiting persons and the creation of families in addition to marriage without divorce regulations and the possibility of freely separating at any time. This contradiction has not received the attention it deserves in the light of the introduction of cohabitation legislation in different states. Even in states that follow the general trend toward no-fault divorce, the actual formal divorce procedure and the specified waiting periods constitute restrictive impediments that have the purpose of reducing family dissolution.[305] As long as states do not entirely capitulate in the effort to prevent hasty divorces and deregulate the entire formal system of marital divorce, there ought to be a reason to introduce comparable regulations for unmarried cohabiting persons. The viability of these reasons must, however, be assessed within the framework for the broader discussions concerning the arguments for and against common law marriage and other cohabitation legislation in general as presented in Chapter 14.

As long as the legal effects of cohabitation legislation clearly differ from those of marriage, they constitute a true alternative to marriage for unmarried cohabiting couples. Cohabitation legislation giving more limited legal effects than marriage in the future may be an attractive alternative for many couples. The legislator then offers the parties a more limited system of regulations that becomes applicable through their cohabitation and a more extensive one that becomes applicable if they formally marry. The more closely the development reaches common law marriage, the less meaningful marriage is from a legal aspect. The legislator who has been criticized for the enactment of the cohabitation legislation usually offers the defense that it is not a question of enacting a new type of marriage or a marriage of a lower dignity.[306] Still, this is exactly what occurs without the addition of any pejorative nuances! It cannot be ruled out that legal systems with limited legal effects for cohabitation in the future can become an attractive alternative to marriage; the effects being a limited financial community, certain regulations concerning property division, and no restrictive divorce regulations for many couples. If the development of the cohabitation legislation in the United States continues in the manner indicated by certain legislative proposals, common law marriage

305 *Compare* Sanford N. Katz, *Marriage and Marriage-Like Relationships: Should They Be Equal,* International Society of Family Law World Conference, unpublished paper, Copenhagen/Oslo, (August 2002), at 2-3.

306 *See* the ALI PRINCIPLES, *supra* note 62, § 6.02, Comment: b) The objectives of this Chapter. "It is not an objective (or a likely effect) of this Chapter to encourage parties to enter a nonmarital relationship as an alternative to marriage." *See also* the Swedish legislator's statements with the enactment of the Act of Cohabitants (1987), Prop. 1986/87:1, at 40 and the new COHABITEES ACT (2003:376), Prop. 2002/03:80, at 25. The committee that presented the basis for the reforms stated that there is no need for legislation which treats cohabitation as an alternative to marriage, *see* SOU 1981:85, at 622.

will return to states in which the doctrine has been repealed,[307] but then the legislation no longer serves as an alternative to marriage with respect to the legal consequences. Only the form of its commencement then differs from formal marriage.

The diverging question about the conditions and legal effects of the cohabitation legislation in different countries has created a legal situation that, for many couples, both heterosexual and same sex, are unclear, difficult to grasp, not to say incomprehensible. It is difficult for an unmarried couple today to know whether they have or do not have a right or an obligation. The requirements often differ within the same jurisdiction from one right to another. Concerning one right, registration is required; concerning another cohabitation; and concerning the cohabitation, the time period requirements and content can vary. This stands in contrast to common law marriage, which, in principle, has a uniform, albeit difficult to interpret, definition within all legal areas and entails all the legal effects of marriage.

4. *Registration as a Basis for Rights and Obligations*

Registration as a basis for rights and obligations within family law is closer to the formal marriage's civil form than common law marriage, which is informal. Because registration requires consent from both parties, there is, as with formal marriage and common law marriage, an agreement between the parties, which is not the case concerning the cohabitations that are regulated by legislation, as seen above. Registration, however, as certain French commentators have expressed the matter, is *un contrat strictement réglementé*.[308]

As can be seen in this chapter, registration as a basis of family law rights and obligations in modern times has developed primarily as a method for persons of the same sex to obtain the same rights and obligations as spouses, in accordance with the principle of separate but equal. Examples of this are the registered partnerships in the Nordic countries and Germany. Even the American legislations in the states of Vermont, Connecticut, and New Jersey concerning civil unions, and in California concerning domestic partnerships have had the same main objective. The question of whether persons of the same sex are to be able to enter into partnerships and even marriage is still highly controversial in the United States.

The development, however, has shown that several jurisdictions, such as New Zealand, the Netherlands, France, Belgium, and several provinces in Canada, have also enacted registered partnerships for persons of different sexes, who consequently can choose between marriage and registered partnerships; both regimes are entered into and *inter vivos* are dissolved

---

307 *See* the ALI Principles, *id.*
308 Carbonnier, *supra* note 90, at 703.

through a formal procedure. When, as in the Netherlands, the legal effects of marriage and registered partnerships are also comparable, we have to question whether registered partnerships for couples of different sexes fulfill any important function in addition to marriage. Since persons of the same sex in the Netherlands have also received the right to enter into marriage, which is a civil marriage, we have to question whether the double formal institutions on top of each other have any function to fulfill. The situation does not appear to be a result of academic legal and structural clarity, but rather arose from a feverish eagerness to respond to strong opinions. The same structural lack of clarity has arisen in New Zealand. There, a cohabiting couple of different sexes can choose between entering into a formal marriage through a church ceremony; entering into a formal marriage through a civil ceremony with the same legal effects; entering into a civil union through a civil ceremony with mostly the same legal effects. Finally, a couple may or may not choose any of these three similar alternatives, but still find that in central issues, the same legal effects are applied, as a result of the regulations concerning de facto relationships. The consequence is that the state, in its capacity as the good provider, has piled benefit upon benefit on couples of different sexes in a manner that has forfeited the parties' part of their true freedom of choice.

This has created a legal situation that is unclear, difficult to grasp, and incomprehensible for heterosexual as well as same sex couples. It must be hazardous for an unmarried couple, today, to know whether they have or do not have a right or an obligation. The requirements differ within the same jurisdiction from one right to another. Concerning one right, registration is required; concerning another, cohabitation; and concerning cohabitation, the time period requirements and the content vary.

To the extent registered partnerships are equipped with different or more limited legal effects than marriage, they are true alternatives. This, as can be seen in this chapter, is the case in France for heterosexual couples and in Belgium for both heterosexual and homosexual couples, since marriage there has been opened also for the latter.

In Chapter 14, where the legal policy motivations behind common law marriage and other cohabitation legislation are discussed, these registered forms of cohabitation will function as comparison objects together with the formal marriage. In Chapter 15, we return to the usefulness of registration forms in describing a future new marriage model.

CHAPTER 13
The Constitutive Requisites in the Future

13.1 Introduction

Every lawmaker who, in the future, intends to enact common law marriage or cohabitation legislation needs to address the elements that will constitute the necessary requisites for the establishment of such relationships. In actuality, the concern is which relationships are to be recognized by the community, regardless of whether they are called *marriages*, *cohabitation relationships*, or something similar.

This chapter focuses on these constitutive requisites, starting with their application within the framework of common law marriage. What functions and effects do the different constructions have? What are the advantages and disadvantages invoked by the different solutions? As common law marriage as a rule gained acceptance through the case law, there has been no critical discussion of the suitability of its different legal technical constructions. In a legal scenario that has been characterized as chaotic, legislation that is "brief, simple, and direct" has been demanded.[1]

Further attention will be given here to the different legislative techniques that have been enacted or proposed since the 1970s for cohabitation law in the Western world. The constitutive elements analyzed below represent the distinction between *animus* and *corpus*, familiar from Roman law; namely, the parties' *consensus* and their cohabitation. In addition, the use of burdens of proof and presumptions is assessed.

The discussion in this chapter can also be of interest with respect to formal marriage, particularly the content of the marriage agreement, which within formal marriage as codified is to a large extent fossilized in its forms, but is sometimes relevant, for example, in assessing sham marriages. Nevertheless, formal marriages, as such, are outside the scope of this analysis, because their conditions are too specific for our purposes.

1 *See* Chester Vernier, American Family Laws I, 108 (1931).

13.2 The Parties' *Consensus* as a Necessary Element

The use of the parties' *consensus* as a necessary element in the establishment of a common law marriage has not been critically discussed in any of the jurisdictions recognizing common law marriage, as examined above. The Roman maxim, *consensus facit nuptias*, was adopted by medieval canon law, and later adopted by American jurisdictions, both judicially and legislatively. As a result, the principle that marriage, whether formal or formless, is based on a contract has been taken for granted by the courts and legislatures, and has not been given further critical examination. The English court's statement in *Dalrymple v. Dalrymple* (1811) is typical: "Marriage being a contract is of course consensual."[2] The United States Supreme Court articulated the general acceptance and breadth of the principle in the United States in *Meister v. Moore* (1877): "Marriage is everywhere regarded as a civil contract."[3]

Therefore, neither the courts nor the legislative bodies have posed the question of whether any contract requisite ought to be generally required for the formation of a common law marriage and its function. Neither has there been any discussion focusing on the formulation of this contract requisite, even though the courts, as seen above, have clearly assumed different constructions. In connection with the analysis of the case law presented in Chapters 6, "The Common Law Marriage Contract," and 7, "Implied Marriage Agreements," we have been critical of the courts' lack of precision in determining the contract's marital intent, a deficiency that has had significant impact on evidentiary proof and valuation, especially if there is a question of an implied agreement.[4]

Neither has any more in-depth analysis of what the parties' *consensus* as a constitutive element should entail occurred in connection with the enactment of the cohabitation legislation in the Western world since the 1970s. This oversight seems strange when assessing, for instance, the importance of the parties' own intentions. The typical answer has been that if the legal relationship has been well established, the parties are given the possibility of contracting out of it, assuming that they are in agreement to do so. On the other hand, ordinarily, it has been possible to establish a cohabitation relationship on objective grounds and against the intent of a party.

---

2 *Dalrymple v. Dalrymple*, (1811) Hagg.Con. 54, 62–64, 161 Eng.Rep. 665, 668–669.

3 *Meister v. Moore*, 96 U.S. 76, 78, 24 L.Ed. 826 (1877). *See also Askew v. Dupree*, 30 Ga. 173, 176, 177, 178, 179, 189 (1869), maintaining the contract principle citing both Scottish and older English law.

4 The significance of the intent of the parties is discussed in Section 14.3.1 *infra* concerning the reasons for and against common law marriage and cohabitation legislation.

In the present section, we will discuss the following issues: (1) The need for a contract, and (2) expressed or implied agreements.

13.2.1 The Need for a Requisite of Contract

To begin, there is reason to question whether a contract element is necessary for the formation of a common law marriage or a legally recognized cohabitation. If the parties cohabit with each other, one could logically surmise that the legal consequences could simply be directly tied to their cohabitation. The parties, if proved to have actually lived together as husband and wife, would then also receive the legal effects of marriage or a legally recognized cohabitation.

If this line of thought is followed, it could be argued that such a system would better reflect reality. The sociological data presented in Chapter 12, "Common Law Marriage and Cohabitation Law," shows that the majority of couples simply "drift into" a formless cohabitation without having entered into any expressed contract,[5] and when the parties at trial are confronted with the question of whether they entered into any contract, they often are confounded. The majority cannot recall entering into any contract, at least not any expressed agreement. Against this background, questions arise about the necessity of this restriction.

Our analysis of the courts' reasoning with respect to implied agreements, as found in Chapter 7, further indicates the contract as a necessary element has suffered considerable erosion. One development can be traced in the courts' reasoning that the cohabitation, whose purpose was actually to prove the existence of a contract, was given increasingly more independent significance, while the importance of the contract receded more and more into the background.[6] This development in the case law is an added reason to question whether the contract requirement should be abandoned, with legal consequences directly resulting from the parties' cohabitation.

A number of legal systems use only the objective requisite of cohabitation as the necessary element for the establishment of a formless marriage. Certain Latin American countries recognize formless marriages, and give the parties marriage-like status and all of marriage's legal consequences, on the condition that certain objective facts are proven.[7] Those legal systems granting unmarried cohabiting couples some of marriage's legal consequences almost always tie them to objective facts as further discussed below under Section 13.2.2, "Expressed or Implied Agreements." Grace Blumberg, who has proposed legislation for unmarried couples

---

5 *See* Section 12.2 *supra.*

6 *See* Section 7.8 *supra.*

7 A joining of a man and a woman characterized by stability and monogamy is comparable to marriage according to Cuban law, *see* Article 18, CUBAN FAMILY CODE, Law No. 1289 (1975).

within the United States, ties the legal consequences to simple, objective elements found in different aspects of the relationship between the parties as well as relationships with third parties and the state, without reference to the parties' subjective intent.[8] The same attitude toward cohabitation and its objective elements characterizes the proposed American Law Institute (ALI) Principles in 2002.[9]

On the other hand, there is a question about whether a tacit agreement existed between the parties concerning their relationship. Or could it really be that they simply woke up one morning without having any intentions with respect to their actions beyond the present? Can they continue to wake up together over the years without having any decided intent with respect to their relationship and their future? Relationships most probably vary considerably from case to case. There are certainly couples who, after a short relationship, have no decided intent as to their relationship. At the same time, there certainly are couples who have a clear, more or less explicit, mutual intent about their relationship.

Certain critics of the ALI Principles have pleaded for the relevance of the parties' intentions. Thus, Marsha Garrison, who has proposed a "revivified common law marriage," has strongly emphasized the significance of regulations based on the parties' free will and commitment. Elizabeth Scott has recommended a presumption that is closely related to the common law marriage presumption as it involves the parties' intentions.[10]

A closer discussion concerning the need for a contract is dependent, *inter alia*, on the marital intent, *essensialia negotii*, that the contract is deemed to have in order for the legal consequences to be invoked.

---

8 Grace Ganz Blumberg, *Cohabitation without Marriage: A Different Perspective*, 28 UCLA L Rev. 1125 (1981). The author, who is critical of the Marvin doctrine and prefers status to contract, distances herself from those theories seeking solutions with the help of property contract constructions. Instead, she proposes legislation creating a "legal status" with rights and obligations for cohabiting couples. Blumberg prefers somewhat different definitions dependent upon the respective laws' purposes, wherewith, a mutual household, children and cohabitation of a certain length can be seen as objective criteria which can lead to the result that unmarried couples in certain situations can be treated as comparable to married spouses. Consequently, a two-year cohabitation or mutual children, according to Blumberg, ought to be sufficient for entitlement to workers' compensation. "Common household" ought to suffice for entitlement to benefits in the social security system. A 60-day-cohabitation ought to have the consequence of a maintenance obligation for a previous spouse and for state support to families with children. Unmarried cohabiting couples ought further to be treated as married spouses from a tax perspective if they previously had been married, or if they have had a mutual household and children, or if the cohabitation was lengthy.

9 *See* American Law Institute (ALI), Principles of the Law of Family Dissolution: Analysis and Recommendations (2002), particularly Chapter 6, Domestic Partners, and Chapter 4. Grace Blumberg, *id.*, was one of ALI's reporters.

10 Marsha Garrison, *Is Consent Necessary? An Evaluation of the Emerging Law of Cohabitant Obligation*, 52 UCLA L. Rev. 815, 884-890 (2005); and Elizabeth S. Scott, *Domestic Partnerships, Implied Contracts, and Law Reform*, in Reconceiving the Family, Critique on the American Law Institute's Principles of the Law of Family Dissolution 331, 342-345 (Robin Fretwell Wilson ed., 2006).

1. *Cohabitation as the Object of the Marital Intent*

If one begins with the view that marriage is based on natural law, and that all human law was created based upon that premise, it becomes predictable that legal consequences are tied to the parties' mutual intent to live together. Most likely, Adam and Eve were not aware of any regulatory system. For them, marriage, most likely, was an agreement to live together. The same thinking can also be found in cultures with developed legal systems. When Gratian spoke of *consensus matrimonialis* in the medieval canon law, it appears that he, as stated above, envisioned a mutual intent to establish a *consortium omnis vitae*, in other words, a fellowship in everything in life. The same thinking can be found in older Scottish and American law, in which the marital contract was a contract "looking to the *consortium vitae*."[11]

If the contract's *essensialia* is determined by the parties' intent to live together, the predictable question is whether it is better, instead, to avoid the contract and tie the legal consequences directly to the cohabitation. In order to answer this question, it is necessary to begin by differentiating between assessments made *ex ante* and *ex post*.

If an assessment is *ex post*, in other words, a proving afterwards of the existence of a common law marriage, it appears that the contract line of thought, with its given marital intent, does not have a function in the majority of cases. If the parties have actually lived together for twenty years, there is scarcely any point to stating afterwards that they also had a contract to live together during this period. If the object of the marital intent is determined by the parties' cohabitation, it is not surprising, as has sometimes been the case, for the courts to have found an implied agreement proven by the long-term cohabitation.[12] With respect to long-term cohabitation, it is generally more consistent in an assessment *ex post* to tie the legal consequences directly to the cohabitation instead of taking a detour in the contract construction.

Nevertheless, if the required intent is stretched over a period longer than the parties' de facto cohabitation, the resulting *subjective surplus* can

---

11 *See* Section 3.3.3 *supra*. Within the framework for a life fellowship between the parties, the canon law has viewed the purpose of marriage to be procreation and the satisfaction of sexual needs, *see* A. ESMEIN, LE MARIAGE EN DROIT CANONIQUE I, 249–250 (R. Génestal ed., 2d ed. 1929). With respect to Scottish law, *see Dalrymple v. Dalrymple*, (1811) 2 Hagg.Con. 54, 161 Eng.Rep. 665, and the cases cited in Section 4.2 and Chapter 11 *supra*. With respect to American law, *see Askew v. Dupre*, 30 Ga. 173, 178 (1860), describing the contract as an agreement "looking to the *consortium vitae*" and speaking of two persons united "by mutual contract to live together."

12 *See* Chapter 7 *supra*. *See also Travers v. Reinhardt*, 205 U.S. 423, 27 S.Ct. 563, 51 L.Ed 865 (1906) (18 years); *Matthews v. Britton*, 112 U.S.App.D.C. 397, 303 F.2d 408 (1962) (22 years); *Boswell v. Boswell*, 497 So.2d 479 (Ala. 1986) (37-38 years); *Campbell v. Christian*, 235 S.C. 102, 110 S.E.2d 1 (1959) (24 years); *In re Marriage of Gebhardt*, 426 N.W.2d 651 (Iowa App. 1988) (16 years); and *Beals v. Beals*, 203 Ga.App. 81, 416 S.E.2d 301 (1992) (7 years).

also have a certain function in proving *ex post*. This can be true in cases of short-term relationships. Consequently, one should distinguish between cases in which the parties simply lived together for a short period and those in which the cohabitation certainly was short, but the parties simultaneously had an intent to continue to live together in the future. If the short-term cohabitation was terminated as a result of the death of a party, the contract can have a function, for example, in an assessment of whether the surviving party is entitled to a portion of the deceased's estate or insurance policy. If the cohabitation was terminated because the parties separated, it can be more difficult to prove the existence of a long-term marital intent after a short-term relationship.

Can a contract also have a function if the cohabitation generally has been insufficient but other reasons exist to grant the parties the legal consequences of marriage? This can be the case if the cohabitation was not possible to its fullest extent on completely legitimate grounds, for example, one party's employment, education, health care, or military duty in another geographic area. The limited cohabitation, alone, cannot be the basis for the granting of a legal consequence, such as the right to inherit. However, if the relationship is viewed as a whole, despite its insufficiencies, it can be justified by viewing the parties as married if they have behaved as a formally married couple would in a comparable situation. A possibility for granting the legal consequences of marriage relies on the use of a contract, according to which the parties had the mutual intent to live together in the future. On the other hand, if the parties continue to not live together in a more complete cohabitation for a long period of time, their contract to live together becomes more illusory, if a lower requirement is not applied to the content of their cohabitation. Another and more certain method is a contract based upon an intent to establish a legal relationship, which also entails overlooking such insufficiencies in the cohabitation and which *ex post* can grant these cases the legal consequences of marriage, as discussed below.

Reason exists, based on a contract for the purpose of a lifelong cohabitation, to grant the legal consequences of marriage to parties who have had a short or insufficient cohabitation. Nevertheless, a plausible objection is that the different legal consequences assume a long and stable cohabitation. The issues of evidentiary and legal certainty are so significant that a couple living together in such a relationship ought to enter into a formal marriage if they desire the legal consequences of marriage.[13]

With an assessment occurring *ex ante*, a contract with an *essensialia* containing the intent to live together appears to have a more important function. The assessment can then address whether the parties should incur the future responsibilities of contributing to each other's maintenance,

---

13 This objection, of course, can be made against the entirety of the institution of common law marriage, for more on this *see* Chapter 14 *infra*.

fidelity, etc. In their relationship with the state and other public authorities, this assessment may extend to whether the parties are entitled to different social benefits in the future.

A system that does not tie the legal consequences to a contract but, instead, directly to the actual cohabitation faces the problem, in an assessment *ex ante*, that neither a currently existing cohabitation nor a past cohabitation speaks to the future and can give indications of that which is and has been, but not what is to be. This is clearly the case if the parties have lived together for a short period of time. They can terminate their cohabitation at any moment. A couple that has spent one night together can terminate the relationship upon awakening; neither of them needs to have any further intentions. This is also true, strictly speaking, in a long-term cohabitation, which similarly indicates nothing certain about the future. If the legal assessment relies simply on the fact that if the parties live or have lived together, they can be granted social benefits in the future despite having already decided to separate within a short period of time. Therefore, the relevant question for the authorities to ask the parties must be: Do you have the intent to live together?

If the parties are in an agreement to live a life together, their mutual *consensus* says something about the future, which is an important function of the contract generally. The contract certainly cannot predict with accuracy what the reality will be. The contract can, of course, be breached. Nevertheless, the parties' intent to be bound and their desire to execute the contract increases the probability that, in comparison with those persons simply living together, they will perform or at least attempt to perform the contract. This is particularly true if the parties have entered into a ceremonial contract, but is also true for formless, though expressed, contracts and even implied agreements. It appears, therefore, with assessments *ex ante*, that tying the legal consequences to the parties' mutual intent to live together instead of the cohabitation is more tailored to the fulfillment of public policy goals. Public authorities, granting a family or a cohabiting couple a social benefit to be awarded monthly into the future, should benefit from the existence of a contract according to which the parties are in agreement to live together for the long term.

Consequently, the purpose of the contract is not so much that the parties have been and are in agreement that the cohabitation has existed and presently exists, but rather that there is a subjective surplus, in other words, an additional mutual intent to live together in the future. This inevitably leads to a question about how long a period of time the subjective surplus must cover. Do the parties, in accordance with Gratian's medieval teachings, have a mutual intent to found an undivided cohabitation for life, *individua vitae consuetudo*? Or, in our society, is it sufficient that the agreement to cohabit exists until further notice, or for the foreseeable future? Should they be allowed to have the opportunity to simply limit their agreement to a cohabitation as long as they have underage children, or as long as they desire, or in any other manner?[14]

One occasionally catches a glimpse in the legal literature of the understanding that, given the high incidence of divorce, it is unrealistic to use the concept of lifetime marriages.[15] However, this viewpoint, as we have seen in Chapter 6, has not been widely accepted in the American case law concerning common law marriage. Instead, it appears that the Christian understanding of marriage as principally a lifelong relationship has led the courts to reject an agreement between the parties to live together "so long as mutual affection shall exist"[16] or "so long as they desired."[17] The courts generally have stressed that the marriage-like relationship at issue principally is lifelong, or at least permanent and durable. The requirement of a lifelong relationship as the object of marital intent appears to have survived the recent, increasing incidence of divorce.[18] Even though marriage as a lifelong relationship often turns out to be a fiction, the fact cannot be disregarded that this fiction is accepted as a reality at the time of the commencement of the marriage, when the contract is actually executed—a fact that cannot be overlooked!

The application of common law marriage, if based on formless marriage of any kind and equipped with all the legal consequences of a formal marriage, should be guided by the legislation and case law on formal marriage. Because common law marriage is a formless reflection of the form-bound marriage, application problems with respect to common law marriage ought to be able to be solved with guidance from the form-bound marriage that appears in the legal system, with support of what we will call the "mirror image theory." This legal method can have different results as a result of differences between legal systems and time periods. However, there is significant agreement about the main characteristics of

---

14 *See* Section 3.3.3 *supra*.

15 Keith G. McWalter, *Marriage as Contract: Towards a Functional Redefinition of the Marital Status*, 9 Col. J.L. & S.P. 607, 637–638 (1973). *See also* Homer H. Clark, Jr., *The New Marriage*, 12 Willamette L.J. 441, 450 (1976), who, with respect to the legal definition of marriage, maintains that "permanence and exclusivity" are no longer characteristics of marriage.

16 *Peck v. Peck*, 155 Mass. 479, 30 N.E. 74 (1892). *Compare Perkins v. Silverman*, 284 Mo. 238, 223 S.W. 895 (1920); *Arnold v. Arnold*, 219 Mo.App. 8, 267 S.W. 950 (1924); and *Perales v. Flores*, 147 S.W.2d 974 (Tex.Civ.App. 1941).

17 *See Swingle v. Keifer*, 105 Tex. 609, 153 S.W. 1132, 1133 (1913), in which the court stated that a contract according to which the parties would live together as husband and wife "so long as they desired" and according to which one of the parties or both "could dissolve the contract at will," could not legally establish a marital contract.

18 *See, e.g.*, from the past thirty-five years, *In re Estate of Hammonds*, 39 Ohio Misc. 96, 315 N.E.2d 843, 847 (1973), in which the court required that the contract be "not merely a temporary arrangement, but an agreement for life." Generally, *see* the extensive case law cited in Section 6.3 *supra*. In Comment, *Fundamental Interests and the Question of Same-Sex Mariage*, 15 Tul. L. Rev. 141, 150 (1979), the statement that marriage is "the public and voluntary commitment of one individual to spend a lifetime with another..." is made.

marriage, including views of marriage as principally lifelong or at least permanent, and as relationships between men and women not limited by time.[19] Therefore, a contract for a more limited relationship appears, in most jurisdictions, to fall outside legal marriage. The requirement of a long-term contract and the need for a contract generally appears somewhat differently if legislation gives only limited legal effects to cohabiting couples.[20] As seen below, the concept of marriage has been the most important model for most of the cohabitation legislation that have been enacted in the Western world over the last thirty years, albeit the model has not been fully realized.

A contract with a long-term intent appears to have a function to fulfill with respect to the concept of marriage and cohabitation, distinguishing relationships that are on a trial basis. It is not uncommon today, and in many cases, is even advisable, for men and women to live together for a trial period to see whether they are compatible. Because the parties have not definitely decided to pursue a long-term relationship together, there is no reason, as a rule, to grant them the legal consequences of marriage or cohabitation.[21] Certainly, after a short period of cohabitation, they can determine whether they are suited for each other. A contract with a long-term intent to live together can contribute to maintaining the distinction between trial relationships and final relationships. The actual cohabitation, as the sole necessary element, does not fulfill this function, because the relationships are similar in the beginning. The difference is subjective! It should be noted that parties who have expressed an intent to truly try need not be considered to have entered into a trial marriage, but, instead, can be seen as expressing a very determined long-term marital intent.[22]

A contract with *essensialia* containing an intent to live together can prevent sham marriages. A common law marriage that has been entered into only for the purpose, for example, of allowing one spouse to immigrate, receive social benefits, or avoid military duty or criminal punishment, but without the parties having any intent to commence a cohabitation, is

---

19 A vow commonly found in the wedding ceremony is that they shall love and be faithful to each other until separated by death: "I, N.N. take thee N.N. to be my lawfully wedded wife (husband) to have and to hold from this day forward, for better, for worse, for richer, for poorer, in sickness and in health, to love and to cherish *till death us do part*" (*italics added*).

20 A legal system containing regulations as to cohabiting unmarried couples today is often based simply on objective circumstances. In a similar manner as that stated above, assessments *ex post* and *ex ante* can derive benefit from the use of a subjective requisite, which however ought to be given a content and a timeframe suitable with respect to the legal consequences being invoked.

21 *Rosetta v. Rosetta*, 525 S.W.2d 255, 261 (Tex.Civ.App.-Tyler 1975); *Leal v. Moreno*, 733 S.W.2d 322 (Tex.Civ.App.-Corpus Christi 1987); *Turner v. Turner*, 251 Ala. 295, 37 So.2d 186 (1948); and *Taylor v. Taylor*, 298 N.Y.S. 912, 164 Misc. 401 (1937).

22 *Benson v. Tom Williams Buick, Inc.*, 551 So.2d 355 (Ala. 1989).

invalid because the contract's required intent does not exist.[23] However, the requirement of an actual cohabitation for a not-too-short time fulfills the same function. In an assessment *ex post*, it is clearly apparent that a requisite of cohabitation is tailored to the goals being sought more than simply an intent to live together. Suppose, however, the cohabitation has been short, or, in an assessment *ex ante*, the parties have, for example, after an immigration, still not moved in together. A contract can, with a requirement of an intent to live together, impede a sham marriage. A contract with an intent to establish a legal relationship does not offer the same protection, an issue that is discussed further below. A contract with an intent to live together naturally does not entail complete protection. Even a marriage based on such a contract can be dissolved after a short period of time.

With the requirement of an intent to live together, the question arises what the intended cohabitation must consist of in order for a marital or cohabitation contract to be considered to exist. A cohabitation can manifest itself in many different ways. The marriage-like togetherness can be greater or lesser, and different couples can, when commencing their cohabitation, have different intents concerning their relationship.

If one begins with the factors most commonly considered by sociologists to be characteristic of a cohabitation, the following are noted: a monogamous sexual relationship, an emotional relationship, mutual children, mutual residence, mutual household, joint economies, and mutual recreation and friends.[24]

However, these factors are based on how the marriage-like relationship actually manifests itself in reality. In contrast, the pertinent question in this section is the *intent* needed by the parties with reference to their cohabitation in order for it to be viewed as a marital contract with legal consequences. Which factors, it can be asked, ought to be necessary and sufficient, respectively, as elements of a marital intent, assuming that these factors can be found in a cohabitation?[25]

---

23 In the case of *Pegg v. Pegg*, 138 Iowa 572, 115 N.W. 1027, 1028 (1908), the parties, according to the record, drafted a written marital contract to prevent being prosecuted for "illicit cohabitation." The court stated: "That a mere written or oral agreement to be husband and wife, without present intention to assume that relationship in fact, does not constitute a marriage between the parties, especially if the agreement is entered into for some other purpose, is well settled."

24 With respect to the element, *see* Blumberg, *supra* note 8, at 1131, who cites Jan Trost, Unmarried Cohabitation, 63-64 (1979): "[J]oint housing, joint economy, joint ownership of real and personal property, children together, meals together, vacations together, recreation together, same friends, same 'language,' feeling of community and belonging together, sexual relation, looking upon themselves and being looked upon by friends and family as having responsibility for each other in case of accident or illness." Most of these elements may be subsumed in the term "economic and social integration."

25 A similar problem arises in the treatment of cohabitation as a necessary requisite. *See* the current state of the law and the future course of the law in Chapter 8 *supra*.

One must begin with the fact that the boundaries of the required intent to live together directly influence the scope of application of common law marriage. If the requirements are set too high, many couples may lose rights they ought to have, while the state may be unable to impose the obligations of marriage or a legally recognized cohabitation on those falling outside of the system. If the requirements for intended cohabitation are set too low, the legal consequences of marriage or a legally recognized cohabitation become applicable to relationships for which they were not intended. Herein lies a considerable problem in the use of an intent to live together.

The concept of a broad cohabitation has a strong historical basis. When Gratian spoke of a *consensus matrimonialis* during the Middle Ages, it contained an intent to establish a *consortium omnis vitae* and *individua vitae consuetudo;* in other words, a companionship in everything for life and an undivided lifelong cohabitation.[26] The primary purpose was to exclude purely sexual relationships from the concept of marriage. This same broad view of cohabitation recurs in older Scottish and American case law, in which a marital contract "looking to the *consortium vitae*" is mentioned.[27] Perhaps the same broad concept of cohabitation was proposed by Ellen Kandoian when she, in modern times, although without reference to any historical sources, defined marriage as a union between two persons "to carry on a shared life."[28]

The question then becomes whether this broad historical concept of cohabitation is archaic in today's modern society. Should a contract, today, encompass a companionship in everything in life? Against the background of the dissolution of family ties occurring in the later half of the 1900s, and the emergence of new family patterns, a number of legal scholars have narrowed the definition of marriage considerably. Homer Clark, consequently, maintains in an article from 1976 that durability and sexual exclusivity no longer characterize marriage, and that its most significant function is "emotional satisfaction."[29] Clark envisions a future development in

---

26 *See* Section 3.3.3 *supra*. Within the framework of a life together between the parties, the canon law posited that the goals of marriage were to procreate and to satisfy sexual needs, *see* ESMEIN, *supra* note 11, at 249-250.

27 With respect to Scottish law, *see* Chapter 11 and American law, *see* Section 6.3 *supra*.

28 Ellen Kandoian, *Cohabitation, Common Law Marriage, and the Possibility of a Shared Moral Life*, 75 GEORG. L.J. 1829, 1870 (1987). *Compare* the new legislation in New Zealand that entered into force 1 February 2002 and to a high degree equates "*de facto* relationships" (both heterosexual and homosexual couples) with married couples. A prerequisite hereto is that the parties "live together as a couple." With the assessment hereof may be considered, in addition to a number of objective elements, also "the degree of mutual commitment to a shared life," however without that any of these elements are necessary, *see* section 2D, PROPERTY (RELATIONSHIPS) ACT (1976). The comparable elements exist also in New South Wales, Australia, *see* section 4(2)(f), THE PROPERTY (RELATIONSHIPS) ACT (1984), Amendment Act (1999).

29 Clark, *supra* note 15, at 442. *See also* David S. Caudill, *Legal Recognition of Unmarried Cohabitation: A Proposal to Update and Reconsider Common-Law Marriage*, 49 TENN. L. REV.

which marriage will be simply redefined as "some sort of relationship" between two individuals of an undetermined length involving "some kind of sexual conduct."[30]

Although Clark does not discuss the content of the marital intent in formless marriages, but rather the development of the concept of marriage in modern times, his definition is still of interest. First, it raises the question of whether his definition, in which marriage lacks durability and sexual exclusivity, challenges the inclusion of these elements in establishing marital intent. With respect to durability, the answer has already been given above, because a distinction must be drawn between what the parties' intent ought to be when they enter into the contract and how the reality later manifests itself. Even though the view of marriage as a lifelong relationship is often a fiction, the fact remains that the legislation is based on an assumption of durable relationships, an assumption that is generally accepted as reality by the parties when they enter the contract by commencing the marriage.

Exclusivity has followed this same development. An essential element of the intent of the marital contract within the Christian tradition is that the parties intend a monogamous relationship, or, as it is often expressed in the American case law, a relationship "exclusive of all others."[31] Perhaps the requirement for a monogamous, lifelong cohabitation is a romantic illusion from the mid-1800s, especially since adultery is being decriminalized and eliminated as a ground for divorce; most states now permit divorce if the parties wish it. Clark's statement that marriage is no longer characterized by durability and exclusivity can, to a considerable degree, be viewed as a correct view of actual relationships. However, the pertinent issue is the intent the parties ought to have when they begin their marriage-like cohabitation, not the actual result. Their intent may be illusory, but with the commencement of the marriage, it ought to be the reality. If we apply the mirror image theory to the problem, formal marriage, as found in different legal systems, reveals a legal concept created for exclusive relationships. Few couples, when they begin their relationship, consider anything other than an exclusive relationship. If they later commit adultery, it is a separate matter that the marriage can be dissolved by divorce. It is notable that the legislation for both unmarried cohabiting couples and formal marriage imposes the same requirement of monogamy.

537, 542 (1982): "Marriage has evolved into a community of moral love involving elements such as intimacy, emotional support, and fidelity..."

30 Clark, *id.* at 450-451. Even more lacking in content is the definition found in the UNIF. MARRIAGE AND DIVORCE ACT § 201, which characterizes marriage as "a personal relationship between man and woman arising out of a civil contract to which the consent of the parties is essential."

31 *See* 6.3 *supra*.

Clark's statement that marriage's most significant task is "emotional satisfaction" and that marriage ought to be redefined as a relationship involving "some kind of sexual conduct," sharply contrasts the early case law, in which loose relationships based only on a sexual relationship were not accepted as common law marriages.[32] Should the intended cohabitation only need to include a sexual relationship, overinclusion would result; it can be argued that a couple entering such a contract, with neither the intent to live together or have a mutual household, does not need the extensive regulatory system of marriage that protects a couple in an extensive and durable marriage-like relationship. In reality, it is precisely the exclusively sexual relationships that the courts have objected to when imposing a requirement of cohabitation for the formation of a common law marriage.[33] A relationship that at first glance seems to be mainly sexual is put in a completely different light if it is shown that the parties had an agreement to live an entire life together.

The courts' clear distancing from purely sexual relationships imposed caution about requiring a sexual relationship in the required intent. Nevertheless, clearly an intent to live as husband and wife also contains a sexual intent and the intent to procreate.[34] Still, it is excessive to include a sexual relationship as an absolute requirement. Older couples most probably would then fall outside of the system. The requirement of monogamy makes it easier to exclude the sexual element as a direct requirement. It makes little difference whether the parties can or will have a sexual relationship; the point is simply that they do not intend to have outside sexual relationships. The goal of procreating, which in the older law was a main element, can scarcely today be seen as a necessary element in the marital or cohabitation intent.[35]

---

32 *Id.*

33 *Id.* The courts have occasionally viewed their task as disclosing relationships hiding behind the description of the parties living together as husband and wife. *See e.g., Thimgan v. Mathews,* 74 Colo. 93, 219 P. 211 (1923). *Compare Foley v. Gavin,* 76 Colo. 286, 230 P. 618 (1924).

34 *See Duggan v. W.C.A.B. (Litchfield TP.),* 569 A.2d 1022, 1023 (Pa.Cmwlth. 1990), in which the court stated that the couple certainly had a very friendly relationship, did many things together, and had a mutual respect for each other, but in which the court did not find that the evidence demonstrated that the deceased "wished to marry and share either his bed or his property with the Claimant." If one spouse expressly declares he or she is willing to attempt to procreate, but later after the marriage has been entered into, refuses to do so, the other spouse, assuming that they do not continue with the cohabitation when this circumstance becomes known, with reference hereto, can not only receive a marital divorce, but also can have the marriage annulled, *see e.g., McCann v. McCann,* 593 N.Y.S.2d 917 (Sup. 1993); and *Rich v. Rich,* 40 A.D.2d 846, 337 N.Y.S.2d 530 (2d Dep't 1972).

35 *Compare* older Scottish law. Lord Stowell stated in *Lindo v. Belisario,* (1795) 1 Hagg. Cons.Rep. 216 that: "A marriage is not every carnal commerce; nor would it be so even in the law of nature; a mere carnal commerce, without the intention of cohabitation and bringing up of children, would not constitute marriage under any supposition. But when two persons agree to have that commerce for the procreation of and bringing up of children, and for such lasting cohabitation—that, in a state of

An element of the intent to live together that can be viewed as having a significant function would be the intent to create a mutual home and household. Already in medieval canon law, the concept of companionship *in lecto et in mensa*, in other words, at bed and board, can be seen, and in Scottish law, as stated in the previous chapters, one speaks of a companionship "at bed and board."[36] The requirement of a companionship at board or a household is designed to distinguish common law marriages from more temporary and/or tenant relationships.

The problem with the requirement of a mutual home and household is that many couples then fall outside the scope of the regulations. An example is that one party, for completely legitimate reasons, such as employment, studies, military duty, or health reasons, has a household in another geographic area. Assume that the parties, when they commenced their relationship, knew that the woman would be working in Texas and the man in Washington for several years. The parties would not, for the foreseeable future, have any mutual residence, household, continuous sexual relations, or mutual children. Their contact will consist mainly of telephone conversations and letters. Certain joint economic matters will exist. They will meet in person as often as they can, however, this will simply be a few times a year. Do they have a marital intent to live together? An even clearer example is the absence of a long-term cohabitation, for example, because one party works at sea.

Clearly, a contract with a requirement of an intent to live together may fail to capture relationships in which the intended cohabitation is very limited. It can certainly be assumed that the couple has a mutual intent to live together more completely but due to the circumstances, is prevented from doing so. This possibility may be feasible for a transition period, but becomes problematical if it continues for many years. Employment in Washington can be for a long period of time. A person can work at sea for a lifetime. In cases of long-term separate living, the mutual intent to live a more complete life together becomes an illusion, a precarious foundation for a marriage. Perhaps, for certain couples, it is already clear when they commence their relationship that, due to the stated circumstances, they will not have a more extensive cohabitation. If there is an interest in giving such couples the possibility of living in a common law marriage, the use of a contract focusing on cohabitation is a questionable way to serve that purpose.

---

nature, would be a marriage; and, in the absence of all civil and religious institutions, might safely be presumed to be, as it is properly called, a marriage in the sight of God."

36 With respect to canon law, *see* Section 3.3.4 *supra*. With respect to Scottish law, *see* Chapter 11 *supra*. Bed and board companionship as a legal conceptual pair can also be found in Germanic law, where they are referred to as a companionship to "*Tisch und Bett*" and in older Nordic law, where it was assumed that the parties "*deler seng*" as well as "*spiser og drikker sammen*." The requirement of household companionship occurs as a particular requisite in French law and also in certain Swedish legislation.

In such a case, the requirement of an intent to live together must be extremely watered down, or an exception must be made for those cases in which, for legitimate reasons, it is not possible for the couple to live together in a more highly developed companionship.

However, one problem arising from a more diluted definition is that it also then includes those cases in which the parties will not live together in a more complete and continuous companionship. Perhaps such parties will only periodically live together or with someone else. However, this problem ought to be limited by a requirement of a mutual intent to establish as broad a companionship as possible, with exceptions for those cases in which a more complete companionship is not possible for legitimate reasons, for example, employment in another geographic area. A contract that is based, instead, on a mutual intent to establish a legal relationship clearly captures, on the other hand, couples willing or forced to live in a more limited cohabitation, as discussed below.

From the parties' perspective, it appears that the most serious objection to a contract with an intent to live together is that they can be included in a regulatory system that they have neither chosen nor desired. A couple may certainly have agreed to live an entire life together, while consciously refraining from formally marrying to avoid marriage and its legal consequences. This can be true of older couples who have been previously married and wish, in the new relationship, to retain their independence by simply living together without any legal ties. This can also be true of young couples living independently within a relationship, with respect to each other and the state's authority and its regulations, at least for several years, until they later decide to marry. From the parties' perspective, a contract based on an intent to live together would therefore pose a danger to legal certainty, especially because many couples are not aware of the fact that a common law marriage invokes the same extensive legal consequences as a ceremonial marriage.

These inconveniences can naturally be limited by informing the parties that an agreement to live together invokes the legal consequences of marriage. For those that have been informed, moving in together becomes a conscious legal action. Further, the party benefiting from the regulatory system, for example, by a division of property through divorce or death, should be more tolerant of the inconveniences of legal certainty; they ought to value economic protection more than legal certainty.

From the state's perspective, however, the views of the parties can be deemed insignificant. With respect to a public law benefit, it can be rational to connect the benefit to the parties' intent to live together regardless of whether they want the legal consequences. This is true, however, also of the private law obligations that the state may want to impose on couples starting families and intending to live a life together. The state may even be seen as a third party to the contract, probably viewing it as advantageous to tie the legal consequences to the parties' mutual intent to live together rather than to their intent to receive legal consequences, if the state will not go so far as to tie the legal consequences directly to the actual cohabitation (*see* section 13.3 below). The stance taken on these issues depends on how the interests of the state and the individuals are weighed against each other.

2. *A Legal Relationship as the Object of the Marital Intent*

As seen in Chapter 6, a number of courts appear to assume that the parties' agreement to live a life together is not sufficient, in itself, for the formation of a common law marriage. The couple must also have had the intent to establish something legal, for example, a *legal relationship* or the *legal status of marriage.*[37] Such formulations of the object for the marital intent are based upon an understanding of marriage as a legal relationship or status relationship invoking a number of legal consequences, and that the parties' goal, or one of their goals, in entering into marriage is to receive these consequences.

The requirement of a legal intent, however, is by no means obvious. In other, similar areas of private law, there is no requirement of a legal intent in order for a contract to be viewed as executed. Parties entering, for example, into a partnership do not need to have an intent to reach the status of partnership. It is considered sufficient that they intend a relationship including "the essential elements of partnership."[38] Accordingly, it has been argued that a status intent is not necessary for the formation of a marriage but rather, an intent encompassing *the essential elements of marriage.*[39]

The requirement of a legal intent, and the issue of its function, however, merits discussion both with respect to common law marriage and a legally recognized cohabitation relationship, beginning with the question of the content of such an intent. A natural solution, against the suggested background, would be to require an intent to obtain legal consequences. The parties entering into a contract become married and receive the legal

---

37 In *Marino v. Anheuser-Bush, Inc.*, 583 N.Y.S.2d 68, 70 (A.D. 1992), no common law marriage was found established as evidence was lacking demonstrating that the parties during their stays in Pennsylvania "sought to establish the legal relationship of husband and wife." *See also State v. Grimes*, 215 Iowa 1287, 247 N.W. at 664-666 (1933), in which the parties in a written contract had agreed "to live as Husband and Wife until such time that we are Lawfully married," but in which the court did not find any common law marriage established as the contract did not contain the intent to assume "the legal relation."

38 J. Crane and A. Blomberg, Partnership 39 note 172 (1968). A business partnership is defined as "an association of two or more persons to carry on as co-owners a business for profit," *see* Uniform Partnership Act § 6(1), 6 U.L.A. 22 (1985).

39 Kandoian, *supra* note 28, at 1871. Kandoian, considering legal solutions for cohabitation, does not more closely discuss which elements constitute "the essential elements of marriage," but appears to assume a joining of two persons "to carry on a shared life." *Id.* at 1870. With respect to cohabitation as the object of the marital intent, *see* Section 6.3.1 *supra.*

consequences of marriage, as desired. If they do not have such a mutual intent to establish a marriage, they are not affected by these legal consequences. The farthest reaching would be to require that the parties be in agreement as to all of the legal consequences of relationship. For example in *Williams v. Williams* (1879), the court maintained that there must be an agreement between the parties that they will hold toward each other the relation of husband and wife, with "all the responsibilities and duties which the law attaches to such relation, otherwise there can be no lawful marriage."[40] The same reasoning would mean that only cohabiting couples intending to receive all the legal effects of the cohabitation legislation would be affected by the legislation. However, such a far-reaching intent appears rather unrealistic because a majority of couples are not aware of all of the legal consequences of a marriage or a cohabitation relationship, and, therefore, make no conscious choice when they marry or refrain from marrying.[41] The legal consequences are certainly neither the result of negotiations between the parties nor accepted in any contract, but follow primarily from the legislation, which may more reflect the lawmaker's agenda. With a requirement of a far-reaching legal intent, the application area of the regulations becomes severely limited.

The issue instead becomes whether it is suitable and possible to limit the requirement of a legal intent to certain legal consequences, for example, those deemed as central to serving the purposes of the requirement. This not in order to facilitate the parties receiving by contract only certain of marriage's legal consequences. The regulatory system on marriage is applied in its entirety. The parties can principally choose either all or none of the legal consequences with certain modifications.[42] The intention is that the mandatory legal consequences of marriage or cohabitation can be required as part of the parties' mutual intent; in other words, the couple cannot contract away those consequences. Such legal consequences, which the parties do not have the ability to change, can be assumed to be so significant that they constitute an essential element in the concept of marriage or the legal recognized cohabitation. This can, for example, concern the requirement of fidelity or the imposition of the laws governing divorce. The parties, it can be argued, ought to agree that these legal consequences are applicable in order for a marriage to be established. A couple may, instead, be in agreement to live in a relationship

40 *Williams v. Williams,* 46 Wisc. 464, 1 N.W. 98, 101, 32 Am.Rep. 722 (1879).

41 With respect to the parties' awareness of the legal regulations, *see* Chapter 14 *infra,* notes 269-270 with references.

42 *Compare* Howard O. Hunter, *An Essay on Contract and Status: Race, Marriage and the Meretricious Spouse,* 64 VA. L. REV. 1039, 1044 (1978). *See also Wright v. Goss,* 229 Ga. App. 393, 494 S.E.2d 23, 25 (1997) and *Baynes v. Baynes,* 219 Ga.App. 848, 467 S.E.2d 195 (1996), in which the court stated that the "legal relationship constituting common law marriage cannot be partial or periodic."

without any requirement of fidelity,[43] or in a relationship terminable at will without any obligation to follow the regulations governing divorce. If so, a marital contract has not been entered into, with the consequence that no common law marriage has been established. The couple has not demonstrated any true marital intent.[44] A completely different perspective would be to find the existence of a marital contract and, thus, the establishment of a common law marriage, based upon their agreement, even though the conditions agreed to concerning fidelity and divorce are invalid. The marriage can then be based on a legal, more general status intent or an intent to live together.

It is probable, given the low level of public awareness, that it is also unrealistic to utilize a legal intent concerning just the mandatory legal consequences. A more limited and realistic ambition can be to require a more general intent to have a marriage-like status or legal relation; in other words, an intent to subjugate oneself to the legal consequences imposed by the state on spouses or cohabitants, or an intent to accept the rights and obligations that result from the regulatory system, without the parties having knowledge of all of them. This appears logical against the background that the legal consequences are automatically invoked without the parties coming to any specific agreement about each legal consequence. This is a result, primarily, of the legislation and case law. Therefore, it may be adequate to speak of a status intent, an intent "to create a marital status," or status as cohabitant, but not more. The depth of the intention does not need be so deep! It is a question of a requirement of a minimum legal intent. Parties having a status intent can be assumed to have an intent to clothe themselves in the rights and obligations that follow from marriage. However, should it be proven that the parties agreed that the mandatory regulations, for example, concerning fidelity and divorce, would not be applicable between them, they can scarcely be seen to have had an intent to have a marriage-like status. The depth of the intention, if the object of the parties' intent is a marriage-like status or a legal relationship, ought to then be comparable to life's reality. Marriage-like status is an indelible concept.[45] The parties may, in principal, chose to either accept the entire regulatory

43 A marriage in which the parties are free to have sexual relationships with other persons has sometimes been termed an "open-ended marriage," *see* R. Mazur, The New Intimacy, Open-ended Marriages and Alternative Life-Styles (1973).

44 In *Perales v. Flores,* 147 S.W.2d 974 (Tex.Civ.App. 1941), the parties had entered into a relationship which was to be "determinable at will" without any interference by public authorities. No contract establishing a common law marriage was found to exist. In *Swingle v. Keifer,* 105 Tex. 609, 153 S.W. 1132, 1133 (1913), the court stated that a contract where one or both of the parties can dissolve the contract "at will" could not legally establish a marriage contract.

45 *Compare In re Estate of Atwood,* 577 N.W.2d 60, 63 (Iowa App. 1998), in which no discussion concerning the use of an intent with respect to legal consequences was made, but in which the Iowa Court of Civil Appeals stated with respect to the woman: "The notion that she was married for some purposes and not for others is in flagrant contradiction of the public policy behind the high standard of proof required to

system or refrain from it, although marital agreements may include some opportunities to refrain from certain legal consequences. This is characteristic of marriage as a status relationship: "Take it or leave it!"

In a comparable manner, a requirement about the parties' *consensus* in a legally recognized cohabitation relationship could be formulated as a requirement to intend to achieve a legal status as a cohabitant or an intent to establish a legal relationship. The choice about the depth of intention can have significant consequences, for example, in the application of the regulations.

A contract, in which the object of the parties' intent is the marital status or a legal relation, is without doubt advantageous to individual freedom and the parties' legal certainty. This becomes even truer if the object is marriage's concrete legal consequences. For couples choosing to live together without formally marrying, specifically to avoid the legal consequences of marriage, it must be viewed as consistent and fair that such regulations do not govern them.[46] This can be the case, for example, with respect to couples with previous marriages who are now older and wish to have more independence in their new relationships. This can also be true of younger couples who choose to live together without marrying in order to remain more independent in relation to each other and the state. If the parties have, as in *State v. Walker* (1887), entered into an express agreement to live together as husband and wife "without any intention of being such in legal contemplation," it would conflict with their individual freedom and legal certainty if they were nevertheless viewed as a married couple because of their cohabitation or their intent to live together.[47] Based on this perception, there was reason for the court's statement in *Collier v. City of Milford* (1988): "One cannot be married unwittingly or accidentally."[48] Here, the requirement of a legal intent in the contract has a significant function.

The strength of this reasoning assumes, however, as indicated above, that the parties know about the legal consequences and that they have made a conscious legal choice by refraining from formal marriage. This is probably true with respect to certain couples.[49] Sociological surveys, however, indicate that most couples have limited knowledge of the legal

establish a valid marriage. We conclude, on this record, that no marriage contract was intended."

46 *Compare* Hunter, *supra* note 42, at 1095, who without directly discussing common law marriage, states: "To impose a marital status on an unmarried couple ... can both embroil the parties in the very obligations they sought to avoid and render legally meaningless the differences between marriage and 'living together'."

47 *State v. Walker*, 36 Kan. 297, 13 P. 279, 288-289 (1887).

48 *Collier v. City of Milford*, 537 A.2d 474, 479 (Conn. 1988). *See also Jennings v. Hurt*, 554 N.Y.S.2d 220, 221 (A.D. 1 Dep't 1990); and *State v. Newman*, 66 Mont. 180, 213 P. 805 (1923).

49 *See* Clark, *supra* note 15, at 452, who appears to assume that couples refraining from formally marrying have made a legal choice.

consequences of marriage and their assessment in determining whether to enter into a formal marriage or refrain from it is not primarily of a legal nature.[50] Despite this, those going through a marriage ceremony become married, and the legal consequences are invoked. Therefore, it has been maintained that a formal marriage can exist without the parties having any knowledge of marriage's legal regulations.[51] These result primarily from the legislation and case law, not from their contract. A separate issue is whether the parties can contractually circumvent the regulations through marital agreements.[52] There is nothing to indicate that persons choosing to enter into a common law marriage have more knowledge of the legal consequences of marriage.[53] The fact that these couples have

---

50 Both American and Swedish sociologists are in agreement that cohabitation without formal marriage is seldom the result of any considered decisions. According to Blumberg, *supra* note 8, at 1139-1140, formal marriage for most couples is not a conscious choice of legal regulations. *See also* Eleanor D Macklin, *Nonmarital Heterosexual Cohabitation*, MAR. FAM. REV, March/April, 1, 6 (1978): "Living together is seldom the result of a considered decision...Most cohabitation evolves from a drift of sleeping more and more frequently together and gradual accumulation of possessions in one residence...." *See also* TROST, *supra* note 24, at 63-64, 82, 101. The foremost reason for the couples the author interviewed as to why Swedish couples formally married was "tradition." Concerning relationships in Australia, the *Tasmania Law Reform Commission*, Report on Obligations Arising from De facto Relationships 5 (1977) stated: "Sometimes two people choose to live together in absolute freedom and choose not to marry, just to avoid the responsibilities of marriage. But, although this is becoming more common, it affects a small minority of *de facto* relationships, and we believe that the vast majority of people who live together without marrying do so without thought of the legal consequences."

51 McWalter, *supra* note 15, at 643: "Current marriage laws require neither familiarity with the laws governing the relationship...." The limited awareness couples have with respect to the legal consequences of marriage is also demonstrated by LEONORE J WEITZMAN, THE MARRIAGE CONTRACT, XV (1981). *See also* Leonore J. Weitzman, *Legal Regulation of Marriage: Tradition and Change.* 62 CAL. L. REV. 1169, 1170 (1974): "The marriage contract is unlike most contracts: its provisions are unwritten, its penalties are unspecified, and the terms of the contract are typically unknown to the 'contracting' parties. Prospective spouses are neither informed of the terms of the contract nor are they allowed any options about these terms. In fact, one wonders how many men and women would agree to the marriage contract if they were given the opportunity to read it and to consider the rights and obligations to which they were committing themselves." McWalter, *supra* note 15, at 643 states: "The empty formalism of present marriage law means that excessive numbers of couples who should not marry will, and that they will enter matrimony ignorant of the array of legal obligations and conditions that accrue to that 'status'." *See also* Carol S. Bruch, *Property Rights of De Facto Spouses Including Thoughts on the Value of Homemakers' Services*, 10 FAM.L.Q. 101, 135 (1977), who stated that unmarried cohabiting couples "enter their relationship...in ignorance of the legal consequences of either marriage or non-marriage (or) under the assumption that some legal protections are available."

52 It is unusual for spouses to exercise the ability to contract away the legal consequences following from the legislation, *see* Kandoian, *supra* note 28, at 1833.

53 The number of parties stating at trial that they generally were not aware of common law marriage prior to the trial is surprising, *see, e.g., State v. Newman*, 66 Mont. 180, 213 P. 805, 807 (1923) in which the man stated: "I first found out that there was such a thing as common law marriage by the authority of my attorney." *See also In re Erickson's Estate*, 75 S.D. 345, 64 N.W.2d 316, 320 (1954); *Taegen v. Taegen*, 61 N.Y.S.2d 869, 873 (1946); and *In re Binger's Estate*, 158 Neb. 444, 63 N.W.2d 784 (1954).

refrained from formally marrying is not, to any significant extent, the result of a legal decision. They simply live together, perhaps an entire lifetime together. The party benefiting from an application of the regulatory system, for example, in the case of a property division based on divorce or death, ought to be tolerant of the inconveniences pertaining to legal certainty. On the other side, the majority of couples, although not aware of all the legal consequences of marriage, know that choosing to have or refrain from a legal wedding ceremony has legal implications.

A contract based upon a legal intent also has a function in certain cases in which the cohabitation is found to be insufficient. Specifically, this is true if the insufficiencies have legitimate causes; for example, employment, education, health reasons, or military duty in a different geographic area, or relationships that prevent a more complete cohabitation.

It is clear that a contract with the requirement of an intent to live together includes difficulties in capturing cases in which the intended cohabitation is limited. The parties can, under such circumstances, establish an informal marriage only if the requirement of the cohabitation is placed at a minimum.[54] A contract based on a mutual intent to establish a legal relationship, on the other hand, can certainly give the parties the possibility of receiving the legal consequences of marriage or a cohabitation relationship.

Herein lies the strength, but also the weakness, of such a contract. A general problem arising from a contract construction based upon a mutual legal intent is that such a marriage or a cohabitation relationship could be entered into without the parties living together or having the intent to live together. This is true of couples involved in a sexual relationship or no relationship at all. The parties could enter into a marriage or cohabitation relationship analogous to a shell corporation only for the purpose of receiving the legal consequences. A man and a woman, as business partners, would be able to utilize property transactions in the form of a property division without the parties ever having lived in a marriage or cohabitation. The regulatory system would be applicable to situations in which it is not materially appropriate. The majority of the legal consequences of marriage or cohabitation are based on an actual

---

Compare Terry v. White, 58 Minn. 268, 59 N.W. 1013 (1894); and *Cross v. Cross*, 55 Mich. 287, 21 N.W. 313 (1884).

54 *Compare Krug v. Krug*, 296 So.2d 715 (1974), where the parties entered into a formal marriage which was, however, invalid due to a marital impediment and during the time from the removal of the impediment until his death, the man was on military duty in Vietnam. However, the parties exchanged letters and the man contributed to the woman's maintenance. Applying a very water-downed requirement of cohabitation, the court found the existence of a common law marriage. *See* Section 8.5.3 *supra*. The problem does not arise in states such as Pennsylvania, which do not have a requirement of cohabitation for the formation of a common law marriage, *see, e.g., Com. v. Amann*, 58 D. & C. 669 (1947), where the man, doing military duty in the Philippines, and the woman, living in Pennsylvania, signed a written contract which established a marriage.

marriage-like cohabitation. It appears that the best solution to this problem would be to have the objective requisite in the form of a requirement of actual cohabitation or a contract containing an intent to live together,

A similar problem is that a marital or cohabitation contract based on a legal intent has difficulty preventing sham marriages or relationships entered into for the purpose of receiving a specific legal consequence, for example, to facilitate immigration. Such relationships are typically entered into through formal weddings, but occasionally are based on a formless marriage.[55] The problem is that the parties actually possess a legal intent, namely, the right to immigrate. If the mutual intent is so limited, the existence of a sham relationship can certainly be prevented if the requirement of a general legal status intent is not fulfilled. Assume, however, that the parties' primary purpose is to allow one party to immigrate, but that, for a short time, they are prepared to completely accept a marital status and all of the legal consequences of marriage, but also intend, soon after the immigration, to dissolve the relationship through divorce. A simple requirement of mutual intent to create a legal relationship does not then prevent the existence of the marriage. Therefore, it is necessary to have either the requirement of an intent to live together or the requirement of actual cohabitation, in addition to the contract.[56]

There is scarcely any doubt that a requirement of an intent to establish a marital status or a legal relation, and, to an even greater degree, an intent to obtain the concrete legal consequences of marriage or cohabitation would considerably limit the scope of common law marriage or cohabitation law. Few contracts are express, and in a contract, either oral or written, it is unusual for the parties to express any legal intent. In the majority of cases in which the contract is an implied agreement based on the parties' actions, it is precarious to conclude the existence of a legal intent from their marriage-like cohabitation. That they live together does not necessarily speak to whether they have a mutual intent to establish a legal relation. The fact that the courts, in the judgments, many times have skimmed over the facts in this sense was noted above in Chapter 7.[57] An even stricter application in the case law of a requirement of an intent to create a legal relationship would further limit the scope of application of common law marriage. Thus, the more precise the requirement of legal intent, for example, the requirement of a more detailed intent as to legal consequences, the more couples will fall outside the concept of common law marriage and outside the rights but also the obligations following from marriage. From the perspective of the parties, this would mean that a number of couples not having made any legal assessments but simply

55 With respect to the treatment of sham marriages in the case law, *see* Section 6.5.3 *supra*.

56 Cohabitation as a necessary requisite and a protection against sham marriages is discussed in the following section.

57 *See* Section 7.8 *supra*.

living together would lose the rights following from marriage or cohabitation, respectively.

From the perspective of the state, it is clear that a requirement of a legal intent, and to a greater extent, an intent as to legal consequences, would limit the state's ability to control its citizens. All couples not possessing such an intent but simply living together would not be affected by the obligations of the legal regulatory system with respect to marriage. A state power, with moral viewpoints about how a man and a woman having a family and living their entire lives together ought to behave during their cohabitation and its dissolution, may no longer be able to influence the family. The state must then accept that the parties have not opted for the regulatory system. For example, a legal intent element would then be an impediment if the state wishes any of the following: the parties having children are to be faithful to each other and contribute to each other's maintenance; the regulations governing divorce are to be applicable upon the dissolution of their relationship; they are to divide their property in a certain manner; the children in the family are to have legitimacy; and the state is able to assess taxes or other official legal obligations based on the existence of a family.

It may be reasonable to tie government benefits to the parties' intent to live together regardless of whether they wish a legal consequence. The greater the requirement placed upon the parties' intent to obtain legal consequences, the more difficult it becomes to capture the lost sheep. This shortcoming frustrates a state with moral viewpoints about how its citizens ought to behave. This is particularly true in areas in which the state has mandatory regulations for formal marriage that cannot be circumvented by contract. For the state, which can even be viewed as a third party to the contract, having ambitions about controlling or influencing families and their lives, it is more advantageous, with an *ex ante* assessment, to tie the legal consequences of marriage to a contract whose intent element is an intent to live together, and with *ex post* assessment to tie them directly to the actual cohabitation as a necessary requisite. A more liberal state, on the other hand, is more disposed to accept the effects of a legal intent element and the free choice of individuals. Any stance taken on these issues is dependent on how the interests of the state and individuals are balanced against each other. There is reason to return to these ideological issues in Chapter 14.3.1, "Limitation of the Freedom of the Parties," in which we discuss the reasons for and against common law marriage and cohabitation legislation.

3. Both Cohabitation and a Legal Relationship as the Object of the Marital Intent

There is also a certain support in the American case law as seen above, for the notion that the parties must have both an intent to live together and an intent to establish a legal relation in order to establish a common law marriage.[58] This double requirement of the content of the intent, founded on good reasons, can be more precisely described as a mutual intent to live together as husband and wife in a monogamous and lifelong, or durable, relationship, to which, according to the spouses, the existing regulatory system is applicable. By this, both the advantages and disadvantages offered by both intent elements are obtained. The requirement of a legal intent exists for the purpose of guaranteeing that neither party in the relationship is forced to accept a regulatory system that he or she has not agreed to and may not desire. This is particularly important because cohabitation without marriage has become more common and more socially acceptable, and many couples face the choice of either living together informally or within marriage's legal regulatory system. The requirement of an intent to live together is designed to prevent sham marriages and ensure that the legal consequences of marriage are given to those for whom they are intended. At the same time, it ought to be noted that the requirement of an intent to establish a legal relationship most probably has the effect that many couples who have quite simply moved in together and continued to live a life together fall outside of the concept of marriage or a legally recognized cohabitation.

13.2.2 Expressed or Implied Agreements

It is not sufficient for the formation of a common law marriage that the parties internally have a mutual intent that is viewed as a marital *consensus* as examined in Chapter 6, "The Common Law Marriage Contract." The intent must also be outwardly manifested: "The law … requires not only consent but an expression of consent."[59] Despite the fact that American case law, with respect to the formless marital contract, has traditionally spoken of a contract *per verba* as such, only the courts in Pennsylvania and the District of Columbia, as we have found, have upheld the requirement of a verbal contract.[60] However, no particular word formulations have

---

58 *See* Section 6.3 *supra.* In *Seuss v. Schukat,* 358 Ill. 27, 192 N.E. 668, 671, 95 A.L.R. 1461 (1934), the court stated: "Marriage is a civil contract, by which man and woman agree to take each other for husband and wife during joint lives, unless it is terminated by law, and to discharge toward each other duties imposed by law on relationship assumed." *See also Lutwak v. United States,* 195 F.2d 748 (7th Cir. 1952), *aff'd,* 344 U.S. 604, 611 (1953), 73 S.Ct. 481, 97 L.Ed. 593 (1953), in which the United States Supreme Court, in dictum, appears to refer to both the actual cohabitation as well as the legal relationship. The Court stated that the common meaning of marriage, which Congress must have intended when enacting the regulations concerning "alien spouses" in the War Brides Act, is that "the two parties have undertaken to establish a life together and assume certain duties and obligations."

59 *In re Erickson's Estate,* 75 S.D. 345, 64 N.W.2d 319 (1954), *see* Section 6.5 *supra.*

60 *See* Section 6.2.2 *supra.* It ought to be noted that a common law marriage in Pennsylvania and the District of Columbia can be established with the support of the marriage presumption, *see* Chapter 9 *supra.* Observe that common law marriage, as was mentioned in Chapter 1, was repealed in Pennsylvania January 1, 2005, however not retroactively, *see* 23 Pa. Cons. Stat. Ann. 1103 (West 2005).

been required.[61] In the majority of cases, an oral contract is entered into in great privacy. There is a wide variety of possible expressions, but commonly, the important verbal act is a conversational utterance, on the fluctuating border between an oral contract and a simple statement.[62] Evidentiary difficulties arise from the absence, in the majority of cases, of written documentation and witnesses. The requirements of great scrutiny and evidence that is clear and convincing, therefore, appear to be well motivated even in the future.

There is no requirement of a verbal contract in the other jurisdictions, as seen in Chapter 7, "Implied Marriage Agreements." It is not necessary for the parties to exchange marital vows in order to constitute a common law marriage. There, the courts today accept inferred or implied agreements. In a proposal for a "revivified common law marriage," Marsha Garrison strongly emphasizes that the application of the regulations should be based on the parties' free will and commitment. Therefore, she is critical of proposals, such as the ALI Principles, which are based on the cohabitation of the parties, but accepts that the parties' *consensus* can be seen from the objective circumstances in the life the parties share.[63] The broad acceptance in the case law of the parties' cohabitation and reputation during the entire 1800s and 1900s as evidence for a marital contract

---

61 *Chambers v. Dickson*, 2 Ser. & R. 475 (Pa. 1816); *Commonwealth v. Haylow*, 17 Pa.Super. 541, 547 f (1901); *Hilton v. Roylance*, 25 Utah 129, 69 P. 660 (1902); *Consolidated Underwriters v. Kelly*, 15 S.W.2d 229 (Tex.Comm'n App. 1929); *In re McKanna's Estate*, 106 Cal.App.2d 126, 234 P.2d 673, 675 (1951); *Nat'l Union Fire Ins. Co. v. Britton*, 187 F.Supp. 359, 364 (C.D.C. 1960); *Com. ex rel. McDermott v. McDermott*, 236 Pa.Super.Ct. 541, 345 A.2d 914, 917 (1975); *Estate of Gavula*, 490 Pa. 535, 417 A.2d 168, 171 (1980); *In re Estate of Stauffer*, 504 Pa. 626, 476 A.2d 354, 355 (1984); *Cann v. Cann*, 632 A.2d 322, 325 (Pa.Super. 1993); *Coates v. Watts*, 622 A.2d 25 (D.C.App. 1993); and *Staudenmayer v. Staudenmayer*, 714 A.2d 1016, 1022 (Pa. 1998).

62 The woman in *Caddy v. Johnstown Firemen's Relief Ass'n of Pennsylvania*, 196 A. 590, 591-592 (Pa.Super. 1938) stated: "He asked me if I was willing to live that way." Thereafter, the man had said: "I am satisfied." Based on this exchange of words between the man and the woman, and the fact that within the relationship from that point until the man's death, they lived together and had a reputation as husband and wife, the court found that a common law marriage had been established. In *Nyhuis v. Pierce*, 114 N.E.2d 75, 76 (Ohio App. 1952), the parties had obtained a "marriage license," after which the man said: "Now we are tied up for good." The woman assumed she was married to him. Thereafter the man said to some fellow workers the couple met later that day: "I want you folks to meet my wife. We were just married this morning." The court found that the parties had entered into a marital contract *in praesenti*.

63 Garrison, *supra* note 10, at 884-890. The author maintains that the proposal, which is inspired by the principles of estoppel, does not rest on "who said what to whom" and on a subjective meeting of the minds as does the traditional common law marriage doctrine (according to that author's view), but on "objective, concrete actions, filing joint tax returns, taking title to property as husband and wife, using marital names, holding a commitment ceremony at which marriage-like vows are exchanged – that would justifiably lead each partner to assume a marital agreement and rely on it," *id.* at 886. These circumstances, however, are well known from 200 years of inferred common law marriage agreements, *see* Chapter 7 and *compare* Chapter 9 as to the common law marriage presumption, *supra*.

has made it possible to capture many relationships that otherwise would have fallen outside marriage's legal system. This coincides with the fact that a majority of couples living together formlessly have never entered into any verbal contract, oral or written. They simply drift into a common law marriage.[64] On the other hand, they often make admissions and declarations concerning their marital status. When such statements are cited as evidence for the existence of a contract, the boundary between express and implied agreements becomes even more unclear.

Despite the development in the case law, there have been no extensive policy discussions on the issue of whether implied agreements should be accepted. A significant exception, however, can be found in Texas, where lawmakers at the end of the 1960s codified the principle that a marital contract could be proven if the parties "lived together as husband and wife" and "represented to others that they were married."[65] However, the Texas legislation was repealed in 1989 as the result of a notorious lawsuit, but without changing the law. The same circumstances can today, without statutory support, be cited as evidence for an inferred agreement.[66]

Against the background given above, there is reason to question how the parties' marital *consensus* on a common law marriage or cohabitation relationship should be expressed. Is it reasonable, looking toward the future, to require a verbal contract (written or oral), or should it be sufficient through a simple implied agreement?

1. Arguments for Implied Agreements

What arguments can be marshaled to support the requirement of an implied agreement with the formation of a common law marriage or a legal recognized cohabitation relationship?

The most striking reason behind the use of implied agreements is the high evidentiary value of the parties' actions in determining the existence of a contract. This is based on the idea that, as the court in the case of *In re Wagner's Estate* (1960) stated, "certain acts may speak as loudly as words."[67]

---

64 *See* Section 7.1 *supra*. *See also* Clarice M. Davis, *Common-Law-Marriage in Texas*, 21 Sw. L.J. 647, 662 (1967); HOMER H. CLARK, JR., THE LAW OF DOMESTIC RELATIONS IN THE UNITED STATES 49 (1968); Kandoian, *supra* note 28, at 1842–1843; *People v. Lucero*, 747 P.2d 660, 664 (Colo. 1987); *Russell v. Russell*, 838 S.W.2d 909, 913 (Tex. App.-Beaumont 1992); TROST, *supra* note 24, at 63–64; Macklin, *supra* note 50, at 6; and Caudill, *supra* note 29, at 565.

65 Act of June 2, 1969, 61 st Leg., R.S. ch. 888, § 1.91, 1969, TEX. GEN. LAWS 2707. 2717: TEX. FAM. CODE ANN. § 1.91 (b) (Vernon 1975).

66 Act of June 14, 1989, 71 st Leg., R.S., ch. 369, § 9, 1989, effective Sept 1 1989, TEX. GEN. LAWS 1459, 1461.

67 *Wagner's Estate*, 398 Pa. 531, 159 A.2d 495, 498 (1960). The fact that the parties' actions can be as significant as their words from an evidentiary perspective can be seen already with JOHN HUBBACK, A TREATISE ON THE EVIDENCE OF SUCCESSION TO REAL AND PERSONAL PROPERTY AND PEERAGES (London W. Benning 1844): "The parties' assertions of marriage and the general reputation of the fact may be evidenced with as much strength and distinctness by actions as by words." *See also Tummalty v. Tummalty*, Bradf. 369, 371 (N.Y. 1855), in which the court gave the ten-year cohabitation a higher

The same high evidentiary value of the actions can be seen in Clark: "It would place a wholly unjustifiable emphasis on form to require the parties to say 'we hereby agree to be husband and wife,' when they are already giving ample evidence by their conduct that this is their understanding."[68] However, the general validity of these statements must be questioned, especially with respect to the content being assumed about the intent.

On the other hand, if the object of the marital intent is "to live together as husband and wife" and the parties actually do this, perhaps for many years, it is clear that the cohabitation ought to be given considerable evidentiary value. With such an object, the outcomes of several of the cases cited in Chapter 7, in which the parties had cohabited for a long period of time, and in which the marital contract was found proven, are unsurprising.[69] Applying the same object for the intent, however, it cannot be assumed that a cohabitation of only a few months expresses an intent to live their entire lives together.[70]

Family patterns and the relationships between men and women since the late 1990s have undergone radical changes. The same stigma is not associated today, as before, with living together without formally having entered into marriage. Such relationships, therefore, have become much more common. The group of persons living together without formally entering into marriage comprises many different relationships. Certain couples live together for a period of time on a trial basis, thereafter separating and perhaps beginning a relationship with someone else. Others live together without any long-term intentions. For others, the first period of cohabitation is followed by a formal marriage or a formless cohabitation for life. Another dimension of this picture is that the number of divorces has increased dramatically.

This increased movement and variety with respect to couples' intentions about their relationships have resulted in the fact that the evidentiary value of their actions, which outwardly can appear to be very similar, has decreased. An actual cohabitation today can certainly encompass both cases, in which the first months of cohabitation are the beginning of a long life together, and the parties cohabit day by day without having any intentions covering a longer period. The new day shows only that the previous one has ended!

---

evidentiary value than the man's "stale conversations and private statements" with reference to the belief that society "would not be safe for a moment."

68 HOMER H. CLARK, JR., THE LAW OF DOMESTIC RELATIONS IN THE UNITED STATES II, 112 (2d ed. 1987). In addition to the representation of the high evidentiary value of the actions, sometimes a closely related argument is added, namely that it would be an expression of an exaggerated formalism to require something additional. MICHAEL GROSSBERG, GOVERNING THE HEART: LAW AND THE FAMILY IN NINETEENTH-CENTURY AMERICA 79–80 (1985), examining the developments during the 1800s, speaks of "a clear policy decision favoring practice over form."

69 With respect to the case law, *see* Section 7.6 *supra*.

70 *Id.*

Add to this picture, however, the fact that the evidentiary evaluations also include statements in the form of admissions and declarations by the parties concerning their marital intention. These are cited as evidence for, as well as against the existence of a contract and can facilitate the evidentiary evaluation.[71]

The evidentiary value of contracts can vary from one to the next, even in contracts in which the cohabitation is the object of the parties' mutual intent. Therefore, the courts have reason to scrutinize the evidence in the light of this variation.

On the other hand, if the object of the intent is a legal element, for example, the intent to change the parties' legal status or to assume the marital duties and obligations of husband and wife,[72] it is clear that the cohabitation, even though it has been long term, ought to be given no more than a limited evidentiary value.[73] The same is true in the application of cohabitation legislation that requires an intent by cohabiting persons to obtain the rights and obligations provided by the legislation. When the content of the intent is determined in this manner, it is not surprising that the courts, in several of the above-cited cases, despite a long-term cohabitation, did not find proof of any marital contract.[74] The cohabitation can certainly indicate promises made by the parties to each other if they, thereafter, fulfill marital obligations. However, the cohabitation need not prove that the parties have decided to apply the central regulations pertaining to marital divorce and property division. The parties can very well have the intent to live entire lives together, but without marital rights and obligations. This intent can even be the reason why they have not formally married!

Nevertheless, whether the parties' conduct may speak as loudly as words can, consequently, in some instances, be questioned if the contract is based on an intent to live together, and especially if the contract is based on a legal intent.

Such doubts should encourage more restrictiveness by the courts in finding the existence of an inferred marital contract, which predictably, as Kathryn Vaughn feared with respect to the legislative development in Texas, should have had the consequence of placing many couples outside of the legal protections offered by common law marriage.[75] This, however,

---

71 With respect to the evidentiary value of admissions and declarations in the case law, *see* Section 7.5.2 *supra.*

72 *Jambrone v. David,* 16 Ill.2d 32, 156 N.E.2d 569, 572 (1959).

73 The court's notation in the case of *In re Erickson's Estate,* 75 S.D. 345, 64 N.W.2d 316, 320 (1954), concerning "the untrustworthiness of mere cohabitation and reputation as proof of marriage" has an increased pertinence today.

74 With respect to the cases where the courts have not found any marital contract proven, despite a long-term cohabitation, *see* Section 7.7 *supra.*

75 Kathryn S. Vaughn, Comment, *The Recent Changes to the Texas Informal Marriage Statute: Limitation or Abolition of Common Law Marriage?,* 28 Hous. L. Rev. 1131, 1161 (1991).

appears to be the inevitable price that must be paid! On one side, it violates the truth to offer protection by pretending that the cohabitation proves something that it does not! If this is not acceptable, but it is still considered desirable to offer, in the new situation, broader legal protection, there are other methods for achieving this goal. Among these is to tie the legal consequences directly to the cohabitation, while eliminating the contract element.

The second significant argument behind the use of an inferred agreement is that it gives legal protection to the majority of couples who do not formalize their relationship with a wedding. This, one of the leading justifications for the entire institution of common law marriage, has great practical significance today, given that the parties, as stated above, often "drift into" a common law marriage without entering into any express contract thereof. Common law marriage, in its current construction, but without the acceptance of implied agreements, would leave many couples outside the legal protections that the institution was created to provide.

The reason for legal protection is given in many of the decisions by the courts. To ignore circumstantial evidence in determining the existence of a common law marriage, according to *Laurence v. Laurence* (1896), would be to "threaten the legitimacy of children and the rights of heirs, and endanger the social fabric which rests on the institution of marriage."[76] Several legal scholars stress the same reasoning. Nancy Shaw, consequently, states: "That the parties be precluded from all protection merely because they have never verbalized their commitment to one another, although their conduct towards one another clearly indicated that such a commitment in fact existed, is unduly rigid."[77] Kathryn Vaughn, who criticized the repeal in Texas in 1989 of the legislation accepting the parties' cohabitation and outward representation as evidence for the existence of a marital contract, maintains that the burden of proving an express agreement is simply too high for most persons attempting to establish a common law marriage to meet, and that the legislative amendments would lead to a number of unjust results.[78]

The legal protection argument, however, must also be assessed in light of the content of the contract. Through the implied agreement, the use of

76 *Laurence v. Laurence*, 164 Ill. 367, 45 N.E. 1071, 1072 (1896). *See also* with more general wording, *In re Estate of Kovalchick*, 345 Pa.Super. 229, 498 A.2d 374, 376 (1985): "Because it is often difficult to prove a civil contract of marriage, the law has permitted that it be established by circumstantial evidence." *See also* with respect to older law, CLARK 1987, *supra* note 70, at 107-108.

77 Nancy Rebecca Shaw, Note, *Common Law Marriage and Unmarried Cohabitation: An Old Solution to a New Problem*, 39 U. PITT. L. REV. 579, 592 (1977).

78 Vaughn, *supra* note 77, at 1155 and 1159. The argumentation is sometimes given a moral overtone. To find, from the parties' cohabitation and reputation as spouses, the existence of a marital contract is consequently, according to the court in *Leibrock v. Leibrock*, 63 Ohio Law Abs. 565, 107 N.E.2d 418, 423 (Ohio Com.Pl. 1952), even compatible with and for the purpose of "morality and decency."

an intent to live together gives legal protection to those who, with the support of the cohabitation and other circumstances, demonstrate that they have a mutual intent to permanently live a life together, but not, in contrast, to those couples simply living together on a trial basis or those living together without truly having a mutual intent with respect to their cohabitation. Proof other than their cohabitation, for example, their declarations and admissions, can indicate something else. Again, if a legal intent is an element of the contract, it is likely that fewer couples would be allowed to enjoy the legal protections of common law marriage or legally recognized cohabitation because the evidentiary value of the parties' cohabitation is then considerably more limited. One method of offering a broader legal protection is to, instead, tie the legal consequences directly to the cohabitation and eliminate the contract element. This approach, however, has disadvantages, as discussed further below.

Yet another argument in favor of the acceptance of implied agreements is that, disregarding the circumstantial evidence would open the door to various forms of fraud and abuse. This argument takes into account the possibility that the parties would easily be able to make oral statements concerning their mutual intention, that lack any basis in reality, but which could nevertheless become the basis of a contract. To ignore circumstantial evidence when determining the existence of a common law marriage has, therefore, been considered to open the door to fraud and imposition, and invite perjury.[79] Another way to prevent misuse is to simply require an actual cohabitation. The danger of abuse and fraud, otherwise, is generally the main reason for not accepting common law marriage and cohabitation legislation. More on this in the next chapter.

An additional argument that supports the acceptance of implied agreements and corresponds to the reasoning behind common law marriage in general is society's interest in capturing as many couples as possible by regulations "in favor of marriage and against concubinage."[80] The efficacy of this function is naturally also dependent upon the content of the contract's intent. The method is more successful if based on an intent to live together, rather than a legal intent, and is probably most effective if the legal consequences are not tied to any contract, but directly to the cohabitation.

2. *Arguments Against Implied Agreements*

Predictably, a contract that can exist without the parties' consideration and without any explicit promises can fail to make it clear to the parties

---

79 *Laurence v. Laurence*, 164 Ill. 367, 45 N.E. 1071, 1072 (1896). *Compare Tummalty v. Tummalty*, 3 Bradf. 369, 371 f (N.Y. 1855), in which the court gave the ten-year cohabitation a higher evidentiary value than the man's "stale conversations and private statements" with reference to the fact that society "would not be safe for a moment."

80 *Linsey v. Jefferson*, 68 Okla. 156, 172 P. 641, 642 (1918).

whether legal regulations are applicable to their relationship. The legal consequences can come as a surprise for one or both of the parties. Employing implied agreements, therefore, creates, first of all, a lack of legal certainty. This argument, the main one against the institution of common law marriage generally, as further discussed in Chapter 14, "Arguments for and Against Common Law Marriage and Cohabitation Law," was cited in connection with the legislative reform concerning common law marriage enacted in Texas in 1989. A proposal concerning the repeal of the institution was submitted,[81] but a compromise was finally adopted.[82] The formless marriage survived, but the legislation was amended on two issues. For the purpose of avoiding the risk that parties would have the threat of litigation hanging over their heads indefinitely into the future, a statute of limitations was enacted. A claim concerning the existence of a common law marriage must be filed within one year, which was later amended to two years, from the dissolution of the relationship, and changed to a presumption. Further, a section of the legislation was repealed that expressly allowed the courts to find the existence of a marital contract from the facts that the parties lived together as husband and wife and that they represented to others that they were married.[83] Despite the repeal of this clause within the marriage legislation, there still is the possibility, as examined in Chapter 7, of proving the existence of a marital *consensus* with the support of general principles concerning circumstantial evidence.[84]

The value of the legal certainty argument is also affected by the intent employed. The requirement of an intent to live together introduces significant legal uncertainty if the parties assume that the formation of a marriage entails a mutual intent to obtain a certain legal status, and the parties may have clearly refrained from formally marrying for the purpose

81 State Representative Patricia Hill from Dallas submitted a proposal in 1989 for the repeal of common law marriage in Texas, House Bill (H.B.) No. 588, 71st Leg.Sess. (1989). The primary reason behind the proposal was the legal uncertainty with respect to the parties' status upon dissolution of a common law marriage, *see* Patricia Hill, floor debate remarks, 71st Leg.Sess., House Recording No. (H.R.) 62 and 78. H.B. 588 was adopted by a bare majority in the House of Representatives (73 votes against 61), but was not voted on by the Senate. The objections with respect to the repeal of common law marriage were based, inter alia, upon reference to the needs of children and women for protection in formless relationships. State Representative Ron Wilson was among the critics, viewing the legislative proposal as "the yuppie shackin' up insurance bill."

82 Senate Bill, (S.B.) No. 307 (Senate Author: Bob Glasgow, House Sponsor: Patricia Hill). Senate Recording No. 127.

83 Act of June 14, 1989, 71 st Leg., R.S., ch. 369 § 9, 1989, effective Sept 1 1989, Tex. Gen. Laws 1459, 1461. The one-year statute of limitations for filing a claim has been extended to two years and is no longer absolute. After the expiration of the period, it is presumed that the parties have not entered into a marital contract, *see* Act of April 17, 1997, 75th Leg., R.S., ch. 7, § 1, 1997 Tex. Sess. Law. Serv. 15 (Vernon 1997), today TEX. FAM. CODE ANN. § 2.401 (a)(2) and in § 6.202 (Vernon Pamph. 1998).

84 For further discussion, *see* Section 7.4 *supra*.

of avoiding the legal consequences of marriage or a legally recognized cohabitation. Most likely, the danger, from a legal certainty perspective, is less if a legal intent is employed, in particular, an intent covering legal consequences.

Second, the review of the cases in Chapter 7 demonstrates clearly that the acceptance of implied agreements creates extensive application problems with both substantive and evidentiary aspects that give rise to unnecessary and expensive litigation. This argument, however, must also be assessed against the background of the content of the intent being employed. The requirement of an intent to live together would most likely entail significant application problems, while a strict requirement of legal intent would most likely minimize application problems in many cases. Generally, considerable application problems should be anticipated in the use of implied agreements.

The application and legal certainty problems that the acceptance of implied agreements creates, however, are not considered sufficient to actually prohibit implied agreements, as attempted by the lawmakers in Texas. We have certainly strongly questioned the general validity of the statement, "certain acts may speak as loudly as words," whose viability is largely dependent on which object is chosen for the mutual intent. However, to forbid implied agreements appears to go too far. This is not so much because they capture and give legal protection to relationships that would otherwise be excluded, but rather, despite everything, they contribute to the proof concerning the parties' intentions. A repeal would be contrary to general principles and hinder the presentation of the best evidence. A prohibition would entail that the courts would have to assess, instead, the oral contract between the parties. As seen in Chapter 6, such contracts are often entered into in privacy and are based on conversational statements, *i.e.*, the evidentiary and application problems would most likely not be reduced.

The boundary between express and implied agreements is not a bright line. The best evidence ought to be produced so that the parties' oral statements can be assessed in a wider context, taking into account the situation in which the statements were made, as well as the parties' actions, their cohabitation and intent as spouses, and other circumstances. In this broader context, a case concerning a statement that is difficult to interpret clearly expresses the parties' mutual marital intentions. In a different case, the consideration of circumstantial evidence allows a clear determination of whether the oral statements made by the parties constitute a contract. A cohabitation that, in a concrete case, does not say too much about the parties' intentions, supplemented by their statements, can demonstrate their mutual intent. It would, therefore, be wrong to forbid circumstantial evidence in the proving of a marital or cohabitation contract.

A reduction of the application and legal certainty problems that the inferred agreement entails ought, instead, occur by narrowing the definition of the object of the marital intent and strictly applying the law. A stricter application of general civil legal principles with respect to the execution of the contract forming the basis of the common law marriage would also be beneficial, even though it must be carried out cautiously.[85] A stricter application of the basic requirements of offer and acceptance would primarily be designed to guarantee that neither party in the relationship was forced to enter an agreement that meant submitting to a regulatory system, an agreement that he or she neither desired nor chose. This is of particular significance in a time in which cohabitation without marriage has become more common and more socially acceptable, and many couples face the choice of living together either formlessly or within the legal regulatory system of marriage or cohabitation.

One effect ought to be that many couples will fall outside of the legal protections offered by common law marriage or cohabitation legislation. This, however, appears to be the inevitable price that one has to pay!

3. The Enactment of a Form Requirement

One logical way to limit application problems is to enact a form requirement with regard to the marital or cohabitation contract. A written contract has a function to fulfill in situations in which the parties are geographically distanced from each other and cannot be present at a wedding ceremony or the formless execution of a contract.[86] A written contract, adequately drafted and signed by both parties, clearly serves the interest of legal certainty. The parties have reason to think through what they actually and legally are doing, as well as the fact that a written contract can simultaneously help avoid evidentiary difficulties and conflicts.[87] However, an inconvenience caused by the requirement of a writing is that it would exclude many couples from common law marriage and cohabitation legislation. As seen in Chapter 6, the use of a written contract is limited, given that the voluntary forms are unattractive to those who have refrained from a wedding ceremony. Naturally, the objection can be made that a requirement of a writing is accepted in other civil legal contexts, for example, in the transfer of the ownership of real estate, and that information as to a requirement of a writing can affect behavior.

85 Despite the general proclamations that common law marriage rests upon a civil legal contract, we found in Chapter 6 that the courts' application of general contractual principles to the executed contract has been rudimentary at best, *see* Section 6.5.1 *supra*.

86 When common law marriage was repealed the first time in New York, a possibility to enter into a marriage through a written contract witnessed by two people was enacted, *see* Laws of 1901, c. 339, § 6; Domestic Relations Law § 19. *See* Fred S. Hall, *Common Law Marriage in New York State*, 30 COLUM. L. REV. 1, 10–11 (1930).

87 *McCoy v. McCoy*, 868 P.2d 527 (Idaho App. 1994) (*dictum*).

A similar, common solution is to enact some form of a registration of the parties' contract.[88] Then, however, we are no longer dealing with formless marriage, but rather a variation of formal marriage, which, strictly speaking, falls outside of the framework of this presentation. A registration procedure, which is well worth considering, would most likely solve a number of the application problems that today are associated with common law marriage and cohabitation legislation. Such a procedure would also effectively serve legal certainty, because the parties then can be assumed to be more aware of what they legally are entering into and when the legal relationship arises. However, it ought to be noted that such a system would most likely result in a considerable group of persons, which common law marriage today is designed to regulate, falling outside of the rights and obligations created within the marital regulatory system. See the relevant proposal in Chapter 14.

If, despite this, the application and legal certainty problems are considered to be too burdensome, the most realistic alternative would be to not forbid implied agreements but rather to consider a repeal of the entire institution of common law marriage, as discussed further in the next chapter.

In certain American states recognizing common law marriage, there is even the possibility of allowing the registration of the relationship. Consequently, the marital legislation in Texas grants cohabiting couples the right to a "Declaration and Registration of Informal Marriage."[89] The declaration, in writing and made on a form before a county clerk, is to contain *inter alia* the following: "I solemnly swear (or affirm) that we, the undersigned, are married to each other by virtue of the following facts: On or about (date) we agreed to be married, and after that date we lived together as husband and wife and in this state we represented to others that we were married. Since that day of marriage to the other party I have not been married to any other person." The parties are also to certify that they have the legal capacity to enter into a marriage. After the declaration is registered, it constitutes *prima facie* evidence of the parties' marriage.[90] This ought, therewith, to break any presumption supporting a later ceremonial marriage or common law marriage.[91]

---

88 *See, e.g.*, Davis, *supra* note 66, at 663, who correctly maintains that the use of "fictional agreements is obviously the most pressing problem," proposing the enactment of some sort of registration process. We return to this issue in Chapter 15 *infra*.

89 Tex. Fam. Code Ann. § 2.402 (Vernon 2005). Even in *Montana*, there is the possibility for a couple, not wishing to enter into a ceremonial marriage, to give a written "declaration of marriage" in front of the county clerk at the district court, *see* Mont. Code Ann. § 40-1-311 (Mont. Leg. Serv. Div. 2003).

90 Tex. Fam. Code Ann. § 2.404 (d) (Vernon 2005).

91 That common law marriages constitute impediments against later ceremonial or common law marriages, *see* Section5.3.1 *supra*.

13.3 COHABITATION AS A NECESSARY REQUISITE

When we discussed, in the previous section, the function that a contract element can have in the formation of a common law marriage or cohabitation relationship, the contract solutions were presented as alternatives to an establishment simply based on the parties' cohabitation, whose consequences were also noted. In contrast, we will discuss the need for and the use of the requisite of cohabitation in addition to the contract. The starting point of this discussion, of course, which was presented in Chapter 8, "Cohabitation, Holding Out, and Reputation as Spouses," where we noted that, with respect to the status of the current law, thirteen of the fifteen American jurisdictions examined now have a requirement of cohabitation in addition to the contract. One of the main purposes of this section is to critically evaluate the reasons behind the pure contract principle, the development of the requisite of cohabitation, and then explore the possible function of such a requisite in the future. Further, based on these reflections, we will then discuss a suitable formulation for the requisite of cohabitation.

13.3.1 The Need for a Requisite of Cohabitation

One of the principal arguments in support of the pure contract principle and against the acceptance of cohabitation as a necessary requisite is that a requirement of cohabitation conflicts with the Justinian and canon law principles of *consensus, non concubitus, facit nuptias,* which, as seen in Chapter 8, historically played an important role in the discussions concerning the current law. However, aside from the fact that the historical validity of the principle cannot be questioned,[92] this argument cannot be given the same weight in a critical discussion about the future. It has certainly been maintained that both the form-bound and the formless marriage are contracts, their only distinction being form. Because no requirement of cohabitation is made with respect to ceremonial marriages, according to Hugh Ross, no such requirement ought to be made with respect to informal marriages.[93] However, the objection can be made that it is precisely the absence of form that creates the need for a substitute capable of serving the same purpose, and that a requisite of cohabitation do just that. Not least, this approach protects against a hasty contract, as discussed later. Another general argument supporting the pure contract

92 With respect to the free Roman marriage, it has been maintained by certain legal historians that for the establishment of such a marriage, in addition to the parties' *consensus,* it was required that the woman enter the man's house, *deductio in domum mariti, see* Section 2.4.2 *supra.*

93 Hugh A. Ross, *The Ohio Law of Marriage,* 14 W. RESERVE L. REV. 724, 732 (1963).

principle, which has its basis in general civil law,[94] is the interest of maintaining a consistent civil law approach. Such an argument, however, must always confront the objection that a marital contract is a contract *sui generis* that has its own terms and conditions.

Another argument supporting the pure contract principle is that it creates inconsistencies in the legal system if the cohabitation, on one side, was given as a condition for the formation of a marriage, and on the other side, was viewed as outside of marriage, and even criminalized before the marriage could be established. This argument is given *inter alia* by Otto Koegel, who somewhat sharply states: "A doctrine that requires two persons to fornicate a number of times before they create a legal status is absurd. Must they live together as husband and wife before they are husband and wife and this too in the face of a provision of the criminal law that persons who do this without first being married are guilty of a crime?"[95]

First, it ought to be noted that, in Koegel's view, the "absurdity" he speaks of has a long history. The combination of penal consequences and civil legal recognition was the church's response to formless marriages, even before the Council of Trent. Through the penal sanctions, the church strongly favored ceremonial marriages, while simultaneously accepting, under the civil law, an actual cohabitation combined with a contract. Through this, the lost sheep were captured not only within the legal system of marriage's rights, but also by its obligations.[96] This same strategy has characterized the policy of the secular legal system.[97] Despite this, one cannot

---

94 Already in *Dalrymple v. Dalrymple,* (1811) 2 Hagg.Cons. 54, 62-64, 161 Eng.Rep. 665, 668-669, the following was stated: "Marriage being a contract is of course consensual ... for it is of the essence of all contracts to be constituted by the consent of parties..." *See also* Blackstone: "Our law considers marriage in no other light than as a civil contract," *see* 1 Black. Com. 433, 439. The understanding that marriage is based on a contract appears again in all of the leading American cases from the 1800s, albeit it is more uncertain whether any additional requirements are made. *See Fenton v. Reed,* 4 Johns. 52, 4 Am.D. 244 (N.Y. 1809): "A contract of marriage made *per verba de praesenti* amounts to an actual marriage, and is as valid as if made *in facie ecclesiae....*" An expressed understanding that common law marriage, comparable to marriage at canon law, is legally qualified as a contract is also established in the later leading case of *Meister v. Moore,* 96 U.S. 76, 78, 24 L.Ed. 826 (1877), in which the Court stated: "Marriage is everywhere regarded as a civil contract." In *Askew v. Dupree,* 30 Ga. 173, 176, 177, 178, 179, 189 (1869), the contract principle is applied, citing both Scottish and older English law.

95 Otto E. Koegel, Common Law Marriage and Its Development in the United States 128 (1922). *See also Davis v. Stouffer,* 132 Mo.App. 555, 112 S.W. 282, 284 (1908); and Ross, *supra* note 95, at 732.

96 *Compare* with respect to the canon law, Section 3.3.2 *supra.*

97 The fact that a violation of the regulations concerning marriage licenses and weddings is criminally punishable does not result in the invalidity of a marriage, *see, e.g., In re Stopps' Estate,* 244 Iowa 931, 57 N.W.2d 221 (1953); and *State v. Ward,* 204 S.C. 210, 28 S.E.2d 785, 786 (1944). In Iowa, the omission of observing certain of the form regulations for marriage can result in fines of up to $50 for both of the parties, *see* Iowa Code Ann. § 595.11 (West 2003). *See, e.g.,* Coleman v. Graves, 122 N.W.2d 853 (Iowa 1963). In Kansas, which also recognizes common law marriage, a comparable

overlook the inherent contradiction that was offset by the decriminalization of nonmarital cohabitation, a ubiquitous development during the second half of the 1900s. A separate issue is the requirement of cohabitation, as maintained by Koegel, which creates application problems, not least with respect to the time for the establishment of the marriage, as discussed later below.

A significant argument behind the pure contract principle that has not received the attention it merits is that a requirement of cohabitation can exclude cases from the marital regulatory system that should, for other reasons, involve the legal consequences of marriage or a legally recognized cohabitation. This can concern cases in which a more complete cohabitation has not been possible, for example, because one of the parties has had a separate residence or household in a different geographical area as a result of employment, military duty, or health reasons. We found in Chapter 8 that the courts, in certain cases, either highly dilute or eliminate the requirement of cohabitation.[98] Such exceptions require a closer analysis and definition of the element of "possibility" and ought to have difficulties in avoiding considerable application difficulties.

To support the application of the pure contract principle in such cases, it can be argued that the parties live together in the same manner as a formally married couple would in a similar situation. However, if the parties do not actually live together, it is debatable whether they should be granted the legal consequences of marriage or a legally recognized cohabitation, which is mostly intended for couples that have lived or live together. The autonomy of the parties is an added reason to base legal effects on the parties' agreement to live together for the long term or legally create a relationship. The difficulties of the contract approach can persist as long as no specific form is required. Moreover, couples in the situation at issue may also obtain the legal effects of marriage by entering into a formal marriage.

As seen from Chapter 8, the idea that cohabitation between the parties ought to be a necessary requisite in addition to the contract is based on the conception of marriage as not simply just a contract between two parties, but also a concern for the entire family and society at large. In *Sheffield v. Sheffield* (1848), the first Chief Justice for the Texas Supreme Court stated: "The parties have pledged themselves, not only for their own happiness, but for purposes important to society ..."[99] The rights and obligations

omission can result in fines between $500-1,000 or a prison sentence of at least one, but not more than three, months of jail, *see* KAN. STAT. ANN. § 23-118 (2002). *See Smith v. Smith*, 161 K.I., 165 P.2d 593 (1946); and *State ex rel. Baird v. Anderson*, 114 Kan. 297, 217 P. 327, 330 (1923). Despite the fact that common law marriage was forbidden in Ohio, the State recognized common law marriages entered into prior to October 10, 1991, as valid, *see* OHIO REV. CODE ANN. § 3105.12 (B)(1-2) (West 1991).

98 *See* Section 8.5.3 *supra*.

99 *Sheffield v. Sheffield*, 3 Tex. 79, 85-86 (1848).

following from marriage are not simply the result of the agreement between the spouses. Marriage constitutes a status relationship with extensive legal consequences that are never regulated in a marital contract but that follow primarily from legislation and case law. A number of these legal consequences cannot be influenced by the parties' intent. A typical consequence is that the establishment of a marriage ought not rest solely on the parties' agreement. Society has an interest in ensuring that the parties' promise to live an entire life together is also followed by a cohabitation that establishes a marriage.[100] A comparable reasoning, to a significant degree, can be viewed as also applicable to cohabitation relationships.

It is clear that this societal intervention minimizes the significance of the contract and opens the door to other requisites. However, it cannot be taken for granted that it is in the best interest of society to always base the legal consequences on a requisite of cohabitation. The formation of a formal marriage, which many view to be the basis of the entire Christian civilization, does not require cohabitation. Even though the legal consequences of marriage or a legally recognized cohabitation are determined by the state, in certain cases, it can serve the goals of public policy to tie legal consequences to the parties' contract. This can be true in the above-cited cases in which cohabitation was not possible in its fullest sense for completely legitimate reasons. Nevertheless, the state can have an interest in placing the obligations of marriage or a legally recognized cohabitation on a couple, including the obligation to pay maintenance, be faithful to each other, observe the regulations governing divorce, etc.

A fundamental reason behind the requirement of cohabitation, as seen in Chapter 8, is that many of the legal consequences of marriage are intended for marriages effected through cohabitation.[101] This factor is based on good reasons, but its importance is dependent upon the legal consequence intended. In the public sphere, consequently, different regulations include a requisite of cohabitation. These can be the regulations through which the state intends to give the couple or the family economic support based on the cohabitation. Thus, it can be purposeful to require cohabitation in addition to the contract as a condition of economic support. That this, alone, is not sufficient in an assessment *ex ante* has been discussed in the previous section, where we stated that the contract has a significant function in speaking to the future. On the other hand, economic support can also be triggered in cases in which the parties, for example, live separately as a result of employment in different geographical areas and, therefore, have a higher cost of living.

100 *Grigsby v. Reib*, 105 Tex. 597, 153 S.W. 1124 (1913); *Catlett v. Chestnut*, 107 Fla. 498, 146 So. 241 (1933); *McChesney v. Johnson*, 79 S.W.2d 658, 659 (Tex.Civ.App. 1934); and *In re McKanna's Estate*, 106 Cal.App.2d 126, 234 P.2d 673, 675 (1951).

101 *Lefkoff v. Sicro*, 189 Ga. 554, 6 S.E.2d 687, 703 (1939).

A number of the civil law ramifications between the parties are especially pertinent to cases in which the parties have actually lived or presently live together. The right to inherit and the right to a division of property arguably are more strongly justified after a long-term cohabitation. From the perspective of the parties it is natural to assume that the cohabitation is a condition of the contract. On the other hand, there certainly are parties who have entered into a marital contract on the assumption that they would gain the legal consequences of marriage or a legally recognized cohabitation, even though the cohabitation, for whatever reasons, has been short term, insufficient, or has not had a chance to be commenced. The lack of cohabitation ought then, it can be argued, not influence the issue of whether the parties generally can be considered married or cohabitants, but instead an allowance should be made for adjusting the rights within the framework of the legal system. With respect to the laws governing divorce and the status of children, it can also be in the interest of the state, as well as the parties, for the legal consequences of marriage or a legally recognized cohabitation to be based on the contract. Cohabiting persons can have agreed to live an entire life together and, based on this, draft their wills. If their relationship is dissolved as a result of death before the cohabitation can be commenced, it may be to their advantage for the contract to be the basis of the legal assessment.

The requirement of cohabitation can also protect the parties themselves against a hasty marital or cohabitation contract. Even though the parties have already entered into a contract, the commencement of the cohabitation can be considered definitive proof that the agreement was serious.[102] It is one thing to enter into a contract and another to carry out its terms. This factor is particularly significant if the contract itself is formless and consists, perhaps, of statements more or less uttered in conversation.[103] The requirement of cohabitation then functions as a substitute for the form requirement. If the parties do not wish to publicize their marriage through a wedding, they must publicize their relationship through outward actions and appearances. In the case law, the parties' outward actions are sometimes referred to as an "acid test," which indicates the weight ascribed to this requirement.[104] If the parties pass this test, they are assumed to have decided to live together simultaneously with the publication that gives the opportunity to assess whether the cohabitation is sufficiently marriage-like. This argument must be viewed as having significant weight.

102 CLARK 1987, *supra* note 70, at 105: "Adding the requirement of open marital cohabitation gives assurance that some objective evidence of the relationship will have to be introduced in every case to establish that the parties did consider themselves husband and wife."

103 With respect to oral contracts in the case law, *see* Section 6.5.1 *supra*.

104 *McChesney v. Johnson*, 79 S.W.2d 658, 659 (Tex.Civ.App. 1934); *Miller v. Sutherland*, 131 Mont. 175, 309 P.2d 322 (1957); *McClish v. Rankin*, 14 So.2d 714 (Fla. 1943); and *In re Schneider's Will*, 206 Misc. 18, 131 N.Y.S.2d 215 (Surr.Ct. 1954).

A longer cohabitation is not necessary for this purpose. It ought to be considered sufficient that the parties demonstrate that the marriage has, so to speak, begun.

The requirement of cohabitation also protects third parties entering into relationships with the parties. This has been considered to be the case primarily in the requirement of holding out; in other words, the parties' outward representations as spouses, which is thought to prevent clandestine marriages, are visible to a third party.[105] The significance of the requisite of cohabitation, in this respect, nowadays, appears rather dubious. Certainly, the parties' holding out as spouses to a third party creates the appearance that they are married to each other. Nevertheless, a third party cannot with certainty know whether the parties also have entered into a contract; the relationship in question could be temporary cohabitation.

One incentive behind the requirement of cohabitation for the formation of a common law marriage has always been that it is desirable to create a protection against fraudulent claims. This is true, to begin with, of relationships between the parties in which there is a danger that one of the parties, without any intent to commence a cohabitation, encourages the other to execute a contract in order to, thereafter, dissolve the marriage and make economic claims against that party. As can be seen in the previous section, a contract in which the object of the intent is the intent to live together can be a restraint. An objective requisite of cohabitation, however, appears more suited to the purpose of discouraging false pretenses. An alternative method is to limit these difficulties in the framework of the marital legal system with the assistance of equitable rules that take into account any lack of a cohabitation.

Fraudulent claims have received the most attention in connection with inheritance cases, in which a claim is brought against the estate of the deceased. It has been argued that a contract without a requirement of cohabitation would make "the estates of wealthy men the prey of the adventuress."[106] With the requirements of cohabitation and holding out, there is a protection against a person, under the claim that they have entered into a marital contract with the deceased and thereby established

---

105 *Lefkoff v. Sicro,* 189 Ga. 554, 6 S.E.2d 687, 703 (1939) ("Even creditors might be injuriously affected, and the State hampered in the enforcement of its penal laws"); and *In re Estate of Vandenhook,* 855 P.2d 518, 520 (Mont. 1993).

106 James Schouler, Marriage, Divorce, Separation & Domestic Relations II, § 1117 (6th ed. 1921). In *Grigsby v. Reib,* 105 Tex. 597, 153 S.W. 1130 (1913), the court maintained in a similar manner with respect to the deceased, that the absence of a requirement of cohabitation would "make their estates the prey of the bawd and the adventuress, with no possible safeguard." *See also* Clark 1987, *supra* note 68, at 105, maintaining that the requirement of cohabitation is "clear and sound" and that the purpose of the requirement "is to prevent, or at least to minimize the fraudulent claims of common law marriage which could be made if an agreement alone were sufficient to prove such a marriage."

a common law marriage, from making an unlawful claim against the estate of the deceased.[107]

A third typical situation in which there is considerable danger of abuse is cases in which a man and a woman, in collusion, make a claim for a public legal right under the premise that they have entered into a common law marriage. This can concern, for example, the right to an economic benefit or the right to immigrate to the country. The risk for sham marriages or relationships is significant.[108] A requirement of cohabitation can be a deterrent.

A further reason for requiring, in addition to the contract for the formation of a common law marriage, cohabitation or the outward appearance as spouses finally can be to avoid evidentiary difficulties and conflicts concerning the existence of the contract. The evidentiary difficulties associated with a marriage commenced, perhaps at night between two parties, without any notice or knowledge of the outside world, can then be avoided.[109] The requirement of cohabitation has even been considered a way to avoid conflict.

---

107 *People v. Lucero*, 747 P.2d 660, 664 (Colo. 1987) ("The reason for this requirement is to guard against fraudulent claims of common law marriage"); and *Schilling v. Parsons*, 110 Ind.App. 52, 36 N.E.2d 958, 961 (1941) ("To hold that a common law marriage is established without public acknowledgment of the marriage status of the contracting parties where there is an unwitnessed oral agreement would open the door to perjury and fraud, deny the parties themselves the protection to which they are each entitled, and jeopardize the sanctity of the basic institution of all civilized society, the home"). The dissident in *Lefkoff v. Sicro*, 189 Ga. 554, 6 S.E.2d 687, 703 (1939) stated: "It would enable a man and woman under a spurious claim of marriage to evade the statutes of frauds, and in virtue of supposed marital relations." In *Grigsby v. Reib*, 105 Tex. 597, 153 S.W. 1124 (1913), the court maintained that the absence of a "holding out" would "open a wide door, with strong imitation to perjury and fraud." *See also Lee v. State*, 44 Tex.Crim.Rep. 354, 72 S.W. 1005 (1902). *Compare In re Callery's Estate*, 75 A. 672 (1910), in which the court with respect to the surviving woman stated: "When Callery was dying ... she not only made no effort to assert the rights of a wife to be with him and care for him, but entered into negotiations for pecuniary settlement." *See also Sharon v. Sharon*, 79 Cal. 633, 22 P. 26, 36 (1889). There naturally is no lack of cases in which several persons simultaneously made claims on an estate based on the claim that they were the deceased's common law wife, *see, e.g., Matter of Estate of Akers*, 541 P.2d 284 (Okla.App. 1975), in which no less than three woman claimed that they were the deceased's widow. *Compare* the following cases in which two women claimed to be the deceased's common law wife: *Chapman v. Chapman*, 88 Tex. 641, 32 S.W. 871 (1895); *Klipfel v. Klipfel*, 41 Colo. 40, 92 P. 26, 124 Am.St.Rep. 96 (1907); *In re Rosenberger's Estate*, 362 Pa. 153, 65 A.2d 377 (1949); *Mitchell v. Smyser*, 236 S.C. 332, 114 S.E.2d 226 (1960); *Rush v. Traveler's Ins. Co.*, 347 S.W.2d 758 (Tex.Civ.App.-Texarkana 1961); *Gary v. Gary*, 490 S.W.2d 929 (Tex.Civ.App.-Tyler 1973); *Beals v. Beals*, 219 Ga.App. 848, 416 S.E.2d 301 (1992); and *Chandler v. Central Oil Corp., Inc.*, 253 Kan. 50, 853 P.2d 649 (1993). *See also Sanders v. Sanders*, 948 P.2d 719 (Okla.App. 1997), in which the woman claimed that she, during the last months of the man's life, was his common law wife and in which there was evidence that she, during this period of time, had a sexual relationship with another man, with whom, a couple months after the deceased's death, she entered into a formal marriage.

108 With respect to sham marriages, *see* Section 6.5.3 *supra*.

109 *See United States v. Simpson*, 4 Utah 227, 7 P. 257, 258 (1885).

However, it can be questioned whether this method is suited to the goal. In the proving whether a contract was entered into, it is an advantage from an evidentiary perspective to be able to consider the cohabitation in addition to other circumstances. This does not, however, render the cohabitation a necessary requisite. It is sufficient, as is the case in all of the examined jurisdictions, that it be admitted as an evidentiary fact as to the contract, as discussed further in Chapter 7. At the same time, it is clear that an unconditional requirement of cohabitation spares the courts and the parties the evidentiary problems concerning the contract in cases in which no cohabitation has existed. All such cases, however, need not be problematical from an evidentiary perspective. The parties can have entered into a written and witnessed contract in which their marital intentions are clearly expressed.

As seen in Chapter 8, a significant simultaneous conclusion of this work has been that the requirement of cohabitation creates extensive application problems. Koegel's criticism is as relevant today as when made: "Again, just where will the line be drawn? When do the parties cease to be fornicators and just when does the sublime institution of matrimony begin?"[110] This uncertainty results in drawn-out and expensive litigation. The examinations of the relevant facts in the cases have been complicated and have threatened personal integrity. A considerable legal uncertainty has followed in the wake of these application problems.[111]

A possibility of reducing these difficulties, assuming the requisite of cohabitation is not entirely abolished, appears to be to limit their role, on one side, by significantly sharpening the application of the contract requisite, in both a substantive and evidentiary manner as discussed in Section 13.2, above, and, on the other side, by applying a more limited requirement of cohabitation intended only to demonstrate that the cohabitation has commenced and, thereby, that the contract was seriously intended. The issue of how the application problems can be overcome depends on the concrete formulation of the requisite of cohabitation, which is discussed further, below. The application problems associated with the requisite of cohabitation, however, are so significant that there is reason to return to them in Chapter 14, "Arguments for and Against Common Law Marriage and Cohabitation Law."

13.3.2 The Formulation of the Requisite of Cohabitation

A discussion of how the requisite of cohabitation ought to be more closely formulated, and which different elements ought to be included, must begin with the purpose of the requisite, and the conceptual environment in which the requisite is to exist. Consequently, the requirement of cohabitation

110 Koegel, *supra* note 97, at 128. *See also* Ross, *supra* note 95, at 732.
111 The application problems are more closely discussed in Section 8.7.6 *supra*.

cannot be viewed in isolation. Entirely different requirements must be applied to the formulation of the requisite if it is to constitute the only ground for the formation of a common law marriage or a legally recognized cohabitation, rather than if it is to be applied in addition to the contract element. The differences are then justified both with respect to the component elements of the requisite and the time frame. Furthermore, it is of great importance to formulate the requisite so that it does not give rise to unnecessary application problems. Defining the concept of cohabitation is also significant because it influences the area of application for common law marriages and cohabitation legislation. The formulation determines the relationships that are to receive the legal rights as well as the obligations, and those that will fall outside of the regulatory system.

1. The Requisites: Cohabitation, Holding Out, and Reputation

The concept of cohabitation as seen in Chapter 8 can be divided into two main approaches, namely, on one side, cohabitation in the more narrow sense encompassing the relationship between the parties; and on the other side, their holding out and reputation as spouses, their outward appearance to others and the reputation they have thus acquired. Both sides of this concept of cohabitation are of interest in discussions concerning the future course of the law. However, the different formulations of both sides, as well as the different component elements, have been thoroughly discussed in Chapter 8, and that discussion will be referred to but not be repeated here. Several aspects, however, are of particular interest here.

Historically, the requirements of cohabitation and holding out have had great significance. By appearing outwardly to family relatives, friends, and to the entire community, as a couple, the parties demonstrated that their relationship is not simply a temporary or purely clandestine sexual relationship undeserving of marital legal effects. As far back as medieval canon law, as seen in Chapter 3, "Informal Marriages in Canon Law," the parties' *publica fama* was given significant evidentiary value in the assessment of whether a formless marriage had been established. With the development of common law marriage in the American case law, as seen in Chapter 8, the parties holding out and reputation were necessary requisites for the establishment of such a marriage.

It can be questioned whether, today, the parties' outward appearance and reputation as spouses should be necessary requisites. Their outward appearance need not be the result of any dramatic decision about their relationship nor speak to the relationship's legal character. Changed attitudes towards cohabitation have made that even cohabiting persons who are together temporarily, without any long-term or legal plans whatsoever, appear outwardly as spouses. A problem recurring in many trials concerning common law marriage is namely that the witnesses testifying as to the parties' reputation as spouses begin with the formal marriage. On the other hand, it is clear that the parties' outward appearance ought to constitute an element in a requisite of cohabitation and that the parties' reputation ought to constitute an evidentiary fact in addition to others.[112] It is also striking how closely these factors conform to the circumstances that, in the American case law, have been considered relevant to common law marriage. These are, e.g., circumstances that have been taken into consideration in the determination of an implied marital agreement, as seen in Chapter 7; in the application of the requirement of cohabitation as spouses, as in Chapter 8; and in the application of the marital presumption examined in Chapter 9. Even the legal capacity requirements included in the cohabitation legislation for the establishment of a legally recognized relationship are usually the same for marriage and common law marriage, with the exception that the latter, today, is not usually applied to couples of the same sex.

2. *The Cohabitation Requisites in the Legislation Concerning Unmarried Cohabitants*

Efforts in countries to enact legislation governing unmarried cohabiting persons since the 1970s that more precisely defines cohabitation requisites have met the same problems that have been typical to common law marriage during the last two hundred years, as seen in Chapter 8. Characteristically, modern concepts of cohabitation are primarily based on objective circumstances. The legislation for unmarried cohabiting persons, therefore, in principle can be said to be more akin to Roman concubinage, while common law marriage is closer to the free Roman marriage based on the principle *consensus, non concubitus, facit matrimonium.* The concepts, however, have become more similar. On one side, cohabitation with the establishment of a common law marriage has been given greater significance, in part as an evidentiary fact of the contract, as seen in Chapter 7; and in part as an independent element in addition to the contract, as shown in Chapter 8. On the other side, cohabitation legislation has not entirely been able to avoid the subjective elements, albeit these have not developed into the requirement of a proper agreement between the parties.[113] In that the cohabitation legislation has refrained from using

112 *Compare* Caudill, *supra* note 29, at 566–567, who suggests that for a "constructive marriage" it could be required that the "the parties hold themselves out as a family, that is, as an intimate, supportive, committed, and enduring social unit."

113 *See* with respect to New Zealand section 2D Property (Relationships) Act (1976), in its new wording that entered into force 1 February 2002, in paragraph (f) is discussed the "the degree of mutual commitment to a shared life." The same element can also be found in section 4 (2) Property (Relationships) Act (1976) (NSW). Even according to the legislative preparatory works to the Swedish cohabitation legislation, consideration ought to be given to the intentions of the parties with respect to the relationship's durability and consequence, and their intent that the relationship be considered as a cohabitation relationship,

the parties' agreeing intent as a necessary requisite for its application, and, instead, tied the legal effects to the cohabitation, the parties cannot themselves decide if and when the legal relationship is to commence. They have, however, ordinarily been given the possibility of contracting out of it. The formation of the cohabitation requisites in the different national laws has been shown to be strikingly similar.

One example is offered by the legislation enacted in **Sweden,** in 1987, for unmarried cohabiting persons, which gave the parties the right to a division of the estate, normally an equal division, as to the residence and household goods acquired during the cohabitation. A prerequisite thereto was that they lived together "under marriage-like conditions."[114] This law according to a different act was also applicable to homosexual couples.[115] The definition has been amended for the purpose of including persons of both the same and different sexes through a new Cohabitation Act in 2003, defining them as "two persons who continually live together in a couple relationship and have a mutual residence."[116] As guidance for the assessment of which relationships are to be included, the Minister of Justice, in connection with both reforms, pointed to a series of relevant factors. No requirement as to a certain period of cohabitation is applied.

---

see Prop. 1986/87:1, at 253, 368, Prop. 2002/03:80, at 43. Also in the case law certain consideration has been taken as to the intentions of the parties, *see* NJA 1994 p. 256, 263, RH 2005:34 and RH 1993:91. *Compare* EVA RYRSTEDT, BODELNING OCH BOSTAD 293–94 (1998). With respect to the United States, the ALI notes, *supra* note 9, among a number of objective circumstances, that consideration also ought to be given to the parties' "statements or promises" to each other. *See also Connell v. Francisco*, 127 Wash.2d 339, 346, 898 P.2d 831, 834 (1995), in which the court finds that "the intent of the parties" and "the purpose of the relationship" ought also to be given relevance.

114 SFS 1987:232 at § 1.

115 SFS 1987:813.

116 SFS 2003:376. The new definition according to the Minister of Justice (*see* prop. 2002/03:80, at 43–44) is not intended to entail any material change except to such an extent that even persons of the same sex are included. The first requirement for a cohabitation relationship is that persons continually live together. Therewith is meant that the relationship is to have a certain durability or in any case to be intended to have that. A guidepost is a six-month cohabitation, but a shorter period of time can be accepted for example if the parties have drafted wills or opened joint bank accounts. If a couple lives together and has mutual children, one can, according to the Minister of Justice, normally assume that a cohabitation relationship exists. In other cases, a mutual registered residential address ought to be indicative that the parties have mutual residence and that their cohabitation is not temporary. Even if the parties formally have different registered residential addresses, it can be sufficient that they clearly actually have a mutual permanent residence. The other requirement is that the parties live together in a couple relationship. Therewith is meant a relationship in which normally is included sexual cohabitation. The third requirement is that the parties have a mutual household, wherewith is meant that they share chores and expenditures, consequently cooperate as to daily tasks in the home, and have mutual economy, in any case such a financial collaboration that one can speak of a shared household. The concept "marriage-like relationship" has caused application difficulties, *see* NJA 1994 p. 256; NJA 1994 p. 61; NJA 1989 p. 682; RH 2005:28; RH 2005:34; RH 1997:98; RH 1993:91; RH 1989:56; and RH 1987: 17.

One guidepost has been six months, however, shorter relationships, under certain circumstances, can also fall within the scope of the law.

In **Norway,** where the Ministry of Justice proposed in 2007 a minimum inheritance right and the right to keep the estate undivided for a surviving cohabitant, the proposed legislation requires the parties to have lived together in a marriage-like relationship during the last five years before the death, or to have, have had, or to expecting, a child.[117]

In **Scotland,** common law marriage "by cohabitation with habit and repute" was repealed in 2006 and, simultaneously, another law was enacted that gave cohabiting couples certain economic rights via separation and death. The law is applicable to couples of different sexes "living together as if they were husband and wife"[118] and to couples of the same sex "living together as if they were civil partners."[119] As guidance for its application, the law includes a series of factors that are seen as relevant in the assessment of whether a relationship falls within the scope of the law.[120] The objective focus of the new legislation does not appear to allow for subjective objections concerning the intentions of the parties with the relationship, as had the repealed presumption "marriage by cohabitation with habit and repute" did.[121] The Scottish law does not contain any time frame for the cohabitation.

According to the legislation enacted in the Spanish province of **Catalonia,** in 1998, unmarried cohabiting persons are partially given the same rights as married persons, although the parties are required to have lived together marriage-like in a stable relationship for an unbroken period of at least two years or to have lived together with a mutual child.[122]

---

117 Høringsnotat, January 2007, Snr. 200405522 EP Høringsnotat, January 2007, Snr. 200405522 EP Høringsnotat, January 2007, Snr. 200405522 EP.

118 *See* section 18, (1)(a), The Family Law (Scotland) Act 2006; Family Law (Scotland) Bill, SP Bill 36B, 18, Session 2 (2005).

119 *Id.*, section 18 (1)(b).

120 By "cohabitant" is meant according to the Scottish law a man and a woman who are or were "living together as if they were husband and wife," *see id.* at section 18, (1)(a), wherewith is to be considered "the length of the period" during which the parties "have been living together (or lived together)," and in addition "the nature of their relationship" as well as "the nature and extent of any financial arrangements" during the period, *see id.* at section 18, (4)(a)(b)(c).

121 With respect to "marriage by cohabitation with habit and repute," *see* Chapter 11 *supra.*

122 The law is applicable as to heterosexual couples "who have executed a public instrument." *See* Act 10/1998 of 15th July, Regarding Stable Pair Relationships, Article 1. The law is also applicable to couples of the same sex who "cohabit matrimonially and who state their will to abide by these provisions in the form that is provided," *see* Article 19; Miquel Martín-Casals, *Same-Sex Partnerships in the Legislation of Spanish Autonomous Communities, EU ERA Conference,* unpublished paper, Uppsala 19–20 (September 2002), p. 2; and Miguel Martin Casals, *Same-Sex Partnerships in the Legislation of Spanish Autonomous Communities,* in Legal Recognition of Same-SexCouples in Europe 54, 60 (Katharina Boele-Woelki and Angelika Fuchs eds. 2003).

The radical development that has occurred in **Australia** and **New Zealand,** in its first stage, meant that cohabiting unmarried couples, to a high degree, were equated with married persons. Later, homosexual couples also received the same rights.[123] For example, in New South Wales in Australia and in New Zealand, in 1999 and 2002, respectively, new legislation was enacted that equates cohabiting unmarried persons, both heterosexual and homosexual, with married persons with respect *inter alia* to the division of property, inheritance, and maintenance. In order for the parties in such a de facto relationship to be equated with spouses, they are required to "live together as a couple" during a period of time that, in New South Wales, is two years[124] and in New Zealand,[125] three years. As guidance for assessing what it means to be living together as a couple, the law gives a series of factors that are relevant but not always necessary.[126] The expression *de facto relationship* that has received a broad dissemination

123 With respect to the development in New Zealand, *see* M. HENEGHAN AND B. ATKIN, FAMILY LAW POLICY IN NEW ZEALAND (2d ed. 2002); Bill Atkin, The Rights of Married and Unmarried Couples in New Zealand: Radical New Laws on Property and Succession, International Society of Family Law World Conference, unpublished paper, Copenhagen/Oslo, (august 2002); Virginia Grainer, *What's Yours Is Mine: Reform of the Property Division Regime for Unmarried Couples in New Zealand*, 11 P.R.L.P. 287 (2002); BILL ATKIN AND WENDY PARKER, RELATIONSHIP PROPERTY IN NEW ZEALAND (2001); Bill Atkin, *Reforming Property Division in New Zealand: From Marriage to Relationships*, 3 E.J.L.R. 349 (2001); and Wendy Parker, *New Zealand property rights legislation: A changing landscape*, 57 FAM. MATT. 62 (2000).

124 Section 17, PROPERTY (RELATIONSHIPS) ACT 1984, New South Wales.

125 New Zealand's PROPERTY (RELATIONSHIPS) ACT 1976, that in February. 2002 became applicable not only to married couples but also to both heterosexual and homosexual cohabiting unmarried couples, requires as a prerequisite hereto that the parties have lived together at least 3 years, *see* sections 4(5) PROPERTY (RELATIONSHIPS) ACT 1976. An exception from the rule is made if any of the parties has children or made "a substantial contribution to the relationship" and the main rule would lead to "serious injustice." The exception is made even if the matter only applies "a specific item" not "a global division of property," *see* section 14A.

126 As examples of relevant elements the new regulations in New Zealand state "(a) the duration of the relationship, (b) the nature and extent of common residence, (c) whether or not a sexual relationship exists, (d) the degree of financial dependence or interdependence, and any arrangements for financial support, between the parties, (e) the ownership, use, and acquisition of property, (f) the degree of mutual commitment to a shared life, (g) the care and support of children, (h) the performance of household duties, (i) the reputation and public aspects of the relationship." *See* section 2D PROPERTY (RELATIONSHIPS) ACT 1976, in its new wording that entered into force the 1st of February 2002. As to case law, *see, e.g. Scragg v. Scott* (2006) N.Z.F.L.R. 1076 and *P.Z. v. J.C.* (2006) N.Z.F.L.R. 97. The definition of a de facto relationship and relevant cases are analysed in Bill Atkin, *Reflections on New Zealand's Property Reforms 'Five Years On'*, in THE INTERNATIONAL SURVEY OF FAMILY LAW 217, 221-225 (Bill Atkin, gen. ed., 2007). The comparable definition and elements can also be found in the legislation from New South Wales, Australia, *see* PROPERTY (RELATIONSHIPS) ACT (1984), N.S.W. ACTS § 4 (1)(2) that *inter alia* for the purpose of including also homosexual couples most recently has been amended through THE PROPERTY (RELATIONSHIPS) AMENDMENT ACT (1999). N.S.W. ACTS § 3. Similar legislation in a number of legal areas has been enacted in Australia's other jurisdictions.

in both the federal and local legislation has been given somewhat varying meanings.[127]

Several provinces in **Canada** have enacted legislation that partially equates cohabiting unmarried couples with married persons. Consequently, with respect to spousal-support obligations, the legislation in Ontario includes in the expression *spouse* "either of a man or a woman who are not married to each other and have cohabited, (a) continuously for a period of not less than three years, or (b) in a relationship of some permanence if they are the natural or adoptive parents of a child."[128] Comparable legislation in British Columbia concerning maintenance includes both couples of different sexes and couples of the same sex that, for three years, lived in a marriage-like relationship.[129] In the province of Manitoba, which has gone farthest in the development of common law marriage in Canada, the new legislation is applicable to a person who is a "common law partner," which ordinarily meant a person who either registered his or her "common law relationship" with another, or who "cohabited with him or her in a conjugal relationship" during a period of at least three years.[130] In several of the laws, e.g., with respect to maintenance obligations and inheritance, at least one year's cohabitation is sufficient if the parties have a mutual child. According to other laws, it is sufficient with less than one year's cohabitation. In contrast to the parties in an American common law marriage, the parties in a common law relationship in Manitoba can be of the same sex. As guidance for the application of the law, factors are given that ought to be deemed relevant.[131]

The regulations based on cohabitation have not simply grown through legislation. In the American state of **Washington,** which does not recognize common law marriage, the courts, without the support of legislation, have granted parties rights based on their cohabitation. In the leading case of *Connell v. Francisco* (1995), in which the community property system

---

127 Reg Graycar, & Jenni Millbank, *The Bride Wore Pink ... to the Property (Relationships) Legislation Amendment 1999: Relationship Law Reform in New South Wales*, 17 CAN. FAM. J. L. 227, 238 (2000).

128 ONTARIO FAMILY LAW REFORM ACT of 1986, R.S.O., ch. F-3, §§ 29, 30 (1990). With respect to the older developments in Canada, *see* Carol S. Bruch, *Nonmarital Cohabitation in the Common Law Countries: A Study in Judicial – Legislative Interaction*, 29 AM.J.COMP.L. 217, 227, 234–235 (1981); and Blumberg, *supra* note 8, at 1176.

129 FAMILY RELATIONS ACT OF BRITISH COLUMBIA, R.S.B.C., ch. 128, § 1 (1996), amended Oct. 1, 1998.

130 THE COMMON-LAW PARTNER'S PROPERTY AND RELATED AMENDMENTS ACT, S.M. 2002, c. 48.

131 With the assessment of that which is a "conjugal relationship," factors such as "whether you live under the same roof; what the sleeping arrangements are; whether you have a sexual relationship; whether you maintain an attitude of fidelity to one another; whether you share household chores or perform any personal services for one another; whether you participate in community or neighbourhood activities as a couple; whether you present yourselves as a couple to others," *see* Manitoba Justice, Changes to Property Laws affecting Common-Law Partners taking effect June 30, 2004.

formally applicable to married spouses was applied to a "meretricious relationship," the latter was defined as "a stable, marital-like relationship where both parties cohabit with knowledge that a lawful marriage between them does not exist…" The court in the case pointed to a series of factors that ought to be relevant with the assessment hereof. Even though durability was considered to be significant, the relationship need not be "long term."[132]

It is not surprising that trials concerning whether both these objective as well as subjective elements exist have entailed application difficulties similar to those that we encountered concerning common law marriage. For example, in the case of *In re Marriage of Pennington* (2000), in which a stable and marital-like relationship was not found proven, the court stated that the relationship between the parties certainly "included companionship, friendship, love, sex, and mutual support and caring," but found nevertheless that "the sporadic cohabitation, the instability of the relationship, Van Pevenage's insistence on marriage, Pennington's refusal to marry, Van Pevenage's absences from the home and relationship with another man, the gaps where no expenses were shared, and the absence of constant or continuous co-payments or investment of time and effort in any significant asset" did not prove the existence of a meretricious relationship.[133]

The development in the Washington case law appears to have influenced the **American Law Institute Principles,** which, in 2002, recommended guidelines for the division of property and compensatory payments in the dissolution of the relationship of domestic partners through separation.[134] The basis of the parties' proposed rights and obligations is their behavior, not a wedding ceremony or, as is the case in principle concerning common law marriage, an agreement between them. The ALI, which has understood the importance of carefully defining what is meant by *domestic partnership*, has made great efforts with the help of different criteria to more closely define the relationship. The principles are illustrated with several examples and supplemented with burdens of proof and legal presumptions.

The objective with the ALI Principles appears to have been to reach relationships that are "indistinguishable from marriage" apart from these formalities.[135] *Domestic partners* are defined as two unmarried persons of

132 *Connell v. Francisco*, 127 Wash.2d 339, 346, 898 P.2d 831, 834 (1995). The relevant factors with the assessment were considered to be "continuous cohabitation, duration of the relationship, purpose of the relationship, pooling of resources and services for joint projects, and the intent of the parties…" *See also* Gavin M. Parr, *What Is a "Meretricious Relationship"?: An Analysis of Cohabitant Property Rights Under Connell v. Francisco*, 74 WASH. L. REV. 1243 (1999); and *In re Marriage of Pennington*, 142 Wash.2d 592, 14 P.3d 764, 770 (2000).

133 *In re Marriage of Pennington*, 142 Wash.2d 592, 14 P.3d 764, 772 (2000).

134 *See* the ALI PRINCIPLES, *supra* note 9, particularly Chapter 6, Domestic Partners.

135 Grace Ganz Blumberg, *The Regularization of Nonmarital Cohabitation: Rights and Responsibilities in the American Welfare State*, 76 NOTRE DAME L. REV. 1265, 1297 (2001).

the same or different sexes, who "for a significant period of time share a primary residence and a life together as a couple."[136] The relationship is commenced when the parties begin to share a primary residence, as long as one of them does not demonstrate that they did not begin a "sharing life together as a couple." The relationship ceases when the parties cease to share the residence. If they have a mutual child, they are considered to have begun to share a life together as a couple no later than when the woman became pregnant.[137] With the assessment of whether two persons can be seen to share a life together as a couple, the ALI gives examples about a number of circumstances that ought to be relevant.[138]

The author was Reporter of the Domestic Partnership chapter of the Principles.

136 The ALI PRINCIPLES, *supra* note 9, § 6.03, paragraph 1. The relationship is defined additionally in six paragraphs as well as the burdens of proof and legal presumptions for its application: "(2) Persons are domestic partners when they have maintained a common household, as defined in Paragraph (4), with their common child, as defined in Paragraph (5), for a continuous period that equals or exceeds a duration, called the *cohabitation parenting period*, set in a rule of statewide application. (3) Persons not related by blood or adoption are presumed to be domestic partners when they have maintained a common household, as defined in Paragraph (4), for a continuous period that equals or exceeds a duration, called the *cohabitation period*, set in a rule of statewide application. The presumption is rebuttable by evidence that the parties did not share life together as a couple, as defined by Paragraph (7). (4) Persons *maintain a common household* when they share a primary residence only with each other and family members; or when, if they share a household with other unrelated persons, they act jointly, rather than as individuals, with respect to management of the household. (5) Persons have a *common child* when each is either the child's legal parent or parent by estoppel, as defined by § 2.03. (6) When the requirements of Paragraph (2) or (3) are not satisfied, a person asserting a claim under this Chapter bears the burden of proving that for a significant period of time the parties shared a primary residence and a life together as a couple, as defined in Paragraph (7). Whether a period of time is significant is determined in light of all the Paragraph (7) circumstances of the parties' relationship and, particularly, the extent to which those circumstances wrought change in the life of one or both parties."

137 *Id.* § 6.04.

138 *Id.* § 6.03, paragraph (7) takes up the following circumstances, which are relevant but not exclusive: "(a) the oral or written statements or promises made to one another, or representations jointly made to third parties, regarding their relationship; (b) the extent to which the parties intermingled their finances; (c) the extent to which their relationship fostered the parties' economic interdependence, or the economic dependence of one party upon the other; (d) the extent to which the parties engaged in conduct and assumed specialized or collaborative roles in furtherance of their life together; (e) the extent to which the relationship wrought change in the life of either or both parties; (f) the extent to which the parties acknowledged responsibilities to each other, as by naming the other the beneficiary of life insurance or of a testamentary instrument, or as eligible to receive benefits under an employee-benefit plan; (g) the extent to which the parties' relationship was treated by the parties as qualitatively distinct from the relationship either party had with any other person; (h) the emotional or physical intimacy of the parties' relationship; (i) the parties' community reputation as a couple; (j) the parties' participation in a commitment ceremony or registration as a domestic partnership; (k) the parties' participation in a void or voidable marriage that, under applicable law, does not give rise to the economic incidents of marriage; (l) the parties' procreation of, adoption of, or joint assumption of parental functions

All these circumstances, however, need not be shown in each individual case. If the parties have had a mutual residence with a mutual child during a certain period that each state is to decide (the Comments suggest two years), they become, according to an absolute rule, domestic partners. If the parties did not have a mutual child but shared a mutual residence during a certain period that each state is to decide, and that has been assumed to be somewhat longer (the Comments suggest three years), they are presumed to be domestic partners (more as to the presumption in a specific section below).[139] If the parties did not have a mutual child or a mutual residence during the prescribed period, it is the duty of the party claiming the existence of a domestic partnership to show that the parties "share a primary residence and a life together as a couple," in accordance with the prescribed guidelines.[140]

It is uncommon that the cohabitation required includes emotional or moral elements. This seems, however, to be the case with regard to the **Italian** proposal of 2007, in which the Italian government proposed new legislation for same-sex and unmarried heterosexual couples. The law, referred to as DICO (*Diritti di coppie conviventi*), would, *inter alia*, give the parties, upon their separation, maintenance rights after three years of cohabitation. In addition, upon the death of one party, the surviving cohabitant receives inheritance rights after nine years of cohabitation. The proposed law requires under its Art. 1 parties who are united by mutual emotional bonds and who cohabit continuously and give each other support and solidarity materially as well as morally. Cohabiting partners will have to go to the registry office to declare their de facto union.[141]

Lawrence Waggoner has also presented a proposal for legislation concerning a legal right to inherit for de facto partners, making an ambitious attempt to more closely define the relationship that the parties must have lived together in order to receive the right to inherit. The author imposes, as requirements, that the surviving party must be unmarried and that he or she, based on family relationships, is not impeded from marrying the deceased. In addition, he requires that the parties have been "regularly living in the same household with the decedent in a marriage-like relationship." For the assessment of whether a relationship is sufficiently marriage-like, the proposed legislative text lists a number of factors that are relevant and do not exclude persons of the same sex.[142] For the purpose of

---

toward a child; (m) the parties' maintenance of a common household, as defined by Paragraph (4)."

139 *Id.* § 6.03 (2)(3).

140 *Id.* § 6.03 (7).

141 Disegno Di Legge, Senato Della Republica, XV Legislatura N. 1339 (2007).

142 Lawrence W. Waggoner, *Marital Property Rights in Transition*, 59 Mo. L. Rev. 21, 78 (1994). The author points to the following factors: "(1) the purpose, duration, constancy, and exclusivity of the relationship; (2) the degree to which the parties pooled their financial resources, such as by maintaining joint checking or other types of accounts, sharing a mortgage or lease on the household in which they lived

preventing disputes, the author supplements the definition with a presumption, discussed further below.

3. The Concept of Marriage as an Ideal Type for the Cohabitation Requisites

A general impression about the above-presented definitions from different parts of the Western world is that they are so similar. The most typical general characteristic in the definitions is that the concept of marriage, in some way, appears to have been the model for the definitions, which can be seen *inter alia* from the frequent use of expressions such as "marriage-like," "living together as if they were in marriage," and "marital-like relationship." This role model discloses that the legislators' purpose has not been to regulate any new social cohabitation. It is the concept of marriage that is the ideal for the legal definitions. Despite the fact that several laws regulating both couples of different sexes and the same sex, instead of using the marriage-related expressions, prescribe that the parties are to live together "as a couple" or that they are to live in a "couple relationship," the role model is still the same. Behind both the terms *marriage-like relationship* and *couple relationship* lies a sexual element that always is relevant, albeit not always necessary.

The circumstance that formal marriage normally does not include any requirement of a marital cohabitation leads to the conclusion that a marriage-like relationship according to the cohabitation legislation must be more marriage-like than marriage itself for the legal effects to be invoked. It is something of a paradox that the legislation and case law with respect to out-of-wedlock relationships has kept alive the image of what marriage is and ought to be, while the formal marriage has largely fossilized in its forms.

The function of marriage as an ideal type for the concepts of cohabitation also appears clearly through all of the factors that the different legislators have considered relevant, albeit not always necessary, for the establishment of an intended relationship. Despite the number of factors that have been emphasized, as seen particularly the notes to the previous section, the similarities are striking. Taken together, they give the impression

---

or on other property, titling the household in which they lived or other property in joint tenancy, or naming the other as primary beneficiary of life insurance or employee benefit plans; (3) the procreation or adoption of children and the degree of mutual care and support given them; (4) whether the couple went through a marriage ceremony; and (5) the degree to which the couple held themselves out to others as married or the degree to which the couple held themselves out to others as emotionally and financially committed to one another on a permanent basis, as exhibited by their acknowledging mutual rights, duties, and obligations toward one another." The list is not complete and all of the recited factors are not necessary. Relevant for the factors "purpose, constancy" and "exclusivity" are whether a sexual relationship existed and to what extent this was monogamous during the cohabitation.

of being the result of one and the same culture. The ideal type is the image of a monogamous and durable relationship with a high degree of a life community in different aspects. To this belongs a community at board and at bed, *mensa et lecto*, a community concerning children and finances, etc. When the ALI Principles speak of "a shared life," it is reminiscent of the Roman jurist Modestinus' ideas as to marriage as a *consortium omnis vitae*, in other words, a community in everything in life.[143]

It is also striking how close these factors concur with the circumstances that, in the American case law, were considered relevant with the application of common law marriage. This concerns, e.g., circumstances taken into consideration with the determination of an inferred marriage agreement as reviewed in Chapter 7, with the application of the requirement of cohabitation as spouses as examined in Chapter 8, and with the application of the marriage presumption as analyzed in Chapter 9. Even the requirements of legal capacity for the relationship's establishment in the cohabitation legislation are ordinarily the same as for marriage and common law marriage with the exception that the latter relationships ordinarily have not yet been granted to couples of the same sex.

A consequence of the high degree of similarity between the cohabitation legislation presented above and marriage-related definitions is that many cohabitation relationships, according to the sociological materials that appear in different countries as included in Chapter 12, fall outside of the scope of this legislation. The problems defining these boundaries that arise from the application of the law are highlighted in the next section.

4. *A Requirement of Cohabitation for a Certain Time*

The idea that cohabitation for a certain period of time is required in order to invoke the legal consequences of marriage has ancient roots. The preclassical Roman *usus*-marriage arose when the woman, after a one-year continuous cohabitation with a man, legally entered into his family and under his marital *manus*.[144] If the woman, after the termination of the *usus*-year, wished to avoid this legal consequence, she could terminate the *usus*-year with an absence of three nights, the *trinoctium*. If she thereafter continued the cohabitation, a new period was commenced.

Even though it can be said to be in the nature of things that requirements of cohabitation and reputation need a certain period of time for all of the component elements to come into existence, no present-day jurisdiction that recognizes common law marriage has been influenced by the Roman construction of applying a requirement of a certain time period of cohabitation. Nevertheless, one state partially recognizing common law

---

143 With respect to the Roman law, *see* Sections 2.2.1. and 2.4.2 *supra*. With respect to the medieval canon law, *see* Sections 3.2.1 and 3.3.3 *supra*.

144 *See* Section 2.2.2 *supra*.

marriage, namely, New Hampshire, imposes a requirement of three years' cohabitation and reputation as spouses up to death of one party. If this requirement is fulfilled, the parties are considered formally married. The surviving party then receives the same rights in the deceased's estate as would a widow or widower in a formal marriage.[145] The courts in other states have emphasized just the opposite, that no minimal time is required but that, instead, the quality of the cohabitation is decisive.[146] As stated in Chapter 8, American courts, in many cases, have accepted remarkably short periods of cohabitation, which can be explained by the fact that the requisite of cohabitation is not viewed in isolation but rather as the performance of the contract.[147] From this perspective, it is appropriate to speak, as in Georgia, of the cohabitation as the "consummation" of the contract.[148] One must demonstrate that the relationship did not stop with the contract and that the marriage commenced, however, nothing more! Clearly, the need for a fixed period of times appears rather limited against this background. If the parties have agreed to live a life together the actual cohabitation is not as important. This assumes, however, that the requirement of a marital contract is actually enforced. In a legal system without a contract requisite, and where the constituting element is only the requisite of cohabitation, a minimum time requirement for the cohabitation can then appear more justified.

As seen above, the cohabitation legislation that has been enacted in several countries during recent years contains no requirement of an agreement, but, on the other hand, does require a certain period of cohabitation. The most common time periods have been two years (Australia, Catalonia) or three years (New Zealand and Canada) of cohabitation. Longer periods have been proposed in Norway (five years) and in Italy (nine years as to inheritance rights). Concerning the proposed American ALI Principles,

---

145 N.H. Rev. Stat. Ann. 457:39 (West 2003): "Persons cohabiting and acknowledging each other as husband and wife, and generally reputed to be such, for the period of 3 years, and until the decease of one of them, shall thereafter be deemed to have been legally married." The legislation has ancient roots, *see* already RS 149:11 (1842). In the case of *In re Estate of Buttrick*, 597 A.2d 74 (N.H. 1991), the parties had lived together for 10 years, which entitled the surviving woman to "spousal share" in the estate. In *Gray v. Gray*, 117 N.H. 826, 379 A.2d 442. 445 (1977), the parties had lived together for more than 16 years, which resulted in that the surviving woman was entitled to "all the rights of a widow in the estate of the decedent." The law has not been seen as applicable other than in cases of death, *see Bisig v. Bisig*, 124 N.H. 372, 469 A.2d 1348 (1983); and *Joan S. v. John S.*, 121 N.H. 96, 427 A.2d 498 (1981).

146 *In re Estate of Burroughs*, 486 N.W.2d 113, 115 (Mich.App. 1992) ("There is no specified length of time the parties must live together, but there must be a constancy of dwelling together.")

147 *See, e.g., In re Estate of Fisher*, 176 N.W.2d 801 (Iowa 1970); *Garduno v. Garduno*, 760 S.W.2d 735 (Tex.App.-Corpus Christi 1988); *Graham v. Graham*, 130 Colo. 225, 274 P.2d 605 (1954); *Dowell v. Welch*, 574 P.2d 1089 (Okla.App. 1978); and *Matter of Estate of Murnion*, 212 Mont. 107, 686 P.2d 893 (1984).

148 *Georgia Osteopathic Hosp. v. O'Neal*, 403 S.E.2d 235, 243 (Ga.App. 1991).

which leave it open to the states to enact a time requirement, Elizabeth Scott has proposed a period of five years.[149] William Reppy, who presented the proposal concerning the enactment of a new status in the United States, which he calls "lawful cohabitation," has suggested that this status should be granted either through a formal registration, or through a short cohabitation if the parties contracted to become lawful cohabitants and outwardly appear as such, or in other situations after a period of time – six months, one year, or two years as specified in the law.[150]

Other countries, for example, Sweden and Scotland, have refrained from enacting a fixed time requirement. As a reason, the Scottish legislature stated that it "would be arbitrary, rigid and unresponsive to individual cases; would create problems of proof; could distort behaviour; and could lead to especially harsh outcomes in relation to discretionary awards on death."[151] According to the principles that have been developed in the case law from the American state of Washington, a certain definite period of cohabitation is not required.

A requirement of a relatively long time period appears to serve several of the goals for which the requisite of cohabitation was designed. This is true with respect to protection against fraudulent claims and abuse of the regulations. Such a requirement is also suitable with respect to the legal consequences intended for relationships executed through a durable cohabitation. With the requirement of a very long cohabitation, application problems would most probably be reduced from a quantitative perspective. The purpose of the requisite of cohabitation, to provide a protection against hasty marital contracts, however, appears to be served without any long-term cohabitation, while protection for third parties can generally be viewed as requiring a longer period of time.

The length of the period has considerable significance in the delineation of the population that the regulations cover. From the sociological materials presented in Chapter 12, "Common Law Marriage and Cohabitation Law," it was seen that many cohabitation relationships last only a few years. This means that the common periods of two to three years, would cut through a large segment of the population of cohabiting persons, making it difficult to justify why all couples who live together one week longer than others are granted all rights while the latter entirely fall outside of the system of regulation. It could be that a couple one week short of the end of the period when one of them died, had planned a long life together, which can be seen *inter alia* from the facts that they had children, drafted wills, and built a house together. The possibility of capturing such cases within the scope of the legislation would be to employ

149 Scott, *supra* note 10, at 343.

150 William A. Reppy, Jr., *Property and Support Rights of Unmarried Cohabitants: A Proposal for Creating a New Legal Status*, 44 LA. L. REV. 1677, 1718 (1984).

151 *See* Policy Memorandum, Family Law (Scotland) Bill (SP Bill 36) (2005), at 14.

a contract requirement, which common law marriage uses and modern cohabitation legislation lacks.

A somewhat longer time requirement, for example, five years, would entail that the majority of the population of cohabiting persons falls outside the regulation systems.[152] Most likely, the need for regulations is less in relationships shorter than this. If, however, such couples do not need all the legal effects of marriage, they may still need more limited protective regulations. If the period is extended, for example, to twenty to thirty years, the system of regulation has entirely other objectives. Giving legal protection is intended only in very exceptional cases and, in general, the parties are left to fill their own needs by regulating their legal situation by drafting a contract or formally marrying.

5. *A Mirror Image Theory for the Application of the Law*

The difficulties associated with applying the requisites of cohabitation and holding out raise the question of whether it is possible, by applying somewhat stricter principles at trial, to facilitate the assessment. If so, it would also be possible to determine, with greater certainty, the component elements that ought to be necessary and sufficient, respectively. One such possibility may be to apply the Mirror Image Theory, according to which the application questions regarding the substantive requisites for a common law marriage could be solved with the guidance of the form-bound marriage as it appears in the legal system. Such a method makes sense to the extent that formless marriage is granted the same legal consequences as formal marriage.

In contrast to sociological methods that explore how a marriage-like existence actually manifests itself,[153] the mirror image theory answers the question of how that reality ought to manifest itself in order to invoke legal consequences. Characteristic of the mirror image theory is that, in the search for answers, it looks for guidance to formal marriage as it appears in the legislation and case law. Common law marriage then becomes a formless mirror image of the form-bound marriage.

Whether the cohabitation in a common law marriage is to reflect a normal or an ideal marriage is open to discussion. The answer is that it is to be a true image of legal marriage, regardless of whether it appears to be ideal or normal.

This legal method can give results that can differ from legal system to legal system and from time to time. Formal marriage and the formless marriage, however, are always comparable within the same legal system. Further, the different legal systems substantially agree with respect to the main characteristics of marriage. Included here is the understanding of marriage as a principally exclusive and lifelong, or at least as a permanent

152 *See* Section 12.2.4 *supra.*

153 *Id.*

and durable relationship between a man and a woman. The fact that the parties contribute to each other's maintenance is a relevant circumstance that falls within the concept of cohabitation.[154]

Another issue is whether the parties' performance of marital obligations can lead to circular reasoning in cases in which the parties are claiming the performance of such obligations. Assume that a woman sues a man, claiming that he has maintenance obligations because they lived in a common law marriage. The man objects, stating that they have never lived in a common law marriage because he has never fulfilled any maintenance obligations. The circle, however, can partially be broken because it is sufficient that the parties, by contributing to each other's maintenance, have established a marriage. If they later do not perform their obligations, a lawsuit can be filed with the marriage as a basis. In addition, the issue of whether a common law marriage was established does not rest simply on this circumstance.

Even though an application of the mirror image theory can contribute a legally systematic relevant argument and factors, it can scarcely be argued that it, in any decisive manner, will aid in reducing the above cited application problems.

6. *A Requirement Concerning Mutual Children*

In the majority of cohabitation laws, seen above, the existence of mutual children constitutes a significant factor in the assessment of whether a legally recognized cohabitation relationship exists, without constituting an absolute requirement.

For the purpose of limiting the application difficulties arising when trying cases concerning common law marriages, while still attempting to satisfy the legal goals behind this institution, Justice Weltner of the Georgia Supreme Court has suggested that the circumstance of the parties having mutual children ought to be given a greater significance when proving whether a common law marriage has been established. Consequently, he suggested in *Ridley v. Grandison* (1990), that, in addition to the requirements that already exist in Georgia today, in other words, of "an actual contract" and "consummation,"[155] two alternative requirements ought to be applied with respect to the required evidence, namely, either (1) "proof of a *bona fide* attempt to contract a valid ceremonial marriage," or (2) "the birth to the parties (after the commencement of an illicit arrangement) of a child or children." According to Weltner, such an expanded rule would aid in not allowing any marriage to be attacked "for a technical deficiency inhering in a *bona fide* attempt to enter into a contract of marriage," and

---

154 *Compare* the expression "assumption of marital rights, duties and obligations" as in Section 8.5 *supra.*

155 It ought to be noted that common law marriage has been repealed in Georgia as of January 1, 1997, but that marriages entered into before that date continue to be recognized, *see* GA. CODE ANN. § 19-3-1.1 (West 2003).

also serve the goal that no child born to unmarried parents should in the future to any significant extent become branded as "illegitimate."[156]

The question, however, is whether Weltner's purpose in minimizing application problems would be achieved by his suggestion. On one side, it is clear that the proof concerning the requirement of children would not likely create any greater application problems. On the other side, the courts would have an additional requisite to review, namely whether the parties have made "a *bona fide* attempt" to enter into a ceremonial marriage, an attempt requisite that does not appear to be totally problem-free from an application perspective. To this must be added the considerable problems connected to the application, as well as to the contract requisite if the requisite of "consummation" is retained. The enactment of the suggestion, on the other hand, would, from a quantitative aspect, minimize the application problems because childless couples not making any "*bona fide* attempt" to enter into a ceremonial marriage would fall outside of the legal framework. Therein also lies the weakness of the proposal. Today, common law marriage serves several purposes, for example, to protect childless women during different stages of their lives or the more vulnerable segments of the population, all of which would become more difficult to achieve.[157] Lawmakers have reason, however, to consider whether this is a price worth paying in order to have a legal system that, at a reasonable cost, is possible to apply.

At the same time, the need for legal protection appears clearest in families having children. The underlying purpose of common law marriage, to protect illegitimate children, can be served, however, without the legal institution of common law marriage, namely, by recognizing the rights of out-of-wedlock children with respect to inheritance and other areas. This would also most probably contribute to reducing the branding of these children. The goal of protecting parties who, in good faith, have attempted to enter into a ceremonial marriage is highly reasonable, and can be achieved within a considerably more limited framework than that of common law marriage. These issues touch upon not only the formulation of the requisite of cohabitation, but the entirety of common law marriage and its future, and are addressed in Chapter 14.

156 *Ridley v. Grandison*, 260 Ga. 6, 389 S.E.2d 746, 749 (1990). Justice Weltner gave a similar proposal in *Johnson v. Green*, 309 S.E.2d 362, 364 (1983). With respect to the application problems, *see* Section 8.7.6 *supra*. *Compare* Blumberg, *supra* note 8, at 1125, who proposes legislation without a contract element and with somewhat different definitions dependent upon the purpose of the law therewith, for example, mutual household, children, and cohabitation of a certain duration are objective criteria which can result in that unmarried cohabiting persons in certain situations are treated as married spouses.

157 With respect to reasons behind common law marriage, *see* Section 4.3 *supra*.

7. *Simply a Requirement of Moving in Together to a Mutual Residence*

The application problems discussed above give us reason to inquire whether these problems could be limited by a different formulation of the requisites. One possible method, well worth considering, is to greatly limit the requirement of cohabitation and simultaneously apply a high requirement with respect to the contract. Instead of the current method of collectively assessing a large number of undetermined factors, as is the case now, the proof would be limited to one single limited factor determined in time and space, which in addition to the contract, would alone be necessary and sufficient.

Ancient Rome appears to have required for the establishment of a free marriage, the marital *consensus* and the women's admission to the man's home, *deductio in domum mariti*. Similarly, the requirement for the formation of a common law marriage, in addition to the contract, could be that the parties have moved in together to a mutual residence.[158] A man and a woman, who have entered into an oral agreement, perhaps before witnesses, to create a family and to live together, and even agreeing that the legal consequences of marriage are to be applicable to their relationship, should receive the legal consequences of marriage on the same day they move into together to a mutual residence. The moving in together would be comparable to publicity in the civil arena. Thus, the parties have shown that the contract was seriously intended and that the marriage has commenced. Both of these requisites ought to be fulfilled simultaneously. If the parties already have an applicable agreement, the legal consequences should be invoked on the day that the moving in together occurs. If they have first moved in together, and then later enter into the contract, the legal consequences should be invoked on the day the contract was executed.

This solution should limit the application problems. The legal considerations should be facilitated. Precarious assessments about the legal relevance of the separate components of cohabitation could thus be avoided. Such a system would be advantageous from an evidentiary perspective. Proving the moving in together of the parties ought not to lead to any great difficulties. As a fairly determined point of time is established, such a system would be beneficial from a legal certainty viewpoint. The parties have the ability beforehand to predict when the legal consequences will be invoked. The commencement of the cohabitation would be viewed as the performance of the contract.[159] One must demonstrate that the relationship did not stop with simply the contract, but that the marriage was also commenced, however, nothing more! Extensive examinations into

---

158 With respect to the requirement of *deductio in domum mariti* with the establishing of a free marriage in ancient Rome, which is debated, *see* Section 2.4.2 *supra*.

159 *Georgia Osteopathic Hosp. v. O'Neal*, 403 S.E.2d 235, 243 (Ga.App. 1991).

the existence of the different elements of cohabitation and holding out would not be necessary. Therewith, difficult and intrusive examinations concerning the parties' sexual relationship could be avoided.[160]

If one wishes to protect the parties against hasty contracts, an agreement before witnesses and the moving in together ought to reasonably give rise to consideration on the part of the parties. The goal of protecting third parties who enter into relationships with the parties, however, is not normally achieved until after a longer period of cohabitation, if at all. This goal ought to be able to be met through the particular regulations governing such third-party relationships.

It appears more dubious whether a requirement of moving in together serves the purpose of the requisite of cohabitation to create a protection against fraudulent claims. Certainly, a strict application of the contract requirement, as well as the requirement for moving in together ought to act as a restraint. Hopefully, few persons would go through this trouble for the purpose of making a claim against another party, the estate of a deceased, or the State. Even if there is no fraudulent intent, one can further object that the legal consequences of marriage are intended for marriages effected through a cohabitation that is longer and more extensive than simply moving in together. Therefore, it appears motivated within the framework of the marital legal system with respect to certain legal consequences to employ an equitable rule that would take into consideration the lack of cohabitation, for example, with respect to claims made on an estate.

Other legal consequences, for example, the parties' marital status, the marital status of the children, the regulations governing divorce, etc., on the other hand should be invoked immediately based on the contract and the moving in together.

There does not appear to be any great need to create a specific exception to the requirement of moving in together where cohabitation has not been possible for example due to employment, education, military duty, health care, etc. To arrange for a moving in together ought to be probable in the majority of cases.

An objective requisite limited to the parties' moving in together needs not facilitate establishing a common law marriage. The emphasis with the proof is centered instead on the issue of whether the contract requisite is fulfilled. To the extent that the parties' cohabitation in concrete cases is limited to simply acquiring a mutual residence, this ought not normally, simply based on this, prove the existence of an implied agreement, regardless of whether the requirement of the parties' intent consists of an intent

160 Neither did free Roman marriages require sexual relations. *Copula carnalis* came first into being with the canon law, *see* Section 3.3.3 *supra*.

to live a life together or the intent to establish a legal relation.[161] In such cases, an express agreement ought to be required. Where the parties consequently have entered into a written or oral contract before witnesses and thereafter have moved in together in a mutual residence, this should establish a common law marriage. If nothing is expressed in a contract, which today appears to be the most common case, the possibility is still open, from the parties' cohabitation in a broader sense, to find the existence of an implied agreement. With respect to the possibilities and difficulties, with the support of a more extensive cohabitation, of finding the existence of a marital *consensus*, see the discussion in Chapter 7 and Section 13.2.3 in the present chapter.

8. *Cohabitation in Relationships Other than Couple Relationships*

One new aspect in the development of the concept of family in the Western world during recent years in several countries has been the enactment of legislation with limited regulations for relationships other than couple relationships, for example cohabiting siblings, or parents and adult children, friends, work acquaintances, or students. From a conceptual perspective, these relationships differ from the formal marriage, common law marriage, and the legally recognized cohabitation relationships, in that the customary requirements as to legal capacity concerning for example family relationships and monogamy are not applicable. On the other hand, a shared household or cohabitation is ordinarily required albeit that the latter does not, as normally is the case concerning the other relationships, include any sexual community. The parties' dependence upon each other or that one without compensation takes care of the other is emphasized instead. Pervasive through all these is that the legal effects of these relationships are limited.

This type of legislation from 1991 in **Norway** is applicable not only to men and women who live together, but also to two or several unmarried persons over 18 years living in a shared residence, for example homosexual couples, siblings, students, or friends. If the parties have lived together at least two years or have mutual children, a member of the household at the relationship's dissolution has the right under certain circumstances to take over the residence and household goods that have been used jointly. If the assets taken over have a value, that party must pay compensation thereto.[162]

---

161 However, there are cases in which the contract is partially expressed, and there the moving in together can be considered sufficient as an implied agreement. Assume that a man asks the woman if she will live a life together with him within the marital legal regulatory system and she is to answer yes by moving in with him. It is clear then that the woman's moving in with the man in such a case could establish a common law marriage.

162 Law No. 45, 4 July 1991. *See* Peter Lødrup, *Family Law in Norway*, in FAMILY LAW IN EUROPE 353 (Carolyn Hamilton et al. eds., 1995).

The legislation enacted in **Belgium** in 1998 and that came into force in January 2000 was made applicable as to both homosexual and heterosexual couples, but in addition also to other relationships, for example, a parent and children or two siblings.[163] The legislation enacted in the province of **Alberta** in Canada in 2002 gives certain rights to "adult interdependent partners," wherewith is meant persons of the same or different sexes living together at least three years, or who have had children in a relationship of a certain durability, or who have entered into a written agreement. The concept also includes relationships between siblings, friends or between a parent and an adult child, that are financial and emotionally dependent upon each other. This legislation gives legal effects concerning *inter alia* maintenance, damages, and workmen's compensation, but does not contain regulations concerning a division of property.[164] According to legislation in **New South Wales,** Australia, there are regulations for "a close personal relationship," that is not marriage or "de facto relationship" between two adult persons who live together, regardless of whether they are related to each other, of whom one or both without compensation "provides the other with domestic support and personal care."[165]

Objections can be made against this type of legislation, that the relationships and needs are so different from one case to another that their legal problems are better solved with private individualized agreements and wills than with general legislation.[166]

9. The Application Problems of the Cohabitation Requisites

Behind all the endeavors in the above-presented cohabitation laws and the proposals to more closely define the relationships and identify relevant factors as support for the application of the concepts of cohabitation used, the objectives of facilitating the assessments, preventing disputes, and creating predictability and legal certainty have been recurrent. The Swedish lawmaker's objective with the enactment of the new Swedish Cohabitees Act in 2003[167] consequently was to create a clearer definition of the term cohabiting persons, and the Scottish lawmaker states with the new regulations for cohabiting persons that came into force in 2006 the intent to obtain "greater certainty, fairness and clarity."[168] A goal of ALI's proposed principles is likewise to create rules that are "consistent and predictable" and Grace Blumberg, who contributed to the drafting of the

---

163 Article 1475, Code Civile.

164 Adult Interdependent Relationships Act, S.A. (2002), c. A-4.5.

165 *See* Property (Relationships) Act (1984), as amended through The Property (Relationships) Amendment Act (1999), section 5 (1)(b).

166 *See, e.g.*, the Swedish government has found that there is no need for a legal regulation for persons in shared households other than cohabiting persons, for example, family relatives, friends and work acquaintances that share residence, *see* Prop. 2002/03:80. at 26.

167 Prop. 2002/03:80, at 27.

168 Policy Memorandum, Family Law (Scotland) Bill (SP Bill 36) (2005), at 13.

proposal, has assumed that the burdensome investigation of facts will no longer be necessary and the application problems will be avoided with the use of the proposed presumption.[169] These efforts are promising, but unfortunately appear unrealistic, an expression of wishful thinking!

Characteristic for the number of factors presented in the legislation as relevant is that they are not always necessary or always sufficient for the establishment of a legally recognized cohabitation relationship. It is left open from case to case to determine which factors are to be used as a basis for the decisions and to contemplate the weight each is to be given. It is alarming when the criteria are based on taking into consideration, as ALI expresses it, "the extent to which" or as Waggoner states, "the degree to which," the parties acted in one or another manner. Such assessments typically never lead to any certain and predictable results.

Marsha Garrison correctly stated that the ALI Principles "direct the fact-finder to consider thirteen different factors that together encompass virtually every aspect of a relationship ... Most of the factors require an incremental assessment; none identifies a threshold level of significance"; and she arrives at the conclusion that many cohabiting couples would be hard-pressed to accurately predict whether their relationship had produced legal obligations or not and that the system produces enormous uncertainty.[170] The criteria applicable in New Zealand have received similar criticism. Thus Bill Atkin has stated that the definition of a de facto relationship is problematic and that there is now a steady stream of cases.[171]

A legitimate question then is whether the requirement of cohabitation for *a certain period* as applied in several legal systems is beneficial for the principle of legal certainty as the parties then have the possibility of predicting at which point of time the regulations, so to say, will strike. To the extent the parties know the time frame, this ought in the best case to give them a possibility upon the approach of its expiration to avoid the legal effects by dissolving the relationship. At the same time, a time frame raises

---

169 Blumberg, *supra* note 137, at 1298–1299.

170 Garrison, *supra* note 10, at 850–52. *See also* David Westfall, *Forcing Incidents of Marriage on Unmarried Cohabitants: The American Law Institute's Principles of Family Dissolution*, 76 NOTRE DAME L. REV. 1467, 1479 (2001), who fears "a troubling degree of uncertainty" in decisions of whether a "domestic partnership status" exists.

171 Bill Atkin, *Reflections, supra* note 126, at 222-223, where he analyses new cases, *e.g.*, *Scragg v. Scott* (2006) N.Z.F.L.R. 1076 and *P.Z. v. J.Z.* (2006) N.Z.F.L.R. 97. *See also* Bill Atkin, *The Rights of Married and Unmarried Couples in New Zealand: Radical New Laws on Property and Succession*, International Society of Family Law World Conference, unpublished paper, Copenhagen/Oslo, (august 2002), at 3, who anticipates that "this reform is a leap into the dark for New Zealand law and is to be heavily litigated." *See also* Bill Atkin, *The Challenge of Unmarried Cohabitation – The New Zealand Response*, 37 FAM. L.Q. 303, 318 (2003); and Virginia Grainer, *What's Yours Is Mine: Reform of the Property Division Regime for Unmarried Couples in New Zealand*, 11 PAC. RIM. L. & POL'Y J. 285, 303 (2002).

a series of issues that do not have any certain answers. From which point of time is the period to begin to be calculated? How many of all of the factors within the concept "cohabitation" as set forth so ambitiously by lawmakers (joint residence, sexual community, shared residence, mutual children, financial support, etc.) must exist in a concrete case in order for the time period to begin to run? When the cohabitation in the meaning of the law has well begun, the question arises of whether the period is to be tolled if any of the relevant factors are weakened or cease during the time period. The cohabitation for a period can have been deficient in one or another manner. The parties perhaps due to work in different places, studies, or military service have not shared a household or residence the entire time. One party at some occasion has had a relationship with someone else, etc. Must it be a consecutive period of a model community or is it sufficient with a consecutive, albeit not ideal, relationship during the prescribed period? Can one combine several short but promising periods of exemplary cohabitation interrupted by periods in which the parties' cohabitation has been deficient or they purely lived apart?

The questions raised have no certain answers and indicate that a requirement of a certain period of cohabitation most likely will give rise to considerable application problems and does not create the predictability that it purports to achieve. The application of the time period required in New Zealand (three years) has been problematic.[172]

In contrast with common law marriage, which must formally be dissolved, cohabitation legislation also raises the question of when a legally recognized cohabitation relationship is to be seen as dissolved. The lawmakers here have ordinarily not employed a contractual element according to which the parties terminate the relationship but rather instead stayed with ties to the objective circumstances, for example a party's move from the mutual residence. These objective constructions have difficulties in solving cases in which a move occurs successively or is more or less definitive, or cases in which the parties are still living together after the relationship is dissolved because of difficulty in acquiring a new residence.

Despite laudable ambitions, the cohabitation concepts that during later years have been launched by the ALI and in the laws in Sweden, Scotland, Australia, New Zealand, Canada, and in the case law from the state of Washington, lead to the very problems that the instigators wished to avoid, namely application problems, unnecessary disputes and costs to society, lack of predictability, and a considerable legal uncertainty. The experiences with the application of the requirement of cohabitation within the framework for common law marriage results in that the risks ought to be taken seriously as further discussed in Chapter 8. The use of presumptions as further discussed in Section 13.4.2, does not ultimately change this assessment.

---

172 Bill Atkin, *Reflections, supra* note 126, at 222.

In addition, the significance attributed the parties' *sexual relationship* causes investigations that entail a danger for personal integrity, adding to the problems.[173] The lawmaker faced with legislation based on a requisite of cohabitation ought to be aware that there is a price that must be paid. Whether this price is worth paying must also be assessed taking into consideration the other arguments for and against the legislation as examined further in Chapter14.

13.4 The Use of Burdens of Proof and Evidentiary Presumptions

The uses of different subjective and objective elements were discussed in the two previous sections in order to examine different suitable constructions of the material requisites concerning the formation of a common law marriage. However, the starting point at trial with respect to the existence of such marriages depends on the procedural rules. More than one thousand cases were examined for this study; the litigation has been extensive, with many witness and evidentiary issues that are difficult to assess. Particularly through the regulations concerning burdens of proof and evidentiary presumptions, lawmakers and the courts are able to influence the outcomes of the cases.

We found in Chapter 9, in which we discussed the current state of the law, that the courts are divided about the required standard of proof. There is a structural contradiction between, on one side, the applied

173 According to ALI's recommendations, *supra* note 9, consideration is to be given to "the emotional or physical intimacy of the parties' relationship," *see* § 6.03, paragraph 7 (h). *See also* Westfall, *id.*, at 1473–1474, who fears a "detailed inquiry into the most intimate aspects of the partner's lives." The parties' sexual relationship and its monogamous character are also relevant with the assessment of the relationship's "purpose, constancy" and "exclusivity" according to Waggoner's list of factors, Westfall *supra* note 144, at 83. Even the legislation in the province of Manitoba in Canada concerning "conjugal relationships" between common-law partners considers factors as the parties' "sleeping arrangements" and "sexual relationship," *see* Manitoba Justice, Changes to Property Laws affecting Common-Law Partners taking effect June 30, 2004. Likewise the legislation in New Zealand and Australia considers "whether or not a sexual relationship exists," section 2D Property (Relationships) Act 1976, in its new wording that entered into force 1 February 2002. In the case of *Scragg v. Scott* (2006) N.Z.F.L.R. 1076 the court held that for there to be a relationship there must be "an emotional association." But a sexual relationship with another did not end the de facto relationsip. The case is analysed in Bill Atkin, *Reflections, supra* note 126, at 223-224.The comparable elements can also be found in the legislation from New South Wales, Australia, *see* section 4(1)(2) Property (Relationships) Act (1984). Even the Swedish Minister of Justice contemplated a cohabitation in which normally is included sexual cohabitation, *see* prop. 1986/87:1, at 252–253, as well as prop. 2002/03:80, at 44. How intrusive the evidence can become can be seen from the Australian case *Bar-Mordecai v. Rotman & others* (2000) N.S.W.C.A. 123, in which video films concerning the parties' sexual activities were cited as evidence. *See also* Section 14.3.7 *infra.*

burden of proof, and, on the other side, the marriage presumption. In this section, we will critically review the reasons behind the current system and discuss the need for and suitability of the applied evidentiary burden of proofs and presumptions with respect to the future course of the law.

13.4.1 The Burden of Proof and the Standard of Evidence

There is good reason, when determining whether a common law marriage exists, to place the burden of proof on the party claiming the existence of such a marriage, consistent with general evidentiary principles.[174] The risk for fraudulent claims and abuse of the regulations are particularly strong justifications for such a rule.[175] This is true with respect to the relationship between the parties, if one party is making a claim against the other or their estate, as well as if the parties collude in making a claim for a public right, under the premise that they have entered into a common law marriage. The burden of proof ought to address each of the necessary requisites; in other words, the parties' legal capacity to enter into marriage, their contract, and, where appropriate, their cohabitation and reputation as spouses or such similar requirement.

With respect to the applicable standard of evidence, the courts, today, are divided, as seen in Chapter 9. Certain courts require clear and convincing evidence, while others, in accordance with the general rules, require a preponderance of the evidence.[176] The adoption of a stance on this issue ought not, as has often been the case, be driven by either a positive or negative view of common law marriage.[177] The decision should, instead, be based on more rational reasoning. Included here would naturally be the risk of fraudulent claims and the abuse of regulations, a risk that can influence not only the placement of the burden of proof but also the required standard of evidence.[178] In addition, it is significant that the standard of evidence is determined in terms of the substantive requisites that are to be proven, as well as their construction. The best situation is

---

174 *Clark v. Cassidy*, 64 Ga. 662, 667 (1880).

175 The need for protection against fraudulent claims appears clearly in the case law, *see* Chapters 9 and 14.3 *supra.*

176 *See* Chapter 9, Burdens of Proof and Legal Presumptions, *supra.*

177 *Metro. Life Ins. Co. v. Johnson,* 103 Idaho 122, 645 P.2d 356, 360 (1982): "Idaho has never viewed the doctrine of common law marriage with disfavor. Together with a small number of other states, Idaho permits a non-ceremonial marriage to be proven by a preponderance of the evidence." Note, however, that Idaho repealed common law marriage beginning 1996 (H.B. 176; Chap. 104, 1995 Idaho Session Laws). In the case of *In re Marriage of Winegard,* 278 N.W.2d 505, 510 (Iowa 1979), the Iowa Supreme Court stated: "The burden of proof lies on the party asserting its existence, and such a claim of marriage will be regarded with suspicion, there being no public policy in Iowa favoring common law marriage." *See also* Chapter 9 *supra.*

178 *See* Chapter 9 *supra.*

substantive requisites that are chosen and formulated so that the normal standard of evidence can be applied.

Nevertheless, if the requisite of cohabitation, in the same manner as today, is a requirement of cohabitation as well as a holding out or reputation with all of the component elements, a high standard of evidence, comparable to clear and convincing evidence, appears to be well justified by the application difficulties that arise. On the other hand, if the requisite of cohabitation is limited, for example, to a requirement of the parties' moving in together, a circumstance that ought to be relatively easy to prove, there is scarcely a reason to depart from the general standard of evidence.

With respect to the contract requisite, it appears that the acceptance of implied agreements justifies the application of a high evidentiary standard, albeit a stricter legal application would then also be desirable.[179] On the other hand, if the contract requisite contains the requirement of an express contract, the normal evidentiary standard should be sufficient. If the contract requisite materially contains only the requirement of a legal intent, the standard of evidence would scarcely need to be above that which is the norm. Consequently, it ought to be difficult to find a legal intent that is supported by the cohabitation. It is important that the burden of proof with respect to the contract remains with the party claiming the existence of a common law marriage. If the contract requisite contains an intent to live together, it appears that the requirement of clear and consistent evidence is better justified. Needless to say, a uniform evidentiary standard is of a value in itself.[180]

If the requisite of cohabitation is limited, for example, to a requirement of the parties' moving in together – a circumstance that ought to be relatively easy to prove – neither is there any reason to depart from the general evidentiary standard.

In terms of the contract requisite, it appears that the acceptance of implied agreements gives rise to a motivation for a higher evidentiary

---

179 *See* the criticism of the legal application as found in Section 7.8 *supra*.

180 It is not difficult to find areas where it can be necessary to heighten the general standard of proof. Simultaneously, there is an advantage, if significant reasons do not exist, in not departing from general evidentiary principles. Another method for achieving a restrictive stance with respect to common law marriage is to sharpen the substantive regulations. This can occur with respect to the contract, where, as seen in the previous section, the content of the contract can have as its object an intent to legally establish a marriage, simply just obtain a few of the legal consequences, or a qualified intent to live together or both. This can occur with respect to the forms of the contract by the requirement of an express contract. A sharpening is also possible with respect to the requisite of cohabitation, which can contain a requirement for a very long-term and qualified cohabitation and an extensive and undivided reputation as spouses. However, lawmakers must be conscious of the fact that every heightening of the material regulations will result in a reduction of the area of application and that couples may therefore fall outside of the system.

standard, albeit a stricter application would also be desirable.[181] If the contract requisite, on the other hand, is given a stricter formulation, for example, by the requirement of an express contract or legal intent, or through a stricter application of the civil legal requirements of offer and acceptance, it ought to be satisfactory to require a preponderance of evidence.

13.4.2 Presumptions

1. *The Marriage Presumption*

As seen in Chapter 9, the marriage presumption can be decisive to the outcome of a case concerning the existence of a common law marriage. If the party claiming the existence of such a marriage is successful in proving cohabitation and reputation, the parties are presumed to have entered into a contract. Consequently, the law concludes that no marital *consensus*, in principle, need be proven. The burden of proof shifts to the other party, who then must prove that a contract was not entered into. Given the difficulties of proving a subjective requisite and, in addition, the negative of a supposition, the presumption contributes to capturing cases in which the parties' marital *consensus* is questionable, within the marital legal framework.

A fundamental is that the elements forming the basis for the application of the presumption, must truly be elements that can indicate the existence of that being presumed, which holds significant legal consequences. Further, another basic condition is that the elements of the presumption be reasonable requirements in terms of determination and predictability. It can be questioned whether the elements of cohabitation and reputation, today, are truly typical of that considered *prima facie* evidence of the existence of a marital *consensus*.

This question is motivated against the background of the development that has occurred in the past few years with respect to patterns of family building and relationships between men and women. In discussing inferred agreements, we stated in Chapter 7 that the stigma of the past no longer exists with respect to living together without formally entering into a marriage. Such relationships have, therefore, become more common. The group of couples living together without formally marrying, however, contains different kinds of relationships. Those who outwardly appear to be rather similar with respect to cohabitation cases can greatly differ greatly with respect to the parties' intentions. Certain couples live together on a trial basis before separating and going on to new relationships with others. Others live together for a time without any long-term intentions at all. For others, the first period of cohabitation is followed by a formal marriage or a formless lifelong cohabitation. Further, different couples can

181 *See* the criticism of the legal application in Section 7.8 *supra*.

have entirely different intentions regarding the legal regulation of their relationship.

This development, as Nancy Shaw has pointed out, naturally affects the credibility and utility of presumptions based upon cohabitation and reputation as elements in assessing whether a marriage exists.[182] However, this question, to a large degree, depends on the content of the contract being presumed.[183]

If the object of the marital intent is to live together as husband and wife, and the parties actually have done this, perhaps for many years, and in addition, have acquired reputation as spouses, it is then clear that the parties' cohabitation and reputation can be used as a basis for the presumption. Shorter periods of cohabitation, of perhaps only one or two years, on the other hand, can be on a trial basis, without any intent to live together on a long-term basis. The application of the presumption then requires American courts to be much stricter than usual in applying the requirement that the cohabitation truly is constant and that the parties' reputation truly is general.

On the other hand, if the object of the marital intent is a legal intent, for example, the intent to change the legal status of the parties, or to assume the marital duties and obligations of husband and wife,[184] it is clear that the parties' actual cohabitation and reputation, even though the cohabitation is long term, can be strongly questioned as a basis of the presumption. The parties can very well have had the intent to live an entire life together, but without any marital rights or obligations. The fact that they have not entered into a formal marriage can indicate this, and trigger the opposite presumption.

The use of a legal marital intent, therefore, is a strong reason not to apply the marriage presumption as stated above, and a strong reason for the burden of proof to remain with the party claiming the existence of a common law marriage!

These circumstances, discussed in Chapter 7 encourage greater caution by the courts than has been the case in proving implied agreements based on the parties' cohabitation and reputation, and drawing conclusions as to their marital intentions, even if we did not recommend a general prohibition.[185] The reasons are, however, stronger and suggest that the marriage presumption should be repealed because the law itself draws conclusions that may lack a basis in reality.

---

182 Shaw, *supra* note 79, at 593, states: "[T]he great weight traditionally accorded to the fact of cohabitation and reputation no longer has rational validity in an age in which the incidence of unmarried cohabitation has increased dramatically."

183 The content of the contract has significance not only with respect to the issue of whether there is a reason to employ legal presumptions based on "cohabitation" and "reputation." In individual cases, the question is pertinent as to which objections can be made as to the existence of a common law marriage.

184 *Jambrone v. David*, 16 Ill.2d 32, 156 N.E.2d 569, 572 (1959).

185 *See* § 13.2.3 *supra.*

A repeal of the marriage presumption raises the question of whether the purpose underlying the presumption can be achieved in a different manner. As seen from Chapter 9, the underlying basis of the marriage presumption is an attempt to save couples living together by granting them a marital status. Traditionally, the interests that are stressed are those of children and their legitimacy; surviving spouses and children in the case of death; and the value of favoring remarriage, have been stressed.[186] These and similar arguments are repeated even in modern case law.[187]

---

186 *Hynes v. McDermott*, 91 N.Y. 451, 459, 43 Am.Rep. 677 (1883) ("The law presumes morality and not immorality; marriage, and not concubinage; legitimacy, and not bastardy.") The reasons narrated above are cited with approval in innumerable cases up to the present day. With respect to the jurisdictions which today recognize common law marriage, *see* the cases particularly from Idaho and South Carolina, *e.g. Huff v. Huff*, 20 Idaho 450, 118 P. 1080 (1911); *Ollschlager's Estate v. Widmer*, 55 Or. 145, 105 P. 717 (1909); *Labonte v. Davidson*, 31 Idaho 644, 175 P. 588 (1918); *Smith v. Smith*, 32 Idaho 478, 482, 185 P. 67, 69 (1919); *Mauldin v. Sunshine Mining Co.*, 61 Idaho 9, 17, 97 P.2d 608, 611 (1939); *Nicholas v. Idaho Power Co.*, 63 Idaho 675, 125 P.2d 321 (1942); *Warner v. Warner*, 76 Idaho 399, 282 P.2d 931, 934 (1955); *Thomey v. Thomey*, 67 Idaho 393, 181 P.2d 777, 779 (1947); *Jeanes v. Jeanes*, 255 S.C. 161, 177 S.E.2d 537, 539-540 (1970); *In re Estate of Brock*, 94 Idaho 111, 482 P.2d 86, 90 (1971); and *Metro. Life Ins. Co. v. Johnson*, 103 Idaho 122, 645 P.2d 356, 361 (1982).

187 In *Johnson v. Lincoln Square Properties*, 571 So.2d 541, 542 (Fla.App. 2 Dist. 1990), the court consequently stated that the presumption "arises out of the concern of all civilized societies over the legitimacy of children, the descent and distribution of property and the sanctity of marriage as the keystone of Christian governments." *See also* the Montana Supreme Court in *Matter of Estate of Murnion*, 212 Mont. 107, 686 P.2d 893, 41 St.Rep. 1627 (1984); and *In re Estate of Swanson*, 160 Mont. 271, 502 P.2d 33, 37 (1972) ("Every intendment of the law is in favor of matrimony which presumes morality and not immorality, marriage and not concubinage, legitimacy and not bastardy"). In *Thomas v. Murphy*, 71 App. D.C. 69, 107 F.2d 268, 269 (1938), the court considered it socially sound to favor marriage between the parties before "concubinage." The marriage presumption was not, however, expressly discussed. *See also Welch v. All Persons*, 78 Mont. 370, 254 P. 179, 182 (1926) ("Every presumption will be indulged in favor of the legality of a common-law marriage in the same way and to the same extent as law indulges them in favor of a ceremonial marriage"); *Coachman v. Sims*, 36 Okla. 536, 129 P. 845, 847 (1913) ("The law is astute to preserve the sanctity of the marriage relation, the legitimacy of children, and stability of descent and distribution, and therefore presumes innocence and virtue, in the absence of proof"); and *compare Gammelgaard v. Gammelgaard* 247 Iowa 978, 77 N.W.2d 479 (1956) ("In doubtful cases, courts prefer that construction of evidence which finds a legitimate marriage rather than a long period of lewd and criminal cohabitation.") The last cited case concerned however an implied agreement rather than a presumption. With respect to the legitimacy of children, *see Dirion v. Brewer*, 20 Ohio App. 298, 151 N.E. 818, 819 (1925). In *Com. ex rel. Rubin v. Rubin*, 201 Pa.Super. 517, 193 A.2d 639, 640 (1963), the Pennsylvania Superior Court stated: "It is highly desirable that the birth of this child be legitimized." With respect to favoring remarriage, *see In re Wagner's Estate*, 398 Pa. 531, 533, 159 A.2d 495, 497 (1960), in which the parties, after their divorce, formlessly moved in together again: "We regard it better to encourage remarriage than to leave such parties under judicial edict that they were living sinfully together for ten years." *See also Com. ex rel. Rubin v. Rubin*, 201 Pa.Super. 517, 193 A.2d 639 (1963). The favoring of remarriage has been criticized, *see* Clark 1987, *supra* note 70, at 106.

The reasons behind the presumption are consequently very similar to the reasons underlying the entire legal doctrine of common law marriage.[188]

These goals, if deemed important, ought to be able to be achieved through the use of the substantive legal regulations, not a legal presumption that today lacks any basis in reality![189] To use a presumption based on cohabitation and reputation to prove something that the elements do not actually prove violates the truth!

The reason stated by Joel Prentiss Bishop that the marriage presumption is an offshoot of a more general presumption, namely, "the presumption of innocence," meaning that a couple is presumed not to be violating the due order of society and breaking the law, has lost its significance in step with reality that cohabitation outside of marriage has been decriminalized.[190]

Rejecting the marriage presumption would entail that the burden of proof with respect to the issue of whether a common law marriage was established, in agreement with the general principles, rests on the party claiming the existence of such a marriage. This ought to be true of all of the necessary requisites, in other words, the parties' legal capacity to enter into a marriage, their contract, and, in appropriate cases, their cohabitation or comparable requisite. Thus, the contradiction existing between the fundamental burden of proof and the marriage presumption is resolved.

2. *The Presumption of Cohabitation*

In the framework of the proposed cohabitation legislation that has grown during recent years, the use of presumptions—whose objective ordinarily is to facilitate the assessment of whether a legally recognized cohabitation relationship exists and limit the number of disputes—has appeared. Characteristic of these legal presumptions is that they, in contrast to the marriage presumption, do not presume that the parties have entered into a marriage contract, but rather that the existence of a cohabitation relationship, which is designated, for example, as a "domestic partnership," "marriage-like relationship," or "constructive marriage." The legal presumptions are ordinarily formulated so that if certain typical criteria exist in the cohabitation, a legally recognized cohabitation relationship is presumed, after which the burden of proof shifts to the opposing party, who

---

188 With respect to the reasons behind the legal institution of common law marriage, *see* Chapter 4 *supra*.

189 Where the lawmaker is prepared to take into consideration the parties' own intentions, the possibility is open to employ a contract that fits. Where the lawmaker does not wish to take into consideration their legal intentions, simply their intent to live together can be considered. If the lawmaker wishes to completely disregard their intentions, the legal consequences can be tied simply to the actual cohabitation. These material legal issues, which fall outside of the framework of this section, are discussed in §§ 14.2 and 14.3 *supra*.

190 JOEL PRENTISS BISHOP, NEW COMMENTARIES ON MARRIAGE, DIVORCE AND SEPARATION (1891), §§ 931–932.

has to rebut the presumption with the support of other circumstances proving that no cohabitation relationship existed.

The above-mentioned ALI Principles contain consequently, as a complement to the substantive regulations concerning "domestic partnership," a presumption according to which the parties are presumed to be domestic partners if they have shared a household during a certain period, which each state decides. (The Comments suggest three years.) The presumption is rebuttable by evidence that the parties "did not share life together as a couple."[191]

Lawrence Waggoner also supplements his above-mentioned definition of a "marriage-like relationship" with a presumption, according to which the relationship is presumed to be marriage-like if: "(1) during the (six) year period next preceding the decedent's death, the decedent and the individual lived together for periods totaling at least (five) years; (2) the decedent and the individual registered as domestic partners with and under procedures established by an organization and neither partner executed a document terminating or purporting to terminate the registration; or (3) the individual is the parent of a child of the decedent who, at the decedent's death, was regularly living in the same household with the decedent and was younger than 18 years of age." If in accordance, the relationship is presumed to be marriage-like, the burden of proof shifts to the opposing party, who has to prove the opposite.[192]

Ellen Kandoian argues that a form of common law marriage could be presumed if a cohabitation relationship has had a certain durability because "it is likely that the early stages of cohabitation represent an experiment on the part of both parties, attaching legal consequences too soon could be contrary to the intention of both." With the determination of the point at which the legal effects of the presumption are invoked, the author speaks of "a substantial period of time, for example after two or more years," at which it becomes probable that one of the parties "feels married."[193] Kandoian's difficulties in defining the point of time of these feelings and the cohabitating couple's difficulties in detecting them do not serve the interest of clarity.

The same problems are faced by David Caudill's proposed presumption, to be applied if (1) the parties have lived together in an intimate relationship for at least two years in a single-family housing unit; and (2) there is evidence of economic interdependence including sharing of financial burdens, pooling of financial resources, or any division of domestic and support functions such that economic dependence of one spouse results; and (3) the parties have represented themselves to be living together as a family unit by, for example, rearing children, renting or purchasing a

191 *See* The ALI Principles, *supra* note 9, § 6.03 (3).
192 Waggoner, *supra* note 144, at 80.
193 Kandoian, *supra* note 28, at 1863.

dwelling together, holding themselves out as husband and wife, or representing that their relationship is like that of a conventional marriage.[194] The presumption termed *constructive marriage* is proposed to be rebuttable. It is obvious that the stated circumstances would lead to application difficulties and make it difficult to predict when the presumption becomes applicable.

It is doubtful that the cohabitation presumption can facilitate the assessment of whether such a relationship exists and reduce the number of disputes to any great extent. There is reason to assume that the opposing party will first contest the existence of the required elements in order to avoid application of the presumption. This assessment, in several cases, can require extensive evidence from both sides concerning whether the parties had been cohabiting and shared a household during the prescribed period. If he or she fails to produce adequate evidence, the party most likely will attempt to rebut the presumption by presenting evidence of all the relevant factors. It is easy to see that a counterpart who, with the application of the ALI Principles, maintains that the parties "did not share life together as a couple" raises questions concerning the significance of "a shared life" and of that living together "as a couple," which neither legally nor evidentiarily will have any certain answers.

Elizabeth Scott has recommended an alteration of the ALI Principles by proposing a presumption that is closely related to the common law marriage presumption because it involves the parties' intentions. Under her model, called "a Contract Default Rule Framework," a five-year relationship establishes a presumption of an intent to undertake marital obligations. The premise of the presumption seems to be that if a couple provides clear evidence through their conduct that the relationship is marriage-like, an agreement to assume marital obligations can be inferred. A couple living together for many years, sharing a life and financial resources, and holding themselves out as husband and wife, can be presumed to intend to share the property acquired during the relationship.[195]

As we found with regard to the common law marriage presumption, it can be questioned today whether legal intentions can generally be inferred from marriage-like cohabitation.[196] Elizabeth Scott's five-year rule, of course, would eliminate many short-term relationships, but even though the cohabitation is long, the parties may have chosen not to marry in order to avoid martial obligations. It can be questioned whether the proposed default rule rests on realistic empirical assumptions about the intentions of couples in long-term informal unions. The model seems to require investigations concerning the cohabitation, when it commenced and ended, and whether it was sufficiently marriage-like during the whole period.

---

194 Caudill, *supra* note 29, at 568.
195 Scott, *supra* note 10, at 342-345.
196 *See supra* in this Chapter, Chapters 9 and 7.

The party who tries to rebut the presumption will probably present evidence about the parties' intentions not to undertake marital obligations but just to cohabit. It is difficult to see how this model avoids litigation and uncertainty.

13.5 Summary and Conclusions

This chapter has focused on a critical discussion concerning the different constructions of the constitutive elements and presumptions applicable in the establishment of a common law marriage and a legally recognized cohabitation. This discussion is appropriate for two reasons. First, common law marriage, as a rule, has been accepted in the case law and, as a result, such discussion has seldom occurred. Second, solutions have been presented during the past thirty years in the cohabitation laws in the Western world. Naturally, the presentation has been directed primarily at lawmakers considering whether to recognize common law marriage or cohabitation.

1. The Parties' Consensus as a Necessary Element

The absence of a critical discussion is felt to the greatest extent with respect to issue of the parties' *consensus* as a necessary element for the establishment of a common law marriage or legally recognized cohabitation, respectively. The Roman maxim, *consensus facit nuptias,* was adopted by the medieval canon law and later incorporated by American jurisdictions in the case law. The principle that marriage, the form-bound as well as the formless, is based on a contract, therefore, was not the object of any thorough critical review. The courts and lawmakers have more or less taken the principle for granted.

We began this chapter by raising the question of whether a general need exists to work with a contract element as a necessary requisite for the formation of a common law marriage. If the parties cohabit with each other, the legal consequences of marriage or a legally recognized cohabitation can be tied as easily directly to their cohabitation.

If this line of reasoning is continued, it can be argued that such a system should better reflect reality. From the presentation in Chapter 7, we saw that the majority of couples drift into a formless cohabitation without entering into any express contract. Against this background, we can question whether there is any need to apply a legal contract construction upon a reality in which it is not apparent to the parties? The risk of a legal fiction then exists, in that the parties concerned are placed in a situation they do not recognize and which simply leads to evidentiary problems and conflicts.

In this chapter, we have found that a more thorough discussion concerning the need for a contract depends on the content of the intent, the *essensialia negotii*, that the parties must have given in order for the legal consequences to be invoked, as well as whether the assessment of these issues is *ex ante* or *ex post*.

2. *An Intent to Live Together*

If the mutual intent must be an intent to live together, we have come to the conclusion that the need for a contract appears to be limited to assessments made *ex post*. If the parties have actually lived together for twenty years, there is scarcely any point in afterwards stating that they also had a contract to live together during this time. Instead of taking a detour from the contract construction, it appears that, for long-term cohabitations, as a rule it is more suitable to tie the legal consequences directly to the cohabitation, for the purpose of assessments made *ex post*. If it is found desirable that even short term or insufficient relationships receive the legal consequences of marriage or a legally recognized cohabitation, we have found that such a contract can have a certain function.

On the other hand, with assessments made *ex ante*, we have come to the conclusion that it can be advantageous to tie the legal consequences to a contract in which the object of the marital intent is constituted of the parties' cohabitation. Such a contract, as opposed to the actual cohabitation, speaks to the future. Based on the mirror image theory, it follows that there should be a long-term intent to live together. A contract with such an intent can also contribute to maintaining the distinction between trial and final relationships. It can also provide a certain protection against formless, sham relationships.

Given a requirement of an intent to live together, the question arises about what the intended cohabitation is to consist of in order for a contract to be considered to exist. The question is significant because the boundaries of the required intent to live together directly influence the scope of application. If the requirement is too high, this will mean, from the perspective of the parties, that they can be denied rights they should have had; from the state's perspective, the obligations of relationship cannot be imposed upon cases that fall outside of the system. If the requirement is too low, the legal consequences of the relationship will apply even to those relationships for which they were not intended. Herein lies the significant problem in the use of an intent to live together.

Despite the rise in the number of divorces, if the commencement of the marriage is used to determine intent, *i.e.*, the point at which the contract was entered into, the majority of couples have a mutual intent to continually live together in a monogamous relationship including companionship as broad as possible. Therefore, it ought to be realistic and also compatible with the intentions of the legal system to use a *consensus* that, if possible, encompasses a *consortium omnis vitae*. A diluted requirement of an intent to live together presents the risk that cases can fall within the marital legal system not intended for them.

From the perspective of the parties, it appears that the most serious objection to a contract based on an intent to live together is that those persons not choosing or desiring to be captured by the legal system may nevertheless fall within it. This negative effect is even stronger if the parties have agreed to live a life together, but refrain from formally marrying just in order to avoid marriage and its legal consequences. Such a contract can, therefore, pose a risk to legal certainty, particularly because many couples are not aware that a common law marriage entails legal consequences as extensive as those of a ceremonial marriage.

From the perspective of a state wishing to control and influence couples living together and creating families, it can be advantageous to tie the legal consequences to the parties' agreement to live together, regardless of whether they desire the legal consequences. This is true, not least, with respect to public benefits.

3. A Legal Intent

On the other hand, the consequences are different if the parties, in order for a contract to be considered established, must have had an intent to establish something legal, for example, "the legal relationship" or "the legal status of marriage." Such formulations of the object of the parties' intent begin with the idea that marriage or cohabitation as a legal or status relationship entails a number of legal consequences and that the parties' purpose, or one of their purposes, in entering into the relationship is to achieve these.

The required intent can be formulated, however, as an intent to receive all or certain of the legal consequences of marriage or a legally recognized cohabitation, for example, those that are mandatory. The legal intent can also be more generally formulated as an intent to accept a marital status or a legal relationship. The choice as to the depth of the intent can have substantial consequences, among other things, in the application of the regulations.

If the parties, by either entering into marriage or refraining from it, make a conscious legal decision, we conclude that a marital contract, in which the object of the parties' intent is a legal element, can preserve individual freedom and legal certainty for the parties. For couples choosing to live together without formally marrying, just for the purpose of avoiding the legal consequences of marriage or a legally recognized cohabitation, it is consistent and fair that the regulations not be imposed on them.

A contract based on a legal intent, as also seen in this chapter, can have a function if the cohabitation has insufficiencies and even though it is appropriate for the parties to accept the legal consequences of marriage or a legally recognized cohabitation. This is true of insufficiencies with completely legitimate causes, such as employment, education, health care, or military service in another geographic area that prevents a more complete cohabitation.

The disadvantage of a contract based upon legal intent, however, is the difficulty of preventing sham marriages or sham relationships, entered into for the purpose of obtaining a specific legal effect and without any intent to live together. A protection against sham relationships can then be created either through the requirement of an intent to live together or the requirement of actual cohabitation as a necessary requisite in addition to the contract.

As seen in this chapter, the requirement of an intent to gain a marital status, a legal relationship, the legal consequences of marriage, or a legally recognized cohabitation – if the evidentiary burden of proof is maintained – ought to considerably limit the scope of common law marriage and cohabitation legislation. The more precise and detailed the requirement of legal intent, for example, the greater the number of couples falling outside of the concepts and, therefore, outside the rights and obligations of these relationships. From the perspective of the parties, this means that a number of couples that have not made any legal decisions, but have simply lived together, would not receive the rights following from marriage or cohabitation legislation.

From the perspective of the state, it is clear that a requirement of a legal intent, and to a greater degree, an intent to invoke legal consequences, limits the ability of the state to control its citizens. All couples not having such an intent, but simply the intent to live together, will not be encompassed by the obligations of the legal system. A state having moral viewpoints about how men and women should actually create families and live their entire lives together, how they ought to act during the cohabitation and its dissolution, will find itself unable to influence the family. The state must then accept that the parties have decided not to participate in the regulatory system. A more liberal state, on the other hand, can be more disposed to accept the effects of the legal intent and the free choice of individuals. Any stance taken on these issues must, as we have seen, depend on how the interests of the state and the individual are weighed against each other.

There is also certain support in American case law, as seen above, for the view that the parties for the establishment of a common law marriage must have both an intent to live together and an intent to establish a legal relationship. This double requirement with respect to intent, based on sound reasons, can be described as a mutual intent to live together as husband and wife in a monogamous and lifelong, or at least durable, relationship that entails application of the regulatory system to the spouses. Thus, the benefits, but also the disadvantages offered by both types of intent can be obtained.

4. *An Expressed or Implied Agreement*

Beginning with the principle that the parties' marital *consensus* must also be manifested outwardly, because the law requires not only consent but an expression of consent, we can pose the question of whether the contract, as is the case in Pennsylvania and the District of Columbia, in principle, ought to be *per verba*, or whether it is sufficient in implied agreements. The question is particularly pertinent against the background of the considerable application problems associated with implied agreements throughout the United States during the entire 1800s and 1900s.

It appears that there is not sufficient reason to attempt to repeal implied agreements, as was the case in Texas. The reason is not so much that this contract type makes it possible to capture and protect relationships that would otherwise fall outside the marital legal system and that would, in many cases, entail the hypothetical existence of a nonexistent contract. Even though the general validity of the principle that the parties' "conduct may speak as loudly as words" can be questioned, it cannot be overlooked that the parties' cohabitation and reputation as well as their admissions and declarations can be significant in the proving their intentions. The implied agreement ought not to be prohibited because such a prohibition would conflict with general principles and create an impediment to the use of the best evidence. Simply, the requirement of a contract *per verba* appears to be no solution because oral contracts also create evidentiary difficulties.

The problems created by implied agreements with respect to application and legal certainty could be limited by a more precise definition of the object of the marital intent and a stricter application of the laws. A more stringent application of the general contractual legal requirements with respect to offer and acceptance ought to also contribute to preventing either party from being forced to accept a legal system which they have not desired. This is of particular importance in a time in which cohabitation without marriage has become more common and more socially acceptable, and many couples face the choice of living together either formlessly or within the marital legal system.

An effect hereof ought to be that many couples will fall outside of the legal protections that the legal system offers. However, this appears to be the inevitable price that must be paid!

The enactment of a form requirement with respect to the marital or cohabitation contract, for example, with a requirement of a writing or registration, which in itself is a type of formal marriage, would probably resolve many application problems, but at the same time would entail a risk that couples to which the state wished to grant rights and impose obligations would fall outside of the system, as examined further below in Chapter 15, "A New Model of Marriage."

5. *The Parties' Cohabitation as a Necessary Element*

The idea that the cohabitation between the parties ought to constitute a necessary requisite in addition to or instead of the marriage contract is based on the idea that marriage is not only a contract between two parties but also concerns the entire family and society on the whole. A natural consequence is society having an interest in the parties also living together in order for the legal effects to be invoked.

A fundamental reason behind the requirement of cohabitation is also that many of the legal effects of marriage are intended for marriages that also are fulfilled through cohabitation. Within the public law sphere, consequently, several rules justify a requisite of cohabitation. These can be rules in which the state intends to give couples or families economic support supported by the actual cohabitation situation.

With respect to the private law effects between the parties, several of these are particularly pertinent if the parties also actually live together or have lived together. The right to inherit and the right to a division of the estate are stronger after a long-term cohabitation. On the other side, there are certainly also parties who have entered into a marriage contract in the expectation that that they would receive legal effects if the cohabitation for different reason was terminated, deficient, or was never commenced. Concerning marital divorce regulations and the status of children, it can also be in the interests of both the state and the parties to apply legal effects already based on the agreement.

The requirement of cohabitation can also constitute a protection for the parties themselves against hasty contracts. The requirement of cohabitation then functions as a substitute for the form requirement.

A reason behind the requirement of cohabitation in the formation of a common law marriage has always been that it is desirable to create a protection against fraudulent claims. A person can feign affection, begin a relationship, and perhaps not be disposed to waste time on a long-term cohabitation to reach his or her goal. The requirement of cohabitation can also prevent the abuse of public benefits based on the parties' actual situation.

A final reason for either cohabitation or outward representation as spouses as a requisite for the formation of a common law marriage, in addition to the contract, is to avoid evidentiary difficulties and conflicts. At the same time, a significant conclusion of the current work is that the requirement of cohabitation itself leads to extensive application problems. This uncertainty has led to long and expensive trials. In the path of these application problems, there has been significant legal uncertainty.

6. *The Formulation of the Requisite of Cohabitation*

The precision of the formulation of the requisite of cohabitation is significant because it influences the scope of the application of the regulations and, therefore, is decisive with respect to the ability or difficulties of applying the regulations.

A specific feature of the cohabitation concept applied within the framework of common law marriage is that it contains, on one side, the requirement of cohabitation in the relationship between the parties and, on the other side, holding out and reputation as spouses, in other words, their outward appearance to others and the reputation they have acquired. Today's changed attitudes towards cohabitation means that even parties living together temporarily without any long-term or legal plans nowadays often outwardly appear to be spouses. It can, therefore, be questioned whether appearance and reputation ought to constitute separate requisites or whether it is sufficient that these merely be included as elements in the cohabitation concept and be considered evidentiary circumstances.

A striking aspect of the cohabitation legislation that has grown since the 1970s in the Western world is the similarity of the various concepts of cohabitation. The definitions and factors that have been considered relevant to defining the concept give witness that they all are the result of one and the same culture, in which the concept of marriage has been the ideal used as the model for the formation of the concepts of cohabitation. The image has been of a cohabitation that must be monogamous, durable, and have a high degree of a life community, a *consortium omnis vitae*.

The circumstance that formal marriage normally does not include any requirement of a marital cohabitation in order to be established has led to the conclusion that a marriage-like relationship, according to the cohabitation legislation, must be more marriage-like than marriage itself needs to be in order for the legal effects to be invoked. It is paradoxical that the legislation and the case law concerning out-of-wedlock relationships have kept alive the image of what marriage is and ought to be, while the formal marriage has become largely fossilized in its forms.

The inconveniences of application resulting from the requisites of cohabitation and holding out give rise to the question of whether it is possible to use the mirror image theory to facilitate the material assessment. Such a theory, according to which the proof of the requisite of cohabitation is made based upon the guidance of the form-bound marriage appearing within the legal system, can contribute by presenting relevant arguments in the assessment, but can scarcely contribute decisively to minimizing application problems.

In this chapter, we have also considered the possibility of limiting application difficulties and guaranteeing that legal consequences are granted only to those for whom they are intended, in a manner similar to that of the Roman *usus*-marriage, through the enactment of a requirement of a certain determined length of cohabitation. The length of the period naturally is decisive for those who are to fall within the scope of the regulations; periods of two to three years, which are common in the modern cohabitation legislation, cut through the population of persons cohabiting in a manner that makes it difficult to decide which couples are inside and outside the line. The result of our assessment is that the requirement of a time period would probably give rise to considerable application problems and fail to create greater predictability and legal certainty. The need for such a requirement appears less in a legal system that includes a contract requirement for the establishment of a common law marriage, than it does in a system employing simply a requirement of cohabitation.

From the presentation above, it can be seen that an unconditional requirement of mutual children for the formation of a common law marriage would probably contribute quantitatively to reducing application problems and giving legal protection to families who need it. However, application problems would remain with respect to the other requisites. At the same time, childless couples living together and in agreement to live a life together would largely fall outside of the rights as well as the obligations of marriage or a legally recognized cohabitation. Even though the need for legal protection is particularly great in families with children, couples without children are also in need of such.

Finally, we have discussed in this chapter the possibility of limiting the requirement of cohabitation in the formation of a common law marriage to simply a requirement that the parties move in together to a mutual residence, in other words, in a fashion similar to that used in ancient Rome for the establishment of the free marriage, which appears to have required, in addition to a marital *consensus*, that the woman enter into the man's house, *deductio in domum mariti*. This moving in together would be comparable to the concept of tradition within property law. With such an action, the parties will have demonstrated that they seriously intend to perform the contract, and that the marriage has commenced. The commencement of the cohabitation would be viewed as the performance of the contract.

An objective requisite limited to the parties' moving in together to a mutual residence would probably limit application problems and be beneficial from a legal certainty aspect, because the point of time for the invocation of the legal consequences would be defined. Extensive investigations concerning the existence of the different elements of cohabitation and holding out would no longer be necessary. Investigations that violate the parties' privacy and integrity, concerning their sexual relationship, could be avoided. The requisite would also give a reasonable level of protection against contracts entered into in haste.

Such a requirement would, however, appear to justify the use of a contract construction and impose a heightened requirement with respect to the contract and as well a rule of equity that would take into consideration any insufficiencies in the cohabitation.

A new aspect of the development of the concept of family in the Western world during recent years is that several countries have enacted legislation with limited rules for relationships other than couple relationships, for example, cohabiting siblings, or parents and adult children, friends, work acquaintances, or students. The basis of this type of legal relationship is ordinarily a shared household or cohabitation in which the parties' dependence upon each other is emphasized or if one takes care of the other without compensation. It is difficult to see the need for such solutions. The needs can be so different that they perhaps are best solved through individual agreements and wills, and not through general legislation.

Despite laudable ambitions, cohabitation concepts launched during recent years in different places in the Western world lead to the very problems that the instigators wished to avoid, namely application problems, unnecessary disputes and costs for society, lack of predictability, and considerable legal uncertainty. The experiences with the application of the requirement of cohabitation within the framework for common law marriage demonstrate that these risks ought to be taken seriously, as evidenced in Chapter 8. Added to the inconveniences is that the significance attributed to the parties' sexual relationship causes investigations that entail a danger for personal integrity. Lawmakers facing legislation that is based on a requisite of cohabitation ought to be aware that there is a price that must be paid. Whether this price is worth paying must also take into consideration the other arguments for and against legislation discussed further in Chapter 14.

7. *The Burden of Proof and Presumptions*

From the over one thousand cases that have been the object of this examination, it appears that the evidentiary issues have been difficult to resolve in the majority of cases. As seen in Chapter 9 and here, lawmakers and the courts have a good possibility, with the regulations governing burdens of proof and the standard of evidence, to control the outcomes of the cases.

When trying the issue of whether a common law marriage has been established, the burden of proof should, according to general principles, rest with the party claiming the existence of such a marriage. This ought to be with respect to all of the necessary requisites, in other words, the legal capacity of the parties, their marital contract, and in the appropriate case, their cohabitation or similar requisite.

The discussion in this chapter has further led to the conclusion that the standard of evidence should be determined with respect to the risk for abuse and fraudulent claims, taking into consideration what must be proven. If the contract and cohabitation requirements are formulated as they are today, there is a need for clear and convincing evidence. The best scenario would be if the substantive requirements were formulated so that the normal standard of evidence could be applied. If the contract requisite received a stricter formulation, for example, by a requirement of an express contract or the requirement of a legal intent, or through a stricter application of the contract laws governing offer and accept, it ought then to be satisfactory to require a preponderance of evidence.

Finally, a conclusion of this chapter is that the legal marriage presumption, according to which the existence of a marital *consensus* is presumed if cohabitation and reputation exist, ought to be abolished, because the given conditions are no longer sufficiently certain. Different couples, today, can have completely different intentions with respect to their cohabitation. The contradiction between the presumption and the fundamental burden of proof resting on the party claiming the existence of a common law marriage would be resolved.

It is doubtful that the legal presumptions that have been launched within the framework of the cohabitation legislation, according to which a cohabitation relationship is presumed if the parties have had a shared household or lived together for a period, actually facilitate the application and decrease the number of disputes. There is reason to assume that the opposing party, in several cases, will contest the required elements and that if unsuccessful, this party will attempt to rebut the presumption by presenting evidence that the parties "did not share life together as a couple," which either legally or evidentiarily will not have any certain answers.

CHAPTER 14

Arguments for and Against Common Law Marriage and Cohabitation Law

14.1 Introduction

Two paradoxical lines of development characterized the family law regulation of informal couple relationships during the 1900s, as shown in Chapter 12, "Common Law Marriage and Cohabitation Law." The first entailed that common law marriage, particularly during the first part of the twentieth century, was mostly in decline. The second development was that many states, because of decreasing rates of marriage and increasing numbers of unmarried cohabitants and children born to such relationships, enacted cohabitation legislation to an increasing extent since the 1970s. Demands from homosexual couples for equality were also addressed through legislation. Jurisdictions in Northern and Western Europe, Australia, New Zealand, Canada, and the United States have enacted regulations, as discussed in Chapter 12, with legal effects that increasingly resemble common law marriage and, thus, formal marriage.

These at times conflicting developments require legislators around the world today to determine the appropriate legislative strategy for the twenty-first century. Is there now good reason to repeal common law marriage or, in contrast, should cohabitation legislation, as a result of decreasing rates of marriage, be further developed as a common law marriage that is entirely comparable with formal marriage? In other words, is common law marriage an anachronism or "an old solution to a new problem?"[1]

This chapter, addressed primarily to legislative bodies considering repealing or enacting common law marriage or other cohabitation legislation, discusses the reasons that support these legal solutions and considers

---

1 Nancy Rebecca Shaw, Note, *Common Law Marriage and Unmarried Cohabitation: An Old Solution to a New Problem*, 39 U. Pitt. L. Rev. 579 (1977); and Caleb Foote et al., Cases and Materials on Family Law 16 (3d ed. 1985) ("The only explanation for its continuation in the 20th century is historical.")

which may be relevant in the future. In Chapter 4, "The Reception of Common Law Marriage in the United States," these reasons were assumed to be the grounds for the reception of common law marriage during the 1800s in the case law. In this chapter, the viability of these options will be discussed. Also the reasoning thought to underlie the repeal of the doctrine during the 1900s will be explored. In addition the reasons behind the new cohabitation legislation enacted in the Western world since the 1970s will be analyzed.

While the discussion in the legal literature concerning the interpretation and application of the current law on common law marriage, as seen in Part II of this book, has been limited, the debates concerning political issues such as the repeal of common law marriage and the enactment of cohabitation legislation have been extensive and intense. The arguments made have sometimes tended to devolve into inflamed rhetoric and resemble a crusade either for or against a given policy, an intensity attributed to the essential and intimate nature of the marital relationship for both citizens and the community. This chapter, therefore, will attempt to objectively present and critically examine the arguments both for and against common law marriage and other cohabitation legislation primarily for the purpose of giving legislators and policymakers a basis for the future assessments.

14.2 Arguments for Common Law Marriage and Cohabitation Law

14.2.1 The Availability of Ceremonial Marriages

Historically, the growth of common law marriage in the American case law was fueled by limited access to persons authorized to perform wedding ceremonies as well as governmental authorities who could issue marriage licenses. During the pioneer period, long distances, sparsely populated settlements, and inadequate transportation systems played a significant role in the United States. The absence of a state church and the diverse faiths that arose in the new world probably limited the possibility of achieving a uniform and unconditional form requirement.[2] Even lack of fluency in English and ignorance about the content of the form requirements have been posited as reasons.[3] Under these conditions, common law marriage is an easily accessible way to formlessly enter into a valid marriage.[4]

2 Alan H., Rothstein, Special Comment, *A New Look at Common Law Marriages in Florida*, 10 Miami L.Q. 87, 95 and 102 (1955): and Note, *The Decline and Fall of Common-law Marriage in Pennsylvania*, 18 Temp. L.Q. 264, 265 (1944).

3 *McChesney v. Johnson*, 79 S.W.2d 658, 659 (Tex.Civ.App.-Ft. Worth 1934).

4 *See Chambers v. Dickson*, 2 S. & R. 475, 476 (1816); *Dumaresly v. Fishly*, 10 Ky. 368 (1821); *Forney v. Hallacher*, S. & R. 159, 162 (1822); *Commonwealth v. Murtagh*, 1 Ashm. 272, 274-275 (1831); *McChesney v. Johnson*, 79 S.W.2d 658, 659 (Tex.Civ.App.-Ft. Worth 1934);

These reasons are no longer relevant in the United States and the developed world in general or, as the court expressed the matter in the case of *In re Estate of Soeder* (1966): "[C]overed wagon days are over ... no person lives, who cannot in some manner easily reach the country court house."[5] An equally vivid description can be found in *Osburne v. Graves* (1948): "The clerk's office is available to all, and none are beyond the sound of church bells."[6] Modern transportation has made the wedding ceremony easily accessible.[7] All states today offer the possibility of choosing between a church and a civil wedding ceremony, with form requirements which do not place unreasonable requirements on the parties, including the license, persons authorized to perform wedding ceremonies, witnesses, and the registration of marriages. In *PNC Bank Corp. v. Workers' Compensation Appeal Board (Stamos)* (2003), the court states with respect to Pennsylvania: "Access to both civil and religious authorities for a ceremonial marriage is readily available in even the most rural areas of the Commonwealth."[8]

If individuals accept form requirements with respect to the purchase of real estate and less important things such as driver's or fishing licenses and tax returns, many argue that individuals ought to be able to accept form requirements with respect to the significant issue of the commencement of a marriage.[9] For those who found accessibility to be the only strong reason behind common law marriage, proposals concerning its repeal were a predictable alternative.[10] The accessibility of formal marriage

---

Middlebrook v. Wideman, 203 S.W.2d 686, 687 (Tex.Civ.App. 1947); *Turner v. Turner*, 251 Ala. 295, 37 So.2d 186, 189 (1948); *Goodman v. McMillan*, 258 Ala. 125, 61 So.2d 55, 60 (1952); *In re Estate of Soeder*, 7 Ohio App. 271, 220 N.E.2d 547, 562 (1966); and *De Santo v. Barnsley*, 476 A.2d 952. 955 (Pa.Super. 1984). For more on this, *see* Section 4.3.4 *supra.*

5 *In re Estate of Soeder*, 7 Ohio App. 271, 220 N.E.2d 547, 562 (1966).

6 *Osburn v. Graves*, 213 Ark. 727, 210 S.W. 496, 498 (1948).

7 *McClish v. Rankin*, 153 Fla. 324, 14 So.2d 714, 717 (1943). In *Turner v. Turner*, 251 Ala. 295, 37 So.2d 186, 189 (1948) the Alabama Supreme Court stated: "The pioneer conditions which fostered the rule no longer obtain in most, if not all, of Alabama." In the case of *In re Erickson's Estate*, 75 S.D. 345, 64 N.W.2d 316, 321 (1954): "[N]o religious differences stood in their way, no scruples against ceremony constituted a bar. There was a church in their immediate vicinity and they took part in its activities the day after decedent arrived." Common law marriage was repealed in South Dakota on July 1, 1959, in other words, five years after *Erickson. See also Anderson v. Anderson*, 235 Ind. 113, 131 N.E.2d 301, 307 (1956); and *In re Robert's Estate*, 58 Wyo. 438, 133 P.2d 492 (1943).

8 *PNC Bank Corp. v. Workers' Compensation Appeal Bd. (Stamos)*, No. 860 C.D. (2003).

9 *See, e.g.*, John R Williams, *Solemnization of Marriage: The common law marriage-never solemn and no longer common-will it remain law?* 13 U. MIAMI L. REV. 447, 453-454 (1959).

10 Note, *supra* note 2, at 265; JOHN W. MORLAND, KEEZER ON THE LAW OF MARRIAGE AND DIVORCE 59 (3d ed. 1946); Rothstein, *supra* note 2, at 95 and 102: "However the court points out that today's conditions differ; distances have shrunk by modern travel, and all facilities for ceremonial marriage are easily available, therefore there is no logical reason for the continued existence of common-law marriage. Common law marriage is no longer necessary in Florida. Licenses and persons who can perform ceremonies are easily obtained throughout the state, so that there is no valid reason why the legislative procedure for the formation of a marriage should

in today's community appears to have been one of the reasons for the repeal of common law marriage, for example, in Ohio in 1991,[11] and in Georgia in 1997. In *Johnson v. Green* (1983), the Georgia Supreme Court expressed an understanding that appears to be fairly extensive, stating that "if marriage is a state 'not to be undertaken lightly' (as observed at almost every wedding) it should not be too burdensome to require of parties who intend to commit their very lives to each other that they make plain to all the world such an intent by undergoing a ceremony of marriage."[12]

The choice of cohabitation form, however, ought not only be a question of convenience or practical and economic reasons of accessibility. No one has ever scientifically explored whether or to what extent the requirement for parties to exchange vows in a formal ritual, before a person

---

be ignored." *See also* Note, *Common Law Marriage - A Legal Anachronism*, 32 IND. L.J. 99, 102 (1956): "With an informed public, no member of which is more than a few hours travel from the county clerk and persons authorized to solemnize marriages, hardships are no longer apparent which might excuse failure to comply with the statutory requirements." *See also* Graham Kirkpatrick, *Common-Law Marriages: Their Common Law Basis and Present Need*, 6 ST. LOUIS U.L.J. 30, 48 (1960); Steven G. Brown, Comment, *Pennsylvania Common Law Marriage and Annulment: Present Law and Proposals for Reform*, 15 VILL. L. REV. 134, 138 (1969); Olen E. Adams, Note, *Common-Law Marriage in Oklahoma*, 14 OKLA. L. REV. 291 (1961); and Nancy Rebecca Shaw, *supra* note 1, at 580.

11 When common law marriage was repealed in Ohio in 1991, Ron Mottl, who presented the legislative proposal (HB 32) and is a practicing attorney, stated in a newspaper interview: "In today's modern society there is no need for common law marriage because most people can easily reach ministers," *see* United Press International, April 4, 1991. Ohio does not recognize common law marriages commenced after October 10, 1991, *see* R.C. § 3105.13(B)1, 2; and *Lyon v. Lyon*, 86 Ohio App.3d 580, 621 N.E.2d 718 (1993). Common law marriage was an object of criticism already in the case of *In re Estate of Maynard*, 117 Ohio App. 315, 192 N.E.2d 281, 287 (1962).

12 *Johnson v. Green*, 251 Ga. 645, 309 S.E.2d 362, 363 (1983). Similar objections appeared already when common law marriage during the 1800s had won an all-greater recognition in the case law. In *Dunbarton v. Franklin*, 19 N.H. 257, 264-265 (1848), the court stated: "It is singular that the most important of all human contracts, on which the rights and duties of the whole community depend, requires less formality for its validity than a conveyance of an acre of land, a policy of insurance, or the agreement which the statute of frauds requires should be in writing." In Kansas, a proposal was presented in 1981 as to the repeal of common law marriage, wherewith the following were stated as reasons: "(1) difficulty in proving the relationship, (2) the availability of causes of actions, other than divorce, to address the division of property between cohabitants, and (3) the ease of availability of obtaining a marriage license," *see* House Bill No. 2689 (1982). *See also* Nancy G. Maxwell, *Can Kansas Live Happily Ever After Without Common Law Marriage?* 20 THE CIRCUIT RIDER No. 3 (1981). *See already State v. Walker*, 36 Kan. 297, 13 P. 279, 286 (1887), in which the court stated: "The consequences of marriage, as to conjugal rights and the rights of heirs, are so momentous that the interests of society may properly require a witness to the marriage, and a record of its acknowledgment. This much is required in the acknowledgment and registration of an ordinary conveyance of real estate." In *McCoy v. District of Columbia*, 256 A.2d 908, 910 (D.C. 1969), the court stated: "Cost is certainly not prohibitory, and a plethora of public and quasi-public officials are available to solemnize such an important and socially significant occasion." *See also Johnson v. Young*, 372 A.2d 992 (D.C. 1977).

authorized to hold a wedding ceremony, is a psychological or ideological impediment to couples who regard the marriage contract as an agreement between them and no one else. If so, it is possible that some less demanding forms, for example, a registration or a written and witnessed contract, could be acceptable alternatives.[13] Many cohabiters, perhaps, would then find that their relationship is worth the trouble. Objectively, no certain conclusions can be made today.

If one only considers the argument of accessibility, certain emergencies that can prevent parties from having a ceremonial wedding may present a need for specific solutions.[14] These limited needs, however, cannot justify common law marriage generally. Variations of emergency marriages in the absence of a person able to perform a wedding ceremony could either be oral contracts with witnesses or written contracts without witnesses.[15] Today, the argument that there is limited access to a wedding ceremony is relevant only in underdeveloped countries. For more developed countries, the argument of accessibility is simply historical.

14.2.2 Ethnic, Cultural, and Social Reasons

Historically, the endeavor in American law, as seen in Chapter 4, has been to place marriage at the disposal of population groups, who, for ethnic or cultural reasons, were prevented from marrying or whose traditions do not include ceremonial marriage.[16] The interest in maintaining a form requirement has taken a backseat to a tolerance toward certain groups and traditions. Thus, Native-American traditions were equated to common

---

13 With respect to registration as an alternative in the future, *see* Chapter 15 *infra.*

14 *Compare Estate of Depasse*, 97 Cal.App.4d 92, 118 Cal.Rptr.2d 143 (2002), in which the parties, the day before the woman's death, had entered into a marriage at the hospital. Due to a shortage of time, they had not acquired a marriage license and the marriage therefore was invalid. As the man was aware of the requirement of a license, he was considered to not be in good faith as to the existence of a valid marriage. The putative marriage doctrine could therefore not offer him any protection. Neither was common law marriage available as it was repealed in California in 1895. A similar case from Missouri is *Nelson v. Marshall*, 869 S.W.2d 132 (Mo.App. 1993).

15 *Compare* HANS FRIEDRICH C. THOMAS, FORMLOSE EHEN 128 (1973), who considers that emergency marriages in individual cases, such as illness, still require the participation of a person in a governmental position (*der Mitwirkung eines Amtsträgers*) and only in collective cases, *e.g.* war, is prepared to abstain from such requirements.

16 As to the spread of common law marriage among African-Americans at the turn of the twentieth century, and concerning the legislator's endeavor to encourage African-Americans to formally marry, *see Renfrow v. Renfrow*, 60 Kan. 277, 72 Am.St.Rep. 350, 56 P. 534 (1899). *See also McAdoo v. Metro. L. Ins. Co*, 233 Mo.App. 900, 110 S.W.2d 845 (1937), concerning two African-Americans who lived together from 1902 to 1909, in which the court stated that they "were living together as husband and wife, as many of their race were wont to do, under a common-law form of marriage." *See also Flores Gonzales v. Viuda de Gonzales*, 466 S.W.2d 839 (Tex.Civ.App. 1971).

law marriage, a possibility that today plays a more minor role.[17] This reason was also later espoused with respect to other population groups, particularly within the slave population.[18] This argument has also been made in more recent times. In the discussions held in Pennsylvania concerning the repeal of common law marriage, a significant argument for retaining the institution was deference to the African-American population and its traditions. Steven Brown stated: "[C]ommentators agree that the common law marriages are most prevalent among lower class Negroes and whites and the poorer segment of society where it is generally accepted. These groups, which compose a significant portion of society, must be taken into consideration before any steps are taken to deny their marriages of their viability."[19]

Formless cohabitation has also been extensive among peoples of Spanish and Mexican descent. Cynthia Bowman, who has researched the consequences of the non-recognition of common law marriage in individual cases, draws the conclusion that it clearly has a disparate impact upon different races and ethnic groups as well, falling particularly hard upon African Americans, Mexican Americans, and Native Americans.[20]

---

17 Adams, *supra* note 10, at 298, states: "The Indian tribes, whose common-law marriages have so often been litigated in the past, are now civilized and it is inconceivable that anyone could be ignorant of this statutory scheme for marriage."

18 *See* Walter O. Weyrauch, *Informal Marriage and Common Law Marriage*, in SEXUAL BEHAVIOUR AND THE LAW 297 (R. Slovenko ed. 1965); Stuart J. Stein, *Common-Law Marriage: Its History and Certain Contemporary Problems*, 9 J. FAM. L. 271, 293 (1969); John R. Valeri, *Informal Marriages and Other Curative Devices*, 17 HOW. L.J. 558 (1972); and Henry H. Foster, *Indian and Common Law Marriages*, 3 AM. INDIAN L. REV. 83 (1975). According to MARY ANN GLENDON, STATE, LAW AND FAMILY. FAMILY LAW IN TRANSITION IN THE UNITED STATES AND WESTERN EUROPE 79 (1977), marriage for certain of these groups is a cultural rather than a legal concept. *See also* HOMER H. CLARK, JR., THE LAW OF DOMESTIC RELATIONS IN THE UNITED STATES I, 121 note 86 (2d ed. 1987). Cynthia Grant Bowman, *A Feminist Proposal to Bring Back Common Law Marriage*, 75 OR. L. REV. 709, 779 (1996), maintains that common law marriage "protects the interests of women, especially poor women and women of colour..."

19 Brown, *supra* note 10, at 140. *See also Shaw, supra* note 1, at 586, in which the author states: "[I]t may be noted that Pennsylvania is a state in which a wide variety of ethnic groups, cultural backgrounds and lifestyles find representation. Marital customs vary among these diverse groups and Pennsylvania's protection of the marital status extends to all of them by means of the common law tradition." Observe that common law marriage was repealed in Pennsylvania January 1, 2005, however not retroactively, *see* PA. CONS. STAT. ANN. § 1103 (West 2005). The reluctance in Florida during the 1950s as to repealing common law marriage appears to a great extent to have depended upon consideration of the African-American population. In 1957, the proposal concerning repeal was rejected, *see* H.B. No. 41, 36th Regular Session, Florida (1957). *See also* Daniel E. Murray, *Domestic Relations*, 12 U. MIAMI L. REV. 428, 429 (1958); Skolnick, *The Social Contexts of Cohabitation*, 29 AM. J. COMP. L. 339, 341 (1981); and William A. Reppy, Jr., *Property and Support Rights of Unmarried Cohabitants: A Proposal for Creating a New Legal Status*, 44 LA. L. REV. 1677, 1679 (1984).

20 Bowman, *supra* note 18, at 744, 747, 767-770. *See also* Jacobus TenBroek, *California's Dual System of Family Law: Its Origin, Development, and Present Status*, 17 STAN. L. REV. 614, 618 (1965), who researched families in California. Another study that was limited to Santa Clara County, California, demonstrated that among Mexican-American women, 27.7% of the marriages were common law and 72.3% formal marriages.

Homer Clark, who has recommended the retention of common law marriage, states: "Without it there would be more injustice and suffering in the world than there is with it. This is particularly true among those social and economic classes who have not accepted middle class standards of marriage. Certainly American marriage law should tolerate this much cultural diversity."[21] The fact that common law marriage offers legal protection to the African-American population appears to have constituted a racial motivation for arguing its repeal.[22]

A more general but distinctive reason for retaining common law is the goal of giving social protection to more vulnerable population groups.[23] Common law marriage offers, regardless of ethnic association, an essential protection for economically, educationally, and socially vulnerable groups who may not formalize their family relationships in a wedding ceremony. These most vulnerable parties, thereby, also enjoy the same series of social benefits that accrue to families in which the parties are or have been married to each other. In the case of *In re Redman's Estate* (1939), the court stated that common law marriages are held valid by courts only to protect the rights of innocent persons.[24] In a close connection, Walter Weyrauch maintained in 1960 with respect to informal marriage that it may aid and protect the poor and the ignorant in their family relations.[25]

The comparable amount among Anglo-American women was 6.2% common law marriages and 93.8% formal marriages, *see* Woodrow Borah & Sherburne F. Cook, *Marriage and Legitimacy in Mexican Culture: Mexico and California*, 54 CAL. L. REV. 946, 987-988 (1966).

21 CLARK, *supra* note 18, at 122. *See also* Kathryn S. Vaughn, Comment, *The Recent Changes to the Texas Informal Marriage Statute: Limitation or Abolition of Common-law Marriage?* 28 HOUS. L. REV. 1131, 1147 (1991), maintains that, considering ethnic and cultural groups that do not use formal marriage, "states should not force these groups to comply with the white middle-class conception of a 'proper' marriage."

22 With respect to the repeal of common law marriage in Mississippi in 1956, *see* Walter O. Weyrauch, *Informal and formal marriage - an appraisal of trends in family organization*, 28 U. CHI. L. REV. 88, 94 (1960). With respect to racial motivations for the repeal or limitation of common law marriage, *see* Bowman, *supra* note 18, at 744 and 747.

23 Even if there is a correlation between social class, race, and ethnicity, with Anglo-Americans being the most privileged economically, *see* Wendy D. Manning & Pamela J. Smock, *Living Together Unmarried in the United States: Demographic Perspectives and Implications for Family Policy*, 26 LAW & POLICY 87, 98 (2004), it should be noted that many Anglo-American couples are not privileged.

24 *In re Redman's Estate*, 135 Ohio St. 554, 558, 21 N.E.2d 659, 661 (1939); *Jolley v. Jolley*, 46 Ohio Misc. 40, 347 N.E.2d 557, 560 (1975); and Williams, *supra* note 9, at 452.

25 Weyrauch, *supra* note 22, at 101. *See also* Williams, *id.* at 453; Martha L. Fineman, *Law and Changing Patterns of Behaviour: Sanctions on Non-Marital Cohabitation*, WIS. L. REV. 275, 322 note 189 (1981); and Thomas Clifford Billig and James Phillip Lynch, *Common-Law Marriage in Minnesota, A Problem in Social Security*, 22 MINN. L. REV. 177, 178 (1938). *See also* TenBroek, *supra* note 20, at 617: "[C]eremonial marriage is often expensive and may not be a part of the cultural mores of various minority groups." *Compare* José E. Arraros, *Concubinage in Latin America*, 3 J. FAM. L. 330, 333 (1963), who states that concubinage is accepted among the poor, who develop their own norms, values and attitudes. *See also* MEYER F. NIMKOFF, MARRIAGE AND THE FAMILY 219 (1947) and JOHN SIRJAMAKI, THE AMERICAN FAMILY IN THE TWENTIETH CENTURY,

Traditionally, cohabitation without formal marriage has been more common in the lower economic classes of society than in the middle class.

The question then becomes whether couples today refrain from ceremonial marriage for economic reasons. It is easy to ascertain that many couples, historically, lacked the economic possibilities of entering into a ceremonial marriage; this circumstance was a primary objection against the enactment of an obligatory form requirement in England in 1753.[26] Something more surprising is that the costs of formal marriage were significant even during the 1900s. The fees for obtaining a marriage license are not unreasonable.[27] Nevertheless, in some circles, the social requirements of an expensive wedding constitute an impediment[28] that should be recognized in the public debate.[29] Research shows that economic instability reduces the likelihood of ceremonial marriage.[30] Social pressure to marry has probably not been as significant in the lower classes of society as in the middle class.

However, formless cohabitation, within the scope of the regulations concerning common law marriage, has expanded during the last twenty years, no longer limited to particular ethnic and social groups. In line with changing attitudes, the phenomenon appears to have spread to all classes

---

69 (1953) (Common law marriage is common among groups with lower socio-economic status).

26 *See* Section 4.2 *supra.*

27 Relatively low fees are required to obtain a marriage license. In *PNC Bank Corp. v. Workers' Compensation Appeal Bd. (Stamos)*, No. 860 C.D. (2003), the court stated: "Under Pennsylvania's statutory scheme, the fee for the issuance of a license is $3.00," *see* 23 PA.C.S. § 1105 (a) (West 2003). *See also* CLARK, *supra* note 18, at 87 fn. 15; Note, *The Passing of Common Law Marriage*, 15 TEMP. L.Q. 541, 547 (1946) ("It is no hardship or disproportionate expense in modern society to comply with wisely-chosen regulations.")

28 A clear testimony that economic impediments exist can be found in *Elliot v. Indus. Accident Bd.*, 101 Mont. 246, 53 P.2d 451, 452-453 (1936), in which the woman witnessed as to a conversation she had had with the man: "Ed. where are we going to get married?' to which he replied, 'Dell, it costs 2.00 dollar for a marriage license and 5.00 dollar for a justice of the peace to marry us, and I have not got a cent and you have very little. If we agree to get married and if we agree that we are married and go ahead and live together as man and wife, it will be a common law marriage ... it will be just as good.'" In the case of *In re Hines's Estate*, 10 Pa.Super. 124, 126 (1894), the woman testified at trial that the man had said: "I will take you for my wife; and asked me if I was satisfied, and I said, 'yes', and he said he would have a ceremony performed, but he did not have any money at that time; he was in bad circumstances at that time." *Compare Trammell v. Trammell*, 196 S.W.2d 209 (Tex.Civ. App. 1946), in which the parties lived together in a common law marriage, but in which they intended sometime in the future, when their economic situation allowed it and from a practical viewpoint it would be appropriate, to solemnize their relationship.

29 *See* TenBroek, *supra* note 20, at 617, who maintained: "[C]eremonial marriage is often expensive and may not be a part of the cultural mores of various minority groups." *See also* Oystein Kravdal, *Does Marriage Require a Stronger Economic Underpinning than Informal Cohabitation?*, 53 POPULATION STUD. 63, 67 (1999).

30 *See* Marin Clarkberg, *The Prize of Partnering: The Role of Economic Well-Being in Young Adults' First Union Experiences*, 77 SOCIAL FORCES 945 (1999).

of society.[31] Today, cohabitation without marriage is commonplace and accepted even in middle-upper class families, in which the parties' objectives in the relationship can vary. Some couples refrain from formal marriage in order to avoid the legal effects of marriage, while others desire the effects, but do not wish to subject themselves to the ceremonial marriage's wedding form. To others, cohabitation is a preliminary stage of marriage. Long standing cohabitation, however, seems to be more frequent among the lower classes, lending itself to the label of "a poor man's marriage."[32]

Naturally, it is difficult to change marital traditions that, for ethnic, cultural, and social reasons, have been rooted in families from different population groups for generations. African-American couples, today, are twice as likely as Anglo-American couples to choose not to marry.[33] In general, however, the frequency of marriage in states recognizing common law marriage is the same as in other states.[34] On the other hand, it should be possible to influence cases in which the tradition is simply parties formlessly moving in together. Therefore, it cannot be taken for granted that common law marriage or extensive cohabitation legislation is the only conceivable solution. A civil wedding, which is neutral to the different cultural forms for the commencement of a marriage and requires more than a simple and inexpensive registration, ought to constitute an acceptable alternative for many individuals. Such a system would give the parties

31 Manning, *supra* note 23, at 97-98, finds that "whites, blacks and Hispanics report similar *levels* of cohabitation experience" and that "cohabitation is commonplace in all these groups." According to the authors, children are more likely to be present in black and Hispanic cohabiting couple households than in white cohabiting households. *See* further Vaughn, *supra* note 21, at 1142, finding that cohabitation has recently become common with middle and upper class couples. *See also* MARY ANN GLENDON, THE TRANSFORMATION OF FAMILY LAW 277 (1989), who maintains that cohabitation is spread in different social groups and notes that it also concerns upper-middle class cohabitation. *Compare* Bowman, *supra* note 18, at 766, who even in 1996 maintained that "informal unions are simply more frequent among lower income groups than among middle class." *Compare also* Reppy, *supra* note 19, at 1681; Barbara Freedman Wand, *The Relevance of Premarital Cohabitation to Property Division Awards in Divorce Proceedings: An Evaluation of Present Trends and a Proposal for Legislative Reform*, 63 B.U. L. REV. 105, 106 (1983); LEONORE WEITZMAN, THE MARRIAGE CONTRACT 361-363 (1981); and Skolnick, *supra* note 19, at 399.

32 Manning, *supra* note 23, at 100.

33 In the United States in 2000, 11.6% of African-American couples were not married while the comparable number for Anglo-American couples was 5.9 %. In absolute numbers, however, there were many more Anglo-American couples, 3.1 million, than African-American couples, 0.6 million, who were not married. There were totally 3.8 million unmarried couples. This estimation is based on the survey, Characteristics of Unmarried Partners and Married Spouses by Sex: March 2000. Bureau of the Census. Table 7. Among Anglo-American cohabiters, the cohabitation was terminated due to marriage in 67% of the cases, while the comparable number for African Americans was 38%. Of the Anglo-American cohabiters, 28% married each other within one year of cohabitation while the comparable number for African Americans was 16%, *see* Wendy D. Manning & Pamela J. Smock, *Why Marry? Race and Transition to Marriage Among Cohabiters*, 32 DEMOGRAPHY 509 (1995).

34 *See* § 14.3.3 *infra*.

themselves the right to determine, with respect to ethnic, cultural, economic, and social factors, the ceremonies in which they choose to participate or not. The parties' choice then is legally meaningless. The legal effects of marriage would be put in place based on the registration, as discussed in detail in Chapter 15.

14.2.3 Protection for the Vulnerable Party

Regardless of ethnic or social association, from the perspective of the parties, the goal of protecting the more vulnerable party in the relationship during the cohabitation, as well as upon its dissolution, is one of the strongest justifications for common law marriage. This reason corresponds, in actuality, to the *ratio legis* behind ceremonial marriage, with its civil and public law effects of providing protection and justice during marriages and their dissolution through divorce or death. The need for protection is greatest in long-term relationships during which the parties formed a family, having children in the same manner as in a formal marriage. Cohabitation causes dependency.

Because the woman is usually the more vulnerable party, common law marriage has come to constitute a protection for her.[35] In the majority of cases researched for this work, it is also the woman in the relationship who has litigated claims based on common law marriage.[36] The need to protect women, therefore, has given rise to feminist proposals supporting both the retention and reinstatement of common law marriage,[37] and the

---

35 Ariela R. Dubler, *Wifely Behaviour: A Legal History of Acting Married*, 100 Colum. L. Rev. 957, 964 (2000), maintains that common law marriage during the 1800s "took as its premise that the law should protect innocent women from the whims and contrivances of irresponsible or rakish men." The same author states: "For over a century in New York, common law marriage essentially functioned to protect women plaintiffs who came to court in search of economic support. In recognizing common law marriage, courts sought to protect innocent women from abandonment and poverty," *id.* at 1002. *See also* Charlotte K. Goldberg, *The Schemes of Adventuresses: The Abolition and Revival of Common-Law Marriage*, 483 Wm. & Mary J. Women & L. 483, 487 (2006-2007), who maintains that "women needed protection from unscrupulous men who would take advantage of their youth and naiveté." In general, women today still earn less than men, *see* Lynne M. Casper & Suzanne M. Bianchi, Continuity and Change in the American Family 53 (2002).

36 *See also* Ariela R. Dubler, Note, *Governing Through Contract: Common Law Marriage in the Nineteenth Century*, 107 Yale L.J. 1885, 1887 (1998), who maintains that the majority of cases concerning the recognition of common law marriage during the 1800s "were claims for the material support of women left, by death or desertion, without male partners to provide for them." *See also* Billig, *supra* note 25, at 190.

37 *See* Bowman, *supra* note 18, at 711-712, who argues that common law marriage "protects the interests of women, especially poor women and women of color..." and who maintains that non-recognition of common law marriage "often results in what appears to be substantial injustices to women who are especially vulnerable," *id.* at 755. The author also notes the possibility for a marital divorce with a division of the estate and maintenance, as common law marriage offers women who are victims of abuse a means for "seeking to escape an abusive marriage," *id.* at 760. *See, e.g.*, *In re Estate of Wagner*, 398 Pa. 531, 159 A.2d 495 (Pa. 1960); Chapter 9 *supra*; and

opposite viewpoint.[38] The legislature in Texas has rejected a proposal to repeal the institution of common law marriage in order to continue giving protection to stable family relationships of long durations and ensure that the surviving party in an informal relationship has the same social benefits as a surviving spouse in a formal marriage.[39] A proposal concerning the repeal of common law marriage was also rejected in Pennsylvania, and the need to protect the surviving party was cited.[40] The Idaho Women Lawyers Association presented similar arguments with less success when common law marriage was repealed in Idaho in 1995.[41] The need to protect the weaker party can also be seen as a reason for retaining the institution of marriage by cohabitation, habit, and repute in Scotland in 1939.[42]

Henderson v. Henderson, 199 Md. 449, 87 A.2d 403 (App. 1952), applying District of Columbia law. Vaughn, *supra* note 21, at 1142, maintains that "an additional inequity in a state's non-recognition of common-law marriage is the fact that, generally, women suffer the adverse consequences." GLENDON, *supra* note 31, at 268, states that the hesitation which the German courts have shown as to intervening in a relationship of cohabitation can be motivated by a respect for the freedom of choice which unmarried cohabiting persons have as to receiving legal protection by formally marrying or to abstain there from. Glendon maintains, however, that "the price of freedom may be high for the socially weaker party, who in most cases will be the woman." According to Ellen Kandoian, women in the nearest predictable future will be the most economically vulnerable party in a cohabitation relationship, *see Cohabitation, Common Law Marriage, and the Possibility of a Shared Moral Life*, 75 GEO. L.J. 1829, 1859 note 132 (1987).

38 *See* Elisabeth Stanton's view, *infra* note 168. *See also* Marsha Garrison, *Is Consent Necessary? An Evaluation of the Emerging Law of Cohabitant Obligation*, 52 UCLA L. REV. 815, 877 (2005), stating that "it is extraordinarily hard to see why cohabitation, without children, would exploit women or even comparatively disadvantage them," but adds: "Cohabitation that leads to childbearing is a different case."

39 Note, 5 TEX. TECH. L. REV. 301 (1974). The most recent proposal as to the repeal of common law marriage in Texas was presented in 1989 by State Representative Patricia Hill from Dallas, House Bill No. 588, 71st Leg.Sess. (1989). The proposal was adopted by the House of Representatives, but defeated as it was not taken up by the Senate. As reason for the proposal was maintained primarily the uncertainty with respect to the parties' status upon the dissolution of a formless marriage. The criticism against the proposal referred *inter alia* to the importance of giving the children and the woman a protection upon the dissolution of the relationship, *see* House Recording Number 62 and 78 (1989). *See also* William W. Morris, *Common Law Marriage and Palimony* 16 (May 1990) (unpublished paper, Marriage Dissolution Institute, Houston).

40 Brown, *supra* note 10, at 141.

41 In the treatment of the legislative proposal as to the repeal of common law marriage in Idaho (HB 176), a Senate Committee conducted an investigation. Judith Holcombe, president of the Idaho Women Lawyers stated that she was opposed to the proposal with respect to the fact that there were "protective purposes to be served." Ann Wheeler also positioned herself as negative to a repeal as she was concerned with respect to the "property rights of women, custody issues and child illegitimacy," *see* Senate Judiciary and Rules Committee, March 1, 1995 – Minutes – page 2. The proposal, however, was adopted primarily with respect to the legal uncertainty that follows with common law marriage. Such marriages cannot be entered into in Idaho after January 1, 1996, *see* H.B. 176; Chap. 104 Idaho Session Laws (1995); and I.C. § 32-201 (1995).

42 HANSARD, VOL. 345, HOUSE OF COMMONS (1938-39) SESSION, col. 2253.

The goal of protecting the economically more vulnerable party is also the primary reason behind all the legislation for cohabiting unmarried persons promulgated since the 1970s. For example, in Sweden[43] and New Zealand,[44] the regulations concerning the division of property among cohabiters primarily purports to give protection upon separation and in cases of death. Both legislations are also applicable to homosexual couples. The proposed American Law Institute (ALI) Principles concerning the division of an estate upon the separation of cohabiting unmarried persons are also based on the idea that their relations closely resemble marriages in function, and their termination therefore poses the same social and legal issues as does the dissolution of a marriage. The primary purpose of the regulations concerning the dissolution of the relationship of "domestic partners" is, therefore, the fair distribution of the economic gains and losses incident to termination of the relationship.[45] In Canada,

---

43 In Sweden, legislation (SFS 1987:232) was enacted in 1987 giving couples living together under marriage-like conditions the right *inter alia* to a division of the residence and its belongings that the parties acquired during the cohabitation. The law was also applicable to homosexual couples (SFS 1987:813). These laws were replaced in 2003 by a new COHABITEES ACT (2003:376) that includes both homosexual and heterosexual cohabiting persons. In contrast to the new legislation in New Zealand, the Swedish law is not applicable to property other than the residence and its belongings. Neither does the Swedish law give any right to inheritance or maintenance. One of the reasons behind the Swedish law was to give protection to the more vulnerable party in the event of separation and/or death. In addition to this, the legislator wished to offer a practical possibility to divide the home they have built up together, *see* Prop. 1986/87:1, pp. 105, 106 and 108. In SOU 1980:81, p. 622, the Commission stated: "What is needed is to find solutions to practical problems and, in particular, to protect the weaker part at the dissolution of cohabitation." Kathleen Kiernan also mentions concerning the development in Europe "protection of weaker and vulnerable family members" as a justification for regulations relating to cohabitation, *see Redrawing the Boundaries of Marriage*, 66 J. MAR. & FAM. 980, 983 (2001).

44 Through amendments in 2001, which came into force February 1, 2002, to New Zealand's MATRIMONIAL PROPERTY ACT of 1976, several exceptions were made to the regulations concerning the division of a marital estate between spouses, making it applicable to heterosexual as well as homosexual cohabiting unmarried couples. Because of this, the law was renamed the PROPERTY (RELATIONSHIPS) ACT of 1976. In order to give cohabiting unmarried persons also the right to maintenance and inheritance, amendments were made at the same time to the Family Protection Act of 1955, the ADMINISTRATION ACT of 1969, and the Family Proceedings Act of 1980. Stated as reasons were *inter alia* the need for protection of women, who for a period leave their careers and take care of children, but with "changing work patterns" also for men, *see* Bill Atkin, *The Rights of Married and Unmarried Couples in New Zealand: Radical New Laws on Property and Succession*, International Society of Family Law World Conference, unpublished paper, Copenhagen/Oslo, (August 2002), at 3. Virginia Grainer, *What's Yours Is Mine: Reform of the Property Division Regime for Unmarried Couples in New Zealand*, 11 P.R.L.P. 287, 300 (2002), argues that the reform was based on the fact that "the property situation of persons in *de facto* relationships were identical to those in marriages" and that they deserved the same treatment.

45 *See* AMERICAN LAW INSTITUTE (ALI), PRINCIPLES OF THE LAW OF FAMILY DISSOLUTION: ANALYSIS AND RECOMMENDATIONS (2002), Chapter 6, Domestic Partners, § 6.02 (1). Comment: a. The basis of this Chapter. *See also* Grace Blumberg, who contributed to the drafting of ALI's principles, who has argued that the principles applied to

the protection of the vulnerable party is also generally the justification for interference into private relationships, such as an imposition of obligations on a former common law partner upon the breakdown of a relationship.[46] Behind the new legislation in Scotland in 2006 for couples "living together as if they were husband and wife" was also the motive to protect vulnerable people either on breakdown of the relationship or when a partner dies. This need for protection can also be seen behind the Norwegian proposal, in 2007, concerning a minimum inheritance right and a right to keep the estate undivided for surviving cohabitants.[47]

If one only looks at the need to protect the economically more vulnerable party, one can question why the majority of jurisdictions enacting regulations for cohabiting unmarried persons have stopped at protective regulations more limited than those applicable to formally married spouses. Long-term cohabitations and the creation of a family between unmarried persons are socially identical to marriage and create the same needs for protection during the relationship and upon its dissolution by separation or death. One can ask why common law marriage is recognized in New Hampshire only in cases of death, while the American Law Institute, in contrast, proposes regulations concerning the division of an estate for domestic partners that are the same as for married couples only upon separation, but not in cases of death?[48] And why does the system concerning the division of an estate for cohabiting persons in Sweden only concern

---

spouses are "equally pertinent at the end of a stable nonmarital cohabitation of substantial duration, whether same-sex or opposite-sex," *see The Regularization of Nonmarital Cohabitation: Rights and Responsibilities in the American Welfare State*, 76 NOTRE DAME L. REV. 1265, 1295 (2001). The goal of providing partners in long-term unions with more effective means of enforcing financial obligations between themselves has been held "laudable," *see* Elizabeth S. Scott, *Domestic Partnerships, Implied Contracts, and Law Reform*, in RECONCEIVING THE FAMILY, CRITIQUE ON THE AMERICAN LAW INSTITUTE'S PRINCIPLES OF THE LAW OF FAMILY DISSOLUTION 331 and 339-340 (Robin Fretwell Wilson ed., 2006).

46 Law Commission of Canada (Personal Relationships) (1999), II A., states that "most Canadians accept that economically vulnerable partners should not be left destitute at the end of a relationship..." *See also* Marguerite Trussler & Ellen Vandergrift, *Changing Relationships: How the Law and Governments Have Accommodated Them. A Canadian Perspective*, June 1 2001, Court of Queen's Bench of Alberta; and Winifred Holland, *Intimate Relationships in the New Millennium: The Assimilation of Marriage and Cohabitation?*, 17 CAN. J. FAM. L. 114, 128 (2000).

47 *See* THE FAMILY LAW (SCOTLAND) ACT 2006; Family Law (Scotland) Bill, SP Bill 36B, 18, Session 2 (2005), sections 18-22; Policy Memorandum, Family Law (Scotland) Bill (SP Bill 36) (2005), at 13. As to the Norwegian proposal, *see* Høringsnotat, January 2007, Snr. 200405522 EP, at 11.

48 N.H. REV. STAT. ANN. 457:39 (West 2003). *See also* the Norwegian proposal, Høringsnotat, January 2007, Snr. 200405522 EP, at 11. *Compare* the ALI PRINCIPLES, *supra* note 47, Chapter 6: Domestic partners. By assuming cohabitation and marriage were similar, but only legislating for the limited purpose of dissolution, it has been argued that the principles create a default rule that few would want, *see* Margaret F. Brinig, *Domestic Partnership and Default Rules*, in RECONCEIVING THE FAMILY. CRITIQUE ON THE AMERICAN LAW INSTITUTE'S PRINCIPLES OF THE LAW OF FAMILY DISSOLUTION 269 (Robin Fretwell Wilson ed., 2006).

the residence and its belongings, and not, in principle, all property as for spouses? If the needs are the same and determinative of policy, one system should suffice. For instance, the state of Washington's case law, in principle, applies the same regulations concerning the division of an estate for long-term cohabitations as for married couples upon both separation and cases of death. New Zealand and New South Wales in Australia go a step further and apply the same regulations concerning maintenance, the division of an estate, and inheritance to both cohabitants and spouses. The common law marriage states in the United States take the step completely and introduce entirely the same regulations as for married persons to the entire legal system.[49]

Legislatures, in general, have not typically and expressly presented well-thought-out explanations about why they did not or have not yet completely toed the line, which may indicate a certain ambivalence about how far to go. A relevant objection may be that the facts of cohabitation tend to be quite different. Many cohabitations are brief and unstable and therefore the needs for legal protection are less or different.[50] On the other hand, long-term and very marriage-like cohabitations may call for the same solutions as marriage provides. However, any final stance with regard to this group must also take into consideration the intentions of the parties. Perhaps everyone does not desire a system of protection and the obligations that the state, as a third party to the contract, imposes on the parties, without their consent. One of the parties can have chosen not to marry formally precisely in order to avoid the regulations of formal marriage.

A number of legislators appear to have attempted to resolve the conflict between the needs for protection and the parties' freedom of choice with a compromise that provides basic or minimal protection concerning certain property. Nevertheless, the parties, in order to reach the same protection as spouses, must actively take legal action by formally marrying.[51]

49 *See, e.g.*, Linda Wilmott et al., *De facto Relationships Property Adjustment Law – A National Direction*, 17 Aust. J. Fam. L. 1, 9 (2003), who contends that "individuals in *de facto* relationships possess interests identical to (those of) married couples" and who argues that the entire marital legal system should be extended to *de facto* couples in Australia. Associate Minister of Justice Margaret Wilson has stated that *de facto* relationships "have a right to the same legal protection" as married couples, *see* Property (Relationship) Amendment Bill: Third Reading (March 29, 2001).

50 Garrison, *supra* note 38, at 839 and 845, who criticizes the equivalence claim, contends that "cohabitants typically behave and describe their relationships very differently than married couples. Even more importantly, it shows that cohabitants rarely make marital commitments or engage in sharing behavior that might induce dependency." With respect to cohabitation as a social phenomenon, *see* Section12.2.4 *supra.*

51 *See* the Swedish Cohabitees Act (2003:376). The reason for giving only a minimal protection can be seen from the legislative proposal, being based on a cohabitation without any express wish from the parties. In order to receive the benefit of a more comprehensive regulation, the Swedish Government advised such persons to marry, *see* Legislative Bill 2002/03:80 at 25.

As with all compromises, the danger is that such a solution fulfills neither objective in a satisfactory manner.

The objection against taking into consideration only the need for protection, in actuality, is one of the strongest arguments against common law marriage and cohabitation legislation, in general, as discussed further below.

14.2.4 Compensation for Contributions and Sacrifices

There are cases in which the surviving cohabitant's rights cannot be justified by a need for protection, for example, if she or he already is wealthy. In such cases, rights can be justified, alternatively, by the surviving party's contributions to the deceased's fortune and to the family's economy as a whole and by the sacrifice, for example, of a professional career in order to take care of the children. The arguments of contribution and sacrifice, often used as legal grounds for property rights outside of family law as examined in Section 12.3, "Property Law Solutions in the Case Law," are a justification for legislation based on a common law marriage or cohabitation. The argument of contributions is more relevant to property acquired during the relationship than to separate property acquired before or during the cohabitation by gift or inheritance.

As in formal marriage, common law marriage in American law has been justified not only by the need for protection but also by the recognition that a spouse, as a result of his or her contributions to their shared lives, is entitled to those rights that follow from marriage. Consequently, it has been argued that the woman in an informal marriage, through work in the home and care of children, has facilitated the acquisition of property by the gainfully employed man during the cohabitation, and that she, therefore, is entitled to a portion of that property.[52] Homer Clark states: "When a woman has performed the obligations of a wife for thirty-five years and then is brutally deprived of all the financial benefits of marriage on the sole ground that the relationship was not signalized by some sort of

52 Shaw, *supra* note 1, at 589, states: "The assumption is the same one that is implicit in the policy considerations underlying the spouse's statutory intestate share and an equitable division of marital property upon divorce—that the homemaking or childrearing efforts of the dependent partner aided the working partner in the accumulation of the assets during the period of cohabitation, thereby entitling the former to an equitable interest in the property jointly accumulated." *See also Seagriff v. Seagriff*, 195 N.Y.S.2d 718, 721 (Dom.Rel.Ct. 1960), in which no common law marriage was found proven, but in which the court stated that one can sympathize with the woman who after having performed "normal wifely duties" for 35 years deemed herself abandoned by the man. The court found, however, that the result ought not to have been entirely unexpected for the woman and that she did not take advantage of all the occasions later available "to legalize her status." The need for protection in New Zealand has been considered especially significant for those who sacrifice a part of their professional career in order to take care of children. As to Swedish law, *see* Legislative Bill 1986/87:1, p. 105.

ceremony, this debases marriage. It is far better in such case to hold that the parties were married."[53]

14.2.5 Protection for Children

One of the primary reasons behind the institution of common law marriage in the United States, similar to those that supported concubinage in postclassical Roman law and the formless marriage of medieval canon law, has been to protect children in such relationships from the stigma of illegitimacy and grant them the rights given to children born in a formal marriage as discussed in Chapter 4, "The Reception of Common Law Marriage in the United States." This reasoning dominated American case law from the 1800s.[54] The same argument can also be found behind the principle presuming "everything in favor of the legitimacy of children,"[55] as well as the presumption applied to the benefit of the latter of two marriages, both of which are applicable to common law marriage.[56]

A number of critics are prepared to disregard the needs of children for protection for the sake of what has been considered a higher societal goal. George Howard, who during the beginning of the 1900s led the criticism against common law marriages, stated: "Far better that children of a delinquent minority should bear the stain of illegitimacy than that the welfare of the whole social body should be endangered."[57] The view that children,

---

53 Clark, *supra* note 18, at 122.

54 *See Rodebaugh v. Sanks*, 2 Watts 9, 11 (Pa. 1833); *Bashaw v. State*, 9 Tenn. (1 Yer.) 177, 197 (1829); *Holmes v. Holmes*, 6 La. 463, 470 (1834); *Graham v. Bennet*, 2 Cal. 503 (1852); *Barnett v. Kimmell*, 35 Pa. 13, 21 (1859); *Commonwealth v. Stump*, 53 Pa. 132, 136, 91 Am.Dec. 198 (1866); *Armaell's Estate*, 2 Brewster 239, 246 (Penn. 1869); *Meister v. Moore*, 96 U.S. 76, 81 (1877); *Markley v. Baldwin*, 112 U.S. 490, 495, 28 L.Ed 822, 824, 5 Sup.Ct.Rep. 278 (1884); *Nixon v. Wichita Land & Cattle Co.*, 84 Tex. 408, 19 S.W. 560, 563 (1892); and *Ingersol v. McWillie*, 9 Tex.Civ.App. 543, 30 S.W. 56, 60-61 (1895). *See also* Joel Prentiss Bishop, New Commentaries on Marriage, Divorce and Separation I, §§ 403, 423 (1891); Robert Black, *Common Law Marriage*, 2 U. Cin. L. Rev. 113, 114, 132 (1928); Note, *Common Law Marriage Abolished*, 3 Brook. L. Rev. 155 (1933); Holland Smith, Note, *Common-law marriage: What it is and how to prove it*, 12 S.C. L.Q. 355, 367 (1960); Michael Grossberg, Governing the Hearth: Law and the Family in Nineteenth-Century America 196 (1985); and Dubler, supra note 36, at 1894. For more on this, *see* Section 4.3 *supra*.

55 *Hynes v. McDermott*, 91 N.Y. 451, 453, 43 Am.Rep. 677 (1883). *Compare Dillon v. Dillon*, 60 Ga. 204 (1878). *See also Megginson's Estate*, 28 P. 388, 389 (Or. 1891).

56 *See* Section 5.3.3 *supra*.

57 *See* George Elliott Howard, A History of Matrimonial Institutions III, 184 (1904). *See also* Gordon A. Stewart, *Our Marriage and Divorce Laws*, 23 PSM 228 (1883), who maintained that common law marriage "bastardizes more children than would enactment of stringent marriage laws, for parties would then be more careful and not enter into such relations without proof of marriage." *Compare Anderson v. Anderson*, 235 Ind. 113, 131 N.E.2d 301, 307 (1956), in which the court stated: "It is regrettable that the parties had a child born out of wedlock, but this court does not sit as the General Assembly to legitimize all children born under such circumstances."

as a third party, should not suffer for the parents' out-of-wedlock "sins" recurs, however, in the case law throughout the 1900s[58] and also appears in the legislative debates both at the beginning of the century and later. One of the primary reasons for the Texas legislature's rejection of a proposal to repeal the institution of common law marriage, during recent years, consequently, was that children born in such relationships would lose their marital legitimacy.[59] Similar motives have played a role in the preservation in 1939 of the marriage by cohabitation with habit and repute in Scotland.[60]

Even though the goal of the modern cohabitation legislation is primarily to protect the vulnerable party and the regulations do not effect the formal status of any children, it also indirectly gives weight to the economic interests of children born in nonmarital relationships. Spousal support and property rights after separation can be seen as benefits to children.[61]

---

58 *Reaves v. Reaves*, 15 Okla. 240, 82 P. 490, 496 (1905); 2 L.R.A., N.S., 353 (1905); *In re McCausland's Estate*, 213 Pa. 189, 62 A. 780 (1906); *Umbenhower v. Labus*, 85 Ohio St. 238, 249, 97 N.E. 832, 834 (1911); *Coachman v. Sims*, 36 Okla. 536, 129 P. 845, 847 (1913); *In re Love's Estate*, 42 Okla. 478, 142 P. 305, 308 (1914); *People v. Spencer*, 199 Mich. 395, 165 N.W. 921, 923 (1917); *In re Sanders' Estate*, 67 Okla. 3, 168 P. 197 (1917); *In re Stevenson's Estate*, 272 Pa. 291, 116 A. 162, 165 (1922); *Dirion v. Brewer*, 20 Ohio App. 298, 301, 151 N.E. 818 (1925); *Welch v. All Persons*, 78 Mont. 370, 254 P. 179, 85 Mont. 114, 278 P. 110, 115 (1929); *Boyd v. Boyd*, 252 N.Y. 422, 169 N.E. 632 (1939); and *Tiuna v. Willmott*, 162 Okla. 42, 19 P.2d 145 (1933). In *Kisla v. Kisla*, 124 W.Va. 220, 19 S.E.2d 609, 611 (1942), it was suggested in dictum that children should be legitimate also if a common law marriage is invalid. *See also Jones v. Kemp*, 144 F.2d 478 (10th Cir. 1944); *Kester v. Kester*, 106 W.Va. 615, 146 S.E. 625 (1929); *Gatterdam v. Gatterdam*, 86 Ohio App. 29, 85 N.E.2d 526, 530 (1949); *In re Rosenberger's Estate*, 362 Pa.153, 65 A.2d 377 (1949); *In re McAnany's Estate*, 91 Pa.Super. 317 (1927); *In re Wagner's Estate*, 398 Pa. 531, 533 f, 159 A.2d 495, 497 (1960); *Reger v. Reger*, 242 Ind. 302, 315, 177 N.E.2d 901 (1961); *Tarter v. Medley*, 356 S.W.2d 255 (Ky. 1962); *Estate of Claveria v. Claveria*, 615 S.W.2d 164 (Tex. 1981); *Johnson v. Green*, 251 Ga. 645, 309 S.E.2d 362, 363 (1983); and *Ridley v. Grandison*, 260 Ga. 6, 389 S.E.2d 746, 748 (1990). *See also Black, supra* note 54, at 114; Weyrauch, *supra* note 22, at 101; Denzil Y. Causey, Jr., Comment, *Domestic Relations - Common Law Marriage in Georgia*, 25 GA. B.J. 225, 229-230 (1962); and CLARK, *supra* note 18, at 112.

59 *See* Warren D. Harris, *The Essentials of a Valid Marriage in Virginia*, 6 VA. L. REG. 437, 444-445 (1900), *supra* Section 4.3 *supra*. *See also* Clarice M. Davis, Comment, *Common-Law Marriage in Texas*, 21 SW. L.J. 647, 660 (1967), who states: "[S]ince Texas has no paternity act, the availability of common-law marriage serves a useful function in reducing the number of children made illegitimate by the failure of their parents to marry." This same reason, as well as others, was presented against a legislative proposal in 1989 to repeal common law marriage in Texas. The proposal was passed by a bare majority in the House of Representatives, but was defeated as the Senate did not take it up. *See* House Bill No. 588, 71st Leg.Sess. (1989); House Recording No. 62 and 78. *See also* Vaughn, *supra* note 21, at 1145, who has argued the legitimacy of children as one of the reasons for retaining common law marriage in Texas. *Compare Boudreaux v. Taylor*, 353 S.W.2d 901, (Tex.Civ.App.-Waco 1962). A child born in a common law marriage can inherit from both parents in Texas, *see Esparza v. Esparza*, 382 S.W.2d 162, 168 (Tex.Civ.App.-Corpus Christi 1964).

60 HANSARD, *supra* note 42, col. 2253.

61 With regard to the ALI PRINCIPLES, *see* Blumberg, *supra* note 47, at 1297; and Scott, *supra* note 47, at 340.

An evaluation of the argument favoring protection, however, must also take into consideration that the demographic picture and the attitudes toward out-of-wedlock children have radically changed in the Western world since the 1970s. The number of children born outside of marriage has greatly increased, as much as threefold in many countries, as a result of decreasing rates of marriage and increasing numbers of cohabitations without marriage. The number of children born outside of marriage in 1998 in England was 38 percent; in Sweden, 54 percent; and in Iceland, 64 percent. In the United States, the comparable number in 1999 was 33 percent, of which 22 percent were Anglo-Americans; 42 percent were Hispanics; and 69 percent were African-Americans.[62] At the same time, the attitude toward children born out of wedlock has undergone significant changes. For more than twenty years, the English legislature's endeavor, for example, has been to repeal the concepts of *legitimacy* and *illegitimacy* among children. In Sweden, there no longer is any stigma to being born outside of marriage and references to *out-of-wedlock children* have been removed from the legislation.[63] The expression that appears to be becoming all the more common both in Europe and the United States is the more neutral term *children of unmarried mothers.*[64]

These demographic developments and changed values have instigated changes in the legal arena. In the United States, the Supreme Court has forbidden discrimination between legitimate and illegitimate children in a series of decisions supported by the equal protection clause of the United States Constitution.[65] Comparable provisions in state constitutions

---

62 *Family Research Report,* 15 J. Fam. Res. Inst. No. 7 (Nov. 2000). The number of births to unmarried mothers in the United States was 18% in 1980, 28% in 1990, and 34% in 2002. *See* National Vital Statistics Reports, Vol. 52, No. 10, December 17, 2003.

63 Stephan Cretney, a member of the Law Commission in London, stated: "We provisionally propose not only the abolition of the remaining legal disadvantages of illegitimacy so far as they affect the child, but the complete removal of the concepts of legitimacy and illegitimacy from the law of family relations," *see The Law Relating to Unmarried Partners From the Perspective of a Law Reform Agency,* in Marriage and Cohabitation in Contemporary Societies 245 (John M. Eekelaar, Sanford N. Katz eds., 1980). In the Family Law Reform Act of 1987 § 1, the fundamental principle that the laws must be construed without taking into consideration whether the father or mother to a child has or had been married to each other nowadays is established. However, there still remain certain legal differences between the two categories. *See also* The Law Reform (Parent and Child) (Scotland) Act 1986 S. 1. In Sweden, in which the majority of children are born outside of marriage, the comparable concept was entirely removed from the law in 1976, albeit that minimal substantive differences remain, *see* Anders Agell, *Cohabitation Without Marriage in Swedish Law,* in Marriage and Cohabitation in Contemporary Societies 252 (John M. Eekelaar, Sanford N. Katz eds., 1980). In modern American case law, the expression "children" has in many cases been considered to cover children regardless of legitimacy, *see, e.g., Green v. Green,* 365 A.2d 610 (D.C. 1976). In Massachusetts, the expression "children born out of wedlock" is used, *see* Chapter 209C Gen. Laws of Massachusetts (West 2003).

64 *See, e.g.,* National Vital Statistics Reports, Vol. 52, No. 10, December 17, 2003.

65 U.S. Const. Amend XIV, § 1. The following Supreme Court cases demonstrate that the step has been taken in order to prevent discrimination of illegitimate children,

have also been cited as support for the rights of illegitimate children.[66] State family legislation, today, contains principle statements prohibiting discrimination against children born outside of marriage and asserting that these children are to be granted the same rights and protections as other children.[67] Similar declarations can also be found in English family legislation.[68]

As regards the choice of methods for granting rights within family law to out-of-wedlock children, the marital status of the parents based on formal marriage or common law marriage has not been proven to be necessary. With respect to rights of inheritance, out-of-wedlock children, increasingly, have been granted a right to inherit from both their fathers and mothers because the requirement of legitimate birth has simply been removed. Thus, rights of inheritance are based solely on parenthood. Originally, illegitimate children in the United States had no right to inherit from either parent. In *Trimble v. Gordon* (1977), the impediment against an illegitimate child's right to inherit from his or her father was found to be unconstitutional.[69] Today, out-of-wedlock children in the majority of states have the right to inherit from both their fathers and mothers.[70] For example, in *PNC Bank Corp. v. Workers' Compensation Appeal Board (Stamos)* (2003), the court stated, with respect to Pennsylvania law, "the marital status of parents no longer determines the inheritance rights of their children."[71] The equal protection clause[72] has also been cited in arguing against any

---

but that differences still remain in relation to legitimate children: *Glona v. American Casualty Co.*, 391 U.S. 73 (1968); *King v. Smith*, 392 U.S. 309 (1968); *Weber v. Aetna Casualty Co.*, 406 U.S. 164 (1972); *Levy v. Louisiana*, 391 U.S. 68 (1968); *Lewis v. Martin*, 397 U.S. 532 (1970); *Labine v. Vincent*, 401 U.S. 532 (1971); *Gomez v. Perez*, 409 U.S. 535 (1973); *Cahill v. New Jersey Welfare Rights Organization*, 411 U.S. 619 (1973); *Jiminez v. Weinberger*, 417 U.S. 628 (1974); *Norton v. Mathews*, 427 U.S. 524 (1976); *Mathews v. Lucas*, 427 U.S. 495 (1976); *Trimble v. Gordon*, 430 U.S. 762, 776 (1977); *Fiallo v. Bell*, 430 U.S. 787 (1977); *Lalli v. Lalli*, 439 U.S. 259 (1978); *Parham v. Hughes*, 441 U.S. 347 (1979); and *Pickett v. Brown*, 462 U.S. 1, 18 (1983).

66 *See* Paul M. Kurtz, *The State Equal Rights Amendments and Their Impact on Domestic Relations Law*, 11 FAM. L.Q. 101 (1977).

67 *See, e.g.*, the legislation of the state of *Massachusetts* which prescribes: "Children born to parents who are not married to each other shall be entitled to the same rights and protections of the law as all other children," *see* MASS. GEN. LAWS, c. 209C § 1 (West 2003). *See also* the state of *Washington's* comparable regulation: "A child to parents who are not married to each other has the same rights under the law as a child born to parents who are married to each other," *see* WASH. REV. CODE § 26.26.106 (West 2003).

68 *See* as to England, the FAMILY LAW REFORM ACT 1987 § 1, and as to Canada, Martha Baily, *Regulation of Cohabitation and Marriage in Canada*, 26 LAW & POLICY 153 (2004).

69 *Trimble v. Gordon*, 430 U.S. 762, 776 (1977).

70 *See* CLARK, *supra* note 18, at 355, with citations.

71 *PNC Bank Corp. v. Workers' Compensation Appeal Bd. (Stamos)*, No. 860 C.D. (2003). *See* 20 PA. C.S. § 2107 (West 2003).

72 *Stanley v. Illinois*, 405 U.S. 645, 92 S.Ct. 1208, 31 L.Ed.2d 551 (1972). *Compare Quilloin v. Walcott*, 434 U.S. 246, 98 S.Ct. 549, 54 L.Ed.2d 511 (1978) and *Lehr v. Robertson*, 463 U.S. 248 (1983). The Equal Rights Amendments in many states also give support to the principle that the mother ought not be given precedence with respect to custody. *Compare* THE UNIFORM PARENTAGE ACT § 25, 9A UNIF. L. ANN.

exclusive right by mothers to the custody of out-of-wedlock children in favor of assessing custody in the same manner as for legitimate children, in other words, in terms of "the child's best interests."[73]

Of the methods that do not assume marital status based on common law marriage, a development in Western Europe during the past few years is of particular interest. Various approaches have been developed to achieve joint custody during the cohabitation of children to unmarried parents. The goals have been to equate out-of-wedlock children with children born in marriages and also to equate the unmarried father with the unmarried mother. These endeavors must be seen against the background that cohabiting unmarried persons have children and create families, just as do married couples.[74] The children, consequently, grow up with their fathers and mothers in families that, sociologically, do not to any great extent deviate from the families in which the parents are married. Joint custody has also been thought to promote good relationships between the child and both parents, regardless of whether they are cohabiting. According to the United Nations Convention on the Rights of the Child (1989), the signatory states are to do their best to ensure recognition of the principle that parents have a joint responsibility for their child's upbringing and development.[75] Joint custody has been assumed to contribute to both parents taking such a responsibility.

One method, most consistent with common law marriage, is that unmarried parents obtain joint custody as soon as paternity is established, assuming that they are living together.[76] Mothers are given no presumptive preference. The basis for the legal consequence consists of the cohabitation. The couple is then equated with married parents. The need for joint custody has been assumed to be greatest among unmarried parents who are living together. This method fits well with the development of all

---

325 (Supp. 1985), which prescribes that when the child's father is identified and petitions for custody, the court is to decide "custodial rights to the child."

73 *Trimble v. Gordon*, 430 U.S. 762, 97 S.Ct. 1459, 52 L.Ed.2d 31 (1977). *See* more closely the analysis of the cases in CLARK, *supra* note 18, at 350-355. *Compare* THE UNIFORM PROBATE CODE § 2-109, 8 UNIF. L. ANN. 67 (1983), which allows an illegitimate child to inherit from or through his or her father if paternity is established.

74 European studies estimate that in most of the Northern and West European countries, 40% or more of unmarried cohabiting couples have a child, *see* Kathleen Kiernan, *Unmarried Cohabitation and Parenthood in Britain and Europe*, 26 LAW & POLICY 33, 43 (2004).

75 Article 18, THE UNITED NATIONS CONVENTION ON THE RIGHTS OF THE CHILD (1989) states: "States Parties shall use their best efforts to ensure recognition of the principle that both parents have common responsibilities for the upbringing and development of the child." As supplements to the United Nations Convention on the Rights of the Child, the Council of Europe has adopted The European Convention on the Exercise of Children's Rights (1996), as well as The Convention on Contact concerning Children (2002).

76 In *Spain*, both parents have legal custody (*patria potestas*) as to their child regardless of whether they are married to each other. If the parents do not live together, custody is exercised by the parent living together with the child, *see* CÓDIGO CIVIL, Article 154.

the cohabitation legislation that, for the invocation of the legal consequences, requires that the parties are cohabiting. As can be seen in Chapter 13, "The Constitutive Requisites in the Future," in practice, this method does not differ very much from common law marriage, because the parties in such a marriage typically do not enter into any expressed contract, and the courts accepted inferred agreements and legal presumptions based on the parties' cohabitation and outward appearance as spouses. The cohabitation is the basis for a status that, *inter alia,* leads to the legal consequence of joint custody.

A disadvantage of this method arises when attempting to establish whether a cohabitation exists in the meaning of the law. With this obstacle in mind, and because it may be important to quickly and certainly establish who is to have custody of a child, certain countries have continued to refuse to tie joint custody to whether the parties are cohabiting even though they have not hesitated to enact cohabitation legislation.[77] One way to reduce such problems is to only accept cohabitations that are registered or confirmed in writing, or can be proven in another unambiguous manner.[78] Registered cohabitations, on the other hand, have been criticized for their resemblance to civil formal marriage.[79]

---

77 The difficulties in establishing when a cohabitation is to be considered to exist has constituted an important reason as to why the Swedish legislator has not wished to introduce automatic joint custody for cohabiting parents nor any presumption of paternity based on the circumstance that the parents live together, *see* the Swedish Report Joint Custody for Unmarried Parents Ds 1999:57, at 57-59, 65. With respect to application difficulties arising with cohabitation legislation, *see* Section 13.3.9 *supra.*

78 Iceland has a register concerning cohabitation relationships. When an unmarried mother has a child, it is presumed that man listed in the register is the father of the child. The parents thereby automatically receive joint custody of the child. As evidence concerning the cohabitation, the parties can also cite other unambiguous evidence, *see* BØRNELOV, nr. 7915, § 29, stk. 1 (2003). In Denmark, a committee in 1997 proposed that parents living together shall at the child's birth be able to give a declaration that they live together, that it is their mutual child, and that they together wish to take care of and be responsible for the child. After this declaration, the man would be viewed as the child's father and the parents receive joint custody, *see* Betænkning om børns retsstilling nr 1350, 1997. The legislator, however, rejected the proposal with respect to the risk for misunderstanding and enacted instead a possibility to make a written care and responsibility declaration. In Norway, there is a regulation that cohabiting persons expecting or having had a child, can confirm in writing that it is their mutual child and that they are cohabiting persons. This confirmation automatically entails that the paternity and maternity are considered established and that the parents receive joint custody as to the child, *see* Samboerne og samfunnet, NOU 1999:25, at 103-108, 139. The Norwegian government has stated its support for the proposed scheme with respect *inter alia* to that a cohabiting father has an equally close relationship to the child as a married father, *see* St. Meld. No. 29 (2002-2003), at 25-26.

79 In Sweden *and* Norway, proposals concerning registration of cohabitation have been rejected with the motivation that such a system would resemble a marriage of a lower dignity and that there is a risk that certain cohabiting persons would still not register and that others would register who are not cohabiting, *see* SOU 1999:104, at 184; Legislative Bill 2002/03:80, at 27; and NOU 1999:25, 2.3.

Another method is for unmarried parents to be given joint custody as a result of a pertinent legal action, for example, a contract or notification leading to registration with a governmental authority or an application to the courts. Some jurisdictions require a review of whether joint custody is appropriate, or in any case, not inappropriate, for the child's best interests. The premise is that the unmarried mother has sole custody of the child at birth. The European Court of Justice has found that this system does not conflict with the prohibition against discrimination based on sex, in accordance to the European Convention of Human Rights, assuming that the father has the right to have custody transferred to himself if this is in the child's best interests.[80] One advantage of an active legal action by the parties is that they thus become aware of the relevant legal effects. In addition, application problems are limited by registration with a governmental authority. Such a joint declaration of intent is most natural if the parents are living together, however, no requirement about this typically exists.[81] It is sufficient that the parents are in agreement. The possibility

80 Article 14, The European Convention on Human Rights (1950).

81 In England, unmarried parents can receive joint custody, which nowadays is called "parental responsibility," in that they enter into a contract that is submitted to the "Principal Registry of the Family Division." Such a contract can also be entered into even if the parents are not living together. The possibility of entering into a contract was enacted in the Children Act of 1989 § 4 (1)(b). If the parents cannot agree, the father can apply to the court for joint custody, which is to be decided with respect to the child's best, *see* § 4 (1)(c). The Adoption and Children Act of 2002, which came into force December 1, 2003, has replaced this law. In 1996, only 3,590 contracts were entered into, which can be compared with approximately 200,000 births outside of marriage, *see* Children Act Advisory Committee, Final Report 1997. London: Lord Chancellor's Department (1997), Appendix 2, commented in Gillian Douglas, *Marriage, Cohabitation, and Parenthood – from Contract to Status?*, in Cross Currents: Family Law and Policy in the US and England 225 (Sanford N. Katz et al. eds., 2000). In Scotland an unmarried father can also get "Parental Responsibilities and Rights" after a registration to which both parties agree. There is no requirement that the parties are cohabiting. The reform is founded on the principle that a child has two parents and is entitled to the loving involvement of both in his or her upbringing. At the same time, the status of illegitimacy was abolished, *see* Family Law (Scotland) Act (2006), sections 15B and 17; Policy Memorandum, Family Law (Scotland) Bill (SP Bill 36)(2005), at 9. In France, parents who are not married to each other can receive joint custody by reporting it. If the child is born after January 8, 1993, the custody becomes joint by the parents acknowledging the child as their own within one year from the child's birth and they at the point of time of the acknowledgment live together, *see* Law No. 93-22 of 8 Jan. 1993. In Germany, unmarried parents can receive joint custody by giving a declaration that they wish to exercise custody jointly, *see* BGB §§ 1626-1698 b. In The Netherlands, unmarried parents can receive joint custody by registration after a joint application. The court can decide upon joint custody between a parent and his/her cohabiting partner, assuming that there is a close relationship between the child and the cohabiting partner, *see* Article 252 of Book 1, Civile Code. If the cohabiting partners have registered the partnership, they have joint custody, *see* Article 253 aa Book 1, Civil Code. In Sweden, unmarried parents, regardless of whether they live together, have the possibility to receive joint custody through a simple notification to the social or tax authorities that the father acknowledges paternity. The cohabiting partners can also apply for joint custody with the court that grants the application if it is not obviously incompatible with the child's best,

that unmarried parents can obtain joint custody through a contract or a judicial decision can also be found in American law.[82]

A third method, which appears to be on the rise, is that unmarried parents automatically receive joint custody of their children as soon as paternity has been established in a certain manner. The mother has no precedence. No active action by the parents is required, nor do they need to be cohabiting. The child is considered to still need both parents' actual and formal participation. The legal, political reason for this method, which is not based on marital status, or on cohabitation and any formal declaration of intent by the parents, actually rests on parenthood and its social and psychological implications. A variation of this method is that joint custody is automatically given a certain period after paternity has been established, as long as neither parent contests. Combinations of these three methods are common.[83]

If parents disagree, there usually is the possibility to enact or revoke joint custody through a judicial decision based on what is in the child's

---

see FÖRÄLDRABALKEN (1949) 6:4. Of unmarried cohabiting parents, 95% register joint custody. For unmarried non-cohabiting parents, the comparable number is 50%, *see* Ds 1999:57 at 40. In Denmark, the parents have the possibility to receive joint custody through a contract registered at a governmental authority. In 1999, 81% of unmarried cohabiting parents contracted as to joint custody upon the birth of the child. Since 2002, they have in addition the possibility to submit a written care and responsibility declaration giving them joint custody (*fælles forældremyndighed*), *see* BØRNELOVEN no. 460, the 7 June 2001 § 2, stk. 1. In Norway, unmarried parents also have the right to receive joint custody through a contract registered at a governmental authority, *see* LOV OM BARN OG FORELDRE (1981) § 35. In all of the Nordic countries, unmarried parents can receive joint custody through a contract, and if the parties are not in agreement, through a court judgment. For more with respect to Nordic law concerning children, *see* SVEND DANIELSEN, NORDISK BØRNERET II (2003). As to the Nordic development, *see also* Anders Agell, *Is There One System of Family Law in the Nordic Countries?*, 3 E.J.L.R. 313, 317-320 (2001).

82 For example, in Massachusetts, a state not recognizing common law marriage, a child of an unmarried mother from birth automatically is under the mother's custody. The parents, however, can receive joint custody through a judicial order, if it is appropriate with respect to the best interests of the child. A contract as to joint custody submitted to and approved by a court has the same effect as a judicial decree, *see* MASS. GEN. LAWS c. 209C § 10 (a)(b) and § 11 (b) (West 2003).

83 Through THE ADOPTION AND CHILDREN ACT of 2002, which came into force December 1, 2003, the legislator in England has enacted automatic shared parental responsibility for unmarried parents, assuming that they upon the birth jointly permit registration of the man as father with Registrar-General, *see* § 4 (1)(a). It appears to have been of significance for the amendments of the laws that ⅘ of all births outside of marriage are registered by the parents jointly and that in ¾ of these cases, the parents are cohabiting. *See The Law on Parental Responsibility for Unmarried Fathers*. London: Lord Chancellor's Department (1998). In *Sweden*, the legislator for a long period of time has considered enacting automatic joint custody for unmarried parents and the discussion continues. According to one proposal, the current regulations concerning the registration ought to be supplemented with a regulation as to automatic joint custody for unmarried parents when three months have gone by from the paternity being established, assuming that neither of the parents within this period have registered that he or she contests joint custody, *see* the report, Ds 1999:57, at 39, 66.

best interests. Consequently, the justifications for common law marriage to protect illegitimate children and equate them with children born in wedlock are very much alive in the Western world today. However, there are many methods other than common law marriage.

14.2.6 Fulfillment of the Parties' Expectations in Good Faith

1. *Common Law Marriage*

A considerably more limited reason behind common law marriage has been to fulfill the parties' good faith expectations about being united in matrimony and, in individual cases, to avoid unjust results.[84] One should distinguish between three different situations.

The first arises if a couple attempts through a wedding ceremony to enter into matrimony that is invalid (void or voidable) as a result of an impediment. If the parties, or in any event one of them, has acted in good faith as regards the existence of the impediment, a common law marriage can be established if the impediment was later removed.[85] The same has been the case if the original marriage has been a common law marriage that was invalid as a result of an impediment. A continued cohabitation after the removal of the impediment, as seen in Chapter 7, "Implied Marriage Agreements," has also, in such cases, given rise to a common law marriage.[86]

A second situation arises if the ceremonial marriage has been invalid because of a mistake in form, for example, because an unauthorized person officiated at the wedding ceremony but the parties proceeded in good faith. A common law marriage has then been able to be established. In *Barron v. Apfel* (2000), the United States Court of Appeals stated that the purpose with common law marriage is "to repair unintended deficiencies in the ceremony, documentation, or other formalities of marriage,

84 Weyrauch, *supra* note 22, at 109, states: "Common law marriage, jointly with other kinds of informal marriages, may assume the function of a safety valve for releasing accumulated pressure and avoiding hardship in individual cases." Vaughn, *supra* note 21, at 1140, views the most important function of common law marriage to be to protect the parties' "good faith expectations." *See also* Clark, *supra* note 18, at 111, who views common law marriage as a means "to make good the bona fide expectations of the parties." *See also* Graham Douthwaite, Unmarried Couples and the Law 19 (1979); Ralph B. Kelley, *Creation and Proof of Common Law Marriage Following Removal of Impediments*, 18 N.Y. Intra. L. Rev. 213, 221 (1963); and Causey, *supra* note 58, at 229-230.

85 Weyrauch, *supra* note 22, at 101; and Albert C. Jacobs & Julius Goebel, Jr., Cases and Other Materials on Domestic Relations 144-147 (3d ed. 1952).

86 *See* Section 7.6 and *compare* with respect to impediments against marriage, Section 5.3, *supra*.

or in the legal capacity to wed (a party might erroneously believe that he or she had been validly divorced from a previous spouse)."[87]

The third situation arises if parties do not enter into a ceremonial marriage, but believe that they have been united in a common law marriage.[88] At times, it is assumed that cohabiting unmarried persons, because they lived as married persons, expect that the law shall treat them as married.[89] A not entirely unusual situation is a man who has a relationship with a woman, enjoys the fruits of that relationship without giving any direct promise of marriage, while raising the expectations of a future ceremonial marriage. Frequently, it is later shown that he "kept putting it off and he never did."[90] The regulations concerning broken promises of marriage have long since languished in American law. Still, common law marriage has been able to provide legal protection to the extent that the parties, through their cohabitation and outward appearance, have still been found to have an agreeing intent to live together.[91] A common law marriage argument for giving legal effects to cohabitation is that cohabitation indicates commitment and that those who live together unmarried are just as committed as those who are married.[92]

Against the acceptance of such a legal protection, it plausibly can be argued that the party working in the home has had the possibility of demanding a formal marriage as a requirement for a continued relationship. In the individual case, however, this is easier said than done. In addition, many young couples do not have any knowledge about the significance of formal marriage in their legal protection.

---

87 *Barron v. Apfel*, 209 F.3d 984, 985 (7th Cir. 2000). *See also* CLARK, *supra* note 18, at 111. Adams, *supra* note 110, at 298, views common law marriage to have its justification in cases of good faith.

88 *Garduno v. Garduno*, 760 S.W.2d 735 (Tex.App.-Corpus Christi 1988); *Rey v. Rey*, 487 S.W.2d 245 (Tex.Civ.App.-El Paso 1972); *Orr v. State*, 129 Fla. 398, 409, 176 So. 510, 514 (1937); and *Brinckle v. Brinckle*, 12 Phila. 232 (1877). *Compare Walker v. Matthews*, 191 Miss. 489, 3 So.2d 820 (1941); and *Travers v. Reinhardt*, 205 U.S. 423 (1906).

89 Vaughn, *supra* note 21, at 1141. According to Stein, *supra* note 18, at 293, many cohabiters in the lower social and economic classes of society believe that their relationships are valid marriages.

90 *Anderson v. Anderson*, 235 Ind. 113, 131 N.E.2d 301 (1956); *Moffat Coal Co. v. Indus. Commission*, 108 Colo. 388, 118 P.2d 769 (1941); and *Kozlowski v. Kozlowski*, 80 N.J. 378, 403 A.2d 902 (1979). With respect to cases in which the intentions of the parties with respect to a future marriage (*per verba de futuro*) prevented the establishment of a common law marriage, *see* Section 6.4.1 *supra*.

91 CLARK, *supra* note 18, at 21. It has been maintained that the repeal of the possibility as to claims with respect to broken promises of marriage in Florida in 1945 increased the number of lawsuits with respect to common law marriage, *see Fincher v. Fincher*, 55 So.2d 800, 802 (Fla. 1952). *Compare* Weyrauch, *supra* note 22, at 99, who argues that the increase was limited. *See also* Rothstein, *supra* note 2, at 104.

92 *See* Milton C. Regan, Jr., *Unmarried Partners and the Legacy of Marvin v. Marvin: Calibrated Commitment: The Legal Treatment of Marriage and Cohabitation*, 76 NOTRE DAME L. REV. 1435, 1437 (2001). Critical is Garrison, *supra* note 38, at 835.

2. *The Doctrine of Putative Marriage*

The limited purpose of fulfilling parties' good faith expectations to be married can be achieved with solutions more narrowly tailored than common law marriage. One such method is the putative marriage doctrine,[93] found in a number of American states in the South and West that do not recognize common law marriage and are community-property states; for example, Louisiana[94] and California.[95] The doctrine is codified in the Uniform Marriage and Divorce Act and is also recognized in

93 *See* Christopher Blakesley, *The Putative Marriage Doctrine*, 60 Tul. L. Rev. 1 (1985); Note, *The Rights of the Putative and Meretricious Spouse in California*, 50 Cal. L. Rev. 866 (1962); Annot., *Rights in Decedent's Estate Between Lawful and Putative Spouses*, 81 A. L.R.3d 6 (1977); Marjorie Dick Rombauer, *Marital Status and Eligibility for Federal Statutory Income Benefits*, 52 Wash. L. Rev. 227 (1977); Ira Mark Ellman et al., Family Law: Cases, Text, Problems 69 (3d ed. 1998); and Clark, *supra* note 18, at 114. *Compare* George L. Blum, *Annotation, Property Rights Arising from Relationship of Couples Cohabiting Without Marriage*, 69 A.L.R.5th 219 (1999), who argues that states not recognizing the putative marriage doctrine instead have opted for different private law solutions.

94 The putative spouse doctrine in Louisiana, influenced by the French Civil Code (1803), can be found in La. Civil Code, art. 117 (2003): "The marriage, which has been declared null, produces nevertheless its civil effects as it relates to the parties and their children, if it has been contracted in good faith." Art. 118 states that: "If only one of the parties acted in good faith, the marriage produces its civil effects only in his or her favor, and in favor of the children born of the marriage." *See Saacks v. Saacks*, 708 So.2d 1077 (La.App. 1998); *Mara v. Mara*, 452 So.2d 329 (App. 1984), 513 So.2d 1220 (App. 1987), 517 So.2d 813 (La. 1988); *Mabry v. Mabry*, 452 So.2d 329 (La.App. 1984); *Super v. Super*, 397 So.2d 1084 (La.App. 1981); *Schaefer v. Schaefer*, 379 So.2d 864 (La.App. 1980); *Super v. Burke*, 367 So.2d 93 (La.App. 1979); *Gathright v. Smith*, 368 So.2d 679 (La. 1978); *Succession of Zinsel*, 360 So.2d 587 (La.App. 1978); *Price v. Price*, 326 So.2d 545 (La.App. 1976); *King v. Cancienne*, 316 So.2d 366 (La. 1975); *Houston v. Mondy*, 306 So.2d 91 (La.App. 1974); *Succession of Barbier*, 296 So.2d 390 (La.App. 1974); *Cortes v. Fleming*, 307 So.2d 611 (La. 1973); *Babineaux v. Pernie-Bailey Drilling Co.*, 261 La. 1080, 262 So.2d 328 (1972); and *Hunter v. Richardson*, 346 F.Supp. 123 (M.D.La. 1972). *See also* Note, *The Putative Marriage Doctrine in Louisiana*, 12 Loy. L. Rev. 89 (1937).

95 Cal. Fam. Code Ann. § 2251 (a) (West 2003) states: "If a determination is made that a marriage is void or voidable and the court finds that either party or both parties believed in good faith that the marriage was valid, the court shall: ... Declare the party or parties to have the status of a putative spouse." *See also Estate of Depasse*, 97 Cal.App.4th 92, 118 Cal.Rptr.2d 143 (2002); *Burks v. Apfel*, 233 F.3d 1220 (10th Cir. 2000); *Welch v. State*, 83 Cal.App.4th 1374, 100 Cal.Rptr.2d 430 (2000); *Centinela Hosp. Med. Ctr. v. Superior Court*, 215 Cal.App.3d 971, 263 Cal.Rptr. 672 (1989); *In re Marriage of Vryonis*, 202 Cal.App.3d 712, 248 Cal.Rptr. 807 (1988); *Marriage of Flores*, 252 Cal.Rptr. 687 (App. 1988); *Estate of Hafner*, 184 Cal.App.3d 1371 (1986); *Estate of Leslie*, 37 Cal.3d 186, 207 Cal.Rptr. 561, 689 P.2d 133 (1984); *Wagner v. County of Imperial*, 145 Cal.App.3d 980, 193 Cal.Rptr. 820 (1983); *In re Marriage of Recknor*, 187 Cal.Rptr. 887, 138 Cal.App.3d 539 (1982); *In re Marriage of Monti*, 135 Cal.App.3d 50, 185 Cal.Rptr. 72 (1982); *Galbraith v. Galbraith*, 396 So.2d 1364 (La.App. 1981); *In re Estate of Vargas*, 36 Cal.App.3d 714, 111 Cal.Rptr. 779 (1974); *Neureither v. Workmen's Compensation Appeals Bd.*, 93 Cal.Rptr. 162, 15 Cal.App.3d 429 (1971); *Adduddell v. Bd. of Admin.*, 8 Cal.App.3d 243, 87 Cal.Rptr. 268 (1970); *Holland America Ins. Co. v. Rogers*, 313 F.Supp. 314 (N.D.Cal. 1970); *Sousa v. Freitas*, 10 Cal.App.3d 660, 89 Cal. Rptr. 485 (1970); and *Miller v. Johnson*, 29 Cal.Rptr. 251, 214 Cal.App.2d 123 (N.D.Cal. 1970). *See also* Laughran and Laughran, *Property and Inheritance Rights of Putative Spouses in California: Selected Problems and Suggested Solutions*, 11 Loy. L.

other states.[96] Putative marriage, sometimes based on legislation and sometimes on case law, can be an alternative to common law marriages, particularly in the first and second of the above-named situations; in other words, if the parties have entered into a ceremonial marriage invalidated by an impediment or a mistake in form, and if one or both the parties were nevertheless in good faith.[97] In such cases, under conditions that may vary among the states, a putative marriage is considered to exist. Good faith is commonly assessed based on an objective standard.[98] Good faith, in some cases, has been presumed until the opposite is proven, but knowledge that one party is married to another person negates the good faith belief required to obtain benefit of putative spouse statute.[99] The party who has had knowledge that a deficiency leads to invalidity has commonly not been able to allege good faith.[100]

REV. 45 (1977); and Note, *The Rights of the Putative and Meretricious Spouse in California*, 50 CAL. R. REV. 866 (1962).

96 THE UNIFORM MARRIAGE AND DIVORCE ACT § 209, 9A U.L.A. 174 (1987). *See, e.g.*, Florida: *Gilvary v. Gilvary*, 648 So.2d 317 (Fla.App. 1995); *Kindle v. Kindle*, 629 So.2d 176 (Fla.App. 1993); Nevada: *Manker v. Manker*, 263 Neb. 944, 644 N.W.2d 522 (1992); *Williams v. Williams*, 97 P.3d 1124 (Nev. 2004) (property division, not spousal support); Minnesota: MINN. STAT. ANN. § 518.055 (West 2003). Illinois: ILL. STAT. ANN., ch. 750, § 5/305 (West 2003); Colorado: COLO. REV. STAT. ANN. § 14-2-111 (2006); *People v. McGuire*, 751 P.2d 1011 (Colo.App. 1987); and *Combs v. Tibbitts*, 148 P.3d 430 (Colo.App. 2006).

97 Putative marriage during the previous century has been sporadically recommended as an alternative to common law marriage by W.J. BROCKELBANK, LA FORMATION DU MARRIAGE DANS LE DROIT DES ETATS-UNIS 265 (1935); OTTO E. KOEGEL, COMMON LAW MARRIAGE AND ITS DEVELOPMENT IN THE UNITED STATES, 170 (1922); and Adams, *supra* note 10, at 298.

98 *People v. McGuire*, 751 P.2d 1011 (Colo.App. 1987); and *Combs v. Tibbitts*, 148 P.3d 430 (Colo.App. 2006). In *Estate of Depasse*, 97 Cal.App.4d 92, 118 Cal.Rptr.2d 143, 156 (2002), the man's statement as to putative spouse status did not rest upon facts which should "cause a reasonable person to harbor a good faith belief that the marriage was lawful, because he lacked a marriage license." *See also Welch v. State*, 83 Cal.App.4th 1374, 1378, 100 Cal.Rptr.2d 430 (2000); *Centinela Hosp. Med. Ctr. v. Superior Court*, 215 Cal.App.3d 971, 975, 263 Cal.Rptr. 672 (1989); *In re Marriage of Vryonis*, 202 Cal.App.3d 712, 720, 248 Cal.Rptr. 807 (1988); and *Galbraith v. Galbraith*, 396 So.2d 1364 (La.App. 1981) ("an honest and reasonable belief").

99 *McDougall v. Gray*, 2003 U.S.Dist. LEXIS 18282, 9 (D.Ill. 2003) applying Texas law; *Whaley v. Peat*, 377 S.W.2d 361 (Tex.Civ.App.-Houston 1964); *Kimball v. Folsom*, 150 F.Supp. 482 (D.C.La. 1957); *Papoutsis v. Trevino*, 167 S.W.2d 777 (Tex.Civ.App.-San Antonio 1942); *Succession of Theriot*, 185 So.2d 361 (La.App. 1966), ??? 249 La. 464, 187 So.2d 443 (1966); *Succession of Zinsel*, 360 So.2d 587 (La.App. 1978); *Succession of Jene*, 173 So.2d 857 (La.App. 1965); *Boudreaux v. Taylor*, 353 S.W.2d 901, (Tex.Civ.App.-Waco 1962) (clear and positive proof to overcome the presumption); *Brown v. Brown*, 274 Cal.App.2d 178, 82 Cal.Rptr. 238 (1961); *Succession of Primus*, 131 So.2d 319 (La.App. 1961); *Christoph v. Sims*, 234 S.W.2d 901 (Tex.Civ.App.-Dallas 1950); *Howard v. Ingle*, 180 So. 248 (La.App. 1938); and *Succession of Chavis*, 211 La. 717, 29 So.2d 860 (La. 1947). The presumption has not been seen to be applicable to a spouse who previously had been married and whose marriage was not dissolved, *see, e.g.*, *Mara v. Mara*, 452 So.2d 329, 332 (La.App. 1984) and *Gathright v. Smith*, 368 So.2d 679 (La. 1978).

100 In *Estate of Depasse*, 97 Cal.App.4d 92, 118 Cal.Rptr.2d 143, 156 (2002), the parties the day before the woman's death had entered into a marriage at the hospital. Due to a lack of time, the parties had not acquired a marriage license. As the man

The doctrine is also applied in some states recognizing common law marriage, for example, Texas.[101] Grounds for a putative marriage can be not only an invalid ceremonial marriage but also an invalid common law marriage.[102] In one and the same case, the question can arise whether a common law marriage or a putative marriage exists. A putative marriage can arise if the parties have entered into a common law marriage invalid because of an impediment, while a common law marriage can be viewed as arising from cases in which the requirements for a putative marriage are not present because the parties are no longer in good faith but the impediment later was removed.[103]

Compared with common law marriage, putative marriage is more limited not only in cases covered by the system, but also in terms of legal effects. In contrast to common law marriage, the spouses do not receive a marital status including all the legal effects of a marriage. Commonly, simply one

---

knew about the requirement for a license, he was considered not to be in good faith.

101 *Cardwell v. Cardwell*, 195 S.W.3d 856 (Tex.App.-Dallas 2006); *McDougall v. Gray*, 2003 U.S.Dist. Lexis 18282 (D.Ill. 2003), applying Texas law; *Weaver v. State*, 855 S.W.2d 116 (Tex.App.-Houston (14th Dist.) 1993); *Jasso v. Robertson*, 771 S.W.2d 231 (Tex. App.-Houston (1st Dist.) 1989); *Garduno v. Garduno*, 760 S.W.2d 735 (Tex.App.-Corpus Christi 1988); *Padon v. Padon*, 670 S.W.2d 354 (Tex.Civ.App.-San Antonio 1984); *R.A.M. a juvenile, v. State*, 599 S.W.2d 841 (Tex.Civ.App.-San Antonio 1980); *Davis v. Davis*, 507 S.W.2d 841 (Tex.Civ.App. 1974), 521 S.W.2d 603 (Tex. 1975); *Dean v. Goldwire*, 480 S.W.2d 494 (Tex.Civ.App.-Waco 1972); *Adams v. Adams*, 456 S.W.2d 222 (Tex.Civ.App.-Houston 1970); *Caruso v. Lucius*, 448 S.W.2d 171 (Tex. Civ.App.-Austin 1969); *Esparza v. Esparza*, 382 S.W.2d 162 (Tex.Civ.App.-Corpus Christi 1964); *Lester v. Celebrezze*, 221 F.Supp. 607 (E.D.Ark. 1963); *Barker v. Lee*, 337 S.W.2d 637 (Tex.Civ.App.-Eastland 1960); *Mathews v. Mathews*, 292 S.W.2d 662 (Tex. Civ.App.-Galveston 1956); *Texas Employer's Ins. Ass'n v. Grimes*, 155 Tex. 356, 269 S. W.2d 332 (1954); *Hupp v. Hupp*, 235 S.W.2d 753 (Tex.Civ.App. 1950); *In re Greathouse's Estate*, 184 S.W.2d 317 (Tex.Civ.App.-San Antonio 1944); *Papoutsis v. Trevino*, 167 S.W.2d 777 (Tex.Civ.App.-San Antonio 1942) (no ceremony was necessary for a valid putative marriage); *Woods v. Hardware Mut. Cas. Co.*, 141 S.W.2d 972 (Tex.Civ.App. 1940); *U.S. Fid. & Guar. Co. v. Henderson*, 53 S.W.2d 811 (Tex.Civ. App. 1932); *Lee v. Lee*, 112 Tex. 392, 247 S.W. 828 (Tex.Comm'n.App. 1923); and *Smith v. Smith*, 1 Tex. 621 (1846). *See also for* Colorado, Colo. Rev. Stat. Ann. § 14-2-111 (West 2003); and *Williams v. Fireman's Fund Ins. Co.*, 670 P.2d 453 (Colo. App. 1983); Montana, *see* Mont. Code Ann. § 40-1-404 (Mont. Leg. Serv. Div. 2003); and *Matter of Estate of Marson*, 328 Mont. 348, 120 P.3d 382 (Mont. 2005), remanded for further proceedings.

102 The putative spouse doctrine has also been seen to be applicable to common law marriage. In *Weaver v. State*, 855 S.W.2d 116, 120 (Tex.App.-Houston (14th Dist.) 1993), the court stated that "a putative marriage is one in which at least one of the parties believed themselves to be married, but because of some encumbrance they are not legally married, either by ceremony or common law." *See also Garduno v. Garduno*, 760 S.W.2d 735 (Tex.App.-Corpus Christi 1988); *Rey v. Rey*, 487 S.W.2d 245 (Tex.Civ.App.-El Paso 1972); *Whaley v. Peat*, 377 S.W.2d 855 (Tex.Civ.App.-Houston 1964); *Esparza v. Esparza*, 382 S.W.2d 162 (Tex.Civ.App.-Corpus Christi 1964); *Curtin v. State*, 155 Tex.Crim. 625, 238 S.W.2d 187 (1950); and *Hupp v. Hupp*, 235 S.W.2d 753 (Tex.Civ.App. 1950). *Compare* older case law, *Greathouse's Estate*, 184 S.W.2d 317 (Tex.Civ.App.-San Antonio 1944); and *Papoutsis v. Trevino*, 167 S.W.2d 777 (Tex.Civ.App.-San Antonio 1942).

103 *Garduno v. Garduno*, 760 S.W.2d 735 (Tex.App.-Corpus Christi 1988).

or a few of the legal effects come into place, for example, the right to a division of the estate,[104] maintenance,[105] inheritance,[106] standing in a wrongful death action,[107] or the right to a social benefit or pension.[108] Not uncommonly, competing demands arise from both a legal spouse and a putative spouse. In some cases, a putative wife in good faith in a marriage invalid due to an impediment is allowed to share the property of a deceased husband along with the legal wife.[109] Any children in a putative marriage are commonly viewed as legitimate.[110] If the parties dissolve the relationship, there is no obligation, to follow the regulations concerning a marital divorce, in contrast to the requirements in a common law marriage. A putative marriage does not constitute an impediment against a new marriage. The legal effects of a putative marriage cease if the parties possess

---

104 CAL. FAM. CODE ANN. §§ 2251, 2254 (West 2003) states that if it is a question as to a division of property, the court is to "divide ... that property acquired during the union ... This property is known as 'quasi-marital property'." *See also Vallera v. Vallera*, 21 Cal.2d 681, 134 P.2d 761 (1943); *Davis v. Davis*, 507 S.W.2d 841 (Tex.Civ. App. 1974); *Schneider v. Schneider*, 183 Cal. 335, 191 P. 533 (1920); *Ray v. Knox*, 164 La. 193, 113 So. 814 (1927); and *Texas Co. v. Stewart*, 101 So.2d 222 (La.App. 1958). *See* LA. CIV. CODE ANN. art. 2336 (West 2003). *Compare* UNIFORM MARRIAGE AND DIVORCE ACT § 209, 9A UNIF. L. ANN. (Part. 1) 192 (1998).

105 *Mabry v. Mabry*, 452 So.2d 329 (La.App. 1984).

106 *Estate of Leslie*, 37 Cal.3d 186, 207 Cal.Rptr. 561, 689 P.2d 133 (1984); *In re Ricci's Estate*, 201 Cal.App.2d 146, 19 Cal.Rptr. 739 (1962); *Kunakoff v. Woods*, 166 Cal. App.2d 59, 332 P.2d 773 (1958); *Succession of Verrett*, 224 La. 461, 70 So.2d 89 (1953); *Succession of Fields*, 222 La. 310, 62 So.2d 495 (1952); *In re Krone's Estate*, 83 Cal. App.2d 766, 189 P.2d 741 (1948); *Parker v. Parker*, 222 F. 186 (5th Cir. 1915); and *Morgan v. Morgan*, 21 S.W. 154 (Tex. Civ. App. 1892) (no right to inherit separate property). *See also* CAL. PROB. CODE § 6400 (West 2003) (intestate succession).

107 CAL. CIV. PROC. CODE § 377.60 (b) (West 2003); *Centinela Hosp. Med. Ctr. v. Superior Court*, 215 Cal.App.3d 971, 263 Cal.Rptr. 672 (1989); and *Wagner v. County of Imperial*, 145 Cal.App.3d 980, 193 Cal.Rptr. 820 (1983).

108 *McDougall v. Gray*, 2003 U.S.Dist. LEXIS 18282 (D.Ill. 2003) (applying Texas law); *Burks v. Apfel*, 233 F.3d 1220 (10th Cir. 2000); *Aubrey v. Folsom*, 151 F.Supp. 836 (N.D.Cal. 1957); *Speedling v. Hobby*, 132 F.Supp. 833 (N.D.Cal. 1955); CAL. LABOR CODE § 3503 (West 2003) (worker's compensation); and *Williams v. Fireman's Fund Ins. Co.*, 670 P.2d 453 (Colo.App. 1983) (worker's compensation).

109 In the case of *In re Estate of Vargas*, 36 Cal.App.3d 714, 111 Cal.Rptr. 779 (1974), the man had lived a double life with two wives and two families. As he married the second wife without dissolving the marriage with the first one, the later marriage was invalid. As the later wife did not know that the first marriage was not dissolved and therefore was in good faith, she shared the estate equally with his legal wife upon the man's death in the capacity as putative spouse. *See also Price v. Price*, 326 So.2d 545 (La.App. 1976); *Sousa v. Freitas*, 10 Cal.App.3d 660, 89 Cal.Rptr. 485 (1970); and *In re Ricci's Estate*, 201 Cal.App.2d 146,19 Cal.Rptr. 739 (1962). *Compare Brown v. Brown*, 274 Cal.App.2d 178, 82 Cal.Rptr. 238 (1961), where the legal wife did not receive any portion of the community property and *In re Estate of Krone*, 83 Cal.App.2d 766, 189 P.2d 741 (1948), in which the deceased's entire "quasi-marital estate" was distributed to his putative wife. *See also United States v. Robinson*, 40 F.2d 14 (5th Cir. 1930) applying Louisiana law, as well as the cases cited therein. THE UNIFORM MARRIAGE AND DIVORCE ACT § 209, 9A UNIF. L. ANN. (Part 1) 192 (1998) suggests a division which is "appropriate."

110 *Texas Co. v. Stewart*, 101 So.2d 222 (La.App. 1958); *Whaley v. Peat*, 377 S.W.2d 855 (Tex.Civ.App.-Houston 1964); and *Curtin v. State*, 155 Tex.Crim. 625, 238 S.W.2d 187 (1950).

knowledge that the marriage is invalid.[111] The burden of proof applied to the benefit of the latter of two marriages that a person has entered into must be distinguished under the putative marriage doctrine.[112] The former can be a ceremonial marriage or a common law marriage. If the existence of the previous marriage cannot be proven, the latter marriage is completely valid, and not just a putative marriage.

Clearly, it will be possible in the future, through legislation, to make putative marriage a stronger alternative than common law marriages by equipping it with some or all of the legal effects of marriage, while retaining the limitation of good faith situations. For the last-named cases, however, this appears a limitation of the legal effects that is fairly reasonable. There are, however, cases in which the courts, without applying the putative marriage doctrine, have also found a ceremonial marriage valid, despite the existence of small errors, such as the lack of registration or a marriage license.[113]

In order to constitute a true alternative to common law marriage and other cohabitation legislation, it appears necessary to make the putative marriage doctrine also applicable to the third of the above-named situations, in other words, in the event that cohabiting parties, who have not married ceremonially, still, for some reason believe that they are legally married.[114] This possibility exists today only as an exception in states not recognizing common law marriage. Thus, in the case law in California, there are several cases in which a formal wedding ceremony was not viewed as constituting an absolute requirement. For example, in *Wagner v. County*

111 *Burks v. Apfel*, 233 F.3d 1220, 1224 (10th Cir. 2000). In *Garduno v. Garduno*, 760 S.W.2d 735, 740 (Tex.App.-Corpus Christi 1988), the court stated: "In the present case appellee was no longer acting in good faith after she learned through appellant's lawyer that the Mexican divorce had been set aside." *See also Dean v. Goldwire*, 480 S.W.2d 494 (Tex.Civ.App.-Waco 1972); *Hunter v. Richardson*, 346 F.Supp. 123 (D.C.La. 1972); *Gallaher v. State Teachers' Retirement Sys.* 237 Cal.App.2d 510, 47 Cal. Rptr. 139 (1965); *Succession of Hopkins*, 114 So.2d 742 (La.App. 1959); *Tatum v. Tatum*, 241 F.2d 401 (9th Cir. 1957); *Curtin v. State*, 155 Tex.Crim. 625, 238 S.W.2d 187 (1950); *Funderburk v. Funderburk*, 214 La. 717, 38 So.2d 502 (1949); *Lazzarevich v. Lazzarevich*, 88 Cal.App.2d 708, 200 P.2d 49 (1948); *Evans v. Eureka Grand Lodge*, 149 So. 305 (La.App. 1933); and *Howard v. Ingle*, 180 So. 248 (La.App. 1938).

112 For more on this *see* Chapter 5 *supra*.

113 *See Accounts Management, Inc. v. Litchfield*, 576 N.W.2d 233 (S.D. 1998) and other cases cited in Homer H. Clark, Jr., Ann Laquer Estin, Cases and Problems on Domestic Relations 103 (6th ed. 2000).

114 In jurisdictions not recognizing common law marriage, the application of the putative marriage doctrine has commonly required that the parties entered into a ceremonial marriage that was invalid. In *Succession of Donohue*, 389 So.2d 879, 880 (La.App. 1980), the court stated that for a putative marriage to exist, there must be "an honest and reasonable belief that all the formalities of a civil ceremony have been complied with..." That the parties had lived in "open concubinage" many years and that the woman was viewed as a spouse was not sufficient. *See also Succession of Rossi*, 214 So.2d 223 (La.App. 1968); *Succession of Theriot*, 185 So.2d 361 (App. 1966), 249 La. 464, 187 So.2d 443 (1966); *Jackson v. Swift & Co.*, 151 So. 816 (La.App. 1934); and *Succession of Cusimano*, 173 La. 539, 138 So. 95 (1932). *Compare Succession of Marinoni*, 183 La. 776, 164 So. 797 (1935).

of Imperial (1983), the parties had privately exchanged marriage vows without going through any wedding ceremony and, thereafter, lived together for approximately two years up to the man's death. The court found that the woman did not need to prove that she participated in a solemnization ceremony in order to obtain the status of a putative spouse. In that capacity, she was awarded wrongful death benefits.[115]

The requirement of good faith, objectively, however, has shown itself to be difficult to fulfill. For example, in *Welch v. State* (2000), the parties made personal marriage vows "wherein they stated that they loved each other and that they were going to spend the rest of their lives together." They had lived together for thirty years and outwardly presented themselves as husband and wife. They had not procured a marriage license and nor had a wedding ceremony because the woman did not believe it was necessary. The court found that a common law marriage could not be established because the relevant doctrine had already been repealed in California in 1895. The court also did not find that a putative marriage existed, because the assessment of good faith must be carried out according to an objective standard. There was, accordingly, no reasonable basis for the woman's subjective faith that a valid marriage existed. She, who previously had been married and divorced twice, according to the court, ought to have been aware of the form requirements.[116]

It is possible that such an extended putative marriage doctrine would be able to constitute a protection among some groups who, for ethnic and cultural reasons, do not enter into ceremonial marriages and who have limited knowledge of the form requirements.[117] It has been assumed that many cohabiting unmarried persons expect the law to treat them as married because they live as if they were married.[118] For the legislator who finds that common law marriage and other general cohabitation legislation is too far-reaching, an acceptable alternative is the putative marriage doctrine's intention to fulfill the parties' good faith expectations. An additional alternative can be to extend the putative marriage doctrine to

115 *Wagner v. County of Imperial*, 145 Cal.App.3d 980, 193 Cal.Rptr. 820 (1983). *See also Sancha v. Arnold*, 114 Cal.App.2d 772, 251 P.2d 67 (1952) and *Santos v. Santos*, 32 Cal.App.2d 62, 89 P.2d 164 (1932).

116 *Welch v. State*, 83 Cal.App.4th 1374, 1378, 100 Cal.Rptr.2d 430 (2000). *See also Centinela Hosp. Med. Ctr. v. Superior Court*, 215 Cal.App.3d 971, 263 Cal.Rptr. 672 (1989), in which the court found that the surviving man's statement that he believed that the parties had entered into a common law marriage "was unreasonable as California abolished common law marriage in 1895." Neither in the case of *In re Marriage of Vryonis*, 202 Cal.App.3d 712, 248 Cal.Rptr. 807 (1988), did the court deem that participation in a wedding ceremony was an absolute requirement for establishing a putative marriage. Despite the fact that the parties privately underwent a Muslim "Muta marriage ceremony" and had poor knowledge as to what California law required, the court did not find that the requirement as to good faith in an objective sense was fulfilled. The parties however were not living together and did not appear outwardly as married.

117 *See Orr v. State*, 129 Fla. 398, 409, 176 So. 510, 514 (1937).

118 *See* note 89 *supra*.

the parties' expectations made in good faith as to being united in a legal cohabiting relation. Each legislator, however, ought to note that extending the putative marriage doctrine to cases of pure cohabitation can entail application problems similar to those arising from common law marriage.[119]

14.2.7 Preventing the Favoring of Cohabiting Unmarried Persons

The justifications for common law marriage mix a number of objectives. One concerns economic justice and is meant to prevent cohabiting couples from receiving benefits that ceremonially married couples do not. The background is that the financial conditions of both spouses are often used in assessing need when married couples apply for social benefits, while cohabiting unmarried persons are considered separate individuals. This, in a number of cases, can be advantageous for an unmarried applicant who is living together with another person. Because married couples are viewed as having lower living costs than a single person living alone, *inter alia,* for the residence, they often receive lower pensions and other benefits that are not awarded on a need basis. Because cohabiting unmarried persons are considered separate persons living alone, they are favored in comparison to married persons.[120] In a number of jurisdictions, this can be the case with respect to taxation; married couples but not cohabiting unmarried persons are taxed jointly.

This economic justice reason appears to have been decisive when the legislator in Utah, after ninety-nine years, reinstated the institution of common law marriage in 1987.[121] The primary goal was to prevent cohabiting unmarried persons from receiving government welfare assistance

119 *Compare Elden v. Sheldon,* 46 Cal.3d 267, 279, 250 Cal.Rptr. 254, 758 P.2d 582 (1988), in which the California Supreme Court was not disposed to extend the possibility to claims concerning the "loss of consortium" to unmarried cohabiting couples with respect to "the difficulty of assessing the emotional, sexual and financial relationship of cohabiting parties to determine whether their arrangement was the equivalent of a marriage." The court cited with approval *Weaver v. G.D. Searle & Co,* 558 F.Supp. 720, 723 (N.D.Ala. 1983), which displayed the same concern for the application problems following from a right based on the parties' cohabitation. The last named court raised several of the issues that are treated in this work: "Would the giving of an engagement ring qualify as creating a significant relationship? If not, how long would the engagement have to exist? Would 'going steady' be sufficient? Is cohabitation sufficient? If it is, how much cohabitation? Would a simple 'rent sharing' do the trick?" *Compare Dunphy v. Gregor,* 136 N.J. 99, 642 A.2d 372 (1994), where the court did not see any problem in allowing a cohabitant recovery for "negligent infliction of emotional distress."

120 *Compare* Kurt J. Bauman, *Shifting Family Definitions: The Effect of Cohabitation and Other Nonfamily Household Relationships on Measures of Poverty,* 36 Demography 315 (1999).

121 Act of Feb. 25, 1987, ch. 246, effective April 27, 1987. Utah Code Ann. § 30-1-4.5 (Supp. 1987).

based on the income of only one party. The underlying purpose was not only to serve economic justice by ensuring that cohabiting unmarried persons do not receive better benefits than married persons, but also to benefit the state's finances by reducing the costs of the welfare system.[122] The purpose, therefore, has sometimes been considered to be to prevent welfare fraud and save money for the various administrative agencies.[123]

In enacting common law marriage in Utah, the scope of the legislation generally widely exceeded the stated objectives. Consequently, cohabiting couples that do not formally marry are equated with formally married couples if the relationship fulfills the requirements of common law marriage in all aspects. Such couples are, quite simply, married, persons and all the legal effects of a marriage, not only social welfare and taxes, but also under penal law and the entirety of public law, as well as family law (including the regulations concerning maintenance obligations, marital divorce, divisions of the estate, inheritance, etc.). The state's financial motive is also provided for by that the economic responsibility for the more vulnerable party, under common law marriage, is construed as a family law maintenance obligation between the parties, which means that the state, in the same manner as for spouses, does not need to shoulder the primary responsibility.[124]

This idea of placing mutual economic responsibilities on individuals in a cohabitation family, and thereby limiting the state's responsibility for social welfare, also appears to be a reason behind the 2002 ALI Principles

---

122 Senator Rees, who was behind the new law, stated during the legislative preparatory stages: "I can't see any practical application for enforcement except in trying to close some loopholes in welfare abuse," *see* Floor Debate, remarks by Sen. Stephen Rees, 47th Utah Leg., Gen.Sess. (Feb. 17, 1987) (Sen. Recording No. 75). Similar views were expressed by Norman Angus, Director of the State Department of Social Services; "[A] woman with children ... may ... be living with an individual who could and in all probability does provide a substantial amount of support to that household and still we cannot consider any of the income or the resources of that individual available and therefore the woman can in fact qualify for full public assistance grant...," *see* Floor Debate, remarks by Norman Angus, Director of State Social Services Adm., 47th Utah Leg., Gen.Sess. (Feb. 17, 1987) (Sen. Recording No. 75). The State Department of Social Services has estimated that approximately 300 families would lose their right to Aid to Families with Dependent Children (AFDC) if common law marriage were enacted, which would mean a savings cost of approximately $ 323,500. No estimation of the additional costs that would arise in that common law marriage couples become entitled to benefits accruing to married persons and as to the administrative costs which lawsuits as to common law marriage cases would entail appear to have been made, a circumstance which has generated criticism, *see In re Marriage of Gonzalez*, 387 Utah adv. Rep. 89, 2000 UT 28, 1 P.3d 1074, 1078 (2000); and David F. Crabtree, *Family Law, Recognition of Common-Law Marriages*, 149 UTAH L. REV. 273, 281 (1988).

123 *Kelley v. Kelley*, 9 P.3d 171, 183 (Utah App. 2000). *See also In re Marriage of Gonzales*, 387 Utah Adv. Rep. 89, 2000 UT 28, 1 P.3d 1074 (2000).

124 Dubler, *supra* note 35, at 969, consequently maintains: "By declaring a woman to be a wife or widow at common law, courts shielded the public fiscal from the potential claims of needy women, effectively deflecting those claims inward to a particular private, family unit."

regarding the dissolution of domestic partnerships. The principles, upon separation, give a cohabiting party the right to a division of the estate and maintenance.[125] The economic reasoning, consequently, has a deep ideological dimension. A circumstance that does not appear to have received the attention it deserves, however, is that cohabiting persons who are recognized as being parties in a common law marriage also become entitled to the benefits granted married couples but not separate individuals, which, in itself imposes to costs on the public.

The goal of not giving cohabiting unmarried persons benefits as if they were married persons can be achieved with more limited methods than common law marriage. Several legal systems in Europe and elsewhere in the world have attempted to achieve the same goal by introducing, in connection to each specific public law right or other rights, regulations that equate cohabiting unmarried persons with married persons. Thus, the assessment of need commonly combines both parties' income and assets. England,[126] Germany,[127] Sweden,[128]

---

125 A secondary objective for the principles regarding the dissolution of relationships between "domestic partners" was said to be the "protection of society from social-welfare burdens that should be borne, in whole or in part, by individuals," *see* the ALI PRINCIPLES, *supra* note 47, § 6.02, (2), Comment: B) The Objectives of this Chapter. *See also* Cynthia Grant Bowman, *Legal Treatment of Cohabitation in the United States*, 26 LAW & POLICY 119, 146 (2004), who points to the function of family law as "privatizing the costs of welfare."

126 *See* the "cohabitation rule" in the SOCIAL SECURITY CONTRIBUTIONS AND BENEFITS ACT (1992), section 137(1), which defines the term "family" as "a married or unmarried couple" and which defines an unmarried couple as "a man and woman who are not married to each other but are living together as husband and wife." In the assessment as to income related benefits, the income and assets of both partners are combined, *see* Section 136(1). The purpose of the rule can be seen from the underlying committee report stating: "It cannot be right to treat unmarried women who have the support of a partner both as if they had no such support and better than if they were married," *see* Finer Committee on One Parent Families (1974) at 269. *See also* David Pearl, *Cohabitation in English Social Security Legislation*, in MARRIAGE AND COHABITATION IN CONTEMPORARY SOCIETIES 337 (John M. Eekelaar, Sanford N. Katz eds., 1980), who states: "Official policy therefore is to ensure that an unmarried couple does not receive more favorable treatment than a married couple." In Great Britain, cohabitation rules are applied in the assessment of different income related benefits such as income support, family credit, disability working allowance and housing benefits. *See also* Nevil Harris, *Unmarried cohabiting couples and Social Security in Great Britain*, 18(2) J. SOC. WELF. FAM. L. 123 (1996).

127 In German law, it is prescribed generally with respect to the right to social assistance that "Personen, die in eheähnlicher Gemeinschaft leben, hinsichtlich der Voraussetzungen sowie des Umfangsder Sozialhilfe nich besser gestellt werden als Ehegatten," *see* BUNDESSOZIALHILFEGESETZ, BSHG, vom 30.6.1961 in BGBl. I 815 § 122. In German law, in the assessment of an unemployed person's need for contributions, considered furthered is not only the spouse's income and assets but also "das Einkommen und das Vermögen einer Person, mit der der Arbeitslose in eheähnlicher Gemeinschaft lebt," *see* GESETZ ÜBER ARBEITSVERMITTLUNG UND ARBEITSLOSENVERSICHERUNG, AVAVG vom 3.4.1957, BGBl., I, 321, § 149 Abs. 5. *See also* VOLKER STÜCKRADT, RECHTSWIRKUNGEN EHEÄHNLICHER VERHÄLTNISSE 116 (1964).

128 Swedish law, which contains many laws concerning cohabiting unmarried couples, has several regulations that have the purpose of ensuring that such persons do not

Australia,[129] and New Zealand[130] can be mentioned as examples. Even in the United States, there are jurisdictions that apply cohabitation legislation or recognize a common law marriage only for this limited purpose.[131] The exploding growth of such regulations has created the need for more uniform or general regulations. Jurisdictions that have taken the step of introducing cohabitation legislation that imposes, on cohabiting persons, the disadvantages that fall on married couples have typically found themselves also giving the advantages enjoyed by spouses. Thus, a step has been taken towards common law marriage. On the other side, granting rights for cohabiting persons has incurred the very costs that constitute the arguments against legislation for cohabiting unmarried persons.[132]

These regulations concerning cohabiting persons have sometimes arisen from the lack of viable alternatives.[133] Another method to avoid favoring cohabiting unmarried persons over married persons in the assessment of pensions and other social benefits is to consider both spouses and unmarried cohabiting persons as separate individuals, which renders cohabitation legislation unnecessary. Each party is assessed individually, taking into consideration their income and assets.[134] Such a procedure

---

receive better economic advantages than married couples. This has its background in that married persons are viewed as having lower costs than separate individuals and receive therefore lower benefits. Because of this, long term cohabiting unmarried couples who previously had been married or who have or have had mutual children are equated with married persons *e.g.* when it comes to financial housing assistance, *see* SFS 1993:737 § 1, and certain pension rights, *see, e.g.*, SFS 1962:381 Chapter 10 § 1; SFS 1998:674 Chapter 10 §§ 1 and 7; and SFS 1998:702 Chapter 1 § 4. Also within Swedish tax law, cohabiting persons have been equated with spouses if the previous have been married or have or have had mutual children, *see e.g.*, SFS 1999:1229 Chapter 2 § 20; SFS 1997:323 § 21, or if they live together under marriage-like conditions, *see, e.g.*, SFS 1941:416 § 3A 16; SFS 1987:1206. With respect to the enactment of rights also for cohabiting persons, *see* Section 12.4 *supra.*

129 One of the primary reasons in accordance to the Australian Social Security Act (1991), section 4 (3)(4)(5) to equate a "marriage-like relationship" with spouses was that cohabiting unmarried persons should not receive better benefits than married couples. This reason can also be found in the investigations from 1975 in Australia and 1972 in New Zealand, *see* T. Carney and P. Hanks, Social Security in Australia 233 (1994).

130 Atkin, *supra* note 46, at 7. With respect to the enactment of rights also for cohabiting persons, see Section 12.4 *supra.*

131 It has been questioned whether the enactment of common law marriage in Utah was necessary with respect to the fact that the stated purpose was already provided for within the framework for the legislation concerning Aid to Families with Dependant Children, *see* Bowman, *supra* note 18, at 750. Already in 1965, Jacobus TenBroek stated that if there was not any common-law husband in California, there was a "common law stepfather" in accordance to the Welfare and Institutions Code, *see* TenBroek, *supra* 20, at 620. In Kentucky, workmen's compensation ceases when an entitled party enters into "a legal or common law marriage," *see* Ky. Rev. Stat. § 342.080 (1959).

132 Sanford N. Katz, *Marriage as Partnership*, 73 Notre Dame L. Rev. 1251, 1269 (1998).

133 Harris, *supra* note 126, at 127-128.

134 Attempts were made in Denmark during the end of the 1980s to introduce this individual principle, *see* Ingrid Lund-Andersen, *Moving Towards an Individual Principle in Danish Law*, 4 IJLPF 328 (1990).

need not entail a total additional cost to the system if the levels of the benefits are simultaneously adjusted.[135] One could avoid the extensive application problems that the regulations concerning cohabiting persons entail, as discussed in the preceding and following chapters. A further argument for an individual review is that it would eliminate the reason for refraining from marriage as well as cohabitation in order to obtain economic benefits. Although such a system has clear advantages with respect to benefits not granted based on need, it exhibits problems if it concerns need-based benefits with regards to investigating and considering the actual economic support that the parties receive from each other and that affects the economic situation for all parties involved.

14.2.8 Moral Reasons

The reasons behind common law marriage have concerned not only substantive rights and obligations within the framework of the legal system. Intangible motivations of a moral nature have also traditionally had considerable significance. As seen in Chapter 4, in the American case law, particularly from the mid and late 1800s, there were attempts by the courts to salvage the honor of the parties, particularly the woman's, through the use of the legal institution of common law marriage, transforming out-of-wedlock relations to legally valid and morally accepted marriages. In *Askew v. Dupree* (1860), the Georgia Supreme Court stated concerning the woman: "Her honor is saved, and this is worth more than everything, even life itself."[136] The community intervened against concubinage and other "loose" relations, armed with moral indignation and criminal measures. Simultaneously, however, the same morality offered salvation to those cases of formless living together that had a marital appearance. As seen in Chapter 9, "Burdens of Proof and Presumptions," the marriage presumption during the 1800s served the same purpose with

135 Individual assessment has been rejected with respect to the risk of costs and an expected reduction of the desire to work, *see* P. Esam and R. Berthoud, Independent Benefits for Men and Women (1991), Chapter 4.

136 *Askew v. Dupree*, 30 Ga. 173, 190 (1860). From the same period, *see Kansas Pac. Ry. Co. v. Miller*, 2 Colo. 442, 463 (1874), in which the Colorado Supreme Court stated with respect to the parties: "Their conduct being susceptible of two opposite explanations, we are bound to assume it to be moral rather than immoral." In *Armaell's Estate*, 2 Brewster 239, 246 (Penn. 1869), in which the Pennsylvania Supreme Court found that a common law marriage existed, the court stated that "marriage, followed by the birth of issue, lies at the very base of the social fabric and of all good morals, and looking at the consequences to society we feel unwilling to suffer an acknowledged marriage and parentage of children..." *In Ingersol v. McWillie*, 9 Tex.Civ.App. 543, 30 S.W. 56, 61 (1895), concerning a surviving woman's rights after the man's death, the Texas Court of Civil Appeals stated that its decisions commonly have been "broad and liberal upon the subject" and continued: "Since his death, we think that public policy, as well as common justice and humanity, demand that the marriage should be sustained, and her rights as survivor protected." *See also* Harris, *supra* note 59, at 444-445.

respect to both spouses and their children.[137] It can scarcely be denied that, for the children, it often is as difficult to bear the stigma of illegitimacy as to lack the rights of legitimacy.[138]

The same morally tinged motivations also recur to a certain extent in the case law during the 1900s.[139] Among those states that today recognize common law marriage, this is clear in the case law from Montana. In the case of *In re Estate of Swanson* (1972), its Supreme Court stated: "Every intendment of the law is in favor of matrimony which presumes morality and not immorality, marriage and not concubinage, legitimacy and not bastardy."[140]

The attitudes towards ceremonial marriage and common law marriage, as seen from Chapter 4, have historically been subject to considerable change. The positive attitude to common law marriage found in the case law of the 1800s is replaced by an altogether more strongly negative

137 In *Hynes v. McDermott*, 91 N.Y. 451, 459, 43 Am.Rep. 677 (1883), concerning a common law marriage, the court stated: "The law presumes morality and not immorality; marriage, and not concubinage; legitimacy and not bastardy." The same statement recurs in *Teter v. Teter*, 101 Ind. 129, 51 Am.R. 742 (1884). *See also Hadley v. Rash*, 21 Mont. 170, 53 P. 312 (1898). In *Cargile v. Wood*, 63 Mo. 501, 512 (1877), the court stated that as the parties had lived together and appeared outwardly as husband and wife, and that there were circumstances from which one could find a contract, a marriage was presumed "in favour of innocence and good morals." The court added: "The law in general presumes against vice and immorality." *Compare Richard v. Brehm*, 73 Pa. 140 (1873); and *Hilton v. Roylance*, 25 Utah 129, 69 P. 660 (1902). A presumption in favor of marriage and against "concubinage" also can be found in *Linsey v. Jefferson*, 68 Okla. 156, 172 P. 641 (1918). *See also Jones v. Jones*, 63 Okla. 208, 164 P. 463, 31 L.R.A. 1917 E (1917) and *Nixon v. Wichita Land & Cattle Co.*, 84 Tex. 408, 19 S.W. 560, 563 (1892).

138 Adams, *supra* note 10, at 297, views that common law marriage saves children from "the stigma of bastardy" and parents from "the sin of fornication." *See also* Weyrauch, *supra* note 22, at 101; J.A. Andrews, *Common Law Marriage*, 22 MOD. L. REV. 396 (1959); and Black, *supra* note 54, at 114.

139 *U.S. Fid. & Guar. Co. v. Dowdle*, 269 S.W. 119, 124, 130 (Tex.Civ.App.-Dallas (1924). In *Trammell v. Trammell*, 196 S.W.2d 209, 210 (Tex.Civ.App. 1946), the court found that a common law marriage was proven instead of "condemning them to a life of unlicensed sin." In *Gammelgaard v. Gammelgaard*, 247 Iowa 978, 77 N.W.2d 479, 481 (1956), the court stated: "In doubtful cases, courts prefer that construction of evidence which finds a legitimate marriage rather than a long period of lewd and criminal cohabitation." *See also In re Wagner's Estate*, 398 Pa. 531, 533, 159 A.2d 495, 497 (1960), in which the parties after a divorce moved in together again, and in which the court stated: "We regard it better to encourage remarriage than to leave such parties under judicial edict that they were living sinfully together for ten years."

140 *In re Estate of Swanson*, 160 Mont. 271, 502 P.2d 33, 37 (1972). *See already Hadley v. Rash*, 21 Mont. 170, 53 P. 312, 314 (1898), in which the court came to the conclusion that a marriage existed "in the interest of morality, innocence, and the sanctity of the marriage relation"; and *State v. Newman*, 66 Mont. 180, 213 P. 805 (1923). In *Welch v. All Persons*, 78 Mont. 370, 254 P. 179, 182 (1926), the Montana Supreme Court stated: "The presumption in favor of matrimony is one of the strongest known to the law ... Every presumption will be indulged in favor of the legality of a common-law marriage in the same way and to the same extent as the law indulges them in favor of a ceremonial marriage." *See also Matter of Estate of Murnion*, 212 Mont. 107, 686 P.2d 893, 897 (1984).

attitude during the first part of the 1900s, a period during which many states repealed the institution. A strongly negative attitude also characterizes many of the proposals for the repeal of common law marriage.[141] Typical of the attitude in those states that retained the institution during this period, for example, Texas and Pennsylvania, was the statement that "the law does not favor, but merely tolerates, common law marriages."[142] In contrast to the other states, however, Idaho has never taken a negative stance to the institution of common law marriage, but nevertheless repealed the same in 1996.[143] It appears that the courts in Alabama also never condemned this form of cohabitation.[144] During the later part of the 1900s, one can again discern a more positive attitude toward common law marriages. The criminalization of cohabitation outside of marriage has gradually ceased. During the years 1970 to 1990, no state abolished common law marriage. In contrast, the institution was enacted in Utah in 1987. At the same time during this period, cohabitation without marriage became even more socially acceptable and spread into all social groups. During the 1990s, three additional states repealed common law marriage, namely, Ohio, Idaho, and Georgia. The explanation appears to be more rational than moral, as discussed in greater detail below.

---

141 With respect to the negative attitude to and criticism against common law marriage, *see infra* under *Argument against common law marriage.*

142 *Texas Employers' Ins. Ass'n v. Elder*, 274 S.W.2d 144, 147 (Tex.Civ.App. 1954); and *Baker v. Mitchell*, 143 Pa.Super. 50, 54, 17 A.2d 738, 741 (1941). The same statement has since recurred in a series of cases from Pennsylvania as well as from other states, *see, e.g.*, In *re Erickson's Estate*, 75 S.D. 345, 64 N.W.2d 316, 318 (1954): "Such marriages are a source of fraud and perjury. They are to be tolerated only and not encouraged"; *Anderson v. Anderson,* 235 Ind. 113, 131 N.E.2d 301, 305 (1956); *In re Blecher's Estate*, 381 Pa. 138, 112 A.2d 129 (1955); *In re Estate of Wagner*, 398 Pa. 531, 159 A.2d 495 (1960); and *In re Estate of Collings*, 405 Pa. 280, 175 A.2d 62, 63 (1961). *See also Jolley v. Jolley*, 46 Ohio Misc. 40, 347 N.E.2d 557, 560 (1975) ("Most cases mention that common law marriage contravenes public policy and should not be accorded any favor. In fact it is generally condemned"); *Com. ex rel. McDermott v. McDermott*, 236 Pa.Super.Ct. 541, 345 A.2d 914, 918 (1975) ("It is true that the courts have in the past looked upon common law marriage with a somewhat jaundiced eye"); *In re Estate of Stauffer*, 505 Pa. 626, 476 A.2d 354, 356 (1984); *Estate of Gavula*, 490 Pa. 535, 417 A.2d 168, 171 (1980); *In re Estate of Kovalchick*, 345 Pa.Super. 229, 498 A.2d 374, 376 (1985); and *Staudenmayer v. Staudenmayer*, 714 A.2d 1016 (Pa. 1998).

143 Idaho Code Ann. § 32-301 (Michie 1983), Analysis, at 374: "Idaho has never viewed the doctrine of common-law marriage with disfavor." The Idaho Supreme Court gives expression to the same stance in *Metro. Life Ins. Co. v. Johnson*, 103 Idaho 122, 645 P.2d 356, 360 (1982).

144 *See* John B. Crawley, *Is the Honeymoon Over for Common Law Marriage: A Consideration of the Continued Viability of the Common Law Marriage Doctrine*, 29 Cumb. L. Rev. 399, 404 (1998/1999), who states that "the Alabama appellate courts have generally not disparaged the doctrine or given it only grudging approval." From the case law, *see, e.g., Morgan v. Richardson*, 325 F.Supp. 128, 129 (D.C.Ala. 1971), in which the Alabama United States District Court stated: "It must be remembered that both plaintiff and Jim Morgan were uneducated and that they were living under conditions or in a community where common-law marriages were not infrequent and no social stigma was cast on such marriages." *See also Kozlowski v. Kozlowski*, 80 N.J. 378, 403 A.2d 902, 908 (1979).

The future moral attitudes toward marital status and births within wedlock are unpredictable. As it has become morally more acceptable to live together as cohabiting unmarried persons, there has been a comparable decline in the desire to salvage the parties' moral reputation through common law marriage. The question of morality will partially depend on which legal regulations are tied to the different forms of living together.

14.2.9 The State's Interest in Capturing the Lost Sheep

The reason for common law marriage that is actually the basis of all others is the legislative interest in capturing the lost sheep and imposing obligations on them. Although marriage commonly is considered as a voluntary contract between independent individuals, there has always been a strong desire to include, within the marital regulations, men and women who live together and create families. As long as the state cannot compel couples to formally marry, a dilemma persists to which common law marriage offers a solution. Regardless of whether the parties choose to formally marry or simply cohabit, they are affected by the marital law system.

This strategy was used already in the medieval canon law, as seen from Chapter 3, "Informal Marriages in Canon Law," within the marital law system to capture, so to speak, men and women who preferred marriage traditions other than those prescribed by the church, or who simply chose to live together formlessly. Because they were considered married to each other, they ended up within marriage's indissoluble sacrament and within the restrictions and prohibitions the canon law legislator laid down for the purpose of legalizing their marital togetherness in accordance to the Christian values. The canon law recognized, in principle, only one system of regulations, marriage, which was intended to be applicable to all marital cohabitation.

The same strategy can be traced behind common law marriage in American law, as seen in Chapter 4, albeit not as tangibly. An example is the court's statement in *Stump v. Stump* (1934): "It is to the interest of the State that persons living together in the family relation should be married and that the relationship of husband and wife and that of the family be preserved and not be lightly destroyed."[145] If a marital relationship

145 *Stump v. Stump,* 111 Pa. Super. 541, 546 (1934); and *Schurler v. Indus. Comm'n,* 86 Utah 284, 43 P.2d 696, 698-699 (1935). The same reason can be traced in older case law, *see, e.g., People v. Spencer,* 199 Mich. 395, 165 N.W. 921, 923 (1917); *Bishop v. Brittain Invest.* Co., 229 Mo. 699, 129 S.W. 668 (1910); *Ingersol v. McWillie,* 9 Tex.Civ. App. 543, 30 S.W. 56, 60 (1895); *Askew v. Dupree,* 30 Ga. 173, 188 (1860); and *Londonderry v. Chester,* 2 N.H. 268, 281, 9 Am.Dec. 61 (1820). In the modern case law, *see, e.g., Laws v. Griep,* 332 N.W.2d 339, 340-341 (Iowa 1983), which holds "that the policy favoring marriage would be subverted if persons could gain marital legal rights without accepting correlative marital legal responsibilities." In the literature, *see also* Harris, *supra* note 59, at 443; and Dubler, *supra* note 36, at 1886. *Compare* Nancy F. Cott, *Giving Character to Our Whole Civil Policy: Marriage and the Public Order*

has been entered into, "the law steps in and holds the parties to various obligations."[146]

The canon law strategy ought to be attractive to present-day legislators who, for religious, moral, or social reasons, have views about how marital family life ought to appear and who, through marriage, have created a goal-oriented system of regulations in order to promote these objectives,[147] but find that the system does not extend to those for whom it was intended because they do not marry. This concerns, for example, religious and conservative powers who usually use propaganda for formal marriage and who often take a negative posture toward common law marriages and other cohabitation legislation.[148] However, it is something of a paradox that many of those who traditionally have had a passion for the need of state intervention and control at the expense of the individual's freedom, at the same time, have pleaded for the repeal of common law marriage.[149] On the other side, proposals are raised in the debates on the basis that the state ought to assume the same responsibility for providing support and

---

in the Late Nineteenth Century, in U.S. HISTORY AS WOMEN'S HISTORY: NEW FEMINIST ESSAYS 107 (Linda K. Kerber et al. eds., 1995). JAMES SCHOULER, A TREATISE ON HUSBAND AND WIFE 47 (1882) states that formless marriage rests upon the idea that "an institution of such fundamental importance to our race ought to be good independently of, and prior to, the formal requirements which human government imposes at an advanced stage of society." *See also* JAMES SCHOULER, MARRIAGE, DIVORCE, SEPARATION & DOMESTIC RELATIONS I, 42 (6th ed. 1921).

146 *Maynard v. Hill*, 125 U.S. 190, 211 (1888).

147 The state's interest has been considered to include "promoting public morality, ensuring family stability, assuring support obligations, and assigning responsibility for the care of children," *see Developments in the Law – The Constitution and the Family*, 93 HARV. L. REV. 1156, 1242 (1980). A proposal was presented already in the 1930s concerning punishment of those who "tamper with marriage," wherewith *inter alia* was referred "those who deny that the state has an enforceable interest in the family and insist that the process of establishing the relationship is a matter of personal contract," *see* John S. Bradway, *Tampering with Marriage*, 6 BROOK. L. REV. 277 (1937).

148 Barbara Mobley, a member of the General Assembly in Georgia, presented with others (Randall, Martin, Falls) legislative proposal (HB 1278), which led to common law marriage being repealed in Georgia in 1997. One of the reasons, albeit not the primary, for the repeal according to Mobley was that "the faith community came out in support of this bill/law, indicating that most religions did not base their recognized family units on just 'living together' or as we call it in the South, 'shacking'," Barbara Mobley, according to an e-mail to this author dated February 26, 2003. GA. CODE ANN. §§ 19-3-1, 19-3-1.1 (1997) prescribes: "No common-law marriage shall be entered into in this state on or after January 1, 1997. Otherwise valid common-law marriages entered into prior to January 1, 1997, shall not be affected by this Code section and shall continue to be recognized in this state." *Compare Wright v. Goss*, 229 Ga.App. 393, 494 S.E.2d 23, 25 (1997); and Brown, *supra* note 10, at 140.

149 George Howard, who in the beginning of the 1900s encouraged a legislative revolution against common law marriages, stated that "the supposed right of the individual must yield to the higher claims of society. In no part of the whole range of human activity is there such imperative need of state interference and control as in the sphere of the matrimonial relations. In this field as in others we are beginning to see more clearly that the highest individual liberty can be secured only when it is subordinated to the highest social good," *see* HOWARD, *supra* note 57, at 184.

imposing obligations on cohabiting persons equal to that assumed for formally married parties.[150]

Common law marriage can constitute a rational instrument within the marital law system to "capture in" couples who formally have not entered into marriage if the state wishes women and men with families to be faithful to each other; contribute to each other's maintenance; that the children in such families have a legitimate status; that upon the dissolution of the relationship, they are to observe certain divorce regulations and divide property in a certain way. Finally, common law marriage is useful if the state intends to levy upon the family taxes or other public law obligations motivated by the fact that they actually live in a family.[151] Through this transformation to a traditional marriage, formless relationships lose their potential subversive and threatening character.[152] This method includes a further ideological dimension. By placing upon the individuals in the family economic obligations to each other, the state can free itself from the responsibility for the social welfare. This reason appears, as can be seen above, behind the reinstatement of common law marriage in Utah and behind the ALI Principles with respect to the dissolution of registered domestic partnerships.[153]

Such a strategy can be natural for a state that views itself as the third party to the marriage contract[154] and, through legislation, assumes responsible for the most of the contract's legal effects. A state acting as *bonus pater familias* and simply wishing persons well does not see any impediment to capturing those who have been left outside of the well-planned pasture the state has created. Rather, it can appear illogical if the legislator, on one side, for strong moral and social reasons, constructs an entire marital law system containing several obligations for spouses; but, on the other side,

---

150 David S. Caudill, *Legal Recognition of Unmarried Cohabitation: A Proposal to Update and Reconsider Common-Law Marriage*, 49 TENN. L. REV. 537, 540 (1982), states that "the state has identical interests in legal marriage and in some unmarried cohabitative relationships" and that the state therefore ought to "provide the same support for and impose the same burdens upon both types of relationships." The author proposes a new form of common law or "constructive" marriage.

151 Caudill, *id.* at 543 and 566, who emphasizes the state's task "to require couples to provide emotional support for one another and their children," maintains that "the traditional burdens and benefits of marriage should be imposed upon all unmarried cohabitators whose relationship have taken on the essential characteristics of marriages," as long as the parties have not expressly agreed to not marry. To not recognize what the author refers to as common law or constructive marriage would "leave many marriage-like relationships without legal protection and may also leave the state's interest in support obligations, care of children, and public morality unserved."

152 Dubler, *supra* note 35, at 969, and *supra* note 36, at 1906.

153 A secondary objective for the principles regarding the dissolution of relationships between domestic partners is said to be the "protection of society from social-welfare burdens that should be borne, in whole or in part, by individuals," *see* the ALI PRINCIPLES, *supra* note 47, § 6.02, (2), Comment: B) The Objectives of this Chapter.

154 For more concerning the marriage contract's character, *see* Section 6.2 *supra*.

declares that the parties can willingly refrain from these obligations by not marrying. There is, without doubt, a contradiction in that a state, on one side, pursues the state's objectives of safeguarding the stability of families by limiting the possibility of receiving a marital divorce while, on the other side, allowing unmarried cohabiting persons who have created a family and acquired children to separate without any further ado. This contradiction in the legal system is particularly marked in states that parallel the formal marriage by enacting legislation for cohabiting unmarried persons without regulations concerning separations.

The efficacy of the canon law strategy, however, is dependent on those requisites that must be fulfilled in order for a common law marriage or a legally recognized cohabitation to be considered to be in existence. If the legal effects are tied not to the existence of a marriage contract, but rather directly to the spouse's cohabitation, the highest degree of efficacy from the state's viewpoint can be reached, as seen in Chapter 13. The parties' own intentions with respect to the cohabitation and to the legal regulations then become irrelevant. Even though the parties themselves did not desire the legal effects of marriage but rather intended a long cohabitation without legal ties, the lost sheep are captured within the legal marital fold. The method of tying the legal consequences only to the parties' cohabitation is applied in most of the cohabitation legislation that has been enacted in Northern and Western Europe, Canada, Australia, and New Zealand.[155] Even the legislation presented by the American Law Institute is based on the principle that legal rights and obligations may arise from the conduct of parties with respect to one another.[156] On the other side the parties are typically given the right, through an expressed contract, to opt out from the system, assuming that they are in agreement.

With respect to common law marriages, the efficacy of the canon law strategy is limited by the requirement of a marriage contract as examined in Chapter 8, "Cohabitation, Holding Out, and Reputation as Spouses." If the contract contains a requirement to live together long term as spouses, those who simply actually live together fall outside of the system and its obligations. The difference as regards tying the legal effects directly to the cohabitation, in practice, however, has not been substantial because the parties typically do not enter into any expressed contracts and the courts have accepted inferred agreements, as discussed in Chapter 7, and legal presumptions, as seen in Chapter 9, based on the parties' cohabitation and outward appearance as spouses. The contractual construction has made it possible, however, for the parties to make the objection that

155 For more with respect to the significance of objective and subjective elements as requisites for the establishment of a common law marriage or a legal cohabitation, *see* Chapter 13 *supra.*

156 *See* the ALI Principles, *supra* note 47, § 6.02, a. Comment: The basis of this Chapter.

no marital *consensus* exists, which as thus prevent the existence of a common law marriage. The efficacy is considerably more limited by the strategy that the contract requires a legal intent, in other words, an intent to reach the legal effects of marriage or, at least, legal status. If both parties do not have a common intent, neither is captured here by the legal regulations. A significant group therefore falls outside of the obligations that the system creates, as discussed further in Chapter 13.

If marriage rates continue to decrease in the Western world, it cannot be ruled out that attitudes to common law marriages and other cohabitation legislation will entirely reverse. Conservative states, protective of the family and marriage, may wish to place different obligations on the parties. They can, with the application of the canon law strategy, introduce common law marriages or other cohabitation legislation for the purpose of capturing the lost sheep. Common law marriages can then appear to be an old solution to a new problem.

14.3 Arguments Against Common Law Marriage and Cohabitation Law

14.3.1 Limitation of the Freedom of the Parties

An ideological argument against common law marriage and cohabitation legislation in general is that such systems can be forced on parties without their choice. Yet, the fact that the parties actually live together, in practice, triggers a system of rights and obligations that becomes applicable to their relationship. The state can be said to infringe upon the parties' individual freedom to decide whether they are to be subjected to the systems of regulation or not, indicating distrust about the capacity of individuals and families to decide the terms and conditions of their cohabitation.[157]

157 Reppy, *supra* note 19, at 1713, states that "[t] he writer cannot see how morality is advanced by the law's telling a couple that it will treat them as married even though they do not want to be." *See also* M. FREEMAN, & C. LYON, COHABITATION WITHOUT MARRIAGE 51-54, 183-185 (1983); and Marjorie Maguire Schultz, *Contractual Ordering of Marriage: A New Model for State Policy*, 70 CAL. L. REV. 204, 287 (1982). Fineman, *supra* note 25, at 325, states: "The choice of cohabitation is, after all, a choice not to marry and it would seem incongruous to attach to it identical consequences." *See also* H. A. Finlay, *The Informal Marriage in Anglo-Australian Law, in* MARRIAGE AND COHABITATION IN CONTEMPORARY SOCIETIES 156, 166 (John M. Eekelaar, Sanford N. Katz eds., 1980); Walter O. Weyrauch, *Metamorphoses of Marriage: Formal and Informal Marriages in the United States*, in MARRIAGE AND COHABITATION IN CONTEMPORARY SOCIETIES 265, 266 (John M. Eekelaar, Sanford N. Katz eds., 1980); Simitian, *Property Rights and the Unmarried Homemaker: Marvin v. Marvin, and the California Experience*, 5 COM. PROP. J. 3, 7, 10 (1978); and Christina M. Fernández, Note, *Beyond Marvin: A Proposal for Quasi-Spousal Support*, 30 STAN. L. REV. 359, 370 (1978). Homer H. Clark, Jr., *The New Marriage*, 12 WILLAMETTE L.J. 441, 452 (1976), appears to assume that couples refraining from formally marrying make a legal choice. *Compare* on the other hand the same author in THE LAW OF DOMESTIC RELATIONS IN THE UNITED STATES 57 (1968), in which the author

This liberal attitude, which places the freedom of the individual in the foreground, is in direct contrast to a strategy favoring common law marriage in order to capture the lost sheep.[158] The liberal philosopher John Stuart Mill has stated: "'If a person possess any tolerable amount of common sense and experience, his own mode of laying out his existence is the best, not because it is the best in itself, but because it is his own mode. Human beings are not like sheep ..."[159] This view safeguards individuals who quite simply do not wish to be captured. A state considering enacting, retaining, or abolishing common law marriage or cohabitation legislation, from this perspective, faces a deeply ideological dilemma in which the state's interests are placed against those of the individual.[160] The freedom to choose and personal autonomy in matters of family life are fundamental values that are guaranteed, e.g., in American and Canadian constitutional doctrines.[161] This dilemma is clearly illustrated by developments in Scotland, in which the legislator pronounced: "Where families are strong and functioning well, the Executive considers the state should play little or no role. Family life should, wherever possible be an issue for families themselves." This policy declaration, however, did not impede the legislature passing a general law giving rights to all couples living together as if they were husband and wife.[162]

Paradoxically, there has been criticism historically against common law marriage that it expresses an unrestrained individualism that neglects the

---

argues that the choice between formal marriage and common law marriages is not any conscious choice. *See also* Valeri, *supra* note 18, at 558.

158 *See* § 14.2.8 *supra.*

159 JOHN STUART MILL, ON LIBERTY 82-83 (London, Longman, Roberts & Green Co., 1859).

160 *See*, Marsha Garrison, *Marriage Matters: What's Wrong with the ALI's Domestic Partnership Proposal*, in RECONCEIVING THE FAMILY, CRITIQUE ON THE AMERICAN LAW INSTITUTE'S PRINCIPLES OF THE LAW OF FAMILY DISSOLUTION 322 (Robin Fretwell Wilson ed., 2006), who holds that the ALI proposal as to domestic partnership based on cohabitation "diminishes personal liberty and privacy; individuals are forced into a marital mold whether or not that family form comports with their own goals and personal choices."

161 With respect to American doctrine, *see, e.g.*, Garrison, *id.* at 320, referring to the Fourteenth Amendment and *Planned Parenthood v. Casey*, 505 U.S. 833, 851 (1992). *See also Santosky v. Kramer*, 455 U.S. 745, 753 (1982); *Zablocki v. Redhail*, 434 U.S. 374 (1978); and *Loving v. Virginia*, 381 U.S. 1, 12 (1967). With respect to Canadian doctrine, *see, e.g., R.. v. Salituro* (1991) 3 S.C.R. 654, 674. The Law Commission of Canada has stated: "The freedom to choose whether and with whom to form close personal relationships is a fundamental value in free and democratic societies," *see* Law Commission of Canada (2001), *Beyond Conjugality* at 17. Ottawa: Law Commission of Canada. The reluctance in the province of Quebec to give the same regulations for cohabitation as for marriage has been based on respect for freedom of choice, *see* Céline Le Bourdais and Évelyne Lapierre-Adamcyk, *Changes in conjugal life in Canada: Is cohabitation progressively replacing marriage?*, 66 J. MAR. & FAM. 929-942 (2004). *See also* Kenneth Karst, *The Freedom of Intimate Association*, 89 YALE L.J. 637 (1980).

162 *See* THE FAMILY LAW (SCOTLAND) ACT 2006; Family Law (Scotland) Bill, SP Bill 36B, 18, Session 2 (2005); Policy Memorandum, Family Law (Scotland) Bill (SP Bill 36), at 1.

community's interests.[163] This paradox is resolved, however, by the fact that this criticism is relevant only with respect to the forms of marriage's commencement. With respect to legal effects, the criticism, in contrast, lacks relevance because the parties can be affected by all of the obligations that marital status entails. The possibility of affecting this coercion through a contract is as limited as for formally married spouses.[164]

The argument that common law marriages and other cohabitation legislation limit freedom appears most clearly in cases in which the parties have chosen to not formally marry simply to avoid the legal effects of marriage.[165] For example, couples who previously had been married and who, in a new formless relationship later in life, *inter alia*, for the sake of the children in the previous marriage, desire a higher degree of financial independence than that formal marriage offers. Others have economic advantages to gain by not formally remarrying. A marriage would perhaps entail a loss of pension, maintenance, or other benefits.[166] This group also includes couples who, for ideological reasons, do not wish to subject themselves to the straitjacket of civil marriage or who wish to be free to leave the relationship if they so desire, without the limitations of divorce regulations.[167]

---

163 *See* HOWARD, *supra* note 57, at 184. *Compare* Weyrauch, *supra* note 22, at 109, who speaks of "[t]he rugged individualism of American frontier days, which favored the growth of common law marriage." For more on this, *see* Section 4.3.2 *supra.*

164 *See also* Dubler, *supra* note 36, at 1907-1908.

165 This argument is brought forward from time to time, *see, e.g.,* Brinig, *supra* note 50, at 269, who holds that "parties who did not want to get married but wanted to cohabit would find themselves with a set of responsibilities on dissolution that they did not want to assume; if they had wanted these responsibilities, they would have married." *See also* Caroline Forder, *European Models of Domestic Partnership Laws: The Field of Choice,* 17 CAN. J. FAM. L. 371, 452 (2000), who argues that: "The possibility of avoiding assimilation with spouses is important, as many unmarried couples have deliberately chosen not to marry and do not wish for assimilation to married couples." The author recommends the Swedish regulation, which creates a "middle way" between being unmarried and being married. *See also* Martha Bailey, *Marriage and Marriage-Like Relationships* (Ottawa: Law Commission of Canada, 1999) at 31, who states that "some object to this as an unjustified interference with the autonomy of parties who may have chosen not to marry in order to avoid responsibility to their partners." *See also* Howard O., Hunter, *An Essay on Contract and Status: Race, Marriage and the Meretricious Spouse,* 64 VA. L. REV. 1039, 1094-1095 (1978), who says that "two people who choose to live together without marriage often may be seeking to avoid that status obligations of marriage itself..." *Compare* Note, *supra* note 10, at 102.

166 *Compare* David S. Caudill who states: "The parties' reasoning for avoiding marriage might include convenience, economic considerations, such as tax benefits or welfare benefits, the desire for a trial period before marriage, the desire to avoid legal obligations, or inability to marry because of an undissolved marriage," *see Legal Recognition of Unmarried Cohabitation: A Proposal to Update and Reconsider Common-Law Marriage,* 49 TENN. L. REV. 537, 566 note 204 (1982); and Leonore Weitzman, *Legal Regulation of Marriage: Tradition and Change,* 62 CAL. L. REV. 1169 (1974).

167 *Compare* the Canadian case of *Dwyer v. Love* (1976) 9 Nfld & PEIR 325 (CA), in which the woman in a *de facto* union claimed compensation for housekeeping services based on *quantum meruit* and in which the court held: "Their union was one of two individuals both wanting to live their lives – wanting a relationship but

A historical example is the prominent feminist Elizabeth Cady Stanton, who was an opponent of common law marriage because the regulations concerning marital divorce limited the parties' freedom.[168] The feminist criticism of marriage as an institution, in which women are subjugated to men, also affects common law marriages.[169] According to this view, legal marriage is an unacceptable limitation on individual freedom.[170] Even though the regulations concerning divorce, nowadays, after the victory of no-fault divorce since the 1970s, are not as restrictive as previously, there still is a point in Stanton's view. Marriage law in most Western legal systems no longer contains rules according to which women are expressly subjugated to men. Nevertheless, it is striking that, today, there are opinions that marriage alters the balance of power in the relationship and that women, therefore, prefer unmarried cohabitation.[171] This does not detract from the fact, seen above, that there are also feminist arguments for common law marriage.[172]

---

could end at any time – no marriage – no ties, no problem to enter and none of divorce to end."

168 *See* Elizabeth Cady Stanton, Address to the Decade Meeting on Marriage and Divorce, reprinted in A HISTORY OF THE NATIONAL WOMAN'S RIGHTS MOVEMENT FOR TWENTY YEARS 59, 68 (photo. Reprint 1971) (Paulina Davis ed., New York, Journeymen Printer's Cooperative Ass'n 1891). A leading feminist during the 1800s, Elizabeth Cady Stanton was an opponent of the courts' recognition of common law marriage, as the regulations concerning marital divorce therewith became applicable to the parties, limiting a woman's freedom of not be captured in a relationship which she did not intend to be abiding. Stanton's views have been the object of much analysis, *see, e.g.*, WILLIAM LEACH, TRUE LOVE AND PERFECT UNION 151 (1980); Fineman, *supra* note 25, at 317; Elisabeth B. Clark, *Matrimonial Bonds: Slavery and Divorce in Nineteenth-Century America*, 8 LAW & HIST. L. REV. 25, 36-41 (1990); Dubler, *supra* note 36, at 1908 and *supra* note 35, at 969, who states that the common law marriage doctrine "allowed judges to efface the potentially threatening nature of nonmarital domestic relationships by labeling them marriages. Common law marriage thus transformed potentially subversive relationships – subversive in their disregard for the social and legal institution of marriage – into completely traditional relationships."

169 *See, e.g.*, Clark, *supra* note 157, at 442; B. FRIEDAN, THE FEMININE MYSTIQUE, Chapters 7 and 10 (1963); K. MILLET, SEXUAL POLITICS, Chapter 3 (1969); and S. FIRESTONE, THE DIALECTIC OF SEX, Chapter 2 (1920).

170 GLENDON, *supra* note 18, at 80.

171 *See, e.g.*, Kiernan, *supra* note 74, at 52, who states: "Cohabitation may symbolize, particularly for women, the avoidance of the notion of dependency that is typically implicit in the marriage contract. Women may be anxious that the legal contract may alter the balance of power in their partnership arrangements and make the relationship less equitable." *See also* K.L. KUFFNER, COMMON LAW AND SAME-SEX RELATIONSHIPS UNDER THE MATRIMONIAL PROPERTY ACT 63 (2000). *Compare* Linda J. Waite, *Trends in Men's and Women's Well-Being in Marriage*, in THE TIES THAT BIND: PERSPECTIVES ON MARRIAGE AND COHABITATION 368, 388-389 (Linda Waite et al. eds., 2000), who states: "We also see little evidence that marriage benefits men more than women, although wives characterize their marriages in slightly more negative terms. Both men and women gain in happiness from marriage and by similar amounts."

172 Dubler, *supra* note 36, at 1916, states that "the doctrine of common law marriage was not necessarily coercive of women in each particular instance. Women plaintiffs who came before nineteenth-century courts seeking financial support through

Consideration about the individual's freedom from state regulation also appears in the Nordic countries, which have high proportions of unmarried cohabitation. In Denmark, a proposal in 1968 concerning common law marriage with all legal effects of marriage for couples living together for three years was rejected by the parliament. The Minister of Justice explained the rejection by citing the parties' freedom of choice. The same argument came to expression when the Ministry of Justice in 2006 rejected a committee proposal concerning legal inheritance rights for surviving cohabitants, *inter alia*, with reference to the parties freedom of choice to marry and to receive the legal effects of marriage, or to cohabit outside marriage without these effects.[173] Similar concerns about autonomy and choice caused Norway to abstain from placing cohabitation on an equal footing with marriage, and also seem to have played a role in Finland.[174] The Canadian legislators have hesitated to extend the application of the marital division of property rules to unmarried cohabitants of the opposite sex, on the argument that the cohabitants have not given their consent thereto.[175] When the Supreme Court of Canada, in a decision from 2002, found that it was not unconstitutional to exclude unmarried cohabitants from the application of the same rules, it held that spouses have freely accepted the rights and obligations of marriage and a decision not to marry should be respected.[176] In the discussion which preceded

judicial recognition of common law marriages were in dire need. In applying the doctrine to their situations, courts afforded these women monumental concrete benefits."

173 *See* the Minister of Justice Knud Thestrup, in the parliamentary debates (folketingets forhandlinger), 24 May 1968, at 3628-3650. As of this writing, no cohabitation legislation between the parties has been enacted in Denmark. One of the reasons has been that the parties have the option to marry and that legislation would be a manifestation of a Big Brother attitude, *see* Betænkning 8, Aegdeskab, Samliv uden ægdeskab I, 50 (nr. 915/1980). As to the rejection of the proposal in 2006 concerning legal inheritance rights, *see* L 100, Forslag til arvelov, Dec. 6, 2006, para. 15.3.1.

174 *See* NOU 1999:25, para. 2.4. On the other hand, it should be noted that in January 2007, the Norwegian Ministry of Justice sent out a proposal to different institutions to get feedback concerning a proposed minimum inheritance right and a right to keep the estate undivided as to residence and household goods for surviving cohabitants, *see* Høringsnotat, January 2007, Snr. 200405522 EP. As to Finland, *see* Forder, *supra* note 165, at 381. Her opinion is supported by professor Urpo Kangas, Faculty of law, University of Helsinki, E-mail communication with Göran Lind, February 2005. The Finnish Ministry of Justice has rejected inheritance rights for surviving cohabitants with reference to the possibility to make a will, *see* Bet. 2004:6.

175 Quebec's Minister of Justice Serge Ménard has stated: "S'il s'est abstenu de le faire, c'est par respect pour la volonté des conjoints: quand ils ne se marient pas, c'est qu'ils ne veulent pas se soumettre au régime légal du marriage," *see* National Assembly *Debates of the National Assembly*, June 18, Bill 84 (1998). *See also* Bailey, *supra* note 68, at 155.

176 *See Attorney Gen. of Nova Scotia v. Walsh*, 4 S.C.R. 325 (2002). Trussler and Vandergrift, *supra* note 48, at 15, state as to the conjugal cohabitation-based approach: "The disadvantage is that it imposes obligations on those that may have chosen not to marry for the express purpose of avoiding those sorts of obligations." *See also* Bailey,

the enactment of extensive regulations for unmarried de facto couples in New Zealand in 2001, objections were made that married persons had chosen not only to live together but also to abide by the system of regulations, while de facto couples, in contrast, had not made any such choice. The critics argued that the parties' freedom to associate without the obligations of matrimonial laws was undermined. These arguments, however, were not accepted by the parliament, which stated that unmarried cohabiting persons were a reality whose practical problems must be resolved.[177] Similar objections have been presented without success concerning the division of estates upon the separation between domestic partners under the ALI Principles that were adopted in 2002, as discussed in greater detail below.[178] It is not surprising that the more deregulated legislation for unmarried cohabitation has been regarded as a combination of "liberty and a trap."[179]

The strength of the coercion to which the parties are exposed depends on how the requisites for the application of the regulations concerning common law marriages and cohabitation legislation, respectively, are formed. The individual's freedom, consequently, appears to be given the greatest protection if the application of the system of regulations requires a legal intent from the parties, in other words, an intent to reach the legal effects of marriage, or in any event, the legal status. If the parties do not have a mutual intent, they are not affected by the legal regulations, but at the same time significant groups fall outside of the legal protections the system offers.[180] If simply a contract with an intent to live together is required, the freedom to avoid the legal effects is limited. If no joint intent is required at all but rather the legal effects are tied directly to the parties' actual cohabitation, then the state's coercion is at its strongest. Already a loose application of implied agreements based on the parties' actions tends to transfer power from the individual.[181] The state's coercion is even clearer with the application of the marriage presumption based on the parties' cohabitation and outward appearance.[182] The individual, however,

---

supra note 68, at 155-156. *Compare* the dissenting opinion by Justice L'Heureux-Dubé.

177 *See* Atkin, *supra* note 46, at 4; and Dubler, *supra* note 35, at 962.

178 *See* David Westfall, *Forcing Incidents of Marriage on Unmarried Cohabitants: The American Law Institute's Principles of Family Dissolution*, 76 NOTRE DAME L. REV. 1467 (2001).

179 Ulla Björnberg, *Cohabitation and Marriage in Sweden - Does Family Form Matter?*, 15 IJLPF 350, 360 (2001).

180 *See, e.g., State v. Walker*, 36 Kan. 297, 13 P. 279, 286 (1887), in which both parties wished to avoid the regulations of formal marriage.

181 In the case of *In re McLaughlin's Estate*, 4 Wash. 570, 30 P. 651, 657 (1892), the Washington Supreme Court, which was very critical to common law marriage, stated that the courts' decisions sometimes resulted "in holding the marriage relation to have been established by the conduct of the parties where there was no real intention to take each other as husband and wife." For more concerning implied agreements, *see* Chapter 7 *supra*.

182 For more concerning the marriage presumption, *see* Section 9.3 *supra*.

has a possibility to rebut the presumption by demonstrating that the parties did not have any marital *consensus*.

In a proposal for a revivified common law marriage, Marsha Garrison strongly emphasizes the importance of basing the application of the regulations on the parties' free will and commitment. She, therefore, is critical of legislation such as the ALI Principles, based on the cohabitation of the parties, but accepts that the parties' *consensus* can be seen from the objective circumstances of the life the parties share.[183]

State coercion is greatest if the application of cohabitation legislation does not take into consideration the intentions of the parties but rather is entirely based on their actual cohabitation. The relationship is not based on a contract between the parties in the same manner as a marriage or a registered partnership. Even the legislation proposed by the American Law Institute is based on the principle that legal rights and obligations may arise from the conduct of parties with respect to one another.[184] As can be seen in Chapter 13, these subjective elements, in the framework of the concept of cohabiting persons, typically have a limited role.[185] However, it should be noted that cohabitation legislation consistently gives fewer legal effects than common law marriage, which completely equates the parties with formally married spouses. Therefore, the coercion concerns certain legal effects considered particularly important, while the parties can freely choose to marry in order to receive the other legal effects. This appears to have been the strategic compromise that the Swedish legislature finally made. The Swedish Cohabitation Act, enacted in 1987 and revised in 2003, consequently offers a minimal protection upon separation and death through a division of an estate encompassing only the residence and household goods acquired during the cohabitation. If the parties wish a more extensive system, they are advised to marry.[186] The parties, consequently, are forced to participate in the fundamental system, but if they wish to obtain the more extensive marriage rights, they must "contract in."

---

183 Garrison, *supra* note 38, at 884-897.

184 *See* the ALI PRINCIPLES, *supra* note 47, § 6.02, a. Comment: The basis of this Chapter.

185 David S. Caudill states that "many unmarried cohabitators meet the minimum requirements for a traditional common law marriage. The additional requirement of a present intent or agreement to be married is, of course, notably absent from some unmarried cohabitants' relationships. Nevertheless, some unmarried cohabitators want to live as *if* they were husband and wife; that is, they want to enjoy a relationship based upon the sharing, commitment, and intimacy that is associated with a good, conventional marriage, even if, for whatever reason, they do not intend to be formally married," *see supra* note 150, at 565.

186 *See* the Swedish COHABITEES ACT (2003:376). The reason for giving only a minimal protection can be seen from the legislative proposal, being based on a cohabitation without any express wishes from the parties. In order to receive the benefit of a more comprehensive regulation, the Swedish Government advised such persons to marry, *see* Prop. 2002/03:80, at 25.

The development appears to be going against a more extensive system based upon cohabitation and, based on the views discussed here, against an altogether higher degree of coercion and an altogether lower degree of freedom of choice for individuals. The regulations proposed by the American Law Institute for the division of an estate between domestic partners correspond to those regulations applied to married persons, but are applicable only upon separation, not death.[187] The system that has been developed in the case law of the state of Washington goes somewhat further and applies similar estate division regulations even in cases of death.[188] The legal systems in New South Wales, Australia, New Zealand, and the Canadian Province of Manitoba go the farthest, equating de facto relationships and common-law relationships[189] with marriage after two and three years' cohabitation, respectively, with respect to essential issues such as the division of an estate (the equal division of property acquired during the relationship), inheritance, and maintenance.

To counter the argument that common law marriage and cohabitation legislation force a system upon the parties that they have not chosen, it should be noted that the parties generally have the possibility to contract out.[190] A common law marriage, once established, can only be dissolved through formal marital divorce, but the parties can enter into a contract containing an economic agreement. Cohabitation legislation, typically, gives the parties the possibility to entirely or partially contract out of the system.[191] This possibility assumes, however, that the parties are aware of and in agreement of this possibility.[192] If only one party does not desire

---

187 *See* the ALI PRINCIPLES, *supra* note 47, particularly Chapter 6, "Domestic Partners" and Chapter 4. With respect to the possibilities to "contract out" of the system, *see* Westfall, *supra* note 178, at 1480.

188 *Marriage of Lindsey*, 101 Wash.2d 299, 678 P.2d 328 (1984); *Warden v. Warden*, 676 P.2d 1037 (Wash.App. 1984); *Foster v. Thilges*, 812 P.2d 523 (Wash.App. 1991); *Connell v. Francisco*, 127 Wash.2d 339, 898 P.2d 831 (1995); and *In re Marriage of Pennington*, 142 Wash.2d 592, 14 P.3d 764 (2000).

189 With respect to New South Wales, Australia, *see* PROPERTY (RELATIONSHIPS) ACT (1984), which was amended through THE PROPERTY (RELATIONSHIPS) AMENDMENT ACT (1999). With respect to New Zealand, *see* PROPERTY (RELATIONSHIPS) ACT (1976), amended through law 2001, which came into force 1 Feb. 2002. With respect to the Canadian Province of Manitoba, *see* THE COMMON-LAW PARTNERS' PROPERTY AND RELATED AMENDMENTS ACT, S.M. 2002, c. 48.

190 Andrews, *supra* note 160, at 37-38; and Reppy, *supra* note 19, at 1718. His proposed status is intended to arise either through "official recordation (or even a ceremony)" or through "common-law cohabitation." The parties however are free to through a contract avoid this status.

191 According to the ALI PRINCIPLES, supra note 47, § 6.01 (2), the parties have the right to contract out of the system as to the division of an estate as between domestic partners. *Compare* the Swedish scheme according to which the parties have the right to contract out of the system as to the division of an estate in accordance with the COHABITEES ACT (2003:376) § 9, but on the other hand, not the right for a cohabiting partner to take over the other's residential apartment, *see* § 22.

192 *See also* The Law Commission of Canada (2001), *Beyond Conjugality*, Ottawa: Law Commission of Canada at 116, stating that treating cohabitants as if they were married "infringes upon the value of autonomy. Although people may opt out of

that the system be applicable to their relation, that party is still forced to subject themselves to the same, due to the cohabitation. In a relationship in which one party is economically stronger, it can be argued that the party is not in need of the marital protective regulations, while the economically more vulnerable desires marriage.[193] A system based on the idea that marriage is a contract, which requires both parties' joint intent in order to receive the legal effects of marriage, then offers no protection. Nor can one argue that the cohabitation was a conscious choice by the woman, in cases in which a man has given a woman expectations of a ceremonial marriage, enjoyed the fruits of the relationship, but later "kept putting it off and he never did."[194]

In the debate in the United States preceding the adoption of the ALI Principles in 2002, according to which a separation between cohabiting unmarried persons offers a system for the division of an estate comparable to that applicable for spouses, the objection was that the parties' failure to marry ought to be interpreted as an agreement that they did not wish any obligations to each other upon the dissolution of the relationship. The prevailing view was that one party certainly could have refrained from marriage in the hope of avoiding marital obligations, but concluded, nevertheless, that the law has no interest in vindicating the intentions of one party only.[195] A party wishing to avoid the obligations must ensure the consent of the other party. In contrast, the ALI viewpoint vindicates the intentions of the other party, the party desiring to subject themselves to a system. The partner is forced into the system based on their cohabitation, but can contract out from it, with the consent of the other party.

However, it ought to be added that the parties in many cohabitations might not have any decided intentions of a legal nature, either to avoid the marital legal effects or obtain them.[196] Relationships can have shifting purposes.[197] Some couples live together for a trial period until they break up and try a different relationship with someone else. For others, the first

---

certain statutory provisions governing their relationships, they are not always aware of this possibility."

193 Ellen Kandoian states: "The problem, again, is that very often both parties do not refuse to be formally married. Only one party refuses. That the party who refuses is often the one in a superior bargaining position both financially (leading to reluctance to assume the support obligations) and emotionally (accounting for success in maintaining the relationship in the absence of legal assurances)," *see supra* note 37, at 1858.

194 *Anderson v. Anderson*, 235 Ind. 113, 131 N.E.2d 301 (1956); *Moffat Coal Co. v. Indus. Comm'n*, 108 Colo 388, 118 P.2d 769 (1941); and *Kozlowski v. Kozlowski*, 80 N.J. 378, 403 A.2d 902 (1979). *See also* Bowman, *supra* note 18, at 757; and Forder, *supra* note 165, at 381.

195 Blumberg, *supra* note 47, at 1296 note 117.

196 *See* Kandoian, *supra* note 37, at 1858.

197 David S. Caudill states: "Obviously there is no single family form that can be termed 'unmarried cohabitants'. Rather, the term encompasses a complex continuum of relationships that range from uncommitted roommates to intimate, monogamous relationships virtually identical to traditional marriages," *see supra* note 150, at 545.

period of cohabitation is followed by a formal marriage or a formless cohabitation that becomes lifelong. Awareness of the legal effects often ought to be limited. Many drift into a common law marriage or cohabitation; the arrangement is not the result of any conscious open assessment and decision.[198] It seems likely that few couples have the knowledge needed to contract out of a cohabitation status.[199] The Swedish Sociologist Jan Trost during the 1970s stated that "couples do not choose to cohabit instead of to marry. They just cohabit."[200] The situation often ought to be the same today in Europe as well as in the United States.[201] Naturally, it is risky to draw conclusions based on this with respect to the parties' legal intentions. Even in those cases in which their wishes are unclear, one can argue that common law marriage and, to a higher degree, cohabitation legislation, based only on cohabitation, imposes on the parties legal effects not chosen or agreed to by both parties.[202] Such legal systems may be acceptable if one thinks that the purpose of family law is not to give effect to the choice of the parties, but to address the needs of parties at the end of a relationship.[203] The most desirable system, naturally, is that the parties themselves consciously freely choose the system of regulations that is to govern their cohabitation, an idea further explored in Chapter 15, "A New Model of Marriage."

---

198 *Compare* Homer H. Clark, Jr., The Law of Domestic Relations in the United States 57 (1968) (not conscious choice, drift into). Carol S. Bruch, *Property Rights of De Facto Spouses Including Thoughts on the Value of Homemakers' services*, 10 Fam. L.Q. 101, 135 (1976), maintains that the majority probably chooses to live together as unmarried "either 1. In ignorance of the legal consequences of either marriage or non-marriage (perhaps the majority of non-lawyers believe that common law marriage exists in all jurisdictions and that protection is granted to stable nonmarital relationships), 2. under the assumption that some legal protections are available, or 3. with absolutely no thought given to the legal consequences of their relationship." *Compare* Atkin, *supra* note 46, at 4, who maintains that *de facto* couples do not make vows in the same manner as spouses, but that they "do make a choice to live together."

199 Garrison, *supra* note 38, at 852-853, maintains: "First, few cohabiting couples currently enter into contracts even though they are legally empowered to do so. Second, because cohabitation often develops over time, there is no obvious event that signals the need to contract out: Some couples, for whom it would be preferable to contract out, may not do so because of ignorance of the need or desirability to do so. Others may be unrealistically optimistic about the chances of the success of their relationship, or may be uncomfortable about raising and addressing issues about property with their partners. Still others will be inhibited by the time and high cost of entering into an agreement."

200 Jan Trost, Unmarried Cohabitation 186 (1979).

201 Blumberg, *supra* note 47, at 1296.

202 Trussler and Vandergrift, *supra* note 48, at 15, state: "The conjugal cohabitation based approach gives, particularly to the more vulnerable partner, the rights that he or, most often, she should have bargained for before entering the relationship."

203 *See, e.g.*, the dissenting opinion by Justice L'Heureux-Dubé in *Attorney Gen.of Nova Scotia v. Walsh*, 4 S.C.R. 325 (2000).

14.3.2 Fraudulent Behavior and Other Abuse

Historically, the most forceful, albeit not most apt, objection against common law marriage is the contention that this doctrine gives rise to perjury, fraudulent behavior, and other abuses. At the same time, given that most courts during the 1800s propagated for the application of common law marriage, there were those who, at the end of the nineteenth century, struck an alarm about the risk of abuse and fraudulent behavior. In several cases, the courts in *dictum* complained, often with moral indignation, of the risk that one party, with baseless statements as to the existence of a common law marriage, sought to reach another's assets. In *Sorensen v. Sorensen* (1904), the court stated that if it would find a marriage based on the evidence presented in the case, the door would be opened to fraud and perjury.[204] Most often, the criticism concerned civil claims presented upon a party's death. The typical example, commonly raised, was the wanton and unscrupulous woman, who upon a wealthy man's death, appears and makes a claim to his estate.[205] There is no absence of

---

204 See *Sorensen v. Sorensen*, 68 Neb. 500, 100 N.W. 930, 934 (1904).

205 *See* already *Milford v. Worchester*, 7 Mass. 48, 52 (1810), one of the first cases refusing to accept common law marriage with reference to that the form requirements were considered to be mandatory. The court stated that marriage is an institution intended to protect against "fraud, surprise, and seduction." *See later Duncan v. Duncan*, 10 Ohio St. 181, 188, 1859 WL 67 (1859), in which the court stated that common law marriage "would obscure the certainty of the rights of inheritance; would be opening a door to false pretenses of marriage, and to the imposition upon estates of suppositious heirs." In the case of *In re Brush*, 49 N.Y.S. 803, 806 (1st Dep't 1898), the court stated with respect to a prostitute, who made claims as to rights as a common law wife, that she "only seeks to assume that relation openly after his death, and when she is impelled to it by the loss of the support he had given her and by a desire to obtain that support by sharing in the proceeds of his property." *See also In re McLaughlin's Estate*, 4 Wash. 570, 30 P. 651, 657 (1892) ("to guard against deception"). In *Hulett v. Carey*, 66 Minn. 327, 69 N.W. 31, 34 (1896), the court stated: "In view of the increasing number of common law widows laying claim (in many instances, doubtless, fraudulently) to the estates of deceased men of wealth, it is a question for the legislature whether the common law should not be changed; but with that the courts have nothing to do." *See also Lorimer v. Lorimer*, 124 Mich. 631, 83 N.W. 609 (1900). In the case of *In re Callery's Estate*, 75 A. 672 (1910), the court stated concerning the surviving woman: "[W]hen Callery was dying ... she not only made no effort to assert the rights of a wife to be with him and care for him, but entered into negotiations for pecuniary settlement..." In *Huard v. McTeigh*, 113 Or. 279, 232 P. 658, 663 (1925), the court stated that common law marriage "places a premium upon illicit cohabitation and offers encouragement to the harlot and to adventuress." In *Matter of Heitman's Estate*, 154 Misc. 838, 279 N.Y.S. 108 (1935), a married man had a relationship with a woman who ran a brothel. When his wife died, he lived together with his sister. He however continued the relationship with the other woman. They did not move in together, but he paid the rent, telephone bills, and for part of the furniture for her apartment. When the man died, the woman claimed that she was the deceased's common law wife and cited as a ground hereto that they had entered into a marriage contract during a short stay in Pennsylvania. The court however found no contract proven. *See also In re Estate of Speeler*, 6 Ohio Op. 529, 1 Ohio Supp. 227, 22 Ohio Law Abst. 223 (P.Ct. 1936). In *Wagner v. Wagner*, 152 Pa.Super 4, 30 A.2d 659, 661-662 (1943), the court stated as to the woman: "She admittedly lied to serve her own ends in

modern cases in which two women compete, each claiming to be the deceased's surviving wife in a common law marriage.[206]

The alleged danger of the undeserving "gold-digging woman" appears to have been exaggerated and at times tinged by a gender bias that turns a blind eye on the man's role in the relationship and the fact that women, sometimes maintain relationships with men under a promise of marriage.[207]

---

securing the marriage license. We believe she would do so again where it would serve her interests to depart from truth." In *McClish v. Rankin*, 153 Fla. 324, 14 So.2d 714, 718 (Fla. 1943), the court describes the situation in accordance to the following: "A man dies; a woman thereupon claims that she and he privately, if not furtively, agreed to be husband and wife. He cannot be heard to deny her story. The testimony being uncontradicted the contract is established and repute becomes immaterial. It is difficult to imagine a readier vehicle of fraud." In *Fisher v. Sweet & McClain*, 154 Pa.Super. 216, 35 A.2d 756, 759, 761 (1944), the court stated: "We think it is clear from the whole record that neither the referee nor the board believed the claimant's testimony of a marriage any more than we would have believed it if we had been the fact-finding body." The court, by applying a requirement for a license, wanted to contribute to "eliminating the fraud and perjury so often occurring with respect to common-law marriages." The requirement of a license was later rejected in *Buradus v. Gen.Cement Products Co.*, 159 Pa.Super. 501, 48 A.2d 883 (1946), *aff'd*, 356 Pa. 349, 52 A.2d 205 (1947), but the court stated that: "There has been a growing judicial impatience of the invitation to perjury in cases depending for recovery on marriage at common law and a progressive change in judicial view requiring higher degrees of proof where such marriages are asserted." *See also Ballenger v. Hazlett*, 4 Fla.Supp. 50 (Cir.Ct. 1950); *In re Erickson's Estate*, 75 S.D. 345, 64 N.W.2d 316, 318 (1954): ("Such marriages are a source of fraud and perjury. They are to be tolerated only and not encouraged"); *Chaachou v. Chaachou*, 73 So.2d 830 (Fla. 1954); *In re Campbell's Estate*. 73 So.2d 883 (Fla. 1954); *In re Klinger's Estate*, 73 So.2d 50 (Fla. 1954); *Dacunzo v. Edgye*, 19 N.J. 443, 117 A.2d 508 (1955); *Jordan v. Jordan*, 89 So.2d 22 (Fla. 1956); *Anderson v. Anderson*, 235 Ind. 113, 131 N.E.2d 301 (1956) ("There is always danger of fraud"); *van Derven v. van Derven*, 105 So.2d 805 (Fla.App. 1958); *In re Estate of Manfredi*, 399 Pa. 285, 159 A.2d 697, 701 (1960); *In re Estate of Soeder*, 7 Ohio App. 271, 220 N.E.2d 547, 562 (1966) (citing *Duncan*); and *Matter of Estate of Willard*, 93 N.M. 352, 600 P.2d 298, 301 (1979).

206 *See, e.g., Int'l Painters and Allied Traders Ind. Pensions Fund v. Calabro*, 312 F.Supp.2d 697 (E.D.Pa. 2004). In *Beals v. Beals*, 203 Ga.App. 81, 416 S.E.2d 301, 302 (1992), the one woman objected that the other's claim was "fraudulent." Also in cases concerning conflicts of laws issues, the courts have warned for "the possibility of fraud arising from claims of common law marriage and the uncertainty which such claims of marriage inject into the affairs of individuals," *see, e.g., In re Estate of Bivians*, 98 N.M. 722, 652 P.2d 744, 749 (1982). In *Whyte v. Blair*, 885 P.2d 791, 795 (Utah 1994), which concerned the right to compensation based on an automobile insurance, the court stated: "Care must be given to guard against fraudulent marriage claims." *Compare Staudenmayer v. Staudenmayer*, 714 A.2d 1016, 1019 (Pa. 1998); and *PNC Bank Corp. v. Workers' Compensation Appeal Bd. (Stamos)*, No. 860 C.D. (2003).

207 *See* Bowman, *supra* note 18, at 733, which in a provocative analysis of the case of *In re Baldwin's Estate*, 162 Cal. 471, 123 P. 267, 733-734 (1912), shows how different perspectives as to a relationship can cast new light over a woman who by some would be considered as a "gold digging-woman" and by others as "a women seduced and abandoned without compensation." In the case, a common law marriage could not be established as the parties did not outwardly present themselves as spouses and the man in addition was married to another woman. *See also* Ariela R. Dubler, *Wifely Behaviour: A Legal History of Acting Married*, 100 COLUM. L. REV. 957, 964 (2000), who maintains that the legislator who repealed common law marriage

The woman then, on her side, runs the risk that the man denies the existence of a common law marriage. Only by exception is this mutual risk of fraudulent behavior raised in the case law.[208] The problem appears, however, to not be primarily moral in nature and does not lie in the parties' more or less fraudulent intentions. Instead, it appears that the problem lies in a system of regulations, which based on its unclear formation, invites disputes.

Even in the academic legal literature, forceful condemnations of common law marriage have referred to the risk of deceit and other abuse. George Howard, who in the beginning of the 1900s led the crusade against common law marriage, considered the legal institution as thoroughly bad, involving social evils of the most dangerous character.[209] Abraham Freedman, who fifty years later, likewise argued for a repeal of common law marriage, maintained that a form requirement would prevent fraudulent claims of marriage, generally made by women seeking to share in the

---

"espoused a vision of a dangerous femininity, of conniving and gold digging women preying on the goodwill of innocent men (or their estates) through false performances of wifely conduct." *See also* Goldberg, *supra* note 35, at 483.

208 *See State v. Walker,* 36 Kan. 297, 13 P. 279, 286 (1887), in which the court stated: "If there be no registration, no officiator, and no eye-witness of the marriage, the woman is placed at the mercy of the man, who may deny the 'consensual relation' and repudiate her; and, on the other hand, a man may be blackmailed by an adventuress, who may declare there was a 'consensual marriage' when there was none." *Compare In re Pratt's Estate,* 233 App.Div. 200, 251 N.Y.S. 424 (1931), in which the man upon the woman's death could not prove the existence of a common law marriage.

209 HOWARD, *supra* not 57, at 171. *See also* SCHOULER, (6th ed. 1921), *supra* note 145, at 1435, who maintains that a requirement for only a contract without a requirement for cohabitation "would open the door to fraud of all kinds and make the estates of wealthy men the prey of the adventuress." *See* further Erroll Clarence Gilkey, *Validity of Common Law Marriage in Oregon,* 3 OREG. L. REV. 28, 46 (1923): "The doctrine of informal marriages favors the harlot and the adventuress and paves the way for them to claim the right of the common law widow upon the death of some man of wealth." In Thomas Clifford Billig and James Phillip Lynch, *Common-Law Marriage in Minnesota, A Problem in Social Security,* 22 MINN. L. REV. 177, 178 (1938), the authors maintain that the majority of judicial decisions concerned a claim which a surviving party addressed to the estate of the deceased, but argue that such conflicts were limited, as common law marriage was not common in the circles in which one had money to litigate. The number of conflicts was assumed to be greater with respect to "social security." *Compare In re Estate of Erlanger,* 145 Misc. 1, 259 N.Y.S. 610 (1932); MORLAND, *supra* note 10, at 59 ("more abuse than use"); and Note, *supra* note 27, at 548 ("To force publicization of the marriage contract will provide against fraud and deception in claims before courts and administrative agencies"). *See also* John W. Roxborough, *Antenuptial Physical Examination on Common Law Marriages in Michigan,* 16 U. DET. L.J. 174, 176 (1953), who maintains that common law marriage altogether too often is used for "purely mercenary reasons." Rothstein, *supra* note 2, at 93, argues that "[t]he plaintiffs often manipulate the events of the particular case..." In Note, *supra* note 10, at 102, the author states: "Heirs and descendents' estates are frequent targets for the claims of bogus common law spouses, since the one party most likely to be able to disprove a marriage is dead."

estates of decedents.[210] Not uncommonly, the debate has been spiced with moral judgments not only about couples living in formless relationships but also about others who have given testimony as support for their case.[211] The problem, however, during the later part of 1900s has also been brought to attention by authors who have taken a stance neutral to or argued for the retention of common law marriage in some form.[212]

Even though the fears concerning abuse sometimes have been baseless, particularly when based on generalizations about women's conspiratorial and fraudulent intentions, it appears that these alleged dangers swayed opinion about common law marriage. From the relatively positive attitude of the 1800s, a more critical view emerged during the end of the century and the first part of the 1900s.[213] The fear of abuse, both in relationships between the parties and in relation to the authorities, have therefore constituted one of the reasons behind the legislators' repeal of common law marriage in several states. California was one of the first.[214] The purpose of preventing fraudulent claims against the estates of a deceased consequently appears to have played a role in the repeal of common law marriage in Nebraska in 1923.[215] When the state of New York repealed common

---

210 ABRAHAM L. FREEDMAN AND MAURICE FREEDMAN, LAW OF MARRIAGE AND DIVORCE IN PENNSYLVANIA I, 103 (2d ed. 1957). *See also* Williams, *supra* note 9, at 449, who maintains that the majority of the cases with respect to common law marriage "involve money claims against the estates of wealthy decedents"; Kirkpatrick, *supra* note 10, at 46; and Causey, *supra* note 58, at 229-230 ("Estates are targets for claims of bogus common law marriages"). *See also* THOMAS, *supra* note 15, at 68.

211 Kirkpatrick, *supra* note 10, at 46-47 stating: "Today, those relying solely upon common-law marriage to sustain their claims to marital benefits generally come from strata of our population where morality and integrity are not always the prevailing virtues. The exceptions are rare. It is unlikely that witnesses called upon to support the claims of a common-law marriage possess any greater claim to morality and integrity than those on whose behalf they testify, particularly, if the estate is substantial enough to make perjury profitable."

212 Weyrauch, *supra* note 22, at 98-99. In Shaw, *supra* note 1, at 581-582, the author states: "These promising pecuniary benefits could lead many meretricious partners to the courthouse to assert a common law marriage where none ever existed. An opportunist could take advantage of a meretricious living arrangement, allege a common law marriage, and bring a divorce action in the hope of forcing a lucrative property settlement. Even more likely would be claims made against the alleged deceased spouse's estate where the only other 'party to the contract' is unavailable to deny the existence of an agreement." *See also* Caudill, *supra* note 150, at 562; and *Dubler, supra* note 36, at 1902.

213 *See* FREEDMAN, *supra* note 210, at 104, with respect to "changing social viewpoint toward common law marriage."

214 *See* Goldberg, *supra* note 35, at 486. *See also* Dubler, *supra* note 35, at 964, who states: "With the rise of the conniving adventuress as the prototypical female in the minds of lawmakers came the fall of common law marriage."

215 In *Collins v. Hoag & Rollins Inc.*, 122 Neb. 805, 241 N.W. 766, 767 (Neb. 1932), the Nebraska Supreme Court stated the following: "It is a matter of common knowledge that for many years the estates of deceased persons have been despoiled by persons claiming to be a common-law spouse of decedent, or an heir-at-law of decedent, born of a common-law marriage. In many cases such claims were in the nature of blackmail. It was no doubt this evil which the legislature sought to correct." Common law marriage was repealed in Nebraska by Chapter 40, Laws (1923).

law marriage for the second time, in 1933, the risk of fraudulent behavior for the purpose of reaching the estate after the deceased persons was cited.[216] The legislature's intervention was preceded by a very well-known and much debated case.[217] Similar reasons appear to have played a role in the repeal in New Jersey, in 1939[218] and in Indiana, in 1958.[219] The same reason recurs even in the repeal in Ohio in 1991 and in Pennsylvania in 2005. The risk of misuse, with cohabiting couples receiving benefits based on their marital status, by sometimes stating to authorities that they are unmarried and, alternatively, that they are spouses in a common law marriage, was also raised.[220] However, it ought to be noted that available

---

216 According to the minority leader in the Senate, Mr. Fearon, who presented the proposal as to the repeal of common law marriage in New York, the Governor stated that its purpose was "to prevent fraudulent claims against estates" and surrogate Foley stated that the members in "the Commission to Investigate Defects in the Law of Estates" were unanimous that "attempts to collect funds from decedents' estates were a fruitful source of litigation," *see Morone v. Morone*, 50 N.Y.2d 481, 429 N.Y.S.2d 592, 596, 407 N.E.2d 438 (1980). In Note, *supra* note 54, at 155, it is argued that common law marriages "have more often been the basis of blackmail and fraudulent claims against the estates of decedents" and that this was the reason for its repeal in New York. *See also* Smith, *supra* note 54, at 366. The same reason was maintained in the literature in the years prior to common law marriage being repealed in Florida in 1968. *See* Williams, *supra* note 9, at 449, who maintains that the majority of cases with respect to common law marriage "involve money claims against the estates of wealthy decedents" and there cited cases.

217 *See In re Estate of Erlanger*, 145 Misc. 1, 259 N.Y.S. 610 (1932). Dubler, *supra* note 35, at 957, maintains, after a thorough analysis of *Erlanger*, that "a revised understanding of femininity – one that viewed women as conniving and deceitful, thus severing the necessary link between wifely performance and a wifely identity – contributed to the demise of common law marriage." *Compare Boyd v. Boyd*, 252 N.Y. 422 (N.Y. 1930), wherein the court held that the validity of a common law marriage "is always open to suspicion. Especially is doubt justified when one of the parties is dead." A common law marriage was found to be established which was an impediment to a later ceremonial marriage.

218 Common law marriage was repealed in New Jersey in 1939, *see* N.J. Stat. Ann. 37:1-10 (West 2003). As commentary to the repeal, the state's Supreme Court stated the following in *Dacunzo v. Edgye*, 19 N.J. 443, 117 A.2d 508, 514 (N.J. 1955): "The many abuses arising from common law marriages, with their effect on public morality, private property rights and the legitimacy of children, called for correction."

219 In *Glasgo v. Glasgo*, 410 N.E.2d 1325 (Ind. App. 1980), the court stated that common law marriage was repealed in Indiana "ostensibly on the grounds that their recognition encouraged fraud and perjury, most notably in actions against decedent's estates and for social security or wrongful death benefits." *See* also Note, *supra* note 10, at 108, which points to the problems with the assessment of cases with respect to workmen's compensation in Indiana.

220 The Supreme Court of Pennsylvania in *Staudenmayer v. Staudenmayer*, 714 A.2d 1016 (Pa. 1998), held that claims for the existence of a marriage in the absence of a certified ceremonial marriage present a fruitful source of perjury and fraud and that Pennsylvania courts have long viewed such claims with hostility. This argument was cited in the legislative materials when common law marriage was abolished in Pennsylvania by legislation effective January 1, 2005. Common law marriages entered into after this date would not be valid, but relationships entered into on or before January 1, 2005, would be recognized. *See* Amendment A3597, House Bill 2719, Senate Bill 985 (2004); 23 PA. CONS. STAT. ANN. § 1103 (West 2005). As to *Ohio*, Ron Mottl, who presented the legislative proposal (HB 32) and who is an attorney with his own practice, stated in a newspaper interview that common law

legislative preparatory works concerning the danger of fraudulent claims and other reasons for the repeal of common law marriage are sparse and caution is required in reaching more general conclusions.[221]

Two objections can be made against the argument that the risk of fraudulent behavior and other misuse is great in the application of common law marriage. First, it ought to be noted that much of the criticism refers to older cases that date from a time when common law marriage could be established on the basis of a simple marriage contract.[222] The development of the requirements of cohabitation and holding out as spouses in addition to the contract, however, was intended to prevent fraudulent claims, as seen in Chapter 8.[223] The idea behind the requirements was that the party who had such objectives was not prepared to sacrifice years of cohabitation in order to reach the other party's wealth. Homer Clark has even stated that if the courts insist on objective proof that the parties openly lived as husband and wife during a longer period,

---

marriage must be repealed "to give some certainty to relationships and to eliminate instances where fraud arises in settling estates." He said in addition that "people always attempt to get part of an estate by claiming a common law arrangement exists," *see* United Press International, April 4, 1991. With an investigation during the legislative work, Judge June Galvin, Lucas County, stated that "people are declaring themselves married for income tax and insurance purposes ... and social security purposes and other times they are single" as when they apply for a credit card, *see* House Civil and Commercial Law 02/05/91. Ohio does not recognize common law marriages commenced after 10 October 1991, *see* R.C. § 3105.13 (B) 1,2 (1991); and *Lyon v. Lyon*, 86 Ohio App.3d 580, 621 N.E.2d 718 (1993).

221 Correct observations concerning the uncertainty in the assertions as to fraudulent claims are made also in Cynthia Grant Bowman, *A Feminist Proposal to Bring Back Common Law Marriage*, 75 Or. L. Rev. 709, 741-742 (1996), who maintains that there is reason "to be suspicious of such generalized claims of fraud."

222 *See, e.g.*, cases in which a cohabitation did not exist, *Matter of Heitman's Estate*, 154 Misc. 838, 279 N.Y.S. 108 (1935) (Pennsylvania law); and *Fisher v. Sweet & McClain*, 154 Pa.Super. 216, 35 A.2d 756, 759, 761 (1944). It ought to be noted that a marriage contract was not found proven and therefore no common law marriage established. *See also Wilmington Trust Co. V. Hendrixen*, 31 Del. 303, 114 A. 215 (1921), which points to the risk for secret marriages.

223 According to *In re Estate of Dallman*, 228 N.W.2d 187, 190 (Iowa 1975), citing *Schilling v. Parsons*, 110 Ind.App. 52, 36 N.E.2d 958, 961 (1941), the establishment of common law marriage without "public acknowledgement" would "open the door to perjury and fraud, deny the parties themselves the protection to which they are each entitled, and jeopardize the sanctity of the basic institution of all civilized society, the home." In *State v. Johnson*, 216 Kan. 445, 532 P.2d 1325 (1975), the court stated that the parties outwardly appeared as husband and wife "only when it was advantageous to assume a marriage posture." Taking this into consideration, the requirement was not proven as to holding out as husband and wife. *See also People v. Lucero*, 747 P.2d 660, 664 (Colo. 1987), where the reason for the requirement of public acknowledgment is "to guard against fraudulent claims of common law marriage." *Compare In re Erickson's Estate*, 75 S.D. 345, 64 N.W.2d 316, 317 (1954), in which the court posited that the parties during a cohabitation which lasted more than 20 years dedicated themselves to "cover[ing] up this socially unacceptable status by falsely representing a marriage relationship to the public." The court continued: "Such marriages are a source of fraud and perjury. They are to be tolerated only and not encouraged," *id.* at 318. More closely with respect to the functions of the requisite of cohabitation, *see* Section 8.3 *supra*.

"there will be no greater risk of fraud or imposition on the court here than in the trial of any other question of fact."[224] No fact ought, however, to be so uncontestable as a registered marriage or partnership, albeit these when entered into *pro forma* can also be problematic.[225]

Second, strictly applied evidentiary requirements can serve the same purpose. As seen in Chapter 9, half of all jurisdictions recognizing common law marriage require clear and convincing evidence for the establishment of such a marriage, an evidentiary requirement that is largely applied to protect against misuse.[226] Even though these requirements, in the case law, do not appear to have been applied very strictly,[227] they have served the stated purpose in many cases. For example, in *Matter of Estate of Atwood* (1998), a woman claimed a portion of the deceased man's estate under the assertion that she was his surviving common law wife. In order to retain a pension after the death of a previous spouse, she had stated that she was unmarried. The court did not find a common law marriage proven and stated: "The notion that she was married for some purposes and not for others is in flagrant contradiction of the public policy behind the high standard of proof required to establish a valid marriage. We conclude, on this record, that no marriage contract was intended."[228]

A particular evidentiary problem arises if a surviving party makes a claim to the estate of the other by citing a common law marriage. In cases in which the survivor is the only witness, there is a risk of perjury. In such cases, a dead man's statute, which forbids the surviving party to testify, can give protection. The policy underlying such a statute is to guard against perjury by living interested witnesses if deceased persons cannot refute the testimony, thus protecting estates against unjust claims. Because few jurisdictions apply the statute, the courts then often refer to information from only one party's side.[229]

---

224 CLARK, *supra* note 18, at 121, who receives support of Vaughn, *supra* note 21, at 1138.

225 The requirement for actual cohabitation has a function to fulfill also with respect to formal marriage, in which the risk for *pro forma* marriages is evident *inter alia* when it comes to the right to immigrate in a country. *Compare* Section 6.5.3 *supra.*

226 *See, e.g., Baker v. Mitchell* (1941), in which the Superior Court in Pennsylvania stated that common law marriages "are a fruitful source of perjury and fraud" and that they therefore ought to be investigated with "great scrutiny." *See also In re Wagner's Estate,* 398 Pa. 531, 59 A.2d 495, 497 (1960). For more concerning the evidentiary requirements, *see* Chapter 9 *supra*; Brown, *supra* note 10, at 139; and *Grossman v. Gangel,* 192 A.D.2d 396, 596 N.Y.S.2d 53, 55, 625 N.E.2d 590 (A.D. 1 Dep't 1993), applying Pennsylvania law. With respect to the evidentiary requirements' application as to implied agreements, *see* Chapter 7 and with temporary visits in common law marriage states, *see* Chapter 10 *supra.*

227 *See* Chapter 9, and the evidentiary requirements' application as to implied agreements in Chapter 7 and with temporary visits in common law marriage states in Chapter 10 *supra.*

228 *Matter of Estate of Atwood,* 577 N.W.2d 60 (Iowa App. 1998).

229 *See also* Kirkpatrick, *supra* note 10, at 46. The Dead Man's Statute was applied in *Matter of Estate of Crenshaw,* 100 P.3d 568 (Colo.App. 2004).

This investigation, though lacking any quantitative statistical investigation, covers more than one thousand American cases from the 1800s and 1900s. The conclusion does not support the premise that fraudulent behavior has been as extensive as claimed, even though one cannot ignore that such a risk always exists within private law and particularly with respect to a claim directed against a deceased's estate. A number of courts have refused to recognize unmarried cohabitating parties' rights to file a lawsuit with respect to loss of consortium with reference to problems of proof and dangers of fraudulent claims.[230]

The risk of misuse appears to be greater within public law in which the parties can have a joint interest in receiving social benefits or tax advantages by submitting incorrect information, to the effect either that they are single or that they are cohabiting, whichever is most beneficial to the goal of claiming the most advantageous status.[231] In *PNC Bank Corp. v. Workers' Compensation Appeal Board (Stamos)* (2003), the Commonwealth Court of Pennsylvania refused to recognize common law marriage any longer, stating: "In hearing cases such as this, we have been struck by the tendency of litigants in these matters to view common law marriage as something rather like a legal raincoat they can put on and take off as changing circumstances dictate. We see records in which couples have told one side of the family that they were married and the other side that they were not, depending upon what each collection of relatives might approve. Other couples may swear in applying for benefits that they are man and wife, but file tax returns averring under penalty of perjury that they are single. One attorney in oral argument, when asked how he could explain affidavits to the IRS inconsistent with the testimony of his client in the litigation then before the court, replied matter-of-factly that he

230 *Elden v. Sheldon*, 46 Cal.3d 267, 279, 250 Cal.Rptr. 254, 758 P.2d 582 (1988). *Compare Dunphy v. Gregor*, 136 N.J. 99, 642 A.2d 372 (1994), where though court did not see any problem by allowing a cohabitant recovery for the negligent infliction of emotional distress.

231 *See United States v. Seay*, 718 F.2d 1279 (4th Cir. 1983) ("fraudulently obtaining federal welfare benefits by claiming the status of widow"); and *Matter of Estate of Brack*, 121 Mich.App. 585, 329 N.W.2d 432 (1982). In *Glasgo v. Glasgo*, 410 N.E.2d 1325 (Ind.App. 1980), the court stated that common law marriage was repealed in Indiana "ostensibly on the grounds that their recognition encouraged fraud and perjury, most notably in actions against decedent's estates and for social security or wrongful death benefits." See *also* Note, *supra* note 10, at 108, which points to the problems with the assessment of cases regarding workmen's compensation in Indiana. *See also In re Gholson's Estate*, 83 Idaho 270, 361 P.2d 791 (1961); *In re Estate of Malli*, 260 Iowa 252, 149 N.W.2d 155, 159 (1967); and *In re Long's Estate*, 251 Iowa 1042, 102 N.W.2d 76, 81 (1960). In *Gammelgaard v. Gammelgaard*, 247 Iowa 979, 77 N.W.2d 479, 483 (1956), the court stated concerning the man's attempts in certain contexts to appear as married and in others as unmarried: "Here is a showing of an apparent attempt by the defendant to secure the advantages of the marital status without its responsibilities." When a common law marriage was found proven, the man also received the responsibility. *See also In re Trope's Estate*, 190 Okla. 453, 124 P.2d 733, 735-736 (1942); and *People v. Spencer*, 85 Mich. 127, 165 N.W. 921, 923 (1917).

assumed it lowered their tax liability. What is truly astonishing is not that parties take inconsistent positions to gain advantage, but that they seem to see nothing particularly inappropriate in their chameleon-like behavior. We must conclude that this court can no longer place its imprimatur on a rule which seems to be a breeding ground for such conduct and its attendant disrespect for the law itself."[232]

Extensive fraud may have been revealed in the assessment of social benefits in England.[233] If the parties have provided different information concerning their marital status, this has sometimes also affected the civil law assessment with the result of no common law marriage being established at civil law. However, there are also cases in which the parties received benefits as single persons but have been found to live in a common law marriage or in a cohabitation.[234] A special form

---

232 *PNC Bank Corp. v. Workers' Compensation Appeal Bd. (Stamos)*, No. 860 C.D. (2003), at 17-18. *Compare Staudenmayer v. Staudenmayer*, 714 A.2d 1016 (Pa. 1998), in which the Pennsylvania Supreme Court applied common law marriage principles but did not find the existence of such a marriage proven. *See also In Fuentes v. Transamerican Nat'l Gas Corp.*, 933 S.W.2d 624, 627-628 (Tex.App.-San Antonio 1999), wherein Judge Rickhoff held: "I would hold that one cannot both declare to be single and married. One cannot drop in and out of marriage based on the financial opportunities or advantages that status presents on different days."

233 In England, 46,000 cases of fraud were found in 1975 concerning the application of "the cohabitation rule" when trying social benefits in accordance with the Supplementary Benefits Act. This disclosure entailed a savings of £ 887,900, *see* Joan Lunn, *Living Together - Is It Worth It?*, 127 N.L.J. 306 (1977). The omission as to stating the commencement of cohabitation was considered in 1990 to be one of "the principal offences," *see* C. Barker, P. Watchman and J. Rowan-Robertson, *Social Security abuse*, Social Policy & Administration 24(2):104. The Secretary of State for Social Security stated in 1995 that "the second largest fraud loss – almost £450 million – is people who claim as if they were single while living as a couple," *see* Harris, *supra* note 126, at 130; FREEMAN & LYON, *supra* note 157, at 79-80; and Note, *supra* note 209, at 547 ("administrative bodies are burdened by superfluous work"). In the United States, the abuse of the right to workmen's compensation for survivors in common law marriages has been criticized, *see* Report of Special Committee on Workmen's Compensation, 20 PA. B. ASS'N Q. 93, 98-99 (1934); and FREEDMAN, *supra* note 210, at 103-104.

234 *See Baynes v. Baynes*, 219 Ga.App. 848, 467 S.E.2d 195 (1996). *See also Matter of Estate of White*, 212 Mont. 228, 686 P.2d 915 (1984), in which the deceased woman received social security benefits as unmarried and the surviving man "listed himself as unmarried or single in his applications for insurance, social security, and other public assistance benefits." The court did not find that a common law marriage had been established. *See also In re Cummings Estate*, 330 Pa.Super. 255, 479 A.2d 537 (1984), in which the surviving woman claimed a part of the deceased man's estate in the capacity as common law wife. At the same time, she had stated that she was single to the Department of Public Welfare from which she received welfare benefits. The man had stated to the tax authorities that he was unmarried. The court did not find a common law marriage proven with clear and convincing evidence. *See also Eagle v. W.C.A.B. (Bahorich)*, 602 A.2d 387, 388 (Pa. Commw. 1992), in which the court stated that if the marriage presumption had been applicable, it had been rebutted by the uncontested evidence concerning the parties' contemporaneous representation to government agencies of their unmarried status. *See also Hamby v. J.R. Simplot Co.*, 94 Idaho 794, 498 P.2d 1267 (1972); and Chapter 9, *supra*. *Compare Oliver v. Landry*, 326 S.W.2d 923 (Tex.Civ.App. 1959), in which the requirement of holding out as spouses was considered fulfilled, despite the fact that the woman

of misuse of common law marriage has also arisen within the penal law.[235]

The courts' application of the requirements of cohabitation and holding out, as well as a higher evidentiary requirement, certainly limit but do not eliminate the risk for fraudulent behavior and other abuse.[236] The same reasoning has triggered criticism against the cohabitation legislation proposed by the American Law Institute in 2002.[237] Though these risks should not be exaggerated, as they were in the American debate during the first part of the 1900s, they should be assessed by each legislator if he or she considers the use of common law marriage or other cohabitation legislation.

14.3.3 Undermining Marriage, the Family, and the Community

Part of the criticism directed against common law marriage at the end of the 1800s and primarily during the first part of the 1900s is the view that common law marriage undermines marriage, the family, and the entire community. This criticism is based on the belief that marriage and the family are the cornerstones upon which the community and the entire civilization rests, an understanding which the United States Supreme Court has expressed on several occasions. For example, in *Maynard v. Hill* (1888), the Court stated that marriage is the most important relationship in life and the foundation of the family and of society, without which there

---

every year to the Veterans Administration of the United States stated that she was unmarried and therefore received a widow's pension after another previously deceased man. *Compare* the Swedish case NJA 1994 p. 256, in which a man and a woman were registered at different addresses, but in which the Swedish Supreme Court nevertheless found that the parties were cohabiting persons as they actually primarily had a joint permanent residence. The woman was found therefore to be entitled to insurance compensation upon the man's death. During the cohabitation, the woman and the man at the same time had received social benefits and tax advantages in the capacity as single persons.

235 A special form of criminal abuse was observed in Chapter 5 *supra*, where the offensive consequences arising in the case law was discussed, particularly when a man prosecuted for sexual relations with a minor could be freed from responsibility by maintaining that they lived in a common law marriage. The explanation hereto lies, as stated, not only in the low age limit but also in the fact that a common law marriage can be established on the basis of an inferred agreement and a limited actual cohabitation. It then can be tempting that as an objection against a prosecution throw out a statement that the parties had been united in a common law marriage. The problem however can to a great extent be solved, as seen from Chapter 7 *supra*, by enacting a marital age exceeding the age that is relevant in the sexual criminal offense.

236 *Compare* Kirkpatrick, *supra* note 10, at 47-48: "Even in those jurisdictions requiring the elements of cohabitation or open assumption of marital obligations and duties, the opportunities for fraud are only slightly reduced."

237 Garrison, *supra* note 38, at 850.

would be neither civilization nor progress.[238] The courts have made similar statements upon different occasions during the 1900s.[239]

Even though the court in *Maynard* did not directly express itself as being against common law marriage, the state courts have invoked similar arguments against the common law marriage doctrine. For example, in *Offield v. Davis* (1902), the Virginia Supreme Court stated: "It is wholly at variance with the ideas of our people as to the requisites of a valid marriage. The question before us involves the best interests of society, the preservation of home and family, the foundation of all society."[240] Other courts, in their criticism, have targeted marriage's moral content and argued that common law marriage is in conflict. For example, in *Huard v. McTeigh* (1925), the Oregon Supreme Court stated that the doctrine of common-law marriage is contrary to public policy and public morals: "It places a premium upon illicit cohabitation and offers encouragement to the harlot and adventuress. We do not sanction loose marriages or easy divorces."[241] One can trace the church's influence on marriage in the moral argument and the concern that relationships outside of formal marriage can negatively affect the stability of families, which was considered to be a misfortune not only for families but also for the community's stability. It would be, according to this logic, unworthy to grant couples rights of marriage if they have refused to give a formal and holy promise

238 *Maynard v. Hill*, 125 U.S. 190, 211, 8 S.Ct. 723, 31 L.Ed. 654 (1888). In the case of *In re McLaughlin's Estate*, 4 Wash. 570, 30 P. 651, 657 (1892), the court stated that marriage encompasses "the best interests of society and the preservation of the home and family – the foundation of all society." *See earlier Dunbarton v. Franklin*, 19 N.H. 257, 264-265 (1848), in which the court speaks of the marriage contract on which the rights and duties of the whole community depend. *See also Parke v. Parke*, 25 Haw. 397 (1920).

239 In *Griswold v. Connecticut*, 381 U.S. 479, 486 (1965), the court stated: "Marriage is a coming together for better and for worse, hopefully enduring, and intimate to the degree of being sacred. It is an association that promotes a way of life, not causes; a harmony in living, not political faiths; a bilateral loyalty, not commercial or social projects. Yet it is an association for as noble a purpose as any involved in our prior decisions." *See also Loving v. Virginia*, 388 U.S. 1, 12 (1967). There marriage is characterized as "one of the 'basic civil rights of man,' fundamental to our very existence and survival." In *Boddie v. Connecticut*, 401 U.S. 371, 374 (1971), the court referred to "the basic position of the marriage relationship in this society's hierarchy of values."

240 *Offield v. Davis*, 100 Va. 250, 40 S.E. 910 (1902). *See also In re McLaughlin's Estate*, 4 Wash. 570, 30 P. 651, 657 (1892), wherein the court referred to "the best interest of society and the preservation of the home and family, —the foundation of all society."

241 *Huard v. McTeigh*, 113 Or. 279, 232 P. 658, 663 (1925). The case is cited in *Bridgman v. Stout*, 5 Ore.App. 558, 485 P.2d 1101, 1102 (1971). *See also In re Robert's Estate*, 58 Wyo. 438, 133 P.2d 492 (1943). Already in *Grisham v. State*, 10 Tenn. 588, 594 (1831), the court stated: "The common law is the guardian of the morals of the people." *See also Dennison v. Dennison*, 35 Md. 361 (1871), wherein the court stated: "These loose and irregular contracts as a general thing, derive no support from morals or religion, but are most generally founded in a wanton and licentious cohabitation. Hence the law of the state has given them no sanction."

of lifelong fidelity to each other and instead chose to commence what is perceived as a loose relationship.[242]

The perception that common law marriage undermines marriage, the family, and the entire community became one of the main arguments against common law marriage in the literature also during the first part of the 1900s. George Howard, who encouraged a legislative revolution against common law marriage, stated in 1904, that "the supposed right of the individual must yield to the higher claims of society. In no part of the whole range of human activity is there such imperative need of state interference and control as in the sphere of the matrimonial relations."[243] Howard considered the threat against the community to be so strong that it weighed heavier than the legitimacy that children received if their parents' relationship was recognized as a common law marriage: "Far better that children of a delinquent minority should bear the stain of illegitimacy than that the welfare of the whole social body should be endangered."[244]

---

242 Already in *Duncan v. Duncan*, 10 Ohio St. 181, 188, 1859 WL 67 (1859), the court stated that common law marriage "would tend to weaken the public estimate of the sanctity of the marriage relation" and would in addition "place honest, God-ordained matrimony, and mere meretricious cohabitation too nearly on a level with each other." Observe that common law marriage was recognized in Ohio two years later, *see Carmichael v. State*, 12 Ohio St. 553 (1861). The same statement as in the case of *Duncan* recurs 65 years later, without reference, in *Sorensen v. Sorensen*, 68 Neb. 500, 504, 100 N.W. 930 (1904). Already during the 1870s there was an organized campaign in order to protect the community from "marital instability," *see* GROSSBERG, *supra* note 54, at 83. In *Furth v. Furth*, 133 S.W. 1037, 1039 (Ark. 1911), the court stated that the formal marriage "will best foster and protect the home, and promote the sacredness of the marriage relation, which is the foundation of the family and the origin of all forms of government." In *McClish v. Rankin*, 153 Fla. 324, 14 So.2d 714, 717 (Fla. 1943), the court stated: "The law universally condemns cohabitation without the bonds of wedlock and every effort has been made by the state and federal law makers to discourage and thwart it. By such precautions the very foundation of society, the home, has been safeguarded; the destructive results of promiscuity such as illegitimacy and tangled property rights have at least been curtailed." *See also In re Robert's Estate*, 58 Wyo. 438, 133 P.2d 492 (1943). Even in the case of *In re Estate of Soeder*, 7 Ohio App. 271, 220 N.E.2d 547, 562 (1966), the court cites the case of *Duncan* above. In *Dunphy v. Gregor*, 136 N.J. 99, 642 A.2d 372 (1994), the court was also concerned as to that the relationship "may dissolve at any time."

243 HOWARD, *supra* note 57, at 184. From the same time, *see* WILLIAM E. BULLOCK, THE LAW OF DOMESTIC RELATIONS OF THE STATE OF NEW YORK 33 (1898), who was advising the repeal *inter alia* as he considered common law marriage to be immoral and that it led to divorces. Somewhat earlier *see also* Frank Gaylord Cook, *The Marriage Celebration in the United States*, 61 Atlantic Monthly 520 (1888). *See later* WILLYSTINE GOODSELL, A HISTORY OF THE FAMILY AS A SOCIAL INSTITUTION 358 (1924), who argued that "no legislative reform is more needed than clear and positive statutes declaring such loosely contracted unions null and void." In Note, *supra* note 27, at 548, it is maintained there that a repeal of common law marriage would have "laid a foundation for greater appreciation of the morals and sanctity surrounding the status of marriage." Kirkpatrick, *supra* note 10, at 48, argues that common law marriages "offend the sense of decency and morality of the overwhelming majority of our citizens."

244 HOWARD, *supra* note 57, at 184. *Compare Anderson v. Anderson*, 235 Ind. 113, 131 N.E.2d 301, 307 (1956), in which the court stated: "It is regrettable that the parties

Similar arguments recur in the 1920s when Frank Keezer stated: "There should always be either a religious ceremony or a civil celebration and all marriages by simple consent should be declared void on the ground of public policy. Such marriages are contrary to the principles of sound morality ..."[245]

The understanding of common law marriage as something immoral also refers back to the notion of a cohabitation commenced prior to and outside a marriage, which was historically condemned and criminalized in many states, as examined in Chapter 8. That the relationship could be recognized as marriage after a period of cohabitation roused moral indignation. Otto Koegel stated in 1922: "A doctrine that requires two persons to fornicate a number of times before they create a legal status is absurd. Must they live together as husband and wife before they are husband and wife and this too in the face of a provision of the criminal law that persons who do this without first being married are guilty of a crime."[246] Even in the 1960s, Graham Kirkpatrick argued that the most potent objection against common law marriage is the fact that they "offend the sense of decency and morality of the overwhelming majority of our citizens."[247]

The above-stated and somewhat sweeping arguments against common law marriages give a basis for the following objections. To the degree that the criticism is directed against common law marriages as a legal construction, it ought be noted that this type of marriage gives the same legal effects as formal marriage. It follows then that spouses in a common law marriage are subjected to the same obligations as formally married spouses. Consequently, they owe each other fidelity. They are obligated to contribute to each other's maintenance and, with respect to certain dispositions, obtain the consent of the other party. They are obligated, in the same manner as formally married spouses, to distribute any property upon the marriage's dissolution by divorce and in the event of death. They are, in addition, subjected to the same restrictive divorce regulations as the latter. Their children are legitimate and have the same rights as the children of formally married parents. Against this background, it cannot reasonably be argued that the system's legal effects and the moral values upon which it rests damage marriage, the family, or the community. Because the legal effects of marriage through common law marriage are also applicable to couples who have not formalized their relationship, it clearly can be argued that, in actuality, common law marriage fulfills a moral function that formal marriage is not capable of. The canon law strategy,

---

had a child born out of wedlock, but this court does not sit as the General Assembly to legitimize all children born under such circumstances."

245 KEEZER, FRANK H., A TREATISE ON THE LAW OF MARRIAGE AND DIVORCE 81-82 (2d ed. 1923); and MORLAND, *supra* note 10, at 59 ("It cheapens marriage and gives instability to the home").

246 KOEGEL, *supra* note 97, at 128. *Compare* Weyrauch, *supra* note 22, at 98.

247 Kirkpatrick, *supra* note 10, at 48.

to capture the lost sheep within marriage's moral system through the use of common law marriage can, in a world of decreasing rates of marriage, be attractive to conservative forces who are protective of the morals of the community.

With respect to the spouses' actual observance of those regulations applicable to common law marriage, there is a considerable lack of clarity. Marriage registers lack information concerning commenced and dissolved common law marriages. Even though, as can be seen herein, parties request marital divorce and all the rights tied to this, they often do not know that they are living in a common law marriage; there is reason to assume that many separate without actually formally requesting a marital divorce.[248]

Objections can also be raised to the extent that the above criticism is directed not against common law marriages as a legal construction and its legal effects, but rather against those who enter into such a marriage and against the immorality of their refusal to enter into a marriage before a church or a civil wedding officiator and in the presence of witnesses. The requirements for a common law marriage to be established entail, consequently, that the parties in principle must have been in agreement to a marital life together or to establish a legal relationship. From Chapter 8, it was seen that the parties to an oral contract sometimes use the words. "Under the eyes of God we are husband and wife." In Chapter 7, we found that the majority of marriage contracts were implied agreements based on the parties' marital actions. We also found, in Chapter 8, that the majority of jurisdictions, in addition to the contract, also require that the parties live together, outwardly appear together and gain a reputation as spouses. Even though the courts sometimes have taken an altogether loose approach to these conditions, it is still a question of moral demands with respect to a marital cohabitation and a marital reputation placed on the parties for them to qualify as spouses. Because no such requirements are placed on couples who formally marry, one can state that a marriage-like common law marriage must be more marriage-like than a marriage itself for the legal effects to be granted. From this perspective, the moral arguments against those who live in common law marriage lose a great deal of their force.

The understanding that common law marriage does not debase marriage but rather strengthens it was expressed during the increase of informal marriages in the beginning of the 1800s[249] and gained added

248 *See* Barbara Mobley, note 148.

249 As against the criticism that common law marriage would damage marriage, the New Hampshire Supreme Court objected already in 1820 that "the purity and sacredness of the marriage contract will remain not less but rather more inviolate", *see Londonderry v. Chester*, 2 N.H. 268, 281 (1820). By way of exception, a similar understanding is expressed in the beginning of the 1900s, *see* Black, *supra* note 54, at 131-132: "The recognition of common law marriage does not involve the

credibility at the end of the 1900s when the attitudes towards unmarried cohabiting persons changed and the legislation began to be enacted. Homer Clark stated, in 1968 and repeated in 1987: "When a woman has performed the obligations of a wife for thirty-five years and then is brutally deprived of all the financial benefits of marriage on the sole ground that the relationship was not signalized by some sort of ceremony, this debases marriage. It is far better in such a case to hold that the parties were married."[250] The moral argument that common law marriage would promote sin was thus transformed to the opposite.[251]

As attitudes towards cohabitation outside of marriage have changed during the past thirty years, and such cohabitations have become much more common, the morally tinged arguments against common law marriages have lost a great deal of their strength. The church's influence on the commencement of marriage has decreased. The feeling that common law marriage would be something unholy and impure is not expressed in the same manner. Attitudes towards sex outside of marriage have radically changed.[252] The legislation criminalizing unmarried cohabiting persons has been repealed in most jurisdictions.[253] Morality does not

---

abandonment of ceremonial marriage. That form is sustained by social pressure and it is only by simulating it that irregular unions escape censure and ostracism".

250 CLARK, *supra* note 18, at 122. Shaw, *supra* note 1, at 585, also argues that two persons who live together "as husband and wife" cannot "debase" marriage. In a similar manner, Caudill argues that the state can work for "public morality" through "a recognition of both formal and informal relationships that develop the moral community of love that is characteristic of traditional marriage" and that "common-law marriage may actually reinforce the institution of marriage by its focus on the essence of a relationship," *see supra* note 150, at 560 and 563. *See also* Bowman, *supra* note 18, at 737. Sonya C. Garza, *Common Law Marriage: A Proposal for the Revival of a Dying Doctrine,* 40 NEW ENG. L. REV. 541 (2005-2006), states that recognition of common law marriage "does not diminish the importance of the institution of marriage but bolsters it."

251 CLARK, *supra* note 198, at 58: "The assertion that common law marriage encourages vice is also fallacious, since common law marriage has precisely the opposite effect. Recognizing non-ceremonial unions gives them status and to that extent reduces vice." This statement is repeated again in the second edition, at 121 (2d ed. 1987).

252 With respect to the changed attitudes towards sex, *see* Bowman, *supra* note 18, at 744 and therein cited literature.

253 Already in 1962, the American Law Institute refrained from defining in the Model Penal Code (Proposed Official Draft, May 4, 1962) unmarried cohabiting persons as a crime, which ought to have been influential as to the development. *See also In re Lane,* 58 Cal.2d 99, 22 Cal.Rptr. 857, 372 P.2d 897 (1967); *State v. Saunders,* 75 N.J. 200, 381 A.2d 333 (1977); H. Jay Folberg, & William P. Buren, *Domestic Partnership: A Proposal for Dividing the Property of Unmarried Families,* 12 WILLAMETTE L.J. 453, 458 (1976); Mary Ann Glendon, *Marriage and the State: The Withering Away of Marriage,* 62 VA. L. REV. 663, 685 note 91 (1976); and Note, *supra* note 157, at 359. In the beginning of the 1980s, the criminalization of unmarried cohabitation in isolated states still existed, *see* Fineman, *supra* note 25; and Kandoian, *supra* note 37, at 1830. Today fornication remains a crime in a few states, *see* IDAHO CODE ANN. § 18-6603 (Michie 2003); MASS. GEN. LAWS 272-18 (2003); S.C. CODE ANN. § 16-15-60 (Law. Coop. 2003); UTAH CODE ANN. §76-7-104 (Michie 2003); W. VA. CODE ANN. § 61-8-3 (2002); MISS. CODE ANN. § 97-29-1 (2003); N.C. GEN. STAT. ANN. § 14-184 (2003); and ILL. COMP. STAT. ANN. § 5/11-8. (2003). The crime is never, or

require formal marriage as strongly as one hundred years ago. It is not commonly considered to be a stigma to live together without marrying.[254] The courts have increasingly rejected morally tinged reasoning. In *Marvin v. Marvin* (1976), the court stated that the attitudes towards persons cohabiting without marriage have radically changed and rejected each "standard based on alleged moral considerations that have apparently been so widely abandoned by so many."[255] At the same time, there are courts denying recovery to surviving cohabitants for the wrongful death of a partner by referring to the fact that such awards would interfere with the state's interest in promoting marriage.[256]

It would be interesting to see academic research concerning the significance of formal vows and the entire ceremonial marriage for the spouses' feelings toward commitment and the stability of families.[257]

---

substantially never, the subject of prosecution, *see, e.g., Fort v. Fort,* 12 Mass.App.Ct. 411, 425 N.E.2d 754 (1971).

254 Smith, *supra* note 54, at 367. *See also* Caudill, *supra* note 150, at 570 ("the shameful aspects of cohabitation are disappearing from our society"); Reppy, *supra* note 19, at 1708 ("Cohabitation has become acceptable in most parts of the country"); and Vaughn, *supra* not 21, at 1139 ("modern society's growing acceptance of unmarried cohabitation").

255 *Marvin v. Marvin,* 134 Cal. Rptr. 815, 18 Cal.3d 660, 557 P.2d 106, 122 (1976). As common law marriage has been repealed in California, this concerned the woman's right "to enforce contracts and to assert her equitable interest in property." *Compare Hewitt v. Hewitt,* 77 Ill.2d 49, 394 N.E.2d 1204, 1207 (1979), which concerned whether a recognition of the cohabitating parties' property rights would affect "our society and the institution of marriage" and whether this would mean a reinstatement of common law marriage. Still in *Jolley v. Jolley,* 46 Ohio Misc. 40, 347 N.E.2d 557, 560 (1975), the court stated: "Most cases mention that common law marriage contravenes public policy and should not be accorded any favor. In fact it is generally condemned." *See also Succession of Batiste,* 145 So.2d 668, 669 (La.App. 4th Cir. 1962).

256 *See Elden v. Sheldon,* 46 Cal.3d 267, 279, 250 Cal.Rptr. 254, 758 P.2d 582 (1988). *Compare Dunphy v. Gregor,* 136 N.J. 99, 642 A.2d 372 (1994)(court did not see any problem allowing a cohabitant recovery for negligent infliction of emotional distress); and *Lozoya v. Sanchez,* 66 P.2d 948 (N.M. 2003)(loss of consortium).

257 Assumptions as to the effects of the promise are not lacking, *see, e.g.,* Anders Agell, *Family forms and legal policies,* 38 Sc. St. L. 197, 205 (1999), who states: "The formation of a marriage might have some beneficial influence on family stability since the partners, by going through with a wedding ceremony making mutual promises to stay together, should have thereby decided upon the character of their relationship." *Compare* Julie Brines and Kara Joyner, *The Ties That Bind: Commitment and Stability in Modern Union,* 64 Am. Soc. Rev. 333 (1999), who argue that the underlying "contract" of cohabitation is more fragile than that of marriage. *See also* Björnberg, *supra* note 179, at 352, who states that the consensual unions' instability could indicate that persons in such unions "have a more individualized commitment to their family unions. It could be an indication of a lower commitment to the relationship or a lower degree of tolerance of a poorly functioning relationship." Nancy F. Cott, Public Vows: A History of Marriage and the Nation 2 (2000), states: "In the marriage ceremony the public recognizes and supports the couple's reciprocal bond..." Elisabeth S. Scott, *Marriage, Social Norms and the Legal Regulation of Marriage,,* 86 Va. L. Rev. 1901, 1907 (1998), finds that the spouses "agree to be subject to a complex set of behavioral expectations defining the roles of spouse and parent..."

To what extent has the *consensus* fossilized in its forms?[258] The rate of marital divorce in the United States does not support the assumption that the significance would be particularly considerable. At the same time, it would be interesting to see what effect the formless promise has on parties who believe that their relationship is not held together by any formal ceremony because they believe that their bond rests on their own love and convictions, and not on social pressures and legal coercion. There are no statistics about the rate of dissolution in common law marriage. On the other hand, there is a certain support for the idea that the frequency of dissolution among unmarried cohabiting persons is higher than that of married persons.[259] Children born to cohabiting parents seem to experience greater risk that their parents will end their relationship than children born to married parents.[260]

If common law marriage, as long as it contains the same legal effects as formal marriage, in principle, cannot be said to constitute a threat, the issue arises whether cohabitation legislation, which has more limited legal effects, does entail such a threat. In a country such as Canada, which has enacted a large body of cohabitation law, there are such opinions, albeit not dominating.[261] Critiques of the ALI Principles have also contended

---

258 *Compare Estate of Neiderhiser*, 2 Pa.D.C.3d 302 (1977), where the man died during the wedding ceremony before the pronouncement of marriage by the minister. As the parties had already exchanged their vows before the collapse of the man, they had entered into a valid contract of marriage. The woman became wife and widow upon the same occasion.

259 European studies estimate that cohabiting unions are more fragile than marital unions and that children born within marriage were less likely to see their parents separate than those born in a cohabiting union, *see* Kiernan, *supra* note 74, at 46-47. Other studies shows that in Sweden, where more than half (54% in 1998) of all children are born outside of marriage and approximately 90% of them are living with their parents, the frequency of dissolution among cohabiting persons with children in 1991 was three times as high as among married persons with children, *see* Be 13, SM 9401, SCB 1994. According to an investigation as to the year 1997, the risk for separation was almost double as large among cohabiting persons as among married persons, *see* SCB, Demografiska rapporter 1999:1. Even according to American studies, cohabitation relations are less stable than marriages. Over 50% of cohabiting relationships in the U.S. end by separation within five years compared to around 20% for marriages, *see* Larry Bumpass & Hsien-Hen Lu, *Trends in Cohabitation and Implications for Children's Family Contexts in the United States,* 54 POPULATION STUD. 29 (2000). *See also* Judith A. Seltzer, *Families Formed Outside of Marriage,* 62 J. MARRIAGE & FAM. 1247, 1252 (2000); Larry L. Bumpass et al., *The Role of Cohabitation in Declining Rates of Marriage,* 53 J. MARRIAGE & FAM. 913, 917 (1991); and Pamela J. Smock, *Cohabitation in the United States: An Appraisal of Research Themes, Findings, and Implications,* 26 ANN. REV. SOC. 1, 13 (2000). Even Canadian investigations shows that marriage is more stable than unmarried cohabitation, *see* Bailey, *supra* note 165, at 30 and 35.

260 *See* Manning & Smock, *supra* note 23, at 94.

261 As to Canada, *see* Bailey *id.* at 11, who states that: "Some take the view that marriage is fundamental to the stability and well-being of the family and that extending marital rights and obligations to unmarried couples undermines the family to the detriment of society. Others argue that some non-marital relationships are equally worthy of support and contribute equally to the stability and well-being of the family and other state objectives." The reluctance in the province of Alberta to give

that the proposed domestic partnership undermines traditional marriage. The strongest criticism has been delivered by Pope Benedict XVI against the Italian proposal in 2007, in which the Italian government proposed new legislation for same-sex and unmarried heterosexual couples, stating: "No man-made law can subvert one made by the Creator without society being dramatically damaged in its very foundation."[262]

A pervading feature in the cohabitation legislation which has grown since the 1970s around the world is that it contains rights with respect to the economic division upon separation, but on the other hand, no regulations as to marital divorce. The parties commonly need not subject themselves to any procedure with restrictive regulations concerning the protection of family stability. If couples creating families choose to simply cohabitate instead of marrying, they are free to at any time leave the relationship even though they have mutual children. It has been assumed that an important reason why couples do not marry is that one or both parties desire an "easy out" if the relationship does not hold.[263]

This possibility must frustrate states that view family stability as a central state interest and have divorce regulations designed to protect marriage, the family, and the community. One can ask, Why shouldn't long-term cohabiting couples who have mutual children observe the same restrictions, upon separating, as married couples who proceed with a marital divorce? For many states, protecting the stability of families must therefore be an argument against cohabitation legislation lacking any regulation of dissolution.[264]

This raises the essential question for each legislator, today, of whether cohabitation legislation, in general, affects the rate of marriage and undermines marriage, because such legislation endeavors to include parties and families within the more extensive legal protections and divorce regulations

---

the same regulations for cohabitation as for marriage has been based on the argument that it would undermine marriage as the basis of family life, *see* Le Bourdais and Lapierre-Adamcyk, *supra* note 161, at 929-942.

262 *La Chiesa sul DICO: Sí o No?*, Whispering in the Loggia, Monday, February 19, 2007; Göran Lind, *Legislation for the Surviving Cohabitant in Comparative Perspective,* in European Challenges in Contemporary Family Law (K. Boele-Woelki and T. Sverdrup eds., European Family Law Series No. 10, Antwerp 2008); Lynn Kohm, *How Will Proliferation and Recognition of Domestic Partnerships Affect Marriage?*, 4 J.L. & Fam. Stud. 105 (2002); and Lynn Wardle, *Deconstructing Family: A Critique of the American Law Institute's "Domestic Partners" Proposal,* 2001 BYU L. Rev. 1189.

263 *Compare* however Reppy, *supra* note 19, at 1719, who proposes a simpler proceeding for the dissolution of "lawful cohabitation." *See also* Freeman, & Lyon, *supra* note 157, at 190; Weitzman, *supra* note 31, at 245; and Robert C. Casad, *Unmarried Couples and Unjust Enrichment: From Status to Contract and Back Again?,* 77 MICH. L. REV. 47, 56 (1978).

264 Caudill, *supra* note 150, at 563; *Developments in the Law – The Constitution and the Family,* 93 Harv. L. Rev. 1156, 1243 (1980). *Compare* Douglas, *supra* note 81, at 225, who underlines marriage's duty in English law to create "stability in family relationships," which is anchored in the Royal Commission on Marriage and Divorce Report (1956) as in the Labour Government consultation paper, Supporting Families (1998).

that formal marriage offers. Anders Agell, with respect to Swedish law, has expressed such a concern, stating: "In my view, it is possible, or even likely, that the decrease in the marriage rate and the weakening of the nuclear family in Sweden has been unintentionally promoted by legislation ... The expansion of laws regulating cohabitation is in itself an incentive to cohabitation instead of marriage."[265] Sweden, as seen in Chapter 12, has since the beginning of the 1970s until 2004 had the lowest rate of marriage and the highest number of persons cohabiting outside of marriage in Europe. At the same time, the Swedish legislature, within its social and tax law, has enacted extensive regulations which equate unmarried cohabiting couples with married couples. Within family law, Sweden has a limited system for the division of an estate, which does not purport to give complete equality with spouses but rather only a minimal protection to the cohabiting persons upon separation and in cases of death. The division of the estate encompasses, therefore, in practice only the permanent residence and household goods acquired by the parties during the cohabitation.[266]

Agell's hypothesis, that the growth of cohabitation legislation affects the rate of marriage, undeniably appears reasonable given that all legal solutions outside of the framework for formal marriage ought to make marriage less necessary and attractive if the parties receive the same or a similar protection without marrying. A concern for such an effect has also been intimated by American court decisions, that have considered private law solutions for cohabiting unmarried persons.[267] It is, however, difficult to find empirical scientific support for Agell's line of thought.[268]

If this hypothesis is correct, the rate of marriage should be lowest in jurisdictions that recognize common law marriage and give cohabiting persons all the legal effects of marriage. The parties in a common law marriage ought not have any legal incentive to formally marry. At the same time, if such a state abolishes common law marriage and the parties thus are excluded from the legal protection of marriage, the rate of marriage ought to increase because the parties then have reason to formally marry.

265 Anders Agell, *Should and Can Family Law Influence Social Behaviour?*, in THE CHANGING FAMILY 125, 136 (John Eekelaar and Thandabantu Nhlapo eds. 1998). *See also* Agell, *supra* note 257, at 205-206.

266 *See* THE Swedish COHABITEES ACT (2003:376).

267 *See Hewitt v. Hewitt*, 77 Ill.2d 49, 31 Ill.Dec. 827, 394 N.E.2d 1204, 1207 (1979), in which the court was concerned that a recognition of the cohabiting parties' property rights would affect "our society and the institution of marriage" and that this would mean a reinstatement of common law marriage. *Compare Kozlowski v. Kozlowski*, 80 N.J. 378, 387, 403 A.2d 902 (1979), in which the court denied that this private law solution would affect the rate of marriage.

268 It can be noted that the rate of marriage per 1,000 inhabitants in Sweden the years prior to the enactment of the most important law for cohabiting unmarried persons, in other words, the law (1987:232) as to cohabitee's mutual home, which came into force 1 Jan 1988, was 4.6% (1986), 4.9% (1987) and the years after the enactment was 5.2% (1988) and 4.8% (1990).

TABLE 1. The Rate of Marriage in States Which Have Repealed Common Law Marriage

	The Number per 1,000 Inhabitants			
	1990	*1995*	*1999*	*2001*
Ohio	9.0	8.1	7.9	7.3
Idaho	13.9	13.3	12.3	11.4
Georgia	10.3	8.5	8.0	6.3
United States	9.8	8.9	8.4	8.5

It can, therefore, be of interest to obtain information about the rate of marriage in the three common law marriage states that most recently repealed the doctrine, namely, Ohio in 1990, Idaho in 1995, and Georgia in 1997.

From the table, it can be seen that the rates of marriage in 1990 in the states of Ohio, Idaho, and Georgia, when all three recognized common law marriage, were not lower than in the United States in general. Despite the fact that the parties in a common law marriage could obtain the same legal protection as married persons by simply cohabiting, they chose, as much as couples in other states, to formally marry. Neither did the rates of marriage increase when these states repealed common law marriage. Despite the fact that cohabiting persons had then lost the legal protection common law marriage offered, they did not choose to marry to any increased extent. Instead, the rates of marriage during the 1990s decreased to a large extent in the same manner as in the United States in general. Marriage habits, consequently, appear to be fairly independent of the existence of common law marriage.[269] As the number of unmarried persons cohabiting increased in the entire United States, there is reason to assume that those couples that previously would have lived in a common law marriage in these states, nowadays, are cohabiting unmarried persons. Perhaps lawyers have an exaggerated belief in the significance of legal regulations on the choice of cohabitation.

269 Similar observations were made in 1960 by *Weyrauch*, who maintained: "For example, one would expect common law marriage states to show statistics on licensed marriages below the national average because of the flow of informal marriages being diverted from the county courthouses. The contrary is true. Many common law marriage jurisdictions show statistics on licensed marriages above the national average." Later he states that: "It is not likely that social patterns of family organization will radically change after abolition of common law marriages," *see* Weyrauch, *supra* note 22, at 95 and 107. *See also* Bowman, *supra* note 125, at 146, who states that "the number of cohabitants has been increasing rapidly over the last decades despite substantial financial disincentives."

On the other side, the value of the statistics about the rates of marriage is restricted by the fact that knowledge in the general population about common law marriage and cohabitation legislation in general can be assumed to be limited.[270] The issue of knowledge ought, however, not be considered based on a static perspective. Legislatures also have a significant responsibility to educate and disseminate knowledge with respect to marriages as well as cohabitations. The value of increased knowledge ought not be contested. It would be somewhat strange if the differences in the systems of regulation did not play a certain role as to the choice of cohabitation for those familiar with the options. The choices in individual cases can certainly vary.

In addition, in this context, it should be noted that cohabitations without formal marriage, according to American and Swedish sociologists, seldom are a result of a conscious decision. The Swedish Sociologist Jan Trost stated during the 1970s, when Sweden and Denmark had the highest frequencies of unmarried cohabitations, that: "In today's Sweden and Denmark couples do not choose to cohabit instead of to marry. They just cohabit."[271] The situation often is the same today in Europe as well as in the United States. Many drift into a common law marriage.[272] Even though the parties' actions are not the result of a considered decision, they may be tinged by hidden social, psychological, and cultural factors.[273] This approach contrasts with the optimism, in the beginning of the 1900s, of American sociologists about the possibilities of influencing family behavior through legislation.[274]

270 Reppy, *supra* note 19, at 1682, speaks of "the dubious assumption that persons considering cohabitation are aware of the negative status rules that the law attaches because of such a living arrangement, but also on the assumption that the couple may actually rely on that state of the law as a reason not to cohabit. That later assumption also is not believable." Andrews, *supra* note 160, at 37, maintains that "the legal rules do not seem to play a significant role in people's decision to marry. So why should we assume that they play a significant role in people's decision NOT to marry?"

271 TROST, *supra* note 200, at 186. *See also* Eleanor D. Macklin, *Nonmarital Heterosexual Cohabitation*, MAR. FAM. REV., March-April 1978 at 1, 6 ("Living together is seldom the result of a considered decision... Most cohabitation evolves from a drift of sleeping more and more frequently together and gradual accumulation of possessions in one residence"); Caudill, *supra* note 150, at 565; Kathleen Kiernan, *The Rise of Cohabitation and Childbearing Outside Marriage in Western Europe*, 15 INT'L J.L. POL'Y & FAM. 1, 3 (2001); Blumberg, *supra* note 47, at 1296; and Wendy Manning & Pamela J. Smock, *Measuring and Modeling Cohabitation: New Perspectives From Qualitative Data 26* (Bowling Green Working Paper 10-03 2003) ("the process of deciding to cohabit is not necessarily planned or deliberate").

272 *Compare* CLARK, *supra* note 198, at 57. Bruch, *supra* note 198, at 135, maintains that the majority probably choose to cohabit as unmarried persons "with absolutely no thought given to the legal consequences of their relationship."

273 Reppy, *supra* note 19, at 1682; and Bowman, *supra* note 18, at 753: "Apparently, the law in a particular state does not dictate whether people enter into formal or informal marriages, so much as other social, economic and cultural factors do."

274 *See, e.g.*, George Elliot Howard, *Social Control of Domestic Relations*, 167 A.J.S. 815 (1910), who stated that a good marriage code "tends to check hasty, clandestine, frivolous, and immature wedlock."

The question is then raised whether, in addition to the other arguments discussed in this chapter, it is disadvantageous for the community for cohabiting couples to refrain from formally marrying. If this occurs in a common law marriage state, the parties have the same rights but also the same obligations as spouses. If this occurs in a state with limited cohabitation legislation, or none at all, it can be argued that the cohabiting persons there do not enjoy complete legal protection if they do not have the same rights as spouses. It can further be maintained that they are not placed under the same obligations as married persons, though they should, if they live as spouses. The significance this difference ought to be given depends on which fundamental ideology one assumes. If the choice of cohabitation form is considered a free choice in which the parties themselves ought to be able to decide which system of regulations they wish to subject themselves to, the differences in the system of regulations constitute no serious problem. The parties have, as we know, themselves made their choices. If the starting point, on the other hand, is that cohabiting persons do not make any conscious choice, or that the state ought not accept such a choice without fulfilling the obligation to create a comprehensive system that is moral and suitable, then a decreasing rate of marriage is a problem. For the state, it remains, then, to either encourage the parties to formally marry or introduce common law marriage. For a state with such ambitions, to stop with a limited system with cohabitation legislation, or nothing at all, must appear as unacceptable.

14.3.4 The Absence of the Form's Protective and Clarifying Functions

The form requirements can be said to have a protective function in that they protect the parties concerned from hasty actions.[275] This function must be seen as material if two parties are facing the choice of cohabitation, perhaps one of the most important decisions in their lives. The ceremonial marriage's form requirements, and to some extent, registered forms of cohabitation, perform this function in that they give reason for reflection and serious consideration to the planned relationship's significance. In states in which the commencement of marriage must be preceded by a waiting period of a few days, this is particularly clear.[276] Even the requirement for a license can have the same function. Parties are also protected against undue influence by the requirement of a written form, participation by a person who is authorized to perform a marriage, and the presence of witnesses.

The absence of form in the establishment of a common law marriage or a formless cohabitation clearly is a deficiency. Couples, who simply drift

275 *Compare* Thomas, *supra* note 15, at 123.
276 Clark, *supra* note 18, at 86 and 88.

into a relationship and who have not made any legal assessments or taken any actual decisions concerning their cohabitation but rather just cohabit, do not get the same protection against hasty actions. The requirement in Pennsylvania of an oral agreement (*per verba*) to a certain extent can be restraining, particularly if the promises are exchanged in a private ceremony resembling the official ritual. From Chapter 6, it was seen, however, how the parties in extremely private situations (e.g., in the bedroom, kitchen, or automobile) can enter into oral agreements, occasions that can give reason to doubt whether the parties closely considered their vows and their legal consequences.[277] The use of a written form naturally would fulfill a protective function, but unfortunately, as seen in Chapter 6, it is very unusual that the parties in a common law marriage use written marriage contracts.[278] In the majority of cases in which such a marriage has been entered into through an implied agreement based on the parties' actions as spouses, the form's protective function is also absent. The parties do not have any reason to pause and more closely consider the legal course of their cohabitation. Often, they are not conscious as to the point at which all the legal effects of common law marriage suddenly came into force.

At the same time, the requirements of cohabitation, outward appearance, and reputation as spouses—which in different variations apply in the majority of states for the establishment of a common law marriage as discussed in Chapter 8—come to serve functions similar to those of the form requirements. The longer the parties have lived together, the more difficult it is to argue that the relationship was rash.[279] However, it cannot be said that the parties have had reason to consider the legal effects, particularly because their knowledge should have been fairly limited. A comparable lack of knowledge ought to apply to spouses, who enter into a ceremonial marriage. The actual moving in together, many times, ought to be understood to be an important step, but scarcely as a triggering alarm in the same manner as a form requirement.

The form requirements' protective function is absent, if possible, to an even higher degree in the cohabitation legislation, which becomes applicable based on the parties' actual cohabitation, without any requirement about the existence of a marriage contract, either orally or inferred.

The observance of a certain form also has a clarifying function in that the legal status is clarified for the parties. The legal effects are not negotiated by the parties in the manner of a civil law contract, but rather, as a rule, follow from the legislation and the parties' often-limited knowledge,

277 *See* Section 6.5.1 *supra.*

278 *See* Section 6.5.2 *supra.*

279 *Compare* the criticism by S.M. CRETNEY AND J.M. MASSON, PRINCIPLES OF FAMILY LAW 13 (6th ed. 1997), against "hasty and ill-considered marriages" which is based on the fact that the agreement is all that is necessary to form a common law marriage, a fact that is not a reality in most jurisdictions today.

and so the legal status is not clarified simply by the parties entering into a ceremonial marriage. However, the observation of formalities ought commonly express the parties' intent to subject themselves to the legal effects that the state offers when they have obtained marital status. Spouses who have entered into a formal marriage ought to not be unconscious of that fact or of the exact time when their new status arose. The witnesses, the person authorized to perform the wedding ceremony and the marriage certificate are unambiguous. For third parties, it is usually fairly simple to check a person's marital status.[280] At the same time, the wedding ceremony clarifies the state's intent to take control of the spouses' marital relationship.

The absence of the protective and clarifying functions of the formless systems naturally constitutes a serious deficiency of legal certainty. Such a lack of clarity should not occur in the invocation of the legal consequences of one of the most important human relationships, with implications of intimacy, length, and economics. Uncertainty about the parties' status is inconvenient to the entire community. However, it is primarily a problem for the parties themselves to be able to predict if and when a common law marriage or a cohabitation is to be seen to be established and if and when the legal effects have come into force.

The absence of legal certainty has long since been maintained as an argument against common law marriages both in the case law[281] and in the academic literature. Chester Vernier, consequently, proposed its repeal as a result of "too much confusion, conflict, and uncertainty."[282] The goal of achieving clarity through a public registration appears to have played a role with the first repeal of common law marriage in New York in 1901.[283] The argument recurs even in modern times. The most important reason behind the repeal of common law marriage in Idaho in 1995, a state which

280 *See also* Douglas, *supra* note 81, at 211.

281 *See, e.g., In re Estate of Bivians,* 98 N.M. 722, 652 P.2d 744 (1982).

282 Chester G. Vernier, American Family Laws I, 108 (1931). *See also* Schouler (1882), *supra* note 145, at 50, who speaks of "the painful uncertainty which hangs about these informal marriages." In Note, *supra* note 10, at 102, the author stated: "Even the parties themselves are seldom certain of the exact nature of the relationship. Little wonder then that the decision cannot have the degree of certainty desirable. To prove or disprove such a marriage is a momentous task." *See also* Morris Ploscowe, *Family Law,* 35 N.Y.U. L. Rev. 388, 389 n. 7 (1960), who maintains that "many persons will not know whether they are or are not married."

283 New York Times, 30 August 1901, p. 1; Laws of 1901, c. 339, § 6; Domestic Relations Law § 19. Common law marriage was reinstated in New York in 1907 by Laws of 1907, c. 742, § 6. *See also Matter of Zeigler v. Cassidy's Sons,* 220 N.Y. 98, 115 N.E. 471 (1917); by mistake according to Fred S. Hall, *Common Law Marriage in New York State,* 30 Colum. L. Rev. 1, 10 (1930); *Matter of Hinman,* 147 App.Div. 452 (3d Dep't 1911); Morton Keller, Regulating a New Society: Public Policy and Social Change in America, 1900-1933, 18 (1994); and Leon A. Plumb, *Marriage: Common-Law Marriage in New York,* 1 Cornell L.Q. 48, 51 (1915). Common law marriage was again repealed in New York in 1933 by Laws of 1933, c. 606, Domestic Relations Law § 11.

generally did not have a negative attitude toward these marriages, appears to have been the legal uncertainty stemming from the difficulties of predicting if and when a couple could be seen to be living in a common law marriage.[284] The argument appears to have played a role even in the repeal of common law marriage in Ohio in 1991[285] and in Georgia in 1997.[286]

The results of the analyses in Chapters 5 to 11 have demonstrated the dangers, from a perspective of legal certainty, arising from common law marriage and other cohabitation legislation. These include the problem of determining the content in the marriage contract, of proving the existence of an oral agreement (Chapter 6) or an implied agreement (Chapter 7), of investigating the circumstances surrounding the parties' cohabitation, outward appearance and reputation with others (Chapter 8), of determining whether the marriage presumption is applicable respectively rebutted (Chapter 9), of considering whether an impediment against the relationship existed

---

284 With the treatment of the legislative proposal as to the repeal of common law marriage in Idaho (HB 176), an investigation in committee in the Idaho House of Representatives treated the proposal. Typical for the witness testimony is Mr. Bob Aldridge's statement that "there is no certainty or predictability to common law marriage," *see* Judiciary, Rules & Administration Committee, February 15, 1995 – Minutes – page 2. Similar views also came to expression in the Senate investigation in which Judge Patricia Flanagan stated that common law marriage "can be used as a powerful weapon and is a fruitful source of fraud and perjury. Many people think they are common-law married but never really know until they get to court," *see* Senate Judiciary and Rules Committee, March 1, 1995 – Minutes – page 2. In a newsletter, Judge Patricia Flanagan stated: "When a lawyer gets two or three phone calls a week from people wanting to know whether or not they are married, something is wrong. What kind of law do we have in Idaho that creates such uncertainty? ...The present situation invites litigation, confusion and gives rise to great opportunity to fraud," *see* Risks of common law marriage, Impact, Lawyers, Inc., 1994 Spring Newsletter. The objections against the legislative proposal concerned women's rights and children's legitimacy, *see supra* note 41. Common law marriage cannot be entered into in Idaho as of January 1, 1996, *see* H.B. 176; Chap. 104 Idaho Session Laws (1995); and I.C. § 32-201 (1995).

285 Ron Mottl, who presented the legislative proposal (HB 32) and who is an attorney with his own practice, stated in a newspaper interview that common law marriage must be repealed "to give some certainty to relationships and to eliminate instances where fraud arises in settling estates," *see* United Press International, April 4, 1991. Ohio does not recognize common law marriages commenced after 10 October 1991, *see* R.C. § 3105.13 (B) 1,2 (1991). *See also Lyon v. Lyon*, 86 Ohio App.3d 580, 621 N.E.2d 718 (1993).

286 Barbara Mobley, a member of the General Assembly in Georgia, presented with others (Randall, Martin, Falls) the legislative proposal (HB 1278) that led to common law marriage being repealed in Georgia in 1997. As a family law attorney, Mobley stated that couples living in common law marriage did not know that their marriage must be dissolved by formal divorce. This led to couples separating and commencing new relationships without taking out a formal divorce. When one of the parties died "their estate would be in a mess." Barbara Mobley, according to e-mail to the author Feb. 26 2003. *See also* GA. CODE ANN. §§ 19-3-1, 19-3-1.1 (West 1997) prescribing that: "No common-law marriage shall be entered into in this state on or after January 1, 1997. Otherwise valid common-law marriages entered into prior to January 1, 1997, shall not be affected by this Code section and shall continue to be recognized in this state." *Compare Wright v. Goss*, 229 Ga.App. 393, 494 S.E.2d 23, 25 (1997).

many years back in time perhaps based on another formless relationship (Chapter 5), and the difficulties in assessing whether the parties during a short stay in a common law marriage state have entered into such a marriage unawares. All these difficulties are not simply problems for the authorities. They also are problems for the parties themselves in predicting their marital status. As can be seen in Chapter 13, the use of statutes of limitations and presumptions can facilitate the assessments of the courts and the authorities, but they do not remove the difficulties for the parties in predicting the invocation of the legal effects. This, of course, is particularly true for parties who are unaware of the legal status and simply drift into a relationship.

The absence of the protective and clarifying functions with formless relationships stands in sharp contrast to the capacity of formal marriage and registered cohabitations to fill these needs. On the other hand, private law solutions, for example, within the framework of the Marvin doctrine, based on formless implied agreements, can be replete with the same deficiencies as common law marriage or other cohabitation legislation. To instead seek solutions in formless alternatives within the private law can, therefore, exchange one set of problems for another.[287] This leads to the conclusion that a repeal of common law marriage or the avoidance of cohabitation legislation does not guarantee increased legal certainty unless the rate of marriage simultaneously increases.

14.3.5 The Absence of Control of Legal Capacity

The marriage form's control functions appear both at the commencement of the marriage and at its dissolution. The possibility of determining which persons are to have the right to enter into a marriage has constituted one of the state's most important instruments of power to influence the creation of families. The state, for the purpose of preventing the existence of unsuitable relationships and the creation of families, have always required, as discussed in Chapter 5, that the parties are to have the legal competence (capacity) to marry. These requirements, which rest on ethical, religious, medical, and social values, address the parties' ages, sex, consanguinity, monogamy, physical and mental status, etc. The trend now appears to be against further limitations in the form of marital impediments, particularly with respect to physical and mental status as well as race and sex. The discussion is in full swing concerning the possibility of

---

287 Weyrauch, *supra* note 22, at 104 fn. 81 and at 109, states the danger of "the exchange of one ambiguity for other ambiguities." In *Carlson v. Olson*, 256 N.W.2d 249, 251 (Minn. 1977), the Minnesota Supreme Court stated that "[t]he elimination of common-law marriage obviously did not eliminate the institution, but only the rules which must be applied to it." Common law marriage was repealed in Minnesota in 1941. Relationships commenced prior to 26 April 1941 however are valid, *see* Laws 1941, c. 459; Minn. Stat. Ann. 517.01 (West 2003); and *Baker v. Baker*, 222 Minn. 169, 23 N.W.2d 582 (1946).

persons of the same sex being able to marry. Despite this development, the states, in the capacity as a third party to the contract, still have a considerable interest with respect to marital impediments.

Legislators have chosen primarily preventive methods to achieve these objectives with respect to ceremonial marriages. Through a licensing procedure, the state seeks to prevent marriages between parties lacking legal capacity.[288]

Even the establishment of a common law marriage assumes that the parties are competent to enter into a marriage with each other. A common law marriage is informal even to the point that it does not require any licensing procedure to be preceded by a review of whether impediments against the marriage exist. Thus, the question of legal capacity is first assessed only after the commencement of the relationship. This question can be raised, for example, if one party upon a separation or death, presents a claim based on a common law marriage. It can also be raised many years later in connection with litigation concerning the legitimacy of a child. Without a review beforehand of whether impediments against the marriage exist, it appears risky to try to prevent unsuitable common law marriages from arising. The possibility of reaching the objectives of the regulations concerning legal capacity are thus jeopardized.

Despite the presumption to the benefit of the later of two marriages, which opens the possibility of a "poor man's divorce," the conclusion in Chapter 5 was that bigamy from a civil law perspective, ought not to be uncommon as parties commence new common law or ceremonial marriages after a common law marriage. The regulations concerning blood tests and physician certificates in connection with the licensing procedure, which exist in certain states and which *inter alia* purport to prevent the spread of venereal diseases and AIDS, are without effect with respect to common law marriage. Attempts by the Pennsylvania courts to have common law marriages declared invalid on the basis that the requirement of a medical examination has not been fulfilled have failed.[289] The legislator in Pennsylvania has prioritized substance over form.[290]

---

288 *Developments in the Law – The Constitution and the Family*, 93 HARV. L. REV. 1156, 1242 (1980).

289 By way of exception, it has been maintained that the requirement of a medical examination in order to receive a marriage license ought to make common law marriages invalid, *see Fisher v. Sweet & McClain*, 154 Pa.Super. 216, 35 A.2d 756, 759, 761 (1944), *overruled in Buradus v. Gen.Cement Products Co.*, 159 Pa.Super. 501, 48 A.2d 883 (1946), *aff'd*, 356 Pa. 349, 52 A.2d 205 (1947). *See also* Roxborough, *supra* note 209, at 178. *Compare Woodward Iron Co. v. Dean*, 217 Ala. 530, 117 So. 52 (1928), in which the court considered the regulations as to this to be simply a "directory." *See also* Adams, *supra* note 10, at 298. In Note, *supra* note 10, at 109, the author maintained that common law marriage "weakens state health control by allowing the licensing procedure to be circumvented." *See also* Note, *supra* note 27, at 548; *Anderson v. Anderson*, 235 Ind. 113, 131 N.E.2d 301, 307 (1956); Kirkpatrick, *supra* note 10, at 47-48; Stein, *supra* note 18, at 296; *McCoy v. District of Columbia*, 256 A.2d 908, 910 (D.C. 1969); Shaw, *supra* note 1, at 581; and Caudill, *supra* note 150, at 562.

290 Shaw *id.* at 580. The legislation in Pennsylvania contains as support for common law marriages the following regulations: "This part shall not be construed to change

It is clear that the difficulties of achieving the preceding objectives without a licensing procedure constitute heavy arguments either for introducing licensing, even for common law marriages, or for repealing the doctrine. The courts began to complain early that the state, by its acceptance of common law marriage, lost control of the commencement of marriage.[291] These reasons have also been stated as support for the repeal of common law marriage.[292] The difficulties in performing health checks and preventing the spread of diseases appear to have played a role with the repeal of common law marriage in New Jersey in 1939[293] and in Georgia in 1997.[294]

---

the existing law with regard to common-law marriage," *see* PA. CONS. STAT. ANN. 23-1103 (West 2003). *Compare PNC Bank Corp. v. Workers' Compensation Appeal Bd. (Stamos),* No. 860 C.D. (2003) at 17, which points to the inability to enact "policies related to public health and welfare" with respect to common law marriage.

291 Dubler, *supra* note 36, at 1911. *See also* Gilkey, *supra* note 209, at 48, who with respect to the laws applying requirements for the parties' health in order to be able to marry states: "Obviously all such laws would be totally ineffective if licenses to marry were not necessary." *See also* Caudill, *supra* note 150, at 562 and Shaw, *supra* note 1, at 581-583.

292 In MORRIS PLOSCOWE, SEX AND THE LAW 23 (1951), the author states: "If two people ... can marry themselves, then there can be ... no bar to the matrimonial entanglements of the immature or the mentally deficient, no requirement that a parent must consent to the marriage of a minor, no prohibition against the marriage of those infected with syphilis and gonorrhea."

293 As commentary to the repeal of common law marriage in New Jersey in 1939, the state's Supreme Court stated the following in *Dacunzo v. Edgye,* 19 N.J. 443, 117 A.2d 508, 514 (N.J. 1955): "Incidental purposes of the statute were to secure the recordation of all marriages and to aid the enforcement of the statute, R.S. 37:1-20, regulating communicable diseases and requiring tests and a health certificate as a prerequisite to the issuance of a marriage license."

294 Barbara Mobley, member of the General Assembly in Georgia, presented with others (Randall, Martin, Falls) the legislative proposal (HB 1278) leading to common law marriage being repealed in Georgia in 1997. As a family law attorney, it was her experience that couples living in a common law marriage did not know that their marriage must be dissolved by formal divorce. This led to couple separating and commencing new relationships without taking out a formal divorce. When one of the parties then died, "their estate would be in a mess." Mobley has also stated for the repeal that the requirements for blood tests and a marriage license are only applicable for ceremonial marriages and that therefore there was a concern for the transfer HIV/AIDS and other venereal diseases with respect to common law marriages, Barbara Mobley, according to e-mail to the author dated Feb. 26, 2003. *See also* GA. CODE ANN. §§ 19-3-1, 19-3-1.1 (West 1997) which states: "No common-law marriage shall be entered into in this state on or after January 1, 1997. Otherwise valid common-law marriages entered into prior to January 1, 1997, shall not be affected by this Code section and shall continue to be recognized in this state." *Compare Wright v. Goss,* 229 Ga.App. 393, 494 S.E.2d 23, 25 (1997); and Causey, *supra* note 58, at 229-230) ("State health control by blood tests are weakened"). THOMAS, *supra* note 15, at 68, points to the possibility of circumventing the requirement for a medical examination by entering into a common law marriage. *See also* Rothstein, *supra* note 2, at 102; and MORLAND, *supra* note 10, at 59. Already in the case of *In re McLaughlin's Estate,* 4 Eash. 570, 4 Wash. 570, 30 P. 651, 658 (1892), the Washington Supreme Court stated that a prohibition against informal marriage would contribute to preventing "pauperism and crime and the transmission of hereditary diseases and defects."

Legislators, however, ought not have any illusions about the effects of a repeal.[295] The possibilities, through family law legislation, to affect the mores associated with the creation of families are limited.[296] It is one thing to prevent a common law marriage from being legally established; it is another to prevent the parties from actually beginning a relationship and starting a family. Men and women can always avoid the requirements for a license, quite simply, by moving in and living together as unmarried persons even though the state views the relationship and the creation of families to be inappropriate. The formless creation of a family also avoids the requirement of a medical examination. The civil law method here has its limitations. The punishment of couples not taking out a marriage license has arisen even in states that recognize common law marriages, but is a blunt instrument of control. In addition, public support for criminal law sanctions in the area of family law has waned in recent years.[297] Today's dilemma for legislators is that, on one side, they have an interest in preventing the creation of unsuitable relationships and families and, on the other, they are able to do this only in relation to parties who formally apply for marriage licenses.

The legislator meets the same dilemma when enacting or considering the enactment of cohabitation legislation, by which long-term cohabitations and the creation of families by unmarried couples are accepted. No prior control addresses an impediment against the relationships unless the cohabitation legislation requires registration.[298] Characteristic of this development is the fact that legislators, to a certain extent, have become resigned to the task of preventing what are understood to be unsuitable relationships and families. In many cases, the requirements have

295 Couples wishing to enter into a ceremonial marriage have always been able to avoid the requirements for health checks and a waiting period by entering into a marriage in a state not applying such requirements. This has given rise to the use of the expression "modern Gretna Greens," in which *e.g.* Elkton in Maryland and Las Vegas in Nevada are usually included, *see* CLARK, *supra* note 18, at 86 and 89 fn. 2.

296 Weyrauch, *supra* note 22, at 107, states: "It is not likely that social patterns of family organization will radically change after abolition of common law marriages." The rate of marriage in those states in which common law marriages have been repealed does not generally appear to have risen by the repeal. Neither do states recognizing common law marriages have a lower rate of marriage than other states.

297 *See* with respect to Florida, Weyrauch *id.* at 97.

298 *See, e.g.*, the legislation in The Netherlands from 1997 concerning registered partnerships including both heterosexual and homosexual couples and which in general takes up marriage impediments similar to those applicable for spouses. Control as to whether the parties are competent occurs prior to the registration, *see* Book 1, Chapter 5a of the NETHERLANDS CIVIL CODE (1988), which came into force 1 January 1988. *See also* the legislation in France from 1999 concerning "Pacte Civil de Solidarité (PACS)" which through registration becomes applicable to heterosexual as well as homosexual cohabiting persons. A partnership can be entered into through a public procedure in front of a "tribunal d'instance." In order to enter into a partnership, the parties are required to be competent in a manner similar to spouses, *see* Du Pacte Civil de Solidarité et du Concubinage (PACS), Law No. 99-944 of 15 November 1999, Recueil Dalloz 1999 L 515-517.

consciously been limited. This concerns, for example, relationships between persons of the same sex, which to an increasing extent are included within cohabitation legislation. Family relationships that constitute impediments against marriage have also been accepted within the framework for cohabitation legislation. This concerns, for example, the ALI Principles as proposed in 2002 with respect to the division of an estate between domestic partners.[299]

The legislator, on one side, places far-reaching requirements on persons intending to start a family and live together for the long term in marriage, and who through a licensing procedure beforehand controls which persons are suitable. The same legislator, on the other side, accepts that other long-term family relationships are established without any such control. It is not a surprise that such a legislative strategy is paradoxical. Such a strategy can be considered a step backwards by the state in its attempt to influence the creation of families to the benefit of the families' autonomy, by which the parties themselves may determine whether they wish to subject themselves to the more extensive marital law system or the less extensive cohabitation legislation. In jurisdictions where the legislation includes impediments to certain cohabitation relationships, the

299 The American Law Institute, which in 2002 recommended principles for the division of an estate and compensatory payments with the dissolution through separation of the relationship of domestic partners, defines "domestic partners" as two persons of the same or different sex, not married to each other, who "for a significant period of time share a primary residence and a life together as a couple." Also parties "related by blood or adoption" are covered by the proposed legislation, but have the evidentiary burden of proof that they are domestic partners, *see* the ALI PRINCIPLES, *supra* note 47, § 6.03, paragraphs (1)(3). In *New South Wales* in Australia, new legislation was enacted in 1999 that to a high degree equates adult cohabiting unmarried persons (both heterosexual and homosexual) with married persons with respect *inter alia* to the division of an estate, inheritance, and maintenance. In order for the parties in such a "*de facto* relationship" to be equated with spouses, they are required to "live together as a couple" and that they "are not married to one another or related by family." At the same time, a new status was introduced, "domestic relationships," which also includes persons who are family with each other, *e.g.* siblings and parents, and who are defined as (a) "a *de facto* relationship," or (b) "a close personal relationship (other than a marriage or a *de facto* relationship) between two adult persons, whether or not related by family, who are living together, one or each of whom provides the other with domestic support and personal care," *see* PROPERTY (RELATIONSHIPS) ACT (1984), N.S.W. ACTS § 4 (1)(2) and § 5 (1)(2), most recently changed by the PROPERTY (RELATIONSHIPS) AMENDMENT ACT (1999), N.S.W. ACTS § 3.

THE COHABITEES ACT (2003:376) enacted in Sweden requires that the parties be unmarried, but is applicable as to relationships of the same sex and lacks regulations concerning family relationships and ages. *See also* Reppy, *supra* note 19, at 1678. His proposed status is intended to arise either through "official recordation (or even a ceremony)" or through "common-law cohabitation." With respect to medical examinations, the author states: "Since child-bearing may not be intended by many cohabitants, blood tests required of marrying couples for the purpose of detecting procreation problems rather than disease might be dispensed with."

lack of control functions creates uncertainty concerning the status of the parties.[300]

14.3.6 The Lack of Control at the Dissolution of the Relationship

Also belonging to the state's control functions is the possibility of determining the terms and conditions of the marriage's dissolution through marital divorce and the control of the pertinent legal procedures. Despite a gradual retreat since the 1970s from defined grounds for divorce, in favor of no-fault divorce, the state still shows an interest in safeguarding the stability of families, not in the least for the sake of children.

It ought herewith be noted that common law marriage is formless only with respect to its commencement, not with respect to its dissolution. The parties in a common law marriage, therefore, are subjected to the same terms and conditions in order to obtain a marital divorce and the same proceedings as formally married persons. Because the parties often do not know that they are living in a common law marriage and therefore commence new relationships without dissolving their marriages, there is, as seen in Chapter 5, chaos and uncertainty with respect to the parties' marital status. The control function, therefore, does not function in reality.

Although common law marriage states, through regulations concerning marital divorce, maintain their interest in the stability of families in such marriages, cohabitation legislation to a great extent can be characterized as a capitulation. Although registered partnerships can be long term and lead to the creation of a family with children, the states commonly have not enacted any divorce procedures with restrictive regulations concerning the dissolution of cohabitations.[301] Usually, only cohabitation legislation containing requirements for registration of the relationship's commencement also take up procedures for its dissolution.[302] A legislative strategy

---

300 The uncertainty as to the parties' capacity in common law unions is also observed in Bailey, *supra* note 165, at 40.

301 Despite the fact that cohabitation legislation in many jurisdictions contains regulations for the economic resolution with the dissolution of long-term cohabitations, divorce procedures for the dissolution of the relationship are often absent, *see, e.g.*, the legislation from Australia, New Zealand, Sweden, Spain, and the legislation proposed by the American Law Institute, which defines "domestic partners" as two persons of the same or different sex, not married to each other, who "for a significant period of time share a primary residence and a life together as a couple," the ALI PRINCIPLES, *supra* note 47, § 6.03, paragraphs (1)(3).

302 Cohabitation legislation containing requirements for registration with the relationship's commencement however also commonly has a procedure for its dissolution upon separation, *e.g.*, the legislation in The Netherlands from 1997 as to "registered partnership," which includes both heterosexual and homosexual couples, *see* Book 1, Chapter 5a of the NETHERLANDS CIVIL CODE (1988), which came into force 1 January 1988. *See also* the legislation in France from 1999 as to "Pacte Civil de Solidarité (PACS)" which through the registration becomes applicable to

that does not protect the stability of families in registered partnerships with children in the same manner as families in which the spouses are formally married can appear contradictory. As the number of cohabiting unmarried persons continues to increase, divorce legislation will become increasingly without effect. Such a development can be justified by the states from a legal-political perspective because the parties gain the freedom to choose the family law system that best fits them. This development can also be seen as a step toward a total capitulation by the state from future attempts to influence the stability of families through regulations of marital divorce, even for formally married spouses. One can then correctly speak of a paradigm shift comparable to the medieval canon law strategy that, *inter alia*, purported, by the use of common law marriage, to capture the lost sheep within the indissoluble sacrament of marriage.

14.3.7 The Absence of the Form's Publicity Function

The form requirements for the commencement of a marriage also have a publicity function that is fulfilled by the registration of marriage licenses and marriage certificates.[303] Before the commencement of the marriage, each party has the possibility of obtaining information from the register about whether the other party previously has been or is married to someone else.[304] Through the wedding ceremony and the ensuing registration of the marriage, the rest of the world also obtains knowledge about the parties' marital status. The form requirements for registered partnerships have a similar function. The information from the register is important for the administration of estates of the deceased and the division of the estate. Any third party who enters into a legal obligation with either of the parties may also obtain information from the register concerning whether the party is married and thus, e.g., the need for the other spouse's consent to different transactions. The register thus contributes to creating order.

No comparable registration is required for common law marriages. With respect to informal marriages, the requirements for cohabitation and outward appearance as spouses, to a certain extent, have a similar function, at least in the circle in which they live. Outside of this circle, it is more difficult to obtain knowledge about the parties' marital status.

---

heterosexual as well as homosexual cohabiting persons, Du Pacte Civil de Solidarité et du Concubinage (PACS), Law no 99-944 of 15 November 1999, Recueil Dalloz 1999 L 515-517. The legislation in Sweden as to registered partnership for homosexual couples also contains regulations for the partnership's dissolution similar to those which are applicable with a divorce between spouses, *see* Chapter 2 of Lag (1994:1117) Om Registrerat Partnerskap. The other Nordic countries have similar laws.

303 All American states have a marriage register, *see* Clark, *supra* note 18, at 92. *Compare* Uniform Marriage and Divorce Act § 206, 9A U.L.A. 107 (1979).

304 Clark, *id.* at 86.

With justification, it has been said that common law marriages often result in a confusion in the public records.[305] Uncertainty about the status of parties has more negative effects on third parties today than when the doctrine was enacted.[306] It has particularly been emphasized that common law marriage causes disorder in real property recording systems. A transfer of real estate can become invalid if it is carried out by one partner in a common law marriage without the consent of the other.[307] It ought not be unusual for such a consent to be absent, because the parties themselves, in many cases, do not know that they are living in a common law marriage. The degree to which the requirement for consent about different dispositions also exists for unmarried cohabiting persons gives rise to similar problems. One method of limiting the problems of real estate transactions has been to give cohabiting persons the right to have their relationship listed in the real estate register.[308]

Several authors have been critical of the chaos entailed by the lack of public control of common law marriages. George Howard has stated: "It is, indeed, marvelous that a progressive people with respect to an institution which is the very basis of the social order should so long neglect the function of proper public control."[309] David Caudill has maintained that the chaos that common law marriages create in the public recording of real property ownership are one of the strongest arguments against them.[310] The argument, that property titles are left in jeopardy, has also been used by several legislators when repealing common law marriages in Illinois, Arizona, Wisconsin, Missouri, and Nebraska. [311] This argument is also relevant even with respect to other cohabitation legislation.

---

305 Caudill, *supra* note 150, at 570, has argued that the disorder which common law marriage creates in "the public recording of real property ownership" is one of the strongest arguments against common law marriages. For the comparable, *see* Weyrauch, *supra* note 22, at 98. *See also* Kirkpatrick, *supra* note 10, at 46; Note, *supra* note 10, at 102; and Fred S. Hall, *Common Law Marriage in New York State,* 30 COLUM. L. REV. 1, 11 (1930).

306 *See PNC Bank Corp. v. Workers' Compensation Appeal Bd. (Stamos),* No. 860 C.D. (2003), at 17. *Compare* Margaret M. Mahoney, *Forces Shaping the Law of Cohabitation for Opposite Sex Couples,* 7 J.L. & FAM. STUD. 135, 183-185 ((2005).

307 In *Romey v. Glass,* 120 Ind. App. 279, 91 N.E.2d 850 (1950), a woman executed a transfer document to a purchaser. As her common law spouse had not consented, the purchase was invalid. *See also* Weyrauch, *supra* note 22, at 99.

308 *See, e.g.,* The Swedish COHABITEES ACT (2003:376) § 5, which gives a cohabiting partner the right in the real estate register to be able to be noted as the cohabiting partner of the person registered as owner to the real estate.

309 HOWARD, *supra* note 57, at 183-184.

310 Caudill, *supra* note 150, at 570. For the comparable, *see* Weyrauch, *supra* note 22, at 98. *See also* Kirkpatrick, *supra* note 10, at 46; Note, *supra* note 10, at 102; and Fred S. Hall, *Common Law Marriage in New York State,* 30 COLUM. L. REV. 1, 11 (1930).

311 *See* Fred S. Hall, *Common law marriage in New York State,* 30 COLUM. L. REV. 1, 11 (1930); Note, *Common Law Marriage - A Legal Anachronism,* 32 IND. L.J. 99, 108-109 (1956): Causey, *supra* note 58, at 229-230 ("Land titles are jeopardized by unrecorded marriages"); Kirkpatrick, *supra* note 10, at 46; and Black, *supra* note 54, at 116-117.

The publicity function also includes the registers' public service function of providing the community with statistical information about marriages and divorces.[312] Even though this service function today appears natural, the United States, in comparison with Europe, was late with establishing a functioning registration, which, *inter alia*, has been explained by deep-seated Anglo-Saxon individualism and its repugnance toward state interference in family life and private affairs.[313] In 1907, only approximately half of all American states had a functioning registration.[314] The absence, today, of information in the register concerning common law marriages and unmarried cohabiting persons clearly inconveniences the community as a whole, even though the register also has its limitations.[315] The difficulties of obtaining certain data concerning the existence of cohabitations and their dissolutions are felt around the world, which is a deficiency not in the least in legal political discussions such as this one.

14.3.8 The Lack of Protection of Personal Privacy

1. Privacy with the Application of Common Law Marriage

Legal regulations, which for their application require investigations into the parties' personal relationships, always threaten personal privacy. This threat is obvious in assessments of those conditions that are to be fulfilled in order for a common law marriage to be viewed as established. Already, the issue of whether the parties have entered into a contract with a marital *consensus* can be sensitive. Investigations into the intentions of the parties about their relationship when they entered into an oral agreement while in private situations (for example, in the bedroom, kitchen, or automobile) treads closely to the parties' personal relationship as discussed in Chapter 6. The investigations in most cases in which common law marriages have been entered into through an implied agreement, based on the parties' marital conduct, can become even more indiscreet, as seen in Chapter 7. The danger, however, is greatest in investigations concerning the requirements for cohabitation and reputation, where either of these requirements constitutes conditions in addition to the contract as

312 *Bates v. State*, 9 Ohio C.C.R. 273, 276, 84 N.E. 1132 (1907).

313 John Wigmore, Treatise on the Law of Evidence 2, 2001 (1905).

314 According Grossberg, *supra* note 54, at 92-93, 27 states had procedures for the registration of marriages and in 1906, New York and South Carolina lacked legislation as to the requirement for a marriage license.

315 Cases from World War II give witness to the belief that the permanency of written documents can be lower than as to other evidence, for example, in *Thomsen v. Thomsen*, 236 Mo.App. 1223, 1232, 163 S.W.2d 792, 797 (1942), the court stated: "All history teaches us that there is no permanency in the preservation of written records, and the present day bombing and total destruction of entire cities and towns ... constitute a cogent argument in support of the wisdom of the ancient rules of evidence which permit proof of marriage by evidence other than that of issuance of a license and of proof of performance of a ceremony."

examined in Chapter 8 or the conditions for an application of the marriage presumption as analyzed in Chapter 9. Questions posed to the parties' circle of acquaintances about whether they had a marital reputation inevitably risk treading too close to their personal privacy.

Particularly sensitive from the viewpoint of individual privacy are the investigations concerning the parties' sexual relationship, which has been shown to be a relevant element in all of the above-stated requirements. As seen in Chapter 8, this element has, *inter alia,* the function of distinguishing between common law marriages and simple friendships or other relationships. Relatives, neighbors, and sometimes private detectives are cited as witnesses. The intrusiveness of the witness testimony can be seen, *inter alia,* from the case of *In re Estate of Soeder* (1966), in which a witness concerning the man stated: "Well, there was times when I saw him in pajamas and a robe and house slippers ..." These cases can be multiplied.[316] Similar experiences can be seen in Scottish case law in the application of marriage by cohabitation with habit and repute.[317]

The requirement that a common law marriage be exclusive has also forced investigations concerning the parties' sexual relationships with others. In certain cases, such actions have prevented or spoken against the existence of a common law marriage.[318] In other cases, the circumstances, such as one party, as in *Hall v. Duster* (1999), who had a girlfriend in every state, or, as in *Russell v. Russell* (1992), a man who had six children with other women in addition to the five he had with his cohabiting partner, have not constituted impediments against the creation of a common law marriage.[319] In all the cases, however, the evidence concerning

316 *See* the following cases which are treated more closely in Chapter 8: *In re Estate of Soeder,* 7 Ohio App. 271, 220 N.E.2d 547, 577 (App. 1966); *Matter of Estate of Foster,* 376 S.E.2d 144, 148 note 3 (W.Va. 1988); *Doyle v. Doyle,* 497 S.W.2d 846, 847 (Mo.App. 1973); *Nestor v. Nestor,* 472 N.E.2d 1091, 1095 (Ohio 1984); *De Shazo v. Christian,* 191 S.W.2d 495, 496-497 (Tex.Civ.App-Amarillo 1946); *Foix v. Jordan,* 421 S.W.2d 481, 484 (Tex.Civ.App.-El Paso 1967); *Smith v. Smith,* 247 Ala.213, 23 So.2d 605 (1945); *In re Long's Estate,* 251 Iowa 1042, 102 N.W.2d 76, 80 (1960); and *Scott v. Jefferson,* 174 Ga.App. 651, 331 S.E.2d 1, 4 (1985).

317 *See Nicol v. Bell,* 1954 S.L.T. 314, 315-316, wherein it was carefully discussed when and in which rooms in the house the man and his maid had been sexually active. The court found that the parties had lived together "at bed and board" and that a marriage was established.

318 *See Middlebrook v. Wideman,* 203 S.W.2d 686, 688 (Tex.Civ.App.-Texarkana 1947); *Marcus v. Director,* 548 F.2d 1044, 1049 (D.C.Cir. 1976); *Gilbreath v. Lewis,* 242 Ala. 510, 7 So.2d 485, 486 and 488 (1942); *Warren v. Canard,* 30 Okla. 514, 120 P. 599 (1911); *Parker v. De Bernardi,* 40 Nev. 361, 164 P. 645 (1917); *Olinghouse v. Olinghouse,* 265 P.2d 711 (Okla. 1954); *Horrigan v. Gibson,* 87 Okla. 1, 206 P. 219 (1922); *In re Stevenson's Estate,* 272 Pa. 291, 116 A. 162, 163 (1922); *In re Callery's Estate,* 226 Pa. 469, 75 A 672, 673 (1910); *Brinckle v. Brinckle,* 12 Phila. 232, 235 (1877); *Winfield v. Renfro,* 821 S.W.2d 640 (Tex.App.-Houston 1991); *Sanders v. Sanders,* 948 P.2d 719, 721 (Okla.Civ.App. Div. 3 1997); *In re Estate of Glover,* 882 S.W.2d 789 (Tenn.App. 1994), *Eaton v. Johnston,* 9 Kan.App. 63, 672 P.2d 10 (1983), *aff'd,* 235 Kan. 323, 681 P.2d 606 (1984); and *Johnson v. Young,* 372 A.2d 992. 993 (D.C.App. 1977).

319 *Hall v. Duster* 727 So.2d 834 (Ala.Civ.App. 1999); *Ballesteros v. Jones,* 985 S.W.2d 485, 490 (Tex.App.-San Antonio 1998); *Crosson v. Crosson,* 668 So.2d 868, 872 (Ala.Civ.

the parties' sexual relations and their reputations has been very intrusive.

The investigations as well as the presentation of the evidence before the courts and other governmental authorities concerning such sensitive questions are often perceived by the parties as violations of personal privacy. Consideration of personal privacy, therefore, is a strong argument against common law marriage.

2. *Personal Privacy within Cohabitation Law*

Issues regarding personal privacy are also raised in the application of all the cohabitation legislation enacted around the world since the 1970s, as seen in Chapter 13. Even though the sexual relationship is not taken up as a necessary requisite for invoking the legal effects, it is consistently considered a relevant factor that normally ought to exist between the parties. If one of them has a sexual relationship with someone else, this commonly speaks against an application of the legislation. At the same time, there are courts that deny recovery to a surviving cohabitant for the wrongful death of a partner with reference, *inter alia,* to the fact that it would require the court to inquire into the details of an intimate relationship.[320]

The problem arises, for example, in the application of the principles recommended by the ALI in 2002 for the division of an estate upon the separation of domestic partners. With the assessment of whether the parties "shared a life together as a couple," the ALI gives examples many of the relevant circumstances, including "(g) the extent to which the parties' relationship was treated by the parties as qualitatively distinct from the relationship either party had with any other person; (h) the emotional or physical intimacy of the parties' relationship; (i) the parties' community reputation as a couple."[321]

The assessment, according to the case law of the state of Washington about whether it was a meretricious relationship, in other words, whether a stable and marriage-like relationship has existed, has also included assessments of the parties' intimate relationships. For example, in the case of *In re Marriage of Pennington* (2000), the court stated that the relationship between the parties "included companionship, friendship, love, sex,

---

App 1995); *Russell v. Russell,* 838 S.W.2d 909 (Tex.App.-Beaumont 1992); *Beals v. Beals,* 203 Ga.App. 81, 416 S.E.2d 301 (1992); *Adams v. Boan,* 559 So.2d 1084, 1087 (Ala. 1990); *Nestor v. Nestor,* 472 N.E.2d 1091, 1096 (Ohio 1984); *Jacoby v. Jacoby,* 132 Kan. 77, 294 P. 857 (1931); and *Walton v. Walton,* 203 S.W. 133 (Tex.Civ.App.-Galveston 1918).

320 *See Elden v. Sheldon,* 46 Cal.3d 267, 279, 250 Cal.Rptr. 254, 758 P.2d 582 (1988). *Compare Dunphy v. Gregor,* 136 N.J. 99, 642 A.2d 372 (1994) (court did not see any problem allowing a cohabitant recovery for negligent infliction of emotional distress); and *Lozoya v. Sanchez,* 66 P.2d 948 (N.M. 2003) (loss of consortium).

321 *See* the ALI PRINCIPLES, *supra* note 47, § 6.03, paragraph (7). The aspects regarding privacy are also emphasized in Westfall, *supra* note 178, at 1473-1474.

and mutual support and caring," but found as well that "the sporadic cohabitation, the instability of the relationship, Van Pevenage's insistence on marriage, Pennington's refusal to marry, Van Pevenage's absences from the home and relationship with another man, the gaps where no expenses were shared, and the absence of constant or continuous co-payments or investment of time and effort in any significant asset" did not prove the existence of a "meretricious relationship."[322]

By the same token, the legislation enacted in New South Wales in Australia in 1999 and in New Zealand in 2002, which to a high degree equates adult cohabiting unmarried persons (both heterosexual and homosexual couples) with married couples with respect, *inter alia*, to the division of an estate, inheritance, and maintenance, was able to avoid taking into consideration highly personal circumstances. In order for the parties in a de facto relationship to be equated with spouses, they must live together as a couple. As guidance for the assessment, the law states a series of elements that are relevant but not always necessary, including whether or not a sexual relationship exists and the reputation and public aspects of the relationship.[323] The danger for personal privacy is illustrated by an Australian case in which the sexual relationship was the object of evidence. Thus, in *Bar-Mordecai v. Rotman & others* (2000) a 37-year-old doctor alleged that he had lived in a de facto relationship with a 72-year old woman, who had died and left a fortune of two million dollars. During the trial, the man introduced video evidence showing the parties' sexual activities. The man also tendered his own notes, according to which the couple had sex four times per week, which was described in detail. The court, however, did not find a de facto relationship proven and held: "The deceased never regarded the appellant as her de facto spouse in any sense and was rather bemused from time to time at his overtures, content to let him experiment with her physically from time to time and content to live in the same house with him over an extended period of time."[324]

---

322 *In re Marriage of Pennington*, 142 Wash.2d 592, 14 P.3d 764, 772 (2000). The aspects regarding privacy are also emphasized in Westfall, *supra* note 178, at 1472, in which the author states that the case of Pennington is a "[a] vivid illustration of the kind of detailed inquiry into the most intimate aspects of Cohabitant's lives that may result from assimilating nonmarital cohabitation to marriage..."

323 *See* NEW ZEALAND'S PROPERTY (RELATIONSHIPS) ACT 1976 section 2D (c) (i), in its new wording which entered into force the 1st of February 2002. In the case of *Scragg v. Scott* (2006) N.Z.F.L.R. 1076 the court held that for there to be a relationship there must be "an emotional association." But a sexual relationship with another did not end the de facto relationship. The definition of a de facto relationship and relevant cases are analyzed in Bill Atkin, *Reflections on New Zealand's Property Reforms 'Five Years On'*, in THE INTERNATIONAL SURVEY OF FAMILY LAW 217, 221-225 (Bill Atkin, gen. ed., 2007). A comparable definition and elements can also be found in the legislation from New South Wales, Australia, *see* PROPERTY (RELATIONSHIPS) ACT (1984), N. S.W. ACTS § 4 (1)(2) which *inter alia* for the purpose of also including homosexual couples latest has been amended through THE PROPERTY (RELATIONSHIPS) AMENDMENT ACT (1999), N.S.W. ACTS § 3.

324 *Bar-Mordecai v. Rotman & others* (2000) N.S.W.C.A. 123.

The same problem arises in the application of the extensive cohabitation law that has been enacted in Canada during recent years. For example, the new legislation of the province of Manitoba, in force as of June 30, 2004, which also to a very high degree equates unmarried cohabiting couples (both heterosexual and homosexual) with married couples, applies to common law partners who cohabit in a conjugal relationship. As examples of relevant factors in the interpretation of these concepts include the sleeping arrangements; whether there is a sexual relationship; whether an attitude of fidelity is maintained to one another.[325]

The comparable exists with respect to the new cohabitation legislation enacted in 2003 in Sweden and which, *inter alia,* gives a limited right to a division of the estate of the residence and household goods between unmarried cohabiting persons. The law includes couples of different sexes or of the same sex, who permanently live together in a couple relationship, which, according to the Minister of Justice means a relationship that normally includes a sexual cohabitation.[326]

Legislation regarding a cohabitation requirement that takes into consideration the relationship's quality, its emotional and physical intimacy, the parties' sexual relationships with each other and with outsiders, and their reputation as a couple in their surroundings, requires investigations and evidence that obviously risk treading on the parties' personal privacy. When Denmark chose to not enact cohabitation legislation, one of deciding factors was that such a measure could violate the right to privacy.[327]

3. Personal Privacy within the Public Law

The problems with personal privacy concern not only common law marriages and cohabitation legislation with respect to the relationship between the parties. It also calls into question all the legislation for cohabiting persons that has grown within the public law around the world. These problems deserve attention not only as a result of the large number of matters affected, but also because the authorities' more or less inquisitorial proceedings render the parties' personal privacy particularly vulnerable.

For example, in Great Britain, an extensive discussion has taken place concerning the application of the cohabitation rule in the assessment of, *inter alia,* the right to social benefits within the framework for the Social Security Contributions and Benefits Act (1992). Particular employees (adjudicating officers) visit the home to investigate the relationships.

325 *See* Manitoba Justice, Changes to Property Laws affecting Common-Law Partners taking effect June 30, 2004.

326 *See* Legislative Bill 2002/03:80, at 43-44. *See also* the Norwegian proposal concerning inheritance rights for cohabitants, Høringsnotat, January 2007, Snr. 200405522 EP, at 40.

327 *See* Betænkning 8, Aegdeskab, Samliv uden ægdeskab I, at 50 (nr. 915/1980).

Nevil Harris has stated: "Tips-offs from the public are still a major source of information on cohabitation ... Thus the investigator might seek to ascertain whether or how frequently the parties stay the night under the same roof, and whether one party leaves the house at the same time each morning ..."[328] Different views have been expressed concerning investigations about the parties' sexual relationship. On one side, officers making home visits have had instructions to not ask questions concerning such matters. On the other side, these guidelines have been considered inappropriate in an inquisitorial system, as long as the sexual relationship is legally relevant, albeit not decisive, in order to distinguish cohabitation from friendships and other relationships.[329] When governmental authorities in Sweden, a country with extensive legislation within social and tax law equating cohabiting unmarried persons with married persons, have made visits to the home for the purpose of ascertaining whether the parties are living in a marriage-like relationship, they have been criticized by the Swedish Parliamentary Ombudsman.[330]

The difficulty and obligation to distinguish between a close friendship and a marriage-like relationship have arisen also in Canada when courts have interpreted the concept of cohabitation. In *Falkiner v. Ontario* (2002), a disabled man applied for social assistance benefits as a single person despite having lived with a woman for ten years. They spent almost all their spare time together. They ate, shopped, visited friends and relatives, and vacationed together, and the woman did laundry for the man. The Court of Appeals of Ontario stated that it is necessary, in such a case, to distinguish between a close friendship and a marriage-like relationship, even though it is difficult, especially because the director is precluded, for reasons of privacy, from investigating or considering sexual factors. The court, however, did not offer any guidance on drawing the line, but awarded the man benefits as a single man.[331]

In Australia, where the sexual relationship appears to have been attributed more significance in the assessment of whether a marriage-like

---

328 *See* Harris, *supra* note 126, at 128-129. *See also* Barker et al., *Social Security abuse,* 24(2) SOC. POL'Y & ADMIN. 104, 106 (1990).

329 *See* Harris, *supra* note 126, at 135-138.

330 In one case, a woman had applied for financial housing assistance. Upon a visit to the woman's home, an official discovered a double bed in her apartment. Taking this into consideration, the authority found that the woman lived in a marriage-like relationship. Her application was rejected with reference to that the combined income of the man and woman was too high. The woman appealed the decision and maintained that the man was only a boarder and that the double bed was from a previous marriage. The woman was found to not live in a marriage-like relationship and was granted financial housing assistance. At the same time, she reported the matter to the Swedish Parliamentary Ombudsman who issued an opinion that a governmental authority may not make a visit to the home for the purpose of investigating whether someone was living in a marriage-like relationship, *see* JO's Official Report 1979/80, at 489.

331 *Falkiner v. Ontario,* 59 O.R.3d 481 (C.App. 2002). The case is also analyzed in Bailey, *supra* note 68, at 153.

relationship exists according to Social Security Act (1991), one does not meet the same restraint as in Great Britain and Sweden. In several cases, the sexual relationship's more exact character has been thoroughly considered by the authorities. Therein, a distinction has been made between a sexual relationship that only "satisfied the physical needs and demands" and a relationship of "a loving or permanent nature."[332]

4. The Assessments

The courts and governmental authorities having the task of applying the law, or the parties citing evidence with respect to the sexual relationship, are naturally not to be blamed if it is legally relevant to the assessment of whether a cohabitation exists in the meaning of the law.[333] At the same time, it is understandable that such investigations and presentations of evidence are perceived as violations of personal privacy.

The question is whether these problems can be limited to the framework of the applicable systems. One method would possibly be to use presumptions based on the existence of objectively, easily determinable facts of a not-so-personal a nature so that no danger arises with respect to personal privacy; for example, a joint residence and household. If such circumstances exist, a marriage-like relationship or a couple relationship is presumed to exist. However, if such a presumption is rebuttable, it is difficult to avoid problems concerning privacy if the opposing party seeks to rebut the same by arguing that no marriage-like relationship existed and the evidence shows that the parties did not have any sexual relationship or that one of them maintained such a relationship with someone else.

A more certain method of avoiding problems concerning privacy is to frame the legal regulation's definitions of the relationships referred to so that no consideration is given to the parties' sexual relationship or such investigations are forbidden. Such a solution, however, results in an expanding circle to which the regulations are applicable, e.g., friendships, cohabitations between relatives or boarders, ordinarily an unintended expansion. It is difficult to avoid that the sexual relationship, even though it is not always necessary, is considered a cornerstone of what we call marriage, marriage-like relationships, or couple relationships. It is not easy to distance oneself from this inheritance from the medieval canon law's informal marriage, as seen in Chapter 3, with roots in Roman law, as explored in Chapter 2.

Consideration of personal privacy, therefore, is an argument against common law marriage as well as cohabitation legislation in general if the

---

332 For more on this, *see* P. SUTHERLAND, ANNOTATIONS TO THE SOCIAL SECURITY ACT 1991, 17 (2d ed. 1994); and Harris, *supra* note 126, at 137-138.

333 In *Walter v. Walter*, 433 S.W.2d 183, 190 (Tex.Civ.App.-Houston 1968), the objections that the evidence concerning the parties' sexual relationships was not lawful were rejected.

parties' sexual relationship and other strictly personal factors are relevant to an assessment of whether such relationships exist. Formal marriage or registered partnerships based on registration ordinarily do not encounter this inconvenience. Even though constitutional and international public law issues fall outside of the framework of this presentation, it bears repeating that the United States Constitution rejects legislation that violates the parties' right to privacy,[334] and that the European Convention of Human Rights requires that the states respect the individuals' right to privacy, and family life.[335] A concrete expression of what the right to privacy requires in legislation for unmarried cohabitants has been given by The Law Commission of Canada (2001): "At its most basic level, privacy requires that the state keep out of the 'bedrooms of the nation.' It also requires that the state avoid, wherever possible, the establishment of legal rules that cannot be administered effectively without intrusive examinations into, or forced disclosure of, the intimate details of personal adult relationships. In particular, absent violence or exploitation, sexual relationships between consenting adults should not be subjected to state investigation."[336] However, the Commission's statement does not seem to have received the attention it deserves during the legislative effort that, in the recent years, has resulted in the extensive body of cohabitation law in Canada.[337]

14.3.9 Application Problems, Disputes, Costs, and Legal Certainty

Even though the lawsuits that common law marriages give rise to ordinarily are not characterized by fraudulent claims, the application problems have been legion when the courts have had to determine whether or not a common law marriage exists. In the legal literature, the assessments here have shifted somewhat. On one side, there are authors, particularly from the first part of the 1900s, who strongly emphasized the application problems. Certain others have emphasized the legal difficulties. Chester Vernier, consequently, in 1930, characterized the state of the law as "chaos" and stated: "There is too much confusion, conflict and uncertainty."[338]

---

334 *Compare Griswold v. Connecticut*, 381 U.S. 479 (1956) and *Eisenstadt v. Baird*, 405 U.S. 438 (1972), in which the Court stated that a prohibition against the use and sales of birth control was in conflict with the Constitution's "right of privacy." *Compare Lawrence v. Texas*, 539 U.S. 558, 123 S.Ct. 2472, 156 L.Ed.2d 508 (2003), where the Court found that the section in the Tex. Pen. Code Ann. § 21.06(a) (West 2003), prohibiting sodomy violated privacy rights protected by the Due Process Clause of the Fourteenth Amendment.

335 *See* D. Feldman, Civil Liberties and Human Rights 366-380 (1993).

336 Law Commission of Canada (2001). *Beyond Conjugality*, at 21. Ottawa: Law Commission of Canada. Available at http://www.lcc.gc.ca/en/themes/pr/cpra/report.asp.

337 *See* Section 12.4.3 *supra*.

338 Vernier, *supra* note 282, at 108.

Thirty years later, Walter Weyrauch maintained: "Whatever hazy notions we have vary not only from jurisdiction to jurisdiction but from case to case within a recognizing jurisdiction."[339] Approximately ten years thereafter, Stuart Stein argued that, "the law is highly uncertain and seemingly in a continued state of flux."[340] Other authors have emphasized the evidentiary problems and the drawn-out and expensive lawsuits that result. Frank Keezer, in 1923, stated that it always entails difficulties in deciding whether persons so loosely united are married or not. He noted that, "it requires very unpleasant and expensive litigation to determine the question" and similar criticism recurs during the 1940s[341] and the 1950s.[342] Even proponents of common law marriage have admitted that the application problems are marked.[343]

On the other side, there are authors, particularly from the latter 1900s, who have wished to downplay the application problems by arguing that they are no greater than in other areas of the law, or can be solved by a more rigorous evidentiary assessment, or simply that the problems do

339 WEYRAUCH, *supra* note 22, at 91; ADAMS, *supra* note 10, at 292: "[T]here is no point of civil law concerning domestic relations, which is more confusing and upon which one will find more contradictory decisions than common-law marriage." The same statement recurs in William Hood, Jr., *Common-law Marriage in Oklahoma: A Survey*, 49 OKLA. B.J. 1505, 1506 (1978). In 1983, Weyrauch-Katz stated as to the concept of common law marriage that "its conceptual equivalents are hazy", *see* WALTER O. WEYRAUCH AND SANFORD N. KATZ, AMERICAN FAMILY LAW IN TRANSITION 118 (1983).

340 The reason for this uncertainty Stein views partially to be "that judges in this field feel a wide latitude in using personal opinions" and further "the fact that presumptions are frequently only an expressions of an individual judge's sentiment on an issue," *see* STEIN, *supra* note 18, at 289. Stein does not cite however convincing support for his assumptions concerning judges.

341 KEEZER, *supra* note 245, at 80-81. The criticism recurs in MORLAND, *supra* note 10, at 59: "It involved in litigation chiefly in claims against the estates of the ones who are claimed have been the common-law husbands." *See also* Note, *supra* note 27, at 547: "It is deplorable that in the treatment of a problem so interwoven with the best interests of society, there should be so little certainty in the law governing it...The status, when it is necessary that it be determined, must be established by expensive and involved litigation. Factual situations arising in this field are myriad and practically inexhaustible."

342 PLOSCOWE, *supra* note 292, at 24, stated that "the only remedy for the uncertainties created by the doctrine of common-law marriage is its total abolition in all states that continue to recognize it." According to Rothstein, *supra* note 2, at 101, the number of disputes increased in Florida from 1869-1954. Of a total of 71 cases, 23 occurred after 1940 and 19 after 1945. Florida repealed common law marriage in 1968. *See also* Williams, *supra* note 9, at 449, who maintains that the majority of the cases with respect to common law marriage "involve money claims against the estates of wealthy decedents" and therein cited cases.

343 Shaw, *supra* note 1, at 581. Bowman, *supra* note 18, at 752, who is positive to a reinstatement of common law marriage, concedes that the strongest arguments for a repeal thereof are "those based upon administrative and judicial efficiency." *See also* Mary D. Feighny, *Common Law Marriage: Civil Contract or "Carnal Commerce"*, 70 KAN. B. J. 20, 25 (2001), who with respect to Kansas case law states that "the evidence can be extremely conflicting" when the marriage contract is to be proven by the parties' "acts and conduct." The evidentiary problems are presented also in FOOTE ET AL., *supra* note 1, at 18.

not exist. Kathryn Vaughn stated, consequently, in 1992, that the evidentiary problems are not unique for common law marriages and that even other legal areas, in which the evidence to a great extent is based on the testimony of witnesses, encounter the same problems.[344] Homer Clark maintained, in 1987, that when a cohabitation is dissolved and one of the parties requests legal advice, the attorney faces such an ambiguous slate of facts that he is unable to respond with any assurance that the parties either were or were not married. Clark considered, however, that the cure for this difficulty is not the repeal of common law marriage but a rigorous insistence by the courts upon proof of all its elements.[345] Least worried, however, is John Crawley, who researched case law from Alabama and, in 1996, maintained that the decisive elements in a common law marriage are "well-established, easy to apply, and predictable in result." With reference to that common law marriages are a realistic and workable concept, he advised that the doctrine be retained in Alabama.[346]

This investigation, encompassing more than one thousand American cases spanning the entire 1800s and 1900s, has arrived at results other than those of Crawley's, not only with respect to Alabama,[347] but also with respect to American case law in its entirety. These results disclose extensive

344 *See* Vaughn, *supra* 21, at 1138, citing *Black*: "The difficulties of proof are not otherwise than those necessarily incurred in litigations involving any other relation of life..." *See* Black, *supra* note 54, at 131-132; and ALBERT C. JACOBS & JULIUS GOEBEL, JR., CASES AND OTHER MATERIALS ON DOMESTIC RELATIONS 94 (4th ed. 1961). *See also* Garza, *supra* note 250, at 552, who argues that if "we were to destroy legal doctrines based merely on the concern of fraudulent claims and administrative and judicial efficiency, we would be lawless."

345 CLARK, *supra* note 18, at 121, states: "The remedy for this difficulty is not abolition of common law marriage but a rigorous insistence by the courts upon proof of all of its elements."

346 Crawley, *supra* note 144, at 400 and 424. *See also* Garza, *supra* note 250, at 552, who states: "Common law marriage provides a clear test and has clear evidentiary requirements." *See further* Bowman, *supra* note 18, at 751, who finds that the courts historically have "handled the case law quite well, although it sometimes required the investment of substantial judicial resources to do so"; and Black, *supra* note 54, at 131.

347 Crawley's statement is somewhat surprising particularly against the background of the application problems that our review of Alabama case law has disclosed. As can be seen from Chapter 6, the courts in Alabama have not consistently defined the content of the concept "marriage relationship." The lack of a clear definition in the definition of the marriage contract's intent created in the Alabama case law has led to difficulties with the application of implied agreements. Judgments from Alabama demonstrate significant deficiencies in the conclusions from the myriads of circumstances to the existence of a marriage contracts as discussed in Section 6.3 *supra*. As can be seen from Chapter 8, the courts in Alabama during the entire 1900s vacillated between different formulations of the requirement of cohabitation. These inconsistencies in the manner of expressing the one requisite necessary for the invocation of the legal consequences has not served the interest of clarity as further discussed in Section 8.4. In Alabama, the requirement of "public assumption of marital duties and obligations" has in addition been considered fulfilled, despite the fact that the man during the parties' approximately one year long cohabitation "dated other women," *see* Section 8.6 *supra*. In another case, only a minimum of cohabitation whose objective facts to a large extent consisted of an exchange of letters and certain economic support was required, *see* Section 8.5.3 *supra*.

application problems that confront the courts when they have to decide whether a common law marriage existed, and refer to the legal as well as the evidentiary assessment.

Desperate statements, consequently, appear more or less in the courts' decisions concerning the applicable principles' lack of legal clarity. For example, in *Ridley v. Grandson* (1990), Justice Weltner of the Georgia Supreme Court exclaims: "Plainly, the law of common law marriage is chaos that cries out for order."[348] In *Russell v. Russell* (1992), Chief Justice Walker of the Court of Appeals in Beaumont, Texas, begins his judgment with the words: "[T]his case is a trial judge's nightmare."[349] In *Kelley v. Kelley* (2000), Judge Jackson finds that "each element becomes a source of dispute."[350] The worry expressed by these judges is typical of the numerous and often drawn-out lawsuits with extensive witness testimony and other evidence that arise from the legal regulations on common law marriage. The examples can be multiplied.[351] One is *PNC*

348 *Ridley v. Grandison,* 260 Ga. 6, 389 S.E.2d 746, 749 (1990). At issue was an application for a marital divorce in June 1988. The trial in the Georgia Supreme Court, which only concerned the issue of whether a common law marriage had been established, lasted three days. During the same, in addition to the parties, seven witnesses were heard, which resulted in 439 pages of trial transcript. In addition, 17 written pieces of evidence were presented. The Supreme Court issued the judgment on March 9, 1990. In the case, it was stated the number of cases concerning common law marriage in Georgia's court of appeals the years 1955-1990 was not less than 129. A similar judgment can also be found in *Dismuke v. C & S Trust Co.*, 407 S.E.2d 739, 741 (Ga. 1991).

349 *Russell v. Russell,* 838 S.W.2d 909, 911 (Tex.App.-Beaumont 1992).

350 *Kelley v. Kelley,* 2000 Utah.App. 236, 9 P.3d 171, 184 (Utah App. 2000).

351 *See, e.g., Harris v. Harris,* 2004 WL 2896422 (Ohio App. 9 Dist.) (conflicting evidence regarding virtually every aspect of the case); *Reyes v. Vasquez,* 2005 WL 1389076 (Ohio App. 6 Dist.) (contradictory evidence regarding most facts); and *In re Ober,* 2003 MT 7, 314 Mont. 20, 62 P.3d 1114 (2003) (over 30 witnesses); *Wilkins v. Wilkins,* 48 P.3d 644, 649 (Idaho 2002) (a voluminous record created relating to the conduct of Charlotte and Albert); *Butler v. Coonrod,* 671 So.2d 750, 751 (Ala.Civ.App. 1995) (22 witnesses); and *Matter of Estate of Alcorn,* 868 P.2d 629 (Mont. 1994) (15 witnesses). As to the parties' tendency to contest each other's information and witnesses, *see In re Marriage of Mosher* 183 Ill.Dec. 911, 243 Ill.App.3d 97, 612 N.E.2d 838 (1993). In *Waller v. Waller,* 567 So.2d 869 (Ala.Civ.App. 1990), the court stated: "As is the situation in the majority of these cases, the facts relevant to the determination of the validity of the common-law marriage are, in large part, disputed." *See also Duggan v. W.C.A.B. (Litchfield TP.),* 569 A.2d 1022 (Pa.Cmwlth. 1990) (14 witnesses). In *Johnson v. Green,* 251 Ga. 645, 309 S.E.2d 362 (1983), in which 20 witnesses were heard (338 pages of transcript), the court stated: "This massive expenditure of energy and of public and private resources was directed to the resolution of such elemental a question as should be answered without cavil: was there a marriage?" *See also In re Marriage of Winegard,* 257 N.W.2d 609, 611 (Iowa 1977) (the court states that the evidence was "voluminous"); *In re Estate of Malli,* 260 Iowa 252, 149 N.W.2d 155, 158 (1967) (approximately 30 witnesses and 160 documents); *In re Estate of Soeder,* 7 Ohio App. 271, 220 N.E.2d 547, 551 (1966) (46 witnesses); *In re Greenfield's Estate,* 245 S.C. 595, 141 S.E.2d 916, 920 (1965) (15 witnesses simply concerning the parties' reputation"); *In re Foster,* 77 Idaho 26, 287 P.2d 282 (1955) (16 witnesses); *Ridgeway v. Logan,* 205 Okla. 603, 239 P.2d 778 (1952); *Bloom v. Willis,* 221 La. 803, 60 So.2d 415, 418 (1952) (the evidence encompassed "a voluminous record of some 2200 pages"); *Goodman v.*

Bank Corp. v. Workers' Compensation Appeal Board (Stamos) (2003), in which the Commonwealth Court of Pennsylvania stated: "Many sound reasons exist to abandon a system that allows the determination of important rights to rest on evidence fraught with inconsistencies, ambiguities and vagaries."[352]

The reasons for these problems ought, with all desirable clarity, to be able to be seen from this treatise. Chapter 6 revealed that a lack of legal clarity prevails with respect to the marriage contract's legal intent. This lack of precision, which concerned the question of whether the marital intent should be an intent to live together or a legal intent, has led to unnecessary and expensive lawsuits with drawn-out witness testimony, in which the parties, legal counsel, and courts tend to speak past each other. There are, in addition, the difficulties of proving the existence of oral marriage contracts, commenced entirely privately at home in the kitchen or bedroom, or in an automobile, without record or witnesses.[353]

McMillan, 258 Ala. 125, 61 So.2d 55, 59 (1952); *In re Blackhawk's Estate*, 195 Okla. 390, 158 P.2d 168 (1944) (more than 60 witnesses were heard and more than 2,000 pages of oral and written evidence); and *In re Trope's Estate*, 190 Okla. 453, 124 P.2d 733, 736 (1942) (the evidence in the trial court was voluminous and encompassed 1124 pages). In *Drummond v. Benson*, 133 S.W.2d 154, 162 (1939), the court stated: "The record in this case is voluminous, many witnesses having testified, consuming several days in the trial court." In *Allen v. State*, 60 Ga.App. 248, 3 S.E.2d 780, 783 (1939), the court stated with respect to common law marriage that "it is too difficult to establish; injustices of various kinds might be done on account of the difficulties in proving such marriages, and the suspicion that more often surrounds them." *See also Cordilla v. Taylor*, 181 Okla. 20, 72 P.2d 375 (1937) (more than 60 witnesses and in which the trial transcript took up almost 860 pages); *Elliot v. Indus. Accident Bd.*, 101 Mont. 246, 53 P.2d 451 (1936) (more than 30 witnesses); *Sam v. Sam*, 172 Okla. 342, 45 P.2d 462 (1935) (more than a dozen witnesses from each side); and *In re Estate of Erlanger*, 145 Misc. 1, 259 N.Y.S. 610 (1932) (three month trial, 149 witnesses, 834 submissions (exhibits), a trial transcript of 6,965 pages, and a judgment of approximately 500 pages). In *White v. White*, 225 Ala. 155, 142 So. 524, 525 (1932), the Alabama Supreme Court stated: "The record is voluminous. The complainant called and examined thirteen witnesses and the respondent examined thirty-seven witnesses. Much of the testimony is in direct conflict." *See also In re Estate of Maher*, 204 Ill. 25, 68 N.E. 159, 161 (1903); *King v. King's Unknown Heirs*, 16 S.W.2d 160 (1929) (23 witnesses); *In re Patterson's Estate*, 85 A. 75 (1912); *In re Callery's Estate*, 75 A. 672, 674 (1910); and *Adger v. Ackerman*, 115 F. 124 (1902) (more than a dozen witnesses). Also in older cases the lawsuits are extensive with amounts of witness testimony, *see, e.g., In re McLaughlin's Estate*, 4 Wash. 570, 30 P. 651, 657 (1892), in which the court stated that: "It is important that publicity should be given to such contracts, to guard against deceptions and to provide accessible evidence to prove the relationship." *See also Jenkins v. Jenkins*, 83 Ga. 286, 9 S.E. 541 (1889); *McFarland v. McFarland* 51 Iowa 565, 2 N.W. 269 (1879) (more than 20 witnesses); *The Guardians of the Poor v. Nathans*, 2 Brewster 149 (1845); *Richard v. Brehm*, 73 Pa. 140 (1873); and *Cargile v. Wood*, 63 Mo, 501 (1876). Already in *Grisham v. Sate*, 10 Tenn. 588 (1831), the court cautioned for "disputes over property rights" and in *Bashaw v. State*, 1 Yrg. 177, 196 (Tenn. 1829), one complained as to "endless property litigations."

352 *PNC Bank Corp. v. Workers' Compensation Appeal Bd. (Stamos)*, No. 860 C.D. (2003).

353 *See* Section 6.5.1 *supra*.

Because the parties in most cases do not enter into an expressed marriage contract, Chapter 7 focuses on an analysis of the courts' conclusions about the application of implied agreements or inferred agreements. The courts, from the myriads of circumstances with respect to cohabitation and reputation as well as admissions and declarations, have found the existence of marriage contracts through the use of conclusions that often appear deficient and demonstrate the substantial application difficulties and the legal uncertainty that results.

From Chapter 8, it can be seen that the separate requirements of cohabitation and/or holding out or reputation as spouses with the marriage contract, requirements which were developed, *inter alia,* for the purpose of preventing secret marriages and to avoid evidentiary difficulties and disputes, in themselves gave rise to extensive application problems. As seen in Chapter 9, neither the heightened evidentiary requirements about clear and convincing evidence nor the application of the marriage presumption have contributed to facilitating the assessments.

In addition, the absence of a licensing procedure with respect to common law marriage creates problems, as seen in Chapter 5, about investigating, afterwards, whether the parties were competent when they, at one time, long ago commenced their relationship. As they themselves often did not know that they lived in a common law marriage, they may have commenced new formless relationships or new ceremonial marriages without formally dissolving previous ones. The new marriage has then been found invalid as a result of an impediment. The presumption to the benefit of the latter of two marriages opens the possibility for the "poor man's divorce." Nevertheless, the conclusion is that bigamy, from a civil law perspective, ought not be uncommon if the parties begin a new common law marriage or a ceremonial marriage. The pertinent lawsuits have been characterized by evidentiary difficulties and a considerable legal uncertainty. One method of reducing these problems is to adopt a short statute of limitations regarding such actions, as has occurred in Utah and Texas.[354] Nevertheless, it is clear that the evidentiary, as well as the legal certainty problems to which assessments afterwards give rise, constitute heavy arguments for either introducing a system of licensing for common law marriage or repealing it.

The application problems are also clearly emphasized in the discussion of the conflict of laws issues in Chapter 10, particularly with respect to the courts' assessments that a common law marriage had been established during a short stay by the parties in a state recognizing such marriages. Even though the parties did not travel to such a state for the purpose of

354 TEX. FAM. CODE ANN. § 2.301(b) (Vernon 2005) (two years); and UTAH CODE ANN. § 30-1-4.5(2) (Michie 2003) (one year). *See* Garrison, supra note 38, at 886. *Compare* CRETNEY AND MASSON, *supra* note 279, at 13, who argue that the intention underlying an assertion of an informal marriage might well be to invalidate the other party's subsequent solemn marriage with a third party.

entering into a common law marriage, or were even conscious that such a marriage could be established, we found cases in which the parties were considered to have had a mutual marital *consensus* as a result of an implied agreement. This naturally must be viewed as a serious deficiency in a legal system if the parties can become married to each other without having knowledge thereof! It then is easy to understand the court's reluctance in the case of *In re Estate of Bivians* (1982) to find a marriage contract proven simply on the basis of the parties' living together during a short visit. The court referred to "the mobility of modern society, the possibility of fraud arising from claims of common law marriage and the uncertainty which such claims of marriage inject into the affairs of individuals."[355]

The requirements in the majority of jurisdictions in which a common law marriage can be entered into by cohabitation, outward appearance, and reputation as spouses in addition to the contract, certainly contribute to preventing couples from other states on short visits to a common law marriage state from becoming married. The effect, however, depends on the requisite's formation. If, as was the case according to Georgia law, the requirement is formulated as a requirement of consummation and there is no separate requirement for holding out or reputation, the doors are open for the creation of a common law marriage in connection with remarkably short visits.[356] The effect is limited by many courts taking into consideration the parties' actions in their state of residence. A long-term cohabitation followed by a short visit to a common law marriage state, however, can then lead to marriage unawares to the parties. A certain period of cohabitation or domicile in the common law marriage state and a requirement for a legal intent to constitute a marriage limit the inconveniences, although the application problems are difficult to avoid entirely.

The application difficulties, the numerous disputes, the costs, and legal uncertainty have also constituted significant reasons for several American states, through legislation, to repeal common law marriage. These reasons recur both in jurisdictions in which a common law marriage could be based simply on an implied agreement and in states which, in addition to this, require cohabitation. One of the reasons for the repeal of common law marriage in California as early as 1895 was to create publicity and facilitate the proving of such a marriage.[357] The repeal in New York, in 1933, was preceded by the very notable and lengthy case of *In re Estate of*

---

355 *In re Estate of Bivians,* 98 N.M. 722, 652 P.2d 744, *cert. quashed,* 652 P.2d 1213, 98 N.M. 762 (1982).

356 *See, e.g.,* a three-day visit, *Coney v. R.S.R. Corp.,* 563 N.Y.S.2d 211 (A.D. 3 Dep't 1990); *Ventura v. Ventura,* 53 Misc.2d 881, 280 N.Y.S.2d 5 (Sup.Ct. 1967).

357 CAL. CIV. CODE § 55 (1895). It has been said that the purpose of the repeal of common law marriage in California was "to facilitate the proof of marriage by requiring their existence to be made public," *see* Note, 7 CAL. L. REV. 279, 282 (1919); and Note, 20 CAL. L. REV. 90, 92 (1931).

Erlanger (1932), in which, during three months of trial, 149 witnesses were heard. It was stated, *inter alia*, that attempts to collect funds from decedents' estates were a fruitful source of litigation.[358] Evidentiary difficulties and extensive lawsuits appear to also have played a role in the repeal of common law marriage in Minnesota in 1941[359] and in Mississippi in 1956.[360] In more recent years, the reforms by which common law marriage was repealed in Ohio in 1991[361] and in Georgia in 1997[362] can be mentioned.

---

358 *See In re Estate of Erlanger*, 145 Misc. 1, 259 N.Y.S. 610 (1932), in which the actress Charlotte Fixel-Erlanger made claims on the estate of theater producer and multimillionaire Abraham Lincoln Erlanger. As basis thereof, she alleged that they lived together in a common law marriage. The court granted her claims and granted her the widow's share, in other words, half of the estate. In order to determine whether a common law marriage existed between the parties, three months of trial was required, wherewith 149 witnesses were heard, 834 submissions (exhibits) were submitted, with a trial transcript of 6,965 pages and a judgment of 500 pages. *See* Ploscowe, *supra* note 292, at 22; William M. Kephart, The Family, Society and the Individual 399 (2d ed. 1966); Dubler, *supra* note 35, at 957; and *Morone v. Morone*, 50 N.Y.2d 481, 429 N.Y.S.2d 592, 596, 407 N.E.2d 438, 442 (1980).

359 *See* Billig and Lynch, *supra* note 25, at 179, in which the authors expected "enormous claims" by alleged widows and widowers. Common law marriage was repealed in Minnesota in 1941. Relationships commenced after 26 April 1941 are invalid, *see* Minn. Stat. Ann. § 517.01 (West 2003).

360 Miss. Code Ann. § 93-1-1 (1956). In *Ladnier v. Ladnier*, 109 So.2d 338 (Miss. 1959), the presentation of evidence took up 1,600 pages. *See also* Ploscowe, *supra* note 282, at 389 fn. 7.

361 Ron Mottl, who presented legislative proposal (H.B. 32), maintained that a repeal of common law marriage would "reduce the amount of litigation the courts experience," *see* Senate Judiciary 05/08/91. Mottl also stated in a newspaper interview that the law "brings legal certainty to the marriage relationship," *see* United Press International, October 10, 1991. In a fiscal note in connection with H.B. 32, it was stated that: "To the extent that the common law provisions reduce the difficulty in determining marriage, there would be a decrease in costs to counties." According to the new law, Ohio does not recognize common law marriages commenced after 10 October 1991, *see* R.C. § 3105.13(B)1 and 2. *See also Lyon v. Lyon*, 86 Ohio App.3d 580, 621 N.E.2d 718 (1993). With respect to the debated requirement of "cohabitation" in Ohio, *see* Section 8.2-4 *supra*.

362 With respect to the criticism in Georgia case law concerning the application problems, *see Johnson v. Green*, 251 Ga. 645, 309 S.E.2d 362, 363 (1983), in which 20 witnesses were heard (338 pages of transcript), and in which the court stated that: "This massive expenditure of energy and of public and private resources was directed to the resolution of such elemental a question as should be answered without cavil: was there a marriage?" In *Ridley v. Grandison*, 260 Ga. 6, 389 S.E.2d 746, 749 (1990), an application for a marital divorce was filed in June 1988. The trial in the Georgia Supreme Court, which only concerned the question of whether a common law marriage had been established, lasted for three days. During the same, in addition to the parties, seven witnesses were heard, which resulted in 439 pages trial transcript. In addition, 17 written pieces of evidence were presented. The Supreme Court issued the judgment on March 9, 1990. In the case, the number of cases concerning common law marriage in Georgia's court of appeals from the years 1955 to 1990 was stated as up to 129. Based on the application problems, Justice Weltner proposed the introduction of a requirement of a child for the establishment of a common law marriage. A similar assessment can also be found in *Dismuke v. C & S Trust Co.*, 407 S.E.2d 739, 741 (Ga. 1991). Barbara Mobley, member of the General Assembly in Georgia, presented with others (Randall, Martin, Falls) the legislative proposal (H.B. 1278), which led to common law marriage being repealed in Georgia in 1997, has referred specifically to the application

The courts in the two last-named states, in addition to the requirement of an expressed or implied marriage contract, applied a requirement of cohabitation or consummation, respectively, for the establishment of such a marriage. Nevertheless, the reforms were justified, *inter alia,* by the application difficulties.

There are also jurisdictions, e.g., Texas,[363] Kansas,[364] District of Columbia,[365] and Pennsylvania,[366] in which legislative proposals have been

---

problems arising when the parties ignorant that they are living in a common law marriage begin new relationships. Barbara Mobley, according to e-mail to the author Feb. 26, 2003. GA. CODE ANN. §§ 19-3-1, 19-3-1.1 (West 1997) states: "No common-law marriage shall be entered into in this state on or after January 1, 1997. Otherwise valid common-law marriages entered into prior to January 1, 1997, shall not be affected by this Code section and shall continue to be recognized in this state." *Compare Wright v. Goss*, 229 Ga.App. 393, 494 S.E.2d 23, 25 (1997).

363 During 1989, State Representative Patricia Hill from Dallas presented a proposal concerning the repeal of common law marriage in Texas, House Bill (H.B.) No. 588, 71st Leg.Sess. (1989). The primary reason for the proposal was the legal uncertainty concerning the parties' status upon the dissolution of a common law marriage (Patricia Hill, floor debate remarks, 71st Leg.Sess., House Recording No. (H.R.) 62 and 78.). H.B. 588 was adopted by a narrow majority (73 votes against 61) by the House of Representatives, but never taken up by the Senate. The objections against the repeal of common law marriage were based *inter alia* on consideration for the needs of the children and the woman as to protection in a formless relationship. To the critics belonged *inter alia* State Representative Ron Wilson, who characterized the legislative proposal as "the yuppie shackin' up insurance bill." The legislative proposal arose after the notorious case of *Winfield v. Renfro,* 821 S.W.2d 640 (Tex.App.-Houston 1991). The legislator stopped finally at a compromise. Common law marriage survived, but a legislative provision prescribing that the marriage contract could be based on that the parties "lived together as husband and wife" and that they "represented to others that they were married" was removed. In addition, a statute of limitations within which the lawsuit must be filed was enacted, *see* Act of June 14, 1989, 71 st Leg., R.S., ch. 369, § 9, 1989, effective Sept 1 1989, Tex.Gen.Laws 1459, 1461; TEX. FAM. CODE ANN. § 1.91(b) (West 1993); Senate Bill, (S.B.) No. 307 (Senate Author: Bob Glasgow, House Sponsor: Patricia Hill), Senate Recording No. 127. For more on this, *see* Section 7.4 concerning Texas *supra.*

364 After the recommendation by the Family Law Advisory Committee, the Judicial Council presented in a proposal as to the repeal of common law marriage in Kansas in 1981. Three reasons were cited as support for the proposal: (1) the difficulty in proving the relationship, (2) the availability of causes of actions, other than divorce, to address the division of property between cohabitants, and (3) the easy availability of obtaining a marriage license, *see* House Bill No. 2689 (1982); and Maxwell, *supra* note 12.

365 The courts in the District of Columbia have suggested the repeal of common law marriage with reference to "[t]he legal complexities" without this leading to any measure by the legislator, *see Johnson v. Young,* 372 A.2d 992, 995-996 (D.C. App. 1977).

366 In Pennsylvania, a proposal concerning the repeal was also rejected with reference to the need for protection of the children and surviving party. A significant argument for a retention of the institution has also been consideration to the African American population and their traditions, *see* House Bill H-404 and Senate Bill S-707 (1941). *See* further Note, *supra* note 2, at 264; and Brown, *supra* note 10, at 140-141. *See also* Shaw, *supra* note 1, at 586-587. In Florida, the legislator during the 1950s also appears to have hesitated as to a repeal common law marriage to a great extent in consideration of the African American population. A proposal was rejected in 1957 concerning a repeal, *see* H.B. No. 41, 36th Regular Session,

presented to repeal common law marriage with reference *inter alia* to the application difficulties, but the proposals have not been adopted for other reasons, e.g., the need to protect the more vulnerable party, ordinarily the woman and any children. According to the court's view in *PNC Bank Corp. v. Workers' Compensation Appeal Board (Stamos)* (2003), a repeal of common law marriage, however, would greatly reduce the need for litigation.[367] The discussion illustrates well the strength of the arguments on both sides.

These legislative and judicial experiences with respect to the application of common law marriage ought to be useful to any legislator considering enacting or repealing cohabitation legislation in general in the future. As found in Chapter 13, enacted and proposed legislation with respect to cohabiting persons in different places in the world proves that it is difficult to avoid evidentiary difficulties and disputes, despite attempts to elaborate criteria to aid in assessments and the use of presumptions. The cohabitation requisites still remain unclear and the absence in the cohabitation legislation addressing a contract requirement, as in common law marriage, makes it risky to distinguish cohabitation in cases in which the parties lived together on a trial basis or in which they did not have an intent to live together long term or to establish a legal relationship.[368]

The application problems and disputes are not simply an inconvenience for the courts and for the community as a whole. They create difficulties primarily for the parties themselves in predicting when the legal regulations will strike, for example, for young couples who are living together in a trial relationship. Even though the cohabitation is incontrovertible, this does not mean that they intend to create a legal relationship. The difficulties in predicting if and when the legal effects arise entail a serious danger to legal certainty. Within the public law, it is also difficult for the parties to predict whether and when they, in the capacity of cohabiting persons, have the right to a social benefit.[369]

Florida (1957). *See* Murray, *supra* note 19, at 429. Common law marriage was repealed in Florida in 1968, *see* Fla. Stat. Ann. § 741.211 (1968) ("no common law marriages entered into after January 1, 1968, shall be valid…").

367 *PNC Bank Corp. v. Workers' Compensation Appeal Bd. (Stamos),* No. 860 C.D. (2003), at 17. Common law marriage was finally abolished in Pennsylvania in 2005, *inter alia,* with reference to *PNC Bank Corp. See* Amendment A3597, House Bill 2719, Senate Bill 985 (2004).

368 *Compare* Vaughn, *supra* note 21, at 1139, who appears to believe that the problem in predicting when a common law marriage exists is resolved with the requirement for cohabitation.

369 When the Fisher Committee in Great Britain in 1973 requested a more precise definition of the expression "cohabiting as man and wife," this was motivated by that many who applied for benefits often were uncertain whether it was cohabitation in the meaning of the law, *see* Fisher Committee, Report of the Committee on Abuse of Social Security benefits (1973), para. 330(b). The new definition "living together as husband and wife" according to Social Security Contributions and Benefits Act (1992), section 136(1), can scarcely be viewed as having minimized uncertainty.

Increased cohabitation without marriage also gives rise to disputes, because these relationships are not publicly registered.[370] To argue, as Homer Clark did, that the application problems are equally significant in other legal areas does not render them less important to common law marriage. A comparison with ceremonial marriage demonstrates that conflicts regarding the existence of such marriages are few and the parties seldom need to find themselves adrift in dubious cases about whether they are married. There is no doubt that the form requirements have an important function to fulfill from an evidentiary perspective and that these requirements facilitate legal certainty.[371]

The ease of proving the existence of a formal marriage in its turn has tempted a certain abuse by pro forma marriage, in which the parties marry without any plans as to living a life together, e.g., for the purpose of facilitating immigration or preventing deportation.[372] This can be countered by a requirement of cohabitation or consummation for the validity of a formal marriage. The enactment of such a requirement has been discussed, but has had difficulties gaining a voice with respect to the relationship between the parties.[373] On the other hand, the absence of a cohabitation can constitute an evidentiary fact because the parties did not have a true marital intent.[374] Within the public law, e.g., with respect to the right to different social benefits, certain legal systems also apply a requirement of cohabitation to spouses. The problems with pro forma marriages, however, appear to be limited compared with the extensive application problems following from common law marriage.

Even though other legal solutions also demonstrate problems,[375] any legislator today considering enacting common law marriage or cohabitation legislation in general has good reason to take into consideration these disputes, the costs, and the legal uncertainty entailed by legislation with respect to formless relationships. When the Danish Ministry of Justice in 2006 rejected a proposal concerning legal inheritance rights for surviving cohabitants, he referred to the risk for litigation with regard to the

370 Glendon, *supra* note 253, at 688; Douglas, *supra* note 81, at 231, maintains that "cohabitation is essentially hard to delineate if justice is to be done to the wide range of circumstances it embraces. The search for certainty in legal terms risks the drawing of arbitrary lines in different contexts, with consequential confusion, complexity, and unfairness."

371 In *PNC Bank Corp. v. Workers' Compensation Appeal Bd. (Stamos)*, No. 860 C.D. (2003), at 15, the court notes that formal marriage creates "certainty and stability" and that it "reduces both the need for litigation to settle rights and the opportunity for fraudulent claims."

372 *Compare* Section 6.5.3 *supra.*

373 CLARK, *supra* note 18, at 93.

374 With respect to marital intent, *see* Section 6.3 *supra.*

375 *See, e.g.*, private law solutions within the framework for the Marvin doctrine, Section 12.3.2 *supra.*

existence of a marriage-like relationship as well as the legal uncertainty.[376] The Law Commission of Canada, in 2001, rightly stated: "Policies should be able to be administered without undue costs, delays or uncertainties. Governments could set out detailed conditions of eligibility to specify the close personal relationships to which law applies." This statement does not seem to have received the attention it deserves during the legislative work that in the recent years has resulted in the extensive body of cohabitation law in Canada.[377] The ALI Proposed Principles have met the same criticism. Marsha Garrison has argued that the multifactor inquiry required by the principles would "ensure uncertainty, expense, fraud, and inconsistency."[378]

What can we learn from history? The application problems caused by formless relationships, such as common law marriage and unmarried cohabitation, are nothing new. In this treatise, we have learned that Emperor Justinian, during the first millennium, presented legislation against the Roman law's formless marriage by *inter alia* laying down requirements for a marriage contract and dowries, the primary objection was numerous and long-term lawsuits (*multae quidem et continuae lites*).[379] When the Catholic Church, during the second millennium in 1563, repealed the canon law's formless marriage, it is worth noting that one of the reasons was precisely the application problems.[380] The same reasons also played a significant role when formless marriage was repealed in England through Lord Hardwicke's Act of 1753.[381] In those states in the United States that later repealed common law marriage, the application difficulties have also constituted one of the reasons. To this can be added that one of the main results of this investigation, which concerned American case law from the entire 1800s and 1900s and more than one thousand cases concerning common law marriage, is to demonstrate extensive application problems, both legal and evidentiary, which to a great extent led to the disputes. Any legislator today who, during the third millennium, is considering enacting common law marriage or cohabitation legislation in general has good

376 *See* L 100, Forslag til arvelov, Dec. 6, 2006, para. 15.3.1 and Betænkning 8, Aegdeskab, Samliv uden ægdeskab I, s. 50 (nr. 915/1980). The evidentiary problems, however, did not prevent the Danish Ministry of Justice from giving a proposal concerning extended cohabitation wills for parties who have lived together in a marriage-like relationship during two years before the death of one party, *see id.* at L 100.

377 Law Commission of Canada (2001), *Beyond Conjugality*, at 24. Ottawa: Law Commission of Canada. Available at http://www.lcc.gc.ca/en/themes/pr/cpra/report.asp. *See also* Section 12.4.3 *supra.*

378 Garrison, *supra* note 160, at 318. *See also* Scott, *supra* note 47, at 340, who as to the ALI Principles argues that the standard to determine whether a union without children qualifies as a domestic partnership is "costly, intrusive and fraught with uncertainty." Her own solution is based on presumptions that are not free from similar problems.

379 Nov. 74, 4. For more on this, *see* Section 2.4.5 *supra.*

380 *See* Section 3.5 *supra.*

381 *See* Section 4.2 *supra.*

reason to take into consideration these disputes, costs, and the legal uncertainty which the legislation entails.

14.4 Summary and Conclusions

14.4.1 The Arguments for Common Law Marriage and Cohabitation Law

1. *The Lack of Availability of Ceremonial Marriages*

Among the historically most significant reasons behind the growth of common law marriage in the American case law during the 1800s was the limited access to persons authorized to perform weddings and governmental authorities issuing marriage licenses. This had its basis in the long distances, low-density population settlements, and insufficient public transportation typical in the pioneer period. Common law marriage, under these conditions, was an easily accessible way to formlessly enter into a valid marriage.

These reasons are no longer relevant in the United States or in the developed world in general. Modern public transportation has made the wedding ceremony easily accessible. All states today offer the possibility of choosing between a church and a civil wedding ceremony with form requirements concerning the license, persons authorized to perform wedding ceremonies, witnesses, and the marriage register, which do not place unreasonable requirements on the parties.

If one only considers the argument of accessibility, only in certain emergency situations, in which the parties do not have the possibility of going through a ceremonial wedding, is there still a need for specific solutions. These limited needs, however, do not justify common law marriage. Only in undeveloped countries can the circumstances today be such that limited access to a wedding ceremony still constitutes a relevant argument for common law marriage. For more developed countries, however, the argument of accessibility purely historical.

2. *Ethnic, Cultural, and Social Reasons*

In American law, there has been an endeavor to make legal marriage available to population groups whose traditions do not require ceremonial marriage. Common law marriage here has played a role particularly within the African-American population. Today, it is still almost twice as common for African-American couples to choose to not ceremonially marry than for Anglo-American couples.

A reason behind common law marriage, which has a close connection with that just mentioned, is to give social protection to the more vulnerable population groups. Traditionally, cohabitation without formal marriage has been more common in the lower economic classes of society than among the economic middle class. The costs of a ceremonial marriage appear to play a role, but probably the social pressures to marry are not as strong as in the middle class.

In this chapter, however, it has been seen that formless cohabitation since the 1970s has so expanded that it is no longer limited to certain ethnic and social groups. Cohabitation without marriage today is commonplace and is accepted even in upper middle class families.

It clearly is not easy to change marital traditions that for ethnic, cultural, and social reasons have been rooted in families from different population groups for generations. However, it cannot be taken for granted that common law marriage or extensive cohabitation legislation constitutes the solution to the problem. A civil wedding for the commencement of a marriage that is neutral to different cultural forms by requiring only a simple and inexpensive registration and that allows the parties to decide the ceremonies to which they wish to subject themselves or entirely refrain from can constitute an alternative as discussed in more detail in Chapter 15.

3. *Protection for the Vulnerable Party*

One of the strongest arguments for common law marriage is that it gives the more vulnerable party in the relationship a protection during the cohabitation as well as upon its dissolution by separation or death. Common law marriage has the same function as formal marriage, a natural consequence as the social family situation and the need for protection, in general, is comparable. Because the woman most often has been the more vulnerable party, common law marriage has come to constitute a protection. The needs of women, therefore, have given rise to feminist proposals regarding both the retention and reinstatement of common law marriage.

The purpose of giving protection to the economically more vulnerable party also constitutes the primary reason behind all the legislation for cohabiting unmarried persons that has grown in the Western world during the past thirty years. The principles proposed by the American Law Institute as to the division of an estate upon a separation between unmarried cohabiting persons is based, therefore, on the idea that their relationship closely resemble marriage in function, and its termination, therefore, poses the same social and legal issues as the dissolution of a marriage.

If one only looks at the need for protection for the economically more vulnerable party, one can ask why the majority of jurisdictions that have enacted regulations for cohabiting unmarried persons have enacted more limited protective regulations than those applicable to formally married spouses. If the needs are the same and decisive, one can imagine that these are best provided for by taking, as in common law marriage states in the United States, the complete step of introducing the same regulations that apply to formally married persons to the entire legal system. Ordinarily, legislators have not answered these principally significant issues with desirable clarity.

The answers to these questions, however, appear to be partially found in the arguments on another plane than the need for protection and also consider the intentions of the parties. Perhaps everyone does not desire a system of protection and the obligations that the state, acting as a third party to the contract, places upon the parties.

4. *Compensation for Contributions and Sacrifices*

There are also cases in which the surviving cohabitant's rights cannot be justified by the need for protection, for example, if she or he is wealthy. In such cases, on the other hand, the rights can be justified by the surviving party's contributions to the deceased's fortune and the family economy as a whole and by the sacrifice, for example, of a professional career in order to take care of children. It should be noted that the arguments of contribution and sacrifice are often used as legal grounds for property rights outside family law, but here they are the justification behind the legislation, where the ground is the common law marriage or the cohabitation.

The argument of contributions is more relevant with regard to property acquired during the relationship than with regard to separate property that the deceased has acquired before or during the cohabitation by gift or inheritance.

5. *Protection for the Children*

Three major motivating factors behind the institution of common law marriage in the United States, similar to those factors motivating concubinage in postclassical Roman law and formless marriage in medieval canon law, has been to protect the children in such a relationship, remove the stigma of illegitimacy, and grant children the same rights granted to children born in marriage. The consideration of children and their legitimacy has also constituted one of the major reasons for the legislature in Texas to reject the proposal to repeal the institution of common law marriage in recent years.

The demographic picture regarding children born of out of wedlock has considerably changed in the entire Western world since the 1970s. The number of children born outside of marriage has increased greatly, partially based on a decreasing rate of marriage and the increasing number of cohabiting persons outside of marriage. At the same time, the attitudes towards out-of-wedlock children have undergone significant changes. It is no longer a stigma to be born outside of marriage.

Marital status based on formal marriage or on common law marriage is not necessary to give children born out of wedlock better legal protection. One method, applied, e.g., in order to grant children the right to inherit, has quite simply meant that the requirement of marital birth has been eliminated. With respect to the possibility for unmarried parents to receive joint custody of children in the same manner as married parents, one method has been for the parents' cohabitation to entail joint custody. This method, therefore, most resembles common law marriage. With respect to the application problems that this method, as well as all that cohabitation legislation, entails, it sometimes has been supplemented with a requirement of a written registration or a confirmation of the cohabitation. A second method has been that the parents receive joint custody after an active legal action, for example, a contract or registration with a governmental authority, or after an application to a court. The advantage of this method is that the parents become aware of its legal effects and the registration with a governmental authority limits application problems. A third method, which appears to be gaining momentum, is that the parents automatically receive joint custody of their children as soon as paternity is established, regardless of whether they cohabit. Combinations of these three methods are not unusual.

6. *Fulfillment of the Parties' Good Faith Expectations*

A considerably more limited reason behind common law marriage has been to fulfill the parties' expectations about being united in marriage and thus, in individual cases, to avoid unjust results. Cases exist in which *inter alia* a couple has entered into a ceremonial marriage, which has been proven invalid due to an impediment. If the parties, or at least one of them, has been in good faith about the existence of the impediment, a common law marriage has been able to be established if the impediment later was removed. The comparable situation has existed when a ceremonial marriage has been invalid on the basis of a mistake in form, for example, because the person holding the wedding ceremony was not so authorized and the parties were acting in good faith. A common law marriage has then been able to be established.

As seen in this chapter, however, the purpose of fulfilling the parties' expectations to be married can be provided for by more limited solutions than common law marriage. One such method is the putative marriage doctrine. Compared with common law marriage, putative marriage is more limited not only with respect to those cases covered by the system, but also with respect to the legal effects.

It is possible that in the future, through legislation, putative marriage will be made a stronger alternative to common law marriage by equipping it with several or all of the legal effects of marriage, while retaining the limitation about good faith.

In order to constitute a true alternative to a common law marriage and other cohabitation legislation, it appears necessary to make the putative marriage doctrine applicable even if the cohabiting parties never have married ceremonially, but still, for some reason, believe that they are legally married.

An additional alternative can extend the putative marriage doctrine to the parties' expectations in good faith about being united in a legal cohabitation relationship. An extended putative marriage doctrine to pure cases of cohabitation entails, however, application problems similar to those of common law marriage.

7. *Preventing that Cohabiting Unmarried Persons are Favored*

When common law marriage was reinstated in Utah in 1987, a decisive reason appears to have been to prevent cohabiting unmarried persons from receiving government welfare assistance based only on one party's income. Herein lies not only an economic justice reason, but also a state financial reason, namely, to reduce the costs of the welfare system.

Because common law marriage in Utah was enacted generally, the legislation was given a breadth that widely exceeded its objective. Unmarried cohabiting couples living in a common law marriage receive all the legal effects of a marriage. The state financial reason is provided for, however, to a certain extent because the economic responsibility for the more vulnerable party through common law marriage is construed as a family law maintenance obligation between the parties, meaning that the state is not required to shoulder the primary responsibility. The idea of placing economic obligations to each other upon the individuals in a cohabitation family law and thereby limiting the state's responsibility for social welfare is one of the reasons behind the principles presented by the ALI in 2002 with respect to the dissolution of domestic partnerships. This economic reasoning has a deep ideological dimension. A circumstance that does not appear to have received the attention it deserves, however, is that cohabiting persons who are recognized as being in a common law marriage become entitled to the benefits granted to married couples and this also leads to costs.

The goal of not giving cohabiting unmarried persons better benefits in relation to married persons, however, can be provided for by more limited methods than common law marriage. Several legal systems, not in the least in Europe, have attempted to fulfill the same purpose by introducing, in connection to each specific public law right or type of rights, regulations equating cohabiting unmarried persons with married persons. Jurisdictions that have taken the step of introducing cohabitation legislation in order to give cohabiting persons the same disadvantages as married couples have ordinarily found themselves also taking the important step of giving them the same advantages as spouses. With this, a step has gradually been taken against common law marriages. An acceptance of public law benefits for cohabiting persons has, on its side, entailed costs that constitute an argument against legislation for cohabiting unmarried persons.

Another way to avoid favoring cohabiting unmarried persons over married persons in the assessment of pensions and other social benefits is to consider both spouses and unmarried cohabiting persons as separate individuals, which would make cohabitation legislation unnecessary. Such an order need not entail a total additional cost to the system if the levels of the benefits are adjusted at the same time. Such an order exhibits problems if it becomes necessary to investigate and consider the actual economic support the parties receive from each other and that affects the economic situation of each.

8. *Moral Reasons*

There was an endeavor by the courts, as seen in Chapter 4, particularly in American case law from the mid to late 1800s, to salvage the honor of the parties, particularly the woman's, through the use of the legal institution of common law marriage, transforming out-of-wedlock relations to legally valid and morally accepted marriages. Even for children, common law marriage means avoiding the stigma of illegitimacy. The marriage presumption during the 1800s served the same purpose, as discussed in Chapter 9, with respect to both spouses and children. The same morally tinged reasons recur, however, to a lesser extent even in the case law during the 1900s.

The positive attitude to common law marriages changed to a more negative posture during the first part of the 1900s, a period during which many states repealed the institution. In the states retaining common law marriage, the most common attitude was to tolerate, not favor, common law marriage. During the later part of the 1900s, one can again discern a more positive attitude toward common law marriages. The criminalization of cohabitation outside of marriage has successively ceased. During the years 1970 to 1990, no state abolished common law marriage. On the other hand, the institution was enacted in Utah, in 1987. At the same time, cohabitation outside of marriage during this period became all the more socially acceptable and spread to all social groups. In states that later repealed common law marriage, it appears that the reasons have been more rational than moral.

It appears highly uncertain, today, what moral tone marital status and marital birth will have in the future. At the same time, because it has become morally more accepted to live together as cohabiting unmarried persons, the reason to salvage the parties' moral reputation through common law marriage has been comparably reduced.

9. *The State's Interest in Capturing the Lost Sheep*

Marriage is not only rights, it is also obligations. The medieval canon law already used informal marriage to capture, within the legal marital system, men and women who preferred marriage traditions other than those prescribed by the church or who entirely formlessly lived together, as seen in Chapter 3. The same strategy can be traced in Chapter 4 to common law marriage in American law, albeit not as tangibly.

If the state desires that women and men starting families demonstrate fidelity to each other, contribute to each other's maintenance, and observe certain divorce regulations and divide property in a certain manner, upon the dissolution of the relationship, then common law marriage can constitute a rational instrument to capture couples who do not formally enter into marriage within the legal marital system.

This method also includes an ideological dimension. By placing on the individuals in the family economic obligations to each other, the state can free itself from the responsibility for the social welfare.

The efficiency of the canon law strategy appears to be maximized by tying the legal effects directly to the spouses' cohabitation in the same manner as ordinarily occurs in accordance with the cohabitation legislation that has grown during the past years. Only express agreements between the parties can prevent the legal effects. The efficiency, from the state's viewpoint, is lessened if the system, such as is the case with respect to common law marriage, also requires a marriage contract, even though the difference in reality is not so considerable as long as the courts accept inferred agreements and legal presumptions based on the parties' cohabitation and outward appearance as spouses. The efficiency becomes even more limited if the contract requires a legal intent, in other words, an intent to reach the legal effects of marriage, or in any case, legal status.

If the rate of marriage continues to decrease in the Western world, it cannot be ruled out that more conservative states, out of protectiveness toward the family and marriage, will place upon the parties different obligations. The application of the canon law strategy could introduce common law marriage or other cohabitation legislation for the purpose of capturing the lost sheep. Common law marriage can then appear as an old solution to a new problem.

14.4.2 The Arguments Against Common Law Marriage and Cohabitation Law

1. *Limitation of the Parties' Freedom*

An ideological argument against common law marriage and cohabitation legislation in general is that such systems, in contrast with marriage and registered partnerships, can be forced upon the parties without their choice. The fact that they actually live together, in reality, subjects them to a system of rights and obligations applicable to their relationship. The state can be said to infringe upon the parties' individual freedom to determine whether they are to be subjected to the systems of regulation or not.

The argument that common law marriage and other cohabitation legislation limits freedom of choice appears most clearly in those cases in which the parties have chosen to not formally marry simply in order to avoid the legal effects of marriage. The degree of coercion the parties are exposed to depends, however, on how the requisites for the application of the regulations concerning common law marriage and cohabitation legislation, respectively, are formulated. The coercion is least if the application of the systems of regulations requires a legal intent from the parties. If a contract with an intent to live together is simply required, their freedom to avoid the legal effects is limited. The state's coercion is greater in the application of a marriage presumption based on the parties' cohabitation and outward appearance. However, individuals then have the possibility to rebut the presumption by demonstrating that the parties did not have any marital *consensus*. The state coercion is greatest in the application of cohabitation legislation that does not take into consideration the intentions of the parties but rather is entirely based on their actual cohabitation. The development appears to be going toward all the more extensive cohabitation legislation and thus, from the views discussed here, toward a higher degree of coercion and lesser freedom of individual choice.

An objection against the argument that common law marriage and cohabitation legislation forces a system on the parties that they have not chosen is that the parties ordinarily can contract out of it. This possibility assumes, however, that the parties are in agreement. If only one of the parties does not desire the system to be applicable to their relationship, that party is forced to subject him- or herself to it based on the cohabitation.

With regard to inheritance, it should be observed that such rights normally can be changed by will and that state coercion exists regardless of who the heirs at law are.

2. *Fraudulent Behavior and Other Abuse*

Historically, the most forceful objection against common law marriage was that the doctrine could give rise to perjury, fraudulent behavior, and other abuse, as discussed in this chapter. The courts, in several cases, often with moral indignation, have complained of the risk that one party, ordinarily the "gold digging woman," through baseless allegations about the existence of a common law marriage, seeks to reach the other's property. Particularly during the first part of the 1900s, this argument was taken up in the academic legal literature, which formed a crusade against common law marriage and came to contribute to the repeal of the institution in many states.

In this investigation, encompassing more than one thousand cases from the 1800 and 1900s, it has been seen that the alleged dangers appear to have been exaggerated and sometimes tinged by a gender bias that turns a blind eye to the man's role in the relationship and the fact that women sometimes maintained relationships with men under the promise of marriage. The problem appears, instead, to lie more in a system of regulations that invites disputes with its unclear formation.

Against the argument that the risk for fraudulent behavior and other abuse is great in the application of common law marriage, we found, in the majority of jurisdictions, the growth of the requirements of cohabitation and holding out as spouses, as well as highly applied evidentiary requirements, was to prevent fraudulent claims.

Even though this investigation does not support a finding that the perjury and fraudulent behavior was extensive as claimed during the first part of the 1900s, one cannot disregard that such a risk always exists within the private law, particularly with respect to claims directed against a deceased's estate. The risk of abuse appears to be greater within the public law in which the parties can have a joint interest in receiving a social benefit or a tax advantage and thus, can submit incorrect information concerning their cohabitation. These risks, even though they ought not be exaggerated, must be considered by any legislator contemplating the use of common law marriage or other cohabitation legislation.

3. *Undermining Marriage, the Family, and the Community*

The primary criticism directed against common law marriage during the first part of the 1900s was that it undermines marriage, the family, and the entire community. This chapter, however, has shown that objections can be raised against these somewhat sweeping arguments. To the degree that the criticism is directed against common law marriage as a legal construction, we found that this marriage entails the same legal effects as formal marriage. The spouses in a common law marriage are consequently subjected to the same morally colored obligations as formally married spouses, even as regards the regulations concerning marital divorce. It, therefore, can clearly be maintained that, in actuality, it is common law marriage that fulfills a moral function if formal marriage is not compelled.

In addition, we found that, to the extent the criticism is directed against those who enter into a common law marriage, it can be objected that the requirements for such a marriage to be established ordinarily mean that the parties must live together, outwardly appear, and gain a reputation as spouses. If no such requirements are placed on couples who formally marry, one can state that a marriage-like common law marriage in actuality must be more marriage-like than a marriage itself needs to be in order for the legal effects to arise. From this perspective, the morally colored arguments against those who live in a common law marriage lose a great deal of force. In step with that, the attitudes towards cohabitation outside of marriage have changed during the past thirty years and such cohabitation has become much more common, so that the moral arguments in general have also received less significance.

In addition, we asked whether cohabitation legislation, which has more limited legal effects than common law marriage, entails a threat against marriage, the family, and the community. A pervasive feature in the cohabitation legislation that has been adopted around the world during the past thirty years is just that it ordinarily contains rights with respect to economic resolution upon separation but, on the other hand, no regulations about divorce. Safeguarding the stability of families must, therefore, for many states be an argument against cohabitation legislation lacking divorce regulations.

This raised the question of whether cohabitation legislation affects the rate of marriage and undermines marriage in that the parties and the families do not come within the more extensive legal protection and the divorce regulations that formal marriage offers. Even though this hypothesis appears reasonable, we have found that the marriage habits in common law marriage states appear to be fairly independent of the existence of common law marriage.

4. The Lack of the Form's Protective and Clarifying Functions

In this chapter, we determined that the form requirements can be said to have a protective function in the sense that they protect the parties concerned from hasty actions. This function must be seen as material if two parties are facing the choice of cohabitation form, perhaps one of the most important decisions in their life. The ceremonial marriage's form requirements and, to some extent the registered forms of cohabitations, fulfill this function in that they give reason for reflection and serious consideration of the planned relationship's significance.

The absence of form in the establishment of a common law marriage or a formless cohabitation naturally is a deficiency. For couples simply drifting into a relationship and not making any legal assessments or any actual decisions concerning their cohabitation, but rather just cohabiting, there is no such protection against hasty actions. The actual moving in together ought many times be understood as an important step, but scarcely as an alarm in the same manner as a form requirement.

The observance of a certain form also provides clarification of the legal status for the parties. Because the legal effects are not negotiated by the parties but rather usually follow from the legislation, and their relevant knowledge is often limited, the legal status is not simply clarified by the parties entering into a ceremonial marriage. However, the observance of marriage's formalities ought to express the parties' intent to subject themselves to the legal effects of marital status that are offered by the state. Spouses who have entered into a formal marriage should not be unaware of their status or when it arose. Moreover, for third parties, it should be easy to check a person's marital status. At the same time, the wedding ceremony clarifies the state's intent to take control over the spouses' marital relationship.

The absence of the protective and clarifying functions with the formless systems naturally constitute serious deficiencies in legal certainty. A lack of clarity ought not prevail regarding the invocation of the legal consequences concerning one of the most important human relationships with respect to intimacy, length, and economic consequences. Uncertainty about the parties' status is inconvenient for the entire community.

However, it is primarily a problem for the parties themselves in predicting if and when a common law marriage or a cohabitation is to be seen as established and if and when the legal effects come into force.

The absence of the protective and clarifying functions in formless relationships stands in sharp contrast to the capacity of formal marriage and registered cohabitations to fulfill these requirements. To search instead for solutions in formless alternatives within the private law, such as the Marvin doctrine, however can be to substitute one set of problems for another. This leads to the conclusion that a repeal of common law marriage or an avoidance of cohabitation legislation does not guarantee an increased legal certainty unless the rate of marriage increases at the same time.

5. *The Lack of Control of Legal Capacity*

One of the state's most important instruments of power in influencing the creation of families and preventing unsuitable relationships has been to determine who is to be given the legal capacity to enter into a marriage. With respect to ceremonial marriages and registered partnerships, the state requires, beforehand, that these conditions be fulfilled. It appears, therefore, somewhat paradoxical that the legislature, at the same time, accepts that other long-term family relationships, such as common law marriage or cohabitations, are established without the same requirements to check legal capacity beforehand. The difficulties of preventing unsuitable relationships constitute, therefore, a strong argument for either introducing a system of licensing even for these cohabitation forms or repealing them. It cannot be ruled out that the states' lowered interest in the requirements of legal capacity for cohabiting persons indicates a more extensive capitulation, even with respect to spouses.

The legislature, however, ought not have any illusions about the effects of repealing formless cohabitation forms. The possibility, through family law, to affect the mores as to the creation of families is limited. Men and women can always avoid the requirements of a license by quite simply moving in and living together as unmarried persons even though the state views the relationship and the creation of families as inappropriate. Criminal law sanctions are a blunt instrument and ought to have waning support in the public consciousness.

6. *The Lack of Control of the Dissolution of the Relationship*

The state's control function also appears clearly in the regulations concerning marital divorce, which *inter alia* purport to safeguard the stability of families, particularly families with children. Despite a gradual retreat since the 1970s from state-defined grounds for divorce in favor of no-fault divorce, the majority of states still show an interest in safeguarding the stability of families, not least for the sake of children. Although common law marriage states, through the regulations concerning marital divorce, maintain their interest in the stability of families in such marriages, cohabitation legislation to a great extent can be characterized as a capitulation. Despite the fact that registered partnerships can be long term and lead to the creation of a family with children, no divorce procedures with restrictive regulations concerning their dissolution have been enacted, which appears contradictory.

If the number of cohabiting unmarried persons continues to increase, divorce legislation will become increasingly without effect. Such a development by the states can be motivated from a legal-political perspective in that they left it to the parties themselves to freely choose the family law system that fit them. Such a development can also be a step towards a total capitulation by the state in attempting to influence the future through the regulations about marital divorce and the stability of families even in marriage. One can then with reason speak of a paradigm shift comparable to the medieval canon law strategy, which *inter alia* purported to capture the lost sheep within the indissoluble sacrament of marriage with the use of common law marriage.

7. *The Lack of the Form's Publicity Function*

The form requirements for the commencement of a marriage also have a publicity function as seen in this chapter. Through the registration, each party prior to the commencement of the marriage can obtain information from the register about whether the other party previously has been or is married to another. Through the wedding ceremony and the ensuing registration of the marriage, third parties who enter into legal obligations with one of the parties can obtain information concerning his or her marital status and the need for the other spouse's consent for different transactions. The register contributes to creating order. The form requirements for registered partnerships have a similar function.

No comparable registration is ordinarily required for a common law marriage or a cohabitation. A transfer of real estate, therefore, can become invalid if carried out by one party in a common law marriage without the consent of the other. For a modern community in need of statistical information with respect to formless relationships, the absence of a register is a considerable inconvenience. The difficulties of fulfilling the publicity function argue against common law marriage as well as other cohabitation legislation.

8. *The Lack of Protection of Personal Privacy*

The legal regulations, which can require investigations of the parties' personal relationships, always constitute a threat to personal privacy. In this chapter, we found that this danger is obvious with respect to the conditions that are to be fulfilled for a common law marriage to be viewed as established. In addition, it has been seen that issues regarding privacy come into question even in the application of all cohabitation law that has grown since the 1970s around the world, both within family law and public law. These problems deserve attention not only based on the significant number of matters in question, but also because the authorities' more or less inquisitorial proceedings render the parties' personal privacy particularly vulnerable.

From the viewpoint of individual integrity, it is predictable that investigations are particularly sensitive if they delve into the parties' sexual relationships with each other and with others. One method of limiting the problems within the framework for the current systems could possibly be to use presumptions based on the existence of objectively, easily determinable facts of a not-so-personal character. However, in this, it is difficult to avoid problems concerning privacy because the other party, in many cases, may attempt to rebut the presumption by citing personal circumstances. A more certain method for avoiding problems concerning personal privacy is to frame the definitions in the legal regulation of the relationships so that the parties' sexual relationship need to be considered. Nevertheless, this solution would expand the circle in which the regulations are applicable, e.g., including even friendships, cohabitations between relatives, and boarders. It is difficult to avoid that the sexual relationship, even though it is not always necessary, is considered a cornerstone of what we call marriage, marriage-like relationships, or couple relationships. It is not easy to distance oneself from this inheritance of the medieval canon law's formless marriage with roots in the Roman law.

Consideration of personal privacy, therefore, is an argument against common law marriage as well as against cohabitation legislation in general as long as the parties' sexual relationship and other strictly personal factors are relevant to the assessment of whether such relationships exist. Formal marriage or registered partnerships based on registration ordinarily do not encounter this inconvenience.

9. *Application Problems, Disputes, Costs, and Legal Certainty*

In this treatise, we have learned that the application problems caused by formless relationships, such as common law marriage and unmarried cohabitation, are nothing new under the sun. Emperor Justinian during the first millennium presented legislation against the Roman law's formless marriage, primarily in reaction to numerous and long-term lawsuits (*multae quidem et continuae lites*). When the Catholic Church during the second millennium in 1563 repealed the canon law's formless marriage, one reason was the application problems. The same reasons also played a significant role when formless marriage was repealed in England through Lord Hardwicke's Act of 1753. In those states in the United States that later repealed common law marriage, the application difficulties have also been among the reasons. To this can be added that one of the main results of this investigation concerning American case law from the entire

1800s and 1900s, and covering more than one thousand cases regarding common law marriage, has been to reveal the extensive application problems, both legal and evidentiary, which to a great extent lead to disputes. Any legislator, today, who during the third millennium is considering enacting common law marriage or cohabitation legislation in general has good reason to take into consideration these disputes, costs, and the legal uncertainty that legislation with respect to formless relationships entails.

14.4.3 The Collective Value of the Arguments

As seen above, there are strong reasons for as well as against common law marriage and other cohabitation legislation. Legislators today certainly have reason, with regard to the differences in the actual relationships and values, to attach greater or lesser weight to the different arguments. Opinions will certainly differ with respect to these issues, which greatly concern the balance of power between the state and the individual. On one side, there probably are many legislators who find it well justified to give protection to the more vulnerable party and children in a formless relationship or to fulfill expectations made in good faith. This is so particularly within ethnic and social groups in which the rate of marriage is low. On the other side, there probably are legislators facing a strongly decreasing rate of marriage who see advantages in capturing the lost sheep within the obligations of the law.

However, few legislators ought to be able to disregard the problems such legislation entails with respect to the limitations of the parties' freedom to determine whether they are to be seen as married persons or in a cohabitation. A number of legislators will presumably consider such legislation to be a danger to the family and the community. Others ought to perceive the difficulties for the state to control the parties' legal capacity to enter into relationships and dissolve them. No legislator can disregard the risks of fraudulent behavior, insufficient legal uncertainty, investigations that violate personal privacy, application difficulties, disputes, and costs. Are all these problems a price worth paying? It appears risky to fulfill all these widely different reasons with one and the same solution. Compromises clearly are conceivable by enacting legislation that is limited and applies in particularly significant areas, and in which the requisites for application are obvious to the parties and the community, as well as easier to apply. Solutions which, under certain conditions, fulfill both the arguments for and against common law marriage and other cohabitation legislation ought not, however, be ruled out. Such a possibility can search for problems as well as their solutions, not only in common law marriage and other cohabitation legislation, but also in formal marriage itself. A reform thereof requires a new balance between the state and the individual as discussed further in the next chapter.

CHAPTER 15
A New Model of Marriage

15.1 Introduction

The decreasing rates of marriage and the increasing number of cohabitations outside of marriage since the 1970s in the United States, Canada, Western Europe, Australia, and New Zealand have unleashed impressive creative forces intent on solving the legal problems of cohabiting unmarried couples, as seen in Chapter 12, "Common Law Marriage and Cohabitation Law." The courts, in the absence of specific legislation, have proven inventive and responsible, for example, by applying property regulations to resolve problems that actually concern family law. Legislative bodies have enacted different types of cohabitation legislation to an increasing extent. The efforts by the courts and legislative bodies, in their turn, have been inspired by a legal scholarship that has devoted great attention and thought to the issues. The development, today, is in an intense phase that Mary Ann Glendon refers to as "a general movement away from formalism in modern law."[1] During this same period, doomsday prophecies about formal marriage abound. Typical questions reflecting the spirit of the age have been: Is marriage an unnecessary legal concept?[2] Are we at the end of an era?[3] Is marriage dead?[4]

Given the extensive problems that stem from common law marriage and cohabitation legislation, in general, revealed in the preceding chapters, it is somewhat surprising that so little attention has been devoted to considering, instead of such legislation, a reform of formal marriage, which can be assumed to be a contributing cause of the growth of the informal relationships. This chapter, therefore, focuses on a new model of formal marriage, one that avoids the problems of cohabitation legislation,

---

1 Mary Ann Glendon, The Transformation of Family Law 290 (1989).

2 E.M. Clive, *Marriage: An Unnecessary Legal Concept?* in Marriage and Cohabitation in Contemporary Societies 71 (John M. Eekelaar, Sanford N. Katz eds., 1980).

3 John Eekelaar, *The end of an era?*, in Cross Currents: Family Law and Policy in the US and England 638 (Sanford N. Katz et al. eds., 2000).

4 Brenda Hale, *The Family Law Act 1996 – the death of marriage?*, in Family Law Towards the Millennium: Essays for P.M. Bromley 1 (Caroline Bridge ed. 1997). *See also* Mary Ann Glendon, who complained of "the withering away of marriage," *supra* note 1, at 197-199.

and can be attractive to couples who will be starting families in the future as well as to the state in its capacity as the third party to the marriage contract. Such reform must take into consideration both the forms for the commencement of marriage as well as its legal effects.

This topic falls somewhat outside of the strict framework of this work, which focuses on informal relationships. This discussion has earned its place, however, because it attempts to reach solutions to the problems arising from the legalization of informal relationships. The intent here is not to exhaustively illustrate all aspects of the subject or present any definitive conclusion. The objective is, rather, to change the perspective by focusing on formal marriage and to initiate a debate concerning an alternative solution to the legal developments in the Western world since the 1970s.

15.2 New Forms for the Commencement of Marriage

15.2.1 A Simple Registration as a Necessary Requisite

The forms for the commencement of a ceremonial marriage have long been mostly unaltered as well as stereotypical. Even though the simplest forms of a wedding ceremony can scarcely be considered particularly onerous, some parties nonetheless experience them as impediments. Marriage vows made as part of a ceremony before a religious or civil officiator, as well as before witnesses, can alienate couples who believe that marriage is primarily an alliance simply between themselves. Today, probably, several young couples associate ceremonial marriage with a social requirement for a large wedding, an obligation that may be discouraging for social, psychological, financial, or other reasons. Naturally, it is important that the forms for the commencement of a marriage, in themselves, do not constitute an impediment against the parties voluntarily obtaining the legal protection marriage offers to benefit the parties themselves as well as the community.

Therefore, one way to increase the rates of marriage can be to minimize the form requirements. This could occur by enacting an obligatory civil wedding based on registration.[5] As seen in Chapter 12, different registration systems have been enacted in the Western world since the 1970s, primarily for same-sex couples, but also for cohabiting unmarried couples of different sexes.[6] A very simple form of marriage registration could be to have the parties sign a written notification or a written

5 In Western Europe, obligatory civil marriages can be found, *inter alia*, in Germany, France, Belgium, the Netherlands, and Switzerland. Nothing prevents the civil ceremony from being followed by a religious ceremony having no legal consequences.

6 *See* Section 12.4.2. Different registration models are discussed in N. Bala, *Alternatives for Extending Spousal Status in Canada*, 17 Can. J. Fam. L. 169 (2000).

standard agreement, drafted by the state and witnessed and submitted to a governmental authority for registration. After the authority checks the legal status of the parties, the registration of the marriage would be complete, valid from the day of the submission of the notification. A more demanding form would be to require that the parties express their consent in person in the presence of an authority and witnesses before registration.[7]

A simple registration should not be viewed as too onerous for a couple who wishes to create a family and establish a lifelong or at least abiding marital relationship. These requirements are actually not any greater than those applicable to a real estate purchase. There should scarcely be any couple who, upon closer consideration, does not deem it worth the trouble to register their relationship. Nothing prevents the notification or the agreement, if the parties so wish, from being signed at a public religious or civil ceremony or at an entirely private ceremony. This, however, ought not to be obligatory. Consequently, ethnic, moral, or social sensitivities should not constitute an impediment against registration as they can against ceremonial marriage.[8] Through the notification, the parties make a conscious choice about cohabitation form. They are not, as may be the case in common law marriage and legislation based on cohabitation, forced into a system they have not chosen. The state does not intrude on the parties' individual freedom to choose whether or not they are subjected to the regulation systems or not. Registration, thus, becomes a "contracting into" the system.

The risks for perjury, fraudulent behavior, and/or other abuse in the use of a registration system are not as great as in the application of informal models of marriage or cohabitation legislation. The requirement of registration also has a protective function in the sense that it protects the concerned parties from hasty legal transactions in an entirely different manner than the formless alternative, albeit a wedding ceremony can be even more effective. The requirement of registration also has a clarification function in that it gives the parties a reason to be informed about the state

7 *Compare* THE UN CONVENTION ON CONSENT TO MARRIAGE, MINIMUM AGE FOR MARRIAGE AND REGISTRATION OF MARRIAGES (1962), which in Article 1 requires the consent of both parties to be "expressed by them in person after due publicity and in the presence of the authority competent to solemnize the marriage and of witnesses." The Convention has not prevented the existence of common law marriage and cohabitation legislation. *See* HANS-FRIEDRICH C. THOMAS, FORMLOSE EHEN 119 (1973).

8 *Compare* Grace Ganz Blumberg, *Unmarried Partners and the Legacy of Marvin v. Marvin: The Regularization of Nonmarital Cohabitation: Rights and Responsibilities in the American Welfare State*, 76 NOTRE DAME L. REV. 1265, 1296-1297 (2001): "Some ethnic and social groups have a substantially lower incidence of marriage and a substantially higher incidence of informal domestic relationships than others." *See also* Grace Ganz Blumberg, *Cohabitation without Marriage: A Different Perspective*, 28 UCLA L. REV. 1125, 1130 (1981); and David Westfall, *Forcing Incidents of Marriage on Unmarried Cohabitants: The American Law Institute's Principles of Family Dissolution*, 76 NOTRE DAME L. REV. 1467, 1477 (2001).

of the law. There need not be any illusions about how knowledgeable the parties are about the marital legal regulations. Nevertheless, the observance of the formalities can be considered an expression of the parties' intent to subject themselves to the legal effects that accompany the marital status. The obligation to choose a system promotes clarity, as discussed further below.

The registration also enables the state to fulfill its verification functions. The state retains the right to influence the creation of families, in advance, by determining which persons are given the legal right to enter into a marriage with each other. The registration, thereby, prevents unsuitable relationships. A compromise that further reduces the form requirements here can be that the legal right is not controlled in advance but rather merely confers the right to a later judicial determination of invalidity. Such a system, however, as can be seen in Chapters 7, "Implied Marriage Agreements," and 14, "Arguments for and Against Common Law Marriage and Cohabitation Law," entails considerable inconveniences. Through the registration, the state also retains the possibility of controlling the dissolution of registered relationships. The procedures for divorce can be retained, which *inter alia* purport to safeguard family stability, particularly for families with children, as examined below. Deregistration can occur after a joint application or at the request of one party upon application of the requirements applicable to the parties. The registration also fulfills the publicity function.[9] Through this, the parties, third parties, and the community in general have the opportunity to obtain information about the parties' marital status from the registry. Verification and publicity functions are facilitated by using the Internet to obtain information concerning the registrations. A third party, such as a bank or a seller, can then easily get information about the kind of marriage model the parties have registered.

A requirement for registration constitutes no danger to personal privacy, unlike the legal regulations, which require investigations into the parties' personal circumstances.[10] No investigations are required into the parties' sexual lives or any relationships with others. A registration also does not have the application problems, disputes, costs, and legal uncertainty of informal relationships. A considerably simplified form for the commencement of a marriage through a registration, neutral in relation to different beliefs, would be able to contribute to increasing the frequency of marriage.

9 *Compare* Law Commission of Canada (2001). *Beyond Conjugality*, at 117. Ottawa: Law Commission of Canada, which states: "Like marriage, registrations have the characteristics of voluntariness, stability, certainty and publicity."

10 *Id.* at 118, which states: "A registration system may also promote the values of equality and autonomy within relationships without compromising the value of privacy." More functional definitions would require an investigation of individual relationships that "necessarily involves some degree of invasion of privacy."

15.2.2 Freely Chosen Ceremonies

An obligatory registration procedure naturally does not prevent the use of ceremonies. All such arrangements, however, become entirely private, nonmandatory special occasions in which the parties themselves, in accordance with religious, social, and cultural traditions, and other preferences, choose and frame the event. It can be a religious, civil, or entirely private occasion. No form was required for the establishment of the free marriage in ancient Rome but, in certain circles, pomp and festivity were common, *pompa nuptialis, nuptiarum festivitas, ritus nuptiarum, celebritas nuptiarum,* as seen in Chapter 2, "Informal Marriages in Roman Law."[11] A couple wishing to have an entirely private ceremony, or none at all, can so choose. The state is neutral in relation to the different cultural expressions that mark the commencement of marriage. For a state advocating freedom of religion, this appears logical. Such a system would also be able to defuse the controversial issue of a homosexual couple's right to marry ceremonially because the state provides the system of regulation but transfers the ceremony to the parties. Every congregation or organization decides how it wishes to contribute.

The possibility of entirely refraining from ceremonies ought to attract couples who consider marriage a private matter and are satisfied with submitting a notification to a governmental authority for registration. The ceremonies, consequently, receive no legal significance; the registration is decisive. Such a system would be able to address whether the expression *marriage* should be reserved only for the religious but legally meaningless ceremony, while the expression *registration* is used for the action invoking the legal effects. Thus, the partnership, family relationship, or whatever, is adequate, particularly if models of registration are also enacted for family relationships in the wider context. Breaking marriage free from the registration, however, may be unsuitable, both from historical and cultural perspectives, at least with respect to relationships between women and men. In addition, marriage has been and ought to be an expression of the legal system to which the parties have agreed. It is, consequently, not a question of "registration instead of marriage," but rather marriage through registration,[12] which does not prevent other relationships from also being registered.

15.2.3 The Monolithic Model's Archaic Structure

A reform purporting to increase the frequency of marriage cannot stop with the forms for the commencement of marriage. It must also make the legal marital system of regulation more attractive to those who start families.

11 *See* Chapter 2.

12 *Compare* Law Commission of Canada (2001), *supra*, note 8, at 123, which speaks of "Registration Instead of Marriage."

A central issue, then, is that the legal effects of marriage be adjusted to different individuals and couples who live under different actual circumstances and have different desires and expectations about the cohabitation and the legal system. The solution can lie in an increased freedom of choice. It may be the case that many states, through their legal marital legislation, have for all too long offered one and the same uniform solution for all spouses. Until the 1970s, in the United States and other places in the world, it conflicted with public policy to enter into a contract before marriage that set out a financial agreement that would take effect in the event of the dissolution of the marriage, because divorce, in principle, was to be neither accepted nor facilitated.[13] Certainly, the parties' possibilities of modifying, through a contract, the economic scheme offered by the state have expanded somewhat in recent years.[14] The parties' autonomy, however, is still limited and the possibilities for contracts all too unknown. The creation of a marriage contract ordinarily requires legal assistance, which is too expensive for many couples. Thus, this option is exercised only to a limited extent. Although the courts have been more disposed to accept contracts concerning the division of an estate and, eventually, maintenance upon the marriage's dissolution, they have been more restrictive toward contracts concerning the legal effects of a continuing

---

13 In *Fricke v. Fricke*, 257 Wis. 124, 42 N.W.2d 500, 502 (1950), the court stated that the agreement "invites dispute, encourages separation and incites divorce." *See also Kahn v. Kahn*, 756 S.W.2d 685 (Tenn. 1988) and *In re Marriage of Dajani*, 204 Cal.App.3d 1387, 251 Cal.Rptr. 871 (1988); *Ching v. Ching*, 7 Haw.App. 221, 751 P.2d 93 (1988); and *Hendrick v. Hendrick*, 976 P.2d 1071 (Okla.App. 1998). *Compare In re Marriage of Goldman*, 196 Ill.App.3d 785, 554 N.E.2d 1016 (1990). *See also* Theodore F. Haas, *The Rationality and Enforceability of Contractual Restrictions on Divorce*, 66 N.C.L. Rev. 879 (1988).

14 With respect to the expanded freedom to before or during a marriage enter into an agreement as to its dissolution, from American case law, *see e.g., Hudson v. Hudson*, 350 P.2d 596 (Okla. 1960); *Posner v. Posner*, 233 So.2d 381 (Fla. 1970); *In re Marriage of Dawley*, 551 P.2d 323 (Cal. 1976); *Osborne v. Osborne*, 384 Mass. 591, 428 N.E.2d 810 (1981); *Newman v. Newman*, 653 P.2d 728 (Colo. 1982); *Scherer v. Scherer*, 249 Ga. 635, 292 S.E.2d 662 (1982); *Marschall v. Marschall*, 195 N.J.Super. 16, 477 A.2d 833 (1984); *McKee-Johnson v. Johnson*, 444 N.W.2d 259 (Minn. 1989); *MacFarlane v. Rich*, 132 N.H. 608, 567 A.2d 585 (1989); *Simeone v. Simeone*, 525 Pa. 392, 581 A.2d 162 (1990); *Bassler v. Bassler*, 157 Vt. 353, 593 A.2d 82 (1991); *Fletcher v. Fletcher*, 68 Ohio St.3d 464, 628 N.E.2d 1343 (1994); and *Rider v. Rider*, 669 N.E.2d 160 (Ind. 1996). *See also* The Uniform Premarital Agreement Act (1983), which has been adopted by more than half the states, 9B U.L.A. 89 (Supp. 2000). The freedom to contract prior to the commencement of marriage is well illustrated in *e.g.* Elisabeth S. Scott and Robert E. Scott, *Marriage as Relational Contract*, 84 Va. L. Rev. 1225 (1998); Sanford N. Katz, *Marriage as Partnership*, 73 Notre Dame L. Rev. 1251, 1256 (1998); Grace Ganz Blumberg, *The Regularization of Nonmarital Cohabitation: Rights and Responsibilities in the American Welfare State*, 76 Notre Dame L. Rev. 1265, 1303 (2001); Homer H. Clark, Jr., Ann Laquer Estin, Cases and Problems on Domestic Relations 15 (6th ed. 2000); Edward L. Winer and Lewis Becker, (eds), Premarital and Marital Contracts: A Lawyer's Guide to Drafting and Negotiating Enforceable Marital and Cohabitation Agreements (1993); and Harry E. Krause et al., Family Law: Cases, Comments, and Questions 33 (5th ed. 2003).

marriage[15] and contracts in which the spouses decide the terms and conditions, and legal effects of obtaining a marital divorce.[16]

The state, consequently, has acted for centuries on the principle that the same legal marital costume should fit everyone equally well. The same monolithic attitude recurs in modern times in legal systems in which the state enacted one and the same status solution for all cohabiting unmarried persons. It does not help that a proposal with respect to such legislation is designated to be a "tailored solution" for "domestic partners."[17] The problem lies in that the legislature is attempting to force all cohabiting couples into the same costume. In actuality, this status strategy is more obligatory because the system scheme becomes applicable without conscious choice by the parties, based on their actual cohabitation.[18] It is difficult to free oneself from the idea that the medieval strategy of capturing the lost sheep lurks in the background. The parties' possibility, when sufficiently sophisticated and in agreement, to contract out of the obligatory scheme does not basically change this strategy.

The basis in actuality can be altogether incorrect. In other contexts, citizens are considered separate individuals with different actual and value-driven perspectives and are given the right to freely choose the legal solutions that best fit them. In this context, however, the state gives the parties one and the same marital uniform solution, regardless of their age, ethnic background, values, class, needs, lifestyle, marital experience, and actual family situation in general.[19] The state offers the parties a prepackaged set of rights and obligations that the state, in the capacity of third party to the contract, following the principle, "Take it or leave it!"[20] It is no wonder that the rate of marriage has been decreasing around the world.

It may not be the case that a monolithic uniform solution fits in our time, given that the concept of family, according to Mary Ann Glendon, is considered to represent a variety of co-existing family types.[21] As a consequence, Marjorie Schultz has maintained that individuals are demanding

---

15 *See, e.g., In re Marriage of Higgason*, 10 Cal.3d 476, 110 Cal.Rptr. 897, 516 P.2d 289 (1973); and *Belcher v. Belcher*, 271 So.2d 7 (Fla. 1972).

16 *See, e.g., Coggins v. Coggins*, 601 So.2d 109 (Ala.Civ.App. 1992); and *Pacelli v. Pacelli*, 319 N.J.Super. 185, 725 A.2d 56 (1999).

17 *See* AMERICAN LAW INSTITUTE (ALI), PRINCIPLES OF THE LAW OF FAMILY DISSOLUTION: ANALYSIS AND RECOMMENDATIONS (2002), Chapter 6 Domestic partners. *See also* Thomas R. Andrews, who proposed a "tailored solution" for domestic partners, despite the fact that the parties "choose not to marry or fail to marry, for a variety of reasons (or no reason) apart from marriage," in *Property Rights of Domestic Partners in the United States and Scandinavia: A Comparative Study* 34-35 (Sept. 7, 2003) (unpublished manuscript, University of Washington).

18 *See, e.g.*, ALI PRINCIPLES, *id. See further* cohabitation legislation in Western Europe, Australia and New Zealand as discussed in Chapter 12 above.

19 *Compare* LEONORE J. WEITZMAN, THE MARRIAGE CONTRACT: SPOUSES, LOVERS, AND THE LAW (1981).

20 *See* Section 6.2, *supra.*

21 MARY ANN GLENDON, THE NEW FAMILY AND THE NEW PROPERTY 4 (1981). *See also* WALTER O. WEYRAUCH & SANFORD N. KATZ, AMERICAN FAMILY LAW IN TRANSITION 115-71 (1983).

greater autonomy and privacy in intimate relationships and a right to tailor their relationships to their needs and preferences.[22] The time ought to be ripe, in a pluralistic society that respects different notions of individuals and families, for the state to give greater freedom to spouses to determine for themselves which costume best fits them. There can be no doubt that the views of citizens are split as to which model they wish.[23] It would be strange if it were otherwise. Certain couples wish, perhaps from the perspective of a religious conviction, for a lifelong commitment, an old-fashioned marriage with restrictive divorce regulations and extensive financial sharing. Why, one can ask, should they be refused such a system? Why must they be forced into a no-fault ideology, according to which divorce is always immediately obtainable, without any need to cite reasons?[24] Other couples wish to have a more limited sharing that is easier to dissolve. Why shouldn't this be the case? Still others prefer an even higher degree of economic and personal independence. Older couples who marry or remarry perhaps have less of a need for a marriage with an extensive economic sharing and rigorous divorce regulations than a family with children. Couples with children from different relationships may desire a system tailored to their needs. Couples of the same sex may need a specific system, *inter alia*, with respect to child-related issues. However, the majority of men and women intending to live together for the long term have in common that they, to a greater or lesser degree, need regulations for their cohabitation and, consequently, for being united in a marriage in some form.

15.2.4 Freely Chosen Models of Marriage

The differences in the actual relationships, needs, and desires of legal solutions predictably raise the issue of whether the parties themselves ought to have an expanded right to enter into private marriage contracts, in which they negotiate the terms and conditions for their cohabitation and its dissolution. Leonore Weitzman has argued for the use of contracts, pointing to the legal advantages and the likelihood that contracts would help the parties to clarify their expectations and to identify and resolve potential conflicts in advance.[25] An increased freedom of contract, in itself, can be an advantage. Private marriage contracts in which the parties

---

22 Marjorie Maguire Schultz, *Contractual Ordering of Marriage: A New Model for State Policy*, 70 Cal. L. Rev. 204, 329-330 (1982).

23 *Compare* Carol S. Bruch, *Nonmarital Cohabitation in the Common Law Countries: A Study in Judicial - Legislative Interaction*, 29 Am. J. Comp. L. 217, 243 (1981).

24 All American states today accept some form of no-fault divorce, however with different divorce grounds, *see* Timothy B. Walker & Linda D. Elrod, *Family Law in the Fifty States*, 25 Fam. L.Q. 417, 439-440 (1992). A summary of a proposal "to limit unilateral divorce" is given in Thomas Oldham, *ALI Principles of Family Dissolution: Some Comments*, 1997 Ill. L. Rev. 801, 818 (1997).

25 Weitzman, *supra* note 18, at 228.

enter into an agreement concerning all of the terms and conditions for their cohabitation and its dissolution, however, hold one danger. In the worst case, these contracts could lead to an anarchistic environment, in which innumerable different private contracts flourish, becoming often difficult to interpret and, at times, dictated by the stronger party. The danger of fraudulent contracts, undue pressure, and indefinite terms would be considerable, as well as the risk of increased litigation and related costs. At the same time, a complete freedom of contract could entail difficulties in setting the boundary between contracts that serve the public policy interests of the community and yet guarantee state influence on the content of the contracts.[26]

The legislature could offer, instead, a number of optional models of marriage, which the parties could choose through registration, for example, an A, B, C, or D type of marriage. Just as an entrepreneur can choose the business form under which he or she wishes to conduct business, e.g., a corporation, partnership, or limited partnership, the spouses would be given the freedom to choose the kind of marriage they prefer. Limited possibilities of choice within marital laws have existed for a long time, e.g., in Germany with respect to the property scheme in which the spouses, instead of the normal order of *Zugewinnengemeinschaft*, can choose a more extensive sharing, *Gütergemeinschaft*.[27] In recent years, several states in the United States have instituted covenant marriage, which gives spouses more restrictive grounds for divorce than is typically the case.[28]

---

26 *Compare* THE UNIFORM PREMARITAL AGREEMENT ACT, U.P.A.A. § 3(a)(8), 9B, UNIF. L. ANN. 373 (1987), prescribing that the parties in a marriage contract may not contract "in violation of public policy or a statute imposing a criminal penalty."

27 *See* concerning *Zugwinnengemeinschaft*. BGB §§ 1363-1390 and concerning *Gütergemeinschaft*, BGB §§ 1408.

28 Legislation as to covenant marriages was enacted in Louisiana in 1997, *see* LA. CIV. CODE ANN., art. 272-275, and 307-309 (2003). In 1998 the legislation with respect to marital divorces was supplemented in Arizona with rules concerning covenant marriages, *see* ARIZ. CIV. CODE ANN., §§ 25-901-906 (2003) and in 2001 the "Covenant Marriage Act" was enacted in Arkansas, *see* ARK. CODE ANN. §§ 9-11-801-810 (2003). The legislation as to covenant marriages has received a rather similar formation in the three states. It emphasizes that marriage is a lifelong relationship and therefore permits only restrictive grounds to receive marital divorce. The spouses must give a "declaration of intent" which demonstrates that they accept the regulations. According to the regulations in Arkansas, the parties are to give a written declaration of the following content: (1) "We do solemnly declare that marriage is a covenant between a man and a woman who agree to live together as husband and wife for so long as they both may live. We have chosen each other carefully and disclose to one another everything which could adversely affect the decision to enter into this marriage. We have received authorized counseling on the nature, purposes, and responsibilities of marriage. We have read the Covenant Marriage Act of 2001, and we understand that a covenant marriage is for life. If we experience marital difficulties, we commit ourselves to take all reasonable efforts to preserve our marriage, including marital counseling. With full knowledge of what this commitment means, we do hereby declare that our marriage will be bound by Arkansas law on covenant marriages, and we promise to love, honor, and care for one another as husband and wife for the rest of our lives," *see* § 9-11-804. This declaration can be made on the spouses'

The problem with these praiseworthy possibilities, however, is that they concern only the aspects of marriage that they specifically address. Moreover, an initiative by the spouses is required, namely, a marriage contract in which they agree that the alternative scheme is to be applicable. They have no obligation to choose the model. Against the background that the parties generally have limited knowledge of marital law, it is not surprising that relatively few couples take such an initiative. In order for the possibilities of choice to be more pertinent, the alternatives must be developed into more all-encompassing models that include additional legal effects so that one can actually speak of a choice between different marriages. In addition, all spouses must be obligated to choose a model when they register their marriage, as discussed further below.

It should be left to each state to determine the number of models and their content with respect to actual circumstances and prevailing values. One model could be intended primarily for couples who, based on religious or other grounds, truly understand marriage to be a lifelong relationship. It could contain more restrictive divorce regulations than those ordinarily applied. A divorce would be possible only upon certain determined grounds and would be able to result in a claim for damages.[29] To such a model could also be tied a more extensive personal and economic sharing, both during the marriage and at its dissolution, e.g., some form of community property system. Such a model would also be attractive to families with children who, until the children are of age, are prepared to commit to a more fixed relationship that is difficult to dissolve. A second model could contain more liberal divorce regulations and a less extensive sharing, both during the marriage and at its dissolution, e.g., some form of separate property system. A third model could also denote the spouses' independence of each other and give the possibility for a divorce without grounds. Nothing prevents a fourth model from being the model that is currently applied, in many countries, to unmarried cohabiting couples, according to which the parties choose through registration. Under this model, cohabitation legislation is incorporated into the marital system. Nothing ought to prevent the parties from living under one marital regime during a period of their lives,

---

application for a marriage license or later during the marriage. The legal effects of a covenant marriage primarily are that it becomes more difficult to dissolve the marriage through marital divorce than is the case with an ordinary marriage, *see* § 9-11-808. James Herbie Difonzo, *Customized Marriage*, 75 IND. L.J. 875 (2000), has stated that "Covenant marriage laws represents the most recent thrust of the movement to undo the excesses of the no-fault revolution" and has mentioned a flurry of covenant marriage bills in different states. Concerning the attitudes towards covenant marriage, *see* Alan J. Hawkens et al., *Attitudes about Covenant Marriage and Divorce: Policy Implications of a Three State Study*, 51 FAM. REL. 166 (2002).

29 *Compare Coggin v. Coggin*, 601 So.2d 109 (Ala.Civ.App. 1992), in which the spouses' contract as to payment of $5,000 from the party who requested a marital divorce was found to be invalid.

for example, while their children are young, and later registering under another. Although the state decides the models of marriage, the parties, in addition to the right and obligation to choose a model, ought, in the same manner as today, have certain possibilities for modifying the models by drafting a marriage contract.

A neutral registration system would also, if a state so wish, contain one or several models concerning partnerships between same-sex couples.[30] An additional step would be to enact the possibility for the registration of family relationships that are not marital or marriage-like in a wider context, as characterized by economic and/or personal dependency relationships, for example, relationships between two or several siblings, a parent with an adult child, two friends, or other closely related parties.[31] Persons in such relationships can need a registration model with limited legal effects. The governmental authorities granting benefits can also use such a registration. A logical objection with regard to these groups is of course that these needs are shifting, at best, and perhaps are best met by the use of individual contracts regarding ownership rights to property, maintenance obligations, care, powers of attorney, cooperation, and the use of a will.[32]

Fundamental to a future registration system with possibilities of choice is that the parties have an obligation to choose the model they wish to have registered. This should not be based on their initiative, as is the case in a premarital agreement. The reasons for this obligation are that the parties, prior to the commencement of marriage, must ascertain for themselves which standard marriage best fits them and the legal regulations that ought to govern their relationship. Such a system would probably create an awareness in the parties about their legal situation far greater than that which generally is the case today. The state's old idea of a single uniform marriage, to which everyone must subject themselves, would then take a backseat. The parties, moreover, would make a more conscious choice than they do today. The Roman legal principle, *consensus, non concubitus, facit matrimonium,* would receive a more substantive content than

30 There are authors who have maintained that it would be better for couples of the same sex to receive a new legal institution rather than try to receive permission to marry, *see* JOHN BOSWELL, SAME-SEX UNIONS IN PREMODERN EUROPE, 281 (1994); Nancy D. Polikoff, *We Will Get What We Ask For: Why Legalizing Gay and Lesbian Marriage Will Not "Dismantle the Legal Structure of Gender in Every Marriage,"* 79 VA. L. REV. 1535 (1993). The literature concerning marriage between persons of the same sex today is extensive and ordinarily advocates that this possibility be opened, *see* CLARK & LAQUER ESTIN, *supra* note 13, at 165. Concerning impediments to marriage, *see* Chapter 5 *supra*. Concerning choice of law issues, *see* Chapter 10 *supra*.

31 *See* Section 12.4, *supra*.

32 *See, e.g.*, HAW. REV. STAT. ANN. (1999), § 572C-1, which is applied to persons who do not have the right to marry. *See also* the province of Catalina in Spain, where whoever wishes to can register their relationship and receive certain rights and/or obligations. *See also* the recommendations regarding "non-conjugal" relationships as by the Law Commission of Canada (2001), *supra*, note 8, at 122.

it ordinarily has within the framework of today's ceremonial marriages, in which the *consensus* is mostly a fossil, and many couples go through the ceremony without contemplating that they are concluding a contract and making a choice about the system of regulations. The parties' *consensus*, as a basis for their legal regime, is contrasted even more strongly against the *concubitus* on which the modern cohabitation legislation commonly rests. Nevertheless, it should be emphasized that the question is not one of individual marriage contracts but rather the choice of marriage model.

15.2.5 A New Balance Between the Interests of the State and the Individual

Marriage's character as status relationship in which the state participates as a third contractual party decreases but is not lost in the scheme sketched above. A new balance is created between the interests of the state and the individual. The state retains influence on the models of marriage by constructing them and giving them content,[33] thereby determining the fundamental regulations that are obligatory for all models. In addition, the state decides the terms and conditions for access through the regulations concerning legal capacity as well as the terms and conditions of divorce. If obligatory regulations based on public policy are required by the state, the parties still have the freedom to choose and somewhat modify a model. It has certainly been said that marriage "is not, is never, and cannot be a private business."[34] However, the balance of power can be readjusted so that the spouses' power increases at the expense of the state's. The sketched scheme is not about property law solutions but rather family law of the highest order. The expanded freedom means that the state recognizes that different cohabiting couples live under different actual circumstances and that they have different wishes and expectations as to marriage. The state recognizes that the citizens are adults, able to make choices.

Such a marriage model aims at satisfying both those who prefer status and those who prefer contract. It would initiate a development, not from status to contract in the manner argued by Henry Maine in the middle of the 1800s, but rather a development towards both status and contracts.[35]

---

33 Concerning marriage as a status relationship, *see* Section 8.2 *supra*. *See also* Keith G. McWalter, *Marriage as Contract: Towards a Functional Redefinition of the Marital Status*, 9 Colum. J.L. & Soc. Probs. 607 (1973), who proposes that with respect to formal marriage "a 'contract' essentially between each party and the state, would be aimed at informing prospective spouses of the considerable and often grave legal obligations and ramifications...that marriage entails, perhaps including a checklist of these effects and requiring a signed acknowledgment of understanding."

34 Claude Lévi-Strauss, *The Family*, in Man, Culture, and Society 142 (Harry L. Shapiro ed. 1956), with agreement by Michael Grossberg, Governing the Heart: Law and the Family in Nineteenth-Century America 64 (1985).

35 Henry Summer Maine, Ancient Law: Its Connection with the early History of Society and its Relation to Modern Times 163-165 (London, Scribner 1861).

The state offers several different statuses. The legislature has decisive influence over these different statuses, and the parties' freedom of contract increases according to their freedom to choose the model that suits them best. The state constructs models in agreement with public policy, and the parties are included within a system sanctioned by the state. The compromise ought to be acceptable for many of the antagonists on both sides as to the line between status and contract. Since the 1970s, legislatures around the world strived to fashion the same status within cohabitation law for all cohabiting couples, based on their actual cohabitation. According to the model discussed here the parties have the opportunity to the freely choose between different formal models. Such a system would contribute to increasing rates of marriage.

15.3 DISPENSING WITH COMMON LAW MARRIAGE AND COHABITATION LEGISLATION

Clearly, a relevant objection to the above-sketched scheme is that cohabiting couples today, as can be seen from the preceding chapter, typically do not refrain from formally marrying by making an intentional choice. They simply live together, as sociologist Jan Trost maintained in 1979.[36] They, therefore, risk falling outside of the regulatory systems if legislation based on actual cohabitation does not exist. It can be argued that, for couples wishing to come in within a regulated system, a simple registration ought not be an impediment to the extent that marriage can be. In addition, the increased possibilities of choice that the above-presented model contains as well as extensive information about them ought to be able to raise couples' awareness of the legal alternatives and entice them to consciously choose the alternative that suit them best. The more vulnerable party becomes informed about the rights offered by the different models and has an incentive to pose the requirements that serve his or her needs. The goal ought to be that the models of marriage are so formed that the majority of couples find reasons to choose one of them. The situation would, consequently, be other than the one Trost described in the 1970s.

Hopefully, a limitation of the form requirements in the manner sketched above, as well as the freedom to choose among the models of marriage, would increase the frequency of marriage or the frequency of registration, and reduce the need for common law marriage and cohabitation legislation. Extensive information concerning the freely chosen alternatives ought to contribute to an entirely new situation that attracts interest and leads more couples to make conscious choices. The requirements for information placed at the commencement of a covenant marriage in certain states in the United States may appear to be a role model,

36 *See* Section 12.2, *supra*.

but should not be solely applicable to such marriages. All couples entering into an ordinary marriage should be subject to the same obligation. Such an information obligation should serve even in the construction of the model sketched here.[37]

The starting point in the new system, therefore, must be that couples who, after extensive information, do not register one of the models of marriage offered choose to stay outside of family law regulations. They can be assumed to have chosen to retain their freedom and to be subject only to the property law applicable to all individuals. Couples who have chosen to remain entirely independent of each other must also have the freedom to stay outside of all systems without the legislature coercing them through legislation based on cohabitation. Somewhere, there must be a boundary where the state intervention ceases and the family and individual responsibility begins. In relation to third parties and within public law, the parties' actual cohabitation situation can be significant without triggering a family law status.

15.3.1 Emergency Solutions

In order to avoid unjust results in relationships in which the parties desire a regulation but still do not register their relationship, there can be a need for protective regulations that are purely exceptional. Such a need would be able to be met through, e.g., the putative marriage doctrine, as discussed in the preceding chapter, and which purports to fulfill the parties' expectations made in good faith about being married or otherwise legally protected.[38] Another need for protection exists in cases in which one party has given the other promises or expectations about marriage or registration that are never kept.[39] There can also be a need to give certain

37 The parties' declaration as to entering into a covenant marriage in Arkansas is to contain, in addition to that mentioned in note 27 above, according to § (2)(A): "An affidavit by the parties that they have received authorized counseling which shall include a discussion of the seriousness of covenant marriage, communication of the fact that a covenant marriage is a commitment for life, a discussion of the obligations to seek marital counseling in times of marital difficulties, and a discussion of the exclusive grounds for legally terminating a covenant marriage by divorce. (B) An attestation, signed by the counselor and attached to or included in the parties' affidavit, confirming that the parties received authorized counseling as to the nature and purpose of the marriage and the grounds for termination of the marriage and an acknowledgment that the counselor provided to the parties the informational pamphlet developed and promulgated by the Administrative Office of the Courts under this subchapter that provides a full explanation of the terms and conditions of a covenant marriage," *see* ARK. CODE ANN. § 9-11-804 (West 2003).

38 *See* Section 14.2.5, *supra*.

39 *See* Marguerite Trussler and Ellen Vandergrift, *Changing Relationships: How the Law and Governments Have Accommodated Them. A Canadian Perspective* 17 (June 1 2001), Court of Queen's Bench of Alberta, which with respect to the registration based approach argues: "The disadvantage is that it may not adequately protect a person who is stuck in a relationship and cannot force her partner to register the relationship, any more than she should force her partner to get married." *See also* Cynthia

protections in order to avoid unjust results in other particularly exceptional situations, for example, if one party, after a very long-term cohabitation of perhaps twenty to thirty years, risks being left with nothing. Such a solution, however, may not appear to be an alternative to the registered models such that the parties do not bother investigating them and making their own choice, in anticipation that the state will provide a solution anyway. The regulations must be pure exceptions. The private law solutions that, since the 1970s, have been applied within the framework include the Marvin doctrine and other similar concepts. These should, in the future, also be able to provide a protection, if considerably more narrow, which does not leave room for pure fictions, as is desirable.

15.3.2 A System Serving Legal Certainty

Registered models of marriage offer a number of advantages compared to cohabitation legislation and common law marriage. The extensive evidentiary and application difficulties of the latter, which occur in the wider context addressed in this work, should be eliminated. The courts would no longer need to tolerate drawn-out lawsuits devoted to more or less metaphysical questions about whether a relationship is sufficiently marriage-like for marital legal effects to arise. This should lead to a reduction in the number of disputes, and the costs for the community would be limited. The risk for abuse of the legal system would be decreased and the violations of personal privacy caused by investigations concerning the parties' most intimate relationships, as touched upon in the preceding chapter, would be avoided. In contrast, legal certainty would primarily be increased. The parties would not need to find themselves adrift in dubious cases about if and when their cohabitation is sufficiently marriage-like for them to enjoy rights. They would not need to live in uncertainty about whether a court in the future would interpret unknown family law or private law implied agreements in their relationship. They would not need to commence their relationship in the expectation of a legal fiction. The parties would not risk being affected, at a future indefinite time, by unforeseen obligations placed on them by the state. A temporary visit to a state recognizing common law marriage would not be able to lead to marriage without the parties' knowledge; parties could not be forced into a system not of their choosing. The parties would, through registration, be conscious of whether and when the legal relationship between them has arisen and when the legal regulations would be applicable to their relationship. The parties themselves have the freedom to choose the marriage model that fits them best while the community's interests are met by the

---

Cynthia Grant Bowman, *Legal Treatment of Cohabitation in the United States*, 26 LAW & POLICY 119, 126 (2004), who believes that there are women who do not have the strength to insist on marriage or common ownership to property.

state's framing of the models. These effects, for many legislators around the world, ought to be laudable objectives for family law legislation in the twenty-first century.

15.4 Summary and Conclusions

Given the decreasing rate of marriage and the extensive problems stemming from common law marriage and cohabitation legislation, this Chapter has been devoted in general to considering a new model of formal marriage that avoids these problems and can become an alternative to informal relationships. The objective has not been to present any definitive conclusions, but rather to initiate a debate concerning an alternative solution to the legal developments in the Western world since the 1970s.

1. A Simple Registration as a Necessary Requisite

The forms for the commencement of a ceremonial marriage have long been mostly unaltered as well as stereotypical. Marriage vows made as part of a ceremony before a religious or civil officiator, as well as before witnesses, can alienate couples who believe that marriage is primarily an alliance simply between themselves. Today, many young couples probably associate ceremonial marriage with a social requirement for a large wedding, an obligation that may be discouraging for social, psychological, financial, or other reasons. Naturally, it is important that the forms for the commencement of a marriage, in themselves, do not constitute an impediment against the parties voluntarily obtaining the legal protection marriage offers to benefit the parties themselves as well as the community.

Therefore, one way to increase the rates of marriage could be to minimize the form requirements. This could occur by enacting an obligatory civil wedding based on registration. A very simple form of marriage registration could be for the parties to sign a written notification or a written standard agreement, drafted by the state and witnessed and submitted to a governmental authority for registration. A more demanding form would be to require that the parties in person in the presence of an authority and witnesses express their consent before registration. A simple registration should not be viewed as too onerous for a couple who wishes to create a family and establish a lifelong or at least law-abiding marital relationship.

An obligatory registration procedure naturally does not prevent the use of ceremonies. All such arrangements, however, become entirely private, nonmandatory special occasions in which the parties themselves, in accordance with religious, social, and cultural traditions, and other preferences, choose and frame the event.

2. *Freely Chosen Models of Marriage*

A reform purporting to increase the frequency of marriage must also make the legal marital system of regulation more attractive to those who start families. A central issue, then, is that the legal effects of marriage be adjusted to different individuals and couples who live under different actual circumstances and have different desires and expectations about the cohabitation and the legal system. The state, consequently, has acted for centuries on the principle that the same legal marital costume should fit everyone equally well. The same monolithic attitude recurs in modern times in legal systems in which the state enacted one and the same status solution for all cohabiting unmarried persons. The parties' possibilities of modifying through a contract the scheme offered by the state is still limited and too unknown.

The legislature could offer, instead, a number of optional models of marriage, which the parties could choose through registration, for example, an A, B, C, or D type of marriage. Just as an entrepreneur can choose the business form under which he or she wishes to conduct business, e.g., a corporation, partnership, or limited partnership, the spouses would be given the freedom to choose the kind of marriage they prefer.

One model could be intended primarily for couples who, based on religious or other grounds, truly understand marriage to be a lifelong relationship. It could contain more restrictive divorce regulations and more extensive personal and economic sharing. A second model could contain more liberal divorce regulations and a less extensive sharing. A third model could also denote the spouses' independence of each other and give the possibility for a divorce without grounds. Nothing prevents a fourth model from being the model that is currently applied, in many countries, to unmarried cohabiting couples, according to which the parties choose through registration. Nothing ought to prevent the parties from living under one marital regime during a period of their lives, for example, while their children are young, and later registering under another. Although the state decides the models of marriage, the parties, in addition to the right and obligation to choose a model, ought, in the same manner as today, have certain possibilities for modifying the models by drafting a marriage contract.

A neutral registration system would also, if a state so wish, contain one or several models concerning partnerships between same-sex couples. An additional step would be to enact the possibility for the registration of family relationships that are not marital or marriage-like in a wider context, as characterized by economic and/or personal dependency relationships,

Fundamental to a future registration system with possibilities of choice is that the parties have an obligation to choose the model they wish to have registered. The reasons for this obligation are that the parties, prior to the commencement of marriage, must ascertain for themselves which standard marriage best fits them and the legal regulations that ought to govern their relationship.

The Roman legal principle, *consensus, non concubitus, facit matrimonium,* would receive a more substantive content than it ordinarily has within the framework of today's ceremonial marriages, in which the *consensus* is mostly a fossil, and many couples go through the ceremony without contemplating that they are concluding a contract and making a choice about the system of regulations.

Marriage's character as a status relationship in which the state participates as a third contractual party decreases but is not lost in the scheme sketched above. A new balance is created between the interests of the state and the individual. The state retains influence on the models of marriage by constructing them and giving them content. The parties get an expanded freedom to choose and somewhat modify the model that they desire.

The registration also fulfills the publicity function. Through this, third parties and the community in general have the opportunity to obtain information about the kind of marriage model the parties have registered.

3. *Emergency Solutions*

In order to avoid unjust results in relationships in which the parties desire a regulation but still do not register their relationship, there can be a need for protective regulations that are purely exceptional. Such a need would be able to be met through, e.g., the putative marriage doctrine, which purports to fulfill the parties' expectations made in good faith about being married or otherwise legally protected. Another need for protection exists in cases in which one party has given the other promises or expectations about marriage or registration that are never kept. There can also be a need to give certain protections in order to avoid unjust results in other particularly exceptional situations, for example, if one party, after a very long-term cohabitation of perhaps twenty to thirty years, risks being left with nothing.

4. *A System Serving Legal Certainty*

The extensive evidentiary and application difficulties of common law marriage and cohabitation legislation should be eliminated by a registration system. This should lead to a reduction in the number of disputes, and the costs for the community would be limited. The risk for abuse of the legal system would be decreased and the violations of personal privacy caused by investigations concerning the parties' most intimate relationships would be avoided. In contrast, legal certainty would primarily be increased.

The parties would, through registration, be conscious of whether and when the legal relationship between them has arisen and when the legal regulations would be applicable to their relationship. The parties themselves have the freedom to choose the marriage model that fits them best while the community's interests are met by the state's framing of the models. These effects, for many legislators around the world, ought to be laudable objectives for family law legislation in the twenty-first century.

In the event that the frequency of marriage or registration, after the enactment of a system of the sort sketched above, does not reach satisfactory levels, certain legislators perhaps will find that there is still a need for common law marriage or cohabitation legislation. The hope, in such cases, is that the knowledge and experiences presented and examined in this work will be of some benefit.

ABBREVIATIONS

1. LEGAL HISTORY

1.1 Roman Law

C.	CODEX IUSTINIANUA
C.I.C.	CORPUS IURIS CIVILIS
D.	DIGESTA
Gai.	GAI INSTITUTIONES
Inst.	INSTITUTIONES
Nov.	NOVELLAE
qu.	QUESTIO
Ulp.	ULPIANI LIBER SINGULARIS REGULARUM
X.	DECRETALES GREGORII

1.2 Canon Law

c.	canon, caput
C.	CAUSAE
C.J.C.	CORPUS JURIS CANONICI
Comp.	QUINQUE COMPILATIONES ANTIQUAE
D.	Distinctio
Sent.	PETRI LOMBARDI LIBRI IV SENTENTIARUM

2. COURTS AND CASE REPORTS

2.1 The United States

A.	Atlantic Reporter
A.D.	Appellate Division Reports (New York)
Ala.	Alabama Reports
Alaska	Alaska Reports
Am.Jur.	American Jurisprudence
App.	Appellate Court

Ariz.	Arizona Reports
Ark.	Arkansas Reports
Binn.	Binney (Pennsylvania)
Cal.	California Reports
C.J.S.	Corpus Juris Secundum
Colo.	Colorado Reports
D.C.	District of Columbia Reports
Del.	Delaware Reports
F.	Federal Reporter
F. Cas.	Federal Cases
F. Supp.	Federal Supplement
Va. (1 Hen. & M.)	Hening & Munford, Virginia Reports
Idaho	Idaho Reports
Ill.	Illinois Reports
Ind.	Indiana Reporter
Iowa	Iowa Reports
Johns.	Johnson's Reports, New York
Kan.	Kansas Reports
Ky.	Kentucky Reports
Ky. (1 B. Mon.)	Monroe Legal Reporter, Kentucky
Ky. (1 J.J. Marsh.)	J.J. Marshall's Kentucky Reports
L.Ed.	Lawyer's Edition (Supreme Court)
La.	Louisiana Reports
Law. Rep. Prob & Div.	Law Reports, Probate and Divorce Cases
Mass.	Massachusetts Reports
Md.	Maryland Reports
Me.	Maine Reports
Mich.	Michigan Reports
Minn.	Minnesota Reports
Miss.	Mississippi Reports
Mo.	Missouri Reports
Mont.	Montana Reports
N.C.	North Carolina Reports
N.D.	North Dakota Reports
N.E.	North Eastern Reporter
N.H.	New Hampshire Reports
N.J.	New Jersey Reports
N.M.	New Mexico Reports
N.W.	North Western Reporter
N.Y.	New York Reports
N.Y.S.	New York Supplement
Neb.	Nebraska Reports
Nev.	Nevada Reports
Ohio	Ohio Reports
Ohio St.	Ohio State Reports

Okla.	Oklahoma Reports
Or.	Oregon Reports
P.	Pacific Reporter
Pa.	Pennsylvania State Reports
Pa. C.	Pennsylvania County Court Reports
Pa. Commw.	Pennsylvania Commonwealth Court Reports
Pa. D.	Pennsylvania District Reports
Pa. D. & C.	Pennsylvania District and County Reports
Pa. Super.	Pennsylvania Superior Court Reports
Pen. Dec.	Pension Decisions from U.S. Interior Department
R.I.	Rhode Island Reports
S. Ct.	Supreme Court Reporter
S.D.	South Dakota Reports
S.E.	South Eastern Reporter
S.W.	South Western Reporter
Serg. & Rawle	Sergeant and Rawle (Pennsylvania)
So.	Southern Reporter
Tenn.	Tennessee Reports
Tex.	Texas Reports
Tex.Crim.	Texas Criminal Reports
U.S.	United States Reports
Utah	Utah Reports
Va.	Virginia Reports
Vet.App.	United States Court of Appeals for Veterans Claims
Vt.	Vermont Reports
W.Va.	West Virginia Reports
Wash.	Washington Reports
Wis.	Wisconsin Reports
Wyo.	Wyoming Reports

2.2 England and Scotland

A.C.	Appeal Cases
All E.R.	All England Law Reports
App. Cas.	Appeal Cases
Ch.	Chancery
Cl. & F.	Clark and Finally Reports
Dow.	Dow's House of Lord Cases 1812-1813
Eng. Rep.	English Reports
EWCA	Court of Appeal (England and Wales)
F.L.R.	Family Law Reports
H.L.	House of Lords
J.C.	Justiciary Cases
L.R.	Law Reports
P.	Probate
R.R.	The Revised Reports

S.C.	Scots Session Cases
S.L.T.	Scots Law Times
Sess. Cas.	Session Cases, Court of Session section
S.	First Series (ed. Shaw)
D.	Second Series (ed. Dunlop)
M.	Third Series (ed. MacPherson)
R.	Fourth Series (ed. Rettie)
Fr.	Fifth Series (ed. Fraser) 1898-1907
W.L.R.	Weekly Law Reports

2.3 Canada

C.A.	Recueils de jurisprudence du Québec, Cour d'appel
E.T.R.	Estate & Trust Reports
D.L.R.	Dominion Law Reports
Nfld. & P.E.I.R.	Newfoundland and Prince Edward Island Reports
R.F.L.	Reports of Family Law
S.C.R.	Supreme Court Reports

2.4 Australia and New Zealand

A.C.	The Law Reports, Appeal Cases
A.L.J.R.	Australian Law Journal Reports
C.A.	Court of Appeals
C.L.R.	Commonwealth Law Reports
F.C.R.	Federal Court Reports
F.L.R.	Federal Law Reports
Fam. L.R.	Family Law Reports
Fed. L.R.	Federal Law Reports
H.C.	High Court
N.S.W.L.R.	New South Wales Law Reports
N.S.W.S.C.	New South Wales Supreme Court Cases
N.S.W. Sup.Ct.	New South Wales Supreme Court Reporter
N.Z. C.A.	New Zealand Court of Appeal Reports
N.Z. C.P.R.	New Zealand Conveyancing and Property Reports
N.Z. F.L.R.	New Zealand Family Law Reports
N.Z. L.R.	New Zealand Law Reports
S.A.S.R.	South Australia State Reports
V.R.	Victorian Reports
W.A.R.	Western Australia Law Reports
W.A.S.C.	Western Australia Supreme Court

2.5 Other Countries

BB	Der Betriebsberater
BGB	Bürgerliches Gesetsbuch
BGH	Bundesgerichtshof
BGHZ	Entscheidungen des Bundesgerichtshofs in Zivilsachen

Bull.	Bulletin des arrêts de la Cour de Cassation. Chambres civiles
Civ.	Cour de Cassation, Chambre civile
Crim.	Cour de Cassation, Chambre crininelle
D.	Recueil Dalloz
D.H.	Recueil hebdomadaire de jurisprudence
D.H.Cronique	Recueil hebdomadaire de jurisprudence cronique
FamRZ	Ehe und Familie im Privaten und öffentlichen Recht. Zeitschrift für das gesamte Familienrecht
GP	Gazette du Palais
J.C.P.	Juris Classeur Périodique, La Semaine Juridique
KG	Kammergericht
LG	Landgericht
NJA	Nytt Juridiskt Arkiv
NJW	Neue Juristische Wohenschrift
OGH	Oberster Gerichtshof
OLG	Oberlandesgericht
RH	Rättsfall från hovrätterna
Rt.	Norsk Retstidende
S.	Recueil Sirey
SZ	Zeitschrift der Savigny-Stiftung für Rechtsgeschichte
trib.	Tribunal civil
UfR	Ugeskrift för Retsvaesen
WM	Wertpapier-Mitteilungen

3. PERIODICALS

A.L.R.	*American Law Reports*
A.M.	*Atlantic Monthly*
AcP	*Archiv für die civilistische Praxis*
Adelphia L.J.	*Adelphia Law Journal*
Alb. L.J.	*Albany Law Journal*
Am. Indian L. Rev	*American Indian Law Review*
Am. J. Comp. L.	*American Journal of Comparative Law*
Am. J. Juris	*American Journal of Jurisprudence*
Am. L. Rev.	*American Law Review*
Am. Soc. Rev.	*American Sociological Review*
Ariz. L. Rev.	*Arizona Law Review*
Aust J. Fam. L.	*Australian Journal of Family Law*
Baylor L. Rev.	*Baylor Law Review*
Benefits L.J.	*Benefits Law Journal*
B.U. L. Rev.	*Boston University Law Review*
Brandeis L.J.	*Brandeis Law Journal*
Brook. L. Rev	*Brooklyn Law Review*
Cal. L. Rev.	*California Law Review*
Cambridge. L.J.	*Cambridge Law Journal*

Can. B.J.	*Canadian Bar Journal*
Can. Fam. L.Q	*Canadian Family Law Quarterly*
Can. J. Fam. L.	*Canadian Journal of Family Law*
Cath. Law.	*Catholic Lawyer*
Cent. L.J.	*Central Law Journal*
Chi. B. Rec.	*Chicago Bar Record*
Chi. L. Rev.	*Chicago Law Review*
C.F.L.Q.	*Child and Family Law Quarterly*
Colo. Law.	*Colorado Lawyer*
Colum. Hum. Rts. L. Rev.	*Columbia Human Rights Law Review*
Colum. J.L. & Soc. Probs.	*Columbia Journal of Law and & Social Problems*
Colum. L. Rev.	*Columbia Law Review*
Com. Prop. J.	*Community Property Journal*
Cornell L. Rev.	*Cornell Law Review*
Cornell L.Q.	*Cornell Law Quarterly*
Cumb. L. Rev.	*Cumberland Law Review*
Current Legal Probs.	*Current Legal Problems*
DePaul L. Rev.	*DePaul Law Review*
Drake L. Rev.	*Drake Law Review*
DriZ	*Deutsche Richterzeitung*
Dublin U. L.J.	*Dublin University Law Journal*
E.J.L.R.	*European Journal of Law Reform*
Fam. L. Rep.	*Family Law Reports*
Fam. L.Q.	*Family Law Quarterly*
Fam. Matt.	*Family Matters*
Fam. Rel.	*Family Relations*
Fla. B.J.	*Florida Baylor Journal*
Hastings L.J.	*Hastings Law Journal*
Hous. L. Rev.	*Houston Law Review*
How. L.J.	*Howard Law Journal*
IJLF	*International Journal of Law and the Family*
Ill. L. Rev.	*Illinois Law Review*
Ind. L. Rev.	*Indiana Law Review*
Ind. L.J.	*Indiana Law Journal*
Int. Fam. L.J.	*International Family Law Journal*
IJLPF	*International Journal of Law, Policy and the Family*
Int'l & Comp. L.Q.	*International and Comparative Law Quarterly*
Iowa L. Rev.	*Iowa Law Review*
J. Fam. L.	*Journal of Family Law*
J. Mar. & Fam.	*Journal of Marriage and Family*
J. Soc. Welfare Fam. L.	*Journal of Social Welfare and Family Law*
Jurid. Rev.	*Juridical Review*
Jurist	*Jurist*

JuS	*Juristische Schulung*
JZ	*Juristenzeitung*
L.Q. Rev.	*Law Quarterly Review*
La. L. Rev.	*Louisiana Law Review*
Law & Hist. Rev.	*Law and History Review*
Law & Ineq. J.	*Law & Inequality Journal*
Law & Policy	*Law & Policy*
Loy. L. Rev.	*Loyola Law Review (New Orleans)*
Mar. Fam. Rev.	*Marriage and Family Review*
Marq. L. Rev.	*Marquette Law Review*
McGill L.J.	*McGill Law Journal*
Md. L. Rev.	*Maryland Law Review*
Melb. U. L. Rev.	*Melbourne University Law Review*
Mem. St.U. L. Rev.	*Memphis State University Law Review*
Miami L.Q.	*Miami Law Quaterly*
Mich. L. Rev.	*Michigan Law Review*
Minn. L. Rev.	*Minnesota Law Review*
Mo. L. Rev.	*Missouri Law Review*
Mod. L. Rev.	*Modern Law Review*
Mont. L. Rev.	*Montana Law Review*
N.C. L. Rev.	*North Carolina Law Review*
N.E.Q	*New England Quarterly*
N.M. L. Rev.	*New Mexico Law Review*
N.Y.U. L. Rev.	*New York University Law Review*
New L.J.	*New Law Journal*
Notre Dame L. Rev.	*Notre Dame Law Review*
Okla. B.J.	*Oklahoma Bar Journal*
Okla. L. Rev.	*Oklahoma Law Review*
Or. L. Rev.	*Oregon Law Review*
Osgoode Hall L.J.	*Osgoode Hall Law Journal*
Pac. Rim. L. & Pol'y J.	*Pacific Rim Law and Policy Journal*
Population Stud.	*Population Studies*
Prac. Law.	*Practical Lawyer*
R.H.D.	*La Nouvelle Revue Historique du Droit Francais et Étranger*
S.C. L. Rev.	*South Carolina Law Review*
S.C. L.Q.	*South Carolina Law Quarterly*
S.Tex. L.J.	*South Texas Law Journal*
San Diego L. Rev.	*San Diego Law Review*
Sc. St. L.	*Scandinavian Studies in Law*
Smu L. Rev.	*Southern Methodist University Law Review*
Soc. Pol'y & Admin.	*Social Policies & Admininstration*
St. John's L. Rev.	*St. John's Law Review*
St. Louis U. L.J.	*Saint Louis University Law Journal*
Stan. L. Rev.	*Stanford Law Review*

Stetson L. Rev.	*Stetson Law Review*
SvJT	*Svensk Juristtidning*
Sw. L.J.	*Southwestern Law Journal*
SZ	*Zeitschrift der Savigny-Stiftung für Rechtsgeschichte*
Tenn. L. Rev.	*Tennessee Law Review*
Tex. B.J.	*Texas Bar Journal*
Tex. J. Women & L.	*Texas Journal of Women and the Law*
Tex. Tech. L. Rev.	*Texas Tech Law Review*
Tru L. I.	*Trust Law International*
Tulsa L.J.	*Tulsa Law Journal*
U.C. Davis L. Rev.	*University of California at Davis Law Review*
U. Cin. L. Rev.	*University of Cincinnati Law Review*
U. Colo. L. Rev.	*University of Colorado Law Review*
U. Det. L.J.	*University of Detroit Law Journal*
U. Ill. L. Rev.	*University of Illinois Law Review*
U. Kan. City L. Rev.	*University of Kansas City Law Review*
U. Miami L. Rev.	*University of Miami Law Review*
U. Mich. J.L. Reform	*University of Michigan Journal of Law Reform*
U. Pa. L. Rev.	*University of Pennsylvania Law Review*
U. Pitt. L. Rev	*University of Pittsburgh Law Review*
U. N.S.W. L.J.	*University of New South Wales Law Journal*
UBC L. Rev.	*University of British Columbia Law Review*
UCLA L. Rev.	*University of California Law Review*
Utah L. Rev.	*Utah Law Review*
VA. J. INT'L L.	*Virginia Journal of International Law*
Va. L.J.	*Virginia Law Journal*
Va. L. Reg.	*Virginia Law Register*
Va. L. Rev.	*Virginia Law Review*
Vand. L. Rev.	*Vanderbilt Law Review*
Vill. L. Rev.	*Villanova Law Review*
W. Reserve L. Rev.	*Western Reserve Law Review*
W.A.L. Rev.	*Western Australia Law Review*
Wash. & Lee L. Rev.	*Washington and Lee Law Review*
Wash. L. Rev.	*Washington Law Review*
Willamette L.J.	*Willamette Law Journal*
Wis. L. Rev.	*Wisconsin Law Review*
Wm. & Mary J. Women & L.	*William and Mary Journal of Women and the Law*
Wm. Mitchell L. Rev.	*William Mitchell Law Review*
Yale L.J.	*Yale Law Journal*
ZHR	*Zeitschrift für das gesamte Handelsrecht*

Bibliography

1. Primary Sources, Legislation and Legislative Materials

1.1 Roman Law

Die Attischen Nächte des Aulus Gellius I-II (Fritz Weiss ed., Darmstadt 1875/76)

Cicero, In Catilinam I-IV, Pro Murena, Pro Flacco, Pro Sulla (Louis E. Lord, Eng. trans. ed., 1953)

Cicero, De Oratore I-II (E.W. Sutton, Eng. trans., intro. H. Rackman, 1942)

Codex Iustinianus (P. Krueger ed., 1900), III

Das Corpus Iuris Civilis (C.E. Otto, B. Schilling & C.F.F. Sintenis, German trans. and, eds., Leipzig 1833)

Corpus Iuris Civilis (S.P. Scott, Eng. trans., 1973)

Corpus Iuris Civilis I, Institutiones, Digesta (P. Krueger & T. Mommsen eds., 1905), II

Fontes Iuris Romani Antiqui, I Leges et Negotia, II Scriptores (C.G. Bruns ed., 1909)

Gagnér, Anders, Gai Institutiones och Corpus Iuris Civilis (1955)

Gai Institutiones (P. Krueger & G. Studemund eds., 5th ed. 1905)

Gaius, The Institutes of Gaius I (crit. notes & trans. by Francis de Zulueta, 1946)

Gaius, The Institutes of Gaius II (comment. by Francis de Zulueta, 1946)

Gaius Institusjoner 23 (Jacob Jorstad, Norwegian trans., 1927)

Gellius A., The Attic Nights of Aulus Gellius I-III (John C. Rolfe trans., 1927).

Gellius, A., Noctes Atticae (Hosius ed., 1903)

Novellae (R. Schoell & G. Kroll eds., 1904)

Plutarch, The Roman Questions of Plutarch (H.J. Rose trans. and comm., 1924)

Ulpiani Liber Singularis Regularum. Pauli Libri quinque Sententiarum. Fragmenta Minora (P. Krueger ed., Berolini 1878)

1.2. Canon Law

Aguirre, Joseph Saenz de, Collectio Maxima Conciliorum omnium Hispaniae et Novi Orbis V (Salamanca 1686)

Aquinas, Thomas S., Thomae Aquinatis Doctoris Angelici Summa Theologica III (Augustae Taurinorum ed., 1903)

Canones et decreta Sacrosanti Oecumenici concilii tridenti sub Paulo III, Iulio III, et Pio IV (1903)

Canons and Decrees of the Sacred and Oecumenical Council of Trent (J. Waterworth trans., Dolman, London 1848)

Corpus Juris Canonici, emendatum et Notis Illustratum. Gregorii XIII. Pontif. Max. Jussu editum Coloniae Munatianae, mdcxcvi. (C.J.C)

Diplomatarium Suecanum (Joh. Gusth. Liljegren ed., Stockholm 1829)

Hardouin, Jean, Acta Conciliorum et Epistolae Decretales ac Constitutiones Summorum Pontificium IX (A. Cotillon et Cie, Paris 1715)

Hartzheim, Joseph, Concilia Germaniae II-IV (Köln 1759-1763)

Labbé, Philippe, Sacrosanta Concilia IX-XV (Lutetise Parisiorum 1671-72)

Launoy, Jean de, Concilia Antiqua Galliae (Paris 1639)

Lombardi, Petri, Libri IV Sententiarum I-II (2 ed. 1916)

Quinque compilationes antiquae I (Aemilius Friedberg ed., Lipsiae 1882)

Rolandus, Die Summa Magistri Rolandi (Friedrich Thaner ed., Innsbruck 1874)

Tancredi Summa de Matrimonio (Agaton Wunderlich ed., Göttingen 1841)

Wilkins, David, Concilia I-IV (London 1737)

1.3 International Conventions

The Council of Europe Convention on Contact concerning Children (2002)

The European Convention for the Protection of Human Rights and Fundamental Freedoms (1950)

The European Convention on the Exercise of Children's Rights (1996)

The United Nations Convention on Consent to Marriage, Minimum Age for Marriage and Registration of Marriages (1962)

The United Nations Convention on the Rights of the Child (1989)

1.4. The United States

Federal Sources

United States Const. Amend. XIV, § 1., XXVI; Art. 4, § 1

Defense of Marriage Act, DOMA, 1 U.S.C.A. § 7 (2000); Pub. L. No. 104-199, 110 Stat. 2419; 28 U.S.C.A. § 1738 C (West 1996); 1 U.S.C. § 7, (Supp. II 1997)

State Legislation

Ala. Code Ann. §§ 13A-13-1, 26-11-2, 30-1-4, 30-1-5, 30-1-10, 30-1-19 (d) (Law. Coop. 2002)

Ariz. Code Ann. §§ 25-901-906 (2003)

Ark. Code Ann. §§ 9-11-801-810 (2003)

Cal. Fam. Code Ann. § 2251 (a) (West 2003), § 308.5 (West 2002)

- Defense of Marriage Act, Cal. Fam. Code § 308.5 (2002) (added by initiative measure, Prop. 22, § 2, eff. Mar. 8, 2000)
- The Domestic Partner Rights and Responsibilities Act (2003); (Stats. 2003, ch. 421 (Assem. Bill No. 205), § 4, eff. Jan. 1, 2005); Cal. Fam. Code § 297 (West 2005), replacing the Domestic Partner Registration Act, former Cal. Fam. Code § 297 (2000), (Stats. 1999, ch. 588 (Assem. Bill No. 26), § 2)

Colo. Rev. Stat. Ann. §§ 14-2-106, 14-2-110, 14-2-110, 14-10-111, 18-6-201, 18-6-202 (West 2003)

Conn. Gen. Stats. § 46b-38pp (2007), eff. October 1, 2005, Senate Bill 963

D.C. Code Ann. §§ 16-97, 16-98, 22-501, 46-401, 46-403, 46-411, 46-417 (West 2001)

- Domestic Partnership Equality Amendment Act of 2006, D.C. Law 16-79, eff. April 4, 2006

GA. CODE ANN. §§ 16-6-20, 19-3-1, 19-3-1.1, 19-3-2 (1)(2)(3), 19-3-3, 19-3-5 (b), 19-3-32, 19-3-37, 19-3-40, 19-4-1 (West 2003)

— H.B. 1278 (Mobley, Randall, Martin), Leg. Sess. 1995/1996

HAW. REV. STAT. ANN. § 572C-1 (1999)

IDAHO CONST. art. 1 § 4 (Michie 2003)

— IDAHO CODE ANN. § 18-1101, 18-1102, 18-1103 and 18-1104, 32-201, 32-202, 32-205, 32-206, 32-207, 32-412A, 32-501(2), 32-503 (Michie 2003);

— H.B. 176; Chap. 104 Idaho Session Laws (1995);

— Senate Judiciary and Rules Committee, Minutes (March 1, 1995);

— House of Representatives Judiciary, Rules & Administration Committee, Minutes (February 15 1995)

ILLINOIS, ILL. STAT. ANN., ch. 750, § 5/305 (West 2003)

IOWA CODE ANN. §§ 595.2, 595.11, 595.19, 598.29, 598.31, 726.1 (West 2003)

KAN. STAT. ANN. §§ 21-3601, 23-101, 23-102, 23-106 (2002); 23-114, 23-118 (2003);

— L. 2002, ch. 143 § 1;

— House Sub. for SB 486 (Sess. 2002); Senate Bill No. 486 (Sess. 2002)

— House Bill No. 2366 (Sess. 2001);

— House Bill No. 2876 (Sess. 2000);

— Kansas, Judicial Council 1981;

— House Bill No. 2689 (1982)

LA. CIV. CODE ANN. art. 272-275, 307-309 (2003)

MASS. GEN. LAWS, c. 209C § 1 (West 2003) and c. 207 (West 2006)

MINN. STAT. ANN. § 518.055 (West 2005)

MONT. CODE ANN. §§ 26-1-602(30), 40-1-202, 40-1-203, 40-1-208, 40-1-213, 40-1-311, 40-1-401 (1)(a)(3), 40-1-402, 40-1-403, 40-1-401, 45-5-611, 45-5-612 (Mont. Leg. Serv. Div. 2003)

N.H. REV. STAT. ANN. 457:39 (WEST 2003);

— RS 149:11 (1842)

N.J. STAT. ANN. § 37:1, 37:2 (2007), eff. February 19 2007;

— Assembly Bill A3787 and Senate Bill S2407 (2006)

OHIO REV. CODE ANN. §§ 2919.01, 3101.01, 3105.12 (B) (1) and (2), 3105.31, 3109.01, 3303, 3305 (West 2003)

OKLA. CONST. art. 1 § 2 (1998)

— OKLA. STAT. tit. 43 § 2, 43 § 3, 43 § 15, 43 § 128 (West 2003)

PA. CONS. STAT. ANN. §§ 1103, 1302 (b) (4), 1304, 18-4301, 23-1304 (b)(c)(e), 3304 (a) (4), 3305 (b) (West 2003);

— Amendment A 3597, House Bill 2719 and Senate Bill 985 (Leg. Pa. 2004);

— THE MARRIAGE LAW, Act of Aug. 22, 1953, P.L. 1344, 48 P.S. § 1-1 et seq.

R.I. GEN. LAWS, §§ 11-6-1, 15-1-1, 15-1-2, 15-1-5, 15-2-11, 15-8-1, 15-12-1 (Michie 2003)

S.C. CODE ANN. §§ 16-15-10, 20-1-15, 20-1-90, 20-1-80, 20-1-100, 20-1-220, 20-1-250, 20-1-360;

— Act 95 of 1997;

— Bill 3861 (Law. Coop. 2003);

— House Bill 3465 (2000)

TEX. FAM. CODE ANN. §§ 1.108, 2.401, 2.402, 2.404 and 6.202 (Vernon Pamph. 1998)(Vernon 2005); Enacted by Act of June 2, 1969, 61 st Leg., R.S. ch. 888, § 1, 1969, effective Jan 1, 1970, Tex.Gen.Laws 2707, 2717;

— Tex. Fam. Code Ann. § 1.91 (b) (Vernon's 1975) Amended by Act of June 14, 1989, 71st Leg., R.S., ch. 369, § 9, 1989, effective Sept 1 1989, Tex.Gen.Laws 1458, 1461;

— House Bill (H.B.) No. 588, 71st Leg.Sess. (1989) (Patricia Hill, floor debate remarks, 71st Leg.Sess., House Recording No. (H.R.) 62 and 78.)

— Senate Bill, (S.B.) No. 307 (Senate Author: Bob Glasgow, House Sponsor: Patricia Hill) Senate Recording No. 127;

— Act of June 14, 1989, 71st Leg., R.S., ch. 369, § 9, 1989, effective Sept 1 1989, Tex.Gen.Laws 1459, 1461. Amended by Act of April 17, 1997, 75th Leg., R.S., ch. 7, § 1, 1997 Tex.Sess. Law.Serv. 15;

— Tex. Fam. Code Ann. §§ 2.010, 2.012, 2.101-2.102; § 6.102, 6.103, 6.106, 6.108, 6.111, 6.201, 160.204(a)(3), (a)(4)(C) (West Supp. 2005);

— Tex. Pen. Code Ann. § 25.01 (West 2002)

Utah Code Ann. § 30-1-4.5 (Supp. 1987), act of Feb. 25, 1987, ch. 246, effective April 27, 1987, floor Debate, remarks by Sen. Stephen Rees, Norman Angus, 47th Utah Leg., Gen.Sess. (Feb. 17, 1987) Sen. Recording No. 75;

— Utah Code Ann. § 30-1-1, 30-1-2, 3-1-2.3, 30-1-9, 30-1-17.1, 76-7-101 (Michie 2003)

15 Vt. Const. Ch. I, art. 7;

— Vt. Stat. Ann. §§ 1201-1206 (1999);

— Vt. Laws 91 (civil unions)

American Uniform Laws and Restatements

American Law Institute, Principles of the Law of Family Dissolution: Analysis and Recommendations (2002)

Restatement (Second) Conflict of Laws, § 283 (2) (1971)

Restatement (Second) of Contracts 190 (1981)

Uniform Commercial code, § 2-206 (A) (1962)

Uniform Marriage and Divorce Act § 209, 9A U.L.A. 174 (1987)

Uniform Marriage Evasion Act § 1, 9A U.L.A. XXI (1957)

Uniform Partnership Act, § 6(1), 6 U.L.A. 22 (1985)

1.5. Other Countries

Australia

— Australian Social Security Act (1991);

— Property (Relationships) Act 1984 NSW;

— The Property (Relationships) Amendment Act (1999) NSW;

— Property (Relationship) Amendment Bill: Third Reading (March 29, 2001);

— Report on Obligations Arising from De Facto Relationships (1977);

— Tasmania Law Reform Commission

Belgium

Code Civil, Art. 1475–1488; Gedr. St., Sen., 1997-1998, nr. 1-916/6, 8 Juillet 1998, eff. 1 Jan. 2000; Loi Fevr. 13, 2003 (M.B. 28.2. 2003), eff. Juin1 2003.

Canada

— Adult Interdependent Relationships Act, S.A. (2002), Alberta, Canada;

— Martha Bailey, *Marriage and Marriage-Like Relationships* (Ottawa: Law Commission of Canada, 1999);

— *Beyond Conjugality*; Law Commission of Canada (Personal Relationships) (Ottawa 1999);

— The Common-Law Partner's Property and Related Amendments Act, S.M. 2002 Manitoba;

— FAMILY RELATIONS ACT OF BRITISH COLUMBIA, R.S.B.C., ch. 128, § 1 (1996), amended Oct. 1, 1998;
— Law Commission of Canada (Ottawa 2001);
— Manitoba Justice, Changes to Property Laws affecting Common-Law Partners (taking effect June 30, 2004);
— MARRIAGE FOR CIVIL PURPOSES ACT c. 33 (2005);
— MODERNIZATION OF BENEFITS AND OBLIGATIONS ACT, S. C. 2000, c. 12;
— National Assembly Debates of the National Assembly. June 18, Bill 84 (1998);
— ONTARIO FAMILY LAW REFORM ACT of 1986, R.S.O., ch. F-3, §§ 29, 30 (1990)

Denmark

— Betænkning 8, Aegdeskab, Samliv uden ægdeskab I, s. 50 (nr. 915/1980);
— Betænkning om børns retsstilling, No. 1350, 1997;
— BØRNELOVEN nr. 460 of June 7, 2001;
— DANMARKS GAMLE LANDSKAPSLOVE I-VIII (J. Brøndum-Nielsen & P.J. Jørgensen eds., 1933-41);
— Folketingets forhandlinger May 24, 1968, 3628-3650;
— Forslag til Arvelov, L. 100 Dec. 6 2006, para. 15.3.1;
— LOV OM REGISTRERET PARTNERSKAB nr. 372 of June 7, 1989, effective Oct. 1, 1989

England

— ADOPTION AND CHILDREN ACT 2002, eff. Dec. 1, 2003;
— Children Act Advisory Committee, Final Report 1997. London: Lord Chancellor's Department (1997);
— CIVIL PARTNERSHIP ACT 2004, Chapter 33, eff. 5 Dec. 2005; Bill 53 (HL), Bill 132 (HC) 2003-2004;
— FAMILY LAW REFORM ACT 1987;
— Finer Committee on One Parent Families (1974);
— Fisher Committee, Report of the Committee on Abuse of Social Security benefits (1973);
— The Law on Parental Responsibility for Unmarried Fathers. London: Lord Chancellor's Department (1998);
— LAW REFORM (SUCCESSION) ACT 1995, Sh. 2.;
— LORD HARDWICKE'S ACT, June 6, 1753, 26 Geo. II c. 33, eff. March 25, (1754);
— SOCIAL SECURITY CONTRIBUTIONS AND BENEFITS ACT (1992)

Finland

LAG OM REGISTRERAT PARTNERSKAP, Nov. 9, 2001 nr. 950, amended Dec. 13, 2001, Nr. 1226

France

DU PACTE CIVIL DE SOLIDARITÉ ET DU CONCUBINAGE (PACS), No 99-944 15 Nov. 1999, CODE CIVILE, Recueil Dalloz 1999 L 515-517.

Germany

— GESETZ ÜBER DIE EINGETRAGENE LEBENSPARTNERSCHAFT, 16 Febr. 2001, BGBl. I 2001, p. 266, eff. 1 Aug. 2001, amended 12 February 2005, BGBl. I 2005, p. 203
— BGB §§ 705 ff.;
— BGB 1626-1698;
— BUNDESSOZIALHILFEGESETZ, BSHG, vom 30.6.1961 in BGBl. I 815 § 122

Iceland

— Ändringslov nr. 52, 2000;
— BØRNELOV, nr. 7915, § 29, para. 1 (2003);
— LOV OM REGISTRERET PARTNERSKAP, nr. 87, June 12 1996, effective June 27, 1996

Italy

Disegno Di Legge, Senato Della Repubblica, XV Legislatura N. 1339 (2007)

The Netherlands

— Book 1 of the Netherlands Civil Code (1988), 5a: Registered partnership; Act of 17th December 1997, Staatsblad 1997, 660, eff. 1 Jan. 1998;

— Article 1:30, Dutch Civil Code, eff. 1 April 2001; Staatsblad 2001, 9-10;

— Act on the Opening of Adoption to Same-Sex Persons of 21 December 2000, Staatsblad 2001

Norway

— Gulatingslovi (Knut Robberstad ed. 1952);

— Lov om barn og foreldre § 35, April 8, 1981 nr. 7;

— Lov om rett til felles bolig og inbo når husstandsfellesskap opphører, 4 July 1991 nr. 45;

— Lov om registrert partnerskap, 30 April 1993 nr. 40;

— NOU 1999:25, Samboere og samfunnet; St. Meld. Nr. 29 (2002-2003);

— Høringsnotat, January 2007, Snr. 200405522 EP

New Zealand

— Administration Act (1969);

— Civil Union Act (2004), eff. 26 April 2005;

— Family Proceedings Act (1980)

— Family Protection Act (1955);

— Property (Relationships) Act (1976), amended by Property (Relationships) Amendment Act, 2001, eff. 1 Feb. 2002

Scotland

— The Family Law (Scotland) Act 2006, Family Law (Scotland) Bill, SP Bill 36B, Session 2 (2005), Policy Memorandum, Family Law (Scotland) Bill (SP Bill 36) (2005);

— Law Reform (Parent and Child) (Scotland) Act 1986 S. 1;

— The Marriage Law of Scotland, Committee Report (1969);

— Marriage (Scotland) Act 1939 (repealed), 2, 3 Geo. VI, c. 34; O.R.(H.L.) Vol. III No. 16, 14th Dec. 1938, Report December 15,1936, Hansard, Vol. 345, House of Commons 1938-39 Session, sp. 2249;

— The Scottish Law Commission, Report on Family Law, No. 135, Part VII (1992)

Spain

— Civil Code, Article 44 (2005) (same sex marriages);

— Ley 10/1998, de 15 de Julio, d'unions estables de parella (DOGC num. 2687, 23.07.1998)

Sweden

— Föräldrabalken § 6.4 (1949);

— Lag (1994:1117) om registrerat partnerskap, eff. 1 Jan. 1995;

— Lagen om sambors gemensamma hem (1987:232), eff. 1 Jan. 1988 (repealed); SFS 1987:813 (repealed); Prop. 1986/87:1; SOU 1981:85;

— Sambolag (2003:376), Cohabitees Act, Prop. 2002/03:80; SOU 1999:104;

— Statskontoret, rapport 1993:24;

— Swedish Ministry of Justice, Abstract of Protocol on Justice Department Matters 4 (1969);

— SFS 2002:603, Prop. 2001/02:123, LU 27; Prop 2004/05:137; Ds 1999:57;

— SFS 1993:737; SFS 1962:381; SFS 1998:674; SFS 1998:702. SFS 1999:1229; SFS 1997:323; SFS 1941:416; SFS 1987:1206; SFS 1973:651 (repealed)

1.6. Statistical Sources

ABS Births Australia (2002);

ABS, Marital Status and Living Arrangements, Marriages and Divorces, Australia 3310.0 (2002);

Be 13, SM 9401, SCB 1994 och Demografiska rapporter, SCB 1999:1 (Sverige);

European Commission, Eurobarometer. esrc Data Archive (1998-2001);

European Observatory on National Famil Policies, Synthesis of National Family Policies (1996);

European Social Statistics: Demography 2002; Demographic Statistics 1997;

Great Britain. Office of National Statistics, Living in Britain: Result from the 2001 general Household Survey (2001);

Legal Studies Research Programme Findings No. 43 (2004) (Scotland);

National Vital Statistics Reports, Vol. 52, No. 10, December 17, 2003 (USA);

Statistics New Zealand, Births and Deaths (March 2002);

U.N. Demographic Year Book;

U.S. Bureau of the Census, Unmarried-Couple Households, by Presence of Children: 1960 to Present (2004);

U.S. Bureau of the Census, Married-Couple and Unmarried-Partner Households: 2000, Census 2000, Special Reports, US Census 2000 (2003)

2. Literature

Agell, Anders, Äganderätten till Fastighet för Makar och Sambor (1985)

— Äktenskap, Samboende, Partnerskap (3d ed. 2004)

Amott, Teresa & Matthaei, Julie, Race, Gender, And Work: A Multicultural Economic History of Woman in the United States (1991)

Anson, William Reynell, The Law of Contract (1995)

Areen, Judith, Cases and Materials on Family Law (3d ed.1992)

Aristotle, The Nicomachean Ethics (H. Rackham ed., 1947)

Atiyah, Patrick S., An Introduction to the Law of Contracts (5th ed. 1995)

Atkin, Bill, Living together Without Marriage (1991)

Atkin, Bill, and Parker, Wendy, Relationship Property in New Zealand (2001)

Austin, John, 2 Lectures on Jurisprudence (5th ed. 1885)

Barton, C., Cohabitation Contracts (1985)

Basch, Norma, In the Eyes of the Law: Women, Marriage, and Property in Nineteenth Century New York (1982)

Baumann, Alexis, Die Zivilrechtliche Bedeutung des Konkubinates (1932)

Becker, Mary, et al., Cases and Materials on Feminist Jurisprudence: Taking Woman Seriously (1994)

Becker, W.G., Platons Gesetze und das griechiche Familienrecht (1932)

Bell, G. J., Principles of the Law of Scotland (Guthrie ed, Edinburgh, 10th ed. 1899)

Bénabent, Alain, Droit Civil, La Famille (7th ed. 1995)

Bishop, Joel Prentiss, Commentaries on the Law of Marriage and Divorce and Evidence in Matrimonial Suits (Boston 1852) (2d ed. 1856)

— New Commentaries on Marriage, Divorce and Separation I-II (Chicago, T.H. Flood and Co. 1891)

Blackstone, William, Commentaries On The Law of England I-IV (R.M. Kerr ed., London 1884)

Bloomfield, Maxwell, American Lawyers in a Changing Society (1976)

Blumstein, Philip & Schwartz, Pepper, American Couples: Money, Work, Sex (1983)

Bonfante, Pietro, Corso di Diritto Romano (1963)

Boswell, John, Same-Sex Unions in Premodern Europe (1994)

Bradley, David, Family Law and Political Culture: Scandinavian Laws in Comparative Perspective (1996)

Bramslett, M.D. & Mosher, W.D., Cohabitation, Marriage, Divorce, and Remarriage in the United States (2002)

Brinig, Margaret F., From Contract to Covenant: Beyond the Law and Economics of the Family (2000)

Brinz, Alois, Lehrbuch der Pandekten III (Erlangen, 2d ed. 1874)

Brockelbank, W.J., La Formation du Mariage dans le Droit des Etats-Unis (1935)

Bromley, P.M., Family Law (4th ed. 1971) (6th ed. 1981)

— Family Law Towards the Millennium: Essays for P.M. Bromley (1997) (Philadelphia 1886)

Brown, Edmund Q., Marriage in Pennsylvania Under the New License Act (Philadelphia 1886)

Bullock, William E., The Law of Domestic Relations of the State of New York (Albany N.Y. 1898)

Bureau of War Risk Ins., Treasury Dep't, Digest of the Law Relating to Common Law Marriage in the States, Territories, and Dependencies of the United States (1919)

Casper, Lynne M. & Bianchi, Suzanne M., Continuity and Change in the American Family (2002)

Calhoun, Arthur, Social History of the American Family I-III (1917)

Carbonnier, Jean, Droit Civil 2, La Famille (20th ed. 1999)

Carlier, Auguste, Marriage in the United States (Boston 1867)

Carlsson, Lizzie, Jag Giver Dig Min Dotter (1965)

Carney, T. and Hanks, P., Social Security in Australia (1994)

Clark, Jr., Homer H., Cases and Problems on Domestic Relations (4th ed. 1990)

— The Law of Domestic Relations in the United States (1968), I-II (2d ed. 1987)

Clark, Jr., Homer H., Estin, Ann Laquer, Cases and Problems on Domestic Relations (6th ed. 2000)

Clive, Eric M., The Law of Husband and Wife in Scotland (4th ed. 1997)

Clive, Eric M. and Wilson, John G., The Law of Husband and Wife in Scotland (1974) (2d ed. 1982)

Corbett, Percy Ellewood, The Roman Law of Marriage (1930)

Cott, Nancy F., Public Vows: A History of Marriage and the Nation (2000)

Crane, J. and Blomberg, A., Partnership (1968)

Cretney, Stephen, Family Law in the Twentieth Century, A History (2003)

Cretney, S.M., and Masson, J.M., Principles of Family Law (6th ed. 1997)

Danielsen, Svend, Nordisk Børneret II (2003)

Dauvillier, Jean, le Mariage dans le Droit Classique de L'Église (1933)

Douthwaite, Graham, Unmarried Couples and the Law (1979)

Ehrenzweig, Albert A., A Treatise on the Conflict of laws (1962)

Eichmann, Eduard, Lehrbuch des Kirchenrechts auf Grund des Codex Iuris Canonici I-II (3d ed. 1929/1930)

Eichmann, Eduard & Mörsdorf, Klaus, Lehrbuch des Kirchenrechts II (11th ed. 1969)

Eisenberg, Melvin Aron, The Nature of the Common Law (1988)

ELLMAN, IRA MARK, ET AL., FAMILY LAW: CASES, TEXT, PROBLEMS (3d ed. 1998) (4th ed. 2004)

ERSKINE, JOHN, AN INSTITUTE OF THE LAW OF SCOTLAND (J.B. Nicholson ed., Edinburgh, 8th ed. 1870)

— PRINCIPLES OF THE LAW OF SCOTLAND (John Rankine ed., 21st ed. 1911)

ESAM, P., AND BERTHOUD, R., INDEPENDENT BENEFITS FOR MEN AND WOMEN (1991)

ESMEIN, A., LE MARIAGE EN DROIT CANONIQUE I (R. Génestal ed., 2d ed. 1929)

— LE MARIAGE EN DROIT CANONIQUE II (R. Génestal & J. Dauvillier eds., 2d ed. 1935)

FERGUSSON, JAMES, A TREATISE ON THE PRESENT STATE OF THE CONSISTORIAL LAW IN SCOTLAND (Edinburgh 1829)

FIRESTONE, S., THE DIALECTIC OF SEX (1920)

FOOTE, CALEB, ET AL., CASES AND MATERIALS ON FAMILY LAW (3d ed.1985)

FRASER, PATRIC, HUSBAND AND WIFE ACCORDING TO THE LAW OF SCOTLAND I (2d ed., Edinburgh 1876)

— A TREATISE ON THE LAW OF SCOTLAND I (Edinburgh, T. & T. Clark, Law-Booksellers 1846)

FREEDMAN, ABRAHAM L., FREEDMAN, MAURICE, LAW OF MARRIAGE AND DIVORCE IN PENNSYLVANIA I (2d ed. 1957)

FREEMAN, M. & LYON, C., COHABITATION WITHOUT MARRIAGE (1983)

FREISEN, JOSEPH, GESCHICHTE DES CANONISCHEN EHERECHTS BIS ZUM VERFALL DER

GLOSSENLITTERATUR (Paderborn, Druck und Verlag von Ferdinand Schöningh, 2d ed. 1893)

FRIEDBERG, EMIL, DAS RECHT DER EHESCHLIESSUNG IN SEINER GESCHICHTLICHEN. ENTWICKLUNG (Leipzig 1865)

— VERLOBUNG UND TRAUUNG (Leipzig 1876)

FRIEDLÄNDER, LUDWIG, DARSTELLUNGEN AUS DER SITTENGESCHICHTE ROMS (Georg Wissowa ed., 10th ed. 1922)

FRIEDMAN, B., THE FEMININE MYSTIQUE (1963)

FRIEDMAN, LAWRENCE M., A HISTORY OF AMERICAN LAW (2nd ed. 1985)

— PRIVATE LIVES: FAMILIES, INDIVIDUALS, AND THE LAW (2004)

GEIS, FRANCES & GEIS, JOSEPH, MARRIAGE AND THE FAMILY IN THE MIDDLE AGE (1987)

GIRARD, PAUL FREDERIC, MANUEL ELEMENTAIRE DE DROIT ROMAIN (1929)

GLENDON, MARY ANN, THE NEW FAMILY AND THE NEW PROPERTY (1981)

— STATE, LAW AND FAMILY. FAMILY LAW IN TRANSITION IN THE UNITED STATES AND WESTERN EUROPE (1977)

— THE TRANSFORMATION OF FAMILY LAW: STATE, LAW, AND FAMILY IN THE UNITED STATES AND WESTERN EUROPE (1997)

GLOAG, W. M., AND HENDERSON, R. CANDLICH, INTRODUCTION TO THE LAW OF SCOTLAND (7th ed. 1968)

GLÜCK, VON, CHRISTIAN FRIEDRICH, AUSFÜRLICHEN ERLÄUTERUNGEN DER PANDECTEN NACH

HELLFELDT, EIN KOMMENTAR, BAND 23 (Erlangen 1822)

GOODSELL, WILLYSTINE, FAMILY IN THE AMERICAN COLONIES (1915)

— A HISTORY OF THE FAMILY AS A SOCIAL AND EDUCATIONAL INSTITUTION (1924) (1930)

GREENLEAF, SIMON, A TREATISE ON THE LAW OF EVIDENCE II (Boston 1842) (2d ed. 1846) (3d ed. 1852) (16th ed. 1899)

GROSSBERG, MICHAEL, GOVERNING THE HEART: LAW AND THE FAMILY IN NINETEENTH-CENTURY AMERICA (1985)

GROSSE, M.C., FREIE RÖMISCHE EHE UND NICHTEHELICHE LEBENSGEMEINSCHAFT (1991)

GUTTERIDGE, H.C., COMPARATIVE LAW (2d ed. 1949)

Hall, Kermit. L, The Magic Mirror: Law in American History (1989)

Hambro, Edward, Den Romerske Familie- og Arveret (1923)

Hanbury, Jill, and Martin, Harold Greville, Modern Equity (15th ed. 1997)

Hartog, Henrik, Man and Wife in America: A History (2000)

Hemard, Joseph, Théorie et Pratique des nullités des Sociétés et Sociétés de fait (1926)

Henaghan, M., and Atkin, B., Family Law Policy in New Zealand (2d ed. 2002)

Hirsch, Barbara B., Living Together. A Guide to the Law for Unmarried Couples (1976)

Holdsworth, William, A History of English Law (7th ed. 1966)

Holmes, Oliver Wendell, The Common Law (Boston, Little, Brown & Co. 1881)

Howard, George Elliott, A History of Matrimonial Institutions I-III (1904)

Hovius, Berend, and Youdan, Timothy G., The Law of Family Property (1991)

Hubback, John, A Treatise on the Evidence of Succession to real and personal Property and Peerages (London, W. Benning 1844)

Huber, Josef, Der Ehekonsens im Römischen Recht (1977)

Hume, David, Lectures on the Law of Scotland 1786-1822 (G.C.H. Paton ed., 1939-1958)

Ihering, Rudolph, Geist des Römischen Rechts auf den verschiedenen Stufen seiner entwicklung I-II (Leibzig, Breitkopf und Härtel, 2d ed. 1866)

Jackson, Joseph, The Formation and Annulment of Marriage (2d ed.1969)

Jacobs, Albert C. & Goebel, JR., Julius, Cases And Other Materials on Domestic Relations (3d ed. 1952) (4th ed. 1961)

Jolowicz, H.F., Roman Foundations of Modern Law (1957)

Joyce, George Hayward, Die Christliche Ehe (1934)

— Christian Marriage: an Historical and Doctrinal Study (2d ed. 1948)

Jörs, Paul & Kunkel, Wolfgang, Römisches Privatrecht (3d ed. 1949)

Karlowa, Otto, Die Formen der Römischen Ehe und Manus (Bonn 1868)

— Römische Rechtsgeschichte II (1901)

Kaser, Max, Das Römische Privatrecht I-II (1966)

Kazen, Barbara A., Family Law: Texas Practice and Procedure (1990)

Keezer, Frank, The Law of Marriage and Divorce (1906) (reprinted 1991)

— A Treatise on the Law of Marriage and divorce (2d ed. 1923)

Kent, James, Commentaries on American Law 2 (New York, William Kent 1826) (2d ed. 1832) (7th ed. 1851) (14th ed. 1896)

Kephart, William M., The Family, Society and the Individual (1961) (2d ed. 1966)

— Legal and Procedural Aspects of Marriage and Divorce. Handbook on Marriage and the Family (1964)

Kessler, Peter-Josef, die Entwicklung der Formvorschriften für die Kanonische Eheschliessung (1934)

King, Morgan D., Cohabitation Handbook. Living together and The Law (1975)

Knecht, August, Handbuch des Katholischen Eherechts (1928)

Koegel, Otto E., Common Law Marriage and its Development in the United States (1922)

Koons, Don, Handbook of Texas Family Law (1996)

Kovacs, Dorothy, De Facto Property Proceedings in Australia (1998)

Krause, Harry D., Family Law, Cases, Comments, and Questions (2d ed. 1983) (3d ed. 1990)

KRAUSE, HARRY D., ET AL., FAMILY LAW, CASES, COMMENTS, AND QUESTIONS (5th ed. 2003)

KUFFNER, K.L., COMMON LAW AND SAME-SEX RELATIONSHIPS UNDER THE MATRIMONIAL PROPERTY ACT (2000)

LAFERRIÉRE, FIRMIN, HISTOIRE DU DROIT CIVIL DE ROME ET DU DROIT FRANCAIS III (Paris 1847)

LASSEN, JUL, LAEREBOG I ROMERSK PRIVATRET (1911)

LAVORI, NORA, LIVING TOGETHER, MARRIED OR SINGLE: YOUR LEGAL RIGHTS (1976)

LAWRENCE, M., A HISTORY OF AMERICAN LAW (1973) (2d ed. 1985)

LEACH, WILLIAM, TRUE LOVE AND PERFECT UNION (1980)

LEVI, EDWARD H., AN INTRODUCTION TO LEGAL REASONING (1948)

LEVY, ERNST, DER HERGANG DERRÖIMISCHEN EHESCHEIDUNG (1925)

LØDRUP, PETER, FAMILIERETTEN (4th ed. 2001)

MADDEN, J.W., HANDBOOK IN THE LAW OF PERSONS AND DOMESTIC RELATIONS (1931)

MAITLAND, FREDERIC W., ROMAN LAW AND CANON LAW IN THE CHURCH OF ENGLAND (London 1898)

MARQUARDT, JOACHIM, DAS PRIVATLEBEN DER RÖMER I (Leibzig, 2d ed. 1886)

MARTIN LUTHER, WERKE (Erlangen 1838)

MAZEAUD, HENRI, ET AL., LECON DE DROIT CIVIL, 4 TOME, 1 VOL. (1969), I TOME, 3 VOL. (1972)

MAZUR, R., THE NEW INTIMACY, OPEN-ENDED MARRIAGES AND ALTERNATIVE LIFE-STYLES (1973)

MEE, JOHN, THE PROPERTY RIGHTS OF COHABITEES (1999)

MEYER, PAUL, DER RÖMISCHE KONKUBINAT NACH DEN RECHTSQUELLEN UND INSCHRIFTEN (Leipzig 1895)

MILL, JOHN STUART, ON LIBERTY (London, Longman, Roberts & Green Co., 1859)

MILLET, K., SEXUAL POLITICS (1969)

MINOR, RALEIGH C., CONFLICT OF LAWS (1901)

MITTEIS, LUDWIG, RÖMISCHES PRIVATRECHT (1908)

MOMMSEN, THEODOR, ABRISS DES RÖMISCHES STAATSRECHT III (Leipzig, Duncker & Humblot 1893)

— RÖMISCHE FORSCHUNGEN I (Berlin 1864)

— RÖMISCHES STRAFRECHT (Leipzig 1899)

MONTESQUIEU, CHARLES DE, L'ÉSPRIT DES LOIS (Genevè, Barillot & Fils 1748)

MORLAND, JOHN W., KEEZER ON THE LAW OF MARRIAGE AND DIVORCE (3d ed. 1946)

MÜLLER-FREIENFELS, WOLFRAM, EHE UND RECHT (1962)

NICHOLAS, BARRY, AN INTRODUCTION TO ROMAN LAW (1962)

NIMKOFF, MEYER F., MARRIAGE AND THE FAMILY (1947)

NOBLE, CHARLES, A COMPENDIUM OF THE LAWS ON MARRIAGE AND DIVORCE (New York, Baker, Voorhis & Co. 1882)

O'DONNELL, J., & JONES, D., THE LAW OF MARRIAGE AND MARITAL ALTERNATIVES (1982)

OAKLEY, A.J., CONSTRUCTIVE TRUSTS (3rd ed. 1997)

OLDHAM, J. THOMAS, DIVORCE, SEPARATION AND THE DISTRIBUTION OF PROPERTY (2002)

OLIVECRONA, S.R.D.K., OM MAKARS GIFTORÄTT I BO (Upsala, 5th ed. 1882)

PARKER, STEPHEN, INFORMAL MARRIAGE, COHABITATION AND THE LAW 1750-1989 (1990)

PARRY, M., THE LAW RELATING TO COHABITATION (3d ed. 1993)

PARSONS, THEOPHILUS, THE LAW OF CONTRACT I-II (Boston 1853)

PEARCE, ROBERT, AND STEVENSON, JOHN, THE LAW OF TRUSTS AND EQUITABLE OBLIGATIONS (1995)

PLASSARD, J., LE CONCUBINAT ROMAIN SOUS LE HAUT EMPIRE (1921)

PLOSCOWE, MORRIS, SEX AND THE LAW (1951)

PLOSCOWE, MORRIS & FREED, DORIS JOHANS, FAMILY LAW. CASES AND MATERIALS (1963)

PLÖCHL, WILLIBALD M., DAS EHERECHT DES MAGISTERS GRATIANUS (1935)

— GESCHICHTE DES KIRCHENRECHTS II (2d ed. 1962)

POLLOCK, FREDERICK, FIRST BOOK OF JURISPRUDENCE (2d ed. 1904)

POLLOCK, FREDERICK & MAITLAND, FREDERIC W., HISTORY OF ENGLISH LAW II (Cambridge, Cambridge University Press, 2d ed. 1898)

POSNER, RICHARD, ECONOMIC ANALYSIS OF LAW (2d ed. 1977)

PUCHTA, GEORG FRIEDRICH, CURSUS DER INSTITUTIONEN I-II (Leipzig,10th ed. 1893)

RABEL, ERNST, THE CONFLICT OF LAWS, A COMPARATIVE STUDY I (1945)

— THE CONFLICT OF LAWS, A COMPARATIVE STUDY I (1958)

RAGE-BROCARD, MADELEINE, RITES DE MARIAGE. LA DEDUCTION IN DOMUM MARITI (1934)

REEVE, TAPPING, DOMESTIC RELATIONS (James W. Eaton, Jr. ed., 4th ed. 1846)

— THE LAW OF BARON AND FEMME (New York 1816)

— THE LAW OF BARON AND FEMME, OF PARENT AND CHILD, GUARDIAN AND WARD, MASTER AND SERVANT, AND OF THE POWERS OF THE COURT OF CHANCERY (Albany, William Gould & Son, 3d ed. 1867)

RICHMOND, MARY E. & HALL, FRED S., MARRIAGE AND THE STATE (1929)

RIPERT, I.G. & BOULANGER, J., TRAITÉ DE DROIT CIVIL I (1956)

RORER, DAVID, AMERICAN INTER-STATE LAW (Chicago, Callaghan 1878)

ROSSBACH, AUGUST, UNTERSUCHUNGEN ÜBER DIE RÖMISCHE EHE (Stuttgart 1853)

RYAN, PHILIP A. & GRANFIELD, DOM DAVID, DOMESTIC RELATIONS. CIVIL AND CANON LAW (1963)

SAMTER, ERNST, FAMILIENFESTE DER GRIECHEN UND RÖMER (1901)

SCHEURL, VON, A., DIE ENTWICKLUNG DES KIRCHLICHEN EHESCHLIESSUNGSRECHT (Erlangen 1877)

SCHLESINGER, RUDOLF B., FORMATION OF CONTRACTS I (1968)

SCHOULER, JAMES, MARRIAGE, DIVORCE, SEPARATION & DOMESTIC RELATIONS I-III (6th ed. 1921)

— A TREATISE ON HUSBAND AND WIFE (Boston, Little, Brown & Co. 1882)

SCHREIBER, G., WELTKONZIL VON TRIENT I-II (1951)

SCHULTE, J. FR., HANDBUCH DES KATOLISCHEN EHERECHTS (Giessen 1855)

SCHULZ, FRITZ S., CLASSICAL ROMAN LAW (1951)

— PRINZIPIEN DER RÖMISCHEN RECHTS (1934)

SCHWIND, FRITZ, RÖMISCHES RECHT I (1950)

SCHÖNSTEINER, FERDINAND, GRUNDRISS DES KIRCHLICHEN EHERECHTS (2d ed. 1937)

SCOLES, EUGENE F. & HAY, PETER, CONFLICT OF LAWS (2d ed. 1992)

SIRJAMAKI, JOHN, THE AMERICAN FAMILY IN THE TWENTIETH CENTURY (1953)

SMITH, T. B., A SHORT COMMENTARY ON THE LAW OF SCOTLAND (1962)

SOHM, RUDOLPH, INSTITUTIONEN (1949)

— DAS RECHT DER EHESCHLIESSUNG AUS DEM DEUTSCHEN UND CANONISCHEN RECHT GESCHICHTLICH ENTWICKELT (Weimar 1875)

SPIESS, HANS-HERMANN, DIE UNGÜLTIGE EHE IM RECHT DER VEREINIGTEN STAATEN (1964)

STAIR, VISCOUNT, THE INSTITUTIONS OF THE LAW OF SCOTLAND I-II (J.S. More ed., Edinburgh, 5th ed. 1832)

STEWARD, DAVID & CAREY, FRANCIS, A DIGEST OF THE LAW OF HUSBAND AND WIFE AS ESTABLISHED IN MARYLAND (Baltimore 1881)

STONE, LAWRENCE, THE FAMILY, SEX AND MARRIAGE IN ENGLAND 1500-1800 (1990)

— UNCERTAIN UNIONS: MARRIAGE IN ENGLAND 1660-1753 (1992)

STORY, JOSEPH, COMMENTARIES ON THE CONFLICTS OF LAWS (Boston, Billiard, Gray, and Co. 1834)

STÜCKRADT, VOLKER, RECHTSWIRKUNGEN EHEÄHNLICHER VERHÄLTNISSE (1964)

SUNDBERG, JACOB W.F., FAMILJERÄTT I OMVANDLING (1969)

SVENSKA LANDSKAPSLAGAR IV, SKÅNELAGEN OCH GUTALAGEN (ÅKE HOLMBÄCK & ELIAS WESSÉN 1979)

SVERDRUP, TONE, STIFTELSE AV SAMEIE I EKTESKAP OG UGIFT SAMLIV (1997)

THOMAS, HANS-FRIEDRICH C., FORMLOSE EHEN (1973)

TREITEL, G.H., THE LAW OF CONTRACT (19th ed. 1995)

TROST, JAN, UNMARRIED COHABITATION (1979)

VANDENBERGHE, H., DEN JURIDISCHE BETEKENIS VAN HET CONCUBINAAT (1970)

VERNIER, CHESTER G., AMERICAN FAMILY LAWS I-III (1931)

VOLTERRA, E., LA CONCEPTION DU MARIAGE D'APRES LES JURISTES ROMAINS (1940)

WADLINGTON, WALTER & O'BRIEN, RAYMOND F., CASES AND MATERIALS ON DOMESTIC RELATIONS (4th ed. 1998)

WAITE, LINDA & GALLAGHER, MAGGIE, THE CASE FOR MARRIAGE: WHY MARRIED PEOPLE ARE HAPPIER (2000)

WALKER, D. M., PRINCIPLES OF SCOTTISH PRIVATE LAW (4th ed. 1988)

WALTON, FREDERICK PARKER, A HANDBOOK OF HUSBAND AND WIFE ACCORDING TO THE LAW OF SCOTLAND (W. E. R. Hendry and Alastair M. Johnston eds., 3d ed. 1951)

WEITZMAN, LEONORE J., THE MARRIAGE CONTRACT: SPOUSES, LOVERS, AND THE LAW (1981)

WESTRUP, C.W., INTRODUCTION TO EARLY ROMAN LAW I (1944)

— RECHERCHES SUR LES FORMES ANTIQUES DE MARIAGE DANS L'ENCIENNE DROIT ROMAINE (1943)

WEYRAUCH, WALTER O. & KATZ, SANFORD N., AMERICAN FAMILY LAW IN TRANSITION (1983)

— FAMILY LAW – LEGAL CONCEPTS AND CHANGING HUMAN RELATIONSHIPS (1994)

WIERSMA, G.E., COHABITATION, AN ALTERNATIVE TO MARRIAGE? A CROSS-NATIONAL STUDY (1983)

WIGMORE, JOHN, TREATISE ON THE LAW OF EVIDENCE 2 (1905) (J. Chadbourn, rev. ed. 1974)

PREMARITAL AND MARITAL CONTRACTS: A LAWYER'S GUIDE TO DRAFTING AND NEGOTIATING ENFORCEABLE MARITAL AND COHABITATION AGREEMENTS (Edward L. Winer & Lewis Becker, eds., 1993)

WOLFF, HANS JULIUS, WRITTEN AND UNWRITTEN MARRIAGES IN HELLENISTIC AND POSTCLASSICAL ROMAN LAW (1939)

YORKE, PHILLIPE, THE LIFE OF LORD CHANCELLOR HARDWICKE (1913)

3. Articles

Abeloff, William H., Note, *The Common Law Wife and Workmen's Compensation*, 16 WASH. & LEE L. REV. 79 (1959)

Adams, Olen E., Note, *Common Law Marriage in Oklahoma*, 14 OKLA. L. REV. 291 (1961)

Adamson, Norman, J., *Lord Brougham's Act and Scottish Irregular Marriages*, JURID. REV. 148 (1958)

Adgate, Robert, *Nineteenth Century Indiana Law on the Formation of Marriage: Contract or Status?*, (Spring 1981) (unpublished seminar paper, Indiana University Law School)

Agell, Anders, *Cohabitation Without Marriage in Swedish Law*, in MARRIAGE AND COHABITATION IN CONTEMPORARY SOCIETIES 245 (John M. Eekelaar, Sanford N. Katz eds., 1980)

— *Family Forms and Legal Policies*, 38 SC. ST. L. 197 (1999)

— *Is There One System of Family Law in the Nordic Countries?*, 3 E.J.L.R. 313 (2001)

— *Should and Can Family Law Influence Social Behaviour?*, in THE CHANGING FAMILY 125 (John Eekelaar and Thandabantu Nhlapo eds., 1998)

— *The Swedish Law on Marriage and Cohabitation: A Journey without a Destination*, 24 SC. ST. L. 9 (1980)

Allen, Robert A., *Presumption of the Validity of a Second Marriage*, 20 BAYLOR L. REV. 206 (1968)

Andrews, J.A., *Common law marriage*, 22 MOD. L. REV. 396 (1959)

Andrews, Thomas, *Property Rights of Domestic Partners in the United States and Scandinavia: A Comparative Study* (2003) (unpublished manuscript, University of Washington)

Annual Report, *Florida Bar Committee in Family Law*, 32 FLA. B.J. 230 (1958)

Appel, Alfred, Note, *Common-law marriage after removal of impediment to valid ceremonial marriage*, 12 Cornell L.Q. 513 (1927)

Arnold, J.C., *Vindication of the common law marriage*, 103 L.J. 293 (1953)

— *Marriage at common law*, 108 L.J. 131 (1958)

— *Marriage by cohabitation and repute*, 111 L.J. 150 (1961)

Arraros, José E., *Concubinage in Latin America*, 3 J. FAM. L. 330 (1963)

Ashton-Cross, D.I.C., *Cohabitation with habit and repute*, JURID. REV. (1961)

Atkin, Bill, *Reflections on New Zealand's Property Reforms 'Five Years On'*, in THE INTERNATIONAL SURVEY OF FAMILY LAW 217 (Bill Atkin, gen. ed., 2007)

— *The Challenge of Unmarried Cohabitation – The New Zealand Response*, 37 FAM. L.Q. 303 (2003)

— *Reforming Property Division in New Zealand: From Marriage to Relationships*, 3 E.J.L.R. (2001)

— *The Rights of Married and Unmarried Couples in New Zealand: Radical New Laws on Property and Succession*, International Society of Family Law World Conference, (Copenhagen/Oslo, August 2002) (unpublished paper)

Axinn, William G. & Thornton, Arland, *The relationship Between Cohabitation and Divorce: Selectivity or Causal Influence?*, 29 DEMOGRAPHY 357 (1992)

Bailey, Martha, *Marriage and Morals*, in THE INTERNATIONAL SURVEY OF FAMILY LAW 53 (Bill Atkin, gen. ed., 2007).

— *Regulation of Cohabitation and Marriage in Canada*, 26 LAW & POLICY 153 (2004)

Bailey-Harris, Rebecca, *A decade of reforms in Australia*, 9 I.J.L.F. 233 (1995)

— *Law and unmarried couple – oppression or liberation*, 8 CHILD FAM. L.Q. 137 (1996)

Bala, Nicholas, *Alternatives for Extending Spousal Status in Canada*, 17 CAN. J. FAM. L. 169 (2000)

— *Controversy Over Couples in Canada: The Evolution of Marriage and Other Adult Interdependent Relationships*, 29 QUEEN'S L.J. 41 (2003)

Barker, C., et al., *Social Security abuse*, 24(2) SOC. POL'Y & ADMIN. 104 (1990)

Barlow, Anne, *Regulation of Cohabitation, Changing Family Policies and Social Attitudes: A Discussion of Britain within Europe*, 26 LAW & POLICY 57 (2004)

Barry, John C., *Tridentine form of marriage: is the law unreasonable?*, 20 JURIST 159 (1960)

Barton, J.L. & Thomson, J.M., *Irregular marriages*, 89 L.Q. REV. 181 (1973)

Basch, Norma, *Relief in the Premises: Divorce as a Woman's Remedy in New York and Indiana*, 1815-1870, 8 LAW HIST. REV. 1 (1990)

Bates, F., *The Presumption of marriages arising from cohabitation*, 13 W.A.L. REV. 341 (1978)

Battes, Robert, *Die rechtliche Behandlung der nichtehelichen Lebensgemeinschaften in der Bundesrepublik Deutschland*, in ENTWICKLUNG IM RECHT DER FAMILIE UND DER AUSSEREHELICHEN LEBENSGEMEINSCHAFT 21 (Uwe Blaurock, Hrsg., 1989)

Billig, Thomas Clifford & Lynch, James Phillip, *Common-Law Marriage in Minnesota, A Problem in Social Security,* 22 MINN. L. REV. 177 (1938)

Björnberg, Ulla, *Cohabitation and Marriage in Sweden - Does Family Form Matter?*, 15 IJLPF 50 (2001)

Black, Robert, *Common Law Marriage,* 2 U. CIN. L. REV. 113 (1928)

Blake, Henry T., *The Gospel of Marriage According to Bishop,* 13 ILL. L. REV. 34 (1918/19)

Blakesley, Christopher, *The Putative Marriage Doctrine,* 60 TUL. L. REV. 1 (1985)

Blanchard, Carlos, Note, *Documentary evidence in informal marriage cases,* 14 JURIST 453 (1953)

Blum, George L., Annotation, *Property Rights Arising from Relationship of Couple Cohabiting Without Marriage,* 69 A.L.R.5th 219 (1999)

Blumberg, Grace Ganz, *Cohabitation without Marriage: A different Perspective,* 28 UCLA L. REV. 1125 (1981)

— *The Regularization of Nonmarital Cohabitation: Rights and Responsibilities in the American Welfare State,* 76 NOTRE DAME L. REV. 1265 (2001)

Boele-Woelki, Katharina, *Registered Partnerships: Legislation of the Netherlands,* CURRENT LEGAL PROBS. 43 (1999)

— *Registered Partnership and Same-Sex Marriage in the* Netherlands, in LEGAL RECOGNITION OF SAME-SEX COUPLES IN EUROPE 41 (Katharina Boele-Woelki and Angelika Fuchs eds., 2003)

Bonesio, Woodrow M., Comment, *Marriage and Divorce Under the Texas Family Code,* 8 HOUS. L. REV. 100 (1970)

Borah, Woodrow & Cook, Sherburne F., *Marriage and Legitimacy in Mexican Culture: Mexico and California,* 54 CAL. L. REV. 946 (1966)

Bowman, Craig A. & Cornish, Blake M., Note, *A More Perfect Union: A Legal and Social Analysis of Domestic Partnership Ordinances,* 92 COLUM. L. REV. 1164 (1992)

Bowman, Cynthia Grant, *A Feminist Proposal To Bring Back Common Law Marriage,* 75 OR. L. REV. 709 (1996)

— *Legal Treatment of Cohabitation in the United States,* 26 LAW & POLICY 119 (2004)

Bradley, David, *Regulation of Unmarried Cohabitation in West-European Jurisdictions – Determinants of Legal Policy,* 15 IJLPF 22 (2001)

Bradway, John S., *Tampering with Marriage,* 6 BROOK. L. REV. 277 (1937)

Brickell, Robert C., *Common-Law Marriage,* 44 AM. L. REV. 256 (1910)

Brines, Julie & Joyner, Kara, *The Ties That Bind: Commitment and Stability in Modern Union,* 64 AM. SOC. REV. 333 (1999)

Brinig, Margaret F., *Domestic Partnership and Default Rules,* in RECONCEIVING THE FAMILY. CRITIQUE ON THE AMERICAN LAW INSTITUTE'S PRINCIPLES OF THE LAW OF FAMILY DISSOLUTION 269 (Robin Fretwell Wilson ed., 2006)

— *Status, Contract and Covenant,* 79 CORNELL L. REV. 1573 (1994)

Brixey, Buddy, Comment, *Texas Legislation on the Statute of Frauds in Palimony Suits: Is an Oral Contract Worth the Paper It's Written On?*, 25 HOUS. L. REV. 979 (1988)

Brock, David H., Note, *Community Property - Division of Property Upon Divorce - Property Acquired During Marriage in A Common Law State Except By Gift, Devise, Or Descent Should Be Treated As Community Property. Cameron v. Cameron,* 641 S.W.2d 210 (Tex. 1982), 14 ST. MARY'S L.J. 789 (1883)

Brown, Jennifer Gerarda, *Competitive Federalism and the Legislative Incentives to Recognize Same-Sex Marriage,* 68 S.C. L. REV. 745 (1995)

Brown, Steven G., Comment, *Pennsylvania Common Law Marriage and Annulment: Present Law and Proposals for Reform,* 15 VILL. L. REV. 134 (1969)

Brown, Susan L., *Relationship Quality Dynamics of Cohabiting Unions,* 24 J. FAM. ISSUES 583 (2003)

Brown, Susan L. & Booth, Alan, *Cohabitation Versus Marriage: A Comparison of Relationship Quality*, 58 J. MAR. & FAM. 668 (1966)

Brownlie, I., Webb, P.R.H., *Belligerent Occupation and Common-law marriages*, 39 BRIT. YEAR BOOK INT.L. 457 (1963)

Bruch, Carol S., *Cohabitation in the Common Law Countries a Decade After Marvin: Settled In or Moving Ahead?*, 22 U.C. DAVIS L. REV. 717 (1989)

— *Nonmarital Cohabitation in the Common Law Countries: A study in Judicial - Legislative Interaction*, 29 AM. J. COMP. L. 217 (1981)

— *Property Rights of De Facto Spouses Including Thoughts on the Value of Homemakers' services*, 10 FAM. L.Q. 101 (1976)

Bryan, Michael, *Constructive Trusts and Unconscionability in Australia: On the Endless Road to Unattainable Perfection*, 8 TRU L. I. 74 (1994)

Buckham, M.H., *The Relation of the Family to the State*, 13 INT. REV. 63 (1882)

Bumpass, Larry L., *The Changing Significance of Marriage in the United States*, in THE CHANGING FAMILY IN COMPARATIVE PERSPECTIVE: ASIA AND THE UNITED STATES 63 (K.O. Mason et al. eds., 1998)

Bumpass, Larry L., et al., *The Role of Cohabitation in Declining Rates of Marriage*, 53 J. MAR. & FAM. 913 (1991)

Bumpass, Larry & Lu, Hsien-Hen, *Trends in Cohabitation and Implications for Children's Family Contexts in the United States*, 54 POPULATION STUDIES 29 (2000)

Casad, Robert C., *Unmarried Couples and Unjust Enrichment: From Status to Contract and Back Again?*, 77 MICH. L. REV. 47 (1978)

Catlin, Nancy, et. al., *Commitment and Relationship Factors in Consensual Cohabitation*, 8 INT. L.J. SOC. FAM. 185 (1978)

Caudill, David S., *Legal Recognition of Unmarried Cohabitation: A proposal to Update and Reconsider Common-Law Marriage*, 49 TENN. L. REV. 537 (1982)

Causey, Jr., Denzil Y., Comment, *Domestic Relations - Common Law Marriage in Georgia*, 25 GA. B.J. 225 (1962)

Chambers, David L., *The "Legalization" of the Family: Towards a Policy of Supportive Neutrality*, 18 U. MICH. J.L. REF. 805 (1985)

Cherlin, Andrew J., *Toward a New Home Socioeconomics of Union Formation*, in THE TIES THAT BIND: PERSPECTIVES ON MARRIAGE AND COHABITATION 126 (Linda Waite et al., eds., 2000)

Clark, Elisabeth B., *Matrimonial Bonds: Slavery and Divorce in Nineteenth-Century America*, 8 LAW & HIST. REV. 25 (1990)

Clark, Jr., Homer H., *The New Marriage*, 12 WILLAMETTE L.J. 441 (1976)

Clarkberg, Marin, *The Prize of Partnering: The Role of Economic Well-Being in Young Adult's First Union Experiences*, 77 SOCIAL FORCES 945 (1999)

Clarkberg, Marin, et al., *Attitudes, Values, and Entrance Into Cohabitational Versus Marital Unions*, 74 SOC. FORCES 609 (1995)

Clive, E.M., *Marriage: An unnecessary legal concept*, in MARRIAGE AND COHABITATION IN CONTEMPORARY SOCIETIES 71 (John M. Eekelaar and Sanford N. Katz, eds. 1980)

Cobb, L. Dean, Comment, *Common Law Marriage in Texas*, 13 BAYLOR L. REV. 168 (1961)

Comment, *Developments - The Law of Marriage and Family*, 116 HARV. L. REV. 1996 (2003)

Comment, *Fundamental Interests and the Question of Same-Sex Marriage*, 15 TULSA L.J. 141 (1979)

Comment, *Marriage and Divorce Under the Texas Family Code*, 8 HOUS. L. REV. 100 (1970)

Comment, *Property Rights Upon Termination of Unmarried Cohabitation: Marvin v. Marvin*, 90 HARV. L. REV. 1708 (1977)

Comment, *Sham marriages*, 20 U. Chi. L. Rev. 710 (1953)

Cook, Frank Gaylord, *The Marriage Celebration in the United States*, 61 A.M. 520 (1888)

— *The Marriage Ceremony in the Colonies*, 61 A.M. 350 (1888)

— *The Patriality of the Law to Married Women*, 58 A.M. 311 (1886)

— *Reform in the Celebration of Marriage*, 61 A.M. 680 (1888)

Cossman, Brenda & Ryder, Bruce, *What is Marriage-Like Like? The Irrelevance of Conjugality*, 18 Can. J. Fam. L. 269 (2001)

Cott, Nancy F., *Giving Character to Our Whole Civil Policy: Marriage and the Public Order in the Late Nineteenth Century*, in U.S. History as Women's History: New Feminist Essays 107 (Linda K. Kerber et al. eds., 1995)

Cox, Barbara, *Same-Sex Marriage and Choice of Law: If We Marry in Hawaii, Are We Still Married When We Return Home?*, 1994 Wis. L. Rev. 1033 (1994)

Crabtree, David F., *Family Law - Recognition of Common-Law Marriages*, 149 Utah L. Rev. 273 (1988)

Crawley, John B., *Is the Honeymoon Over for Common Law Marriage: A Consideration of the Continued Viability of the Common Law Marriage Doctrine*, 29 Cumb. L. Rev. 399 (1998/1999)

Crutchfield, Charles F., *Nonmarital Relationships and Their Impact on the Institution of Marriage and the Traditional Family Structure,* 19 J. Fa. L. 247 (1980-1981)

Cunningham, John D. & Antill, John K., *Cohabitation and Marriage: Retrospective and Predictive Comparisons,* 11 J. Soc. & Pers. Rel. 77 (1994)

Dalton, Clare, *An Essay in the Deconstruction of Contract Doctrine*, 94 Yale L.J. 997 (1985)

Daube, David, *Consortium in Roman and Hebrew Law*, 62 Jurid. Rev. 71 (1950)

— *Historical Aspects of Informal Marriage*, 15 rev. Int. Droits de L'Antiquité 95 (1978)

Davies, C., *The Extension of Marital Rights and Obligations to the Unmarried: Registered Domestic Partnerships and Other Methods*, 17 Can. Fam. L.Q. 247(1999)

Davis, Clarice M., Comment, *Common-Law Marriage in Texas*, 21 Sw. L.J. 647 (1967)

Davis, Noah, *Marriage and Divorce*, 139 N. Am. Rev. 31 (1884)

Deech, Ruth, *The Case Against Legal Recognition of Cohabitation*, 29 Int'l & Comp. L.Q. 480 (1980)

Difonzo, James Herbie, *Customized Marriage,* 75 Ind. L.J. 875 (2000)

Dillon, Robert E., *Proof of common law marriage*, 8 Jurist 393 (1948)

Dion, M. Robin & Devaney, Barbara, *Strengthening Relationships and Supporting Healthy Marriage Among Unwed Parents,* 1 Building Strong Families In Brief 1 (2003)

Dodds, J., *The New Constructive Trust: An Analysis of its Nature and Scope*, 16 Melb. U. L. Rev. 482 (1988)

Dubler, Ariela R., Note: *Governing Through Contract: Common Law Marriage in the Nineteenth Century*, 107 Yale L.J. 1885 (1998)

— *Wifely Behaviour: A Legal History of Acting Married*, 100 Colum. L. Rev. 957 (2000)

Douglas, Gillian, *Marriage, Cohabitation, and Parenthood – from Contract to Status?*, in Cross Currents: Family Law And Policy In The US And England 211 (Sanford N. Katz et. al. eds., 2000)

Edin, Kathryn, et al., *A Peek Inside the Black Box: What Marriage Means for Poor Unmarried Parents*, 66 J. Mariage & Fam. 1007 (2004)

Edwards, Laura F., *The Marriage Covenant Is at the Foundation of All Our Rights: The Politics of Slave Marriages in North Carolina After Emancipation*, 14 Law & Hist. Rev. 81 (1996)

Eekelaar, John, *The End of an Era?*, in Cross Currents: Family Law And Policy In The US And England (Sanford N. Katz et. al. eds., 2000)

Ehrhardt, Arnold, *Consortium omnis vitae*, 57 SZ 357 (1937)

Ellman, Ira Mark, *Contract Thinking Was Marvin's Fatal Flaw,* 76 NOTRE DAME L. REV. 1365 (2001)

— *The Theory of Alimony,* 77 CAL. L. REV. 1 (1989)

Engdahl, D., *Proposal for a Benign in Marriage Law and Marriage Conflicts Law,* 55 IOWA L. REV. 56 (1969)

Enquist, Per Olov, *On the Art of Flying Backward with Dignity,* in NORDEN-THE PASSION FOR EQUALITY (Stephen R. Graubard, ed., 1986)

Fawcett, Matthew, *Taking the Middle Path: Recent Swedish Legislation Grants Minimal Property Rights to Unmarried Cohabitants,* 24 FAM. L.Q. 179 (1990)

Feighny, Mary D., *Common Law Marriage: Civil Contract or "Carnal Commerce",* 70 KAN. B. J. 20 (2001)

Fellows, Mary Louise, et. al., *Committed Partners and Inheritance: An Empirical Study,* 16 LAW & INEQUALITY 1 (1998)

Fernández, Christina M., Note, *Beyond Marvin: A Proposal for Quasi-Spousal Support,* 30 STAN. L. REV. STAN. L. REV. 359 (1978)

Finch, Michael S., & Smeltzly, Lora J., *The Restatement Second and Conflict of Laws: Extending The Bishop Approach to Problems in Contracts,* 16 STETSON L. REV. 261 (1987)

Fineman, Martha L., *Law and Changing Patterns of Behaviour: Sanctions on Non-Marital Cohabitation,* WIS. L. REV. 275 (1981)

— *Masking Dependency: The Political Role of Family Rhetoric,* 81 VA. L. REV. 2181 (1995)

Finlay, H.A., *Defining the informal marriage,* 3 U. N.S.W. L.J. 279 (1980)

— *The Informal Marriage in Anglo-Australian Law,* in MARRIAGE AND COHABITATION IN CONTEMPORARY SOCIETIES (John M. Eekelaar, Sanford N. Katz eds., 1980)

Fitch, Douglas F., *As Grounds for Divorce, Let's Abolish Matrimonial Offences,* CAN. B.J. 9 (1966)

Fitzgibbon, Scott, *Marriage and the good of obligation,* 44 AM. J. JURIS 41 (2002)

Fridman, G.H.L., *When does a marriage become a marriage?,* 104 L.J. 293 (1953)

Folberg, H. Jay & Buren, William P., *Domestic Partnership: A Proposal for Dividing the Property of Unmarried Families,* 12 WILLAMETTE L.J. 453 (1976)

Forder, Caroline, *European Models of Domestic Partnership Laws: The Field of Choice,* 17 CAN. J. FAM. L. 371 (2000)

— *To Marry or Not to Marry: That is the Question,* in THE INTERNATIONAL SURVEY OF FAMILY LAW 301 (A. Bainham ed., 2001)

Forste, Renata & Tanfer, Koray, *Sexual Exclusivity Among Dating, Cohabiting, and Married Women,* 58 J. MAR. & FAM. 33 (1996)

Foster, Henry H., *Indian and Common Law Marriage,* 3 AM. INDIAN L. REV. 83 (1975)

Foster, Henry H., & Freed, Doris Jonas, *Marvin v. Marvin: New Wine in Old Bottles,* 5 FAM. L. REP. 4001 (1979)

Frank, Rainer, *The Status of Cohabitation in the Legal Systems of West Germany and Other West European Countries,* 33 AM. J. COMP. L. 185 (1985)

Freeman, Michael, *Family Values and Family Justice,* in CURRENT LEGAL PROBLEMS. LAW AND OPINION AT THE END OF THE TWENTIETH CENTURY (Michael Freeman ed., 1997)

Friedmann, Wolfgang G., *Some Reflections on Status and Freedom,* in ESSAYS IN JURISPRUDENCE IN HONOR OF ROSCOE POUND (Ralph A. Newman ed., 1962)

Fulton, Alexander J., Note, *The Contract of Marriage,* 9 ALB. L.J. 401 (1874)

Furlong, Robert, *Youthful Marriages and Parenthood: A Threat to Family Stability,* 19 HASTINGS L.J. 105 (1967)

Garrison, Marsha, *Is Consent Necessary? An Evaluation of the Emerging Law of Cohabitant Obligation,* 52 UCLA L. REV. 815 (2005)

— *Marriage Matters: What's Wrong with the ALI's Domestic Partnership Proposal,* in RECONCEIVING THE FAMILY, CRITIQUE ON THE AMERICAN LAW INSTITUTE'S PRINCIPLES OF THE LAW OF FAMILY DISSOLUTION 305 (Robin Fretwell Wilson ed., 2006)

Garza, Sonya C., *Common Law Marriage: A Proposal for the Revival of a Dying Doctrine*, 40 NEW ENG. L. REV. 541 (2005-2006)

Getty, Jr., Clair, Note, *Marriage - Presumption in favour of a subsequent common law marriage - Evidence - Texas Employers' Ins. Ass'n v. Elder, 282 S.W.2d 371 (Tex.Sup.Ct., rehearing den'd 1955)*, 2 S. TEX. L.J. 191 (1956)

Gide, Paul, *De la Condition de l'enfant naturel et de la concubine dans la législation romaine*, R.H.D. 337(1880)

Gilfoyle, Timothy J., *The Hearts of Nineteenth-Century Men: Bigamy and Working Class Marriage in New York City, 1800-1890*, 19 PROSPECTS 135 (1994)

Gilkey, Erroll Clarence, *Validity of Common Law Marriage in Oregon*, 3 OR. L. REV. 28 (1923)

Glendon, Mary Ann, *Marriage and the State: The Withering Away of Marriage*, 62 VA. L. REV. 663 (1976)

— *Patterns of Contemporary Legal Response to the Social Phenomenom of De Facto Marriage*, in KONFLIKT UND ORDNUNG, FESTSCHRIFT FÜR MURAD FERID ZUM 70. GEBURSTTAG (1978)

Glenn, Norval, *Is the Current Concern About American Marriage Warranted?*, 9 VA. J. SOC. POL'Y & L. 5 (2001)

Glezer, Helen & Mills, Eva, *Controlling the Purse String*, 29 FAM. MATT. 35 (1991)

Glick, Paul C., *American Household Structure in Transition*, 16 FAM. PLAN. PERSP. 205 (1984)

Goldberg, Charlotte K., *The Schemes of Adventuresses: The Abolition and Revival of Common-Law Marriage*, 483 WM. & MARY J. WOMEN & L. 483 (2006-2007)

Goodhart, Arthur, *Determining the Ratio Decidendi of a Case*, 40 YALE L.J. 161 (1930)

Goodman, Robert, *In Sickness or in Health: The Right to Marry and the Case of HIV Antibody Testing*, 38 DEPAUL L. REV. 87 (1988)

Gordon, Katherine, Note, *The Necessity and Enforcement of Cohabitation Agreements: When Strings Will Attach and How to Prevent Them – A State Survey*, 37 BRANDEIS L.J. 245 (1998-1999)

Gottlieb, Arthur H., Note, *Living Together: The Need for a Uniform Nonmarital Cohabitation Act*, 2 Adelphia L.J. 79 (1983)

Grainer, Virginia, *What's Yours is Mine: Reform of the Property Division Regime for Unmarried Couples in New Zealand*, 11 PAC. RIM. L. & POL'Y J. 285 (2002)

Graycar, Reg & Millbank, Jenni, *The Bride Wore Pink...to the Property (Relationships) Legislation Amendment 1999: Relationship Law Reform in New South Wales*, 17 CAN. FAM. J. L. 227 (2000)

Green, J., Note, *Problems in common law marriages*, 15 JURIST 301 (1955)

Grossberg, Michael, *Balancing Acts: Crisis, Change, and Continuity in American Family Law, 1890-1990*, 28 IND. L. REV. 273 (1995)

Gwartney-Gibbs, Patricia A., *The Institution of Premarital Cohabitation: Estimates from Marriage License Applications, 1970 and 1980*, 48 J. MAR. & FAM. 423 (1986)

Haas, Theodore F., *The Rationality and Enforceability of Contractual Restrictions on Divorce*, 66 N.C. L. REV. 879 (1988)

Habegger, Dee Ann, *Living in Sin and the Law: Benefits for Unmarried Couples Dependent Upon Sexual Orientation?*, 33 IND. L. REV. 991 (2000)

Hale, Brenda, *The Family Law Act 1996 – the death of marriage?*, in FAMILY LAW TOWARDS THE MILLENNIUM: ESSAYS FOR P.M. BROMLEY 1 (Caroline Bridge ed., 1997)

Hall, Fred S., *Common Law Marriage in New York State*, 30 COLUM. L. REV. 1 (1930)

Hall, J.C., *Common Law Marriage*, 46 CAMBRIDGE L.J. 106 (1987)

Hamilton, Robert R., Note, *Presumption of Marriage in Oklahoma*, 14 OKLA. L. REV. 299 (1961)

Harris, Nevil, *Unmarried cohabiting couples and Social Security in Great Britain*, 18(2) J. SOC. WELFARE FAM. L. 123 (1996)

Harris, Warren D., *The Essentials of a Valid Marriage in Virginia*, 6 VA. L. REV. 437 (1900)

Hartog, Henrik, *Marital Exits and Marital Expectations in Nineteenth-Century America*, 80 GEO. L.J. 95 (1991)

Haskey, J., *Demographic Aspects of Cohabitation in Great Britain*, 15 IJLPF 51 (2001)

D'Haucour, L., *L'Évolution Historique du Concubinat Romain*, 16 R.H.D. 730 (1894)

Hawkens, Alan J. et al., *Attitudes about Covenant Marriage and Divorce: Policy Implications of a Three State Study*, 51 FAM. REL. 166 (2002)

Heimdal, Kristen R. & Houseknecht, Sharon K., *Cohabiting and Married Couples' Income Organization: Approaches in Sweden and the United States*, 65 J. MAR. & FAM. 525 (2003)

Hein, Jonathan Andrew, *Caring for the Evolving American Family: Cohabiting Partners and Employer Sponsored Health Care*, 30 N.M. L. REV. 19 (2000)

Helitzer, Jack B., *State Developments in Employee Benefits: Common-Law Marriage*, 4 BENEFITS L.J. 95 (1991)

Hill, Martha S., et al., *Childhood Family Structure and Young Adult Behaviours*, 14 J. POP. ECON. 271 (2001)

Hilton, A., *The Validity of "Common Law" Marriages*, 19 MCGILL L. J. 577 (1973)

Hodson, F.L.C., *Common law marriage*, 7 INT'L. & COMP. L.Q. 205 (1958)

Hoem, Jan & Hoem, Brita, *The Swedish Family: Aspects of Contemporary Developments*, 9 J. FAM. ISS. 397 (1988)

Holland, Winifred, *Intimate Relationships in the New Millennium: The Assimilation of Marriage and Cohabitation*? 17 CAN. J. FAM. L. 114 (2000)

Hood, Jr., William W., *Common-law marriage in Oklahoma: A Survey*, 49 OKLA. B.J. 1505 (1978)

Howard, George Elliot, *Social Control of Domestic Relations*, 167 A.J.S. 815 (1910)

Howard, Lowell B., Note, *Common law marriage*, 10 OHIO ST. L.J. 405 (1949)

Hovermill, Joseph, A., *Conflict of Law and Morals: The Choice of Law Implications of Hawaii's Recognition of Same-Sex Marriages*, 53 MD. L. REV. 450 (1994)

Howery, W.H., *Marriage by Proxy and Other Informal Marriages*, 13 U. KAN. CITY L. REV. 48 (1944-45)

Huet-Weiller, Danielle, *La Cessation du concubinage*, in LES CONCUBINAGES: APPROCHE SOCIO-JURIDIQUE II 107 (Jaqueline Rubellin-Devichi ed., 1986)

Hunter, Howard O., *An Essay on Contract and Status: Race, Marriage and the Meretricious Spouse*, 64 VA. L. REV. 1039 (1978)

Hübner, Heinz, *Eheschliessung und allgemeine Wirkungen der Ehe als dogmatische Problem*, FamRZ 1(1962)

Jackson, J., *Consent of the parties to their marriage*, 14 MOD. L. REV. 1 (1951)

Jackson, Malcolm, *Validity of Common Law Marriage as Affected by Statute*, 12 VA. L.J. 1 (1888)

Kahn-Freund, Otto, *On Uses and Misuses of Comparative Law*, 37 MOD. L. REV. 1 (1974)

Kandoian, Ellen, *Cohabitation, Common Law Marriage, and the Possibility of a Shared Moral Life*, 75 GEO. L.J. 1829 (1987)

Kantorowicz, Kim, Comment, *Contracts – Cohabitation in Minnesota: From Love to Contract-Public Policy Gone Away in In Re Estate of Palmen, 588 N.W.2d 493 (Minn. 2000)*, 26 WM. MITCHELL L. REV. 213 (1999)

Kaser, Max, *Ehe und "conventio in manum"*, 1 IURA 64 (1960)

— *Recensiones librorum*, 18 STUDIA ET DOCUMENTA HISTORIAE ET IURIS 300 (1952)

Katz, Sanford N., *Emerging Models for Alternatives to Marriage*, 33 FAM. L.Q. 663 (1999)

— Marriage and Marriage-Like Relationships: Should They Be Equal, International Society of Family Law World Conference (Copenhagen/Oslo, August 2002) (unpublished paper)

— *Marriage as Partnership*, 73 NOTRE DAME L. REV. 1251 (1998)

Kay, Herma & Amyx, Carol, *Marvin v. Marvin: Preserving the Options,* 65 CAL. L. REV. 937 (1977)

Keefe, Jr., J. E., Annotation, *Presumption as to Validity of Second Marriage,* 14 A.L.R.2d 7 (1950)

Kelley, Ralph B., *Creation and Proof of Common Law Marriage Following Removal of Impediments,* 18 N.Y. INTRA. L. REV. 213 (1963)

Kendrick, Robert E., Note, *Informal Marriages in Tennessee - Marriage by Estoppel, by Prescription and by Ratification,* 3 VAND. L. REV. 610 (1950)

Keyes, Gary Murray, *The Validity of the Common Law Marriage in Ontario,* 1 OSGOODE HALL L.J. 58 (1958)

Kiernan, Kathleen, *Redrawing the Boundaries of Marriage,* 66 J. MAR. & FAM. 980 (2001)

— *The Rise of Cohabitation and Childbearing Outside Marriage in Western Europe,* 15 INT'L J.L. POL'Y & FAM. 1 (2001)

— *Unmarried Cohabitation and Parenthood in Britain and Europé,* 26 LAW & POLICY 33 (2004)

Kingsley, Robert, *The law of infants' marriages,* 9 VAND. L. REV. 593 (1956)

Kirkpatrick, Graham, *Common-Law Marriages: Their Common Law Basis and Present Need,* 6 ST. LOUIS U. L.J. 30 (1960)

Knittel, Wilhelm, *Die formlose Ehe (Common-Law Marriage) in den USA,* FamRZ 57 (1965)

Knoblauch, Mary L., *Minnesota's Cohabitation Statute,* 2 LAW & INEQ. J. 335 (1984)

Kohm, Lynne, *How Will Proliferation and Recognition of Domestic Partnerships Affect Marriage?,* 4 J.L. & FAM. STUD. 105 (2002)

Kramer, Larry, *Same-Sex Marriage, Conflict of Laws, and the Unconstitutional Public Policy Exception,* 106 YALE L.J. 1965 (1997)

Krause, Harry D., Private and Public Ordering of Intimate Relationships, International Society of Family Law World Conference (Copenhagen/Oslo, August 2002) (unpublished paper)

Kravdal, Oystein, *Does Marriage Require a Stronger Economic Underpinning than Informal Cohabitation?,* 53 POPULATION STUD. 63 (1999)

Kroll, Wilhelm, *Die Kultur der Ciceronischen Zeit,* in DAS ERBE DER ALTEN XII (1933)

Kunkel, Wolfgang, *Matrimonium,* 14 PAULUS REAL-ENZYKLOPÄDIE DER CLASSISCHEN ALTERTUMS WISSENSCHAFT sp. 2259 (1930)

Kurtz, Paul M., *The State Equal Rights Amendments and Their Impact on Domestic Relations Law,* 11 FAM. L.Q. 101 (1977)

Kübler, B., Recention av: *Paul Meyer, Der römische Concubinat nach den Rechtsquellen und den Innschriften (1895),* 17 SZ 357 (1896)

Köstler, Rudolf, *Raub - und Kaufehe bei den Römern,* 65 SZ 43 (1947)

Laquer Estin, Ann, *Ordinary Cohabitation,* 76 NOTRE DAME L. REV. 1381 (2000-2001)

— *When Baehr Meets Romer: Family Law Issues After Amendment 2,* 68 U. COLO. L. REV. 349 (1997)

Lavarato, Louis A., Note, *The Elements of a Common-Law Marriage,* 11 DRAKE L. REV. 64 (1962)

La Violette, Nicole, *Registered Partnerships: A Model for Relationship Recognition* (Ottawa: Law Commission of Canada 2001)

Le Bourdais, Céline & Lapierre-Adamcyk, Évelyne, *Changes in conjugal life in Canada: Is cohabitation progressively replacing marriage?,* 66 J. MAR. & FAM. 929 (2004)

Lemouland, Jean-Jacques, *Présentation de la loi No. 99-944 du 15 novembre 1999 relative au pacte civil de solidarité,* 43 RECUEIL DALLOZ 483 (1999)

Lévi-Strauss, Claude, *The Family,* in MAN, CULTURE, AND SOCIETY 142 (Harry L. Shapiro ed., 1956)

Levy & Bruhl, Henri, *Les origines du mariage sine manu,* 14 TIJDSCHRIFT VOOR RECHTSGESCHIEDENIS 453 (1936)

Lightner, J.A.C., *Common Law Marriages in Wisconsin,* 6 MARQ. L. REV. 82 (1922)

Lim, Amy, Comment, *In Defense of Washington's Equitable Treatment of Pseudomarital Property,* 29 IDAHO L. REV. 975 (1992)

Lind, Göran, *Legislation for the Surviving Cohabitant in Comparative Perspective,* in EUROPEAN CHALLENGES IN CONTEMPORARY FAMILY LAW (K. Boele-Woelki and T. Sverdrup eds., European Family Law Series No. 10, Antwerp 2008)

Linford, Orma, *The Mormons and the Law: The Polygamy Cases,* 9 UTAH L. REV. 308 (1964)

Lorio, Kathryn Venturatos, *Concubinage and Its Alternatives: A Proposal for a More Perfect Union,* 26 LOY. L. REV. 1 (1980)

Lovas, Sol, *When is a Family Not a Family?,* 24 IDAHO L. REV. 353 (1987)

Lucas, Peter, *Common Law Marriage,* 49 C.L.J. 117 (1990)

Lund-Andersen, Ingrid, *Moving Towards an Individual Principle in Danish Law,* 4 INT. J.L. FAM. 328 (1990)

— *Cohabitation and Registered Partnership in Scandinavia: The Legal Position of Homosexuals,* in THE CHANGING FAMILY 397 (John Eekelaar and Thandabantu Nhlapo eds., 1998)

— *The Danish Registered Partnership Act,* in LEGAL RECOGNITION OF SAME-SEX COUPLES IN EUROPE 13 (Katharina Boele-Woelki and Angelika Fuchs eds., 2003)

Lunn, Joan, *Living Together – Is it Worth It?,* 127 NEW L.J. 306 (1977)

Lynch, James P., *Social Security Encounters Common Law Marriage in North Carolina,* 16 N.C. L. REV. 259 (1938)

Lødrup, Peter, *Family law in Norway,* in FAMILY LAW IN EUROPE 353 (Carolyn Hamilton et al. eds., 1995)

Macklin, Eleanor D., *Nonmarital Heterosexual Cohabitation,* MAR. FAM. REV. 1 (March-April 1978)

McConnell, Harley Wayne, Note, *Void and Voidable Marriages,* 14 OKLA. L. REV. 304 (1961)

McKnight, Joseph W., *Family Law: Husband and Wife,* 44 SW. L.J. 1 (1990)

— *Family Law: Husband and Wife,* 38 SW. L.J. 131 (1984)

— *Family Law: Husband and Wife,* 37 SW. L.J. 65 (1983)

— *Husband and Wife,* 21 TEX. TECH. L. REV. 911 (1990)

— *Recodification and Reform of the Law of Husband and Wife,* 33 TEX. B.J. 34 (1970)

McWalter, Keith G., *Marriage as Contract: Towards a Functional Redefinition of the Marital Status,* 9 COLUM. J.L. & SOC. PROBS. 607 (1973)

Madison, George W., *Marital and Nonmarital Relationships: the Right to Alternative Lifestyles,* 11 COLUM. HUM. RTS. L. REV. 189 (1979/80)

Mahoney, Margaret M., *Forces Shaping the Law of Cohabitation for Opposite Sex Couples,* 7 J. L. & FAM. STUD. 135 (2005)

Maitland, Frederic W., *Magistri Vacarii Summa de Matrimonio,* 13 L.Q. REV. 133 (1897)

Manning, Wendy D. & Smock, Pamela J., *Living Together Unmarried in the United States: Demographic Perspectives and Implications for Family Policy,* 26 LAW & POLICY 87 (2004)

— *Measuring and Modeling Cohabitation: New Perspectives from Qualitative Data,* 67 J. MARRIAGE S. FAM. 989 (2005)

— *Why Marry? Race and the Transition to Marriage Among Cohabitors,* 32 DEMOGRAPHY 509 (1995)

Martin, Claude and Thery, Irène, *The PACS and Marriage and Cohabitation in France,* 15 IJLPF 35 (2001)

Martín-Casals, Miquel, *Same-Sex Partnerships in the Legislation of Spanish Autonomous Communities,* EU ERA Conference (Uppsala 19-20 September 2002) (unpublished paper)

— *Same-Sex Partnerships in the Legislation of Spanish Autonomous Communities,* in LEGAL RECOGNITION OF SAME-SEX COUPLES IN EUROPE 54 (Katharina Boele-Woelki and Angelika Fuchs eds., 2003)

Maxwell, Nancy G., *Can Kansas Live Happily Ever After Without Common Law Marriage?*, 20 THE CIRCUIT RIDER NO. 3 (1981)

Meade, David, *Consortium Rights of the Unmarried: Time for a Reappraisal*, 15 FAM. L.Q. 223 (1981)

Miller, Myron, Note, *Common-Law Marriage*, 31 DICTA 451 (1954)

Mills, Catherine Augusta, Comment, *Implications of the Repeal of Louisiana Civil Code Article 1481*, 48 LA. L. REV. 1201 (1988)

Mills, Denise K., *Common Law Marriage in Colorado*, 16 COLO. LAW. 252 (1987)

Mitteis, Ludwig, *Romanistische Papyrusstudien*, 23 SZ 274 (1902)

Morris, William W., *Common Law Marriage and Palimony* (May 1990) (unpublished paper, Marriage Dissolution Institute, Houston)

Moynahan, *Common Law Marriage in Ohio*, OHIO ST. L.J. 26 (1938)

Murray, Daniel E., *Domestic Relations*, 12 U. MIAMI L. REV. 428 (1958)

Myerberg, Herbert, *Common Law Marriage*, 29 GEO.L.J. 858 (1941)

Neave, M., *The New Unconscionability Principle – Property Disputes Between de Facto* Partners, 6 AUSTRALIAN J. FAM. L. 185 (1991)

Nerson, R., *Les couples non-mariés en France*, in MARRIAGE AND COHABITATION IN CONTEMPORARY SOCIETIES 198, 207 (John M. Eekelaar, Sanford N. Katz eds., 1980)

Newcomb, Paul R., *Cohabitation in America: An Assessment of Consequences*, 41 J. MAR. & FAM. 597 (1979)

Nielsen, Linda, *Family Law in Denmark*, in FAMILY LAW IN EUROPE 33 (Carolyn Hamilton et al. eds., 1995)

— *Family Law in Denmark*, in FAMILY LAW IN EUROPE 90 (Carolyn Hamilton and Alison Perry, eds., 2d ed. 2002)

— *Family Rights and the "Registered Partnership" in Denmark*, IJLPF 297 (1990)

Nielson, Patrick A., Note, *In re Cary: A Judicial Recognition of Illicit Cohabitation*, 25 HASTINGS L.J. 1226 (1974)

Nock, Steven L., *A Comparison of Marriages and Cohabiting Relationships*, 16 J. FAM. ISSUES 53 (1995)

Note, *Beyond Marvin: A Proposal for Quasi-Spousal Support*, 30 STAN. L. REV. 359 (1978)

Note, *Cohabitation as Essential to a Common Law Marriage*, 3 MINN.L.REV. 426 (1918/1919)

Note, *Common Law Marriage - A Legal Anachronism*, 32 IND. L.J. 99 (1956)

Note, *Common Law Marriage Abolished*, 3 BROOK. L. REV. 155 (1933)

Note, *The Constituents of Common Law Marriage*, 1 BROOK. L. REV. 79 (1932)

Note, *The Decline and Fall of Common-law Marriage in Pennsylvania*, 18 TEMP. L.Q. 264 (1944)

Note, *Domestic Relations-Proxy Marriage-Validity as a Common Law-Marriage*, 32 IOWA L. REV. 774 (1947)

Note, *Family Law, Common-Law Marriage*, 44 OHIO JURISPRUDENCE 3d 428 (1983)

Note, *Idaho courts holds common-law marriage valid in workmen's compensation case*, 5 UTAH L. REV. 125 (1956)

Note, *Marriage, Contracts and Public Policy*, 54 HARV. L. REV. 473 (1941)

Note, *A More Perfect Union: A Legal and Social Analysis of Domestic Partnership Ordinances*, 92 COLUM. L. REV. 1164 (1992)

Note, *Necessity of Cohabitation in Common Law Marriage*, 23 IOWA L. REV. 75 (1937)

Note, *The Passing of Common Law Marriage*, 15 TEMP. L.Q. 541 (1946)

Note, *Presumptions in Common Law Marriage*, 14 IOWA L. REV. 215 (1929)

Note, *The Uniform Marriage and Divorce Act - Marital Age Provisions*, 57 MINN. L. REV. 179 (1972)

Note, *Use of Presumptions in Proving the Existence of Marriage Relationships in Tennessee,* 5 MEM. ST.U. L. REV. 409 (1975)

Note, V*alidity - Marriage contracted for sole purpose of evading immigration laws held valid in annulment proceeding,* 69 HARV. L. REV. 768 (1956)

O'Brien, Raymond F., *Domestic Partnership: Recognition and Responsibility,* 32 SAN DIEGO L. REV. 163 (1995)

Oldham, Thomas, *ALI Principles of Family Dissolution: Some Comments,* 1997 ILL. L. REV. 801 (1997)

— *The American Law Institute's Principles of the Law of Family Dissolution: Its Impact on Family Law,* 7 TEX. J. WOMEN & L. (1997)

Oldham, Thomas & Caudill, David S., *A Reconnaissance of Public Policy Restrictions upon Enforcement of Contracts Between Cohabitants,* 18 FAM. L.Q. 93 (1984)

Oppenheimer, Valerie K., *Cohabiting and Marriage During Men's Career-Development Process,* 40 DEMOGRAPHY 127 (2003)

Parker, Wendy, *New Zealand property rights legislation: A changing landscape,* 57 FAM. MATT. 62 (2000)

Parkman, Allen M., *To What "Marriage" Do We Have a Right?,* International Society of Family Law, World Conference (Copenhagen/Oslo, August 2002) (unpublished paper)

Parr, Gavin M., *What is a "Meretricious relationship"?: An Analysis of Cohabitant Property Rights Under Connell v. Francisco,* 74 WASH. L. REV. 1243 (1999)

Patterson, Paul L., Note, *Common Law Marriages in Oregon,* 4 OR. L. REV. 308 (1925)

Perry, Joseph N., *Canonical Concept of Marital Consent: Roman Law Influence,* 25 CATHOLIC LAW 228 (1980)

Perry, Twila L., *Dissolution Planning in Family Law: A Critique of Current Analyses and a Look Toward the Future,* 24 FAM. L.Q. 77 (1990)

Ploscowe, Morris, *Family Law,* 35 N.Y.U. L. REV. 388 (1960)

Plumb, Leon, A., *Marriage: Common-Law Marriage in New York,* 1 CORNELL L.Q. 48 (1915)

Polikoff, Nancy D., *We Will Get What we Ask For: Why Legalizing Gay and Lesbian Marriage Will Not "Dismantle the Legal Structure of Gender in Every Marriage",* 79 VA. L. REV. 1535 (1993)

Powell, Chilton, *Marriage in Early New England,* 1 N.E.Q. 331 (1928)

Powell, Raphael, *The Concept of Marriage in Ancient and Modern Law,* 3 CURRENT LEGAL PROBS. 46 (1950)

Pringsheim, Fritz, *Animus in Roman Law,* 49 L.Q. REV. 43 (1933)

Qu, Lixia, *Expectations of Marriage Among Cohabiting Couples,* 64 FAM. MATT. 35 (2003)

Quinn, John S., *Roman Replies and Recent Jurisprudence,* 17 JURIST 441 (1957)

Raley, Kelly, *Recent Trends and Differentials in Marriage and Cohabitation: The United States,* in THE TIES THAT BIND: PERSPECTIVES ON MARRIAGE AND COHABITATION (Linda Waite et al. eds., 2000)

Ramage, C.J., *What is a Common Law Marriage?,* 90 CENT. L.J. 263 (1920)

Reese, Willis L.M., *Marriage in American Conflict of Laws,* 26 INT'L & COMP. L.Q. 952 (1977)

— Note, *The Hague Convention on Celebration and Recognition of the Validity of Marriages,* 20 VA. J. INT'L L. 23 (1979)

Regan, Jr., Milton C., *Unmarried Partners and the Legacy of Marvin v. Marvin: Calibrated Commitment: The Legal Treatment of Marriage and Cohabitation,* 76 NOTRE DAME L. REV. 1435 (2001)

Reiland, *Hewitt v. Hewitt: Middle America, Marvin and Common-Law Marriage,* 60 CHI. B. REC. 84 (1978)

Reppy, Jr., William A., *Choice of Law Problems Arising When Unmarried Cohabitants Change Domicile,* 55 SMU L. REV. 273 (2002)

— *Property and Support Rights of Unmarried Cohabitants: A Proposal for Creating a New Legal Status,* 44 LA. L. REV. 1677 (1984)

Riverend-Brusone, Eduardo, *Anomalous Marriages,* 10 MIAMI L.Q. 481 (1956)

Richardson, Nicky, *Defeating De Facto Partner's Claims to Property in New Zealand,* INT. FAM. L.J. 107 (2003)

— *Dishonesty, Constructive Trusts and De Facto Relationships,* INT. FAM. L.J. 182 (2002)

— *The New Property (Relationships) Act in Practise,* INT. FAM. L.J. 221 (2003)

Robbenholt, Jennifer K. & Kirkpatrick Johnson, Monica, *Legal Planning for Unmarried Committed Partners: Empirical Lessons for a Preventive and Therapeutic Approach,* 41 ARIZ. L. REV. 417 (1999)

Rombauer, Marjorie Dick, *Marital Status and Eligibility for Federal Statutory Income Benefits: A Historical Survey,* 52 WASH. L. REV. 227 (1977)

Ross, Hugh A., *The Ohio Law of Marriage,* 14 W. RESERVE L. REV. 724 (1963)

Rothstein, Alan H., *A New Look at Common Law Marriages in Florida,* 10 MIAMI L.Q. 87 (1955)

Roxborough, John W., *Antenuptial Physical Examination on Common Law Marriages in Michigan,* 16 U. DET. L.J. 174 (1953)

Salari, Miner & Baldwin, Bret M., *Verbal, Physical, and Injurious Aggression Among Intimate Couples Over Time,* 23 J. FAM. ISSUES 523 (2002)

Sampson, John J., *Legislation Affecting Family Law Practice - The 71st Legislature, Regular Session,* 89-1 ST. BAR.SEC. FAM. L. REPT. 1,7 (1989)

Savolainen, Matti, *The Finnish and the Swedish Partnership Acts – Similarities and Divergencies,* in LEGAL RECOGNITION OF SAME-SEX COUPLES IN EUROPE 24 (Katharina Boele-Woelki and Angelika Fuchs eds., 2003).

Schrama, Wendy M., *Registered Partnership in the Netherlands,* 13 IJLPF 315 (1999)

Schultz, Marjorie Maguire, *Contractual Ordering of Marriage: A New Model for State Policy,* 70 CAL. L. REV. 204 (1982)

Scott, Elizabeth, *Domestic Partnerships, Implied Contracts, and Law Reform,* in RECONCEIVING THE FAMILY, CRITIQUE ON THE AMERICAN LAW INSTITUTE'S PRINCIPLES OF THE LAW OF FAMILY DISSOLUTION 331 (Robin Fretwell Wilson ed., 2006)

— *Marriage, Social Norms and the Legal Regulation of Marriage,* 86 VA. L. REV. 1901 (1998)

Scott, Elisabeth S. & Scott, Robert E., *Marriage as Relational Contract,* 84 VA. L. REV. 1225 (1998)

Sellar, W.D.H., *Marriage by cohabitation with habit and repute: review and requiem?,* in COMPARATIVE AND HISTORICAL ESSAYS IN SCOTS LAW 117 (D.L. Carey Miller and D.W. Meyers eds., 1992)

Seltzer, Judith A., *Families formed Outside of Marriage,* 62 J. MAR. & FAM. 1247 (2000)

Semonche, John E., *Common Law Marriage in North Carolina: A Study in Legal History,* 9 AM. J. LEGAL HIST. 320 (1965)

Setaro, Franklin C., *A History of English Ecclesiastical Law (Part I),* 18 B.U. L. REV. 102 (1938)

Shackelford, Todd K., *Cohabitation, Marriage and Murder: Woman-Killing by Male Romantic Partners,* 27 AGGRESSIVE BEHAVIOR 284 (2001)

Shaw, Nancy Rebecca, Note, *Common Law Marriage and Unmarried Cohabitation: An old Solution to a New Problem,* 39 U. PITT. L. REV. 579 (1977)

Shultz, Marjorie Maguire, *Contractual Ordering of Marriage: A New Model for State Policy,* 70 CAL. L. REV. 204 (1982)

Simitian, J., *Property Rights and the Unmarried Homemaker: Marvin v. Marvin, and the California Experience,* 5 COM. PROP. J. 3 (1978)

Skolnick, Arlene, *The Social Contexts of Cohabitation*, 29 AM. J. COMP. L. 339 (1981)

Slovenko, Ralph, *The De Facto Decriminalization of Bigamy*, 17 J. FAM. L. 297 (1978)

Smith, J.C., *Economic Loss And the Common Law Marriage of Contracts and Torts*, 18 UBC L. REV. 95 (1984)

Smith, Holland, Note, *Common-law marriage: What it is and how to prove it*, 12 S.C. L.Q. 355 (1960)

Smock, Pamela J., *Cohabitation in the United States: An Appraisal of Research Themes, Findings, and Implications*, 26 ANN. REV. SOC. 1 (2000)

Smock, Pamela J. & Manning, Wendy D., *Living together Unmarried in the United States: Demographic Perspectives and Implications for Family Policy*, 26 LAW & POLICY 87 (2004)

Spanier, Graham B., *Married and Unmarried Cohabitation in the United States: 1980*, 45 J. MAR. & FAM. 277 (1983)

Stanley, Scott M., *Maybe I Do: Interpersonal Commitment and Premarital or Nonmarital Cohabitation*, 25 J. FAM. ISSUES 496 (2004)

Stanton, Elisabeth Cady, *Address to the Decade Meeting on Marriage and Divorce*, in A HISTORY OF THE NATIONAL WOMAN'S RIGHTS MOVEMENT FOR TWENTY YEARS (Paulina Davis ed., New York, Journeymen Printers' Cooperative Ass'n 1871)

Stein, Stuart J., *Common-Law Marriage: Its History and Certain Contemporary Problems*, 9 J. FAM. L. 271 (1969)

Steiner, Eva, *The Spirit of the new French registered partnership law – promoting autonomy and pluralism or weakening marriage?*, 12 C. F. L.Q. 1 (2000)

Stets, Jan E., *Cohabiting and Marital Aggression: The Role of Social Isolation*, 53 J. MAR. & FAM. 669 (1991)

Stewart, Gordon A., *Our Marriage and Divorce Laws*, 23 P.S.M. 228 (1883)

Strøm-Bull, Kirsti, *Non marital cohabitation in Norway*, 30 SC. ST. L. (1986)

Strömholm, Stig, *Användningen av utländskt material i juridiska mongrafier. Några anteckningar och förslag*, SvJT 251 (1971)

Sverdrup, Tone, *Maintenance as a Separate Issue – The Relationship between Maintenance and Matrimonial Property*, in COMMON CORE AND BETTER LAW IN EUROPEAN FAMILY LAW 119 (K. Boele-Woelki, ed., European Family Law Series No. 10, Antwerp 2005)

— *Marriage and Cohabitation: Community of Life or Community of Work?*, Working Papers in Women's Law No. 51 (Nov. 1999) (unpublished paper, Institute of Women's Law Department of Public and International Law, University of Oslo)

Swisher, Peter Nash & Jones, Melanie Diana, *The Last-in-time Marriage Presumption*, 29 FAM. L.Q. 409 (1995)

Sykes, Edward I., *The Essential Validity of Marriage*, 4 INT'L & COMP. L.Q. 159 (1955)

Taintor, Charles W., *Marriage in the Conflict of Laws*, 9 VAND. L. REV. 607 (1956)

Teachman, Jay D., et al., *The Changing Demography of America's Families*, 62 J. MAR. & FAM. 1234 (2000)

TenBroek, Jacobus, *California's Dual System of Family Law: Its Origin, Development, and Present Status*, 17 STAN. L. REV. 614 (1965)

Thomas, Milton, *The consortium vitae coniugalis*, 38 JURIST 171 (1978)

Thomson, Elisabeth & Colella, Ugo, *Cohabitation and Marital Stability: Quality or Commitment*, 54 J. MAR. & FAM. 259 (1992)

Thorn, Karsten, *The German Law on Same-Sex Partnerships*, in LEGAL RECOGNITION OF SAME-SEX COUPLES IN EUROPE 84 (Katharina Boele-Woelki and Angelika Fuchs eds., 2003).

Thornton, Arland & Young-Demarco, Linda, *Four Decades of Trends in Attitudes Toward Family Issues in the United States: The 1960s through the 1990s*, 63 J. MAR. & FAM. 1009 (2001)

Townsend, Karen, *The Uniform Marriage and Divorce Act: New Statutory Solutions to old Problems*, 37 MONT. L. REV. 119 (1976)

Tracol, Xavier, *The Pacte Civil de Solidarité (PACS)*, in LEGAL RECOGNITION OF SAME-SEX COUPLES IN EUROPE 68 (Katharina Boele-Woelki and Angelika Fuchs eds., 2003)

Treas, Judith & Giesen, Deidre, *Sexual Infidelity Among Married and Cohabiting Americans*, 62 J. MAR. & FAM. 48 (2000)

Trost, Jan, *Cohabitation without Marriage in Sweden*, in MARRIAGE AND COHABITATION IN CONTEMPORARY SOCIETIES 16 (John M. Eekelaar, Sanford N. Katz eds., 1980)

— *A Renewed Social Institution: Non Marital Cohabitation*, 21 ACTA SOCIOLOGICA 303 (1978)

Trussler, Marguerite & Vandergrift, Ellen, *Changing Relationships: How the Law and Governments Have Accommodated Them. A Canadian Perspective* (June 1 2001), Court of Queen's Bench of Alberta

Turner, Sharon, *Family law - Marriage at common law*, 9 DUBLIN U. L.J. 126 (1987)

Valeri, John R., *Informal Marriages and Other Curative Devices*, 17 HOW. L.J. 558 (1972)

Vaughn, Kathryn S., Comment, *The Recent Changes to the Texas Informal Marriage Statute: Limitation or Abolition of Common Law Marriage?*, 28 HOUS. L. REV. 1131 (1991)

Waaldijk, K., *Civil Developments: Patterns of Reform in the Legal Position of Same-Sex Partners in Europe*, 17 CAN. J. FAM. L. 62 (2000)

Wacke, Andreas, *Zivilrechtsfragen der nichtehelichen Lebensgemeinschaft*, in MÜNSCHENER KOMMENTAR 7, BGB, 100 (4th ed. 2000)

Wadlington, Walter J., *Divorce Without Fault Without Perjury*, 52 VA. L. REV. 84 (1966)

— *Marriage: An Institution in Transition and Redefinition*, in CROSS CURRENTS: FAMILY LAW AND POLICY IN THE US AND ENGLAND 235 (Sanford N. Katz et. al. eds., 2000)

Waggoner, Lawrence W., *Marital Property Rights in Transition*, 59 MO. L. REV. 21 (1994)

Waite, Linda J., *Trends in Men's and Women's Well-Being in Marriage*, in THE TIES THAT BIND: PERSPECTIVES ON MARRIAGE AND COHABITATION 368 (Linda Waite et al. eds., 2000)

Waite, Linda J. & Joyner, Kara, *Emotional and Physical Satisfaction With Sex*, in SEX, LOVE, AND HEALTH IN AMERICA 239 (Edward O. Laumann & Robert T. Michael eds., 2001)

Walker, Sue Sheridan, *Common law Juries and feudal marriage customs in medieval England: The Pleas of Ravishment*, U. ILL. L. REV. 705 (1984)

Walker, Timothy B. & Elrod, Linda D., *Family Law in the Fifty States*, 25 FA. L.Q. 417 (1992)

Walsh, Michael F., *Marriage and Civil Law*, 23 ST. JOHN'S L. REV. 209 (1949)

Wand, Barbara Freedman, *The Relevance of Premarital Cohabitation to Property Division Awards in Divorce Proceedings: An Evaluation of Present Trends and a Proposal for Legislative Reform*, 63 B.U. L. REV. 105 (1983)

Wardle, Lynn, *Deconstructing Family: A Critique of the American Law Institute's "Domestic Partners" Proposal*, 2001 B.U. L. REV. 1189.

— *Rethinking Marital Age Restrictions*, 22 J. FAM. L. 1 (1983-84)

Webb, P.R.H., *Common law marriage and the principle of validation*, 26 MOD. L. REV. 191 (1963)

Weinberg, Meyer, *"Concubinage" and common law marriage*, 37 CHI. B. REC. 436 (1956)

Weiss, Warren W. & Collada, Henry B., *Judicial Consent to Marry - Its Complex Demands*, 3 FAM. L.Q. 288 (1969)

Weitzman, Leonore J., *Changing Families, Changing Laws*, 5 FAM. ADVOC. 2 (1982)

— *Legal Regulation of Marriage: Tradition and Change*, 62 CAL. L. REV. 1169 (1974)

Westfall, David, *Forcing incidents of Marriage on Unmarried cohabitants: The American Law Institute's Principles of Family Dissolution*, 76 NOTRE DAME L. REV. 1467 (2001)

Weyrauch, Walter O., *Informal and formal marriage - an appraisal of trends in family organization*, 28 U. CHI. L. REV. 88 (1960)

— *Informal Marriage and Common Law Marriage*, in SEXUAL BEHAVIOUR AND THE LAW 297 (R. Slovenko ed., 1965)

— *Metamorphoses of Marriage: Formal and Informal Marriages in the United States,* in MARRIAGE AND COHABITATION IN CONTEMPORARY SOCIETIES 265 (John M. Eekelaar, Sanford N. Katz eds., 1980)

Williams, John R., *Solemnization of Marriages: The Common Law Marriage - Never Solemn and No Longer Common - Will it Remain Law?*, 13 U. MIAMI L. REV. 447 (1959)

Wilmott, Linda, et. al., *De facto Relationships Property Adjustment Law – A National Direction,* 17 AUST. J. FAM. L. 1 (2003)

Winkler, Anna E., *Economic Decision-Making by Cohabitors: Findings Regarding Income Pooling,* 29 APPLIED ECON. 1079 (1997)

Woodhouse, J.T., *Lack of consent as a ground for nullity and the conflict of laws,* 3 INT'L & COMP. L.Q. 454 (1954)

Xie, Yu, et al., *Economic Potential and Entry into Marriage and Cohabitation,* 40 DEMOGRAPHY 351 (2003)

Younger, Judith T., *Marital Regimes: A Story of Compromise and Demoralization, Together with Criticism and Suggestions for Reform,* 67 CORNELL L. REV. 45 (1981)

Table of Cases

United States

Australia

Canada

Denmark

England och Scotland

France

Germany

New Zealand

Norway

Sweden

Index